The
Complete
World Hockey Association, 10e

The Complete World Hockey Association, 10e

by Scott Surgent

First Edition: March 1995; Second Edition: October 1995; Third Edition: October 1998; Fourth Edition: October 1999; Fifth Edition: September 2001; Sixth Edition, October 2003; Seventh Edition, October 2004; Eighth Edition, January 2008; Ninth Edition, September 2013.

Previously titled "The Complete Historical and Statistical Reference to the World Hockey Association".

ISBN-13: 978-1518754760
ISBN-10: 1518754767

www.surgent.net/wha

Manuscript development assisted by www.docupub.com and www.pdfmerge.com.

Minor updates and typographical and other error corrections made, August 2016.

Author's Note

This is the 10th edition of *The Complete World Hockey Association*. Twenty years ago, in March 1995, the first edition of this book was released. That I am still doing this twenty years later is very surprising to me, but the support I have received from hockey fans over the past two decades has been very strong, and I sincerely thank everyone who has purchased a copy and offered constructive criticism since the beginning! In many ways, this book is a team effort, and I'm just the guy who gets to type it all up.

My thanks to **Ed Nudge** (Glendale, Arizona): Ed's nearly complete collection of hockey media guides going back to the 1960s helped fill in the many holes I had remaining in my research. I met him in 1994 when I was about 50% done with the original draft. It was Ed's collection that helped me to solve the dozens of statistical inconsistencies I encountered in my research up to that date. I now own most of the WHA component of his collection. **Ted Martin** (Kingston, Ontario): Ted compiled the 1972 general player draft information and graciously allowed me to use it in this book. To me, it is one of the most valuable portions of the entire book. **Morey Holzman** (Escondido, California): Morey has been a great help to me in many facets of this book. His research area concentrates on hockey's early origins, but Morey knows literally everything about the sport and has it stored in his mind. **Mike Franzese** (Bethel, Connecticut): Mike contributed significantly to the International Series information contained in this book. **Timothy Gassen** (Tucson, Arizona, formerly of Indianapolis): A long-time writer and editor himself, Tim recently completed and published a detailed history of the Indianapolis Racers. Tim has proofread and edited the text in previous versions of this book.

I'd like to also thank **Ginger Malone** (early proofreading and editing), **Bill Tuele** (Director of public relations, Edmonton Oilers, lots of great information, support), **Lee Zats** (supplier of old Hockey News issues), **Mike McDonald** (his Tucson shop, "The Sports Page", had lots of old WHA items), **Stu McMurray** (1978-79 player statistics assistance), **James Felton** (Cleveland hockey and arenas expert), **Wayne Kewin**, **Ralph Slate** (hockeydb.com mastermind), **Mean Gene Dupras** (general information), **Don Buchanan** (Mariners information), **James Berwick**, **Robert Browning** (library research in Toronto), **Richard Bendell** and **Anthony Buccongello** (statistics error corrections), **Pat Houda** (international information), **Doug Holste** (lots of general information, player statistics), **Gregg Inkpen** (general information), **Randy Peters** (Blazers and Cowboys expert), **Phil Kessel, Mel Bailey** (uniform numbers), **Jason Kasiorek** (Oilers information, uniform numbers, transactions), **Benoit Clairoux** (Nordiques expert), **Steve Mauws** (Jets information), **Robert Schulz** (biographical information), **Guy Villeneuve** (statistics), **Jan Vesely** (Czechoslovakian information), **John Chapman** (error corrections), **Frank Williams** (general information), **Bob Friedlander** (general information, tapes), **Joseph Nieforth** (Denver Spurs & Ottawa Civics Information), **Bill Wentworth** (statistics, including the 1974-75 +/- stats), **Jonathan Wiener** (statistics error corrections), **Alex Baranov** (Russian player names), **Stephane Harvey, Budd Bailey, John Stager, John Landers** and many, many others.

I would also like to extend my eternal thanks and love to my wife **Beth**, who is thoroughly supportive of my project over the years.

All information contained in this book is as accurate as best as can be determined from the sources, and is verifiable. I am responsible for all typing, so all typographical errors are mine and mine alone. Errors in statistics and information are regrettable but unavoidable, and I take full responsibility for all such instances. I have made great pains to cross-check information, ensure internal self-consistency, and in a few cases, correct long-standing errors from way back.

If you have any information regarding an error, typographical mistake, or omission, please feel free to send along a copy (with source information, please) to me at the address below. I am always grateful for all assistance and it is the efforts of eagle-eyed readers such as yourself that have helped make this book what it is today!

Sincerely,

Scott Surgent
MC 1804
Tempe, AZ 85287-1804 USA
October 2015

* * * * * * * *

Dedicated to a friend, Jane Kaveney, who passed on way too soon (1968-1994). -SAS

Table of Contents

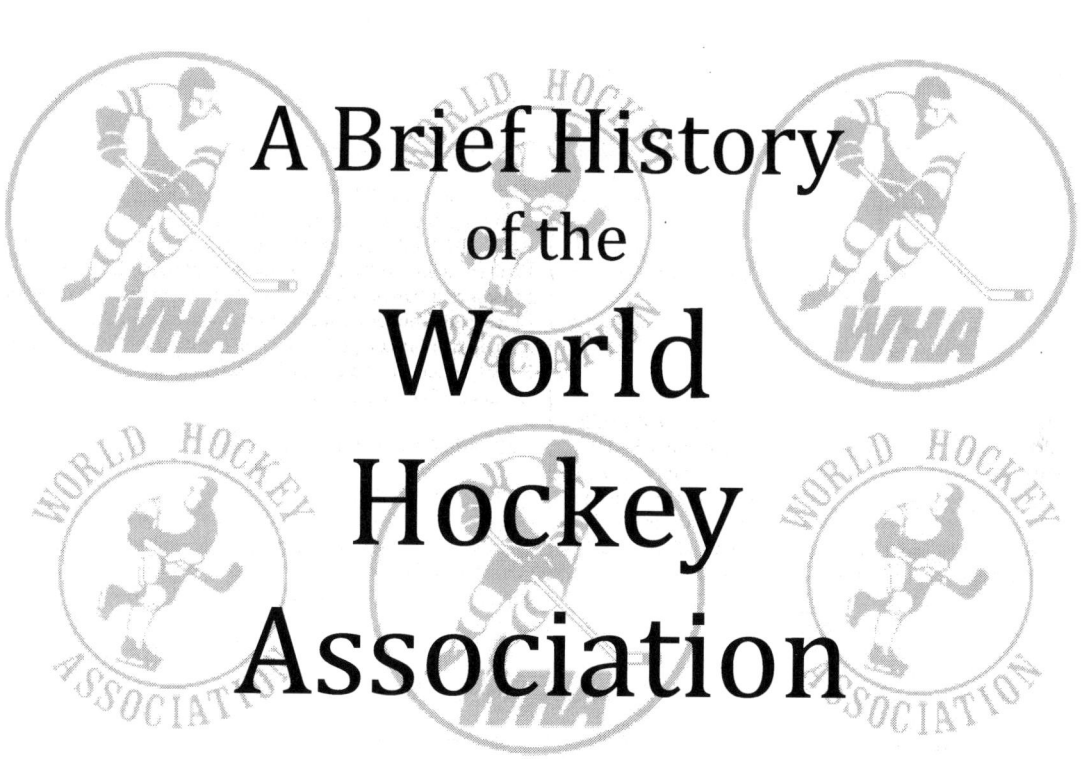

A Brief History

of the

World

Hockey

Association

Clause and Effect:
The Birth of the
World Hockey Association

The World Hockey Association (WHA) was established in 1971 by California-based sports entrepreneur and politician Dennis A. Murphy, and his friend and business partner, attorney Gary L. Davidson. They created the WHA as a major professional hockey league to compete against the established National Hockey League (NHL), with plans to start play in October 1972 with 12 teams.

The National Hockey League met this news with little regard for what seemed to be a foolish endeavor. Since its own inception in 1917, the NHL had fought off would-be challengers such as the Pacific Coast Hockey League of the 1920s, the American Hockey League of the 1950s, and the Western League of the 1960s. The NHL featured North America's best hockey players and was run by extremely wealthy and powerful men. The NHL also controlled virtually all of Junior and minor-league hockey in North America. The NHL had a firm monopoly on all facets of the North American game when the WHA formed in 1971.

However, the NHL had an exploitable weakness: a fixture included in player contracts known as the Reserve Clause. The Reserve Clause allowed a team to renew a player's contract at the previous year's terms without the player's approval. The effect of the clause was twofold: players were bound to their teams indefinitely as long as the team opted to renew the contract, and by limiting player movement, salaries could be suppressed. Free agency did not exist, and a player wishing to renegotiate the terms of his contract was at a disadvantage since the team could invoke the clause at will. The player's only option was to sit out the season. Lawsuits challenging the Reserve Clause in other sports (for example, Curt Flood's lawsuit against Major League Baseball in 1969-70) had set in motion a series of court rulings and other lawsuits that would eventually lead to the Reserve Clause's demise a few years later. However, as of 1971, it was a feature in virtually all NHL player contracts.

The WHA was a repeat of a similar experiment, the formation of the American Basketball Association (ABA) in 1967, also by Dennis Murphy. By banning the Reserve Clause, Murphy hoped to attract the attention of players from the NBA. A few jumped to the new league, while many used the ABA as leverage to negotiate better terms with teams in the NBA. Players in the NBA had viable options, and salaries in the NBA rose dramatically in a short period of time.

It was in the early ABA that Murphy and Davidson met. Through mutual friends, Davidson learned of the new league and bought into the Dallas team, quickly involving himself with the league's operations and serving as the league's president during the 1967-68 season. Emboldened by the success of the early ABA, both reasoned the same model could be applied to hockey. Living not too far apart in Orange County, California, both absolved themselves of the ABA by the early 1970s to devote their time to their new project, the WHA.

The World Hockey Association planned to move into cities not represented in the NHL, notably in Canadian cities passed by in recent NHL expansion, as well as the media centers of New York, Los Angeles and Chicago. Despite hockey's popularity, the NHL was still a six-team league as late as 1967, when the league doubled in size, adding six more teams for the 1967-68 season. In 1970, two more teams were added, increasing the league to 14 teams. Canadian fans were incensed that of the eight new teams added in 1967 and 1970, just one—Vancouver—was based in Canada, and it was owned by American interests. Both Murphy and Davidson saw potential in non-traditional major-league markets in the Southern United States and the Canadian Prairie.

The World Hockey Association moved forward during the summer of 1971. Articles of incorporation were filed in Delaware on June 10, 1971, and the summer was spent seeking interested owners and possible sites to house its clubs. To facilitate meetings between Murphy and Davidson with potential investors in Canada, Walt Marlow, a long-time writer for the *Los Angeles Herald Examiner* (and transplanted Canadian), took it upon himself to introduce them to selected heavyweights of Canadian Junior hockey. Quickly, the new WHA had W. D. ("Wild Bill") Hunter in Edmonton, Ben Hatskin in Winnipeg, and Scotty Munro and Robert Brownridge in Calgary on board. Hunter, in particular, was a man of considerable gravitas and who was not afraid to go up against the NHL, having run his Junior Edmonton Oil Kings "outlaw" for a few years in the 1960s to protest the NHL's stranglehold on the Junior system. Marlow was soon hired as the league's publicist and would be involved with the WHA through 1977.

By September 1971, the World Hockey Association was holding the first of many official meetings and press conferences. The Los Angeles meetings of September 23 and 24 gave the WHA its first significant amount of publicity, and the new league followed with more meetings and announcements designed to set the stage for its debut the following October. The WHA officially announced its plan to outlaw the Reserve Clause October 20, 1971 in Chicago. On November 1 at the Americana Hotel in New York City, the WHA held its formal organizational meeting with the announcement of 10 teams: Edmonton, Calgary, New York, Winnipeg, Chicago, St. Paul, Miami, Dayton, Los Angeles and San Francisco. Two more teams were announced on November 21: in the

New England region (later to settle in Boston) and in Ontario Province (later to settle in Ottawa).

The Miami team was a bold concept in 1971, arguably the least "traditional" place for a major-league hockey team, but Murphy liked the area, had co-owned the Miami Floridians of the ABA, and saw potential, given the high number of wealthy northerners (and presumed hockey fans) who had settled in southern Florida. However, Miami lacked a decent major-league quality arena. Developer Herb Martin won the rights to the team, but could not secure funding nor support to get a new arena built. Within months, the Miami franchise was dead, and the rights were sold to Bernard Brown and James Cooper, who settled the team to Philadelphia. Meanwhile, the Calgary franchise also became an early casualty when its owner, Bob Brownridge, fell ill in late 1971. The team was replaced by a Cleveland franchise headed by Cleveland attorney and sports mogul Nick Mileti, who also owned the Cavaliers of the NBA and the Indians of Major League Baseball.

Many other men who would have a large effect on the league's future came aboard during 1971. Howard Baldwin emerged from the Philadelphia Flyers' front office to buy into and secure the New England franchise along with Robert Schmertz, who had made his fortune building retirement communities. Baldwin later served as league president and was instrumental in the eventual 1979 merger between the two leagues. Paul Deneau, a builder of skyscrapers and based in Ohio, oversaw the Dayton entrant, which later moved to Texas as the Houston Aeros. In Alberta, Bill Hunter surrounded himself with wealthy investors and set about establishing the Edmonton franchise, while Ben Hatskin did the same in Winnipeg. Dennis Murphy awarded himself the Los Angeles franchise, with the main financial backing from Dr. Arthur Rhoades. Gary Davidson assumed the rights to the San Francisco franchise, but sold out in February 1972 to a six-member group headed by Jean Dacres, Paul Racine and the former Premier of Quebec, the Honorable Jean Lesage, which established a team in Quebec.

By late 1971, the National Hockey League finally began paying more attention to World Hockey Association. President Clarence Campbell of the NHL declared his league would "man the ramparts" to repel a full-scale player raid by the WHA on its talent, but in truth, the NHL had no cohesive plan to do battle with the WHA. As Murphy and Davidson had gambled, the National Hockey League's lack of internal coordination to secure its positions and protect its players would prove to be a significant benefit to the early World Hockey Association.

The New Kids on the Block:
The WHA Looks
For Places to Play

Central to the WHA's plans for success was to be represented in regions where the NHL was not. The WHA had grand plans for its Miami franchise, as it would be the first major league hockey team in the Deep South. Also of great importance to the WHA was to be well represented in the media capital of New York, and at the time, a new arena was being built in Nassau on Long Island without a planned hockey tenant. The WHA wanted to place its New York franchise in the new Nassau Coliseum, hoping that a strong New York-based franchise would serve as an anchor for the league. Attorney Neil Shayne, the owner of the New York team, met with the Nassau Coliseum representative William Shea to discuss a potential partnership, but Shea and the Nassau Coliseum were reluctant to commit to a new team from an unestablished league. The owners of the Nassau Coliseum desired an NHL franchise instead. This set the stage for the NHL to make its first counter-moves.

The NHL had not planned to expand again until 1974, but the arrival of the WHA dashed those plans. Not long after the WHA announced its twelve franchise locations in 1971, the NHL announced the addition of two new teams, to be based in Atlanta, Georgia, and Long Island, New York, to begin play in 1972. Placing a team in Atlanta was a counter-gesture to the WHA's Miami team, and the Long Island franchise was the NHL's way of blocking the WHA from the Nassau Coliseum. The Long Island move hurt the WHA, for its New York team was now forced to negotiate with the expensive Madison Square Garden in Manhattan for a home site. Eventually, the WHA would fail in New York City—the high rental fees for use of the Garden being a main cause—and the National Hockey League rang up an early victory in one of the first battles of what was to be a very long and arduous war.

The WHA exacted a measure of revenge on the new Long Island franchise a few months later: seven of the twenty picks made by the New York Islanders in their expansion draft were signed by teams in the WHA, causing the 1972-73 Islanders to suffer the worst season ever (60 losses) for any team in the NHL's history to that time. The California Golden Seals were also hit hard, as its players were more than eager to consider the WHA as a way to escape the floundering situation in Oakland.

In Los Angeles, the Sharks had the option of playing at the Long Beach Arena or the Los Angeles Sports Arena; they settled for the Sports Arena, but played selected games at Long Beach. Houston and Cleveland had older, smaller arenas that would suffice until more modern facilities, The Summit in

Houston and The (Richfield) Coliseum in Cleveland, were completed. The St. Paul (Minnesota) club would play in the new St. Paul Civic Center Arena, scheduled to open in January 1973.

On the East Coast, the New England Whalers were able to secure playing dates at the Boston Garden, home to the NHL Bruins and NBA Celtics. When the Garden was booked for an evening, the Whalers moved into the smaller Boston Arena for the night. However, competing against the Bruins and Celtics for prime playing dates, and often losing the battle, motivated the Whalers to make Hartford their permanent home in early 1975.

All of the Canadian cities had hockey facilities ready for use, though most of the arenas were older buildings with low capacities. The Winnipeg Arena and Le Colisee in Quebec both sat around 10,000, while the Edmonton Gardens sat barely 5,000 and served as a temporary building while the new Edmonton Coliseum was being built. The city of Ottawa had the fine new Civic Centre Arena, which sat just under 10,000, to house the Nationals.

The Chicago Cougars stood no chance of sharing the Chicago Stadium, home of the Blackhawks, and instead pinned their hopes on a planned (but still unbuilt) arena in suburban Rosemont. In the meantime, the team played its home games at the antiquated International Amphitheater, which was intended to be a temporary home, a year or two at most. However, the Rosemont Arena, which was originally to be built by 1973 or 1974, remained unbuilt until 1980, by which time the Cougars had long since folded.

Later, when the World Hockey Association started admitting expansion teams and considering relocations of established teams, a large, major-league arena was a requirement for the league to grant its approval. At the least, the team needed a commitment from its host city that a new arena was to be built soon, if one was not already present. Expansion teams in Cincinnati, Phoenix, Denver and Indianapolis could all boast major-league quality playing sites upon entry into the league.

The Scramble for Players:
The Signing of Bobby Hull

The advent of the twelve new teams in World Hockey Association meant there were now nearly 250 player positions to be filled. The new teams were stocked with journeymen NHL veterans and career minor leaguers who were never quite able to crack NHL lineups. Also, the WHA scouted American collegiate hockey for talent—a source historically ignored by the NHL—as well as players from the Canadian junior ranks, the primary source for NHL players. An ethical question arose regarding the new league drafting players from the Canadian Juniors, as these leagues were financially supported by the NHL through the Canadian Amateur Hockey Association (CAHA). However, a player drafted by an NHL club was not bound to that club until he signed an NHL contract. The WHA felt drafting from the juniors was within its rights, and the new league did so yearly.

However, the WHA desired star NHL performers for its new league, and many top name NHL players were selected at the WHA's General Player Draft held in February 1972 at Anaheim, California. At the General Player Draft, over one thousand players were selected in the hundred-plus rounds of selections. No one was off-limits, and the teams did not limit themselves to players from North America. A large number of players from Europe and from behind the Iron Curtain—the Soviet Union and Czechoslovakia—were selected. Also among those drafted were a handful of former and current football players, the Governor of Minnesota, and the Premier of the Soviet Union.

The WHA began signing players to contracts in February 1972, and the first player of significant stature, Toronto Maple Leaf goaltender Bernie Parent, signed with the Miami Screaming Eagles that month. Parent's plunge emboldened other players in the NHL to look toward the WHA, and many were in serious negotiations with WHA clubs by March. Parent's jump also served as a barometer on how the NHL would react to a star player's defection. The Maple Leafs made no effort to retain Parent, content to let him go instead of challenging the Miami offers. The Maple Leafs were under intense pressure from the rest of the NHL owners not to give in to the WHA, for if one team started signing players to more expensive contracts the rest would certainly be forced to do the same. The Maple Leafs may have established a point on principle by quietly letting Parent go to the Miami team, but it cost the team the services of one of the finest goaltenders in the game.

However, the signing that ensured the survival of the fledgling league occurred on June 27, 1972, when Bobby Hull—the second leading scorer in NHL history and the league's most visible superstar—signed a 10-year, $2.5-million contract to play and coach for the Winnipeg Jets. In 1971, Bobby Hull was the highest paid player in the NHL, making over $100,000 per year, but that figure was only achieved through arduous and bitter yearly negotiations with Chicago management. Being drafted by Winnipeg gave Hull the opportunity to finally free himself of the vicious cycle in Chicago as well as a chance to forge a path for other players in a similar bind. Naturally, Hull was aware of the risks of leaving the security of Chicago for the uncertainty of a renegade league, but Winnipeg's Ben Hatskin was quite sincere with his offers, and Hull and his lawyers and agents listened carefully.

The importance of securing a performer of Hull's fame was not lost on the World Hockey Association, and the league stepped in on behalf of the Jets and helped negotiate the $1 million signing bonus, a sum to which all twelve of the WHA clubs contributed. The other $1.5 million was to be paid out over ten years, with Hull eventually joining the executive ranks of the Winnipeg Jets. With Hull's signature, the WHA had captured one of the all-time great players in hockey history as well as capturing itself the much-needed legitimacy as a true major hockey league. The survival of the WHA was virtually guaranteed with Hull on board, at least through its first season.

Hull's signing opened the floodgates for a full-scale assault on NHL players by the WHA clubs. Cleveland, the twelfth club to be formed in the wake of the demise of Calgary and led by its aggressive owner Nick Mileti, attempted to make up for lost time by negotiating with the star trio of Vic Hadfield, Rod Gilbert and Brad Park of the New York Rangers. The Rangers countered by signing the three to wealthy long-term contracts. In doing so, the Rangers kept the heart of its team intact but incurred the wrath of the other NHL owners who were coming to the unpleasant realization that they, too, would be forced to follow suit and open the checkbooks wider than ever before. Mileti did not get his Rangers, but he was able sign the Bruins' star Stanley Cup goaltender Gerry Cheevers to a long-term contract. As the 1972-73 season drew near, the player signings continued, though most of the jumpers were not of the stature of Hull, Cheevers or Parent, but a few were prize catches nevertheless. Montreal Canadien star defenseman J.-C. Tremblay signed with Quebec, while New England picked up former Bruin Ted Green to anchor its defense. After Miami dropped from the league, the Philadelphia team honored Bernie Parent's contract and also signed Bruins' stars John McKenzie and Derek Sanderson. Most teams made do with one or two marquee players, and stocked the remaining roster spots with players from all backgrounds.

The World Hockey Association altered some rules to present a slightly different product from the National Hockey League. Tie games at the end of regulation play would go into a 10-minute sudden-death overtime. Restrictions against maximum blade curvature were relaxed, allowing players to use a blade with a 1.25 inch (3 cm) bend, as opposed to the NHL's maximum 0.5 inch (1.27 cm). Also, a two-line pass, normally an offside pass outlawed in the NHL, was allowed under certain conditions in the WHA. A player in his defensive zone was allowed to pass across the blue line and the center red line to a teammate as long as his teammate was preceded by the puck across the red line. These "breakout" passes often produced breakaways when used skillfully. Also during 1972-

73 and 1973-74, icing the puck by a short-handed team was not allowed, unless the puck was brought out past the defensive blue-line first. This requirement was dropped for 1974-75. A shootout to decide tie games after the overtime period was considered and tried once in a 1972 preseason game, but voted down, while removal of the center red line in 1974 was considered, but not implemented.

An Icy Reception:
WHA Play Gets Underway

After a year and a half of growth and controversy, the World Hockey Association put its product on ice in October 1972. The grand plans of opening night in Miami were scrapped and replaced with a more sedate Oilers-Nationals contest in Ottawa. Still, the brand new league had to grapple with problems as they continually arose. Opening night in Philadelphia featured the ice-resurfacing vehicle crashing through the ice at the Philadelphia Civic Center, and an ensuing near riot when the game was postponed. Souvenir orange pucks given out to the fans became projectiles, and the players and referees were forced to take cover from the barrage. The Blazers were also struggling as their heralded trio of ex-NHL stars, Bernie Parent, John McKenzie and Derek Sanderson, were out with injuries. McKenzie and Parent returned to have respectable seasons, but Sanderson grew sour toward the Blazers and the feeling was mutual. Sanderson's contract was bought out in January 1973, and he was back in Boston of the NHL by season's end. The Blazers lasted only one year in Pennsylvania before moving to Vancouver in 1973 after a change in ownership.

Bobby Hull was forced to sit out the first three weeks of the season while his status was adjudicated. A suit filed by John McKenzie attempted to argue the Reserve Clause was a violation of antitrust laws. A previous suit filed in Illinois by the Chicago Blackhawks and the National Hockey League claimed that Bobby Hull was still Blackhawk property under the aegis of the clause, and its immediate effect was to bar Hull from participating in the WHA until a court would make a decision. McKenzie's suit was acted upon by Judge A. Leon Higginbotham in a Philadelphia Federal District Court on November 8, 1972 when Judge Higginbotham placed a temporary restraint on the NHL, barring it from using the Reserve Clause to prohibit its players from jumping to the WHA. Higginbotham's ruling superseded the Illinois injunction, and Hull was free to play his first games for Winnipeg as of that evening. The injunction against the NHL was not a ruling on the Reserve Clause's legality, for the suit had yet to go to trial, but it did serve notice to the NHL that in all likelihood, the Reserve Clause would be found

illegal in the event of a trial. The NHL quietly accepted the decision, and from that point forward, the Reserve Clause had lost its power.

Most of the first-year problems for the WHA involved teams under-financed by owners with the less than necessary wealth to run a big league team. Neil Shayne, who originally owned the New York franchise, sold out as soon as the NHL had cut him off from the Nassau Coliseum. His successors, Sy Siegel and Dick Wood, lasted through November 1972. The team's meager resources were drained by the horrible rent agreement with the Madison Square Garden, and the league stepped in to support them team through mid-1973. Even the dreadful Islanders, losers of 60 games in 1972-73, significantly outdrew the Raiders. The situation in New York was dire and would eventually wear out the second-year New York Golden Blades—the team formed to replace the Raiders—after just six weeks in November 1973.

The Ottawa Nationals also had to contend with a bad lease arrangement with the city of Ottawa, which owned the Civic Centre. Very few people went to the games, and at the midpoint of the season, it appeared that the team had been purchased by Marv Fishman, who would then move it to Milwaukee, Wisconsin. Fishman could not close the deal, and the Nationals played out the string in Ottawa, fortunately on a high note with a rush of wins that saw them make the playoffs, before the city strong-armed the team and the owners out of town, permanently, for Toronto the following season.

Despite the various problems, the WHA had a successful inaugural season, if only because all the teams survived and the league did not lose as much money as expected. The league was getting by on its novelty interest, and the performances of its star players Hull, Cheevers and Tremblay. A few fringe performers in the NHL also found their niche in the WHA. Players such as Andre Lacroix, Ron Ward and Tom Webster turned in outstanding seasons for the first-year league. The New England Whalers, led by Webster's 53-goal season, captured the WHA's first championship, beating out Bobby Hull and the Winnipeg Jets for the World Trophy.

Meanwhile, the NHL would have nothing to do with the WHA. The WHA's surprisingly successful lifting of top talent from the NHL further soured the NHL on its rival, and the elder league was content to wait out the WHA, which it believed was going to collapse under the weight of its fat contracts and mismanagement. Still, despite the hopes and wishes of the ardent anti-WHA crowd in the NHL, the year-old league was almost certainly going to play a second season, and more players from the NHL were sure to jump.

The Howes Sign Up and The First Hints of Merger

No one could have predicted that the biggest name to sign in 1973 would be the game's all-time leading goal and point leader, the remarkable Gordie Howe, who had retired as a player in 1971 after 25 seasons playing for Detroit. By 1973, his sons, Marty and Mark, were 19 and 18 years old, respectively, while dad Gordie was 45, still in top shape, and bored with his figurehead executive position with the Red Wings. The prospect of playing again, especially alongside his sons, was too enticing to ignore. Although the younger Howes were too young for the NHL Amateur draft, the Howe family had a plan.

Colleen Howe, Gordie's wife, queried the WHA about her sons signing professionally with the WHA, arguing that they were technically profess-ionals after receiving weekly stipends while playing for the Toronto Marlboros (OHA Jr). When she received word that she had a strong argument for her case, the Houston Aeros, coached by Gordie's old teammate and friend Bill Dineen, selected Mark and Marty in the 1973 Professional Player Draft, thus bypassing the amateur draft and its age restrictions.

The plan, of course, was to have Gordie Howe himself come out of retirement and play alongside his sons. When the 45-year old star signed with Houston on June 5, 1973, many viewed it as a mere publicity stunt, afraid that the older Howe might embarrass himself after two years away from the ice. But Gordie played brilliantly, no doubt thrilled to be throwing elbows again and sliding pucks to his sons. He accrued 100 points in 1973-74, leading the Aeros to the league's second championship in 1974. The Howes would eventually stay together as a unit for six seasons, and in 1979, Gordie Howe would play a full season in the NHL, aged 52, alongside his sons in Hartford.

With Howe's signing, the WHA had another player of enormous star status and fan appeal on which it could rest its fortunes. Wherever the Jets (Hull) or the Aeros (Howe) went, the media followed and the games were usually sold out. Certainly, having the two all-time leading NHL scorers in its league was a scenario not even the most visionary WHA builder could have foreseen. The league ended its second year having improved on its attendance from the first year, and in healthy spirits.

The WHA still had the day-to-day concern of financially weak teams, often on the brink of insolvency. The two weakest were in the two largest cities, New York and Los Angeles. After the New York Golden Blades went bankrupt and folded shortly into the 1973-74 season, the league again jumped in to support the franchise, relocating it to a bandbox arena in Cherry Hill, New Jersey. The

Los Angeles Sharks were not drawing at the Sports Arena and were moribund for most of the season. By the start of the 1974-75 season, both franchises had been sold and relocated, to San Diego and Detroit, respectively. Still, the WHA was confident enough to expand by three more teams in 1973, adding Cincinnati, Phoenix and Indianapolis. Phoenix and Indianapolis began play in 1974 while Cincinnati was forced to wait until 1975 before taking to the ice.

Meanwhile, the two leagues lobbed volleys at one another through the courts. The WHA filed a $50-million lawsuit against the NHL, decrying the NHL's monopoly of power and restraint of trade practices. The NHL had no desire to go to court, sensing the WHA might actually win on its arguments. In February 1974, the two leagues settled the suit out of the same Philadelphia court headed by Judge Higginbotham. The settlement marked the first time the WHA and NHL had ever met face to face in discussing or resolving an issue. The NHL agreed to pay the WHA $1.75 million to convince the WHA to drop its lawsuit. In return, the WHA won some concessions from the NHL, including agreements to play interleague exhibition games during the preseason, and agreements by the NHL to not block access of its arenas to the WHA. The first interleague game ever held was played the following preseason, when the Houston Aeros defeated the St. Louis Blues 5-3 on September 26, 1974 in Houston.

After the February 1974 settlement, the two leagues ceased the lawsuit battles and agreed to coexist in the best possible fashion. Serious merger negotiations were still a couple of years away, and some in the NHL were content to sit still and wait for the WHA to self-destruct. However, the settlement did indirectly bring about the end of the NHL presidency of Clarence Campbell. Campbell, who directed the NHL from a post-World War II six-team league to a 16 (soon to be 18) team circuit, viewed the settlement as a signal that his thirty-year tenure was nearly over, and he made plans to retire from his post within a couple of years. Only upon the retirement of Campbell would formal NHL-WHA merger negotiations be possible.

The WHA had established itself by 1974 such that the most hard-lined NHL executive had to admit the younger league was not going to quickly vanish. Although the two leagues maintained very little direct contact during these years, they were very much at war for talent, which meant bidding wars and large contracts. Financially weak teams in both leagues suffered, unable to keep up with salaries. In the WHA, these weaker clubs would eventually fold. The bidding wars also burdened the weaker NHL clubs, notably the California Golden Seals, which lost an inordinate number of players to the WHA during 1972-74, and the 1974 NHL expansion franchises Washington and Kansas

City. By 1976, California and Kansas City would be out of the NHL, having moved to Cleveland and Denver respectively, with the Cleveland team folding outright in 1978.

During the 1974-75 season, the first overtures of a resolution began to appear. The NHL and WHA together consisted of 32 teams in 1974-75, up from 14 teams three years earlier. Officially, the NHL had no contact with the WHA, and as long as Campbell remained president of the league this policy was not going to change. A minority of NHL executives, however, thought differently and realized the importance of keeping a line open with the WHA. The WHA, in turn, preferred to chart its own course, at least while it was young and had lots of energy and could better gain leverage, before seriously considering a consolidation of the two leagues. Many in the WHA felt as their NHL counterparts did: that the two leagues could very well price themselves out of existence in a few years if a solution was not found. However, the issue was essentially tabled until 1977 and the retirement of President Campbell from the NHL.

Meanwhile during 1974, the WHA was still busy luring top-flight NHL stars to its league. The Toronto Toros (formerly the Ottawa Nationals) were able to sign long-time NHL star Frank Mahovlich, making him the third former NHL player with 500 career goals to join the WHA (Hull and Howe were the other two). Also in 1974, the WHA bid farewell to Gary Davidson, as he stepped down from his presidency to concentrate his efforts on his newest project, the World Football League. Dennis Murphy succeeded Davidson as president, although only on an interim basis. Murphy stepped aside and left the WHA altogether in 1975. By now, the "new guard", led by Phoenix' William MacFarland and New England's Howard Baldwin, were charting the course for the evolving WHA.

Putting the "World" in World Hockey Association: *The WHA Goes European*

On the ice, the show went on. The 14 WHA clubs attracted over 4 million customers in 1974-75 to its rinks for the third straight year of growth. Gordie Howe led the Aeros to another championship, and Bobby Hull scored 77 goals in 78 games to break Phil Esposito's NHL record of 76 in a season. Hull also matched Maurice Richard's hallowed NHL feat of 50 goals in 50 games set during 1944-45. For good measure, Andre Lacroix of the San Diego Mariners collected 106 assists to break another NHL record, Bobby Orr's 102.

It was in 1974 that the WHA fundamentally and forevermore altered the composition of teams in North America. Teams such as the Jets, Toros and Whalers signed a handful of European stars,

the biggest catches being Vaclav Nedomansky from Czechoslovakia, signed by Toronto, and Anders Hedberg and Ulf Nilsson from Sweden, signed by Winnipeg. The "Hot Line" of Hull-Nilsson-Hedberg would become arguably one of the finest forward lines ever in professional hockey. More European players followed, opening wide the opportunities for European players to play in North America, continuing to this day. In 1975, Winnipeg and Toronto held training camps in Europe, as did Phoenix a year later. The WHA was henceforth inextricably linked to Europe, cleverly recognizing this enormous and untapped source of talent.

The fast and flowing European style was a sharp contrast to the grinding style that was popular in the NHL and the WHA during the mid-1970s. The 1974-75 Philadelphia Flyers had used muscle combined with talent to win the Stanley Cup. Immediately, many teams—in both leagues—tried to emulate the Flyers. Players of marginal talent but willing to fight were plentiful and cheap, and virtually every team had one or two "goons" on its roster. The rough-house tactics could occasionally nullify the advantage of a speedier team, and the fights also attracted fans to the games, a fact not lost on the teams always looking for any source of revenue. Colorful characters such as Gordie Gallant, Curt Brackenbury, Paul Baxter, the Carlson Brothers, Gilles "Bad News" Bilodeau and Bill Goldthorpe would, for a time, draw regular paychecks in the WHA.

The 1975-76 season was the year of the fighter for both leagues, but it was especially apparent in the WHA, which was not as blessed with the depth of talent as the NHL. The fighting and unnecessary violence reached its nadir in the 1976 playoffs between Calgary and Quebec, when Quebec's Marc Tardif was leveled with a high-stick check to the head by Calgary's Rick Jodzio, knocking him out of the series and into a nearby hospital with severe head injuries. The ensuing brawl carried on for nearly 30 minutes, and required police to quell the fighting. Jodzio would face criminal assault charges as a result of his hit on Tardif. The embarrassing incident brought about stricter rule changes for 1976, although fighters (and line brawls) remained in both leagues for years to come. With all the tough guys in the two leagues during 1976, it was pleasantly ironic that both championships of 1976 were won by swift-skating, high scoring, strong but clean teams, the Jets in the WHA and the Canadiens in the NHL.

The WHA's fourth year was the start of the decline of the league. Salaries had risen so high in the past three years that many of the WHA's teams were near bankruptcy. Two teams folded in 1975, the Chicago Cougars and the Baltimore Blades, reducing the WHA to 12 members. Waiting in the wings to replace one of the fallen teams was the expansion Cincinnati Stingers. But to give the

league an even 14 teams again, the WHA hastily granted a franchise to Denver a mere four months before the start of the next season. As the 1975-76 season began, the Denver Spurs quickly fell into the red and despite a brief stop in Ottawa in January, the Denver-Ottawa franchise folded at the All-Star break. The sting of the Denver-Ottawa collapse had barely subsided when the Minnesota Fighting Saints, one of the better drawing teams in the league, folded six weeks later. The quick failure of two of its teams severely shook the credibility of the WHA. The decision was made to not expand for a period of time, and to concentrate on ensuring the survival of those remaining teams that were teetering on the brink of closure.

During its first four years, the WHA also learned that none of its teams could survive in a city already represented in the NHL, no matter how inferior that NHL team might have been. Six of the twelve WHA clubs shared a city with an NHL club in 1972-73, but by the start of the 1976-77 season, eleven of the twelve WHA teams were in no direct competition with the NHL. The exception was a short-lived second incarnation of the Minnesota Fighting Saints. The "new" Fighting Saints were previously the Cleveland Crusaders, who left Cleveland in 1976 when the NHL came to town with the new Barons. By the following January, the new Minnesota Fighting Saints had also disbanded, leaving the WHA with eleven teams, and its third contraction in a year. By August 1977, three more teams had folded: Phoenix, San Diego and Calgary. The league had shed six teams in a two-year period, and clearly it knew its salvation rested on a successful resolution with the NHL.

Fortunately for the WHA, Clarence Campbell retired from his presidency of the NHL in June 1977, replaced by the more pragmatic John Ziegler. Ziegler was well aware of the WHA's troubles, but he was also acutely aware of the faltering teams in his own league, teams unable to keep up financially during the now five-year old NHL-WHA money war. In the NHL, the Minnesota, Cleveland, Pittsburgh, St. Louis and Atlanta franchises were all near broke at times during 1976-78. During the months prior to June 1977, when Campbell's planned retirement from the league presidency was a fait accompli, pro-merger figures in both leagues met behind the scenes to begin discussions toward a resolution. Immediately after Ziegler's ascension to the presidency, the two leagues met for the first time officially to discuss merger, possibly in time for the 1977-78 season.

Detente:
The WHA and NHL Hold
Merger Negotiations

Various proposals were considered at the June 1977 merger negotiations, including plans to consolidate some of the weaker NHL clubs to make room for the WHA teams. The strongest proposal was for six of the eight WHA clubs—Cincinnati, Edmonton, Houston, Winnipeg, New England and Quebec—to apply for NHL membership, placing all six teams in a new NHL division. In June 1977, the NHL gave permission for an expansion exploratory committee to be formed to consider bringing the clubs from the WHA. The formal applications would be due August 9, 1977.

A significant issue was the distribution of players from the WHA teams that would fold, or those players whose rights were also held by an NHL team. Also, the WHA featured underage (under 20 years old) players who would normally enter the NHL's player draft in their 20th year. Again, at issue would be the WHA team's willingness, or probable lack thereof, to give up an underage player. Lastly, the NHL and WHA Players Associations would have a say in any deals struck at the negotiating table, to ensure the owners would not collude to regain their pre-WHA hold on the players, nor to infringe on the players' new autonomy.

A three-quarters majority was required on a vote of the NHL owners to permit merger. When the vote took place in August 1977, twelve voted in favor of merger, while six voted against, short of the three-quarter majority. Thus, merger in 1977 failed. The six teams voting against merger had their reasons. Toronto's Harold Ballard, a long-time opponent of the WHA, felt the NHL should be concentrating its efforts on saving its own insolvent clubs instead of taking in teams from the WHA. West Coast teams Vancouver and Los Angeles feared longer travel schedules and less visits by the big draws (Montreal and Boston, for example). Montreal enjoyed large television revenues and a religion-like status in Quebec Province and the team was not about to give up its standing. The old-guard ownership of Boston, a team that was decimated by the 1972 WHA player raids, voted against merger, as did the New York Islanders, a team borne of the WHA formation and another victim of the WHA player raids.

By the August 1977 vote, the WHA was down to nine teams. San Diego's franchise reverted to the league after a sale fell through, and was disbanded in June. Meanwhile, Calgary held on in the barest sense of the word, placing all its hopes in the 1977 merger. When it failed, Calgary formally dropped out of the WHA. The six spurned WHA clubs committed to play for the 1977-78 season, while the two clubs that stayed out of the merger plans,

Indianapolis and Birmingham, also committed to icing teams for the WHA's sixth season. Nevertheless, officials from both leagues continued to meet to hammer out an agreement. The WHA was heartened by the twelve positive votes, and the league worked to reach a deal with some of the anti-merger teams. And despite the near agreement for 1977 merger, many of the details regarding the handling and distribution of players had yet to be worked out satisfactorily, so the two leagues worked at those topics as well.

Although virtually all of the executives associated with the WHA believed that merger was simply a matter of time, they also realized they needed to offer competitive hockey to remain afloat, or merger would be a moot proposition. The league had been getting by in its early years on the strength of its star NHL defectors, but by 1977 the novelty of signing big name NHL players had worn off. Any strength the WHA was to gain had to be done through scouting the junior ranks and competing with the NHL for available talent. The WHA did not feel compelled to honor the Canadian Amateur Hockey Association's (CAHA) request that players be in their 20th year to be eligible for the amateur draft, as the agreement was largely an unwritten one between the CAHA and the NHL. Hence, many of the WHA owners (particularly John Bassett in Birmingham) enticed teenage junior stars to go professional with relatively attractive offers. The NHL, on the other hand, rarely drafted and signed underage juniors, so in essence the WHA was beating the NHL to the young talent. The NHL would exact some revenge by drafting the WHA teenage stars a year or two later and luring them to the NHL. Such was the case with Birmingham's Mark Napier and Ken Linseman, who both left the Bulls when more attractive NHL offers came along. Many of the teenagers performed well in the WHA, and along with the heavy European influence, the WHA's caliber of play was nearly comparable with that of the midstream NHL, and considerably better than its own level a few years previously.

No new big name NHL stars had jumped to the WHA for 1977-78, but the league's first family, the Howes, had moved on to Hartford to join the Whalers. The Whalers started the season white hot, winning 13 of its first 15 games, but injuries to key players and the collapse of its home arena in January 1978 slowed the Whalers, who were forced to play their remaining home games in Springfield, Massachusetts. Winnipeg won the 1978 crown after posting 50 wins during the regular season with winning streaks of 11 and 15 games, the latter a league record. The 1977-78 season also featured two touring clubs from Europe, the Soviet "All-Stars" and the Czechoslovakian national team. Both clubs played each of the eight WHA teams once, with the games

counting in the standings. On the downside, three clubs were experiencing trouble. The once-mighty Houston Aeros limped along without the Howes in front of small home crowds, and the team nearly folded in late 1977, but managed to play out the season. The Indianapolis Racers nearly folded in 1977, but the entrance of new owner Nelson Skalbania kept the team afloat—albeit tenuously—as the team nearly folded again in early 1978. Cincinnati did not come as near as Houston or Indianapolis to folding, but the Stingers played to frustratingly sparse crowds at the Riverfront Coliseum. The Birmingham Bulls also suffered poor attendance, but the deep pockets of owner John Bassett usually kept the team running relatively problem free.

The Merger Negotiations:
The Arrival of Wayne Gretzky
and the Beer Boycott

The two leagues met to consider merger again in 1978, but there was no longer a unified six-team bloc hoping to enter the NHL all at once. Houston had won the right to negotiate on its own terms for entry into the NHL. Owner Kenneth Schnitzer tried to purchase the NHL's Colorado Rockies, whom he would rebrand as the new Aeros and resume play in 1978-79 in the NHL. However, his scheme fell through, the Rockies stayed in Denver and Houston disbanded in July 1978. Birmingham and Indianapolis were once again the teams that would be left out, joined now by Cincinnati, whose financial troubles made them less attractive to the NHL. The remaining four teams—Winnipeg, New England, Edmonton and Quebec—now comprised the merger bloc.

Meanwhile, the NHL had dissolved the Cleveland Barons, merging them with the Minnesota North Stars. Now a 17-team league, the NHL wanted three teams to bring its rolls to an even 20 teams. New England and Edmonton were the likeliest teams to gain admittance, but the collapse of New England's home rink earlier in the year caused concern, although Hartford took advantage of the unfortunate collapse to rebuild the arena to NHL standards, but not until 1980 at the earliest. Winnipeg and Quebec also had arenas too small by NHL standards. Ultimately, there were too many unresolved issues—whether three or four teams would be admitted, and the situation with Hartford's rink—on how the 1978 merger would occur, and it was voted down once again.

Thus, the WHA convened for its seventh season, now a seven-team league, of which two were very unhealthy financially. Some in the NHL insisted that given time, the WHA would fold outright, while the WHA still talked big, even discussing expansion into Europe in the 1980s. Realistically, the WHA knew it would not likely survive to see an eighth season, while the NHL saw some value in taking in the WHA's strongest teams. When not playing games of brinksmanship, the negotiations pressed forward. Fourteen of the 17 NHL teams needed to approve merger, but five of the teams consistently voted against merger in any form. Essentially, the negotiations centered on winning over enough votes from the anti-merger subset to accumulate the necessary 14 approvals.

The WHA needed a better bargaining position, and it found one: a skinny high-school senior named Wayne Gretzky. The prodigy had drawn attention and a level of fame as early as 1971, and by 1978, had shown he was clearly heads and shoulders above his Junior mates, and ready for better competition. The NHL balked at signing a 17-year old child, so Gretzky's agent, Gus Badali, shopped Gretzky to the teams in the WHA. The situation was delicate as signing Gretzky would potentially anger the NHL, who naturally wanted him in their league, and potentially scuttle the negotiations. Yet, clearly, someone was going to sign him—he was simply too good to be forced to repeat a season in the Juniors.

In June 1978, Wayne Gretzky signed a personal services contract with Nelson Skalbania, the owner of the Indianapolis Racers. Indianapolis was not going to be part of any merger, and Skalbania was enough of an iconoclast to sidestep the negative reaction he might receive. Skalbania's motives were not entirely altruistic: he wanted his Racers to survive the season to recoup costs when he would be paid to fold. In October 1978, the Gretzky-Indianapolis experiment unfolded. The Racers were barely hanging on, a dreadful team that would be lucky to win 10 games. But his teammates took to the kid, and in return, Gretzky responded well, with 3 goals and 3 assists in 8 games. But no one came to the games, there was no money, and in November, Skalbania sold Gretzky to Edmonton; the cash he received lasted until mid-December, when the Racers finally folded. But Gretzky was now firmly in the WHA, on one of its strongest franchises. The NHL realized that the only way to get Gretzky into its league would be to let the whole team in.

In Birmingham, the Bulls' new crop of Baby Bulls this time featured defensemen Rob Ramage, Gaston Gingras and Craig Hartsburg, forwards Michel Goulet and Rick Vaive, and goaltender Pat Riggin. The teenagers performed well for the Bulls, much to the delight of Birmingham fans. Cincinnati was signed forward Mike Gartner, and later Mark Messier from the failed Indianapolis team. Gartner had a good rookie season for the Stingers while Messier did not, but both later went on to enjoy brilliant NHL careers.

Merger negotiations continued during the winter of 1978-79, leading up to another vote in early March 1979. By this time the major details of

merger (or "expansion" as the NHL termed it, to avoid antitrust issues) had already been worked out to both leagues' satisfaction. Yet when the vote was taken in Key Largo, Florida, on March 8, 1979, the proposition again failed by a 12-5 vote, two votes short of approval. The five clubs voting against merger were the same clubs that consistently voted against it: Boston, Los Angeles, Montreal, Toronto and Vancouver. The new Islanders ownership (1978) was pro-merger.

The Montreal and Vancouver vetoes upset the three Canadian-based WHA clubs hoping for NHL admission. The Montreal Canadiens, citing concerns about loss of television revenue, came under a backlash of criticism from all over Canada, and the Canadiens ownership, Molson Breweries, faced a boycott of its products in the three Canadian WHA cities. Many Canadians, upset that one of its own teams would block entrance of three other fellow cities to the NHL, supported the Molson boycott. Particularly upset were the Quebec Nordiques, owned by Molson's rival O'Keefe Breweries. Molson Breweries moved quickly to shore up a severe public relations disaster, as well as to avoid a full-scale boycott and loss of business to another brewery, and decided to change their stance on merger. The Vancouver Canucks, one of the other Canadian-based teams to vote against merger, did not come under the fire that Montreal experienced, but were convinced to change their stance when promises were made for a more balanced schedule to ensure the big East Coast draws would come to the West Coast as often as before. Somehow, Toronto stayed out of the fray, everyone recognizing that as long as Harold Ballard was in charge, Toronto would never support merger.

Nearly two weeks after the failed vote, the NHL Board of Governors reconvened in Chicago at the behest of Washington Capitals' owner Abe Pollin. With two more "yes" votes committed for merger, the NHL finally agreed to accept the plan on March 22, 1979 by a 14-3 vote in time for the 1979-80 season. The last hurdle was the NHL Players Association, which held the option of vetoing the plan, but the NHLPA voted 30-1 in favor of the merger in return for increased benefits in their pension plans and insurance policies.

The WHA was to fold while four of its clubs—Edmonton, Quebec, New England and Winnipeg—would become members of the NHL, formally as expansion teams. The two remaining WHA clubs, Cincinnati and Birmingham, would be bought out by the other four clubs. The NHL levied a $6 million expansion fee per team for entrance to the NHL, plus another $1.5 million "clean up" fee per team, essentially the buyout money for the Cincinnati and Birmingham ownerships.

Redistributing the players required a series of dispersals and drafts. A special draft was held by the WHA (in one of its last official acts ever) to disperse the players from the Cincinnati and Birmingham franchises to the four surviving WHA teams. The NHL then held a reclamation draft, which allowed for NHL teams to reclaim players from the WHA whose rights they held. The four ex-WHA clubs then had the right to keep four players from their 1978-79 rosters as priority selections, which would protect the player from being reclaimed or placed into the amateur draft. It was in this manner that Wayne Gretzky became a member of the NHL, as a priority selection of the Edmonton Oilers. Interestingly, Gretzky was never formally drafted by a WHA or an NHL team, a unique distinction for such a unique player.

Once these preliminary drafts and dispersals were completed, the four now-ex-WHA clubs participated in the actual expansion draft, selecting up to 15 skaters and two goaltenders from the 17 NHL clubs' unprotected lists. Exactly four players were selected from each of the NHL clubs. To placate Vancouver and Los Angeles, the league adopted a balanced 80-game schedule in which each team played the other four times, two at home and two away. Because of the balanced schedule, realignment of the four divisions was deemed unnecessary for 1979-80, and the four ex-WHA clubs were placed in three of the divisions essentially at random. Quebec went to the Adams Division, Edmonton and Winnipeg to the Smythe Division, and Hartford (New England) to the Norris Division. Meanwhile, some NHL clubs were moved to other divisions to keep a semblance of balance. The NHL realigned geographically and dropped the balanced schedule in time for the 1981-82 season.

The Merging of Two Leagues:
The Newly Expanded
National Hockey League

For years, hockey fans in Edmonton, Quebec, Winnipeg and Hartford longed to pit their respective teams against those in the NHL. As the quality of play in the WHA rose considerably over its last three seasons, many fans felt that the best teams in the WHA could easily hold their own, if not succeed, against regular competition from the NHL. The 1979 merger of the two leagues seemed to offer the opportunity for these much longed-for battles to take place, but the various drafts of June 1979 effectively knocked the talent of the incoming clubs down a level. The 1979 WHA AVCO Cup champion Winnipeg Jets lost star forwards Kent Nilsson, Rich Preston and Terry Ruskowski, and the gutted Jets suffered from a terrible offense (shut out 13 times) and won just 20 games during 1979-80. Quebec won just 25 games and finished last in their division, while Hartford and Edmonton won 27 and 28 games respectively, both eligible for the 1980 Stanley Cup Playoffs. Unfortunately, the

Whalers and Oilers were both swept in the Preliminary Round, by Montreal and Philadelphia respectively.

Still, 1979-80 was an interesting season as many former NHL stars returned to the NHL after years in the WHA. Bobby Hull, retired for most of the 1978-79 season, returned to play for the Jets for their first NHL season. Hartford featured Gordie Howe, returning nine years after his last NHL game, along with his sons Mark and Marty. The Whalers also featured 39-year old center Dave Keon, back in the NHL after his five-year hiatus in the WHA. Later in the season, Hull was traded to the Whalers where he played alongside Gordie Howe and Dave Keon as the oldest forward line in NHL history. Edmonton's Wayne Gretzky immediately established himself as the best player of the NHL when he tied for the league scoring title with Los Angeles' Marcel Dionne with 137 points, though he lost out for the Art Ross Trophy due to scoring 51 goals to Dionne's 53. The Oilers did not distinguish themselves in 1979-80, but shrewd drafts in the upcoming years by general manager-coach Glen Sather resulted in a team that won five Stanley Cups from 1984-90. Among his 1979 acquisitions was Cincinnati's Mark Messier, whose one-goal campaign for the Stingers in 1978-79 hid the enormous talent the teenager held.

Many of the other teenagers from the WHA's 1978-79 season had respectable to outstanding inaugural NHL seasons in 1979-80. Mike Gartner scored 36 goals, the first of 18 consecutive seasons of scoring in excess of 30 goals, an NHL record. Rob Ramage moved to Colorado (later New Jersey) where he starred for the Rockies and other teams before finally retiring in 1993. Michel Goulet went to the Nordiques before moving on to Chicago, retiring in 1994. Some of the scoring stars of the WHA found the NHL defenses harder to manage, and saw a drop in their output. Quebec's Real Cloutier and Marc Tardif hovered around the 80-point range, far off their usual WHA production. Robbie Ftorek never neared the 100-point plateau in the NHL that he accomplished four times in the WHA. On the other hand, Mike Rogers, who had never scored more than 83 points in five seasons in the WHA, exceeded 100 points in each of his first three seasons in the NHL, playing for Hartford and later, the Rangers.

Epilogue:
The War Is Over

Ultimately, the expansion by the NHL to accept the four WHA teams proved to be one of the wisest moves the elder league ever made. By taking in the four clubs and effectively ending the WHA, the NHL was free of the constant battles for talent and salaries that it waged with the WHA for seven years. The four WHA teams now made for a 21-team NHL, and aside from a couple franchise shifts (Atlanta to Calgary in 1980, Colorado to New Jersey in 1982), a strong, stable league. In many ways, the WHA achieved what it originally set out to do from its inception. The WHA gave players rights and leveraging power that they never had before in the days of the Reserve Clause. The ensuing salary wars pushed the average player's salary to a level comparable to those of the other major sports.

The WHA also proved to quite a visionary league. In actively signing European players, the WHA showed conclusively that top talent did not have to necessarily come from Canada or the handful of United States along the Great Lakes. The graceful European style of play became trademark for some of the WHA clubs, a fact not lost on the NHL, which began pursuing European talent aggressively after absorbing the WHA. The WHA also succeeded in cities that the NHL historically overlooked. The WHA showed that hockey could draw a following in the seemingly unlikely locales of Birmingham, Houston and Phoenix. Indeed, Phoenix later joined the NHL in an ironic turn of events, as the Winnipeg Jets moved to Arizona in 1996. Houston has been seriously considered as an expansion site, while the Deep South now boasts four clubs: Tampa Bay, Miami (Florida), Raleigh-Durham (Carolina), and Nashville. The Carolina team is the relocated Hartford Whalers, who left Connecticut in 1997. A new expansion team in Atlanta (2000) relocated to Winnipeg in 2011, resurrecting the Jets nickname.

Hockey in North America has seen a steady growth in popularity in the years since the demise of the World Hockey Association. The NHL has enjoyed increased prosperity since 1979, adding five new teams during the early 1990s and four more during 1998-2000. The World Hockey Association will likely fade from the memories of most hockey fans, or be remembered for its inefficiently run teams, sometimes low quality of play (especially in its early years), and its contributions to the anecdotal history of the sport. Its appropriate legacy, however, should be for its pioneering forays into Europe, its adoption of rules (such as overtime periods) now in use in the NHL, its efforts in "non-traditional" markets such as Phoenix, Houston and Birmingham, and, most importantly, its choice to abolish the Reserve Clause and the resultant rise in players' freedoms and salaries. The World Hockey Association has earned its appreciation: the league served a progressive, innovative purpose, and it served it well.

The Teams of the World Hockey Association

When the World Hockey Association drew to a close in 1979 after its seven-year existence, it had represented itself in 30 cities with 32 teams. Some teams never took to the ice, some played very briefly, while others survived for the full duration. In the league's formative stages of 1971, rights to a WHA team could be purchased for as little as $25,000. This figure, a tiny fraction compared to the cost of an NHL expansion franchise, attracted many would-be owners who ultimately could not cover the costs of actually assembling a team of players and securing a home arena. The results were poorly run and under-financed franchises that either folded or moved out of town, and a league whose image was tarnished as being a haven for fly-by-night owners with little regard for the integrity of the sport. The league did have its share of responsible owners who fervently cared for their teams and the league's well being.

In the early years, the World Hockey Association tried to compete head to head with established NHL clubs, and in every instance where a city included teams in both the NHL and WHA, the WHA lost the rivalry. Eventually, the WHA found establishment and success in the mid-sized cities far from an NHL. Most WHA franchises attracted a solid core of fans, but average game attendances for any one team rarely neared 10,000. Phoenix, Minnesota and Houston were prime examples of successful hockey clubs with a solid core of fans but not quite popular enough with the general public to attract more casual fans. These three teams seemingly folded before their times were up, each an unfortunate loss to the league.

The WHA started with twelve teams, went as high as fourteen before shrinking to eight in eighteen months during 1976-77. When the WHA finally folded in 1979, only six teams remained, the sole survivors from the heady heyday of the mid-1970s when the WHA entertained thoughts of actually meeting, if not superceding, the NHL in eminence. Ultimately, the sheer wealth and establishment of the NHL helped it stave off the challenges from the WHA. Absorption of four WHA clubs into the NHL in 1979 finally closed the book on the WHA.

Alberta Oilers
Edmonton Oilers

For years, hockey in Edmonton (and for that matter, all of Alberta and neighboring Saskatchewan) was dominated the colorful W. D. (Wild Bill) Hunter. By the mid-1960s, Hunter was owner and occasional coach of the junior Edmonton Oil Kings, which played in the ancient Edmonton Gardens. He was a key figure in the creation of the Western Canada Hockey League in 1967, a Junior circuit that eventually grew enough in stature to be considered on equal footing with the established Ontario and Quebec leagues. However, the creation of the WCHL did not come without some controversy, but Hunter always enjoyed a good battle in taking on the hockey "establishment". Thus, when Dennis Murphy and Gary Davidson came to Canada seeking support for the new WHA in 1971, Hunter was immediately interested, and with his connections and background, helped launch the WHA in Canada.

Hunter's involvement came through the efforts of a beat writer for the *Los Angeles Herald-Examiner*, a transplanted Canadian named Walt Marlow, who took it upon himself to bring together Murphy and Davidson with the heavy hitters in western Canada. With Hunter on board, the WHA awarded one of the ten franchises to him on November 1, 1971. Local businessmen Zane Feldman and Charles Allard entered in with Hunter as the bankrollers and the new team adopted the Oilers nickname. Hunter would be the team's general manager, building it from scratch.

The first-year Oilers pursued NHL players with Alberta connections including former players for the Edmonton Junior Oil Kings. Ray Kinasewich, an Alberta native who played and coached for the various incarnations of the Edmonton minor-league squads of the 1950s and 1960s, was hired as coach. Helping him in an unofficial role as assistant was the great goaltender Glenn Hall. Under Kinasewich, the Oilers played break-even hockey for most of the season. Jim Harrison was the most productive forward, leading the team in goals with 39 and points with 86. Former Buffalo Sabres' defenseman Al Hamilton chipped in 50 assists to lead the club. Ross Perkins (21 g, 37 a, 58 pts), Ron Walters (28-26-54) and Rusty Patenaude (29-27-56) also posted good offensive numbers. However, Kinasewich was not around for the end: he had been replaced in early February by Hunter himself, a habit of Hunter's, carrying over from his days managing his Junior clubs. The two coaches had a combined 38-37-3 record, the team tying for fourth place with Minnesota in the Western Division. Although the two teams had identical records and also had four wins apiece against one another, the Oilers should have been declared the fourth-place team by their advantage in goals. However, the league decided at the last minutes to hold a one-game playoff between the two teams to break the tie. The game was held in Calgary, and the Oilers were beaten 4-2 by the Fighting Saints.

Another former Edmonton Oil Kings coach, Brian Shaw, became the coach of the Oilers in 1973-74, and despite 13 wins in the first 14 games, the second-year team finished again with a 38-37-3 record. Newcomer Ron Climie led the team with 38 goals and 74 points, and second-year men Hamilton and Harrison tied for the team lead in assists with 45. This time, the Oilers' record was good enough for third place in the Western Division, but they were eliminated in the first round of the playoffs by nemesis Minnesota.

The 1974-75 club, playing in the new Edmonton Coliseum, slipped to a record of 36-38-4, and finished last in the new Canadian Division. Jacques Plante left his coaching job with Quebec to play a season in goal for the Oilers. The 46-year old legend won 15 games and posted a shutout, part of a three-man rotation in goal. Seven players scored at least 20 goals, led by rookie Mike Rogers' 35. Hunter repeated history and fired coach Shaw, who left with a winning record. Under Hunter, the Oilers won just 6 of 19 games and finished last in the Canadian Division and out of the playoffs.

The Oilers bottomed out in 1975-76, finishing 27-49-5. Rusty Patenaude (42 g, 72 pts), Tim Sheehy (34 g, 65 pts) and long-time NHL vet Norm Ullman (31 g, 87 pts) led the offense, but a lack of depth hurt the team. New coach Clare Drake, a successful college coach at the University of Alberta, lasted half the season before falling victim to Bill Hunter's axe, and for the third time in four seasons Hunter finished the season as the Oiler bench boss. Hunter had a 9-21-3 mark in his third tenure behind the bench. Despite a near 50-loss season, the Oilers made the playoffs, managing to finish ahead of the woeful Toronto Toros. Their fourth-place finish in the new Canadian Division was good enough for the tenth and last playoff spot in the WHA's liberal playoff format. Not surprisingly, the Oilers were no match for the powerful Jets, losing in four straight.

In 1976, new owners Nelson Skalbania and Mitch Klimove took over, releasing Bill Hunter from his duties and association with the team. The Hunter era had ended. Skalbania hired former Boston Bruin and Kansas City Scout coach Armand "Bep" Guidolin to rebuild the struggling Oilers for 1976-77. Guidolin was a busy man as general manager, making deal after deal, but the transient Oilers failed to gel under Guidolin the coach. He stepped aside as coach in February 1977 and selected forward Glen Sather to assume the role. Sather, who would assemble and coach a superior Oilers team to five NHL Stanley Cups during the 1980s, cut his teeth by leading the Oilers to a fourth place finish in the Western Division and an early exit in the playoffs. Bep Guidolin's involvement with the Oilers ended after the 1976-77 season.

Ownership changed again during 1977 when Peter Pocklington purchased majority control of the team from Skalbania, who in turn bought into the Indianapolis franchise (while keeping a minority stake with Edmonton). The 1977-78 club continued its rebuilding program and the Oilers finished a respectable 38-39-3 under Sather before being eliminated in the playoffs in the first round. The offense was led by Bill "Cowboy" Flett's 41 goals, with Ron Chipperfield and Blair MacDonald each meeting the 30-goal mark. The defense was anchored by the capable corps of Paul Shmyr, Dave Langevin and Al Hamilton, while Dave Dryden and Don McLeod blocked the pucks in goal.

The 1978-79 club was once again playing break-even hockey when Pocklington made the most significant move in the franchise's history, purchasing 17-year old Wayne Gretzky from the faltering Indianapolis Racers in November. Nelson Skalbania's situation in Indianapolis was so desperate he chose to sell off his prized scoring star, along with valuable teammates Peter Driscoll and Ed Mio, to the Oilers for cash. Gretzky responded by setting Oiler records with 43 goals, 61 assists and 104 points. Chipperfield, MacDonald and winger Brett Callighen rounded out the offense, while Dave Dryden had a superlative year in goal, posting 41 wins, three shutouts and a 2.89 average. The upstart Oilers went as far as the finals of the 1979 playoffs, but a more experienced Winnipeg team proved too formidable and the Oilers were beaten in six games.

The Oilers have been members of the National Hockey League since 1979, coming into the NHL as part of that year's merger between the two leagues. During the latter half of the 1980s, the Oilers were the dominant team in the NHL, winning five Stanley Cups ('84, '85, '87, '88, '90), with Gretzky and Mark Messier heading an all-star cast of players. The Oilers continue to represent Edmonton in the NHL to this day.

Chicago Cougars

Although placing a team in an established NHL market could be risky, the WHA deemed Chicago to be a reasonably safe gamble. The city was big enough to possibly support two teams (akin to the Cubs and White Sox of Major League Baseball). Furthermore, a new arena was in the drawing stages in the suburb of Rosemont. These factors suggested that it was worth the risk, and a franchise was awarded to Chicago in November, 1971. However, the team went through a series of ownership changes during 1971 and early 1972, and in the meantime, no action was taken to actually build a team. It was not until late Spring of 1972 when brothers Jordon and Walter Kaiser, real-estate developers in the Chicagoland area, took control of the team. The Cougars would play at the International Amphitheatre for the time being. The older arena had poor sightlines and was merely a

temporary home until the Rosemont arena was completed.

While the Kaisers had money and connections, the delay in getting them on board meant that the team had not signed anyone. This put the Cougars at a disadvantage, forcing them to scramble for players. Most of the first-year team came from the minor-professional ranks, and a few from the NHL. Rosaire Paiement had shown he could score in the NHL with Vancouver, and he would be the team's star player that first season, scoring 33 goals to lead the team. Minor-leaguer Bobby Sicinski proved to be a bright spot, leading the team with 88 points (25 g, 63 a). Former Blackhawk Reggie Fleming also joined, having his best season as a pro with 23 goals. Marcel Pronovost did the best he could with a weak squad in his first major-league coaching job, but the heroics were too few and far between. The Cougars started the season on a 2-12-1 run, then closed out on another 2-12-1 skid. They finished 26-50-2 and were the only team not to compete for a playoff berth that first season.

The Cougars made amends over the summer of 1973 by signing two former Blackhawk stars, Pat Stapleton and Ralph Backstrom. Backstrom was a member of the Stanley Cup winning Montreal teams of the late 1960s, but he had spent the last couple of years shuffling from the Canadiens to the Kings, and then onto the Blackhawks. Stapleton, however, was an established Blackhawk star for many seasons, and a Chicago fan favorite. Wearing the jungle green and gold of the Cougars, Backstrom responded with 33 goals while Stapleton, serving as player-coach, scored 58 points on 52 assists while giving the defense some credibility. When Stapleton was on the ice, the bench boss was a young Jacques Demers, in his first of many coaching roles he would assume in the WHA and later, the NHL.

The Cougars improved significantly over their previous year's effort, and the team finished 38-35-5, squeaking into the playoffs barely ahead of the Quebec Nordiques. The Cougars then caught fire, eliminating Toronto and New England in grueling seven game series, each time winning the decisive seventh game on the road. The Cinderella Cougars then proceeded into the final round, only to lose in four straight to the Houston Aeros. The Cougars were forced to play their two home games of the Houston series at a smaller residential rink, the Randhurst Twin Arena, after the Amphitheatre was booked by other tenants.

Buoyed by their success in 1973-74, the Cougars had reason to expect better days in 1974-75 after signing highly-touted center Gary MacGregor, who scored 100 goals as a Junior for Cornwall. MacGregor responded with a team-record 42 goals, and another rookie, Francois Rochon, added 27. Dave Dryden was lured away from the Buffalo Sabres to tend the nets, but the winning charm was gone ... not to mention the financial backing and the team owners after a

certain point. A weak defense and a lack of scoring depth doomed the Cougars to a 30-47-1 record and out of the playoffs.

By late 1974, the Kaisers wanted out. The Rosemont arena (to be called the Horizon) was still in the planning stages (construction would not actually begin until 1978). The team was losing money and going under fast. When no takers came forward to buy the team, three Chicago players—Ralph Backstrom, Pat Stapleton and Dave Dryden—achieved a sports first by purchasing controlling interest of the Cougars on December 28, 1974. The Kaiser brothers retained the season ticket revenue, and the player-owners could only hope to recoup their investment by the walk-up crowds and a hopeful sale of the team. Unfortunately, attendance to the Cougar games was always low, and the three player-owners lost heavily.

It was clear that the WHA had played out its string in Chicago. No substantive offers were made to purchase the team, and there was no way it could survive continuing to play in Chicago at the Amphi-theater. Instead, a new team, the Denver Spurs, was created in May 1975, stocked with most of the remaining roster of the Cougars team. In June 1975, the Cougars were formally dissolved by the league.

Cincinnati Stingers

The final game of the first WHA Championship Series took place on May 6, 1973, and it was also on that day that the WHA admitted a new franchise, awarded to Brian Heekin III and Bill DeWitt Jr, to be housed in Cincinnati, Ohio, and called the Stingers. The owners had money and experience. DeWitt himself was the son of Bill DeWitt, former owner of the St. Louis Browns of Major League Baseball who also sat on the Board of Directors of the new Cincinnati hockey club (in 1995, DeWitt Jr would assume majority ownership of baseball's St. Louis Cardinals). A new arena, the Riverfront Coliseum, was being built along the Ohio River, part of the Riverfront Complex. The new Cincinnati team would have began play in 1974-75, as part of a three-team expansion bringing the league to fifteen teams, but the Riverfront Coliseum would not be completed in time. Thus, their debut was delayed until the Fall of 1975.

In the meantime, the Stingers assembled a front office and participated in the 1973 and 1974 Amateur Drafts. Their prize catch was Dennis Sobchuk, a highly-regarded center from Regina. He was signed in 1974 and loaned to the new Phoenix Roadrunners for the 1974-75 season. Another scorer from the Juniors, Jacques Locas, was signed and subsequently loaned to Michigan for 1974-75. Terry Slater was the team's first coach. Along with their Junior stars and prospects, the Stingers also signed Rick Dudley from Buffalo of the NHL. Dudley was a fan favorite in Cincinnati, having starred for the AHL Swords during 1971-73. Under Slater, the Stingers started 1975-76 respectably well, playing above break-even for most of the first half before cooling at the end. In fact, the Stingers were still battling for a playoff spot as late as mid-March. The offense was strong, with Dudley scoring 43 goals, Sobchuk 32, top draft pick Claude Larose 28, and Jacques Locas 27. But keeping opponent goals outside their own net was difficult. Still, their first year record of 35-44-1 was impressive and something to build upon.

Before 1976-77, the Stingers signed center Richie Leduc from Cleveland and winger Blaine Stoughton from the NHL Maple Leafs, and both rewarded the Stingers with 52-goal seasons. With Dennis Sobchuk scoring 44 goals and Rick Dudley 41 more, the Stingers amassed an impressive team total of 354 goals for, compared to 303 against. The Stingers finished the season with a 39-37-5 record, but were upset in the divisional semifinals of the playoffs by nemesis Indianapolis in four straight. Terry Slater was relieved from his coaching job immediately after the end of Cincinnati's playoff run.

In a pre-arranged deal with the faltering Phoenix Roadrunners toward the end of the 1976-77 season, the Stingers had agreed to purchase star forward Robbie Ftorek, who would join Cincinnati for the 1977-78 season. The Stingers hired Jacques Demers, formerly of Chicago and Indianapolis, to coach, and goalie Michel Dion, also formerly of Indianapolis, to tend the nets. However, the Stingers experienced a high turnover as previous year's stars Richie Leduc, Dennis Sobchuk, Blaine Stoughton, defenseman Ron Plumb and forward Claude Larose all left the team in midseason trades. Ftorek had another fantastic season with 59 goals and 109 points, and Dion collected four shutouts but also a bloated goals-against average. The Stingers spent most of the season near the bottom of the standings, and subsequently, the Stingers missed the 1978 playoffs with a 35-42-3 record.

Like many WHA clubs, the Stingers did not draw large crowds, and the team was struggling financially. The Stingers nearly folded during the summer of 1978, but an aggressive save-the-team campaign generated enough revenue to ensure another season. Robbie Ftorek again led all Cincinnati scorers in 1978-79 with 116 points on 39 goals and 77 assists. Second-year man Jamie Hislop scored 30 goals while Peter Marsh, in his third year, had a career best 43 goals but was a defensive liability. The squad's top rookie was Mike Gartner, who scored 27 goals, a hint of the 700 goals he would eventually score in the NHL. With big Mike Liut in goal and Dion as his backup, the Stingers were able to secure a playoff spot despite losing a point from the previous season's total. They were eliminated in three games by New England.

Cincinnati's fate had been sealed two months earlier after the NHL agreed to absorb four WHA clubs for 1979-80, but not Cincinnati. The lame-duck

franchise played out its string of games in front of its usual core of devoted fans and thousands of empty seats. The Stingers, it seemed, did everything right except draw fans. Cincinnati had applied for admission into the NHL as part of the bloc of six WHA clubs trying to get in through the planned NHL-WHA merger of 1977, which ultimately failed. The 1978 crisis and the team's ongoing struggle to win over the Cincinnati public prompted owners DeWitt and Heekin to close shop and accept a cash settlement to fold. The Stingers received $3.15 million as a settlement figure, and its players were disbursed to their appropriate rights-holding NHL teams or into the pool of the unsigned, hoping to latch on somewhere for the 1979-80 season.

Cleveland Crusaders
Minnesota Fighting Saints II

The Cleveland Crusaders were the twelfth and final franchise to be granted its charter from the World Hockey Association in time for the 1972-73 season. The league originally planned to base a team in Calgary, Alberta. The Calgary Broncos were one of the original ten charter franchises granted at the league's November 1971 introduction, with Scotty Munro in charge of building the team, but when the Broncos' principal owner, Bob Brownridge, fell ill and passed away, the team was left to wither until April 1972, when the WHA dropped Calgary.

Enter Nick Mileti, a Cleveland attorney and sports mogul of the Northern Ohio port city. By 1972 Mileti owned the MLB Indians, NBA Cavaliers, AHL Barons—and the Cleveland Arena—home of the Cavs and Barons. Mileti hoped to add major league hockey to his portfolio and applied for one of the two planned National Hockey League expansion franchises to be granted for the 1974-75 season. When the NHL chose Kansas City and Washington over Cleveland, Mileti immediately turned his attentions toward the WHA. The World Hockey Association, eager to salvage the failed franchise in Calgary and impressed by Mileti's background, granted him the rights to the Calgary franchise on June 21, 1972, a mere three months before the start of the following season. The new Crusaders assumed the rights to the draft choices made by the Calgary team a few months earlier. Calgary, however, had signed no one, and Mileti was forced to construct a team from near scratch.

A star player is what the team needed, Mileti believed, especially given the limited time he had to gather together a team. To that end, Mileti offered the New York Rangers' star trio of Vic Hadfield, Rod Gilbert and Brad Park generous offers to come to Cleveland. The Rangers matched the Cleveland offers and kept the players, but Mileti had made it known that he was willing to open his checkbook wide to attract the stars. While he didn't get his Rangers, he did sign Bruins' goaltender Gerry Cheevers, fresh from two Stanley Cups playing in Boston and one of the NHL's top goaltenders. With Cheevers now in Cleveland, Mileti could boast having the best goaltender in the WHA, and few would argue.

Bill Needham had spent 15 seasons playing for the Cleveland Barons, and had played as a player-coach for Toledo during 1971-72. Now age 40, he retired as a player and assumed the coaching role for the Crusaders. Having Cheevers naturally meant that the Cleveland team would build from the net outward, emphasizing defense. Veterans Paul Shmyr, Wayne Muloin and John Hanna led the defense, and together, the Crusaders allowed just 239 goals, the fewest in the league during 1972-73. The offense was a pleasant surprise, the team scoring 287 goals. Ron Buchanan led the team in points with 81, with ex-Seals Gary Jarrett and Gerry Pinder scoring 40 and 30 goals, respectively. Jim Wiste's 71 points placed him among the team's leaders. The Crusaders finished the season in second place in the Eastern Division behind New England, and in the playoffs Cleveland swept Philadelphia before losing to the eventual champion Whalers in the divisional finals.

The 1973-74 season, however, was a disappointment for the Crusaders. Ron Buchanan's ailing knees (and a near-tragic head-first crash into the boards that left him temporarily paralyzed) limited him to 45 points in 49 games, and Gary Jarrett led a very average offense with 31 goals and 70 points. Gerry Cheevers posted four shutouts, but also a 3.03 average. Unfortunately, the offense declined while the defense allowed more goals than the year before. The result was a 37-32-9 record, and a fast exit from the 1974 Playoffs. Bill Needham's tenure as the team's coach ended soon thereafter.

The Crusaders played their games at the antiquated Cleveland Arena, which was too small for modern-day hockey and still featured chain-link fencing around the rink rather than plexiglass. In the meantime, the new Coliseum (as it was known) was being built in suburban Richfield Township. When it opened in fall 1974, it was by far the most modern arena in the WHA. But it was also far from Cleveland with an inadequate highway system to support it. The move would eventually play a factor in the team's demise two years later.

The early signs were not good: their first two home games of 1974-75 were cancelled due to bad ice. The Richfield Coliseum was an attractive and well-designed arena, and a relatively event free facility after its initial ice troubles, but the arena turned out to be too distant to attract fans from Cleveland, while the hoped-for crowds from Akron to the south never materialized. It was soon painfully clear that the Coliseum, the most modern of its time, had become a liability almost as soon as its doors opened.

On the ice, the Crusaders' lack of offense undermined the usual steady efforts of the defense. For the season, the Crusaders scored just 236 goals, with

newcomers Al McDonough and Richie Leduc leading the attack with 34 goals each. Former player John Hanna had assumed the coaching duties from Bill Needham before the season began, but he was in turn replaced by Jack Vivian, who finished the season behind the bench before resigning to return to his role as general manager after the season's end. The Crusaders 35-40-3 record barely earned them a playoff berth, but they were eliminated by Houston in five games, another first-round exit

The Crusaders' situation in Cleveland had soured considerably by 1975-76, and the weak attendance at the Richfield Coliseum put the Crusaders in an unpleasant financial situation. Nick Mileti had surrendered his controlling interests of the Crusaders to Jay Moore in 1975, but the new owner did not endear himself to the fans or the players with his disinterested manner toward the team and his open desire to buy and relocate an NHL team to Cleveland. The Crusaders were dealt another blow in January 1976, when its star and foundation, Gerry Cheevers, settled his contract and returned to the Boston Bruins. The Crusaders finished the season with a near identical mark of 35-40-5 under Coach John Wilson, with Ron Ward's 82 points leading the team and Jim Harrison's 34 goals setting the pace. In the playoffs, Cleveland rolled over for New England, losing three times in three games in three nights.

At the close of the 1975-76 season, the Crusaders were a team without a home. They were evicted because the NHL was coming to Cleveland (though Jay Moore was not involved) with the Barons, formerly the California Seals. For a few weeks, the franchise seemed to have found a home in Hollywood, Florida, under the ownership of Bill Putnam. The Florida Breakers (as they were to be called) would have played at the Sportatorium, a suspect venue that had been built expressly for music and other entertainment events, but not for professional sports. The arena was partially open to the air, and similar to the Coliseum in Richfield, too far from the major cities and serviced by scant roads that were famous for its traffic jams. The WHA wisely steered the team away from the Sportatorium. Instead, the nomadic club with no hometown or name was offered a chance to assume the role of the recently-failed Minnesota Fighting Saints, setting up shop in St. Paul, Minnesota, as the second incarnation of the Fighting Saints for 1976-77.

The first incarnation of the Minnesota Fighting Saints had iced quality teams, but suffered financially, folding in February of 1976. This second version, featuring a few holdovers from the Cleveland days and a few from the original Saints such as Dave Keon and Mike Antonovich, and coached by Glen Sonmor, skated to a 19-18-5 record for the first half of the 1976-77 season. However, if fans in the Twin Cities weren't supporting the original team, there was no reason to expect them to support a second version, and they did not.

Attendance was spotty, and the team was losing money severely. In January 1977, the Fighting Saints started selling its players to other WHA clubs, formally folding on January 18 when the WHA allowed the Saints to liquidate, rather than face lawsuits from the floundering team.

Denver Spurs
Ottawa Civics

The Denver Spuirs were a rushed franchise, granted to Ivan Mullenix, who was based in St. Louis, who had previously owned the Denver Spurs of the Western League, and who had applied for, and received, a conditional expansion franchise by the NHL for Denver, to start play in 1976. However, that franchise was revoked (along with a franchise for Seattle) by the NHL in 1975, when the NHL dropped its plans to expand in 1976. Meanwhile, the WHA had disbanded its Chicago and Baltimore operations, was admitting a new team in Cincinnati for Fall of 1975, and sought to include another team to bring the league rolls back to 14 teams. Thus, the WHA offered Mullenix the rights to a Denver-based team, and he accepted. The new Denver Spurs were stocked with players from the Chicago Cougars, most notably, Ralph Backstrom.

On paper, the Denver situation looked promising. Mullenix had a track record in Denver with the Western League's Spurs, and if the NHL had once liked him, he certainly would have looked attractive to the WHA. The team would play in the brand-new McNichols Arena, and the team itself had some history, being together in Chicago for most of the past three seasons, rather than as a rag-tag team of castoffs, as many expansion teams tend to be. Jean-Guy Talbot, recently retired as a player for the great Montreal squads of the 1960s, was the team's first coach, assuming the same role he held for the Spurs when they were in the WHL, 1974-75. Although the team had just a few months to get its act together, there was some reason to believe it could work.

Unfortunately, hockey fans in Denver never got the memo, and they stayed away in impressive numbers. After teased with a possible NHL team for over a year, then to have it yanked and replaced with a WHA version, Denver fans felt no kinship with this edition of the Spurs. Attendance was often around 3,000, being generous. The team itself didn't impress the fans, going winless in its first eight home games. A "guaranteed win" promotion on November 21, 1975 backfired as the Spurs lost to the visiting Calgary Cowboys. Fans received free passes to a future Spurs game, which few redeemed, partly due to their general disinterest in the team, partly due to there being relatively few people at the guaranteed-win game in the first place, but mostly due to the team's abandonment of Denver altogether a month later.

18

The Spurs played their last game in Denver on December 30, 1975, then embarked on an extended road trip, never to return to Colorado. Mullenix had given up on Denver and was seeking a sale to a group in Ottawa. The Founders Club was an aggregate of Ottawa businessmen and fans who wanted to see hockey return to the city, and they negotiated with Mullenix, acting as an intermediary to find a buyer for the team. In the meantime, the Founders Club would cover some costs and smooth the way for the team to play two "home" games in Ottawa. But the Founders Club was itself not going to own the team.

The two home games in Ottawa went over well. Still smarting from losing the Nationals in 1973, Ottawa fans wanted to show they could support a major-league team, and both games drew sell-out crowds, something the Spurs never saw in Denver and the Nationals rarely saw back in 1972-73. During these two weeks of early January 1976, the team was nicknamed the Ottawa Civics. For home games, they wore their orange Denver sweaters minus the Spurs logo, while on the road, they wore their normal Spurs duds. Uniform issues aside, Mullenix was feeling the heat from Denver, being sued by the city for back-taxes and monies owed. He wanted hard cash now, and would not (or could not) wait a few months for a possible buyer down the line. Despite the best efforts of the Founders Club, a buyer could not be found, and in mid-January 1976, Mullenix pulled the plug on the whole operation. The Spurs-Civics were defunct, its players either sold to various teams in the WHA, or made free agents.

Lost in all this were the efforts of its players. Ralph Backstrom scored 21 goals and had 50 points, playing in all 41 games that the team existed. Don Borgeson, a long-time minor-leaguer given a chance to play on the big stage, also scored 21 goals, on pace to easily be his best effort of his career. Gary MacGregor scored 16 and Jim Sherrit 11. Bob Johnson won 8 games in goal, while Cam Newton registered the team's one shutout.

The NHL would actually come to Denver in 1976, relocating its Kansas City operation to Denver as the new Rockies. The fans in Denver seemed to show similar interest in the Rockies, as they soon moved to New Jersey in 1982. Finally, in a round-about way, the "WHA" came to Denver in 1995, when the Quebec Nordiques moved to town as the Avalanche. The new Avs were quick to impress, winning the Stanley Cup their first season in Colorado (and again in 2001). Finally, major-league hockey had roots in Denver.

Houston Aeros

Paul Deneau, a real-estate developer based on Dayton, Ohio, secured the rights to a World Hockey Association franchise in November 1971. Within months, Deneau lost his bid to receive municipal help in building a new stadium in Dayton, and the team relocated to Houston, Texas, in April of 1972. Jim Smith and Robert Tate joined with Deneau to fund the club after its move to Texas. The Houston Aeros would play at the old Sam Houston Coliseum for a couple seasons, until the newer Summit Arena was completed in 1975. Deneau hired Bill Dineen to coach, and under Dineen, the team assembled a squad composed mostly of second- and third-line players with NHL experience or from the high minors. With this approach, the first-year Aeros were a tight unit that played effective hockey, winning more than they lost. Lacking star players, the Aeros got by with capable veterans like Ted Taylor (34 goals), Duke Harris (30 goals) and Murray Hall (28 goals). Gord Labossiere led all scorers with 36 goals and 96 points, while long-time Western Leaguer Larry Lund proved he belonged in the big time with a 66-point campaign. The Aeros finished second in the Western Division, but lost the 1973 divisional finals to the Winnipeg Jets.

Seeking the extra edge needed to contend for the league championship, the Aeros signed 45-year old Gordie Howe to a contract over the summer of 1973. Howe had been retired from active status since 1971, but was unhappy as a figurehead executive for the Detroit Red Wings. When the Aeros drafted his sons, 18-year old Mark and 19-year old Marty in the 1973 Professional Draft (these selections also a source of controversy: the sons were members of the Ontario League's Toronto Marlboros but because they received a weekly stipend, were perceived as "professionals", at least for the purposes of the draft), Gordie jumped at the chance to play alongside his sons. Despite his two-year layoff and his advanced age, he had stayed in shape and quickly dispelled any concerns that he was not ready to rejoin the fray on the ice. The Howes meshed perfectly with an already sound team, and the 1973-74 Aeros captured the league's best record at 48-25-5. Gordie scored 31 goals and 100 points to capture the league's Most Valuable Player award. Mark Howe scored 38 goals, while second-year men Larry Lund (33-53-86) and Frank Hughes (42-42-84) contributed well. The Aeros sailed through the playoffs to capture the 1974 AVCO World Trophy, beating a tired but inspired Chicago team in four straight for the crown.

The 1974-75 club remained unchanged from the previous year, the principal new addition being goaltender Ron Grahame, who replaced the departed Don McLeod. The Aeros enjoyed an injury free year (no skater played in less than 70 games, except for rookie Bill Prentice) and finished atop the heap again with a sparkling 53-25-0 record. The offense scored 369 goals, with 15 of the 17 regulars scoring goals in the double digits, led by Frank Hughes' 48. Houston easily defended its crown, losing only once in 13 postseason games, and remaining undefeated during the final 10 contests.

The 1975-76 club moved its home contests to the newly-completed Summit, and finished with a

near-identical 53-27-0 mark from the previous season and another first-place berth. Gordie Howe surpassed the 100-point mark for the second time in three years, and was one of five 30-goal scorers on the club. However, the Aeros were no longer the clear favorites to win the World Trophy. The much improved Winnipeg Jets were up to the challenge and Houston was beaten in four straight in the final round.

The Aeros finished the following year with another outstanding record of 50-24-6. Youngsters Terry Ruskowski, Rich Preston, John Tonelli and Morris Lukowich replaced some of the old guard and played extremely competent hockey. Sophomore Preston led the club with 38-41-79 numbers. Houston was eliminated in the playoff semifinals by Winnipeg. This was also the end of the Howe era in Houston, as the three Howes signed with the New England Whalers over the summer of 1977. To pick up some of the slack, the Aeros signed Andre Lacroix from the recently-defunct San Diego Mariners, and the 1977-78 club finished a respectable 42-34-4 and third place overall. Coach Bill Dineen was awarded his second Coach of the Year Award for guiding a club that many felt would not contend after the departure of the Howes.

The Aeros were clearly one of the classiest teams of the WHA, but attendance at the Summit was consistently below average, and the Aeros suffered financially. Ownership changed hands three times after 1974, and none of the three subsequent owners was wealthy (or willing) enough to overcome the losses the team incurred each year. The Aeros placed their bid to be included in the 1977 merger, but when that plan failed, Aeros owner Kenneth Schnitzer (1977) won the right from the league to negotiate his own agreement for NHL admittance.

The 1977-78 season was a make or break year for Schnitzer, for the Aeros were near collapse the entire season, almost folding near Christmas of 1977. Schnitzer campaigned hard, and his plan was broad: Either his Aeros would be admitted to the NHL as an expansion team independent of any WHA-NHL merger, or an existing NHL team would relocate to Houston under Schnitzer's ownership. Regardless, Houston's involvement in the WHA would be finished after the 1977-78 season. Schnitzer almost succeeded in bringing the NHL's Colorado Rockies to the Summit, but the plan failed and the Rockies stayed put in Denver. The rebuff by Colorado effectively dashed the hopes of Schnitzer and his plan for major league hockey in Houston. The Aeros made their demise official when thirteen Aero players' contracts were purchased by the Winnipeg Jets in early July 1978. The remaining players were released, and the Aeros ceased existence.

Hockey in Houston languished after the Aeros' fold. The Houston Apollos played for two seasons as a member of the Central Hockey League before folding midway through the 1980-81 season. For the next thirteen years, Houston was without a team. In 1994, the Houston Aeros were reborn as members of the International Hockey League, and Terry Ruskowski was hired as the coach the new team. The Aeros continue to play, now as members of the American Hockey League.

Indianapolis Racers

Indianapolis was granted an expansion franchise on September 14, 1973, when the World Hockey Association expanded by two teams for the 1974-75 season. The franchise was granted to John Weissert and Dick Tinkham, who also owned the American Basketball Association's Indiana Pacers. Weissert and Tinkham soon sold out to former Houston Aeros owner Paul Deneau, who assumed majority ownership in December 1974. The Racers planned to make the new Market Square Arena in downtown Indianapolis their home. The multi-level, state-of-the-art arena was still under construction during 1973-74, and it was completed barely in time for the Racers' inaugural season in September 1974.

Gerry Moore coached the expansion club, having proved his worth by guiding Dallas to the 1973-74 CHL Adams Cup Championship. Unlike their expansion brothers in Phoenix, Indianapolis did not have an established minor league team from which to build. As a result, the Racers built through the expansion draft and the signing of available talent, competing against the new NHL expansion teams Washington and Kansas City as well. Former Crusader Jim Wiste and Shark Bobby Whitlock were the most notable of the new Racers. Andy Brown, the last of the maskless goalies, was signed from the NHL's Pittsburgh Penguins to tend the nets. However, the rest of the squad was a motley collection of career minor-leaguers, teenagers and other unknowns. Jim Browitt came aboard midway into the season as the General Manager in an effort to raise the level of competency of the brand-new team.

The Racers staggered through their inaugural season, winning just 6 of their first 40 games (and losing their final ten), to finish 18-57-3, a league record for fewest wins and most losses. Wiste and Whitlock turned in respectable scoring figures, as did winger Kerry Bond and former Pittsburgh Penguin Nick Harbaruk. Still, Indianapolis employed 37 players during the season, and the team lacked strength in all areas. The defense was not only unable to spare goalie Brown from a nightly barrage of shots, but no one defenseman could manage more than two goals during the entire season. Andy Brown lost a league-record 35 games during the season, but his nightly acts of bravery earned him the nomination as the lone Indianapolis representative to the 1975 All-Star Game in Edmonton. Brown also held the distinction of finishing second on the club in penalty minutes with 75, which set an all-time major league hockey record (up to that time) for goaltender

penalty minutes in a season. Former Vancouver Canuck Ed Dyck served as Brown's understudy, but he was gone by the next season in favor of the young prospect Michel Dion.

As bad as the first season had been, the Racers improved dramatically in their second season. Former Chicago Cougar general manager and bench coach Jacques Demers replaced Gerry Moore early in the season behind the bench. Pat Stapleton joined Demers in Indianapolis and became the second-year club's defensive anchor. The Racers defense was also helped by midseason arrivals Bryon Baltimore and Darryl Maggs from the defunct Denver-Ottawa franchise. Aided by holdovers Ken Block and Dick Proceviat, the suddenly-competent defense made life easier for rookie goaltender Michel Dion. Dion turned in a league leading 2.74 goals against average, helping the Racers achieve the lowest team goals against total for 1975-76. Despite the sparkling play of the defense, the Racers were below break-even for most of the season, due to a powerless attack. A second wave of free agents made available by the recent fold of the Minnesota franchise put long-time NHL star Dave Keon in a Racers uniform. Keon's arrival coincided with a ten-game unbeaten streak during March 1976, which vaulted the Racers to the top of the weak Eastern Division. After a mad scramble in the season's waning days, the Racers finished in first place with a 35-39-6 record, a point ahead of second place Cleveland. Michel Parizeau and Rene Leclerc, both midseason arrivals from Quebec, gave the Racers' attack some punch. Nick Harbaruk and newcomer Reg Thomas tied for team honors with 23 goals apiece. The Racers' season ended one round into the playoffs, but not before extending the Whalers seven games in a series that featured two shutouts by each team. The Racers' shutouts were turned in by another rookie goaltender, Jim Park.

The Racers improved slightly to 36-37-8 in 1976-77. Jacques Demers still called the shots, with former Ottawa National Brian Conacher assuming the role of general manager, having served an apprenticeship as coach of the Racers' affiliate in Mohawk Valley of the NAHL. Dave Keon was gone, but Rene Leclerc, Blair MacDonald and Reg Thomas all collected at least 25 goals while Gene Peacosh netted 22 playing in a partial season. Defenseman Darryl Maggs paced the club in scoring with 71 points. However, the Racers' defense permitted 305 goals against, and the team could only manage a third place finish in the Eastern Division. In the playoffs, the Racers upset rival Cincinnati in four straight, including an exciting three-overtime endurance contest in which the Racers came from three separate one-goal deficits to overcome the Stingers. However, the Racers were eliminated by eventual champion Quebec in the semifinals.

The Racers were not a financially strong organization in Indianapolis. In 1976, owner Paul Deneau allowed a group of investors headed by Harold Ducote to purchase the team. They defaulted and by June 1977, the Racers were wards of the creditors, ready to be folded if a buyer could not be found. In July, Nelson Skalbania assumed principal ownership of the team while still holding onto a minority share of the Edmonton Oilers. The ongoing financial crises that beset the team, as well as the merger discussions during the summer of 1977, seemed to portend that the Racers would fold, so much so that many of its players—and coach Demers—bolted for Cincinnati, who were likely to enter into the NHL. When the merger failed in August, the Racers pieced together a team for the 1977-78 season, minus its favorite stars, now playing for nemesis Cincinnati. Ron Ingram, most recently coach of the Mariners, was hired to be the bench boss.

Not surprisingly, the Racers struggled all season, losing twice as many games as they won. Coach Ingram lasted half the season before being replaced by the tandem of Bill Goldsworthy (player-coach) and Rosaire Paiement (injured, served as bench coach). Ex-Penguin Gary Inness and promising rookie Ed Mio tended the nets, and Claude St. Sauveur came aboard and set the team record with 36 goals. Peter Driscoll and Richie Leduc provided help up front in partial seasons with the team, but the defense, severely hurt by the loss of Stapleton and Dion, lagged all season and allowed a league-high 351 goals against. With a 24-51-5 record, the Racers finished last in the league and out of the playoffs.

As in the previous summer, the team was close to folding in mid-1978, but Skalbania signed 17-year old Wayne Gretzky to a personal services contract that July. The budding superstar was clearly ready for top-level competition, although still very young. He was ostensibly the "savior" of the franchise. Realistically, no player could have saved the Racers by then. Skalbania hoped to stay afloat for the year and collect on the buy-out money should the WHA and NHL merge, or possibly leverage the young Gretzky for immediate cash in the near future.

Wayne Gretzky was pivotal to the long-term survival of the WHA as part of the NHL. The NHL certainly knew of him and wanted him in their league, but would not draft a 17-year old, no matter the circumstances. The WHA knew that having him in its league helped their bargaining position considerably, but had he gone directly to one of the teams most likely to be admitted into the NHL, it could have ruined the negotiations. Thus, having Gretzky play in Indianapolis was "convenient" for everyone involved. Indianapolis was not going to be part of any merger, and Skalbania had a reputation for being a maverick so that his actions would not necessarily stall the talks between the two leagues.

In any case, Gretzky skated for eight games with the Racers in October 1978, scoring three goals and assisting on three others. On November 2, 1978, he was sold to Edmonton along with Ed Mio and Peter Driscoll for $850,000. He was on a stable franchise

likely to be admitted into the NHL, and Skalbania was suddenly richer. Unfortunately, the Racers could barely keep up with the rest of the league, winning just five of 25 games, and on pace to allow over 400 goals. Pat Stapleton coached the team, knowing full well the likely outcome, giving the young skaters a chance to play so that they might find work on another team down the line. In mid-December 1978, Skalbania folded the Racers.

Mark Messier, who would join Wayne Gretzky in Edmonton during the 1980s and win a total of six Stanley Cups with the Oilers and Rangers, and who would play through the 2003-04 season as one of the all-time greats on the sport, started his illustrious career with the Racers in late November of 1978. He was pointless in five games, then scored one lone goal playing for Cincinnati the remainder of the year. The Racers may have lingered on for four and a half years with a few good months during 1976 and 1977, but their imprint on hockey history is profound, as the team that included Gretzky and Messier among its ranks, if just for a few games each.

Los Angeles Sharks
Michigan Stags
Baltimore Blades

The Los Angeles Sharks gained its charter on November 1, 1971. The new league planned to mimic the NHL by placing teams in Los Angeles and San Francisco, despite the fact that the NHL had already done so and (to this point) without much success. When the San Francisco franchise rights were re-granted to Quebec in February 1972, Los Angeles was left alone in the West, their closest rivals being the Alberta Oilers and the Houston Aeros.

In 1972, fans in Los Angeles were still getting used to the idea of one (alleged) major-league hockey team, just five years after the Kings had entered the NHL in 1967. In those five years, the Kings had hardly smoothed the way for the Sharks. The Kings had finished last overall twice and had not made the playoffs since 1969, and were lucky to draw 7,000 fans to its games at the Forum in Inglewood. The Sharks would play at the cross-town Sports Arena, nearby the Los Angeles Memorial Coliseum. Clearly, Los Angeles received a team to give the WHA leverage for seeking media exposure, not for its history of supporting major-league hockey. The fact that Dennis Murphy lived close by certainly played a role. Murphy would run and own a small stake in the team. Dr. Arthur Rhoades, an old connection of Murphy's from his ABA days, would assume the larger share of the costs. Terry Slater, formerly coach of Des Moines in the Central League, was signed in February to coach the new Sharks.

The Sharks stocked their squad with journeymen and minor leaguers for the inaugural season. No one on the 1972-73 roster could claim any actual fame as a hockey player, none ever having established any significant numbers in the NHL. However, the no-name Sharks played competitive hockey and drew better than expected. Average attendance settled near the 6,000 mark, with a few games drawing crowds over 10,000, including an unlikely crowd of 12,000 for a Sunday game in March against Ottawa, televised live to Canada, in which the opening face-off took place at 11 a.m. local time.

Winger Gary Veneruzzo, formerly of the St. Louis Blues, blossomed into a scorer, leading the team with 43 goals and 73 points. Center J.P. LeBlanc was second with 69 points. When the team was not scoring goals, they resorted to a tight defense and their fists to keep the opponents away from the net. Five regulars had more than 100 minutes in penalties, led by Tom Gilmore's 191, and the Sharks led the league in team penalty minutes. The Sharks had the distinction of being the only winning hockey team, NHL included, to post a losing home record. On the other hand, their road record was the best in the league. The Sharks' overall 37-35-6 record gave them third place in the West, but they were bumped after one round in the playoffs by Houston.

The Sharks entered their second season with high expectations, but little money, as Rhoades had walked away from the team in early 1973. In his place, Dr. Leonard Bloom of San Diego purchased control of the team, but his motives were mixed. Bloom also owned the San Diego Conquistadors of the ABA and purchased the Sharks as leverage to have a new sports arena built in suburban Chula Vista, the assumption being that the Sharks would relocate to the San Diego area. However, for the time being, the official party line was that the Sharks were staying put in Los Angeles.

The Sharks had reason to be excited entering the 1973-74 season. They had posted a better record than the Kings, and signed a legitimate front-line scorer, Marc Tardif from Montreal. Tardif responded with 40 goals and Veneruzzo added 39 more, but supporting cast was thin, and the Sharks managed just 239 goals for the season, worst in the league. The defense did not hold up, allowing 339 enemy goals, causing the Sharks to stumble to a last-place finish at 25-53-0, losing 24 of their final 29 games. By mid-season, the Sharks were in severe turmoil. Bloom had lost his bid to have community support to build his arena, and he simply wanted out. Murphy had left the team to assume the presidency of the WHA on an interim basis. Coach Slater had assumed the general manager's role, relinquishing the coaching role to Ted McCaskill. In February 1974, Charles Nolton and Pete Shagena, both from the Detroit area, purchased the team, keeping alive the illusion that the team was staying in Los Angeles. However, the new owners cut costs, returned Slater to the coaching role, stopped radio broadcasts, and effectively squashed any support the team may have had in Los Angeles. To no one's surprise, Nolton and Shagena announced the transfer of the Sharks to Detroit within a week after

the end of the 1973-74 season, and the team was renamed the Michigan Stags.

The Stags were intending to compete against the established Red Wings, playing its home games at the Cobo Arena. The Red Wings had been around for decades, had won numerous Stanley Cups, and had many great players in its storied history, but in recent years had fallen on lean times. Nolton and Shagena hoped that Stags could draw fans away from the Red Wings, but it became clear that no matter how bad the Red Wings may be in any given season, its fans were loyal and not interested in the WHA squad down the road. The Stags had over-extended themselves on player contracts and had little money to promote the team. Its inaugural game (in Indianapolis) was televised—and they won—but that would be the only game shown on television. Only 2,500 people attended the home-opener a few nights later, which also happened to be the same night as the Ali-Foreman "Rumble in the Jungle" championship boxing match. The Stags won, but then lost their next home game, with less than 1,500 in attendance. This was the theme for the next three months, crowds too small to support the team financially. Surprisingly, the schedule maker chose not to book the Houston Aeros, and Gordie Howe, into Detroit until February, by which time the team had left town altogether.

By January 1975, the Stags were finished in Detroit. For two weeks the team did not function, except for one game in which the team wore generic sweaters with no name or crest. Folding the team and distributing the players was financially unwise, as few teams were willing to take on these players and their over-sized contracts. Since the WHA was on the hook for the contracts anyway, it was cheaper to play out the schedule (rather than fold) by forming a replacement team in Baltimore, called the Blades. Not surprisingly, the new Blades played as well as they had in Detroit, winning rarely, the team finishing 21-53-4. Even when the Stags/Blades won, it wasn't easy: every one of the team's 21 wins was by at most two goals.

The league tried to peddle the franchise to anyone willing to purchase it, but no substantive offers came forth. The league then formally disbanded the Blades on June 19, 1975. A dispersal draft and auction was held allowing for the remaining WHA teams to claim the former Stags and Blades players.

Minnesota Fighting Saints

Placing a team in the Twin Cities meant going up against the established NHL, although in this case, the North Stars had only been "established" since 1967. A group of nine Twin Cities businessmen led by Lou Kaplan, Fred Grothe and Frank Marzitelli applied for and received a franchise in November 1971. In view of Minnesota's reputation for support-

ing hockey at all levels, placing a second team in the Twin Cities seemed to be a reasonably sound business decision. The new Fighting Saints would play in St. Paul, to leverage its natural rivalry with fellow Twin City Minneapolis. A new arena was being built in St. Paul, which the Fighting Saints would inhabit starting in January 1973. In the meantime, they played at the St. Paul Auditorium.

Glen Sonmor, the long-time coach of the University of Minnesota hockey team, was hired to be the general manager and coach. Realizing that there would be fourteen new teams starting play in the fall of 1972 (twelve in the WHA and two expansion teams in the NHL), Sonmor recognized that he would need to be clever in scouting players for the Fighting Saints. He knew the program well in Minnesota, and set about tracking down as many Minnesota-born players as possible. In an era when just a handful of major-league hockey players were born in the United States, the first-year Fighting Saints featured nearly half a roster of American-born or trained players. Among them were Mike Antonovich, a quick center who had become a legend at the secondary and collegiate levels in Minnesota, Mike Curran, goaltender for the 1972 Men's Olympic Silver-medal hockey team, and Jack McCartan, who was the goalie for the 1960 Men's Olympic Gold hockey champs.

The 1972-73 Fighting Saints finished 38-37-3, in a fourth-place tie with Alberta, forcing a one-game playoff to decide the last playoff berth. Minnesota won, but lost in five games against Winnipeg in the ensuing round. Center Mike Antonovich and winger Bill Klatt turned in good seasons, with Klatt's 36 goals second on the team behind Wayne Connelly's 40. Connelly's 70 points paced the club, followed by fellow NHL expatriate Ted Hampson's 62. Mike Curran's four shutouts were good enough for a second-place tie among league goalies. John Arbour and Dick Paradise kept opponents honest, collecting 188 and 189 penalty minutes, respectively. Glen Sonmor handed over the coaching reins to Harry Neale for the last quarter of the season. Sonmor assumed the general manager's role full time, while Neale would be the team's coach through their end, four years later.

Under Neale as full-time coach (and Sonmor as general manager), the 1973-74 Saints matured into a high-powered scoring threat. Wayne Connelly scored 42 goals while second-year man George Morrison scored 40, but the real star of 1973-74 was Mike Walton, previously of Toronto and Boston in the NHL. Taking advantage of the WHA's two-line pass rule to promote breakaways, Walton scored 57 goals and 117 points to lead the league. With newcomer John Garrett in the nets to complement Curran, the Saints raced to a 44-32-2 finish, good enough for second place behind the Houston Aeros. Unfortunately, the Saints were eliminated in the second round of the playoffs by eventual champion Houston. In the boardroom, Wayne Belisle, a lawyer based in

the twin cities, assumed ownership of the team in late 1974.

The 1974-75 club finished 44-33-3, a third place finish in the competitive Western Division. The team was once again paced by Mike Walton (48 goals, 93 points), Wayne Connelly (38 goals) and George Morrison (31 goals). Mike Antonovich, Fran Huck and Don Tannahill all exceeded the 20-goal mark. The 1975 playoffs got off to a bizarre start as strongman Gord Gallant leveled coach Neale with a punch to the eye after the first game. The fan favorite and the WHA's leading penalty minute getter for the past two seasons was immediately suspended by the team. The Fighting Saints once again could go no further than the second round before elimination.

The 1975-76 Saints welcomed long-time Maple Leaf Dave Keon and ex-Blazer John McKenzie, adding to an already potent lineup. Five Saints were already past the 20-goal mark just 59 games into the season, and the team was coasting along at a comfortable 30-25-4 clip. Fan support was solid but not enough to cover the costs. The Saints were in a desperate financial situation, as some investors had pulled out of the team before the start of the season. Missed paychecks were common, and on February 27, 1976, the Fighting Saints conceded defeat and folded. The team simply could not meet its financial demands, and the loss proved to be a crushing blow to the WHA, which was still recovering from the loss of the Denver Spurs-Ottawa Civics franchise six weeks earlier.

Many of the 1975-76 squad found work elsewhere. Mike Antonovich, who was enjoying his best season to date before the collapse, signed with the North Stars but could only collect two assists in 12 games of NHL action. Dave Keon went to Indianapolis and helped the Racers to a surprising first place finish and a brief run through the playoffs. Coach Harry Neale moved onto New England.

In 1976, the Crusaders moved into the vacant St. Paul Civic Center after abandoning Cleveland. The second incarnation of the Fighting Saints were coached by Glen Sonmor and featured original Saints favorites Antonovich and Keon, but that team could barely last half the season before folding in mid-January, 1977.

New England Whalers

Howard Baldwin, who had been with the Philadelphia Flyers in various front-office roles since 1967, decided to set out on his own, and along with his friend John Coburn, convinced the WHA that Boston should be awarded a WHA franchise, with Baldwin and Coburn the nominal owners. The WHA awarded the rights to the Boston-area franchise to the two men on November 21, 1971. Neither Baldwin nor Coburn had the immediate means to launch the team, but they were savvy businessmen with a knack for finding investors. Soon, Robert Schmertz (eventual owner of the NBA's Boston Celtics) came on as the principal investor, and the new "New England Whalers" were taking shape, aiming to establish itself in a region devoted to the NHL's Bruins and a very strong collegiate hockey scene.

Baldwin hired Jack Kelley, long-time hockey coach at Boston University, to find players and coach. Rather than sign one or two big-name stars, Kelley concentrated on players buried on the various NHL squads, plus the abundance of players available from the many colleges surrounding Boston. The biggest name to jump from the NHL to sign with the Whalers was defenseman Ted Green, a Bruins star and member of the 1970 and 1972 Stanley Cup squads, who signed with New England in the summer of 1972. Meanwhile, Tom Webster was more than happy to leave the NHL's Seals to sign with New England. Goaltender Al Smith came to New England after sharing net duties for three seasons in Pittsburgh and Detroit. Led by Webster's offense, Green's defense, and Smith's puck-stopping, New England finished its inaugural season with the league's best record at 46-30-2, defeating Winnipeg in the playoffs for the first World Trophy. Webster led the team with 53 goals and 103 points, while rookie-of-the-year Terry Caffery scored 39 goals and 100 points. Former Canadien Larry Pleau chipped in 39 goals and Tim Sheehy had 33. Ted Green, Jim Dorey, Brad Selwood and Rick Ley formed the core of a very solid defense that changed very little over the first few years of the team.

The 1973-74 club again finished first in the East despite the loss of Terry Caffery to a damaged knee. Tom Webster scored 43 times to lead the club, but the Whalers were eliminated in the playoffs by the surging Chicago Cougars in the semifinals. Boston fans generally supported the Whalers, but sharing the Boston Garden with the Bruins and Celtics proved difficult for the Whalers, who were often stuck with the least-preferable playing dates. After having among the league's highest average attendance in 1972-73, the figures dropped significantly in 1973-74, by which time Baldwin and Schmertz were already looking for a new home. In 1974, the Whalers made plans to vacate Boston and settle in Hartford, Connecticut, at a brand-new arena that, for the moment, was without a prime tenant. The move was beneficial for everyone: the Whalers had Hartford to itself, and the city's many insurance corporations banded together to buy into the team, ensuring a strong financial foundation for years to come (Robert Schmertz unfortunately had fallen ill in the meantime and passed away in 1975). The arena would not be ready until January 1975. Until then, the Whalers played at the Eastern States Coliseum in Springfield, Massachusetts. The 1974-75 team played well, won first place in their division, but like the year before, could not get past the first round of the playoffs. In his first season as a Whaler, Wayne Carleton scored 35 goals and led the team with 74 points.

The Whalers would experience their worst WHA season in 1975-76, with just 73 points and a third-place finish. Tom Webster continued to play well, aided by Mike Rogers, obtained in a trade with Edmonton, and Ralph Backstrom, a refugee from the failed Denver-Ottawa franchise. However, the Whalers would enjoy an unlikely run through the 1976 playoffs, lasting two rounds, and almost single-handedly the result of strong goaltending from a minor-league call-up named Cap Raeder. Although he would never reach such heights again as a player, Raeder became a local legend for his three weeks of hard work in the spring of 1976.

The 1976-77 club finished fourth in the six-team Eastern Division and were bumped one round into the playoffs. Tom Webster's 36 goals and 85 points paced the club, while Mike Rogers was not far behind with 82 points on a team leading 57 assists. The principal midseason arrival was veteran Dave Keon, who was now playing for his fourth team in two years of WHA participation. Keon arrived as a result of the second passing of the Minnesota Fighting Saints in January 1977, and he responded with 39 points in 34 games as a Whaler. Fortunately for the center, New England would be his team for the remainder of his career, which would extend through 1982.

By 1977, Howard Baldwin had rose to the role of President of the WHA, and he was a principal figure in the merger negotiations between the WHA and the NHL. The Whalers were well supported by its fans in Hartford as well as being healthy financially and consistently one of the league's most stable franchises. There was no doubt that should the two leagues merge, the Whalers would be included into an expanded NHL. To help their case, the Whalers signed the Howe trio – father Gordie, sons Mark and Marty – in the summer of 1977. The Howes signed with New England specifically because of its stability and its healthy chances for admission into the NHL in the event of a merger. However, the 1977 merger plan failed. The Whalers, now with the Howes, geared up for another season as members of the WHA.

The 1977-78 Whalers started the year on a tear, winning fifteen of their first seventeen games, including thirteen games in a row. Tom Webster, their most consistent scorer since 1972 and who had 15 goals during the initial month, was lost for the season with a recurring back injury in November. From that point on, the Whalers played average hockey, winning and losing about equally often. The season took a bizarre turn when the roof of the Hartford Civic Center collapsed in January 1978, under the weight of heavy snow. This forced the team to relocate to Springfield for the remainder of the season (and through January 1980). Despite these dramas, the Whalers finished second in the league behind Winnipeg, and the two teams met in the final round for the Avco Cup, in which the Jets

prevailed. Gordie and Mark Howe lead the team in scoring, finishing first and second respectively.

Merger negotiations took place again in 1978, but failed. Once again, the Whalers convened to play another season in the WHA, which by now was reduced to seven teams, and would lose another one in a matter of months. The 1978-79 club finished fourth in the reduced six-team league. Mark Howe had a breakthrough season, setting club records with 65 assists and 107 points. Andre Lacroix arrived from Houston and chipped in 88 points, while former Birmingham Bull John Garrett shared net duties with Al Smith. The Whalers defeated Cincinnati in the playoffs before being eliminated in the semifinal round by Wayne Gretzky and the surging Edmonton Oilers.

New England became one of four WHA teams to be admitted to the NHL in 1979. Now known as the Hartford Whalers, they played at the enlarged Hartford Civic Center II arena. before moving south to Raleigh, North Carolina, becoming the Carolina Hurricanes in 1997. In 2006, the Hurricanes won the Stanley Cup, joining Quebec/Colorado as the only teams to win championships in the WHA and the NHL.

New York Raiders
New York Golden Blades
Jersey Knights
San Diego Mariners

New York was certain to receive a WHA franchise, given the city's size and media imprint. In early 1972, a new arena was being built in Nassau on Long Island, and the WHA hoped to place its team there. There was no intention to go directly into battle with the established Rangers, but New York and its suburbs were so big, it was reasonable to assume two New York teams could co-exist side by side.

The franchise rights went to Neal Shayne, a New York-based lawyer, in November 1971. Meanwhile, the Nassau Coliseum directors hired William Shea, who was best known for directing baseball's New York Mets to Flushing Meadows, New York in 1964 (and for whom the baseball stadium was named), to secure an NHL franchise for the new arena. The NHL obliged by granting two expansion teams to start play in Fall 1972. One would be based at the Nassau Coliseum, to be called the New York Islanders. Checkmated, Shayne sold out as soon as he could, to Dick Wood and Sy Siegel. The two new owners had no choice but to look downtown and wrangle a deal to play its games at Madison Square Garden, home of the Rangers. The WHA's New York team adopted the Raiders nickname.

Two teams in New York might have worked, but three almost certainly would not. The new Islanders outsold season tickets over the Raiders by a 4 to 1 margin. The 1972-73 season had yet to start, and the fans had aleady shown their allegiances. The "deal"

between the Raiders and Madison Square Garden was so rotten from the Raiders' standpoint, it was bound to sink the Raiders financially. The Raiders paid USD$15,000 per game to rent the Garden (By comparison, the Houston Aeros paid less than USD$1,000 per game to rent the Sam Houston Coliseum). By November 1972, Wood and Siegel were out, and the league took over the costs and operation of the team.

On the ice, the Raiders were a collection of NHL veterans and minor leaguers, coached by former Ranger Camille Henry. Ron Ward, formerly of the Vancouver Canucks for whom he scored two goals in 1971-72, erupted for 53 goals for the Raiders. The 6,000 fans who regularly attended Raider games saw lots of goals by the Raiders and just as many by the opposition. The Raiders defence consisted of older 1960s-era NHL defencemen who had lost a step or two since their hey-days. The Raiders scored and surrendered over 300 goals, the first team ever to achieve the feat. They finished last in the Eastern Division. In April 1973, the league found a buyer for the franchise, a group headed by Lee Matison, Jerry DeLise and Ralf Brent, to take over the team for the following season.

The new owners renamed the team the Golden Blades, crafted the worst-looking sweaters in WHA history, required the players to wear white skates, and reportedly squandered a part of their budget on a team song. But they were also working under the same rent arrangement with the Madison Square Garden as the Raiders had the year before. The new owners could not meet the team's first payroll, and the league immediately seized the team, and a few weeks later, gave up on New York and placed the team in Cherry Hill, New Jersey, to play out the season as the Jersey Knights. The Golden Blades-Knights team went a combined 32-42-4. Their lone highlight was Andre Lacroix, acquired when the Philadelphia team moved to Vancouver to start the season. Playing for the Blades and Knights, he scored 31 goals and 80 assists for 111 points. Wayne Rivers collected 30 goals, while long-time NHL defensive great Harry Howell played on the blue line as the player-coach. Despite the rough season, the franchise won a reprieve when Joseph Schwartz, a businessman based in Baltimore, purchased the team in January 1974. At season's end, he uprooted the team to San Diego, California, now doing business as the San Diego Mariners.

The San Diego Gulls were one of the more successful teams in the Western Hockey League between 1966 and 1974, often leading the league in attendance. Owner Bob Breitbard attempted to leverage this fact when applying for an NHL franchise in 1974. However, Vancouver-based Peter Graham, who owned the Sports Arena, worked a deal on his own with Schwartz in April 1974 to bring the WHA to his arena, nixing the NHL application. The Gulls were evicted, and the Western League folded that summer.

Hockey fans in San Diego were unhappy about the proceedings and were very skeptical of the Mariners when they first came to town.

At first, Schwartz was a savior, whose backing allowed the team to finally play without fear of extinction. The Mariners started the 1974-75 season playing break-even, but then gained steam after acquiring goaltender Ernie Wakely midway through the season. Andre Lacroix collected a record 106 assists, Wayne Rivers scored 54 goals, while Gene Peacosh and Dick Sentes joined Lacroix in the 40-goal club. The improved club finished second in the Western Division at 43-31-4, and went two rounds before losing to Houston in the playoffs.

The Mariners slipped to 36 wins in 1975-76. Lacroix collected 101 points and Ernie Wakely accounted for 35 of the team's 36 wins. Wayne Rivers dropped to 19 goals, but Ray Adduono picked up the slack with a 90-point season. However, Schwartz walked away from the team in March 1976, effectively folding the Mariners. The players voted to stay together and play out the schedule. Assuming they made the playoffs, they could recoup some lost pay through their playoff salaries, which were covered by the league. The Mariners lasted two rounds, then went into limbo, waiting to see if the team would be purchased or be folded. As late as June 1976, it appeared the Mariners had all but folded, but Ray Kroc, owner of the San Diego Padres of major League Baseball and of the McDonalds fast-food chain, stepped in at the last possible moment to assume control of the team. The Mariners would live to play for 1976-77.

The 1976-77 team played strongly for the first two-thirds, before enduring a 14-game winless string in February and March. The team finished 40-37-4 and played one round in the playoffs. Lacroix and Wakely were the two stars, with Joe Noris and his 92 points helping considerably. But Kroc's patronage would end very soon. He had grown sour on the Mariners operation well before the end of the season and planned to fold the team, but on May 1, 1977, he sold the team to Jerry Saperstein, heading a group of about a dozen investors, who planned to move the team to south Florida and play at the Sportatorium. The league, however, was already in heavy negotiations for merger with the NHL, and opted not to approve the sale. The Mariners were then returned to the league, which disbanded it.

Ottawa Nationals
Toronto Toros
Birmingham Bulls

The WHA granted a "regional" franchise on November 21, 1971, to be placed somewhere in Ontario Province. Doug Michel, a businessman with a background in construction, convinced the WHA to grant him the franchise while he would take care of finding a place to play. Hamilton was everyone's preferred

26

choice, but the city at the time did not have a major-league arena. Toronto was the next logical choice, and Michel negotiated—without success—with Maple Leafs owner Harold Ballard, for use of the Maple Leaf Gardens. Ballard was already an outspoken foe of the WHA but still heard Michel's case to place a WHA team in Toronto if for no other reason than to cut off a potential bid by another well-connected, wealthy Toronto family, the Bassetts, to bid for a Toronto-based WHA club. Ultimately, negotiations between Ballard and Michel waned, with Ballard's attentions being side-tracked by personal and legal troubles that would land him a spell in prison.

Ottawa became the franchise's home once Michel was able to wrangle a deal with the city to use the Ottawa Civic Centre Arena, which he did in February 1972. The Civic Centre was brand new and sat just over 10,000 people, but the populace did not exactly warm to Michel or the WHA when it was known that Ottawa was his third choice for a home site. With still nine months before the start of play, Michel faced an uphill battle to maintain funding, sign players and convince a skeptical Ottawa public that his team was for real. The new team was named the Nationals, a nod to Ottawa's status as the national capital and to Michel's previous role as co-founder of the amateur Young Nationals during the 1960s.

Spending most of his time and money searching for a home left Michel short on funds and the possibility of having to withdraw from the league if outside help could not be secured. Through league channels, Buffalo industrialist Nick Trbovich joined the team in May as a co-owner. Trbovich controlled the money, and Michel oversaw the operations, assembling it from scratch and hiring the coaching staff. A. J. "Buck" Houle signed on as the General Manager, and former player and Swedish Nationals coach Billy Harris assumed the same role with Ottawa. A few players were signed, but until Trbovich's role was solidified, none of the contract guarantees could be made until August 1972, at which time the Ottawa Nationals were presented to the public. Wayne Carleton and Les Binkley were the biggest names, the rest of the roster a collection of fringe NHLers, minor-league players, and amateurs from the college and Junior ranks.

Michel realized he needed to sign a big name to launch the new team, and to that end, he pursued Toronto's Dave Keon. Negotiations carried on for weeks during the summer of 1972, at times Keon virtually a National, and at other tames the parties back to square one. Ultimately, Keon used this as leverage to secure a better deal with the Maple Leafs, and the Nationals were back to where they were at the start of the summer: no star players and an Ottawa crowd thoroughly unimpressed.

The WHA debuted, playing its first game in Ottawa on October 11, 1972, the Nationals hosting the Alberta Oilers. The game was to be televised nationally across Canada, but the same luck that had dogged the Nationals appeared again. The arena was just half-filled, and a few minutes into the game, an electrical transformer blew, blacking out the broadcast. And the Nats lost the game. The Ottawa fans remained wary of this team, and the Nationals didn't help their cause by losing consistently, often to home crowds in the hundreds.

By early February 1973, the Nationals were playing down to everyone's expectations, sporting a 19-31-4 record and a tight hold on last place. Attendance was growing but still very low, and in January, the team was nearly sold to Marv Fishman, who would have uprooted the team immediately to Milwaukee, Wisconsin. The deal fell through and the team stayed in Ottawa, facing an even more skeptical audience. Then, the team caught fire. The Nats won 16 of their next 22 games to vault into a playoff berth, and for the first time, had developed a small but devoted following of fans in the Canadian Capital. Wayne Carleton led scorers with 42 goals and 91 points, Gavin Kirk was the best of the no-name rookies with 28 goals and 68 points, while Gilles Gratton won 25 games in goal.

While the public may have shown some belated affection for the Nationals, the city's government, especially the group that controlled the lease on the Civic Centre and the arena, did not. The city demanded a full payment of $100,000 on March 15, 1973 to secure dates for the following season, a steep sum and money that Michel and Trbovich weren't willing to pay. Particularly troubling to the owners was that while the Nationals could play out their 1972-73 home schedule at the Civic Centre, there was no guarantee they could play their home playoff games there unless they paid the money for the next season. Viewing this as a strong-arm tactic, Trbovich sent Michel down to Toronto to aggressively work a deal with the Maple Leaf Gardens, at the very least for its possible 1973 playoff dates. A deal was struck (helped by the fact the Maple Leafs missed the 1973 playoffs), and the team played its two home playoff games in Toronto. Almost immediately, the team was sold to John F. Bassett Jr, heading a group of over 20 investors. The team was relocated to Toronto in May 1973 and renamed the Toros.

Bassett housed the Toros at the University of Toronto's Varsity Arena during 1973-74, with selected games in Ottawa. More significantly, Bassett sought underage Junior players (younger than 20 years of age), signing them to small but attractive contracts and circumventing the league's self-imposed age restrictions. Bassett was unapologetic, reasoning that if an 18-year old man can vote and fight in wars, he can play hockey professionally. In 1973, he signed Wayne Dillon, who scored 30 goals for the 1973-74 Toros. Vet Wayne Carleton led with 37 goals, and seven other Toros scored at least 20 goals. The Toros finished second in the Eastern Division, lasting two rounds in the 1974 Playoffs.

The 1974-75 Toros added Frank Mahovlich and his 500 NHL career goals, 1972 Summit Series hero Paul Henderson, Czech defector Vaclav "Big Ned" Nedomansky, and youngster Pat Hickey to the attack, and the Toros finished second again, winning 43 games. Tom Simpson, an original National from 1972, broke through with 52 goals. Their 1975 Playoffs lasted just one round, bumped by San Diego. Toronto fans had embraced the team on a conditional basis, certainly not ready to abandon the Maple Leafs quite yet. Attendance for the Toros, now playing at the Maple Leaf Gardens, was above 10,000 per game, but the per-game rental fee demanded by Ballard was one of the highest in the league.

Bassett signed another youngster, Mark Napier, for the following season, and hired former Leaf great Bobby Baun to coach, but the bottom fell out from beneath the team in 1975-76. The Toros lost 52 games, endured a 17-game winless streak which cost Baun his job, and surrendered a league-record 398 goals. Toronto fans showed little support for the team and Bassett was already looking for greener pastures, a home rink where his team would be the principal tenant. In June 1976, Bassett uprooted the Toros, moved them south to Birmingham, Alabama, and rebranded them as the Bulls.

The 1976-77 Bulls performed better than the previous year's team, but missed the playoffs. Mark Napier potted 60 goals, Nedomansky 36 more, giving the team some footing in the Deep South. By summer 1977, the two leagues were discussing merger on a serious level, but the NHL was not interested in Birmingham, given the situation in Atlanta where the Flames were struggling. Bassett was ready to fold his club, but when merger failed, he reassembled the Bulls for the 1977-78 season. After a year off from raiding the Juniors, he signed two of note, Ken Linseman and Rod Langway, for 1977-78.

The 1977-78 Bulls started poorly, winning just twice in fourteen games. A wholesale change in the team's identity was needed. In early November, the Bulls unloaded Vaclav Nedomansky and Tim Sheehy to Detroit of the NHL in return for Dave "Killer" Hanson and Steve "Mental Case" Durbano. Frank "Seldom" Beaton was signed as a free agent, and the three new tough guys joined Gilles "Bad News" Bilodeau to form the core of the new Bulls, a team eager to hit, fight and brawl. Coached by Glen Sonmor, The Bulls became the villains of the league, setting numerous penalty-minute records (the top four individual slots were occupied by a Bull), and engaging in a few notorious incidences, including a line-brawl against Cincinnati on November 24, 1977 which occurred less than a minute into the game and resulted in the Bulls winning, 12-2.

The rough-house tactics worked, as the Bulls played above break-even for the remainder of the season. Scoring (and agitation) was led by Ken Linseman, who collected 38 goals and 76 points, Paul Henderson with 37 goals, and Mark Napier, who contributed 33 goals. John Garrett won 24 games in goal, and the team was rewarded with the last playoff position in the Eastern Division, where they lasted one round against Winnipeg. That series was notable for a brawl in which Dave Hanson inadvertently yanked off Bobby Hull's hairpiece during the scuffling. At the close of the 1978 season, Linseman and Langway had graduated to the NHL, to Philadelphia and Montreal, respectively.

To assemble a squad for the 1978-79 season, Bassett unabashedly raided the Juniors for six top-level players, collectively known as the Baby Bulls. Led by teenagers Rick Vaive, Michel Goulet, Louis Sleigher, Rob Ramage, Gaston Gingras and Pat Riggin, and their dependable veterans including Paul Henderson and goaltender Ernie Wakely, the 1978-79 Bulls played well, but not well enough to secure a playoff berth. Coached by legendary minor-league fighter John Brophy, the Bulls played hard but with restraint, not engaging in all-out brawls as in the previous season. Still, Vaive led the league in penalty minutes with 248, and Dave Hanson was fourth with 212. However, the fate of the Bulls was sealed in March 1979, when the NHL agreed to absorb four of the WHA teams the following season. The Bulls were not part of the merger, and were folded at the season's close, one of just five teams to endure for the entire seven-year run of the WHA.

Although the Bulls never had a winning record, their legacy lived on for many years, as many of the teenagers who once skated for Birmingham went on to illustrious careers in the NHL. Ken Linseman played many seasons in Philadelphia and later with Edmonton, winning the Stanley Cup in 1984. Rob Ramage would play for many teams, retiring in 1994 and the only former WHA player to play with a 1990s-era expansion team. Rick Vaive would score 50 goals in three successive seasons for Toronto in the 1980s, and a total of 441 goals in his NHL career. Gaston Gingras, Pat Riggin and Craig Hartsburg would all have lengthy and productive careers in the NHL.

However, two Bulls in particular deserve mention: Rod Langway (a member of the 1977-78 team) and Michel Goulet (a Baby Bull of 1978-79). Both had long and very productive careers in the NHL, and both were rewarded with induction into the Hockey Hall of Fame in Toronto, a lasting legacy of the short-lived Birmingham Bulls.

Philadelphia Blazers
Vancouver Blazers
Calgary Cowboys

Miami received a franchise in November 1971, part of an ambitious plan by the league to play its first game ever on national television from southern Florida. League co-founder Dennis Murphy had co-owned the Miami Floridians of the American Basketball Association in the early 1970s, and

through his influence, made sure Miami received a team, the recipient being Herb Martin, a local businessman and builder who then sought to win public funds to build a new arena (to be called the Executive Square Garden) to house the new team.

The Screaming Eagles moved fast, signing the first star-caliber player, Toronto goaltender Bernie Parent, as well as pursuing Boston Bruins' forward Derek Sanderson. These moves (and the flashy nickname) garnered the team and the league a little press during this time, but it soon became clear Martin could not pull off a new arena. The franchise quickly went moribund, losing its charter on April 28, 1972 after failing to post a required performance bond to the league.

In June 1972, the Philadelphia Blazers were born when businessmen Bernard Brown and James Cooper were granted the rights to the former Miami team. The new owners assumed Parent's contract and continued the pursuit of Sanderson, signing him to a $2.65 million contract, the largest contract of its time. For good measure, the Blazers signed another Bruin, John McKenzie, as a player-coach. The team would play its home games at the Philadelphia Civic Center, and attempt to lure fans away from the Flyers.

Despite the presence of Parent, Sanderson and McKenzie, the 1972-73 season started badly for Philadelphia. McKenzie injured himself in a pre-season game while Parent and Sanderson suffered injuries in the season's first three weeks. The first home game was cancelled when the Zamboni crashed through the ice. Derek Sanderson, already wondering what he had gotten himself into, announced the cancellation to the fans, and survived a barrage of commemorative orange pucks thrown his way. When the Blazers actually did play, they lost regularly, sporting a 4-16-0 record after six weeks.

The situation in Philadelphia was dire. No one was coming to the games and the team was bleeding money. When Brown learned of just how his money was being spent, Cooper was eased aside from his role. While Parent and McKenzie would return and play well for the team, Sanderson was another matter. He had injured his back early in the season, and tried to come back too quickly, re-injuring it. His large contract and his naturally outgoing—and sometimes confrontational—personality made him an easy target of fans who accused him of not trying hard enough, to put it kindly. Sanderson was openly unhappy, and he and the team's owners worked out a deal to cut their losses, release him, allowing him to return to Boston by the end of the 1972-73 season.

Remarkably, the Blazers began to win often. A healthy Bernie Parent played nearly every game in nets, McKenzie was solid as he had always been, but it was a surprising pair of forwards, Andre Lacroix and Danny Lawson, who carried the team. Lawson scored 61 goals to lead the league, turning many of Lacroix's passes into scores. Lacroix assisted on 74 goals and led the league with 124 points. The Blazers finished the season with a 34-24-0 run to make the playoffs. However, the magic ended fast when Parent walked out on the team after the first game of the playoffs, claiming the team had defaulted on his contract. The Blazers lost in the first round of the postseason, and abandoned Philadelphia immediately thereafter.

In May 1973, Brown sold the team to Canadian industrialist Jim Pattison, who moved the team to Vancouver. The move into Canada cost the Blazers the services of Lacroix, whose contract did not bind him to play for a Canadian-based team. Lacroix left for New York, but Danny Lawson continued to develop into a legitimate scoring star, while forwards Claude St. Sauveur and Bryan Campbell also served as very capable help. Nevertheless, the Blazers missed the playoffs both years in Vancouver. The Blazers actually drew quite well at the Pacific Coliseum, but an improving Canucks team was slowly phasing the Blazers out of town. In May 1975, owner Pattison relocated his club to Calgary, renamed the Cowboys, playing at the famous, but tiny, Stampede Corral.

The move seemed to do the trick for the new Cowboys, as they finished with their best record in four years of existence. Coached by Joe Crozier, and with ironman Don McLeod in the nets and 40-goal seasons from Lawson and Ron Chipperfield, the 1975-76 Cowboys finished 41-35-4, good for third place in the Canadian Division and a playoff spot. Calgary was able to defeat Quebec in the quarterfinals, but the Cowboys were themselves eliminated in the semifinals. The 1976-77 club finished a disappointing fifth place in the Western Division with a 31-43-7 record, including a miserable 5-31-5 road mark and a badly-timed ten-game losing streak in March that sunk any hopes of a playoff berth for 1977.

The future of the Cowboys in Calgary grew increasingly dim as the 1976-77 season drew to its close. The Stampede Corral was too small to support a major-league hockey team, and plans to erect a modern arena kept being pushed back. Fan support was usually strong, but even with sell-out crowds every night (which did not happen), the Cowboys would lose money playing at the Corral. The team was all-but-dead after the 1976-77 season closed, but did not formally close shop for a few more months.

A self-imposed deadline to achieve a certain number of season ticket sales by May 31, 1977, came and went without meeting the goal. Next on the horizon was the possible merger of the two leagues. Calgary was interested, but the NHL was not, and although Calgary was usually not mentioned as one of the six teams to be considered for acceptance into the NHL, they stayed in business (in the barest sense) to see how the vote would go. The NHL's vote took place August 9, 1977, and was against merger. For all intents, The Cowboys folded as of that date.

The modern Saddledome Arena would not be completed until the 1988 Olympics. In the meantime, the NHL moved the Atlanta Flames into the Stampede Corral beginning in 1980. By this time, the arena plans were certain, and the Flames could count on a modern arena in the future, something the Cowboys could not.

Phoenix Roadrunners

Phoenix had developed a solid reputation for supporting hockey after the Roadrunners arrived in 1967, members of the Western Hockey League. With its large winter-time population of "snowbirds" who migrate to Arizona from the colder climes, there was no shortage of hockey fans to adopt the 'runners as their team. The Roadrunners played seven seasons in the Western Hockey League, and won the 1972-73 and 1973-74 Patrick Cup as league champions. In September 1973, the WHA awarded one of its two expansion franchises to Phoenix, a group headed by William MacFarland and Karl Eller. The new WHA Roadrunners would begin play in 1974-75. There was a lot of continuity between the 1973-74 Western League club and the 1974-75 WHA edition. Sandy Hucul, who coached the Western League team, remained as coach, while nearly a dozen players on the 1974-75 club had played for Phoenix the previous season. This gave the expansion team a head-start, which would benefit the team immediately.

The first-year Roadrunners featured strong players at every position: Gary Kurt (from New Jersey) and Jack Norris (from Edmonton via Indianapolis) in goal, Bob Barlow (WHL Roadrunners) and all-star Gerry Odrowski (from Los Angeles) on defense, and forwards Michel Cormier, Murray Keogan (both of the WHL Roadrunners), Jim Boyd, John Gray (both of the CHL Oklahoma City Blazers), Dennis Sobchuk (on loan for the year from the Cincinnati Stingers) and Robbie Ftorek (late of NHL Detroit). The Roadrunners finished the first year with an impressive 39-31-8 record and a fourth place finish in the tough Western Division. Five players scored at least 30 goals, while Boyd and Don Borgeson helped out respectively with 26 and 29 goals each. Fourteen rookies played at least 50 games, the defense was third stingiest in the league with only 265 goals against, and coach Hucul was named Coach of the Year by the league. Despite the successful season, Phoenix lasted only one round in the playoffs, beaten in five games by the Quebec Nordiques.

The team experienced personnel changes over the summer of 1975, with Barlow retiring, Odrowski moving to Minnesota, and Sobchuk leaving for the Stingers. In their places, Garry Lariviere and Pekka Rautakallio took up the defensive slack, while new scorers Del Hall, Ron Huston and Gary Veneruzzo stepped in with strong seasons. Holdovers John Gray

(35 goals) and Jim Boyd (23) contributed well, while center Robbie Ftorek broke through with 41 goals and 72 assists for 113 points. Del Hall led all scorers with 47 goals. The second year club finished 39-35-4, good enough for second place and a playoff berth. Again, Phoenix could only last one round in the playoffs, bumped this time by San Diego. Sandy Hucul stepped down as coach at the season's close, replaced by general manager Al Rollins.

After two 39-win seasons, the 1976-77 Roadrunners ground to a 28-48-4 finish. Led by Ftorek's 117 points, the offense was respectable, scoring 281 goals, with a trio of former Finnish Olympians lending a helping hand. Seppo Repo, Lauri Mononen and Juha Tamminen combined for 60 goals while countryman Pekka Rautakallio led all defensemen with 35 points. Del Hall scored 38 goals, second to Ftorek's 46. However, the defense surrendered 383 goals to easily lead the league. Not surprisingly, the Roadrunners missed the playoffs. Robbie Ftorek provided the lone bright spot as he was awarded the 1976-77 Most Valuable Player trophy in honor of his superb season. Ftorek's victory (by one point in the balloting over Winnipeg's Anders Hedberg) represented the first time a United States born player was named the MVP of a major hockey league, and only the second instance in which a player from a last place team was so awarded. Coincidentally, the first was his coach, Al Rollins, who won the NHL's Hart Trophy in 1954 playing for the last-place Blackhawks.

The 1976-77 season proved to be very trying on the club financially. Attendance at the Veterans Memorial Coliseum was consistently light, and the club was losing nearly $2 million annually. Many of the club's top young prospects were traded away early during the 1976-77 season for immediate cash, contributing to the team's dismal record, and unfortunately not helping the financial picture significantly as the team continued to lose money. Finally in March 1977, principal owner Eller announced that the Roadrunners would fold immediately on the season's end. The lame-duck Roadrunners played out the schedule, winning their final game on April 6, 1977, a 7-3 victory at home over the Indianapolis Racers.

Center Robbie Ftorek moved to Cincinnati for the remaining two years of the league's operation and later played with Quebec and the New York Rangers in the NHL. No other Roadrunner went on to great success, although many did play in the National Hockey League for varying periods of time.

Between 1977 and 1996, the Roadrunners were resurrected a handful of times. In fall 1977, the Roadrunners lasted just 27 games in the Central League before folding, then reforming a month later, now in the low-rent Pacific League, where they lasted for two seasons. From 1989 to 1997, the Roadrunners played in the International League as the top minor-league affiliate of the Los Angeles Kings. In

1996, the Winnipeg Jets relocated to Phoenix, renamed the Coyotes, and the two teams co-existed for one season. However, unlike their cartoon counterparts, the Coyotes won this battle, easing the Roadrunners from the scene after 1997.

Québec Nordiques

The Quebec Nordiques were one of the strongest teams, both on the ice and financially, during the seven-year run of the WHA. They featured high-powered offense, regularly finished at the top of the standings, and even won a championship, capturing the crown in 1977. For their efforts, the Nordiques were admitted into the NHL when the two leagues merged in 1979.

When the WHA was seeking owners for its teams in 1971, Quebec was immediately interested. A group of businessmen, some who owned the Junior Quebec Remparts, formed together to garner a team for Quebec City. The group took a little while to get its finances in order and to win over city officials. To this end, the Honorable Jean Lesage, former Premier of Quebec Province, came aboard as a co-owner.

In the meantime, the WHA liked what they saw in Quebec, but could not immediately grant a franchise to the group. Thus, in November 1971, Gary Davidson awarded himself a team, ostensibly to be based in San Francisco, California. Given how badly the NHL Seals were doing in the Bay Area, there was no realistic chance that another major-league hockey team would encounter success there. Davidson held the team until the Quebec group was ready. In February 1972, the franchise rights were awarded to this group, and Quebec now had a team. Paul Racine and Jean Dacres were the principals of the ownership team, and the new Nordiques would play its home games at Le Colisee, a return of major-league hockey to Quebec after an absence of 50 years.

The Nordiques actively sought players of French-Canadian background, scouting the Quebec Junior ranks for talent, as well as seeing what was available in the minor-pro circuits and the NHL. Most of the first-year team were relative unknowns, except for one: former Montreal Canadien great, J.-C. Tremblay. For the next seven years, Tremblay would be the face of the franchise, a perennial all-star, and the focus around which the team would build. Another former Canadien great, Maurice "Rocket" Richard, was hired to coach the 1972-73 squad.

The team was well-received by Quebec fans. The Nordiques lost their first game ever, a road loss in Cleveland, then came home to a sell-out crowd and defeated Alberta. And that was the end of Richard's tenure as coach. He resigned immediately following the game, citing his discomfort in the role. General Manager Maurice Filion stepped in and assumed the duties. The first-year Nordiques finished 33-40-5, but in fifth place and out of the playoffs. Not surprisingly, J.-C. Tremblay was the team's star, leading the team in assists (75) and points (89). Winger Alain "Boom Boom" Caron led the team in goals with 36.

Another former Montreal great, Jacques Plante, joined the Nordiques in 1973-74, to be the team's head coach. This was Plante's first (and only) head coaching job, having retired as a player just a few months earlier. Up front, Serge Bernier signed from Los Angeles (NHL) led the team with 37 goals and 86 points, with Caron and Bob Guindon scoring 31 goals apiece. The Nordiques improved to 38-36-4, but frustratingly, missed the playoffs once again. Plante hadn't exactly taken to the coaching role, sometimes being absent from the team, where Maurice Filion would again step in to coach. After the season's end, Plante stepped down as coach and would return as a player in 1974-75, tending goal for the Edmonton Oilers. Former player Jean-Guy Gendron was hired to coach for the 1974-75 season.

The Nordiques started strong in 1974-75, with Rejean Houle (formerly of Montreal) being the most recognizable new face, but a pair of trades made in early December of 1974 would set the tone for this season and those to follow. First, the Nordiques traded for Christian Bordeleau, trading defenseman Alain Beaule to Winnipeg, then a couple days later, acquired Marc Tardif from Michigan for Alain Caron. Immediately, the offense exploded, and the Nordiques coasted to a 46-win season, a first-place finish, and an eventual berth in the AVCO Cup championship round, where they ultimately lost to Houston. Bernier scored 54 goals, Houle 40, and Tardif 38 (and 50 for the season counting his Michigan totals). Michel Parizeau contributed 28 goals, and a rookie, Real "Buddy" Cloutier, added 26. Despite the loss to Houston in the AVCO Cup Finals, the Nordiques were highly optimistic heading into 1975-76.

The high-powered Nordiques of 1975-76 featured five 100-point performers who paced the offense to a record 371 goals for the season. Led by Marc Tardif (71 g, 148 pts), Real Cloutier (60 g, 114 pts), Christian Bordeleau (37 g, 109 pts), Rejean Houle (51 g, 103 pts) and Serge Bernier (34 g, 102 pts), the Nordiques breezed to a 50-27-4 mark, although it was only good enough for second place behind the Winnipeg Jets. Goaltender Richard Brodeur posted a 3.69 average, winning 44 games backing up a defense that was not particularly defensive. The Nordiques were quite literally bumped from the 1976 playoffs in the first round by Calgary. The Cowboys' Rick Jodzio checked the Nordiques' Marc Tardif with a strike to the head that put the Quebec star out of the playoffs and into the hospital. After the tremendous brawl that ensued, the shaken and leaderless Nordiques were dismissed by Calgary in five games.

The Nordiques finally broke through in 1976-77 when they posted a 47-31-3 mark and a first place finish in the Eastern Division under new coach Marc Boileau. Real Cloutier's 66 goals, 141 point season led the Nordiques, and Marc Tardif returned from his head injuries to score 49 goals in 62 games. Christian Bordeleau (107 pts), his brother Paulin Bordeleau (42 goals) and Serge Bernier (43 goals) rounded out the offense. The healthy and hungry Nordiques eliminated New England and Indianapolis in the playoffs before squaring off against Winnipeg for the AVCO Cup. In the only championship series to go the full seven games, the Nordiques outlasted the Jets to capture their first and only championship. Serge Bernier emerged as the scoring star of the playoffs, scoring 36 points on 14 goals and 22 assists. Real Cloutier also scored 14 goals.

The 1977-78 and 1978-79 editions were moderately successful, but a generous defense prevented the Nordiques from duplicating their 1977 championship form. Marc Tardif set a league record in 1978 with 154 points, and Real Cloutier continued to score piles of goals, but the Nordiques were eliminated early in both the 1978 and 1979 playoffs.

The Nordiques were clearly one of the WHA's strongest and better supported teams during the seven year life of the league, and indeed the Nordiques were considered every time the two leagues discussed merger during 1977-79. Quebec's home arena, Le Colisee, proved to be a sticking point in the talks, as its capacity was below that mandated by the NHL. The Nordiques, however, could guarantee improvements to the site in the event of admittance into the NHL. In 1976, the O'Keefe Breweries bought into the Nordiques, ensuring the team a strong financial base. The fact that the Nordiques was owned by a beer company proved to be pivotal in the 1979 merger negotiations. When merger was once again voted down by the NHL in early March 1979, one of the teams voting against merger was the Montreal Canadiens, owned by the Molson Breweries. The Nordiques viewed the Canadiens' veto as a direct insult, and supporters of the Nordiques, as well as fans in Edmonton, Winnipeg and other parts of Canada, staged a beer strike against Molson Breweries in a show of solidarity against the Montreal "no" vote. Whether consumption of Molson Brewery products went down is debatable, but the public relations fiasco was plainly obvious. When another merger vote by the NHL was held on March 22, 1979, the Canadiens had changed their vote to "yes," and it was instrumental in passing the merger for 1979-80. The Nordiques were admitted to the NHL as an expansion franchise for the 1979-80 season.

The Nordiques played in Quebec through the 1994-95 season, but the economics of hockey in the 1990s—and the nearly-obsolete Le Colisee—prompted the team to relocate to Denver, Colorado that summer. In Denver, the new Avalanche won the Stanley Cup in 1996 and again in 2001. Quebec's hopes for a new NHL team have risen in recent years with the construction of the new Centre Videotron arena, completed in September 2015, with a group committed to securing an expansion franchise in the coming years.

Winnipeg Jets

The Winnipeg Jets were one of the original twelve franchises, and awarded to a group led by Ben Hatskin and David Simkin. Hatskin, like his counterpart Bill Hunter in Edmonton, was a big thinker and not afraid of jumping in head-first to create interest in his team and the new league.

Hatskin selected Chicago Blackhawks' star Bobby Hull as a priority draftee in 1971, although at the time, winning over the game's most visible superstar seemed like wishful thinking at best, folly at worst. However, Hull was interested. Although Hull was the highest paid player in the NHL in 1971-72 with a salary just over $100,000 per year, he was tiring of the annual contract negotiations with Blackhawk management that seemed to grow bitter in recent years. Hull's exasperation with Chicago management was evident by the simple fact that he listened to what Hatskin, Winnipeg and the WHA had to offer. Apparently impressed by the earnestness of Hatskin, Hull was ready to sign with the Jets as long as they could produce the money to sign him. When it became apparent that Hull was heeding Winnipeg's advances, the WHA, excited that the NHL's second all-time leading goal scorer might actually defect to its operation, stepped in on behalf of Winnipeg and helped negotiate the $1 million signing bonus, a sum to which all twelve WHA clubs contributed. Hull made his jump official when he signed his Winnipeg contract on June 27, 1972, thus severing his ties to the NHL and giving the WHA the bedrock of legitimacy it so desperately needed.

Court injunctions kept Hull on the sidelines until mid-November, but when he returned, he was a man on fire, scoring 51 goals and 103 in his abbreviated season. With center Christian Bordeleau and right-winger Norm Beaudin, the threesome formed a powerful line, each collecting 100 or more points, leading the Jets to 43 victories and a first-place finish in the Western Division. In the playoffs, the Jets went as far as the finals, losing to New England in five games.

The 1973-74 club didn't fare as well. With essentially the same team as the year before, the Jets won 9 fewer games and were swept in the opening round of the 1974 Playoffs. The rest of the league had caught up to the Jets' act, and realized that shutting down the Jets top line was sufficient to shut down the whole team. To correct this, the Jets got creative and scouted Europe for its talent. In doing so, the Jets would be the first North American major-league hockey team to actively pursue European players,

forever changing the style and the philosophy of the game. The Jets signed Swedes Anders Hedberg, Ulf Nilsson, Lars-Erik Sjoberg and Curt Larsson, and Finns Heikki Riihiranta and Veli-Pekka Ketola, and all contributed well for the 1974-75 club that improved to 38-35-5 and third place in the new Canadian Division. Bobby Hull scored a league-record 77 goals, including 50 in the first 50 games, equaling Rocket Richard's feat from 1944-45. Ironically, despite the improvements, the Jets failed to qualify for the 1975 Playoffs, the only season in their seven years in the WHA the Jets would stay home in April.

For the remaining four seasons, the Jets would be the class of the WHA. Bobby Hull gave up on his coaching duties, with Bobby Kromm now assuming the role. Willy Lindstrom and Mats Lindh joined in 1975-76, and the high-powered Jets won 52 games that season. Both Hull and Hedberg scored 50 or more goals, while linemate Nilsson joined the other two as 100-point producers. In the 1976 Playoffs, the Jets took apart all challengers and defeated defending champ Houston in four straight in the final round, securing their first Avco Cup Championship.

The 1976-77 club fared well, but lost Bobby Hull for half the season as he suffered a broken wrist early in the year. Anders Hedberg scored 70 goals, including 51 in the Jets' first 49 games. The Jets had no trouble with the rest of the league, and went as far as the final round. However, an inspired Quebec Nordiques club bested the Jets in seven games for the 1977 crown, arguably the best final round in the league's history.

The Jets spent December 1976 participating in the Izvestia Tournament in Moscow, the first North American team to take part in the USSR's most prestigious hockey tournament. It would be the start of a series of visits between teams from the WHA to Europe, and teams from Europe playing in North America. The Jets did not fare well in the Izvestia Tournament. Promised a few extra quality players from the other WHA clubs, they got none, and the travel and extra time for what was essentially an exhibition series wore on the Jets. In their first game back from Europe, the Jets were pounded 12-3 by Quebec. Bobby Kromm left the team upon the season's end.

The 1977-78 team might have been the best Jets team of the WHA. The Hull-Nilsson-Hedberg "Hot Line" produced hundred-point seasons for each, and a deep supporting cast included Willy Lindstrom (30 goals) and Kent Nilsson (42 goals, 107 points). Coached now by Larry Hillman, the Jets scored a league-record 381 goals and reeled off winning streaks of 11 and 15 games to run away with the league's best record. In the playoffs, the Jets put aside New England in five games to win the 1978 crown and their second in three years. Unfortunately for Winnipeg fans, Anders Hedberg and Ulf Nilsson signed to play for the New York Rangers the following season.

In July 1978, the Jets essentially merged with the Houston Aeros franchise, purchasing thirteen players including Morris Lukowich, Terry Ruskowski, Rich Preston and Scott Campbell. These quality players would help balance the loss of Ulf Nilsson and Anders Hedberg, and after just a few games into the 1978-79 season, the loss of Bobby Hull, who decided to retire. Not unsurprisingly, the "Aero-Jets" took time to meld into a cohesive unit, winning and losing games equally often. Other players stepped up: Lukowich (65 goals), Preston and Ruskowski had strong seasons, as did Kent Nilsson (107 points) and Peter Sullivan, who broke through for 46 goals. Late in the season, Tom McVie took over as coach, and the Jets signed veteran netminder Gary Smith from the failed Indianapolis club. The changes seemed to give the Jets some spark, and the team finished strongly, with 39 wins and third place. In the 1979 playoffs, the exciting Edmonton Oilers seemed to have the inside track on the championship, but the Jets channeled their winning knowledge, as well as that of the Aeros, to outplay the Oilers, and win their third Avco Cup, the last the league would offer.

The Jets had strong community support, but struggled financially at times, the situation direst in 1974 when it appeared the team might fold. That summer, a "Save the Jets" campaign allowed for individuals to buy shares for as low as $25 to own part of the team. The revenue helped keep the Jets solvent, and in February 1978, the Jets were purchased by Hockey 8 Ventures, a consortium of eight men led by Barry Shenkarow, Bob Graham and Michael Gobuty, and including Bobby Hull.

In 1979, the Jets entered the NHL along with Edmonton, New England and Quebec. At first, the Jets performed poorly, including a 9-win season in 1980-81, but in time, built a strong club led by Dale Hawerchuk that made the Jets competitive, albeit with a frustrating tendency to lose in the first round of the Stanley Cup Playoffs every year. In 1996, the Jets left Winnipeg and relocated to Phoenix, Arizona, becoming the Coyotes. The NHL would not return to Winnipeg until 2011, when the Atlanta Thrashers transferred and assumed the Jets nickname.

The World Hockey Association

Gary Davidson

Dennis Murphy

James Browitt

Norman "Bud" Poile

Larry Gordon

Edward Fitkin

Donald Regan

Lee Meade

Frank Polnaszek

Walt Marlow

Alberta Oilers • Edmonton Oilers

year	record	points	finish
1972-73:	38-37-3	79 pts	4th (tie), Western
1973-74:	38-37-3	79 pts	3rd, Western
1974-75:	36-38-4	76 pts	5th, Canadian
1975-76:	27-49-5	59 pts	4th, Canadian
1976-77:	34-43-4	72 pts	4th, Western
1977-78:	38-39-3	79 pts	5th, League
1978-79:	48-30-2	98 pts	1st, League

Home Rinks: Edmonton Gardens (5,200, 1972-74); Edmonton Coliseum (15,513-17,000, 1974-79). **Colors:** Royal Blue, Orange, White. **Formation:** November 1, 1971. **Dissolution:** None, entered NHL 1979. **Ownerships:** Dr. Charles Allard, Zane Feldman, Bill Hunter (1972-76); Nelson Skalbania, Mitch Klimove (1976-77); Peter Pocklington (1977-1990s). **General Managers:** Bill Hunter (1972-76), Armand Guidolin (1976-77), Brian Conacher (1977-78), Larry Gordon (1978-79). **Coaches:** Ray Kinasewich (1972-73), Bill Hunter (1973, 1975, 1976), Brian Shaw (1973-75), Clare Drake (1975-76), Armand Guidolin (1976-77), Glen Sather (1977-79).

Longest Streaks

Winning: 11, October 21 to November 13, 1973; **Undefeated:** 13 (12-0-1), February 6 to March 3, 1979; **Losing & Winless:** 9, December 19, 1975 to January 4, 1976.

Statistical Leaders

Season: Goals: 43, Wayne Gretzky (1978-79); **Assists:** 61, Wayne Gretzky (1978-79); **Points:** 104, Wayne Gretzky (1978-79); **Penalty minutes:** 274, Frank Beaton (1976-77); **Wins:** 41, Dave Dryden (1978-79); **Shutouts:** 4, Ken Broderick (1976-77); **Goals against average:** 2.89, Dave Dryden (1978-79).

All time: Games: 454, Al Hamilton (1972-79); **Goals:** 136, Rusty Patenaude (1972-77); **Assists:** 258, Al Hamilton (1972-79); **Points:** 311, Al Hamilton (1972-79); **Penalty minutes:** 620, Doug Barrie (1972-77); **Wins:** 94, Dave Dryden (1975-79); **Shutouts:** 7, Dave Dryden (1975-79); **Goals against average:** 3.13, Jack Norris (1972-74).

Dr. Charles Allard

Zane Feldman

Bill Hunter

Peter Pocklington

Chicago Cougars

year	record	points	finish
1972-73:	26-50-2	54 pts	6th, Eastern
1973-74:	38-35-5	81 pts	4th, Eastern
1974-75:	30-47-1	61 pts	3rd, Eastern

Home Rinks: International Amphitheater (9,000); Randhurst Twin Ice Arena (3,000, 1974 playoffs selected dates). **Colors:** Dark Green, Gold, White. **Formation:** November 1, 1971. **Dissolution:** May 19, 1975 (most of team chosen by Denver in expansion draft); June 19, 1975 (formal dissolution). **Ownerships:** John Tierney (1971), H. Anderson, A. J. Syke (1971), John Ladner (1971-72), Jordon H. Kaiser, Walter Kaiser (1972-74); Ralph Backstrom, Dave Dryden, Pat Stapleton, Jeff Rosen (1974-75). **General Managers:** Edwin Short (1972), Walter Kaiser (1972-74), Jacques Demers (Director of Player Personnel (1973-75). **Coaches:** Marcel Pronovost (1972-73), Pat Stapleton (1973-75, player-coach. Jacques Demers was bench coach).

Longest Streaks

Winning & Undefeated: 6, October 25 to November 10, 1973, and March 7 to March 17, 1974; **Losing & Winless:** 7, November 1 to November 17, 1972; December 30, 1972 to January 18, 1973; March 22 to April 1, 1973; November 24 to December 11, 1973.

Statistical Leaders

Season: Goals: 42, Gary MacGregor (1974-75); **Assists:** 63, Bob Sicinski (1972-73); **Points:** 88, Bob Sicinski (1972-73); **Penalty minutes:** 157, Larry Mavety (1973-74); **Wins:** 25, Cam Newton (1973-74); **Shutouts:** 1, Jim McLeod (1972-73), Cam Newton (1973-74), Dave Dryden (1974-75); **Goals against average:** 3.14, Cam Newton (1973-74).

All-time: Games: 234, Rosaire Paiement (1972-75); **Goals:** 89, Rosaire Paiement (1972-75); **Assists:** 127, Rosaire Paiement (1972-75); **Points:** 216, Rosaire Paiement (1972-75); **Penalty minutes:** 356, Larry Mavety (1972-75); **Wins:** 37, Cam Newton (1973-75); **Shutouts:** 1, Jim McLeod (1972-73), Cam Newton (1973-74), Dave Dryden (1974-75); **Goals against average:** 3.32, Jim McLeod (1972-73).

Jordon Kaiser

Walter Kaiser

Cincinnati Stingers

year	record	points	finish
1975-76:	35-44-1	71 pts	4th, Eastern
1976-77:	39-37-5	83 pts	2nd, Eastern
1977-78:	35-42-3	73 pts	7th, League
1978-79:	33-41-6	72 pts	5th, League

Home Rink: Riverfront Coliseum (15,820); **Colors:** Yellow, Black, White; **Formation:** May 6, 1973; **Dissolution:** June 13, 1979; **Ownerships:** William DeWitt Jr, Brian Heekin + others; **General Managers:** Jerry Rafter (Director Player Personnel 1975-78), Floyd Smith (1978-79); **Coaches:** Terry Slater (1975-77), Jacques Demers (1977-78), Floyd Smith (1978-79).

Longest Streaks

Winning & Undefeated: 7, February 13 to February 25, 1976; **Losing:** 8, November 16 to November 29, 1975; **Winless:** 8 (0-8-0), November 16 to November 29, 1975; (0-6-2), December 5 to December 20, 1976.

Statistical Leaders

Season: Goals: 59, Robbie Ftorek (1977-78); **Assists:** 77, Robbie Ftorek (1978-79); **Points:** 116, Robbie Ftorek (1978-79); **Penalty Minutes:** 241, Paul Stewart (1977-78); **Wins:** 23, Mike Liut (1978-79); **Shutouts:** 4, Michel Dion (1977-78); **Goals against average:** 3.32, Michel Dion (1978-79), 2.83, Jacques Caron (1976-77, 24 games played).

All-time: Games: 270, Rick Dudley (1975-79); **Goals:** 131, Rick Dudley (1975-79); **Assists:** 146, Rick Dudley (1975-79); **Points:** 278, Rick Dudley (1975-79); **Penalty Minutes:** 516, Rick Dudley (1975-79); **Wins:** 31, Mike Liut (1977-79), Michel Dion (1977-79); **Shutouts:** 4, Michel Dion (1977-79); **Goals against average:** 3.46, Michel Dion (1977-79).

Bill DeWitt, Jr.   Brian Heekin

Cleveland Crusaders
Minnesota Fighting Saints II

year	record	points	finish
1972-73:	43-32-3	89 pts	2nd, Eastern
1973-74:	37-32-9	83 pts	3rd, Eastern
1974-75:	35-40-3	73 pts	2nd, Eastern
1975-76:	35-40-5	75 pts	2nd, Eastern
1976-77:	19-18-5	43 pts	folded

Home Rinks: Cleveland Arena (9,847, 1972-74); The Coliseum (Richfield OH, 19,861, 1974-76); St. Paul Civic Center (15,705, 1976-77); **Colors:** Purple, Black, White (Cleveland); Scarlet, Gold, White (Minnesota); **Formation:** November 1, 1971 (Calgary); June 21, 1972 (Cleveland); June 1976 (transfer to Minnesota); **Dissolution:** April 28, 1972 (Calgary); June 1976 (Cleveland); January 17, 1977 (Minnesota); **Ownerships:** Robert Brownridge (Calgary, 1971-72), Nick Mileti (Cleveland, 1972-75), Jay Moore (1975-76), Nick Mileti, Robert Brown (1976-77); **General Managers:** Scotty Munro (1971-72), Chuck Catto (Director of Player Personnel 1972-73), Jack Vivian (1973-76), Glen Sonmor (1976-77); **Coaches:** Bill Needham (1972-74), John Hanna (1974-75), Jack Vivian (1975), John Wilson (1975-76), Glen Sonmor (1976-77).

Longest Streaks

Winning: 6, December 21, 1972 to January 11, 1973; **Undefeated:** 6 (6-0-0), December 21, 1972 to January 11, 1973, and 5-0-1, November 20 to November 28, 1976; **Losing:** 6, December 10 to December 19, 1974; **Winless:** 7 (0-5-2), October 28 to November 11, 1976.

Statistical Leaders

Season: Goals: 40, Gary Jarrett (1972-73); **Assists:** 50, Ron Ward (1975-76); **Points:** 82, Ron Ward (1975-76); **Penalty Minutes:** 201, Baxter (1975-76); **Wins:** 32, Gerry Cheevers (1972-73); **Shutouts:** 5, Gerry Cheevers (1972-73); **Goals against average:** 2.84, Gerry Cheevers (1972-73).

All-time: Games: 304, Gerry Pinder (1972-76); **Goals:** 104, Gary Jarrett (1972-76); **Assists:** 132, Paul Shmyr (1972-76); **Points:** 222, Gary Jarrett (1972-76); **Penalty Minutes:** 538, Paul Shmyr (1972-76); **Wins:** 99, Gerry Cheevers (1972-76); **Shutouts:** 14, Gerry Cheevers (1972-76); **Goals against average:** 3.12, Gerry Cheevers (1972-76).

Nick Mileti   Jay Moore

Bob Brown

Denver Spurs
Ottawa Civics

year	record	points	finish
1975-76:	14-26-1	29 pts	folded

Home Rinks: McNichols Arena (16,800, 1975); Ottawa Civic Centre (10,500, 1976); **Colors:** Orange, Gold, Black, White; **Formation:** May 19, 1975 (Denver); January 2, 1976 (transfer to Ottawa); **Dissolution:** January 17, 1976; **Ownership:** Ivan Mullenix; **General Manager:** Jean-Guy Talbot; **Coach:** Jean-Guy Talbot.

Longest Streaks

Winning & Undefeated: 3, October 17 to October 22, 1975; **Losing:** 4, November 6 to November 13, 1975; December 23 to December 28, 1975, and January 7 to January 15, 1976; **Winless:** 8 (0-7-1), October 24 to November 13, 1975.

Statistical Leaders

Season and All-time: Games: 41, Ralph Backstrom, Bryon Baltimore, Larry Bignell, Darryl Maggs, Francois Rochon; **Goals:** 21, Ralph Backstrom, Don Borgeson; **Assists:** 29, Ralph Backstrom; **Points:** 50, Ralph Backstrom; **Penalty Minutes:** 58, Rick Morris; **Wins:** 8, Bob Johnson; **Shutouts:** 1, Cam Newton; **Goals against average:** 3.66, Cam Newton.

Ivan Mullenix

Houston Aeros

year	record	points	finish
1972-73:	39-35-4	82 pts	2nd, Western
1973-74:	48-25-5	101 pts	1st, Western
1974-75:	53-25-0	106 pts	1st, Western
1975-76:	53-27-0	106 pts	1st, Western
1976-77:	50-24-6	106 pts	1st, Western
1977-78:	42-34-4	88 pts	3rd, League

AVCO Cup Champions: 1974, 1975

Home Rinks: Sam Houston Coliseum (9,300, 1972-75); The Summit (14,906, 1975-78); **Colors:** Dark Blue, Powder Blue, White; **Formation:** November 1, 1971 (Dayton OH); April 15, 1972 (transfer to Houston); **Dissolution:** July 6, 1978; **Ownerships:** Paul Deneau, Jim Smith (1972-74), Irv Kaplan (1974-75), George Bolin (1975-77), Harrison Vickers, Ken Schnitzer (1977-78); **General Manager:** Bill Dineen; **Coach:** Bill Dineen

Longest Streaks

Winning & Undefeated: 9, January 14 to February 1, 1977; **Losing:** 4, December 3 to December 8, 1972; October 18 to October 23, 1974; December 5 to December 11, 1976; May 20 to May 27, 1976 (AVCO Cup Finals); January 4 to January 8, 1978; February 4 to March 1, 1978; **Winless:** 6 (0-4-2), November 26 to December 11, 1976.

Statistical Leaders

Season: Goals: 48, Frank Hughes (1974-75); **Assists:** 77, Andre Lacroix (1977-78); **Points:** 113, Andre Lacroix (1977-78); **Penalty Minutes:** 239, John Schella (1972-73); **Wins:** 39, Ron Grahame (1974-75); **Shutouts:** 4, Ron Grahame (1974-75, 1976-77); **Goals against average:** 2.56, Don McLeod (1973-74).

All-time: Games: 468, Poul Popiel (1972-78); **Goals:** 149, Larry Lund (1972-78), Frank Hughes (1972-78); **Assists:** 277, Larry Lund (1972-78); **Points:** 426, Larry Lund (1972-78); **Penalty Minutes:** 844, John Schella (1972-78); **Wins:** 102, Ron Grahame (1974-77); **Shutouts:** 12, Ron Grahame (1974-77); **Goals against average:** 2.99, Ron Grahame (1974-77).

Paul Deneau

Jim Smith

George Bolin

Harrison Vickers

Indianapolis Racers

year	record	points	finish
1974-75:	18-57-3	39 pts	4th, Eastern
1975-76:	35-39-6	76 pts	1st, Eastern
1976-77:	36-37-8	80 pts	3rd, Eastern
1977-78:	24-51-5	53 pts	8th, League
1978-79:	5-18-2	12 pts	folded

Home Rink: Market Square Arena (16,500); **Colors:** Red, Blue, White; **Formation:** September 14, 1973; **Dissolution:** December 15, 1978; **Ownerships:** Richard Tinkham Jr., John Weissert (1973-74), Paul Deneau (1974-76), Harold DuCote & others (1976-77), Nelson Skalbania & others (1977-78); **General Managers:** Chuck Catto (Director of Player Personnel, 1974), James Browitt (1974-76), Brian Conacher (1976-77), Ron Ingram (1977-78), Pat Stapleton (1978); **Coaches:** Gerry Moore (1974-75), Jacques Demers (1975-77), Ron Ingram (1977-78), Bill Goldsworthy (1978, player-coach. Rosaire Paiement was bench coach), Pat Stapleton (1978).

Longest Streaks

Winning: 6, November 14 to November 24, 1976, and November 27 to December 10, 1976; **Undefeated:** 10 (7-0-3), March 11 to March 28, 1976 (the streak included three consecutive tie games, a league record); **Losing & Winless:** 13, November 13 to December 7, 1974 (The 13-game losing streak is the league record).

Statistical Leaders

Season: Goals: 36, Claude St. Sauveur (1977-78); **Assists:** 55, Darryl Maggs (1976-77); **Points:** 78, Claude St. Sauveur (1977-78); **Penalty Minutes:** 351, Kim Clackson (1975-76); **Wins:** 17, Michel Dion (1976-77); **Shutouts:** 2, Andy Brown (1974-75); **Goals against average:** 2.74, Michel Dion (1975-76).

All-time: Games: 267, Ken Block (1974-78); **Goals:** 63, Reg Thomas (1975-78); **Assists:** 92, Bob Sicinski (1974-77); **Points:** 136, Michel Parizeau (1976-78); **Penalty Minutes:** 519, Kim Clackson (1975-77); **Wins:** 31, Michel Dion (1975-77); **Shutouts:** 3, Andy Brown (1974-76); **Goals Against Average:** 3.10, Michel Dion (1975-77)

John Weissert

Paul Deneau

Nelson Skalbania

Los Angeles Sharks • Michigan Stags
Baltimore Blades

year	record	points	finish
1972-73:	37-35-6	80 pts	3rd, Western
1973-74:	25-53-0	50 pts	6th, Western
1974-75:	21-53-4	46 pts	6th, Western

Home Rinks: Los Angeles Sports Arena (14,700, 1972-74); Long Beach Arena (11,325, Selected dates during 1972-73); Cobo (Detroit) Hall (10,200, 1974-75); Baltimore Civic Center (11,000, 1975); **Colors:** Red, Black, White (Los Angeles and Baltimore); Red, Black, Gold, White (Michigan); **Formation:** November 1, 1971 (Los Angeles); April 11, 1974 (Detroit); January 23, 1975 (Baltimore); **Dissolution:** January 18, 1975 (Michigan); June 19, 1975 (Baltimore); **Ownerships:** Dennis Murphy, Arthur Rhoades (1971-74), Leonard Bloom (1972-74), Charles Nolton, Peter Shagena (1974-75). Baltimore was league-owned. **General Managers:** Dennis Murphy (1972-73), Terry Slater (1973-74), John Wilson (1974-75); **Coaches:** Terry Slater (1972-73, 1974), Ted McCaskill (1973-74), John Wilson (1974-75).

Longest Streaks

Winning: 5, November 30 to December 10, 1972, January 28 to February 8, 1973; **Undefeated:** 6 (5-0-1), November 30 to December 12, 1972; **Losing & Winless:** 10, January 10 to February 6, 1975.

Statistical Leaders

Season: Goals: 43, Gary Veneruzzo (1972-73); **Assists:** 50, J.-P. Leblanc (1973-74); **Points:** 73, Gary Veneruzzo (1972-73); **Penalty Minutes:** 191, Tom Gilmore (1972-73); **Wins:** 19, George Gardner (1972-73); **Shutouts:** 2, Russ Gillow (72-73), Paul Hoganson (1974-75); **Goals against average:** 2.91, Russ Gillow (1972-73).

All-time: Games: 233, J.-P. Leblanc (1972-75), 233, Gary Veneruzzo (1972-75); **Goals:** 115, Gary Veneruzzo (1972-75); **Assists:** 129, J.-P. Leblanc (1972-75); **Points:** 201, Gary Veneruzzo (1972-75); **Penalty Minutes:** 317, Steve Sutherland (1972-74); **Wins:** 21, Russ Gillow (1972-74); **Shutouts:** 3, Russ Gillow (1972-74); **Goals against average:** 3.38, Russ Gillow (1972-74).

Dennis Murphy

Arthur Rhoades

Charles Nolton

Peter Shagena

Minnesota Fighting Saints

year	record	points	finish
1972-73:	38-37-3	79 pts	4th, Western
1973-74:	44-32-2	90 pts	2nd, Western
1974-75:	42-33-3	87 pts	3rd, Western
1975-76:	30-25-4	65 pts	folded

Home Rink: St. Paul Civic Center (15,705); (Played briefly at St. Paul Auditorium during first season while new St Paul Civic Center was being built.); **Colors:** Blue, Gold, White; **Formation:** November 1, 1971; **Dissolution:** February 27, 1976; **Ownerships:** MidWestern Saints Inc. (1972-74, headed by Louis Kaplan, Frank Marzitelli, Fred Grothe & others), Wayne Belisle (1974-76), Frank Marzitelli and others (1976); **General Manager:** Glen Sonmor (1972-76); **Coaches:** Glen Sonmor (1972-73), Harry Neale (1973-76).

Longest Streaks

Winning: 6, February 13 to February 27, 1974, January 24 to February 5, 1975; **Undefeated:** 11 (10-0-1), February 13 to March 9, 1974; **Losing:** 5, January 13 to January 23, 1974; **Winless:** 5 (0-5-0), January 13 to January 23, 1974; (0-4-1) February 6 to February 14, 1975; (0-4-1) February 1 to February 8, 1976.

Statistical Leaders

Season: Goals: 57, Mike Walton (1973-74); **Assists:** 60, Mike Walton (1973-74); **Points:** 117, Mike Walton (1973-74); **Penalty minutes:** 254, Curt Brackenbury (1975-76); **Wins:** 30, John Garrett (1974-75); **Shutouts:** 4, Mike Curran (1972-73); **Goals against average:** 3.09, Mike Curran (1972-73).

All-time: Games: 291, Ted Hampson (1972-76); **Goals:** 144, Wayne Connelly (1973-76); **Assists:** 145, Mike Walton (1973-76); **Points:** 283, Wayne Connelly (1973-76); **Penalty minutes:** 461, John Arbour (1972-75, 1976); **Wins:** 77, John Garrett (1973-76); **Shutouts:** 7, Mike Curran (1972-76); **Goals against average:** 3.38, John Garrett (1973-76).

Fred Grothe

Lou Kaplan

Frank Marzitelli

Wayne Belisle

New England Whalers

year	record	points	finish
1972-73:	46-30-2	94 pts	1st, Eastern
1973-74:	43-31-4	90 pts	1st, Eastern
1974-75:	43-30-5	91 pts	1st, Eastern
1975-76:	33-40-7	73 pts	3rd, Eastern
1976-77:	35-40-6	76 pts	4th, Eastern
1977-78:	44-31-5	93 pts	2nd, League
1978-79:	37-34-9	83 pts	4th, League

AVCO Cup Champions: 1973

Home Rinks: Boston Garden (14,442, 1972-74); Boston Arena (6,000, 1972-73); Eastern States Coliseum (W. Springfield MA, 5,513, 1974-75); Hartford Civic Center (Hartford CT, 10,507, 1975-76); Springfield Civic Center (Springfield MA, 7,725, 1978-80); Hartford Civic Center II (14,250, 1980-97); **Colors:** Green, Black, White (1972-74); Green, Gold, White (1975-79); **Formation:** November 21, 1971 (New England regional franchise); February 1972 (Boston); January 11, 1975 (transfer to Hartford CT); **Dissolution:** None, entered NHL 1979. Transferred to North Carolina, 1997; **Ownerships:** Howard Baldwin (Principal, & others, 1971-79), Robert Schmertz (1971-c.73), various Hartford-area businesses held a 50% stake in the team from 1974 onward; **General Managers:** Jack Kelley (1972-76), Ron Ryan (1976-78); **Coaches:** Jack Kelley (1972-73, 1974-76), Ron Ryan (1973-75), Don Blackburn (1975, 1979), Harry Neale (1976-78), Bill Dineen (1978-79).

Longest Streaks:

Winning: 13, October 19 to November 20, 1977; **Undefeated:** 14 (13-0-1), October 18 to November 20, 1977; **Losing:** 8, January 4 to January 20, 1977; **Winless:** 9 (0-8-1), January 4 to January 22, 1977.

Statistical Leaders

Season: Goals: 53, Tom Webster (1972-73); **Assists:** 65, Mark Howe (1978-79); **Points:** 107, Mark Howe (1978-79); **Penalty minutes:** 192, Jack Carlson (1977-78); **Wins:** 33, Al Smith (1974-75); **Shutouts:** 3, Al Smith (1972-73), Louis Levasseur (1977-78); **Goals against average:** 3.08, Al Smith (1973-74).

All-time: Games: 479, Rick Ley (1972-79); **Goals:** 220, Tom Webster (1972-77); **Assists:** 215, Larry Pleau (1972-79); **Points:** 425, Tom Webster (1972-77); **Penalty minutes:** 716, Rick Ley (1972-79); **Wins:** 141, Al Smith (1972-75, 1977-79); **Shutouts:** 10, Al Smith (1972-75, 1977-79); **Goals against average:** 3.25, Al Smith (1972-75, 1977-79).

Robert Schmertz

Howard Baldwin

New York Raiders • New York Golden Blades
Jersey Knights • San Diego Mariners

year	record	points	finish
1972-73:	33-43-2	68 pts	6th, Eastern
1973-74:	32-42-4	68 pts	6th, Eastern
1974-75:	43-31-4	90 pts	2nd, Western
1975-76:	36-38-6	78 pts	3rd, Western
1976-77:	40-37-4	84 pts	3rd, Western

Home Rinks: Madison Square Garden (17,500, 1972-73); Cherry Hill NJ Arena (4,000, 1973-74); San Diego Sports Arena (13,039, 1974-77); **Colors:** Raiders: Gold, Blue, Red, White; Blades: Purple, Gold, Black, White; Knights: Gold, Blue, Red, White; Mariners: Blue, Orange, White; **Formation:** November 1, 1971; November 20, 1973 (New Jersey); April 30, 1974 (transfer to San Diego); **Dissolution:** November 18, 1973 (New York); June 1977 (San Diego); **Ownerships:** Neil Shayne (1971-72), Richard Wood, Seymour Siegel (1972), Lee Matison, Ralf Brent, Jerry Delise (1973), Joseph Schwartz (1974-76), Ray Kroc (1976-77), Jerry Saperstein (1977). The league ran the franchise in segments during 1972-74; **General Managers:** Marvin Milkes (1972-73), Bill McDermott (1973), Skip Feldman (1974-75), Ron Ingram (1975-76), Ballard Smith (1976-77); **Coaches:** Camille Henry (1972-73), Harry Howell (1973-75), player-coach. Ron Ingram bench coach), Ron Ingram (1975-77).

Longest Streaks

Winning & Undefeated: 7, March 22 to March 31, 1975; **Losing:** 8, February 26 to March 12, 1977; **Winless:** 14 (0-12-2), February 16 to March 19, 1977.

Statistical Leaders

Season: Goals: 54, Wayne Rivers (1975-76); **Assists:** 106, Andre Lacroix (1974-75); **Points:** 147, Andre Lacroix (1974-75); **Penalty minutes:** 159, Hal Willis (1972-73); **Wins:** 35, Ernie Wakely (1975-76); **Shutouts:** 3, Ernie Wakely (1975-76, 1976-77); **Goals against average:** 3.09, Ernie Wakely (1976-77).

All-time: Games: 365, Norm Ferguson (1972-77); **Goals:** 158, Wayne Rivers (1972-77); **Assists:** 340, Andre Lacroix (1973-77); **Points:** 473, Andre Lacroix (1973-77); **Penalty minutes:** 399, Kevin Morrison (1973-77); **Wins:** 77, Ernie Wakely (1974-77); **Shutouts:** 8, Ernie Wakely (1974-77); **Goals against average:** 3.23, Ernie Wakely (1974-77).

Richard Wood

Seymour Siegel

Joseph Schwartz

Ray Kroc

Ottawa Nationals • Toronto Toros
Birmingham Bulls

year	record	points	finish
1972-73:	35-39-4	74 pts	4th, Eastern
1973-74:	41-33-4	86 pts	2nd, Eastern
1974-75:	43-33-2	88 pts	2nd, Canadian
1975-76:	24-52-5	53 pts	5th, Canadian
1976-77:	31-46-4	66 pts	5th, Eastern
1977-78:	36-41-3	75 pts	5th, League
1978-79:	32-42-6	70 pts	6th, League

Home Rinks: Ottawa Civic Center (10,500, 1972-73 and selected dates in 1973-74); Varsity Arena (4,860, 1973-74); Maple Leaf Gardens (16,316, 1973 Playoffs, 1974-76); Jefferson County Civic Center (16,753, 1976-79); **Colors:** Red, White, Blue (All three teams); **Formation:** November 21, 1971 (Ontario regional franchise); February 17, 1972 (Ottawa); May 1973 (transfer to Toronto); June 30, 1976 (transfer to Birmingham); **Dissolution:** June 13, 1979; **Ownerships:** Doug Michel (1971-73), Nick Trbovich (1972-73), John F. Bassett Jr, John C. Eaton & others (1973-75), John F. Bassett, Jr. (1975-79); **General Managers:** A. J. "Buck" Houle (1972-75), Gilles Leger (1975-79); **Coaches:** Bill Harris (1972-75), Bob Leduc (1975), Bob Baun (1975-76), Gilles Leger (1976), Pat Kelly (1976-77), Glen Sonmor (1977-78), John Brophy (1978-79).

Longest Streaks

Winning & Undefeated: 12, March 21 to October 28, 1974 (2 seasons), 7, March 15 to March 29, 1973; **Losing:** 12, January 31 to February 27, 1976; **Winless:** 17 (0-15-2, league record), January 22 to February 27, 1976.

Statistical Leaders

Season: Goals: 60, Mark Napier (1976-77); **Assists:** 66, Wayne Dillon (1974-75); **Points:** 98, Vaclav Nedomansky (1975-76); **Penalty minutes:** 284, Steve Durbano (1977-78); **Wins:** 30, Gilles Gratton (1974-75); **Shutouts:** 4, John Garrett (1976-77); **Goals against average:** 3.27, Les Binkley (1973-74).

All-time: Games: 392, Jim Turkiewicz (1974-79); **Goals:** 140, Paul Henderson (1974-79); **Assists:** 207, Gavin Kirk (1972-77); **Points:** 309, Gavin Kirk (1972-77); **Penalty minutes:** 458, Rick Cunningham (1972-77); **Wins:** 81, Gilles Gratton (1972-75); **Shutouts:** 7, John Garrett (1976-78); **Goals against average:** 3.66, John Garrett (1976-78).

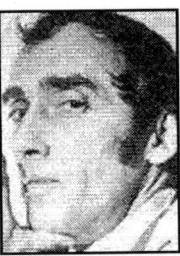
Doug Michel

Nick Trbovich

John Bassett

Philadelphia Blazers • Vancouver Blazers
Calgary Cowboys

year	record	points	finish
1972-73:	38-40-0	76 pts	3rd, Eastern
1973-74:	27-50-1	55 pts	5th, Western
1974-75:	37-39-2	76 pts	4th, Canadian
1975-76:	41-35-4	86 pts	3rd, Canadian
1976-77:	31-43-7	69 pts	5th, Western

Home Rinks: Philadelphia Civic Center (8,000, 1972-73); Pacific Coliseum, Vancouver (15,569, 1973-75); Calgary Stampede Corral (8,945, 1975-77); **Colors:** Philadelphia and Vancouver: Yellow, Burnt Orange; Calgary: Red, White; **Formation:** November 1, 1971 (Miami); June 3, 1972 (Philadelphia); May 1973 (Vancouver); May 7, 1975 (Calgary); **Dissolution:** April 28, 1972 (Miami); August 9, 1977 (Calgary); **Ownerships:** Herb Martin (1971-72), James L. Cooper (1972), Bernard A. Brown (1972-73), Jim Pattison (1973-75), Bill Sleeman, B. Hay, June Sifton (1975-77); **General Managers:** Les Patrick (1971-72), Barry Mendelson (1972), Jerry Rafter (1972-73), Phil Watson (1973-74), Joe Crozier (1974-77); **Coaches:** John McKenzie (1972, 1973), Phil Watson (1972-73), Andy Bathgate (1973-74), Joe Crozier (1974-77).

Longest Streaks

Winning: 7, October 24 to November 11, 1976; **Undefeated:** 8 (7-0-1), October 22 to November 11, 1976; **Losing & Winless:** 10, October 21 to November 10, 1973, and March 11 to March 26, 1977.

Statistical Leaders

Season: Goals: 61, Danny Lawson (1972-73); **Assists:** 74, Andre Lacroix (1972-73); **Points:** 124, Andre Lacroix (1972-73); **Penalty minutes:** 196, Butch Deadmarsh (1975-76); **Wins:** 33, Parent (1972-73), Don McLeod (1974-75); **Shutouts:** 3, Peter Donnelly (1973-74), Don McLeod (1974-75); **Goals against average:** 3.34, Don McLeod (1974-75).

All-time: Games: 378, Danny Lawson (1972-77); **Goals:** 212, Danny Lawson (1972-77); **Assists:** 197, Danny Lawson (1972-77); **Points:** 409, Danny Lawson (1972-77); **Penalty minutes:** 401, Butch Deadmarsh (1974-77); **Wins:** 88, Don McLeod (1974-77); **Shutouts:** 5, Don McLeod (1974-77); **Goals against average:** 3.41, Don McLeod (1974-77).

Bernard Brown

James Cooper

Jim Pattison

Bill Sleeman

Phoenix Roadrunners

year	record	points	finish
1974-75:	39-31-8	86 pts	4th, Western
1975-76:	39-35-4	82 pts	2nd, Western
1976-77:	28-48-4	60 pts	6th, Western

Home Rink: Veterans Memorial Coliseum (12,600); **Colors:** Dark Blue, Copper, Gold, White; **Formation:** September 14, 1973; **Dissolution:** April 6, 1977; **Ownerships:** William H. MacFarland, Karl Eller, Bert A. Getz, Steven W. Craig, J. G. Wells, Dr. H. J. Louis, L. G. Hooker Jr., Brian O'Neill (1976); **General Manager:** Al Rollins (1974-77); **Coaches:** Sandy Hucul (1974-76), Al Rollins (1976-77).

Longest Streaks

Winning & Undefeated: 6, December 10 to December 26, 1974; **Losing & Winless:** 8, November 30 to December 14, 1976.

Statistical Leaders

Season: Goals: 47, Del Hall (1975-76); **Assists:** 72, Robbie Ftorek (1975-76); **Points:** 117, Robbie Ftorek (1976-77); **Penalty minutes:** 295, Cam Connor (1975-76); **Wins:** 25, Gary Kurt (1974-75); **Shutouts:** 2, Gary Kurt (1974-75); **Goals against average:** 3.18, Jack Norris (1975-76).

All-time: Games: 229, Jim Niekamp (1974-77); **Goals:** 118, Robbie Ftorek (1974-77); **Assists:** 180, Robbie Ftorek (1974-77); **Points:** 298, Robbie Ftorek (1974-77); **Penalty minutes:** 463, Cam Connor (1974-76); **Wins:** 54, Gary Kurt (1974-77); **Shutouts:** 3, Gary Kurt (1974-77); **Goals against average:** 3.22, Jack Norris (1974-76).

William MacFarland

Karl Eller

Brian O'Neill

Québec Nordiques

year	record	points	finish
1972-73:	33-40-5	71 pts	5th, Eastern
1973-74:	38-36-4	80 pts	5th, Eastern
1974-75:	46-32-0	92 pts	1st, Canadian
1975-76:	50-27-4	104 pts	2nd, Canadian
1976-77:	47-31-3	97 pts	1st, Eastern
1977-78:	40-37-3	83 pts	4th, League
1978-79:	41-34-5	87 pts	2nd, League

AVCO Cup Champions: 1977

Home Rink: Le Colisee (10,004); Colors: Powder Blue, Red, White. Later sweaters emphasized a deeper shade of blue and de-emphasized the red; **Formation:** November 1, 1971 (San Francisco); February 11, 1972 (Quebec); **Dissolution:** None, entered NHL 1979; Transferred to Denver, 1995; **Ownerships:** Gary Davidson (1971-72), Paul Racine, Hon. Jean Lesage, Jean Dacres & others (1972-78), Marcel Aubut (1978-95); **General Managers:** Marius Fortier (1972), Maurice Filion (1972-73, 1974-79), Jacques Plante (1973-74); **Coaches:** Maurice Richard (1972), Maurice Filion (1972-73, 1977-78), Jacques Plante (1973-74), Jean-Guy Gendron (1974-76), Marc Boileau (1976-78), Jacques Demers (1978-79).

Longest Streaks

Winning & Undefeated: 11, March 25 to October 16, 1976 (2 seasons); 9, January 1 to January 19, 1975, December 22, 1976 to January 25, 1977; **Losing:** 7, March 14 to March 29, 1975, February 9 to February 19, 1978; **Winless:** 8 (0-6-2), February 8 to February 22, 1973.

Statistical Leaders

Season: Goals: 75, Real Cloutier (1978-79); **Assists:** 89, Marc Tardif (1977-78); **Points:** 154, Marc Tardif (1977-78); **Penalty minutes:** 297, Gordie Gallant (1975-76); **Wins:** 44, Richard Brodeur (1975-76); **Shutouts:** 3, Richard Brodeur (1978-79), Jim Corsi (1978-79); **Goals against average:** 3.11, Richard Brodeur (1978-79).

All-time: Games: 451, J.-C. Tremblay (1972-79); **Goals:** 283, Real Cloutier (1974-79); **Assists:** 358, J.-C. Tremblay (1972-79); **Points:** 579, Marc Tardif (1974-79); **Penalty minutes:** 732, Pierre Roy (1972-77); **Wins:** 165, Richard Brodeur (1972-79); **Shutouts:** 8, Richard Brodeur (1972-79); **Goals against average:** 3.64, Richard Brodeur (1972-79).

Winnipeg Jets

year	record	points	finish
1972-73:	43-31-4	90 pts	1st, Western
1973-74:	34-39-5	73 pts	4th, Western
1974-75:	38-35-5	81 pts	3rd, Canadian
1975-76:	52-27-2	106 pts	1st, Canadian
1976-77:	46-32-2	94 pts	2nd, Western
1977-78:	50-28-2	102 pts	1st, League
1978-79:	39-35-6	84 pts	3rd, League

AVCO Cup Champions: 1976, 1978, 1979

Home Rink: Winnipeg Arena (10,131); **Colors:** Blue, Red, White; Formation: November 1, 1971; December 27, 1971 (formal organization); **Dissolution:** None, entered NHL 1979; Transferred to Phoenix, 1996; Atlanta Thrashers (NHL) transferred to Winnipeg in 2011, assuming Jets nickname; **Ownerships:** Ben Hatskin (1971-74), Dave Simkin (1971-72), Robert G. Graham, Jack McKeag (& others, 1974-78; the Jets were community-owned with shares starting at $25), Michael Gobuty (1978-79); **General Managers:** Annis Stukus (1972-74), Rudy Pilous (1974-78), John Ferguson (1978-79); **Coaches:** Bobby Bobby Hull (1972-75, player-coach. Nick Mikoski was bench coach), Rudy Pilous (1974-75), Bobby Kromm (1975-77), Larry Hillman (1977-79), Tom McVie (1979).

Longest Streaks

Winning & Undefeated: 15, January 29 to February 26, 1978 (the 15-game winning streak is the league record); **Losing:** 5, March 10 to March 18, 1973; **Winless:** 6 (0-5-1), March 10 to March 22, 1973.

Statistical Leaders

Season: Goals: 77, Bobby Hull (1974-75); **Assists:** 94, Ulf Nilsson (1974-75); **Points:** 142, Bobby Hull (1974-75); **Penalty minutes:** 248, Scott Campbell (1978-79); **Wins:** 41, Joe Daley (1975-76); **Shutouts:** 5, Joe Daley (1975-76); **Goals against average:** 2.84, Joe Daley (1975-76).

All-time: Games: 411, Bobby Hull (1972-78); **Goals:** 303, Bobby Hull (1972-78); **Assists:** 344, Ulf Nilsson (1974-78); **Points:** 638, Bobby Hull (1972-78); **Penalty minutes:** 413, Kim Clackson (1977-79); **Wins:** 167, Joe Daley (1972-79); **Shutouts:** 12, Joe Daley (1972-79); **Goals against average:** 3.37, Joe Daley (1972-79).

Hon. Jean Lesage

Marius Fortier

Ben Hatskin

Bob Graham

Jean Dacres

Marcel Aubut

John McKeag

Michael Gobuty

Origins of the Team Names

How were the team names chosen? Every team name has its own history; some of the more interesting ones are given below.

Alberta/Edmonton Oilers: The Oilers were named after the Junior Western Canada Hockey League's Edmonton Oil Kings. Bill Hunter owned and operated the Oil Kings for many seasons before entering into the World Hockey Association in 1971.

Birmingham Bulls: When the Toronto Toros moved to Birmingham in 1976, "Bulls" was the natural choice for the new Birmingham club, as "Bull" and "Toro" translate back and forth between English and Spanish. There is speculation the name "Bulls" might have been given to the club by the Birmingham media, when the team was referred to as such in the Birmingham papers announcing the planned move of the Toros to Alabama in May, 1976. The Toros' owner, John Bassett, at the time would not confirm or deny the reports, but when the move was made final a month later, the team was known officially as the Birmingham Bulls.

Calgary Cowboys: "Cowboys" is a reference to the cowboy-western image of Calgary. The city is host to many rodeo competitions, many of them held at the old Stampede Corral.

Chicago Cougars: The name was adopted by the original owners in 1971, and kept after the Kaiser brothers bought the team.

Cincinnati Stingers: Chosen by the owners based on suggestions from the public.

Cleveland Crusaders: "Crusaders" was chosen by a fan vote to name the team.

Denver Spurs: The WHA Spurs were named after the defunct WHL and CHL Denver Spurs teams of the late 1960s-early 1970s. The minor-league Spurs were owned by Ivan Mullenix, who was also granted the rights to the WHA team in 1975.

Houston Aeros: The Aeros nickname was given to the team while it was still based in Dayton, Ohio. It was a personal choice of team owner Paul Deneau, reportedly inspired by the "Aero-Mexico" logo painted on the tail of an airliner.

Indianapolis Racers: "Racers" is a reference to the famous Indianapolis-500 race, and was chosen as the result of a fan vote to name the team. The name also made for a clever pairing with the Indiana Pacers of the American Basketball Association (later NBA in 1976). Both teams played at the Market Square Arena.

Jersey Knights: An unconfirmed story indicates that when the WHA sought to place a temporary team in Cherry Hill, New Jersey after the collapse of the New York Golden Blades, a local uniform supplier had a set of "Knights" patches available for a reasonable price. The WHA took the offer and the team became the Knights by default. The underlying jerseys were used by the Raiders the previous year.

Los Angeles Sharks: In the early days of the WHA the Los Angeles team was to be named the Aces, in a clever reference at the NHL Kings (Aces beat Kings in cards). The team adopted the Sharks moniker, a personal choice of Dennis Murphy's.

Minnesota Fighting Saints: Named after the International League's St. Paul Saints of the 1960s, the WHA team added the "Fighting" as a form of identity. Nevertheless, the WHA team was often referred to as the Saints.

New England Whalers: Chosen partly to honor the men of New England who make their living as whalers, the name was also chosen because the first three letters are "WHA", and was suggested by the wife of original coach Jack Kelley.

Ottawa Nationals: Original owner Doug Michel had previously run a youth team known as the Young Nationals before buying into the WHA. "Nationals" was his first choice for his WHA team, and a natural choice considering the team's home city of Ottawa is the Canadian capital.

Philadelphia Blazers: The name was chosen by the team owners, Bernard Brown and James Cooper. The team colors of red and orange were suggested by the wife of James Cooper.

Phoenix Roadrunners: Originally chosen by a fan vote, carried over from the WHL team of 1967-74. Roadrunners are small birds that prefer to run across, rather than fly over, the Arizona deserts.

Quebec Nordiques: Nordiques translates as "Northmen", referencing Quebec City's northern setting.

San Diego Mariners: The Gulls had been a popular nickname for the San Diego entrant in the Western League, but it was not available for use by Joseph Schwartz, owner of the San Diego WHA club. Instead, Mariners was chosen in honor of San Diego's role as a leading shipping port.

Toronto Toros: "Toros" is a shortened version of "Toronto", and Spanish for "bull", the team logo.

Winnipeg Jets: Named after the Winnipeg Jets of the Western Canada Hockey (Jr) League.

Abbreviation Key

Yearly Standings

The yearly standings list each team's record of **gp** (games played), **w**ins, **l**osses and **t**ies, **pts** (points), **gf** (goals for) and **ga** (goals against). The teams are grouped by appropriate division and are listed according to their finish, determined by point total. Teams that folded in midseason are also included, although no finish is indicated nor applicable. The date of fold is indicated. After each team's seasonal record are two rows indicating home and away records, points, percentage, and goals for and against.

Game by Game Linescore Results

Linescores are given for every regular-season and playoff game. The visiting team is listed in the top row, home team on the bottom row. Goals by period, plus game totals, then shots by period, and game totals are given, followed by goaltenders and goal scorers.

Goal scorers are generally listed in the order in which the goals were scored. However, players who scored more than one goal in the game are moved to the front of the list. Notable facts about game-tying and game-winning goals are given using the following protocol:

- All overtime goal scorers are denoted by "OT", with the time of the goal;
- All third-period game winning goals which were the result of breaking a tie are denoted by "WG" and the time of the goal;
- Any notable game-tying goals that occurred late in the third period are denoted "TG" with time of the goal;
- Any shutout that was broken in the last five minutes is mentioned;
- All shutouts by goaltenders are mentioned;
- Any other notable fact about the game is mentioned, space permitting.

Due to space limitations, first initials are used only where confusion would be impossible to avoid, or in some cases for aesthetic reasons. The following illustrate examples of its usage:

- If two players on the same team with the same last name scored goals relatively often, first initials are used. For example, C. Bordeleau and P. Bordeleau are used to identify Christian and Paulin Bordeleau, both playing for Quebec during 1976-77 and 1977-78.

- If two players on the same team had the same last name but one of the players scored rarely, only his first initial is used. For example, in the 1974-75 table, "Sobchuk" always refers to Dennis Sobchuk. His brother, Gene Sobchuk, scored just one goal and is listed as G. Sobchuk.
- If two players on the same team had the same last name but one did not score a goal, no first initial is necessary when mentioning the one who did score.
- Players on the same team who share a last name with the goaltender do not have their first initial included. Thus, references to Abrahamsson in the goal-scoring tables refer to Thommie, not to his brother, goaltender Christer.
- Goaltenders with same last names have first initials included, since it is possible (and did occur) that they would face one another. This was done for aesthetic reasons. For example, D. McLeod and J. McLeod are listed as such in the 1972-73 through 1974-75 tables. However, from 1975-76 onward, all references to McLeod refer to Don McLeod, his brother Jim having retired.

Line scores were collated from multiple resources including The Sporting News, The Hockey News, Le Journal de Quebec, the Calgary Herald, the Edmonton Journal, the New York Times, the Chicago Tribune and the Arizona Republic.

Following the linescores are charts for each team, showing that team's game-by-game progress. The list features the **date**, **opponent** (@ indicates an away game), **score** (* indicates an overtime game, with all tie games understood to be overtime games, and thus not marked redundantly), **result** (W win, L loss, T tie), **record** to date (w-l-t), current **pts** (points total) to date, and cumulative **gf** (goals for) and **ga** (goals against) to date. All teams are indicated by city or region, since no confusion should occur in the case of different teams in the same city (e.g. "Ottawa" in a 1975-76 chart refers to the Ottawa Civics, in a 1972-73 chart to the Ottawa Nationals.) Further notation is defined elsewhere as needed.

In the case of the teams that played in more than one location during a season (New York and Jersey in 1973-74, Michigan and Baltimore in 1974-75 and Denver and Ottawa in 1975-76), a separate table is included that shows the breakdown of the season, home and away records, point totals and goals for/against totals in each locale. Teams that folded during midseason (Minnesota and Denver-Ottawa in 1975-76, Minnesota in 1976-77 and Indianapolis in 1978-79) include a note indicating date of fold after the abbreviated game-by-game chart.

Individual Scoring and Goaltending

All players' statistics are grouped according to team and year. All players are represented, and names are listed alphabetically by last name. Each player's **pos**ition is noted beside his **name** (C center, LW left wing, RW rightwing, D defenseman and G goaltender, with F forward used when the exact forward position was unknown). The players uniform number is listed under the column headed "#" The player's statistics include **gp** (games played), **g**oals, **a**ssists, **pts** (points), **ppg** (power-play goals), **shg** (short-handed goals), **sog** (shots on goal) and **sc%** (scoring percentage, calculated by dividing goals by shots on goal) for the regular season, followed by the scoring information for playoffs. For the 1974-75, 1975-76, 1976-77, 1977-78 and 1978-79 seasons, each players' even strength plus/minus (**+/-**) figure is also included. The +/- figures and the shots on goal and scoring percentage figures were not available for the 1972-73 and 1973-74 seasons. Power play and short-handed goal information was often inconsistently available and in many cases, does not sum with the player totals. I have sought to correct these inconsistencies whenever possible but a few remain.

Goaltenders' records include the goaltender's **name**, **gp** (games played), **min** (minutes played), **ga** (goals against), **en** (empty net goals), **so** (shutouts), **w**ins, **l**osses, **t**ies, **gaa** (goals against average), **sog** (shots on goal by opposing players) and **sv%** (save percent-tage).

Place Name Abbreviations

The following is a list of the abbreviations used throughout the book for each WHA team:

Alb Alberta Oilers; **Balt** Baltimore Blades; **Bir** Birmingham Bulls; **Cgy** Calgary Cowboys; **Chi** Chicago Cougars; **Cin** Cincinnati Stingers; **Cle** Cleveland Crusaders; **Den** Denver Spurs; **D-O** Denver-Ottawa; **Edm** Edmonton Oilers; **Hou** Houston Aeros; **Ind** Indianapolis Racers; **Jer** Jersey Knights; **LA** Los Angeles Sharks; **M-B** Michigan-Baltimore; **Mich** Michigan Stags; **Min** Minnesota Fighting Saints; **NE** New England Whalers; **NY** New York Raiders; **NY-J** New York-Jersey; **Ott** Ottawa Nationals; **Phi** Philadelphia Blazers; **Phx** Phoenix Roadrunners; **Que** Quebec Nordiques; **SD** San Diego Mariners; **Tor** Toronto Toros; **Van** Vancouver Blazers; **Wpg** Winnipeg Jets.

Formula Calculations

Certain statistics are calculated by using standard formulas as noted here:

A team's seasonal point total is arrived at multiplying the win total by 2, then adding the number of ties to this figure, or pts = (2w) + t. Winning percentage is found by dividing the pts figure by 2 times the number of games played, or pct = pts ÷ (2gp). A player's seasonal point total is found by adding the number of goals and assists together.

A goaltender's goals against average (gaa) is found by multiplying the number of goals against by 60, and then dividing by the number of minutes played, or gaa = (60 × ga) ÷ min. Empty net goals (en) are not counted against a goaltender's goals against average, nor are they counted toward the team's cumulative goals against average. Save percentage is calculated by dividing total saves (sog minus ga) by total shots on goal. For goaltenders who faced no shots on goal, a save percentage is meaningless and is noted by a hyphen (-).

Player Uniform Numbers

The uniform numbers listed for the players is as accurate as can best be determined from the various sources. Unfortunately, not all player uniform numbers could be determined, in which case the space is left blank. Players who changed numbers during the season may not be noted.

Statistical Inconsistencies

All statistical information contained within this book has been checked and cross-referenced against multiple sources. Not all information was released in contemporary public forums, or was released in incomplete form.

It is possible that the frequency of a player's name in the goal-scoring section of the linescore sheets may not add to his presumed "official" totals. When conflicts arose, I rechecked the validity of the game summary against multiple sources, but not all conflicts can be resolved. In such cases, the conflicting information is provided, until further clarification can be found to resolve these issues.

Season I

1972-1973

After 17 months of promises, controversies and setbacks, the World Hockey Association achieved its first truly historic goal: it survived to see the start of its first season.

Twelve teams found enough willing NHL stars and journeymen to jump to the new league, and plenty of career minor leaguers and college players happy to play at salaries comparable to that of a seasoned NHL veteran. The twelve teams settled into two divisions: The Western Division counted the Alberta (Edmonton) Oilers, Chicago Cougars, Houston Aeros, Los Angeles Sharks, Minnesota (St. Paul) Fighting Saints and Winnipeg Jets as members, while the Eastern Division included the Cleveland Crusaders, New England (Boston) Whalers, New York Raiders, Ottawa Nationals, Philadelphia Blazers and Quebec Nordiques. The controversies did not stop: Lawsuits kept Bobby Hull from playing in the Jets' first fourteen games, while the highly-paid Derek Sanderson lasted eight games for the Blazers before leaving on less-than-amicable terms. By the sheer determination of its teams and players, the World Hockey Association played the 78-game schedule to its completion. Not one team folded, and attendance figures proved encouraging for the brand-new league.

The 78 game schedule had a team play each of the six teams in the other division six times (three home and away), four of the five teams in its own division eight times (four and four), with the remaining fifth .

team, the "designated rival", being played ten times (five and five). The playoff system allowed for the top four teams in each division to advance to the postseason. Divisional semifinals led to divisional finals, where the winners vied for the World Trophy, underwritten by the AVCO Financial Services Corporation. Two teams, the Oilers and Fighting Saints, tied for fourth place in the West with identical records and were forced to play a one-game mini-playoff to decide the final playoff spot. The New England Whalers beat out the Golden Jet's Winnipeg Jets in five games for the first championship. However, a one-game, neutral ice challenge issued by the Whalers' president, Howard Baldwin, to the NHL champion Montreal Canadiens for the Stanley Cup went unheeded.

Top individual performances included the Blazers' Danny Lawson's 61 goals and teammate Andre Lacroix's 124 points. The Crusaders' Gerry Cheevers led all goaltenders with 5 shutouts and a 2.84 average. Houston's John Schella was the league's most penalized player with 239 minutes. Bobby Hull, the league's foundation, came back to score 51 goals and 103 points after being cleared by the courts to play. Alberta's Ron Anderson scored the league's first goal on opening night, October 11th, and teammate Bill Hicke attempted the league's first penalty shot a mere 16:37 into the first period the same night. Gerry Cheevers turned in the first shutout a few hundred miles away, also on October 11th, blanking the Quebec Nordiques.

Standings

Eastern Division

	team		gp	w	l	t	pts	pct	gf	ga
1.	New England WHALERS		78	46	30	2	94	.603	318	263
		home	39	30	8	1	61	.782	169	112
		away	39	16	22	1	33	.423	149	151
2.	Cleveland CRUSADERS		78	43	32	3	89	.571	287	239
		home	39	26	11	2	54	.692	164	115
		away	39	17	21	1	35	.449	123	124
3.	Philadelphia BLAZERS		78	38	40	0	76	.487	288	305
		home	39	24	15	0	48	.615	172	144
		away	39	14	25	0	28	.359	116	161
4.	Ottawa NATIONALS		78	35	39	4	74	.474	279	301
		home	39	21	15	3	45	.577	146	130
		away	39	14	24	1	29	.372	133	171
5.	Québec NORDIQUES		78	33	40	5	71	.455	276	313
		home	39	22	12	5	49	.628	155	126
		away	39	11	28	0	22	.282	121	187
6.	New York RAIDERS		78	33	43	2	68	.436	303	334
		home	39	23	15	1	47	.603	176	144
		away	39	10	28	1	21	.269	127	190

Western Division

	team		gp	w	l	t	pts	pct	gf	ga
1.	Winnipeg JETS		78	43	31	4	90	.577	285	249
		home	39	26	11	2	54	.692	156	112
		away	39	17	20	2	36	.462	129	137
2.	Houston AEROS		78	39	35	4	82	.526	284	269
		home	39	22	16	1	45	.577	162	139
		away	39	17	19	3	37	.474	122	130
3.	Los Angeles SHARKS		78	37	35	6	80	.513	259	250
		home	39	18	20	1	37	.474	117	122
		away	39	19	15	5	43	.551	142	128
4.	Minnesota FIGHTING SAINTS		78	38	37	3	79	.506	250	269
		home	39	24	14	1	49	.628	129	117
		away	39	14	25	2	30	.385	121	152
5.	Alberta OILERS		78	38	37	3	79	.506	269	256
		home	39	25	12	2	52	.667	161	116
		away	39	13	25	1	27	.346	108	140
6.	Chicago COUGARS		78	26	50	2	54	.346	245	295
		home	39	17	22	0	34	.436	129	130
		away	39	9	28	2	20	.256	116	165

Award Winners

Most Valuable Player
Gary Davidson Trophy
Bobby Hull, Wpg

Rookie of the Year
Lou Kaplan Trophy
Terry Caffery, NE

Best Goaltender
Ben Hatskin Trophy
Gerry Cheevers, Cle

Best Defeseman
Dennis Murphy Trophy
J.-C. Tremblay, Que

Coach of the Year
Howard Baldwin Trophy
Jack Kelley, NE

Most Gentlemanly
Paul Deneau Trophy
Ted Hampson, Min

1973 World Hockey Association Champions
New England Whalers

1973 Playoff Series Results

Tiebreaker Playoff

Apr 4   Minnesota 4, Alberta 2
        (at Calgary, Alberta)

Eastern Division Semifinals

Cleveland vs. Philadelphia
Apr 4   Philadelphia 2 at Cleveland 3
        (ot: Ron Buchanan 9:49)
Apr 7   Philadelphia 1 at Cleveland 7
Apr 8   Cleveland 3 at Philadelphia 1
Apr 11 Cleveland 6 at Philadelphia 2

New England vs. Ottawa
Apr 7   Ottawa 3 at New England 6
Apr 8   Ottawa 3 at New England 4
        (ot: Brit Selby 3:37)
Apr 9   New England 2 vs Ottawa 4
Apr 12 New England 7 vs Ottawa 3
Apr 14 Ottawa 4 at New England 5
        (ot: Mike Byers 5:47)

Ottawa's home games
played in Toronto

Western Division Semifinals

Winnipeg vs. Minnesota
Apr 6   Minnesota 1 at Winnipeg 3
Apr 8   Minnesota 2 at Winnipeg 5
Apr 10 Winnipeg 4 at Minnesota 6
Apr 11 Winnipeg 3 at Minnesota 2
        (ot: Norm Beaudin 3:12)
Apr 15 Minnesota 5 at Winnipeg 8

Houston vs. Los Angeles
Apr 5   Los Angeles 2 at Houston 7
Apr 7   Los Angeles 4 at Houston 2
Apr 11 Houston 2 at Los Angeles 3
Apr 13 Houston 3 at Los Angeles 2
        (ot: Murray Hall 3:38)
Apr 15 Los Angeles 3 at Houston 6
Apr 17 Houston 3 at Los Angeles 2

Eastern Division Finals

New England vs. Cleveland
Apr 18 Cleveland 2 at New England 3
Apr 19 Cleveland 2 at New England 3
Apr 21 New England 5 at Cleveland 4
Apr 22 New England 2 at Cleveland 5
Apr 26 Cleveland 1 at New England 3

Western Division Finals

Winnipeg vs. Houston
Apr 20 Houston 1 at Winnipeg 5
Apr 22 Houston 0 at Winnipeg 2
        (so: Ernie Wakely, 28 saves)
Apr 24 Winnipeg 4 at Houston 2
Apr 26 Winnipeg 3 at Houston 0
        (so: Ernie Wakely, 25 saves)

AVCO World Trophy Championship

New England vs. Winnipeg
Apr 29 Winnipeg 2 at New England 7
May 2   New England 7 at Winnipeg 4
May 3   New England 3 at Winnipeg 4
May 5   Winnipeg 2 at New England 4
May 6   Winnipeg 6 at New England 9

Playoff Standings

Overall Team	w	l	gf	ga
New England	12	3	70	49
Winnipeg	9	5	55	49
Cleveland	5	4	33	22
Houston	4	6	26	30
Minnesota*	2	4	20	25
Los Angeles	2	4	16	23
Ottawa	1	4	17	24
Philadelphia	0	4	6	19
Alberta*	0	1	2	4

Home Team	w	l	gf	ga
New England	9	0	44	25
Winnipeg	6	1	31	19
Cleveland	3	1	19	10
Houston	2	3	17	16
Minnesota	1	1	8	7
Ottawa	1	1	7	9
Los Angeles	1	2	7	8
Philadelphia	0	2	3	9

Away Team	w	l	gf	ga
New England	3	3	26	24
Winnipeg	3	4	24	30
Cleveland	2	3	14	12
Houston	2	3	9	14
Los Angeles	1	2	9	15
Philadelphia	0	2	3	10
Minnesota	0	3	8	16
Ottawa	0	3	10	15

* The one-game tiebreaker between Minnesota and Alberta is included in both teams' total standings, but not in the home and away standings, as the game was held at a neutral site. Statistics from this game are not included in the individual players' and goaltenders' statistics.

48

Championship Series Summaries

The first World Hockey Association Championship was claimed by the New England Whalers, who had compiled the league's best record during the season. The Winnipeg Jets, led by Bobby Hull, made a game effort but were easily cast aside in five games. New England's balanced attack included four goals from both Larry Pleau and Tom Webster. Larry Pleau's hat-trick in the deciding game helped seal the championship for the Whalers.

Game 1 • April 29, 1973
New England 7, Winnipeg 2

| Winnipeg | 1 | 0 | 1 | - | 2 |
| New England | 4 | 2 | 1 | - | 7 |

1st period: 1. Wpg: Beaudin (Bordeleau, Hull) 10:02; 2. NE: Ley (Dorey, Webster) 12:10; 3. NE: Webster (Williams, Hurley) 14:07; 4. NE: Earl (Sheehy, Green) 16:13; 5. NE: French 19:37.
2nd period: 6. NE: Webster (Williams, Hurley) 10:55; 7. NE: Williams (French) 16:01.
3rd period: 8. NE: Dorey (Sheehy, Earl) 3:45; 9. Wpg: Hull 11:07.
Shots on goal

| Wpg on Smith | 14 | 6 | 7 | - | 27 |
| NE on Daley | 7 | 13 | 5 | - | 25 |

Game 2 • May 2, 1973
New England 7, Winnipeg 4

| New England | 1 | 1 | 5 | - | 7 |
| Winnipeg | 2 | 2 | 0 | - | 4 |

1st period: 1. Wpg: Beaudin (Hull, Hornung) 0:33; 2. Wpg: Bordeleau (Hull, Beaudin) 19:20; 3. NE: Williams (Webster, Dorey) 19:46.
2nd period: 4. NE: Selwood (Williams) 1:47; 5. Wpg: Boyer (Rousseau, Zanussi) 5:59; 6. Wpg: Bordeleau (Hull, Woytowich) 7:37.
3rd period: 7. NE: Dorey (Williams, Webster) 2:19; 8. NE: Selby (Williams, Webster) 3:08; 9. NE: French (Ley, Sheehy) 9:03 10. NE: Cunniff (Byers) 10:16; 11. NE: French (Hurley, Pleau) 18:59
Shots on goal

| NE on Wakely | 13 | 6 | 6 | - | 25 |
| Wpg on Smith | 13 | 11 | 12 | - | 36 |

Game 3 • May 3, 1973
Winnipeg 4, New England 3

| New England | 0 | 1 | 2 | - | 3 |
| Winnipeg | 2 | 1 | 1 | - | 4 |

1st period: 1. Wpg: Hull (Bordeleau, Beaudin) 15:23; 2. Wpg: McDonald (Beaudin, Hornung) 19:34.
2nd period: 3. Wpg: Johnson (Hull, Hornung) 5:21; 4. NE: Ley (Byers) 14:44.
3rd period: 5. NE: Green (Ley, Webster) 4:23; 6. NE: Sheehy (French, Dorey) 18:56; 7. Wpg: Hull (Beaudin, Ash) 19:33.
Shots on goal

| NE on Daley | 12 | 4 | 11 | - | 27 |
| Wpg on Smith | 8 | 14 | 6 | - | 28 |

Game 4 • May 5, 1973
New England 4, Winnipeg 2

| Winnipeg | 1 | 0 | 1 | - | 2 |
| New England | 0 | 3 | 1 | - | 4 |

1st period: 1. Wpg: Hull (Bordeleau) 15:50
2nd period: 2. NE: Pleau (Sheehy, Ley) 0:47; 3. NE: Byers (Earl, Dorey) 14:11 4. NE: Sheehy (Dorey, Selwood) 16:17
3rd period: 5. NE: Byers (Earl) 7:17; 6. Wpg: Rousseau (Ash) 19:54.
Shots on goal

| Wpg on Smith | 9 | 11 | 10 | - | 30 |
| NE on Wakely | 13 | 8 | 11 | - | 32 |

Game 5 • May 6, 1973
New England 9, Winnipeg 6

| Winnipeg | 2 | 2 | 2 | - | 6 |
| New England | 5 | 1 | 3 | - | 9 |

1st period: 1. NE: Webster (Williams, Ley) 0:21; 2. NE: Pleau 4:43; 3. Wpg: Johnson (Sutherland) 7:07; 4. NE: G. Smith (Williams, Webster) 11:47; 5. NE: Ley 15:43; 6. Wpg: Beaudin (Hull) 17:53; 7. NE: Sheehy (Webster, Pleau) 18:41
2nd period: 8. NE: Webster (Williams, Green) 0:15; 9. Wpg: Beaudin (Bordeleau, McDonald) 3:15; 10. Wpg: Black (Shmyr) 4:02
3rd period: 11. Wpg: Woytowich (Swenson, Asmundson) 4:59; 12. NE: Pleau (Sheehy, French) 5:24; 13. NE: Pleau (Sheehy, French) 7:31; 14. NE: Byers (Green, Williams) 17:20; 15. Wpg: Asmundson (Swenson, Cuddie) 18:10
Shots on goal

| Wpg on Smith | 17 | 12 | 13 | - | 42 |
| NE on Daley | 11 | 6 | 10 | - | 27 |

Statistical Leaders

Goals: 13, Norm Beaudin (Wpg); 12, Larry Pleau (NE), Tom Webster (NE); 9, Bobby Hull (Wpg), Tim Sheehy (NE).

Assists: 16, Jim Dorey (NE), Bobby Hull (Wpg); 15, Norm Beaudin (Wpg); 14, Tim Sheehy (NE), Tom Webster (NE).

Points: 28, Norm Beaudin (Wpg); 26, Tom Webster (NE); 25, Bobby Hull (Wpg).

Penalty Minutes: 41, Jim Dorey (NE), 30, Gerry Pinder (Cle); 27, Skip Krake (Cle).

Goaltending Wins: 12, Al Smith (NE); 5, Joe Daley (Wpg), Gerry Cheevers (Cle).

Goals Against Average: 2.41, Gerry Cheevers (Cle); 2.84, Wayne Rutledge (Hou); 2.91, Russ Gillow (LA).

Splits by Opponent and by Month, Home and Away

Alb Alberta, **Chi** Chicago, **Cle** Cleveland, **Hou** Houston, **LA** Los Angeles, **Min** Minnesota,
NE New England, **NY** New York, **Ott** Ottawa, **Phi** Philadelphia, **Que** Quebec, **Wpg** Winnipeg

ALBERTA

Opp.	overall	gf-ga	home	gf-ga	away	gf-ga
Chi	4-3-1	28-23	2-1-1	16-11	2-2-0	12-12
Cle	2-4-0	15-21	2-1-0	9-7	0-3-0	6-14
Hou	3-5-0	28-31	2-2-0	15-15	1-3-0	13-16
LA	5-3-0	32-25	3-1-0	21-14	2-2-0	11-11
Min	4-4-0	34-27	3-1-0	22-14	1-3-0	12-13
NE	3-3-0	18-21	2-1-0	10-9	1-2-0	8-12
NY	3-3-0	31-26	3-0-0	23-10	0-3-0	8-16
Ott	3-3-0	20-18	1-2-0	9-10	2-1-0	11-8
Phi	3-3-0	15-12	2-1-0	8-4	1-2-0	7-8
Que	3-3-0	15-23	2-1-0	9-8	1-2-0	9-15
Wpg	5-3-2	30-29	3-1-1	19-14	2-2-1	11-15
Oct	5-5-1	33-39	2-1-1	13-10	3-4-0	20-29
Nov	7-7-1	46-47	6-2-1	33-23	1-5-0	13-24
Dec	3-8-0	33-44	2-3-0	17-21	1-5-0	16-23
Jan	7-4-0	48-33	5-3-0	41-25	2-1-0	7-8
Feb	6-9-0	59-56	5-3-0	37-28	1-6-0	22-28
Mar	10-4-1	50-37	5-0-0	20-9	5-4-1	30-28

HOUSTON

Opp.	overall	gf-ga	home	gf-ga	away	gf-ga
Alb	5-3-0	31-28	3-1-0	16-13	2-2-0	15-15
Chi	7-1-0	34-19	4-0-0	18-11	3-1-0	16-8
Cle	3-3-0	15-17	1-2-0	6-11	2-1-0	9-6
LA	3-6-1	28-43	1-3-1	18-25	2-3-0	10-18
Min	5-2-1	31-20	3-1-0	19-9	2-1-1	12-11
NE	3-2-1	26-21	1-2-0	12-14	2-0-1	14-7
NY	2-4-0	21-22	1-2-0	11-12	1-2-0	10-10
Ott	4-1-0	36-19	3-0-0	23-8	1-1-1	13-11
Phi	4-2-0	26-20	2-1-0	15-11	2-1-0	11-9
Que	1-5-0	15-24	1-2-0	10-11	0-3-0	5-13
Wpg	2-6-0	21-36	2-2-0	14-14	0-4-0	7-22
Oct	5-5-0	32-33	3-2-0	17-15	2-3-0	15-18
Nov	5-6-1	36-42	2-2-0	16-17	3-4-1	20-25
Dec	6-6-2	56-52	3-2-1	30-25	3-4-1	26-27
Jan	10-2-1	66-41	6-2-0	40-29	4-0-1	26-12
Feb	7-7-0	46-47	6-3-0	36-25	1-4-0	10-22
Mar	5-9-0	42-51	2-5-0	23-28	3-4-0	19-23
Apr	1-0-0	6-3	0-0-0	0-0	1-0-0	6-3

CHICAGO

Opp.	overall	gf-ga	home	gf-ga	away	gf-ga
Alb	3-4-1	23-28	2-2-0	12-12	1-2-1	11-16
Cle	2-4-0	19-21	1-2-0	8-7	1-2-0	11-14
Hou	1-7-0	19-34	1-3-0	8-16	0-4-0	11-18
LA	2-6-0	23-28	0-4-0	12-20	2-2-0	11-8
Min	4-6-0	32-39	2-3-0	16-20	2-3-0	16-19
NE	1-5-0	15-22	1-2-0	11-11	0-3-0	4-11
NY	3-2-1	33-27	3-0-0	19-7	0-2-1	14-20
Ott	2-4-0	21-21	1-2-0	7-8	1-2-0	14-13
Phi	3-3-0	21-24	2-1-0	11-8	1-2-0	10-16
Que	3-3-0	22-18	2-1-0	14-7	1-2-0	8-11
Wpg	2-6-0	17-33	2-2-0	11-14	0-4-0	6-19
Oct	2-5-1	19-26	1-0-0	3-1	1-5-1	16-25
Nov	3-8-0	31-37	0-4-0	8-14	3-4-0	23-23
Dec	8-10-0	59-71	7-5-0	43-39	1-5-0	16-32
Jan	4-9-0	47-57	3-5-0	31-32	1-4-0	16-25
Feb	7-5-0	45-39	4-2-0	19-15	3-3-0	26-24
Mar	2-12-1	43-60	2-6-0	25-29	0-6-1	18-31
Apr	0-1-0	1-5	0-0-0	0-0	0-1-0	1-5

LOS ANGELES

Opp.	overall	gf-ga	home	gf-ga	away	gf-ga
Alb	3-5-0	25-32	2-2-0	11-11	1-3-0	14-21
Chi	6-2-0	28-23	2-2-0	8-11	4-0-0	20-12
Cle	2-3-1	15-19	1-2-0	6-11	1-1-1	9-8
Hou	6-3-1	43-28	3-2-0	18-10	3-1-1	25-18
Min	5-2-1	29-19	2-1-1	13-10	3-1-0	16-9
NE	3-3-0	20-22	2-1-0	9-9	1-2-0	11-13
NY	5-1-0	31-15	2-1-0	15-8	3-0-0	16-7
Ott	2-2-2	19-20	1-2-0	10-13	1-0-2	9-7
Phi	2-4-0	19-22	1-2-0	8-12	1-2-0	11-10
Que	3-2-1	17-15	2-1-0	10-9	1-1-1	7-6
Wpg	0-8-0	13-35	0-4-0	9-18	0-4-0	4-17
Oct	5-4-0	35-29	1-3-0	13-17	4-1-0	22-12
Nov	6-10-1	49-63	3-3-0	18-18	3-7-1	31-45
Dec	6-5-3	50-47	3-3-1	22-22	3-2-2	28-25
Jan	6-5-0	45-38	2-4-0	19-19	4-1-0	26-19
Feb	6-5-1	38-38	4-4-0	23-27	2-1-1	15-11
Mar	8-6-1	42-35	5-3-0	22-19	3-3-1	20-16

CLEVELAND

Opp.	overall	gf-ga	home	gf-ga	away	gf-ga
Alb	4-2-0	21-15	3-0-0	14-6	1-2-0	7-9
Chi	4-2-0	21-19	2-1-0	14-11	2-1-0	7-8
Hou	3-3-0	17-15	1-2-0	6-9	2-1-0	11-6
LA	3-2-1	19-15	1-1-1	8-9	2-1-0	11-6
Min	2-4-0	17-22	1-2-0	7-10	1-2-0	10-12
NE	3-5-0	20-23	3-1-0	15-10	0-4-0	5-13
NY	6-2-0	40-29	4-0-0	26-11	2-2-0	14-18
Ott	4-3-1	28-24	2-1-1	15-12	2-2-0	13-12
Phi	6-4-0	52-39	3-2-0	30-19	3-2-0	22-20
Que	5-2-1	26-19	4-0-0	18-9	1-2-1	8-10
Wpg	3-3-0	26-19	2-1-0	11-9	1-2-0	15-10
Oct	7-2-1	40-23	4-2-0	20-13	3-0-1	20-10
Nov	7-7-0	43-40	4-3-0	24-21	3-4-0	19-19
Dec	9-5-0	57-39	7-1-0	42-17	2-4-0	15-22
Jan	7-5-0	38-36	2-1-0	12-13	5-4-0	26-23
Feb	6-6-1	55-57	5-2-1	40-32	1-4-0	15-25
Mar	6-7-1	49-43	3-2-1	21-18	3-5-0	28-25
Apr	1-0-0	5-1	1-0-0	5-1	0-0-0	0-0

MINNESOTA

Opp.	overall	gf-ga	home	gf-ga	away	gf-ga
Alb	4-4-0	27-34	3-1-0	13-12	1-3-0	14-22
Chi	6-4-0	39-32	3-2-0	19-16	3-2-0	20-16
Cle	4-2-0	22-17	2-1-0	12-10	2-1-0	10-7
Hou	2-5-1	20-31	1-2-1	11-12	1-3-0	9-19
LA	2-5-1	19-29	1-3-0	9-16	1-2-1	10-13
NE	3-3-0	20-23	3-0-0	14-8	0-3-0	6-15
NY	4-2-0	21-22	2-1-0	11-11	2-1-0	10-11
Ott	3-3-0	16-19	3-0-0	10-4	0-3-0	6-15
Phi	4-2-0	20-17	2-1-0	8-7	2-1-0	12-10
Que	3-3-0	27-25	2-1-0	11-11	1-2-0	16-14
Wpg	3-4-1	19-20	2-2-0	11-10	1-2-1	8-10
Oct	2-5-1	19-31	1-2-0	7-11	1-3-1	12-20
Nov	10-4-0	52-40	7-2-0	32-23	3-2-0	20-17
Dec	8-7-1	53-51	5-3-0	27-22	3-4-1	26-29
Jan	5-7-1	43-49	3-4-1	24-29	2-3-0	19-20
Feb	6-6-0	41-46	4-0-0	18-9	2-6-0	23-37
Mar	7-8-0	42-52	4-3-0	21-23	3-5-0	21-29

NEW ENGLAND

Opp.	overall	gf-ga	home	gf-ga	away	gf-ga
Alb	3-3-0	21-18	2-1-0	12-8	1-2-0	9-10
Chi	5-1-0	22-15	3-0-0	11-4	2-1-0	11-11
Cle	5-3-0	23-20	4-0-0	13-5	1-3-0	10-15
Hou	2-3-1	21-26	0-2-1	7-14	2-1-0	14-12
LA	3-3-0	22-20	2-1-0	13-11	1-2-0	9-9
Min	3-3-0	23-20	3-0-0	15-6	0-3-0	8-14
NY	7-3-0	47-36	5-0-0	23-17	2-3-0	24-19
Ott	5-3-0	33-29	3-1-0	21-16	2-2-0	12-13
Phi	4-4-0	38-33	3-1-0	19-13	1-3-0	19-20
Que	4-3-1	36-27	2-2-0	19-12	2-1-1	17-15
Wpg	5-1-0	32-19	3-0-0	16-6	2-1-0	16-13
Oct	5-4-0	34-29	3-2-0	17-13	2-2-0	17-16
Nov	8-4-1	56-42	8-0-1	48-26	0-4-0	8-16
Dec	11-7-0	84-65	5-3-0	34-27	6-4-0	50-38
Jan	6-4-0	39-30	3-1-0	15-8	3-3-0	24-22
Feb	5-6-1	42-45	2-1-0	14-14	3-5-1	28-31
Mar	10-5-0	55-49	8-1-0	33-21	2-4-0	22-28
Apr	1-0-0	8-3	1-0-0	8-3	0-0-0	0-0

PHILADELPHIA

Opp.	overall	gf-ga	home	gf-ga	away	gf-ga
Alb	3-3-0	12-15	2-1-0	8-7	1-2-0	4-8
Chi	3-3-0	24-21	2-1-0	16-10	1-2-0	8-11
Cle	4-6-0	39-52	2-3-0	20-22	2-3-0	19-30
Hou	2-4-0	20-26	1-2-0	9-11	1-2-0	11-15
LA	4-2-0	22-19	2-1-0	10-11	2-1-0	12-8
Min	2-4-0	17-20	1-2-0	10-12	1-2-0	7-8
NE	4-4-0	33-38	3-1-0	20-19	1-3-0	13-19
NY	4-4-0	22-26	2-2-0	15-14	2-2-0	7-12
Ott	5-3-0	33-27	3-1-0	18-11	2-2-0	15-16
Que	4-4-0	40-35	3-1-0	29-17	1-3-0	11-18
Wpg	3-3-0	26-26	3-0-0	17-10	0-3-0	9-16
Oct	1-8-0	22-45	1-2-0	10-17	0-6-0	12-28
Nov	4-8-0	40-54	2-3-0	20-22	2-5-0	20-32
Dec	9-8-0	72-79	6-3-0	47-39	3-5-0	25-40
Jan	8-4-0	48-37	3-3-0	24-21	5-1-0	24-16
Feb	7-6-0	51-48	6-1-0	36-22	1-5-0	15-26
Mar	8-6-0	51-40	5-3-0	31-21	3-3-0	20-19
Apr	1-0-0	4-2	1-0-0	4-2	0-0-0	0-0

NEW YORK

Opp.	overall	gf-ga	home	gf-ga	away	gf-ga
Alb	3-3-0	26-31	3-0-0	16-8	0-3-0	10-23
Chi	2-3-1	27-33	2-0-1	20-14	0-3-0	7-19
Cle	2-6-0	29-40	2-2-0	18-14	0-4-0	11-26
Hou	4-2-0	22-21	2-1-0	10-10	2-1-0	12-11
LA	1-5-0	15-31	0-3-0	7-16	1-2-0	8-15
Min	2-4-0	22-21	1-2-0	11-10	1-2-0	11-11
NE	3-7-0	36-47	3-2-0	29-19	0-5-0	17-23
Ott	6-2-0	36-28	4-0-0	27-17	2-2-0	9-11
Phi	4-4-0	26-22	2-2-0	12-7	2-2-0	14-15
Que	4-3-1	40-31	3-1-0	26-12	1-2-1	14-19
Wpg	2-4-0	24-29	1-2-0	10-12	1-2-0	14-17
Oct	5-5-0	45-38	5-4-0	42-34	0-1-0	3-4
Nov	8-6-0	59-48	6-1-0	33-18	2-5-0	26-30
Dec	8-8-0	66-61	4-4-0	36-33	4-4-0	30-28
Jan	3-8-1	40-62	1-3-0	16-16	2-5-1	24-46
Feb	5-6-0	44-59	4-0-0	22-15	1-6-0	22-44
Mar	4-10-1	49-66	3-3-1	27-28	1-7-0	22-38

QUEBEC

Opp.	overall	gf-ga	home	gf-ga	away	gf-ga
Alb	3-3-0	23-18	2-1-0	15-9	1-2-0	8-9
Chi	3-3-0	18-22	2-1-0	11-8	1-2-0	7-14
Cle	2-5-1	19-26	2-1-1	10-8	0-4-0	9-18
Hou	5-1-0	24-15	3-0-0	13-5	2-1-0	11-10
LA	2-3-1	15-17	1-1-1	6-7	1-2-0	9-10
Min	3-3-0	25-27	2-1-0	14-16	1-2-0	11-11
NE	3-4-1	27-36	1-2-1	15-17	2-2-0	12-19
NY	3-4-1	31-40	2-1-1	19-14	1-3-0	12-26
Ott	3-7-0	42-50	3-2-0	25-20	0-5-0	17-30
Phi	4-4-0	35-40	3-1-0	18-11	1-3-0	17-29
Wpg	2-3-1	17-22	1-1-1	9-11	1-2-0	8-11
Oct	5-3-1	32-25	4-2-1	28-20	1-1-0	4-5
Nov	6-6-0	42-44	6-0-0	28-14	0-6-0	14-30
Dec	8-9-0	62-71	5-3-0	31-25	3-6-0	31-46
Jan	3-6-1	41-58	1-2-1	20-26	2-4-0	21-32
Feb	3-8-2	38-48	2-3-2	20-22	1-5-0	18-26
Mar	8-7-1	58-59	4-2-1	28-19	4-5-0	30-40
Apr	0-1-0	3-8	0-0-0	0-0	0-1-0	3-8

OTTAWA

Opp.	overall	gf-ga	home	gf-ga	away	gf-ga
Alb	3-3-0	18-20	1-2-0	8-11	2-1-0	10-9
Chi	4-2-0	21-21	2-1-0	13-14	2-1-0	8-7
Cle	3-4-1	24-28	2-2-0	12-13	1-2-1	12-15
Hou	1-4-1	19-36	1-1-1	11-13	0-3-0	8-23
LA	2-2-2	20-19	0-1-2	7-9	2-1-0	13-10
Min	3-3-0	19-16	3-0-0	15-6	0-3-0	4-10
NE	3-5-0	29-33	2-2-0	13-12	1-3-0	16-21
NY	2-6-0	28-36	2-2-0	11-9	0-4-0	17-27
Phi	3-5-0	27-33	2-2-0	16-15	1-3-0	11-18
Que	7-3-0	50-42	5-0-0	30-17	2-3-0	20-25
Wpg	4-2-0	24-17	1-2-0	10-11	3-0-0	14-6
Oct	5-4-0	45-44	1-2-0	15-16	4-2-0	30-28
Nov	5-6-1	31-41	4-3-1	16-22	1-3-0	15-19
Dec	6-8-2	58-74	3-2-2	30-27	3-6-0	28-47
Jan	3-11-0	49-68	3-3-0	27-23	0-8-0	22-45
Feb	6-7-1	42-42	3-4-0	21-22	3-3-1	21-20
Mar	10-2-0	51-26	7-0-0	34-14	3-2-0	17-12
Apr	0-1-0	3-6	0-1-0	3-6	0-0-0	0-0

WINNIPEG

Opp.	overall	gf-ga	home	gf-ga	away	gf-ga
Alb	3-5-2	29-30	2-2-1	15-11	1-3-1	14-19
Chi	6-2-0	33-17	4-0-0	19-6	2-2-0	14-11
Cle	3-3-0	19-26	2-1-0	10-15	1-2-0	9-11
Hou	6-2-0	36-21	4-0-0	22-7	2-2-0	14-14
LA	8-0-0	35-13	4-0-0	17-4	4-0-0	18-9
Min	4-3-1	20-19	2-1-1	10-8	2-2-0	10-11
NE	1-5-0	19-32	1-2-0	13-16	0-3-0	6-16
NY	4-2-0	29-24	2-1-0	17-14	2-1-0	12-10
Ott	2-4-0	17-24	0-3-0	6-14	2-1-0	11-10
Phi	3-3-0	26-26	3-0-0	16-9	0-3-0	10-17
Que	3-2-1	22-17	2-1-0	11-8	1-1-1	11-9
Oct	6-3-1	36-30	4-1-1	23-17	2-2-0	13-13
Nov	10-7-1	65-52	6-2-0	35-21	4-5-1	30-31
Dec	6-7-0	46-42	4-2-0	26-14	2-5-0	20-28
Jan	7-4-1	46-41	5-1-0	25-15	2-3-1	21-26
Feb	9-2-0	50-26	4-1-0	24-10	5-1-0	26-16
Mar	5-7-1	40-54	3-4-1	23-35	2-3-0	17-19
Apr	0-1-0	2-4	0-0-0	0-0	0-1-0	2-4

1973 All-Star Game

Le Colisée
Quebec City, Quebec
January 6, 1973

East

Coach: Jack Kelley (New England).
Goaltenders: Gerry Cheevers (Cleveland), Al Smith (New England), Serge Aubry (Quebec)
Defensemen: Paul Shmyr, John Hanna (Cleveland), Ken Block (New York), J. C. Tremblay (Quebec), Rick Ley, Jim Dorey (New England)
Forwards: Gary Jarrett, Gerry Pinder (Cleveland), Ron Ward, Norm Ferguson (New York), Larry Pleau, Tom Webster, Terry Caffery (New England), Wayne Carleton, Guy Trottier, Bob Charlebois, Ron Climie (Ottawa), Danny Lawson, John McKenzie (Philadelphia), Michel Parizeau (Quebec)

West

Coach: Bobby Hull (Winnipeg)
Goaltenders: Ernie Wakely (Winnipeg), Jack Norris (Alberta), Mike Curran (Minnesota)
Defensemen: Gerry Odrowski, Bart Crashley (Los Angeles), Al Hamilton, Bob Wall (Alberta), Ron Anderson (Chicago), Larry Hornung (Winnipeg), Mike McMahon, Terry Ball (Minnesota)
Forwards: Bobby Hull, Christian Bordeleau, Norm Beaudin (Winnipeg), Ted Hampson, Wayne Connelly (Minnesota), Jim Harrison (Alberta), Gord Labossiere, Ted Taylor (Houston), Mike Byers, Gary Veneruzzo (Los Angeles), Jan Popiel (Chicago)

East 6, West 2				
West	1	0	1	- 2
East	1	3	2	- 6

1st period: 1. West: Odrowski (Beaudin) 10:39; 2. East: Jarrett (Ward) 10:51.
2nd period: 3. East: McKenzie (Carleton, Block) 3:37; 4. East: Pleau (Webster, Caffery) 12:47; 5. East: Dorey (Ward, Lawson) 19:43.
3rd period: 6. West: Hull (Connelly, Bordeleau) 3:05; 7. East: Lawson (Jarrett, Tremblay) 7:29; 8. East: Carleton (Charlebois, Dorey) 8:00.

Shots on goal

West	8	13	12	- 33
East	18	14	15	- 47

MVP: Wayne Carleton, Ottawa
Attendance 5,435
Did not play: Bart Crashley, Serge Aubry

1972-1973 Year End All-Star Teams

First Team: Goaltender: Gerry Cheevers, Cleveland; Defensemen: J.-C. Tremblay, Quebec and Paul Shmyr, Cleveland; Center: Andre Lacroix, Philadelphia; Right Wing: Danny Lawson, Philadelphia; Left Wing: Bobby Hull, Winnipeg.

Second Team: Goaltender: Bernie Parent, Philadelphia; Defensemen: Jim Dorey, New England and Larry Hornung, Winnipeg; Center: Ron Ward, New York; Right Wing: Tom Webster, New England; Left Wing: Garry Jarrett, Cleveland.

Penalty Shots

date	player, team	goaltender, team	period	time	result
Oct 11	Bill Hicke, Alberta	Les Binkley, Ottawa	1	16:37	Score
Nov 29	Ron Ward, New York	Al Smith, New England	1	5:24	Save
Jan 16	Rene Leclerc, Quebec	Gilles Gratton, Ottawa	3	8:17	Score
Mar 22	Bobby Hull, Winnipeg	Jack Norris, Alberta	-	-	Save
Mar 25	Rene Leclerc, Quebec	Jack Norris, Alberta	3	6:15	Score

Attendance Figures

Each team played 39 home games

team	season total	avg	g	playoff total	avg	team	season total	avg	g	playoff total	avg
Alberta	149,280	3,828	-	-	-	New England	272,255	6,981	9	79,866	8,874
Chicago	178,960	4,589	-	-	-	New York	228,857	5,868	-	-	-
Cleveland	206,202	5,287	4	24,460	6,115	Ottawa	125,802	3,226	2	8,820	4,410
Houston	180,037	4,616	5	33,098	6,620	Philadelphia	168,680	4,325	2	7,234	3,617
Los Angeles	233,285	5,982	3	17,695	5,898	Quebec	269,979	6,923	-	-	-
Minnesota	228,360	5,855	2	12,133	6,067	Winnipeg	237,982	6,102	7	52,559	7,508

Total Attendance: 2,479,679   **Average Attendance:** 5,298

1972-1973 Team Thumbnails

Alberta: Bill Hunter's Oilers started strong and boasted a solid defense headed by Al Hamilton and assisted by Bob Wall, Ken Baird, Doug Barrie and Bob Falkenberg, but a middling offense generally meant the Oilers lost about as often as they won. Up front, the Oilers were led by ex-Leaf Jim Harrison, who when hot, could carry the team by himself. Harrison led the team in goals (39) and points (86), highlighted by a January contest against New York in which he had an amazing 10 points: a hat trick and seven assists. After Harrison, the goals were generally scored by Rusty Patenaude, Ron Walters, Eddie "The Jet" Joyal and Ross Perkins, who all exceeded 20 goals for the season. Ray Kinasewish was the team's first coach, but he was relieved by Hunter in early February. The Oilers suffered through two long losing streaks: a 1-10-1 run in November and December, and an 8-game losing skid in February, that negated stretched in which the Oilers played very well. Their 38-37-3 record tied them with Minnesota for fourth place in the West, but Minnesota prevailed in a one-game playoff to advance to the playoffs, leaving the Oilers shut-out for the post-season.

Chicago: The Cougars had to endure three ownership changes prior to the start of the season, and by the time the Kaiser brothers assumed control, the team had no players and were by far the least-prepared team of the twelve. The Cougars had to quickly assemble a squad, but lacked any big-name stars. Rosaire Paiement had shown he was a legitimate scorer in the NHL with Vancouver, and he was by default the best known of the new Cougars. To appeal to old-time Blackhawks fans, Reggie Fleming also signed up to play for the new Cougars. Hall-of-Famer Marcel Pronovost was selected to be the team's first coach. Alas, the late start and lack of depth doomed the Cougars from the get-go: the Cougars started the season 2-12-1, and also finished the season on a 2-12-1 skid. The Cougars were never in contention, and finished last in the league with a 26-50-2 mark. Goal-scoring was led by Rosie Paiement's 33, with Rick Morris and Jan Popiel each tabbing 31. Bobby Sicinski (25-63-88) led the Cougars in assists and points, while Bob Liddington, Reg Fleming and Bobby Whitlock also met the 20-goal mark. And that was it—the Cougars scored a league-worst 245 goals and gave up 295. Veteran Larry "Hank" Cahan, led the no-name defense, while goaltending was handled by Jimmy McLeod and Andre Gill.

Cleveland: Nick Mileti's Crusaders were built from the goal outward, boasting one of the best in the business in Gerry Cheevers. Fronting him were defensemen Paul Shmyr and Ray Clearwater, both effective defensemen and capable puck-movers who regularly created chances and collected their share of assists. Cheevers was superlative in the nets, with the league's best average (2.84), most shutouts (5) and second in wins with 32; as a team, the Crusaders allowed the fewest goals in the WHA, with just 239 against. Their offense was solid, led by Gary Jarrett's 40 goals and 78 points. Ron Buchanan collected 37 goals, and former Seal Gerry Pinder had 30, with three other Crusaders scoring at least 20 goals; collectively, the Crusaders had 287 goals as a team. Coached by Bill Needham, the Crusaders finished second in the East with a 43-32-3 record. After dismissing Philadelphia in four straight to open the playoffs, the Crusaders could not do much against New England, losing in five games against the eventual champs.

Houston: The Aeros landed in Houston under the guidance of Bill "Foxy" Dineen, who put together a strong squad made up of many mid-line NHLers and a number of capable yet unknown players from the Western League. The result was a team lacking any major stars, but a solid club with three-line depth, solid defense and goaltending. Gord Labossiere was the leading scorer with 36 goals and 96 points. Former Vancouver Canuck Ted Taylor contributed 34 goals, Duke Harris 30, and five others with at least 20 goals. The defense was manned by John Schella, who led the league in penalty minutes with 239, Larry Hale, and Poul Popiel. Don McLeod and Wayne Rutledge shared netminding duties. The Aeros finished 38-35-5, good for second in the West. After beating Los Angeles in the first round, the Aeros were swept by Winnipeg in the semifinals.

Los Angeles: Coached by Terry Slater, the Sharks played rough-and-tumble hockey, featuring five players with over 100 minutes in penalties, partly to hide a thin offense. Scoring was led by Gary Veneruzzo, with 43 goals and 73 points. Alton White, with 20 goals exactly, was second in goals, although eleven other players scored ten or more goals. Playmaking was the job of former Red Wing J.-P. Leblanc, who collected 50 assists. The defense was tight and often belligerent, with Gerry Odrowski, Jim Niekamp, Ralph MacSweyn, Jim Watson and Bart Crashley manning the blue line. In goal were George Gardner and Russ Gillow, the latter sporting a sharp 2.82 average as Gardner's back-up. Somehow, the Sharks managed a very respectable finish, with 37 wins against 35 losses (and 6 ties), for a third-place finish in the Western Division. In the playoffs, Los Angeles lost to Houston in six games.

Minnesota: The Fighting Saints cleverly built their team through the colleges and American junior and amateur ranks. A number of Saints skaters had played for the United States in the 1968 and/or 1972 Olympics (and one, goaltender Jack McCartan, played for the 1960 Gold Medalists). Coached by Glen

Sonmor, the Saints were a quick-skating, smallish club that relied on speed and playmaking. Wayne Connelly scored 40 goals to lead the team, Bill Klatt had 36, and eight other players scored in double figures. When things got rough, the Saints could turn to defensemen John Arbour (188 penalty minutes), Dick Paradise (189 penalty minutes) and Frank Sanders to keep the opponents at bay. Goal was the domain of McCartan and 1972 Olympian Mike "Lefty" Curran. The Saints finished tied with Alberta for fourth place in the West, and won the one-game special playoff game to advance to the post-season. However, Minnesota's run didn't last long, losing to Winnipeg in five games.

New England: The Whalers took a more conservative approach to building their club, foregoing the big splashy names and opting for a squad of seasoned pros that gave the Whalers major-league talent and three-line depth. The approach paid significant dividends as the Whalers were the first champions of the World Hockey Association, winning the World Trophy in a five-game battle with Winnipeg. Tom Webster bolted from the California Golden Seals to the Whalers and provided 53 goals and 103 points, while Terry Caffery earned the Rookie-of-the-Year award with 39 goals and 100 points. Larry Pleau and Tim Sheehy also provided 30-goal seasons, leading a balanced attack that produced 318 goals for the season. The defense was anchored by ex-Leafs Rick Ley, Brad Selwood and Jim Dorey, and ex-Bruins Ted Green and Paul Hurley. Al Smith handled the bulk of the goaltending, winning 31 games, and the team was ably coached by former Boston University coach Jack Kelley.

New York: The WHA felt a need to have a team in New York, and at first, desired to place their team in the new Nassau Coliseum being built on Long Island. However, the NHL quickly cut the WHA off at the pass, forming the expansion Islanders to play at Nassau, starting in 1972. This forced the WHA Raiders to look back to downtown and the Madison Square Garden, which had no objection to gouging the under-funded ownership for steep per-game rental fees. Ultimately, the Raiders would wear out two ownership groups before being league-run for the remainder of the 1972-73 season. Long-time Rangers forward Camille Henry was the team's first coach, but it was a former two-goal scorer who would run away with the team's offense: Ron Ward, who had scored two goals for the Canucks in 1971-72, scored 51 with the Raiders, finishing with 118 points, second best in the league. Scoring was not the team's problem: Wayne Rivers, Gene Peacosh and Bobby Sheehan all scored 35 or more goals, and the Raiders scored 303 for the season. However, keeping the other team from scoring was the team's downfall. The Raiders gave up 334 goals (becoming the first team ever to score and give up 300 or more goals in the same season). The

end result was a last-place finish in the Eastern Division.

Ottawa: The formation of the Ottawa franchise seemed to encounter every conceivable road-block, from under-funded ownership to finding a place to play to a city (Ottawa) that at first would have nothing to do with the Nationals. Despite these set-backs, the Nationals managed to start the season, which was a minor miracle by itself. Not surprisingly, the Nats did not play well and drew even worse at the new Civic Centre Arena. Goaltender Les Binkley and forward Wayne Carleton were the Nats' best-known players, most of the rest of the team being composed of fringe NHLers, career minor-leaguers and untested juniors, all coached by former Leaf Billy Harris. The situation in Ottawa was so bad that the team was looking to move to Toronto in mid-season when the Nats caught fire on the ice. Sporting a 19-31-4 record in early February, the Nationals reeled off 16 wins in its next 22 games, which vaulted them into fourth place in the East and the final playoff spot. The fans in Ottawa had come around and were starting to support the team, but the arena landlords nixed the groundswell by shutting the team out of the arena for the playoffs. The Nats were forced to play its home games in Toronto, and ultimately, moved to Toronto for the following season.

Philadelphia: The Blazers seemed to be the joke of the league at first. Its first home game was cancelled when the ice-surfacer tore up the ice. A near-riot ensued as fans threw their commemorative orange hockey pucks at Derek Sanderson, who bravely stood at center ice to announce the cancellation of the game. Sanderson himself was openly unhappy being in Philadelphia, and lasted just eight games before getting injured and eventually being bought out from his contract and released. Meanwhile, the Blazers' other stars, goaltender Bernie Parent and forward Johnny "Pie" McKenzie, were out with injuries. All this conspired to give the Blazers a 4-16-0 start, and it looked like a long season for the Philadelphia skaters. It would be a relatively obscure centerman and his winger who would save the season for the Blazers: ex-Flyer Andre Lacroix, who had never scored above 24 goals in the NHL, erupted for 50 goals, 74 assists and a league-leading 124 points. Many of his assists went to his slick right-winger, Danny Lawson, whose 61 goals led the league. John McKenzie did come back to score 28 goals, and Bernie Parent was a work-horse in goal, leading the league with 33 wins. McKenzie was a player-coach, but veteran coach Phil Watson would assume most of the coaching duties for the season. The reward: the Blazers finished on a 16-9-0 run, good for third place in the Eastern Division. Alas, the playoffs went quickly, as the Blazers lost in four straight to Cleveland, after Bernie Parent had left the team when his contract was voided. After a rocky year in Philadelphia, Parent stayed in Philly, now

tending goal again for the Flyers, while the Blazers had moved across the continent to Vancouver.

Quebec: The Nordiques sought to build a team composed of French-Canadian players, and succeeded nicely in luring the great Canadiens' defenseman Jean-Claude Tremblay away from Montreal to anchor the new Nordique squad. Even Jean Beliveau, who had retired from playing in 1971, was offered a chance to join with Quebec, but he declined. The team was to be coached by perhaps the greatest-known Canadien, Maurice "Rocket" Richard. But Richard's tenure lasted just two games (replaced by Maurice Filion), quickly realizing he had no desire to coach. After that rocky start, the Nordiques skated through a disappointing inaugural season, finishing 33-40-5, fifth place in the East, and out of the playoffs. Their top scorer was Alain "Boom-Boom" Caron, with 36 goals. Bobby Guindon (28 goals), Andre Gaudette (27), Michel Parizeau (25) and Renald Leclerc (24) were the only other Nordiques to surpass 20 goals. On defense, J.-C. Tremblay was superlative, leading the team with 75 assists and 89 points, often skating more than half of each game. Ex-Seal Francois Lacombe was perhaps the best-known of the other defenseman. In goal, Serge Aubry handled the majority of the workload, with a promising rookie, Richard Brodeur, as his back-up.

Winnipeg: Simply having Bobby Hull on the roster vaulted the Jets to the top tier of the league, but it would be fifteen games before Hull actually suited up for a game, once he was cleared to play by the courts. Hull made up for lost time and turned in an excellent season, scoring 51 goals and collecting 103 points. His linemates—center Christian Bordeleau and right-wing Norm Beaudin—each surpassed 100 points. A strong second half vaulted the Jets to a 43-31-4 record and first place in the Western Division. The Jets lacked offensive depth after their top line—Danny Johnson's 19 goals was next best—but a solid defense and a strong one-two goaltending tandem of Ernie Wakely and Joe Daley permitted just 249 goals against. In the playoffs, the Jets dismissed Minnesota and Houston, losing just once in nine games, before meeting the Whalers in the finals. However, the Whalers were able to defeat Winnipeg in the final round, denying the Jets the first league crown.

First Season Fun Facts

Len Lilyholm not only played in the new St. Paul Civic Center as a member of the Minnesota Fighting Saints in 1972-73, he helped design it. An architect and builder, Lilyholm participated in the design of the Saints' home arena, which was completed in January, 1973.

Alton White scored a hat trick for the Los Angeles Sharks against the Minnesota Fighting Saints on March 1, 1973, while being credited with only two shots on goal for the game. He scored on his only two shots. On a breakaway late in the game against an empty net, a sure third goal was thwarted when Saints coach Harry Neale threw a stick onto the ice in White's path. White was awarded the goal, completing his most unusual hat trick.

Minnesota won two consecutive games in overtime by identical 2-1 scores, March 22 at Chicago, and March 24 at Cleveland. In both games, the Fighting Saints scored the winning goals in the last possible seconds. Bob MacMillan won the first game scoring with just 3 seconds remaining, while Bill Klatt won the second game, scoring with just 17 seconds on the clock.

1972-1973 Game by Game Line Scores

Date & Teams	Scoring 1 2 3 ot F	Shots 1 2 3 ot F	Goaltenders	Goals & Other Scoring Highlights
October 11				
Alberta	3 3 1 - 7	14 8 9 - 31	Brown	Hicke 2, Anderson 2, Harrison, Walters, Joyal
Ottawa	1 1 2 - 4	8 12 12 - 32	Binkley	Charlebois 2, Carleton, Trottier
Quebec	0 0 0 - 0	6 9 6 - 21	Aubry	▸ Cheevers: shutout (1), 21 saves
Cleveland	0 1 1 - 2	13 9 12 - 34	Cheevers	Dillabough, Buchanan
October 12				
Chicago	0 1 1 - 2	8 12 10 - 30	J. McLeod	Fleming, Popiel
Houston	1 0 2 - 3	10 8 9 - 27	D. McLeod	Lund, Taylor, Hughes
Philadelphia	2 0 1 - 3	12 7 10 - 29	Parent	Sanderson, Plumb, Migneault
New England	1 2 1 - 4	6 8 9 - 23	Smith	Williams, Sarrazin, Cunniff, Pleau (WG 17:49)
Winnipeg	3 1 2 - 6	14 11 8 - 33	Wakely	Bordeleau 4, McDonald, Asmundson
New York	1 2 1 - 4	12 11 7 - 30	Kurt	Ward 2, Sheehan 2
October 13				
Alberta	0 0 0 - 0	6 16 6 - 28	Norris	▸ Aubry: shutout (1), 28 saves
Quebec	3 1 2 - 6	15 8 12 - 35	Aubry	Leclerc 2, Lacombe, Bergeron, Guindon, Tremblay
Houston	0 2 1 - 3	11 7 9 - 27	Rutledge	Hall, Lund, McCallum
Los Angeles	0 1 1 - 2	13 10 7 - 30	Gardner	Sutherland, Young
Winnipeg	1 1 2 - 4	8 6 13 - 27	Daley	Bordeleau, Johnson, McDonald, Asmundson (WG 18:31)
Minnesota	2 1 0 - 3	14 9 8 - 31	Curran	Connelly, Speck, McMahon
October 14				
Alberta	1 1 0 - 2	13 7 7 - 27	Norris	Anderson, Harrison
Cleveland	0 1 2 - 3	11 12 16 - 39	Cheevers	Pinder 2 (WG 11:25), Hanna
Ottawa	1 1 4 - 6	8 14 11 - 33	Binkley, Gratton	Kirk, Leduc, Warr, Carleton, Sentes, Climie
New York	4 2 2 - 8	14 8 8 - 30	Kurt	Sheehan 2, Laughton 2, Perry, Ward, Bradley, Morenz
October 15				
Alberta	2 1 2 - 5	10 7 9 - 26	Brown	Cote, Fonteyne, Walters, Hicke, Joyal
Winnipeg	0 1 1 - 2	13 11 5 - 29	Wakely	Johnson, Bordeleau
Chicago	1 1 0 - 2	9 9 14 - 32	Gill	Sicinski, Whitlock
Minnesota	2 0 1 - 3	16 10 13 - 39	McCartan	Pearson, Klatt, Antonovich (WG 12:22)
Cleveland	4 1 2 - 7	8 8 6 - 22	Whidden	Hardy 3, Shmyr, Krake, Brindley, Hanna
Ottawa	1 3 1 - 5	7 16 7 - 30	Gratton	Carleton 2, Martin, Climie, Trottier
Los Angeles	3 1 1 - 5	8 12 11 - 31	Gillow	Leblanc 2, Sutherland, Heiskala, Szura
Houston	1 0 0 - 1	12 10 8 - 30	D. McLeod	Harris
Philadelphia	0 0 0 - 0	8 12 9 - 29	Parent, Paille	▸ Donnelly: shutout (1), 29 saves
New York	2 2 1 - 5	8 8 16 - 32	Donnelly	Rivers, Ward, Perry, Sheehan, Morenz
October 16				
Chicago	0 1 0 - 1	6 9 8 - 23	J. McLeod	Paiement
New England	0 3 1 - 4	11 11 10 - 32	Smith	Sarrazin, French, Green, Caffery
October 17				
Los Angeles	1 2 2 - 5	10 14 9 - 33	Gillow	Odrowski, Crashley, Byers, Slater, Veneruzzo
Minnesota	0 0 1 - 1	15 12 12 - 39	Curran	Connelly
New York	0 1 2 0 3	13 13 8 1 35	Kurt	Morenz, Laughton, White
Cleveland	2 1 0 1 4	14 4 13 3 34	Cheevers	Pumple, Dillabough, Buchanan, Krake (OT 6:09)
Winnipeg	1 0 1 0 2	15 8 11 2 36	Daley	Ash, Beaudin
Alberta	1 1 0 1 3	9 9 10 3 31	Norris	Harrison 2, Walters (OT 4:53)
October 18				
New England	1 2 1 - 4	10 12 7 - 29	Landon	Webster 3, Cunniff
Houston	1 0 0 - 1	9 10 4 - 23	Rutledge	Taylor
October 19				
Chicago	0 1 1 - 2	12 12 9 - 33	Gill, J. McLeod	Proceviat, Paiement
Ottawa	2 1 3 - 6	8 10 14 - 32	Gratton	Climie 2, Donnelly, Trottier, Martin, Carleton
Cleveland	1 1 1 - 3	6 13 6 - 25	Cheevers	Pumple, Krake, Jarrett
New York	0 1 0 - 1	8 12 7 - 27	Donnelly	Ferguson
Minnesota	0 1 0 - 1	10 13 11 - 34	McCartan	Antonovich
Houston	2 1 2 - 5	12 11 10 - 33	D. McLeod	Labossiere 3, Harris 2
Philadelphia	0 0 2 - 2	10 10 9 - 29	Parent	Plante, Lawson
Los Angeles	1 2 1 - 4	9 13 11 - 33	Gillow	Veneruzzo 2, Young, Crashley
Quebec	0 1 3 - 4	7 7 15 - 29	Aubry	Leclerc 2 (WG 16:06), Gendron, Guindon
New England	0 1 2 - 3	18 13 16 - 47	Smith	Pleau, Ley, Webster
October 20				
Minnesota	0 0 1 0 1	6 7 6 3 22	Curran	Speck
Winnipeg	1 0 0 0 1	15 9 6 8 38	Daley	Zanussi
Philadelphia	1 0 0 - 1	9 7 8 - 24	Parent	Bennett
Alberta	1 2 1 - 4	17 18 11 - 46	Brown	Walters 3, Patenaude
October 21				
Houston	1 1 0 - 2	7 10 12 - 29	Rutledge	Harris, Labossiere
New York	1 1 1 - 3	9 8 12 - 29	Donnelly	Sheehan 2 (WG 3:14), Rivers
New England	1 2 1 - 4	6 13 4 - 23	Smith	Pleau, Selwood, Caffery
Quebec	4 2 0 - 6	10 6 11 - 27	Aubry	Leclerc 2, Tremblay, Payette, Guite, Parizeau
Ottawa	2 2 1 - 5	13 12 12 - 37	Gratton	Trottier 2, Carleton, Climie, Kirk
Cleveland	2 1 0 - 3	15 13 11 - 39	Whidden	Buchanan, Pinder, Hanna
October 22				
Chicago	1 1 2 - 4	8 5 6 - 19	J. McLeod	Whitlock, Popiel, Blanchette, Proceviat
Los Angeles	0 1 1 - 2	7 17 4 - 28	Gillow	Mavety, Crashley
Minnesota	2 2 1 - 5	12 11 3 - 26	McCartan	Connelly 2, Christiansen, MacMillan, Hampson
New York	3 0 1 - 4	15 3 7 - 25	Donnelly	Ward 2, Chartre, Douglas
Ottawa	1 2 0 - 3	10 7 9 - 26	Gratton	Martin, Leduc, Charlebois
Quebec	1 1 0 - 2	16 7 15 - 38	Aubry	Gendron, Dufour
Philadelphia	0 1 2 - 3	2 7 8 - 17	Parent	Lacroix, Meloche, Herriman
Winnipeg	3 3 0 - 6	17 10 11 - 38	Wakely	Bordeleau 2, Rizzuto, Black, McDonald, Cadle

1972-1973 Game by Game Line Scores

Date & Teams	Scoring 1 2 3 ot F	Shots 1 2 3 ot F	Goaltenders	Goals & Other Scoring Highlights
October 23				
Minnesota	0 0 1 - 1	8 11 15 - 34	Curran	Konik
New England	1 2 2 - 5	17 6 7 - 30	Landon	Pleau, Earl, Caffery, Sheehy, Danby
October 24				
Chicago	1 0 2 0 3	10 7 13 5 35	J. McLeod	Whitlock, Glenwright, Popiel
Alberta	0 2 1 0 3	8 11 9 3 31	Norris	Carlin 2, Harrison
Houston	0 1 2 - 3	11 11 12 - 34	D. McLeod	Hall, McCallum, Popiel
Quebec	2 2 1 - 5	12 10 11 - 33	Aubry	Leclerc 2, Parizeau 2, Guindon
New England	1 1 0 1 3	7 5 7 2 21	Smith	Webster, French, Sheehy (OT 5:27)
Cleveland	0 1 1 0 2	17 14 14 2 47	Cheevers	Jarrett, Wiste (TG 17:04)
Philadelphia	1 1 1 - 3	7 4 8 - 19	Paille	Sanderson, Herriman, Lacroix
Winnipeg	0 2 3 - 5	7 8 19 - 34	Daley	Beaudin 2, Rizzuto, Bordeleau, Boyer
October 25				
Cleveland	2 4 2 - 8	14 11 8 - 33	Cheevers	Hodgson 3, Pinder 2, Clearwater, Erickson, Andrea
Philadelphia	2 0 0 - 2	8 8 5 - 21	Parent, Paille	Burgess, Campbell
Ottawa	2 3 3 - 8	8 9 7 - 24	Gratton	Trottier 2, Kirk 2, Carleton, Climie, Conacher, Leduc
Los Angeles	1 2 2 - 5	15 10 9 - 34	Gardner, Gillow	Veneruzzo, Niekamp, Serviss, Heiskala, McCaskill
October 26				
Minnesota	0 3 1 - 4	11 12 12 - 35	Curran	Connelly 2, Konik, Antonovich
Quebec	4 0 1 - 5	6 6 11 - 23	Aubry	Lacombe, Bergeron, Gaudette, Desjardine, Parizeau
New England	3 2 1 - 6	8 10 7 - 25	Smith	French, Sheehy, Caffery, Williams, Ahearn, Pleau
New York	2 2 3 - 7	12 7 14 - 33	Kurt	Rivers 3, Reichmuth, Perry, Ferguson, Laughton
Ottawa	1 2 0 - 3	11 8 15 - 34	Gratton	Carleton, King, Conacher
Houston	1 5 1 - 7	19 10 13 - 42	Rutledge	Labossiere 2, Taylor 2, Hall 2, Lund
October 27				
Alberta	0 0 0 - 0	9 6 5 - 20	Brown	▶ Cheevers: shutout (2), 20 saves
Cleveland	0 4 2 - 6	7 16 11 - 34	Cheevers	Buchanan 2, Krake, Jarrett, Clearwater, Hodgson
Chicago	0 0 2 - 2	11 9 12 - 32	J. McLeod	Fleming, Popiel
Winnipeg	0 3 1 - 4	8 16 7 - 31	Wakely	Beaudin 2, Black, Rizzuto
Los Angeles	3 1 0 - 4	10 10 13 - 33	Gillow	Crashley 2, Young
Philadelphia	1 2 2 - 5	9 10 11 - 30	Archambault	Lacroix 2 (WG 4:32), Cardiff, Lawson, Paiement
October 28				
Alberta	1 1 2 - 4	14 11 18 - 43	Norris	Kassian, Carlin, Patenaude, Hicke
New England	0 0 1 - 1	16 9 9 - 34	Landon	Pleau (spoiled Norris' shutout at 18:10)
Los Angeles	3 0 0 1 4	11 11 8 2 32	Gardner	Byers 2, Gilmore, Slater (OT 1:56)
New York	1 1 1 0 3	8 11 5 0 24	Kurt, Donnelly	Chartre, Kennedy, Ferguson
Ottawa	3 1 1 - 5	10 13 4 - 27	Gratton	Martin 3, Trottier, Climie
Philadelphia	0 2 1 - 3	5 16 14 - 35	Archambault	Migneault, Lawson, Campbell
October 29				
Alberta	1 0 1 - 2	2 9 11 - 22	Brown	Anderson, Perkins
New York	1 3 3 - 7	17 15 12 - 44	Donnelly	Ward 2, Sheehan 2, Morenz, Ferguson, Laughton
Cleveland	0 1 1 0 2	7 5 6 6 24	Cheevers	Hodgson, Jarrett
Quebec	0 0 2 0 2	10 11 10 4 35	Brodeur	Guindon, Leclerc
Houston	2 1 0 - 3	11 9 4 - 24	Rutledge	Labossiere, Taylor, Harris
Winnipeg	1 0 4 - 5	10 7 25 - 42	Daley	Beaudin 2, Gratton, Black, Hornung
October 31				
Houston	1 2 1 - 4	16 13 7 - 36	D. McLeod	Labossiere, Lund, Hale, Taylor (WG 7:09)
Alberta	2 1 0 - 3	12 12 12 - 36	Norris	Harrison, Hicke, Perkins
Los Angeles	1 1 2 - 4	6 10 13 - 29	Gardner	Serviss, MacNeil, Crashley, McCaskill
Quebec	1 1 0 - 2	9 10 14 - 33	Brodeur	Leclerc, Payette
Winnipeg	0 1 0 - 1	8 10 8 - 26	Wakely	Rousseau (Hull: first game back in Chicago, DNP)
Chicago	0 0 3 - 3	7 7 11 - 25	J. McLeod	Whitlock 2, Sicinski
November 1				
Chicago	1 1 0 - 2	14 10 13 - 37	J. McLeod	Glenwright, Sicinski
New England	0 2 2 - 4	10 8 10 - 28	Smith	Ahearn 2, Caffery, Earl
Philadelphia	2 3 2 - 7	10 11 13 - 34	Paille	Lawson 4, Bennett, Sanderson, Herriman
Cleveland	0 3 2 - 5	16 18 13 - 47	Cheevers	Erickson 2, Buchanan, Krake, Jarrett
Winnipeg	0 0 0 - 0	12 18 11 - 41	Daley	▶ Curran: shutout (1), 41 saves
Minnesota	0 2 1 - 3	6 12 8 - 26	Curran	Falkman, Konik, Antonovich
November 2				
Los Angeles	0 0 1 0 1	6 5 8 2 21	Gardner	Veneruzzo
Ottawa	0 0 1 0 1	7 13 8 3 31	Gratton	King (TG, spoiled Gardner's shutout at 17:56)
New York	0 2 2 - 4	16 13 12 - 41	Donnelly	Olds, Rivers, Ward, Morenz
Minnesota	1 0 1 - 2	12 10 11 - 33	Curran	MacMillan, Sanders
Philadelphia	0 0 3 - 3	11 8 10 - 29	Paille	O'Donoghue 2, Campbell
Quebec	2 3 1 - 6	11 14 11 - 36	Lemelin	Archambault 2, Guindon 2, Giroux, Tremblay
November 3				
Houston	1 1 1 - 3	11 10 9 - 30	D. McLeod	Popiel 2, Taylor
Alberta	1 3 0 - 4	6 17 7 - 30	Norris	Carlin, Barrie, Kassian, Wall
New York	4 3 2 - 9	11 7 6 - 24	Donnelly	Sheehan 2, Ward 2, Ferguson, Rivers, Bradley, Perry, Block
Winnipeg	1 2 3 - 6	16 20 13 - 49	Wakely	Black 2, Johnson, Bordeleau, Cadle, Beaudin
November 4				
Los Angeles	0 0 2 1 3	18 14 12 7 51	Gardner	Niekamp 2 (OT 9:27), Veneruzzo
Chicago	1 0 1 0 2	10 11 7 3 31	J. McLeod	Whitlock, Liddington
Philadelphia	1 2 1 - 4	11 6 9 - 26	Paille, Archambault	Lacroix, Campeau, Burgess, Campbell
New England	2 5 1 - 8	13 15 19 - 47	Landon	French 2, Pleau 2, Caffery, Ahearn, Danby, Sheehy
Quebec	2 0 1 - 3	20 6 7 - 33	Aubry	Gendron, Payette, Tremblay
Cleveland	1 1 3 - 5	7 18 16 - 41	Cheevers	Pumple, Hodgson, Pinder, Krake, Wiste

1972-1973 Game by Game Line Scores

Date & Teams	Scoring 1 2 3 ot F	Shots 1 2 3 ot F	Goaltenders	Goals & Other Scoring Highlights
November 5				
Chicago	2 0 0 - 2	11 3 7 - 21	J. McLeod	Sicinski, Whitlock
Quebec	0 2 1 - 3	16 16 10 - 42	Aubry	Caron, Parizeau, Giroux (WG 7:26)
Houston	0 0 0 - 0	6 9 8 - 23	Rutledge	▶ Gillow: shutout (1), 23 saves
Los Angeles	1 2 1 - 4	10 9 20 - 39	Gillow	Crashley, Odrowski, Young, Sutherland
New York	0 0 1 - 1	0 11 7 - 18	Kurt	Perry
Winnipeg	3 0 0 - 3	17 9 9 - 35	Daley	Hornung, Johnson, McDonald
Ottawa	0 2 3 - 5	10 13 15 - 38	Gratton	Leduc, Climie, Carleton, Meloff, Charlebois
Alberta	2 1 0 - 3	11 7 12 - 30	Brown	Walters, Perkins, Wall
Philadelphia	1 0 0 - 1	9 10 5 - 24	Paille	Lawson
Minnesota	1 1 1 - 3	20 12 11 - 43	McCartan	Speck 2, Morrison
November 6				
Winnipeg	1 0 1 - 2	8 5 12 - 25	Wakely	Black, Boyer
New England	2 0 4 - 6	6 7 7 - 20	Smith	Webster 3, Pleau, Green, Williams
November 7				
Houston	0 1 2 - 3	16 13 10 - 39	Rutledge	Taylor, Hoekstra, Stanfield
Chicago	0 1 1 - 2	15 13 5 - 33	J. McLeod, Gill	Paiement, Fleming
New York	1 0 1 - 2	10 3 6 - 19	Wilkie	Ferguson, Reichmuth
Alberta	1 1 2 - 4	10 16 14 - 40	Norris	Hicke, Walters, Hamilton, Carlyle
November 8				
New York	0 0 1 - 1	6 9 6 - 21	Donnelly	Ferguson
Los Angeles	0 0 2 - 2	12 6 14 - 32	Gillow	Byers, Krupicka (WG 19:26)
Winnipeg	1 0 1 - 2	16 11 17 - 44	Wakely	Rousseau, Johnson (Hull: league debut)
Quebec	2 1 0 - 3	14 8 4 - 26	Aubry	Roy, Payette, Bergeron
November 9				
Los Angeles	2 0 0 - 2	14 6 9 - 29	Gardner	Sutherland, Heiskala
Alberta	3 1 3 - 7	12 13 14 - 39	Brown	Harrison 2, Baird, Fonteyne, Hicke, Joyal, Barrie
Winnipeg	1 3 0 - 4	8 12 10 - 30	Wakely	Hornung, Beaudin, Cuddie, Rousseau
Ottawa	0 1 0 - 1	11 4 13 - 28	Gratton	Leduc
November 10				
Minnesota	2 1 2 - 5	14 8 11 - 33	Curran	Klatt, Christiansen, Hampson, Antonovich, Morrison
Winnipeg	0 1 0 - 1	6 18 7 - 31	Daley	Gratton
November 11				
Cleveland	0 1 3 - 4	12 12 10 - 34	Cheevers	Pinder 3, Andrea
Chicago	0 1 0 - 1	12 9 5 - 26	Gill	Hatoum
Houston	1 0 0 - 1	15 9 13 - 37	Rutledge	Harris
Quebec	1 0 2 - 3	13 9 13 - 35	Aubry	Gaudette 2, Parizeau
Los Angeles	0 2 1 - 3	9 13 10 - 32	Gillow	Leblanc, Crashley, Serviss
Alberta	2 0 3 - 5	10 7 10 - 27	Norris	Harrison 2, Carlyle, Barrie, Falkenberg
New York	2 2 1 - 5	5 4 9 - 18	Kurt	Peacosh 2, Olds, Rivers, Ferguson
New England	1 1 4 - 6	8 9 8 - 25	Smith	Webster 2 (WG 19:20), Sheehy, Selby, Williams, Pleau
November 12				
Cleveland	3 0 0 - 3	11 10 6 - 27	Whidden	Buchanan, Erickson, Jarrett
Alberta	0 1 0 - 1	1 15 9 - 25	Brown, Norris	Walters
Los Angeles	1 0 1 - 2	14 7 8 - 29	Gardner	MacNeil, Veneruzzo
Winnipeg	1 1 3 - 5	9 13 10 - 32	Wakely	Hull 2 (first WHA goals), Johnson, McDonald, Bordeleau
Philadelphia	1 0 0 - 1	12 8 8 - 28	Archambault	Plante
Ottawa	0 1 1 - 2	10 6 4 - 20	Gratton	Climie, Conacher (WG 17:40)
November 13				
Houston	3 1 0 0 4	15 6 13 5 39	Hughes	Harris, Hall, Labossiere, McDonald
New England	0 2 2 0 4	6 18 12 14 50	Landon	Sheehy 2 (TG 19:00), Webster, French
November 14				
Cleveland	2 1 0 - 3	8 11 7 - 26	Cheevers	Jarrett 2, Hardy
Minnesota	1 1 3 - 5	14 7 12 - 33	Curran	Speck 2, MacMillan, Konik, Christiansen
Los Angeles	0 0 0 - 0	9 8 7 - 24	Gardner, Gillow	▶ Wakely: shutout (1), 24 saves
Winnipeg	4 3 1 - 8	13 10 12 - 35	Wakely	Bordeleau 2, Hornung 2, Hull, Johnson, Rousseau, Cadle
Philadelphia	1 0 3 - 4	11 15 12 - 38	Paille	Burgess, Lawson, Plante, Lacroix (WG 19:50)
Chicago	1 2 0 - 3	8 15 13 - 36	Gill	Lodboa 2, Liddington
November 15				
Los Angeles	2 2 2 - 6	14 17 7 - 38	Gillow	Szura 2, Jones 2, Byers, McCaskill
Houston	2 1 1 - 4	11 10 8 - 29	Hughes	Hall, Popiel, Hoekstra, Labossiere
New York	2 2 0 - 4	11 8 3 - 22	Donnelly	Peacosh 2, Sheehan, Ward
Quebec	2 1 4 - 7	14 15 8 - 37	Aubry	Caron 3, Archambault, Gendron, Gaudette, Guindon
Winnipeg	1 0 0 - 1	9 10 8 - 27	Wakely	Bordeleau
Alberta	0 1 2 - 3	11 5 6 - 22	Norris	Walters 2, Fonteyne
November 16				
Ottawa	0 2 1 - 3	15 13 11 - 39	Binkley	Climie, Trottier, King
Cleveland	0 2 4 - 6	10 10 8 - 28	Whidden	Buchanan 4, Jarrett, Andrea
Quebec	0 3 1 - 4	4 10 12 - 26	Aubry	Rouleau, Bergeron, Golembrosky, Caron
Minnesota	2 2 1 - 5	13 12 15 - 40	Curran	Connelly 2, Hampson, Klatt, Ryan
November 17				
Chicago	0 1 0 - 1	12 15 11 - 38	J. McLeod, Gill	Sicinski
Alberta	0 0 3 - 3	7 15 14 - 36	Norris	Harrison, Joyal (WG 16:57), Walters
New England	0 0 0 - 0	4 4 8 - 16	Smith	▶ Cheevers: shutout (3), 16 saves
Cleveland	0 0 3 - 3	4 9 8 - 21	Cheevers	Wiste, Dillabough, Clearwater
Winnipeg	2 2 1 - 5	14 14 6 - 34	Wakely	Rizzuto, Cadle, Bordeleau, Beaudin, Swenson
Los Angeles	1 0 0 - 1	9 12 6 - 27	Gillow	Leblanc

1972-1973 Game by Game Line Scores

Date & Teams	Scoring 1 2 3 ot F	Shots 1 2 3 ot F	Goaltenders	Goals & Other Scoring Highlights
November 18				
Minnesota	0 3 1 1 5	8 12 9 2 31	McCartan	Antonovich, Connelly, Hampson, Morrison, MacMillan (OT 1:23)
Philadelphia	2 1 1 0 4	13 9 15 0 37	Paille	McKenzie, Lacroix, Herriman, Gravel
Ottawa	1 1 0 - 2	14 21 10 - 45	Binkley	Carleton, Trottier
New England	1 2 0 - 3	8 12 14 - 34	Landon	Hyndman, Selwood, Caffery
Quebec	0 1 0 - 1	11 7 6 - 24	Aubry	Caron
New York	4 3 0 - 7	14 6 9 - 29	Donnelly	Sheehan 2, Ward 2, Peacosh 2, Ferguson
November 19				
Chicago	0 2 2 - 4	9 15 18 - 42	J. McLeod	Morris, Sicinski, Fleming, Popiel (WG 17:29)
Minnesota	0 3 0 - 3	4 15 14 - 33	Curran	Klatt, Arbour, Morrison
Cleveland	1 0 1 - 2	8 6 8 - 22	Cheevers	Hardy, Shmyr
Houston	1 1 2 - 4	6 7 10 - 23	D. McLeod	Mortson 3, Harris
Philadelphia	0 0 0 - 0	7 9 3 - 19	Archambault, Paiile	▶ Donnelly: shutout (2), 19 saves
New York	1 3 1 - 5	8 13 15 - 36	Donnelly	Laughton 2, Gauthier, Peters, Reichmuth
Winnipeg	1 3 0 - 4	5 9 5 - 19	Wakely	Hull 2, Beaudin, McDonald
Los Angeles	0 1 2 - 3	12 13 18 - 43	Gardner	Veneruzzo, Crashley, Byers
November 20				
Ottawa	3 1 1 - 5	14 6 5 - 25	Gratton	Carleton, Cunningham, Kirk, Martin, Leduc
New England	3 4 0 - 7	16 11 8 - 35	Smith	French 2, Green 2, Webster 2, Caffery
November 21				
Alberta	2 1 0 0 3	10 14 10 4 38	Norris	Carlin, Patenaude, Walters
Minnesota	0 3 0 1 4	14 18 10 6 48	McCartan	Christiansen, Morrison, Speck, Hampson (OT 6:42)
Cleveland	2 3 0 - 5	12 8 5 - 25	Cheevers	Buchanan 2, Pumple 2, Pinder
Los Angeles	0 1 1 - 2	20 16 12 - 48	Gillow	Byers, Young
Quebec	0 2 0 - 2	4 13 7 - 24	Aubry	Caron, Archambault
Ottawa	3 1 0 - 4	15 15 13 - 43	Binkley	Sentes, Trottier, Climie, Carleton
Winnipeg	2 1 1 - 4	14 12 6 - 32	Wakely	Bordeleau 2, McDonald, Swenson
Houston	1 0 1 - 2	8 9 10 - 27	D. McLeod	Labossiere 2
November 22				
Alberta	1 1 2 0 4	8 9 11 0 28	Norris	Hicke, Patenaude, Carlin, Walters
Philadelphia	0 1 3 1 5	12 17 12 1 42	Cottringer	Lawson 2, Campbell, Herriman, Lacroix (OT 1:59)
New England	0 0 1 - 1	6 7 8 - 21	Landon	Green
New York	0 2 1 - 3	2 8 11 - 21	Donnelly	Ward 2, Sheehan
November 23				
Chicago	5 1 2 - 8	13 10 8 - 31	J. McLeod	Morris 2, Lodboa, Paiement, Popiel, Fleming, Anderson, Liddington
Ottawa	1 0 0 - 1	9 9 14 - 32	Binkley	Conacher
Los Angeles	0 1 2 - 3	12 22 15 - 49	Gardner	Young 2, Byers
Minnesota	2 2 0 - 4	17 11 9 - 37	Curran	Hampson, Pearson, Christiansen, Connelly
Winnipeg	0 4 1 0 5	13 13 8 2 36	Wakely	Cuddie, Rousseau, McDonald, Beaudin, Hull
Houston	1 1 3 1 6	7 8 10 2 27	D. McLeod	Labossiere 2, Taylor, Harris, McDonald, Mortson (OT 4:03)
November 24				
Alberta	2 0 0 - 2	11 10 10 - 31	Norris, Brown	Perkins 2
New England	2 5 0 - 7	13 18 13 - 44	Smith	Caffery, Webster, Selby, Earl, Green, Ahearn, Pleau
Los Angeles	1 1 0 0 2	15 10 12 1 38	Gardner	Heiskala, Young
Cleveland	0 0 2 1 3	8 11 11 7 37	Cheevers	Pinder 2 (OT 4:44), Jarrett
Minnesota	2 1 3 - 6	11 8 11 - 30	McCartan	Klatt 2, Speck, Morrison, Ryan (WG 13:36), Pearson
Philadelphia	0 3 1 - 4	10 14 16 - 40	Paille	Lacroix 2, McKenzie, Herriman
Quebec	0 2 1 - 3	6 10 5 - 21	Aubry, Lemelin	Rouleau, Gendron, Archambault
Winnipeg	3 0 2 - 5	12 10 12 - 34	Wakely	Hull 2, Bordeleau, Gratton, McDonald
November 25				
Alberta	0 2 0 - 2	7 11 5 - 23	Brown	Perkins, Anderson
New York	1 1 2 - 4	9 9 10 - 28	Donnelly	Kennedy, Sheehan, Ferguson, Laughton
Chicago	1 0 3 - 4	13 10 14 - 37	J. McLeod	Fleming 2, Morris, Popiel (WG 18:05)
Philadelphia	1 1 1 - 3	8 17 15 - 40	Cottringer	Campbell, Herriman, Lacroix
Houston	3 0 0 - 3	13 10 9 - 32	D. McLeod	Labossiere, McCallum, Hall
Cleveland	0 0 1 - 1	13 6 11 - 30	Whidden	Hanna (spoiled McLeod's shutout at 16:52)
November 26				
Alberta	0 1 1 - 2	6 16 9 - 31	Norris	Baird, Walters (WG 7:02)
Ottawa	1 0 0 - 1	8 8 9 - 25	Binkley	Kirk
Los Angeles	3 2 1 - 6	6 9 7 - 22	Gardner	Veneruzzo, Slater, White, Byers, Young, McCaskill
New York	2 0 0 - 2	5 10 13 - 28	Donnelly	Morenz, Peacosh
New England	0 1 0 - 1	12 11 14 - 37	Landon	Pleau
Minnesota	2 1 0 - 3	12 13 6 - 31	Curran	Pearson, Speck, Paradise
Quebec	1 0 0 - 1	11 8 6 - 25	Lemelin	Archambault
Winnipeg	3 1 0 - 4	15 7 13 - 35	Wakely	Rousseau 2, Swenson, Hull
November 27				
Cleveland	0 0 0 - 0	11 11 9 - 31	Cheevers	▶ Smith: shutout (1), 31 saves
New England	1 1 1 - 3	6 6 12 - 24	Smith	Ley, Pleau, Caffery
November 28				
Alberta	0 0 0 - 0	8 8 12 - 28	Norris	▶ Wakely: shutout (2), 28 saves
Winnipeg	1 1 1 - 3	10 12 17 - 39	Wakely	Black, Rousseau, Boyer
Chicago	1 0 1 - 2	9 9 6 - 24	J. McLeod	Fleming, Paiement
Quebec	1 3 2 - 6	12 20 18 - 50	Aubry	Guindon 2, Payette 2, Archambault, Giroux
Houston	2 1 0 - 3	13 13 8 - 34	D. McLeod	Hughes, Stanfield, Lund
Cleveland	1 0 0 - 1	13 13 13 - 39	Whidden	Wiste
Los Angeles	1 1 1 - 3	13 10 11 - 34	Gardner	Slater, Gilmore, White
Philadelphia	0 3 1 - 4	6 7 7 - 20	Sullivan	Lawson 2, McKenzie, Lacroix
Minnesota	1 1 0 0 2	13 7 12 1 33	McCartan	Arbour, Ball
Ottawa	2 0 0 1 3	14 6 8 1 29	Binkley	Gibson, Warr, Cunningham (OT 1:11)

1972-1973 Game by Game Line Scores

Date & Teams	Scoring 1 2 3 ot F	Shots 1 2 3 ot F	Goaltenders	Goals & Other Scoring Highlights
November 29				
New England	1 3 2 - 6	13 14 6 - 33	Smith	Pleau, Webster, French, Earl, Ahearn, Selwood
New York	2 4 1 - 7	10 14 9 - 33	Donnelly, Kurt	Ward 3, Rivers 2 (WG 11:05), Ferguson, Jones
Winnipeg	2 1 0 0 3	14 8 9 6 37	Wakely	Rousseau 2, Swenson
Alberta	0 1 2 0 3	17 11 10 5 43	Norris	Patenaude, McAneeley, Walters
November 30				
Cleveland	1 0 1 - 2	7 7 11 - 25	Cheevers	Andrea, Jarrett
Ottawa	2 0 1 - 3	8 17 10 - 35	Binkley	Carleton, Sentes, King
Houston	0 2 1 - 3	4 14 17 - 35	D. McLeod	Taylor, Hall, Popiel
Los Angeles	4 1 1 - 6	14 9 11 - 34	Gardner	Odrowski, Crashley, Veneruzzo, McCaskill, White, Leblanc
Minnesota	0 0 2 - 2	10 9 8 - 27	Curran	Connelly 2 (scored at 0:07)
New York	3 1 1 - 5	15 11 11 - 37	Kurt	Ward 2, Sheehan, Krupicka, Ferguson
December 1				
Los Angeles	1 2 2 - 5	13 12 5 - 30	Gardner, Gillow	Heiskala, White, MacNeil, Leblanc, Crashley
Chicago	1 1 1 - 3	6 5 8 - 19	J. McLeod	Lodboa, Whitlock, Sicinski
Minnesota	2 1 3 - 6	12 9 11 - 32	McCartan	Klatt 2, MacMillan, McMahon, Speck, Connelly
Alberta	2 1 1 - 4	10 17 9 - 36	Norris	McAneeley, Walters, Perkins, Wall
New England	1 1 1 - 3	7 13 13 - 33	Landon	Caffery, Williams, Webster
Philadelphia	1 2 2 - 5	11 7 12 - 30	Parent	Boudreau 2, Lacroix, Plante, McKenzie
Ottawa	1 1 2 - 4	6 11 7 - 24	Gratton	Gibson, Martin, Sentes, Simpson
Winnipeg	0 2 1 - 3	5 14 10 - 29	Tumilson	Bordeleau, Beaudin, Johnson
December 2				
Houston	1 6 0 - 7	5 13 5 - 23	D. McLeod	Grierson 2, Hoekstra, Hall, Harris, McCallum, McDonald
New York	1 0 1 - 2	11 10 9 - 30	Kurt, Donnelly	Peacosh 2
Los Angeles	2 1 1 - 4	9 8 8 - 25	Gillow	Veneruzzo 3, Szura
Chicago	0 0 2 - 2	2 5 9 - 16	J. McLeod, Gill	Whitlock, Fleming
Philadelphia	0 0 2 - 2	10 9 11 - 30	Parent	Burgess, Campbell
Cleveland	2 2 4 - 8	14 19 15 - 48	Cheevers	Pumple 2, Pinder, Hodgson, Hardy, Andrea, Erickson, Clearwater
Quebec	0 1 1 - 2	9 12 9 - 30	Aubry	Gaudette, Gendron
New England	4 1 2 - 7	18 9 11 - 38	Smith	Danby 2, Pleau, Webster, Sheehy, Earl, Williams
December 3				
Cleveland	1 1 0 - 2	12 13 13 - 38	Cheevers	Hodgson, Hanna
New York	4 0 1 - 5	17 7 3 - 27	Donnelly	Ward 2, Rivers, Perry, Morenz
Houston	2 1 1 0 4	9 16 9 1 35	D. McLeod	Popiel, Stanfield, Hall, Grierson
Ottawa	2 0 2 1 5	13 9 16 1 39	Gratton	Carleton 3, Trottier, Charlebois (OT 4:32)
Minnesota	0 1 0 - 1	7 5 7 - 19	Curran	Christiansen
Winnipeg	3 0 2 - 5	16 19 5 - 40	Wakely	Hornung 2, Johnson, Woytowich, Black
Quebec	3 1 2 - 6	12 12 11 - 35	Aubry	Guindon 2, Golembrosky, Bergeron, Giroux, Payette
Alberta	0 2 0 - 2	11 9 13 - 33	Norris	Hamilton, Anderson
December 4				
Ottawa	1 0 1 - 2	13 11 9 - 33	Gratton	Carleton, Leduc
New England	4 1 2 - 7	17 18 19 - 54	Smith	Sheehy 2, French, Pleau, Caffery, Webster, Danby
December 5				
Chicago	2 0 0 1 3	14 7 11 5 37	Gill	Whitlock, Popiel, Anderson (OT 7:01)
Minnesota	1 1 0 0 2	14 17 17 6 54	McCartan	Antonovich, Pearson
Cleveland	1 1 1 1 4	11 7 5 2 25	Whidden	Buchanan 2, Hodgson, Jarrett (OT 0:30)
Philadelphia	1 1 1 0 3	13 13 14 0 40	Parent	Lawson, McKenzie, O'Donoghue
New York	4 0 2 - 6	13 10 7 - 30	Donnelly	Peacosh 3, Ward 2, Ferguson
Houston	1 1 2 - 4	6 10 7 - 23	D. McLeod, Hughes	Popiel, Labossiere, Hall, McDonald
Quebec	0 4 0 - 4	9 13 6 - 28	Aubry	Bergeron, Payette, Roy, Gendron
Winnipeg	1 0 1 - 2	9 9 15 - 33	Wakely	Beaudin, Hull
December 6				
Chicago	0 1 0 - 1	7 7 14 - 28	Gill, J. McLeod	Liddington
Winnipeg	3 4 0 - 7	14 11 7 - 32	Wakely	Gratton 3, Bordeleau, Hornung, Hull, Rousseau
New York	1 2 0 - 3	5 6 6 - 17	Donnelly	Reichmuth, Douglas, Ward
New England	0 2 2 - 4	9 16 15 - 40	Landon	Sarrazin 2, Ahearn, Danby (WG 16:26)
December 7				
Cleveland	1 1 1 - 3	10 8 9 - 27	Cheevers	Jarrett 2, Pinder
Quebec	1 0 0 - 1	11 7 7 - 25	Aubry	Golembrosky
Houston	0 0 0 - 0	14 9 14 - 37	D. McLeod	▶ Curran: shutout (2), 37 saves
Minnesota	1 0 2 - 3	9 11 13 - 33	Curran	Antonovich 2, Connelly
New England	1 3 0 - 4	5 9 6 - 20	Smith	Webster, Caffery, Green, Sheehy
Ottawa	0 1 1 - 2	11 11 15 - 37	Binkley	King, Charlebois
December 8				
Alberta	1 1 0 - 2	5 4 11 - 20	Norris	Anderson 2
Los Angeles	1 2 1 - 4	14 18 6 - 38	Gillow	McCaskill 2, Slater, Niekamp
Houston	2 0 0 - 2	5 6 13 - 24	D. McLeod	Hoekstra, Stanfield
Winnipeg	2 0 4 - 6	20 7 11 - 38	Wakely	Cuddie 2, Hull 2, Bordeleau, Gratton
Minnesota	0 2 1 0 3	6 7 10 0 23	McCartan	Ball, Connelly, Lilyholm
Chicago	1 1 1 1 4	10 13 12 1 36	J. McLeod, Gill	Fleming 2 (OT 4:10), Popiel, Sicinski
New York	1 0 0 - 1	13 13 8 - 34	Donnelly	Bradley
Philadelphia	1 1 1 - 3	11 8 12 - 31	Parent	Herriman, Lacroix, Campbell
December 9				
New York	1 1 0 - 2	13 14 8 - 35	Donnelly	Peacosh, Reichmuth
New England	2 0 2 - 4	14 11 17 - 42	Landon	Selwood, Hyndman, Caffery, Dorey
Ottawa	0 1 0 - 1	6 8 10 - 24	Gratton	Kirk
Philadelphia	2 2 3 - 7	18 10 12 - 40	Parent, Paille	Herriman 2, Plumb, Lacroix, Lawson, Bennett, Burgess
Quebec	2 1 1 - 4	13 15 9 - 37	Lemelin	Caron, Roy, Desjardine, Gaudette
Chicago	1 1 0 - 2	9 9 10 - 28	Gill	Morris, Zaine
Winnipeg	0 0 2 1 3	8 12 16 4 40	Wakely	Hull, Johnson, Black (OT 3:15)
Cleveland	1 1 0 0 2	11 20 7 2 40	Cheevers	Erickson, Jarrett

1972-1973 Game by Game Line Scores

Date & Teams	Scoring 1 2 3 ot F	Shots 1 2 3 ot F	Goaltenders	Goals & Other Scoring Highlights
December 10				
Alberta	1 1 1 - 3	18 11 7 - 36	Norris	Hamilton, Anderson, Patenaude
Los Angeles	0 1 4 - 5	7 14 13 - 34	Gardner	Byers 3, Veneruzzo 2
Cleveland	0 1 2 0 3	6 9 14 2 31	Whidden	Jarrett 2, Hardy
Minnesota	1 1 1 1 4	13 9 10 3 35	Curran	Connelly, Klatt, McMahon (TG 19:31), Hampson (OT 2:29)
Quebec	1 2 3 0 6	11 10 10 0 31	Lemelin	Caron 2, Golembrosky, Tremblay, Gaudette, Parizeau
Ottawa	1 3 2 1 7	9 12 10 1 32	Binkley	King 2, Carleton 2 (OT 0:23), Climie, Gibson, Leduc
December 11				
Chicago	0 3 0 - 3	9 13 14 - 36	J. McLeod	Whitlock, Barber, Fleming
New York	1 3 4 - 8	4 11 14 - 29	Donnelly	Rivers 2, Ferguson, Laughton, Ward, Reichmuth, Willis, Jones
Winnipeg	0 1 2 - 3	9 9 8 - 26	Wakely	Black, Beaudin, Bordeleau
New England	0 1 3 - 4	10 8 6 - 24	Smith	Webster, Dorey, Hyndman, Ahearn
December 12				
Alberta	1 1 2 - 4	8 13 13 - 34	Norris	Patenaude, Anderson, Perkins, McAneeley
Houston	3 1 2 - 6	13 7 8 - 28	D. McLeod	Hughes 2, Taylor, Lund, Harris, Grierson
Minnesota	0 2 1 0 3	9 10 10 6 35	McCartan	Klatt, Antonovich, Christiansen
Los Angeles	1 1 1 0 3	13 15 8 6 42	Gardner	White, Veneruzzo, Byers
Philadelphia	0 1 1 - 2	8 3 7 - 18	Parent	Plumb, Boudreau
Quebec	2 1 2 - 5	12 11 13 - 36	Lemelin	Gaudette 3, Golembrosky, Caron
December 13				
Alberta	0 1 2 - 3	9 12 10 - 31	Brown	Baird, Patenaude, Benzelock (WG 6:54)
Houston	1 1 0 - 2	13 4 7 - 24	D. McLeod	Grierson, Harris
New England	0 0 3 - 3	6 9 9 - 24	Landon	Jordan, Danby, Webster
Chicago	3 1 2 - 6	11 8 11 - 30	Gill	Popiel 3, Whitlock, Knibbs, Sicinski
Quebec	0 0 1 - 1	8 17 3 - 28	Brodeur	Caron
New York	5 1 3 - 9	13 11 10 - 34	Donnelly	Sheehan 3, Jones, Ferguson, Peters, Ward, Speer, Rivers
Winnipeg	0 2 2 - 4	9 11 15 - 35	Wakely, Tumilson	Rousseau, Hull, Bordeleau, Zanussi
Philadelphia	0 3 4 - 7	8 12 7 - 27	Parent	Plante 2, Cardiff, McKenzie, Plumb, Lawson, Campbell
December 14				
Minnesota	2 3 1 - 6	13 9 8 - 30	Curran	McMahon 2, Morrison, Christiansen, Hampson, Klatt
Chicago	0 3 0 - 3	8 16 12 - 36	Gill	Liddington 2, Paiement
New England	2 3 0 - 5	3 7 3 - 13	Smith	Sheehy, Green, Pleau, Dorey, Hurley
Los Angeles	1 0 1 - 2	13 12 11 - 36	Gardner	Leblanc, Serviss
New York	1 0 3 - 4	14 12 11 - 37	Wilkie	Reichmuth, Rivers, Bradley, Jones (WG 15:05)
Ottawa	0 1 2 - 3	9 12 11 - 32	Binkley	Gibson, Sentes, Gibbons
December 15				
Houston	1 1 1 - 3	11 10 4 - 25	Rutledge	Hall, McCallum, Stanfield (WG 12:50)
Minnesota	0 2 0 - 2	8 12 14 - 34	McCartan	Sanders, Connelly
Ottawa	1 3 0 - 4	5 11 9 - 25	Gratton	Charlebois, Trottier, Leduc, Boland
Alberta	1 1 1 - 3	11 12 16 - 39	Norris, Brown	Carlin, Walters, Anderson
Quebec	1 1 1 - 3	6 15 10 - 31	Aubry	Caron 2, Giroux
Cleveland	1 3 2 - 6	14 13 18 - 45	Cheevers	Buchanan 2, Horton, Hopiavuori, Shmyr, Dillabough
Winnipeg	0 0 4 - 4	6 17 11 - 34	Wakely	Bordeleau, Hull 3
Philadelphia	0 3 3 - 6	7 11 10 - 28	Parent	Plante 2, Campbell 2, O'Donoghue, Lawson
December 16				
New England	1 4 5 - 10	14 10 14 - 38	Landon	French 2, Selby 2, Green, Ahearn, Webster, Pleau, Caffery, Earl
Philadelphia	0 2 4 - 6	6 11 20 - 37	Parent, Paille	McKenzie 2, Lawson 2, Plante, Cardiff
December 17				
Chicago	0 2 0 - 2	11 13 9 - 33	J. McLeod	Fleming, Morris
Minnesota	2 1 1 - 4	18 11 8 - 37	Curran	Christiansen 2, Morrison, Klatt
Cleveland	0 1 1 - 2	7 8 7 - 22	Cheevers	Buchanan, Wiste
Quebec	1 0 2 - 3	11 11 8 - 30	Aubry	Payette, Parizeau, Caron
Los Angeles	3 0 1 0 4	14 7 7 3 31	Gillow	Slater, Heggedal, Niekamp, Veneruzzo
Houston	2 1 1 0 4	10 7 8 3 28	Rutledge	Harris, Hoekstra, Taylor, Lund
Ottawa	0 1 0 - 1	12 9 8 - 29	Binkley	King
Alberta	0 1 2 - 3	8 15 12 - 35	Norris	Perkins, Patenaude, Joyal
December 17				
Philadelphia	0 3 3 - 6	15 6 14 - 35	Parent	Herriman 3, Lawson, Boudreau, Bennett
New England	2 0 1 - 3	14 9 3 - 26	Smith	Pleau, Webster, Caffery
Winnipeg	0 1 3 - 4	11 8 14 - 33	Wakely	Bordeleau, Hull, Black, Boyer
New York	0 2 1 - 3	11 10 6 - 27	Donnelly	Bradley, Ferguson, Rivers
December 19				
Cleveland	1 0 0 - 1	14 12 13 - 39	Whidden	Pumple
Chicago	2 1 3 - 6	11 7 11 - 29	J. McLeod	Popiel 2, Paiement, Morris, Sicinski, Liddington
Los Angeles	0 2 3 - 5	11 8 15 - 34	Gillow, Gardner	Watson 2, Crashley, Veneruzzo, Heggedal
Houston	2 2 3 - 7	12 12 11 - 35	D. McLeod	McDonald 4, Labossiere, Taylor, Hoekstra
New England	3 2 0 - 5	10 20 4 - 34	Smith	Webster 2, Caffery 2, Selwood
Minnesota	1 3 3 - 7	9 10 15 - 34	McCartan	Connelly 2, Christiansen, Speck, Klatt, Ball, McMahon
New York	4 3 0 - 7	20 9 8 - 37	Donnelly	Peacosh 2, Sheehan 2, Laughton, Bradley, Reichmuth
Philadelphia	0 0 2 - 2	14 9 15 - 38	Parent, Paille	McKenzie, Lacroix
Ottawa	1 1 1 - 3	10 6 8 - 24	Gratton	Carleton, Gibbons, Gibson
Quebec	3 0 4 - 7	15 7 16 - 38	Aubry	Parizeau 2, Giroux, Tremblay, Guite, Caron, Rouleau
December 20				
Chicago	2 2 1 - 5	19 7 9 - 35	Gill	Knibbs 2, Lodboa, Fleming, Barber
Philadelphia	1 2 5 - 8	10 16 13 - 39	Parent	Lawson 4, Lacroix 2, O'Donoghue, Henry

1972-1973 Game by Game Line Scores

Date & Teams	Scoring (1 2 3 ot F)	Shots (1 2 3 ot F)	Goaltenders	Goals & Other Scoring Highlights
December 21				
Los Angeles	2 0 2 0 4	11 18 13 6 48	Gardner	Veneruzzo, Watson, White, Heiskala
Ottawa	2 2 0 0 4	8 9 6 7 30	Gratton	Stephanson, Gibson, Charlebois, Carleton
New England	2 2 0 - 4	10 10 12 - 32	Landon	Webster 2, Caffery, Sheehy
Alberta	1 2 2 - 5	9 8 13 - 30	Norris	Harrison 2, Walters, Patenaude, Hickey (WG 16:04)
New York	1 1 0 - 2	13 8 14 - 35	Wilkie	Rivers, Peacosh
Cleveland	1 2 3 - 6	13 15 14 - 42	Cheevers	Jarrett 2, Buchanan, Pinder, Hodgson, Erickson
Winnipeg	0 0 0 - 0	10 17 5 - 32	Wakely	▶ McCartan: shutout (1), 32 saves
Minnesota	0 0 3 - 3	4 6 11 - 21	McCartan	Pearson 2, Connelly
December 22				
Ottawa	1 3 1 - 5	11 8 7 - 26	Gratton, Binkley	Carleton 2, Simpson, Trottier, Gibbons
New York	2 4 1 - 7	16 16 10 - 42	Donnelly	Sheehan 2, Bradley 2, Peacosh 2, Ferguson
Winnipeg	2 0 0 - 2	10 11 7 - 28	Daley	Gratton, Hull
Chicago	2 0 1 - 3	10 10 8 - 28	J. McLeod	Paiement, Morris, Barber (WG 2:16)
December 23				
Alberta	0 1 1 - 2	16 8 10 - 34	Norris	Barrie, Harrison
Chicago	2 1 0 - 3	8 9 5 - 22	J. McLeod	Popiel, Mavety, Liddington
Los Angeles	0 0 1 - 1	11 11 18 - 40	Gardner	White
Quebec	2 0 0 - 2	8 8 8 - 24	Aubry	Parizeau, Caron
Minnesota	0 0 1 - 1	15 9 10 - 34	Wetzel	Antonovich
Cleveland	0 2 1 - 3	8 15 12 - 35	Cheevers	Wiste 2, Jarrett
Philadelphia	2 0 1 - 3	7 9 5 - 21	Parent	Lacroix, O'Donoghue, Plumb
Houston	1 2 4 - 7	14 13 10 - 37	D. McLeod	Grierson 3, Popiel, Lund, Hall, Hughes
December 24				
Los Angeles	2 1 2 - 5	15 7 17 - 39	Gardner	Veneruzzo 2, Byers 2, Gilmore
New England	1 1 1 - 3	10 9 8 - 27	Smith	Pleau 3
Quebec	2 0 0 - 2	9 8 2 - 19	Aubry	Parizeau, Rouleau
Ottawa	1 3 2 - 6	17 16 17 - 50	Gratton	Carleton 2, Sentes, Charlebois, Simpson, King
December 25				
Alberta	0 1 1 - 2	11 10 14 - 35	Norris	Patenaude, Hamilton
Chicago	1 1 1 - 3	12 5 7 - 24	J. McLeod	Paiement, Mavety, Fleming
New England	3 2 3 - 8	8 9 9 - 26	Landon	Webster 2, French, Caffery, Ahearn, Sheehy, Danby, Selby
New York	1 0 1 - 2	6 6 13 - 25	Donnelly, Wilkie	Sheehan, Reichmuth
Philadelphia	0 0 0 - 0	12 5 5 - 22	Paille, Parent	▶ Cheevers: shutout (4), 22 saves
Cleveland	3 3 2 - 8	15 19 16 - 50	Cheevers	Andrea 2, Dillabough, Pinder, Jarrett, Hardy, Erickson, Hodgson
December 26				
Chicago	0 2 0 - 2	4 8 5 - 17	D. McLeod	Blanchette, Zaine
Winnipeg	1 1 1 - 3	17 20 10 - 47	Daley	Bordeleau, McDonald, Gratton (WG 8:17)
Houston	0 1 2 0 3	12 10 12 4 38	D. McLeod	Hall, Popiel, Mortson
Ottawa	1 0 2 0 3	16 10 16 3 45	Gratton	King, Sentes, Gibson
New York	1 2 2 - 5	12 9 15 - 36	Donnelly	Ferguson 2, Peacosh, Willis, Perry
Quebec	1 1 0 - 2	17 12 14 - 43	Aubry	Roy, Leclerc
Philadelphia	2 4 0 - 6	14 15 13 - 42	Parent	Lawson 3, Herriman, Lacroix, Henry
Minnesota	0 2 0 - 2	6 13 11 - 30	McCartan	Paradise, Connelly
December 28				
Minnesota	2 1 1 - 4	8 7 12 - 27	Curran	Morrison 2, Hampson, Klatt
Los Angeles	0 1 1 - 2	11 11 13 - 35	Gardner	Serviss, Veneruzzo
New England	2 1 2 - 5	8 13 14 - 35	Landon	Webster 2, Sheehy, Pleau, Green
Quebec	0 0 3 - 3	12 10 11 - 33	Brodeur	Gendron, Tremblay, Caron
Philadelphia	2 1 0 - 3	18 16 7 - 41	Parent	Lawson, Lacroix, Herriman
Chicago	3 0 3 - 6	12 6 8 - 26	J. McLeod	Paiement 2, Popiel, Mavety, Morris, Sicinski
December 29				
Houston	1 2 1 - 4	10 11 10 - 31	Rutledge	Lund 2, Hughes, Labossiere
New England	1 0 1 - 2	13 12 11 - 36	Landon	Selwood, Pleau
Minnesota	0 1 1 - 2	6 8 7 - 21	McCartan	Connelly, Ryan
Los Angeles	3 0 2 - 5	14 8 19 - 41	Gillow	Odrowski, Leblanc, Gilmore, Young, Heiskala
Quebec	0 0 3 - 3	12 14 21 - 47	Brodeur	Parizeau, Caron, Giroux
Cleveland	2 3 0 - 5	21 15 14 - 50	Cheevers	Andrea 2, Brindley, Hardy, Jarrett
December 30				
Houston	1 2 0 0 3	8 17 9 0 34	D. McLeod	Taylor, Hughes, Smith
Cleveland	1 0 2 1 4	12 16 4 4 36	Whidden	Brindley, Hardy, Erickson (TG 16:43), Andrea (OT 6:06)
Ottawa	0 3 1 - 4	7 11 6 - 24	Gratton	Conacher, Kirk, King, Gibson
Chicago	0 0 2 - 2	3 10 15 - 28	J. McLeod	Lodboa 2
December 31				
New England	1 0 2 - 3	14 3 5 - 22	Smith	Webster, Ahearn, Hurley
New York	0 0 0 - 0	8 10 10 - 28	Donnelly	▶ Smith: shutout (2), 28 saves
Ottawa	1 2 1 - 4	8 11 10 - 29	Gratton, Blum	Sentes 2, Stephanson, Carleton
Quebec	3 3 2 - 8	14 12 12 - 38	Brodeur	Gendron 2, Guite, Parizeau, Tremblay, Leclerc, Caron, Gaudette
Philadelphia	1 1 1 - 3	7 8 7 - 22	Parent	Herriman, McKenzie, Campbell
Los Angeles	1 0 0 - 1	13 10 11 - 34	Gillow	White
January 1				
Houston	1 2 1 0 4	10 12 10 6 38	Rutledge	Harris 2, Lund, Hoekstra
Minnesota	1 2 1 0 4	16 14 12 2 44	Curran	Johnson, Hampson, Antonovich, Klatt (TG 12:32)
Winnipeg	1 0 2 - 3	8 10 8 - 26	Wakely, Daley	Rousseau, McDonald, Hull
Alberta	2 3 2 - 7	11 18 5 - 34	Norris	Perkins 3, Joyal 2, Patenaude, Harrison
Philadelphia	1 1 1 - 3	11 12 10 - 33	Parent	St. Sauveur, Lacroix, Burgess
New York	0 0 0 - 0	14 11 14 - 39	Kurt	▶ Parent: shutout (1), 39 saves
January 4				
Ottawa	0 3 1 - 4	9 11 8 - 28	Gratton	Cunningham 2, Gibson, Trottier
New York	2 4 3 - 9	6 17 17 - 40	Kurt	Ward 5 (WHA record), Bradley 2, Kennedy, Ferguson

1972-1973 Game by Game Line Scores

Date & Teams	Scoring 1	2	3	ot	F	Shots 1	2	3	ot	F	Goaltenders	Goals & Other Scoring Highlights
January 7												
Winnipeg	0	3	3	-	6	18	20	15	-	53	Daley	Bordeleau 2, Rousseau 2, McDonald, Black
Minnesota	1	0	1	-	2	8	9	9	-	26	McCartan	Morrison, Speck
January 8												
Quebec	3	1	1	1	6	7	6	10	1	24	Brodeur	Payette, Giroux, Gaudette, Parizeau, Lacombe, Bergeron (OT 2:35)
New York	1	1	3	0	5	7	6	9	0	22	Donnelly	Ward, Peacosh, Bradley, Perry, Laughton
January 9												
Los Angeles	2	0	1	1	4	10	12	10	2	34	Gillow	Young 2, Leblanc, Veneruzzo (OT 1:57)
Minnesota	2	1	0	0	3	9	14	8	1	32	Curran	McMahon, Ryan, Connelly
New England	2	0	3	-	5	11	12	11	-	34	Smith	Caffery 2, Sheehy, Ahearn, French
Houston	2	2	3	-	7	7	12	11	-	30	Rutledge	Labossiere 3, Hughes 2, Grierson, Larose
Quebec	4	0	1	-	5	9	9	11	-	29	Brodeur	Gendron, Guite, Gaudette, Caron, Payette
Ottawa	5	0	2	-	7	19	11	16	-	46	Gratton	Gibson 2, Charlebois 2, Conacher, Trottier, Leduc
January 10												
Alberta	0	0	1	-	1	4	8	10	-	22	Norris	Blanchette
Winnipeg	4	2	0	-	6	14	11	10	-	35	Wakely	Beaudin 2, Black 2, Gratton, Bordeleau
Los Angeles	3	4	1	-	8	10	14	12	-	36	Gillow	White 3, Veneruzzo 2, Leblanc, Byers, McCaskill
Chicago	0	3	2	-	5	10	10	7	-	27	J. McLeod	Morris 3, Popiel, Mavety
New York	0	2	2	-	4	8	10	13	-	31	Kurt	Ferguson 2, Jones, Perry
Philadelphia	1	0	0	-	1	15	9	13	-	37	Parent	Lawson
January 11												
Cleveland	2	0	2	-	4	8	11	10	-	29	Cheevers	Buchanan 2 (WG 18:59), Brindley, Shmyr
Minnesota	1	0	2	-	3	10	8	14	-	32	McCartan	Johnson, Klatt, Hampson
Houston	0	3	2	-	5	10	16	9	-	35	D. McLeod	McCallum, Hoekstra, Hall, Hale, Harris
Chicago	0	0	0	-	0	8	10	6	-	24	Gill	▶ McLeod: shutout (1), 24 saves
New York	0	0	1	-	1	9	10	7	-	26	Kurt	Jones
Ottawa	2	2	0	-	4	9	9	9	-	27	Gratton	Sentes, Charlebois, Trottier, Leduc
January 12												
Alberta	1	1	0	-	2	11	4	10	-	25	Norris	Blanchette, Walters
Los Angeles	0	1	0	-	1	7	9	5	-	21	Gillow	Sutherland
Cleveland	2	0	1	-	3	5	5	9	-	19	Cheevers	Wiste, Hardy, Clearwater
Winnipeg	3	0	2	-	5	20	12	12	-	44	Daley	Bordeleau 2, Hull, Rizzuto, Beaudin
Ottawa	1	1	1	-	3	11	4	7	-	22	Gratton	Sentes 2, Simpson
Philadelphia	0	4	0	-	4	5	16	8	-	29	Parent	Lawson 2, Plante, Lacroix
Quebec	0	1	1	-	2	6	10	11	-	27	Brodeur	Gaudette, Guite
Minnesota	1	1	1	-	3	10	12	19	-	41	Curran	Johnson 2, Lilyholm
January 13												
Alberta	2	2	0	-	4	12	6	8	-	26	Norris	Harrison, Patenaude, Carlin, Baird
Los Angeles	0	0	1	-	1	8	12	14	-	34	Gillow, Gardner	Young (spoiled Norris' shutout at 18:23)
Chicago	0	0	2	-	2	14	14	11	-	39	Menard, Gill	Fleming 2
Houston	3	2	1	-	6	8	12	11	-	31	Rutledge	Harris 2, Hall, Popiel, Taylor, Labossiere
New York	1	1	1	-	3	13	6	16	-	35	Kurt	Ward 2, Ferguson
New England	0	4	0	-	4	14	24	15	-	53	Landon	Caffery 2, Green, Pleau
Quebec	1	3	0	-	4	15	13	13	-	41	Brodeur	Guindon 2, Gendron, Bergeron
Philadelphia	4	3	2	-	9	16	9	11	-	36	Parent	Lacroix 4, Lawson 3, McKenzie 2
January 14												
Cleveland	0	1	0	-	1	8	11	6	-	25	Whidden	Hodgson
Winnipeg	1	0	2	-	3	9	9	15	-	33	Wakely	Rizzuto, Ash, Cuddie
Ottawa	1	0	1	0	2	9	12	9	6	36	Gratton	Kirk, Sentes
Minnesota	1	0	1	1	3	11	14	11	7	43	Curran	Lilyholm 2 (OT 5:58), Antonovich
January 15												
Chicago	1	2	1	-	4	11	10	6	-	27	Gill	Mavety 2, Liddington, Popiel
Houston	1	1	3	-	5	9	18	12	-	39	D. McLeod	Labossiere, McCallum, Hale, Harris, Smith (WG 16:34)
Los Angeles	1	2	1	-	4	14	12	7	-	33	Gardner	Heiskala 2 (WG 13:55 3rd), Veneruzzo, Sutherland
Alberta	2	1	0	-	3	9	7	8	-	24	Norris	Wall, Walters, Harrison
January 16												
Cleveland	2	1	1	-	4	9	9	9	-	27	Cheevers	Wiste, Brindley, Andrea, Pumple (WG 17:03)
Philadelphia	1	1	1	-	3	14	9	9	-	32	Parent	Herriman, McKenzie, Lacroix
Los Angeles	2	1	2	0	5	7	9	14	1	31	Gardner	Szura 2, Crashley, Leblanc, Byers
Alberta	0	1	4	1	6	6	6	13	1	26	Norris	Hamilton, Fonteyne, Patenaude, Wall, Carlin, Falkenberg (OT 1:06)
Minnesota	0	0	1	-	1	8	15	5	-	28	McCartan	Connelly
Winnipeg	0	0	3	-	3	9	13	9	-	31	Daley	Hull, Johnson, Beaudin
Ottawa	3	1	0	0	4	20	7	8	0	35	Gratton	Carleton, Cunningham, Stephanson, Trottier
Quebec	1	2	1	1	5	9	9	14	2	34	Brodeur	Leclerc 2, Lacombe, Gaudette, Harvey (OT 0:48)
January 17												
Cleveland	1	2	2	-	5	14	9	3	-	26	Cheevers	Wiste 2, Pumple, Muloin, Brindley
Houston	0	0	0	-	0	9	9	5	-	23	Rutledge	▶ Cheevers: shutout (5), 23 saves
New England	1	1	2	-	4	11	6	7	-	24	Smith	Sheehy, Pleau, Danby, Ahearn
Chicago	0	1	1	-	2	4	7	8	-	19	Gill	Morris, Sicinski
January 18												
Houston	3	3	2	-	8	7	14	6	-	27	D. McLeod	Lund 2, Labossiere, Mortson, Hall, McDonald, Smith, Grierson
Chicago	1	1	1	-	3	13	14	9	-	36	Gill, J. McLeod	Benzelock, Popiel, Sicinski
Minnesota	1	1	1	-	3	5	13	8	-	26	Curran	Connelly, MacMillan, Antonovich
Ottawa	3	1	2	-	6	13	15	14	-	42	Gratton	Amodeo, King, Gibson, Martin, Simpson, Trottier
New York	3	1	0	0	4	11	17	8	5	41	Donnelly	Willis, Laughton, Ward, Perry
Quebec	3	1	0	0	4	10	10	9	8	37	Brodeur	Payette 2, Parizeau, Tremblay

1972-1973 Game by Game Line Scores

Date & Teams	Scoring 1 2 3 ot F	Shots 1 2 3 ot F	Goaltenders	Goals & Other Scoring Highlights
January 19				
Cleveland	2 1 1 - 4	11 4 7 - 22	Cheevers	Wiste 2, Brindley, Andrea
Los Angeles	0 1 0 - 1	10 20 10 - 40	Gardner	Veneruzzo
New England	1 0 1 - 2	9 9 11 - 29	Landon	Hyndman, French
Winnipeg	1 2 3 - 6	8 12 12 - 32	Wakely	Beaudin 2, Bordeleau 2, McDonald, Gratton
Ottawa	0 1 1 - 2	4 8 12 - 24	Gratton	Kirk, Gibson
Philadelphia	1 1 2 - 4	14 10 16 - 40	Parent	Lacroix 2, Migneault, Campbell
January 20				
Chicago	1 3 2 - 6	6 5 13 - 24	J. McLeod	Paiement 2, Lodboa, Benzelock, Sicinski, Liddington
Alberta	3 0 1 - 4	9 14 15 - 38	Brown, Norris	Fonteyne, Wall, Hicke, Patenaude
Houston	0 4 0 - 4	11 15 9 - 35	Rutledge	Hall 2, Hughes, Grierson
Philadelphia	2 1 0 - 3	14 11 7 - 32	Parent	Lawson 2, Lacroix
Minnesota	1 6 3 - 10	13 14 9 - 36	McCartan	Antonovich 3, Lilyholm 2, Ryan 2, Sanders, Arbour, Johnson
Quebec	1 2 2 - 5	10 7 7 - 24	Aubry	Gendron 2, Guindon, Payette, Leclerc
January 21				
Cleveland	1 0 1 - 2	4 10 6 - 20	Whidden	Buchanan, Erickson
Los Angeles	2 0 1 - 3	8 12 8 - 28	Gillow	Odrowski, Veneruzzo, Byers
New England	2 3 2 - 7	10 10 8 - 28	Smith	Ahearn 2, French, Danby, Pleau, Webster, Sheehy
Winnipeg	1 0 1 - 2	6 7 7 - 20	Daley	Rizzuto, Gratton
Ottawa	1 1 0 - 2	6 10 14 - 30	Gratton, Blum	Cunningham, Martin
Houston	0 3 2 - 5	12 10 10 - 32	D. McLeod	Grierson 2, Taylor, Labossiere, Harris
January 22				
Chicago	0 1 0 - 1	14 9 6 - 29	J. McLeod	Morris
Alberta	2 1 3 - 6	8 14 15 - 37	Norris	Fonteyne, Hicke, Anderson, Joyal, Perkins, Walters
Minnesota	2 0 1 - 3	9 5 10 - 24	Curran	Ryan, Speck, Klatt (WG 0:50)
New York	0 2 0 - 2	12 12 8 - 32	Kurt	Laughton, Bradley
January 23				
Ottawa	2 0 1 - 3	8 15 10 - 33	Gratton, Binkley	Simpson, Sentes, King
Houston	4 4 3 - 11	10 21 12 - 43	Rutledge	Taylor 2, Lund 2, Popiel 2, McDonald, Hughes, Hale, Hall, Grierson
Quebec	0 0 1 - 1	11 5 16 - 32	Brodeur, Lemelin	Blain
Chicago	3 2 2 - 7	5 15 13 - 33	J. McLeod	Paiement 3, Liddington 2, Sicinski, Whitlock
Winnipeg	1 2 1 0 4	15 13 13 0 41	Wakely	Bordeleau, Hull, Swenson, Hornung
Cleveland	1 3 0 1 5	19 7 5 2 33	Cheevers	Clearwater 2 (OT 0:29), Buchanan, Pinder, Wiste
January 24				
Philadelphia	3 0 3 - 6	22 6 15 - 43	Parent	McKenzie 3, Lacroix 2, Migneault
Quebec	1 2 1 - 4	11 19 15 - 45	Aubry	Golembrosky, Archambault, Parizeau, Gendron
Winnipeg	0 1 0 - 1	21 11 9 - 41	Daley	Hornung
New England	2 3 1 - 6	9 8 8 - 25	Smith	Selwood 2, Webster, Caffery, Pleau, Selby
January 25				
Houston	1 3 1 - 5	11 10 6 - 27	D. McLeod	Popiel, Labossiere, Hall, Stanfield, Taylor
Minnesota	1 0 1 - 2	14 10 7 - 31	Curran	Sanders, Arbour
New England	1 1 2 - 4	4 8 6 - 18	Smith	Webster 2, Caffery, Danby
Ottawa	1 1 0 - 2	6 8 9 - 23	Binkley	Charlebois, Sentes
New York	1 0 1 - 2	8 5 13 - 26	Kurt, Donnelly	Rivers, Laughton
Chicago	2 1 6 - 9	14 16 20 - 50	J. McLeod	Lodboa 3, Whitlock 2, Morris 2, Popiel, Benzelock
Philadelphia	3 2 2 - 7	14 14 14 - 42	Parent	Lawson, Burgess 2, O'Donoghue, Migneault, Campbell
Cleveland	1 2 1 - 4	8 10 19 - 37	Cheevers	Jarrett 2, Andrea 2
January 26				
New York	1 2 1 1 5	9 6 15 10 40	Kurt	Rivers 2 (OT 9:41), Sheehan, Jones, Peacosh
Los Angeles	0 2 2 0 4	5 14 20 5 44	Gillow, Gardner	Odrowski, Szura, Slater, Veneruzzo
Ottawa	0 0 2 - 2	8 8 19 - 35	Binkley	Gibson, Carleton
Minnesota	1 2 1 - 4	13 8 13 - 34	McCartan	MacMillan 2, Johnson 2
Winnipeg	1 1 0 0 2	10 10 11 7 38	Wakely	Bordeleau, Cuddie
Quebec	1 1 0 0 2	10 10 8 4 32	Aubry	Caron, Gaudette
January 27				
Cleveland	1 0 1 - 2	5 10 10 - 25	Whidden	Andrea, Pumple (WG 10:22)
Chicago	0 1 0 - 1	10 12 11 - 33	J. McLeod	Liddington
Philadelphia	0 0 0 1 1	9 9 10 1 29	Parent	Lawson (OT 2:39)
Alberta	0 0 0 0 0	11 3 8 1 23	Norris	▸ Parent: shutout (2), 23 saves
Quebec	2 0 1 - 3	9 9 11 - 29	Brodeur	Parizeau, Guindon, Bergeron
New England	1 0 0 - 1	15 9 17 - 41	Smith	Sheehy
January 28				
Chicago	3 0 0 - 3	12 6 12 - 30	J. McLeod	Morris 2, Popiel
Houston	2 1 1 - 4	18 8 6 - 32	Rutledge	Lund, Stanfield, Harris, Hughes (WG 12:02)
New York	0 0 2 - 2	13 11 8 - 32	Donnelly	Laughton (spoiled Gardner's shutout at 17:17), Peacosh
Los Angeles	3 4 2 - 9	14 17 17 - 48	Gardner	White 2, Watson, Serviss, Gilmore, Niekamp, Byers, Young, Leblanc
Philadelphia	1 0 1 - 2	10 9 10 - 29	Parent	Lacroix, Boudreau
Alberta	1 2 1 - 4	10 11 4 - 25	Norris	Joyal, Barrie, Cote, Harrison
Winnipeg	0 3 2 - 5	7 19 7 - 33	Daley	Beaudin 2, Sutherland, McDonald, Hull (WG 13:31)
Ottawa	1 3 0 - 4	12 9 14 - 35	Gratton	Martin, Trottier, Conacher, Leduc
January 29				
New England	1 1 0 - 2	7 11 14 - 32	Smith	French, Webster
Cleveland	1 0 2 - 3	7 12 12 - 31	Cheevers	Clearwater, Jarrett, Wiste (WG 16:26)

1972-1973 Game by Game Line Scores

Date & Teams	Scoring 1 2 3 ot F	Shots 1 2 3 ot F	Goaltenders	Goals & Other Scoring Highlights
January 30				
Los Angeles	1 3 1 - 5	7 6 4 - 17	Gardner	Szura, Serviss, White, Veneruzzo, Crashley
Houston	0 2 0 - 2	14 9 4 - 27	D. McLeod	Smith, Grierson
Minnesota	0 1 1 - 2	11 10 13 - 34	McCartan	Arbour, Hampson
Chicago	2 0 2 - 4	13 9 8 - 30	J. McLeod	Paiement 2, Morris, Popiel
New York	2 0 1 - 3	10 6 4 - 20	Wilkie, Kurt	Peacosh, Kennedy, Laughton Blanchette, Patenaude. Barrie
Alberta	3 2 6 - 11	11 18 23 - 52	Norris	Harrison 3 (7 assists, 10 points), Carlyle 2, Fonteyne, Hamilton, Wall,
Philadelphia	1 2 1 1 5	9 13 7 1 30	Parent	Campbell 2 (OT 5:45), Lacroix, Boudreau, Burgess
Ottawa	1 1 2 0 4	11 16 14 2 43	Binkley	Carleton, Martin, Leduc, Gibson
Cleveland	0 0 1 - 1	11 9 11 - 31	Cheevers	Pumple
New England	1 2 1 - 4	17 17 12 - 46	Smith	Caffery, Ahearn, Sheehy, Green
February 1				
Minnesota	0 0 2 - 2	10 11 11 - 32	Curran	Ryan, Klatt
Quebec	1 2 1 - 4	15 7 6 - 28	Aubry	Archambault, Caron, Leclerc, Guindon
New England	1 0 3 1 5	4 7 9 3 23	Landon	Selby 3 (OT 2:43), Dorey, Caffery
Houston	1 0 3 0 4	12 11 16 1 40	Rutledge	Hall, Lund, McCallum, McDonald (TG 19:34)
New York	3 0 2 - 5	15 3 10 - 28	Kurt, Donnelly	Reichmuth, Ward, Rivers, Block, Perry
Alberta	5 2 1 - 8	16 14 7 - 37	Norris	Harrison 2, Perkins 2, Carlin, Hamilton, Blanchette, Wall
Ottawa	1 1 0 0 2	11 7 10 4 32	Binkley	Kirk, Carleton
Cleveland	1 0 1 0 2	16 19 10 7 52	Whidden	Hanna, Jarrett (TG, 18:34)
February 2				
Alberta	2 1 1 - 4	12 6 8 - 26	Norris	Patenaude, Joyal, Wall, Harrison (WG 16:41)
Winnipeg	1 0 2 - 3	10 5 16 - 31	Wakely	Gratton 2, Hull
New England	0 0 1 - 1	7 2 5 - 14	Smith	Hurley
Los Angeles	1 2 0 - 3	9 23 9 - 41	Gardner	Veneruzzo, Heiskala, Gilmore
Ottawa	0 1 0 - 1	15 11 12 - 38	Gratton	Warr
Chicago	1 1 2 - 4	11 13 10 - 34	J. McLeod	Whitlock 2, Benzelock, Liddington
Philadelphia	2 1 0 - 3	12 12 10 - 34	Parent	McKenzie, Lacroix, Lawson
Cleveland	2 2 1 - 5	13 18 14 - 45	Cheevers	Pinder, Andrea, Erickson, Muloin, Brindley
February 3				
Minnesota	0 0 1 - 1	15 13 12 - 40	Curran	MacMillan
Houston	3 2 2 - 7	14 9 8 - 31	Rutledge	Mortson 2, Hughes, Popiel, Smith, Schella, Taylor
New York	2 0 0 - 2	9 13 15 - 37	Kurt	Ferguson, Bradley
Chicago	2 0 2 - 4	15 4 12 - 31	J. McLeod	Sicinski 2, Liddington, Paiement
February 4				
Cleveland	0 1 2 - 3	13 12 10 - 35	Cheevers	Jarrett, Andrea, Pumple
Ottawa	1 0 1 - 2	8 5 12 - 25	Binkley	Charlebois, Gibson
New England	1 1 1 - 3	8 9 6 - 23	Smith	Webster, Selby, Caffery
Los Angeles	2 1 1 - 4	9 6 10 - 25	Gillow	Veneruzzo, Crahsley, Heiskala, Slater
Quebec	1 2 1 - 4	8 8 9 - 25	Aubry	Leclerc 2, Golembrosky, Guite
New York	2 2 1 - 5	10 13 9 - 32	Donnelly	Rivers 2, Bradley, Peacosh, Ward
Winnipeg	0 3 2 - 5	9 13 7 - 29	Daley, Wakely	Hull 3, Bordeleau, Sutherland
Alberta	1 1 1 - 3	13 6 10 - 29	Norris	Joyal, Wall, Blanchette
February 5				
Chicago	1 3 1 - 5	6 16 12 - 34	J. McLeod	Paiement 2, Lodboa, Sicinski, Morris
Cleveland	3 2 2 - 7	24 12 13 - 49	Whidden	Wiste 2, Jarrett 2, Hodgson, Brindley, Buchanan
Minnesota	3 1 2 - 6	16 4 14 - 34	McCartan	Sanders, Lilyholm, Morrison, Young, McMahon, Johnson
Houston	0 1 2 - 3	11 8 16 - 35	D. McLeod	Grierson, Taylor, Harris
February 6				
New England	2 2 0 - 4	6 9 6 - 21	Landon, Smith	Pleau 2, Webster, Sheehy
Alberta	1 0 1 - 2	9 11 9 - 29	Norris	Wall, Patenaude
New York	0 2 2 - 4	14 16 19 - 49	Kurt	Ferguson 2, Peacosh 2
Minnesota	2 3 0 - 5	19 13 8 - 40	Curran	Klatt 2, Connelly 2, Hampson
Philadelphia	2 1 0 - 3	12 8 9 - 29	Parent	Plante, Campbell, Boudreau
Ottawa	0 2 3 - 5	13 10 14 - 37	Binkley	Gibson, Charlebois, Carleton, Simpson, King
February 7				
New England	0 1 0 - 1	7 9 7 - 23	Smith	Caffery
Alberta	1 1 1 - 3	6 6 9 - 21	Norris	Baird, Perkins, Walters
Philadelphia	0 0 0 - 0	8 12 9 - 29	Parent	▶ Aubry/Brodeur, shutout, Aubry 8 saves, Brodeur 21 saves
Quebec	1 2 0 - 3	13 14 13 - 40	Aubry, Brodeur	Caron 2, Tremblay
Winnipeg	2 0 0 - 2	19 9 6 - 34	Wakely	Rizzuto, Zanussi
Houston	1 2 2 - 5	8 16 6 - 30	Rutledge	Hughes, Stanfield, Hall, Grierson, McDonald
February 8				
Minnesota	0 0 1 - 1	9 7 8 - 24	McCartan	Klatt (spoiled Gardner's shutout at 18:38)
Los Angeles	0 1 2 - 3	10 8 8 - 26	Gardner	Veneruzzo 2, McCaskill
New York	2 0 1 - 3	11 7 8 - 26	Donnelly	Ferguson, Block, Peacosh (WG 14:09)
Ottawa	1 0 1 - 2	17 12 8 - 37	Binkley	Kirk, King
Quebec	0 1 1 - 2	9 15 17 - 41	Brodeur, Aubry	Tremblay, Lacombe
Chicago	3 1 1 - 5	9 9 15 - 33	J. McLeod	Morris 2, Whitlock, Liddington, Benzelock
Winnipeg	0 1 2 - 3	10 11 11 - 32	Daley	Johnson, Hull, Beaudin
Houston	0 0 1 - 1	4 17 17 - 38	Rutledge	Hall (spoiled Daley's shutout at 15:26)
February 9				
Minnesota	0 0 0 - 0	7 10 10 - 27	Curran	▶ Norris: shutout (1), 27 saves
Alberta	2 0 4 - 6	12 12 15 - 39	Norris	Harrison 2, Joyal, Patenaude, Walters, Barrie
Ottawa	1 3 3 - 7	14 16 8 - 38	Gratton	Gibson 2, Simpson 2, Leduc, Sentes, Kirk
New England	1 1 2 - 4	14 9 20 - 43	Landon	Caffery 2, Pleau, Webster

1972-1973 Game by Game Line Scores

Date & Teams	Scoring 1 2 3 ot F	Shots 1 2 3 ot F	Goaltenders	Goals & Other Scoring Highlights
February 10				
Houston	0 0 0 - 0	15 12 10 - 37	D. McLeod	▶ J. McLeod: shutout (1), 37 saves
Chicago	0 1 2 - 3	7 10 11 - 28	J. McLeod	Lodboa, Popiel, Anderson
New York	2 1 1 - 4	16 18 9 - 43	Kurt	Peacosh 2, Ferguson, Scharf
Cleveland	3 1 4 - 8	16 15 12 - 43	Cheevers	Buchanan 2, Hodgson, Pinder, Erickson, Clearwater, Wiste, Brindley
Quebec	1 3 0 0 4	9 10 9 7 35	Aubry, Brodeur	Caron, Gendron, Guindon, Lacombe
Philadelphia	3 1 0 1 5	14 10 10 9 43	Parent	Plumb, Herriman, Lawson, Spencer, McKenzie (OT 9:42)
Winnipeg	3 0 2 1 6	8 8 7 8 31	Wakely	Hull 2, Black, McDonald, Rousseau, Beaudin (OT 6:07)
Los Angeles	1 2 2 0 5	8 5 6 2 21	Gardner	MacNeil, Leblanc, Gilmore, Veneruzzo, Szura
February 11				
Cleveland	0 1 0 - 1	8 8 12 - 28	Cheevers	Jarrett
Philadelphia	0 3 3 - 6	10 11 11 - 32	Parent	Burgess, Lawson, O'Donoghue, Migneault, Spencer, Herriman
Minnesota	2 3 0 - 5	15 11 6 - 32	McCartan	Connelly, Klatt, Young, Antonovich, Morrison
Alberta	0 1 6 - 7	4 22 17 - 43	Norris, Brown	Joyal 2, Baird, Barrie, Perkins, Harrison, Hamilton (6 goals in 7:02)
New England	1 0 1 0 2	11 19 11 9 50	Smith	Pleau, Caffery (TG 19:13)
Quebec	1 1 0 0 2	7 9 6 5 27	Brodeur	Gaudette, Guite
Ottawa	0 1 1 - 2	11 5 6 - 22	Gratton	Sentes, Gibbons
New York	0 2 1 - 3	7 15 8 - 30	Donnelly	Rivers, Sheehan, Scharf
Winnipeg	0 2 1 - 3	5 8 6 - 19	Daley	Johnson 2, Hull
Los Angeles	0 0 0 - 0	13 6 13 - 32	Gardner	▶ Daley: shutout (1), 31 saves
February 12				
New York	0 1 1 - 2	10 17 11 - 38	Donnelly	Ward, Speer
Cleveland	2 1 5 - 8	14 12 15 - 41	Whidden	Hardy 2, Andrea 2, Pumple, Buchanan, Wiste, Pinder
February 13				
Chicago	2 3 1 - 6	9 13 14 - 36	J. McLeod	Mavety, Morris, Paiement, Lodboa, Sicinski, Whitlock
Los Angeles	0 1 0 - 1	6 8 15 - 29	Gardner, Gillow	Szura
Houston	1 0 2 - 3	12 9 14 - 35	Rutledge	Harris 2, Grierson
Alberta	1 3 1 - 5	11 8 11 - 30	Norris	Joyal 2, Hicke, Falkenberg, Harrison
New England	1 2 1 - 4	6 15 9 - 30	Smith	Earl 2, Green, Selby
Philadelphia	4 1 0 - 5	14 7 5 - 26	Parent	Lawson 4, O'Donoghue
February 14				
Cleveland	3 2 0 - 5	11 8 12 - 31	Cheevers	Pumple, Buchanan, Andrea, Wiste, Hardy
Philadelphia	3 1 2 - 6	11 16 14 - 41	Parent	O'Donoghue 2, Lawson 2 (WG 19:45), Lacroix, Burgess
Ottawa	1 1 4 - 6	13 17 9 - 39	Binkley	Charlebois 2, Kirk, Sentes, Trottier, Gibson
Quebec	1 1 1 - 3	10 6 10 - 26	Brodeur	Leclerc 2, Gaudette
February 15				
Houston	0 2 3 - 5	5 9 10 - 24	D. McLeod	Taylor 2, McDonald, Labossiere, Hughes
Alberta	0 0 3 - 3	12 9 10 - 31	Norris	Hicke, Falkenberg, Patenaude
Los Angeles	2 1 2 - 5	9 16 13 - 38	Gardner	Veneruzzo, White, Leblanc, Sutherland, McCaskill
New England	3 1 2 - 6	11 11 9 - 31	Smith	Sheehy 2, Pleau, Earl, French, Cunniff
Ottawa	0 0 0 - 0	6 7 7 - 20	Binkley	▶ Curran: shutout (3), 20 saves
Minnesota	1 1 1 - 3	10 14 9 - 33	Curran	Antonovich 2, Paradise
Winnipeg	3 1 3 - 7	18 10 10 - 38	Wakely	Hull 4, Beaudin 2, Cuddie
Chicago	1 1 0 - 2	10 11 9 - 30	J. McLeod	Morris 2
February 16				
Houston	0 0 0 - 0	9 11 11 - 31	D. McLeod	▶ Daley: shutout (2), 31 saves
Winnipeg	3 1 3 - 7	19 8 11 - 38	Daley	Sutherland 2, McDonald 2, Hull 2, Bordeleau
Los Angeles	1 1 0 0 2	15 15 13 8 51	Gardner	Szura, Serviss
Quebec	0 0 2 0 2	2 2 9 4 17	Aubry	Guindon, Rouleau
New York	2 0 0 - 2	9 9 6 - 24	Donnelly	Rivers, Sheehan
Philadelphia	0 6 3 - 9	10 17 12 - 39	Parent	McKenzie 3, O'Donoghue 2, Burgess 2, Lawson, Lapierre
February 17				
Minnesota	4 2 1 - 7	10 15 15 - 40	McCartan	Morrison 2, Klatt 2, McMahon, Connelly, Hampson
Cleveland	0 2 1 - 3	7 8 15 - 30	Cheevers	Wiste, Brindley, Pinder
New England	1 4 1 - 6	10 14 20 - 44	Smith	Ahearn 2, Sheehy 2, Williams, Selby
Quebec	1 1 2 - 4	10 6 10 - 26	Aubry	Guindon, Caron, Lacombe, Tremblay
Ottawa	1 0 2 - 3	6 16 11 - 33	Gratton	Cunningham, King, Charlebois
Chicago	0 0 1 - 1	5 6 11 - 22	J. McLeod	Sicinski
February 18				
Chicago	1 1 3 - 5	9 13 14 - 36	Gill, J. McLeod	Sicinski 2, Benzelock, Fleming, Mavety
Minnesota	3 3 1 - 7	14 13 14 - 41	Curran	Connelly 2, Ryan 2, Morrison, Klatt, Ball
Houston	0 1 1 - 2	7 6 12 - 25	Rutledge	Harris, McCallum
Winnipeg	0 1 3 - 4	3 10 6 - 19	Wakely	Beaudin, Black, Bordeleau, Sutherland
Los Angeles	0 3 1 - 4	5 13 10 - 28	Gardner	Veneruzzo, Hyndman, Serviss, Heiskala
Philadelphia	0 1 0 - 1	8 7 11 - 26	Parent	Lapierre
February 20				
Alberta	2 1 1 - 4	14 12 15 - 41	Brown	Patenaude 2, Hamilton, Harrison
Cleveland	3 1 1 - 5	12 18 10 - 40	Whidden	Hardy, Clearwater, Jarrett, Dillabough, Buchanan
Chicago	1 1 2 - 4	8 9 8 - 25	Gill	Popiel, Paiement, Morris
Quebec	0 1 1 - 2	10 21 9 - 40	Aubry	Harvey, Tremblay
Los Angeles	1 1 2 - 4	11 5 9 - 25	Gardner	White 2, Veneruzzo, Speck
Ottawa	1 1 0 - 2	8 13 7 - 28	Gratton	King, Kirk
New England	0 1 1 - 2	7 6 7 - 20	Smith	Smith, Webster
Philadelphia	1 1 2 - 4	10 11 4 - 25	Parent	Migneault, Plumb, McKenzie, Plante
February 21				
Alberta	1 3 0 - 4	9 16 1 - 26	Norris	Perkins 2, Joyal, Falkenberg
New York	0 3 2 - 5	9 11 15 - 35	Kurt	Peacosh, Jones, Sheehan, Ward, Rivers (WG 18:56)

1972-1973 Game by Game Line Scores

Date & Teams	Scoring 1 2 3 ot F	Shots 1 2 3 ot F	Goaltenders	Goals & Other Scoring Highlights
February 22				
Philadelphia	1 3 2 - 6	12 10 11 - 33	Parent	Burgess 2, Plante, O'Donoghue, Herriman, Lawson (WG 18:08)
Ottawa	2 0 3 - 5	14 9 21 - 44	Gratton	Carleton 2, Kirk 2, Charlebois
Quebec	1 0 0 - 1	9 14 11 - 34	Brodeur	Harvey
Houston	1 0 3 - 4	17 9 11 - 37	McLeod, Rutledge	Grierson, Harris, Mortson, Hoekstra
February 23				
Alberta	1 0 1 - 2	13 4 9 - 26	Norris	Patenaude, Joyal
New England	0 2 2 - 4	9 11 15 - 35	Smith	Webster 2, Sheehy, French
February 24				
Chicago	1 2 2 - 5	11 15 15 - 41	Gill	Morris, Lodboa, Paiement, Whitlock, Liddington
Cleveland	0 2 0 - 2	10 9 14 - 33	Whidden	McMasters, Pinder
Quebec	2 2 1 - 5	3 11 9 - 23	Aubry	Guindon 2, Archambault, Caron, Payette
Los Angeles	0 1 2 - 3	15 19 21 - 55	Gardner	Watson, Leblanc, Serviss
February 25				
Alberta	0 2 0 - 2	12 18 11 - 41	Norris	Falkenberg, Walters
Ottawa	2 0 1 - 3	16 6 9 - 31	Binkley	Leduc 2 (WG 7:10 3rd), Charlebois
Cleveland	1 2 2 - 5	12 9 5 - 26	Cheevers	Jarrett, Brindley, Wiste, Buchanan, Pinder
New York	2 3 4 - 9	8 16 15 - 39	Kurt	Peacosh 3, Rivers 3, Ward 2, Bradley
Minnesota	1 0 0 - 1	12 16 15 - 43	McCartan	Klatt
Houston	3 0 1 - 4	10 4 17 - 31	Rutledge	Taylor 2, McDonald, Harris
Philadelphia	2 1 0 - 3	12 9 7 - 28	Parent	Migneault 2, Lawson
Winnipeg	1 1 3 - 5	12 9 13 - 34	Daley	Beaudin 3 (all in 3rd period), Hull 2
Quebec	1 0 1 - 2	4 6 7 - 17	Brodeur	Bergeron, Giroux
Los Angeles	1 1 2 - 4	22 9 15 - 46	Perreault	Gilmore 2, Veneruzzo, Leblanc
February 27				
Alberta	2 2 0 - 4	8 7 10 - 25	Norris	McAneeley, Baird, Carlin, Cote
Houston	1 0 4 - 5	14 11 13 - 38	Rutledge	Grierson 2, Schella, Mortson, Popiel (WG 10:54)
Chicago	0 1 0 - 1	8 4 9 - 21	Gill	Paiement
Winnipeg	1 3 1 - 5	14 13 12 - 39	Wakely	Hull 2, Black 2, Bordeleau
Cleveland	1 0 0 - 1	6 3 6 - 15	Cheevers	Hardy
Ottawa	1 0 1 - 2	17 8 5 - 30	Binkley	Kirk, Trottier (WG 7:46)
Philadelphia	0 0 0 - 0	11 10 16 - 37	Parent	▶ Curran: shutout (4), 37 saves
Minnesota	1 0 2 - 3	14 7 15 - 36	Curran	MacMillan, Hampson, Young
February 28				
Alberta	1 1 0 0 2	8 5 6 0 19	Norris	Patenaude, Harrison
Houston	0 1 1 1 3	12 7 18 2 39	D. McLeod	Taylor 2, Harris (OT 1:48)
March 1				
Los Angeles	0 2 2 - 4	10 10 9 - 29	Gardner	White 3, Speck
Minnesota	1 0 0 - 1	8 7 15 - 30	McCartan	MacMillan
New York	0 1 0 - 1	7 12 8 - 27	Kurt	Bradley
Ottawa	0 1 1 - 2	13 12 6 - 31	Binkley	Trottier, Carleton
March 2				
Los Angeles	0 1 0 - 1	5 8 8 - 21	Gillow	Slater
Winnipeg	1 1 0 - 2	7 11 8 - 26	Daley	Beaudin, Swenson
March 3				
Cleveland	1 2 1 - 4	6 7 11 - 24	Whidden	Erickson 2, Hardy, Pinder (WG 11:47)
New York	1 1 1 - 3	10 11 13 - 34	Kurt	Sheehan, Ward, Rivers
Quebec	1 2 1 - 4	9 11 6 - 26	Aubry	Bergeron, Guite 2, Guindon (WG 15:47)
Houston	2 1 0 - 3	16 13 15 - 44	Rutledge	Harris, Labossiere, Mortson
March 4				
Chicago	2 1 1 - 4	9 7 8 - 24	Gill, J. McLeod	Liddington, Fleming, Popiel, Benzelock
Ottawa	1 3 2 - 6	11 16 7 - 34	Binkley	Carleton 2, Trottier, Kirk, Leduc, Charlebois
Los Angeles	0 0 1 - 1	5 5 11 - 21	Gillow	Hyndman
Winnipeg	1 1 0 - 2	13 8 8 - 29	Wakely	Bordeleau, Hornung
New England	0 0 2 - 2	8 6 6 - 20	Smith	Byers, Selwood
Minnesota	1 0 3 - 4	16 9 11 - 36	Curran	Sanders, Johnson, Connelly, MacMillan
Philadelphia	1 0 3 - 4	13 5 20 - 38	Parent	Lawson, Campbell, Burgess, McKenzie
New York	0 1 1 - 2	7 9 9 - 25	Kurt	Sheehan, Bradley
Quebec	1 2 3 - 6	10 11 11 - 32	Brodeur	Caron, Golembrosky, Guindon, Rouleau, Bergeron
Houston	0 2 1 - 3	8 7 10 - 25	D. McLeod	McDonald, Hughes, Lund
March 5				
Chicago	1 3 0 0 4	15 2 11 8 36	J. McLeod	Popiel, Paiement, Sarrazin, Benzelock
New York	0 2 2 0 4	11 11 12 4 38	Donnelly	Rivers 2, Ward, Jones (TG 19:23) (NY: 2 goals in last 0:50 to tie)
March 6				
Alberta	3 0 0 0 3	13 6 9 1 29	Norris	Baird, Carlyle, Patenaude
Minnesota	1 1 1 1 4	10 16 12 1 39	McCartan	Klatt 2, Connelly, McMahon (OT 1:25)
Philadelphia	1 0 0 0 1	12 8 12 4 36	Parent	McKenzie
Chicago	1 0 0 1 2	13 5 8 5 31	J. McLeod	Whitlock, Paiement (OT 4:00)
Quebec	1 1 0 0 2	12 5 3 0 20	Aubry	Gaudette, Lacombe
Los Angeles	1 0 1 1 3	19 15 13 1 48	Gillow	Gilmore, Szura, Leblanc (OT 1:05)
Winnipeg	1 1 0 - 2	9 9 5 - 23	Daley	Beaudin, Ash
Ottawa	2 2 1 - 5	14 11 17 - 42	Gratton	Carleton 2, Kirk, Charlebois, Martin
March 7				
Cleveland	0 0 0 0 0	10 6 5 1 22	Cheevers	▶ Smith: shutout (3), 22 saves
New England	0 0 0 1 1	14 11 10 4 39	Smith	French (OT 7:57)
Houston	0 1 2 - 3	8 9 9 - 26	Rutledge	Hughes 2, Labossiere
Los Angeles	0 1 0 - 1	12 14 12 - 38	Gillow	Slater

1972-1973 Game by Game Line Scores

Date & Teams	Scoring 1	2	3	ot	F	Shots 1	2	3	ot	F	Goaltenders	Goals & Other Scoring Highlights
March 8												
Alberta	1	1	0	1	3	7	10	6	9	32	Norris	Hamilton, Carlyle, Wall (OT 5:04)
Chicago	0	1	1	0	2	11	15	11	0	37	J. McLeod	Mavety, Popiel
Minnesota	0	1	0	-	1	9	9	8	-	26	McCartan	Young
Philadelphia	1	1	0	-	2	10	9	8	-	27	Parent	Lawson, Herriman
Winnipeg	2	3	2	-	7	7	17	15	-	39	Wakely	Bordeleau 2, Hornung, Beaudin, Johnson, Boyer, Hull
Quebec	2	1	1	-	4	11	8	9	-	28	Brodeur	Guindon, Leclerc, Gaudette, Harvey
March 9												
Cleveland	2	1	1	-	4	9	10	15	-	34	Whidden	Pinder 2, Pumple, Wiste
New England	3	2	0	-	5	17	6	6	-	29	Smith	Green, Danby, Pleau, Williams, Smith
Houston	0	0	1	-	1	5	12	11	-	28	Rutledge	Taylor
Los Angeles	2	2	1	-	5	16	9	7	-	32	Gardner	Gilmore 3, Niekamp, Hyndman
Quebec	2	1	0	-	3	6	9	6	-	21	Brodeur, Aubry	Gaudette, Caron, Guindon McKenzie
Philadelphia	3	4	4	-	11	17	17	19	-	53	Parent	Lacroix 3, Herriman 2, Campbell 2, O'Donoghue, Lawson, Burgess,
March 10												
Alberta	0	4	0	1	5	9	19	12	7	47	Brown	Joyal 2, Walters 2 (OT 5:39), Wall
Chicago	2	2	0	0	4	15	5	8	-	28	J. McLeod	Paiement 2, Benzelock, Popiel
Minnesota	0	0	1	-	1	5	13	19	-	37	McCartan	Klatt
New England	2	1	0	-	3	14	8	6	-	28	Landon	Webster, Ahearn, Pleau
Winnipeg	1	0	1	0	2	12	8	10	0	30	Daley	Bordeleau, Hull
New York	1	0	1	1	3	10	11	9	3	33	Donnelly	Peacosh, Block (TG 18:12), Bradley (OT 7:41)
March 11												
Alberta	0	0	1	-	1	7	10	14	-	31	Norris	Baird
Minnesota	1	1	0	-	2	18	11	8	-	37	Curran	Hampson, Young
Cleveland	2	4	5	-	11	11	15	8	-	34	Cheevers	Buchanan 3, Jarrett 2, Dillabough 2, Pumple, Horton, Clearwater, Brindley
Winnipeg	1	1	0	-	2	12	7	11	-	30	Wakely	Beaudin, Gratton
Houston	3	0	1	-	4	14	12	6	-	32	D. McLeod	Grierson, Labossiere, Lund, Taylor
Philadelphia	0	1	1	-	2	5	8	18	-	31	Parent	Lapierre, Burgess
New York	0	1	0	-	1	9	10	10	-	29	Donnelly	Gauthier
Quebec	1	3	2	-	6	15	19	18	-	52	Aubry	Leclerc 2, Caron, Tremblay, Parizeau, Guindon
Ottawa	0	1	1	-	2	9	4	9	-	22	Gratton	Kirk, Leduc
Los Angeles	3	1	0	-	4	11	13	9	-	33	Gardner	Veneruzzo 2, Gilmore, Slater
March 12												
Chicago	3	2	2	-	7	11	10	7	-	28	J. McLeod	Fleming 3, Morris, Paiement, Whitlock, Barber
New York	2	3	3	-	8	9	18	15	-	42	Kurt	Reichmuth 2, Sheehan 2, Bradley 2 (WG 19:10), Peacosh, Ward
Quebec	2	2	2	-	6	8	11	9	-	28	Aubry	Lacombe 2, Giroux, Gaudette, Archambault, Parizeau
Philadelphia	2	1	1	-	4	15	15	14	-	44	Parent	Campbell 2, Plumb, Lacroix
March 13												
Cleveland	0	1	1	-	2	7	4	15	-	26	Cheevers	Hopiavuori, Pinder
Alberta	2	2	0	-	4	13	13	6	-	32	Norris	Kassian 2, Wall, Baird
Houston	0	3	0	-	3	5	12	11	-	28	D. McLeod	Labossiere, Smith, Taylor
Philadelphia	1	3	0	-	4	17	15	11	-	43	Parent	Lawson 2, O'Donoghue, McKenzie
New England	2	0	1	1	4	6	4	20	4	34	Smith	French, Sheehy, Webster, Dorey (OT 6:57)
Chicago	0	2	1	0	3	7	4	9	4	24	Gill	Sicinski, Sarrazin, Paiement
Ottawa	3	0	0	-	3	13	6	6	-	25	Gratton	Carleton 2, Sentes
Los Angeles	0	0	1	-	1	12	12	12	-	36	Gardner	Hyndman
March 14												
Cleveland	0	2	0	-	2	7	7	15	-	29	Whidden	Krake, jarrett
Alberta	1	2	1	-	4	14	6	8	-	28	Brown	Wall, McAneeley, Harrison, Perkins
Houston	1	0	0	-	1	11	18	6	-	35	Rutledge	Mortson
New York	3	0	2	-	5	19	10	12	-	41	Donnelly	Rivers 2, Sheehan, Ward, Olds
New England	4	1	2	-	7	8	8	9	-	25	Landon	Sheehy 2, Selwood 2, Williams, Green, Byers
Winnipeg	2	1	2	-	5	8	10	9	-	27	Daley	Hull 3, Boyer, Zanussi
March 15												
Los Angeles	2	2	2	-	6	11	8	7	-	26	Gardner	Gilmore 2, Hyndman 2, McCaskill, Sutherland
New York	1	1	0	-	2	7	8	12	-	27	Donnelly	Peacosh, Olds
Minnesota	2	4	1	-	7	10	10	11	-	31	Curran	Connelly 2, Klatt, Ryan, Lilyholm, McMahon, Sanders
Chicago	1	1	2	-	4	15	11	10	-	36	Gill	Whitlock, Morris, Liddington, Paiement
March 16												
Minnesota	1	3	0	-	4	9	11	6	-	26	Curran, McCartan	Ball 2, McMahon, Sanders
New England	5	0	2	-	7	22	12	12	-	46	Smith	Pleau 2, Sheehy, Danby, Webster, French, Byers
Ottawa	3	1	2	-	6	16	9	9	-	34	Gratton	Martin 4, Sentes, Carleton
Winnipeg	1	0	0	-	1	7	12	10	-	29	Wakely	Johnson
Quebec	1	0	1	-	2	8	8	7	-	23	Aubry	Guite, Bergeron
Alberta	1	1	2	-	4	9	9	7	-	25	Norris	Joyal, Hamilton, Harrison, Patenaude
March 17												
Los Angeles	0	1	1	-	2	10	8	12	-	30	Gardner	Gilmore, Sutherland
Cleveland	0	0	0	-	0	11	8	8	-	27	Cheevers	▸ Gardner: shutout (1), 27 saves
New York	1	1	1	-	3	12	19	16	-	47	Kurt	Bradley, Rivers, Speer
Chicago	3	0	3	-	6	13	9	12	-	34	J. McLeod	Sicinski 2, Liddington, Morris, Sarrazin, Fleming
Philadelphia	0	0	0	-	0	14	12	8	-	34	Parent	▸ Landon: shutout (1), 34 saves
New England	0	2	2	-	4	13	10	14	-	37	Landon	Danby, Williams, Webster, Sheehy
Quebec	0	0	0	-	0	11	11	10	-	32	Aubry	▸ Brown: shutout (1): 31 saves
Alberta	1	1	1	-	3	13	21	16	-	50	Brown	Walters, Carlin, Harrison
March 18												
New York	1	0	1	1	3	12	11	14	4	41	Donnelly	Douglas, Ward, Block (OT 4:18)
Houston	1	1	0	0	2	14	9	10	0	33	D. McLeod	Hughes, McDonald
Ottawa	2	1	1	-	4	14	8	3	-	25	Gratton	Leduc, King, Cunningham, Martin
Winnipeg	0	2	0	-	2	13	11	14	-	38	Daley	Hornung, Hull

1972-1973 Game by Game Line Scores

Date & Teams	Scoring 1	2	3	ot	F	Shots 1	2	3	ot	F	Goaltenders	Goals & Other Scoring Highlights
March 19												
Los Angeles	1	0	4	0	5	8	9	13	7	37	Gardner, Gillow	Leblanc 2, Crashley, Szura, Speck (TG 18:07)
Cleveland	1	4	0	0	5	11	15	10	4	40	Whidden	Buchanan 2, Brindley, Pumple, Pinder
Philadelphia	0	1	0	-	1	12	15	17	-	44	Parent	McKenzie
Houston	2	1	2	-	5	16	11	14	-	41	Rutledge	McDonald 2, Harris, Hughes, Hoekstra
March 20												
Cleveland	0	1	0	-	1	11	9	8	-	28	Whidden	Wiste
Quebec	0	1	3	-	4	21	12	14	-	47	Aubry	Gaudette 2, Parizeau, Archambault
Los Angeles	1	0	0	-	1	14	7	12	-	33	Gillow	Crashley
New England	2	1	1	-	4	6	9	11	-	26	Smith	Caffery, Ley, Byers, Dorey
Minnesota	1	1	1	-	3	8	11	10	-	29	Curran	Klatt 2, Ryan
Alberta	1	2	2	-	5	13	10	14	-	37	Brown	Harrison 2, Barrie, Carlyle, Anderson
March 21												
Philadelphia	2	1	4	-	7	16	9	12	-	37	Parent	Lacroix 3, Lapierre 2, Burgess, Plumb
Houston	1	0	2	-	3	16	9	9	-	34	D. McLeod	Labossiere, Hughes, McDonald
March 22												
Alberta	0	1	0	0	1	6	12	5	2	25	Norris	Baird
Winnipeg	0	0	1	0	1	11	9	10	4	34	Wakely	Beaudin (TG 19:44)
Minnesota	1	0	0	1	2	5	3	12	7	27	McCartan	Hampson, MacMillan (OT 9:57)
Chicago	0	0	1	0	1	5	8	9	7	29	Gill	Popiel
New England	0	1	1	-	2	4	11	7	-	22	Landon	Pleau, Ahearn
Ottawa	3	0	1	-	4	10	7	13	-	30	Gratton	Simpson, Leduc, Kirk, Gibbons
March 23												
Chicago	0	1	0	-	1	9	7	7	-	23	Gill	Paiement
New England	0	2	1	-	3	15	13	14	-	42	Smith	Webster 2, Green
Philadelphia	3	1	3	-	7	14	11	7	-	32	Parent	Lacroix 2, Lawson, Migneault, Burgess, Herriman, McKenzie
Los Angeles	1	0	2	-	3	6	12	12	-	30	Gardner	Hyndman 2, Slater
March 24												
Alberta	0	3	1	-	4	20	15	7	-	42	Brown, Norris	Kassian 2, Hicke, Harrison
Quebec	0	4	1	-	5	10	16	17	-	43	Aubry	Parizeau 2, Harvey, Caron, Gaudette
Minnesota	0	1	0	1	2	12	9	4	10	35	Curran	Ryan, Klatt (OT 9:43)
Cleveland	1	0	0	0	1	14	13	8	3	38	Whidden	Shmyr
March 25												
Alberta	1	1	3	-	5	12	9	11	-	32	Norris	Patenaude 2 (WG 9:07), Harrison, Perkins, Joyal
Quebec	1	1	2	-	4	16	14	14	-	44	Aubry	Guindon 2, Leclerc, Caron
Chicago	0	0	0	-	0	6	9	14	-	29	Gill	▶ Gillow: shutout (2): 29 saves
Los Angeles	1	0	0	-	1	9	10	13	-	32	Gillow	Sutherland
Cleveland	2	2	0	-	4	9	9	5	-	23	Cheevers	Jarrett, Hopiavuori, Krake, Buchanan
Houston	2	0	0	-	2	11	13	15	-	39	Rutledge	Labossiere 2
Minnesota	0	1	0	-	1	8	10	8	-	26	McCartan	Christiansen
Ottawa	3	3	0	-	6	15	11	5	-	31	Gratton	Kirk 2, Sentes, Cunningham, Gibbons, Gibson
New York	4	0	0	-	4	17	7	3	-	27	Donnelly, Kurt	Rivers 2, Sheehan, Perry
Winnipeg	3	4	1	-	8	9	14	12	-	35	Daley	Bordeleau 2, Beaudin 2, Johnson 2, Woytowich, Hull
March 26												
New England	1	3	1	-	5	10	12	11	-	33	Smith	Caffery 2, Earl, Selwood, Byers
Cleveland	3	0	4	-	7	11	10	21	-	42	Cheevers	Wiste 2, Buchanan, Erickson, Pumple, Jarrett, Krake
March 27												
Chicago	0	0	1	-	1	6	6	9	-	21	Gill	Zaine
Los Angeles	1	2	1	-	4	22	12	9	-	43	Gillow	Serviss, Crashley, Veneruzzo, Sutherland
Houston	3	0	3	-	6	14	10	10	-	34	Rutledge	Hughes, Popiel, Taylor, Labossiere, Smith, Mortson
New England	0	1	0	-	1	9	12	14	-	35	Landon	Selby
New York	1	0	2	-	3	4	11	13	-	28	Kurt	Ward 2, Bradley
Minnesota	2	2	0	-	4	16	16	6	-	38	Curran	Arbour, Connelly, Pearson, Klatt
Quebec	1	0	1	-	2	6	10	10	-	26	Aubry	Dufour, Roy
Ottawa	0	3	3	-	6	6	12	18	-	36	Gratton	Leduc 2, Trottier, Gibson, Sentes, Charlebois
March 28												
Alberta	1	0	1	-	2	12	6	8	-	26	Norris	Patenaude, Harrison (WG 11:01)
Philadelphia	1	0	0	-	1	6	10	16	-	32	Parent	Lacroix
Winnipeg	0	3	0	1	4	9	22	4	1	36	Daley	Hull 2 (OT 0:55), Swenson, Johnson
Chicago	1	0	2	0	3	9	7	16	0	32	Gill	Proceviat, Cahan, Morris
March 29												
Alberta	0	1	0	-	1	6	7	7	-	20	Norris	Baird
Philadelphia	0	0	2	-	2	10	10	12	-	32	Parent	Campbell, Lacroix (WG 14:30)
New England	2	0	0	-	2	10	6	6	-	22	Smith	Webster, Sheehy
Ottawa	2	1	2	-	5	14	8	10	-	32	Gratton	Kirk 3, Gibbons, Trottier
New York	2	1	0	-	3	12	13	8	-	33	Kurt	Perry, Olds, Ward
Houston	2	1	2	-	5	12	13	4	-	29	Rutledge	Hall 3, Lund, McDonald
Quebec	2	2	1	-	5	17	9	9	-	35	Aubry	Caron 2, Roy, Dufour, Parizeau
Minnesota	0	2	1	-	3	15	12	17	-	44	McCartan, Curran	Connelly 2, Klatt
March 30												
Alberta	1	2	2	-	5	12	14	13	-	39	Norris	Baird 2, Harrison, Wall, Anderson
Minnesota	2	1	0	-	3	17	9	7	-	33	McCartan, Curran	Connelly 2, Klatt
New York	0	2	2	0	4	5	20	18	2	45	Kurt	Jones 2, Peacosh, Reichmuth
New England	1	1	2	1	5	12	14	9	7	42	Landon	Caffery 3 (OT 7:30), French, Sheehy
Winnipeg	1	0	1	-	2	12	13	12	-	37	Daley	Rizzuto, Bordeleau
Cleveland	3	0	1	-	4	10	11	12	-	33	Cheevers	Jarrett 2, Wiste, Andrea

1972-1973 Game by Game Line Scores

Date & Teams	Scoring 1 2 3 ot F	Shots 1 2 3 ot F	Goaltenders	Goals & Other Scoring Highlights
March 31				
Chicago	0 0 1 - 1	6 8 8 - 22	Gill	Popiel
Philadelphia	1 2 2 - 5	9 15 9 - 33	Parent	Lawson 3, Campbell, Lacroix
Houston	0 0 1 - 1	13 7 10 - 30	D. McLeod	Lund
Quebec	2 1 2 - 5	12 17 13 - 42	Aubry	Rouleau, Gaudette, Bergeron, Parizeau, Gendron
Ottawa	1 0 1 - 2	12 7 12 - 31	Binkley, Gratton	Kirk, Charlebois
Cleveland	0 2 2 - 4	12 15 12 - 39	Whidden	Hodgson, Pumple, Hopiavuori, Pinder
April 1				
Chicago	0 0 1 - 1	13 16 13 - 42	Gill	Proceviat
Cleveland	0 2 3 - 5	20 13 15 - 48	Cheevers	Jarrett, Brindley, Pinder, Pumple, Wiste
Houston	0 1 5 - 6	18 12 15 - 45	Rutledge	Taylor 3, Hoekstra, Labossiere, Hall
Ottawa	2 1 0 - 3	8 10 7 - 25	Gratton	Carleton, Martin, Conacher
Quebec	1 1 1 - 3	12 14 11 - 37	Brodeur	Harvey, Gaudette, Roy
New England	2 2 4 - 8	11 13 20 - 44	Smith	Webster 3, Selwood, Dorey, Byers, French, Smith
Winnipeg	0 2 0 - 2	10 11 11 - 32	Tumilson	Rizzuto, Sutherland
Philadelphia	0 1 3 - 4	13 6 12 - 31	Parent	Plumb, Campbell, Lawson, Lacroix

End of Regular Season

1973 Playoffs Game by Game Line Scores

Date & Teams	Scoring 1 2 3 ot F	Shots 1 2 3 ot F	Goaltenders	Goals & Other Scoring Highlights
April 4				
Minnesota	1 1 2 - 4	5 11 8 - 24	Curran	Pearson, Connelly, Antonovich, Young
Alberta	0 0 2 - 2	11 8 6 - 25	Norris	Walters, Baird (Game played in Calgary)
Philadelphia	0 0 2 0 2	14 10 8 7 39	Parent	McKenzie 2
Cleveland	0 2 0 1 3	7 18 16 4 45	Cheevers	Shmyr, Clearwater, Buchanan (OT 9:44)
April 5				
Los Angeles	0 1 1 - 2	12 8 10 - 30	Gardner, Gillow	Niekamp 2
Houston	3 1 3 - 7	8 12 11 - 31	Rutledge	Taylor 2, Hale, McDonald, McCallum, Hoekstra, Lund
April 6				
Minnesota	0 0 1 - 1	8 12 9 - 29	McCartan	Antonovich
Winnipeg	1 0 2 - 3	9 11 9 - 29	Wakely	Hull 2, Bordeleau
April 7				
Ottawa	0 1 2 - 3	7 5 16 - 28	Binkley	Charlebois, Gibson, Cunningham
New England	1 2 3 - 6	19 19 20 - 58	Smith	Pleau, Ahearn, Williams, Byers, Selby, Caffery
Philadelphia	0 0 1 - 1	4 15 11 - 30	Paille, Archambault	Campeau (spoiled Cheevers' shutout at 16:04)
Cleveland	2 4 1 - 7	13 16 9 - 38	Cheevers	Jarrett 3, Wiste 2, Pinder, Erickson
Los Angeles	1 0 3 - 4	8 10 10 - 28	Gardner	Veneruzzo 2, McCaskill, Gilmore
Houston	1 1 0 - 2	13 10 6 - 29	Rutledge	Hall, McDonald
April 8				
Ottawa	2 0 1 0 3	15 6 6 2 29	Gratton	Conacher, Kirk, Climie (TG 19:06)
New England	0 2 1 1 4	16 22 15 4 57	Smith	Webster 2, Selwood, Selby (OT 3:37)
Cleveland	1 1 1 - 3	9 5 7 - 21	Cheevers	Andrea, Erickson, Jarrett
Philadelphia	0 1 0 - 1	10 8 6 - 24	Archambault	Burgess
Minnesota	1 1 0 - 2	7 11 9 - 27	McCartan	Morrison, Hampson
Winnipeg	1 2 2 - 5	17 17 13 - 47	Daley	Bordeleau, Johnson, Boyer, Beaudin, Hull
April 10				
New England	0 1 1 - 2	11 10 9 - 30	Smith	Webster 2
Ottawa	2 1 1 - 4	6 8 11 - 25	Binkley	Sentes 2, Stephanson, Trottier (Game played in Toronto)
Winnipeg	2 1 1 - 4	16 14 10 - 40	Wakely	Sutherland, Rousseau, Swenson, Gratton
Minnesota	4 0 2 - 6	13 9 8 - 30	McCartan	Johnson 2, Klatt, Young, Connelly, Lilyholm
April 11				
Winnipeg	1 0 1 1 3	12 9 16 4 41	Daley	Hornung, Sutherland (TG 19:15), Beaudin (OT 3:12)
Minnesota	1 1 0 0 2	13 13 7 1 34	Curran	Hampson, Ball
Cleveland	1 4 1 - 6	10 12 10 - 32	Cheevers	Pinder, Andrea, Krake, Wiste, Dillabough, Pumple
Philadelphia	1 1 0 - 2	10 11 13 - 34	Archambault	Herriman, McKenzie
Houston	2 0 0 - 2	7 12 12 - 31	D. McLeod	McCallum, McDonald
Los Angeles	3 0 0 - 3	10 13 5 - 28	Gillow	White, Speck, Odrowski
April 12				
New England	3 3 1 - 7	11 13 11 - 35	Smith	Williams 3, Caffery 2, Pleau, Byers
Ottawa	0 2 1 - 3	5 5 8 - 18	Binkley	Carleton 3 (Game played in Toronto)
April 13				
Houston	0 1 1 1 3	6 10 5 3 24	Rutledge	Lund, Popiel, Hall (OT 3:38)
Los Angeles	0 1 1 0 2	14 12 10 1 37	Gillow	McCaskill, Speck
April 14				
Ottawa	1 1 2 0 4	7 10 13 0 30	Gratton, Binkley	Kirk, Simpson, Sentes, Gibbons
New England	2 2 0 1 5	14 10 9 6 39	Smith	Webster 3, Pleau, Byers (OT 3:47)
April 15				
Minnesota	2 2 1 - 5	8 14 20 - 42	Curran, McCartan	Pearson 2, Christiansen, Antonovich, Hampson
Winnipeg	2 5 1 - 8	13 12 9 - 34	Wakely	Beaudin 3, Sutherland 2, Ash, McDonald, Zanussi
Los Angeles	2 0 1 - 3	16 11 14 - 41	Gardner, Gillow	Heiskala, Veneruzzo, Zrymiak
Houston	3 2 1 - 6	11 9 7 - 27	Rutledge	Hughes 2, Popiel, Lund, Labossiere, Hall
April 17				
Houston	2 1 0 - 3	9 11 10 - 30	Rutledge	Hughes 2, Hall
Los Angeles	0 1 1 - 2	11 11 10 - 32	Gillow	MacSweyn, Speck

1973 Playoffs Game by Game Line Scores

Date & Teams	Scoring 1	2	3	ot	F	Shots 1	2	3	ot	F	Goaltenders	Goals & Other Scoring Highlights
April 18												
Cleveland	0	0	2	-	2	10	11	5	-	26	Cheevers	Buchanan, Pumple
New England	1	0	2	-	3	5	8	19	-	32	Smith	Sheehy 2 (WG 19:35), Pleau
April 19												
Cleveland	2	0	0	-	2	11	11	9	-	31	Cheevers	Buchanan, Muloin
New England	1	2	0	-	3	13	12	9	-	34	Smith	Pleau 2, Webster
April 20												
Houston	0	1	0	-	1	6	8	8	-	22	Rutledge	Harris
Winnipeg	3	1	1	-	5	12	9	8	-	29	Daley	Boyer 2, Sutherland, Johnson, Hull
April 21												
New England	2	1	2	-	5	6	12	9	-	27	Smith	Sheehy 2, Smith, Dorey, Pleau
Cleveland	1	1	2	-	4	5	10	6	-	21	Cheevers	Buchanan 2, Jarrett, Hodgson
April 22												
New England	1	0	1	-	2	8	17	11	-	36	Smith	Sheehy, Pleau
Cleveland	2	1	2	-	5	13	9	11	-	33	Cheevers	Jarrett 3, Buchanan 2
Houston	0	0	0	-	0	4	13	11	-	28	D. McLeod	▸ Wakely: shutout (1), 28 saves
Winnipeg	0	0	2	-	2	10	7	10	-	27	Wakely	Rousseau, Beaudin
April 24												
Winnipeg	2	1	1	-	4	8	5	9	-	22	Daley	Zanussi, Beaudin, Hull, Bordeleau
Houston	0	0	2	-	2	19	12	9	-	40	D. McLeod	Taylor, Stanfield
April 26												
Cleveland	1	0	0	-	1	12	10	9	-	31	Cheevers	Pumple
New England	1	1	1	-	3	9	16	7	-	32	Smith	Sheehy, Earl, Selwood
Winnipeg	1	0	2	-	3	11	12	9	-	32	Wakely	Beaudin 2, Hornung
Houston	0	0	0	-	0	8	12	5	-	25	Rutledge	▸ Wakely: shutout (2), 25 saves
April 29												
Winnipeg	1	0	1	-	2	14	6	7	-	27	Daley	Beaudin, Hull
New England	4	2	1	-	7	7	13	5	-	25	Smith	Webster 2, Ley, Earl, French, Williams, Dorey
May 2												
New England	1	1	5	-	7	13	6	6	-	25	Smith	French 2, Williams, Selwood, Dorey, Selby, Cunniff
Winnipeg	2	2	0	-	4	13	11	12	-	36	Wakely	Bordeleau 2, Beaudin, Boyer
May 3												
New England	0	1	2	-	3	12	4	11	-	27	Smith	Ley, Green, Sheehy
Winnipeg	2	1	1	-	4	8	14	6	-	28	Daley	Hull 2 (WG 18:56), McDonald, Johnson
May 5												
Winnipeg	1	0	1	-	2	9	11	10	-	30	Wakely	Hull, Rousseau
New England	0	3	1	-	4	13	8	11	-	32	Smith	Byers 2, Pleau, Sheehy
May 6												
Winnipeg	2	2	2	-	6	17	12	13	-	42	Daley	Beaudin 2, Johnson, Black, Woytowich, Asmundson
New England	5	1	3	-	9	11	6	10	-	27	Smith	Pleau 3, Webster 2, Smith, Ley, Sheehy, Byers

New England is League Champion

Gallery

Kent Douglas

George Gardner

Al Globensky

Danny Geoffrion

Craig Reichmuth

Danny Spring

Bob Winograd

Paul Larose

Mike Hyndman

Dave Gilmour

1972-1973 ALBERTA OILERS

Coach
Ray Kinasewich
24-26-2

Coach
Bill Hunter
14-11-1

Summary of Games (@ Away, * Overtime)

#	date	opponent	score		record	pts	gf-ga
1.	Oct 11 @	Ottawa	7-4	W	1-0-0	2	7-4
2.	Oct 13 @	Quebec	0-6	L	1-1-0	2	7-10
3.	Oct 14 @	Cleveland	2-3	L	1-2-0	2	9-13
4.	Oct 15 @	Winnipeg	5-2	W	2-2-0	4	14-15
5.	Oct 17	Winnipeg	*3-2	W	3-2-0	6	17-17
6.	Oct 20	Philadelphia	4-1	W	4-2-0	8	21-18
7.	Oct 24	Chicago	3-3	T	4-2-1	9	24-21
8.	Oct 27 @	Cleveland	0-6	L	4-3-1	9	24-27
9.	Oct 28 @	New England	4-1	W	5-3-1	11	28-28
10.	Oct 29 @	New York	2-7	L	5-4-1	11	30-35
11.	Oct 31	Houston	3-4	L	5-5-1	11	33-39
12.	Nov 3	Houston	4-3	W	6-5-1	13	37-42
13.	Nov 5	Ottawa	3-5	L	6-6-1	13	40-47
14.	Nov 7	New York	4-2	W	7-6-1	15	44-49
15.	Nov 9	Los Angeles	7-2	W	8-6-1	17	51-51
16.	Nov 11	Los Angeles	5-3	W	9-6-1	19	56-54
17.	Nov 12	Cleveland	1-3	L	9-7-1	19	57-57
18.	Nov 15	Winnipeg	3-1	W	10-7-1	21	60-58
19.	Nov 17	Chicago	3-1	W	11-7-1	23	63-59
20.	Nov 21 @	Minnesota	*3-4	L	11-8-1	23	66-63
21.	Nov 22 @	Philadelphia	*4-5	L	11-9-1	23	70-68
22.	Nov 24 @	New England	2-7	L	11-10-1	23	72-75
23.	Nov 25 @	New York	2-4	L	11-11-1	23	74-79
24.	Nov 26 @	Ottawa	2-1	W	12-11-1	25	76-80
25.	Nov 28 @	Winnipeg	0-3	L	12-12-1	25	76-83
26.	Nov 30	Winnipeg	3-3	T	12-12-2	26	79-86
27.	Dec 1	Minnesota	4-6	L	12-13-2	26	83-92
28.	Dec 3	Quebec	2-6	L	12-14-2	26	85-98
29.	Dec 8 @	Los Angeles	2-4	L	12-15-2	26	87-102
30.	Dec 10 @	Los Angeles	3-5	L	12-16-2	26	90-107
31.	Dec 12 @	Houston	4-6	L	12-17-2	26	94-113
32.	Dec 13 @	Houston	3-2	W	13-17-2	28	97-115
33.	Dec 15	Ottawa	3-4	L	13-18-2	28	100-119
34.	Dec 17	Ottawa	3-1	W	14-18-2	30	103-120
35.	Dec 21	New England	5-4	W	15-18-2	32	108-124
36.	Dec 23 @	Chicago	2-3	L	15-19-2	32	110-127
37.	Dec 25 @	Chicago	2-3	L	15-20-2	32	112-130
38.	Jan 1	Winnipeg	7-3	W	16-20-2	34	119-133
39.	Jan 10 @	Winnipeg	1-6	L	16-21-2	34	120-139
40.	Jan 12 @	Los Angeles	2-1	W	17-21-2	36	122-140
41.	Jan 13 @	Los Angeles	4-1	W	18-21-2	38	126-141
42.	Jan 15	Los Angeles	3-4	L	18-22-2	38	129-145
43.	Jan 16	Los Angeles	*6-5	W	19-22-2	40	135-150
44.	Jan 20	Chicago	4-6	L	19-23-2	40	139-156
45.	Jan 22	Chicago	6-1	W	20-23-2	42	145-157
46.	Jan 27	Philadelphia	*0-1	L	20-24-2	42	145-158
47.	Jan 28	Philadelphia	4-2	W	21-24-2	44	149-160
48.	Jan 30	New York	11-3	W	22-24-2	46	160-163
49.	Feb 1	New York	8-5	W	23-24-2	48	168-168
50.	Feb 2 @	Winnipeg	4-3	W	24-24-2	50	172-171
51.	Feb 4	Winnipeg	3-5	L	24-25-2	50	175-176
52.	Feb 6	New England	2-4	L	24-26-2	50	177-180
53.	Feb 7	New England	3-1	W	25-26-2	52	180-181
54.	Feb 9	Minnesota	6-0	W	26-26-2	54	186-181
55.	Feb 11	Minnesota	7-5	W	27-26-2	56	193-186
56.	Feb 13	Houston	5-3	W	28-26-2	58	198-189
57.	Feb 15	Houston	3-5	L	28-27-2	58	201-194
58.	Feb 20 @	Cleveland	4-5	L	28-28-2	58	205-199
59.	Feb 21 @	New York	4-5	L	28-29-2	58	209-204
60.	Feb 23 @	New England	2-4	L	28-30-2	58	211-208
61.	Feb 25 @	Ottawa	2-3	L	28-31-2	58	213-211
62.	Feb 27 @	Houston	4-5	L	28-32-2	58	217-216
63.	Feb 28 @	Houston	*2-3	L	28-33-2	58	219-219
64.	Mar 6 @	Minnesota	*3-4	L	28-34-2	58	222-223
65.	Mar 8 @	Chicago	*3-2	W	29-34-2	60	225-225
66.	Mar 10 @	Chicago	*5-4	W	30-34-2	62	230-229
67.	Mar 11 @	Minnesota	1-2	L	30-35-2	62	231-231
68.	Mar 13	Cleveland	4-2	W	31-35-2	64	235-233
69.	Mar 14	Cleveland	4-2	W	32-35-2	66	239-235
70.	Mar 16	Quebec	4-2	W	33-35-2	68	243-237
71.	Mar 17	Quebec	3-0	W	34-35-2	70	246-237
72.	Mar 20	Minnesota	5-3	W	35-35-2	72	251-240
73.	Mar 22 @	Winnipeg	1-1	T	35-35-3	73	252-241
74.	Mar 24	Quebec	4-5	L	35-36-3	73	256-246
75.	Mar 25 @	Quebec	5-4	W	36-36-3	75	261-250
76.	Mar 28 @	Philadelphia	2-1	W	37-36-3	77	263-251
77.	Mar 29 @	Philadelphia	1-2	L	37-37-3	77	264-253
78.	Mar 30 @	Minnesota	5-3	W	38-37-3	79	269-256

Oilers Stars of 1972-1973

Jim Harrison
Led team in scoring

Al Hamilton
Blueline leader

Rusty Patenaude
29 goals as rookie

Eddie Joyal
"The Jet" scores 22

Ross Perkins
21 goals, 58 points

Jack Norris
28 wins in nets

Scoring

pos	#	player	Regular Season gp	g	a	pts	pim	ppg	shg	Playoffs gp	g	a	pts	pim
RW	10	Anderson, Ron C.	73	14	15	29	43	3	0	-	-	-	-	-
D	19	Baird, Ken	75	14	15	29	112	1	0	-	-	-	-	-
D	5	Barrie, Doug	54	9	22	31	111	0	1	-	-	-	-	-
RW	21	Benzelock, Jim	26	1	1	2	10	0	0	-	-	-	-	-
RW	21	Blanchette, Bernie	23	5	4	9	2	3	0	-	-	-	-	-
G	1	Brown, Ken	20	0	0	0	2	0	0	-	-	-	-	-
LW	14	Carlin, Brian	65	12	22	34	6	1	0	-	-	-	-	-
D	20	Carlyle, Steve	67	7	10	17	35	0	0	-	-	-	-	-
D	2	Cote, Roger	61	3	5	8	46	1	0	-	-	-	-	-
D	6	Falkenberg, Bob	76	6	23	29	44	2	0	-	-	-	-	-
D	9/22	Fisher, John	39	0	5	5	0	0	0	-	-	-	-	-
LW	8	Fonteyne, Val	77	7	32	39	2	1	0	-	-	-	-	-
D	3	Hamilton, Al	78	11	50	61	124	2	1	-	-	-	-	-
D	27	Harker, Derek	1	0	0	0	0	0	0	-	-	-	-	-
C	7	Harrison, Jim	66	39	47	86	93	8	6	-	-	-	-	-
RW	12	Hicke, Bill	73	14	24	38	16	4	0	-	-	-	-	-
C	16	Joyal, Eddie	71	22	16	38	16	6	0	-	-	-	-	-
LW	15	Kassian, Dennis	50	6	7	13	14	1	0	-	-	-	-	-
C	18	McAneeley, Bob	51	5	7	12	24	0	0	-	-	-	-	-
G	30	Norris, Jack	64	0	3	3	2	0	0	-	-	-	-	-
RW	17	Patenaude, Rusty	78	29	27	56	55	4	0	-	-	-	-	-
C	9	Perkins, Ross	71	21	37	58	19	5	0	-	-	-	-	-
D	4	Wall, Bob	78	16	29	45	20	5	2	-	-	-	-	-
RW	11	Walters, Ron	78	28	26	54	37	1	3	-	-	-	-	-

Power Play: 48 goals scored in 248 opportunities (19.4%) with 7 short-handed goals allowed.
Penalty Killing: 56 goals allowed in 252 opportunities (77.8%) with 13 short-handed goals scored.

Goaltending

goaltender	gp	min	ga	en	so	record	gaa	sog	sv%	gp	min	ga	record	gaa
Brown, Ken	20	1034	63	1	1	10-8-0	3.66	540	0.883	-	-	-	-	-
Norris, Jack	64	3702	189	3	1	28-29-3	3.06	1947	0.902	-	-	-	-	-

Transactions: Rights to Jim Harrison and Dennis Kassian acquired from Calgary, May 1972 • Al Hamilton, Eddie Joyal, Doug Barrie, Bob Wall, Ross Perkins, Roger Cote and Brian Carlin signed to contracts, Jun 1972 • Jack Norris' rights acquired from Calgary/Cleveland Jun 1972, subsequently signed to contract • Derek Harker, Bob McAneeley signed to contracts, Jul 1972 • Rights to Ken Brown acquired from Cleveland, Jul 1972 • Rights to Steve Carlyle acquired from Cleveland, Jul 1972 • Dennis Kassian, Bill Hicke signed to contracts, Sep 1972 • Jim Benzelock traded to Chicago for Bernie Blanchette, Dec 1972 • Derek Harker sold to Philadelphia, Nov 1972

1972-1973 CHICAGO COUGARS

**Coach
Marcel Pronovost**

Summary of Games (@ Away, * Overtime)

	date	opponent	score		record	pts	gf-ga		date	opponent	score		record	pts	gf-ga
1.	Oct 12 @	Houston	2-3	L	0-1-0	0	2-3	40.	Jan 13 @	Houston	2-6	L	13-26-1	27	116-153
2.	Oct 15 @	Minnesota	2-3	L	0-2-0	0	4-6	41.	Jan 15 @	Houston	4-5	L	13-27-1	27	120-158
3.	Oct 16 @	New England	1-4	L	0-3-0	0	5-10	42.	Jan 17	New England	2-4	L	13-28-1	27	122-162
4.	Oct 19 @	Ottawa	2-6	L	0-4-0	0	7-16	43.	Jan 18	Houston	3-8	L	13-29-1	27	125-170
5.	Oct 22 @	Los Angeles	4-2	W	1-4-0	2	11-18	44.	Jan 20 @	Alberta	6-4	W	14-29-1	29	131-174
6.	Oct 24 @	Alberta	3-3	T	1-4-1	3	14-21	45.	Jan 22 @	Alberta	1-6	L	14-30-1	29	132-180
7.	Oct 27 @	Winnipeg	2-4	L	1-5-1	3	16-25	46.	Jan 23	Quebec	7-1	W	15-30-1	31	139-181
8.	Oct 31	Winnipeg	3-1	W	2-5-1	5	19-26	47.	Jan 25	New York	9-2	W	16-30-1	33	148-183
9.	Nov 1 @	New England	2-4	L	2-6-1	5	21-30	48.	Jan 27	Cleveland	1-2	L	16-31-1	33	149-185
10.	Nov 4	Los Angeles	*2-3	L	2-7-1	5	23-33	49.	Jan 28 @	Houston	3-4	L	16-32-1	33	152-189
11.	Nov 5 @	Quebec	2-3	L	2-8-1	5	25-36	50.	Jan 30	Minnesota	4-2	W	17-32-1	35	156-191
12.	Nov 7	Houston	2-3	L	2-9-1	5	27-39	51.	Feb 2	Ottawa	4-1	W	18-32-1	37	160-192
13.	Nov 11	Cleveland	1-4	L	2-10-1	5	28-43	52.	Feb 3	New York	4-2	W	19-32-1	39	164-194
14.	Nov 14	Philadelphia	3-4	L	2-11-1	5	31-47	53.	Feb 5 @	Cleveland	5-7	L	19-33-1	39	169-201
15.	Nov 17 @	Alberta	1-3	L	2-12-1	5	32-50	54.	Feb 8	Quebec	5-2	W	20-33-1	41	174-203
16.	Nov 19 @	Minnesota	4-3	W	3-12-1	7	36-53	55.	Feb 10	Houston	3-0	W	21-33-1	43	177-203
17.	Nov 23 @	Ottawa	8-1	W	4-12-1	9	44-54	56.	Feb 13 @	Los Angeles	6-1	W	22-33-1	45	183-204
18.	Nov 25 @	Philadelphia	4-3	W	5-12-1	11	48-57	57.	Feb 15	Winnipeg	2-7	L	22-34-1	45	185-211
19.	Nov 28 @	Quebec	2-6	L	5-13-1	11	50-63	58.	Feb 17	Ottawa	1-3	L	22-35-1	45	186-214
20.	Dec 1	Los Angeles	3-5	L	5-14-1	11	53-68	59.	Feb 18 @	Minnesota	5-7	L	22-36-1	45	191-221
21.	Dec 2	Los Angeles	2-4	L	5-15-1	11	55-72	60.	Feb 20 @	Quebec	4-2	W	23-36-1	47	195-223
22.	Dec 5 @	Minnesota	*3-2	W	6-15-1	13	58-74	61.	Feb 24 @	Cleveland	5-2	W	24-36-1	49	200-225
23.	Dec 6 @	Winnipeg	1-7	L	6-16-1	13	59-81	62.	Feb 27 @	Winnipeg	1-5	L	24-37-1	49	201-230
24.	Dec 8	Minnesota	*4-3	W	7-16-1	15	63-84	63.	Mar 4 @	Ottawa	4-6	L	24-38-1	49	205-236
25.	Dec 9	Quebec	2-4	L	7-17-1	15	65-88	64.	Mar 5 @	New York	4-4	T	24-38-2	50	209-240
26.	Dec 11 @	New York	3-8	L	7-18-1	15	68-96	65.	Mar 6	Philadelphia	*2-1	W	25-38-2	52	211-241
27.	Dec 13	New England	6-3	W	8-18-1	17	74-99	66.	Mar 8	Alberta	*2-3	L	25-39-2	52	213-244
28.	Dec 14	Minnesota	3-6	L	8-19-1	17	77-105	67.	Mar 10	Alberta	*4-5	L	25-40-2	52	217-249
29.	Dec 17 @	Minnesota	2-4	L	8-20-1	17	79-109	68.	Mar 12 @	New York	7-8	L	25-41-2	52	224-257
30.	Dec 19	Cleveland	6-1	W	9-20-1	19	85-110	69.	Mar 13	New England	*3-4	L	25-42-2	52	227-259
31.	Dec 20 @	Philadelphia	5-8	L	9-21-1	19	90-118	70.	Mar 15	Minnesota	4-7	L	25-43-2	52	231-266
32.	Dec 22	Winnipeg	3-2	W	10-21-1	21	93-120	71.	Mar 17	New York	6-3	W	26-43-2	54	237-269
33.	Dec 23	Alberta	3-2	W	11-21-1	23	96-122	72.	Mar 22	Minnesota	*1-2	L	26-44-2	54	238-271
34.	Dec 25	Alberta	3-2	W	12-21-1	25	99-124	73.	Mar 23 @	New England	1-3	L	26-45-2	54	239-274
35.	Dec 26 @	Winnipeg	2-3	L	12-22-1	25	101-127	74.	Mar 25 @	Los Angeles	0-1	L	26-46-2	54	239-275
36.	Dec 28	Philadelphia	6-3	W	13-22-1	27	107-130	75.	Mar 27 @	Los Angeles	1-4	L	26-47-2	54	240-276
37.	Dec 30	Ottawa	2-4	L	13-23-1	27	109-134	76.	Mar 28	Winnipeg	*3-4	L	26-48-2	54	243-280
38.	Jan 10	Los Angeles	5-8	L	13-24-1	27	114-142	77.	Mar 31 @	Philadelphia	1-5	L	26-49-2	54	244-285
39.	Jan 11	Houston	0-5	L	13-25-1	27	114-147	78.	Apr 1 @	Cleveland	1-5	L	26-50-2	54	245-295

Cougars Stars of 1972-1973

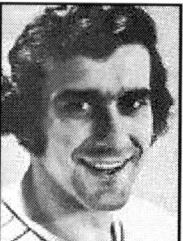

Rosaire Paiement	**Jan Popiel**	**Rick Morris**	**Bob Sicinski**	**Ron F. Anderson**	**Jim McLeod**
33 goals led team	31 goals, 65 points	31 goals	88 points led team	All-star defenseman	22 wins in goal

Scoring

				Regular Season							Playoffs			
pos	#	player	gp	g	a	pts	pim	ppg	shg	gp	g	a	pts	pim
D	18	Anderson, Ron F.	73	3	26	29	34	0	1	-	-	-	-	-
D	2	Barber, Butch	75	4	19	23	39	0	0	-	-	-	-	-
RW	12	Benzelock, Jim	43	9	12	21	23	3	0	-	-	-	-	-
RW	22	Blanchette, Bernie	24	2	3	5	8	0	0	-	-	-	-	-
D	5	Cahan, Larry	75	1	10	11	44	0	0	-	-	-	-	-
LW	6	Fleming, Reggie	74	23	45	68	95	7	1	-	-	-	-	-
G	30	Gill, Andre	33	0	0	0	6	0	0	-	-	-	-	-
LW	27	Glenwright, Brian	48	2	5	7	0	0	0	-	-	-	-	-
RW	12	Hatoum, Ed	15	1	1	2	2	0	0	-	-	-	-	-
RW	22	Knibbs, Darrel	41	3	8	11	0	0	0	-	-	-	-	-
LW	7	Liddington, Bob	78	20	11	31	24	1	0	-	-	-	-	-
LW	14	Lodboa, Dan	59	15	18	33	16	4	0	-	-	-	-	-
D	21	Mavety, Larry	67	9	40	49	73	2	1	-	-	-	-	-
D	4	McGlynn, Dick	30	0	0	0	12	0	0	-	-	-	-	-
G	1	McLeod, Jim	54	0	1	1	2	0	0	-	-	-	-	-
G	24	Menard, Paul	1	0	0	0	0	0	0	-	-	-	-	-
LW	10	Morris, Rick	76	31	17	48	84	4	0	-	-	-	-	-
RW	9	Paiement, Rosaire	78	33	36	69	137	5	0	-	-	-	-	-
LW	19	Popiel, Jan	76	31	34	65	77	6	0	-	-	-	-	-
D	3	Proceviat, Dick	56	4	14	18	33	1	0	-	-	-	-	-
RW	20	Sarrazin, Dick	33	3	8	11	2	2	0	-	-	-	-	-
C	17	Sicinski, Bob	77	25	63	88	18	7	1	-	-	-	-	-
C		Trooien, Jerry	2	0	0	0	0	0	0	-	-	-	-	-
D	20	Viau, Pierre	4	0	0	0	0	0	0	-	-	-	-	-
C	16	Whitlock, Bobby	75	23	28	51	53	3	2	-	-	-	-	-
C	8	Zaine, Rod	74	3	14	17	25	0	0	-	-	-	-	-

Power Play: 45 goals scored in 248 opportunities (18.1%) with 11 short-handed goals allowed.
Penalty Killing: 57 goals allowed in 253 opportunities (77.5%) with 6 short-handed goals scored.

Goaltending

goaltender	gp	min	ga	en	so	record	gaa	sog	sv%	gp	min	ga	record	gaa
Gill, Andre	33	1709	118	2	0	4-24-0	4.24	982	0.879	-	-	-	-	-
McLeod, Jim	54	2996	166	4	1	22-25-2	3.32	1742	0.904	-	-	-	-	-
Menard, Paul	1	45	5	0	0	0-1-0	6.67	23	0.782	-	-	-	-	-

Transactions: Rights to Jan Popiel acquired from Ottawa, May 1972 • Rights to Darrel Knibbs purchased from Cleveland, Jun 1972 • Rosaire Paiement, Rick Morris, Reg Fleming signed to contracts, Jun 1972 • Rights to Bob Liddington, Larry Cahan and Bobby Whitlock acquired in trade with Los Angeles for Bill Young, Jul 1972 • Darrel Knibbs, Dan Lodboa, Dick Proceviat, Rod Zaine signed to contracts, Jul 1972 • Dick McGlynn, Jan Popiel, Bob Sicinski, Bobby Whitlock signed to contracts, Aug 1972 • Pierre Viau, Paul Menard, Andre Gill, Ron F. Anderson, Brian Glenwright, Bob Liddington signed to contracts, Sep 1972 • Ed Hatoum released, Oct 1972 • Larry Mavety purchased from Philadelphia, Nov 1972 • Bernie Blanchette traded to Alberta for Jim Benzelock, Dec. 1972 • Dick Sarrazin purchased from New England, Jan 1973

1972-1973 CLEVELAND CRUSADERS

Coach
Bill Needham

Summary of Games (@ Away, * Overtime)

	date	opponent	score		record	pts	gf-ga		date	opponent	score		record	pts	gf-ga
1.	Oct 11	Quebec	2-0	W	1-0-0	2	2-0	40.	Jan 12 @	Winnipeg	3-5	L	24-15-1	49	147-110
2.	Oct 14	Alberta	3-2	W	2-0-0	4	5-2	41.	Jan 14 @	Winnipeg	1-3	L	24-16-1	49	148-113
3.	Oct 15 @	Ottawa	7-5	W	3-0-0	6	12-7	42.	Jan 16 @	Philadelphia	4-3	W	25-16-1	51	152-116
4.	Oct 17	New York	*4-3	W	4-0-0	8	16-10	43.	Jan 17 @	Houston	5-0	W	26-16-1	53	157-116
5.	Oct 19 @	New York	3-1	W	5-0-0	10	19-11	44.	Jan 19 @	Los Angeles	4-1	W	27-16-1	55	161-117
6.	Oct 21	Ottawa	3-5	L	5-1-0	10	22-16	45.	Jan 21 @	Los Angeles	2-3	L	27-17-1	55	163-120
7.	Oct 24	New England	2-3	L	5-2-0	10	24-19	46.	Jan 23	Winnipeg	*5-4	W	28-17-1	57	168-124
8.	Oct 25 @	Philadelphia	8-2	W	6-2-0	12	32-21	47.	Jan 25	Philadelphia	4-7	L	28-18-1	57	172-131
9.	Oct 27	Alberta	6-0	W	7-2-0	14	38-21	48.	Jan 27 @	Chicago	2-1	W	29-18-1	59	174-132
10.	Oct 29 @	Quebec	2-2	T	7-2-1	15	40-23	49.	Jan 29	New England	3-2	W	30-18-1	61	177-134
11.	Nov 1	Philadelphia	5-7	L	7-3-1	15	45-30	50.	Jan 31 @	New England	1-4	L	30-19-1	61	178-138
12.	Nov 4	Quebec	5-3	W	8-3-1	17	50-33	51.	Feb 1	Ottawa	2-2	T	30-19-2	62	180-140
13.	Nov 11 @	Chicago	4-1	W	9-3-1	19	54-34	52.	Feb 2	Philadelphia	5-3	W	31-19-2	64	185-143
14.	Nov 12 @	Alberta	3-1	W	10-3-1	21	57-35	53.	Feb 4 @	Ottawa	3-2	W	32-19-2	66	188-145
15.	Nov 14 @	Minnesota	3-5	L	10-4-1	21	60-40	54.	Feb 5	Chicago	7-5	W	33-19-2	68	195-150
16.	Nov 16	Ottawa	6-3	W	11-4-1	23	66-43	55.	Feb 10	New York	8-4	W	34-19-2	70	203-154
17.	Nov 17	New England	3-0	W	12-4-1	25	69-43	56.	Feb 11 @	Philadelphia	1-6	L	34-20-2	70	204-160
18.	Nov 19 @	Houston	2-4	L	12-5-1	25	71-47	57.	Feb 12	New York	8-2	W	35-20-2	72	212-162
19.	Nov 21 @	Los Angeles	5-2	W	13-5-1	27	76-49	58.	Feb 14 @	Philadelphia	5-6	L	35-21-2	72	217-168
20.	Nov 24	Los Angeles	*3-2	W	14-5-1	29	79-51	59.	Feb 17	Minnesota	3-7	L	35-22-2	72	220-175
21.	Nov 25	Houston	1-3	L	14-6-1	29	80-54	60.	Feb 20	Alberta	5-4	W	36-22-2	74	225-179
22.	Nov 27 @	New England	0-3	L	14-7-1	29	80-57	61.	Feb 24	Chicago	2-5	L	36-23-2	74	227-184
23.	Nov 28	Houston	1-3	L	14-8-1	29	81-60	62.	Feb 25 @	New York	5-9	L	36-24-2	74	232-193
24.	Nov 30 @	Ottawa	2-3	L	14-9-1	29	83-63	63.	Feb 27 @	Ottawa	1-2	L	36-25-2	74	233-195
25.	Dec 2	Philadelphia	8-2	W	15-9-1	31	91-65	64.	Mar 3 @	New York	4-3	W	37-25-2	76	237-198
26.	Dec 3 @	New York	2-5	L	15-10-1	31	93-70	65.	Mar 7 @	New England	*0-1	L	37-26-2	76	237-199
27.	Dec 5 @	Philadelphia	*4-3	W	16-10-1	33	97-73	66.	Mar 9 @	New England	4-5	L	37-27-2	76	241-204
28.	Dec 7 @	Quebec	3-1	W	17-10-1	35	100-74	67.	Mar 11 @	Winnipeg	11-2	W	38-27-2	78	252-206
29.	Dec 9	Winnipeg	*2-3	L	17-11-1	35	102-77	68.	Mar 13 @	Alberta	2-4	L	38-28-2	78	254-210
30.	Dec 10 @	Minnesota	*3-4	L	17-12-1	35	105-81	69.	Mar 14 @	Alberta	2-4	L	38-29-2	78	256-214
31.	Dec 15	Quebec	6-3	W	18-12-1	37	111-84	70.	Mar 17	Los Angeles	0-2	L	38-30-2	78	256-216
32.	Dec 17 @	Quebec	2-3	L	18-13-1	37	113-87	71.	Mar 19	Los Angeles	5-5	T	38-30-3	79	261-221
33.	Dec 19 @	Chicago	1-6	L	18-14-1	37	114-93	72.	Mar 20 @	Quebec	1-4	L	38-31-3	79	262-225
34.	Dec 21	New York	6-2	W	19-14-1	39	120-95	73.	Mar 24	Minnesota	*1-2	L	38-32-3	79	263-227
35.	Dec 23	Minnesota	3-1	W	20-14-1	41	123-96	74.	Mar 25 @	Houston	4-2	W	39-32-3	81	267-229
36.	Dec 25	Philadelphia	8-0	W	21-14-1	43	131-96	75.	Mar 26	New England	7-5	W	40-32-3	83	274-234
37.	Dec 29	Quebec	5-3	W	22-14-1	45	136-99	76.	Mar 30	Winnipeg	4-2	W	41-32-3	85	278-236
38.	Dec 30	Houston	*4-3	W	23-14-1	47	140-102	77.	Mar 31	Ottawa	4-2	W	42-32-3	87	282-238
39.	Jan 11 @	Minnesota	4-3	W	24-14-1	49	144-105	78.	Apr 1	Chicago	5-1	W	43-32-3	89	287-239

Crusaders Stars of 1972-1973

Gerry Cheevers
League's top goalie

Gary Jarrett
40 goals led team

Ron Buchanan
37 goals, 81 points

Gerry Pinder
30 goals

Bob Dillabough
6 shorthanded goals

Jim Wiste
28 goals, 71 points

Scoring

pos	#	player	gp	g	a	pts	pim	ppg	shg	gp	g	a	pts	pim
RW	21	Andrea, Paul	66	21	30	51	12	7	0	9	2	8	10	2
D	8	Ball, Blake	0	-	-	-	-	-	-	2	0	0	0	2
C	9	Brindley, Doug	73	15	11	26	6	2	0	9	0	0	0	0
C	10	Buchanan, Ron	75	37	44	81	20	6	0	9	7	3	10	0
G	30	Cheevers, Gerry	52	0	1	1	30	0	0	9	0	0	0	0
D	6	Clearwater, Ray	78	11	36	47	41	1	0	9	1	2	3	8
C	24	Dillabough, Bob	72	8	8	16	8	1	6	9	1	0	1	0
LW	16	Erickson, Grant	77	15	29	44	23	2	1	9	2	1	3	2
D	2	Hanna, John	65	6	20	26	68	3	0	-	-	-	-	-
C	25	Hardy, Joe	72	17	33	50	80	1	0	7	0	2	2	0
RW	11	Hodgson, Ted	74	15	23	38	93	2	0	9	1	3	4	13
D	4	Hopiavuori, Ralph	31	4	5	9	44	0	0	8	0	1	1	6
D	26	Horton, Bill	73	2	17	19	55	0	0	9	0	1	1	10
LW	12	Jarrett, Gary	77	40	38	78	79	8	0	9	8	3	11	19
C	17	Krake, Skip	26	9	10	19	61	2	0	9	1	2	3	27
D	22	McMasters, Jim	76	1	7	8	37	0	0	9	0	1	1	6
D	5	Muloin, Wayne	70	2	13	15	64	0	0	9	1	3	4	14
LW	7	Pinder, Gerry	78	30	36	66	21	7	3	9	2	9	11	30
LW	23	Pumple, Rich	78	21	20	41	45	5	0	9	3	5	8	11
RW	19	Rycroft, Al	7	0	2	2	0	0	0	-	-	-	-	-
D	3	Shmyr, Paul	73	5	43	48	169	0	1	8	1	3	4	19
G	1	Whidden, Bob	26	0	0	0	5	0	0	-	-	-	-	-
C	14	Wiste, Jim	70	28	43	71	24	4	0	9	3	8	11	13

Power Play: 51 goals scored in 272 opportunities (18.8%) with 5 short-handed goals allowed.
Penalty Killing: 59 goals allowed in 338 opportunities (82.5%) with 11 short-handed goals scored.

Goaltending

goaltender	gp	min	ga	en	so	record	gaa	sog	sv%	gp	min	ga	record	gaa
Cheevers, Gerry	52	3144	149	2	5	32-20-2	2.84	1695	0.912	9	548	22	5-4	2.41
Whidden, Bob	26	1609	88	0	0	11-12-3	3.28	886	0.900	-	-	-	-	-

Transactions: Rights to Gary Jarrett purchased from Alberta, Jun 1972 • Rights to Gerry Cheevers acquired from New England, Jun 1972 • Rights to Paul Andrea acquired from Houston, Jun 1972 • Rights to Bob Whidden acquired from Alberta, Jul 1972 • Ron Buchanan, Tom Edur, Grant Erickson signed to contracts, Jul 1972 • Rights to Joe Hardy, Bill Horton, and Doug Brindley acquired from Alberta, Jul and Aug 1972 • Joe Hardy, Ralph Hopiavuori, Rich Pumple, Al Rycroft signed to contracts, Aug 1972 • Jim Wiste signed to contract, Aug 1972, after being dropped from New York's negotiating list • Ray Clearwater signed to contract, Sep 1972 • Blake Ball signed to contract, Apr 1973

1972-1973 HOUSTON AEROS

Coach
Bill Dineen

Summary of Games (@ Away, * Overtime)

	date	opponent	score		record	pts	gf-ga
1.	Oct 12	Chicago	3-2	W	1-0-0	2	3-2
2.	Oct 13 @	Los Angeles	3-2	W	2-0-0	4	6-4
3.	Oct 15	Los Angeles	1-5	L	2-1-0	4	7-9
4.	Oct 18	New England	1-4	L	2-2-0	4	8-13
5.	Oct 19	Minnesota	5-1	W	3-2-0	6	13-14
6.	Oct 21 @	New York	2-3	L	3-3-0	6	15-17
7.	Oct 24 @	Quebec	3-5	L	3-4-0	6	18-22
8.	Oct 26	Ottawa	7-3	W	4-4-0	8	25-25
9.	Oct 29 @	Winnipeg	3-5	L	4-5-0	8	28-30
10.	Oct 31 @	Alberta	4-3	W	5-5-0	10	32-33
11.	Nov 3 @	Alberta	3-4	L	5-6-0	10	35-37
12.	Nov 5 @	Los Angeles	0-4	L	5-7-0	10	35-41
13.	Nov 7 @	Chicago	3-2	W	6-7-0	12	38-43
14.	Nov 11 @	Quebec	1-3	L	6-8-0	12	39-46
15.	Nov 13 @	New England	4-4	T	6-8-1	13	43-50
16.	Nov 15	Los Angeles	4-6	L	6-9-1	13	47-56
17.	Nov 19	Cleveland	4-2	W	7-9-1	15	51-58
18.	Nov 21	Winnipeg	2-4	L	7-10-1	15	53-62
19.	Nov 23	Winnipeg	6-5	W	8-10-1	17	59-67
20.	Nov 25 @	Cleveland	3-1	W	9-10-1	19	62-68
21.	Nov 28 @	Cleveland	3-1	W	10-10-1	21	65-69
22.	Nov 30 @	Los Angeles	3-6	L	10-11-1	21	68-75
23.	Dec 2 @	New York	7-2	W	11-11-1	23	75-77
24.	Dec 3 @	Ottawa	*4-5	L	11-12-1	23	79-82
25.	Dec 5	New York	4-6	L	11-13-1	23	83-88
26.	Dec 7 @	Minnesota	0-3	L	11-14-1	23	83-91
27.	Dec 8 @	Winnipeg	2-6	L	11-15-1	23	85-97
28.	Dec 12	Alberta	6-4	W	12-15-1	25	91-101
29.	Dec 13	Alberta	2-3	L	12-16-1	25	93-104
30.	Dec 15 @	Minnesota	3-2	W	13-16-1	27	96-106
31.	Dec 17	Los Angeles	4-4	T	13-16-2	28	100-110
32.	Dec 19	Los Angeles	7-5	W	14-16-2	30	107-115
33.	Dec 23	Philadelphia	7-3	W	15-16-2	32	114-118
34.	Dec 26 @	Ottawa	3-3	T	15-16-3	33	117-121
35.	Dec 29 @	New England	4-2	W	16-16-3	35	121-123
36.	Dec 30 @	Cleveland	*3-4	L	16-17-3	35	124-127
37.	Jan 1 @	Minnesota	4-4	T	16-17-4	36	128-131
38.	Jan 9	New England	7-5	W	17-17-4	38	135-136
39.	Jan 11 @	Chicago	5-0	W	18-17-4	40	140-136
40.	Jan 13	Chicago	6-2	W	19-17-4	42	146-138
41.	Jan 15	Chicago	5-4	W	20-17-4	44	151-142
42.	Jan 17	Cleveland	0-5	L	20-18-4	44	151-147
43.	Jan 18 @	Chicago	8-3	W	21-18-4	46	159-150
44.	Jan 20 @	Philadelphia	4-3	W	22-18-4	48	163-153
45.	Jan 21	Ottawa	5-2	W	23-18-4	50	168-155
46.	Jan 23	Ottawa	11-3	W	24-18-4	52	179-158
47.	Jan 25 @	Minnesota	5-2	W	25-18-4	54	184-160
48.	Jan 28	Chicago	4-3	W	26-18-4	56	188-163
49.	Jan 30	Los Angeles	2-5	L	26-19-4	56	190-168
50.	Feb 1	New England	*4-5	L	26-20-4	56	194-173
51.	Feb 3	Minnesota	7-1	W	27-20-4	58	201-174
52.	Feb 5	Minnesota	3-6	L	27-21-4	58	204-180
53.	Feb 7	Winnipeg	5-2	W	28-21-4	60	209-182
54.	Feb 8	Winnipeg	1-3	L	28-22-4	60	210-185
55.	Feb 10 @	Chicago	0-3	L	28-23-4	60	210-188
56.	Feb 13 @	Alberta	3-5	L	28-24-4	60	213-193
57.	Feb 15 @	Alberta	5-3	W	29-24-4	62	218-196
58.	Feb 16 @	Winnipeg	0-7	L	29-25-4	62	218-203
59.	Feb 18 @	Winnipeg	2-4	L	29-26-4	62	220-207
60.	Feb 22	Quebec	4-1	W	30-26-4	64	224-208
61.	Feb 25	Minnesota	4-1	W-	31-26-4	66	228-209
62.	Feb 27	Alberta	5-4	W	32-26-4	68	233-213
63.	Feb 28	Alberta	*3-2	W	33-26-4	70	236-215
64.	Mar 3	Quebec	3-4	L	33-27-4	70	239-219
65.	Mar 4	Quebec	3-6	L	33-28-4	70	242-225
66.	Mar 7 @	Los Angeles	3-1	W	34-28-4	72	245-226
67.	Mar 9 @	Los Angeles	1-5	L	34-29-4	72	246-231
68.	Mar 11 @	Philadelphia	4-2	W	35-29-4	74	250-233
69.	Mar 13 @	Philadelphia	3-4	L	35-30-4	74	253-237
70.	Mar 14 @	New York	1-5	L	35-31-4	74	254-242
71.	Mar 18	New York	*2-3	L	35-32-4	74	256-245
72.	Mar 19	Philadelphia	5-1	W	36-32-4	76	261-246
73.	Mar 21	Philadelphia	3-7	L	36-33-4	76	264-253
74.	Mar 25	Cleveland	2-4	L	36-34-4	76	266-257
75.	Mar 27 @	New England	6-1	W	37-34-4	78	272-258
76.	Mar 29	New York	5-3	W	38-34-4	80	277-261
77.	Mar 31 @	Quebec	1-5	L	38-35-4	80	278-266
78.	Apr 1 @	Ottawa	6-3	W	39-35-4	82	284-269

Aeros Stars of 1972-1973

Ted Taylor	Gord Labossiere	Don Grierson	Murray Hall	Larry Hale	John Schella
34 goals, 76 points	96 points led team	22 goals	28 goals	Anchored defense	Most penalty minutes

Scoring

pos	#	player	gp	g	a	pts	pim	ppg	shg	gp	g	a	pts	pim
						Regular Season							**Playoffs**	
RW	21	Grierson, Don	78	22	22	44	83	5	0	3	0	0	0	6
D	17	Hale, Larry	68	4	26	30	65	0	0	10	1	2	3	2
C	11	Hall, Murray	76	28	42	70	84	7	2	10	4	4	8	18
RW	15	Harris, Duke	75	30	12	42	14	4	5	10	1	1	2	4
C	12	Hoekstra, Ed	78	11	28	39	12	0	1	9	1	2	3	0
G	29	Hughes, Bill	3	0	0	0	2	0	0	-	-	-	-	-
LW	7	Hughes, Frank	76	22	19	41	41	4	0	10	4	4	8	2
D	5	Kannegiesser, Gord	45	0	10	10	32	0	0	9	0	1	1	11
C	10	Labossiere, Gord	77	36	60	96	56	10	0	6	1	4	5	8
D	3	Larose, Ray	68	1	10	11	25	0	0	8	0	0	0	2
C	13	Lund, Larry	77	21	45	66	120	4	0	10	3	7	10	24
D	4	McCallum, Dunc	69	9	20	29	112	2	0	10	2	3	5	6
RW	8	McDonald, Brian	71	20	20	40	78	0	0	10	3	0	3	16
G	1	McLeod, Don	41	0	0	0	6	0	0	3	0	0	0	0
RW	9	Mortson, Keke	69	13	16	29	95	2	0	10	0	3	3	16
D	6	Popiel, Poul	74	16	48	64	158	5	0	10	2	9	11	23
D	22	Prentice, Bill	3	0	1	1	0	0	0	-	-	-	-	-
G	30	Rutledge, Wayne	36	0	0	0	11	0	0	7	0	0	0	0
D	2	Schella, John	77	2	24	26	239	0	1	10	0	2	2	12
LW	19	Smith, Brian	48	7	6	13	19	2	0	10	0	2	2	0
LW	18	Stanfield, Jack	71	8	12	20	8	0	0	9	1	0	1	0
LW	14	Taylor, Ted	72	34	42	76	101	5	1	10	3	1	4	10

Power Play: 50 goals scored in 188 opportunities (26.6%) with 2 short-handed goals allowed.
Penalty Killing: 63 goals allowed in 330 opportunities (80.9%) with 10 short-handed goals scored.

Goaltending

goaltender	gp	min	ga	en	so	record	gaa	sog	sv%	gp	min	ga	record	gaa
Hughes, Bill	3	170	11	1	0	0-1-1	3.88	88	0.875	-	-	-	-	-
McLeod, Don	41	2410	145	2	1	19-20-1	3.61	1230	0.883	3	178	8	0-3	2.70
Rutledge, Wayne	36	2163	110	0	0	20-14-2	3.05	1192	0.907	7	422	20	4-3	2.84

Transactions: Larry Lund, Wayne Rutledge, Larry Hale, Frank Hughes, Gord Labossiere, John Schella, Ted Taylor, Don Grierson, Murray Hall, Poul Popiel, Duke Harris, Ed Hoekstra, Brian Smith, Ray Larose, Don McLeod, Keke Mortson, Brian McDonald and Jack Stanfield all selected during 1972 general player draft and signed to contracts, summer 1972 (exact dates not available).

1972-1973 LOS ANGELES SHARKS

Coach
Terry Slater

Summary of Games (@ Away, * Overtime)

#	date	opponent	score		record	pts	gf-ga
1.	Oct 13	Houston	2-3	L	0-1-0	0	2-3
2.	Oct 15 @	Houston	5-1	W	1-1-0	2	7-4
3.	Oct 17 @	Minnesota	5-1	W	2-1-0	4	12-5
4.	Oct 19	Philadelphia	4-2	W	3-1-0	6	16-7
5.	Oct 22	Chicago	2-4	L	3-2-0	6	18-11
6.	Oct 25	Ottawa	5-8	L	3-3-0	6	23-19
7.	Oct 27 @	Philadelphia	4-5	L	3-4-0	6	27-24
8.	Oct 28 @	New York	*4-3	W	4-4-0	8	31-27
9.	Oct 31 @	Quebec	4-2	W	5-4-0	10	35-29
10.	Nov 2 @	Ottawa	1-1	T	5-4-1	11	36-30
11.	Nov 4 @	Chicago	*3-2	W	6-4-1	13	39-32
12.	Nov 5	Houston	4-0	W	7-4-1	15	43-32
13.	Nov 8	New York	2-1	W	8-4-1	17	45-33
14.	Nov 9 @	Alberta	2-7	L	8-5-1	17	47-40
15.	Nov 11 @	Alberta	3-5	L	8-6-1	17	50-45
16.	Nov 12 @	Winnipeg	2-5	L	8-7-1	17	52-50
17.	Nov 14 @	Winnipeg	0-8	L	8-8-1	17	52-58
18.	Nov 15 @	Houston	6-4	W	9-8-1	19	58-62
19.	Nov 17	Winnipeg •	1-5	L	9-9-1	19	59-67
20.	Nov 19	Winnipeg	3-4	L	9-10-1	19	62-71
21.	Nov 21	Cleveland	2-5	L	9-11-1	19	64-76
22.	Nov 23 @	Minnesota	3-4	L	9-12-1	19	67-80
23.	Nov 24 @	Cleveland	2-3	L	9-13-1	19	69-83
24.	Nov 26 @	New York	6-2	W	10-13-1	21	75-85
25.	Nov 28 @	Philadelphia	3-4	L	10-14-1	21	78-89
26.	Nov 30	Houston	6-3	W	11-14-1	23	84-92
27.	Dec 1 @	Chicago	5-3	W	12-14-1	25	89-95
28.	Dec 2 @	Chicago	4-2	W	13-14-1	27	93-97
29.	Dec 8	Alberta	4-2	W	14-14-1	29	97-99
30.	Dec 10	Alberta	5-3	W	15-14-1	31	102-102
31.	Dec 12	Minnesota	3-3	T	15-14-2	32	105-105
32.	Dec 14	New England	2-5	L	15-15-2	32	107-110
33.	Dec 17 @	Houston	4-4	T	15-15-3	33	111-114
34.	Dec 19 @	Houston	5-7	L	15-16-3	33	116-121
35.	Dec 21 @	Ottawa	4-4	T	15-16-4	34	120-125
36.	Dec 23 @	Quebec	1-2	L	15-17-4	34	121-127
37.	Dec 24 @	New England	5-3	W	16-17-4	36	126-130
38.	Dec 28	Minnesota •	2-4	L	16-18-4	36	128-134
39.	Dec 29	Minnesota	5-2	W	17-18-4	38	133-136
40.	Dec 31	Philadelphia	1-3	L	17-19-4	38	134-139
41.	Jan 9 @	Minnesota	*4-3	W	18-19-4	40	138-142
42.	Jan 10 @	Chicago	8-5	W	19-19-4	42	146-147
43.	Jan 12	Alberta	1-2	L	19-20-4	42	147-149
44.	Jan 13	Alberta	1-4	L	19-21-4	42	148-153
45.	Jan 15 @	Alberta	4-3	W	20-21-4	44	152-156
46.	Jan 16 @	Alberta	*5-6	L	20-22-4	44	157-162
47.	Jan 19	Cleveland	1-4	L	20-23-4	44	158-166
48.	Jan 21	Cleveland	3-2	W	21-23-4	46	161-168
49.	Jan 26	New York	*4-5	L	21-24-4	46	165-173
50.	Jan 28	New York	9-2	W	22-24-4	48	174-175
51.	Jan 30 @	Houston	5-2	W	23-24-4	50	179-177
52.	Feb 2	New England	3-1	W	24-24-4	52	182-178
53.	Feb 4	New England	4-3	W	25-24-4	54	186-181
54.	Feb 8	Minnesota	3-1	W	26-24-4	56	189-182
55.	Feb 10	Winnipeg	5-6	L	26-25-4	56	194-188
56.	Feb 11	Winnipeg	0-3	L	26-26-4	56	194-191
57.	Feb 13	Chicago	1-6	L	26-27-4	56	195-197
58.	Feb 15 @	New England	5-6	L	26-28-4	56	200-203
59.	Feb 16 @	Quebec	2-2	T	26-28-5	57	202-205
60.	Feb 18 @	Philadelphia	4-1	W	27-28-5	59	206-206
61.	Feb 20 @	Ottawa	4-2	W	28-28-5	61	210-208
62.	Feb 24	Quebec	3-5	L	28-29-5	61	213-213
63.	Feb 25	Quebec	4-2	W	29-29-5	63	217-215
64.	Mar 1 @	Minnesota	4-1	W	30-29-5	65	221-216
65.	Mar 2 @	Winnipeg	1-2	L	30-30-5	65	222-218
66.	Mar 4 @	Winnipeg	1-2	L	30-31-5	65	223-220
67.	Mar 6	Quebec	*3-2	W	31-31-5	67	226-222
68.	Mar 7	Houston	1-3	L	31-32-5	67	227-225
69.	Mar 9	Houston •	5-1	W	32-32-5	69	232-226
70.	Mar 11	Ottawa	4-2	W	33-32-5	71	236-228
71.	Mar 13	Ottawa	1-3	L	33-33-5	71	237-231
72.	Mar 15 @	New York	6-2	W	34-33-5	73	243-233
73.	Mar 17 @	Cleveland	2-0	W	35-33-5	75	245-233
74.	Mar 19 @	Cleveland	5-5	T	35-33-6	76	250-238
75.	Mar 20 @	New England	1-4	L	35-34-6	76	251-242
76.	Mar 23	Philadelphia	3-7	L	35-35-6	76	254-249
77.	Mar 25	Chicago	1-0	W	36-35-6	78	255-249
78.	Mar 27	Chicago •	4-1	W	37-35-6	80	259-250

• Home games played at the Long Beach Arena, Long Beach, California

Sharks Stars of 1972-1973

Gary Veneruzzo
43 goals led team

Alton White
20 goals

Russ Gillow
2.91 average

J.-P. Leblanc
50 assists

Jim Niekamp
Blueline leader

Gerry Odrowski
All-Star defenseman

Scoring

pos	#	player	gp	g	a	pts	pim	ppg	shg	gp	g	a	pts	pim
RW	9	Byers, Mike	56	19	17	36	20	2	0	-	-	-	-	-
D	7	Crashley, Bart	70	18	27	45	10	7	0	6	0	2	2	2
G	30	Gardner, George	49	0	0	0	0	0	0	3	0	0	0	0
G	1	Gillow, Russ	38	0	0	0	6	0	0	5	0	0	0	0
LW	12	Gilmore, Tom	70	17	18	35	191	6	0	5	1	3	4	2
LW	22	Heggedal, Howie	8	2	1	3	0	1	0	1	0	0	0	0
LW	16	Heiskala, Earl	70	12	17	29	150	2	0	5	1	1	2	4
RW	17	Hyndman, Mike	19	8	7	15	11	1	0	6	0	3	3	17
C	21	Jakubo, Mike	7	0	0	0	0	0	0	-	-	-	-	-
LW	8	Jones, Bob	20	2	7	9	8	1	0	-	-	-	-	-
RW	23	Krupicka, Jarda	6	1	0	1	2	0	0	-	-	-	-	-
C	10	Leblanc, J. P.	77	19	50	69	49	2	1	6	0	5	5	2
LW	20	MacNeil, Bernie	42	4	7	11	48	0	0	3	0	0	0	4
D	4	MacSweyn, Ralph	78	0	23	23	39	0	0	6	1	2	3	4
D	5	Mavety, Larry	2	1	0	1	2	1	0	-	-	-	-	-
C	11	McCaskill, Ted	73	11	11	22	150	0	2	6	2	3	5	12
D	3	Niekamp, Jim	78	7	22	29	155	0	1	6	2	1	3	10
D	6	Odrowski, Gerry	78	6	31	37	89	0	1	6	1	2	3	6
G	26	Perreault, Bob	1	0	0	0	0	0	0	-	-	-	-	-
RW	24	Serviss, Tom	73	11	26	37	32	0	3	6	0	0	0	0
RW	14	Slater, Peter	72	12	12	24	87	3	0	6	0	0	0	2
C	8	Speck, Fred	28	3	13	16	22	0	0	6	3	2	5	2
RW	19	Sutherland, Steve	43	11	6	17	98	0	0	6	0	2	2	8
C	15	Szura, Joe	72	13	32	45	25	3	0	2	0	0	0	0
LW	18	Veneruzzo, Gary	78	43	30	73	34	13	0	6	3	0	3	4
D	2	Watson, Jim	75	5	15	20	123	1	0	4	0	1	1	2
RW	23	White, Alton	57	20	17	37	22	2	0	6	1	0	1	0
LW	17	Young, Bill	50	14	12	26	46	6	0	-	-	-	-	-
D	23	Zrymiak, Jerry	1	0	0	0	0	0	0	2	1	0	1	0

Power Play: 51 goals scored in 259 opportunities (19.7%) with 11 short-handed goals allowed.
Penalty Killing: 59 goals allowed in 315 opportunities (81.3%) with 8 short-handed goals scored.

Goaltending

goaltender	gp	min	ga	en	so	record	gaa	sog	sv%	gp	min	ga	record	gaa
Gardner, George	49	2713	149	0	1	19-22-4	3.30	1238	0.879	3	116	11	1-2	5.69
Gillow, Russ	38	1892	96	3	2	17-13-2	2.91	851	0.887	5	247	12	1-2	2.91
Perreault, Bob	1	60	2	0	0	1-0-0	2.00	17	0.882	-	-	-	-	-

Transactions: Steve Sutherland signed to contract, Feb 1972 • George Gardner signed to contract, May 1972 • Rights to Bill Young acquired in trade with Chicago for rights to Larry Cahan, Bob Liddington and Bobby Whitlock, Jul 1972 • Ralph Macsweyn signed to contract, Jul 1972 • Bob Jones, Tom Serviss signed to contracts, Sep 1972 • Mike Byers traded to New England for Mike Hyndman, Feb 1973 • Bob Jones and Jarda Krupicka traded to New York for Alton White, Nov 1972 • Larry Mavety sold to Philadelphia, Oct 1972 • Bill Young traded to Minnesota for Fred Speck, Jan 1973

1972-1973 MINNESOTA FIGHTING SAINTS

Coach
Glen Sonmor
28-28-3

Coach
Harry Neale
10-9-0

Summary of Games (@ Away, * Overtime)

	date	opponent	score		record	pts	gf-ga
1.	Oct 13	Winnipeg	3-4	L	0-1-0	0	3-4
2.	Oct 15	Chicago	3-2	W	1-1-0	2	6-6
3.	Oct 17	Los Angeles	1-5	L	1-2-0	2	7-11
4.	Oct 19 @	Houston	1-5	L	1-3-0	2	8-16
5.	Oct 20 @	Winnipeg	1-1	T	1-3-1	3	9-17
6.	Oct 22 @	New York	5-4	W	2-3-1	5	14-21
7.	Oct 23 @	New England	1-5	L	2-4-1	5	15-26
8.	Oct 26 @	Quebec	4-5	L	2-5-1	5	19-31
9.	Nov 1	Winnipeg	3-0	W	3-5-1	7	22-31
10.	Nov 2	New York	2-4	L	3-6-1	7	24-35
11.	Nov 5	Philadelphia	3-1	W	4-6-1	9	27-36
12.	Nov 10 @	Winnipeg	5-1	W	5-6-1	11	32-37
13.	Nov 14	Cleveland	5-3	W	6-6-1	13	37-40
14.	Nov 16	Quebec	5-4	W	7-6-1	15	42-44
15.	Nov 18 @	Philadelphia	*5-4	W	8-6-1	17	47-48
16.	Nov 19	Chicago	3-4	L	8-7-1	17	50-52
17.	Nov 21	Alberta	*4-3	W	9-7-1	19	54-55
18.	Nov 23	Los Angeles	4-3	W	10-7-1	21	58-58
19.	Nov 24 @	Philadelphia	6-4	W	11-7-1	23	64-62
20.	Nov 26	New England	3-1	W	12-7-1	25	67-63
21.	Nov 28 @	Ottawa	*2-3	L	12-8-1	25	69-66
22.	Nov 30 @	New York	2-5	L	12-9-1	25	71-71
23.	Dec 1 @	Alberta	6-4	W	13-9-1	27	77-75
24.	Dec 3 @	Winnipeg	1-5	L	13-10-1	27	78-80
25.	Dec 5	Chicago	*2-3	L	13-11-1	27	80-83
26.	Dec 7	Houston	3-0	W	14-11-1	29	83-83
27.	Dec 8 @	Chicago	*3-4	L	14-12-1	29	86-87
28.	Dec 10	Cleveland	*4-3	W	15-12-1	31	90-90
29.	Dec 12 @	Los Angeles	3-3	T	15-12-2	32	93-93
30.	Dec 14 @	Chicago	6-3	W	16-12-2	34	99-96
31.	Dec 15	Houston	2-3	L	16-13-2	34	101-99
32.	Dec 17	Chicago	4-2	W	17-13-2	36	105-101
33.	Dec 19	New England	7-5	W	18-13-2	38	112-106
34.	Dec 21	Winnipeg	3-0	W	19-13-2	40	115-106
35.	Dec 23 @	Cleveland	1-3	L	19-14-2	40	116-109
36.	Dec 26	Philadelphia	2-6	L	19-15-2	40	118-115
37.	Dec 28 @	Los Angeles	4-2	W	20-15-2	42	122-117
38.	Dec 29 @	Los Angeles	2-5	L	20-16-2	42	124-122
39.	Jan 1	Houston	4-4	T	20-16-3	43	128-126
40.	Jan 7	Winnipeg	2-6	L	20-17-3	43	130-132
41.	Jan 9	Los Angeles	*3-4	L	20-18-3	43	133-136
42.	Jan 11	Cleveland	3-4	L	20-19-3	43	136-140
43.	Jan 12	Quebec	3-2	W	21-19-3	45	139-142
44.	Jan 14	Ottawa	*3-2	W	22-19-3	47	142-144
45.	Jan 16 @	Winnipeg	1-3	L	22-20-3	47	143-147
46.	Jan 18 @	Ottawa	3-6	L	22-21-3	47	146-153
47.	Jan 20 @	Quebec	10-5	W	23-21-3	49	156-158
48.	Jan 22 @	New York	3-2	W	24-21-3	51	159-160
49.	Jan 25	Houston	2-5	L	24-22-3	51	161-165
50.	Jan 26	Ottawa	4-2	W	25-22-3	53	165-167
51.	Jan 30 @	Chicago	2-4	L	25-23-3	53	167-171
52.	Feb 1 @	Quebec	2-4	L	25-24-3	53	169-175
53.	Feb 3 @	Houston	1-7	L	25-25-3	53	170-182
54.	Feb 5 @	Houston	6-3	W	26-25-3	55	176-185
55.	Feb 6	New York	5-4	W	27-25-3	57	181-189
56.	Feb 8 @	Los Angeles	1-3	L	27-26-3	57	182-192
57.	Feb 9 @	Alberta	0-6	L	27-27-3	57	182-198
58.	Feb 11 @	Alberta	5-7	L	27-28-3	57	187-205
59.	Feb 15	Ottawa	3-0	W	28-28-3	59	190-205
60.	Feb 17 @	Cleveland	7-3	W	29-28-3	61	197-208
61.	Feb 18	Chicago	7-5	W	30-28-3	63	204-213
62.	Feb 25 @	Houston	1-4	L	30-29-3	63	205-217
63.	Feb 27	Philadelphia	3-0	W	31-29-3	65	208-217
64.	Mar 1	Los Angeles	1-4	L	31-30-3	65	209-221
65.	Mar 4	New England	4-2	W	32-30-3	67	213-223
66.	Mar 6	Alberta	*4-3	W	33-30-3	69	217-226
67.	Mar 8 @	Philadelphia	1-2	L	33-31-3	69	218-228
68.	Mar 10 @	New England	1-3	L	33-32-3	69	219-231
69.	Mar 11	Alberta	2-1	W	34-32-3	71	221-232
70.	Mar 15 @	Chicago	7-4	W	35-32-3	73	228-236
71.	Mar 16 @	New England	4-7	L	35-33-3	73	232-243
72.	Mar 20 @	Alberta	3-5	L	35-34-3	73	235-248
73.	Mar 22 @	Chicago	*2-1	W	36-34-3	75	237-249
74.	Mar 24 @	Cleveland	*2-1	W	37-34-3	77	239-250
75.	Mar 25 @	Ottawa	1-6	L	37-35-3	77	240-256
76.	Mar 27	New York	4-3	W	38-35-3	79	244-259
77.	Mar 29	Quebec	3-5	L	38-36-3	79	247-264
78.	Mar 30	Alberta	3-5	L	38-37-3	79	250-269

Home games after January 1, 1973, played at St. Paul Civic Center

Fighting Saints Stars of 1972-1973

Wayne Connelly
40 goals, 70 points

Bill Klatt
36 goals

Terry Ryan
6 short-handed goals

Mike Curran
4 shutouts

John Arbour
188 penalty minutes

Mike McMahon
Blueline All-Star

Scoring

pos	#	player	gp	g	a	pts	pim	ppg	shg	gp	g	a	pts	pim
						Regular Season						**Playoffs**		
C	12	Antonovich, Mike	75	20	19	39	44	1	0	5	2	0	2	0
D	17	Arbour, John	76	6	27	33	188	1	0	5	0	1	1	12
D	21	Ball, Terry	76	6	34	40	66	1	0	5	1	2	3	4
C	6	Christiansen, Keith	64	12	30	42	24	2	0	5	1	0	1	0
RW	7	Connelly, Wayne	78	40	30	70	16	10	0	5	1	3	4	0
G	1	Curran, Mike	43	0	1	1	26	0	0	2	0	0	0	0
RW	16	Falkman, Craig	44	1	5	6	12	0	0	-	-	-	-	-
C	10	Hampson, Ted	77	17	45	62	20	4	0	5	3	1	4	0
C	20	Johnson, Jim	33	9	14	23	12	0	0	5	2	1	3	2
RW	8	Klatt, Bill	78	36	22	58	22	12	0	5	1	3	4	5
LW	19	Konik, George	54	4	12	16	34	0	0	-	-	-	-	-
LW	15	Lilyholm, Len	77	8	13	21	37	0	0	5	1	0	1	0
RW	14	MacMillan, Bob	75	13	27	40	48	1	0	5	0	3	3	0
G	30	McCartan, Jack	38	0	0	0	19	0	0	4	0	1	1	0
D	23	McMahon, Mike	75	12	39	51	87	4	0	5	0	5	5	2
LW	9	Morrison, George	70	16	24	40	20	9	0	5	1	1	2	2
D	2	Paradise, Dick	77	3	15	18	189	0	0	5	0	1	1	2
LW	26	Pearson, Mel	70	8	12	20	12	0	0	5	2	0	2	0
D	18	Ryan, Terry	76	13	6	19	13	1	6	5	0	2	2	0
D	22	Rydman, Blaine	29	0	1	1	65	0	0	1	0	0	0	0
D	4	Sanders, Frank	78	8	8	16	94	1	0	4	0	1	1	0
C	11	Speck, Fred	47	13	16	29	52	5	0	-	-	-	-	-
G	35	Wetzel, Carl	1	0	0	0	0	0	0	-	-	-	-	-
LW	24	Young, Bill	23	5	6	11	20	2	0	5	1	1	2	4

Power Play: 54 goals scored in 300 opportunities (18.0%) with 12 short-handed goals allowed.
Penalty Killing: 48 goals allowed in 269 opportunities (82.2%) with 6 short-handed goals scored.

Goaltending

goaltender	gp	min	ga	en	so	record	gaa	sog	sv%	gp	min	ga	record	gaa
Curran, Mike	43	2540	131	3	4	23-17-2	3.09	1437	0.908	2	90	9	0-2	6.00
McCartan, Jack	38	2160	129	3	1	15-19-1	3.58	1181	0.890	4	213	14	1-2	3.94
Wetzel, Carl	1	60	3	0	0	0-1-0	3.00	35	0.914	-	-	-	-	-

Transactions: Dick Paradise signed to contract, Jun 1972 • Ted Hampson signed to contract, Aug 1972 • Blaine Rydman purchased from New York, Jan 1973 • Fred Speck to Los Angeles for Bill Young, Jan 1973 • Carl Wetzel signed to contract, Jan 1973

1972-1973 NEW ENGLAND WHALERS

Coach
Jack Kelley

Summary of Games (@ Away, * Overtime)

	date	opponent	score		record	pts	gf-ga		date	opponent	score		record	pts	gf-ga
1.	Oct 12	Philadelphia	4-3	W	1-0-0	2	4-3	40.	Dec 31 @	New York	3-0	W	24-15-1	49	174-136
2.	Oct 16	Chicago	4-1	W	2-0-0	4	8-4	41.	Jan 9 @	Houston	5-7	L	24-16-1	49	179-143
3.	Oct 18 @	Houston	4-1	W	3-0-0	6	12-5	42.	Jan 13	New York •	4-3	W	25-16-1	51	183-146
4.	Oct 19	Quebec	3-4	L	3-1-0	6	15-9	43.	Jan 17 @	Chicago	4-2	W	26-16-1	53	187-148
5.	Oct 21 @	Quebec	4-6	L	3-2-0	6	19-15	44.	Jan 19 @	Winnipeg	2-6	L	26-17-1	53	189-154
6.	Oct 23	Minnesota	5-1	W	4-2-0	8	24-16	45.	Jan 21 @	Winnipeg	7-2	W	27-17-1	55	196-156
7.	Oct 24 @	Cleveland	*3-2	W	5-2-0	10	27-18	46.	Jan 24	Winnipeg	6-1	W	28-17-1	57	202-157
8.	Oct 26 @	New York	6-7	L	5-3-0	10	33-25	47.	Jan 25 @	Ottawa	4-2	W	29-17-1	59	206-159
9.	Oct 28	Alberta •	1-4	L	5-4-0	10	34-29	48.	Jan 27	Quebec •	1-3	L	29-18-1	59	207-162
10.	Nov 1	Chicago •	4-2	W	6-4-0	12	38-31	49.	Jan 29 @	Cleveland	2-3	L	29-19-1	59	209-165
11.	Nov 4	Philadelphia	8-4	W	7-4-0	14	46-35	50.	Jan 30	Cleveland	4-1	W	30-19-1	61	213-166
12.	Nov 6	Winnipeg	6-2	W	8-4-0	16	52-37	51.	Feb 1 @	Houston	*5-4	W	31-19-1	63	218-170
13.	Nov 11	New York	6-5	W	9-4-0	18	58-42	52.	Feb 2 @	Los Angeles	1-3	L	31-20-1	63	219-173
14.	Nov 13	Houston	4-4	T	9-4-1	19	62-46	53.	Feb 4 @	Los Angeles	3-4	L	31-21-1	63	222-177
15.	Nov 17 @	Cleveland	0-3	L	9-5-1	19	62-49	54.	Feb 6 @	Alberta	4-2	W	32-21-1	65	226-179
16.	Nov 18	Ottawa •	3-2	W	10-5-1	21	65-51	55.	Feb 7 @	Alberta	1-3	L	32-22-1	65	227-182
17.	Nov 20	Ottawa	7-5	W	11-5-1	23	72-56	56.	Feb 9	Ottawa •	4-7	L	32-23-1	65	231-189
18.	Nov 22 @	New York	1-3	L	11-6-1	23	73-59	57.	Feb 11 @	Quebec	2-2	T	32-23-2	66	233-191
19.	Nov 24	Alberta •	7-2	W	12-6-1	25	80-61	58.	Feb 13 @	Philadelphia	4-5	L	32-24-2	66	237-196
20.	Nov 26 @	Minnesota	1-3	L	12-7-1	25	81-64	59.	Feb 15	Los Angeles •	6-5	W	33-24-2	68	243-201
21.	Nov 27	Cleveland	3-0	W	13-7-1	27	84-64	60.	Feb 17 @	Quebec	6-4	W	34-24-2	70	249-205
22.	Nov 29 @	New York	6-7	L	13-8-1	27	90-71	61.	Feb 20 @	Philadelphia	2-4	L	34-25-2	70	251-209
23.	Dec 1 @	Philadelphia	3-5	L	13-9-1	27	93-76	62.	Feb 23	Alberta	4-2	W	35-25-2	72	255-211
24.	Dec 2	Quebec	7-2	W	14-9-1	29	100-78	63.	Mar 4 @	Minnesota	2-4	L	35-26-2	72	257-215
25.	Dec 4	Ottawa	7-2	W	15-9-1	31	107-80	64.	Mar 7	Cleveland	*1-0	W	36-26-2	74	258-215
26.	Dec 6	New York	4-3	W	16-9-1	33	111-83	65.	Mar 9	Cleveland	5-4	W	37-26-2	76	263-219
27.	Dec 7 @	Ottawa	4-2	W	17-9-1	35	115-85	66.	Mar 10	Minnesota •	3-1	W	38-26-2	78	266-220
28.	Dec 9	New York	4-2	W	18-9-1	37	119-87	67.	Mar 13 @	Chicago	*4-3	W	39-26-2	80	270-223
29.	Dec 11	Winnipeg	4-3	W	19-9-1	39	123-90	68.	Mar 14 @	Winnipeg	7-5	W	40-26-2	82	277-228
30.	Dec 13 @	Chicago	3-6	L	19-10-1	39	126-96	69.	Mar 16	Minnesota •	7-4	W	41-26-2	84	284-232
31.	Dec 14 @	Los Angeles	5-2	W	20-10-1	41	131-98	70.	Mar 17	Philadelphia •	4-0	W	42-26-2	86	288-232
32.	Dec 16 @	Philadelphia	10-6	W	21-10-1	43	141-104	71.	Mar 20	Los Angeles •	4-1	W	43-26-2	88	292-233
33.	Dec 17	Philadelphia	3-6	L	21-11-1	43	144-110	72.	Mar 22 @	Ottawa	2-4	L	43-27-2	88	294-237
34.	Dec 19 @	Minnesota	5-7	L	21-12-1	43	149-117	73.	Mar 23	Chicago •	3-1	W	44-27-2	90	297-238
35.	Dec 21 @	Alberta	4-5	L	21-13-1	43	153-122	74.	Mar 26 @	Cleveland	5-7	L	44-28-2	90	302-245
36.	Dec 24	Los Angeles	3-5	L	21-14-1	43	156-127	75.	Mar 27	Houston •	1-6	L	44-29-2	90	303-251
37.	Dec 25 @	New York	8-2	W	22-14-1	45	164-129	76.	Mar 29 @	Ottawa	2-5	L	44-30-2	90	305-256
38.	Dec 28 @	Quebec	5-3	W	23-14-1	47	169-132	77.	Mar 30	New York •	*5-4	W	45-30-2	92	310-260
39.	Dec 29	Houston •	2-4	L	23-15-1	47	171-136	78.	Apr 1	Quebec •	8-3	W	46-30-2	94	318-263

• Home games played at the Boston Arena

84

Whalers Stars of 1972-1973

Tom Webster
53 goals

Terry Caffery
100 points as rookie

Larry Pleau
39 goals, 87 points

Al Smith
12 wins in playoffs

Tim Sheehy
33 goals

Rick Ley
Defense chief

Scoring

pos	#	player	gp	g	a	pts	pim	ppg	shg	gp	g	a	pts	pim
						Regular Season							Playoffs	
LW	14	Ahearn, Kevin	78	20	22	42	18	1	0	14	1	2	3	9
RW	21	Byers, Mike	19	6	4	10	4	0	0	12	6	5	11	6
C	7	Caffery, Terry	74	39	61	100	14	9	1	8	3	7	10	0
LW	17	Cunniff, John	32	3	5	8	16	0	0	13	1	1	2	2
C	12	Danby, John	77	14	23	37	10	1	0	8	0	0	0	0
D	10	Dorey, Jim	75	7	56	63	95	0	1	15	3	16	19	41
RW	27	Earl, Tom	76	10	13	23	4	0	4	15	2	3	5	10
LW	11	French, John	74	24	35	59	43	2	0	15	3	11	14	2
D	6	Green, Ted	78	16	30	46	47	2	0	12	1	5	6	25
D	5	Hurley, Paul	78	3	15	18	58	1	0	15	0	7	7	14
RW	21	Hyndman, Mike	59	4	14	18	21	0	0	-	-	-	-	-
D	20	Jordan, Ric	34	1	5	6	12	0	0	7	0	0	0	6
G	30	Landon, Bruce	30	0	1	1	8	0	0	0	0	0	0	0
D	2	Ley, Rick	76	3	27	30	108	0	0	15	3	7	10	24
C	4	Pleau, Larry	78	39	48	87	42	10	0	15	12	7	19	15
RW	16	Sarrazin, Dick	35	4	7	11	0	1	0	-	-	-	-	-
LW	18	Selby, Brit	65	13	29	42	48	2	0	13	3	4	7	13
D	3	Selwood, Brad	75	13	21	34	114	1	0	15	3	5	8	22
RW	15	Sheehy, Tim	78	33	38	71	30	5	0	15	9	14	23	13
G	1	Smith, Al	51	0	3	3	39	0	0	15	0	1	1	12
RW	19	Smith, Guy	22	3	3	6	6	0	0	11	2	0	2	4
RW	8	Webster, Tom	77	53	50	103	89	12	0	15	12	14	26	6
C	9	Williams, Tom	69	10	21	31	14	2	0	15	6	11	17	2

Power Play: 49 goals scored in 272 opportunities (18.0%) with 6 short-handed goals allowed.
Penalty Killing: 48 goals allowed in 234 opportunities (80.8%) with 6 short-handed goals scored.

Goaltending

goaltender	gp	min	ga	en	so	record	gaa	sog	sv%	gp	min	ga	record	gaa
Landon, Bruce	30	1671	100	0	1	15-11-1	3.59	888	0.887	-	-	-	-	-
Smith, Al	51	3059	162	1	3	31-19-1	3.18	1535	0.894	15	909	49	12-3	3.23

Transactions: Larry Pleau signed to contract, Apr 1972 • Brad Selwood, Tim Sheehy, Bruce Landon, Dick Sarrazin, Tom Earl and Terry Caffrey signed to contracts, May 1972 • Rick Ley, John Cunniff, Mike Hyndman, John French, Bob Brown, Ric Jordan, Tom Webster, John Danby, Paul Hurley and Kevin Ahearn signed to contracts, Jun 1972 • Jim Dorey, Ted Green, Al Smith and Guy Smith signed to contracts, Aug 1972 • Tommy Williams signed to contract, Sep 1972 • Bob Brown traded to Philadelphia for Brit Selby, Nov 1972 • Dick Sarrazin sold to Chicago, Jan 1973 • Mike Hyndman traded to Los Angeles for Mike Byers, Feb 1973

1972-1973 NEW YORK RAIDERS

**Coach
Camille Henry**

Summary of Games (@ Away, * Overtime)

	date	opponent	score		record	pts	gf-ga		date	opponent	score		record	pts	gf-ga
1.	Oct 12	Winnipeg	4-6	L	0-1-0	0	4-6	40.	Dec 31	New England	0-3	L	21-19-0	42	170-147
2.	Oct 14	Ottawa	8-6	W	1-1-0	2	12-12	41.	Jan 1	Philadelphia	0-3	L	21-20-0	42	170-150
3.	Oct 15	Philadelphia	5-0	W	2-1-0	4	17-12	42.	Jan 4	Ottawa	9-4	W	22-20-0	44	179-154
4.	Oct 17 @	Cleveland	*3-4	L	2-2-0	4	20-16	43.	Jan 8	Quebec	*5-6	L	22-21-0	44	184-160
5.	Oct 19	Cleveland	1-3	L	2-3-0	4	21-19	44.	Jan 10 @	Philadelphia	4-1	W	23-21-0	46	188-161
6.	Oct 21	Houston	3-2	W	3-3-0	6	24-21	45.	Jan 11 @	Ottawa	1-4	L	23-22-0	46	189-165
7.	Oct 22	Minnesota	4-5	L	3-4-0	6	28-26	46.	Jan 13 @	New England	3-4	L	23-23-0	46	192-169
8.	Oct 26	New England	7-6	W	4-4-0	8	35-32	47.	Jan 18 @	Quebec	4-4	T	23-23-1	47	196-173
9.	Oct 28	Los Angeles	*3-4	L	4-5-0	8	38-36	48.	Jan 22	Minnesota	2-3	L	23-24-1	47	198-176
10.	Oct 29	Alberta	7-2	W	5-5-0	10	45-38	49.	Jan 25 @	Chicago	2-9	L	23-25-1	47	200-185
11.	Nov 2 @	Minnesota	4-2	W	6-5-0	12	49-40	50.	Jan 26 @	Los Angeles	*5-4	W	24-25-1	49	205-189
12.	Nov 3 @	Winnipeg	9-6	W	7-5-0	14	58-46	51.	Jan 28 @	Los Angeles	2-9	L	24-26-1	49	207-198
13.	Nov 5 @	Winnipeg	1-3	L	7-6-0	14	59-49	52.	Jan 30 @	Alberta	3-11	L	24-27-1	49	210-209
14.	Nov 7 @	Alberta	2-4	L	7-7-0	14	61-53	53.	Feb 1 @	Alberta	5-8	L	24-28-1	49	215-217
15.	Nov 8 @	Los Angeles	1-2	L	7-8-0	14	62-55	54.	Feb 3 @	Chicago	2-4	L	24-29-1	49	217-221
16.	Nov 11 @	New England	5-6	L	7-9-0	14	67-61	55.	Feb 4	Quebec	5-4	W	25-29-1	51	222-225
17.	Nov 15 @	Quebec	4-7	L	7-10-0	14	71-68	56.	Feb 6 @	Minnesota	4-5	L	25-30-1	51	226-230
18.	Nov 18	Quebec	7-1	W	8-10-0	16	78-69	57.	Feb 8 @	Ottawa	3-2	W	26-30-1	53	229-232
19.	Nov 19	Philadelphia	5-0	W	9-10-0	18	83-69	58.	Feb 10 @	Cleveland	4-8	L	26-31-1	53	233-240
20.	Nov 22	New England	3-1	W	10-10-0	20	86-70	59.	Feb 11	Ottawa	3-2	W	27-31-1	55	236-242
21.	Nov 25	Alberta	4-2	W	11-10-0	22	90-72	60.	Feb 12 @	Cleveland	2-8	L	27-32-1	55	238-250
22.	Nov 26	Los Angeles	2-6	L	11-11-0	22	92-78	61.	Feb 16 @	Philadelphia	2-9	L	27-33-1	55	240-259
23.	Nov 29	New England	7-6	W	12-11-0	24	99-84	62.	Feb 21	Alberta	5-4	W	28-33-1	57	245-263
24.	Nov 30	Minnesota	5-2	W	13-11-0	26	104-86	63.	Feb 25	Cleveland	9-5	W	29-33-1	59	254-268
25.	Dec 2	Houston	2-7	L	13-12-0	26	106-93	64.	Mar 1 @	Ottawa	1-2	L	29-34-1	59	255-270
26.	Dec 3	Cleveland	5-2	W	14-12-0	28	111-95	65.	Mar 3	Cleveland	3-4	L	29-35-1	59	258-274
27.	Dec 5 @	Houston	6-4	W	15-12-0	30	117-99	66.	Mar 4	Philadelphia	2-4	L	29-36-1	59	260-278
28.	Dec 6 @	New England	3-4	L	15-13-0	30	120-103	67.	Mar 5	Chicago	4-4	T	29-36-2	60	264-282
29.	Dec 8 @	Philadelphia	1-3	L	15-14-0	30	121-106	68.	Mar 10	Winnipeg	*3-2	W	30-36-2	62	267-284
30.	Dec 9 @	New England	2-4	L	15-15-0	30	123-110	69.	Mar 11 @	Quebec	1-6	L	30-37-2	62	268-290
31.	Dec 11	Chicago	8-3	W	16-15-0	32	131-113	70.	Mar 12	Chicago	8-7	W	31-37-2	64	276-297
32.	Dec 13	Quebec	9-1	W	17-15-0	34	140-114	71.	Mar 14	Houston	5-1	W	32-37-2	66	281-298
33.	Dec 14 @	Ottawa	4-3	W	18-15-0	36	144-117	72.	Mar 15	Los Angeles	2-6	L	32-38-2	66	283-304
34.	Dec 17	Winnipeg	3-4	L	18-16-0	36	147-121	73.	Mar 17 @	Chicago	3-6	L	32-39-2	66	286-310
35.	Dec 19	Philadelphia	7-2	W	19-16-0	38	154-123	74.	Mar 18 @	Houston	*3-2	W	33-39-2	68	289-312
36.	Dec 21 @	Cleveland	2-6	L	19-17-0	38	156-129	75.	Mar 25 @	Winnipeg	4-8	L	33-40-2	68	293-320
37.	Dec 22	Ottawa	7-5	W	20-17-0	40	163-134	76.	Mar 27 @	Minnesota	3-4	L	33-41-2	68	296-324
38.	Dec 25	New England	2-8	L	20-18-0	40	165-142	77.	Mar 29 @	Houston	3-5	L	33-42-2	68	299-329
39.	Dec 26 @	Quebec	5-2	W	21-18-0	42	170-144	78.	Mar 30 @	New England	*4-5	L	33-43-2	68	303-334

Raiders Stars of 1972-1973

Ron Ward	**Bobby Sheehan**	**Pete Donnelly**	**Wayne Rivers**	**Hal Willis**	**Brian Bradley**
51 goals, 118 points	35 goals, 88 points	22 wins, 2 shutouts	37 goals	Hard-hitting defense	22 goals

Scoring

pos	#	player	gp	g	a	pts	pim	ppg	shg	gp	g	a	pts	pim
					Regular Season							Playoffs		
D	17	Block, Ken	78	5	53	58	43	0	1	-	-	-	-	-
LW	14	Bradley, Brian	78	22	33	55	20	1	2	-	-	-	-	-
D	26	Brown, Bob	17	0	4	4	6	0	0	-	-	-	-	-
C	22	Chartre, Claude	12	2	3	5	0	2	0	-	-	-	-	-
G	23	Donnelly, Pete	47	0	0	0	2	0	0	-	-	-	-	-
D	21	Douglas, Kent	60	3	15	18	74	0	0	-	-	-	-	-
RW	9	Ferguson, Norm	56	28	40	68	8	8	1	-	-	-	-	-
D	3	Gauthier, Jean	31	2	1	3	21	0	0	-	-	-	-	-
LW	10	Jones, Bob	56	11	12	23	24	0	1	-	-	-	-	-
RW	16	Kennedy, Jamie	52	4	6	10	11	0	0	-	-	-	-	-
RW	28	Krupicka, Jarda	30	1	2	3	4	0	0	-	-	-	-	-
G	30	Kurt, Gary	36	0	1	1	2	0	0	-	-	-	-	-
C	18	Laughton, Mike	67	16	20	36	44	1	0	-	-	-	-	-
C	15	Morenz, Brian	32	7	1	8	23	1	2	-	-	-	-	-
D	4	Olds, Wally	61	5	7	12	4	0	0	-	-	-	-	-
LW	25	Peacosh, Gene	67	37	34	71	25	10	1	-	-	-	-	-
C	19	Perry, Brian	74	13	20	33	30	3	1	-	-	-	-	-
C	8	Peters, Garry	23	2	7	9	24	0	0	-	-	-	-	-
LW	11	Reichmuth, Craig	73	13	14	27	127	0	0	-	-	-	-	-
RW	12	Rivers, Wayne	75	37	40	77	47	4	0	-	-	-	-	-
D	27	Rydman, Blaine	2	0	0	0	4	0	0	-	-	-	-	-
RW	20	Scharf, Ted	29	2	2	4	72	0	0	-	-	-	-	-
C	7	Sheehan, Bobby	75	35	53	88	17	18	0	-	-	-	-	-
D	24	Speer, Bill	69	3	23	26	40	0	0	-	-	-	-	-
C	6	Ward, Ron	77	51	67	118	28	12	1	-	-	-	-	-
RW	10	White, Alton	13	1	4	5	2	0	0	-	-	-	-	-
G	1	Wilkie, Ian	5	0	0	0	0	0	0	-	-	-	-	-
D	5	Willis, Hal	74	3	21	24	159	0	0	-	-	-	-	-
D	2	Winograd, Bob	52	0	12	12	23	0	0	-	-	-	-	-

Power Play: 60 goals scored in 305 opportunities (19.7%) with 12 short-handed goals allowed.
Penalty Killing: 63 goals allowed in 268 opportunities (76.5%) with 10 short-handed goals scored.

Goaltending

goaltender	gp	min	ga	en	so	record	gaa	sog	sv%	gp	min	ga	record	gaa
Donnelly, Pete	47	2606	155	1	2	22-19-2	3.57	1328	0.883	-	-	-	-	-
Kurt, Gary	36	1881	150	1	0	10-21-0	4.78	1034	0.854	-	-	-	-	-
Wilkie, Ian	5	253	27	0	0	1-3-0	6.40	172	0.843	-	-	-	-	-

Transactions: Peter Donnelly signed to contract, May 1972 • Rights to Wayne Rivers acquired in trade with Ottawa, Jul 1972 • Brian Bradley signed to contract, Jul 1972 • Craig Reichmuth signed to contract, Aug 1972 • Rights to Hal Willis acquired from Houston for 1974 draft pick, Aug 1972 • Rights to Bobby Sheehan acquired in trade with New England for 1973 draft picks, Aug 1972 • Blaine Rydman signed to contract, Aug 1972 • Jean Gauthier signed to contract, Sep 1972 • Alton White traded to Los Angeles for Bob Brown and Jarda Krupicka, Nov 1972 • Blaine Rydman sold to Minnesota, Jan 1973 • Bob Brown purchased from Philadelphia, Feb 1973

1972-1973 OTTAWA NATIONALS

Coach
Billy Harris

Summary of Games (@ Away, * Overtime)

	date	opponent	score		record	pts	gf-ga		date	opponent	score		record	pts	gf-ga
1.	Oct 11	Alberta	4-7	L	0-1-0	0	4-7	40.	Jan 11	New York	4-1	W	18-19-3	39	149-174
2.	Oct 14 @	New York	6-8	L	0-2-0	0	10-15	41.	Jan 12 @	Philadelphia	3-4	L	18-20-3	39	152-178
3.	Oct 15	Cleveland	5-7	L	0-3-0	0	15-22	42.	Jan 14 @	Minnesota	*2-3	L	18-21-3	39	154-181
4.	Oct 19	Chicago	6-2	W	1-3-0	2	21-24	43.	Jan 16 @	Quebec	*4-5	L	18-22-3	39	158-186
5.	Oct 21 @	Cleveland	5-3	W	2-3-0	4	26-27	44.	Jan 18	Minnesota	6-3	W	19-22-3	41	164-189
6.	Oct 22 @	Quebec	3-2	W	3-3-0	6	29-29	45.	Jan 19 @	Philadelphia	2-4	L	19-23-3	41	166-193
7.	Oct 25 @	Los Angeles	8-5	W	4-3-0	8	37-34	46.	Jan 21 @	Houston	2-5	L	19-24-3	41	168-198
8.	Oct 26 @	Houston	3-7	L	4-4-0	8	40-41	47.	Jan 23 @	Houston	3-11	L	19-25-3	41	171-209
9.	Oct 28 @	Philadelphia	5-3	W	5-4-0	10	45-44	48.	Jan 25	New England	2-4	L	19-26-3	41	173-213
10.	Nov 2	Los Angeles	1-1	T	5-4-1	11	46-45	49.	Jan 26 @	Minnesota	2-4	L	19-27-3	41	175-217
11.	Nov 5 @	Alberta	5-3	W	6-4-1	13	51-48	50.	Jan 28	Winnipeg	4-5	L	19-28-3	41	179-222
12.	Nov 9	Winnipeg	1-4	L	6-5-1	13	52-52	51.	Jan 30	Philadelphia	*4-5	L	19-29-3	41	183-227
13.	Nov 12	Philadelphia	2-1	W	7-5-1	15	54-53	52.	Feb 1 @	Cleveland	2-2	T	19-29-4	42	185-229
14.	Nov 16 @	Cleveland	3-6	L	7-6-1	15	57-59	53.	Feb 2 @	Chicago	1-4	L	19-30-4	42	186-233
15.	Nov 18 @	New England	2-3	L	7-7-1	15	59-62	54.	Feb 4	Cleveland	2-3	L	19-31-4	42	188-236
16.	Nov 20 @	New England	5-7	L	7-8-1	15	64-69	55.	Feb 6	Philadelphia	5-3	W	20-31-4	44	193-239
17.	Nov 21	Quebec	4-2	W	8-8-1	17	68-71	56.	Feb 8	New York	2-3	L	20-32-4	44	195-242
18.	Nov 23	Chicago	1-8	L	8-9-1	17	69-79	57.	Feb 9 @	New England	7-4	W	21-32-4	46	202-246
19.	Nov 26	Alberta	1-2	L	8-10-1	17	70-81	58.	Feb 11 @	New York	2-3	L	21-33-4	46	204-249
20.	Nov 28	Minnesota	*3-2	W	9-10-1	19	73-83	59.	Feb 14 @	Quebec	6-3	W	22-33-4	48	210-252
21.	Nov 30	Cleveland	3-2	W	10-10-1	21	76-85	60.	Feb 15 @	Minnesota	0-3	L	22-34-4	48	210-255
22.	Dec 1 @	Winnipeg	4-3	W	11-10-1	23	80-88	61.	Feb 17 @	Chicago	3-1	W	23-34-4	50	213-256
23.	Dec 3	Houston	*5-4	W	12-10-1	25	85-92	62.	Feb 20	Los Angeles	2-4	L	23-35-4	50	215-260
24.	Dec 4 @	New England	2-7	L	12-11-1	25	87-99	63.	Feb 22	Philadelphia	5-6	L	23-36-4	50	220-266
25.	Dec 7	New England	2-4	L	12-12-1	25	89-103	64.	Feb 25	Alberta	3-2	W	24-36-4	52	223-268
26.	Dec 9 @	Philadelphia	1-7	L	12-13-1	25	90-110	65.	Feb 27	Cleveland	2-1	W	25-36-4	54	225-269
27.	Dec 10	Quebec	*7-6	W	13-13-1	27	97-116	66.	Mar 1	New York	2-1	W	26-36-4	56	227-270
28.	Dec 14	New York	3-4	L	13-14-1	27	100-120	67.	Mar 4	Chicago	6-4	W	27-36-4	58	233-274
29.	Dec 15 @	Alberta	4-3	W	14-14-1	29	104-123	68.	Mar 6	Winnipeg	5-2	W	28-36-4	60	238-276
30.	Dec 17 @	Alberta	1-3	L	14-15-1	29	105-126	69.	Mar 11 @	Los Angeles	2-4	L	28-37-4	60	240-280
31.	Dec 19 @	Quebec	3-7	L	14-16-1	29	108-133	70.	Mar 13 @	Los Angeles	3-1	W	29-37-4	62	243-281
32.	Dec 21	Los Angeles	4-4	T	14-16-2	30	112-137	71.	Mar 16 @	Winnipeg	6-1	W	30-37-4	64	249-282
33.	Dec 22 @	New York	5-7	L	14-17-2	30	117-144	72.	Mar 18 @	Winnipeg	4-2	W	31-37-4	66	253-284
34.	Dec 24	Quebec	6-2	W	15-17-2	32	123-146	73.	Mar 22	New England	4-2	W	32-37-4	68	257-286
35.	Dec 26	Houston	3-3	T	15-17-3	33	126-149	74.	Mar 25	Minnesota	6-1	W	33-37-4	70	263-287
36.	Dec 30 @	Chicago	4-2	W	16-17-3	35	130-151	75.	Mar 27	Quebec	6-2	W	34-37-4	72	269-289
37.	Dec 31 @	Quebec	4-8	L	16-18-3	35	134-159	76.	Mar 29	New England	5-2	W	35-37-4	74	274-291
38.	Jan 4 @	New York	4-9	L	16-19-3	35	138-168	77.	Mar 31 @	Cleveland	2-4	L	35-38-4	74	276-295
39.	Jan 9	Quebec	7-5	W	17-19-3	37	145-173	78.	Apr 1	Houston	3-6	L	35-39-4	74	279-301

Nationals Stars of 1972-1973

Gilles Gratton
25 wins

Guy Trottier
26 goals, 58 points

Wayne Carleton
42 goals led team

Bob Charlebois
64 points

Gavin Kirk
28 goals

Jack Gibson
22 goals

Scoring

pos	#	player	Regular Season gp	g	a	pts	pim	ppg	shg	Playoffs gp	g	a	pts	pim
D	5	Amodeo, Mike	61	1	14	15	77	0	0	5	0	1	1	10
G	30	Binkley, Les	30	0	0	0	0	0	0	4	0	0	0	0
G	1	Blum, Frank	2	0	0	0	0	0	0	-	-	-	-	-
RW	10	Boland, Mike	41	1	15	16	44	0	0	1	0	0	0	12
LW	9	Carleton, Wayne	75	42	49	91	42	6	1	3	3	3	6	4
LW	16	Charlebois, Bob	78	24	40	64	28	5	1	5	1	1	2	4
LW	23	Climie, Ron	31	12	19	31	2	4	0	4	1	0	1	2
LW	20	Conacher, Brian	69	8	19	27	32	0	0	5	1	3	4	4
D	3	Cunningham, Rick	78	9	31	40	121	2	0	5	1	1	2	2
D	24	Donnelly, John	15	1	1	2	44	0	0	-	-	-	-	-
D	6	Gibbons, Brian	73	7	35	42	62	2	0	5	1	2	3	12
LW	21	Gibson, Jack	59	22	12	34	48	3	0	1	1	0	1	5
G	33	Gratton, Gilles	51	0	1	1	10	0	0	2	0	0	0	0
D	22	Haney, Merv	7	0	1	1	4	0	0	-	-	-	-	-
RW	12	King, Steve	69	18	34	52	28	3	4	5	0	1	1	7
C	11	Kirk, Gavin	78	28	40	68	54	6	0	5	2	3	5	12
LW	19	Leduc, Bob	78	22	33	55	71	6	0	5	0	2	2	4
RW	17	Martin, Tom	75	19	27	46	27	6	0	5	0	5	5	2
D	22	Meloff, Chris	28	1	6	7	40	0	0	-	-	-	-	-
LW	15	Riley, Ron	22	0	5	5	2	0	0	2	0	0	0	0
RW	8	Sentes, Dick	74	22	19	41	78	2	0	5	3	1	4	2
RW	14	Simpson, Tom	57	10	7	17	44	0	0	5	1	0	1	0
D	4	Stephanson, Ken	77	3	16	19	93	1	0	5	1	1	2	8
RW	7	Trottier, Guy	72	26	32	58	25	11	0	5	1	2	3	0
D	2	Warr, Steve	72	3	8	11	79	2	0	2	0	0	0	0

Power Play: 59 goals scored in 321 opportunities (18.4%) with 7 short-handed goals allowed.
Penalty Killing: 51 goals allowed in 278 opportunities (81.7%) with 6 short-handed goals scored.

Goaltending

goaltender	gp	min	ga	en	so	record	gaa	sog	sv%	gp	min	ga	record	gaa
Binkley, Les	30	1709	106	1	0	10-17-1	3.72	900	0.882	4	223	17	1-3	4.57
Blum, Frank	2	28	3	0	0	0-0-0	4.78	17	0.823	-	-	-	-	-
Gratton, Gilles	51	3021	187	4	0	25-22-3	3.71	1591	0.882	2	87	7	0-1	4.83

Transactions: Steve King signed to contract, Jul 1972 • Rights to Gavin Kirk purchased from Quebec, Jul 1972 • Rights to Steve Warr acquired from New England, Jul 1972 • Rights to Gilles Gratton acquired from Alberta, Aug 1972 • Wayne Carleton, Bob Charlebois, Ron Climie, Bob Leduc, Guy Trottier signed to contracts, Aug 1972. Many players had signed prior to Aug 1972, but contracts were not guaranteed until August • Mike Amodeo, Les Binkley signed to contract, Sep 1972 • Gilles Gratton signed to contract, Oct 1972

1972-1973 PHILADELPHIA BLAZERS

Coach
John McKenzie
1-6-0

Coach
Phil Watson
34-33-4

Summary of Games (@ Away, * Overtime)

	date	opponent	score		record	pts	gf-ga		date	opponent	score		record	pts	gf-ga
1.	Oct 12 @	New England	3-4	L	0-1-0	0	3-4	40.	Jan 10	New York	1-4	L	15-25-0	30	138-182
2.	Oct 15 @	New York	0-5	L	0-2-0	0	3-9	41.	Jan 12	Ottawa	4-3	W	16-25-0	32	142-185
3.	Oct 19 @	Los Angeles	2-4	L	0-3-0	0	5-13	42.	Jan 13	Quebec	9-4	W	17-25-0	34	151-189
4.	Oct 20 @	Alberta	1-4	L	0-4-0	0	6-17	43.	Jan 16	Cleveland	3-4	L	17-26-0	34	154-193
5.	Oct 22 @	Winnipeg	3-6	L	0-5-0	0	9-23	44.	Jan 19	Ottawa	4-2	W	18-26-0	36	158-195
6.	Oct 24 @	Winnipeg	3-5	L	0-6-0	0	12-28	45.	Jan 20	Houston	3-4	L	18-27-0	36	161-199
7.	Oct 25	Cleveland	2-8	L	0-7-0	0	14-36	46.	Jan 24 @	Quebec	6-4	W	19-27-0	38	167-203
8.	Oct 27	Los Angeles	5-4	W	1-7-0	2	19-40	47.	Jan 25 @	Cleveland	7-4	W	20-27-0	40	174-207
9.	Oct 28	Ottawa	3-5	L	1-8-0	2	22-45	48.	Jan 27 @	Alberta	*1-0	W	21-27-0	42	175-207
10.	Nov 1 @	Cleveland	7-5	W	2-8-0	4	29-50	49.	Jan 28 @	Alberta	2-4	L	21-28-0	42	177-211
11.	Nov 2 @	Quebec	3-6	L	2-9-0	4	32-56	50.	Jan 30 @	Ottawa	*5-4	W	22-28-0	44	182-215
12.	Nov 4 @	New England	4-8	L	2-10-0	4	36-64	51.	Feb 2 @	Cleveland	3-5	L	22-29-0	44	185-220
13.	Nov 5 @	Minnesota	1-3	L	2-11-0	4	37-67	52.	Feb 6 @	Ottawa	3-5	L	22-30-0	44	188-225
14.	Nov 12 @	Ottawa	1-2	L	2-12-0	4	38-69	53.	Feb 7 @	Quebec	0-3	L	22-31-0	44	188-228
15.	Nov 14 @	Chicago	4-3	W	3-12-0	6	42-72	54.	Feb 10	Quebec	*5-4	W	23-31-0	46	193-232
16.	Nov 18	Minnesota	*4-5	L	3-13-0	6	46-77	55.	Feb 11	Cleveland	6-1	W	24-31-0	48	199-233
17.	Nov 19 @	New York	0-5	L	3-14-0	6	46-82	56.	Feb 13	New England	5-4	W	25-31-0	50	204-237
18.	Nov 22	Alberta	*5-4	W	4-14-0	8	51-86	57.	Feb 14	Cleveland	6-5	W	26-31-0	52	210-242
19.	Nov 24	Minnesota	4-6	L	4-15-0	8	55-92	58.	Feb 16	New York	9-2	W	27-31-0	54	219-244
20.	Nov 25	Chicago	3-4	L	4-16-0	8	58-96	59.	Feb 18	Los Angeles	1-4	L	27-32-0	54	220-248
21.	Nov 28	Los Angeles	4-3	W	5-16-0	10	62-99	60.	Feb 20	New England	4-2	W	28-32-0	56	224-250
22.	Dec 1	New England	5-3	W	6-16-0	12	67-102	61.	Feb 22 @	Ottawa	6-5	W	29-32-0	58	230-255
23.	Dec 2 @	Cleveland	2-8	L	6-17-0	12	69-110	62.	Feb 25 @	Winnipeg	3-5	L	29-33-0	58	233-260
24.	Dec 5	Cleveland	*3-4	L	6-18-0	12	72-114	63.	Feb 27 @	Minnesota	0-3	L	29-34-0	58	233-263
25.	Dec 8	New York	3-1	W	7-18-0	14	75-115	64.	Mar 4 @	New York	4-2	W	30-34-0	60	237-265
26.	Dec 9	Ottawa	7-1	W	8-18-0	16	82-116	65.	Mar 6 @	Chicago	*1-2	L	30-35-0	60	238-267
27.	Dec 12 @	Quebec	2-5	L	8-19-0	16	84-121	66.	Mar 8	Minnesota	2-1	W	31-35-0	62	240-268
28.	Dec 13	Winnipeg	7-4	W	9-19-0	18	91-125	67.	Mar 9	Quebec	11-3	W	32-35-0	64	251-271
29.	Dec 15	Winnipeg	6-4	W	10-19-0	20	97-129	68.	Mar 11	Houston	2-4	L	32-36-0	64	253-275
30.	Dec 16	New England	6-10	L	10-20-0	20	103-139	69.	Mar 12	Quebec	4-6	L	32-37-0	64	257-281
31.	Dec 17 @	New England	6-3	W	11-20-0	22	109-142	70.	Mar 13	Houston	4-3	W	33-37-0	66	261-284
32.	Dec 19	New York	2-7	L	11-21-0	22	111-149	71.	Mar 17 @	New England	0-4	L	33-38-0	66	261-288
33.	Dec 20	Chicago	8-5	W	12-21-0	24	119-154	72.	Mar 19 @	Houston	1-5	L	33-39-0	66	262-293
34.	Dec 23 @	Houston	3-7	L	12-22-0	24	122-161	73.	Mar 21 @	Houston	7-3	W	34-39-0	68	269-296
35.	Dec 25 @	Cleveland	0-8	L	12-23-0	24	122-169	74.	Mar 23 @	Los Angeles	7-3	W	35-39-0	70	276-299
36.	Dec 26 @	Minnesota	6-2	W	13-23-0	26	128-171	75.	Mar 28	Alberta	1-2	L	35-40-0	70	277-301
37.	Dec 28 @	Chicago	3-6	L	13-24-0	26	131-177	76.	Mar 29	Alberta	2-1	W	36-40-0	72	279-302
38.	Dec 31 @	Los Angeles	3-1	W	14-24-0	28	134-178	77.	Mar 31	Chicago	5-1	W	37-40-0	74	284-303
39.	Jan 1 @	New York	3-0	W	15-24-0	30	137-178	78.	Apr 1	Winnipeg	4-2	W	38-40-0	76	288-305

Blazers Stars of 1972-1973

 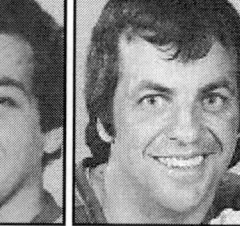    

Danny Lawson	Andre Lacroix	Bernie Parent	John McKenzie	Jim Cardiff	Ron Plumb
61 goals led league	124 points led league	33 wins	78 points	185 penalty minutes	51 points on defense

Scoring

pos	#	player	Regular Season							Playoffs				
			gp	g	a	pts	pim	ppg	shg	gp	g	a	pts	pim
G	30	Archambault, Yves	6	0	1	1	0	0	0	3	0	0	0	0
LW	20	Bennett, John	34	4	6	10	18	1	0	-	-	-	-	-
D	9	Boudreau, Michel	33	7	7	14	4	1	0	2	0	0	0	0
D		Brown, Bob	4	0	0	0	2	0	0	-	-	-	-	-
LW	8	Burgess, Don	74	20	22	42	15	1	3	4	1	0	1	0
C	14	Campbell, Bryan	75	25	48	73	85	6	0	3	0	1	1	8
D	6	Campeau, Rychard	75	1	18	19	72	1	0	4	1	0	1	17
D	5	Cardiff, Jim	78	3	24	27	185	0	2	4	0	0	0	11
D		Chipchase, Jack	3	0	0	0	2	0	0	-	-	-	-	-
G		Cottringer, Tom	2	0	0	0	0	0	0	-	-	-	-	-
LW	21	Gellard, Sam	5	0	0	0	0	0	0	-	-	-	-	-
RW	10	Golembrosky, Frank	8	0	0	0	0	0	0	-	-	-	-	-
D	23	Gravel, John	8	1	3	4	0	0	0	-	-	-	-	-
D	22	Harker, Derek	27	0	5	5	46	0	0	-	-	-	-	-
LW	10	Henry, Pierre	19	2	3	5	13	0	0	-	-	-	-	-
LW	17	Herriman, Don	78	24	48	72	63	9	0	4	1	0	1	14
D	3	Hutchison, Dave	28	0	2	2	34	0	0	3	0	0	0	2
C	7	Lacroix, Andre	78	50	74	124	83	16	0	4	0	2	2	18
C	15	Lapierre, Camille	24	5	9	14	2	0	0	4	0	2	2	0
RW	11	Lawson, Danny	78	61	45	106	35	20	3	4	0	1	1	0
D	3	Mavety, Larry	4	0	0	0	14	0	0	-	-	-	-	-
RW	19	McKenzie, John	60	28	50	78	157	8	1	4	3	1	4	8
C	15	Meloche, Denis	4	1	1	2	0	0	0	-	-	-	-	-
LW	18	Migneault, John	55	10	8	18	38	1	0	4	0	0	0	0
D	21	Mosdell, Wayne	9	0	1	1	12	0	0	-	-	-	-	-
LW		Mott, Darwin	1	0	0	0	0	0	0	-	-	-	-	-
RW	9	Myers, Murray	7	0	0	0	0	0	0	-	-	-	-	-
RW	12	O'Donoghue, Don	74	16	23	39	43	1	0	4	0	1	1	0
D	25	Paiement, Pierre	8	1	0	1	18	0	0	-	-	-	-	-
G	1	Paille, Marcel	15	0	0	0	0	0	0	1	0	0	0	0
G	0	Parent, Bernie	63	0	1	1	36	0	0	1	0	0	0	0
LW	24	Plante, Michel	70	13	12	25	35	0	0	4	0	0	0	2
D	4	Plumb, Ron	78	10	41	51	66	6	0	4	0	2	2	13
D	2	Polano, Nick	17	0	3	3	24	0	0	-	-	-	-	-
C	9	Rouleau, Michel	6	0	1	1	15	0	0	-	-	-	-	-
LW	22	St. Sauveur, Claude	2	1	0	1	0	0	0	-	-	-	-	-
C	16	Sanderson, Derek	8	3	3	6	69	0	1	-	-	-	-	-
D	23	Spencer, Irv	54	2	27	29	43	0	0	4	0	0	0	4
G	34	Sullivan, Danny	1	0	0	0	0	0	0	-	-	-	-	-

Power Play: 71 goals scored in 293 opportunities (24.2%) with 10 short-handed goals allowed.
Penalty Killing: 60 goals allowed in 295 opportunities (80.7%) with 10 short-handed goals scored.

Goaltending

goaltender	gp	min	ga	en	so	record	gaa	sog	sv%	gp	min	ga	record	gaa
Archambault, Yves	6	260	17	0	0	1-3-0	3.92	122	0.861	3	153	11	0-2	4.31
Cottringer, Tom	2	122	8	0	0	1-1-0	3.93	65	0.877	-	-	-	-	-
Paille, Marcel	15	611	49	3	0	2-8-0	4.81	377	0.865	1	26	5	0-1	11.54
Parent, Bernie	63	3653	220	5	2	33-28-0	3.61	1936	0.886	1	70	3	0-1	2.57
Sullivan, Danny	1	60	3	0	0	1-0-0	3.00	34	0.912	-	-	-	-	-

Transactions: Rights to Andre Lacroix acquired from Quebec, Mar 1972 • Rights to Bryan Campbell acquired from Chicago, May 1972; signed to contract, Jun 1972 • Bernie Parent, Jim Cardiff, Don Burgess signed to contracts, Jun 1972 • Don Herriman, Irv Spencer signed to contracts, Jun 1972 • Rights to Don O'Donoghue acquired from New England, Jun 1972 • Ron Plumb, Danny Lawson signed to contracts, Jul 1972 • John McKenzie, Derek Sanderson, Don O'Donoghue signed to contracts, Aug 1972 • John Migneault signed to contract, Sep 1972 • Wayne Mosdell signed to contract, Oct 1972 • Frank Golembrosky and Michel Rouleau traded to Quebec for Jean Gravel and Brit Selby, Nov 1972 • Larry Mavety purchased from Los Angeles, Oct 1972, sold to Chicago, Nov 1972 • Brit Selby traded to New England for Bob Brown, Nov 1972 • Derek Sanderson released, Jan 1973 • Bob Brown sold to New York, Feb 1973

1972-1973 QUEBEC NORDIQUES

**Coach
Maurice Richard
1-1-0**

**Coach
Maurice Filion
32-39-5**

Summary of Games (@ Away, * Overtime)

	date		opponent	score		record	pts	gf-ga		date		opponent	score		record	pts	gf-ga
1.	Oct 11	@	Cleveland	0-2	L	0-1-0	0	0-2	40.	Jan 9	@	Ottawa	5-7	L	20-19-1	41	147-152
2.	Oct 13		Alberta	6-0	W	1-1-0	2	6-2	41.	Jan 12	@	Minnesota	2-3	L	20-20-1	41	149-155
3.	Oct 19	@	New England	4-3	W	2-1-0	4	10-5	42.	Jan 13	@	Philadelphia	4-9	L	20-21-1	41	153-164
4.	Oct 21		New England	6-4	W	3-1-0	6	16-9	43.	Jan 16		Ottawa	5-4	W	21-21-1	43	158-168
5.	Oct 22		Ottawa	2-3	L	3-2-0	6	18-12	44.	Jan 18		New York	4-4	T	21-21-2	44	162-172
6.	Oct 24		Houston	5-3	W	4-2-0	8	23-15	45.	Jan 20		Minnesota	5-10	L	21-22-2	44	167-182
7.	Oct 26		Minnesota	5-4	W	5-2-0	10	28-19	46.	Jan 23	@	Chicago	1-7	L	21-23-2	44	168-189
8.	Oct 29		Cleveland	2-2	T	5-2-1	11	30-21	47.	Jan 24		Philadelphia	4-6	L	21-24-2	44	172-195
9.	Oct 31		Los Angeles	2-4	L	5-3-1	11	32-25	48.	Jan 26		Winnipeg	2-2	T	21-24-3	45	174-196
10.	Nov 2		Philadelphia	6-3	W	6-3-1	13	38-28	49.	Jan 27	@	New England	3-1	W	22-24-3	47	177-198
11.	Nov 4	@	Cleveland	3-5	L	6-4-1	13	41-33	50.	Feb 1		Minnesota	4-2	W	23-24-3	49	181-200
12.	Nov 5		Chicago	3-2	W	7-4-1	15	44-35	51.	Feb 4	@	New York	4-5	L	23-25-3	49	185-205
13.	Nov 8		Winnipeg	3-2	W	8-4-1	17	47-37	52.	Feb 7		Philadelphia	3-0	W	24-25-3	51	188-205
14.	Nov 11		Houston	3-1	W	9-4-1	19	50-38	53.	Feb 8	@	Chicago	2-5	L	24-26-3	51	190-210
15.	Nov 15		New York	7-4	W	10-4-1	21	57-42	54.	Feb 10	@	Philadelphia	*4-5	L	24-27-3	51	194-215
16.	Nov 16	@	Minnesota	4-5	L	10-5-1	21	61-47	55.	Feb 11		New England	2-2	T	24-27-4	52	196-217
17.	Nov 18	@	New York	1-7	L	10-6-1	21	62-54	56.	Feb 14		Ottawa	3-6	L	24-28-4	52	199-223
18.	Nov 21	@	Ottawa	2-4	L	10-7-1	21	64-58	57.	Feb 16		Los Angeles	2-2	T	24-28-5	53	201-225
19.	Nov 24	@	Winnipeg	3-5	L	10-8-1	21	67-63	58.	Feb 17		New England	4-6	L	24-29-5	53	205-231
20.	Nov 26	@	Winnipeg	1-4	L	10-9-1	21	68-67	59.	Feb 20		Chicago	2-4	L	24-30-5	53	207-235
21.	Nov 28		Chicago	6-2	W	11-9-1	23	74-69	60.	Feb 22	@	Houston	1-4	L	24-31-5	53	208-239
22.	Dec 2	@	New England	2-7	L	11-10-1	23	76-76	61.	Feb 24	@	Los Angeles	5-3	W	25-31-5	55	213-242
23.	Dec 3	@	Alberta	6-2	W	12-10-1	25	82-78	62.	Feb 25	@	Los Angeles	2-4	L	25-32-5	55	215-246
24.	Dec 5	@	Winnipeg	4-2	W	13-10-1	27	86-80	63.	Mar 3	@	Houston	4-3	W	26-32-5	57	219-249
25.	Dec 7		Cleveland	1-3	L	13-11-1	27	87-83	64.	Mar 4	@	Houston	6-3	W	27-32-5	59	225-252
26.	Dec 9	@	Chicago	4-2	W	14-11-1	29	91-85	65.	Mar 6	@	Los Angeles	*2-3	L	27-33-5	59	227-255
27.	Dec 10	@	Ottawa	*6-7	L	14-12-1	29	97-92	66.	Mar 8		Winnipeg	4-7	L	27-34-5	59	231-262
28.	Dec 12		Philadelphia	5-2	W	15-12-1	31	102-94	67.	Mar 9	@	Philadelphia	3-11	L	27-35-5	59	234-273
29.	Dec 13	@	New York	1-9	L	15-13-1	31	103-103	68.	Mar 11		New York	6-1	W	28-35-5	61	240-274
30.	Dec 15	@	Cleveland	3-6	L	15-14-1	31	106-109	69.	Mar 12	@	Philadelphia	6-4	W	29-35-5	63	246-278
31.	Dec 17		Cleveland	3-2	W	16-14-1	33	109-111	70.	Mar 16	@	Alberta	2-4	L	29-36-5	63	248-282
32.	Dec 19		Ottawa	7-3	W	17-14-1	35	116-114	71.	Mar 17	@	Alberta	0-3	L	29-37-5	63	248-285
33.	Dec 23		Los Angeles	2-1	W	18-14-1	37	118-115	72.	Mar 20		Cleveland	4-1	W	30-37-5	65	252-286
34.	Dec 24	@	Ottawa	2-6	L	18-15-1	37	120-121	73.	Mar 24		Alberta	5-4	W	31-37-5	67	257-290
35.	Dec 26		New York	2-5	L	18-16-1	37	122-126	74.	Mar 25		Alberta	4-5	L	31-38-5	67	261-295
36.	Dec 28		New England	3-5	L	18-17-1	37	125-131	75.	Mar 27	@	Ottawa	2-6	L	31-39-5	67	263-301
37.	Dec 29	@	Cleveland	3-5	L	18-18-1	37	128-136	76.	Mar 29	@	Minnesota	5-3	W	32-39-5	69	268-304
38.	Dec 31		Ottawa	8-4	W	19-18-1	39	136-140	77.	Mar 31		Houston	5-1	W	33-39-5	71	273-305
39.	Jan 8	@	New York	*6-5	W	20-18-1	41	142-145	78.	Apr 1	@	New England	3-8	L	33-40-5	71	276-313

Nordiques Stars of 1972-1973

J.-C. Tremblay 75 assists, 89 points	**Alain Caron** 36 goals led team	**Andre Gaudette** Top penalty killer	**Bob Guindon** 28 goals	**Serge Aubry** 25 wins	**Michel Parizeau** 73 points

Scoring

pos	#	player	gp	g	a	pts	pim	ppg	shg	gp	g	a	pts	pim
LW	9	Archambault, Michel	57	12	25	37	36	3	0	-	-	-	-	-
G	1	Aubry, Serge	52	0	0	0	54	0	0	-	-	-	-	-
RW	17	Bergeron, Yves	65	14	19	33	32	3	0	-	-	-	-	-
D	5	Blain, Jacques	70	1	10	11	78	0	0	-	-	-	-	-
G	30	Brodeur, Richard	24	0	0	0	4	0	0	-	-	-	-	-
RW	19	Caron, Alain	68	36	27	63	14	15	0	-	-	-	-	-
D	20	Cartier, Jean-Yves	15	0	3	3	8	0	0	-	-	-	-	-
D	24	Descoteaux, Norm	2	0	1	1	0	0	0	-	-	-	-	-
D	22	Desjardine, Ken	57	2	6	8	36	0	0	-	-	-	-	-
RW	20	Dufour, Guy	9	3	2	5	2	1	0	-	-	-	-	-
C	16	Gaudette, Andre	76	27	44	71	12	0	5	-	-	-	-	-
LW	7	Gendron, Jean-Guy	63	17	33	50	113	5	0	-	-	-	-	-
RW	18	Giroux, Rejean	59	10	12	22	41	4	0	-	-	-	-	-
D	11	Globensky, Alan	4	0	0	0	0	0	0	-	-	-	-	-
RW	11	Golembrosky, Frank	52	8	12	20	44	0	0	-	-	-	-	-
LW	25	Guindon, Bob	71	28	28	56	31	3	1	-	-	-	-	-
LW	6	Guite, Pierre	66	10	8	18	136	1	0	-	-	-	-	-
C	10	Harvey, Michel	40	6	13	19	14	2	0	-	-	-	-	-
D	4	Lacombe, Francois	62	10	18	28	123	0	0	-	-	-	-	-
RW	14	Larose, Paul	28	0	7	7	7	0	0	-	-	-	-	-
RW	15	Leclerc, Rene	60	24	28	52	111	8	2	-	-	-	-	-
G	21	Lemelin, Jacques	9	0	1	1	0	0	0	-	-	-	-	-
D	24	McNamara, Mike	19	0	0	0	5	0	0	-	-	-	-	-
C	12	Parizeau, Michel	75	25	48	73	50	10	1	-	-	-	-	-
C	8	Payette, Jean	71	15	29	44	46	8	0	-	-	-	-	-
C	23	Rouleau, Michel	52	7	14	21	142	0	1	-	-	-	-	-
D	2	Roy, Pierre	64	7	12	19	169	1	0	-	-	-	-	-
LW	11	Selby, Brit	7	0	1	1	4	0	0	-	-	-	-	-
D	3	Tremblay, J. C.	76	14	75	89	32	4	0	-	-	-	-	-

Power Play: 68 goals scored in 317 opportunities (21.5%) with 15 short-handed goals allowed.
Penalty Killing: 58 goals allowed in 289 opportunities (79.9%) with 10 short-handed goals scored.

Goaltending

goaltender	gp	min	ga	en	so	record	gaa	sog	sv%	gp	min	ga	record	gaa
Aubry, Serge	52	3036	182	0	1	25-22-2	3.60	1781	0.897	-	-	-	-	-
Brodeur, Richard	24	1288	102	0	0	5-14-2	4.75	733	0.860	-	-	-	-	-
Lemelin, Jacques	9	435	29	0	0	3-4-1	4.00	199	0.854	-	-	-	-	-

Transactions: Bob Guindon signed to contract, May 1972 • Rights to J. C. Tremblay acquired from Los Angeles, Jun 1972 • Serge Aubry, Richard Brodeur signed to contracts, Jun 1972 • Pierre Guite, Michel Parizeau signed to contracts, Jul 1972 • Rights to Francois Lacombe acquired from Alberta, Jun 1972 • J. C. Tremblay, Alain Caron, Andre Gaudette signed to contracts, Aug 1972 • Jean Gravel signed to contract, Sep 1972 • Jean Gravel and Brit Selby traded to Philadelphia for Frank Golembrosky and Michel Rouleau, Nov 1972

93

1972-1973 WINNIPEG JETS

**Player-Coach
Bobby Hull**

**Bench Coach
Nick Mickoski**

Summary of Games (@ Away, * Overtime)

	date	opponent	score		record	pts	gf-ga		date	opponent	score		record	pts	gf-ga
1.	Oct 12 @	New York	6-4	W	1-0-0	2	6-4	40.	Dec 22 @	Chicago	2-3	L	21-17-2	44	144-122
2.	Oct 13 @	Minnesota	4-3	W	2-0-0	4	10-7	41.	Dec 26	Chicago	3-2	W	22-17-2	46	147-124
3.	Oct 15	Alberta	2-5	L	2-1-0	4	12-12	42.	Jan 1 @	Alberta	3-7	L	22-18-2	46	150-131
4.	Oct 17 @	Alberta	*2-3	L	2-2-0	4	14-15	43.	Jan 7 @	Minnesota	6-2	W	23-18-2	48	156-133
5.	Oct 20	Minnesota	1-1	T	2-2-1	5	15-16	44.	Jan 10	Alberta	6-1	W	24-18-2	50	162-134
6.	Oct 22	Philadelphia	6-3	W	3-2-1	7	21-19	45.	Jan 12	Cleveland	5-3	W	25-18-2	52	167-137
7.	Oct 24	Philadelphia	5-3	W	4-2-1	9	26-22	46.	Jan 14	Cleveland	3-1	W	26-18-2	54	170-138
8.	Oct 27	Chicago	4-2	W	5-2-1	11	30-24	47.	Jan 16	Minnesota	3-1	W	27-18-2	56	173-139
9.	Oct 29	Houston	5-3	W	6-2-1	13	35-27	48.	Jan 19	New England	6-2	W	28-18-2	58	179-141
10.	Oct 31 @	Chicago	1-3	L	6-3-1	13	36-30	49.	Jan 21	New England	2-7	L	28-19-2	58	181-148
11.	Nov 1 @	Minnesota	0-3	L	6-4-1	13	36-33	50.	Jan 23 @	Cleveland	*4-5	L	28-20-2	58	185-153
12.	Nov 3	New York	6-9	L	6-5-1	13	42-42	51.	Jan 24 @	New England	1-6	L	28-21-2	58	186-159
13.	Nov 5	New York	3-1	W	7-5-1	15	45-43	52.	Jan 26 @	Quebec	2-2	T	28-21-3	59	188-161
14.	Nov 6 @	New England	2-6	L	7-6-1	15	47-49	53.	Jan 28 @	Ottawa	5-4	W	29-21-3	61	193-165
15.	Nov 8 @	Quebec	2-3	L	7-7-1	15	49-52	54.	Feb 2	Alberta	3-4	L	29-22-3	61	196-169
16.	Nov 9 @	Ottawa	4-1	W	8-7-1	17	53-53	55.	Feb 4 @	Alberta	5-3	W	30-22-3	63	201-172
17.	Nov 10	Minnesota	1-5	L	8-8-1	17	54-58	56.	Feb 7 @	Houston	2-5	L	30-23-3	63	203-177
18.	Nov 12	Los Angeles	5-2	W	9-8-1	19	59-60	57.	Feb 8 @	Houston	3-1	W	31-23-3	65	206-178
19.	Nov 14	Los Angeles	8-0	W	10-8-1	21	67-60	58.	Feb 10 @	Los Angeles	*6-5	W	32-23-3	67	212-183
20.	Nov 15 @	Alberta	1-3	L	10-9-1	21	68-63	59.	Feb 11 @	Los Angeles	3-0	W	33-23-3	69	215-183
21.	Nov 17 @	Los Angeles	5-1	W	11-9-1	23	73-64	60.	Feb 15 @	Chicago	7-2	W	34-23-3	71	222-185
22.	Nov 19 @	Los Angeles	4-3	W	12-9-1	25	77-67	61.	Feb 16	Houston	7-0	W	35-23-3	73	229-185
23.	Nov 21 @	Houston	4-2	W	13-9-1	27	81-69	62.	Feb 18	Houston	4-2	W	36-23-3	75	233-187
24.	Nov 23 @	Houston	*5-6	L	13-10-1	27	86-75	63.	Feb 25	Philadelphia	5-3	W	37-23-3	77	238-190
25.	Nov 24	Quebec	5-3	W	14-10-1	29	91-78	64.	Feb 27	Chicago	5-1	W	38-23-3	79	243-191
26.	Nov 26	Quebec	4-1	W	15-10-1	31	95-79	65.	Mar 2	Los Angeles	2-1	W	39-23-3	81	245-192
27.	Nov 28	Alberta	3-0	W	16-10-1	33	98-79	66.	Mar 4	Los Angeles	2-1	W	40-23-3	83	247-193
28.	Nov 29 @	Alberta	3-3	T	16-10-2	34	101-82	67.	Mar 6 @	Ottawa	2-5	L	40-24-3	83	249-198
29.	Dec 1	Ottawa	3-4	L	16-11-2	34	104-86	68.	Mar 8 @	Quebec	7-4	W	41-24-3	85	256-202
30.	Dec 3	Minnesota	5-1	W	17-11-2	36	109-87	69.	Mar 10 @	New York	*2-3	L	41-25-3	85	258-205
31.	Dec 5	Quebec	2-4	L	17-12-2	36	111-91	70.	Mar 11	Cleveland	2-11	L	41-26-3	85	260-216
32.	Dec 6	Chicago	7-1	W	18-12-2	38	118-92	71.	Mar 14	New England	5-7	L	41-27-3	85	265-223
33.	Dec 8	Houston	6-2	W	19-12-2	40	124-94	72.	Mar 16	Ottawa	1-6	L	41-28-3	85	266-229
34.	Dec 9 @	Cleveland	*3-2	W	20-12-2	42	127-96	73.	Mar 18	Ottawa	2-4	L	41-29-3	85	268-233
35.	Dec 11 @	New England	3-4	L	20-13-2	42	130-100	74.	Mar 22	Alberta	1-1	T	41-29-4	86	269-234
36.	Dec 13 @	Philadelphia	4-7	L	20-14-2	42	134-107	75.	Mar 25	New York	8-4	W	42-29-4	88	277-238
37.	Dec 15 @	Philadelphia	4-6	L	20-15-2	42	138-113	76.	Mar 28 @	Chicago	*4-3	W	43-29-4	90	281-241
38.	Dec 17 @	New York	4-3	W	21-15-2	44	142-116	77.	Mar 30 @	Cleveland	2-4	L	43-30-4	90	283-245
39.	Dec 21 @	Minnesota	0-3	L	21-16-2	44	142-119	78.	Apr 1 @	Philadelphia	2-4	L	43-31-4	90	285-249

Jets Stars of 1972-1973

Bobby Hull	**Christian Bordeleau**	**Norm Beaudin**	**Ernie Wakely**	**Larry Hornung**	**Bill Sutherland**
51 goals, 103 points	47 goals, 101 points	38 goals, 103 points	26 wins, 2 shutouts	All-star defenseman	14 playoff points

Scoring

pos	#	player	gp	g	a	pts	pim	ppg	shg	gp	g	a	pts	pim
						Regular Season						**Playoffs**		
D	3	Ash, Bob	75	3	14	17	39	0	0	13	1	3	4	4
D/F	21	Asmundson, Duke	78	2	14	16	54	1	0	12	1	2	3	8
RW	11	Beaudin, Norm	78	38	65	103	15	5	0	14	13	15	28	2
RW	19	Black, Milt	77	18	16	34	31	1	0	14	1	3	4	2
C	7	Bordeleau, Christian	78	47	54	101	12	6	3	12	5	8	13	4
C	8	Boyer, Walter	69	6	28	34	27	2	0	14	4	2	6	4
LW	20	Cadle, Brian	56	4	4	8	39	1	0	3	0	0	0	0
D	6	Cuddie, Steve	77	7	13	20	121	0	0	12	0	1	1	10
G	1	Daley, Joe	29	0	1	1	10	0	0	7	0	0	0	0
RW	16	Gratton, Jean-Guy	71	15	12	27	37	1	0	12	1	1	2	4
D	5	Hornung, Larry	77	13	45	58	28	5	2	14	2	9	11	0
LW	9	Hull, Bobby	63	51	52	103	37	14	2	14	9	16	25	16
C	17	Johnson, Dan	76	19	23	42	17	4	0	14	4	1	5	0
LW	14	McDonald, Ab	77	17	24	41	16	7	0	14	2	5	7	2
C	15	Rizzuto, Garth	61	10	10	20	32	4	0	14	0	1	1	14
LW	12	Rousseau, Dunc	75	16	17	33	75	2	0	14	3	2	5	2
D	22	Shmyr, John	7	0	0	0	2	0	0	3	0	1	1	2
C	10	Sutherland, Bill	48	6	16	22	34	1	0	14	5	9	14	9
C	18	Swenson, Cal	75	7	21	28	19	2	0	14	1	5	6	7
G	28	Tumilson, Gord	3	0	0	0	0	0	0	-	-	-	-	-
G	30	Wakely, Ernie	49	0	0	0	0	0	0	7	0	0	0	0
D	2	Woytowich, Bob	62	2	4	6	47	0	0	14	1	1	2	4
D	4	Zanussi, Joe	73	4	21	25	53	1	0	14	2	5	7	6

Power Play: 57 goals scored in 292 opportunities (19.5%) with 5 short-handed goals allowed.
Penalty Killing: 43 goals allowed in 230 opportunities (81.3%) with 7 short-handed goals scored.

Goaltending

goaltender	gp	min	ga	en	so	record	gaa	sog	sv%	gp	min	ga	record	gaa
Daley, Joe	29	1718	83	2	2	17-10-1	2.90	776	0.893	7	422	25	5-2	3.55
Tumilson, Gord	3	138	10	0	0	0-2-0	4.34	65	0.846	-	-	-	-	-
Wakely, Ernie	49	2889	152	2	2	26-19-3	3.14	1411	0.892	7	420	22	4-3	3.14

Transactions: Rights to Danny Johnson acquired in trade with New York, Jun 1972 • Bobby Hull signed to contract, Jun 1972 • Rights to Bob Ash acquired from Minnesota, Jun 1972 • Christian Bordeleau signed to contract, Aug 1972 • Steve Cuddie, Garth Rizzuto signed to contracts, Aug 1972.

1972-1973 Statistical Leaders

Top five in each category.

Goals: 61, Danny Lawson (Philadelphia); 53, Tom Webster (New England); 51, Bobby Hull (Winnipeg), Ron Ward (New York); 50, Andre Lacroix (Philadelphia); 47, Christian Bordeleau (Winnipeg).

Assists: 75, J.-C. Tremblay (Quebec); 74, Andre Lacroix (Philadelphia); 67, Ron Ward (New York); 65, Norm Beaudin (Winnipeg); 63, Bob Sicinski (Chicago)

Points: 124, Andre Lacroix (Philadelphia); 118, Ron Ward (New York); 106, Danny Lawson (Philadelphia); 103, Norm Beaudin (Winnipeg), Bobby Hull (Winnipeg), Tom Webster (New England); 101, Christian Bordeleau (Winnipeg).

Penalty Minutes: 239, John Schella (Houston); 191, Tom Gilmore (Los Angeles); 189, Dick Paradise (Minnesota); 188, John Arbour (Minnesota); 185, Jim Cardiff (Philadelphia).

Power-play Goals: 20, Danny Lawson (Philadelphia); 18, Bobby Sheehan (New York); 16, Andre Lacroix (Philadelphia); 15, Alain Caron (Quebec); 14, Bobby Hull (Winnipeg).

Short-handed Goals: 6, Bob Dillabough (Cleveland), Jim Harrison (Alberta), Terry Ryan (Minnesota); 5, Andre Gaudette (Quebec), Duke Harris (Houston); 4, Tom Earl (New England), Steve King (Ottawa); 3, Christian Bordeleau (Winnipeg), Don Burgess (Philadelphia), Danny Lawson (Philadelphia), Gerry Pinder (Cleveland), Tom Serviss (Los Angeles); 2, shared by many.

Goaltending Minutes: 3702, Jack Norris (Alberta); 3653, Bernie Parent (Philadelphia); 3144, Gerry Cheevers (Cleveland); 3059, Al Smith (New England); 3036, Serge Aubry (Quebec).

Goals Against Average: 2.84, Gerry Cheevers (Cleveland); 2.90, Joe Daley (Winnipeg); 2.91, Russ Gillow (Los Angeles); 3.05, Wayne Rutledge (Houston); 3.06, Jack Norris (Alberta).

Wins: 33, Bernie Parent (Philadelphia); 32, Gerry Cheevers (Cleveland); 31, Al Smith (New England); 28, Jack Norris (Alberta); 26, Ernie Wakely (Winnipeg).

Shutouts: 5, Gerry Cheevers (Cleveland); 4, Mike Curran (Minnesota); 3, Al Smith (New England); 2, shared by many.

Totals for Players With Two or More Teams During 1972-1973

player	teams	gp	g	a	pts	pim	ppg	shg
Benzelock, Jim	Alb, Chi	69	10	13	23	33	3	0
Blanchette, Bernie	Chi, Alb	47	7	7	14	10	3	0
Brown, Bob	Phi, NY	21	0	4	4	8	0	0
Byers, Mike	LA, NE	75	25	21	46	24	2	0
Golembrosky, Frank	Phi, Que	60	8	12	20	44	0	0
Harker, Derek	Alb, Phi	28	0	5	5	46	0	0
Hyndman, Mike	NE, LA	78	12	21	33	32	1	0
Jones, Bob	LA, NY	76	13	19	32	32	1	1
Krupicka, Jarda	LA, NY	36	2	2	4	6	0	0
Mavety, Larry	LA, Phi, Chi	73	10	40	50	89	3	1
Rouleau, Michel	Phi, Que	58	7	15	22	157	0	1
Rydman, Blaine	NY, Min	31	0	1	1	69	0	0
Sarrazin, Dick	NE, Chi	68	7	15	22	2	3	0
Selby, Brit	Que, NE	72	13	30	43	52	2	0
Speck, Fred	Min, LA	75	16	29	45	74	5	0
White, Alton	NY, LA	70	21	21	42	24	2	0
Young, Bill	LA, Min	73	19	18	37	66	8	0

Scoring for the Tiebreaker Game between Minnesota and Alberta at Calgary, Alberta, on April 4, 1973

These statistics do not appear under either teams' regular season or playoff charts.

MINNESOTA: Goals: Connelly, Antonovich, Young, Pearson. **Assists:** Connelly, McMahon, Ball, Young, Arbour 2. **Penalty minutes:** Connelly 2, McMahon 4, Arbour 10. **Goaltending:** Curran 60 minutes, 2 ga, 23 saves.

ALBERTA: Goals: Walters, Baird. **Assists:** Harrison, Patenaude, Wall, Kassian. **Penalty Minutes:** Harrison 2, Hamilton 2, Perkins 2, Patenaude 4, Barrie 22, Baird 6. **Goaltending:** Norris 59 minutes, 4 ga, 20 saves.

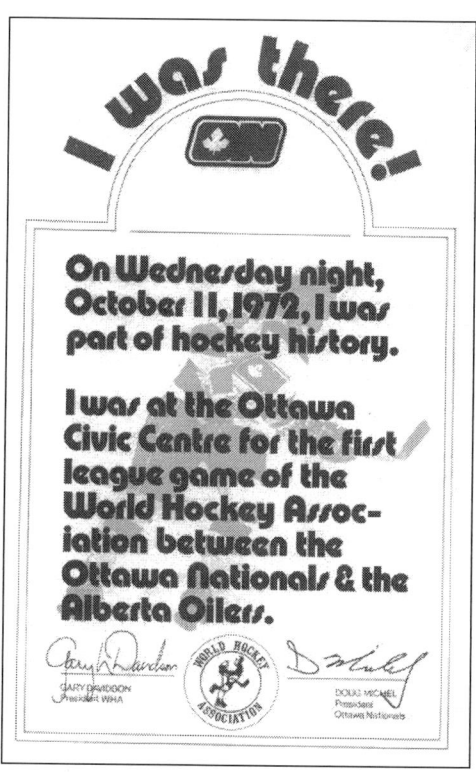

Souvenir keepsake handed out at the first WHA game ever,
Alberta at Ottawa, October 11, 1972.

The Ottawa Nationals and The Lucky Half-Eaten Corn Cob

Athletes are notoriously superstitious, adopting the same rituals if there is any reason to believe it will help their cause. For the players of the Ottawa Nationals at the tail end of the 1972-73 season, their charm was an unlikely object: a half-eaten cob of corn.

By the end of February, the Nats were mired in the cellar at 23-36-4 and coming off an extended slump which saw them lose 14 of their previous 19 games. Before a game against the Oilers on February 25th, Nats trainer Peter Unwin spotted a corn cob lying in a hallway and picked it up. According to *Left Wing and a Prayer*, Doug Michel's account of his team's year in Ottawa,

> He [Unwin] walked into the dressing room and threw it at the first player he saw, who happened to be Gavin Kirk. "Hey," he said, "here's a good luck charm I got from an old Indian."
> "If that's a good luck charm," Kirk said in mock seriousness, "then I guess I better hang onto it."
> ...That night, the club went out and beat the Alberta Oilers on a freak goal scored by Bobby Leduc when his shot caromed off the stick of Oiler Bob Wall.
> ...That dumb corncob became the focal point of a pre-game ceremony. Before going on the ice, Kirk would solemnly remove it from his glove, have six players rub it for luck, and then pry out one single kernel and throw it to Ken Stephanson. Then everybody'd hoot and holler and charge out onto the ice.

With the corncob tradition now firmly established, the rejuvenated Nats went on to win 12 of their next 13 games, broken only by a loss in Los Angeles when they didn't perform their pregame corncob ceremony. Nevertheless, the hot streak helped the team's fortunes immensely and the Nats were rewarded with the fourth and final playoff position in the East when the season came to an end. All thanks to someone's half-eaten cob of corn!

Minor League Affiliations

1972-1973 Affiliations

Alberta Oilers: none. **Chicago Cougars:** Rhode Island Eagles (EHL). **Cleveland Crusaders:** Syracuse Blazers (EHL). **Houston Aeros:** none. **Los Angeles Sharks:** Greensboro Generals (EHL). **Minnesota Fighting Saints:** none. **New England Whalers:** none. **New York Raiders:** Long Island Ducks (EHL). **Ottawa Nationals:** Clinton Comets (EHL). **Philadelphia Blazers:** Roanoke Valley Rebels (EHL). **Quebec Nordiques:** none. **Winnipeg Jets:** none.

1973-1974 Affiliations

Chicago Cougars: Long Island Cougars (NAHL). **Cleveland Crusaders:** Jacksonville Barons (AHL), shared with Winnipeg, Toronto and New England. **Edmonton Oilers:** Winston-Salem Polar Twins (SHL). **Houston Aeros:** Macon Whoopies (SHL, folded midseason). **Los Angeles Sharks:** Greensboro Generals (SHL). **Minnesota Fighting Saints:** Suncoast Suns (SHL, folded midseason). **New England Whalers:** Jacksonville Barons (AHL), shared with Winnipeg, Cleveland and Toronto. **New York Golden Blades - Jersey Knights:** Syracuse Blazers (NAHL). **Quebec Nordiques:** Maine Nordiques (NAHL). **Toronto Toros:** Mohawk Valley Comets (NAHL); Jacksonville Barons (AHL), shared with Winnipeg, Cleveland and New England. **Vancouver Blazers:** Roanoke Valley Rebels (SHL). **Winnipeg Jets:** Jacksonville Barons (AHL), shared with Toronto, Cleveland and New England.

1974-1975 Affiliations

Chicago Cougars: Long Island Cougars (NAHL). **Cleveland Crusaders:** Tulsa Oilers (CHL), shared with Winnipeg, Houston, Indianapolis and Phoenix; Cape Codders (NAHL), shared with New England; Roanoke Valley Rebels (SHL), shared with Winnipeg, Houston, Indianapolis and Phoenix. **Edmonton Oilers:** Flint Generals (IHL), shared with Chicago (NHL); Winston-Salem Polar Twins (SHL), shared with NY Rangers (NHL). **Houston Aeros:** Tulsa Oilers (CHL), shared with Winnipeg, Cleveland, Indianapolis and Phoenix; Roanoke Valley Rebels (SHL), shared with Winnipeg, Cleveland, Indianapolis and Phoenix. **Indianapolis Racers:** Columbus Owls (IHL), shared with St. Louis (NHL); Mohawk Valley Comets (NAHL), shared with Toronto (WHA); Tulsa Oilers (CHL), shared with Winnipeg, Houston, Cleveland and Phoenix; Roanoke Valley Rebels (SHL), shared with Winnipeg, Houston, Cleveland and Phoenix. **Michigan Stags-Baltimore Blades:** Syracuse Blazers (NAHL), shared with San Diego; Greensboro Generals (SHL), shared with Quebec and NY Islanders (NHL); Philadelphia Firebirds (NAHL), shared with San Diego and Philadelphia (NHL). **Minnesota Fighting Saints:** Johnstown Jets (NAHL), shared with Pittsburgh (NHL). **New England Whalers:** Cape Codders (NAHL), shared with Cleveland. **Phoenix Roadrunners:** Tulsa Oilers (CHL), shared with Winnipeg, Houston, Indianapolis and Cleveland; Roanoke Valley Rebels (SHL), shared with Winnipeg, Houston, Indianapolis and Cleveland. **Quebec Nordiques:** Maine Nordiques (NAHL); Greensboro Generals (SHL), shared with Michigan-Baltimore and NY Islanders (NHL). **San Diego Mariners:** Syracuse Blazers (NAHL), shared with Michigan-Baltimore; Philadelphia Firebirds (NAHL), shared with Michigan-Baltimore and Philadelphia (NHL). **Toronto Toros:** Mohawk Valley Comets (NAHL), shared with Indianapolis. **Vancouver Blazers:** Charlotte Checkers (SHL), shared with Buffalo and California (NHL). **Winnipeg Jets:** Tulsa Oilers (CHL), shared with Cleveland, Houston, Indianapolis and Phoenix; Roanoke Valley Rebels (SHL), shared with Cleveland, Houston, Indianapolis and Phoenix. **Cincinnati Stingers:** Hampton Gulls (SHL), as preparation for the Stingers' 1975-76 debut.

1975-1976 Affiliations

Calgary Cowboys: Johnstown Jets (NAHL), shared with Minnesota (WHA) and Kansas City (NHL); Charlotte Checkers (SHL), shared with Buffalo (NHL). **Cincinnati Stingers:** Hampton Gulls (SHL). **Cleveland Crusaders:** Syracuse Blazers (NAHL); Tidewater Sharks (SHL), shared with Buffalo (NHL). **Denver Spurs-Ottawa Civics:** Tucson Mavericks (CHL), shared with Phoenix, San Diego and Houston. **Edmonton Oilers:** Greensboro Generals (SHL), shared with Detroit (NHL). **Houston Aeros:** Tucson Mavericks (CHL), shared with Phoenix, Denver and San Diego. **Indianapolis Racers:** Mohawk Valley Comets (NAHL). **Minnesota Fighting Saints:** Johnstown Jets (NAHL), shared with Calgary and Kansas City (NHL). **New England Whalers:** Cape Codders (NAHL, folded midseason); Baltimore Clippers (AHL), shared with Washington (NHL). **Phoenix Roadrunners:** Tucson Mavericks (CHL), shared with Houston, Denver and San Diego. **Quebec Nordiques:** Maine Nordiques (NAHL). **San Diego Mariners:** Tucson Mavericks (CHL), shared with Denver, Houston and Phoenix; Binghamton Dusters (NAHL), shared with Boston (NHL). **Toronto Toros:** Buffalo Norsemen (NAHL), shared with Buffalo (NHL); Beauce Jaros (NAHL), shared with Montreal (NHL). **Winnipeg Jets:** Roanoke Valley Rebels (SHL).

1976-1977 Affiliations

Birmingham Bulls: Charlotte Checkers (SHL), shared with Winnipeg and Buffalo (NHL). **Calgary Cowboys:** Tidewater Sharks (SHL); Erie Blades (NAHL), shared with Los Angeles and NY Islanders (NHL); **Cincinnati Stingers:** Hampton Gulls (SHL), shared with Minnesota (WHA). **Edmonton Oilers:** Baltimore Clippers (SHL). **Houston Aeros:** Oklahoma City Blazers (CHL), shared with Phoenix; Johnstown Jets (NAHL), shared with Washington (NHL). **Indianapolis Racers:** Mohawk Valley Comets (NAHL), shared with Buffalo (NHL). **Minnesota Fighting Saints:** Syracuse Blazers (NAHL); Hampton Gulls (SHL), shared with Cincinnati. **New England Whalers:** Rhode Island Reds (AHL), shared with Colorado (NHL). **Phoenix Roadrunners:** Oklahoma City Blazers (CHL), shared with Houston. **Quebec Nordiques:** Maine Nordiques (NAHL), shared with Colorado (NHL). **San Diego Mariners:** Port Huron Flags (IHL); Binghamton Dusters (NAHL), shared with Boston (NHL). **Winnipeg Jets:** Charlotte Checkers (SHL), shared with Birmingham and Buffalo (NHL).

1977-1978 Affiliations

Birmingham Bulls: Hampton Gulls (AHL), shared with Cincinnati, New England and Quebec. **Cincinnati Stingers:** Hampton Gulls (AHL), shared with Birmingham, New England and Quebec. **Edmonton Oilers:** none. **Houston Aeros:** Binghamton Dusters (AHL), shared with Pittsburgh (NHL). **Indianapolis Racers:** none. **New England Whalers:** Springfield Indians (AHL), shared with Los Angeles (NHL); Hampton Gulls (AHL), shared with Cincinnati, Birmingham and Quebec. **Quebec Nordiques:** Hampton Gulls (AHL), shared with Cincinnati, New England and Birmingham. **Winnipeg Jets:** none.

1978-1979 Affiliations

Birmingham Bulls, Cincinnati Stingers and Quebec Nordiques: Binghamton Dusters (AHL), shared with Pittsburgh (NHL). **Edmonton Oilers, New England Whalers and Winnipeg Jets:** Springfield Indians (AHL), shared with Los Angeles (NHL). Edmonton was also affiliated with the Dallas Black Hawks (CHL), whom they shared with Vancouver and Los Angeles (NHL). **Indianapolis Racers:** none.

Officials: Referees and Linesmen

Veteran National Hockey League referee Vern Buffey joined the World Hockey Association in early 1972 and was named Chief of Officials and Referee-In-Chief for the new league. In 1975, Bill Friday assumed the Referee-In-Chief post and Bob Frampton the Chief of Officials. Art Skov succeeded Friday in 1977. The remainder of the officiating staff was culled from all areas of major, minor and junior league hockey. Upon the demise of the WHA in 1979, a few of the officials found work in the newly-expanded NHL.

Vern Buffey

Bob Frampton

Bill Friday

Chief of Officials

Vern Buffey (1972-75), Bob Frampton (1975-79).

Referee In Chief

Vern Buffey (1972-75), Bill Friday (1975-77), Art Skov (1977-79).

Referees

Bill Friday, *Steve Dowling, Ron Ego, Bob Kolari, Ron Harris, Wayne Mundey, Peter Moffat,
Ron Fournier, Alan Glaspell, Bob Sloan, Brent Casselman, *Ron Asselstine
(* also served as linesmen).

Linesmen

Dennis Dahlman, Gord Kerr, Ross Keenan, Graham Hern, Michel Chartre, Frank Larochelle, Wayne Bonney,
Jim Brunelle, Ron Foyt, Joe Dame, Dennis Fonteyne, Ken Pierce, Darryl Havrelock, Ron Renneberg,
Steve Barry, Dave Madsen, Bob McPherson, Pierre Belanger, Eric Manship, Gene Kusy, Paul Corcoran,
Mike Pritchard, Don Koharski, Ray Laing, Dan Stone, Gordon Cresswell, Mike Entwistle, Tom Shamshak,
Max Hansen, Tom Marek, Glen Sherwood, Kevin Weatherby, Mike Chee, Dick Haigh, Ray Thomas, Willie Papp

Season II
1973-1974

Flush from the success of season one, the World Hockey Association desperately hoped to avoid any sort of sophomore slump. All twelve teams were back for action, albeit some in different locations than before. The Ottawa Nationals moved to Toronto, becoming the Toros. Philadelphia's Blazers were sold to Canadian interests led by Jim Pattison and relocated across the continent to Vancouver, British Columbia. The struggling New York Raiders were sold and renamed the New York Golden Blades; they would later move to the tiny rink at Cherry Hill, New Jersey, in November, one step ahead of the Madison Square Garden rent collector. The now-renamed Jersey Knights played out the season as wards of the league. Lastly, the Oilers dropped the Alberta prefix in favor of their hometown Edmonton.

The league again featured a Western Division, consisting of Edmonton, Houston, Los Angeles, Minnesota, Vancouver and Winnipeg, while the Eastern Division listed Chicago, Cleveland, New England, New York-Jersey, Quebec and Toronto. The teams played a 78 game schedule under the same scheme as the year before, and the playoffs took in the top four teams from each division.

The league achieved another public relations coup in June 1973, when all-time NHL leading scorer Gordie Howe, a man of near mythical stature, agreed to come out of retirement to play alongside his sons Mark and Marty for the Houston Aeros. Any doubts as to his abilities at age 45 were quickly dispelled when Old Man Howe scored 31 goals and 100 points. The Howes led the tight and well balanced Aeros to their first of two AVCO World Trophies.

The Saints' Mike Walton led all scorers with 57 goals and 117 points, and Andre Lacroix of the nomad Golden Blades-Knights saw 80 of his passes go in the net to lead the league in assists. Gerry Cheevers posted a league-leading four shutouts, but Houston's Don McLeod captured the goals-against race at 2.56 per game, and the league lead in wins with 33. Minnesota's Gord Gallant was chief troublemaker with 223 penalty minutes.

Attendance increased to 2.7 million as the upstart league continued to attract attention and gain respect from all around the sport.

Standings

Eastern Division

	team		gp	w	l	t	pts	pct	gf	ga
1.	**New England WHALERS**		**78**	**43**	**31**	**4**	**90**	**.576**	**291**	**260**
		home	39	26	11	2	54	.692	155	118
		away	39	17	20	2	36	.462	136	142
2.	**Toronto TOROS**		**78**	**41**	**33**	**4**	**86**	**.551**	**304**	**272**
		home	39	25	11	3	53	.679	167	118
		away	39	16	22	1	33	.423	137	154
3.	**Cleveland CRUSADERS**		**78**	**37**	**32**	**9**	**83**	**.532**	**266**	**264**
		home	39	27	8	4	58	.744	147	105
		away	39	10	24	5	25	.321	119	159
4.	**Chicago COUGARS**		**78**	**38**	**35**	**5**	**81**	**.519**	**271**	**273**
		home	39	23	13	3	49	.628	153	132
		away	39	15	22	2	32	.410	118	141
5.	**Québec NORDIQUES**		**78**	**38**	**36**	**4**	**80**	**.513**	**306**	**280**
		home	39	25	10	4	54	.692	179	115
		away	39	13	26	0	26	.333	127	165
6.	**New York GOLDEN BLADES -**		**78**	**32**	**42**	**4**	**68**	**.436**	**268**	**313**
	Jersey KNIGHTS	home	39	22	16	1	45	.577	161	139
		away	39	10	26	3	23	.295	107	174

Western Division

	team		gp	w	l	t	pts	pct	gf	ga
1.	**Houston AEROS**		**78**	**48**	**25**	**5**	**101**	**.647**	**318**	**219**
		home	39	28	9	2	58	.744	170	90
		away	39	20	16	3	43	.551	148	129
2.	**Minnesota FIGHTING SAINTS**		**78**	**44**	**32**	**2**	**90**	**.576**	**332**	**275**
		home	39	26	12	1	53	.679	194	132
		away	39	18	20	1	37	.474	138	143
3.	**Edmonton OILERS**		**78**	**38**	**37**	**3**	**79**	**.506**	**268**	**269**
		home	39	24	14	1	49	.628	152	120
		away	39	14	23	2	30	.385	116	149
4.	**Winnipeg JETS.**		**78**	**34**	**39**	**5**	**73**	**.468**	**264**	**296**
		home	39	26	11	2	54	.692	164	109
		away	39	8	28	3	19	.243	100	187
5.	**Vancouver BLAZERS**		**78**	**27**	**50**	**1**	**55**	**.353**	**278**	**345**
		home	39	19	20	0	38	.487	154	152
		away	39	8	30	1	17	.218	124	193
6.	**Los Angeles SHARKS**		**78**	**25**	**53**	**0**	**50**	**.321**	**239**	**339**
		home	39	17	22	0	34	.436	126	153
		away	39	8	31	0	16	.205	113	186

Award Winners

Most Valuable Player
Gary L. Davidson Trophy
Gordie Howe, Hou

Rookie of the Year
Lou Kaplan Trophy
Mark Howe, Hou

Best Goaltender
Ben Hatskin Trophy
Don McLeod, Hou

Best Defeseman
Dennis Murphy Trophy
Pat Stapleton, Chi

Coach of the Year
Howard Baldwin Trophy
Billy Harris, Tor

Most Gentlemanly
Paul Deneau Trophy
Ralph Backstrom, Chi

1974 World Hockey Association AVCO Cup Champions
Houston Aeros

1974 Playoff Series Results

Eastern Division Semifinals

New England vs. Chicago
Apr 6	Chicago 4 at New England 6
Apr 7	Chicago 3 at New England 4
	(ot: John French, 2:51)
Apr 9	New England 6 at Chicago 8
Apr 10	New England 1 at Chicago 2
	(ot: Ralph Backstrom, 17:45)
Apr 12	Chicago 4 at New England 2
Apr 14	New England 2 at Chicago 0
	(so: Al Smith, 31 saves)
Apr 16	Chicago 3 at New England 2

Toronto vs. Cleveland
Apr 7	Cleveland 0 at Toronto 4
	(so: Gilles Gratton, 29 saves)
Apr 9	Cleveland 3 at Toronto 4
Apr 12	Toronto 4 at Cleveland 2
Apr 13	Toronto 2 at Cleveland 3
	(ot: Wayne Muloin, 4:17)
Apr 15	Cleveland 1 at Toronto 4

Eastern Division Final

Toronto vs. Chicago
Apr 19	Chicago 4 at Toronto 6
Apr 22	Chicago 4 at Toronto 3
Apr 28	Toronto 2 at Chicago 3
Apr 30	Toronto 7 at Chicago 6
May 1	Chicago 3 at Toronto 5
May 4	Toronto 2 at Chicago 9
May 6	Chicago 5 at Toronto 2

Western Division Semifinals

Houston vs. Winnipeg
Apr 8	Houston 5 at Winnipeg 2
Apr 10	Houston 3 at Winnipeg 2
Apr 13	Winnipeg 1 at Houston 10
Apr 14	Winnipeg 4 at Houston 5

Minnesota vs. Edmonton
Apr 6	Edmonton 1 at Minnesota 2
Apr 7	Edmonton 5 at Minnesota 8
Apr 10	Minnesota 6 at Edmonton 2
Apr 12	Minnesota 1 at Edmonton 2
Apr 14	Edmonton 4 at Minnesota 5

Western Division Final

Houston vs. Minnesota
Apr 18	Minnesota 5 at Houston 4
	(ot: Mike Walton, 1:40)
Apr 20	Minnesota 2 at Houston 5
Apr 21	Houston 1 at Minnesota 4
Apr 28	Houston 4 at Minnesota 1
Apr 29	Minnesota 4 at Houston 9
May 1	Houston 3 at Minnesota 1

AVCO World Trophy Championship

Houston vs. Chicago
May 12	Chicago 2 at Houston 3
May 15	Chicago 1 at Houston 6
May 17	Houston 7 at Chicago 4
May 19	Houston 6 at Chicago 2

Penalty Shot: Apr 19: Wayne Dillon (Tor) scored on Cam Newton, Chi

Playoff Standings

Overall Team	w	l	gf	ga	Home Team	w	l	gf	ga	Away Team	w	l	gf	ga
Houston	12	2	71	35	Houston	6	1	42	19	Houston	6	1	29	16
Chicago	8	10	67	72	Toronto	5	2	28	20	Chicago	4	6	33	39
Toronto	7	5	45	43	Minnesota	4	2	21	18	Toronto	2	3	17	23
Minnesota	6	5	39	40	Chicago	4	4	34	33	Minnesota	2	3	18	22
New England	3	4	23	24	New England	2	2	14	14	New England	1	2	9	10
Edmonton	1	4	14	22	Edmonton	1	1	4	7	Winnipeg	0	2	5	15
Cleveland	1	4	9	18	Cleveland	1	1	5	6	Edmonton	0	3	10	15
Winnipeg	0	4	9	23	Winnipeg	0	2	4	8	Cleveland	0	3	4	12

Championship Series Summaries

The Houston Aeros won their first AVCO Championship with a four-game sweep of the Chicago Cougars. Gordie Howe had 8 assists, while Murray Hall had five goals and two assists. The Cougars were the season's Cinderella story: after compiling the league's worst record in 1972-73, they improved to fourth place and the final playoff berth in the Eastern Division. The Cougars then proceeded to achieve two enormous seven-game upsets of New England and Toronto, each time winning the decisive seventh game on the road. However, the Aeros were waiting, having had 11 days of rest before the start of the finals.

Game 1 • May 12, 1974
Houston 3, Chicago 2

Houston	2	0	1	- 3
Chicago	0	0	2	- 2

1st period: 1. Hou: Hale (Hall, Labossiere) 6:31; 2. Hou: Labossiere (Taylor, Grierson) 9:15
2nd period: No Scoring.
3rd period: 3. Chi: Liddington (Stapleton, Backstrom) 5:42; 4. Chi: Gordon (Mavety, Proceviat) 13:45; 5. Hou: Hughes 15:48.
Shots on goal

Hou on Gill	10	8	11	- 29
Chi on McLeod	8	12	11	- 31

Game 2 • May 15, 1974
Houston 6, Chicago 1

Houston	2	1	3	- 6
Chicago	0	0	1	- 1

1st period: 1. Hou: Hall (Taylor, Lund) 13:21; 2. Hou: Labossiere (P. Popiel, Taylor) 18:08
2nd period: 3. Hou: Hinse (G. Howe, Hughes) 16:50
3rd period: 4. Hou: Sherrit (Mark Howe, G. Howe) 1:59; 5. Hou: Hinse (Lund, Hughes) 2:23; 6. Hou: Taylor (Hall) 13:16; 7. Chi: Rochon 19:44
Shots on goal

Hou on Gill & Newton	12	10	10	- 32
Chi on McLeod	8	11	8	- 27

Game 3 • May 17, 1974
Houston 7, Chicago 4

Chicago	1	3	0	- 4
Houston	3	3	1	- 7

1st period: 1. Hou: Hall 5:19; 2. Hou: Hughes (G. Howe, Hinse) 10:51; 3. Chi: Backstrom 12:17; 4. Hou: Mark Howe (Sherrit, G. Howe) 13:22
2nd period: 5. Hou: Hinse (G. Howe, P. Popiel) 1:34; 6. Hou: Hale (Sherrit) 3:21; 7. Chi: Paiement 5:01; 8. Chi: Morris (Hardy, Gordon) 11:38; 9. Hou: Hinse (Lund, P. Popiel) 14:08; 10. Chi: Mavety (Stapleton, Sicinski) 15:34
3rd period: 11. Hou: Hughes (Hinse) 0:48
Shots on goal

Chi on McLeod	9	10	9	- 28
Hou on Gill & Newton	9	10	11	- 30

Game 4 • May 19, 1974
Houston 6, Chicago 2

Chicago	0	1	1	- 2
Houston	3	3	0	- 6

1st period: 1. Hou: Lund (Hinse, Hale) 14:34; 2. Hou: Hall 15:47; 3. Hou: Hall (P. Popiel, G. Howe) 16:55
2nd period: 4. Hou: Hinse (G. Howe, P. Popiel) 12:40; 5. Hou Labossiere (P. Popiel, Schella) 13:58; 6. Hou: Lund (G. Howe, P. Popiel) 15:52; 7. Chi: J. Popiel (Paiement, Sicinski) 17:29
3rd period: 8. Chi: Morris (Mavety) 10:12
Shots on goal

Chi on McLeod	7	7	16	- 30
Hou on Newton	13	13	7	- 33

Statistical Leaders

Goals: 10, Mike Walton (Min); 9, Murray Hall (Hou), Mark Howe (Hou), Frank Hughes (Hou), Larry Lund (Hou), Rosaire Paiement (Chi); 8, Andre Hinse (Hou), Jan Popiel (Chi)

Assists: 14, Ralph Backstrom (Chi), Gordie Howe (Hou), Larry Lund (Hou), Poul Popiel (Hou); 13, Pat Stapleton (Chi); 12, Wayne Carleton (Tor)

Points: 23, Larry Lund (Hou); 19, Ralph Backstrom (Chi), Mark Howe (Hou); 18, Mike Walton (Min)

Penalty Minutes: 71, Darryl Maggs (Chi); 67, Gord Gallant (Min); 60, Ted Taylor (Hou)

Goaltending Wins: 12, Don McLeod (Hou); 6, Andre Gill (Chi); 5, Gilles Gratton (Tor)

Goals Against Average: 2.49, Don McLeod (Hou); 2.78, Gilles Gratton (Tor); 2.91, Mike Curran (Min)

Splits by Opponent and by Month, Home and Away

Chi Chicago, **Cle** Cleveland, **Edm** Edmonton, **Hou** Houston, **LA** Los Angeles, **Min** Minnesota,
NE New England, **NY-J** New York-Jersey, **Que** Quebec, **Tor** Toronto, **Van** Vancouver, **Wpg** Winnipeg

CHICAGO

Opp.	season	gf-ga	home	gf-ga	away	gf-ga
Cle	2-4-2	30-32	1-2-1	13-16	1-2-1	17-16
Edm	2-4-0	11-17	2-1-0	7-6	0-3-0	4-11
Hou	2-4-0	16-24	2-1-0	12-13	0-3-0	4-11
LA	5-1-0	28-18	2-1-0	13-11	3-0-0	15-7
Min	2-4-0	24-31	1-2-0	15-15	1-2-0	9-16
NE	4-4-0	27-26	2-2-0	12-12	2-2-0	15-14
NY-J	4-4-0	28-26	3-1-0	17-9	1-3-0	11-17
Que	5-3-0	26-28	3-1-0	18-14	2-2-0	8-14
Tor	5-2-1	33-27	2-2-0	16-14	3-0-1	17-13
Van	4-1-1	27-21	2-0-1	15-13	2-1-0	12-8
Wpg	3-4-1	21-23	3-0-1	15-9	0-4-0	6-14
Oct	5-4-1	36-31	1-0-0	4-1	4-4-1	32-30
Nov	6-3-0	35-32	4-1-0	18-15	2-2-0	17-17
Dec	5-9-1	43-56	2-4-1	22-24	3-5-0	21-32
Jan	5-4-1	32-32	3-1-1	20-15	2-3-0	12-17
Feb	6-10-0	50-62	5-4-0	31-33	1-6-0	19-29
Mar	10-4-2	67-54	7-3-1	51-41	3-1-1	16-13
Apr	1-1-0	8-6	1-0-0	7-3	0-1-0	1-3

HOUSTON

Opp.	season	gf-ga	home	gf-ga	away	gf-ga
Chi	4-2-0	24-16	3-0-0	11-4	1-2-0	13-12
Cle	2-2-2	14-18	1-1-1	6-7	1-1-1	8-11
Edm	5-3-0	29-22	3-1-0	15-9	2-2-0	14-13
LA	8-2-0	50-28	4-1-0	25-13	4-1-0	25-15
Min	5-3-0	28-24	2-2-0	13-14	3-1-0	15-10
NE	2-4-0	17-21	1-2-0	9-10	1-2-0	8-11
NY-J	5-1-0	27-9	3-0-0	16-4	2-1-0	11-5
Que	2-3-1	22-22	2-1-0	12-5	0-2-1	10-17
Tor	2-4-0	18-22	2-1-0	12-8	0-3-0	6-14
Van	8-0-0	49-18	4-0-0	25-10	4-0-0	24-8
Wpg	5-1-2	40-19	3-0-1	26-6	2-1-1	14-13
Oct	4-3-1	29-20	2-2-0	14-8	2-1-1	15-12
Nov	7-4-1	48-41	5-1-1	33-21	2-3-0	15-20
Dec	8-5-2	60-41	4-1-1	30-10	4-4-1	30-31
Jan	9-4-0	53-30	7-1-0	39-14	2-3-0	14-16
Feb	11-2-1	67-33	6-1-0	32-14	5-1-1	35-19
Mar	7-7-0	54-52	3-3-0	19-22	4-4-0	35-30
Apr	2-0-0	7-2	1-0-0	3-1	1-0-0	4-1

CLEVELAND

Opp.	season	gf-ga	home	gf-ga	away	gf-ga
Chi	4-2-2	32-30	2-1-1	16-17	2-1-1	16-13
Edm	3-2-1	18-16	3-0-0	10-3	0-2-1	8-13
Hou	2-2-2	18-14	1-1-1	11-8	1-1-1	7-6
LA	5-1-0	26-19	3-0-0	13-9	2-1-0	13-10
Min	3-4-1	24-27	2-2-0	9-9	1-2-1	15-19
NE	3-5-0	17-23	3-1-0	8-6	0-4-0	9-17
NY-J	2-4-2	21-27	1-1-2	11-10	1-3-0	10-17
Que	3-4-1	32-30	3-1-0	18-12	0-3-1	14-18
Tor	5-3-0	25-28	4-0-0	16-11	1-3-0	9-17
Van	3-3-0	30-27	2-1-0	21-11	1-2-0	9-16
Wpg	4-2-0	23-23	3-0-0	14-9	1-2-0	9-14
Oct	6-1-2	33-22	5-0-2	28-18	1-1-0	5-4
Nov	4-7-1	41-54	2-2-0	12-13	2-5-1	29-41
Dec	7-7-1	38-39	6-2-0	23-16	1-5-1	15-23
Jan	6-6-1	42-42	5-0-0	26-10	1-6-1	16-32
Feb	5-6-1	44-46	5-3-0	30-24	0-3-1	14-22
Mar	9-5-3	68-61	4-1-2	28-24	5-4-1	40-37

LOS ANGELES

Opp.	season	gf-ga	home	gf-ga	away	gf-ga
Chi	1-5-0	18-28	0-3-0	7-15	1-2-0	11-13
Cle	1-5-0	19-26	1-2-0	10-13	0-3-0	9-13
Edm	4-4-0	23-28	3-1-0	13-9	1-3-0	10-19
Hou	2-8-0	28-50	1-4-0	15-25	1-4-0	13-25
Min	2-6-0	27-40	2-2-0	15-17	0-4-0	12-23
NE	1-5-0	15-31	1-2-0	7-12	0-3-0	8-19
NY-J	3-3-0	30-30	1-2-0	15-19	2-1-0	15-11
Que	2-4-0	16-31	2-1-0	12-10	0-3-0	4-21
Tor	2-4-0	19-22	2-1-0	8-6	0-3-0	11-16
Van	3-5-0	20-28	1-3-0	7-15	2-2-0	13-13
Wpg	4-4-0	24-25	3-1-0	17-12	1-3-0	7-13
Oct	3-7-0	23-36	1-4-0	13-23	2-3-0	10-13
Nov	6-9-0	47-56	4-4-0	26-26	2-5-0	21-30
Dec	4-8-0	40-56	2-3-0	16-22	2-5-0	24-34
Jan	7-7-0	45-51	5-1-0	20-12	2-6-0	25-39
Feb	1-10-0	27-50	1-6-0	19-32	0-4-0	8-18
Mar	3-12-0	51-86	3-4-0	26-34	0-8-0	25-52
Apr	1-0-0	6-4	1-0-0	6-4	0-0-0	0-0

EDMONTON

Opp.	season	gf-ga	home	gf-ga	away	gf-ga
Chi	4-2-0	17-11	3-0-0	11-4	1-2-0	6-7
Cle	2-3-1	16-18	2-0-1	13-8	0-3-0	3-10
Hou	3-5-0	22-29	2-2-0	13-14	1-3-0	9-15
LA	4-4-0	28-23	3-1-0	19-10	1-3-0	9-13
Min	5-3-0	33-30	2-2-0	14-14	3-1-0	19-16
NE	2-3-1	21-24	1-2-0	11-15	1-1-1	10-9
NY-J	5-1-0	31-19	2-1-0	17-10	3-0-0	14-9
Que	2-3-1	22-24	1-2-0	11-12	1-1-1	11-12
Tor	4-2-0	22-18	3-0-0	11-7	1-2-0	11-11
Van	4-6-0	28-42	3-2-0	16-13	1-4-0	12-29
Wpg	3-5-0	28-31	2-2-0	16-13	1-3-0	12-18
Oct	6-1-0	33-19	5-1-0	27-17	1-0-0	6-2
Nov	9-5-0	48-39	5-1-0	28-15	4-4-0	20-24
Dec	5-9-0	42-52	3-3-0	23-22	2-6-0	19-30
Jan	5-8-0	48-56	3-4-0	25-25	2-4-0	23-31
Feb	5-7-0	36-50	4-3-0	23-24	1-4-0	13-26
Mar	7-6-3	53-45	4-2-1	26-17	3-4-2	27-28
Apr	1-1-0	8-8	0-0-0	0-0	1-1-0	8-8

MINNESOTA

Opp.	season	gf-ga	home	gf-ga	away	gf-ga
Chi	4-2-0	31-24	2-1-0	16-9	2-1-0	15-15
Cle	4-3-1	27-24	2-1-1	18-15	2-2-0	9-9
Edm	3-5-0	30-33	1-3-0	16-19	2-2-0	14-14
Hou	3-5-0	24-28	1-3-0	10-15	2-2-0	14-13
LA	6-2-0	40-27	4-0-0	23-12	2-2-0	17-15
NE	4-1-1	26-21	3-0-0	16-11	1-1-1	10-10
NY-J	2-4-0	23-21	2-1-0	17-9	0-3-0	6-12
Que	4-2-0	32-23	2-1-0	17-11	1-2-0	15-12
Tor	2-4-0	22-34	1-2-0	12-17	1-2-0	10-17
Van	5-3-0	36-25	4-0-0	20-6	1-3-0	16-19
Wpg	7-1-0	41-15	4-0-0	29-8	3-1-0	12-7
Oct	4-4-1	27-29	3-1-0	15-11	1-3-1	12-18
Nov	7-6-0	57-46	5-2-0	34-21	2-4-0	23-25
Dec	8-7-0	50-55	4-4-0	30-30	4-3-0	20-25
Jan	9-4-0	50-49	3-3-0	35-26	1-4-0	15-23
Feb	11-2-1	68-39	5-1-1	37-21	6-1-0	31-18
Mar	9-6-0	71-57	5-1-0	34-23	4-5-0	37-34
Apr	1-0-0	9-0	1-0-0	9-0	0-0-0	0-0

NEW ENGLAND

Opp.	season	gf-ga	home	gf-ga	away	gf-ga
Chi	4-4-0	26-27	2-2-0	14-15	2-2-0	12-12
Cle	5-3-0	23-17	4-0-0	17-9	1-3-0	6-8
Edm	3-2-1	24-21	1-1-1	9-10	2-1-0	15-11
Hou	4-2-0	21-17	2-1-0	11-8	2-1-0	10-9
LA	5-1-0	31-15	3-0-0	19-8	2-1-0	12-7
Min	1-4-1	21-26	1-1-1	10-10	0-3-0	11-16
NY-J	8-1-1	39-21	5-0-0	18-8	3-1-1	21-13
Que	3-5-0	22-31	2-2-0	10-17	1-3-0	12-14
Tor	3-4-1	33-36	2-2-0	19-17	1-2-1	14-19
Van	4-2-0	33-27	3-0-0	18-9	1-2-0	15-18
Wpg	3-3-0	18-22	1-2-0	10-7	2-1-0	8-15
Oct	7-3-1	36-26	4-1-1	20-14	3-2-0	16-12
Nov	7-6-0	57-53	5-3-0	39-34	2-3-0	18-19
Dec	8-5-0	45-40	6-2-0	29-23	2-3-0	16-17
Jan	6-5-1	50-49	5-1-0	32-22	1-4-1	18-27
Feb	6-6-1	39-41	2-2-0	12-13	4-4-1	27-28
Mar	9-5-1	63-47	4-1-1	22-8	5-4-0	41-39
Apr	0-1-0	1-4	0-1-0	1-4	0-0-0	0-0

TORONTO

Opp.	season	gf-ga	home	gf-ga	away	gf-ga
Chi	2-5-1	27-33	0-3-1	13-17	2-2-0	14-16
Cle	3-5-0	28-25	3-1-0	17-9	0-4-0	11-16
Edm	2-4-0	18-22	2-1-0	11-11	0-3-0	7-11
Hou	4-2-0	22-18	3-0-0	14-6	1-2-0	8-12
LA	4-2-0	22-19	3-0-0	16-11	1-2-0	6-8
Min	4-2-0	34-22	2-1-0	17-10	2-1-0	17-12
NE	4-3-1	36-33	2-1-1	19-14	2-2-0	17-19
NY-J	4-3-1	32-33	2-1-1	16-10	2-2-0	16-23
Que	5-5-0	31-30	2-3-0	15-16	3-2-0	16-14
Van	6-0-0	30-19	3-0-0	15-10	3-0-0	15-9
Wpg	3-2-1	24-18	3-0-0	14-4	0-2-1	10-14
Oct	2-7-3	36-45	0-4-2	15-23	2-3-1	21-22
Nov	8-5-0	43-37	4-1-0	20-12	4-4-0	23-25
Dec	9-6-0	72-49	6-2-0	38-18	3-4-0	34-31
Jan	6-6-1	53-56	5-2-1	43-32	1-4-0	12-24
Feb	8-5-0	48-40	4-0-0	16-8	4-5-0	32-32
Mar	7-4-0	47-43	5-2-0	32-23	2-2-0	15-20
Apr	1-0-0	3-2	1-0-0	3-2	0-0-0	0-0

NEW YORK-JERSEY

Opp.	season	gf-ga	home	gf-ga	away	gf-ga
Chi	4-4-0	26-28	3-1-0	17-11	1-3-0	9-17
Cle	4-2-2	27-21	3-1-0	17-10	1-1-2	10-11
Edm	1-5-0	19-31	0-3-0	9-14	1-2-0	10-17
Hou	1-5-0	9-27	1-2-0	5-11	0-3-0	4-16
LA	3-3-0	30-30	1-2-0	11-15	2-1-0	19-15
Min	4-2-0	21-23	3-0-0	12-6	1-2-0	9-17
NE	1-8-1	21-39	1-3-1	13-21	0-5-0	8-18
Que	4-4-0	31-35	4-0-0	21-10	0-4-0	10-25
Tor	3-4-1	33-32	2-2-0	23-16	1-2-1	10-16
Van	5-1-0	29-21	2-1-0	16-14	3-0-0	13-7
Wpg	2-4-0	22-26	2-1-0	17-11	0-3-0	5-15
Oct	2-7-2	24-44	2-5-0	17-27	0-2-2	7-17
Nov	5-7-0	30-44	3-2-0	16-13	2-5-0	14-31
Dec	8-6-0	45-40	6-1-0	33-19	2-5-0	12-21
Jan	7-6-0	49-50	3-2-0	19-14	4-4-0	30-36
Feb	4-8-1	48-60	3-3-1	30-28	1-5-0	18-32
Mar	6-6-1	65-62	5-3-0	46-38	1-3-1	19-24
Apr	0-2-0	7-13	0-0-0	0-0	0-2-0	7-13

VANCOUVER

Opp.	season	gf-ga	home	gf-ga	away	gf-ga
Chi	1-4-1	21-27	1-2-0	8-12	0-2-1	13-15
Cle	3-3-0	27-30	2-1-0	16-9	1-2-0	11-21
Edm	6-4-0	42-28	4-1-0	29-12	2-3-0	13-16
Hou	0-8-0	18-49	0-4-0	8-24	0-4-0	10-25
LA	5-3-0	28-20	2-2-0	13-13	3-1-0	15-7
Min	3-5-0	25-36	3-1-0	19-16	0-4-0	6-20
NE	2-4-0	27-33	2-1-0	18-15	0-3-0	9-18
NY-J	1-5-0	21-29	0-3-0	7-13	1-2-0	14-16
Que	2-4-0	18-29	2-1-0	10-9	0-3-0	8-20
Tor	0-6-0	19-30	0-3-0	9-15	0-3-0	10-15
Wpg	4-4-0	32-34	3-1-0	17-14	1-3-0	15-20
Oct	3-8-0	33-54	2-5-0	18-35	1-3-0	15-19
Nov	6-6-0	46-42	5-3-0	36-25	1-3-0	10-17
Dec	6-8-0	48-52	4-3-0	26-25	2-5-0	22-27
Jan	4-10-0	56-71	2-4-0	24-24	2-6-0	32-47
Feb	4-6-0	46-43	3-1-0	28-12	1-5-0	18-31
Mar	3-11-1	45-72	2-4-0	18-29	1-7-1	27-43
Apr	1-1-0	4-11	1-0-0	4-2	0-1-0	0-9

QUEBEC

Opp.	season	gf-ga	home	gf-ga	away	gf-ga
Chi	3-5-0	28-26	2-2-0	14-8	1-3-0	14-18
Cle	4-3-1	30-32	3-0-1	18-14	1-3-0	12-18
Edm	3-2-1	24-22	1-1-1	12-11	2-1-0	12-11
Hou	3-2-1	22-22	2-0-1	17-10	1-2-0	5-12
LA	4-2-0	31-16	3-0-0	21-4	1-2-0	10-12
Min	2-4-0	23-32	1-2-0	12-15	1-2-0	11-17
NE	5-3-0	31-22	3-1-0	14-12	2-2-0	17-10
NY-J	4-4-0	35-31	4-0-0	25-10	0-4-0	10-21
Tor	5-5-0	30-31	2-3-0	14-16	3-2-0	16-15
Van	4-2-0	29-18	3-0-0	20-8	1-2-0	9-10
Wpg	1-4-1	23-28	1-1-1	12-7	0-3-0	11-21
Oct	8-4-0	50-34	3-1-0	19-9	5-3-0	31-25
Nov	4-8-2	49-53	2-3-2	25-24	2-5-0	24-29
Dec	5-6-1	41-41	3-2-1	24-18	2-4-0	17-23
Jan	7-5-0	44-37	7-0-0	36-14	0-5-0	8-23
Feb	9-5-0	64-58	6-1-0	40-24	3-4-0	24-34
Mar	5-8-1	58-57	4-3-1	35-26	1-5-0	23-31

WINNIPEG

Opp.	season	gf-ga	home	gf-ga	away	gf-ga
Chi	4-3-1	23-21	4-0-0	14-6	0-3-1	9-15
Cle	2-4-0	23-23	2-1-0	14-9	0-3-0	9-14
Edm	5-3-0	31-28	3-1-0	18-12	2-2-0	13-16
Hou	1-5-2	19-40	1-2-1	13-14	0-3-1	6-26
LA	4-4-0	25-24	3-1-0	13-7	1-3-0	12-17
Min	1-7-0	15-41	1-3-0	7-12	0-4-0	8-29
NE	3-3-0	22-18	1-2-0	15-8	2-1-0	7-10
NY-J	4-2-0	26-22	3-0-0	15-5	1-2-0	11-17
Que	4-1-1	28-23	3-0-0	21-11	1-1-1	7-12
Tor	2-3-1	18-24	2-0-1	14-10	0-3-0	4-14
Van	4-4-0	34-32	3-1-0	20-15	1-3-0	14-17
Oct	4-5-1	34-34	2-0-1	11-7	2-5-0	23-27
Nov	5-8-2	53-57	5-2-0	31-17	0-6-2	22-40
Dec	8-5-1	41-44	6-2-0	27-17	2-3-1	14-27
Jan	7-4-0	47-48	4-1-0	29-15	3-3-0	18-33
Feb	5-8-1	31-46	4-2-1	22-15	1-6-0	9-31
Mar	5-7-0	51-57	5-3-0	39-32	0-4-0	12-25
Apr	0-2-0	7-10	0-1-0	5-6	0-1-0	2-4

1974 All-Star Game

St. Paul Civic Center
St. Paul, Minnesota
January 3, 1974

East

Coach: Jack Kelley (New Engalnd).
Goaltenders: Gerry Cheevers (Cleveland), Gilles Gratton (Toronto), Al Smith (New England)
Defensemen: Jim Dorey, Rick Ley, Brad Selwood (New England), J.C. Tremblay (Quebec), Paul Shmyr (Cleveland), Pat Stapleton (Chicago)
Forwards: Andre Lacroix, Bobby Sheehan (Jersey), Tom Webster, Larry Pleau, Hugh Harris (New England), Serge Bernier, Rejean Houle (Quebec), Rosaire Paiement, Ralph Backstrom (Chicago), Wayne Carleton, Tom Simpson (Toronto), Gerry Pinder, Gary Jarrett (Cleveland)

West

Coach: Bobby Hull (Winnipeg)
Goaltenders: Jack Norris (Edmonton), Ernie Wakely (Winnipeg), John Garrett (Minnesota)
Defensemen: Poul Popiel (Houston), Al Hamilton (Edmonton), Rick Smith (Minnesota), Ralph MacSweyn (Vancouver), Larry Hornung (Winnipeg), Bart Crashley, Gerry Odrowski (Los Angeles).
Forwards: Gordie Howe, Larry Lund, Frank Hughes (Houston), Mike Walton, Wayne Connelly (Minnesota), Marc Tardif (Los Angeles), Ron Climie, Jim Harrison (Edmonton), Fran Huck, Bobby Hull (Winnipeg), Danny Lawson, Bryan Campbell (Vancouver)

MVP: Mike Walton, Minnesota
Did not play: Al Smith, Larry Hornung, Jim Harrison

East 8, West 4

East	5	1	2	- 8
West	1	3	0	- 4

1st period: 1. East: Houle (Bernier, Paiement) 2:11; 2. East: Backstrom (Carleton, Stapleton) 8:02; 3. East: Pleau 10:39; 4. West: Walton (Lawson) 14:55; 5. East: Pinder (Lacroix, Shmyr) 18:38; 6. East: Lacroix (Pinder, Jarrett) 19:12.
2nd period: 7. West: Walton (Hull, Tardif) 7:27; 8. East: Paiement (Backstrom) 9:15; 9. West: Walton (Hamilton, Climie) 16:04; 10. West: Lund (Hughes, Hamilton) 17:28.
3rd period: 11. East: Lacroix (Jarrett, Pinder) 9:17; 12. East: Pleau (Harris, Webster) 18:59.

Shots on goal

East	10	12	10	- 32
West	10	13	7	- 30

Attendance 13,196

1973-1974 Year End All-Star Teams

First Team: Goaltender: Don McLeod, Houston; Defensemen: Pat Stapleton, Chicago and Paul Shmyr, Cleveland; Center: Andre Lacroix, New York-Jersey; Right Wing: Gordie Howe, Houston; Left Wing: Bobby Hull, Winnipeg.

Second Team: Goaltender: Gerry Cheevers, Cleveland; Defensemen: J.-C. Tremblay, Quebec and Al Hamilton, Edmonton; Center: Wayne Carleton, Toronto; Right Wing: Mike Walton, Minnesota; Left Wing: Mark Howe, Houston.

Penalty Shots

date	player, team	goaltender, team	period	time	result
Oct 11	Andre Lacroix, New York	Cam Newton, Chicago	3	18:28	Save
Oct 19	Denis Meloche, Vancouver	Jack Norris, Edmonton	3	15:19	Save
Oct 25	Andre Lacroix, New York	Al Smith, New England	2	8:57	Save
Nov 3	Ron Buchanan, Cleveland	Andre Gill, Chicago	2	7:46	Save
Nov 22	Wayne Connelly, Minnesota	Al Smith, New England	2	10:34	Save
Nov 23	Marc Tardif, Los Angeles	Jack Norris, Edmonton	3	18:12	Save
Dec 22	Gary Veneruzzo, Los Angeles	Don McLeod, Houston	3	15:08	Save
Dec 29	Andre Lacroix, Jersey	Gerry Cheevers, Cleveland	1	19:09	Save
Mar 1	Brian Carlin, Edmonton	Don McLeod, Houston	3	19:50	Score
Mar 10	Ron Garwasiuk, Los Angeles	Mike Curran, Minnesota	2	19:38	Save
Mar 14	Tom Martin, Toronto	Cam Newton, Chicago	2	3:39	Save
Mar 31	Brian Morenz, Jersey	Gerry Cheevers, Cleveland	3	12:22	Save
Apr 1	Frank Hughes, Houston	Al Smith, New England	2	7:10	Save

Attendance Figures

Each team played 39 regular season home games.

team	season total	season avg	g	playoffs total	avg	team	season total	season avg	g	playoffs total	avg
Chicago	192,048	4,924	8	25,093	3,137	New England	232,814	5,970	4	22,064	5,516
Cleveland	242,277	6,212	2	16,203	8,102	NY - Jersey	100,810	2,585	-	-	-
Edmonton	172,737	4,429	2	9,806	4,903	Quebec	311,352	7,983	-	-	-
Houston	265,622	6,811	7	65,356	9,337	Toronto	167,432	4,291	7	51,801	7,400
Los Angeles	208,175	5,338	-	-	-	Vancouver	364,903	9,356	-	-	-
Minnesota	256,772	6,584	6	81,569	13,595	Winnipeg	249,654	6,401	2	17,138	8,569

Total Attendance: 2,764,506   **Average Attendance:** 5,907

1973-1974 Team Thumbnails

Chicago: What a difference a year makes—and the addition of an all-star defenseman. The Cougars went from the league's worst team in 1972-73 to the Cinderella-story of 1974, advancing to the Championship round before falling to the Houston Aeros. Much of this credit can be given to the signing of long-time Blackhawk blueliner Pat "Whitey" Stapleton, who immediately elevated the Cougars' game and made the team competitive. Joining him was former Canadien Ralph Backstrom, who led the team in scoring with 33 goals and 83 points. Rosie Paiement, the team's star performer from 1972-73, came through with 30 goals, while newcomers Bob Liddington and Joe Hardy added 26 and 24 goals respectively. Still, the Cougars started slowly and played at break-even for most of the season before ending the season on a 10-3-2 run, clinching fourth-place (and the final playoff position) in the Eastern Division on the second-to-last game of the year. In the playoffs, the Cougars endured two grueling seven-game series, defeating both New England and Toronto—both times on the road—to advance to the finals. Scoring was balanced as ten players scored ten or more points, while an unlikely hero, backup goaltender Andre Gill, came through with six wins. However, the Aeros burst the Cougars' bubble, defeating Chicago in four straight, to capture the second World Hockey Association championship.

Cleveland: As in 1972-73, the Crusaders were one of the league's best defensive squads, allowing just 264 goals—the third-lowest total in the league—with star goaltender Gerry Cheevers leading the league in games played and shutouts, and second in average and wins. But a pop-gun offense—266 goals, third worst in the league—meant the Crusaders were in a lot of low-scoring games, many ending in ties (their 9 ties would be the most by any WHA team). Only Gary Jarrett scored above 30 goals—he had 31—while Jim Wiste, Gerry Pinder and Grant Erickson each scored 23 goals. Even 1972-73 scoring star Ron Ward, who played for the Crusaders for the last third of the season, could not shake the Crusader attack from the doldrums, despite his 19 goals in 23 games. The Crusaders finished in third place in the Eastern Division with a 37-32-9 record, but were no match for Toronto in the first round of the playoffs, losing the series in five games in which the Crusaders scored just 9 goals.

Edmonton: It was a repeat performance for the Oilers in 1973-74, finishing with a 38-37-3 record, identical to their 1972-73 record. The offense was led by Ron Climie's 38 goals and 74 points, with Jim Harrison's 24 goals and 69 points not far behind. Veteran Len Lunde added 26 goals, while Blair MacDonald (21) and Rusty Patenaude (20) rounded out the offense. Al Hamilton was the best of the backliners, co-leading the team with 45 assists and making the league's all-star squad for the second time in two years. Goaltender Jack Norris—also an all-star nominee—contributed 23 wins and 2 shutouts. Under new bench boss Brian Shaw (and the ever-present watchful eye of Bill Hunter), the Oilers finished third in the Western Division, and a spot in the post-season. Their run for the championship ended quickly, however, with a five-game loss against Minnesota. Blair MacDonald led the Oilers in the playoffs with 4 goals.

Houston: Texas' biggest city became known as the Howes' Town after the Aeros pulled off the biggest signing of 1973, inking all-time scoring great Gordie Howe to a contract to play along-side his two sons, Mark and Marty. Already a solid team with many of the 1972-73 squad carrying over into 1973-74, the addition of the Howes catapulted the Aeros to the top of the league, their 48-25-5 record the league's best, and their 219 goals against by far the league's lowest total. Coached again by Gordie's old linemate in Detroit, Bill Dineen, the Aeros featured a balanced attack led by Frank Hughes' 42 goals, with five others reaching the 30-goal barrier. Young Mark Howe, just 18 years old and alternating on offense and defense, was second with 38 goals. Larry Lund, Murray Hall, Jim Sherrit and Gordie Howe also collected at least 30 scores, with Gordie's 100 points leading the team, dispelling any notions the 45-year old had lost his touch after two years away from the ice. The smothering defense was led by the steady backliners Larry Hale, Gord Kannegiesser, John Schella and Poul Popiel, with Marty Howe (and occasionally Mark) making sure enemy skaters stayed away from the Houston net. On the rare occasion someone got through, Don McLeod was there to kick away the puck, his 2.56 average by far the league's best, and his 33 wins leading the league as well. In the playoffs, Houston swept Winnipeg in the first round, put aside a small challenge by Minnesota in the semifinal round, and swept Chicago in the finals to capture their first World Hockey Association championship, showing the rest of the league Howe it was done.

Los Angeles: After an encouraging 1972-73 in which the Sharks had a winning record and a solid, ornery squad that liked to fight as often as score goals, the bottom fell out from under the team in 1973-74. Certainly, expectations were high, with the signing of the Canadiens' Marc Tardif to a contract, but the team got off to a 5-15-0 start and never recovered. Tardif came through with 40 goals and 70 points, and Gary Veneruzzo added 39 goals, but the Sharks lacked depth and finished with just 239 goals as a team, the league's worst offense. There were injuries, minor-league call-ups and trades, a revolving door of new faces that kept the team from forming any sense

of continuity. There was also the inconvenient fact the team was bankrupt and had lost what few fans it had as the cross-town NHL Kings for once were playing competitive hockey. In February, the team was sold to a pair of Detroit businessmen, and the Sharks played out the string in front of empty seats, their 5-24-0 finish and lame-duck status ensuring no one would come to its games. The Sharks finished a league-worst 25-53-0 and gave up 339 goals. Within a week of the season's end, the team uprooted from Los Angeles and attempted to make a go of it in Detroit the following season.

Minnesota: The Fighting Saints added Mike Walton to the attack in 1973, and the former Maple Leaf liked the wide-open nature of the WHA so much he led the league with 57 goals and 117 points. As a whole, Coach Harry Neale's squad was the league's most potent with the puck, scoring 332 goals. After Walton, both Wayne Connelly and George Morrison cracked the 40-goal mark, while ten other skaters scored in double figures. The Fighting Saints were also capable without the puck, as backliners John Arbour, Terry Ball, Mike McMahon and newcomer Rick Smith (formerly of the Bruins) kept the other teams honest. Goaltending was handled by veteran Mike Curran and rookie John Garrett, both appearing in 40 games and winning at least 20 apiece. Despite the solid line-up, the Fighting Saints had a losing record as late as January, before catching fire and reeling off 17 victories over a 20-game stretch in February and March. Overall, the Saints finished an impressive 44-32-2 and second in the Western Division. After turning aside Edmonton in the first round, the Saints could not overcome the Houston Aeros, losing in six games against the eventual champs.

New England: The reigning champs once again had one of the league's best and deepest teams, and once again finished atop the Eastern Division with 43 wins and 90 points. Under new coach Ron Ryan, the Whalers won consistently behind a three-line deep attack led by Tom Webster's 43 goals, and supported by eight other players who scored 20 or more goals. Mike Byers and Tim Sheehy both collected 29 goals to place second behind Webster. On the defense, it was the same solid set of blueliners as from 1972-73, led by Rick Ley, Jim Dorey, Brad Selwood, Paul Hurley and Ted Green. Al Smith handled the bulk of net duties, winning 30 games and finishing third in average with 3.08 goals allowed per game. The one blemish for the 1973-74 Whalers was the loss of second-year man Terry Caffery, who injured his knee and missed the entire season, the Whalers obviously missing his potent offense. In the playoffs, the Whalers faced off against the Chicago Cougars, who were riding a strong finish into the post-season. The Whalers and Cougars fought for seven games, the Cougars upsetting the Whalers—on Whaler home

ice, no less—in the decisive seventh game. Both John French and Tim Sheehy scored 4 goals to lead the Whaler offense.

New York-Jersey: The Raiders of 1972-73 had failed financially in New York, but the league desired a franchise in the America's biggest city so badly it gambled again, resurrecting the Raiders as the new Golden Blades, again set to play in the Madison Square Garden. The new owners, Lee Matison, Jerry DeLise and Ralf Brent, decked the Blades in purple jerseys and white skates, gimmicks that could not cover the reality of a bankrupt organization. The Golden Blades lasted just 20 games, folding in late November of 1973, and finally, the WHA and New York divorced from one another for good. Within a week, the Jersey Knights were born, playing out of the tiny Cherry Hill arena across the river from Philadelphia. The arena was completely inadequate for major-league hockey, featuring an uneven playing surface, cramped bench-seating for the players, dressing rooms that were so foul many teams opted to change at their hotel, and little seating for the fans, which proved not to be an issue since no one came to see the team anyway. Despite this, the Blades-Knights somehow played the full 78-game schedule. Scoring was led by Andre Lacroix' 31 goals, 80 assists and 111 points. Wayne Rivers also scored 30 goals, and Mike Laughton, Kevin Morrison, Brian Perry, Gene Peacosh and Brian Morenz all collected at least 20 goals. Preventing goals was the team's biggest problem, allowing 313 enemy scores. Long-time defensive great—and former Ranger—Harry Howell was the notable new addition on the blue line, but he could not single-handedly solve the defensive woes of the club. Howell also served as the team's coach while in Cherry Hill. The team would uproot altogether and move to San Diego, California, upon the season's end.

Quebec: The Nordiques made a splash by signing goaltending great Jacques Plante to serve as the team's coach for 1973-74, while Serge Bernier was rescued from hockey Siberia in Los Angeles to come home and play for his kinsmen. Overall, the Nordiques improved by nine points, finishing with a 38-36-4 mark and 80 points, but painfully missing out on the playoffs once again, this time being pushed aside by the Chicago Cougars. On offense, the Nordiques showed hints of what they were capable of, scoring 306 goals (third best in the league), led by Bernier's 37 scores, followed by Alain Caron and Bobby Guindon, who both scored 31. Ex-Canadien Rejean Houle added 27 goals, as did Guy Dufour. J.-C. Tremblay once again was the star of the blue line, assisted ably by Francois Lacombe and newcomer Dale "Red" Hoganson. The goaltending was once again handled by Serge Aubry and Richard Brodeur, with Michel Deguise rotating in nets. Although the record shows Plante was the team's coach for the

entire season, he seemed to lose his drive to coach midway into the season, sometimes leaving the team for short periods and turning over the reins to Maurice Filion. Plante would actually return to the WHA in 1974-75, this time as a player tending the nets for the Oilers. The Nordiques would seek to solve the puzzle of making the playoffs and becoming a force in the league the following year.

Toronto: The Former Nationals by now had escaped the draconian lease arrangement in Ottawa and were now settled in Toronto under the ownership team of John F. Bassett as principal. For this season, however, the new Toros would play their home games at a local university's rink, and ironically, even a handful of games back in Ottawa. Bassett was hedging his hopes on Toronto's well-known hockey fanaticism, where the Maple Leafs were a regional religion. It had long been argued that Toronto could support two major-league hockey teams, and now this claim would be put to the test. The team that had shown talent and late-season improvement while in Ottawa blossomed while in Toronto, still essentially a squad of unknowns. Wayne Carleton, the closest thing on the Toros to a star, was once again the team's leading goal scorer with 37, and point-getter with 92. Tom "Shotgun" Simpson scored 33 goals, while two promising rookies, Wayne Dillon and Pat Hickey, scored 30 and 26 goals respectively, to lead an attack that put in 304 goals for the season. A familiar face, ex-Leaf Carl Brewer, joined up to lead the defense, which retained many of the same blueliners from Ottawa, including Brian Gibbons, Rick Cunningham and Mike Amodeo. Steve Cuddie, a hard-hitting defenseman, came over from Winnipeg to lend help. In goal, the duties were handled again by colorful Gilles Gratton, with vet Les Binkley playing back-up. Coach Billy Harris' boys finished a strong 41-33-4, good for second in the East. In the playoffs, the Toros beat up on Cleveland in the first round before falling to the juggernaut Cougars in seven games.

Vancouver: If Toronto was being tested for its ability to host two major-league hockey teams, so was Vancouver, now host to the Blazers, late of Philadelphia. In Vancouver, the Blazers would go up against the four-year old Canucks, who had done little in their short tenure in the NHL. By now, Bernie Parent and Andre Lacroix were gone, but John McKenzie and Danny Lawson were still around to lead the attack, augmented now by promising rookie Claude St. Sauveur. Lawson proved he wasn't just Lacroix' finisher by scoring 50 goals essentially on his own. St. Sauveur scored 38, with Don Burgess also meeting the 30-goal mark, but the supporting attack was spotty, while the defense was the worst in the league, allowing 345 goals against. Ron Plumb was the best of blueliners, and in goal, Pete Donnelly actually put together a solid season with 21 wins, 3 shutouts and a 3.80 average. Coaching was handled by McKenzie at first, who gave up the role to General Manager Phil Watson, who in turn was replaced by Andy Bathgate. Nothing worked, and the Blazers ended the year on a 4-18-1 streak and a 27-50-1 overall record, well out of a playoff spot. Bathgate would relinquish his coaching role to try and help as a player in 1974-75. The saving grace was that the Canucks had not done well either; whether Vancouver could support two major-league teams still remained an open question.

Winnipeg: The best of the West in 1972-73, the Jets backslid considerably to an unimpressive 34-39-5 record in 1973-74, despite another superb season from Bobby Hull, whose 53 goals and 95 points led the team. But after Hull, there was little to put fear into the opposition. Hull's linemates, Christian Bordeleau and Norm Beaudin, had solid seasons but both fell off their 1972-73 numbers. The Jets were essentially a one-line team; shut them down, or just Bordeleau and Beaudin, and the Jets could be beat. Remarkably, the Jets had the second-worst offense in the WHA, while the defense, consisting mainly of low-scoring conser-vative types, gave the team neither much of a transition game nor much defense, as the team allowed 296 goals against. The goaltending was the team's strong suit, with Joe Daley and Ernie Wakely forming a potent pairing, although both suffered bloated statistics for 1973-74. The Jets did make the playoffs, luckily being in the same division as Vancouver and Los Angeles, but the Aeros tossed Winnipeg aside in four straight. Clearly, Winnipeg realized having Hull alone was not sufficient; the Jets would need to get creative to solve this dilemma, and would look across the Atlantic to make their big moves for 1974-75.

The One and Only...
Hockey Spectacular!

On September 25, 1973, four teams engaged in a unique hockey match at New York's Madison Square Garden, billed as the *World's First Hockey Spectacular*.

The Hockey Spectacular was a promotional ploy cooked up by the New York Golden Blades front office over the summer of 1973, in an attempt to introduce the new Golden Blades (previously the Raiders) in grand fashion. Originally, the date was set for an exhibition match against the Winnipeg Jets and Bobby Hull. But the Blades staff wanted something big, unique and outrageous. The New England Whalers agreed to participate in the exhibition, bringing along with them the AVCO World Trophy to display to the fans. The final piece of the puzzle was the Houston Aeros. With Gordie Howe recently signed, the Aeros agreed to participate, sensing an excellent chance for media exposure. With all parties in agreement, the stage was set for a most unusual match: four teams, one rink, one "game". Not all four teams would play at the same time. A modified series of periods, each fifteen minutes long, was established, each team playing three periods against each opponent once, for a total of six periods.

The Hockey Spectacular featured the first appearance of Gordie Howe and his sons Mark and Marty in Aeros uniforms. In period three, Elder Howe scored a goal 21 seconds into the frame with assists from son Mark and linemate Ed Hoekstra.

The extravaganza featured a number of gimmicks: Snoopy of *Peanuts* fame made an appearance on skates, and model Avril Lund presented Hull and Howe with ceremonial keys and a kiss on the cheek for each.

There were no "winners" in the match, although the Whalers and the Aeros each accounted for three goals. A little over 7,000 people were in attendance.

Winnipeg's Goaltending Woes

For virtually all of the 1973-74 season, Joe Daley and Ernie Wakely provided Winnipeg with dependable goaltending, helping lead the Jets into the 1974 playoffs. Late in the season, Joe Daley became ill and had to be relieved. The Jets did not have a minor league team from which to summon a replacement, so the Toronto Toros loaned the Jets a youngster named Billy Holden to lend a hand. Holden appeared in the Jets' final game of the season, a 4-2 loss against Vancouver. In the game, Holden broke a finger making a save, although the break was not noticed until after the game.

With Holden out, Daley recovered and returned, but now Ernie Wakely became ill. Needing another backup, the Toros again stepped in, loaning another prospect named Frank Blum to the Jets. Daley performed in two playoff games but was not able to play otherwise, allowing Blum an opportunity to play. Blum played the final two games of the series against Houston, allowing 15 goals as the Jets went down in four straight.

Joe Daley, c. 1973. Daley was one of the last goaltenders in professional hockey to go maskless.

Gallery

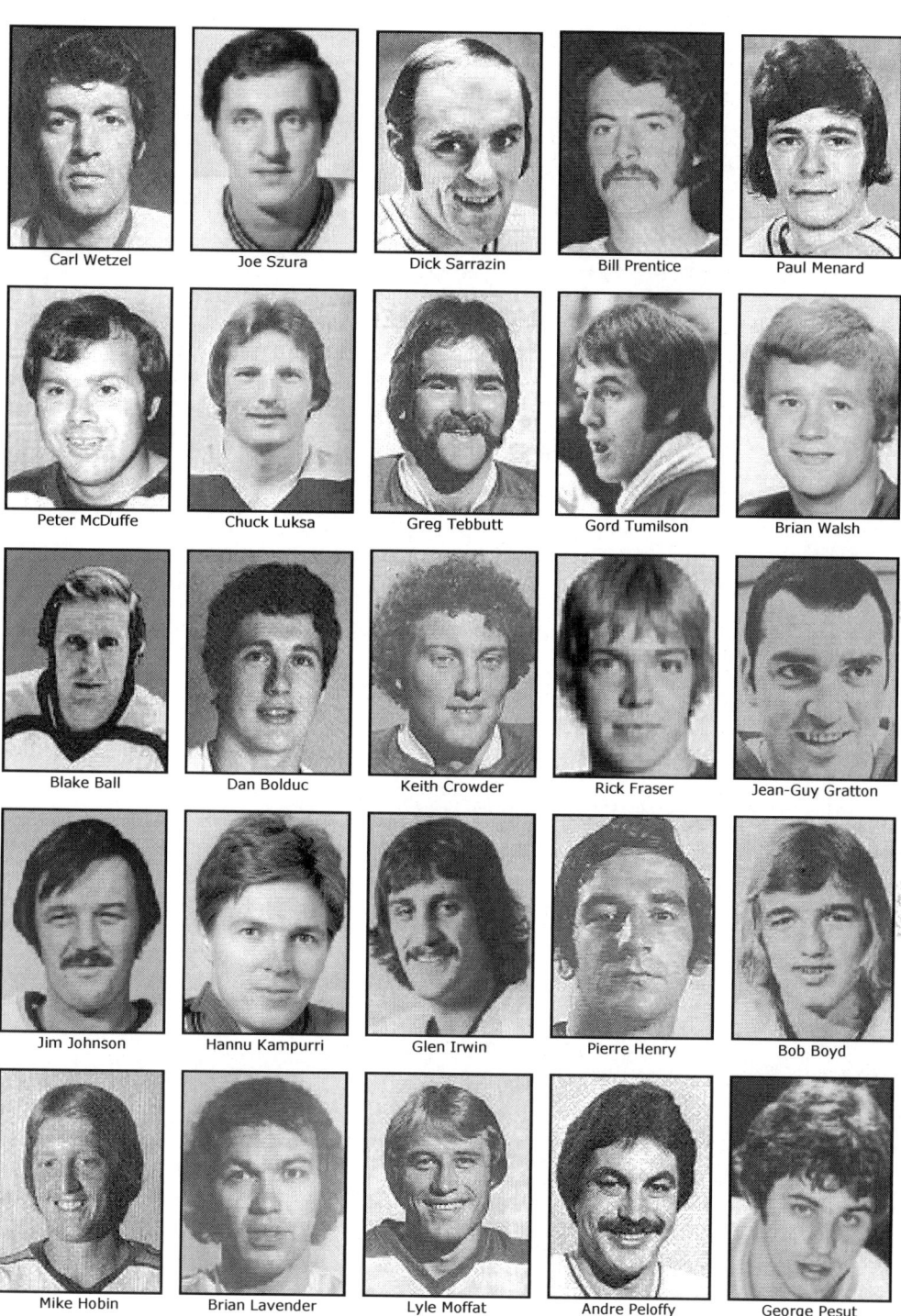

Carl Wetzel   Joe Szura   Dick Sarrazin   Bill Prentice   Paul Menard

Peter McDuffe   Chuck Luksa   Greg Tebbutt   Gord Tumilson   Brian Walsh

Blake Ball   Dan Bolduc   Keith Crowder   Rick Fraser   Jean-Guy Gratton

Jim Johnson   Hannu Kampurri   Glen Irwin   Pierre Henry   Bob Boyd

Mike Hobin   Brian Lavender   Lyle Moffat   Andre Peloffy   George Pesut

1973-1974 Game by Game Line Scores

Date & Teams	Scoring 1 2 3 ot F	Shots 1 2 3 ot F	Goaltenders	Goals & Other Scoring Highlights
October 6				
New York	1 1 0 0 2	5 12 12 2 31	Junkin	Rivers, Sheehan
Cleveland	1 1 0 0 2	11 14 16 4 45	Cheevers	Andrea, Jarrett
October 7				
Chicago	0 2 2 0 4	10 12 16 7 45	Newton	Popiel 2, Zaine, Morris
Toronto	1 2 1 0 4	11 8 14 6 39	Binkley	Simpson 2, Dillon, Gibson
New England	0 2 0 - 2	7 12 5 - 24	Smith	Williams, Pleau
Quebec	0 2 2 - 4	7 12 9 - 28	Aubry	Bernier 2, Caron, Payette
October 9				
Quebec	0 2 0 - 2	6 11 7 - 24	Brodeur	Lacombe, Houle
New England	1 1 1 - 3	8 13 14 - 35	Smith	Sheehy 2, Harris (WG 14:27)
New York	0 1 2 0 3	5 13 13 4 35	Junkin	Sheehan, Perry, Jones
Toronto	0 3 0 0 3	16 14 11 7 48	Gratton	Sentes, Dillon, Selby
October 10				
Winnipeg	1 1 1 0 3	13 13 12 1 39	Wakely	Gratton, McDonald, Beaudin
Vancouver	2 0 1 1 4	9 14 12 5 40	Archambault	Adair 2 (OT 3:50), Lawson, St. Sauveur
October 11				
Quebec	1 1 2 - 4	10 7 15 - 32	Aubry	Houle, Gilbert, Descoteaux, Bernier
Toronto	1 0 0 - 1	11 14 9 - 34	Binkley	Carleton
Chicago	2 2 0 - 4	15 9 7 - 31	Newton	Glenwright, Rochon, Hardy, Popiel
New York	1 0 2 - 3	5 3 9 - 17	Junkin	Rivers, Morrison, Laughton
October 12				
Vancouver	1 2 1 - 4	6 13 14 - 33	Archambault	St. Sauveur, Lawson, O'Donoghue, Gellard
Minnesota	2 2 1 - 5	18 23 10 - 51	Curran	M. Walton, Gallant, Antonovich, Connelly, Heatley
Winnipeg	1 2 1 - 4	11 7 9 - 27	Daley	Beaudin 2, Hull, J. Hargreaves
Edmonton	3 2 1 - 6	19 14 9 - 42	Norris	Harrison 3, McDonald, Climie, Fonteyne
October 13				
Chicago	2 0 2 - 4	6 5 7 - 18	Newton	Morris, Whitlock, Coates, Maggs
New England	2 0 4 - 6	10 4 12 - 26	Landon	Selwood, Blackburn, Sheehy, Ley, Webster, Byers
Quebec	0 3 0 - 3	3 10 11 - 24	Aubry	Houle, Guindon, Dufour
Cleveland	2 1 3 - 6	12 9 8 - 29	Cheevers	Buchanan 2, Wiste, L. Hillman, Pinder, Young
Houston	0 2 2 - 4	12 6 6 - 24	Rutledge	Hughes 2, Hinse, Labossiere (G. Howe: WHA debut, 3 assists)
Los Angeles	0 2 1 - 3	8 7 9 - 24	Gillow	Gordon, Speck, Veneruzzo
October 14				
New England	0 1 0 1 2	6 10 12 1 29	Smith	Byers, Williams (OT 0:18)
New York	0 0 1 0 1	5 7 10 0 22	J. McLeod	Laughton (TG 17:30)
Houston	0 0 2 - 2	4 10 11 - 25	D. McLeod	Hughes 2
Edmonton	4 0 1 - 5	10 12 6 - 28	Norris	Climie 2, Harrison, Baird, Patenaude
Minnesota	1 3 1 - 5	13 13 10 - 36	Garrett	Christiansen, Heatley, McMahon, Klatt, Arbour
Toronto	0 0 2 - 2	9 13 11 - 33	Gratton	Martin, Trottier
Chicago	0 1 1 0 2	11 10 13 3 37	Gill	Hardy, Backstrom
Cleveland	1 1 0 1 3	11 15 13 5 44	Whidden	Krake, Muloin, Buchanan (OT 3:39)
Vancouver	0 2 1 - 3	6 12 7 - 25	Donnelly	St. Sauveur, O'Donoghue, Gellard
Winnipeg	3 2 1 - 6	14 12 12 - 38	Wakely	Hull 2, Bordeleau, Beaudin, Johnson, Gratton
October 15				
Minnesota	2 1 0 0 3	11 14 8 7 40	Curran	M. Walton, Connelly, Christiansen
New England	0 0 3 0 3	10 9 16 8 43	Landon	Pleau 2, Williams
October 16				
Toronto	2 1 0 - 3	13 7 3 - 23	Binkley, Gratton	Simpson, Sentes, Gibson
Los Angeles	0 0 0 - 0	3 15 9 - 27	Gillow	▶ Shutout: Binkley (9 saves), Gratton (18 saves)
October 17				
Winnipeg	0 0 3 - 3	11 11 11 - 33	Daley	Johnson, Bordeleau, Beaudin
New England	1 0 0 - 1	5 6 10 - 21	Smith	Webster
Houston	4 1 2 - 7	17 8 12 - 37	Grahame	Hughes 2, Mk Howe 2, Hinse, Taylor, Labossiere
Vancouver	0 0 2 - 2	5 6 16 - 27	Archambault	Lawson 2
October 18				
Toronto	2 0 0 - 2	8 6 9 - 23	Gratton	Martin, Sentes
Quebec	3 1 1 - 5	11 12 12 - 35	Aubry	Dufour, Guindon, Caron, Bernier, Guite
Winnipeg	2 2 2 - 6	12 11 8 - 31	Wakely	Huck 2, Johnson, Rousseau, Spring, Bordeleau
New York	0 0 1 - 1	10 7 9 - 26	Junkin	Lacroix
Chicago	1 2 4 - 7	10 8 13 - 31	Gill	Nesterenko 2, Backstrom 2, Paiement, Morris, Liddington
Los Angeles	1 0 1 - 2	20 5 13 - 38	Gardner	McDonald, McCaskill
October 19				
New England	0 0 0 - 0	11 11 8 - 30	Landon, Smith	▶ Garrett: shutout (1), 30 saves
Minnesota	0 1 0 - 1	7 7 10 - 24	Garrett	Connelly
Vancouver	1 1 1 - 3	11 11 9 - 31	Donnelly	McKenzie, O'Donoghue, Lawson
Edmonton	1 0 0 - 1	8 13 17 - 38	Norris	Perkins
October 20				
Chicago	0 1 2 - 3	8 11 12 - 31	Gill	Glenwright, Morris, Rochon
Vancouver	2 1 1 - 4	10 12 13 - 35	Donnelly	Burgess 2, C. Campbell, Lawson
New York	1 0 0 - 1	7 10 10 - 27	J. McLeod	Lacroix
Quebec	5 2 1 - 8	14 11 20 - 45	Aubry, Deguise	Parizeau 2, Gendron 2, Bernier, Tremblay, Caron, Houle
Toronto	1 2 1 - 4	10 15 8 - 33	Binkley	Gibson, Carleton, King, Simpson
Cleveland	1 1 4 - 6	8 17 20 - 45	Cheevers	Wiste, Krake, Jarrett, Buchanan, Walker, Young

1973-1974 Game by Game Line Scores

Date & Teams	Scoring 1	2	3	ot	F	Shots 1	2	3	ot	F	Goaltenders	Goals & Other Scoring Highlights
October 21												
Quebec	1	1	1	-	3	8	14	15	-	37	Deguise	Dufour, Parizeau, Bernier
New York	1	1	2	-	4	7	14	13	-	34	Junkin	Lacroix, Perry, Block, Ferguson (WG 10:34)
New England	1	1	2	-	4	10	12	6	-	28	Smith	Byers 2, Webster 2 (WG 16:25)
Toronto	1	0	2	-	3	9	8	13	-	30	Gratton	Trottier 2, King
Cleveland	0	1	1	-	2	7	13	5	-	25	Cheevers	Buchanan, Wiste
Houston	0	0	0	-	0	9	8	22	-	39	Rutledge	▸ Cheevers: shutout (1), 39 saves
Los Angeles	0	3	1	-	4	9	16	10	-	35	Gillow	Veneruzzo 2, McDonald, Serviss
Vancouver	0	0	1	-	1	8	15	10	-	33	Donnelly	Lawson (spoiled Gillow's shutout at 15:08)
Minnesota	1	0	0	0	1	11	10	10	4	35	Curran	Connelly
Winnipeg	1	0	0	1	2	9	11	14	8	42	Daley	Hull, Bordeleau (OT 7:17)
Chicago	0	0	1	-	1	10	12	14	-	36	Newton	Harris (spoiled Norris' shutout at 19:09)
Edmonton	3	0	1	-	4	13	8	11	-	32	Norris	Perkins, Harrison, Gilmore, Fitchner
October 22												
New York	0	0	1	-	1	8	7	15	-	30	Junkin	Laughton
New England	2	2	0	-	4	14	17	12	-	43	Smith	Harris, Hurley, Selwood, French
October 23												
Toronto	1	1	0	-	2	9	9	11	-	29	Binkley, Gratton	King, Simpson
Edmonton	1	1	2	-	4	10	20	16	-	46	Norris, Worthy	Fonteyne, Hamilton, Patenaude, Climie
Cleveland	0	3	0	-	3	10	8	7	-	25	Whidden	Pinder, L. Hillman, Jarrett
Los Angeles	1	1	2	-	4	18	8	12	-	38	Gillow	McDonald 2, Sutherland, Thomas (WG 14:17)
October 24												
Los Angeles	1	0	1	-	2	8	10	9	-	27	Gardner	Walters, Veneruzzo
Houston	1	2	3	-	6	10	11	13	-	34	D. McLeod	Lund 2, Hall, Labossiere, Mk Howe, Hughes
Minnesota	0	1	1	-	2	17	14	11	-	42	Garrett	Gallant, Connelly
New York	2	2	1	-	5	11	15	14	-	40	J. McLeod	Sheehan 2, Lacroix, Ferguson, Morrison
Toronto	0	3	4	-	7	14	5	14	-	33	Gratton	Carleton, Kirk, Brewer, Martin, Simpson, Sentes, King
Vancouver	0	2	2	-	4	4	9	12	-	25	A'bault, Donnelly	B. Campbell, McKenzie, Burgess, Migneault
October 25												
New England	1	3	4	-	8	9	11	9	-	29	Smith	Harris 2, Green, Karlander, Webster, Dorey, Byers, Earl
New York	1	2	0	-	3	10	12	9	-	31	J. McLeod	Jones, Sheehan, Brown
Chicago	1	2	1	-	4	10	7	7	-	24	Newton	Paiement 2, Whitlock, Zaine
Quebec	0	2	0	-	2	12	13	13	-	38	Aubry, Deguise	Bernier, Hoganson
October 26												
Toronto	0	0	3	0	3	8	13	17	3	41	Gratton	Simpson 2, Carleton (TG 19:29)
Winnipeg	0	2	1	0	3	9	13	8	6	36	Wakely	Pratt, Hull, Rousseau
Los Angeles	0	1	0	-	1	10	14	11	-	35	Gillow	Crashley
Cleveland	1	0	2	-	3	13	8	6	-	27	Whidden	Jarrett, Buchanan (WG 14:39), Clearwater
Quebec	1	2	2	-	5	11	9	9	-	29	Deguise	Caron 2, Guite, Dufour, Houle
Minnesota	1	1	2	-	4	5	14	9	-	28	Curran	Heatley, Morrison, Hampson, MacMillan
October 27												
Edmonton	3	0	3	-	6	18	8	10	-	36	Worthy	McKenzie, Patenaude, Gilmore, Harrison, Barrie, MacDonald
Vancouver	0	1	1	-	2	15	18	15	-	48	Donnelly	Lawson, Meloche
Winnipeg	0	1	1	-	2	8	8	5	-	21	Daley	T. Hargreaves, Huck
Minnesota	2	2	1	-	5	12	11	13	-	36	Garrett	MacMillan, Morrison, Klatt, M. Walton, Heatley
Houston	0	2	0	0	2	13	10	13	8	44	Rutledge	Hughes, Lund
Cleveland	1	1	0	0	2	6	11	8	1	26	Cheevers	Edur, Buchanan
Los Angeles	0	1	0	-	1	6	8	12	-	26	Gillow	Veneruzzo
New England	2	1	0	-	3	13	6	6	-	25	Smith	Webster 3
October 28												
Chicago	2	0	1	-	3	11	7	7	-	25	Newton	Maggs, Liddington, Whitlock
Toronto	0	2	0	-	2	12	11	9	-	32	Gratton	Carleton, Simpson
Los Angeles	2	0	0	-	2	19	6	8	-	33	Gillow	Walters, Veneruzzo
New York	0	0	0	-	0	8	4	6	-	18	Junkin	▸ Gillow: shutout (1), 18 saves
Vancouver	0	3	2	-	5	9	17	8	-	34	Gardner	Lawson 3, Tetreault, O'Donoghue
Edmonton	3	2	2	-	7	21	15	14	-	50	Norris	Climie 2, Gilmore, Fonteyne, Falkenberg, Patenaude, Joyal
Quebec	0	2	1	-	3	8	10	9	-	27	Deguise	Beaule, Gaudette, Desjardine (WG 5:51)
Houston	1	0	1	-	2	15	10	10	-	35	D. McLeod	Popiel, Hall
October 30												
Minnesota	1	0	0	-	1	8	8	6	-	22	Curran	Paradise
Houston	2	0	4	-	6	18	11	15	-	44	Rutledge	Grierson 2, Hall 2, Lund, Hughes
Winnipeg	0	1	0	-	1	11	8	12	-	31	Wakely	Snell
Chicago	1	1	2	-	4	7	12	9	-	28	Newton	Hardy 2, Sicinski, Morris
Quebec	0	5	1	-	6	10	11	7	-	28	Aubry	Gilbert 2, Bernier, Gendron, Hoganson, Dufour
Los Angeles	2	1	1	-	4	13	6	13	-	32	Gillow	White, Tardif, Odrowski, McDonald
October 31												
Quebec	3	0	2	-	5	12	4	8	-	24	Deguise	Gilbert, Houle, Caron, Gendron, Beaule
Vancouver	0	1	0	-	1	6	9	4	-	19	Gardner	Gellard
Winnipeg	1	2	1	-	4	8	11	12	-	31	Daley	Snell, Hull, Spring, Johnson
Cleveland	0	4	2	-	6	8	13	11	-	32	Cheevers	Walker 2, Pinder, Buchanan, Wiste, W. Hillman
November 2												
New York	0	0	1	-	1	4	6	6	-	16	J. McLeod	Morrison (spoiled Wakely's shutout at 17:50)
Winnipeg	1	1	1	-	3	10	12	16	-	38	Wakely	Snell 2, Hull
Minnesota	0	2	3	-	5	10	14	18	-	42	Garrett	Connelly 2, Heatley, Morrison, M. Walton
Los Angeles	0	0	1	-	1	5	9	5	-	19	Gillow, Hoganson	Ward
Quebec	0	2	2	-	4	8	6	9	-	23	Aubry	Guite 2, Dufour, Gaudette
Edmonton	1	1	3	-	5	12	16	9	-	37	Worthy	McKenzie 2, Joyal, Patenaude, Harrison (WG 17:04)

1973-1974 Game by Game Line Scores

Date & Teams	Scoring 1 2 3 ot F	Shots 1 2 3 ot F	Goaltenders	Goals & Other Scoring Highlights
November 3				
Vancouver	0 0 0 - 0	10 13 9 - 32	Donnelly, Gardner	▸ Junkin: shutout (1), 32 saves
New York	0 2 2 - 4	8 10 16 - 34	Junkin	Scharf, Lacroix, Morenz, Morrison
Los Angeles	0 1 3 - 4	15 8 10 - 33	Gillow, Hoganson	Ward, McCaskill, Serviss, Gordon
Houston	2 2 2 - 6	8 13 13 - 34	Rutledge	Hughes 3, Hall, G. Howe (first WHA goal), Lund
Chicago	4 1 2 - 7	20 10 8 - 38	Gill	Hardy 2, Whitlock 2, Proceviat, Backstrom, Maggs
Cleveland	1 1 2 - 4	5 14 9 - 28	Whidden	Young, Pinder, Edur, Muloin
Toronto	0 3 2 - 5	4 13 10 - 27	Binkley	Gibson, King, Kirk, Dillon, Trottier (WG 14:51)
New England	1 1 2 - 4	14 12 9 - 35	Smith	Webster 2, Pleau, Selwood
November 4				
Cleveland	1 2 2 - 5	14 10 7 - 31	Cheevers	Pumple, Pinder, Erickson, Jarrett, Buchanan
New England	2 4 1 - 7	12 16 11 - 39	Smith	French 2, Byers 2, Sheehy, Pleau, Harris
New York	1 2 1 - 4	13 7 11 - 31	Junkin	Sheehan, Laughton, Reichmuth, Perry (WG 16:02)
Vancouver	2 0 1 - 3	14 18 23 - 55	Gardner	Gellard, Adair, Burgess
Quebec	2 0 0 - 2	11 9 5 - 25	Deguise	Guindon, Caron
Winnipeg	2 4 2 - 8	9 18 24 - 51	Daley	Hull 4, Gratton, Snell, Woytowich, Beaudin
Los Angeles	2 1 0 - 3	13 11 10 - 34	Gilow	Ward 2, McDonald
Toronto	2 3 1 - 6	12 16 12 - 40	Binkley	King 2, Carleton 2, Sentes, Gibson
Minnesota	2 1 0 - 3	10 14 9 - 33	Garrett	Morrison, M. Walton, MacMillan
Edmonton	0 2 2 - 4	10 17 9 - 36	Norris	McKenzie 2, Patenaude, Joyal (WG 12:09)
November 6				
Winnipeg	1 0 1 0 2	8 6 6 6 26	Wakely	Beaudin, Gratton
Quebec	0 1 1 0 2	9 11 11 2 33	Aubry	Guite, Gilbert
Edmonton	2 2 4 - 8	9 14 17 - 40	Norris	Climie 5, MacDonald, Perkins, Carlyle
New York	0 0 0 - 0	16 10 5 - 31	Junkin	▸ Norris: shutout (1), 31 saves
Los Angeles	1 2 1 0 4	15 9 14 0 38	Hoganson	Tardif 2, Veneruzzo, Sutherland
Chicago	2 1 1 1 5	9 8 13 3 33	Newton	Whitlock, Rochon, Paiement, Harris, Hardy (OT 1:53)
November 7				
New York	0 0 1 - 1	11 14 14 - 39	J. McLeod, Junkin	Rivers Morrison, Gallant
Minnesota	5 1 4 - 10	13 9 14 - 36	Curran	M. Walton 3, Connelly, Arbour, MacMillan, R. Walton, Antonovich,
Los Angeles	0 2 1 - 3	8 7 5 - 20	Hoganson	Tardif, Veneruzzo, White
Vancouver	0 0 1 - 1	8 6 15 - 29	Gardner	Gellard
Winnipeg	1 1 0 - 2	8 9 6 - 23	Daley	Snell, McDonald Harris
New England	6 1 2 - 9	17 11 17 - 45	Landon	Blackburn 2, Sheehy, Pleau, Karlander, Webster, Charlebois, Byers,
Toronto	3 0 2 - 5	9 7 6 - 22	Binkley	Simpson, Sentes, Dillon, Kirk, Hickey (WG 6:11)
Houston	1 2 1 - 4	11 12 6 - 29	Rutledge	Sherrit 2, G. Howe, Labossiere
November 8				
Edmonton	2 1 1 - 4	19 9 12 - 40	Worthy	Joyal, Patenaude, Fonteyne, Climie
Quebec	1 1 1 - 3	14 11 8 - 33	Deguise	Guite 2, Parizeau
November 9				
Toronto	1 1 0 - 2	9 10 9 - 28	Gratton	Dillon, Kirk
Los Angeles	1 3 0 - 4	12 11 8 - 31	Hoganson	Gordon 2, Tardif, Crashley
Vancouver	0 0 1 - 1	10 12 16 - 38	Gardner	Chernoff
Minnesota	0 1 2 - 3	8 15 13 - 36	Garrett	R. Walton, Connelly, Hampson
November 10				
Edmonton	2 4 0 - 6	15 9 5 - 29	Norris	Perkins 2, Gilmore, MacDonald, Patenaude, Joyal
New England	1 1 1 - 3	11 13 5 - 29	Smith	Webster, Sheehy, Ley
Winnipeg	0 1 1 - 2	6 9 12 - 27	Wakely	Hornung, Beaudin
Cleveland	1 1 2 - 4	17 13 10 - 40	Whidden	Buchanan, Jarrett, Krake, Erickson
Quebec	0 3 0 - 3	9 15 6 - 30	Deguise	Houle, Lacombe, Gilbert
New York	0 1 3 - 4	7 7 15 - 29	Junkin, J. McLeod	Jones, Morenz, Lacroix, Laughton (WG 17:12)
Toronto	0 1 1 - 2	8 9 6 - 23	Gratton, Binkley	Martin, Trottier
Chicago	1 1 1 - 3	18 8 13 - 39	Gill	Whitlock, Backstrom, Morris
Vancouver	1 1 1 - 3	8 13 5 - 26	Gardner	Lawson 2, Gellard
Houston	2 1 5 - 8	8 11 11 - 30	D. McLeod	Hughes 2, Hinse 2, Schella, Hall, G. Howe, Sherrit
November 11				
Edmonton	1 3 0 - 4	8 21 9 - 38	Worthy	Gilmore, Joyal, Harrison, Climie
Toronto	2 0 0 - 2	16 14 9 - 39	Gratton, Binkley	B. Gibbons, Carleton
New England	0 0 2 - 2	10 8 10 - 28	Landon	Webster, Smith
Quebec	1 1 1 - 3	17 9 15 - 41	Aubry	Lacombe, Bernier, Guindon
Los Angeles	1 1 0 - 2	11 14 8 - 33	Hoganson, Gillow	Crashley, Tardif
Winnipeg	3 0 3 - 6	7 7 13 - 27	Daley	Johnson 2, Hull, Snell, Spring, Pratt
Cleveland	0 2 2 - 4	11 6 16 - 33	Whidden	Pinder, Krake, Shmyr, Buchanan
Minnesota	2 2 2 - 6	18 14 12 - 44	Curran	Morrison 2, MacMillan, Heatley, R. Walton, Hampson
November 12				
New York	0 1 1 0 2	13 7 8 1 29	J. McLeod	Lacroix, Perry
New England	0 0 2 1 3	12 9 11 3 35	Landon	Pleau, Blackburn, Harris (OT 3:21)
November 13				
Winnipeg	1 1 1 - 3	14 8 13 - 35	Gardner	Johnson, Bordeleau, Pratt
Vancouver	3 0 2 - 5	14 11 14 - 39	Wakely	Gellard, Lawson, St. Sauveur, Adair, O'Donoghue
Los Angeles	0 0 0 - 0	13 5 8 - 26	Wilkie	▸ Norris: shutout (2), 26 saves
Edmonton	2 2 0 - 4	17 11 8 - 36	Norris	Climie 2, McKenzie, Hamilton (Edm: 11th straight win)
Houston	2 1 2 - 5	9 11 20 - 40	Rutledge	Hinse 2, Taylor, Hughes, Hall
Minnesota	0 1 1 - 2	13 9 14 - 36	Garrett	Connelly 2
Cleveland	2 1 2 - 5	5 9 6 - 20	Cheevers	Jarrett 2, Erickson, Wiste, Pinder
Chicago	0 1 1 - 2	12 11 11 - 34	Gill	Paiement, Backstrom

1973-1974 Game by Game Line Scores

Date & Teams	Scoring 1 2 3 ot F	Shots 1 2 3 ot F	Goaltenders	Goals & Other Scoring Highlights
November 15				
New England	2 2 1 - 5	9 11 10 - 30	Smith	Blackburn, Sheehy, Pleau, Harris, Hurley
Quebec	2 0 1 - 3	5 8 6 - 19	Aubry	Tremblay, Gaudette, Bernier
Houston	1 1 0 - 2	8 8 5 - 21	D. McLeod	Hughes, Mk Howe
Chicago	3 0 0 - 3	14 8 16 - 38	Newton	Paiement 2, Whitlock
Minnesota	2 2 1 - 5	17 10 12 - 39	Curran	Ball, M. Walton, Heatley, Smith, Morrison
Vancouver	1 2 4 - 7	16 15 11 - 42	Gardner	St. Sauveur 3 (WG 18:20), Burgess 2, Meloche, Adair
November 16				
Cleveland	2 1 0 1 4	5 2 7 2 16	Cheevers	Jarrett, Buchanan, Edur, Clearwater (OT 3:45)
Los Angeles	1 1 1 0 3	12 5 5 0 22	Gillow	McDonald, Tardif, Ward (TG 19:45)
Edmonton	0 0 1 - 1	8 10 11 - 29	Norris	Harrison
Winnipeg	1 0 2 - 3	16 22 6 - 44	Daley	Hull 2 (WG 17:57), Rousseau
November 17				
Quebec	5 4 1 - 10	17 6 13 - 36	Aubry	Caron 2, Guindon 2, Bernier 2, Gilbert, Guite, Gaudette, Dufour
New England	1 1 2 - 4	11 9 11 - 31	Landon, Smith	Karlander, Harris, Dorey, Pleau
Toronto	0 1 1 - 2	10 14 5 - 29	Gratton	Gibson, Leduc
Chicago	2 3 0 - 5	10 9 11 - 30	Newton	Sicinski, Liddington, Rochon, Whitlock, Coates
Houston	3 0 0 - 3	9 8 10 - 27	Rutledge	Schella, Hall, G. Howe
New York	0 2 0 - 2	8 12 5 - 25	Junkin	Morrison, Lacroix
November 18				
Chicago	0 3 0 - 3	5 17 13 - 35	Newton	Hardy, Mavety, Harris
New York	1 2 2 - 5	11 8 10 - 29	J. McLeod	Morrison, Lacroix, Jones, Laughton, Perry
Winnipeg	2 0 0 - 2	16 6 7 - 29	Wakely	Hull, Woytowich
Toronto	0 3 3 - 6	8 11 18 - 37	Binkley, Gratton	Trottier 2, Selby, Kirk, Gibson, Carleton
Houston	1 0 2 - 3	8 9 10 - 27	Rutledge	Mk Howe, Williamson, Hughes
Quebec	1 4 3 - 8	11 10 12 - 33	Deguise	Guindon 2, Lacombe, Parizeau, Dufour, Caron, Houle
New England	1 2 2 - 5	10 12 11 - 33	Smith	Pleau, Selwood, Byers, Sheehy, Webster
Los Angeles	0 0 2 - 2	7 10 18 - 35	Hoganson	Tardif, McDonald
Minnesota	2 2 1 - 5	13 10 10 - 33	Garrett	Cardwell 2, Heatley, McMahon, Smith
Edmonton	2 0 0 - 2	15 16 14 - 45	Worthy, Norris	Gilmore, MacDonald
Cleveland	0 1 1 - 2	2 11 6 - 19	Cheevers	Buchanan, Walker
Vancouver	0 3 5 - 8	12 12 14 - 38	Gardner	B. Campbell 2, Meloche, Myers, Migneault, Hatoum, Lawson, St. Sauv'r
November 20 ▶ New York franchise transfers to Cherry Hill, New Jersey				
Cleveland	1 2 0 - 3	7 11 10 - 28	Cheevers	Clearwater, Edur, Pumple
Edmonton	1 3 1 - 5	13 16 8 - 37	Norris	Climie 2, Joyal, McCrimmon, MacDonald
Minnesota	1 1 0 - 2	4 6 2 - 12	Curran	Ball, Connelly
Los Angeles	0 3 3 - 6	16 16 10 - 42	Gillow	Odrowski, Walters, Ward, Garwasiuk, Heiskala, Thomas
November 21				
Cleveland	0 1 1 - 2	9 11 11 - 31	Whidden	Krake, Cournoyer
Winnipeg	2 1 3 - 6	13 10 9 - 32	Daley	Bordeleau 3, Beaudin, Huck, Rousseau
New England	1 0 0 - 1	7 5 5 - 17	Landon	Webster
Houston	3 1 0 - 4	11 10 6 - 27	D. McLeod	Sherrit, Szura, G. Howe, Hall
November 22				
Edmonton	1 0 0 - 1	10 12 12 - 34	Worthy	Climie
Vancouver	0 4 3 - 7	6 6 13 - 25	Gardner	Lawson 2, Myers, Migneault, Adair, B. Campbell, St. Sauveur
Chicago	1 1 2 - 4	13 9 10 - 32	Newton	Hardy, Mavety, Glenwright
Los Angeles	0 1 2 - 3	8 11 11 - 30	Gillow	McDonald 3
Toronto	0 1 3 - 4	8 11 11 - 30	Gratton	Carleton 2, Simpson, Trottier
Quebec	1 1 0 - 2	17 13 24 - 54	Aubry	Houle, Tremblay
New England	1 1 3 - 5	12 12 13 - 37	Smith	Pleau 2, Blackburn, Earl, Karlander
Minnesota	0 5 2 - 7	9 19 9 - 37	Garrett	Morrison 2, Cardwell, Connelly, Heatley, Johnson, M. Walton
November 23				
Quebec	1 1 1 - 3	13 9 8 - 30	Deguise	Dufour, Bernier, Gaudette (WG 10:51)
Cleveland	2 0 0 - 2	13 12 9 - 34	Cheevers	Jarrett, Pinder
Edmonton	0 0 0 - 0	5 2 6 - 13	Norris	▶ Wilkie: shutout (1), 13 saves
Los Angeles	1 0 1 - 2	13 12 13 - 38	Wilkie	Tardif, Leblanc
Vancouver	2 0 1 1 4	11 8 8 3 30	Donnelly	Burgess 2 (TG 16:12), Myers, B. Campbell (OT 5:25)
Winnipeg	0 2 1 0 3	11 9 9 0 29	Wakely	Hull, Rousseau, Beaudin
November 24				
Chicago	1 2 0 - 3	15 12 9 - 36	Newton	Backstrom 2, Paiement
Houston	3 1 1 - 5	10 9 10 - 29	D. McLeod	Schella 2, Lund, Mk Howe, Hinse
Toronto	0 1 0 - 1	11 11 6 - 28	Gratton	Gibson
Cleveland	0 0 2 - 2	11 4 12 - 27	Cheevers	Andrea, Pinder (WG 4:00)
November 25				
Winnipeg	1 1 1 - 3	16 14 8 - 38	Daley	Rousseau, Woytowich, Bordeleau
Minnesota	1 2 2 - 5	7 15 16 - 38	Curran	Cardwell 2, Heatley 2 (WG 8:20), M. Walton
Edmonton	1 0 0 - 1	10 7 9 - 26	Norris	McKenzie
Houston	0 1 1 - 2	8 13 13 - 34	D. McLeod	Szura, Hoekstra (WG 2:23)
Quebec	0 0 1 - 1	5 9 12 - 26	Deguise	Bernier
Jersey	0 0 3 - 3	8 11 13 - 32	Junkin	Reichmuth, Morenz, Lacroix
Vancouver	1 1 0 0 2	9 13 19 3 44	Gardner	Adair, B. Campbell
Toronto	1 1 0 1 3	14 10 19 7 50	Gratton	Martin, Dillon, Kirk (OT 8:34)
November 26				
Jersey	0 1 1 - 2	12 13 11 - 36	J. McLeod	Perry, Lacroix
New England	1 3 0 - 4	13 9 8 - 30	Smith	Webster, Harris, Williams, Karlander

1973-1974 Game by Game Line Scores

Date & Teams	Scoring 1 2 3 ot F	Shots 1 2 3 ot F	Goaltenders	Goals & Other Scoring Highlights
November 27				
Quebec	1 0 0 - 1	11 9 8 - 28	Deguise	Dufour
Toronto	1 1 1 - 3	10 9 9 - 28	Gratton	Kirk, Brewer, Martin
Winnipeg	0 2 2 0 4	8 10 9 1 28	Wakely	Rousseau, Spring, Huck, Zanussi
Los Angeles	1 3 0 1 5	14 9 7 3 33	Wilkie	Tardif 2, Leblanc, Veneruzzo, McDonald (OT 1:59)
November 28				
Minnesota	1 1 1 - 3	8 15 8 - 31	Garrett	Smith, McMahon, Hampson
Vancouver	2 1 2 - 5	16 12 7 - 35	Donnelly	St. Sauveur 3 (WG 15:55), Hatoum, Lawson
Winnipeg	0 1 3 0 4	7 15 7 5 34	Daley	Snell 2, Rizzuto, McDonald
Houston	0 3 1 0 4	11 19 10 4 44	D. McLeod	Hughes 2 (TG 19:13), Hall, Sherrit
November 29				
Edmonton	1 1 1 - 3	13 14 7 - 34	Norris	Harrison, McKenzie, MacDonald
Jersey	0 0 2 - 2	17 6 16 - 39	Junkin	Sheehan, Bradley
Houston	1 0 1 - 2	7 6 11 - 24	Rutledge	Hinse, Sherrit
New England	1 1 3 - 5	12 15 15 - 42	Smith	Pleau, Byers, Ley, Selwood, Karlander
Cleveland	3 0 1 0 4	11 7 12 6 36	Cheevers	Heindl, Cournoyer, Shmyr, L. Hillman
Quebec	0 3 1 0 4	10 14 13 7 44	Aubry	Parizeau, Gendron, Dufour, Houle
November 30				
Toronto	0 0 2 - 2	10 4 13 - 27	Gratton	Carleton, Martin (WG 9:35)
Minnesota	0 1 0 - 1	8 7 13 - 28	Curran, Garrett	Connelly
Los Angeles	1 1 3 - 5	11 10 14 - 35	Wilkie	Heiskala, Thomas, Sutherland, Walters, Ward
Winnipeg	0 1 1 - 2	8 10 12 - 30	Wakely	Rizzuto, Hull
December 1				
Los Angeles	1 2 1 1 5	11 13 18 6 48	Wilkie	Ward 3 (OT 7:37), Veneruzzo, McDonald
Chicago	1 2 1 0 4	8 13 9 5 35	Newton	Sicinski, Hardy, Whitlock, Paiement
Edmonton	0 1 1 - 2	6 12 10 - 28	Worthy	Perkins, Harrison
Cleveland	0 2 2 - 4	12 16 17 - 45	Cheevers	Clearwater, Krake, Pinder, Young
Houston	2 1 0 0 3	17 11 4 3 35	D. McLeod	G. Howe, Taylor, Mk Howe
Quebec	1 0 2 0 3	7 10 23 8 48	Deguise	Caron 2 (TG 19:51), Tremblay
December 2				
Edmonton	0 0 0 - 0	9 7 16 - 32	Norris	▶ Whidden: shutout (1), 32 saves
Cleveland	1 2 0 - 3	11 12 7 - 30	Whidden	Wiste 2, Jarrett
Houston	2 0 0 - 2	12 10 10 - 32	Rutledge	Hoekstra, Popiel
Toronto	2 2 1 - 5	11 12 13 - 36	Gratton	Martin 2, Kirk, Leduc, Carleton
Minnesota	1 0 0 - 1	11 3 10 - 24	Garrett	Antonovich
Jersey	0 2 0 - 2	12 10 5 - 27	Junkin	Morrison, Brown
Chicago	1 2 0 - 3	8 16 9 - 33	Newton	Rochon, Mavety, Liddington
New England	2 2 0 - 4	16 15 7 - 38	Smith	Webster 2, Williams, Pleau
Quebec	2 1 0 - 3	10 10 7 - 27	Aubry	Dufour, Gaudette, Lacombe
Winnipeg	0 3 2 - 5	21 11 13 - 45	Daley	Huck 3, Gratton 2
December 4				
Los Angeles	0 0 2 - 2	7 7 14 - 28	Hoganson, Wilkie	Tardif, Slater
Minnesota	5 2 2 - 9	15 9 9 - 33	Garrett	M. Walton 3, Antonovich, Cardwell, R. Walton, McMahon, Johnson, Connelly
Edmonton	1 0 1 - 2	12 10 11 - 33	Worthy	Lunde, McKenzie
Chicago	0 0 0 - 0	8 9 10 - 27	Coutu	▶ Worthy: shutout (1), 27 saves
December 5				
Toronto	0 0 3 - 3	15 12 16 - 43	Gratton	Trottier, Gibson, Carleton
Vancouver	0 1 0 - 1	11 10 10 - 31	Gardner	Myers
Edmonton	0 1 0 - 1	11 8 5 - 24	Norris	Fonteyne
Winnipeg	0 1 2 - 3	6 13 17 - 36	Wakely	Asmundson, Hull, Johnson
Jersey	1 1 0 - 2	6 10 7 - 23	Junkin	Morrison, Sheehan
Houston	1 2 2 - 5	10 14 12 - 36	D. McLeod	Szura 3, Hinse 2
December 6				
Toronto	2 0 1 - 3	13 8 12 - 33	Gratton	Trottier, Hickey, Carleton
Edmonton	1 1 2 - 4	12 17 11 - 40	Worthy	Harrison 2 (WG 18:07), Lunde, Perkins
Cleveland	2 0 0 - 2	20 5 13 - 38	Cheevers	Wiste, Cournoyer
Jersey	1 1 1 - 3	9 13 11 - 33	Junkin	Sheehan, Laughton, Ferguson (WG 11:08)
Houston	0 1 2 - 3	5 4 12 - 21	Rutledge	Mk Howe 2, Lund
Los Angeles	0 3 1 - 4	7 12 9 - 28	Wilkie	Veneruzzo 2, McDonald, Leblanc
December 7				
Vancouver	0 1 0 - 1	11 8 11 - 30	Donnelly	B. Campbell
Minnesota	0 1 2 - 3	8 18 10 - 36	Garrett	Heatley, Morrison (WG 12:03), M. Walton
Toronto	2 0 2 - 4	14 12 12 - 38	Gratton, Blum	Gibson, Simpson, Carleton, B. Gibbons
Winnipeg	2 5 0 - 7	16 14 4 - 34	Daley, Wakely	Johnson 2, Rizzuto, Bordeleau, Huck, Rousseau, Black
December 8				
Quebec	0 1 0 - 1	11 15 14 - 40	Deguise	Guindon
Minnesota	2 2 0 - 4	13 14 15 - 42	Curran	Morrison, Heatley, McMahon, M. Walton
New England	0 1 0 0 1	4 5 9 2 20	Smith	Harris
Cleveland	0 1 0 1 2	15 11 12 5 43	Cheevers	Krake, Wiste (OT 6:29)
Jersey	1 0 2 - 3	7 4 10 - 21	Junkin	Reichmuth, Rivers, Perry
Chicago	0 1 0 - 1	9 9 8 - 26	Coutu	Backstrom
December 9				
Chicago	0 1 0 - 1	6 5 9 - 20	Newton	Morris
Quebec	3 3 0 - 6	11 21 11 - 43	Aubry, Deguise	Payette 2, Parizeau, Caron, Gaudette, Gilbert
Jersey	1 0 0 - 1	10 11 8 - 29	Junkin	Rivers
Winnipeg	0 2 1 - 3	7 11 6 - 24	Wakely	Johnson, Spring, Beaudin

116

1973-1974 Game by Game Line Scores

Date & Teams	Scoring 1 2 3 ot F	Shots 1 2 3 ot F	Goaltenders	Goals & Other Scoring Highlights
December 9				
Cleveland	0 0 2 - 2	4 8 15 - 27	Cheevers	Pinder, Shmyr
New England	3 0 0 - 3	12 17 7 - 36	Smith	Byers 2, Pleau
Houston	3 2 0 - 5	19 9 7 - 35	D. McLeod	Hughes 3, Schella, Lund
Vancouver	1 0 2 - 3	13 6 9 - 28	Gardner, Donnelly	B. Campbell, Myers, Migneault
Minnesota	0 1 0 - 1	12 15 9 - 36	Garrett	McMahon
Toronto	1 1 8 - 10	7 14 18 - 39	Gratton	Hickey 4, Simpson 2, Sentes 2, Dillon, Nistico
December 11				
Minnesota	2 1 2 - 5	10 7 11 - 28	Curran	Antonovich 2, Morrison, Connelly, Hampson
Chicago	1 1 1 - 3	19 17 11 - 47	Newton	Benzelock, Maggs, Whitlock
December 12				
Quebec	0 1 0 0 1	5 12 8 1 26	Brodeur	Gendron
Vancouver	1 0 0 1 2	10 11 19 5 45	Donnelly	Migneault, Plante (OT 3:30)
Los Angeles	4 2 1 - 7	10 11 11 - 32	Wilkie	Gordon 2, Tardif, Walters, Thomas, Veneruzzo, Leblanc
Edmonton	0 1 1 - 2	13 12 11 - 36	Norris, Worthy	Lunde, Perkins
Houston	2 0 1 - 3	10 5 5 - 20	D. McLeod	Hughes, Mk Howe, Labossiere
Winnipeg	0 1 1 - 2	14 8 8 - 30	Daley	Woytowich, Bordeleau
Jersey	3 0 1 - 4	15 5 13 - 33	Junkin	Bradley 2, Brown, Perry
Cleveland	1 1 0 - 2	13 9 3 - 25	Whidden, Cheevers	Jarrett 2
Toronto	3 2 1 - 6	12 5 15 - 32	Gratton	Simpson 2, Gibson, Sentes, Carleton, Trottier
New England	1 2 5 - 8	11 14 19 - 44	Landon, Smith	French 4, Karlander, Harris, Sheehy, Hurley
December 13				
Cleveland	0 1 0 - 1	10 11 10 - 31	Cheevers	Erickson
Toronto	2 0 1 - 3	11 8 10 - 29	Binkley	Simpson, Leduc, Martin
December 14				
Jersey	0 0 1 - 1	13 13 12 - 38	Junkin	Morenz
New England	0 1 2 - 3	9 9 7 - 25	Landon	Earl, Pleau, Sheehy
Houston	3 2 0 - 5	12 9 8 - 29	Rutledge	Sherrit 2, Mk Howe, Lund, Taylor
Minnesota	0 2 0 - 2	10 7 10 - 27	Garrett	Ball 2
Los Angeles	0 0 0 - 0	13 7 12 - 32	Wilkie	▶ Wakely: shutout (1), 32 saves
Winnipeg	0 1 0 - 1	7 12 6 - 25	Wakely	Hull
Quebec	1 3 0 - 4	14 12 8 - 34	Deguise	Caron 2, Leclerc, Guindon
Edmonton	0 0 3 - 3	12 11 18 - 41	Worthy	Gilmore 2, Harrison
December 15				
Los Angeles	0 0 4 - 4	11 7 12 - 30	Gillow	Sutherland 2, Speck, Thomas
Vancouver	2 3 1 - 6	10 10 14 - 34	Donnelly	Myers 2, St. Sauveur, C. Campbell, Chernoff, Lawson
Houston	0 2 0 - 2	4 11 9 - 24	D. McLeod	Popiel, Sherrit
Chicago	4 0 1 - 5	9 7 13 - 29	Coutu	Stapleton 2, Paiement, Mavety, Benzelock
Toronto	0 0 3 - 3	8 9 14 - 31	Binkley, Blum	Simpson, Leduc, Kirk
Cleveland	1 2 1 - 4	14 11 11 - 36	Cheevers	Andrea, Jarrett, L. Hillman, Erickson
December 16				
Chicago	0 0 3 - 3	12 9 14 - 35	Coutu	Hardy, Liddington, Backstrom (WG 14:20)
New England	1 1 0 - 2	9 15 6 - 30	Landon	Williams, Green
Edmonton	1 4 2 - 7	10 15 11 - 36	Norris, Worthy	Harrison 2, MacDonald, Wall, McCrimmon, Baird, Perkins
Jersey	4 1 1 - 6	15 12 17 - 44	Junkin	Rivers 2, Lacroix 2, Laughton, Jones
Cleveland	0 1 1 0 2	11 9 9 4 33	Cheevers	Andrea, Wiste
Houston	0 0 2 0 2	16 10 8 4 38	Grahame	Popiel, Taylor (TG 17:43)
Vancouver	0 1 2 - 3	5 9 13 - 27	Gardner	B. Campbell , Burgess, Lawson
Los Angeles	3 1 1 - 5	18 6 7 - 31	Wilkie	Sutherland, Walters, McDonald, Serviss, Thomas
Quebec	2 0 1 1 4	8 4 9 3 24	Brodeur	Gendron, Dufour, Guindon, Gaudette (OT 4:39)
Toronto	1 1 1 0 3	10 13 10 2 35	Gratton	Kirk 2, Carleton
Minnesota	1 1 1 - 3	17 9 9 - 35	Curran	Connelly 2 (WG 8:53), Heatley
Winnipeg	1 1 0 - 2	7 7 13 - 27	Daley	Beaudin, Snell
December 18				
Edmonton	0 1 1 - 2	11 19 13 - 43	Worthy	Baird, MacDonald
Quebec	1 2 1 - 4	13 7 15 - 35	Deguise	Dufour, Caron, Lacombe, Desjardine
Winnipeg	1 1 1 0 3	4 13 13 4 34	Wakely	Huck, Beaudin, Snell
Chicago	0 0 3 0 3	9 10 13 2 34	Coutu	Backstrom, Sicinski, Liddington (TG 19:18)
Jersey	0 0 1 - 1	5 10 10 - 25	Kurt	Scharf
Toronto	2 0 2 - 4	14 12 10 - 36	Binkley	Hickey, Simpson, Leduc, Selby
Vancouver	2 2 1 - 5	10 9 8 - 27	Donnelly	Plumb 2, Meloche, Plante, Migneault
Los Angeles	2 0 0 - 2	9 16 9 - 34	Wilkie	Veneruzzo 2
December 19				
Edmonton	0 1 1 - 2	9 9 8 - 26	Norris	MacDonald, Climie
New England	2 1 1 - 4	11 12 13 - 36	Smith	French 2, Blackburn, Webster
Winnipeg	0 0 0 - 0	7 7 5 - 19	Daley	▶ D. McLeod: shutout (1), 19 saves
Houston	4 1 5 - 10	10 12 16 - 38	D. McLeod	Mk Howe 2, Hall 2, Grierson 2, Sherrit, G. Howe, Taylor, Lund
Minnesota	1 1 2 - 4	8 11 10 - 29	Garrett	Connelly, Antonovich, Morrison, Klatt
Vancouver	1 1 0 - 2	6 10 9 - 25	Donnelly	St. Sauveur, Burgess
December 21				
Vancouver	1 0 0 - 1	9 8 13 - 30	Gardner	Chernoff
Edmonton	2 1 1 - 4	12 11 9 - 32	Norris	Lunde, McKenzie, Hamilton, Harrison
Los Angeles	0 3 0 - 3	9 15 11 - 35	Gillow	Walters, Tardif, Garwasiuk
Minnesota	1 1 2 - 4	11 15 13 - 39	Curran	Morrison 2, Johnson, R. Walton (WG 8:51)
Houston	1 0 0 - 1	11 13 10 - 34	Rutledge	Lund
Toronto	1 2 0 - 3	16 9 5 - 30	Binkley	Leduc, Carleton, Simpson
Chicago	0 1 0 - 1	7 9 14 - 30	Coutu	Rochon
Jersey	3 2 0 - 5	13 9 10 - 32	Junkin	Sheehan, Ferguson, Bradley, Jones, Reichmuth

117

1973-1974 Game by Game Line Scores

Date & Teams	Scoring 1 2 3 ot F	Shots 1 2 3 ot F	Goaltenders	Goals & Other Scoring Highlights
December 22				
Toronto	1 2 3 - 6	8 9 13 - 30	Gratton	Gibson, Selby, Leduc, Simpson, Cuddie (WG 16:04), Carleton
Quebec	0 2 2 - 4	13 21 16 - 50	Brodeur	Caron 2, Dufour, Gilbert
Winnipeg	1 1 0 - 2	10 8 12 - 30	Wakely	Rousseau, Huck
New England	0 0 0 - 0	8 8 9 - 25	Smith	▸ Wakely: shutout (2), 25 saves
Minnesota	0 0 1 - 1	12 10 6 - 28	Garrett, McCartan	Connelly (spoiled Cheevers' shutout at 19:58)
Cleveland	1 0 1 - 2	17 11 15 - 43	Cheevers	Erickson, Heindl
Los Angeles	2 1 0 - 3	12 13 18 - 43	Gillow	Walters, Ward, Leblanc
Houston	4 3 1 - 8	16 14 11 - 41	D. McLeod	G. Howe 4, Taylor 2, Hughes, Hall
Edmonton	0 1 2 - 3	6 12 13 - 31	Worthy, Norris	Lunde, Gilmore, Baird
Vancouver	4 0 2 - 6	15 8 12 - 35	Donnelly	B. Campbell 2, St. Sauveur 2, Migneault, Plumb
December 23				
Cleveland	0 1 3 - 4	12 8 10 - 30	Whidden	Wiste, Pinder, Erickson, Walker
Minnesota	0 1 1 - 2	13 12 15 - 40	Garrett	Morrison, Cardwell
Winnipeg	1 1 1 - 3	13 11 4 - 28	Daley	Huck, Black, Beaudin
Jersey	1 3 2 - 6	10 11 10 - 31	Junkin	Bradley 2, Ferguson, Brown, Jones, Morenz
Chicago	2 2 2 - 6	12 7 13 - 32	Coutu	Hardy 2, Mavety, Rochon, Stapleton, Backstrom (WG 19:40)
Toronto	1 4 0 - 5	18 20 13 - 51	Binkley	Carleton, Trottier, Gibson, Leduc, Simpson
December 24				
Vancouver	1 0 3 0 4	5 6 9 6 26	Gardner	St. Sauveur 2, MacSweyn, Plumb
New England	3 1 0 1 5	12 8 12 5 37	Landon	Blackburn 2 (OT 8:11), Byers, Webster, Sheehy
December 26				
Chicago	0 2 0 - 2	6 7 14 - 27	Newton	Rochon, Liddington
Winnipeg	2 0 2 - 4	19 10 12 - 41	Wakely	Black, Snell, Hull, T. Hargreaves
New England	0 1 1 1 3	9 11 9 1 30	Landon	Williams, Sheehy, Selwood (OT 2:23)
Houston	2 0 0 0 2	4 13 15 0 32	D. McLeod	Lund, Hinse
Vancouver	0 2 3 - 5	10 8 15 - 33	Donnelly	Burgess, B. Campbell, Chernoff, St. Sauveur, Lawson
Cleveland	1 0 2 - 3	9 11 6 - 26	Whidden	Neale, Erickson, Krake
December 27				
Cleveland	0 1 1 - 2	6 5 6 - 17	Cheevers	Andrea, Shmyr
Quebec	0 3 1 - 4	7 16 16 - 39	Deguise	Leclerc, Dufour, Bernier, Guindon
New England	1 1 3 - 5	14 9 6 - 29	Smith, Landon	Karlander, Selwood, French, Webster, Pleau
Los Angeles	0 1 0 - 1	16 9 5 - 30	Wilkie	Veneruzzo
Minnesota	2 3 0 - 5	16 10 7 - 33	Garrett	Paradise, Klatt, R. Walton, Connelly, Hampson
Edmonton	3 1 0 - 4	13 18 14 - 45	Norris	Baird, Gilmore, McKenzie, Harrison
December 28				
Quebec	1 2 1 - 4	13 12 13 - 38	Brodeur	Gilbert, Parizeau, Bernier, Payette
Chicago	2 2 2 - 6	13 16 13 - 42	Coutu	Rochon 2, Paiement, Hardy, Benzelock, Shmyr
Vancouver	1 1 1 - 3	8 10 13 - 31	Gardner	Migneault, St. Sauveur, Lawson
Jersey	1 1 3 - 5	8 13 18 - 39	Junkin	Lacroix, Peacosh, Rivers, Ferguson, Morenz
December 29				
Winnipeg	0 3 1 - 4	10 15 10 - 35	Daley	Gratton, Hull, McDonald, Huck
Quebec	2 0 1 - 3	8 10 10 - 28	Aubry	Caron 2, Leclerc
Jersey	0 0 0 - 0	12 10 6 - 28	Kurt	▸ Cheevers: shutout (2), 28 saves
Cleveland	1 2 0 - 3	8 13 17 - 38	Cheevers	Andrea, Wiste, Krake
New England	1 1 0 - 2	16 7 10 - 33	Landon	Byers, Blackburn
Edmonton	3 1 2 - 6	13 11 11 - 35	Worthy	Fonteyne, Patenaude, Perkins, Lunde, McAneeley, Climie
Houston	0 1 2 - 3	9 8 9 - 26	Grahame	Mk Howe, G. Howe, Labossiere
Chicago	0 0 0 - 0	15 6 11 - 32	Newton	▸ Grahame: shutout (1), 32 saves
Toronto	4 2 3 - 9	16 14 12 - 42	Binkley	Sentes 2, Dillon 2, Leduc, Martin, Cuddie, Marrin, Carleton
Minnesota	0 1 2 - 3	8 9 16 - 33	Garrett, McCartan	Morrison 2, Connelly
December 30				
Houston	3 2 1 - 6	10 5 8 - 23	D. McLeod	Hall 2, Taylor, Schella, Mk Howe, Labossiere
Los Angeles	1 3 0 - 4	10 7 7 - 24	Wilkie	Veneruzzo 2, Thomas, Leblanc
Winnipeg	0 2 0 - 2	7 11 14 - 32	Wakely	Huck 2
Toronto	0 4 1 - 5	7 14 19 - 40	Gratton	Carleton, Leduc, Dillon, Cuddie, Trottier
Cleveland	1 1 0 - 2	12 11 6 - 29	Whidden	Jarrett, Heindl
Jersey	1 3 2 - 6	11 19 11 - 41	Junkin	Peacosh 2, Morenz, Rivers, Lacroix, Morrison
New England	1 4 0 0 5	13 14 4 5 36	Smith	Sheehy 2, Webster, Byers, Earl
Vancouver	2 2 1 1 6	14 8 6 6 34	Donnelly	Lawson 3 (OT 8:45), Myers, Migneault, Meloche
Chicago	1 1 3 - 5	10 11 7 - 28	Coutu	Liddington 2, Hardy, Paiement, Fleming
Minnesota	1 1 1 - 3	13 7 17 - 37	Garrett	Johnson, Connelly, Klatt
January 1				
Cleveland	0 0 0 - 0	6 8 13 - 27	Cheevers	▸ Binkley: shutout (1), 27 saves
Toronto	1 2 0 - 3	17 12 16 - 45	Binkley	Carleton 2, Dillon
Winnipeg	1 1 1 1 4	15 11 9 1 36	Daley	Johnson, Woytowich, Hull, Huck (OT) 0:46
Edmonton	0 3 0 0 3	6 15 8 0 29	Norris	MacDonald, Baird, Lunde
Vancouver	0 2 2 - 4	7 8 6 - 21	Donnelly	Burgess, Migneault, St. Sauveur, Lawson
Chicago	3 0 2 - 5	10 9 8 - 27	Newton	Whitlock, Stapleton, Morris, P'ment (TG 19:25), B'kstrom (WG 19:38)
January 4				
Edmonton	2 1 0 - 3	8 9 7 - 24	Worthy, Norris	Climie 2, Patenaude
Los Angeles	1 2 1 - 4	7 11 5 - 23	Wilkie	Tardif 2 (WG 4:46), Sutherland, Leblanc
New England	1 3 0 - 4	11 11 8 - 30	Berglund	Pleau, Harris, French, Webster
Winnipeg	1 0 2 - 3	7 4 7 - 18	Wakely	Beaudin, Hull, T. Hargreaves

1973-1974 Game by Game Line Scores

Date & Teams	Scoring 1 2 3 ot F	Shots 1 2 3 ot F	Goaltenders	Goals & Other Scoring Highlights
January 5				
Minnesota	2 1 3 - 6	10 5 11 - 26	Curran	Morrison, Ball, Connelly, Klatt, Hampson, Antonovich (WG 14:25)
Chicago	0 2 3 - 5	14 11 16 - 41	Coutu	Backstrom, Benzelock, Liddington, Hardy, Mavety
New England	0 0 0 - 0	10 6 8 - 24	Berglund	▶ Cheevers: shutout (3), 24 saves
Cleveland	1 0 0 - 1	13 13 11 - 37	Cheevers	Jarrett
Houston	0 0 1 - 1	9 19 9 - 37	D. McLeod	Schella
Jersey	2 0 0 - 2	11 6 7 - 24	Junkin	Peacosh, Morenz
Vancouver	1 0 1 - 2	6 13 10 - 29	Donnelly	Lawson 2
Quebec	3 2 0 - 5	17 14 6 - 37	Brodeur	Caron 2, Houle 2, Leclerc
January 6				
Chicago	0 0 0 - 0	7 12 8 - 27	Gill	▶ Deguise: shutout (1), 27 saves
Quebec	1 1 2 - 4	17 12 10 - 39	Deguise	Bernier, Leclerc, Gaudette, Gilbert
Edmonton	2 2 2 - 6	16 13 11 - 40	Norris	Climie, McAneeley, Hamilton, Patenaude, Baird
Minnesota	2 0 2 - 4	10 8 11 - 29	Garrett	MacMillan, Arbour, R. Walton, Johnson
Houston	3 2 2 - 7	6 20 20 - 46	Rutledge	Mk Howe 2, Taylor, Lund, Hughes, Labossiere, Sherrit
Winnipeg	0 0 1 - 1	7 14 4 - 25	Daley	Huck
Jersey	1 2 1 - 4	13 14 8 - 35	Kurt	Rivers 2, Winograd, Laughton
Toronto	2 0 0 - 2	10 15 15 - 40	Gratton	Hickey, Simpson
Vancouver	1 2 0 - 3	6 10 12 - 28	Gardner	Burgess, Lawson, Cardiff Young, Pinder
Cleveland	4 6 1 - 11	6 12 9 - 27	Cheevers	Jarrett 2, Clearwater 2, Walker, Wiste, L. Hillman, Neale, Andrea,
January 7				
Vancouver	2 2 1 - 5	15 12 6 - 33	Donnelly	Lawson 3, Myers, Burgess
Jersey	0 2 2 - 4	9 13 12 - 34	Junkin	Rivers 2, Boylan, Lacroix
January 8				
Toronto	0 1 2 - 3	18 13 6 - 37	Gratton	Leduc, King, Selby
New England	2 0 0 - 2	11 9 10 - 30	Landon	Williams, Byers
Cleveland	0 0 0 0 - 0	6 7 12 2 - 27	Cheevers	▶ Cheevers: shutout (4), 39 saves
Chicago	0 0 0 0 - 0	8 13 14 4 - 39	Newton	▶ Newton: shutout (1), 27 saves
Winnipeg	0 1 0 - 1	13 7 8 - 28	Wakely	Gratton
Los Angeles	0 2 2 - 4	8 10 10 - 28	Wilkie	Ward, Veneruzzo, Serviss, Leblanc
Edmonton	1 0 1 - 2	6 11 8 - 25	Norris, Worthy	Lunde 2
Houston	4 1 1 - 6	14 12 11 - 37	D. McLeod	Hall 2, Hinse, Mk Howe, Sherrit, Hughes
January 9				
Winnipeg	3 1 2 - 6	10 12 10 - 32	Daley	Hull 2, Bordeleau 2, Asmundson, Beaudin
Vancouver	3 0 1 - 4	10 2 8 - 20	Donnelly	Lawson, St. Sauveur, McKenzie, Burgess
Edmonton	2 2 2 - 6	13 12 12 - 37	Norris	MacDonald, Harrison, McKenzie, Climie, Hamilton, Lunde
Minnesota	2 0 2 - 4	13 10 8 - 31	Curran	Johnson, Christiansen, Morrison, Connelly
January 10				
New England	0 2 4 0 6	9 7 9 2 27	Landon	Harris 2, Dorey, Blackburn, Byers, Webster
Toronto	3 2 1 0 6	9 11 8 1 29	Gratton	Hickey 2, Orr, Dillon, Leduc, Sentes
Los Angeles	1 0 0 - 1	18 8 11 - 37	Wilkie	Veneruzzo
Quebec	1 2 4 - 7	9 9 11 - 29	Brodeur	Houle 3, Dufour 2, Bernier, Leclerc
January 11				
Edmonton	1 0 3 - 4	9 13 13 - 35	Worthy	Harrison, McAneeley, Climie, MacDonald
Winnipeg	3 2 2 - 7	16 14 13 - 43	Wakely	Hull 2, Beaudin, Swenson, Snell, Johnson, Asmundson
January 12				
Los Angeles	1 2 1 - 4	10 6 13 - 29	Hoganson	Tardif 3, Garwasiuk
Cleveland	2 2 1 - 5	9 10 9 - 28	Cheevers	Jarrett 2, Buchanan, Erickson, Wiste
Houston	1 1 3 - 5	7 4 9 - 20	Rutledge	Lund, Mty Howe, Popiel, Hughes, Labossiere
Quebec	0 0 1 - 1	6 8 8 - 22	Deguise	Gilbert (spoiled Rutledge's shutout at 17:53)
Toronto	4 2 0 - 6	13 12 7 - 32	Gratton	Sentes 2, Leduc 2, Hickey, Trottier
Minnesota	1 1 6 - 8	17 15 15 - 47	Curran, Garrett	M. Walton 2, Hampson, Connelly, Smith, R. Walton, Ant'vich, Cardwell
January 13				
Chicago	0 1 0 - 1	8 10 9 - 27	Coutu	Backstrom
Winnipeg	1 1 1 - 3	7 12 9 - 28	Daley	Bordeleau, Snell, Hull
Jersey	1 1 0 - 2	12 13 10 - 35	Kurt	Ferguson, Morrison
Toronto	4 3 0 - 7	16 13 11 - 40	Gratton	Dillon 2, B. Gibbons, Martin, Cuddie, Simpson, Trottier
Minnesota	0 1 1 - 2	10 12 11 - 33	Garrett	M. Walton, Klatt
Cleveland	0 2 2 - 4	12 19 10 - 41	Cheevers	Shmyr, Walker, Krake, Buchanan
Edmonton	0 0 2 - 2	9 8 10 - 27	Norris	McAneeley, MacDonald
Vancouver	3 1 2 - 6	9 7 13 - 29	Donnelly	St. Sauveur 2, Meloche, Myers, Adair, Lawson
Los Angeles	4 2 0 - 6	11 11 10 - 32	Hoganson	Sutherland, Ward, Tardif, Leblanc, White, Veneruzzo
New England	5 1 3 - 9	17 14 14 - 45	Berglund	Webster 2, Blackburn 2, Williams, Danby, Ley, Sheehy, French
January 15				
Minnesota	1 0 0 - 1	11 3 7 - 21	Garrett	Arbour
Edmonton	2 0 2 - 4	7 17 18 - 42	Norris	Wall, Lunde, Hamilton, Gilmore
Quebec	2 2 0 - 4	8 10 8 - 26	Brodeur	Guindon, Lacombe, Gaudette, Bernier
Los Angeles	1 1 4 - 6	15 11 15 - 41	Hoganson	Tardif 2, Walters 2, Thomas, Leblanc
January 16				
Jersey	0 0 2 - 2	6 12 10 - 28	Junkin	Morenz, Howell
New England	1 1 2 - 4	5 8 12 - 25	Landon	Karlander, Williams, French, Harris
Toronto	0 0 1 - 1	9 8 13 - 30	Gratton, Holden	Martin
Houston	2 1 1 - 4	13 20 13 - 46	Rutledge	Mk Howe, G. Howe, Labossiere, Sherrit
January 17				
Vancouver	3 0 1 - 4	6 7 13 - 26	Donnelly	Burgess 2, Hatoum, B. Campbell
Houston	2 2 3 - 7	14 11 9 - 34	D. McLeod	Mk Howe 2, G. Howe, Lund, Schella, Hinse, Sherrit
Chicago	2 3 0 - 5	11 16 4 - 31	Gill	Backstrom 2, Stapleton, Morris, Harris
New England	1 0 1 - 2	9 5 13 - 27	Landon	Sheehy, Webster

1973-1974 Game by Game Line Scores

Date & Teams	Scoring 1 2 3 ot F	Shots 1 2 3 ot F	Goaltenders	Goals & Other Scoring Highlights
January 18				
Cleveland	2 1 0 - 3	11 6 7 - 24	Whidden	Erickson, Jarrett, Krake
Winnipeg	2 3 2 - 7	13 13 11 - 37	Wakely	Hull 2, Snell, Black, Bordeleau, Huck, Zanussi
Toronto	1 0 0 - 1	8 4 11 - 23	Gratton	Kirk
Los Angeles	2 1 1 - 4	9 12 9 - 30	Hoganson	Tardif 2, Sutherland, Ward
Jersey	1 2 1 - 4	10 19 9 - 38	Kurt, Junkin	Block, Scharf, Peacosh, Perry
Edmonton	3 4 0 - 7	14 12 10 - 36	Doyle	Wall, Fonteyne, Climie, McKenzie, Lunde, Patenaude, Harrison
January 19				
Los Angeles	0 2 1 - 3	5 11 8 - 24	J. McLeod	Sutherland 2 (WG 8:09), Leblanc
Houston	0 1 1 - 2	14 17 9 - 40	Rutledge	Hall, Hinse
Minnesota	0 0 2 - 2	5 12 13 - 30	Curran	Hampson, Antonovich
New England	2 1 2 - 5	9 14 12 - 35	Smith	Karlander, French, Harris, Williams, Sheehy
Quebec	1 1 0 - 2	3 11 6 - 20	Deguise	Houle, Parizeau
Chicago	1 1 3 - 5	12 9 19 - 40	Newton	Backstrom 2, Rochon, Coates, Rombough,
Jersey	1 2 1 1 5	13 9 7 1 30	Junkin	Perry 2 (OT 2:36), Laughton, Lacroix, Morrison
Vancouver	1 1 2 0 4	11 13 10 0 34	Gardner	Myers 3 (TG 19:36), Chernoff
January 20				
Vancouver	1 1 1 - 3	12 7 6 - 25	Donnelly	St. Sauveur, Burgess, Chernoff
Los Angeles	0 0 0 - 0	10 7 12 - 29	J. McLeod	▸ Peter Donnelly (1), 29 saves
New England	2 0 2 - 4	7 8 13 - 28	Smith	Sheehy, Ley, Karlander, French
Toronto	2 2 4 - 8	11 19 10 - 40	Gratton	Carleton 2, Martin 2, Hickey 2, Dillon, Leduc
Minnesota	1 1 2 0 4	5 14 15 2 36	Garrett	Klatt 2, M. Walton, Christiansen
Quebec	2 2 0 1 5	26 14 7 7 54	Brodeur	Guite 2, Caron, Dufour, Bernier (OT 7:22)
Cleveland	1 0 1 - 2	5 4 14 - 23	Cheevers	Wiste, Pinder
Edmonton	0 3 2 - 5	6 17 6 - 29	Norris	Hamilton 2, Gilmore 2, Harrison
Jersey	2 0 1 - 3	9 7 16 - 32	Junkin	Perry, Morenz, Laughton
Winnipeg	4 3 2 - 9	14 15 13 - 42	Daley	Hull 3, Gratton 2, Bordeleau, Rousseau, T. Hargreaves, Snell
January 22				
Los Angeles	0 0 1 - 1	6 7 9 - 22	Hoganson	Veneruzzo
Houston	1 0 2 - 3	11 14 7 - 32	D. McLeod	Hughes, Lund, Mk Howe
Jersey	3 2 1 - 6	17 8 8 - 33	Junkin	Peacosh 3, Lacroix 2, Herriman
Edmonton	0 2 0 - 2	8 18 14 - 40	Worthy	Baird, MacDonald
New England	2 1 0 - 3	10 10 6 - 26	Smith	Green, Blackburn, Karlander
Chicago	1 1 3 - 5	12 10 9 - 31	Coutu	Hardy, Morris, Backstrom, Mavety, Popiel
January 23				
Jersey	1 1 2 - 4	16 7 7 - 30	Kurt	Scharf, Laughton, Lacroix, Morrison
Minnesota	0 1 0 - 1	12 13 8 - 33	Garrett	Hampson
Cleveland	1 0 2 - 3	6 14 12 - 32	Whidden, Cheevers	Young 3
Vancouver	4 0 2 - 6	16 7 11 - 34	Donnelly	Chernoff 2, McKenzie, St. Sauveur, Burgess, Lawson
January 24				
Cleveland	3 1 1 - 5	12 5 8 - 25	Cheevers	Neale 2, Erickson, Pinder, Shmyr
Toronto	0 1 2 - 3	18 9 16 - 43	Gratton	Carleton, Sentes, Cunningham
Quebec	0 1 0 - 1	13 12 9 - 34	Aubry	Guindon
Houston	2 2 1 - 5	13 11 5 - 29	D. McLeod	Mk Howe 2, Hinse, Popiel, G. Howe
January 25				
Winnipeg	2 0 2 - 4	15 10 10 - 35	Wakely	Johnson 2 (WG 14:34), Swenson, Hull
Edmonton	1 1 1 - 3	10 14 11 - 35	Norris	Patenaude 2, Gilmore
Quebec	0 0 0 - 0	4 10 10 - 24	Brodeur	▸ J. McLeod: shutout (1), 24 saves
Los Angeles	0 1 1 - 2	9 11 8 - 28	J. McLeod	Walters, Tardif
Chicago	1 1 0 - 2	10 5 15 - 30	Gill	Coates, Hardy
Minnesota	3 2 1 - 6	7 18 7 - 32	Curran	Cardwell 3, McMahon 2, Connelly
January 26				
Cleveland	0 0 0 - 0	4 5 10 - 19	Cheevers	▸ Smith: shutout (1), 19 saves
New England	3 1 0 - 4	10 13 7 - 30	Smith	Webster 2, Green, French
Houston	2 1 1 - 4	7 8 9 - 24	D. McLeod	Hughes, Taylor, Mk Howe, G. Howe
Vancouver	0 1 1 - 2	9 9 11 - 29	Donnelly	Migneault, R. Walton
January 27				
Houston	1 2 1 - 4	7 8 7 - 22	D. McLeod	Hall 2, Taylor, Lund
Edmonton	0 0 1 - 1	9 11 12 - 32	Norris	Climie
Winnipeg	1 0 1 - 2	10 10 9 - 29	Daley	Zanussi, Hornung • Antonovich, Christiansen, Heatley
Minnesota	3 6 3 - 12	14 21 16 - 51	Curran	Connelly 2, M. Walton 2, Morrison 2, Cardwell, Klatt, Johnson,
Cleveland	0 2 1 - 3	14 5 8 - 27	Cheevers	Buchanan 2, Edur
Quebec	2 2 0 - 4	18 15 9 - 42	Deguise	Dufour, Gilbert, Bernier, Tremblay
Los Angeles	3 1 2 - 6	11 11 12 - 34	J. McLeod	Willis, Tardif, McDonald, Sutherland, White, Thomas
Jersey	2 1 0 - 3	11 7 13 - 31	Junkin	Rivers, Bradley, Ferguson
Vancouver	2 2 3 - 7	16 6 21 - 43	A'bault, Donnelly	Chernoff 2, Lawson, R. Walton, B. Campbell, McKenzie, Burgess
Toronto	5 4 0 - 9	21 16 4 - 41	Gratton	Dillon 2, Kirk 2, Sentes 2, Simpson, Leduc, Hickey
January 28				
Vancouver	3 0 1 - 4	8 4 15 - 27	Donnelly	C. Campbell, McKenzie, R. Walton, Migneault
New England	0 1 5 - 6	10 12 15 - 37	Smith	Webster, Selwood, Earl, Byers, French, Ley
January 29				
Los Angeles	0 0 0 - 0	14 7 7 - 28	J. McLeod	▸ Brodeur: shutout (1), 28 saves
Quebec	2 2 1 - 5	11 12 17 - 40	Brodeur	Tremblay 2, Dufour 2, Gaudette
Toronto	1 0 0 - 1	14 13 5 - 32	Gratton	Martin
Jersey	4 0 2 - 6	17 15 15 - 47	Kurt	Rivers, Jones, Peacosh, Reichmuth, Herriman, Laughton

1973-1974 Game by Game Line Scores

Date & Teams	Scoring 1 2 3 ot F	Shots 1 2 3 ot F	Goaltenders	Goals & Other Scoring Highlights
January 30				
Houston	0 1 0 - 1	11 11 10 - 31	D. McLeod	Hall
Cleveland	3 2 0 - 5	11 12 9 - 32	Cheevers	Clearwater 2, Walker, Andrea, Shmyr
Chicago	1 1 2 - 4	7 15 10 - 32	Newton	Zaine, Liddington, Fleming, Backstrom
Vancouver	1 1 0 - 2	8 8 5 - 21	Donnelly	Chernoff, B. Campbell
January 31				
New England	0 1 0 - 1	5 11 4 - 20	Smith	French
Jersey	1 2 1 - 4	8 13 6 - 27	Kurt	Rivers, Lacroix, Howell, Jones
Houston	0 3 1 - 4	9 15 8 - 32	Rutledge	Sherrit 2, G. Howe, Lund
Quebec	2 1 3 - 6	13 7 9 - 29	Aubry	Guindon 2, Tremblay, Gaudette, Parizeau, Leclerc
Los Angeles	1 1 2 0 4	5 7 11 2 25	Hoganson	Leblanc 3, Sutherland
Toronto	1 1 2 1 5	9 13 19 4 45	Binkley	King, Leduc, Carleton, Dillon (TG 19:34), Martin (OT, 3:46)
February 1				
Toronto	1 0 0 - 1	8 11 7 - 26	Gratton	Simpson
Quebec	1 0 1 - 2	11 9 12 - 32	Deguise	Roy, Leclerc (WG 18:31)
Los Angeles	0 0 0 - 0	11 8 19 - 38	J. McLeod	▶ Wakely: shutout (3), 38 saves
Winnipeg	2 2 0 - 4	8 11 11 - 30	Wakely	Beaudin 2, Bordeleau, Ash
Chicago	0 1 1 - 2	12 12 10 - 34	Newton	Hardy, Benzelock
Edmonton	0 1 2 - 3	13 6 13 - 32	Norris	Lunde, Hamilton, Harrison
February 2				
Minnesota	2 0 2 - 4	12 12 8 - 32	Curran	Cardwell 2, Christiansen, Antonovich
Cleveland	2 0 0 - 2	14 11 9 - 34	Cheevers	Jarrett, Brindley
Houston	0 1 1 - 2	6 10 9 - 25	D. McLeod	Taylor, Hinse
New England	3 1 1 - 5	9 9 7 - 25	Smith	Green, Earl, French, Williams, Webster
February 3				
Jersey	2 1 0 - 3	16 11 8 - 35	Junkin	Peacosh, Perry, Bradley
Quebec	1 1 3 - 5	7 15 15 - 37	Brodeur	Caron 3, Guite, Parizeau
Chicago	0 2 0 - 2	2 19 11 - 32	Newton	Sicinski, Backstrom
Winnipeg	1 1 2 - 4	12 6 4 - 22	Daley	Snell, Asmundson, Spring, Hull
Los Angeles	0 2 0 - 2	9 12 10 - 31	J. McLeod	Thomas, Veneruzzo
Edmonton	1 3 1 - 5	9 12 16 - 37	Norris	Climie 2, Harrison, McKenzie, Barrie
New England	0 1 0 - 1	6 8 15 - 29	Smith	Earl
Cleveland	3 0 0 - 3	14 8 10 - 32	Cheevers	Brindley, Wiste, Clearwater
Minnesota	2 2 0 - 4	14 10 6 - 30	Garrett, Curran	Cardwell 2, Heatley, Morrison
Toronto	2 1 2 - 5	9 10 8 - 27	Gratton	Dillon, Selby, Sentes, B. Gibbons, Trottier (WG 14:56)
February 4				
Houston	3 1 3 - 7	9 17 7 - 33	D. McLeod	Hughes 2, Lund, Hinse, Taylor, Mty Howe, Hall
Jersey	1 0 0 - 1	7 5 9 - 21	Kurt	Herriman
February 5				
Winnipeg	0 0 1 - 1	5 9 7 - 21	Wakely	Swenson
Chicago	2 1 0 - 3	16 8 11 - 35	Coutu	Harris, Proceviat, Whitlock
Edmonton	0 0 0 - 0	6 12 11 - 29	Norris, Worthy	▶ Donnelly: shutout (2), 29 saves
Vancouver	3 2 3 - 8	11 13 12 - 36	Donnelly	B. Campbell 3, R. Walton 2, Lawson, St. Sauveur, Burgess
Cleveland	1 0 0 - 1	14 9 9 - 32	Cheevers	Brindley
Minnesota	0 2 2 - 4	13 13 9 - 35	Curran	M. Walton 2, Cardwell, Morrison
Jersey	0 0 0 - 0	3 8 14 - 25	Junkin	▶ D. McLeod: shutout (2), 25 saves
Houston	1 3 0 - 4	12 11 9 - 32	D. McLeod	G. Howe 2, Szura, Hall
February 6				
Quebec	0 2 1 - 3	10 4 10 - 24	Aubry	Guindon, Leclerc, Gaudette
New England	0 0 0 - 0	13 14 7 - 34	Smith	▶ Aubry: shutout (1), 34 saves
Chicago	1 0 1 - 2	11 16 14 - 41	Coutu	Mavety, Hardy
Minnesota	2 1 4 - 7	19 13 15 - 47	Curran	Morrison 2, Boyd, Connelly, Hampson, MacMillan, Cardwell
February 7				
Jersey	3 2 2 - 7	10 9 15 - 34	Kurt	Morenz 3, Morrison, Perry, Speer, Jones
Los Angeles	3 1 0 - 4	19 4 8 - 31	J. McLeod, Wilkie	Veneruzzo, Garwasiuk, Walters, White
February 8				
Houston	4 1 1 - 6	9 13 12 - 34	D. McLeod	Hinse 2, Labossiere, Mty Howe, G. Howe, Hughes
Edmonton	1 0 1 - 2	12 17 19 - 48	Norris	Baird, Lunde
Minnesota	2 0 1 1 4	13 13 6 4 36	Curran	Morrison 2, McMahon, M. Walton (OT 7:05)
Winnipeg	1 1 1 0 3	13 14 10 4 41	Daley	Hull 3
Quebec	3 0 0 - 3	13 6 8 - 27	Deguise	Hoganson, Bernier, Parizeau
Vancouver	2 2 3 - 7	8 17 13 - 38	Donnelly	St. Sauveur 2, Migneault 2, B. Campbell, R. Walton, McKenzie
New England	2 1 1 - 4	11 7 8 - 26	Smith	Byers, Pleau, Charlebois, Sheehy
Cleveland	1 1 0 - 2	12 6 7 - 25	Cheevers	Erickson, Neale
February 9				
Jersey	1 1 0 - 2	10 4 8 - 22	Junkin	Lacroix, Herriman
Chicago	3 1 1 - 5	15 8 5 - 28	Newton	Liddington 2, Harris, Popiel, Paiement
Toronto	2 1 0 - 3	17 12 10 - 39	Binkley	Orr, Sentes, Trottier
Cleveland	1 2 1 - 4	6 15 10 - 31	Cheevers	Andrea 2 (WG 3:18), Shmyr, Brindley
February 10				
Chicago	3 0 1 - 4	10 13 8 - 31	Coutu	Morris, Coates, Maggs, Harris
Los Angeles	0 1 1 - 2	8 9 11 - 28	Wilkie, Hoganson	Veneruzzo, Gordon
Minnesota	1 3 1 - 5	8 14 7 - 29	Curran	M. Walton 2, Smith, Morrison, Antonovich
New England	1 1 0 - 2	9 7 11 - 27	Smith	Pleau, Dorey
Quebec	2 1 1 - 4	11 12 9 - 32	Aubry	Guindon, Houle, Beaule, Bernier
Edmonton	0 2 1 - 3	9 14 8 - 31	Worthy	Lunde, Patenaude, McKenzie

1973-1974 Game by Game Line Scores

Date & Teams	Scoring 1 2 3 ot F	Shots 1 2 3 ot F	Goaltenders	Goals & Other Scoring Highlights
February 10				
Houston	1 1 0 0 2	11 10 10 5 36	D. McLeod	Hall, G. Howe
Winnipeg	0 0 2 0 2	6 8 14 3 31	Wakely	Beaudin (18:04, broke shutout), Bordeleau (TG 19:17)
Toronto	1 1 3 - 5	14 11 11 - 36	Gratton	Trottier 2 (WG 14:18), Hickey, Sentes, Gibson
Jersey	0 2 2 - 4	7 10 25 - 42	Kurt	Ferguson 2, Jones, Bradley
February 12				
Edmonton	1 1 0 - 2	4 9 8 - 21	Worthy	Gilmore, Lunde
Chicago	1 1 1 - 3	14 11 14 - 39	Newton	Liddington, Paiement, Morris (WG 10:19)
Winnipeg	0 2 2 - 4	6 12 6 - 24	Daley	Hornung, Bordeleau, Beaudin, Snell
Los Angeles	0 0 2 - 2	11 8 8 - 27	J. McLeod	Niekamp, Gordon
Houston	0 1 2 - 3	9 16 13 - 38	D. McLeod	Hughes, Lund, Taylor
Minnesota	0 1 0 - 1	14 11 11 - 36	Curran	M. Walton
Quebec	3 0 1 - 4	8 7 9 - 24	Aubry	Bernier, Guindon, Lacombe
Toronto	0 3 3 - 6	8 12 18 - 38	Binkley	Simpson 3, Leduc, Dillon, Trottier
February 13				
Winnipeg	1 0 0 - 1	9 5 11 - 25	Wakely	Huck
Houston	3 1 1 - 5	16 11 13 - 40	D. McLeod	Lund, Taylor, G. Howe, Hinse, Hale
Edmonton	1 1 2 - 4	5 5 10 - 20	Norris	Hamilton, Perkins, MacDonald, Lunde
Minnesota	3 3 1 - 7	16 12 5 - 33	Curran	Antonovich 2, Connelly, M. Walton, MacMillan, Cardwell, Heatley
New England	1 1 2 - 4	13 12 15 - 40	Landon	Williams 3, Harris
Vancouver	1 6 2 - 9	9 11 8 - 28	Donnelly	McKenzie 3, Myers 2, R. Walton, St. Sauveur, B. Campbell, Burgess
February 14				
Toronto	1 3 1 - 5	15 7 8 - 30	Gratton	Sentes 2, Simpson, Dillon, Martin
Jersey	0 1 1 - 2	8 14 15 - 37	Junkin	Block, Morrison
Quebec	1 1 3 - 5	9 16 9 - 34	Brodeur	Parizeau 2, Hoganson, Houle, Giroux
Chicago	1 0 2 - 3	9 8 11 - 28	Coutu	Popiel, Harris, Whitlock
February 15				
Cleveland	1 1 0 - 2	10 12 10 - 32	Whidden	Erickson, Shmyr
Jersey	2 1 3 - 6	9 13 14 - 36	Junkin	Peacosh 2, Jones, Rivers, Perry, Bradley
New England	4 1 2 - 7	19 4 9 - 32	Smith	Earl 2, Pleau, Cunniff, Sheehy, Harris, French
Edmonton	0 0 3 - 3	6 11 14 - 31	Worthy, Norris	McKenzie, Baird, Wall
Winnipeg	1 0 0 - 1	10 7 13 - 30	Daley	McDonald
Minnesota	3 1 3 - 7	12 18 19 - 49	Curran	M. Walton 3, Heatley, MacMillan, Christiansen, Cardwell
Houston	3 2 1 - 6	16 12 8 - 36	D. McLeod	G. Howe 3, Sherrit 2, Mk Howe
Los Angeles	1 2 1 - 4	7 9 10 - 26	Hoganson	Garwasiuk, Veneruzzo, Thomas, Serviss
February 16				
Quebec	0 1 1 - 2	9 6 5 - 20	Aubry, Deguise	Gilbert, Leclerc
Cleveland	4 0 1 - 5	15 9 10 - 34	Cheevers	Wiste 3 (all scored within first 5:03 of game), Jarrett 2
Toronto	0 4 1 - 5	11 12 9 - 32	Binkley	Martin 3, Sentes, Simpson
Chicago	2 1 1 - 4	9 11 14 - 34	Newton	Whitlock 2, Liddington, Popiel
February 17				
Chicago	3 2 0 - 5	16 8 6 - 30	Coutu	Popiel 2, Paiement 2, Mavety
Cleveland	3 1 2 - 6	11 17 13 - 41	Cheevers	Ward 3, Brindley, Jarrett, Erickson
Vancouver	1 2 1 - 4	8 10 7 - 25	Donnelly	Myers, Burgess, B. Campbell, McKenzie
Los Angeles	0 0 0 - 0	6 4 8 - 18	J. McLeod	▶ Donnelly: shutout (3), 18 saves
Minnesota	1 3 2 - 6	13 6 13 - 32	Curran	Connelly 3, Johnson 2, Christiansen
Houston	1 0 0 - 1	13 11 14 - 38	D. McLeod	G. Howe
New England	1 0 1 1 3	4 8 18 2 32	Smith	Cunniff 2 (OT 5:52), Sheehy
Winnipeg	0 1 1 0 2	8 11 8 3 30	Wakely	McDonald, Hull
Quebec	1 2 0 - 3	13 9 8 - 30	Deguise, Brodeur	Gaudette 2, Guindon
Jersey	3 4 3 - 10	13 14 15 - 42	Junkin	Rivers 2, Morenz 2, Laughton 2, Bradley 2, Brown, Reichmuth
Toronto	0 2 0 0 2	10 6 5 3 24	Gratton, Binkley	G. Gibbons, Cuddie
Edmonton	0 1 1 1 3	8 19 13 7 47	Norris	Hamilton 2 (OT 9:58, latest OT goal, WHA history), MacDonald
February 18				
Chicago	0 1 2 - 3	7 23 19 - 49	Newton	Hardy, Benzelock, Liddington
Jersey	3 0 1 - 4	11 9 12 - 32	Junkin	Peacosh 2 (WG 12:12), Brown, Morenz
February 19				
Cleveland	1 2 2 0 5	5 8 13 2 28	Cheevers	Pinder 2, Clearwater, Erickson, Jarrett
Quebec	1 3 1 1 6	19 13 11 2 45	Deguise	Parizeau 3 (OT 5:01), Gaudette 2, Hoganson
Toronto	0 0 4 1 5	11 10 15 2 38	Gratton	Selby 2 (TG 16:19, OT 5:53), Hickey, Simpson, Carleton
Vancouver	0 2 2 0 4	11 16 8 0 35	Donnelly	Beaudoin, McKenzie, Migneault, Lawson (Van: led 4-0 at 10:00, 3rd)
February 20				
New England	0 1 1 - 2	4 8 6 - 18	Smith	Blackburn 2
Los Angeles	1 2 1 - 4	11 8 6 - 25	J. McLeod	White 2, Whitlock, Thomas
Winnipeg	0 0 1 - 1	7 8 4 - 19	Daley	Bordeleau
Edmonton	1 0 3 - 4	14 21 14 - 49	Norris	Baird, Lunde, Climie, Fonteyne
Jersey	0 2 0 - 2	6 8 10 - 24	Junkin, Kurt	Herriman, Laughton
Houston	3 2 2 - 7	16 20 14 - 50	Rutledge	Hughes, Hall, Lund, Mk Howe, G. Howe, Sherrit, Mty Howe
February 21				
Vancouver	1 2 1 - 4	9 8 11 - 28	Donnelly	Jones, Migneault, St. Sauveur, Myers
Chicago	1 3 1 - 5	8 24 14 - 46	Coutu	Gordon 2, Paiement, Morris, Popiel
February 22				
Toronto	1 0 2 - 3	10 7 15 - 32	Gratton	Dillon, Trottier, King
Winnipeg	2 1 1 - 4	14 11 6 - 31	Wakely	Huck, T. Hargreaves, McDonald, Hull (WG 18:00)
Minnesota	2 2 2 - 6	20 9 8 - 37	Garrett	M. Walton 2, Johnson, MacMillan, Christiansen, Antonovich (WG 14:48)
Quebec	1 1 2 - 4	7 16 21 - 44	Aubry	Bernier 2, Gaudette, Caron

1973-1974 Game by Game Line Scores

Date & Teams	Scoring 1 2 3 ot F	Shots 1 2 3 ot F	Goaltenders	Goals & Other Scoring Highlights
February 23				
New England	2 1 0 - 3	8 8 2 - 18	Smith	Byers 2, Karlander
Chicago	0 0 0 - 0	7 11 10 - 28	Coutu	▸ Smith: shutout (2), 28 saves
Edmonton	1 1 0 - 2	7 9 8 - 24	Worthy	Anderson, Wall
Houston	2 2 1 - 5	11 11 18 - 40	D. McLeod	Lund 2, Hinse, Schella, G. Howe
Vancouver	1 2 0 - 3	11 14 10 - 35	Donnelly	Lawson 2, McKenzie
Cleveland	3 1 3 - 7	12 16 14 - 42	Cheevers	Krake 2, Jarrett, Clearwater, Pinder, Erickson, Heindl
February 24				
Minnesota	1 1 0 - 2	5 9 15 - 29	Curran	Arbour, M. Walton
Cleveland	1 0 0 - 1	12 14 12 - 38	Cheevers	Ward
New England	0 0 0 - 0	6 7 8 - 21	Smith	▸ Gratton: shutout (1), 21 saves
Toronto	0 0 2 - 2	5 11 18 - 34	Gratton	Sentes 2
Vancouver	0 0 1 - 1	9 8 12 - 29	Gardner	Jones
Houston	2 2 3 - 7	12 8 14 - 34	Rutledge	Popiel, Schella, Lund, Mk Howe, Hale, Hall, Taylor
Chicago	0 1 0 - 1	16 13 13 - 42	Newton	Sicinski
Winnipeg	1 1 1 - 3	15 17 17 - 49	Daley	Hull 2, Beaudin
Jersey	3 1 0 - 4	12 4 13 - 29	Junkin	Lacroix 2, Bradley, Morenz
Quebec	1 4 2 - 7	16 12 14 - 42	Brodeur	Bernier, Hoganson, Parizeau, Beaule, Tremblay, Guindon, Dufour
Edmonton	2 3 0 - 5	11 7 6 - 24	Norris	McAneeley 2, Fonteyne, Anderson, Climie
Los Angeles	1 1 1 - 3	7 9 8 - 24	J. McLeod, Hog'son	Veneruzzo, Hodgson, Garwasiuk
February 26				
Winnipeg	0 1 0 - 1	13 8 4 - 25	Wakely	McDonald
Quebec	4 2 1 - 7	14 15 15 - 44	Brodeur	Leclerc 2, Parizeau, Houle, Bernier, Lacombe, Guindon
Los Angeles	0 1 1 - 2	11 14 7 - 32	J. McLeod	Leblanc, Tardif
Chicago	0 2 2 - 4	11 7 10 - 28	Newton	Harris 2, Stapleton, Coates
Vancouver	0 1 1 - 2	9 9 5 - 23	Donnelly	Jones, Lawson
Houston	0 1 2 - 3	15 9 10 - 34	D. McLeod	Taylor, Labossiere, Hall (WG 12:12)
February 27				
Toronto	1 1 1 - 3	11 9 9 - 29	Gratton	Hickey 2, Kirk
New England	1 2 2 - 5	9 11 10 - 30	Smith	Cunniff 2, Sheehy, Karlander, Byers
Los Angeles	1 1 2 - 4	10 16 8 - 34	Hoganson	Serviss, Whitlock, Veneruzzo, Niekamp
Minnesota	2 2 1 - 5	7 14 9 - 30	Garrett	Connelly 2, Heatley, Morrison, Hampson (WG 8:26)
February 28				
Houston	4 2 3 - 9	11 9 14 - 34	Rutledge	Mk Howe 3, Hughes 3, Hall, Sherrit, Hinse
Chicago	2 1 1 - 4	15 9 16 - 40	Coutu	Popiel, Paiement, Backstrom, Hardy
Winnipeg	0 0 0 - 0	13 10 5 - 28	Daley	▸ Gratton: shutout (2), 28 saves
Toronto	2 1 0 - 3	13 9 10 - 32	Gratton	Carleton, Trottier, Hickey
Vancouver	0 1 3 - 4	3 19 16 - 38	Donnelly	B. Campbell 2, McKenzie, Migneault
Quebec	2 5 2 - 9	17 14 12 - 43	Brodeur	Houle 2, Dufour, Leclerc, Gilbert, Bernier, Guindon, Roy, Gaudette
New England	0 1 2 0 3	10 9 7 4 30	Smith	Blackburn, Earl, Sheehy
Jersey	2 1 0 0 3	12 11 6 4 33	Junkin	Reichmuth, Sheehan, Lacroix
Cleveland	1 4 1 0 6	16 14 5 2 37	Whidden	Walker 2, Andrea, Ward, Neale, Edur
Minnesota	2 2 2 0 6	14 8 12 3 37	Curran	Smith, Arbour, Klatt, Johnson, M. Walton, Cardwell
March 1				
Houston	1 0 1 - 2	19 12 9 - 40	D. McLeod	Hinse, Sherrit
Edmonton	1 2 2 - 5	9 11 10 - 30	Norris	Climie, Hamilton, Perkins, Lunde, Carlin
Cleveland	3 1 0 - 4	10 11 9 - 30	Cheevers	Brindley 2, Buchanan, Jarrett
Chicago	3 1 3 - 7	18 12 12 - 42	Newton	Paiement 2, Harris, Backstrom, Gordon, Liddington, Sicinski
Minnesota	3 0 1 - 4	8 6 13 - 27	Curran	Connelly, Johnson, M. Walton, Gallant
Winnipeg	0 0 0 - 0	17 13 11 - 41	Wakely	▸ Curran: shutout (1), 41 saves
March 2				
Los Angeles	3 1 3 - 7	6 7 17 - 33	J. McLeod, Hog'son	Veneruzzo 4, Tardif 2, Thomas
Jersey	2 4 2 - 8	6 18 10 - 34	Junkin	Lacroix 2, Peacosh, Sheehan, Herriman, Brown, Morrison, Ferguson
Vancouver	0 1 0 - 1	5 11 7 - 23	Sullivan	Myers
New England	2 1 4 - 7	8 16 14 - 38	Smith	Williams, Green, Cunniff, Sheehy, Webster, Dorey, Pleau
March 3				
Toronto	1 2 2 - 5	11 7 9 - 27	Gratton	Trottier 2 (WG 14:57), Carleton, Selby, Hickey
Chicago	2 1 1 - 4	13 10 14 - 37	Newton	Morris, Paiement, Sicinski, Liddington
Los Angeles	2 0 1 - 3	18 9 12 - 39	Hoganson	Leblanc 3
Minnesota	0 1 4 - 5	9 13 15 - 37	Garrett	M. Walton 3, Morrison, MacMillan
Cleveland	0 0 3 0 3	1 10 14 3 28	Whidden	Neale, Erickson, Wiste
Edmonton	2 1 0 0 3	16 11 12 8 47	Norris	Lunde, Patenaude, Wall
New England	2 2 2 - 6	14 3 5 - 22	Smith	Williams 2, Karlander 2, French, Webster
Houston	1 1 1 - 3	8 12 15 - 35	Rutledge	Grierson, G. Howe, Sherrit
Quebec	1 2 3 - 6	12 14 19 - 45	Brodeur	Caron 2, Gilbert, Dufour, Bernier, Guindon (Hull: 700th
Winnipeg	3 3 2 - 8	17 17 15 - 49	Daley	Hull 3, Beaudin, Hornung, McDonald, Snell, Bordeleau career goal)
March 4				
Vancouver	1 4 1 0 6	9 13 10 3 35	Gardner	Myers 2, Lawson, Migneault, Adair, Plumb
Jersey	3 2 1 1 7	17 11 13 1 42	Junkin	Peacosh 2, Ferguson, Peters, Lacroix, Morrison, Morenz (OT 5:33)
March 5				
Cleveland	1 4 1 - 6	7 8 7 - 22	Cheevers	Wiste, Clearwater, Walker, Brindley, Krake, Edur
Los Angeles	1 2 0 - 3	9 10 16 - 35	Hoganson, Wilkie	Veneruzzo, Sutherland, Tardif
New England	1 0 2 - 3	12 8 9 - 29	Smith	Byers, Webster, Williams (WG 8:05)
Chicago	0 2 0 - 2	12 13 10 - 35	Newton	Mavety, Paiement
March 6				
New England	1 3 2 - 6	9 14 15 - 38	Smith	Byers 2, Charlebois, Dorey, Pleau, Karlander
Minnesota	2 3 3 - 8	11 8 11 - 30	Curran	M. Walton 4, MacMillan, Klatt, Smith, Antonovich
Edmonton	1 1 2 - 4	9 10 9 - 28	Norris	Lunde, McAneeley, Climie, Anderson
Houston	1 1 0 - 2	11 14 11 - 36	D. McLeod	Hughes, Labossiere

1973-1974 Game by Game Line Scores

Date & Teams	Scoring 1 2 3 ot F	Shots 1 2 3 ot F	Goaltenders	Goals & Other Scoring Highlights
March 7				
Chicago	2 0 1 - 3	10 11 12 - 33	Newton	Sicinski, Popiel, Paiement
Quebec	0 1 1 - 2	21 13 15 - 49	Brodeur, Deguise	Gaudette, Gilbert
Cleveland	1 0 3 - 4	14 13 11 - 38	Whidden	Ward 2, Erickson, Krake
Vancouver	0 2 0 - 2	12 7 9 - 28	Donnelly	Burgess, O'Donoghue
March 8				
Edmonton	0 1 0 - 1	5 7 13 - 25	Norris	Anderson
Los Angeles	2 1 1 - 4	15 3 7 - 25	Wilkie	McDonald, Zrymiak, Crashley, Tardif
Cleveland	2 1 1 - 4	12 7 11 - 30	Cheevers	Ward, Erickson, Brindley, Walker
Winnipeg	1 0 0 - 1	13 9 10 - 32	Wakely	Beaudin
New England	3 1 3 - 7	7 12 13 - 32	Landon	Sheehy, Blackburn, French, Karlander, Byers, Webster, Cunniff
Jersey	0 1 1 - 2	4 8 8 - 20	Junkin	Peacosh, Morrison
March 9				
Winnipeg	2 1 1 0 4	13 9 9 3 34	Daley	Black, Gratton, Huck, Bordeleau
Chicago	2 2 0 1 5	13 20 11 8 52	Newton	Paiement, Rochon, Popiel, Liddington, Mavety (OT 7:46)
Toronto	1 0 1 - 2	3 7 9 - 19	Gratton, Blum	Gibson, Carleton
Houston	1 1 2 - 4	13 11 13 - 37	D. McLeod	Mk Howe 2, Lund, Grierson
Quebec	2 1 2 - 5	14 17 6 - 37	Aubry, Brodeur	Caron 2, Guindon, Dufour, Leclerc
Minnesota	5 2 2 - 9	20 13 14 - 47	Garrett	M. Walton 4, Hampson, Christiansen, Johnson, Antonovich, Smith
March 10				
Jersey	1 1 0 - 2	17 13 19 - 49	Kurt	Jones 2
Quebec	1 1 3 - 5	10 9 12 - 31	Brodeur	Gaudette 2, Guindon, Hoganson, Gendron
Cleveland	0 1 2 - 3	9 11 11 - 31	Cheevers	Wiste, Pinder, Walker
Toronto	2 4 2 - 8	12 15 19 - 46	Binkley	Hickey 2, Cunningham, Martin, Kirk, Sentes, Dillon, Simpson
Minnesota	0 3 2 - 5	8 13 6 - 27	Curran	Ball, Antonovich, MacMillan, Johnson, Morrison
Los Angeles	2 1 3 - 6	10 19 12 - 41	Wilkie	Sutherland, Odrowski, Hodgson, Veneruzzo, Leblanc, McDonald
Vancouver	0 0 1 1 2	9 14 9 1 33	Donnelly	Burgess, Myers (OT 1:32)
Edmonton	1 0 0 0 1	15 18 15 1 49	Norris	Falkenberg
March 11				
Winnipeg	1 1 0 - 2	8 7 14 - 29	Wakely	Bordeleau, Sutherland
Jersey	3 5 2 - 10	17 12 12 - 41	Kurt	Peacosh 2, Reichmuth 2, Rivers 2, Lacroix, Morrison, Laughton, Jones
March 12				
New England	1 1 1 - 3	10 8 7 - 25	Smith	Webster, Green, Pleau
Chicago	0 2 3 - 5	12 17 10 - 39	Newton	Harris 2, Backstrom 2. Gordon
Minnesota	0 2 0 - 2	11 8 4 - 23	Curran	Johnson, Ball
Houston	1 1 1 - 3	11 20 15 - 46	D. McLeod	Lund, Hinse, Labossiere (WG 6:48)
Los Angeles	0 1 0 - 1	18 14 1 - 33	Wilkie	Odrowski
Edmonton	3 1 4 - 8	14 15 19 - 48	Worthy	McKenzie 2, Lunde, MacDonald, Hamilton, Perkins, McAn'ley, Schraefel
March 13				
Los Angeles	0 1 1 - 2	6 7 6 - 19	J. McLeod	Zrymiak, Veneruzzo
Vancouver	1 1 3 - 5	11 14 9 - 34	Donnelly	St. Sauveur 3, Myers, B. Campbell
Winnipeg	0 0 3 - 3	10 7 10 - 27	Daley	Bordeleau, Huck, Sutherland
Cleveland	2 1 1 - 4	9 13 11 - 33	Cheevers	Pinder, Walker, Andrea, Wiste (WG 12:28)
March 14				
Quebec	2 1 0 - 3	6 9 5 - 20	Brodeur	Guindon, Bernier, Parizeau
Toronto	1 1 0 - 2	13 15 10 - 38	Gratton	Leduc, Trottier
Minnesota	1 3 0 - 4	8 10 6 - 24	Curran	Heatley 2, Connelly, Hampson
Chicago	2 3 2 - 7	25 11 10 - 46	Newton	Coates 3, Backstrom 2, Mavety, Liddington
Houston	1 3 2 - 6	9 16 8 - 33	D. McLeod	Labossiere 2, Sherrit, G. Howe, Szura, Lund
Los Angeles	0 0 0 - 0	9 12 5 - 26	Wilkie	▶ D. McLeod: shutout (3), 26 saves
New England	2 1 3 - 6	7 8 6 - 21	Smith	Harris 2, Sheehy, Selwood, Blackburn, Webster
Vancouver	2 0 1 - 3	8 11 8 - 27	Donnelly	St. Sauveur, Adair, Plumb
March 15				
New England	0 2 4 - 6	8 12 14 - 34	Landon	Sheehy 2, Charlebois, Williams, Pleau, French
Edmonton	0 2 0 - 2	14 14 10 - 38	Norris	McAneeley 2
Minnesota	1 1 1 - 3	6 7 4 - 17	Garrett	Christiansen, Morrison, M. Walton
Jersey	0 4 1 - 5	9 18 14 - 41	Kurt	Rivers 2, Herriman, Howell, Lacroix
Vancouver	0 2 3 - 5	3 11 14 - 28	Donnelly	Lawson 2, Burgess 2, Boudreau
Winnipeg	0 3 4 - 7	15 17 12 - 44	Wakely	Hull 2, McDonald 2, Beaudin, Huck, Snell
March 16				
Chicago	0 1 2 1 4	15 17 13 1 46	Newton	Backstrom 2 (TG 17:39, OT 1:24), Morris, Liddington
Quebec	2 1 0 0 3	10 5 6 0 21	Brodeur	Houle, Dufour, Bernier
Jersey	1 3 0 0 4	9 8 4 2 23	Junkin, Kurt	Jones, Rivers, Laughton, Morrison
Cleveland	1 0 3 0 4	16 18 19 7 60	Cheevers, Whidden	Ward 2, Krake, Shmyr (TG 17:08)
March 17				
Cleveland	2 1 0 - 3	13 8 5 - 26	Whidden	Shmyr, Ward, Andrea
Houston	1 1 2 - 4	9 8 7 - 24	D. McLeod	Taylor, Labossiere, Schella, G. Howe (WG 7:40)
Minnesota	1 2 2 - 5	9 6 12 - 27	Garrett	Morrison, M. Walton 2, Ball
Quebec	1 1 1 - 3	21 19 13 - 53	Deguise	Leclerc, Gendron, Houle
Chicago	1 2 1 - 4	9 13 7 - 29	Newton	Popiel, Mavety, Backstrom, Paiement
Toronto	1 0 1 - 2	8 14 14 - 36	Binkley	Martin, Leduc
Vancouver	1 0 1 - 2	8 7 11 - 26	Gardner	Adair, Plante
Edmonton	1 1 1 - 3	19 13 14 - 46	Worthy	Lunde, Baird, Barrie (WG 16:15)
New England	1 0 0 - 1	13 10 4 - 27	Smith	Byers · · · · · · · · · Gratton, Sutherland
Winnipeg	2 3 5 - 10	16 13 11 - 40	Daley	Snell 2, Huck, Woytowich, Black, Hull, Bordeleau, Asmundson,

124

1973-1974 Game by Game Line Scores

Date & Teams	Scoring 1 2 3 ot F	Shots 1 2 3 ot F	Goaltenders	Goals & Other Scoring Highlights
March 18				
Toronto	1 3 1 - 5	6 9 8 - 23	Gratton	Kirk 2, Hickey, Gibson, King
Jersey	4 3 4 - 11	13 17 13 - 43	Kurt	Herriman 3, Morrison 3, Rivers 2, Bradley, Lacroix, Laughton
March 19				
Cleveland	2 1 4 - 7	12 6 11 - 29	Cheevers	Ward 2, Brindley 2, Neale, Krake, Walker
Chicago	1 1 2 - 4	8 9 14 - 31	Newton	Paiement, Mavety, Liddington, Popiel
Minnesota	1 1 2 - 4	10 6 8 - 24	Curran	Gallant, Antonovich, M. Walton, MacMillan
Vancouver	2 2 1 - 5	15 8 13 - 36	Donnelly	B. Campbell, St. Sauveur, Migneault, Burgess, Lawson (WG 18:35)
March 20				
Edmonton	0 2 0 0 2	6 11 10 4 31	Wilkie	Patenaude, Joyal
New England	1 1 0 0 2	13 8 7 4 32	Smith	Blackburn, Webster
Houston	2 0 3 - 5	17 6 15 - 38	D. McLeod	Sherrit 2, Mk Howe, Lund, Hall
Cleveland	2 0 2 - 4	12 7 15 - 34	Cheevers	Pinder, Muloin, Krake, Erickson
Jersey	2 3 3 - 8	14 10 15 - 39	Junkin	Rivers 2, Perry 2, Ferguson, Herriman, Bradley, Morenz
Los Angeles	1 4 0 - 5	11 12 6 - 29	Hoganson	Sutherland 2, Veneruzzo, Walters, Tardif
March 21				
Vancouver	0 3 2 0 5	8 10 12 3 33	Gardner	Lawson, Migneault, St. Sauveur, Burgess, O'Donoghue
Chicago	1 4 0 0 5	9 13 16 8 46	Gill	Maggs, Paiement, Hardy, Liddington, Sicinski
Houston	0 3 0 - 3	8 10 10 - 28	Rutledge	Lund, Mk Howe, Grierson
Toronto	1 4 1 - 6	13 19 8 - 40	Binkley, Blum	Dillon 4, Kirk, Carleton
Edmonton	2 1 2 0 5	11 10 7 4 32	Worthy	MacDonald, Patenaude, Baird, Climie, Lunde
Quebec	1 2 2 0 5	24 11 17 5 57	Brodeur	Guite 2 (TG 17:20), Hoganson, Leclerc, Giroux
March 22				
Houston	2 2 0 - 4	9 14 6 - 29	D. McLeod	Labossiere 2, Schella, Mk Howe
Winnipeg	2 0 0 - 2	13 5 9 - 27	Daley	Hull, Swenson
Minnesota	2 0 3 - 5	10 8 15 - 33	Garrett	Connelly 2, Hampson, Gallant, Heatley
Los Angeles	0 1 1 - 2	15 11 11 - 37	J. McLeod	Tardif, McDonald
March 23				
Jersey	0 1 0 - 1	8 14 9 - 31	Junkin	Peters
Chicago	3 0 1 - 4	17 9 9 - 35	Newton	Popiel 2, Paiement, Zaine
Edmonton	1 0 0 - 1	9 3 4 - 16	Norris	Climie
Cleveland	1 2 0 - 3	12 20 14 - 46	Whidden	Ward, Erickson, Brindley
Vancouver	1 0 1 - 2	12 10 17 - 39	Donnelly	Migneault, Lawson
Quebec	0 5 1 - 6	21 18 5 - 44	Brodeur	Houle 2, Bernier, Gaudette, Guindon, Leclerc
March 24				
New England	1 2 0 - 3	15 10 5 - 30	Smith	Webster, French, Sheehy
Quebec	2 2 0 - 4	15 9 12 - 36	Brodeur	Parizeau, Guindon, Gendron, Bernier
Vancouver	1 0 0 - 1	10 5 9 - 24	Gardner	Lawson
Toronto	0 0 3 - 3	14 14 20 - 48	Gratton	Hickey, Dillon, King
Winnipeg	0 1 2 - 3	9 8 13 - 30	Daley	Swenson, Spring, Snell
Los Angeles	1 3 2 - 6	14 9 11 - 34	Hoganson	Tardif 4, Whitlock, Sutherland
Chicago	1 1 1 0 3	9 9 14 5 37	Gill	Maggs, Popiel, Liddington
Cleveland	0 1 2 0 3	5 9 10 6 30	Cheevers	Jarrett, Pinder, Ward (TG 14:27)
Minnesota	2 1 2 - 5	10 10 9 - 29	Garrett	Heatley, Connelly, McMahon, Gallant, M. Walton
Houston	1 2 0 - 3	17 18 15 - 50	D. McLeod	Sherrit 2, Lund
March 25				
Edmonton	1 2 1 - 4	8 9 9 - 26	Wilkie	McAneeley, Barrie, Lunde, Perkins
Jersey	0 0 1 - 1	4 6 8 - 18	Kurt	Rivers
March 26				
Edmonton	1 0 1 - 2	6 9 6 - 21	Norris	Patenaude, Perkins
Chicago	0 1 3 - 4	15 8 18 - 41	Newton	Paiement, Morris, Backstrom, Liddington
March 27				
Los Angeles	0 0 1 - 1	9 10 13 - 32	Hoganson	McDonald (spoiled Landon's shutout at 17:24)
New England	3 1 3 - 7	14 6 17 - 37	Landon	Karlander 2, Byers 2, Williams, Webster, Danby
Quebec	0 2 2 0 4	7 13 10 2 32	Brodeur	Parizeau, Gendron, Guindon (TG 16:18)
Cleveland	2 1 1 1 5	10 11 11 4 36	Cheevers	Ward 3 (OT 6:33), Jarrett, Brindley
Jersey	0 3 1 - 4	13 19 11 - 43	Kurt	Perry, Reichmuth, Ferguson, Peacosh
Minnesota	3 2 1 - 6	9 9 5 - 23	Garrett	Heatley 2, Klatt, Hampson, Cardwell, M. Walton
Houston	2 4 2 - 8	11 13 13 - 37	D. McLeod	Grierson, Hughes 2, Williamson, Sherrit, Hall, Szura
Vancouver	0 0 1 - 1	11 10 7 - 28	Gardner, Donnelly	B. Campbell
March 28				
Edmonton	0 2 3 0 5	10 6 11 1 28	Norris	McAneeley, Climie, Lunde, MacDonald, Perkins (TG 19:50)
Toronto	1 3 1 1 6	11 13 11 5 40	Gratton	Dillon 2 (OT 9:32), Carleton, Hickey, Leduc, Martin
Los Angeles	0 2 1 - 3	9 14 4 - 27	Hoganson	Tardif 2, Hodgson
Quebec	3 2 4 - 9	18 15 16 - 49	Brodeur	Giroux 3, Bernier 2, Houle 2, Parizeau 2
Cleveland	0 0 2 - 2	10 9 12 - 31	Whidden	Shmyr, Erickson
New England	2 1 0 - 3	7 7 8 - 22	Landon	Webster 2, Pleau
March 29				
Houston	0 2 3 - 5	8 11 10 - 29	D. McLeod	Lund 2, Sherrit, Taylor, Mk Howe (Huck: TG 19:10)
Winnipeg	0 1 6 - 7	18 15 15 - 48	Daley	Beaudin 2 (WG 19:55), Ash, T. Hargreaves, Sutherland, Hull, Huck
Chicago	1 2 2 - 5	13 19 13 - 45	Newton	Maggs, Popiel, Mavety, Harris, Backstrom
Vancouver	2 0 0 - 2	7 7 11 - 25	Gardner	MacSweyn, Burgess
Edmonton	1 2 0 - 3	14 10 11 - 35	Wilkie	Sheehan, Anderson, MacDonald
Minnesota	0 0 1 - 1	9 9 10 - 28	Curran	Smith

1973-1974 Game by Game Line Scores

Date & Teams	Scoring 1 2 3 ot F	Shots 1 2 3 ot F	Goaltenders	Goals & Other Scoring Highlights
March 30				
Los Angeles	1 1 2 0 4	11 7 9 1 28	J. McLeod	Sutherland 2, Young, Veneruzzo
Cleveland	1 1 2 1 5	5 18 12 3 38	Cheevers	Shmyr, Andrea, Erickson, Pinder, Jarrett (OT 4:36)
Toronto	2 1 0 - 3	5 11 4 - 20	Gratton	King, Trottier, Martin
Quebec	0 0 1 - 1	20 15 14 - 49	Brodeur, Deguise	Guite (spoiled Gratton's shutout at 19:34)
March 31				
Vancouver	0 2 1 0 3	11 15 16 1 43	Donnelly	Adair, O'Donoghue, B. Campbell
Winnipeg	1 2 0 1 4	10 11 4 1 26	Daley	Hull 2, Bordeleau, Huck (OT 2:00)
Chicago	0 0 1 - 1	12 7 15 - 34	Gill	Liddington
Edmonton	1 1 2 - 4	15 17 9 - 41	Norris	Baird, Carlyle, Climie, Patenaude
Houston	0 1 1 - 2	9 8 15 - 32	Rutledge	Taylor, Sherrit
Minnesota	3 1 1 - 5	18 16 8 - 42	Garrett	Heatley, Connelly, M. Walton, Klatt, Hampson
Los Angeles	1 2 1 - 4	6 11 5 - 22	Hoganson	Leblanc, Thomas, Veneruzzo, White
Toronto	3 1 1 - 5	16 13 11 - 40	Gratton	Leduc, King, Trottier, Orr, Hickey (WG 14:11)
Cleveland	1 1 2 - 4	9 6 10 - 25	Cheevers	Krake 2, Andrea, Ward
Jersey	1 0 1 - 2	13 7 11 - 31	Junkin	Ferguson, Morrison
Quebec	1 0 1 0 2	9 9 6 2 26	Deguise, Brodeur	Gaudette, Parizeau
New England	1 1 0 1 3	18 10 12 4 44	Smith	Harris 2, Webster (OT 7:20)
April 1				
Houston	0 2 2 - 4	4 17 5 - 26	Grahame	Grierson 2, Prentice, Stanfield
New England	1 0 0 - 1	10 11 10 - 31	Smith	Harris
April 2				
Edmonton	0 1 1 - 2	12 12 12 - 36	Worthy, Wilkie	Baird 2
Toronto	1 1 1 - 3	17 16 16 - 49	Blum	Carleton 2 (WG 17:11), Kirk
Jersey	0 0 3 - 3	9 11 14 - 34	Kurt	Morrison, Rivers, Morenz
Chicago	3 1 3 - 7	14 9 8 - 31	Newton	Popiel 3, Gordon, Sicinski, Coates, Zaine
April 3				
Edmonton	2 1 2 1 6	12 17 12 1 42	Wilkie, Worthy	Gilmore 4 (TG 16:00, OT 3:13), Falkenberg, Baird
Winnipeg	2 2 1 0 5	12 10 14 4 40	Daley	Hull, Pratt, Snell, T. Hargreaves, Johnson
Vancouver	0 0 0 - 0	12 16 12 - 40	Gardner	▸ Curran: shutout (2), 40 saves
Minnesota	4 3 2 - 9	18 13 8 - 39	Curran	Morrison 4, M. Walton 2, Smith, Antonovich, Cardwell
Chicago	0 1 0 - 1	16 11 12 - 39	Gill	Morris
Houston	2 0 1 - 3	14 7 8 - 29	D. McLeod	Hughes 2, Mk Howe
April 4				
Winnipeg	1 1 0 - 2	9 7 10 - 26	Holden	McDonald, Spring
Vancouver	2 1 1 - 4	13 9 6 - 28	Donnelly	Lawson 2, St. Sauveur, R. Walton
Jersey	1 2 1 - 4	10 12 10 - 32	Junkin	Perry 2, Laughton, Jones
Los Angeles	2 0 4 - 6	10 8 14 - 32	Hoganson	McDonald 2, Whitlock, Veneruzzo, Walters, Tardif

End of Regular Season

Gallery

Jordy Douglas

Mike Harvey

Bengt-Ake Gustafsson

Markus Mattsson

Alex Tidey

Danny O'Shea

Mats Lindh

Tony Featherstone

Richard David

Doug Berry

1974 Playoffs Game by Game Line Scores

Date & Teams	Scoring 1 2 3 ot F	Shots 1 2 3 ot F	Goaltenders	Goals & Other Scoring Highlights
April 6				
Chicago	3 1 0 - 4	11 18 11 - 40	Newton	Hardy, Sicinski, Maggs, Harris
New England	1 3 2 - 6	10 11 9 - 30	Smith	Pleau 2, Webster 2, Danby, Blackburn
Edmonton	0 1 0 - 1	10 12 12 - 34	Norris	MacDonald
Minnesota	0 2 0 - 2	12 16 9 - 37	Garrett	Heatley, M. Walton
April 7				
Chicago	1 1 1 0 3	12 15 9 1 37	Gill	Mavety, Popiel, Hardy
New England	1 1 1 1 4	13 9 12 3 37	Smith	Webster, Sheehy, Karlander, French (OT 2:51)
Cleveland	0 0 0 - 0	14 6 9 - 29	Cheevers	▶ Gratton: shutout (1), 29 saves
Toronto	1 1 2 - 4	13 13 13 - 39	Gratton	Dillon 2, Kirk, Trottier
Edmonton	0 1 4 - 5	7 19 16 - 42	Norris	MacDonald 2, McAneeley, Climie, Sheehan
Minnesota	2 3 3 - 8	13 14 9 - 36	Curran	Arbour 2, M. Walton 2, Morrison, Ball, Gallant, Hampson
April 8				
Houston	2 0 3 - 5	14 8 13 - 35	D. McLeod	Hall 2, Hughes, Sherrit, Mk Howe
Winnipeg	0 0 2 - 2	6 10 3 - 19	Daley	Johnson, Beaudin
April 9				
New England	0 4 2 - 6	9 9 11 - 29	Smith, Landon	Sheehy 2, Byers, Blackburn, Cunniff, French
Chicago	5 3 0 - 8	12 9 7 - 28	Newton	Liddington 2, Gordon, Hardy, Paiement, Watson, Popiel, Sicinski
Cleveland	0 3 0 - 3	12 9 6 - 27	Cheevers	Ward, Edur, Andrea
Toronto	0 1 3 - 4	14 14 16 - 44	Gratton	Martin 3 (TG 13:28, WG 16:49), Carleton
April 10				
New England	0 0 1 0 1	7 6 9 8 30	Smith	Sheehy
Chicago	0 0 1 1 2	7 12 14 15 48	Newton	Popiel (TG 19:35), Backstrom (OT 17:45)
Houston	0 1 2 - 3	3 9 10 - 22	D. McLeod	Mty Howe, Mk Howe, Hinse
Winnipeg	1 0 1 - 2	6 9 7 - 22	Daley	Beaudin, Black
Minnesota	1 2 3 - 6	9 11 9 - 29	Garrett	MacMillan, Klatt 2, Morrison, Connelly
Edmonton	0 1 1 - 2	12 15 14 - 41	Wilkie, Norris	Hamilton, Perkins
April 12				
Chicago	1 1 2 - 4	6 6 11 - 23	Gill	Harris 2, Mavety, Sicinski
New England	0 2 0 - 2	10 13 4 - 27	Smith	Byers, French
Toronto	1 3 0 - 4	8 15 7 - 30	Gratton	Sentes 3, Kirk
Cleveland	1 1 0 - 2	14 5 15 - 34	Cheevers	Jarrett, Morgan
Minnesota	0 0 1 - 1	8 5 12 - 25	Curran	Connelly (spoiled Worthy's shutout at 19:22)
Edmonton	0 1 1 - 2	10 12 14 - 36	Worthy	Fonteyne, Joyal
April 13				
Toronto	1 0 1 0 2	8 10 14 2 34	Gratton	B. Gibbons, Martin (TG 15:05)
Cleveland	0 2 0 1 3	9 11 16 3 39	Cheevers	Walker, Ward, Muloin (WG 4:17)
Winnipeg	0 1 0 - 1	7 11 13 - 31	Blum	Bordeleau
Houston	5 1 4 - 10	18 8 18 - 44	D. McLeod	Lund 4, Hughes 2, G. Howe, Labossiere, Taylor, Grierson
April 14				
New England	0 0 2 - 2	14 9 8 - 31	Smith	French, Ley
Chicago	0 0 0 - 0	11 11 9 - 31	Newton	▶ Smith: shutout (1), 31 saves
Winnipeg	0 1 3 - 4	10 8 8 - 26	Blum	Bordeleau 2, Beaudin, Hull
Houston	2 2 1 - 5	12 13 5 - 30	D. McLeod	Schella, Hale, Hall, Taylor, Mk Howe
Edmonton	0 2 2 - 4	7 13 20 - 40	Worthy	Baird, Joyal, Barrie, MacDonald
Minnesota	2 2 1 - 5	19 9 7 - 35	Garrett	M. Walton 3, Morrison, Connelly
April 15				
Cleveland	0 1 0 - 1	6 9 13 - 28	Cheevers	Ward
Toronto	3 0 1 - 4	18 19 12 - 49	Gratton	Simpson 2, Hickey 2
April 16				
Chicago	1 0 2 - 3	7 12 24 - 43	Gill	Hardy, Backstrom, Popiel (WG 13:26)
New England	0 2 0 - 2	12 8 7 - 27	Smith	Webster 2
April 18				
Minnesota	2 1 1 1 5	9 8 13 3 33	Garrett	Arbour, Klatt, Johnson, McMahon, M. Walton (OT 1:40)
Houston	1 1 2 0 4	19 11 14 0 44	D. McLeod	Mk Howe, Popiel, Lund, Taylor
April 19				
Chicago	1 2 1 - 4	10 17 7 - 34	Newton	Benzelock, Harris, Morris, Zaine
Toronto	1 2 3 - 6	12 9 16 - 37	Gratton, Binkley	Dillon 2, Cuddie, Martin, Sentes, Leduc
April 20				
Minnesota	1 1 0 - 2	4 8 2 - 14	Garrett	Connelly, M. Walton
Houston	3 2 0 - 5	20 18 12 - 50	D. McLeod	Hinse, Lund, Hall, Sherrit, Labossiere
April 21				
Minnesota	0 3 1 - 4	6 15 15 - 36	Curran	Morrison 2, Hampson, Connelly
Houston	1 0 0 - 1	10 5 5 - 20	D. McLeod	Hughes
April 22				
Chicago	1 2 1 - 4	6 13 10 - 29	Gill	Backstrom 2, Gordon, Rochon (WG 9:28)
Toronto	0 3 0 - 3	11 16 11 - 38	Binkley	Leduc, Martin, Dillon
April 28				
Toronto	2 0 0 - 2	7 8 9 - 24	Gratton, Binkley	Leduc, B. Gibbons
Chicago	1 0 2 - 3	11 10 11 - 32	Gill	Paiement 2 (WG 6:42), Sicinski
Houston	1 1 2 - 4	11 7 16 - 34	D. McLeod	Schella, G. Howe, Labossiere, Hughes
Minnesota	0 1 0 - 1	9 9 14 - 32	Curran	Connelly
April 29				
Minnesota	0 1 3 - 4	5 10 9 - 24	Garrett	M. Walton 2, Antonovich, Hampson
Houston	3 4 2 - 9	25 11 15 - 51	D. McLeod	Mk Howe 2, Hinse, G. Howe, Labossiere, Hughes, Lund, Hall, Sherrit

127

1974 Playoffs Game by Game Line Scores

Date & Teams	Scoring 1 2 3 ot F	Shots 1 2 3 ot F	Goaltenders	Goals & Other Scoring Highlights
April 30				
Toronto	2 5 0 - 7	9 12 9 - 30	Binkley, Gratton	Trottier 3, Carleton, Simpson, Leduc, Sentes (WG 19:49 2nd)
Chicago	2 2 2 - 6	15 11 10 - 36	Gill, Newton	Mavety, Paiement, Benzelock, Popiel, Morris, Liddington
May 1				
Houston	0 1 2 - 3	13 11 13 - 37	D. McLeod	Mk Howe 2, Sherrit
Minnesota	0 1 0 - 1	13 12 6 - 31	Curran, Garrett	Hampson
Chicago	0 3 0 - 3	6 12 8 - 26	Newton	Chicago, Harris, Watson
Toronto	2 1 2 - 5	8 9 17 - 34	Gratton	Orr, Selby, Hickey, Gibson, Trottier
May 4				
Toronto	1 0 1 - 2	9 10 8 - 27	Binkley	Martin, Sentes
Chicago	4 3 2 - 9	14 12 12 - 38	Gill	Paiement 3, Liddington, Sicinski, Maggs, Gordon, Zaine, Popiel
May 6				
Chicago	0 4 1 - 5	12 9 7 - 28	Gill	Liddington, Popiel, Sicinski, Maggs, Harris
Toronto	1 0 1 - 2	17 8 13 - 38	Gratton	Simpson, Sentes
May 12				
Houston	2 0 1 - 3	10 8 11 - 29	D. McLeod	Hale, Labossiere, Hughes (WG 15:48)
Chicago	0 0 2 - 2	8 12 11 - 31	Gill	Liddington, Gordon
May 15				
Houston	2 1 3 - 6	12 10 10 - 32	D. McLeod	Hinse 2, Hall, Labossiere, Sherrit, Taylor
Chicago	0 0 1 - 1	8 11 8 - 27	Gill, Newton	Rochon (spoiled McLeod's shutout at 19:44)
May 17				
Chicago	1 3 0 - 4	9 10 9 - 28	Gill, Newton	Backstrom, Paiement, Morris, Mavety
Houston	3 3 1 - 7	9 10 11 - 30	D. McLeod	Hinse 2, Hughes 2, Hall, Mk Howe, Hale
May 19				
Chicago	0 1 1 - 2	7 7 16 - 30	Newton	Popiel, Morris
Houston	3 3 0 - 6	13 13 7 - 33	D. McLeod	Hall 2, Lund 2, Hinse, Labossiere

Houston is League Champion

"Peter Pan" Causes Scheduling Trouble

The Chicago Cougars and Houston Aeros were both affected by the travelling production of *Peter Pan*, which caused a week-long delay of games for the Aeros while the show was being held at the Sam Houston Coliseum, and forced the Cougars out of the International Amphitheater in Chicago for their series against Toronto. The Cougars played at the Randhurst Twin Ice Arena in suburban Mount Prospect, then returned to the Randhurst for its two home games against Houston in the Finals when the ice at the Amphitheater could not be restored to game-playing conditions.

George Morrison's 43-Second Hat Trick

George Morrison of Minnesota scored a natural hat trick in 43 seconds, the fastest hat trick in WHA history and just 22 seconds "slower" than Bill Mosienko's memorable 1952 feat in the NHL. Morrison scored his three goals in the second period as the Saints demolished the Vancouver Blazers, 9-0, on April 3, 1974. The second fastest hat trick in the WHA was scored by Indy's Randy Wyrozub, who scored his three goals in just under two minutes of action against Calgary, October 30, 1975.

Gallery

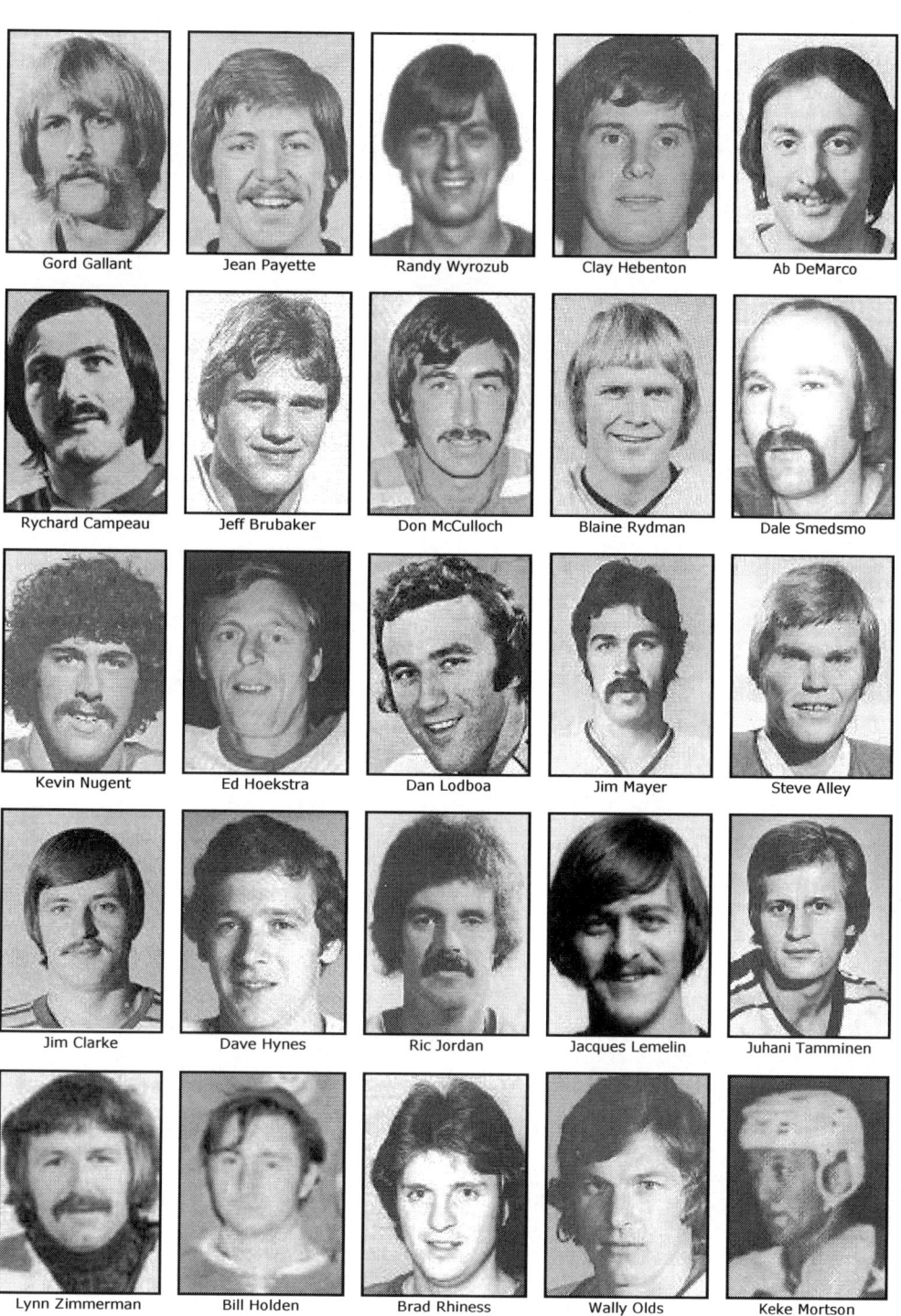

Gord Gallant   Jean Payette   Randy Wyrozub   Clay Hebenton   Ab DeMarco

Rychard Campeau   Jeff Brubaker   Don McCulloch   Blaine Rydman   Dale Smedsmo

Kevin Nugent   Ed Hoekstra   Dan Lodboa   Jim Mayer   Steve Alley

Jim Clarke   Dave Hynes   Ric Jordan   Jacques Lemelin   Juhani Tamminen

Lynn Zimmerman   Bill Holden   Brad Rhiness   Wally Olds   Keke Mortson

1973-1974 CHICAGO COUGARS

**Player-Coach
Pat Stapleton**

**Bench Coach
Jacques Demers**

Summary of Games (@ Away, * Overtime)

	date	opponent	score		record	pts	gf-ga
1.	Oct 7 @	Toronto	4-4	T	0-0-1	1	4-4
2.	Oct 11 @	New York	4-3	W	1-0-1	3	8-7
3.	Oct 13 @	New England	4-6	L	1-1-1	3	12-13
4.	Oct 14 @	Cleveland	*2-3	L	1-2-1	3	14-16
5.	Oct 15 @	Los Angeles	7-2	W	2-2-1	5	21-18
6.	Oct 20 @	Vancouver	3-4	L	2-3-1	5	24-22
7.	Oct 22 @	Edmonton	1-4	L	2-4-1	5	25-26
8.	Oct 25 @	Quebec	4-2	W	3-4-1	7	29-28
9.	Oct 28 @	Toronto	3-2	W	4-4-1	9	32-30
10.	Oct 30	Winnipeg	4-1	W	5-4-1	11	36-31
11.	Nov 3 @	Cleveland	7-4	W	6-4-1	13	43-35
12.	Nov 6	Los Angeles	*5-4	W	7-4-1	15	48-39
13.	Nov 10	Toronto	3-2	W	8-4-1	17	51-41
14.	Nov 13	Cleveland	2-5	L	8-5-1	17	53-46
15.	Nov 15	Houston	3-2	W	9-5-1	19	56-48
16.	Nov 17	Toronto	5-2	W	10-5-1	21	61-50
17.	Nov 18 @	New York	3-5	L	10-6-1	21	64-55
18.	Nov 22 @	Los Angeles	4-3	W	11-6-1	23	68-58
19.	Nov 24 @	Houston	3-5	L	11-7-1	23	71-63
20.	Dec 1	Los Angeles	*4-5	L	11-8-1	23	75-68
21.	Dec 2 @	New England	3-4	L	11-9-1	23	78-72
22.	Dec 4	Edmonton	0-2	L	11-10-1	23	78-74
23.	Dec 8	Jersey	1-3	L	11-11-1	23	79-77
24.	Dec 9 @	Quebec	1-6	L	11-12-1	23	80-83
25.	Dec 11	Minnesota	3-5	L	11-13-1	23	83-88
26.	Dec 15	Houston	5-2	W	12-13-1	25	88-90
27.	Dec 16 @	New England	3-2	W	13-13-1	27	91-92
28.	Dec 18	Winnipeg	3-3	T	13-13-2	28	94-95
29.	Dec 21 @	Jersey	1-5	L	13-14-2	28	95-100
30.	Dec 23 @	Toronto	6-5	W	14-14-2	30	101-105
31.	Dec 26 @	Winnipeg	2-4	L	14-15-2	30	103-109
32.	Dec 28	Quebec	6-4	W	15-15-2	32	109-113
33.	Dec 29 @	Houston	0-3	L	15-16-2	32	109-116
34.	Dec 30 @	Minnesota	5-3	W	16-16-2	34	114-119
35.	Jan 1	Vancouver	5-4	W	17-16-2	36	119-123
36.	Jan 5	Minnesota	5-6	L	17-17-2	36	124-129
37.	Jan 6 @	Quebec	0-4	L	17-18-2	36	124-133
38.	Jan 8	Cleveland	0-0	T	17-18-3	37	124-133
39.	Jan 13 @	Winnipeg	1-3	L	17-19-3	37	125-136
40.	Jan 17 @	New England	5-2	W	18-19-3	39	130-138
41.	Jan 19	Quebec	5-2	W	19-19-3	41	135-140
42.	Jan 22	New England	5-3	W	20-19-3	43	140-143
43.	Jan 25 @	Minnesota	2-6	L	20-20-3	43	142-149
44.	Jan 30 @	Vancouver	4-2	W	21-20-3	45	146-151
45.	Feb 1 @	Edmonton	2-3	L	21-21-3	45	148-154
46.	Feb 3 @	Winnipeg	2-4	L	21-22-3	45	150-158
47.	Feb 5	Winnipeg	3-1	W	22-22-3	47	153-159
48.	Feb 6 @	Minnesota	2-7	L	22-23-3	47	155-166
49.	Feb 9	Jersey	5-2	W	23-23-3	49	160-168
50.	Feb 10 @	Los Angeles	4-2	W	24-23-3	51	164-170
51.	Feb 12	Edmonton	3-2	W	25-23-3	53	167-172
52.	Feb 14	Quebec	3-5	L	25-24-3	53	170-177
53.	Feb 16	Toronto	4-5	L	25-25-3	53	174-182
54.	Feb 17 @	Cleveland	5-6	L	25-26-3	53	179-188
55.	Feb 18 @	Jersey	3-4	L	25-27-3	53	182-192
56.	Feb 21	Vancouver	5-4	W	26-27-3	55	187-196
57.	Feb 23	New England	0-3	L	26-28-3	55	187-199
58.	Feb 24 @	Winnipeg	1-3	L	26-29-3	55	188-202
59.	Feb 26	Los Angeles	4-2	W	27-29-3	57	192-204
60.	Feb 28	Houston	4-9	L	27-30-3	57	196-213
61.	Mar 1	Cleveland	7-4	W	28-30-3	59	203-217
62.	Mar 3	Toronto	4-5	L	28-31-3	59	207-222
63.	Mar 5	New England	2-3	L	28-32-3	59	209-225
64.	Mar 7 @	Quebec	3-2	W	29-32-3	61	212-227
65.	Mar 9	Winnipeg	*5-4	W	30-32-3	63	217-231
66.	Mar 12	New England	5-3	W	31-32-3	65	222-234
67.	Mar 14	Minnesota	7-4	W	32-32-3	67	229-238
68.	Mar 16	Quebec	*4-3	W	33-32-3	69	233-241
69.	Mar 17 @	Toronto	4-2	W	34-32-3	71	237-243
70.	Mar 19	Cleveland	4-7	L	34-33-3	71	241-250
71.	Mar 21	Vancouver	5-5	T	34-33-4	72	246-255
72.	Mar 23	Jersey	4-1	W	35-33-4	74	250-256
73.	Mar 24 @	Cleveland	3-3	T	35-33-5	75	253-259
74.	Mar 26	Edmonton	4-2	W	36-33-5	77	257-261
75.	Mar 29 @	Vancouver	5-2	W	37-33-5	79	262-263
76.	Mar 31 @	Edmonton	1-4	L	37-34-5	79	263-267
77.	Apr 2	Jersey	7-3	W	38-34-5	81	270-270
78.	Apr 3 @	Houston	1-3	L	38-35-5	81	271-273

Cougars Stars of 1973-1974

Pat Stapleton
Leadership

Ralph Backstrom
33 goals, 83 points

Bob Liddington
26 goals

Joe Hardy
24 goals

Andre Gill
6 wins in playoffs

Larry Mavety
51 points, 157 minutes

Scoring

pos	#	player	Regular Season							Playoffs				
			gp	g	a	pts	pim	ppg	shg	gp	g	a	pts	pim
D	18	Anderson, Ron F.	2	0	0	0	0	0	0	-	-	-	-	-
C	14	Backstrom, Ralph	78	33	50	83	26	6	2	18	5	14	19	4
RW	22	Benzelock, Jim	53	6	7	13	19	0	0	18	2	2	4	36
RW	18	Brackenbury, Curt	4	0	1	1	11	0	0	-	-	-	-	-
D	5	Cahan, Larry	3	0	0	0	2	0	0	-	-	-	-	-
LW	11	Coates, Brian	50	10	3	13	14	0	1	17	0	3	3	35
RW	5/18	Connelly, Gary	4	0	1	1	2	0	0	-	-	-	-	-
G	31	Coutu, Rich	20	0	0	0	0	0	0	-	-	-	-	-
LW	6	Fleming, Reggie	45	2	12	14	49	1	0	12	0	4	4	12
LW	24	Forey, Connie	1	0	0	0	0	0	0	-	-	-	-	-
LW	24	Glenwright, Brian	15	3	2	5	0	0	0	-	-	-	-	-
G	1	Gill, Andre	13	0	0	0	0	0	0	11	0	0	0	0
RW	16	Gordon, Don	23	5	4	9	9	3	0	18	4	8	12	4
C	25	Hardy, Joe	77	24	35	59	55	4	0	17	4	8	12	13
RW	20	Harris, Duke	64	14	16	30	20	3	0	18	6	6	12	2
D		Jones, James W.	1	0	0	0	0	0	0	-	-	-	-	-
LW	7	Liddington, Bob	73	26	21	47	20	4	1	18	6	5	11	11
D	5	MacKenzie, Al	2	0	0	0	0	0	0	-	-	-	-	-
D	4	Maggs, Darryl	78	8	22	30	148	0	0	18	3	5	8	71
D	21	Mavety, Larry	77	15	36	51	157	4	0	18	4	8	12	46
LW	10	Morris, Rick	76	17	16	33	140	1	0	18	4	3	7	42
RW	15	Nesterenko, Eric	29	2	5	7	8	1	0	-	-	-	-	-
G	30	Newton, Cam	45	0	1	1	0	0	0	10	0	0	0	0
RW	9	Paiement, Rosaire	78	30	43	73	87	7	0	18	9	6	15	16
LW	19	Popiel, Jan	63	22	17	39	36	6	0	18	8	5	13	12
D	3	Proceviat, Dick	77	2	20	22	53	0	0	13	0	4	4	10
LW	23	Rochon, Francois	71	12	11	23	27	1	0	9	2	1	3	0
LW	18	Rombough, Lorne	3	1	2	3	0	1	0	-	-	-	-	-
D	2	Shmyr, John	43	1	3	4	13	0	0	-	-	-	-	-
C	17	Sicinski, Bob	69	11	29	40	8	1	0	18	6	8	14	0
D	12	Stapleton, Pat	78	6	52	58	44	2	1	18	0	13	13	36
C	18	Walter, Dave	4	0	1	1	2	0	0	-	-	-	-	-
D	5	Watson, Jim	23	0	5	5	22	0	0	18	2	3	5	18
C	16	Whitlock, Bobby	52	16	19	35	44	6	1	-	-	-	-	-
C	8	Zaine, Rod	78	5	13	18	17	0	1	18	2	1	3	2

Power Play: 51 goals scored in 245 opportunities (20.8%) with 8 short-handed goals allowed.
Penalty Killing: 45 goals allowed in 289 opportunities (84.4%) with 7 short-handed goals scored.

Goaltending

goaltender	gp	min	ga	en	so	record	gaa	sog	sv%	gp	min	ga	record	gaa
Coutu, Rich	20	1207	75	3	0	9-10-1	3.73	628	0.881	-	-	-	-	-
Gill, Andre	13	803	46	1	0	4-7-2	3.44	418	0.890	11	614	38	6-5	3.71
Newton, Cam	45	2732	143	5	1	25-18-2	3.14	1352	0.894	10	486	34	2-5	4.20

Transactions: Dave Walter signed to contract, Feb 1973 • Butch Barber traded to New York for Wally Olds, May 1973 • Francois Rochon signed to contract, Jun 1973 • Darryl Maggs, Cam Newton signed to contracts, May 1973 • Pat Stapleton signed to contract, Jul 1973 • Rights to Ralph Backstrom acquired from Los Angeles Sharks, signed to contract, Aug 1973 • Joe Hardy acquired from Cleveland for rights to Larry Hillman, Sep 1973 • Duke Harris purchased from Houston, Sep 1973 • Eric Nesterenko signed a free agent, Oct 1973 • Al MacKenzie signed to contract, Dec 1973 • Bobby Whitlock traded to Los Angeles for Don Gordon and Jim Watson, Feb 1974.

131

1973-1974 CLEVELAND CRUSADERS

**Coach
Bill Needham**

Summary of Games (@ Away, * Overtime)

	date	opponent	score		record	pts	gf-ga			date	opponent	score		record	pts	gf-ga
1.	Oct 6	New York	2-2	T	0-0-1	1	2-2		40.	Jan 8 @	Chicago	0-0	T	19-16-5	43	124-121
2.	Oct 13	Quebec	6-3	W	1-0-1	3	8-5		41.	Jan 12	Los Angeles	5-4	W	20-16-5	45	129-125
3.	Oct 14	Chicago	*3-2	W	2-0-1	5	11-7		42.	Jan 13	Minnesota	4-2	W	21-16-5	47	133-127
4.	Oct 20	Toronto	6-4	W	3-0-1	7	17-11		43.	Jan 18 @	Winnipeg	3-7	L	21-17-5	47	136-134
5.	Oct 21 @	Houston	2-0	W	4-0-1	9	19-11		44.	Jan 20 @	Edmonton	2-5	L	21-18-5	47	138-139
6.	Oct 23 @	Los Angeles	3-4	L	4-1-1	9	22-15		45.	Jan 23 @	Vancouver	3-6	L	21-19-5	47	141-145
7.	Oct 26	Los Angeles	3-1	W	5-1-1	11	25-16		46.	Jan 24 @	Toronto	5-3	W	22-19-5	49	146-148
8.	Oct 27	Houston	2-2	T	5-1-2	12	27-18		47.	Jan 26 @	New England	0-4	L	22-20-5	49	146-152
9.	Oct 31	Winnipeg	6-4	W	6-1-2	14	33-22		48.	Jan 27 @	Quebec	3-4	L	22-21-5	49	149-156
10.	Nov 3	Chicago	4-7	L	6-2-2	14	37-29		49.	Jan 30	Houston	5-1	W	23-21-5	51	154-157
11.	Nov 4 @	New England	5-7	L	6-3-2	14	42-36		50.	Feb 2	Minnesota	2-4	L	23-22-5	51	156-161
12.	Nov 10	Winnipeg	4-2	W	7-3-2	16	46-38		51.	Feb 3	New England	3-1	W	24-22-5	53	159-162
13.	Nov 11 @	Minnesota	4-6	L	7-4-2	16	50-44		52.	Feb 5 @	Minnesota	1-4	L	24-23-5	53	160-166
14.	Nov 13 @	Chicago	5-2	W	8-4-2	18	55-46		53.	Feb 8	New England	2-4	L	24-24-5	53	162-170
15.	Nov 16 @	Los Angeles	*4-3	W	9-4-2	20	59-49		54.	Feb 9	Toronto	4-3	W	25-24-5	55	166-173
16.	Nov 18 @	Vancouver	2-8	L	9-5-2	20	61-57		55.	Feb 15 @	Jersey	2-6	L	25-25-5	55	168-179
17.	Nov 20 @	Edmonton	3-5	L	9-6-2	20	64-62		56.	Feb 16	Quebec	5-2	W	26-25-5	57	173-181
18.	Nov 21 @	Winnipeg	2-6	L	9-7-2	20	66-68		57.	Feb 17	Chicago	6-5	W	27-25-5	59	179-186
19.	Nov 23	Quebec	2-3	L	9-8-2	20	68-71		58.	Feb 19 @	Quebec	*5-6	L	27-26-5	59	184-192
20.	Nov 24	Toronto	2-1	W	10-8-2	22	70-72		59.	Feb 23	Vancouver	7-3	W	28-26-5	61	191-195
21.	Nov 29 @	Quebec	4-4	T	10-8-3	23	74-76		60.	Feb 24	Minnesota	1-2	L	28-27-5	61	192-197
22.	Dec 1	Edmonton	4-2	W	11-8-3	25	78-78		61.	Feb 28 @	Minnesota	6-6	T	28-27-6	62	198-203
23.	Dec 2	Edmonton	3-0	W	12-8-3	27	81-78		62.	Mar 1 @	Chicago	4-7	L	28-28-6	62	202-210
24.	Dec 6 @	Jersey	2-3	L	12-9-3	27	83-81		63.	Mar 3 @	Edmonton	3-3	T	28-28-7	63	205-213
25.	Dec 8	New England	*2-1	W	13-9-3	29	85-82		64.	Mar 5 @	Los Angeles	6-3	W	29-28-7	65	211-216
26.	Dec 9 @	New England	2-3	L	13-10-3	29	87-85		65.	Mar 7 @	Vancouver	4-2	W	30-28-7	67	215-218
27.	Dec 12	Jersey	2-4	L	13-11-3	29	89-89		66.	Mar 8 @	Winnipeg	4-1	W	31-28-7	69	219-219
28.	Dec 13 @	Toronto	1-3	L	13-12-3	29	90-92		67.	Mar 10 @	Toronto	3-8	L	31-29-7	69	222-227
29.	Dec 15	Toronto	4-3	W	14-12-3	31	94-95		68.	Mar 13	Winnipeg	4-3	W	32-29-7	71	226-230
30.	Dec 16 @	Houston	2-2	T	14-12-4	32	96-97		69.	Mar 16	Jersey	4-4	T	32-29-8	72	230-234
31.	Dec 22	Minnesota	2-1	W	15-12-4	34	98-98		70.	Mar 17 @	Houston	3-4	L	32-30-8	72	233-238
32.	Dec 23 @	Minnesota	4-2	W	16-12-4	36	102-100		71.	Mar 19 @	Chicago	7-4	W	33-30-8	74	240-242
33.	Dec 26	Vancouver	3-5	L	16-13-4	36	105-105		72.	Mar 20	Houston	4-5	L	33-31-8	74	244-247
34.	Dec 27 @	Quebec	2-4	L	16-14-4	36	107-109		73.	Mar 23	Edmonton	3-1	W	34-31-8	76	247-248
35.	Dec 29	Jersey	3-0	W	17-14-4	38	110-109		74.	Mar 24	Chicago	3-3	T	34-31-9	77	250-251
36.	Dec 30 @	Jersey	2-6	L	17-15-4	38	112-115		75.	Mar 27	Quebec	*5-4	W	35-31-9	79	255-255
37.	Jan 1 @	Toronto	0-3	L	17-16-4	38	112-118		76.	Mar 28 @	New England	2-3	L	35-32-9	79	257-258
38.	Jan 5	New England	1-0	W	18-16-4	40	113-118		77.	Mar 30	Los Angeles	*5-4	W	36-32-9	81	262-262
39.	Jan 6	Vancouver	11-3	W	19-16-4	42	124-121		78.	Mar 31 @	Jersey	4-2	W	37-32-9	83	266-264

Crusaders Stars of 1973-1974

Paul Shmyr
44 points, 165 minutes

Grant Erickson
23 goals

Wayne Muloin
Defensive shot-blocker

Gerry Cheevers
4 shutouts, 30 wins

Gary Jarrett
70 points led team

Skip Krake
20 goals, 56 points

Scoring

pos	#	player	gp	g	a	pts	pim	ppg	shg	gp	g	a	pts	pim
						Regular Season							**Playoffs**	
C		Adduono, Ray	2	0	0	0	0	0	0	-	-	-	-	-
RW	21	Andrea, Paul	69	15	18	33	14	6	3	5	1	0	1	0
C	9	Brindley, Doug	30	13	9	22	13	1	0	5	0	1	1	2
C	10	Buchanan, Ron	49	18	27	45	2	6	0	5	0	0	0	2
LW	27	Buetow, Brad	25	0	0	0	4	0	0	-	-	-	-	-
G	30	Cheevers, Gerry	59	0	0	0	30	0	0	5	0	0	0	0
D	6	Clearwater, Ray	68	12	23	35	47	3	0	5	0	0	0	2
C	19	Cournoyer, Norm	13	3	5	8	6	1	0	-	-	-	-	-
D	18	Edur, Tom	76	7	31	38	26	1	0	5	1	2	3	0
LW	16	Erickson, Grant	78	23	27	50	26	3	2	5	0	2	2	0
LW	15	Heindl, William	67	4	14	18	4	1	0	5	0	1	1	2
D	2	Hillman, Larry	44	5	21	26	37	1	0	-	-	-	-	-
D	8	Hillman, Wayne	66	1	7	8	51	0	0	5	0	0	0	16
RW	24	Hodgson, Ted	10	0	2	2	6	0	0	-	-	-	-	-
D	4	Hopiavuori, Ralph	13	0	2	2	6	0	0	4	0	1	1	0
LW	12	Jarrett, Gary	75	31	39	70	68	11	0	5	1	1	2	13
C	17	Krake, Skip	69	20	36	56	94	5	0	5	0	1	1	39
D	22	McMasters, Jim	9	0	0	0	4	0	0	-	-	-	-	-
LW	11	Morgan, Ron	4	0	1	1	7	0	0	2	1	0	1	0
D	5	Muloin, Wayne	76	3	7	10	39	1	0	5	1	0	1	0
C	29	Neale, Robbie	43	8	9	17	30	1	0	5	0	0	0	4
LW	7	Pinder, Gerry	73	23	33	56	90	3	1	1	0	0	0	0
LW	23	Pumple, Rich	17	2	2	4	16	0	0	-	-	-	-	-
D	26	Shirton, Glen	4	0	0	0	0	0	0	-	-	-	-	-
D	3	Shmyr, Paul	78	13	31	44	165	3	0	5	0	4	4	31
RW	28	Walker, Russ	76	15	14	29	117	1	0	5	1	0	1	11
C	24	Ward, Ron	23	19	7	26	7	4	0	5	3	0	3	2
G	1	Whidden, Bob	22	0	1	1	2	0	0	-	-	-	-	-
C	14	Wiste, Jim	76	23	35	58	26	4	0	5	0	1	1	0
LW	20	Young, Bill	53	8	9	17	73	0	0	-	-	-	-	-

Power Play: 56 goals scored in 245 opportunities (22.9%) with 12 short-handed goals allowed.
Penalty Killing: 59 goals allowed in 237 opportunities (75.1%) with 6 short-handed goals scored.

Goaltending

goaltender	gp	min	ga	en	so	record	gaa	sog	sv%	gp	min	ga	record	gaa
Cheevers, Gerry	59	3562	180	4	4	30-20-6	3.03	1911	0.906	5	303	18	1-4	3.56
Whidden, Bob	22	1232	80	0	1	7-12-3	3.90	680	0.882	-	-	-	-	-

Transactions: Robbie Neale signed to contract, May 1973 • Russ Walker signed to contract, Jul 1973 • Bill Heindl signed to contract, Aug 1973 • Bill Young acquired from Minnesota for rights to Rick Smith, Sep 1973 • Wayne Hillman's rights acquired from New York, Sep 1973 • Larry Hillman, Wayne Hillman signed to contract, Sep 1973 • Ted Hodgson and Bill Young traded to Los Angeles for Ron Ward, Feb 1974

1973-1974 EDMONTON OILERS

Coach
Brian Shaw

Summary of Games (@ Away, * Overtime)

	date	opponent	score		record	pts	gf-ga		date	opponent	score		record	pts	gf-ga
1.	Oct 12	Winnipeg	6-4	W	1-0-0	2	6-4	40.	Jan 9 @	Minnesota	6-4	W	22-18-0	44	143-132
2.	Oct 14	Houston	5-2	W	2-0-0	4	11-6	41.	Jan 11 @	Winnipeg	4-7	L	22-19-0	44	147-139
3.	Oct 19	Vancouver	1-3	L	2-1-0	4	12-9	42.	Jan 13 @	Vancouver	2-6	L	22-20-0	44	149-145
4.	Oct 21	Chicago	4-1	W	3-1-0	6	16-10	43.	Jan 15	Minnesota	4-1	W	23-20-0	46	153-146
5.	Oct 23	Toronto	4-2	W	4-1-0	8	20-12	44.	Jan 18	Jersey	7-4	W	24-20-0	48	160-150
6.	Oct 27 @	Vancouver	6-2	W	5-1-0	10	26-14	45.	Jan 20	Cleveland	5-2	W	25-20-0	50	165-152
7.	Oct 28	Vancouver	7-5	W	6-1-0	12	33-19	46.	Jan 22	Jersey	2-6	L	25-21-0	50	167-158
8.	Nov 2	Quebec	5-4	W	7-1-0	14	38-23	47.	Jan 25	Winnipeg	3-4	L	25-22-0	50	170-162
9.	Nov 4	Minnesota	4-3	W	8-1-0	16	42-26	48.	Jan 27	Houston	1-4	L	25-23-0	50	171-166
10.	Nov 6	New York	8-0	W	9-1-0	18	50-26	49.	Feb 1	Chicago	3-2	W	26-23-0	52	174-168
11.	Nov 8 @	Quebec	4-3	W	10-1-0	20	54-29	50.	Feb 3	Los Angeles	5-2	W	27-23-0	54	179-170
12.	Nov 10 @	New England	6-3	W	11-1-0	22	60-32	51.	Feb 5 @	Vancouver	0-8	L	27-24-0	54	179-178
13.	Nov 11 @	Toronto	4-2	W	12-1-0	24	64-34	52.	Feb 8	Houston	2-6	L	27-25-0	54	181-184
14.	Nov 13	Los Angeles	4-0	W	13-1-0	26	68-34	53.	Feb 10	Quebec	3-4	L	27-26-0	54	184-188
15.	Nov 16 @	Winnipeg	1-3	L	13-2-0	26	69-37	54.	Feb 12 @	Chicago	2-3	L	27-27-0	54	186-191
16.	Nov 18	Minnesota	2-5	L	13-3-0	26	71-42	55.	Feb 13 @	Minnesota	4-7	L	27-28-0	54	190-198
17.	Nov 20	Cleveland	5-3	W	14-3-0	28	76-45	56.	Feb 15	New England	3-7	L	27-29-0	54	193-205
18.	Nov 22 @	Vancouver	1-7	L	14-4-0	28	77-52	57.	Feb 17	Toronto	*3-2	W	28-29-0	56	196-207
19.	Nov 23 @	Los Angeles	0-2	L	14-5-0	28	77-54	58.	Feb 20	Winnipeg	4-1	W	29-29-0	58	200-208
20.	Nov 25 @	Houston	1-2	L	14-6-0	28	78-56	59.	Feb 23 @	Houston	2-5	L	29-30-0	58	202-213
21.	Nov 29 @	Jersey	3-2	W	15-6-0	30	81-58	60.	Feb 24 @	Los Angeles	5-3	W	30-30-0	60	207-216
22.	Dec 1 @	Cleveland	2-4	L	15-7-0	30	83-62	61.	Mar 1	Houston	5-2	W	31-30-0	62	212-218
23.	Dec 2 @	Cleveland	0-3	L	15-8-0	30	83-65	62.	Mar 3	Cleveland	3-3	T	31-30-1	63	215-221
24.	Dec 4 @	Chicago	2-0	W	16-8-0	32	85-65	63.	Mar 6 @	Houston	4-2	W	32-30-1	65	219-223
25.	Dec 5 @	Winnipeg	1-3	L	16-9-0	32	86-68	64.	Mar 8 @	Los Angeles	1-4	L	32-31-1	65	220-227
26.	Dec 6	Toronto	4-3	W	17-9-0	34	90-71	65.	Mar 10	Vancouver	*1-2	L	32-32-1	65	221-229
27.	Dec 12	Los Angeles	2-7	L	17-10-0	34	92-78	66.	Mar 12	Los Angeles	8-1	W	33-32-1	67	229-230
28.	Dec 14	Quebec	3-4	L	17-11-0	34	95-82	67.	Mar 15	New England	2-6	L	33-33-1	67	231-236
29.	Dec 16 @	Jersey	7-6	W	18-11-0	36	102-88	68.	Mar 17	Vancouver	3-2	W	34-33-1	69	234-238
30.	Dec 18 @	Quebec	2-4	L	18-12-0	36	104-92	69.	Mar 20 @	New England	2-2	T	34-33-2	70	236-240
31.	Dec 19 @	New England	2-4	L	18-13-0	36	106-96	70.	Mar 21 @	Quebec	5-5	T	34-33-3	71	241-245
32.	Dec 21	Vancouver	4-1	W	19-13-0	38	110-97	71.	Mar 23 @	Cleveland	1-3	L	34-34-3	71	242-248
33.	Dec 22 @	Vancouver	3-6	L	19-14-0	38	113-103	72.	Mar 25 @	Jersey	4-1	W	35-34-3	73	246-249
34.	Dec 27	Minnesota	4-5	L	19-15-0	38	117-108	73.	Mar 26 @	Chicago	2-4	L	35-35-3	73	248-253
35.	Dec 29	New England	6-2	W	20-15-0	40	123-110	74.	Mar 28 @	Toronto	*5-6	L	35-36-3	73	253-259
36.	Jan 1	Winnipeg	*3-4	L	20-16-0	40	126-114	75.	Mar 29 @	Minnesota	3-1	W	36-36-3	75	256-260
37.	Jan 4 @	Los Angeles	3-4	L	20-17-0	40	129-118	76.	Mar 31	Chicago	4-1	W	37-36-3	77	260-261
38.	Jan 6 @	Minnesota	6-4	W	21-17-0	42	135-122	77.	Apr 2 @	Toronto	2-3	L	37-37-3	77	262-264
39.	Jan 8 @	Houston	2-6	L	21-18-0	42	137-128	78.	Apr 3 @	Winnipeg	*6-5	W	38-37-3	79	268-269

Oilers Stars of 1973-1974

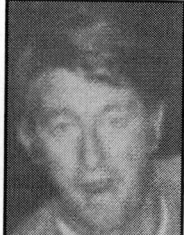

Ron Climie
38 goals, 74 points

Ken Baird
17 goals, 115 minutes

Jack Norris
23 wins, 2 shutouts

Doug Barrie
214 minutes

Tom Gilmore
19 goals

Len Lunde
26 goals

Scoring

pos	#	player	gp	g	a	pts	pim	ppg	shg	gp	g	a	pts	pim
RW	21	Anderson, Ron C.	19	5	2	7	6	0	0	-	-	-	-	-
D	19	Baird, Ken	68	17	19	36	115	2	0	5	1	1	2	7
D	5	Barrie, Doug	69	4	27	31	214	0	0	4	1	0	1	16
LW	14	Carlin, Brian	5	1	0	1	0	0	0	-	-	-	-	-
D	20	Carlyle, Steve	50	2	13	15	18	0	0	5	0	1	1	4
LW	11	Climie, Ron	76	38	36	74	22	9	0	5	0	0	0	0
LW		Colborne, Howie	2	0	0	0	0	0	0	-	-	-	-	-
D	2	Cote, Roger	59	0	3	3	34	0	0	2	0	0	0	0
D	22	Cunningham, Gary	2	0	0	0	0	0	0	-	-	-	-	-
G		Doyle, Gary	1	0	0	0	0	0	0	-	-	-	-	-
D	6	Falkenberg, Bob	78	3	14	17	32	0	0	5	0	2	2	14
C	21	Fitchner, Bob	31	1	2	3	21	0	0	-	-	-	-	-
LW	8	Fonteyne, Val	72	9	13	22	2	0	4	5	1	0	1	0
LW	10	Gilmore, Tom	57	19	23	42	164	2	0	5	1	4	5	15
D	3	Hamilton, Al	77	14	45	59	104	6	0	4	1	1	2	15
C	7	Harrison, Jim	46	24	45	69	99	3	2	-	-	-	-	-
C	16	Joyal, Eddie	45	8	10	18	2	0	0	5	2	0	2	4
C	27	Lunde, Len	71	26	22	48	8	7	2	5	0	1	1	0
RW	14	MacDonald, Blair	78	21	24	45	34	5	0	5	4	2	6	2
C	18	McAneeley, Bob	52	12	11	23	49	0	0	4	1	0	1	0
D	22	McCrimmon, Jim	75	2	3	5	106	0	0	-	-	-	-	-
LW	12	McKenzie, Brian	78	18	20	38	66	0	0	5	0	1	1	0
G	30	Norris, Jack	53	0	3	3	0	0	0	3	0	0	0	0
RW	17	Patenaude, Rusty	71	20	23	43	55	2	0	4	0	2	2	2
C	9	Perkins, Ross	78	16	40	56	43	0	0	5	1	3	4	2
C	25	Schraefel, Jim	34	1	1	2	0	0	0	5	0	3	3	0
C	15	Sheehan, Bobby	10	1	3	4	6	1	0	5	1	3	4	0
D	4	Wall, Bob	74	6	31	37	46	2	1	-	-	-	-	-
G	38	Wilkie, Ian	5	0	0	0	0	0	0	1	0	0	0	0
G	1	Worthy, Chris	29	0	0	0	0	0	0	3	0	0	0	0
C	15	Zuk, Wayne	2	0	0	0	0	0	0	-	-	-	-	-

Power Play: 39 goals scored in 245 opportunities (15.9%) with 4 short-handed goals allowed.
Penalty Killing: 66 goals allowed in 295 opportunities (77.6%) with 9 short-handed goals scored.

Goaltending

goaltender	gp	min	ga	en	so	record	gaa	sog	sv%	gp	min	ga	record	gaa
Doyle, Gary	1	60	4	0	0	1-0-0	4.00	38	0.895	-	-	-	-	-
Norris, Jack	53	2954	158	5	2	23-24-1	3.21	1546	0.898	3	111	9	0-2	4.86
Wilkie, Ian	5	256	9	0	0	3-1-1	2.11	128	0.930	1	41	4	0-1	5.85
Worthy, Chris	29	1452	92	1	1	11-12-1	3.80	866	0.894	3	146	8	1-1	3.29

Transactions: Ron Climie acquired from Toronto for rights to Darryl Sittler, Jun 1973 • Brian McKenzie signed to contract, Jun 1973 • Bob Fitchner, Chris Worthy signed to contracts, Aug 1973 • Gary Doyle signed to contract, Sep 1973 • Ron Walters traded to Los Angeles for Tom Gilmore, Oct 1973 • Ian Wilkie signed to contract, Sep 1973, sold to Los Angeles, Nov 1973 • Bobby Sheehan acquired for future considerations (Bob Falkenberg) from Jersey, Mar 1974 • Wayne Zuk traded to Los Angeles for Ian Wilkie, Mar 1974

1973-1974 HOUSTON AEROS

Coach
Bill Dineen

Summary of Games (@ Away, * Overtime)

	date	opponent	score		record	pts	gf-ga
1.	Oct 13 @	Los Angeles	4-3	W	1-0-0	2	4-3
2.	Oct 14 @	Edmonton	2-5	L	1-1-0	2	6-8
3.	Oct 17 @	Vancouver	7-2	W	2-1-0	4	13-10
4.	Oct 21	Cleveland	0-2	L	2-2-0	4	13-12
5.	Oct 24	Los Angeles	6-2	W	3-2-0	6	19-14
6.	Oct 27 @	Cleveland	2-2	T	3-2-1	7	21-16
7.	Oct 28	Quebec	2-3	L	3-3-1	7	23-19
8.	Oct 30	Minnesota	6-1	W	4-3-1	9	29-20
9.	Nov 3	Los Angeles	6-4	W	5-3-1	11	35-24
10.	Nov 7	Toronto	4-5	L	5-4-1	11	39-29
11.	Nov 10	Vancouver	8-3	W	6-4-1	13	47-32
12.	Nov 13 @	Minnesota	5-2	W	7-4-1	15	52-34
13.	Nov 15 @	Chicago	2-3	L	7-5-1	15	54-37
14.	Nov 17 @	New York	3-2	W	8-5-1	17	57-39
15.	Nov 18 @	Quebec	3-8	L	8-6-1	17	60-47
16.	Nov 21	New England	4-1	W	9-6-1	19	64-48
17.	Nov 24	Chicago	5-3	W	10-6-1	21	69-51
18.	Nov 25	Edmonton	2-1	W	11-6-1	23	71-52
19.	Nov 28	Winnipeg	4-4	T	11-6-2	24	75-56
20.	Nov 29 @	New England	2-5	L	11-7-2	24	77-61
21.	Dec 1 @	Quebec	3-3	T	11-7-3	25	80-64
22.	Dec 2 @	Toronto	2-5	L	11-8-3	25	82-69
23.	Dec 5	Jersey	5-2	W	12-8-3	27	87-71
24.	Dec 6 @	Los Angeles	3-4	L	12-9-3	27	90-75
25.	Dec 9 @	Vancouver	5-3	W	13-9-3	29	95-78
26.	Dec 12 @	Winnipeg	3-2	W	14-9-3	31	98-80
27.	Dec 14 @	Minnesota	5-2	W	15-9-3	33	103-82
28.	Dec 15 @	Chicago	2-5	L	15-10-3	33	105-87
29.	Dec 16	Cleveland	2-2	T	15-10-4	34	107-89
30.	Dec 19	Winnipeg	10-0	W	16-10-4	36	117-89
31.	Dec 21 @	Toronto	1-3	L	16-11-4	36	118-92
32.	Dec 22	Los Angeles	8-3	W	17-11-4	38	126-95
33.	Dec 26	New England	*2-3	L	17-12-4	38	128-98
34.	Dec 29	Chicago	3-0	W	18-12-4	40	131-98
35.	Dec 30 @	Los Angeles	6-4	W	19-12-4	42	137-102
36.	Jan 5 @	Jersey	1-2	L	19-13-4	42	138-104
37.	Jan 6	Winnipeg	7-1	W	20-13-4	44	145-105
38.	Jan 8	Edmonton	6-2	W	21-13-4	46	151-107
39.	Jan 12	Quebec	5-1	W	22-13-4	48	156-108
40.	Jan 16	Toronto	4-1	W	23-13-4	50	160-109
41.	Jan 17	Vancouver	7-4	W	24-13-4	52	167-113
42.	Jan 19	Los Angeles	2-3	L	24-14-4	52	169-116
43.	Jan 22	Los Angeles	3-1	W	25-14-4	54	172-117
44.	Jan 24	Quebec	5-1	W	26-14-4	56	177-118
45.	Jan 26 @	Vancouver	4-2	W	27-14-4	58	181-120
46.	Jan 27 @	Edmonton	4-1	W	28-14-4	60	185-121
47.	Jan 30 @	Cleveland	1-5	L	28-15-4	60	186-126
48.	Jan 31 @	Quebec	4-6	L	28-16-4	60	190-132
49.	Feb 2 @	New England	2-5	L	28-17-4	60	192-137
50.	Feb 4 @	Jersey	7-1	W	29-17-4	62	199-138
51.	Feb 5	Jersey	4-0	W	30-17-4	64	203-138
52.	Feb 8 @	Edmonton	6-2	W	31-17-4	66	209-140
53.	Feb 10 @	Winnipeg	2-2	T	31-17-5	67	211-142
54.	Feb 12 @	Minnesota	3-1	W	32-17-5	69	214-143
55.	Feb 13	Winnipeg	5-1	W	33-17-5	71	219-144
56.	Feb 15 @	Los Angeles	6-4	W	34-17-5	73	225-148
57.	Feb 17	Minnesota	1-6	L	34-18-5	73	226-154
58.	Feb 20	Jersey	7-2	W	35-18-5	75	233-156
59.	Feb 23	Edmonton	5-2	W	36-18-5	77	238-158
60.	Feb 24	Vancouver	7-1	W	37-18-5	79	245-159
61.	Feb 26	Vancouver	3-2	W	38-18-5	81	248-161
62.	Feb 28 @	Chicago	9-4	W	39-18-5	83	257-165
63.	Mar 1 @	Edmonton	2-5	L	39-19-5	83	259-170
64.	Mar 3	New England	3-6	L	39-20-5	83	262-176
65.	Mar 6	Edmonton	2-4	L	39-21-5	83	264-180
66.	Mar 9	Toronto	4-2	W	40-21-5	85	268-182
67.	Mar 12	Minnesota	3-2	W	41-21-5	87	271-184
68.	Mar 14 @	Los Angeles	6-0	W	42-21-5	89	277-184
69.	Mar 17	Cleveland	4-3	W	43-21-5	91	281-187
70.	Mar 20 @	Cleveland	5-4	W	44-21-5	93	286-191
71.	Mar 21 @	Toronto	3-6	L	44-22-5	93	289-197
72.	Mar 22 @	Winnipeg	4-2	W	45-22-5	95	293-199
73.	Mar 24	Minnesota	3-5	L	45-23-5	95	296-204
74.	Mar 27 @	Vancouver	8-1	W	46-23-5	97	304-205
75.	Mar 29 @	Winnipeg	5-7	L	46-24-5	97	309-212
76.	Mar 31 @	Minnesota	2-5	L	46-25-5	97	311-217
77.	Apr 1 @	New England	4-1	W	47-25-5	99	315-218
78.	Apr 3	Chicago	3-1	W	48-25-5	101	318-219

Aeros Stars of 1973-1974

Gordie Howe	**Mark Howe**	**Marty Howe**	**Don McLeod**	**Poul Popiel**	**Jim Sherrit**
100 points led team	38 goals, 79 points	24 points, 90 minutes	33 wins, 3 shutouts	7 goals, 126 minutes	30 goals

Scoring

| pos | # | player | Regular Season | | | | | | | Playoffs | | | | |
			gp	g	a	pts	pim	ppg	shg	gp	g	a	pts	pim
G	29	Grahame, Ron	4	0	0	0	0	0	0	-	-	-	-	-
RW	21	Grierson, Don	65	11	18	29	45	0	0	14	1	5	6	23
D	17	Hale, Larry	69	2	14	16	35	0	0	14	3	2	5	6
C	11	Hall, Murray	78	30	28	58	25	8	2	14	9	6	15	6
LW	16	Hinse, Andre	69	24	56	80	39	10	0	14	8	9	17	18
C	12	Hoekstra, Ed	19	2	0	2	0	0	0	-	-	-	-	-
RW	9	Howe, Gordie	76	31	69	100	46	9	3	13	3	14	17	34
D/F	4	Howe, Mark	76	38	41	79	20	5	5	14	9	10	19	4
D	3	Howe, Marty	73	4	20	24	90	0	0	14	1	5	6	31
LW	7	Hughes, Frank	73	42	42	84	47	13	0	14	9	5	14	9
D	5	Kannegiesser, Gord	78	0	20	20	26	0	0	3	0	2	2	2
C	10	Labossiere, Gord	67	19	36	55	30	4	0	14	7	9	16	20
C	13	Lund, Larry	75	33	53	86	109	7	2	14	9	14	23	56
G	1	McLeod, Don	49	0	3	3	6	0	0	14	0	0	0	0
D	6	Popiel, Poul	78	7	41	48	126	1	0	14	1	14	15	22
D	22	Prentice, Bill	55	1	2	3	35	0	0	10	0	0	0	5
G	30	Rutledge, Wayne	25	0	1	1	14	0	0	-	-	-	-	-
D	2	Schella, John	73	12	19	31	170	0	2	14	2	6	8	42
C	23	Sherrit, Jim	76	30	28	58	18	4	0	14	5	7	12	2
LW	18	Stanfield, Jack	41	1	3	4	2	1	0	7	0	0	0	2
C	8	Szura, Joe	42	8	7	15	4	0	0	10	0	0	0	0
LW	14	Taylor, Ted	75	21	23	44	143	1	3	14	4	8	12	60
LW	25	Williamson, Gary	9	2	6	8	0	1	0	12	0	0	0	0

Power Play: 64 goals scored in 223 opportunities (28.7%) with 3 short-handed goals allowed.
Penalty Killing: 47 goals allowed in 288 opportunities (83.7%) with 17 short-handed goals scored.

Goaltending

goaltender	gp	min	ga	en	so	record	gaa	sog	sv%	gp	min	ga	record	gaa
Grahame, Ron	4	250	5	0	1	3-0-1	1.20	123	0.959	-	-	-	-	-
McLeod, Don	49	2971	127	3	3	33-13-3	2.56	1432	0.911	14	842	35	12-2	2.49
Rutledge, Wayne	25	1509	84	0	0	12-12-1	3.34	653	0.886	-	-	-	-	-

Transactions: Mark Howe and Marty Howe signed to contracts, Jun 1973 • Gordie Howe signed to contract, Jul 1973 • Rights to Ron Grahame acquired from New York, Jul 1973 • Andre Hinse signed to contract, Sep 1973 • Brian McDonald traded to Los Angeles for Joe Szura, Sep 1973

1973-1974 LOS ANGELES SHARKS

Coach
Terry Slater
10-34-0

Coach
Ted McCaskill
15-19-0

(McCaskill coached from November 18, 1973 to February 3, 1974)

Summary of Games (@ Away, * Overtime)

	date	opponent	score		record	pts	gf-ga		date	opponent	score		record	pts	gf-ga
1.	Oct 13	Houston	3-4	L	0-1-0	0	3-4	40.	Jan 10 @	Quebec	1-7	L	15-25-0	30	119-159
2.	Oct 16	Toronto	0-3	L	0-2-0	0	3-7	41.	Jan 12 @	Cleveland	4-5	L	15-26-0	30	123-164
3.	Oct 18	Chicago	2-7	L	0-3-0	0	5-14	42.	Jan 13 @	New England	6-9	L	15-27-0	30	129-173
4.	Oct 21 @	Vancouver	4-1	W	1-3-0	2	9-15	43.	Jan 15	Quebec	6-4	W	16-27-0	32	135-177
5.	Oct 23	Cleveland	4-3	W	2-3-0	4	13-18	44.	Jan 18	Toronto	4-1	W	17-27-0	34	139-178
6.	Oct 24 @	Houston	2-6	L	2-4-0	4	15-24	45.	Jan 19 @	Houston	3-2	W	18-27-0	36	142-180
7.	Oct 26 @	Cleveland	1-3	L	2-5-0	4	16-27	46.	Jan 20	Vancouver	0-3	L	18-28-0	36	142-183
8.	Oct 27 @	New England	1-3	L	2-6-0	4	17-30	47.	Jan 22 @	Houston	1-3	L	18-29-0	36	143-186
9.	Oct 28 @	New York	2-0	W	3-6-0	6	19-30	48.	Jan 25	Quebec	2-0	W	19-29-0	38	145-186
10.	Oct 30	Quebec	4-6	L	3-7-0	6	23-36	49.	Jan 27 @	Jersey	6-3	W	20-29-0	40	151-189
11.	Nov 2	Minnesota	1-5	L	3-8-0	6	24-41	50.	Jan 29 @	Quebec	0-5	L	20-30-0	40	151-194
12.	Nov 3 @	Houston	4-6	L	3-9-0	6	28-47	51.	Jan 31 @	Toronto	*4-5	L	20-31-0	40	155-199
13.	Nov 4 @	Toronto	3-6	L	3-10-0	6	31-53	52.	Feb 1 @	Winnipeg	0-4	L	20-32-0	40	155-203
14.	Nov 6 @	Chicago	*4-5	L	3-11-0	6	35-58	53.	Feb 3 @	Edmonton	2-5	L	20-33-0	40	157-208
15.	Nov 7 @	Vancouver	3-1	W	4-11-0	8	38-59	54.	Feb 7	Jersey	4-7	L	20-34-0	40	161-215
16.	Nov 9	Toronto	4-2	W	5-11-0	10	42-61	55.	Feb 10	Chicago	2-4	L	20-35-0	40	163-219
17.	Nov 11 @	Winnipeg	2-6	L	5-12-0	10	44-67	56.	Feb 12	Winnipeg	2-4	L	20-36-0	40	165-223
18.	Nov 13 @	Edmonton	0-4	L	5-13-0	10	44-71	57.	Feb 15	Houston	4-6	L	20-37-0	40	169-229
19.	Nov 16	Cleveland	*3-4	L	5-14-0	10	47-75	58.	Feb 17	Vancouver	0-4	L	20-38-0	40	169-233
20.	Nov 18	New England	2-5	L	5-15-0	10	49-80	59.	Feb 20	New England	4-2	W	21-38-0	42	173-235
21.	Nov 20	Minnesota	6-2	W	6-15-0	12	55-82	60.	Feb 24	Edmonton	3-5	L	21-39-0	42	176-240
22.	Nov 22	Chicago	3-4	L	6-16-0	12	58-86	61.	Feb 26 @	Chicago	2-4	L	21-40-0	42	178-244
23.	Nov 23	Edmonton	2-0	W	7-16-0	14	60-86	62.	Feb 27 @	Minnesota	4-5	L	21-41-0	42	182-249
24.	Nov 27	Winnipeg	*5-4	W	8-16-0	16	65-90	63.	Mar 2 @	Jersey	7-8	L	21-42-0	42	189-257
25.	Nov 30 @	Winnipeg	5-2	W	9-16-0	18	70-92	64.	Mar 3 @	Minnesota	3-5	L	21-43-0	42	192-262
26.	Dec 1 @	Chicago	*5-4	W	10-16-0	20	75-96	65.	Mar 5	Cleveland	3-6	L	21-44-0	42	195-268
27.	Dec 4 @	Minnesota	2-9	L	10-17-0	20	77-105	66.	Mar 8	Edmonton	4-1	W	22-44-0	44	199-269
28.	Dec 6	Houston	4-3	W	11-17-0	22	81-108	67.	Mar 10	Minnesota	6-5	W	23-44-0	46	205-274
29.	Dec 12 @	Edmonton	7-2	W	12-17-0	24	88-110	68.	Mar 12 @	Edmonton	1-8	L	23-45-0	46	206-282
30.	Dec 14 @	Winnipeg	0-1	L	12-18-0	24	88-111	69.	Mar 13 @	Vancouver	2-5	L	23-46-0	46	208-287
31.	Dec 15 @	Vancouver	4-6	L	12-19-0	24	92-117	70.	Mar 14	Houston	0-6	L	23-47-0	46	208-293
32.	Dec 16	Vancouver	5-3	W	13-19-0	26	97-120	71.	Mar 20	Jersey	5-8	L	23-48-0	46	213-301
33.	Dec 18	Vancouver	2-5	L	13-20-0	26	99-125	72.	Mar 22	Minnesota	2-5	L	23-49-0	46	215-306
34.	Dec 21 @	Minnesota	3-4	L	13-21-0	26	102-129	73.	Mar 24	Winnipeg	6-3	W	24-49-0	48	221-309
35.	Dec 22 @	Houston	3-8	L	13-22-0	26	105-137	74.	Mar 27 @	New England	1-7	L	24-50-0	48	222-316
36.	Dec 27	New England	1-5	L	13-23-0	26	106-142	75.	Mar 28 @	Quebec	3-9	L	24-51-0	48	225-325
37.	Dec 30	Houston	4-6	L	13-24-0	26	110-148	76.	Mar 30 @	Quebec	*4-5	L	24-52-0	48	229-330
38.	Jan 4	Edmonton	4-3	W	14-24-0	28	114-151	77.	Mar 31 @	Toronto	4-5	L	24-53-0	48	233-335
39.	Jan 8	Winnipeg	4-1	W	15-24-0	30	118-152	78.	Apr 4	Jersey	6-4	W	25-53-0	50	239-339

Sharks Stars of 1973-1974

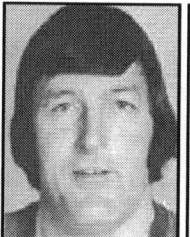

Ian Wilkie	**Marc Tardif**	**Tom Serviss**	**Steve Sutherland**	**Brian McDonald**	**Bart Crashley**
11-9-0 record	40 goals	Penalty killer	182 minutes	22 goals	Blueline offense

Scoring

pos	#	player	gp	g	a	pts	pim	ppg	shg	gp	g	a	pts	pim
LW	16	Bowman, Kirk	10	0	2	2	0	0	0	-	-	-	-	-
D	7	Crashley, Bart	78	4	26	30	16	2	0	-	-	-	-	-
D	4	Derksen, Brian	1	0	0	0	2	0	0	-	-	-	-	-
G	30	Gardner, George	2	0	0	0	0	0	0	-	-	-	-	-
LW	22	Garwasiuk, Ron	51	6	13	19	100	0	1	-	-	-	-	-
G	1	Gillow, Russ	18	0	0	0	2	0	0	-	-	-	-	-
RW	20	Gordon, Don	29	8	6	14	24	1	0	-	-	-	-	-
LW	16	Heiskala, Earl	24	2	6	8	45	0	0	-	-	-	-	-
RW	16	Hodgson, Ted	23	3	9	12	22	2	0	-	-	-	-	-
G	25	Hoganson, Paul	27	0	0	0	0	0	0	-	-	-	-	-
D	5	Horton, Bill	60	0	9	9	46	0	0	-	-	-	-	-
RW	4	Hyndman, Mike	8	0	1	1	0	0	0	-	-	-	-	-
C	10	LeBlanc, J. P.	78	20	46	66	58	7	0	-	-	-	-	-
D	4	MacSweyn, Ralph	13	0	3	3	6	0	0	-	-	-	-	-
C	11	McCaskill, Ted	18	2	2	4	63	0	1	-	-	-	-	-
RW	17	McDonald, Brian	56	22	30	52	54	4	0	-	-	-	-	-
G	1	McLeod, Jim	17	0	0	0	0	0	0	-	-	-	-	-
D	3	Niekamp, Jim	76	2	19	21	95	0	0	-	-	-	-	-
D	6	Odrowski, Gerry	77	4	32	36	48	2	0	-	-	-	-	-
RW	24	Serviss, Tom	74	6	15	21	37	0	2	-	-	-	-	-
RW	13	Slater, Peter	19	1	1	2	2	0	0	-	-	-	-	-
C	8	Speck, Fred	18	2	5	7	4	0	0	-	-	-	-	-
LW	19	Sutherland, Steve	72	20	12	32	182	4	0	-	-	-	-	-
LW	9	Tardif, Marc	75	40	30	70	47	10	0	-	-	-	-	-
LW	21	Thomas, Reg	77	14	21	35	22	1	0	-	-	-	-	-
LW	18	Veneruzzo, Gary	78	39	29	68	68	5	0	-	-	-	-	-
RW	15	Walters, Ron	71	14	14	28	28	1	0	-	-	-	-	-
C	12	Ward, Ron	40	14	19	33	16	3	0	-	-	-	-	-
D	2	Watson, Jim	48	0	6	6	28	0	0	-	-	-	-	-
RW	23	White, Alton	48	8	13	21	13	0	0	-	-	-	-	-
C	20	Whitlock, Bobby	14	4	10	14	4	1	0	-	-	-	-	-
G	30	Wilkie, Ian	23	0	0	0	2	0	0	-	-	-	-	-
D	4	Willis, Hal	18	1	2	3	24	0	0	-	-	-	-	-
LW		Young, Bill	16	1	3	4	4	0	0	-	-	-	-	-
D	8/2/4	Zrymiak, Jerry	27	2	8	10	8	0	0	-	-	-	-	-

Power Play: 43 goals scored in 255 opportunities (16.9%) with 8 short-handed goals allowed.
Penalty Killing: 62 goals allowed in 234 opportunities (73.5%) with 4 short-handed goals scored.

Goaltending

goaltender	gp	min	ga	en	so	record	gaa	sog	sv%	gp	min	ga	record	gaa
Gardner, George	2	120	13	0	0	0-2-0	6.50	65	0.800	-	-	-	-	-
Gillow, Russ	18	1041	69	1	0	4-13-0	3.98	483	0.851	-	-	-	-	-
Hoganson, Paul	27	1308	102	2	0	6-16-0	4.68	711	0.857	-	-	-	-	-
McLeod, Jim	17	969	69	1	1	4-13-0	4.27	481	0.857	-	-	-	-	-
Wilkie, Ian	23	1257	82	0	1	11-9-0	3.91	592	0.861	-	-	-	-	-

Transactions: Marc Tardif signed to contract, Jun 1973 • Don Gordon, Paul Hoganson signed to contracts, Jul 1973 • Joe Szura traded to Houston for Brian McDonald, Sep 1973 • Bill Horton purchased from Cleveland, Oct 1973 • Tom Gilmore traded to Edmonton for Ron Walters, Oct 1973 • George Gardner and Ralph MacSweyn traded to Vancouver for Ron Ward, Oct 1973 • Ian Wilkie purchased from Edmonton, Nov 1973 • Mike Hyndman sold to Phoenix (WHL), Dec 1973 • Peter Slater sold to Denver (WHL), Dec 1973 • Russ Gillow and Earl Heiskala traded to Jersey for Jim McLeod, Jan 1974 • Don Gordon and Jim Watson traded to Chicago for Bobby Whitlock, Feb 1974 • Ron Ward traded to Cleveland for Bill Young and Ted Hodgson, Feb 1974 • Ian Wilkie traded to Edmonton for Wayne Zuk, Mar 1974

1973-1974 MINNESOTA FIGHTING SAINTS

Coach
Harry Neale
42-32-2

Coach
Jack McCartan
2-0-0

Summary of Games (@ Away, * Overtime)

	date	opponent	score		record	pts	gf-ga
1.	Oct 12	Vancouver	5-4	W	1-0-0	2	5-4
2.	Oct 14 @	Toronto	5-2	W	2-0-0	4	10-6
3.	Oct 15 @	New England	3-3	T	2-0-1	5	13-9
4.	Oct 19	New England	1-0	W	3-0-1	7	14-9
5.	Oct 21 @	Winnipeg	*1-2	L	3-1-1	7	15-11
6.	Oct 24 @	New York	2-5	L	3-2-1	7	17-16
7.	Oct 26	Quebec	4-5	L	3-3-1	7	21-21
8.	Oct 27	Winnipeg	5-2	W	4-3-1	9	26-23
9.	Oct 30 @	Houston	1-6	L	4-4-1	9	27-29
10.	Nov 1 @	Los Angeles	5-1	W	5-4-1	11	32-30
11.	Nov 4 @	Edmonton	3-4	L	5-5-1	11	35-34
12.	Nov 7	New York	10-1	W	6-5-1	13	45-35
13.	Nov 9	Vancouver	3-1	W	7-5-1	15	48-36
14.	Nov 11	Cleveland	6-4	W	8-5-1	17	54-40
15.	Nov 13	Houston	2-5	L	8-6-1	17	56-45
16.	Nov 15 @	Vancouver	5-7	L	8-7-1	17	61-52
17.	Nov 18 @	Edmonton	5-2	W	9-7-1	19	66-54
18.	Nov 20 @	Los Angeles	2-6	L	9-8-1	19	68-60
19.	Nov 22	New England	7-5	W	10-8-1	21	75-65
20.	Nov 25	Winnipeg	5-3	W	11-8-1	23	80-68
21.	Nov 28 @	Vancouver	3-5	L	11-9-1	23	83-73
22.	Nov 30	Toronto	1-2	L	11-10-1	23	84-75
23.	Dec 2 @	Jersey	1-2	L	11-11-1	23	85-77
24.	Dec 4	Los Angeles	9-2	W	12-11-1	25	94-79
25.	Dec 7	Vancouver	3-1	W	13-11-1	27	97-80
26.	Dec 8	Quebec	4-1	W	14-11-1	29	101-81
27.	Dec 9 @	Toronto	1-10	L	14-12-1	29	102-91
28.	Dec 11 @	Chicago	5-3	W	15-12-1	31	107-94
29.	Dec 14	Houston	2-5	L	15-13-1	31	109-99
30.	Dec 16 @	Winnipeg	3-2	W	16-13-1	33	112-101
31.	Dec 19 @	Vancouver	4-2	W	17-13-1	35	116-103
32.	Dec 21	Los Angeles	4-3	W	18-13-1	37	120-106
33.	Dec 22 @	Cleveland	1-2	L	18-14-1	37	121-108
34.	Dec 23	Cleveland	2-4	L	18-15-1	37	123-112
35.	Dec 27 @	Edmonton	5-4	W	19-15-1	39	128-116
36.	Dec 29	Toronto	3-9	L	19-16-1	39	131-125
37.	Dec 30	Chicago	3-5	L	19-17-1	39	134-130
38.	Jan 5 @	Chicago	6-5	W	20-17-1	41	140-135
39.	Jan 6	Edmonton	4-6	L	20-18-1	41	144-141
40.	Jan 9	Edmonton	4-6	L	20-19-1	41	148-147
41.	Jan 12	Toronto	8-6	W	21-19-1	43	156-153
42.	Jan 13 @	Cleveland	2-4	L	21-20-1	43	158-157
43.	Jan 15 @	Edmonton	1-4	L	21-21-1	43	159-161
44.	Jan 19 @	New England	2-5	L	21-22-1	43	161-166
45.	Jan 20 @	Quebec	*4-5	L	21-23-1	43	165-171
46.	Jan 23	Jersey	1-4	L	21-24-1	43	166-175
47.	Jan 25	Chicago	6-2	W	22-24-1	45	172-177
48.	Jan 27	Winnipeg	12-2	W	23-24-1	47	184-179
49.	Feb 2 @	Cleveland	4-2	W	24-24-1	49	188-181
50.	Feb 3 @	Toronto	4-5	L	24-25-1	49	192-186
51.	Feb 5	Cleveland	4-1	W	25-25-1	51	196-187
52.	Feb 6	Chicago	7-2	W	26-25-1	53	203-189
53.	Feb 8 @	Winnipeg	4-3	W	27-25-1	55	207-192
54.	Feb 10 @	New England	5-2	W	28-25-1	57	212-194
55.	Feb 12	Houston	1-3	L	28-26-1	57	213-197
56.	Feb 13	Edmonton	7-4	W	29-26-1	59	220-201
57.	Feb 15	Winnipeg	7-1	W	30-26-1	61	227-202
58.	Feb 17 @	Houston	6-1	W	31-26-1	63	233-203
59.	Feb 22 @	Quebec	6-4	W	32-26-1	65	239-207
60.	Feb 24 @	Cleveland	2-1	W	33-26-1	67	241-208
61.	Feb 27	Los Angeles	5-4	W	34-26-1	69	246-212
62.	Feb 28	Cleveland	6-6	T	34-26-2	70	252-218
63.	Mar 1 @	Winnipeg	4-0	W	35-26-2	72	256-218
64.	Mar 3	Los Angeles	5-3	W	36-26-2	74	261-221
65.	Mar 6	New England	8-6	W	37-26-2	76	269-227
66.	Mar 9	Quebec	9-5	W	38-26-2	78	278-232
67.	Mar 10 @	Los Angeles	5-6	L	38-27-2	78	283-238
68.	Mar 12 @	Houston	2-3	L	38-28-2	78	285-241
69.	Mar 14 @	Chicago	4-7	L	38-29-2	78	289-248
70.	Mar 15 @	Jersey	3-5	L	38-30-2	78	292-253
71.	Mar 17 @	Quebec	5-3	W	39-30-2	80	297-256
72.	Mar 19 @	Vancouver	4-5	L	39-31-2	80	301-261
73.	Mar 22 @	Los Angeles	5-2	W	40-31-2	82	306-263
74.	Mar 24 @	Houston	5-3	W	41-31-2	84	311-266
75.	Mar 27	Jersey	6-4	W	42-31-2	86	317-270
76.	Mar 29	Edmonton	1-3	L	42-32-2	86	318-273
77.	Mar 31	Houston	5-2	W	43-32-2	88	323-275
78.	Apr 3	Vancouver	9-0	W	44-32-2	90	332-275

Fighting Saints Stars of 1973-1974

Mike Antonovich
21 goals

Ted Hampson
55 points

Mike Walton
57 goal, 117 points

Murray Heatley
26 goals

Wayne Connelly
42 goals, 95 points

Rick Smith
38 points from blueline

Scoring

| pos | # | player | Regular Season | | | | | | | Playoffs | | | | |
			gp	g	a	pts	pim	ppg	shg	gp	g	a	pts	pim
C	12	Antonovich, Mike	68	21	29	50	4	2	0	11	1	4	5	4
D	17	Arbour, John	77	6	43	49	192	0	0	11	3	6	9	27
D	21	Ball, Terry	71	8	28	36	34	4	0	11	1	2	3	6
D	24	Boyd, Bob	41	1	14	15	14	0	0	7	0	0	0	4
LW	33	Cardwell, Steve	77	23	23	46	100	1	1	10	0	0	0	20
C	6	Christiansen, Keith	74	11	25	36	36	4	0	10	0	1	1	2
RW	7	Connelly, Wayne	78	42	53	95	16	15	0	11	6	7	13	4
G	1	Curran, Mike	40	0	0	0	6	0	0	5	0	0	0	0
LW	16	Gallant, Gord	72	7	15	22	223	0	0	11	1	2	3	67
G	35	Garrett, John	40	0	0	0	10	0	0	7	0	0	0	0
LW	18	Goldthorpe, Bill	0	-	-	-	-	-	-	3	0	0	0	25
C	10	Hampson, Ted	77	17	38	55	9	2	4	11	4	4	8	8
RW	11	Heatley, Murray	71	26	32	58	23	3	0	10	1	0	1	2
C	20	Johnson, Jim	71	15	39	54	30	1	1	11	1	4	5	4
RW	8	Klatt, Bill	65	14	6	20	12	3	0	11	3	2	5	18
RW	14	MacMillan, Bob	78	14	34	48	81	3	0	11	2	3	5	4
G	30	McCartan, Jack	2	0	0	0	0	0	0	-	-	-	-	-
D	23	McMahon, Mike	71	10	35	45	82	1	3	11	1	7	8	9
LW	9	Morrison, George	73	40	38	78	37	12	1	11	5	5	10	12
D	2	Paradise, Dick	67	2	7	9	71	0	0	7	0	0	0	6
D	22	Rydman, Blaine	8	0	0	0	21	0	0	-	-	-	-	-
D	3	Smith, Rick	71	10	28	38	98	0	1	11	0	1	1	22
C	4	Walton, Mike	78	57	60	117	88	9	9	11	10	8	18	16
C	5	Walton, Rob	45	8	23	31	24	1	0	-	-	-	-	-

Power Play: 61 goals scored in 262 opportunities (23.3%) with 11 short-handed goals allowed.
Penalty Killing: 53 goals allowed in 265 opportunities (80.0%) with 20 short-handed goals scored.

Goaltending

goaltender	gp	min	ga	en	so	record	gaa	sog	sv%	gp	min	ga	record	gaa
Curran, Mike	40	2382	130	2	2	23-14-2	3.27	1444	0.910	5	289	14	2-3	2.91
Garrett, John	40	2290	137	1	1	21-18-0	3.59	1414	0.903	7	372	25	4-2	4.03
McCartan, Jack	2	42	5	0	0	0-0-0	7.14	26	0.808	-	-	-	-	-

Transactions: Don Tannahill, Rick Smith, Steve Cardwell signed to contracts, May 1973 • Mike Walton and Rob Walton signed to contracts, Jun 1973 • Bob Boyd, Gary Gambucci, John Garrett signed to contracts, Jul 1973 • Gord Gallant signed to contract, Oct 1973 • Rob Walton traded to Vancouver for Jean Tetreault, Jan 1974 • Bill Goldthorpe signed to contract, April 1974

141

1973-1974 NEW ENGLAND WHALERS

**Coach
Jack Kelley**

Summary of Games (@ Away, * Overtime)

	date		opponent	score		record	pts	gf-ga
1.	Oct 7	@	Quebec	2-4	L	0-1-0	0	2-4
2.	Oct 9		Quebec	3-2	W	1-1-0	2	5-6
3.	Oct 13		Chicago	6-4	W	2-1-0	4	11-10
4.	Oct 14	@	New York	*2-1	W	3-1-0	6	13-11
5.	Oct 15		Minnesota	3-3	T	3-1-1	7	16-14
6.	Oct 17		Winnipeg	1-3	L	3-2-1	7	17-17
7.	Oct 19	@	Minnesota	0-1	L	3-3-1	7	17-18
8.	Oct 21	@	Toronto	4-3	W	4-3-1	9	21-21
9.	Oct 22		New York	4-1	W	5-3-1	11	25-22
10.	Oct 25		New York	8-3	W	6-3-1	13	33-25
11.	Oct 27		Los Angeles	3-1	W	7-3-1	15	36-26
12.	Nov 3		Toronto	4-5	L	7-4-1	15	40-31
13.	Nov 4		Cleveland	7-5	W	8-4-1	17	47-36
14.	Nov 7		Winnipeg	9-2	W	9-4-1	19	56-38
15.	Nov 10		Edmonton	3-6	L	9-5-1	19	59-44
16.	Nov 11	@	Quebec	2-3	L	9-6-1	19	61-47
17.	Nov 12		New York	*3-2	W	10-6-1	21	64-49
18.	Nov 15	@	Quebec	5-3	W	11-6-1	23	69-52
19.	Nov 17		Quebec	4-10	L	11-7-1	23	73-62
20.	Nov 18	@	Los Angeles	5-2	W	12-7-1	25	78-64
21.	Nov 21	@	Houston	1-4	L	12-8-1	25	79-68
22.	Nov 22	@	Minnesota	5-7	L	12-9-1	25	84-75
23.	Nov 26		Jersey	4-2	W	13-9-1	27	88-77
24.	Nov 29		Houston	5-2	W	14-9-1	29	93-79
25.	Dec 2		Chicago	4-3	W	15-9-1	31	97-82
26.	Dec 8	@	Cleveland	*1-2	L	15-10-1	31	98-84
27.	Dec 9		Cleveland	3-2	W	16-10-1	33	101-86
28.	Dec 12		Toronto	8-6	W	17-10-1	35	109-92
29.	Dec 14		Jersey	3-1	W	18-10-1	37	112-93
30.	Dec 16		Chicago	2-3	L	18-11-1	37	114-96
31.	Dec 19		Edmonton	4-2	W	19-11-1	39	118-98
32.	Dec 22		Winnipeg	0-2	L	19-12-1	39	118-100
33.	Dec 24		Vancouver	*5-4	W	20-12-1	41	123-104
34.	Dec 26	@	Houston	*3-2	W	21-12-1	43	126-106
35.	Dec 27	@	Los Angeles	5-1	W	22-12-1	45	131-107
36.	Dec 29	@	Edmonton	2-6	L	22-13-1	45	133-113
37.	Dec 30	@	Vancouver	*5-6	L	22-14-1	45	138-119
38.	Jan 4	@	Winnipeg	4-3	W	23-14-1	47	142-122
39.	Jan 5	@	Cleveland	0-1	L	23-15-1	47	142-123
40.	Jan 8		Toronto	2-3	L	23-16-1	47	144-126
41.	Jan 10	@	Toronto	6-6	T	23-16-2	48	150-132
42.	Jan 13		Los Angeles	9-6	W	24-16-2	50	159-138
43.	Jan 16		Jersey	4-2	W	25-16-2	52	163-140
44.	Jan 17		Chicago	2-5	L	25-17-2	52	165-145
45.	Jan 19		Minnesota	5-2	W	26-17-2	54	170-147
46.	Jan 20	@	Toronto	4-8	L	26-18-2	54	174-155
47.	Jan 22	@	Chicago	3-5	L	26-19-2	54	177-160
48.	Jan 26		Cleveland	4-0	W	27-19-2	56	181-160
49.	Jan 28		Vancouver	6-4	W	28-19-2	58	187-164
50.	Jan 31	@	Jersey	1-4	L	28-20-2	58	188-168
51.	Feb 2		Houston	5-2	W	29-20-2	60	193-170
52.	Feb 3	@	Cleveland	1-3	L	29-21-2	60	194-173
53.	Feb 6		Quebec	0-3	L	29-22-2	60	194-176
54.	Feb 8	@	Cleveland	4-2	W	30-22-2	62	198-178
55.	Feb 10		Minnesota	2-5	L	30-23-2	62	200-183
56.	Feb 13	@	Vancouver	4-9	L	30-24-2	62	204-192
57.	Feb 15	@	Edmonton	7-3	W	31-24-2	64	211-195
58.	Feb 17	@	Winnipeg	*3-2	W	32-24-2	66	214-197
59.	Feb 20	@	Los Angeles	2-4	L	32-25-2	66	216-201
60.	Feb 23	@	Chicago	3-0	W	33-25-2	68	219-201
61.	Feb 24	@	Toronto	0-2	L	33-26-2	68	219-203
62.	Feb 27		Toronto	5-3	W	34-26-2	70	224-206
63.	Feb 28	@	Jersey	3-3	T	34-26-3	71	227-209
64.	Mar 2		Vancouver	7-1	W	35-26-3	73	234-210
65.	Mar 3	@	Houston	6-3	W	36-26-3	75	240-213
66.	Mar 5	@	Chicago	3-2	W	37-26-3	77	243-215
67.	Mar 6	@	Minnesota	6-8	L	37-27-3	77	249-223
68.	Mar 8		Jersey	7-2	W	38-27-3	79	256-225
69.	Mar 12	@	Chicago	3-5	L	38-28-3	79	259-230
70.	Mar 14	@	Vancouver	6-3	W	39-28-3	81	265-233
71.	Mar 15	@	Edmonton	6-2	W	40-28-3	83	271-235
72.	Mar 17	@	Winnipeg	1-10	L	40-29-3	83	272-245
73.	Mar 20		Edmonton	2-2	T	40-29-4	84	274-247
74.	Mar 24		Quebec	3-4	L	40-30-4	84	277-251
75.	Mar 27		Los Angeles	7-1	W	41-30-4	86	284-252
76.	Mar 28		Cleveland	3-2	W	42-30-4	88	287-254
77.	Mar 31		Quebec	*3-2	W	43-30-4	90	290-256
78.	Apr 1		Houston	1-4	L	43-31-4	90	291-260

Whalers Stars of 1973-1974

Mike Byers
29 goals

Al Karlander
20 goals, 61 points

Tom Webster
43 goals

John French
72 points

Tom Earl
Defesinve forward

Tommy Williams
21 goals, 58 points

Scoring

pos	#	player	gp	g	a	pts	pim	ppg	shg	gp	g	a	pts	pim
					Regular Season							**Playoffs**		
G	30	Berglund, Bill	3	0	0	0	0	0	0	-	-	-	-	-
LW	22	Blackburn, Don	75	20	39	59	18	9	0	7	2	4	6	4
RW	21	Byers, Mike	78	29	21	50	6	4	0	7	2	4	6	12
LW	18	Charlebois, Bob	74	4	7	11	6	0	2	7	0	0	0	4
LW	17	Cunniff, John	30	7	5	12	14	0	0	5	1	1	2	6
C	12	Danby, John	72	2	2	4	6	0	0	7	1	0	1	0
D	10	Dorey, Jim	77	6	40	46	134	0	0	6	0	6	6	26
RW	27	Earl, Tom	78	10	10	20	29	2	0	7	0	2	2	2
LW	11	French, John	77	24	48	72	31	5	1	7	4	2	6	2
D	6	Green, Ted	75	7	26	33	42	3	0	7	0	4	4	7
C	16	Harris, Hugh	75	24	28	52	78	1	0	3	0	0	0	0
D	5	Hurley, Paul	52	3	11	14	21	0	0	-	-	-	-	-
D	20/23	Jordan, Ric	34	0	3	3	14	0	0	-	-	-	-	-
C	14	Karlander, Al	77	20	41	61	46	4	0	7	1	3	4	2
D	20	Keeler, Mike	1	0	0	0	0	0	0	1	0	0	0	0
G	30	Landon, Bruce	24	0	0	0	24	0	0	1	0	0	0	0
D	2	Ley, Rick	72	6	35	41	148	3	0	7	1	5	6	18
C	4	Pleau, Larry	77	26	43	69	35	6	0	2	2	0	2	0
D	3	Selwood, Brad	76	9	28	37	91	0	0	7	0	2	2	11
RW	15	Sheehy, Tim	77	29	29	58	22	2	0	7	4	2	6	4
G	1	Smith, Al	55	0	3	3	33	0	0	7	0	0	0	0
RW	19	Smith, Guy	16	1	5	6	25	0	0	-	-	-	-	-
RW	8	Webster, Tom	64	43	27	70	28	5	0	3	5	0	5	7
C	9	Williams, Tom	70	21	37	58	6	3	0	4	0	3	3	10

Power Play: 47 goals scored in 228 opportunities (20.6%) with 7 short-handed goals allowed.
Penalty Killing: 36 goals allowed in 197 opportunities (81.7%) with 3 short-handed goals scored.

Goaltending

goaltender	gp	min	ga	en	so	record	gaa	sog	sv%	gp	min	ga	record	gaa
Berglund, Bill	3	180	10	0	0	2-1-0	3.33	87	0.885	-	-	-	-	-
Landon, Bruce	24	1386	82	0	0	11-9-2	3.55	692	0.882	1	40	3	0-0	4.50
Smith, Al	55	3194	164	4	2	30-21-2	3.08	1569	0.895	7	399	21	3-4	3.16

Transactions: Don Blackburn, Hugh Harris, Al Karlander signed to contracts, Jun 1973 • Brit Selby traded to Toronto for Bob Charlebois, Jul 1973

143

1973-1974 NEW YORK GOLDEN BLADES – JERSEY KNIGHTS

Coach
Camille Henry
6-12-2

Player-Coach
Harry Howell
26-30-2

Summary of Games (@ Away, * Overtime)

#	date		opponent	score		record	pts	gf-ga
1.	Oct 6	@	Cleveland	2-2	T	0-0-1	1	2-2
2.	Oct 9	@	Toronto	3-3	T	0-0-2	2	5-5
3.	Oct 11		Chicago	3-4	L	0-1-2	2	8-9
4.	Oct 14		New England	*1-2	L	0-2-2	2	9-11
5.	Oct 18		Winnipeg	1-6	L	0-3-2	2	10-17
6.	Oct 20	@	Quebec	1-8	L	0-4-2	2	11-25
7.	Oct 21		Quebec	4-3	W	1-4-2	4	15-28
8.	Oct 22	@	New England	1-4	L	1-5-2	4	16-32
9.	Oct 24		Minnesota	5-2	W	2-5-2	6	21-34
10.	Oct 25		New England	3-8	L	2-6-2	6	24-42
11.	Oct 28		Los Angeles	0-2	L	2-7-2	6	24-44
12.	Nov 2	@	Winnipeg	1-3	L	2-8-2	6	25-47
13.	Nov 3	@	Vancouver	4-0	W	3-8-2	8	29-47
14.	Nov 4	@	Vancouver	4-3	W	4-8-2	10	33-50
15.	Nov 6	@	Edmonton	0-8	L	4-9-2	10	33-58
16.	Nov 7	@	Minnesota	1-10	L	4-10-2	10	34-68
17.	Nov 10		Quebec	4-3	W	5-10-2	12	38-71
18.	Nov 12	@	New England	*2-3	L	5-11-2	12	40-74
19.	Nov 17		Houston	2-3	L	5-12-2	12	42-77
20.	Nov 18		Chicago	5-3	W	6-12-2	14	47-80
21.	Nov 25		Quebec	3-1	W	7-12-2	16	50-81
22.	Nov 26	@	New England	2-4	L	7-13-2	16	52-85
23.	Nov 29		Edmonton	2-3	L	7-14-2	16	54-88
24.	Dec 2		Minnesota	2-1	W	8-14-2	18	56-89
25.	Dec 5	@	Houston	2-5	L	8-15-2	18	58-94
26.	Dec 6		Cleveland	3-2	W	9-15-2	20	61-96
27.	Dec 8	@	Chicago	3-1	W	10-15-2	22	64-97
28.	Dec 9	@	Winnipeg	1-3	L	10-16-2	22	65-100
29.	Dec 12	@	Cleveland	4-2	W	11-16-2	24	69-102
30.	Dec 14	@	New England	1-3	L	11-17-2	24	70-105
31.	Dec 16		Edmonton	6-7	L	11-18-2	24	76-112
32.	Dec 18	@	Toronto	1-4	L	11-19-2	24	77-116
33.	Dec 21		Chicago	5-1	W	12-19-2	26	82-117
34.	Dec 23		Winnipeg	6-3	W	13-19-2	28	88-120
35.	Dec 28		Vancouver	5-3	W	14-19-2	30	93-123
36.	Dec 29	@	Cleveland	0-3	L	14-20-2	30	93-126
37.	Dec 30		Cleveland	6-2	W	15-20-2	32	99-128
38.	Jan 5		Houston	2-1	W	16-20-2	34	101-129
39.	Jan 6	@	Toronto	4-2	W	17-20-2	36	105-131
40.	Jan 7		Vancouver	4-5	L	17-21-2	36	109-136
41.	Jan 13	@	Toronto	2-7	L	17-22-2	36	111-143
42.	Jan 16	@	New England	2-4	L	17-23-2	36	113-147
43.	Jan 18	@	Edmonton	4-7	L	17-24-2	36	117-154
44.	Jan 19	@	Vancouver	*5-4	W	18-24-2	38	122-158
45.	Jan 20	@	Winnipeg	3-9	L	18-25-2	38	125-167
46.	Jan 22	@	Edmonton	6-2	W	19-25-2	40	131-169
47.	Jan 23	@	Minnesota	4-1	W	20-25-2	42	135-170
48.	Jan 27		Los Angeles	3-6	L	20-26-2	42	138-176
49.	Jan 29		Toronto	6-1	W	21-26-2	44	144-177
50.	Jan 31		New England	4-1	W	22-26-2	46	148-178
51.	Feb 3	@	Quebec	3-5	L	22-27-2	46	151-183
52.	Feb 4		Houston	1-7	L	22-28-2	46	152-190
53.	Feb 5	@	Houston	0-4	L	22-29-2	46	152-194
54.	Feb 7	@	Los Angeles	7-4	W	23-29-2	48	159-198
55.	Feb 9	@	Chicago	2-5	L	23-30-2	48	161-203
56.	Feb 10		Toronto	4-5	L	23-31-2	48	165-208
57.	Feb 14		Toronto	2-5	L	23-32-2	48	167-213
58.	Feb 15		Cleveland	6-2	W	24-32-2	50	173-215
59.	Feb 17		Quebec	10-3	W	25-32-2	52	183-218
60.	Feb 18		Chicago	4-3	W	26-32-2	54	187-221
61.	Feb 20	@	Houston	2-7	L	26-33-2	54	189-228
62.	Feb 24	@	Quebec	4-7	L	26-34-2	54	193-235
63.	Feb 28		New England	3-3	T	26-34-3	55	196-238
64.	Mar 2		Los Angeles	8-7	W	27-34-3	57	204-245
65.	Mar 4		Vancouver	*7-6	W	28-34-3	59	211-251
66.	Mar 8		New England	2-7	L	28-35-3	59	213-258
67.	Mar 10	@	Quebec	2-5	L	28-36-3	59	215-263
68.	Mar 11		Winnipeg	10-2	W	29-36-3	61	225-265
69.	Mar 15		Minnesota	5-3	W	30-36-3	63	230-268
70.	Mar 16	@	Cleveland	4-4	T	30-36-4	64	234-272
71.	Mar 18		Toronto	11-5	W	31-36-4	66	245-277
72.	Mar 20	@	Los Angeles	8-5	W	32-36-4	68	253-282
73.	Mar 23	@	Chicago	1-4	L	32-37-4	68	254-286
74.	Mar 25		Edmonton	1-4	L	32-38-4	68	255-290
75.	Mar 27	@	Minnesota	4-6	L	32-39-4	68	259-296
76.	Mar 31		Cleveland	2-4	L	32-40-4	68	261-300
77.	Apr 2	@	Chicago	3-7	L	32-41-4	68	264-307
78.	Apr 4	@	Los Angeles	4-6	L	32-42-4	68	268-313

As New York (October 6 to November 18, 1973): 6-12-2, 14 points, 47 gf, 80 ga
As Jersey (November 25, 1973 to April 4, 1974): 26-30-2, 54 points, 221 gf, 233 ga

Golden Blades-Knights Stars of 1973-1974

Andre Lacroix
111 points

Kevin Morrison
67 points from blueline

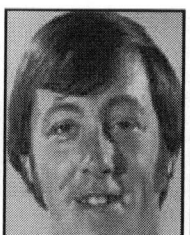
Joe Junkin
21 wins, 1 shutout

Wayne Rivers
30 goals

Bob Jones
17 goals, 45 points

Brian Perry
20 goals

Scoring

| | | | | Regular Season | | | | | | | Playoffs | | | | |
pos	#	player	gp	g	a	pts	pim	ppg	shg	gp	g	a	pts	pim
D	28	Barber, Butch	3	0	0	0	2	0	0	-	-	-	-	-
D	17	Block, Ken	74	3	43	46	22	1	0	-	-	-	-	-
D	5	Boylan, Dean	61	1	5	6	112	0	0	-	-	-	-	-
LW	14	Bradley, Brian	78	15	23	38	12	3	1	-	-	-	-	-
D	26	Brown, Bob	59	7	13	20	38	1	0	-	-	-	-	-
C	22	Chartre, Claude	5	0	0	0	0	0	0	-	-	-	-	-
RW	9	Ferguson, Norm	75	15	21	36	12	3	0	-	-	-	-	-
LW	21	Herriman, Don	44	11	21	32	59	2	0	-	-	-	-	-
D	3	Howell, Harry	65	3	23	26	24	0	0	-	-	-	-	-
LW	19	Inglis, Lee	5	0	0	0	0	0	0	-	-	-	-	-
LW	10	Jones, Bob	78	17	28	45	20	6	0	-	-	-	-	-
G	36	Junkin, Joe	53	0	1	1	7	0	0	-	-	-	-	-
G	30	Kurt, Gary	20	0	1	1	0	0	0	-	-	-	-	-
C	7	Lacroix, Andre	78	31	80	111	54	11	0	-	-	-	-	-
D	23	Larose, Ray	18	0	1	1	20	0	0	-	-	-	-	-
C	18	Laughton, Mike	71	20	18	38	34	1	1	-	-	-	-	-
G	1	McLeod, Jim	10	0	0	0	2	0	0	-	-	-	-	-
C	15	Morenz, Brian	75	20	30	50	44	1	2	-	-	-	-	-
D	4	Morrison, Kevin	78	24	43	67	132	5	2	-	-	-	-	-
LW	25	Peacosh, Gene	68	21	32	53	17	5	0	-	-	-	-	-
C	19	Perry, Brian	71	20	11	31	19	3	1	-	-	-	-	-
C	8	Peters, Garry	34	2	5	7	18	0	0	-	-	-	-	-
LW	11	Reichmuth, Craig	72	10	8	18	114	0	0	-	-	-	-	-
RW	12	Rivers, Wayne	73	30	27	57	20	5	0	-	-	-	-	-
RW	20	Scharf, Ted	63	4	2	6	107	0	0	-	-	-	-	-
C	6	Sheehan, Bobby	50	12	8	20	8	5	0	-	-	-	-	-
D	24	Speer, Bill	66	1	3	4	30	0	0	-	-	-	-	-
D	2	Winograd, Bob	7	1	0	1	0	0	0	-	-	-	-	-

Power Play: 52 goals scored in 213 opportunities (24.4%) with 4 short-handed goals allowed.
Penalty Killing: 55 goals allowed in 241 opportunities (77.2%) with 7 short-handed goals scored.

Goaltending

goaltender	gp	min	ga	en	so	record	gaa	sog	sv%	gp	min	ga	record	gaa
Junkin, Joe	53	3122	197	3	1	21-25-4	3.79	1762	0.888	-	-	-	-	-
Kurt, Gary	20	1089	75	1	0	8-10-0	4.13	566	0.867	-	-	-	-	-
McLeod, Jim	10	517	36	1	0	3-7-0	4.18	296	0.878	-	-	-	-	-

Transactions: Ron Ward and Peter Donnelly traded to Philadelphia/Vancouver for Andre Lacroix and Don Herriman, May 1973 • Butch Barber acquired in trade with Chicago for Wally Olds, May 1973 • Harry Howell signed to contract, Jul 1973 • Jim McLeod traded to Los Angeles for Earl Heiskala and Russ Gillow, Jan 1974 (McLeod's rights purchased by New York from Chicago, Jul 1973). Heiskala refused to report and was suspended • Bobby Sheehan traded to Edmonton for future considerations (Bob Falkenberg), Mar 1974

1973-1974 QUEBEC NORDIQUES

Coach
Jacques Plante

Summary of Games (@ Away, * Overtime)

	date	opponent	score		record	pts	gf-ga		date	opponent	score		record	pts	gf-ga
1.	Oct 7	New England	4-2	W	1-0-0	2	4-2	40.	Jan 6	Chicago	4-0	W	19-18-3	41	149-130
2.	Oct 9 @	New England	2-3	L	1-1-0	2	6-5	41.	Jan 10	Los Angeles	7-1	W	20-18-3	43	156-131
3.	Oct 11 @	Toronto	4-1	W	2-1-0	4	10-6	42.	Jan 12 @	Houston	1-5	L	20-19-3	43	157-136
4.	Oct 13 @	Cleveland	3-6	L	2-2-0	4	13-12	43.	Jan 15 @	Los Angeles	4-6	L	20-20-3	43	161-142
5.	Oct 18	Toronto	5-2	W	3-2-0	6	18-14	44.	Jan 19 @	Chicago	2-5	L	20-21-3	43	163-147
6.	Oct 20	New York	8-1	W	4-2-0	8	26-15	45.	Jan 20	Minnesota	*5-4	W	21-21-3	45	168-151
7.	Oct 21 @	New York	3-4	L	4-3-0	8	29-19	46.	Jan 24 @	Houston	1-5	L	21-22-3	45	169-156
8.	Oct 25	Chicago	2-4	L	4-4-0	8	31-23	47.	Jan 25 @	Los Angeles	0-2	L	21-23-3	45	169-158
9.	Oct 26 @	Minnesota	5-4	W	5-4-0	10	36-27	48.	Jan 27	Cleveland	4-3	W	22-23-3	47	173-161
10.	Oct 28 @	Houston	3-2	W	6-4-0	12	39-29	49.	Jan 29	Los Angeles	5-0	W	23-23-3	49	178-161
11.	Oct 30 @	Los Angeles	6-4	W	7-4-0	14	45-33	50.	Jan 31	Houston	6-4	W	24-23-3	51	184-165
12.	Oct 31 @	Vancouver	5-1	W	8-4-0	16	50-34	51.	Feb 1	Toronto	2-1	W	25-23-3	53	186-166
13.	Nov 2 @	Edmonton	4-5	L	8-5-0	16	54-39	52.	Feb 3	Jersey	5-3	W	26-23-3	55	191-169
14.	Nov 4 @	Winnipeg	2-8	L	8-6-0	16	56-47	53.	Feb 6 @	New England	3-0	W	27-23-3	57	194-169
15.	Nov 6	Winnipeg	2-2	T	8-6-1	17	58-49	54.	Feb 8 @	Vancouver	3-7	L	27-24-3	57	197-176
16.	Nov 8	Edmonton	3-4	L	8-7-1	17	61-53	55.	Feb 10 @	Edmonton	4-3	W	28-24-3	59	201-179
17.	Nov 10 @	New York	3-4	L	8-8-1	17	64-57	56.	Feb 12 @	Toronto	4-6	L	28-25-3	59	205-185
18.	Nov 11	New England	3-2	W	9-8-1	19	67-59	57.	Feb 14 @	Chicago	5-3	W	29-25-3	61	210-188
19.	Nov 15	New England	3-5	L	9-9-1	19	70-64	58.	Feb 16 @	Cleveland	2-5	L	29-26-3	61	212-193
20.	Nov 17 @	New England	10-4	W	10-9-1	21	80-68	59.	Feb 17 @	Jersey	3-10	L	29-27-3	61	215-203
21.	Nov 18	Houston	8-3	W	11-9-1	23	88-71	60.	Feb 19	Cleveland	*6-5	W	30-27-3	63	221-208
22.	Nov 22	Toronto	2-4	L	11-10-1	23	90-75	61.	Feb 22	Minnesota	4-6	L	30-28-3	63	225-214
23.	Nov 23 @	Cleveland	3-2	W	12-10-1	25	93-77	62.	Feb 24	Jersey	7-4	W	31-28-3	65	232-218
24.	Nov 25 @	Jersey	1-3	L	12-11-1	25	94-80	63.	Feb 26	Winnipeg	7-1	W	32-28-3	67	239-219
25.	Nov 27 @	Toronto	1-3	L	12-12-1	25	95-83	64.	Feb 28	Vancouver	9-4	W	33-28-3	69	248-223
26.	Nov 29	Cleveland	4-4	T	12-12-2	26	99-87	65.	Mar 3 @	Winnipeg	6-8	L	33-29-3	69	254-231
27.	Dec 1	Houston	3-3	T	12-12-3	27	102-90	66.	Mar 7	Chicago	2-3	L	33-30-3	69	256-234
28.	Dec 2 @	Winnipeg	3-5	L	12-13-3	27	105-95	67.	Mar 9 @	Minnesota	5-9	L	33-31-3	69	261-243
29.	Dec 8 @	Minnesota	1-4	L	12-14-3	27	106-99	68.	Mar 10	Jersey	5-2	W	34-31-3	71	266-245
30.	Dec 9	Chicago	6-1	W	13-14-3	29	112-100	69.	Mar 14 @	Toronto	3-2	W	35-31-3	73	269-247
31.	Dec 12 @	Vancouver	*1-2	L	13-15-3	29	113-102	70.	Mar 16 @	Chicago	*3-4	L	35-32-3	73	272-251
32.	Dec 14 @	Edmonton	4-3	W	14-15-3	31	117-105	71.	Mar 17	Minnesota	3-5	L	35-33-3	73	275-256
33.	Dec 16 @	Toronto	*4-3	W	15-15-3	33	121-108	72.	Mar 21	Edmonton	5-5	T	35-33-4	74	280-261
34.	Dec 18	Edmonton	4-2	W	16-15-3	35	125-110	73.	Mar 23	Vancouver	6-2	W	36-33-4	76	286-263
35.	Dec 22	Toronto	4-6	L	16-16-3	35	129-116	74.	Mar 24	New England	4-3	W	37-33-4	78	290-266
36.	Dec 27	Cleveland	4-2	W	17-16-3	37	133-118	75.	Mar 27 @	Cleveland	*4-5	L	37-34-4	78	294-271
37.	Dec 28 @	Chicago	4-6	L	17-17-3	37	137-124	76.	Mar 28	Los Angeles	9-3	W	38-34-4	80	303-274
38.	Dec 29	Winnipeg	3-4	L	17-18-3	37	140-128	77.	Mar 30	Toronto	1-3	L	38-35-4	80	304-277
39.	Jan 5	Vancouver	5-2	W	18-18-3	39	145-130	78.	Mar 31 @	New England	*2-3	L	38-36-4	80	306-280

Nordiques Stars of 1973-1974

| Jeannot Gilbert | J.-C. Tremblay | Bob Guindon | Francois Lacombe | Andre Gaudette | Serge Bernier |
| 56 points | 53 points | 31 goals, 70 points | 35 points from blueline | 24 goals | 86 points |

Scoring

pos	#	player	gp	g	a	pts	pim	ppg	shg	gp	g	a	pts	pim
					Regular Season							Playoffs		
G	1	Aubry, Serge	26	0	1	1	8	0	0	-	-	-	-	-
LW	9	Balon, David	22	0	0	0	2	0	0	-	-	-	-	-
D	2	Beaule, Alain	78	4	36	40	93	1	0	-	-	-	-	-
C	21	Bernier, Serge	74	37	49	86	107	7	0	-	-	-	-	-
G	30	Brodeur, Richard	30	0	1	1	0	0	0	-	-	-	-	-
RW	19	Caron, Alain	59	31	15	46	10	9	0	-	-	-	-	-
G	23	Deguise, Michel	32	0	1	1	0	0	0	-	-	-	-	-
D	24	Descoteaux, Norm	35	1	6	7	6	0	0	-	-	-	-	-
D	22	Desjardine, Ken	70	2	10	12	44	1	0	-	-	-	-	-
RW	20	Dufour, Guy	74	27	23	50	30	6	0	-	-	-	-	-
C	16	Gaudette, Andre	78	24	44	68	76	3	1	-	-	-	-	-
LW	7	Gendron, Jean-Guy	64	11	8	19	42	1	0	-	-	-	-	-
C	17	Gilbert, Jeannot	75	17	39	56	20	4	0	-	-	-	-	-
RW	18	Giroux, Rejean	12	5	6	11	14	0	0	-	-	-	-	-
LW	25	Guindon, Bob	71	31	39	70	30	5	0	-	-	-	-	-
LW	6	Guite, Pierre	72	14	20	34	106	0	0	-	-	-	-	-
D	33	Hoganson, Dale	62	8	33	41	27	2	0	-	-	-	-	-
RW	5	Houle, Rejean	69	27	35	62	17	6	0	-	-	-	-	-
D	4	Lacombe, Francois	71	9	26	35	41	4	0	-	-	-	-	-
RW	15	Leclerc, Rene	58	17	27	44	84	2	0	-	-	-	-	-
C	12	Parizeau, Michel	78	26	34	60	39	5	0	-	-	-	-	-
C	8	Payette, Jean	41	4	11	15	6	1	0	-	-	-	-	-
C	14	Rouleau, Michel	4	0	4	4	2	0	0	-	-	-	-	-
D	2	Roy, Pierre	44	2	7	9	137	0	0	-	-	-	-	-
D	3	Tremblay, J. C.	68	9	44	53	10	4	0	-	-	-	-	-

Power Play: 61 goals scored in 280 opportunities (21.8%) with 6 short-handed goals allowed.
Penalty Killing: 44 goals allowed in 194 opportunities (77.3%) with 1 short-handed goal scored.

Goaltending

goaltender	gp	min	ga	en	so	record	gaa	sog	sv%	gp	min	ga	record	gaa
Aubry, Serge	26	1395	90	1	1	11-11-2	3.87	751	0.880	-	-	-	-	-
Brodeur, Richard	30	1607	89	3	1	15-12-1	3.32	900	0.901	-	-	-	-	-
Deguise, Michel	32	1750	96	1	1	12-13-1	3.29	919	0.896	-	-	-	-	-

Transactions: Dale Hoganson signed to contract, May 1973 • Michel Deguise signed to contract, Jun 1973 • Rejean Houle signed to contract, Jul 1973

147

1973-1974 TORONTO TOROS

**Coach
Billy Harris**

Summary of Games (@ Away, * Overtime)

	date	opponent	score		record	pts	gf-ga		date	opponent	score		record	pts	gf-ga
1.	Oct 7	Chicago	4-4	T	0-0-1	1	4-4	40.	Dec 30	Winnipeg	5-2	W	19-18-3	41	151-131
2.	Oct 9	New York	3-3	T	0-0-2	2	7-7	41.	Jan 1	Cleveland	3-0	W	20-18-3	43	154-131
3.	Oct 11	Quebec	1-4	L	0-1-2	2	8-11	42.	Jan 6	Jersey	2-4	L	20-19-3	43	156-135
4.	Oct 14	Minnesota	2-5	L	0-2-2	2	10-16	43.	Jan 8	@ New England	3-2	W	21-19-3	45	159-137
5.	Oct 16	@ Los Angeles	3-0	W	1-2-2	4	13-16	44.	Jan 10	New England •	6-6	T	21-19-4	46	165-143
6.	Oct 18	@ Quebec	2-5	L	1-3-2	4	15-21	45.	Jan 12	@ Minnesota	6-8	L	21-20-4	46	171-151
7.	Oct 20	@ Cleveland	4-6	L	1-4-2	4	19-27	46.	Jan 13	Jersey	7-2	W	22-20-4	48	178-153
8.	Oct 21	New England	3-4	L	1-5-2	4	22-31	47.	Jan 16	@ Houston	1-4	L	22-21-4	48	179-157
9.	Oct 23	@ Edmonton	2-4	L	1-6-2	4	24-35	48.	Jan 18	@ Los Angeles	1-4	L	22-22-4	48	180-161
10.	Oct 24	@ Vancouver	7-4	W	2-6-2	6	31-39	49.	Jan 20	New England	8-4	W	23-22-4	50	188-165
11.	Oct 26	@ Winnipeg	3-3	T	2-6-3	7	34-42	50.	Jan 24	Cleveland •	3-5	L	23-23-4	50	191-170
12.	Oct 28	Chicago	2-3	L	2-7-3	7	36-45	51.	Jan 27	Vancouver	9-7	W	24-23-4	52	200-177
13.	Nov 3	@ New England	5-4	W	3-7-3	9	41-49	52.	Jan 29	@ Jersey	1-6	L	24-24-4	52	201-183
14.	Nov 4	Los Angeles	6-3	W	4-7-3	11	47-52	53.	Jan 31	Los Angeles •	*5-4	W	25-24-4	54	206-187
15.	Nov 7	@ Houston	5-4	W	5-7-3	13	52-56	54.	Feb 1	@ Quebec	1-2	L	25-25-4	54	207-189
16.	Nov 9	@ Los Angeles	2-4	L	5-8-3	13	54-60	55.	Feb 3	Minnesota	5-4	W	26-25-4	56	212-193
17.	Nov 10	@ Chicago	2-3	L	5-9-3	13	56-63	56.	Feb 9	@ Cleveland	3-4	L	26-26-4	56	215-197
18.	Nov 11	Edmonton	2-4	L	5-10-3	13	58-67	57.	Feb 10	@ Jersey	5-4	W	27-26-4	58	220-201
19.	Nov 17	@ Chicago	2-5	L	5-11-3	13	60-72	58.	Feb 12	Quebec •	6-4	W	28-26-4	60	226-205
20.	Nov 18	Winnipeg	6-2	W	6-11-3	15	66-74	59.	Feb 14	@ Jersey	5-2	W	29-26-4	62	231-207
21.	Nov 22	@ Quebec	4-2	W	7-11-3	17	70-76	60.	Feb 16	@ Chicago	5-4	W	30-26-4	64	236-211
22.	Nov 24	@ Cleveland	1-2	L	7-12-3	17	71-78	61.	Feb 17	@ Edmonton	*2-3	L	30-27-4	64	238-214
23.	Nov 25	Vancouver	*3-2	W	8-12-3	19	74-80	62.	Feb 19	@ Vancouver	5-4	W	31-27-4	66	243-218
24.	Nov 27	Quebec •	3-1	W	9-12-3	21	77-81	63.	Feb 22	@ Winnipeg	3-4	L	31-28-4	66	246-222
25.	Nov 30	@ Minnesota	2-1	W	10-12-3	23	79-82	64.	Feb 24	New England	2-0	W	32-28-4	68	248-222
26.	Dec 2	Houston	5-2	W	11-12-3	25	84-84	65.	Feb 27	@ New England	3-5	L	32-29-4	68	251-227
27.	Dec 5	@ Vancouver	3-1	W	12-12-3	27	87-85	66.	Feb 28	Winnipeg •	3-0	W	33-29-4	70	254-227
28.	Dec 6	@ Edmonton	3-4	L	12-13-3	27	90-89	67.	Mar 3	@ Chicago	5-4	W	34-29-4	72	259-231
29.	Dec 7	@ Winnipeg	4-7	L	12-14-3	27	94-96	68.	Mar 9	@ Houston	2-4	L	34-30-4	72	261-235
30.	Dec 9	Minnesota	10-1	W	13-14-3	29	104-97	69.	Mar 10	Cleveland	8-3	W	35-30-4	74	269-238
31.	Dec 12	@ New England	6-8	L	13-15-3	29	110-105	70.	Mar 14	Quebec •	2-3	L	35-31-4	74	271-241
32.	Dec 13	Cleveland	3-1	W	14-15-3	31	113-106	71.	Mar 17	Chicago	2-4	L	35-32-4	74	273-245
33.	Dec 15	Cleveland	3-4	L	14-16-3	31	116-110	72.	Mar 18	@ Jersey	5-11	L	35-33-4	74	278-256
34.	Dec 16	Quebec	3-4	L	14-17-3	31	119-114	73.	Mar 21	Houston •	6-3	W	36-33-4	76	284-259
35.	Dec 18	Jersey	4-1	W	15-17-3	33	123-115	74.	Mar 24	Vancouver	3-1	W	37-33-4	78	287-260
36.	Dec 21	Houston	3-1	W	16-17-3	35	126-116	75.	Mar 28	Edmonton •	*6-5	W	38-33-4	80	293-265
37.	Dec 22	@ Quebec	6-4	W	17-17-3	37	132-120	76.	Mar 30	@ Quebec	3-1	W	39-33-4	82	296-266
38.	Dec 23	Chicago	5-6	L	17-18-3	37	137-126	77.	Mar 31	Los Angeles	5-4	W	40-33-4	84	301-270
39.	Dec 29	@ Minnesota	9-3	W	18-18-3	39	146-129	78.	Apr 2	Edmonton	3-2	W	41-33-4	86	304-272

• Home games played at the Ottawa Civic Centre

148

Toros Stars of 1973-1974

Wayne Carleton	**Tom Martin**	**Wayne Dillon**	**Tom Simpson**	**Les Binkley**	**Pat Hickey**
92 points led team	25 goals	30 goals	33 goals for "Shotgun"	3.27 average	26 goals for rookie

Scoring

pos	#	player	gp	g	a	pts	pim	ppg	shg	gp	g	a	pts	pim
					Regular Season							**Playoffs**		
D	5	Amodeo, Mike	77	0	11	11	82	0	0	12	0	2	2	26
G	30	Binkley, Les	27	0	0	0	0	0	0	5	0	0	0	0
G	29	Blum, Frank	5	0	0	0	0	0	0	-	-	-	-	-
D	2	Brewer, Carl	77	2	23	25	42	1	0	12	0	4	4	11
LW	9	Carleton, Wayne	78	37	55	92	31	5	0	12	2	12	14	4
D	4	Cuddie, Steve	74	5	18	23	65	0	0	8	1	4	5	14
D	3	Cunningham, Rick	75	2	19	21	88	1	0	11	0	4	4	31
C	18	Dillon, Wayne	71	30	35	65	13	7	0	12	5	6	11	9
LW	10	Dupras, Rich	2	0	0	0	0	0	0	-	-	-	-	-
D	6	Gibbons, Brian	78	4	31	35	84	3	0	12	2	5	7	10
D	22	Gibbons, Gerard	26	1	4	5	23	0	0	1	0	0	0	0
LW	21	Gibson, Jack	61	16	9	25	60	4	0	12	1	3	4	11
G	33	Gratton, Gilles	57	0	4	4	28	0	0	10	0	0	0	0
LW	16	Hickey, Pat	78	26	29	55	52	3	4	12	3	3	6	12
G		Holden, Bill	1	0	0	0	0	0	0	-	-	-	-	-
RW	12	King, Steve	67	14	22	36	26	4	0	12	0	3	3	11
C	11	Kirk, Gavin	78	20	48	68	44	3	0	12	2	4	6	4
LW	19	Leduc, Bob	61	22	29	51	29	4	0	12	4	6	10	42
C	20	Marrin, Peter	31	1	4	5	4	0	0	3	0	1	1	2
RW	17	Martin, Tom	74	25	32	57	14	7	0	12	7	3	10	2
C	10	Nistico, Lou	13	1	3	4	14	0	0	-	-	-	-	-
D	23	Orr, Bill	46	3	9	12	16	1	0	12	1	0	1	6
LW	15	Selby, Brit	64	9	17	26	21	1	0	10	1	3	4	2
RW	8	Sentes, Dick	64	26	34	60	46	6	0	12	7	4	11	19
RW	14	Simpson, Tom	74	33	20	53	27	5	1	12	4	1	5	5
RW	7	Trottier, Guy	71	27	35	62	58	4	0	12	5	5	10	4
D		Warr, Steve	0	-	-	-	-	-	-	2	0	0	0	0

Power Play: 60 goals scored in 257 opportunities (23.3%) with 4 short-handed goals allowed.
Penalty Killing: 42 goals allowed in 249 opportunities (83.1%) with 5 short-handed goals scored.

Goaltending

goaltender	gp	min	ga	en	so	record	gaa	sog	sv%	gp	min	ga	record	gaa
Binkley, Les	27	1412	77	1	1	14-9-1	3.27	776	0.901	5	182	17	2-2	5.93
Blum, Frank	5	130	5	0	0	1-0-0	2.31	66	0.924	-	-	-	-	-
Gratton, Gilles	57	3200	188	1	2	26-24-3	3.53	1786	0.895	10	539	25	5-3	2.78
Holden, Bill	1	10	0	0	0	0-0-0	0.00	7	1.000	-	-	-	-	-

Transactions: Steve Cuddie from Winnipeg for Ken Stephenson, Jun 1973 • Bob Charlebois traded to New England for Brit Selby, Jun 1973 • Carl Brewer signed to contract, Jul 1973 • Bill Orr signed to contract, Oct 1973 • Frank Blum loaned to Winnipeg for playoffs under emergency conditions, Apr 1974 • Bill Holden loaned to Winnipeg under emergency conditions, Apr 1974

149

1973-1974 VANCOUVER BLAZERS

Coach
John McKenzie
3-4-0

Coach
Phil Watson
3-9-0

Coach
Andy Bathgate
21-37-1

Summary of Games (@ Away, * Overtime)

	date	opponent	score		record	pts	gf-ga		date	opponent	score		record	pts	gf-ga
1.	Oct 10	Winnipeg	*4-3	W	1-0-0	2	4-3	40.	Jan 6 @	Cleveland	3-11	L	15-25-0	30	136-169
2.	Oct 12 @	Minnesota	4-5	L	1-1-0	2	8-8	41.	Jan 7 @	Jersey	5-4	W	16-25-0	32	141-173
3.	Oct 14 @	Winnipeg	3-6	L	1-2-0	2	11-14	42.	Jan 9	Winnipeg	4-6	L	16-26-0	32	145-179
4.	Oct 17	Houston	2-7	L	1-3-0	2	13-21	43.	Jan 13	Edmonton	6-2	W	17-26-0	34	151-181
5.	Oct 19 @	Edmonton	3-1	W	2-3-0	4	16-22	44.	Jan 17 @	Houston	4-7	L	17-27-0	34	155-188
6.	Oct 20	Chicago	4-3	W	3-3-0	6	20-25	45.	Jan 19	Jersey	*4-5	L	17-28-0	34	159-193
7.	Oct 21	Los Angeles	1-4	L	3-4-0	6	21-29	46.	Jan 20 @	Los Angeles	3-0	W	18-28-0	36	162-193
8.	Oct 24	Toronto	4-7	L	3-5-0	6	25-36	47.	Jan 23	Cleveland	6-3	W	19-28-0	38	168-196
9.	Oct 27	Edmonton	2-6	L	3-6-0	6	27-42	48.	Jan 26	Houston	2-4	L	19-29-0	38	170-200
10.	Oct 28 @	Edmonton	5-7	L	3-7-0	6	32-49	49.	Jan 27 @	Toronto	7-9	L	19-30-0	38	177-209
11.	Oct 31	Quebec	1-5	L	3-8-0	6	33-54	50.	Jan 28 @	New England	4-6	L	19-31-0	38	181-215
12.	Nov 3	New York	0-4	L	3-9-0	6	33-58	51.	Jan 30	Chicago	2-4	L	19-32-0	38	183=219
13.	Nov 4	New York	3-4	L	3-10-0	6	36-62	52.	Feb 5	Edmonton	8-0	W	20-32-0	40	191-219
14.	Nov 7	Los Angeles	1-3	L	3-11-0	6	37-65	53.	Feb 8	Quebec	7-3	W	21-32-0	42	198=222
15.	Nov 9 @	Minnesota	1-3	L	3-12-0	6	38-68	54.	Feb 13	New England	9-4	W	22-32-0	44	207-226
16.	Nov 10 @	Houston	3-8	L	3-13-0	6	41-76	55.	Feb 17 @	Los Angeles	4-0	W	23-32-0	46	211-226
17.	Nov 13	Winnipeg	5-3	W	4-13-0	8	46-79	56.	Feb 19	Toronto	4-5	L	23-33-0	46	215=231
18.	Nov 15	Minnesota	7-5	W	5-13-0	10	53-84	57.	Feb 21 @	Chicago	4-5	L	23-34-0	46	219=236
19.	Nov 18	Cleveland	8-2	W	6-13-0	12	61-86	58.	Feb 23 @	Cleveland	3-7	L	23-35-0	46	222-243
20.	Nov 22	Edmonton	7-1	W	7-13-0	14	68-87	59.	Feb 24 @	Houston	1-7	L	23-36-0	46	223=250
21.	Nov 23 @	Winnipeg	*4-3	W	8-13-0	16	72-90	60.	Feb 26 @	Houston	2-3	L	23-37-0	46	225=253
22.	Nov 25 @	Toronto	*2-3	L	8-14-0	16	74-93	61.	Feb 28 @	Quebec	4-9	L	23-38-0	46	229=262
23.	Nov 28	Minnesota	5-3	W	9-14-0	18	79-96	62.	Mar 2 @	New England	1-7	L	23-39-0	46	230-269
24.	Dec 5	Toronto	1-3	L	9-15-0	18	80-99	63.	Mar 4 @	Jersey	*6-7	L	23-40-0	46	236=276
25.	Dec 7 @	Minnesota	1-3	L	9-16-0	18	81-102	64.	Mar 7	Cleveland	2-4	L	23-41-0	46	238-280
26.	Dec 9	Houston	3-5	L	9-17-0	18	84-107	65.	Mar 10 @	Edmonton	*2-1	W	24-41-0	48	240-281
27.	Dec 12	Quebec	*2-1	W	10-17-0	20	86-108	66.	Mar 13	Los Angeles	5-2	W	25-41-0	50	245-283
28.	Dec 15	Los Angeles	6-4	W	11-17-0	22	92-112	67.	Mar 14	New England	3-6	L	25-42-0	50	248-289
29.	Dec 16 @	Los Angeles	3-5	L	11-18-0	22	95-117	68.	Mar 15 @	Winnipeg	5-7	L	25-43-0	50	253-296
30.	Dec 18 @	Los Angeles	5-2	W	12-18-0	24	100-119	69.	Mar 17 @	Edmonton	2-3	L	25-44-0	50	255-299
31.	Dec 19	Minnesota	2-4	L	12-19-0	24	102-123	70.	Mar 19	Minnesota	5-4	W	26-44-0	52	260-303
32.	Dec 21 @	Edmonton	1-4	L	12-20-0	24	103-127	71.	Mar 21 @	Chicago	5-5	T	26-44-1	53	265=308
33.	Dec 22	Edmonton	6-3	W	13-20-0	26	109-130	72.	Mar 23 @	Quebec	2-6	L	26-45-1	53	267=314
34.	Dec 24 @	New England	*4-5	L	13-21-0	26	113-135	73.	Mar 24 @	Toronto	1-3	L	26-46-1	53	268=317
35.	Dec 26 @	Cleveland	5-3	W	14-21-0	28	118-138	74.	Mar 27	Houston	1-8	L	26-47-1	53	269=325
36.	Dec 28 @	Jersey	3-5	L	14-22-0	28	121-143	75.	Mar 29	Chicago	2-5	L	26-48-1	53	271=330
37.	Dec 30	New England	*6-5	W	15-22-0	30	127-148	76.	Mar 31 @	Winnipeg	*3-4	L	26-49-1	53	274-334
38.	Jan 1 @	Chicago	4-5	L	15-23-0	30	131-153	77.	Apr 3 @	Minnesota	0-9	L	26-50-1	53	274-343
39.	Jan 5 @	Quebec	2-5	L	15-24-0	30	133-158	78.	Apr 4	Winnipeg	4-2	W	27-50-1	55	278-345

Blazers Stars of 1973-1974

Claude St. Sauveur
38 goals

Don Burgess
30 goals

Danny Lawson
50 goals, 88 points

Pete Donnelly
22 wins, 3 shutouts

Dave Hutchison
151 minutes

Colin Campbell
3 goals, 191 minutes

Scoring

pos	#	player	gp	Regular Season g	a	pts	pim	ppg	shg	Playoffs gp	g	a	pts	pim
C	7	Adair, Jim	70	12	17	29	10	2	0	-	-	-	-	-
G	30	Archambault, Yves	5	0	0	0	0	0	0	-	-	-	-	-
D	23	Beaudoin, Serge	26	1	11	12	37	0	0	-	-	-	-	-
D		Boudreau, Michel	3	1	0	1	0	0	0	-	-	-	-	-
LW	8	Burgess, Don	78	30	36	66	8	5	3	-	-	-	-	-
C	14	Campbell, Bryan	76	27	62	89	50	8	1	-	-	-	-	-
D	2	Campbell, Colin	78	3	20	23	191	0	0	-	-	-	-	-
D	6	Campeau, Rychard	7	0	0	0	2	0	0	-	-	-	-	-
D	5	Cardiff, Jim	78	1	21	22	188	1	0	-	-	-	-	-
LW	16	Chernoff, Mike	36	11	10	21	4	0	1	-	-	-	-	-
G	1	Donnelly, Pete	49	0	1	1	9	0	0	-	-	-	-	-
G	35	Gardner, George	28	0	0	0	0	0	0	-	-	-	-	-
LW	20/21	Gellard, Sam	23	7	4	11	15	3	0	-	-	-	-	-
RW	25	Hatoum, Ed	37	3	12	15	8	0	0	-	-	-	-	-
D	3	Hutchison, Dave	69	0	13	13	151	0	0	-	-	-	-	-
C	20	Jones, James H.	18	3	2	5	23	2	0	-	-	-	-	-
C	25	Lapierre, Camille	9	0	3	3	0	0	0	-	-	-	-	-
RW	11	Lawson, Danny	78	50	38	88	14	10	0	-	-	-	-	-
D	6	MacSweyn, Ralph	56	2	18	20	52	0	0	-	-	-	-	-
RW	19	McKenzie, John	45	14	38	52	71	3	0	-	-	-	-	-
D	6	McNamee, Pete	3	0	0	0	0	0	0	-	-	-	-	-
C	15	Meloche, Denis	41	6	13	19	18	1	0	-	-	-	-	-
LW	18	Migneault, John	74	21	26	47	27	2	0	-	-	-	-	-
RW	17	Myers, Murray	61	22	20	42	28	2	0	-	-	-	-	-
RW	12	O'Donoghue, Don	49	8	6	14	20	0	0	-	-	-	-	-
LW	24	Plante, Michel	22	3	2	5	2	0	0	-	-	-	-	-
D	4	Plumb, Ron	78	6	32	38	40	1	0	-	-	-	-	-
LW	22	St. Sauveur, Claude	70	38	30	68	55	6	2	-	-	-	-	-
D	23	Spencer, Irv	19	0	1	1	6	0	0	-	-	-	-	-
G	34	Sullivan, Danny	1	0	0	0	0	0	0	-	-	-	-	-
F	10	Tetreault, Jean	6	1	1	2	0	0	0	-	-	-	-	-
C	10	Walton, Rob	28	8	15	23	2	1	0	-	-	-	-	-
C	10	Ward, Ron	7	0	2	2	2	0	0	-	-	-	-	-

Power Play: 47 goals scored in 289 opportunities (16.3%) with 12 short-handed goals allowed.
Penalty Killing: 66 goals allowed in 286 opportunities (76.9%) with 7 short-handed goals scored.

Goaltending

goaltender	gp	min	ga	en	so	record	gaa	sog	sv%	gp	min	ga	record	gaa
Archambault, Yves	5	263	27	0	0	1-4-0	6.16	183	0.852	-	-	-	-	-
Donnelly, Pete	49	2824	179	4	3	22-24-0	3.80	1525	0.883	-	-	-	-	-
Gardner, George	28	1590	125	3	0	4-21-1	4.72	957	0.869	-	-	-	-	-
Sullivan, Danny	1	60	7	0	0	0-1-0	7.00	38	0.816	-	-	-	-	-

Transactions: Andre Lacroix and Don Herriman traded to New York for Ron Ward and Peter Donnelly, May 1973 • Jim Adair signed to contract, Sep 1973 • Ron Ward traded to Los Angeles for George Gardner and Ralph MacSweyn, Oct 1973 • Denis Meloche, Claude St. Sauveur signed to contracts, Oct 1973 • Jean Tetreault traded to Minnesota for Rob Walton, Jan 1974

1973-1974 WINNIPEG JETS

**Player-Coach
Bobby Hull**

**Bench Coach
Nick Mickoski**

Summary of Games (@ Away, * Overtime)

	date		opponent	score		record	pts	gf-ga		date		opponent	score		record	pts	gf-ga
1.	Oct 10	@	Vancouver	*3-4	L	0-1-0	0	3-4	40.	Jan 1	@	Edmonton	*4-3	W	18-18-4	40	132-138
2.	Oct 12	@	Edmonton	4-6	L	0-2-0	0	7-10	41.	Jan 4		New England	3-4	L	18-19-4	40	135-142
3.	Oct 14		Vancouver	6-3	W	1-2-0	2	13-13	42.	Jan 6	@	Houston	1-7	L	18-20-4	40	136-149
4.	Oct 17	@	New England	3-1	W	2-2-0	4	16-14	43.	Jan 8	@	Los Angeles	1-4	L	18-21-4	40	137-153
5.	Oct 18	@	New York	6-1	W	3-2-0	6	22-15	44.	Jan 9	@	Vancouver	6-4	W	19-21-4	42	143-157
6.	Oct 21		Minnesota	*2-1	W	4-2-0	8	24-16	45.	Jan 11		Edmonton	7-4	W	20-21-4	44	150-161
7.	Oct 26		Toronto	3-3	T	4-2-1	9	27-19	46.	Jan 13		Chicago	3-1	W	21-21-4	46	153-162
8.	Oct 27	@	Minnesota	2-5	L	4-3-1	9	29-24	47.	Jan 18		Cleveland	7-3	W	22-21-4	48	160-165
9.	Oct 30	@	Chicago	1-4	L	4-4-1	9	30-28	48.	Jan 20		Jersey	9-3	W	23-21-4	50	169-168
10.	Oct 31	@	Cleveland	4-6	L	4-5-1	9	34-34	49.	Jan 25	@	Edmonton	4-3	W	24-21-4	52	173-171
11.	Nov 2		New York	3-1	W	5-5-1	11	37-35	50.	Jan 27	@	Minnesota	2-12	L	24-22-4	52	175-183
12.	Nov 4		Quebec	8-2	W	6-5-1	13	45-37	51.	Feb 1		Los Angeles	4-0	W	25-22-4	54	179-183
13.	Nov 6	@	Quebec	2-2	T	6-5-2	14	47-39	52.	Feb 3		Chicago	4-2	W	26-22-4	56	183-185
14.	Nov 7	@	New England	2-9	L	6-6-2	14	49-48	53.	Feb 5	@	Chicago	1-3	L	26-23-4	56	184-188
15.	Nov 10	@	Cleveland	2-4	L	6-7-2	14	51-52	54.	Feb 8		Minnesota	3-4	L	26-24-4	56	187-192
16.	Nov 11		Los Angeles	6-2	W	7-7-2	16	57-54	55.	Feb 10		Houston	2-2	T	26-24-5	57	189-194
17.	Nov 13	@	Vancouver	3-5	L	7-8-2	16	60-59	56.	Feb 11	@	Los Angeles	4-2	W	27-24-5	59	193-196
18.	Nov 16		Edmonton	3-1	W	8-8-2	18	63-60	57.	Feb 13	@	Houston	1-5	L	27-25-5	59	194-201
19.	Nov 18	@	Toronto	2-6	L	8-9-2	18	65-66	58.	Feb 15	@	Minnesota	1-7	L	27-26-5	59	195-208
20.	Nov 21		Cleveland	6-2	W	9-9-2	20	71-68	59.	Feb 17		New England	*2-3	L	27-27-5	59	197-211
21.	Nov 23		Vancouver	*3-4	L	9-10-2	20	74-72	60.	Feb 20	@	Edmonton	1-4	L	27-28-5	59	198-215
22.	Nov 25	@	Minnesota	3-5	L	9-11-2	20	77-77	61.	Feb 22		Toronto	4-3	W	28-28-5	61	202-218
23.	Nov 27	@	Los Angeles	*4-5	L	9-12-2	20	81-82	62.	Feb 24		Chicago	3-1	W	29-28-5	63	205-219
24.	Nov 28	@	Houston	4-4	T	9-12-3	21	85-86	63.	Feb 26	@	Quebec	1-7	L	29-29-5	63	206-226
25.	Nov 30		Los Angeles	2-5	L	9-13-3	21	87-91	64.	Feb 28	@	Toronto	0-3	L	29-30-5	63	206-229
26.	Dec 2		Quebec	5-3	W	10-13-3	23	92-94	65.	Mar 1		Minnesota	0-4	L	29-31-5	63	206-233
27.	Dec 5		Edmonton	3-1	W	11-13-3	25	95-95	66.	Mar 3		Quebec	8-6	W	30-31-5	65	214-239
28.	Dec 7		Toronto	7-4	W	12-13-3	27	102-99	67.	Mar 8		Cleveland	1-4	L	30-32-5	65	215-243
29.	Dec 9		Jersey	3-1	W	13-13-3	29	105-100	68.	Mar 9	@	Chicago	*4-5	L	30-33-5	65	219-248
30.	Dec 12		Houston	2-3	L	13-14-3	29	107-103	69.	Mar 11	@	Jersey	2-10	L	30-34-5	65	221-258
31.	Dec 14		Los Angeles	1-0	W	14-14-3	31	108-103	70.	Mar 13	@	Cleveland	3-4	L	30-35-5	65	224-262
32.	Dec 16		Minnesota	2-3	L	14-15-3	31	110-106	71.	Mar 15		Vancouver	7-5	W	31-35-5	67	231-267
33.	Dec 18	@	Chicago	3-3	T	14-15-4	32	113-109	72.	Mar 17		New England	10-1	W	32-35-5	69	241-268
34.	Dec 19	@	Houston	0-10	L	14-16-4	32	113-119	73.	Mar 22		Houston	2-4	L	32-36-5	69	243-272
35.	Dec 22	@	New England	2-0	W	15-16-4	34	115-119	74.	Mar 24	@	Los Angeles	3-6	L	32-37-5	69	246-278
36.	Dec 23	@	Jersey	3-6	L	15-17-4	34	118-125	75.	Mar 29		Houston	7-5	W	33-37-5	71	253-283
37.	Dec 26		Chicago	4-2	W	16-17-4	36	122-127	76.	Mar 31		Vancouver	*4-3	W	34-37-5	71	257-286
38.	Dec 29	@	Quebec	4-3	W	17-17-4	38	126-130	77.	Apr 3		Edmonton	*5-6	L	34-38-5	71	262-292
39.	Dec 30	@	Toronto	2-5	L	17-18-4	38	128-135	78.	Apr 4	@	Vancouver	2-4	L	34-39-5	71	264-296

Jets Stars of 1973-1974

Ernie Wakely
3 shutouts

Fran Huck
26 goals, 74 points

Ron Snell
24 goals

Joe Zanussi
Steady defense

Duke Asmundson
85 minutes

Bobby Hull
53 goals, 95 points

Scoring

pos	#	player	gp	g	a	pts	pim	ppg	shg	gp	g	a	pts	pim
					Regular Season							Playoffs		
D	3	Ash, Bob	60	2	18	20	30	0	0	4	0	1	1	2
D	21	Asmundson, Duke	72	5	14	19	85	0	0	4	0	1	1	2
RW	11	Beaudin, Norm	74	27	28	55	8	5	0	4	3	1	4	2
RW	19	Black, Milt	47	6	9	15	14	0	0	4	1	1	2	0
G	27	Blum, Frank	0	-	-	-	-	-	-	2	0	0	0	0
C	7	Bordeleau, Christian	75	26	49	75	22	5	1	3	3	2	5	0
G	1	Daley, Joe	41	0	1	1	4	0	0	2	0	0	0	0
RW	16	Gratton, Jean-Guy	68	12	21	33	13	4	0	2	0	0	0	0
D	6	Hargreaves, Jim	53	1	4	5	50	0	0	-	-	-	-	-
LW	8	Hargreaves, Ted	74	7	12	19	15	0	2	4	0	1	1	10
G	28	Holden, Bill	1	0	0	0	0	0	0	-	-	-	-	-
D	5	Hornung, Larry	51	4	19	23	18	1	1	4	0	0	0	0
C	25	Huck, Fran	74	26	48	74	68	2	2	4	0	0	0	2
LW	9	Hull, Bobby	75	53	42	95	38	9	1	4	1	1	2	4
C	17	Johnson, Dan	78	16	21	37	20	2	0	4	1	0	1	5
LW	14	McDonald, Ab	70	12	17	29	8	2	0	4	0	1	1	2
RW	24	Pratt, Kelly	46	4	6	10	50	1	0	-	-	-	-	-
C	15	Rizzuto, Garth	41	3	4	7	8	1	1	-	-	-	-	-
LW	12	Rousseau, Dunc	60	10	8	18	39	0	0	4	0	0	0	0
RW	20	Snell, Ron	70	24	25	49	32	5	0	4	0	0	0	0
C	22	Spring, Dan	66	8	16	24	8	1	0	4	0	1	1	0
D	10	Stephanson, Ken	29	0	7	7	74	0	0	3	0	2	2	10
C	10/27	Sutherland, Bill	12	4	5	9	6	0	0	4	0	0	0	4
C	12/18	Swenson, Cal	25	5	4	9	2	0	0	1	0	0	0	0
G	30	Wakely, Ernie	37	0	0	0	0	0	0	-	-	-	-	-
D	2	Woytowich, Bob	72	6	28	34	43	1	0	4	0	0	0	0
D	4	Zanussi, Joe	76	3	22	25	53	0	0	4	0	0	0	0

Power Play: 39 goals scored in 240 opportunities (16.3%) with 15 short-handed goals allowed.
Penalty Killing: 45 goals allowed in 207 opportunities (78.3%) with 8 short-handed goals scored.

Goaltending

goaltender	gp	min	ga	en	so	record	gaa	sog	sv%	gp	min	ga	record	gaa
Blum, Frank	0	-	-	-	-	-	-	-	-	2	120	15	0-2	7.50
Daley, Joe	41	2454	163	4	0	19-20-1	3.99	1402	0.884	2	119	8	0-2	4.03
Holden, Bill	1	60	4	0	0	0-1-0	4.00	28	0.857	-	-	-	-	-
Wakely, Ernie	37	2254	123	2	3	15-18-4	3.27	1184	0.896	-	-	-	-	-

Transactions: Ron Snell signed to contract, Jun 1973 • Dan Spring signed to contract, Jul 1973 • Bill Holden loaned to Winnipeg from Toronto under emergency conditions, Apr 1974 • Frank Blum loaned to Winnipeg from Toronto under emergency conditions, Apr 1974.

1973-1974 Statistical Leaders

Top five in each category.

Goals: 57, Mike Walton (Minnesota); 53, Bobby Hull (Winnipeg); 50, Danny Lawson (Vancouver); 43, Tom Webster (New England); 42, Wayne Connelly (Minnesota), Frank Hughes (Houston).

Assists: 80, Andre Lacroix (New York-Jersey); 69, Gordie Howe (Houston); 62, Bryan Campbell (Vancouver); 60, Mike Walton (Minnesota); 56, Andre Hinse (Houston).

Points: 117, Mike Walton (Minnesota); 111, Andre Lacroix (New York-Jersey); 100, Gordie Howe (Houston); 95, Wayne Connelly (Minnesota), Bobby Hull (Winnipeg); 92, Wayne Carleton (Toronto)

Penalty Minutes: 223, Gord Gallant (Minnesota); 214, Doug Barrie (Edmonton); 192, John Arbour (Minnesota); 191, Colin Campbell (Vancouver); 188, Jim Cardiff (Vancouver).

Power-play Goals: 15, Wayne Connelly (Minnesota); 13, Frank Hughes (Houston); 12, George Morrison (Minnesota); 11, Gary Jarrett (Cleveland), Andre Lacroix (New York-Jersey); 10, Andre Hinse (Houston), Marc Tardif (Los Angeles), Danny Lawson (Vancouver)

Short-handed Goals: 9, Mike Walton (Minnesota); 4, Val Fonteyne (Edmonton), Ted Hampson (Minnesota), Pat Hickey (Toronto); 3, Paul Andrea (Cleveland), Don Burgess (Vancouver), Mike McMahon (Minnesota), Ted Taylor (Houston); 2, shared by many.

Goaltending Minutes: 3562, Gerry Cheevers (Cleveland); 3200, Gilles Gratton (Toronto); 3194, Al Smith (New England); 3122, Joe Junkin (New York–Jersey); 2971, Don McLeod (Houston).

Goals Against Average: 2.56, Don McLeod (Houston); 3.03, Gerry Cheevers (Cleveland); 3.08 Al Smith (New England); 3.21, Jack Norris (Edmonton); 3.27, Les Binkley (Toronto), Ernie Wakely (Winnipeg), Mike Curran (Minnesota).

Wins: 33, Don McLeod (Houston); 30, Gerry Cheevers (Cleveland), Al Smith (New England); 26, Gilles Gratton (Toronto); 25, Cam Newton (Chicago); 23, Mike Curran (Minnesota), Jack Norris (Edmonton).

Shutouts: 4, Gerry Cheevers (Cleveland); 3, Pete Donnelly (Vancouver), Don McLeod (Houston), Ernie Wakely (Winnipeg); 2, shared by many.

Totals for Players With Two or More Teams During 1973-1974

player	teams	gp	g	a	pts	pim	ppg	shg
Gardner, George	LA, Van	30	0	0	0	0	0	0
Gordon, Don	LA, Chi	52	13	10	23	33	4	0
Hodgson, Ted	Cle, LA	33	3	11	14	28	2	0
Holden, Bill	Wpg, Tor	2	0	0	0	0	0	0
MacSweyn, Ralph,	LA, Van	69	2	21	23	58	0	0
McLeod, Jim	NY-J, LA	27	0	0	0	2	0	0
Sheehan, Bobby	NY-J, Edm	60	13	11	24	14	6	0
Walton, Rob	Min, Van	73	16	38	54	26	2	0
Ward, Ron	Van, LA, Cle	70	33	28	61	25	7	0
Watson, Jim	LA, Chi	71	0	11	11	50	0	0
Whitlock, Bobby	Chi, LA	66	20	29	49	48	7	1
Wilkie, Ian	LA, Edm	28	0	0	0	2	0	0
Young, Bill	Cle, LA	69	9	12	21	74	0	0

Totals for Goaltenders With Two or More Teams During 1973-1974

goaltender	teams	gp	min	ga	en	so	record	gaa	sog	sv%
George Gardner	LA, Van	30	1710	138	3	0	4-23-1	4.84	1022	0.865
Bill Holden	Tor, Wpg	2	70	4	0	0	0-1-0	3.43	35	0.886
Jim McLeod	NY-J, LA	27	1486	105	2	1	7-20-0	4.24	777	0.865
Ian Wilkie	LA, Edm	28	1513	91	0	1	14-10-0	3.61	720	0.874

One Game at a Time

Eddie Hatoum of the Vancouver Blazers had perhaps the most unique contract arrangement of any player in either league during 1973-74: he signed a series of one-game contracts, 37 in all for 1973-74, with no guarantee that he would be around after the end of any given game. This arrangement persisted for over half the season, finally ending when the Blazers released him in February 1974.

1974 Canada-USSR Summit Challenge
Team Canada (WHA All-Stars) vs. Soviet National Team

The historic 1972 series pitting the NHL's all-stars, known collectively as Team Canada, against the USSR's finest, was followed in 1974 with another Team Canada, this time composed of the WHA's top players. Notable members of the 1974 Canadian squad were Gordie Howe, who missed the 1972 series as he was retired from hockey, and his two sons, Mark and Marty. Bobby Hull also played, having been omitted from the 1972 team after he had signed with the WHA that summer. Paul Henderson, who scored the famous late goal in the final game to give Canada the series win in 1972, also played for the WHA squad. Toronto's Billy Harris served as coach, with Edmonton's Bill Hunter as general manager. Boris Kulagin coached the 1974 Soviet team, which had changed very little from 1972. The WHA all-stars were unable to repeat as series champs, with the Soviets winning four games to Canada's one lone win, with three ties serving as little consolation.

Richard Bendell, a researcher who recently published an extensive account of the 1972 Canada-USSR Summit Series, has also studied game films of the 1974 Series, and has noted many instances where errors or omissions were made in the scoring summaries. He has graciously allowed this information to be included in this book. What follows are the "official" game summaries as reported by the media in 1974, with the presumptive errors included, and following each, a summary of the scoring revisions as determined by Mr Bendell. The accumulated scoring totals for both teams lists the official statistics as based on the 1974 game summaries, then a revised account which takes into Mr Bendell's research. Game films from the 1974 Series vary in quality, especially those games played in Moscow. Many segments are missing and almost half of Game 5 is unavailable.

This is an ongoing research project, and Mr Bendell can be reached at thesummitseries1972@yahoo.com.

The Summaries

Game 1 • September 17, 1974
Le Colisee, Quebec

Bobby Hull scored two goals, including the game-tying goal in the third period, to allow Canada a tie against the Soviets in the first game of the series. Canada pressed the attack and had many opportunities to score during the final five minutes, but key saves by Soviet goaltender Vladislav Tretiak, and missed shots by the Canadian attackers, kept the score unchanged.

USSR 3, Canada 3

USSR	0	3	0	-	3
Canada	1	1	1	-	3

1st period: 1. Can: McKenzie (Lacroix, Hull) 12:13.
2nd period: 2. USSR: Lutchenko (Tsygankov, Kapustin) 7:46. 3. Can: Hull (Walton, G. Howe) 12:07. 4. USSR: Kharlamov (Vasilyev) 14:04. 5. USSR: Petrov (Gusev, Kharlamov) 17:10.
3rd period: 6. Can: Hull (Lacroix, McKenzie) 14:18.
Shots on goal

USSR on Cheevers	8	11	9 -	28
Canada on Tretiak	9	10	15 -	34

Scoring revision: Alexander Gusev should also be awarded an assist on Valeri Kharlamov's 2nd period goal.

Game 2 • September 19, 1974
Maple Leaf Gardens, Toronto

Canada won its first game of the series with an even attack and a little luck. A goal by the Soviets early in the 2nd period was waved off. Canada scored soon thereafter, and led wire-to-wire for the win. Gordie Howe missed almost the entire game after bruising his ribs early in the 1st period.

Canada 4, USSR 1

USSR	0	1	0	-	1
Canada	2	1	1	-	4

1st period: 1. Can: Backstrom (Mark Howe, G. Howe) 4:31. 2. Can: Lacroix (McKenzie, Tremblay) 10:49.
2nd period: 3. Can: Hull (Lacroix, McKenzie) 2:50. 4. USSR: Yakushev (Shadrin, Lebedev) 13:09.
3rd period: 5. Can: Tremblay (Lacroix, Hull) 17:03.
Shots on goal

USSR on Cheevers	13	8	9 -	30
Canada on Tretiak	10	16	7 -	33

Scoring revisions: Bobby Hull should be awarded an assist on Andre Lacroix' 1st period goal, in place of John McKenzie. Pat Stapleton should be awarded an assist on J.-C. Tremblay's 3rd period goal, in place of Andre Lacroix.

Game 3 • September 21, 1974
Winnipeg Arena, Winnipeg

Coach Harris rested six of his stars: Gordie Howe (who was still smarting from the previous game), Frank Mahovlich, Rejean Houle, Rick Ley, Gerry Cheevers and Brad Selwood all got the night off, and the understudies had a difficult time holding back the Soviets, who skated circles around the Canadians. Two late goals by Paul Henderson made the score respectable for Team Canada.

USSR 8, Canada 5

USSR	1	3	4	-	8
Canada	1	1	3	-	5

1st period: 1. Can: MacGregor (Henderson) 14:58. 2. USSR: Yakushev (Sahdrin) 17:25.
2nd period: 3. USSR: Mikhailov (Petrov) 1:23. 4. Can: Webster (Bernier, Tardif) 12:40. 5. USSR: Vasilyev (Mikhailov, Petrov) 15:14. 6. USSR: Maltsev (Anisin) 15:31.
3rd period: 7. USSR: Yakushev (Shadrin) 2:35. 8. USSR: Bodunov 8:44. 9. USSR: Yakushev 11:27. 10. Can: Henderson (Harrison) 14:31. 11. Can: Henderson (Harrison, MacGregor) 15:04. 12. Can: Bernier (Webster, Hamilton) 16:01. 13. USSR: Lebedev (Lutchenko) 18:05.
Shots on goal

USSR on McLeod	11	16	12 -	39
Canada on Tretiak	8	14	12 -	34

Game 3 (continued)

Scoring revisions: Al Hamilton should be awarded an assist on Tom Webster's 2nd period goal, in place of Marc Tardif. Marc Tardif should be awarded an assist on Serge Bernier's 3rd period goal, in place of Tom Webster. Gennady Tsygankov should also be awarded an assist on Boris Mikhailov's 2nd period goal. Vladimir Vasiliev's 2nd period goal should be awarded to Vladimir Petrov, while Vasiliev gets an assist. Victor Kuznetsov should also be awarded an assist on Boris Maltsev's 2nd period goal. Yuri Lebedev should also be awarded an assist on Vladimir Yakushev's 3rd period goal. Alexander Bodunov's 3rd period goal should have assists awarded to Alexander Maltsev and Viacheslav Anisin.

Game 4 • September 23, 1974
Pacific Coliseum, Vancouver

The Canadians scored four goals in five minutes, including three by Bobby Hull, late in the 1st period to take a 5-2 lead. The Soviets then pecked away at the lead, tying with two late goals in the 3rd period. The Canadians then had a late power play, but could not convert.

USSR 5, Canada 5

USSR	2	1	2	-	5
Canada	5	0	0	-	5

1st period: 1. USSR: Vasilyev (Kharlamov) 3:34. 2. Can: G. Howe (Stapleton, Backstrom) 4:20. 3. USSR: Mikhailov (Petrov) 5:59. 4. Can: Hull (Mahovlich) 12:45. 5. Can: Hull (Stapleton) 15:11. 6. Can: Mahovlich (Bernier, Houle) 17:10. 7. Can: Hull (Lacroix) 17:45.
2nd period: 8. USSR: Yakushev (Lebedev) 11:04.
3rd period: 9. USSR: Maltsev 16:08. 10. USSR: Gusev (Mikhailov, Petrov) 16:59.
Shots on goal

USSR on Cheevers	12	8	6	-	26
Canada on Tretiak	11	8	8	-	27

Scoring revisions: Mark Howe should be awarded an assist on Gordie Howe's 1st period goal, in place of Ralph Backstrom. Assists on Bobby Hull's 1st period goal at 12:45 should be awarded to Rejean Houle and Paul Shmyr, in place of Frank Mahovlich. John McKenzie should also be awarded an assist on Hull's 1st period goal at 15:11. Alexander Gusev should also be awarded an assist on Boris Mikhailov's 1st period goal. Vladimir Shadrin and Yuri Lyapkin should be awarded assists on Alexander Yakushev's 2nd period goal in place of Yuri Lebedev. Shots on goal should be revised to 10 shots for USSR in the 2nd period for a total of 28 in the game, and 9 shots for Canada in the 3rd period, for a total of 28 in the game.

Game 5 • October 1, 1974
Luzhniki Arena, Moscow

The Soviets played a hard-hitting game which kept the Canadians effectively bottled up in their own end, producing just 16 shots against Tretiak. Ralph Backstrom received a rare misconduct for arguing a call, and while he was cooling his heels, Alexander Gusev scored what would be the game winner for the Soviets.

USSR 3, Canada 2

Canada	0	1	1	-	2
USSR	1	1	1	-	3

1st period. 1. USSR: Maltsev (Vikulov, Anisin) 5:34.
2nd period: 2. Can: G. Howe (Backstrom, Mark Howe) 0:15. 3. USSR: Maltsev (Shadrin, Vikulov) 15:04.
3rd period: 4. USSR: Gusev 11:48. 5. Can: Mark Howe (Shmyr) 18:10.
Shots on goal

Canada on Tretiak	4	4	8	-	16
USSR on Cheevers	9	10	8	-	27

Scoring revisions: Mark Howe should be awarded an assist on Gordie Howe's 2nd period goal, in place of Marty Howe. Bobby Hull and Gordie Howe should be awarded assists on Mark Howe's 3rd period goal, in place of Paul Shmyr. Valeri Kharlamov and Boris Mikhailov should be awarded assists on Alexander Gusev's 3rd period goal.

Game 6 • October 3, 1974
Luzhniki Arena, Moscow

The Soviets took advantage of a blown penalty call that should have given Canada a man-advantage midway through the 2nd period. Instead, the Soviets put the game out of reach against an angered Canadian squad.

USSR 5, Canada 2

Canada	1	1	0	-	2
USSR	2	2	1	-	5

1st period: 1. USSR: Mikhailov (Kharlamov) 0:34. 2. USSR: Vasilyev (Kharlamov) 2:43. 3. Can: Houle (Shmyr) 15:56.
2nd period: 4. Can: G. Howe (Mark Howe) 2:55. 5. USSR: Anisin (Vikulov) 8:22. 6. USSR: Shatalov (Tsygankov) 13:57.
3rd period: 7. USSR: Kharlamov (Vikulov) 13:00
Shots on goal

Canada on Tretiak	13	9	6	-	28
USSR on Cheevers	14	8	7	-	29

Scoring revisions: Serge Bernier should also be awarded an assist on Rejean Houle's 1st period goal. Vladimir Petrov and Alexander Gusev should be awarded assists on Vladimir Vasiliev's 1st period goal, in place of Valeri Kharlamov. Sergei Kapustin should also be awarded an assist on Viacheslav Anisin's 2nd period goal.

Game 7 • October 5, 1974
Luzhniki Arena, Moscow

Bobby Hull scored an apparent game-winning goal as time expired, but the goal was disallowed. The timekeeper had allowed time to pass during other stoppages, adding to the Canadians' ire.

Canada 4, USSR 4

Canada	1	2	1	-	4
USSR	2	2	0	-	4

1st period: 1. USSR: Anisin (Lutchenko) 3:34. 2. USSR: Tyurin (Lebedev, Yakushev) 6:47. 3. Can: Webster (Lacroix) 17:42.
2nd period: 4. Can: Backstrom (G. Howe, Mark Howe) 2:55. 5. Can: Mark Howe (Tremblay, Backstrom) 6:38. 6. USSR: Gusev (Petrov, Kharlamov) 7:20. 7. USSR: Mikhailov (Petrov, Kharlamov) 7:59.
3rd period: 8. Can: Backstrom (Tremblay) 6:38.
Shots on goal

Canada on Tretiak	10	13	7	-	30
USSR on Cheevers	11	7	3	-	21

Scoring revisions: Gordie Howe should be awarded an assist on Mark Howe's 2nd period goal in place of Ralph Backstrom.

Game 8 • October 6, 1974
Luzhniki Arena, Moscow

Victor Shalimov scored two goals, his first coming with a two-man advantage early in the third period, to lead the Soviets, who closed out the eight-game set with their fourth victory.

USSR 3, Canada 2

Canada	1	0	1	-	2
USSR	0	1	2	-	3

1st period: 1. Can: Hull (Backstrom, Tremblay) 13:47.
2nd period: 2. USSR: Yakushev (Shadrin) 6:27.
3rd period: 3. USSR: Shalimov 0:53. 4. USSR: Shalimov (Yakushev) 6:59. 5. Can: Backstrom (G. Howe, Ley) 12:42.
Shots on goal

Canada on Sidelnikov	10	8	6	-	24
USSR on Cheevers	10	12	8	-	30

Scoring revisions: Gordie Howe should be awarded an assist on Bobby Hull's 1st period goal in place of Ralph Backstrom. Victor Shalimov should also be awarded an assist on Alexander Yakushev's 2nd period goal. Vladimir Shadrin and Victor Kuznetsov should be awarded assists on Victor Shalimov's goal at 0:53 of the 3rd period.

Final Standings

	w	l	t	pts	gf	ga
USSR	4	1	3	11	32	27
Canada	1	4	3	5	27	32

Scoring

USSR

	#	name	gp	g	a	pt	pm	g	a	pt
				Historical				**Revised**		
F	22	Vyacheslav Anisin	8	2	2	4	0	2	3	5
F	24	Alexander Bodunov	7	1	0	1	4	1	0	1
D	26	Alexander Filippov	1	0	0	0	0	0	0	0
D	36	Yuri Fyodorov	1	0	0	0	0	0	0	0
D	2	Alexander Gusev	8	3	1	4	4	3	4	7
F	8	Sergei Kapustin	5	0	1	1	6	0	2	2
F	17	Valeri Kharlamov	8	2	6	8	4	2	5	7
F	30	Konstantin Klimov	1	0	0	0	0	0	0	0
F	29	Sergei Kotov	5	0	0	0	0	0	0	0
F	12	Victor Kuznetsov	8	0	0	0	4	0	2	2
F	11	Yuri Lebedev	8	1	3	4	6	1	3	4
D	5	Yuri Lyapkin	5	0	0	0	2	0	1	1
D	3	Vladimir Lutchenko	8	1	2	3	4	1	1	2
F	10	Alexander Maltsev	8	4	0	4	0	4	1	5
F	13	Boris Mikhailov	7	4	2	6	0	4	3	7
F	16	Vladimir Petrov	7	1	6	7	4	2	6	8
F	14	Vladimir Popov	1	0	0	0	0	0	0	0
D	27	Alexander Sapyolkin	1	0	0	0	0	0	0	0
F	19	Vladimir Shadrin	8	0	5	5	11	0	6	6
F	31	Victor Shalimov	4	2	0	2	0	2	1	3
D	32	Yuri Tyurin	4	1	0	1	4	1	0	1
D	7	Gennady Tsygankov	6	0	2	2	2	0	3	3
D	6	Valeri Vasilyev	8	3	1	4	7	2	2	4
F	21	Vladimir Vikulov	4	0	4	4	0	0	4	4
F	9	Alexander Volchkov	2	0	0	0	4	0	0	0
F	15	Alexander Yakushev	7	6	2	8	2	6	2	8

Also on roster (pos, no): Alexei Volchenkov (D, 18); Sergei Glukhov (D, 28); Sergei Korotkov (D, 33); Alexander Kulikov (D, 37); Vladimir Repnyov (F, 23); Mikhail Titov (F, 32); Alexander Golikov (F, 34); Victor Afonin (G, 25).
Coaches: Boris Kulagin, Konstantin Loktev, Vladimir Yurzinov.

Canada

	#	name	gp	g	a	pt	pm	g	a	pt
				Historical				**Revised**		
F	14	Ralph Backstrom	8	4	4	8	10	4	1	5
F	21	Serge Bernier	8	1	2	3	4	1	2	3
D	24	Al Hamilton	3	0	1	1	4	0	2	2
F	15	Jim Harrison	3	0	2	2	0	0	1	1
F	19	Paul Henderson	7	2	1	3	0	2	1	3
F	9	Gordie Howe	7	3	4	7	2	3	7	10
F	11	Mark Howe	7	2	4	6	4	2	5	7
D	10	Marty Howe	4	0	0	0	12	0	0	0
F	5	Rejean Houle	7	1	1	2	2	1	2	3
F	16	Bobby Hull	8	7	2	9	0	7	3	10
F	7	Andre Lacroix	8	1	6	7	6	1	5	6
D	2	Rick Ley	7	0	1	1	14	0	1	1
F	20	Bruce MacGregor	5	1	1	2	5	1	1	2
F	27	Frank Mahovlich	6	1	1	2	6	1	0	1
F	23	John McKenzie	7	1	3	4	12	1	3	4
D	6	Brad Selwood	4	0	0	0	2	0	0	0
D	18	Paul Shmyr	7	0	2	2	4	0	2	2
D	17	Rick Smith	7	0	0	0	14	0	1	1
D	12	Pat Stapleton	8	0	2	2	12	0	3	3
F	22	Marc Tardif	5	0	1	1	10	0	1	1
D	3	J.-C. Tremblay	8	1	4	5	2	1	4	5
F	4	Mike Walton	6	0	1	1	2	0	1	1
F	8	Tom Webster	4	2	1	3	6	2	0	2

Also on roster (pos, no): Ron Chipperfield (F, 32), Wayne Dillon (F, 28), Gilles Gratton (G, 33), Gavin Kirk (F, 29), Barry Long (D, 25), Pat Price (D, 26), Dennis Sobchuk (F, 31).
Coach: Billy Harris.

Goaltending

	no.	name	gp	ga	record	gaa
G	1	Alexander Sidelnikov	1	2	1-0-0	2.00
G	20	Vladislav Tretiak	7	25	3-1-3	3.57

	no.	name	gp	ga	record	gaa
G	30	Gerry Cheevers	7	24	1-3-3	3.44
G	1	Don McLeod	1	8	0-1-0	8.14

Players of the Soviet Union

Viacheslav Anisin

Alexander Gusev

Valeri Kharlamov

Alexander Yakushev

Vladimir Vikulov

Vladimir Petrov

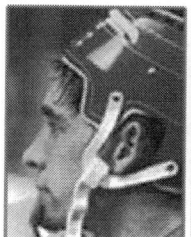
Yuri Shatalov

Vladislav Tretiak

Yuri Shadrin

Boris Mikhailov

Alexander Maltsev

Coach Boris Kulagin

157

Season III

1974-1975

The World Hockey Association's third season opened with two new teams, the Phoenix Roadrunners and Indianapolis Racers, joining the original twelve for a fourteen-team circuit. Three teams from the previous season found new homes: The Los Angeles Sharks moved to Detroit and became the Michigan Stags, the Jersey Knights went West and became the San Diego Mariners, and the Whalers left Boston for temporary digs in Springfield, then to their new permanent home in Hartford. The fourteen teams were placed into three divisions. The Canadian Division consisted of Edmonton, Quebec, Toronto, Vancouver and Winnipeg; the Eastern Division included Chicago, Cleveland, Indianapolis and New England, while Houston, Michigan, Minnesota, Phoenix and San Diego made up the Western Division.

The league would not be without its troubles as the Michigan Stags became insolvent in a hurry and folded in mid-January of 1975. A week later, the league formed the Baltimore Blades to replace the Stags for the remainder of the season. The Chicago Cougars were facing a mid-season fold when three of its players, Ralph Backstrom, Dave Dryden and Pat Stapleton, purchased the team. Unfortunately, the move gave the Cougars life only until the season's end. Both Baltimore and Chicago folded soon after the close of the 1974-75 season.

Keeping the 78-game season, each team played a perfectly balanced schedule, playing the thirteen other teams six times, three home and three away. The playoffs admitted the top two teams from each of the three divisions, plus two wild-card spots based on point standings. First-year Phoenix made the playoffs as a wild-card entrant, while fellow expansionists Indianapolis finished 18-57-3. The Houston Aeros breezed to their second consecutive AVCO World Trophy, losing only once in thirteen games.

Venerable offensive records from the NHL were broken when Bobby Hull scored 77 goals to beat Phil Esposito's NHL mark of 76, with 50 of Hull's goals coming in his team's first 50 games. San Diego's Andre Lacroix collected 106 assists to break Bobby Orr's record of 102, while also leading the league in points with 147. Houston's Ron Grahame led all goaltenders with a 3.03 goals against average while tying Cleveland's Gerry Cheevers with four shutouts. Grahame also notched a league high 33 wins, a feat matched by Vancouver's Don McLeod. McLeod, getting his ice time, also suffered a league high 35 defeats, as did Indianapolis' Andy Brown. Minnesota's Gord Gallant again led the league in penalty minutes with 203, just a minor call ahead of Phoenix's John Hughes.

Award Winners

Most Valuable Player
Gordie Howe Trophy
Bobby Hull, Wpg

Rookie of the Year
Lou Kaplan Trophy
Andres Hedberg, Wpg

Best Goaltender
Ben Hatskin Trophy
Ron Grahame, Hou

Standings

Canadian Division

#	team		gp	w	l	t	pts	pct	gf	ga
1.	Québec NORDIQUES		78	46	32	0	92	.590	331	299
		home	39	27	12	0	54	.692	184	140
		away	39	19	20	0	38	.487	147	159
2.	Toronto TOROS		78	43	33	2	88	.564	349	304
		home	39	24	15	0	48	.615	175	139
		away	39	19	18	2	40	.513	174	165
3.	Winnipeg JETS		78	38	35	5	81	.519	322	293
		home	39	23	13	3	49	.628	171	121
		away	39	15	22	2	32	.410	151	172
4.	Vancouver BLAZERS		78	37	39	2	76	.487	256	270
		home	39	25	12	2	52	.667	138	115
		away	39	12	27	0	24	.308	118	155
5.	Edmonton OILERS		78	36	38	4	76	.487	279	279
		home	39	25	12	2	52	.667	174	130
		away	39	11	26	2	24	.308	105	149

Eastern Division

#	team		gp	w	l	t	pts	pct	gf	ga
1.	New England WHALERS		78	43	30	5	91	.583	274	279
		home	39	28	8	3	59	.756	157	118
		away	39	15	22	2	32	.410	117	161
2.	Cleveland CRUSADERS		78	35	40	3	73	.467	236	258
		home	39	23	15	1	47	.603	130	109
		away	39	12	25	2	26	.333	106	149
3.	Chicago COUGARS		78	30	47	1	61	.391	261	312
		home	39	18	20	1	37	.474	138	153
		away	39	12	27	0	24	.308	123	159
4.	Indianapolis RACERS		78	18	57	3	39	.250	216	338
		home	39	13	26	0	26	.333	106	149
		away	39	5	31	3	13	.167	110	189

Western Division

#	team		gp	w	l	t	pts	pct	gf	ga
1.	Houston AEROS		78	53	25	0	106	.679	369	247
		home	39	28	11	0	56	.718	205	120
		away	39	25	14	0	50	.641	164	127
2.	San Diego MARINERS		78	43	31	4	90	.576	326	268
		home	39	26	11	2	54	.692	192	126
		away	39	17	20	2	36	.452	134	142
3.	Minnesota FIGHTING SAINTS		78	42	33	3	87	.558	308	279
		home	39	26	13	0	52	.667	176	136
		away	39	16	20	3	35	.449	132	143
4.	Phoenix ROADRUNNERS		78	39	31	8	86	.551	300	265
		home	39	23	11	5	51	.654	170	115
		away	39	16	20	3	35	.449	130	150
5.	Michigan STAGS - Baltimore BLADES		78	21	53	4	46	.295	205	341
		home	39	15	21	3	33	.423	103	142
		away	39	6	32	1	13	.167	102	199

Award Winners

Best Defeseman
Dennis Murphy Trophy
J.-C. Tremblay, Que

Coach of the Year
Howard Baldwin Trophy
Sandy Hucul, Phx

Most Gentlemanly
Paul Deneau Trophy
Mike Rogers, Edm

1975 World Hockey Association AVCO Cup Champions
Houston Aeros

1975 Playoff Series Results

Quarterfinals

Houston vs. Cleveland
Apr 10 Cleveland 5 at Houston 8
Apr 12 Cleveland 3 at Houston 5
Apr 13 Houston 1 at Cleveland 3
Apr 15 Houston 7 at Cleveland 2
Apr 17 Cleveland 1 at Houston 3

Quebec vs. Phoenix
Apr 8   Phoenix 2 at Quebec 5
Apr 10 Phoenix 2 at Quebec 6
Apr 12 Quebec 3 at Phoenix 0
        (so: Richard Brodeur, 32 saves)
Apr 15 Quebec 5 at Phoenix 6
        (ot: Michel Cormier, 7:21)
Apr 17 Phoenix 2 at Quebec 4

New England vs. Minnesota
Apr 9   Minnesota 6 at New England 5
Apr 11 Minnesota 2 at New England 3
        (ot: Rick Ley, 6:46)
Apr 13 New England 3 at Minnesota 8
Apr 15 New England 5 at Minnesota 2
Apr 18 Minnesota 4 at New England 0
        (so: John Garrett, 27 saves)
Apr 19 New England 1 at Minnesota 6

San Diego vs. Toronto
Apr 9   Toronto 3 at San Diego 5
Apr 12 Toronto 6 at San Diego 7
Apr 14 San Diego 2 at Toronto 5
Apr 16 San Diego 5 at Toronto 6
Apr 18 Toronto 3 at San Diego 4
Apr 21 San Diego 6 at Toronto 4

Semifinals

Quebec vs. Minnesota
Apr 22 Minnesota 1 at Quebec 4
Apr 23 Minnesota 5 at Quebec 3
Apr 26 Quebec 6 at Minnesota 1
Apr 27 Quebec 2 at Minnesota 4
Apr 29 Minnesota 3 at Quebec 6
May 1   Quebec 4 at Minnesota 2

Houston vs. San Diego
Apr 25 Houston 4 at San Diego 0
        (so: Ron Grahame, 25 saves)
Apr 27 Houston 2 at San Diego 1
Apr 29 San Diego 0 at Houston 6
        (so: Ron Grahame, 34 saves)
May 1   San Diego 4 at Houston 5
        (ot: Jim Sherrit, 0:27)

AVCO World Trophy Championship

Houston vs. Quebec
May 3   Quebec 2 at Houston 6
May 6   Quebec 3 at Houston 5
May 10 Houston 2 at Quebec 0
        (so: Ron Grahame, 34 saves)
May 12 Houston 7 at Quebec 2

Playoff Standings

Overall

Team	w	l	gf	ga
Houston	12	1	61	26
Quebec	8	7	55	48
Minnesota	6	6	44	42
San Diego	4	6	34	44
New England	2	4	17	28
Toronto	2	4	27	29
Cleveland	1	4	14	24
Phoenix	1	4	12	23

Home

Team	w	l	gf	ga
Houston	7	0	38	18
Quebec	5	3	30	24
Minnesota	3	3	23	21
San Diego	3	2	17	18
Toronto	2	1	15	13
Cleveland	1	1	5	8
Phoenix	1	1	6	8
New England	1	2	8	12

Away

Team	w	l	gf	ga
Houston	5	1	23	8
Minnesota	3	3	21	21
Quebec	3	4	25	24
New England	1	2	9	16
San Diego	1	4	17	26
Toronto	0	3	12	16
Cleveland	0	3	9	16
Phoenix	0	3	6	15

160

Championship Series Summaries

The Houston Aeros breezed to their second consecutive AVCO Cup with a four-game sweep of the Quebec Nordiques. Houston dominated in the playoffs, winning losing only once and winning their final 10 games. Ron Grahame sported a sharp 1.75 average and a 94.3 save percentage, stopping 116 of 123 Quebec shots. Gordie Howe paced the Aero offense, with 5 goals and 3 assists in the four games.

Game 1 • May 3, 1975
Houston 6, Quebec 2

Quebec	0	1	1	- 2
Houston	4	1	1	- 6

1st period: 1. Hou: Labossiere (Popiel, Schella) 1:26; 2. Hou: Lund (Mark Howe, G. Howe) 2:36; 3. Hou: G. Howe (Schella, Preston) 12:13; 4. Hou: Ruskowski (Popiel, Larway) 17:54
2nd period: 5. Hou: Larway (Ruskowski) 4:37; 6. Que: Tardif (Bordeleau, Hoganson) 17:51
3rd period: 7. Hou: Labossiere (Taylor, Hughes) 1:45; 8. Que: Guindon (Bordeleau) 3:45
Shots on goal

Que on Grahame	7	8	10	- 25
Hou on Brodeur	11	10	15	- 36

Game 2 • May 6, 1975
Houston 5, Quebec 3

Quebec	1	1	1	- 3
Houston	1	1	3	- 5

1st period: 1. Hou: G. Howe (Mark Howe, Sherrit) 4:44; 2. Que: Hoganson (S. Bernier, Houle) 16:34
2nd period: 3. Hou: G. Howe (Lund, Hughes) 1:19; 4. Que: Tardif (Guindon, Bordeleau) 2:57
3rd period: 5. Hou: Labossiere (Hall, Taylor) 2:06; 6. Que: Tardif (Bordeleau) 2:37; 7. Hou: Ruskowski (Preston, Irwin) 3:04; 8. Hou: Hinse (Lund, Schella) 11:08
Shots on goal

Que on Grahame	8	9	9	- 26
Hou on Brodeur	10	15	22	- 47

Game 3 • May 10, 1975
Houston 2, Quebec 0

Houston	0	1	1	- 2
Quebec	0	0	0	- 0

1st period: No scoring.
2nd period: 1. Hou: Hughes (G. Howe, Mark Howe) 0:14
3rd period: 2. Hou: Popiel (Schella) 13:48
Shots on goal

Hou on Brodeur	5	8	11	- 24
Que on Grahame	13	6	15	- 34

Game 4 • May 12, 1975
Houston 7, Quebec 2

Houston	3	2	2	- 7
Quebec	1	1	0	- 2

1st period: 1. Hou: G. Howe (Hinse, Lund) 2:41; 2. Que: Houle (Tardif, S. Bernier) 6:01; 3. Hou: Mark Howe (Hinse, Lund) 12:18; 4. Hou: Labossiere (Schella, Hall) 19:53
2nd period: 5. Hou: G. Howe (Lund) 7:36; 6. Que: Houle (S. Bernier, Brodeur) 14:51; 7. Hou: Hughes (Mark Howe, Sherrit) 16:52
3rd period: 8. Hou: Lund (Popiel) 14:07; 9. Hou: Hughes (G. Howe, Lund) 18:30
Shots on goal

Hou on Brodeur	12	11	8	- 31
Que on Grahame	12	18	8	- 38

Statistical Leaders

Goals: 10, Rejean Houle (Que), Mark Howe (Hou), Marc Tardif (Que), Mike Walton (Min); 8, Serge Bernier (Que), Wayne Connelly (Min), Gordie Howe (Hou).

Assists: 13, Christian Bordeleau (Que), Fran Huck (Min), Larry Lund (Hou); 12, Gordie Howe (Hou), Mark Howe (Hou); 11, Marc Tardif (Que).

Points: 22, Mark Howe (Hou); 21, Marc Tardif (Que); 20, Gordie Howe (Hou); 18, Larry Lund (Hou); 17, Mike Walton (Min)

Penalty Minutes: 63, Ron Busniuk (Min); 59, Curt Brackenbury (Min); 41, Jack Carlson (NE), Rene Leclerc (Que), Garry Swain (NE).

Goaltending Wins: 12, Ron Grahame (Hou); 8, Richard Brodeur (Que); 6, John Garrett (Min); 4, Ernie Wakely (SD)

Goals Against Average: 2.00, Ron Grahame (Hou); 3.18, Richard Brodeur (Que); 3.39, John Garrett (Min)

Splits by Opponent and by Month, Home and Away

Chi Chicago, **Cle** Cleveland, **Edm** Edmonton, **Hou** Houston, **Ind** Indianapolis, **M-B** Michigan-Baltimore, **Min** Minnesota, **NE** New England, **Phx** Phoenix, **Que** Quebec, **SD** San Diego, **Tor** Toronto, **Van** Vancouver, **Wpg** Winnipeg

CHICAGO

Opp.	season	gf-ga	home	gf-ga	away	gf-ga
Cle	4-2-0	23-22	3-0-0	10-7	1-2-0	13-15
Edm	2-4-0	14-23	1-2-0	5-11	1-2-0	9-12
Hou	0-6-0	15-26	0-3-0	11-15	0-3-0	4-11
Ind	3-2-1	24-24	2-0-1	16-13	1-2-0	8-11
M-B	4-2-0	26-16	3-0-0	16-5	1-2-0	10-11
Min	3-3-0	25-24	2-1-0	10-9	1-2-0	15-15
NE	2-4-0	23-28	1-2-0	12-15	1-2-0	11-13
Phx	2-4-0	19-28	1-2-0	10-13	1-2-0	9-15
Que	1-5-0	19-32	0-3-0	5-16	1-2-0	14-16
SD	3-3-0	20-20	1-2-0	10-12	2-1-0	10-8
Tor	3-3-0	21-25	2-1-0	13-13	1-2-0	8-12
Van	2-4-0	14-19	1-2-0	9-11	1-2-0	5-8
Wpg	1-5-0	18-25	1-2-0	11-13	0-3-0	7-12
Oct	1-5-0	13-19	0-1-0	2-4	1-4-0	11-15
Nov	6-8-0	50-62	3-5-0	30-40	3-3-0	20-22
Dec	6-7-0	46-46	3-3-0	23-19	3-4-0	23-27
Jan	5-8-1	49-59	4-4-1	30-32	1-4-0	19-27
Feb	7-7-0	50-53	4-2-0	26-24	3-5-0	24-29
Mar	3-11-0	44-64	2-5-0	21-31	1-6-0	23-33
Apr	2-1-0	9-9	2-0-0	6-3	0-1-0	3-6

HOUSTON

Opp.	season	gf-ga	home	gf-ga	away	gf-ga
Chi	6-0-0	26-15	3-0-0	11-4	3-0-0	15-11
Cle	5-1-0	29-18	2-1-0	20-16	3-0-0	9-2
Edm	4-2-0	32-21	3-0-0	18-4	1-2-0	14-17
Ind	5-1-0	35-19	2-1-0	14-13	3-0-0	21-6
M-B	4-2-0	27-19	2-1-0	15-11	2-1-0	12-8
Min	5-1-0	31-16	3-0-0	19-6	2-1-0	12-10
NE	4-2-0	30-18	2-1-0	16-7	2-1-0	14-11
Phx	3-3-0	30-22	2-1-0	18-12	1-2-0	12-10
Que	3-3-0	26-23	2-1-0	18-11	1-2-0	8-12
SD	1-5-0	25-29	1-2-0	15-11	0-3-0	10-18
Tor	4-2-0	28-21	2-1-0	14-10	2-1-0	14-11
Van	4-2-0	22-12	1-2-0	8-9	3-0-0	14-3
Wpg	5-1-0	28-14	3-0-0	19-6	2-1-0	9-8
Oct	4-4-0	26-28	2-0-0	4-2	2-4-0	22-26
Nov	10-4-0	76-39	5-4-0	46-28	5-0-0	30-11
Dec	10-3-0	57-32	5-2-0	33-18	5-1-0	24-14
Jan	5-5-0	48-42	4-1-0	30-18	1-4-0	18-24
Feb	12-4-0	80-50	4-3-0	38-26	8-1-0	42-24
Mar	9-4-0	60-42	6-1-0	39-20	3-3-0	21-22
Apr	3-1-0	22-14	2-0-0	15-8	1-1-0	7-6

CLEVELAND

Opp.	season	gf-ga	home	gf-ga	away	gf-ga
Chi	2-4-0	22-23	2-1-0	15-13	0-3-0	7-10
Edm	4-2-0	16-10	2-1-0	10-5	2-1-0	6-5
Hou	1-5-0	18-29	0-3-0	2-9	1-2-0	16-20
Ind	4-2-0	23-23	3-0-0	15-8	1-2-0	8-15
M-B	4-2-0	12-7	2-1-0	4-4	2-1-0	8-3
Min	1-5-0	11-24	0-3-0	6-11	1-2-0	5-13
NE	2-3-1	17-16	2-1-0	10-5	0-2-1	7-11
Phx	4-1-1	23-16	3-0-0	15-8	1-1-1	8-8
Que	3-3-0	19-19	2-1-0	10-8	1-2-0	9-11
SD	3-3-0	16-21	2-1-0	6-5	1-2-0	10-16
Tor	2-4-0	23-25	1-2-0	12-13	1-2-0	11-12
Van	3-3-0	17-17	2-1-0	13-10	1-2-0	4-7
Wpg	2-3-1	19-28	2-0-1	12-10	0-3-0	7-18
Oct	2-2-1	14-16	0-0-0	0-0	2-2-1	14-16
Nov	7-4-0	36-33	3-2-0	19-17	4-2-0	17-16
Dec	4-11-0	36-51	3-4-0	18-18	1-7-0	18-33
Jan	8-8-1	51-53	6-3-1	33-25	2-5-0	18-28
Feb	5-8-0	34-49	4-4-0	23-25	1-4-0	11-24
Mar	8-5-1	52-44	6-2-0	32-22	2-3-1	20-22
Apr	1-2-0	13-12	1-0-0	5-2	0-2-0	8-10

INDIANAPOLIS

Opp.	season	gf-ga	home	gf-ga	away	gf-ga
Chi	2-3-1	24-24	2-1-0	11-8	0-2-1	13-16
Cle	2-4-0	23-23	2-1-0	15-8	0-3-0	8-15
Edm	1-4-1	13-17	1-2-0	5-7	0-2-1	8-10
Hou	1-5-0	19-35	0-3-0	6-21	1-2-0	13-14
M-B	4-2-0	30-19	1-2-0	13-12	3-0-0	17-7
Min	1-5-0	17-26	1-2-0	7-11	0-3-0	10-15
NE	1-5-0	10-27	1-2-0	3-11	0-3-0	7-16
Phx	0-6-0	7-31	0-3-0	2-8	0-3-0	5-23
Que	1-5-0	18-32	1-2-0	11-12	0-3-0	7-20
SD	2-4-0	16-24	2-1-0	10-8	0-3-0	6-16
Tor	1-5-0	16-33	1-2-0	9-16	0-3-0	7-17
Van	1-4-1	13-24	1-2-0	8-14	0-2-1	5-10
Wpg	1-5-0	10-23	1-2-0	6-13	0-3-0	4-10
Oct	1-6-0	13-29	1-3-0	10-16	0-3-0	3-13
Nov	3-12-0	32-72	1-7-0	11-40	2-5-0	21-32
Dec	2-10-1	31-53	2-6-0	19-33	0-4-1	12-20
Jan	4-7-2	31-43	3-3-0	16-14	1-4-2	15-29
Feb	4-7-0	43-43	3-3-0	21-18	1-4-0	22-25
Mar	4-12-0	59-79	3-4-0	29-28	1-8-0	30-51
Apr	0-3-0	7-19	0-0-0	0-0	0-3-0	7-19

EDMONTON

Opp.	season	gf-ga	home	gf-ga	away	gf-ga
Chi	4-2-0	23-14	2-1-0	12-9	2-1-0	11-5
Cle	2-4-0	10-16	1-2-0	5-6	1-2-0	5-10
Hou	2-4-0	21-32	2-1-0	17-14	0-3-0	4-18
Ind	4-1-1	17-13	2-0-1	10-8	2-1-0	7-5
M-B	4-1-1	26-11	3-0-0	20-4	1-1-1	6-7
Min	3-3-0	19-23	2-1-0	10-11	1-2-0	9-12
NE	2-3-1	24-24	2-1-0	16-11	0-2-1	8-13
Phx	1-4-1	20-21	0-2-1	11-14	1-2-0	9-7
Que	2-4-0	23-25	1-2-0	12-13	1-2-0	11-12
SD	3-3-0	21-24	2-1-0	11-10	1-2-0	10-14
Tor	3-3-0	33-26	2-1-0	18-15	1-2-0	15-11
Van	3-3-0	23-23	3-0-0	15-6	0-3-0	8-17
Wpg	3-3-0	19-27	3-0-0	17-9	0-3-0	2-18
Oct	0-2-0	6-12	0-0-0	0-0	0-2-0	6-12
Nov	8-4-0	42-32	5-1-0	24-16	3-3-0	18-16
Dec	9-4-0	57-44	5-1-0	33-19	4-3-0	24-25
Jan	6-7-2	53-54	5-4-2	41-38	1-3-0	12-16
Feb	6-7-1	52-49	5-3-0	40-31	1-4-1	12-18
Mar	5-12-1	53-74	3-2-0	22-15	2-10-1	31-59
Apr	2-2-0	16-14	2-1-0	14-11	0-1-0	2-3

MICHIGAN-BALTIMORE

Opp.	season	gf-ga	home	gf-ga	away	gf-ga
Chi	2-4-0	16-26	2-1-0	11-10	0-3-0	5-16
Cle	2-4-0	7-12	1-2-0	3-8	1-2-0	4-4
Edm	1-4-1	11-26	1-1-1	4-6	0-3-0	4-20
Hou	2-4-0	19-27	1-2-0	8-12	1-2-0	11-15
Ind	2-4-0	19-30	0-3-0	7-17	2-1-0	12-13
Min	2-4-0	20-24	2-1-0	12-11	0-3-0	8-13
NE	1-4-1	11-19	1-1-1	5-9	0-3-0	6-10
Phx	2-3-1	14-26	1-1-1	4-5	1-2-0	10-21
Que	1-5-0	15-24	1-2-0	9-10	0-3-0	6-14
SD	2-3-1	18-30	1-2-0	8-14	1-1-1	10-16
Tor	0-6-0	17-37	0-3-0	8-19	0-3-0	9-18
Van	2-4-0	14-25	2-1-0	8-9	0-3-0	6-16
Wpg	2-4-0	24-35	2-1-0	13-12	0-3-0	11-23
Oct	2-5-0	18-26	1-1-0	6-7	1-4-0	12-19
Nov	3-10-0	36-65	3-5-0	18-32	0-5-0	18-33
Dec	6-7-3	35-62	6-1-2	25-22	0-6-1	10-40
Jan	2-9-0	25-38	2-1-0	10-8	0-8-0	15-30
Feb	2-11-0	29-61	1-9-0	20-43	1-2-0	9-18
Mar	3-9-1	40-63	1-3-1	15-22	2-6-0	25-41
Apr	3-2-0	22-26	1-1-0	9-8	2-1-0	13-18

MINNESOTA

Opp.	season	gf-ga	home	gf-ga	away	gf-ga
Chi	3-3-0	24-25	2-1-0	15-15	1-2-0	9-10
Cle	5-1-0	24-11	2-1-0	13-5	3-0-0	11-6
Edm	3-3-0	23-19	2-1-0	12-9	1-2-0	11-10
Hou	1-5-0	16-31	1-2-0	10-12	0-3-0	6-19
Ind	5-1-0	26-17	3-0-0	15-10	2-1-0	11-7
M-B	4-2-0	24-20	3-0-0	13-8	1-2-0	11-12
NE	4-2-0	26-18	3-0-0	20-9	1-2-0	6-9
Phx	2-3-1	21-19	2-1-0	15-9	0-2-1	6-10
Que	4-2-0	29-21	1-2-0	12-16	3-0-0	17-5
SD	2-3-1	21-23	1-2-0	9-9	1-1-1	12-14
Tor	4-2-0	28-30	2-1-0	16-15	2-1-0	12-15
Van	3-3-0	21-18	2-1-0	12-7	1-2-0	9-11
Wpg	2-3-1	25-27	2-1-0	14-12	0-2-1	11-15
Oct	2-4-0	17-28	1-1-0	7-8	1-3-0	10-20
Nov	4-7-0	53-49	2-4-0	33-34	2-3-0	20-15
Dec	10-5-0	66-43	6-1-0	36-21	4-4-0	30-22
Jan	8-4-0	51-30	5-2-0	36-19	3-2-0	15-11
Feb	7-7-2	50-61	5-2-0	22-21	2-5-2	28-40
Mar	9-3-1	54-46	6-1-0	33-24	3-2-1	21-22
Apr	2-3-0	17-22	1-2-0	9-9	1-1-0	8-13

QUEBEC

Opp.	season	gf-ga	home	gf-ga	away	gf-ga
Chi	5-1-0	32-19	2-1-0	16-14	3-0-0	16-5
Cle	3-3-0	19-19	2-1-0	11-9	1-2-0	8-10
Edm	4-2-0	25-23	2-1-0	12-11	2-1-0	13-12
Hou	3-3-0	23-26	2-1-0	12-8	1-2-0	11-18
Ind	5-1-0	32-18	3-0-0	20-7	2-1-0	12-11
M-B	5-1-0	24-15	3-0-0	14-6	2-1-0	10-9
Min	2-4-0	21-29	0-3-0	5-17	2-1-0	16-12
NE	2-4-0	28-25	2-1-0	21-8	0-3-0	7-17
Phx	4-2-0	25-24	2-1-0	13-12	2-1-0	12-12
SD	2-4-0	20-33	2-1-0	14-11	0-3-0	6-22
Tor	3-3-0	22-25	1-2-0	9-15	2-1-0	13-10
Van	4-2-0	30-26	3-0-0	18-13	1-2-0	12-13
Wpg	4-2-0	30-17	3-0-0	19-9	1-2-0	11-8
Oct	4-1-0	24-11	4-0-0	21-6	0-1-0	3-5
Nov	8-6-0	56-57	5-4-0	36-38	3-2-0	20-19
Dec	7-8-0	59-52	6-3-0	38-26	1-5-0	21-26
Jan	11-2-0	62-34	5-1-0	30-18	6-1-0	32-16
Feb	9-4-0	57-59	3-1-0	23-19	6-3-0	34-40
Mar	4-10-0	53-71	3-3-0	27-28	1-7-0	26-43
Apr	3-1-0	20-15	1-0-0	9-5	2-1-0	11-10

NEW ENGLAND

Opp.	season	gf-ga	home	gf-ga	away	gf-ga
Chi	4-2-0	28-23	2-1-0	13-11	2-1-0	15-12
Cle	3-2-1	16-17	2-0-1	11-7	1-2-0	5-10
Edm	3-2-1	24-24	2-0-1	13-8	1-2-0	11-16
Hou	2-4-0	18-30	1-2-0	11-14	1-2-0	7-16
Ind	5-1-0	27-10	3-0-0	16-7	2-1-0	11-3
M-B	4-1-1	19-11	3-0-0	10-6	1-1-1	9-5
Min	2-4-0	18-26	2-1-0	9-6	0-3-0	9-20
Phx	1-3-2	17-23	1-1-1	12-12	0-2-1	5-11
Que	4-2-0	25-28	3-0-0	17-7	1-2-0	8-21
SD	3-3-0	20-22	2-1-0	8-9	1-2-0	12-13
Tor	5-1-0	25-20	3-0-0	14-8	2-1-0	11-12
Van	3-3-0	14-20	3-0-0	11-6	0-3-0	3-14
Wpg	4-2-0	23-25	1-2-0	12-17	3-0-0	11-8
Oct	5-1-0	26-15	4-0-0	18-8	1-1-0	8-7
Nov	9-4-0	53-41	3-1-0	12-8	6-3-0	41-33
Dec	5-8-1	41-56	3-1-0	21-13	2-7-1	20-43
Jan	8-6-1	45-56	7-1-0	28-20	1-5-1	17-36
Feb	8-4-1	33-35	3-1-1	17-13	3-3-0	16-22
Mar	8-5-2	64-64	6-4-2	52-52	2-1-0	12-12
Apr	2-2-0	12-12	2-0-0	9-4	0-2-0	3-8

SAN DIEGO

Opp.	season	gf-ga	home	gf-ga	away	gf-ga
Chi	3-3-0	20-20	1-2-0	8-10	2-1-0	12-10
Cle	3-3-0	21-16	2-1-0	16-10	1-2-0	5-6
Edm	3-3-0	24-21	2-1-0	14-10	1-2-0	10-11
Hou	5-1-0	29-25	3-0-0	18-10	2-1-0	11-15
Ind	4-2-0	24-16	3-0-0	16-6	1-2-0	8-10
M-B	3-2-1	30-18	1-1-1	16-10	2-1-0	14-8
Min	3-2-1	23-21	1-1-1	14-12	2-1-0	9-9
NE	3-3-0	22-20	2-1-0	13-12	1-2-0	9-8
Phx	3-3-0	19-23	2-1-0	13-6	1-2-0	6-17
Que	4-2-0	33-20	3-0-0	22-6	1-2-0	11-14
Tor	3-3-0	28-25	2-1-0	15-11	1-2-0	13-14
Van	5-1-0	24-10	3-0-0	10-3	2-1-0	14-7
Wpg	1-3-2	29-33	1-2-0	17-20	0-1-2	12-13
Oct	4-1-0	19-16	4-0-0	17-8	0-1-0	2-8
Nov	7-6-0	41-46	2-3-0	15-18	5-3-0	26-28
Dec	4-9-1	46-52	2-4-1	29-28	2-5-0	17-24
Jan	8-4-0	50-37	6-1-0	38-25	2-3-0	12-12
Feb	6-7-1	65-53	5-0-1	39-14	1-7-0	26-39
Mar	12-3-1	80-50	5-2-0	34-24	7-1-1	46-26
Apr	2-1-1	25-14	2-1-0	20-9	0-0-1	5-5

PHOENIX

Opp.	season	gf-ga	home	gf-ga	away	gf-ga
Chi	4-2-0	28-19	2-1-0	15-9	2-1-0	13-10
Cle	1-4-1	16-23	1-1-1	8-8	0-3-0	8-15
Edm	4-1-1	21-20	2-1-0	7-9	2-0-1	14-11
Hou	3-3-0	22-30	2-1-0	10-12	1-2-0	12-18
Ind	6-0-0	31-7	3-0-0	23-5	3-0-0	8-2
M-B	3-2-1	26-14	2-1-0	21-10	1-1-1	5-4
Min	3-2-1	19-21	2-0-1	10-6	1-2-0	9-15
NE	3-1-2	23-17	2-0-1	11-5	1-1-1	12-12
Que	2-4-0	24-25	1-2-0	12-12	1-2-0	12-13
SD	3-3-0	23-19	2-1-0	17-6	1-2-0	6-13
Tor	1-3-2	21-30	0-1-2	11-14	1-2-0	10-16
Van	3-3-0	22-19	3-0-0	13-7	0-3-0	9-12
Wpg	3-3-0	24-21	1-2-0	12-12	2-1-0	12-9
Oct	2-4-1	28-29	2-0-1	18-10	0-4-0	10-19
Nov	5-5-1	36-40	1-2-1	13-13	4-3-0	23-27
Dec	10-4-1	53-39	6-3-0	30-23	4-1-1	23-16
Jan	7-7-3	54-56	4-2-2	31-25	3-5-1	23-31
Feb	6-5-0	47-41	3-3-0	29-20	3-2-0	18-21
Mar	8-4-2	71-47	7-0-1	43-17	1-4-1	28-30
Apr	1-2-0	11-13	0-1-0	6-7	1-1-0	5-6

TORONTO

Opp.	season	gf-ga	home	gf-ga	away	gf-ga
Chi	3-3-0	25-21	2-1-0	12-8	1-2-0	13-13
Cle	4-2-0	25-23	2-1-0	12-11	2-1-0	13-12
Edm	3-3-0	26-33	2-1-0	11-15	1-2-0	15-18
Hou	2-4-0	21-28	1-2-0	11-14	1-2-0	10-14
Ind	5-1-0	33-16	3-0-0	17-7	2-1-0	16-9
M-B	6-0-0	37-17	3-0-0	18-9	3-0-0	19-8
Min	2-4-0	30-28	1-2-0	15-12	1-2-0	15-16
NE	1-5-0	20-25	1-2-0	12-11	0-3-0	8-14
Phx	3-1-2	30-21	2-1-0	16-10	1-0-2	14-11
Que	3-3-0	25-22	1-2-0	10-13	2-1-0	15-9
SD	3-3-0	25-28	2-1-0	14-13	1-2-0	11-15
Van	4-2-0	30-21	2-1-0	16-10	2-1-0	14-11
Wpg	4-2-0	22-21	2-1-0	11-6	2-1-0	11-15
Oct	6-1-0	36-17	6-0-0	34-12	0-1-0	2-5
Nov	8-7-1	72-67	0-4-0	9-25	8-3-1	63-42
Dec	6-5-0	42-41	3-4-0	24-27	3-1-0	18-14
Jan	7-6-1	58-52	3-2-0	21-15	4-4-1	37-37
Feb	6-7-0	54-59	4-1-0	24-17	2-6-0	30-42
Mar	8-6-0	71-61	6-3-0	47-36	2-3-0	24-25
Apr	2-1-0	16-7	2-1-0	16-7	0-0-0	0-0

VANCOUVER

Opp.	season	gf-ga	home	gf-ga	away	gf-ga
Chi	4-2-0	19-14	2-1-0	8-5	2-1-0	11-9
Cle	3-3-0	17-17	2-1-0	7-4	1-2-0	10-13
Edm	3-3-0	23-23	3-0-0	17-8	0-3-0	6-15
Hou	2-4-0	12-22	0-3-0	3-14	2-1-0	9-8
Ind	4-1-1	24-13	2-0-1	10-5	2-1-0	14-8
M-B	4-2-0	25-14	3-0-0	16-6	1-2-0	9-8
Min	3-3-0	18-21	2-1-0	11-9	1-2-0	7-12
NE	3-3-0	20-14	3-0-0	14-3	0-3-0	6-11
Phx	3-3-0	19-22	3-0-0	12-9	0-3-0	7-13
Que	2-4-0	26-30	2-1-0	13-12	0-3-0	13-18
SD	1-5-0	10-24	1-2-0	7-14	0-3-0	3-10
Tor	2-4-0	21-30	1-2-0	11-14	1-2-0	10-16
Wpg	3-2-1	22-26	1-1-1	9-12	2-1-0	13-14
Oct	3-3-0	18-22	3-3-0	18-22	0-0-0	0-0
Nov	4-7-1	38-40	1-5-1	17-25	3-2-0	21-15
Dec	8-4-1	41-34	5-0-1	21-8	3-4-0	20-26
Jan	6-9-0	42-57	3-1-0	14-12	3-8-0	28-45
Feb	7-5-0	52-39	5-1-0	26-17	2-4-0	26-22
Mar	6-9-0	47-59	6-2-0	35-26	0-7-0	12-33
Apr	3-2-0	18-19	2-0-0	7-5	1-2-0	11-14

WINNIPEG

Opp.	season	gf-ga	home	gf-ga	away	gf-ga
Chi	5-1-0	25-18	3-0-0	12-7	2-1-0	13-11
Cle	3-2-1	28-19	3-0-0	18-7	0-2-1	10-12
Edm	3-3-0	27-19	3-0-0	18-2	0-3-0	9-17
Hou	1-5-0	14-28	1-2-0	8-9	0-3-0	6-19
Ind	5-1-0	23-10	2-1-0	10-4	3-0-0	13-6
M-B	4-2-0	35-24	3-0-0	23-11	1-2-0	12-13
Min	3-2-1	27-25	2-0-1	15-11	1-2-0	12-14
NE	2-4-0	25-23	0-3-0	8-11	2-1-0	17-12
Phx	3-3-0	21-24	1-2-0	9-12	2-1-0	12-12
Que	2-4-0	17-30	2-1-0	8-11	0-3-0	9-19
SD	3-1-2	33-29	1-0-2	13-12	2-1-0	20-17
Tor	2-4-0	21-22	1-2-0	15-11	1-2-0	6-11
Van	2-3-1	26-22	1-2-0	14-13	1-1-1	12-9
Oct	4-1-0	22-12	3-0-0	15-7	1-1-0	7-5
Nov	7-5-1	61-39	6-2-0	44-21	1-3-1	17-18
Dec	6-8-0	45-50	2-3-0	15-15	4-5-0	30-35
Jan	3-7-1	42-50	1-4-0	14-20	2-3-1	28-30
Feb	7-6-1	56-50	5-3-1	36-30	2-3-0	20-20
Mar	11-5-1	81-65	6-0-1	38-17	5-5-0	43-48
Apr	0-3-1	15-27	0-1-1	9-11	0-2-0	6-16

1975 All-Star Game

Edmonton Coliseum
Edmonton, Alberta
January 21, 1975

West

Coach: Bill Dineen (Houston)
Goaltenders: Don McLeod (Vancouver), Wayne Rutledge (Houston), Joe Daley (Winnipeg)
Defensemen: Barry Long, Doug Barrie, Al Hamilton (Edmonton), John Schella, Poul Popiel (Houston), Lars-Erik Sjoberg (Winnipeg), Gerry Odrowski (Phoenix)
Forwards: Bobby Hull, Ulf Nilsson (Winnipeg), Gordie Howe, Mark Howe, Larry Lund, Andre Hinse, Frank Hughes, Ted Taylor (Houston), Andre Lacroix (San Diego), Danny Lawson (Vancouver), Fran Huck, Mike Walton (Minnesota)

East

Coach: Ron Ryan (New England)
Goaltenders: Al Smith (New England), Gerry Cheevers (Cleveland), Andy Brown (Indianapolis).
Defensemen: Pat Stapleton (Chicago), Brad Selwood, Rick Ley (New England), Dale Hoganson, J.-C. Tremblay (Quebec), Jim Dorey (Toronto), Paul Shmyr (Cleveland).
Forwards: Serge Bernier, Rejean Houle, Marc Tardif (Quebec), Pierre Guite, Gary Veneruzzo (Michigan), Wayne Dillon, Frank Mahovlich, Paul Henderson, Tom Simpson (Toronto), Larry Pleau, Tom Webster (New England), Ralph Backstrom (Chicago).

MVP: Rejean Houle, Quebec
Did Not Play: Mike Walton, Paul Shmyr, Pierre Guite

West 6, East 4

East	2	1	1	- 4
West	2	4	0	- 6

1st period: 1. West: Mark Howe (G. Howe, Lacroix) 7:08; 2. West: Hinse (Lund, Hughes) 8:18; 3. East: Tardif (Houle, Selwood) 13:32; 4. East: Houle (Pleau, Dorey) 17:37.
2nd period
5. West: Hull (Lawson) 4:23; 6. West: Hinse (Hughes, Odrowski) 6:35; 7. West: Taylor (Lacroix, Schella) 10:07; 8. West: G. Howe (Lacroix, Mark Howe) 11:53; 9. East: Houle (Selwood, Dorey) 14:32.
3rd period: 10. East: Bernier (Tardif, Houle) 11:20.
Shots on goal

East:	11	9	8	- 28
West:	7	11	12	- 30

Attendance 15,326

1974-1975 Year End All-Star Teams

First Team: Goaltender: Ron Grahame, Houston; Defensemen: J.-C. Tremblay, Quebec and Kevin Morrison, San Diego; Center: Andre Lacroix, San Diego; Right Wing: Gordie Howe, Houston; Left Wing: Bobby Hull, Winnipeg.

Second Team: Goaltender: Gerry Cheevers, Cleveland; Defensemen: Poul Popiel, Houston and Barry Long, Edmonton; Center: Serge Bernier, Quebec; Right Wing: Anders Hedberg, Winnipeg; Left Wing: Marc Tardif, Quebec.

Penalty Shots

date	player, team	goaltender, team	period	time	result
Oct 24	Wayne Connelly, Minnesota	Andy Brown, Indianapolis	1	11:44	Save
Nov 12	Gary MacGregor, Chicago	Joe Junkin, San Diego	1	10:19	Save
Dec 4	Eddie Joyal, Edmonton	Don McLeod, Vancouver	2	6:45	Score
Dec 26	Wayne Connelly, Minnesota	Jacques Plante, Edmonton	1	7:44	Save
Jan 4	Danny Lawson, Calgary	Al Smith, New England	3	19:42	Score
Jan 5	Bob LeDuc, Toronto	Bob Whidden, Cleveland	1	9:49	Save
Jan 28	Norm Ferguson, San Diego	Joe Daley, Winnipeg	3	12:46	Save
Feb 11	Rejean Houle, Quebec	Ernie Wakely, San Diego	2	8:33	Score
Mar 1	Bob Mowat, Phoenix	Andy Brown, Indianapolis	2	19:36	Score
Mar 12	Jim Harrison, Cleveland	Paul Hoganson, Baltimore	2	5:34	Save

Attendance Figures

Each team played 39 regular season home games.

team	season total	avg	g	playoff total	avg	team	season total	avg	g	playoff total	avg
Chicago	123,543	3,168	-	-	-	New England	305,959	7,845	3	30,521	10,174
Cleveland	270,304	6,931	2	13,784	6,892	Phoenix	290,277	7,443	2	14,767	7,384
Edmonton	418,150	10,722	-	-	-	Quebec	366,848	9,406	8	77,788	9,724
Houston	265,230	6,801	7	52,938	7,563	San Diego	237,118	6,080	5	54,906	10,981
Indianapolis	309,005	7,923	-	-	-	Toronto	407,006	10,436	3	28,162	9,387
Michigan-Baltimore	127,072	3,258	-	-	-	Vancouver	312,563	8,014	-	-	-
Minnesota	327,979	8,410	6	63,177	10,530	Winnipeg	334,857	8,586	-	-	-

Total Attendance: 4,095,911; **Average Attendance:** 7,502

Third Season Fun Facts

Six Roadrunner players scored two goals apiece as Phoenix thrashed Indianapolis, 12-2, on March 1, 1975. Jim Boyd, Michel Cormier, Robbie Ftorek, John Gray, Bob Mowat and Dennis Sobchuk each tallied twice, with one of Mowat's coming on a penalty shot.

Walter "Bud" Gulka had a perfect shooting percentage, connecting on his only shot attempt during 1974-75. Gulka was a late-comer to hockey, picking up the game in his 20s. He was signed from a local men's amateur league in Vancouver by the Blazers and kept around for most of the season as an extra tough guy, playing sparingly. Gulka's goal came on January 4, 1975, against Al Smith of New England.

Jeff Jacques scored four goals in his WHA debut, as his Toronto Toros defeated Houston, 7-4, on January 12, 1975. He scored three of his goals in the third period.

Bill Evo scored the last goal in the abbreviated history of the Michigan Stags, January 18, 1975, then scored the first goal of the similarly-abbreviated history of the Baltimore Blades, January 25, 1975.

Steve West of Baltimore completed a hat trick by scoring a game-winning overtime goal against Phoenix on April 5, 1975 – into an empty net. The Roadrunners, playing their last regular-season game and assured a fourth-place finish and a playoff berth, gambled for a win which would vault them into third place by pulling goaltender Gary Kurt with less than a minute remaining in the extra period.

165

1974-1975 Team Thumbnails

Chicago: As surprising as the Cougars' rise from last place in 1973 to Eastern Division champs in 1974 was, their drop back toward the rear of the pack in 1975 had to be similarly surprising, given their high expectations entering 1974-75. With Pat Stapleton leading the defense and calling the shots as coach (assisted by a young Jacques Demers), the Cougars had also signed veteran goaltender Dave Dryden, and highly-regarded junior forward Gary MacGregor (100 goals in 1973-74 for Cornwall), to contracts. On the positive side, Stapleton, MacGregor and Dryden all performed very well: MacGregor's 42 goals led the team, with fellow rookie Francois "Frankie" Rochon's 27 goals placing second. Rosie Paiement had another solid 26-48-74 season, but Ralph Backstrom's 15 goals and 39 points in 70 games was a disappointment. Preventing goals ruined the Cougars, who allowed 312 for the season. Of greater concern was the fate of the team itself. The Kaiser's pulled out in mid-season when it was clear their planned new arena would not be built for many years (The Rosemont Horizon would not be completed until 1980). Rather than fold the club, Backstrom, Stapleton and Dryden achieved a sports' first by buying controlling interest in the team, thus becoming player-owners, and staving off a fold at least until season's end. The team struggled to a 30-47-1 finish and a far sight back from the playoffs. In June 1975, the Chicago Cougars franchise was dissolved, with most of its players being chosen by the expansion Denver Spurs for the 1975-76 season.

Cleveland: Once again the Crusaders were one of the best in the league at keeping goals out of their net, permitting just 258 against, second-best in the league. Once again Gerry Cheevers was at or near the top in the goaltending statistical categories. And once again, the Crusaders couldn't buy a goal, scoring just 236, ahead of only expansion Indianapolis and the woeful Stags-Blades. The Crusaders certainly made an effort to enhance their offense, acquiring Jim Harrison in a trade and signing rookie Richie Leduc, whose 35 goals led the team. Veteran Al McDonough was one back with 34, and Ron Ward contributed 30, but Harrison missed 18 games and turned in a 20-goal, 42-point season. There was no depth beyond the top line, and as in 1973-74, the Crusaders played a lot of low-scoring games, their stellar defense the only thing keeping Cleveland in most games. The Crusaders ended the season with a 35-40-5 record, second place in the Eastern Division. However, as in the previous season, Cleveland barely put up a fight in the playoffs, losing to Houston in the first round in five games.

Edmonton: The big news for the Oilers in 1974-75 was their new home, the modern Northlands Coliseum, the showcase arena for all of Alberta when it opened its doors—a month into the season. Delays kept the Oilers idle for most of October, forcing all home contests to be postponed. By November 10th, the Oilers had played just four games on the season, all on the road. Finally, the Oilers could move in to their new digs, and for the rest of the season the Oilers played as they had their previous two seasons: break-even hockey, finishing 36-38-4, with 279 goals for and against. Rookie Mike Rogers led the scorers with 35 goals and 83 points, and Ken Baird also scored 30 goals playing mostly on defense. Five other Oilers collected at least 20 goals, while the defense was led by Barry Long, who was one of the five to score 20 goals. The Oilers also featured the venerable Jacques Plante in goal, and the 46-year old star produced 15 wins and a 3.32 average in what would be his last season as a player. Behind the bench, Brian Shaw had led the team to a strong 18-10-0 start, but extended periods of average play meant a mid-season exit for Shaw, who was replaced by Bill Hunter for the remaining month of the season. Unfortunately, the Oilers finished last in the new Canadian Division, and did not participate in the playoffs.

Houston: Like a well-oiled machine, the Aeros hummed quietly, with impressive efficiency, in finishing with the league's best record at 53-25-0, leading the lead in goals (369) and permitting the fewest (247). The deep and well-balanced club benefited from nearly no man-games lost to injury (17 regulars played in 70 or more games). Larry Lund, the pride of the Western Hockey League, used his long stick and face-off skills to collect 33 goals, 75 assists and 108 points, which led the team. Not far behind was ageless Gordie Howe, whose 99 points placed second. Frank Hughes led all goal scorers with 48, with Andre Hinse (39) and Mark Howe (36) also potting at least 30 goals. Ten other players scored in double figures. The Aeros were not afraid to get physical, featuring diggers such as Ted Taylor and rookie Terry Ruskowski, who established himself as a smart offensive threat who could also fight (and often beat) the worst goons in the league. Goal was the domain of rookie Ron Grahame, whose 33 wins and 3.03 average led the league. Wayne Rutledge was his capable understudy. In the playoffs, Houston lost just once in thirteen games to easily win its second league crown, sweeping the Quebec Nordiques in the final round.

Indianapolis: The brand-new Racers were one of two new clubs added to the league in 1974 (Phoenix being the other). The Racers were originally owned by John Weissert and Dick Tinkham of the American Basketball Association's Indiana Pacers team, and the new Racers would be co-tenants in the brand-new Market Square Arena, opened just in September 1974. Shortly into the season, Weissert and Tinkham

sold out to ex-Aeros owner Paul Deneau. Unfortunately, talent was hard to come by, with the NHL also expanding by two new teams. Thus, the new Indianapolis Racers were initially composed of a few name players, some past their prime, a few rookies with credentials, and a bunch of warm bodies. Gerry Moore, who had coached in the Central League, was the team's first coach. Building from the goal outward, Andy Brown was the biggest name to sign with the Racers, and he would prove to be the team's lone all-star, facing a barrage of shots every night, all the while not wearing any face protection. The defense was manned by Bob Ash, Bob Woytowich, Bill Horton, Roger Cote and a number of minor-leaguers who came and went. None of them was much of a playmaker, and no defenseman scored more than two goals the entire campaign. Keeping the puck out of their own end also proved equally troubling, and the Racers allowed 338 enemy scores, second-worst in the league. Up front, Bobby Whitlock had 31 goals, Kerry Bond 22 and ex-Penguin Nick Harbaruk 20. Bob Sicinski was the team's main playmaker, with 34 assists. There was no depth or cohesion; the Racers potted just 216 goals as a team. All of this added up to a dreadful inaugural season in which the team started 5-27-0 and finished 18-57-3, setting league records for fewest wins and most losses. At least there was nowhere to go but up.

Michigan-Baltimore: The Michigan Stags were new to the WHA in 1974-75, having moved to Detroit after two seasons in Los Angeles as the Sharks. Detroit-area chemical industrialists Charles Nolton and Peter Shagena purchased the moribund franchise while it was playing out the string in California, then opened shop as the Michigan Stags entering the 1974-75 season. The Stags would play at the Cobo Arena, with Nolton and Shagena banking on attracting fans away from the Red Wings, who were going through a long stretch of mediocrity of their own. The Stags had inherited most of the Sharks roster, which included Marc Tardif, Gary Veneruzzo, J.-P. Leblanc and Tom Serviss, but this was the same team that had lost 53 games the year before. Not surprisingly, the Stags started poorly and lost often while based in Detroit. The money ran out, the owners were forced to trade Marc Tardif to Quebec for cash and players, but the team was completely bankrupt by January. The Detroit fans universally ignored the Stags, with home attendances typically between 1,000 and 2,000 spectators. On January 10, 1975, the Stags played their last game representing Michigan, and another on January 18th wearing generic sweaters as the league moved to avoid a complete fold. On January 25, the new Baltimore Blades came into existence, formed out of the Stags franchise and league-run for the duration of the season. The team did not fare any better in Baltimore, winning just 8 of 35 games. Overall, the Stags-Blades team finished 21-53-4, scored the fewest goals (205) and gave up the most

(341). Gary Veneruzzo was the lone star, scoring 33 goals, with no one else breaking the 20-goal barrier. In goal, Gerry Desjardins had come over from the NHL, gave his best efforts and bolted back to the NHL when the Stags folded. Paul Hoganson had 9 wins and 2 shutouts. John Wilson coached both incarnations of the team, an admirable performance despite his poor first-year record. The league could find no buyers for the team, and officially disbanded the Blades in June 1975.

Minnesota: The Fighting Saints turned in another strong team performance in 1974-75, finishing with 41 wins after a slow start, and a third-place finish in the Western Division. Mike Walton had another superlative season, scoring 48 goals and 93 points to lead the team in both categories. As in 1973-74, the Saints boasted a deep offense, with Wayne Connelly and George Morrison contributing 38 and 31 goals, respectively, and Mike Antonovich, Fran Huck and Don Tannahill scoring above the 20-goal mark. The defense was led by Rick Smith, with John Arbour, Terry Ball and Mike McMahon plugging up the middle and also providing a strong transition game, as Arbour (45 assists) and Ball (37 assists) became experts at advancing the puck quickly to the speedy forwards. When things got rough, Gordie Gallant once again led the league in penalty minutes with 203. Ron Busniuk (176 minutes) also liked to get into the mix. John Garrett and Mike Curran manned the nets. The Saints fared the same as did the 1974 edition, winning the first round in the playoffs before losing the semifinals, this time to the Quebec Nordiques.

New England: Another strong season by the Whalers, winning 43 and tying 5 for 91 points and an easy first-place finish in the Eastern Division. Tom Webster scored 40 goals, and new addition Wayne Carleton added 35, but as a team, the Whalers' offense dipped, scoring 274 goals collectively, and actually being outscored on the season by the opposition, giving up 279 enemy goals. Terry Caffery returned and contributed a solid campaign, with 52 points in 67 games coming back from major knee surgery. The defense was once again in the charge of Rick Ley, Brad Selwood, Ted Green and Paul Hurley, with newcomer Thommie Abrahamsson coming over from Sweden and turning in a solid season. Thommie's twin brother Christer played as a back-up goaltender to veteran Al Smith. However, New England made an early exit from the postseason, losing in the first round to Minnesota in six games.

Phoenix: The Roadrunners were the surprise of the season, as the expansion team won 39 games, scored 300 goals, and played like a team of veterans, which, in a manner of speaking, they were. The Roadrunners were two-time defending champions of the Western Hockey League, and were able to keep many of their players from the 1973-74 squad as the team made the

transition to the major leagues. Coached by Sandy Hucul, who had guided the team in the WHL, the Roadrunners featured veterans Gary Kurt and Jack Norris in goal, a defense led by Jim Niekamp and Gerry Odrowski, and a solid offense featuring Robbie Ftorek, who joined the team from Detroit and showed even the little skaters can make a big contribution, scoring 31 goals and 68 points. The scoring was evenly spread, with Michel Cormier leading with 36 goals, and both John Gray and Murray Keogan adding 35. Dennis Sobchuk, property of the Cincinnati Stingers but on loan to Phoenix during 1974-75, scored 32, while Don Borgeson and Jim Boyd scored 29 and 26, respectively. Getting the puck from the corners was the hard work of unsung diggers such as Bob Mowat, Bob Barlow, Wendell Bennett and Mike Stevens, all carry-overs from the Western League champs of 1974. The Roadrunners earned a trip to the playoffs, but the magic ended quickly as they lost in five games to the Quebec Nordiques. Nevertheless, Sandy Hucul won Coach of the Year for his efforts.

Quebec: The Nordiques had assembled a solid club during their first two seasons, but with much aggravation, had missed the playoffs in both 1973 and 1974, despite a solid core of scorers and a mobile defense led by J.-C. Tremblay and Francois Lacombe. Former player Jean-Guy Gendron became the new head coach, their fourth in three years. Entering 1974-75, the Nordiques made a couple of early-season trades that vaulted the team into the upper tier of teams, acquiring Marc Tardif from the Michigan Stags and Christian Bordeleau from Winnipeg. The Nordiques raced out of the gate, winning 11 of their first 15 games, and scoring goals in bunches. The scoring star for 1974-75 was Serge Bernier, whose 54 goals and 122 points led the Nords, while Marc Tardif also scored 50—38 playing for Quebec—to help the potent attack. Rejean Houle quietly put in 40 goals of his own, Michel Parizeau added 28, and a promising rookie named Real Cloutier added 26, as Quebec scored 331 goals for the season. The wide-open style of play was perfect for the talented collection of forwards, but also exposed the team's weakness of allowing goals in bunches, permitting 299 for the season. Nevertheless, the Nordiques won 46 games and the top spot in the Canadian Division, finally securing their long-awaited trip to the post-season. Quebec turned aside Phoenix and Minnesota to advance to the Championship round against Houston. Unfortunately, Quebec's run would come to a halt, as the Aeros' superlative defense completely shut down the Quebec gunners. The Nordiques scored just 7 goals while being swept in four straight.

San Diego: All attempts of putting a team in New York proved to be a complete disaster for the WHA, so the league finally conceded defeat and moved the team across the country, to the sunny beach city of San Diego, California, where the new Mariners would play out of the San Diego Sports Arena under much friendlier conditions, in a city that had shown it could support hockey as it had done for the Gulls of the Western League. The Mariners quickly established themselves in Southern California, winning their first four home games and getting off to a strong start with an 11-6-0 mark. Coach Harry Howell called the shots and also skated his shift, and free from the distractions of their first two seasons, the Mariners enjoyed a very strong year, winning 43 and finishing second in the Western Division. The high-powered offense was led by Andre Lacroix, who set a major-league record with 106 assists. Linemate Wayne Rovers' 54 goals led the team, while three others—Dick Sentes (44), Gene Peacosh (43) and Lacroix (41)—each scored 40 goals. As a team, the Mariners knocked in 326 goals, and only permitted 268 behind a strong defense led by Howell, Ron Plumb, Bob Wall and Bob Falkenberg. Ernie Wakely was acquired in an early-season trade with Winnipeg and established himself as the team's number one goaltender, winning 20 games. Ex-Shark Russ Gillow backed him and won 15. San Diego met Toronto in the playoffs and were able to eliminate the Toros in a hard-fought six-game set, but the effort depleted the Mariners, who then lost in four quick games against the Aeros, being shut out twice.

Toronto: Intending on making as big an impact in Toronto as possible, John Bassett went all out to sign big names, both from near and afar. Long-time Maple Leafs Frank Mahovlich and Paul Henderson were signed to contracts; in signing Mahovlich, the WHA could now boast three of the top five goal scorers of all time (Howe and Hull being the others, of course). Henderson was a solid second-line forward with nimble hands, most famous for his last-minute goal in the 1972 Canada-USSR series that gave Canada the eighth-game win and the series win. From afar the Toros signed Czechoslovakian defectors Richard Farda and Vaclav Nedomansky. "Big Ned" was an established star in Europe and one of the first significant European stars to make the jump to North America. The result was the second-most potent offense in the WHA, as the Toros scored 349 goals and had their best season to date, with 43 wins and 88 points. Tom "Shotgun" Simpson scored 52 goals to lead the attack, with Nedomansky second at 41. Mahovlich turned in 38 goals, second-year man Pat Hickey scored 35, and Henderson knocked in 30. The relentless offense masked a porous defense, as the Toros gave up 304 goals against. Nevertheless, this plan worked more than it failed, and the Toros were able to finish second in the Canadian Division behind Quebec. The high was short-lived, as Toronto fell to San Diego in six games in the first round of the post-season.

Vancouver: After a dreadful first season in Vancouver, the Blazers came under the control of Joe "The Crow" Crozier, who assumed both general manager and coach duties while rebuilding the Blazers. Danny Lawson once again showed he was one of the best natural goal-scorers, leading the team with 33 goals and in points with 76. Supporting him were five 20-goal men: Bryan Campbell with 29, Claude St. Sauveur and Rob Walton with 24 each, and John McKenzie and Hugh Harris with 23 each. Mike Pelyk, Duane Rupp, Paul Terbenche and rookie Pat Price led the defense, which permitted just 270 goals against, a 75-goal improvement over 1973-74. The defense certainly deserves credit, but some must also go to new goaltender Don McLeod, late of Houston, who appeared in 72 games, led the league in both wins and losses, and even contributed 8 assists to the offense. Overall, the Blazers finished 37-39-2, a fourth-place finish in the Canadian Division and out of a playoff spot. Nevertheless, it was a significant improvement over the previous year, and gave the team hope for 1975-76, albeit while relocated in Calgary, Alberta, as the Cowboys.

Winnipeg: The Jets had been at the vanguard in 1972, signing Bobby Hull to a contract and giving the WHA a fighting chance to survive and succeed during its first years. But Hull alone could not win championships, and after a poor showing in 1973-74,

the Jets sought to make amends for 1974-75. Instead of looking for another big-name NHLer to sign, the Jets looked east to Europe, and signed a handful of star performers, thereby becoming the first team in North American major-league hockey to aggressively sign European players and build a team around the European style of play. From Sweden the Jets signed right-wing Anders Hedberg and center Ulf Nilsson, who would team with Hull on left wing to form one of the best forward lines ever. Each would have 100-point seasons, with Hedberg scoring 53 and assisting on 47, while Nilsson scored "just" 26 but assisted on an amazing 94 goals, many of them Hull's, who set the major-league record with 77 goals (and his own personal best with 142 points). Helping out was a Finn, Veli-Pekka Ketola, who scored 26 goals, while fellow Finn Heikki "Hexi" Riihiranta and another Swede, Lars-Erik Sjoberg, anchored the defense. Joe Daley was now the main man in nets, and he won 23 games, spelled occasionally by Swede Curt Larsson. The Jets finished 38-35-5, an improvement over 1973-74, but frustratingly, out of a playoff berth. This would be the lone blemish on a much-improved season, one on which the Jets would build upon in the coming years as they rose to the top of the league behind the jet-powered attack of Hull, Hedberg and Nilsson.

Gallery

| Dave Gorman | Charles Constantin | Reg Fleming | Bruce Boudreau | Dick Paradise |
| Phil Roberto | Rich Pumple | Jim Shaw | Wayne Wood | Jim Troy |

1974-1975 Game by Game Line Scores

Date & Teams	Scoring 1 2 3 ot F	Shots 1 2 3 ot F	Goaltenders	Goals & Other Scoring Highlights
October 15				
New England	0 0 2 - 2	7 12 15 - 34	Smith	Webster, Swain
Toronto	4 1 1 - 6	17 6 13 - 36	Gratton	Mahovlich 3, Leduc, Henderson, Dillon
Winnipeg	2 2 2 - 6	11 11 10 - 32	Daley	Nilsson, Johnson, Hedberg, Spring, Beaudin, Riihiranta
Vancouver	0 1 1 - 2	16 9 10 - 35	D. McLeod	St. Sauveur, Pelyk
October 16				
San Diego	2 0 0 - 2	9 10 13 - 32	Gillow	Adduono, Ferguson
Phoenix	2 2 4 - 8	11 16 8 - 35	Kurt	Ftorek 3, Boyd, Harris, McLeod, Cormier, Keogan
Houston	2 4 0 - 6	13 14 8 - 35	Grahame	Mk Howe, Lund, Sherrit, Hall, Hughes, Labossiere
Vancouver	0 0 0 - 0	5 10 14 - 29	D. McLeod	▶ Grahame: shutout (1), 29 saves
October 17				
Michigan	2 0 2 - 4	6 11 7 - 24	Desjardins	Johnstone, West, Gruen, Tardif
Indianapolis	0 1 1 - 2	13 11 9 - 33	A. Brown	Richardson, Whitlock
October 18				
Indianapolis	0 1 0 - 1	5 9 8 - 22	A. Brown	Whitlock
Toronto	1 1 1 - 3	10 7 10 - 27	Shaw	Dillon, Henderson, Selby
Edmonton	0 0 0 - 0	6 7 15 - 28	K. Brown	▶ Daley: shutout (1), 28 saves
Winnipeg	1 1 2 - 4	9 9 11 - 29	Daley	Nilsson, Ketola, Bordeleau, Ford
Houston	1 3 0 - 4	15 19 9 - 43	Grahame	Hughes 2, Sherrit, Larway
Phoenix	1 1 4 - 6	11 8 11 - 30	Norris	Borgeson 2, Cormier, Barlow, Odrowski, Gorman
Chicago	0 1 1 - 2	7 2 8 - 17	Newton	Liddington, Rochon (WG 18:19)
Vancouver	0 1 0 - 1	5 8 10 - 23	D. McLeod	Rupp
October 19				
Houston	2 0 0 - 2	9 10 7 - 26	Rutledge	G. Howe, Schella
San Diego	1 2 3 - 6	12 12 7 - 31	Junkin	Rivers 2, Plumb, Lacroix, Adduono. Morenz
Michigan	0 1 0 0 1	15 12 12 7 46	Desjardins	Veneruzzo
New England	1 0 0 1 2	9 11 8 4 32	A. Smith	Abrahamsson, Pleau (OT 9:13)
Cleveland	2 0 1 - 3	12 12 10 - 34	Cheevers	Ward 2, McDonough
Minnesota	1 0 0 - 1	11 11 14 - 36	Garrett	D. O'Shea
October 20				
Michigan	2 0 1 - 3	8 5 7 - 20	Desjardins	Speck, Johnstone, Veneruzzo
Toronto	2 0 2 - 4	15 17 15 - 47	Binkley	Nedomansky, Featherstone, Trottier, Dillon (WG 18:08)
Indianapolis	0 0 1 - 1	10 13 13 - 36	Dyck	Walters (spoiled Brodeur's shutout at 17:05)
Quebec	3 1 0 - 4	10 10 6 - 26	Brodeur	Caron, Bernier, Hoganson, Houle
Chicago	0 1 0 - 1	6 10 8 - 24	Dryden	Backstrom
Vancouver	0 1 2 - 3	10 12 14 - 36	D. McLeod	Campbell, McKenzie, Lawson
Cleveland	3 1 0 0 4	11 10 4 6 31	Whidden	McDonough 3, Leduc
Phoenix	0 3 1 0 4	6 9 8 2 25	Kurt	Cormier, Gray, Borgeson, Keogan (TG 13:54)
October 22				
Minnesota	0 1 1 - 2	10 7 13 - 30	Garrett	Antonovich, Heatley
Toronto	5 2 4 - 11	14 13 17 - 44	Gratton, Shaw	Simpson 4, Hickey 3, Nedomansky, Mahovlich, Dillon, Henderson
Cleveland	1 1 0 - 2	8 13 11 - 32	Cheevers	Pinder, Buchanan
San Diego	0 3 2 - 5	10 10 18 - 38	Junkin	Lacroix 2, Sentes, Morrison, Peacosh
Houston	1 1 0 - 2	14 9 7 - 30	Grahame	Lund, Mty Howe
Quebec	2 2 3 - 7	9 17 9 - 35	Brodeur	Guite 2, Houle, Cloutier, Parizeau, Beaule, Caron
October 23				
Michigan	0 2 0 - 2	9 10 6 - 25	Desjardins	McDonald, Tardif
Quebec	2 0 4 - 6	8 11 14 - 33	Brodeur	Bernier 2, Gilbert, Houle, Guite, Constantin
Houston	1 2 1 - 4	9 11 11 - 31	Rutledge	Lund, Larway, Taylor, Sherrit
New England	1 2 2 - 5	11 15 14 - 40	Smith	O'Donnell 2 (WG 12:03), Dorey, Byers, Webster
Cleveland	0 0 1 - 1	7 9 7 - 23	Whidden	Buchanan (spoiled McLeod's shutout at 17:46)
Vancouver	1 2 1 - 4	14 12 11 - 37	D. McLeod	McKenzie 2, Campbell, Rupp
October 24				
Phoenix	0 0 1 - 1	6 8 10 - 24	Norris	Barlow
San Diego	0 1 1 - 2	17 12 20 - 49	Gillow	Rivers, Ferguson (WG 15:03)
Minnesota	1 1 1 - 3	9 8 6 - 23	Garrett	D. O'Shea, Huck, Heatley
Indianapolis	1 0 1 - 2	16 12 7 - 35	A. Brown	Bredin, Whitlock
October 25				
Winnipeg	1 0 0 - 1	11 8 9 - 28	Daley	Hull
Toronto	0 2 1 - 3	11 17 10 - 38	Shaw	Dillon, Simpson, Nedomansky
October 26				
Minnesota	1 0 1 - 2	7 15 6 - 28	Garrett, McCartan	Tannahill, Walton
Houston	1 2 0 - 3	13 10 13 - 36	Rutledge	Labossiere, Hughes, Preston
Indianapolis	0 1 0 - 1	6 11 11 - 28	Dyck	Andrascik
New England	2 2 2 - 6	6 11 11 - 28	Smith	Abrahamsson, Ley, Caffery, Pleau, Karlander, Sheehy
Phoenix	1 0 0 - 1	12 11 5 - 28	Kurt	Connor
Quebec	3 0 1 - 4	15 16 14 - 45	Brodeur	Houle, Cloutier, Lacombe, Bernier
October 27				
Quebec	1 0 2 - 3	8 10 12 - 30	Brodeur	Parizeau, Guite, Gaudette
Indianapolis	1 3 1 - 5	15 9 10 - 34	A. Brown	Andrascik, Pumple, Robertson, Sicinski, Whitlock
Michigan	0 1 1 - 2	6 7 10 - 23	Desjardins	West, Curtis
Winnipeg	0 2 3 - 5	12 15 15 - 42	Daley	Riihiranta, Nilsson, Sjoberg, Johnson, Hull
Chicago	2 1 2 0 5	15 12 9 1 37	Dryden	Popiel 2, Paiement 2, MacGregor
Minnesota	1 2 2 1 6	11 11 13 6 41	Garrett	Walton 2, Morrison, Ball, D. O'Shea (TG 19:53), Connelly (OT 7:53)
October 28				
Phoenix	2 0 1 - 3	16 10 10 - 36	Norris	Harris, Sobchuk, Boyd
Toronto	3 2 2 - 7	18 13 13 - 44	Gratton	Simpson 2, Featherstone, Nedomansky, Dillon, Henderson, Trottier

1974-1975 Game by Game Line Scores

Date & Teams	Scoring 1 2 3 ot F	Shots 1 2 3 ot F	Goaltenders	Goals & Other Scoring Highlights
October 29				
Houston	1 1 2 - 4	12 13 13 - 38	Rutledge	Popiel, Hinse, Lund, Labossiere
Chicago	1 1 0 - 2	10 9 8 - 27	Dryden	Morris, Liddington
Minnesota	2 1 0 0 3	8 17 5 2 32	Curran	Tannahill, Heatley, Morrison
Michigan	2 1 0 1 4	15 11 11 1 38	Desjardins	Veneruzzo, R. Legge, Tardif, Gruen (OT 4:22)
October 30				
Chicago	0 0 0 - 0	5 10 9 - 24	Newton	▶ Rutledge: shutout (1), 24 saves
Houston	0 0 1 - 1	12 15 11 - 38	Rutledge	Hall (WG 11:14)
Toronto	1 0 1 - 2	8 10 10 - 28	Shaw	Nedomansky, Hickey
New England	0 2 3 - 5	13 12 17 - 42	Smith	Dorey, Karlander, Webster, Abrahamsson, Byers
Phoenix	2 2 1 0 5	7 6 8 3 24	Kurt	Cormier 3, Sobchuk, Young
Winnipeg	1 1 3 1 6	13 7 14 8 42	Larsson	Hull 3 (OT 9:19), Spring, Hedberg, Ford
Edmonton	3 3 0 - 6	9 9 12 - 30	K. Brown	Patenaude 2, Baird 2, MacDonald, Climie
Vancouver	2 3 3 - 8	13 6 13 - 32	D. McLeod	Campbell 3, Lawson 2, St. Sauveur 2, Chipperfield
October 31				
New England	3 1 2 - 6	8 7 9 - 24	Abrahamsson	Webster 2, Pleau 2, French, Carleton
Indianapolis	0 1 0 - 1	7 11 12 - 30	A. Brown	Whitlock
Cleveland	0 2 2 - 4	12 8 10 - 30	Cheevers	Krake 2, Pinder 2
Michigan	0 1 1 - 2	9 9 9 - 27	Desjardins	West, Veneruzzo
Chicago	0 1 2 - 3	4 15 14 - 33	Newton	MacGregor, Paiement, Harris
San Diego	3 0 1 - 4	19 11 12 - 42	Junkin	Lacroix 2, Rivers, Peacosh
November 1				
Toronto	1 0 0 - 1	14 8 9 - 31	Gratton	Hickey
Winnipeg	5 1 4 - 10	17 18 12 - 47	Daley	Hull 3, Bordeleau 2, Ford 2, Spring, Asmundson, Beaudin
November 2				
Toronto	0 1 2 0 3	14 15 10 2 41	Binkley	Nedomansky, Simpson, Dillon
Chicago	0 3 0 1 4	9 9 11 3 32	Dryden	Liddington, Harris, Backstrom, Walter (OT 1:24)
Michigan	2 0 1 - 3	10 8 12 - 30	Desjardins	Tardif, Speck, Leblanc
Minnesota	1 1 4 - 6	20 13 11 - 44	Garrett, Curran	Smith, Connelly, Hampson, Huck, Morrison, Antonovich
Edmonton	1 0 3 - 4	12 6 13 - 31	Worthy	Buchanan 2, Baird, MacGregor
Cleveland	0 2 0 - 2	12 10 7 - 29	Cheevers	Ward, McDonough
Phoenix	0 2 0 - 2	5 18 4 - 27	Norris	Keogan, Barlow
Houston	3 0 5 - 8	14 9 15 - 38	Grahame	Lund 2, Sherrit, G. Howe, Schella, Larway, Hughes, Mty Howe
Quebec	0 1 1 - 2	8 11 11 - 30	Brodeur	Parizeau, Gaudette
New England	2 0 2 - 4	16 7 14 - 37	Smith	Carleton, Pleau, Karlander, Caffery
November 3				
San Diego	2 2 2 - 6	10 10 9 - 29	Junkin	Lacroix 2, Ferguson, Rivers, Howell, Morrison
Vancouver	0 1 1 - 2	17 7 10 - 34	D. McLeod	Campbell, Migneault
Edmonton	0 1 2 - 3	7 4 8 - 19	Worthy	Climie 2, Baird
Indianapolis	0 1 0 - 1	14 13 7 - 34	A. Brown	Robertson
Michigan	0 1 2 - 3	7 9 12 - 28	J.McLeod, Des'dins	Veneruzzo, McDonald, Locas
Winnipeg	3 3 5 - 11	13 14 15 - 42	Wakely	Hull 2, Hedberg 2, Ketola 2, Spring 2, Johnson, Ford, Beaudin
November 4				
Quebec	1 2 2 - 5	9 11 9 - 29	Brodeur	Parizeau, Guite, Hoganson, Tremblay, Bernier
Toronto	1 2 0 - 3	14 8 10 - 32	Shaw	Dillon 2, Hickey
November 5				
Toronto	1 2 2 - 5	13 16 14 - 43	Gratton	Hickey 2, Henderson, Kirk, Leduc
Michigan	0 2 0 - 2	6 14 9 - 29	Desjardins	Tardif, Veneruzzo
Phoenix	0 1 2 - 3	14 3 12 - 29	Kurt	Harris, Stevens, Cormier
Indianapolis	0 0 0 - 0	5 11 8 - 24	Dyck	▶ Kurt: shutout (1), 24 saves
Vancouver	2 1 2 - 5	14 16 15 - 45	Wood	McKenzie, Lawson, Burgess, St. Sauveur, Israelson (WG 11:56)
Chicago	3 0 1 - 4	7 8 6 - 21	Dryden	MacGregor 2, Backstrom, Stapleton
San Diego	0 3 0 - 3	5 11 6 - 22	Junkin	Sentes, Peacosh, Lacroix
Houston	3 2 4 - 9	10 9 10 - 29	Rutledge	Hughes 2, Sherrit 2, Larway, G. Howe, Lund, Labossiere, Hall
Minnesota	0 2 2 - 4	12 8 13 - 33	Curran	D. O'Shea, Tannahill, Walton, Morrison
Winnipeg	2 1 3 - 6	9 24 17 - 50	Daley	Bordeleau 2, Nilsson 2, Hedberg, Hull
November 6				
Vancouver	0 2 1 - 3	7 13 12 - 32	D. McLeod	Walton 2, Chipperfield
Quebec	0 2 3 - 5	8 16 14 - 38	Brodeur	Houle 2, Leclerc, Guite, Bernier
November 7				
San Diego	0 0 0 - 0	8 9 18 - 35	Gillow	▶ A. Brown: shutout (1), 35 saves
Indianapolis	0 3 0 - 3	13 11 7 - 31	A. Brown	Walters, Whitlock, McKenzie
November 8				
Cleveland	1 0 1 - 2	12 4 5 - 21	Cheevers	Shmyr, Erickson (WG 16:35)
Vancouver	0 1 0 - 1	5 12 9 - 26	Wood	Lawson
San Diego	0 0 0 - 0	11 13 6 - 30	Junkin	▶ Smith: shutout (1), 30 saves
New England	1 1 1 - 3	16 11 10 - 37	Smith	Ley, Caffery, French
November 9				
Indianapolis	1 0 3 1 5	12 6 13 3 34	Dyck	Pumple, Whitlock, Sicinski, Robertson (TG 19:59), Bredin (OT 3:50)
Houston	2 1 1 0 4	11 12 11 1 35	Grahame	Lund 2, Taylor, Hale
Phoenix	1 2 1 - 4	6 15 13 - 34	Norris	Gorman 2, Sobchuk, Harris
New England	2 0 0 - 2	12 5 11 - 28	Abrahamsson	Abrahamsson, Earl
Toronto	2 1 4 - 7	12 10 15 - 37	Gratton	Henderson 3, Mahovlich 2, Nedomansky, Simpson
Minnesota	2 2 0 - 4	12 14 12 - 38	Curran	Walton 2, Morrison, Connelly
Winnipeg	1 1 1 0 3	10 10 4 4 28	Daley	Ketola, Hull, Hornung
Vancouver	1 1 1 0 3	10 11 11 2 34	D. McLeod	Walton, Driscoll, McKenzie

1974-1975 Game by Game Line Scores

Date & Teams	Scoring 1 2 3 ot F	Shots 1 2 3 ot F	Goaltenders	Goals & Other Scoring Highlights
November 10				
Cleveland	1 0 0 - 1	10 9 2 - 21	Cheevers	Clearwater (Plante: WHA debut, opening
Edmonton	1 0 3 - 4	11 8 14 - 33	Plante	Long 2, Buchanan, Barrie night, Edmonton Coliseum)
San Diego	0 2 2 - 4	12 8 10 - 30	Gillow	Rivers 2, Adduono, Morenz
Quebec	1 1 1 - 3	11 6 10 - 27	Brodeur	Guindon, Parizeau, Houle
Indianapolis	1 2 3 - 6	5 7 13 - 25	A. Brown	Hargreaves, Bredin, Fitchner, Wiste, Whitlock, Robertson
Michigan	0 1 0 - 1	12 11 10 - 33	Desjardins	Gruen
Phoenix	0 4 0 - 4	12 10 14 - 36	Kurt	Boyd, Young, Bennett, Gray
Minnesota	4 2 4 - 10	11 10 11 - 32	Garrett	Walton 3, D. O'Shea 2, Arbour, McMahon, Connelly, Morrison, Heatley
Toronto	2 2 3 - 7	11 10 11 - 32	Gratton	Simpson, Dillon, Nedomansky, Martin, Kirk, Henderson, Mahovlich
Chicago	0 0 0 - 0	9 9 7 - 25	Newton	▶ Gratton: shutout (1), 25 saves
November 12				
San Diego	2 1 1 - 4	14 10 11 - 35	Junkin	Ferguson 2, Lacroix, Plumb
Chicago	1 1 0 - 2	14 10 11 - 35	Dryden	MacGregor, Harris
New England	0 1 0 - 1	8 8 7 - 23	Smith	Carleton
Houston	2 4 0 - 6	14 15 15 - 44	Rutledge	Hughes, Taylor, Lund, Sherrit, Hinse, Ruskowski
Quebec	2 2 1 - 5	11 19 8 - 38	Brodeur	Parizeau 2, Houle, Caron, Gaudette
Michigan	3 0 1 - 4	16 11 11 - 38	Desjardins	Veneruzzo 2, Sutherland, Trottier
November 13				
Toronto	0 3 2 - 5	5 14 14 - 33	Gratton	Featherstone 2, Dillon, Simpson (WG 18:57), Henderson
Vancouver	0 3 0 - 3	18 8 8 - 34	D. McLeod	McKenzie 2, Walton
Houston	5 1 2 - 8	10 9 7 - 26	Rutledge	Lund 3, G. Howe, Ruskowski, Mk Howe, Hinse, Hughes
Minnesota	0 3 2 - 5	9 10 14 - 33	Garrett	Tannahill 2, Connelly, Johnson, Morrison
Winnipeg	0 1 2 - 3	12 5 14 - 31	Daley	Hull, Bordeleau, Hedberg
Edmonton	1 2 2 - 5	10 11 9 - 30	Plante	Baird 3, Barrie, Patenaude
Indianapolis	0 3 0 - 3	9 15 12 - 36	A. Brown	Pumple, Whitlock, Bond
Quebec	4 1 5 - 10	14 9 12 - 35	Brodeur	Beaule 2, Gaudette, Caron, Constantin, Tremblay, Bernier, Jordan, Hoganson, Parizeau
November 14				
Chicago	1 0 1 - 2	8 12 16 - 36	Newton	Harris, Maggs
Michigan	2 0 2 - 4	17 13 14 - 44	Desjardins	Tardif 2, Trottier, Gruen
New England	4 2 1 - 7	8 8 6 - 22	Abrahamsson	Webster 2, Dorey, Caffery, Carleton, Sheehy, French
San Diego	1 1 0 - 2	16 10 11 - 37	Gillow, Junkin	Rivers 2
Cleveland	1 0 0 1 2	11 5 13 3 32	Whidden	Pinder, Harrison (OT 7:00)
Phoenix	1 0 0 0 1	6 8 4 2 20	Norris	Keogan
November 15				
Toronto	1 2 1 - 4	9 9 4 - 22	Gratton	Farda 2, Featherstone, Dillon
Edmonton	2 3 0 - 5	12 15 17 - 44	Plante	Patenaude, MacDonald, McKay, Herriman, Climie
Cleveland	1 3 1 - 5	5 13 9 - 27	Whidden	Ward 2, Leduc, Jarrett, Edur
San Diego	1 2 0 - 3	17 15 13 - 45	Junkin	Rivers, Morenz, Lacroix
Indianapolis	0 0 0 - 0	16 16 7 - 39	Dyck	▶ Wakely: shutout (1), 39 saves
Winnipeg	2 0 3 - 5	10 6 14 - 30	Wakely	Hornung, Hedberg, Asmundson, Nilsson, Ketola
November 16				
Michigan	0 2 1 - 3	11 12 9 - 32	J. McLeod	Johnstone, Speck, Veneruzzo
Quebec	0 3 1 - 4	9 17 13 - 39	Brodeur	Bernier, Parizeau, Jordan, Leclerc (TG 18:26)
Chicago	2 0 0 - 2	7 7 14 - 28	Dryden	Paiement, MacGregor
Houston	1 4 1 - 6	12 16 7 - 35	Rutledge	Preston 2, Larway 2, Lund, Ruskowski
New England	0 1 2 - 3	8 8 10 - 26	Abrahamsson	French, O'Donnell, Sheehy
Phoenix	0 2 4 - 6	9 9 10 - 28	Norris	Keogan 2, Harris 2, Sobchuk, Gray
November 17				
New England	2 0 4 - 6	14 12 17 - 43	Smith	Pleau 2, Webster 2, Fotiu, Swain
Michigan	1 0 0 - 1	7 8 8 - 23	Desjardins	Johnstone
Indianapolis	1 0 0 - 1	9 13 10 - 32	A. Brown	Bond
Edmonton	0 0 2 - 2	4 5 15 - 24	Worthy	MacDonald, Buchanan
Minnesota	2 3 2 - 7	11 12 13 - 36	Garrett	Walton 2, Busniuk, Huck, Antonovich, D. O'Shea, Morrison
Quebec	0 1 0 - 1	14 16 9 - 39	Brodeur	Caron (Morrison: 8th straight game with goal)
San Diego	0 2 2 - 4	11 15 10 - 36	Gillow	Peacosh 2, Ferguson, Sentes
Houston	0 1 2 - 3	8 10 14 - 32	Rutledge	Preston, Hinse, G. Howe
Toronto	0 1 2 - 3	14 12 11 - 37	Shaw	Henderson, Simpson, Featherstone
Winnipeg	0 0 1 - 1	6 10 15 - 31	Daley	Johnson
November 18				
Winnipeg	1 2 0 - 3	9 10 9 - 28	Daley, Wakely	Hull 2, Sjoberg
Edmonton	1 3 1 - 5	11 21 18 - 50	Plante	Rogers 2, Baird, Patenaude, Barrie
November 19				
Houston	2 6 2 - 10	11 20 10 - 41	Grahame	Mk Howe 3, Hinse 2, Hughes 2, Sherrit, Mty Howe, Lund
Indianapolis	0 0 0 - 0	8 4 10 - 22	A. Brown, Dyck	▶ Grahame: shutout (2), 22 saves
Toronto	1 4 1 - 6	12 13 12 - 37	Shaw	Hickey 2, Simpson, Mahovlich, Cuddie, Henderson
Cleveland	2 1 2 - 5	20 11 10 - 41	Cheevers, Whidden	McDonough 2, Erickson, Holbrook, Walker
New England	2 1 2 - 5	15 15 11 - 41	Smith	Webster 2 (WG 13:38), Byers, Pleau, O'Donnell
Chicago	3 1 0 - 4	11 10 4 - 25	Dryden	Rochon 3, MacGregor
Vancouver	1 0 1 - 2	8 4 11 - 23	Wood	Migneault, Lawson
San Diego	2 1 0 - 3	17 14 6 - 37	Gillow	Peacosh 2, Morrison
November 20				
Minnesota	0 0 1 - 1	10 10 15 - 35	Curran	Heatley
Winnipeg	1 0 2 - 3	15 6 12 - 33	Wakely	Hull 2, Johnson
Indianapolis	2 2 0 - 4	10 15 12 - 37	A. Brown	Bond 2, Hopiavuori, Whitlock
Chicago	3 1 2 - 6	14 10 8 - 32	Dryden	Harris 2, Rochon 2, Popiel, Lomenda
Edmonton	1 1 0 - 2	5 8 5 - 18	Worthy	Rogers, Patenaude
Quebec	2 2 0 - 4	13 17 6 - 36	Brodeur	Caron, Guite, Leclerc, Bernier

1974-1975 Game by Game Line Scores

Date & Teams	Scoring 1 2 3 ot F	Shots 1 2 3 ot F	Goaltenders	Goals & Other Scoring Highlights
November 21				
New England	1 3 0 - 4	6 14 8 - 28	Abrahamsson	Sheehy, Carleton, Caffery, Webster
Indianapolis	0 0 0 - 0	15 8 12 - 35	Dyck, A. Brown	▶ Abrahamsson: shutout (1), 35 saves
Phoenix	0 1 0 - 1	8 14 6 - 28	Kurt	Sobchuk
Michigan	0 2 0 - 2	15 7 9 - 31	J. McLeod	Gruen, Fontaine
November 22				
Houston	0 2 2 - 4	8 15 11 - 34	Grahame	G. Howe, Sherrit, Schella, Hughes
Vancouver	0 0 1 - 1	8 10 10 - 28	D. McLeod	Walton
Edmonton	2 6 0 - 8	12 17 7 - 36	Plante, K. Brown	Climie 2, Carlyle, Joyal, Rogers, Gilmore, MacGregor, Baird
Toronto	0 1 1 - 2	10 8 13 - 31	Shaw, Gratton	Mahovlich, Hickey
Cleveland	1 0 1 - 2	14 7 15 - 36	Whidden	Ward, Krake
Quebec	0 2 1 - 3	10 11 10 - 31	Brodeur	Bernier, Guite, Parizeau (WG 8:08)
Michigan	1 2 0 - 3	11 9 17 - 37	J. McLeod, Des'dins	Tardif. McDonald, West
Chicago	2 1 2 - 5	15 22 11 - 48	Dryden	Rochon 2, Paiement, Liddington, Watson
November 23				
Chicago	1 1 0 - 2	12 8 9 - 29	Newton	Mara, Lomenda
New England	1 1 1 - 3	10 22 17 - 49	Smith	Webster 2 (WG 15:30), Byers
San Diego	0 3 2 - 5	13 22 10 - 45	.Gillow	Peacosh 3, Morenz, Morrison
Minnesota	1 1 1 - 3	9 10 14 - 33	Curran	Morrison, Antonovich, Connelly
Houston	1 1 2 - 4	12 11 10 - 33	Rutledge	Ruskowski, Hinse, Hughes, G. Howe
Vancouver	0 0 2 - 2	8 13 11 - 32	D. McLeod	Campbell, Chipperfield
Toronto	3 4 2 - 9	10 9 12 - 31	Gratton	Simpson 4, Nedomansky 2, Henderson, Featherstone, Hickey
Quebec	1 1 0 - 2	14 17 14 - 45	Brodeur, Aubry	Gilbert, Tremblay
November 24				
Toronto	1 4 4 - 9	9 15 17 - 41	Binkley	Mahovlich 2, H'derson 2, F'therstone, Nedomansky, Farda, Kirk, Hickey
Indianapolis	0 1 1 - 2	8 6 18 - 32	A. Brown, Dyck	Harbaruk, Whitlock
Phoenix	1 1 1 - 3	10 10 12 - 32	Norris	Keogan 2, Sobchuk
Winnipeg	1 0 0 - 1	6 9 5 - 20	Wakely	Ketola
Houston	1 2 0 1 4	12 13 10 1 36	Grahame	Hughes 2 (OT 2:49), Labossiere, G. Howe
Edmonton	2 1 0 0 3	14 7 6 0 27	Plante	Patenaude 2, Sheehan
Quebec	0 1 0 - 1	8 12 14 - 34	Aubry	Lacombe
Cleveland	1 1 1 - 3	17 15 9 - 41	Cheevers	Krake, Pinder, Leduc
Minnesota	0 0 2 - 2	13 15 17 - 45	Garrett, Curran	Walton, Smith
Michigan	1 2 0 - 3	14 9 8 - 31	Desjardins	Tardif, Miszuk, West
New England	1 4 4 - 9	11 14 16 - 41	Abrahamsson	Carleton 3, O'Donnell 2, Sheehy, Abrahamsson, Swain, French
Chicago	2 1 2 - 5	14 12 14 - 40	Dryden	Liddington, Rochon, Popiel, Backstrom, Baltimore
November 26				
Winnipeg	2 2 0 - 4	9 12 9 - 30	Larsson	Hull, Nilsson, Bordeleau, Ford
Indianapolis	0 0 0 - 0	17 9 13 - 39	A. Brown	▶ Larsson: shutout (1), 39 saves
New England	1 2 1 1 5	10 12 14 1 37	Smith	French 2 (OT 0:04, center-ice slapshot), Sheehy, Ley, Webster
Quebec	0 2 2 0 4	13 18 12 0 43	Aubry	Guite 2, Guindon, Beaule
Minnesota	1 3 2 - 6	11 7 17 - 35	Curran, Garrett	Walton 2, Ball, Connelly, K. O'Shea, Huck
Toronto	1 0 1 - 2	11 11 9 - 31	Gratton, Binkley	Simpson, Farda
Vancouver	3 1 1 - 5	15 7 4 - 26	D. McLeod	Burgess, St. Sauveur, Chipperfield, McNamee, Pelyk
Michigan	0 0 1 - 1	9 10 10 - 29	Desjardins	Tardif
Phoenix	3 2 1 - 6	10 15 7 - 32	Kurt	Harris 3, Keogan, Cormier, Niekamp
Houston	3 0 1 - 4	17 8 16 - 41	Grahame	Preston 2, Lund, Popiel
Edmonton	0 1 0 - 1	7 8 4 - 19	Worthy	Baird
San Diego	2 2 1 - 5	9 22 12 - 43	Gillow, Junkin	Peacosh 2, Reichmuth, Adduono, Morrison
November 27				
Winnipeg	1 3 0 0 4	10 12 14 3 39	Wakely	Beaudin 2, Hull, Bordeleau
Cleveland	2 2 0 1 5	6 14 13 6 39	Cheevers	Jarrett 2, Harrison 2 (OT 9:54), Walker
Chicago	2 0 2 - 4	9 5 10 - 24	Newton	Liddington 2, Paiement, MacGregor
Phoenix	0 1 1 - 2	4 7 11 - 22	Norris	Odrowski, Connor
November 28				
Quebec	2 3 2 - 7	10 16 6 - 32	Brodeur	Cloutier 3, Leclerc 2, Guite, Caron
Indianapolis	2 1 2 - 5	8 11 14 - 33	Dyck	Bond, Smith, Kennett, Hopiavuori, Harbaruk
Vancouver	1 4 1 - 6	19 15 15 - 49	D. McLeod	Lawson, McNamee, Walton, Campbell, Migneault
Toronto	0 2 0 - 2	8 17 13 - 38	Binkley	Mahovlich, Kirk
Chicago	1 1 1 - 3	9 10 13 - 32	Newton	Mara 2, Popiel
San Diego	1 0 1 - 2	11 13 14 - 38	Junkin	Lacroix, Ferguson
Edmonton	0 0 0 - 0	3 6 6 - 15	K. Brown	▶ Rutledge: shutout (2), 15 saves
Houston	0 1 1 - 2	15 8 13 - 36	Rutledge	G. Howe, Mk Howe
November 29				
New England	1 0 0 - 1	10 7 8 - 25	Abrahamsson	Carleton
Vancouver	0 3 2 - 5	5 11 10 - 26	D. McLeod	Chipperfield 2, Pelyk, Lawson, McKenzie
Indianapolis	0 2 0 - 2	6 14 8 - 28	A. Brown	Pumple, Sicinski
Cleveland	2 2 0 - 4	6 10 10 - 26	Whidden	Pinder, Erickson, Shmyr, Clearwater
Michigan	3 1 2 - 6	14 18 21 - 53	Des'dins, J.McLeod	Serviss, Veneruzzo, Gruen, Tardif, Trottier, West
Winnipeg	3 2 2 - 7	24 17 13 - 54	Larsson	Hull 4, Riihiranta, Miller Spring (Teams: 107 shots, WHA record)
Toronto	3 0 1 0 4	7 3 9 3 22	Gratton	Featherstone, Hickey, Nedomansky, Simpson
Phoenix	1 0 3 0 4	13 9 17 4 43	Kurt	Harris, Keogan, Mowat, Sobchuk (TG 15:04)
November 30				
Cleveland	1 1 3 - 5	11 8 15 - 34	Cheevers	Jarrett, Ward, Leduc, Pinder, Erickson
Houston	2 1 1 - 4	11 11 12 - 34	Rutledge	Hughes 3, Hinse
Chicago	4 0 3 - 7	10 11 12 - 33	Newton	Lomenda, Hardy, Mavety, Maggs, MacGregor, Backstrom, Popiel
Minnesota	1 3 1 - 5	16 11 9 - 36	Curran, Garrett	Gallant 2, Walton, Huck, Antonovich

1974-1975 Game by Game Line Scores

Date & Teams	Scoring 1 2 3 ot F	Shots 1 2 3 ot F	Goaltenders	Goals & Other Scoring Highlights
December 1				
Toronto	1 1 1 - 3	12 4 4 - 20	Gratton	Nedomansky 3
San Diego	0 0 1 - 1	13 10 14 - 37	Gillow	Rivers
Phoenix	1 2 0 - 3	6 15 7 - 28	Norris	Gray 2, Mowat
Minnesota	3 0 1 - 4	15 10 8 - 33	Garrett	Antonovich 2, Hampson, D. O'Shea (WG 15:49)
New England	2 1 1 - 4	8 15 17 - 40	Smith	French, Pleau, O'Donnell, Sheehy
Edmonton	2 5 1 - 8	6 15 13 - 34	Plante, K. Brown	MacGregor, Gilmore, Climie, Sheehan, Long, Baird, Rogers, Patenaude
Houston	2 3 2 - 7	10 13 5 - 28	Grahame	Hughes 2, G. Howe, Preston, Taylor, Sherrit, Hall
Indianapolis	1 1 1 - 3	16 11 7 - 34	A. Brown	Sheridan 2, Bond
Quebec	1 0 1 - 2	9 10 11 - 30	Brodeur	Cloutier, Hoganson
Winnipeg	3 0 0 - 3	14 13 8 - 35	Daley	Nilsson, Ketola, Hedberg
December 3				
New England	0 0 1 - 1	6 13 8 - 27	Abrahamsson	Dorey
Michigan	1 0 1 - 2	12 17 10 - 39	Desjardins	Richardson, Zrymiak (WG 5:28)
Phoenix	1 0 3 1 5	10 7 16 1 34	Kurt	Keogan, Sobchuk, Barlow, Hughes (TG 19:34), Cormier (OT 6:01)
San Diego	0 3 1 0 4	12 10 8 3 33	Gillow	Plumb, Morrison, Adduono, Ferguson
Houston	1 2 2 - 5	8 12 10 - 30	Rutledge	Hughes 2, Larway 2 (WG 10:46), Hinse
Toronto	3 1 0 - 4	10 8 8 - 26	Gratton	Mahovlich 2, Kirk, Hickey
December 4				
San Diego	2 0 0 - 2	6 1 5 - 12	Junkin	Block, Adduono
Phoenix	0 0 0 - 0	9 6 12 - 27	Norris	▸ Junkin: shutout (1), 27 saves
Minnesota	3 2 1 - 6	12 11 14 - 37	Garrett	Walton, D. O'Shea, Huck, Antonovich, Hampson, K. O'Shea
Quebec	1 1 1 - 3	6 8 7 - 21	Brodeur	Cloutier, Tremblay, Guite
Houston	0 2 1 - 3	11 16 7 - 34	Grahame	Hinse 2, G. Howe (WG 9:29)
Winnipeg	2 0 0 - 2	12 11 6 - 29	Daley	Riihiranta, Ketola
New England	2 1 0 - 3	10 7 9 - 26	Abrahamsson	Carleton, Dorey, Byers
Cleveland	1 0 1 - 2	18 16 8 - 42	Cheevers, Whidden	Walker, Ward
Vancouver	1 1 1 - 3	11 15 11 - 37	D. McLeod	Walton, Lawson, Migneault
Edmonton	2 3 1 - 6	9 9 11 - 29	Plante, K. Brown	Joyal 2, Barrie, Hamilton, Sheehan, Perkins
December 5				
New England	1 0 0 - 1	8 6 4 - 18	Ab'sson, Ouimet	Charlebois (Que: 5 goals in 5:14, 2nd period)
Quebec	1 5 3 - 9	12 10 13 - 35	Aubry	Cloutier 2, Bernier 2, Lacombe, Tremblay, Rouleau, Guite, Leclerc
San Diego	2 0 1 - 3	12 11 8 - 31	Junkin, Gillow	Rivers 2, Morrison
Michigan	1 3 1 - 5	9 11 15 - 35	Desjardins	Zrymiak, Tardif, Leblanc, Gruen, Veneruzzo
Chicago	2 0 3 - 5	4 9 11 - 24	Newton	Rochon, Liddington, Mara, MacGregor, Popiel
Indianapolis	1 2 0 - 3	12 15 10 - 37	Dyck	Johnson, Sicinski, Whitlock
December 6				
Winnipeg	0 1 1 - 2	10 9 13 - 32	Daley	Spring 2
Minnesota	1 2 1 - 4	10 17 7 - 34	Curran	Morrison, Hampson, Busniuk, Connelly
Edmonton	0 1 0 - 1	5 3 7 - 15	Worthy	Rogers
Phoenix	1 0 2 - 3	9 10 14 - 33	Kurt	Boyd, Barlow, Ftorek
December 7				
Michigan	0 2 0 - 2	7 11 9 - 27	Desjardins	Gruen, Bredin
Vancouver	2 1 1 - 4	13 10 16 - 39	Wood, D. McLeod	Chipperfield 2, Campbell, St. Sauveur
Indianapolis	2 0 1 - 3	17 6 10 - 33	A. Brown	Sheridan, Whitlock, Bond (Ind: 13th straight defeat)
New England	1 2 3 - 6	12 11 16 - 39	Abrahamsson	Pleau 3, Sheehy, Green, O'Donnell
San Diego	0 1 0 - 1	13 11 12 - 36	Gillow	Rivers
Cleveland	1 1 1 - 3	16 10 14 - 40	Whidden	McDonough, Krake, Jarrett
Toronto	3 0 0 - 3	12 16 7 - 35	Gratton	Dillon, Mahovlich, Kirk
Chicago	1 4 4 - 9	12 10 8 - 30	Newton	Mara 3, Liddington 2, Harris, Zaine, Backstrom, MacGregor
December 8				
Chicago	1 0 1 - 2	7 6 18 - 31	Newton	Rochon, Maggs
Winnipeg	2 2 1 - 5	15 16 6 - 37	Daley	Beaudin 2, Black, Johnson, Sjoberg
Minnesota	2 0 0 - 2	8 7 5 - 20	Garrett	Tannahill, Hampson
Vancouver	0 3 1 - 4	8 8 15 - 31	D. McLeod	Campbell, Lawson, Jones, Walton
Houston	1 0 0 - 1	11 6 8 - 25	Rutledge	Hinse
Quebec	0 0 2 - 2	9 18 14 - 41	Aubry	Bernier, Parizeau
Toronto	1 2 2 - 5	6 13 8 - 27	Binkley	Simpson 2, Cuddie, Nedomansky, Hickey
Phoenix	1 1 0 - 2	9 8 6 - 23	Norris	Keogan, Sobchuk
Michigan	0 0 0 - 0	10 7 7 - 24	Des'dins, J.McLeod	▸ Plante: shutout (1), 24 saves
Edmonton	3 0 4 - 7	7 7 11 - 25	Plante	Rogers 2, Climie 2, McCrimmon, MacDonald, Perkins
San Diego	1 1 1 - 3	14 8 11 - 33	Junkin	Morrison, Ferguson
Indianapolis	3 1 1 - 5	11 12 9 - 32	A. Brown	Sheridan 2, Wiste, Bond, Hargreaves
December 10				
Vancouver	2 2 0 - 4	11 11 8 - 30	D. McLeod	Campbell 2, Shmyr, Bathgate
Cleveland	0 1 2 - 3	9 13 17 - 39	Whidden	Pinder, McDonough, Leduc
Michigan	0 1 3 0 4	12 8 11 2 33	J. McLeod	Serviss, Veneruzzo, Curtis, Andrascik (TG 17:41)
San Diego	0 1 3 0 4	18 15 14 4 51	Gilow	Peacosh, Sentes, Rivers, Falkenberg
Minnesota	1 1 2 - 4	17 6 13 - 36	Curran	Connelly 2, Hampson, Walton
Toronto	1 1 0 - 2	13 15 13 - 41	Gratton	Nedomansky, Gibbons
Phoenix	1 2 1 - 4	13 19 4 - 36	Kurt	Cormier 2, Keogan, Sobchuk
Chicago	0 1 1 - 2	6 10 10 - 26	Newton	MacGregor, Liddington
Winnipeg	3 1 1 - 5	11 11 6 - 28	Larsson	Riihiranta 2, Ketola 2, Hull
Indianapolis	0 2 1 - 3	11 10 13 - 34	A. Brown	Sheridan 2, Harbaruk

1974-1975 Game by Game Line Scores

Date & Teams	Scoring 1 2 3 ot F	Shots 1 2 3 ot F	Goaltenders	Goals & Other Scoring Highlights
December 11				
Minnesota	0 0 1 - 1	8 15 13 - 36	Garrett	Walton
New England	2 1 0 - 3	13 8 16 - 37	Abrahamsson	Sheehy 2, Byers
Vancouver	1 1 0 - 2	6 11 7 - 24	D. McLeod	McKenzie, McCulloch
Houston	1 2 2 - 5	18 18 7 - 43	Grahame	Hughes 2, Mk Howe, G. Howe, Hinse
Edmonton	1 0 2 0 3	16 8 12 1 37	K. Brown	Baird, MacGregor, Rogers (TG 17:08)
Quebec	2 1 0 1 4	13 16 11 1 41	Aubry	Tardif, Cloutier, Bernier, Sutherland (OT 0:56)
December 12				
Winnipeg	1 0 2 - 3	8 9 5 - 22	Larsson, Daley	Nilsson 2, Hull
Michigan	1 2 2 - 5	17 8 9 - 34	Desjardins	Guite 3, Trottier 2
Vancouver	1 0 1 - 2	6 9 6 - 21	D. McLeod	Harris, McKenzie
Phoenix	1 1 2 - 4	8 9 11 - 28	Kurt	Gray 2, Sobchuk, Mowat
Cleveland	1 1 0 - 2	13 10 5 - 28	Cheevers	Shmyr, Erickson
Quebec	1 1 3 - 5	22 16 13 - 51	Aubry	Bernier 2, Roy, Bordeleau, Tardif
December 13				
Cleveland	2 2 2 0 6	6 9 14 0 29	Cheevers	Krake, Walker, Holbrook, Jarrett, Harrison, Leduc
Toronto	3 2 1 1 7	15 20 8 3 46	Gratton	H'derson 2, F'therstone, Ned'sky, Hickey, Cunning'm, Martin (OT 2:11)
Edmonton	0 3 2 - 5	6 9 8 - 23	Worthy	Rogers 2, MacDonald, Barrie, Patenaude (WG 18:14)
Minnesota	0 2 2 - 4	9 17 14 - 40	Curran, Garrett	K. O'Shea, Walton, Connelly, Smith
December 14				
Michigan	0 0 0 - 0	18 15 13 - 46	J. McLeod	▶ Dryden: shutout (1), 46 saves
Chicago	1 3 2 - 6	15 14 15 - 44	Dryden	Backstrom 2, Harris, Stapleton, Liddington, Mavety
Quebec	0 2 2 - 4	9 17 15 - 41	Aubry	Cloutier, Tremblay, Bernier, Guindon
New England	2 3 4 - 9	12 17 17 - 46	Abrahamsson	Blackburn 3, Caffery 3, Byers, Sheehy, Pleau
Winnipeg	1 0 2 - 3	7 7 13 - 27	Daley	Hull, Riihiranta, Gratton
Houston	1 3 1 - 5	10 13 9 - 32	Grahame	G. Howe 2, Hinse, Taylor, Hughes
Indianapolis	0 0 0 - 0	2 5 7 - 14	A. Brown	▶ Blanchet: shutout (1), 14 saves (league debut)
San Diego	2 0 0 - 2	14 8 9 - 31	Blanchet	Lacroix, Rivers
Minnesota	2 1 0 - 3	12 9 7 - 28	Garrett	Connelly, Gambucci, Huck
Phoenix	1 0 3 - 4	8 9 12 - 29	Kurt	Mowat, Keogan, Boyd, Connor (WG 18:58)
December 15				
Toronto	3 3 1 - 7	11 16 16 - 43	Gratton	Simpson 3, Cunningham, Featherstone, Dillon, Martin
Michigan	1 1 0 - 2	12 10 5 - 27	J. McLeod, Des'dins	Bredin, Thomas
Cleveland	0 1 0 - 1	12 11 16 - 39	Whidden	Cardwell
Vancouver	1 1 0 - 2	17 5 6 - 28	D. McLeod	Campbell, Terbenche
Edmonton	0 1 2 - 3	13 7 8 - 28	K. Brown	Baird, Sheehan, MacGregor
Indianapolis	0 0 1 - 1	16 15 7 - 38	Dyck	Harbaruk
Quebec	0 1 3 - 4	14 11 10 - 35	Brodeur	Bernier 2, Leclerc, Parizeau
Minnesota	4 1 1 - 6	15 17 10 - 42	Garrett	Huck, Morrison, Antonovich, Connelly, K. O'Shea, Hampson
San Diego	1 1 2 - 4	10 13 9 - 32	Gillow	Ferguson, Peacosh, Rivers, Lacroix (WG 15:19)
Houston	1 1 1 - 3	13 14 10 - 37	Rutledge	Labossiere, Preston, Lund
New England	1 3 0 - 4	6 17 7 - 30	Smith	Byers 2, Ley, Carleton
Winnipeg	2 1 0 - 3	8 10 14 - 32	Daley	Hull, Miller, Black
December 17				
Winnipeg	2 0 2 - 4	11 8 14 - 33	Daley	Hull 2, Ketola, Asmundson
Toronto	0 0 1 - 1	10 4 13 - 27	Gratton	Simpson
New England	1 0 1 0 2	6 13 17 4 40	Abrahamsson	Sheehy 2 (TG 18:11)
Michigan	1 1 0 0 2	12 5 9 5 31	Hoganson	Guite, Veneruzzo
Quebec	2 2 2 - 6	11 11 7 9 - 37	Brodeur	Bernier 2, Jordan, Cloutier, Gaudette, Tardif
Chicago	0 1 0 - 1	14 8 13 - 35	Dryden	MacGregor
Vancouver	1 1 1 - 3	11 8 6 - 25	D. McLeod	McKenzie 2 (WG 0:41), Lawson
Indianapolis	2 0 0 - 2	11 9 9 - 29	A. Brown	Sicinski, Harbaruk
Cleveland	0 2 1 - 3	4 14 6 - 24	Cheevers	Holbrook, Muloin, Walker
San Diego	1 5 2 - 8	15 17 18 - 50	Blanchet	Ferguson 2, Rivers 2, Morenz, Peacosh, Reichmuth, Lacroix
Edmonton	1 1 0 - 2	10 13 11 - 34	Worthy, K. Brown	Rogers, Buchanan
Houston	5 2 0 - 7	19 14 14 - 47	Grahame	G. Howe 2, Labossiere 2, Larway, Ruskowski, Preston
December 18				
Winnipeg	0 0 1 - 1	11 11 13 - 35	Larsson	Johnson (spoiled Brodeur's shutout at 16:13)
Quebec	3 0 2 - 5	18 11 9 - 38	Brodeur	Lacombe 2, Jordan, Guindon, Bernier
Vancouver	1 2 0 - 3	8 12 7 - 27	D. McLeod	Harris, Deadmarsh, Campbell
Phoenix	1 2 2 - 5	5 7 13 - 25	Kurt	Cormier 3, Borgeson 2
December 19				
Minnesota	2 3 1 - 6	8 9 3 - 20	Garrett	Tannahill, Walton, Antonovich, Huck, K. O'Shea, Hampson
Indianapolis	0 0 0 - 0	8 8 13 - 29	Dyck	▶ Garrett: shutout (2), 29 saves
San Diego	3 2 1 0 6	16 7 11 1 35	Gillow	Rivers 2, Lacroix, Ferguson, Laughton, Morrison
Edmonton	1 1 4 1 7	6 8 13 2 29	K. Brown	MacDonald 2, Baird, Barrie, Patenaude, Joyal, Rogers (OT 2:49)
Vancouver	1 1 1 - 3	12 13 7 - 32	D. McLeod	Lawson, St. Sauveur, Harris
Houston	1 0 0 - 1	13 12 11 - 36	Rutledge	Lund
Cleveland	0 0 0 - 0	7 12 13 - 32	Whidden	▶ Hoganson: shutout (1), 32 saves
Michigan	1 0 0 - 1	16 7 3 - 26	Hoganson	Gruen
December 20				
New England	0 0 0 - 0	8 14 8 - 30	Smith	▶ Cheevers: shutout (1), 30 saves
Cleveland	3 0 0 - 3	15 9 16 - 40	Cheevers	Ward, Erickson, Walker
Indianapolis	1 1 2 - 4	16 9 6 - 31	A. Brown	Whitlock, Wiste, Johnson, Sheridan
Minnesota	2 2 2 - 6	14 9 13 - 36	Garrett	Huck, Ball, Antonovich, Walton, Gambucci, Smith
Chicago	1 1 3 - 5	11 11 11 - 33	Newton	Rochon 2, Morris, Lomenda, Baltimore
Quebec	1 0 2 - 3	17 11 17 - 45	Brodeur	Bernier, Tardif, Jordan
Michigan	1 0 1 - 2	5 6 8 - 19	J.McLeod, Hog'son	Veneruzzo, Serviss
Phoenix	1 3 3 - 7	7 9 9 - 25	Kurt	Gray 2, Keogan 2, Borgeson 2, Cormier

1974-1975 Game by Game Line Scores

Date & Teams	Scoring 1 2 3 ot F	Shots 1 2 3 ot F	Goaltenders	Goals & Other Scoring Highlights
December 21				
San Diego	1 0 0 - 1	7 10 17 - 34	Junkin	Howell
Vancouver	2 0 0 - 2	13 10 5 - 28	D. McLeod	Jones 2 (both short-handed)
Edmonton	1 1 1 - 3	13 10 15 - 38	Worthy	Baird, Gilmore, Climie
Chicago	0 0 0 - 0	12 6 13 - 31	Dryden	▸ Worthy: shutout (1), 31 saves
Houston	2 0 3 - 5	9 10 14 - 33	Grahame	Preston 2, Mk Howe, Lund, Larway
New England	0 2 1 - 3	7 10 12 - 29	Smith	Sheehy, Pleau, Karlander
December 22				
Phoenix	2 1 1 - 4	11 7 6 - 24	Kurt	Cormier 2, Bennett, Barlow
Winnipeg	1 1 0 - 2	10 13 20 - 43	Daley	Nilsson, Hull
Quebec	0 0 2 0 2	9 10 18 2 39	Aubry	Bernier 2
Michigan	2 0 0 1 3	12 7 5 2 26	Hoganson	Veneruzzo, Leblanc, Andrascik (OT 2:54)
Chicago	1 0 1 - 2	6 6 11 - 23	Newton	Paiement, Popiel
Toronto	0 2 3 - 5	15 10 16 - 41	Gratton	Cunningham 2, Nedomansky, Dillon, Henderson
New England	0 0 1 - 1	8 3 6 - 17	Smith	Carleton
Indianapolis	2 0 0 - 2	8 8 7 - 23	A. Brown	Hanmer, Whitlock
Houston	0 2 1 - 3	18 11 8 - 37	Grahame	Taylor 2, Labossiere
Cleveland	0 0 0 - 0	9 13 11 - 33	Cheevers	▸ Grahame: shutout (3), 33 saves
San Diego	0 2 1 - 3	5 12 12 - 29	Blanchet	Ferguson, Devine, Lacroix
Edmonton	2 0 4 - 6	10 9 14 - 33	Plante, K. Brown	Barrie 2, MacGregor, Baird, Buchanan, Long
December 23				
Cleveland	2 1 1 - 4	19 6 12 - 37	Whidden	Cardwell, Pinder, Erickson, Krake
Toronto	0 0 1 - 1	12 9 14 - 35	Shaw	Simpson
December 26				
Minnesota	1 3 1 - 5	7 7 5 - 19	Garrett	Tannahill 2, Walton, Gallant, Antonovich
Edmonton	1 0 0 - 1	18 17 19 - 54	Plante, Worthy	Climie
Michigan	0 0 1 - 1	7 7 15 - 29	Desjardins	Serviss (spoiled D. McLeod's shutout at 19:54)
Vancouver	3 4 1 - 8	18 14 13 - 45	D. McLeod	Walton 2, Chipperfield 2, St. Sauveur, Pelyk, Burgess, Lawson
Winnipeg	1 0 2 - 3	6 6 12 - 24	Larsson	Johnson, Hedberg, Ford (WG 11:09)
Phoenix	0 1 1 - 2	10 9 10 - 29	Norris	Cormier, Gray
December 27				
Chicago	0 2 0 - 2	9 9 5 - 23	Newton	Mavety, Popiel
Toronto	1 2 1 - 4	13 11 17 - 41	Gratton	Leduc, Simpson, Henderson, Mahovlich
New England	2 1 0 - 3	11 11 12 - 34	Smith	Carleton, Pleau, Webster
Minnesota	1 1 4 - 6	7 9 11 - 27	Garrett	Walton 2, Huck, Smith, Hampson, Morrison
Quebec	0 1 2 - 3	11 14 13 - 38	Aubry	Gaudette, Bernier, Tardif (Bernier: 11 straight games with a goal)
Cleveland	2 0 2 - 4	8 12 11 - 31	Cheevers	Leduc 3, Ward
Indianapolis	1 0 0 0 1	8 4 5 3 20	Dyck	Wiste
Vancouver	0 1 0 0 1	8 4 9 7 28	D. McLeod	Price
December 28				
Michigan	0 0 1 - 1	4 7 7 - 18	Hoganson	Veneruzzo
Quebec	0 3 1 - 4	15 21 13 - 49	Brodeur	Tardif 2, Parizeau, Tremblay
Winnipeg	2 1 3 - 6	10 7 12 - 29	Larsson	Hull 2, Hedberg 2, Johnson, Ashton (WG 18:52)
San Diego	1 2 1 - 4	11 15 7 - 33	Junkin, Gillow	Morenz, Rivers, Ferguson, Peacosh
Cleveland	1 1 0 0 2	10 12 5 2 29	Whidden	Erickson, Stewart
Phoenix	0 2 0 1 3	8 13 7 4 32	Kurt	Sobchuk 2 (OT 5:49), Bennett
Minnesota	0 1 2 - 3	8 13 18 - 39	Garrett	Tannahill, Hampson, Huck
Chicago	3 1 1 - 5	18 12 15 - 45	Newton	Popiel 2, Mavety, MacGregor, Angotti
New England	0 1 0 - 1	8 6 11 - 25	Smith	Caffery
Houston	1 3 2 - 6	11 10 6 - 27	Grahame	Sherrit 2, Hughes, Lund, Irwin, Popiel
December 29				
Chicago	2 1 0 - 3	5 10 7 - 22	Newton	Paiement, Mara, Rochon
Michigan	0 1 3 - 4	10 12 15 - 37	Hoganson	Leblanc, Serviss, Guite, Evo (WG 18:47)
Indianapolis	2 0 2 0 4	9 12 11 0 32	Dyck	Sheridan, Sicinski, McDonald, Harbaruk (TG 18:54)
Edmonton	3 1 0 1 5	10 14 8 4 36	Plante	Gilmore 2 (OT 3:37), Climie, Patenaude, Joyal
Winnipeg	1 2 0 - 3	5 20 5 - 30	Larsson	Hull 2, Nilsson
Houston	1 0 5 - 6	15 8 18 - 41	Rutledge	Taylor 3, Hughes, Mk Howe, Hall
Cleveland	0 0 0 - 0	10 7 6 - 23	Cheevers	▸ Garrett: shutout (2), 23 saves
Minnesota	4 0 2 - 6	16 9 12 - 37	Garrett	Morrison 3, Tannahill, Connelly, Walton
December 30				
Phoenix	3 1 2 - 6	12 15 11 - 38	Kurt	Borgeson 3, Boyd, Sobchuk, Odrowski
Quebec	3 0 0 - 3	12 3 25 - 40	Brodeur	Bernier, Houle, Hoganson
December 31				
Phoenix	0 1 0 0 1	9 9 12 5 35	Norris	Gray
Michigan	0 1 0 0 1	11 7 11 3 32	Desjardins	Miszuk
Chicago	0 3 1 - 4	6 16 8 - 30	Dryden	Popiel, Liddington, Mara, Backstrom (WG 7:59)
Cleveland	0 2 1 - 3	11 12 21 - 44	Cheevers	W. Hillman, Ward, Harrison
January 1				
San Diego	1 0 1 0 2	9 8 7 4 28	Gillow	Sentes, Peacosh
Edmonton	1 1 0 1 3	10 11 5 5 31	Plante	Gilmore, MacGregor, Patenaude (OT 5:26)
Cleveland	1 1 0 - 2	20 6 12 - 38	Whidden	Harrison, McDonough
Minnesota	2 2 2 - 6	8 13 18 - 39	Garrett	Hampson 2, Connelly, Walton, D. O'Shea, Smith
Indianapolis	0 2 1 - 3	5 13 8 - 26	A. Brown	Whitlock 2, Fitchner
Quebec	1 2 3 - 6	16 16 11 - 43	Aubry	Cloutier 2, Houle 2, Tardif, Guindon

1974-1975 Game by Game Line Scores

Date & Teams	Scoring 1 2 3 ot F	Shots 1 2 3 ot F	Goaltenders	Goals & Other Scoring Highlights
January 2				
Indianapolis	0 1 0 - 1	8 14 10 - 32	Dyck	Wiste
Cleveland	1 1 2 - 4	9 13 17 - 39	Cheevers	Leduc 2, McDonough, Harrison
Michigan	1 2 0 - 3	8 8 5 - 21	Desjardins	Caron 2, Veneruzzo
Houston	2 1 3 - 6	7 19 12 - 38	Grahame	Lund 3, Hale, Taylor, Schella
Phoenix	0 1 1 0 2	6 7 10 0 23	Kurt	Stevens, Sobchuk
Vancouver	1 1 0 1 3	5 11 9 2 27	D. McLeod	Jones 2 (OT 2:17), Price
January 3				
New England	2 1 2 - 5	7 12 5 - 24	Smith	Pleau 2, Carleton, Caffery, O'Donnell
Toronto	3 0 0 - 3	10 11 10 - 31	Gratton	Featherstone, Mahovlich, Dillon (Tor: led 3-0 at 5:37)
San Diego	1 1 0 - 2	9 12 6 - 27	Junkin	Bradley, Sentes
Minnesota	0 1 0 - 1	9 13 8 - 30	Garrett	Tannahill
Phoenix	1 1 1 0 3	9 8 13 4 34	Norris, Kurt	Borgeson, Migneault, McNamee
Edmonton	2 1 0 0 3	14 12 8 2 36	Worthy	Baird, Long, Climie
January 4				
Michigan	1 1 0 - 2	10 5 7 - 22	Hoganson	Veneruzzo, Brown
Houston	3 1 1 - 5	15 15 7 - 37	Rutledge	Hinse, Mty Howe, Taylor, Mk Howe, Popiel
San Diego	0 0 2 - 2	10 10 12 - 32	Gillow	Morenz, Scharf
Cleveland	0 0 0 - 0	14 11 10 - 35	Cheevers	▸ Gillow: shutout (1), 35 saves
Indianapolis	1 2 1 0 4	11 11 9 4 35	A. Brown, Dyck	Whitlock 3, McDonald
Chicago	1 2 1 0 4	9 8 14 4 35	Dryden	Maggs 2, Mara, Paiement
Vancouver	0 2 1 0 3	9 16 8 0 33	D. McLeod	Gulka, Jones, Lawson (TG 19:42)
New England	0 1 2 1 4	10 13 16 2 41	Smith	Blackburn 2 (OT 1:25), Webster, Byers
Toronto	0 1 0 - 1	3 16 8 - 27	Gratton	Dillon
Quebec	0 0 3 - 3	13 20 12 - 45	Aubry	Sutherland, Bordeleau, Guindon
January 5				
Vancouver	0 1 0 - 1	7 6 8 - 21	D. McLeod	St. Sauveur
Michigan	0 0 3 - 3	9 15 13 - 37	Hoganson	Leblanc 2, Bredin (all 3 goals scored in last 4:56 of game)
Chicago	0 2 1 - 3	8 11 5 - 24	Dryden	Lomenda, Backstrom, Popiel
Edmonton	0 0 2 - 2	20 9 14 - 43	Plante	Sheehan, Long
New England	1 0 2 - 3	16 11 15 - 42	Smith, Ab'sson	Webster, French, Carleton
Minnesota	1 7 1 - 9	14 18 15 - 47	Garrett	Huck 3, Walton 2, Gambucci, Morrison, Connelly, Robertson
Phoenix	1 0 1 - 2	12 9 7 - 28	Kurt	Keogan, Young (WG 9:34)
Indianapolis	0 1 0 - 1	5 5 9 - 19	Dyck	Fitchner
Toronto	2 1 1 - 4	12 12 8 - 32	Shaw	Kirk, Nedomansky, Mahovlich, Simpson
Cleveland	0 1 2 - 3	17 10 17 - 44	Whidden	Jarrett, Muloin
January 7				
Winnipeg	2 0 2 0 4	12 6 10 5 33	Daley	Hedberg 2, Asmundson, Hull
Cleveland	0 3 1 0 4	8 20 7 4 39	Cheevers	Leduc 2 (TG 19:29), Holbrook, Harrison
New England	2 1 0 - 3	6 9 8 - 23	Ab'sson, Smith	Webster, Sheehy, Swain
San Diego	3 1 1 - 5	12 11 9 - 32	Gillow	Lacroix, Rivers, Ferguson, Peacosh, Sentes
Minnesota	3 1 0 - 4	17 11 7 - 35	Garrett	Arbour, Morrison, Walton, Ball
Chicago	1 0 1 - 2	10 13 20 - 43	Dryden	MacGregor, Paiement
Vancouver	1 0 1 - 2	8 10 14 - 32	D. McLeod	St. Sauveur 2
Indianapolis	1 2 1 - 4	11 10 7 - 28	A. Brown	Harbaruk, Sicinski, Bond, Johnson
Quebec	1 0 1 1 3	13 10 13 1 37	Brodeur	Tardif, Bernier, Bordeleau (OT 3:04)
Michigan	1 1 0 0 2	17 19 8 1 45	Desjardins	Caron, Bredin
Phoenix	2 0 1 - 3	12 8 13 - 33	Kurt	McNamee, Cormier, Migneault
Toronto	1 0 1 - 2	13 8 9 - 30	Shaw, Binkley	Kirk, Featherstone
January 8				
Vancouver	1 0 2 - 3	13 11 8 - 32	D. McLeod	Deadmarsh, Jones, Harris
Quebec	2 1 1 - 4	16 9 16 - 41	Aubry	Houle 2, Guindon, Bernier (WG 18:48)
January 9				
Minnesota	0 1 1 - 2	5 19 8 - 32	Garrett	Arbour, Hampson
Edmonton	0 0 3 - 3	10 15 9 - 34	Plante	MacGregor, Patenaude (TG 18:23), Rogers (WG 19:48)
Winnipeg	3 1 0 0 4	11 9 10 1 31	Daley	Ketola 2, Nilsson, Hull
Michigan	1 2 1 1 5	10 17 15 2 44	Hoganson	Serviss 2, Thomas, Evo, West (OT 4:40)
New England	1 0 0 0 1	6 10 3 2 21	Smith	Abrahamsson
Phoenix	1 0 0 0 1	9 8 7 6 30	Kurt	Cormier
January 10				
San Diego	2 1 0 - 3	10 8 14 - 32	Wakely	Lacroix, Sentes, Rivers
Toronto	1 1 2 - 4	19 13 12 - 44	Gratton	Kirk, Simpson, Martin, Nedomansky (WG 10:15)
Vancouver	1 2 1 - 4	6 14 20 - 40	D. McLeod, Wood	Lawson 2, Chipperfield, Jones
Cleveland	3 2 1 - 6	18 8 16 - 42	Whidden	Krake, Harrison, Stewart, McDonough, Leduc
Indianapolis	0 2 1 0 3	8 11 6 1 26	Dyck	Whitlock, Fitchner, Bond
Edmonton	0 0 3 0 3	3 8 16 9 36	Worthy	McKay, Sheehan, Patenaude
Quebec	3 1 2 - 6	13 9 8 - 30	Brodeur	Leclerc, Sutherland, Parizeau, Tremblay, Tardif, Houle
Winnipeg	1 0 0 - 1	12 18 11 - 41	Daley	Spring
Michigan	2 0 0 - 2	8 12 11 - 31	Desjardins	West, Bredin
Chicago	2 2 1 - 5	17 11 13 - 41	Newton	MacGregor 2, Stapleton, Mavety, Rochon
January 11				
San Diego	1 1 1 0 3	12 9 10 3 34	Wakely	Sentes 2, Rouleau
New England	2 1 0 1 4	13 11 12 2 38	Smith	Blackburn, O'Donnell, Carleton, Swain (OT 5:47)
Phoenix	2 0 2 - 4	24 4 12 - 40	Norris	Connor, Cormier, Keogan, Gray
Houston	2 1 3 - 6	9 16 19 - 44	Grahame	Lund, Hall, Hughes, Larway, Hinse, Mty Howe

1974-1975 Game by Game Line Scores

Date & Teams	Scoring 1 2 3 ot F	Shots 1 2 3 ot F	Goaltenders	Goals & Other Scoring Highlights
January 12				
Phoenix	0 2 0 - 2	7 13 11 - 31	Kurt	Borgeson, McNamee
Cleveland	0 2 2 - 4	17 8 6 - 31	Cheevers	Pinder, Jarrett, Krake, Holbrook
Toronto	2 0 5 - 7	13 9 18 - 40	Gratton	Jacques 4 (debut game), Simpson, Featherstone, Hickey
Houston	3 0 1 - 4	15 14 14 - 43	Rutledge	Hinse, Sherrit, Hughes, Mk Howe
Quebec	1 0 2 - 3	15 12 15 - 42	Brodeur	Bernier, Leclerc (WG 16:19), Tremblay
Edmonton	1 0 0 - 1	15 11 8 - 34	Plante	Long
January 14				
Toronto	2 0 2 - 4	7 10 11 - 28	Gratton, Binkley	Hickey 2, Cuddie 2
San Diego	2 4 0 - 6	15 10 7 - 32	Wakely	Bradley 2, Peacosh, Morenz, Ferguson, Rivers
Quebec	2 1 3 - 6	7 10 10 - 27	Brodeur	Bernier, Parizeau, Sutherland, Houle, Bordeleau, Tardif
Vancouver	0 2 0 - 2	12 12 17 - 41	D. McLeod	St. Sauveur, Campbell
Phoenix	1 0 1 - 2	9 10 9 - 28	Norris	Keogan 2
Chicago	2 1 2 - 5	17 15 14 - 46	Dryden	Liddington 2, Popiel, Mara, MacGregor
January 15				
Edmonton	0 1 1 - 2	6 10 4 - 20	K. Brown, Worthy	Barrie, McKay
Houston	4 1 4 - 9	19 9 14 - 42	Grahame	Hinse 5, Labossiere, Larway, G. Howe, Hughes
Chicago	1 3 1 - 5	6 11 6 - 23	Dryden	Morris 2, Backstrom, Mavety, Paiement
New England	4 1 2 - 7	20 10 9 - 39	Smith	Pleau 2, Sheehy, Webster, French, Green, Carleton
Vancouver	1 1 2 - 4	6 6 10 - 22	D. McLeod	Israelson, Lawson, Deadmarsh, Campbell
Winnipeg	1 1 0 - 2	14 15 13 - 42	Larsson	Hedberg, Nilsson
Minnesota	2 2 0 - 4	14 11 9 - 34	Curran	Huck, Gambucci, Morrison
Cleveland	0 2 0 - 2	15 15 10 - 40	Cheevers	McDonough, Leduc
Toronto	2 0 3 0 5	6 5 16 4 31	Shaw	Cuddie, Gibbons, Nedomansky, Simpson, Henderson
Phoenix	2 2 1 0 5	9 11 10 3 33	Kurt	Boyd 2, Connor, Sobchuk, Cormier
January 16				
Cleveland	0 0 2 - 2	11 10 23 - 44	Whidden	Ward, Clearwater
Indianapolis	2 1 1 - 4	11 18 8 - 37	A. Brown	Sicinski, Sheridan, McDonald, Johnson
Edmonton	0 1 1 - 2	10 4 3 - 17	K. Brown	Sheehan, MacDonald
San Diego	2 0 1 - 3	10 13 13 - 36	Wakely	Peacosh, Sentes, Lacroix (WG 16:02)
January 17				
Edmonton	2 2 3 - 7	8 10 13 - 31	Plante, K. Brown	Baird 2, Joyal, MacDonald, Sheehan, MacGregor, Rogers
Phoenix	0 0 1 - 1	7 16 15 - 38	Kurt	Boyd
Toronto	0 0 1 - 1	11 8 12 - 31	Gratton	Henderson
New England	0 1 1 - 2	8 9 14 - 31	Abrahamsson	Byers, Webster (WG 18:48)
January 18				
Houston	2 2 0 0 4	16 13 9 0 38	Grahame	Mk Howe, Lund, Hughes, Labossiere
San Diego	0 3 1 1 5	12 16 9 1 38	Wakely	Morenz 2, Ferguson, Peacosh (TG 19:49), Rivers (WG 0:35)
Edmonton	1 0 0 - 1	7 4 4 - 15	Worthy	Sheehan
Phoenix	0 3 0 - 3	12 11 6 - 29	Norris	Ftorek, G. Sobchuk, Borgeson
New England	0 1 1 - 2	11 11 29 - 32	A. Smith, Berglund	Carleton 2
Quebec	2 4 2 - 8	16 17 12 - 45	Brodeur	Houle 3, Gaudette 2, Bernier, Tardif, Tremblay
Michigan	0 1 0 - 1	16 8 11 - 35	Hoganson	Evo
Cleveland	0 2 0 - 2	8 19 11 - 38	Cheevers	Pinder, Harrison
Minnesota	1 0 1 - 2	17 14 12 - 43	Curran	McMahon, Arbour
Chicago	0 3 0 - 3	9 13 11 - 33	Newton	Rochon, Mara, MacGregor
January 19				
Quebec	1 1 3 - 5	17 9 13 - 39	Aubry	Bernier, Sutherland, Leclerc, Tremblay, Tardif
Chicago	1 0 1 - 2	5 19 9 - 33	Newton	Mavety, Angotti
Cleveland	1 3 0 - 4	13 9 8 - 30	Cheevers	Ward 2, Leduc, McDonough
Winnipeg	1 1 7 - 9	15 14 21 - 50	Daley	Hedberg 4, Hull 2, Young, Spring, Gratton
Indianapolis	0 1 0 - 1	7 6 7 - 20	Dyck	Sheridan
Vancouver	2 2 1 - 5	10 13 12 - 35	D. McLeod	Harris 2, Campbell 2, Deadmarsh
Minnesota	0 0 3 - 3	17 11 9 - 37	Garrett	Walton, Gallant, Tannahill
New England	1 0 0 - 1	9 15 11 - 35	Smith	Webster
January 22				
Vancouver	1 1 0 - 2	8 9 8 - 25	D. McLeod	Chipperfield, Harris
Minnesota	1 0 0 - 1	17 10 8 - 35	Garrett	Gallant
Chicago	2 2 1 - 5	16 5 11 - 32	Dryden	Coates, Gordon, Paiement, Mavety, MacGregor
Phoenix	3 2 3 - 8	13 14 17 - 44	Kurt	Borgeson 3, Keogan 2, Mowat, Cormier, Gray
Indianapolis	0 1 2 - 3	9 8 10 - 27	A. Brown	McDonald, Sicinski (WG 8:12), Harbaruk
Winnipeg	1 0 0 - 1	16 12 9 - 37	Larsson, Daley	Hull
January 23				
Cleveland	1 2 2 - 5	11 11 12 - 34	Whidden	McDonough 2, Harrison 2, Ward
Quebec	1 1 1 - 3	16 17 11 - 44	Brodeur	Bernier, Houle, Tardif
Chicago	1 1 0 - 2	10 10 2 - 22	Newton	MacGregor, Baltimore
Indianapolis	1 3 0 - 4	19 11 10 - 40	A. Brown	Johnson 2, Buchanan, Sicinski
Winnipeg	0 2 1 - 3	13 14 8 - 35	Daley	Hull 2, Riihiranta
Edmonton	3 0 4 - 7	14 8 10 - 32	Plante	MacDonald 3, Rogers 2, Climie, MacGregor
Vancouver	0 1 0 - 1	10 10 15 - 35	D. McLeod, Wood	Pelyk
San Diego	2 1 3 - 6	12 16 15 - 43	Wakely	Lacroix, Ferguson, Hargreaves. Rivers, Adduono, Plumb
January 24				
New England	0 1 0 - 1	5 13 8 - 26	Smith	Carleton
Phoenix	1 1 2 - 4	12 8 8 - 28	Kurt	Boyd, Cormier, Odrowski, Bennett
Houston	1 0 4 - 5	20 16 16 - 52	Rutledge	G. Howe, Preston, Labossiere, Hinse, Popiel
Edmonton	3 2 2 - 7	11 7 5 - 23	K. Brown	MacDonald 2, Perkins, MacGregor, Long, Sheehan, Joyal
Toronto	1 1 3 - 5	13 15 13 - 41	Gratton	Hickey 2, Nedomansky, Henderson, Martin
Minnesota	1 2 4 - 7	12 9 9 - 30	Curran	Connelly 2, Smith, D. O'Shea, Gambucci, McMahon, Arbour
Winnipeg	1 1 1 0 3	13 7 3 3 26	Larsson	Johnson, Hedberg, Sjoberg
Vancouver	0 1 2 1 4	7 13 12 3 35	D. McLeod	Walton, Israelson, Pelyk (TG 17:49), Deadmarsh (OT 4:22)

1974-1975 Game by Game Line Scores

Date & Teams	Scoring 1 2 3 ot F	Shots 1 2 3 ot F	Goaltenders	Goals & Other Scoring Highlights
January 25	▶ Baltimore formed to replace defunct Michigan franchise			
New England	1 0 1 - 2	6 11 8 - 25	Smith	Sheehy, O'Donnell
San Diego	0 4 2 - 6	8 18 9 - 35	Wakely	Rivers, Morenz, Sentes, Rouleau, Hargreaves, Ferguson
Baltimore	1 0 0 - 1	12 9 12 - 33	Desjardins	Evo
Cleveland	0 1 1 - 2	16 12 11 - 39	Cheevers	Leduc, McDonough (WG 14:34)
Chicago	0 3 1 - 4	5 8 5 - 18	Newton	MacGregor 3, Paiement
Quebec	1 3 2 - 6	10 11 14 - 35	Aubry	Tardif 2, Bordeleau, Bernier, Gilbert, Houle
January 26				
Indianapolis	0 0 0 - 0	8 11 11 - 30	Dyck	▶ Kurt: shutout (2), 30 saves
Phoenix	2 3 1 - 6	7 15 9 - 31	Kurt	Boyd 2, Connor, Mowat, Keogan, Cormier
Vancouver	2 1 2 - 5	9 9 13 - 31	D. McLeod	Campbell 2, McKenzie, Israelson, Harris
Chicago	0 2 1 - 3	7 9 13 - 29	Dryden	Rochon, Mara, Baltimore
Toronto	1 3 3 - 7	15 12 11 - 38	Gratton	Mahovlich 2, Hickey 2, Jacques 2, Henderson
Edmonton	1 2 2 - 5	10 15 9 - 34	Plante	Patenaude 2, Long, Joyal, Baird
Baltimore	0 1 0 - 1	8 17 10 - 35	Hoganson	Brown
Minnesota	0 2 0 - 2	7 15 9 - 31	Garrett	Ball, Tannahill
Houston	0 2 1 - 3	15 16 9 - 40	Grahame	Mty Howe, G. Howe, Hall
Winnipeg	0 0 1 - 1	10 9 11 - 30	Daley	Spring
January 27				
Cleveland	0 0 0 - 0	10 11 14 - 35	Cheevers	▶ Smith: shutout (2), 35 saves
New England	0 1 1 - 2	6 12 8 - 26	Smith	Webster, Swain
January 28				
Quebec	0 1 3 - 4	10 6 13 - 29	Brodeur	Tardif 3, Bordeleau
Toronto	2 3 1 - 6	21 19 11 - 51	Gratton	Mahovlich 3, Martin, Henderson, Hickey
Winnipeg	2 4 3 - 9	12 20 13 - 45	Larsson, Daley	Hedberg 3, Hull 2, Spring, Johnson, Beaudin, Ketola
San Diego	1 4 2 - 7	14 21 11 - 46	Wakely	Lacroix 2, Ferguson, Morenz, Peacosh, Morrison, Sentes
Cleveland	1 1 1 - 3	10 9 14 - 33	Whidden	Erickson, Leduc, Jarrett
Chicago	2 1 1 - 4	19 9 11 - 39	Newton	Coates, Popiel, Lomenda, Liddington (WG 19:56)
Houston	0 4 1 - 5	10 13 14 - 37	Grahame	Hinse 4, Larway 2
Edmonton	3 2 2 - 7	13 9 10 - 32	Worthy	Long, Rogers, Patenaude, MacGregor, Gilmore, Baird, Joyal
Phoenix	2 0 1 - 3	13 7 14 - 34	Kurt	Sobchuk, Borgeson, Connor
Indianapolis	0 0 1 - 1	9 12 7 - 28	A. Brown	Buchanan (spoiled Kurt's shutout at 18:37)
January 29				
Baltimore	0 2 1 - 3	8 8 5 - 21	Desjardins	Bredin, West, Leblanc
New England	2 0 2 - 4	9 21 17 - 47	Smith	Sheehy, Caffery, Webster, Pleau (WG 15:23)
Phoenix	1 0 1 - 2	12 10 14 - 36	Norris	Gray, Cormier
Cleveland	2 2 2 - 6	7 9 9 - 25	Cheevers	McDonough 2, Walker 2, Neale, Stewart
January 30				
Toronto	0 2 1 - 3	14 13 16 - 43	Gratton	Nedomansky, Henderson, Hickey
Indianapolis	1 0 1 - 2	9 6 11 - 26	A. Brown	Whitlock, Harbaruk
Quebec	2 1 2 - 5	12 11 10 - 33	Aubry	Parizeau 3, Bernier, Houle
Chicago	1 1 0 - 2	8 12 15 - 35	Newton	Mavety, Paiement
Winnipeg	3 0 2 - 5	10 11 5 - 26	Daley	Hedberg 2, Miller, Spring, Hull
Phoenix	3 0 0 - 3	17 7 12 - 36	Norris	Ftorek, Borgeson, Sobchuk
Vancouver	0 1 2 - 3	9 11 13 - 33	D. McLeod	Jones, Walton, Deadmarsh
Minnesota	3 1 2 - 6	9 12 3 - 24	Garrett	Tannahill 2, Gambucci, Huck, K. O'Shea, Antonovich
January 31				
Vancouver	0 0 0 - 0	8 15 10 - 33	D. McLeod	▶ Gratton: shutout (2), 33 saves
Toronto	2 3 1 - 6	22 14 6 - 42	Gratton	Featherstone 2, Turkiewicz, Simpson, Nedomansky, Dillon
Cleveland	1 0 1 - 2	9 14 8 - 31	Cheevers	McDonough, Krake
Edmonton	0 0 0 - 0	13 6 9 - 28	Plante	▶ Cheevers: shutout (2), 28 saves
Baltimore	1 1 0 - 2	3 6 6 - 15	Hoganson	Thomas, Curtis
New England	0 2 2 - 4	13 14 14 - 41	Smith	Carleton, Blackburn, Byers, Webster
Houston	0 0 1 - 1	8 12 14 - 34	Grahame	Labossiere
Minnesota	1 2 1 - 4	11 9 11 - 31	Garrett	Gambucci, Huck, McMahon, Connelly
February 1				
Baltimore	1 0 0 - 1	7 5 14 - 26	Desjardins	Speck
Phoenix	3 4 1 - 8	16 16 7 - 39	Kurt	Ftorek 2, Borgeson, Gray, Sobchuk, McLeod, Keogan, Hughes
Quebec	1 1 0 - 2	9 10 14 - 33	Aubry	Tremblay, Gaudette
Indianapolis	1 0 0 - 1	15 8 9 - 32	A. Brown	Ash
Houston	2 3 1 - 6	12 20 14 - 46	Grahame	G. Howe, Larway, Hinse, Ruskowski, Preston, Hall
Chicago	3 0 2 - 5	13 7 9 - 29	Newton	Liddington 2, Zaine, Morris, MacGregor
February 2				
Winnipeg	2 0 2 0 4	8 13 14 1 36	Larsson	Hedberg, Hull, Sjoberg, Young
Minnesota	2 1 1 1 5	17 11 19 3 50	Garrett	Morrison 2 (OT 2:16), D. O'Shea 2, Hampson
Toronto	0 1 1 - 2	10 7 13 - 30	Gratton	Martin, Hickey
Vancouver	1 0 3 - 4	13 11 16 - 40	D. McLeod	Walton, Terbenche, Harris, McKenzie
Quebec	2 2 0 - 4	10 16 9 - 35	Brodeur	Bernier 2, Houle, Sutherland
Cleveland	1 2 0 - 3	8 15 14 - 37	Whidden	Leduc, McDonough
Houston	1 3 1 - 5	16 13 8 - 37	Rutledge	Preston 2, Mty Howe, Sherrit, Taylor
Baltimore	0 1 1 - 2	9 11 10 - 30	Hoganson	Leblanc, West
Chicago	2 0 1 0 3	15 8 10 0 33	Dryden	Harris, Zaine, Liddington
Edmonton	1 1 1 1 4	8 7 12 2 29	Worthy	Rogers, Long, Kennett, Gilmore (OT 3:16)
February 4				
Edmonton	0 0 0 1 1	9 7 7 4 27	K. Brown	Joyal (OT 4:15)
Baltimore	0 0 0 0 0	5 12 11 1 29	Desjardins	▶ K. Brown: shutout (1), 29 saves
Toronto	2 1 1 - 4	13 9 9 - 31	Binkley	Nedomansky 2, Featherstone, Gibbons
San Diego	2 1 5 - 8	11 21 14 - 46	Gillow	Rivers 3, Morrison 2, Adduono, Ferguson, Lacroix
Houston	0 2 1 1 4	9 17 7 1 34	Grahame	G. Howe, Mk Howe, Hinse, Sherrit (OT 1:08)
Indianapolis	0 1 2 0 3	10 12 13 0 35	A. Brown	Buchanan, Heatley, Hardy

1974-1975 Game by Game Line Scores

Date & Teams	Scoring 1 2 3 ot F	Shots 1 2 3 ot F	Goaltenders	Goals & Other Scoring Highlights
February 5				
San Diego	1 1 0 - 2	8 13 6 - 27	Wakely, Gillow	Lacroix, Rivers
Phoenix	2 3 4 - 9	13 17 10 - 40	Kurt	Ftorek 2, Cormier 2, Sobchuk 2, Migneault, Borgeson, Boyd
Edmonton	0 2 0 - 2	11 12 5 - 28	Plante	MacDonald, Climie
Minnesota	2 1 1 - 4	13 10 11 - 34	Garrett	Gallant, Walton, Gambucci, Hampson
Chicago	1 1 0 - 2	9 3 4 - 16	Newton	Paiement, MacGregor
Vancouver	1 1 2 - 4	6 15 14 - 35	D. McLeod	McKenzie, Pelyk, Lawson, Harris
Toronto	0 0 2 - 2	6 8 7 - 21	Gratton	Jacques, Dillon
Houston	3 1 1 - 5	18 9 8 - 35	Rutledge	Hinse, Mk Howe, Hall, Larway, Hughes
Winnipeg	1 0 1 - 2	8 11 11 - 30	Daley	Ford, Hornung
Cleveland	0 1 2 - 3	6 15 15 - 36	Cheevers	Leduc, McDonough, Ward
February 6				
Minnesota	0 1 1 0 2	16 15 6 3 40	Garrett	McMahon, Walton
San Diego	0 1 1 0 2	8 5 8 6 27	Wakely	Rivers, Sentes
Cleveland	0 2 2 - 4	11 19 13 - 43	Cheevers	Walker 2, Ward, Cardwell
Baltimore	0 0 0 - 0	13 13 9 - 35	Hoganson	▸ Cheevers: shutout (3), 35 saves
Quebec	2 1 1 - 4	10 10 7 - 27	Brodeur	Bordeleau 2, Parizeau, Guindon (WG 10:41)
Houston	2 1 0 - 3	11 14 8 - 33	Rutledge	G. Howe, Sherrit, Taylor
February 7				
Cleveland	0 1 0 - 1	8 13 8 - 29	Cheevers	McDonough
Toronto	0 2 2 - 4	17 16 12 - 45	Gratton	Henderson, Simpson, Nedomansky, Amodeo
Minnesota	0 1 0 - 1	14 6 9 - 29	Garrett	J. Carlson
Phoenix	2 1 1 - 4	8 9 15 - 32	Kurt	Borgeson, Boyd, Ftorek, Keogan *(Teams combined for 204 penalty minutes in game)*
New England	3 0 1 1 5	10 6 12 3 31	Smith	Sheehy, Webster, Selwood, Byers, Hurley (OT 8:02)
Winnipeg	1 2 1 0 4	17 14 8 3 42	Larsson	Hedberg, Hull, Nilsson, Gruen
February 8				
New England	0 0 1 - 1	4 3 12 - 19	Smith	Karlander
Vancouver	1 2 1 - 4	9 11 4 - 24	D. McLeod	Harris, Price, Chipperfield, McKenzie
Winnipeg	2 1 0 - 3	13 10 14 - 37	Daley, Larsson	Nilsson, Hull, Hedberg
Chicago	4 2 0 - 6	12 7 10 - 29	Dryden	MacGregor 2, Mara, Morris, Liddington, Rochon
Baltimore	2 2 2 - 6	6 6 12 - 24	Desjardins	Veneruzzo 2, Evo 2, White, Brown
Houston	0 2 2 - 4	8 14 8 - 30	Rutledge	Popiel 2, Mk Howe, Larway
Quebec	2 1 0 1 4	7 8 12 2 29	Aubry	Bordeleau, Bernier, Houle, Sutherland (OT 5:56)
Phoenix	2 1 0 0 3	13 9 12 5 39	Kurt	Connor 2, McLeod
Minnesota	3 1 0 - 4	10 17 13 - 40	Garrett	Carlson 2, Connelly, Arbour
San Diego	4 2 2 - 8	15 4 15 - 34	Wakely	Ferguson 2, Rivers 2, Sentes, Adduono, Hargreaves, Peacosh
February 9				
Chicago	0 2 0 - 2	5 7 14 - 26	Dryden	Rochon, Lomenda
Winnipeg	2 1 0 - 3	9 16 10 - 35	Larsson	Hedberg, Gruen, Johnson
Houston	1 2 1 - 4	12 12 6 - 30	Grahame	Taylor 2, G. Howe, Mk Howe
Cleveland	0 0 1 - 1	15 10 11 - 36	Whidden	Leduc
Phoenix	2 1 3 - 6	10 7 7 - 24	Norris	Ftorek 2, Sobchuk, McNamee, Keogan, Cormier
Edmonton	0 1 3 - 4	15 7 19 - 41	Plante	Long 2, Rogers, Baird
New England	0 0 1 - 1	12 7 7 - 26	Smith	Earl
Vancouver	2 1 2 - 5	7 19 9 - 35	D. McLeod	Pelyk, Terbenche, Myers, Chipperfield, Lawson
Indianapolis	2 0 3 - 5	11 17 8 - 36	A. Brown	Bond, Heatley, Buchanan, Fitchner, Sicinski
Toronto	0 3 4 - 7	11 24 17 - 52	Gratton	Cunningham 2, Dorey 2, Martin, Hickey, Henderson
February 10				
Chicago	1 0 0 - 1	9 7 13 - 29	Dryden	MacGregor
Indianapolis	0 3 1 - 4	7 19 9 - 35	A. Brown	Harbaruk, Buchanan, Sicinski, Johnson
February 11				
Edmonton	1 1 1 - 3	5 8 10 - 23	Plante	Long 2, Patenaude
Toronto	1 3 0 - 4	12 15 12 - 39	Gratton	Martin, Henderson, Mahovlich, Gibbons
Houston	2 2 1 - 5	8 12 14 - 34	Grahame	Labossiere, Mk Howe, Schella, Sherrit, G. Howe
Baltimore	1 0 1 - 2	10 13 7 - 30	Hoganson	Veneruzzo, White
Quebec	0 1 1 - 2	7 13 4 - 24	Brodeur	Houle, Bernier
San Diego	4 1 4 - 9	14 5 14 - 33	Wakely	Lacroix 2, Add'no, Rouleau, Sentes, Morrison, P'cosh, Rivers, Laughton
February 12				
Edmonton	1 0 1 0 2	12 12 9 4 37	Worthy	Joyal 2
New England	1 1 0 0 2	7 10 17 7 41	Smith	Swain, Sheehy
Houston	0 1 2 - 3	6 11 17 - 34	Grahame	Larway, Hinse, Schella
Minnesota	0 1 0 - 1	9 13 11 - 33	Garrett	Connelly
Toronto	2 2 3 - 7	7 11 13 - 31	Gratton	Simpson 2, Mahovlich, Dorey, Nistico, Martin, Hickey
Winnipeg	1 3 0 - 4	16 8 9 - 33	Daley	Gruen, Hedberg, Spring, Gratton
Chicago	1 0 2 - 3	10 8 11 - 29	Dryden	Lomenda 2, Rochon
Cleveland	2 2 1 - 5	12 12 15 - 39	Cheevers	Walker, Ward, Krake, Erickson, Cardwell
Phoenix	1 3 0 - 4	7 7 3 - 17	Kurt	Keogan 2, Cormier, Borgeson
Vancouver	3 1 1 - 5	6 12 3 - 21	D. McLeod, Wood	Lawson 2, Campbell, Chipperfield, Harris (WG 18:56)
February 13				
Quebec	2 1 2 - 5	9 5 8 - 22	Aubry	Parizeau, Gilbert, Tardif, Tremblay, Bernier
Phoenix	2 1 0 - 3	7 10 11 - 28	Kurt	Borgeson 2, Gray
San Diego	1 1 4 - 6	9 10 16 - 35	Wakely	Peacosh 2, Lacroix, Sentes, Rivers, Scharf
Baltimore	0 1 0 - 1	10 8 13 - 31	Desjardins	White

1974-1975 Game by Game Line Scores

Date & Teams	Scoring 1 2 3 ot F	Shots 1 2 3 ot F	Goaltenders	Goals & Other Scoring Highlights
February 14				
Houston	2 1 0 - 3	14 10 16 - 40	Grahame	Popiel, Taylor, Mk Howe
Winnipeg	1 3 1 - 5	9 19 11 - 39	Larsson	Hull 3, Nilsson, Ford (Hull: 50th goal in 50 games)
San Diego	1 0 1 - 2	13 15 10 - 38	Gillow	Sentes, Lacroix
Cleveland	1 1 1 - 3	10 14 16 - 40	Cheevers	Ward, Krake, McDonough
Indianapolis	1 1 1 0 3	6 7 9 4 26	A. Brown	Whitlock, Buchanan, Heatley
New England	2 0 1 1 4	17 10 15 5 47	Smith	Carleton, Sheehy, Ley, Webster (OT 4:22)
Quebec	0 4 3 - 7	6 15 11 - 32	Brodeur	Sutherland 3, Tardif 2, Houle, Parizeau
Minnesota	1 2 0 - 3	11 15 14 - 40	Garrett	Antonovich, Walton, Connelly
Toronto	2 1 1 - 4	8 9 7 - 24	Gratton, Shaw	Farda, Mahovlich, Featherstone, Cunningham
Edmonton	4 3 1 - 8	19 16 15 - 50	Plante, K. Brown	Rogers 2, Sheehan 2, Gilmore, Patenaude, MacGregor, Kennett
February 15				
Chicago	0 2 3 - 5	13 10 17 - 40	Newton	MacGregor 2, Baltimore, Lomenda, Coates
Baltimore	1 1 1 - 3	10 17 20 - 47	Desjardins	Serviss, Evo, Bredin
Cleveland	1 0 0 - 1	7 8 8 - 23	Whidden	Muloin
Winnipeg	2 1 2 - 5	13 12 6 - 31	Daley	Sjoberg, Spring, Gruen, Hedberg, Nilsson
February 16				
Phoenix	2 1 2 - 5	10 15 20 - 45	Norris	Boyd 2, Ftorek, Gray, McNamee (WG 18:20, disputed, in crease)
Edmonton	1 0 3 - 4	10 5 8 - 23	Plante, K. Brown	Kennett, MacDonald, Morris, Rogers
Toronto	2 1 4 - 7	13 11 11 - 35	Binkley	Simpson 2, Nedomansky, Henderson, Mahovlich, Dillon, Martin
Vancouver	0 3 1 - 4	7 19 12 - 38	D. McLeod	Campbell, Burgess, St. Sauveur, Deadmarsh
San Diego	0 1 1 - 2	8 15 13 - 36	Wakely	Peacosh, Sentes
Minnesota	1 2 2 - 5	10 8 14 - 32	Garrett	Connelly 2, Morrison, Walton, Arbour
Winnipeg	5 0 1 - 6	17 9 11 - 37	Daley	Johnson 3, Spring, Ketola, Gratton
Chicago	1 1 1 - 3	12 17 14 - 43	Newton	Liddington, Lomenda, Paiement
February 17				
Houston	3 1 1 - 5	13 9 10 - 32	Grahame	Sherrit, Preston, Mk Howe, Schella, Labossiere
Quebec	1 1 1 - 3	15 15 8 - 38	Aubry, Brodeur	Bordeleau, Houle, Jordan
Indianapolis	3 0 2 0 5	13 11 7 2 33	A. Brown	Bond, Heatley, Wiste, Whitlock, Hardy
Chicago	2 2 1 1 6	6 11 16 4 37	Dryden	Paiement, Coates, Baltimore, Lomenda, Morris, Mara (OT 5:48)
Minnesota	1 1 0 - 2	6 11 10 - 27	Curran	Gambucci, Connelly
Cleveland	0 1 0 - 1	9 12 8 - 29	Cheevers	Cardwell
February 18				
Phoenix	0 0 0 - 0	6 8 14 - 28	Kurt	▶ Wakely: shutout (1), 28 saves
San Diego	1 4 2 - 7	14 7 13 - 34	Wakely	Sentes 4, Rouleau, Ferguson, Rivers
Vancouver	5 1 3 - 9	15 11 13 - 39	D. McLeod	Israelson 2, Harris, St. Sauveur, Chipperfield, Burgess, Lawson,
Indianapolis	0 1 1 - 2	11 8 14 - 33	A. Brown, Dyck	Bond, Harbaruk McKenzie, Campbell
Winnipeg	0 2 3 - 5	3 10 22 - 35	Daley	Hull 2, Hedberg 2, Gruen
Baltimore	2 1 0 - 3	8 10 10 - 28	Hoganson	Evo, Leblanc, Veneruzzo
New England	0 2 1 - 3	14 14 10 - 38	Smith	O'Donnell, Earl, Carleton
Edmonton	5 1 0 - 6	18 7 10 - 35	K. Brown	Gilmore, Baird, Rogers, Sheehan, Morris, Joyal
February 19				
Edmonton	1 0 0 - 1	6 15 11 - 32	Worthy	Joyal
Winnipeg	2 1 1 - 4	13 16 7 - 36	Daley	Spring, Bergman, Young, Hedberg
Minnesota	3 1 1 - 5	15 8 6 - 29	Curran	Morrison, Arbour, Walton, D. O'Shea, Connelly
Cleveland	3 0 0 - 3	13 13 8 - 34	Cheevers	Walker (at 0:05), Edur, Harrison
Quebec	1 0 3 - 4	14 7 7 - 28	Brodeur, Aubry	Tardif 3, Guindon
Houston	2 3 5 - 10	11 15 16 - 42	Grahame	Mk Howe 2, Ruskowski 2, Lund 2, Taylor 2, Hall, G. Howe
February 20				
Chicago	2 1 0 1 4	15 6 12 1 34	Dryden	Lomenda, Coates, Rochon, Paiement (OT 5:42)
Toronto	1 1 1 0 3	8 11 10 6 35	Binkley, Shaw	Simpson, Featherstone, Nedomansky
Quebec	1 1 0 - 2	11 9 14 - 34	Aubry	Guindon, Cloutier
San Diego	1 2 2 - 5	17 17 13 - 47	Wakely	Peacosh 2, Rouleau, Rivers, Ferguson
Vancouver	2 0 1 - 3	13 10 11 - 34	D. McLeod	Israelson, St. Sauveur, Harris
Baltimore	3 1 0 - 4	16 6 10 - 32	Desjardins	Veneruzzo 2, Caron, Thomas
February 21				
Minnesota	1 0 1 - 2	11 2 10 - 23	Garrett	Morrison, K. O'Shea
Indianapolis	1 3 1 - 5	13 21 15 - 49	A. Brown	Wiste 2, Harbaruk, Horton, Bond
New England	1 1 2 - 4	5 8 8 - 21	Smith	Carleton 2, Caffery, Webster
Edmonton	0 1 1 - 2	8 9 11 - 28	Plante, K. Brown	Gilmore, Sheehy
February 22				
Toronto	0 1 2 - 3	9 15 16 - 40	Shaw	Kirk 2, Mahovlich
Cleveland	2 1 1 - 4	7 14 7 - 28	Cheevers	Harrison 2, Ward, Shmyr
Phoenix	0 1 2 - 3	14 13 11 - 38	Kurt	Cormier, Keogan, Ftorek
Baltimore	1 0 0 - 1	8 10 12 - 30	Desjardins	White
Vancouver	2 0 2 - 4	11 10 8 - 29	D. McLeod	Lawson, St. Sauveur, Campbell, McKenzie
Houston	1 0 1 - 2	9 16 10 - 35	Grahame	Taylor, G. Howe
February 23				
Minnesota	2 2 0 - 4	10 14 12 - 36	Garrett	Connelly 2, Walton, D. O'Shea
Edmonton	4 2 0 - 6	19 12 10 - 41	K. Brown	Long 2, Sheehy, Patenaude, Sheehan, MacGregor
San Diego	1 2 1 - 4	6 14 10 - 30	Wakely	Rivers 3, Morenz
Quebec	3 1 2 - 6	20 11 7 - 38	Aubry	Leclerc 2, Cloutier, Bordeleau, Tardif, Houle
Cleveland	0 0 0 - 0	11 10 15 - 36	Whidden	▶ A. Brown: shutout (2), 36 saves
Indianapolis	2 3 1 - 6	11 9 9 - 29	A. Brown	Heatley 2, Bond, Sheridan, Buchanan, Wiste
Vancouver	0 0 1 - 1	6 11 14 - 31	D. McLeod	McKenzie
Chicago	0 1 1 - 2	10 12 19 - 41	Dryden	Coates, MacGregor (WG 5:46)
Toronto	0 0 1 - 1	6 9 13 - 28	Gratton, Binkley	Nedomansky
Houston	2 2 1 - 5	24 15 15 - 54	Rutledge	Hinse 2, Mk Howe, Lund, Preston
New England	0 0 1 1 2	7 6 8 2 23	Smith	Blackburn, Webster (OT 5:21)
Winnipeg	0 1 0 0 1	12 6 16 2 36	Daley	Hedberg

1974-1975 Game by Game Line Scores

Date & Teams	Scoring 1	2	3	ot	F	Shots 1	2	3	ot	F	Goaltenders	Goals & Other Scoring Highlights
February 24												
San Diego	0	0	3	-	3	7	8	15	-	30	Gillow	Rivers, Howell, Morrison
Quebec	1	0	4	-	5	10	13	15	-	38	Brodeur	Bordeleau, Tardif, Gilbert, Houle, Cloutier
February 25												
Edmonton	1	1	1	0	3	15	15	12	0	42	Worthy	Rogers 2, MacDonald
Chicago	0	2	1	1	4	11	11	15	1	38	Dryden	Mara, Mavety, Rochon, MacGregor (OT 0:11)
Indianapolis	0	4	2	-	6	5	10	7	-	22	A. Brown	Bond, Sicinski, Buchanan, Harbaruk, McDonald, Whitlock
Baltimore	1	3	0	-	4	20	17	9	-	46	Hoganson, Des'dins	White, Caron, B. Legge, Evo
Vancouver	0	1	1	-	2	6	11	9	-	26	D. McLeod	St. Sauveur, Harris
New England	0	1	2	-	3	8	9	14	-	31	Smith	Webster, Fotiu, Blackburn
Minnesota	2	3	1	0	6	13	12	10	4	39	Curran	Walton, Morrison, Connelly, Carlson, Hampson, Ball
Winnipeg	1	3	2	0	6	15	11	12	4	42	Daley	Hedberg 2, Hornung, Johnson, Hull, Nilsson
San Diego	2	1	1	-	4	9	5	15	-	29	Wakely	Lacroix 2, Peacosh, Morrison
Toronto	2	3	1	-	6	16	17	7	-	40	Gratton	Mahovlich 2, Nistico, Nedomansky, Hickey, Dorey
February 26												
Chicago	2	0	2	-	4	11	7	12	-	30	Dryden	Coates 2 (WG 19:54), Morris, MacGregor
New England	1	0	2	-	3	17	10	13	-	40	Landon	Karlander, Carleton, Byers
Indianapolis	0	1	2	0	3	5	11	15	2	33	Dyck	McDonald, Wiste, Sheridan (TG 19:42)
Minnesota	1	0	2	1	4	14	12	10	5	41	Garrett	Gambucci, Walton, Morrison, K. O'Shea (OT 4:58)
Cleveland	1	2	2	-	5	6	15	7	-	28	Cheevers, Whidden	McDonough 2, Ward, Leduc, Holbrook
Houston	5	3	1	-	9	11	13	9	-	33	Grahame	Hughes 2, Labossiere 2, Popiel, Sherrit, Mk Howe, Preston, G. Howe
February 27												
Houston	3	2	2	-	7	7	11	12	-	30	Rutledge	Mk Howe 2, Larway 2, Hughes 2, Preston
Phoenix	1	0	1	-	2	11	9	19	-	39	Kurt	Gray 2
Minnesota	1	1	0	-	2	10	10	11	-	31	Curran	Carlson, Walton
New England	1	3	1	-	5	12	15	15	-	42	Smith	Blackburn, Climie, Green, Carleton, Caffery
Vancouver	2	4	1	-	7	13	9	13	-	35	D. McLeod	St. Sauveur 3, Israelson, Walton, Harris, Campbell
Quebec	2	4	3	-	9	11	21	15	-	47	Brodeur	Cloutier 3, S. Bernier 2, Parizeau, J. Bernier, Tardif, Leclerc
February 28												
Baltimore	1	1	0	-	2	12	10	9	-	31	Desjardins	Thomas, Serviss
Edmonton	2	2	2	-	6	6	8	11	-	25	K. Brown	MacGregor 2, Rogers 2, Sheehy, Kerslake
San Diego	1	1	1	-	3	11	8	11	-	30	Wakely	Rivers, Morenz, Sentes
Winnipeg	1	1	2	-	4	10	15	11	-	36	Daley	Hull 2 (WG 17:17), Young 2
March 1												
Indianapolis	2	0	0	-	2	6	10	5	-	21	A. Brown	Fitchner, Buchanan
Phoenix	3	6	3	-	12	12	17	15	-	44	Norris	Sobchuk 2, Ftorek 2, Cormier 2, Boyd 2, Gray 2, Mowat 2
Minnesota	2	1	1	-	4	10	12	8	-	30	Garrett	Tannahill, Gallant, Antonovich, Morrison
Quebec	0	1	0	-	1	11	17	8	-	36	Aubry	Parizeau
Chicago	0	1	1	-	2	14	9	13	-	36	Dryden	MacGregor, Backstrom
Houston	0	2	2	-	4	12	14	10	-	36	Rutledge	Taylor 2, Hughes, Larway
Cleveland	0	2	2	0	4	11	13	8	2	34	Cheevers	Leduc, Walker, Harrison, Shmyr (TG 19:39)
New England	1	1	2	0	4	12	8	10	9	39	Smith	Climie, Webster, O'Donnell, Pleau
March 2												
Vancouver	0	0	1	-	1	9	8	5	-	22	D. McLeod	Price
New England	2	1	1	-	4	4	7	10	-	21	Landon	Pleau, Webster, Green, French
Indianapolis	0	1	2	0	3	13	5	8	1	27	Dyck	Sheridan, Whitlock, Sicinski
Houston	0	1	2	1	4	15	11	10	4	40	Grahame	Ruskowski, Labossiere, Lund, Hinse (OT 3:00)
Chicago	0	0	0	-	0	7	12	8	-	27	Dryden	▸ Norris: shutout (1), 27 saves
Phoenix	2	2	1	-	5	8	13	8	-	29	Norris	Ftorek 2, Sobchuk 2, Keogan
San Diego	1	1	2	0	4	12	8	9	4	33	Wakely	Hargreaves, Peacosh, Ferguson, Sentes
Winnipeg	1	3	0	0	4	21	11	5	5	42	Daley	Johnson, Hull, Beaudin, Hedberg
Toronto	1	2	0	-	3	10	10	8	-	28	Gratton, Binkley	Nedomansky, Hickey, Kirk
Minnesota	1	4	0	-	5	9	17	6	-	32	Curran	Tannahill 2, Walton, Antonovich, Morrison
Baltimore	0	2	0	-	2	10	7	12	-	29	Hoganson	Thomas, Caron
Edmonton	1	3	3	-	7	11	14	13	-	38	Worthy	Sheehy 2, Rogers, Kerslake, Baird, MacDonald, Barrie
March 4												
Cleveland	1	1	1	-	3	5	10	5	-	20	Cheevers	McDonough, Ward, Pinder
Edmonton	0	0	1	-	1	14	10	11	-	35	K. Brown	Morris
Baltimore	1	1	2	-	4	11	11	10	-	32	Hog'son, J. McLeod	B. Legge, Sittler, Thomas, Leblanc
Toronto	2	1	3	-	6	13	13	17	-	43	Binkley	Nedomansky 2, Dorey, Jacques, Mahovlich, Nistico
Quebec	1	0	1	-	2	13	12	8	-	33	Brodeur, Aubry	Gilbert, Bernier
San Diego	4	3	1	-	8	18	11	12	-	41	Wakely	Morenz 2, Plumb 2, Adduono, Rivers, Lacroix, Peacosh
March 5												
Edmonton	0	0	0	-	0	6	11	9	-	26	Plante, K. Brown	▸ D. McLeod: shutout (1), 26 saves
Vancouver	2	3	1	-	6	11	13	9	-	33	D. McLeod	Walton 2, Lawson, Campbell, McKenzie, Burgess
Indianapolis	1	2	2	-	5	9	10	11	-	30	A. Brown	Harbaruk 2, McDonald, Whitlock, Wiste
Baltimore	0	1	1	-	2	15	9	12	-	36	J. McLeod	Bredin, Leblanc
Quebec	2	0	1	-	3	6	11	8	-	25	Aubry	Leclerc, Bernier, Guindon
Phoenix	2	2	2	-	6	14	18	16	-	48	Norris	Sobchuk 2, Gray, Ftorek, Borgeson, Cormier
Cleveland	0	1	1	-	2	11	7	7	-	25	Cheevers	Ward, Jarrett
Winnipeg	1	1	2	-	4	11	9	15	-	35	Daley	Nilsson 2, Black, Hull
New England	1	1	1	-	3	10	5	16	-	31	Smith	Byers, Carleton, Blackburn
Minnesota	1	1	3	-	5	7	10	11	-	28	Garrett	Antonovich 2, Morrison 2, Connelly
March 6												
Houston	0	3	1	-	4	7	13	8	-	28	Rutledge	Labossiere, Hughes, Preston, Hinse
San Diego	2	2	3	-	7	5	11	12	-	28	Wakely	Rivers 2, Adduono 2, Laughton, Peacosh, Sentes

1974-1975 Game by Game Line Scores

Date & Teams	Scoring 1 2 3 ot F	Shots 1 2 3 ot F	Goaltenders	Goals & Other Scoring Highlights
March 7				
Winnipeg	2 1 1 - 4	6 7 7 - 20	Daley	Hull 2, Hedberg 2
Phoenix	2 2 3 - 7	13 10 14 - 37	Kurt	Sobchuk 2, Hughes, Keogan, Gray, Odrowski, Borgeson
Quebec	0 3 1 - 4	14 16 12 - 42	Brodeur	Leclerc 2, Houle, Tremblay
Toronto	1 0 0 - 1	8 16 16 - 40	Gratton	Martin
Vancouver	0 0 0 - 0	13 9 9 - 31	D. McLeod	▸ K. Brown: shutout (2), 31 saves
Edmonton	0 1 3 - 4	7 7 14 - 28	K. Brown	Joyal, Baird, Laing, McKay
Baltimore	1 2 1 1 5	11 12 10 2 35	Hoganson	Veneruzzo 2, Bredin, White, Thomas (OT 2:48)
Indianapolis	0 1 3 0 4	11 13 12 0 36	A. Brown	Fitchner 2 (TG 18:29), Buchanan, Sheridan
March 8				
Winnipeg	2 0 3 - 5	14 7 12 - 33	Larsson	Young, Hornung, Ford, Hedberg, Beaudin
San Diego	1 3 2 - 6	12 21 6 - 39	Wakely	Sentes 3, Plumb, Bradley, Ferguson
New England	0 2 3 - 5	5 14 10 - 29	Smith	Green, Selwood, Abrahamsson, Carleton, Pleau
Houston	3 0 1 - 4	8 10 13 - 31	Grahame	Hinse 2, Schella, Mty Howe
Toronto	2 2 3 - 7	14 14 12 - 40	Shaw, Gratton	Mahovlich 2, Nistico 2, Dillon, Nedomansky, Simpson
Baltimore	1 1 2 - 4	17 6 9 - 32	Hoganson	Bredin, Caron, B. Legge, Veneruzzo
Cleveland	1 3 2 - 6	15 15 6 - 36	Cheevers	McDonough 2, Leduc, Shmyr, Erickson, W. Hillman (WG 15:41)
Indianapolis	1 3 1 - 5	9 19 10 - 38	A. Brown	Heatley 2, Fitchner, Bond, Sicinski
March 9				
Winnipeg	1 1 3 1 6	5 14 18 4 41	Daley	Ketola 2 (TG 19:50, OT 3:02), Young, Hull, Hornung, Miller
Minnesota	2 2 1 0 5	10 14 12 2 38	Curran	Walton 2, Smith, Gambucci, Tannahill
Chicago	1 2 2 - 5	9 12 12 - 33	Newton	Paiement 2, Morris, Coates, Gordon
Quebec	1 4 2 - 7	7 18 16 - 41	Brodeur	Parizeau 2, Houle, Cloutier, Bernier, Sutherland, Tardif
Phoenix	0 1 2 - 3	9 10 8 - 27	Norris	Ftorek 2, Gray
Vancouver	2 1 1 - 4	7 15 9 - 31	D. McLeod	Walton 2, Harris, Burgess
Baltimore	0 1 1 - 2	14 7 11 - 32	Hog'son, J. McLeod	Veneruzzo 2
Toronto	0 5 3 - 8	11 22 13 - 46	Gratton	Nedomansky 2, Jacques, Dillon, H'derson, Mahovlich, Simpson, Dorey
March 10				
Edmonton	1 1 1 - 3	12 9 10 - 31	K. Brown	Joyal 2, McKay
Baltimore	0 2 3 - 5	12 7 8 - 27	Hoganson	Caron, Serviss, Bredin, Leblanc, Richardson
March 11				
Winnipeg	1 0 1 - 2	12 5 10 - 27	Daley	Young 2
New England	0 3 3 - 6	16 11 10 - 37	Smith	O'Donnell 3, Hurley, Carleton, Selwood
Edmonton	4 1 0 - 5	17 11 8 - 36	Worthy	Perkins, MacDonald, MacGregor, Sheehan, Long
Chicago	0 0 1 - 1	9 17 15 - 41	Coutu	Morris
Minnesota	3 0 3 - 6	9 4 8 - 21	Garrett	Gallant 2, D. O'Shea, Gambucci, Antonovich, Huck
San Diego	0 2 2 - 4	14 17 9 - 40	Wakely	Rivers, Morenz, Lacroix, Sentes
Phoenix	4 0 0 - 4	12 10 10 - 32	Kurt	Migneault, Borgeson, Boyd, Gray
Toronto	1 3 3 - 7	10 11 17 - 38	Binkley, Gratton	Simpson 2, Featherstone 2, Hickey, Dillon, Dorey
March 12				
Baltimore	0 2 0 - 2	11 15 6 - 32	Hoganson	Bredin, Veneruzzo
Cleveland	0 0 0 - 0	9 8 10 - 27	Whidden	▸ Hoganson: shutout (2), 27 saves
Winnipeg	1 2 0 - 3	9 8 13 - 30	Larsson	Hull 2, Miller
Quebec	3 1 1 - 5	20 14 16 - 50	Aubry	Cloutier 2, Sutherland, Parizeau, Gilbert
Minnesota	0 1 1 - 2	11 6 9 - 26	Garrett	Walton, Butters
Vancouver	0 1 3 - 4	3 12 12 - 27	D. McLeod	Burgess, Walton, St. Sauveur, Lawson
March 13				
Toronto	3 1 0 - 4	10 12 15 - 37	Shaw	Jacques, Hickey, Nistico, Kirk
Indianapolis	2 2 1 - 5	19 17 12 - 48	Dyck	Whitlock 2, Buchanan 2 (WG 8:38), Proceviat
Phoenix	2 2 1 0 5	10 10 5 2 27	Norris	Ftorek 2, Sobchuk, Gray, Mowat
New England	2 1 2 0 5	8 12 12 4 36	Landon, Smith	Webster 2, Blackburn, Pleau, Carleton
March 14				
Edmonton	0 0 0 - 0	10 13 6 - 29	Worthy	▸ Cheevers: shutout (4), 29 saves
Cleveland	1 1 1 - 3	5 13 7 - 25	Cheevers	Shmyr, Krake, Leduc
San Diego	1 2 3 - 6	14 15 19 - 48	Wakely, Gillow	Peacosh 2, Laughton, Ferguson, Rivers, Falkenberg
Toronto	1 2 1 - 4	18 22 19 - 59	Gratton, Shaw	Simpson 2, Nistico, Dillon
Houston	2 2 1 - 5	9 18 11 - 38	Grahame	Mk Howe, Hughes, G. Howe, Popiel, Hinse
Chicago	3 1 0 - 4	18 8 8 - 34	Newton	Backstrom 2, Lomenda, Liddington
Quebec	1 2 0 - 3	10 8 8 - 26	Brodeur	Bordeleau 2, Hoganson
Winnipeg	1 2 1 - 4	12 20 19 - 51	Daley	Young, Hedberg, Gruen, Hull (WG 11:36)
March 15				
Baltimore	1 1 1 - 3	11 9 6 - 26	Hoganson	Leblanc, Bredin, White
Indianapolis	1 3 3 - 7	9 10 10 - 29	Dyck	Bond 2, Buchanan 2, Sicinski, Kannegiesser, McDonald
Edmonton	0 0 2 - 2	6 15 6 - 27	Plante, K. Brown	Rogers, Morris
New England	2 1 3 - 6	6 9 10 - 25	Smith, Berglund	Pleau 3, Caffery, Climie, Webster
Quebec	0 2 2 - 4	15 6 9 - 30	Aubry	Parizeau, Lacombe, Houle, Cloutier
Vancouver	1 3 3 - 7	8 17 19 - 44	D. McLeod	Walton 2, Pelyk 2, Harris, Campbell, Chipperfield
March 16				
Quebec	0 1 1 - 2	4 12 15 - 31	Brodeur	Bernier 2
Vancouver	1 2 1 - 4	8 11 15 - 34	D. McLeod	Walton, Chipperfield, Harris, Rupp
Houston	1 1 0 - 2	7 8 7 - 22	Grahame	Hughes, Mty Howe
Cleveland	0 1 0 - 1	10 17 8 - 35	Cheevers	Krake
San Diego	1 0 1 - 2	9 10 11 - 30	Wakely	Sentes, Morenz
Chicago	1 2 1 - 4	8 6 8 - 22	Dryden	Rochon 3, MacGregor
Edmonton	0 0 1 - 1	13 8 6 - 27	Worthy, K. Brown	Sheehy
Winnipeg	4 3 3 - 10	12 10 16 - 38	Larsson	Hull 3, Ketola 2, Black, Nilsson, Beaudin, Spring, Ford
Toronto	2 2 1 - 5	11 17 12 - 40	Shaw	Dillon, Kirk, Dorey, Hickey, Farda
New England	4 2 1 - 7	20 7 9 - 36	Smith	Byers 2, O'Donnell, Karlander, Ley, Climie, Pleau

1974-1975 Game by Game Line Scores

Date & Teams	Scoring 1 2 3 ot F	Shots 1 2 3 ot F	Goaltenders	Goals & Other Scoring Highlights
March 17				
Cleveland	1 1 0 - 2	17 16 7 - 40	Cheevers	McDonough, Erickson
Chicago	0 1 2 - 3	14 11 20 - 45	Dryden	MacGregor, Morris, Gordon (WG 10:23)
Houston	1 2 1 - 4	8 12 9 - 29	Rutledge	G. Howe 2, Labossiere, Mty Howe
Toronto	4 0 1 - 5	13 13 11 - 37	Gratton	Simpson 2, Featherstone, Nistico, Turkiewicz (WG 18:58)
March 18				
Phoenix	3 2 2 - 7	9 15 14 - 38	Norris, Kurt	Keogan 2, Gray 2, McNamee 2, Boyd
Chicago	1 1 1 - 3	11 8 15 - 34	Newton	Lomenda, Morris, MacGregor
Quebec	1 3 1 - 5	4 13 8 - 25	Brodeur	Tardif 2, Hoganson, Bernier, Houle
Edmonton	4 2 2 - 8	10 15 13 - 38	Worthy	Kerslake 2 (0:12 apart, 1st), MacGregor 2, Joyal 2, Sheehan, Laing
Minnesota	3 0 2 - 5	13 8 7 - 28	Curran	Connelly, Morrison, K O'Shea, Hampson, Walton
Vancouver	1 0 2 - 3	8 8 15 - 31	D. McLeod	Lawson, Israelson, McKenzie
March 19				
Vancouver	1 1 1 - 3	8 11 6 - 25	D. McLeod	Harris, Walton, McKenzie
Winnipeg	4 1 3 - 8	17 8 18 - 43	Larsson	Hull 2, Bergman, Sjoberg, Beaudin, Nilsson, Young, Hedberg
San Diego	3 2 1 - 6	9 9 9 - 27	Gillow	Ferguson, Laughton, Hargreaves, Lacroix, Peacosh, Plumb
New England	0 0 1 - 1	8 14 12 - 34	Smith, Landon	Webster (Lacroix: points in 32 straight games)
Phoenix	1 3 0 - 4	8 18 8 - 34	Kurt	Boyd 2, Migneault, Cormier
Cleveland	2 1 2 - 5	10 10 13 - 33	Cheevers	Leduc 2, Jarrett, Pinder, Holbrook (WG 18:16)
Indianapolis	3 1 1 - 5	12 6 7 - 25	Dyck	Heatley 2, Whitlock, Wiste, Buchanan
Houston	1 2 3 - 6	12 15 14 - 41	Grahame	Schella 2, Mk Howe 2, Popiel, Hughes
March 20				
Quebec	2 0 1 - 3	8 8 13 - 29	Brodeur	Bernier, Houle, Cloutier
Houston	1 2 2 - 5	11 17 13 - 41	Rutledge	Hall 2, Taylor, Labossiere, Mk Howe
Chicago	0 1 3 - 4	5 5 10 - 20	Dryden	Rochon, MacGregor, Lomenda, Paiement
San Diego	2 0 0 - 2	9 10 9 - 28	Wakely	Laughton, Ferguson
Edmonton	0 1 0 - 1	10 11 5 - 26	Plante	McKay
Indianapolis	1 0 2 - 3	7 6 8 - 21	A. Brown	Harbaruk, McDonald, Fitchner
March 21				
Winnipeg	0 2 4 - 6	9 12 13 - 34	Daley	Hedberg 3, Spring, Hull, Miller
New England	1 1 1 - 3	15 12 10 - 37	Smith	Carleton, Climie, Byers
March 22				
Houston	2 3 0 - 5	14 19 17 - 50	Grahame	Mk Howe 2, Hall 2, Mty Howe
New England	2 1 0 - 3	10 10 5 - 25	Landon	Webster, Byers, Blackburn
Edmonton	1 0 0 - 1	13 12 10 - 35	Worthy	MacDonald
Cleveland	2 0 3 - 5	21 9 12 - 42	Cheevers	Ward 2, Leduc 2, Jarrett
Vancouver	1 1 0 - 2	6 10 6 - 22	D. McLeod	Lawson, Chipperfield
Phoenix	1 1 2 - 4	11 8 10 - 29	Kurt	Boyd, Gray, Ftorek, Sobchuk
Winnipeg	0 2 2 - 4	8 18 11 - 37	Daley	Hull, Gruen, Johnson, Beaudin
Chicago	1 0 1 - 2	13 14 13 - 40	Dryden	Paiement 2
Indianapolis	1 0 2 - 3	7 4 8 - 19	A. Brown	Bond, Harbaruk, Heatley
San Diego	3 3 0 - 6	12 10 5 - 27	Wakely	Sentes 3, Hardy, Lacroix, Rivers
March 23				
Edmonton	0 2 0 - 2	14 16 12 - 42	K. Brown	Rogers, McKay
Minnesota	0 1 3 - 4	15 13 19 - 47	Garrett	Gambucci 2, Connelly, Arbour
Chicago	0 1 2 - 3	6 6 10 - 22	Dryden	Popiel, Coates, Backstrom
Winnipeg	0 1 3 - 4	10 9 13 - 32	Daley	Hedberg 2, Beaudin, Ketola (WG 18:50)
Indianapolis	0 2 1 - 3	8 9 10 - 27	Dyck	Sheridan, Heatley, Bond
Phoenix	2 2 1 - 5	10 8 7 - 25	Norris	Gray 2, McNamee, Ftorek, Borgeson
Vancouver	0 0 0 0 - 0	6 7 10 0 23	D. McLeod	▶ Wakely: shutout (3), 23 saves
San Diego	0 0 0 1 - 1	19 12 10 2 43	Wakely	Lacroix (OT 0:59)
March 25				
Vancouver	1 3 0 - 4	19 10 10 - 39	D. McLeod, Wood	St. Sauveur, Lawson, Driscoll, Price
Toronto	3 1 4 - 8	9 10 16 - 35	Gratton	Simpson 4, Dorey, Featherstone, Dillon, Martin
Baltimore	1 2 1 - 4	9 12 5 - 26	J. McLeod	Evo, Richardson, Leblanc, Curtis
Minnesota	3 2 0 - 5	7 10 11 - 28	Curran	Connelly 2, Walton 2, Arbour
Edmonton	1 0 3 - 4	9 8 11 - 28	K. Brown	Rogers 3, Perkins
New England	2 1 2 - 5	11 14 8 - 33	Smith	Abrahamsson, Carleton, Climie, Byers, O'Donnell
Winnipeg	2 1 0 1 4	12 13 4 1 30	Larsson	Hull 2, Gruen, Beaudin (OT 1:32)
Indianapolis	0 1 2 0 3	16 8 15 - 39	A. Brown	Horton, Harbaruk, Sheridan
San Diego	2 4 0 - 6	12 13 14 - 39	Wakely	Peacosh 3 (in 6:01, 2nd), Rivers, Morenz, Ferguson
Chicago	1 2 1 - 4	17 7 14 - 38	Dryden	Liddington, Coates, Morris, MacGregor
March 26				
Edmonton	0 3 3 - 6	13 10 13 - 36	Worthy	Perkins 2, Baird, MacGregor, Gilmore, Joyal
Quebec	1 0 3 - 4	13 8 4 - 25	Brodeur	Tremblay, Houle, Patry, Tardif
Chicago	1 2 0 - 3	8 10 7 - 25	Dryden	Maggs, Mara, Paiement
Minnesota	1 1 2 - 4	15 13 12 - 40	Garrett	Tannahill, Gallant, Gambucci, Connelly (WG 13:59)
Houston	0 1 0 - 1	14 8 5 - 27	Rutledge	Lund
Phoenix	0 1 1 - 2	11 13 9 - 33	Norris	Gray, Hughes (WG 12:52)
Vancouver	2 0 0 - 2	8 4 8 - 20	Wood	McKenzie, Driscoll
Cleveland	1 1 2 - 4	9 10 14 - 33	Cheevers	Harrison, Cardwell, Ward, Leduc
San Diego	3 0 2 - 5	16 11 17 - 44	Gillow	Hargreaves 2, Devine, Morrison, Adduono
Baltimore	0 1 1 - 2	5 14 7 - 26	Hoganson	Evo, Bredin

1974-1975 Game by Game Line Scores

Date & Teams	Scoring 1 2 3 ot F	Shots 1 2 3 ot F	Goaltenders	Goals & Other Scoring Highlights
March 27				
Winnipeg	0 0 0 - 0	10 9 7 - 26	Larsson	▸ Grahame: shutout (4), 26 saves (G. Howe: 2000th career point)
Houston	1 2 5 - 8	1310 9 - 32	Grahame	G. Howe 2, Irwin, Hall, Lund, Sherrit, Taylor, Mk Howe
San Diego	2 2 1 - 5	1713 8 - 38	Wakely	Morrison, Peacosh, Scharf, Lacroix, Devine
Indianapolis	1 0 1 - 2	111117 - 39	Dyck	Heatley, McDonald
Edmonton	1 1 0 0 2	8 1211 3 34	Plante	Baird, Sheehy
Baltimore	0 0 2 0 2	1315 8 8 44	Hoganson	Veneruzzo, Bredin
Cleveland	0 3 0 - 3	9 1610 - 35	Cheevers	McDonough, Krake, Ward
New England	1 3 1 - 5	1315 9 - 37	Smith	Carleton, Selwood, O'Donnell, French, Green
March 28				
Edmonton	1 2 1 - 4	9 11 7 - 27	Worthy	MacGregor, Sheehy, MacDonald, Baird
Toronto	2 1 2 - 5	16 8 11 - 35	Gratton	Dillon 2, Nedomansky, Mahovlich, Simpson
Minnesota	0 0 2 0 2	12 8 171047	Garrett	Tannahill, Antonovich
Phoenix	1 0 1 0 2	10 9 16 5 40	Norris	Keogan, Ftorek
March 29				
Indianapolis	2 2 1 - 5	171214 - 43	A. Brown, Dyck	Heatley 2, Sicinski 2, McDonald
Cleveland	2 3 2 - 7	191710 - 46	Whidden	Harrison, Muloin, McDonough, Jarrett, Stewart, Leduc, Holbrook
San Diego	4 1 2 - 7	8 8 7 - 23	Wakely	Sentes 3, Morrison, Hargreaves, Peacosh, Laughton
Vancouver	1 2 0 - 3	161016 - 42	D. McLeod	St. Sauveur, Jones, Pelyk
Winnipeg	1 4 4 - 9	6 149 - 29	Daley	Hull 3, Miller 2, Hedberg, Bergman, Ketola, Beaudin
New England	1 1 1 - 3	121213 - 37	Smith	Hurley, Climie, Pleau
Minnesota	2 0 0 - 2	9 8 9 - 26	Curran	Ball, Gambucci
Houston	1 4 3 - 8	172021 - 58	Rutledge	Hinse, Mk Howe, Taylor, G. Howe, Hall, Ruskowski, Mty Howe
Toronto	1 1 2 1 5	1411 13 3 41	Gratton	Martin 2, Hickey, Kirk, Mahovlich (OT 7:55)
Quebec	1 2 1 0 4	121214 7 45	Brodeur	Cloutier, Bernier, Tardif, Houle (TG 19:26)
March 30				
Chicago	0 3 3 - 6	3 1515 - 33	Dryden	Coates, Morris, Gordon, Baltimore, Rochon, Paiement
Cleveland	1 4 2 - 7	121117 - 40	Cheevers	Leduc 2, Jarrett 2, Cardwell 2, Edur
Baltimore	1 1 1 - 3	8 159 - 32	Hoganson	White, Richardson, Veneruzzo
Vancouver	1 1 2 - 4	8 4 15 - 27	Wood	Campbell, Jones, Israelson, Walton (WG 14:38)
Indianapolis	0 2 1 - 3	6 9 13 - 28	Dyck	Fitchner, Whitlock, Bond
Minnesota	1 3 1 - 5	1613 9 - 38	Garrett	Ball, Walton, K O'Shea, Smith, Arbour
New England	3 1 0 - 4	1210 4 - 26	Landon	Blackburn 2, Caffery, Climie
Toronto	1 0 2 - 3	15 9 16 - 40	Gratton, Binkley	Nedomansky, Dorey, Nistico
Phoenix	2 2 1 - 5	151510 3 43	Kurt	Ftorek 2, Hughes, Keogan, Boyd
Quebec	2 3 0 1 6	9 14 5 2 30	Aubry	Houle 2, Tardif 2, Tremblay, Leclerc (OT 3:34)
March 31				
Indianapolis	1 0 0 - 1	4 6 9 - 19	A. Brown, Dyck	Wiste
Winnipeg	2 1 1 - 4	1012 6 - 28	Daley	Young 2, Ketola, Hedberg
San Diego	3 2 0 - 5	10 7 7 - 24	Gillow	Peacosh, Ferguson, Sentes, Devine, Hardy
Edmonton	1 1 0 - 2	11 4 11 - 26	Plante, K. Brown	MacDonald, Kennett
April 1				
Quebec	1 2 2 - 5	131014 - 37	Aubry	Gaudette 2, Tardif, Leclerc, Bernier
Edmonton	0 2 1 - 3	6 8 13 - 27	Worthy	MacGregor, Carlyle, Joyal
Phoenix	0 3 0 - 3	9 11 5 - 25	Norris	McNamee, Cormier, Gray
New England	3 1 1 - 5	12 6 8 - 26	Smith	O'Donnell 2, Byers 2, Blackburn
Indianapolis	0 0 1 - 1	8 14 5 - 27	A. Brown	McDonald
Toronto	1 2 4 - 7	141113 - 38	Binkley	Nedomansky, Dorey, Jacques, Marrin, F'therstone, Nistico, Turkiewicz
Cleveland	0 1 1 0 2	121615 0 43	Whidden	Holbrook, Cardwell (TG 19:02)
Chicago	0 2 0 1 3	1117 6 3 37	Dryden	MacGregor 2, Morris (OT 3:37)
Vancouver	0 1 1 - 2	19 5 10 - 34	D. McLeod	Jodzio, Lawson
Minnesota	0 2 3 - 5	101111 - 32	Curran, Garrett	Huck, Connelly, Tannahill, Morrison, Antonovich
Baltimore	1 3 0 - 4	8 9 5 - 22	Hoganson	Andrascik, Richardson, West, White
San Diego	0 2 1 - 3	9 16 6 - 31	Wakely	Rivers 2, Lacroix
April 2				
Vancouver	2 4 0 - 6	5 15 6 - 26	D. McLeod	Lawson 3, Israelson 2, Burgess
Winnipeg	0 4 0 - 4	9 1617 - 42	Daley	Ketola, Gruen, Hedberg, Nilsson
Cleveland	1 2 3 - 6	9 9 11 - 29	Cheevers	Harrison 2, Jarrett, McDonough, Ward, Holbrook
Houston	4 1 2 - 7	151712 - 44	Grahame	Hughes 2, Taylor, Labossiere, Lund, Larway, Mk Howe
Quebec	0 2 3 - 5	111713 - 41	Brodeur	Bernier, Bordeleau, Hoganson, Tardif, Houle
Minnesota	1 2 0 - 3	1516 6 - 37	Garrett	Huck, Antonovich, Walton
April 3				
Baltimore	0 0 2 - 2	8 9 9 - 26	Hoganson	Serviss, Richardson
San Diego	2 4 3 - 9	221015 - 47	Wakely	Ferguson 2, Plumb 2, Sentes, Laughton, Lacroix, Adduono, Rivers
Quebec	0 0 1 - 1	3 6 11 - 20	Aubry	Lacombe
New England	1 2 1 - 4	1213 6 - 34	Smith	Blackburn 2, Carleton, Webster
April 4				
Vancouver	1 0 2 - 3	11 7 12 - 30	Wood	Burgess, Pelyk, Campbell
Edmonton	1 3 1 - 5	8 1112 - 31	K. Brown	Joyal, Sheehan, Long, Baird, Barrie
New England	0 0 1 - 1	5 2019 - 44	Landon	Webster
Chicago	2 1 0 - 3	13 7 9 - 29	Dryden	Watson, Stapleton, Paiement
Winnipeg	0 0 1 - 1	10 7 11 - 28	Larsson	Hedberg
Toronto	1 2 4 - 7	181618 - 52	Shaw	Marrin 2, Featherstone, Nistico, Jacques, Mahovlich, Simpson
Phoenix	1 1 0 - 2	121212 - 36	Norris	Borgeson, Niekamp
Minnesota	0 1 0 - 1	8 8 8 - 24	Garrett	Connelly

1974-1975 Game by Game Line Scores

Date & Teams	Scoring 1 2 3 ot F	Shots 1 2 3 ot F	Goaltenders	Goals & Other Scoring Highlights
April 5				
Indianapolis	1 1 1 - 3	11 8 6 - 25	Dyck	McDonald 2, Buchanan
San Diego	2 2 4 - 8	14 19 25 - 58	Wakely	Sentes 3, Lacroix 2, Peacosh, Morrison, Morenz
Winnipeg	1 1 3 - 5	15 11 16 - 42	Daley	Bergman, Nilsson, Hedberg, Miller, Hull
Quebec	3 3 3 - 9	14 11 17 - 42	Brodeur	Houle 2, Sutherland 2, Bernier, Tardif, Parizeau, Hoganson, Guindon
Baltimore	1 4 1 1 7	7 10 11 6 34	J. McLeod, Hog'son	West 3 (OT 9:28, e.n.), Richardson, Serviss, Andrascik, Veneruzzo
Phoenix	2 2 2 0 6	11 11 10 5 37	Kurt	Boyd 2, Ftorek 2, Migneault, Gray (TG 19:45)
Minnesota	0 1 1 - 2	10 7 12 - 29	Garrett	Butters, Antonovich
Houston	1 5 2 - 8	11 22 15 - 48	Rutledge	Hughes 3, Hall, Labossiere, Mty Howe, Mk Howe, Lund
New England	1 0 1 - 2	7 16 11 - 34	Smith	Pleau, Webster
Cleveland	2 2 1 - 5	9 15 6 - 30	Whidden	Ward 2, Leduc, McDonough, Clearwater
Edmonton	0 1 1 - 2	8 10 5 - 23	Worthy	McKay, Barrie
Vancouver	0 0 3 - 3	6 8 17 - 31	D. McLeod	Harris, Pelyk (TG 18:33), St. Sauveur (WG 19:40)
April 6				
San Diego	1 2 2 0 5	10 9 13 3 35	Gillow	Sentes 2 (TG 18:40), Howell, Ferguson, Lacroix
Winnipeg	1 2 2 0 5	13 8 8 8 37	Larsson	Nilsson, Hedberg, Hull (77th goal), Hornung, Ford
Houston	2 2 1 - 5	18 10 8 - 36	Grahame	Sherrit 2, Hughes 2, Mk Howe
Toronto	0 1 1 - 2	14 10 17 - 41	Shaw	Mahovlich, Dillon
Indianapolis	1 1 1 - 3	6 8 12 - 26	Dion	Harbaruk, Sicinski, Proceviat
Vancouver	2 2 0 - 4	11 13 14 - 38	D. McLeod	Harris 2, Pelyk, Burgess
Minnesota	2 1 2 1 6	14 9 6 1 30	McCartan	Gambucci 3 (OT 0:21), Antonovich, Arbour, Connelly (TG 19:52)
Baltimore	3 1 1 0 5	14 13 11 0 38	Hoganson	Richardson, West, Veneruzzo, Leblanc, Evo
Chicago	0 1 2 - 3	10 15 9 - 34	Dryden, Dumas	Popiel 2, Baltimore
Edmonton	3 0 3 - 6	17 9 19 - 45	K. Brown	MacGregor 2, Long, Baird, Sheehan, Rogers
April 7				
Houston	0 1 1 - 2	9 22 13 - 44	Rutledge	Hall, G. Howe
Baltimore	1 3 0 - 4	14 13 11 - 38	J. McLeod	Evo, Larose, Veneruzzo, Zrymiak

End of Regular Season

1975 Playoffs Game by Game Line Scores

Date & Teams	Scoring 1 2 3 ot F	Shots 1 2 3 ot F	Goaltenders	Goals & Other Scoring Highlights
April 8				
Phoenix	0 1 1 - 2	10 8 21 - 39	Norris	Ftorek, Sobchuk
Quebec	2 3 0 - 5	10 8 6 - 24	Brodeur	Houle 2, Leclerc 2, Parizeau
April 9				
Toronto	2 1 0 - 3	10 14 4 - 28	Shaw	Nistico, Nedomansky, Kirk
San Diego	1 2 2 - 5	16 12 16 - 44	Wakely	Adduono 2, Peacosh, Rivers, Lacroix
Minnesota	2 3 1 - 6	13 15 8 - 36	Garrett	Connelly 2, Gallant, Butters, Gambucci, Walton
New England	2 2 1 - 5	13 13 10 - 36	Smith	Pleau 2, Climie, Carleton, French
April 10				
Phoenix	1 0 1 - 2	14 12 17 - 43	Norris, Kurt	Boyd, McNamee
Quebec	1 4 1 - 6	7 8 7 - 22	Brodeur	Bernier 2, Tardif, Guindon, Bordeleau, Houle
Cleveland	2 1 2 - 5	8 6 11 - 25	Cheevers	Shmyr 2, Harrison, Edur, Pinder
Houston	3 1 4 - 8	14 13 9 - 36	Grahame	Mk Howe 3, Hughes 2, Ruskowski, Taylor, Hall
April 11				
Minnesota	0 1 1 0 2	9 9 10 4 32	Garrett	Morrison, Busniuk
New England	1 1 0 1 3	10 11 10 3 34	Smith	Carlton, Selwood, Ley (OT 6:46)
April 12				
Toronto	0 2 4 - 6	15 12 13 - 40	Gratton, Shaw	Mahovlich, Nedomansky, Kirk, Dorey, Nistico, Martin
San Diego	3 3 1 - 7	13 23 10 - 46	Wakely	Peacosh 2, Hargreaves, Lacroix, Ferguson, Howell, Rivers
Quebec	1 2 0 - 3	7 4 7 - 18	Brodeur	Bernier, Tardif, Houle
Phoenix	0 0 0 - 0	6 8 18 - 32	Kurt	▸ Brodeur: shutout (1), 32 saves
Cleveland	1 0 2 - 3	15 11 11 - 37	Cheevers	McDonough, Pinder, Walker
Houston	1 1 3 - 5	10 17 8 - 35	Grahame	Hall 2, Larway, Lund, Mk Howe
April 13				
New England	0 2 1 - 3	8 10 10 - 28	Smith	Climie 2, Byers
Minnesota	3 3 2 - 8	10 11 10 - 31	Garrett	Morrison 2, Ball 2, Huck, Walton, Smith, Busniuk
Houston	0 1 0 - 1	8 13 15 - 36	Grahame	Mk Howe
Cleveland	0 1 2 - 3	9 10 18 - 37	Cheevers	McDonough, L. Hillman, Edur
April 14				
San Diego	0 2 0 - 2	11 7 10 - 28	Wakely, Gillow	Ferguson 2
Toronto	2 2 1 - 5	17 12 12 - 41	Binkley	Nistico 2, Kirk, Simpson, Dillon

1975 Playoffs Game by Game Line Scores

Date & Teams	Scoring 1 2 3 ot F	Shots 1 2 3 ot F	Goaltenders	Goals & Other Scoring Highlights
April 15				
Houston	2 0 5 - 7	13 13 9 - 35	Grahame	Mk Howe 3, Hall 2, Hinse, Hughes
Cleveland	0 0 2 - 2	12 9 15 - 36	Cheevers	Krake, Clearwater
Quebec	2 3 0 0 5	10 9 6 3 28	Brodeur	Bernier 2, Guindon 2, Houle
Phoenix	4 1 0 1 6	10 15 7 6 38	Kurt	Sobchuk 2, Grayt, Ftorek, Bennett, Cormier (OT 7:21)
New England	0 1 4 - 5	6 8 14 - 28	Smith	Fotiu 2, Carleton, Earl, Blackburn
Minnesota	1 1 0 - 2	12 11 10 - 33	Garrett	Gambucci, Connelly
April 16				
San Diego	1 1 3 - 5	8 14 9 - 31	Wakely	Laughton 2, Ferguson. Peacosh, Perry
Toronto	0 4 2 - 6	10 17 18 - 45	Shaw	Dillon 2, Nistico, Featherstone, Mahovlich, Kirk
April 17				
Cleveland	0 1 0 - 1	10 9 9 - 28	Cheevers	Pinder
Houston	2 0 1 - 3	19 7 14 - 40	Grahame	G. Howe, Lund, Taylor
Phoenix	0 2 0 - 2	14 15 10 - 39	Kurt	Gray, Sobchuk
Quebec	0 2 2 - 4	8 11 13 - 32	Brodeur	Leclerc, Gilbert, Tardif, Bernier
April 18				
Toronto	1 1 1 - 3	9 13 15 - 37	Shaw	Mahovlich, Nedomansky, Kirk
San Diego	0 2 2 - 4	14 19 22 - 55	Wakely	Peacosh 2 (WG 11:59), Laughton, Adduono
Minnesota	0 1 3 - 4	6 13 10 - 29	Garrett	Connelly 2, Huck, Walton
New England	0 0 0 - 0	9 5 13 - 27	Smith	▶ Garrett: shutout (1), 27 saves
April 19				
New England	0 0 1 - 1	7 15 11 - 33	Smith	Byers
Minnesota	2 1 3 - 6	9 10 12 - 31	Garrett	Walton 2, Gambucci, Connelly, Tannahill
April 21				
San Diego	2 2 2 - 6	13 14 12 - 39	Wakely	Ferguson 2, Adduono, Devine, Peacosh, Lacroix
Toronto	0 2 2 - 4	15 13 17 - 45	Binkley	Nistico, Dillon, Dorey, Featherstone
April 22				
Minnesota	0 0 1 - 1	12 9 10 - 31	Garrett	Walton (spoiled Brodeur's shutout at 19:27)
Quebec	1 0 3 - 4	15 17 6 - 38	Brodeur	Gilbert 2, Leclerc, Houle
April 24				
Minnesota	0 4 1 - 5	17 20 10 - 47	Garrett	Walton 2, Morrison, Smith, Antonovich
Quebec	2 1 0 - 3	9 9 8 - 26	Brodeur	Tardif 2, Globensky
April 25				
Houston	1 2 1 - 4	11 13 11 - 35	Grahame	Hinse, Hall, Ruskowski, Labossiere
San Diego	0 0 0 - 0	14 12 9 - 35	Wakely	▶ Grahame: shutout (1), 35 saves
April 26				
Quebec	3 1 2 - 6	12 13 15 - 40	Brodeur	Tardif, Houle, Bernier, Cloutier, Guindon, Leclerc
Minnesota	1 0 0 - 1	11 5 12 - 28	Garrett	Hampson
April 27				
Houston	0 2 0 - 2	6 9 8 - 23	Grahame	Hall, Sherrit
San Diego	0 0 1 - 1	18 11 19 - 48	Wakely	Rivers
Quebec	1 1 0 - 2	14 16 11 - 41	Brodeur	Bernier, Guindon
Minnesota	1 1 2 - 4	14 15 9 - 38	Garrett	Ball, Tannahill, Huck, Connelly
April 29				
Minnesota	0 2 1 - 3	8 18 12 - 38	Garrett	Connelly, Walton, Morrison
Quebec	2 2 2 - 6	17 10 14 - 41	Brodeur	Cloutier 2, Guindon, Bordeleau, Tardif, Leclerc
San Diego	0 0 0 - 0	16 6 12 - 34	Wakely, Gillow	▶ Grahame: shutout (2), 34 saves
Houston	2 2 2 - 6	12 12 13 - 37	Grahame	Hinse 2, Mk Howe, Labossiere, Lund, G. Howe
May 1				
Quebec	2 0 2 - 4	14 6 14 - 34	Brodeur	Cloutier, Leclerc, Parizeau, Houle
Minnesota	1 0 1 - 2	13 14 11 - 38	Garrett	Gambucci, Carlson
San Diego	2 1 1 0 4	17 8 12 0 37	Gillow, Wakely	Plumb 2, Adduono, Laughton
Houston	1 1 2 1 5	11 16 22 1 50	Grahame	Sherrit 2 (OT 0:27), Preston, Larway, G. Howe
May 3				
Quebec	0 1 1 - 2	7 8 10 - 25	Brodeur	Tardif, Guindon
Houston	4 1 1 - 6	11 10 15 - 36	Grahame	Labossiere 2, Lund, G. Howe, Ruskowski, Larway
May 6				
Quebec	1 1 1 - 3	8 9 9 - 26	Brodeur	Tardif 2, Hoganson
Houston	1 1 3 - 5	10 15 22 - 47	Grahame	G. Howe 2, Labossiere, Ruskowski, Hinse
May 10				
Houston	0 1 1 - 2	5 8 11 - 24	Grahame	Hughes, Popiel
Quebec	0 0 0 - 0	13 6 15 - 34	Brodeur	▶ Grahame: shutout (3), 34 saves
May 12				
Houston	3 2 2 - 7	12 11 8 - 31	Grahame	G. Howe 2, Hughes 2, Mk Howe, Labossiere, Lund
Quebec	1 1 0 - 2	12 18 8 - 38	Brodeur	Houle 2

Houston is League Champion

187

1974-1975 CHICAGO COUGARS

Player-Coach
Pat Stapleton

Bench Coach
Jacques Demers

Summary of Games (@ Away, * Overtime)

	date	opponent	score		record	pts	gf-ga
1	Oct 18 @	Vancouver	2-1	W	1-0-0	2	2-1
2	Oct 20 @	Vancouver	1-3	L	1-1-0	2	3-4
3	Oct 27 @	Minnesota	*5-6	L	1-2-0	2	8-10
4	Oct 29	Houston	2-4	L	1-3-0	2	10-14
5	Oct 30	Houston	0-1	L	1-4-0	2	10-15
6	Oct 31 @	San Diego	3-4	L	1-5-0	2	13-19
7	Nov 2	Toronto	4-3	W	2-5-0	4	17-22
8	Nov 5	Vancouver	4-5	L	2-6-0	4	21-27
9	Nov 10	Toronto	0-7	L	2-7-0	4	21-34
10	Nov 12	San Diego	2-4	L	2-8-0	4	23-38
11	Nov 14 @	Michigan	2-4	L	2-9-0	4	25-42
12	Nov 16 @	Houston	2-6	L	2-10-0	4	27-48
13	Nov 19	New England	4-5	L	2-11-0	4	31-53
14	Nov 20	Indianapolis	6-4	W	3-11-0	6	37-57
15	Nov 22	Michigan	5-3	W	4-11-0	8	42-60
16	Nov 23 @	New England	2-3	L	4-12-0	8	44-63
17	Nov 24	New England	5-9	L	4-13-0	8	49-72
18	Nov 27 @	Phoenix	4-2	W	5-13-0	10	53-74
19	Nov 28 @	San Diego	3-2	W	6-13-0	12	56-76
20	Nov 30 @	Minnesota	7-5	W	7-13-0	14	63-81
21	Dec 5 @	Indianapolis	5-3	W	8-13-0	16	68-84
22	Dec 7	Toronto	9-3	W	9-13-0	18	77-87
23	Dec 8 @	Winnipeg	2-5	L	9-14-0	18	79-92
24	Dec 10	Phoenix	2-4	L	9-15-0	18	81-96
25	Dec 14	Michigan	6-0	W	10-15-0	20	87-96
26	Dec 17	Quebec	1-6	L	10-16-0	20	88-102
27	Dec 20 @	Quebec	5-3	W	11-16-0	22	93-105
28	Dec 21	Edmonton	0-3	L	11-17-0	22	93-108
29	Dec 22 @	Toronto	2-5	L	11-18-0	22	95-113
30	Dec 27 @	Toronto	2-4	L	11-19-0	22	97-117
31	Dec 28	Minnesota	5-3	W	12-19-0	24	102-120
32	Dec 29 @	Michigan	3-4	L	12-20-0	24	105-124
33	Dec 31 @	Cleveland	4-3	W	13-20-0	26	109-127
34	Jan 4	Indianapolis	4-4	T	13-20-1	27	113-131
35	Jan 5 @	Edmonton	3-2	W	14-20-1	29	116-133
36	Jan 7	Minnesota	2-4	L	14-21-1	29	118-137
37	Jan 10	Michigan	5-2	W	15-21-1	31	123-139
38	Jan 14	Phoenix	5-2	W	16-21-1	33	128-141
39	Jan 15 @	New England	5-7	L	16-22-1	33	133-148
40	Jan 18	Minnesota	3-2	W	17-22-1	35	136-150
41	Jan 19	Quebec	2-5	L	17-23-1	35	138-155
42	Jan 22 @	Phoenix	5-8	L	17-24-1	35	143-163
43	Jan 23 @	Indianapolis	2-4	L	17-25-1	35	145-167
44	Jan 25 @	Quebec	4-6	L	17-26-1	35	149-173
45	Jan 26	Vancouver	3-5	L	17-27-1	35	152-178
46	Jan 28	Cleveland	4-3	W	18-27-1	37	156-181
47	Jan 30	Quebec	2-5	L	18-28-1	37	158-186
48	Feb 1	Houston	5-6	L	18-29-1	37	163-192
49	Feb 2 @	Edmonton	*3-4	L	18-30-1	37	166-196
50	Feb 5 @	Vancouver	2-4	L	18-31-1	37	168-200
51	Feb 8	Winnipeg	6-3	W	19-31-1	39	174-203
52	Feb 9 @	Winnipeg	2-3	L	19-32-1	39	176-206
53	Feb 10 @	Indianapolis	1-4	L	19-33-1	39	177-210
54	Feb 12 @	Cleveland	3-5	L	19-34-1	39	180-215
55	Feb 15 @	Baltimore	5-3	W	20-34-1	41	185-218
56	Feb 16	Winnipeg	3-6	L	20-35-1	41	188-224
57	Feb 17	Indianapolis	6-5	W	21-35-1	43	194-229
58	Feb 20 @	Toronto	4-3	W	22-35-1	45	198-232
59	Feb 23	Vancouver	2-1	W	23-35-1	47	200-233
60	Feb 25	Edmonton	*4-3	W	24-35-1	49	204-236
61	Feb 26 @	New England	4-3	W	25-35-1	51	208-239
62	Mar 1 @	Houston	2-4	L	25-36-1	51	210-243
63	Mar 2 @	Phoenix	0-5	L	25-37-1	51	210-248
64	Mar 9 @	Quebec	5-7	L	25-38-1	51	215-255
65	Mar 11	Edmonton	1-5	L	25-39-1	51	216-260
66	Mar 14	Houston	4-5	L	25-40-1	51	220-265
67	Mar 16	San Diego	4-2	W	26-40-1	53	224-267
68	Mar 17	Cleveland	3-2	W	27-40-1	55	227-269
69	Mar 18	Phoenix	3-7	L	27-41-1	55	230-276
70	Mar 20 @	San Diego	4-2	W	28-41-1	57	234-278
71	Mar 22	Winnipeg	2-4	L	28-42-1	57	236-282
72	Mar 23 @	Winnipeg	3-4	L	28-43-1	57	239-286
73	Mar 25	San Diego	4-6	L	28-44-1	57	243-292
74	Mar 26 @	Minnesota	3-4	L	28-45-1	57	246-296
75	Mar 30 @	Cleveland	6-7	L	28-46-1	57	252-303
76	Apr 1	Cleveland	*3-2	W	29-46-1	59	255-305
77	Apr 4	New England	3-1	W	30-46-1	61	258-306
78	Apr 6 @	Edmonton	3-6	L	30-47-1	61	261-312

Cougars Stars of 1974-1975

| **Gary MacGregor** | **Darryl Maggs** | **Francois Rochon** | **Dave Dryden** | **Peter Mara** | **Mark Lomenda** |
| 42 goals | +17 rating | 27 goals | 18 wins, shutout | 38 points, +7 rating | 16 goals |

Scoring

pos	#	player	gp	g	a	pts	pim	+/-	ppg	shg	sog	sc%	gp	g	a	pts	pim
C	17	Angotti, Lou	26	2	5	7	9	-1	0	1	14	0.143	-	-	-	-	-
C	14	Backstrom, Ralph	70	15	24	39	28	-28	6	0	161	0.093	-	-	-	-	-
D	18	Baltimore, Bryon	77	8	12	20	110	-24	0	0	104	0.077	-	-	-	-	-
RW	22	Benzelock, Jim	10	0	2	2	14		0	0	5	0.000	-	-	-	-	-
LW	11	Coates, Brian	35	12	9	21	26	-6	1	0	62	0.194	-	-	-	-	-
G	25	Coutu, Rich	1	0	0	0	0		0	0	0	-	-	-	-	-	-
G	1	Dryden, Dave	45	0	1	1	4		0	0	0	-	-	-	-	-	-
G		Dumas, Rich	1	0	0	0	0		0	0	0	-	-	-	-	-	-
RW	16	Gordon, Don	42	4	5	9	10	-14	1	0	49	0.082	-	-	-	-	-
C	25	Hardy, Joe	17	1	6	7	8		0	0	14	0.071	-	-	-	-	-
RW	20	Harris, Duke	54	9	19	28	18	-13	4	0	109	0.083	-	-	-	-	-
D	3	Kokkola, Keith	33	0	2	2	69	-4	0	0	47	0.000	-	-	-	-	-
LW	7	Liddington, Bob	78	23	18	41	27	-31	5	0	155	0.148	-	-	-	-	-
RW	24	Lomenda, Mark	69	16	33	49	21	-2	2	0	128	0.125	-	-	-	-	-
C	6	MacGregor, Gary	78	42	34	76	26	+3	8	0	269	0.164	-	-	-	-	-
D	4	Maggs, Darryl	77	6	27	33	137	+17	0	1	213	0.028	-	-	-	-	-
C	23	Mara, Peter	57	17	21	38	16	+7	1	0	90	0.189	-	-	-	-	-
D	21	Mavety, Larry	57	10	22	32	126	-3	3	0	169	0.059	-	-	-	-	-
D	2	McCallum, Dunc	31	0	10	10	24	-6	0	0	28	0.000	-	-	-	-	-
LW	10	Morris, Rick	78	15	13	28	110	-14	0	2	115	0.130	-	-	-	-	-
G	30	Newton, Cam	32	0	0	0	0		0	0	0	-	-	-	-	-	-
RW	9	Paiement, Rosaire	78	26	48	74	97	0	3	0	256	0.101	-	-	-	-	-
LW	19	Popiel, Jan	60	18	22	40	74	-1	3	0	97	0.186	-	-	-	-	-
D	23	Pritchard, Jim	2	0	0	0	0		0	0	2	0.000	-	-	-	-	-
D	3	Proceviat, Dick	11	0	3	3	11	-6	0	0	11	0.000	-	-	-	-	-
LW	15	Rochon, Francois	69	27	29	56	19	+8	5	0	160	0.169	-	-	-	-	-
D	12	Stapleton, Pat	68	4	30	34	38	-9	2	0	105	0.038	-	-	-	-	-
C	17	Walter, Dave	6	1	0	1	2		0	0	14	0.071	-	-	-	-	-
D	5	Watson, Jim	37	2	6	8	31	-8	0	0	62	0.048	-	-	-	-	-
C	8	Zaine, Rod	68	3	6	9	16	-6	0	1	28	0.107	-	-	-	-	-

Power Play: 46 goals scored in 237 opportunities (19.4%) with 11 short-handed goals allowed.
Penalty Killing: 58 goals allowed in 282 opportunities (79.4%) with 6 short-handed goals scored.

Goaltending

goaltender	gp	min	ga	en	so	record	gaa	sog	sv%	gp	min	ga	record	gaa
Coutu, Rich	1	60	5	0	0	0-1-0	5.00	36	0.861	-	-	-	-	-
Dryden, Dave	45	2728	176	3	1	18-26-1	3.87	1679	0.895	-	-	-	-	-
Dumas, Rich	1	1	0	0	0	0-0-0	0.00	0	-	-	-	-	-	-
Newton, Cam	32	1905	126	2	0	12-20-0	3.97	1196	0.895	-	-	-	-	-

Transactions: Peter Mara signed to contract, Sep 1974 • Dunc McCallum signed to contract, Nov 1974 • Joe Hardy to Indianapolis for future considerations, Dec. 1974 • Dick Proceviat to Indianapolis for future considerations, Dec. 1974 • Larry Mavety to Toronto for draft picks, Feb. 1975

1974-1975 CLEVELAND CRUSADERS

**Coach
John Hanna
14-18-1**

**Coach
Jack Vivian
21-22-1**

Summary of Games (@ Away, * Overtime)

	date	opponent	score		record	pts	gf-ga		date	opponent	score		record	pts	gf-ga
1	Oct 19 @	Minnesota	3-1	W	1-0-0	2	3-1	40	Jan 16 @	Indianapolis	2-4	L	16-22-2	34	113-131
2	Oct 20 @	Phoenix	4-4	T	1-0-1	3	7-5	41	Jan 18	Michigan	2-1	W	17-22-2	36	115-132
3	Oct 22 @	San Diego	2-5	L	1-1-1	3	9-10	42	Jan 19 @	Winnipeg	4-9	L	17-23-2	36	119-141
4	Oct 23 @	Vancouver	1-4	L	1-2-1	3	10-14	43	Jan 23 @	Quebec	5-3	W	18-23-2	38	124-144
5	Oct 31 @	Michigan	4-2	W	2-2-1	5	14-16	44	Jan 25	Baltimore	2-1	W	19-23-2	40	126-145
6	Nov 2	Edmonton	2-4	L	2-3-1	5	16-20	45	Jan 27 @	New England	0-2	L	19-24-2	40	126-147
7	Nov 8 @	Vancouver	2-1	W	3-3-1	7	18-21	46	Jan 28 @	Chicago	3-4	L	19-25-2	40	129-151
8	Nov 10 @	Edmonton	1-4	L	3-4-1	7	19-25	47	Jan 29	Phoenix	6-2	W	20-25-2	42	135-153
9	Nov 14 @	Phoenix	2-1	W	4-4-1	9	21-26	48	Jan 31 @	Edmonton	2-0	W	21-25-2	44	137-153
10	Nov 15 @	San Diego	5-3	W	5-4-1	11	26-29	49	Feb 2	Quebec	3-4	L	21-26-2	44	140-157
11	Nov 19	Toronto	5-6	L	5-5-1	11	31-35	50	Feb 5	Winnipeg	3-2	W	22-26-2	46	143-159
12	Nov 22 @	Quebec	2-3	L	5-6-1	11	33-38	51	Feb 6 @	Baltimore	4-0	W	23-26-2	48	147-159
13	Nov 24	Quebec	3-1	W	6-6-1	13	36-39	52	Feb 7 @	Toronto	1-4	L	23-27-2	48	148-163
14	Nov 27	Winnipeg	*5-4	W	7-6-1	15	41-43	53	Feb 9	Houston	1-4	L	23-28-2	48	149-167
15	Nov 29	Indianapolis	4-2	W	8-6-1	17	45-45	54	Feb 12	Chicago	5-3	W	24-28-2	50	154-170
16	Nov 30 @	Houston	5-4	W	9-6-1	19	50-49	55	Feb 14	San Diego	3-2	W	25-28-2	52	157-172
17	Dec 4	New England	2-3	L	9-7-1	19	52-52	56	Feb 15 @	Winnipeg	1-5	L	25-29-2	52	158-177
18	Dec 7	San Diego	3-1	W	10-7-1	21	55-53	57	Feb 17	Minnesota	1-2	L	25-30-2	52	159-179
19	Dec 10	Vancouver	3-4	L	10-8-1	21	58-57	58	Feb 19	Minnesota	3-5	L	25-31-2	52	162-184
20	Dec 12 @	Quebec	2-5	L	10-9-1	21	60-62	59	Feb 22	Toronto	4-3	W	26-31-2	54	166-187
21	Dec 13 @	Toronto	*6-7	L	10-10-1	21	66-69	60	Feb 23 @	Indianapolis	0-6	L	26-32-2	54	166-193
22	Dec 15 @	Vancouver	1-2	L	10-11-1	21	67-71	61	Feb 26 @	Houston	5-9	L	26-33-2	54	171-202
23	Dec 17 @	San Diego	3-8	L	10-12-1	21	70-79	62	Mar 1 @	New England	4-4	T	26-33-3	55	175-206
24	Dec 19 @	Michigan	0-1	L	10-13-1	21	70-80	63	Mar 4 @	Edmonton	3-1	W	27-33-3	57	178-207
25	Dec 20	New England	3-0	W	11-13-1	23	73-80	64	Mar 5 @	Winnipeg	2-4	L	27-34-3	57	180-211
26	Dec 22	Houston	0-3	L	11-14-1	23	73-83	65	Mar 8 @	Indianapolis	6-5	W	28-34-3	59	186-216
27	Dec 23 @	Toronto	4-1	W	12-14-1	25	77-84	66	Mar 12	Baltimore	0-2	L	28-35-3	59	186-218
28	Dec 27	Quebec	4-3	W	13-14-1	27	81-87	67	Mar 14	Edmonton	3-0	W	29-35-3	61	189-218
29	Dec 28 @	Phoenix	*2-3	L	13-15-1	27	83-90	68	Mar 16	Houston	1-2	L	29-36-3	61	190-220
30	Dec 29 @	Minnesota	0-6	L	13-16-1	27	83-96	69	Mar 17 @	Chicago	2-3	L	29-37-3	61	192-223
31	Dec 31	Chicago	3-4	L	13-17-1	27	86-100	70	Mar 19	Phoenix	5-4	W	30-37-3	63	197-227
32	Jan 1 @	Minnesota	2-6	L	13-18-1	27	88-106	71	Mar 22	Edmonton	5-1	W	31-37-3	65	202-228
33	Jan 2	Indianapolis	4-1	W	14-18-1	29	92-107	72	Mar 26	Vancouver	4-2	W	32-37-3	67	206-230
34	Jan 4	San Diego	0-2	L	14-19-1	29	92-109	73	Mar 27 @	New England	3-5	L	32-38-3	67	209-235
35	Jan 5	Toronto	3-4	L	14-20-1	29	95-113	74	Mar 29	Indianapolis	7-5	W	33-38-3	69	216-240
36	Jan 7	Winnipeg	4-4	T	14-20-2	30	99-117	75	Mar 30	Chicago	7-6	W	34-38-3	71	223-246
37	Jan 10	Vancouver	6-4	W	15-20-2	32	105-121	76	Apr 1 @	Chicago	2-3	L	34-39-3	71	225-249
38	Jan 12	Phoenix	4-2	W	16-20-2	34	109-123	77	Apr 2 @	Houston	6-7	L	34-40-3	71	231-256
39	Jan 15	Minnesota	2-4	L	16-21-2	34	111-127	78	Apr 5	New England	5-2	W	35-40-3	73	236-258

Crusaders Stars of 1974-1975

Al McDonough
34 goals, 64 points

Richie Leduc
35 goals, 66 points

Ron Ward
30 goals, 62 points

Ray Clearwater
+4 rating on defense

Paul Shmyr
+11 rating

Gerry Cheevers
26 wins, 4 shutouts

Scoring

pos	#	player	gp	g	a	pts	pim	+/-	ppg	shg	sog	sc%	gp	g	a	pts	pim
D	27	Anderson, Ron F.	39	0	9	9	10	+7	0	0	34	0.000	-	-	-	-	-
D	4	Baxter, Paul	5	0	0	0	37	+1	0	0	3	0.000	-	-	-	-	-
C	10	Buchanan, Ron	4	2	0	2	2		1	0	6	0.333	-	-	-	-	-
LW	11	Cardwell, Steve	75	9	13	22	127	-3	0	1	110	0.082	5	0	1	1	14
G	30	Cheevers, Gerry	52	0	1	1	59		0	0	0	-	5	0	0	0	0
D	6	Clearwater, Ray	66	4	18	22	51	+4	0	0	104	0.038	4	1	1	2	0
D	18	Edur, Tom	61	3	20	23	28	-4	0	0	107	0.028	5	2	0	2	0
LW	16	Erickson, Grant	78	12	15	27	24	+2	0	2	128	0.094	-	-	-	-	-
C	9	Harrison, Jim	60	20	22	42	106	-8	6	0	152	0.132	5	1	2	3	4
D	2	Hillman, Larry	77	0	16	16	83	-6	0	0	151	0.000	5	1	3	4	8
D	8	Hillman, Wayne	60	2	9	11	37	+3	0	0	30	0.067	5	0	2	2	2
RW	20	Holbrook, Terry	78	10	13	23	7	-10	0	0	86	0.116	5	0	1	1	0
LW	12	Jarrett, Gary	77	17	24	41	70	+8	1	0	233	0.073	5	0	1	1	0
C	17	Krake, Skip	71	15	23	38	108	+9	1	0	157	0.096	5	1	1	2	0
C	22	Leduc, Richie	78	35	31	66	122	+12	5	0	299	0.117	5	0	2	2	2
RW	14	McDonough, Al	78	34	30	64	27	-11	12	0	257	0.132	5	2	1	3	2
D	5	Muloin, Wayne	78	4	17	21	5	-6	0	1	89	0.045	5	0	1	1	4
C	29	Neale, Robbie	9	1	3	4	4		0	0	13	0.077	-	-	-	-	-
LW	7	Pinder, Gerry	74	13	28	41	71	-6	4	0	180	0.072	5	3	1	4	6
D	3	Shmyr, Paul	49	7	14	21	103	+11	3	0	87	0.080	5	2	1	3	15
C	19	Stewart, John C.	59	4	7	11	8	+5	0	0	52	0.077	1	0	0	0	0
RW	28	Walker, Russ	66	14	11	25	80	+16	0	0	131	0.107	5	1	0	1	17
C	24	Ward, Ron	73	30	32	62	18	+7	5	0	208	0.144	5	0	2	2	2
G	1	Whidden, Bob	29	0	0	0	2		0	0	0	-	-	-	-	-	-

Power Play: 38 goals scored in 226 opportunities (16.8%) with 6 short-handed goals allowed.
Penalty Killing: 61 goals allowed in 275 opportunities (77.8%) with 4 short-handed goals scored.

Goaltending

goaltender	gp	min	ga	en	so	record	gaa	sog	sv%	gp	min	ga	record	gaa
Cheevers, Gerry	52	3076	167	2	4	26-24-2	3.26	1763	0.905	5	300	23	1-4	4.60
Whidden, Bob	29	1654	89	0	0	9-16-1	3.23	918	0.903	-	-	-	-	-

Transactions: Ray McKay traded to Edmonton for future consideration, May 1974 • Terry Holbrook, Al McDonough signed to contracts, May 1974 • Richie Leduc signed to contract, Aug(?) 1974 • Steve Cardwell acquired from Indianapolis for future consitions, Aug 1974 • Ron Buchanan traded to Edmonton for Jim Harrison, Oct 1974 • Ron Anderson signed as free agent after release by Phoenix, Oct 1974 • Robbie Neale traded to Winnipeg for cash, future considerations, Feb. 1975

191

1974-1975 EDMONTON OILERS

Coach
Brian Shaw
30-26-3

Coach
Bill Hunter
6-12-1

Summary of Games (@ Away, * Overtime)

	date	opponent	score		record	pts	gf-ga		date	opponent	score		record	pts	gf-ga
1	Oct 18 @	Winnipeg	0-4	L	0-1-0	0	0-4	40	Jan 26	Toronto	5-7	L	22-16-2	46	151-135
2	Oct 30 @	Vancouver	6-8	L	0-2-0	0	6-12	41	Jan 28	Houston	7-5	W	23-16-2	48	158-140
3	Nov 2 @	Cleveland	4-2	W	1-2-0	2	10-14	42	Jan 31	Cleveland	0-2	L	23-17-2	48	158-142
4	Nov 3 @	Indianapolis	3-1	W	2-2-0	4	13-15	43	Feb 2	Chicago	*4-3	W	24-17-2	50	162-145
5	Nov 10	Cleveland	4-1	W	3-2-0	6	17-16	44	Feb 4 @	Baltimore	*1-0	W	25-17-2	52	163-145
6	Nov 13	Winnipeg	5-3	W	4-2-0	8	22-19	45	Feb 5 @	Minnesota	2-4	L	25-18-2	52	165-149
7	Nov 15	Toronto	5-4	W	5-2-0	10	27-23	46	Feb 9	Phoenix	4-6	L	25-19-2	52	169-155
8	Nov 17	Indianapolis	2-1	W	6-2-0	12	29-24	47	Feb 11 @	Toronto	3-4	L	25-20-2	52	172-159
9	Nov 18	Winnipeg	5-3	W	7-2-0	14	34-27	48	Feb 12 @	New England	2-2	T	25-20-3	53	174-161
10	Nov 20 @	Quebec	2-4	L	7-3-0	14	36-31	49	Feb 14	Toronto	8-4	W	26-20-3	55	182-165
11	Nov 22 @	Toronto	8-2	W	8-3-0	16	44-33	50	Feb 16	Phoenix	4-5	L	26-21-3	55	186-170
12	Nov 24	Houston	*3-4	L	8-4-0	16	47-37	51	Feb 18	New England	6-3	W	27-21-3	57	192-173
13	Nov 26 @	San Diego	1-5	L	8-5-0	16	48-42	52	Feb 19 @	Winnipeg	1-4	L	27-22-3	57	193-177
14	Nov 28 @	Houston	0-2	L	8-6-0	16	48-44	53	Feb 21	New England	2-4	L	27-23-3	57	195-181
15	Dec 1	New England	8-4	W	9-6-0	18	56-48	54	Feb 23	Minnesota	6-4	W	28-23-3	59	201-185
16	Dec 4	Vancouver	6-3	W	10-6-0	20	62-51	55	Feb 25 @	Chicago	*3-4	L	28-24-3	59	204-189
17	Dec 6 @	Phoenix	1-3	L	10-7-0	20	63-54	56	Feb 28	Baltimore	6-2	W	29-24-3	61	210-191
18	Dec 8	Michigan	7-0	W	11-7-0	22	70-54	57	Mar 2	Baltimore	7-2	W	30-24-3	63	217-193
19	Dec 11 @	Quebec	*3-4	L	11-8-0	22	73-58	58	Mar 4	Cleveland	1-3	L	30-25-3	63	218-196
20	Dec 13 @	Minnesota	5-4	W	12-8-0	24	78-62	59	Mar 5 @	Vancouver	0-6	L	30-26-3	63	218-202
21	Dec 15 @	Indianapolis	3-1	W	13-8-0	26	81-63	60	Mar 7	Vancouver	4-0	W	31-26-3	65	222-202
22	Dec 17 @	Houston	2-7	L	13-9-0	26	83-70	61	Mar 10 @	Baltimore	3-5	L	31-27-3	65	225-207
23	Dec 19 @	San Diego	*7-6	W	14-9-0	28	90-76	62	Mar 11 @	Chicago	5-1	W	32-27-3	67	230-208
24	Dec 21 @	Chicago	3-0	W	15-9-0	30	93-76	63	Mar 14 @	Cleveland	0-3	L	32-28-3	67	230-211
25	Dec 22	San Diego	6-3	W	16-9-0	32	99-79	64	Mar 15 @	New England	2-6	L	32-29-3	67	232-217
26	Dec 26	Minnesota	1-5	L	16-10-0	32	100-84	65	Mar 16 @	Winnipeg	1-10	L	32-30-3	67	233-227
27	Dec 29	Indianapolis	*5-4	W	17-10-0	34	105-88	66	Mar 18	Quebec	8-5	W	33-30-3	69	241-232
28	Jan 1	San Diego	*3-2	W	18-10-0	36	108-90	67	Mar 20 @	Indianapolis	1-3	L	33-31-3	69	242-235
29	Jan 3	Phoenix	3-3	T	18-10-1	37	111-93	68	Mar 22 @	Cleveland	1-5	L	33-32-3	69	243-240
30	Jan 5	Chicago	2-3	L	18-11-1	37	113-96	69	Mar 23 @	Minnesota	2-4	L	33-33-3	69	245-244
31	Jan 9	Minnesota	3-2	W	19-11-1	39	116-98	70	Mar 25 @	New England	4-5	L	33-34-3	69	249-249
32	Jan 10	Indianapolis	3-3	T	19-11-2	40	119-101	71	Mar 26 @	Quebec	6-4	W	34-34-3	71	255-253
33	Jan 12	Quebec	1-3	L	19-12-2	40	120-104	72	Mar 27 @	Baltimore	2-2	T	34-34-4	72	257-255
34	Jan 15 @	Houston	2-9	L	19-13-2	40	122-113	73	Mar 28 @	Toronto	4-5	L	34-35-4	72	261-260
35	Jan 16 @	San Diego	2-3	L	19-14-2	40	124-116	74	Mar 31	San Diego	2-5	L	34-36-4	72	263-265
36	Jan 17 @	Phoenix	7-1	W	20-14-2	42	131-117	75	Apr 1	Quebec	3-5	L	34-37-4	72	266-270
37	Jan 18 @	Phoenix	1-3	L	20-15-2	42	132-120	76	Apr 4	Vancouver	5-3	W	35-37-4	74	271-273
38	Jan 23	Winnipeg	7-3	W	21-15-2	44	139-123	77	Apr 5 @	Vancouver	2-3	L	35-38-4	74	273-276
39	Jan 24	Houston	7-5	W	22-15-2	46	146-128	78	Apr 6	Chicago	6-3	W	36-38-4	76	279-279

Oilers Stars of 1974-1975

Jacques Plante	Ken Brown	Ken Baird	Mike Rogers	Bruce MacGregor	Barry Long
15 wins, shutout	10 wins, 2 shutouts	30 goals	35 goals as rookie	24 goals	20 goals on defense

Scoring

							Regular Season								Playoffs				
pos	#	player	gp	g	a	pts	pim	+/-	ppg	shg	sog	sc%			gp	g	a	pts	pim
D	19	Baird, Ken	77	30	28	58	151	-19	8	0	173	0.173			-	-	-	-	-
D	5	Barrie, Doug	78	12	33	45	122	-11	1	2	152	0.079			-	-	-	-	-
G	27	Brown, Ken	32	0	1	1	2		0	0	0	-			-	-	-	-	-
C	15	Buchanan, Ron	22	6	9	15	4		1		60	0.100			-	-	-	-	-
D	20	Carlyle, Steve	73	2	25	27	46	-13	0	0	118	0.034			-	-	-	-	-
LW	11	Climie, Ron	49	15	27	42	15	+3	3	0	90	0.167			-	-	-	-	-
LW	10	Gilmore, Tom	74	12	19	31	84	-22	0	0	140	0.086			-	-	-	-	-
D	3	Hamilton, Al	25	1	13	14	62	+5	1	0	49	0.020			-	-	-	-	-
LW	8	Herriman, Don	33	1	2	3	21	-6	0	0	24	0.042			-	-	-	-	-
C	16	Joyal, Eddie	78	22	25	47	2	-10	0	2	183	0.120			-	-	-	-	-
D	6/15	Kennett, Murray	50	4	14	18	17	+16	0	0	47	0.085			-	-	-	-	-
RW	23	Kerslake, Doug	10	4	0	4	10	+3	0	0	17	0.235			-	-	-	-	-
C	21	Laing, Bill	43	2	4	6	32	-3	0	0	26	0.077			-	-	-	-	-
D	2	Long, Barry	78	20	40	60	116	-8	7	1	167	0.120			-	-	-	-	-
RW	14	MacDonald, Blair	72	22	24	46	14	+4	1	0	155	0.142			-	-	-	-	-
RW	12	MacGregor, Bruce	72	24	28	52	10	-11	3	3	151	0.159			-	-	-	-	-
D	22	McCrimmon, Jim	34	1	5	6	50	+9	0	0	27	0.037			-	-	-	-	-
D	4	McKay, Ray	69	8	20	28	47	+18	1	0	208	0.038			-	-	-	-	-
LW	6/11	Morris, Bill	36	4	8	12	6	+5	0	0	34	0.118			-	-	-	-	-
RW	17	Patenaude, Rusty	56	20	16	36	38	+1	3	0	92	0.217			-	-	-	-	-
C	9	Perkins, Ross	76	7	16	23	33	+7	0	1	89	0.079			-	-	-	-	-
G	1	Plante, Jacques	31	0	1	1	2		0	0	0	-			-	-	-	-	-
C	18	Rogers, Mike	78	35	48	83	2	+2	4	0	189	0.185			-	-	-	-	-
C	7/15	Sheehan, Bobby	77	19	39	58	8	+7	2	0	178	0.107			-	-	-	-	-
RW	15	Sheehy, Tim	29	8	20	28	4	-5	2	0	81	0.099			-	-	-	-	-
G	30	Worthy, Chris	29	0	0	0	7		0	0	0	-			-	-	-	-	-

Power Play: 40 goals scored in 262 opportunities (15.3%) with 4 short-handed goals allowed.
Penalty Killing: 52 goals allowed in 236 opportunities (78.0%) with 10 short-handed goals scored.

Goaltending

goaltender	gp	min	ga	en	so	record	gaa	sog	sv%	gp	min	ga	record	gaa
Brown, Ken	32	1466	86	2	2	10-11-0	3.49	844	0.899	-	-	-	-	-
Plante, Jacques	31	1592	88	4	1	15-14-1	3.32	803	0.890	-	-	-	-	-
Worthy, Chris	29	1660	99	0	1	11-13-3	3.58	929	0.893	-	-	-	-	-

Transactions: Barry Long signed to contract, Apr 1974 • Ray McKay acquired from Cleveland for future considerations, signed to contract, May 1974 • Bruce MacGregor, Jacques Plante signed to contracts, Jun 1974 • Steve Andrascik's rights traded to Cincinnati, Jul 1974 • Don Herriman from San Diego for Bob Wall, Aug 1974 • Mike Rogers signed to contract, Aug 1974 • Ron Buchanan from Cleveland for Jim Harrison, Oct 1974 • Jim Harrison to Cleveland for Ron Buchanan, Oct 1974 • Bill Morris signed to contract, Oct 1974 • Ron Buchanan to Indianapolis for Murray Kennett, Jan. 1975 • Ron Climie to New England for Tim Sheehy, Feb 1975 • Doug Kerslake signed to contract, Feb 1975 • Jim McCrimmon sold to St. Louis (NHL), Mar 1975

1974-1975 HOUSTON AEROS

Coach
Bill Dineen

Summary of Games (@ Away, * Overtime)

	date	opponent	score		record	pts	gf-ga		date	opponent	score		record	pts	gf-ga
1	Oct 16 @	Vancouver	6-0	W	1-0-0	2	6-0	40	Jan 15	Edmonton	9-2	W	28-12-0	56	189-117
2	Oct 18 @	Phoenix	4-6	L	1-1-0	2	10-6	41	Jan 18 @	San Diego	*4-5	L	28-13-0	56	193-122
3	Oct 19 @	San Diego	2-6	L	1-2-0	2	12-12	42	Jan 24 @	Edmonton	5-7	L	28-14-0	56	198-129
4	Oct 22 @	Quebec	2-7	L	1-3-0	2	14-19	43	Jan 26 @	Winnipeg	3-1	W	29-14-0	58	201-130
5	Oct 23 @	New England	4-5	L	1-4-0	2	18-24	44	Jan 28 @	Edmonton	5-7	L	29-15-0	58	206-137
6	Oct 26	Minnesota	3-2	W	2-4-0	4	21-26	45	Jan 31 @	Minnesota	1-4	L	29-16-0	58	207-141
7	Oct 29 @	Chicago	4-2	W	3-4-0	6	25-28	46	Feb 1 @	Chicago	6-5	W	30-16-0	60	213-146
8	Oct 30	Chicago	1-0	W	4-4-0	8	26-28	47	Feb 2 @	Baltimore	5-2	W	31-16-0	62	218-148
9	Nov 2	Phoenix	8-2	W	5-4-0	10	34-30	48	Feb 4 @	Indianapolis	*4-3	W	32-16-0	64	222-151
10	Nov 5	San Diego	9-3	W	6-4-0	12	43-33	49	Feb 5	Toronto	5-2	W	33-16-0	66	227-153
11	Nov 9	Indianapolis	*4-5	L	6-5-0	12	47-38	50	Feb 6	Quebec	3-4	L	33-17-0	66	230-157
12	Nov 12	New England	6-1	W	7-5-0	14	53-39	51	Feb 8	Baltimore	4-6	L	33-18-0	66	234-163
13	Nov 13 @	Minnesota	8-5	W	8-5-0	16	61-44	52	Feb 9 @	Cleveland	4-1	W	34-18-0	68	238-164
14	Nov 16	Chicago	6-2	W	9-5-0	18	67-46	53	Feb 11 @	Baltimore	5-2	W	35-18-0	70	243-166
15	Nov 17	San Diego	3-4	L	9-6-0	18	70-50	54	Feb 12 @	Minnesota	3-1	W	36-18-0	72	246-167
16	Nov 19 @	Indianapolis	10-0	W	10-6-0	20	80-50	55	Feb 14 @	Winnipeg	3-5	L	36-19-0	72	249-172
17	Nov 22 @	Vancouver	4-1	W	11-6-0	22	84-51	56	Feb 17 @	Quebec	5-3	W	37-19-0	74	254-175
18	Nov 23 @	Vancouver	4-2	W	12-6-0	24	88-53	57	Feb 19	Quebec	10-4	W	38-19-0	76	264-179
19	Nov 24 @	Edmonton	*4-3	W	13-6-0	26	92-56	58	Feb 22	Vancouver	2-4	L	38-20-0	76	266-183
20	Nov 26	Phoenix	4-6	L	13-7-0	26	96-62	59	Feb 23	Toronto	5-1	W	39-20-0	78	271-184
21	Nov 28	Edmonton	2-0	W	14-7-0	28	98-62	60	Feb 26	Cleveland	9-5	W	40-20-0	80	280-189
22	Nov 30	Cleveland	4-5	L	14-8-0	28	102-67	61	Feb 27 @	Phoenix	7-2	W	41-20-0	82	287-191
23	Dec 1 @	Indianapolis	7-3	W	15-8-0	30	109-70	62	Mar 1	Chicago	4-2	W	42-20-0	84	291-193
24	Dec 3 @	Toronto	5-4	W	16-8-0	32	114-74	63	Mar 2	Indianapolis	*4-3	W	43-20-0	86	295-196
25	Dec 4 @	Winnipeg	3-2	W	17-8-0	34	117-76	64	Mar 6 @	San Diego	4-7	L	43-21-0	86	299-203
26	Dec 8 @	Quebec	1-2	L	17-9-0	34	118-78	65	Mar 8	New England	4-5	L	43-22-0	86	303-208
27	Dec 11	Vancouver	5-2	W	18-9-0	36	123-80	66	Mar 14 @	Chicago	5-4	W	44-22-0	88	308-212
28	Dec 14	Winnipeg	5-3	W	19-9-0	38	128-83	67	Mar 16 @	Cleveland	2-1	W	45-22-0	90	310-213
29	Dec 15	San Diego	3-4	L	19-10-0	38	131-87	68	Mar 17 @	Toronto	4-5	L	45-23-0	90	314-218
30	Dec 17	Edmonton	7-2	W	20-10-0	40	138-89	69	Mar 19	Indianapolis	6-5	W	46-23-0	92	320-223
31	Dec 19	Vancouver	1-3	L	20-11-0	40	139-92	70	Mar 20	Quebec	5-3	W	47-23-0	94	325-226
32	Dec 21 @	New England	5-3	W	21-11-0	42	144-95	71	Mar 22 @	New England	5-3	W	48-23-0	96	330-229
33	Dec 22 @	Cleveland	3-0	W	22-11-0	44	147-95	72	Mar 26 @	Phoenix	1-2	L	48-24-0	96	331-231
34	Dec 28	New England	6-1	W	23-11-0	46	153-96	73	Mar 27	Winnipeg	8-0	W	49-24-0	98	339-231
35	Dec 29	Winnipeg	6-3	W	24-11-0	48	159-99	74	Mar 29	Minnesota	8-2	W	50-24-0	100	347-233
36	Jan 2	Michigan	6-3	W	25-11-0	50	165-102	75	Apr 2	Cleveland	7-6	W	51-24-0	102	354-239
37	Jan 4	Michigan	5-2	W	26-11-0	52	170-104	76	Apr 5	Minnesota	8-2	W	52-24-0	104	362-241
38	Jan 11	Phoenix	6-4	W	27-11-0	54	176-108	77	Apr 6 @	Toronto	5-2	W	53-24-0	106	367-243
39	Jan 12	Toronto	4-7	L	27-12-0	54	180-115	78	Apr 7 @	Baltimore	2-4	L	53-25-0	106	369-247

Aeros Stars of 1974-1975

Larry Lund
108 points led team

Ron Grahame
33 wins, 4 shutouts

Larry Hale
+35 rating

Frank Hughes
48 goals

Gordie Howe
99 points, +40 rating

Andre Hinse
39 goals

Scoring

pos	#	player	Regular Season										Playoffs				
			gp	g	a	pts	pim	+/-	ppg	shg	sog	sc%	gp	g	a	pts	pim
G	29	Grahame, Ron	43	0	1	1	0		0	0	0	-	13	0	0	0	0
D	17	Hale, Larry	76	2	18	20	40	+35	0	0	51	0.039	13	0	4	4	0
C	11	Hall, Murray	78	18	29	47	28	+2	0	0	127	0.141	13	7	3	10	8
LW	16	Hinse, Andre	75	39	47	86	12	+34	13	0	190	0.205	11	5	4	9	8
RW	9	Howe, Gordie	75	34	65	99	84	+40	8	3	255	0.133	13	8	12	20	20
D/F	4	Howe, Mark	74	36	40	76	30	+40	7	4	256	0.141	13	10	12	22	0
D	3	Howe, Marty	75	13	21	34	89	+46	0	1	158	0.082	11	0	2	2	11
LW	7	Hughes, Frank	70	48	35	83	35	+32	15	0	206	0.233	13	6	6	12	2
D	24	Irwin, Glen	70	2	11	13	153	+38	0	0	61	0.033	13	0	2	2	8
C	10	Labossiere, Gord	76	23	34	57	40	+5	4	0	171	0.135	13	6	7	13	4
RW	27	Larway, Don	75	22	14	36	59	+26	0	0	140	0.157	13	3	1	4	8
C	13	Lund, Larry	78	33	75	108	68	+28	13	0	188	0.176	13	5	13	18	13
D	6	Popiel, Poul	78	11	53	64	22	+41	4	2	236	0.047	13	1	10	11	34
D	22	Prentice, Bill	17	0	3	3	19	+3	0	0	13	0.000	-	-	-	-	-
RW	21	Preston, Rich	78	20	21	41	10	+25	1	0	137	0.146	13	1	6	7	6
C	8	Ruskowski, Terry	71	10	36	46	134	+30	3	0	105	0.095	13	4	2	6	15
G	30	Rutledge, Wayne	35	0	0	0	0		0	0	0	-	-	-	-	-	-
D	2	Schella, John	78	10	42	52	176	+43	0	0	222	0.045	13	0	8	8	12
C	23	Sherrit, Jim	77	22	25	47	25	+36	1	0	135	0.163	13	3	3	6	6
LW	14	Taylor, Ted	73	26	27	53	130	+7	2	3	201	0.126	11	2	5	7	22

Power Play: 71 goals scored in 254 opportunities (28.0%) with 6 short-handed goals allowed.
Penalty Killing: 64 goals allowed in 372 opportunities (82.8%) with 18 short-handed goals scored.

Goaltending

goaltender	gp	min	ga	en	so	record	gaa	sog	sv%	gp	min	ga	record	gaa
Grahame, Ron	43	2590	131	3	4	33-10-0	3.03	1307	0.900	13	780	26	12-1	2.00
Rutledge, Wayne	35	2098	113	0	2	20-15-0	3.23	1045	0.892	-	-	-	-	-

Transactions: Glen Irwin, Rich Preston signed to contracts, Jun 1974 • Rights to Don Larway from Cincinnati for rights to Dick Spannbauer, Jul 1974

195

1974-1975 INDIANAPOLIS RACERS

Coach
Gerry Moore

Summary of Games (@ Away, * Overtime)

	date	opponent	score		record	pts	gf-ga		date	opponent	score		record	pts	gf-ga
1	Oct 17	Michigan	2-4	L	0-1-0	0	2-4	40	Jan 7	Vancouver	4-2	W	7-31-2	16	89-172
2	Oct 18 @	Toronto	1-3	L	0-2-0	0	3-7	41	Jan 10 @	Edmonton	3-3	T	7-31-3	17	92-175
3	Oct 20 @	Quebec	1-4	L	0-3-0	0	4-11	42	Jan 16	Cleveland	4-2	W	8-31-3	19	96-177
4	Oct 24	Minnesota	2-3	L	0-4-0	0	6-14	43	Jan 19 @	Vancouver	1-5	L	8-32-3	19	97-182
5	Oct 26 @	New England	1-6	L	0-5-0	0	7-20	44	Jan 22 @	Winnipeg	3-1	W	9-32-3	21	100-183
6	Oct 27	Quebec	5-3	W	1-5-0	2	12-23	45	Jan 23	Chicago	4-2	W	10-32-3	23	104-185
7	Oct 31	New England	1-6	L	1-6-0	2	13-29	46	Jan 26 @	Phoenix	0-6	L	10-33-3	23	104-191
8	Nov 3	Edmonton	1-3	L	1-7-0	2	14-32	47	Jan 28	Phoenix	1-3	L	10-34-3	23	105-194
9	Nov 5	Phoenix	0-3	L	1-8-0	2	14-35	48	Jan 30	Toronto	2-3	L	10-35-3	23	107-197
10	Nov 7	San Diego	3-0	W	2-8-0	4	17-35	49	Feb 1	Quebec	1-2	L	10-36-3	23	108-199
11	Nov 9 @	Houston	*5-4	W	3-8-0	6	22-39	50	Feb 4	Houston	*3-4	L	10-37-3	23	111-203
12	Nov 10 @	Michigan	6-1	W	4-8-0	8	28-40	51	Feb 9 @	Toronto	5-7	L	10-38-3	23	116-210
13	Nov 13 @	Quebec	3-10	L	4-9-0	8	31-50	52	Feb 10	Chicago	4-1	W	11-38-3	25	120-211
14	Nov 15 @	Winnipeg	0-5	L	4-10-0	8	31-55	53	Feb 14 @	New England	*3-4	L	11-39-3	25	123-215
15	Nov 17 @	Edmonton	1-2	L	4-11-0	8	32-57	54	Feb 17 @	Chicago	5-6	L	11-40-3	25	128-221
16	Nov 19	Houston	0-10	L	4-12-0	8	32-67	55	Feb 18	Vancouver	2-9	L	11-41-3	25	130-230
17	Nov 20 @	Chicago	4-6	L	4-13-0	8	36-73	56	Feb 21	Minnesota	5-2	W	12-41-3	27	135-232
18	Nov 21	New England	0-4	L	4-14-0	8	36-77	57	Feb 23	Cleveland	6-0	W	13-41-3	29	141-232
19	Nov 24	Toronto	2-9	L	4-15-0	8	38-86	58	Feb 25 @	Baltimore	6-4	W	14-41-3	31	147-236
20	Nov 26	Winnipeg	0-4	L	4-16-0	8	38-90	59	Feb 26 @	Minnesota	*3-4	L	14-42-3	31	150-240
21	Nov 28	Quebec	5-7	L	4-17-0	8	43-97	60	Mar 1 @	Phoenix	2-12	L	14-43-3	31	152-252
22	Nov 29 @	Cleveland	2-4	L	4-18-0	8	45-101	61	Mar 2 @	Houston	*3-4	L	14-44-3	31	155-256
23	Dec 1	Houston	3-7	L	4-19-0	8	48-108	62	Mar 5 @	Baltimore	5-2	W	15-44-3	33	160-258
24	Dec 5	Chicago	3-5	L	4-20-0	8	51-113	63	Mar 7	Baltimore	*4-5	L	15-45-3	33	164-263
25	Dec 7 @	New England	3-6	L	4-21-0	8	54-119	64	Mar 8	Cleveland	5-6	L	15-46-3	33	169-269
26	Dec 8	San Diego	5-3	W	5-21-0	10	59-122	65	Mar 13	Toronto	5-4	W	16-46-3	35	174-273
27	Dec 10	Winnipeg	3-5	L	5-22-0	10	62-127	66	Mar 15	Baltimore	7-3	W	17-46-3	37	181-276
28	Dec 14 @	San Diego	0-2	L	5-23-0	10	62-129	67	Mar 19 @	Houston	5-6	L	17-47-3	37	186-282
29	Dec 15	Edmonton	1-3	L	5-24-0	10	63-132	68	Mar 20	Edmonton	3-1	W	18-47-3	39	189-283
30	Dec 17	Vancouver	2-3	L	5-25-0	10	65-135	69	Mar 22 @	San Diego	3-6	L	18-48-3	39	192-289
31	Dec 19	Minnesota	0-6	L	5-26-0	10	65-141	70	Mar 23 @	Phoenix	3-5	L	18-49-3	39	195-294
32	Dec 20 @	Minnesota	4-6	L	5-27-0	10	69-147	71	Mar 25	Winnipeg	*3-4	L	18-50-3	39	198-298
33	Dec 22	New England	2-1	W	6-27-0	12	71-148	72	Mar 27	San Diego	2-5	L	18-51-3	39	200-303
34	Dec 27 @	Vancouver	1-1	T	6-27-1	13	72-149	73	Mar 29 @	Cleveland	5-7	L	18-52-3	39	205-310
35	Dec 29 @	Edmonton	*4-5	L	6-28-1	13	76-154	74	Mar 30 @	Minnesota	3-5	L	18-53-3	39	208-315
36	Jan 1 @	Quebec	3-6	L	6-29-1	13	79-160	75	Mar 31 @	Winnipeg	1-4	L	18-54-3	39	209-319
37	Jan 2 @	Cleveland	1-4	L	6-30-1	13	80-164	76	Apr 1 @	Toronto	1-7	L	18-55-3	39	210-326
38	Jan 4 @	Chicago	4-4	T	6-30-2	14	84-168	77	Apr 5 @	San Diego	3-8	L	18-56-3	39	213-334
39	Jan 5	Phoenix	1-2	L	6-31-2	14	85-170	78	Apr 6 @	Vancouver	3-4	L	18-57-3	39	216-338

Racers Stars of 1974-1975

Andy Brown
All-Star goalie

Nick Harbaruk
20 goals

Kerry Bond
22 goals

Ron Buchanan
16 goals

Bobby Whitlock
31 goals led team

John Sheridan
17 goals

Scoring

pos	#	player	gp	g	a	pts	pim	+/-	ppg	shg	sog	sc%	gp	g	a	pts	pim
RW	17	Andrascik, Steve	20	2	4	6	16		0	0	56	0.036	-	-	-	-	-
D	3	Ash, Bob	64	1	14	15	19	-30	1	0	53	0.019	-	-	-	-	-
D	24	Block, Ken	37	0	17	17	18	-10	0	0	48	0.000	-	-	-	-	-
LW	21	Bond, Kerry	71	22	15	37	23	-30	5	0	204	0.108	-	-	-	-	-
RW	19	Bredin, Gary	10	3	2	5	8	-3	0	0	12	0.250	-	-	-	-	-
G	1	Brown, Andy	52	0	1	1	75		0	0	0	-	-	-	-	-	-
C	9	Buchanan, Ron	32	16	15	31	16	-12	9		89	0.180	-	-	-	-	-
D	23	Cote, Roger	36	0	6	6	24	-9	0	0	33	0.000	-	-	-	-	-
D	2	Desjardine, Ken	46	0	8	8	68	-24	0	0	60	0.000	-	-	-	-	-
G		Dion, Michel	1	0	0	0	0		0	0	0	-	-	-	-	-	-
G	31	Dyck, Ed	32	0	0	0	6		0	0	0	-	-	-	-	-	-
C	16	Fitchner, Bob	78	11	19	30	96	-26	2	0	108	0.102	-	-	-	-	-
D	5	Fraser, Rick	4	0	0	0	2		0	0	5	0.000	-	-	-	-	-
D	4	Hanmer, Craig	27	1	0	1	15				28	0.036	-	-	-	-	-
RW	10	Harbaruk, Nick	78	20	23	43	52	-22	3	1	157	0.127	-	-	-	-	-
C	12	Hardy, Joe	32	2	17	19	36		0	0	64	0.031	-	-	-	-	-
D	6	Hargreaves, Jim	37	2	5	7	30	-19	0	0	63	0.032	-	-	-	-	-
RW	26	Heatley, Murray	29	15	8	23	25	-7	5	0	83	0.181	-	-	-	-	-
D	18	Hopiavuori, Ralph	28	2	8	10	21	-17	1	0	64	0.031	-	-	-	-	-
D	25	Horton, Bill	59	2	9	11	30	-28	0	0	42	0.048	-	-	-	-	-
C	15	Johnson, Jim	42	7	15	22	12	-15	2	0	62	0.112	-	-	-	-	-
D	8	Kannegiesser, Gord	4	1	4	5	4	+4	0	0	6	0.167	-	-	-	-	-
D	26	Kennett, Murray	28	1	3	4	8	-11	1	0	9	0.111	-	-	-	-	-
C	8	Locas, Jacques	11	0	1	1	2		0	0	8	0.000	-	-	-	-	-
RW	20	McDonald, Brian	47	14	15	29	19	-10	2	0	104	0.135	-	-	-	-	-
LW	12	McKenzie, Brian	9	1	0	1	6				9	0.111	-	-	-	-	-
D	19	Proceviat, Dick	52	1	28	29	51	-13	0	0	65	0.015	-	-	-	-	-
LW	27	Pumple, Rich	34	4	8	12	29	-12	0	0	72	0.056	-	-	-	-	-
C	8	Richardson, Steve	19	1	4	5	16	-2	0	0	39	0.026	-	-	-	-	-
C	15	Robertson, Joe	18	4	4	8	23	-6	0	0	31	0.129	-	-	-	-	-
C	22	Sheridan, John	58	17	11	28	20	-15	3	0	137	0.124	-	-	-	-	-
C	17	Sicinski, Bob	77	19	34	53	12	-32	4	2	206	0.092	-	-	-	-	-
LW	9	Smith, Ross	15	1	6	7	19		1	0	23	0.043	-	-	-	-	-
RW	11	Walters, Ron	17	2	1	3	9				18	0.111	-	-	-	-	-
C	7	Whitlock, Bobby	73	31	26	57	56	-27	5	0	290	0.107	-	-	-	-	-
C	14	Wiste, Jim	75	13	28	41	30	-19	0	0	114	0.114	-	-	-	-	-
D	5	Woytowich, Bob	42	0	8	8	28	-26	0	0	30	0.000	-	-	-	-	-

Power Play: 45 goals scored in 290 opportunities (15.5%) with 14 short-handed goals allowed.
Penalty Killing: 55 goals allowed in 256 opportunities (78.5%) with 4 short-handed goals scored.

Goaltending

goaltender	gp	min	ga	en	so	record	gaa	sog	sv%	gp	min	ga	record	gaa
Brown, Andy	52	2979	206	1	2	15-35-0	4.15	1627	0.873	-	-	-	-	-
Dion, Michel	1	59	4	0	0	0-1-0	4.07	38	0.895	-	-	-	-	-
Dyck, Ed	32	1692	123	4	0	3-21-3	4.36	913	0.865	-	-	-	-	-

Transactions: Ed Dyck signed to contract, Apr 1974 • Steve Richardson signed to contract, Jun 1974 • Nick Harbaruk acquired from New England, Jun 1974 • Steve Andrascik on loan to Indianapolis by Cincinnati for 1974-75 season, Jul 1974 • Andy Brown signed to contract, Jul 1974 • Kerry Bond purchased from San Diego (WHL), Oct 1974 • Steve Andrascik and Steve Richardson traded to Michigan for Jacques Locas and Brian McDonald, Nov 1974 • Gary Bredin traded to Michigan for Bill Horton, Nov 1974 • Joe Robertson traded to Minnesota for Jim Johnson, Nov 1974 • Dick Proceviat acquired from Chicago for future considerations, Dec 1974 • Bob Woytowich purchased from Winnipeg, Dec 1974 • Murray Kennett traded to Edmonton for Ron Buchanan, Jan 1975 • Jim Hargreaves traded to San Diego for Ken Block, Jan 1975 • Murray Heatley acquired from Minnesota for future considerations, Feb 1975 • Joe Hardy traded to San Diego for future considerations (Ted Scharf), Mar 1975

1974-1975 MICHIGAN STAGS-BALTIMORE BLADES

**Coach
John Wilson**

Summary of Games (@ Away, * Overtime)

	date	opponent	score		record	pts	gf-ga		date	opponent	score		record	pts	gf-ga
1	Oct 17 @	Indianapolis	4-2	W	1-0-0	2	4-2	40	Jan 7	Quebec	*2-3	L	12-25-3	27	99-168
2	Oct 19 @	New England	1-2	L	1-1-0	2	5-4	41	Jan 9	Winnipeg	*5-4	W	13-25-3	29	104-172
3	Oct 20 @	Toronto	3-4	L	1-2-0	2	8-8	42	Jan 10 @	Chicago	2-5	L	13-26-3	29	106-177
4	Oct 23 @	Quebec	2-6	L	1-3-0	2	10-14	43	Jan 18 @	Cleveland	1-2	L	13-27-3	29	107-179
5	Oct 27 @	Winnipeg	2-5	L	1-4-0	2	12-19	44	Jan 25 @	Cleveland	1-2	L	13-28-3	29	108-181
6	Oct 29	Minnesota	*4-3	W	2-4-0	4	16-22	45	Jan 26 @	Minnesota	1-2	L	13-29-3	29	109-183
7	Oct 31	Cleveland	2-4	L	2-5-0	4	18-26	46	Jan 29 @	New England	3-4	L	13-30-3	29	112-187
8	Nov 2 @	Minnesota	3-6	L	2-6-0	4	21-32	47	Jan 31 @	New England	2-4	L	13-31-3	29	114-191
9	Nov 3 @	Winnipeg	3-11	L	2-7-0	4	24-43	48	Feb 1 @	Phoenix	1-8	L	13-32-3	29	115-199
10	Nov 5	Toronto	2-5	L	2-8-0	4	26-48	49	Feb 2	Houston	2-5	L	13-33-3	29	117-204
11	Nov 10	Indianapolis	1-6	L	2-9-0	4	27-54	50	Feb 4	Edmonton	*0-1	L	13-34-3	29	117-205
12	Nov 12	Quebec	4-5	L	2-10-0	4	31-59	51	Feb 6	Cleveland	0-4	L	13-35-3	29	117-209
13	Nov 14	Chicago	4-2	W	3-10-0	6	35-61	52	Feb 8 @	Houston	6-4	W	14-35-3	31	123-213
14	Nov 16 @	Quebec	3-4	L	3-11-0	6	38-65	53	Feb 11	Houston	2-5	L	14-36-3	31	125-218
15	Nov 17	New England	1-6	L	3-12-0	6	39-71	54	Feb 13	San Diego	1-6	L	14-37-3	31	126-224
16	Nov 21	Phoenix	2-1	W	4-12-0	8	41-72	55	Feb 15	Chicago	3-5	L	14-38-3	31	129-229
17	Nov 22 @	Chicago	3-5	L	4-13-0	8	44-77	56	Feb 18	Winnipeg	3-5	L	14-39-3	31	132-234
18	Nov 24	Minnesota	3-2	W	5-13-0	10	47-79	57	Feb 20	Vancouver	4-3	W	15-39-3	33	136-237
19	Nov 26	Vancouver	1-5	L	5-14-0	10	48-84	58	Feb 22	Phoenix	1-3	L	15-40-3	33	137-240
20	Nov 29 @	Winnipeg	6-7	L	5-15-0	10	54-91	59	Feb 25	Indianapolis	4-6	L	15-41-3	33	141-246
21	Dec 3	New England	2-1	W	6-15-0	12	56-92	60	Feb 28 @	Edmonton	2-6	L	15-42-3	33	143-252
22	Dec 5	San Diego	5-3	W	7-15-0	14	61-95	61	Mar 2 @	Edmonton	2-7	L	15-43-3	33	145-259
23	Dec 7 @	Vancouver	2-4	L	7-16-0	14	63-99	62	Mar 4 @	Toronto	4-6	L	15-44-3	33	149-265
24	Dec 8 @	Edmonton	0-7	L	7-17-0	14	63-106	63	Mar 5	Indianapolis	2-5	L	15-45-3	33	151-270
25	Dec 10 @	San Diego	4-4	T	7-17-1	15	67-110	64	Mar 7 @	Indianapolis	*5-4	W	16-45-3	35	156-274
26	Dec 12	Winnipeg	5-3	W	8-17-1	17	72-113	65	Mar 8	Toronto	4-7	L	16-46-3	35	160-281
27	Dec 14 @	Chicago	0-6	L	8-18-1	17	72-119	66	Mar 9 @	Toronto	2-8	L	16-47-3	35	162-289
28	Dec 15	Toronto	2-7	L	8-19-1	17	74-126	67	Mar 10	Edmonton	5-3	W	17-47-3	37	167-292
29	Dec 17	New England	2-2	T	8-19-2	18	76-128	68	Mar 12 @	Cleveland	2-0	W	18-47-3	39	169-292
30	Dec 19	Cleveland	1-0	W	9-19-2	20	77-128	69	Mar 15 @	Indianapolis	3-7	L	18-48-3	39	172-299
31	Dec 20 @	Phoenix	2-7	L	9-20-2	20	79-135	70	Mar 25 @	Minnesota	4-5	L	18-49-3	39	176-304
32	Dec 22	Quebec	*3-2	W	10-20-2	22	82-137	71	Mar 26	San Diego	2-5	L	18-50-3	39	178-309
33	Dec 26 @	Vancouver	1-8	L	10-21-2	22	83-145	72	Mar 27	Edmonton	2-2	T	18-50-4	40	180-311
34	Dec 28 @	Quebec	1-4	L	10-22-2	22	84-149	73	Mar 30 @	Vancouver	3-4	L	18-51-4	40	183-315
35	Dec 29	Chicago	4-3	W	11-22-2	24	88-152	74	Apr 1 @	San Diego	4-3	W	19-51-4	42	187-318
36	Dec 31	Phoenix	1-1	T	11-22-3	25	89-153	75	Apr 3 @	San Diego	2-9	L	19-52-4	42	189-327
37	Jan 2 @	Houston	3-6	L	11-23-3	25	92-159	76	Apr 5 @	Phoenix	*7-6	W	20-52-4	44	196-333
38	Jan 4 @	Houston	2-5	L	11-24-3	25	94-164	77	Apr 6	Minnesota	*5-6	L	20-53-4	44	201-339
39	Jan 5	Vancouver	3-1	W	12-24-3	27	97-165	78	Apr 7	Houston	4-2	W	21-53-4	46	205-341

As Michigan (October 17, 1974 to January 18, 1975): 13-27-3, 29 pts, 107 gf, 179 ga.
As Baltimore (January 25 to April 7, 1975): 8-26-1, 17 pts, 98 gf, 162 ga.

Stags-Blades Stars of 1974-1975

     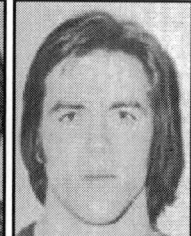

Gary Veneruzzo	**Paul Hoganson**	**Steve West**	**Gary Bredin**	**Larry Johnston**	**Bill Evo**
33 goals led team	2 shutouts	15 goals	15 goals	Veterzn blueliner	13 goals

Scoring

pos	#	player	gp	g	a	pts	pim	+/-	ppg	shg	sog	sc%	gp	g	a	pts	pim
RW	17	Andrascik, Steve	57	4	7	11	42	-18	0	0	118	0.034	-	-	-	-	-
RW	6	Bredin, Gary	67	15	21	36	29	-37	1	0	113	0.133	-	-	-	-	-
D	4	Brown, Arnie	50	3	4	7	27	-32	1	0	63	0.048	-	-	-	-	-
RW	19	Caron, Alain	47	8	5	13	4	-15	5	0	98	0.082	-	-	-	-	-
C		Chartre, Claude	1	0	0	0	0		0	0	2	0.000	-	-	-	-	-
D	15	Curtis, Paul	76	4	15	19	32	-63	1	0	110	0.036	-	-	-	-	-
G	88/1	Desjardins, Gerry	41	0	1	1	13		0	0	0		-	-	-	-	-
RW	14/7	Evo, Bill	49	13	9	22	32	-25			99	0.131	-	-	-	-	-
C	11	Fontaine, Len	21	1	8	9	6				28	0.036	-	-	-	-	-
LW	9	Goldthorpe, Bill	7	0	0	0	26				6	0.000	-	-	-	-	-
LW	8	Gruen, Danny	34	10	16	26	73	-12	3	0	92	0.109	-	-	-	-	-
LW	22	Guite, Pierre	13	5	4	9	11				36	0.139	-	-	-	-	-
G	33/30	Hoganson, Paul	32	0	0	0	12		0	0	0		-	-	-	-	-
D	3	Johnston, Larry	49	0	9	9	93		0	0	51	0.000	-	-	-	-	-
RW	22	Johnstone, Ed	23	4	4	8	43				43	0.093	-	-	-	-	-
LW	11	Jones, Bob	5	0	1	1	8		0	0	10	0.000	-	-	-	-	-
RW	8	Larose, Paul	5	1	1	2	2	-2	0	0	5	0.200	-	-	-	-	-
C	10	Leblanc, J. P.	78	16	33	49	100	-52	3	3	207	0.077	-	-	-	-	-
D	14	Legge, Barry	36	3	18	21	20	-19	3	0	66	0.045	-	-	-	-	-
D	2	Legge, Randy	78	1	14	15	69	-40	0	0	73	0.014	-	-	-	-	-
C	12	Locas, Jacques	12	1	4	5	4				18	0.056	-	-	-	-	-
RW	17	McDonald, Brian	18	3	5	8	15	-11	2	0	39	0.077	-	-	-	-	-
G	30/1	McLeod, Jim	16	0	0	0	0		0	0	0	-	-	-	-	-	-
D	5	Miszuk, John	66	2	19	21	56	-29	0	0	98	0.020	-	-	-	-	-
D	4/20	Reed, Bill	11	0	0	0	12		0	0	14	0.000	-	-	-	-	-
LW	26	Reichmuth, Craig	16	0	2	2	6		0	0	18	0.000	-	-	-	-	-
C	12/9	Richardson, Steve	47	8	18	26	58	-16			107	0.075	-	-	-	-	-
C	9	Rouleau, Michel	7	0	3	3	25		0	0	14	0.000	-	-	-	-	-
RW	25/22	Serviss, Tom	61	12	17	29	18	-35	2	0	134	0.090	-	-	-	-	-
D		Sittler, Gary	5	1	1	2	14		0	0	10	0.100	-	-	-	-	-
C	20/23	Speck, Fred	30	4	8	12	18				65	0.062	-	-	-	-	-
LW	19	Sutherland, Steve	22	1	5	6	37	-10	0	0	25	0.040	-	-	-	-	-
LW	9	Tardif, Marc	23	12	5	17	9	-1	2	0	79	0.152	-	-	-	-	-
LW	21	Thomas, Reg	50	8	13	21	42	-23	2	0	147	0.054	-	-	-	-	-
RW	14	Trottier, Guy	17	5	4	9	2				34	0.147	-	-	-	-	-
LW	18	Veneruzzo, Gary	77	33	27	60	57	-45	9	0	244	0.135	-	-	-	-	-
C	16	West, Steve	50	15	18	33	4	-5	5	0	116	0.129	-	-	-	-	-
RW	12	White, Alton	27	9	12	21	8	-15	4	0	52	0.173	-	-	-	-	-
D	23/24	Zrymiak, Jerry	49	3	9	12	53	-23	0	0	45	0.067	-	-	-	-	-

Power Play: 52 goals scored in 279 opportunities (18.6%) with 12 short-handed goals allowed.
Penalty Killing: 50 goals allowed in 278 opportunities (82.0%) with 4 short-handed goals scored.

Goaltending

goaltender	gp	min	ga	en	so	record	gaa	sog	sv%	gp	min	ga	record	gaa
Desjardins, Gerry	41	2282	162	3	0	9-28-1	4.26	1391	0.884	-	-	-	-	-
Hoganson, Paul	32	1776	121	1	2	9-19-2	4.09	1010	0.880	-	-	-	-	-
McLeod, Jim	16	694	53	1	0	3-6-1	4.58	421	0.874	-	-	-	-	-

Transactions: Daniel Gruen signed to contract, Apr 1974 • Len Fontaine, Gerry Desjardins signed to contracts, May 1974 • Rights to Bill Evo acquired from Edmonton, May 1974 • Steve West signed to contract, Jun 1974 • Paul Curtis, Barry Legge, Larry Johnston signed to contracts, Jul 1974 • Brian McDonald and Jacques Locas traded to Indianapolis for Steve Andrascik and Steve Richardson, Nov. 1974 • Bill Horton to Indianapolis for Gary Bredin, Nov. 1974 • Guy Trottier purchased from Toronto, Nov. 1974 • Marc Tardif and Steve Sutherland traded to Quebec for Alain Caron, Pierre Guite and Michel Rouleau, Dec. 1974 • Michel Rouleau traded to San Diego for Craig Reichmuth, Dec. 1974 • Danny Gruen traded to Winnipeg for future considerations, Feb. 1975. Returned to Baltimore end of season • Arnie Brown and Gary Desjardins made free agents, Mar. 1975; Brown signed by Vancouver, Mar. 1975 • Pierre Guite sold to Cincinnati, Mar 1975

1974-1975 MINNESOTA FIGHTING SAINTS

Coach
Harry Neale
42-32-3

Coach
Jack McCartan
0-1-0

Summary of Games (@ Away, * Overtime)

	date	opponent	score		record	pts	gf-ga		date	opponent	score		record	pts	gf-ga
1	Oct 19	Cleveland	1-3	L	0-1-0	0	1-3	40	Jan 19 @	New England	3-1	W	21-19-0	42	167-138
2	Oct 22 @	Toronto	2-11	L	0-2-0	0	3-14	41	Jan 22	Vancouver	1-2	L	21-20-0	42	168-140
3	Oct 24 @	Indianapolis	3-2	W	1-2-0	2	6-16	42	Jan 24	Toronto	7-5	W	22-20-0	44	175-145
4	Oct 26 @	Houston	2-3	L	1-3-0	2	8-19	43	Jan 26	Baltimore	2-1	W	23-20-0	46	177-146
5	Oct 27	Chicago	*6-5	W	2-3-0	4	14-24	44	Jan 30	Vancouver	6-3	W	24-20-0	48	183-149
6	Oct 29 @	Michigan	*3-4	L	2-4-0	4	17-28	45	Jan 31	Houston	4-1	W	25-20-0	50	187-150
7	Nov 2	Michigan	6-3	W	3-4-0	6	23-31	46	Feb 2	Winnipeg	*5-4	W	26-20-0	52	192-154
8	Nov 5 @	Winnipeg	4-6	L	3-5-0	6	27-37	47	Feb 5	Edmonton	4-2	W	27-20-0	54	196-156
9	Nov 9	Toronto	4-7	L	3-6-0	6	31-44	48	Feb 6 @	San Diego	2-2	T	27-20-1	55	198-158
10	Nov 10	Phoenix	10-4	W	4-6-0	8	41-48	49	Feb 7 @	Phoenix	1-4	L	27-21-1	55	199-162
11	Nov 13	Houston	5-8	L	4-7-0	8	46-56	50	Feb 8 @	San Diego	4-8	L	27-22-1	55	203-170
12	Nov 17 @	Quebec	7-1	W	5-7-0	10	53-57	51	Feb 12	Houston	1-3	L	27-23-1	55	204-173
13	Nov 20 @	Winnipeg	1-3	L	5-8-0	10	54-60	52	Feb 14	Quebec	3-7	L	27-24-1	55	207-180
14	Nov 23	San Diego	3-5	L	5-9-0	10	57-65	53	Feb 16	San Diego	5-2	W	28-24-1	57	212-182
15	Nov 24 @	Michigan	2-3	L	5-10-0	10	59-68	54	Feb 17 @	Cleveland	2-1	W	29-24-1	59	214-183
16	Nov 26 @	Toronto	6-2	W	6-10-0	12	65-70	55	Feb 19 @	Cleveland	5-3	W	30-24-1	61	219-186
17	Nov 30	Chicago	5-7	L	6-11-0	12	70-77	56	Feb 21 @	Indianapolis	2-5	L	30-25-1	61	221-191
18	Dec 1	Phoenix	4-3	W	7-11-0	14	74-80	57	Feb 23 @	Edmonton	4-6	L	30-26-1	61	225-197
19	Dec 4 @	Quebec	6-3	W	8-11-0	16	80-83	58	Feb 25 @	Winnipeg	6-6	T	30-26-2	62	231-203
20	Dec 6	Winnipeg	4-2	W	9-11-0	18	84-85	59	Feb 26	Indianapolis	*4-3	W	31-26-2	64	235-206
21	Dec 8 @	Vancouver	2-4	L	9-12-0	18	86-89	60	Feb 27 @	New England	2-5	L	31-27-2	64	237-211
22	Dec 10 @	Toronto	4-2	W	10-12-0	20	90-91	61	Mar 1 @	Quebec	4-1	W	32-27-2	66	241-212
23	Dec 11 @	New England	1-3	L	10-13-0	20	91-94	62	Mar 2	Toronto	5-3	W	33-27-2	68	246-215
24	Dec 13	Edmonton	4-5	L	10-14-0	20	95-99	63	Mar 5	New England	5-3	W	34-27-2	70	251-218
25	Dec 14 @	Phoenix	3-4	L	10-15-0	20	98-103	64	Mar 9 @	Winnipeg	*5-6	L	34-28-2	70	256-224
26	Dec 15	Quebec	6-4	W	11-15-0	22	104-107	65	Mar 11 @	San Diego	6-4	W	35-28-2	72	262-228
27	Dec 19 @	Indianapolis	6-0	W	12-15-0	24	110-107	66	Mar 12 @	Vancouver	2-4	L	35-29-2	72	264-232
28	Dec 20	Indianapolis	6-4	W	13-15-0	26	116-111	67	Mar 18 @	Vancouver	5-3	W	36-29-2	74	269-235
29	Dec 26 @	Edmonton	5-1	W	14-15-0	28	121-112	68	Mar 23	Edmonton	4-2	W	37-29-2	76	273-237
30	Dec 27	New England	6-3	W	15-15-0	30	127-115	69	Mar 25	Baltimore	5-4	W	38-29-2	78	278-241
31	Dec 28 @	Chicago	3-5	L	15-16-0	30	130-120	70	Mar 26	Chicago	4-3	W	39-29-2	80	282-244
32	Dec 29	Cleveland	6-0	W	16-16-0	32	136-120	71	Mar 28 @	Phoenix	2-2	T	39-29-3	81	284-246
33	Jan 1	Cleveland	6-2	W	17-16-0	34	142-122	72	Mar 29 @	Houston	2-8	L	39-30-3	81	286-254
34	Jan 3	San Diego	1-2	L	17-17-0	34	143-124	73	Mar 30	Indianapolis	5-3	W	40-30-3	83	291-257
35	Jan 5	New England	9-3	W	18-17-0	36	152-127	74	Apr 1	Vancouver	5-2	W	41-30-3	85	296-259
36	Jan 7 @	Chicago	4-2	W	19-17-0	38	156-129	75	Apr 2	Quebec	3-5	L	41-31-3	85	299-264
37	Jan 9 @	Edmonton	2-3	L	19-18-0	38	158-132	76	Apr 4	Phoenix	1-2	L	41-32-3	85	300-266
38	Jan 15 @	Cleveland	4-2	W	20-18-0	40	162-134	77	Apr 5 @	Houston	2-8	L	41-33-3	85	302-274
39	Jan 18 @	Chicago	2-3	L	20-19-0	40	164-137	78	Apr 6 @	Baltimore	*6-5	W	42-33-3	87	308-279

Fighting Saints Stars of 1974-1975

George Morrison
31 goals, +11

Wayne Connelly
38 goals

Don Tannahill
23 goals, +13

John Garrett
30 wins, 2 shutouts

Ron Busniuk
176 minutes, +12

Gary Gambucci
19 goals, +14

Scoring

pos	#	player		Regular Season										Playoffs				
			gp	g	a	pts	pim	+/-	ppg	shg	sog	sc%		gp	g	a	pts	pim
C	12	Antonovich, Mike	67	24	26	50	20	+9	4	0	147	0.163		12	1	4	5	2
D	17	Arbour, John	70	12	43	55	67	-1	4	0	220	0.055		12	0	6	6	23
D	21	Ball, Terry	76	8	37	45	36	+3	2	0	143	0.056		12	3	4	7	4
D	24	Boyd, Bob	13	0	0	0	21		0	0	9	0.000		-	-	-	-	-
RW	19	Brackenbury, Curt	7	0	0	0	22		0	0	0	-		12	0	2	2	59
RW	15	Busniuk, Ron	73	2	21	23	176	+12	0	0	76	0.026		12	2	1	3	63
D	2	Butters, Bill	24	2	2	4	58	-8	0	0	16	0.125		12	1	0	1	21
LW	20	Carlson, Jack	32	5	5	10	85	-1	0	0	50	0.100		10	1	2	3	41
RW	7	Connelly, Wayne	76	38	33	71	16	+14	13	1	260	0.146		12	8	4	12	10
G	1	Curran, Mike	26	0	0	0	18		0	0	0	-		-	-	-	-	-
OLW	16	Gallant, Gord	66	10	13	23	203	-3	1	0	91	0.110		1	1	0	1	0
C	14	Gambucci, Gary	67	19	18	37	19	+14	2	0	121	0.157		12	4	0	4	6
G	35	Garrett, John	58	0	0	0	6		0	0	0	-		12	0	0	0	0
C	10	Hampson, Ted	78	17	36	53	6	-8	1	3	117	0.145		12	1	7	8	0
RW	11	Heatley, Murray	22	5	9	14	31	0	1	0	27	0.185		-	-	-	-	-
C	25	Huck, Fran	78	22	45	67	26	+7	2	3	184	0.120		12	3	13	16	6
C	20	Johnson, Jim	11	1	3	4	0	-4	0	0	16	0.063		-	-	-	-	-
G	30	McCartan, Jack	2	0	0	0	0		0	0	0	-		-	-	-	-	-
D	23	McMahon, Mike	54	5	15	20	42	+6	1	0	78	0.064		7	0	1	1	0
LW	9	Morrison, George	76	31	29	60	30	+11	9	0	177	0.175		12	5	9	14	0
C	22	O'Shea, Danny	76	16	25	41	42	-22	3	0	161	0.099		-	-	-	-	-
RW	8	O'Shea, Kevin	68	10	10	20	42	-9	0	0	106	0.094		-	-	-	-	-
C	26	Robertson, Joe	11	1	4	5	4	+5	0	0	7	0.143		-	-	-	-	-
D	3	Smith, Rick	78	9	29	38	112	+12	1	0	158	0.057		12	2	7	9	6
C	5	Tannahill, Don	72	23	30	53	20	+13	2	4	141	0.163		10	2	4	6	0
C	4	Walton, Mike	75	48	45	93	33	-11	7	4	300	0.160		12	10	7	17	10
D	6	Westrum, Pat	23	0	3	3	48		0	0	10	0.000		-	-	-	-	-

Power Play: 53 goals scored in 228 opportunities (23.2%) with 9 short-handed goals allowed.
Penalty Killing: 47 goals allowed in 256 opportunities (81.6%) with 16 short-handed goals scored.

Goaltending

goaltender	gp	min	ga	en	so	record	gaa	sog	sv%		gp	min	ga	record	gaa
Curran, Mike	26	1367	90	1	0	11-10-1	3.95	836	0.892		-	-	-	-	-
Garrett, John	58	3294	180	3	2	30-23-2	3.28	1890	0.905		12	726	41	6-6	3.39
McCartan, Jack	2	61	5	0	0	1-0-0	4.92	38	0.868		-	-	-	-	-

Transactions: Fran Huck purchased from Winnipeg, Jun 1974 • DonTannahill signed to contract, Jun 1974 • Rights to Danny O'Shea acquired from Winnipeg for future considerations, Jun 1974 • Ron Busniuk, Gary Gambucci signed to contracts, Jul 1974 • Jim Johnson traded to Indianapolis for Joe Robertson, Nov 1974 • Curt Brackenbury purchased from Chicago, Nov 1974 • Murray Heatley traded to Indianapolis for future considerations, Feb. 1975 • Gord Gallant released after altercation with Coach Neale, Apr 1975

1974-1975 NEW ENGLAND WHALERS

Coach
Ron Ryan
40-28-5

Coach
Jack Kelley
3-2-0

Summary of Games (@ Away, * Overtime)

	date	opponent	score		record	pts	gf-ga		date	opponent	score		record	pts	gf-ga
1	Oct 15 @	Toronto	2-6	L	0-1-0	0	2-6	40	Jan 15	Chicago	7-5	W	23-15-2	48	147-141
2	Oct 19	Michigan	2-1	W	1-1-0	2	4-7	41	Jan 17	Toronto	2-1	W	24-15-2	50	149-142
3	Oct 23	Houston	5-4	W	2-1-0	4	9-11	42	Jan 18 @	Quebec	2-8	L	24-16-2	50	151-150
4	Oct 26	Indianapolis	6-1	W	3-1-0	6	15-12	43	Jan 19	Minnesota	1-3	L	24-17-2	50	152-153
5	Oct 30	Toronto	5-2	W	4-1-0	8	20-14	44	Jan 24 @	Phoenix	1-4	L	24-18-2	50	153-157
6	Oct 31 @	Indianapolis	6-1	W	5-1-0	10	26-15	45	Jan 25 @	San Diego	2-6	L	24-19-2	50	155-163
7	Nov 2	Quebec	4-2	W	6-1-0	12	30-17	46	Jan 27	Cleveland	2-0	W	25-19-2	52	157-163
8	Nov 8	San Diego	3-0	W	7-1-0	14	33-17	47	Jan 29	Baltimore	4-3	W	26-19-2	54	161-166
9	Nov 9	Phoenix	2-4	L	7-2-0	14	35-21	48	Jan 31	Baltimore	4-2	W	27-19-2	56	165-168
10	Nov 11 @	Houston	1-6	L	7-3-0	14	36-27	49	Feb 7 @	Winnipeg	*5-4	W	28-19-2	58	170-172
11	Nov 14 @	San Diego	7-2	W	8-3-0	16	43-29	50	Feb 8 @	Vancouver	1-4	L	28-20-2	58	171-176
12	Nov 16 @	Phoenix	3-6	L	8-4-0	16	46-35	51	Feb 9 @	Vancouver	1-5	L	28-21-2	58	172-181
13	Nov 17 @	Michigan	6-1	W	9-4-0	18	52-36	52	Feb 12	Edmonton	2-2	T	28-21-3	59	174-183
14	Nov 19 @	Chicago	5-4	W	10-4-0	20	57-40	53	Feb 14	Indianapolis	*4-3	W	29-21-3	61	178-186
15	Nov 21 @	Indianapolis	4-0	W	11-4-0	22	61-40	54	Feb 18 @	Edmonton	3-6	L	29-22-3	61	181-192
16	Nov 23	Chicago	3-2	W	12-4-0	24	64-42	55	Feb 21 @	Edmonton	4-2	W	30-22-3	63	185-194
17	Nov 24 @	Chicago	9-5	W	13-4-0	26	73-47	56	Feb 23 @	Winnipeg	2-1	W	31-22-3	65	187-195
18	Nov 26 @	Quebec	*5-4	W	14-4-0	28	78-51	57	Feb 25	Vancouver	3-2	W	32-22-3	67	190-197
19	Nov 29 @	Vancouver	1-5	L	14-5-0	28	79-56	58	Feb 26	Chicago	3-4	L	32-23-3	67	193-201
20	Dec 1 @	Edmonton	4-8	L	14-6-0	28	83-64	59	Feb 27	Minnesota	5-2	W	33-23-3	69	198-203
21	Dec 3 @	Michigan	1-2	L	14-7-0	28	84-66	60	Mar 1	Cleveland	4-4	T	33-23-4	70	202-207
22	Dec 4 @	Cleveland	3-2	W	15-7-0	30	87-68	61	Mar 2	Vancouver	4-1	W	34-23-4	72	206-208
23	Dec 5 @	Quebec	1-9	L	15-8-0	30	88-77	62	Mar 5 @	Minnesota	3-5	L	34-24-4	72	209-213
24	Dec 7	Indianapolis	6-3	W	16-8-0	32	94-80	63	Mar 8 @	Houston	5-4	W	35-24-4	74	214-217
25	Dec 11	Minnesota	3-1	W	17-8-0	34	97-81	64	Mar 11	Winnipeg	6-2	W	36-24-4	76	220-219
26	Dec 14	Quebec	9-4	W	18-8-0	36	106-85	65	Mar 13	Phoenix	5-5	T	36-24-5	77	225-224
27	Dec 15 @	Winnipeg	4-3	W	19-8-0	38	110-88	66	Mar 15	Edmonton	6-2	W	37-24-5	79	231-226
28	Dec 17 @	Michigan	2-2	T	19-8-1	39	112-90	67	Mar 16	Toronto	7-5	W	38-24-5	81	238-231
29	Dec 20 @	Cleveland	0-3	L	19-9-1	39	112-93	68	Mar 19	San Diego	1-6	L	38-25-5	81	239-237
30	Dec 21	Houston	3-5	L	19-10-1	39	115-98	69	Mar 21	Winnipeg	3-6	L	38-26-5	81	242-243
31	Dec 22 @	Indianapolis	1-2	L	19-11-1	39	116-100	70	Mar 22	Houston	3-5	L	38-27-5	81	245-248
32	Dec 27 @	Minnesota	3-6	L	19-12-1	39	119-106	71	Mar 25	Edmonton	5-4	W	39-27-5	83	250-252
33	Dec 28 @	Houston	1-6	L	19-13-1	39	120-112	72	Mar 27	Cleveland	5-3	W	40-27-5	85	255-255
34	Jan 3 @	Toronto	5-3	W	20-13-1	41	125-115	73	Mar 29	Winnipeg	3-9	L	40-28-5	85	258-264
35	Jan 4	Vancouver	*4-3	W	21-13-1	43	129-118	74	Mar 30 @	Toronto	4-3	W	41-28-5	87	262-267
36	Jan 5 @	Minnesota	3-9	L	21-14-1	43	132-127	75	Apr 1	Phoenix	5-3	W	42-28-5	89	267-270
37	Jan 7 @	San Diego	3-5	L	21-15-1	43	135-132	76	Apr 3	Quebec	4-1	W	43-28-5	91	271-271
38	Jan 9 @	Phoenix	1-1	T	21-15-2	44	136-133	77	Apr 4 @	Chicago	1-3	L	43-29-5	91	272-274
39	Jan 11	San Diego	*4-3	W	22-15-2	46	140-136	78	Apr 5 @	Cleveland	2-5	L	43-30-5	91	274-279

Whalers Stars of 1974-1975

Wayne Carleton
35 goals, 74 points

Tom Webster
40 goals

Al Smith
33 wins

Jim Dorey
+6 from blueline

T. Abrahamsson
30 points, +8

Ted Green
Vetern blueliner

Scoring

pos	#	player	gp	g	a	pts	pim	+/-	ppg	shg	sog	sc%	gp	g	a	pts	pim
G	29	Abrahamsson, Christer	15	0	0	0	0		0	0	0	-	-	-	-	-	-
D	19	Abrahamsson, Thommie	76	8	22	30	46	+8	2	0	151	0.053	-	-	-	-	-
G	30	Berglund, Bill	2	0	0	0	0		0	0	0	-	-	-	-	-	-
LW	22	Blackburn, Don	50	18	32	50	16	+9	7	0	78	0.231	5	1	2	3	2
RW	21	Byers, Mike	72	22	26	48	10	+6	1	0	157	0.140	6	2	2	4	2
C	7	Caffery, Terry	67	15	37	52	12	-8	2	0	133	0.113	-	-	-	-	-
LW	9	Carleton, Wayne	73	35	39	74	50	+8	3	0	323	0.109	6	2	5	7	14
LW	18	Charlebois, Bob	8	1	0	1	0	-4	0	0	6	0.167	4	1	0	1	0
LW	15	Climie, Ron	25	8	4	12	12	0	0	0	43	0.186	6	3	0	3	2
C	12	Danby, John	0	-	-	-	-	-	-	-	-	-	4	0	1	1	0
D	10	Dorey, Jim	31	5	17	22	43	+6	1	1	85	0.059	-	-	-	-	-
RW	27	Earl, Tom	72	3	8	11	20	-13	0	1	52	0.057	6	1	1	2	12
LW	23	Fotiu, Nick	61	2	2	4	144	-14	0	0	40	0.050	4	2	0	2	27
LW	11	French, John	75	12	41	53	28	-5	2	1	140	0.086	4	1	2	3	0
D	6	Green, Ted	57	6	14	20	29	-13	1	0	75	0.080	-	-	-	-	-
D	17	Hangsleben, Alan	26	0	4	4	8	-14	0	0	25	0.000	6	0	3	3	19
D	5	Hurley, Paul	75	3	26	29	36	-10	0	0	149	0.020	6	0	1	1	4
C	14	Karlander, Al	48	7	14	21	2	-4	0	0	64	0.109	5	0	3	3	0
G	30	Landon, Bruce	7	0	0	0	0		0	0	0	-	-	-	-	-	-
D	2	Ley, Rick	62	6	36	42	50	0	1	1	125	0.048	6	1	1	2	32
LW	18	Methe, Gerry	5	0	1	1	4	-2	0	0	2	0.000	-	-	-	-	-
RW	16	O'Donnell, Fred	76	21	15	36	84	-6	0	0	131	0.160	-	-	-	-	-
G	30	Ouimet, Ted	1	0	0	0	0		0	0	0	-	-	-	-	-	-
C	4	Pleau, Larry	78	30	34	64	50	+3	6	0	208	0.144	6	2	3	5	14
D	3	Selwood, Brad	77	4	35	39	117	+1	3	0	148	0.027	5	1	0	1	11
RW	10	Sheehy, Tim	52	21	13	34	18	-10	3	0	131	0.160	-	-	-	-	-
G	1	Smith, Al	59	0	0	0	18		0	0	0	-	6	0	0	0	0
C	20	Swain, Garry	66	7	15	22	18	-7	0	2	71	0.099	6	0	3	3	41
RW	8	Webster, Tom	66	40	24	64	52	+1	7	0	212	0.189	3	0	2	2	0

Power Play: 38 goals scored in 225 opportunities (17.3%) with 5 short-handed goals allowed.
Penalty Killing: 29 goals allowed in 215 opportunities (86.5%) with 6 short-handed goals scored.

Goaltending

goaltender	gp	min	ga	en	so	record	gaa	sog	sv%	gp	min	ga	record	gaa
Abrahamsson, C.	15	870	47	0	1	8-6-1	3.24	504	0.907	-	-	-	-	-
Berglund, Bill	2	36	3	0	0	0-0-0	5.00	16	0.813	-	-	-	-	-
Landon, Bruce	7	339	19	0	0	2-3-0	3.36	190	0.900	-	-	-	-	-
Ouimet, Ted	1	20	3	0	0	0-0-0	9.00	13	0.769	-	-	-	-	-
Smith, Al	59	3494	202	5	2	33-21-4	3.47	1725	0.883	6	366	28	2-4	4.59

Transactions: Fred O'Donnell signed to contract, Feb 1974 • Nick Fotiu, Gerry Methe, Thommie and Christer Abrahamsson signed to contracts, Jun 1974 • Thommie Abrahamsson and Christer Abrahamsson signed to contracts, Aug 1974 • Jim Dorey traded to Toronto for Sep 1974 Wayne Carleton trade, Dec 1974 • Ted Ouimet purchased from Cleveland, Dec 1974 • Tim Sheehy traded to Edmonton for Ron Climie, Feb 1975

1974-1975 PHOENIX ROADRUNNERS

Coach
Sandy Hucul

Summary of Games (@ Away, * Overtime)

	date	opponent	score		record	pts	gf-ga		date	opponent	score		record	pts	gf-ga
1	Oct 16	San Diego	8-2	W	1-0-0	2	8-2	40	Jan 12 @	Cleveland	2-4	L	19-16-5	43	134-128
2	Oct 18	Houston	6-4	W	2-0-0	4	14-6	41	Jan 14 @	Chicago	2-5	L	19-17-5	43	136-133
3	Oct 20	Cleveland	4-4	T	2-0-1	5	18-10	42	Jan 15	Toronto	5-5	T	19-17-6	44	141-138
4	Oct 24 @	San Diego	1-2	L	2-1-1	5	19-12	43	Jan 17	Edmonton	1-7	L	19-18-6	44	142-145
5	Oct 26 @	Quebec	1-4	L	2-2-1	5	20-16	44	Jan 18	Edmonton	3-1	W	20-18-6	46	145-146
6	Oct 28 @	Toronto	3-7	L	2-3-1	5	23-23	45	Jan 22	Chicago	8-5	W	21-18-6	48	153-151
7	Oct 30 @	Winnipeg	*5-6	L	2-4-1	5	28-29	46	Jan 24	New England	4-1	W	22-18-6	50	157-152
8	Nov 2 @	Houston	2-8	L	2-5-1	5	30-37	47	Jan 26	Indianapolis	6-0	W	23-18-6	52	163-152
9	Nov 5 @	Indianapolis	3-0	W	3-5-1	7	33-37	48	Jan 28 @	Indianapolis	3-1	W	24-18-6	54	166-153
10	Nov 9 @	New England	4-2	W	4-5-1	9	37-39	49	Jan 29 @	Cleveland	2-6	L	24-19-6	54	168-159
11	Nov 10 @	Minnesota	4-10	L	4-6-1	9	41-49	50	Jan 30	Winnipeg	3-5	L	24-20-6	54	171-164
12	Nov 14	Cleveland	1-2	L	4-7-1	9	42-51	51	Feb 1	Baltimore	8-1	W	25-20-6	56	179-165
13	Nov 16	New England	6-3	W	5-7-1	11	48-54	52	Feb 5	San Diego	9-2	W	26-20-6	58	188-167
14	Nov 21 @	Michigan	1-2	L	5-8-1	11	49-56	53	Feb 7	Minnesota	4-1	W	27-20-6	60	192-168
15	Nov 24 @	Winnipeg	3-1	W	6-8-1	13	52-57	54	Feb 8	Quebec	*3-4	L	27-21-6	60	195-172
16	Nov 26 @	Houston	6-4	W	7-8-1	15	58-61	55	Feb 9 @	Edmonton	6-4	W	28-21-6	62	201-176
17	Nov 27	Chicago	2-4	L	7-9-1	15	60-65	56	Feb 12 @	Vancouver	4-5	L	28-22-6	62	205-181
18	Nov 29	Toronto	4-4	T	7-9-2	16	64-69	57	Feb 13	Quebec	3-5	L	28-23-6	62	208-186
19	Dec 1 @	Minnesota	3-4	L	7-10-2	16	67-73	58	Feb 16 @	Edmonton	5-4	W	29-23-6	64	213-190
20	Dec 3 @	San Diego	*5-4	W	8-10-2	18	72-77	59	Feb 18 @	San Diego	0-7	L	29-24-6	64	213-197
21	Dec 4	San Diego	0-2	L	8-11-2	18	72-79	60	Feb 22 @	Baltimore	3-1	W	30-24-6	66	216-198
22	Dec 6	Edmonton	3-1	W	9-11-2	20	75-80	61	Feb 27	Houston	2-7	L	30-25-6	66	218-205
23	Dec 8	Toronto	2-5	L	9-12-2	20	77-85	62	Mar 1	Indianapolis	12-2	W	31-25-6	68	230-207
24	Dec 10 @	Chicago	4-2	W	10-12-2	22	81-87	63	Mar 2	Chicago	5-0	W	32-25-6	70	235-207
25	Dec 12	Vancouver	4-2	W	11-12-2	24	85-89	64	Mar 5	Quebec	6-3	W	33-25-6	72	241-210
26	Dec 14	Minnesota	4-3	W	12-12-2	26	89-92	65	Mar 7	Winnipeg	7-4	W	34-25-6	74	248-214
27	Dec 18	Vancouver	5-3	W	13-12-2	28	94-95	66	Mar 9 @	Vancouver	3-4	L	34-26-6	74	251-218
28	Dec 20	Michigan	7-2	W	14-12-2	30	101-97	67	Mar 11 @	Toronto	4-7	L	34-27-6	74	255-225
29	Dec 22 @	Winnipeg	4-2	W	15-12-2	32	105-99	68	Mar 13 @	New England	5-5	T	34-27-7	75	260-230
30	Dec 26	Winnipeg	2-3	L	15-13-2	32	107-102	69	Mar 18 @	Chicago	7-3	W	35-27-7	77	267-233
31	Dec 28	Cleveland	*3-2	W	16-13-2	34	110-104	70	Mar 19 @	Cleveland	4-5	L	35-28-7	77	271-238
32	Dec 30 @	Quebec	6-3	W	17-13-2	36	116-107	71	Mar 22	Vancouver	4-2	W	36-28-7	79	275-240
33	Dec 31 @	Michigan	1-1	T	17-13-3	37	117-108	72	Mar 23	Indianapolis	5-3	W	37-28-7	81	280-243
34	Jan 2 @	Vancouver	2-3	L	17-14-3	37	119-111	73	Mar 26	Houston	2-1	W	38-28-7	83	282-244
35	Jan 3 @	Edmonton	3-3	T	17-14-4	38	122-114	74	Mar 28	Minnesota	2-2	T	38-28-8	84	284-246
36	Jan 5 @	Indianapolis	2-1	W	18-14-4	40	124-115	75	Mar 30 @	Quebec	*5-6	L	38-29-8	84	289-252
37	Jan 7 @	Toronto	3-2	W	19-14-4	42	127-117	76	Apr 1 @	New England	3-5	L	38-30-8	84	292-257
38	Jan 9	New England	1-1	T	19-14-5	43	128-118	77	Apr 4 @	Minnesota	2-1	W	39-30-8	86	294-258
39	Jan 11 @	Houston	4-6	L	19-15-5	43	132-124	78	Apr 5	Baltimore	*6-7	L	39-31-8	86	300-265

204

Roadrunners Stars of 1974-1975

Robbie Ftorek	Michel Cormier	John Gray	Dennis Sobchuk	John Hughes	Gary Kurt
31 goals, +49	36 goals	35 goals	32 goals, +35	+49 on defense	25 wins, 2 shutouts

Scoring

pos	#	player	Regular Season										Playoffs				
			gp	g	a	pts	pim	+/-	ppg	shg	sog	sc%	gp	g	a	pts	pim
LW	12	Barlow, Bob	51	6	20	26	8	-9	0	0	94	0.064	-	-	-	-	-
RW	19	Bennett, Wendell	67	4	15	19	92	+5	0	0	58	0.069	5	1	2	3	6
LW	22	Borgeson, Don	74	29	28	57	38	+20	3	2	205	0.141	5	0	1	1	2
C	14	Boyd, Jim	76	26	44	70	18	+29	7	3	188	0.138	5	1	1	2	2
RW	17	Connor, Cam	57	9	19	28	168	+20	0	0	91	0.099	5	0	0	0	2
LW	16	Cormier, Michel	78	36	38	74	26	+18	5	1	242	0.149	5	1	0	1	2
C	8	Ftorek, Robbie	53	31	37	68	29	+49	4	0	155	0.200	5	2	5	7	2
RW	10	Gorman, Dave	13	3	5	8	10		0	0	15	0.200	-	-	-	-	-
LW	15	Gray, John	75	35	33	68	107	+28	4	0	155	0.226	5	2	3	5	12
C	7	Harris, Hugh	22	10	10	20	15	+2	1	0	53	0.189	-	-	-	-	-
D	24	Hughes, John	72	4	25	29	201	+49	2	0	91	0.044	-	-	-	-	-
C	11	Keogan, Murray	78	35	29	64	68	-12	11	0	225	0.156	5	0	1	1	0
G	1	Kurt, Gary	47	0	2	2	4		0	0	0	-	4	0	0	0	0
D	4	Lariviere, Garry	4	0	1	1	28		0	0	14	0.000	1	0	0	0	0
D	3	McLeod, Al	77	3	16	19	98	+12	0	0	75	0.040	5	0	4	4	4
D	7	McNamee, Pete	55	9	19	28	77	+5	1	0	90	0.100	5	1	0	1	2
LW	20	Migneault, John	47	6	13	19	16	-4	1	0	63	0.095	1	0	0	0	0
RW	18	Mowat, Bob	53	9	10	19	34	-4	0	1	56	0.161	3	0	0	0	0
D	5	Newell, Rick	25	0	4	4	39	+3	0	0	24	0.000	5	0	1	1	2
D	2	Niekamp, Jim	71	2	26	28	66	+12	1	0	78	0.026	-	-	-	-	-
G	30	Norris, Jack	33	0	1	1	2		0	0	0	-	2	0	0	0	0
D	6	Odrowski, Gerry	77	5	38	43	77	+23	2	0	143	0.035	5	0	2	2	0
C	9	Sobchuk, Dennis	78	32	45	77	36	+35	4	0	242	0.132	5	4	1	5	2
LW		Sobchuk, Gene	3	1	0	1	0		1	0	9	0.111	5	0	0	0	0
D	23	Stevens, Mike	70	2	16	18	69	+15	0	0	86	0.023	5	0	1	1	0
D	4	Young, Howie	30	3	12	15	44	-2	1	0	46	0.065	-	-	-	-	-

Power Play: 50 goals scored in 304 opportunities (16.4%) with 6 short-handed goals allowed.
Penalty Killing: 76 goals allowed in 315 opportunities (75.9%) with 7 short-handed goals scored.

Goaltending

goaltender	gp	min	ga	en	so	record	gaa	sog	sv%	gp	min	ga	record	gaa
Kurt, Gary	47	2841	156	1	2	25-16-4	3.29	1356	0.885	4	207	12	1-2	3.48
Norris, Jack	33	1962	107	1	1	14-15-4	3.27	979	0.891	2	100	10	0-2	6.00

Transactions: Rights to Jim Niekamp acquired from Michigan for rights to Danny Gruen, May 1974 • Robbie Ftorek, Rick Newell signed to contracts, Jun 1974 • Garry Lariviere acquired from Chicago for future considerations, Jun 1974 • John Hughes, Dennis Sobchuk and Gene Sobchuk on loan from Cincinnati for 1974-75 season, Jul 1974 (Hughes to Cincinnati from Houston for future considerations, May 1974) • John Gray signed to contract, Jul 1974 • Hugh Harris purchased from New England, Aug 1974 • Al McLeod signed to contract, Aug 1974 • Jack Norris acquired from Indianapolis, Sep 1974 (Indianapolis had acquired Norris from Edmonton for future considerations, Jun 1974) • Hugh Harris traded to Vancouver for John Migneault, Serge Beaudoin and Pete McNamee, Nov 1974 • Howie Young sold to Winnipeg, Jan 1975 • Bob Barlow, Wendell Bennett, Michel Cormier, Murray Keogan, Bob Mowat and Howie Young holdover members of 1973-74 WHL club.

1974-1975 QUEBEC NORDIQUES

**Coach
Jean-Guy Gendron**

Summary of Games (@ Away, * Overtime)

	date	opponent	score		record	pts	gf-ga		date	opponent	score		record	pts	gf-ga
1	Oct 20	Indianapolis	4-1	W	1-0-0	2	4-1	40	Jan 12 @	Edmonton	3-1	W	25-15-0	50	164-131
2	Oct 22	Houston	7-2	W	2-0-0	4	11-3	41	Jan 14 @	Vancouver	6-2	W	26-15-0	52	170-133
3	Oct 23	Michigan	6-2	W	3-0-0	6	17-5	42	Jan 18	New England	8-2	W	27-15-0	54	178-135
4	Oct 26	Phoenix	4-1	W	4-0-0	8	21-6	43	Jan 19 @	Chicago	5-2	W	28-15-0	56	183-137
5	Oct 27 @	Indianapolis	3-5	L	4-1-0	8	24-11	44	Jan 23	Cleveland	3-5	L	28-16-0	56	186-142
6	Nov 2 @	New England	2-4	L	4-2-0	8	26-15	45	Jan 25	Chicago	6-4	W	29-16-0	58	192-146
7	Nov 4 @	Toronto	5-3	W	5-2-0	10	31-18	46	Jan 28 @	Toronto	4-6	L	29-17-0	58	196-152
8	Nov 6	Vancouver	5-3	W	6-2-0	12	36-21	47	Jan 30 @	Chicago	5-2	W	30-17-0	60	201-154
9	Nov 10	San Diego	3-4	L	6-3-0	12	39-25	48	Feb 1 @	Indianapolis	2-1	W	31-17-0	62	203-155
10	Nov 12 @	Michigan	5-4	W	7-3-0	14	44-29	49	Feb 2 @	Cleveland	4-3	W	32-17-0	64	207-158
11	Nov 13	Indianapolis	10-3	W	8-3-0	16	54-32	50	Feb 6 @	Houston	4-3	W	33-17-0	66	211-161
12	Nov 16	Michigan	4-3	W	9-3-0	18	58-35	51	Feb 8 @	Phoenix	*4-3	W	34-17-0	68	215-164
13	Nov 17	Minnesota	1-7	L	9-4-0	18	59-42	52	Feb 11 @	San Diego	2-9	L	34-18-0	68	217-173
14	Nov 20	Edmonton	4-2	W	10-4-0	20	63-44	53	Feb 13 @	Phoenix	5-3	W	35-18-0	70	222-176
15	Nov 22	Cleveland	3-2	W	11-4-0	22	66-46	54	Feb 14 @	Minnesota	7-3	W	36-18-0	72	229-179
16	Nov 23	Toronto	2-9	L	11-5-0	22	68-55	55	Feb 17	Houston	3-5	L	36-19-0	72	232-184
17	Nov 24 @	Cleveland	1-3	L	11-6-0	22	69-58	56	Feb 19 @	Houston	4-10	L	36-20-0	72	236-194
18	Nov 26	New England	*4-5	L	11-7-0	22	73-63	57	Feb 20 @	San Diego	2-5	L	36-21-0	72	238-199
19	Nov 28 @	Indianapolis	7-5	W	12-7-0	24	80-68	58	Feb 23	San Diego	6-4	W	37-21-0	74	244-203
20	Dec 1 @	Winnipeg	2-3	L	12-8-0	24	82-71	59	Feb 24	San Diego	5-3	W	38-21-0	76	249-206
21	Dec 4	Minnesota	3-6	L	12-9-0	24	85-77	60	Feb 27	Vancouver	9-7	W	39-21-0	78	258-213
22	Dec 5	New England	9-1	W	13-9-0	26	94-78	61	Mar 1	Minnesota	1-4	L	39-22-0	78	259-217
23	Dec 8	Houston	2-1	W	14-9-0	28	96-79	62	Mar 4	San Diego	2-8	L	39-23-0	78	261-225
24	Dec 11	Edmonton	*4-3	W	15-9-0	30	100-82	63	Mar 5 @	Phoenix	3-6	L	39-24-0	78	264-231
25	Dec 12	Cleveland	5-2	W	16-9-0	32	105-84	64	Mar 7 @	Toronto	4-1	W	40-24-0	80	268-232
26	Dec 14 @	New England	4-9	L	16-10-0	32	109-93	65	Mar 9	Chicago	7-5	W	41-24-0	82	275-237
27	Dec 15 @	Minnesota	4-6	L	16-11-0	32	113-99	66	Mar 12	Winnipeg	5-3	W	42-24-0	84	280-240
28	Dec 17 @	Chicago	6-1	W	17-11-0	34	119-100	67	Mar 14 @	Winnipeg	3-4	L	42-25-0	84	283-244
29	Dec 18	Winnipeg	5-1	W	18-11-0	36	124-101	68	Mar 15 @	Vancouver	4-7	L	42-26-0	84	287-251
30	Dec 20	Chicago	3-5	L	18-12-0	36	127-106	69	Mar 16 @	Vancouver	2-4	L	42-27-0	84	289-255
31	Dec 22 @	Michigan	*2-3	L	18-13-0	36	129-109	70	Mar 18 @	Edmonton	5-8	L	42-28-0	84	294-263
32	Dec 27 @	Cleveland	3-4	L	18-14-0	36	132-113	71	Mar 20 @	Houston	3-5	L	42-29-0	84	297-268
33	Dec 28	Michigan	4-1	W	19-14-0	38	136-114	72	Mar 26	Edmonton	4-6	L	42-30-0	84	301-274
34	Dec 30	Phoenix	3-6	L	19-15-0	38	139-120	73	Mar 29	Toronto	*4-5	L	42-31-0	84	305-279
35	Jan 1	Indianapolis	6-3	W	20-15-0	40	145-123	74	Mar 30	Phoenix	*6-5	W	43-31-0	86	311-284
36	Jan 4	Toronto	3-1	W	21-15-0	42	148-124	75	Apr 1 @	Edmonton	5-3	W	44-31-0	88	316-287
37	Jan 7 @	Michigan	*3-2	W	22-15-0	44	151-126	76	Apr 2 @	Minnesota	5-3	W	45-31-0	90	321-290
38	Jan 8	Vancouver	4-3	W	23-15-0	46	155-129	77	Apr 3 @	New England	1-4	L	45-32-0	90	322-294
39	Jan 10 @	Winnipeg	6-1	W	24-15-0	48	161-130	78	Apr 5	Winnipeg	9-5	W	46-32-0	92	331-299

Nordiques Stars of 1974-1975

Marc Tardif	Rejean Houle	Serge Bernier	Real Cloutier	Richard Brodeur	J.-C. Tremblay
38 goals as Nordique	40 goals, 92 points	54 goals, 122 points	26 goals as rookie	29 wins, 8 in playoffs	72 points, +27

Scoring

pos	#	player	gp	g	a	pts	pim	+/-	ppg	shg	sog	sc%	gp	g	a	pts	pim
G	1	Aubry, Serge	31	0	1	1	22		0	0	0	-	-	-	-	-	-
D	2	Beaule, Alain	22	4	7	11	19	+5	0	0	29	0.138	-	-	-	-	-
D	24	Bernier, Jean	34	1	13	14	13	+9	0	0	55	0.018	9	0	1	1	2
C	21	Bernier, Serge	76	54	68	122	75	+27	11	3	335	0.161	16	8	8	16	6
C	11	Bordeleau, Christian	53	15	33	48	24	+2	2	2	187	0.080	15	2	13	15	2
G	30	Brodeur, Richard	51	0	0	0	5		0	0	0	-	15	0	0	0	0
RW	19	Caron, Alain	21	7	3	10	2	-1	6		35	0.200	-	-	-	-	-
RW	9	Cloutier, Real	63	26	27	53	36	+16	5		154	0.169	12	4	3	7	2
LW	14	Constantin, Charlie	20	2	4	6	9	0	0	0	14	0.143	-	-	-	-	-
LW	7	Garneau, J. C.	17	0	5	5	27		0	0			-	-	-	-	-
C	16	Gaudette, Andre	67	10	17	27	6	-4	0	0	88	0.114	9	0	1	1	0
C	17	Gilbert, Jeannot	58	7	21	28	12	-10	1	0	46	0.152	11	3	6	9	2
D	2	Globensky, Alan	5	0	0	0	5		0	0	2	0.000	2	1	0	1	0
LW	25	Guindon, Robert	69	12	18	30	23	-11	1	0	134	0.090	15	7	6	13	10
LW	6	Guite, Pierre	22	14	8	22	59		1		50	0.280	-	-	-	-	-
D	33	Hoganson, Dale	78	9	35	44	47		3	1	221	0.041	13	1	3	4	4
RW	5	Houle, Rejean	64	40	52	92	37	+20	13	1	275	0.145	15	10	6	16	2
D	20	Jordan, Ric	56	6	8	14	75	-26	0	0	79	0.076	-	-	-	-	-
D	4	Lacombe, Francois	55	7	17	24	54	+13	0	0	109	0.064	15	0	2	2	4
RW	15	Leclerc, Rene	72	18	32	50	85	-10	2	0	206	0.087	14	7	7	14	41
C	12	Parizeau, Michel	78	28	46	74	69	+9	5	2	145	0.193	15	2	4	6	10
RW	21	Patry, Denis	3	1	2	3	2		0	0	4	0.250	-	-	-	-	-
C	27	Rouleau, Michel	19	1	7	8	63		0	0	21	0.048	-	-	-	-	-
D	10	Roy, Pierre	61	1	18	19	118	-3	0	0	57	0.018	15	0	9	9	40
LW	19	Sutherland, Steve	56	14	15	29	114	-3	0	0	110	0.127	13	0	3	3	34
LW	8	Tardif, Marc	53	38	34	72	70	+13	9	0	207	0.184	15	10	11	21	10
D	3	Tremblay, J. C.	68	16	56	72	18	+27	2	0	176	0.091	11	0	10	10	2

Power Play: 62 goals scored in 284 opportunities (21.8%) with 12 short-handed goals allowed.
Penalty Killing: 51 goals allowed in 237 opportunities (78.5%) with 11 short-handed goals scored.

Goaltending

goaltender	gp	min	ga	en	so	record	gaa	sog	sv%	gp	min	ga	record	gaa
Aubry, Serge	31	1762	109	0	0	17-11-0	3.71	959	0.886	-	-	-	-	-
Brodeur, Richard	51	2938	188	2	0	29-21-0	3.90	1737	0.892	15	906	48	8-7	3.18

Transactions: Ric Jordan acquired from New England for Guy Dufour, May 1974 • Alain Beaule traded to Winnipeg for Christian Bordeleau, Nov 1974 • Alain Caron, Michel Rouleau and Pierre Guite traded to Michigan for Marc Tardif and Steve Sutherland, Dec 1974

207

1974-1975 SAN DIEGO MARINERS

Player-Coach
Harry Howell

Bench Coach
Ron Ingram

Summary of Games (@ Away, * Overtime)

	date	opponent	score		record	pts	gf-ga
1	Oct 16 @	Phoenix	2-8	L	0-1-0	0	2-8
2	Oct 19	Houston	6-2	W	1-1-0	2	8-10
3	Oct 22	Cleveland	5-2	W	2-1-0	4	13-12
4	Oct 24	Phoenix	2-1	W	3-1-0	6	15-13
5	Oct 31	Chicago	4-3	W	4-1-0	8	19-16
6	Nov 3 @	Vancouver	6-2	W	5-1-0	10	25-18
7	Nov 5 @	Houston	3-9	L	5-2-0	10	28-27
8	Nov 7 @	Indianapolis	0-3	L	5-3-0	10	28-30
9	Nov 8 @	New England	0-3	L	5-4-0	10	28-33
10	Nov 10 @	Quebec	4-3	W	6-4-0	12	32-36
11	Nov 12 @	Chicago	4-2	W	7-4-0	14	36-38
12	Nov 14	New England	2-7	L	7-5-0	14	38-45
13	Nov 15	Cleveland	3-5	L	7-6-0	14	41-50
14	Nov 17 @	Houston	4-3	W	8-6-0	16	45-53
15	Nov 19	Vancouver	3-2	W	9-6-0	18	48-55
16	Nov 23 @	Minnesota	5-3	W	10-6-0	20	53-58
17	Nov 26	Edmonton	5-1	W	11-6-0	22	58-59
18	Nov 28	Chicago	2-3	L	11-7-0	22	60-62
19	Dec 1	Toronto	1-3	L	11-8-0	22	61-65
20	Dec 3	Phoenix	*4-5	L	11-9-0	22	65-70
21	Dec 4 @	Phoenix	2-0	W	12-9-0	24	67-70
22	Dec 5 @	Michigan	3-5	L	12-10-0	24	70-75
23	Dec 7 @	Cleveland	1-3	L	12-11-0	24	71-78
24	Dec 8 @	Indianapolis	3-5	L	12-12-0	24	74-83
25	Dec 10	Michigan	4-4	T	12-12-1	25	78-87
26	Dec 14	Indianapolis	2-0	W	13-12-1	27	80-87
27	Dec 15 @	Houston	4-3	W	14-12-1	29	84-90
28	Dec 17	Cleveland	8-3	W	15-12-1	31	92-93
29	Dec 19	Edmonton	*6-7	L	15-13-1	31	98-100
30	Dec 21 @	Vancouver	1-2	L	15-14-1	31	99-102
31	Dec 22 @	Edmonton	3-6	L	15-15-1	31	102-108
32	Dec 28	Winnipeg	4-6	L	15-16-1	31	106-114
33	Jan 1 @	Edmonton	*2-3	L	15-17-1	31	108-117
34	Jan 3 @	Minnesota	2-1	W	16-17-1	33	110-118
35	Jan 4 @	Cleveland	2-0	W	17-17-1	35	112-118
36	Jan 7	New England	5-3	W	18-17-1	37	117-121
37	Jan 10 @	Toronto	3-4	L	18-18-1	37	120-125
38	Jan 11 @	New England	*3-4	L	18-19-1	37	123-129
39	Jan 14	Toronto	6-4	W	19-19-1	39	129-133
40	Jan 16	Edmonton	3-2	W	20-19-1	41	132-135
41	Jan 18	Houston	*5-4	W	21-19-1	43	137-139
42	Jan 23	Vancouver	6-1	W	22-19-1	45	143-140
43	Jan 25	New England	6-2	W	23-19-1	47	149-142
44	Jan 28	Winnipeg	7-9	L	23-20-1	47	156-151
45	Feb 4	Toronto	8-4	W	24-20-1	49	164-155
46	Feb 5 @	Phoenix	2-9	L	24-21-1	49	166-164
47	Feb 6	Minnesota	2-2	T	24-21-2	50	168-166
48	Feb 8	Minnesota	8-4	W	25-21-2	52	176-170
49	Feb 11	Quebec	9-2	W	26-21-2	54	185-172
50	Feb 13 @	Baltimore	6-1	W	27-21-2	56	191-173
51	Feb 14 @	Cleveland	2-3	L	27-22-2	56	193-176
52	Feb 16 @	Minnesota	2-5	L	27-23-2	56	195-181
53	Feb 18	Phoenix	7-0	W	28-23-2	58	202-181
54	Feb 20	Quebec	5-2	W	29-23-2	60	207-183
55	Feb 23 @	Quebec	4-6	L	29-24-2	60	211-189
56	Feb 24 @	Quebec	3-5	L	29-25-2	60	214-194
57	Feb 25 @	Toronto	4-6	L	29-26-2	60	218-200
58	Feb 28 @	Winnipeg	3-4	L	29-27-2	60	221-204
59	Mar 2 @	Winnipeg	4-4	T	29-27-3	61	225-208
60	Mar 4	Quebec	8-2	W	30-27-3	63	233-210
61	Mar 6	Houston	7-4	W	31-27-3	65	240-214
62	Mar 8	Winnipeg	6-5	W	32-27-3	67	246-219
63	Mar 11	Minnesota	4-6	L	32-28-3	67	250-225
64	Mar 14 @	Toronto	6-4	W	33-28-3	69	256-229
65	Mar 16 @	Chicago	2-4	L	33-29-3	69	258-233
66	Mar 19 @	New England	6-1	W	34-29-3	71	264-234
67	Mar 20	Chicago	2-4	L	34-30-3	71	266-238
68	Mar 22	Indianapolis	6-3	W	35-30-3	73	272-241
69	Mar 23	Vancouver	*1-0	W	36-30-3	75	273-241
70	Mar 25 @	Chicago	6-4	W	37-30-3	77	279-245
71	Mar 26 @	Baltimore	5-2	W	38-30-3	79	284-247
72	Mar 27 @	Indianapolis	5-2	W	39-30-3	81	289-249
73	Mar 29 @	Vancouver	7-3	W	40-30-3	83	296-252
74	Mar 31 @	Edmonton	5-2	W	41-30-3	85	301-254
75	Apr 1	Baltimore	3-4	L	41-31-3	85	304-258
76	Apr 3	Baltimore	9-2	W	42-31-3	87	313-260
77	Apr 5	Indianapolis	8-3	W	43-31-3	89	321-263
78	Apr 6 @	Winnipeg	5-5	T	43-31-4	90	326-268

Mariners Stars of 1974-1975

Andre Lecroix
106 assists

Wayne Rivers
54 goals, 107 points

Gene Peacosh
43 goals

Kevin Morrison
81 points, +29

Ernie Wakely
20 wins, 2 shutouts

Dick Sentes
44 goals

Scoring

pos	#	player	gp	g	a	pts	pim	+/-	ppg	shg	sog	sc%	gp	g	a	pts	pim
C	10	Adduono, Ray	78	15	59	74	23	+27	1	0	129	0.116	10	5	9	14	13
D	22	Bateman, Jamie	24	0	3	3	96	-4	0	0	17	0.000	-	-	-	-	-
G	30	Blanchet, Bob	3	0	0	0	0		0	0	0	-	-	-	-	-	-
D	17	Block, Ken	36	1	11	12	12	-4	1	0	43	0.023	-	-	-	-	-
D	23	Boylan, Dean	3	0	0	0	10		0	0	1	0.000	-	-	-	-	-
LW	29	Bradley, Brian	24	4	5	9	6	-7	0	0	40	0.100	6	0	1	1	2
LW	16	Devine, Kevin	46	4	10	14	48	-4	1	0	60	0.067	10	1	0	1	14
D	6	Falkenberg, Bob	78	2	18	20	42	+4	0	0	95	0.021	10	0	1	1	4
RW	9	Ferguson, Norm	78	36	33	69	6	+22	2	0	227	0.159	10	6	5	11	0
G	1	Gillow, Russ	30	0	1	1	4		0	0	0	-	3	0	0	0	0
C	19	Hardy, Joe	12	2	3	5	22	0	0	0	6	0.333	-	-	-	-	-
D	17	Hargreaves, Jim	41	8	10	18	45	+4	0	0	52	0.154	10	1	0	1	6
D	3	Howell, Harry	74	4	10	14	28	+28	0	1	78	0.051	5	1	0	1	10
LW	19	Inglis, Lee	5	0	2	2	0		0	0	11	0.000	-	-	-	-	-
G	36	Junkin, Joe	16	0	1	1	2		0	0	0	-	-	-	-	-	-
D		Krezanski, Reg	2	0	0	0	2		0	0	2	0.000	-	-	-	-	-
C	7	Lacroix, Andre	78	41	106	147	63	+40	12	0	275	0.149	10	3	9	12	2
C	18	Laughton, Mike	65	8	9	17	22	-12	0	3	92	0.076	10	4	1	5	0
C	15	Morenz, Brian	78	20	19	39	76	-5	0	2	133	0.150	10	0	3	3	6
D	4	Morrison, Kevin	78	20	61	81	143	+29	7	1	280	0.071	10	0	7	7	2
LW	25	Peacosh, Gene	78	43	36	79	22	+13	12	0	269	0.160	10	7	5	12	4
C	19	Perry, Brian	0	-	-	-	-		-	-	-	-	6	1	2	3	6
D	2	Plumb, Ron	78	10	38	48	56	+18	1	1	215	0.047	10	2	3	5	11
LW	11	Reichmuth, Craig	28	2	1	3	58		0	0	35	0.057	-	-	-	-	-
RW	12	Rivers, Wayne	78	54	53	107	52	+29	13	0	323	0.167	5	3	1	4	8
C	28	Rouleau, Michel	27	5	6	11	42	+1	0	0	42	0.119	-	-	-	-	-
RW	20	Scharf, Ted	67	3	1	4	94	-6	0	0	37	0.081	-	-	-	-	-
RW	8	Sentes, Dick	74	44	41	85	52	+44	6	1	217	0.203	10	0	2	2	0
C	21	Trevelyn, Tom	20	0	2	2	4		0	0	17	0.000	-	-	-	-	-
RW	23	Volmar, Doug	10	0	1	1	4		0	0	17	0.000	-	-	-	-	-
G	31	Wakely, Ernie	35	0	0	0	0		0	0	0	-	10	0	0	0	0
D	5	Wall, Bob	33	0	9	9	15	+13	0	0	39	0.000	10	0	3	3	2

Power Play: 60 goals scored in 218 opportunities (27.5%) with 8 short-handed goals allowed.
Penalty Killing: 53 goals allowed in 275 opportunities (80.7%) with 11 short-handed goals scored.

Goaltending

goaltender	gp	min	ga	en	so	record	gaa	sog	sv%	gp	min	ga	record	gaa
Blanchet, Bob	3	179	7	2	1	2-1-0	2.35	70	0.900	-	-	-	-	-
Gillow, Russ	30	1653	94	1	1	15-11-2	3.41	864	0.891	3	79	5	0-0	3.80
Junkin, Joe	16	839	46	0	1	6-7-0	3.29	416	0.889	-	-	-	-	-
Wakely, Ernie	35	2062	115	3	2	20-12-2	3.35	1091	0.895	10	520	39	4-6	4.50

Transactions: Dick Sentes acquired from Toronto in intra-league draft, May 1974 • Doug Volmar signed to contract, Jun 1974 • Bob Wall from Edmonton for Don Herriman, Aug 1974 • Ron Plumb loaned to San Diego by Cincinnati for 1974-75 season, Aug 1974 • Craig Reichmuth traded to Michigan for Michel Rouleau, Dec. 1974 • Ernie Wakely purchased from Winnipeg, Jan. 1975 • Ken Block traded to Indianapolis for Jim Hargreaves, Jan. 1975 • Joe Hardy acquired from Indianapolis for future considerations, Mar. 1975

1974-1975 TORONTO TOROS

Coach
Billy Harris
23-17-1

Coach
Bob Leduc
20-16-1

Summary of Games (@ Away, * Overtime)

	date	opponent	score		record	pts	gf-ga		date	opponent	score		record	pts	gf-ga
1	Oct 15	New England	6-2	W	1-0-0	2	6-2	40	Jan 12 @	Houston	7-4	W	23-16-1	47	171-146
2	Oct 18	Indianapolis	3-1	W	2-0-0	4	9-3	41	Jan 14 @	San Diego	4-6	L	23-17-1	47	175-152
3	Oct 20	Michigan	4-3	W	3-0-0	6	13-6	42	Jan 15 @	Phoenix	5-5	T	23-17-2	48	180-157
4	Oct 22	Minnesota	11-2	W	4-0-0	8	24-8	43	Jan 17 @	New England	1-2	L	23-18-2	48	181-159
5	Oct 25	Winnipeg	3-1	W	5-0-0	10	27-9	44	Jan 24 @	Minnesota	5-7	L	23-19-2	48	186-166
6	Oct 28	Phoenix	7-3	W	6-0-0	12	34-12	45	Jan 26 @	Edmonton	7-5	W	24-19-2	50	193-171
7	Oct 30 @	New England	2-5	L	6-1-0	12	36-17	46	Jan 28	Quebec	6-4	W	25-19-2	52	199-175
8	Nov 1 @	Winnipeg	1-10	L	6-2-0	12	37-27	47	Jan 30 @	Indianapolis	3-2	W	26-19-2	54	202-177
9	Nov 2 @	Chicago	3-4	L	6-3-0	12	40-31	48	Jan 31	Vancouver	6-0	W	27-19-2	56	208-177
10	Nov 4	Quebec	3-5	L	6-4-0	12	43-36	49	Feb 2 @	Vancouver	2-4	L	27-20-2	56	210-181
11	Nov 5 @	Michigan	5-2	W	7-4-0	14	48-38	50	Feb 4 @	San Diego	4-8	L	27-21-2	56	214-189
12	Nov 9 @	Minnesota	7-4	W	8-4-0	16	55-42	51	Feb 5 @	Houston	2-5	L	27-22-2	56	216-194
13	Nov 10 @	Chicago	7-0	W	9-4-0	18	62-42	52	Feb 7	Cleveland	4-1	W	28-22-2	58	220-195
14	Nov 13 @	Vancouver	5-3	W	10-4-0	20	67-45	53	Feb 9	Indianapolis	7-5	W	29-22-2	60	227-200
15	Nov 15 @	Edmonton	4-5	L	10-5-0	20	71-50	54	Feb 11	Edmonton	4-3	W	30-22-2	62	231-203
16	Nov 17 @	Winnipeg	3-1	W	11-5-0	22	74-51	55	Feb 12 @	Winnipeg	7-4	W	31-22-2	64	238-207
17	Nov 19 @	Cleveland	6-5	W	12-5-0	24	80-56	56	Feb 14 @	Edmonton	4-8	L	31-23-2	64	242-215
18	Nov 22	Edmonton	2-8	L	12-6-0	24	82-64	57	Feb 16 @	Vancouver	7-4	W	32-23-2	66	249-219
19	Nov 23 @	Quebec	9-2	W	13-6-0	26	91-66	58	Feb 20	Chicago	*3-4	L	32-24-2	66	252-223
20	Nov 24 @	Indianapolis	9-2	W	14-6-0	28	100-68	59	Feb 22 @	Cleveland	3-4	L	32-25-2	66	255-227
21	Nov 26	Minnesota	2-6	L	14-7-0	28	102-74	60	Feb 23 @	Houston	1-5	L	32-26-2	66	256-232
22	Nov 28	Vancouver	2-6	L	14-8-0	28	104-80	61	Feb 25	San Diego	6-4	W	33-26-2	68	262-236
23	Nov 29 @	Phoenix	4-4	T	14-8-1	29	108-84	62	Mar 2 @	Minnesota	3-5	L	33-27-2	68	265-241
24	Dec 1 @	San Diego	3-1	W	15-8-1	31	111-85	63	Mar 4	Baltimore	6-4	W	34-27-2	70	271-245
25	Dec 3	Houston	4-5	L	15-9-1	31	115-90	64	Mar 7	Quebec	1-4	L	34-28-2	70	272-249
26	Dec 7 @	Chicago	3-9	L	15-10-1	31	118-99	65	Mar 8 @	Baltimore	7-4	W	35-28-2	72	279-253
27	Dec 8 @	Phoenix	5-2	W	16-10-1	33	123-101	66	Mar 9	Baltimore	8-2	W	36-28-2	74	287-255
28	Dec 10	Minnesota	2-4	L	16-11-1	33	125-105	67	Mar 11	Phoenix	7-4	W	37-28-2	76	294-259
29	Dec 13	Cleveland	*7-6	W	17-11-1	35	132-111	68	Mar 13 @	Indianapolis	4-5	L	37-29-2	76	298-264
30	Dec 15 @	Michigan	7-2	W	18-11-1	37	139-113	69	Mar 14	San Diego	4-6	L	37-30-2	76	302-270
31	Dec 17	Winnipeg	1-4	L	18-12-1	37	140-117	70	Mar 16 @	New England	5-7	L	37-31-2	76	307-277
32	Dec 22	Chicago	5-2	W	19-12-1	39	145-119	71	Mar 17	Houston	5-4	W	38-31-2	78	312-281
33	Dec 23	Cleveland	1-4	L	19-13-1	39	146-123	72	Mar 25	Vancouver	8-4	W	39-31-2	80	320-285
34	Dec 27	Chicago	4-2	W	20-13-1	41	150-125	73	Mar 28	Edmonton	5-4	W	40-31-2	82	325-289
35	Jan 3	New England	3-5	L	20-14-1	41	153-130	74	Mar 29 @	Quebec	*5-4	W	41-31-2	84	330-293
36	Jan 4 @	Quebec	1-3	L	20-15-1	41	154-133	75	Mar 30	New England	3-4	L	41-32-2	84	333-297
37	Jan 5 @	Cleveland	4-3	W	21-15-1	43	158-136	76	Apr 1	Indianapolis	7-1	W	42-32-2	86	340-298
38	Jan 7	Phoenix	2-3	L	21-16-1	43	160-139	77	Apr 4	Winnipeg	7-1	W	43-32-2	88	347-299
39	Jan 10	San Diego	4-3	W	22-16-1	45	164-142	78	Apr 6	Houston	2-5	L	43-33-2	88	349-304

Toros Stars of 1974-1975

Tom Simpson
52 goals

Frank Mahovlich
38 goals, 82 points

Paul Henderson
30 goals, +18

Gilles Gratton
30 wins, 2 shutouts

Rick Cunningham
+23 rating

Vaclav Nedomansky
41 goals

Scoring

pos	#	player	gp	g	a	pts	pim	+/-	ppg	shg	sog	sc%	gp	g	a	pts	pim
D	5	Amodeo, Mike	64	1	13	14	50	+10	0	0	55	0.018	3	0	1	1	4
G	30	Binkley, Les	17	0	0	0	0		0	0	0	-	1	0	0	0	0
D	4	Cuddie, Steve	70	5	16	21	49	+3	1	0	92	0.054	6	0	4	4	8
D	3	Cunningham, Rick	71	7	18	25	117	+23	1	0	113	0.062	5	0	1	1	0
C	9	Dillon, Wayne	77	29	66	95	22	+17	6	0	250	0.116	6	4	4	8	4
D	7	Dorey, Jim	43	11	23	34	69	+18	3	0	114	0.096	6	2	6	8	2
C	8	Farda, Richard	66	6	25	31	2	-7	2	1	85	0.071	-	-	-	-	-
RW	26	Featherstone, Tony	76	25	38	63	26	+12	3	2	194	0.129	6	2	1	3	2
D	6	Gibbons, Brian	73	4	22	26	105	0	0	0	103	0.039	-	-	-	-	-
G	33	Gratton, Gilles	53	0	4	4	8		0	0	1	0.000	1	0	0	0	0
LW	10/19	Henderson, Paul	58	30	33	63	18	+18	4	2	146	0.205	-	-	-	-	-
LW	16	Hickey, Pat	74	35	34	69	50	+8	5	0	215	0.163	5	0	1	1	4
C	25	Jacques, Jeff	39	12	8	20	26	+9	1	0	54	0.222	6	0	4	4	2
C	11	Kirk, Gavin	78	15	58	73	69	+19	1	2	149	0.101	6	5	6	11	2
D	23	Kuzmicz, George	34	0	12	12	22	-3	0	0	27	0.000	-	-	-	-	-
LW	19	Leduc, Bob	19	3	4	7	9		0	0	31	0.097	-	-	-	-	-
C	27	Mahovlich, Frank	73	38	44	82	27	+8	8	0	268	0.142	6	3	0	3	2
C	20	Marrin, Peter	4	3	1	4	0		0	0	6	0.500	6	0	4	4	2
RW	17	Martin, Tom	64	15	17	32	50	-3	0	0	184	0.082	5	1	5	6	0
D	21	Mavety, Larry	17	0	9	9	24	+6	0	0	28	0.000	6	0	3	3	6
RW	14	Nedomansky, Vaclav	78	41	40	81	19	+7	5	0	306	0.134	6	3	1	4	9
C	15	Nistico, Lou	29	11	11	22	75	+12	0	0	68	0.162	6	6	1	7	19
LW	15	Selby, Brit	17	1	4	5	0		0	0	14	0.071	-	-	-	-	-
G	1	Shaw, Jim	21	0	0	0	0		0	0	0	-	5	0	0	0	0
RW	12	Simpson, Tom	70	52	28	80	48	+25	11	0	228	0.228	5	1	1	2	0
LW	24	Titcomb, Gord	2	0	1	1	0		0	0	5	0.000	-	-	-	-	-
RW	7	Trottier, Guy	6	2	2	4	2		1	0	5	0.400	-	-	-	-	-
D	2	Turkiewicz, Jim	78	3	27	30	28	+18	0	0	113	0.027	6	0	2	2	6

Power Play: 57 goals scored in 285 opportunities (20.0%) with 9 short-handed goals allowed.
Penalty Killing: 50 goals allowed in 233 opportunities (78.5%) with 7 short-handed goals scored.

Goaltending

goaltender	gp	min	ga	en	so	record	gaa	sog	sv%	gp	min	ga	record	gaa
Binkley, Les	17	772	47	0	0	6-4-0	3.59	419	0.888	1	59	5	0-1	5.08
Gratton, Gilles	53	2881	185	1	2	30-20-1	3.85	1632	0.887	1	36	5	0-1	8.33
Shaw, Jim	21	1055	70	1	0	7-9-1	3.98	611	0.885	5	262	18	2-2	4.12

Transactions: Jim Dorey acquired from New England as "future considerations" in Sep 1974 Wayne Carleton trade, Dec 1974 • Rights to Paul Henderson purchased from Quebec, Jun 1974 • Tony Featherstone, Jim Shaw signed to contracts, Jun 1974 • Frank Mahovlich signed to contract, Jun 1974 • Richard Farda and Vaclav Nedomansky signed to contracts, Jul 1974 • Guy Trottier sold to Michigan, Nov 1974 • Larry Mavety acquired for draft picks from Chicago, Feb 1975

1974-1975 VANCOUVER BLAZERS

**Coach
Joe Crozier**

Summary of Games (@ Away, * Overtime)

	date	opponent	score		record	pts	gf-ga			date	opponent	score		record	pts	gf-ga
1	Oct 15	Winnipeg	2-6	L	0-1-0	0	2-6		40	Jan 19	Indianapolis	5-1	W	18-20-2	38	124-128
2	Oct 16	Houston	0-6	L	0-2-0	0	2-12		41	Jan 22 @	Minnesota	2-1	W	19-20-2	40	126-129
3	Oct 18	Chicago	1-2	L	0-3-0	0	3-14		42	Jan 23 @	San Diego	1-6	L	19-21-2	40	127-135
4	Oct 20	Chicago	3-1	W	1-3-0	2	6-15		43	Jan 24	Winnipeg	*4-3	W	20-21-2	42	131-138
5	Oct 23	Cleveland	4-1	W	2-3-0	4	10-16		44	Jan 26 @	Chicago	5-3	W	21-21-2	44	136-141
6	Oct 30	Edmonton	8-6	W	3-3-0	6	18-22		45	Jan 30 @	Minnesota	3-6	L	21-22-2	44	139-147
7	Nov 3	San Diego	2-6	L	3-4-0	6	20-28		46	Jan 31 @	Toronto	0-6	L	21-23-2	44	139-153
8	Nov 5 @	Chicago	5-4	W	4-4-0	8	25-32		47	Feb 2	Toronto	4-2	W	22-23-2	46	143-155
9	Nov 6 @	Quebec	3-5	L	4-5-0	8	28-37		48	Feb 5	Chicago	4-2	W	23-23-2	48	147-157
10	Nov 8	Cleveland	1-2	L	4-6-0	8	29-39		49	Feb 8	New England	4-1	W	24-23-2	50	151-158
11	Nov 9	Winnipeg	3-3	T	4-6-1	9	32-42		50	Feb 9	New England	5-1	W	25-23-2	52	156-159
12	Nov 13	Toronto	3-5	L	4-7-1	9	35-47		51	Feb 12	Phoenix	5-4	W	26-23-2	54	161-163
13	Nov 19 @	San Diego	2-3	L	4-8-1	9	37-50		52	Feb 16	Toronto	4-7	L	26-24-2	54	165-170
14	Nov 22	Houston	1-4	L	4-9-1	9	38-54		53	Feb 18 @	Indianapolis	9-2	W	27-24-2	56	174-172
15	Nov 23	Houston	2-4	L	4-10-1	9	40-58		54	Feb 20 @	Baltimore	3-4	L	27-25-2	56	177-176
16	Nov 26 @	Michigan	5-1	W	5-10-1	11	45-59		55	Feb 22 @	Houston	4-2	W	28-25-2	58	181-178
17	Nov 28 @	Toronto	6-2	W	6-10-1	13	51-61		56	Feb 23 @	Chicago	1-2	L	28-26-2	58	182-180
18	Nov 29	New England	5-1	W	7-10-1	15	56-62		57	Feb 25 @	New England	2-3	L	28-27-2	58	184-183
19	Dec 4 @	Edmonton	3-6	L	7-11-1	15	59-68		58	Feb 27 @	Quebec	7-9	L	28-28-2	58	191-192
20	Dec 7	Michigan	4-2	W	8-11-1	17	63-70		59	Mar 2 @	New England	1-4	L	28-29-2	58	192-196
21	Dec 8	Minnesota	4-2	W	9-11-1	19	67-72		60	Mar 5	Edmonton	6-0	W	29-29-2	60	198-196
22	Dec 10 @	Cleveland	4-3	W	10-11-1	21	71-75		61	Mar 7 @	Edmonton	0-4	L	29-30-2	60	198-200
23	Dec 11 @	Houston	2-5	L	10-12-1	21	73-80		62	Mar 9	Phoenix	4-3	W	30-30-2	62	202-203
24	Dec 12 @	Phoenix	2-4	L	10-13-1	21	75-84		63	Mar 12	Minnesota	4-2	W	31-30-2	64	206-205
25	Dec 15	Cleveland	2-1	W	11-13-1	23	77-85		64	Mar 15	Quebec	7-4	W	32-30-2	66	213-209
26	Dec 17 @	Indianapolis	3-2	W	12-13-1	25	80-87		65	Mar 16	Quebec	4-2	W	33-30-2	68	217-211
27	Dec 18 @	Phoenix	3-5	L	12-14-1	25	83-92		66	Mar 18	Minnesota	3-5	L	33-31-2	68	220-216
28	Dec 19 @	Houston	3-1	W	13-14-1	27	86-93		67	Mar 19 @	Winnipeg	3-8	L	33-32-2	68	223-224
29	Dec 21	San Diego	2-1	W	14-14-1	29	88-94		68	Mar 22 @	Phoenix	2-4	L	33-33-2	68	225-228
30	Dec 26	Michigan	8-1	W	15-14-1	31	96-95		69	Mar 23 @	San Diego	*0-1	L	33-34-2	68	225-229
31	Dec 27	Indianapolis	1-1	T	15-14-2	32	97-96		70	Mar 25 @	Toronto	4-8	L	33-35-2	68	229-237
32	Jan 2	Phoenix	3-2	W	16-14-2	34	100-98		71	Mar 26 @	Cleveland	2-4	L	33-36-2	68	231-241
33	Jan 4 @	New England	*3-4	L	16-15-2	34	103-102		72	Mar 29	San Diego	3-7	L	33-37-2	68	234-248
34	Jan 5 @	Michigan	1-3	L	16-16-2	34	104-105		73	Mar 30	Baltimore	4-3	W	34-37-2	70	238-251
35	Jan 7 @	Indianapolis	2-4	L	16-17-2	34	106-109		74	Apr 1 @	Minnesota	2-5	L	34-38-2	70	240-256
36	Jan 8 @	Quebec	3-4	L	16-18-2	34	109-113		75	Apr 2 @	Winnipeg	6-4	W	35-38-2	72	246-260
37	Jan 10 @	Cleveland	4-6	L	16-19-2	34	113-119		76	Apr 4 @	Edmonton	3-5	L	35-39-2	72	249-265
38	Jan 14	Quebec	2-6	L	16-20-2	34	115-125		77	Apr 5	Edmonton	3-2	W	36-39-2	74	252-267
39	Jan 15 @	Winnipeg	4-2	W	17-20-2	36	119-127		78	Apr 6	Indianapolis	4-3	W	37-39-2	76	256-270

Blazers Stars of 1974-1975

Don McLeod
33 wins

Bryan Campbell
29 goals

Danny Lawson
33 goals

Mike Pelyk
40 points

John McKenzie
23 goals, +11

Duane Rupp
+20 on defense

Scoring

pos	#	player	gp	g	a	pts	pim	+/-	ppg	shg	sog	sc%	gp	g	a	pts	pim
RW	9	Bathgate, Andy	11	1	6	7	2		0	0	12	0.083	-	-	-	-	-
D	23	Beaudoin, Serge	4	0	0	0	2		0	0	1	0.000	-	-	-	-	-
D	23	Brown, Arnie	10	0	1	1	13	-8	0	0	14	0.000	-	-	-	-	-
LW	8	Burgess, Don	62	11	18	29	19	+2	2	0	131	0.084	-	-	-	-	-
C	14	Campbell, Bryan	78	29	34	63	24	-15	10	1	251	0.116	-	-	-	-	-
D	5	Cardiff, Jim	44	0	2	2	25	-7	0	0	15	0.000	-	-	-	-	-
LW	16	Chernoff, Mike	3	0	0	0	0		0	0	3	0.000	-	-	-	-	-
C	7	Chipperfield, Ron	78	19	20	39	30	-2	7	0	238	0.080	-	-	-	-	-
LW	15	Deadmarsh, Butch	38	7	8	15	128	-4	1	0	44	0.159	-	-	-	-	-
RW		Delorenzi, Ray	3	0	0	0	0		0	0	4	0.000	-	-	-	-	-
LW	24	Driscoll, Peter	21	3	2	5	40	-2	0	0	18	0.167	-	-	-	-	-
RW	17	Given, David	1	0	0	0	0		0	0	0	-	-	-	-	-	-
RW	23	Gulka, Bud	5	1	0	1	10		0	0	1	1.000	-	-	-	-	-
C	18	Harris, Hugh	58	23	34	57	19	+6	6	0	186	0.124	-	-	-	-	-
LW	12	Israelson, Larry	46	12	9	21	10	-2	1	0	63	0.190	-	-	-	-	-
LW	16	Jodzio, Rick	44	1	3	4	159	-12	0	0	22	0.045	-	-	-	-	-
C	20	Jones, James H.	63	11	7	18	39	-5	0	3	98	0.112	-	-	-	-	-
RW	11	Lawson, Danny	78	33	43	76	19	-5	3	1	298	0.111	-	-	-	-	-
D	6	McCulloch, Don	51	1	9	10	42	-12	0	0	93	0.011	-	-	-	-	-
RW	19	McKenzie, John	74	23	37	60	84	+11	5	0	107	0.215	-	-	-	-	-
G	1	McLeod, Don	72	0	8	8	14		0	0	3	0.000	-	-	-	-	-
D	25	McNamee, Pete	11	2	1	3	15	+3	1	0	6	0.333	-	-	-	-	-
LW	18	Migneault, John	14	4	2	6	12	-1	0	0	16	0.250	-	-	-	-	-
RW	17	Myers, Murray	24	1	1	2	4	-4	0	0	18	0.056	-	-	-	-	-
RW	12	O'Donoghue, Don	4	0	0	0	0		0	0	4	0.000	-	-	-	-	-
D	4	Pelyk, Mike	75	14	26	40	121	-2	1	3	167	0.084	-	-	-	-	-
D	3	Price, Pat	68	5	29	34	15	+6	1	0	96	0.052	-	-	-	-	-
D	2	Rupp, Duane	72	3	26	29	45	+20	1	0	101	0.030	-	-	-	-	-
LW	22	St. Sauveur, Claude	76	24	23	47	28	-8	11	0	200	0.120	-	-	-	-	-
D	25	Shmyr, John	39	1	5	6	43	-9	0	0	13	0.077	-	-	-	-	-
D	21	Terbenche, Paul	60	3	14	17	10	-7	0	0	81	0.037	-	-	-	-	-
C	10	Walton, Rob	75	24	33	57	28	+1	7	0	159	0.151	-	-	-	-	-
G	35	Wood, Wayne	11	0	0	0	0		0	0	0	-	-	-	-	-	-

Power Play: 59 goals scored in 271 opportunities (21.8%) with 7 short-handed goals allowed.
Penalty Killing: 62 goals allowed in 267 opportunities (76.8%) with 8 short-handed goals scored.

Goaltending

goaltender	gp	min	ga	en	so	record	gaa	sog	sv%	gp	min	ga	record	gaa
McLeod, Don	72	4184	233	7	1	33-35-2	3.34	2106	0.889	-	-	-	-	-
Wood, Wayne	11	512	30	0	0	4-4-0	3.52	263	0.886	-	-	-	-	-

Transactions: Duane Rupp, Wayne Wood signed to contracts, Jun 1974 • Paul Terbenche, Rick Jodzio signed to contracts, Jul 1974 • Mike Pelyk loaned to Vancouver by Cincinnati for 1974-75 season, Jun 1974 • Don McCulloch signed to contract, Jun 1974 • Pete McNamee, Serge Beaudoin and John Migneault to Phoenix for Hugh Harris, Nov 1974 • Rick Jodzio signed to contract, Jan 1975 • Arnie Brown signed as free agent, Mar 1975

1974-1975 WINNIPEG JETS

Player-Coach
Bobby Hull
4-9-0

Coach
Rudy Pilous
34-26-5

(Hull coached from January 22 to February 14, 1975)

Summary of Games (@ Away, * Overtime)

#	date	opponent	score		record	pts	gf-ga
1	Oct 15	@ Vancouver	6-2	W	1-0-0	2	6-2
2	Oct 18	Edmonton	4-0	W	2-0-0	4	10-2
3	Oct 25	@ Toronto	1-3	L	2-1-0	4	11-5
4	Oct 27	Michigan	5-2	W	3-1-0	6	16-7
5	Oct 30	Phoenix	*6-5	W	4-1-0	8	22-12
6	Nov 1	Toronto	10-1	W	5-1-0	10	32-13
7	Nov 3	Michigan	11-3	W	6-1-0	12	43-16
8	Nov 5	Minnesota	6-4	W	7-1-0	14	49-20
9	Nov 9	@ Vancouver	3-3	T	7-1-1	15	52-23
10	Nov 13	@ Edmonton	3-5	L	7-2-1	15	55-28
11	Nov 15	Indianapolis	5-0	W	8-2-1	17	60-28
12	Nov 17	Toronto	1-3	L	8-3-1	17	61-31
13	Nov 18	@ Edmonton	3-5	L	8-4-1	17	64-36
14	Nov 20	Minnesota	3-1	W	9-4-1	19	67-37
15	Nov 24	Phoenix	1-3	L	9-5-1	19	68-40
16	Nov 26	@ Indianapolis	4-0	W	10-5-1	21	72-40
17	Nov 27	@ Cleveland	*4-5	L	10-6-1	21	76-45
18	Nov 29	Michigan	7-6	W	11-6-1	23	83-51
19	Dec 1	Quebec	3-2	W	12-6-1	25	86-53
20	Dec 4	Houston	2-3	L	12-7-1	25	88-56
21	Dec 6	@ Minnesota	2-4	L	12-8-1	25	90-60
22	Dec 8	Chicago	5-2	W	13-8-1	27	95-62
23	Dec 10	@ Indianapolis	5-3	W	14-8-1	29	100-65
24	Dec 12	@ Michigan	3-5	L	14-9-1	29	103-70
25	Dec 14	@ Houston	3-5	L	14-10-1	29	106-75
26	Dec 15	New England	3-4	L	14-11-1	29	109-79
27	Dec 17	@ Toronto	4-1	W	15-11-1	31	113-80
28	Dec 18	@ Quebec	1-5	L	15-12-1	31	114-85
29	Dec 22	Phoenix	2-4	L	15-13-1	31	116-89
30	Dec 26	@ Phoenix	3-2	W	16-13-1	33	119-91
31	Dec 28	@ San Diego	6-4	W	17-13-1	35	125-95
32	Dec 29	@ Houston	3-6	L	17-14-1	35	128-101
33	Jan 7	@ Cleveland	4-4	T	17-14-2	36	132-105
34	Jan 9	@ Michigan	*4-5	L	17-15-2	36	136-110
35	Jan 10	Quebec	1-6	L	17-16-2	36	137-116
36	Jan 15	Vancouver	2-4	L	17-17-2	36	139-120
37	Jan 19	Cleveland	9-4	W	18-17-2	38	148-124
38	Jan 22	Indianapolis	1-3	L	18-18-2	38	149-127
39	Jan 23	@ Edmonton	3-7	L	18-19-2	38	152-134
40	Jan 24	@ Vancouver	*3-4	L	18-20-2	38	155-138
41	Jan 26	Houston	1-3	L	18-21-2	38	156-141
42	Jan 28	@ San Diego	9-7	W	19-21-2	40	165-148
43	Jan 30	@ Phoenix	5-3	W	20-21-2	42	170-151
44	Feb 2	@ Minnesota	*4-5	L	20-22-2	42	174-156
45	Feb 5	@ Cleveland	2-3	L	20-23-2	42	176-159
46	Feb 7	New England	*4-5	L	20-24-2	42	180-164
47	Feb 8	@ Chicago	3-6	L	20-25-2	42	183-170
48	Feb 9	Chicago	3-2	W	21-25-2	44	186-172
49	Feb 12	Toronto	4-7	L	21-26-2	44	190-179
50	Feb 14	Houston	5-3	W	22-26-2	46	195-182
51	Feb 15	Cleveland	5-1	W	23-26-2	48	200-183
52	Feb 16	@ Chicago	6-3	W	24-26-2	50	206-186
53	Feb 18	@ Baltimore	5-3	W	25-26-2	52	211-189
54	Feb 19	Edmonton	4-1	W	26-26-2	54	215-190
55	Feb 23	New England	1-2	L	26-27-2	54	216-192
56	Feb 25	Minnesota	6-6	T	26-27-3	55	222-198
57	Feb 28	San Diego	4-3	W	27-27-3	57	226-201
58	Mar 2	San Diego	4-4	T	27-27-4	58	230-205
59	Mar 5	Cleveland	4-2	W	28-27-4	60	234-207
60	Mar 7	@ Phoenix	4-7	L	28-28-4	60	238-214
61	Mar 8	@ San Diego	5-6	L	28-29-4	60	243-220
62	Mar 9	@ Minnesota	*6-5	W	29-29-4	62	249-225
63	Mar 11	@ New England	2-6	L	29-30-4	62	251-231
64	Mar 12	@ Quebec	3-5	L	29-31-4	62	254-236
65	Mar 14	Quebec	4-3	W	30-31-4	64	258-239
66	Mar 16	Edmonton	10-1	W	31-31-4	66	268-240
67	Mar 19	Vancouver	8-3	W	32-31-4	68	276-243
68	Mar 21	@ New England	6-3	W	33-31-4	70	282-246
69	Mar 22	@ Chicago	4-2	W	34-31-4	72	286-248
70	Mar 23	Chicago	4-3	W	35-31-4	74	290-251
71	Mar 25	@ Indianapolis	*4-3	W	36-31-4	76	294-254
72	Mar 27	@ Houston	0-8	L	36-32-4	76	294-262
73	Mar 29	@ New England	9-3	W	37-32-4	78	303-265
74	Mar 31	Indianapolis	4-1	W	38-32-4	80	307-266
75	Apr 2	Vancouver	4-6	L	38-33-4	80	311-272
76	Apr 4	@ Toronto	1-7	L	38-34-4	80	312-279
77	Apr 5	@ Quebec	5-9	L	38-35-4	80	317-288
78	Apr 6	San Diego	5-5	T	38-35-5	81	322-293

Jets Stars of 1974-1975

Bobby Hull	**Anders Hedberg**	**Ulf Nilsson**	**Veli-Pekka Ketola**	**Mike Ford**	**Lars-Erik Sjoberg**
Record 77 goals	53 goals, 100 points	94 assists, 120 points	23 goals	+40 on defense	60 points, +43

Scoring

pos	#	player	gp	g	a	pts	pim	+/-	ppg	shg	sog	sc%	gp	g	a	pts	pim
LW	10	Ashton, Ron	36	1	3	4	66	-11	0	0	36	0.028	-	-	-	-	-
D	21	Asmundson, Duke	38	4	15	19	53	-3	0	0	49	0.082	-	-	-	-	-
RW	11	Beaudin, Norm	77	16	31	47	8	-17	1	2	202	0.079	-	-	-	-	-
D	28/18	Beaule, Alain	54	0	14	14	24	-19	0	0	36	0.000	-	-	-	-	-
D	2/25	Bergman, Thommie	49	4	15	19	70	-16	3	0	85	0.047	-	-	-	-	-
RW	19	Black, Milt	65	4	6	10	10	-2	0	0	37	0.108	-	-	-	-	-
C	7	Bordeleau, Christian	18	8	8	16	0	-1	0	2	52	0.154	-	-	-	-	-
G	1	Daley, Joe	51	0	1	1	6		0	0	0	-	-	-	-	-	-
D	3	Ford, Mike	73	12	22	34	68	+43	3	0	205	0.059	-	-	-	-	-
RW	16	Gratton, Jean-Guy	49	4	8	12	2	+2	0	0	57	0.070	-	-	-	-	-
LW	18	Gruen, Danny	32	9	12	21	21	0	3	0	64	0.141	-	-	-	-	-
RW	15	Hedberg, Anders	65	53	47	100	45	+38	20	0	271	0.196	-	-	-	-	-
D	5	Hornung, Larry	69	7	25	32	21	-17	1	0	80	0.088	-	-	-	-	-
LW	9	Hull, Bobby	78	77	65	142	41	+55	27	0	556	0.138	-	-	-	-	-
C	17	Johnson, Dan	78	18	14	32	25	-32	2	4	111	0.162	-	-	-	-	-
C	12	Ketola, Veli-Pekka	74	23	28	51	25	-18	2	0	154	0.149	-	-	-	-	-
G	24	Larsson, Curt	26	0	1	1	4		0	0	0	-	-	-	-	-	-
D	8	Miller, Perry	67	9	19	28	133	-22	0	1	99	0.091	-	-	-	-	-
C	10	Neale, Robbie	7	0	2	2	4		0	0	14	0.000	-	-	-	-	-
C	14	Nilsson, Ulf	78	26	94	120	79	+47	7	0	147	0.177	-	-	-	-	-
D	6	Riihiranta, Heikki	64	8	14	22	30	-40	2	0	102	0.078	-	-	-	-	-
D	4	Sjoberg, Lars-Erik	75	7	53	60	30	+43	0	1	123	0.057	-	-	-	-	-
RW	20	Snell, Ron	20	0	0	0	8	-10	0	0	15	0.000	-	-	-	-	-
C	22	Spring, Dan	60	19	24	43	22	-14	1	0	123	0.154	-	-	-	-	-
G	30	Wakely, Ernie	6	0	0	0	0		0	0	0	-	-	-	-	-	-
D	2	Woytowich, Bob	24	0	4	4	8	-3	0	0	11	0.000	-	-	-	-	-
D	7	Young, Howie	42	13	10	23	42	-9	2	0	81	0.160	-	-	-	-	-

Power Play: 74 goals scored in 362 opportunities (20.4%) with 16 short-handed goals allowed.
Penalty Killing: 37 goals allowed in 221 opportunities (83.3%) with 10 short-handed goals scored.

Goaltending

goaltender	gp	min	ga	en	so	record	gaa	sog	sv%	gp	min	ga	record	gaa
Daley, Joe	51	2902	175	0	1	23-21-4	3.99	1550	0.887	-	-	-	-	-
Larsson, Curt	26	1514	100	2	1	12-11-1	3.96	887	0.887	-	-	-	-	-
Wakely, Ernie	6	355	16	0	1	3-3-0	2.70	213	0.925	-	-	-	-	-

Transactions: Anders Hedberg, Ulf Nilsson, Lars-Erik Sjoberg signed to contracts, May 1974 • Heikki Riihiranta signed to contract, summer 1974 • Rights to Veli-Pekka Ketola acquired from Cleveland for future considerations, Aug 1974 • Perry Miller signed to contract, Sep 1974 • Christian Bordeleau to Quebec for Alain Beaule, Nov 1974 • Bob Woytowich sold to Indianapolis, Dec 1974 • Thommie Bergman purchased from Detroit (NHL), Dec 1974 • Ernie Wakely sold to San Diego, Jan 1975 • Howie Young purchased from Phoenix, Jan 1975 • Robbie Neale acquired from Cleveland for cash, future considerations, Feb 1975 • Danny Gruen acquired for future considerations from Baltimore, Feb 1975. Returned to Baltimore end of season.

1974-1975 Statistical Leaders

Top five in each category.

Goals: 77, Bobby Hull (Winnipeg); 54, Serge Bernier (Quebec), Wayne Rivers (San Diego); 53, Anders Hedberg (Winnipeg); 52, Tpm Simpson (Toronto); 50, Marc Tardif (Michigan-Quebec).

Assists: 106, Andre Lacroix (San Diego); 94, Ulf Nilsson (Winnipeg); 75, Larry Lund (Houston); 68, Serge Bernier (Quebec); 66, Wayne Dillon (Toronto).

Points: 147, Andre Lacroix (San Diego); 142, Bobby Hull (Winnipeg); 122, Serge Bernier (Quebec); 120, Ulf Nilsson (Winnipeg); 108, Larry Lund (Houston).

Penalty Minutes: 203, Gord Gallant (Minnesota); 201, John Hughes (Phoenix); 176, Ron Busniuk (Minnesota); John Schella (Houston); 168, Cam Connor (Phoenix); 159, Rick Jodzio (Vancouver).

Power-play Goals: 27, Bobby Hull (Winnipeg); 20, Anders Hedberg (Winnipeg); 15, Frank Hughes (Houston), 13, Wayne Connelly (Minnesota), Andre Hinse (Houston); Rejean Houle (Quebec), Larry Lund (Houston), Wayne Rivers (San Diego); 12, Andre Lacroix (San Diego), Al McDonough (Cleveland), Gene Peacosh (San Diego).

Short-handed Goals: 5, Murray Hall (Houston); 4, Christian Bordeleau (Winnipeg-Quebec), Mark Howe (Houston), Danny Johnson (Winnipeg), Don Tannahill (Minnesota), Mike Walton (Minnesota); 3, shared by many.

Goaltending Minutes: 4184, Don McLeod (Vancouver); 3494, Al Smith (New England); 3294, John Garrett (Minnesota); 3076, Gerry Cheevers (Cleveland); 2979, Andy Brown (Indianapolis).

Goals Against Average: 3.03, Ron Grahame (Houston); 3.23, Bob Whidden (Cleveland, 3.228), Wayne Rutledge (Houston, 3.232); 3.25, Ernie Wakely (Winnipeg-San Diego); 3.26, Gerry Cheevers (Cleveland); 3.27, Jack Norris (Phoenix).

Wins: 33, Ron Grahame (Houston), Don McLeod (Vancouver), Al Smith (New England); 30, John Garrett (Minnesota), Gilles Gratton (Toronto); 29, Richard Brodeur (Quebec); 26, Gerry Cheevers (Cleveland); 25, Gary Kurt (Phoenix).

Shutouts: 4, Gerry Cheevers (Cleveland), Ron Grahame (Houston); 3, Ernie Wakely (Winnipeg-San Diego); 2, shared by many.

Totals for Players With Two or More Teams During 1974-1975

player	teams	gp	g	a	pts	pim	+/-	ppg	shg	sog	sc%
Andrascik, Steve	Ind, M-B	77	6	11	17	58				174	0.034
Beaule, Alain	Que, Wpg	76	4	21	25	43	-14	0	0	65	0.062
Block, Ken	SD, Ind	73	1	28	29	30	-14	1	0	91	0.011
Bordeleau, Christian	Wpg, Que	71	23	41	64	24	+1	2	4	239	0.096
Bredin, Gary	Ind, M-B	77	18	23	41	37	-40	1	0	125	0.144
Brown, Arnie	M-B, Van	60	3	5	8	40	-40	1	0	77	0.039
Buchanan, Ron	Cle, Edm, Ind	58	24	24	48	22	-13	11		155	0.155
Caron, Alain	Que, M-B	68	15	8	23	6	-16	11	0	133	0.113
Climie, Ron	Edm, NE	74	23	31	54	27	+3	3	0	133	0.173
Dorey, Jim	NE, Tor	74	16	40	56	112				199	0.080
Gruen, Danny	Mich, Wpg	66	19	28	47	94	-12	3	0	156	0.122
Guite, Pierre	Que, M-B	35	19	12	31	70				86	0.221
Hardy, Joe	Chi, Ind, SD	61	5	26	31	66	-14	0	0	84	0.060
Hargreaves, Jim	Ind, SD	78	10	15	25	75	-15	0	0	115	0.087
Harris, Hugh	Phx, Van	80	33	44	77	34	+8	7	0	239	0.138
Heatley, Murray	Min, Ind	51	20	17	37	56	-7	6	0	110	0.182
Johnson, Jim	Min, Ind	53	8	18	26	12	-19	2	0	78	0.103
Kennett, Murray	Ind, Edm	78	5	17	22	25	+5	1	0	56	0.089
Locas, Jacques	Mich, ind	23	1	5	6	6				26	0.038
Mavety, Larry	Chi, Tor	74	10	31	41	150	+3	3	0	197	0.051
McDonald, Brian	Mich, Ind	66	17	20	37	34	-21	4	0	143	0.119
McNamee, Pete	Van, Phx	66	11	20	31	92	+8	2	0	96	0.115
Migneault, John	Van, Phx	61	10	15	25	28	-5	1	0	79	0.127
Neale, Robbie	Cle, Wpg	16	1	5	6	8				27	0.037
Proceviat, Dick	Chi, Ind	63	1	31	32	62	-19	0	0	76	0.013
Reichmuth, Craig	SD, M-B	44	2	3	5	81				53	0.038
Richardson, Steve	Ind, M-B	66	9	22	31	74	-18	0	0	146	0.062
Robertson, Joe	Ind, Min	29	5	8	13	27	-1	0	0	38	0.132
Rouleau, Michel	Que, Mich, SD	53	6	16	22	130	0	0	0	77	0.078
Sheehy, Tim	NE, Edm	81	29	33	62	22	-15	5	0	212	0.137
Sutherland, Steve	Mich, Que	78	15	20	35	151	-13	0	0	135	0.111
Tardif, Marc	Mich, Que	76	50	39	89	79	+12	11	0	286	0.175
Trottier, Guy	Tor, Mich	23	7	6	13	4				39	0.179
Wakely, Ernie	Wpg, SD	41	0	0	0	0		0	0	0	-
Woytowich, Bob	Wpg, Ind	66	0	12	12	36	-29	0	0	41	0.000
Young, Howie	Phx, Wpg	72	16	22	38	86	-11	3	0	127	0.126

Totals for Goaltenders With Two or More Teams During 1974-1975

goaltender	teams	gp	min	ga	en	so	record	gaa	sog	sv%
Ernie Wakely	Wpg, SD	41	2417	131	3	3	23-15-2	3.25	1304	0.900

Andre Lacroix's Record Scoring Streak

Between January 4th and March 19th of 1975, San Diego's Andre Lacroix accounted for at least one point in every Mariner game, a streak that reached 32 consecutive games. During his scoring skein, Lacroix scored 16 goals and assisted on 53 others for a total of 69 points on his way to leading the league in scoring. Dave Dryden and the Chicago Cougars put an end to his streak on March 20th. The details of his streak follow (goals-assists):

1.	Jan 4	at Cleveland (0-1)	12.	Feb 5	at Phoenix (1-1)	23.	Feb 25	at Toronto (2-0)
2.	Jan 7	New England (1-2)	13.	Feb 6	Minnesota (0-2)	24.	Feb 28	at Winnipeg (0-1)
3.	Jan 10	at Toronto (1-2)	14.	Feb 8	Minnesota (0-4)	25.	Mar 2	at Winnipeg (0-1)
4.	Jan 11	at New England (0-2)	15.	Feb 11	Quebec (2-2)	26.	Mar 4	Quebec (1-1)
5.	Jan 14	Toronto (0-1)	16.	Feb 13	at Baltimore (1-2)	27.	Mar 6	Houston (0-2)
6.	Jan 16	Edmonton (1-0)	17.	Feb 14	at Cleveland (1-1)	28.	Mar 8	Winnipeg (0-3)
7.	Jan 18	Houston (0-2)	18.	Feb 16	at Minnesota (0-1)	29.	Mar 11	Minnesota (0-2)
8.	Jan 23	Vancouver (1-1)	19.	Feb 18	Phoenix (0-4)	30.	Mar 14	at Toronto (0-2)
9.	Jan 25	New England (0-2)	20.	Feb 20	Quebec (0-1)	31.	Mar 16	at Chicago (0-1)
10.	Jan 28	Winnipeg (2-2)	21.	Feb 23	at Quebec (0-3)	32.	Mar 19	at New England (1-0)
11.	Feb 4	Toronto (1-3)	22.	Feb 24	at Quebec (0-1)			

He Is His Father's Son

Mark and Marty Howe are the most well-known examples of sons following their old man in the family business. Both had long careers as players, just like their dad Gordie, with Mark finally retiring as a player in 1995, after 22 seasons. Bobby Hull's son Brett also had a long and very productive career in the NHL, scoring 741 career regular season goals. Murray Heatley had a brief, unmemorable run in the WHA, but his son Dany was a top star of the National Hockey League during the 2000s. Pat Stapleton's son Mike also played in the NHL, from 1986 through 2001, and a couple more seasons in Europe. Other WHA players and coaches whose sons played in the NHL include Paulin Bordeleau (Sebastian), Norm Dube (Christian), Ron Grahame (John), Matti Hagman (Niklas), Bernie Lukowich (Brad), Kent Nilsson (Robert), Ted Hampson (Gord), Bobby Kromm (Richard), Bill Dineen (Gord, Peter & Kevin), Frank Spring (Corey), and Dale Smedsmo (step-father to Dustin Byfuglien). Ted McCaskill's son Kirk also played hockey as a youth, but Kirk's greatest fame would come as a pitcher for the California Angels and Chicago White Sox of Major League Baseball, from 1985 to 1996. (*source*: Wikipedia)

Gallery

John Fisher   Bengt Eriksson   Frank Beaton   Claude Chartre   Bill Laing

Dunc McCallum   Len Lilyholm   Gord Kannegiesser   Dave Hunter   Billy Steele

Goaltender Face Masks

Below are some examples of the various face masks worn by goaltenders in the World Hockey Association.

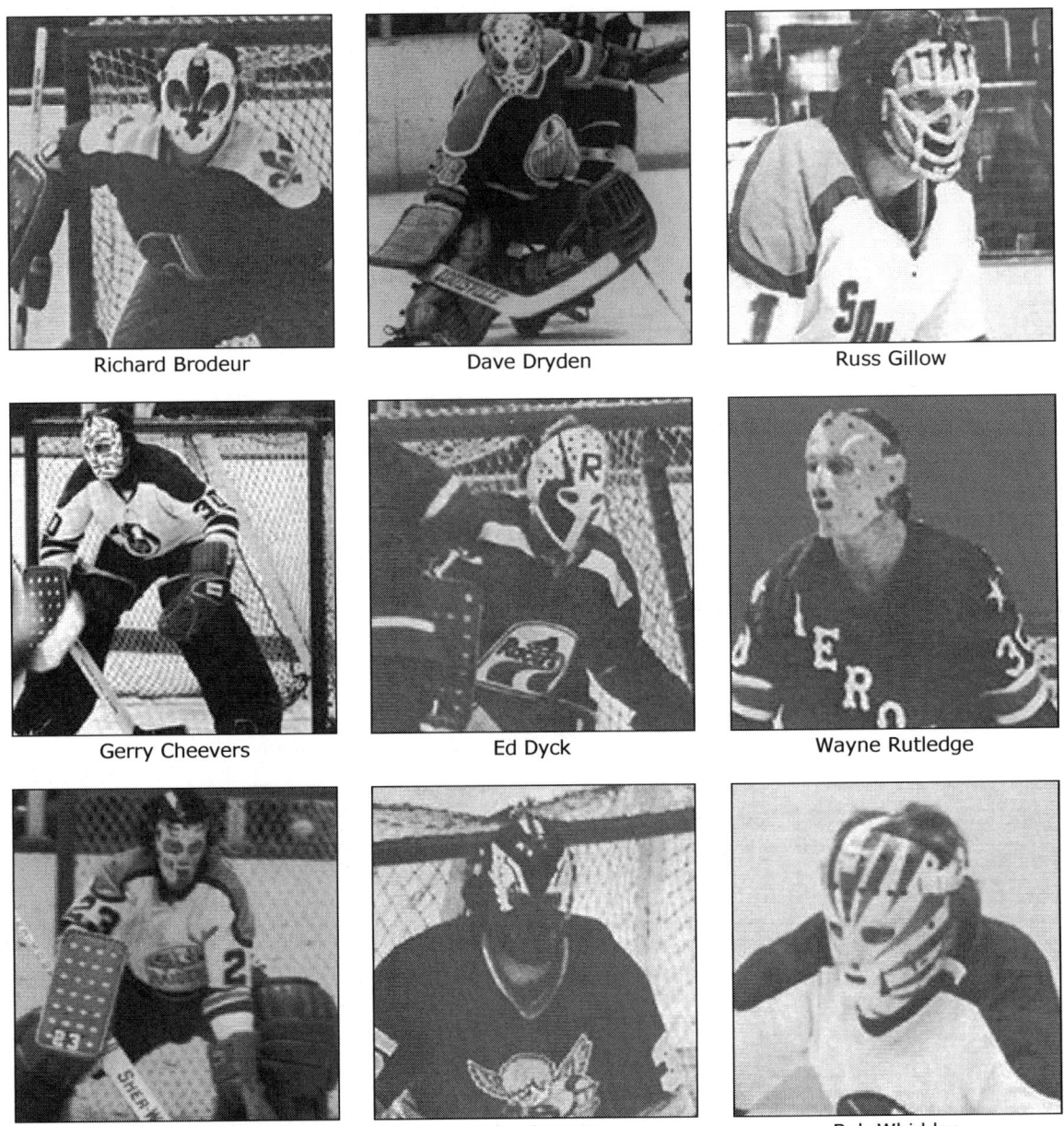

Richard Brodeur

Dave Dryden

Russ Gillow

Gerry Cheevers

Ed Dyck

Wayne Rutledge

Peter Donnelly

John Garrett

Bob Whidden

Don McLeod, Houston   Bernie Parent   Ken Brown

Don McLeod, Vancouver   Gary Kurt   Jack Norris

Don McLeod, Calgary   Bill Berglund   Mike Liut

Season IV

1975-1976

The World Hockey Association opened its fourth season with high hopes after three previous seasons of steadily increasing attendance figures. Two teams would not be back for the 1975-76 campaign: the Chicago Cougars folded immediately after the previous season's end, and the Baltimore Blades ceased operations not long after. In their places were two expansion franchises: the Cincinnati Stingers (In operation since 1973) and the Denver Spurs. The Vancouver Blazers moved across the Rockies to Calgary, becoming the Cowboys.

The fourteen teams were again divided into three divisions. Calgary, Edmonton, Quebec, Toronto and Winnipeg made up the Canadian Division; Cincinnati, Cleveland, Indianapolis and New England comprised the Eastern Division, while the Western Division included Denver, Houston, Minnesota, Phoenix and San Diego.

Denver's Spurs could not make it to the new year; they were moved to Ottawa on January 2, 1976 and disbanded altogether two weeks later. Six weeks after Ottawa's departure, the Minnesota Fighting Saints folded, paring the league to twelve teams. The patchwork schedule used for the

remainder of the season saw some teams play 81 games so that other teams could reach 80. Disparities abounded: Quebec and Toronto tangled 16 times, while Winnipeg and San Diego squared off on only three occasions. Ten teams were admitted to the playoffs, where the slick, European-influenced Jets denied Houston its third straight World Trophy, sweeping the Aeros in four straight.

Quebec's Marc Tardif led all scorers with 71 goals and 148 points, and he tied with teammate J.-C. Tremblay for the league lead in assists with 77. Curt Brackenbury collected a league-record 365 penalty minutes playing for Minnesota and Quebec. The Racers' Kim Clackson had 351 penalty minutes, while the leader the past two season, Gord Gallant, had 297 playing for Quebec.

The Nordiques' Richard Brodeur led all goalies with 69 games and 44 wins. Joe Daley of the Jets turned in five shutouts and also collected 41 wins himself. Michel Dion of the surprisingly defensive Indianapolis Racers had a 2.74 average, the best in the league.

Award Winners

Most Valuable Player
Gordie Howe Trophy
Marc Tardif, Que

Rookie of the Year
Lou Kaplan Trophy
Mark Napier, Bir

Best Goaltender
Ben Hatskin Trophy
Michel Dion, Ind

Standings

Canadian Division

team		gp	w	l	t	pts	pct	gf	ga
1. Winnipeg JETS		81	52	27	2	106	.654	345	254
	home	40	29	11	0	58	.725	171	106
	away	41	23	16	2	48	.585	174	148
2. Québec NORDIQUES		81	50	27	4	104	.642	371	316
	home	40	33	7	0	66	.825	216	136
	away	41	17	20	4	38	.463	155	180
3. Calgary COWBOYS		80	41	35	4	86	.538	307	282
	home	40	25	13	2	52	.650	162	120
	away	40	16	22	2	34	.425	145	162
4. Edmonton OILERS		81	27	49	5	59	.364	268	345
	home	40	20	17	3	43	.538	151	145
	away	41	7	32	2	16	.195	117	200
5. Toronto TOROS		81	24	52	5	53	.327	335	398
	home	40	16	20	4	36	.450	184	180
	away	41	8	32	1	17	.207	151	218

Eastern Division

team		gp	w	l	t	pts	pct	gf	ga
1. Indianapolis RACERS		80	35	39	6	76	.475	245	247
	home	40	21	17	2	44	.550	127	117
	away	40	14	22	4	32	.400	118	130
2. Cleveland CRUSADERS		80	35	40	5	75	.469	273	279
	home	40	23	15	2	48	.600	145	112
	away	40	12	25	3	27	.338	128	167
3. New England WHALERS		80	33	40	7	73	.456	255	290
	home	40	22	16	2	46	.575	148	130
	away	40	11	24	5	27	.338	107	160
4. Cincinnati STINGERS		80	35	44	1	71	.444	285	340
	home	40	26	14	0	52	.650	170	152
	away	40	9	30	1	19	.238	115	188

Western Division

team		gp	w	l	t	pts	pct	gf	ga
1. Houston AEROS		80	53	27	0	106	.663	341	263
	home	40	33	7	0	66	.825	207	126
	away	40	20	20	0	40	.500	134	137
2. Phoenix ROADRUNNERS		80	39	35	6	84	.525	302	287
	home	40	20	14	6	46	.575	163	135
	away	40	19	21	0	38	.475	139	152
3. San Diego MARINERS		80	36	38	6	78	.488	303	290
	home	40	24	12	4	52	.650	171	110
	away	40	12	26	2	26	.325	132	180
Minnesota FIGHTING SAINTS		59	30	25	4	64	.542	211	212
• Disbanded Feb 27, 1976	home	29	16	11	2	34	.586	111	108
	away	30	14	14	2	30	.500	100	104
Denver SPURS-Ottawa CIVICS		41	14	26	1	29	.354	134	172
• Disbanded Jan 17, 1976	home	23	8	14	1	17	.370	79	93
	away	18	6	12	0	12	.333	55	79

Award Winners

Best Defeseman
Dennis Murphy Trophy
Paul Shmyr, Cle

Coach of the Year
Howard Baldwin Trophy
Bobby Kromm, Wpg

Most Gentlemanly
Paul Deneau Trophy
Vaclav Nedomansky, Tor

221

1976 World Hockey Association AVCO Cup Champions
Winnipeg Jets

1976 Playoff Series Results

Preliminary Rounds

Cleveland vs. New England
Apr 9   Cleveland 3 at New England 5
Apr 10   New England 6 at Cleveland 1
Apr 11   New England 3 at Cleveland 2

Phoenix vs. San Diego
Apr 9   San Diego 2 at Phoenix 3
         (ot: Del Hall, 0:31)
Apr 10   Phoenix 2 at San Diego 4
Apr 13   San Diego 4 at Phoenix 6
Apr 15   Phoenix 1 at San Diego 5
Apr 17   San Diego 2 at Phoenix 1

Quarterfinals

Winnipeg vs. Edmonton
Apr 9   Edmonton 3 at Winnipeg 7
Apr 11   Edmonton 4 at Winnipeg 5
         (ot: Ulf Nilsson, 0:54)
Apr 14   Winnipeg 3 at Edmonton 2
Apr 16   Winnipeg 7 at Edmonton 2

Quarterfinals (continued)

Quebec vs. Calgary
Apr 10   Calgary 3 at Quebec 1
Apr 11   Calgary 8 at Quebec 4
Apr 14   Quebec 2 at Calgary 3
Apr 16   Quebec 4 at Calgary 3
Apr 18   Calgary 6 at Quebec 4

Indianapolis vs. New England
Apr 16   New England 4 at Indianapolis 1
Apr 17   New England 0 at Indianapolis 4
         (so: Jim Park 29 saves)
Apr 21   Indianapolis 0 at New England 3
         (so: Cap Raeder, 22 saves)
Apr 23   Indianapolis 1 at New England 2
Apr 24   New England 0 at Indianapolis 4
         (so: Jim Park, 30 saves)
Apr 27   Indianapolis 5 at New England 3
Apr 29   New England 6 at Indianapolis 0
         (so: Cap Raeder, 26 saves)

Houston vs. San Diego
Apr 21   San Diego 6 at Houston 8
Apr 23   San Diego 1 at Houston 3
Apr 25   Houston 8 at San Diego 4
Apr 27   Houston 2 at San Diego 3
Apr 28   San Diego 3 at Houston 2
Apr 30   Houston 3 at San Diego 2

Semifinals

Winnipeg vs. Calgary
Apr 23   Calgary 1 at Winnipeg 6
Apr 25   Calgary 2 at Winnipeg 3
Apr 28   Winnipeg 6 at Calgary 3
Apr 30   Winnipeg 3 at Calgary 7
May 2   Calgary 0 at Winnipeg 4
         (so: Joe Daley, 17 saves)

Houston vs. New England
May 5   New England 4 at Houston 2
May 7   New England 2 at Houston 5
May 9   Houston 1 at New England 4
May 11   Houston 4 at New England 3
May 13   New England 2 at Houston 4
May 15   Houston 1 at New England 6
May 16   New England 0 at Houston 2
         (so: Ron Grahame, 21 saves)

AVCO World Trophy Championship

Houston vs. Winnipeg
May 20   Winnipeg 4 at Houston 3
May 23   Winnipeg 5 at Houston 4
May 25   Houston 3 at Winnipeg 6
May 27   Houston 1 at Winnipeg 9

Playoff Standings

Overall

Team	w	l	gf	ga
Winnipeg	12	1	68	35
New England	10	7	53	40
Houston	8	9	56	64
Calgary	5	5	36	37
San Diego	5	6	36	39
Indianapolis	3	4	15	18
Phoenix	2	3	13	17
Quebec	1	4	15	23
Cleveland	0	3	6	14
Edmonton	0	4	11	22

Home

Team	w	l	gf	ga
Winnipeg	7	0	40	14
New England	5	2	26	15
Houston	5	4	33	27
San Diego	3	2	18	16
Phoenix	2	1	10	8
Calgary	2	2	16	15
Indianapolis	2	2	9	10
Cleveland	0	2	3	9
Edmonton	0	2	4	10
Quebec	0	3	9	17

Away

Team	w	l	gf	ga
Winnipeg	5	1	28	21
New England	5	5	27	25
Calgary	3	3	20	22
Houston	3	5	23	37
San Diego	2	4	18	23
Quebec	1	1	6	6
Indianapolis	1	2	6	8
Cleveland	0	1	3	5
Phoenix	0	2	3	9
Edmonton	0	2	7	12

Championship Series Summaries

The Aeros received a dose of their own medicine by being swept in four straight as the Winnipeg Jets won their first AVCO Cup Championship, and stopping Houston's two-year hold on the trophy. The line of Hull-Nilsson-Hedberg accounted for 25 points as Ulf Nilsson paced all scorers with 4 goals and 6 assists. Anders Hedberg chipped in with 6 goals and 2 assists, while Bobby Hull had 3 goals and 4 assists.

Game 1 • May 20, 1976
Winnipeg 4, Houston 3

Winnipeg	2	1	1	-	4
Houston	2	0	1	-	3

1st period 1. Hou: Hughes (Butters, Hale) 9:37; 2. Wpg: Hedberg (Hull, Nilsson) 13:08; 3. Wpg: Moffat (Beaudin, Lindh) 15:36; 4. Hou: Mark Howe (West, Hale) 19:35
2nd period 5. Wpg: Hedberg (Bergman) 16:10
3rd period 6. Hou: Mark Howe (Preston) 0:46; 7. Wpg: Hull (Nilsson) 16:43
Shots on goal

Wpg on Grahame	9	11	9	-	29
Hou on Daley	11	7	11	-	29

Game 2 • May 23, 1976
Winnipeg 5, Houston 4

Winnipeg	1	2	2	-	5
Houston	0	2	2	-	4

1st period 1. Wpg: Hedberg (Nilsson) 13:52
2nd period 2. Hou: G. Howe (Mark Howe, Schella) 1:22; 3. Wpg: Lindstrom (Sullivan, Bergman) 2:17; 4. Hou: Marty Howe (Hall) 12:44; 5. Wpg: Asmundson (Lesuk, Guindon) 16:53
3rd period 6. Hou: Ruskowski (Preston, Popiel) 1:29; 7. Hou: Marty Howe (Taylor, Popiel) 3:23; 8. Wpg: Bergman 5:19; 9. Wpg: Hull (Bergman, Hedberg) 18:06
Shots on goal

Wpg on Grahame	8	9	9	-	26
Hou on Daley	8	11	13	-	32

Game 3 • May 25, 1976
Winnipeg 6, Houston 3

Houston	1	1	1	-	3
Winnipeg	4	1	1	-	6

1st period 1. Wpg: Ketola (Lindstrom, Riihiranta) 2:24; 2. Wpg: Nilsson (Hedberg) 3:23; 3. Hou: Mark Howe (Schella) 3:48; 4. Wpg: Hedberg (Ford, Ketola) 8:49; 5. Wpg: Sullivan (Hull, Lindstrom) 11:33
2nd period 6. Wpg: Nilsson (Sjoberg) 7:46; 7. Hou: Larway (Marty Howe, Tonelli) 14:28
3rd period 8. Wpg: Nilsson 1:44; 9. Hou: Larway (Tonelli, Ruskowski) 13:22
Shots on goal

Hou on Daley	7	4	7	-	18
Wpg on Grahame	13	7	5	-	25

Game 4 • May 27, 1976
Winnipeg 9, Houston 1

Houston	1	0	0	-	1
Winnipeg	3	4	2	-	9

1st period 1. Wpg: Hull (Ford, Nilsson) 5:37; 2. Hou: Taylor (Labossiere, Marty Howe) 9:45; 3. Wpg: Ketola (Ford, Hull) 10:22; 4. Wpg: Moffat (Sjoberg, Ford) 11:21
2nd period 5. Wpg: Ketola (Lindstrom, Sullivan) 1:07; 6. Wpg: Hedberg (Nilsson, Hull) 3:11; 7. Wpg: Hedberg (Nilsson) 9:19; 8. Wpg: Sullivan (Hillman) 12:14
3rd period 9. Wpg: Sullivan (Ford, Riihiranta) 1:33; 10. Wpg: Guindon (Riihiranta, Ketola) 9:30.
Shots on goal

Hou on Daley	7	5	5	-	17
Wpg on Grahame	12	12	9	-	33

Statistical Leaders

Goals: 13, Anders Hedberg (Wpg); 12, Bobby Hull (Wpg); 10, Tom Webster (NE); 7, Veli-Pekka Ketola (Wpg), Don Larway (Hou), Ulf Nilsson (Wpg), John Tonelli (Hou)

Assists: 21, Ulf Nilsson (Wpg); 12, Mike Ford (Wpg); 11, Rosaire Paiement (NE); 10, Thommie Bergman (Wpg), Mark Howe (Hou), Terry Ruskowski (Hou)

Points: 26, Ulf Nilsson (Wpg); 20, Bobby Hull (Wpg); 19, Anders Hedberg (Wpg), Tom Webster (NE); 16, Mark Howe (Hou), Terry Ruskowski (Hou)

Penalty Minutes: 64, Terry Ruskowski (Hou); 57, Nick Fotiu (NE); 51, Bill Butters (NE); 49, Rick Ley (NE)

Goaltending Wins: 10, Joe Daley (Wpg); 7, Cap Raeder (NE); 6, Ron Grahame (Hou); 5, Don McLeod (Cgy), Ernie Wakely (SD)

Goals Against Average: 2.27, Cap Raeder (NE); 2.45, Jim Park (Ind); 2.59, Joe Daley (Wpg); 3.42, Jack Norris (Phx). Note: Bruce Landon (NE) 2.13 in 4 games

Penalty Shots: April 21: Gord Labossiere, Houston, scored on Ernie Wakely, San Diego; May 5, Tom Earl, new England, did not score on Ron Grahame, Houston

Splits by Opponent and by Month, Home and Away

CALGARY

Opp.	season	gf-ga	home	gf-ga	away	gf-ga
Cin	1-3-0	11-16	1-1-0	5-8	0-2-0	6-8
Cle	3-1-0	13-11	2-0-0	10-6	1-1-0	3-5
D-O	1-1-0	7-4	0-1-0	1-2	1-0-0	6-2
Edm	10-3-1	65-39	6-1-0	34-15	4-2-1	31-24
Hou	2-2-0	12-12	2-0-0	9-5	0-2-0	3-7
Ind	4-0-0	19-12	2-0-0	8-4	2-0-0	11-8
Min	1-2-0	9-12	0-2-0	3-8	1-0-0	6-4
NE	2-3-0	17-22	1-1-0	8-9	1-2-0	9-13
Phx	1-3-0	10-15	0-2-0	5-9	1-1-0	5-6
Que	5-4-1	48-45	4-0-1	23-12	1-4-0	25-33
SD	1-2-1	11-15	0-1-1	6-10	1-1-0	5-5
Tor	6-3-1	47-33	4-1-0	27-12	2-2-1	20-21
Wpg	4-8-0	38-46	3-3-0	23-20	1-5-0	15-26
Oct	3-5-0	22-26	1-4-0	11-17	2-1-0	11-9
Nov	9-4-1	58-45	5-2-1	32-27	4-2-0	26-18
Dec	7-5-1	63-49	4-2-0	33-16	3-3-1	30-33
Jan	6-7-0	40-36	4-1-0	20-10	2-6-0	20-26
Feb	6-6-2	49-57	5-3-1	34-34	1-3-1	15-23
Mar	9-7-0	68-63	5-0-0	25-10	4-7-0	43-53
Apr	1-1-0	7-6	1-1-0	7-6	0-0-0	0-0

DENVER-OTTAWA

Opp.	season	gf-ga	home	gf-ga	away	gf-ga
Cgy	1-1-0	4-7	0-1-0	2-6	1-0-0	2-1
Cin	2-2-0	11-10	2-0-0	8-5	0-2-0	3-5
Cle	3-0-1	16-9	2-0-1	13-9	1-0-0	3-0
Edm	1-0-0	6-3	1-0-0	6-3	0-0-0	0-0
Hou	0-5-0	14-24	0-2-0	6-8	0-3-0	8-16
Ind	3-1-0	13-14	1-1-0	3-8	2-0-0	10-6
Min	1-2-0	12-11	0-1-0	4-5	1-1-0	8-6
NE	1-2-0	10-11	1-1-0	7-4	0-1-0	3-7
Phx	1-5-0	15-34	0-3-0	5-12	1-2-0	10-22
Que	0-1-0	3-5	0-1-0	3-5	0-0-0	0-0
SD	1-2-0	9-11	1-1-0	8-6	0-1-0	1-5
Tor	0-1-0	8-11	0-1-0	8-11	0-0-0	0-0
Wpg	0-4-0	13-22	0-2-0	6-11	0-2-0	7-11
Oct	3-4-0	21-31	0-3-0	6-17	3-1-0	15-14
Nov	5-8-1	48-57	3-5-1	35-40	2-3-0	13-17
Dec	5-8-0	41-54	5-4-0	32-28	0-4-0	9-26
Jan	1-6-0	24-30	0-2-0	6-8	1-4-0	18-22

CINCINNATI

Opp.	season	gf-ga	home	gf-ga	away	gf-ga
Cgy	3-1-0	16-11	2-0-0	8-6	1-1-0	8-5
Cle	6-5-0	38-36	4-1-0	24-14	2-4-0	14-22
D-O	2-2-0	10-11	2-0-0	5-3	0-2-0	5-8
Edm	2-2-0	17-13	2-0-0	13-4	0-2-0	4-9
Hou	3-4-0	27-32	3-1-0	19-14	0-3-0	8-18
Ind	3-8-0	25-38	2-3-0	14-17	1-5-0	11-21
Min	1-3-0	15-19	0-2-0	6-10	1-1-0	9-9
NE	6-5-0	43-41	5-1-0	25-17	1-4-0	18-24
Phx	3-3-0	19-26	1-2-0	9-13	2-1-0	10-13
Que	1-3-0	22-31	1-1-0	17-16	0-2-0	5-15
SD	3-2-1	22-28	3-0-0	15-9	0-2-1	7-19
Tor	2-2-0	26-27	1-1-0	10-13	1-1-0	16-14
Wpg	0-4-0	5-27	0-2-0	5-16	0-2-0	0-11
Oct	5-3-0	28-29	2-0-0	13-8	3-3-0	15-21
Nov	4-9-0	58-77	4-4-0	38-45	0-5-0	20-32
Dec	7-7-1	54-55	5-1-0	28-18	2-6-1	26-37
Jan	5-8-0	45-59	4-3-0	31-27	1-5-0	14-32
Feb	8-6-0	52-44	6-2-0	31-20	2-4-0	21-24
Mar	5-10-0	40-68	4-4-0	24-32	1-6-0	16-36
Apr	1-1-0	8-8	1-0-0	5-2	0-1-0	3-6

EDMONTON

Opp.	season	gf-ga	home	gf-ga	away	gf-ga
Cgy	3-10-1	39-65	2-4-1	24-31	1-6-0	15-34
Cin	2-2-0	13-17	2-0-0	9-4	0-2-0	4-13
Cle	2-2-0	11-13	1-1-0	6-6	1-1-0	5-7
D-O	0-1-0	3-6	0-0-0	0-0	0-1-0	3-6
Hou	0-4-0	14-22	0-2-0	8-11	0-2-0	6-11
Ind	3-1-0	15-10	2-0-0	9-5	1-1-0	6-5
Min	2-1-0	8-8	1-1-0	5-7	1-0-0	3-1
NE	1-2-1	12-11	1-0-1	6-2	0-2-0	6-9
Phx	1-3-0	11-15	1-1-0	9-7	0-2-0	2-8
Que	2-10-0	49-69	2-4-0	25-26	0-6-0	24-43
SD	3-1-0	16-15	2-0-0	11-6	1-1-0	5-9
Tor	4-4-2	44-45	4-1-0	24-16	0-3-2	20-29
Wpg	4-8-1	33-49	2-3-1	15-24	2-5-0	18-25
Oct	4-6-2	45-49	3-1-1	20-16	1-5-1	25-33
Nov	6-8-0	46-58	5-1-0	27-17	1-7-0	19-41
Dec	5-9-0	46-61	2-4-0	23-24	3-5-0	26-37
Jan	3-8-1	39-56	2-5-0	21-35	1-3-1	18-21
Feb	4-8-2	41-54	4-3-2	33-29	0-5-0	8-25
Mar	4-9-0	41-58	3-3-0	22-22	1-6-0	19-36
Apr	1-1-0	7-9	1-0-0	5-2	0-1-0	2-7

CLEVELAND

Opp.	season	gf-ga	home	gf-ga	away	gf-ga
Cgy	1-3-0	11-13	1-1-0	5-3	0-2-0	6-10
Cin	5-6-0	36-38	4-2-0	22-14	1-4-0	14-24
D-O	0-3-1	9-16	0-1-0	0-3	0-2-1	9-13
Edm	2-2-0	13-11	1-1-0	7-5	1-1-0	6-6
Hou	2-5-0	25-29	1-3-0	12-14	1-2-0	13-15
Ind	5-5-0	31-28	3-2-0	15-14	2-3-0	16-14
Min	4-0-0	19-12	2-0-0	5-3	2-0-0	14-9
NE	3-6-1	28-34	2-2-1	14-13	1-4-0	14-21
Phx	3-2-2	25-25	2-1-0	10-7	1-1-2	15-18
Que	3-1-0	16-16	2-0-0	11-6	1-1-0	5-10
SD	2-4-0	21-19	2-1-0	14-8	0-3-0	7-11
Tor	3-2-0	24-24	2-1-0	20-15	1-1-0	4-9
Wpg	2-1-1	15-14	1-0-1	10-7	1-1-0	5-7
Oct	3-3-0	25-18	2-3-0	17-14	1-0-0	8-4
Nov	6-6-2	47-51	4-2-0	26-23	2-4-2	21-28
Dec	3-11-0	36-54	3-4-0	20-19	0-7-0	16-35
Jan	7-5-2	54-52	5-0-1	26-17	2-5-1	28-35
Feb	7-6-1	48-43	4-1-1	19-12	3-5-0	29-31
Mar	7-7-0	49-48	3-4-0	25-19	4-3-0	24-29
Apr	2-2-0	14-13	2-1-0	12-8	0-1-0	2-5

HOUSTON

Opp.	season	gf-ga	home	gf-ga	away	gf-ga
Cgy	2-2-0	12-12	2-0-0	7-3	0-2-0	5-9
Cin	4-3-0	32-27	3-0-0	18-8	1-3-0	14-19
Cle	5-2-0	29-25	2-1-0	15-13	3-1-0	14-12
D-O	5-0-0	24-14	3-0-0	16-8	2-0-0	8-6
Edm	4-0-0	22-14	2-0-0	11-6	2-0-0	11-8
Ind	4-3-0	20-17	3-0-0	12-6	1-3-0	8-11
Min	4-2-0	27-17	3-0-0	19-8	1-2-0	8-9
NE	4-2-0	26-17	2-1-0	15-11	2-1-0	11-6
Phx	9-1-0	58-34	5-0-0	30-18	4-1-0	28-16
Que	1-3-0	9-11	1-1-0	6-4	0-2-0	3-7
SD	7-5-0	50-37	5-2-0	40-21	2-3-0	10-16
Tor	2-2-0	20-23	1-1-0	10-11	1-1-0	10-12
Wpg	2-2-0	12-15	1-1-0	8-9	1-1-0	4-6
Oct	3-4-0	24-27	0-0-0	0-0	3-4-0	24-27
Nov	11-3-0	61-45	9-0-0	46-24	2-3-0	15-21
Dec	7-6-0	53-47	5-3-0	36-28	2-3-0	17-19
Jan	10-5-0	63-50	6-1-0	38-23	4-4-0	25-27
Feb	9-4-0	51-41	5-1-0	28-19	4-3-0	23-22
Mar	9-5-0	64-43	6-2-0	46-25	3-3-0	18-18
Apr	4-0-0	25-10	2-0-0	13-7	2-0-0	12-3

INDIANAPOLIS

Opp.	season	gf-ga	home	gf-ga	away	gf-ga
Cgy	0-4-0	12-19	0-2-0	8-11	0-2-0	4-8
Cin	8-3-0	38-25	5-1-0	21-11	3-2-0	17-14
Cle	5-5-0	28-31	3-2-0	14-16	2-3-0	14-15
D-O	1-3-0	14-13	0-2-0	6-10	1-1-0	8-3
Edm	1-3-0	10-15	1-1-0	5-6	0-2-0	5-9
Hou	3-4-0	17-20	3-1-0	11-8	0-3-0	6-12
Min	0-4-0	14-20	0-2-0	6-8	0-2-0	8-12
NE	7-2-3	44-31	3-1-1	20-13	4-1-2	24-18
Phx	3-3-0	18-24	2-1-0	13-11	1-2-0	5-13
Que	1-3-0	10-13	1-1-0	6-7	0-2-0	4-6
SD	0-3-3	17-23	0-2-1	6-9	0-1-2	11-14
Tor	4-0-0	16-7	2-0-0	7-4	2-0-0	9-3
Wpg	2-2-0	7-6	1-1-0	4-3	1-1-0	3-3
Oct	3-6-0	33-33	2-3-0	18-18	1-3-0	15-15
Nov	6-6-0	37-37	3-2-0	14-14	3-4-0	23-23
Dec	5-6-2	33-39	4-1-1	20-13	1-5-1	13-26
Jan	5-10-0	32-46	4-4-0	19-23	1-6-0	13-23
Feb	5-7-1	48-38	4-4-0	32-22	1-3-1	16-16
Mar	9-2-3	52-42	4-1-1	21-18	5-1-2	31-24
Apr	2-2-0	10-12	0-2-0	3-9	2-0-0	7-3

PHOENIX

Opp.	season	gf-ga	home	gf-ga	away	gf-ga
Cgy	3-1-0	15-10	1-1-0	6-5	2-0-0	9-5
Cin	3-3-0	26-19	1-2-0	13-10	2-1-0	13-9
Cle	2-3-2	25-25	1-1-2	18-15	1-2-0	7-10
D-O	5-1-0	34-15	2-1-0	22-10	3-0-0	12-5
Edm	3-1-0	15-11	2-0-0	8-2	1-1-0	7-9
Hou	1-9-0	34-58	1-4-0	16-28	0-5-0	18-30
Ind	3-3-0	24-18	2-1-0	13-5	1-2-0	11-13
Min	3-3-1	25-22	2-1-1	12-10	1-2-0	13-12
NE	3-2-1	23-24	1-1-1	12-13	2-1-0	11-11
Que	1-2-1	12-14	0-1-1	5-6	1-1-0	7-8
SD	9-3-0	46-41	5-0-0	24-16	4-3-0	22-25
Tor	2-1-1	14-12	1-0-1	8-6	1-1-0	6-6
Wpg	1-3-0	9-18	1-1-0	6-9	0-2-0	3-9
Oct	5-4-0	30-38	2-2-0	16-19	3-2-0	14-19
Nov	2-7-3	33-47	1-2-3	15-18	1-5-0	18-29
Dec	8-4-0	54-32	5-3-0	38-22	3-1-0	16-10
Jan	8-5-2	64-52	6-1-2	46-28	2-4-0	18-24
Feb	8-4-1	47-35	4-1-1	22-14	4-3-0	25-21
Mar	8-9-0	67-67	2-4-0	24-26	6-5-0	43-41
Apr	0-2-0	7-16	0-1-0	2-8	0-1-0	5-8

MINNESOTA

Opp.	season	gf-ga	home	gf-ga	away	gf-ga
Cgy	2-1-0	12-9	0-1-0	4-6	2-0-0	8-3
Cin	3-1-0	19-15	1-1-0	9-9	2-0-0	10-6
Cle	0-4-0	12-19	0-2-0	9-14	0-2-0	3-5
D-O	2-1-0	11-12	1-1-0	6-8	1-0-0	5-4
Edm	1-2-0	8-8	0-1-0	1-3	1-1-0	7-5
Hou	2-4-0	17-27	2-1-0	9-8	0-3-0	8-19
Ind	4-0-0	20-14	2-0-0	12-8	2-0-0	8-6
NE	2-1-1	7-5	1-0-1	3-2	1-1-0	4-3
Phx	3-3-1	22-25	2-1-0	12-13	1-2-1	10-12
Que	1-1-1	16-16	1-0-1	10-8	0-1-0	6-8
SD	3-6-1	29-40	2-3-0	15-19	1-3-1	14-21
Tor	4-0-0	20-11	2-0-0	9-5	2-0-0	11-6
Wpg	3-1-0	18-11	2-0-0	12-5	1-1-0	8-6
Oct	3-4-1	22-29	0-3-0	9-17	3-1-1	13-12
Nov	7-5-0	49-48	5-1-0	28-23	2-4-0	21-25
Dec	6-4-2	34-32	3-1-2	19-15	3-3-0	15-17
Jan	9-5-0	57-52	6-3-0	35-33	3-2-0	22-19
Feb	5-7-1	49-51	2-3-0	20-20	3-4-1	29-31

QUEBEC

Opp.	season	gf-ga	home	gf-ga	away	gf-ga
Cgy	4-5-1	45-48	4-1-0	33-25	0-4-1	12-23
Cin	3-1-0	31-22	2-0-0	15-5	1-1-0	16-17
Cle	1-3-0	16-16	1-1-0	10-5	0-2-0	6-11
D-O	1-0-0	5-3	0-0-0	0-0	1-0-0	5-3
Edm	10-2-0	69-49	6-0-0	43-24	4-2-0	26-25
Hou	3-1-0	11-9	2-0-0	7-3	1-1-0	4-6
Ind	3-1-0	13-10	2-0-0	6-4	1-1-0	7-6
Min	1-1-1	16-16	1-0-0	8-6	0-1-1	8-10
NE	4-1-0	20-7	3-0-0	15-2	1-1-0	5-5
Phx	2-1-1	14-12	1-1-0	8-7	1-1-0	6-5
SD	2-2-0	14-20	2-0-0	9-5	0-2-0	5-15
Tor	10-5-1	76-60	7-1-0	44-25	3-4-1	32-35
Wpg	6-4-0	41-44	2-3-0	18-20	4-1-0	23-24
Oct	5-4-0	38-34	5-1-0	30-18	0-3-0	8-16
Nov	11-4-1	62-51	4-1-0	26-18	7-3-1	36-33
Dec	8-6-1	78-74	6-0-0	41-22	2-6-1	37-52
Jan	7-2-1	48-34	7-1-0	41-26	0-1-1	7-8
Feb	7-3-1	46-35	4-1-0	21-11	3-2-1	25-24
Mar	8-8-0	72-75	4-3-0	35-27	4-5-0	37-48
Apr	4-0-0	27-13	3-0-0	22-9	1-0-0	5-4

NEW ENGLAND

Opp.	season	gf-ga	home	gf-ga	away	gf-ga
Cgy	3-2-0	22-17	2-1-0	13-9	1-1-0	9-8
Cin	5-6-0	41-43	4-1-0	24-18	1-5-0	17-25
Cle	6-3-1	34-28	4-1-0	21-14	2-2-1	13-14
D-O	2-1-0	11-10	1-0-0	7-3	1-1-0	4-7
Edm	2-1-1	11-12	2-0-0	9-6	0-1-1	2-6
Hou	2-4-0	17-26	1-2-0	6-11	1-2-0	11-15
Ind	2-7-3	31-44	1-4-2	18-24	1-3-1	13-20
Min	1-2-1	5-7	1-1-0	3-4	0-1-1	2-3
Phx	2-3-1	24-23	1-2-0	11-11	1-1-1	13-12
Que	1-4-0	7-20	1-1-0	5-5	0-3-0	2-15
SD	3-3-0	23-27	2-1-0	16-12	1-2-0	7-15
Tor	4-0-0	22-13	2-0-0	10-4	2-0-0	12-9
Wpg	0-4-0	7-20	0-2-0	5-9	0-2-0	2-11
Oct	5-2-1	23-25	4-1-0	15-13	1-1-1	8-12
Nov	4-10-0	43-43	4-5-0	33-26	0-5-0	10-17
Dec	8-4-2	44-37	6-0-0	25-14	2-4-2	19-23
Jan	5-7-2	48-61	4-2-0	28-23	1-5-2	20-38
Feb	4-8-1	39-61	1-3-1	15-23	3-5-0	24-38
Mar	6-8-1	51-57	3-4-1	30-27	3-4-0	21-30
Apr	1-1-0	7-6	0-1-0	2-4	1-0-0	5-2

SAN DIEGO

Opp.	season	gf-ga	home	gf-ga	away	gf-ga
Cgy	2-1-1	15-11	1-1-0	5-5	1-0-1	10-6
Cin	2-3-1	28-22	2-0-1	19-7	0-3-0	9-15
Cle	4-2-0	19-21	3-0-0	11-7	1-2-0	8-14
D-O	2-1-0	11-9	1-0-0	5-1	1-1-0	6-8
Edm	1-3-0	15-16	1-1-0	9-5	0-2-0	6-11
Hou	5-7-0	37-50	3-2-0	16-10	2-5-0	21-40
Ind	3-0-3	23-17	1-0-2	14-11	2-0-1	9-6
Min	6-3-1	40-29	3-1-1	21-14	3-2-0	19-15
NE	3-3-0	27-23	2-1-0	15-7	1-2-0	12-16
Phx	3-9-0	41-46	3-4-0	25-22	0-5-0	16-24
Que	2-2-0	20-14	2-0-0	15-5	0-2-0	5-9
Tor	2-2-0	20-20	1-1-0	10-10	1-1-0	10-10
Wpg	1-2-0	7-12	1-1-0	6-6	0-1-0	1-6
Oct	3-3-1	24-20	3-2-1	19-14	0-1-0	5-6
Nov	6-7-1	57-53	4-3-0	30-19	2-4-1	27-34
Dec	7-4-2	52-40	5-1-2	38-22	2-3-0	14-18
Jan	8-8-0	67-65	5-1-0	26-17	3-7-0	41-48
Feb	6-6-0	37-38	6-1-0	14-8	3-5-0	23-30
Mar	5-8-2	59-63	4-4-1	44-30	1-4-1	15-33
Apr	1-2-0	7-11	0-0-0	0-0	1-2-0	7-11

TORONTO

Opp.	season	gf-ga	home	gf-ga	away	gf-ga
Cgy	3-6-1	33-47	2-2-1	21-20	1-4-0	12-27
Cin	2-2-0	27-26	1-1-0	14-16	1-1-0	13-10
Cle	2-3-0	24-24	1-1-0	9-4	1-2-0	15-20
D-O	1-0-0	11-8	0-0-0	0-0	1-0-0	11-8
Edm	4-4-2	45-44	3-0-2	29-20	1-4-0	16-24
Hou	2-2-0	23-20	1-1-0	12-10	1-1-0	11-10
Ind	0-4-0	7-16	0-2-0	3-9	0-2-0	4-7
Min	0-4-0	11-20	0-2-0	6-11	0-2-0	5-9
NE	0-4-0	13-22	0-2-0	9-12	0-2-0	4-10
Phx	1-2-1	12-14	1-1-0	6-6	0-1-1	6-8
Que	5-10-1	60-76	4-3-1	35-32	1-7-0	25-44
SD	2-2-0	20-20	1-1-0	10-10	1-1-0	10-10
Wpg	2-9-0	49-61	2-4-0	30-30	0-5-0	19-31
Oct	2-4-1	26-29	2-1-1	20-16	0-3-0	6-13
Nov	4-9-1	70-74	1-3-0	16-22	3-6-1	54-52
Dec	6-9-1	59-79	4-4-1	40-40	2-5-0	19-39
Jan	3-7-2	46-59	2-0-2	17-12	1-7-0	29-47
Feb	1-11-0	58-76	1-6-0	41-49	0-5-0	17-27
Mar	8-8-0	64-58	6-4-0	45-33	2-4-0	19-25
Apr	0-4-0	12-23	0-2-0	5-8	0-2-0	7-15

WINNIPEG

Opp.	season	gf-ga	home	gf-ga	away	gf-ga
Cgy	8-4-0	46-38	5-1-0	26-15	3-3-0	20-23
Cin	4-0-0	27-5	2-0-0	11-0	2-0-0	16-5
Cle	1-2-1	14-15	1-1-0	7-5	0-1-1	7-10
D-O	4-0-0	22-13	2-0-0	11-7	2-0-0	11-6
Edm	8-4-1	49-33	5-2-0	25-18	3-2-1	24-15
Hou	2-2-0	15-12	1-1-0	6-4	1-1-0	9-8
Ind	2-2-0	6-7	1-1-0	3-3	1-1-0	3-4
Min	1-3-0	11-18	1-1-0	6-6	0-2-0	5-12
NE	4-0-0	20-7	2-0-0	11-2	2-0-0	9-5
Phx	3-1-0	18-9	2-0-0	9-3	1-1-0	9-6
Que	4-6-0	44-41	1-4-0	24-23	3-2-0	20-18
SD	2-1-0	12-7	1-0-0	6-1	1-1-0	6-6
Tor	9-2-0	61-49	5-0-0	31-19	4-2-0	30-30
Oct	7-2-0	43-16	4-0-0	21-2	3-2-0	22-14
Nov	10-5-0	55-38	5-3-0	25-17	5-2-0	30-21
Dec	8-7-0	59-56	2-3-0	17-18	6-4-0	42-38
Jan	10-4-0	63-38	6-2-0	36-18	4-2-0	27-20
Feb	9-3-2	68-60	6-1-0	36-26	3-2-2	32-34
Mar	7-4-0	49-34	6-2-0	41-25	1-2-0	8-9
Apr	1-2-0	8-12	0-0-0	0-0	1-2-0	8-12

1976 All-Star Game

The Coliseum
Richfield, Ohio
January 13, 1976

Canada

Coach: Jean Guy Gendron (Quebec)
Goaltenders: Jim Shaw (Toronto), Joe Daley (Winnipeg), Don McLeod (Calgary)
Defensemen: Lars-Erik Sjoberg, Larry Hornung, Thommie Bergman (Winnipeg), J.-C. Tremblay (Quebec), Barry Long (Edmonton), John Miszuk, Paul Terbenche (Calgary)
Forwards: Marc Tardif, Real Cloutier, Serge Bernier, Christian Bordeleau, Rejean Houle (Quebec), Vaclav Nedomansky, Frank Mahovlich (Toronto), Bobby Hull, Anders Hedberg, Ulf Nilsson (Winnipeg), Danny Lawson (Calgary), Rusty Patenaude (Edmonton)

United States

Coach: Bill Dineen (Houston)
Goaltenders: Christer Abrahamsson (New England), Gerry Cheevers (Cleveland)
Defensemen: Paul Shmyr (Cleveland), John Schella, Marty Howe (Houston), Pat Stapleton (Indianapolis), Rick Ley (New England), Kevin Morrison (San Diego)
Forwards: Andre Lacroix, Gene Peacosh (San Diego), Gordie Howe, Mark Howe (Houston), Dave Keon, Mike Walton (Minnesota), Claude Larose (Cincinnati), Ralph Backstrom, Don Borgeson (Denver-Ottawa), Robbie Ftorek (Phoenix), Wayne Carleton, Tom Webster (New England)

MVPs: Canada: Real Cloutier, Quebec
U. S.: Paul Shmyr, Cleveland
Did Not Play: Joe Daley, J.-C. Tremblay

Canada 6, United States 1

Canada	0	3	3	- 6
United States	0	0	1	- 1

1st period: No scoring.
2nd period: 1. Can: Cloutier (Tardif) 1:45; 2. Can: Mahovlich (Bergman) 11:50; 3. Can: Cloutier (Sjoberg, Bordeleau) 16:44.
3rd period: 4. Can: Lawson 3:50; 5. US: Lacroix (Ley) 13:26; 6. Can: Nilsson (Hedberg, Miszuk) 15:33; 7. Can: Cloutier (Bordeleau, Tardif) 18:04.

Shots on goal

Canada	8	9	13	- 30
United States	9	9	7	- 25

Attendance 15,491

1975-1976 Year End All-Star Teams

First Team: Goaltender: Joe Daley, Winnipeg; Defensemen: Paul Shmyr, Cleveland, and J.-C. Tremblay, Quebec; Center: Ulf Nilsson, Winnipeg; Right Wing: Anders Hedberg, Winnipeg; Left Wing: Marc Tardif, Quebec.

Second Team: Goaltender: Ron Grahame, Houston; Defensemen: Kevin Morrison, San Diego, and Pat Stapleton, Indianapolis; Center: Robbie Ftorek, Phoenix; Right Wing: Real Cloutier, Quebec; Left Wing: Bobby Hull, Winnipeg.

Penalty Shots

date	player, team	goaltender, team	period	time	result
Oct 10	Kevin Devine, San Diego	Gary Kurt, Phoenix	2	6:01	save
Oct 28	Serge Bernier, Quebec	Mario Vien, Toronto	1	13:45	score
Feb 6	Mark Napier, Toronto	Joe Daley, Winnipeg	3	13:43	score
Feb 18	Al McDonough, Cleveland	Don McLeod, Calgary	3	2:48	save
Feb 18	Danny Gruen, Cleveland	Don McLeod, Calgary	3	11:47	save
Mar 2	Rick Morris, Edmonton	Don McLeod, Calgary	1	18:33	score
Mar 20	Christian Bordeleau, Quebec	Don McLeod, Calgary	1	8:46	save
Mar 20	Rejean Houle, Quebec	Don McLeod, Calgary	1	10:21	save
Mar 30	Florent Fortier, Quebec	Chris Worthy, Edmonton	3	14:46	save

Attendance Figures

g indicates the number of home games played

team	g	season total	avg	playoff g	total	avg	team	g	season total	avg	playoff g	total	avg
Calgary	40	197,913	4,948	4	28,959	7,240	Minnesota	29	243,488	8,396	-	-	-
Cincinnati	40	309,630	7,741	-	-	-	New England	40	372,334	9,308	7	700,633	10,090
Cleveland	40	254,224	6,356	2	7,827	3,914	Phoenix	40	258,576	6,464	3	22,556	7,519
Denver-Ottawa	23	99,394	4,321	-	-	-	Quebec	40	395,383	9,885	3	33,229	11,076
Edmonton	40	317,234	7,931	2	20,884	10,442	San Diego	40	249,488	6,237	6	45,832	7,639
Houston	40	367,187	9,180	8	98,945	12,368	Toronto	40	359,305	8,983	-	-	-
Indianapolis	40	351,127	8,778	4	48,346	12,087	Winnipeg	40	347,838	8,696	7	67,339	9,620

Total Attendance: 4,123,121   **Average Attendance:** 7,750

1975-1976 Team Thumbnails

Calgary: Three years after the Broncos were forced to drop out of the WHA, Calgary was once again a member of the World Hockey Association, now host to the Cowboys, late of Vancouver. The old Blazers had given up their fight in Vancouver and moved across the Rocky Mountains to Calgary, playing out of the tiny yet raucous Stampede Corral. The move seemed to be a tonic, as the Cowboys skated to the best record of the four-year old franchise, finishing 41-35-4 and a third-place finish in the Canadian Division. Joe Crozier's boys broke through for 307 goals, led by the talented Danny Lawson's 44 goals and 96 points. Sophomore Ron Chipperfield scored 42, while tough-guy Butch Deadmarsh scored 26, apart from his 196 minutes spent in the box. A trio of 25-goal scorers—George Morrison, Don Tannahill and Dick Sentes—rounded out the offense. The defense was led by veterans Duane Rupp, Chris Evans and Paul Terbenche, with Francois Lacombe joining the Cowboys for this season. Unheralded John Miszuk made the team as a spare and eventually worked his way to a spot in the all-star game. Don McLeod handled goaltending, and even assisted on an impressive 13 goals during the season, while failing in his bid to be the first goaltender in major-league hockey to score a goal, going 0 for 6 on the season in shot attempts. The Cowboy were well-suited for the smaller rink dimensions of the Corral, often stifling speedier teams against the boards. In the playoffs, the Cowboys faced off against Quebec. In the second game at Quebec, the Cowboys' Rick Jodzio cross-checked Nordiques' Marc Tardif, severely injuring Tardif and touching off perhaps the worst brawl in WHA history, a free-for-all that was only quelled by the presence of police. The Cowboys would defeat Quebec in the series, then lose to Winnipeg in the semifinals. However, Jodzio's hit and the ensuing brawl would be the low-point of the overly-violent brand of goon hockey that had become popular in the middle 1970s. The Cowboys, whether fairly or not, would be viewed as the league's bad guys as a result, and many rule-changes would be adopted for 1976-77, directly as a result of this brawl.

Cincinnati: The Stingers were welcomed to the league as an expansion franchise, playing in the new Riverfront Arena complex, which had just been completed. The Stingers had existed on paper since 1973, and had been participating in drafts and player-signings, putting together a strong squad of young players and veterans, in the hope of avoiding the usual dreadful first year of many expansion clubs. Coached by former Sharks' coach Terry Slater, the new Stingers featured a core of scorers and a bit of toughness. Most notable of the new Stingers was Rick Dudley, a fan favorite from his days with the Cincinnati Swords in the early 1970s, and recently of the Buffalo Sabres. Also on the roster was prized youngster Dennis Sobchuk, who had signed with Cincinnati in 1974 but was loaned to Phoenix for 1974-75. Joining them were veterans Bryan Campbell and Pierre Guite, youngsters Claude Larose and Jacques Locas, and later in the season, John McKenzie, late of the failed Minnesota franchise. Dudley would score 43 goals and 81 points to lead the team, while Sobchuk and Campbell each produced 72 points, Sobchuk with 32 goals and Campbell with 22. Dennis' brother, Gene Sobchuk, scored 23. Larose put in 28 and Locas 27, and overall, Cincinnati scored 285 goals. Keeping them out of their own net was another thing, as they gave up 340 on the season. The Stingers started strongly with a 9-4-0 record, and while they eventually played at just under break-even hockey for most of the year, they were in the race for a playoff position as late as mid-March in the weak Eastern Division, before fading at the end. Nevertheless, the Stingers finished with a 35-44-1 record, a very impressive mark for a first-year club.

Cleveland: In its first three years the Crusaders were a low-scoring defensive club built around Gerry Cheevers. The results were middling records and early playoff exits. In 1974, Nick Mileti moved the team to the brand-new Richfield Coliseum, a state-of-the-art arena built in the suburbs of Cleveland. Despite the arena's attractions, the move may have hastened the demise of the Crusaders as a franchise. The crowds simply didn't materialize as Mileti would have liked, and the team found itself on shaky financial footing. In 1975, he sold a sizable portion of the team to Jay Moore, and the two went about running the Crusaders hockey club. Now coached by John Wilson, the Crusaders were able to increase their goal scoring

behind Richie Leduc's 36 goals, with Jim Harrison rebounding for 34 goals. Ron Ward scored 32 and led the team with 82 points. However, the Crusaders started poorly, sporting a 10-18-2 mark in mid-December. Gerry Cheevers was released from his contract about this time and bid the WHA farewell, returning to his old haunts in Boston. With their star gone and the team faltering financially, the Crusaders actually had a stronger second half to finish 35-40-5, but by the end of the season it was clear the team's days in Cleveland were over. The Crusaders made the playoffs, but lost again in the first round, losing in three straight to New England. And so it was, the end of the line for the Crusaders in Cleveland. For part of the summer of 1976 the Crusaders sat in limbo, Mileti intent on placing the team somewhere. Florida looked like a possibility, but since the Minnesota Fighting Saints had folded, Mileti was induced to move his team to St. Paul and become the second incarnation of the Fighting Saints for 1976-77. Alas, Mileti's new Fighting Saints would be history by January 1977. The NHL would try its luck in Richfield, housing the Barons there through 1978.

Denver-Ottawa: In 1974, the NHL announced two new expansion franchises for 1976: Denver and Seattle. The Denver franchise was granted to St. Louis-based businessman Ivan Mullenix, who had run the Denver Spurs of the Western League. However, both franchises were revoked in early 1975 when required payments and bonds were not made in time. Meanwhile, in 1975 the WHA had lost two of its teams and gained one, the Cincinnati Stingers. Intending to forestall an awkward 13-team league for 1975-76, the WHA approached Mullenix about placing a team in Denver, to be housed in the brand-new McNichols Arena. Mullenix went for the offer, and in May 1975, he was granted the rights to the Denver franchise. The team itself was essentially the re-incarnation of the failed Chicago Cougars, featuring Ralph Backstrom, Frankie Rochon and former Roadrunner Don Borgeson, while ex-Canadien Jean-Guy Talbot would coach. Unfortunately, the new Spurs played poorly, not winning at home until their ninth game, with the Denver fans universally disinterested in the team after being teased with an NHL franchise. The Spurs played to tiny crowds, often just a thousand fans, and lost often. The financial drain was so severe that the Spurs had essentially folded in December 1975. Mullenix wanted out, and the league stepped in to broker a deal with an Ottawa group called the Founders Club, who would purchase the team and play out the schedule as the Ottawa Civics. In early January 1976, the Spurs left Denver for good, playing an extended road trip while the deal was being negotiated. During this period the Spurs played two "home" games in Ottawa, to sell-out crowds no less, but despite the enthusiastic support, the Founders Club simply did not have the means nor the money to close the purchase. Mullenix had no choice but to fold the operation. On January 17, 1976, the Spurs-Civics were defunct, having played just half the schedule, finishing 14-26-1. Ralph Backstrom and Don Borgeson led the team with 21 goals, with Gary MacGregor chipping in 16. The highlights were few for this ephemeral squad. A year later the NHL would move the Kansas City Scouts to Denver as the new Rockies, only to see them leave town in 1982.

Edmonton: 1975-76 would be the end of an era in Oiler hockey: the last year of the Bill Hunter regime. The Oilers had been an average club in its first three seasons, wearing out two coaches, Ray Kinasewich in 1973 and Brian Shaw in 1975, each time Bill Hunter replacing them in the season's final weeks. This time, former University of Alberta coach Clare Drake would be given the reins, but he could only make it into February before Hunter once again stepped in, replacing Drake as the team's coach. The Oilers were thin, with a solid first line and no depth, and a porous defense. Rusty Patenaude was always good for a couple dozen goals, and this year was his best, with a team-leading 42. Ex-Whaler Tim Sheehy scored 34, and former Maple Leaf Norm Ullman scored 31, with a team-leading 82 points. Al Hamilton was lost for 28 games and scored just twice. The sieve-like defense allowed 345 goals against, and the Oilers finished a poor 27-49-5, with Hunter's record 9-21-3. Despite their poor record, the Oilers did make the playoffs, but were soundly clobbered in the opening round by eventual champs Winnipeg. At season's end, the team was struggling financially, and Hunter's heavy-handed tactics had worn thin. The team was purchased by Nelson Skalbania and Mitch Klimove, and would teeter financially for another season before getting its act together in 1977 under Peter Pocklington and Glen Sather.

Houston: The Aeros were once again the class of the WHA, winning 53 games for the second year in a row, and easily winning the Western Division crown with 106 points. The offense was strong and balanced, with 341 goals as a team despite no one reaching the 40-goal mark. Mark Howe's 39 goals led the team, with Andre Hinse (35), Gordie Howe (32), Frank Hughes (31) and Don Larway (30) also reaching 30 goals. Behind them were four 20-goal scorers. Gordie Howe led the team in overall scoring with 102 points, while Terry Ruskowski, Ted Taylor and Rich Preston did the grunt work in the corners. Larry Hale, Poul Popiel, Marty Howe and John Schella once again formed the core of the defense, while Ron Grahame and Wayne Rutledge tended the nets. However, in the post-season, Houston found the going a little more challenging than in previous years. A grueling seven-game semifinal series against New England tired the Aeros enough, and an up-and-coming Jets squad— who had been rested for 18 days before the first game of the final round—proved too much for the Aeros. The Aeros were swept in the finals by Winnipeg; the

first two games decided by one goal each, but the remaining two games blow-out wins by the Jets.

Indianapolis: The WHA's worst team in 1974-75 borrowed a page from the Chicago Cougars' playbook from two years ago: sign Pat Stapleton and get Jacques Demers to coach. Stapleton alone vaulted Indianapolis' defense into one of the league's elite, while Demers (who replaced Gerry Moore six games into the season) instituted a tight, defense-first game plan. The dividends were immediate: the low-scoring Racers won their share of games, or at least made the opposition sweat for their two points. The offense was still extremely weak, with Nick Harbaruk and Reg Thomas leading in goal scoring, with just 23 apiece. Two mid-season trades with Quebec brought over two valuable second-line forwards, Michel Parizeau and Renald Leclerc, both who would stay with Indianapolis through 1978, and who fit perfectly with the new Racers' style of play. The Racers were also beneficiaries of the two failed franchises, receiving defensemen Bryon Baltimore and Darryl Maggs, and forward Francois Rochon, from Denver-Ottawa, and notably, Dave Keon from Minnesota. Key additions from within were goaltender Michel Dion and rugged defenseman Kim Clackson, whose 351 penalty minutes were second in the league and who gave the other Racers room to roam. The result was a surprising 35-39-6 finish, including a ten-game unbeaten streak in March. In fact, the Racers' record was good enough for first place in the Eastern Division, and their 247 goals-against was the lowest in the league. In the playoffs, Indianapolis spotted New England a three-games-to-one advantage before winning twice to even the series. The magic finally ran out, as New England prevailed in the seventh game, but the Racers had proven to the rest of the league that the patsies of 1974-75 were now a long-distant memory.

Minnesota: The Fighting Saints were always strong, and 1975-76 started out as the seasons of before, with the Saints winning more than they lost, often piling up the goals in the process. But there were storm clouds building. The financial situation had been tenuous for over a year, the team being supported by a large group of owners fronted by Wayne Belisle. But in 1975, most pulled out, leaving Belisle essentially alone. The money ran out about midway through the season, with the team missing paychecks. The team pressed forward, attempting to last the season, and especially trying to avoid a fold, as the Ottawa Civics had recently experienced in January. But it was not to be; in February, the Fighting Saints closed shop, which was a shame given the strong on-ice performance and the perception that Minneapolis-St. Paul was the one city where the WHA clearly had the better product than the NHL. In the 59 games the Saints did play, Mike Walton had 31 goals and 71 points, on pace for a possible 100-point season; he would leave the WHA altogether once the team folded. Mike Antonovich had 25 goals, and would end the season playing for Minnesota—the North Stars—but would return to the WHA the following year. Minnesota-native Paul Holmgren made his big-league debut and scored 14 goals with 121 penalty minutes, before departing to the Flyers in the NHL. There was considerable toughness: Curt Bracken-bury had accumulated 254 penalty minutes; he would move on to Quebec, while Jack Carlson had 189 before moving to Edmonton. The demise of the Saints helped other teams, with Dave Keon giving Indianapolis a lift, Perry Miller and Gerry Odrowski augmenting the Winnipeg defense, and John McKenzie helping out the new Cincinnati skaters. The following year there would be another Fighting Saints team, as Cleveland relocated to St. Paul. However, the "new Fighting Saints" would last just half the season.

New England: The Whalers suffered through their worst season, finishing 33-40-7, just two points ahead of expansion Cincinnati in the Eastern Division. The offense, once one of the league's deepest and best, was now very ordinary, scoring just 255 goals. Tom Webster was again the leader, with 33 goals and 83 points, despite missing 25 games. Helping him were Larry Pleau (29 goals, 74 points) and newcomer Rosaire Paiement (28 goals, 71 points). Ron Climie added 25 goals, but after that, it was a thin crowd. Mike Rogers came over in a mid-season trade and scored 18 goals in 36 games. The defense seemed to lose its edge, allowing 290 goals. Rick Ley was again the anchor, supported by Brad Selwood and Alan Hangsleben. The Whalers also welcomed veteran Doug Roberts and his 18-year old brother, Gordie, to the backline. The Whalers went through three coaches: Jack Kelley started the season but gave way to former player Don Blackburn, who in turn was replaced by Harry Neale, recently left without a job when Minnesota folded. Despite their poor regular-season showing, the Whalers did squeak into the playoffs, where they caught fire, sweeping Cleveland in the preliminary round, beating Indianapolis in a seven-game duel, and taking the defending champs Houston to another seven games before finally being eliminated. The unlikely hero was goaltender Robert "Cap" Raeder, who had seen action in just three regular-season games, but due to injuries to the team's main goaltenders, played in 14 of the post-season games, turning in an outstanding 2.27 average and two shutouts in carrying the Whalers almost single-handedly to the final round.

Phoenix: Intent on proving 1974-75's successful inaugural season was no fluke, the Roadrunners once again won 39 games behind a strong attack led by the remarkable Robbie Ftorek, a solid defense, and the team-first philosophy of coach Sandy Hucul. Ftorek came through with 41 goals and 113 points, while Del Hall led the team with 47 goals and was second to Ftorek with 91 points. John Gray had 35 goals and the

Roadrunners scored 302 as a team. The Roadrunners also sought help from across the Atlantic, signing defenseman Pekka Rautakallio and forward Lari Mononen, both from Finland. Rautakallio joined a defense that was almost entirely changed from the previous season, with Jim Niekamp the only returnee to play a significant role in 1975-76. Serge Beaudoin, Jim Clarke and Garry Lariviere rounded out the defense. In goal, Gary Kurt and Jack Norris were once again a solid one-two tandem. The Roadrunners liked the physical game, with Cam Connor accumulating 295 penalty minutes, and four other players—including Ftorek—collecting at least 100 minutes in the box. Phoenix finished second in the Western Division and met rivals San Diego in the best-of-three preliminary round. Despite taking a two-games-to-one advantage, San Diego prevailed in five games, another frustrating early exit from the playoffs for the desert birds.

Quebec: The Nordiques gave up 316 goals—yet won 50 games behind an awesome offense in which five players scored 100 or more points, led by Marc Tardif's 71 goals and 148 points. Real Cloutier scored 60 and collected 114 points, and Rejean Houle had 51 goals and 103 points. Christian Bordeleau came through for 109 points, while last season's scoring leader, Serge Bernier, was fifth, with 102 points. As a team, the Nordiques scored 371 goals and successfully played the wide-open, no-defense style of play, generally winning by battering their opponents with goals. The defense was again led by J.-C. Tremblay, who had 77 assists and 89 points. Dale Hoganson and Jean Bernier also skated a regular shift, and Richard Brodeur led the league with 44 wins in nets. Along with the other-worldly offense, the Nordiques also played the fighting game, signing Gordie Gallant (297 penalty minutes), and giving Pierre Roy (258 minutes) a regular shift. Late in the season, the Nordiques also picked up Curt Brackenbury from Minnesota. He would collect 111 minutes in his short stay, and set a league-mark with 365 total for the season. After reaching the final round in 1975, expectations were the same for 1976. In the first round, Quebec squared off against the slower-skating Calgary Cowboys, who likely felt the only way to stop the Nordiques was to fight. To that end, Tardif would be felled by the Cowboy's Rick Jodzio in the second game, setting off a tremendous brawl. Tardif was hospitalized, and with their star injured and their spirit broken, the Nordiques fell to the Cowboys in five games. As appalling as the brawl and outcome were to the Nordiques, they would regain their star Tardif in time for the 1976-77 season, and a more satisfying form of redemption in the spring of 1977.

San Diego: The Mariners won 36 games in 1975-76, a remarkable feat for a team that went bankrupt in February, had no owner thereafter, and went without being paid for weeks as the season closed. The WHA, stinging from two recent folds in Ottawa and Minnesota, could do little to help the San Diego franchise financially except to hope it survived and would find a buyer over the summer. To that end, the Mariners gutted it out behind a strong offense led by Andre Lacroix' 101 points, and a total of eight players who scored at least 20 goals, led by Gene Peacosh and Norm Ferguson, who each scored 37. As a team, the Mariners scored 303 goals, and gave up 290. The defense was manned by returnees Bob Falkenberg and Bob Wall, and new additions Mike McMahon and Brent Hughes. Ernie Wakely was again the workhorse in goal, in nets for 35 of the team's 36 wins. San Diego earned a playoff berth as a wild-card, and beat Phoenix in five games to advance to the quarterfinal round, where they lost to Houston in six games. Perhaps the hearty showing of the team, playing against the odds, won favor with the San Diego community; in the summer of 1976 the Mariners would get a reprieve, being purchased by hamburger-baron Ray Kroc and living to see another season.

Toronto: The Toros had experienced a very promising, successful season during 1974-75, arguably icing a better team than the NHL's Maple Leafs. The Toros won behind a relentless attack and essentially no defense, which had worked in 1974-75, but would fail miserably in 1975-76. Old-time Leaf favorite Bobby Baun was named as the new coach, and he certainly knew a thing or two about playing defense, but the message did not seem to register with the players. The offense was just fine, scoring 335 goals behind Vaclav Nedomansky's 56 and Mark Napier's 43, but the defense, which was led (in a manner of speaking) by Jim Dorey, Jim Turkiewicz and a revolving door of minor-league call-ups, allowed 398 goals against, a WHA record. The Toros found themselves playing some remarkable games, including an 11-8 shootout against Denver, and a 10-9 loss against Cleveland in a game that Toronto led 8-2 with just over a period to play. The Toros used six goaltenders during the season. Gratton was gone, to the Rangers of the NHL, and Binkley retired early, leaving the duties mainly to Jim Shaw and Mario Vien, with Dave Tataryn appearing in a few games. None were satisfactory, but John Garrett came over late in the season from the defunct Fighting Saints and performed well, with a sub-4.00 average; he would be the franchise's top netminder for the following two seasons. The nadir was a seventeen-game winless streak in February and March that cost Baun his job (replaced by Gilles Leger), and a last-place finish in the Canadian Division with a 24-52-5 record. Not surprisingly, the Toronto fans abandoned the Toros and in turn, the Toros abandoned Toronto at season's end, moving to Birmingham, Alabama, in June of 1976. John Bassett had conceded defeat in Toronto, but the iconoclastic owner would embark on a truly unique hockey experiment, attempting to build interest in hockey deep in Dixie country.

Winnipeg: The great European experiment paid dividends in 1975-76, as the new-look Jets assaulted the other teams with a 345-goal attack led by the amazing line of Ulf Nilsson, Anders Hedberg and Bobby Hull, each of whom collected at least 100 points on the season. Hull scored 53 goals and Hedberg 50, while Nilsson had 76 assists. Finn returnee Veli-Pekka Ketola scored 32, as did Peter "Silky" Sullivan. New players from Europe also helped the offense, with Willy Lindstrom scoring 23, and Mats Lindh with 19. Lars-Erik Sjoberg played a sound defense and was a +46. The defense improved considerably with Ted Green bringing his experience and talent to the back line. Mike Ford and Thommie Bergman rounded out the defense, who limited opponents to 254 goals against. In nets, Joe Daley won 41 games against 17 losses, and leading the league with 5 shutouts. Coached by Bobby Kromm, the Jets finished with 52 wins and 106 points, and a first-place finish in the Canadian Division. In the post-season, the Jets overwhelmed the competition, losing just once in thirteen contests, including a satisfying four-game sweep of the defending champs Houston in the final round. The Jets had risen to the elite of the league, claiming their first of three AVCO Cup championship.

Gallery

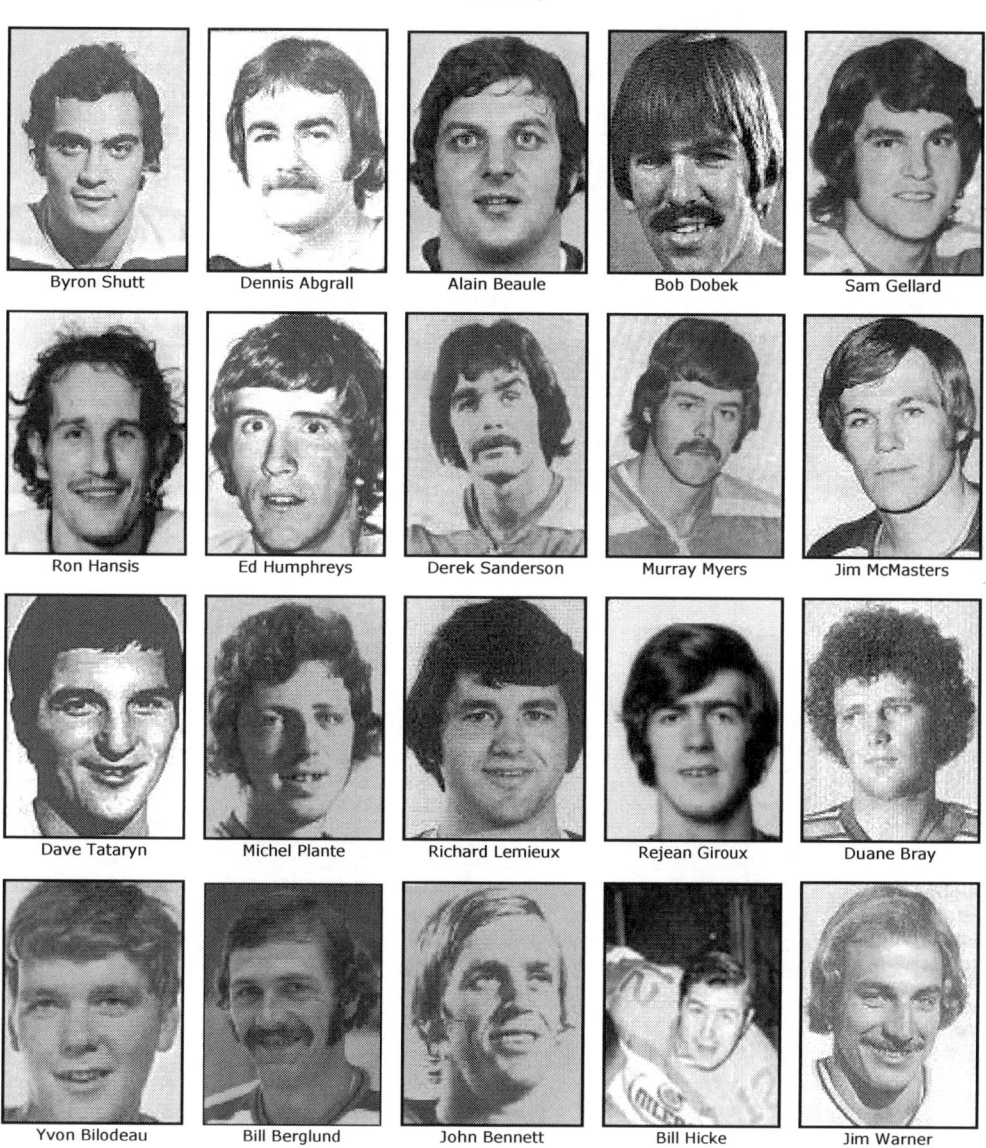

Byron Shutt	Dennis Abgrall	Alain Beaule	Bob Dobek	Sam Gellard
Ron Hansis	Ed Humphreys	Derek Sanderson	Murray Myers	Jim McMasters
Dave Tataryn	Michel Plante	Richard Lemieux	Rejean Giroux	Duane Bray
Yvon Bilodeau	Bill Berglund	John Bennett	Bill Hicke	Jim Warner

1975-1976 Game by Game Line Scores

Date & Teams	Scoring 1 2 3 ot F	Shots 1 2 3 ot F	Goaltenders	Goals & Other Scoring Highlights
October 9				
Winnipeg	3 1 1 - 5	17 12 13 - 42	Daley	Nilsson 2, Green, Hedberg, Ford
Quebec	2 0 1 - 3	9 7 9 - 25	Brodeur	Bordeleau, Parizeau, Tardif
October 10				
San Diego	2 2 1 - 5	9 8 6 - 23	Wakely	Peacosh 2, Rivers, Ferguson, Morenz
Phoenix	1 2 3 - 6	11 13 13 - 37	Kurt	Ftorek 2, Boyd, Rautakallio, Gray, Migneault
Minnesota	2 1 1 - 4	14 5 7 - 26	Garrett	Hampson, McKenzie, Antonovich, Huck
Edmonton	0 1 0 - 1	6 6 12 - 24	Dryden	MacDonald
Indianapolis	1 3 3 - 7	6 12 16 - 34	Brown	Wyrozub 2, Buchanan, Fitchner, Thomas, Karlander, Whitlock
Denver	1 0 0 - 1	17 5 5 - 27	Johnson	Rochon
October 11				
Toronto	1 2 0 - 3	14 10 13 - 37	Shaw, Vien	Nedomansky 2, Simpson
Quebec	2 1 4 - 7	8 12 19 - 39	Brodeur	S. Bernier 3, Cloutier 2, Leclerc, Houle
Houston	1 1 3 - 5	10 6 12 - 28	Grahame	Labossiere, G. Howe, Mk Howe, Taylor, Ruskowski
New England	0 0 0 - 0	9 7 11 - 27	Hoganson	▸ Grahame: shutout (1), 27 saves
Cincinnati	0 1 0 - 1	9 12 7 - 28	Aubry	Larose
Cleveland	0 0 0 - 0	24 4 10 - 38	Cheevers	▸ Aubry: shutout (1), 38 saves
Phoenix	1 0 3 - 4	11 11 7 - 29	Kurt	Hall 2, Boyd, Rautakallio
San Diego	0 1 1 - 2	15 14 13 - 42	Wakely	Morrison, Peacosh
October 12				
Winnipeg	0 2 2 - 4	9 10 12 - 31	Daley	Hull 2, Nilsson, Hornung
Phoenix	0 0 0 - 0	7 7 11 - 25	Kurt	▸ Daley: shutout (1), 25 saves
Indianapolis	2 1 2 - 5	16 11 15 - 42	Brown	Buchanan 2, Fitchner, Coates, Thomas
Edmonton	2 3 1 - 6	8 12 8 - 28	Worthy	Joyal 2, Patenaude 2, MacGregor, Spring
Minnesota	2 0 0 - 2	7 6 13 - 26	Curran	Walton, Huck
Calgary	0 0 0 - 0	9 11 11 - 31	McLeod	▸ Curran: shutout (1), 31 saves
October 14				
Houston	1 0 2 - 3	8 15 16 - 39	Grahame	Hinse, Ruskowski, Hughes
Toronto	1 3 2 - 6	15 11 9 - 35	Vien	Nedomansky 2, Farda, Simpson, D'Alvise, Napier
Edmonton	0 3 2 - 5	9 10 8 - 27	Dryden	P. Morris 2, Ullman, Spring, Kennett
Quebec	3 4 1 - 8	15 16 10 - 41	Brodeur	Tardif 2, Cloutier 2, Houle 2, Parizeau, Bordeleau
Indianapolis	0 2 1 - 3	6 12 9 - 27	Holmquist	Dubois, Whitlock, Fitchner
Calgary	2 2 1 - 5	10 6 7 - 23	McLeod	Haas 2, Chipperfield, Morrison, Harris
October 15				
Cleveland	4 3 1 - 8	12 17 15 - 44	Cheevers	Harrison 2, Walker 2, McDonough, McKay, Holbrook, Ward
Minnesota	4 0 0 - 4	13 12 16 - 41	Curran	Walton, Hampson, Westrum, Keon
Edmonton	2 2 0 0 4	9 16 8 0 33	Worthy	Patenaude, MacDonald, Ullman, Baird
New England	2 0 2 1 5	8 18 14 8 48	Hoganson	Climie 2 (OT 6:52), Webster, Earl, Byers
October 16				
Indianapolis	0 0 0 - 0	8 14 8 - 30	Brown	▸ Wakely: shutout (1), 30 saves
San Diego	0 1 2 - 3	12 10 10 - 32	Wakely	Tidey 2, Peacosh
Winnipeg	6 0 1 - 7	11 7 8 - 26	Larsson	Ketola 2, Lindstrom, Lesuk, Bergman, Hedberg, Nilsson
Denver	2 0 1 - 3	9 7 10 - 26	Newton, Johnson	Rochon, Bignell, Sherrit
October 17				
Denver	1 2 2 - 5	6 13 6 - 25	Johnson	Borgeson 3, MacGregor, Bredin
Phoenix	1 0 3 - 4	8 7 14 - 29	Norris	Hall, Mononen, Huston, Ftorek
Cincinnati	3 1 2 - 6	14 9 6 - 29	Aubry	G. Sobchuk 2, Larose, Locas, Plumb, Dudley
Calgary	0 1 1 - 2	7 7 8 - 22	McLeod	Morrison, Lawson
Edmonton	1 1 2 0 4	13 14 11 5 43	Dryden	MacDonald, Spring, Barrie, Ketter (TG 17:46)
Toronto	0 3 1 0 4	9 15 15 11 50	Vien	Henderson 2, Jacques, Farda
October 18				
Toronto	0 0 1 - 1	10 6 10 - 26	Binkley	Nedomansky
New England	1 1 1 - 3	12 11 8 - 31	Landon	Webster, O'Donnell, Earl
Edmonton	0 1 2 - 3	6 13 8 - 27	Worthy	Joyal, Patenaude, M. Rogers
Minnesota	1 0 0 - 1	6 10 9 - 25	Garrett	Walton
Winnipeg	0 1 0 - 1	11 14 5 - 30	Daley	Hedberg
San Diego	1 1 0 - 2	10 7 9 - 26	Wakely	Ferguson, Peacosh
Denver	3 2 1 - 6	13 9 15 - 37	Johnson	Bredin, Rochon 2, MacGregor, Backstrom
Indianapolis	1 1 2 - 4	11 12 12 - 35	Brown	Sheridan, Thomas, Proceviat, Fitchner
Houston	0 0 2 - 2	8 15 12 - 35	Grahame	Larway, Hughes
Quebec	2 0 1 - 3	16 9 10 - 35	Brodeur	Cloutier 2, Gallant
October 19				
Houston	2 1 3 - 6	8 18 15 - 41	Grahame	Preston, Larway, Labossiere, Hall, Taylor, Hinse (WG 10:01)
Cleveland	1 3 1 - 5	14 16 10 - 40	Cheevers	JA Stewart 2, McDonough, Pinder, Walker
Winnipeg	2 2 1 - 5	9 6 6 - 21	Daley	Hedberg, Miller, Lindstrom, Beaudin, Ketola
Phoenix	5 0 1 - 6	13 7 10 - 30	Kurt	Mononen 3, Huston, Cormier, Ftorek
Cincinnati	0 1 1 - 2	14 9 14 - 37	Aubry	Veneruzzo, MacNeil
Edmonton	0 2 2 - 4	9 8 10 - 27	Dryden	Baird 2, MacDonald, Long
October 21				
Cincinnati	0 0 0 - 0	7 7 8 - 22	Aubry, Lapointe	▸ Daley: shutout (2), 22 saves
Winnipeg	4 2 1 - 7	20 17 10 - 47	Daley	Hedberg 2, Nilsson, Ketola, Beaudin, Lindh, Sullivan
Minnesota	1 0 1 - 2	10 6 6 - 22	Garrett	Keon, Carlson (WG 4:58)
Indianapolis	1 0 0 - 1	9 12 8 - 29	Holmquist	Stapleton
New England	0 0 1 - 1	9 16 10 - 35	Hoganson	Carleton
Quebec	2 1 3 - 6	11 6 14 - 31	Brodeur	Hoganson, Houle, Leclerc, Parizeau, Serviss, Tardif
October 22				
Denver	0 2 0 - 2	8 16 6 - 30	Johnson	Maggs, Morris
Calgary	0 1 0 - 1	8 3 12 - 23	McLeod	Hull

1975-1976 Game by Game Line Scores

Date & Teams	Scoring 1 2 3 ot F	Shots 1 2 3 ot F	Goaltenders	Goals & Other Scoring Highlights
October 23				
Houston	0 0 0 - 0	13 14 8 - 35	Grahame	▸ Brown: shutout (1), 35 saves
Indianapolis	0 1 3 - 4	10 14 15 - 39	Brown	Thomas 2, Whitlock, Harbaruk
Minnesota	0 3 1 0 4	6 16 12 8 42	Garrett	Connelly 2, Keon 2 (TG 17:25)
San Diego	2 1 1 0 4	13 7 6 2 28	Wakely	Peacosh 2, Noris 2
Edmonton	1 3 0 - 4	13 7 5 - 25	Worthy	Krake 2, Spring, Patenaude
Cincinnati	0 4 2 - 6	9 15 20 - 44	Aubry	Dudley 2, Andrascik, Larose, G. Sobchuk, Campbell
October 24				
Denver	2 0 0 - 2	11 7 10 - 28	Johnson	Borgeson 2
Winnipeg	1 3 1 - 5	10 14 9 - 33	Daley	Green, Sullivan, Nilsson, Lindstrom, Riihiranta
New England	3 0 2 - 5	12 13 10 - 35	Abrahamsson	Fotiu, Swain, Hangsleben, Carleton, Arndt
Toronto	1 1 2 - 4	7 11 12 - 30	Vien	Featherstone, Mahovlich, Simpson, Jacques
Phoenix	2 0 2 - 4	5 10 10 - 25	Norris	Gray, Cormier, McNamee, Dean
Calgary	2 0 1 - 3	11 6 13 - 30	McLeod	Haas, Deadmarsh, Evans
October 25				
Toronto	0 0 2 - 2	8 6 15 - 29	Vien	Kirk 2
Quebec	3 0 0 - 3	15 15 15 - 45	Brodeur	Bordeleau, Tardif, Roy
Edmonton	1 1 0 - 2	9 10 6 - 25	Dryden	Baird, M. Rogers
Cleveland	1 2 2 - 5	12 24 15 - 51	Whidden	McDonough 2, Walker, Gruen, Harrison
Minnesota	1 0 0 - 1	8 7 10 - 25	Curran	McKenzie
San Diego	2 1 3 - 6	4 13 20 - 37	Wakely	Ferguson 2, Noris, Lacroix, Peacosh, Goldthorpe
Houston	1 1 2 - 4	8 11 9 - 28	Grahame	Larway, Hall, Tonelli, Taylor
Cincinnati	0 3 4 - 7	15 9 14 - 38	Aubry	MacNeil 2, Guite 2, Veneruzzo, Larose, Campbell
October 26				
Phoenix	0 0 0 - 0	18 14 7 - 39	Kurt	▸ Daley: shutout (3), 39 saves
Winnipeg	2 3 0 - 5	13 9 9 - 31	Daley	Hull, Nilsson, Ford, Ketola. Hedberg
Edmonton	0 1 2 - 3	8 10 10 - 28	Worthy	B. McAneeley 2, Kennett
Indianapolis	0 3 1 - 4	11 9 8 - 28	Holmquist	Prentice, Fitchner, Harbaruk, Sicinski
Calgary	1 0 0 - 1	7 12 9 - 28	McLeod	Israelson
New England	1 1 1 - 3	12 8 10 - 30	Landon	Abrahamsson, Webster, Paiement
October 28				
Phoenix	2 0 1 - 3	9 11 10 - 30	Norris	Boyd, Ftorek, Hall
Edmonton	3 2 2 - 7	10 5 13 - 28	Dryden	Sheehy 2, Baird, Long, Joyal, Ullman, B. McAneeley
Quebec	2 1 1 - 4	11 13 19 - 43	Brodeur	Cloutier, S. Bernier, J. Bernier, Tardif
Toronto	2 2 2 - 6	12 9 7 - 28	Vien	Kirk 2, Nedomansky 2, Rollins, D'Alvise
October 29				
Cincinnati	2 3 1 - 6	9 10 6 - 25	Aubry	Larose 2, Campbell, MacNeil, Locas, Guite
Minnesota	0 2 2 - 4	4 12 7 - 23	Garrett	Boucha 2, Antonovich, Connelly
Quebec	0 1 1 - 2	11 7 6 - 24	Deguise	Cloutier, Parizeau
New England	1 1 2 - 4	15 9 16 - 40	Abrahamsson	Climie 2, Webster, Carleton
Calgary	0 1 2 - 3	9 9 10 - 28	McLeod	Israelson, Harris, Morrison
Cleveland	1 0 0 - 1	11 13 9 - 33	Whidden	Walker
October 30				
Phoenix	2 0 1 - 3	8 8 8 - 24	Kurt	Cormier, Connor, Ftorek
Denver	0 1 1 - 2	11 14 9 - 34	Johnson	Mara, Morris
Cincinnati	0 0 0 - 0	11 8 8 - 27	Lapointe	▸ Daley: shutout (4), 27 saves
Winnipeg	0 2 2 - 4	13 16 14 - 43	Daley	Hull, Sullivan, Hedberg, Beaudin
Calgary	4 2 1 - 7	13 8 15 - 36	McLeod	Lawson 3, Harris, Israelson, Tannahill, Morrison
Indianapolis	2 2 1 - 5	12 19 14 - 45	Brown	Wyrozub 3 (18:48 & 19:02 2nd, 0:28 3rd), Scharf, Coates
Houston	0 3 1 - 4	10 11 9 - 30	Grahame	Tonelli, Taylor, Ruskowski, Schella
San Diego	1 0 1 - 2	9 10 18 - 37	Wakely	Noris, Ferguson
October 31				
Quebec	0 1 1 - 2	12 7 3 - 22	Brodeur, Deguise	Sutherland, Houle
Cleveland	1 3 2 - 6	17 14 12 - 43	Cheevers	Leduc 3, McDonough 2, Gruen
New England	1 0 1 0 2	10 4 10 4 28	Hoganson, Landon	Arndt, Climie
Edmonton	0 1 1 0 2	9 8 11 2 30	Dryden	Long, MacGregor
November 1				
Quebec	1 1 3 - 5	10 9 9 - 28	Brodeur	Tardif 2, Houle, Jordan, Leclerc
Indianapolis	0 2 0 - 2	13 10 9 - 32	Holmquist	Scharf, Coates
Calgary	0 1 1 - 2	8 9 8 - 25	McLeod	Lawson, Chipperfield
Cincinnati	0 0 3 - 3	6 9 10 - 25	Aubry	MacNeil, D. Sobchuk, G. Sobchuk (WG 17:55)
Houston	1 1 1 - 3	11 5 9 - 25	Grahame	Larway, P. Popiel, Hall
Denver	0 1 1 - 2	10 19 10 - 39	Newton	Bignell, Backstrom
Phoenix	0 1 1 - 2	7 10 11 - 28	Norris	Ftorek, Mononen
Minnesota	1 2 0 - 3	9 10 8 - 27	Garrett	Walton, Keon, Huck
November 2				
Quebec	0 0 1 - 1	6 10 8 - 24	Brodeur	Sutherland (WG 16:35)
Winnipeg	0 0 0 - 0	12 11 9 - 32	Daley	▸ Brodeur: shutout (1), 32 saves
San Diego	2 1 0 - 3	13 16 6 - 35	Wakely, Gillow	Ferguson, Rivers, Burgess
Edmonton	1 2 2 - 5	7 9 9 - 25	Dryden	Patenaude 2, Ullman, Barrie, Sheehy
Phoenix	0 0 2 - 2	12 7 13 - 32	Kurt, Norris	Niekamp, Cormier
Cleveland	2 2 1 - 5	16 15 8 - 39	Cheevers	Moffat, Gruen, Ward, Pinder
New England	0 2 1 0 3	7 9 7 3 26	Landon	Fotiu, Byers, Carleton
Calgary	1 0 2 1 4	14 6 13 3 36	McLeod	Deadmarsh 2, Driscoll, Keogan (OT 4:11)

1975-1976 Game by Game Line Scores

Date & Teams	Scoring 1 2 3 ot F	Shots 1 2 3 ot F	Goaltenders	Goals & Other Scoring Highlights
November 4				
Cleveland	2 0 0 0 2	14 10 10 5 39	Whidden	Ward, JC Stewart
Denver	1 0 1 0 2	10 9 10 8 37	Johnson	Sherrit, Lomenda
Quebec	2 0 2 - 4	9 10 7 - 26	Brodeur	Tardif 2, Cloutier, Serviss (WG 18:57)
Edmonton	2 0 1 - 3	12 8 14 - 34	Worthy	Patenaude 2, Ullman
Toronto	3 0 0 - 3	10 13 7 - 30	Vien	Mahovlich, Featherstone, Amodeo
Indianapolis	2 1 1 - 4	13 16 10 - 39	Brown	Thomas, Buchanan, Prentice, Coates (WG 14:52)
San Diego	0 4 0 0 4	7 8 4 5 24	Gillow	French, Ferguson, Tidey, Burgess
Calgary	0 3 1 0 4	8 10 12 3 33	McLeod	Sentes 2, Israelson, Harris
New England	0 0 2 0 2	9 14 4 1 28	Abrahamsson	O'Donnell, Abrahamsson
Winnipeg	0 2 0 1 3	5 16 13 4 38	Larsson	Hull, Hedberg, Ford (OT 4:06)
November 5				
Minnesota	1 2 1 - 4	12 9 11 - 32	Garrett	McKenzie 2, Antonovich, Holmgren
Houston	5 1 0 - 6	11 13 8 - 32	Grahame	Mk Howe 3, Hughes, Preston, G. Howe
Quebec	0 1 1 - 2	5 9 17 - 31	Brodeur	Leclerc, Bordeleau
Calgary	0 1 3 - 4	9 10 8 - 27	McLeod	Sentes 2, Tannahill, Caffery
November 6				
Quebec	0 2 3 - 5	6 7 7 - 20	Deguise	Houle 2, Tremblay, Cloutier, Leclerc
Denver	2 0 1 - 3	12 12 13 - 37	Johnson	Backstrom 2, MacGregor
Cincinnati	1 2 0 - 3	17 11 11 - 39	Aubry	MacNeil, Andrascik, O'Donoghue
New England	3 1 4 - 8	9 9 15 - 33	Abrahamsson	Abrahamsson 3, Carleton 2, Webster, Paiement, Arndt
November 7				
San Diego	1 0 1 1 3	7 7 13 5 32	Wakely	Peacosh 2 (OT 8:42), Lacroix
Denver	0 0 2 0 2	10 9 16 3 38	Newton	MacGregor 2
Toronto	0 1 3 0 4	10 11 10 1 32	Shaw	Kirk 2, Napier, Farda
Edmonton	0 2 2 1 5	14 6 15 2 37	Dryden	Joyal, Sheehy, Spring, Krake, B. McAneeley (OT 3:36)
Cleveland	0 2 0 - 2	8 11 4 - 23	Cheevers	Maxwell, Walker
Calgary	1 1 3 - 5	8 7 14 - 29	McLeod	Lawson 2, Sentes, Keogan, Tannahill
Phoenix	2 1 0 - 3	8 12 15 - 35	Kurt	Gray, Hall, McLeod
Houston	2 2 1 - 5	16 10 16 - 42	Grahame	Hughes 2, Taylor, Mk Howe, Preston
November 8				
Toronto	1 0 2 - 3	9 7 12 - 28	Vien	Farda, Cunningham, Foley
Minnesota	1 3 0 - 4	13 17 8 - 38	Garrett	Walton 2, Antonovich, Holmgren
San Diego	1 3 0 - 4	9 11 8 - 28	Wakely, Gillow	Noris, Peacosh, Devine, Lacroix
Cincinnati	0 6 1 - 7	12 17 8 - 37	Lapointe	Locas 2, Dudley 2, Guite, Inkpen, Pelyk
Phoenix	0 1 2 - 3	12 3 6 - 21	Norris	Gray, Huston, Niekamp
New England	0 0 2 - 2	9 12 13 - 34	Landon	Climie, Webster (both goals in last 1:29)
Indianapolis	0 1 1 0 2	10 8 9 0 27	Dion	Coates, Fitchner
Quebec	0 1 1 1 3	9 15 12 1 37	Brodeur	Hoganson, Leclerc, Cloutier (OT 1:07)
November 9				
Cleveland	1 0 0 - 1	14 12 10 - 36	Cheevers	Pinder
Edmonton	0 3 1 - 4	6 15 5 - 26	Dryden	Patenaude 2, M. Rogers 2
Phoenix	0 2 1 - 3	9 8 9 - 26	Kurt	Rautakallio, Connor, Gorman
Quebec	2 4 1 - 7	10 11 12 - 33	Brodeur	Houle 2, Sutherland 2, Tardif, Cloutier, S. Bernier
New England	0 1 1 - 2	9 10 10 - 29	Abrahamsson	Climie, Blackburn
Cincinnati	2 0 2 - 4	13 10 11 - 34	Lapointe	Plumb, Dudley, Locas, Guite
Toronto	0 0 3 - 3	5 6 16 - 27	Shaw	Nedomansky 3 (all in last 8 minutes of game)
Winnipeg	2 2 1 - 5	14 20 6 - 40	Daley	Beaudin 2, Hedberg 2, Nilsson
Denver	2 0 0 - 2	7 11 7 - 25	Newton	Lavender, Borgeson
Houston	1 0 2 - 3	14 11 13 - 38	Grahame	G. Howe, Tonelli, Hall (WG 9:35)
November 11				
Cleveland	1 0 2 - 3	9 9 17 - 35	Cheevers	McDonough, Gruen, Shmyr (WG 19:52)
Winnipeg	1 1 0 - 2	11 9 8 - 28	Daley	Hedberg, Beaudin
Minnesota	2 2 2 - 6	11 10 15 - 36	Garrett	Boucha 2, Walton 2, Carlson, Connelly
Quebec	3 3 2 - 8	15 17 9 - 41	Brodeur	Houle 2, S. Bernier 2, Tardif, Bordeleau, Sutherland
Edmonton	1 2 0 - 3	9 9 6 - 24	Worthy	MacDonald, Long, Sheehy
Calgary	2 2 2 - 6	13 11 12 - 36	McLeod	Harris, Hull, Lawson, Caffery, Morrison, Tannahill
Toronto	1 1 2 - 4	15 11 10 - 36	Vien	Dorey 2, Marrin, Mahovlich
Houston	3 2 0 - 5	22 14 10 - 46	Rutledge	Hall 2, Hughes, Mty Howe, Taylor
November 12				
Houston	0 1 0 - 1	13 9 10 - 32	Grahame	G. Howe
New England	0 1 3 - 4	7 7 9 - 23	Abrahamsson	Abrahamsson, Webster, Earl, Byers
November 13				
Toronto	3 3 5 - 11	9 6 12 - 27	Shaw	Nedomansky 5, Kirk 2, Mahovlich 2, D'Alvise, Amodeo
Denver	2 3 3 - 8	14 13 11 - 38	Johnson, Sanza	Arbour, MacGregor, Legge, Leblanc, Borgeson, Mara, Sherrit, Bredin
Cleveland	0 1 0 - 1	10 12 8 - 30	Whidden	McDonough
San Diego	1 0 2 - 3	9 6 13 - 28	Wakely	Devine, Lacroix, Ferguson
Winnipeg	2 0 2 - 4	11 5 8 - 24	Daley	Ford, Nilsson, Lesuk, Ketola
Calgary	0 2 0 - 2	11 12 13 - 36	McLeod	Tannahill, Driscoll
November 14				
Edmonton	0 1 0 - 1	6 2 5 - 13	Dryden	Long
Winnipeg	3 1 2 - 6	16 11 14 - 41	Daley	Hull 2, Sullivan 2, Ford, Hornung
Toronto	2 0 0 0 2	10 6 7 1 24	Vien	Jacques, Mahovlich
Phoenix	1 1 0 0 2	8 15 15 4 42	Norris	Lariviere, Mononen

234

1975-1976 Game by Game Line Scores

Date & Teams	Scoring 1	2	3	ot	F	Shots 1	2	3	ot	F	Goaltenders	Goals & Other Scoring Highlights
November 15												
Cleveland	1	2	1	0	4	7	17	11	1	36	Whidden	Ward, Pinder, Moffat, Leduc (TG 17:20)
Denver	1	2	1	1	5	16	12	14	1	43	Newton	MacGregor 2, Bignell, Borgeson, Backstrom (OT 2:23)
Houston	2	3	0	-	5	11	14	9	-	34	Grahame	Taylor, Hall, Labossiere, J. Popiel, Larway
Cincinnati	4	2	2	-	8	9	8	8	-	25	Lapointe	Larose 2, Dudley 2, Campbell, Veneruzzo, Guite, D. Sobchuk
Quebec	1	1	1	-	3	11	10	3	-	24	Brodeur	S. Bernier, Houle, Tardif
New England	0	1	0	-	1	11	10	14	-	35	Abrahamsson	Carleton
Indianapolis	1	2	4	-	7	11	16	13	-	40	Brown	Wyrozub 2, Stapleton 2, Scharf, Thomas, Harbaruk
Minnesota	1	6	2	-	9	9	17	16	-	42	Curran	Holmgren 3, Walton 2, McKenzie 2, Keon, Smith
Toronto	1	3	2	-	6	7	14	5	-	26	Vien	Kirk 2, Mahovlich, Farda, Dorey, Marrin (WG 15:22)
San Diego	2	1	1	-	4	13	11	18	-	42	Wakely	Lacroix, Ferguson, Rivers, Noris
November 16												
Houston	2	0	1	-	3	6	8	7	-	21	Rutledge	Lund 2, Tonelli
Calgary	1	3	1	-	5	10	10	6	-	26	McLeod	Caffery, Hull, Lacombe, Lawson, Morrison
Cleveland	3	1	0	0	4	15	10	8	3	36	Cheevers	Walker 2, JC Stewart, Shmyr
Phoenix	1	2	1	0	4	16	12	13	5	46	Norris	Connor, Niekamp, Gray, Boyd (TG 13:51)
Indianapolis	0	0	1	-	1	7	7	9	-	23	Holmquist	Harbaruk
Winnipeg	0	1	1	-	2	8	12	10	-	30	Larsson	Sullivan, Hedberg
Minnesota	1	2	0	-	3	9	19	16	-	44	Garrett	Boucha, Keon
Cincinnati	1	1	0	-	2	11	17	8	-	36	Aubry, Lapointe	D. Sobchuk 2
November 17												
San Diego	1	1	1	-	3	7	11	11	-	29	Gillow, Wakely	Peacosh, Lacroix, Walter
Edmonton	1	2	3	-	6	7	11	10	-	28	Dryden	M. Rogers 2, Ullman, Sheehy, MacDonald, Baird
Indianapolis	1	2	3	-	6	9	11	17	-	37	Brown	Harbaruk 2, Woytowich, Prentice, Scharf, Thomas
Toronto	1	0	1	-	2	14	9	9	-	32	Vien	Turkiewicz, Marrin
November 18												
Edmonton	0	1	2	-	3	4	8	12	-	24	Worthy	Baird, Kennett, Patenaude
Denver	2	2	2	-	6	18	4	5	-	27	Newton	Borgeson 2, Liddington 2, Sherrit, Backstrom
Cincinnati	0	1	3	-	4	7	10	11	-	28	Lapointe	Plumb, Inkpen, Smedsmo, G. Sobchuk
Quebec	1	3	2	-	6	15	12	15	-	42	Brodeur	Cloutier 2, Tardif 2, Leclerc, S. Bernier
San Diego	1	3	2	-	6	9	11	11	-	31	Wakely	French 2, Devine, Ferguson, Adduono, Tidey
Calgary	0	2	0	-	2	10	20	10	-	40	McLeod, Wood	Haas, Deadmarsh
Houston	1	0	2	-	3	18	4	13	-	35	Grahame	Lund 2, Hall
Winnipeg	0	0	2	-	2	11	9	10	-	30	Daley	Sullivan, Hull
November 19												
Minnesota	1	1	1	0	3	10	12	7	3	32	Garrett	Boudreau 2, Boucha
Cleveland	3	0	0	1	4	14	20	11	8	53	Cheevers	McDonough, Ball, Edur, JA Stewart (OT 5:36)
New England	0	1	0	-	1	11	12	6	-	29	Landon	Carleton
Indianapolis	1	2	0	-	3	4	16	6	-	26	Holmquist	Thomas, Coates, Harbaruk
November 20												
Minnesota	1	0	1	-	2	12	5	5	-	22	Garrett	Keon, Connelly
New England	0	0	0	-	0	11	6	7	-	24	Abrahamsson	▶ Garrett: shutout (2), 24 saves
Edmonton	0	0	1	-	1	5	6	6	-	17	Dryden	Patenaude
Phoenix	0	2	1	-	3	9	17	10	-	36	Norris	Huston 2, Gray
Denver	0	1	0	-	1	4	11	6	-	21	Johnson	Morris
San Diego	3	0	2	-	5	11	8	13	-	32	Wakely	Noris 2, Hughes, Tidey, Adduono
Winnipeg	1	1	0	1	3	10	11	14	1	36	Daley	Ketola, Lindh, Nilsson (OT 1:13)
Quebec	0	1	1	0	2	17	8	9	1	35	Brodeur	Cloutier, S. Bernier
November 21												
Edmonton	0	1	1	-	2	8	11	9	-	28	Dryden	MacGregor, Ullman
Houston	3	0	1	-	4	12	7	10	-	29	Grahame	Schella, Lund, Tonelli, Larway
Calgary	2	2	2	-	6	10	8	12	-	30	Wood	Chipperfield 2, Hull, Morrison, Driscoll, Lacombe
Denver	0	2	0	-	2	9	10	6	-	25	Newton	MacGregor, Morris (Denver: "Guaranteed Win" night)
Cincinnati	0	2	5	-	7	9	9	20	-	38	Coutu	G. Sobchuk 2, Smedsmo 2, Larose, Pelyk, Andrascik
Toronto	2	5	1	-	8	14	15	7	-	36	Vien	Turk'cz 2, Marrin, Kirk, M'vlich, Nedom'sky, Rollins, Napier (WG 19:44)
November 22												
Winnipeg	0	2	1	-	3	8	10	12	-	30	Larsson	Ketola 2, Miller
Cleveland	4	2	0	-	6	12	13	9	-	34	Cheevers	Pinder, McDonough, Harrison, Leduc, Tamminen, JA Stewart
Quebec	2	5	2	-	9	13	17	5	-	35	Brodeur	Tardif 3, Cloutier 2, Bordeleau, Sutherland, Houle, S. Bernier
Cincinnati	3	2	1	-	6	14	13	8	-	35	Lapointe	Larose 2, Smedsmo, Hughes, Plumb, Abbey
Phoenix	1	1	3	-	5	9	10	15	-	34	Kurt	Cormier, Gray, Ftorek, Rautakallio
New England	4	2	1	-	7	9	12	5	-	26	Landon	O'Donnell 2, D. Roberts, Carleton, Abrahamsson, Byers, Climie
Calgary	2	2	2	-	6	10	14	11	-	35	Wood	Driscoll, Chipperfield, Deadmarsh, Keogan, Tannahill, Caffery
Minnesota	1	2	1	-	4	9	9	8	-	26	Garret, Curran	Walton 2, Boucha, Holmgren
Edmonton	2	0	0	1	3	11	6	6	1	24	Dryden	MacGregor, MacDonald, Patenaude (OT 2:39)
San Diego	0	0	2	0	2	6	15	24	1	46	Wakely, Gillow	Bateman, Morrison
November 23												
Winnipeg	1	1	1	-	3	11	9	12	-	32	Daley	Hull, Sullivan, Nilsson (WG 5:52)
New England	0	2	0	-	2	6	8	11	-	25	Abrahamsson	Climie, Selwood
Cincinnati	3	0	0	-	3	12	7	5	-	24	Lapointe	MacNeil, D. Sobchuk, Larose
Denver	1	2	2	-	5	12	8	14	-	34	Johnson	Borgeson 2, MacGregor, Bignell, Lavender
Quebec	0	0	0	-	0	9	13	9	-	31	Brodeur	▶ Grahame: shutout (2), 31 saves
Houston	2	2	0	-	4	15	11	10	-	36	Grahame	Tonelli 2, Mty Howe, Irwin

1975-1976 Game by Game Line Scores

Date & Teams	Scoring 1 2 3 ot F	Shots 1 2 3 ot F	Goaltenders	Goals & Other Scoring Highlights
November 25				
New England	1 0 1 0 2	8 10 11 5 34	Abrahamsson	Swain, Climie (TG 19:50)
Minnesota	0 0 2 1 3	10 7 7 3 27	Garrett	McKenzie, Connelly, Antonovich (OT 6:22)
Indianapolis	0 1 0 - 1	13 5 10 - 28	Brown	Thomas
Houston	2 1 1 - 4	13 11 8 - 32	Grahame	Larway, Ruskowski, G. Howe, Hughes
Edmonton	1 0 1 - 2	12 10 11 - 33	Dryden	M. Rogers, MacGregor
San Diego	2 2 3 - 7	12 17 12 - 41	Wakely	Peacosh 2, Devine 2, Morrison, Lacroix, Tidey
Cleveland	2 0 1 1 4	17 10 9 3 39	Cheevers	McDonough 2, Gruen, Pinder (OT 2:36)
Toronto	2 0 1 0 3	10 11 12 2 35	Shaw	Jacques, Nedomansky, Mahovlich
November 26				
Winnipeg	4 3 4 - 11	10 10 16 - 36	Daley	Hedberg 3, Lesuk 2, Miller 2, Hull, Nilsson, Sullivan, Ford
Cincinnati	2 1 0 - 3	16 8 9 - 33	Lapointe, Aubry	Larose, G. Sobchuk, Locas
Denver	0 2 1 - 3	7 14 8 - 29	Newton	Delorme, Sherrit, Rochon
Cleveland	0 0 0 - 0	11 5 7 - 23	Cheevers	▶ Newton: shutout (1), 23 saves
November 27				
Quebec	1 0 0 - 1	11 11 4 - 26	Brodeur	Parizeau
San Diego	0 3 2 - 5	12 19 14 - 45	Wakely	Burgess, Bredin, Peacosh, French, Ferguson
Winnipeg	1 0 0 - 1	7 8 7 - 22	Larsson, Daley	Hull
Indianapolis	1 2 0 - 3	8 8 8 - 24	Holmquist	Heatley, Wyrozub, Clackson
Cincinnati	1 1 1 - 3	9 16 15 - 40	Coutu	G. Sobchuk, D. Sobchuk, Larose
Minnesota	2 2 1 - 5	9 8 8 - 25	Garrett	Connelly 5
Calgary	1 2 2 - 5	15 11 9 - 35	McLeod	Delorenzi 2, Lawson, Tannahill, Morrison
Phoenix	1 0 0 - 1	7 14 6 - 27	Norris	Boyd
November 28				
Edmonton	1 1 2 - 4	8 10 9 - 27	Dryden	Baird, Patenaude, Ullman, Sheehy
Houston	3 2 2 - 7	10 14 8 - 32	Grahame	Hughes 3, Lund 2, Larway, Hinse
Winnipeg	1 2 2 - 5	13 15 10 - 38	Daley	Hedberg 2, Lesuk, Beaudin, Lindh
Toronto	1 2 0 - 3	11 13 11 - 35	Shaw	Nedomansky 2, Farda
Denver	0 1 2 - 3	6 10 14 - 30	Johnson	Liddington 2, Backstrom
New England	2 4 1 - 7	14 10 10 - 34	Abrahamsson	Climie 3, Paiement, Webster, Pleau, Carleton
Indianapolis	0 2 1 - 3	14 8 5 - 27	Brown	Sicinski 2, Proceviat
Cleveland	1 0 0 - 1	11 16 14 - 41	Cheevers	Walker
November 29				
Indianapolis	0 2 1 - 3	14 15 5 - 34	Brown	Harbaruk 2 (WG 15:21), Coates
New England	2 0 0 - 2	10 6 11 - 27	Abrahamsson	Pleau, Webster
Toronto	1 4 4 - 9	8 13 14 - 35	Vien, Shaw	Mahovlich 2, Kirk, Nedomansky, Turkiewicz, Marrin, Farda, Featherstone, Henderson
Cincinnati	3 0 2 - 5	19 15 16 - 50	Lapointe, Coutu	Donnelly 2, MacNeil, Guite, Pelyk
Quebec	0 3 1 0 4	8 12 7 5 32	Deguise	Houle, Tremblay, Bordeleau, Tardif
Phoenix	2 2 0 0 4	13 13 12 11 49	Kurt	Migneault 2, Cormier, McLeod
Calgary	1 1 2 1 5	9 10 12 1 32	Wood	Tannahill, Driscoll, Hull, Israelson, Lawson (OT 2:21)
San Diego	1 2 1 0 4	16 11 16 1 44	Gillow	Rivers, Devine, Ferguson, Hughes (TG 18:49)
November 30				
Toronto	4 4 1 - 9	13 10 7 - 30	Shaw, Vien	Marrin 2, F'therstone, C'ngham, Simpson, Dorey, Henderson, M'vlich, Nedomansky
Cleveland	2 2 6 - 10	24 23 16 - 63	Cheevers, Whidden	Ward 5, JA Stewart 2 (WG 19:48), Edur, Ball, Pinder
Calgary	2 0 0 - 2	11 12 10 - 33	McLeod	Deadmarsh, Hull
Edmonton	1 2 1 - 4	4 15 9 - 28	Dryden	Krake 2, Baird, Sheehy
Quebec	0 1 1 - 2	4 9 11 - 24	Brodeur	Tardif 2 (WG 8:19)
Phoenix	0 1 0 - 1	8 10 10 - 28	Kurt	Connor
San Diego	2 1 1 - 4	9 11 15 - 35	Wakely, Gillow	Adduono, Hughes, Noris, Morrison
Houston	5 3 0 - 8	18 10 9 - 37	Rutledge	P. Popiel 2, Hinse 2, Preston, Tonelli, Taylor, Ruskowski
Denver	3 0 1 - 4	12 11 10 - 33	Newton	Backstrom, MacGregor, Arbour
Indianapolis	2 0 0 - 2	10 9 18 - 37	Holmquist	Harbaruk, Karlander
Minnesota	0 2 1 - 3	11 9 6 - 26	Garrett	Boucha, McKenzie, Huck
Winnipeg	3 2 0 - 5	17 14 7 - 38	Larsson	Hull, Nilsson, Lindstrom, Beaudin, Hedberg
December 2				
Winnipeg	3 0 0 1 4	9 12 8 2 31	Larsson	Lindh, Hedberg, Sullivan, Hull (OT 4:00)
Denver	2 0 1 0 3	4 10 8 1 23	Johnson	Sherrit 2 (TG 18:53), Lomenda
New England	1 0 4 - 5	9 8 8 - 25	Abrahamsson	D. Roberts, Selwood, Earl, Pleau, Ley
Houston	1 0 1 - 2	11 9 9 - 29	Grahame	Hughes, Mty Howe
Toronto	2 0 0 - 2	8 9 14 - 31	Vien, Tataryn	Napier, Nedomansky
Edmonton	2 3 2 - 7	13 13 14 - 40	Dryden	Sheehy 2, Patenaude 2, Long, P. Morris, Barrie
Cleveland	0 2 0 - 2	14 8 12 - 34	Whidden	Leduc, Ward
Quebec	3 1 5 - 9	12 6 17 - 35	Brodeur	Bordeleau 2, S. Bernier 2, Sutherland 2, Cloutier 2, Houle
December 3				
Toronto	0 1 3 - 4	9 9 6 - 24	Tataryn	Mahovlich 2 (WG 18:57), Simpson, Cunningham
Calgary	1 0 2 - 3	12 6 13 - 31	McLeod	Delorenzi, Lacombe, Hull
Cincinnati	0 1 4 - 5	9 10 15 - 34	Kiely	G. Sobchuk, Dudley, Larose, Locas, D. Sobchuk
Cleveland	2 0 1 - 3	14 12 13 - 39	Whidden	Ward, Leduc, Shmyr
December 4				
New England	1 2 1 - 4	8 8 6 - 22	Abrahamsson	Webster 2, Paiement, Carleton
Phoenix	3 1 1 - 5	14 7 6 - 27	Kurt	Hall 2, Ftorek, Gray, Cormier
Cincinnati	0 1 0 - 1	6 7 14 - 27	Kiely	D. Sobchuk
Indianapolis	3 2 2 - 7	14 12 8 - 34	Holmquist	Sicinski 2, Scharf 2, Harbaruk, McDonald, Whitlock (Stapleton: 6 as'ts)
Winnipeg	0 3 2 - 5	10 11 9 - 30	Daley	Hull 2, Bergman, Lindh, Lindstrom (WG 19:03)
San Diego	0 2 2 - 4	8 8 6 - 22	Wakely	Adduono, Devine, French, Ferguson

1975-1976 Game by Game Line Scores

Date & Teams	Scoring 1	2	3	ot	F	Shots 1	2	3	ot	F	Goaltenders	Goals & Other Scoring Highlights
December 5												
Winnipeg	3	0	1	-	4	13	11	6	-	30	Larsson	Hull 2, Sjoberg, Nilsson (Hou: 3 goals
Houston	1	1	3	-	5	6	19	14	-	39	Grahame, Rutledge	P. Popiel, G. Howe, Hall, Taylor, Hale (WG 19:58) in last 1:23)
Toronto	2	0	5	-	7	11	11	15	-	37	Tataryn	Marrin 2, Simpson, Kirk, Dorey, Amodeo, Nedomansky
Quebec	1	1	2	-	4	19	10	13	-	42	Deguise	Tardif 2, Cloutier, Tremblay
Edmonton	2	0	1	-	3	8	7	9	-	24	Dryden, Worthy	MacGregor 2, Sheehy
Calgary	3	3	2	-	8	8	14	11	-	33	Wood, McLeod	Lawson 3, Tannahill 2, Deadmarsh, Caffery, Morrison
Denver	1	1	1	-	3	13	8	5	-	26	Johnson	Mara, Morris, Rochon
Minnesota	1	1	2	-	4	20	6	17	-	43	Garrett	Huck, Antonovich, Walton, Boucha (WG 15:57)
December 6												
Houston	2	1	2	0	5	10	9	12	0	31	Rutledge	Mk Howe 2 (TG 19:28), Lund, Taylor, Hinse
Phoenix	0	3	2	1	6	6	14	8	1	29	Kurt	Ftorek 3, Hall 2 (OT 0:42), Connor
New England	0	0	1	-	1	9	9	7	-	25	Landon	Paiement
San Diego	0	3	1	-	4	8	12	12	-	32	Wakely	Peacosh, Lacroix, Ferguson, Adduono
Denver	0	0	2	-	2	7	14	13	-	34	Johnson	Backstrom, Legge
Cincinnati	0	2	1	-	3	19	15	7	-	41	Kiely	Dudley, Campbell, Donnelly
Cleveland	1	0	1	-	2	18	14	9	-	41	Cheevers	Leduc 2
Indianapolis	1	0	2	-	3	7	4	12	-	23	Brown	Whitlock, Coates, Prentice
December 7												
Quebec	0	3	0	-	3	9	15	6	-	30	Brodeur	Houle, J. Bernier, Bordeleau
Winnipeg	1	0	1	-	2	11	14	11	-	36	Daley	Lesuk, Ketola
Cleveland	0	0	1	-	1	11	10	10	-	31	Cheevers, Whidden	Jarrett
Cincinnati	2	1	0	-	3	12	13	13	-	38	Kiely	D. Sobchuk, Larose, Campbell
Calgary	3	1	1	-	5	13	13	12	-	38	McLeod	Tannahill 2, Israelson, Evans, Chipperfield
Edmonton	0	2	2	-	4	6	15	4	-	25	Dryden	Laing, J. Rogers, P. Morris, B. McAneeley
New England	0	1	0	-	1	3	12	7	-	22	Abrahamsson	Climie
Denver	2	1	2	-	5	11	10	7	-	28	Johnson	Borgeson 2, Maggs, Backstrom, Rochon
December 9												
Quebec	1	0	0	-	1	10	9	9	-	28	Brodeur	S. Bernier
Calgary	1	1	2	-	4	12	17	6	-	35	McLeod	Israelson 2, Chipperfield, Keogan
Minnesota	2	1	2	-	5	12	13	18	-	43	Garrett	McKenzie, Holmgren, Connelly, Walton, Antonovich
Toronto	1	1	1	-	3	12	7	12	-	31	Tataryn	Kirk, Mahovlich, Napier
Cincinnati	2	1	1	-	4	13	14	23	-	50	Kiely	D. Sobchuk, Campbell, Locas, Guite
Houston	2	1	3	-	6	12	13	9	-	34	Grahame	Mk Howe 2, Mty Howe, Hinse, Preston, Ruskowski
Cleveland	1	2	0	-	3	9	11	7	-	27	Whidden, Cheevers	Jarrett 2, Pinder
Denver	2	1	3	-	6	6	10	14	-	30	Johnson	Backstrom 2, Borgeson 2, Rochon, Liddington
December 10												
Quebec	0	1	3	-	4	6	10	7	-	23	Donnelly	Sutherland, Houle, Bordeleau, Tardif
Edmonton	2	2	3	-	7	17	15	11	-	43	Dryden	Sheehy 4, Ullman 2, M. Rogers (Ullman: 500th career goal)
Indianapolis	0	1	1	-	2	8	6	4	-	18	Brown	Wyrozub, MacDonald (WG 9:32)
Phoenix	0	0	1	-	1	7	9	7	-	23	Kurt	Veneruzzo
Minnesota	1	1	0	-	2	12	13	3	-	28	Garrett	Gambucci, Keon
New England	0	2	1	-	3	15	17	11	-	43	Abrahamsson	Paiement, Pleau, Webster (WG 9:25)
Toronto	1	1	3	0	5	9	12	9	0	30	Vien, Tataryn	Napier 2, Mahovlich, Henderson, Marrin
Winnipeg	3	1	1	1	6	13	19	16	1	49	Daley	Sullivan, Nilsson, Beaudin, Hedberg, Ford (TG 17:21), Hull (OT 0:44)
December 11												
Edmonton	0	1	2	-	3	6	6	5	-	17	Worthy	Patenaude, Sheehy, Ullman (WG 5:38)
Calgary	1	1	0	-	2	12	14	14	-	40	McLeod	Deadmarsh 2
Indianapolis	1	0	2	0	3	12	12	13	3	40	Brown	Karlander, MacDonald, Harbaruk
San Diego	2	1	0	0	3	14	12	13	4	43	Wakely	Adduono 2, Ferguson
December 12												
Minnesota	0	0	0	-	0	7	5	2	-	14	Garrett	▶ Cheevers: shutout (1), 14 saves
Cleveland	0	0	1	-	1	7	13	12	-	32	Cheevers	Leduc (WG 15:18)
Calgary	1	0	1	-	2	10	5	14	-	29	McLeod, Wood	Leiter, Lawson
Winnipeg	0	2	2	-	4	5	7	9	-	21	Daley	Lindh 2, Nilsson, Beaudin
Quebec	1	1	2	-	4	15	16	16	-	47	Brodeur	Tardif 2, Bordeleau, Cloutier
Toronto	2	2	2	-	6	10	10	13	-	33	Tataryn	Napier 2, Simpson, Turkiewicz, Nedomansky, Mahovlich
Cincinnati	2	2	0	-	4	7	14	6	-	27	Kiely	G. Sobchuk, Myers, Campbell, Locas
Phoenix	0	2	0	-	2	11	17	11	-	39	Kurt	Gray, Hall
Indianapolis	0	1	1	-	2	8	8	14	-	30	Brown	Thomas, MacDonald
Houston	3	0	1	-	4	7	12	10	-	29	Grahame	Lund, Schella, Hughes, Mty Howe
December 13												
Cleveland	2	1	1	-	4	9	13	10	-	32	Whidden	Harrison, Leduc, Moffat, Baxter
New England	1	4	0	-	5	11	17	11	-	39	Abrahamsson	Paiement, McManama, D. Roberts, G. Roberts, Webster
Cincinnati	1	1	1	0	3	12	7	12	1	32	Kiely	Donnelly, Dudley, Larose (TG 17:31)
San Diego	1	2	0	0	3	10	16	14	4	44	Gillow	Lacroix 2, Morrison
Toronto	2	1	0	-	3	9	17	10	-	36	Tataryn	Nedomansky 3
Quebec	2	2	2	-	6	7	10	12	-	29	Brodeur	Houle 3, Tardif, Parizeau, Leclerc
Houston	0	2	1	-	3	12	13	16	-	41	Rutledge	G. Howe, P. Popiel, Hinse
Minnesota	0	2	2	-	4	12	14	12	-	38	Garrett	Huck 2, Walton, McKenzie
Phoenix	2	1	1	-	4	8	5	16	-	29	Norris	Connor, Gray, Gorman, Cormier
Denver	0	1	0	-	1	12	10	9	-	31	Johnson	Lomenda

1975-1976 Game by Game Line Scores

Date & Teams	Scoring 1 2 3 ot F	Shots 1 2 3 ot F	Goaltenders	Goals & Other Scoring Highlights
December 14				
Houston	0 1 3 - 4	9 14 19 - 42	Grahame	Hughes, Schella, P. Popiel, Preston (WG 7:13)
Cleveland	0 3 0 - 3	14 8 9 - 31	Cheevers	Tamminen, Harrison, Leduc
San Diego	2 0 0 - 2	12 8 6 - 26	Wakely	Noris 2
Phoenix	1 2 1 - 4	10 11 12 - 33	Norris	Gray 2, Veneruzzo, Mononen
Calgary	1 1 1 0 3	14 11 16 4 45	Wood	Delorenzi 2, Leiter
Toronto	1 2 0 0 3	10 13 8 2 33	Vien	Napier 2, Amodeo
New England	1 1 0 0 2	10 9 7 5 31	Landon	McManama, Swain
Indianapolis	1 0 1 0 2	6 11 9 9 35	Brown	Fitchner, Karlander
Winnipeg	1 1 1 - 3	14 19 10 - 43	Daley	Hull, Bergman, Hedberg
Edmonton	0 1 0 - 1	6 8 6 - 20	Worthy	Baird
December 16				
Calgary	0 1 2 - 3	5 12 12 - 29	McLeod	Driscoll, Hull, Israelson
Quebec	3 2 2 - 7	11 7 10 - 28	Brodeur	Tardif 2, Bordeleau 2, Leclerc, S. Bernier, Cloutier
Edmonton	1 0 2 - 3	12 14 9 - 35	Dryden	J. Rogers, Patenaude, B. McAneeley
Indianapolis	0 1 0 - 1	10 10 13 - 33	Holmquist	Thomas
San Diego	1 1 2 - 4	14 9 9 - 32	Wakely	Noris 2, Burgess, Peacosh
Houston	1 1 0 - 2	6 16 9 - 31	Grahame	J. Popiel, Hinse
Cincinnati	1 1 0 0 2	8 15 2 1 26	Kiely	Larose, Dudley
Denver	0 0 2 1 3	6 8 11 3 28	Johnson	Morris, Backstrom, Legge (OT 5:25)
Winnipeg	1 2 1 - 4	11 16 15 - 42	Larsson	Sullivan 2, Lesuk, Hedberg (WG 19:45)
Toronto	1 2 0 - 3	10 14 19 - 43	Tataryn	Napier 2, Henderson
December 17				
New England	0 0 0 0 0	9 6 7 4 26	Abrahamsson	▸ Abrahamsson: shutout (1), 39 saves
Minnesota	0 0 0 0 0	13 10 7 9 39	Garrett	▸ Garrett: shutout (2), 26 saves
Edmonton	1 1 1 - 3	9 5 10 - 24	Dryden	Krake 2 (WG 2:15), B. McAneeley
Cleveland	0 2 0 - 2	14 10 12 - 36	Whidden	Tamminen 2
December 18				
Cincinnati	1 1 1 - 3	12 7 13 - 32	Kiely, Aubry	Campbell, Dudley, Locas
San Diego	1 3 3 - 7	10 10 14 - 34	Wakely	Morrison 2, Noris, Rivers, Peacosh, Hughes, McMahon
Indianapolis	1 0 0 - 1	4 4 3 - 11	Brown	Fitchner
Phoenix	2 3 2 - 7	10 12 14 - 36	Norris	Hall 2, Ftorek, Dean, Clarke, Veneruzzo, Gorman
Winnipeg	3 1 0 - 4	21 15 7 - 43	Daley	Sullivan, Sjoberg, Hedberg, Lesuk
Quebec	1 2 2 - 5	6 10 11 - 27	Brodeur	Houle, Bordeleau, Parizeau, Tardif, Jordan (WG 16:31)
December 19				
San Diego	2 0 1 - 3	10 13 5 - 28	Gillow	Noris, Burgess, French
Denver	2 0 4 - 6	12 10 17 - 39	Johnson	Sherrit 2, Backstrom 2, Bignell, Morris
Cleveland	1 1 2 0 4	12 9 16 1 38	Cheevers	Leduc, Edur, Harrison, Maxwell
Indianapolis	3 0 1 1 5	12 13 7 2 34	Brown	Wyrozub, Scharf, Sicinski, Whitlock, Fitchner (OT 1:44)
Edmonton	1 1 0 - 2	11 13 6 - 30	Dryden	J. Rogers, Russell
New England	1 1 2 - 4	7 9 9 - 25	Abrahamsson	Webster 2, Pleau, Paiement
Calgary	1 2 2 - 5	23 11 10 - 44	Wood	Chipperfield, Driscoll 2, Hull
Toronto	1 1 1 - 3	12 14 7 - 33	Tataryn	Napier, Kirk, Cunningham
December 20				
Calgary	2 2 3 - 7	12 7 9 - 28	Wood, McLeod	Morrison 3, Deadmarsh, Leiter, Tannahill, Lawson
Quebec	3 3 2 - 8	14 14 11 - 39	Brodeur	Cloutier 3, Houle, Roy, Globensky, Leclerc, Tardif
New England	0 1 1 - 2	4 11 13 - 28	Landon	Webster, Pleau
Cincinnati	1 0 3 - 4	13 9 14 - 36	Kiely	Pelyk, Guite, Dudley, Donnelly
Winnipeg	0 2 1 - 3	18 14 5 - 37	Daley	Asmundson, Ketola, Lindstrom
Minnesota	1 1 4 - 6	14 19 14 - 47	Garrett	Connelly 3, Gambucci, Boucha, Huck
Houston	2 0 2 - 4	12 7 9 - 28	Rutledge	Tonelli, Larway, Hinse, Hughes (WG 13:56)
Phoenix	1 2 0 - 3	8 8 11 - 27	Norris	Gray, Cormier, Rautakallio
Indianapolis	0 3 0 - 3	15 11 6 - 32	Holmquist	Coates 2, Dubois
Cleveland	2 1 2 - 5	9 11 9 - 29	Whidden	Gruen, Edur, Walker, JA Stewart, Harrison
December 21				
Toronto	0 4 0 - 4	7 8 13 - 28	Tataryn	Kirk, Farda, Nistico, Jacques
Edmonton	1 1 0 - 2	16 10 10 - 36	Worthy	MacGregor, M. Rogers
Minnesota	2 1 0 - 3	15 9 9 - 33	Garrett	Keon 2, Huck
Winnipeg	1 0 0 - 1	9 4 7 - 20	Daley	Hull
Houston	0 1 0 - 1	5 14 10 - 29	Grahame	Hinse
San Diego	0 2 1 - 3	11 19 6 - 36	Wakely	Ferguson, Burgess, Noris
Quebec	3 3 1 - 7	14 8 14 - 36	Brodeur, Deguise	Bordeleau 2, Leclerc 2, Parizeau, Cloutier, Tardif
Cincinnati	1 7 3 - 11	7 23 9 - 39	Aubry, Kiely	Myers 3, Campbell 2, Guite 2, Plumb, Larose, Dudley, Locas
December 22				
New England	1 2 1 - 4	5 13 7 - 25	Landon	Webster 3, Blackburn
Cleveland	0 1 0 - 1	6 9 10 - 25	Whidden	Ward
December 23				
Quebec	1 1 2 - 4	7 12 9 - 28	Brodeur	Houle, Benzelock, S. Bernier, Leclerc
San Diego	4 2 4 - 10	32 15 17 - 64	Wakely	Tidey 3, Ferguson 2, Lacroix 2, Burgess, Rivers, Peacosh
Toronto	0 1 0 - 1	7 5 3 - 15	Vien, Tataryn	Kirk
Calgary	5 3 2 - 10	13 9 14 - 36	McLeod	Deadmarsh 2, Leiter 2, Lawson 2, Evans, Morrison, Delorenzi, Sentes
Phoenix	0 1 4 - 5	10 9 15 - 34	Norris	Cormier 2, Dean, Gorman, Hall
Cincinnati	0 2 1 - 3	12 11 8 - 31	Kiely	Dudley 2, Larose
Winnipeg	2 2 2 - 6	11 7 10 - 28	Larsson	Sullivan 3, Hull 2, Ketola
Edmonton	0 1 1 - 2	13 11 10 - 34	Dryden	Russell 2
Minnesota	1 1 3 - 5	7 9 8 - 24	Garrett	Boucha, Keon, Walton, Gambucci, Antonovich (WG 17:21)
Denver	1 1 2 - 4	13 8 11 - 32	Johnson	Borgeson, MacGregor, Liddington, Lomenda

1975-1976 Game by Game Line Scores

Date & Teams	Scoring 1 2 3 ot F	Shots 1 2 3 ot F	Goaltenders	Goals & Other Scoring Highlights
December 26				
Cincinnati	1 0 2 - 3	14 10 12 - 36	Kiely, Hoganson	Guite 2, Plumb
New England	4 0 0 - 4	10 9 9 - 28	Abrahamsson	Webster 2, Pleau, Climie
Calgary	0 4 1 - 5	9 15 3 - 27	McLeod	Israelson, Lawson, Deadmarsh, Morrison, Driscoll
Winnipeg	1 1 2 - 4	15 10 14 - 39	Daley	Hull 2, Miller, Nilsson
Phoenix	1 0 1 - 2	9 8 12 - 29	Norris	Connor, Gorman
San Diego	3 1 0 - 4	16 9 11 - 36	Wakely	French, Adduono, Tidey, Lacroix
Edmonton	1 1 4 - 6	13 14 10 - 37	Dryden	Patenaude 2, M. Rogers, Ullman, Russell, Baird
Toronto	1 4 3 - 8	13 13 13 - 39	Tataryn	Henderson 3, Farda 2, Jacques, Atkinson, Kirk
Denver	1 2 1 - 4	7 9 9 - 25	Johnson, Grigg	Legge, Liddington, Morris, Backstrom
Houston	4 1 4 - 9	11 9 23 - 43	Grahame	G. Howe 2, Larway 2, Mk Howe, Hughes, Irwin, Labossiere, Hinse
December 27				
Minnesota	0 0 0 - 0	5 7 11 - 23	Garrett	▸ Rutledge: shutout (1), 23 saves
Houston	1 3 1 - 5	10 12 14 - 36	Rutledge	Larway, Ruskowski, Hinse, Hughes, Tonelli
Toronto	0 0 0 - 0	5 12 8 - 25	Shaw	▸ Whidden: shutout (1), 25 saves
Cleveland	1 3 1 - 5	14 21 12 - 47	Whidden	Baxter, Harrison, Gruen, McDonough, Leduc
Cincinnati	0 1 0 - 1	10 8 14 - 32	Hoganson	Dudley
Indianapolis	1 0 1 - 2	11 14 5 - 30	Holmquist	Harbaruk 2 (WG 2:08)
Denver	0 0 0 - 0	8 11 11 - 30	Johnson, Grigg	▸ Norris: shutout (1), 30 saves
Phoenix	2 4 4 - 10	12 15 11 - 38	Norris	Boyd 3, Hall 2, Dean 2, Veneruzzo, Gray, Huston
Edmonton	1 0 2 - 3	11 7 8 - 26	Worthy	J. Rogers, Laing, Ullman
Quebec	1 3 2 - 6	7 12 16 - 35	Brodeur	Bordeleau 2, Cloutier 2, Parizeau, S. Bernier
December 28				
Winnipeg	2 1 1 - 4	13 10 13 - 36	Larsson	Ketola 3, Lindstrom
Calgary	4 2 0 - 6	8 7 1 - 16	Wood	Lawson 2 (0:36 & 0:51, 1st), Chipperfield 2, Sentes, Keogan
Cleveland	0 0 0 - 0	7 4 6 - 17	Whidden	▸Abrahamsson: shutout (2), 17 saves
New England	2 2 0 - 4	14 12 5 - 31	Abrahamsson	Webster, Arndt, Paiement, Pleau
Quebec	2 3 1 - 6	15 19 15 - 49	Brodeur	Tardif 2, S. Bernier, Bordeleau, Cloutier, Jordan
Toronto	0 0 1 - 1	4 10 16 - 30	Tataryn	Nistico
Indianapolis	0 1 0 - 1	9 12 12 - 33	Holmquist	Harbaruk
Cincinnati	2 2 0 - 4	16 9 8 - 33	Hoganson	Guite, Plumb, Campbell, Myers
San Diego	0 2 0 - 2	9 10 7 - 26	Wakely	Bredin, Adduono
Minnesota	0 1 0 - 1	15 14 9 - 38	Garrett	Walton
Phoenix	1 2 2 - 5	10 14 8 - 32	Norris	Hall 2, Cormier, Mononen, Huston
Denver	0 1 1 - 2	13 8 9 - 30	Zimmerman	Borgeson, Legge
December 30				
Winnipeg	1 3 1 - 5	10 8 8 - 26	Larsson	Hedberg, Nilsson, Ford, Hull, Lindstrom
Houston	1 1 1 - 3	11 13 11 - 35	Grahame	Hughes, Hinse, Lund
Indianapolis	0 1 0 0 1	10 12 5 3 30	Dion	Whitlock
Denver	1 0 0 1 2	7 7 9 6 29	Zimmerman	Rochon, Backstrom (OT 9:42)
Edmonton	2 1 0 - 3	8 8 11 - 27	Dryden	Sheehy, M. Rogers, J. Rogers
Toronto	3 2 1 - 6	17 19 11 - 47	Shaw	Henderson 2, Farda 2, Atkinson, Nedomansky
Quebec	4 0 0 0 4	15 16 9 6 46	Brodeur	Sutherland 2, Leclerc, Tardif
Minnesota	2 1 1 0 4	19 13 14 6 52	Garrett	Odrowski, Gambucci, Keon, Carlson
San Diego	1 1 1 - 3	13 10 8 - 31	Wakely, Gillow	French, Tidey, Hargreaves
New England	1 3 1 - 5	10 8 14 - 32	Abrahamsson	Pleau 3, Abrahamsson, D. Roberts
January 1				
Edmonton	0 1 0 - 1	3 10 8 - 21	Worthy	MacGregor
Calgary	1 1 3 - 5	14 10 13 - 37	McLeod	Chipperfield 2, Sentes, Driscoll, Deadmarsh
January 2	▸ Denver franchise relocates to Ottawa.			
Quebec	1 1 2 0 4	11 13 17 0 41	Brodeur	Sutherland 2, Bordeleau, S. Bernier
Cleveland	2 1 1 1 5	22 9 9 3 43	Cheevers	Harrison 2, Ward, JA Stewart, Walker (OT 3:02)
San Diego	1 0 1 - 2	10 12 6 - 28	Wakely	Rivers, Burgess
Indianapolis	0 0 0 - 0	8 10 17 - 35	Dion	▸ Wakely: shutout (2), 35 saves
Phoenix	0 1 0 - 1	11 10 12 - 33	Kurt	Cormier
Toronto	1 2 1 - 4	10 10 8 - 28	Tataryn	Henderson 2, Nistico, Mahovlich
Calgary	1 0 2 - 3	10 8 8 - 26	Wood	Sentes, Chipperfield, Deadmarsh
Edmonton	1 0 0 - 1	11 7 7 - 25	Dryden	Patenaude
Ottawa	0 0 1 - 1	15 3 9 - 27	Zimmerman	Sherrit
Cincinnati	1 1 0 - 2	12 15 15 - 42	Hoganson	Dudley, Larose
January 3				
Cleveland	1 1 0 - 2	3 7 6 - 16	Cheevers	Jarrett, Ward
New England	1 1 1 - 3	14 7 10 - 31	Abrahamsson	Climie, Abrahamsson, G. Roberts (WG 19:26)
San Diego	3 0 0 - 3	19 4 9 - 32	Gillow, Wakely	Ferguson, Bredin, Devine
Cincinnati	0 2 3 - 5	10 14 16 - 40	Hoganson	Locas, Dudley, Myers, Larose, D. Sobchuk
Ottawa	0 0 2 - 2	15 8 7 - 30	Zimmerman	MacGregor, Lomenda
Houston	2 2 0 - 4	16 16 15 - 47	Rutledge	Hinse 2, G. Howe, Lund
Phoenix	1 1 2 - 4	17 11 10 - 38	Norris	Veneruzzo 2, Cormier, Hall
Quebec	0 0 1 - 1	1 6 10 - 17	Brodeur	Leclerc
Indianapolis	1 0 0 - 1	13 12 9 - 34	Dion	McDonald
Minnesota	3 0 0 - 3	10 5 13 - 28	Garrett	Carlson, Gambucci, Connelly
Winnipeg	1 3 2 - 6	11 11 4 - 27	Daley	Ketola 2, Hedberg, Sullivan, Bergman, Hull
Calgary	2 1 0 - 3	15 6 3 - 24	McLeod	Lawson, Sentes, Leiter

1975-1976 Game by Game Line Scores

Date & Teams	Scoring 1 2 3 ot F	Shots 1 2 3 ot F	Goaltenders	Goals & Other Scoring Highlights
January 4				
Winnipeg	2 2 4 - 8	16 10 6 - 32	Daley	Sullivan 3, Hedberg 2, Nilsson, Green, Miller
Edmonton	1 0 0 - 1	10 7 16 - 33	Dryden	Ullman
Ottawa	2 1 2 - 5	14 7 13 - 34	Zimmerman	Borgeson 2, MacGregor, Morris, Lavender
Minnesota	1 0 1 - 2	10 21 9 - 40	Garrett	Walton, McKenzie
Phoenix	0 0 2 - 2	13 17 12 - 42	Norris	Huston, Ftorek
Cleveland	2 1 0 - 3	7 13 12 - 32	Whidden	Harrison 2, Pinder
New England	1 1 0 - 2	6 8 8 - 22	Landon	Paiement, Pleau
Indianapolis	0 1 2 - 3	12 12 14 - 38	Dion	Heatley, Wyrozub, Block (WG 5:54)
January 6				
Indianapolis	0 0 0 - 0	6 6 11 - 23	Dion	▶ Worthy: shutout (1), 23 saves
Edmonton	1 1 1 - 3	9 8 5 - 22	Worthy	T. McAneeley, MacGregor, M. Rogers
San Diego	1 2 1 - 4	13 14 16 - 43	Wakely	Lacroix, Peacosh, French, Noris
Toronto	2 3 1 - 6	11 11 14 - 36	Shaw	Phaneuf 2, Nedomansky, Mahovlich, Nistico, Jacques
Cincinnati	1 2 0 - 3	15 17 13 - 45	Hoganson, Kiely	Pelyk, Campbell, Smedsmo
Houston	2 4 1 - 7	12 13 11 - 36	Rutledge	Lund 3, Hughes, Hall, Mk Howe, Taylor
Winnipeg	0 0 0 - 0	7 7 7 - 21	Larsson	▶ Wood: shutout (1), 21 saves
Calgary	2 2 1 - 5	11 12 10 - 33	Wood	Lawson 2, Keogan, Leiter, Sentes
January 7				
New England	2 0 1 - 3	8 7 5 - 20	Abrahamsson	Webster 2 (WG 17:34), Paiement
Ottawa	1 1 0 - 2	7 13 14 - 34	Zimmerman	Lavender 2
Phoenix	0 5 1 0 6	14 11 15 2 42	Norris	Hall 2, Connor, Ftorek, Gorman, Mononen Gambucci (OT 3:32)
Minnesota	1 1 4 1 7	4 19 19 4 46	Garrett	Keon, Antonovich, Boucha, Boudreau, McKenzie, Huck (TG 19:59),
San Diego	2 0 1 - 3	11 18 12 - 41	Blanchet, Gillow	French, Falkenberg, Ferguson
Cleveland	1 5 2 - 8	12 19 13 - 44	Whidden	McDonough, Walker 2, Leduc 2, Ward, Pinder
Toronto	1 0 1 - 2	8 5 16 - 29	Tataryn	Dorey, Mahovlich
Winnipeg	4 2 2 - 8	16 19 7 - 42	Daley	Nilsson 3, Hedberg 2, Lesuk, Miller, Moffat
Indianapolis	1 0 0 - 1	11 4 8 - 23	Dion	MacDonald
Calgary	2 0 1 - 3	7 12 14 - 33	Wood	Lawson 2, Sentes
January 8				
Cincinnati	1 0 0 - 1	8 8 13 - 29	Kiely	Hughes
Phoenix	1 3 3 - 7	13 15 11 - 39	Kurt	Hall 2, Gray 2, Connor, Rautakallio, Lariviere
January 9				
Indianapolis	0 1 0 1 2	9 11 7 2 29	Dion	Thomas, Karlander (OT 5:44)
Winnipeg	0 0 1 0 1	3 9 9 3 24	Daley	Ford (TG 17:51)
Cleveland	1 3 1 - 5	11 11 8 - 30	Cheevers	Leduc 2, McDonough, Harrison, Ward
Houston	1 3 2 - 6	8 11 10 - 29	Grahame	Larway 2 (WG 11:11), G. Howe, Hall, Irwin, Tonelli
San Diego	1 1 3 - 5	10 10 16 - 36	Wakely	Morrison 2, Burgess, Noris, Rivers (WG 16:56)
New England	1 1 1 - 3	10 8 7 - 25	Landon	Abrahamsson, Paiement, G. Roberts
Toronto	1 2 0 - 3	2 14 11 - 27	Shaw, Tataryn	Nedomansky, Nistico, Dorey
Edmonton	2 2 1 - 5	12 7 10 - 29	Worthy	Ullman 2, Patenaude, Krake, MacGregor
January 10				
San Diego	0 1 2 0 3	7 13 7 1 28	Gillow	Lacroix, Morrison, Peacosh (TG 18:05)
Quebec	0 2 1 1 4	10 10 10 1 31	Brodeur	Tremblay, Bordeleau, Sutherland, Tardif (OT 1:43)
Houston	0 3 1 - 4	11 11 5 - 27	Rutledge	Hughes, Hall, Hinse, Mk Howe
Minnesota	0 0 1 - 1	15 11 20 - 46	Garrett	Keon
Ottawa	2 0 3 - 5	13 7 6 - 26	Zimmerman	Backstrom 2, Legge, Maggs, Sherrit
Phoenix	3 3 2 - 8	11 15 14 - 40	Kurt	Ftorek 3, Hall 2, Mononen, Huston, Boyd
January 11				
San Diego	1 1 2 - 4	5 15 12 - 32	Wakely	Hughes, Tidey, Adduono, Burgess
New England	4 1 3 - 8	15 7 7 - 29	Abrahamsson	Paiement 3, Pleau 2, Swain, Abrahamsson, Carleton
Indianapolis	1 0 2 - 3	8 6 14 - 28	Dion	MacDonald, Harris, McDonald
Cleveland	1 1 2 - 4	20 6 5 - 31	Cheevers	Harrison 2, McDonough, Pinder
Ottawa	2 1 2 0 5	13 9 8 2 32	Zimmerman	MacGregor 2, Rochon, Baltimore, Lomenda
Winnipeg	2 1 2 1 6	10 18 14 7 49	Daley	Moffat, Sjoberg, Nilsson, Beaudin, Hull (TG 14:28), Hedberg (OT 8:01)
Minnesota	0 3 4 - 7	11 8 12 - 31	Garrett	Connelly 2, Antonovich, Walton, Huck, Boucha, McKenzie
Cincinnati	1 1 2 - 4	10 10 15 - 35	Hoganson	Smedsmo, Dudley, G. Sobchuk, Guite
Houston	2 1 2 - 5	8 4 6 - 18	Rutledge	Hinse 2, Tonelli, Mk Howe, Lund
Edmonton	0 1 2 - 3	8 6 10 - 24	Worthy	Laing, Spring, Long
January 14				
Houston	1 0 0 - 1	7 6 3 - 16	Grahame	Lund
Winnipeg	2 0 2 - 4	11 14 14 - 39	Larsson	Ketola 2, Hedberg, Sullivan
January 15				
Cincinnati	1 0 1 - 2	10 11 15 - 36	Hoganson	D. Sobchuk, G. Sobchuk
New England	2 0 3 - 5	8 10 11 - 29	Abrahamsson	Paiement 2, Webster, Climie, Pleau
Cleveland	0 2 1 - 3	5 19 12 - 36	Dion	Gruen 2, Edur
Indianapolis	1 0 0 - 1	13 14 11 - 38	Whidden	Harbaruk
Calgary	1 1 1 - 3	9 14 10 - 33	Wood	Morrison 2, Chipperfield
Quebec	1 2 2 - 5	10 12 11 - 33	Deguise	Tardif 2, Parizeau, S. Bernier, J. Bernier
Minnesota	2 1 1 0 4	7 9 6 0 22	Garrett	Antonovich, McKenzie, Carlson, Connelly
San Diego	2 2 0 1 5	16 11 8 4 39	Wakely	Morrison 2, Ferguson, Tidey, Rivers (OT 1:07)
Houston	0 1 3 1 5	18 17 19 1 55	Rutledge	Labossiere 2 (OT 1:37), Hinse, Mty Howe, Preston
Ottawa	1 1 2 0 4	10 6 9 0 25	Newton	Rochon, Borgeson, Backstrom, Maggs
January 16				
New England	2 1 0 - 3	11 17 6 - 34	Abrahamsson	Ley, Pleau, Arndt (Webster: 21 game scoring streak)
Cleveland	2 1 1 - 4	17 14 9 - 40	Cheevers	Harrison 2 (WG 19:21), Leduc 2
Minnesota	1 0 0 - 1	10 5 5 - 20	Garrett	Keon
Phoenix	1 0 2 - 3	15 8 13 - 36	Norris	Ftorek 2 (WG 12:23), Cormier
Edmonton	1 0 4 - 5	10 4 14 - 28	Dryden	Long 2, Russell, Muloin, Spring
Winnipeg	1 0 0 - 1	12 10 10 - 32	Larsson	Hillman

1975-1976 Game by Game Line Scores

Date & Teams	Scoring 1 2 3 ot F	Shots 1 2 3 ot F	Goaltenders	Goals & Other Scoring Highlights
January 17	▸ Denver-Ottawa folds			
Cleveland	2 1 1 - 4	5 9 7 - 21	Whidden	JA Stewart 2, Harrison, Pinder
San Diego	2 1 2 - 5	5 10 11 - 26	Wakely	Rivers 2, Noris 2 (WG 14:38), Burgess
Houston	2 0 0 - 2	7 11 6 - 24	Rutledge	Larway, Mty Howe
Calgary	1 1 2 - 4	16 11 11 - 38	McLeod	Chipperfield, Morrison, Tannahill, Deadmarsh
Toronto	1 2 0 0 3	8 13 5 4 30	Shaw	Napier, Henderson, Simpson
Quebec	2 1 0 1 4	8 18 16 6 48	Brodeur	Cloutier, S. Bernier, Bordeleau, Houle (OT 9:45)
Cincinnati	0 3 1 - 4	11 12 9 - 32	Hoganson	Guite, Larose, Campbell, Myers
Indianapolis	0 0 0 - 0	14 13 13 - 40	Dion	▸ Hoganson: shutout (1), 40 saves
Minnesota	2 1 1 - 4	8 5 8 - 21	Garrett	McKenzie, Gambucci, Huck, Keon
Phoenix	1 0 1 - 2	9 13 9 - 31	Norris	Migneault, Rautakallio
January 18				
New England	0 0 0 - 0	7 10 9 - 26	Landon	▸ Daley: shutout (5), 26 saves
Winnipeg	2 2 4 - 8	13 11 17 - 41	Daley	Hull 3, Lindstrom 2, Sullivan, Bergman, Ketola
January 20				
New England	0 3 1 0 4	11 15 10 3 39	Landon	O'Donnell, Paiement, Rogers, Backstrom
Phoenix	0 3 1 0 4	13 13 8 3 37	Kurt	Connor 2, Migneault, Boyd
Toronto	1 3 3 - 7	10 5 12 - 27	Tataryn	Kirk 2, Cunningham, Turkiewicz, Farda, Nedomansky, Mahovlich
Houston	3 1 1 - 5	12 9 10 - 31	Rutledge	Larway 2, Hinse, Labossiere, P. Popiel
Calgary	4 1 5 - 10	10 16 13 - 39	McLeod, Wood	Chipperfield 2, Leiter 2, Sentes 2, Tannahill, Lawson, Morrison, Keogan
Edmonton	2 0 1 - 3	12 7 2 - 21	Dryden, Worthy	Ullman, Patenaude, Kerslake
January 21				
New England	0 1 2 - 3	9 10 8 - 27	Abrahamsson	Ley 2, Paiement
Houston	1 3 5 - 9	11 11 16 - 38	Grahame	Labossiere 3, Larway 2, Hughes, P. Popiel, Mk Howe, Hinse
San Diego	0 3 2 0 5	9 11 15 1 36	Wakely	Rivers 2, Bredin, French, Peacosh
Minnesota	1 1 3 1 6	7 7 12 3 29	Garrett	Keon 2 (OT 4:22), McKenzie, Huck, Carlson, Walton
Cleveland	2 0 0 - 2	8 10 15 - 33	Cheevers	Leduc, McDonough
Cincinnati	3 1 4 - 8	15 11 10 - 36	Hoganson	Dudley 2, Pelyk, Campbell, D. Sobchuk, Hughes, Myers, Ball
Indianapolis	0 0 2 - 2	10 5 8 - 23	Dion	Karlander, Proceviat
Quebec	1 2 0 - 3	10 7 11 - 28	Brodeur	Sutherland, Tremblay, Jordan
Calgary	1 0 0 - 1	8 5 9 - 22	McLeod	Lawson
Winnipeg	1 2 1 - 4	14 11 6 - 31	Daley	Hedberg, Moffat, Lindh, Nilsson
January 22				
Toronto	2 2 0 - 4	12 12 13 - 37	Shaw, Tataryn	Phaneuf 2, Nedomansky, Napier
Phoenix	2 1 3 - 6	11 14 11 - 36	Norris	Connor, Ftorek, Cormier, Huston, Dean, Hobin
January 23				
Edmonton	2 0 0 - 2	11 6 8 - 25	Dryden	Sheehy, Patenaude
Winnipeg	0 2 2 - 4	8 12 16 - 36	Daley	Hull, Lesuk, Nilsson, Hedberg
Calgary	0 0 0 - 0	11 9 13 - 33	McLeod	▸ Grahame: shutout (3), 33 saves
Houston	1 1 0 - 2	11 18 6 - 35	Grahame	Labossiere, Larway (No penalties called during game)
Cincinnati	0 2 1 - 3	5 17 8 - 30	Hoganson	Locas, Campbell, G. Sobchuk
Indianapolis	1 2 1 - 4	14 11 9 - 34	Holmquist	Fitchner 2, MacDonald, Harris (WG 19:24)
San Diego	2 2 3 - 7	10 16 12 - 38	Wakely	Devine 3, French 2, Morenz, Lacroix
Minnesota	0 1 0 - 1	10 16 10 - 36	Garrett	Brackenbury
New England	1 1 0 0 2	8 14 10 3 35	Abrahamsson	Rogers, O'Donnell
Cleveland	0 2 0 0 2	9 11 13 6 39	Whidden	Leduc, Tamminen
January 24				
New England	0 0 3 - 3	10 8 16 - 34	Landon, Ab'sson	McManama, Pleau, Borgeson
Cincinnati	1 5 0 - 6	8 10 15 - 33	Hoganson	Dudley 2, D. Sobchuk 2, Larose, Guite
Toronto	3 1 0 - 4	12 9 8 - 29	Tataryn	Nedomansky 2, Mahovlich, Henderson
San Diego	1 3 2 - 6	9 15 18 - 42	Gillow	Adduono 2, Peacosh, Burgess, Devine, Lacroix
January 25				
San Diego	1 4 0 - 5	11 16 9 - 36	Wakely	French 2, Morenz, Adduono, Ferguson
Phoenix	3 3 1 - 7	13 19 9 - 41	Kurt	Huston, Lariviere, Ftorek, Boyd, Connor, Hall, Cormier
Calgary	2 0 1 - 3	11 12 14 - 37	McLeod	Lawson, Sentes
Houston	1 3 1 - 5	10 12 7 - 29	Grahame	Hughes 2, Schella, Mk Howe, Preston
Cleveland	2 0 0 - 2	13 5 7 - 25	Cheevers	Walker, Leduc (Cheevers: final game with Cleveland)
Indianapolis	1 2 1 - 4	14 14 10 - 38	Dion	Leclerc 2, Sicinski, Harris
Toronto	1 0 1 - 2	5 8 12 - 25	Tataryn	Kirk, Simpson
Minnesota	2 2 1 - 5	8 12 16 - 36	Garrett	Hampson, Boucha, McKenzie, Walton, Antonovich
Edmonton	2 3 1 - 6	12 13 4 - 29	Worthy	Ullman 2, Sheehy 2, R. Morris
Quebec	2 2 3 - 7	14 9 12 - 35	Brodeur	S. Bernier 2 (WG 13:25), Cloutier 2, Tardif 2, Tremblay
January 27				
Phoenix	0 2 1 1 4	7 8 6 3 24	Norris	Cormier 3, Boyd (OT 0:17)
San Diego	2 1 0 0 3	14 7 8 0 29	Wakely	Tidey, Morrison, Peacosh
Cincinnati	0 0 1 - 1	9 8 14 - 31	Hoganson, Kiely	Locas
Quebec	2 4 3 - 9	11 13 9 - 33	Brodeur	Serviss 3, Cloutier 2, Tardif 2, S. Bernier, Benzelock
Edmonton	0 4 0 0 4	11 11 5 7 34	Dryden	Patenaude, Ullman, B. McAneeley, Sheehy
Toronto	1 1 2 0 4	13 8 9 5 35	Shaw	Simpson 2, Farda, Rollins
January 28				
Houston	1 3 2 - 6	15 9 4 - 28	Grahame	Lund 2, G. Howe, J. Popiel, Larway, Preston (WG 19:20)
Edmonton	2 1 2 - 5	13 17 13 - 43	Dryden	Hamilton, Sheehy, Laing, J. Rogers, Barrie
Calgary	0 0 0 - 0	3 9 10 - 22	Wood, McLeod	▸ Kurt: shutout (1), 22 saves
Phoenix	2 1 2 - 5	14 10 15 - 39	Kurt	Veneruzzo, Boyd, Huston, Ftorek, Rautakallio
Winnipeg	1 1 0 - 2	5 11 11 - 27	Daley	Nilsson 2
Minnesota	0 2 4 - 6	15 15 12 - 42	Garrett	Walton 2, Holmgren 2, Miller, Antonovich
Cleveland	1 2 3 - 6	8 13 14 - 35	Caron	Ward 2, Pinder, Walker, Leduc, Gruen
Cincinnati	1 1 2 - 4	14 15 10 - 39	Hoganson	D. Sobchuk 2, G. Sobchuk, Locas
Indianapolis	1 2 1 - 4	10 11 10 - 31	Holmquist	Harris, Fitchner, MacDonald, Karlander
New England	2 2 2 - 6	10 11 13 - 34	Abrahamsson	Pleau 3, Abrahamsson, Borgeson, Climie

1975-1976 Game by Game Line Scores

Date & Teams	Scoring 1 2 3 ot F	Shots 1 2 3 ot F	Goaltenders	Goals & Other Scoring Highlights
January 29				
Minnesota	1 3 1 1 6	10 14 12 2 38	Levasseur	Antonovich 2, Westrum, Holmgren, Brackenbury, Walton (OT 4:17)
Indianapolis	1 2 2 0 5	11 5 11 1 28	Brown, Park	Harris 2, MacDonald 2, Harbaruk
Calgary	0 0 0 - 0	8 8 13 - 29	Wood	▶ Wakely: shutout (3), 29 saves
San Diego	1 0 0 - 1	6 11 8 - 25	Wakely	Morrison
January 30				
Houston	1 0 0 - 1	16 9 13 - 38	Rutledge	J. Popiel
Indianapolis	0 1 1 - 2	12 5 15 - 32	Park	Leclerc, McDonald (WG 7:20)
Quebec	1 0 2 0 3	5 14 14 7 40	Brodeur	Cloutier 2, Tardif
Toronto	2 0 1 0 3	18 12 7 7 44	Tataryn	Farda, Marrin, Nistico (TG 17:50)
Cleveland	1 2 1 0 4	7 11 8 4 30	Caron	Jarrett 2, Leduc, Pinder
Phoenix	2 1 1 0 4	10 9 10 4 33	Norris	Veneruzzo 2, Hall, Lariviere
Winnipeg	1 2 3 - 6	10 12 17 - 39	Daley	Hull 2, Hedberg 2, Moffat, Sjoberg
New England	1 2 0 - 3	11 13 7 - 31	Abrahamsson	Rogers 2, Pleau
January 31				
Phoenix	0 1 0 - 1	4 7 9 - 20	Kurt	Huston
San Diego	1 2 3 - 6	9 14 9 - 32	Wakely	Adduono, Rivers, Devine, Peacosh, Morrison, Ferguson
Winnipeg	1 1 3 - 5	12 12 14 - 38	Daley	Lindstrom 2, Hornung, Hedberg, Asmundson
Cincinnati	2 0 0 - 2	15 12 9 - 36	Hoganson	Dudley, Campbell
Toronto	1 2 1 - 4	12 14 8 - 34	Vien	Mahovlich 3, Henderson
Quebec	3 2 3 - 8	14 12 14 - 40	Brodeur	Houle 3, Cloutier 3, Sutherland, Roy
Houston	1 0 0 - 1	11 9 10 - 30	Rutledge	Labossiere
Minnesota	1 2 1 - 4	11 12 7 - 30	Garrett	Walton 2, Connelly, Westrum
February 1				
New England	1 0 6 - 7	6 14 14 - 34	Landon	Climie 3, Pleau, Ley, Rogers, Earl
Toronto	1 2 2 - 5	10 7 5 - 22	Tataryn	Napier 2, Kirk 2, Farda
Winnipeg	1 1 0 - 2	8 9 5 - 22	Larsson	Ketola, Sullivan
Indianapolis	0 1 0 - 1	5 22 12 - 39	Park	Thomas
Cincinnati	1 1 0 - 2	12 6 6 - 24	Hoganson	Campbell, Locas
Edmonton	1 2 2 - 5	11 16 7 - 34	Dryden	Patenaude 2, R. Morris, Sheehy, Ullman
Cleveland	3 1 2 - 6	15 7 10 - 32	Johnson	Harrison 2, Gruen, Shmyr, Walker, McDonough
Minnesota	1 0 4 - 5	9 6 21 - 36	Garrett	Antonovich, Busniuk, Walton, Hampson
February 3				
Winnipeg	1 2 1 - 4	11 9 15 - 35	Daley	Moffat, Nilsson, Ketola, Bergman
Quebec	1 3 1 - 5	6 10 11 - 27	Brodeur	Hoganson, Houle, Tardif, Roy, Constantin
New England	0 0 0 - 0	7 10 5 - 22	C. Abrahamsson	▶ Dryden: shutout (1), 22 saves
Edmonton	1 2 1 - 4	7 10 8 - 25	Dryden	Laing, R. Morris, J. Rogers, Patenaude
Cincinnati	1 1 0 - 2	9 9 5 - 23	Hoganson	Myers, D. Sobchuk
Calgary	1 0 2 - 3	10 11 14 - 35	McLeod	Leiter, Deadmarsh, Driscoll (WG 16:29)
Minnesota	0 1 3 - 4	6 7 9 - 22	Garrett	Gambucci, Antonovich, Carlson, Walton
Houston	3 1 4 - 8	23 6 14 - 43	Grahame	Hughes 2, Taylor, Preston, Larway, Mk Howe, Labossiere, G. Howe
February 4				
Minnesota	0 0 1 - 1	8 7 11 - 26	Garrett	Holmgren
San Diego	0 3 1 - 4	9 10 10 - 29	Wakely	Lacroix 3, Peacosh
Cleveland	0 0 1 - 1	5 8 13 - 26	Johnson	Gruen
Phoenix	1 3 1 - 5	13 16 8 - 37	Kurt	Gray, Dean, Connor, Ftorek, Mononen
February 5				
New England	1 2 3 - 6	7 6 11 - 24	Abrahamsson	Rogers 2, Arndt, Climie, Earl, Backstrom
Calgary	2 1 1 - 4	11 7 12 - 30	McLeod	Leiter 2, Morrison, Tannahill
Edmonton	0 1 0 - 1	11 8 7 - 26	Dryden, Worthy	Ullman
Phoenix	1 4 0 - 5	16 14 13 - 43	Norris	Huston 2, Dean, Hall, Boyd
Cleveland	1 1 0 - 2	12 7 8 - 27	Newton	Pinder, Gruen
San Diego	1 1 1 - 3	13 10 7 - 30	Wakely	Rivers, Wall, Noris (WG 11:25)
Quebec	1 1 0 - 2	17 9 9 - 35	Brodeur	Gallant, Tardif
Indianapolis	1 2 1 - 4	8 12 7 - 27	Dion	Karlander 2, Fitchner 2
February 6				
Edmonton	0 0 0 - 0	4 4 6 - 14	Worthy	▶ Hoganson: shutout (2), 14 saves
Cincinnati	0 4 3 - 7	11 19 11 - 41	Hoganson	Locas 2, Larose, Inkpen, D. Sobchuk, Guite, MacNeil
Winnipeg	3 2 2 - 7	12 9 11 - 32	Larsson, Daley	Hedberg 2, Guindon, Sullivan, Nilsson, Hull, Ford (WG 19:05)
Toronto	1 3 2 - 6	7 21 12 - 40	Shaw, Binkley	Simpson 2, Henderson, Nedomansky, Kirk, Napier
Indianapolis	0 3 0 - 3	8 13 12 - 33	Brown, Holmquist	Leclerc, MacDonald, McDonald
Houston	0 3 1 - 4	9 12 14 - 35	Rutledge	Mk Howe, Labossiere, Preston, Hinse (WG 0:18)
February 7				
Quebec	1 3 0 0 4	7 5 6 4 22	Brodeur, Deguise	Cloutier 2, Gallant, S. Bernier
Calgary	1 0 3 0 4	9 7 11 7 34	Wood, McLeod	Leiter, Sentes, Lawson, Tannahill (TG 15:53)
Minnesota	1 1 0 - 2	10 11 9 - 30	Garrett, Levasseur	Connelly, Huck
Phoenix	2 1 1 - 4	13 11 17 - 41	Kurt	Hall 2, Sleep, Ftorek
Cincinnati	0 0 1 - 1	14 11 14 - 39	Hoganson	Myers
Indianapolis	3 1 1 - 5	18 5 7 - 30	Dion	Karlander 3, Stapleton, MacDonald
Toronto	1 2 0 - 3	6 4 6 - 16	Tataryn	Marrin, Henderson, Napier
New England	2 0 5 - 7	17 10 16 - 43	Abrahamsson	Swain, Backstrom, Hangsleben, Borgeson, Rogers, Arndt, Pleau
Winnipeg	1 2 1 0 4	4 10 15 8 37	Daley	Beaudin, Hull, Hedberg, Ketola
Cleveland	2 1 1 0 4	16 6 8 6 36	Newton	Harrison, McDonough, Leduc, MacGregor

1975-1976 Game by Game Line Scores

Date & Teams	Scoring 1 2 3 ot F	Shots 1 2 3 ot F	Goaltenders	Goals & Other Scoring Highlights
February 8				
Quebec	1 2 2 - 5	7 8 9 - 24	Brodeur	Tardif 2, Cloutier, Sutherland, Parizeau
Edmonton	1 2 1 - 4	7 7 10 - 24	Dryden	Patenaude 2, Russell, Ullman
Calgary	3 0 1 - 4	14 2 12 - 28	McLeod	Chipperfield 3, Morrison
Winnipeg	3 4 1 - 8	14 19 4 - 37	Daley	Nilsson 2, Lindh 2, Ketola, Hull, Lindstrom, Guindon
San Diego	1 0 1 - 2	5 6 6 - 17	Wakely, Gillow	Ferguson, Peacosh
Houston	1 2 2 - 5	16 17 12 - 45	Grahame	Hughes, Hinse, Mk Howe, G. Howe, Schella
Minnesota	1 1 1 0 3	14 8 12 6 40	Garrett	Keon, Carlson, Connelly
Phoenix	2 1 0 0 3	13 14 10 4 41	Norris	Gray, Boyd, Huston
Cleveland	3 0 3 - 6	11 9 8 - 28	Johnson	Jarrett 2, Shmyr, MacGregor, Tamminen, Walker
New England	0 0 1 - 1	7 8 9 - 24	Abrahamsson	Backstrom
February 10				
San Diego	0 1 2 - 3	8 11 9 - 28	Gillow	Noris 2, Morenz
Minnesota	2 3 1 - 6	16 12 9 - 37	Garrett	Keon 2, Walton 2, Antonovich, Gambucci
Toronto	0 3 0 - 3	7 11 3 - 21	Vien	Mahovlich, Simpson, Kirk
Calgary	2 1 1 - 4	12 20 8 - 40	McLeod	Lawson 2, Chipperfield, Deadmarsh (WG 10:35)
February 11				
Quebec	2 2 2 - 6	15 6 13 - 34	Brodeur	Cloutier 2, Tardif 2, Serviss, S. Bernier
Winnipeg	1 2 1 - 4	9 14 15 - 38	Daley	Sjoberg, Lindh, Hedberg, Bergman
Cincinnati	0 1 1 - 2	9 12 13 - 34	Hoganson	Dudley, Larose
Cleveland	2 1 1 - 4	8 14 6 - 28	Johnson	Walker 2, Gruen, Ward
Phoenix	1 0 0 - 1	8 15 3 - 26	Kurt	Rautakallio
Indianapolis	1 1 0 - 2	4 7 10 - 21	Dion	Thomas, Stapleton
Minnesota	1 2 1 - 4	6 11 8 - 25	Garrett	Keon 3, Huck
San Diego	0 1 1 - 2	13 7 9 - 29	Wakely	Morrison, Noris
February 12				
Quebec	2 1 1 - 4	9 8 14 - 31	Brodeur	Tardif 2, Houle, Bordeleau
Minnesota	0 5 1 - 6	10 19 12 - 41	Garrett	Antonovich 2, Hampson, Connelly, McKenzie, Huck
Houston	3 1 0 - 4	13 8 8 - 29	Grahame	Mk Howe, Hall, Lund, Hinse
Phoenix	0 0 1 - 1	6 14 12 - 32	Kurt	Hall
February 13				
Calgary	1 0 2 1 4	11 13 10 3 37	McLeod	Sentes 2 (TG 19:21, OT 1:18), Delorenzi, Lawson
Indianapolis	1 2 0 0 3	10 13 6 0 29	Dion	McDonald, Harbaruk, Rochon
Toronto	0 2 1 - 3	8 7 12 - 27	Binkley	Jacques 2, Nedomansky
Edmonton	2 1 2 - 5	11 12 9 - 32	Dryden	Russell 2, R. Morris, Spring, Sheehy
Cincinnati	4 1 0 - 5	15 7 12 - 34	Hoganson	Plumb, Dudley, MacNeil, Campbell, Guite
New England	1 0 0 - 1	21 11 11 - 43	Abrahamsson	Ley
February 14				
Indianapolis	0 2 0 - 2	15 9 4 - 28	Brown	Harbaruk, Maggs
Cincinnati	1 0 2 - 3	7 7 16 - 30	Hoganson	Dudley, Guite, Larose (WG 19:19)
Houston	0 0 1 - 1	7 11 8 - 26	Rutledge	G. Howe
San Diego	1 4 0 - 5	16 15 10 - 41	Wakely	McMahon, Lacroix, Ferguson, Devine, Peacosh
Phoenix	3 1 1 - 5	17 11 10 - 38	Kurt, Norris	Boyd 2, Hall, Ftorek, Veneruzzo
Minnesota	1 0 1 - 2	12 19 15 - 46	Garrett	Gambucci, Huck
February 15				
Toronto	2 1 3 - 6	11 6 14 - 31	Vien	Nistico 2, Kirk, Syvret, Jacques, Mahovlich
Winnipeg	2 2 3 - 7	16 13 12 - 41	Daley	Hedberg 2, Lesuk, Ketola, Lindstrom, Guindon, Sullivan
New England	0 1 2 - 3	7 11 9 - 27	Landon	Swain, Pleau, Charlebois (WG 13:43)
Cleveland	2 0 0 - 2	7 9 7 - 23	Newton	MacGregor, Ward
San Diego	1 1 1 - 3	7 11 9 - 27	Wakely	Hughes, McNamee, French
Indianapolis	1 0 1 - 2	10 9 11 - 30	Dion	Rochon, Fitchner
Quebec	2 1 1 - 4	13 8 4 - 25	Brodeur	S. Bernier 2, Bordeleau, Cloutier
Houston	1 1 0 - 2	11 9 12 - 32	Grahame	Preston, G. Howe
Calgary	1 3 0 0 4	8 14 8 1 31	Humphreys	Leiter 2, Sentes, Chipperfield
Cincinnati	2 0 2 1 5	14 9 30 6 59	Hoganson	MacNeil, Pelyk, D. Sobchuk, G. Sobchuk, Smedsmo (OT 4:42)
Phoenix	0 1 3 - 4	5 9 9 - 23	Norris	Mononen, Ftorek, Migneault, Huston
Edmonton	1 0 1 - 2	16 5 14 - 35	Dryden	Patenaude, Ullman
February 17				
Minnesota	3 2 1 - 6	16 16 13 - 45	Levasseur	Antonovich 2, Busniuk, McKenzie, Walton, Connelly
Toronto	1 1 1 - 3	7 11 9 - 27	Binkley, Vien	Napier, Rollins, Kirk
Winnipeg	0 2 2 0 4	8 12 9 5 34	Larsson	Nilsson 2 (TG 17:48), Sullivan, Hedberg
Edmonton	0 2 0 4	4 4 10 2 20	Dryden	R. Morris, Carleton, Spring
San Diego	0 2 0 - 2	7 10 7 - 24	Wakely, Gillow	Adduono, Devine
Quebec	3 2 0 - 5	17 13 11 - 41	Brodeur	Bordeleau 2, Houle, Tardif, Parizeau
New England	0 0 3 - 3	9 5 12 - 26	Landon	Borgeson, Charlebois, Paiement · (Teams combined for 5
Houston	0 1 3 - 4	10 12 11 - 33	Grahame	G. Howe, Lund, Taylor, Hinse (WG 19:49) · goals in 2:35, 3rd)
February 18				
Calgary	0 0 0 - 0	7 8 10 - 25	McLeod, H'phreys	▶ Johnson: shutout (1), 25 saves
Cleveland	0 1 3 - 4	16 13 13 - 42	Johnson	Ward 2, Walker, Gruen
Phoenix	0 0 3 - 3	15 8 13 - 36	Kurt	Hall, Sleep, Gray
Winnipeg	1 2 1 - 4	8 9 7 - 24	Daley	Ford, Sullivan, Hedberg, Lindstrom
February 19				
New England	0 1 2 - 3	6 9 8 - 23	Landon, Ab'sson	Charlebois, Borgeson, Swain · Leclerc
Indianapolis	3 5 2 - 10	13 13 19 - 45	Dion	McDonald 2, Sicinski 2, Rochon, Proceviat, MacDonald, Thomas, Harris,
Cleveland	3 0 0 - 3	13 9 10 - 32	Newton	Gruen 2, Harrison
Houston	2 3 0 - 5	10 10 5 - 25	Grahame	Hall 2, Larway, Hinse, G. Howe

1975-1976 Game by Game Line Scores

Date & Teams	Scoring 1 2 3 ot F	Shots 1 2 3 ot F	Goaltenders	Goals & Other Scoring Highlights
February 20				
Phoenix	0 1 0 - 1	8 9 9 - 26	Norris	Huston
Cincinnati	0 2 2 - 4	7 10 10 - 27	Hoganson	G. Sobchuk, Smedsmo, Dudley, Plumb
Minnesota	2 1 3 - 6	10 9 8 - 27	Garrett	Holmgren 2, McKenzie 2, Antonovich, Brackenbury
Calgary	2 0 1 - 3	21 7 9 - 37	McLeod	Delorenzi, Driscoll, Chipperfield
Edmonton	0 1 1 - 2	10 9 9 - 28	Dryden	Sheehy, Ullman
Winnipeg	1 2 1 - 4	13 13 16 - 42	Daley	Nilsson, Beaudin, Sullivan, Hull
San Diego	1 4 1 - 6	16 11 19 - 46	Wakely	Ferguson 2, French, Morenz, Devine, Peacosh
Toronto	2 1 1 - 4	15 10 13 - 38	Vien	Napier, Marrin, Nedomansky, Mahovlich
February 21				
Indianapolis	1 0 1 - 2	10 5 17 - 32	Brown	Rochon, Leclerc
Cleveland	0 0 3 - 3	10 7 3 - 20	Johnson	Harrison 2, Maxwell
San Diego	1 0 1 - 2	8 11 10 - 29	Gillow	Peacosh, Morrison
Cincinnati	3 0 0 - 3	12 9 6 - 27	Hoganson	Dudley, Myers, Locas
February 22				
New England	0 0 0 - 0	4 5 8 - 17	Abrahamsson	▸ Brodeur: shutout (2), 17 saves
Quebec	0 2 2 - 4	8 7 11 - 26	Brodeur	Tardif 2, Tremblay, Serviss
Houston	1 0 0 - 1	16 10 11 - 37	Grahame	Mty Howe
Cleveland	0 0 2 - 2	8 18 16 - 42	Newton	Baxter, MacGregor (WG 15:57)
Phoenix	2 2 2 - 6	13 11 10 - 34	Kurt	Ftorek 2, Gray, Boyd, Veneruzzo, Hall (WG 19:09)
Indianapolis	1 1 3 - 5	8 11 14 - 33	Dion, Brown	MacDonald 2, Harris, Thomas, Rochon
Minnesota	1 1 1 - 3	10 3 11 - 24	Garrett	Antonovich, Brackenbury, Holmgren
Edmonton	0 2 2 - 4	14 13 8 - 35	Dryden	Russell, Ullman, Patenaude, Long (WG 17:07)
Toronto	0 1 1 - 2	6 7 8 - 21	Binkley	Nedomansky, Marrin
Calgary	0 1 3 - 4	13 13 20 - 46	McLeod	Lawson, Sentes, Deadmarsh, Hull
February 24				
Houston	0 0 1 - 1	13 8 6 - 27	Grahame	Hinse
Quebec	1 1 2 - 4	12 12 18 - 42	Brodeur	Tardif 2, Cloutier, S. Bernier
Cincinnati	3 5 1 - 9	15 12 17 - 44	Hoganson	Myers 3, D. Sobchuk 2, Beaton, Dudley, G. Sobchuk, Pelyk
Toronto	2 3 1 - 6	18 13 10 - 41	Binkley, Vien	Simpson 3, Marrin 2, Napier
Calgary	1 1 1 0 3	15 13 11 6 45	Wood, McLeod	Lawson, Powis, Hull (TG 16:32)
Edmonton	2 0 1 0 3	12 7 5 3 27	Dryden	R. Morris, B. McAneeley, T. McAneeley
February 25				
New England	0 2 0 - 2	6 17 10 - 33	Abrahamsson	Rogers, Borgeson
Cincinnati	1 2 2 - 5	13 13 7 - 33	Hoganson	Locas 2, D. Sobchuk, G. Sobchuk, Byers
Cleveland	0 0 2 - 2	2 11 11 - 24	Johnson	Gruen, Walker
Winnipeg	2 2 1 - 5	14 8 10 - 32	Daley	Nilsson, Ford, Lindh, Lesuk, Ketola
San Diego	0 0 1 1 2	13 8 5 6 32	Wakely	Peacosh, Ferguson (OT 8:13)
Minnesota	1 0 0 0 1	13 9 6 4 32	Levasseur	Keon
Edmonton	1 0 1 - 2	8 9 8 - 25	Dryden	Russell, Laing
Calgary	0 3 2 - 5	12 8 13 - 33	Turnbull	Tannahill 2, Morrison, Sentes, Deadmarsh
February 26				
Houston	2 1 2 - 5	11 10 8 - 29	Grahame	Labossiere, Hughes, Preston, Hinse, G. Howe
New England	0 0 2 - 2	11 11 14 - 36	Abrahamsson	O'Donnell, Webster
February 27				
Houston	2 2 2 1 7	11 10 11 1 33	Grahame	Mk Howe 3, Hinse 2, Taylor, G. Howe (OT 0:41, 1st OT goal – career)
Toronto	1 4 1 0 6	12 9 6 1 28	Wood	Napier 2, Marrin, Nedomansky, Jacques, Gibbons (Tor: 0-15-2 streak)
San Diego	2 0 1 - 3	9 9 5 - 23	Wakely	French 2, Morrison
Phoenix	0 1 3 - 4	17 11 11 - 39	Norris	Gray, Veneruzzo, Gorman, Boyd (WG 18:18) (3 goals in 3:40 to win)
Cleveland	1 2 1 - 4	7 9 10 - 26	Newton	McDonough, Edur, Ward, MacGregor
Calgary	2 1 2 - 5	18 13 11 - 42	McLeod	Chipperfield, Jodzio, Sentes, Tannahill, Driscoll (WG 12:26)
Edmonton	1 1 1 - 3	10 11 9 - 30	Dryden	Russell, J. Rogers, Ullman
Winnipeg	3 1 0 - 4	14 7 14 - 35	Daley	Green, Hull, Asmundson, Ketola
February 28				
Winnipeg	0 0 3 1 4	9 12 12 3 36	Daley	Lesuk, Sullivan, Ketola, Moffat (OT 1:51)
Quebec	1 0 2 0 3	10 13 13 0 36	Brodeur	S. Bernier, Bordeleau, Houle
Indianapolis	2 0 2 0 4	7 13 9 3 32	Holmquist	Proceviat, Rochon, MacDonald, Leclerc (TG 18:40)
New England	2 2 0 0 4	9 15 9 4 37	Landon	Borgeson 2, O'Donnell, Webster
Houston	1 2 1 - 4	13 9 12 - 34	Rutledge	Taylor, Lund, Mk Howe, Labossiere
Cincinnati	2 0 0 - 2	12 10 9 - 31	Hoganson	D. Sobchuk, G. Sobchuk
February 29	▸ Minnesota folds			
Winnipeg	3 2 2 - 7	15 15 14 - 44	Daley, Larsson	Ketola 2, Bergman, Moffat, Beaudin, Hull, Hedberg
Toronto	4 2 5 - 11	15 15 15 - 45	Wood	Napier 3, Nedomansky 2, Jacques 2, Kirk 2, Nistico, Marrin
Phoenix	2 0 3 - 5	6 5 8 - 19	Kurt	Gray, Hall, Veneruzzo, Connor
Calgary	1 0 1 - 2	7 10 10 - 27	McLeod	Jodzio 2
Cleveland	2 2 1 - 5	5 10 9 - 24	Johnson	Leduc 2, Tamminen, Gruen, Jarrett
Edmonton	1 1 0 - 2	10 10 6 - 26	Dryden, Turnbull	P. Morris, Russell
Indianapolis	1 0 4 - 5	8 18 8 - 34	Park	Harris 2, Coates, Leclerc, Proceviat
Cincinnati	0 0 2 - 2	15 12 9 - 36	Hoganson	Dudley, Larose
March 2				
Indianapolis	1 0 1 - 2	12 7 7 - 26	Park	Thomas, MacDonald
Phoenix	1 2 2 - 5	14 12 12 - 38	Norris	Gray, Erickson, Mononen, Ftorek, Gorman
Edmonton	1 0 2 - 3	8 9 7 - 24	Turnbull	Sheehy 2, R. Morris
Calgary	2 3 1 - 6	17 12 12 - 41	McLeod	Tannahill 2, Chipperfield 2, Lawson, Terbenche
Quebec	0 2 0 - 2	9 23 12 - 44	Brodeur	S. Bernier, Constantin
Toronto	1 3 1 - 5	13 8 9 - 30	Wood	Farda 2, Mahovlich 2, Napier (Mahovlich: 600th career goal)
New England	2 1 1 - 4	4 11 9 - 24	Landon	Swain, Ley, Arndt, Rogers (WG 19:57)
San Diego	0 2 1 - 3	5 10 8 - 23	Wakely	French 2, Rivers

1975-1976 Game by Game Line Scores

Date & Teams	Scoring 1 2 3 ot F	Shots 1 2 3 ot F	Goaltenders	Goals & Other Scoring Highlights
March 3				
Calgary	2 1 1 - 4	10 12 13 - 35	Humphreys	Deadmarsh 2, Chipperfield, Powis
Edmonton	3 0 3 - 6	11 1 13 - 25	Dryden	Sheehy 2, Ullman 2, Patenaude, R. Morris
Cleveland	1 1 1 0 3	8 8 14 0 30	Johnson	Ward 2, Harrison
Cincinnati	1 2 0 1 4	15 11 7 2 35	Hoganson	Locas 2, MacNeil 2 (OT 0:23)
March 4				
Quebec	1 0 0 - 1	7 8 8 - 23	Brodeur, Deguise	Tardif
Calgary	1 3 0 - 4	9 14 8 - 31	McLeod, H'phreys	Jodzio 2, Tannahill, Chipperfield
New England	1 1 0 - 2	5 16 10 - 31	Landon	Webster, Paiement
San Diego	2 3 3 - 8	13 10 10 - 33	Wakely	Noris, Ferguson, French, Peacosh, Rivers, Morrison, Burgess, Adduono
Cincinnati	1 0 0 - 1	6 9 10 - 25	Hoganson	Campbell
Indianapolis	1 2 0 - 3	7 11 6 - 24	Park	McDonald 2, Parizeau
March 5				
Quebec	1 2 1 1 5	11 12 8 2 33	Deguise	Cloutier 2, Roy, Bordeleau (TG 18:07), Tremblay (OT 2:05)
Edmonton	2 1 1 0 4	15 10 12 0 37	Dryden	Patenaude 3, MacGregor
Phoenix	0 3 0 - 3	12 15 8 - 35	Kurt	Hall, Veneruzzo, Niekamp
Houston	1 2 3 - 6	11 11 14 - 36	Grahame	Mk Howe 3 (all in 3rd), Ruskowski, G. Howe, Larway
March 6				
Cleveland	2 1 2 - 5	11 7 10 - 28	Newton	Ward 2, Harrison 2, Leduc
Houston	2 0 2 - 4	6 5 13 - 24	Rutledge	Preston 2, Tonelli 2
Calgary	1 1 0 - 2	11 16 12 - 39	Humphreys	Jodzio, Lukowich
Toronto	1 3 1 - 5	8 11 18 - 37	Wood	Nedomansky, Farda, Turkiewicz, Henderson, Jacques
New England	1 1 3 - 5	7 6 8 - 21	Ab'sson, Landon	Paiement 2, Climie 2, Rogers
Phoenix	2 1 0 - 3	8 10 12 - 30	Norris	Dean, Ftorek, Connor
Indianapolis	1 1 1 - 3	11 10 6 - 27	Park	McDonald, Harbaruk, Baltimore (WG 9:42)
Cincinnati	1 1 0 - 2	8 14 13 - 35	Hoganson	Dudley, MacNeil
March 7				
Quebec	1 1 0 - 2	8 9 12 - 29	Deguise	Cloutier, S. Bernier
Edmonton	0 0 4 - 4	8 3 8 - 19	Dryden	Carleton, Patenaude, R. Morris, Ullman
New England	1 0 2 - 3	10 5 14 - 29	Landon	Climie, O'Donnell, Paiement
Cincinnati	2 1 2 - 5	13 13 12 - 38	Hoganson	Locas, Ball, Pelyk, Dudley, G. Sobchuk
Calgary	1 0 0 - 1	5 9 8 - 22	McLeod	Chipperfield
Winnipeg	2 0 1 - 3	12 9 14 - 35	Daley	Hull, Lindh, Lindstrom
Cleveland	1 1 3 - 5	7 7 11 - 25	Johnson	Ward, Harrison, Evo, Leduc, Jarrett
Indianapolis	0 1 0 - 1	16 17 9 - 42	Park	Thomas
Phoenix	0 0 2 - 2	1 7 19 - 27	Kurt	Gray, Hall
San Diego	4 1 0 - 5	9 7 7 - 23	Wakely	Hughes, Noris, Ferguson, Peacosh, Lacroix
March 9				
San Diego	1 1 0 - 2	9 5 12 - 26	Wakely, Gillow	Devine, Tidey
Houston	2 1 6 - 9	12 14 20 - 46	Grahame	Hughes 2, Tonelli, Mk Howe, Rusk'ski, Labossiere, Larway, Hinse, Hall
Quebec	1 1 2 - 4	8 6 8 - 22	Brodeur	Tardif 2, Bordeleau, Houle
Calgary	3 2 2 - 7	13 6 10 - 29	McLeod	Chipperfield 3, Deadmarsh 2, Kirk, Lawson
Winnipeg	0 3 2 - 5	12 21 15 - 48	Larsson	Lindh 2, Hull, Hedberg, Nilsson
Toronto	0 1 1 - 2	8 13 7 - 28	Garrett	Napier 2
March 10				
Quebec	1 2 0 - 3	12 9 1 - 22	Brodeur	Bordeleau, Tardif, Sutherland Nilsson, Ketola
Winnipeg	2 4 4 - 10	12 16 12 - 40	Daley	Lindh 2, Hedberg, Bergman, Beaudin, Lindstrom, Hull, Sullivan,
Cincinnati	1 0 1 - 2	9 12 11 - 32	Hoganson	Campbell, Ball (Cle: wore black armbands to
Cleveland	0 2 3 - 5	12 16 15 - 43	Johnson, Newton	Pinder 2, Harrison, Gruen, Ward protest owner's plans for team)
Phoenix	1 2 0 - 3	9 12 5 - 26	Norris	Ftorek, Boyd, Hall
New England	0 2 0 - 2	7 11 13 - 31	Landon	Pleau 2
March 11				
Houston	1 0 0 - 1	7 11 14 - 32	Grahame	Mty Howe
San Diego	3 1 0 - 4	14 12 7 - 33	Wakely	Dobek, Morenz, Ferguson, Devine
Edmonton	0 0 0 - 0	4 8 4 - 16	Dryden	▶ McLeod: shutout (1), 16 saves
Calgary	0 2 0 - 2	13 12 11 - 36	McLeod	Jodzio, Kirk
Toronto	1 0 0 - 1	10 10 9 - 29	Wood	Napier
Indianapolis	0 2 1 - 3	8 14 13 - 35	Dion	Harbaruk, Leclerc, Parizeau
March 12				
Phoenix	0 2 3 - 5	6 9 9 - 24	Kurt	Veneruzzo 3, Hall, Migneault
Toronto	0 0 2 - 2	10 7 10 - 27	Garrett	Henderson, Turkiewicz
Quebec	6 2 2 - 10	11 6 8 - 25	Brodeur	Houle 3, Cloutier 3, Constantin, Sutherland, Tremblay, Tardif
Winnipeg	1 5 2 - 8	12 25 12 - 49	Larsson, Daley	Lindstrom 3, Hedberg 2, Lesuk, Sullivan, Green
Indianapolis	5 1 0 - 6	12 12 8 - 32	Dion	Leclerc 2, Bond, Karlander, Proceviat, Thomas
Cincinnati	1 0 2 - 3	9 16 16 - 41	Hoganson, Kiely	Dudley, Pelyk, McKenzie
Cleveland	0 1 1 - 2	5 6 13 - 24	Newton	Edur, Walker
New England	1 5 2 - 8	12 11 11 - 34	Landon	Backstrom 3, Earl, Paiement, Webster, Swain, Rogers
March 13				
New England	2 1 2 - 5	11 6 7 - 24	Landon	Rogers, Paiement, Abrahamsson, Earl, Backstrom
Cincinnati	0 0 1 - 1	8 11 9 - 28	Hoganson, Kiely	McKenzie
Phoenix	2 2 0 - 4	10 16 9 - 35	Norris	Gray, Connor, Lariviere
Indianapolis	1 1 4 - 6	18 12 18 - 48	Dion	Parizeau 2, McDonald, Leclerc, Thomas, Harris
Houston	1 0 2 - 3	11 6 10 - 27	Rutledge	Hinse, Mk Howe, G. Howe (WG 18:07)
San Diego	1 1 0 - 2	9 7 8 - 24	Wakely	Adduono 2

1975-1976 Game by Game Line Scores

Date & Teams	Scoring 1 2 3 ot F	Shots 1 2 3 ot F	Goaltenders	Goals & Other Scoring Highlights
March 14				
Toronto	1 0 2 - 3	6 6 6 - 18	Wood	Nedomansky 3
Quebec	0 1 0 - 1	11 11 6 - 28	Brodeur	Tardif
Edmonton	0 1 1 - 2	8 17 4 - 29	Dryden	B. McAneeley, Spring
Winnipeg	3 0 1 - 4	10 7 4 - 21	Daley	Lindh 2, Nilsson, Hull
Phoenix	0 0 2 1 3	9 17 17 2 45	Kurt	Gorman, Lariviere, Rautakallio (OT 2:49)
Cleveland	0 0 2 0 2	7 4 7 0 18	Johnson	Gruen, Leduc (TG 19:48)
March 16				
New England	0 1 0 - 1	7 4 8 - 19	Landon	Bolduc
Quebec	2 3 0 - 5	11 8 7 - 26	Deguise	Tardif 2, Houle 2, Brackenbury
Calgary	1 2 0 1 4	15 10 7 3 35	McLeod	Chipperfield 2 (OT 8:58), Kirk, Lawson
Edmonton	0 2 1 0 3	6 12 13 6 37	Dryden	Carlson, Carleton, Hamilton (TG 19:48)
Cleveland	0 0 0 - 0	8 11 17 - 36	Newton	▶ Garrett: shutout (3), 36 saves
Toronto	1 2 3 - 6	8 10 14 - 32	Garrett	Napier 2, Nedomansky 2, Henderson, Dorey
March 17				
Houston	3 1 3 - 7	11 10 11 - 32	Grahame	G. Howe 4, Mk Howe, Mty Howe, Lund
Phoenix	1 1 2 - 4	10 10 9 - 29	Norris	Hall 2, Ftorek 2
Toronto	0 1 3 - 4	7 7 9 - 23	Wood	Turkiewicz, Phaneuf, Nistico, Nedomansky
Cincinnati	1 3 1 - 5	20 16 13 - 49	Lapointe	Dudley 3, Byers, McKenzie
Indianapolis	3 1 1 - 5	15 9 7 - 31	Dion	Parizeau 2, Karlander, MacDonald, Maggs
New England	1 0 1 - 2	9 10 8 - 27	Raeder	Pleau, Backstrom
Calgary	0 0 2 - 2	15 9 12 - 36	McLeod	Morrison, Lukowich
Winnipeg	0 1 2 - 3	8 6 8 - 22	Daley	Ketola, Ford, Lindstrom
March 18				
San Diego	2 2 0 0 4	11 11 10 4 36	Wakely	Morrison, Adduono, Lacroix, Rivers
Indianapolis	2 1 1 0 4	14 9 9 8 40	Holmquist	Leclerc, McDonald, Bond, Keon
March 19				
Cincinnati	2 1 2 0 5	11 12 10 0 33	Hoganson	D. Sobchuk 2, MacNeil, G. Sobchuk, Byers
New England	2 2 1 6	15 12 4 3 34	Landon	Backstrom 3 (OT 4:33), Swain, Rogers, Abrahamsson
San Diego	1 1 1 - 3	9 7 6 - 22	Gillow	McNamee, Adduono, Lacroix
Houston	3 4 1 - 8	10 19 15 - 44	Grahame	Mk Howe 3, Preston 2, Ruskowski, Mty Howe, Larway
Quebec	1 1 1 4	14 15 11 3 43	Brodeur	Fitchner 2, Brackenbury, Houle (OT 6:29)
Toronto	1 2 0 0 3	12 11 14 5 42	Garrett	Napier 2, Mahovlich
Winnipeg	0 0 1 - 1	5 9 8 - 22	Daley	Beaudin
Edmonton	0 0 2 - 2	17 15 7 - 39	Dryden	Sheehy, Carleton (WG 15:39)
Cleveland	1 2 2 1 6	9 7 12 1 29	Johnson	Jarrett 3, McDonough, Walker, Leduc (OT 2:20)
Phoenix	2 2 1 0 5	14 14 14 0 42	Kurt	Hall 2, Boyd, Migneault, Ftorek
March 20				
Phoenix	1 1 1 1 4	9 9 6 2 26	Norris	Gray 2 (OT 1:29), Erickson, Hall
San Diego	0 1 2 0 3	10 6 13 0 29	Wakely	Peacosh, Lacroix, Adduono (TG 19:25)
Houston	0 0 1 - 1	9 6 7 - 22	Rutledge	Mk Howe
Cincinnati	1 0 1 - 2	12 8 15 - 35	Hoganson	D. Sobchuk, Inkpen
Indianapolis	0 1 0 0 1	9 16 11 8 44	Dion	MacDonald
New England	1 0 0 0 1	16 10 10 5 41	Landon	Rogers
Toronto	3 0 3 - 6	11 11 13 - 35	Shaw	Nedomansky, Phaneuf, Nistico, Jacques, Atkinson, Henderson
Cleveland	2 3 0 - 5	15 13 9 - 37	Johnson	McDonough, Stewart, Pinder, Legge, Ward (WG 16:10)
Calgary	2 4 2 - 8	11 16 9 - 36	McLeod	Miszuk 2, Morrison, Kirk, Sentes, Chipperfield, Lukowich, Driscoll
Quebec	3 1 3 - 7	12 8 8 - 28	Deguise	Houle 4, Bordeleau 2, Fitchner (WG 18:03)
March 21				
Winnipeg	0 1 1 - 2	17 18 11 - 46	Daley	Hull, Moffat
Toronto	0 2 3 - 5	8 9 17 - 34	Garrett	Nedomansky 2, Henderson, Napier, Mahovlich
Phoenix	0 3 0 - 3	4 12 10 - 26	Kurt	Ftorek, Boyd, Huston
Houston	0 2 2 - 4	17 14 5 - 36	Grahame	Hall, Mty Howe, G. Howe, Hinse (WG 14:22)
Cincinnati	0 0 1 - 1	9 11 10 - 30	Kiely	Campbell (spoiled Newton's shutout at 19:13)
Cleveland	3 1 0 - 4	19 8 11 - 38	Newton	Leduc 2, Gruen, Shmyr
Quebec	3 1 2 - 6	9 12 9 - 30	Brodeur	Houle 2, Fitchner, Cloutier, Hampson, Sutherland
Edmonton	1 0 2 - 3	10 13 6 - 29	Dryden	Patenaude, P. Morris, Carleton
March 23				
Cleveland	0 1 2 - 3	9 13 7 - 29	Newton	Connelly 3
Quebec	0 0 1 - 1	12 5 14 - 31	Brodeur	Brackenbury
Calgary	1 4 0 0 5	13 14 5 0 32	Humphreys	Sentes, Morrison, Jodzio, Lawson, Chipperfield
Toronto	2 1 2 1 6	5 21 16 2 44	Wood	Napier 2, Nedomansky, D'Alvise, Dorey, Marrin (OT 1:32)
Indianapolis	3 0 5 0 8	11 0 11 3 25	Dion, Holmquist	Parizeau 3, Leclerc 2, Keon, Thomas, Maggs
San Diego	3 3 2 0 8	8 14 6 5 33	Wakely	Ferguson 2, French 2, Devine, Noris, Morrison, Tidey
March 24				
Calgary	3 2 2 - 7	15 9 12 - 36	McLeod	Chipperfield 2, Driscoll, Kirk, Sentes, Powis, Lukowich (WG 19:56)
New England	2 4 0 - 6	11 15 7 - 33	Landon	Rogers 2, Paiement 2, Webster 2
Cincinnati	1 3 1 - 5	9 12 9 - 30	Hoganson	Dudley 2, Locas 2, G. Sobchuk
Phoenix	0 2 2 - 4	8 16 10 - 34	Norris	Hall 2, Gray, Ftorek
Houston	1 1 1 - 3	17 14 12 - 43	Grahame	G. Howe, Lund, P. Popiel (WG 10:55)
Cleveland	1 1 0 - 2	12 13 9 - 34	Johnson	Gruen, JA Stewart
Edmonton	0 2 1 - 3	14 8 6 - 28	Dryden	Sheehy 2 (WG 13:55), Russell
Winnipeg	1 0 1 - 2	8 9 15 - 32	Daley	Moffat, Bergman
March 25				
Edmonton	4 0 1 - 5	15 12 8 - 35	Worthy, Dryden	Patenaude 2, Spring, MacGregor, Baird
Quebec	4 3 0 - 7	11 10 10 - 31	Deguise, Brodeur	Tardif 2, Houle, Bordeleau, Fitchner, Hampson, Tremblay
Cincinnati	0 1 0 - 1	9 11 10 - 30	Hoganson, Kiely	Beaton Noris
San Diego	3 1 5 - 9	11 18 14 - 43	Wakely	Ferguson 2, Falkenberg, Morrison, Lacroix, Rivers, Dobek, Peacosh,
Houston	0 1 2 0 3	5 8 15 2 30	Grahame	Mk Howe, Preston, Larway
Indianapolis	1 1 1 1 4	19 2 9 1 31	Dion	Leclerc 2 (OT 5:07), Parizeau, Keon

1975-1976 Game by Game Line Scores

Date & Teams	Scoring 1 2 3 ot F	Shots 1 2 3 ot F	Goaltenders	Goals & Other Scoring Highlights
March 26				
Cincinnati	1 0 0 - 1	16 11 7 - 34	Hoganson	D. Sobchuk
Houston	4 0 1 - 5	15 7 7 - 29	Rutledge	Hall 3, Labossiere 2
Edmonton	0 1 2 - 3	8 10 17 - 35	Dryden	Sheehy, Laing, J. Rogers
Toronto	3 3 1 - 7	18 16 8 - 42	Garrett	Heaver, Folco, D'Alvise, Marrin, Napier, Nedomansky, Simpson
Indianapolis	1 0 2 - 3	8 10 15 - 33	Dion	Leclerc, Parizeau, Thomas
Cleveland	1 0 1 - 2	16 13 11 - 40	Johnson	Connelly, Ward
Calgary	0 1 0 - 1	4 10 9 - 23	Humphreys	Leiter
New England	2 1 1 - 4	12 21 5 - 38	Landon	Backstrom 2, O'Donnell, Rogers
San Diego	1 0 0 - 1	16 6 14 - 36	Wakely	Peacosh
Phoenix	0 2 1 - 3	9 10 18 - 37	Kurt	Mononen, Huston, Rautakallio
March 27				
Calgary	1 2 1 - 4	13 12 11 - 36	McLeod	Tannahill, Lawson, Chipperfield, Jodzio
Quebec	1 2 3 - 6	8 9 14 - 31	Brodeur	Constantin 2, Tardif, Fitchner, Gallant, Houle
Phoenix	0 2 3 - 5	9 10 7 - 26	Norris	Ftorek 2, Gray, Gorman, Veneruzzo
San Diego	0 0 2 - 2	10 7 16 - 33	Wakely	Burgess, Peacosh
March 28				
San Diego	1 0 0 - 1	12 10 11 - 33	Gillow	Adduono
Winnipeg	2 4 0 - 6	13 14 12 - 39	Daley	Hull 2, Bergman, Moffat, Lesuk, Lindstrom
Indianapolis	1 1 1 - 3	11 14 7 - 32	Dion	Karlander 2, McDonald
New England	0 1 0 - 1	8 9 9 - 26	Landon, Raeder	Ley
Phoenix	3 1 0 - 4	11 8 8 - 27	Kurt	Gray 2, Huston, Ftorek
Houston	4 1 2 - 7	7 17 12 - 36	Grahame	Ruskowski 2, Mty Howe, Lund, P. Popiel, Labossiere, Hughes
Calgary	1 1 3 - 5	11 12 16 - 39	McLeod	Lawson 2, Morrison, Terbenche, Kirk
Toronto	0 3 1 - 4	9 10 12 - 31	Wood	Henderson 2, Marrin, Rollins
March 30				
Edmonton	1 1 1 - 3	10 6 9 - 25	Dryden, Worthy	Baird, Spring, B. McAneeley
Quebec	5 2 1 - 8	17 13 10 - 40	Brodeur, Donnelly	Cloutier 2, Bordeleau 2, Fortier, Houle, Tardif, Sutherland
Toronto	0 2 0 - 2	9 13 11 - 33	Garrett	Napier, Nedomansky
Calgary	2 0 4 - 6	16 7 15 - 38	McLeod	Lukowich, Tannahill, Chipperfield, Haas, Leiter, Jodzio
San Diego	3 0 1 - 4	11 12 9 - 32	Wakely	Ferguson, Falkenberg, Lacroix, Devine (WG 14:54)
Houston	0 1 2 - 3	11 10 13 - 34	Grahame	Labossiere, Mk Howe, G. Howe
March 31				
Phoenix	4 2 1 - 7	13 6 9 - 28	Norris	Erickson, Boyd, Veneruzzo, Ftorek, Mononen, Gorman, Hall
Cincinnati	0 1 1 - 2	9 13 10 - 32	Hoganson, Kiely	Locas, Dudley
New England	1 0 0 - 1	16 11 7 - 34	Landon	O'Donnell
Cleveland	1 3 1 - 5	14 19 5 - 38	Newton	Jarrett 2, Pinder 2, Ward
Toronto	1 1 1 - 3	12 7 3 - 22	Wood	Jacques, Napier, Phaneuf
Winnipeg	2 1 2 - 5	11 10 13 - 34	Daley	Hull 3, Moffat, Lindstrom
April 1				
Edmonton	0 0 2 - 2	9 5 7 - 21	Dryden	B. McAneeley, Patenaude
Quebec	2 1 4 - 7	16 11 12 - 39	Brodeur, Donnelly	Prentice, Roy, Tremblay, Fitchner, Constantin, Cloutier, Houle
Houston	0 3 1 - 4	14 11 7 - 32	Rutledge, Grahame	G. Howe 2, Labossiere, Mty Howe
Indianapolis	1 0 0 - 1	15 13 19 - 47	Dion, Park	Parizeau
April 2				
Cleveland	1 1 0 - 2	10 10 8 - 28	Johnson	Connelly, McKay
Cincinnati	1 3 1 - 5	12 16 8 - 36	Hoganson	D. Sobchuk 3, Steele, Plumb
Winnipeg	1 0 0 - 1	10 4 6 - 20	Larsson	Asmundson
Calgary	3 1 0 - 4	11 13 3 - 27	Humphreys	Kirk, Driscoll, Deadmarsh, Lawson
Indianapolis	1 1 1 - 3	17 11 10 - 38	Park	McDonald 2, Harbaruk
Toronto	0 1 0 - 1	9 17 5 - 31	Garrett	Mahovlich
April 3				
Houston	2 5 1 - 8	14 23 11 - 48	Grahame	Larway 2, Hughes 2, Mk Howe 2, Labossiere, Tonelli
Phoenix	2 0 0 - 2	11 12 9 - 32	Norris, Hebenton	Erickson, Huston
New England	1 2 2 - 5	7 13 9 - 29	Landon	Pleau, Borgeson, Webster, Bolduc
Indianapolis	0 2 0 - 2	9 6 4 - 19	Dion	Maggs, Harris
Toronto	0 1 0 - 1	12 9 11 - 32	Wood	Napier
Quebec	2 1 2 - 5	8 12 6 - 26	Brodeur, Deguise	Prentice, Tardif, Tremblay, Constantin, Hampson
San Diego	0 2 0 - 2	18 12 9 - 39	Gillow	French, Lacroix
Cleveland	1 0 3 - 4	9 11 16 - 36	Newton	Gruen 2, McKay, Harrison
April 4				
Quebec	2 1 1 1 5	6 13 14 2 35	Deguise	Brackenbury, Sutherland, J. Bernier, S. Bernier, Tardif (OT 4:25)
Toronto	2 1 1 0 4	15 8 14 2 39	Garrett	Mahovlich, Jacques, Marrin, Simpson
San Diego	1 0 1 - 2	12 3 9 - 24	Gillow	Ferguson, Dobek
Houston	2 0 3 - 5	11 14 9 - 34	Grahame	Hughes, Preston, Tonelli, Labossiere, Larway
Indianapolis	2 1 1 - 4	8 15 13 - 36	Park	MacDonald, Maggs, Parizeau, Harbaruk
New England	0 2 0 - 2	7 12 10 - 29	Landon	Webster, Fotiu
Cincinnati	3 0 0 - 3	15 9 11 - 35	Hoganson	Dudley, Steele, D. Sobchuk
Cleveland	2 2 2 - 6	10 13 12 - 35	Johnson	Harrison 2, Gruen, Jarrett, Leduc, Pinder
Winnipeg	1 1 0 - 2	10 11 2 - 23	Larsson	Asmundson, Hull
Edmonton	1 3 1 - 5	14 10 12 - 36	Dryden	R. Morris, Hurley, Sheehy, P. Morris, Laing
April 6				
Toronto	2 2 2 - 6	12 9 8 - 29	Wood	Nedomansky 2, Henderson, Simpson, Turkiewicz, Phaneuf
Quebec	1 4 5 - 10	9 15 12 - 36	Deguise, Donnelly	Cloutier 4, Houle, Tardif, Bordeleau, Constantin, S. Bernier, Hampson
Phoenix	3 1 1 - 5	11 8 8 - 27	Hebenton	Gray 2, Hall, Lariviere, Connor
Houston	3 2 3 - 8	15 13 9 - 37	Grahame	Preston 3, Ruskowski 2, Hinse, Mk Howe, G. Howe
San Diego	0 2 0 1 3	7 10 1 3 21	Wakely	Lacroix, Devine, Adduono (OT 7:49)
Cleveland	1 0 1 0 2	19 16 20 4 59	Newton	Harrison, Leduc
Winnipeg	1 2 2 - 5	13 9 4 - 26	Daley	Hull 3, Moffat 2
Calgary	1 1 1 - 3	10 12 3 - 25	McLeod	Chipperfield 2, Powis

End of Regular Season

247

1976 Playoffs Game by Game Line Scores

Date & Teams	Scoring 1 2 3 ot F	Shots 1 2 3 ot F	Goaltenders	Goals & Other Scoring Highlights
April 9				
San Diego	1 1 0 0 2	10 9 6 0 25	Wakely	Rivers, Falkenberg
Phoenix	2 0 0 1 3	9 7 12 1 29	Norris	Veneruzzo, Beaudoin, Hall (OT 0:31)
Edmonton	1 1 1 - 3	7 6 8 - 21	Dryden	Russell, Baird, Sheehy
Winnipeg	3 2 2 - 7	18 13 17 - 48	Daley	Hull, Guindon, Lindh, Ketola, Bergman, Beaudin, Sullivan
Cleveland	1 1 1 - 3	10 10 11 - 31	Johnson	Leduc, Connelly, Gruen
New England	3 1 1 - 5	10 16 7 - 33	Landon	Backstrom, G. Roberts, Fotiu, Pleau, Rogers
April 10				
Calgary	1 1 1 - 3	9 5 10 - 24	McLeod	Evans 2, Chipperfield
Quebec	0 0 1 - 1	10 7 11 - 28	Brodeur	Cloutier
Phoenix	1 0 1 - 2	7 13 4 - 24	Norris	Boyd 2
San Diego	1 1 2 - 4	9 12 16 - 37	Wakely	French, Noris, Ferguson, Lacroix
New England	1 2 3 - 6	13 9 18 - 40	Landon	Pleau, O'Donnell, Webster, Selwood, Rogers
Cleveland	1 0 0 - 1	11 11 8 - 30	Newton	Leduc
April 11				
Calgary	2 0 6 - 8	8 8 13 - 29	McLeod	Morrison 2, Kirk 2, Tannahill, Lukowich, Chipperfield, Powis
Quebec	2 2 0 - 4	8 8 9 - 25	Brodeur	S. Bernier 2, Tardif, Fitchner
Edmonton	1 2 1 0 4	10 11 3 0 24	Dryden	Spring, Patenaude, Baird, Sheehy (TG 18:10)
Winnipeg	1 2 1 1 5	24 16 21 1 62	Daley, Larsson	Nilsson 2 (OT 0:54), Moffat, Hull, Lindstrom
New England	0 1 2 - 3	12 11 13 - 36	Landon	McManama, Backstrom, Rogers (WG 16:38)
Cleveland	2 0 0 - 2	16 9 10 - 35	Johnson	Gruen, McDonough
April 13				
San Diego	4 0 0 - 4	10 6 8 - 24	Wakely	Hughes, Peacosh, Adduono, French
Phoenix	1 4 1 - 6	16 14 10 - 40	Norris	Hall, Boyd, Ftorek, Veneruzzo, Huston, Mononen
April 14				
Winnipeg	2 0 1 - 3	10 10 9 - 29	Larsson	Hedberg, Sullivan, Hull (WG 10:22)
Edmonton	0 2 0 - 2	12 12 5 - 29	Dryden	B. McAneeley, Baird
Quebec	0 1 1 - 2	5 8 7 - 20	Brodeur	Cloutier, Hoganson
Calgary	1 1 1 - 3	14 9 4 - 27	McLeod	Powis 2, Lukowich
April 15				
Phoenix	0 0 1 - 1	3 7 11 - 21	Norris	Connor
San Diego	2 1 2 - 5	11 15 7 - 33	Wakely	Devine, Morenz, Lacroix, Tidey, Wall
April 16				
Winnipeg	1 5 1 - 7	13 14 11 - 38	Daley	Hull 2, Ketola, Lesuk, Lindh, Beaudin, Asmundson
Edmonton	1 1 0 - 2	5 13 2 - 20	Worthy	Carleton, Ullman
Quebec	0 4 0 - 4	8 12 5 - 25	Brodeur	Cloutier 2, Houle 2
Calgary	1 0 2 - 3	8 9 12 - 29	McLeod	Chipperfield, Kirk, Lawson
New England	1 1 2 - 4	15 7 10 - 32	Landon	Pleau, Paiement, D. Roberts, Backstrom
Indianapolis	1 0 0 - 1	8 8 8 - 24	Dion	Parizeau
April 17				
San Diego	1 1 0 - 2	9 11 3 - 23	Wakely	Tidey, Ferguson (No penalties were
Phoenix	0 1 0 - 1	10 10 10 - 30	Gray	called during the game)
New England	0 0 0 - 0	11 6 12 - 29	Raeder	▸ Park: shutout (1), 29 saves
Indianapolis	2 1 1 - 4	11 6 8 - 25	Park	Bond, Parizeau, Harris, Leclerc
April 18				
Calgary	2 1 3 - 6	11 6 11 - 28	McLeod	Evans 2, Driscoll, Morrison, Lukowich, Lawson
Quebec	0 3 1 - 4	13 15 13 - 41	Brodeur	Sutherland 2, Bordeleau, Roy
April 21				
San Diego	2 2 2 - 6	6 7 14 - 27	Wakely, Gillow	French 2, Lacroix, Morenz, Adduono, Rivers
Houston	6 2 0 - 8	14 6 19 - 39	Grahame	Preston 3, Ruskowski 2, Labossiere 2, Hughes
Indianapolis	0 0 0 - 0	9 5 8 - 22	Dion	▸ Raeder: shuout (1), 22 saves
New England	1 1 1 - 3	10 14 10 - 34	Raeder	Hangsleben 2, Swain
April 23				
San Diego	0 0 1 - 1	10 8 8 - 26	Wakely	Lacroix (spoiled Grahame's shutout at 17:21)
Houston	0 2 1 - 3	8 8 11 - 27	Grahame	Tonelli, Hughes, G. Howe
Indianapolis	0 0 1 - 1	9 14 10 - 33	Dion	Harris
New England	0 1 1 - 2	8 16 15 - 39	Raeder	Pleau, Rogers (WG 19:03)
Calgary	0 0 1 - 1	4 8 5 - 17	McLeod, H'phreys	Evans
Winnipeg	3 3 0 - 6	9 11 9 - 29	Daley	Lindstrom, Nilsson, Sullivan, Hull, Guindon, Ketola
April 24				
New England	0 0 0 - 0	13 5 12 - 30	Raeder	▸ Park: shutout (2), 30 saves
Indianapolis	1 2 1 - 4	14 11 9 - 34	Park	Parizeau 2, Thomas, Keon
April 25				
Houston	1 4 3 - 8	10 12 12 - 34	Grahame	Larway 3, Tonelli 2, Mty Howe, Schella, G. Howe
San Diego	1 2 1 - 4	10 10 12 - 32	Wakely	Tidey, Morrison, Adduono, Noris
Calgary	1 1 0 - 2	10 7 5 - 22	McLeod	Chipperfield, Miller
Winnipeg	2 0 1 - 3	15 15 15 - 45	Daley	Hull 2, Hedberg (WG 1:32)
April 27				
Houston	1 0 1 - 2	10 15 11 - 36	Grahame	Larway, Tonelli
San Diego	0 1 2 - 3	21 8 10 - 39	Wakely	Rivers, Dobek, Devine
Indianapolis	0 4 1 - 5	10 12 9 - 31	Park	Harbaruk 2, Maggs, Leclerc, Keon
New England	0 1 2 - 3	7 15 15 - 37	Raeder	Webster, Fotiu, McManama
April 28				
Houston	0 1 1 - 2	14 7 7 - 28	Grahame	Tonelli, G. Howe
San Diego	1 2 0 - 3	7 8 12 - 27	Wakely	Adduono, Peacosh, Devine
Winnipeg	1 1 4 - 6	10 12 13 - 35	Daley	Hedberg 2, Hull, Nilsson, Ketola, Lesuk
Calgary	0 3 0 - 3	6 17 9 - 32	McLeod	Powis (4:08), Tannahill (4:11, fastest 2 goals, WHA record), Driscoll

248

1976 Playoffs Game by Game Line Scores

Date & Teams	Scoring 1 2 3 ot F	Shots 1 2 3 ot F	Goaltenders	Goals & Other Scoring Highlights
April 29				
New England	1 3 2 - 6	10 9 10 - 29	Raeder	Bolduc, Webster, O'Donnell, Swain, Paiement, Backstrom
Indianapolis	0 0 0 - 0	7 11 8 - 26	Park	▸ Raeder: shutout (2), 26 saves
April 30				
Houston	1 1 1 - 3	7 10 6 - 23	Rutledge	Hughes, Preston, Hall
San Diego	0 0 2 - 2	12 17 14 - 43	Wakely	Burgess, Rivers
Winnipeg	1 1 1 - 3	11 7 13 - 31	Daley	Hedberg, Nilsson, Bergman
Calgary	3 2 2 - 7	11 8 7 - 26	McLeod	Lawson 2, Leiter 2, Kirk, Powis, Chipperfield
May 2				
Calgary	0 0 0 - 0	6 7 4 - 17	McLeod	▸ Daley: shutout (1), 17 saves
Winnipeg	0 1 3 - 4	13 10 8 - 31	Daley	Hedberg 2, Lindstrom, Asmundson
May 5				
New England	0 3 1 - 4	5 10 3 - 18	Raeder	Webster 3, Paiement
Houston	0 2 0 - 2	9 10 11 - 30	Grahame	Mty Howe, Lund
May 7				
New England	1 0 1 - 2	6 6 9 - 21	Raeder, Cooley	Abrahamsson, McManama
Houston	0 4 1 - 5	10 12 10 - 32	Rutledge	Ruskowski, Tonelli, Taylor, Mk Howe, Hinse
May 9				
Houston	0 0 1 - 1	9 7 14 - 30	Rutledge	Mk Howe (spoiled Raeder's shutout at 16:20)
New England	2 1 1 - 4	16 10 8 - 34	Raeder	Paiement, Borgeson, Abrahamsson, McManama
May 11				
Houston	3 1 0 - 4	11 6 8 - 25	Grahame	P. Popiel 2, J. Popiel, Ruskowski
New England	0 1 2 - 3	8 15 12 - 35	Raeder	Selwood, Webster, G. Roberts
May 13				
New England	1 0 1 - 2	10 7 10 - 27	Raeder, Ab'sson	Webster, Ley
Houston	0 2 2 - 4	15 16 14 - 45	Grahame	Tonelli, Hughes, Ruskowski, Hinse
May 15				
Houston	0 0 1 - 1	9 13 18 - 40	Grahame, Rutledge	Larway
New England	1 3 2 - 6	11 10 7 - 28	Raeder	Webster 2, Rogers, Fotiu, Backstrom, Swain
May 16				
New England	0 0 0 - 0	9 5 7 - 21	Raeder	▸ Grahame: shutout (1), 21 saves
Houston	1 0 1 - 2	10 16 11 - 37	Grahame	P. Popiel, Mk Howe
May 20				
Winnipeg	2 1 1 - 4	9 11 9 - 29	Daley	Hedberg 2, Moffat, Hull (WG 16:43)
Houston	2 0 1 - 3	11 7 11 - 29	Grahame	Mk Howe 2, Hughes
May 23				
Winnipeg	1 2 2 - 5	8 9 9 - 26	Daley	Hedberg, Lindstrom, Asmundson, Bergman, Hull (WG 18:06)
Houston	0 2 2 - 4	8 11 13 - 32	Grahame	Mty Howe 2, G. Howe, Ruskowski
May 25				
Houston	1 1 1 - 3	7 4 7 - 18	Grahame	Larway 2, Mk Howe
Winnipeg	4 1 1 - 6	13 7 5 - 25	Daley	Nilsson 3, Ketola, Hedberg, Sullivan
May 27				
Houston	1 0 0 - 1	7 5 5 - 17	Grahame	Taylor
Winnipeg	3 4 2 - 9	12 12 9 - 33	Daley	Ketola 2, Hedberg 2, Sullivan 2, Hull, Moffat, Guindon

Winnipeg is League Champion

Don McLeod Almost Scores a Goal

Don McLeod was known for his stickhandling and passing ability, resulting in numerous assists for the goaltender. Over his six years in the WHA, McLeod collected 43 assists, including 13 during 1975-76. However, he almost became the first major-league goaltender to score a goal. In a game against Edmonton on March 2, 1976, Oilers' goaltender Frank Turnbull was skating out of his crease, the Oilers planning for an extra attacker. McLeod collected the loose puck and heaved it on target. Turnbull realized his defenders could not reach it in time, so he bolted back for the crease, and made a diving stick safe to knock the puck aside, saving the goal, but denying McLeod immediate fame in the process.

1975-1976 CALGARY COWBOYS

**Coach
Joe Crozier**

Summary of Games (@ Away, * Overtime)

	date		opponent	score		record	pts	gf-ga
1.	Oct 12		Minnesota	0-2	L	0-1-0	0	0-2
2.	Oct 14		Indianapolis	5-3	W	1-1-0	2	5-5
3.	Oct 17		Cincinnati	2-6	L	1-2-0	2	7-11
4.	Oct 22		Denver	1-2	L	1-3-0	2	8-13
5.	Oct 24		Phoenix	3-4	L	1-4-0	2	11-17
6.	Oct 26	@	New England	1-3	L	1-5-0	2	12-20
7.	Oct 29	@	Cleveland	3-1	W	2-5-0	4	15-21
8.	Oct 30	@	Indianapolis	7-5	W	3-5-0	6	22-26
9.	Nov 1	@	Cincinnati	2-3	L	3-6-0	6	24-29
10.	Nov 2		New England	*4-3	W	4-6-0	8	28-32
11.	Nov 4		San Diego	4-4	T	4-6-1	9	32-36
12.	Nov 5		Quebec	4-2	W	5-6-1	11	36-38
13.	Nov 7		Cleveland	5-2	W	6-6-1	13	41-40
14.	Nov 11		Edmonton	6-3	W	7-6-1	15	47-43
15.	Nov 13		Winnipeg	2-4	L	7-7-1	15	49-47
16.	Nov 16		Houston	5-3	W	8-7-1	17	54-50
17.	Nov 18		San Diego	2-6	L	8-8-1	17	56-56
18.	Nov 21	@	Denver	6-2	W	9-8-1	19	62-58
19.	Nov 22	@	Minnesota	6-4	W	10-8-1	21	68-62
20.	Nov 27	@	Phoenix	5-1	W	11-8-1	23	73-63
21.	Nov 29	@	San Diego	5-4	W	12-8-1	25	78-67
22.	Nov 30	@	Edmonton	2-4	L	12-9-1	25	80-71
23.	Dec 3		Toronto	3-4	L	12-10-1	25	83-75
24.	Dec 5		Edmonton	8-3	W	13-10-1	27	91-78
25.	Dec 7	@	Edmonton	5-4	W	14-10-1	29	96-82
26.	Dec 9		Quebec	4-1	W	15-10-1	31	100-83
27.	Dec 11		Edmonton	2-3	L	15-11-1	31	102-86
28.	Dec 12	@	Winnipeg	2-4	L	15-12-1	31	104-90
29.	Dec 14	@	Toronto	3-3	T	15-12-2	32	107-93
30.	Dec 16	@	Quebec	3-7	L	15-13-2	32	110-100
31.	Dec 19	@	Toronto	5-3	W	16-13-2	34	115-103
32.	Dec 20	@	Quebec	7-8	L	16-14-2	34	122-111
33.	Dec 23		Toronto	10-1	W	17-14-2	36	132-112
34.	Dec 26	@	Winnipeg	5-4	W	18-14-2	38	137-116
35.	Dec 28		Winnipeg	6-4	W	19-14-2	40	143-120
36.	Jan 1		Edmonton	5-1	W	20-14-2	42	148-121
37.	Jan 2	@	Edmonton	3-1	W	21-14-2	44	151-122
38.	Jan 3		Winnipeg	3-6	L	21-15-2	44	154-128
39.	Jan 6		Winnipeg	5-0	W	22-15-2	46	159-128
40.	Jan 7		Indianapolis	3-1	W	23-15-2	48	162-129
41.	Jan 15	@	Quebec	3-5	L	23-16-2	48	165-134
42.	Jan 17		Houston	4-2	W	24-16-2	50	169-136
43.	Jan 20	@	Edmonton	10-3	W	25-16-2	52	179-139
44.	Jan 21	@	Winnipeg	1-4	L	25-17-2	52	180-143
45.	Jan 23	@	Houston	0-2	L	25-18-2	52	180-145
46.	Jan 25	@	Houston	3-5	L	25-19-2	52	183-150
47.	Jan 28	@	Phoenix	0-5	L	25-20-2	52	183-155
48.	Jan 29	@	San Diego	0-1	L	25-21-2	52	183-156
49.	Feb 3		Cincinnati	3-2	W	26-21-2	54	186-158
50.	Feb 5		New England	4-6	L	26-22-2	54	190-164
51.	Feb 7		Quebec	4-4	T	26-22-3	55	194-168
52.	Feb 8	@	Winnipeg	4-8	L	26-23-3	55	198-176
53.	Feb 10		Toronto	4-3	W	27-23-3	57	202-179
54.	Feb 13	@	Indianapolis	*4-3	W	28-23-3	59	206-182
55.	Feb 15	@	Cincinnati	*4-5	L	28-24-3	59	210-187
56.	Feb 18	@	Cleveland	0-4	L	28-25-3	59	210-191
57.	Feb 20		Minnesota	3-6	L	28-26-3	59	213-197
58.	Feb 22		Toronto	4-2	W	29-26-3	61	217-199
59.	Feb 24	@	Edmonton	3-3	T	29-26-4	62	220-202
60.	Feb 25		Edmonton	5-2	W	30-26-4	64	225-204
61.	Feb 27		Cleveland	5-4	W	31-26-4	66	230-208
62.	Feb 29		Phoenix	2-5	L	31-27-4	66	232-213
63.	Mar 2		Edmonton	6-3	W	32-27-4	68	238-216
64.	Mar 3	@	Edmonton	4-6	L	32-28-4	68	242-222
65.	Mar 4		Quebec	4-1	W	33-28-4	70	246-223
66.	Mar 6	@	Toronto	2-5	L	33-29-4	70	248-228
67.	Mar 7	@	Winnipeg	1-3	L	33-30-4	70	249-231
68.	Mar 9		Quebec	7-4	W	34-30-4	72	256-235
69.	Mar 11		Edmonton	2-0	W	35-30-4	74	258-235
70.	Mar 16	@	Edmonton	*4-3	W	36-30-4	76	262-238
71.	Mar 17	@	Winnipeg	2-3	L	36-31-4	76	264-241
72.	Mar 20	@	Quebec	8-7	W	37-31-4	78	272-248
73.	Mar 23	@	Toronto	5-6	L	37-32-4	78	277-254
74.	Mar 24	@	New England	7-6	W	38-32-4	80	284-260
75.	Mar 26	@	New England	1-4	L	38-33-4	80	285-264
76.	Mar 27	@	Quebec	4-6	L	38-34-4	80	289-270
77.	Mar 28	@	Toronto	5-4	W	39-34-4	82	294-274
78.	Mar 30		Toronto	6-2	W	40-34-4	84	300-276
79.	Apr 2		Winnipeg	4-1	W	41-34-4	86	304-277
80.	Apr 6		Winnipeg	3-5	L	41-35-4	86	307-282

250

Cowboys Stars of 1975-1976

Don McLeod
30 wins, 13 assists

Butch Deadmarsh
26 goals, 196 minutes

Ron Chipperfield
42 goals, +13

John Miszuk
+31 rating

Danny Lawson
44 goals, 96 points

Chris Evans
+12 rating

Scoring

pos	#	player	gp	g	a	pts	pim	+/-	ppg	shg	sog	sc%	gp	g	a	pts	pim	+/-
D		Bilodeau, Yvon	4	0	0	0	2	-4	0	0	2	0.000	-	-	-	-	-	-
C	10	Caffery, Terry	21	5	13	18	4	+3	1	0	38	0.132	-	-	-	-	-	-
C	7	Chipperfield, Ron	75	42	41	83	32	+13	19	0	228	0.184	10	5	4	9	6	+2
LW	15	Deadmarsh, Butch	79	26	28	54	196	+5	5	2	215	0.122	8	0	1	1	14	-1
RW	19	Delorenzi, Ray	39	8	12	20	4	+7	0	1	56	0.143	-	-	-	-	-	-
D		Desjardine, Ken	1	0	0	0	0	0	0	0	0	-	-	-	-	-	-	-
LW	24	Driscoll, Peter	75	16	18	34	127	+12	2	0	118	0.136	10	2	5	7	41	-1
D	4	Evans, Chris	75	3	20	23	50	+12	1	0	146	0.021	10	5	5	10	4	-2
LW		Gilmour, Dave	1	0	0	0	0	-2	0	0	0	-	-	-	-	-	-	-
LW	17	Gratton, Bill	6	0	1	1	2	-2	0	0	4	0.000	-	-	-	-	-	-
LW	14/25	Haas, Derek	30	5	9	14	6	+5	0	0	34	0.147	1	0	0	0	0	0
C	18	Harris, Hugh	30	5	9	14	19	-7	0	0	66	0.076	-	-	-	-	-	-
D	3	Howell, Harry	31	0	3	3	6	+4	0	0	26	0.000	2	0	0	0	2	+1
LW	17	Hull, Steve	58	11	15	26	6	-2	0	0	81	0.136	-	-	-	-	-	-
G	0	Humphreys, Ed	8	0	0	0	0		0	0	0	-	1	0	0	0	0	-
LW	12	Israelson, Larry	57	10	22	32	26	+10	1	0	69	0.145	3	0	0	0	0	-2
LW	16/18	Jodzio, Rick	47	10	7	17	137	+5	0	0	44	0.227	2	0	0	0	14	+1
C	20	Keogan, Murray	38	7	11	18	19		0	0	61	0.115	-	-	-	-	-	-
C	20	Kirk, Gavin	15	7	8	15	14	+8	1	0	37	0.189	10	4	6	10	19	+3
D	6	Lacombe, Francois	71	3	28	31	62	+11	1	0	100	0.030	8	0	0	0	2	0
RW	11	Lawson, Danny	80	44	52	96	46	+13	7	4	381	0.115	9	4	4	8	19	-3
C	16	Leiter, Bob	51	17	17	34	8	+6	6	0	94	0.181	3	2	0	2	0	0
RW	22	Lukowich, Bernie	15	5	2	7	18	-5	0	0	24	0.208	10	4	3	7	8	+1
D		McCrimmon, Jim	5	0	0	0	2	+1	0	0	0	-	-	-	-	-	-	-
G	1	McLeod, Don	63	0	13	13	4		0	0	6	0.000	10	0	1	1	4	-
C	10	Mercredi, Victor	3	0	0	0	29	0	0	0	1	0.000	-	-	-	-	-	-
RW	17	Miller, Warren	3	0	0	0	0	0	0	0	4	0.000	10	1	0	1	28	-1
D	23	Miszuk, John	69	2	21	23	66	+31	0	0	77	0.026	10	0	1	1	10	-4
LW	9	Morrison, George	79	25	32	57	13	+5	7	1	145	0.172	10	3	2	5	0	2
D	22	Olds, Wally	28	0	5	5	6	+4	0	0	17	0.000	9	0	2	2	4	0
C	10	Powis, Lynn	21	4	10	14	2	+2	0	1	63	0.063	10	5	4	9	12	+1
D	3	Reed, Bill	29	0	5	5	14	+3	0	0	29	0.000	-	-	-	-	-	-
D	2	Rupp, Duane	42	0	16	16	33	-6	0	0	61	0.000	7	0	2	2	8	+2
RW	8	Sentes, Dick	72	25	24	49	33	+9	7	0	139	0.180	8	0	1	1	8	+1
LW	5	Tannahill, Don	78	25	24	49	10	+6	1	5	174	0.144	10	2	5	7	8	-2
D	21	Terbenche, Paul	58	2	4	6	22	-3	0	1	58	0.034	10	0	6	6	6	-2
C	10	Walton, Rob	2	0	0	0	0	0	0	0	1	0.000	-	-	-	-	-	-
D	19	Westrum, Pat	9	0	2	2	23	+2	0	0	8	0.000	6	0	1	1	19	+1
G	30	Wood, Wayne	19	0	0	0	4		0	0	0	-	-	-	-	-	-	-

Power Play: 59 goals scored in 271 opportunities (21.8%) with 13 short-handed goals allowed.
Penalty Killing: 70 goals allowed in 297 opportunities (76.4%) with 15 short-handed goals scored.

Goaltending

goaltender	gp	min	ga	en	so	record	gaa	sog	sv%	gp	min	ga	record	gaa
Humphreys, Ed	8	441	27	2	0	2-5-0	3.67	255	0.894	1	20	0	0-0	0.00
McLeod, Don	63	3534	206	2	1	30-27-3	3.50	1600	0.871	10	579	37	5-5	3.83
Wood, Wayne	19	880	45	0	1	9-3-1	3.07	415	0.892	-	-	-	-	-

Transactions: Dick Sentes acquired from San Diego for rights to Joe Noris, Aug 1975 • Rights to Chris Evans purchased from New England, Aug 1975 • George Morrison, Don Tannahill, Joe Micheletti and Wally Olds acquired from Minnesota for John McKenzie and cash, Sep 1975 • Terry Caffery acquired from New England for future considerations, Oct 1975 • Keith McCreary and Vic Mercredi acquired from Atlanta (NHL) for Claude St. Sauveur, Oct 1975. McCreary announced retirement immediately, Mercredi left team after third game and was subsequently released • Murray Keogan purchased from Phoenix, Oct 1975 • Hugh Harris traded to Indianapolis for future considerations, Jan 1976 • Harry Howell signed to contract, Jan 1976 • Wayne Wood traded to Toronto for Gavin Kirk, Mar 1976 • Pat Westrum signed as free agent from defunct Minnesota, Mar 1976

1975-1976 CINCINNATI STINGERS

**Coach
Terry Slater**

Summary of Games (@ Away, * Overtime)

	date	opponent	score		record	pts	gf-ga		date	opponent	score		record	pts	gf-ga
1.	Oct 11 @	Cleveland	1-0	W	1-0-0	2	1-0	41.	Jan 11	Minnesota	4-7	L	18-22-1	37	155-186
2.	Oct 17 @	Calgary	6-2	W	2-0-0	4	7-2	42.	Jan 15 @	New England	2-5	L	18-23-1	37	157-191
3.	Oct 19 @	Edmonton	2-4	L	2-1-0	4	9-6	43.	Jan 17 @	Indianapolis	4-0	W	19-23-1	39	161-191
4.	Oct 21 @	Winnipeg	0-7	L	2-2-0	4	9-13	44.	Jan 21	Cleveland	8-2	W	20-23-1	41	169-193
5.	Oct 23	Edmonton	6-4	W	3-2-0	6	15-17	45.	Jan 23 @	Indianapolis	3-4	L	20-24-1	41	172-197
6.	Oct 25	Houston	7-4	W	4-2-0	8	22-21	46.	Jan 24	New England	6-3	W	21-24-1	43	178-200
7.	Oct 29 @	Minnesota	6-4	W	5-2-0	10	28-25	47.	Jan 27 @	Quebec	1-9	L	21-25-1	43	179-209
8.	Oct 30 @	Winnipeg	0-4	L	5-3-0	10	28-29	48.	Jan 28	Cleveland	4-6	L	21-26-1	43	183-215
9.	Nov 1	Calgary	3-2	W	6-3-0	12	31-31	49.	Jan 31	Winnipeg	2-5	L	21-27-1	43	185-220
10.	Nov 6 @	New England	3-8	L	6-4-0	12	34-39	50.	Feb 1 @	Edmonton	2-5	L	21-28-1	43	187-225
11.	Nov 8	San Diego	7-4	W	7-4-0	14	41-43	51.	Feb 3 @	Calgary	2-3	L	21-29-1	43	189-228
12.	Nov 9	New England	4-2	W	8-4-0	16	45-45	52.	Feb 6	Edmonton	7-0	W	22-29-1	45	196-228
13.	Nov 15	Houston	8-5	W	9-4-0	18	53-50	53.	Feb 7 @	Indianapolis	1-5	L	22-30-1	45	197-233
14.	Nov 16	Minnesota	2-3	L	9-5-0	18	55-53	54.	Feb 11 @	Cleveland	2-4	L	22-31-1	45	199-237
15.	Nov 18 @	Quebec	4-6	L	9-6-0	18	59-59	55.	Feb 13 @	New England	5-1	W	23-31-1	47	204-238
16.	Nov 21 @	Toronto	7-8	L	9-7-0	18	66-67	56.	Feb 14	Indianapolis	3-2	W	24-31-1	49	207-240
17.	Nov 22	Quebec	6-9	L	9-8-0	18	72-76	57.	Feb 15	Calgary	*5-4	W	25-31-1	51	212-244
18.	Nov 23 @	Denver	3-5	L	9-9-0	18	75-81	58.	Feb 20	Phoenix	4-1	W	26-31-1	53	216-245
19.	Nov 26	Winnipeg	3-11	L	9-10-0	18	78-92	59.	Feb 21	San Diego	3-2	W	27-31-1	55	219-247
20.	Nov 27 @	Minnesota	3-5	L	9-11-0	18	81-97	60.	Feb 24 @	Toronto	9-6	W	28-31-1	57	228-253
21.	Nov 29	Toronto	5-9	L	9-12-0	18	86-106	61.	Feb 25	New England	5-2	W	29-31-1	59	233-255
22.	Dec 3 @	Cleveland	5-3	W	10-12-0	20	91-109	62.	Feb 28	Houston	2-4	L	29-32-1	59	235-259
23.	Dec 4 @	Indianapolis	1-7	L	10-13-0	20	92-116	63.	Feb 29	Indianapolis	2-5	L	29-33-1	59	237-264
24.	Dec 6	Denver	3-2	W	11-13-0	22	95-118	64.	Mar 3	Cleveland	*4-3	W	30-33-1	61	241-267
25.	Dec 7	Cleveland	3-1	W	12-13-0	24	98-119	65.	Mar 4 @	Indianapolis	1-3	L	30-34-1	61	242-270
26.	Dec 9 @	Houston	4-6	L	12-14-0	24	102-125	66.	Mar 6	Indianapolis	2-3	L	30-35-1	61	244-273
27.	Dec 12	Phoenix	4-2	W	13-14-0	26	106-127	67.	Mar 7	New England	5-3	W	31-35-1	63	249-276
28.	Dec 13 @	San Diego	3-3	T	13-14-1	27	109-130	68.	Mar 10 @	Cleveland	2-5	L	31-36-1	63	251-281
29.	Dec 16 @	Denver	*2-3	L	13-15-1	27	111-133	69.	Mar 12	Indianapolis	3-6	L	31-37-1	63	254-287
30.	Dec 18 @	San Diego	3-7	L	13-16-1	27	114-140	70.	Mar 13	New England	1-5	L	31-38-1	63	255-292
31.	Dec 20	New England	4-2	W	14-16-1	29	118-142	71.	Mar 17	Toronto	5-4	W	32-38-1	65	260-296
32.	Dec 21	Quebec	11-7	W	15-16-1	31	129-149	72.	Mar 19 @	New England	*5-6	L	32-39-1	65	265-302
33.	Dec 23	Phoenix	3-5	L	15-17-1	31	132-154	73.	Mar 20	Houston	2-1	W	33-39-1	67	267-303
34.	Dec 26 @	New England	3-4	L	15-18-1	31	135-158	74.	Mar 21 @	Cleveland	1-4	L	33-40-1	67	268-307
35.	Dec 27 @	Indianapolis	1-2	L	15-19-1	31	136-160	75.	Mar 24 @	Phoenix	5-4	W	34-40-1	69	273-311
36.	Dec 28	Indianapolis	4-1	W	16-19-1	33	140-161	76.	Mar 25 @	San Diego	1-9	L	34-41-1	69	274-320
37.	Jan 2	Ottawa	2-1	W	17-19-1	35	142-162	77.	Mar 26 @	Houston	1-5	L	34-42-1	69	275-325
38.	Jan 3	San Diego	5-3	W	18-19-1	37	147-165	78.	Mar 31	Phoenix	2-7	L	34-43-1	69	277-332
39.	Jan 6 @	Houston	3-7	L	18-20-1	37	150-172	79.	Apr 2	Cleveland	5-2	W	35-43-1	71	282-334
40.	Jan 8 @	Phoenix	1-7	L	18-21-1	37	151-179	80.	Apr 4 @	Cleveland	3-6	L	35-44-1	71	285-340

Stingers Stars of 1975-1976

Bryan Campbell
50 assists, 72 pts

Claude Larose
28 goals

Dennis Sobchuk
32 goals, +5

Rick Dudley
43 goals, 81 points

Jacques Locas
27 goals

Gene Sobchuk
23 goals

Scoring

pos	#	player	gp	g	a	pts	pim	+/-	ppg	shg	sog	sc%	gp	g	a	pts	pim	+/-
D	5	Abbey, Bruce	17	1	0	1	12	-3	0	0	2	0.500	-	-	-	-	-	-
G	35	Aubry, Serge	12	0	1	1	4		0	0	0	-	-	-	-	-	-	-
RW	23	Andrascik, Steve	20	3	2	5	21	0	0	0	44	0.068	-	-	-	-	-	-
D	19	Ball, Terry	36	3	14	17	12	-1	1	0	63	0.048	-	-	-	-	-	-
LW	20	Beaton, Frank	29	2	3	5	61	+1	0	0	19	0.105	-	-	-	-	-	-
RW	15	Byers, Mike	20	3	3	6	0	-5	0	0	42	0.071	-	-	-	-	-	-
C	7	Campbell, Bryan	77	22	50	72	24	-10	6	1	191	0.115	-	-	-	-	-	-
G	31	Coutu, Rich	3	0	0	0	0		0	0	0	-	-	-	-	-	-	-
C	21	Donnelly, Pat	23	5	7	12	4	-18	0	0	54	0.093	-	-	-	-	-	-
LW	9	Dudley, Rick	74	43	38	81	156	+5	13	0	218	0.197	-	-	-	-	-	-
LW	13	Guite, Pierre	52	20	24	44	80	-1	5	0	114	0.175	-	-	-	-	-	-
G	1	Hoganson, Paul	45	0	1	1	4		0	0	0	-	-	-	-	-	-	-
D	10	Hughes, John	79	3	34	37	204	-3	0	0	171	0.018	-	-	-	-	-	-
D	6	Inkpen, Dave	80	4	24	28	95	-10	0	0	120	0.033	-	-	-	-	-	-
D	3	Justin, Dan	17	0	0	0	2	-10	0	0	19	0.000	-	-	-	-	-	-
G	25	Kiely, John	22	0	1	1	6		0	0	0	-	-	-	-	-	-	-
G	1	Lapointe, Norm	12	0	0	0	0		0	0	0	-	-	-	-	-	-	-
LW	8	Larose, Claude	79	28	24	52	19	-13	1	0	195	0.144	-	-	-	-	-	-
C	11	Locas, Jacques	80	27	46	73	70	-14	7	0	200	0.135	-	-	-	-	-	-
LW	16	MacNeil, Bernie	77	15	12	27	83	-14	0	5	122	0.123	-	-	-	-	-	-
RW	19	McKenzie, John	12	3	10	13	6	-1	1	0	17	0.176	-	-	-	-	-	-
RW	18	Myers, Murray	56	14	15	29	12	+2	2	0	108	0.130	-	-	-	-	-	-
RW	12	O'Donoghue, Don	20	1	8	9	0	-3	0	0	11	0.091	-	-	-	-	-	-
D	4	Pelyk, Mike	75	10	23	33	117	-5	2	0	176	0.057	-	-	-	-	-	-
D	2	Plumb, Ron	80	10	36	46	31	-8	6	0	287	0.035	-	-	-	-	-	-
D	15	Serafini, Ron	16	0	2	2	15	-11	0	0	15	0.000	-	-	-	-	-	-
LW	17	Smedsmo, Dale	66	8	14	22	187	-8	0	0	67	0.119	-	-	-	-	-	-
C	14	Sobchuk, Dennis	79	32	40	72	74	+5	5	2	254	0.126	-	-	-	-	-	-
LW	22	Sobchuk, Gene	78	23	19	42	37	-6	4	0	184	0.125	-	-	-	-	-	-
RW	12	Steele, Billy	3	2	0	2	0	+1	0	0	4	0.500	-	-	-	-	-	-
LW	18	Veneruzzo, Gary	14	3	2	5	8	+5	0	0	30	0.100	-	-	-	-	-	-

Power Play: 54 goals scored in 317 opportunities (17.0%) with 8 short-handed goals allowed.
Penalty Killing: 83 goals allowed in 321 opportunities (74.1%) with 8 short-handed goals scored.

Goaltending

goaltender	gp	min	ga	en	so	record	gaa	sog	sv%	gp	min	ga	record	gaa
Aubry, Serge	12	549	38	0	1	6-4-0	4.15	267	0.858	-	-	-	-	-
Coutu, Rich	3	149	17	1	0	0-2-0	6.85	81	0.790	-	-	-	-	-
Hoganson, Paul	45	2392	145	3	2	19-24-0	3.64	1270	0.886	-	-	-	-	-
Kiely, John	22	1087	78	1	0	6-8-1	4.31	604	0.871	-	-	-	-	-
Lapointe, Norm	12	641	55	2	0	4-6-0	5.15	377	0.854	-	-	-	-	-

Transactions: Rick Dudley, Bernie MacNeil signed to contracts, May 1975 • Dale Smedsmo signed to contract, Jun 1975 • Serge Aubry purchased from Quebec, Jul 1975, subsequently released, Dec 1975 • Bryan Campbell and Murray Myers acquired in trade from Calgary for future considerations (Murray Myers himself, returned to Calgary Jun 1976), Aug 1975 • Frank Beaton signed to contract, Aug 1975 • Dale Smedsmo claimed on waivers from Minnesota, Sep 1975 • Gary Veneruzzo traded to Phoenix for Ron Serafini, Nov 1975 • Paul Hoganson signed as free agent after release from New England, Dec 1975 • Terry Ball acquired from Cleveland for future considerations, Jan 1976 • Mike Byers signed as free agent after release from New England, Feb 1976 • John McKenzie signed as free agent from defunct Minnesota, Mar 1976

1975-1976 CLEVELAND CRUSADERS

Coach
John Wilson

Summary of Games (@ Away, * Overtime)

#	date	opponent	score		record	pts	gf-ga
1.	Oct 11	Cincinnati	0-1	L	0-1-0	0	0-1
2.	Oct 15 @	Minnesota	8-4	W	1-1-0	2	8-5
3.	Oct 19	Houston	5-6	L	1-2-0	2	13-11
4.	Oct 25	Edmonton	5-2	W	2-2-0	4	18-13
5.	Oct 29	Calgary	1-3	L	2-3-0	4	19-16
6.	Oct 31	Quebec	6-2	W	3-3-0	6	25-18
7.	Nov 2	Phoenix	5-2	W	4-3-0	8	30-20
8.	Nov 4 @	Denver	2-2	T	4-3-1	9	32-22
9.	Nov 6 @	Calgary	2-5	L	4-4-1	9	34-27
10.	Nov 9 @	Edmonton	1-4	L	4-5-1	9	35-31
11.	Nov 11 @	Winnipeg	3-2	W	5-5-1	11	38-33
12.	Nov 13 @	San Diego	1-3	L	5-6-1	11	39-36
13.	Nov 15 @	Denver	*4-5	L	5-7-1	11	43-41
14.	Nov 16 @	Phoenix	4-4	T	5-7-2	12	47-45
15.	Nov 19	Minnesota	*4-3	W	6-7-2	14	51-48
16.	Nov 22	Winnipeg	6-3	W	7-7-2	16	57-51
17.	Nov 25 @	Toronto	*4-3	W	8-7-2	18	61-54
18.	Nov 26	Denver	0-3	L	8-8-2	18	61-57
19.	Nov 28	Indianapolis	1-3	L	8-9-2	18	62-60
20.	Nov 30	Toronto	10-9	W	9-9-2	20	72-69
21.	Dec 2 @	Quebec	2-9	L	9-10-2	20	74-78
22.	Dec 3	Cincinnati	3-5	L	9-11-2	20	77-83
23.	Dec 6 @	Indianapolis	2-3	L	9-12-2	20	79-86
24.	Dec 7 @	Cincinnati	1-3	L	9-13-2	20	80-89
25.	Dec 9 @	Denver	3-6	L	9-14-2	20	83-95
26.	Dec 12	Minnesota	1-0	W	10-14-2	22	84-95
27.	Dec 13 @	New England	4-5	L	10-15-2	22	88-100
28.	Dec 14	Houston	3-4	L	10-16-2	22	91-104
29.	Dec 17	Edmonton	2-3	L	10-17-2	22	93-107
30.	Dec 19 @	Indianapolis	*4-5	L	10-18-2	22	97-112
31.	Dec 20	Indianapolis	5-3	W	11-18-2	24	102-115
32.	Dec 22	New England	1-4	L	11-19-2	24	103-119
33.	Dec 27	Toronto	5-0	W	12-19-2	26	108-119
34.	Dec 28 @	New England	0-4	L	12-20-2	26	108-123
35.	Jan 2	Quebec	*5-4	W	13-20-2	28	113-127
36.	Jan 3 @	New England	2-3	L	13-21-2	28	115-130
37.	Jan 4	Phoenix	3-2	W	14-21-2	30	118-132
38.	Jan 7	San Diego	8-3	W	15-21-2	32	126-135
39.	Jan 9 @	Houston	5-6	L	15-22-2	32	131-141
40.	Jan 11	Indianapolis	4-3	W	16-22-2	34	135-144
41.	Jan 15 @	Indianapolis	3-1	W	17-22-2	36	138-145
42.	Jan 16	New England	4-3	W	18-22-2	38	142-148
43.	Jan 17 @	San Diego	4-5	L	18-23-2	38	146-153
44.	Jan 21 @	Cincinnati	2-8	L	18-24-2	38	148-161
45.	Jan 23	New England	2-2	T	18-24-3	39	150-163
46.	Jan 25 @	Indianapolis	2-4	L	18-25-3	39	152-167
47.	Jan 28 @	Cincinnati	6-4	W	19-25-3	41	158-171
48.	Jan 30	Phoenix	4-4	T	19-25-4	42	162-175
49.	Feb 1 @	Minnesota	6-5	W	20-25-4	44	168-180
50.	Feb 4 @	Phoenix	1-5	L	20-26-4	44	169-185
51.	Feb 5 @	San Diego	2-3	L	20-27-4	44	171-188
52.	Feb 7	Winnipeg	4-4	T	20-27-5	45	175-192
53.	Feb 8 @	New England	6-1	W	21-27-5	47	181-193
54.	Feb 11	Cincinnati	4-2	W	22-27-5	49	185-195
55.	Feb 15	New England	2-3	L	22-28-5	49	187-198
56.	Feb 18	Calgary	4-0	W	23-28-5	51	191-198
57.	Feb 19 @	Houston	3-5	L	23-29-5	51	194-203
58.	Feb 21	Indianapolis	3-2	W	24-29-5	53	197-205
59.	Feb 22	Houston	2-1	W	25-29-5	55	199-206
60.	Feb 25 @	Winnipeg	2-5	L	25-30-5	55	201-211
61.	Feb 27 @	Calgary	4-5	L	25-31-5	55	205-216
62.	Feb 29 @	Edmonton	5-2	W	26-31-5	57	210-218
63.	Mar 3 @	Cincinnati	*3-4	L	26-32-5	57	213-222
64.	Mar 6 @	Houston	5-4	W	27-32-5	59	218-226
65.	Mar 7 @	Indianapolis	5-1	W	28-32-5	61	223-227
66.	Mar 10	Cincinnati	5-2	W	29-32-5	63	228-229
67.	Mar 12 @	New England	2-8	L	29-33-5	63	230-237
68.	Mar 14	Phoenix	*2-3	L	29-34-5	63	232-240
69.	Mar 16 @	Toronto	0-6	L	29-35-5	63	232-246
70.	Mar 19 @	Phoenix	*6-5	W	30-35-5	65	238-251
71.	Mar 20	Toronto	5-6	L	30-36-5	65	243-257
72.	Mar 21	Cincinnati	4-1	W	31-36-5	67	247-258
73.	Mar 23 @	Quebec	3-1	W	32-36-5	69	250-259
74.	Mar 24	Houston	2-3	L	32-37-5	69	252-262
75.	Mar 26	Indianapolis	2-3	L	32-38-5	69	254-265
76.	Mar 31	New England	5-1	W	33-38-5	71	259-266
77.	Apr 2 @	Cincinnati	2-5	L	33-39-5	71	261-271
78.	Apr 3	San Diego	4-2	W	34-39-5	73	265-273
79.	Apr 4	Cincinnati	6-3	W	35-39-5	75	271-276
80.	Apr 6	San Diego	*2-3	L	35-40-5	75	273-279

Crusaders Stars of 1975-1976

Ron Ward	Richie Leduc	Danny Gruen	Tom Edur	Russ Walker	Jim Harrison
82 points	36 goals, +7	26 goals, +9	+15 rating	23 goals	72 points, +4

Scoring

pos	#	player	gp	g	a	pts	pim	+/-	ppg	shg	sog	sc%	gp	g	a	pts	pim	+/-
D	21	Ball, Terry	23	2	15	17	18	-21	2	0	62	0.032	-	-	-	-	-	-
D	4	Baxter, Paul	67	3	7	10	201	-7	1	0	65	0.046	3	0	0	0	10	-2
D		Bowles, Brian	3	0	0	0	0	-2	0	0	0	-	-	-	-	-	-	-
G	30	Caron, Jacques	2	0	1	1	0		0	0	0	-	-	-	-	-	-	-
G	30	Cheevers, Gerry	28	0	0	0	15		0	0	0	-	-	-	-	-	-	-
RW	25	Connelly, Wayne	12	5	2	7	4	-1	3	0	39	0.128	3	1	0	1	2	-2
LW		Conroy, Mike	4	0	1	1	0	0	0	0	0	-	-	-	-	-	-	-
D	18	Edur, Tom	80	7	28	35	62	+15	3	0	151	0.046	3	0	2	2	0	-3
RW	27	Evo, Bill	40	1	5	6	32	-15	0	0	30	0.033	-	-	-	-	-	-
LW	23	Gruen, Danny	80	26	24	50	72	+9	5	0	173	0.150	3	2	0	2	0	-1
C	15	Harrison, Jim	59	34	38	72	62	+4	9	2	216	0.157	3	0	1	1	9	-2
RW	20	Holbrook, Terry	15	1	2	3	6	-1	0	1	17	0.059	3	0	0	0	0	-5
LW	12	Jarrett, Gary	69	16	17	33	22	-4	1	0	128	0.125	3	0	3	3	2	-1
G	31	Johnson, Bob	18	0	0	0	0		0	0	0	-	2	0	0	0	0	
C	22	Leduc, Richie	79	36	22	58	76	+7	8	2	286	0.126	3	2	1	3	2	-3
D	6	Legge, Barry	35	0	7	7	22	-8	0	0	28	0.000	3	0	1	1	12	-3
D	8	Legge, Randy	44	1	8	9	28	-7	0	0	41	0.024	3	0	0	0	0	-2
C	16	MacGregor, Gary	35	5	3	8	6	-16	4	0	45	0.111	3	0	0	0	4	0
D	26	Maxwell, Bryan	73	3	14	17	177	-13	0	0	67	0.045	2	0	1	1	4	-1
RW	14	McDonough, Al	80	23	22	45	19	+1	4	0	229	0.100	3	1	0	1	2	-2
D	2	McKay, Ray	68	3	10	13	44	-8	1	0	50	0.060	3	0	0	0	4	-3
LW	10	Moffat, Lyle	33	4	7	11	33	+10	1	0	57	0.070	-	-	-	-	-	-
D	5	Muloin, Wayne	27	0	5	5	12	-7	0	0	16	0.000	-	-	-	-	-	-
G	35	Newton, Cam	15	0	1	1	0		0	0	0	-	1	0	0	0	0	
LW	7	Pinder, Gerry	79	21	30	51	118	-8	8	3	201	0.104	3	0	0	0	4	-2
D	3	Shmyr, Paul	70	6	44	50	101	+16	4	1	165	0.036	-	-	-	-	-	-
LW	17	Stewart, John A.	79	12	21	33	42	-3	0	0	166	0.072	3	0	0	0	0	0
C	19	Stewart, John C.	42	2	9	11	15	-2	0	0	68	0.029	-	-	-	-	-	-
RW	9/16	Tamminen, Juhani	65	7	14	21	12	-8	2	0	101	0.069	1	0	0	0	0	0
RW	28	Walker, Russ	72	23	15	38	122	-7	5	0	161	0.143	3	0	0	0	18	+1
C	24	Ward, Ron	75	32	50	82	24	+14	11	2	172	0.186	3	0	2	2	0	-3
G	1	Whidden, Bob	21	0	0	0	2		0	0	0	-	-	-	-	-	-	-

Power Play: 69 goals scored in 292 opportunities (23.6%) with 14 short-handed goals allowed.
Penalty Killing: 49 goals allowed in 294 opportunities (83.3%) with 11 short-handed goals scored.

Goaltending

goaltender	gp	min	ga	en	so	record	gaa	sog	sv%	gp	min	ga	record	gaa
Caron, Jacques	2	130	8	0	0	1-0-1	3.69	77	0.896	-	-	-	-	-
Cheevers, Gerry	28	1570	95	1	1	11-14-1	3.63	834	0.886	-	-	-	-	-
Johnson, Bob	18	1043	56	0	1	9-8-0	3.22	601	0.907	2	120	8	0-2	4.00
Newton, Cam	15	896	48	0	0	7-7-1	3.21	468	0.897	1	60	6	0-1	6.00
Whidden, Bob	21	1230	70	1	1	7-11-2	3.41	650	0.892	-	-	-	-	-

Transactions: John A. Stewart rights acquired from Edmonton, signed to contract, Jun 1975 • Lyle Moffat signed to contract, Jul 1975 • Skip Krake traded to Edmonton for Ray McKay, Aug 1975 • Grant Erickson traded to Phoenix for Rick Newell and Rob Watt, Nov 1975 • Terry Ball traded to Cincinnati for future considerations, Jan 1976 • Wayne Muloin traded to Edmonton for Bill Evo, Jan 1976 • Gary MacGregor and Barry Legge purchased from Ottawa, Jan 1976 • Bob Johnson and Cam Newton signed as free agents from defunct Ottawa, Jan 1976 • Lyle Moffat traded to Winnipeg for Randy Legge, Jan 1976 • Gerry Cheevers released, Jan 1976 • Jacques Caron signed to contract, Feb 1976 • Wayne Connelly signed as free agent from defunct Minnesota, Mar 1976

1975-1976 DENVER SPURS-OTTAWA CIVICS

**Coach
Jean-Guy Talbot**

Summary of Games (@ Away, * Overtime)

	date	opponent	score		record	pts	gf-ga		date	opponent	score		record	pts	gf-ga
1.	Oct 10	Indianapolis	1-7	L	0-1-0	0	1-7	22.	Dec 2	Winnipeg	*3-4	L	8-13-1	17	72-92
2.	Oct 16	Winnipeg	3-7	L	0-2-0	0	4-14	23.	Dec 5 @	Minnesota	3-4	L	8-14-1	17	75-96
3.	Oct 17 @	Phoenix	5-4	W	1-2-0	2	9-18	24.	Dec 6 @	Cincinnati	2-3	L	8-15-1	17	77-99
4.	Oct 18 @	Indianapolis	6-4	W	2-2-0	4	15-22	25.	Dec 7	New England	5-1	W	9-15-1	19	82-100
5.	Oct 22 @	Calgary	2-1	W	3-2-0	6	17-23	26.	Dec 9	Cleveland	6-3	W	10-15-1	21	88-103
6.	Oct 24 @	Winnipeg	2-5	L	3-3-0	6	19-28	27.	Dec 13	Phoenix	1-4	L	10-16-1	21	89-107
7.	Oct 30	Phoenix	2-3	L	3-4-0	6	21-31	28.	Dec 16	Cincinnati	*3-2	W	11-16-1	23	92-109
8.	Nov 1	Houston	2-3	L	3-5-0	6	23-34	29.	Dec 19	San Diego	6-3	W	12-16-1	25	98-112
9.	Nov 4	Cleveland	2-2	T	3-5-1	7	25-36	30.	Dec 23	Minnesota	4-5	L	12-17-1	25	102-117
10.	Nov 6	Quebec	3-5	L	3-6-1	7	28-41	31.	Dec 26 @	Houston	4-9	L	12-18-1	25	106-126
11.	Nov 7	San Diego	*2-3	L	3-7-1	7	30-44	32.	Dec 27 @	Phoenix	0-10	L	12-19-1	25	106-136
12.	Nov 9 @	Houston	2-3	L	3-8-1	7	32-47	33.	Dec 28	Phoenix	2-5	L	12-20-1	25	108-141
13.	Nov 13	Toronto	8-11	L	3-9-1	7	40-58	34.	Dec 30	Indianapolis	*2-1	W	13-20-1	27	110-142
14.	Nov 15	Cleveland	*5-4	W	4-9-1	9	45-62	35.	Jan 2 @	Cincinnati	1-2	L	13-21-1	27	111-144
15.	Nov 18	Edmonton	6-3	W	5-9-1	11	51-65	36.	Jan 3 @	Houston	2-4	L	13-22-1	27	113-148
16.	Nov 20 @	San Diego	1-5	L	5-10-1	11	52-70	37.	Jan 4 @	Minnesota	5-2	W	14-22-1	29	118-150
17.	Nov 21	Calgary	2-6	L	5-11-1	11	54-76	38.	Jan 7	New England	2-3	L	14-23-1	29	120-153
18.	Nov 23	Cincinnati	5-3	W	6-11-1	13	59-79	39.	Jan 10 @	Phoenix	5-8	L	14-24-1	29	125-161
19.	Nov 26 @	Cleveland	3-0	W	7-11-1	15	62-79	40.	Jan 11 @	Winnipeg	*5-6	L	14-25-1	29	130-167
20.	Nov 28 @	New England	3-7	L	7-12-1	15	65-86	41.	Jan 15	Houston	*4-5	L	14-26-1	29	134-172
21.	Nov 30 @	Indianapolis	4-2	W	8-12-1	17	69-88			**Franchise folded January 17, 1976**					

As Denver (October 10 to December 30, 1975): 13-20-1, 27 points, 110 gf and 142 ga.
As Ottawa (January 2 to January 15, 1976): 1-6-0, 2 points, 24 gf and 30 ga.

256

Spurs-Civics Stars of 1975-1976

Ralph Backstrom	**Don Borgeson**	**Jim Sherrit**	**Bob Johnson**	**Cam Newton**	**Francois Rochon**
50 points led team	21 goals	11 goals	8 wins	3.66 gaa, shutout	11 goals

Scoring

pos	#	player	gp	g	a	pts	pim	+/-	ppg	shg	sog	sc%	gp	g	a	pts	pim	+/-
D	5	Arbour, John	34	2	13	15	49	-14			62	0.032	-	-	-	-	-	-
C	14	Backstrom, Ralph	41	21	29	50	14	+9	8	0	142	0.148	-	-	-	-	-	-
D	18	Baltimore, Bryon	41	1	8	9	32	-13	0	0	47	0.021	-	-	-	-	-	-
D	2	Bignell, Larry	41	5	5	10	43	-4			40	0.125	-	-	-	-	-	-
LW	12	Borgeson, Don	40	21	16	37	26	+7	5	0	119	0.176	-	-	-	-	-	-
RW	17	Bredin, Gary	16	4	3	7	2	-7	1	0	25	0.160	-	-	-	-	-	-
C	11	Delorme, Ron	22	1	3	4	28	-3			10	0.100	-	-	-	-	-	-
D	5	Gibbons, Brian	2	0	0	0	0	-2	0	0	0	-	-	-	-	-	-	-
LW	16	Goldthorpe, Bill	12	0	0	0	31	-5	0	0	7	0.000	-	-	-	-	-	-
G	31	Grigg, Chris	2	0	0	0	0		0	0	0	-	-	-	-	-	-	-
G	1	Johnson, Bob	24	0	0	0	0		0	0	0	-	-	-	-	-	-	-
D	24	Kokkola, Keith	16	0	3	3	40	-2	0	0	26	0.000	-	-	-	-	-	-
LW	21	Lavender, Brian	37	5	6	11	37	-15			..	..	-	-	-	-	-	-
C	16	LeBlanc, J. P.	15	1	5	6	25	-7			26	0.038	-	-	-	-	-	-
D	3	Legge, Barry	40	6	8	14	15	-11	4	0	59	0.102	-	-	-	-	-	-
LW	7	Liddington, Bob	35	7	8	15	14	-2	1	0	63	0.111	-	-	-	-	-	-
RW	8	Lomenda, Mark	37	6	16	22	11	-6	5	0	66	0.091	-	-	-	-	-	-
C	9	MacGregor, Gary	38	16	14	30	18	-2	3	0	127	0.126	-	-	-	-	-	-
D	4	Maggs, Darryl	41	4	23	27	42	-9	1	0	98	0.041	-	-	-	-	-	-
C	23	Mara, Peter	40	3	7	10	8	-15			41	0.073	-	-	-	-	-	-
D	6	Mavety, Larry	14	0	4	4	14	-12	0	0	20	0.000	-	-	-	-	-	-
LW	10	Morris, Rick	40	9	6	15	58	-19			75	0.120	-	-	-	-	-	-
G	30	Newton, Cam	10	0	0	0	0		0	0	0	-	-	-	-	-	-	-
D	22	Pizunski, Ed	1	0	0	0	0		0	0	0	-	-	-	-	-	-	-
LW	19	Popiel, Jan	1	0	0	0	2		0	0	0	-	-	-	-	-	-	-
LW	15	Rochon, Francois	41	11	10	21	10	-18	3	0	78	0.141	-	-	-	-	-	-
G	1	Sanza, Nick	1	0	0	0	0		0	0	0	-	-	-	-	-	-	-
C	19	Sherrit, Jim	40	11	19	30	16	-4			91	0.121	-	-	-	-	-	-
G	31	Zimmerman, Lynn	8	0	0	0	0		0	0	0	-	-	-	-	-	-	-

Power Play: 25 goals scored in 149 opportunities (16.8%) with 6 short-handed goals allowed.
Penalty Killing: 31 goals allowed in 148 opportunities (79.1%) with 2 short-handed goals scored.

Goaltending

goaltender	gp	min	ga	en	so	record	gaa	sog	sv%	gp	min	ga	record	gaa
Grigg, Chris	2	80	13	0	0	0-0-0	9.75	59	0.780	-	-	-	-	-
Johnson, Bob	24	1334	88	0	0	8-14-1	3.96	689	0.872	-	-	-	-	-
Newton, Cam	10	573	35	0	1	4-6-0	3.66	314	0.889	-	-	-	-	-
Sanza, Nick	1	20	5	0	0	0-1-0	15.00	12	0.583	-	-	-	-	-
Zimmerman, Lynn	8	495	31	0	0	2-5-0	3.76	301	0.897	-	-	-	-	-

Transactions: Larry Bignell, Bob Johnson signed to contracts, Sep 1975 • Rights to Brian Lavender purchased from Edmonton, Sep 1975 • Jan Popiel traded to Houston for Don Borgeson and Jim Sherrit, Oct 1975 • John Arbour acquired from Minnesota for draft picks, Oct 1975, subsequently declared free agent, Jan 1976 • Gary Bredin traded to San Diego for Bill Goldthorpe, Nov 1975 • Lynn Zimmerman purchased from Erie (NAHL), Dec 1975 • Ralph Backstrom and Don Borgeson sold to New England, Jan 1976 • Bryon Baltimore, Mark Lomenda, Francois Rochon and Darryl Maggs sold to Indianapolis, Jan 1976 • Gary MacGregor and Barry Legge sold to Cleveland, Jan 1976 • Remaining players declared free agents, Jan 1976, upon demise of Ottawa

1975-1976 EDMONTON OILERS

Coach
Clare Drake
18-28-2

Coach
Bill Hunter
9-21-3

Summary of Games (@ Away, * Overtime)

	date	opponent	score		record	pts	gf-ga		date	opponent	score		record	pts	gf-ga
1.	Oct 10	Minnesota	1-4	L	0-1-0	0	1-4	41.	Jan 1 @	Calgary	1-5	L	15-24-2	32	141-173
2.	Oct 12	Indianapolis	6-5	W	1-1-0	2	7-9	42.	Jan 2	Calgary	1-3	L	15-25-2	32	142-176
3.	Oct 14 @	Quebec	5-8	L	1-2-0	2	12-17	43.	Jan 4	Winnipeg	1-8	L	15-26-2	32	143-184
4.	Oct 15 @	New England	*4-5	L	1-3-0	2	16-22	44.	Jan 6	Indianapolis	3-0	W	16-26-2	34	146-184
5.	Oct 17 @	Toronto	4-4	T	1-3-1	3	20-26	45.	Jan 9	Toronto	5-3	W	17-26-2	36	151-187
6.	Oct 18 @	Minnesota	3-1	W	2-3-1	5	23-27	46.	Jan 11	Houston	3-5	L	17-27-2	36	154-192
7.	Oct 19	Cincinnati	4-2	W	3-3-1	7	27-29	47.	Jan 16 @	Winnipeg	5-1	W	18-27-2	38	159-193
8.	Oct 23 @	Cincinnati	4-6	L	3-4-1	7	31-35	48.	Jan 20	Calgary	3-10	L	18-28-2	38	162-203
9.	Oct 25 @	Cleveland	2-5	L	3-5-1	7	33-40	49.	Jan 23 @	Winnipeg	2-4	L	18-29-2	38	164-207
10.	Oct 26 @	Indianapolis	3-4	L	3-6-1	7	36-44	50.	Jan 25 @	Quebec	6-7	L	18-30-2	38	170-214
11.	Oct 28	Phoenix	7-3	W	4-6-1	9	43-47	51.	Jan 27 @	Toronto	4-4	T	18-30-3	39	174-218
12.	Oct 31	New England	2-2	T	4-6-2	10	45-49	52.	Jan 28	Houston	5-6	L	18-31-3	39	179-224
13.	Nov 2	San Diego	5-3	W	5-6-2	12	50-52	53.	Feb 1	Cincinnati	5-2	W	19-31-3	41	184-226
14.	Nov 4	Quebec	3-4	L	5-7-2	12	53-56	54.	Feb 3	New England	4-0	W	20-31-3	43	188-226
15.	Nov 7	Toronto	5-4	W	6-7-2	14	58-60	55.	Feb 5 @	Phoenix	1-5	L	20-32-3	43	189-231
16.	Nov 9	Cleveland	4-1	W	7-7-2	16	62-61	56.	Feb 6 @	Cincinnati	0-7	L	20-33-3	43	189-238
17.	Nov 11 @	Calgary	3-6	L	7-8-2	16	65-67	57.	Feb 8	Quebec	4-5	L	20-34-3	43	193-243
18.	Nov 14 @	Winnipeg	1-6	L	7-9-2	16	66-73	58.	Feb 13	Toronto	5-3	W	21-34-3	45	198-246
19.	Nov 17	San Diego	6-3	W	8-9-2	18	72-76	59.	Feb 15	Phoenix	2-4	L	21-35-3	45	200-250
20.	Nov 18 @	Denver	3-6	L	8-10-2	18	75-82	60.	Feb 17	Winnipeg	4-4	T	21-35-4	46	204-254
21.	Nov 20 @	Phoenix	1-3	L	8-11-2	18	76-85	61.	Feb 20 @	Winnipeg	2-4	L	21-36-4	46	206-258
22.	Nov 21 @	Houston	2-4	L	8-12-2	18	78-89	62.	Feb 22	Minnesota	4-3	W	22-36-4	48	210-261
23.	Nov 22 @	San Diego	*3-2	W	9-12-2	20	81-91	63.	Feb 24	Calgary	3-3	T	22-36-5	49	213-264
24.	Nov 25 @	San Diego	2-7	L	9-13-2	20	83-98	64.	Feb 25 @	Calgary	2-5	L	22-37-5	49	215-269
25.	Nov 28 @	Houston	4-7	L	9-14-2	20	87-105	65.	Feb 27 @	Winnipeg	3-4	L	22-38-5	49	218-273
26.	Nov 30	Calgary	4-2	W	10-14-2	22	91-107	66.	Feb 29	Cleveland	2-5	L	22-39-5	49	220-278
27.	Dec 2	Toronto	7-2	W	11-14-2	24	98-109	67.	Mar 2 @	Calgary	3-6	L	22-40-5	49	223-284
28.	Dec 5 @	Calgary	3-8	L	11-15-2	24	101-117	68.	Mar 3	Calgary	6-4	W	23-40-5	51	229-288
29.	Dec 7	Calgary	4-5	L	11-16-2	24	105-122	69.	Mar 5	Quebec	*4-5	L	23-41-5	51	233-293
30.	Dec 10	Quebec	7-4	W	12-16-2	26	112-126	70.	Mar 7	Quebec	4-2	W	24-41-5	53	237-295
31.	Dec 11 @	Calgary	3-2	W	13-16-2	28	115-128	71.	Mar 11 @	Calgary	0-2	L	24-42-5	53	237-297
32.	Dec 14	Winnipeg	1-3	L	13-17-2	28	116-131	72.	Mar 14 @	Winnipeg	2-4	L	24-43-5	53	239-301
33.	Dec 16 @	Indianapolis	3-1	W	14-17-2	30	119-132	73.	Mar 16	Calgary	*3-4	L	24-44-5	53	242-305
34.	Dec 17 @	Cleveland	3-2	W	15-17-2	32	122-134	74.	Mar 19	Winnipeg	2-1	W	25-44-5	55	244-306
35.	Dec 19 @	New England	2-4	L	15-18-2	32	124-138	75.	Mar 21	Quebec	3-6	L	25-45-5	55	247-312
36.	Dec 21	Toronto	2-4	L	15-19-2	32	126-142	76.	Mar 24 @	Winnipeg	3-2	W	26-45-5	57	250-314
37.	Dec 23	Winnipeg	2-6	L	15-20-2	32	128-148	77.	Mar 25 @	Quebec	5-7	L	26-46-5	57	255-321
38.	Dec 26 @	Toronto	5-8	L	15-21-2	32	133-156	78.	Mar 26 @	Toronto	3-7	L	26-47-5	57	258-328
39.	Dec 27 @	Quebec	3-6	L	15-22-2	32	136-162	79.	Mar 30 @	Quebec	3-8	L	26-48-5	57	261-336
40.	Dec 30 @	Toronto	4-6	L	15-23-2	32	140-168	80.	Apr 1 @	Quebec	2-7	L	26-49-5	57	263-343
								81.	Apr 4	Winnipeg	5-2	W	27-49-5	59	268-345

Oilers Stars of 1975-1976

Norm Ullman	**Tim Sheehy**	**Rusty Patenaude**	**Bob McAneeley**	**Mike Rogers**	**Barry Long**
31 goals, 87 points	34 goals	42 goals	12 goals	12 goals, +5	42 points from blueline

Scoring

pos	#	player	gp	g	a	pts	pim	+/-	ppg	shg	sog	sc%	gp	g	a	pts	pim	+/-
						Regular Season										**Playoffs**		
D	19	Baird, Ken	48	13	24	37	87	-6	3	0	93	0.140	4	3	1	4	16	+1
D	5	Barrie, Doug	79	4	21	25	81	-42	0	0	109	0.037	4	0	1	1	6	-2
LW	8	Carleton, Wayne	26	5	16	21	6	-3	2	0	86	0.058	4	1	1	2	2	-6
LW	20	Carlson, Jack	10	1	1	2	31	-2	0	0	13	0.077	4	0	0	0	4	-4
D	20	Carlyle, Steve	28	0	11	11	10	-3	0	0	27	0.000	-	-	-	-	-	-
G	28	Dryden, Dave	62	0	2	2	2		0	0	0	-	3	0	0	0	0	-
RW	8	Evo, Bill	8	0	4	4	0	0	0	0	4	0.000	-	-	-	-	-	-
D	3	Hamilton, Al	54	2	32	34	78	-8	1	0	83	0.024	4	0	1	1	6	-2
D	6	Hurley, Paul	26	1	4	5	14	-5	0	0	47	0.021	4	0	0	0	0	-2
C	16	Joyal, Eddie	45	5	4	9	6	-19	0	0	53	0.094	-	-	-	-	-	-
D	6	Kennett, Murray	28	3	4	7	14	-8	1	0	22	0.136	-	-	-	-	-	-
RW	14	Kerslake, Doug	13	1	1	2	4	-2	0	0	4	0.250	-	-	-	-	-	-
D	4	Ketter, Kerry	48	1	9	10	20	-12	0	0	48	0.021	-	-	-	-	-	-
C	11	Krake, Skip	41	8	8	16	55	-3	2	1	64	0.125	-	-	-	-	-	-
C	21	Laing, Bill	54	8	12	20	67	-10	0	1	62	0.129	-	-	-	-	-	-
D	2	Long, Barry	78	10	32	42	66	-49	5	0	214	0.047	4	0	0	0	4	-2
RW	14	MacDonald, Blair	29	7	5	12	8	-8	3	0	72	0.097	-	-	-	-	-	-
RW	12	MacGregor, Bruce	63	13	10	23	13	-33	2	1	65	0.200	-	-	-	-	-	-
C	18	McAneeley, Bob	71	12	16	28	60	-11	2	0	84	0.143	3	1	0	1	0	+1
D	23	McAneeley, Ted	79	2	17	19	71	-9	0	0	63	0.032	4	0	0	0	0	-1
LW	22	Morris, Pete	75	7	13	20	34	-16	1	0	62	0.113	3	0	1	1	7	0
LW	7	Morris, Rick	33	11	15	26	52	-14	0	4	89	0.124	4	0	1	1	4	-1
D	26	Muloin, Wayne	10	1	1	2	0	-6	0	0	2	0.500	1	0	0	0	0	-1
RW	17	Patenaude, Rusty	77	42	30	72	88	-3	11	0	202	0.208	4	1	4	5	12	+2
RW	10	Rogers, John	77	9	8	17	34	-13	0	0	59	0.153	-	-	-	-	-	-
C	7	Rogers, Mike	44	12	15	27	10	+5	0	0	96	0.125	-	-	-	-	-	-
C	25	Russell, Bob	58	13	18	31	19	-12	0	0	118	0.110	4	1	0	1	0	-3
RW	15	Sheehy, Tim	81	34	31	65	17	-4	6	0	223	0.152	4	2	2	4	0	-5
C	24	Spring, Dan	75	12	11	23	8	-25	1	0	72	0.167	2	1	1	2	0	0
G	1/27	Turnbull, Frank	3	0	0	0	0		0	0	0	-	-	-	-	-	-	-
C	9	Ullman, Norm	77	31	56	87	12	-21	13	1	158	0.196	4	1	3	4	2	+3
G	30	Worthy, Chris	24	0	0	0	7		0	0	0	-	1	0	0	0	0	-

Power Play: 53 goals scored in 293 opportunities (18.1%) with 10 short-handed goals allowed.
Penalty Killing: 58 goals allowed in 273 opportunities (78.8%) with 8 short-handed goal scored.

Goaltending

goaltender	gp	min	ga	en	so	record	gaa	sog	sv%	gp	min	ga	record	gaa
Dryden, Dave	62	3567	235	2	1	22-34-5	3.95	1927	0.878	3	180	15	0-3	5.00
Turnbull, Frank	3	106	9	0	0	0-1-0	5.09	65	0.862	-	-	-	-	-
Worthy, Chris	24	1256	98	1	1	5-14-0	4.68	711	0.862	1	60	7	0-1	7.00

Transactions: Kerry Ketter, Bob McAneeley and Ted McAneeley (whose rights were acquired from Houston for future considerations) signed to contracts, Jun 1975 • Ray McKay traded to Cleveland for Skip Krake, Aug 1975 • Dan Spring, Norm Ullman signed to contracts, Sep 1975 • Blair MacDonald traded to Indianapolis for draft picks, Dec 1975 • Mike Rogers traded to New England for Wayne Carleton, Jan 1976 • Bill Evo traded to Cleveland for Wayne Muloin, Jan 1976 • Rick Morris signed as free agent from defunct Ottawa, Jan 1976 • Steve Carlyle and Kerry Ketter traded to New England for Paul Hurley, Feb 1976 • Jack Carlson signed as free agent from defunct Minnesota, Mar 1976

1975-1976 HOUSTON AEROS

Coach
Bill Dineen

Summary of Games (@ Away, * Overtime)

	date	opponent	score		record	pts	gf-ga		date	opponent	score		record	pts	gf-ga
1.	Oct 11 @	New England	5-0	W	1-0-0	2	5-0	41.	Jan 15 @	Ottawa	*5-4	W	27-14-0	54	170-141
2.	Oct 14 @	Toronto	3-6	L	1-1-0	2	8-6	42.	Jan 17 @	Calgary	2-4	L	27-15-0	54	172-145
3.	Oct 18 @	Quebec	2-3	L	1-2-0	2	10-9	43.	Jan 20	Toronto	5-7	L	27-16-0	54	177-152
4.	Oct 19 @	Cleveland	6-5	W	2-2-0	4	16-14	44.	Jan 21	New England	9-3	W	28-16-0	56	186-155
5.	Oct 23 @	Indianapolis	0-4	L	2-3-0	4	16-18	45.	Jan 23	Calgary	2-0	W	29-16-0	58	188-155
6.	Oct 25 @	Cincinnati	4-7	L	2-4-0	4	20-25	46.	Jan 25	Calgary	5-3	W	30-16-0	60	193-158
7.	Oct 30 @	San Diego	4-2	W	3-4-0	6	24-27	47.	Jan 28 @	Edmonton	6-5	W	31-16-0	62	199-163
8.	Nov 1 @	Denver	3-2	W	4-4-0	8	27-29	48.	Jan 30 @	Indianapolis	1-2	L	31-17-0	62	200-165
9.	Nov 5	Minnesota	6-4	W	5-4-0	10	33-33	49.	Jan 31 @	Minnesota	1-4	L	31-18-0	62	201-169
10.	Nov 7	Phoenix	5-3	W	6-4-0	12	38-36	50.	Feb 3	Minnesota	8-4	W	32-18-0	64	209-173
11.	Nov 9	Denver	3-2	W	7-4-0	14	41-38	51.	Feb 6	Indianapolis	4-3	W	33-18-0	66	213-176
12.	Nov 11	Toronto	5-4	W	8-4-0	16	46-42	52.	Feb 8	San Diego	5-2	W	34-18-0	68	218-178
13.	Nov 12 @	New England	1-4	L	8-5-0	16	47-46	53.	Feb 12 @	Phoenix	4-1	W	35-18-0	70	222-179
14.	Nov 15 @	Cincinnati	5-8	L	8-6-0	16	52-54	54.	Feb 14 @	San Diego	1-5	L	35-19-0	70	223-184
15.	Nov 16 @	Calgary	3-5	L	8-7-0	16	55-59	55.	Feb 15	Quebec	2-4	L	35-20-0	70	225-188
16.	Nov 18 @	Winnipeg	3-2	W	9-7-0	18	58-61	56.	Feb 17	New England	4-3	W	36-20-0	72	229-191
17.	Nov 21	Edmonton	4-2	W	10-7-0	20	62-63	57.	Feb 19	Cleveland	5-3	W	37-20-0	74	234-194
18.	Nov 23	Quebec	4-0	W	11-7-0	22	66-63	58.	Feb 22 @	Cleveland	1-2	L	37-21-0	74	235-196
19.	Nov 25	Indianapolis	4-1	W	12-7-0	24	70-64	59.	Feb 24 @	Quebec	1-4	L	37-22-0	74	236-200
20.	Nov 28	Edmonton	7-4	W	13-7-0	26	77-68	60.	Feb 26 @	New England	5-2	W	38-22-0	76	241-202
21.	Nov 30	San Diego	8-4	W	14-7-0	28	85-72	61.	Feb 27 @	Toronto	*7-6	W	39-22-0	78	248-208
22.	Dec 2	New England	2-5	L	14-8-0	28	87-77	62.	Feb 28 @	Cincinnati	4-2	W	40-22-0	80	252-210
23.	Dec 5	Winnipeg	5-4	W	15-8-0	30	92-81	63.	Mar 5	Phoenix	6-3	W	41-22-0	82	258-213
24.	Dec 6 @	Phoenix	*5-6	L	15-9-0	30	97-87	64.	Mar 6	Cleveland	4-5	L	41-23-0	82	262-218
25.	Dec 9	Cincinnati	6-4	W	16-9-0	32	103-91	65.	Mar 9	San Diego	9-2	W	42-23-0	84	271-220
26.	Dec 12	Indianapolis	4-2	W	17-9-0	34	107-93	66.	Mar 11 @	San Diego	1-4	L	42-24-0	84	272-224
27.	Dec 13 @	Minnesota	3-4	L	17-10-0	34	110-97	67.	Mar 13 @	San Diego	3-2	W	43-24-0	86	275-226
28.	Dec 14 @	Cleveland	4-3	W	18-10-0	36	114-100	68.	Mar 17 @	Phoenix	7-4	W	44-24-0	88	282-230
29.	Dec 16	San Diego	2-4	L	18-11-0	36	116-104	69.	Mar 19	San Diego	8-3	W	45-24-0	90	290-233
30.	Dec 20 @	Phoenix	4-3	W	19-11-0	38	120-107	70.	Mar 20 @	Cincinnati	1-2	L	45-25-0	90	291-235
31.	Dec 21 @	San Diego	1-3	L	19-12-0	38	121-110	71.	Mar 21	Phoenix	4-3	W	46-25-0	92	295-238
32.	Dec 26	Denver	9-4	W	20-12-0	40	130-114	72.	Mar 24 @	Cleveland	3-2	W	47-25-0	94	298-240
33.	Dec 27	Minnesota	5-0	W	21-12-0	42	135-114	73.	Mar 25 @	Indianapolis	*3-4	L	47-26-0	94	301-244
34.	Dec 30	Winnipeg	3-5	L	21-13-0	42	138-119	74.	Mar 26	Cincinnati	5-1	W	48-26-0	96	306-245
35.	Jan 3	Ottawa	4-2	W	22-13-0	44	142-121	75.	Mar 28	Phoenix	7-4	W	49-26-0	98	313-249
36.	Jan 6	Cincinnati	7-3	W	23-13-0	46	149-124	76.	Mar 30	San Diego	3-4	L	49-27-0	98	316-253
37.	Jan 9	Cleveland	6-5	W	24-13-0	48	155-129	77.	Apr 1 @	Indianapolis	4-1	W	50-27-0	100	320-254
38.	Jan 10 @	Minnesota	4-1	W	25-13-0	50	159-130	78.	Apr 3 @	Phoenix	8-2	W	51-27-0	102	328-256
39.	Jan 11 @	Edmonton	5-3	W	26-13-0	52	164-133	79.	Apr 4	San Diego	5-2	W	52-27-0	104	333-258
40.	Jan 14 @	Winnipeg	1-4	L	26-14-0	52	165-137	80.	Apr 6	Phoenix	8-5	W	53-27-0	106	341-263

Aeros Stars of 1975-1976

Andre Hinse
35 goals

Gordie Howe
32 goals, 102 points

Marty Howe
+40 led team

Ron Grahame
39 wins, 3 shutouts

Don Larway
30 goals

Larry Lund
73 points

Scoring

pos	#	player	gp	g	a	pts	pim	+/-	ppg	shg	sog	sc%	gp	g	a	pts	pim	+/-
D	22	Butters, Bill	14	0	4	4	18	+8	0	0	11	0.000	17	0	3	3	51	-6
G	29	Grahame, Ron	57	0	1	1	0		0	0	0	-	14	0	0	0	0	-
D	17	Hale, Larry	77	1	14	15	32	+7	0	0	49	0.020	17	0	5	5	8	-1
C	11	Hall, Murray	80	20	26	46	18	-3	3	0	118	0.169	17	1	4	5	0	-5
LW	16	Hinse, Andre	70	35	38	73	6	+12	12	0	158	0.222	17	2	3	5	2	-10
RW	9	Howe, Gordie	78	32	70	102	76	+14	12	1	241	0.133	17	4	8	12	31	+1
D/F	4	Howe, Mark	72	39	37	76	38	+29	13	6	270	0.144	17	6	10	16	18	0
D	3	Howe, Marty	80	14	23	37	51	+40	0	0	179	0.078	16	4	4	8	12	-1
LW	7	Hughes, Frank	80	31	45	76	26	+12	12	0	165	0.188	17	5	1	6	20	-6
D	24	Irwin, Glen	72	3	8	11	116	+3	0	0	59	0.051	5	0	0	0	9	0
C	10	Labossiere, Gord	80	24	32	56	18	-1	4	0	151	0.159	17	2	8	10	14	-4
RW	27	Larway, Don	79	30	20	50	56	+9	3	0	196	0.153	16	7	5	12	21	+5
LW	22	Liddington, Bob	2	0	0	0	2	0	0	1	0.000	-	-	-	-	-	-	
C	13	Lund, Larry	73	24	49	73	50	+3	6	1	146	0.164	5	1	1	2	4	-4
LW	19	Popiel, Jan	67	4	7	11	59	-13	0	0	68	0.059	8	1	1	2	4	-2
D	6	Popiel, Poul	78	10	36	46	71	+29	2	2	162	0.062	17	3	5	8	16	-2
RW	21	Preston, Rich	77	22	33	55	33	+30	1	2	159	0.138	17	4	6	10	8	-1
C	8	Ruskowski, Terry	65	14	35	49	100	+18	3	0	105	0.133	16	6	10	16	64	+8
G	30	Rutledge, Wayne	35	0	0	0	6		0	0	0	-	4	0	0	0	0	-
D	2	Schella, John	74	6	32	38	106	+8	0	0	193	0.031	17	1	6	7	38	-2
D	22	Stevens, Mike	6	0	0	0	2	-2	0	0	7	0.000	-	-	-	-	-	-
LW	14	Taylor, Ted	68	15	26	41	80	-10	3	0	130	0.115	11	2	2	4	17	-5
LW	18	Tonelli, John	79	17	14	31	66	+11	3	1	123	0.138	17	7	7	14	8	+8
C	12	West, Steve	0	-	-	-	-	-	-	-	-	-	7	0	1	1	0	-1

Power Play: 77 goals scored in 254 opportunities (30.3%) with 10 short-handed goals allowed.
Penalty Killing: 43 goals allowed in 301 opportunities (85.7%) with 13 short-handed goals scored.

Goaltending

goaltender	gp	min	ga	en	so	record	gaa	sog	sv%	gp	min	ga	record	gaa
Grahame, Ron	57	3343	182	3	3	39-17-0	3.27	1752	0.896	14	817	54	6-8	3.97
Rutledge, Wayne	25	1456	77	1	1	14-10-0	3.17	780	0.901	4	200	10	2-1	3.00

Transactions: John Tonelli signed to contract, Mar 1975 (Tonelli was never drafted by Houston and as a result, Houston was penalized their first-round draft choice in the 1975 Amateur Draft) • Mike Stevens purchased from Phoenix, Aug 1975 • Jim Sherrit and Don Borgeson traded to Denver for Jan Popiel, Oct 1975 • Bob Liddington signed as free agent from defunct Ottawa, Feb 1976 • Bill Butters signed as free agent from defunct Minnesota, Mar 1976

1975-1976 INDIANAPOLIS RACERS

**Coach
Gerry Moore
1-4-0**

**Coach
Jacques Demers
34-35-6**

Summary of Games (@ Away, * Overtime)

	date	opponent	score		record	pts	gf-ga		date	opponent	score		record	pts	gf-ga
1.	Oct 10 @	Denver	7-1	W	1-0-0	2	7-1	41.	Jan 11 @	Cleveland	3-4	L	16-23-2	34	113-127
2.	Oct 12 @	Edmonton	5-6	L	1-1-0	2	12-7	42.	Jan 15	Cleveland	1-3	L	16-24-2	34	114-130
3.	Oct 14 @	Calgary	3-5	L	1-2-0	2	15-12	43.	Jan 17	Cincinnati	0-4	L	16-25-2	34	114-134
4.	Oct 16 @	San Diego	0-3	L	1-3-0	2	15-15	44.	Jan 21 @	Quebec	2-3	L	16-26-2	34	116-137
5.	Oct 18	Denver	4-6	L	1-4-0	2	19-21	45.	Jan 23	Cincinnati	4-3	W	17-26-2	36	120-140
6.	Oct 21	Minnesota	1-2	L	1-5-0	2	20-23	46.	Jan 25	Cleveland	4-2	W	18-26-2	38	124-142
7.	Oct 23	Houston	4-0	W	2-5-0	4	24-23	47.	Jan 28 @	New England	4-6	L	18-27-2	38	128-148
8.	Oct 26	Edmonton	4-3	W	3-5-0	6	28-26	48.	Jan 29	Minnesota	5-6	L	18-28-2	38	133-154
9.	Oct 30	Calgary	5-7	L	3-6-0	6	33-33	49.	Jan 30	Houston	2-1	W	19-28-2	40	135-155
10.	Nov 1	Quebec	2-5	L	3-7-0	6	35-38	50.	Feb 1	Winnipeg	1-2	L	19-29-2	40	136-157
11.	Nov 4	Toronto	4-3	W	4-7-0	8	39-41	51.	Feb 5	Quebec	4-2	W	20-29-2	42	140-159
12.	Nov 8 @	Quebec	2-3	L	4-8-0	8	41-44	52.	Feb 6 @	Houston	3-4	L	20-30-2	42	143-163
13.	Nov 15 @	Minnesota	7-9	L	4-9-0	8	48-53	53.	Feb 7	Cincinnati	5-1	W	21-30-2	44	148-164
14.	Nov 16 @	Winnipeg	1-2	L	4-10-0	8	49-55	54.	Feb 11	Phoenix	2-1	W	22-30-2	46	150-165
15.	Nov 17 @	Toronto	6-2	W	5-10-0	10	55-57	55.	Feb 13	Calgary	*3-4	L	22-31-2	46	153-169
16.	Nov 19	New England	3-1	W	6-10-0	12	58-58	56.	Feb 14 @	Cincinnati	2-3	L	22-32-2	46	155-172
17.	Nov 25 @	Houston	1-4	L	6-11-0	12	59-62	57.	Feb 15	San Diego	2-3	L	22-33-2	46	157-175
18.	Nov 27	Winnipeg	3-1	W	7-11-0	14	62-63	58.	Feb 19	New England	10-3	W	23-33-2	48	167-178
19.	Nov 28 @	Cleveland	3-1	W	8-11-0	16	65-64	59.	Feb 21 @	Cleveland	2-3	L	23-34-2	48	169-181
20.	Nov 29 @	New England	3-2	W	9-11-0	18	68-66	60.	Feb 22	Phoenix	5-6	L	23-35-2	48	174-187
21.	Nov 30	Denver	2-4	L	9-12-0	18	70-70	61.	Feb 28 @	New England	4-4	T	23-35-3	49	178-191
22.	Dec 4	Cincinnati	7-1	W	10-12-0	20	77-71	62.	Feb 29 @	Cincinnati	5-2	W	24-35-3	51	183-193
23.	Dec 6	Cleveland	3-2	W	11-12-0	22	80-73	63.	Mar 2 @	Phoenix	2-5	L	24-36-3	51	185-198
24.	Dec 10 @	Phoenix	2-1	W	12-12-0	24	82-74	64.	Mar 4	Cincinnati	3-1	W	25-36-3	53	188-199
25.	Dec 11 @	San Diego	3-3	T	12-12-1	25	85-77	65.	Mar 6 @	Cincinnati	3-2	W	26-36-3	55	191-201
26.	Dec 12 @	Houston	2-4	L	12-13-1	25	87-81	66.	Mar 7	Cleveland	1-5	L	26-37-3	55	192-206
27.	Dec 14	New England	2-2	T	12-13-2	26	89-83	67.	Mar 11	Toronto	3-1	W	27-37-3	57	195-207
28.	Dec 16	Edmonton	1-3	L	12-14-2	26	90-86	68.	Mar 12 @	Cincinnati	6-3	W	28-37-3	59	201-210
29.	Dec 18 @	Phoenix	1-7	L	12-15-2	26	91-93	69.	Mar 13	Phoenix	6-4	W	29-37-3	61	207-214
30.	Dec 19	Cleveland	*5-4	W	13-15-2	28	96-97	70.	Mar 17 @	New England	5-2	W	30-37-3	63	212-216
31.	Dec 20 @	Cleveland	3-5	L	13-16-2	28	99-102	71.	Mar 18	San Diego	4-4	T	30-37-4	64	216-220
32.	Dec 27	Cincinnati	2-1	W	14-16-2	30	101-103	72.	Mar 20 @	New England	1-1	T	30-37-5	65	217-221
33.	Dec 28 @	Cincinnati	1-4	L	14-17-2	30	102-107	73.	Mar 23 @	San Diego	8-8	T	30-37-6	66	225-229
34.	Dec 30 @	Denver	*1-2	L	14-18-2	30	103-109	74.	Mar 25	Houston	*4-3	W	31-37-6	68	229-232
35.	Jan 2	San Diego	0-2	L	14-19-2	30	103-111	75.	Mar 26 @	Cleveland	3-2	W	32-37-6	70	232-234
36.	Jan 3 @	Minnesota	1-3	L	14-20-2	30	104-114	76.	Mar 28 @	New England	3-1	W	33-37-6	72	235-235
37.	Jan 4	New England	3-2	W	15-20-2	32	107-116	77.	Apr 1	Houston	1-4	L	33-38-6	72	236-239
38.	Jan 6 @	Edmonton	0-3	L	15-21-2	32	107-119	78.	Apr 2 @	Toronto	3-1	W	34-38-6	74	239-240
39.	Jan 7 @	Calgary	1-3	L	15-22-2	32	108-122	79.	Apr 3	New England	2-5	L	34-39-6	74	241-245
40.	Jan 9 @	Winnipeg	*2-1	W	16-22-2	34	110-123	80.	Apr 4 @	New England	4-2	W	35-39-6	76	245-247

Racers Stars of 1975-1976

Michel Dion
Top goaltender

Reg Thomas
23 goals led team

Brian McDonald
16 goals

Jim Park
2 playoff shutouts

Ken Block
26 points, +4

Dick Proceviat
+7 rating

Scoring

			Regular Season										Playoffs					
pos	#	player	gp	g	a	pts	pim	+/-	ppg	shg	sog	sc%	gp	g	a	pts	pim	+/-
D	5	Baltimore, Bryon	37	1	10	11	30	+8	0	0	44	0.023	7	0	1	1	4	0
D	24	Block, Ken	79	1	25	26	28	+4	0	0	104	0.010	-	-	-	-	-	-
LW	21	Bond, Kerry	15	2	0	2	9	-7	0	0	20	0.100	7	1	0	1	11	0
G	1	Brown, Andy	24	0	3	3	17		0	0	0	-	-	-	-	-	-	-
C	9	Buchanan, Ron	23	4	7	11	4	-5	1	0	60	0.067	-	-	-	-	-	-
D	4	Clackson, Kim	77	1	12	13	351	-10	1	0	71	0.014	6	0	0	0	25	-2
ILW	18	Coates, Brian	59	11	16	27	24	-5	2	1	72	0.153	4	0	0	0	6	-2
D		Critch, Glen	3	0	0	0	0	0	0	0	0	-	-	-	-	-	-	-
G	31	Dion, Michel	31	0	0	0	2		0	0	0	-	3	0	0	0	0	-
D	25	Dubois, Michel	34	2	2	4	104	-11	1	0	29	0.069	-	-	-	-	-	-
C	16	Fitchner, Bob	52	15	16	31	112	0	5	0	74	0.203	-	-	-	-	-	-
RW	10	Harbaruk, Nick	76	23	19	42	26	+10	2	2	170	0.135	7	2	0	2	10	+2
C	7	Harris, Hugh	41	12	28	40	23	+1	3	0	166	0.072	7	2	5	7	8	-3
RW	26	Heatley, Murray	34	2	5	7	7	-7	0	0	46	0.043	-	-	-	-	-	-
G	30	Holmquist, Leif	19	0	0	0	4		0	0	0	-	-	-	-	-	-	-
LW		Jones, Bob	2	0	0	0	0	-1	0	0	3	0.000	-	-	-	-	-	-
C	15	Karlander, Al	79	16	28	44	36	+15	4	0	121	0.132	3	0	0	0	4	0
C	6	Keon, Dave	12	3	7	10	2	+2	1	0	40	0.075	7	2	2	4	2	0
IRW	8	Leclerc, Rene	40	18	21	39	52	+1	7	0	152	0.118	7	2	5	7	7	-3
RW	25	Lomenda, Mark	2	0	0	0	0	-1	0	0	4	0.000	-	-	-	-	-	-
RW	14	MacDonald, Blair	56	19	11	30	14	+2	1	0	142	0.134	7	0	0	0	0	-3
D	2	Maggs, Darryl	36	5	16	21	40	+5	1	0	90	0.056	7	1	0	1	20	-2
RW	11	McDonald, Brian	63	16	17	33	58	-6	1	2	117	0.137	7	0	1	1	12	-1
C	16	Parizeau, Michel	23	13	15	28	20	+9	8	0	58	0.224	7	4	4	8	6	-3
G	28	Park, Jim	11	0	1	1	2		0	0	0	-	6	0	0	0	0	-
D	2	Prentice, Bill	38	4	2	6	92	-5	0	0	47	0.085	-	-	-	-	-	-
D	3	Proceviat, Dick	73	7	13	20	31	+7	0	0	65	0.108	7	0	0	0	2	-3
LW	19	Rochon, Francois	19	6	2	8	31	0	2	0	21	0.286	-	-	-	-	-	-
LW		Roselle, Bob	1	0	0	0	0	-1	0	0	1	0.000	-	-	-	-	-	-
RW	20	Scharf, Ted	74	7	13	20	56	-8	2	0	90	0.078	7	0	0	0	5	0
C	22	Sheridan, John	11	1	2	3	0	-5	0	0	9	0.111	-	-	-	-	-	-
C	17	Sicinski, Bob	70	9	34	43	4	-2	3	0	140	0.064	7	0	0	0	2	-1
D	12	Stapleton, Pat	80	5	40	45	48	-7	3	0	205	0.024	7	0	2	2	2	-3
LW	8/21	Thomas, Reg	80	23	17	40	23	+1	4	0	192	0.120	7	1	0	1	4	-1
C	7	Whitlock, Bobby	30	7	15	22	16	+1	2	0	111	0.063	-	-	-	-	-	-
C	14	Wiste, Jim	7	0	2	2	0	-2	0	0	3	0.000	-	-	-	-	-	-
D	5	Woytowich, Bob	42	1	7	8	14	0	0	0	23	0.043	-	-	-	-	-	-
C	6	Wyrozub, Randy	55	11	14	25	8	-4	5	1	79	0.139	-	-	-	-	-	-

Power Play: 59 goals scored in 254 opportunities (23.2%) with 9 short-handed goals allowed.
Penalty Killing: 52 goals allowed in 251 opportunities (79.4%) with 6 short-handed goals scored.

Goaltending

goaltender	gp	min	ga	en	so	record	gaa	sog	sv%	gp	min	ga	record	gaa
Brown, Andy	24	1368	82	0	1	9-11-2	3.60	751	0.891	-	-	-	-	-
Dion, Michel	31	1860	85	1	0	14-15-1	2.74	942	0.910	3	126	5	0-2	2.38
Holmquist, Leif	19	1079	54	2	0	6-9-3	3.00	522	0.897	-	-	-	-	-
Park, Jim	11	572	23	0	0	6-4-0	2.41	297	0.923	6	293	12	3-2	2.45

Transactions: Jim Park signed to contract, Oct 1974 • Leif Holmquist signed to contract, Jun 1975 • Rights to Randy Wyrozub acquired from Edmonton, Jul 1975 • Brian Coates acquired from Denver for future considerations, Sep 1975 • Randy Wyrozub signed to contract, Sep 1975 • Blair MacDonald acquired from Edmonton for draft picks, Dec 1975 • Bill Prentice traded to Quebec for Rene Leclerc, Jan 1976 • Bob Fitchner and Michel Dubois traded to Quebec for Michel Parizeau, Feb 1976 • Bryon Baltimore, Mark Lomenda, Gary MacGregor and Darryl Maggs purchased from Ottawa, Jan 1976 • Dave Keon signed as free agent from defunct Minnesota, Mar 1976

1975-1976 MINNESOTA FIGHTING SAINTS

Coach
Harry Neale

Summary of Games (@ Away, * Overtime)

	date		opponent	score		record	pts	gf-ga		date		opponent	score		record	pts	gf-ga
1.	Oct 10	@	Edmonton	4-1	W	1-0-0	2	4-1	31.	Dec 28		San Diego	1-2	L	16-13-2	34	101-105
2.	Oct 12	@	Calgary	2-0	W	2-0-0	4	6-1	32.	Dec 30		Quebec	4-4	T	16-13-3	35	105-109
3.	Oct 15		Cleveland	4-8	L	2-1-0	4	10-9	33.	Jan 3		Indianapolis	3-1	W	17-13-3	37	108-110
4.	Oct 18		Edmonton	1-3	L	2-2-0	4	11-12	34.	Jan 4		Ottawa	2-5	L	17-14-3	37	110-115
5.	Oct 21	@	Indianapolis	2-1	W	3-2-0	6	13-13	35.	Jan 7		Phoenix	*7-6	W	18-14-3	39	117-121
6.	Oct 23	@	San Diego	4-4	T	3-2-1	7	17-17	36.	Jan 10		Houston	1-4	L	18-15-3	39	118-125
7.	Oct 25	@	San Diego	1-6	L	3-3-1	7	18-23	37.	Jan 11	@	Cincinnati	7-4	W	19-15-3	41	125-129
8.	Oct 29		Cincinnati	4-6	L	3-4-1	7	22-29	38.	Jan 15	@	San Diego	*4-5	L	19-16-3	41	129-134
9.	Nov 1		Phoenix	3-2	W	4-4-1	9	25-31	39.	Jan 16	@	Phoenix	1-3	L	19-17-3	41	130-137
10.	Nov 5	@	Houston	4-6	L	4-5-1	9	29-37	40.	Jan 17	@	Phoenix	4-2	W	20-17-3	43	134-139
11.	Nov 8		Toronto	4-3	W	5-5-1	11	33-40	41.	Jan 21		San Diego	6-5	W	21-17-3	45	140-144
12.	Nov 11	@	Quebec	6-8	L	5-6-1	11	39-48	42.	Jan 23		San Diego	1-7	L	21-18-3	45	141-151
13.	Nov 15		Indianapolis	9-7	W	6-6-1	13	48-55	43.	Jan 25		Toronto	5-2	W	22-18-3	47	146-153
14.	Nov 16	@	Cincinnati	3-2	W	7-6-1	15	51-57	44.	Jan 28		Winnipeg	6-2	W	23-18-3	49	152-155
15.	Nov 19	@	Cleveland	*3-4	L	7-7-1	15	54-61	45.	Jan 29	@	Indianapolis	6-5	W	24-18-3	51	158-160
16.	Nov 20	@	New England	2-0	W	8-7-1	17	56-61	46.	Jan 31		Houston	4-1	W	25-18-3	53	162-161
17.	Nov 22		Calgary	4-6	L	8-8-1	17	60-67	47.	Feb 1		Cleveland	5-6	L	25-19-3	53	167-167
18.	Nov 25		*New England	3-2	W	9-8-1	19	63-69	48.	Feb 3	@	Houston	4-8	L	25-20-3	53	171-175
19.	Nov 27		Cincinnati	5-3	W	10-8-1	21	68-72	49.	Feb 4	@	San Diego	1-4	L	25-21-3	53	172-179
20.	Nov 30	@	Winnipeg	3-5	L	10-9-1	21	71-77	50.	Feb 7	@	Phoenix	2-4	L	25-22-3	53	174-183
21.	Dec 5		Denver	4-3	W	11-9-1	23	75-80	51.	Feb 8	@	Phoenix	3-3	T	25-22-4	54	177-186
22.	Dec 9	@	Toronto	5-3	W	12-9-1	25	80-83	52.	Feb 10		San Diego	6-3	W	26-22-4	56	183-189
23.	Dec 10		New England	2-3	L	12-10-1	25	82-86	53.	Feb 11	@	San Diego	4-2	W	27-22-4	58	187-191
24.	Dec 12	@	Cleveland	0-1	L	12-11-1	25	82-87	54.	Feb 12		Quebec	6-4	W	28-22-4	60	193-195
25.	Dec 13		Houston	4-3	W	13-11-1	27	86-90	55.	Feb 14		Phoenix	2-5	L	28-23-4	60	195-200
26.	Dec 17		New England	0-0	T	13-11-2	28	86-90	56.	Feb 17	@	Toronto	6-3	W	29-23-4	62	201-203
27.	Dec 20		Winnipeg	6-3	W	14-11-2	30	92-93	57.	Feb 20	@	Calgary	6-3	W	30-23-4	64	207-206
28.	Dec 21	@	Winnipeg	3-1	W	15-11-2	32	95-94	58.	Feb 22	@	Edmonton	3-4	L	30-24-4	64	210-210
29.	Dec 23	@	Denver	5-4	W	16-11-2	34	100-98	59.	Feb 25		San Diego	*1-2	L	30-25-4	64	211-212
30.	Dec 27	@	Houston	0-5	L	16-12-2	34	100-103		**Franchise folded February 27, 1976**							

264

Fighting Saints Stars of 1975-1976

| **Dave Keon** | **John McKenzie** | **Mike Antonovich** | **Paul Holmgren** | **Mike Walton** | **Henry Boucha** |
| 26 goals, +14 | 21 goals, +10 | 25 goals, +21 | 121 minutes | 71 points | 15 goals, 35 points |

Scoring

pos	#	player	gp	g	a	pts	pim	+/-	ppg	shg	sog	sc%	gp	g	a	pts	pim	+/-
C	12	Antonovich, Mike	57	25	21	46	18	+21		0	166	0.151	-	-	-	-	-	-
D	17	Arbour, John	7	0	4	4	14	+4	0	0	15	0.000	-	-	-	-	-	-
C	16	Boucha, Henry	36	15	20	35	47	+3		0	85	0.176	-	-	-	-	-	-
C	18	Boudreau, Bruce	30	3	6	9	4	-1		0	36	0.083	-	-	-	-	-	-
RW	9	Brackenbury, Curt	59	4	9	13	254	+7	0	0	52	0.077	-	-	-	-	-	-
RW	5	Busniuk, Ron	59	2	11	13	150	+9	2	0	76	0.026	-	-	-	-	-	-
D	2	Butters, Bill	59	0	15	15	120	+19	0	0	82	0.000	-	-	-	-	-	-
LW	20	Carlson, Jack	58	8	10	18	189	-14	0	0	68	0.117	-	-	-	-	-	-
RW	22	Carlson, Jeff	7	0	1	1	14	0	0	0	10	0.000	-	-	-	-	-	-
C	21	Carlson, Steve	10	0	1	1	23	-1	0	0	7	0.000	-	-	-	-	-	-
RW	7	Connelly, Wayne	59	24	23	47	19	+9	4	0	203	0.118	-	-	-	-	-	-
G	1	Curran, Mike	5	0	0	0	2		0	0	0	-	-	-	-	-	-	-
C	8	Gambucci, Gary	45	10	6	16	14	+5		0	92	0.109	-	-	-	-	-	-
G	35	Garrett, John	52	0	0	0	6		0	0	0	-	-	-	-	-	-	-
C	10	Hampson, Ted	59	5	15	20	14	-3	0	1	46	0.109	-	-	-	-	-	-
RW	24	Holmgren, Paul	51	14	16	30	121	-7		0	97	0.144	-	-	-	-	-	-
C	25	Huck, Fran	59	17	32	49	27	+9		0	115	0.110	-	-	-	-	-	-
C	14	Keon, Dave	57	26	38	64	4	+14	5	2	144	0.181	-	-	-	-	-	-
G	30	Levasseur, Louis	4	0	0	0	0		0	0	0	-	-	-	-	-	-	-
RW	19	McKenzie, John	57	21	26	47	48	+10	4	2	125	0.168	-	-	-	-	-	-
D	11	Miller, Perry	13	1	4	5	11	-5	0	0	15	0.067	-	-	-	-	-	-
D	15	Odrowski, Gerry	37	1	12	13	10	-9	0	0	69	0.014	-	-	-	-	-	-
D	26	Ouimet, Francois	9	0	2	2	2	0	0	0	3	0.000	-	-	-	-	-	-
RW		Sarner, Craig	1	0	0	0	0	0	0	0	1	0.000	-	-	-	-	-	-
D	3	Smith, Rick	51	1	32	33	50	+1		0	101	0.010	-	-	-	-	-	-
C	11	Tetreault, Jean	3	0	0	0	0	0	0	0	1	0.000	-	-	-	-	-	-
C	4	Walton, Mike	58	31	40	71	27	+7		0	210	0.148	-	-	-	-	-	-
D	6	Westrum, Pat	54	3	10	13	98	0	0	0	55	0.055	-	-	-	-	-	-
D	23	Zrymiak, Jerry	22	0	8	8	16	+2	0	0	18	0.000	-	-	-	-	-	-

Power Play: 40 goals scored in 185 opportunities (21.6%) with 9 short-handed goals allowed.
Penalty Killing: 58 goals allowed in 245 opportunities (76.3%) with 5 short-handed goals scored.

Goaltending

goaltender	gp	min	ga	en	so	record	gaa	sog	sv%	gp	min	ga	record	gaa
Curran, Mike	5	240	22	0	1	2-2-0	5.50	153	0.856	-	-	-	-	-
Garrett, John	52	3179	177	3	2	26-22-4	3.34	1673	0.894	-	-	-	-	-
Levasseur, Louis	4	193	10	0	0	2-1-0	3.11	87	0.885	-	-	-	-	-

Transactions: Henry Boucha signed to contract, May 1975 • Rights to Paul Holmgren purchased from Edmonton, Jul 1975 • Dave Keon signed to contract, Aug 1975 • John McKenzie acquired from Calgary for George Morrison, Wally Olds, Don Tannahill and Joe Micheletti, Sep 1976 • John Arbour traded to Denver for draft pick, Oct 1975, subsequently resigned as free agent from defunct Ottawa, Feb 1976 • Gerry Odrowski traded to Winnipeg for Perry Miller, Jan 1976 • Remaining players declared free agents, Mar 1976

1975-1976 NEW ENGLAND WHALERS

**Coach
Jack Kelley
14-16-3**

**Coach
Don Blackburn
14-18-3**

**Coach
Harry Neale
5-6-1**

Summary of Games (@ Away, * Overtime)

#	date	opponent	score		record	pts	gf-ga
1.	Oct 11	Houston	0-5	L	0-1-0	0	0-5
2.	Oct 15	Edmonton	*5-4	W	1-1-0	2	5-9
3.	Oct 18	Toronto	3-1	W	2-1-0	4	8-10
4.	Oct 21 @	Quebec	1-6	L	2-2-0	4	9-16
5.	Oct 24 @	Toronto	5-4	W	3-2-0	6	14-20
6.	Oct 26	Calgary	3-1	W	4-2-0	8	17-21
7.	Oct 29	Quebec	4-2	W	5-2-0	10	21-23
8.	Oct 31 @	Edmonton	2-2	T	5-2-1	11	23-25
9.	Nov 2 @	Calgary	*3-4	L	5-3-1	11	26-29
10.	Nov 4 @	Winnipeg	*2-3	L	5-4-1	11	28-32
11.	Nov 6	Cincinnati	8-3	W	6-4-1	13	36-35
12.	Nov 8	Phoenix	2-3	L	6-5-1	13	38-38
13.	Nov 9 @	Cincinnati	2-4	L	6-6-1	13	40-42
14.	Nov 12	Houston	4-1	W	7-6-1	15	44-43
15.	Nov 15	Quebec	1-3	L	7-7-1	15	45-46
16.	Nov 19 @	Indianapolis	1-3	L	7-8-1	15	46-49
17.	Nov 20	Minnesota	0-2	L	7-9-1	15	46-51
18.	Nov 22	Phoenix	7-5	W	8-9-1	17	53-56
19.	Nov 23	Winnipeg	2-3	L	8-10-1	17	55-59
20.	Nov 25 @	Minnesota	*2-3	L	8-11-1	17	57-62
21.	Nov 28	Denver	7-3	W	9-11-1	19	64-65
22.	Nov 29	Indianapolis	2-3	L	9-12-1	19	66-68
23.	Dec 2 @	Houston	5-2	W	10-12-1	21	71-70
24.	Dec 4 @	Phoenix	4-5	L	10-13-1	21	75-75
25.	Dec 6 @	San Diego	1-4	L	10-14-1	21	76-79
26.	Dec 7 @	Denver	1-5	L	10-15-1	21	77-84
27.	Dec 10	Minnesota	3-2	W	11-15-1	23	80-86
28.	Dec 13	Cleveland	5-4	W	12-15-1	25	85-90
29.	Dec 14 @	Indianapolis	2-2	T	12-15-2	26	87-92
30.	Dec 17 @	Minnesota	0-0	T	12-15-3	27	87-92
31.	Dec 19	Edmonton	4-2	W	13-15-3	29	91-94
32.	Dec 20 @	Cincinnati	2-4	L	13-16-3	29	93-98
33.	Dec 22 @	Cleveland	4-1	W	14-16-3	31	97-99
34.	Dec 26	Cincinnati	4-3	W	15-16-3	33	101-102
35.	Dec 28	Cleveland	4-0	W	16-16-3	35	105-102
36.	Dec 30	San Diego	5-3	W	17-16-3	37	110-105
37.	Jan 3	Cleveland	3-2	W	18-16-3	39	113-107
38.	Jan 4 @	Indianapolis	2-3	L	18-17-3	39	115-110
39.	Jan 7 @	Ottawa	3-2	W	19-17-3	41	118-112
40.	Jan 9	San Diego	3-5	L	19-18-3	41	121-117

#	date	opponent	score		record	pts	gf-ga
41.	Jan 11	San Diego	8-4	W	20-18-3	43	129-121
42.	Jan 15	Cincinnati	5-2	W	21-18-3	45	134-123
43.	Jan 16 @	Cleveland	3-4	L	21-19-3	45	137-127
44.	Jan 18 @	Winnipeg	0-8	L	21-20-3	45	137-135
45.	Jan 20 @	Phoenix	4-4	T	21-20-4	46	141-139
46.	Jan 21 @	Houston	3-9	L	21-21-4	46	144-148
47.	Jan 23 @	Cleveland	2-2	T	21-21-5	47	146-150
48.	Jan 24 @	Cincinnati	3-6	L	21-22-5	47	149-156
49.	Jan 28	Indianapolis	6-4	W	22-22-5	49	155-160
50.	Jan 30	Winnipeg	3-6	L	22-23-5	49	158-166
51.	Feb 1 @	Toronto	7-5	W	23-23-5	51	165-171
52.	Feb 3 @	Edmonton	0-4	L	23-24-5	51	165-175
53.	Feb 5 @	Calgary	6-4	W	24-24-5	53	171-179
54.	Feb 7	Toronto	7-3	W	25-24-5	55	178-182
55.	Feb 8	Cleveland	1-6	L	25-25-5	55	179-188
56.	Feb 13	Cincinnati	1-5	L	25-26-5	55	180-193
57.	Feb 15 @	Cleveland	3-2	W	26-26-5	57	183-195
58.	Feb 17 @	Houston	3-4	L	26-27-5	57	186-199
59.	Feb 19 @	Indianapolis	3-10	L	26-28-5	57	189-209
60.	Feb 22 @	Quebec	0-4	L	26-29-5	57	189-213
61.	Feb 25 @	Cincinnati	2-5	L	26-30-5	57	191-218
62.	Feb 26	Houston	2-5	L	26-31-5	57	193-223
63.	Feb 28	Indianapolis	4-4	T	26-31-6	58	197-227
64.	Mar 2 @	San Diego	4-3	W	27-31-6	60	201-230
65.	Mar 4 @	San Diego	2-8	L	27-32-6	60	203-238
66.	Mar 6 @	Phoenix	5-3	W	28-32-6	62	208-241
67.	Mar 7 @	Cincinnati	3-5	L	28-33-6	62	211-246
68.	Mar 10	Phoenix	2-3	L	28-34-6	62	213-249
69.	Mar 12	Cleveland	8-2	W	29-34-6	64	221-251
70.	Mar 13 @	Cincinnati	5-1	W	30-34-6	66	226-252
71.	Mar 16 @	Quebec	1-5	L	30-35-6	66	227-257
72.	Mar 17	Indianapolis	2-5	L	30-36-6	66	229-262
73.	Mar 19	Cincinnati	*6-5	W	31-36-6	68	235-267
74.	Mar 20	Indianapolis	1-1	T	31-36-7	69	236-268
75.	Mar 24	Calgary	6-7	L	31-37-7	69	242-275
76.	Mar 26	Calgary	4-1	W	32-37-7	71	246-276
77.	Mar 28	Indianapolis	1-3	L	32-38-7	71	247-279
78.	Mar 31 @	Cleveland	1-5	L	32-39-7	71	248-284
79.	Apr 3 @	Indianapolis	5-2	W	33-39-7	73	253-286
80.	Apr 4	Indianapolis	2-4	L	33-40-7	73	255-290

Whalers Stars of 1975-1976

Rosaire Paiement — 28 goals, 71 points   **Cap Raeder** — Playoff hero   **Larry Pleau** — 29 goals, 74 points   **Tom Webster** — 33 goals, 83 points   **Christer Abrahamsson** — 18 wins, 2 shutouts   **Brad Selwood** — +5 rating

Scoring

pos	#	player	gp	g	a	pts	pim	+/-	ppg	shg	sog	sc%	gp	g	a	pts	pim	+/-
G	1	Abrahamsson, C.	41	0	1	1	6		0	0	0	-	1	0	0	0	0	-
D	6	Abrahamsson, T.	63	14	21	35	47	-11	3	2	150	0.093	17	2	4	6	15	+2
LW	19	Arndt, Danny	69	8	8	16	10	-16	1	0	89	0.090	8	0	0	0	0	+3
C	9	Backstrom, Ralph	38	14	19	33	6		0	1	94	0.149	17	5	4	9	8	+4
LW	22	Blackburn, Don	21	2	3	5	6	-5	0	0	15	0.133	-	-	-	-	-	-
LW	21	Bolduc, Dan	14	2	5	7	14	+5	0	0	27	0.074	16	1	6	7	4	+4
LW	22	Borgeson, Don	31	9	8	17	4	-2	1	0	62	0.145	3	1	1	2	0	+2
RW	5	Busniuk, Ron	11	0	3	3	55	0	0	0	18	0.000	17	0	2	2	14	+1
RW	21	Byers, Mike	21	4	3	7	0	-2	0	0	25	0.160	-	-	-	-	-	-
C	7	Caffery, Terry	2	0	0	0	0	-1	0	0	2	0.000	-	-	-	-	-	-
LW	9	Carleton, Wayne	35	12	21	33	6	-3	2	0	107	0.112	-	-	-	-	-	-
LW	18	Charlebois, Bob	28	3	3	6	0	-1	0	0	19	0.158	-	-	-	-	-	-
LW	15	Climie, Ron	65	25	20	45	17	-8	6	0	118	0.212	-	-	-	-	-	-
G	29	Cooley, Gaye	0	-	-	-	-	0	0	0	-	-	1	0	0	0	0	-
C	24	Danby, John	1	0	0	0	0	0	0	0	0	-	-	-	-	-	-	-
RW	27	Earl, Tom	66	8	11	19	26	-7	0	6	63	0.127	17	0	5	5	4	0
LW	23	Fotiu, Nick	49	3	2	5	94	-5	0	0	44	0.068	16	3	2	5	57	+2
D	26	Gateman, J. Marty	12	0	1	1	6	-8	0	0	6	0.000	-	-	-	-	-	-
D	10	Hangsleben, Alan	78	2	23	25	62	-3	0	0	118	0.017	13	2	3	5	20	+2
G	29	Hoganson, Paul	4	0	1	1	0		0	0	0	-	-	-	-	-	-	-
D	5	Hurley, Paul	46	0	14	14	20	-6	0	0	98	0.000	-	-	-	-	-	-
G	30	Landon, Bruce	38	0	1	1	0		0	0	0	-	4	0	0	0	0	-
D	2	Ley, Rick	67	8	30	38	78	-20	2	0	130	0.062	17	1	4	5	49	+3
C	11	McManama, Rob	37	3	10	13	28	-12	1	0	39	0.077	12	4	3	7	4	+6
RW	16	O'Donnell, Fred	79	11	11	22	81	-19	0	0	100	0.110	17	2	5	7	20	-2
RW	12	Paiement, Rosaire	80	28	43	71	89	-6	4	1	200	0.140	17	4	11	15	41	+3
C	4	Pleau, Larry	75	29	45	74	21	+1	12	2	192	0.151	14	5	7	12	0	+5
G	35	Raeder, Cap	3	0	0	0	0		0	0	0	-	14	0	0	0	0	-
C	18	Richardson, Steve	6	0	0	0	0	-1	0	0	5	0.000	-	-	-	-	-	-
D	14	Roberts, Doug	76	4	13	17	51	-3	0	0	109	0.037	17	1	1	2	8	+8
D	7	Roberts, Gordie	77	3	19	22	102	-17	0	0	115	0.026	17	2	9	11	36	+10
C	17	Rogers, Mike	36	18	14	32	10	-5	1	0	88	0.205	17	5	8	13	2	+1
D	3	Selwood, Brad	40	2	10	12	28	+5	0	0	55	0.036	17	2	2	4	27	+5
C	20	Swain, Garry	79	10	16	26	46	-30	1	3	118	0.085	17	3	2	5	15	+3
RW	25	Troy, Jim	14	0	0	0	43	-5	0	0	7	0.000	2	0	0	0	29	0
RW	8	Webster, Tom	55	33	50	83	24	+14	9	0	195	0.169	17	10	9	19	6	+3

Power Play: 46 goals scored in 259 opportunities (17.8%) with 4 short-handed goals allowed.
Penalty Killing: 56 goals allowed in 271 opportunities (79.3%) with 15 short-handed goals scored.

Goaltending

goaltender	gp	min	ga	en	so	record	gaa	sog	sv%	gp	min	ga	record	gaa
Abrahamsson, C.	41	2385	136	1	2	18-18-2	3.42	1221	0.889	1	1	0	0-0	0.00
Cooley, Gaye	0	-	-	-	-	-	-	-	-	1	1	0	0-0	0.00
Hoganson, Paul	4	224	16	0	0	1-2-0	4.29	108	0.852	-	-	-	-	-
Landon, Bruce	38	2181	126	3	0	14-19-5	3.47	1094	0.885	4	197	7	3-0	2.13
Raeder, Cap	3	100	8	0	0	0-1-0	4.80	46	0.826	14	819	31	7-7	2.27

Transactions: Rosaire Paiement acquired from Denver for 1976 draft choice, Jun 1975 • Marty Gateman, Doug Roberts and Gordie Roberts signed to contracts, Sep 1975 • Terry Caffery traded to Calgary for future considerations, Oct 1975 • Mike Byers and Paul Hoganson released, Nov 1975. Both subsequently signed by Cincinnati • Ralph Backstrom and Don Borgeson purchased from Ottawa, Jan 1976 • Wayne Carleton traded to Edmonton for Mike Rogers, Jan 1976 • Paul Hurley traded to Edmonton for Kerry Ketter and Steve Carlyle, Feb 1976 • Ron Busniuk signed as free agent from defunct Minnesota, Mar 1976 • Dan Bolduc signed to contract, Mar 1976 • Gaye Cooley signed as emergency goaltender, Apr 1976

1975-1976 PHOENIX ROADRUNNERS

Coach
Sandy Hucul

Summary of Games (@ Away, * Overtime)

	date	opponent	score		record	pts	gf-ga		date	opponent	score		record	pts	gf-ga
1.	Oct 10	San Diego	6-5	W	1-0-0	2	6-5	41.	Jan 17	Minnesota	2-4	L	19-19-3	41	150-143
2.	Oct 11 @	San Diego	4-2	W	2-0-0	4	10-7	42.	Jan 20	New England	4-4	T	19-19-4	42	154-147
3.	Oct 12	Winnipeg	0-4	L	2-1-0	4	10-11	43.	Jan 22	Toronto	6-4	W	20-19-4	44	160-151
4.	Oct 17	Denver	4-5	L	2-2-0	4	14-16	44.	Jan 25	San Diego	7-5	W	21-19-4	46	167-156
5.	Oct 19	Winnipeg	6-5	W	3-2-0	6	20-21	45.	Jan 27 @	San Diego	*4-3	W	22-19-4	48	171-159
6.	Oct 24 @	Calgary	4-3	W	4-2-0	8	24-24	46.	Jan 28	Calgary	5-0	W	23-19-4	50	176-159
7.	Oct 26 @	Winnipeg	0-5	L	4-3-0	8	24-29	47.	Jan 30	Cleveland	4-4	T	23-19-5	51	180-163
8.	Oct 28 @	Edmonton	3-7	L	4-4-0	8	27-36	48.	Jan 31 @	San Diego	1-6	L	23-20-5	51	181-169
9.	Oct 30 @	Denver	3-2	W	5-4-0	10	30-38	49.	Feb 4	Cleveland	5-1	W	24-20-5	53	186-170
10.	Nov 1 @	Minnesota	2-3	L	5-5-0	10	32-41	50.	Feb 5	Edmonton	5-1	W	25-20-5	55	191-171
11.	Nov 2 @	Cleveland	2-5	L	5-6-0	10	34-46	51.	Feb 7	Minnesota	4-2	W	26-20-5	57	195-173
12.	Nov 7 @	Houston	3-5	L	5-7-0	10	37-51	52.	Feb 8	Minnesota	3-3	T	26-20-6	58	198-176
13.	Nov 8 @	New England	3-2	W	6-7-0	12	40-53	53.	Feb 11 @	Indianapolis	1-2	L	26-21-6	58	199-178
14.	Nov 9 @	Quebec	3-7	L	6-8-0	12	43-60	54.	Feb 12	Houston	1-4	L	26-22-6	58	200-182
15.	Nov 14	Toronto	2-2	T	6-8-1	13	45-62	55.	Feb 14 @	Minnesota	5-2	W	27-22-6	60	205-184
16.	Nov 16	Cleveland	4-4	T	6-8-2	14	49-66	56.	Feb 15 @	Edmonton	4-2	W	28-22-6	62	209-186
17.	Nov 20	Edmonton	3-1	W	7-8-2	16	52-67	57.	Feb 18 @	Winnipeg	3-4	L	28-23-6	62	212-190
18.	Nov 22 @	New England	5-7	L	7-9-2	16	57-74	58.	Feb 20 @	Cincinnati	1-4	L	28-24-6	62	213-194
19.	Nov 27	Calgary	1-5	L	7-10-2	16	58-79	59.	Feb 22 @	Indianapolis	6-5	W	29-24-6	64	219-199
20.	Nov 29	Quebec	4-4	T	7-10-3	17	62-83	60.	Feb 27	San Diego	4-3	W	30-24-6	66	223-202
21.	Nov 30	Quebec	1-2	L	7-11-3	17	63-85	61.	Feb 29 @	Calgary	5-2	W	31-24-6	68	228-204
22.	Dec 4	New England	5-4	W	8-11-3	19	68-89	62.	Mar 2	Indianapolis	5-2	W	32-24-6	70	233-206
23.	Dec 6	*Houston	*6-5	W	9-11-3	21	74-94	63.	Mar 5 @	Houston	3-6	L	32-25-6	70	236-212
24.	Dec 10	Indianapolis	1-2	L	9-12-3	21	75-96	64.	Mar 6	New England	3-5	L	32-26-6	70	239-217
25.	Dec 12	Cincinnati	2-4	L	9-13-3	21	77-100	65.	Mar 7 @	San Diego	2-5	L	32-27-6	70	241-222
26.	Dec 13 @	Denver	4-1	W	10-13-3	23	81-101	66.	Mar 10 @	New England	3-2	W	33-27-6	72	244-224
27.	Dec 14	San Diego	4-2	W	11-13-3	25	85-103	67.	Mar 12 @	Toronto	5-2	W	34-27-6	74	249-226
28.	Dec 18	Indianapolis	7-1	W	12-13-3	27	92-104	68.	Mar 13 @	Indianapolis	4-6	L	34-28-6	74	253-232
29.	Dec 20	Houston	3-4	L	12-14-3	27	95-108	69.	Mar 14 @	Cleveland	*3-2	W	35-28-6	76	256-234
30.	Dec 23 @	Cincinnati	5-3	W	13-14-3	29	100-111	70.	Mar 17	Houston	4-7	L	35-29-6	76	260-241
31.	Dec 26 @	San Diego	2-4	L	13-15-3	29	102-115	71.	Mar 19	Cleveland	*5-6	L	35-30-6	76	265-247
32.	Dec 27	Denver	10-0	W	14-15-3	31	112-115	72.	Mar 20 @	San Diego	*4-3	W	36-30-6	78	269-250
33.	Dec 28 @	Denver	5-2	W	15-15-3	33	117-117	73.	Mar 21 @	Houston	3-4	L	36-31-6	78	272-254
34.	Jan 2 @	Toronto	1-4	L	15-16-3	33	118-121	74.	Mar 24	Cincinnati	4-5	L	36-32-6	78	276-259
35.	Jan 3 @	Quebec	4-1	W	16-16-3	35	122-122	75.	Mar 26	San Diego	3-1	W	37-32-6	80	279-260
36.	Jan 4 @	Cleveland	2-3	L	16-17-3	35	124-125	76.	Mar 27 @	San Diego	5-2	W	38-32-6	82	284-262
37.	Jan 7 @	Minnesota	*6-7	L	16-18-3	35	130-132	77.	Mar 28 @	Houston	4-7	L	38-33-6	82	288-269
38.	Jan 8	Cincinnati	7-1	W	17-18-3	37	137-133	78.	Mar 31 @	Cincinnati	7-2	W	39-33-6	84	295-271
39.	Jan 10	Ottawa	8-5	W	18-18-3	39	145-138	79.	Apr 3	Houston	2-8	L	39-34-6	84	297-279
40.	Jan 16	Minnesota	3-1	W	19-18-3	41	148-139	80.	Apr 6 @	Houston	5-8	L	39-35-6	84	302-287

Roadrunners Stars of 1975-1976

Pekka Rautakallio
+25 rating

John Gray
35 goals, +22

Robbie Ftorek
113 points

Del Hall
47 goals, 91 points

Michel Cormier
21 goals

Cam Connor
295 minutes, +23

Scoring

			Regular Season										**Playoffs**						
pos	#	player	gp	g	a	pts	pim	+/-	ppg	shg	sog	sc%	gp	g	a	pts	pim	+/-
D	5	Beaudoin, Serge	76	0	21	21	102	+4	0	0	96	0.000	5	1	0	1	10	-2
C	14	Boyd, Jim	80	23	34	57	44	+3	8	2	189	0.122	5	3	2	5	2	+4
D	26	Clarke, Jim	59	1	9	10	57	+3	0	0	56	0.018	-	-	-	-	-	-
RW	17	Connor, Cam	73	18	21	39	295	+23	0	0	153	0.118	5	1	0	1	21	+2
LW	16	Cormier, Michel	46	21	15	36	4	+5	4	0	120	0.175	-	-	-	-	-	-
LW	21	Dean, Barry	71	9	25	34	110	+17	1	0	126	0.071	-	-	-	-	-	-
LW	7	Erickson, Grant	33	4	4	8	6	0	0	1	64	0.063	5	0	2	2	0	+1
C	8	Ftorek, Robbie	80	41	72	113	109	+36	10	0	232	0.177	5	1	3	4	2	-3
RW	10	Gorman, Dave	67	11	20	31	28	0	1	0	120	0.092	5	0	2	2	24	+1
LW	15	Gray, John	79	35	45	80	136	+22	6	0	192	0.182	5	1	1	2	7	+2
C	9	Hall, Del	80	47	44	91	10	+21	12	0	249	0.189	5	2	3	5	0	-5
G	25	Hebenton, Clay	2	0	0	0	0		0	0	0	-	-	-	-	-	-	-
C	20	Hobin, Mike	9	1	1	2	2	+1	0	0	13	0.077	-	-	-	-	-	-
C	12	Huston, Ron	79	22	44	66	4	0	4	4	185	0.119	5	1	1	2	0	+1
C	11	Keogan, Murray	8	0	2	2	4		0	0	14	0.000	-	-	-	-	-	-
G	1	Kurt, Gary	40	0	4	4	4		0	0	0	-	-	-	-	-	-	-
D	4	Lariviere, Garry	79	7	17	24	100	+15	1	0	102	0.069	5	0	2	2	2	+7
RW	3	McLeod, Al	80	2	17	19	82	+12	1	0	83	0.024	5	0	2	2	4	-1
D	7	McNamee, Pete	14	1	2	3	32	-6	0	0	22	0.045	-	-	-	-	-	-
LW	18	Migneault, John	68	8	12	20	14	-9	0	0	69	0.116	3	0	0	0	0	+1
RW	24	Mononen, Lauri	75	15	21	36	19	+9	2	0	135	0.111	5	1	3	4	2	-2
D	2	Niekamp, Jim	79	4	14	18	77	+21	1	0	87	0.046	5	0	1	1	0	-4
G	30	Norris, Jack	41	0	2	2	6		0	0	0	-	5	0	0	0	0	-
D	19	Rautakallio, Pekka	73	11	39	50	8	+25	3	0	191	0.058	5	0	2	2	0	+4
D	31	Sleep, Mike	9	2	0	2	0	-4	0	0	5	0.40	-	-	-	-	-	-
LW	11	Veneruzzo, Gary	61	19	24	43	27	+22	3	1	130	0.146	5	2	0	2	7	+3

Power Play: 57 goals scored in 276 opportunities (20.7%) with 3 short-handed goals allowed.
Penalty Killing: 89 goals allowed in 330 opportunities (73.0%) with 8 short-handed goals scored.

Goaltending

goaltender	gp	min	ga	en	so	record	gaa	sog	sv%	gp	min	ga	record	gaa
Hebenton, Clay	2	80	9	0	0	0-1-0	6.75	48	0.813	-	-	-	-	-
Kurt, Gary	40	2369	147	1	1	18-20-2	3.72	1162	0.873	-	-	-	-	-
Norris, Jack	41	2412	128	2	1	21-14-4	3.18	1177	0.891	5	298	17	2-3	3.42

Transactions: Del Hall and Ron Huston acquired from California (NHL) for rights to Gary Holt, Jun 1975 • Lauri Mononen, Pekka Rautakallio signed to contracts, Jun 1975 • Rights to Barry Dean acquired from Edmonton for two 1976 draft choices, Aug 1975 • Murray Keogan sold to Calgary, Oct 1975 • Gary Veneruzzo acquired from Cincinnati for Ron Serafini, Nov 1975 • Grant Erickson acquired from Cleveland for Rick Newell and Rob Watt, Nov 1975 • Pete McNamee traded to San Diego for Dave Walter, Dec 1975

1975-1976 QUEBEC NORDIQUES

**Coach
Jean-Guy Gendron**

Summary of Games (@ Away, * Overtime)

	date	opponent	score		record	pts	gf-ga
1.	Oct 9	Winnipeg	3-5	L	0-1-0	0	3-5
2.	Oct 11	Toronto	7-3	W	1-1-0	2	10-8
3.	Oct 14	Edmonton	8-5	W	2-1-0	4	18-13
4.	Oct 18	Houston	3-2	W	3-1-0	6	21-15
5.	Oct 21	New England	6-1	W	4-1-0	8	27-16
6.	Oct 25	Toronto	3-2	W	5-1-0	10	30-18
7.	Oct 28 @	Toronto	4-6	L	5-2-0	10	34-24
8.	Oct 29 @	New England	2-4	L	5-3-0	10	36-28
9.	Oct 31 @	Cleveland	2-6	L	5-4-0	10	38-34
10.	Nov 1 @	Indianapolis	5-2	W	6-4-0	12	43-36
11.	Nov 2 @	Winnipeg	1-0	W	7-4-0	14	44-36
12.	Nov 4 @	Edmonton	4-3	W	8-4-0	16	48-39
13.	Nov 5 @	Calgary	2-4	L	8-5-0	16	50-43
14.	Nov 6 @	Denver	5-3	W	9-5-0	18	55-46
15.	Nov 8	Indianapolis	3-2	W	10-5-0	20	58-48
16.	Nov 9	Phoenix	7-3	W	11-5-0	22	65-51
17.	Nov 11	Minnesota	8-6	W	12-5-0	24	73-57
18.	Nov 15 @	New England	3-1	W	13-5-0	26	76-58
19.	Nov 18	Cincinnati	6-4	W	14-5-0	28	82-62
20.	Nov 20	Winnipeg	*2-3	L	14-6-0	28	84-65
21.	Nov 22 @	Cincinnati	9-6	W	15-6-0	30	93-71
22.	Nov 23 @	Houston	0-4	L	15-7-0	30	93-75
23.	Nov 27 @	San Diego	1-5	L	15-8-0	30	94-80
24.	Nov 29 @	Phoenix	4-4	T	15-8-1	31	98-84
25.	Nov 30 @	Phoenix	2-1	W	16-8-1	33	100-85
26.	Dec 2	Cleveland	9-2	W	17-8-1	35	109-87
27.	Dec 5 @	Toronto	4-7	L	17-9-1	35	113-94
28.	Dec 7 @	Winnipeg	3-2	W	18-9-1	37	116-96
29.	Dec 9 @	Calgary	1-4	L	18-10-1	37	117-100
30.	Dec 10 @	Edmonton	4-7	L	18-11-1	37	121-107
31.	Dec 12 @	Toronto	4-6	L	18-12-1	37	125-113
32.	Dec 13	Toronto	6-3	W	19-12-1	39	131-116
33.	Dec 16	Calgary	7-3	W	20-12-1	41	138-119
34.	Dec 18	Winnipeg	5-4	W	21-12-1	43	143-123
35.	Dec 20	Calgary	8-7	W	22-12-1	45	151-130
36.	Dec 21 @	Cincinnati	7-11	L	22-13-1	45	158-141
37.	Dec 23 @	San Diego	4-10	L	22-14-1	45	162-151
38.	Dec 27	Edmonton	6-3	W	23-14-1	47	168-154
39.	Dec 28 @	Toronto	6-1	W	24-14-1	49	174-155
40.	Dec 30 @	Minnesota	4-4	T	24-14-2	50	178-159
41.	Jan 2 @	Cleveland	*4-5	L	24-15-2	50	182-164
42.	Jan 3	Phoenix	1-4	L	24-16-2	50	183-168
43.	Jan 10	San Diego	*4-3	W	25-16-2	52	187-171
44.	Jan 15	Calgary	5-3	W	26-16-2	54	192-174
45.	Jan 17	Toronto	4-3	W	27-16-2	56	196-177
46.	Jan 21	Indianapolis	3-2	W	28-16-2	58	199-179
47.	Jan 25	Edmonton	7-6	W	29-16-2	60	206-185
48.	Jan 27	Cincinnati	9-1	W	30-16-2	62	215-186
49.	Jan 30 @	Toronto	3-3	T	30-16-3	63	218-189
50.	Jan 31	Toronto	8-4	W	31-16-3	65	226-193
51.	Feb 3	Winnipeg	5-4	W	32-16-3	67	231-197
52.	Feb 5 @	Indianapolis	2-4	L	32-17-3	67	233-201
53.	Feb 7 @	Calgary	4-4	T	32-17-4	68	237-205
54.	Feb 8 @	Edmonton	5-4	W	33-17-4	70	242-209
55.	Feb 11 @	Winnipeg	6-4	W	34-17-4	72	248-213
56.	Feb 12 @	Minnesota	4-6	L	34-18-4	72	252-219
57.	Feb 15 @	Houston	4-2	W	35-18-4	74	256-221
58.	Feb 17	San Diego	5-2	W	36-18-4	76	261-223
59.	Feb 22	New England	4-0	W	37-18-4	78	265-223
60.	Feb 24	Houston	4-1	W	38-18-4	80	269-224
61.	Feb 28	Winnipeg	*3-4	L	38-19-4	80	272-228
62.	Mar 2 @	Toronto	2-5	L	38-20-4	80	274-233
63.	Mar 4 @	Calgary	1-4	L	38-21-4	80	275-237
64.	Mar 5 @	Edmonton	*5-4	W	39-21-4	82	280-241
65.	Mar 7 @	Edmonton	2-4	L	39-22-4	82	282-245
66.	Mar 9 @	Calgary	4-7	L	39-23-4	82	286-252
67.	Mar 10 @	Winnipeg	3-10	L	39-24-4	82	289-262
68.	Mar 12 @	Winnipeg	10-8	W	40-24-4	84	299-270
69.	Mar 14	Toronto	1-3	L	40-25-4	84	300-273
70.	Mar 16	New England	5-1	W	41-25-4	86	305-274
71.	Mar 19 @	Toronto	*4-3	W	42-25-4	88	309-277
72.	Mar 20	Calgary	7-8	L	42-26-4	88	316-285
73.	Mar 21 @	Edmonton	6-3	W	43-26-4	90	322-288
74.	Mar 23	Cleveland	1-3	L	43-27-4	90	323-291
75.	Mar 25	Edmonton	7-5	W	44-27-4	92	330-296
76.	Mar 27	Calgary	6-4	W	45-27-4	94	336-300
77.	Mar 30	Edmonton	8-3	W	46-27-4	96	344-303
78.	Apr 1	Edmonton	7-2	W	47-27-4	98	351-305
79.	Apr 3	Toronto	5-1	W	48-27-4	100	356-306
80.	Apr 4 @	Toronto	*5-4	W	49-27-4	102	361-310
81.	Apr 6	Toronto	10-6	W	50-27-4	104	371-316

Nordiques Stars of 1975-1976

Marc Tardif
71 goals, 148 points

Serge Bernier
102 points

Christian Bordeleau
109 points

Rejean Houle
103 points

Real Cloutier
60 goals, 114 points

Richard Brodeur
44 wins

Scoring

pos	#	player	gp	g	a	pts	pim	+/-	ppg	shg	sog	sc%	gp	g	a	pts	pim	+/-
							Regular Season									**Playoffs**		
RW	7	Benzelock, Jim	34	2	5	7	6	-1	0	0	37	0.054	3	0	0	0	0	-1
D	24	Bernier, Jean	81	4	26	30	10	+25	0	0	111	0.036	4	0	1	1	0	-5
C	21	Bernier, Serge	70	34	68	102	91	+26	4	2	283	0.120	5	2	6	8	6	+1
C	11	Bordeleau, Christian	74	37	72	109	42	+16	11	1	243	0.152	5	1	1	2	4	-1
RW	15	Brackenbury, Curt	15	4	5	9	111	+8	0	0	24	0.167	5	0	0	0	18	-1
G	30	Brodeur, Richard	69	0	3	3	0		0	0	0	-	5	0	0	0	0	-
RW	9	Cloutier, Real	80	60	54	114	27	+33	16	0	246	0.244	5	4	5	9	0	-3
LW	14	Constantin, Charles	41	8	7	15	77	-1	0	1	60	0.133	5	0	1	1	4	-4
LW	25	Cunniff, John	2	0	0	0	5	-2	0	0	0	-	-	-	-	-	-	-
G	23	Deguise, Michel	18	0	1	1	0		0	0	0	-	-	-	-	-	-	-
G	1	Donnelly, Pete	4	0	0	0	0		0	0	0	-	-	-	-	-	-	-
D	4	Dubois, Michel	21	0	3	3	23	+2	0	0	13	0.000	-	-	-	-	-	-
C	12	Fitchner, Bob	21	7	9	16	22	+8	0	0	34	0.206	5	1	0	1	8	-3
D	25	Fortier, Florent	4	1	1	2	0	+1	0	0	2	0.500	1	0	0	0	0	0
LW	16	Gallant, Gord	64	4	15	19	297	+5	0	0	90	0.044	2	0	0	0	31	0
D	2	Globensky, Alan	34	1	2	3	13	-2	0	0	7	0.143	-	-	-	-	-	-
D	2	Gresdal, Gary	2	0	1	1	5	+2	0	0	0	-	1	0	0	0	14	0
C	18	Hampson, Ted	14	4	10	14	2	+7	0	0	18	0.222	5	0	2	2	10	+1
D	33	Hoganson, Dale	45	3	14	17	18	+21	1	0	64	0.047	5	1	3	4	2	-1
RW	5	Houle, Rejean	81	51	52	103	61	+20	19	0	256	0.172	5	2	0	2	8	-2
D	20	Jordan, Ric	54	4	7	11	25	+5	0	0	49	0.082	-	-	-	-	-	-
RW	15	Leclerc, Rene	42	15	17	32	35	+9	0	1	100	0.150	-	-	-	-	-	-
C	12	Parizeau, Michel	58	12	27	39	24	+6	0	0	79	0.152	-	-	-	-	-	-
D	6	Prentice, Bill	21	2	5	7	89	+7	1	0	22	0.091	5	0	0	0	17	-1
D	10	Roy, Pierre	78	6	30	36	258	+12	0	0	100	0.060	5	1	2	3	29	-1
RW	17	Serviss, Tom	71	7	19	26	12	+3	1	0	76	0.092	5	0	0	0	0	-1
LW	19	Sutherland, Steve	74	22	19	41	197	-10	0	0	159	0.138	4	2	1	3	17	0
LW	8	Tardif, Marc	81	71	77	148	79	+35	21	1	359	0.198	2	1	0	1	2	0
D	3	Tremblay, J. C.	80	12	77	89	16	+40	3	0	161	0.075	5	0	3	3	0	-2
D	4	Watson, Jim	28	0	1	1	24	-21	0	0	17	0.000	-	-	-	-	-	-

Power Play: 77 goals scored in 249 opportunities (30.9%) with 10 short-handed goals allowed.
Penalty Killing: 69 goals allowed in 305 opportunities (77.4%) with 5 short-handed goals scored.

Goaltending

goaltender	gp	min	ga	en	so	record	gaa	sog	sv%	gp	min	ga	record	gaa
Brodeur, Richard	64	3967	244	1	2	44-21-2	3.69	2216	0.890	5	299	22	1-4	4.41
Deguise, Michel	18	535	60	1	0	6-5-2	4.35	460	0.870	-	-	-	-	-
Donnelly, Pete	4	129	10	0	0	0-1-0	4.65	65	0.846	-	-	-	-	-

Transactions: Gord Gallant purchased from Minnesota, Jun 1975 • Rene Leclerc traded to Indianapolis for Bill Prentice, Jan 1976 • Michel Parizeau traded to Indianapolis for Michel Dubois and Bop Fitchner, Feb 1976 • Curt Brackenbury and Ted Hampson signed as free agents from defunct Minnesota, Mar 1976

1975-1976 SAN DIEGO MARINERS

**Coach
Ron Ingram**

Summary of Games (@ Away, * Overtime)

	date		opponent	score		record	pts	gf-ga		date		opponent	score		record	pts	gf-ga
1.	Oct 10	@	Phoenix	5-6	L	0-1-0	0	5-6	41.	Jan 11	@	New England	4-8	L	18-19-4	40	157-147
2.	Oct 11		Phoenix	2-4	L	0-2-0	0	7-10	42.	Jan 15		Minnesota	*5-4	W	19-19-4	42	162-151
3.	Oct 16		Indianapolis	3-0	W	1-2-0	2	10-10	43.	Jan 17		Cleveland	5-4	W	20-19-4	44	167-155
4.	Oct 18		Winnipeg	2-1	W	2-2-0	4	12-11	44.	Jan 21	@	Minnesota	5-6	L	20-20-4	44	172-161
5.	Oct 23		Minnesota	4-4	T	2-2-1	5	16-15	45.	Jan 23	@	Minnesota	7-1	W	21-20-4	46	179-162
6.	Oct 25		Minnesota	6-1	W	3-2-1	7	22-16	46.	Jan 24		Toronto	6-4	W	22-20-4	48	185-166
7.	Oct 30		Houston	2-4	L	3-3-1	7	24-20	47.	Jan 25	@	Phoenix	5-7	L	22-21-4	48	190-173
8.	Nov 2	@	Edmonton	3-5	L	3-4-1	7	27-25	48.	Jan 27		Phoenix	*3-4	L	22-22-4	48	193-177
9.	Nov 4	@	Calgary	4-4	T	3-4-2	8	31-29	49.	Jan 29		Calgary	1-0	W	23-22-4	50	194-177
10.	Nov 7	@	Denver	*3-2	W	4-4-2	10	34-31	50.	Jan 31		Phoenix	6-1	W	24-22-4	52	200-178
11.	Nov 8	@	Cincinnati	4-7	L	4-5-2	10	38-38	51.	Feb 4		Minnesota	4-1	W	25-22-4	54	204-179
12.	Nov 13		Cleveland	3-1	W	5-5-2	12	41-39	52.	Feb 5		Cleveland	3-2	W	26-22-4	56	207-181
13.	Nov 15		Toronto	4-6	L	5-6-2	12	45-45	53.	Feb 8	@	Houston	2-5	L	26-23-4	56	209-186
14.	Nov 17	@	Edmonton	3-6	L	5-7-2	12	48-51	54.	Feb 10	@	Minnesota	3-6	L	26-24-4	56	212-192
15.	Nov 18	@	Calgary	6-2	W	6-7-2	14	54-53	55.	Feb 11		Minnesota	2-4	L	26-25-4	56	214-196
16.	Nov 20		Denver	5-1	W	7-7-2	16	59-54	56.	Feb 14		Houston	5-1	W	27-25-4	58	219-197
17.	Nov 22		Edmonton	*2-3	L	7-8-2	16	61-57	57.	Feb 15	@	Indianapolis	3-2	W	28-25-4	60	222-199
18.	Nov 25		Edmonton	7-2	W	8-8-2	18	68-59	58.	Feb 17	@	Quebec	2-5	L	28-26-4	60	224-204
19.	Nov 27		Quebec	5-1	W	9-8-2	20	73-60	59.	Feb 20	@	Toronto	6-4	W	29-26-4	62	230-208
20.	Nov 29		Calgary	4-5	L	9-9-2	20	77-65	60.	Feb 21	@	Cincinnati	2-3	L	29-27-4	62	232-211
21.	Nov 30	@	Houston	4-8	L	9-10-2	20	81-73	61.	Feb 25	@	Minnesota	*2-1	W	30-27-4	64	234-212
22.	Dec 4		Winnipeg	4-5	L	9-11-2	20	85-78	62.	Feb 27	@	Phoenix	3-4	L	30-28-4	64	237-216
23.	Dec 6		New England	4-1	W	10-11-2	22	89-79	63.	Mar 2		New England	3-4	L	30-29-4	64	240-220
24.	Dec 11		Indianapolis	3-3	T	10-11-3	23	92-82	64.	Mar 4		New England	8-2	W	31-29-4	66	248-222
25.	Dec 13		Cincinnati	3-3	T	10-11-4	24	95-85	65.	Mar 7		Phoenix	5-2	W	32-29-4	68	253-224
26.	Dec 14	@	Phoenix	2-4	L	10-12-4	24	97-89	66.	Mar 9	@	Houston	2-9	L	32-30-4	68	255-233
27.	Dec 16	@	Houston	4-2	W	11-12-4	26	101-91	67.	Mar 11		Houston	4-1	W	33-30-4	70	259-234
28.	Dec 18		Cincinnati	7-3	W	12-12-4	28	108-94	68.	Mar 13		Houston	2-3	L	33-31-4	70	261-237
29.	Dec 19	@	Denver	3-6	L	12-13-4	28	111-100	69.	Mar 18	@	Indianapolis	4-4	T	33-31-5	71	265-241
30.	Dec 21		Houston	3-1	W	13-13-4	30	114-101	70.	Mar 19	@	Houston	3-8	L	33-32-5	71	268-249
31.	Dec 23		Quebec	10-4	W	14-13-4	32	124-105	71.	Mar 20		Phoenix	*3-4	L	33-33-5	71	271-253
32.	Dec 26		Phoenix	4-2	W	15-13-4	34	128-107	72.	Mar 23		Indianapolis	8-8	T	33-33-6	72	279-261
33.	Dec 28	@	Minnesota	2-1	W	16-13-4	36	130-108	73.	Mar 25		Cincinnati	9-1	W	34-33-6	74	288-262
34.	Dec 30	@	New England	3-5	L	16-14-4	36	133-113	74.	Mar 26	@	Phoenix	1-3	L	34-34-6	74	289-265
35.	Jan 2	@	Indianapolis	2-0	W	17-14-4	38	135-113	75.	Mar 27		Phoenix	2-5	L	34-35-6	74	291-270
36.	Jan 3	@	Cincinnati	3-5	L	17-15-4	38	138-118	76.	Mar 28	@	Winnipeg	1-6	L	34-36-6	74	292-276
37.	Jan 6	@	Toronto	4-6	L	17-16-4	38	142-124	77.	Mar 30	@	Houston	4-3	W	35-36-6	76	296-279
38.	Jan 7	@	Cleveland	3-8	L	17-17-4	38	145-132	78.	Apr 3	@	Cleveland	2-4	L	35-37-6	76	298-283
39.	Jan 9	@	New England	5-3	W	18-17-4	40	150-135	79.	Apr 4	@	Houston	2-5	L	35-38-6	76	300-288
40.	Jan 10	@	Quebec	*3-4	L	18-18-4	40	153-139	80.	Apr 6	@	Cleveland	*3-2	W	36-38-6	78	303-290

Mariners Stars of 1975-1976

Ray Adduono	Gene Peacosh	Ernie Wakely	Kevin Morrison	Norm Ferguson	Andre Lacroix
90 points, +29	37 goals	35 wins	65 points on defense	37 goals, +14	101 points

Scoring

pos	#	player	|| Regular Season										|| Playoffs					
			gp	g	a	pts	pim	+/-	ppg	shg	sog	sc%	gp	g	a	pts	pim	+/-
C	10	Adduono, Ray	80	23	67	90	22	+29	6	0	92	0.250	11	4	7	11	6	0
D	22	Bateman, Jamie	7	1	0	1	4	-1	0	0	6	0.167	-	-	-	-	-	-
G	30	Blanchet, Bob	1	0	0	0	0		0	0	0	-	-	-	-	-	-	-
RW	27	Bredin, Gary	50	4	5	9	10	-12	0	0	55	0.073	-	-	-	-	-	-
LW	8	Burgess, Don	73	14	11	25	35	-17	2	0	122	0.115	11	1	7	8	4	-3
C		Bye, Brian	1	0	0	0	0	0	0	0	1	0.000	-	-	-	-	-	-
LW	16	Devine, Kevin	80	21	28	49	102	+2	3	0	109	0.193	11	3	1	4	36	0
C	19	Dobek, Bob	14	3	1	4	2	+1	0	0	23	0.130	11	1	2	3	0	-1
D	6	Falkenberg, Bob	79	3	13	16	31	-18	0	0	71	0.042	11	1	2	3	6	-3
RW	9	Ferguson, Norm	79	37	37	74	12	+14	4	0	253	0.146	4	2	0	2	9	-1
LW	11	French, John	76	25	39	64	16	-2	6	0	110	0.227	11	4	7	11	0	0
G	1	Gillow, Russ	23	0	0	0	0		0	0	0	-	-	-	-	-	-	-
LW	18	Goldthorpe, Bill	14	1	0	1	30	0	0	0	12	0.083	-	-	-	-	-	-
D	17	Hargreaves, Jim	43	1	1	2	26	-3	0	0	34	0.029	5	0	0	0	2	+1
D	2	Hughes, Brent	78	7	28	35	63	+6	1	0	104	0.067	10	1	5	6	6	-9
D		Jacquith, Gary	2	0	0	0	0	0	0	0	0	-	-	-	-	-	-	-
C	7	Lacroix, Andre	80	29	72	101	42	-29	12	3	274	0.106	11	4	6	10	4	-4
D	3	Lalonde, Rick	2	0	0	0	0	-1	0	0	0	-	-	-	-	-	-	-
D	23	McMahon, Mike	69	2	12	14	38	-5	0	0	79	0.025	9	0	1	1	2	+3
D	18	McNamee, Pete	51	2	3	5	27	-10	0	0	52	0.038	11	0	1	1	28	-2
C	15	Morenz, Brian	40	6	7	13	22	-9	0	0	38	0.158	11	2	1	3	11	-3
D	4	Morrison, Kevin	80	22	43	65	56	0	7	0	334	0.066	11	1	5	6	12	-3
C	21	Noris, Joe	80	28	40	68	24	+4	5	3	194	0.144	11	2	4	6	6	-1
LW	25	Peacosh, Gene	79	37	33	70	35	-5	8	0	214	0.173	11	2	1	3	21	-5
RW	12	Rivers, Wayne	71	19	25	44	24	-18	10	0	188	0.101	11	4	4	8	4	-2
RW	14	Tidey, Alex	74	16	11	27	46	+7	2	0	160	0.100	11	3	6	9	10	+2
D	5	Wall, Bob	68	1	20	21	32	+3	0	0	73	0.014	11	1	3	4	4	0
G	31	Wakely, Ernie	67	0	0	0	0		0	0	0	-	11	0	0	0	0	-
C	11	Walter, Dave	16	1	2	3	6	+2	0	0	13	0.077	-	-	-	-	-	-

Power Play: 66 goals scored in 287 opportunities (23.0%) with 10 short-handed goals allowed.
Penalty Killing: 42 goals allowed in 220 opportunities (80.9%) with 6 short-handed goals scored.

Goaltending

goaltender	gp	min	ga	en	so	record	gaa	sog	sv%	gp	min	ga	record	gaa
Blanchet, Bob	1	32	4	0	0	0-1-0	7.50	24	0.833	-	-	-	-	-
Gillow, Russ	23	1037	74	1	0	1-10-2	4.28	568	0.870	1	20	0	0-0	0.00
Wakely, Ernie	67	3824	208	3	3	35-27-4	3.26	1980	0.895	11	640	39	5-6	3.66

Transactions: Don Burgess acquired from Calgary for future considerations, Jun 1975 • Rights to Joe Noris acquired from Calgary for Dick Sentes, Aug 1975 • John French acquired from New England for future considerations, Oct 1975 • Bill Goldthorpe traded to Denver for Gary Bredin, Nov 1975 • Dave Walter traded to Phoenix for Pete McNamee, Dec 1975

1975-1976 TORONTO TOROS

**Coach
Bob Baun
15-35-5**

**Coach
Gilles Leger
9-17-0**

Summary of Games (@ Away, * Overtime)

	date	opponent	score		record	pts	gf-ga		date	opponent	score		record	pts	gf-ga
1.	Oct 11 @	Quebec	3-7	L	0-1-0	0	3-7	41.	Jan 9 @	Edmonton	3-5	L	14-24-3	31	170-200
2.	Oct 14	Houston	6-3	W	1-1-0	2	9-10	42.	Jan 17 @	Quebec	*3-4	L	14-25-3	31	173-204
3.	Oct 17	Edmonton	4-4	T	1-1-1	3	13-14	43.	Jan 20 @	Houston	7-5	W	15-25-3	33	180-209
4.	Oct 18 @	New England	1-3	L	1-2-1	3	14-17	44.	Jan 22 @	Phoenix	4-6	L	15-26-3	33	184-215
5.	Oct 24	New England	4-5	L	1-3-1	3	18-22	45.	Jan 24 @	San Diego	4-6	L	15-27-3	33	188-221
6.	Oct 25 @	Quebec	2-3	L	1-4-1	3	20-25	46.	Jan 25 @	Minnesota	2-5	L	15-28-3	33	190-226
7.	Oct 28	Quebec	6-4	W	2-4-1	5	26-29	47.	Jan 27	Edmonton	4-4	T	15-28-4	34	194-230
8.	Nov 4 @	Indianapolis	3-4	L	2-5-1	5	29-33	48.	Jan 30	Quebec	3-3	T	15-28-5	35	197-233
9.	Nov 7 @	Edmonton	4-5	L	2-6-1	5	33-38	49.	Jan 31 @	Quebec	4-8	L	15-29-5	35	201-241
10.	Nov 8 @	Minnesota	3-4	L	2-7-1	5	36-42	50.	Feb 1	New England	5-7	L	15-30-5	35	206-248
11.	Nov 9 @	Winnipeg	3-5	L	2-8-1	5	39-47	51.	Feb 6	Winnipeg	6-7	L	15-31-5	35	212-255
12.	Nov 11 @	Houston	4-5	L	2-9-1	5	43-52	52.	Feb 7 @	New England	3-7	L	15-32-5	35	215-262
13.	Nov 13 @	Denver	11-8	W	3-9-1	7	54-60	53.	Feb 10 @	Calgary	3-4	L	15-33-5	35	218-266
14.	Nov 14 @	Phoenix	2-2	T	3-9-2	8	56-62	54.	Feb 13 @	Edmonton	3-5	L	15-34-5	35	221-271
15.	Nov 15 @	San Diego	6-4	W	4-9-2	10	62-66	55.	Feb 15 @	Winnipeg	6-7	L	15-35-5	35	227-278
16.	Nov 17	Indianapolis	2-6	L	4-10-2	10	64-72	56.	Feb 17	Minnesota	3-6	L	15-36-5	35	230-284
17.	Nov 21	Cincinnati	8-7	W	5-10-2	12	72-79	57.	Feb 20	San Diego	4-6	L	15-37-5	35	234-290
18.	Nov 25	Cleveland	*3-4	L	5-11-2	12	75-83	58.	Feb 22 @	Calgary	2-4	L	15-38-5	35	236-294
19.	Nov 28	Winnipeg	3-5	L	5-12-2	12	78-88	59.	Feb 24	Cincinnati	6-9	L	15-39-5	35	242-303
20.	Nov 29 @	Cincinnati	9-5	W	6-12-2	14	87-93	60.	Feb 27	Houston	*6-7	L	15-40-5	35	248-310
21.	Nov 30 @	Cleveland	9-10	L	6-13-2	14	96-103	61.	Feb 29	Winnipeg	11-7	W	16-40-5	37	259-317
22.	Dec 2 @	Edmonton	2-7	L	6-14-2	14	98-110	62.	Mar 2	Quebec	5-2	W	17-40-5	39	264-319
23.	Dec 3 @	Calgary	4-3	W	7-14-2	16	102-113	63.	Mar 6	Calgary	5-2	W	18-40-5	41	269-321
24.	Dec 5	Quebec	7-4	W	8-14-2	18	109-117	64.	Mar 9	Winnipeg	2-5	L	18-41-5	41	271-326
25.	Dec 9	Minnesota	3-5	L	8-15-2	18	112-122	65.	Mar 11 @	Indianapolis	1-3	L	18-42-5	41	272-329
26.	Dec 10 @	Winnipeg	*5-6	L	8-16-2	18	117-128	66.	Mar 12	Phoenix	2-5	L	18-43-5	41	274-334
27.	Dec 12	Quebec	6-4	W	9-16-2	20	123-132	67.	Mar 14 @	Quebec	3-1	W	19-43-5	43	277-335
28.	Dec 13 @	Quebec	3-6	L	9-17-2	20	126-138	68.	Mar 16	Cleveland	6-0	W	20-43-5	45	283-335
29.	Dec 14	Calgary	3-3	T	9-17-3	21	129-141	69.	Mar 17 @	Cincinnati	4-5	L	20-44-5	45	287-340
30.	Dec 16	Winnipeg	3-4	L	9-18-3	21	132-145	70.	Mar 19	Quebec	*3-4	L	20-45-5	45	290-344
31.	Dec 19	Calgary	3-5	L	9-19-3	21	135-150	71.	Mar 20 @	Cleveland	6-5	W	21-45-5	47	296-349
32.	Dec 21 @	Edmonton	4-2	W	10-19-3	23	139-152	72.	Mar 21	Winnipeg	5-2	W	22-45-5	49	301-351
33.	Dec 23 @	Calgary	1-10	L	10-20-3	23	140-162	73.	Mar 23	Calgary	6-5	W	23-45-5	51	307-356
34.	Dec 26	Edmonton	8-5	W	11-20-3	25	148-167	74.	Mar 26	Edmonton	7-3	W	24-45-5	53	314-359
35.	Dec 27 @	Cleveland	0-5	L	11-21-3	25	148-172	75.	Mar 28	Calgary	4-5	L	24-46-5	53	318-364
36.	Dec 28	Quebec	1-6	L	11-22-3	25	149-178	76.	Mar 30 @	Calgary	2-6	L	24-47-5	53	320-370
37.	Dec 30	Edmonton	6-4	W	12-22-3	27	155-182	77.	Mar 31 @	Winnipeg	3-5	L	24-48-5	53	323-375
38.	Jan 2	Phoenix	4-1	W	13-22-3	29	159-183	78.	Apr 2	Indianapolis	*1-3	L	24-49-5	53	324-378
39.	Jan 6	San Diego	6-4	W	14-22-3	31	165-187	79.	Apr 3	Quebec	1-5	L	24-50-5	53	325-383
40.	Jan 7 @	Winnipeg	2-8	L	14-23-3	31	167-195	80.	Apr 4	Quebec	*4-5	L	24-51-5	53	329-388
								81.	Apr 6 @	Quebec	6-10	L	24-52-5	53	335-398

Toros Stars of 1975-1976

Vaclav Nedomansky	**John Garrett**	**Richard Farda**	**Mark Napier**	**Jim Dorey**	**Rick Cunningham**
56 goals	3.59 average, shutout	19 goals, 54 points	43 goals	60 points on defense	+1 rating

Scoring

pos	#	player	gp	g	a	pts	pim	+/-	ppg	shg	sog	sc%	gp	g	a	pts	pim	+/-
D	5	Amodeo, Mike	31	4	8	12	35	-7	1	0	33	0.121	-	-	-	-	-	-
RW	24	Atkinson, Steve	52	2	6	8	22	-7	0	0	35	0.057	-	-	-	-	-	-
LW	8	Bilodeau, Gilles	14	0	1	1	38	0	0	0	5	0.000	-	-	-	-	-	-
G	30	Binkley, Les	7	0	0	0	0		0	0	0	-	-	-	-	-	-	-
RW	17	Crowley, Paul	4	0	0	0	0	0	0	0	5	0.000	-	-	-	-	-	-
D	3	Cunningham, Rick	36	5	14	19	57	+1	0	0	58	0.086	-	-	-	-	-	-
C	16	D'Alvise, Bob	59	5	8	13	10	-13	1	2	61	0.082	-	-	-	-	-	-
D	7	Dorey, Jim	74	9	51	60	134	-21	3	2	163	0.055	-	-	-	-	-	-
C	8	Farda, Richard	63	19	35	54	8	-5	2	0	109	0.174	-	-	-	-	-	-
RW	26	Featherstone, Tony	32	4	7	11	5	-10	1	0	33	0.121	-	-	-	-	-	-
D	5	Folco, Peter	19	1	8	9	15	-7	0	0	18	0.056	-	-	-	-	-	-
D	6	Foley, Rick	11	1	2	3	6	-8	1	0	15	0.067	-	-	-	-	-	-
G	35	Garrett, John	9	0	1	1	0		0	0	0	-	-	-	-	-	-	-
D		Gibbons, Gerard	5	1	0	1	7	-1	0	0	3	0.333	-	-	-	-	-	-
LW	23	Gibson, Jack	2	0	0	0	0	-2	0	0	5	0.000	-	-	-	-	-	-
D	22	Heaver, Paul	66	2	12	14	83	-4	0	0	42	0.048	-	-	-	-	-	-
LW	19	Henderson, Paul	65	26	29	55	22	-20	8	1	179	0.145	-	-	-	-	-	-
C	25	Jacques, Jeff	81	17	33	50	113	-8	1	0	101	0.168	-	-	-	-	-	-
C	11	Kirk, Gavin	62	29	38	67	32	-6	3	0	142	0.204	-	-	-	-	-	-
D	23	Kuzmicz, George	1	0	0	0	0	0	0	0	0	-	-	-	-	-	-	-
LW	29	Mahovlich, Frank	75	34	55	89	14	-16	6	1	239	0.142	-	-	-	-	-	-
C	20	Marrin, Peter	64	22	16	38	16	-12	2	0	105	0.209	-	-	-	-	-	-
RW	9	Napier, Mark	78	43	50	93	20	0	10	3	245	0.176	-	-	-	-	-	-
RW	14	Nedomansky, Vaclav	81	56	42	98	8	-2	6	0	328	0.171	-	-	-	-	-	-
D	6	Neeld, Greg	17	0	1	1	18	-16	0	0	10	0.000	-	-	-	-	-	-
C	15	Nistico, Lou	65	12	22	34	120	-20	1	0	154	0.078	-	-	-	-	-	-
C	28	Phaneuf, Jean-Luc	48	8	8	16	4	-16	1	0	65	0.123	-	-	-	-	-	-
D	4	Rollins, Jerry	52	5	7	12	185	-20	0	0	59	0.084	-	-	-	-	-	-
G	1	Shaw, Jim	16	0	0	0	0		0	0	0	-	-	-	-	-	-	-
RW	12	Simpson, Tom	73	20	21	41	15	-15	5	0	159	0.126	-	-	-	-	-	-
D	10	Syvret, Dave	50	1	11	12	14	-15	0	0	36	0.028	-	-	-	-	-	-
G	21	Tataryn, Dave	23	0	0	0	0		0	0	0	-	-	-	-	-	-	-
D	2	Turkiewicz, Jim	77	9	29	38	55	-13	2	0	111	0.081	-	-	-	-	-	-
D	17	Van Horlick, John	2	0	0	0	12	-1	0	0	0	-	-	-	-	-	-	-
G	33	Vien, Mario	26	0	0	0	0		0	0	0	-	-	-	-	-	-	-
G	1	Wood, Wayne	13	0	1	1	0		0	0	0	-	-	-	-	-	-	-
D	23	Zrymiak, Jerry	17	0	5	5	11	-14	0	0	13	0.000	-	-	-	-	-	-

Power Play: 54 goals scored in 279 opportunities (19.4%) with 7 short-handed goals allowed.
Penalty Killing: 59 goals allowed in 251 opportunities (76.5%) with 9 short-handed goals scored.

Goaltending

goaltender	gp	min	ga	en	so	record	gaa	sog	sv%	gp	min	ga	record	gaa
Binkley, Les	7	335	32	0	0	0-6-0	5.73	212	0.849	-	-	-	-	-
Garrett, John	9	551	33	0	1	3-6-0	3.59	349	0.905	-	-	-	-	-
Shaw, Jim	16	777	63	0	0	4-7-1	4.86	506	0.875	-	-	-	-	-
Tataryn, Dave	23	1261	100	3	0	7-12-1	4.76	786	0.872	-	-	-	-	-
Vien, Mario	26	1228	105	0	0	4-14-3	5.13	830	0.873	-	-	-	-	-
Wood, Wayne	13	781	62	0	0	6-7-0	4.76	474	0.869	-	-	-	-	-

Transactions: Mark Napier signed to contract, May 1975 • Rick Foley, Dave Tataryn signed to contracts, Jun 1975 • Rights to Bob D'Alvise acquired from Cleveland for 1976 draft choice, Aug 1975 • Steve Atkinson purchased from Buffalo (NAHL), Jan 1976 • John Garrett and Jerry Zrymiak signed as free agents from defunct Minnesota, Mar 1976 • Gavin Kirk traded to Calgary for Wayne Wood, Mar 1976

1975-1976 WINNIPEG JETS

**Coach
Bobby Kromm**

Summary of Games (@ Away, * Overtime)

	date		opponent	score		record	pts	gf-ga		date		opponent	score		record	pts	gf-ga
1.	Oct 9	@	Quebec	5-3	W	1-0-0	2	5-3	41.	Jan 4	@	Edmonton	8-1	W	27-14-0	54	171-114
2.	Oct 12	@	Phoenix	4-0	W	2-0-0	4	9-3	42.	Jan 6	@	Calgary	0-5	L	27-15-0	54	171-119
3.	Oct 16	@	Denver	7-3	W	3-0-0	6	16-6	43.	Jan 7		Toronto	8-2	W	28-15-0	56	179-121
4.	Oct 18	@	San Diego	1-2	L	3-1-0	6	17-8	44.	Jan 9		Indianapolis	*1-2	L	28-16-0	56	180-123
5.	Oct 19	@	Phoenix	5-6	L	3-2-0	6	22-14	45.	Jan 11		Ottawa	*6-5	W	29-16-0	58	186-128
6.	Oct 21		Cincinnati	7-0	W	4-2-0	8	29-14	46.	Jan 14		Houston	4-1	W	30-16-0	60	190-129
7.	Oct 24		Denver	5-2	W	5-2-0	10	34-16	47.	Jan 16		Edmonton	1-5	L	30-17-0	60	191-134
8.	Oct 26		Phoenix	5-0	W	6-2-0	12	39-16	48.	Jan 18		New England	8-0	W	31-17-0	62	199-134
9.	Oct 30		Cincinnati	4-0	W	7-2-0	14	43-16	49.	Jan 21		Calgary	4-1	W	32-17-0	64	203-135
10.	Nov 2		Quebec	0-1	L	7-3-0	14	43-17	50.	Jan 23		Edmonton	4-2	W	33-17-0	66	207-137
11.	Nov 4		New England	*3-2	W	8-3-0	16	46-19	51.	Jan 28	@	Minnesota	2-6	L	33-18-0	66	209-143
12.	Nov 9		Toronto	5-3	W	9-3-0	18	51-22	52.	Jan 30	@	New England	6-3	W	34-18-0	68	215-146
13.	Nov 11		Cleveland	2-3	L	9-4-0	18	53-25	53.	Jan 31	@	Cincinnati	5-2	W	35-18-0	70	220-148
14.	Nov 13	@	Calgary	4-2	W	10-4-0	20	57-27	54.	Feb 1	@	Indianapolis	2-1	W	36-18-0	72	222-149
15.	Nov 14		Edmonton	6-1	W	11-4-0	22	63-28	55.	Feb 3	@	Quebec	4-5	L	36-19-0	72	226-154
16.	Nov 16		Indianapolis	2-1	W	12-4-0	24	65-29	56.	Feb 6	@	Toronto	7-6	W	37-19-0	74	233-160
17.	Nov 18		Houston	2-3	L	12-5-0	24	67-32	57.	Feb 7	@	Cleveland	4-4	T	37-19-1	75	237-164
18.	Nov 20	@	Quebec	*3-2	W	13-5-0	26	70-34	58.	Feb 8		Calgary	8-4	W	38-19-1	77	245-168
19.	Nov 22	@	Cleveland	3-6	L	13-6-0	26	73-40	59.	Feb 11		Quebec	4-6	L	38-20-1	77	249-174
20.	Nov 23	@	New England	3-2	W	14-6-0	28	76-42	60.	Feb 15		Toronto	7-6	W	39-20-1	79	256-180
21.	Nov 26	@	Cincinnati	11-3	W	15-6-0	30	87-45	61.	Feb 17	@	Edmonton	4-4	T	39-20-2	80	260-184
22.	Nov 27	@	Indianapolis	1-3	L	15-7-0	30	88-48	62.	Feb 18		Phoenix	4-3	W	40-20-2	82	264-187
23.	Nov 28	@	Toronto	5-3	W	16-7-0	32	93-51	63.	Feb 20		Edmonton	4-2	W	41-20-2	84	268-189
24.	Nov 30		Minnesota	5-3	W	17-7-0	34	98-54	64.	Feb 25		Cleveland	5-2	W	42-20-2	86	273-191
25.	Dec 2	@	Denver	*4-3	W	18-7-0	36	102-57	65.	Feb 27		Edmonton	4-3	W	43-20-2	88	277-194
26.	Dec 4	@	San Diego	5-4	W	19-7-0	38	107-61	66.	Feb 28	@	Quebec	*4-3	W	44-20-2	90	281-197
27.	Dec 5	@	Houston	4-5	L	19-8-0	38	111-66	67.	Feb 29	@	Toronto	7-11	L	44-21-2	90	288-208
28.	Dec 7		Quebec	2-3	L	19-9-0	38	113-69	68.	Mar 7		Calgary	3-1	W	45-21-2	92	291-209
29.	Dec 10		Toronto	*6-5	W	20-9-0	40	119-74	69.	Mar 9	@	Toronto	5-2	W	46-21-2	94	296-211
30.	Dec 12		Calgary	4-2	W	21-9-0	42	123-76	70.	Mar 10		Quebec	10-3	W	47-21-2	96	306-214
31.	Dec 14	@	Edmonton	3-1	W	22-9-0	44	126-77	71.	Mar 12		Quebec	8-10	L	47-22-2	96	314-224
32.	Dec 16	@	Toronto	4-3	W	23-9-0	46	130-80	72.	Mar 14		Edmonton	4-2	W	48-22-2	98	318-226
33.	Dec 18	@	Quebec	4-5	L	23-10-0	46	134-85	73.	Mar 17		Calgary	3-2	W	49-22-2	100	321-228
34.	Dec 20	@	Minnesota	3-6	L	23-11-0	46	137-91	74.	Mar 19	@	Edmonton	1-2	L	49-23-2	100	322-230
35.	Dec 21		Minnesota	1-3	L	23-12-0	46	138-94	75.	Mar 21	@	Toronto	2-5	L	49-24-2	100	324-235
36.	Dec 23	@	Edmonton	6-2	W	24-12-0	48	144-96	76.	Mar 24		Edmonton	2-3	L	49-25-2	100	326-238
37.	Dec 26		Calgary	4-5	L	24-13-0	48	148-101	77.	Mar 28		San Diego	6-1	W	50-25-2	102	332-239
38.	Dec 28	@	Calgary	4-6	L	24-14-0	48	152-107	78.	Mar 31		Toronto	5-3	W	51-25-2	104	337-242
39.	Dec 30	@	Houston	5-3	W	25-14-0	50	157-110	79.	Apr 2	@	Calgary	1-4	L	51-26-2	104	338-246
40.	Jan 3	@	Calgary	6-3	W	26-14-0	52	163-113	80.	Apr 4	@	Edmonton	2-5	L	51-27-2	104	340-251
									81.	Apr 6	@	Calgary	5-3	W	52-27-2	106	345-254

Jets Stars of 1975-1976

Ulf Nilsson	**Joe Daley**	**Bobby Hull**	**Anders Hedberg**	**Ted Green**	**Lars-Erik Sjoberg**
76 assists, 114 points	41 wins, 5 shutouts	53 goals, 123 points	105 points, +60	+32 on defense	+46 on defense

Scoring

						Regular Season								**Playoffs**					
pos	#	player	gp	g	a	pts	pim	+/-	ppg	shg	sog	sc%	gp	g	a	pts	pim	+/-
D	21	Asmundson, Duke	72	5	11	16	19	+1	0	0	50	0.100	13	3	2	5	11	+2
RW	11	Beaudin, Norm	80	16	31	47	38	-1	2	0	155	0.103	13	2	3	5	10	-5
D	2	Bergman, Thommie	81	11	30	41	111	+9	1	0	183	0.060	13	3	10	13	8	10
G	1	Daley, Joe	62	0	1	1	17		0	0	0	-	12	0	0	0	10	-
D	3	Ford, Mike	81	13	43	56	70	+39	2	0	245	0.053	12	1	12	13	8	+8
D	6	Green, Ted	79	5	23	28	73	+32	0	0	61	0.082	11	0	2	2	16	+6
LW	7	Guindon, Robert	39	3	3	6	14	-7	1	0	26	0.115	13	3	3	6	9	+7
RW	15	Hedberg, Anders	76	50	55	105	48	+60	9	6	271	0.185	13	13	6	19	15	+16
D	16	Hillman, Larry	71	1	12	13	62	-3	0	0	67	0.015	12	0	2	2	32	+2
D	5	Hornung, Larry	76	3	18	21	26	-6	1	0	50	0.060	13	0	3	3	6	+1
LW	9	Hull, Bobby	80	53	70	123	30	+62	14	0	416	0.127	13	12	8	20	4	+15
C	12	Ketola, Veli-Pekka	80	32	36	68	32	-4	8	0	339	0.094	13	7	5	12	2	+7
G	30	Larsson, Curt	23	0	1	1	6		0	0	0	-	2	0	0	0	0	-
D	7	Legge, Randy	1	0	0	0	0	+1	0	0	0	-	-	-	-	-	-	-
LW	17	Lesuk, Bill	81	15	21	36	92	+1	0	0	120	0.125	13	2	2	4	8	+1
D	19	Lindh, Mats	65	19	15	34	12	+7	4	0	99	0.192	13	2	2	4	4	-6
RW	20	Lindstrom, Willy	81	23	36	59	32	+4	5	1	151	0.152	11	4	7	11	2	+9
D	8/25	Miller, Perry	47	7	6	13	41	+8	1	0	42	0.167	-	-	-	-	-	-
LW	22	Moffat, Lyle	42	13	9	22	44	+3	4	0	61	0.213	13	3	3	6	9	-5
C	14	Nilsson, Ulf	78	38	76	114	84	+65	7	3	152	0.250	13	7	19	26	6	+15
D	8	Odrowski, Gerry	13	0	1	1	6	-8	0	0	13	0.000	-	-	-	-	-	-
D	18	Riihiranta, Heikki	70	1	8	9	26	0	0	0	38	0.026	4	0	4	4	5	+7
D	4	Sjoberg, Lars-Erik	81	5	36	41	12	+46	1	0	120	0.042	13	0	5	5	12	+7
C	10	Sullivan, Peter	78	32	39	71	22	-4	5	0	161	0.199	13	6	7	13	0	+7

Power Play: 68 goals scored in 394 opportunities (17.3%) with 8 short-handed goals allowed.
Penalty Killing: 45 goals allowed in 251 opportunities (72.1%) with 10 short-handed goals scored.

Goaltending

goaltender	gp	min	ga	en	so	record	gaa	sog	sv%	gp	min	ga	record	gaa
Daley, Joe	62	3612	171	0	5	41-17-1	2.84	1771	0.903	12	671	29	10-1	2.59
Larsson, Curt	23	1287	83	0	0	11-10-1	3.87	635	0.869	2	110	6	2-0	3.27

Transactions: Ted Green acquired from New England for future considerations, May 1975 • Rights to Bill Lesuk acquired from Edmonton for future considerations, Jul 1975 • Willy Lindstrom signed to contract, Jul 1975 • Peter Sullivan signed to contract, Aug 1975 • Bobby Guindon signed to contract, Nov 1975 • Randy Legge traded to Cleveland for Lyle Moffat, Jan 1976 • Perry Miller traded to Minnesota for Gerry Odrowski, Jan 1976, subsequently re-signed as a free agent from defunct Minnesota, Mar 1976 • Morris Mott signed to contract, Mar 1976

1975-1976 Statistical Leaders

Top five in each category.

Goals: 71, Marc Tardif (Quebec); 60, Real Cloutier (Quebec); 56, Vaclav Nedomansky (Toronto); 53, Bobby Hull (Winnipeg); 51, Rejean Houle (Quebec).

Assists: 77, Marc Tardif (Quebec), J.-C. Tremblay (Quebec); 76, Ulf Nilsson (Winnipeg); 72, Christian Bordeleau (Quebec), Robbie Ftorek (Phoenix), Andre Lacroix (San Diego); 70, Gordie Howe (Houston), Bobby Hull (Winnipeg).

Points: 148, Marc Tardif (Quebec); 123, Bobby Hull (Winnipeg); 114, Real Cloutier (Quebec), Ulf Nilsson (Winnipeg); 113, Robbie Ftorek (Phoenix); 109, Christian Bordeleau (Quebec)

Penalty Minutes: 365, Curt Brackenbury (Minnesota-Quebec); 351, Kim Clackson (Indianapolis); 297, Gord Gallant (Quebec); 295, Cam Connor (Phoenix); 258, Pierre Roy (Quebec).

Power-play Goals: 21, Marc Tardif (Quebec); 19, Ron Chipperfield (Calgary); Rejean Houle (Quebec); 16, Real Cloutier (Quebec); 14, Bobby Hull (Winnipeg); 13, Rick Dudley (Cincinnati), Mark Howe (Houston), Norm Ullman (Edmonton).

Short-handed Goals: 6, Anders Hedberg (Winnipeg), Mark Howe (Houston), Rick Morris (Denver-Ottawa-Edmonton); 5, Bernie MacNeil (Cincinnati), Don Tannahill (Calgary); 4, Danny Lawson (Calgary), Ron Huston (Phoenix).

Goaltending Minutes: 3967, Richard Brodeur (Quebec); 3824, Ernie Wakely (San Diego); 3730, John Garrett (Minnesota-Toronto); 3612, Joe Daley (Winnipeg); 3567, Dave Dryden (Edmonton).

Goals Against Average: 2.74, Michel Dion (Indianapolis); 2.84, Joe Daley (Winnipeg); 3.17, Wayne Rutledge (Houston); 3.18, Jack Norris (Phoenix); 3.26, Ernie Wakely (San Diego).

Wins: 44, Richard Brodeur (Quebec); 41, Joe Daley (Winnipeg); 39, Ron Grahame (Houston); 35, Ernie Wakely (San Diego); 30, Don McLeod (Calgary).

Shutouts: 5, Joe Daley (Winnipeg); 3, John Garrett (Minnesota-Toronto), Ron Grahame (Houston); Ernie Wakely (San Diego); 2, Christer Abrahamsson (New England), Richard Brodeur (Quebec), Paul Hoganson (Cincinnati).

Totals for Players With Two or More Teams During 1975-1976

player	teams	gp	g	a	pts	pim	+/-	ppg	shg	sog	sc%
Arbour, John	D-O, Min	42	2	17	19	63	-10			77	0.026
Backstrom, Ralph	D-O, NE	79	35	48	83	20	+16	8	1	236	0.148
Ball, Terry	Cle, Cin	59	5	29	34	30	-22	3	0	125	0.040
Baltimore, Bryon	D-O, Ind	78	2	18	20	62	-5	0	0	91	0.022
Borgeson, Don	D-O, NE	71	30	24	54	30	+5	6	0	181	0.166
Brackenbury, Curt	Min, Que	74	8	14	22	365	+15	0	0	76	0.105
Bredin, Gary	Den, SD	66	8	8	16	12	-19	1	0	70	0.114
Busniuk, Ron	Min, NE	70	2	14	16	205	+9	2	0	94	0.021
Butters, Bill	Min, Hou	73	0	19	19	138	+27	0	0	93	0.000
Byers, Mike	NE, Cin	41	7	6	13	0	-7	0	0	67	0.104
Caffery, Terry	NE, Cgy	23	5	13	18	4	+2	1	0	40	0.125
Carleton, Wayne	NE, Edm	61	17	37	54	12	-6	4	0	193	0.088
Carlson, Jack	Min, Edm	68	9	11	20	220	-16	0	0	81	0.111
Connelly, Wayne	Min, Cle	71	29	25	54	23	+8	7	0	242	0.120
Dubois, Michel	Ind, Que	51	2	5	7	127	-9	1	0	42	0.048
Evo, Bill	Edm, Cle	48	1	9	10	32	-15	0	0	34	0.029
Fitchner, Bob	Ind, Que	73	22	25	47	134	+8	5	0	108	0.204
Garrett, John	Min, Tor	61	0	1	1	6		0	0	0	-
Goldthorpe, Bill	SD, Den	26	1	0	1	61	-5	0	0	19	0.053
Hampson, Ted	Min, Que	73	9	25	34	16	+4	0	1	84	0.107
Harris, Hugh	Cgy, Ind	71	17	37	54	42	-6	3	0	232	0.073
Hoganson, Paul	NE, Cin	49	0	2	2	4		0	0	0	-
Hurley, Paul	NE, Edm	72	1	18	19	34	-11	0	0	145	0.007
Johnson, Bob	D-O, Cle	42	0	0	0	0		0	0	0	-
Keogan, Murray	Phx, Cgy	46	7	13	20	23	+4	0	0	75	0.093
Keon, Dave	Min, Ind	69	29	45	74	6	+16	6	2	184	0.158
Kirk, Gavin	Tor, Cgy	77	36	46	82	46	+2	4	0	179	0.201
Leclerc, Rene	Que, Ind	82	33	38	71	87	+10	7	1	252	0.131
Legge, Barry	D-O, Cle	75	6	15	21	37	-19	4	0	87	0.069
Legge, Randy	Wpg, Cle	45	1	8	9	28	-6	0	0	41	0.024
Liddington, Bob	Den, Hou	37	7	8	15	16	+2	1	0	64	0.109
Lomenda, Mark	D-O, Ind	39	6	16	22	11	-7	5	0	70	0.086
MacDonald, Blair	Edm, Cle	85	26	16	42	22	-6	4	0	214	0.121
MacGregor, Gary	D-O, Cle	73	21	17	38	24	-18	7	0	172	0.122
Maggs, Darryl	D-O, Ind	78	9	39	48	82	-4	2	0	188	0.048
McKenzie, John	Min, Cin	69	24	36	60	54	+9	5	2	142	0.169
McNamee, Pete	Phx, SD	65	3	5	8	59	-16	0	0	70	0.043
Miller, Perry	Min, Wpg	60	8	10	18	52	+3	1	0	57	0.140
Moffat, Lyle	Cle, Wpg	75	17	16	33	77	+13	5	0	118	0.144
Morris, Rick	D-O, Edm	73	20	21	41	110	-33	0	6	164	0.122

Totals for Players With Two or More Teams During 1975-1976
(continued)

player	teams	gp	g	a	pts	pim	+/-	ppg	shg	sog	sc%
Muloin, Wayne	Cle, Edm	37	1	6	7	12	-13	0	0	18	0.056
Newton, Cam	D-O, Cle	25	0	1	1	0		0	0	0	-
Odrowski, Gerry	Min, Wpg	50	1	13	14	16	-17	0	0	82	0.012
Parizeau, Michel	Que, Ind	81	25	42	67	44	+15	8	0	137	0.182
Popiel, Jan	Den, Hou	68	4	7	11	61	-13	0	0	68	0.059
Prentice, Bill	Ind, Que	59	6	7	13	181	+2	1	0	69	0.087
Rochon, Francois	D-O, Ind	60	17	12	29	41	-18	5	0	99	0.172
Rogers, Mike	Edm, NE	80	30	29	59	20	0	1	0	184	0.163
Veneruzzo, Gary	Cin, Phx	75	22	26	48	35	+27	3	1	160	0.138
Westrum, Pat	Min, Cgy	63	3	12	15	121	+2	0	0	63	0.048
Wood, Wayne	Cgy, Tor	32	0	1	1	4		0	0	0	-
Zrymiak, Jerry	Min, Tor	39	0	13	13	27	-12	0	0	31	0.000

Totals for Goaltenders With Two or More Teams During 1975-1976

goaltender	teams	gp	min	ga	en	so	record	gaa	sog	sv%
John Garrett	Min, Tor	61	3730	210	3	3	29-28-4	3.38	2022	0.896
Paul Hoganson	NE, Cin	49	2616	161	3	2	20-26-0	3.69	1378	0.883
Bob Johnson	D-O, Cle	42	2377	144	0	1	17-22-1	3.63	1290	0.888
Cam Newton	D-O, Cle	25	1469	83	0	1	11-13-1	3.39	782	0.894
Wayne Wood	Cgy, Tor	32	1661	107	0	1	15-10-1	3.87	889	0.880

Gaye Cooley's Busy Playoffs

Gaye Cooley was a career minor-league goaltender, a graduate of Michigan State University who was a member of the Spartans' 1966 NCAA Championship team. In 1976, he was the principal goaltender for the Charlotte Checkers, who won the EHL Championship. Shortly thereafter, he was called up as an injury-replacement for the Philadelphia Firebirds, as they went on to win the NAHL Championship, giving Cooley the unique distinction of playing for two championship teams in the same post-season. But his busy spring wasn't yet over: the New England Whalers of the WHA called on Cooley as a back-up after Christer Abrahamsson was lost for the playoffs. Cooley mainly sat and watched, but did manage to see action for one three-second stretch, in what would be his only big-league appearance. He retired from professional hockey in 1977. In 2010, he was inducted into the Charlotte Hockey Hall of Fame, in honor of his goaltending that led the Checkers to three championships during the early 1970s.

Penalty Shot Parade

Don McLeod of the Calgary Cowboys faced five penalty shots between February 18 and March 20, 1976, including two games (the February 18 and March 20 games) in which he faced two penalty shots apiece – in a single period, no less. In the February 18 game against Cleveland, McLeod had been relieved two minutes into the third period by back-up Ed Humphreys. However, when the penalty shots were called, he returned to the game to face each shot, only to return to the bench afterwards. In the March 20 game against Quebec, the two teams played a chippy, fight-filled game that not only resulted in numerous penalties, but another two free shots for the Nordiques, barely two minutes apart. McLeod was up to the task and stopped each of the shots.

Slap Shot: Based on a True Story

The motion picture *Slap Shot* was released in early 1977, starring Paul Newman as the player-coach of the fictional minor-league Charlestown Chiefs. The movie is a classic example of the maxim "the truth is stranger than fiction". Were the film entirely fictional, it would be nothing more than Hollywood nonsense. Unbelievably, the characters and events in *Slap Shot* are based on actual players and an actual team!

The Charlestown Chiefs were the fictionalized version of the Johnstown Jets, the principal minor-league affiliate of the Minnesota Fighting Saints. The Jets played in the North American Hockey League, which lasted from 1973 until 1977. During the 1974-75 season, the Jets, mired in the middle of the standings midway through the season, suddenly caught fire and eventually won the league's Lockhart Trophy despite only finishing fourth in the standings. A turning point for the Jets, and somewhat faithfully recreated for the film, was a January game in Utica in which Jets players went into the stands to confront some belligerent fans. The incident brought the team much notoriety and helped spur them to their strong finish. The screenplay for *Slap Shot* was written by Nancy Dowd, sister of Ned Dowd, a player on that Johnstown team.

Jack Carlson

Jeff Carlson

Steve Carlson

The film, and the team, featured the Hanson brothers. In the film, they are portrayed as three bruising brothers with long hair, plastic glasses taped at the bridge and an amazing penchant for fighting and rough-housing, which, for the most part, was exactly how they were in real life. The Hansons are based on the three Carlson brothers,

Jeff, Jack and Steve, from Virginia, Minnesota. Playing for the Jets, Jack and Jeff produced 246 and 250 penalty minutes respectively, but also added 49 and 47 points to the attack. Steve was an 88-point man and accounted for 84 minutes in penalties. The Carlson brothers were all property of the Fighting Saints and all three saw action in the WHA with the Saints and other teams. Jeff's career was the shortest, 7 games, but Jack and Steve played for a few seasons including time in the NHL.

The Hansons were intended to be portrayed by the three Carlson brothers, but during filming, Jack was unavailable and the role was filled by Dave Hanson. Other members of the Johnstown Jets to play in the film were Jean Tetreault as Bergeron, Ron Docken as the back-up goaltender Lebrun, and Guido Tenesi as Billy Charlebois. Tetreault had a brief career in the WHA with Vancouver and Minnesota, but Docken and Tenesi never made it to the big-time. The Jets' coach, Dick Roberge, plays referee Ecker in the film. Another Jet, John Gofton, plays the drunk Presidents player who suffers an "accident" after a hard check to the boards. Some players on the fictional Chiefs were likely inspired by actual Jets players, although their parts were played by actors. "Moe" of the Chiefs may have been inspired by Pat Westrum, while goaltender Lemieux was likely based on Louis Levasseur. The fictional Chiefs were filmed at the real-life Jets' home arena, the Cambria County War Memorial, in Johnstown, Pennsylvania. Even the Chiefs' jerseys wore identical in color and design to those of the Jets.

Bill Goldthorpe

Dave Hanson

Every story needs a villain, and in *Slap Shot*, it was "Ogie" Oglethorpe. Oglethorpe was based on Bill Goldthorpe, a notorious fighter who played for numerous teams in the minor leagues—and a few in the WHA—during a six-year career. Goldthorpe was absolutely fearless, amassing remarkable penalty minute totals wherever he played, and leveraging his fearsome reputation with a fearsome appearance—a full blond afro hairstyle, long sideburns, and a menacing sneer. In the movie, his character was supposedly "banned for life", only to return for the championship game. In the movie, Oglethorpe is played by Ned Dowd, wearing a wig.

Several skating scenes in the film featured actual NAHL players, including a few who played in the WHA. Blake Ball, who had a brief two-game stint with Cleveland in the 1973 playoffs, played Gilmore Tuttle (from Mile-40, Saskatchewan) in the film's championship game. Alton White appears very briefly skating behind the net as a player for the Presidents. Ted McCaskill, Ross Smith, Reg Krezanski and Louis Levasseur all skated as extras in uncredited roles. A non-WHA player who may rate some familiarity is Connie Madigan (the NHL's oldest rookie ever at age 38 in 1973), who plays Ross "Mad Dog" Madison in the championship game.

The acting bug seemed to take hold in Ned Dowd. He retired from professional hockey in 1977 and had roles in films such as *Popeye* (1980), *Southern Comfort* (1981, playing one of the hunters tracking the National Guardsmen through the Louisiana bayou), and *48 Hrs* (1982, playing a policeman). He appeared in a few other films during the 1980s, and has remained in the motion picture industry as an assistant director, producer and production head. He has over 30 films to his credit in various roles. Nancy Dowd has worked on a few films as a writer, sometimes uncredited, and often using male *nommes de plume*. Films she has worked on include *Coming Home* (1978), *North Dallas Forty* (1979) and *Swing Shift* (1984).

The 1974–75 Johnstown Jets, inspiration for the fictional Charlestown Chiefs.

Front Row (L-R): Ron Docken, Pat Westrum, Mike Chernoff, John Mitchell (Executive Director), Galen Head, Dick Roberge, Louis Levasseur.

Middle Row: Gary Kazmierczyk (Trainer), Jerry Welsh, Bob Boyd, Dave Hanson, Jeff Carlson, Steve Carlson, Ned Dowd, Francois Ouimet.

Back Row: Ed Neisner (Assistant trainer), Vern Campigotto, Reg Bechtold, Guido Tenesi, John Gofton, Jean Tetreault.

Season V

1976-1977

The World Hockey Association turned five years old during 1976, slightly worse for wear after a rocky 1975-76 which saw two teams fold in midseason. The Toronto Toros moved south to Birmingham, Alabama, where they became the Bulls; while the Cleveland Crusaders moved to St. Paul, Minnesota, where they became the second incarnation of the Minnesota Fighting Saints. The twelve teams were grouped into Eastern and Western Divisions. Birmingham, Cincinnati, Indianapolis, Minnesota, New England and Quebec were placed in the East, while Calgary, Edmonton, Houston, Phoenix, San Diego and Winnipeg comprised the West.

Alas, the Minnesota (new) Fighting Saints resembled the old Fighting Saints in more ways than just the name. The team folded halfway through the season, and in less than a year, the league was zero for two in St. Paul.

An 80-game schedule was planned, modeled after the style used in 1972-73 and 1973-74. A team would play each of the six teams in the other division six times, three at home and three as guests, and it would play its own division rivals eight or ten times, split evenly home and away. The demise of Minnesota once again required some creative restructuring on the part of the league's schedule maker. As in the previous season, some teams played 81 games so that others could reach

80, with a proper balance of home and away games. (The eight teams that played 81 games played 40 at home and 41 away, since Minnesota left having played eight more home games than away.)

Winnipeg took a two-week trip to tour Europe during December as a reward for winning the 1976 World Trophy. As ambassadors for the league, the Jets paved the way for touring European teams to visit North America the following season. After their sojourn, the jet-lagged Jets were welcomed home with a 12-3 bombing administered by Quebec. The Nordiques would go on to win the 1977 World Trophy by beating the same Jets in a seven-game duel.

Winnipeg's Anders Hedberg scored more goals than anybody else with 70, while teammate Ulf Nilsson collected a league leading 85 assists, but Quebec's Real Cloutier accumulated the most points with 141, on 66 goals and 75 assists. Edmonton's Frank Beaton spent 274 minutes in the penalty box as the league's top troublemaker. Winnipeg's Joe Daley won the most games with 39, but Houston's Ron Grahame regularly permitted the fewest goals per outing with a 2.74 average. Grahame, with Edmonton's Ken Broderick and Birmingham's John Garrett, tied for the league high in shutouts, with 4 apiece.

Standings

Eastern Division

	team		gp	w	l	t	pts	pct	gf	ga
1.	Québec NORDIQUES		81	47	31	3	97	.599	353	295
		home	40	29	10	1	59	.738	186	117
		away	41	18	21	2	38	.463	167	178
2.	Cincinnati STINGERS		81	39	37	5	83	.512	354	303
		home	40	29	10	1	59	.738	207	115
		away	41	10	27	4	24	.293	147	188
3.	Indianapolis RACERS		81	36	37	8	80	.493	276	305
		home	40	24	13	3	51	.638	157	134
		away	41	12	24	5	29	.354	119	171
4.	New England WHALERS		81	35	40	6	76	.469	275	290
		home	40	20	16	4	44	.550	150	133
		away	41	15	24	2	32	.390	125	157
5.	Birmingham BULLS		81	31	46	4	66	.407	289	309
		home	40	22	15	3	47	.588	177	131
		away	41	9	31	1	19	.232	112	178
	Minnesota FIGHTING SAINTS		42	19	18	5	43	.512	136	129
	• Disbanded Jan 17, 1977	home	25	14	8	3	31	.620	94	69
		away	17	5	10	2	12	.353	42	60

Western Division

	team		gp	w	l	t	pts	pct	gf	ga
1.	Houston AEROS		80	50	24	6	106	.663	320	241
		home	40	33	3	4	70	.875	180	88
		away	40	17	21	2	36	.450	140	153
2.	Winnipeg JETS		80	46	32	2	94	.588	366	291
		home	40	30	9	1	61	.763	207	119
		away	40	16	23	1	33	.413	159	172
3.	San Diego MARINERS		81	40	37	4	84	.519	284	283
		home	40	26	10	4	56	.700	164	122
		away	41	14	27	0	28	.341	120	161
4.	Edmonton OILERS		81	34	43	4	72	.444	243	304
		home	40	24	15	1	49	.613	148	131
		away	41	10	28	3	23	.280	95	173
5.	Calgary COWBOYS		81	31	43	7	69	.426	252	296
		home	40	26	12	2	54	.675	160	117
		away	41	5	31	5	15	.183	92	179
6.	Phoenix ROADRUNNERS		80	28	48	4	60	.375	281	383
		home	40	20	18	2	42	.525	164	159
		away	40	8	30	2	18	.225	117	224

Award Winners

Most Valuable Player
Gordie Howe Trophy
Robbie Ftorek, Phx

Rookie of the Year
Lou Kaplan Trophy
George Lyle, NE

Best Goaltender
Ben Hatskin Trophy
Ron Grahame, Hou

Best Defeseman
Dennis Murphy Trophy
Ron Plumb, Cin

Coach of the Year
Howard Baldwin Trophy
Bill Dineen, Hou

Most Gentlemanly
Paul Deneau Trophy
Dave Keon, NE

1977 World Hockey Association AVCO Cup Champions
Quebec Nordiques

1977 Playoff Series Results

Eastern Division Semifinals

Quebec vs. New England
Apr 9	New England 2 at Quebec 5
Apr 12	New England 3 at Quebec 7
Apr 14	Quebec 4 at New England 3
	(ot: Paul Baxter, 1:50)
Apr 16	Quebec 4 at New England 6
Apr 19	New England 0 at Quebec 3
	(so: Richard Brodeur, 19 saves)

Cincinnati vs. Indianapolis
Apr 9	Indianapolis 4 at Cincinnati 3
	(ot: Gene Peacosh, 48:40)
Apr 12	Indianapolis 7 at Cincinnati 2
Apr 14	Cincinnati 3 at Indianapolis 5
Apr 16	Cincinnati 1 at Indianapolis 3

Eastern Division Final

Quebec vs. Indianapolis
Apr 23	Indianapolis 1 at Quebec 3
Apr 25	Indianapolis 3 at Quebec 8
Apr 28	Quebec 6 at Indianapolis 5
	(ot: Paulin Bordeleau, 5:29)
Apr 30	Quebec 0 at Indianapolis 2
	(so: Paul Hoganson, 22 saves)
May 2	Indianapolis 3 at Quebec 8

Western Division Semifinals

Houston vs. Edmonton
Apr 13	Edmonton 3 at Houston 4
	(ot: Morris Lukowich, 13:11)
Apr 15	Edmonton 2 at Houston 6
Apr 17	Houston 2 at Edmonton 7
Apr 20	Houston 4 at Edmonton 1
Apr 22	Edmonton 3 at Houston 4

Winnipeg vs. San Diego
Apr 10	San Diego 1 at Winnipeg 5
Apr 12	San Diego 1 at Winnipeg 4
Apr 16	Winnipeg 4 at San Diego 5
Apr 17	Winnipeg 4 at San Diego 6
Apr 20	San Diego 0 at Winnipeg 3
	(so: Joe Daley, 25 saves)
Apr 22	Winnipeg 1 at San Diego 3
Apr 24	San Diego 3 at Winnipeg 7

Western Division Final

Houston vs. Winnipeg
Apr 26	Winnipeg 4 at Houston 3
	(ot: Peter Sullivan, 8:05)
Apr 28	Winnipeg 2 at Houston 7
Apr 30	Houston 3 at Winnipeg 4
May 1	Houston 4 at Winnipeg 6
May 3	Winnipeg 2 at Houston 3
May 5	Houston 3 at Winnipeg 6

AVCO World Trophy Championship

Winnipeg vs. Quebec
May 11	Winnipeg 2 at Quebec 1
May 15	Winnipeg 1 at Quebec 6
May 18	Quebec 1 at Winnipeg 6
May 20	Quebec 4 at Winnipeg 2
May 22	Winnipeg 3 at Quebec 8
May 24	Quebec 3 at Winnipeg 12
May 26	Winnipeg 2 at Quebec 8

Playoff Standings

Overall Team	w	l	gf	ga	Home Team	w	l	gf	ga	Away Team	w	l	gf	ga
Quebec	12	5	79	56	Quebec	9	1	57	20	Quebec	3	4	22	36
Winnipeg	11	9	80	73	Winnipeg	9	1	55	23	Indianapolis	2	3	18	24
Houston	6	5	43	40	Houston	5	1	27	16	Winnipeg	2	8	25	50
Indianapolis	5	4	33	34	San Diego	3	0	14	9	Houston	1	4	16	24
San Diego	3	4	19	28	Indianapolis	3	1	15	10	Cincinnati	0	2	4	8
Edmonton	1	4	16	20	Edmonton	1	1	8	6	Edmonton	0	3	8	14
New England	1	4	14	23	New England	1	1	9	8	New England	0	3	5	15
Cincinnati	0	4	9	19	Cincinnati	0	2	5	11	San Diego	0	4	5	19

Championship Series Summaries

The 1977 AVCO Championship pitted two high-flying, high-scoring teams against one another, and for the first time in the league's short history, featured two Canadian-based teams. The action lived up to the hype as the series went the full seven games. Winnipeg was defending its hold on the throne against a very motivated Quebec Nordique squad. Led by Marc Tardif, who had been felled in last year's playoffs, the Nordiques fought furiously to stave off the equally potent Jets club. The Jets forced a game 7 with a 12-3 thrashing in game 6, but a 6-goal period in game 7 sealed the Quebec victory. Serge Bernier had 4 goals and 8 assists to lead the scoring, and he was supported by Real Cloutier (4-7), Marc Tardif (2-5) and Christian and Paulin Bordeleau (both 4-3).

Game 1 • May 11, 1977
Winnipeg 2, Quebec 1

Winnipeg	0	2	0	-	2
Quebec	0	0	1	-	1

1st period: No Scoring.
2nd period: 1. Wpg: Labraaten (Dunn) 2:22; 2. Wpg: Lindstrom (Labraaten, Sullivan) 13:30
3rd period: 3. Que: P. Bordeleau 7:00
Shots on goal

Wpg on Brodeur	12	6	9	-	27
Que on Daley	6	17	9	-	32

Game 2 • May 15, 1977
Quebec 6, Winnipeg 1

Winnipeg	0	0	1	-	1
Quebec	4	1	1	-	6

1st period: 1. Que: Guite (Boudrias, Lacombe) 4:32; 2. Que: P. Bordeleau (S. Bernier, Dube) 13:25; 3. Que: Sutherland 15:17; 4. Que: S. Bernier (Dube, Brackenbury) 18:23
2nd period: 5. Que: Brackenbury (S. Bernier, Weir) 17:02
3rd period: 6. Wpg: Labraaten (Lindstrom) 2:47; 7. Que: Sutherland (Fitchner, Brackenbury) 13:00
Shots on goal

Wpg on Brodeur	5	15	7	-	27
Que on Daley	9	12	13	-	34

Game 3 • May 18, 1977
Winnipeg 6, Quebec 1

Quebec	1	0	0	-	1
Winnipeg	0	2	4	-	6

1st period: 1. Que: Brackenbury (Fitchner) 2:08
2nd period: 2. Wpg: Lindstrom (Labraaten) 4:42; 3. Wpg: Labraaten (Lindstrom) 13:16
3rd period: 4. Wpg: Hedberg (Ford, Daley) 0:31; 5. Wpg: Nilsson 6:16; 6. Wpg: Lesuk (Lindh, Long) 9:30; 7. Wpg: Lindstrom (Sullivan, Labraaten) 16:33
Shots on goal

Que on Daley	8	8	8	-	24
Wpg on Brodeur	5	8	8	-	21

Game 4 • May 20, 1977
Quebec 4, Winnipeg 2

Quebec	1	2	1	-	4
Winnipeg	2	0	0	-	2

1st period: 1. Que: S. Bernier (P. Bordeleau, J. Bernier) 7:33; 2. Wpg: Miller (Sullivan, Labraaten) 11:38; 3. Wpg: Nilsson (Hull, Hedberg) 17:17
2nd period: 4. Que: Lacombe (Cloutier, Tremblay) 1:50; 5. Que: Tardif (S. Bernier, C. Bordeleau) 14:53
3rd period: 6. Que: S. Bernier (P. Bordeleau) 4:32
Shots on goal

Que on Daley	11	9	7	-	27
Wpg on Brodeur, Aubry	9	8	12	-	29

Game 5 • May 23, 1977
Quebec 8, Winnipeg 3

Winnipeg	1	2	0	-	3
Quebec	4	3	1	-	8

1st period: 1. Que: Guite (Boudrias, J. Bernier) 4:23; 2. Que: Cloutier (Tardif, Tremblay) 8:49; 3. Que: C. Bordeleau (Cloutier) 12:10; 4. Que: P. Bordeleau (Dube, S. Bernier) 14:20; 5. Wpg: Nilsson (Miller, Hull) 17:04
2nd period: 6. Que: Cloutier (C. Bordeleau) 4:18; 7. Que: P. Bordeleau (S. Bernier, Tremblay) 6:01; 8. Wpg: Ford (Sullivan, Labraaten) 6:39; 9. Que: C. Bordeleau (Cloutier, S. Bernier) 11:37; 10: Wpg: Hull 13:43
3rd period: 11. Que: S. Bernier (P. Bordeleau) 8:49
Shots on goal

Wpg on Brodeur	14	9	9	-	32
Que on Daley	8	7	7	-	22

Game 6 • May 24, 1977
Winnipeg 12, Quebec 3

Quebec	3	0	0	-	3
Winnipeg	4	4	4	-	12

1st period: 1. Wpg: Hull (Nilsson, Ford) 1:26; 2. Que: Cloutier 3:02; 3. Que: Cloutier (Tardif, C. Bordeleau) 4:28; 4. Wpg: Labraaten (Sullivan, Lindstrom) 9:17; 5. Wpg: Hedberg (Nilsson) 12:09; 6. Wpg: Guindon (Huck, Miller) 13:47; 7. Que: C. Bordeleau (Tardif, Cloutier) 16:35
2nd period: 8. Wpg: Hull (Guindon, Dunn) 6:28; 9. Wpg: Sullivan (Labraaten) 8:04; 10. Wpg: Ford (Sjoberg, Hedberg) 16:57; 11. Wpg: Guindon (Long, Huck) 17:30
3rd period: 12. Wpg: Sullivan (Labraaten) 2:21; 13: Wpg: Hedberg (Nilsson, Miller) 3:37; 14. Wpg: Lindstrom (Sullivan) 5:20; 15. Wpg: Hull (Nilsson, Hedberg) 12:36
Shots on goal

Que on Daley	7	9	8	-	24
Wpg on Brodeur, Aubry	11	17	14	-	42

Game 7 • May 26, 1977
Quebec 8, Winnipeg 2

Winnipeg	0	1	1	-	2
Quebec	0	6	2	-	8

1st period: No Scoring
2nd period: 1. Que: Fitchner 0:11; 2. Que: Tardif (Cloutier, C. Bordeleau) 1:10; 3. Que: Cloutier (Tardif, Lariviere) 6:27; 4. Wpg: Labraaten (Ford, Sullivan) 8:39; 5. Que: Tremblay (Cloutier, Tardif) 9:24; 6. Que: P. Bordeleau (S. Bernier, Lacombe) 18:41
3rd period: 8. Que: C. Bordeleau (Cloutier, Lacombe) 1:39; 9. Que: S. Bernier (Dube, Lariviere) 3:39; 10. Wpg: Miller (Nilsson, Hedberg) 14:09
Shots on goal

Wpg on Brodeur	12	8	7	-	27
Que on Daley	7	11	7	-	25

Statistical Leaders

Goals: 14, Serge Bernier (Que), Real Cloutier (Que); 13, Anders Hedberg (Wpg), Bobby Hull (Wpg); 12, Paulin Bordeleau (Que)

Assists: 22, Serge Bernier (Que); 21, Ulf Nilsson (Wpg); 17, Dan Labraaten (Wpg); 16, Anders Hedberg (Wpg); 13, Real Cloutier (Que), Mike Ford (Wpg)

Points: 36, Serge Bernier (Que); 29, Anders Hedberg (Wpg); 27, Real Cloutier (Que); 24, Dan Labraaten (Wpg)

Penalty Minutes: 67, Terry Ruskowski (Hou); 51, Curt Brackenbury (Que); 47, Cam Connor (Hou); 37, Ron Busniuk (Edm); 35, Paul Baxter (Que)

Goaltending Wins: 12, Richard Brodeur (Que); 11, Joe Daley (Wpg); 4, Ron Grahame (Hou); 3, Paul Hoganson (Ind)

Goals Against Average: 2.93, Paul Hoganson (Ind); 3.28, Richard Brodeur (Que); 3.59, Joe Daley (Wpg); 3.85, Ron Grahame (Hou). Note: Ken Broderick (Edm) had 3.35 gaa in 3 games, Norm Lapointe (Cin) had 3.52 gaa in 4 games

Splits by Opponent and by Month, Home and Away

Bir Birmingham, **Cgy** Calgary, **Cin** Cincinnati, **Edm** Edmonton, **Hou** Houston, **Ind** Indianapolis, **Min** Minnesota, **NE** New England, **Phx** Phoenix, **Que** Quebec, **SD** San Diego, **Wpg** Winnipeg

BIRMINGHAM

Opp.	season	gf-ga	home	gf-ga	away	gf-ga
Cgy	3-2-1	25-24	3-0-0	16-7	0-2-1	9-17
Cin	5-4-2	42-39	3-1-2	27-19	2-3-0	15-20
Edm	1-6-0	21-27	0-3-0	8-11	1-3-0	13-16
Hou	4-3-0	26-26	3-0-0	18-9	1-3-0	8-17
Ind	3-6-1	28-35	2-2-1	19-15	1-4-0	9-20
Min	1-4-0	9-19	0-2-0	3-7	1-2-0	6-12
NE	4-5-0	34-38	3-2-0	21-19	1-3-0	13-19
Phx	4-2-0	32-20	3-0-0	20-10	1-2-0	12-10
Que	3-5-0	39-33	3-1-0	25-14	0-4-0	14-19
SD	1-5-0	15-24	1-2-0	9-10	0-3-0	6-14
Wpg	2-4-0	18-24	1-2-0	11-10	1-2-0	7-14
Oct	4-8-1	48-61	3-2-1	33-26	1-6-0	15-35
Nov	4-11-0	43-53	4-6-0	30-31	0-5-0	13-22
Dec	5-7-0	43-43	2-3-0	16-15	3-4-0	27-28
Jan	5-6-0	37-41	4-0-0	24-8	1-6-0	13-33
Feb	7-4-2	54-38	4-0-2	34-17	3-4-0	20-21
Mar	6-8-0	51-57	5-3-0	35-28	1-5-0	16-29
Apr	0-2-1	13-16	0-1-0	5-6	0-1-1	8-10

EDMONTON

Opp.	season	gf-ga	home	gf-ga	away	gf-ga
Bir	6-1-0	27-21	3-1-0	16-13	3-0-0	11-8
Cgy	3-5-2	23-27	3-1-1	15-8	0-4-1	8-19
Cin	3-3-0	21-24	2-1-0	12-12	1-2-0	9-12
Hou	1-7-1	20-29	1-3-0	12-13	0-4-1	8-16
Ind	3-3-0	24-22	2-1-0	14-8	1-2-0	10-14
Min	1-2-0	5-12	1-0-0	4-2	0-2-0	1-10
NE	4-2-0	21-19	2-1-0	9-7	2-1-0	12-12
Phx	4-4-0	26-26	3-1-0	20-13	1-2-0	6-13
Que	3-2-1	24-22	1-2-0	12-13	2-0-1	12-9
SD	2-6-0	19-30	2-2-0	14-14	0-4-0	5-16
Wpg	4-8-0	33-72	4-2-0	20-28	0-6-0	13-44
Oct	4-5-0	26-38	3-3-0	18-21	1-2-0	8-17
Nov	6-9-0	44-53	5-1-0	24-16	1-8-0	20-37
Dec	6-6-1	29-36	3-2-0	16-15	3-4-1	13-21
Jan	5-8-0	41-51	3-2-1	23-16	2-6-0	17-35
Feb	4-7-0	31-47	4-5-0	28-40	0-2-0	3-7
Mar	7-7-1	56-66	4-1-0	26-14	3-6-1	30-52
Apr	2-1-1	17-13	2-1-0	13-9	0-0-1	4-4

CALGARY

Opp.	season	gf-ga	home	gf-ga	away	gf-ga
Bir	2-3-1	24-25	2-0-1	17-9	0-3-0	7-16
Cin	2-4-0	23-32	2-1-0	14-13	0-3-0	9-19
Edm	5-3-2	27-23	4-0-1	19-8	1-3-1	8-15
Hou	2-6-0	22-32	2-2-0	16-16	0-4-0	6-16
Ind	2-3-1	12-14	2-1-0	9-8	0-2-1	3-6
Min	2-2-1	11-15	2-0-0	6-4	0-2-1	5-11
NE	1-5-0	11-30	1-2-0	6-10	0-3-0	5-20
Phx	7-0-1	41-21	4-0-0	27-12	3-0-1	14-9
Que	2-4-0	15-25	2-1-0	10-7	0-3-0	5-18
SD	4-4-0	27-24	3-1-0	14-7	1-3-0	13-17
Wpg	2-9-1	39-55	2-4-0	22-23	0-5-1	17-32
Oct	3-6-1	33-34	3-1-0	23-11	0-5-1	10-23
Nov	6-5-1	32-33	5-2-0	23-17	1-3-1	9-16
Dec	5-6-0	35-34	5-1-0	23-10	0-5-0	12-24
Jan	5-7-2	50-54	3-4-0	29-26	2-3-2	21-28
Feb	5-7-1	35-48	4-3-0	18-22	1-4-1	17-26
Mar	6-10-0	48-72	6-0-0	32-17	0-10-0	16-55
Apr	1-2-2	19-21	0-1-2	12-14	1-1-0	7-7

HOUSTON

Opp.	season	gf-ga	home	gf-ga	away	gf-ga
Bir	3-4-0	26-26	3-1-0	17-8	0-3-0	9-18
Cgy	6-2-0	32-22	4-0-0	16-6	2-2-0	16-16
Cin	4-2-0	27-25	3-0-0	16-9	1-2-0	11-16
Edm	7-1-1	29-20	4-0-1	16-8	3-1-0	13-12
Ind	4-1-1	30-17	2-1-0	15-9	2-0-1	15-8
Min	0-0-2	2-2	0-0-1	1-1	0-0-1	1-1
NE	2-3-1	17-18	2-0-1	12-5	0-3-0	5-13
Phx	9-2-0	66-35	5-0-0	36-13	4-2-0	30-22
Que	3-3-0	20-24	3-0-0	15-8	0-3-0	5-16
SD	8-3-0	44-30	5-0-0	21-10	3-3-0	23-20
Wpg	4-3-1	27-22	2-1-1	15-11	2-2-0	12-11
Oct	5-5-2	37-39	4-0-2	18-10	1-5-0	19-29
Nov	7-2-1	42-22	5-0-1	30-10	2-2-0	12-12
Dec	6-7-1	47-52	4-1-1	27-15	2-6-0	20-37
Jan	10-2-1	54-31	5-0-0	24-10	5-2-1	30-21
Feb	9-3-1	60-38	6-0-0	30-12	3-3-1	30-26
Mar	10-4-0	64-44	7-1-0	40-19	3-3-0	24-25
Apr	3-1-0	16-15	2-1-0	11-12	1-0-0	5-3

CINCINNATI

Opp.	season	gf-ga	home	gf-ga	away	gf-ga
Bir	4-5-2	39-42	3-2-0	20-15	1-3-2	19-27
Cgy	4-2-0	32-23	3-0-0	19-9	1-2-0	13-14
Edm	3-3-0	24-21	2-1-0	12-9	1-2-0	12-12
Hou	2-4-0	25-27	2-1-0	16-11	0-3-0	9-16
Ind	4-5-1	50-35	4-1-0	34-11	0-4-1	16-24
Min	3-2-0	19-12	2-0-0	12-2	1-2-0	7-10
NE	4-5-0	38-30	3-2-0	28-18	1-3-0	10-12
Phx	3-3-0	36-29	3-0-0	21-6	0-3-0	15-23
Que	5-4-1	35-37	3-1-1	21-14	2-3-0	14-23
SD	3-2-1	24-24	2-1-0	7-9	1-1-1	17-15
Wpg	4-2-0	32-23	2-1-0	17-11	2-1-0	15-12
Oct	6-3-2	59-44	3-0-0	20-7	3-3-2	39-37
Nov	6-6-0	45-40	5-1-0	32-17	1-5-0	13-23
Dec	5-7-0	52-46	5-3-0	39-26	0-4-0	13-20
Jan	6-7-0	56-54	4-0-0	21-6	2-7-0	35-48
Feb	8-5-1	67-47	6-3-0	45-25	2-2-1	22-22
Mar	8-7-1	66-59	6-3-0	48-32	2-4-1	18-27
Apr	0-2-1	9-13	0-0-1	2-2	0-2-0	7-11

INDIANAPOLIS

Opp.	season	gf-ga	home	gf-ga	away	gf-ga
Bir	6-3-1	35-28	4-1-0	20-9	2-2-1	15-19
Cgy	3-2-1	14-12	2-0-1	6-3	1-2-0	8-9
Cin	5-4-1	35-50	4-0-1	24-16	1-4-0	11-34
Edm	3-3-0	22-24	2-1-0	14-10	1-2-0	8-14
Hou	1-4-1	14-30	0-2-1	8-15	1-2-0	9-15
Min	1-3-0	13-21	1-1-0	7-8	0-2-0	6-13
NE	7-1-2	41-25	3-1-0	15-7	4-0-2	26-18
Phx	2-3-1	21-23	2-1-0	12-9	0-2-1	9-14
Que	5-6-0	40-42	3-3-0	22-28	2-3-0	18-14
SD	2-3-1	16-20	2-1-0	11-11	0-2-1	5-9
Wpg	1-5-0	22-30	1-2-0	18-18	0-3-0	4-12
Oct	3-5-1	26-41	3-2-0	18-20	0-3-1	8-21
Nov	9-5-1	57-55	5-1-0	26-17	4-4-1	31-38
Dec	6-4-0	29-28	4-2-0	17-16	2-2-0	12-12
Jan	5-7-2	47-46	4-1-1	25-12	1-6-1	22-34
Feb	4-8-3	50-63	2-3-1	26-29	2-5-2	24-34
Mar	8-6-1	55-59	6-3-1	43-37	2-3-0	12-22
Apr	1-2-0	12-13	0-1-0	2-3	1-1-0	10-10

MINNESOTA

Opp.	season	gf-ga	home	gf-ga	away	gf-ga
Bir	4-1-0	19-9	2-1-0	12-6	2-0-0	7-3
Cgy	2-2-1	15-11	2-0-1	11-5	0-2-0	4-6
Cin	2-3-0	12-19	2-1-0	10-7	0-2-0	2-12
Edm	2-1-0	12-5	2-0-0	10-1	0-1-0	2-4
Hou	0-0-2	2-2	0-0-1	1-1	0-0-1	1-1
Ind	3-1-0	21-13	2-0-0	13-6	1-1-0	8-7
NE	3-1-2	20-16	2-0-1	12-9	1-1-1	8-7
Phx	0-2-0	4-7	0-1-0	1-3	0-1-0	3-4
Que	2-3-0	17-22	1-2-0	12-15	1-1-0	5-7
SD	1-2-0	9-12	1-2-0	9-12	0-0-0	0-0
Wpg	0-2-0	5-13	0-1-0	3-4	0-1-0	2-9
Oct	3-6-2	31-37	3-2-1	21-16	0-4-1	10-21
Nov	6-5-2	42-42	3-2-0	22-18	3-3-1	20-24
Dec	7-6-0	42-39	5-3-0	30-24	2-3-0	12-15
Jan	3-1-1	21-11	3-1-1	21-11	0-0-0	0-0

QUEBEC

Opp.	season	gf-ga	home	gf-ga	away	gf-ga
Bir	5-3-0	33-39	4-0-0	19-14	1-3-0	14-25
Cgy	4-2-0	25-15	3-0-0	18-5	1-2-0	7-10
Cin	4-5-1	37-35	3-2-0	23-14	1-3-1	14-21
Edm	2-3-1	22-24	0-2-1	9-12	2-1-0	13-12
Hou	3-3-0	24-20	3-0-0	16-5	0-3-0	8-15
Ind	6-5-0	42-40	3-2-0	14-18	3-3-0	28-22
Min	3-2-0	22-17	1-1-0	7-5	2-1-0	15-12
NE	8-2-1	52-33	5-1-0	25-13	3-1-1	27-20
Phx	5-1-0	38-22	2-1-0	23-10	3-0-0	15-12
SD	4-2-0	24-20	3-0-0	17-6	1-2-0	7-14
Wpg	3-3-0	34-30	2-1-0	15-15	1-2-0	19-15
Oct	9-2-0	61-35	6-1-0	39-20	3-1-0	22-15
Nov	6-8-0	53-60	4-4-0	27-33	2-4-0	26-27
Dec	7-5-1	54-42	3-2-0	18-13	4-3-1	36-29
Jan	8-1-0	46-28	5-1-0	28-16	3-0-0	18-12
Feb	6-8-0	50-62	4-1-0	22-17	2-7-0	28-45
Mar	9-6-1	74-52	6-1-1	45-16	3-5-0	29-36
Apr	2-1-1	15-16	1-0-0	7-2	1-1-1	8-14

NEW ENGLAND

Opp.	season	gf-ga	home	gf-ga	away	gf-ga
Bir	5-4-0	38-34	3-1-0	19-13	2-3-0	19-21
Cgy	5-1-0	30-11	3-0-0	20-5	2-1-0	10-6
Cin	5-4-0	30-38	3-1-0	12-10	2-3-0	18-28
Edm	2-4-0	19-21	1-2-0	12-12	1-2-0	7-9
Hou	3-2-1	18-17	3-0-0	13-5	0-2-1	5-12
Ind	1-7-2	25-41	0-4-2	18-26	1-3-0	7-15
Min	1-3-2	16-20	1-1-1	7-8	0-2-1	9-12
Phx	4-2-0	25-14	2-1-0	12-7	2-1-0	13-7
Que	2-8-1	33-52	1-3-1	20-27	1-5-0	13-25
SD	5-1-0	21-14	2-1-0	6-4	3-0-0	15-10
Wpg	2-4-0	20-28	1-2-0	11-16	1-2-0	9-12
Oct	4-4-1	28-31	4-2-0	22-20	0-2-1	6-11
Nov	4-8-2	44-52	1-3-1	16-21	3-5-1	28-31
Dec	8-6-1	57-53	5-2-1	36-27	3-4-0	21-26
Jan	4-10-1	43-62	2-5-1	24-31	2-5-0	19-31
Feb	6-6-1	44-46	2-2-1	18-18	4-4-0	26-28
Mar	8-5-0	54-37	6-2-0	34-16	2-3-0	20-21
Apr	1-1-0	5-9	0-0-0	0-0	1-1-0	5-9

SAN DIEGO

Opp.	season	gf-ga	home	gf-ga	away	gf-ga
Bir	5-1-0	24-15	3-0-0	14-6	2-1-0	10-9
Cgy	4-4-0	24-27	3-1-0	17-13	1-3-0	7-14
Cin	2-3-1	24-24	1-1-1	15-17	1-2-0	9-7
Edm	6-2-0	30-19	4-0-0	16-5	2-2-0	14-14
Hou	3-8-0	30-44	3-3-0	20-23	0-5-0	10-21
Ind	3-2-1	20-16	2-0-1	9-5	1-2-0	11-11
Min	2-1-0	12-9	0-0-0	0-0	2-1-0	12-9
NE	1-5-0	14-21	0-3-0	10-15	1-2-0	4-6
Phx	8-3-2	62-47	4-1-2	33-21	4-2-0	29-26
Que	2-4-0	20-24	2-1-0	14-7	0-3-0	6-17
Wpg	4-4-0	24-37	4-0-0	16-10	0-4-0	8-27
Oct	4-5-2	41-44	2-0-2	18-14	2-5-0	23-30
Nov	8-5-0	54-39	5-0-0	20-8	3-5-0	18-31
Dec	11-3-0	54-35	6-1-0	25-18	5-2-0	29-17
Jan	4-7-0	31-42	3-4-0	23-29	1-3-0	8-13
Feb	6-6-1	48-50	4-2-1	28-21	2-4-0	20-29
Mar	5-9-1	55-62	4-2-1	34-24	1-7-0	21-38
Apr	2-2-0	17-11	2-1-0	16-8	0-1-0	1-3

PHOENIX

Opp.	season	gf-ga	home	gf-ga	away	gf-ga
Bir	2-4-0	20-32	2-1-0	10-12	0-3-0	10-20
Cgy	0-7-1	21-41	0-3-1	9-14	0-4-0	12-27
Cin	3-3-0	29-36	3-0-0	23-15	0-3-0	6-21
Edm	4-4-0	26-26	3-1-0	13-6	1-3-0	13-20
Hou	2-9-0	35-66	2-4-0	22-30	0-5-0	13-36
Ind	3-2-1	23-21	2-0-1	14-9	1-2-0	9-12
Min	2-0-0	7-4	1-0-0	4-3	1-0-0	3-1
NE	2-4-0	14-25	1-2-0	7-13	1-2-0	7-12
Que	1-5-0	22-38	0-3-0	12-15	1-2-0	10-23
SD	3-8-2	47-62	2-4-0	26-29	1-4-2	21-33
Wpg	6-2-0	37-32	4-0-0	24-13	2-2-0	13-19
Oct	5-5-0	41-54	3-0-0	18-13	2-5-0	23-41
Nov	7-5-2	46-45	4-2-2	27-21	3-3-0	19-24
Dec	2-10-0	33-59	2-5-0	25-29	0-5-0	8-30
Jan	6-7-0	54-68	5-2-0	37-28	1-5-0	17-40
Feb	4-9-1	45-65	3-4-0	26-32	1-5-1	19-33
Mar	3-11-1	50-83	2-4-0	19-27	1-7-1	31-56
Apr	1-1-0	12-9	1-1-0	12-9	0-0-0	0-0

WINNIPEG

Opp.	season	gf-ga	home	gf-ga	away	gf-ga
Bir	4-2-0	24-18	2-1-0	14-7	2-1-0	10-11
Cgy	9-2-1	55-39	5-0-1	32-17	4-2-0	23-22
Cin	2-4-0	23-32	1-2-0	12-15	1-2-0	11-17
Edm	8-4-0	72-33	6-0-0	44-13	2-4-0	28-20
Hou	3-4-1	22-27	2-2-0	11-12	1-2-1	11-15
Ind	5-1-0	30-22	3-0-0	12-4	2-1-0	18-18
Min	2-0-0	13-5	1-0-0	9-2	1-0-0	4-3
NE	4-2-0	28-20	2-1-0	12-9	2-1-0	16-11
Phx	2-6-0	32-37	2-2-0	19-13	0-4-0	13-24
Que	3-3-0	30-34	2-1-0	15-19	1-2-0	15-15
SD	4-4-0	37-24	4-0-0	27-8	0-4-0	10-16
Oct	7-3-0	33-26	6-1-0	42-16	1-2-0	11-10
Nov	7-7-1	67-59	5-3-0	41-26	2-4-1	26-33
Dec	4-5-0	34-42	1-2-0	10-19	3-3-0	24-23
Jan	7-5-0	55-46	6-1-0	40-22	1-4-0	15-24
Feb	9-5-1	70-50	5-1-1	29-17	4-4-0	41-33
Mar	9-6-0	67-49	6-1-0	39-15	3-5-0	28-34
Apr	3-1-0	20-19	1-0-0	6-4	2-1-0	14-15

1977 All-Star Game

Hartford Civic Center
Hartford, Connecticut
January 18, 1977

East

Coach: Jacques Demers (Indianapolis)
Goaltenders: Louis Levasseur (Minnesota), John Garrett (Birmingham)
Defensemen: Pat Stapleton (Indianapolis), J.C. Tremblay (Quebec), Ron Plumb, John Hughes (Cincinnati), Gordie Roberts, Thommie Abrahamsson (New England)
Forwards: Serge Bernier, Real Cloutier, Marc Tardif (Quebec), Richie Leduc, Dennis Sobchuk (Cincinnati), Michel Parizeau, Hugh Harris, Blair MacDonald (Indianapolis), Mike Rogers, George Lyle, Ralph Backstrom (New England), Mark Napier (Birmingham)

West

Coach: Bobby Kromm (Winnipeg)
Goaltenders: Wayne Rutledge (Houston), Joe Daley (Winnipeg)
Defensemen: Thommie Bergman (Winnipeg), Paul Shmyr, Kevin Morrison (San Diego), Barry Wilkins (Edmonton), Poul Popiel (Houston), Paul Terbenche (Calgary)
Forwards: Bobby Hull, Ulf Nilsson, Anders Hedberg, Willy Lindstrom (Winnipeg), Robbie Ftorek, Del Hall (Phoenix), Cam Connor, Gordie Howe (Houston), Joe Noris, Andre Lacroix, Norm Ferguson (San Diego), Danny Lawson (Calgary)

MVPs: West: Willy Lindstrom, Winnipeg
East: Louis Levasseur, Minnesota

East 4, West 2

West	1	0	1	- 2
East	2	0	2	- 4

1st period: 1. East: Tremblay (Leduc, Sobchuk) 11:17; 2. West: Shmyr (Lindstrom, Lacroix) 11:58; 3. East: Tardif (Stapleton, Bernier) 14:56.
2nd period: No scoring.
3rd period: 4. West: Lindstrom (Wilkins) 4:07; 5. East: Cloutier (Tardif, Hughes) 7:57; 6. East: Lyle (Rogers, Abrahamsson) 8:35.

Shots on goal

West	18	20	13	- 51
East	7	11	9	- 27

Attendance: 10,337

1976-1977 Year End All-Star Teams

First Team: Goaltender: John Garrett, Birmingham; Defensemen: Darryl Maggs, Indianapolis, and Ron Plumb, Cincinnati; Center: Robbie Ftorek, Phoenix; Right Wing: Anders Hedberg, Winnipeg; Left Wing: Marc Tardif, Quebec.

Second Team: Goaltender: Joe Daley, Winnipeg; Defensemen: Poul Popiel, Houston and Mark Howe, Houston; Center: Ulf Nilsson, Winnipeg; Right Wing: Real Cloutier, Quebec; Left Wing: Rick Dudley, Cincinnati.

Penalty Shots

date	player, team	goaltender, team	period	time	result
Oct 17	Daniel Gruen, Minnesota	Wayne Wood, Birmingham	2	6:49	Save
Nov 11	Danny Lawson, Calgary	Curt Larsson, Winnipeg	2	14:30	Save
Dec 17	Robbie Ftorek, Phoenix	Ken Broderick, Edmonton	1	17:53	Save
Dec 26	Mark Napier, Birmingham	Wayne Rutledge, Houston	3	17:44	Score
Jan 20	Frank Hughes, Phoenix	Paul Hoganson, Cincinnati	3	15:56	Save
Feb 18	Bruce Greig, Calgary	Norm Lapointe, Cincinnati	2	16:46	Score

Attendance Figures

g indicates the number of home games played

team	g	season total	avg	g	playoff total	avg	team	g	season total	avg	g	playoff total	avg
Birmingham	40	338,711	8,468	-	-	-	Minnesota	25	155,280	6,211	-	-	-
Calgary	40	172,535	4,313	-	-	-	New England	40	356,726	8,918	2	10,730	9,865
Cincinnati	40	305,860	7,647	2	21,396	10,698	Phoenix	40	279,384	6,985	-	-	-
Edmonton	40	334,805	8,370	2	30,098	15,049	Quebec	40	343,922	8,598	10	91,420	9,142
Houston	40	353,209	8,830	6	57,430	9,572	San Diego	40	240,508	6,013	3	31,388	10,463
Indianapolis	40	371,787	9,295	4	50,867	12,717	Winnipeg	40	337,874	8,447	10	98,608	9,861

Total Attendance: 3,590,511; **Average Attendance:** 7,722

Birmingham: John Bassett moved his Toronto Toros to Birmingham, Alabama, for the 1976-77 season, renaming the team the "Bulls", conveniently keeping the same uniforms as the old Toros. Birmingham was the WHA's first foray into the deep south, and would promise to be an interesting challenge to sell hockey in Alabama. The actual team wasn't the best, but they were improved over the previous season's squad, winning 31 and tying 4, a thirteen-point improvement. Notably, the defense "only" gave up 309 goals, an 89-goal improvement, thanks to solid goaltending by John Garrett, and the addition of Dale Hoganson to the blue line. Up front, Mark Napier scored 60 goals and 96 points, with Vaclav Nedomansky trailing him with 36 goals. Five other Bulls scored 20 or more goals. The fans seemed to pick up on the Bulls, averaging over 8,000 per game at the Jefferson County Civic Center. Although the Bulls did not make the playoffs, the team was much improved and year one of the Alabama hockey experiment had gone very well.

Calgary: There were two Cowboys teams in 1976-77: the club that played a tight-checking, pesky game at home, taking advantage of the Corral's small dimensions and loud, supportive fans to win 26 games, and the malingerers who could not buy a road win, winning just 5 games all year on enemy ice (except in Phoenix for some reason, where the Cowboys were undefeated in four games). As a result, the club was very streaky, depending on where they were playing: an 0-6-1 start segued into a seven-game home win streak. Such was their season, the team playing break-even hockey before a 10-game road losing streak in March sank any hopes of a post-season berth. Joe Crozier's club finished 31-43-7, fifth in the Western Division. Star Danny Lawson finally bid farewell, traded to Winnipeg in mid-season. Lynn Powis led the team in goals with 30 and points with 60. Behind him was Ron Chipperfield with 27 goals, and Peter Driscoll with 23. The defense was led by Paul Terbenche, John Miszuk and Chris Evans, and as always, Don McLeod played nearly every game in goal, also collecting 9 assists. Off the ice, the team was in trouble, unable to survive in the long term in the Corral, despite strong community support. The Cowboys folded in May 1977, leaving Calgary without major-league hockey until 1980, when the Atlanta Flames relocated to Calgary, also playing in the Corral until the Saddledome was completed in time for the 1984 Winter Olympics.

Cincinnati: The second-year Stingers made a dramatic improvement overall, especially on offense where the team was second in the league with 354 goals. The Stingers featured two 50-goal scorers— Richie Leduc and Blaine Stoughton, both with 52— and two 40-goal scorers: Dennis Sobchuk with 44,

Rick Dudley with 41. Terry Slater's club started fast with a 17-10-2 record, then played break-even for the rest of the season. Despite the impressive offense, the Stingers still played a weak defense, permitting 303 goals, although defenseman Ron Plumb had his best season, with a league-leading +64 rating, 58 assists and winning the league's best defenseman award. Overall, the Stingers finished 39-37-5, second place in the Eastern Division. In their first playoff series, the Stingers lost a heart-breaking three-overtime contest against Indianapolis in the first game, then were swept by the Racers, a sudden end to a promising year.

Edmonton: Coming off a horrible 49-loss season from the year before, and a shake-up in ownership when Bill Hunter stepped aside and Nelson Skalbania came aboard, the Oilers hoped merely to play a full season in what would be their weakest year financially as a team. Armand "Bep" Guidolin was hired as general manager and coach, coming over from the NHL where he had experienced a high calling the shots as the Bruins' coach from 1972 to 1974, and a low as the coach of the Kansas City Scouts the year before. The Oilers were still thin, with no depth beyond their top line. Bill Flett scored 34 goals to lead the team, and Rusty Patenaude was behind him with 25. Flett's 54 points led the team, tied with Bryan Campbell. Trailing by a point was Glen Sather, a journeyman forward for most of his NHL career. Guidolin was busy as general manager, making trades and call-ups from the minors; 42 players wore an Oilers sweater in 1976-77. Not surprisingly, there was little cohesiveness and the Oilers finished 34-43-4 in the Western Division, but still a solid improvement over 1975-76. The Oilers played one round in the playoffs, losing to Houston in five games. Although hardly earth-shaking news at the time, the Oilers elevated Glen Sather to player-coach in February 1977. He would retire as a player in 1977 and coach the team to significant glory in the National Hockey League. The Oilers were on the rise, ever so slowly.

Houston: The Aeros turned in another 50-win, 106-point season, almost on autopilot, featuring a deep, talented roster of scorers, diggers, fighters, a stifling defense, and top-notch goaltending. Terry Ruskowski led the team in points with 84, was a +31 on the ice, fought the tough guys and had emerged as the team's heart. Gordie Howe dropped to 68 points, and son Mark dipped to 23 goals but did total 75 points, second on the team. Rich Preston was the goal-leader with 38, and Cam Connor had 35 when he wasn't whiling away 224 minutes in the penalty box. The defense was again in the charge of veterans Larry Hale, Marty Howe and Poul Popiel. John Schella played just 20 games, but veteran Al McLeod came

over from Phoenix to lend a hand. Glen Irwin took up some of the slack when Schella was felled by injuries. Goaltending was rock-solid, with Ron Grahame winning 27 and collecting 4 shutouts. Backup Wayne Rutledge won 23 and had 3 shutouts. Despite all the heroics, the Aeros were shown to be human after last-season's defeat in the final round. In the 1977 post-season, the Aeros had little trouble with Edmonton in the first round, but lost in six games to Winnipeg in the semifinal round. The golden age of the Aeros had come to an end: the team was never healthy financially, wearing out many owners. As merger talks gained momentum in 1977, Houston seemed like a strong candidate, given its overall merits as a city and its arena; certainly, the NHL was interested. But when merger in 1977 failed, and the Howes had left for Hartford, the immediate future seemed to dim. The Aeros would play one more season and attempt its own independent entry into the NHL, but unfortunately, come up short.

Indianapolis: Jacques Demers' crew entered the 1976-77 season buoyed by last season's dramatic improvement and exciting playoff run, but got started slowly with a 4-9-2 record before reeling off 12 wins in 13 games in November and December. The Racers were effective when they played a pressing, defense-first game for which they were well-suited. Pat Stapleton was again the on-ice leader and most visible star performer for the Racers. Blair Mac-Donald gave the team some offense with 34 goals, with Reg Thomas and Renald Leclerc netting 25 apiece. Hugh Harris had 21 goals and 56 points in 46 games before suffering a season-ending injury. Nine other players reached double figures in goals, and the Racers, never an offensive force, set the team mark with 276 goals for. Injuries plagued the team and the Racers suffered through a frustrating second half but still finished with a 36-37-8 record, good for third place in the Eastern Division. In the first round, the Racers played rivals Cincinnati. The first game went three overtime periods before Gene Peacosh won it for Indianapolis, a rousing victory that portended a four-game sweep of the Stingers. However, in the Eastern Division final, the Racers were overmatched by the powerful Quebec Nordiques, losing in five games.

Minnesota: After the original Fighting Saints folded in February 1976, the Cleveland Crusaders came to town and were reborn as the new Fighting Saints. In an attempt to lend some continuity between the old and the new versions of the Saints, some original Saints players returned, including Dave Keon, Mike Antonovich, John McKenzie, John Arbour, Gordie Gallant, Mike Curran, and the Carlson brothers: Jack and Steve. Glen Sonmor returned as coach. After a 3-10-3 start, the new Fighting Saints started to win often, working their record over the break-even point in early January. Mike Antonovich was having his best

season, with 27 goals in 42 games, with John McKenzie behind him with 17. Former Crusader Ron Ward had 15 goals and 36 points. All this was for naught as the new Fighting Saints could not solve the financial riddle that had plagued the original team. Over the All-Star break in mid-January, the new Fighting Saints folded, playing just 42 games of the schedule. There would be no mid-season replacement team. The players scattered among the other WHA teams, with New England being helped considerably with the addition of seven former Saints, including Dave Keon, John McKenzie and Mike Antonovich.

New England: The Whalers turned in a near-repeat of 1975-76's performance, winning 35, losing 40 and tying 6, a three-point improvement from the previous year. The defense was average, allowing 290 goals, the same as the year before, while the offense improved slightly, buoyed by Rookie-of-the-Year George Lyle's team-leading 39 goals. Tom Webster was good for 36 goals and a team-leading 85 points, while Mike Rogers scored 25 and came in second with 82 points. There was considerable turn-over in personnel, as the Whalers took on seven of the former Fighting Saints in a complicated series of claims and trades with the Edmonton Oilers, who had claimed the batch first. In the end, New England finished fourth in the Eastern Division and made an early exit from the playoffs, losing in the first round to eventual champs Quebec. However, the Whalers now featured a solid core of young and veteran players, positioning themselves for a strong 1977-78 campaign that would feature newcomers Gordie Howe and sons Mark and Marty.

Phoenix: The luster rubbed off the Roadrunners in 1976-77: after two impressive 39-win seasons in their first two seasons, the Roadrunners lost coach Sandy Hucul and a number of key players at key positions. Much of the loss was motivated by financial problems, the team pressured to sell off talent for immediate cash. Up front, Robbie Ftorek had no problems, scoring 46 goals and accumulating 117 points and an impressive +26 rating on a team that gave up 102 more goals than it scored. For his efforts, Ftorek won the league's Most Valuable Player award, the first American-born player to win the award in either the WHA or the NHL. Del Hall also turned in a solid offensive season, scoring 38 goals. Finn star Seppo "The Fox" Repo came over for the season, scored 29 goals but was a -35. He was one of four Finns on the Roadrunners, joining Juhani Tamminen, Lauri Mononen and Pekka Rautakallio. The defense was the team's weak area. With veteran goaltender Jack Norris gone, and Gary Kurt giving up 5.55 goals per game, rookie Clay Hebenton shouldered the bulk of the games but was 17-29-3. Overall, the Roadrunners gave up 383 goals, the second-worst showing in WHA history. The financial strain was severe enough that the team announced it would fold

immediately upon the season's end. An April 6th win over Indianapolis was the team's final contest as members of the WHA.

Quebec: The Nordiques were still angry over last April's brawl against Calgary which severely injured star Marc Tardif and drove the Nordiques out of the playoffs. Tardif was able to recover in time to start the 1976-77 season, and the Nordiques picked up on last season's theme: lots of goals and lots of wins. Real Cloutier scored an amazing 66 goals and led the league with 141 points. Tardif had 49 goals and 109 points in just 62 games, while Christian Bordeleau scored 32 goals with 107 points. Serge Bernier turned in 43 goals, and Paulin Bordeleau scored 42 as the Nordiques collected 353 goals and skated to 47 wins and the top spot in the Eastern Division. New coach Marc Boileau was able to get his team to play a little defense—not much—but enough to keep the goals against below 300. J.-C. Tremblay was the team leader on the ice but appeared in just 53 games. Francois Lacombe returned from a year in Calgary and was solid, while new additions Paul Baxter and Wally Weir showed skill in their own end and plenty of toughness, Baxter with 244 minutes in the box, Weir with 197. Goaltender Richard Brodeur continued to show the world he was a rising star, winning 29 games and a very impressive 3.45 average, considering his team's style of play. But the regular season was just something to do for six months until April could come around, where the Nordiques had a lot to prove and a lot of frustration to exorcise. They won their first two rounds against New England and Indianapolis convincingly, beating each in five games, and facing off against the powerful Winnipeg Jets in the final round. The Quebec-Winnipeg showdown was arguably the best of the league's seven-year run, with the series going the full seven games. Winnipeg gave the Nordiques all it could handle, including a 12-3 blowout in game six that returned the series to Quebec for a decisive game seven. After a scoreless first period, unheralded digger Bob Fitchner surprised the Jets and gave the Nordiques a lift with a goal eleven seconds into the second frame. In all, the Nordiques scored six goals and seemed to completely break the Jets' spirit. For example, one of the goals was a mid-ice clearing shot by J.-C. Tremblay that somehow tumbled past Jets goaltender Joe Daley into the net. There was no doubt: the luck of the puck was on Quebec's side, and the Nordiques celebrated a series win and the WHA's championship, their first and with no doubt, most satisfying win in franchise history.

San Diego: After essentially being abandoned and left to die on the vine by previous owner Joseph Schwartz, the Mariners gained a last-minute reprieve over the summer of 1976 when McDonald's magnate Ray Kroc purchased the team, guaranteeing it at least a solid footing for the 1976-77 campaign. The team itself was largely the same as the year before: a solid squad of scorers led by Andre Lacroix, a capable defense and the strong goaltending of Ernie Wakely. Lacroix had another 100-point season, scoring 32 goals and assisting on 82 for 114 total points. Norm Ferguson led the team with 39 goals, and Joe Noris had a surprising year with 35 goals and 92 points from the blue-line. Kevin Devine was the other Mariner to meet the 30-goal barrier. The defense was bolstered by Paul Shmyr, aided by fellow WHA defense stalwarts Larry Hornung and Randy Legge. Ernie Wakely won 22 games and allowed just 3.09 goals per game. Former Canuck Ken Lockett backed him with 18 wins. The Mariners were eleven games above break-even before enduring a 14-game winless streak in March that watered down what could have been a superlative year. Their reward was a third-place finish in the Western Division and a seven-game battle against Winnipeg in the first round, which they ultimately lost. This was also the end of Kroc's involvement; once he pulled back, the Mariners were finished in San Diego. In May 1977, the team seemingly had been sold to a group including Jerry Saperstein, with intentions to move the team to Florida. But the move never happened and in June 1977, the WHA disbanded the Mariners.

Winnipeg: There was nothing wrong with the Jets in 1976-77: the reigning champs had the league's best offense, scoring 366 goals, and despite the loss of Bobby Hull to injuries, still finished a strong 46-32-2, second place in the Western Division. The scoring star was Anders Hedberg, who scored 70 goals to lead the league, and who scored his 50th goal in his 47th game (and the Jets' 49th game) to better Maurice Richard's legendary feat from 1945 by one game. Hedberg was second in the league with 131 points, and linemate Ulf Nilsson right behind him with 124 points on 85 assists. Willy Lindstrom had 44 goals, Peter Sullivan 31, Veli-Pekka Ketola 25 and Dan Labraaten 24. Even Bobby Hull netted 21 in his abbreviated season. Lars-Erik Sjoberg and Ted Green led a solid defense, while goaltender Joe Daley led the league with 39 wins. Coach Kromm's team eagerly sought to retain the Cup, but to do so they took seven games to defeat a pesky San Diego squad, and six more games to set aside the talented Houston team. In the final round, the Jets met the Nordiques, two high-powered offenses squaring off. The action lived up to the hype, as the series went the full seven, the Jets finally falling to the Nordiques. Despite the setback, the Jets were eyeing the next season and the return of a healthy Bobby Hull.

1976-1977 Game by Game Line Scores

Date & Teams	Scoring 1 2 3 ot F	Shots 1 2 3 ot F	Goaltenders	Goals & Other Scoring Highlights
October 7				
Minnesota	0 0 2 - 2	3 7 10 - 20	Curran	McKenzie, Antonovich
Cincinnati	2 4 1 - 7	14 17 12 - 43	Hoganson	Dudley 2, Stoughton, Guite, Locas, Sobchuk, Leduc
October 8				
Houston	0 1 1 - 2	12 5 6 - 23	Graham	Preston, G. Howe
Birmingham	1 2 1 - 4	6 14 8 - 28	Garrett	Simpson, Phaneuf, Napier, Nistico
Minnesota	0 2 1 - 3	11 11 8 - 30	Levasseur	McKenzie, Keon, Antonovich
Indianapolis	0 2 2 - 4	12 7 6 - 25	Brown	Lomenda, Rochon, Thomas, Stapleton (WG 11:41)
New England	0 0 0 - 0	8 8 9 - 25	Abrahamsson	▶ Dryden: shutout (1), 25 saves
Edmonton	1 0 1 - 2	9 11 4 - 24	Dryden	Baird, Sheehy
Calgary	0 1 0 - 1	13 15 7 - 35	McLeod, Bromley	Powis
Winnipeg	0 3 1 - 4	12 9 8 - 29	Daley	Lindstrom 2, Hedberg, Ruhnke
Cincinnati	1 2 3 - 6	9 12 15 - 36	Lapointe, Hoganson	Larose 2, Locas, Leduc, Stoughton, Guite
Phoenix	2 3 3 - 8	15 11 9 - 35	Kurt	Hall 3, Ftorek 2, Mononen 2, Huston
October 9				
Calgary	1 1 0 - 2	9 7 5 - 21	Bromley	Pesut, Driscoll
Quebec	2 2 1 - 5	14 6 9 - 29	Brodeur	Bernier 2, P. Bordeleau, Cloutier, Grenier
Phoenix	2 1 0 - 3	12 6 9 - 27	Kurt	Gray, Ftorek, Beaudoin
Houston	4 1 0 - 5	13 10 10 - 33	Rutledge	Preston 2, Ruskowski, Lund, Tonelli
Cincinnati	3 3 1 0 7	13 9 8 1 31	Hoganson	Ouimet, Stoughton, Sobchuk, Larose, Guite, Leduc, Abgrall (TG 16:49)
San Diego	3 3 1 0 7	7 12 6 6 31	Wakely, Lockett	Veneruzzo 3, Noris, Rhiness, Rivers, Lacroix
October 10				
Birmingham	0 2 1 0 3	9 9 4 2 24	Garrett	Napier, Kirk, Nedomansky
Quebec	0 1 2 1 4	6 12 18 8 44	Brodeur	Cloutier 2, Bernier, C. Bordeleau (OT 9:19)
Indianapolis	0 0 1 - 1	9 12 9 - 30	Park	Campbell
Minnesota	0 2 2 - 4	5 18 11 - 34	Curran	Stewart, Keon, Gallant, Ward
New England	2 0 0 - 2	10 9 3 - 22	Abrahamsson	Paiement, Selwood
Winnipeg	3 1 1 - 5	17 13 13 - 43	Daley	Nilsson 2, Ketola, Moffat, Sjoberg
October 12				
San Diego	4 0 0 - 4	13 4 8 - 25	Lockett	Ferguson 2, Noris, Morrison
Quebec	2 1 3 - 6	8 11 11 - 30	Aubry, Brodeur	C. Bordeleau 2, P. Bordeleau, Cloutier, Grenier, Fitchner
Calgary	1 1 0 - 2	10 10 7 - 27	McLeod, Bromley	Lawson, Serviss
Birmingham	3 2 1 - 6	10 5 7 - 22	Wood, Garrett	Mahovlich, Kirk, Nedomansky, Jacques, Farda, Henderson
October 13				
Calgary	1 0 0 - 1	11 8 4 - 23	McLeod	Pesut
Houston	0 2 0 - 2	6 10 8 - 24	Grahame	Connor, Mty Howe
October 14				
Minnesota	1 2 0 - 3	9 15 11 - 35	Curran	Adduono, McKenzie, Keon
Phoenix	1 1 2 - 4	7 11 10 - 28	Kurt	Ftorek, Hall, Repo, Cormier (WG 19:45)
Cincinnati	3 2 2 0 7	12 16 12 7 47	Hoganson, Lapointe	Guite 2, Leduc 2, Stoughton, Dudley
Birmingham	5 0 2 0 7	14 8 9 6 37	Garrett	Napier 3, Henderson 2, Nedomansky, Simpson
October 15				
San Diego	3 3 1 - 7	12 13 10 - 35	Wakely	French 2, Lacroix, Noris, Devine, Shmyr, Veneruzzo
Minnesota	2 0 2 - 4	11 9 14 - 34	Curran, Levasseur	Deadmarsh, Stewart, McKenzie, Keon
Winnipeg	1 3 2 - 6	6 14 11 - 31	Daley	Ruhnke 2, Lindstrom, Nilsson, Hedberg, Lesuk
Edmonton	1 0 0 - 1	10 8 10 - 28	Dryden	Peacosh
Cincinnati	1 2 2 0 5	11 10 8 4 33	Hoganson	Hughes, Dudley, Sobchuk, Guite, Abgrall
Indianapolis	1 2 2 1 6	9 12 7 4 32	Park	MacDonald, Harris, Stapleton, Harbaruk, Parizeau, Rochon (OT 4:36)
October 16				
Winnipeg	3 0 1 - 4	8 7 6 - 21	Larsson, Daley	Lindstrom, Hedberg, Ketola, Guindon
Phoenix	1 2 3 - 6	8 11 13 - 32	Kurt	Repo 2, Huston, Beaudoin, Hall, Ftorek
Quebec	4 4 0 - 8	14 7 6 - 27	Aubry	Bernier 2, Constantin, Tardif, Boudrias, Grenier, P. Bordeleau, Cloutier
New England	0 2 0 - 2	6 20 8 - 34	Ab'sson, Landon	Arndt, Pleau
Birmingham	0 0 0 - 0	5 11 8 - 24	Garrett	▶ Grahame: shutout (1), 24 saves
Houston	0 0 3 - 3	19 14 6 - 39	Grahame	Mk Howe, Preston, Popiel
Calgary	0 1 1 - 2	10 4 9 - 23	McLeod	Powis, Lawson
San Diego	0 3 1 - 4	7 12 7 - 26	Lockett	French, Rivers, Veneruzzo, Lacroix
October 17				
Birmingham	1 0 0 - 1	13 9 17 - 39	Wood	Nedomansky
Minnesota	1 4 1 - 6	13 19 11 - 43	Levasseur	Ward 2, Keon, McDonough, Antonovich, Stewart
Indianapolis	1 0 1 - 2	3 5 13 - 21	Brown, Park	MacDonald, McDonald
Edmonton	2 2 3 - 7	11 11 12 - 34	Broderick	Ullman 2, Patenaude, Sheehy, Peacosh, Sather, Hamilton
Cincinnati	2 1 2 - 5	9 9 14 - 32	Lapointe	Sobchuk, Locas 2, Stoughton
Quebec	2 0 0 - 2	9 13 3 - 25	Brodeur	Cloutier, Constantin
Winnipeg	0 0 1 - 1	5 6 3 - 14	Daley	Hedberg
San Diego	1 0 2 - 3	6 4 9 - 19	Wakely	Veneruzzo, French, Noris
October 19				
Phoenix	1 0 3 0 4	7 12 10 0 29	Kurt, Hebenton	Hall, Repo, Liddington, Ftorek
Edmonton	3 1 0 1 5	13 13 5 1 32	Broderick	Sather 2 (OT 0:22), Morris, Merrell, Hornung
Cincinnati	2 2 0 - 4	12 10 7 - 29	Lapointe	Abgrall 2, Dudley, Stoughton
Minnesota	1 0 1 - 2	15 13 15 - 43	Levasseur	Adduono, Antonovich
Indianapolis	0 1 0 - 1	10 9 6 - 25	Dion	McDonald
Winnipeg	1 3 2 - 6	15 17 13 - 45	Daley	Lindstrom 2, Sullivan, Lesuk, Hedberg, Lindh
New England	2 1 1 0 4	13 12 17 5 47	Abrahamsson	Earl 2, Lyle, Selwood
Houston	1 3 0 0 4	8 14 4 5 31	Rutledge	Mk Howe 2, Connor, Hughes
Quebec	2 3 0 1 6	17 16 13 1 47	Aubry	Tardif, Bernier, Cloutier, Lacombe, P. Bordeleau, Grenier (OT 0:10)
Birmingham	2 1 2 0 5	11 8 9 0 28	Garrett	Napier 2, Kirk, Farda, Nistico

1976-1977 Game by Game Line Scores

Date & Teams	Scoring 1 2 3 ot F	Shots 1 2 3 ot F	Goaltenders	Goals & Other Scoring Highlights
October 21				
Houston	3 0 2 - 5	12 10 11 - 33	Grahame	Mk Howe, Tonelli, Larway, Mty Howe, Lukowich
Birmingham	3 2 3 - 8	12 9 10 - 31	Garrett, Wood	Marrin 2, Kirk 2, Nistico, Napier, Farda, Nedomansky
Indianapolis	2 2 0 0 4	13 7 8 3 31	Brown	Harris 2, MacDonald 2
San Diego	1 2 1 0 4	10 16 5 2 33	Lockett, Wakely	Noris, Lacroix, Ferguson, Devine
Quebec	2 0 2 - 4	11 8 13 - 32	Brodeur	Cloutier 2, Bernier 2
Calgary	0 0 2 - 2	10 10 10 - 30	McLeod	Jodzio, Tannahill
October 22				
Phoenix	0 2 2 - 4	11 10 9 - 30	Kurt	Tamminen, Huston, Repo, Ftorek (WG 15:27)
Winnipeg	1 1 1 - 3	8 7 11 - 26	Daley	Hedberg 2, Nilsson
Calgary	2 0 0 0 2	7 11 10 3 31	McLeod	Miller, Powis
Minnesota	2 0 0 0 2	17 9 11 4 41	Curran	Ward, Keon
Houston	1 0 1 - 2	6 9 14 - 29	Rutledge	Preston, G. Howe
New England	3 1 1 - 5	13 13 2 - 28	Landon	Earl, Webster, Backstrom, Arndt, Paiement
October 23				
Cincinnati	1 2 1 - 4	10 14 18 - 42	Lapointe	Steele, Sobchuk, Stoughton, Legge
New England	2 2 1 - 5	8 12 8 - 28	Abrahamsson	Arndt, Hangsleben, Lyle, Backstrom
Houston	0 2 0 - 2	8 12 7 - 27	Grahame	Mty Howe, Larway
Quebec	2 2 2 - 6	12 12 8 - 32	Brodeur	Tardif 2, Tremblay, P. Bordeleau, Grenier, Bernier
Birmingham	1 2 0 - 3	7 13 8 - 28	Garrett	Napier 2, Kirk
Indianapolis	0 1 0 - 1	14 14 13 - 41	Brown	Karlander
October 24				
Phoenix	2 1 2 - 5	7 7 7 - 21	Kurt	Ftorek 3, Mononen, Liddington
Edmonton	1 1 1 - 3	5 6 14 - 25	Broderick	Williams, Peacosh, Sheehy
Birmingham	0 0 1 - 1	11 4 10 - 25	Wood	Nedomansky (spoiled Daley's shutout at 16:28)
Winnipeg	1 2 4 - 7	11 10 17 - 38	Daley	Lindstrom 2, Lesuk, Dunn, Hedberg, Labraaten, Lindh
San Diego	0 0 0 - 0	9 6 8 - 23	Lockett	▶ McLeod: shutout (1), 23 saves
Calgary	2 1 3 - 6	13 9 12 - 34	McLeod	Terbenche 2, Connelly, Powis, Lawson, Chipperfield
October 26				
Phoenix	1 2 0 - 3	9 14 7 - 30	Kurt, Hebenton	Ftorek, Huston, Liddington
Quebec	4 5 2 - 11	11 12 19 - 42	Brodeur	Cloutier 5, Sutherland 2, Bernier 2, Brackenbury, Tardif
Cincinnati	0 0 1 - 1	11 11 9 - 31	Hoganson	Sobchuk (WG 5:12)
New England	0 0 0 - 0	10 4 10 - 24	Ab'sson, Landon	▶ Hoganson: shutout (1) 24 saves
Birmingham	0 2 1 - 3	8 10 5 - 23	Garrett, Wood	Nistico, Nedomansky, Marrin
Calgary	0 5 4 - 9	13 11 18 - 42	McLeod	Chipperfield 2, Lemieux 2, Sentes 2, Lawson, Driscoll, Powis
San Diego	0 1 0 - 1	8 21 8 - 37	Wakely	Ferguson
Minnesota	1 1 1 - 3	11 7 8 - 26	Levasseur	Westrum, Ward, McDonough
Edmonton	0 1 0 - 1	9 7 9 - 25	Dryden	Peacosh
Houston	1 0 2 - 3	6 3 9 - 18	Grahame	Popiel, Ruskowski, Preston
October 27				
San Diego	3 1 1 - 5	12 10 8 - 30	Wakely	Veneruzzo 2, Noris, Ferguson, Lacroix
Indianapolis	1 0 0 - 1	8 5 13 - 26	Brown	Parizeau
October 28				
Edmonton	1 1 1 1 4	10 12 7 5 34	Dryden	Peacosh, Sheehy, Sather, Hamilton (OT 7:10)
Birmingham	1 1 1 0 3	4 5 8 4 21	Garrett	Marrin, Nistico, Nedomansky (TG 19:37)
Minnesota	0 0 1 0 1	11 5 12 3 31	Curran	Ward
Houston	0 1 0 0 1	8 11 5 1 25	Rutledge	Larway
October 29				
Edmonton	2 1 0 - 3	10 4 6 - 20	Broderick	Hornung, Sheehy, Williams
Winnipeg	6 1 4 - 11	14 14 12 - 40	Daley	Ketola 4, Lindstrom 2, Nilsson, Long. Lesuk, Sullivan. Lindh, Labraaten
San Diego	0 0 2 - 2	9 9 7 - 25	Lockett, Wakely	Burgess, Cassolato
Cincinnati	3 1 0 - 4	11 12 10 - 33	Lapointe	Leduc, Abgrall, Dudley, Stoughton
Quebec	0 2 2 - 4	4 18 10 - 32	Aubry	Tardif 3, Grenier
Indianapolis	1 2 3 - 6	10 10 12 - 32	Dion	Clackson, McDonald, Lomenda, Block, Stapleton, Harris
Phoenix	1 0 0 - 1	6 8 7 - 21	Hebenton	Repo
New England	0 3 2 - 5	12 13 18 - 43	Landon	Lyle 2, Webster, Paiement, Rogers
October 30				
Phoenix	1 1 1 - 3	7 8 5 - 20	Kurt, Hebenton	Hall 2, Liddington
Cincinnati	2 4 3 - 9	18 11 17 - 46	Hoganson	Locas 2, Sobchuk 2, Marsh 2, Stoughton, Abgrall, Larose
Houston	2 1 1 - 4	5 2 13 - 20	Grahame	Connor, Preston, Mty Howe, Ruskowski
Calgary	2 1 3 - 6	9 11 9 - 29	McLeod	Powis, Evans, Lawson, Terbenche, Miller, Chipperfield
Birmingham	1 2 1 - 4	18 14 12 - 44	Garrett	Napier 2, Simpson, Mahovlich
New England	3 1 1 - 5	12 12 14 - 38	Abrahamsson	Lyle, Busniuk, Hynes, Webster, Backstrom
Minnesota	0 0 1 - 1	4 17 8 - 29	Levasseur	Ward
Quebec	2 3 0 - 5	19 11 8 - 38	Brodeur	Grenier 2, Boudrias, P. Bordeleau, Cloutier
October 31				
Houston	2 1 1 - 4	9 8 8 - 25	Rutledge	Mk Howe, Connor, Lund, Hinse
Edmonton	0 0 0 - 0	3 12 7 - 22	Dryden	▶ Rutledge: shutout (1), 22 saves
San Diego	3 0 1 - 4	11 4 10 - 25	Lockett	Burgess, Veneruzzo, Ferguson, Devine
Winnipeg	1 3 2 - 6	9 16 10 - 35	Daley	Hedberg, Ketola, Lesuk, Nilsson, Guindon, Sullivan
November 2				
Phoenix	0 3 2 - 5	6 12 14 - 32	Hebenton	Liddington 2, Gray, Cormier, Mononen
Quebec	1 0 2 - 3	10 10 14 - 34	Brodeur	Boudrias, P. Bordeleau, Bernier
Houston	1 0 2 - 3	11 8 10 - 29	Rutledge	Popiel, Lund, Preston
Winnipeg	0 0 1 - 1	8 16 13 - 37	Daley	Lindh
Minnesota	3 0 0 - 3	10 5 8 - 23	Curran	Keon, Deadmarsh, Ward
Calgary	2 1 1 - 4	15 16 14 - 45	McLeod	Terbenche, Chipperfield, Sentes, Powis (WG 18:16)
San Diego	1 0 2 1 4	9 9 9 4 31	Wakely	French, Rivers, Dobek, Veneruzzo (OT 6:53)
Birmingham	0 1 2 0 3	12 9 7 3 31	Garrett	Napier, Simpson, Kirk

1976-1977 Game by Game Line Scores

Date & Teams	Scoring 1 2 3 ot F	Shots 1 2 3 ot F	Goaltenders	Goals & Other Scoring Highlights
November 3				
Minnesota	1 1 0 - 2	10 7 6 - 23	Levasseur	Keon, McKenzie
Edmonton	1 0 3 - 4	8 14 9 - 31	Dryden	Patenaude 3, Morris
Indianapolis	0 0 2 - 2	9 7 11 - 27	Park, Brown	MacDonald, Harris
Cincinnati	4 4 0 - 8	10 15 7 - 32	Lapointe	Larose 2, Marsh 2, Leduc, Stoughton, Abgrall, Locas
November 4				
Edmonton	0 1 1 - 2	4 10 5 - 19	Broderick	Beaton, Wilkins
Calgary	0 1 3 - 4	9 8 9 - 26	McLeod	Chipperfield 2, Lawson, Miller
Phoenix	0 0 3 - 3	5 9 11 - 25	Hebenton	Repo, Hall, Gray
Birmingham	1 3 1 - 5	18 14 12 - 44	Garrett	Napier, Nedomansky, Jacques, Mahovlich, Marrin
Cincinnati	1 0 1 - 2	10 16 15 - 41	Hoganson, Lapointe	Stoughton, Carroll
Indianapolis	3 1 1 - 5	14 15 6 - 35	Dion	MacDonald 2, Parizeau 2, Lomenda
November 5				
Phoenix	0 1 0 - 1	8 8 4 - 20	Kurt	Mononen
Houston	4 1 4 - 9	10 10 11 - 31	Rutledge	Ruskowski 4, Lund 3, Mk Howe, Lukowich
New England	0 2 2 - 4	9 11 8 - 28	Abrahamsson	Backstrom, Paiement, Lyle, Webster (WG 17:11)
Edmonton	1 1 1 - 3	4 9 12 - 25	Dryden	Sheehy 2, Langevin
Minnesota	1 0 1 - 2	11 9 9 - 29	Curran	Keon, S. Carlson
Winnipeg	3 2 4 - 9	8 8 12 - 28	Larsson	Hedberg 2, Sjoberg, Labr'ten, Lindstrom, Green, Ketola, Miller, G'ndon
November 6				
Birmingham	4 0 1 - 5	16 9 6 - 31	Garrett	Henderson 2, Phaneuf, Jacques, Kirk
Quebec	1 3 2 - 6	9 15 13 - 37	Brodeur, Aubry	Cloutier 2 (WG 19:26), Tardif, Bernier, P. Bordeleau, Constantin
Houston	0 0 1 - 1	9 11 8 - 28	Rutledge	Ruskowski
San Diego	2 1 1 - 4	10 10 7 - 27	Lockett	Veneruzzo, Noris, Ferguson, Rivers
Winnipeg	0 2 1 - 3	13 8 4 - 25	Daley	Sullivan 2, Nilsson
Cincinnati	1 0 6 - 7	16 13 20 - 49	Lapointe	Locas 3, Leduc, Abgrall, Hughes, Dudley
November 7				
Indianapolis	0 0 0 - 0	6 4 6 - 16	Brown	▸ Wakely: shutout (1), 16 saves
San Diego	0 0 3 - 3	6 10 6 - 22	Wakely	Hughes, Lacroix, Devine
New England	0 1 1 - 2	9 9 5 - 23	Landon	Hangsleben, Rogers
Calgary	0 1 3 - 4	8 8 13 - 29	McLeod	Driscoll, Connelly, Sentes, Morrison
Phoenix	0 2 1 - 3	11 16 11 - 38	Hebenton	Liddington 2, Ftorek
Minnesota	0 0 1 - 1	15 7 11 - 33	Levasseur	Adduono
Edmonton	0 0 2 - 2	11 6 9 - 26	Broderick	Morris 2
Winnipeg	1 4 0 - 5	16 13 8 - 37	Daley	Labraaten 2, Nilsson 2, Moffat
November 9				
Indianapolis	2 0 0 - 2	10 7 12 - 29	Brown	Thomas, MacDonald
Houston	1 1 5 - 7	8 3 9 - 20	Grahame	Preston 2, Larway 2, Mk Howe, Hinse, Lund
New England	1 3 0 0 4	7 13 2 6 28	Abrahamsson	Paiement, Earl, Rogers, Lyle
Winnipeg	1 3 0 1 5	10 15 10 5 40	Larsson	Labraaten, Long, Hedberg, Green, Nilsson (OT 8:53)
Birmingham	1 2 0 - 3	8 6 5 - 19	Garrett	Simpson, Nedomansky, Farda
Quebec	1 2 1 - 4	11 10 22 - 43	Brodeur	C. Bordeleau 2, Grenier, Bernier (WG 3:24)
November 10				
Edmonton	1 1 0 - 2	6 6 7 - 19	Broderick	Campbell, Sheehy
Cincinnati	2 1 1 - 4	13 17 8 - 38	Lapointe	Steele, Leduc, Larose, Stoughton
Indianapolis	0 2 1 0 3	7 12 6 2 27	Dion, Brown	Sicinski, Parizeau, Harris
Phoenix	1 0 2 0 3	9 3 11 7 30	Hebenton	Hall 2, Lariviere
November 11				
San Diego	0 2 1 - 3	12 14 7 - 33	Lockett	Morrison, Pinder, Ferguson (WG 15:03)
Birmingham	0 1 1 - 2	13 9 8 - 30	Garrett	Nedomansky, Napier
Winnipeg	3 2 0 - 5	16 8 12 - 36	Larsson	Ketola 2, Hedberg, Sullivan, Lindstrom
Calgary	1 4 2 - 7	10 16 7 - 33	McLeod	Chipperfield 2, Lawson 2, Powis, Connelly, Miller (WG 17:21)
New England	3 0 0 0 3	13 5 7 2 27	Abrahamsson	Abrahamsson, Hangsleben, Rogers
Minnesota	1 0 2 0 3	11 9 16 3 39	Curran	Antonovich 3 (TG 19:45)
November 12				
New England	0 1 0 - 1	7 19 9 - 35	Landon	Bolduc
Phoenix	2 0 1 - 3	9 7 15 - 31	Hebenton	Ftorek 2, Tamminen
San Diego	1 0 0 - 1	11 15 10 - 36	Wakely	Devine
Houston	2 1 1 - 4	12 12 7 - 31	Grahame	Connor 2, Mk Howe, Hughes
November 13				
Indianapolis	0 1 2 - 3	10 10 4 - 24	Dion, Brown	Leclerc 3
Cincinnati	2 2 3 - 7	13 8 11 - 32	Lapointe	Dudley 2, Leduc 2, Carroll, Stoughton, Inkpen
Edmonton	1 0 2 - 3	8 4 18 - 30	Dryden	Ullman, Sather, Morris
Birmingham	0 0 2 - 2	9 11 10 - 30	Garrett	Napier, Ball
Minnesota	1 2 1 - 4	8 12 6 - 26	Levasseur	McKenzie 2, S. Carlson, Gruen
Quebec	1 0 1 - 2	14 13 10 - 37	Aubry	Cloutier, Constantin
November 14				
San Diego	0 0 3 - 3	11 8 12 - 31	Lockett	Devine 2, Ferguson
Phoenix	1 2 3 - 6	9 10 10 - 29	Hebenton	Gray 2, Tamminen, Cormier, Ftorek
Indianapolis	0 1 2 - 3	5 10 15 - 30	Dion	Leclerc, Harris, Karlander
Quebec	0 0 1 - 1	4 9 8 - 21	Brodeur	Tardif
Winnipeg	1 0 1 - 2	10 5 11 - 26	Daley	Lesuk, Lindh
Calgary	0 0 0 - 0	15 10 6 - 31	McLeod	▸ Daley: shutout (1), 31 saves

1976-1977 Game by Game Line Scores

Date & Teams	Scoring 1 2 3 ot F	Shots 1 2 3 ot F	Goaltenders	Goals & Other Scoring Highlights
November 16				
Calgary	0 2 0 - 2	9 10 10 - 29	McLeod	Lemieux, Miller
Houston	1 1 2 - 4	5 13 15 - 33	Rutledge	Popiel, Lukowich, Mk Howe, G. Howe
New England	1 1 3 - 5	9 12 11 - 32	Abrahamsson	Webster 2, G. Roberts, Hangsleben, Backstrom (WG 18:11),
Birmingham	0 4 0 - 4	10 11 6 - 27	Garrett	Marrin 3, Napier
Quebec	2 2 0 - 4	10 15 6 - 31	Aubry, Brodeur	Bernier, Tardif, Cloutier, C. Bordeleau
Winnipeg	2 1 5 - 8	13 8 21 - 42	Daley	Hedberg 2, Labraaten 2, Ketola, Nilsson, Lindstrom, Guindon
Edmonton	0 2 0 - 2	10 12 7 - 29	Dryden	Sheehy 2
Phoenix	1 3 1 - 5	12 18 12 - 42	Hebenton	Gray 2, Cormier 2, Ftorek
Cincinnati	0 1 2 - 3	18 5 10 - 33	Lapointe	Locas 2, Inkpen
Indianapolis	2 3 0 - 5	19 10 13 - 42	Dion	Peacosh 2, MacDonald, Parizeau. Thomas
November 17				
Birmingham	1 2 1 - 4	10 12 16 - 38	Wood	Napier 2, Turkiewicz, Simpson
New England	1 1 4 - 6	10 12 16 - 38	Abrahamsson	Webster, Lyle, MacGregor, Backstrom, Rogers, Hangsleben
Edmonton	1 0 1 - 2	10 6 5 - 21	Broderick	Patenaude 2
San Diego	2 0 2 - 4	14 6 16 - 36	Wakely	Ferguson 2, Noris, French
November 18				
Quebec	2 2 5 - 9	17 11 16 - 44	Brodeur	Tardif 4, P. Bordeleau 3, Cloutier, C. Bordeleau
Minnesota	1 3 1 - 5	13 10 13 - 36	Levasseur	Deadmarsh 2, Ward, Gruen, Patrick
Calgary	0 0 1 1 2	8 7 10 9 34	Bromley	Lawson, Powis (OT 9:56)
Phoenix	0 0 1 0 1	9 8 9 2 28	Hebenton	Mononen
November 19				
Cincinnati	1 1 1 0 3	8 7 8 5 28	Lapointe	Sobchuk, Dudley, Leduc
Edmonton	1 1 1 1 4	8 9 18 3 38	Broderick	Campbell 2 (OT 6:33), Barrie, Patenaude
Winnipeg	1 3 3 - 7	11 11 8 - 30	Daley	Hedberg 2, Sullivan, Nilsson, Lindstrom, Ketola, Moffat
New England	1 0 2 - 3	15 7 11 - 33	Ab'sson, Landon	Hangsleben, Webster, G. Roberts
Quebec	0 0 1 - 1	9 15 11 - 35	Brodeur	Sutherland (spoiled McLeod's shutout at 19:18)
Calgary	2 1 1 - 4	9 4 12 - 25	McLeod	Tannahill, Lawson, Lemieux, Miller
Birmingham	0 0 0 - 0	9 11 7 - 27	Garrett	▸ Dion: shutout (1), 27 saves
Indianapolis	2 2 0 - 4	13 9 11 - 33	Dion	Parizeau, Paiement, Thomas
Houston	0 0 3 - 3	13 16 9 - 38	Grahame	Mty Howe 2, Tonelli
San Diego	2 1 2 - 5	14 6 10 - 30	Lockett	Rivers, Boddy, Lacroix, French, Morrison
November 20				
Minnesota	1 0 2 0 3	8 8 11 4 31	Curran	Antonovich 2, Zrymiak
New England	1 0 2 0 3	12 13 11 7 43	Landon	D. Roberts, G. Roberts, Rogers
Houston	0 2 3 - 5	9 13 9 - 31	Rutledge	Lund 2, Mk Howe, Tonelli, Lukowich
Phoenix	2 0 0 - 2	7 7 10 - 24	Hebenton	Gray 2
Winnipeg	2 0 2 - 4	8 11 15 - 34	Larsson	Lesuk, Ruhnke, Hedberg, Ketola
Indianapolis	3 3 2 - 8	15 10 8 - 33	Dion	Thomas 3, Leclerc 2, Harris, Sicinski. Peacosh
November 21				
San Diego	2 1 0 - 3	7 8 13 - 28	Wakely	Veneruzzo, Rivers, Hughes
Birmingham	2 0 2 - 4	10 12 8 - 30	Wood	Napier, Marrin, Nedomansky, Jacques (WG 5:03)
Quebec	3 0 2 - 5	13 11 6 - 30	Brodeur, Aubry	Dorey, Bernier, C. Bordeleau, Tremblay, Sutherland
Edmonton	1 3 2 - 6	9 12 10 - 31	Broderick	Ullman 2 (WG 18:50), Williams, Russell, Sheehy, Morris
Calgary	0 0 1 - 1	7 19 20 - 46	McLeod, Bromley	Sentes (spoiled Levasseur's shutout at 19:56)
Minnesota	2 2 1 - 5	8 11 3 - 22	Levasseur	Patrick 2, Deadmarsh 2, Antonovich
Cincinnati	1 2 1 - 4	15 12 15 - 42	Lapointe	Leduc, Dudley, Sobchuk, Stoughton
Winnipeg	0 0 2 - 2	9 11 10 - 30	Daley	Hedberg, Lindstrom
November 23				
Winnipeg	2 0 2 - 4	13 5 6 - 24	Daley	Nilsson, Ketola, Sullivan, Lindstrom
Quebec	2 2 3 - 7	8 8 9 - 25	Aubry	Cloutier 3, C. Bordeleau 2, Tardif, Lacombe
Cincinnati	0 0 0 - 0	11 16 21 - 48	Lapointe	▸ Levasseur: shutout (1), 48 saves (WHA record, most saves, shutout)
Minnesota	3 0 1 - 4	12 11 9 - 32	Levasseur	Deadmarsh, Keon, Antonovich, Arbour
Edmonton	0 1 2 - 3	10 11 8 - 29	Dryden	Patenaude, Ullman, Langevin
Houston	1 4 0 - 5	13 14 9 - 36	Rutledge	Lukowich 2, Connor 2, Hughes
New England	0 3 0 - 3	10 12 9 - 31	Landon	Lyle 2, Webster
Indianapolis	1 1 2 - 4	14 14 13 - 41	Dion	Parizeau, Karlander, Leclerc, Harris (WG 9:48)
Calgary	0 1 0 - 1	16 8 13 - 37	McLeod	Lemieux
Birmingham	0 2 1 - 3	8 14 4 - 26	Garrett	Nedomansky, Farda, Napier
November 24				
Indianapolis	1 4 1 - 6	9 15 8 - 32	Park	MacDonald 3, Thomas, Harris, Lomenda
Cincinnati	2 1 1 - 4	11 13 13 - 37	Lapointe	Larose 2, Stoughton, Dudley
Calgary	2 0 1 0 3	9 4 9 7 29	Bromley	Miller 2, Powis
Phoenix	0 0 3 0 3	4 7 12 4 27	Hebenton	Ftorek, Huston, Hall (TG 19:31)
Edmonton	1 1 0 - 2	10 2 7 - 19	Broderick	Ullman, Morris
San Diego	0 0 4 - 4	14 11 9 - 34	Lockett	Shmyr, Devine, Ferguson, Noris
November 25				
New England	1 2 2 - 5	7 11 8 - 26	Abrahamsson	Rogers 2, Hangsleben, Pleau, Webster
Birmingham	2 1 0 - 3	15 10 9 - 34	Wood	Napier, Jacques, Farda
Quebec	2 0 3 - 5	15 12 12 - 39	Aubry	Bernier 2, Tardif, C. Bordeleau, P. Bordeleau
Indianapolis	0 0 0 - 0	6 8 13 - 27	Park	▸ Aubry: shutout (1), 27 saves
November 26				
Quebec	1 1 0 - 2	11 10 9 - 30	Aubry	Tardif 2
Minnesota	2 0 2 - 4	10 9 4 - 23	Levasseur	Patrick, McDonough, Gruen, Antonovich
Winnipeg	0 1 0 0 1	8 9 10 3 30	Daley	Sullivan
Houston	0 1 0 0 1	13 10 5 5 33	Grahame	Connor (Both goals of game scored 32 seconds apart)
Edmonton	0 0 2 - 2	5 2 10 - 17	Dryden	Sheehy 2
Phoenix	1 1 2 - 4	4 13 7 - 24	Hebenton	Hall, Mononen, Sleep, Huston

295

1976-1977 Game by Game Line Scores

Date & Teams	Scoring 1 2 3 ot F	Shots 1 2 3 ot F	Goaltenders	Goals & Other Scoring Highlights
November 27				
Birmingham	0 1 0 - 1	16 8 4 - 28	Garrett	Simpson
Cincinnati	1 1 0 - 2	13 8 17 - 38	Hoganson	Stoughton, Abgrall
San Diego	1 0 1 - 2	7 6 3 - 16	Wakely	Rivers, Ferguson
Calgary	0 0 0 - 0	7 17 10 - 34	McLeod	▶ Wakely: shutout (2), 34 saves
Minnesota	2 0 1 - 3	10 7 10 - 27	Curran	Patrick, Antonovich, Keon
New England	0 1 0 - 1	12 10 11 - 33	Ab'sson, Landon	Webster
Indianapolis	3 3 2 - 8	8 12 10 - 30	Dion, Park	Harris 2, Maggs 2, Block, Karlander, Parizeau, Lomenda
Quebec	0 1 1 - 2	6 12 12 - 30	Brodeur, Aubry	Brackenbury, P. Bordeleau
November 28				
Phoenix	3 0 2 - 5	10 10 11 - 31	Hebenton	Ftorek 2, Rautakallio 2, Hall (Ftorek: points on all five goals)
Winnipeg	3 0 0 - 3	16 18 6 - 40	Daley	Hedberg, Ketola, Nilsson (Hull: season debut, assist)
Minnesota	2 1 0 - 3	6 9 4 - 19	Levasseur	McDonough, Ward, McKay
Birmingham	0 1 0 - 1	6 19 15 - 40	Wood	Kirk
Indianapolis	1 1 2 - 4	6 9 9 - 24	Park	Harris 2, Paiement, Karlander (WG 13:23)
New England	2 0 1 - 3	11 10 15 - 36	Landon, Ab'sson	Lyle 2, Selwood
San Diego	0 0 0 - 0	6 13 12 - 31	Lockett	▶ Broderick: shutout (1), 31 saves
Edmonton	1 1 2 - 4	5 7 13 - 25	Broderick	Sheehy, Russell, Sather, Beaton
November 30				
San Diego	0 0 2 - 2	8 4 8 - 20	Wakely	Cassolato, Morrison
Winnipeg	1 5 2 - 8	12 18 9 - 39	Daley	Hedberg 4, Long, Hull, Guindon, Ketola
Phoenix	1 0 1 0 2	9 4 7 0 20	Hebenton	Rollins 2 (TG 19:35)
Edmonton	0 0 2 1 3	10 11 10 6 37	Broderick	Russell, Patenaude, Ullman (OT 7:42)
Cincinnati	1 0 0 - 1	10 14 10 - 34	Lapointe	Marsh
Birmingham	1 0 2 - 3	10 5 10 - 25	Garrett	Nedomansky, Jacques, Napier
New England	0 0 1 - 1	9 3 10 - 22	Abrahamsson	Swain
Quebec	1 1 0 - 2	9 20 10 - 39	Brodeur	C. Bordeleau, Weir
December 1				
Calgary	3 1 0 - 4	16 11 12 - 39	Bromley, McLeod	Miller 2, Evans, Lawson
New England	3 3 2 - 8	13 13 12 - 38	Abrahamsson	MacG'gor 2, Backstrom, Swain, Selwood, Hangsleben, G. Roberts, Lyle
December 2				
Phoenix	1 2 0 - 3	5 8 6 - 19	Hebenton	Repo, Ftorek, Rautakallio
San Diego	1 0 3 - 4	18 10 9 - 37	Lockett, Wakely	Dobek, Ferguson, Devine, Cassolato (WG 9:47)
Edmonton	1 0 3 - 4	10 8 17 - 35	Dryden	Morris, Campbell, Sheehy, Ullman
Birmingham	0 2 1 - 3	6 11 9 - 26	Garrett	Henderson, Napier, Stewart
Calgary	0 0 1 - 1	8 11 17 - 36	McLeod	Powis
Indianapolis	0 1 1 - 2	11 12 9 - 32	Park	Paiement, Leclerc (WG 17:20)
December 3				
Quebec	2 2 1 0 5	19 23 10 6 58	Brodeur	Tardif, Grenier, Brackenbury, Constantin, C. Bordeleau (TG 19:30)
New England	2 2 1 0 5	14 12 10 4 40	Abrahamsson	MacGregor, Pleau, G. Roberts, Webster, Hangsleben
Calgary	0 3 1 - 4	5 9 15 - 29	McLeod	Powis, Driscoll, Jodzio, Lawson
Cincinnati	2 2 2 - 6	15 7 11 - 33	Hoganson	Abgrall 2, Stoughton, Locas, Dudley, Plumb
Winnipeg	1 3 0 - 4	6 19 10 - 35	Daley	Miller, Lindstrom, Hedberg, Labraaten
Minnesota	2 1 0 - 3	21 7 12 - 40	Levasseur	Ward, Keon, Antonovich
Edmonton	0 0 0 0 0	7 8 6 3 24	Broderick	▶ Broderick: shutout (2), 31 saves
Houston	0 0 0 0 0	12 4 9 6 31	Rutledge	▶ Rutledge: shutout (2), 24 saves
December 4				
Winnipeg	2 1 3 - 6	10 9 14 - 33	Daley	Green, Sullivan, Nilsson, Lindstrom, Ketola, Hedberg
New England	1 1 0 - 2	7 9 11 - 27	Abrahamsson	Swain, Lyle
Edmonton	0 1 2 - 3	8 10 10 - 28	Dryden	Barrie 2, Rota
Indianapolis	0 0 5 - 5	18 13 15 - 46	Park	MacDonald 2, Harris, Parizeau, Paiement
San Diego	2 1 1 - 4	7 15 6 - 28	Wakely	Lacroix, Shmyr, Devine, Burgess (WG 14:48)
Phoenix	2 1 0 - 3	16 7 7 - 30	Hebenton	Huston 2, Ftorek
December 5				
Phoenix	0 0 0 - 0	10 8 10 - 28	Kurt	▶ McLeod: shutout (2), 28 saves
Calgary	1 5 0 - 6	8 17 5 - 30	McLeod	Chipperfield 2, Connelly, Miller, Powis, Sentes
Winnipeg	2 0 2 - 4	6 12 14 - 32	Larsson	Sullivan, Hedberg, Moffat, Nilsson
Quebec	1 4 1 - 6	10 11 11 - 32	Brodeur	Tardif 2, Cloutier, Brackenbury, Bernier, Lacombe
Houston	0 2 0 - 2	11 9 10 - 30	Grahame	Connor, Mty Howe
Cincinnati	1 3 3 - 7	13 8 15 - 36	Lapointe	Sobchuk 2, Locas, Plumb, Leduc, Steele, Marsh
Edmonton	0 0 1 - 1	7 8 12 - 27	Broderick	Campbell
Minnesota	3 0 2 - 5	9 8 11 - 28	Curran	Antonovich 2, Arbour, McDonough, Patrick
December 7				
Phoenix	0 1 1 - 2	4 8 10 - 22	Hebenton	Repo, Mononen
Winnipeg	1 1 2 - 4	7 10 9 - 26	Daley	Miller 2, Hedberg, Moffat
New England	2 0 0 - 2	8 6 11 - 25	Abrahamsson	Backstrom, Webster
Minnesota	0 2 2 - 4	12 13 13 - 38	Levasseur	Gallant, Deadmarsh, Antonovich, McDonough
Edmonton	0 2 2 - 4	7 16 7 - 30	Dryden	Morris, Boddy, Ullman, Russell
Quebec	1 1 0 - 2	6 10 12 - 28	Brodeur	Tardif 2
Indianapolis	0 2 0 1 3	5 7 14 6 32	Dion	MacDonald, Maggs, Harris (OT 7:17)
Birmingham	1 1 0 0 2	14 10 7 4 35	Wood	Marrin, Jacques
December 8				
Winnipeg	0 0 4 - 4	13 11 19 - 43	Daley	Labraaten, Sullivan, Hull, Hedberg
Calgary	0 1 1 - 2	14 12 15 - 41	McLeod	Tannahill, Sentes
Houston	1 0 0 - 1	12 9 16 - 37	Rutledge	Hansis
New England	1 4 0 - 5	12 17 10 - 39	Raeder	Lyle 3, G. Roberts, Bolduc
San Diego	3 1 2 - 6	14 7 9 - 30	Lockett	Ferguson 3, Dobek, Cassolato, Lacroix
Cincinnati	0 0 1 - 1	14 15 6 - 35	Hoganson, Lapointe	Plumb

1976-1977 Game by Game Line Scores

Date & Teams	Scoring 1 2 3 ot F	Shots 1 2 3 ot F	Goaltenders	Goals & Other Scoring Highlights
December 9				
Quebec	0 2 3 - 5	12 14 10 - 36	Brodeur	Cloutier 3, Bernier, P. Bordeleau
Phoenix	0 1 3 - 4	3 10 8 - 21	Hebenton	Cormier 2, McLeod, Repo
December 10				
Birmingham	1 3 1 - 5	8 8 5 - 21	Garrett	Nedomansky 2, Jacques, Napier, Henderson
Winnipeg	0 1 2 - 3	10 16 15 - 41	Larsson	Hedberg, Miller, Labraaten
San Diego	1 0 1 - 2	9 7 7 - 23	Wakely	Dobek, Lacroix
Indianapolis	0 1 2 - 3	10 8 10 - 28	Park	MacDonald, Sicinski, Leclerc
Calgary	1 1 0 - 2	12 10 16 - 38	McLeod	Lawson, Chipperfield
Minnesota	0 3 1 - 4	10 12 9 - 31	Curran	McKenzie 2, McKay, Gruen
Houston	0 1 1 - 2	7 17 2 - 26	Grahame	Tonelli, Connor
Cincinnati	2 1 3 - 6	11 10 9 - 30	Lapointe	Legge, Locas, Guite, Larose, Stoughton, Carroll
December 11				
Houston	0 1 0 - 1	7 13 10 - 30	Rutledge	Taylor
Quebec	1 0 3 - 4	6 11 13 - 30	Brodeur	C. Bordeleau, Baxter, P. Bordeleau. Bernier
San Diego	0 2 0 - 2	12 7 11 - 30	Lockett	Noris, Ferguson
New England	0 2 1 - 3	6 9 6 - 21	Raeder	Rogers 2, Lyle (WG 5:09)
Edmonton	0 0 0 - 0	8 8 3 - 19	Broderick	▶ McLeod: shutout (3), 19 saves
Calgary	0 1 2 - 3	8 6 8 - 22	McLeod	Morrison, Driscoll, Miller
December 12				
Phoenix	0 0 0 - 0	7 8 8 - 23	Hebenton	▶ Lapointe: shutout (1), 23 saves
Cincinnati	4 3 1 - 8	17 14 15 - 46	Lapointe	Stoughton 2, Larose 2, Abgrall, Dudley, Leduc, Carroll
New England	0 1 0 - 1	7 6 9 - 22	Raeder, Ab'sson	Webster
Quebec	3 1 1 - 5	18 15 10 - 43	Brodeur	J. Bernier 2, C. Bordeleau, Constantin, P. Bordeleau
Houston	0 2 1 - 3	10 9 8 - 27	Grahame	Popiel, G. Howe, Hansis
Indianapolis	0 1 0 - 1	13 16 5 - 34	Dion	Harris
San Diego	1 1 2 - 4	10 12 10 - 32	Wakely	Legge, Cassolato, Shmyr, McNamee
Minnesota	1 0 1 - 2	12 11 13 - 36	Levasseur	Antonovich, Gallant
Birmingham	2 1 0 - 3	7 11 10 - 28	Garrett	Henderson, Napier, Sheehy
Edmonton	3 1 1 - 5	14 6 16 - 36	Dryden	Russell, Simpson, Rota, Patenaude, Barrie
December 14				
New England	1 0 2 - 3	8 8 11 - 27	Abrahamsson	Bolduc, Webster, Smedsmo
Quebec	0 1 0 - 1	16 12 12 - 40	Brodeur	Bernier
Phoenix	2 0 1 - 3	8 4 7 - 19	Hebenton	Hall 2, Ftorek
Houston	2 0 6 - 8	10 8 14 - 32	Grahame	G. Howe 2, Connor 2, Larway 2, Irwin, Taylor
San Diego	3 3 0 - 6	13 7 8 - 28	Lockett	Noris 2, Burgess 2, Ferguson, Morrison
Edmonton	0 0 1 - 1	3 8 9 - 20	Broderick	Nevin
December 15				
Minnesota	0 0 0 - 0	8 13 10 - 31	Curran	▶ Lapointe: shutout (2), 31 saves
Cincinnati	3 1 1 - 5	15 12 12 - 39	Lapointe	Plumb 2, Abgrall, Leduc, Dudley
Birmingham	2 1 2 - 5	11 8 15 - 34	Wood	Henderson, Stewart, Nistico, Sheehy, Turkiewicz
Phoenix	2 3 1 - 6	11 11 14 - 36	Kurt	Liddington 2, Tamminen, Ftorek, Rautakallio, Cormier
December 16				
Edmonton	0 0 0 - 0	3 2 6 - 11	Dryden	▶ Wakely: shutout (3), 11 saves (WHA record, fewest saves, shutout)
San Diego	2 0 1 - 3	18 7 6 - 31	Wakely	Noris 2, Burgess
Minnesota	2 3 0 - 5	12 13 9 - 34	Levasseur	Antonovich 3, McKenzie, Keon
Indianapolis	1 1 1 - 3	27 14 6 - 47	Park, Dion	Maggs, Parizeau, Rochon
December 17				
Edmonton	0 1 0 - 1	8 11 11 - 30	Broderick	Flett
Phoenix	0 0 0 - 0	13 10 10 - 33	Hebenton	▶ Broderick: shutout (3), 33 saves
Birmingham	3 0 1 - 4	9 7 6 - 22	Garrett	Nedomansky 2, Napier 2 (WG 18:01)
Houston	1 0 2 - 3	11 19 15 - 45	Rutledge	G. Howe, Taylor, Ruskowski
Indianapolis	0 3 1 1 5	12 10 5 3 30	Park	Harris, Karlander, Peacosh, Clackson, Sicinski (OT 5:31)
New England	1 2 1 0 4	7 6 12 1 26	Raeder	Webster 3, Lyle
December 18				
Birmingham	1 1 0 - 2	14 9 8 - 31	Garrett	Farda, Carleton
New England	2 2 2 - 6	10 14 19 - 43	Abrahamsson	Bolduc, Webster, Backstrom, Lyle, MacGregor, Smedsmo
Cincinnati	1 1 1 - 3	13 13 12 - 38	Lapointe	Sobchuk, Guite, Steele
Minnesota	2 1 1 - 4	11 12 12 - 35	Levasseur	Gallant, McKenzie, McDonough, Adduono
Quebec	0 2 0 - 2	11 11 8 - 30	Brodeur	Bernier 2
Calgary	1 1 2 - 4	16 9 9 - 34	Bromley	Connelly, Tannahill, Powis, Lemieux
Houston	0 2 1 - 3	8 10 7 - 25	Grahame	Popiel, Ruskowski, McLeod
San Diego	0 3 1 - 4	10 10 11 - 31	Lockett	Rivers, Cassolato, Ferguson, Dobek (WG 15:44)
December 19				
Houston	1 3 2 - 6	13 12 8 - 33	Rutledge	G. Howe 2, Connor, Taylor, Preston, Lund
Phoenix	1 0 3 - 4	9 10 9 - 28	Hebenton	Mononen, Repo, Cormier, Huston
Cincinnati	0 0 2 - 2	8 4 15 - 27	Hoganson	Larose, Sobchuk
Edmonton	1 2 1 - 4	14 13 7 - 34	Broderick	Flett, Morris, Nevin, Sather
Quebec	0 1 2 - 3	11 10 9 - 30	Brodeur	P. Bordeleau, Tremblay, Boudrias
San Diego	2 1 2 - 5	12 11 6 - 29	Wakely	Rivers, Burgess, Devine, Noris, Ferguson
Birmingham	0 1 1 0 2	10 6 9 0 25	Garrett	Sheehy, Nedomansky (TG 18:22)
Indianapolis	0 2 0 1 3	16 13 13 3 45	Dion	Sicinski, Lomenda, Karlander (OT 2:11)
December 21				
New England	0 0 0 - 0	4 8 6 - 18	Abrahamsson	▶ Grahame: shutout (2), 18 saves
Houston	1 0 3 - 4	9 11 12 - 32	Grahame	Connor 2, Lund, Tonelli
Quebec	1 1 0 - 2	9 12 9 - 30	Brodeur	Bernier, Sutherland
Birmingham	1 1 1 - 3	7 6 8 - 21	Garrett	Sheehy, Jacques, Lagace (WG 5:18)
Calgary	1 0 0 - 1	10 2 11 - 23	Bromley	Ford
Edmonton	1 2 1 - 4	12 16 5 - 33	Dryden	Sather, Nevin, Langevin, Kirk

1976-1977 Game by Game Line Scores

Date & Teams	Scoring (1 2 3 ot F)	Shots (1 2 3 ot F)	Goaltenders	Goals & Other Scoring Highlights
December 22				
San Diego	1 2 1 1 5	11 6 9 1 27	Lockett	Noris 2, Burgess, Lacroix, Ferguson (OT 0:21)
Phoenix	2 0 2 0 4	13 12 11 - 36	Hebenton	Hall, Ftorek, Lariviere, Beaudoin
Birmingham	3 1 2 - 6	10 10 10 - 30	Garrett	Hoganson, Henderson, Marrin, Nedomansky, Gorman, Napier
Cincinnati	0 1 1 - 2	14 16 4 - 34	Lapointe, Hoganson	Sobchuk, Dudley
Quebec	0 2 2 - 4	12 16 13 - 41	Brodeur	P. Bordeleau, Grenier, Dorey, Constantin (WG 18:19)
Minnesota	1 1 1 - 3	11 8 14 - 33	Curran, Levasseur	McKenzie, Gallant, McDonough
December 23				
Cincinnati	1 3 1 0 5	8 11 10 0 29	Lapointe	Leduc 2, Abgrall, Stoughton, Guite
Houston	2 2 1 1 6	15 11 4 1 31	Grahame	Preston 2 (OT 1:04), Ruskowski 2, Popiel, Mty Howe
New England	0 2 3 - 5	8 9 12 - 29	Raeder	Lyle, Arndt, Backstrom, Pleau, Webster
San Diego	1 2 0 - 3	7 13 9 - 29	Wakely	Ferguson, Cassolato, Rhiness
Minnesota	1 0 0 - 1	10 5 4 - 19	Levasseur, Curran	Gruen
Calgary	2 0 0 - 2	12 12 8 - 32	McLeod	Miszuk, Sentes
December 26				
Quebec	7 3 2 - 12	17 12 11 - 40	Brodeur	Cloutier 3, Constantin 3, Bernier 2, Sutherland, Roy, C. Bordeleau, P. Bordeleau
Winnipeg	1 1 1 - 3	7 5 12 - 24	Daley, Larsson	Hedberg, Nilsson, Ruhnke
Houston	1 0 1 - 2	12 10 15 - 37	Rutledge	Larway 2
Birmingham	4 1 1 - 6	14 10 10 - 34	Garrett	Marrin, Farda, Henderson, Stewart, Sheehy, Napier
Cincinnati	0 1 2 - 3	5 10 6 - 21	Lapointe, Hoganson	Carroll, Marsh, Sobchuk
Calgary	5 0 1 - 6	13 9 5 - 27	McLeod, Bromley	Sentes, Jodzio, Chipperfield, Morrison, Driscoll, Mayer
Indianapolis	1 0 0 - 1	14 10 9 - 33	Park	Peacosh
San Diego	0 0 2 - 2	7 4 7 - 18	Lockett	Pinder, Shmyr (WG 14:00)
Minnesota	1 0 1 - 2	6 6 12 - 24	Levasseur	McKenzie, S. Carlson
New England	2 1 0 - 3	14 11 8 - 33	Abrahamsson	Lyle 2, Callighen
December 28				
New England	0 1 3 - 4	10 8 13 - 31	Abrahamsson	MacGregor 3, Arndt
Minnesota	4 0 1 - 5	20 13 13 - 46	Levasseur	Antonovich 3, McKenzie, S. Carlson
Quebec	1 2 0 - 3	8 7 6 - 21	Brodeur, Aubry	Cloutier, Bernier, Fitchner
Edmonton	0 0 2 - 2	8 12 6 - 26	Dryden	Patenaude, Barrie
Indianapolis	0 2 1 - 3	9 17 8 - 34	Dion	Maggs 2, MacDonald
Phoenix	2 1 1 - 4	10 15 10 - 35	Kurt	Mononen 2, Hall, Hobin
Winnipeg	1 0 2 - 3	7 2 6 - 15	Daley	Hull, Lesuk, Sullivan
Houston	1 3 2 - 6	7 13 9 - 29	Grahame	Tonelli 2, Preston, Mty Howe, Hansis, Gray
December 30				
Minnesota	2 0 2 - 4	10 12 12 - 34	Levasseur	Gruen, McDonough, McKenzie, Antonovich
Birmingham	1 1 0 - 2	8 13 6 - 27	Garrett	Jacques, Henderson
Winnipeg	1 0 2 - 3	5 4 6 - 15	Daley	Hedberg, Moffat, Ketola
San Diego	2 0 2 - 4	10 10 22 - 42	Wakely	Noris, Ferguson, Burgess, Pinder
New England	2 2 2 - 6	15 8 10 - 33	Raeder	Bolduc 2, G. Roberts, Rogers, Swain, Callighen
Cincinnati	1 1 2 - 4	10 12 18 - 40	Hoganson	Sobchuk 2, Stoughton, Larose
January 1				
Edmonton	1 0 0 - 1	15 5 9 - 29	Broderick	Barrie
Calgary	1 3 1 - 5	12 7 15 - 34	McLeod	Ford, Driscoll, Sentes, Serviss, Lawson
January 2				
Houston	0 0 2 - 2	4 7 9 - 20	Grahame	G. Howe, Tonelli
Winnipeg	1 1 3 - 5	18 14 13 - 45	Daley	Hedberg, Labraaten, Ruhnke, Hull, Moffat (Kromm: sat out game)
Phoenix	0 0 1 - 1	10 8 12 - 30	Kurt	Repo
Indianapolis	1 2 1 - 4	10 14 10 - 34	Park, Dion	Maggs, MacDonald, Karlander, Thomas
Cincinnati	1 0 1 - 2	9 14 13 - 36	Lapointe	Plumb, Larose
New England	1 1 1 - 3	16 16 13 - 45	Abrahamsson	Backstrom, Lyle, Earl (WG 15:04)
Birmingham	0 0 1 - 1	10 13 15 - 38	Wood	Stewart
Minnesota	0 1 2 - 3	16 12 8 - 36	Levasseur	Antonovich, Ward, Deadmarsh
January 4				
New England	2 1 0 - 3	8 8 7 - 23	Raeder	Rogers, Pleau, Earl
Quebec	2 2 1 - 5	11 14 7 - 32	Brodeur	Tardif, Dorey, C. Bordeleau, Roy
Phoenix	3 2 0 - 5	11 9 9 - 29	Kurt, Hebenton	Liddington, Huston, Ftorek, Repo, Beaudoin
Birmingham	3 1 4 - 8	15 11 14 - 40	Garrett, Wood	Sheehy 2, Napier 2, Henderson, Jacques, Nistico, Bilodeau
Houston	1 1 3 - 5	5 5 12 - 22	Grahame	Larway, Taylor, Connor, Tonelli, Preston
Edmonton	2 0 1 - 3	13 11 4 - 28	Dryden	Flett, Connelly, Campbell
Indianapolis	0 0 1 - 1	7 8 8 - 23	Dion	Paiement
Winnipeg	0 1 1 - 2	7 9 7 - 23	Daley	Lindstrom, Guindon
January 5				
Houston	0 3 1 - 4	10 9 7 - 26	Rutledge	Ruskowski, Irwin, Tonelli, Preston
Calgary	0 2 1 - 3	4 7 7 - 18	McLeod	Powis, Tannahill, Driscoll
San Diego	1 1 0 - 2	14 10 7 - 31	Wakely	Morrison, Ferguson
New England	0 1 0 - 1	8 17 10 - 35	Raeder	Earl
January 7				
Quebec	2 2 3 - 7	9 10 16 - 35	Humphreys	Cloutier 3, Bernier, Roy, P. Bordeleau, C. Bordeleau
New England	1 0 2 - 3	10 14 15 - 39	Abrahamsson	Pleau, Rogers, Callighen
Birmingham	0 0 1 - 1	4 7 7 - 18	Garrett	Nedomansky
Cincinnati	4 2 1 - 7	14 14 11 - 39	Lapointe	Leduc 2, Sobchuk, Legge, Abgrall, Marsh, Stoughton
Houston	0 0 1 0 1	7 8 14 8 37	Grahame	Connor
Minnesota	0 0 1 0 1	10 15 8 4 37	Levasseur	Gruen
Calgary	1 0 0 - 1	8 17 8 - 33	McLeod, Bromley	Kryskow
Edmonton	3 1 0 - 4	6 9 6 - 21	Broderick, Dryden	Wilkins, Sather, Rota, Kirk

1976-1977 Game by Game Line Scores

Date & Teams	Scoring 1 2 3 ot F	Shots 1 2 3 ot F	Goaltenders	Goals & Other Scoring Highlights
January 8				
Indianapolis	0 0 3 - 3	8 6 9 - 23	Dion	Proceviat, Karlander, Maggs
Calgary	2 2 0 - 4	16 17 11 - 44	McLeod	Lawson 2, Powis, Kryskow
Phoenix	1 1 2 - 4	7 13 13 - 33	Hebenton	Lariviere, Hinse, Liddington, Niekamp (WG 18:56)
New England	0 2 1 - 3	11 12 9 - 32	Raeder	Callighen, Arndt, Bolduc
Edmonton	0 0 0 - 0	11 9 11 - 31	Dryden	▶ Levasseur: shutout (2), 31 saves
Minnesota	1 1 3 - 5	13 11 16 - 40	Levasseur	Arbour, Gruen, S. Carlson, J. Carlson, Antonovich
San Diego	1 0 0 - 1	6 9 14 - 29	Lockett	Hornung
Cincinnati	1 0 1 - 2	14 8 13 - 35	Lapointe	Leduc, Dudley (WG 3:58)
January 9				
Indianapolis	2 0 1 - 3	12 6 11 - 29	Dion	Thomas 2, Karlander
Edmonton	1 1 3 - 5	6 10 9 - 25	Dryden	Patenaude 2, Sather, Flett, Connelly
San Diego	2 0 0 - 2	12 8 5 - 25	Wakely	Ferguson, Devine
Quebec	1 1 3 - 5	11 13 7 - 31	Humphreys	Cloutier, Tardif, Dorey, C. Bordeleau, Constantin
Birmingham	0 0 1 - 1	10 7 11 - 28	Garrett	Napier
Winnipeg	0 2 2 - 4	17 15 12 - 44	Daley	Lesuk, Sullivan, Miller, Guindon
January 11				
New England	1 0 1 - 2	6 14 7 - 27	Raeder, Ab'sson	Earl, Arndt
Cincinnati	3 0 5 - 8	10 12 25 - 47	Lapointe	Marsh 3, Leduc 2, Hislop 2, Stoughton
Phoenix	0 2 0 - 2	6 14 7 - 27	Kurt	Ftorek, Cormier
Winnipeg	3 4 2 - 9	17 10 15 - 42	Daley	Labraaten 2, Lesuk, Nilsson, Hull, Ketola, Hedberg, Sullivan, Lindstrom
Indianapolis	1 1 1 1 4	6 4 10 1 21	Park	Thomas 2, Block, Harris (OT 7:01)
Calgary	2 0 1 0 3	6 11 5 2 24	McLeod	Evans, Miller, Chipperfield
January 12				
Birmingham	1 1 2 - 4	5 15 11 - 31	Wood	Nedomansky, Sheehy, Farda, Henderson (WG 8:53)
Minnesota	1 0 2 - 3	17 15 9 - 41	Levasseur	J. Carlson 3
Houston	1 0 1 - 2	9 6 9 - 24	Grahame	Preston, Lukowich
Phoenix	1 1 2 - 4	7 8 11 - 26	Hebenton	Huston 2, Ftorek, Cormier
January 13				
New England	0 0 1 - 1	8 7 11 - 26	Abrahamsson	Webster
Indianapolis	2 1 1 - 4	11 15 13 - 39	Park	Rochon 2, Thomas, Sicinski
Cincinnati	1 3 3 - 7	8 15 12 - 35	Lapointe	Carroll 2, Sobchuk 2, Larose, Hislop, Leduc
San Diego	1 1 0 - 2	11 8 11 - 30	Wakely, Lockett	Hughes, Cassolato
January 14				
Edmonton	2 1 2 - 5	11 11 12 - 34	Dryden	Rota 2, Flett, Connelly, Beaton
New England	2 1 0 - 3	8 14 12 - 34	Raeder	Hynes, Lyle, Abrahamsson
Birmingham	1 1 1 - 3	4 10 10 - 24	Garrett	Sheehy, Hoganson, Jacques
Houston	3 1 1 - 5	18 7 5 - 30	Rutledge	Popiel, Lukowich, Connor, Mk Howe, Ruskowski
Indianapolis	2 0 3 - 5	9 9 11 - 29	Dion, Burchell	Thomas 2, Maggs, Rochon, Harris
Minnesota	3 3 3 - 9	12 20 7 - 39	Levasseur	Ward 3, McKenzie 2, Gruen 2, Gallant, Zrymiak
Winnipeg	3 1 1 - 5	12 12 5 - 29	Daley	Hedberg 2, Sullivan, Nilsson, Labraaten
Calgary	1 0 2 - 3	9 7 17 - 33	McLeod, Bromley	Miller, Kryskow, Morrison
Cincinnati	1 0 4 0 5	9 9 19 0 37	Lapointe	Larose, Hughes, Stoughton, Leduc, Steele
Phoenix	1 3 1 1 6	9 14 10 2 35	Hebenton	Hall 3, Hughes 2 (OT 1:05), Repo
January 15				
Edmonton	3 0 0 - 3	12 17 13 - 42	Dryden	Patenaude, Flett, Kirk
Indianapolis	2 1 3 - 6	15 18 14 - 47	Park	Karlander 3, Thomas, Maggs, Lomenda
Calgary	0 2 3 - 5	7 10 9 - 26	Bromley	Tannahill 2, Evans, Lawson, Driscoll
San Diego	0 1 2 - 3	9 12 16 - 37	Wakely, Lockett	Lacroix, Burgess, Dobek
January 16				
Cincinnati	3 1 2 - 6	18 9 7 - 34	Lapointe	Stoughton 4, Sobchuk, Dudley
Winnipeg	3 0 1 - 4	12 11 11 - 34	Daley	Lindstrom 2, Hedberg, Nilsson
Edmonton	0 1 0 - 1	4 13 7 - 24	Broderick	Sather
Houston	1 0 2 - 3	10 5 13 - 28	Grahame	Popiel, G. Howe, Gray
Birmingham	0 0 2 - 2	4 6 10 - 20	Wood	Bilodeau, Turkiewicz
San Diego	1 4 0 - 5	13 13 13 - 39	Lockett	Lacroix, Devine, French, Rivers, Burgess
Calgary	1 3 1 - 5	15 15 11 - 41	Bromley, McLeod	Miller 2, Deschamps, Deadmarsh, Driscoll
Phoenix	1 1 2 - 4	8 12 17 - 37	Hebenton	Hughes, Ftorek, Cormier, Beaudoin
January 20	▶ Minnesota folded, January 17			
Edmonton	0 0 1 - 1	13 5 11 - 29	Levasseur	Connelly
San Diego	2 1 2 - 5	11 10 10 - 31	Wakely	Ferguson 2, Devine, Shmyr, Noris
Cincinnati	0 2 2 - 4	10 14 19 - 43	Lapointe, Hoganson	Stoughton, Leduc, Sobchuk, Hislop
Phoenix	2 2 5 - 9	19 16 16 - 51	Kurt	Lariviere 2, Repo 2, Hobin 2, Hinse, Cormier, Huston (Kurt: 3 assists)
Quebec	2 2 1 - 5	8 7 8 - 23	Humphreys	Cloutier, Brackenbury, C. Bordeleau, P. Bordeleau, Tardif (WG 7:35)
New England	3 1 0 - 4	13 9 13 - 35	Ab'sson, Raeder	G. Roberts 2, Hynes, Rogers
January 21				
Birmingham	1 0 0 - 1	12 8 14 - 34	Garrett	Marrin (scored at 0:20 in 1st)
Houston	3 2 1 - 6	7 13 12 - 32	Grahame	Lukowich 3, Mk Howe, Connor, Gray
Cincinnati	2 1 2 0 5	14 9 9 1 33	Lapointe	Leduc, Dudley, Marsh, Locas, Inkpen
Winnipeg	1 4 0 1 6	13 9 9 4 35	Daley	Hedberg 2 (WG 3:57), Long, Lindstrom, Ketola, Ruhnke
Calgary	0 1 0 0 1	5 5 7 2 19	Bromley	Chipperfield
Indianapolis	0 0 1 0 1	8 12 16 6 42	Park	Thomas
January 22				
Edmonton	0 1 0 - 1	10 9 8 - 27	Broderick	Barrie
Phoenix	0 1 3 - 4	9 12 12 - 33	Hebenton	Huston 2, Hughes, Hobin
Calgary	2 0 1 - 3	7 9 11 - 27	McLeod	Kryskow, Driscoll, Ford
Quebec	0 1 4 - 5	17 11 10 - 38	Brodeur	C. Bordeleau 2, Dorey 2, P. Bordeleau
Houston	1 3 2 - 6	9 10 7 - 26	Grahame	Mk Howe 2, Gray 2, McLeod, Taylor
San Diego	0 0 0 - 0	4 7 6 - 17	Lockett	▶ Grahame: shutout (3), 26 saves
Indianapolis	0 2 1 0 3	13 9 16 4 42	Park	MacDonald 2, Proceviat
New England	2 0 1 0 3	9 12 13 2 36	Raeder	Lyle 2, Keon

1976-1977 Game by Game Line Scores

Date & Teams	Scoring 1 2 3 ot F	Shots 1 2 3 ot F	Goaltenders	Goals & Other Scoring Highlights
January 23				
Phoenix	1 1 0 - 2	10 8 7 - 25	Kurt	Hughes, Hobin Simpson
Edmonton	1 2 6 - 9	15 8 13 - 36	Levasseur	Sather 2, Flett, Connelly, Antonovich, Patenaude, Hamilton, Wilkins,
San Diego	2 1 0 - 3	7 6 4 - 17	Wakely	Cournoyer, Pinder, Adduono
Houston	4 1 0 - 5	17 9 14 - 40	Rutledge	Lukowich, Lund, Tonelli, Mk Howe, Connor
Indianapolis	0 1 1 - 2	7 12 10 - 29	Dion	Thomas, Harris
Birmingham	2 1 3 - 6	12 7 13 - 32	Garrett	Sheehy 2, Stewart 2, Napier, Hoganson
Cincinnati	2 1 0 0 3	12 14 11 2 39	Lapointe	Sobchuk, Stoughton, Steele
New England	1 2 0 1 4	16 10 15 3 44	Abrahamsson	Keon, S. Carlson, J. Carlson, Hynes (OT 4:43)
Calgary	2 2 1 - 5	14 9 7 - 30	Bromley, McLeod	Driscoll 2, Lawson, Deadmarsh, Chipperfield • Lesuk, Lindh, Hedberg
Winnipeg	4 4 2 - 10	14 16 11 - 41	Daley	Lindstrom, Bergman, Sullivan, Nilsson, Riihiranta, Ketola, Guindon,
January 25				
Indianapolis	1 0 0 0 1	10 11 12 1 34	Dion	Thomas
Quebec	0 1 0 1 2	9 16 6 5 36	Brodeur	Cloutier 2 (OT 4:55)
Winnipeg	0 2 0 - 2	7 12 12 - 31	Daley	Lindh, Nilsson
Houston	0 1 4 - 5	5 9 13 - 27	Grahame	Lukowich 2, Gray, Tonelli, Taylor
New England	2 0 0 - 2	6 9 11 - 26	Abrahamsson	Keon, Callighen
Cincinnati	1 1 2 - 4	11 6 10 - 27	Lapointe	Stoughton 2, Steele, Locas
Phoenix	2 0 1 - 3	6 10 5 - 21	Hebenton	Bray, Hughes, Ftorek
Calgary	2 2 3 - 7	11 9 17 - 37	McLeod	Driscoll 3, Deadmarsh 2, Gruen, Lawson
January 26				
Edmonton	1 1 2 1 5	16 6 10 1 33	Levasseur	Campbell 2, Wilkins, Flett, Sather (OT 2:01)
Quebec	0 0 4 0 4	11 10 12 0 33	Humphreys	C. Bordeleau, Tardif, Boudrias, Fitchner
January 27				
Winnipeg	0 0 0 - 0	4 7 10 - 21	Daley	▶ Garrett: shutout (1), 21 saves
Birmingham	1 0 2 - 3	14 6 11 - 31	Garrett	Marrin, Napier, Jacques
New England	1 0 4 - 5	10 6 11 - 27	Abrahamsson	Earl, Backstrom, Lyle, Ley (WG 17:50), Keon
San Diego	0 2 1 - 3	7 11 6 - 24	Lockett	Hornung 2, Burgess
January 28				
Quebec	2 1 3 - 6	7 10 15 - 32	Brodeur	Tardif 3 (WG 10:57), Cloutier, C. Bordeleau, P. Bordeleau
Indianapolis	0 3 2 - 5	8 13 11 - 32	Park	Leclerc 2, Karlander, Stapleton, Peacosh
New England	2 3 1 - 6	14 11 6 - 31	Abrahamsson	McKenzie, S. Carlson, Callighen, Keon, Webster, Hynes
Phoenix	0 1 1 - 2	8 8 10 - 26	Hebenton	Ftorek, Repo
Houston	2 2 0 - 4	14 10 5 - 29	Grahame	Gray, Lund, Lukowich, Mk Howe
Edmonton	0 0 1 - 1	7 7 9 - 23	Levasseur	Hamilton
January 29				
Winnipeg	1 1 1 - 3	21 10 12 - 43	Daley	Lindstrom 2, Sullivan
San Diego	3 2 0 - 5	10 11 8 - 29	Wakely	Rhiness 2, Sentes 2, Adduono
Houston	2 3 1 - 6	14 9 6 - 29	Rutledge	Preston, Ruskowski, Connor, Gray, Mty Howe, G. Howe
Calgary	1 0 3 - 4	6 6 10 - 22	McLeod	Kryskow 2, Miller, Chipperfield
Cincinnati	1 0 1 - 2	9 9 10 - 28	Lapointe	Sobchuk, Roy
Quebec	1 1 5 - 7	11 9 14 - 34	Brodeur	Fitchner, P.Bordeleau, Brackenbury, Tardif, Cloutier, C.Bordeleau, Weir
January 30				
Cincinnati	0 1 0 - 1	10 10 10 - 30	Hoganson	Locas
Birmingham	3 1 3 - 7	12 9 12 - 33	Garrett	Napier, Hoganson, Nistico, Henderson, Sheehy, Turkiewicz, Stewart
Calgary	1 0 0 0 1	8 5 7 5 25	McLeod	Kryskow
Edmonton	0 0 1 0 1	5 10 14 1 30	Levasseur	Connelly
New England	0 0 0 - 0	7 8 18 - 33	Abrahamsson	▶ Park: shutout (1), 33 saves
Indianapolis	1 3 1 - 5	13 13 11 - 37	Park	Peacosh, Paiement, Leclerc, Zuke, Mavety
Winnipeg	2 1 2 - 5	16 11 8 - 35	Larsson, Daley	Lindstrom, Sullivan, Nilsson, Moffat, Lesuk
Phoenix	1 7 0 - 8	12 15 10 - 37	Hebenton	Hall 3, Repo 3, Hughes, Sleep
February 1				
Winnipeg	2 6 3 - 11	9 13 12 - 34	Daley	Miller 4, Hedberg 4, Lindstrom 2, Moffat (Wpg: 11 consecutive goals)
Edmonton	1 0 0 - 1	10 11 11 - 32	Levasseur	Campbell
Indianapolis	2 2 0 - 4	11 11 7 - 29	Park	McDonald, Coates, Paiement, Stapleton
Quebec	2 0 3 - 5	11 10 15 - 36	Brodeur	Tremblay, Weir, Tardif, Dorey, Bernier (WG 3:53)
New England	2 0 1 - 3	15 7 10 - 32	Ab'sson, Raeder	Hangsleben 2. G. Roberts
Birmingham	2 0 2 - 4	15 8 11 - 34	Garrett	Sheehy, Nistico, Gallant, Jacques (WG 11:48)
Calgary	0 1 0 - 1	10 6 5 - 21	McLeod, Bromley	Jodzio
Houston	2 3 1 - 6	5 13 11 - 29	Grahame, Rutledge	Connor 2, Popiel, Lund, Mty Howe, Lukowich
Phoenix	1 0 0 - 1	7 7 8 - 22	Hebenton	Hughes
San Diego	3 2 0 - 5	15 9 10 - 34	Lockett	Lacroix 2, Cassolato, Rivers, Pinder
February 2				
Birmingham	1 0 2 - 3	7 6 6 - 19	Wood	Stewart, Nistico, Napier (WG 14:38)
Cincinnati	1 0 1 - 2	12 7 15 - 34	Lapointe	Leduc, Roy
Quebec	2 3 0 - 5	10 8 8 - 26	Brodeur	Tardif 2, Brackenbury, Fitchner, P. Bordeleau
Indianapolis	3 1 2 - 6	17 9 17 - 43	Park	Leclerc 2, Paiement, McDonald, Mavety, Sicinski (WG 12:05)
Calgary	2 1 1 - 4	15 12 8 - 35	Bromley, McLeod	Locas, Lawson, Miller, Kryskow
San Diego	3 1 2 - 6	10 6 11 - 27	Wakely	Burgess 2, Cassolato 2, Lacroix, Devine
February 3				
Houston	2 1 0 - 3	10 17 16 - 43	Rutledge	Mty Howe, Tonelli, Taylor
Phoenix	3 1 1 - 5	10 9 8 - 27	Hebenton	Ftorek 2, Hall 2, Hobin
February 4				
New England	0 0 1 - 1	9 9 14 - 32	Raeder	Lyle
Houston	1 2 1 - 4	15 12 9 - 36	Rutledge	Popiel, Mk Howe, Preston, Tonelli
San Diego	2 0 0 - 2	13 6 12 - 31	Lockett	Sentes, Pinder
Winnipeg	2 4 2 - 8	15 15 17 - 47	Daley	Hedberg 4, Bergman, Lesuk, Nilsson, Moffat
Quebec	0 0 0 - 0	8 9 7 - 24	Brodeur	▶ Garrett: shutout (2), 24 saves
Birmingham	1 3 3 - 7	9 13 11 - 33	Garrett	Sheehy 2, Stewart, Nistico, Marrin, Napier, Jacques

1976-1977 Game by Game Line Scores

Date & Teams	Scoring 1 2 3 ot F	Shots 1 2 3 ot F	Goaltenders	Goals & Other Scoring Highlights
February 5				
Calgary	1 1 2 - 4	13 13 9 - 35	Bromley	Terbenche, Chipperfield, Miller, Lawson
Phoenix	0 0 1 - 1	9 7 9 - 25	Kurt	Ftorek
Birmingham	0 0 2 - 2	7 9 13 - 29	Wood	Stewart, Nistico
Indianapolis	2 0 3 - 5	23 13 12 - 48	Park	Peacosh 2, Inkpen, Sicinski, Leclerc
New England	2 0 1 - 3	11 10 5 - 26	Abrahamsson	Webster, Pleau, Backstrom
Cincinnati	2 4 2 - 8	11 13 13 - 37	Caron	Dudley 4, Leduc 2, Larose, Sobchuk
February 6				
San Diego	1 0 1 - 2	12 8 11 - 31	Wakely	Burgess, Shmyr
Edmonton	2 2 0 - 4	11 13 10 - 34	Levasseur	Patenaude, Beaton, Flett, Morris
Indianapolis	2 2 1 0 5	17 10 11 2 40	Park	Thomas 2, MacDonald, Paiement, McDonald
New England	1 2 2 0 5	13 12 10 5 40	Abrahamsson	Webster, Hangsleben, Rogers, Backstrom, J. Carlson (TG 17:22)
Calgary	2 0 2 - 4	8 12 12 - 32	Bromley	Kryskow 2, Driscoll, Evans
Winnipeg	0 4 2 - 6	11 15 11 - 37	Daley	Hedberg 3 (51 goals in team's 49th game), Ward, Ketola, Sullivan
Cincinnati	0 0 1 - 1	6 5 11 - 22	Lapointe	Dudley
Quebec	2 3 1 - 6	13 17 7 - 37	Brodeur	Brackenbury 2, Cloutier, Tardif, Dube, P. Bordeleau
February 8				
Winnipeg	2 2 3 - 7	5 11 11 - 27	Larsson	Nilsson 3, Ruhnke, Sullivan, Ketola, Lindstrom
Quebec	0 0 2 - 2	13 11 6 - 30	Brodeur, Aubry	Bernier, Dorey
San Diego	2 3 1 - 6	10 10 7 - 27	Lockett	Ferguson 2, Devine, Rhiness, McNamee, Burgess
Edmonton	2 0 3 - 5	18 12 17 - 47	Levasseur, Brod'ck	Connelly 2, Flett 2, Ullman
Houston	1 1 2 0 4	13 13 8 8 42	Rutledge	Lund, Gray, Lukowich, Tonelli
Indianapolis	1 2 1 0 4	5 9 12 6 32	Park	MacDonald 2 (TG 19:18), Parizeau, Karlander
February 9				
Birmingham	1 0 2 0 3	13 9 15 2 39	Garrett	Gorman, Sheehy, Nedomansky (TG 19:32)
Phoenix	0 0 3 1 4	9 9 15 10 43	Hebenton	Bray, Hall, Beaudoin, Hughes (OT 8:41)
Indianapolis	0 0 0 - 0	7 8 4 - 19	Park, Burchell	▶ Caron: shutout (1), 19 saves
Cincinnati	4 4 1 - 9	12 19 10 - 41	Caron	Leduc 3, Dudley 2, Sobchuk, Abgrall, Stoughton, Larose
February 10				
Winnipeg	1 2 0 - 3	12 12 9 - 33	Larsson	Ruhnke 2, Sullivan
New England	2 3 1 - 6	13 16 15 - 44	Landon	McKenzie, Webster, Antonovich, Backstrom, Rogers, Keon
February 11				
Winnipeg	0 0 0 - 0	5 7 9 - 21	Daley	▶ Caron: shutout (2), 21 saves
Cincinnati	1 0 3 - 4	17 10 18 - 45	Caron	Dudley 2, Abgrall, Hislop
San Diego	1 1 3 - 5	11 11 25 - 47	Wakely	Lacroix 3, Burgess, Sentes
Phoenix	1 1 1 - 3	17 13 12 - 42	Kurt	Huston, Ftorek, Hall
Edmonton	0 1 0 - 1	6 2 8 - 16	Broderick	Flett
Calgary	0 2 1 - 3	7 11 12 - 30	McLeod	Chipperfield, Tannahill, Terbenche
Quebec	1 2 2 - 5	12 7 14 - 33	Humphreys	Cloutier 2, Brackenbury, Constantin, Tardif
Indianapolis	0 1 0 - 1	9 6 7 - 22	Park	MacDonald
February 12				
Birmingham	0 2 0 0 2	5 5 2 0 12	Garrett	Napier, Stewart
San Diego	1 0 1 1 3	6 16 9 2 33	Lockett	Sentes, Shmyr, Ferguson (OT 0:50)
Quebec	1 1 1 - 3	13 12 14 - 39	Humphreys, Aubry	Cloutier 3
Houston	3 2 2 - 7	24 10 9 - 43	Rutledge	G. Howe 2, Preston 2, Taylor, Popiel, Gray
Indianapolis	2 2 1 - 5	20 11 10 - 41	Burchell	Stapleton, Leclerc, Maggs, Paiement, Inkpen
New England	1 0 0 - 1	15 17 14 - 46	Ab'sson, Landon	Webster
February 13				
Winnipeg	2 3 2 - 7	11 8 9 - 28	Daley	Nilsson 3, Sullivan, Dunn, Moffat, Miller
Indianapolis	3 1 1 - 5	8 11 10 - 29	Burchell, Park	Thomas, McDonald, Paiement, Parizeau, Zuke
Phoenix	0 2 0 - 2	6 9 8 - 23	Kurt	Hobin 2
San Diego	0 4 1 - 5	6 13 11 - 30	Wakely	Noris 2, Sentes, Lacroix, Rhiness
New England	0 2 3 - 5	9 11 13 - 33	Landon	Butters, Backstrom, Keon, McKenzie, Antonovich
Cincinnati	0 3 1 - 4	10 12 10 - 32	Caron	Dudley, Marsh, Leduc, Carroll
Calgary	1 0 1 - 2	8 9 12 - 29	McLeod	Ford, Arbour
Edmonton	2 3 0 - 5	9 8 10 - 27	Levasseur	Flett 2, Kirk, Hamilton, Morris
February 15				
Quebec	1 0 1 - 2	12 17 14 - 43	Humphreys	Bernier, C. Bordeleau
Houston	2 0 2 - 4	12 9 14 - 35	Rutledge	Preston, Mk Howe, Lund, G. Howe
Cincinnati	2 3 2 - 7	13 11 12 - 36	Caron	Larose, Sobchuk, Melrose, Abgrall, Stoughton, Steele
Edmonton	1 2 1 - 4	9 12 12 - 33	Levasseur	Simpson, Patenaude, Campbell, Flett
Calgary	1 1 0 0 2	8 12 10 2 32	McLeod	Miszuk, Locas
Winnipeg	1 0 1 0 2	11 11 9 4 35	Daley	Labraaten, Moffat
February 16				
Phoenix	0 2 0 - 2	8 11 14 - 33	Garrett	Hall, Lariviere
Birmingham	3 2 2 - 7	11 10 10 - 31	Kurt, Hebenton	Gallant 2, Nedomansky 2, Napier, Sheehy, Henderson
Cincinnati	3 1 3 - 7	13 11 12 - 36	Lapointe	Leduc 3, Plumb, Dudley, Sobchuk, Carroll
Calgary	1 0 2 - 3	7 9 10 - 26	McLeod	Locas, Kryskow, Lawson
Quebec	0 4 0 - 4	4 14 4 - 22	Humphreys	Tardif 2, Cloutier, P. Bordeleau
San Diego	0 1 1 - 2	9 3 8 - 20	Lockett	Cassolato, Ferguson
February 17				
Phoenix	1 0 1 - 2	13 12 12 - 37	Kurt	Liddington, Ftorek
New England	0 2 2 - 4	13 10 14 - 37	Landon	Rogers, McKenzie, Webster, Abrahamsson
Indianapolis	1 1 0 - 2	13 13 9 - 35	Dion	Rochon, Inkpen
Winnipeg	0 3 1 - 4	16 11 9 - 36	Larsson	Lindh 2, Lindstrom, Ketola

1976-1977 Game by Game Line Scores

Date & Teams	Scoring 1 2 3 ot F	Shots 1 2 3 ot F	Goaltenders	Goals & Other Scoring Highlights
February 18				
Birmingham	1 1 1 - 3	7 10 14 - 31	Garrett	Napier 3 (WG 1:48)
New England	1 1 0 - 2	19 11 16 - 46	Landon	Lyle, Webster
San Diego	2 0 0 - 2	11 4 7 - 22	Wakely, Lockett	Noris, Ferguson
Houston	1 1 2 - 4	7 15 14 - 36	Rutledge	Gray, Taylor, Lund, Connor (Mk Howe: 4 assists)
Winnipeg	1 0 1 - 2	7 1 9 - 17	Daley	Ketola, Ward
Edmonton	0 2 1 - 3	9 9 7 - 25	Broderick	Patenaude, Rota, Campbell
Cincinnati	1 1 1 - 3	8 9 9 - 26	Lapointe	Abgrall 2, Carroll
Calgary	0 2 3 - 5	11 12 9 - 32	Bromley	Chipperfield, Greig, Terbenche, Deadmarsh, Tannahill
February 19				
San Diego	1 1 1 - 3	13 8 11 - 32	Lockett	Lacroix, Devine, Sentes
Houston	2 0 3 - 5	11 17 15 - 43	Rutledge	Taylor 2, Preston 2 (both in last 2:16), Gray
Quebec	0 1 0 - 1	14 15 10 - 39	Humphreys	Lacombe
Cincinnati	1 1 1 - 3	8 5 8 - 21	Caron	Hislop, Larose, Leduc
Phoenix	2 2 2 - 6	15 14 8 - 37	Kurt	Mononen 2, Repo 2, Hall 2
Indianapolis	2 1 2 - 5	15 10 10 - 35	Dion	Maggs, Zuke, Lomenda, Leclerc, MacDonald
February 20				
Indianapolis	1 0 1 0 2	5 11 8 5 29	Dion	Lomenda, Parizeau
Birmingham	1 1 0 0 2	12 16 5 6 39	Garrett	Henderson, Nistico
Edmonton	1 1 0 - 2	6 9 10 - 25	Broderick	Flett, Langevin
Winnipeg	1 1 2 - 4	9 6 11 - 26	Daley	Ward 2, Ruhnke, Labraaten
New England	1 1 3 - 5	6 7 10 - 23	Landon	Antonovich 2, Rogers, McKenzie, Webster
Calgary	0 0 0 - 0	7 8 3 - 18	Bromley	▶ Landon: shutout (1), 18 saves
Phoenix	3 0 0 - 3	14 4 2 - 20	Hebenton	Popiel 2, Hughes
Cincinnati	2 1 1 - 4	15 11 15 - 41	Lapointe, Caron	Sobchuk, Legge, Steele, Abgrall (WG 18:08)
February 22				
Cincinnati	0 0 4 0 4	12 10 8 3 33	Caron	Dudley, Stoughton, Larose, Plumb
Birmingham	1 2 1 0 4	13 14 5 0 32	Garrett	Marrin, Stewart, Nistico, Napier (TG 19:40)
Houston	0 0 2 - 2	10 17 12 - 39	Rutdledge	Mk Howe, Gray
Winnipeg	1 0 2 - 3	13 11 16 - 40	Daley	Lindstrom, Green, Lindh
New England	2 0 1 - 3	7 8 10 - 25	Landon	J. Carlson, Abrahamsson, G. Roberts
Edmonton	0 3 1 - 4	12 11 10 - 33	Broderick	Flett, Morris, Rota, Hamilton
Indianapolis	0 2 0 - 2	11 7 4 - 22	Dion	Peacosh, MacDonald
Quebec	2 1 1 - 4	14 12 9 - 35	Humphreys	P. Bordeleau, C. Bordeleau, Dorey, Brackenbury
February 23				
Houston	1 1 0 - 2	13 15 6 - 34	Rutledge	Ruskowski, Mk Howe
Calgary	1 2 0 - 3	9 7 10 - 26	McLeod	Miller, Lawson, Chipperfield
Winnipeg	2 1 0 - 3	9 7 7 - 23	Larsson	Labraaten, Lindh, Moffat
Phoenix	2 3 1 - 6	17 11 10 - 38	Kurt	Hughes 4, Repo 2
February 24				
Phoenix	1 1 1 0 3	4 9 7 2 22	Hebenton	Hughes, Hall, Hobin
San Diego	0 1 2 0 3	13 8 10 6 37	Wakely	Sentes, Devine, Ferguson
Quebec	2 3 1 - 6	7 13 14 - 34	Brod'r, Humphreys	Bernier 2, Baxter, Cloutier, Tardif, Dube
Birmingham	1 4 5 - 10	9 21 16 - 46	Garrett	Sheehy 3, Marrin 2, Stewart, Jacques, Gorman, Nedomansky, Napier
February 25				
New England	0 1 2 - 3	9 9 13 - 31	Landon	J. Carlson, Abrahamsson, G. Roberts (WG 15:19)
Calgary	0 2 0 - 2	11 11 7 - 29	McLeod	Kryskow, Chipperfield
Houston	3 2 4 - 9	9 13 15 - 37	Rutledge	Lukowich 2, Connor 2, Tonelli 2, Taylor, Preston, Gray
Phoenix	1 2 0 - 3	14 11 3 - 28	Kurt, Hebenton	Hall, Ftorek, Huston
Indianapolis	1 1 0 1 3	10 12 6 3 31	Dion	Maggs, Parizeau, Peacosh (OT 4:55)
Edmonton	1 1 0 0 2	10 9 11 0 30	Broderick	Campbell, Morris
Quebec	1 0 1 - 2	13 7 7 - 27	Brodeur	P. Bordeleau, Boudrias
Cincinnati	2 2 1 - 5	15 7 12 - 34	Caron	Marsh 2, Larose 2, Carroll
February 26				
Winnipeg	1 2 5 - 8	9 6 11 - 26	Daley	Lindstrom 3 (WG 18:46), Hedberg, Lindh, Guindon, Labraaten, Long
Cincinnati	1 2 3 - 6	9 19 12 - 40	Lapointe	Leduc 2, Marsh, Stoughton, Dudley, Legge
Birmingham	0 1 2 - 3	4 6 10 - 20	Wood	Marrin, Napier, Nistico
Quebec	2 0 3 - 5	11 14 14 - 39	Humphreys	Tardif 2, P. Bordeleau, Cloutier, Boudrias
Houston	0 2 3 - 5	8 6 12 - 26	Grahame	Lund, Connor, Preston, Tonelli, Ruskowski (WG 17:05)
San Diego	1 2 1 - 4	5 9 11 - 25	Lockett	Noris, Rivers, Shmyr, Devine
February 27				
Houston	1 3 1 - 5	16 17 10 - 43	Rutledge	G. Howe, Lund, Taylor, Connor, Ruskowski
Phoenix	3 0 1 - 4	9 3 9 - 21	Hebenton	Mononen, Huston, Lariviere, Ftorek
Birmingham	2 1 1 - 4	11 9 4 - 24	Garrett	Napier 2, Marrin, Westrum
Edmonton	0 0 0 - 0	10 10 11 - 31	Levasseur	▶ Garrett: shutout (3), 31 saves
Indianapolis	0 0 1 - 1	8 4 12 - 24	Dion	Peacosh
Calgary	1 1 0 - 2	6 12 8 - 26	McLeod	Deadmarsh, Kryskow
New England	1 0 2 - 3	10 6 11 - 27	Landon	Pleau, Rogers, Webster (WG 12:40)
Winnipeg	1 1 0 - 2	10 12 12 - 34	Daley	Sullivan 2
March 1				
Phoenix	2 1 0 - 3	11 12 10 - 33	Kurt, Hebenton	Ftorek, Repo, Hall (G. Howe: 900th career reg. season goal)
Houston	4 2 2 - 8	13 10 11 - 34	Grahame	Lund 3, G. Howe, Taylor, Pentland, Preston, Ruskowski
Winnipeg	0 0 1 - 1	6 7 12 - 25	Daley, Larsson	Miller (spoiled McLeod's shutout at 18:54)
Calgary	2 4 0 - 6	13 19 5 - 37	McLeod	Chipperfield 2, Powis 2, Terbenche, Driscoll
Quebec	2 1 2 - 5	12 10 9 - 31	Brod'r, Humphreys	Brackenbury, C. Bordeleau, P. Bordeleau, Tardif, Lacombe
Edmonton	2 1 1 - 4	8 11 5 - 24	Levasseur	Langevin, Callighen, Ullman, Russell
March 2				
Quebec	0 0 3 0 3	11 8 8 6 33	Humphreys	Baxter, Tardif, C. Bordeleau
Winnipeg	1 1 1 1 4	13 17 13 5 48	Daley	Lindstrom 2, Guindon, Hedberg (OT 9:19)
San Diego	0 0 0 - 0	5 13 11 - 29	Wakely	▶ Raeder: shutout (1), 29 saves
New England	0 0 2 - 2	10 15 17 - 42	Raeder	Antonovich, Webster

1976-1977 Game by Game Line Scores

Date & Teams	Scoring 1 2 3 ot F	Shots 1 2 3 ot F	Goaltenders	Goals & Other Scoring Highlights
March 3				
Birmingham	0 1 1 - 2	9 6 14 - 29	Garrett	Gallant, Henderson
Calgary	3 0 1 - 4	17 5 12 - 34	McLeod	Powis 3, Deadmarsh
Winnipeg	2 0 2 - 4	5 6 6 - 17	Larsson	Hedberg, Ketola, Long, Miller
Edmonton	1 3 1 - 5	7 14 9 - 30	Broderick	Flett 2, Sather, Patenaude, Ullman (WG 13:09)
March 4				
Houston	0 1 1 - 2	10 16 9 - 35	Rutledge	Mty Howe, Tonelli
New England	0 1 2 - 3	5 12 11 - 28	Raeder	Lyle 2, Rogers (WG 18:35)
San Diego	2 0 2 - 4	18 13 12 - 43	Lockett	Lacroix 2, Devine, Sentes
Indianapolis	1 2 4 - 7	11 13 13 - 37	Dion	MacDonald 2, Inkpen, Karlander, Leclerc, Clackson, Peacosh
March 5				
Indianapolis	0 0 0 - 0	11 11 5 - 27	Dion, Hoganson	▸ Caron: shutout (3), 27 saves
Cincinnati	1 3 2 - 6	10 7 4 - 21	Caron	Sobchuk 2, Dudley, Stoughton, Abgrall, Leduc
San Diego	0 0 0 - 0	11 6 9 - 26	Wakely	▸ Humphreys: shutout (1), 26 saves
Quebec	1 2 3 - 6	16 18 15 - 49	Humphreys	Constantin, P. Bordeleau, Baxter, Cloutier, Dube
Winnipeg	0 1 0 - 1	12 12 11 - 35	Daley	Sullivan
Phoenix	0 3 1 - 4	14 13 7 - 34	Hebenton	Ftorek 2, Mononen, Hughes
March 6				
Birmingham	0 0 2 - 2	8 11 5 - 24	Garrett	Napier, Nedomansky
Edmonton	2 1 2 - 5	11 7 6 - 24	Broderick	Callighen 3, Ullman, Flett
San Diego	1 0 1 - 2	5 14 7 - 26	Lockett, Shmyr	Lacroix, Shmyr
Calgary	1 2 1 - 4	13 4 7 - 24	McLeod	Ford, Morin, Morrison, Powis
Quebec	0 1 1 - 2	6 9 9 - 24	Humphreys	P. Bordeleau, Dube
New England	3 0 3 - 6	17 9 8 - 34	Raeder	Antonovich 2, D. Roberts, Lyle, Keon, Webster
Phoenix	2 0 0 0 2	12 7 7 2 28	Hebenton	Tamminen, Rollins
Indianapolis	0 2 0 1 3	7 20 11 4 42	Dion	Rochon, Leclerc, Maggs (OT 8:44)
Houston	3 1 3 - 7	14 6 10 - 30	Grahame	Mty Howe, Preston, Lund, Ruskowksi, Larway, Hansis, Gray
Cincinnati	0 2 1 - 3	16 17 5 - 38	Caron	Sobchuk, Carroll, Stoughton
March 8				
San Diego	0 0 0 - 0	12 11 10 - 33	Wakely, Lockett	▸ Daley: shutout (2), 33 saves
Winnipeg	2 2 1 - 5	11 12 13 - 36	Daley	Hedberg, Hull, Labraaten, Lindstrom, Nilsson
Edmonton	0 3 0 - 3	9 9 7 - 25	Levasseur	Flett, Ullman, Morris (3 goals in 0:53)
Houston	0 3 2 - 5	14 16 8 - 38	Rutledge	Gray, Preston, G. Howe, Ruskowski, Lund
Phoenix	1 1 0 - 2	7 8 11 - 26	Hebenton	Hughes, Tamminen Brackenbury
Quebec	3 1 5 - 9	10 19 15 - 44	Humphreys	Cloutier 3, C. Bordeleau, Baxter, Fitchner, Guite, P. Bordeleau,
March 9				
New England	1 0 2 0 3	15 7 6 1 29	Raeder	McKenzie, Rogers, D. Roberts
Birmingham	2 0 1 1 4	13 8 8 2 31	Garrett	Nedomansky, Stewart, Sheehy, Jacques (OT 1:27)
San Diego	0 1 2 - 3	12 15 16 - 43	Wakely	Morrison, Noris, Devine
Calgary	1 0 3 - 4	10 10 6 - 26	McLeod	Powis, Morrison, Morin, Lawson (WG 14:32)
Edmonton	2 1 0 - 3	9 8 1 - 18	Levasseur	Flett 2, Hamilton
Cincinnati	3 0 2 - 5	20 9 15 - 44	Caron	Sobchuk 2, Plumb, Hislop, Marsh
March 10				
Edmonton	2 2 0 - 4	6 13 5 - 24	Brod'ck, Levasseur	Russell, Callighen, Connelly, Flett
Indianapolis	1 1 1 - 3	15 11 14 - 40	Dion	Peacosh, Leclerc, MacDonald
March 11				
Cincinnati	0 0 0 - 0	10 10 11 - 31	Lapointe	▸ Grahame: shutout (4), 31 saves
Houston	1 2 2 - 5	7 13 9 - 29	Grahame	Tonelli 2, Gray 2, G. Howe
New England	3 0 0 - 3	7 4 6 - 17	Landon	Keon 2, Lyle
Birmingham	2 3 1 - 6	8 17 10 - 35	Garrett	Sheehy 2, Marrin, Hoganson, Nedomansky, Nistico
Calgary	0 0 1 - 1	5 6 13 - 24	Bromley	Driscoll (spoiled Daley's shutout at 16:49)
Winnipeg	0 1 3 - 4	11 10 13 - 34	Daley	Hedberg 2, Labraaten 2
March 12				
Phoenix	1 3 2 1 7	8 9 8 4 29	Hebenton	Hughes 3 (OT 2:42), Hobin 2, Mononen, Huston
San Diego	2 3 1 0 6	8 10 10 0 28	Lockett, Wakely	Burgess 2, Devine, Hornung, Noris, Lacroix
Edmonton	1 1 1 0 3	7 9 11 5 32	Levasseur	Kirk, Sather, Langevin
Quebec	1 1 1 0 3	13 10 15 8 46	Humphreys	Brackenbury, P. Bordeleau, Dube
Birmingham	0 1 1 - 2	6 7 8 - 21	Garrett	Lagace, Sheehy
Indianapolis	1 2 4 - 7	14 11 20 - 45	Dion	Paiement, Parizeau, Harbaruk, Peacosh, Thomas, Rochon, MacDonald
Calgary	2 0 0 - 2	11 9 9 - 29	McLeod, Bromley	Powis, Ketola
Cincinnati	2 3 4 - 9	15 7 16 - 38	Caron, Lapointe	Leduc, Sobchuk 2, Dudley 2, Larose, Marsh, Stoughton
March 13				
Birmingham	2 2 0 - 4	9 10 9 - 28	Garrett	Napier, Nedomansky, Henderson, Gorman
Cincinnati	2 3 2 - 7	12 20 16 - 48	Lapointe	Leduc 2, Dudley, Abgrall, Larose, Sobchuk, Carroll
New England	0 1 2 - 3	5 9 7 - 21	Landon	S. Carlson 2, Antonovich
Quebec	1 0 4 - 5	14 6 20 - 40	Humphreys	Cloutier 2, Tardif, Dorey, C. Bordeleau
Indianapolis	0 0 0 - 0	12 8 14 - 34	Hoganson	▸ Rutledge: shutout (3), 34 saves
Houston	2 2 1 - 5	13 9 3 - 25	Rutledge	G. Howe, McLeod, Connor, Preston, Gray
Edmonton	0 2 1 - 3	3 8 10 - 21	Broderick	Langevin, Callighen, Ullman
Winnipeg	2 5 2 - 9	13 10 12 - 35	Daley	Lindstrom 2, Hull, Nilsson, Hedberg, Huck, Sullivan, Ford, Miller
March 15				
Edmonton	0 0 0 - 0	11 6 7 - 24	Levasseur	▸ Daley: shutout (3), 24 saves
Winnipeg	3 4 0 - 7	18 12 10 - 40	Daley	Hedberg 3, Lawson 2, Huck, Long
Phoenix	2 1 1 0 4	8 5 5 3 21	Kurt	Hall, Liddington, Repo, Hughes
San Diego	1 1 2 0 4	9 12 6 3 30	Wakely	French 2 (TG 16:21), McNamee, Devine
Cincinnati	0 1 1 - 2	11 24 13 - 48	Lapointe	Stoughton, Sobchuk
Birmingham	3 1 0 - 4	14 11 10 - 35	Garrett	Napier 2, Jacques, Stewart
Quebec	3 0 0 - 3	10 3 8 - 21	Humphreys, Aubry	Dube, Cloutier, Fitchner
Houston	0 1 3 - 4	8 16 9 - 33	Grahame	Lukowich 2 (WG 4:53), McLeod, Mk Howe
Calgary	1 0 0 - 1	5 12 8 - 25	McLeod	Kryskow
Indianapolis	1 1 1 - 3	9 9 9 - 27	Hoganson	Leclerc 2, MacDonald

1976-1977 Game by Game Line Scores

Date & Teams	Scoring 1 2 3 ot F	Shots 1 2 3 ot F	Goaltenders	Goals & Other Scoring Highlights
March 16				
Calgary	1 0 2 - 3	6 6 10 - 22	Bromley	Morrison, Mayer, Miller
Cincinnati	1 0 3 - 4	8 7 15 - 30	Caron	Roy, Stoughton, Legge, Marsh
March 17				
Indianapolis	1 4 0 - 5	11 22 14 - 47	Dion	Rochon 2, Paiement, Maggs, Karlander
Birmingham	0 0 2 - 2	10 6 13 - 29	Garrett, Wood	Napier, Sheehy
Winnipeg	1 0 2 - 3	5 6 11 - 22	Daley	Sullivan, Labraaten, Lindh
Edmonton	2 0 2 - 4	12 8 8 - 28	Broderick	Kirk 2, Busniuk, Flett
Quebec	2 1 1 - 4	15 9 14 - 38	Aubry	Dube 2 (WG 14:28), Brackenbury, Tardif
Phoenix	0 2 1 - 3	3 9 11 - 23	Kurt	Hobin, Tamminen, Liddington
March 18				
Phoenix	0 2 1 - 3	5 10 8 - 23	Hebenton	Young, Tamminen, Rollins
Houston	1 4 1 - 6	17 15 13 - 45	Rutledge	G. Howe, Mty Howe, Lund, Connor, Taylor, McLeod
Calgary	0 1 0 - 1	8 13 6 - 27	McLeod	Powis
New England	2 1 0 - 3	9 16 10 - 35	Raeder	Lyle, J. Carlson, Keon
Winnipeg	4 2 1 - 7	13 9 9 - 31	Larsson	Hull 2, Hedberg 2, Labraaten, Lindh, Nilsson
Indianapolis	2 1 2 - 5	12 11 10 - 33	Dion	McDonald 3, Rochon, Thomas
Quebec	2 1 0 - 3	8 11 6 - 25	Brodeur	Cloutier 3
Cincinnati	1 4 2 - 7	13 13 14 - 40	Caron	Stoughton 2, Larose, Carroll, Leduc, Plumb, Marsh
March 19				
San Diego	2 1 2 - 5	17 11 10 - 38	Lockett	Burgess, Shmyr, Devine, Dobek, Lacroix
Phoenix	2 3 2 - 7	13 11 17 - 41	Kurt	Ftorek 2, Repo, Hobin, Hughes, Liddington, Hall
Calgary	0 0 0 - 0	14 11 10 - 35	McLeod, Bromley	▶ Brodeur: shutout (1), 35 saves
Quebec	1 4 3 - 8	10 15 14 - 39	Brodeur	Bernier 3, P. Bordeleau 2, Cloutier, C. Bordeleau, Dube
March 20				
Houston	1 1 6 - 8	11 16 17 - 44	Grahame	Lukowich 2, Preston 2, G. Howe 2, Gray, Connor
Indianapolis	2 1 0 - 3	14 9 8 - 31	Park	MacDonald, Sicinski, Stapleton
Phoenix	0 0 1 - 1	6 6 14 - 26	Hebenton	Tamminen
San Diego	2 3 1 - 6	13 9 6 - 28	Wakely	Lacroix, French, Noris, Veneruzzo, Ferguson, Shmyr
Calgary	0 0 0 - 0	12 7 8 - 27	McLeod, Bromley	▶ Raeder: shutout (1), 27 saves
New England	3 3 3 - 9	15 17 18 - 50	Raeder	McKenzie 3, Pleau, Lyle, Antonovich, Backstrom, Keon, Webster
Winnipeg	2 0 1 1 4	9 8 15 1 33	Daley	Hull, Lindstrom, Ford (TG 19:41), Nilsson (OT 0:35)
Birmingham	2 0 1 0 3	13 13 3 0 29	Garrett	Turkiewicz, Napier, Hoganson
March 22				
Houston	0 2 0 - 2	13 12 9 - 34	Rutledge	G. Howe, Preston
Quebec	0 3 3 - 6	11 10 12 - 33	Brodeur	Cloutier 2, Boudrias 2, Bernier, P. Bordeleau
Edmonton	1 1 1 - 3	11 9 9 - 29	Levasseur	Flett, St. Sauveur, Barrie
Winnipeg	3 2 3 - 8	11 9 11 - 31	Daley	Hedberg 2, Nilsson 2, Lawson 2, Hull, Lindstrom
Calgary	0 0 4 - 4	14 13 17 - 44	McLeod	Ketola, Powis, Deadmarsh, Kryskow
Birmingham	2 2 3 - 7	9 11 13 - 33	Wood	Napier 2, Gorman 2, Nistico, Jacques, Nedomansky
Cincinnati	0 1 0 - 1	9 9 14 - 32	Caron	Maxwell
Indianapolis	0 3 0 - 3	5 17 6 - 28	Hoganson	McDonald, MacDonald, Rochon
March 23				
Quebec	0 3 3 - 6	10 7 9 - 26	Brodeur, Aubry	Dube 2, Bernier 2, Dorey, Boudrias
Cincinnati	1 3 0 - 4	12 9 10 - 31	Caron	Larose, Stoughton, Sobchuk, Leduc
Birmingham	1 2 1 - 4	11 11 3 8 - 32	Garrett	Napier, Henderson, Nistico, Gorman
Phoenix	0 0 0 - 0	12 19 12 - 43	Hebenton	▶ Garrett: shutout (4), 43 saves
March 24				
Birmingham	1 0 1 - 2	10 7 8 - 25	Garrett, Wood	Napier, Stewart
San Diego	3 3 0 - 6	9 6 8 - 23	Lockett	Rhiness 2, Veneruzzo, Devine, Rivers, Lacroix
Quebec	1 0 2 - 3	4 9 7 - 20	Aubry, Brodeur	Boudrias, Guite, Cloutier
Indianapolis	1 0 3 - 4	12 15 7 - 34	Dion, Hoganson	Paiement 2 (WG 19:41), Peacosh, McDonald
Edmonton	3 1 1 - 5	8 8 9 - 25	Broderick	Flett 3, Sather, Morris
New England	1 2 1 - 4	15 16 6 - 37	Raeder. Ab'sson	Backstrom, J. Carlson, Lyle, Pleau
March 25				
Calgary	1 0 1 - 2	11 11 10 - 32	McLeod	Ketola, Driscoll
Houston	2 2 0 - 4	9 10 8 - 27	Grahame	Preston, Lukowich, Gray, Tonelli
Edmonton	0 2 1 1 4	13 15 6 4 38	Levaseur	St. Sauveur, Flett, Connelly, Patenaude (OT 6:10)
Cincinnati	0 2 1 0 3	5 14 14 5 38	Caron	Leduc, Dudley, Stoughton (TG 18:48)
San Diego	2 3 2 - 7	17 18 10 - 45	Wakely	Noris, Devine, Shmyr, Rivers, Morrison, Lacroix, Ferguson
Phoenix	1 1 1 - 3	8 19 12 - 39	Hebenton	Hall, Ftorek, Repo
March 26				
Indianapolis	0 3 1 - 4	17 10 8 - 35	Hoganson, Dion	Peacosh 2, Rochon, MacDonald
New England	1 0 1 - 2	11 8 15 - 34	Abrahamsson	Rogers, McKenzie
Cincinnati	0 2 4 - 6	8 8 8 - 24	Lapointe	Stoughton 2, Leduc 2, Plumb, Larose
Quebec	1 1 2 - 4	10 9 12 - 31	Brodeur, Aubry	Tardif 2, Brackenbury, Dube
Calgary	0 0 2 - 2	12 3 7 - 22	Bromley	Ward, Ketola
San Diego	1 0 3 - 4	6 9 8 - 23	Lockett	Devine 2, Lacroix, Rivers (Ward & Rivers goals 4 second apart, 3rd)
March 27				
Winnipeg	1 2 2 - 5	8 6 11 - 25	Daley	Hull 3, Sullivan, Hedberg
Houston	0 1 2 - 3	7 8 7 - 22	Rutledge	Lund 2, Tonelli
Indianapolis	2 0 1 - 3	7 5 12 - 24	Dion, Hoganson	Leclerc 2, Stapleton
Birmingham	4 0 3 - 7	16 12 10 - 38	Garrett	Gorman 2, Henderson, Nedomansky, Hoganson, Stewart, Marrin
Edmonton	0 0 2 - 2	13 12 16 - 41	Levasseur	Kirk, Patenaude
New England	1 1 3 - 5	10 15 12 - 37	Raeder	Webster 2, Antonovich, Ley, Rogers
Phoenix	3 0 1 - 4	10 5 9 - 24	Kurt	Mononen 2, Hughes, Ftorek
Calgary	1 2 2 - 5	12 14 12 - 38	McLeod	Powis 2 (WG 19:33), Morrison, Ward, Miller
Cincinnati	0 0 0 - 0	12 4 5 - 21	Lapointe	▶ Brodeur: shutout (2), 21 saves
Quebec	2 1 1 - 4	10 8 7 - 25	Brodeur	P. Bordeleau, Cloutier, Bernier, Dube

1976-1977 Game by Game Line Scores

Date & Teams	Scoring 1 2 3 ot F	Shots 1 2 3 ot F	Goaltenders	Goals & Other Scoring Highlights
March 29				
Phoenix	1 4 0 - 5	9 16 5 - 30	Hebenton	Popiel, Ftorek, Hall, Liddington, Repo
Calgary	3 2 4 - 9	12 7 9 - 28	McLeod	Driscoll 2, Ward 2, Deadmarsh 2, Morrison, Powis, Evans
Houston	3 0 2 - 5	9 8 10 - 27	Grahame	Preston 2, McLeod, Connor, Ruskowski
Winnipeg	1 1 0 - 2	5 9 8 - 22	Daley	Lesuk, Nilsson
Cincinnati	1 2 1 - 4	12 18 7 - 37	Caron	Leduc 2, Dudley, Stoughton
Birmingham	1 0 1 - 2	7 6 2 - 15	Garrett	Turkiewicz, Nedomansky
New England	3 2 0 - 5	13 11 7 - 31	Raeder	Keon, Pleau, Webster, McKenzie, Lyle
San Diego	1 2 1 - 4	5 7 12 - 24	Wakely, Lockett	Lacroix 2, French, Noris
March 30				
Houston	0 0 0 - 0	9 7 12 - 28	Rutledge	▸ Broderick: shutout (4), 28 saves
Edmonton	2 4 2 - 8	14 12 10 - 36	Broderick	St. Sauveur 2, Connelly 2, Patenaude 2, Hamilton, Callighen
Cincinnati	0 3 2 0 5	12 10 12 4 38	Lapointe	Stoughton 3, Dudley, Legge
Indianapolis	2 3 0 0 5	15 12 13 5 45	Hoganson	Peacosh 3, McDonald, Sicinski (Ind: led 5-0)
March 31				
Winnipeg	0 2 1 - 3	12 8 9 - 29	Daley	Hull 2, Sullivan
San Diego	0 2 2 - 4	10 9 9 - 28	Lockett	Noris 2 (WG 19:34), French, Rivers
New England	1 1 4 - 6	15 11 20 - 46	Abrahamsson	Antonovich 2, J. Carlson, Lyle, Rogers, Keon
Phoenix	1 1 0 - 2	9 7 11 - 27	Hebenton, Kurt	Hobin 2
April 1				
Calgary	1 0 2 - 3	8 12 14 - 34	McLeod	Terbenche, Micheletti (WG 18:14), Powis
Edmonton	1 0 0 - 1	8 10 8 - 26	Broderick	Callighen
Cincinnati	1 0 3 - 4	7 14 6 - 27	Caron	Marsh 3, Carroll
Houston	1 3 1 - 5	11 7 6 - 24	Grahame	Lukowich, McLeod, Mty Howe, Preston, Lund
April 2				
Winnipeg	2 3 1 - 6	12 15 15 - 42	Larsson	Hull 2, Nilsson, Lawson, Sullivan, Hedberg
Birmingham	3 1 1 - 5	12 13 13 - 38	Wood	Napier, Jacques, Sheehy, Nistico, Nedomansky
Cincinnati	2 1 0 - 3	14 4 8 - 26	Lapointe, Caron	Dudley 2, Sobchuk
San Diego	3 1 2 - 6	8 7 7 - 22	Wakely	Noris 2, Ferguson 2, Cassolato, Rivers
Quebec	2 0 3 1 6	14 12 14 3 43	Humphreys	P. Bordeleau 2, Boudrias, Baxter, Cloutier, Fitchner (OT 2:03)
Phoenix	1 1 3 0 5	10 15 9 3 37	Kurt, Hebenton	Liddington 2, Huston, Ftorek, Hobin
New England	0 1 1 1 3	5 11 8 3 27	Raeder	Selwood, G. Roberts (TG 19:58), Rogers (OT 0:15)
Indianapolis	1 1 0 0 2	7 6 10 0 23	Dion	McDonald, Peacosh
Edmonton	2 2 0 - 4	7 12 5 4 28	Levasseur	Patenaude 2, Connelly, Busniuk
Calgary	1 1 2 0 4	9 11 17 6 43	McLeod	Micheletti 2 (TG 19:43), Ward, Deadmarsh
April 3				
Calgary	0 1 3 - 4	7 6 13 - 26	McLeod	Kryskow, Chipperfield, Deadmarsh, Miller
Winnipeg	2 2 2 - 6	10 8 9 - 27	Daley	Hedberg 2, Hull, Lindstrom, Long, Ford
Quebec	0 0 0 - 0	4 7 5 - 16	Humphreys	▸ Lockett: shutout (1), 16 saves
San Diego	1 4 2 - 7	10 8 7 - 25	Lockett	Noris 2, Sentes, Rivers, Ferguson, Rhiness, Devine
Indianapolis	0 2 5 - 7	10 12 14 - 36	Dion	Paiement 3, Leclerc, Sicinski, Parizeau, McDonald
Houston	1 2 0 - 3	7 13 7 - 27	Rutledge	Connor, Ruskowski, Lund
April 4				
Winnipeg	0 1 1 - 2	10 6 10 - 26	Larsson	Hull, Dunn
Edmonton	1 3 2 - 6	17 7 14 - 38	Broderick	Rota 2, Flett, Sather, St. Sauveur, Callighen
April 5				
San Diego	0 0 1 - 1	5 10 7 - 22	Wakely	Noris (spoiled Grahame's shutout at 18:57)
Houston	1 1 1 - 3	8 7 15 - 30	Grahame	Lukowich 2, Connor
Birmingham	1 0 3 0 4	6 5 10 5 26	Garrett	Henderson 2, Napier, Marrin (TG 19:29)
Calgary	3 1 0 0 4	15 6 10 9 40	McLeod	Morrison 2, Evans, Chipperfield
New England	1 0 1 - 2	7 4 9 - 20	Landon, Ab'sson	Swain, Hangsleben
Quebec	0 4 3 - 7	14 20 12 - 46	Brodeur	Bernier 2, Dorey 2, P. Bordeleau, Cloutier, Dube
April 6				
Indianapolis	0 2 1 - 3	10 11 14 - 35	Hoganson	Maggs, Sicinski, Rochon
Phoenix	2 2 3 - 7	12 15 16 - 43	Hebenton	Mononen 3, Tamminen, Liddington, Hobin, Hughes
Birmingham	1 3 0 - 4	4 9 10 - 23	Garrett	Nedomansky 2, Nistico, Jacques
Edmonton	3 0 3 - 6	13 8 23 - 44	Broderick	Flett 3 (all in 3rd period), Morris 2, Sather
Houston	2 0 3 - 5	9 10 8 - 27	Rutledge	Mk Howe 2, Preston, Ruskowski, Mty Howe
San Diego	1 2 0 - 3	6 15 6 - 27	Lockett	Hughes, French, Devine
Quebec	1 0 1 0 2	10 6 11 7 34	Brodeur	Dube, Fitchner (TG 18:08)
Cincinnati	0 1 1 0 2	9 12 6 6 33	Caron	Sobchuk
April 7				
Winnipeg	3 2 1 - 6	10 16 10 - 36	Larsson	Hedberg, Hull, Nilsson, Lawson, Long, Lindstrom
Calgary	1 2 1 - 4	10 14 9 - 33	McLeod	Deadmarsh, Driscoll, Chipperfield, Tannahill

End of Regular Season

1977 Playoffs Game by Game Line Scores

Date & Teams	Scoring 1 2 3 ot F	Shots 1 2 3 ot F	Goaltenders	Goals & Other Scoring Highlights
April 9				
New England	0 2 0 - 2	6 7 7 - 20	Landon	G. Roberts, Webster
Quebec	2 0 3 - 5	7 6 8 - 21	Brodeur	Weir, Boudrias, Lacombe, Guite, Cloutier
Indianapolis	1 1 1 0 0 1 4	12 10 5 8 12 5 52	Hoganson	Lomenda 2, Thomas, Peacosh (3rd OT, 8:40)
Cincinnati	1 1 1 0 0 0 3	9 15 13 8 11 3 59	Lapointe	Leduc, Abgrall, Larose
April 10				
San Diego	0 0 1 - 1	11 6 10 - 27	Lockett	Adduono
Winnipeg	2 2 1 - 5	13 20 6 - 39	Daley	Hull 2, Hedberg, Lawson, Lindstrom
April 12				
Indianapolis	3 2 2 - 7	7 14 10 - 31	Dion	Thomas 2, Lomenda, Leclerc, Harbaruk, Parizeau, MacDonald
Cincinnati	0 1 1 - 2	14 10 8 - 32	Caron, Lapointe	Abgrall, Plumb
Quebec	2 3 2 - 7	12 7 9 - 28	Brodeur	Cloutier 2, Tremblay, P. Bordeleau, S. Bernier, Brackenbury, Guite
New England	1 0 2 - 3	8 11 15 - 34	Raeder	Keon 2, McKenzie
San Diego	1 0 0 - 1	11 5 4 - 20	Lockett	Ferguson
Winnipeg	1 0 3 - 4	5 12 14 - 31	Daley	Hull 2, Dun, Miller
April 13				
Edmonton	1 1 1 0 3	8 5 8 6 27	Levasseur	Boddy, Rota, Sather
Houston	0 2 1 1 4	11 8 14 12 45	Grahame	Preston, Lund, Taylor, Lukowich (OT 13:11)
April 14				
Cincinnati	1 0 2 - 3	14 4 15 - 33	Lapointe	Marsh 2, Larose
Indianapolis	2 1 2 - 5	6 9 8 - 23	Hoganson	MacDonald 3, McDonald 2
Quebec	1 2 0 1 4	11 13 8 4 36	Brodeur	S. Bernier 2, P. Bordeleau, Baxter (OT 1:50)
New England	1 1 1 0 3	13 18 7 0 38	Abrahamsson	G. Roberts, Antonovich, McKenzie
April 15				
Edmonton	0 1 1 - 2	6 8 10 - 24	Levasseur	Callighen 2
Houston	1 3 2 - 6	9 12 8 - 29	Grahame	Larway, McLeod, Mty Howe, Preston, Ruskowski, Connor
April 16				
Cincinnati	0 0 1 - 1	7 13 6 - 26	Lapointe	Carroll
Indianapolis	1 1 1 - 3	8 5 11 - 24	Dion	Thomas, McDonald, Karlander
Quebec	2 0 2 - 4	10 9 14 - 33	Brodeur, Aubry	Cloutier 2, Fitchner
New England	3 1 2 - 6	10 8 13 - 31	Landon	Keon, J. Carlson, Pleau, Rogers, Lyle, Antonovich
Winnipeg	3 1 0 - 4	8 10 10 - 28	Daley	Moffat 2, Sullivan, Lindstrom
San Diego	0 2 3 - 5	9 10 14 - 33	Lockett	Noris, Lacroix, Burgess, Rivers, Sentes (WG 13:46)
April 17				
Houston	1 1 0 - 2	7 12 8 - 27	Grahame	G. Howe, Mk Howe
Edmonton	3 2 2 - 7	14 17 9 - 40	Broderick	Callighen 2, Campbell 2, Langevin, Kirk, Rota
Winnipeg	1 3 0 - 4	9 13 5 - 27	Daley	Lawson, Guindon, Hull, Labraaten
San Diego	3 1 2 - 6	11 12 4 - 27	Wakely	Sentes 2, Burgess, Adduono, Ferguson, Devine
April 19				
New England	0 0 0 - 0	5 6 8 - 19	Landon, Ab'sson	▶ Brodeur: shutout (1), 19 saves
Quebec	1 1 1 - 3	12 14 10 - 36	Brodeur	Boudrias, S. Bernier, Fitchner
April 20				
Houston	2 1 1 - 4	7 8 12 - 27	Rutledge	Lukowich 3, Taylor
Edmonton	1 0 0 - 1	14 9 11 - 34	Broderick	St. Sauveur
San Diego	0 0 0 - 0	14 4 7 - 25	Lockett	▶ Daley: shutout (1), 25 saves
Winnipeg	1 0 2 - 3	12 12 17 - 41	Daley	Lindh 2, Lindstrom
April 22				
Edmonton	1 2 0 - 3	9 8 3 - 20	Broderick	Campbell, Langevin, Rota
Houston	2 1 1 - 4	15 6 7 - 28	Rutledge	Preston, Taylor, G. Howe, Hansis (WG 0:32)
Winnipeg	0 1 0 - 1	2 6 7 - 15	Daley	Hedberg
San Diego	0 3 0 - 3	11 10 9 - 30	Wakely	Morrison, Sentes, French
April 23				
Indianapolis	0 1 0 - 1	7 11 3 - 21	Hoganson	Parizeau
Quebec	0 3 0 - 3	18 12 7 - 37	Brodeur	S. Bernier 2, Baxter
April 24				
San Diego	1 1 1 - 3	8 11 12 - 31	Lockett	Adduono, Noris, French
Winnipeg	3 1 3 - 7	19 8 13 - 40	Daley	Hull 2, Hedberg 2, Guindon, Nilsson, Dunn
April 25				
Indianapolis	1 1 1 - 3	10 7 8 - 25	Dion	McDonald, Stapleton, Thomas
Quebec	2 4 2 - 8	10 17 10 - 37	Brodeur	Sutherland 2, Coutier, Tardif, Lacombe, S. Bernier, Weir, Dube
April 26				
Winnipeg	2 0 1 1 4	9 8 4 5 26	Daley	Sullivan 2 (OT 8:05), Hedberg, Nilsson
Houston	1 2 0 0 3	15 13 8 2 38	Grahame	Mty Howe, Tonelli, Ruskowski
April 28				
Winnipeg	1 1 0 - 2	9 4 10 - 23	Daley, Larsson	Green, Hedberg
Houston	1 5 1 - 7	21 11 6 - 38	Grahame	Mk Howe 3, G. Howe 2, Lund, Schella
Quebec	1 4 0 1 6	9 19 11 6 45	Brodeur	P. Bordeleau 3 (OT 5:29), Boudrias, Tardif, S. Bernier
Indianapolis	3 1 1 0 5	14 11 10 2 37	Dion	Thomas 2, Peacosh 2, Karlander
April 30				
Houston	1 1 1 - 3	9 8 8 - 25	Grahame	Ruskowski, Tonelli, G. Howe
Winnipeg	1 2 1 - 4	12 10 16 - 38	Daley	Sullivan 2 (WG 18:24), Hull, Dunn
Quebec	0 0 0 - 0	4 10 8 - 22	Brodeur	▶ Hoganson: shutout (1), 22 saves
Indianapolis	0 1 1 - 2	8 15 3 - 26	Hoganson	Parizeau, Maggs

1977 Playoffs Game by Game Line Scores

Date & Teams	Scoring 1 2 3 ot F	Shots 1 2 3 ot F	Goaltenders	Goals & Other Scoring Highlights
May 1				
Houston	0 3 1 - 4	11 10 12 - 33	Grahame	Lukowich 2, Connor, Mty Howe
Winnipeg	2 3 1 - 6	7 16 8 - 31	Daley	Hedberg 3, Nilsson, Labraaten, Dunn
May 2				
Indianapolis	1 0 2 - 3	5 11 17 - 33	Hoganson	MacDonald 2, Stapleton
Quebec	3 2 3 - 8	8 10 10 - 28	Brodeur	Cloutier 3, P. Bordeleau 2, S. Bernier, Lacombe, Dube
May 3				
Winnipeg	0 1 1 - 2	8 7 4 - 19	Daley	Ford, Miller
Houston	0 2 1 - 3	7 7 10 - 24	Grahame	Ruskowski 2, Taylor (WG 6:01)
May 5				
Houston	0 1 2 - 3	11 3 10 - 24	Grahame	Ruskowski, Connor, Tonelli
Winnipeg	1 3 2 - 6	10 11 16 - 37	Daley	Lindstrom 2, Long, Lesuk, Hull, Hedberg
May 11				
Winnipeg	0 2 0 - 2	12 6 9 - 27	Daley	Labraaten, Lindstrom
Quebec	0 0 1 - 1	6 17 9 - 32	Brodeur	P. Bordeleau
May 15				
Winnipeg	0 0 1 - 1	5 15 7 - 27	Daley	Labraaten
Quebec	4 1 1 - 6	9 12 13 - 34	Brodeur	Sutherland 2, Guite, P. Bordeleau, S. Bernier, Brackenbury
May 18				
Quebec	1 0 0 - 1	8 8 8 - 24	Brodeur	Brackenbury
Winnipeg	0 2 4 - 6	5 8 8 - 21	Daley	Lindstrom 2, Labraaten, Hedberg, Nilsson, Lesuk
May 20				
Quebec	1 2 1 - 4	11 9 7 - 27	Brodeur, Aubry	S. Bernier 2, Lacombe, Tardif
Winnipeg	2 0 0 - 2	9 8 12 - 29	Daley	Miller, Nilsson
May 22				
Winnipeg	1 2 0 - 3	8 7 7 - 22	Daley	Nilsson, Ford, Hull
Quebec	4 3 1 - 8	14 9 9 - 32	Brodeur	Cloutier 2, C. Bordeleau 2, P. Bordeleau 2, Guite, S. Bernier
May 24				
Quebec	3 0 0 - 3	7 9 8 - 24	Brodeur, Aubry	Cloutier 2, C. Bordeleau
Winnipeg	4 4 4 - 12	11 17 14 - 42	Daley	Hull 3, Guindon 2, Hedberg 2, Sullivan 2, Labraaten, Ford, Lindstrom
May 26				
Winnipeg	0 1 1 - 2	2 8 7 - 17	Daley	Labraaten, Miller
Quebec	0 6 2 - 8	7 11 6 - 24	Brodeur	Fitchner, Tardif, Cloutier, Tremblay, Dube, P. Bordeleau, C. Bordeleau, S. Bernier

Quebec is League Champion

Waving the White Towel

The third game of the 1977 Western Division Semifinals between Winnipeg and San Diego – and the first game of the series to be played at the San Diego Sports Arena – went perfectly ... except ...

... the goal lights did not work. Instead of the familiar red light when a goal was scored, goal judges were given white towels to wave in the event of a goal ...

... and the game clock also failed. The task of keeping time fell to two minor game officials who kept track of time and stoppages using a stopwatch. Winnipeg's Rudy Pilous was an observer, in order to avoid any possible hometown advantage.

Whatever gremlin had gotten into the goal lights and game clock then went for the main arena lights, causing a twenty-minute outage. Somehow, the game was played in its entirely, San Diego winning 5-4.

1976-1977 BIRMINGHAM BULLS

Coach
Gilles Leger
7-16-1

Coach
Pat Kelly
24-30-3

Summary of Games (@ Away, * Overtime)

	date	opponent	score		record	pts	gf-ga
1.	Oct 8	Houston	4-2	W	1-0-0	2	4-2
2.	Oct 10 @	Quebec	*3-4	L	1-1-0	2	7-6
3.	Oct 12	Calgary	6-2	W	2-1-0	4	13-8
4.	Oct 14	Cincinnati	7-7	T	2-1-1	5	20-15
5.	Oct 16 @	Houston	0-3	L	2-2-1	5	20-18
6.	Oct 17 @	Minnesota	1-6	L	2-3-1	5	21-24
7.	Oct 19	Quebec	*5-6	L	2-4-1	5	26-30
8.	Oct 21	Houston	8-5	W	3-4-1	7	34-35
9.	Oct 23 @	Indianapolis	3-1	W	4-4-1	9	37-36
10.	Oct 24 @	Winnipeg	1-7	L	4-5-1	9	38-43
11.	Oct 26 @	Calgary	3-9	L	4-6-1	9	41-52
12.	Oct 28	Edmonton	*3-4	L	4-7-1	9	44-56
13.	Oct 30 @	New England	4-5	L	4-8-1	9	48-61
14.	Nov 2	San Diego	*3-4	L	4-9-1	9	51-65
15.	Nov 4	Phoenix	5-3	W	5-9-1	11	56-68
16.	Nov 6 @	Quebec	5-6	L	5-10-1	11	61-74
17.	Nov 9 @	Quebec	3-4	L	5-11-1	11	64-78
18.	Nov 11	San Diego	2-3	L	5-12-1	11	66-81
19.	Nov 13	Edmonton	2-3	L	5-13-1	11	68-84
20.	Nov 16	New England	4-5	L	5-14-1	11	72-89
21.	Nov 17 @	New England	4-6	L	5-15-1	11	76-95
22.	Nov 19 @	Indianapolis	0-4	L	5-16-1	11	76-99
23.	Nov 21	San Diego	4-3	W	6-16-1	13	80-102
24.	Nov 23	Calgary	3-1	W	7-16-1	15	83-103
25.	Nov 25	New England	3-5	L	7-17-1	15	86-108
26.	Nov 27 @	Cincinnati	1-2	L	7-18-1	15	87-110
27.	Nov 28	Minnesota	1-3	L	7-19-1	15	88-113
28.	Nov 30	Cincinnati	3-1	W	8-19-1	17	91-114
29.	Dec 2	Edmonton	3-4	L	8-20-1	17	94-118
30.	Dec 7	Indianapolis	*2-3	L	8-21-1	17	96-121
31.	Dec 10 @	Winnipeg	5-3	W	9-21-1	19	101-124
32.	Dec 12 @	Edmonton	3-5	L	9-22-1	19	104-129
33.	Dec 15 @	Phoenix	5-6	L	9-23-1	19	109-135
34.	Dec 17 @	Houston	4-3	W	10-23-1	21	113-138
35.	Dec 18 @	New England	2-6	L	10-24-1	21	115-144
36.	Dec 19 @	Indianapolis	*2-3	L	10-25-1	21	117-147
37.	Dec 21	Quebec	3-2	W	11-25-1	23	120-149
38.	Dec 22 @	Cincinnati	6-2	W	12-25-1	25	126-151
39.	Dec 26	Houston	6-2	W	13-25-1	27	132-153
40.	Dec 30	Minnesota	2-4	L	13-26-1	27	134-157
41.	Jan 2 @	Minnesota	1-3	L	13-27-1	27	135-160
42.	Jan 4	Phoenix	8-5	W	14-27-1	29	143-165
43.	Jan 7 @	Cincinnati	1-7	L	14-28-1	29	144-172
44.	Jan 9 @	Winnipeg	1-4	L	14-29-1	29	145-176
45.	Jan 12 @	Minnesota	4-3	W	15-29-1	31	149-179
46.	Jan 14 @	Houston	3-5	L	15-30-1	31	152-184
47.	Jan 16 @	San Diego	2-5	L	15-31-1	31	154-189
48.	Jan 21 @	Houston	1-6	L	15-32-1	31	155-195
49.	Jan 23	Indianapolis	6-2	W	16-32-1	33	161-197
50.	Jan 27	Winnipeg	3-0	W	17-32-1	35	164-197
51.	Jan 30	Cincinnati	7-1	W	18-32-1	37	171-198
52.	Feb 1	New England	4-3	W	19-32-1	39	175-201
53.	Feb 2 @	Cincinnati	3-2	W	20-32-1	41	178-203
54.	Feb 4	Quebec	7-0	W	21-32-1	43	185-203
55.	Feb 5 @	Indianapolis	2-5	L	21-33-1	43	187-208
56.	Feb 9 @	Phoenix	3-4	L	21-34-1	43	190-212
57.	Feb 12 @	San Diego	*2-3	L	21-35-1	43	192-215
58.	Feb 16	Phoenix	7-2	W	22-35-1	45	199-217
59.	Feb 18 @	New England	3-2	W	23-35-1	47	202-219
60.	Feb 20	Indianapolis	2-2	T	23-35-2	48	204-221
61.	Feb 22	Cincinnati	4-4	T	23-35-3	49	208-225
62.	Feb 24	Quebec	10-6	W	24-35-3	51	218-231
63.	Feb 26 @	Quebec	3-5	L	24-36-3	51	221-236
64.	Feb 27 @	Edmonton	4-0	W	25-36-3	53	225-236
65.	Mar 3 @	Calgary	2-4	L	25-37-3	53	227-240
66.	Mar 6 @	Edmonton	2-5	L	25-38-3	53	229-245
67.	Mar 9	New England	*4-3	W	26-38-3	55	233-248
68.	Mar 11	New England	6-3	W	27-38-3	57	239-251
69.	Mar 12 @	Indianapolis	2-7	L	27-39-3	57	241-258
70.	Mar 13 @	Cincinnati	4-7	L	27-40-3	57	245-265
71.	Mar 15	Cincinnati	4-2	W	28-40-3	59	249-267
72.	Mar 17	Indianapolis	2-5	L	28-41-3	59	251-272
73.	Mar 20	Winnipeg	3-4	L	28-42-3	59	254-276
74.	Mar 22	Calgary	7-4	W	29-42-3	61	261-280
75.	Mar 23 @	Phoenix	4-0	W	30-42-3	63	265-280
76.	Mar 24 @	San Diego	2-6	L	30-43-3	63	267-286
77.	Mar 27	Indianapolis	7-3	W	31-43-3	65	274-289
78.	Mar 29	Cincinnati	2-4	L	31-44-3	65	276-293
79.	Apr 2	Winnipeg	5-6	L	31-45-3	65	281-299
80.	Apr 5 @	Calgary	4-4	T	31-45-4	66	285-303
81.	Apr 6 @	Edmonton	4-6	L	31-46-4	66	289-309

Bulls Stars of 1976-1977

John Garrett
24 wins, 4 shutouts

Mark Napier
60 goals

Peter Marrin
23 goals, 60 points

J.C. Stewart
41 points, +11

Lou Nistico
56 points

Vaclav Nedomansky
36 goals

Scoring

pos	#	player	gp	g	a	pts	pim	+/-	ppg	shg	sog	sc%	gp	g	a	pts	pim	+/-
						Regular Season										Playoffs		
D	21	Ball, Terry	23	1	6	7	8	+2	0	0	33	0.030	-	-	-	-	-	-
LW	8	Bilodeau, Gilles	34	2	6	8	133	+1	0	0	10	0.200	-	-	-	-	-	-
LW	12	Carleton, Wayne	3	1	0	1	0	-2	0	0	4	0.250	-	-	-	-	-	-
D	3	Cunningham, Rick	63	0	8	8	75	-18	0	0	90	0.000	-	-	-	-	-	-
C	8	Farda, Richard	48	9	26	35	2	-23	1	0	76	0.118	-	-	-	-	-	-
D	5	Folco, Peter	2	0	0	0	0	-3	0	0	1	0.000	-	-	-	-	-	-
LW	23	Gallant, Gord	34	4	13	17	62	+8	1	0	50	0.080	-	-	-	-	-	-
G	35	Garrett, John	65	0	3	3	21		0	0	0	-	-	-	-	-	-	-
RW	18	Gorman, David	52	9	13	22	38	+2	0	1	62	0.145	-	-	-	-	-	-
D		Hart, Dick	4	0	0	0	0	+1	0	0	0	-	-	-	-	-	-	-
D	22	Heaver, Paul	5	0	0	0	0	0	0	0	1	0.000	-	-	-	-	-	-
LW	19	Henderson, Paul	81	23	25	48	30	-9	1	0	176	0.131	-	-	-	-	-	-
D	33	Hoganson, Dale	81	7	48	55	48	+1	3	0	129	0.054	-	-	-	-	-	-
C	25	Jacques, Jeff	79	21	27	48	92	-1	1	0	139	0.151	-	-	-	-	-	-
C	11	Kirk, Gavin	29	9	18	27	34	-6	5	0	46	0.196	-	-	-	-	-	-
D	4	Kokkola, Keith	5	0	0	0	21	-3	0	0	1	0.000	-	-	-	-	-	-
LW	26	Lagace, Jean-Guy	78	2	25	27	110	-8	0	0	78	0.026	-	-	-	-	-	-
RW	27	Mahovlich, Frank	17	3	20	23	12	-1	2	0	45	0.067	-	-	-	-	-	-
C	20	Marrin, Peter	79	23	37	60	36	-7	4	1	148	0.156	-	-	-	-	-	-
D		Marsh, Jim	1	0	0	0	0	-3	0	0	0	-	-	-	-	-	-	-
D	4	McKay, Ray	19	0	1	1	11	-5	0	0	7	0.000	-	-	-	-	-	-
RW	9	Napier, Mark	80	60	36	96	24	+16	9	1	254	0.236	-	-	-	-	-	-
RW	14	Nedomansky, Vaclav	81	36	33	69	10	-13	9	0	306	0.118	-	-	-	-	-	-
C	15	Nistico, Lou	79	20	36	56	166	-9	1	1	200	0.100	-	-	-	-	-	-
C	28	Phaneuf, Jean	30	2	7	9	2	-4	0	0	43	0.047	-	-	-	-	-	-
D	10	Rollins, Jerry	8	0	0	0	17	-2	0	0	7	0.000	-	-	-	-	-	-
LW		Schneider, Buzz	4	0	0	0	2	-2	0	0	0	-	-	-	-	-	-	-
RW	16	Sheehy, Tim	50	26	21	47	44	-2	7	0	177	0.147	-	-	-	-	-	-
RW	12	Simpson, Tom	25	7	6	13	11	-12	4	0	62	0.113	-	-	-	-	-	-
LW	18	Stewart, John A.	1	0	0	0	0	0	0	0	2	0.000	-	-	-	-	-	-
C	18	Stewart, John C.	52	17	24	41	33	+11	2	0	91	0.187	-	-	-	-	-	-
D	10	Syvret, Dave	8	0	0	0	0	-4	0	0	10	0.000	-	-	-	-	-	-
D	2	Turkiewicz, Jim	80	6	25	31	54	+5	0	2	90	0.067	-	-	-	-	-	-
D	6	Westrum, Pat	34	1	11	12	48	+8	0	0	24	0.042	-	-	-	-	-	-
G	1	Wood, Wayne	23	0	0	0	0		0	0	0	-	-	-	-	-	-	-

Power Play: 50 goals scored in 261 opportunities (19.2%) with 7 short-handed goals allowed.
Penalty Killing: 54 goals allowed in 231 opportunities (76.6%) with 6 short-handed goals scored.

Goaltending

goaltender	gp	min	ga	en	so	record	gaa	sog	sv%	gp	min	ga	record	gaa
Garrett, John	65	3803	224	4	4	24-34-4	3.53	2218	0.899	-	-	-	-	-
Wood, Wayne	23	1132	78	3	0	7-12-0	4.13	667	0.883	-	-	-	-	-

Transactions: Dale Hoganson acquired from Quebec for future considerations (Jim Dorey), Jun 1976 • Jean-Guy Lagace signed to contract, Aug 1976 • Terry Ball claimed on waivers, Oct 1976 • Jerry Rollins traded to Phoenix for Dave Gorman, Nov 1976 • Gavin Kirk and Tom Simpson traded to Edmonton for Tim Sheehy, Dec 1976 • Peter Folco sold to Philadelphia (NAHL), Dec 1976 • Gord Gallant, Ray McKay, John A. Stewart and Pat Westrum signed from defunct Minnesota, Jan 1977 • Wayne Carleton signed to contract, Jan 1977

1976-1977 CALGARY COWBOYS

Coach
Joe Crozier

Summary of Games (@ Away, * Overtime)

#	date	opponent	score		record	pts	gf-ga
1.	Oct 8	@ Winnipeg	1-4	L	0-1-0	0	1-4
2.	Oct 9	@ Quebec	2-5	L	0-2-0	0	3-9
3.	Oct 12	@ Birmingham	2-6	L	0-3-0	0	5-15
4.	Oct 13	@ Houston	1-2	L	0-4-0	0	6-17
5.	Oct 16	@ San Diego	2-4	L	0-5-0	0	8-21
6.	Oct 21	Quebec	2-4	L	0-6-0	0	10-25
7.	Oct 22	@ Minnesota	2-2	T	0-6-1	1	12-27
8.	Oct 24	San Diego	6-0	W	1-6-1	3	18-27
9.	Oct 26	Birmingham	9-3	W	2-6-1	5	27-30
10.	Oct 30	Houston	6-4	W	3-6-1	7	33-34
11.	Nov 2	Minnesota	4-3	W	4-6-1	9	37-37
12.	Nov 4	Edmonton	4-2	W	5-6-1	11	41-39
13.	Nov 7	New England	4-2	W	6-6-1	13	45-41
14.	Nov 11	Winnipeg	7-5	W	7-6-1	15	52-46
15.	Nov 14	Winnipeg	0-2	L	7-7-1	15	52-48
16.	Nov 16	@ Houston	2-4	L	7-8-1	15	54-52
17.	Nov 18	@ Phoenix	*2-1	W	8-8-1	17	56-53
18.	Nov 19	Quebec	4-1	W	9-8-1	19	60-54
19.	Nov 21	@ Minnesota	1-5	L	9-9-1	19	61-59
20.	Nov 23	@ Birmingham	1-3	L	9-10-1	19	62-62
21.	Nov 24	@ Phoenix	3-3	T	9-10-2	20	65-65
22.	Nov 27	San Diego	0-2	L	9-11-2	20	65-67
23.	Dec 1	@ New England	4-8	L	9-12-2	20	69-75
24.	Dec 2	@ Indianapolis	1-2	L	9-13-2	20	70-77
25.	Dec 3	@ Cincinnati	4-6	L	9-14-2	20	74-83
26.	Dec 5	Phoenix	6-0	W	10-14-2	22	80-83
27.	Dec 8	Winnipeg	2-4	L	10-15-2	22	82-87
28.	Dec 10	@ Minnesota	2-4	L	10-16-2	22	84-91
29.	Dec 11	Edmonton	3-0	W	11-16-2	24	87-91
30.	Dec 18	Quebec	4-2	W	12-16-2	26	91-93
31.	Dec 21	@ Edmonton	1-4	L	12-17-2	26	92-97
32.	Dec 23	Minnesota	2-1	W	13-17-2	28	94-98
33.	Dec 26	Cincinnati	6-3	W	14-17-2	30	100-101
34.	Jan 1	Edmonton	5-1	W	15-17-2	32	105-102
35.	Jan 5	Houston	3-4	L	15-18-2	32	108-106
36.	Jan 7	@ Edmonton	1-4	L	15-19-2	32	109-110
37.	Jan 8	Indianapolis	4-3	W	16-19-2	34	113-113
38.	Jan 11	Indianapolis	*3-4	L	16-20-2	34	116-117
39.	Jan 14	Winnipeg	3-5	L	16-21-2	34	119-122
40.	Jan 15	@ San Diego	5-3	W	17-21-2	36	124-125
41.	Jan 16	@ Phoenix	5-4	W	18-21-2	38	129-129
42.	Jan 21	@ Indianapolis	1-1	T	18-21-3	39	130-130
43.	Jan 22	@ Quebec	3-5	L	18-22-3	39	133-135
44.	Jan 23	@ Winnipeg	5-10	L	18-23-3	39	138-145
45.	Jan 25	Phoenix	7-3	W	19-23-3	41	145-148
46.	Jan 29	Houston	4-6	L	19-24-3	41	149-154
47.	Jan 30	@ Edmonton	1-1	T	19-24-4	42	150-155
48.	Feb 1	@ Houston	1-6	L	19-25-4	42	151-161
49.	Feb 2	@ San Diego	4-6	L	19-26-4	42	155-167
50.	Feb 5	@ Phoenix	4-1	W	20-26-4	44	159-168
51.	Feb 6	@ Winnipeg	4-6	L	20-27-4	44	163-174
52.	Feb 11	Edmonton	3-1	W	21-27-4	46	166-175
53.	Feb 13	@ Edmonton	2-5	L	21-28-4	46	168-180
54.	Feb 15	@ Winnipeg	2-2	T	21-28-5	47	170-182
55.	Feb 16	Cincinnati	3-7	L	21-29-5	47	173-189
56.	Feb 18	Cincinnati	5-3	W	22-29-5	49	178-192
57.	Feb 20	New England	0-5	L	22-30-5	49	178-197
58.	Feb 23	Houston	3-2	W	23-30-5	51	181-199
59.	Feb 25	New England	2-3	L	23-31-5	51	183-202
60.	Feb 27	Indianapolis	2-1	W	24-31-5	53	185-203
61.	Mar 1	Winnipeg	6-1	W	25-31-5	55	191-204
62.	Mar 3	Birmingham	4-2	W	26-31-5	57	195-206
63.	Mar 6	San Diego	4-2	W	27-31-5	59	199-208
64.	Mar 9	San Diego	4-3	W	28-31-5	61	203-211
65.	Mar 11	@ Winnipeg	1-4	L	28-32-5	61	204-215
66.	Mar 12	@ Cincinnati	2-9	L	28-33-5	61	206-224
67.	Mar 15	@ Indianapolis	1-3	L	28-34-5	61	207-227
68.	Mar 16	@ Cincinnati	3-4	L	28-35-5	61	210-231
69.	Mar 18	@ New England	1-3	L	28-36-5	61	211-234
70.	Mar 19	@ Quebec	0-8	L	28-37-5	61	211-242
71.	Mar 20	@ New England	0-9	L	28-38-5	61	211-251
72.	Mar 22	@ Birmingham	4-7	L	28-39-5	61	215-258
73.	Mar 25	@ Houston	2-4	L	28-40-5	61	217-262
74.	Mar 26	@ San Diego	2-4	L	28-41-5	61	219-266
75.	Mar 27	Phoenix	5-4	W	29-41-5	63	224-270
76.	Mar 29	Phoenix	9-5	W	30-41-5	65	233-275
77.	Apr 1	@ Edmonton	3-1	W	31-41-5	67	236-276
78.	Apr 2	Edmonton	4-4	T	31-41-6	68	240-280
79.	Apr 3	@ Winnipeg	4-6	L	31-42-6	68	244-286
80.	Apr 5	Birmingham	4-4	T	31-42-7	69	248-290
81.	Apr 7	Winnipeg	4-6	L	31-43-7	69	252-296

Cowboys Stars of 1976-1977

Lynn Powis
30 goals led team

Peter Driscoll
23 goals

Ron Chipperfield
27 goals

Dave Kryskow
16 goals, 33 points

Warren Miller
23 goals, +11

Don McLeod
25 wins, 3 shutouts

Scoring

					Regular Season										**Playoffs**				
pos	#	player	gp	g	a	pts	pim	+/-	ppg	shg	sog	sc%	gp	g	a	pts	pim	+/-	
D	25	Arbour, John	37	1	15	16	38	-26	1	0	69	0.015	-	-	-	-	-	-	
D	20	Baird, Ken	7	0	0	0	2	-2	0	0	3	0.000	-	-	-	-	-	-	
C	20	Boyd, Jim	13	0	2	2	6	-7	0	0	11	0.000	-	-	-	-	-	-	
G	29	Bromley, Gary	28	0	0	0	2		0	0	0	-	-	-	-	-	-	-	
C	7	Chipperfield, Ron	81	27	27	54	32	-10	5	0	209	0.129	-	-	-	-	-	-	
RW	12	Connelly, Wayne	25	5	6	11	4	-2	1	0	51	0.098	-	-	-	-	-	-	
LW	15	Deadmarsh, Butch	38	13	17	30	77	-5	3	0	79	0.165	-	-	-	-	-	-	
LW	12	Deschamps, Andre	9	1	2	3	19	-2	0	0	4	0.250	-	-	-	-	-	-	
LW	24	Driscoll, Peter	76	23	29	52	120	-8	4	0	130	0.177	-	-	-	-	-	-	
D	4	Evans, Chris	81	7	27	34	60	+12	0	0	174	0.040	-	-	-	-	-	-	
D	3	Ford, Mike	54	5	20	25	14	-8	2	0	144	0.034	-	-	-	-	-	-	
LW	6	Greig, Bruce	7	1	1	2	10	-1	0	0	4	0.250	-	-	-	-	-	-	
LW		Gruen, Danny	1	1	0	1	0	+2	0	0	3	0.333	-	-	-	-	-	-	
LW		Hull, Steve	2	0	2	2	0	+1	0	0	3	0.000	-	-	-	-	-	-	
D	6	Hurley, Paul	34	0	6	6	32	-8	0	0	51	0.000	-	-	-	-	-	-	
LW	12	Israelson, Larry	2	0	0	0	0	-2	0	0	3	0.000	-	-	-	-	-	-	
LW	18	Jodzio, Rick	46	4	6	10	61	-13	0	0	39	0.103	-	-	-	-	-	-	
D	6	Jordan, Ric	5	0	0	0	4	-9	0	0	3	0.000	-	-	-	-	-	-	
C	12	Ketola, Veli-Pekka	17	4	6	10	2	-17	1	0	58	0.069	-	-	-	-	-	-	
LW	16	Kryskow, Dave	45	16	17	33	47	-14	3	1	124	0.130	-	-	-	-	-	-	
RW	11	Lawson, Danny	64	24	19	43	26	-13	2	2	248	0.097	-	-	-	-	-	-	
C	15	Lemieux, Richard	33	6	11	17	9	-4	1	0	62	0.097	-	-	-	-	-	-	
LW	22	Lindskog, Doug	2	0	0	0	2	-1	0	0	2	0.000	-	-	-	-	-	-	
C	8	Locas, Jacques	22	3	4	7	2	-5	1	0	29	0.103	-	-	-	-	-	-	
F	25	Lukowich, Bernie	6	0	1	1	0	+2	0	0	10	0.000	-	-	-	-	-	-	
RW	22	Mayer, James	21	2	3	5	0	-9	0	0	12	0.167	-	-	-	-	-	-	
G	1	McLeod, Don	67	0	9	9	2		0	0	3	0.000	-	-	-	-	-	-	
D	3	Micheletti, Joe	14	3	3	6	10	-5	2	0	41	0.073	-	-	-	-	-	-	
RW	17	Miller, Warren	80	23	32	55	51	+11	2	0	183	0.126	-	-	-	-	-	-	
D	23	Miszuk, John	79	2	26	28	57	+5	0	0	61	0.033	-	-	-	-	-	-	
D	2	Morin, Wayne	13	2	0	2	25	-3	0	0	11	0.182	-	-	-	-	-	-	
LW	9	Morrison, George	63	11	19	30	10	-10	2	0	99	0.111	-	-	-	-	-	-	
D	2	Pesut, George	17	2	0	2	2	-7	2	0	12	0.167	-	-	-	-	-	-	
C	10	Powis, Lynn	63	30	30	60	46	+4	4	1	168	0.179	-	-	-	-	-	-	
LW	16	St. Sauveur, Claude	17	0	3	3	2	-3	0	0	21	0.000	-	-	-	-	-	-	
RW	8	Sentes, Dick	29	10	14	24	8	+17	1	0	53	0.189	-	-	-	-	-	-	
RW	20	Serviss, Tom	8	2	1	3	2	-1	0	0	10	0.200	-	-	-	-	-	-	
LW	5	Tannahill, Don	77	10	22	32	4	-9	0	4	129	0.078	-	-	-	-	-	-	
D	21	Terbenche, Paul	80	9	24	33	30	-14	0	0	130	0.069	-	-	-	-	-	-	
C	19	Walsh, Brian	5	0	2	2	12	-3	0	0	7	0.000	-	-	-	-	-	-	
C	6/11	Ward, Ron	9	5	5	10	0	+2	1	0	18	0.278	-	-	-	-	-	-	

Power Play: 38 goals scored in 258 opportunities (14.7%) with 10 short-handed goals allowed.
Penalty Killing: 47 goals allowed in 228 opportunities (79.4%) with 8 short-handed goals scored.

Goaltending

goaltender	gp	min	ga	en	so	record	gaa	sog	sv%	gp	min	ga	record	gaa
Bromley, Gary	28	1237	79	2	0	6-9-2	3.83	622	0.873	-	-	-	-	-
McLeod, Don	67	3701	210	5	3	25-34-5	3.40	1736	0.879	-	-	-	-	-

Transactions: Rights to Bruce Greig purchased from Cleveland, Jul 1976 • Gary Bromley, Richard Lemieux signed to contracts, Aug 1976 • Paul Hurley, Jim Mayer, George Pesut, Claude St Sauveur signed to contracts, Sep 1976 • Rights to Dave Kryskow acquired from Edmonton for future considerations, Sep 1976 • Mike Ford acquired from Winnipeg for draft picks, Oct 1976 • Ken Baird signed as free agent, Nov 1976 • John Arbour, Butch Deadmarsh and Danny Gruen signed from defunct Minnesota, Jan 1977 • Claude St. Sauveur and Wayne Connelly sold to Edmonton, Jan 1977 • Dick Sentes released, Jan 1977, subsequently signed by San Diego • Jacques Locas acquired from Cincinnati for future considerations, Feb 1977 (Returned to Cincinnati, May 1977) • Mike Ford and Danny Lawson traded to Winnipeg for Veli-Pekka Ketola and Ron Ward, Mar 1977

1976-1977 CINCINNATI STINGERS

Coach
Terry Slater

Summary of Games (@ Away, * Overtime)

#	date		opponent	score		record	pts	gf-ga
1.	Oct 7		Minnesota	7-2	W	1-0-0	2	7-2
2.	Oct 8	@	Phoenix	6-8	L	1-1-0	2	13-10
3.	Oct 9	@	San Diego	7-7	T	1-1-1	3	20-17
4.	Oct 14	@	Birmingham	7-7	T	1-1-2	4	27-24
5.	Oct 15	@	Indianapolis	*5-6	L	1-2-2	4	32-30
6.	Oct 17	@	Quebec	5-2	W	2-2-2	6	37-32
7.	Oct 19	@	Minnesota	4-2	W	3-2-2	8	41-34
8.	Oct 23	@	New England	4-5	L	3-3-2	8	45-39
9.	Oct 26	@	New England	1-0	W	4-3-2	10	46-39
10.	Oct 29		San Diego	4-2	W	5-3-2	12	50-41
11.	Oct 30		Phoenix	9-3	W	6-3-2	14	59-44
12.	Nov 3		Indianapolis	8-2	W	7-3-2	16	67-46
13.	Nov 4	@	Indianapolis	2-5	L	7-4-2	16	69-51
14.	Nov 6		Winnipeg	7-3	W	8-4-2	18	76-54
15.	Nov 10		Edmonton	4-2	W	9-4-2	20	80-56
16.	Nov 13		Indianapolis	7-3	W	10-4-2	22	87-59
17.	Nov 16	@	Indianapolis	3-5	L	10-5-2	22	90-64
18.	Nov 19	@	Edmonton	*3-4	L	10-6-2	22	93-68
19.	Nov 21	@	Winnipeg	4-2	W	11-6-2	24	97-70
20.	Nov 23	@	Minnesota	0-4	L	11-7-2	24	97-74
21.	Nov 24		Indianapolis	4-6	L	11-8-2	24	101-80
22.	Nov 27		Birmingham	2-1	W	12-8-2	26	103-81
23.	Nov 30	@	Birmingham	1-3	L	12-9-2	26	104-84
24.	Dec 3		Calgary	6-4	W	13-9-2	28	110-88
25.	Dec 5		Houston	7-2	W	14-9-2	30	117-90
26.	Dec 8		San Diego	1-6	L	14-10-2	30	118-96
27.	Dec 10		Houston	6-2	W	15-10-2	32	124-98
28.	Dec 12		Phoenix	8-0	W	16-10-2	34	132-98
29.	Dec 15		Minnesota	5-0	W	17-10-2	36	137-98
30.	Dec 18	@	Minnesota	3-4	L	17-11-2	36	140-102
31.	Dec 19	@	Edmonton	2-4	L	17-12-2	36	142-106
32.	Dec 22		Birmingham	2-6	L	17-13-2	36	144-112
33.	Dec 23	@	Houston	*5-6	L	17-14-2	36	149-118
34.	Dec 26	@	Calgary	3-6	L	17-15-2	36	152-124
35.	Dec 30		New England	4-6	L	17-16-2	36	156-130
36.	Jan 2	@	New England	2-3	L	17-17-2	36	158-133
37.	Jan 7		Birmingham	7-1	W	18-17-2	38	165-134
38.	Jan 8		San Diego	2-1	W	19-17-2	40	167-135
39.	Jan 11		New England	8-2	W	20-17-2	42	175-137
40.	Jan 13	@	San Diego	7-2	W	21-17-2	44	182-139
41.	Jan 14	@	Phoenix	*5-6	L	21-18-2	44	187-145
42.	Jan 16	@	Winnipeg	6-4	W	22-18-2	46	193-149
43.	Jan 20	@	Phoenix	4-9	L	22-19-2	46	197-158
44.	Jan 21	@	Winnipeg	*5-6	L	22-20-2	46	202-164
45.	Jan 23	@	New England	3-4	L	22-21-2	46	205-168
46.	Jan 25		New England	4-2	W	23-21-2	48	209-170
47.	Jan 29	@	Quebec	2-7	L	23-22-2	48	211-177
48.	Jan 30	@	Birmingham	1-7	L	23-23-2	48	212-184
49.	Feb 2		Birmingham	2-3	L	23-24-2	48	214-187
50.	Feb 5		New England	8-3	W	24-24-2	50	222-190
51.	Feb 6	@	Quebec	1-6	L	24-25-2	50	223-196
52.	Feb 9		Indianapolis	9-0	W	25-25-2	52	232-196
53.	Feb 11		Winnipeg	4-0	W	26-25-2	54	236-196
54.	Feb 13		New England	4-5	L	26-26-2	54	240-201
55.	Feb 15	@	Edmonton	7-4	W	27-26-2	56	247-205
56.	Feb 16	@	Calgary	7-3	W	28-26-2	58	254-208
57.	Feb 18	@	Calgary	3-5	L	28-27-2	58	257-213
58.	Feb 19		Quebec	3-1	W	29-27-2	60	260-214
59.	Feb 20		Phoenix	4-3	W	30-27-2	62	264-217
60.	Feb 22	@	Birmingham	4-4	T	30-27-3	63	268-221
61.	Feb 25		Quebec	5-2	W	31-27-3	65	273-223
62.	Feb 26		Winnipeg	6-8	L	31-28-3	65	279-231
63.	Mar 5		Indianapolis	6-0	W	32-28-3	67	285-231
64.	Mar 6		Houston	3-7	L	32-29-3	67	288-238
65.	Mar 9		Edmonton	5-3	W	33-29-3	69	293-241
66.	Mar 11	@	Houston	0-5	L	33-30-3	69	293-246
67.	Mar 12		Calgary	9-2	W	34-30-3	71	302-248
68.	Mar 13		Birmingham	7-4	W	35-30-3	73	309-252
69.	Mar 15	@	Birmingham	2-4	L	35-31-3	73	311-256
70.	Mar 16		Calgary	4-3	W	36-31-3	75	315-259
71.	Mar 18		Quebec	7-3	W	37-31-3	77	322-262
72.	Mar 22	@	Indianapolis	1-3	L	37-32-3	77	323-265
73.	Mar 23		Quebec	4-6	L	37-33-3	77	327-271
74.	Mar 25		Edmonton	*3-4	L	37-34-3	77	330-275
75.	Mar 26	@	Quebec	6-4	W	38-34-3	79	336-279
76.	Mar 27	@	Quebec	0-4	L	38-35-3	79	336-283
77.	Mar 29	@	Birmingham	4-2	W	39-35-3	81	340-285
78.	Mar 30	@	Indianapolis	5-5	T	39-35-4	82	345-290
79.	Apr 1	@	Houston	4-5	L	39-36-4	82	349-295
80.	Apr 2	@	San Diego	3-6	L	39-37-4	82	352-301
81.	Apr 6		Quebec	2-2	T	39-37-5	83	354-303

Stingers Stars of 1976-1977

Richie Leduc	**Blaine Stoughton**	**Dennis Sobchuk**	**Jacques Caron**	**Norm Lapointe**	**Ron Plumb**
52 goals, 107 points	52 goals, 104 points	44 goals, 96 points	3 shutouts	21 wins, 2 shutouts	+64 rating led league

Scoring

						Regular Season										Playoffs				
pos	#	player	gp	g	a	pts	pim	+/-	ppg	shg	sog	sc%	gp	g	a	pts	pim	+/-
RW	15	Abgrall, Dennis	80	23	39	62	22	+26	4	0	125	0.184	4	2	0	2	5	-3
G	35	Caron, Jacques	24	0	1	1	0		0	0	0	-	1	0	0	0	0	
C	26	Carroll, Greg	77	15	39	54	53	+16	0	0	125	0.120	4	1	2	3	0	0
LW	9	Dudley, Rick	77	41	47	88	102	+25	7	0	229	0.179	4	0	1	1	7	-7
LW	13	Guite, Pierre	27	10	8	18	32	-2	2	0	69	0.145	-	-	-	-	-	-
RW	24	Hislop, Jamie	46	7	19	26	6	+11	1	0	60	0.117	4	0	1	1	5	+1
G	1	Hoganson, Paul	17	0	0	0	2		0	0	0	-	-	-	-	-	-	-
D	10	Hughes, John	79	3	27	30	113	+15	0	0	107	0.028	4	0	0	0	8	-5
D	5	Inkpen, Dave	48	3	14	17	61	+6	0	0	81	0.037	-	-	-	-	-	-
D	3	Justin, Dan	6	0	2	2	4	+3	0	0	5	0.000	-	-	-	-	-	-
G	30	Lapointe, Norm	52	0	0	0	2		0	0	0	-	4	0	0	0	0	
LW	8	Larose, Claude	81	30	46	76	8	+18	1	0	273	0.110	4	2	1	3	0	-1
C	25	Leduc, Richie	81	52	55	107	75	+28	11	0	357	0.146	4	1	3	4	16	-9
D	21	Legge, Barry	74	7	22	29	39	+20	0	0	107	0.065	4	0	0	0	0	-7
C	11	Locas, Jacques	45	18	13	31	27	0	5	0	89	0.202	-	-	-	-	-	-
D	3	Long, Ted	1	0	0	0	0	-1	0	0	4	0.000	-	-	-	-	-	-
RW	18	Marsh, Peter	76	23	28	51	52	+11	3	0	186	0.124	4	2	0	2	0	-4
D	6	Maxwell, Bryan	34	1	8	9	29	+2	0	0	44	0.023	4	0	0	0	29	-3
D	4	Melrose, Barry	29	1	4	5	8	-22	0	0	17	0.059	-	-	-	-	-	-
D	23	Ouimet, Francois	16	1	8	9	10	+12	0	0	11	0.091	-	-	-	-	-	-
D	2	Plumb, Ron	79	11	58	69	52	+64	1	0	223	0.049	4	1	2	3	0	-3
D	3	Roy, Pierre	39	3	12	15	126	+19	0	0	65	0.046	3	0	1	1	7	-3
LW	16	Smedsmo, Dale	23	0	5	5	43	-7	0	0	21	0.000	2	0	1	1	0	0
C	14	Sobchuk, Dennis	81	44	52	96	38	+14	6	5	312	0.141	3	0	1	1	2	-1
RW	12	Steele, Billy	81	9	22	31	21	+11	3	1	76	0.118	2	0	0	0	0	-1
RW	17	Stoughton, Blaine	81	52	52	104	39	+24	11	0	284	0.183	4	0	3	3	2	-5

Power Play: 54 goals scored in 283 opportunities (19.1%) with 7 short-handed goals allowed.
Penalty Killing: 58 goals allowed in 259 opportunities (77.6%) with 6 short-handed goals scored.

Goaltending

goaltender	gp	min	ga	en	so	record	gaa	sog	sv%	gp	min	ga	record	gaa
Caron, Jacques	24	1292	61	1	3	13-6-2	2.83	565	0.892	1	14	3	0-1	12.86
Hoganson, Paul	17	823	64	0	1	5-6-1	4.67	401	0.840	-	-	-	-	-
Lapointe, Norm	52	2817	175	2	2	21-25-2	3.73	1434	0.878	4	273	16	0-3	3.52

Transactions: Dennis Abgrall signed to contract, Jun 1976 • Mike Pelyk sold to Toronto (NHL), Jun 1976 • Richie Leduc purchased from Cleveland, Jun 1976 • Rights to Gilles Marotte acquired from Edmonton, Jul 1976 • Jacques Caron, Jamie Hislop signed to contracts, Jul 1976 • Blaine Stoughton signed to contract, Aug 1976 • Bryan Maxwell acquired from Minnesota for John McKenzie, Sep 1976 • Barry Legge purchased from Minnesota, Oct 1976 • Pierre Guite traded to Quebec for Pierre Roy, Jan 1977 • Jacques Locas traded to Calgary for future considerations, Feb 1977 (Calgary returned Locas to Cincinnati, May 1977) • Dale Smedsmo acquired from New England, Feb 1977 • Paul Hoganson and Dave Inkpen sold to Indianapolis, Feb 1977.

1976-1977 EDMONTON OILERS

Coach
Bep Guidolin, 25-36-2

Coach
Glen Sather, 9-7-2

Summary of Games (@ Away, * Overtime)

	date	opponent	score		record	pts	gf-ga		date	opponent	score		record	pts	gf-ga
1.	Oct 8	New England	2-0	W	1-0-0	2	2-0	41.	Jan 8 @	Minnesota	0-5	L	17-23-1	35	107-143
2.	Oct 15	Winnipeg	1-6	L	1-1-0	2	3-6	42.	Jan 9	Indianapolis	5-3	W	18-23-1	37	112-146
3.	Oct 17	Indianapolis	7-2	W	2-1-0	4	10-8	43.	Jan 14 @	New England	5-3	W	19-23-1	39	117-149
4.	Oct 19	Phoenix	*5-4	W	3-1-0	6	15-12	44.	Jan 15 @	Indianapolis	3-6	L	19-24-1	39	120-155
5.	Oct 24	Phoenix	3-5	L	3-2-0	6	18-17	45.	Jan 16 @	Houston	1-3	L	19-25-1	39	121-158
6.	Oct 26 @	Houston	1-3	L	3-3-0	6	19-20	46.	Jan 20 @	San Diego	1-5	L	19-26-1	39	122-163
7.	Oct 28 @	Birmingham	*4-3	W	4-3-0	8	23-23	47.	Jan 22 @	Phoenix	1-4	L	19-27-1	39	123-167
8.	Oct 29 @	Winnipeg	3-11	L	4-4-0	8	26-34	48.	Jan 23	Phoenix	9-2	W	20-27-1	41	132-169
9.	Oct 31	Houston	0-4	L	4-5-0	8	26-38	49.	Jan 26 @	Quebec	*5-4	W	21-27-1	43	137-173
10.	Nov 3	Minnesota	4-2	W	5-5-0	10	30-40	50.	Jan 28	Houston	1-4	L	21-28-1	43	138-177
11.	Nov 4 @	Calgary	2-4	L	5-6-0	10	32-44	51.	Jan 30	Calgary	1-1	T	21-28-2	44	139-178
12.	Nov 5	New England	3-4	L	5-7-0	10	35-48	52.	Feb 1	Winnipeg	1-11	L	21-29-2	44	140-189
13.	Nov 7 @	Winnipeg	2-5	L	5-8-0	10	37-53	53.	Feb 6	San Diego	4-2	W	22-29-2	46	144-191
14.	Nov 10 @	Cincinnati	2-4	L	5-9-0	10	39-57	54.	Feb 8	San Diego	5-6	L	22-30-2	46	149-197
15.	Nov 13 @	Birmingham	3-2	W	6-9-0	12	42-59	55.	Feb 11 @	Calgary	1-3	L	22-31-2	46	150-200
16.	Nov 16 @	Phoenix	2-5	L	6-10-0	12	44-64	56.	Feb 13	Calgary	5-2	W	23-31-2	48	155-202
17.	Nov 17 @	San Diego	2-4	L	6-11-0	12	46-68	57.	Feb 15	Cincinnati	4-7	L	23-32-2	48	159-209
18.	Nov 19	Cincinnati	*4-3	W	7-11-0	14	50-71	58.	Feb 18	Winnipeg	3-2	W	24-32-2	50	162-211
19.	Nov 21	Quebec	6-5	W	8-11-0	16	56-76	59.	Feb 20 @	Winnipeg	2-4	L	24-33-2	50	164-215
20.	Nov 23 @	Houston	3-5	L	8-12-0	16	59-81	60.	Feb 22	New England	4-3	W	25-33-2	52	168-218
21.	Nov 24 @	San Diego	2-4	L	8-13-0	16	61-85	61.	Feb 25	Indianapolis	2-3	L	25-34-2	52	170-221
22.	Nov 26 @	Phoenix	2-4	L	8-14-0	16	63-89	62.	Feb 27	Birmingham	0-4	L	25-35-2	52	170-225
23.	Nov 28	San Diego	4-0	W	9-14-0	18	67-89	63.	Mar 1	Quebec	4-5	L	25-36-2	52	174-230
24.	Nov 30	Phoenix	*3-2	W	10-14-0	20	70-91	64.	Mar 3	Winnipeg	5-4	W	26-36-2	54	179-234
25.	Dec 2 @	Birmingham	4-3	W	11-14-0	22	74-94	65.	Mar 6	Birmingham	5-2	W	27-36-2	56	184-236
26.	Dec 3 @	Houston	0-0	T	11-14-1	23	74-94	66.	Mar 8 @	Houston	3-5	L	27-37-2	56	187-241
27.	Dec 4 @	Indianapolis	3-5	L	11-15-1	23	77-99	67.	Mar 9 @	Cincinnati	3-5	L	27-38-2	56	190-246
28.	Dec 5 @	Minnesota	1-5	L	11-16-1	23	78-104	68.	Mar 10 @	Indianapolis	4-3	W	28-38-2	58	194-249
29.	Dec 7 @	Quebec	4-2	W	12-16-1	25	82-106	69.	Mar 12 @	Quebec	3-3	T	28-38-3	59	197-252
30.	Dec 11 @	Calgary	0-3	L	12-17-1	25	82-109	70.	Mar 13 @	Winnipeg	3-9	L	28-39-3	59	200-261
31.	Dec 12	Birmingham	5-3	W	13-17-1	27	87-112	71.	Mar 15 @	Winnipeg	0-7	L	28-40-3	59	200-268
32.	Dec 14	San Diego	1-6	L	13-18-1	27	88-118	72.	Mar 17	Winnipeg	4-3	W	29-40-3	61	204-271
33.	Dec 16 @	San Diego	0-3	L	13-19-1	27	88-121	73.	Mar 22 @	Winnipeg	3-8	L	29-41-3	61	207-279
34.	Dec 17 @	Phoenix	1-0	W	14-19-1	29	89-121	74.	Mar 24 @	New England	5-4	W	30-41-3	63	212-283
35.	Dec 19	Cincinnati	4-2	W	15-19-1	31	93-123	75.	Mar 25 @	Cincinnati	*4-3	W	31-41-3	65	216-286
36.	Dec 21	Calgary	4-1	W	16-19-1	33	97-124	76.	Mar 27 @	New England	2-5	L	31-42-3	65	218-291
37.	Dec 28	Quebec	2-3	L	16-20-1	33	99-127	77.	Mar 30	Houston	8-0	W	32-42-3	67	226-291
38.	Jan 1 @	Calgary	1-5	L	16-21-1	33	100-132	78.	Apr 1	Calgary	1-3	L	32-43-3	67	227-294
39.	Jan 4	Houston	3-5	L	16-22-1	33	103-137	79.	Apr 2 @	Calgary	4-4	T	32-43-4	68	231-298
40.	Jan 7	Calgary	4-1	W	17-22-1	35	107-138	80.	Apr 4	Winnipeg	6-2	W	33-43-4	70	237-300
								81.	Apr 6	Birmingham	6-4	W	34-43-4	72	243-304

Transactions: Rights to Barry Wilkins acquired from Houston, Jun 1976 • Pete Laframboise, Barry Merrell, Glen Sather signed to contracts, Aug 1976 • Gene Peacosh acquired from San Diego for future considerations, Aug 1976 • Ken Broderick, Dennis Patterson, Barry Wilkins, Butch Williams signed to contracts, Sep 1976 • Frank Beaton purchased from Cincinnati, Oct 1976 • Barry Long traded to Winnipeg for future considerations, Oct 1976 • Bob Nevin, Paul Stewart signed to contracts, Oct 1976 • Ken Baird released, Oct 1976, signed by Calgary, Nov 1976 • Randy Rota purchased from Colorado (NHL), Nov 1976 • Tim Sheehy traded to Birmingham for Tom Simpson and Gavin Kirk, Dec 1976 • Bill Flett purchased from Atlanta (NHL), Dec 1976 • Gene Peacosh traded to Indianapolis for Bryan Campbell, Nov 1976 • Larry Hornung traded to San Diego for Greg Boddy, Nov 1976 • Mike Antonovich, Dave Keon, John McKenzie, Steve Carlson, Jack Carlson, Bill Butters and Louis Levasseur purchased from defunct Minnesota, Jan 1977 • Dave Keon, John McKenzie, Steve Carlson and Jack Carlson sold to New England, Jan 1977 • Claude St. Sauveur and Wayne Connelly purchased from Calgary, Jan 1977 • Danny Arndt acquired from New England for future considerations, Jan 1977 • Mike Antonovich and Bill Butters traded to New England for Brett Callighen and Ron Busniuk, Feb 1977 • Glenn Patrick signed to contract, Feb 1977

Oilers Stars of 1976-1977

Bill Flett	**Al Hamilton**	**Ken Broderick**	**Rusty Patenaude**	**Bryan Campbell**	**Rick Morris**
34 goals	45 points	4 shutouts led league	25 goals	54 points	18 goals

Scoring

| | | | | | | | Regular Season | | | | | | | | Playoffs | | | | |
pos	#	player	gp	g	a	pts	pim	+/-	ppg	shg	sog	sc%	gp	g	a	pts	pim	+/-
C	18	Antonovich, Mike	7	1	1	2	0	-3	0	0	16	0.063	-	-	-	-	-	-
LW	24	Arndt, Danny	1	0	0	0	0	-2	0	0	0	-	-	-	-	-	-	-
D	19	Baird, Ken	2	1	2	3	0	+2	0	0	7	0.143	-	-	-	-	-	-
D	5	Barrie, Doug	70	8	19	27	92	-4	2	0	102	0.078	4	0	0	0	0	0
LW	19/27	Beaton, Frank	68	4	9	13	274	-12	0	0	63	0.063	5	0	2	2	21	+2
D	2	Boddy, Greg	46	1	17	18	41	-1	1	0	42	0.024	4	1	2	3	14	+2
G	1	Broderick, Ken	40	0	3	3	2		0	0	0	-	3	0	0	0	0	
RW	8	Busniuk, Ron	22	2	2	4	83	0	0	0	37	0.054	5	0	2	2	37	-4
D	8	Butters, Bill	7	0	2	2	17	-2	0	0	7	0.000	-	-	-	-	-	-
C	18	Callighen, Brett	29	9	16	25	48	+6	2	0	48	0.186	5	4	1	5	7	+1
C	21	Campbell, Bryan	66	12	42	54	18	-10	0	1	149	0.081	5	3	1	4	0	-4
RW	12	Connelly, Wayne	38	13	15	28	18	0	4	0	111	0.117	5	0	1	1	0	-4
G	28	Dryden, Dave	24	0	2	2	0		0	0	0	-	-	-	-	-	-	-
RW	19	Flett, Bill	48	34	20	54	20	+7	7	0	177	0.192	5	0	2	2	2	-3
LW	10	Fortunato, Joe	1	0	0	0	0	0	0	0	0	-	-	-	-	-	-	-
D	3	Hamilton, Al	81	8	37	45	60	-19	3	0	140	0.057	5	0	4	4	4	+1
D	4	Hornung, Larry	21	2	1	3	0	-6	0	0	21	0.095	-	-	-	-	-	-
C	10	Kirk, Gavin	52	8	28	36	16	-4	3	0	87	0.092	5	1	0	1	4	+5
C	20	Laframboise, Pete	17	0	5	5	12	-6	0	0	28	0.000	-	-	-	-	-	-
D	26	Langevin, Dave	77	7	16	23	94	-16	2	0	133	0.053	5	2	1	3	9	-6
G	30	Levasseur, Louis	21	0	0	0	0		0	0	0	-	2	0	0	0	2	
D	2	Long, Barry	2	0	1	1	2	-4	0	0	3	0.000	-	-	-	-	-	-
C	11	Merrell, Barry	10	1	3	4	0	-2	0	0	15	0.067	-	-	-	-	-	-
LW	22	Morris, Pete	3	0	1	1	7	-2	0	0	1	0.000	-	-	-	-	-	-
LW	7	Morris, Rick	79	18	17	35	76	-1	1	0	198	0.091	-	-	-	-	-	-
RW	8	Nevin, Bob	13	3	2	5	0	-8	1	0	15	0.200	-	-	-	-	-	-
RW	17	Patenaude, Rusty	73	25	16	41	57	-23	8	0	201	0.124	2	0	0	0	8	0
D	24	Patrick, Glenn	23	0	4	4	62	-10	0	0	25	0.000	2	0	0	0	0	-1
D	23	Patterson, Dennis	23	0	2	2	2	-18	0	0	11	0.000	-	-	-	-	-	-
LW	21	Peacosh, Gene	11	5	4	9	14	+2	2	0	28	0.179	-	-	-	-	-	-
D	4	Prentice, Bill	3	0	0	0	2	+2	0	0	4	0.000	-	-	-	-	-	-
LW	20	Rota, Randy	40	9	6	15	8	-10	1	0	80	0.113	5	3	2	5	0	+2
C	25	Russell, Bob	57	7	6	13	41	-10	0	0	79	0.089	1	0	0	0	0	+1
LW	15	St. Sauveur, Claude	15	5	7	12	2	-1	0	0	24	0.208	5	1	0	1	0	-3
LW	14	Sather, Glen	81	19	34	53	77	-17	2	0	124	0.153	5	1	1	2	2	-3
RW	10	Scharf, Ted	5	0	2	2	14	-1	0	0	11	0.000	-	-	-	-	-	-
RW	15	Sheehy, Tim	28	15	8	23	4	-7	4	0	85	0.176	-	-	-	-	-	-
RW	16	Simpson, Tom	15	3	2	5	16	+2	0	0	23	0.130	-	-	-	-	-	-
LW	16	Stewart, Paul	2	0	0	0	2	0	0	0	1	0.000	-	-	-	-	-	-
C	9	Ullman, Norm	67	16	27	43	28	-23	4	0	107	0.150	5	0	3	3	0	-2
D	6	Wilkins, Barry	51	4	24	28	75	-7	0	0	65	0.062	4	0	1	1	2	+2
RW	12	Williams, Butch	29	3	10	13	16	-9	1	0	37	0.081	-	-	-	-	-	-

Power Play: 50 goals scored in 242 opportunities (20.7%) with 11 short-handed goals allowed.
Penalty Killing: 58 goals allowed in 278 opportunities (79.1%) with 1 short-handed goal scored.

Goaltending

goaltender	gp	min	ga	en	so	record	gaa	sog	sv%	gp	min	ga	record	gaa
Broderick, Ken	40	2301	134	1	4	18-18-1	3.49	1098	0.878	3	179	10	1-2	3.35
Dryden, Dave	24	1416	77	3	1	10-13-0	3.76	694	0.889	-	-	-	-	-
Levasseur, Louis	21	1213	88	1	0	6-12-3	4.35	658	0.866	2	133	10	0-2	4.51

1976-1977 HOUSTON AEROS

Coach
Bill Dineen

Summary of Games (@ Away, * Overtime)

	date		opponent	score		record	pts	gf-ga		date		opponent	score		record	pts	gf-ga
1.	Oct 8	@	Birmingham	2-4	L	0-1-0	0	2-4	41.	Jan 12	@	Phoenix	2-4	L	20-16-5	45	140-129
2.	Oct 9		Phoenix	5-3	W	1-1-0	2	7-7	42.	Jan 14		Birmingham	5-3	W	21-16-5	47	145-132
3.	Oct 13		Calgary	2-1	W	2-1-0	4	9-8	43.	Jan 16		Edmonton	3-1	W	22-16-5	49	148-133
4.	Oct 16		Birmingham	3-0	W	3-1-0	6	12-8	44.	Jan 21		Birmingham	6-1	W	23-16-5	51	154-134
5.	Oct 19		New England	4-4	T	3-1-1	7	16-12	45.	Jan 22	@	San Diego	6-0	W	24-16-5	53	160-134
6.	Oct 21	@	Birmingham	5-8	L	3-2-1	7	21-20	46.	Jan 23		San Diego	5-3	W	25-16-5	55	165-137
7.	Oct 22	@	New England	2-5	L	3-3-1	7	23-25	47.	Jan 25		Winnipeg	5-2	W	26-16-5	57	170-139
8.	Oct 23	@	Quebec	2-6	L	3-4-1	7	25-31	48.	Jan 28	@	Edmonton	4-1	W	27-16-5	59	174-140
9.	Oct 26		Edmonton	3-1	W	4-4-1	9	28-32	49.	Jan 29	@	Calgary	6-4	W	28-16-5	61	180-144
10.	Oct 28		Minnesota	1-1	T	4-4-2	10	29-33	50.	Feb 1		Calgary	6-1	W	29-16-5	63	186-145
11.	Oct 30	@	Calgary	4-6	L	4-5-2	10	33-39	51.	Feb 3	@	Phoenix	3-5	L	29-17-5	63	189-150
12.	Oct 31	@	Edmonton	4-0	W	5-5-2	12	37-39	52.	Feb 4		New England	4-1	W	30-17-5	65	193-151
13.	Nov 2	@	Winnipeg	3-1	W	6-5-2	14	40-40	53.	Feb 8	@	Indianapolis	4-4	T	30-17-6	66	197-155
14.	Nov 5		Phoenix	9-1	W	7-5-2	16	49-41	54.	Feb 12		Quebec	7-3	W	31-17-6	68	204-158
15.	Nov 6	@	San Diego	1-4	L	7-6-2	16	50-45	55.	Feb 15		Quebec	4-2	W	32-17-6	70	208-160
16.	Nov 9		Indianapolis	7-2	W	8-6-2	18	57-47	56.	Feb 18		San Diego	4-2	W	33-17-6	72	212-162
17.	Nov 12		San Diego	4-1	W	9-6-2	20	61-48	57.	Feb 19		San Diego	5-3	W	34-17-6	74	217-165
18.	Nov 16		Calgary	4-2	W	10-6-2	22	65-50	58.	Feb 22	@	Winnipeg	2-3	L	34-18-6	74	219-168
19.	Nov 19	@	San Diego	3-5	L	10-7-2	22	68-55	59.	Feb 23	@	Calgary	2-3	L	34-19-6	74	221-171
20.	Nov 20	@	Phoenix	5-2	W	11-7-2	24	73-57	60.	Feb 25	@	Phoenix	9-3	W	35-19-6	76	230-174
21.	Nov 23		Edmonton	5-3	W	12-7-2	26	78-60	61.	Feb 26	@	San Diego	5-4	W	36-19-6	78	235-178
22.	Nov 26		Winnipeg	1-1	T	12-7-3	27	79-61	62.	Feb 27	@	Phoenix	5-4	W	37-19-6	80	240-182
23.	Dec 3		Edmonton	0-0	T	12-7-4	28	79-61	63.	Mar 1		Phoenix	8-3	W	38-19-6	82	248-185
24.	Dec 5	@	Cincinnati	2-7	L	12-8-4	28	81-68	64.	Mar 4	@	New England	2-3	L	38-20-6	82	250-188
25.	Dec 8	@	New England	1-5	L	12-9-4	28	82-73	65.	Mar 6	@	Cincinnati	7-3	W	39-20-6	84	257-191
26.	Dec 10	@	Cincinnati	2-6	L	12-10-4	28	84-79	66.	Mar 8		Edmonton	5-3	W	40-20-6	86	262-194
27.	Dec 11	@	Quebec	1-4	L	12-11-4	28	85-83	67.	Mar 11		Cincinnati	5-0	W	41-20-6	88	267-194
28.	Dec 12	@	Indianapolis	3-1	W	13-11-4	30	88-84	68.	Mar 13		Indianapolis	5-0	W	42-20-6	90	272-194
29.	Dec 14		Phoenix	8-3	W	14-11-4	32	96-87	69.	Mar 15		Quebec	4-3	W	43-20-6	92	276-197
30.	Dec 17		Birmingham	3-4	L	14-12-4	32	99-91	70.	Mar 18		Phoenix	6-3	W	44-20-6	94	282-200
31.	Dec 18	@	San Diego	3-4	L	14-13-4	32	102-95	71.	Mar 20	@	Indianapolis	8-3	W	45-20-6	96	290-203
32.	Dec 19	@	Phoenix	6-4	W	15-13-4	34	108-99	72.	Mar 22	@	Quebec	2-6	L	45-21-6	96	292-209
33.	Dec 21		New England	4-0	W	16-13-4	36	112-99	73.	Mar 25		Calgary	4-2	W	46-21-6	98	296-211
34.	Dec 23		Cincinnati	*6-5	W	17-13-4	38	118-104	74.	Mar 27		Winnipeg	3-5	L	46-22-6	98	299-216
35.	Dec 26	@	Birmingham	2-6	L	17-14-4	38	120-110	75.	Mar 29	@	Winnipeg	5-2	W	47-22-6	100	304-218
36.	Dec 28		Winnipeg	6-3	W	18-14-4	40	126-113	76.	Mar 30	@	Edmonton	0-8	L	47-23-6	100	304-226
37.	Jan 2	@	Winnipeg	2-5	L	18-15-4	40	128-118	77.	Apr 1		Cincinnati	5-4	W	48-23-6	102	309-230
38.	Jan 4	@	Edmonton	5-3	W	19-15-4	42	133-121	78.	Apr 3		Indianapolis	3-7	L	48-24-6	102	312-237
39.	Jan 5	@	Calgary	4-3	W	20-15-4	44	137-124	79.	Apr 5		San Diego	3-1	W	49-24-6	104	315-238
40.	Jan 7	@	Minnesota	1-1	T	20-15-5	45	138-125	80.	Apr 6	@	San Diego	5-3	W	50-24-6	106	320-241

Aeros Stars of 1976-1977

Terry Ruskowski	**Rich Preston**	**John Tonelli**	**Wayne Rutledge**	**Ron Grahame**	**Cam Connor**
84 points, +31	38 goals	24 goals	23 wins, 3 shutouts	27 wins, 4 shutouts	35 goals, 224 mins

Scoring

pos	#	player	gp	g	a	pts	pim	+/-	ppg	shg	sog	sc%	gp	g	a	pts	pim	+/-
RW	15	Connor, Cam	76	35	32	67	224	+23	6	1	217	0.161	11	3	4	7	47	-1
RW	27	Donaldson, Gary	5	0	0	0	6	-3	0	0	14	0.000	-	-	-	-	-	-
D		Fedorko, Mike	4	0	0	0	0	-4	0	0	4	0.000	-	-	-	-	-	-
G	29	Grahame, Ron	39	0	1	1	2		0	0	0	-	9	0	2	2	0	
LW	10	Gray, John	47	21	20	41	25	+22	3	0	120	0.175	6	0	1	1	8	-3
D	17	Hale, Larry	67	0	14	14	18	+9	0	0	45	0.000	11	0	2	2	6	+5
RW	26	Hansis, Ron	22	4	3	7	6	-4	0	0	24	0.167	8	1	1	2	4	0
LW	16	Hinse, Andre	26	2	3	5	8	-9	0	0	33	0.061	-	-	-	-	-	-
RW	9	Howe, Gordie	62	24	44	68	57	+27	5	1	162	0.148	11	5	3	8	11	+1
D/F	4	Howe, Mark	57	23	52	75	46	+41	5	3	220	0.105	11	4	10	14	2	+3
D	3	Howe, Marty	80	17	28	45	103	+29	3	0	226	0.075	11	3	1	4	10	-3
LW	7	Hughes, Frank	27	3	8	11	2	-5	0	0	40	0.075	-	-	-	-	-	-
D	24	Irwin, Glen	44	2	4	6	168	-12	0	0	38	0.053	-	-	-	-	-	-
RW	27	Larway, Don	75	11	13	24	112	+5	3	0	152	0.072	3	1	0	1	0	0
LW	12	Lukowich, Morris	68	27	18	45	67	+20	6	0	119	0.227	11	6	4	10	19	+4
C	13	Lund, Larry	80	29	38	67	36	+20	7	0	109	0.266	11	2	8	10	17	-2
D	5	McLeod, Al	51	7	21	28	20	+19	1	0	69	0.101	10	1	3	4	9	-2
D	19	Pentland, Dwayne	29	1	2	3	6	+3	0	0	13	0.077	2	0	0	0	0	0
D	6	Popiel, Poul	80	12	56	68	87	+53	2	0	177	0.068	11	0	7	7	10	+4
RW	21	Preston, Rich	80	38	41	79	54	+37	6	5	216	0.176	11	3	5	8	10	+6
C	8	Ruskowski, Terry	80	24	60	84	143	+31	7	0	162	0.148	11	6	11	17	67	+8
G	30	Rutledge, Wayne	42	0	3	3	63		0	0	0	-	2	0	0	0	0	
D	2	Schella, John	20	0	6	6	28	+8	0	0	30	0.000	6	1	2	3	6	+1
LW	14	Taylor, Ted	78	16	35	51	90	+28	4	0	145	0.110	11	4	4	8	28	-2
LW	18	Tonelli, John	80	24	31	55	109	+14	6	1	179	0.134	11	3	4	7	12	-1
C	19	West, Steve	3	0	0	0	2	-3	0	0	3	0.000	6	0	0	0	0	+1

Power Play: 64 goals scored in 227 opportunities (28.2%) with 4 short-handed goals allowed.
Penalty Killing: 61 goals allowed in 361 opportunities (83.1%) with 11 short-handed goals scored.

Goaltending

goaltender	gp	min	ga	en	so	record	gaa	sog	sv%	gp	min	ga	record	gaa
Grahame, Ron	39	2345	107	1	4	27-10-2	2.74	1081	0.901	9	561	36	4-5	3.85
Rutledge, Wayne	42	2512	132	1	3	23-14-4	3.15	1294	0.898	2	120	4	2-0	2.00

Transactions: Bob Liddington to Phoenix for Cam Connor, Oct 1976 • Andre Hinse and Frank Hughes to Phoenix for Al McLeod and John Gray, Dec 1976

1976-1977 INDIANAPOLIS RACERS

Coach
Jacques Demers

Summary of Games (@ Away, * Overtime)

#	date	opponent	score		record	pts	gf-ga		#	date	opponent	score		record	pts	gf-ga
1.	Oct 8	Minnesota	4-3	W	1-0-0	2	4-3		41.	Jan 14 @	Minnesota	5-9	L	21-18-2	44	136-149
2.	Oct 10 @	Minnesota	1-4	L	1-1-0	2	5-7		42.	Jan 15	Edmonton	6-3	W	22-18-2	46	142-152
3.	Oct 15	Cincinnati	*6-5	W	2-1-0	4	11-12		43.	Jan 21	Calgary	1-1	T	22-18-3	47	143-153
4.	Oct 17 @	Edmonton	2-7	L	2-2-0	4	13-19		44.	Jan 22 @	New England	3-3	T	22-18-4	48	146-156
5.	Oct 19 @	Winnipeg	1-6	L	2-3-0	4	14-25		45.	Jan 23 @	Birmingham	2-6	L	22-19-4	48	148-162
6.	Oct 21 @	San Diego	4-4	T	2-3-1	5	18-29		46.	Jan 25 @	Quebec	*1-2	L	22-20-4	48	149-164
7.	Oct 23	Birmingham	1-3	L	2-4-1	5	19-32		47.	Jan 28	Quebec	5-6	L	22-21-4	48	154-170
8.	Oct 27	San Diego	1-5	L	2-5-1	5	20-37		48.	Jan 30	New England	5-0	W	23-21-4	50	159-170
9.	Oct 29	Quebec	6-4	W	3-5-1	7	26-41		49.	Feb 1 @	Quebec	4-5	L	23-22-4	50	163-175
10.	Nov 3 @	Cincinnati	2-8	L	3-6-1	7	28-49		50.	Feb 2	Quebec	6-5	W	24-22-4	52	169-180
11.	Nov 4	Cincinnati	5-2	W	4-6-1	9	33-51		51.	Feb 5	Birmingham	5-2	W	25-22-4	54	174-182
12.	Nov 7 @	San Diego	0-3	L	4-7-1	9	33-54		52.	Feb 6 @	New England	5-5	T	25-22-5	55	179-187
13.	Nov 9 @	Houston	2-7	L	4-8-1	9	35-61		53.	Feb 8	Houston	4-4	T	25-22-6	56	183-191
14.	Nov 10 @	Phoenix	3-3	T	4-8-2	10	38-64		54.	Feb 9 @	Cincinnati	0-9	L	25-23-6	56	183-200
15.	Nov 13 @	Cincinnati	3-7	L	4-9-2	10	41-71		55.	Feb 11	Quebec	1-5	L	25-24-6	56	184-205
16.	Nov 14 @	Quebec	3-1	W	5-9-2	12	44-72		56.	Feb 12 @	New England	5-1	W	26-24-6	58	189-206
17.	Nov 16	Cincinnati	5-3	W	6-9-2	14	49-75		57.	Feb 13	Winnipeg	5-7	L	26-25-6	58	194-213
18.	Nov 19	Birmingham	4-0	W	7-9-2	16	53-75		58.	Feb 17 @	Winnipeg	2-4	L	26-26-6	58	196-217
19.	Nov 20	Winnipeg	8-4	W	8-9-2	18	61-79		59.	Feb 19	Phoenix	5-6	L	26-27-6	58	201-223
20.	Nov 23	New England	4-3	W	9-9-2	20	65-82		60.	Feb 20 @	Birmingham	2-2	T	26-27-7	59	203-225
21.	Nov 24 @	Cincinnati	6-4	W	10-9-2	22	71-86		61.	Feb 22 @	Quebec	2-4	L	26-28-7	59	205-229
22.	Nov 25	Quebec	0-5	L	10-10-2	22	71-91		62.	Feb 25 @	Edmonton	3-2	W	27-28-7	61	208-231
23.	Nov 27 @	Quebec	8-2	W	11-10-2	24	79-93		63.	Feb 27 @	Calgary	1-2	L	27-29-7	61	209-233
24.	Nov 28 @	New England	4-3	W	12-10-2	26	83-96		64.	Mar 4	San Diego	7-4	W	28-29-7	63	216-237
25.	Dec 2	Calgary	2-1	W	13-10-2	28	85-97		65.	Mar 5 @	Cincinnati	0-6	L	28-30-7	63	216-243
26.	Dec 4	Edmonton	5-3	W	14-10-2	30	90-100		66.	Mar 6	Phoenix	*3-2	W	29-30-7	65	219-245
27.	Dec 7 @	Birmingham	*3-2	W	15-10-2	32	93-102		67.	Mar 10	Edmonton	3-4	L	29-31-7	65	222-249
28.	Dec 10	San Diego	3-2	W	16-10-2	34	96-104		68.	Mar 12	Birmingham	7-2	W	30-31-7	67	229-251
29.	Dec 12	Houston	1-3	L	16-11-2	34	97-107		69.	Mar 13 @	Houston	0-5	L	30-32-7	67	229-256
30.	Dec 16	Minnesota	3-5	L	16-12-2	34	100-112		70.	Mar 15	Calgary	3-1	W	31-32-7	69	232-257
31.	Dec 17 @	New England	*5-4	W	17-12-2	36	105-116		71.	Mar 17 @	Birmingham	5-2	W	32-32-7	71	237-259
32.	Dec 19	Birmingham	*3-2	W	18-12-2	38	108-118		72.	Mar 18	Winnipeg	5-7	L	32-33-7	71	242-266
33.	Dec 26 @	San Diego	1-2	L	18-13-2	38	109-120		73.	Mar 20	Houston	3-8	L	32-34-7	71	245-274
34.	Dec 28 @	Phoenix	3-4	L	18-14-2	38	112-124		74.	Mar 22	Cincinnati	3-1	W	33-34-7	73	248-275
35.	Jan 2	Phoenix	4-1	W	19-14-2	40	116-125		75.	Mar 24	Quebec	4-3	W	34-34-7	75	252-278
36.	Jan 4 @	Winnipeg	1-2	L	19-15-2	40	117-127		76.	Mar 26 @	New England	4-2	W	35-34-7	77	256-280
37.	Jan 8 @	Calgary	3-4	L	19-16-2	40	120-131		77.	Mar 27 @	Birmingham	3-7	L	35-35-7	77	259-287
38.	Jan 9 @	Edmonton	3-5	L	19-17-2	40	123-136		78.	Mar 30	Cincinnati	5-5	T	35-35-8	78	264-292
39.	Jan 11 @	Calgary	*4-3	W	20-17-2	42	127-139		79.	Apr 2	New England	*2-3	L	35-36-8	78	266-295
40.	Jan 13	New England	4-1	W	21-17-2	44	131-140		80.	Apr 3 @	Houston	7-3	W	36-36-8	80	273-298
									81.	Apr 6 @	Phoenix	3-7	L	36-37-8	80	276-305

318

Racers Stars of 1976-1977

Darryl Maggs	**Michel Parizeau**	**Hugh Harris**	**Blair MacDonald**	**Rene Leclerc**	**Dave Inkpen**
71 points led team	55 points	56 points	34 goals	25 goals	+10 rating

Scoring

pos	#	player	gp	g	a	pts	pim	+/-	ppg	shg	sog	sc%	gp	g	a	pts	pim	+/-
D	5	Baltimore, Bryon	55	0	15	15	63	-22	0	0	37	0.000	9	0	0	0	5	+1
D	24	Block, Ken	52	3	10	13	25	-12	0	0	34	0.088	9	0	2	2	6	+4
G	1	Brown, Andy	10	0	0	0	0		0	0	0	-	-	-	-	-	-	-
G	1	Burchell, Randy	5	0	1	1	0		0	0	0	-	-	-	-	-	-	-
C	21	Campbell, Bryan	8	1	4	5	6	-8	1	0	21	0.048	-	-	-	-	-	-
D	4	Clackson, Kim	71	3	8	11	168	-9	0	0	44	0.068	9	0	1	1	24	+2
LW	18	Coates, Brian	16	1	5	6	4	-2	0	0	24	0.042	-	-	-	-	-	-
G	31	Dion, Michel	42	0	0	0	0		0	0	0	-	4	0	0	0	0	
RW	20	Harbaruk, Nick	27	2	2	4	21	-16	0	0	28	0.071	6	1	1	2	0	-1
C	7	Harris, Hugh	46	21	35	56	21	+10	4	4	182	0.115	2	0	0	0	0	-1
G	30	Hoganson, Paul	11	0	0	0	2		0	0	0	-	5	0	0	0	0	
D	10	Inkpen, Dave	32	4	12	16	20	+10	0	0	43	0.093	9	0	2	2	8	-4
C	15	Karlander, Al	65	17	28	45	23	+5	4	0	98	0.173	6	2	1	3	0	0
RW	8	Leclerc, Rene	68	25	30	55	43	-7	2	0	174	0.144	9	1	1	2	4	-7
RW	25	Lomenda, Mark	56	9	12	21	14	-11	0	0	99	0.091	9	3	1	4	17	-3
RW	14	MacDonald, Blair	81	34	30	64	28	+10	8	0	253	0.134	9	7	8	15	4	+11
C	6	MacGregor, Gary	16	0	5	5	4	-11	0	0	33	0.000	-	-	-	-	-	-
D	2	Maggs, Darryl	81	16	55	71	114	+4	5	1	310	0.052	9	1	4	5	4	-3
D	21	Mavety, Larry	10	2	2	4	8	-1	0	0	13	0.154	-	-	-	-	-	-
RW	11	McDonald, Brian	50	15	13	28	48	-20	5	2	89	0.169	9	3	4	7	33	-5
RW	6	Paiement, Rosaire	67	18	25	43	91	-3	2	0	144	0.125	9	0	5	5	15	-3
G	28	Park, Jim	31	0	1	1	6		0	0	0	-	-	-	-	-	-	-
C	16	Parizeau, Michel	75	18	37	55	39	+6	8	0	139	0.129	8	3	6	9	8	+7
LW	22	Peacosh, Gene	64	22	26	48	21	-1	6	0	124	0.177	9	3	3	6	2	-2
D	3	Proceviat, Dick	55	2	12	14	33	-7	0	0	65	0.031	-	-	-	-	-	-
LW	19	Rochon, Francois	67	15	8	23	8	-13	2	0	122	0.123	5	0	1	1	0	-1
C	17	Sicinski, Bob	60	12	24	36	14	-8	1	0	141	0.085	9	0	3	3	4	-5
D	12	Stapleton, Pat	81	8	45	53	29	-28	4	0	156	0.051	9	2	6	8	0	-1
LW	9	Thomas, Reg	79	25	30	55	34	-9	5	0	241	0.104	9	7	9	16	4	+8
C	23	Zuke, Mike	15	3	4	7	2	-2	0	0	24	0.125	-	-	-	-	-	-

Power Play: 57 goals scored in 259 opportunities (22.0%) with 2 short-handed goals allowed.
Penalty Killing: 62 goals allowed in 251 opportunities (75.3%) with 7 short-handed goals scored.

Goaltending

goaltender	gp	min	ga	en	so	record	gaa	sog	sv%	gp	min	ga	record	gaa
Brown, Andy	10	430	26	0	0	1-4-1	3.63	195	0.867	-	-	-	-	-
Burchell, Randy	5	136	8	0	0	1-0-0	3.53	89	0.910	-	-	-	-	-
Dion, Michel	42	2286	128	4	1	17-19-3	3.36	1174	0.891	4	245	17	2-2	4.16
Hoganson, Paul	11	395	24	0	0	3-2-0	3.65	199	0.879	5	348	17	3-2	2.93
Park, Jim	31	1727	114	1	1	14-12-4	3.96	898	0.873	-	-	-	-	-

Transactions: Bryan Campbell acquired from Cincinnati for future considerations, Jun 1976 • Gary MacGregor acquired from Minnesota for Dave Keon, Sep 1976 • Bryan Campbell traded to Edmonton for Gene Peacosh, Nov 1976 • Gary MacGregor traded to New England for Rosaire Paiement, Nov 1976 • Paul Hoganson and Dave Inkpen purchased from Cincinnati, Feb 1977

1976-1977 MINNESOTA FIGHTING SAINTS

Coach
Glen Sonmor

Summary of Games (@ Away, * Overtime)

	date		opponent	score		record	pts	gf-ga
1.	Oct 7	@	Cincinnati	2-7	L	0-1-0	0	2-7
2.	Oct 8	@	Indianapolis	3-4	L	0-2-0	0	5-11
3.	Oct 10		Indianapolis	4-1	W	1-2-0	2	9-12
4.	Oct 14	@	Phoenix	3-4	L	1-3-0	2	12-16
5.	Oct 15		San Diego	4-7	L	1-4-0	2	16-23
6.	Oct 17		Birmingham	6-1	W	2-4-0	4	22-24
7.	Oct 19		Cincinnati	2-4	L	2-5-0	4	24-28
8.	Oct 22		Calgary	2-2	T	2-5-1	5	26-30
9.	Oct 26		San Diego	3-1	W	3-5-1	7	29-31
10.	Oct 28	@	Houston	1-1	T	3-5-2	8	30-32
11.	Oct 30	@	Quebec	1-5	L	3-6-2	8	31-37
12.	Nov 2	@	Calgary	3-4	L	3-7-2	8	34-41
13.	Nov 3	@	Edmonton	2-4	L	3-8-2	8	36-45
14.	Nov 5	@	Winnipeg	2-9	L	3-9-2	8	38-54
15.	Nov 7		Phoenix	1-3	L	3-10-2	8	39-57
16.	Nov 11		New England	3-3	T	3-10-3	9	42-60
17.	Nov 13	@	Quebec	4-2	W	4-10-3	11	46-62
18.	Nov 18		Quebec	5-9	L	4-11-3	11	51-71
19.	Nov 20	@	New England	3-3	T	4-11-4	12	54-74
20.	Nov 21		Calgary	5-1	W	5-11-4	14	59-75
21.	Nov 23		Cincinnati	4-0	W	6-11-4	16	63-75

	date		opponent	score		record	pts	gf-ga
22.	Nov 26		Quebec	4-2	W	7-11-4	18	67-77
23.	Nov 27	@	New England	3-1	W	8-11-4	20	70-78
24.	Nov 28	@	Birmingham	3-1	W	9-11-4	22	73-79
25.	Dec 3		Winnipeg	3-4	L	9-12-4	22	76-83
26.	Dec 5		Edmonton	5-1	W	10-12-4	24	81-84
27.	Dec 7		New England	4-2	W	11-12-4	26	85-86
28.	Dec 10		Calgary	4-2	W	12-12-4	28	89-88
29.	Dec 12		San Diego	2-4	L	12-13-4	28	91-92
30.	Dec 15	@	Cincinnati	0-5	L	12-14-4	28	91-97
31.	Dec 16	@	Indianapolis	5-3	W	13-14-4	30	96-100
32.	Dec 18		Cincinnati	4-3	W	14-14-4	32	100-103
33.	Dec 22		Quebec	3-4	L	14-15-4	32	103-107
34.	Dec 23	@	Calgary	1-2	L	14-16-4	32	104-109
35.	Dec 26	@	New England	2-3	L	14-17-4	32	106-112
36.	Dec 28		New England	5-4	W	15-17-4	34	111-116
37.	Dec 30	@	Birmingham	4-2	W	16-17-4	36	115-118
38.	Jan 2		Birmingham	3-1	W	17-17-4	38	118-119
39.	Jan 7		Houston	1-1	T	17-17-5	39	119-120
40.	Jan 8		Edmonton	5-0	W	18-17-5	41	124-120
41.	Jan 12		Birmingham	3-4	L	18-18-5	41	127-124
42.	Jan 14		Indianapolis	9-5	W	19-18-5	43	136-129

Franchise folded January 17, 1977

Fighting Saints Stars of 1976-1977

Louis Levasseur	**Mike Antonovich**	**John McKenzie**	**John Arbour**	**Ray McKay**	**Pat Westrum**
15 wins, 2 shutouts	27 goals	30 points, +14	+14 rating	+19 rating	+15 rating

Scoring

pos	#	player	gp	g	a	pts	pim	+/-	ppg	shg	sog	sc%	gp	g	a	pts	pim	+/-
C	10	Adduono, Ray	40	4	19	23	17	-14	3	0	47	0.085	-	-	-	-	-	-
C	12	Antonovich, Mike	42	27	21	48	28	+20	6	0	157	0.172	-	-	-	-	-	-
D	17	Arbour, John	33	3	19	22	22	+14	0	0	89	0.034	-	-	-	-	-	-
D	2	Butters, Bill	42	0	7	7	133	+5	0	0	48	0.000	-	-	-	-	-	-
LW	20	Carlson, Jack	36	4	3	7	55	-1	0	0	50	0.080	-	-	-	-	-	-
C	25	Carlson, Steve	21	5	8	13	8	+3	0	0	38	0.132	-	-	-	-	-	-
D		Clearwater, Ray	2	0	0	0	2	-3	0	0		-	-	-	-	-	-	-
G	1	Curran, Mike	16	0	0	0	6		0	0	0	-	-	-	-	-	-	-
LW	15	Deadmarsh, Butch	35	9	4	13	51	-5	2	0	82	0.110	-	-	-	-	-	-
LW	16	Gallant, Gord	37	6	3	9	64	-1	0	0	55	0.109	-	-	-	-	-	-
LW	23	Gruen, Danny	34	10	9	19	19	+7	2	0	82	0.122	-	-	-	-	-	-
D	5	Hanson, Dave	1	0	0	0	9	0	0	0	0	-	-	-	-	-	-	-
C	14	Keon, Dave	42	13	38	51	2	+25	1	1	151	0.086	-	-	-	-	-	-
D	21	Legge, Barry	2	0	0	0	0	-1	0	0	1	0.000	-	-	-	-	-	-
G	30	Levasseur, Louis	30	0	1	1	4		0	0	0	-	-	-	-	-	-	-
RW	26	McDonough, Al	42	9	21	30	6	+13				-	-	-	-	-	-	-
D	4	McKay, Ray	42	2	9	11	28	+19	0	0	52	0.038	-	-	-	-	-	-
RW	19	McKenzie, John	40	17	13	30	52	+14	3	0	98	0.173	-	-	-	-	-	-
RW		Milani, Tom	2	0	0	0	0	-2	0	0		-	-	-	-	-	-	-
RW	9	Patrick, Craig	30	6	11	17	6	+4				-	-	-	-	-	-	-
LW	7	Stewart, John A.	15	3	3	6	2	-6	0	0	37	0.081	-	-	-	-	-	-
C	24	Ward, Ron	41	15	21	36	6	+9	4	1	96	0.156	-	-	-	-	-	-
D	6	Westrum, Pat	40	1	9	10	42	+15	0	0	46	0.022	-	-	-	-	-	-
D	8	Zrymiak, Jerry	40	2	10	12	14	+7				-	-	-	-	-	-	-

Power Play: 22 goals scored in 107 opportunities (20.6%) with 7 short-handed goals allowed.
Penalty Killing: 33 goals allowed in 130 opportunities (74.8%) with 3 short-handed goals scored.

Goaltending

goaltender	gp	min	ga	en	so	record	gaa	sog	sv%	gp	min	ga	record	gaa
Curran, Mike	16	848	50	0	0	4-7-3	3.54	476	0.895	-	-	-	-	-
Levasseur, Louis	30	1715	78	1	2	15-11-2	2.73	974	0.920	-	-	-	-	-

Transactions: Rights to Bill Butters acquired from Birmingham, Jun 1976 • Rights to Craig Patrick acquired from Calgary for future considerations, Jun 1976 • Barry Legge signed to contract, Jul 1976 • Rights to Gord Gallant acquired from Quebec for rights to Andre Boudrias, Sep 1976 • Dave Keon acquired from Indianapolis for Gary MacGregor, Sep 1976 • John McKenzie acquired from Cincinnati for Bryan Maxwell, Sep 1976 • Paul Shmyr and Gerry Pinder traded to San Diego for Ray Adduono and Bob Wall, Sep 1976 • Butch Deadmarsh acquired in trade with Calgary for rights to Jim Harrison, Sep 1976 • Barry Legge sold to Edmonton, Oct 1976 • Butch Deadmarsh, John Arbour and Danny Gruen sold to Calgary, Jan 1977 • Mike Antonovich, Bill Butters, Steve Carlson, Jack Carlson, Dave Keon, John McKenzie, Louis Levasseur sold to Edmonton, Jan 1977 • Remaining players declared free agents, Jan 1977

1976-1977 NEW ENGLAND WHALERS

Coach
Harry Neale

Summary of Games (@ Away, * Overtime)

	date		opponent	score		record	pts	gf-ga
1.	Oct 8	@	Edmonton	0-2	L	0-1-0	0	0-2
2.	Oct 10	@	Winnipeg	2-5	L	0-2-0	0	2-7
3.	Oct 16		Quebec	2-8	L	0-3-0	0	4-15
4.	Oct 19	@	Houston	4-4	T	0-3-1	1	8-19
5.	Oct 22		Houston	5-2	W	1-3-1	3	13-21
6.	Oct 23		Cincinnati	5-4	W	2-3-1	5	18-25
7.	Oct 26		Cincinnati	0-1	L	2-4-1	5	18-26
8.	Oct 29		Phoenix	5-1	W	3-4-1	7	23-27
9.	Oct 30		Birmingham	5-4	W	4-4-1	9	28-31
10.	Nov 5	@	Edmonton	4-3	W	5-4-1	11	32-34
11.	Nov 7	@	Calgary	2-4	L	5-5-1	11	34-38
12.	Nov 9	@	Winnipeg	*4-5	L	5-6-1	11	38-43
13.	Nov 11	@	Minnesota	3-3	T	5-6-2	12	41-46
14.	Nov 12	@	Phoenix	1-3	L	5-7-2	12	42-49
15.	Nov 16	@	Birmingham	5-4	W	6-7-2	14	47-53
16.	Nov 17		Birmingham	6-4	W	7-7-2	16	53-57
17.	Nov 19		Winnipeg	3-7	L	7-8-2	16	56-64
18.	Nov 20		Minnesota	3-3	T	7-8-3	17	59-67
19.	Nov 23	@	Indianapolis	3-4	L	7-9-3	17	62-71
20.	Nov 25	@	Birmingham	5-3	W	8-9-3	19	67-74
21.	Nov 27		Minnesota	1-3	L	8-10-3	19	68-77
22.	Nov 28		Indianapolis	3-4	L	8-11-3	19	71-81
23.	Nov 30	@	Quebec	1-2	L	8-12-3	19	72-83
24.	Dec 1		Calgary	8-4	W	9-12-3	21	80-87
25.	Dec 3		Quebec	5-5	T	9-12-4	22	85-92
26.	Dec 4		Winnipeg	2-6	L	9-13-4	22	87-98
27.	Dec 7	@	Minnesota	2-4	L	9-14-4	22	89-102
28.	Dec 8		Houston	5-1	W	10-14-4	24	94-103
29.	Dec 11		San Diego	3-2	W	11-14-4	26	97-105
30.	Dec 12	@	Quebec	1-5	L	11-15-4	26	98-110
31.	Dec 14	@	Quebec	3-1	W	12-15-4	28	101-111
32.	Dec 17		Indianapolis	*4-5	L	12-16-4	28	105-116
33.	Dec 18	@	Birmingham	6-2	W	13-16-4	30	111-118
34.	Dec 21	@	Houston	0-4	L	13-17-4	30	111-122
35.	Dec 23	@	San Diego	5-3	W	14-17-4	32	116-125
36.	Dec 26		Minnesota	3-2	W	15-17-4	34	119-127
37.	Dec 28		Minnesota	4-5	L	15-18-4	34	123-132
38.	Dec 30	@	Cincinnati	6-4	W	16-18-4	36	129-136
39.	Jan 2		Cincinnati	3-2	W	17-18-4	38	132-138
40.	Jan 4	@	Quebec	3-5	L	17-19-4	38	135-143
41.	Jan 5		San Diego	1-2	L	17-20-4	38	136-145
42.	Jan 7		Quebec	3-7	L	17-21-4	38	139-152
43.	Jan 8		Phoenix	3-4	L	17-22-4	38	142-156
44.	Jan 11	@	Cincinnati	2-8	L	17-23-4	38	144-164
45.	Jan 13	@	Indianapolis	1-4	L	17-24-4	38	145-168
46.	Jan 14		Edmonton	3-5	L	17-25-4	38	148-173
47.	Jan 20		Quebec	4-5	L	17-26-4	38	152-178
48.	Jan 22		Indianapolis	3-3	T	17-26-5	39	155-181
49.	Jan 23		Cincinnati	4-3	W	18-26-5	41	159-184
50.	Jan 25	@	Cincinnati	2-4	L	18-27-5	41	161-188
51.	Jan 27	@	San Diego	5-3	W	19-27-5	43	166-191
52.	Jan 28	@	Phoenix	6-2	W	20-27-5	45	172-193
53.	Jan 30	@	Indianapolis	0-5	L	20-28-5	45	172-198
54.	Feb 1	@	Birmingham	3-4	L	20-29-5	45	175-202
55.	Feb 4	@	Houston	1-4	L	20-30-5	45	176-206
56.	Feb 5	@	Cincinnati	3-8	L	20-31-5	45	179-214
57.	Feb 6		Indianapolis	5-5	T	20-31-6	46	184-219
58.	Feb 10		Winnipeg	6-3	W	21-31-6	48	190-222
59.	Feb 12		Indianapolis	1-5	L	21-32-6	48	191-227
60.	Feb 13	@	Cincinnati	5-4	W	22-32-6	50	196-231
61.	Feb 17		Phoenix	4-2	W	23-32-6	52	200-233
62.	Feb 18		Birmingham	2-3	L	23-33-6	52	202-236
63.	Feb 20	@	Calgary	5-0	W	24-33-6	54	207-236
64.	Feb 22	@	Edmonton	3-4	L	24-34-6	54	210-240
65.	Feb 25	@	Calgary	3-2	W	25-34-6	56	213-242
66.	Feb 27	@	Winnipeg	3-2	W	26-34-6	58	216-244
67.	Mar 2		San Diego	2-0	W	27-34-6	60	218-244
68.	Mar 4		Houston	3-2	W	28-34-6	62	221-246
69.	Mar 6		Quebec	6-2	W	29-34-6	64	227-248
70.	Mar 9	@	Birmingham	*3-4	L	29-35-6	64	230-252
71.	Mar 11	@	Birmingham	3-6	L	29-36-6	64	233-258
72.	Mar 13	@	Quebec	3-5	L	29-37-6	64	236-263
73.	Mar 18		Calgary	3-1	W	30-37-6	66	239-264
74.	Mar 20		Calgary	9-0	W	31-37-6	68	248-264
75.	Mar 24		Edmonton	4-5	L	31-38-6	68	252-269
76.	Mar 26		Indianapolis	2-4	L	31-39-6	68	254-273
77.	Mar 27		Edmonton	5-2	W	32-39-6	70	259-275
78.	Mar 29	@	San Diego	5-4	W	33-39-6	72	264-279
79.	Mar 31	@	Phoenix	6-2	W	34-39-6	74	270-281
80.	Apr 2	@	Indianapolis	*3-2	W	35-39-6	76	273-283
81.	Apr 5	@	Quebec	2-7	L	35-40-6	76	275-290

Whalers Stars of 1976-1977

George Lyle	Mike Rogers	Rick Ley	Bill Butters	T. Abrahamsson	Tom Webster
39 goals led team	82 points, +11	102 minutes	+13 rating	+6 rating	36 goals

Scoring

						Regular Season									Playoffs				
pos	#	player	gp	g	a	pts	pim	+/-	ppg	shg	sog	sc%	gp	g	a	pts	pim	+/-
G	1	Abrahamsson, C.	45	0	0	0	0		0	0	0	-	2	0	0	0	0	
D	6	Abrahamsson, T.	64	6	24	30	33	+6	0	0	174	0.034	5	0	3	3	0	-3
C	12	Antonovich, Mike	26	12	9	21	10	+11	1	0	83	0.145	5	2	2	4	4	+5
LW	19	Arndt, Danny	46	8	14	22	11	-13	1	0	87	0.092	-	-	-	-	-	-
C	9	Backstrom, Ralph	77	17	31	48	30	+1	0	0	162	0.105	3	0	0	0	0	-1
LW	21	Bolduc, Dan	33	8	3	11	15	-13	0	0	57	0.140	-	-	-	-	-	-
RW	5	Busniuk, Ron	59	1	9	10	141	-10	0	0	78	0.013	-	-	-	-	-	-
D	22	Butters, Bill	26	1	8	9	65	+13	0	0	38	0.026	5	0	3	3	15	-1
C	22	Callighen, Brett	33	6	10	16	41	-1	1	0	49	0.122	-	-	-	-	-	-
RW	23	Carlson, Jack	35	7	5	12	81	-2	0	0	46	0.152	5	1	1	2	9	-2
C	26	Carlson, Steve	31	4	9	13	40	0	0	0	51	0.078	5	0	0	0	9	-2
LW	15	Climie, Ron	3	0	0	0	0	-1	0	0	4	0.000	-	-	-	-	-	-
RW	27	Earl, Tom	54	9	14	23	37	-7	0	1	69	0.130	1	0	0	0	0	0
D	10	Hangsleben, Alan	74	13	9	22	79	-24	0	0	118	0.110	4	0	0	0	9	-1
D	24	Hanson, Dave	7	0	2	2	35	-9	0	0	4	0.000	1	0	0	0	0	0
LW	11	Hynes, Dave	22	5	4	9	4	+5	0	1	41	0.122	-	-	-	-	-	-
C	14	Keon, Dave	34	14	25	39	8	+13	5	1	107	0.131	5	3	1	4	0	+4
G	30	Landon, Bruce	23	0	0	0	4		0	0	0	-	3	0	0	0	0	
D	2	Ley, Rick	55	2	21	23	102	-6	0	0	98	0.020	5	0	4	4	4	+1
LW	16	Lyle, George	75	39	33	72	62	+30	12	0	229	0.170	5	1	0	1	4	-4
C	12	MacGregor, Gary	30	8	8	16	4	-14	3	0	67	0.119	-	-	-	-	-	-
RW	19	McKenzie, John	34	11	19	30	25	+10	0	3	63	0.175	5	2	1	3	8	+4
RW	12	Paiement, Rosaire	13	5	2	7	12	+2	1	0	32	0.156	-	-	-	-	-	-
C	4	Pleau, Larry	78	11	21	32	22	-17	0	0	146	0.075	5	1	0	1	0	-4
G	35	Raeder, Cap	26	0	0	0	2		0	0	0	-	1	0	0	0	0	
D	14	Roberts, Doug	64	3	18	21	33	-6	0	0	107	0.028	2	0	0	0	0	-1
D	7	Roberts, Gordie	77	13	33	46	169	+16	2	0	199	0.065	5	2	2	4	6	-2
C	17	Rogers, Mike	78	25	57	82	10	+11	6	0	212	0.118	5	1	1	2	2	-4
D	3	Selwood, Brad	41	4	12	16	71	-8	2	0	60	0.067	5	0	0	0	2	-1
LW	24	Smedsmo, Dale	15	2	0	2	54	-6	1	0	12	0.167	-	-	-	-	-	-
C	20	Swain, Garry	26	5	2	7	6	-6	1	2	30	0.167	2	0	0	0	0	0
RW	25	Troy, Jim	7	0	0	0	7	-3	0	0	4	0.000	-	-	-	-	-	-
RW	8	Webster, Tom	70	36	49	85	43	+18	11	0	188	0.191	5	1	1	2	0	-5

Power Play: 47 goals scored in 245 opportunities (19.2%) with 10 short-handed goals allowed.
Penalty Killing: 65 goals allowed in 281 opportunities (76.9%) with 8 short-handed goals scored.

Goaltending

goaltender	gp	min	ga	en	so	record	gaa	sog	sv%	gp	min	ga	record	gaa
Abrahamsson, C.	45	2484	159	0	0	15-22-4	3.84	1432	0.889	2	90	5	0-1	3.33
Landon, Bruce	23	1118	59	3	1	8-8-1	3.17	567	0.896	3	152	11	1-2	4.34
Raeder, Cap	26	1328	69	0	2	12-10-1	3.12	704	0.902	1	60	7	0-1	7.00

Transactions: Wayne Carleton acquired in trade with Cleveland for Rob McManama and Fred O'Donnell, Jun 1976 • George Lyle signed to contract, Jul 1976 • Dave Hynes signed to contract, Aug 1976 • Rosaire Paiement traded to Indianapolis for Gary MacGregor, Nov 1976 • Danny Arndt traded to Edmonton for future considerations, Jan 1977 • Dave Keon, John McKenzie, Steve Carlson, Jack Carlson purchased from Edmonton, Jan 1977 • Dave Hanson signed from defunct Minnesota, Jan 1977 • Brett Callighen and Ron Busniuk traded to Edmonton for Mike Antonovich and Bill Butters, Feb 1977 • Dale Smedsmo traded to Cincinnati for future considerations, Feb 1977

1976-1977 PHOENIX ROADRUNNERS

Coach
Al Rollins

Summary of Games (@ Away, * Overtime)

#	date		opponent	score		record	pts	gf-ga		#	date		opponent	score		record	pts	gf-ga
1.	Oct 8		Cincinnati	8-6	W	1-0-0	2	8-6		41.	Jan 12		Houston	4-2	W	16-23-2	34	136-184
2.	Oct 9	@	Houston	3-5	L	1-1-0	2	11-11		42.	Jan 14		Cincinnati	*6-5	W	17-23-2	36	142-189
3.	Oct 14		Minnesota	4-3	W	2-1-0	4	15-14		43.	Jan 16		Calgary	4-5	L	17-24-2	36	146-194
4.	Oct 16		Winnipeg	6-4	W	3-1-0	6	21-18		44.	Jan 20		Cincinnati	9-4	W	18-24-2	38	155-198
5.	Oct 19	@	Edmonton	*4-5	L	3-2-0	6	25-23		45.	Jan 22		Edmonton	4-1	W	19-24-2	40	159-199
6.	Oct 22	@	Winnipeg	4-3	W	4-2-0	8	29-26		46.	Jan 23	@	Edmonton	2-9	L	19-25-2	40	161-208
7.	Oct 24	@	Edmonton	5-3	W	5-2-0	10	34-29		47.	Jan 25	@	Calgary	3-7	L	19-26-2	40	164-215
8.	Oct 26	@	Quebec	3-11	L	5-3-0	10	37-40		48.	Jan 28		New England	2-6	L	19-27-2	40	166-221
9.	Oct 27	@	New England	1-5	L	5-4-0	10	38-45		49.	Jan 30		Winnipeg	8-5	W	20-27-2	42	174-226
10.	Oct 30	@	Cincinnati	3-9	L	5-5-0	10	41-54		50.	Feb 1	@	San Diego	1-5	L	20-28-2	42	175-231
11.	Nov 2	@	Quebec	5-3	W	6-5-0	12	46-57		51.	Feb 3		Houston	5-3	W	21-28-2	44	180-234
12.	Nov 4	@	Birmingham	3-5	L	6-6-0	12	49-62		52.	Feb 5		Calgary	1-4	L	21-29-2	44	181-238
13.	Nov 5	@	Houston	1-9	L	6-7-0	12	50-71		53.	Feb 9		Birmingham	4-3	W	22-29-2	46	185-241
14.	Nov 7	@	Minnesota	3-1	W	7-7-0	14	53-72		54.	Feb 11		San Diego	3-5	L	22-30-2	46	188-246
15.	Nov 10		Indianapolis	3-3	T	7-7-1	15	56-75		55.	Feb 13	@	San Diego	2-5	L	22-31-2	46	190-251
16.	Nov 12		New England	3-1	W	8-7-1	17	59-76		56.	Feb 16	@	Birmingham	2-7	L	22-32-2	46	192-258
17.	Nov 14		San Diego	6-3	W	9-7-1	19	65-79		57.	Feb 17	@	New England	2-4	L	22-33-2	46	194-262
18.	Nov 16		Edmonton	5-2	W	10-7-1	21	70-81		58.	Feb 19	@	Indianapolis	6-5	W	23-33-2	48	200-267
19.	Nov 18		Calgary	*1-2	L	10-8-1	21	71-83		59.	Feb 20	@	Cincinnati	3-4	L	23-34-2	48	203-271
20.	Nov 20		Houston	2-5	L	10-9-1	21	73-88		60.	Feb 23		Winnipeg	6-3	W	24-34-2	50	209-274
21.	Nov 24		Calgary	3-3	T	10-9-2	22	76-91		61.	Feb 24	@	San Diego	3-3	T	24-34-3	51	212-277
22.	Nov 26		Edmonton	4-2	W	11-9-2	24	80-93		62.	Feb 25		Houston	3-9	L	24-35-3	51	215-286
23.	Nov 28	@	Winnipeg	5-3	W	12-9-2	26	85-96		63.	Feb 27		Houston	4-5	L	24-36-3	51	219-291
24.	Nov 30	@	Edmonton	*2-3	L	12-10-2	26	87-99		64.	Mar 1	@	Houston	3-8	L	24-37-3	51	222-299
25.	Dec 2	@	San Diego	3-4	L	12-11-2	26	90-103		65.	Mar 5		Winnipeg	4-1	W	25-37-3	53	226-300
26.	Dec 4		San Diego	3-4	L	12-12-2	26	93-107		66.	Mar 6	@	Indianapolis	*2-3	L	25-38-3	53	228-303
27.	Dec 5	@	Calgary	0-6	L	12-13-2	26	93-113		67.	Mar 8	@	Quebec	2-9	L	25-39-3	53	230-312
28.	Dec 7	@	Winnipeg	2-4	L	12-14-2	26	95-117		68.	Mar 12	@	San Diego	7-6	W	26-39-3	55	237-318
29.	Dec 9		Quebec	4-5	L	12-15-2	26	99-122		69.	Mar 15	@	San Diego	4-4	T	26-39-4	56	241-322
30.	Dec 12	@	Cincinnati	0-8	L	12-16-2	26	99-130		70.	Mar 17		Quebec	3-4	L	26-40-4	56	244-326
31.	Dec 14	@	Houston	3-8	L	12-17-2	26	102-138		71.	Mar 18	@	Houston	3-6	L	26-41-4	56	247-332
32.	Dec 15		Birmingham	6-5	W	13-17-2	28	108-143		72.	Mar 19		San Diego	7-5	W	27-41-4	58	254-337
33.	Dec 17		Edmonton	0-1	L	13-18-2	28	108-144		73.	Mar 20	@	San Diego	1-6	L	27-42-4	58	255-343
34.	Dec 19		Houston	4-6	L	13-19-2	28	112-150		74.	Mar 23		Birmingham	0-4	L	27-43-4	58	255-347
35.	Dec 22		San Diego	*4-5	L	13-20-2	28	116-155		75.	Mar 25		San Diego	3-7	L	27-44-4	58	258-354
36.	Dec 28		Indianapolis	4-3	W	14-20-2	30	120-158		76.	Mar 27	@	Calgary	4-5	L	27-45-4	58	262-359
37.	Jan 2	@	Indianapolis	1-4	L	14-21-2	30	121-162		77.	Mar 29	@	Calgary	5-9	L	27-46-4	58	267-368
38.	Jan 4	@	Birmingham	5-8	L	14-22-2	30	126-170		78.	Mar 31		New England	2-6	L	27-47-4	58	269-374
39.	Jan 8	@	New England	4-3	W	15-22-2	32	130-173		79.	Apr 2		Quebec	*5-6	L	27-48-4	58	274-380
40.	Jan 11	@	Winnipeg	2-9	L	15-23-2	32	132-182		80.	Apr 6		Indianapolis	7-3	W	28-48-4	60	281-383

Roadrunners Stars of 1976-1977

Robbie Ftorek
League MVP

Del Hall
38 goals

Seppo Repo
29 goals

Lauri Mononen
21 goals

Bob Liddington
20 goals

Ron Huston
20 goals

Scoring

| | | | | | | Regular Season | | | | | | | | | Playoffs | | | | |
pos	#	player	gp	g	a	pts	pim	+/-	ppg	shg	sog	sc%	gp	g	a	pts	pim	+/-
D	5	Beaudoin, Serge	77	6	24	30	136	-11	0	0	136	0.044	-	-	-	-	-	-
D	29	Bray, Duane	46	2	6	8	62	-41	0	0	40	0.050	-	-	-	-	-	-
LW	16	Cormier, Michel	58	13	16	29	22	-26	0	0	105	0.124	-	-	-	-	-	-
D		Davidson, Blair	2	0	0	0	2	-1	0	0	0	-	-	-	-	-	-	-
C	8	Ftorek, Robbie	80	46	71	117	86	+26	11	0	284	0.162	-	-	-	-	-	-
RW	10	Gorman, David	5	0	0	0	0	-2	0	0	6	0.000	-	-	-	-	-	-
LW	15	Gray, John	28	10	10	20	59	-1	0	0	54	0.185	-	-	-	-	-	-
C	9	Hall, Del	80	38	41	79	30	+6	9	1	259	0.147	-	-	-	-	-	-
G	25	Hebenton, Clay	56	0	0	0	2		0	0	0	-	-	-	-	-	-	-
LW	15	Hinse, Andre	16	2	7	9	14	-7	0	0	19	0.105	-	-	-	-	-	-
C	20	Hobin, Mike	68	17	18	35	14	-43	2	0	132	0.129	-	-	-	-	-	-
LW	17	Hughes, Frank	48	24	29	53	20	+5	3	0	158	0.152	-	-	-	-	-	-
C	12	Huston, Ron	80	20	39	59	10	-57	6	4	198	0.101	-	-	-	-	-	-
G	1	Kurt, Gary	33	0	3	3	6		0	0	0	-	-	-	-	-	-	-
D	4	Lariviere, Garry	61	7	23	30	48	-19	3	0	107	0.065	-	-	-	-	-	-
LW	7	Liddington, Bob	80	20	24	44	28	-22	0	0	142	0.141	-	-	-	-	-	-
D	3	McLeod, Al	29	1	5	6	35	-10	0	0	23	0.043	-	-	-	-	-	-
RW	24	Mononen, Lauri	67	21	29	50	10	-20	2	0	118	0.178	-	-	-	-	-	-
D	2	Niekamp, Jim	79	1	15	16	91	-32	0	0	61	0.016	-	-	-	-	-	-
LW	18	Popiel, Jan	28	3	2	5	8	-24	1	0	31	0.097	-	-	-	-	-	-
D	19	Rautakallio, Pekka	78	4	31	35	8	-24	2	0	147	0.027	-	-	-	-	-	-
C	22	Repo, Seppo	80	29	31	60	10	-35	5	0	143	0.203	-	-	-	-	-	-
D	6	Rollins, Jerry	63	4	10	14	169	-25	1	0	70	0.057	-	-	-	-	-	-
D	27	Sleep, Mike	13	2	2	4	6	-3	0	0	16	0.125	-	-	-	-	-	-
RW	23	Tamminen, Juhani	65	10	29	39	72	-23	2	0	131	0.076	-	-	-	-	-	-
D	44	Young, Howie	26	1	3	4	23	-8	0	0	28	0.036	-	-	-	-	-	-

Power Play: 47 goals scored in 246 opportunities (19.1%) with 10 short-handed goals allowed.
Penalty Killing: 62 goals allowed in 243 opportunities (74.5%) with 5 short-handed goals scored.

Goaltending

goaltender	gp	min	ga	en	so	record	gaa	sog	sv%	gp	min	ga	record	gaa
Hebenton, Clay	56	3129	220	1	0	17-29-3	4.22	1760	0.875	-	-	-	-	-
Kurt, Gary	33	1752	162	0	0	11-19-1	5.55	1000	0.838	-	-	-	-	-

Transactions: Dave Gorman traded to Birmingham for Jerry Rollins, Nov 1976 • Al McLeod and John Gray traded to Houston for Frank Hughes and Andre Hinse, Dec 1976 • Howie Young signed to contract, Feb 1977 • Garry Lariviere sold to Quebec, Mar 1977

1976-1977 QUEBEC NORDIQUES

Coach
Marc Boileau

Summary of Games (@ Away, * Overtime)

	date	opponent	score		record	pts	gf-ga
1.	Oct 9	Calgary	5-2	W	1-0-0	2	5-2
2.	Oct 10	Birmingham	*4-3	W	2-0-0	4	9-5
3.	Oct 12	San Diego	6-4	W	3-0-0	6	15-9
4.	Oct 16 @	New England	8-2	W	4-0-0	8	23-11
5.	Oct 17	Cincinnati	2-5	L	4-1-0	8	25-16
6.	Oct 19 @	Birmingham	*6-5	W	5-1-0	10	31-21
7.	Oct 21 @	Calgary	4-2	W	6-1-0	12	35-23
8.	Oct 23	Houston	6-2	W	7-1-0	14	41-25
9.	Oct 26	Phoenix	11-3	W	8-1-0	16	52-28
10.	Oct 29 @	Indianapolis	4-6	L	8-2-0	16	56-34
11.	Oct 30	Minnesota	5-1	W	9-2-0	18	61-35
12.	Nov 2	Phoenix	3-5	L	9-3-0	18	64-40
13.	Nov 6	Birmingham	6-5	W	10-3-0	20	70-45
14.	Nov 9	Birmingham	4-3	W	11-3-0	22	74-48
15.	Nov 13	Minnesota	2-4	L	11-4-0	22	76-52
16.	Nov 14	Indianapolis	1-3	L	11-5-0	22	77-55
17.	Nov 16 @	Winnipeg	4-8	L	11-6-0	22	81-63
18.	Nov 18 @	Minnesota	9-5	W	12-6-0	24	90-68
19.	Nov 19 @	Calgary	1-4	L	12-7-0	24	91-72
20.	Nov 21 @	Edmonton	5-6	L	12-8-0	24	96-78
21.	Nov 23	Winnipeg	7-4	W	13-8-0	26	103-82
22.	Nov 25 @	Indianapolis	5-0	W	14-8-0	28	108-82
23.	Nov 26 @	Minnesota	2-4	L	14-9-0	28	110-86
24.	Nov 27	Indianapolis	2-8	L	14-10-0	28	112-94
25.	Nov 30	New England	2-1	W	15-10-0	30	114-95
26.	Dec 3 @	New England	5-5	T	15-10-1	31	119-100
27.	Dec 5	Winnipeg	6-4	W	16-10-1	33	125-104
28.	Dec 7	Edmonton	2-4	L	16-11-1	33	127-108
29.	Dec 9 @	Phoenix	5-4	W	17-11-1	35	132-112
30.	Dec 11	Houston	4-1	W	18-11-1	37	136-113
31.	Dec 12	New England	5-1	W	19-11-1	39	141-114
32.	Dec 14	New England	1-3	L	19-12-1	39	142-117
33.	Dec 18 @	Calgary	2-4	L	19-13-1	39	144-121
34.	Dec 19 @	San Diego	3-5	L	19-14-1	39	147-126
35.	Dec 21 @	Birmingham	2-3	L	19-15-1	39	149-129
36.	Dec 22 @	Minnesota	4-3	W	20-15-1	41	153-132
37.	Dec 26 @	Winnipeg	12-3	W	21-15-1	43	165-135
38.	Dec 28 @	Edmonton	3-2	W	22-15-1	45	168-137
39.	Jan 4	New England	5-3	W	23-15-1	47	173-140
40.	Jan 7 @	New England	7-3	W	24-15-1	49	180-143
41.	Jan 9	San Diego	5-2	W	25-15-1	51	185-145
42.	Jan 20 @	New England	5-4	W	26-15-1	53	190-149
43.	Jan 22	Calgary	5-3	W	27-15-1	55	195-152
44.	Jan 25	Indianapolis	*2-1	W	28-15-1	57	197-153
45.	Jan 26	Edmonton	*4-5	L	28-16-1	57	201-158
46.	Jan 28 @	Indianapolis	6-5	W	29-16-1	59	207-163
47.	Jan 29	Cincinnati	7-2	W	30-16-1	61	214-165
48.	Feb 1	Indianapolis	5-4	W	31-16-1	63	219-169
49.	Feb 2 @	Indianapolis	5-6	L	31-17-1	63	224-175
50.	Feb 4 @	Birmingham	0-7	L	31-18-1	63	224-182
51.	Feb 6	Cincinnati	6-1	W	32-18-1	65	230-183
52.	Feb 8	Winnipeg	2-7	L	32-19-1	65	232-190
53.	Feb 11 @	Indianapolis	5-1	W	33-19-1	67	237-191
54.	Feb 12 @	Houston	3-7	L	33-20-1	67	240-198
55.	Feb 15 @	Houston	2-4	L	33-21-1	67	242-202
56.	Feb 16 @	San Diego	4-2	W	34-21-1	69	246-204
57.	Feb 19 @	Cincinnati	1-3	L	34-22-1	69	247-207
58.	Feb 22	Indianapolis	4-2	W	35-22-1	71	251-209
59.	Feb 24 @	Birmingham	6-10	L	35-23-1	71	257-219
60.	Feb 25 @	Cincinnati	2-5	L	35-24-1	71	259-224
61.	Feb 26	Birmingham	5-3	W	36-24-1	73	264-227
62.	Mar 1 @	Edmonton	5-4	W	37-24-1	75	269-231
63.	Mar 2 @	Winnipeg	*3-4	L	37-25-1	75	272-235
64.	Mar 5	San Diego	6-0	W	38-25-1	77	278-235
65.	Mar 6 @	New England	2-6	L	38-26-1	77	280-241
66.	Mar 8	Phoenix	9-2	W	39-26-1	79	289-243
67.	Mar 12	Edmonton	3-3	T	39-26-2	80	292-246
68.	Mar 13	New England	5-3	W	40-26-2	82	297-249
69.	Mar 15 @	Houston	3-4	L	40-27-2	82	300-253
70.	Mar 17 @	Phoenix	4-3	W	41-27-2	84	304-256
71.	Mar 18 @	Cincinnati	3-7	L	41-28-2	84	307-263
72.	Mar 19	Calgary	8-0	W	42-28-2	86	315-263
73.	Mar 22	Houston	6-2	W	43-28-2	88	321-265
74.	Mar 23 @	Cincinnati	6-4	W	44-28-2	90	327-269
75.	Mar 24 @	Indianapolis	3-4	L	44-29-2	90	330-273
76.	Mar 26	Cincinnati	4-6	L	44-30-2	90	334-279
77.	Mar 27	Cincinnati	4-0	W	45-30-2	92	338-279
78.	Apr 2 @	Phoenix	*6-5	W	46-30-2	94	344-284
79.	Apr 3 @	San Diego	0-7	L	46-31-2	94	344-291
80.	Apr 5	New England	7-2	W	47-31-2	96	351-293
81.	Apr 6 @	Cincinnati	2-2	T	47-31-3	97	353-295

Nordiques Stars of 1976-1977

Real Cloutier	**Richard Brodeur**	**Christian Bordeleau**	**Pailin Bordeleau**	**Paul Baxter**	**Serge Bernier**
141 points led league	29 wins, 12 in playoffs	107 points	42 goals	244 minutes, +14	Playoff-leading 36 pts

Scoring

						Regular Season								**Playoffs**					
pos	#	player	gp	g	a	pts	pim	+/-	ppg	shg	sog	sc%	gp	g	a	pts	pim	+/-
G	25	Aubry, Serge	21	0	1	1	0		0	0	0	-	3	0	0	0	0	0
D	4	Baxter, Paul	66	6	17	23	244	+14	0	0	123	0.049	12	2	2	4	35	+1
D	24	Bernier, Jean	72	2	13	15	23	+2	1	0	115	0.017	9	0	2	2	0	+3
C	21	Bernier, Serge	74	43	53	96	94	+1	11	4	293	0.147	17	14	22	36	10	+16
C	11	Bordeleau, Christian	72	32	75	107	34	+28	6	0	230	0.139	8	4	5	9	0	+3
RW	17	Bordeleau, Paulin	80	42	41	83	52	+7	8	0	210	0.200	16	12	9	21	12	+12
LW	18	Boudrias, Andre	74	12	31	43	12	+3	1	0	92	0.130	17	3	12	15	6	+5
RW	15	Brackenbury, Curt	77	16	13	29	146	+2	0	0	112	0.143	17	3	5	8	51	-1
G	1	Brodeur, Richard	53	0	1	1	0		0	0	0	-	17	0	2	2	0	
RW	9	Cloutier, Real	76	66	75	141	39	+47	25	1	332	0.199	17	14	13	27	10	+11
LW	14	Constantin, Charlie	77	14	19	33	93	+1	1	0	117	0.120	15	0	1	1	15	+4
D	7	Dorey, Jim	73	13	34	47	102	+26	1	3	135	0.096	10	0	2	2	28	+10
LW	20	Dube, Norm	39	15	18	33	8	+11	1	0	75	0.200	14	3	12	15	11	+12
D	20	Dubois, Michel	4	0	0	0	0	0	0	0	2	0.000	2	0	1	1	0	+1
C	12	Fitchner, Bob	81	9	30	39	105	+1	1	0	110	0.082	17	3	3	6	16	+1
C	16	Grenier, Richard	34	11	9	20	4	-6	2	0	60	0.183	-	-	-	-	-	-
LW	6	Guite, Pierre	35	2	6	8	67	-3	0	0	48	0.042	17	5	0	5	9	+1
G	30	Humphreys, Ed	22	0	1	1	0		0	0	0	-	-	-	-	-	-	-
D	22	Lacombe, Francois	81	5	22	27	86	+17	0	0	141	0.035	17	4	3	7	16	+6
D	5	Lariviere, Garry	15	0	3	3	8	+7	0	0	18	0.000	17	0	10	10	10	+13
D	10	Roy, Pierre	29	3	5	8	50	+10	0	0	35	0.086	-	-	-	-	-	-
LW	19	Sutherland, Steve	36	6	9	15	34	+6	0	0	60	0.100	17	5	0	5	16	-4
LW	8	Tardif, Marc	62	49	60	109	65	+29	10	0	220	0.223	12	4	10	14	8	+5
D	3	Tremblay, J.C.	53	4	31	35	10	+2	2	0	75	0.053	17	2	9	11	2	+8
D	2	Weir, Wally	69	3	17	20	197	+13	0	0	123	0.024	17	1	5	6	13	+3

Power Play: 70 goals scored in 258 opportunities (27.1%) with 6 short-handed goals allowed.
Penalty Killing: 66 goals allowed in 316 opportunities (79.1%) with 16 short-handed goals scored.

Goaltending

goaltender	gp	min	ga	en	so	record	gaa	sog	sv%	gp	min	ga	record	gaa
Aubry, Serge	21	769	51	2	1	6-8-0	3.98	370	0.862	3	18	1	0-0	3.33
Brodeur, Richard	53	2906	167	1	2	29-18-2	3.45	1392	0.880	17	1007	55	12-5	3.28
Humphreys, Ed	22	1240	74	0	1	12-8-1	3.58	617	0.880	-	-	-	-	-

Transactions: Paul Baxter signed to contract, Jun 1976 • Richard Grenier acquired from Calgary for future considerations, Jul 1976 • Francois Lacombe acquired from Calgary for future considerations, Aug 1976 • Rights to Paulin Bordeleau acquired from Birmingham for future considerations, Aug 1976 • Jim Corsi, Wally Weir signed to contracts, Sep 1976 • Rights to Andre Boudrias acquired from Minnesota for rights to Gord Gallant, Sep 1976 • Jim Dorey acquired from Birmingham as future consideration of trade for Dale Hoganson, Sep 1976 • Pierre Roy traded to Cincinnati for Pierre Guite, Jan 1977 • Garry Lariviere purchased from Phoenix, Mar 1977

1976-1977 SAN DIEGO MARINERS

**Coach
Ron Ingram**

Summary of Games (@ Away, * Overtime)

	date		opponent	score		record	pts	gf-ga		date		opponent	score		record	pts	gf-ga
1.	Oct 9		Cincinnati	7-7	T	0-0-1	1	7-7	41.	Jan 9	@	Quebec	2-5	L	24-15-2	50	138-126
2.	Oct 12	@	Quebec	4-6	L	0-1-1	1	11-13	42.	Jan 13		Cincinnati	2-7	L	24-16-2	50	140-133
3.	Oct 15	@	Minnesota	7-4	W	1-1-1	3	18-17	43.	Jan 15		Calgary	3-5	L	24-17-2	50	143-138
4.	Oct 16		Calgary	4-2	W	2-1-1	5	22-19	44.	Jan 16		Birmingham	5-2	W	25-17-2	52	148-140
5.	Oct 17		Winnipeg	3-1	W	3-1-1	7	25-20	45.	Jan 20		Edmonton	5-1	W	26-17-2	54	153-141
6.	Oct 21		Indianapolis	4-4	T	3-1-2	8	29-24	46.	Jan 22		Houston	0-6	L	26-18-2	54	153-147
7.	Oct 24	@	Calgary	0-6	L	3-2-2	8	29-30	47.	Jan 23	@	Houston	3-5	L	26-19-2	54	156-152
8.	Oct 26	@	Minnesota	1-3	L	3-3-2	8	30-33	48.	Jan 27		New England	3-5	L	26-20-2	54	159-157
9.	Oct 27	@	Indianapolis	5-1	W	4-3-2	10	35-34	49.	Jan 29		Winnipeg	5-3	W	27-20-2	56	164-160
10.	Oct 29	@	Cincinnati	2-4	L	4-4-2	10	37-38	50.	Feb 1		Phoenix	5-1	W	28-20-2	58	169-161
11.	Oct 31	@	Winnipeg	4-6	L	4-5-2	10	41-44	51.	Feb 2		Calgary	6-4	W	29-20-2	60	175-165
12.	Nov 2	@	Birmingham	*4-3	W	5-5-2	12	45-47	52.	Feb 4	@	Winnipeg	2-8	L	29-21-2	60	177-173
13.	Nov 6		Houston	4-1	W	6-5-2	14	49-48	53.	Feb 6	@	Edmonton	2-4	L	29-22-2	60	179-177
14.	Nov 7		Indianapolis	3-0	W	7-5-2	16	52-48	54.	Feb 8	@	Edmonton	6-5	W	30-22-2	62	185-182
15.	Nov 11	@	Birmingham	3-2	W	8-5-2	18	55-50	55.	Feb 11	@	Phoenix	5-3	W	31-22-2	64	190-185
16.	Nov 12	@	Houston	1-4	L	8-6-2	18	56-54	56.	Feb 12		Birmingham	*3-2	W	32-22-2	66	193-187
17.	Nov 14	@	Phoenix	3-6	L	8-7-2	18	59-60	57.	Feb 13		Phoenix	5-2	W	33-22-2	68	198-189
18.	Nov 17		Edmonton	4-2	W	9-7-2	20	63-62	58.	Feb 16		Quebec	2-4	L	33-23-2	68	200-193
19.	Nov 19		Houston	5-3	W	10-7-2	22	68-65	59.	Feb 18	@	Houston	2-4	L	33-24-2	68	202-197
20.	Nov 21	@	Birmingham	3-4	L	10-8-2	22	71-69	60.	Feb 19	@	Houston	3-5	L	33-25-2	68	205-202
21.	Nov 24		Edmonton	4-2	W	11-8-2	24	75-71	61.	Feb 24		Phoenix	3-3	T	33-25-3	69	208-205
22.	Nov 27	@	Calgary	2-0	W	12-8-2	26	77-71	62.	Feb 26		Houston	4-5	L	33-26-3	69	212-210
23.	Nov 28	@	Edmonton	0-4	L	12-9-2	26	77-75	63.	Mar 2	@	New England	0-2	L	33-27-3	69	212-212
24.	Nov 30	@	Winnipeg	2-8	L	12-10-2	26	79-83	64.	Mar 4	@	Indianapolis	4-7	L	33-28-3	69	216-219
25.	Dec 2		Phoenix	4-3	W	13-10-2	28	83-86	65.	Mar 5	@	Quebec	0-6	L	33-29-3	69	216-225
26.	Dec 4	@	Phoenix	4-3	W	14-10-2	30	87-89	66.	Mar 6	@	Calgary	2-4	L	33-30-3	69	218-229
27.	Dec 8	@	Cincinnati	6-1	W	15-10-2	32	93-90	67.	Mar 8	@	Winnipeg	0-5	L	33-31-3	69	218-234
28.	Dec 10	@	Indianapolis	2-3	L	15-11-2	32	95-93	68.	Mar 9	@	Calgary	3-4	L	33-32-3	69	221-238
29.	Dec 11	@	New England	2-3	L	15-12-2	32	97-96	69.	Mar 12		Phoenix	6-7	L	33-33-3	69	227-245
30.	Dec 12	@	Minnesota	4-2	W	16-12-2	34	101-98	70.	Mar 15		Phoenix	4-4	T	33-33-4	70	231-249
31.	Dec 14	@	Edmonton	6-1	W	17-12-2	36	107-99	71.	Mar 19	@	Phoenix	5-7	L	33-34-4	70	236-256
32.	Dec 16		Edmonton	3-0	W	18-12-2	38	110-99	72.	Mar 20		Phoenix	6-1	W	34-34-4	72	242-257
33.	Dec 18		Houston	4-3	W	19-12-2	40	114-102	73.	Mar 24		Birmingham	6-2	W	35-34-4	74	248-259
34.	Dec 19		Quebec	5-3	W	20-12-2	42	119-105	74.	Mar 25	@	Phoenix	7-3	W	36-34-4	76	255-262
35.	Dec 22	@	Phoenix	*5-4	W	21-12-2	44	124-109	75.	Mar 26		Calgary	4-2	W	37-34-4	78	259-264
36.	Dec 23		New England	3-5	L	21-13-2	44	127-114	76.	Mar 29		New England	4-5	L	37-35-4	78	263-269
37.	Dec 26		Indianapolis	2-1	W	22-13-2	46	129-115	77.	Mar 31		Winnipeg	4-3	W	38-35-4	80	267-272
38.	Dec 30		Winnipeg	4-3	W	23-13-2	48	133-118	78.	Apr 2		Cincinnati	6-3	W	39-35-4	82	273-275
39.	Jan 5	@	New England	2-1	W	24-13-2	50	135-119	79.	Apr 3		Quebec	7-0	W	40-35-4	84	280-275
40.	Jan 8	@	Cincinnati	1-2	L	24-14-2	50	136-121	80.	Apr 5	@	Houston	1-3	L	40-36-4	84	281-278
									81.	Apr 6		Houston	3-5	L	40-37-4	84	284-283

328

Mariners Stars of 1976-1977

Norm Ferguson
39 goals

Andre Lacroix
82 assists, 114 points

Joe Noris
35 goals, 92 points

Paul Shmyr
103 minutes

Kevin Devine
30 goals

Tony Cassolato
team best +9

Scoring

pos	#	player	gp	g	a	pts	pim	+/-	ppg	shg	sog	sc%	gp	g	a	pts	pim	+/-
C	10	Adduono, Ray	13	2	5	7	5	+1	1	0	47	0.043	7	3	2	5	19	0
D	18	Boddy, Greg	18	1	2	3	19	-6	0	0	15	0.067	-	-	-	-	-	-
W	8	Burgess, Don	77	20	22	42	8	-8	4	1	167	0.120	7	2	2	4	0	-2
RW	22	Cassolato, Tony	43	13	12	25	26	+9	2	0	54	0.241	3	0	0	0	4	-4
C	27	Cournoyer, Norm	19	1	2	3	8	-14	0	0	30	0.033	-	-	-	-	-	-
LW	16	Devine, Kevin	81	30	20	50	114	-12	7	1	182	0.165	7	1	3	4	14	-5
C	19	Dobek, Bob	58	7	17	24	17	-9	2	0	87	0.080	5	0	0	0	4	-2
D	6	Falkenberg, Bob	64	0	6	6	34	-11	0	0	25	0.000	2	0	0	0	0	0
RW	9	Ferguson, Norm	77	39	32	71	5	-5	10	0	217	0.180	7	2	4	6	0	+2
LW	11	French, John	44	14	21	35	6	-3	2	0	79	0.177	7	2	3	5	2	+1
D	29	Hornung, Larry	58	4	9	13	8	-7	0	0	42	0.095	6	0	0	0	0	-12
D	2	Hughes, Brent	62	4	13	17	48	-3	0	0	54	0.074	7	0	4	4	0	+5
C	7	Lacroix, Andre	81	32	82	114	79	+2	11	3	231	0.139	7	1	6	7	6	-1
D	5	Legge, Randy	69	1	9	10	69	-18	0	0	29	0.034	7	0	0	0	18	-6
G	1	Lockett, Ken	45	0	0	0	0		0	0	0	-	5	0	0	0	0	
D	18	McNamee, Pete	41	3	6	9	38	-7	0	0	26	0.115	2	0	0	0	2	-1
D	4	Morrison, Kevin	75	8	30	38	68	-30	4	0	247	0.032	7	1	3	4	8	+6
D	21	Noris, Joe	73	35	57	92	30	+2	9	6	243	0.144	7	2	1	3	6	-5
RW	20	O'Connell, Tim	16	0	3	3	4	-12	0	0	13	0.000	-	-	-	-	-	-
LW	14	Pinder, Gerry	44	6	13	19	36	-24	2	0	90	0.067	-	-	-	-	-	-
C	10	Rhiness, Brad	58	9	14	23	14	-17	0	0	66	0.136	5	0	1	1	0	+1
RW	12	Rivers, Wayne	60	18	31	49	40	+5	7	0	168	0.107	7	1	1	2	2	-4
RW	28	Sentes, Dick	24	10	11	21	16	+7	2	0	56	0.179	5	4	0	4	12	-3
D	3	Shmyr, Paul	81	13	37	50	103	-4	3	0	206	0.063	7	0	2	2	8	-12
LW	17	Veneruzzo, Gary	40	14	11	25	18	+4	3	0	94	0.149	7	0	0	0	0	-1
G	31	Wakely, Ernie	46	0	0	0	0		0	0	0	-	3	0	0	0	0	
D		Winograd, Bob	1	0	0	0	0	+1	0	0	1	0.000	-	-	-	-	-	-

Power Play: 69 goals scored in 257 opportunities (26.8%) with 6 short-handed goals allowed.
Penalty Killing: 43 goals allowed in 204 opportunities (78.9%) with 11 short-handed goals scored.

Goaltending

goaltender	gp	min	ga	en	so	record	gaa	sog	sv%	gp	min	ga	record	gaa
Lockett, Ken	45	2397	148	4	1	18-19-1	3.70	1147	0.871	5	260	19	1-3	4.38
Wakely, Ernie	46	2506	129	2	3	22-18-3	3.09	1240	0.896	3	160	9	2-1	3.38

Transactions: Randy Legge signed to contract, Jul 1976 • Gary Veneruzzo acquired from Phoenix for future considerations, Aug 1976 • Greg Boddy, Ken Lockett signed to contracts, Sep 1976 • Ray Adduono and Bob Wall traded to Minnesota for Paul Shmyr and Gerry Pinder, Sep 1976 • Greg Boddy traded to Edmonton for Larry Hornung, Nov 1976 • Ray Adduono signed from defunct Minnesota, Jan 1977 • Dick Sentes signed as free agent, Jan 1977

1976-1977 WINNIPEG JETS

**Coach
Bobby Kromm**

Summary of Games (@ Away, * Overtime)

	date	opponent	score		record	pts	gf-ga		date	opponent	score		record	pts	gf-ga
1.	Oct 8	Calgary	4-1	W	1-0-0	2	4-1	41.	Jan 21	Cincinnati	*6-5	W	24-16-1	49	189-147
2.	Oct 10	New England	5-2	W	2-0-0	4	9-3	42.	Jan 23	Calgary	10-5	W	25-16-1	51	199-152
3.	Oct 15 @	Edmonton	6-1	W	3-0-0	6	15-4	43.	Jan 25 @	Houston	2-5	L	25-17-1	51	201-157
4.	Oct 16 @	Phoenix	4-6	L	3-1-0	6	19-10	44.	Jan 27 @	Birmingham	0-3	L	25-18-1	51	201-160
5.	Oct 17 @	San Diego	1-3	L	3-2-0	6	20-13	45.	Jan 29 @	San Diego	3-5	L	25-19-1	51	204-165
6.	Oct 19	Indianapolis	6-1	W	4-2-0	8	26-14	46.	Jan 30 @	Phoenix	5-8	L	25-20-1	51	209-173
7.	Oct 22	Phoenix	3-4	L	4-3-0	8	29-18	47.	Feb 1 @	Edmonton	11-1	W	26-20-1	53	220-174
8.	Oct 24	Birmingham	7-1	W	5-3-0	10	36-19	48.	Feb 4	San Diego	8-2	W	27-20-1	55	228-176
9.	Oct 29	Edmonton	11-3	W	6-3-0	12	47-22	49.	Feb 6	Calgary	6-4	W	28-20-1	57	234-180
10.	Oct 31	San Diego	6-4	W	7-3-0	14	53-26	50.	Feb 8 @	Quebec	7-2	W	29-20-1	59	241-182
11.	Nov 2	Houston	1-3	L	7-4-0	14	54-29	51.	Feb 10 @	New England	3-6	L	29-21-1	59	244-188
12.	Nov 5	Minnesota	9-2	W	8-4-0	16	63-31	52.	Feb 11 @	Cincinnati	0-4	L	29-22-1	59	244-192
13.	Nov 6 @	Cincinnati	3-7	L	8-5-0	16	66-38	53.	Feb 13 @	Indianapolis	7-5	W	30-22-1	61	251-197
14.	Nov 7	Edmonton	5-2	W	9-5-0	18	71-40	54.	Feb 15	Calgary	2-2	T	30-22-2	62	253-199
15.	Nov 9	New England	*5-4	W	10-5-0	20	76-44	55.	Feb 17	Indianapolis	4-2	W	31-22-2	64	257-201
16.	Nov 11 @	Calgary	5-7	L	10-6-0	20	81-51	56.	Feb 18 @	Edmonton	2-3	L	31-23-2	64	259-204
17.	Nov 14 @	Calgary	2-0	W	11-6-0	22	83-51	57.	Feb 20	Edmonton	4-2	W	32-23-2	66	263-206
18.	Nov 16	Quebec	8-4	W	12-6-0	24	91-55	58.	Feb 22	Houston	3-2	W	33-23-2	68	266-208
19.	Nov 19 @	New England	7-3	W	13-6-0	26	98-58	59.	Feb 23 @	Phoenix	3-6	L	33-24-2	68	269-214
20.	Nov 20 @	Indianapolis	4-8	L	13-7-0	26	102-66	60.	Feb 26 @	Cincinnati	8-6	W	34-24-2	70	277-220
21.	Nov 21	Cincinnati	2-4	L	13-8-0	26	104-70	61.	Feb 27	New England	2-3	L	34-25-2	70	279-223
22.	Nov 23 @	Quebec	4-7	L	13-9-0	26	108-77	62.	Mar 1 @	Calgary	1-6	L	34-26-2	70	280-229
23.	Nov 26 @	Houston	1-1	T	13-9-1	27	109-78	63.	Mar 2	Quebec	*4-3	W	35-26-2	72	284-232
24.	Nov 28	Phoenix	3-5	L	13-10-1	27	112-83	64.	Mar 3 @	Edmonton	4-5	L	35-27-2	72	288-237
25.	Nov 30	San Diego	8-2	W	14-10-1	29	120-85	65.	Mar 5 @	Phoenix	1-4	L	35-28-2	72	289-241
26.	Dec 3 @	Minnesota	4-3	W	15-10-1	31	124-88	66.	Mar 8	San Diego	5-0	W	36-28-2	74	294-241
27.	Dec 4 @	New England	6-2	W	16-10-1	33	130-90	67.	Mar 11	Calgary	4-1	W	37-28-2	76	298-242
28.	Dec 5 @	Quebec	4-6	L	16-11-1	33	134-96	68.	Mar 13	Edmonton	9-3	W	38-28-2	78	307-245
29.	Dec 7	Phoenix	4-2	W	17-11-1	35	138-98	69.	Mar 15	Edmonton	7-0	W	39-28-2	80	314-245
30.	Dec 8 @	Calgary	4-2	W	18-11-1	37	142-100	70.	Mar 17 @	Edmonton	3-4	L	39-29-2	80	317-249
31.	Dec 10	Birmingham	3-5	L	18-12-1	37	145-105	71.	Mar 18 @	Indianapolis	7-5	W	40-29-2	82	324-254
32.	Dec 26	Quebec	3-12	L	18-13-1	37	148-117	72.	Mar 20 @	Birmingham	4-3	W	41-29-2	84	328-257
33.	Dec 28 @	Houston	3-6	L	18-14-1	37	151-123	73.	Mar 22	Edmonton	8-3	W	42-29-2	86	336-260
34.	Dec 30 @	San Diego	3-4	L	18-15-1	37	154-127	74.	Mar 27 @	Houston	5-3	W	43-29-2	88	341-263
35.	Jan 2	Houston	5-2	W	19-15-1	39	159-129	75.	Mar 29	Houston	2-5	L	43-30-2	88	343-268
36.	Jan 4	Indianapolis	2-1	W	20-15-1	41	161-130	76.	Mar 31 @	San Diego	3-4	L	43-31-2	88	346-272
37.	Jan 9	Birmingham	4-1	W	21-15-1	43	165-131	77.	Apr 2 @	Birmingham	6-5	W	44-31-2	90	352-277
38.	Jan 11	Phoenix	9-2	W	22-15-1	45	174-133	78.	Apr 3	Calgary	6-4	W	45-31-2	92	358-281
39.	Jan 14 @	Calgary	5-3	W	23-15-1	47	179-136	79.	Apr 4 @	Edmonton	2-6	L	45-32-2	92	360-287
40.	Jan 16	Cincinnati	4-6	L	23-16-1	47	183-142	80.	Apr 7 @	Calgary	6-4	W	46-32-2	94	366-291

Jets Stars of 1976-1977

Andres Hedberg	Ulf Nilsson	Joe Daley	Willy Lindstrom	Perry Miller	Dan Labraaten
70 goals, 131 points	85 assists, 124 points	39 wins, 3 shutouts	44 goals	+27 rating	24 goals, 51 points

Scoring

pos	#	player	gp	g	a	pts	pim	+/-	ppg	shg	sog	sc%	gp	g	a	pts	pim	+/-
						Regular Season									**Playoffs**			
D	2	Bergman, Thommie	42	2	24	26	37	+3	0	0	74	0.027	-	-	-	-	-	-
LW	21	Cole, Jim	2	0	1	1	0	-1	0	0	5	0.000	-	-	-	-	-	-
G	1	Daley, Joe	65	0	4	4	6		0	0	0	-	20	0	0	0	0	
D	8	Dunn, Dave	40	3	11	14	129	-1	0	0	30	0.100	20	4	4	8	23	-7
D	5	Ford, Mike	22	3	14	17	20	+14	0	0	57	0.053	20	3	13	16	12	+7
D	6	Green, Ted	70	4	21	25	45	+12	2	0	59	0.068	20	1	3	4	12	-4
LW	18	Guindon, Robert	69	10	17	27	19	-12	3	0	75	0.133	20	4	4	8	9	-4
RW	15	Hedberg, Anders	68	70	61	131	48	+48	22	0	313	0.224	20	13	16	29	13	+6
C	7	Huck, Fran	12	2	2	4	10	-1	0	0	15	0.133	7	0	2	2	6	-1
LW	9	Hull, Bobby	34	21	32	53	14	+16	7	0	102	0.206	20	13	9	22	2	+6
C	12	Ketola, Veli-Pekka	64	25	29	54	59	-13	6	0	210	0.119	-	-	-	-	-	-
LW	21	Labraaten, Dan	64	24	27	51	21	-11	8	0	134	0.179	20	7	17	24	15	+8
G	30	Larsson, Curt	19	0	1	1	4		0	0	0	-	1	0	0	0	0	
RW	11	Lawson, Danny	14	6	7	13	2	0	2	2	46	0.130	13	2	4	6	6	-1
LW	17	Lesuk, Bill	78	14	27	41	85	+23	2	0	90	0.156	18	2	1	3	22	-7
D	19	Lindh, Mats	73	14	17	31	2	-13	1	2	101	0.139	20	2	7	9	2	0
RW	20	Lindstrom, Willy	79	44	36	80	37	-2	11	0	235	0.187	20	9	6	15	22	+5
D	3	Long, Barry	71	9	38	47	54	-1	4	0	178	0.051	20	1	5	6	10	-1
D	25	Miller, Perry	74	14	31	45	124	+27	5	1	154	0.091	20	4	6	10	27	-6
LW	22	Moffat, Lyle	74	13	11	24	90	-7	2	0	86	0.151	17	2	0	2	6	-6
RW	11	Mott, Morris	2	0	1	1	5	+1	0	0	1	0.000	-	-	-	-	-	-
C	14	Nilsson, Ulf	71	39	85	124	89	+57	8	3	193	0.202	20	6	21	27	33	+5
D	5	Riihiranta, Heikki	53	1	16	17	28	-1	0	0	49	0.020	-	-	-	-	-	-
RW	23	Ruhnke, Kent	51	11	11	22	2	-12	0	0	87	0.126	-	-	-	-	-	-
D	4	Sjoberg, Lars-Erik	52	2	38	40	31	+9	1	1	77	0.026	20	0	5	5	12	+11
D	10	Sullivan, Peter	78	31	52	83	18	+11	6	0	176	0.176	20	7	12	19	2	+5
C	11	Ward, Ron	14	4	7	11	2	-2	2	0	24	0.167	-	-	-	-	-	-

Power Play: 90 goals scored in 370 opportunities (24.3%) with 11 short-handed goals allowed.
Penalty Killing: 49 goals allowed in 231 opportunities (78.8%) with 9 short-handed goals scored.

Goaltending

goaltender	gp	min	ga	en	so	record	gaa	sog	sv%	gp	min	ga	record	gaa
Daley, Joe	65	3818	206	1	3	39-23-2	3.24	1907	0.892	20	1186	71	11-9	3.59
Larsson, Curt	19	1019	82	2	0	7-9-0	4.83	547	0.850	1	20	1	0-0	3.00

Transactions: Fran Huck signed to contract, Jun 1976 • Dave Dunn signed to contract, Sep 1976 • Mike Ford traded to Calgary for draft picks, Oct 1976 • Barry Long acquired for future considerations from Edmonton, Nov 1976 • Morris Mott and Jim Cole signed to contracts, Jan 1977 • Ron Ward and Veli-Pekka Ketola traded to Calgary for Mike Ford and Danny Lawson, Mar 1977 (Heikki Riihiranta was originally to be traded, but he refused to report and Ron Ward was sent to Calgary to complete the trade)

1976-1977 Statistical Leaders

Top five in each category.

Goals: 70, Anders Hedberg (Winnipeg); 66, Real Cloutier (Quebec); 60, Mark Napier (Birmingham); 52, Richie Leduc (Cincinnati), Blaine Stoughton (Cincinnati); 49, Marc Tardif (Quebec).

Assists: 85, Ulf Nilsson (Winnipeg); 82, Andre Lacroix (San Diego); 75, Christian Bordeleau (Quebec), Real Cloutier (Quebec); 71, Robbie Ftorek (Phoenix); 63, Dave Keon (Minnesota-New England).

Points: 141, Real Cloutier (Quebec); 131, Anders Hedberg (Winnipeg); 124, Ulf Nilsson (Winnipeg); 117, Robbie Ftorek (Phoenix); 114, Andre Lacroix (San Diego).

Penalty Minutes: 274, Frank Beaton (Edmonton); 244, Paul Baxter (Quebec); 224, Ron Busniuk (Minnesota-Edmonton), Cam Connor (Houston); 215, Bill Butters (Minnesota-Edmonton-New England); 197, Wally Weir (Quebec).

Power-play Goals: 25, Real Cloutier (Quebec); 22, Anders Hedberg (Winnipeg); 12, George Lyle (New England); 11, Serge Bernier (Quebec), Robbie Ftorek (Phoenix), Andre Lacroix (San Diego), Richie Leduc (Cincinnati), Willy Lindstrom (Winnipeg), Tim Sheehy (Edmonton-Birmingham), Tom Webster (New England).

Short-handed Goals: 8, Paulin Bordeleau (Quebec); 6, Joe Noris (San Diego); 5, Rich Preston (Houston), Dennis Sobchuk (Cincinnati); 4, Serge Bernier (Quebec), Hugh Harris (Indianapolis), Ron Huston (Phoenix), Danny Lawson (Calgary-Winnipeg), Don Tannahill (Calgary).

Goaltending Minutes: 3818, Joe Daley (Winnipeg); 3803, John Garrett (Birmingham); 3701, Don McLeod (Calgary); 3129, Clay Hebenton (Phoenix); 2928, Louis Levasseur (Minnesota-Edmonton).

Goals Against Average: 2.74, Ron Grahame (Houston); 3.09, Ernie Wakely (San Diego); 3.12, Cap Raeder (New England); 3.15, Wayne Rutledge (Houston); 3.36, Michel Dion (Indianapolis). (Note: Jacques Caron (Cincinnati), 2.84 average in 24 games; Dave Dryden (Edmonton), 3.26 average in 24 games).

Wins: 39, Joe Daley (Winnipeg); 29, Richard Brodeur (Quebec); 27, Ron Grahame (Houston); 25, Don McLeod (Calgary); 24, John Garrett (Birmingham).

Shutouts: 4, Ken Broderick (Edmonton); John Garrett (Birmingham); Ron Grahame (Houston); 3, Joe Daley (Winnipeg), Don McLeod (Calgary), Wayne Rutledge (Houston), Ernie Wakely (San Diego); 2, shared by many.

Totals for Players With Two or More Teams During 1976-1977

player	teams	gp	g	a	pts	pim	+/-	ppg	shg	sog	sc%
Adduono, Ray	Min, SD	53	6	24	30	22	-13	4	0	55	0.109
Antonovich, Mike	Min, Edm, NE	75	40	31	71	38	+28	7	0	256	0.156
Arbour, John	Min, Cgy	70	4	34	38	60	-12	1	0	158	0.025
Arndt, Danny	NE, Edm	47	8	14	22	11	-15	1	0	87	0.092
Baird, Ken	Edm, Cgy	9	1	2	3	2	0	0	0	10	0.100
Boddy, Greg	SD, Edm	64	2	19	21	60	+5	1	0	57	0.035
Butters, Biil	Min, Edm, NE	75	1	17	18	215	+16	0	0	93	0.011
Busniuk, Ron	NE, Edm	81	3	11	14	224	-10	0	0	115	0.026
Callighen, Brett	NE, Edm	62	15	26	41	89	+5	3	0	97	0.155
Campbell, Bryan	Ind, Edm	74	13	46	59	24	-18	1	1	170	0.076
Carlson, Jack	Min, NE	71	11	8	19	136	-3	0	0	96	0.115
Carlson, Steve	Min, NE	52	9	17	26	48	+3	0	0	89	0.101
Connelly, Wayne	Cgy, Edm	63	18	21	39	22	-2	5	0	162	0.111
Deadmarsh, Butch	Min, Cgy	73	22	21	43	128	-10	5	0	161	0.137
Ford, Mike	Cgy, Wpg	76	8	34	42	34	+8	2	0	201	0.040
Gallant, Gord	Min, Bir	71	10	16	26	126	+7	1	0	105	0.095
Gorman, David	Phx, Bir	57	9	13	22	38	+2	0	1	68	0.132
Gray, John	Phx, Hou	75	31	30	61	84	+21	3	0	174	0.178
Gruen, Danny	Min, Cgy	35	11	9	20	19	+9	2	0	85	0.129
Guite, Pierre	Cin, Que	62	12	14	26	99	-5	2	0	117	0.103
Hanson, Dave	Min, NE	8	0	2	2	44	-9	0	0	4	0.000
Hinse, Andre	Hou, Phx	42	4	10	14	22	-16	0	0	52	0.077
Hoganson, Paul	Cin, Ind	28	0	0	0	2		0	0	0	-
Hornung, Larry	Edm, SD	79	6	10	16	8	-13	0	0	63	0.095
Hughes, Frank	Hou, Phx	75	27	37	64	22	+5	3	0	198	0.136
Inkpen, Dave	Cin, Ind	80	7	26	33	81	+16	0	0	124	0.056
Keon, Dave	Min, NE	76	27	63	90	10	+38	6	2	258	0.105
Ketola, Veli-Pekka	Wpg, Cgy	81	29	35	64	61	-30	7	0	268	0.108
Kirk, Gavin	Bir, Edm	81	17	46	63	50	-10	8	0	133	0.128
Lawson, Danny	Cgy, Wpg	78	30	26	56	28	-13	4	4	294	0.102
Lariviere, Garry	Phx, Que	76	7	26	33	56	-12	3	0	125	0.056
Legge, Barry	Min, Cin	76	7	22	29	39	+19	0	0	108	0.065
Levasseur, Louis	Min, Edm	51	0	1	1	4		0	0	0	-
Locas, Jacques	Cin, Cgy	67	21	17	38	29	-5	6	0	118	0.178
Long, Barry	Edm, Wpg	73	9	39	48	56	-5	3	0	181	0.050
MacGregor, Gary	Ind, NE	46	8	13	21	8	-25	3	0	100	0.080
McKay, Ray	Min, Bir	61	2	10	12	39	+14	0	0	59	0.034
McKenzie, John	Min, NE	74	28	32	60	77	+24	3	3	161	0.174
McLeod, Al	Phx, Hou	80	8	26	34	55	+9	1	0	92	0.087
Paiement, Rosaire	NE, Ind	80	23	27	50	103	-1	3	0	176	0.131
Peacosh, Gene	Edm, Ind	75	27	30	57	35	+1	9	0	152	0.178
Rollins, Jerry	Bir, Phx	71	4	10	14	186	-27	1	0	77	0.052

Totals for Players With Two or More Teams During 1976-1977

(continued)

player	teams	gp	g	a	pts	pim	+/-	ppg	shg	sog	sc%
Roy, Pierre	Que, Cin	68	6	17	23	176	+29	0	0	100	0.060
St Sauveur, Claude	Cgy, Edm	32	5	10	15	4	-2	0	0	45	0.111
Sentes, Dick	Cgy, SD	53	20	25	45	24	+24	3	0	109	0.183
Sheehy, Tim	Edm, Bir	78	41	29	70	48	-9	11	0	260	0.158
Simpson, Tom	Bir, Edm	40	10	8	18	26	-10	4	0	85	0.118
Smedsmo, Dale	NE, Cin	38	2	5	7	97	-13	1	0	33	0.061
Stewart, John A.	Min, Bir	16	3	3	6	2	-6	0	0	39	0.077
Ward, Ron	Min, Wpg, Cgy	64	24	33	57	8	+9	7	1	138	0.174
Westrum, Pat	Min, Bir	74	2	20	22	90	+23	0	0	70	0.029

Totals for Goaltenders With Two or More Teams During 1976-1977

goaltender	teams	gp	min	ga	en	so	record	gaa	sog	sv%
Paul Hoganson	Cin, Ind	28	1218	88	0	1	8-8-1	4.33	600	0.853
Louis Levasseur	Min, Edm	51	2928	166	2	2	21-23-5	3.40	1632	0.898

Shorthanded

In a penalty-filled game between the touring Soviet All-Stars and the Houston Aeros on December 28, 1977, the Aeros played almost half the game shorthanded, a whopping 25:42 with at least one player in the penalty box. In the game, the Soviets had 24 man-advantages, compared to two for the Aeros. The Soviets scored four power-play goals in winning the exhibition game, 7-3. The WHA record for man-advantages by one team was 13, set three times by Winnipeg in wins over Cincinnati (October 21, 1975), Quebec (March 10, 1976) and Houston (March 27, 1977).

San Diego and Phoenix participated in a gentlemanly game, their final playoff tangle on April 17, 1976, in which no penalties were called. It is the only game in which both teams combined for zero penalties and penalty minutes. San Diego won, 2-1.

Gallery

Ralph MacSweyn

Fred Speck

Brit Selby

Dunc Rousseau

Irv Spencer

Rudy Tajcnar

Jim Turkiewicz

Bob Whidden

Rod Zaine

Jean-Luc Phaneuf

Arenas of the World Hockey Association

Northlands Coliseum
Edmonton, Alberta

Opened: November 1974. Delays at the last moments forced Edmonton to reschedule its October 1974 contests to later dates. Known as Northlands Coliseum until 1995, then Skyreach Centre through 2003, and currently as Rexall Place. The Oilers played their final game here in April 2016, at which time Rexall Arena was the second-oldest arena in the NHL, behind Madison Square Garden in New York. It is expected that Rexall Place will still be used for other attractions after the Oilers vacate.

Le Colisee
Quebec City, Quebec

Opened: 1949. Long-time home to the minor-pro and major-junior Quebec Aces and later, the Quebec Remparts, and to the Nordiques during 1972 through 1995. The arena underwent a massive expansion in 1979 after the Nordiques were admitted to the NHL. Known as Colisee Pepsi, the arena continued to host hockey tournaments as well as many other sporting events and attractions. The new Centre Videotron Arena opened September 2015 and was built nearby Le Colisee, with hopes that an NHL franchise will move to Quebec City soon. Le Colisee hosted its last attraction in September 2015, and will eventually be demolished.

Hartford Civic Center Arena
Hartford, Connecticut

Opened: January, 1975. Home to the New England Whalers during 1975 through January 1978, and the Hartford Whalers of the NHL from 1980 through 1997. On January 18, 1978, the roof collapsed under the weight of heavy snow, forcing the Whalers to play in Springfield, Massachusetts for three years. The arena was rebuilt and expanded, now known as the XL Center. Multiple professional and college sports teams continue to use the XL Center.

Winnipeg Arena
Winnipeg, Manitoba

Opened: 1955. Home to the Winnipeg Jets from 1972 through 1996. Like other WHA arenas, it was expanded in size in 1979 as the Jets transferred to the NHL. The Winnipeg Arena was home to many sports teams and host to many attractions until it ceased to be used in November 2004. It was finally demolished in 2006. The newer MTS Centre, completed in 2004, is home to the newer incarnation of the Winnipeg Jets of the NHL, after the Atlanta Thrashers moved to Winnipeg in 2011.

International Amphitheater
Chicago, Illinois

Opened: 1934. The arena was state-of-the-art for its time and was host to many sports teams as well as other attractions beyond its original intended use. It may be most famous in American history as the location of the 1968 Democratic Presidential Convention and the riots that took place immediately outside. It became obsolete by the early 1980s and was demolished in 1999.

Riverfront Coliseum
Cincinnati, Ohio

Opened: September 1975. Built adjacent to the old Riverfront Stadium, old home of the Reds (MLB) and Bengals (NFL). The arena has been continuously used by multiple college and professional sports teams since its inception, as well as for other attractions. It is known today as the U. S. Bank Arena.

Market Square Arena
Indianapolis, Indiana

Opened: September 1974. Home to the Racers from 1974 through 1978, and the Pacers of the ABA and NBA from 1974 through 1999. Market Square Arena was unique in that its playing surface was elevated—indeed, the whole building was elevated—over Market Street. The arena was imploded in 2001.

Los Angeles Memorial Sports Arena
Los Angeles, California

Opened: 1959. Home to the Lakers of the NBA from 1960 through 1967, when the Forum in Inglewood was completed. It also hosted the Kings of the NHL briefly during 1967. The Clippers of the NBA then played here from 1984 through 1999, while many USC and UCLA sporting events have been held here. It was closed and demolished over the summer of 2016.

Cobo Hall
Detroit, Michigan

Opened: 1960. Home to the Detroit Pistons of the NBA through 1978, and to the Stags during their short life, October 1974 through January 1975. The site has undergone many renovations and is currently known as the Cobo Center. Professional sports no longer use the site, which is strictly used these days for expositions and fairs.

San Diego Sports Arena
San Diego, California

Opened: 1966. Home to the San Diego Gulls of the Western Hockey League, and the Mariners from 1974 through 1977. Also home to the Rockets (1967-71) and Clippers (1978-84) of the NBA, and the Conquistadors and Sails of the ABA (1974-75). Still is use for sports and other attractions, it is currently known as the Valley View Casino Center.

Ottawa Civic Centre
Ottawa, Ontario

Opened: 1967. Built alongside—and partially within—the Lansdowne Football Stadium. Home to the Ottawa 67's of the OHA nearly continuously since 1967, also home to the Ottawa Senators of the NHL from 1992-95. The Nationals (1972-73), and the Toronto Toros (selected games during 1973-74), played here, as did the Ottawa Civics for two games in January 1976. It is still is use and called the TD Place Arena.

Maple Leaf Gardens
Toronto, Ontario

Opened: 1931. The hallowed "shrine" of hockey, run by avowed WHA-foe Harold Ballard, actually hosted the Ottawa Nationals during the 1973 playoffs, and the Toronto Toros from 1974-76. Of course, the Maple Leafs of the NHL called the Gardens their home through 1999, when they moved into the Air Canada Centre. Even the Toronto Raptors of the NBA played a handful of games here. It is currently retrofitted as a multi-use retail center with some limited sporting facilities, mainly for local universities.

Jefferson County Civic Center
Birmingham, Alabama

Opened: 1976. The Bulls were its first principal tenants, from 1976 through 1979. It is currently known as the Birmingham-Jefferson Convention Complex and is still used for minor-pro and college sports, concerts, expositions, and other attractions.

Philadelphia Civic Center
Philadelphia. Pennsylvania

Opened: 1931. State of the art for its time and an architectural attraction in its own right, the Civic Center hosted all sorts of sports teams such as the old Warriors of the NBA and for a time, the 76ers, as well as minor-pro hockey during the 1960s and 1970s. Many historically famous figures gave speeches within the Civic Center as well as featuring musical acts such as the Beatles. However, by the 1970s, it had become obsolete. It was demolished in 1995.

Stampede Corral
Calgary, Alberta

Opened: 1950. When it was built, it was the largest arena in Western Canada, but by the time the Cowboys moved in, in 1975, it was the smallest arena in the WHA. The Corral has also hosted the Flames when they first moved to Calgary in 1980, and innumerable rodeos—for which it was originally built and is most famous for—over the years. It still stands, is regularly used for a variety of events, and is a landmark in Calgary.

Veterans Memorial Coliseum
Phoenix, Arizona

Opened: 1965. Home to the NBA Suns from 1968 through 1992, and various incarnations of the Roadrunners from 1967 through 1997. Located on the State Fairgrounds, the arena is still used for Fair-related events and occasional local sporting events. Its saddle-shaped roof was unique for its time, and at one time, featured the largest mural in the world that could only be seen from the air.

Pacific Coliseum
Vancouver, British Columbia

Opened: 1968. The Canucks of the WHL played here from 1968-70, then the Canucks of the NHL from 1970 through 1995. The Blazers also played here between 1973-75. The arena has undergone two renovations and is currently used for a variety of attractions, including hosting some events during the 2010 Winter Olympics.

St. Paul Civic Center
St. Paul, Minnesota

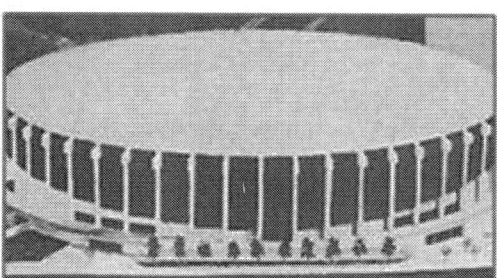

Opened: January 1973. The arena was unique in that its boards were entirely plexiglass. The arena hosted the Saints as well as multiple sports and other attractions. It was demolished in 1998 and the new Xcel Center, home to the Minnesota Wild of the NHL, was built in 2000.

Cherry Hill Arena
Cherry Hill, New Jersey

Opened: 1959. A small, inadequate arena for big-league hockey, used more for local Philadelphia-area sporting events, even hosting the Warriors of the NBA on rare occasions. The arena had limited seating for fans and players, no visitor's dressing rooms, an uneven playing surface, chain-link fence above the boards instead of plexiglass, and undependable plumbing. It was mercifully demolished in the 1980s.

Baltimore Civic Center
Baltimore, Maryland

Opened: 1962. Home to the Clippers of the AHL through 1976, and to the Bullets of the NBA through 1973. It has hosted many sporting and non-sporting events over the years and is still used today, now known as the Royal Farms Arena.

338

Sam Houston Coliseum
Houston, Texas

The Summit
Houston, Texas

Cleveland Arena
Cleveland, Ohio

The Coliseum
Richfield, Ohio

Opened: The Sam Houston Coliseum opened in 1937 and hosted its first hockey team, the Skippers of the USHL, as far back as 1946. The Houston Mavericks of the ABA played here during 1967-69, followed by the Aeros from 1972 through 1975. The arena was also used by other professional and collegiate sports teams as well as host to many musical acts and other attractions. By the late 1970s, the Coliseum had become obsolete and was rarely used. It was finally demolished in 1998.

The Summit was completed in November 1975, and the Aeros immediately moved in, as did the Houston Rockets of the NBA. It remained Houston's premier indoor arena through the late 1990s, featuring many sports and other attractions. It has since been sold and renovated as a "mega church" site.

Opened: The Cleveland Arena was opened in 1937 and housed the Barons of the AHL continuously through the 1970s, as well as the Crusaders from 1972-74. It was also home to the NBA Cavaliers from 1970-74. For hockey, the rink was surrounded by chain-link fence and was merely a temporary site for the Crusaders as ground had been broken for the new Richfield Coliseum in 1972. The Arena was demolished in 1977.

The Richfield Coliseum (known simply as "The Coliseum" at the time) was as state-of-the-art as a new arena could be in 1974, and was the league's showcase arena. However, it was built too far from Cleveland and the local roads could not handle the traffic. It hosted its last events in 1994 and was demolished in 1999. By design, nothing has been built at its old location. It is now a wildland park.

Season VI

1977-1978

In some ways, the World Hockey Association hoped this season would not convene. Six of the clubs had applied for admission to the National Hockey League as the two leagues negotiated for the first time for a merger. The vote of the NHL owners was close, but not close enough for approval, and the WHA, down but not quite out, picked itself up off the mat for another year of action.

Phoenix, Calgary and San Diego ceased operations over the Spring and Summer of 1977, and the remaining eight teams were lumped into one division. Birmingham, Cincinnati, Edmonton, Houston, Indianapolis, New England, Quebec and Winnipeg were left to fight it out for the top spot, although a liberal playoff system allowed six teams into the postseason.

An 80-game schedule was used, with each team playing its opponents 11 or 12 times. Czechoslovakia and the Soviet Union sent teams to tour the league, playing each team once, with the results counting in the standings. As a result, each team played 41 home games and 39 away. For a change, all eight clubs survived the entire year, although Indianapolis came close to folding on two occasions, and Houston once.

The Howes left Houston for Hartford over the Summer of 1977. The Aeros, perennially the league's strongest team, played out the season but folded after the season closed. The Whalers survived a collapsed home arena and managed to advance to the 1978 finals, where they lost to the speedy Winnipeg Jets, led by the amazing Hull-Hedberg-Nilsson line. The Jets cruised to the championship behind 50 wins, 381 goals as a team, and win streaks of 11 games and a league-record 15 games.

The Nordiques' Marc Tardif exploded for 65 goals, 89 assists and 154 points, leading the league in all three categories. Winnipeg's Ulf Nilsson also had 89 assists. Birmingham iced a team of fighters, and the top four penalty minute leaders were Bulls, led by Steve Durbano with 284. The Whalers' Al Smith led all goalies with 30 wins and a 3.22 average, while Cincinnati's Michel Dion put up 4 shutouts to lead the league.

Standings

team		League gp	w	l	t	pts	pct	gf	ga
1. **Winnipeg JETS**		80	50	28	2	102	.638	381	270
	home	41	28	11	2	58	.707	213	124
	away	39	22	17	0	44	.564	168	146
2. **New England WHALERS**		80	44	31	5	93	.581	335	269
	home	41	26	14	1	53	.646	180	120
	away	39	18	17	4	40	.513	155	149
3. **Houston AEROS**		80	42	34	4	88	.550	296	302
	home	41	26	13	2	54	.659	165	139
	away	39	16	21	2	34	.436	131	163
4. **Québec NORDIQUES**		80	40	37	3	83	.519	349	347
	home	41	29	10	2	60	.732	210	150
	away	39	11	27	1	23	.295	139	197
5. **Edmonton OILERS**		80	38	39	3	79	.494	309	307
	home	41	24	15	2	50	.610	186	147
	away	39	14	24	1	29	.372	123	160
6. **Birmingham BULLS**		80	36	41	3	75	.469	287	314
	home	41	23	16	2	48	.585	171	127
	away	39	13	25	1	27	.346	116	187
7. **Cincinnati STINGERS**		80	35	42	3	73	.456	298	332
	home	41	21	19	1	43	.524	163	154
	away	39	14	23	2	30	.385	135	178
8. **Indianapolis RACERS**		80	24	51	5	53	.331	267	353
	home	41	17	21	3	37	.451	159	162
	away	39	7	30	2	16	.205	108	191
Soviet All Stars		8	3	4	1	7	.438	27	36
Czechoslovakia		8	1	6	1	3	.188	21	40

Award Winners

Most Valuable Player
Gordie Howe Trophy
Marc Tardif, Que

Rookie of the Year
Lou Kaplan Trophy
Kent Nilsson, Wpg

Best Goaltender
Ben Hatskin Trophy
Al Smith, NE

Best Defeseman
Dennis Murphy Trophy
Lars-Erik Sjoberg, Wpg

Coach of the Year
Robert Schmertz Trophy
Bill Dineen, Hou

Most Gentlemanly
Paul Deneau Trophy
Dave Keon, NE

1978 World Hockey Association AVCO World Trophy Champions
Winnipeg Jets

1978 Playoff Series Results

Quarterfinals

New England vs. Edmonton

Apr 14	Edmonton 4 at New England 6
Apr 16	Edmonton 1 at New England 4
Apr 19	New England 0 at Edmonton 2
	(so: Don McLeod, 19 saves)
Apr 21	New England 9 at Edmonton 1
Apr 23	Edmonton 1 at New England 4

Houston vs. Quebec

Apr 16	Quebec 3 at Houston 4
	(ot: Ted Taylor, 7:19)
Apr 18	Quebec 5 at Houston 4
	(ot: Marc Tardif, 2:59)
Apr 20	Houston 1 at Quebec 5
Apr 21	Houston 0 at Quebec 3
	(so: Richard Brodeur, 26 saves)
Apr 23	Quebec 2 at Houston 5
Apr 25	Houston 2 at Quebec 11

Quarterfinals (Continued)

Winnipeg vs. Birmingham

Apr 14	Birmingham 3 at Winnipeg 9
Apr 16	Birmingham 3 at Winnipeg 8
Apr 19	Winnipeg 2 at Birmingham 3
Apr 21	Winnipeg 5 at Birmingham 1
Apr 23	Birmingham 2 at Winnipeg 5

Semifinal (Winnipeg: bye)

New England vs. Quebec

Apr 28	Quebec 1 at New England 5
Apr 30	Quebec 3 at New England 2
May 3	New England 5 at Quebec 4
May 5	New England 7 at Quebec 3
May 7	Quebec 3 at New England 6

AVCO World Trophy Championship

Winnipeg vs. New England

May 12	Winnipeg 4 at New England 1
May 14	Winnipeg 5 at New England 2
May 19	New England 2 at Winnipeg 10
May 22	New England 3 at Winnipeg 5

Penalty Shot: April 14: Anders Hedberg (Winnipeg) scored on John Garrett (Birmingham).

Playoff Standings

Overall Team	w	l	gf	ga	Home Team	w	l	gf	ga	Away Team	w	l	gf	ga
Winnipeg	8	1	53	20	Winnipeg	5	0	37	13	Winnipeg	3	1	16	7
New England	8	6	56	47	New England	5	3	30	22	New England	3	3	26	25
Quebec	5	6	43	41	Quebec	3	2	26	15	Quebec	2	4	17	26
Houston	2	4	16	29	Houston	2	1	13	10	Houston	0	3	3	19
Birmingham	1	4	12	29	Birmingham	1	1	4	7	Birmingham	0	3	8	22
Edmonton	1	4	9	23	Edmonton	1	1	3	9	Edmonton	0	3	6	15

Championship Series Summaries

In a season that saw the Winnipeg Jets reel off victory streaks of 6, 10 and a record 15, and dominate the World Hockey Association like no other team ever had, nothing short of a convincing AVCO Cup Championship would be expected, and the Jets delivered. After quickly dispatching the Birmingham Bulls in the quarterfinals, the Jets rested for almost three weeks, then swept the New England Whalers for their second WHA Championship in three years. Lyle Moffatt had 3 goals and 4 assists, while linemate Bobby Guindon had 4 goals and 1 assist, to lead a balanced attack.

Game 1 • May 12, 1978
Winnipeg 4, New England 1

Winnipeg	0	0	4	-	4
New England	0	0	1	-	1

1st period: No Scoring.
2nd period: No Scoring.
3rd period: 1. Wpg: Guindon (Moffat) 4:31; 2. Wpg: Sullivan 4:53; 3. NE: Pleau (Hangsleben, Bolduc) 8:07; 4. Wpg: Guindon (Lesuk) 13:55; 5. Wpg: Sullivan (Moffat) 19:45
Shots on goal

Wpg on Levasseur	12	6	12	-	30
NE on Bromley	8	11	14	-	33

Game 2 • May 14, 1978
Winnipeg 5, New England 2

Winnipeg	2	2	1	-	5
New England	0	0	2	-	2

1st period: 1. Wpg: Labraaten (Lindstrom) 14:02; 2. Wpg: Moffat (Amodeo) 19:32
2nd period: 3. Wpg: Guindon (Lesuk, Moffat) 1:21; 4. Wpg: Hedberg (U. Nilsson) 17:10
3rd period: 5. NE: G. Howe (Plumb, Rogers) 6:28; 6. NE: Mark Howe (J. Carlson) 15:17; 7. Wpg: U. Nilsson (Hedberg) 16:35
Shots on goal

Wpg on Levasseur	12	8	7	-	27
NE on Daley	2	13	9	-	24

Game 3 • May 19, 1978
Winnipeg 10, New England 2

New England	0	0	2	-	2
Winnipeg	6	2	2	-	10

1st period: 1. Wpg: Lindstrom 4:56; 2. Wpg: Guindon (Lesuk, Moffat) 5:09; 3. Wpg: Hull (U. Nilsson, Hedberg) 6:32; 4. Wpg: Lindstrom (Sullivan, Long) 7:31; 5. Wpg: K. Nilsson (Kryskow, Baird) 7:46; 6. Wpg: K. Nilsson (Lindstrom, Clackson) 17:36
2nd period: 7. Wpg: Powis (Kryskow, K. Nilsson) 4:55; 8. Wpg: Moffat (Dunn, Sullivan) 16:28.
3rd period: 9. NE: McKenzie (Keon, Marty Howe) 4:07; 10. NE: Sheehy (Lyle, Selwood) 5:10; 11. Wpg: Powis (K. Nilsson, Kryskow) 8:30; 12. Wpg: Lindstrom (Labraaten, Sullivan) 12:12
Shots on goal

NE on Bromley	12	7	11	-	30
Wpg on Smith	12	11	10	-	33

Game 4 • May 22, 1978
Winnipeg 5, New England 3

New England	2	0	1	-	3
Winnipeg	0	3	2	-	6

1st period: 1. NE: Antonovich (Keon, McKenzie) 1:37; 2. NE: Ley (Sheehy) 1:59
2nd period: 3. Wpg: Kryskow (Hedberg, K. Nilsson) 3:26; 4. Wpg: Moffat (Guindon) 3:38; 5. Wpg: Hedberg (Sjoberg, U. Nilsson) 17:59
3rd period: 6. Wpg: Hull (U. Nilsson, Hedberg) 3:26; 7. NE: Lyle (Hangsleben, S. Carlson) 11:25; 8. Wpg: Hedberg (U. Nilsson, Green) 19:28
Shots on goal

NE on Daley	8	6	13	-	27
Wpg on Smith	8	12	8	-	28

Statistical Leaders

Goals: 10, Mike Antonovich (NE); 9, Real Cloutier (Que), Anders Hedberg (Wpg); 8, Bob Guindon (Wpg), Mark Howe (NE), Bobby Hull (Wpg).

Assists: 13, Ulf Nilsson (Wpg); 11, Dave Keon (NE); 10, Serge Bernier (Que); 9, Lars-Erik Sjoberg (Wpg), Marc Tardif (Que).

Points: 17, Mike Antonovich (NE), 16, Real Cloutier (Que), Dave Keon (NE); 15, Anders Hedberg (Wpg), Mark Howe (NE), Marc Tardif (Que)

Penalty Minutes: 61, Kim Clackson (Wpg); 50, Wally Weir (Que); 48, Dave Hanson (Bir); 46, Serge Beaudoin (Bir).

Goaltending Wins: 8, Louis Levassuer (NE); 5, Richard Brodeur (Que); 4, Gary Bromley (Wpg), Joe Daley (Wpg)

Goals Against Average: 1.57, Gary Bromley (Wpg); 2.59, Louis Levasseur (NE); 2.88, Joe Daley (Wpg); 3.76, Richard Brodeur (Que

Splits by Opponent and by Month, Home and Away

Bir Birmingham, **Cin** Cincinnati, **Edm** Edmonton, **Hou** Houston, **Ind** Indianapolis, **NE** New England, **Que** Quebec, **Wpg** Winnipeg, **TT** Touring Teams

BIRMINGHAM

Opp.	season	gf-ga	home	gf-ga	away	gf-ga
Cin	7-4-0	53-31	5-0-0	32-9	2-4-0	21-22
Edm	5-5-1	34-38	3-2-1	19-15	2-3-0	15-23
Hou	7-5-0	42-39	4-2-0	24-20	3-3-0	18-19
Ind	5-5-1	38-44	3-2-1	23-20	2-3-0	15-24
NE	2-9-0	28-54	0-5-0	13-23	2-4-0	15-31
Que	4-7-0	47-52	3-3-0	28-22	1-4-0	19-30
Wpg	4-6-1	34-55	3-2-0	21-17	1-4-1	13-38
TT	2-0-0	11-1	2-0-0	11-1	0-0-0	0-0
Oct	1-6-0	23-40	1-2-0	11-11	0-4-0	12-29
Nov	5-7-2	43-42	3-2-1	27-18	2-5-1	16-24
Dec	8-4-0	48-37	5-2-0	26-14	3-2-0	22-23
Jan	7-7-0	52-61	5-3-0	34-29	2-4-0	18-32
Feb	5-9-0	44-65	4-3-0	31-25	1-6-0	13-40
Mar	7-7-1	54-53	3-4-1	32-26	4-3-0	22-27
Apr	3-1-0	23-16	2-0-0	10-4	1-1-0	13-12

HOUSTON

Opp.	season	gf-ga	home	gf-ga	away	gf-ga
Bir	5-7-0	39-42	3-3-0	19-18	2-4-0	20-24
Cin	6-4-1	40-40	4-1-1	27-21	2-3-0	13-19
Edm	8-3-0	47-42	4-1-0	25-19	4-2-0	22-23
Ind	5-5-1	38-35	3-2-0	19-13	2-3-1	20-22
NE	6-4-1	37-42	3-2-1	20-21	3-2-0	17-21
Que	5-5-1	45-49	4-1-0	26-20	1-4-1	19-29
Wpg	6-5-0	44-44	4-2-0	24-19	2-3-0	20-25
TT	1-1-0	5-8	1-1-0	5-8	0-0-0	0-0
Oct	3-4-0	28-33	3-1-0	19-16	0-3-0	9-17
Nov	5-5-1	41-43	5-1-1	31-22	0-4-0	10-21
Dec	6-6-2	51-50	2-4-1	24-30	4-2-1	27-20
Jan	10-5-0	51-46	5-3-0	23-20	5-2-0	28-26
Feb	6-7-0	51-53	3-3-0	25-24	3-4-0	26-29
Mar	9-4-1	48-46	6-1-0	32-20	3-3-1	16-26
Apr	3-3-0	26-31	2-0-0	11-7	1-3-0	15-24

CINCINNATI

Opp.	season	gf-ga	home	gf-ga	away	gf-ga
Bir	4-7-0	31-53	4-2-0	22-21	0-5-0	9-32
Edm	4-6-1	40-41	3-2-0	15-12	1-4-1	25-29
Hou	4-6-1	40-40	3-2-0	19-13	1-4-1	21-27
Ind	9-3-0	53-35	5-1-0	27-12	4-2-0	26-23
NE	3-8-0	41-55	2-4-0	28-32	1-4-0	13-23
Que	8-3-0	50-43	4-1-0	25-18	4-2-0	25-25
Wpg	3-8-0	34-55	0-6-0	18-36	3-2-0	16-19
TT	0-1-1	9-10	0-1-1	9-10	0-0-0	0-0
Oct	1-5-0	22-26	1-2-0	14-12	0-3-0	8-14
Nov	7-8-0	46-61	3-3-0	14-18	4-5-0	32-43
Dec	5-6-2	49-52	2-4-1	24-31	3-2-1	25-21
Jan	6-8-0	50-60	4-5-0	35-41	2-3-0	15-19
Feb	5-6-1	50-55	4-4-0	35-29	1-2-1	15-26
Mar	8-5-0	55-46	5-1-0	30-17	3-4-0	25-29
Apr	3-4-0	26-32	2-0-0	11-6	1-4-0	15-26

INDIANAPOLIS

Opp.	season	gf-ga	home	gf-ga	away	gf-ga
Bir	5-5-1	44-38	3-2-0	24-15	2-3-1	20-23
Cin	3-9-0	35-53	2-4-0	23-26	1-5-0	12-27
Edm	2-9-0	34-52	1-4-0	15-21	1-5-0	19-31
Hou	5-5-1	35-39	3-2-1	22-20	2-3-0	13-19
NE	2-7-2	31-49	2-2-1	16-17	0-5-1	15-32
Que	4-6-1	44-53	4-1-1	29-24	0-5-0	15-29
Wpg	3-8-0	38-60	2-4-0	24-30	1-4-0	14-30
TT	0-2-0	6-9	0-2-0	6-9	0-0-0	0-0
Oct	4-2-2	29-33	2-0-2	17-11	2-2-0	12-22
Nov	2-9-1	37-52	2-4-0	25-28	0-5-1	12-24
Dec	3-11-1	42-67	2-4-1	21-29	1-7-0	21-38
Jan	5-7-0	36-43	3-5-0	25-28	2-2-0	11-15
Feb	4-7-0	44-52	3-2-0	24-20	1-5-0	20-32
Mar	5-10-1	55-71	4-3-0	29-24	1-7-1	26-47
Apr	1-5-0	24-35	1-3-0	18-22	0-2-0	6-13

EDMONTON

Opp.	season	gf-ga	home	gf-ga	away	gf-ga
Bir	5-5-1	38-34	3-2-0	23-15	2-3-1	15-19
Cin	6-4-1	41-40	4-1-1	29-25	2-3-0	12-15
Hou	3-8-0	42-47	2-4-0	23-22	1-4-0	19-25
Ind	9-2-0	52-34	5-1-0	31-19	4-1-0	21-15
NE	3-7-1	35-41	1-3-1	17-21	2-4-0	18-20
Que	5-6-0	48-57	4-1-0	31-19	1-5-0	17-38
Wpg	5-7-0	42-51	3-3-0	21-23	2-4-0	21-28
TT	2-0-0	11-3	2-0-0	11-3	0-0-0	0-0
Oct	2-5-0	24-36	1-2-0	10-15	1-3-0	14-21
Nov	8-5-1	52-45	6-2-0	35-24	2-3-1	17-21
Dec	6-5-0	52-42	5-3-0	43-31	1-2-0	9-11
Jan	8-7-0	49-48	3-3-0	21-18	5-4-0	28-30
Feb	7-5-1	63-50	5-2-1	42-30	2-3-0	21-20
Mar	5-11-0	56-70	3-3-0	27-23	2-8-0	29-47
Apr	2-1-1	13-16	1-0-1	8-6	1-1-0	5-10

NEW ENGLAND

Opp.	season	gf-ga	home	gf-ga	away	gf-ga
Bir	9-2-0	54-28	4-2-0	31-15	5-0-0	23-13
Cin	8-3-0	55-41	4-1-0	23-13	4-2-0	32-28
Edm	7-3-1	41-35	4-2-0	20-18	3-1-1	21-17
Hou	4-6-1	42-37	2-3-0	21-17	2-3-1	21-20
Ind	7-2-2	49-31	5-0-1	32-15	2-2-1	17-16
Que	4-8-0	48-45	3-3-0	27-21	1-5-0	21-24
Wpg	3-7-1	34-47	2-3-0	14-16	1-4-1	20-31
TT	2-0-0	12-5	2-0-0	12-5	0-0-0	0-0
Oct	6-1-1	37-18	3-0-0	19-5	3-1-1	18-13
Nov	9-3-2	56-47	4-2-1	23-23	5-1-1	33-24
Dec	8-4-0	53-39	6-2-0	40-23	2-2-0	13-16
Jan	6-8-1	58-53	3-3-0	25-22	3-5-1	33-31
Feb	5-6-0	44-47	2-2-0	13-12	3-4-0	31-35
Mar	7-8-0	59-44	5-5-0	40-25	2-3-0	19-19
Apr	3-1-1	28-21	3-0-0	20-10	0-1-1	8-11

QUEBEC

Opp.	season	gf-ga	home	gf-ga	away	gf-ga
Bir	7-4-0	52-47	4-1-0	30-19	3-3-0	22-28
Cin	3-8-0	43-50	2-4-0	25-25	1-4-0	18-25
Edm	6-5-0	57-48	5-1-0	38-17	1-4-0	19-31
Hou	5-5-1	49-45	4-1-1	29-19	1-4-0	20-26
Ind	6-4-1	53-44	5-0-0	29-15	1-4-1	24-29
NE	8-4-0	45-48	5-1-0	24-21	3-3-0	21-27
Wpg	4-7-0	39-58	3-2-0	24-27	1-5-0	15-31
TT	1-0-1	11-7	1-0-1	11-7	0-0-0	0-0
Oct	4-3-1	33-32	4-0-0	24-12	0-3-1	9-20
Nov	8-6-0	66-57	5-3-0	38-32	3-3-0	28-25
Dec	4-3-0	34-38	4-0-0	23-15	0-3-0	11-23
Jan	7-8-1	66-70	3-3-1	29-32	4-5-0	37-38
Feb	5-10-0	60-76	4-1-0	29-19	1-9-0	31-57
Mar	8-6-1	60-61	5-3-1	39-33	3-3-0	21-28
Apr	4-1-0	30-13	4-0-0	28-17	0-1-0	2-6

WINNIPEG

Opp.	season	gf-ga	home	gf-ga	away	gf-ga
Bir	6-4-1	55-34	4-1-1	38-13	2-3-0	17-21
Cin	8-3-0	55-34	2-3-0	19-16	6-0-0	36-18
Edm	7-5-0	51-42	4-2-0	28-21	3-3-0	23-21
Hou	5-6-0	44-44	3-2-0	25-20	2-4-0	19-24
Ind	8-3-0	60-38	4-1-0	30-14	4-2-0	30-24
NE	7-3-1	47-34	4-1-1	31-20	3-2-0	16-14
Que	7-4-0	58-39	5-1-0	31-15	2-3-0	27-24
TT	2-0-0	11-5	2-0-0	11-5	0-0-0	0-0
Oct	7-2-0	49-27	5-1-0	34-15	2-1-0	15-12
Nov	5-6-1	45-39	1-3-1	13-15	4-3-0	32-24
Dec	9-4-0	66-42	6-2-0	44-22	3-2-0	22-20
Jan	7-6-1	66-47	3-2-1	31-18	4-4-0	35-29
Feb	13-0-0	78-36	8-0-0	54-22	5-0-0	24-14
Mar	8-6-0	59-55	4-2-0	26-23	4-4-0	33-32
Apr	1-4-0	18-24	1-1-0	11-9	0-3-0	7-15

1978 All-Star Game

Le Colisee
Quebec City, Quebec
January 17, 1978

WHA All-Stars
Coach: Bill Dineen (Houston)
Goaltenders: Al Smith (New England), John Garrett (Birmingham)
Defensemen: Rick Ley, Gordie Roberts (New England), Al Hamilton, Barry Long (Edmonton), Lars-Erik Sjoberg (Winnipeg), Pat Stapleton (Cincinnati)
Forwards: Bobby Hull, Anders Hedberg, Ulf Nilsson (Winnipeg), Bill Flett (Edmonton), Mark Napier (Birmingham), Mark Howe, Mike Antonovich, Gordie Howe (New England), Andre Lacroix, Morris Lukowich (Houston), Rusty Patenaude (Indianapolis), Robbie Ftorek (Cincinnati)

Quebec Nordiques
Coach: Marc Boileau
Goaltenders: Ken Broderick, Jim Corsi
Defensemen: Paul Baxter, Jean Bernier, Garry Lariviere, J.-C. Tremblay, Chris Evans, Jim Dorey
Forwards: Paulin Bordeleau, Andre Boudrias, Curt Brackenbury, Real Cloutier, Warren Miller, Marc Tardif, Steve Sutherland, Bob Fitchner, Norm Dube, Matti Hagman, Serge Bernier, Charles Constantin

MVPs: WHA: Mark Howe, New England
Que: Marc Tardif

Quebec 5, WHA All-Stars 4

WHA All-Stars	3	1	0	-	4
Quebec	1	3	1	-	5

1st period 1. Que: Hagman (Tardif) 12:56; 2. WHA: Mark Howe (Flett, Sjoberg) 14:50; 3. WHA: Hedberg (Hull) 18:57; 4. WHA: Lukowich (Lacroix, Long) 19:10.
2nd period 5. WHA: Flett (Mark Howe) 7:07; 6. Que: Miller (Hagman, Tardif) 10:01; 7. Que: Baxter (Tardif, Fitchner) 12:14; 8. Que: Tardif (Boudrias) 17:51.
3rd period 9. Que: Hagman (Tardif, Tremblay) 14:12.
Shots on goal

WHA	10	14	8	-	32
Quebec	9	12	11	-	32

Attendance 6,413

1977-1978 Year End All-Star Teams

First Team: Goaltender: Al Smith, New England; Defensemen: Lars-Erik Sjoberg, Winnipeg, and Al Hamilton, Edmonton; Center: Ulf Nilsson, Winnipeg; Right Wing: Anders Hedberg, Winnipeg; Left Wing: Marc Tardif, Quebec.

Second Team: Goaltender: Ernie Wakely, Houston; Defensemen: Rick Ley, New England, and Barry Long, Winnipeg; Center: Robbie Ftorek, Cincinnati; Right Wing: Real Cloutier, Quebec; Left Wing: Bobby Hull, Winnipeg.

Penalty Shots

None awarded during 1977-78

Attendance Figures

team	g	season total	avg	g	playoff total	avg	team	g	season total	avg	g	playoff total	avg
Birmingham	41	359,860	8.777	2	20,807	10,404	Indianapolis	41	301,891	7,363	-	-	-
Cincinnati	41	303,404	7,400	-	-	-	New England	41	381,075	9,294	8	58,555	7,319
Edmonton	41	429,862	10,484	2	26,812	13,406	Quebec	41	372,336	9,081	5	57,569	11,514
Houston	41	314,698	7,676	3	17,286	5,762	Winnipeg	41	397,085	9,685	5	49,971	9,958

Total Attendance: 2,860,211 **Average Attendance:** 8,720

Ed Mio, Streakstopper

The Quebec Nordiques had never been shut out at home during their first six regular seasons in the WHA, while the Indianapolis Racers had never administered a shutout on enemy ice during their first four terms. Early in the 1978-79 season, both streaks came to a tidy end when Racers goaltender Ed Mio stopped 37 Nordiques shots at Le Colisee. It was Mio's first career shutout, as the Racers prevailed 4-0 at Quebec. The game was also notable as Wayne Gretzky collected his first big-league point, an assist on Richie Leduc's first period goal.

The Ottawa-Toronto-Birmingham franchise had also not been shutout at home during its first six seasons in the WHA. The Bulls were close to making it a perfect seven entering a late-season March 1979 contest, hosting Edmonton. However, the Oilers blanked the Bulls, 4-0. Tending nets that night for Edmonton was Ed Mio, getting a rare start to spell Dave Dryden. It was Mio's second shutout of the season, and his first since coming to the Oilers along with Wayne Gretzky the previous November.

1977-1978 Team Thumbnails

Birmingham: Somewhere along the line, the magic had escaped the Toro-Bull franchise, which lurched through two dreadful seasons during 1975-76 (in Toronto) and 1976-77 (in Birmingham). There was no fear of the team going under, as owner John Bassett had the wherewithal to keep the Bulls alive seemingly forever. Nevertheless, the on-ice performance needed to change. 1977-78 seemed to be more of the same, with the team enduring an eight-game losing streak and a 2-10-2 mark to start the season. In November, Bassett, his general manager Gilles Leger, and new coach Glen Sonmor decided to strip the Bulls down, trade away some of their scorers, and put together a team of some of the roughest, most notorious fighters in the game. Tim Sheehy and Vaclav Nedomansky were gone. In their stead were Steve Durbano, Gilles Bilodeau, Frank Beaton, Dave Hanson (of Slap Shot fame), and Serge Beaudoin. The "new" Bulls gave notice to the rest of the league that playing Birmingham would no longer be a walk in the park. In one of their first games together, the revamped Bulls obliterated Cincinnati by a 12-2 score, in a game known as the Thanksgiving Day Massacre. Coach Sonmor put out his tough guys to start the game against Cincinnati's slick (and small) skaters. A line brawl ensued within the first minute of the game. The Bulls literally scared the Stingers into the dressing room, scoring 7 goals in the third period alone. The new line-up, and the energizing victory, gave the Bulls enough life to intimidate their way to 36 wins and their first playoff appearance since 1975. Steve Durbano led all players with 284 minutes in penalties (in just 45 games). Frank Beaton was second with 279, Gilles "Bad News" Bilodeau third with 258, and Dave Hanson fourth with 241. The team was not without talent: Ken Linseman had a solid rookie season as an under-age signee, leading the team with 38 goals and 76 points. Future Hall-of-Famer Rod Langway also made his pro debut with the Bulls. Veterans Paul Henderson (37 goals) and Peter Marrin (28 goals) gave the offense life, while second-year man Mark Napier put in 33 goals. Dale Hoganson, Brent Hughes, Jim Turkiewicz and Serge Beaudoin anchored a solid defense, while goaltending was in the good hands of John Garrett.

Cincinnati: The Stingers' third season was lost within the first month: a 1-8-0 start put the team too far back to overcome, although a strong second half gave the Stingers 35 wins, but no playoff appearance. There were high hopes, after the Stingers were able to gut the core of their rivals Indianapolis by signing coach Jacques Demers, goaltender Michel Dion and defenseman Pat Stapleton. However, the new "Cincinnapolis Ringers" never formed a cohesive unit, and numerous trades and minor-league call-ups did not help to maintain a sense of consistency.

Individually, many players turned in fine seasons: Center Robbie Ftorek scored 59 goals and 109 points. Rick Dudley scored 30 goals and collected 156 penalty minutes, while Jamie Hislop, Peter Marsh and Richie Leduc all scored at least 20 goals. Pat Stapleton was the best of the blueliners, a +6 and often the point-man on the attack. Ron Plumb had a solid year, partly reduced by injuries. Michel Dion led the league with 4 shutouts, with a young Mike Liut backing him, but ultimately, the Stingers gave up too many goals (332) and were forced to watch the 1978 playoffs on the television.

Edmonton: The Oilers were just glad to be here, now under the stable ownership of Peter Pocklington after a handful of seasons of uncertainty and a near-fold over summer 1977. The team itself was unspectacular, a handful of solid, seasoned players and a seeming cast of hundreds trying out for the remaining jobs. "Cowboy" Bill Flett led the team with 41 goals, while Ron Chipperfield hit for 33 goals and a team-leading 85 points. Blair MacDonald also met the 30-goal barrier, collecting 34 for the season. Brett Callighen, Norm Ferguson and Mike Zuke each were good for at least 20 goals. Paul Shmyr and Dave Langevin anchored the defense, with long-time star Al Hamilton putting in a solid season, despite losing a third of it to injuries. Dave Dryden and Don McLeod formed a solid one-two goaltending tandem. The Oilers' 38-39-3 mark was good for fourth place and a quick five-game appearance in the playoffs. While not a great season by most standards, it was the first year of a new life for the Oilers, now under an ownership with money, and a young Glen Sather honing his craft behind the bench. There would be much rosier days ahead for the Edmonton skaters.

Houston: After losing the Howes to New England and enduring a summer (and winter) of financial uncertainty, the Aeros entered 1977-78 a team that might win another 50 games, as they'd done in 1976-77, or a team that might win half that many, given the loss of many key players. Aside from the Howes, the Aeros also lost star goaltender Ron Grahame to Boston of the NHL. However, the Aeros did acquire Andre Lacroix from the defunct San Diego Mariners, and early in the season, acquired steady goaltender Ernie Wakely from Cincinnati. The Aeros played average hockey through the first half of the season, sporting a 15-19-3 record at one point. But afterward, the Aeros played like the championship teams of old, finishing the season on a 27-15-1 run to capture third place in the league. Lacroix had another fine season, with 77 assists and a team-leading 113 points, while youngster Morris Lukowich led the team with 40 goals. Depth was the key: the Aeros relied on their unheralded second and third lines to cobble together a very effective attack. John Gray had

35 goals, while Rich Preston, Don Larway, John Tonelli and Cam Connor each contributed at least 20 goals apiece. Terry Ruskowski was the emotional on-ice leader, with a strong 72 points and 170 penalty minutes, often fearlessly fighting the league's worst goons. The defense was its usual solid unit, with Poul Popiel, John Schella and Larry Hale—all with the team since 1972—anchoring the blueline. In goal, Ernie Wakely was second in the league with 28 victories. The Aeros lasted just the first round in the playoffs, losing in six games to Quebec. Unfortunately, this was the end of the line for the Aeros. The financial situation was simply too much to overcome, and the Aeros formally folded on July 6, 1978. However, thirteen Aeros would go on to join Winnipeg for 1978-79, and help lead the Jets to the 1979 Championship.

Indianapolis: The Racers could not withstand the loss of their core—coach Demers, defenseman Stapleton and goaltender Dion—to Cincinnati, and a dire financial situation forced the team to scrimp by, always on the verge of total collapse. There was still some guarded hope that the solid, low-scoring diggers who played such an important role for the Racers during 1975-76 and 1976-77 would be enough to squeak out a few wins for the 1977-78 edition. But injuries, numerous trades and a revolving-door of new faces meant the Racers could never gel, which was bad news for a team already severely depleted. In the end, the Racers finished 24-51-5, wore out two coaches (Ron Ingram, fired, and Bill Goldsworthy, who went back to playing full time), and finished dead last in the league. Just three players reached 20 goals, led by Claude St. Sauveur's 36 goals and 78 points. Rusty Patenaude, Peter Driscoll, Michel Parizeau and Renald Leclerc rounded out the attack, while Kevin Morrison scored 57 points from the blueline, but with a –32 rating.

New England: With the Howes now on board, the New England Whalers raced out to the best start ever in the WHA's history, riding a 13-game winning streak to a 15-1-1 start. Remarkably, ageless Gordie Howe set the pace for scoring, leading the Whalers with 96 points behind 34 goals and 62 assists, both of which led the team. Mark Howe was second behind his pop with 91 points on the strength of 30 goals and 61 assists. George Lyle and Mike Antonovich also met the 30-goal mark, while Mike Rogers, Dave Keon and John McKenzie scored at least 20 goals. Injuries cost the Whalers a strong season from Tom Webster, who had 15 goals in 20 games before being felled. The defense behind Rick Ley, Brad Selwood and Al Hangsleben allowed 269 goals, the fewest in the WHA, while goaltender Al Smith won 30 games and had a league-best 3.22 goals-against average. The Whaler's season took a bizarre turn, when the roof of their home arena in Hartford collapsed in January 1978 under the weight of a heavy accumulation of snow. The Whalers played their remaining home games in Springfield, Massachusetts. The Whalers finished somewhat flat, playing sub-.500 hockey during the second half of the season, but still managed a 2nd-place finish when the season closed. After defeating Edmonton and Quebec in the playoffs, the Whalers were no match for the fast-skating Jets in the finals, losing in four straight to Winnipeg.

Quebec: The reigning champs found defending the crown to be a thankless task, and the Nordiques never got untracked during all of 1977-78, winning 40 but losing 37, and never in the hunt for the league's top spot. The offense was led, as usual, by the remarkable pair of Marc Tardif and Real Cloutier. Tardif scored a league-leading 65 goals, assisted on 89 (sharing the league-lead in assists with teammate J.-C. Tremblay), for a cumulative 154 points, which set a major-league record for points in a season. Cloutier was deadly near the net again, potting 53 goals and 129 total points. It was the supporting cast that saw a decline: Serge Bernier went from 43 goals in 1976-77 to 26 in 1977-78, while Christian Bordeleau dropped from 32 goals and 107 points in 1976-77 to 9 goals and 31 points in just 26 games, a season cut short by injury. Despite scoring 349 goals as a team, the Nordiques gave up 347. Richard Brodeur won 18 and had a 3.70 average, easily the best marks of the five men to man the nets for Quebec during the season. The Nordiques won their first-round playoff series over Houston, but lost to New England in the semifinal round.

Winnipeg: The Jets were the class of the league in 1977-78, riding winning streaks of 15 (a league record) and 11 games to a league-best 50 wins and 102 points, and their second AVCO Cup Championship. The remarkable line of Ulf Nilsson, Bobby Hull and Anders Hedberg skated circles around the opponents, each accruing over 100 points and cementing their argument as one of the best forward lines in pro hockey during the season, and possibly ever. Hedberg scored 63 goals and 122 points while Hull accounted for 46 goals and 117 points. Meanwhile, center Ulf Nilsson scored 37 goals but slid 89 assists to his teammates, for 126 points. Even the secondary lines were potent: Rookie-of-the-year Kent Nilsson scored 42 goals and 107 points, while steady veteran Willy Lindstrom knocked in 30 goals, as the Jets scored a league-leading 381 goals. On defense, the Jets were second to the Whalers in fewest goals allowed. Veterans Ted Green and Lars-Erik Sjoberg paced the defense, assisted by Dave Dunn, Thommie Bergman, Barry Long, and new acquisition tough-guy Kim Clackson. The goaltending was evenly split between Joe Daley and newcomer Gary Bromley, who both turned in 3.30 goals-against averages and over 20 wins apiece.

1977-1978 Game by Game Line Scores

Date & Teams	Scoring 1 2 3 ot F	Shots 1 2 3 ot F	Goaltenders	Goals & Other Scoring Highlights
October 12				
Winnipeg	1 1 5 - 7	5 9 13 - 27	Bromley	Hull 3, Labraaten 2, Moffat, Hornung
Edmonton	1 1 1 - 3	10 13 14 - 37	Broderick	Ferguson 2, Zuke
Indianapolis	2 2 1 - 5	11 8 5 - 24	Inness	Patenaude 2, Fortier, Burgess, Paiement
Cincinnati	2 1 1 - 4	11 10 17 - 38	Wakely	Leduc 4
New England	0 2 1 - 3	10 6 4 - 20	Smith	Webster 2, Keon
Houston	0 0 0 - 0	7 7 8 - 22	Rutledge	▶ Smith: shutout (1), 22 saves
October 13				
Quebec	0 0 2 - 2	4 16 8 - 28	McLeod	P. Bordeleau, Brackenbury
Winnipeg	3 0 2 - 5	13 11 9 - 33	Daley	K. Nilsson 2, Hull, Hedberg, Bergman
October 14				
Quebec	2 0 0 - 2	9 3 5 - 17	McLeod	Lacombe, Guite
Edmonton	1 1 2 - 4	13 11 13 - 37	Broderick	MacDonald 2, Miller, Baird
Houston	1 0 2 - 3	10 15 13 - 38	Rutledge	Ruskowski, Connor, Lund
Birmingham	2 1 2 - 5	10 13 13 - 36	Garrett	Noris 2, Evans, Nedomansky, Sheehy
October 15				
Birmingham	1 0 1 - 2	11 9 10 - 30	Garrett	Henderson 2
New England	3 0 2 - 5	10 13 10 - 33	Smith	G. Howe, J. Carlson, Webster, Hangsleben, Keon
Indianapolis	0 1 0 - 1	8 16 12 - 36	Inness, Park	St. Sauveur
Houston	3 1 1 - 5	8 9 3 - 20	Zimmerman	Lukowich 3, Preston, Ruskowski
Winnipeg	2 2 1 - 5	8 7 10 - 25	Mattsson	K. Nilsson, U. Nilsson, Ruhnke, Hedberg, Moffat (WG 19:03)
Cincinnati	2 2 0 - 4	13 10 10 - 33	Wakely	Leduc 2, Ftorek, Plumb
Edmonton	1 0 1 - 2	12 8 12 - 32	Broderick	Callighen, Chipperfield
Quebec	2 3 1 - 6	13 17 6 - 36	Brodeur, McLeod	Tardif 2, Cloutier, Brackenbury, S. Bernier, P. Bordeleau
October 16				
Indianapolis	1 0 0 - 1	12 16 9 - 37	Inness	Powis
Winnipeg	3 2 4 - 9	7 8 9 - 24	Daley	Hull 2, Sjoberg 2, Ruhnke 2, Dunn, Long, Hedberg
New England	0 1 1 - 2	10 16 8 - 34	Levasseur	Carroll, Webster
Cincinnati	5 0 1 - 6	13 7 13 - 33	Liut	Ftorek 2, Dudley 2, Abgrall, Larose
October 18				
Cincinnati	1 0 0 - 1	12 10 7 - 29	Liut, Wakely	Ftorek
Quebec	0 1 4 - 5	7 16 17 - 40	McLeod	Fitchner, Cloutier, S. Bernier, Dube, Tardif
New England	2 0 0 0 2	20 7 7 4 38	Smith	McKenzie, Ley
Indianapolis	2 0 0 0 2	15 7 8 3 33	Inness	Thomas, St. Sauveur
October 19				
New England	2 3 1 - 6	4 10 10 - 24	Levasseur	Webster 3, Rogers 2, Mk Howe
Edmonton	0 0 3 - 3	9 11 13 - 33	Turnbull	Callighen, Baird, MacDonald
October 21				
Cincinnati	1 2 2 - 5	8 17 6 - 31	Wakely	Ftorek 2, Leduc 2, Hall
Houston	2 3 1 - 6	8 12 10 - 30	Zimmerman	F. Hughes 2, Gray, Lund, Lacroix, Connor (WG 11:59)
New England	3 0 2 - 5	10 2 7 - 19	Smith	Pleau 2, Webster, Rogers, J. Carlson
Winnipeg	1 1 0 - 2	7 11 5 - 23	Daley	K. Nilsson, Hedberg
Quebec	2 2 0 0 4	10 14 11 4 39	Brodeur	P. Bordeleau 2 (TG 19:59 2nd) Sutherland, S. Bernier
Indianapolis	0 4 0 0 4	16 9 13 6 44	Inness	Burgess, Thomas, Paiement, Devine
October 22				
Birmingham	1 4 0 - 5	11 12 11 - 34	Wood	Noris 2, Gorman, Hughes, Napier
Quebec	3 2 3 - 8	11 8 13 - 32	McLeod	Cloutier 2, Dube, Baxter, Constantin, Brackenbury, P.Bordeleau, Tardif
October 23				
Birmingham	2 1 0 - 3	3 4 7 - 14	Garrett, Wood	Napier, Noris, Henderson
Winnipeg	4 3 3 - 10	10 12 14 - 36	Bromley	Hull 3, Sullivan 2, K. Nilsson 2, Labraaten, U. Nilsson, Ruhnke
October 25				
Indianapolis	0 3 2 - 5	6 20 12 - 38	Park	Thomas 2, St. Sauveur, Patenaude, Baltimore (WG 8:13)
Birmingham	2 1 1 - 4	16 12 4 - 32	Garrett	Sheehy, Marrin, Cassolato, Napier
October 26				
Edmonton	1 2 4 0 7	8 9 9 4 30	Broderick, Dryden	MacGregor 2, Ferguson 2, Zuke, Chipperfield, Flett
Houston	5 2 0 1 8	13 5 3 1 22	Rutledge	Schella 2, Larway 2 (OT 4:39), F. Hughes, Gray, Lund, Lukowich
Quebec	1 0 0 - 1	10 13 8 - 31	McLeod	Sutherland
New England	2 3 2 - 7	11 11 9 - 31	Smith	Antonovich 2, Roberts, Webster, Mk Howe, G. Howe, Rogers
Winnipeg	0 2 1 - 3	11 12 7 - 30	Mattsson	K. Nilsson, Labraaten, Dunn
Indianapolis	2 1 2 - 5	12 10 9 - 31	Inness	St. Sauveur 3, Sheehan 2
October 28				
Cincinnati	0 1 1 - 2	7 8 9 - 24	Wakely	Leduc, Ftorek
Winnipeg	2 1 0 - 3	9 15 10 - 34	Mattsson	Hull, Lindstrom, Labraaten
Edmonton	1 1 1 - 3	12 6 12 - 30	Dryden, Broderick	Campbell 3
Birmingham	0 0 2 - 2	7 10 12 - 29	Garrett	Sheehy, Linseman
October 29				
Houston	1 1 0 - 2	7 9 6 - 22	Zimmerman	Lukowich, Connor
New England	1 3 3 - 7	8 12 19 - 39	Smith	Pleau 2, Webster, Mty Howe, Antonovich, McKenzie, Mk Howe
Birmingham	0 0 2 - 2	13 6 6 - 25	Garrett	Linseman, Terbenche
Indianapolis	4 1 1 - 6	14 19 18 - 51	Park	Sheehan 3, St. Sauveur, Thomas, French
October 30				
Houston	1 1 2 - 4	7 11 13 - 31	Rutledge	Gray 3, Lacroix
Quebec	3 1 1 - 5	21 10 14 - 45	Brodeur	Tardif 2, Driscoll, Fitchner, Tremblay
Edmonton	1 0 1 - 2	10 9 6 - 25	Broderick	Chipperfield 2
Winnipeg	0 2 3 - 5	8 10 14 - 32	Daley	Hull 2, Sjoberg, Hedberg, Lindstrom
November 1				
New England	3 2 1 - 6	10 12 6 - 28	Smith	Antonovich, J. Carlson, G. Howe, Mty Howe, McKenzie, S. Carlson
Quebec	0 3 0 - 3	16 19 9 - 44	Brodeur	Tardif, S. Bernier, Sutherland
Houston	0 2 1 - 3	7 12 16 - 35	Zimmerman	Popiel, Hansis, Lacroix
Indianapolis	2 3 1 - 6	9 10 13 - 32	Inness	Sheehan 2, Rhiness, Patenaude, Thomas, St. Sauveur

1977-1978 Game by Game Line Scores

Date & Teams	Scoring 1	2	3	ot	F	Shots 1	2	3	ot	F	Goaltenders	Goals & Other Scoring Highlights
November 2												
Winnipeg	2	1	3	-	6	7	9	5	-	21	Bromley	Labraaten, Long, U. Nilsson, Hull, Sullivan, Hedberg
Edmonton	2	0	1	-	3	12	10	15	-	37	Broderick	Shmyr, Micheletti, MacGregor
Birmingham	2	0	1	-	3	10	1	12	-	23	Wood	Hughes, Napier, Marrin
Houston	1	1	3	-	5	11	10	13	-	34	Rutledge	Ruskowski, Connor, Campbell, Lukowich, Schella
November 4												
Cincinnati	1	0	2	-	3	6	4	14	-	24	Liut	Ftorek 2, Sobchuk
New England	2	2	0	-	4	11	14	11	-	36	Smith	Lyle 2, Webster, Keon
Winnipeg	0	2	2	-	4	6	12	8	-	26	Daley	U. Nilsson, Hedberg, Lindstrom, Lesuk
Birmingham	0	1	1	-	2	7	10	9	-	26	Garrett	Marrin, Napier
Indianapolis	1	0	0	-	1	8	9	9	-	26	McDuffe	Patenaude
Edmonton	0	3	0	-	3	12	18	13	-	43	Dryden	MacGregor, Callighen, Campbell
Quebec	1	4	2	-	7	6	19	6	-	31	Corsi	Dube 2 (WG 17:29), Sutherland, Driscoll, Cloutier, Boudrias, S.Bernier
Houston	1	1	4	-	6	13	8	10	-	31	Rutledge	Gray, Connor, Popiel, Lacroix, Lund, Lukowich
November 5												
Quebec	1	1	2	0	4	11	7	18	5	41	Corsi	S. Bernier 2 (TG 19:55), Cloutier, Baxter
Birmingham	1	1	2	1	5	7	6	11	3	27	Garrett	Napier 2, Mahovlich, Noris, Sheehy (WG 4:35)
Winnipeg	2	1	3	-	6	8	9	8	-	25	Mattsson	U. Nilsson 2, Moffat 2, Hedberg, Guindon
Cincinnati	1	0	0	-	1	11	11	17	-	39	Wakely	Sobchuk
November 6												
Houston	0	0	1	-	1	4	9	11	-	24	Zimmerman	Ruskowski
Edmonton	4	2	1	-	7	14	11	10	-	35	Dryden	Ferguson 3, MacGregor, Langevin, Morris, Zuke
New England	1	4	0	-	5	2	11	7	-	20	Smith	Rogers, Mk Howe, McKenzie, G. Howe, Lyle
Cincinnati	1	0	1	-	2	13	5	9	-	27	Liut	Leduc, Marotte
November 8												
Edmonton	1	2	0	-	3	9	15	9	-	33	Dryden	Flett 2, MacGregor
Quebec	0	4	3	-	7	7	19	15	-	41	Corsi	Tardif 2, Dube 2, J. Bernier, S. Bernier, P. Bordeleau
New England	1	3	0	-	4	15	11	12	-	38	Smith	Rogers, Antonovich, Mayer, Webster
Birmingham	1	2	0	-	3	7	8	14	-	29	Garrett	Henderson 2, Napier
November 9												
Birmingham	1	0	0	-	1	3	9	4	-	16	Garrett	Nedomansky
Cincinnati	1	0	1	-	2	10	13	14	-	37	Dion	Plumb, Abgrall (WG 14:23)
Houston	2	1	0	-	3	11	8	9	-	28	Zimmerman	Campbell, Lukowich, West
Winnipeg	2	1	1	-	4	7	12	5	-	24	Bromley	Clackson, U. Nilsson, K. Nilsson, Hull (WG 8:01)
November 10												
Edmonton	0	1	2	-	3	5	14	10	-	29	Dryden	Hamilton 2, MacGregor
New England	1	0	4	-	5	12	11	12	-	35	Smith	Mayer, Antonovich, Webster, G. Howe, Roberts
November 11												
Edmonton	0	2	1	-	3	12	14	7	-	33	Broderick	MacGregor, Rota, Flett (WG 6:19)
Cincinnati	1	1	0	-	2	6	7	5	-	18	Dion	Ftorek, Larose
Indianapolis	1	1	1	-	3	10	10	5	-	25	Inness	Paiement, Maggs, Patenaude
Houston	0	5	0	-	5	8	11	3	-	22	Zimmerman	Preston, Lacroix, Gray, Hansis, Larway
Quebec	0	1	1	1	3	10	5	7	2	24	Corsi	Tardif 2 (OT 6:32), S. Bernier
Winnipeg	1	1	0	0	2	9	16	13	6	44	Daley	Labraaten, Hedberg
November 12												
Indianapolis	2	0	1	-	3	8	6	7	-	21	McDuffe	Morrison, Powis, French
New England	0	3	2	-	5	14	15	12	-	41	Smith	Keon 2, Lyle 2, Webster
Edmonton	1	0	0	0	1	13	6	17	3	39	Dryden	Zuke
Birmingham	1	0	0	0	1	10	12	10	3	35	Garrett	Cassolato
Cincinnati	3	1	1	1	6	11	8	11	1	31	Dion	Ftorek 3, Sobchuk, Plumb, Abgrall (OT 1:41)
Quebec	1	3	1	0	5	15	15	17	0	47	McLeod	P. Bordeleau 2, Cloutier, Tardif, Boudrias
November 13												
Cincinnati	1	0	2	-	3	4	13	7	-	24	Liut	Dudley, Leduc, Stoughton (WG 18:32)
Winnipeg	2	0	0	-	2	16	13	8	-	37	Mattsson	Hull, Labraaten
November 15												
New England	0	4	2	-	6	7	9	8	-	24	Levasseur	Antonovich 3, Mayer, Rogers, McKenzie
Indianapolis	0	3	1	-	4	7	8	7	-	22	Inness	St. Sauveur, Harris, Spring, Patenaude
Winnipeg	2	1	3	0	6	10	15	16	3	44	Daley, Mattsson	U. Nilsson 2, Hedberg 2, Moffat, Hull
Quebec	2	4	0	1	7	11	19	12	1	43	Corsi	Guite 2 (OT 1:11), Cloutier 2, Tardif, P. Bordeleau, Sutherland
November 16												
Cincinnati	1	2	1	-	4	8	7	12	-	27	Dion, Liut	Hall, Sobchuk, Dudley, Hislop
Edmonton	2	2	2	-	6	7	15	14	-	36	Dryden	Flett 2, Hamilton, Chipperfield, Campbell, MacGregor
Birmingham	0	2	0	0	2	3	10	9	5	27	Wood	Linseman, Mahovlich
Winnipeg	1	0	1	0	2	7	7	11	3	28	Bromley	Kryskow, Labraaten
November 18												
Quebec	2	2	1	-	5	8	11	15	-	34	Corsi, Brodeur	Tardif 3, P. Bordeleau, Dube
Houston	4	2	0	-	6	14	12	6	-	32	Zimmerman	West 2, Lacroix, Preston, Larway, Connor
Winnipeg	0	1	1	-	2	8	12	5	-	25	Daley	K. Nilsson, Hedberg
New England	0	0	3	-	3	9	12	16	-	37	Levasseur	McKenzie, Hangsleben, Antonovich (WG 15:55)
Birmingham	1	1	0	-	2	5	8	9	-	22	Garrett	Beaton, Cassolato
Indianapolis	1	0	0	-	1	16	12	6	-	34	Park	St. Sauveur
Cincinnati	2	1	0	0	3	4	8	8	1	21	Liut	Plumb, Ftorek, Hall
Edmonton	1	1	1	1	4	9	5	11	3	28	Dryden	Chipperfield 2, Widing, Flett (OT 2:00)
November 19												
Winnipeg	0	2	4	-	6	7	11	6	-	24	Bromley	Hedberg 2, Kryskow 2, Labraaten 2
Indianapolis	0	2	2	-	4	12	10	11	-	33	Inness	Maggs, Devine, St. Sauveur, Paiement
Houston	2	1	0	-	3	8	3	8	-	19	Wakely	Preston, Lacroix, Hansis
Birmingham	1	1	2	-	4	10	6	13	-	29	Garrett	Turkiewicz, Durbano, Marrin, Napier (WG 16:07)

1977-1978 Game by Game Line Scores

Date & Teams	Scoring 1 2 3 ot F	Shots 1 2 3 ot F	Goaltenders	Goals & Other Scoring Highlights
November 20				
New England	1 1 2 1 5	8 4 6 3 21	Levasseur	McKenzie, Carroll, Webster, Mty Howe, Hangsleben (OT 7:53)
Edmonton	0 4 0 0 4	6 23 7 2 38	Broderick	Micheletti 2, MacDonald, Flett (NE: 13th straight win)
Indianapolis	1 0 1 - 2	7 9 9 - 25	McDuffe	Sheehan, Devine
Quebec	1 2 2 - 5	7 16 11 - 34	Corsi	P. Bordeleau 3, Tardif, J. Bernier
November 22				
New England	2 0 2 - 4	9 9 15 - 33	Levasseur	Lyle, Mayer, Carroll, Pleau
Quebec	1 3 1 - 5	10 8 15 - 33	Corsi	Boudrias 2, Fitchner, Tardif, P. Bordeleau
Winnipeg	1 1 0 - 2	4 10 6 - 20	Daley	Hedberg 2
Edmonton	1 1 2 - 4	25 8 14 - 47	Dryden	Miller, MacDonald, Chipperfield, MacGregor
November 23				
Birmingham	0 0 0 - 0	15 6 4 - 25	Garrett	▶ Wakely: shutout (1), 25 saves
Houston	0 3 0 - 3	6 10 8 - 24	Wakely	Lacroix 2, Campbell
Indianapolis	2 0 1 0 3	12 11 6 3 32	Inness	Burgess 2 (TG 19:11), Morrison
New England	0 1 2 0 3	9 16 12 2 39	Smith	Lyle, Rogers, McKenzie
Quebec	1 0 2 - 3	5 7 14 - 26	Brodeur	Guite, Sutherland, S. Bernier
Cincinnati	1 3 0 - 4	9 11 11 - 31	Dion	Ftorek 2, Legge, Leduc
November 24				
Edmonton	0 2 2 0 4	6 16 13 5 40	Dryden	Rota 2, Micheletti, Callighen
Indianapolis	2 2 0 1 5	12 9 7 4 32	McDuffe	Patenaude 3 (OT 9:36), St. Sauveur, Devine
Cincinnati	1 0 1 - 2	9 10 11 - 30	Liut, Dion	Leduc, Stapleton Henderson, Gorman, Marrin
Birmingham	3 2 7 - 12	6 16 14 - 36	Wood	Stephenson 2, Linseman 2, Beaudoin 2, Cassolato 2, Mahovlich,
November 25				
Quebec	2 2 2 - 6	11 14 17 - 42	Brodeur	Cloutier 2, Tardif 2, S. Bernier, P. Bordeleau
New England	0 2 0 - 2	11 13 21 - 45	Smith	Pleau, Lyle
Cincinnati	1 0 0 - 1	9 8 13 - 30	Dion, Liut	Stoughton
Houston	0 0 3 - 3	10 8 12 - 30	Wakely	Preston 2, Lukowich
November 26				
Edmonton	0 1 2 - 3	14 13 10 - 37	Dryden	Chipperfield, Callighen, Flett
New England	0 0 1 - 1	8 5 13 - 26	Levasseur	Keon
Birmingham	1 1 0 - 2	12 11 8 - 31	Garrett	Linseman, Gorman
Quebec	1 1 2 - 4	12 12 6 - 30	Brodeur	Tardif, Cloutier, J. Bernier, S. Bernier
Cincinnati	1 2 4 - 7	10 11 11 - 32	Dion	Norwich 2, Leduc 2, Legge, Stoughton, Hislop
Indianapolis	2 2 1 - 5	11 12 13 - 36	Park	Powis 2, St. Sauveur, Patenaude, Leclerc
November 27				
Birmingham	1 0 2 1 4	10 5 7 2 24	Wood	Linseman, Stewart, Hughes, Stephenson (OT 2:57)
Winnipeg	0 2 1 0 3	8 8 15 0 31	Daley	Guindon, Kryskow, Hedberg
November 29				
Cincinnati	1 2 0 - 3	9 11 9 - 29	Liut	Larose 2, Sobchuk
Quebec	0 1 1 - 2	14 6 16 - 36	Brodeur	Brackenbury, Tardif
November 30				
Indianapolis	0 0 0 - 0	6 9 7 - 22	Inness	▶ Dion: shutout (1), 22 saves
Cincinnati	2 0 1 - 3	4 7 6 - 17	Dion	Ftorek, Legge, Hall
Birmingham	1 0 1 - 2	10 12 6 - 28	Garrett	Hughes, Cassolato
Edmonton	1 0 3 - 4	11 11 14 - 36	Dryden	Ferguson, Guite, MacDonald, Chipperfield
New England	1 1 1 0 3	5 5 13 5 28	Smith	Carroll, Rogers, Pleau
Houston	1 1 1 0 3	7 11 10 2 30	Wakely	Larway, Lukowich, Connor
December 1				
Quebec	2 1 1 - 4	7 9 16 - 32	Brodeur	Tardif 3, Driscoll
Indianapolis	2 1 2 - 5	14 11 14 - 39	McDuffe, Inness	Block, Devine, Maggs, Parizeau, St. Sauveur (WG 17:09)
December 2				
Winnipeg	0 1 0 - 1	9 12 8 - 29	Daley	Long
New England	1 1 2 - 4	9 7 10 - 26	Smith	Pleau, McKenzie, Hangsleben, Mayer
Birmingham	1 2 4 - 7	12 11 17 - 40	Garrett	Cassolato 2 (WG 18:27), Henderson 2, Napier, Gorman, Marrin
Edmonton	3 2 0 - 5	9 18 8 - 35	Dryden, McLeod	Chipperfield, Hamilton, Widing, Callighen, Deadmarsh
Indianapolis	1 3 0 - 4	5 9 10 - 24	Inness	Devine, St. Sauveur, Patenaude, Spring
Houston	0 1 1 - 2	7 6 12 - 25	Wakely	Lacroix, Lukowich
December 3				
Cincinnati	1 1 3 - 5	9 10 17 - 36	Dion, Liut	Leduc 2, Stoughton, Marsh, Gilligan
New England	0 1 1 - 2	9 14 10 - 33	Smith	Antonovich, Roberts
Winnipeg	1 2 2 - 5	14 16 6 - 36	Bromley	Hedberg, Lindstrom, Kryskow, Hull, Guindon
Quebec	3 3 0 - 6	10 14 8 - 32	Brodeur, Corsi	Cloutier 2, Miller, P. Bordeleau, J. Bernier, Tardif
December 4				
Edmonton	1 1 1 - 3	6 6 7 - 19	McLeod	Ferguson, MacDonald, Widing
Winnipeg	1 0 1 - 2	13 5 7 - 25	Daley	Lindstrom, Labraaten
Houston	1 1 1 - 3	11 8 7 - 26	Wakely	Lacroix, Preston, Connor (WG 13:15)
Cincinnati	0 1 1 - 2	14 13 11 - 38	Liut	Dudley, Stapleton
Indianapolis	0 0 0 - 0	10 7 6 - 23	Park	▶ Garrett: shutout (1), 23 saves
Birmingham	1 0 2 - 3	10 2 15 - 27	Garrett	Henderson, Durbano, Napier
December 6				
Houston	1 0 2 0 3	10 13 8 2 33	Rutledge	Lukowich, Lacroix, Connor
Quebec	0 2 1 1 4	12 14 11 4 41	Broderick	Cloutier 2 (OT 4:55), Sutherland, Tardif
New England	0 1 1 - 2	13 7 13 - 33	Levasseur	Antonovich, Lyle
Indianapolis	2 3 0 - 5	5 13 8 - 26	Inness	Patenaude 2, Burgess 2, Goldsworthy
December 7				
New England	2 3 1 - 6	12 11 2 - 25	Smith	G. Howe, Rogers, Pleau, McKenzie, Roberts, J. Carlson
Birmingham	1 0 2 - 3	9 12 10 - 31	Garrett	Stephenson, Linseman, Napier (Howe: 1000th career goal)
Winnipeg	3 0 2 - 5	9 9 9 - 27	Daley	Hull 2, Kryskow, Hedberg, Labraaten
Houston	0 1 1 - 2	4 7 12 - 23	Wakely	Lukowich, Larway
Cincinnati	1 2 1 0 4	8 12 9 0 29	Dion	Leduc 2, Marsh, Gilligan
Edmonton	1 1 2 1 5	15 11 14 1 41	McLeod	Flett 2 (OT 0:54), Ferguson 2, Shmyr

1977-1978 Game by Game Line Scores

Date & Teams	Scoring 1	2	3	ot	F	Shots 1	2	3	ot	F	Goaltenders	Goals & Other Scoring Highlights
December 9												
Cincinnati	0	2	1	1	4	10	9	9	1	29	Liut	Larose 2, Melrose (TG 18:57), Ftorek (OT 3:25)
Winnipeg	1	1	1	0	3	13	12	14	0	39	Bromley	Sjoberg, Sullivan, Hedberg
New England	0	0	1	1	2	9	1	6	2	18	Smith	Roberts, Lyle (OT 7:55)
Birmingham	0	1	0	0	1	5	12	3	3	23	Wood	Marrin
Houston	0	3	2	-	5	5	10	10	-	25	Wakely	Tonelli 2, Gray, Larway, Lacroix
Edmonton	0	1	2	-	3	19	14	12	-	45	Dryden	DeMarco, Hamilton, MacGregor
Czechoslovakia	2	0	3	-	5	8	11	16	-	35	Dzurilla	Richter 3, Vlcek, Mec
Indianapolis	0	2	1	-	3	3	12	10	-	25	Inness	St. Sauveur 2, Patenaude
December 10												
Indianapolis	0	2	1	-	3	6	14	8	-	28	McDuffe	Devine, Patenaude, Burgess
Quebec	0	1	4	-	5	10	10	9	-	29	Broderick	Hagman 4, Tardif
December 11												
Houston	1	0	3	-	4	4	5	11	-	20	Wakely	Schella, Ruskowski, Larway, Lacroix
Edmonton	2	0	0	-	2	12	11	9	-	32	McLeod	Chipperfield 2
Indianapolis	0	0	1	-	1	11	8	11	-	30	Inness	Leclerc
Winnipeg	2	1	4	-	7	14	8	14	-	36	Bromley	Baird 3, U. Nilsson 2, Hull, Bergman
Czechoslovakia	2	1	1	-	4	18	10	16	-	44	Dzurilla	Cernik 2, Kokrment, Duris
Quebec	3	1	4	-	8	12	19	11	-	42	Broderick	Hagman 2, Cloutier 2, Miller, Baxter, Tardif, P. Bordeleau
December 13												
Czechoslovakia	0	1	0	-	1	10	10	10	-	30	Kapoun	Vlcek
Winnipeg	0	4	1	-	5	11	13	15	-	39	Daley	Sullivan, Hedberg, Hull, Labraaten, U. Nilsson
Birmingham	0	4	1	-	5	6	8	4	-	18	Garrett	Roberto, Hughes, Beaton, Napier, Linseman
Houston	3	0	0	-	3	16	6	4	-	26	Wakely	Lukowich 2, Tonelli
December 14												
Soviet All-Stars	1	0	1	-	2	11	9	14	-	34	Vaselyonok	Bilyaletdinov 2
New England	3	3	1	-	7	17	11	6	-	34	Smith	Pleau 2, Rogers, Antonovich, Keon, Lyle, Mk Howe
Czechoslovakia	1	0	0	-	1	7	13	12	-	32	Kapoun	Kolar
Edmonton	1	1	4	-	6	14	8	14	-	36	Dryden	Flett 4, Micheletti, MacDonald
Indianapolis	1	0	0	-	1	8	7	8	-	23	Inness	Burgess
Cincinnati	1	1	1	-	3	12	11	14	-	37	Dion	Ftorek 2, Hislop
December 15												
Houston	1	2	0	0	3	9	8	6	4	27	Wakely	Tonelli, Preston, Lukowich
Indianapolis	1	0	2	0	3	9	12	12	3	36	McDuffe	Leclerc, Rhiness, Parizeau (TG 19:33)
Cincinnati	0	1	2	-	3	8	8	15	-	31	Liut	Stoughton, Larose, Hislop
Birmingham	0	3	2	-	5	6	7	14	-	27	Garrett	Henderson 2, Napier, Marrin, Hanson
December 16												
Czechoslovakia	2	1	0	-	3	16	9	5	-	30	Podesva	Duris 2, Tarant
New England	1	0	4	-	5	15	10	15	-	40	Smith	J. Carlson, Pleau, G. Howe, McKenzie, Rogers
December 17												
Soviet All-Stars	1	2	2	-	5	9	8	11	-	28	Babariko	Volchenkov 2, Volchkov, Popov, I. Gimayev
Cincinnati	2	0	2	-	4	10	6	9	-	25	Liut, Dion	Hislop, Leduc, Stoughton, Ftorek
Winnipeg	2	2	2	-	6	9	9	9	-	27	Bromley	Sullivan 2, Hull, Lindstrom, Sjoberg, Kryskow
New England	1	0	2	-	3	10	10	11	-	31	Smith	J. Carlson 3
December 18												
New England	1	1	1	-	3	12	10	12	-	34	Levasseur	Antonovich 2, G. Howe
Winnipeg	1	3	3	-	7	6	8	12	-	26	Daley	Hedberg 2, Dunn, Hull, Green, Guindon, Baird
Edmonton	0	2	0	-	2	10	15	10	-	35	Dryden	Hamilton, Micheletti
Birmingham	1	0	2	-	3	9	11	13	-	33	Wood	Napier, Mahovlich, Stewart (WG 12:05)
Czechoslovakia	1	0	1	-	2	8	10	7	-	25	Dzurilla, Podesva	Lycka, Duris
Houston	0	2	1	-	3	4	4	7	-	15	Wakely	McLeod, Taylor, Popiel
Soviet All-Stars	0	2	2	-	4	4	10	9	-	23	Babariko	Tyumenev, Yemelianenko, Bilyaletdinov, Popov (WG 12:27)
Indianapolis	2	1	0	-	3	10	6	4	-	20	Inness	Goldsworthy, Driscoll, Thomas
December 20												
Soviet All-Stars	1	1	2	-	4	8	12	13	-	33	Vaselyonok	Yemelianenko, Romashin, Volchkov, Makarov
Winnipeg	2	3	1	-	6	9	13	9	-	31	Daley	Kryskow 2, K. Nilsson, Hull, Sjoberg, Sullivan
Edmonton	1	1	2	-	4	6	11	15	-	32	McLeod, Dryden	Hamilton, Ferguson, Semenko, Widing
Houston	1	3	2	-	6	5	11	8	-	24	Wakely	Lukowich 2, Gray 2, J. Hughes, Tonelli
Czechoslovakia	1	2	2	0	5	11	8	12	3	34	Kapoun	Cernik 2, Klabouch, Mec, Duris
Cincinnati	2	3	0	0	5	11	12	11	5	39	Dion	Norwich, Hislop, Marsh, Plumb, Leduc
December 21												
Soviet All-Stars	0	1	1	-	2	3	5	6	-	14	Babariko	Tyumenev, Semyonov
Edmonton	1	2	2	-	5	18	9	12	-	39	Dryden	Widing 3, DeMarco, Callighen
Czechoslovakia	0	0	0	-	0	10	8	6	-	24	Podesva, Kapoun	▶ Garrett: shutout (2), 24 saves
Birmingham	0	5	0	-	5	18	15	9	-	42	Garrett	Linseman 2, Henderson, Marrin, Roberto
Winnipeg	3	1	0	-	4	13	5	10	-	28	Bromley	Kryskow, Hedberg, Lesuk, Hull
Houston	2	1	0	-	3	13	5	4	-	22	Wakely	Lukowich, Ruskowski, Connor
December 22												
Cincinnati	2	1	1	-	4	10	11	5	-	26	Lapointe	Dudley, Ftorek, Plumb, Marsh
Indianapolis	0	0	1	-	1	8	12	13	-	33	McDuffe	Thomas
December 23												
Winnipeg	3	2	1	-	6	13	8	10	-	31	Daley	Hedberg 2, Lindstrom, Moffat, Labraaten, Sullivan
Cincinnati	2	1	1	-	4	14	11	10	-	35	Lapointe	Dudley 2, Plumb, Larose
Indianapolis	2	1	0	-	3	11	11	10	-	32	Inness	Maggs, Thomas, Parizeau
New England	1	1	3	-	5	14	8	16	-	38	Smith	Roberts, McKenzie, Ley, G. Howe, Lyle
Soviet All-Stars	2	2	2	-	6	5	13	11	-	29	Babariko	Bilyaletdinov 2, Romashin, Volchenkov, Golubovich, Shostak
Houston	0	0	2	-	2	12	1	11	-	24	Wakely	Preston, Hansis

1977-1978 Game by Game Line Scores

Date & Teams	Scoring 1 2 3 ot F	Shots 1 2 3 ot F	Goaltenders	Goals & Other Scoring Highlights
December 26				
Soviet All-Stars	0 1 0 - 1	10 6 11 - 27	Vaselyonok	Golubovich
Birmingham	3 2 1 - 6	6 9 7 - 22	Wood	Marrin 2, Beaudoin, Durbano, Mahovlich, Hughes
Quebec	1 2 1 - 4	9 1411 - 34	Corsi, Broderick	P. Bordeleau 2, Sutherland, Cloutier
Winnipeg	4 3 2 - 9	12 9 9 - 30	Daley	Hedberg 4, Guindon, Green, Labraaten, Kryskow, K. Nilsson
December 27				
Birmingham	1 0 0 - 1	9 11 3 - 23	Garrett, Wood	Linseman
New England	3 1 4 - 8	111314 - 38	Smith	Selwood 2, McKenzie 2, Lyle, Antonovich, Mk Howe, Rogers
Quebec	1 0 2 - 3	7 1310 - 30	Broderick, Corsi	Tardif, S. Bernier, Cloutier
Edmonton	5 3 1 - 9	261418 - 58	McLeod	MacDonald 2, Guite, Widing, Chipperfield, Semenko, Rota, Zuke, Flett
December 28				
Indianapolis	1 1 2 0 4	7 7 12 0 26	Inness	Rhiness, Goldsworthy, Stoughton, Patenaude
Cincinnati	1 0 3 1 5	13 6 13 1 33	Dion	Marsh 2, Dudley, Melrose (TG 19:10), Hislop (4:36)
December 29				
Houston	2 4 1 - 7	101911 - 40	Wakely	Preston 2, Gray 2, Ruskowski, Connor, Lund
Indianapolis	0 0 1 - 1	121212 - 36	Inness, McDuffe	Marotte
Birmingham	2 3 2 - 7	141010 - 34	Wood	Napier 3, Henderson, Stephenson, Stewart, Linseman
Cincinnati	0 0 1 - 1	12 6 10 - 28	Dion	Ftorek
December 30				
Indianapolis	3 0 2 - 5	7 1011 - 28	McDuffe, Inness	Morrison 2, Paiement, Stoughton, Goldsworthy
Edmonton	3 3 2 - 8	181613 - 47	McLeod	Sobchuk 3, Flett, MacDonald, Callighen, Widing, Chipperfield
Birmingham	1 1 0 - 2	1210 3 - 25	Wood	Beaudoin, Marrin
New England	2 3 1 - 6	131912 - 44	Smith	G. Howe 2, Pleau 2, Mk Howe, Antonovich
Cincinnati	3 1 1 0 5	12 8 9 6 35	Lapointe	Coates 2, Leduc, Ftorek, Marsh
Houston	2 2 1 0 5	1510 7 3 35	Wakely	Connor, Lacroix, Hale, Tonelli, Ruskowski
January 1				
Quebec	2 2 1 - 5	1812 8 - 38	Broderick	Cloutier 4, Hagman
Birmingham	0 1 1 - 2	6 1410 - 30	Wood	Napier, Mahovlich
Houston	1 0 1 - 2	1010 6 - 26	Zimmerman	Hansis, Schella (WG 8:49)
Edmonton	0 1 0 - 1	121810 - 40	Dryden	Semenko
New England	1 1 1 1 4	6 9 5 4 24	Smith	G. Howe 2 (OT 5:16), Lyle, Maxwell (TG 19:44)
Cincinnati	1 1 1 0 3	9 9 9 2 29	Dion	Ftorek 2, Hislop
January 3				
Soviet All-Stars	0 2 1 - 3	6 127 - 25	Babariko	Romashin, Lavrentiev, Volchkov
Quebec	2 0 1 - 3	108 3 - 21	Broderick	Tardif 2, Fitchner (no OT played)
January 4				
Birmingham	0 1 0 - 1	4 4 5 - 13	Wood	Beaudoin
Indianapolis	2 0 2 - 4	8 1116 - 35	Inness	Devine, Maggs, Patenaude, Driscoll
Houston	2 0 1 - 3	10 6 13 - 29	Wakely	Lacroix, Taylor, Tonelli
Cincinnati	3 1 1 - 5	14 9 11 - 34	Dion	Harris 2, Leduc, Abgrall, Ftorek
Quebec	2 2 2 - 6	11 7 11 - 29	Corsi	Hagman 2, Dube, Cloutier, Fitchner, Sutherland
New England	2 2 0 - 4	111610 - 37	Smith	Maxwell, Pleau, Lyle, Roberts
January 6				
Houston	1 2 1 - 4	7 4 13 - 24	Zimmerman	Campbell 2, Lukowich, Tonelli
Birmingham	0 3 3 - 6	131412 - 39	Garrett	Hughes, Mahovlich, Hanson, Gorman, Marrin, Cassolato
New England	0 1 2 - 3	1213 9 - 34	Smith	Carroll, Lyle, G. Howe
Indianapolis	2 2 0 - 4	14 9 4 - 27	Park	Stoughton, St. Sauveur, Patenaude, Goldsworthy
Quebec	0 0 3 - 3	7 1132 - 50	Broderick	Hagman, Tardif, Sutherland
Cincinnati	1 1 3 - 5	16 9 8 - 33	Dion	Coates 2, Harris 2, Hislop
Winnipeg	2 1 1 - 4	11 7 7 - 25	Bromley	U. Nilsson 2, Baird, Hull
Edmonton	0 1 0 - 1	9 1413 - 36	McLeod	Holland
January 7				
Indianapolis	0 1 0 1 2	10 9 11 1 31	Inness	Morrison, Devine (OT 0:21)
Houston	0 0 1 0 1	7 7 5 0 19	Wakely	Taylor
Cincinnati	2 1 0 - 3	10 7 8 - 25	Lapointe	Stewart, Gilligan, Hislop
New England	2 1 2 - 5	141412 - 40	Levasseur	Roberts, Mk Howe, Mty Howe, Carroll, Hangsleben
January 8				
Birmingham	4 1 0 - 5	14 7 11 - 32	Garrett	Durbano, Henderson, Marrin, Mahovlich, Hoganson
New England	1 2 1 - 4	8 136 - 27	Smith	Mty Howe, Keon, Antonovich, Rogers
Edmonton	2 1 1 - 4	131910 - 42	McLeod	Guite, Sobchuk, MacDonald, Hamilton
Houston	1 0 1 - 2	5 5 9 - 19	Rutledge	Preston, Gray
Indianapolis	1 1 0 - 2	4 9 5 - 18	Inness	Maggs, Driscoll
Winnipeg	1 3 0 - 4	101311 - 34	Daley	Labraaten, K. Nilsson, Hull, U. Nilsson
January 10				
Birmingham	2 2 0 - 4	6 7 6 - 19	Garrett	Linseman 3, Roberto
Quebec	1 3 2 - 6	151216 - 43	Broderick	Hagman, P. Bordeleau, J. Bernier, Fitchner, Dube, Tardif
January 11				
Edmonton	0 0 2 - 2	8 1114 - 33	McLeod	Micheletti (spoiled Dion's shutout at 18:50), Flett
Cincinnati	0 0 0 - 0	9 5 14 - 28	Dion	▶ McLeod: shutout (1), 28 saves
Quebec	0 0 1 - 1	101211 - 33	Corsi	Fitchner (spoiled Inness/Park shutout at 18:49)
Indianapolis	0 2 0 - 2	9 1113 - 33	Inness, Park	Goldsworthy, Parizeau
Winnipeg	4 4 3 - 11	161310 - 39	Daley	Hedberg 2, Hull 2, Baird 2, Sjoberg 2, Bergman, Lindstrom, Green
Birmingham	1 1 0 - 2	7 1310 - 30	Wood, Garrett	Durbano, Stephenson (Wpg: 11th straight victory)
January 13				
Winnipeg	1 1 0 - 2	10 6 7 - 23	Bromley	K. Nilsson, Kryskow
Houston	0 3 0 - 3	1112 8 - 31	Wakely	Hale, Larway, Connor
Edmonton	0 0 0 - 0	12 5 10 - 27	Dryden	▶ Levasseur: shutout (1), 27 saves
New England	1 1 0 - 2	6 9 8 - 23	Levasseur	Lyle, Mk Howe

1977-1978 Game by Game Line Scores

Date & Teams	Scoring 1 2 3 ot F	Shots 1 2 3 ot F	Goaltenders	Goals & Other Scoring Highlights
January 14				
Winnipeg	2 3 1 - 6	11 17 14 - 42	Daley	Hedberg, Powis, Lindstrom, Lesuk, U. Nilsson, K. Nilsson
Indianapolis	3 0 0 - 3	10 4 15 - 29	Inness	Driscoll, St. Sauveur, Thomas
Birmingham	1 2 1 - 4	12 8 10 - 30	Garrett	Henderson, Napier, Linseman, Gorman
Cincinnati	1 1 1 - 3	16 5 4 - 25	Dion	Leduc, Ftorek, Plumb
Houston	1 3 0 1 5	9 9 9 2 29	Wakely	Larway, J. Hughes, Lukowich, McLeod, Preston (OT 6:09)
New England	1 2 1 0 4	3 10 13 4 30	Smith	G. Howe 2, Selwood, Hangsleben
Edmonton	0 0 4 - 4	9 10 21 - 40	McLeod	Chipperfield, Zuke, Micheletti, Ferguson
Quebec	1 3 3 - 7	8 22 10 - 40	Corsi	Miller 2, Fitchner, Lariviere, S. Bernier, Tardif, Dube
January 15				
Edmonton	1 1 1 1 4	8 12 7 5 32	Dryden	Chipperfield 2 (OT 6:04), Guite, Langevin
Winnipeg	2 0 1 0 3	9 10 12 4 35	Daley	Lindstrom, Hull, Powis
Cincinnati	1 4 1 - 6	10 10 11 - 31	Lapointe	Abgrall 2, Leduc, Coates, Dudley, Hislop
Quebec	1 1 1 - 3	12 11 14 - 37	Corsi, Broderick	P. Bordeleau, Tardif, Miller
January 18				
Cincinnati	0 0 0 - 0	9 4 5 - 18	Dion	▶ Wood: shutout (1), 18 saves
Birmingham	0 2 1 - 3	11 10 10 - 31	Wood	Marrin, Westrum, Henderson
Quebec	1 0 0 - 1	10 5 6 - 21	Corsi	Constantin
Winnipeg	2 1 2 - 5	14 13 15 - 42	Daley	Labraaten, K. Nilsson, Hull, Hedberg, Guindon
New England	0 0 0 - 0	12 9 6 - 27	Levasseur	▶ Dryden: shutout (1), 27 saves
Edmonton	1 0 0 - 1	16 9 10 - 35	Dryden	MacDonald
January 20				
Edmonton	0 1 2 - 3	8 13 9 - 30	Dryden, McLeod	Guite, Hamilton, Campbell
Birmingham	2 3 0 - 5	11 9 4 - 24	Garrett	Langway 2, Marrin, Cassolato, Stewart
Quebec	2 4 2 - 8	13 14 12 - 39	Mattsson	Hagman 2, Tardif, Dube, P. Bordeleau, Fitchner, Sutherland, Lariviere
Cincinnati	0 2 0 - 2	14 12 6 - 32	Lapointe, Dion	Trognitz, Ftorek
New England	1 2 1 0 4	10 10 5 4 29	Levasseur	Lyle, Rogers, Mayer, Mk Howe
Winnipeg	3 1 0 0 4	11 7 12 3 33	Daley	K. Nilsson 2, Hull, Lindstrom
Houston	0 2 2 - 4	8 11 11 - 30	Wakely	Preston 2, Larway, Lacroix
Indianapolis	1 0 2 - 3	16 12 17 - 45	Inness	Parizeau, Morrison, Thomas
January 21				
Cincinnati	1 1 0 - 2	16 11 4 - 31	Lapointe	Plumb, Abgrall
Houston	1 2 2 - 5	5 8 11 - 24	Wakely	Lukowich, Schella, West, Preston, Ruskowski (WG 17:09)
Edmonton	3 0 0 - 3	13 5 5 - 23	McLeod	Chipperfield 2, Flett
Indianapolis	1 1 0 - 2	6 15 13 - 34	Inness	Morrison, Driscoll
New England	0 0 2 - 2	9 8 12 - 29	Levasseur	Mk Howe, G. Howe
Quebec	0 0 3 - 3	16 10 10 - 36	Corsi	Tremblay, Hagman, Lariviere (WG 14:20)
January 22				
Indianapolis	1 3 1 - 5	15 11 6 - 32	Inness	Thomas 2, Driscoll, St. Sauveur, Goldsworthy
Winnipeg	1 2 1 - 4	5 8 15 - 28	Bromley, Daley	Lesuk, Guindon, Lindstrom, Powis
Quebec	3 0 0 - 3	11 11 7 5 - 33	Mattsson	Tardif, Lariviere, P. Bordeleau
New England	0 2 4 - 6	16 13 15 - 44	Levasseur	Mty Howe, Peloffy, Lyle, G. Howe, Antonovich, Bolduc
Birmingham	1 0 1 - 2	3 7 13 - 23	Garrett	Linseman, Henderson
Houston	1 2 1 - 4	7 13 7 - 27	Wakely	Preston 2, Ruskowski, Gray
Edmonton	1 0 1 - 2	11 14 14 - 39	McLeod	Ferguson, Guite
Cincinnati	0 4 1 - 5	8 10 5 - 23	Lapointe	Ftorek 2, Deadmarsh, Plumb, Hislop
January 24				
Houston	3 1 2 - 6	17 6 12 - 35	Wakely	Tonelli 2 (WG 9:41), Campbell, Hansis, Lukowich, Preston
Quebec	2 3 0 - 5	18 16 6 - 40	Mattsson, Brod'ck	Hagman 2, Miller, Cloutier, P. Bordeleau
January 25				
Indianapolis	0 1 1 - 2	10 7 8 - 25	Inness, McDuffe	Driscoll, Morrison
Edmonton	4 2 0 - 6	16 19 14 - 49	McLeod	Hamilton, Zuke, Shmyr, Guite, Widing, Flett
Winnipeg	1 0 1 - 2	5 19 12 - 36	Daley	Lindstrom, K. Nilsson
Birmingham	2 2 2 - 6	6 8 5 - 19	Garrett	Linseman 2, Henderson, Beaudoin, Mahovlich, Marrin
New England	1 3 3 0 7	5 8 11 4 28	Levasseur	G. Howe 2, Mk Howe 2, Keon 2, Lyle (OT 6:11)
Cincinnati	2 2 3 1 8	20 9 13 3 45	Lapointe	Ftorek 2, Harris, Deadmarsh, Dudley, Baltimore, Abgrall, Legge
January 26				
Winnipeg	0 0 1 0 1	8 15 11 0 34	Bromley	Hull
Houston	0 0 1 1 2	3 8 10 1 22	Wakely	Tonelli 2 (OT 0:19)
January 27				
Quebec	3 2 1 - 6	9 8 11 - 28	Mattsson	Cloutier 2, Miller, Tardif, Sutherland, Hagman
Edmonton	3 4 2 - 9	13 15 15 - 43	Dryden, McLeod	Zuke 2 (2 s.h. in 0:29), Chipperfield 2, Callighen 2, Flett, Langevin
New England	2 2 2 - 6	3 5 13 - 21	Smith	Keon 2, Mayer, Hangsleben, Lyle, Mk Howe
Birmingham	2 0 0 - 2	11 3 3 - 17	Garrett	Marrin, Mahovlich
January 28				
New England	0 2 1 - 3	8 10 8 - 26	Smith	Mayer, Roberts, Carroll
Houston	0 0 0 - 0	12 6 10 - 28	Wakely	▶ Smith: shutout (2), 28 saves
Winnipeg	3 2 0 - 5	7 10 4 - 21	Daley	Hedberg 2, K. Nilsson, Powis, U. Nilsson
Birmingham	2 2 4 - 8	7 13 11 - 31	Wood, Garrett	Henderson 3, Linseman 2, Cassolato, Napier, Durbano
January 29				
Quebec	1 2 1 - 4	10 6 8 - 24	Broderick	Tremblay, Cloutier, Dube, Lariviere
Edmonton	0 2 1 - 3	11 14 10 - 35	McLeod	Callighen, Zuke, Rota
New England	2 1 1 - 4	12 6 15 - 33	Smith	Lyle, Peloffy, Roberts, G. Howe
Houston	1 4 1 - 6	11 15 10 - 36	Wakely	Lukowich, Taylor, Lacroix, Popiel, Gray, Preston
Winnipeg	2 3 3 - 8	7 9 15 - 31	Bromley	K. Nilsson 2, U. Nilsson 2, Ruhnke 2, Lindstrom, Sullivan
Cincinnati	1 1 2 - 4	10 7 6 - 23	Lapointe, Dion	Coates, Ftorek, Harris, Plumb
January 30				
Cincinnati	1 2 1 - 4	17 9 14 - 40	Dion, Lapointe	Dudley, Marsh, Larose, Hislop (WG 19:39)
Indianapolis	1 2 0 - 3	15 15 10 - 40	Inness	Thomas, St. Sauveur, Driscoll

1977-1978 Game by Game Line Scores

Date & Teams	Scoring 1 2 3 ot F	Shots 1 2 3 ot F	Goaltenders	Goals & Other Scoring Highlights
January 31				
Winnipeg	3 2 2 - 7	10 15 10 - 35	Daley	U. Nilsson 3, Lindstrom 2, Dunn, Guindon
Quebec	1 0 1 - 2	12 7 13 - 32	Brod'ck, Corsi	Hagman, P. Bordeleau
Houston	1 2 1 - 4	11 5 9 - 25	Rutledge	Tonelli, Gray, Ruskowski, Hansis
Birmingham	1 1 0 - 2	5 11 25 - 41	Garrett	Marrin, Linseman
Edmonton	3 1 2 - 6	13 23 14 - 50	Dryden	Zuke 2, Flett, Widing, Micheletti, Busniuk
Indianapolis	2 1 1 - 4	14 13 7 - 34	Park	Thomas, French, Burgess, Morrison
February 1				
Indianapolis	0 0 0 - 0	3 12 11 - 26	Inness	▸ Dion: shutout (2), 26 saves
Cincinnati	1 4 3 - 8	11 18 16 - 45	Dion	Abgrall 3, Ftorek, Dudley, Marsh, Coates, Leduc
Edmonton	0 1 2 - 3	12 6 16 - 34	Dryden	Campbell, Flett, Ferguson
New England	1 2 1 - 4	7 7 12 - 26	Smith	Rogers, Keon, Carroll, Mk Howe (WG 16:56)
February 2				
Quebec	0 4 0 - 4	4 10 4 - 18	Corsi	Cloutier 2, Lagace 2
Birmingham	1 0 1 - 2	17 4 17 - 38	Garrett	Linseman, Marrin
February 3				
Houston	0 0 0 - 0	6 6 11 - 23	Wakely	▸ Dion: shutout (3), 23 saves
Cincinnati	0 1 0 - 1	10 13 10 - 33	Dion	Dudley
Quebec	1 1 2 0 4	8 13 16 2 39	Corsi	Hagman, P. Bordeleau, Sutherland, Tardif
Indianapolis	2 1 1 1 5	10 16 10 2 38	Inness	St. Sauveur 2 (OT 5:26), French, Devine, Adduono
Edmonton	2 2 2 - 6	12 10 14 - 36	Dryden	MacDonald 4, Micheletti, Flett
New England	0 2 1 - 3	9 9 5 - 23	Levasseur	Mayer, Selwood, Bolduc
February 4				
Winnipeg	4 2 1 - 7	8 11 9 - 28	Bromley	Hedberg 2, Hull, K. Nilsson, U. Nilsson, Ruhnke, Baird
Cincinnati	2 0 3 - 5	14 6 12 - 32	Dion	Ftorek 2, Coates, Hislop, Dudley
New England	0 2 2 - 4	7 13 11 - 31	Smith	Lyle 2, Roberts, Rogers
Houston	3 0 2 - 5	7 3 8 - 18	Wakely	Lukowich 2, Lacroix, Taylor, Gray
Edmonton	0 0 3 1 4	7 17 14 2 40	McLeod	Langevin, Flett, Widing (TG 17:57), Zuke (OT 2:56)
Quebec	0 3 0 0 3	8 7 8 1 24	Broderick	Baxter, Cloutier, Fitchner
Indianapolis	1 0 1 - 2	10 8 9 - 27	Inness, McDuffe	Driscoll, French
Birmingham	4 0 1 - 5	14 8 7 - 29	Wood	Cassolato 2, Napier 2, Mahovlich
February 5				
Edmonton	1 1 1 - 3	11 9 5 - 25	Dryden	Flett, MacDonald, Langevin
Winnipeg	1 1 2 - 4	14 9 10 - 33	Daley	Sullivan, Lindstrom, Powis, Bergman
Birmingham	1 0 0 - 1	4 11 7 - 22	Garrett	Napier
Indianapolis	1 3 2 - 6	8 11 8 - 27	Inness	Driscoll 2, Stoughton, Goldsworthy, French, St. Sauveur
February 7				
Birmingham	2 0 1 - 3	9 4 7 - 20	Wood	Henderson, Stephenson, Stewart
Quebec	2 3 3 - 8	19 14 7 - 40	Broderick	Hagman 3, Sutherland 2, Cloutier, Miller, Tardif
February 8				
Birmingham	0 0 0 - 0	6 6 7 - 19	Garrett	▸ Bromley: shutout (1), 19 saves
Winnipeg	3 2 4 - 9	11 9 16 - 36	Bromley	Hedberg 3, Lindstrom 2, U. Nilsson, K. Nilsson, Hull, Bergman
Cincinnati	1 2 3 0 6	4 8 8 6 26	Hoganson	Marsh 3, Leduc, Larose, Plumb (Cin: 3 goals in 1:34, 3rd, to tie)
Edmonton	2 2 2 0 6	12 12 6 2 32	McLeod	Flett 2, Widing, Shmyr, MacDonald, Troy
February 9				
Quebec	1 0 0 - 1	12 9 6 - 27	Brodeur	Hagman
Houston	0 1 1 - 2	12 8 13 - 33	Wakely	Connor, Taylor (WG 16:08)
February 10				
Cincinnati	0 1 1 - 2	13 7 19 - 39	Lapointe, Hog'son	Harris, Hislop
Winnipeg	5 2 3 - 10	10 8 9 - 27	Bromley	Guindon 2, U. Nilsson 2, K. Nilsson 2, Lesuk, Lindstrom, Long, Baird
February 11				
New England	3 2 3 - 8	10 13 13 - 36	Smith	Antonovich, Keon, Butters, Bolduc, Ley, McKenzie, Carroll, Mk Howe
Cincinnati	2 1 4 - 7	10 3 12 - 25	Dion	Ftorek 2, Plumb, Marsh, Abgrall, Dudley
Winnipeg	0 1 4 - 5	11 8 11 - 30	Bromley	K. Nilsson 3 (WG 17:48), Powis, Hedberg
Indianapolis	2 1 0 - 3	9 8 15 - 32	Inness	French, Leclerc, Morrison
Quebec	2 1 1 - 4	9 4 5 - 18	Brodeur	Hagman 2, Fitchner, Tremblay
Houston	4 2 2 - 8	18 12 18 - 48	Wakely	Connor 2, Gray, Tonelli, West, Preston, Ruskowski, Lukowich
February 12				
Winnipeg	0 3 3 - 6	4 12 15 - 31	Daley	Hedberg 2 (WG 18:31), Sjoberg, Baird, Hull, Ruhnke
Houston	2 2 1 - 5	15 9 7 - 31	Wakely	Lukowich, Ruskowski, Gray, Connor, Lacroix
Birmingham	0 0 0 - 0	15 7 12 - 34	Garrett	▸ Dryden: shutout (2), 34 saves
Edmonton	2 2 3 - 7	21 9 16 - 46	Dryden	Micheletti, MacDonald, Widing, Chipperfield, Holland, Zuke, Ferguson
Quebec	0 1 1 - 2	8 10 8 - 26	Mattsson	P. Bordeleau
Cincinnati	3 1 4 - 8	19 9 7 - 35	Hoganson	Marsh 2, Hislop 2, Ftorek, Baltimore, Norwich, Carroll
February 14				
Quebec	0 0 1 - 1	11 5 14 - 30	Brodeur	J. Bernier (spoiled Smith's shutout at 18:24)
New England	2 1 2 - 5	8 13 15 - 36	Smith	Antonovich, S. Carlson, Keon, Lyle, McKenzie
Birmingham	0 0 1 - 1	5 9 11 - 25	Garrett	Marrin
Edmonton	2 0 2 - 4	5 13 19 - 37	Dryden	MacDonald 2, Hamilton, Langevin
February 15				
Quebec	1 3 2 - 6	8 13 11 - 32	Brod'ck, Mattsson	P. Bordeleau 3, Miller, Cloutier, Boudrias
Indianapolis	3 5 1 - 9	10 8 8 - 26	Mio	Leclerc 2, St. Sauveur 2, Devine 2, Driscoll, Leduc, French
Edmonton	1 2 2 - 5	8 8 14 - 30	Dryden	Ferguson 2, Micheletti 2, Widing
Winnipeg	0 3 3 - 6	12 16 11 - 39	Daley	Lesuk 2, Sjoberg, K. Nilsson, Hedberg, Hull
Houston	2 2 1 - 5	7 7 8 - 22	Zimmerman	Taylor 2, Larway 2, Tonelli
Cincinnati	2 0 0 - 2	19 8 6 - 33	Hoganson	Thomas, Marsh

Date & Teams	Scoring 1 2 3 ot F	Shots 1 2 3 ot F	Goaltenders	Goals & Other Scoring Highlights
February 16				
Winnipeg	0 0 1 1 2	8 11 6 4 29	Bromley	Guindon, Lindstrom (OT 3:15)
New England	0 1 0 0 1	11 12 9 1 33	Smith	Plumb
Birmingham	2 1 2 - 5	12 6 5 - 23	Wood	Turkiewicz, Gorman, Cassolato, Napier, Hanson
Houston	0 0 2 - 2	12 14 12 - 38	Rutledge, Z'man	Lacroix, Larway
February 17				
Cincinnati	0 2 1 1 4	8 8 13 3 32	Dion	Dudley 2, Ftorek, Marsh (OT 4:02)
Houston	1 1 1 0 3	6 8 6 1 21	Z'man, Rutledge	Lacroix, Tonelli, Lukowich
Quebec	1 2 1 - 4	11 13 5 - 29	Brodeur	Dube, Boudrias, Sutherland, S. Bernier
Edmonton	1 0 5 - 6	13 10 14 - 37	McLeod	Zuke 2, Ferguson 2, Chipperfield, Callighen
Indianapolis	0 4 0 0 4	11 11 12 2 37	Mio	Larose, St. Sauveur, Stoughton, Patenaude
Birmingham	2 1 1 1 5	13 7 13 1 34	Garrett	Henderson 3 (TG 10:16, OT 3:23), Bilodeau, Hanson
February 18				
Houston	0 3 0 - 3	9 16 2 - 27	Wakely	Gray, Taylor, Lukowich
Birmingham	1 0 1 - 2	12 10 11 - 33	Garrett	Bilodeau, Roberto
New England	1 1 2 - 4	11 17 8 - 36	Smith	Mty Howe, G. Howe, Sheehy, Keon
Indianapolis	1 0 0 - 1	9 11 8 - 28	Inness	Stoughton
Winnipeg	1 1 2 - 4	12 11 7 - 30	Daley	Hedberg 4
Cincinnati	0 0 0 - 0	11 9 12 - 32	Hoganson	▶ Daley: shutout (1), 32 saves
February 19				
Birmingham	1 1 1 0 3	12 13 9 6 40	Garrett	Cassolato, Marrin, Turkiewicz
Cincinnati	0 3 0 1 4	8 14 10 3 35	Dion	Dudley, Greig, Ftorek, Maggs (OT 9:38)
Indianapolis	2 1 0 0 3	9 12 6 2 29	Inness	Prentice, Driscoll, Morrison
Edmonton	1 0 2 1 4	11 13 14 4 42	McLeod, Dryden	Widing, Callighen, Guite, Zuke (OT 7:08)
Quebec	1 0 1 - 2	12 6 8 - 26	Brodeur	Fitchner, Sutherland
Winnipeg	2 0 3 - 5	13 9 9 - 31	Bromley	Sullivan 2, Lindstrom, Hedberg, Hull
February 21				
New England	1 3 1 0 5	10 14 8 1 33	Smith	Hangsleben, McKenzie, Pleau, G. Howe, Keon
Quebec	2 1 2 1 6	12 9 15 1 37	Brodeur	Cloutier 2, Dube, Miller, Boudrias, Tremblay (OT 3:38)
February 22				
New England	1 1 0 - 2	11 8 2 - 21	Smith	Rogers, G. Howe
Winnipeg	1 1 2 - 4	8 10 16 - 34	Daley	Lindstrom 2, Hull, K. Nilsson
Houston	2 2 2 - 6	9 14 3 - 26	Wakely	Connor 2 (WG 13:52), Gray 2, Lacroix, Larway
Edmonton	2 2 1 - 5	19 11 17 - 47	Dryden	MacDonald 2, Semenko, Troy, Flett
February 23				
Quebec	2 0 1 - 3	15 10 13 - 38	Corsi	Cloutier 2, Miller
Birmingham	2 3 2 - 7	10 16 17 - 43	Wood	Henderson 3, Linseman, Napier, Cassolato, Gorman
February 24				
New England	0 1 1 - 2	8 8 8 - 24	Smith	Mk Howe, G. Howe
Winnipeg	3 2 2 - 7	14 9 10 - 33	Bromley	Hedberg 2, Powis 2, U. Nilsson, Moffat, Kryskow
Houston	0 3 1 0 4	8 13 8 0 29	Wakely	Lacroix, Taylor, Hansis
Edmonton	1 2 1 1 5	11 16 11 4 42	McLeod	MacDonald 3 (OT 1:50), Ferguson, Callighen (TG 18:38)
February 25				
Indianapolis	0 1 4 - 5	11 8 10 - 29	Inness	Driscoll, Larose, Leclerc, Stoughton, Morrison
Quebec	2 3 2 - 7	13 12 17 - 42	Brodeur, Corsi	Cloutier 2, P. Bordeleau, C. Bordeleau, Boudrias, Tardif, Miller
Cincinnati	0 2 1 - 3	6 7 4 - 17	Dion, Liut	Deadmarsh, Norwich, Gilligan
Birmingham	4 2 1 - 7	14 13 10 - 37	Wood	Napier 2, Linseman 2, Beaton, Marrin, Henderson
February 26				
New England	3 3 0 - 6	13 9 4 - 26	Smith	Antonovich 2, Hangsleben, Sheehy, Rogers, G. Howe
Edmonton	1 1 3 - 5	4 12 14 - 30	Dryden, McLeod	Shmyr, DeMarco, Flett, Zuke, Guite
Indianapolis	3 0 3 - 6	6 3 12 - 21	Mio	Driscoll 2, Larose, Wilkins, Leduc, Parizeau
Birmingham	0 1 2 - 3	16 9 11 - 36	Wood, Garrett	Marrin, Napier, Linseman
Houston	1 1 4 - 6	6 7 12 - 25	Zimmerman	Gray 3, Hansis, Popiel, Lukowich (Wpg: 15th straight win)
Winnipeg	3 3 3 - 9	16 12 15 - 43	Daley, Bromley	K. Nilsson 2, U. Nilsson 2, Hull 2, Lesuk, Green, Baird
February 28				
Houston	1 1 0 - 2	12 9 10 - 31	Wakely	Connor, Lacroix
Quebec	2 0 3 - 5	14 17 8 - 39	Brodeur	Cloutier 3, Tardif, J. Bernier
March 1				
Houston	0 1 0 - 1	5 8 10 - 23	Zimmerman	Campbell
Indianapolis	2 1 2 - 5	7 13 11 - 31	Mio	Larose 2, St. Sauveur, Devine, Patenaude
Quebec	0 2 1 1 4	13 11 11 4 39	Brodeur	Tardif 2 (OT 5:51), C. Bordeleau, S. Bernier (TG 19:00)
New England	1 1 1 0 3	13 19 13 4 49	Smith	McKenzie 2, Keon
Winnipeg	1 1 1 - 3	6 8 12 - 26	Bromley	Hedberg, Guindon, Hull
Birmingham	1 2 1 - 4	8 13 8 - 29	Garrett	Henderson, Cassolato, Beaton, Hanson
Cincinnati	1 2 3 - 6	6 9 6 - 21	Liut	Marsh 2, Hislop, Deadmarsh, Handrahan (WG 16:02), Harris
Edmonton	0 1 3 - 4	11 16 18 - 45	McLeod	Zuke, MacDonald, Chipperfield, Flett
March 3				
Cincinnati	1 1 3 - 5	8 6 11 - 25	Liut	Ftorek 3, Marsh, Carroll
Winnipeg	1 0 0 - 1	6 15 7 - 28	Bromley	Hull
Indianapolis	1 5 2 - 8	10 15 10 - 35	Inness	Driscoll 2, Morrison 2, Larose 2, Stoughton, Wilkins
Edmonton	3 3 0 - 6	17 9 10 - 36	Dryden	Flett 2, Chipperfield, Ferguson, Jarry, Callighen
Houston	1 1 0 1 3	15 6 5 4 30	Wakely	Lukowich, Lund, Preston (OT 7:11)
New England	0 0 2 0 2	10 15 15 7 47	Smith	Hangsleben, G. Howe

1977-1978 Game by Game Line Scores

Date & Teams	Scoring 1 2 3 ot F	Shots 1 2 3 ot F	Goaltenders	Goals & Other Scoring Highlights
March 4				
Birmingham	2 2 1 - 5	9 7 5 - 21	Garrett, Wood	Linseman 2, Henderson, Mahovlich, Marrin
New England	2 0 0 - 2	9 11 12 - 32	Smith	G. Howe, Mayer
Winnipeg	0 5 1 - 6	6 14 11 - 31	Mattsson	Lindstrom, Kryskow, K. Nilsson, U. Nilsson, Hedberg, Guindon
Indianapolis	1 4 3 - 8	5 10 11 - 26	Mio	St. Sauv'r 2, Marotte, Paten'de, Larose, Parizeau, Constantin, St'ghton
Houston	1 1 1 0 3	16 11 13 6 46	Wakely	Lacroix, Gray, Lund
Quebec	0 2 1 0 3	7 15 12 8 42	Brodeur	Tardif, Dorey, S. Bernier
March 5				
Houston	0 3 1 - 4	9 12 6 - 27	Zimmerman	West, Lukowich, Gray, Lund
Winnipeg	1 2 0 - 3	13 13 16 - 42	Bromley	Kryskow, Lindstrom, Guindon
Cincinnati	0 0 2 - 2	11 11 13 - 35	Liut	Maggs, Hislop
Indianapolis	1 2 1 - 4	9 9 7 - 25	Mio	Leduc 2, Constantin, Leclerc
Edmonton	1 0 3 - 4	19 5 7 - 31	Dryden	Flett 2 (WG 14:04), Shmyr, Zuke
Birmingham	0 3 0 - 3	9 13 8 - 30	Garrett	Henderson 2, Roberto
New England	1 0 0 - 1	7 11 10 - 28	Smith	Mayer
Quebec	0 2 0 - 2	10 8 9 - 27	Brodeur	Tardif, C. Bordeleau
March 7				
Edmonton	2 0 1 - 3	14 7 7 - 28	McLeod	Chipperfield, Shmyr, Flett
Houston	0 2 2 - 4	9 17 10 - 36	Wakely	Preston 2, Lacroix, Ruskowski
Cincinnati	1 2 2 - 5	11 11 9 - 31	Dion	Dudley 2 (WG 11:24), Hislop, Ftorek, Gilligan
Quebec	1 1 2 - 4	14 19 15 - 48	Brodeur	P. Bordeleau, J. Bernier, Tardif, Miller
March 8				
Quebec	2 0 2 1 5	11 5 16 1 33	Brodeur	Boudrias, C. Bordeleau, Sutherland, Tardif (TG 19:55), P. Bordeleau
Indianapolis	1 1 2 0 4	11 19 9 0 39	Mio	Leduc 2, Devine, St. Sauveur (OT 2:06)
March 9				
Edmonton	2 1 2 - 5	16 14 9 - 39	Dryden	Flett 2, Chipperfield, Callighen, Guite
Cincinnati	1 4 1 - 6	5 13 11 - 29	Liut	Dudley 2, Gilligan, Deadmarsh, Harris, Marsh
New England	2 1 1 - 4	7 8 9 - 24	Smith	Rogers 2, S. Carlson, Mk Howe
Houston	2 2 2 - 6	13 7 4 - 24	Wakely	Lukowich 2, Gray, J. Hughes, Lacroix, Connor
Quebec	0 1 1 - 2	3 8 11 - 22	Brodeur, Brod'ck	Tardif, P. Bordeleau Beaudoin
Birmingham	5 4 0 - 9	12 12 7 - 31	Garrett, Wood	Henderson 2, Linseman, Noris, Roberto, Cassolato, Hanson, Marrin,
Indianapolis	1 1 3 - 5	11 6 16 - 33	Mio, Inness	Devine, Inkpen, Larose, Burgess, Leclerc (Wpg: 3 goals
Winnipeg	0 3 3 - 6	10 9 8 - 27	Bromley	Powis, Lindstrom, Kryskow, Dunn, U. Nilsson, Guindon in final 3:53)
March 10				
New England	1 1 2 1 5	11 10 12 3 36	Levasseur, Smith	G. Howe 2, Sheehy, McKenzie (TG 17:54), Rogers (OT 3:54)
Birmingham	2 2 0 0 4	4 11 7 3 25	Garrett	Stewart 2, Linseman, Napier
March 11				
Winnipeg	2 2 3 - 7	7 9 8 - 24	Bromley	K. Nilsson 3, Hull, Sullivan, Baird, Moffat (Hull: 1000th career goal)
Quebec	0 1 3 - 4	19 10 8 - 37	Brodeur	S. Bernier, Sutherland, Cloutier, C. Bordeleau
Edmonton	0 0 0 - 0	9 9 6 - 24	Dryden	▸ Dion: shutout (4), 24 saves
Cincinnati	0 0 2 - 2	8 7 10 - 25	Dion	Gilligan, Stapleton
Houston	1 1 0 - 2	5 11 7 - 23	Wakely	Lukowich, Schella
Indianapolis	2 1 1 - 4	13 8 8 - 29	Mio	St. Sauveur, Larose, Driscoll, Burgess
March 12				
Birmingham	1 0 1 - 2	7 6 8 - 21	Garrett, Wood	Alley, Westrum
Winnipeg	1 0 2 - 3	8 11 10 - 29	Bromley	Long, Hedberg, Sullivan
Indianapolis	1 1 1 - 3	6 4 13 - 23	Mio, Inness	Leclerc, Parizeau, Driscoll
Houston	3 2 1 - 6	14 9 10 - 33	Zimmerman	Schella 2, Larway, Preston, West, Lukowich
March 14				
Birmingham	0 0 0 - 0	9 4 5 - 18	Garrett, Wood	▸ Levasseur: shutout (2), 18 saves
New England	2 2 2 - 6	4 22 15 - 41	Levasseur	G. Howe 2, Mk Howe, Sheehy, Bolduc, S. Carlson
Edmonton	2 0 1 - 3	16 13 12 - 41	McLeod, Dryden	Flett, Zuke, MacDonald
Quebec	3 1 2 - 6	16 11 14 - 41	Brodeur	Cloutier 3, P. Bordeleau, Baxter, Dube
March 15				
Indianapolis	0 0 0 - 0	11 7 3 - 21	Inness	▸ Levasseur: shutout (3), 21 saves
New England	4 2 1 - 7	14 18 17 - 49	Levasseur	Antonovich 3, Keon, Sheehy, Roberts, Rogers
Edmonton	1 1 2 - 4	10 11 10 - 31	Dryden	Ferguson, Zuke, MacDonald, Chipperfield
Winnipeg	2 2 4 - 8	14 9 11 - 34	Bromley	Hedberg 2, K. Nilsson 2, U. Nilsson 2, Lindstrom, Guindon
Birmingham	1 0 1 - 2	10 14 9 - 33	Garrett, Wood	Napier, Noris
Cincinnati	3 2 2 - 7	17 17 14 - 48	Dion, Liut	Dudley, Hislop, Carroll, Ftorek, Deadmarsh, Trognitz, Stapleton
March 16				
Indianapolis	1 1 0 - 2	18 13 7 - 38	Mio	Driscoll, Morrison
Quebec	1 2 2 - 5	9 20 12 - 41	Brodeur	Cloutier 2, S. Bernier 2, P. Bordeleau
March 17				
New England	1 4 1 - 6	12 9 9 - 30	Levasseur	Sheehy, McKenzie, Mty Howe, Roberts, Lyle, Keon
Cincinnati	2 0 0 - 2	8 9 6 - 23	Liut, Dion	Dudley, Hislop
Winnipeg	2 0 0 - 2	5 8 4 - 17	Bromley, Mattsson	Hedberg 2
Edmonton	2 1 3 - 6	18 15 12 - 45	Dryden	Ferguson 3, MacDonald 2, Widing
Birmingham	2 0 1 - 3	11 8 9 - 28	Wood	Noris, Gorman, Henderson (WG 5:59)
Houston	1 0 1 - 2	4 7 13 - 24	Wakely	Gray, Lund
March 18				
New England	0 2 1 - 3	9 13 6 - 28	Levasseur	G. Howe, Mk Howe, Rogers
Quebec	0 3 2 - 5	5 8 9 - 22	Brodeur, Brod'ck	S. Bernier 2, P. Bordeleau, Miller, Tardif
Indianapolis	1 0 1 - 2	10 8 10 - 28	Mio	Stoughton, Morrison
Cincinnati	1 3 0 - 4	7 11 3 - 21	Dion	Legge, Deadmarsh, Thomas, Carroll

1977-1978 Game by Game Line Scores

Date & Teams	Scoring 1 2 3 ot F	Shots 1 2 3 ot F	Goaltenders	Goals & Other Scoring Highlights
March 19				
Cincinnati	1 1 0 - 2	14 10 7 - 31	Liut	Thomas, Dudley
Edmonton	0 2 2 - 4	9 11 13 - 33	Dryden	Flett 2 (WG 11:15), Chipperfield, Shmyr
Quebec	1 2 0 - 3	8 7 16 - 31	Broderick	J. Bernier, Cloutier, Sutherland
Winnipeg	3 1 1 - 5	13 13 8 - 34	Bromley	U. Nilsson, Sjoberg, K. Nilsson, Dunn, Lindstrom
Indianapolis	0 3 0 0 3	7 12 7 1 27	Inness	Devine, Parizeau, French
Birmingham	1 0 2 0 3	19 6 15 2 42	Wood	Gorman, Hughes, Stewart
March 21				
Birmingham	1 2 2 - 5	5 7 9 - 21	Garrett	Alley 2, Hughes, Stewart, Gorman
Quebec	1 1 2 - 4	15 13 12 - 40	Brodeur	Tardif 2, Dube, P. Bordeleau
Indianapolis	1 2 0 - 3	6 11 5 - 22	Inness, Mio	Leduc, Patenaude, Larose
New England	2 4 0 - 6	5 21 14 - 40	Levasseur	Hangsleben, Keon, Mty Howe, G. Howe, Antonovich, McKenzie
March 22				
Winnipeg	2 1 2 - 5	9 10 10 - 29	Bromley	Hull 2, Sullivan, U. Nilsson, Long (WG 19:11, shg)
New England	1 1 1 - 3	11 11 14 - 36	Levasseur	McKenzie, Sheehy, Selwood
Houston	0 2 0 - 2	11 16 9 - 36	Wakely	Tonelli 2
Cincinnati	3 3 3 - 9	12 15 12 - 39	Dion	Dudley 3, Hislop, Carroll, Harris, Marsh, Gilligan, Greig
Birmingham	1 1 3 - 5	9 12 7 - 28	Wood	Stewart 2, Napier, Henderson, Beaton
Edmonton	1 0 2 - 3	11 5 16 - 32	Dryden	Rota, Callighen, MacDonald
March 24				
Houston	0 1 0 - 1	1 11 9 - 21	Wakely	Larway
New England	0 0 0 - 0	12 5 7 - 24	Smith	▸ Wakely: shutout (2), 24 saves
Quebec	1 2 0 1 4	7 11 4 2 24	Brodeur	Cloutier, Fitchner, S. Bernier, C. Bordeleau (OT 3:11)
Birmingham	1 2 0 0 3	9 11 8 0 28	Wood	Linseman, Roberto, Larose
Indianapolis	0 0 0 - 0	7 7 7 - 21	Park	▸ McLeod: shutout (2), 21 saves
Edmonton	0 3 1 - 4	12 16 10 - 38	McLeod	Chipperfield, Callighen, Semenko, Rota
March 25				
Winnipeg	1 0 2 - 3	8 9 13 - 30	Bromley	Hedberg 2 (WG 11:09), Guindon
Birmingham	0 1 0 - 1	8 10 7 - 25	Garrett	Beaton
Quebec	1 0 2 0 3	10 6 14 9 39	Broderick	Tardif 3 (TG 19:33)
Houston	3 0 0 1 4	11 6 8 7 32	Zimmerman	Lacroix 2, Larway, Lukowich (OT 8:17)
March 26				
Edmonton	1 0 2 - 3	10 13 12 - 35	McLeod	Semenko, Shmyr, Sobchuk
New England	1 3 1 - 5	6 12 9 - 27	Levasseur	Mk Howe 3, Rogers, McKenzie
March 28				
Cincinnati	3 0 1 - 4	12 15 12 - 39	Dion, Hoganson	Ftorek 2, Greig, Legge
Quebec	3 2 1 - 6	16 12 12 - 40	Brod'ck, Brodeur	C. Bordeleau, Cote, Boudrias, S. Bernier, Sutherland, Lariviere
Winnipeg	2 0 1 - 3	8 7 10 - 25	Bromley	Guindon, Kryskow, U. Nilsson
Houston	1 2 2 - 5	9 11 3 - 23	Wakely	West, Lacroix, Ruskowski, Larway, Hansis
Edmonton	0 2 1 1 4	11 8 10 1 30	McLeod	Guite, Sobchuk, Chipperfield, Jarry (OT 1:49)
Indianapolis	0 1 2 0 3	1 8 9 2 20	Mio	Driscoll 2, Leduc
March 29				
Cincinnati	0 0 1 - 1	7 4 11 - 22	Dion, Hoganson	Ftorek
New England	3 1 2 - 6	14 11 15 - 40	Smith	Rogers 3, Mk Howe, Antonovich, Roberts
March 30				
Edmonton	0 0 1 - 1	8 6 15 - 29	McLeod	Sandbeck
Houston	0 2 3 - 5	15 8 11 - 34	Wakely	Hansis 2, Gray, Lukowich, Campbell
Winnipeg	2 2 0 - 4	10 12 4 - 26	Mattsson	Hedberg, Baird, Guindon, U. Nilsson
Indianapolis	1 0 0 - 1	7 10 8 - 25	Park	Leduc
March 31				
Edmonton	0 0 2 - 2	10 9 8 - 27	Dryden	Rota, Callighen
Birmingham	2 1 2 - 5	8 13 11 - 32	Garrett	Alley, Stewart, Gorman, Napier, Mahovlich
April 1				
Edmonton	2 1 1 - 4	8 3 9 - 20	McLeod	Chipperfield, Jarry, McKay, Micheletti
Indianapolis	1 0 0 - 1	8 6 4 - 18	Mio, Inness	Driscoll
Winnipeg	0 1 1 - 2	9 12 11 - 32	Mattsson	Powis, Hedberg
Quebec	0 2 3 - 5	11 13 15 - 39	Brodeur, Brod'ck	C. Bordeleau, Tardif, Cloutier, J. Bernier, Fitchner
Cincinnati	1 0 0 - 1	9 9 10 - 28	Dion	Ftorek
Birmingham	2 1 2 - 5	7 6 7 - 20	Garrett	Linseman 2, Mahovlich, Gorman, Stewart
April 2				
Houston	1 0 0 - 1	9 10 6 - 25	Wakely	West
Quebec	1 2 4 - 7	17 12 14 - 43	Broderick	Tardif 3, Cloutier 2, Fitchner, Sutherland
Cincinnati	2 0 1 - 3	7 10 11 - 28	Liut	Gilligan, Ftorek, Debol
Indianapolis	3 1 2 - 6	9 10 11 - 30	Inness	Driscoll, St. Sauveur, Leduc, Morrison, Larose, Leclerc
April 3				
Houston	2 2 2 - 6	7 9 12 - 28	Zimmerman	Gray 2, Tonelli, Larway, Hansis, Lukowich
New England	4 1 3 - 8	9 11 11 - 31	Smith	McKenzie 3, Lyle 2, Mk Howe 2, Antonovich
April 4				
Edmonton	0 0 1 - 1	10 12 9 - 31	Dryden, McLeod	Jarry; P. Bordeleau, S. Bernier
Quebec	2 4 3 - 9	17 15 10 - 42	Brodeur	Tardif 2, Cote, Sutherland, Cloutier, Lariviere, C. Bordeleau,
Winnipeg	0 0 3 - 3	12 9 23 - 44	Daley	K. Nilsson 2, Lindstrom
Houston	4 1 1 - 6	11 8 6 - 25	Wakely	Lacroix 2, Tonelli 2, West, Taylor
April 5				
New England	1 2 1 0 4	4 10 12 4 30	Levasseur	Keon 2, Antonovich, Roberts
Edmonton	1 0 3 0 4	9 7 17 8 41	Dryden, McLeod	DeMarco 3 (TG 19:55), Guite (0:05, 1st)
Birmingham	2 1 1 - 4	9 5 10 - 24	Garrett	Marrin, Alley, Gorman
Cincinnati	1 3 1 - 5	17 16 16 - 49	Dion	Ftorek 2, Hislop, Debol, Marsh
April 6				
New England	0 1 3 - 4	6 13 13 - 32	Smith	J. Carlson, Mk Howe, Sheehy, Lyle
Winnipeg	4 3 0 - 7	12 18 5 - 35	Bromley	K. Nilsson, Lesuk, Clackson, Moffat, Kryskow, Long, Baird

1977-1978 Game by Game Line Scores

Date & Teams	Scoring 1 2 3 ot F	Shots 1 2 3 ot F	Goaltenders	Goals & Other Scoring Highlights
April 7				
Cincinnati	1 2 3 - 6	9 15 10 - 34	Dion	Ftorek 2, Carroll, Marsh, Dudley, Harris
Indianapolis	1 2 1 - 4	7 8 9 - 24	Inness	St. Sauveur 2, Larose, Parizeau
Houston	2 1 0 - 3	13 9 9 - 31	Wakely	Gray, Tonelli, Popiel
Birmingham	2 2 1 - 5	13 9 11 - 33	Garrett	Linseman 2, Gorman, Hanson, Roberto
Winnipeg	2 0 0 - 2	10 6 8 - 24	Daley	Guindon, Kryskow
Edmonton	4 0 0 - 4	15 20 8 - 43	Dryden	Widing, Busniuk, Callighen, MacDonald
April 8				
Indianapolis	2 1 0 - 3	11 16 17 - 44	Mio	Stoughton, Leclerc, Parizeau
Quebec	1 3 3 - 7	10 8 9 - 27	Brodeur	P. Bordeleau 2, Tardif 2, Baxter, S. Bernier, Cloutier
Cincinnati	2 1 1 - 4	5 10 16 - 31	Dion	Ftorek 2, Debol, Norwich
Houston	0 3 2 - 5	11 10 12 - 33	Wakely, Z'man	Larway 2, Gray 2, Lacroix
April 9				
Birmingham	2 5 2 - 9	16 22 11 - 49	Garrett	Alley 3, Gorman 3, Beaudoin, Langway, Linseman
Indianapolis	2 2 3 - 7	6 8 12 - 26	Park, Inness	Parizeau 2, Devine 2, Larose, Stoughton, St. Sauveur
Houston	3 2 0 - 5	11 12 8 - 31	Rutledge	Larway 2, Lacroix, West, Tonelli
Winnipeg	1 2 1 - 4	9 14 10 - 33	Bromley, Daley	Powis 2, Amodeo, Kryskow
Quebec	1 0 1 - 2	6 7 3 - 16	Brodeur, Corsi	Cote, Tardif
Cincinnati	2 1 3 - 6	16 16 10 - 42	Liut	Legge, Gilligan, Marsh, Ftorek, Norwich, Thomas
April 10				
Cincinnati	0 1 0 - 1	7 5 7 - 19	Liut	Abgrall
New England	0 2 4 - 6	13 19 24 - 56	Levasseur	Mk Howe 2, Antonovich, Mty Howe, Keon, Selwood
April 11				
Indianapolis	1 0 2 - 3	6 3 6 - 15	Inness	Stoughton, Devine, Paiement
New England	4 0 2 - 6	18 10 11 - 39	Smith	S. Carlson 2, Antonovich, Mk Howe, Bolduc, Lyle

End of Regular Season

1978 Playoffs Game by Game Line Scores

Date & Teams	Scoring 1 2 3 ot F	Shots 1 2 3 ot F	Goaltenders	Goals & Other Scoring Highlights
April 14				
Birmingham	1 2 0 - 3	3 4 5 - 12	Garrett	Linseman, Beaton, Gorman
Winnipeg	4 0 5 - 9	21 13 14 - 48	Daley, Bromley	Hedberg 2, Hull 2, Guindon 2, Amodeo, Moffat, Ruhnke
Edmonton	1 0 3 - 4	6 4 13 - 23	McLeod	Jarry, Chipperfield, Zuke, Rota
New England	1 3 2 - 6	7 15 17 - 39	Levasseur	Antonovich 2, Keon, G. Howe, Pleau, Mty Howe
April 16				
Birmingham	1 2 0 - 3	6 6 8 - 20	Garrett, Wood	Henderson, Beaton, Mahovlich
Winnipeg	3 3 2 - 8	15 16 13 - 44	Bromley	Hull 2, Kryskow 2, Sullivan, Ruhnke, Guindon, Lesuk
Edmonton	0 0 1 - 1	9 10 7 - 26	McLeod	MacDonald
New England	2 0 2 - 4	12 9 14 - 35	Levasseur	Rogers, Mckenzie, Mk Howe, S. Carlson
Quebec	2 0 1 0 3	19 5 8 3 35	Brodeur	J. Bernier, Baxter, Cloutier
Houston	1 0 2 1 4	9 8 18 3 38	Zimmerman	Lacroix, McLeod, Larway (TG 15:49), Taylor (OT 7:19)
April 18				
Quebec	1 0 3 1 5	12 6 10 1 29	Brodeur	Tardif 2 (OT 2:59), Fitchner, Cloutier, Baxter
Houston	1 0 3 0 4	10 13 8 0 31	Zimmerman	Tonelli, Lacroix, Hansis, Lukowich (TG 19:19)
April 19				
New England	0 0 0 - 0	6 8 5 - 19	Levasseur	▶ McLeod: shutout (1), 19 saves
Edmonton	1 0 1 - 2	9 12 7 - 28	McLeod	Guite, Zuke
Winnipeg	0 2 0 - 2	5 10 6 - 21	Daley	Hedberg, Hull
Birmingham	2 1 0 - 3	11 14 10 - 35	Garrett	Linseman, Turkiewicz, Stewart
April 20				
Houston	0 0 1 - 1	7 10 13 - 30	Zimmerman	J. Hughes
Quebec	1 2 2 - 5	14 10 8 - 32	Brodeur	Sutherland, Tardif, Dube, Lacombe, Cloutier
April 21				
Houston	0 0 0 - 0	11 9 6 - 26	Rutledge	▶ Brodeur: shutout (1), 26 saves
Quebec	1 1 1 - 3	14 9 18 - 41	Brodeur	S. Bernier, Tardif, P. Bordeleau
New England	4 4 1 - 9	13 11 8 - 32	Levasseur	Antonovich 3, McKenzie, G. Howe, Keon, S. Carlson, Pleau, Bolduc
Edmonton	1 0 0 - 1	9 10 10 - 29	McLeod, Dryden	Sobchuk
Winnipeg	2 2 1 - 5	7 6 8 - 21	Bromley	Hedberg 2, Kryskow, Moffat, Hull
Birmingham	0 1 0 - 1	5 7 14 - 26	Garrett	Alley
April 23				
Edmonton	0 0 1 - 1	5 10 11 - 26	Dryden	Shmyr
New England	0 1 3 - 4	15 13 11 - 39	Levasseur	G. Howe, Antonovich, McKenzie, Keon
Birmingham	1 0 1 - 2	7 7 4 - 18	Garrett	Beaudoin, Roberto
Winnipeg	2 1 2 - 5	17 8 12 - 37	Daley	Lesuk, Ford, Hedberg, Dunn, Guindon
Quebec	0 2 0 - 2	4 14 6 - 24	Brodeur	P. Bordeleau 2
Houston	2 1 2 - 5	6 5 15 - 26	Rutledge	Taylor 2, Terbenche, Connor, Campbell
April 26				
Houston	0 0 2 - 2	8 13 16 - 37	Rutledge, Z'man	West, Ruskowski … Dube, Baxter
Quebec	4 2 5 - 11	14 9 10 - 33	Brodeur	Cloutier 4, Lariviere, Brackenbury, J. Bernier, Weir, P. Bordeleau,
April 28				
Quebec	0 0 1 - 1	6 7 11 - 24	Brodeur, Brod'ck	Lariviere
New England	2 1 2 - 5	14 14 11 - 39	Levasseur	M. Howe, Plumb, Rogers, Lyle, J. Carlson
April 30				
Quebec	1 1 1 - 3	13 15 5 - 33	Brodeur	Tardif, Cloutier, Sutherland
New England	1 0 1 - 2	15 7 18 - 40	Levasseur	Rogers, Bolduc

1978 Playoffs Game by Game Line Scores

Date & Teams	Scoring 1 2 3 ot F	Shots 1 2 3 ot F	Goaltenders	Goals & Other Scoring Highlights
May 3				
New England	3 1 1 - 5	15 6 4 - 25	Levasseur, Smith	McKenzie, Antonovich, Mk Howe, Rogers, Pleau
Quebec	0 1 3 - 4	10 19 15 - 44	Brodeur, Brod'ck	S. Bernier 2, C. Bordeleau, Baxter
May 5				
New England	4 2 1 - 7	16 10 13 - 39	Levasseur	Keon 2, Hangsleben, Mk Howe, Rogers, Antonovich, Pleau
Quebec	2 0 1 - 3	8 6 8 - 22	Brodeur	Tardif, Cloutier
May 7				
Quebec	1 1 1 - 3	7 5 8 - 20	Brodeur	S. Bernier, J. Bernier, Lariviere
New England	1 3 2 - 6	16 16 13 - 45	Levasseur	Mk Howe 2, McKenzie, Antonovich, G. Howe
May 12				
Winnipeg	0 0 4 - 4	12 6 12 - 30	Bromley	Guindon 2, Sullivan 2
New England	0 0 1 - 1	8 11 14 - 33	Levasseur	Pleau
May 14				
Winnipeg	2 2 1 - 5	12 8 7 - 27	Daley	Labraaten, Moffat, Guindon, Hedberg, U. Nilsson
New England	0 0 2 - 2	2 13 9 - 24	Levasseur	G. Howe, Mk Howe
May 19				
New England	0 0 2 - 2	12 7 11 - 30	Smith	McKenzie, Sheehy (Wpg: 5 goals in 2:50, 1st)
Winnipeg	6 2 2 - 10	12 11 10 - 33	Bromley	Lindstrom 3, K. Nilsson 2, Powis 2, Guindon, Hull, Moffat
May 22				
New England	2 0 1 - 3	8 6 14 - 28	Smith	Antonovich, Ley, Lyle
Winnipeg	0 3 2 - 5	8 12 8 - 28	Daley	Hedberg 2, Kryskow, Moffat, Hull

Winnipeg is League Champion

The Tale of Willie Trognitz

Willie Trognitz may have played in utter obscurity were it not for a stick-swinging incident in a minor-league game that earned him a "ban for life", and his subsequent signing by the Cincinnati Stingers less than a week later. The series of events in Fall 1977 brought scrutiny and some sense of notoriety onto the WHA, the Stingers and to Trognitz.

Trognitz was never more than a fringe player, a 1973 draft pick of the California Golden Seals who toiled in the low minors, amassing a number of fights and penalty minutes upwards of 300 per season. He was a member of an infamous line put together in Toledo (International League) by coach Ted Garvin—the Murder, Inc. line—with fellow rumblers Paul Tantardini and Doug Mahood. As the name suggests, this line was not meant for scoring, and during the height of goon-era hockey, even the Murder, Inc. line seemed to be on the periphery of what was considered acceptable.

Playing for Dayton in the IHL, Trognitz was involved in a brawl in a game against Port Huron on October 29, 1977. At the end of the fracas, Trognitz was charged by Port Huron's Archie Henderson: Trognitz reacted with a swing of his stick that clocked Henderson and sent him to the hospital. In the game Trognitz was assessed 63 minutes in penalties, and was given a lifetime suspension afterwards. Meanwhile, the Cincinnati Stingers had got off to a slow start and needed some muscle to protect their skaters. In early November, Trognitz was signed to a ten-game contract. The WHA was concerned enough to force the Stingers to post a bond as a means to ensure Trognitz would behave. Most definitely, Trognitz' reputation had preceded him to Cincinnati. His stay in Cincinnati ultimately stretched to 29 games, during which he scored 2 goals and collected 94 minutes. This would be it for his major-league career; he retired after two more seasons in the minor leagues.

After hockey, Trognitz went on to a career with the Canadian Coast Guard, stationed in Thunder Bay. As a crew member of the *Westfort*, Trognitz participated in the daring rescues of the stranded vessels *Glenada* and *Grampa Woo* on Lake Superior, during a tremendous fall squall. For his heroism, he was given awards for bravery by the Canadian Coast Guard as well as from the United States Coast Guard.

The date of this event? October 29, 1996.

1977-1978 BIRMINGHAM BULLS

Coach
Glen Sonmor

Summary of Games (@ Away, * Overtime)

	date	opponent	score		record	pts	gf-ga		date	opponent	score		record	pts	gf-ga
1	Oct 14	Houston	5-3	W	1-0-0	2	5-3	41	Jan 18	Cincinnati	3-0	W	18-21-2	38	141-156
2	Oct 15	@ New England	2-5	L	1-1-0	2	7-8	42	Jan 20	Edmonton	5-3	W	19-21-2	40	146-159
3	Oct 22	@ Quebec	5-8	L	1-2-0	2	12-16	43	Jan 22	@ Houston	2-4	L	19-22-2	40	148-163
4	Oct 23	@ Winnipeg	3-10	L	1-3-0	2	15-26	44	Jan 25	Winnipeg	6-2	W	20-22-2	42	154-165
5	Oct 25	Indianapolis	4-5	L	1-4-0	2	19-31	45	Jan 27	New England	2-6	L	20-23-2	42	156-171
6	Oct 28	Edmonton	2-3	L	1-5-0	2	21-34	46	Jan 28	Winnipeg	8-5	W	21-23-2	44	164-176
7	Oct 29	@ Indianapolis	2-6	L	1-6-0	2	23-40	47	Jan 31	Houston	2-4	L	21-24-2	44	166-180
8	Nov 2	@ Houston	3-5	L	1-7-0	2	26-45	48	Feb 2	Quebec	2-4	L	21-25-2	44	168-184
9	Nov 4	Winnipeg	2-4	L	1-8-0	2	28-49	49	Feb 4	Indianapolis	5-2	W	22-25-2	46	173-186
10	Nov 5	Quebec	*5-4	W	2-8-0	4	33-53	50	Feb 5	@ Indianapolis	1-6	L	22-26-2	46	174-192
11	Nov 8	New England	3-4	L	2-9-0	4	36-57	51	Feb 7	@ Quebec	3-8	L	22-27-2	46	177-200
12	Nov 9	@ Cincinnati	1-2	L	2-10-0	4	37-59	52	Feb 8	@ Winnipeg	0-9	L	22-28-2	46	177-209
13	Nov 12	Edmonton	1-1	T	2-10-1	5	38-60	53	Feb 12	@ Edmonton	0-7	L	22-29-2	46	177-216
14	Nov 16	@ Winnipeg	2-2	T	2-10-2	6	40-62	54	Feb 14	@ Edmonton	1-4	L	22-30-2	46	178-220
15	Nov 18	@ Indianapolis	2-1	W	3-10-2	8	42-63	55	Feb 16	@ Houston	5-2	W	23-30-2	48	183-222
16	Nov 19	Houston	4-3	W	4-10-2	10	46-66	56	Feb 17	Indianapolis	*5-4	W	24-30-2	50	188-226
17	Nov 23	@ Houston	0-3	L	4-11-2	10	46-69	57	Feb 18	Houston	2-3	L	24-31-2	50	190-229
18	Nov 24	Cincinnati	12-2	W	5-11-2	12	58-71	58	Feb 19	@ Cincinnati	*3-4	L	24-32-2	50	193-233
19	Nov 26	@ Quebec	2-4	L	5-12-2	12	60-75	59	Feb 23	Quebec	7-3	W	25-32-2	52	200-236
20	Nov 27	@ Winnipeg	*4-3	W	6-12-2	14	64-78	60	Feb 25	Cincinnati	7-3	W	26-32-2	54	207-239
21	Nov 30	@ Edmonton	2-4	L	6-13-2	14	66-82	61	Feb 26	Indianapolis	3-6	L	26-33-2	54	210-245
22	Dec 2	@ Edmonton	7-5	W	7-13-2	16	73-87	62	Mar 1	Winnipeg	4-3	W	27-33-2	56	214-248
23	Dec 4	Indianapolis	3-0	W	8-13-2	18	76-87	63	Mar 4	@ New England	5-2	W	28-33-2	58	219-250
24	Dec 7	New England	3-6	L	8-14-2	18	79-93	64	Mar 5	Edmonton	3-4	L	28-34-2	58	222-254
25	Dec 9	New England	1-2	L	8-15-2	18	80-95	65	Mar 9	Quebec	9-2	W	29-34-2	60	231-256
26	Dec 13	@ Houston	5-3	W	9-15-2	20	85-98	66	Mar 10	New England	*4-5	L	29-35-2	60	235-261
27	Dec 15	Cincinnati	5-3	W	10-15-2	22	90-101	67	Mar 12	@ Winnipeg	2-3	L	29-36-2	60	237-264
28	Dec 18	Edmonton	3-2	W	11-15-2	24	93-103	68	Mar 14	@ New England	0-6	L	29-37-2	60	237-270
29	Dec 21	Czechoslovakia	5-0	W	12-15-2	26	98-103	69	Mar 15	@ Cincinnati	2-7	L	29-38-2	60	239-277
30	Dec 26	Soviet All-Stars	6-1	W	13-15-2	28	104-104	70	Mar 17	@ Houston	3-2	W	30-38-2	62	242-279
31	Dec 27	New England	1-8	L	13-16-2	28	105-112	71	Mar 19	Indianapolis	3-3	T	30-38-3	63	245-282
32	Dec 29	@ Cincinnati	7-1	W	14-16-2	30	112-113	72	Mar 21	@ Quebec	5-4	W	31-38-3	65	250-286
33	Dec 30	@ New England	2-6	L	14-17-2	30	114-119	73	Mar 22	@ Edmonton	5-3	W	32-38-3	67	255-289
34	Jan 1	Quebec	2-5	L	14-18-2	30	116-124	74	Mar 24	Quebec	*3-4	L	32-39-3	67	258-293
35	Jan 4	@ Indianapolis	1-4	L	14-19-2	30	117-128	75	Mar 25	Winnipeg	1-3	L	32-40-3	67	259-296
36	Jan 6	Houston	6-4	W	15-19-2	32	123-132	76	Mar 31	Edmonton	5-2	W	33-40-3	69	264-298
37	Jan 8	@ New England	5-4	W	16-19-2	34	128-136	77	Apr 1	Cincinnati	5-1	W	34-40-3	71	269-299
38	Jan 10	@ Quebec	4-6	L	16-20-2	34	132-142	78	Apr 5	@ Cincinnati	4-5	L	34-41-3	71	273-304
39	Jan 11	@ Winnipeg	2-11	L	16-21-2	34	134-153	79	Apr 7	Houston	5-3	W	35-41-3	73	278-307
40	Jan 14	@ Cincinnati	4-3	W	17-21-2	36	138-156	80	Apr 9	@ Indianapolis	9-7	W	36-41-3	75	287-314

Bulls Stars of 1977-1978

Rod Langway
Future HOFer, +10

Ken Linseman
38 goals, 76 points

Paul Henderson
37 goals

Serge Beaudoin
+14 rating

John Garrett
24 wins

Dave Hanson
241 minutes, +10 rating

Scoring

pos	#	player	gp	g	a	pts	pim	+/-	ppg	shg	sog	sc%	gp	g	a	pts	pim	+/-
LW	11	Alley, Steve	27	8	12	20	11	+17	1	0	43	0.186	5	1	0	1	10	-3
LW	17	Arndt, Danny	4	0	1	1	0	1	0	0	0	-	-	-	-	-	-	-
LW	16	Beaton, Frank	56	6	9	15	279	-8	0	1	63	0.095	5	2	0	2	10	-2
D	5	Beaudoin, Serge	64	8	25	33	105	+14	1	0	95	0.084	5	1	0	1	46	-2
LW	8	Bilodeau, Gilles	59	2	2	4	258	-14	0	0	20	0.100	3	0	0	0	27	+1
RW	24	Cassolato, Tony	77	18	25	43	59	-3	4	0	124	0.145	4	0	0	0	4	-2
D	14	Durbano, Steve	45	6	4	10	284	-12	1	0	64	0.094	4	0	2	2	16	0
D	12	Evans, Chris	12	1	2	3	4	-7	0	0	8	0.125	-	-	-	-	-	-
G	35	Garrett, John	58	0	3	3	26		0	0	0	-	5	0	0	0	0	-
RW	7	Gorman, Dave	63	19	21	40	93	+18	2	0	108	0.176	4	1	1	2	0	-2
D	15	Hanson, Dave	42	7	16	23	241	+10	0	0	39	0.179	5	0	1	1	48	-1
LW	19	Henderson, Paul	80	37	29	66	22	+4	11	1	212	0.175	5	1	1	2	0	-4
D	33	Hoganson, Dale	43	1	12	13	29	-6	0	0	54	0.019	5	0	0	0	7	-1
D	3	Hughes, Brent	80	9	35	44	48	+12	3	0	109	0.083	5	0	0	0	12	-3
D	4	Langway, Rod	52	3	18	21	52	+10	0	0	75	0.040	4	0	0	0	9	-2
C	10	Linseman, Ken	71	38	38	76	126	+6	5	4	216	0.176	5	2	2	4	15	+1
RW	27	Mahovlich, Frank	72	14	24	38	22	-5	6	0	125	0.112	3	1	1	2	0	+2
C	20	Marrin, Peter	80	28	43	71	53	+9	7	1	187	0.150	5	0	3	3	2	-2
RW	9	Napier, Mark	79	33	32	65	9	-11	14	0	194	0.170	5	0	2	2	14	+2
RW	14	Nedomansky, Vaclav	12	2	3	5	6	-9	1	0	29	0.069	-	-	-	-	-	-
D	21	Noris, Joe	45	9	19	28	6	-9	0	0	83	0.108	-	-	-	-	-	-
RW	17	Roberto, Phil	53	8	20	28	91	+7	0	0	91	0.088	4	1	0	1	20	-2
RW	16	Sheehy, Tim	13	4	2	6	5	-14	2	0	43	0.093	-	-	-	-	-	-
D	30	Stephenson, Bob	39	7	6	13	33	-2	0	0	51	0.137	-	-	-	-	-	-
C	18	Stewart, John C.	48	13	26	39	52	+13	2	1	86	0.151	5	1	1	2	6	-3
D	4	Terbenche, Paul	11	1	0	1	0	+1	0	0	4	0.250	-	-	-	-	-	-
D	2	Turkiewicz, Jim	78	3	21	24	45	+10	0	0	83	0.036	5	1	1	2	0	-2
D	6	Westrum, Pat	77	2	10	12	97	-7	0	0	72	0.028	3	0	1	1	0	+1
G	1	Wood, Wayne	32	0	3	3	22		0	0	0	-	1	0	0	0	0	-

Power Play: 60 goals scored in 286 opportunities (21.0%) with 13 short-handed goals allowed.
Penalty Killing: 84 goals allowed in 355 opportunities (76.3%) with 8 short-handed goals scored.

Goaltending

goaltender	gp	min	ga	en	so	record	gaa	sog	sv%	gp	min	ga	record	gaa
Garrett, John	58	3306	210	5	2	24-31-1	3.81	1714	0.877	5	271	26	1-4	5.76
Wood, Wayne	32	1551	99	0	1	12-10-2	3.83	794	0.875	1	29	3	0-0	6.21

Transactions: Paul Terbenche signed to contract, May 1977 • Rights to Steve Durbano purchased from Quebec, Jun 1977 • Brent Hughes signed to contract, Jun 1977 • Steve Alley acquired from New England for future considerations, Jul 1977 • Phil Roberto signed to contract, Jul 1977 • Bob Stephenson signed to contract, Sep 1977 • Serge Beaudoin signed to contract, Nov 1977 • Tim Sheehy and Vaclav Nedomansky traded to Detroit (NHL) for Steve Durbano and Dave Hanson, Nov 1977. Sheehy later released, signed by New England. Hanson returned to Detroit at close of season • Frank Beaton signed to contract, Nov 1977 • Chris Evans waived, Nov 1977, claimed by Quebec • Paul Terbenche traded to Houston for future considerations, Mar 1978 (Playoffs only)

1977-1978 CINCINNATI STINGERS

Coach
Jacques Demers

Summary of Games (@ Away, * Overtime)

	date	opponent	score		record	pts	gf-ga
1	Oct 12	Indianapolis	4-5	L	0-1-0	0	4-5
2	Oct 15	Winnipeg	4-5	L	0-2-0	0	8-10
3	Oct 16	New England	6-2	W	1-2-0	2	14-12
4	Oct 18 @	Quebec	1-5	L	1-3-0	2	15-17
5	Oct 21 @	Houston	5-6	L	1-4-0	2	20-23
6	Oct 28 @	Winnipeg	2-3	L	1-5-0	2	22-26
7	Nov 4 @	New England	3-4	L	1-6-0	2	25-30
8	Nov 5	Winnipeg	1-6	L	1-7-0	2	26-36
9	Nov 6	New England	2-5	L	1-8-0	2	28-41
10	Nov 9	Birmingham	2-1	W	2-8-0	4	30-42
11	Nov 11	Edmonton	2-3	L	2-9-0	4	32-45
12	Nov 12 @	Quebec	*6-5	W	3-9-0	6	38-50
13	Nov 13 @	Winnipeg	3-2	W	4-9-0	8	41-52
14	Nov 16 @	Edmonton	4-6	L	4-10-0	8	45-58
15	Nov 18 @	Edmonton	*3-4	L	4-11-0	8	48-62
16	Nov 23	Quebec	4-3	W	5-11-0	10	52-65
17	Nov 24 @	Birmingham	2-12	L	5-12-0	10	54-77
18	Nov 25 @	Houston	1-3	L	5-13-0	10	55-80
19	Nov 26 @	Indianapolis	7-5	W	6-13-0	12	62-85
20	Nov 29 @	Quebec	3-2	W	7-13-0	14	65-87
21	Nov 30	Indianapolis	3-0	W	8-13-0	16	68-87
22	Dec 3 @	New England	5-2	W	9-13-0	18	73-89
23	Dec 4	Houston	2-3	L	9-14-0	18	75-92
24	Dec 7 @	Edmonton	*4-5	L	9-15-0	18	79-97
25	Dec 9 @	Winnipeg	*4-3	W	10-15-0	20	83-100
26	Dec 14	Indianapolis	3-1	W	11-15-0	22	86-101
27	Dec 15 @	Birmingham	3-5	L	11-16-0	22	89-106
28	Dec 17	Soviet All-Stars	4-5	L	11-17-0	22	93-111
29	Dec 20	Czechoslovakia	5-5	T	11-17-1	23	98-116
30	Dec 22 @	Indianapolis	4-1	W	12-17-1	25	102-117
31	Dec 23	Winnipeg	4-6	L	12-18-1	25	106-123
32	Dec 28	Indianapolis	*5-4	W	13-18-1	27	111-127
33	Dec 29	Birmingham	1-7	L	13-19-1	27	112-134
34	Dec 30 @	Houston	5-5	T	13-19-2	28	117-139
35	Jan 1	New England	*3-4	L	13-20-2	28	120-143
36	Jan 4	Houston	5-3	W	14-20-2	30	125-146
37	Jan 6	Quebec	5-3	W	15-20-2	32	130-149
38	Jan 7 @	New England	3-5	L	15-21-2	32	133-154
39	Jan 11	Edmonton	0-2	L	15-22-2	32	133-156
40	Jan 14	Birmingham	3-4	L	15-23-2	32	136-160
41	Jan 15 @	Quebec	6-3	W	16-23-2	34	142-163
42	Jan 18 @	Birmingham	0-3	L	16-24-2	34	142-166
43	Jan 20	Quebec	2-8	L	16-25-2	34	144-174
44	Jan 21 @	Houston	2-5	L	16-26-2	34	146-179
45	Jan 22	Edmonton	5-2	W	17-26-2	36	151-181
46	Jan 25	New England	*8-7	W	18-26-2	38	159-188
47	Jan 29	Winnipeg	4-8	L	18-27-2	38	163-196
48	Jan 30 @	Indianapolis	4-3	W	19-27-2	40	167-199
49	Feb 1	Indianapolis	8-0	W	20-27-2	42	175-199
50	Feb 3	Houston	1-0	W	21-27-2	44	176-199
51	Feb 4	Winnipeg	5-7	L	21-28-2	44	181-206
52	Feb 8 @	Edmonton	6-6	T	21-28-3	45	187-212
53	Feb 10 @	Winnipeg	2-10	L	21-29-3	45	189-222
54	Feb 11	New England	7-8	L	21-30-3	45	196-230
55	Feb 12	Quebec	8-2	W	22-30-3	47	204-232
56	Feb 15	Houston	2-5	L	22-31-3	47	206-237
57	Feb 17 @	Houston	*4-3	W	23-31-3	49	210-240
58	Feb 18	Winnipeg	0-4	L	23-32-3	49	210-244
59	Feb 19	Birmingham	*4-3	W	24-32-3	51	214-247
60	Feb 25 @	Birmingham	3-7	L	24-33-3	51	217-254
61	Mar 1 @	Edmonton	6-4	W	25-33-3	53	223-258
62	Mar 3 @	Winnipeg	5-1	W	26-33-3	55	228-259
63	Mar 5 @	Indianapolis	2-4	L	26-34-3	55	230-263
64	Mar 7 @	Quebec	5-4	W	27-34-3	57	235-267
65	Mar 9	Edmonton	6-5	W	28-34-3	59	241-272
66	Mar 11	Edmonton	2-0	W	29-34-3	61	243-272
67	Mar 15	Birmingham	7-2	W	30-34-3	63	250-274
68	Mar 17	New England	2-6	L	30-35-3	63	252-280
69	Mar 18	Indianapolis	4-2	W	31-35-3	65	256-282
70	Mar 19 @	Edmonton	2-4	L	31-36-3	65	258-286
71	Mar 22	Houston	9-2	W	32-36-3	67	267-288
72	Mar 28 @	Quebec	4-6	L	32-37-3	67	271-294
73	Mar 29 @	New England	1-6	L	32-38-3	67	272-300
74	Apr 1 @	Birmingham	1-5	L	32-39-3	67	273-305
75	Apr 2 @	Indianapolis	3-6	L	32-40-3	67	276-311
76	Apr 5	Birmingham	5-4	W	33-40-3	69	281-315
77	Apr 7 @	Indianapolis	6-4	W	34-40-3	71	287-319
78	Apr 8 @	Houston	4-5	L	34-41-3	71	291-324
79	Apr 9	Quebec	6-2	W	35-41-3	73	297-326
80	Apr 10 @	New England	1-6	L	35-42-3	73	298-332

Stingers Stars of 1977-1978

Robbie Ftorek	**Richie Leduc**	**Michel Dion**	**Rick Dudley**	**Pat Stapleton**	**Jamie Hislop**
59 goals, 109 points	27 goals	4 shutouts led league	30 goals, 156 minutes	Defensive leadership	+20 rating

Scoring

												Regular Season		Playoffs					
pos	#	player	gp	g	a	pts	pim	+/-	ppg	shg	sog	sc%	gp	g	a	pts	pim	+/-
LW	15	Abgrall, Dennis	65	13	11	24	13	-2	2	0	79	0.165	-	-	-	-	-	-
D	6	Allen, Jeff	2	0	0	0	0	0	0	0	1	0.000	-	-	-	-	-	-
D	5	Baltimore, Bryon	28	2	9	11	23	-9	0	0	32	0.063	-	-	-	-	-	-
D	5	Beaudoin, Serge	13	0	1	1	10	-11	0	0	19	0.000	-	-	-	-	-	-
C	7	Carroll, Greg	26	6	13	19	36	+3	0	1	48	0.125	-	-	-	-	-	-
LW	21	Coates, Brian	42	8	10	18	18	+7	2	0	53	0.151	-	-	-	-	-	-
LW	11	Deadmarsh, Butch	45	7	6	13	86	+6	0	0	71	0.099	-	-	-	-	-	-
C	6	Debol, Dave	9	3	2	5	2	+2	0	0	15	0.200	-	-	-	-	-	-
G	31	Dion, Michel	45	0	0	0	26		0	0	0	-	-	-	-	-	-	-
LW	9	Dudley, Rick	72	30	41	71	156	-1	5	1	204	0.147	-	-	-	-	-	-
C	8	Ftorek, Robbie	80	59	50	109	54	+31	20	2	262	0.225	-	-	-	-	-	-
C	16	Gilligan, Bill	54	10	14	24	59	-13	1	0	80	0.125	-	-	-	-	-	-
LW	27	Greig, Bruce	32	3	1	4	57	-1	1	0	10	0.300	-	-	-	-	-	-
C	27	Hall, Del	25	4	3	7	4	-3	0	0	35	0.114	-	-	-	-	-	-
RW	22	Handrahan, Alf	14	1	3	4	42	+2	0	0	9	0.111	-	-	-	-	-	-
C	20	Harris, Hugh	45	11	23	34	30	+1	0	0	95	0.116	-	-	-	-	-	-
G	22	Hoganson, Paul	7	0	0	0	0		0	0	0	-	-	-	-	-	-	-
RW	24	Hislop, Jamie	80	24	43	67	17	+20	3	0	132	0.182	-	-	-	-	-	-
D	6	Lahache, Floyd	11	0	3	3	13	-6	0	0	11	0.000	-	-	-	-	-	-
G	35	Lapointe, Norm	13	0	1	1	4		0	0	0	-	-	-	-	-	-	-
LW	8	Larose, Claude	51	11	20	31	6	-11	1	0	100	0.110	-	-	-	-	-	-
C	7	Leduc, Richie	54	27	31	58	44	-27	7	1	184	0.147	-	-	-	-	-	-
D	21/25	Legge, Barry	78	7	17	24	114	-7	2	0	103	0.068	-	-	-	-	-	-
G	1	Liut, Mike	27	0	1	1	0		0	0	0	-	-	-	-	-	-	-
C	11	Locas, Jacques	17	0	2	2	6	-7	0	0	9	0.000	-	-	-	-	-	-
D	2	Maggs, Darryl	11	2	5	7	7	+9	0	0	33	0.061	-	-	-	-	-	-
D	3	Marotte, Gilles	29	1	7	8	58	-6	0	0	49	0.020	-	-	-	-	-	-
RW	18	Marsh, Peter	74	25	25	50	123	-17	4	0	234	0.107	-	-	-	-	-	-
D	4	Melrose, Barry	69	2	9	11	113	-10	0	0	51	0.039	-	-	-	-	-	-
D	6/10	Norwich, Craig	65	7	23	30	48	+3	2	0	100	0.070	-	-	-	-	-	-
D	2	Plumb, Ron	54	13	34	47	45	-18	8	0	150	0.087	-	-	-	-	-	-
C	14	Sobchuk, Dennis	23	5	9	14	22	-11	1	1	62	0.081	-	-	-	-	-	-
D	12	Stapleton, Pat	65	4	45	49	28	+6	1	1	103	0.039	-	-	-	-	-	-
LW	17	Stewart, Paul	40	1	5	6	241	-7	0	0	15	0.067	-	-	-	-	-	-
RW	17	Stoughton, Blaine	30	6	13	19	36	-13	1	0	75	0.080	-	-	-	-	-	-
LW	23	Thomas, Reg	18	4	2	6	36	-5	0	0	44	0.091	-	-	-	-	-	-
LW	19	Trognitz, Willie	29	2	1	3	94	-3	1	0	20	0.100	-	-	-	-	-	-
G	35	Wakely, Ernie	6	0	0	0	0		0	0	0	-	-	-	-	-	-	-

Power Play: 62 goals scored in 295 opportunities (21.0%) with 10 short-handed goals allowed.
Penalty Killing: 76 goals allowed in 256 opportunities (70.3%) with 7 short-handed goals scored.

Goaltending

goaltender	gp	min	ga	en	so	record	gaa	sog	sv%	gp	min	ga	record	gaa
Dion, Michel	45	2356	140	2	4	21-17-1	3.57	1220	0.885	-	-	-	-	-
Hoganson, Paul	7	326	24	0	0	1-2-1	4.42	153	0.843	-	-	-	-	-
Lapointe, Norm	13	647	50	2	0	5-6-1	4.64	345	0.855	-	-	-	-	-
Liut, Mike	27	1215	86	2	0	8-12-0	4.25	663	0.870	-	-	-	-	-
Wakely, Ernie	6	311	26	0	0	0-5-0	5.02	146	0.822	-	-	-	-	-

Transactions: Robbie Ftorek, Del Hall purchased from Phoenix, May 1977 • Rights to Mike Liut acquired from New England for Bryan Maxwell and Greg Carroll, May 1977 • Ernie Wakely signed to contract, Aug 1977 • Serge Beaudoin signed to contract, Sep 1977, released, Oct 1977 • Michel Dion, Dave Forbes signed to contracts, Oct 1977 • Ernie Wakely traded to Houston for future considerations, Oct 1977 • Pat Stapleton, Willie Trognitz signed to contracts, Nov 1977 • Paul Stewart signed to contract, Dec 1977 • Del Hall and Dennis Sobchuk traded to Edmonton for Butch Deadmarsh, Dec 1977 • Gilles Marotte and Blaine Stoughton traded to Indianapolis for Bryon Baltimore and Hugh Harris, Jan 1978 • Bruce Greig signed to contract, Jan 1978 • Rich Leduc and Claude Larose traded to Indianapolis for Darryl Maggs and Reg Thomas, Feb 1978 • Ron Plumb traded to New England for Greg Carroll, Feb 1978 • Paul Hoganson signed to contract, Feb 1978 • Darryl Maggs suspended after leaving team, Mar 1978

1977-1978 EDMONTON OILERS

**Coach
Glen Sather**

Summary of Games (@ Away, * Overtime)

	date	opponent	score		record	pts	gf-ga			date	opponent	score		record	pts	gf-ga
1	Oct 12	Winnipeg	3-7	L	0-1-0	0	3-7		41	Jan 20 @	Birmingham	3-5	L	20-20-1	41	148-148
2	Oct 14	Quebec	4-2	W	1-1-0	2	7-9		42	Jan 21 @	Indianapolis	3-2	W	21-20-1	43	151-150
3	Oct 15 @	Quebec	2-6	L	1-2-0	2	9-15		43	Jan 22 @	Cincinnati	2-5	L	21-21-1	43	153-155
4	Oct 19	New England	3-6	L	1-3-0	2	12-21		44	Jan 25	Indianapolis	6-2	W	22-21-1	45	159-157
5	Oct 26 @	Houston	*7-8	L	1-4-0	2	19-29		45	Jan 27	Quebec	9-6	W	23-21-1	47	168-163
6	Oct 28 @	Birmingham	3-2	W	2-4-0	4	22-31		46	Jan 29	Quebec	3-4	L	23-22-1	47	171-167
7	Oct 30 @	Winnipeg	2-5	L	2-5-0	4	24-36		47	Jan 31 @	Indianapolis	6-4	W	24-22-1	49	177-171
8	Nov 2	Winnipeg	3-6	L	2-6-0	4	27-42		48	Feb 1 @	New England	3-4	L	24-23-1	49	180-175
9	Nov 4	Indianapolis	3-1	W	3-6-0	6	30-43		49	Feb 3 @	New England	6-3	W	25-23-1	51	186-178
10	Nov 6	Houston	7-1	W	4-6-0	8	37-44		50	Feb 4 @	Quebec	*4-3	W	26-23-1	53	190-181
11	Nov 8 @	Quebec	3-7	L	4-7-0	8	40-51		51	Feb 5 @	Winnipeg	3-4	L	26-24-1	53	193-185
12	Nov 10 @	New England	3-5	L	4-8-0	8	43-56		52	Feb 8	Cincinnati	6-6	T	26-24-2	54	199-191
13	Nov 11 @	Cincinnati	3-2	W	5-8-0	10	46-58		53	Feb 12	Birmingham	7-0	W	27-24-2	56	206-191
14	Nov 12 @	Birmingham	1-1	T	5-8-1	11	47-59		54	Feb 14	Birmingham	4-1	W	28-24-2	58	210-192
15	Nov 16	Cincinnati	6-4	W	6-8-1	13	53-63		55	Feb 15 @	Winnipeg	5-6	L	28-25-2	58	215-198
16	Nov 18	Cincinnati	*4-3	W	7-8-1	15	57-66		56	Feb 17	Quebec	6-4	W	29-25-2	60	221-202
17	Nov 20	New England	*4-5	L	7-9-1	15	61-71		57	Feb 19	Indianapolis	4-3	W	30-25-2	62	225-205
18	Nov 22	Winnipeg	4-2	W	8-9-1	17	65-73		58	Feb 22	Houston	5-6	L	30-26-2	62	230-211
19	Nov 24 @	Indianapolis	*4-5	L	8-10-1	17	69-78		59	Feb 24	Houston	*5-4	W	31-26-2	64	235-215
20	Nov 26 @	New England	3-1	W	9-10-1	19	72-79		60	Feb 26	New England	5-6	L	31-27-2	64	240-221
21	Nov 30	Birmingham	4-2	W	10-10-1	21	76-81		61	Mar 1	Cincinnati	4-6	L	31-28-2	64	244-227
22	Dec 2	Birmingham	5-7	L	10-11-1	21	81-88		62	Mar 3	Indianapolis	6-8	L	31-29-2	64	250-235
23	Dec 4 @	Winnipeg	3-2	W	11-11-1	23	84-90		63	Mar 5 @	Birmingham	4-3	W	32-29-2	66	254-238
24	Dec 7	Cincinnati	*5-4	W	12-11-1	25	89-94		64	Mar 7 @	Houston	3-4	L	32-30-2	66	257-242
25	Dec 9	Houston	3-5	L	12-12-1	25	92-99		65	Mar 9 @	Cincinnati	5-6	L	32-31-2	66	262-248
26	Dec 11	Houston	2-4	L	12-13-1	25	94-103		66	Mar 11 @	Cincinnati	0-2	L	32-32-2	66	262-250
27	Dec 14	Czechoslovakia	6-1	W	13-13-1	27	100-104		67	Mar 14 @	Quebec	3-6	L	32-33-2	66	265-256
28	Dec 18 @	Birmingham	2-3	L	13-14-1	27	102-107		68	Mar 15 @	Winnipeg	4-8	L	32-34-2	66	269-264
29	Dec 20 @	Houston	4-6	L	13-15-1	27	106-113		69	Mar 17	Winnipeg	6-2	W	33-34-2	68	275-266
30	Dec 21	Soviet All-Stars	5-2	W	14-15-1	29	111-115		70	Mar 19	Cincinnati	4-2	W	34-34-2	70	279-268
31	Dec 27	Quebec	9-3	W	15-15-1	31	120-118		71	Mar 22	Birmingham	3-5	L	34-35-2	70	282-273
32	Dec 30	Indianapolis	8-5	W	16-15-1	33	128-123		72	Mar 24	Indianapolis	4-0	W	35-35-2	72	286-273
33	Jan 1	Houston	1-2	L	16-16-1	33	129-125		73	Mar 26 @	New England	3-5	L	35-36-2	72	289-278
34	Jan 6	Winnipeg	1-4	L	16-17-1	33	130-129		74	Mar 28 @	Indianapolis	*4-3	W	36-36-2	74	293-281
35	Jan 8 @	Houston	4-2	W	17-17-1	35	134-131		75	Mar 30 @	Houston	1-5	L	36-37-2	74	294-286
36	Jan 11 @	Cincinnati	2-0	W	18-17-1	37	136-131		76	Mar 31 @	Birmingham	2-5	L	36-38-2	74	296-291
37	Jan 13 @	New England	0-2	L	18-18-1	37	136-133		77	Apr 1 @	Indianapolis	4-1	W	37-38-2	76	300-292
38	Jan 14 @	Quebec	4-7	L	18-19-1	37	140-140		78	Apr 4 @	Quebec	1-9	L	37-39-2	76	301-301
39	Jan 15 @	Winnipeg	*4-3	W	19-19-1	39	144-143		79	Apr 5	New England	4-4	T	37-39-3	77	305-305
40	Jan 18	New England	1-0	W	20-19-1	41	145-143		80	Apr 7	Winnipeg	4-2	W	38-39-3	79	309-307

Transactions: Ron Chipperfield, Warren Miller, Ken Baird and Butch Deadmarsh signed from defunct Calgary, May 1977 • Norm Ferguson signed to contract, May 1977 • Gerry Pinder, Juha Widing signed to contracts, Jun 1977 • Kevin Devine, Paul Shmyr signed to contracts, Aug 1977 • Kevin Devine, Blair MacDonald, Barry Wilkins, Rusty Patenaude and Claude St Sauveur traded to Indianapolis for Dave Inkpen and Mike Zuke, Sep 1977 • Jerry Holland signed to contract, Sep 1977 • Rights to Joe Micheletti acquired from Winnipeg for future considerations, Sep 1977 (Winnipeg had acquired his rights from Calgary a month earlier) • Bob Falkenberg, Dave Semenko (rights acquired from Houston) signed to contracts, Oct 1977 • Ken Baird released, Dec 1977, signed by Winnipeg • Dave Inkpen, Ken Broderick, Warren Miller and Rick Morris traded to Quebec for Don McLeod and Pierre Guite, Dec 1977 • Butch Deadmarsh and Dave Debol traded to Cincinnati for Del Hall and Dennis Sobchuk, Dec 1977 • Chris Ahrens and Pierre Jarry acquired from Minnesota (NHL) for future considerations, Mar 1978; Ahrens returned to Minnesota after failing physical (hernia) • Ray McKay, Kevin Primeau signed to contracts, Mar 1978

Oilers Stars of 1977-1978

Ron Chipperfield
33 goals, 85 points

Bill Flett
41 goals led team

Blair MacDonald
34 goals

Joe Micheletti
48 points, +8 rating

Al Hamilton
+24 rating

Mike Zuke
57 points

Scoring

pos	#	player	gp	g	a	pts	pim	+/-	ppg	shg	sog	sc%	gp	g	a	pts	pim	+/-
						Regular Season										**Playoffs**		
D	2	Ahrens, Chris	4	0	0	0	15	-5	0	0	4	0.000	-	-	-	-	-	-
D	24	Baird, Ken	6	2	4	6	2	0	0	0	10	0.200	-	-	-	-	-	-
G	1	Broderick, Ken	9	0	0	0	0		0	0	0		-	-	-	-	-	-
RW	8	Busniuk, Ron	59	2	18	20	157	-8	0	0	69	0.029	5	0	0	0	18	-2
C	18	Callighen, Brett	80	20	30	50	112	+5	1	0	201	0.100	5	0	2	2	16	-1
C	21	Campbell, Bryan	53	7	13	20	12	-17	2	0	81	0.086	-	-	-	-	-	-
C	7/10	Chipperfield, Ron	80	33	52	85	48	+1	11	1	212	0.156	5	1	1	2	0	-1
D	17	Cross, Jim	2	0	0	0	0	-3	0	0	1	0.000	-	-	-	-	-	-
LW	15	Deadmarsh, Butch	20	1	3	4	32	-1	0	0	27	0.037	-	-	-	-	-	-
D	5	DeMarco, Ab	47	6	8	14	20	-7	3	0	101	0.059	1	0	0	0	0	-1
G	28	Dryden, Dave	48	0	1	1	0		0	0	0	-	2	0	0	0	0	-
D	2	Falkenberg, Bob	2	0	0	0	0	-1	0	0	0	-	-	-	-	-	-	-
RW	9	Ferguson, Norm	71	26	21	47	2	+14	8	0	159	0.164	5	0	0	0	0	-2
RW	19	Flett, Bill	74	41	28	69	34	+9	8	1	224	0.183	-	-	-	-	-	-
LW	16	Guite, Pierre	60	12	21	33	71	-7	2	0	118	0.102	5	1	1	2	20	-3
C	15	Hall, Del	1	0	0	0	0	0	0	0	1	0.000	-	-	-	-	-	-
D	3	Hamilton, Al	59	11	43	54	46	+24	6	0	183	0.060	-	-	-	-	-	-
LW	24	Holland, Jerry	22	2	1	3	14	-1	1	0	28	0.071	-	-	-	-	-	-
D	5	Inkpen, Dave	19	0	1	1	16	-6	0	0	7	0.000	-	-	-	-	-	-
LW	22	Jarry, Pierre	18	4	10	14	4	-1	0	0	45	0.089	5	1	0	1	4	-3
D	26	Langevin, Dave	62	6	22	28	90	+11	1	0	132	0.045	5	0	2	2	10	-4
D	30	Lloyd, Owen	3	0	1	1	4	-1	0	0	1	0.000	-	-	-	-	-	-
RW	14/16	MacDonald, Blair	80	34	34	68	11	-12	7	4	237	0.143	5	1	1	2	0	-2
C	17	MacGregor, Gary	37	11	2	13	29	-2	2	0	77	0.143	-	-	-	-	-	-
D	17	McKay, Ray	14	1	4	5	4	+3	0	0	20	0.050	4	0	1	1	4	-1
G	1	McLeod, Don	33	0	7	7	2		0	0	1	0.000	4	0	0	0	0	-
LW	22	McMullen, Dale	1	0	0	0	0	0	0	0	2	0.000	-	-	-	-	-	-
D	4	Micheletti, Joe	56	14	34	48	56	+8	3	0	141	0.099	5	0	2	2	4	0
RW	22	Miller, Warren	18	2	4	6	18	+1	0	0	28	0.071	-	-	-	-	-	-
LW	7	Morris, Rick	5	1	1	2	7	-7	0	1	4	0.250	-	-	-	-	-	-
LW	15	Pinder, Gerry	5	0	1	1	0	-1	0	0	4	0.000	-	-	-	-	-	-
RW	15/23	Primeau, Kevin	7	0	1	1	0	-1	0	0	7	0.000	2	0	0	0	2	-2
LW	20	Rota, Randy	53	8	22	30	12	+11	0	0	93	0.086	5	1	1	2	4	-1
D	2	Sandbeck, Cal	11	1	2	3	39	+1	1	0	19	0.053	5	0	0	0	10	-1
LW	27	Semenko, Dave	65	6	6	12	140	-4	0	0	47	0.128	5	0	0	0	8	-1
D	6	Shmyr, Paul	80	9	40	49	100	-9	3	0	169	0.053	5	1	3	4	11	-3
C	10	Sobchuk, Dennis	13	6	3	9	4	-4	1	0	30	0.200	5	1	0	1	4	-2
D	25	Topolnisky, Craig	10	0	2	2	4	-1	0	0	16	0.000	-	-	-	-	-	-
G	25	Turnbull, Frank	1	0	0	0	0		0	0	0	-	-	-	-	-	-	-
RW	23	Troy, Jim	47	2	0	2	124	-11	0	0	19	0.105	2	0	0	0	0	0
C	11	Widing, Juha	71	18	24	42	8	+10	0	1	153	0.118	5	0	1	1	0	-4
C	12	Zuke, Mike	71	23	34	57	47	+1	2	3	188	0.122	5	2	3	5	0	-2

Power Play: 62 goals scored in 283 opportunities (21.9%) with 8 short-handed goals allowed.
Penalty Killing: 60 goals allowed in 292 opportunities (79.5%) with 11 short-handed goals scored.

Goaltending

goaltender	gp	min	ga	en	so	record	gaa	sog	sv%	gp	min	ga	record	gaa
Broderick, Ken	9	497	42	0	0	2-5-0	5.07	206	0.796	-	-	-	-	-
Dryden, Dave	48	2578	150	5	2	21-23-2	3.49	1239	0.879	2	91	6	0-1	3.96
McLeod, Don	33	1723	102	2	2	15-10-1	3.55	750	0.864	4	207	16	1-3	4.64
Turnbull, Frank	1	60	6	0	0	0-1-0	6.00	24	0.750	-	-	-	-	-

1977-1978 HOUSTON AEROS

**Coach
Bill Dineen**

Summary of Games (@ Away, * Overtime)

	date	opponent	score		record	pts	gf-ga		date	opponent	score		record	pts	gf-ga
1	Oct 12	New England	0-3	L	0-1-0	0	0-3	41	Jan 21	Cincinnati	5-2	W	19-19-3	41	149-155
2	Oct 14 @	Birmingham	3-5	L	0-2-0	0	3-8	42	Jan 22	Birmingham	4-2	W	20-19-3	43	153-157
3	Oct 15	Indianapolis	5-1	W	1-2-0	2	8-9	43	Jan 24 @	Quebec	6-5	W	21-19-3	45	159-162
4	Oct 21	Cincinnati	6-5	W	2-2-0	4	14-14	44	Jan 26	Winnipeg	*2-1	W	22-19-3	47	161-163
5	Oct 26	Edmonton	*8-7	W	3-2-0	6	22-21	45	Jan 28	New England	0-3	L	22-20-3	47	161-166
6	Oct 29 @	New England	2-7	L	3-3-0	6	24-28	46	Jan 29	New England	6-4	W	23-20-3	49	167-170
7	Oct 30 @	Quebec	4-5	L	3-4-0	6	28-33	47	Jan 31 @	Birmingham	4-2	W	24-20-3	51	171-172
8	Nov 1 @	Indianapolis	3-6	L	3-5-0	6	31-39	48	Feb 3 @	Cincinnati	0-1	L	24-21-3	51	171-173
9	Nov 2	Birmingham	5-3	W	4-5-0	8	36-42	49	Feb 4	New England	5-4	W	25-21-3	53	176-177
10	Nov 4	Quebec	6-7	L	4-6-0	8	42-49	50	Feb 9	Quebec	2-1	W	26-21-3	55	178-178
11	Nov 6 @	Edmonton	1-7	L	4-7-0	8	43-56	51	Feb 11	Quebec	8-4	W	27-21-3	57	186-182
12	Nov 9 @	Winnipeg	3-4	L	4-8-0	8	46-60	52	Feb 12	Winnipeg	5-6	L	27-22-3	57	191-188
13	Nov 11	Indianapolis	5-3	W	5-8-0	10	51-63	53	Feb 15 @	Cincinnati	5-2	W	28-22-3	59	196-190
14	Nov 18	Quebec	6-5	W	6-8-0	12	57-68	54	Feb 16	Birmingham	2-5	L	28-23-3	59	198-195
15	Nov 19 @	Birmingham	3-4	L	6-9-0	12	60-72	55	Feb 17	Cincinnati	*3-4	L	28-24-3	59	201-199
16	Nov 23	Birmingham	3-0	W	7-9-0	14	63-72	56	Feb 18 @	Birmingham	3-2	W	29-24-3	61	204-201
17	Nov 25	Cincinnati	3-1	W	8-9-0	16	66-73	57	Feb 22 @	Edmonton	6-5	W	30-24-3	63	210-206
18	Nov 30	New England	3-3	T	8-9-1	17	69-76	58	Feb 24 @	Edmonton	*4-5	L	30-25-3	63	214-211
19	Dec 2	Indianapolis	2-4	L	8-10-1	17	71-80	59	Feb 26 @	Winnipeg	6-9	L	30-26-3	63	220-220
20	Dec 4 @	Cincinnati	3-2	W	9-10-1	19	74-82	60	Feb 28 @	Quebec	2-5	L	30-27-3	63	222-225
21	Dec 6 @	Quebec	*3-4	L	9-11-1	19	77-86	61	Mar 1 @	Indianapolis	1-5	L	30-28-3	63	223-230
22	Dec 7 @	Winnipeg	2-5	L	9-12-1	19	79-91	62	Mar 3 @	New England	*3-2	W	31-28-3	65	226-232
23	Dec 9 @	Edmonton	5-3	W	10-12-1	21	84-94	63	Mar 4 @	Quebec	3-3	T	31-28-4	66	229-235
24	Dec 11 @	Edmonton	4-2	W	11-12-1	23	88-96	64	Mar 5 @	Winnipeg	4-3	W	32-28-4	68	233-238
25	Dec 13	Birmingham	3-5	L	11-13-1	23	91-101	65	Mar 7	Edmonton	4-3	W	33-28-4	70	237-241
26	Dec 15 @	Indianapolis	3-3	T	11-13-2	24	94-104	66	Mar 9	New England	6-4	W	34-28-4	72	243-245
27	Dec 18	Czechoslovakia	3-2	W	12-13-2	26	97-106	67	Mar 11 @	Indianapolis	2-4	L	34-29-4	72	245-249
28	Dec 20	Edmonton	6-4	W	13-13-2	28	103-110	68	Mar 12	Indianapolis	6-3	W	35-29-4	74	251-252
29	Dec 21	Winnipeg	3-4	L	13-14-2	28	106-114	69	Mar 17	Birmingham	2-3	L	35-30-4	74	253-255
30	Dec 23	Soviet All-Stars	2-6	L	13-15-2	28	108-120	70	Mar 22 @	Cincinnati	2-9	L	35-31-4	74	255-264
31	Dec 29 @	Indianapolis	7-1	W	14-15-2	30	115-121	71	Mar 24 @	New England	1-0	W	36-31-4	76	256-264
32	Dec 30	Cincinnati	5-5	T	14-15-3	31	120-126	72	Mar 25	Quebec	4-3	W	37-31-4	78	260-267
33	Jan 1 @	Edmonton	2-1	W	15-15-3	33	122-127	73	Mar 28	Winnipeg	5-3	W	38-31-4	80	265-270
34	Jan 4 @	Cincinnati	3-5	L	15-16-3	33	125-132	74	Mar 30	Edmonton	5-1	W	39-31-4	82	270-271
35	Jan 6 @	Birmingham	4-6	L	15-17-3	33	129-138	75	Apr 2 @	Quebec	1-7	L	39-32-4	82	271-278
36	Jan 7	Indianapolis	1-2	L	15-18-3	33	130-140	76	Apr 3 @	New England	6-8	L	39-33-4	82	277-286
37	Jan 8	Edmonton	2-4	L	15-19-3	33	132-144	77	Apr 4	Winnipeg	6-3	W	40-33-4	84	283-289
38	Jan 13	Winnipeg	3-2	W	16-19-3	35	135-146	78	Apr 7 @	Birmingham	3-5	L	40-34-4	84	286-294
39	Jan 14 @	New England	*5-4	W	17-19-3	37	140-150	79	Apr 8	Cincinnati	5-4	W	41-34-4	86	291-298
40	Jan 20 @	Indianapolis	4-3	W	18-19-3	39	144-153	80	Apr 9 @	Winnipeg	5-4	W	42-34-4	88	296-302

Aeros Stars of 1977-1978

  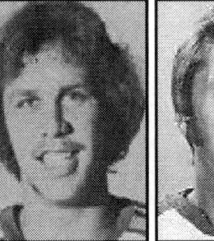    

Andre Lacroix	**Cam Connor**	**Ernie Wakely**	**Morris Lukowich**	**Terry Ruskowski**	**John Gray**
113 points	217 minutes, +4 rating	28 wins, 2 shutouts	40 goals	72 points, +13 rating	35 goals

Scoring

						Regular Season							Playoffs				
pos	#	player	gp	g	a	pts	pim	+/-	ppg	shg	sog	sc%	gp	g	a	pts	pim	+/-
D	4	Campbell, Scott	75	8	29	37	116	+10	1	0	113	0.071	6	1	1	2	8	-2
RW	15	Connor, Cam	68	21	16	37	217	+4	0	0	152	0.138	2	1	0	1	22	+1
LW	10	Gray, John	77	35	23	58	80	+15	6	0	151	0.232	6	0	3	3	10	+2
D	17	Hale, Larry	56	2	11	13	22	+4	0	0	16	0.125	-	-	-	-	-	-
RW	26	Hansis, Ron	78	13	9	22	51	0	1	0	62	0.210	6	1	1	2	4	0
LW	16	Hughes, Frank	11	3	2	5	2	-10	0	0	29	0.103	-	-	-	-	-	-
D	20	Hughes, John	79	3	25	28	130	+20	1	0	62	0.048	6	1	1	2	6	+2
D	24	Irwin, Glen	3	0	0	0	0		0	0			-	-	-	-	-	-
C	7	Lacroix, Andre	78	36	77	113	57	+8	7	0	193	0.187	6	2	2	4	0	-4
RW	27	Larway, Don	69	24	35	59	52	+1	5	0	176	0.136	6	1	2	3	4	-3
LW	12	Lukowich, Morris	80	40	35	75	131	+13	13	0	199	0.201	6	1	2	3	17	-3
C	13	Lund, Larry	76	9	17	26	36	-22	1	0	60	0.150	6	0	2	2	2	-1
LW	16	Mazur, John	1	0	0	0	0	-1	0	0	0	-	-	-	-	-	-	-
D	5	McLeod, Al	80	2	22	24	54	+18	0	0	85	0.024	6	1	0	1	2	-9
RW	24	Mortson, Keke	6	0	1	1	7	-1	0	0	2	0.000	2	0	1	1	0	+1
D	6	Popiel, Poul	80	6	31	37	53	-6	1	1	126	0.048	6	0	2	2	13	+4
RW	21	Preston, Rich	73	25	25	50	52	+3	7	3	213	0.117	-	-	-	-	-	-
C	8	Ruskowski, Terry	78	15	57	72	170	+13	3	1	144	0.104	4	1	1	2	5	-1
G	30	Rutledge, Wayne	12	0	0	0	2		0	0	0	-	3	0	0	0	2	-
D	2	Schella, John	63	9	20	29	125	-2	4	0	139	0.065	6	0	1	1	33	-8
LW	14	Taylor, Ted	54	11	11	22	46	+8	1	1	74	0.149	6	3	1	4	10	+2
D	3	Terbenche, Paul	0	-	-	-	-	-	-	-	-	-	6	1	1	2	0	0
LW	18	Tonelli, John	65	23	41	64	103	+13	5	0	146	0.158	6	1	3	4	8	-4
G	31	Wakely, Ernie	51	0	0	0	0		0	0	0	-	-	-	-	-	-	-
C	19	West, Steve	71	11	21	32	23	+4	0	0	60	0.183	6	1	0	1	0	+2
G	1	Zimmerman, Lynn	20	0	0	0	0		0	0	0	-	4	0	0	0	6	-

Power Play: 56 goals scored in 270 opportunities (20.7%) with 8 short-handed goals allowed.
Penalty Killing: 77 goals allowed in 366 opportunities (79.0%) with 6 short-handed goals scored.

Goaltending

goaltender	gp	min	ga	en	so	record	gaa	sog	sv%	gp	min	ga	record	gaa
Rutledge, Wayne	12	634	47	0	0	4-7-0	4.45	360	0.869	3	131	8	1-2	3.66
Wakely, Ernie	51	3070	166	3	2	28-18-4	3.24	1608	0.897	-	-	-	-	-
Zimmerman, Lynn	20	1166	84	2	0	10-9-0	4.32	641	0.869	4	239	21	1-2	5.27

Transactions: John Hughes acquired from Cincinnati for rights to Craig Norwich, May 1977 • Andre Lacroix signed to contract from defunct San Diego, May 1977 • Frank Hughes signed to contract, Jul 1977, released Nov 1977 • Ernie Wakely acquired from Cincinnati for future considerations, Nov 1977 • Paul Terbenche acquired from Birmingham for future considerations, Mar 1978 • Glenn Irwin traded to Indianapolis for future considerations, Mar 1978

1977-1978 INDIANAPOLIS RACERS

Coach
Ron Ingram
16-31-4

Player-Coach
Bill Goldsworthy
8-20-1

Bench Coach
Rosaire Paiement

Summary of Games (@ Away, * Overtime)

	date	opponent	score		record	pts	gf-ga
1	Oct 12 @	Cincinnati	5-4	W	1-0-0	2	5-4
2	Oct 15 @	Houston	1-5	L	1-1-0	2	6-9
3	Oct 16 @	Winnipeg	1-9	L	1-2-0	2	7-18
4	Oct 18	New England	2-2	T	1-2-1	3	9-20
5	Oct 21	Quebec	4-4	T	1-2-2	4	13-24
6	Oct 25 @	Birmingham	5-4	W	2-2-2	6	18-28
7	Oct 26	Winnipeg	5-3	W	3-2-2	8	23-31
8	Oct 29	Birmingham	6-2	W	4-2-2	10	29-33
9	Nov 1	Houston	6-3	W	5-2-2	12	35-36
10	Nov 4 @	Edmonton	1-3	L	5-3-2	12	36-39
11	Nov 11 @	Houston	3-5	L	5-4-2	12	39-44
12	Nov 12 @	New England	3-5	L	5-5-2	12	42-49
13	Nov 15	New England	4-6	L	5-6-2	12	46-55
14	Nov 18	Birmingham	1-2	L	5-7-2	12	47-57
15	Nov 19	Winnipeg	4-6	L	5-8-2	12	51-63
16	Nov 20 @	Quebec	2-5	L	5-9-2	12	53-68
17	Nov 23 @	New England	3-3	T	5-9-3	13	56-71
18	Nov 24	Edmonton	*5-4	W	6-9-3	15	61-75
19	Nov 26	Cincinnati	5-7	L	6-10-3	15	66-82
20	Nov 30 @	Cincinnati	0-3	L	6-11-3	15	66-85
21	Dec 1	Quebec	5-4	W	7-11-3	17	71-89
22	Dec 2 @	Houston	4-2	W	8-11-3	19	75-91
23	Dec 4 @	Birmingham	0-3	L	8-12-3	19	75-94
24	Dec 6	New England	5-2	W	9-12-3	21	80-96
25	Dec 9	Czechoslovakia	3-5	L	9-13-3	21	83-101
26	Dec 10 @	Quebec	3-5	L	9-14-3	21	86-106
27	Dec 11 @	Winnipeg	1-7	L	9-15-3	21	87-113
28	Dec 14 @	Cincinnati	1-3	L	9-16-3	21	88-116
29	Dec 15	Houston	3-3	T	9-16-4	22	91-119
30	Dec 18	Soviet All-Stars	3-4	L	9-17-4	22	94-123
31	Dec 22	Cincinnati	1-4	L	9-18-4	22	95-127
32	Dec 23 @	New England	3-5	L	9-19-4	22	98-132
33	Dec 28 @	Cincinnati	*4-5	L	9-20-4	22	102-137
34	Dec 29	Houston	1-7	L	9-21-4	22	103-144
35	Dec 30 @	Edmonton	5-8	L	9-22-4	22	108-152
36	Jan 4	Birmingham	4-1	W	10-22-4	24	112-153
37	Jan 6	New England	4-3	W	11-22-4	26	116-156
38	Jan 7 @	Houston	2-1	W	12-22-4	28	118-157
39	Jan 8 @	Winnipeg	2-4	L	12-23-4	28	120-161
40	Jan 11	Quebec	2-1	W	13-23-4	30	122-162
41	Jan 14	Winnipeg	3-6	L	13-24-4	30	125-168
42	Jan 20	Houston	3-4	L	13-25-4	30	128-172
43	Jan 21	Edmonton	2-3	L	13-26-4	30	130-175
44	Jan 22 @	Winnipeg	5-4	W	14-26-4	32	135-179
45	Jan 25 @	Edmonton	2-6	L	14-27-4	32	137-185
46	Jan 30	Cincinnati	3-4	L	14-28-4	32	140-189
47	Jan 31	Edmonton	4-6	L	14-29-4	32	144-195
48	Feb 1 @	Cincinnati	0-8	L	14-30-4	32	144-203
49	Feb 3	Quebec	*5-4	W	15-30-4	34	149-207
50	Feb 4 @	Birmingham	2-5	L	15-31-4	34	151-212
51	Feb 5	Birmingham	6-1	W	16-31-4	36	157-213
52	Feb 11	Winnipeg	3-5	L	16-32-4	36	160-218
53	Feb 15	Quebec	9-6	W	17-32-4	38	169-224
54	Feb 17 @	Birmingham	*4-5	L	17-33-4	38	173-229
55	Feb 18	New England	1-4	L	17-34-4	38	174-233
56	Feb 19 @	Edmonton	3-4	L	17-35-4	38	177-237
57	Feb 25 @	Quebec	5-7	L	17-36-4	38	182-244
58	Feb 26 @	Birmingham	6-3	W	18-36-4	40	188-247
59	Mar 1	Houston	5-1	W	19-36-4	42	193-248
60	Mar 3 @	Edmonton	8-6	W	20-36-4	44	201-254
61	Mar 4	Winnipeg	8-6	W	21-36-4	46	209-260
62	Mar 5	Cincinnati	4-2	W	22-36-4	48	213-262
63	Mar 8	Quebec	*4-5	L	22-37-4	48	217-267
64	Mar 9 @	Winnipeg	5-6	L	22-38-4	48	222-273
65	Mar 11	Houston	4-2	W	23-38-4	50	226-275
66	Mar 12 @	Houston	3-6	L	23-39-4	50	229-281
67	Mar 15 @	New England	0-7	L	23-40-4	50	229-288
68	Mar 16 @	Quebec	2-5	L	23-41-4	50	231-293
69	Mar 18 @	Cincinnati	2-4	L	23-42-4	50	233-297
70	Mar 19 @	Birmingham	3-3	T	23-42-5	51	236-300
71	Mar 21 @	New England	3-6	L	23-43-5	51	239-306
72	Mar 24 @	Edmonton	0-4	L	23-44-5	51	239-310
73	Mar 28	Edmonton	*3-4	L	23-45-5	51	242-314
74	Mar 30	Winnipeg	1-4	L	23-46-5	51	243-318
75	Apr 1	Edmonton	1-4	L	23-47-5	51	244-322
76	Apr 2	Cincinnati	6-3	W	24-47-5	53	250-325
77	Apr 7	Cincinnati	4-6	L	24-48-5	53	254-331
78	Apr 8 @	Quebec	3-7	L	24-49-5	53	257-338
79	Apr 9	Birmingham	7-9	L	24-50-5	53	264-347
80	Apr 11 @	New England	3-6	L	24-51-5	53	267-353

Racers Stars of 1977-1978

Claude St. Sauveur	Peter Driscoll	Kevin Devine	Barry Wilkins	Gilles Marotte	Michel Parizeau
36 goals led team	25 goals, 130 minutes	19 goals, 141 minutes	23 points on blueline	Hard-hitting defenseman	40 points

Scoring

pos	#	player	gp	g	a	pts	pim	+/-	ppg	shg	sog	sc%	gp	g	a	pts	pim	+/-
C	26	Adduono, Ray	8	1	2	3	0	-5	0	0	10	0.100	-	-	-	-	-	-
D	5	Baltimore, Bryon	22	1	7	8	47	0	0	0	14	0.071	-	-	-	-	-	-
D	25	Blackwood, Bill	3	0	0	0	0		0	0	4	0.000	-	-	-	-	-	-
D	24	Block, Ken	77	1	25	26	34	-39	1	0	30	0.033	-	-	-	-	-	-
LW	15	Burgess, Don	79	11	12	23	2	-30	2	0	100	0.110	-	-	-	-	-	-
LW	26	Constantin, Charles	6	2	1	3	0	+1	2	0	7	0.286	-	-	-	-	-	-
LW	12	Devine, Kevin	76	19	23	42	141	-24	1	0	143	0.133	-	-	-	-	-	-
D	26	Dornseif, Dave	3	0	1	1	0	+1	0	0	1	0.000	-	-	-	-	-	-
LW	23	Driscoll, Peter	56	25	21	46	130	0	5	0	122	0.205	-	-	-	-	-	-
D	22	Fortier, Dave	54	1	15	16	86	-17	0	0	69	0.014	-	-	-	-	-	-
LW	11	French, John	74	9	8	17	6	-25	2	2	67	0.134	-	-	-	-	-	-
RW	19	Goldsworthy, Bill	32	8	10	18	10	+2	0	0	51	0.157	-	-	-	-	-	-
C	7	Harris, Hugh	19	1	7	8	6	-4	0	0	23	0.043	-	-	-	-	-	-
D	2	Inkpen, Dave	24	1	9	10	24	-5	0	0	26	0.038	-	-	-	-	-	-
G	30	Inness, Gary	52	0	0	0	42		0	0	0	-	-	-	-	-	-	-
D	3	Irwin, Glen	20	0	0	0	72		0	0		-	-	-	-	-	-	-
LW	9	Larose, Claude	28	14	16	30	12	-15	3	0	68	0.206	-	-	-	-	-	-
RW	8	Leclerc, Rene	60	12	15	27	31	-7	2	0	110	0.109	-	-	-	-	-	-
C	10	Leduc, Richie	28	10	15	25	38	-16	3	0	70	0.143	-	-	-	-	-	-
D	2	Maggs, Darryl	51	6	15	21	30	-27	3	0	116	0.052	-	-	-	-	-	-
D	5	Marotte, Gilles	44	2	13	15	18	-17	0	0	49	0.041	-	-	-	-	-	-
G	1	McDuffe, Pete	12	0	0	0	0		0	0	0	-	-	-	-	-	-	-
G	31	Mio, Ed	17	0	0	0	0		0	0	0	-	-	-	-	-	-	-
D	4	Morrison, Kevin	75	17	40	57	49	-32	6	1	206	0.083	-	-	-	-	-	-
RW	6	Paiement, Rosaire	61	6	24	30	81	-13	1	0	84	0.071	-	-	-	-	-	-
C	16	Parizeau, Michel	70	13	27	40	47	-13	2	0	75	0.173	-	-	-	-	-	-
G	28	Park, Jim	12	0	0	0	6		0	0	0	-	-	-	-	-	-	-
RW	17	Patenaude, Rusty	73	23	19	42	71	-20	1	0	197	0.117	-	-	-	-	-	-
C	21	Powis, Lynn	14	4	6	10	2	-5	0	0	34	0.118	-	-	-	-	-	-
D	21	Prentice, Bill	71	1	1	2	28	-4	0	0	28	0.036	-	-	-	-	-	-
C	10	Rhiness, Brad	12	3	3	6	12	-4	0	0	14	0.214	-	-	-	-	-	-
LW	20	St. Sauveur, Claude	72	36	42	78	24	-5	7	0	218	0.165	-	-	-	-	-	-
C	18	Sheehan, Bobby	29	8	7	15	6	-19	1	3	70	0.114	-	-	-	-	-	-
LW	26	Smedsmo, Dale	6	0	3	3	7	+3	0	0	9	0.000	-	-	-	-	-	-
RW	19	Spring, Frank	13	2	4	6	2	+1	1	0	20	0.100	-	-	-	-	-	-
RW	7	Stoughton, Blaine	47	13	13	26	28	-24	5	0	102	0.127	-	-	-	-	-	-
LW	9	Thomas, Reg	49	15	16	31	44	-11	7	0	120	0.125	-	-	-	-	-	-
D	14	Wilkins, Barry	79	2	21	23	79	-35	1	0	89	0.022	-	-	-	-	-	-

Power Play: 56 goals scored in 317 opportunities (17.7%) with 13 short-handed goals allowed.
Penalty Killing: 51 goals allowed in 241 opportunities (78.8%) with 6 short-handed goals scored.

Goaltending

goaltender	gp	min	ga	en	so	record	gaa	sog	sv%	gp	min	ga	record	gaa
Inness, Gary	52	2850	200	6	0	14-30-4	4.21	1543	0.870	-	-	-	-	-
McDuffe, Peter	12	539	39	1	0	1-6-1	4.34	313	0.875	-	-	-	-	-
Mio, Ed	17	900	64	1	0	6-8-0	4.27	470	0.864	-	-	-	-	-
Park, Jim	12	589	41	1	0	3-7-0	4.21	323	0.873	-	-	-	-	-

Transactions: Lynn Powis signed to contract, May 1977 • Kevin Morrison signed to contract, Jul 1977 • Mike Zuke and Dave Inkpen traded to Edmonton for Kevin Devine, Blair MacDonald, Barry Wilkins, Rusty Patenaude and Claude St Sauveur, Sep 1977 • Dave Fortier, Gary Inness, Pete McDuffe, Frank Spring signed to contracts, Sep 1977 • Dave Inkpen and Peter Driscoll purchased from Quebec, Dec 1977 • Lynn Powis released, signed by Winnipeg, Dec 1977 • Bill Goldsworthy acquired from NY Rangers (NHL) for Frank Spring, Dec 1977 • Bryon Baltimore and Hugh Harris traded to Cincinnati for Gilles Marotte and Blaine Stoughton, Jan 1978 • Darryl Maggs and Reg Thomas traded to Cincinnati for Rich Leduc and Claude Larose, Feb 1978 • Ed Mio purchased from Birmingham, Feb 1978 • Glenn Irwin acquired from Houston for future considerations, Mar 1978 • Charles Constantin acquired from Quebec for future considerations, Mar 1978 • Dale Smedsmo, Bill Blackwood signed to contracts, Mar 1978

1977-1978 NEW ENGLAND WHALERS

Coach
Harry Neale

Summary of Games (@ Away, * Overtime)

	date	opponent	score		record	pts	gf-ga		date	opponent	score		record	pts	gf-ga
1	Oct 12 @	Houston	3-0	W	1-0-0	2	3-0	41	Jan 14	Houston	*4-5	L	26-12-3	55	172-130
2	Oct 15	Birmingham	5-2	W	2-0-0	4	8-2	42	Jan 18 @	Edmonton	0-1	L	26-13-3	55	172-131
3	Oct 16 @	Cincinnati	2-6	L	2-1-0	4	10-8	43	Jan 20 @	Winnipeg	4-4	T	26-13-4	56	176-135
4	Oct 18 @	Indianapolis	2-2	T	2-1-1	5	12-10	44	Jan 21 @	Quebec	2-3	L	26-14-4	56	178-138
5	Oct 19 @	Edmonton	6-3	W	3-1-1	7	18-13	45	Jan 22	Quebec	6-3	W	27-14-4	58	184-141
6	Oct 21 @	Winnipeg	5-2	W	4-1-1	9	23-15	46	Jan 25 @	Cincinnati	*7-8	L	27-15-4	58	191-149
7	Oct 26	Quebec	7-1	W	5-1-1	11	30-16	47	Jan 27 @	Birmingham	6-2	W	28-15-4	60	197-151
8	Oct 29	Houston	7-2	W	6-1-1	13	37-18	48	Jan 28 @	Houston	3-0	W	29-15-4	62	200-151
9	Nov 1 @	Quebec	6-3	W	7-1-1	15	43-21	49	Jan 29 @	Houston	4-6	L	29-16-4	62	204-157
10	Nov 4	Cincinnati	4-3	W	8-1-1	17	47-24	50	Feb 1	Edmonton	4-3	W	30-16-4	64	208-160
11	Nov 6 @	Cincinnati	5-2	W	9-1-1	19	52-26	51	Feb 3	Edmonton	3-6	L	30-17-4	64	211-166
12	Nov 8 @	Birmingham	4-3	W	10-1-1	21	56-29	52	Feb 4 @	Houston	4-5	L	30-18-4	64	215-171
13	Nov 10	Edmonton	5-3	W	11-1-1	23	61-32	53	Feb 11 @	Cincinnati	8-7	W	31-18-4	66	223-178
14	Nov 12	Indianapolis	5-3	W	12-1-1	25	66-35	54	Feb 14	Quebec	5-1	W	32-18-4	68	228-179
15	Nov 15 @	Indianapolis	6-4	W	13-1-1	27	72-39	55	Feb 16	Winnipeg	*1-2	L	32-19-4	68	229-181
16	Nov 18	Winnipeg	3-2	W	14-1-1	29	75-41	56	Feb 18 @	Indianapolis	4-1	W	33-19-4	70	233-182
17	Nov 20 @	Edmonton	*5-4	W	15-1-1	31	80-45	57	Feb 21 @	Quebec	*5-6	L	33-20-4	70	238-188
18	Nov 22 @	Quebec	4-5	L	15-2-1	31	84-50	58	Feb 22 @	Winnipeg	2-4	L	33-21-4	70	240-192
19	Nov 23	Indianapolis	3-3	T	15-2-2	32	87-53	59	Feb 24 @	Winnipeg	2-7	L	33-22-4	70	242-199
20	Nov 25	Quebec	2-6	L	15-3-2	32	89-59	60	Feb 26 @	Edmonton	6-5	W	34-22-4	72	248-204
21	Nov 26	Edmonton	1-3	L	15-4-2	32	90-62	61	Mar 1	Quebec	*3-4	L	34-23-4	72	251-208
22	Nov 30 @	Houston	3-3	T	15-4-3	33	93-65	62	Mar 3	Houston	*2-3	L	34-24-4	72	253-211
23	Dec 2	Winnipeg	4-1	W	16-4-3	35	97-66	63	Mar 4	Birmingham	2-5	L	34-25-4	72	255-216
24	Dec 3	Cincinnati	2-5	L	16-5-3	35	99-71	64	Mar 5 @	Quebec	1-2	L	34-26-4	72	256-218
25	Dec 6 @	Indianapolis	2-5	L	16-6-3	35	101-76	65	Mar 9 @	Houston	4-6	L	34-27-4	72	260-224
26	Dec 7 @	Birmingham	6-3	W	17-6-3	37	107-79	66	Mar 10 @	Birmingham	*5-4	W	35-27-4	74	265-228
27	Dec 9 @	Birmingham	2-1	W	18-6-3	39	109-80	67	Mar 14	Birmingham	6-0	W	36-27-4	76	271-228
28	Dec 14	Soviet All-Stars	7-2	W	19-6-3	41	116-82	68	Mar 15	Indianapolis	7-0	W	37-27-4	78	278-228
29	Dec 16	Czechoslovakia	5-3	W	20-6-3	43	121-85	69	Mar 17 @	Cincinnati	6-2	W	38-27-4	80	284-230
30	Dec 17	Winnipeg	3-6	L	20-7-3	43	124-91	70	Mar 18 @	Quebec	3-5	L	38-28-4	80	287-235
31	Dec 18 @	Winnipeg	3-7	L	20-8-3	43	127-98	71	Mar 21	Indianapolis	6-3	W	39-28-4	82	293-238
32	Dec 23	Indianapolis	5-3	W	21-8-3	45	132-101	72	Mar 22	Winnipeg	3-5	L	39-29-4	82	296-243
33	Dec 27	Birmingham	8-1	W	22-8-3	47	140-102	73	Mar 24	Houston	0-1	L	39-30-4	82	296-244
34	Dec 30	Birmingham	6-2	W	23-8-3	49	146-104	74	Mar 26	Edmonton	5-3	W	40-30-4	84	301-247
35	Jan 1 @	Cincinnati	*4-3	W	24-8-3	51	150-107	75	Mar 29	Cincinnati	6-1	W	41-30-4	86	307-248
36	Jan 4	Quebec	4-6	L	24-9-3	51	154-113	76	Apr 3	Houston	8-6	W	42-30-4	88	315-254
37	Jan 6 @	Indianapolis	3-4	L	24-10-3	51	157-117	77	Apr 5 @	Edmonton	4-4	T	42-30-5	89	319-258
38	Jan 7	Cincinnati	5-3	W	25-10-3	53	162-120	78	Apr 6 @	Winnipeg	4-7	L	42-31-5	89	323-265
39	Jan 8	Birmingham	4-5	L	25-11-3	53	166-125	79	Apr 10	Cincinnati	6-1	W	43-31-5	91	329-266
40	Jan 13	Edmonton	2-0	W	26-11-3	55	168-125	80	Apr 11	Indianapolis	6-3	W	44-31-5	93	335-269

Home games after January 18, 1978, played at Springfield, Massachusetts.

Whalers Stars of 1977-1978

Gordie Howe	Mark Howe	Mike Rogers	Dave Keon	Al Smith	George Lyle
96 points led team	91 points	28 goals	62 points	30 wins	30 goals

Scoring

pos	#	player	gp	g	a	pts	pim	+/-	ppg	shg	sog	sc%	gp	g	a	pts	pim	+/-
C	12	Antonovich, Mike	75	32	35	67	32	+17	5	0	243	0.132	14	10	7	17	4	+1
LW	21	Bolduc, Dan	41	5	5	10	22	+6	0	0	37	0.135	14	2	4	6	4	+2
D	22	Butters, Bill	45	1	13	14	69	+21	0	0	37	0.027	-	-	-	-	-	-
LW	23	Carlson, Jack	67	9	20	29	192	+9	0	0	81	0.111	9	1	1	2	14	+4
C	26	Carlson, Steve	38	6	7	13	11	+7	1	1	41	0.146	13	2	7	9	2	+4
C	11	Carroll, Greg	48	9	14	23	27	+3	0	2	70	0.129	-	-	-	-	-	-
D	10	Hangsleben, Alan	79	11	18	29	140	+17	0	0	152	0.072	14	1	4	5	37	+2
RW	9	Howe, Gordie	76	34	62	96	85	+46	16	0	163	0.209	14	5	5	10	15	0
D/F	5	Howe, Mark	70	30	61	91	32	+30	4	0	220	0.136	14	8	7	15	18	0
D	18	Howe, Marty	75	10	10	20	66	+10	1	0	146	0.068	14	1	1	2	13	-2
C	14	Keon, Dave	77	24	38	62	2	-4	1	5	169	0.142	14	5	11	16	4	+2
G	30	Levasseur, Louis	27	0	0	0	2		0	0	0	-	12	0	1	1	2	-
D	2	Ley, Rick	73	3	41	44	95	+36	0	0	106	0.028	14	1	8	9	4	+2
LW	16	Lyle, George	68	30	24	54	74	+12	3	0	161	0.186	12	2	1	3	13	+5
D	24	Maxwell, Bryan	17	2	1	3	11	+9	0	0	30	0.067	-	-	-	-	-	-
RW	27	Mayer, Jim	51	11	9	20	21	+1	1	0	57	0.193	-	-	-	-	-	-
RW	19	McKenzie, John	79	27	29	56	61	+15	9	0	135	0.200	14	6	6	12	6	-2
C	20	Peloffy, Andre	10	2	0	2	2	-2	0	0	6	0.333	2	0	0	0	0	-1
C	4	Pleau, Larry	54	16	18	34	4	+12	2	0	91	0.176	14	5	4	9	8	-2
D	6	Plumb, Ron	27	1	9	10	18	+6	0	0	74	0.014	14	1	5	6	16	+2
D	7	Roberts, Gordie	78	15	46	61	118	+17	5	0	135	0.111	14	0	5	5	29	+1
C	17	Rogers, Mike	80	28	43	71	46	+22	4	1	204	0.137	14	5	6	11	8	-2
D	3	Selwood, Brad	80	6	25	31	88	+11	2	0	109	0.055	14	0	3	3	8	+4
RW	15	Sheehy, Tim	25	8	11	19	12	-2	3	0	43	0.186	13	1	3	4	9	+1
G	1	Smith, Al	55	0	3	3	4		0	0	0	-	3	0	0	0	0	-
RW	8	Webster, Tom	20	15	5	20	5	+8	5	0	70	0.214	-	-	-	-	-	-

Power Play: 62 goals scored in 239 opportunities (25.9%) with 4 short-handed goals allowed.
Penalty Killing: 65 goals allowed in 315 opportunities (79.4%) with 9 short-handed goals scored.

Goaltending

goaltender	gp	min	ga	en	so	record	gaa	sog	sv%	gp	min	ga	record	gaa
Levasseur, Louis	27	1655	91	1	3	14-11-2	3.30	796	0.886	12	719	31	8-4	2.59
Smith, Al	55	3246	174	3	2	30-20-3	3.22	2306	0.885	3	120	14	0-2	7.00

Transactions: Bryan Maxwell and Greg Carroll acquired from Cincinnati for rights to Mike Liut, May 1977 • Gordie Howe, Mark Howe and Marty Howe signed to contracts, Jun 1977 • Brett Callighen acquired from Edmonton for future considerations, Jun 1977. Traded back to Edmonton with Dave Dryden for Louis Levasseur, Sep 1977 • Jim Mayer signed to contract, Jul 1977 • Andre Peloffy, Al Smith signed to contracts, Aug 1977 • Greg Carroll traded to Cincinnati for Ron Plumb, Feb 1978 • Bryan Maxwell released, Feb 1978 • Tim Sheehy signed as free agent, Feb 1978 • Bill Butters waived, Mar 1978

1977-1978 QUEBEC NORDIQUES

Coach
Marc Boileau
27-30-2

Coach
Maurice Filion
13-7-1

Summary of Games (@ Away, * Overtime)

	date	opponent	score		record	pts	gf-ga
1	Oct 13 @	Winnipeg	2-5	L	0-1-0	0	2-5
2	Oct 14 @	Edmonton	2-4	L	0-2-0	0	4-9
3	Oct 15	Edmonton	6-2	W	1-2-0	2	10-11
4	Oct 18	Cincinnati	5-1	W	2-2-0	4	15-12
5	Oct 21 @	Indianapolis	4-4	T	2-2-1	5	19-16
6	Oct 22	Birmingham	8-5	W	3-2-1	7	27-21
7	Oct 26 @	New England	1-7	L	3-3-1	7	28-28
8	Oct 30	Houston	5-4	W	4-3-1	9	33-32
9	Nov 1	New England	3-6	L	4-4-1	9	36-38
10	Nov 4 @	Houston	7-6	W	5-4-1	11	43-44
11	Nov 5 @	Birmingham	*4-5	L	5-5-1	11	47-49
12	Nov 8	Edmonton	7-3	W	6-5-1	13	54-52
13	Nov 11 @	Winnipeg	*3-2	W	7-5-1	15	57-54
14	Nov 12	Cincinnati	*5-6	L	7-6-1	15	62-60
15	Nov 15	Winnipeg	*7-6	W	8-6-1	17	69-66
16	Nov 18 @	Houston	5-6	L	8-7-1	17	74-72
17	Nov 20	Indianapolis	5-2	W	9-7-1	19	79-74
18	Nov 22	New England	5-4	W	10-7-1	21	84-78
19	Nov 23 @	Cincinnati	3-4	L	10-8-1	21	87-82
20	Nov 25 @	New England	6-2	W	11-8-1	23	93-84
21	Nov 26	Birmingham	4-2	W	12-8-1	25	97-86
22	Nov 29	Cincinnati	2-3	L	12-9-1	25	99-89
23	Dec 1 @	Indianapolis	4-5	L	12-10-1	25	103-94
24	Dec 3	Winnipeg	6-5	W	13-10-1	27	109-99
25	Dec 6	Houston	*4-3	W	14-10-1	29	113-102
26	Dec 10	Indianapolis	5-3	W	15-10-1	31	118-105
27	Dec 11	Czechoslovakia	8-4	W	16-10-1	33	126-109
28	Dec 26 @	Winnipeg	4-9	L	16-11-1	33	130-118
29	Dec 27 @	Edmonton	3-9	L	16-12-1	33	133-127
30	Jan 1 @	Birmingham	5-2	W	17-12-1	35	138-129
31	Jan 3	Soviet All-Stars	3-3	T	17-12-2	36	141-132
32	Jan 4 @	New England	6-4	W	18-12-2	38	147-136
33	Jan 6 @	Cincinnati	3-5	L	18-13-2	38	150-141
34	Jan 10	Birmingham	6-4	W	19-13-2	40	156-145
35	Jan 11 @	Indianapolis	1-2	L	19-14-2	40	157-147
36	Jan 14	Edmonton	7-4	W	20-14-2	42	164-151
37	Jan 15	Cincinnati	3-6	L	20-15-2	42	167-157
38	Jan 18 @	Winnipeg	1-5	L	20-16-2	42	168-162
39	Jan 20 @	Cincinnati	8-2	W	21-16-2	44	176-164
40	Jan 21	New England	3-2	W	22-16-2	46	179-166
41	Jan 22 @	New England	3-6	L	22-17-2	46	182-172
42	Jan 24	Houston	5-6	L	22-18-2	46	187-178
43	Jan 27 @	Edmonton	6-9	L	22-19-2	46	193-187
44	Jan 29 @	Edmonton	4-3	W	23-19-2	48	197-190
45	Jan 31	Winnipeg	2-7	L	23-20-2	48	199-197
46	Feb 2 @	Birmingham	4-2	W	24-20-2	50	203-199
47	Feb 3 @	Indianapolis	*4-5	L	24-21-2	50	207-204
48	Feb 4	Edmonton	*3-4	L	24-22-2	50	210-208
49	Feb 7	Birmingham	8-3	W	25-22-2	52	218-211
50	Feb 9 @	Houston	1-2	L	25-23-2	52	219-213
51	Feb 11 @	Houston	4-8	L	25-24-2	52	223-221
52	Feb 12 @	Cincinnati	2-8	L	25-25-2	52	225-229
53	Feb 14 @	New England	1-5	L	25-26-2	52	226-234
54	Feb 15 @	Indianapolis	6-9	L	25-27-2	52	232-243
55	Feb 17 @	Edmonton	4-6	L	25-28-2	52	236-249
56	Feb 19 @	Winnipeg	2-5	L	25-29-2	52	238-254
57	Feb 21	New England	*6-5	W	26-29-2	54	244-259
58	Feb 23 @	Birmingham	3-7	L	26-30-2	54	247-266
59	Feb 25	Indianapolis	7-5	W	27-30-2	56	254-271
60	Feb 28	Houston	5-2	W	28-30-2	58	259-273
61	Mar 1 @	New England	*4-3	W	29-30-2	60	263-276
62	Mar 4	Houston	3-3	T	29-30-3	61	266-279
63	Mar 5	New England	2-1	W	30-30-3	63	268-280
64	Mar 7	Cincinnati	4-5	L	30-31-3	63	272-285
65	Mar 8 @	Indianapolis	*5-4	W	31-31-3	65	277-289
66	Mar 9 @	Birmingham	2-9	L	31-32-3	65	279-298
67	Mar 11	Winnipeg	4-7	L	31-33-3	65	283-305
68	Mar 14	Edmonton	6-3	W	32-33-3	67	289-308
69	Mar 16	Indianapolis	5-2	W	33-33-3	69	294-310
70	Mar 18	New England	5-3	W	34-33-3	71	299-313
71	Mar 19 @	Winnipeg	3-5	L	34-34-3	71	302-318
72	Mar 21	Birmingham	4-5	L	34-35-3	71	306-323
73	Mar 24 @	Birmingham	*4-3	W	35-35-3	73	310-326
74	Mar 25 @	Houston	3-4	L	35-36-3	73	313-330
75	Mar 28	Cincinnati	6-4	W	36-36-3	75	319-334
76	Apr 1	Winnipeg	5-2	W	37-36-3	77	324-336
77	Apr 2	Houston	7-1	W	38-36-3	79	331-337
78	Apr 4	Edmonton	9-1	W	39-36-3	81	340-338
79	Apr 8	Indianapolis	7-3	W	40-36-3	83	347-341
80	Apr 9 @	Cincinnati	2-6	L	40-37-3	83	349-347

Nordiques Stars of 1977-1978

Marc Tardif	**Real Cloutier**	**Paulin Bordeleau**	**Matti Hagman**	**Jean Bernier**	**Garry Lariviere**
Record 154 points	129 points	42 goals	25 goals	+22 rating	56 points, +3 rating

Scoring

					Regular Season								**Playoffs**						
pos	#	player	gp	g	a	pts	pim	+/-	ppg	shg	sog	sc%	gp	g	a	pts	pim	+/-
D	4	Baxter, Paul	76	6	29	35	240	-37	0	0	145	0.041	11	4	7	11	42	0
D	24	Bernier, Jean	74	10	32	42	4	+22	1	1	135	0.074	10	3	4	7	2	+2
C	21	Bernier, Serge	58	26	52	78	48	-1	9	1	180	0.144	11	4	10	14	17	-1
C	11	Bordeleau, Christian	26	9	22	31	28	+6	3	0	72	0.125	10	1	5	6	6	0
RW	17	Bordeleau, Paulin	77	42	23	65	29	-13	7	2	217	0.194	11	4	6	10	2	+1
LW	18	Boudrias, Andre	66	10	17	27	22	+4	1	2	70	0.143	11	0	2	2	4	-2
RW	15	Brackenbury, Curt	33	4	9	13	54	+4	0	0	41	0.098	10	1	1	2	31	-2
G	30	Broderick, Ken	24	0	0	0	0		0	0	0		2	0	0	0	0	-
G	1	Brodeur, Richard	36	0	2	2	0		0	0	1	0.000	11	0	0	0	0	-
RW	9	Cloutier, Real	73	56	73	129	19	+14	20	0	312	0.179	10	9	7	16	15	0
LW	14	Constantin, Charles	48	2	4	6	50	-3	0	0	42	0.048	-	-	-	-	-	-
G	25	Corsi, Jim	23	0	1	1	2		0	0	0		-	-	-	-	-	-
LW	26	Cote, Alain	27	3	5	8	8	-9	1	0	19	0.158	11	1	2	3	0	-3
D	7	Dorey, Jim	26	1	9	10	23	-5	0	0	32	0.031	11	0	3	3	34	-2
LW	10	Driscoll, Peter	21	3	7	10	28	-1	1	0	32	0.094	-	-	-	-	-	-
LW	20	Dube, Norm	73	16	31	47	17	-10	3	0	148	0.108	10	2	2	4	6	+4
D	16	Evans, Chris	36	0	2	2	22	-4	0	0	36	0.000	-	-	-	-	-	-
C	12	Fitchner, Bob	72	15	28	43	76	-5	2	1	125	0.120	11	1	6	7	10	-3
LW	13	Guite, Pierre	8	4	5	9	15	+6	1	0	29	0.138	-	-	-	-	-	-
C	10	Hagman, Matti	53	25	31	56	16	-14	9	0	108	0.231	-	-	-	-	-	-
D	6	Inkpen, Dave	24	0	1	1	20	-6	0	0	8	0.000	-	-	-	-	-	-
D	22	Lacombe, Francois	22	1	7	8	12	+1	0	0	27	0.037	10	1	4	5	2	0
LW	28	Lagace, Pierre	17	2	4	6	12	+1	0	0	11	0.182	1	0	0	0	0	-1
D	5	Lariviere, Garry	80	7	49	56	78	+3	2	0	149	0.047	11	3	2	5	4	-7
G	31	Mattsson, Markus	6	0	0	0	0		0	0	0	-	-	-	-	-	-	-
G	30	McLeod, Don	7	0	3	3	0		0	0	0	-	-	-	-	-	-	-
RW	23	Miller, Warren	60	14	24	38	50	-26	2	1	121	0.116	11	0	2	2	0	-3
LW	27	Morris, Rick	25	0	5	5	40	+1	0	0	22	0.000	-	-	-	-	-	-
LW	19	Sutherland, Steve	75	23	10	33	143	-15	1	2	138	0.167	11	2	0	2	37	-4
LW	8	Tardif, Marc	78	65	89	154	50	+15	16	1	375	0.173	11	6	9	15	11	-2
D	3	Tremblay, J. C.	54	5	37	42	26	-14	0	0	106	0.047	1	0	1	1	0	-2
D	2	Weir, Wally	13	0	0	0	47	-5	0	0	21	0.000	11	1	2	3	50	-4

Power Play: 79 goals scored in 277 opportunities (28.5%) with 10 short-handed goals allowed.
Penalty Killing: 60 goals allowed in 269 opportunities (77.7%) with 11 short-handed goals scored.

Goaltending

goaltender	gp	min	ga	en	so	record	gaa	sog	sv%	gp	min	ga	record	gaa
Broderick, Ken	24	1140	83	0	0	9-8-1	4.37	590	0.859	2	48	2	0-1	2.50
Brodeur, Richard	36	1962	121	1	0	18-15-2	3.70	1120	0.892	11	622	38	5-5	3.67
Corsi, Jim	23	1089	82	1	0	10-7-0	4.52	647	0.873	-	-	-	-	-
Mattsson, Markus	6	266	30	0	0	1-3-0	6.77	166	0.819	-	-	-	-	-
McLeod, Don	7	403	28	1	0	2-4-0	4.17	215	0.870	-	-	-	-	-

Transactions: Don McLeod signed to contract, Aug 1977 • Chris Evans claimed on waivers, Nov 1977 • Matti Hagman purchased from Boston (NHL), Dec 1977 • Pierre Guite and Don McLeod traded to Edmonton for Dave Inkpen, Ken Broderick, Warren Miller and Rick Morris, Dec 1977 • Peter Driscoll and Dave Inkpen sold to Indianapolis, Dec 1977 • Markus Mattsson acquired from Winnipeg for cash and draft picks, Jan 1978. Returned to Winnipeg, Mar 1978 • Charlie Constantin traded to Indianapolis for future considerations, Mar 1978

1977-1978 WINNIPEG JETS

Coach
Larry Hillman

Summary of Games (@ Away, * Overtime)

	date	opponent	score		record	pts	gf-ga		date	opponent	score		record	pts	gf-ga
1	Oct 12 @	Edmonton	7-3	W	1-0-0	2	7-3	41	Jan 18	Quebec	5-1	W	26-14-1	53	195-124
2	Oct 13	Quebec	5-2	W	2-0-0	4	12-5	42	Jan 20	New England	4-4	T	26-14-2	54	199-128
3	Oct 15 @	Cincinnati	5-4	W	3-0-0	6	17-9	43	Jan 22	Indianapolis	4-5	L	26-15-2	54	203-133
4	Oct 16	Indianapolis	9-1	W	4-0-0	8	26-10	44	Jan 23 @	Birmingham	2-6	L	26-16-2	54	205-139
5	Oct 21	New England	2-5	L	4-1-0	8	28-15	45	Jan 26 @	Houston	*1-2	L	26-17-2	54	206-141
6	Oct 23	Birmingham	10-3	W	5-1-0	10	38-18	46	Jan 28 @	Birmingham	5-8	L	26-18-2	54	211-149
7	Oct 26 @	Indianapolis	3-5	L	5-2-0	10	41-23	47	Jan 29 @	Cincinnati	8-4	W	27-18-2	56	219-153
8	Oct 28	Cincinnati	3-2	W	6-2-0	12	44-25	48	Jan 31 @	Quebec	7-2	W	28-18-2	58	226-155
9	Oct 30	Edmonton	5-2	W	7-2-0	14	49-27	49	Feb 4 @	Cincinnati	7-5	W	29-18-2	60	233-160
10	Nov 2 @	Edmonton	6-3	W	8-2-0	16	55-30	50	Feb 5	Edmonton	4-3	W	30-18-2	62	237-163
11	Nov 4 @	Birmingham	4-2	W	9-2-0	18	59-32	51	Feb 8	Birmingham	9-0	W	31-18-2	64	246-163
12	Nov 5 @	Cincinnati	6-1	W	10-2-0	20	65-33	52	Feb 10	Cincinnati	10-2	W	32-18-2	66	256-165
13	Nov 9	Houston	4-3	W	11-2-0	22	69-36	53	Feb 11 @	Indianapolis	5-3	W	33-18-2	68	261-168
14	Nov 11	Quebec	*2-3	L	11-3-0	22	71-39	54	Feb 12 @	Houston	6-5	W	34-18-2	70	267-173
15	Nov 13	Cincinnati	2-3	L	11-4-0	22	73-42	55	Feb 15	Edmonton	6-5	W	35-18-2	72	273-178
16	Nov 15 @	Quebec	*6-7	L	11-5-0	22	79-49	56	Feb 16 @	New England	*2-1	W	36-18-2	74	275-179
17	Nov 16	Birmingham	2-2	T	11-5-1	23	81-51	57	Feb 18 @	Cincinnati	4-0	W	37-18-2	76	279-179
18	Nov 18 @	New England	2-3	L	11-6-1	23	83-54	58	Feb 19	Quebec	5-2	W	38-18-2	78	284-181
19	Nov 19 @	Indianapolis	6-4	W	12-6-1	25	89-58	59	Feb 22	New England	4-2	W	39-18-2	80	288-183
20	Nov 22 @	Edmonton	2-4	L	12-7-1	25	91-62	60	Feb 24	New England	7-2	W	40-18-2	82	295-185
21	Nov 27	Birmingham	3-4	L	12-8-1	25	94-66	61	Feb 26	Houston	9-6	W	41-18-2	84	304-191
22	Dec 2 @	New England	1-4	L	12-9-1	25	95-70	62	Mar 1 @	Birmingham	3-4	L	41-19-2	84	307-195
23	Dec 3 @	Quebec	5-6	L	12-10-1	25	100-76	63	Mar 3	Cincinnati	1-5	L	41-20-2	84	308-200
24	Dec 4	Edmonton	2-3	L	12-11-1	25	102-79	64	Mar 4 @	Indianapolis	6-8	L	41-21-2	84	314-208
25	Dec 7	Houston	5-2	W	13-11-1	27	107-81	65	Mar 5	Houston	3-4	L	41-22-2	84	317-212
26	Dec 9	Cincinnati	*3-4	L	13-12-1	27	110-85	66	Mar 9	Indianapolis	6-5	W	42-22-2	86	323-217
27	Dec 11	Indianapolis	7-1	W	14-12-1	29	117-86	67	Mar 11 @	Quebec	7-4	W	43-22-2	88	330-221
28	Dec 13	Czechoslovakia	5-1	W	15-12-1	31	122-87	68	Mar 12	Birmingham	3-2	W	44-22-2	90	333-223
29	Dec 17 @	New England	6-3	W	16-12-1	33	128-90	69	Mar 15	Edmonton	8-4	W	45-22-2	92	341-227
30	Dec 18	New England	7-3	W	17-12-1	35	135-93	70	Mar 17 @	Edmonton	2-6	L	45-23-2	92	343-233
31	Dec 20	Soviet All-Stars	6-4	W	18-12-1	37	141-97	71	Mar 19	Quebec	5-3	W	46-23-2	94	348-236
32	Dec 21 @	Houston	4-3	W	19-12-1	39	145-100	72	Mar 22 @	New England	5-3	W	47-23-2	96	353-239
33	Dec 23 @	Cincinnati	6-4	W	20-12-1	41	151-104	73	Mar 25 @	Birmingham	3-1	W	48-23-2	98	356-240
34	Dec 26	Quebec	9-4	W	21-12-1	43	160-108	74	Mar 28 @	Houston	3-5	L	48-24-2	98	359-245
35	Jan 6 @	Edmonton	4-1	W	22-12-1	45	164-109	75	Mar 30 @	Indianapolis	4-1	W	49-24-2	100	363-246
36	Jan 8	Indianapolis	4-2	W	23-12-1	47	168-111	76	Apr 1 @	Quebec	2-5	L	49-25-2	100	365-251
37	Jan 11	Birmingham	11-2	W	24-12-1	49	179-113	77	Apr 4 @	Houston	3-6	L	49-26-2	100	368-257
38	Jan 13 @	Houston	2-3	L	24-13-1	49	181-116	78	Apr 6	New England	7-4	W	50-26-2	102	375-261
39	Jan 14 @	Indianapolis	6-3	W	25-13-1	51	187-119	79	Apr 7 @	Edmonton	2-4	L	50-27-2	102	377-265
40	Jan 15	Edmonton	*3-4	L	25-14-1	51	190-123	80	Apr 9	Houston	4-5	L	50-28-2	102	381-270

Jets Stars of 1977-1978

Andres Hedberg
63 goals, 122 points

Ulf Nilsson
89 assists, 126 points

Bobby Hull
117 points

Gary Bromley
1.57 average in playoffs

Joe Daley
21 wins

Kent Nilsson
107 points as rookie

Scoring

						Regular Season									Playoffs				
pos	#	player	gp	g	a	pts	pim	+/-	ppg	shg	sog	sc%	gp	g	a	pts	pim	+/-
D	2	Amodeo, Mike	3	1	1	2	0	+3	0	0	4	0.250	7	1	3	4	19	-2
D	26	Baird, Ken	49	14	7	21	29	+5	2	0	66	0.212	7	0	4	4	7	+1
D	2	Bergman, Thommie	65	5	28	33	43	+22	0	0	139	0.036	-	-	-	-	-	-
G	30	Bromley, Gary	39	0	1	1	0		0	0	0	-	5	0	0	0	2	-
D	5	Clackson, Kim	52	2	7	9	203	+6	0	0	42	0.048	9	0	1	1	61	+6
G	1	Daley, Joe	37	0	2	2	2		0	0	0	-	5	0	1	1	20	-
D	7	Davis, Bill	12	0	0	0	2	-9	0	0	9	0.000	-	-	-	-	-	-
D	8	Dunn, David	66	6	20	26	79	+20	1	0	53	0.113	9	1	2	3	0	+8
D	24	Ford, Mike	3	0	0	0	0	-5	0	0	6	0.000	2	1	0	1	0	-1
D	6	Green, Ted	73	4	22	26	52	+19	2	0	88	0.045	8	0	2	2	2	+4
LW	18	Guindon, Robert	71	20	22	42	18	-1	0	4	127	0.157	9	8	5	13	5	+9
RW	15	Hedberg, Anders	77	63	59	122	60	+60	17	6	290	0.217	9	9	6	15	2	+5
D	24	Hornung, Larry	19	1	4	5	2	+17	0	0	13	0.077	-	-	-	-	-	-
C	25	Huck, Fran	5	0	0	0	2	-2	0	0	4	0.000	-	-	-	-	-	-
LW	9	Hull, Bobby	77	46	71	117	23	+55	10	0	257	0.179	9	8	3	11	12	+5
LW	16	Kryskow, Dave	71	20	21	41	16	+12	3	0	103	0.194	9	4	4	8	2	+1
LW	21	Labraaten, Dan	47	18	16	34	30	+7	5	0	81	0.222	4	1	1	2	8	+4
LW	17	Lesuk, Bill	80	9	18	27	48	-4	0	0	85	0.106	9	2	5	7	12	+9
RW	20	Lindstrom, Willy	77	30	30	60	42	+4	7	0	151	0.199	8	3	4	7	17	+3
D	3	Long, Barry	78	7	24	31	42	+10	1	1	159	0.044	9	0	5	5	6	+11
G	35	Mattsson, Markus	10	0	0	0	2		0	0	0	-	-	-	-	-	-	-
LW	22	Moffat, Lyle	57	9	16	25	39	-6	0	0	58	0.155	9	5	7	12	9	+3
C	11	Nilsson, Kent	80	42	65	107	8	+27	18	0	212	0.198	9	2	8	10	10	+2
C	14	Nilsson, Ulf	73	37	89	126	89	+41	7	3	180	0.206	9	1	13	14	12	+5
C	19	Powis, Lynn	55	12	19	31	16	+2	2	0	68	0.176	3	2	1	3	7	+2
RW	23	Ruhnke, Kent	21	8	9	17	2	+9	0	0	26	0.308	5	2	0	2	0	-2
D	4	Sjoberg, Lars-Erik	78	11	39	50	72	+60	0	1	133	0.083	9	0	9	9	4	+8
C	10	Sullivan, Peter	77	16	39	55	43	-12	3	1	130	0.123	9	3	4	7	4	+3

Power Play: 78 goals scored in 330 opportunities (23.6%) with 10 short-handed goals allowed.
Penalty Killing: 44 goals allowed in 233 opportunities (81.1%) with 16 short-handed goals scored.

Goaltending

goaltender	gp	min	ga	en	so	record	gaa	sog	sv%	gp	min	ga	record	gaa
Bromley, Gary	39	2250	124	0	1	25-12-1	3.31	1090	0.886	5	268	7	4-0	1.57
Daley, Joe	37	2075	114	1	1	21-11-1	3.30	971	0.883	5	271	13	4-1	2.88
Mattsson, Markus	10	511	30	1	0	4-5-0	3.52	257	0.883	-	-	-	-	-

Transactions: Gary Bromley, Larry Hornung signed to contracts, May 1977 • Kent Nilsson signed to contract, Jul 1977 • Kim Clackson signed to contract, Aug 1977 • Dave Kryskow signed to contract, Nov 1977 • Ken Baird, Lynn Powis signed to contracts, Dec 1977 • Markus Mattsson traded to Quebec for cash, draft picks, Jan 1978. Reacquired from Quebec, Mar 1978 • Mike Ford and Mike Amodeo signed to contracts, Mar 1978 • Thommie Bergman released, Mar 1978

1977-1978 Statistical Leaders

Top five in each category.

Goals: 65, Marc Tardif (Quebec); 63, Anders Hedberg (Winnipeg); 59, Robbie Ftorek (Cincinnati); 56, Real Cloutier (Quebec); 46, Bobby Hull (Winnipeg)

Assists: 89, Ulf Nilsson (Winnipeg), Marc Tardif (Quebec); 77, Andre Lacroix (Houston); 73, Real Cloutier (Quebec); 71, Bobby Hull (Winnipeg); 65, Kent Nilsson (Winnipeg).

Points: 154, Marc Tardif (Quebec); 129, Real Cloutier (Quebec); 126, Ulf Nilsson (Winnipeg); 122, Anders Hedberg (Winnipeg); 117, Bobby Hull (Winnipeg).

Penalty Minutes: 284, Steve Durbano (Birmingham); 279, Frank Beaton (Birmingham); 256, Gilles Bilodeau (Birmingham); 241, Dave Hanson (Birmingham), Paul Stewart (Cincinnati); 240, Paul Baxter (Quebec).

Power-play Goals: 20, Real Cloutier (Quebec), Robbie Ftorek (Cincinnati); 18, Kent Nilsson (Winnipeg); 17, Anders Hedberg (Winnipeg); 16, Gordie Howe (New England), Marc Tardif (Quebec); 14, Mark Napier (Birmingham).

Short-handed Goals: 6, Anders Hedberg (Winnipeg); 5, Dave Keon (New England); 4, Bob Guindon (Winnipeg); Ken Linseman (Birmingham), Blair MacDonald (Edmonton); 3, Greg Carroll (New England-Cincinnati), Ulf Nilsson (Winnipeg); Rich Preston (Houston), Bobby Sheehan (Indianapolis), Mike Zuke (Edmonton).

Goaltending Minutes: 3381, Ernie Wakely (Cincinnati-Houston); 3306, John Garrett (Birmingham); 3246, Al Smith (New England); 2850, Gary Inness (Indianapolis); 2578, Dave Dryden (Edmonton).

Goals Against Average: 3.22, Al Smith (New England); 3.30, Louis Levasseur (New England, 3.299), Joe Daley (Winnipeg, 3.296); 3.31, Gary Bromley (Winnipeg, 3.307); 3.41, Ernie Wakely (Cincinnati-Houston); 3.57, Michel Dion (Cincinnati).

Wins: 30, Al Smith (New England); 28, Ernie Wakely (Houston; Wakely was winless with Cincinnati); 25, Gary Bromley (Winnipeg); 24, John Garrett (Birmingham); 21, Joe Daley (Winnipeg), Michel Dion (Cincinnati), Dave Dryden (Edmonton).

Shutouts: 4, Michel Dion (Cincinnati); 3, Louis Levasseur (New England); 2, Dave Dryden (Edmonton), John Garrett (Birmingham), Don McLeod (Edmonton), Al Smith (New England), Ernie Wakely (Houston); 1, shared by many.

Totals for Players With Two or More Teams During 1977-1978

player	teams	gp	g	a	pts	pim	+/-	ppg	shg	sog	sc%
Baird, Ken	Edm, Wpg	55	16	11	27	31	+5	2	0	76	0.211
Baltimore, Bryon	Ind, Cin	50	3	16	19	70	-9	0	0	46	0.065
Beaudoin, Serge	Cin, Bir	77	8	26	34	115	+3	1	0	114	0.070
Broderick, Ken	Edm, Que	33	0	0	0	0		0	0	0	-
Carroll, Greg	NE, Cin	74	15	27	42	63	+6	0	3	118	0.127
Constantin, Charles	Que, Ind	54	4	5	9	50	-2	2	0	49	0.082
Deadmarsh, Butch	Edm, Cin	65	8	9	17	118	+5	0	0	98	0.082
Driscoll, Peter	Que, Ind	77	28	28	56	158	-1	6	0	154	0.182
Evans, Chris	Bir, Que	48	1	4	5	26	-11	0	0	44	0.023
Guite, Pierre	Que, Edm	78	16	26	42	86	-1	3	0	147	0.109
Hall, Del	Cin, Edm	26	4	3	7	4	-3	0	0	36	0.111
Harris, Hugh	Ind, Cin	64	12	30	42	36	-3	0	0	118	0.102
Inkpen, Dave	Edm, Que, Ind	67	1	11	12	60	-17	0	0	41	0.024
Irwin, Glen	Hou, Ind	23	0	0	0	72	-3	0	0	17	0.000
Larose, Claude	Cin, Ind	79	25	36	61	18	-26	4	0	168	0.149
Leduc, Richie	Cin, Ind	82	37	46	83	82	-43	10	1	254	0.146
Maggs, Darryl	Ind, Cin	62	8	20	28	37	-18	3	0	149	0.054
Marotte, Gilles	Cin, Ind	73	3	20	23	76	-23	0	0	80	0.038
Mattsson, Markus	Que, Wpg	16	0	0	0	2		0	0	0	-
McLeod, Don	Que, Edm	40	0	10	10	2		0	0	1	0.000
Miller, Warren	Edm, Que	78	16	28	44	68	-25	2	1	149	0.107
Morris, Rick	Edm, Que	30	1	6	7	47	-6	0	1	26	0.038
Plumb, Ron	Cin, NE	81	14	43	57	63	-12	8	0	224	0.063
Powis, Lynn	Ind, Wpg	69	16	25	41	18	-3	2	0	102	0.157
Sheehy, Tim	Bir, NE	38	12	13	25	17	-16	5	0	71	0.169
Sobchuk, Dennis	Cin, Edm	36	11	12	23	26	-15	2	1	92	0.120
Stoughton, Blaine	Cin, Ind	77	19	26	45	64	-37	6	0	177	0.107
Thomas, Reg	Ind, Cin	67	19	18	37	56	-16	7	0	164	0.116
Wakely, Ernie	Cin, Hou	57	0	0	0	0		0	0	0	-

Totals for Goaltenders With Two or More Teams During 1977-1978

goaltender	teams	gp	min	ga	en	so	record	gaa	sog	sv%
Ken Broderick	Edm, Que	33	1637	125	0	0	11-13-1	4.58	796	0.843
Markus Mattsson	Que, Wpg	16	777	60	1	0	5-8-0	4.63	423	0.858
Don McLeod	Que, Edm	40	2126	130	3	2	17-14-1	3.67	965	0.865
Ernie Wakely	Cin, Hou	57	3381	192	3	2	28-23-4	3.41	1754	0.891

1977-1978 Touring Team Statistics

For games that counted in the regular season.

Soviet All-Stars
Coach: Boris Maiorov

	date	opponent	score		record	pts
1.	Dec 14	New England	2-7	L	0-1-0	0
2.	Dec 17	Cincinnati	5-4	W	1-1-0	2
3.	Dec 18	Indianapolis	4-3	W	2-1-0	4
4.	Dec 20	Winnipeg	4-6	L	2-2-0	4
5.	Dec 21	Edmonton	2-5	L	2-3-0	4
6.	Dec 23	Houston	6-2	W	3-3-0	6
7.	Dec 26	Birmingham	1-6	L	3-4-0	6
8.	Jan 3	Quebec	3-3	T	3-4-1	7

(No overtime was played in January 3rd game)

Scoring

Pos	#	player	g	a	pts	pim
G	22	Babariko, Sergei	0	1	1	0
D	7	Bilyaletdinov, Zinetula	5	2	7	6
LW	21	Bragin, Valeri	0	2	2	2
C	5	Gimayev, Irek	1	2	3	28
D		Gimayev, Sergei	0	0	0	-
RW	24	Golubovich, Vladimir	2	0	2	0
D	4	Korotkov, Sergei	0	0	0	2
RW	8	Kostylev, Alexei	0	0	0	0
RW	10	Lavrentiev, Vladimir	1	7	8	8
D	3	Lokotko, Vladimir	0	0	0	2
D	6	Makarov, Nikolai	1	3	4	2
D	13	Nazarov, Vyacheslav	0	4	4	2
LW	9	Podgortsev, Sergei	0	1	1	0
C	14	Popov, Vladimir	2	3	5	0
C	12	Romashin, Igor	3	3	6	0
LW	26	Semyonov, Vladimir	1	2	3	4
C	23	Shostak, Mikhail	1	1	2	16
D	19	Spiridonov, Vasili	0	1	1	4
LW	11	Tyumenev, Viktor	2	3	5	8
G	1	Vaselyonok, Mikhail	0	0	0	0
D	20	Volchenkov, Alexei	3	1	4	14
LW	16	Volchkov, Alexander	3	4	7	0
RW	15	Yemelianenko, Anatoli	2	4	6	10

Goaltending

Goaltender	gp	min	ga	record	gaa
Babariko, Sergei	5	300	17	3-1-1	3.20
Vaselyonok, Mikhail	3	180	19	0-3-0	6.33

Czechoslovakia
Coach: Stanislav Nevesely

	date	opponent	score		record	pts
1.	Dec 9	Indianapolis	5-3	W	1-0-0	2
2.	Dec 11	Quebec	4-8	L	1-1-0	2
3.	Dec 13	Winnipeg	1-5	L	1-2-0	2
4.	Dec 14	Edmonton	1-6	L	1-3-0	2
5.	Dec 16	New England	3-5	L	1-4-0	2
6.	Dec 18	Houston	2-3	L	1-5-0	2
7.	Dec 20	Cincinnati	5-5	T	1-5-1	3
8.	Dec 21	Birmingham	0-5	L	1-6-1	3

Scoring

Pos	#	player	g	a	pts	pim
RW	14	Cernik, Franticek	4	3	7	4
D	2	Duris, Vitezslav	5	0	5	12
G	1	Dzurilla, Vladimir	0	0	0	0
D	5	Figala, Milan	0	0	0	4
C	15	Honc, Vaclav	0	1	1	2
G	25	Kapoun, Miroslav	0	0	0	0
LW	12	Klabouch, Jan	1	0	1	0
D	24	Kocer, Jaroslav	0	1	1	8
C	23	Kokrment, Jindrich	1	2	3	12
C	11	Kolar, Jiri	1	2	3	0
C	19	Kraft, Milan	0	0	0	0
D	3	Kveton, Josef	0	1	1	6
D	4	Lycka, Jaroslav	1	0	1	2
C	9	Mec, Jaroslav	2	5	7	0
LW	16	Novak, Milos	0	2	2	6
D	6	Oslizlo, Lubomir	0	0	0	6
D	18	Pazourek, Pavel	0	0	0	0
LW	17	Penicka, Lubomir	0	3	3	4
G	22	Podesva, Ivan	0	0	0	7
RW	8	Richter, Pavel	3	1	4	2
RW	20	Slavik, Rudolf	0	0	0	2
LW	10	Tarant, Milos	1	1	2	2
D	7	Vlcek, Vladislav	2	7	9	4
LW	21	Vyborny, Frantisek	0	1	1	0

Goaltending

Goaltender	gp	min	ga	record	gaa
Dzurilla, Vladimir	3	163	14	1-2-0	5.15
Kapoun, Miroslav	4	191	16	0-2-0	5.03
Podesva, Ivan	3	136	10	0-2-1	4.41

1977-78 Fun Facts

Paul Stewart collected 241 penalty minutes in just 40 games for Cincinnati during 1977-78. He seemed to save his best for the Birmingham Bulls, collecting 105 penalty minutes alone while fighting the rogue's gallery of tough guys the Bulls iced each game.

Dave Fortier scored the first Racers' goal of the 1977-78 season, on opening night against Cincinnati. It would be Fortier's only goal of the season.

The Story of the Pacific Hockey League

The Pacific Hockey League was conceived in January 1977 by Dennis Murphy and Walt Marlow, and gained traction later in the year when Peter Graham, operator of the San Diego Sports Arena, expressed interest after the San Diego Mariners had left town. Along with Jim Browitt, the PHL organized over Summer 1977, intending to play its first games in late December. By design, the PHL was a low-budget league with a salary cap and a short schedule. Teams had to sign a certain minimum number of American-born players. The teams could not enter into affiliations with major-league teams. If a team in the NHL or WHA wanted a player, they had to purchase him outright.

James Browitt was to be the first commiss-ioner, but he resigned the position before the start of the season to buy into the Long Beach Sharks team. Taking his place was Walt Marlow, who as commissioner, ran all aspects of the league including scheduling, statistics, and officiating. Peter Graham formed the San Diego Mariners, while Dennis Murphy controlled the San Francisco Shamrocks, co-owned by Jerry Saperstein of the Harlem Globetrotters. A fourth team was to be based in Los Angeles, but when Nike Skerlak, owner of the Phoenix Roadrunners, expressed interest in joining the PHL, the Los Angeles team was abandoned in favor of Phoenix. The Roadrunners had been reformed after the WHA team folded in April, this time as a member of the Central League. However, the financial strain was too much playing in a far-away league, and Skerlak withdrew the team from the CHL in early December of 1977, entering the PHL afterwards. The Pacific Hockey League played its first game on December 25, 1977. Each team in the four-team league would play a 42-game schedule.

Finding players for the new league was not difficult. With the WHA scaling back by four teams in 1977, and the demise of the North American and Southern Hockey Leagues in 1976-77, there were many players available. The PHL did not offer big contracts, but players signed anyway, hoping for another chance at the major leagues. The rosters of the four PHL clubs featured many former WHA players. Frank Hughes led all scorers with 74 points (33g, 41a) playing for Phoenix. Randy Wyrozub (SF), Bob Sicinski (SD), Steve Cardwell (SF), Dale Smedsmo (LB), Jeff Carlson (Phx) and Bill Evo (SF) rounded out the top scorers. Other notable players to play in the PHL were Wayne Rivers, Keith Kokkola, John Miszuk, John Kiely and Paul Hoganson with San Francisco; Bob Liddington, John Sheridan, Bill Horton and Peter Donnelly in Long Beach; Clay Hebenton and Bill Reed in San Diego; and Kerry Bond, Howie Young and Jim Niekamp in Phoenix. The league survived its first season with all of the teams playing a full schedule. In the lone playoff series, San Francisco defeated Phoenix to capture the PHL championship.

The Pacific Hockey League expanded by three teams for 1978-79. The Tucson Rustlers were added to provide a rival for Phoenix, and the Spokane Flyers marked the league's first northern foray, with the eventual plan of adding teams in between and creating Northern and Southern divisions. A new team was also placed in Los Angeles, while the Long Beach team dropped out. The San Diego Mariners were sold to Pittsburgh businessman Elmer Jonnet and renamed the Hawks. Now a six-team circuit, the schedule was expanded to 60 games.

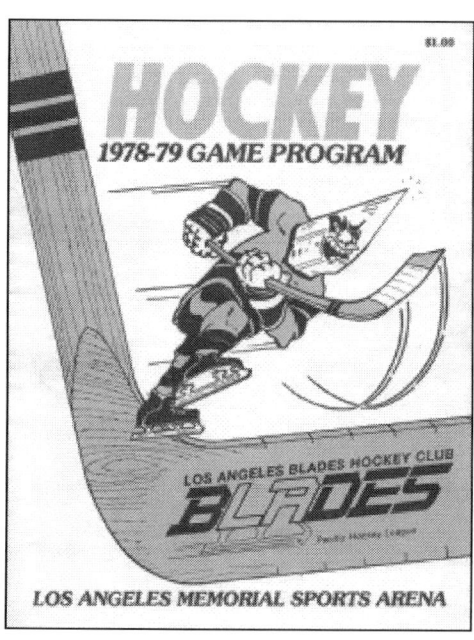

The second season was a disaster. Elmer Jonnet violated the league's salary cap rules and signed a team of former WHA veterans, while performing a power-play of his own to wrest control of the league. Walt Marlow resigned as comm.-issioner in December 1978, and was succeeded by Ken Broderick, the former WHA goaltender. Less than two months later, Alf Cadman, owner of the Tucson team, abandoned the Rustlers. The Los Angeles and San Francisco teams had zero fan support and less money, and both folded in early January 1979. Most of the Los Angeles squad were absorbed into the Tucson Rustlers, who somehow managed to play out the schedule.

Jonnet was determined to change the league to a minor league in full affiliation with the NHL and WHA. In the meanwhile, there were no affiliations, and therefore, no financial assistance from the big leagues. By signing so many WHA players, Jonnet had thrown the league's salary structure off kilter, and the rest of the owners were either unwilling or

unable to keep up. Upon completion of the regular season, the PHL cancelled the playoffs for financial reasons. Phoenix was declared champions as a result of their first place finish. The PHL was finished.

The San Diego Hawks boasted a roster in which every player had at least some WHA experience. Joe Noris led all scorers with 104 points (27 g, 77 a), with Ray Adduono, Kevin Devine and Brian Morenz not far behind. Other WHA veterans to play with San Diego included Don Burgess, Dwayne Pentland, Bill Goldthorpe, John Schella, Glenn Irwin, John Miszuk and Jerry Rollins. Wayne Wood and Clay Hebenton were the goalies. San Diego also employed 40-year old Willie O'Ree, who was the first black man to play in the NHL when he played with Boston in 1958. Despite the presence of these players, the Hawks still finished seven points behind Phoenix. The Roadrunners were led by Jim Boyd and Don Borgeson, with Chris Evans, Bob Liddington, Michel Cormier, Jeff Carlson and Jim Park augmenting the roster. Sandy Hucul was the coach. The Tucson Rustlers included Frank Hughes, with help coming from Jerry Holland, Pete McNamee, Randy Wyrozub and Willie Trognitz. Ron Huston was the big gun for Spokane, with Larry Hale, Ted McAneely and Peter Morris offering assistance. Familiar names for Los Angeles included Dale Smedsmo, Howie Young and Bill Horton, while Wayne Rivers, Keith Kokkola and Pat Donnelly played for San Francisco.

Preceding page: Game program for the Los Angeles Blades.
Below: Earl Sargent of San Diego releases a slapshot;
The "San Diego's Mariners" game program, 1978;
Logos for Spokane, San Francisco and Tucson

San Diego's Mariners

SHAMROCKS

Season VII

1978-1979

Fresh off another summer of hopeful yet unsuccessful negotiations for merger with the National Hockey League, the World Hockey Association teams pulled themselves together to play a seventh season. One member, the Houston Aeros, folded during the summer while another, Indianapolis, was on the brink. The seven teams formed into one division consisting of Birmingham, Cincinnati, Edmonton, Indianapolis, New England, Quebec and Winnipeg.

The schedule had each team play its rivals 13 times, plus one game each against the touring Soviet All-Stars and Czechoslovakia. Shortly into the season, the Indianapolis Racers ceased operations, leaving the league with six survivors. Adjustments in the schedule were made to be as fair as possible to the remaining teams. However, in order for Edmonton to reach 80 games without forcing another team to play an 81st game, a March game against the touring Finland team counted in the standings for the Oilers.

The WHA's final season was enlivened by the emergence of the Oilers' Wayne Gretzky, who scored 46 goals and 110 points as an 18-year old rookie. His arrival to the Oilers from the defunct Racers spurred Edmonton to its only WHA division title, although the equally potent Winnipeg Jets, featuring many ex-

.

Aeros on the roster, dropped the Oilers in six games for the last World Trophy.

The Nordiques' Real Cloutier put in 75 goals to easily lead the league, while his 129 total points were also the league's best. The Stingers' Robbie Ftorek led with 77 assists, while the Bulls' Rick Vaive and the Jets' Scott Campbell tied for the league lead with 248 penalty minutes each. Dave Dryden turned in a brilliant season in goal for the Oilers, winning 41 games and permitting only 2.89 goals per game. His three shutouts tied him with the Stingers' Mike Liut and the Nordiques' tandem of Richard Brodeur and Jim Corsi for the league high.

The WHA sealed its fate on March 22, 1979 when the NHL agreed to take in four of its teams as part of an merger deal struck by the two leagues. After paying their dues for seven years in the WHA, the Edmonton Oilers, Winnipeg Jets, Quebec Nordiques and New England Whalers were rewarded with membership in the NHL for the 1979-80 season. The Birmingham Bulls and Cincinnati Stingers were paid to fold, and the WHA played out its string, with Dave Semenko's goal at 19:48 in the third period of the final game of the championship round closing out the final game of the league's history.

Standings

team		League gp	w	l	t	pts	pct	gf	ga
1. Edmonton OILERS		80	48	30	2	98	.613	340	266
	home	41	29	11	1	59	.720	192	120
	away	39	19	19	1	39	.500	148	146
2. Québec NORDIQUES		80	41	34	5	87	.544	288	271
	home	41	24	13	4	52	.634	166	132
	away	39	17	21	1	35	.449	122	139
3. Winnipeg JETS		80	39	35	6	84	.525	307	306
	home	41	22	15	4	48	.585	163	143
	away	39	17	20	2	36	.462	144	163
4. New England WHALERS		80	37	34	9	83	.519	298	287
	home	41	22	19	0	44	.537	161	135
	away	39	15	15	9	39	.500	137	152
5. Cincinnati STINGERS		80	33	41	6	72	.450	274	284
	home	41	21	16	4	46	.561	156	135
	away	39	12	25	2	26	.333	118	149
6. Birmingham BULLS		80	32	42	6	70	.438	286	311
	home	41	20	16	5	45	.549	155	140
	away	39	12	26	1	25	.321	131	171
Indianapolis RACERS		25	5	18	2	12	.240	78	130
• Disbanded Dec. 15, 1978	home	13	4	8	1	9	.346	50	68
	away	12	1	10	1	3	.125	28	62
Soviet All-Stars		6	4	1	1	9	.750	27	20
Czechoslovakia		6	1	4	1	3	.250	14	33
Finland		1	0	1	0	0	.000	4	8

Award Winners

Most Valuable Player
Gordie Howe Trophy
Dave Dryden, Edm

Rookie of the Year
Lou Kaplan Trophy
Wayne Gretzky, Edm

Best Goaltender
Ben Hatskin Trophy
Dave Dryden, Edm

Best Defeseman
Dennis Murphy Trophy
Rick Ley, NE

Coach of the Year
Rob't Schmertz Trophy
John Brophy, Bir

Most Gentlemanly
Paul Deneau Trophy
Kent Nilsson, Wpg

1979 World Hockey Association AVCO World Trophy Champions
Winnipeg Jets

1979 Playoff Series Results

Quarterfinal

New England vs. Cincinnati
Apr 21   Cincinnati 3 at New England 5
Apr 22   New England 3 at Cincinnati 6
Apr 24   Cincinnati 1 at New England 2

Semifinals

Quebec vs. Winnipeg
Apr 23   Winnipeg 6 at Quebec 3
Apr 25   Winnipeg 9 at Quebec 2
Apr 27   Quebec 5 at Winnipeg 9
Apr 29   Quebec 2 at Winnipeg 6

Edmonton vs. New England
Apr 26   New England 2 at Edmonton 6
Apr 27   New England 5 at Edmonton 9
Apr 29   Edmonton 1 at New England 4
May 1   Edmonton 4 at New England 5
May 3   New England 2 at Edmonton 5
May 6   Edmonton 4 at New England 8
May 8   New England 3 at Edmonton 6

AVCO World Trophy Championship

Edmonton vs. Winnipeg
May 11   Winnipeg 3 at Edmonton 1
May 13   Winnipeg 3 at Edmonton 2
May 15   Edmonton 8 at Winnipeg 3
May 16   Edmonton 2 at Winnipeg 3
May 18   Winnipeg 2 at Edmonton 10
May 20   Edmonton 3 at Winnipeg 7

Playoff Standings

Overall Team	w	l	gf	ga	Home Team	w	l	gf	ga	Away Team	w	l	gf	ga
Winnipeg	8	2	51	38	New England	5	0	24	13	Winnipeg	4	1	23	18
Edmonton	6	7	61	50	Edmonton	5	2	39	20	Edmonton	1	5	22	30
New England	5	5	39	45	Winnipeg	4	1	28	20	Cincinnati	0	2	4	7
Cincinnati	1	2	10	10	Cincinnati	1	0	6	3	Quebec	0	2	7	15
Quebec	0	4	12	30	Quebec	0	2	5	15	New England	0	5	15	32

Championship Series Summaries

The Winnipeg Jets won their third AVCO Cup Championship with a 6-game victory over the Edmonton Oilers, who were making their first appearance in the finals. The Oilers had dominated the league during the regular season, led by 18-year old star Wayne Gretzky, but a grueling 7-game semifinal series against the Whalers tired the Oilers. The Jets, on the other hand, had been rested for almost two weeks. Morris Lukowich had 4 goals and 5 assists to lead Winnipeg. Edmonton's Ron Chipperfield had 7 goals, including 5 in the sixth game.

Game 1 • May 11, 1979
Winnipeg 3, Edmonton 1

Winnipeg	2	0	1	-	3
Edmonton	1	0	0	-	1

1st period: 1. Wpg: Preston (Sullivan) 3:29; 2. Wpg: Lesuk (Eriksson, Moffat) 15:23; 3. Edm: Flett (Shmyr) 17:48.
2nd period: No Scoring.
3rd period: 4. Wpg: Preston (Nilsson) 16:24.
Shots on goal

Wpg on Dryden	11	9	8	-	28
Edm on Smith	5	9	10	-	24

Game 2 • May 13, 1979
Winnipeg 3, Edmonton 2

Winnipeg	0	0	3	-	3
Edmonton	0	1	1	-	2

1st period: No Scoring.
2nd period: 1. Edm: Sobchuk (Driscoll) 6:12.
3rd period: 2. Wpg: Sullivan (Terbenche) 1:17; 3. Edm: Hamilton 4:10; 4. Wpg: Lukowich (Campbell, Ruskowski) 11:53; 5. Wpg: Lindstrom (Long, Lukowich) 15:24.
Shots on goal

Wpg on Dryden	8	8	11	-	27
Edm on Smith	5	9	7	-	21

Game 3 • May 15, 1979
Edmonton 8, Winnipeg 3

Edmonton	4	0	4	-	8
Winnipeg	2	1	0	-	3

1st period: 1. Wpg: Lukowich (Ruskowski, Nilsson) 4:54; 2. Edm: Hamilton (Gretzky, Callighen) 9:03; 3. Edm: Driscoll (Goldsworthy) 9:44; 4. Edm: Chipperfield (Shmyr, Driscoll) 12:45; 5. Wpg: Lindstrom 15:53; 6. Edm: Goldsworthy (Hamilton, Chipperfield) 16:01.
2nd period: 7. Wpg: Lukowich (MacKinnon, Eriksson) 11:56
3rd period: 8. Edm: MacDonald (Siltanen) 1:42; 9. Edm: Callighen (MacDonald, Gretzky) 4:14; 10. Edm: Gustafsson (Hunter, Weir) 9:52; 11. Edm: Hunter (Gustafsson, Hamilton) 11:00.
Shots on goal

Edm on Smith, Daley	12	5	10	-	27
Wpg on Dryden	8	8	10	-	26

Game 4 • May 16, 1979
Winnipeg 3, Edmonton 2

Edmonton	1	1	0	-	2
Winnipeg	1	0	2	-	3

1st period: 1. Edm: Gretzky (MacDonald, Callighen) 7:41; 2. Wpg: Preston (Sullivan) 12:54
2nd period: 3. Edm: Callighen (Gretzky, Gustafsson) 13:42
3rd period: 4. Wpg: Lukowich (Nilsson, Lindstrom) 9:24; 5. Wpg: Moffat (Lesuk, Eriksson) 13:34
Shots on goal

Edm on Smith	5	10	7	-	22
Wpg on Dryden	11	10	6	-	27

Game 5 • May 18, 1979
Edmonton 10, Winnipeg 2

Winnipeg	0	1	1	-	2
Edmonton	4	4	2	-	10

1st period: 1. Edm: Sobchuk (Chipperfield, Shmyr) 4:23; 2. Edm: Gretzky (Callighen, Chipperfield) 16:28; 3. Edm: Weir (Micheletti, Sobchuk) 17:29; 4. Edm: Chipperfield (Langevin) 18:01
2nd period: 5. Wpg: Preston (Lukowich, Nilsson) 0:22; 6. Edm: Sobchuk (Shmyr, Weir) 2:58; 7. Edm: Chipperfield (Siltanen, Micheletti) 4:51; 8. Edm: Chipperfield (Driscoll, Semenko) 10:45; 9. Edm: Hughes (Sobchuk) 14:23
3rd period: 10. Wpg: Nilsson 3:14; 11. Edm: Chipperfield (Semenko) 7:45; 12. Edm: Chipperfield (Micheletti, Siltanen) 14:31
Shots on goal

Wpg on Dryden, Mio	5	8	8	-	21
Edm on Smith, Daley	16	13	13	-	42

Game 6 • May 20, 1979
Winnipeg 7, Edmonton 3

Edmonton	0	1	2	-	3
Winnipeg	2	3	2	-	7

1st period: 1. Wpg: Lindstrom (Ruskowski, Lukowich) 2:14; 2. Wpg: Long (Ruskowski, Lukowich) 13:42
2nd period: 3. Wpg: MacKinnon (Sullivan, Hicks) 5:22; 4. Wpg: Moffat (Eriksson, Lukowich) 6:35; 5. Wpg: Long (Ruskowski, MacKinnon) 9:23; 6. Edm: Chipperfield (Driscoll, Siltanen) 18:45
3rd period: 7. Edm: Flett (Hamilton) 1:48; 8. Wpg: Nilsson (Sullivan) 2:09; 9. Wpg: Lindstrom (Ruskowski) 13:38; 10. Edm: Semenko (Chipperfield, Siltanen) 19:48
Shots on goal

Edm on Smith	11	8	11	-	30
Wpg on Dryden, Mio	10	13	11	-	34

Playoff Statistical Leaders

Goals: 10, Wayne Gretzky (Edm), Willy Lindstrom (Wpg); 9, Ron Chipperfield (Edm); 8 Blair MacDonald (Edm), Morris Lukowich (Wpg), Rich Preston (Wpg).

Assists: 12, Terry Ruskowski (Wpg); 11, Kent Nilsson (Wpg); 10, Brett Callighen (Edm), Ron Chipperfield (Edm), Wayne Gretzky (Edm), Blair MacDonald (Edm).

Points: 20, Wayne Gretzky (Edm), 19, Ron Chipperfield (Edm), 18, Blair MacDonald (Edm).

Penalty Minutes: 42, Dave Hunter (Edm), 35, John Hughes (Edm); 29, Dave Semenko (Edm).

Goaltending Wins: 8, Gary Smith (Wpg); 6, Dave Dryden (Edm); 4, John Garrett (NE)

Goals Against Average: 3.35, Mike Liut (Cin, 3 games); 3.67, Dave Dryden (Edm), 3.73, Gary Smith (Wpg).

Splits by Opponent and by Month, Home and Away

Bir Birmingham, **Cin** Cincinnati, **Edm** Edmonton, **Ind** Indianapolis, **NE** New England, **Que** Quebec, **Wpg** Winnipeg, **TT** Touring Teams

BIRMINGHAM

Opp.	season	gf-ga	home	gf-ga	away	gf-ga
Cin	7-7-1	50-53	5-2-0	22-15	2-5-1	28-38
Edm	4-10-1	52-74	2-5-1	29-38	2-5-0	23-36
Ind	3-1-0	20-13	2-0-0	8-4	1-1-0	12-9
NE	7-5-3	56-57	3-1-3	30-27	4-4-0	26-35
Que	4-11-1	50-64	3-5-0	26-35	1-6-0	24-29
Wpg	6-8-0	46-46	4-3-0	28-22	2-5-0	18-24
TT	1-0-1	12-4	1-0-1	12-4	0-0-0	0-0
Oct	4-3-0	32-29	1-1-0	8-7	3-2-0	24-22
Nov	4-8-1	48-59	2-4-1	27-27	2-4-0	21-32
Dec	6-7-2	42-48	5-2-1	24-20	1-5-1	18-28
Jan	4-6-0	38-46	3-3-0	24-20	1-3-0	14-26
Feb	5-6-1	49-46	3-2-1	26-22	2-4-0	23-24
Mar	6-8-2	50-55	4-3-2	30-29	2-5-0	20-26
Apr	3-4-0	27-28	2-1-0	16-15	1-3-0	11-13

CINCINNATI

Opp.	season	gf-ga	home	gf-ga	away	gf-ga
Bir	7-7-1	53-50	5-2-1	38-28	2-5-0	15-22
Edm	4-10-0	44-59	3-4-0	26-29	1-6-0	18-30
Ind	3-1-0	19-13	2-0-0	12-5	1-1-0	7-8
NE	7-6-2	45-39	3-2-2	20-17	4-4-0	25-22
Que	5-8-2	49-46	4-4-0	29-24	1-4-2	20-22
Wpg	7-7-1	60-68	4-2-1	27-23	3-5-0	33-45
TT	0-2-0	4-9	0-2-0	4-9	0-0-0	0-0
Oct	5-3-1	35-29	3-1-0	14-10	2-2-1	21-19
Nov	7-5-1	55-54	6-1-1	38-27	1-4-0	17-27
Dec	4-9-2	42-51	2-3-2	22-23	2-6-0	20-28
Jan	4-6-1	39-37	2-3-1	22-22	2-3-0	17-15
Feb	4-5-1	31-37	4-2-0	23-17	0-3-1	8-20
Mar	6-10-0	53-59	3-5-0	30-29	3-5-0	23-30
Apr	3-3-0	19-17	1-1-0	7-7	2-2-0	12-10

EDMONTON

Opp.	season	gf-ga	home	gf-ga	away	gf-ga
Bir	10-4-1	74-52	5-2-0	36-23	5-2-1	38-29
Cin	10-4-0	59-44	6-1-0	30-18	4-3-0	29-26
Ind	3-1-0	22-12	2-0-0	14-3	1-1-0	8-9
NE	9-4-1	53-35	4-2-1	30-17	5-2-0	23-18
Que	6-10-0	51-60	5-3-0	31-24	1-7-0	20-36
Wpg	7-7-0	63-55	4-3-0	33-27	3-4-0	30-28
TT	3-0-0	18-8	3-0-0	18-8	0-0-0	0-0
Oct	3-5-0	25-27	1-4-0	12-18	2-1-0	13-9
Nov	8-3-0	47-34	6-0-0	32-13	2-3-0	15-21
Dec	6-7-0	52-53	4-2-0	27-21	2-5-0	25-32
Jan	6-4-0	42-27	4-2-0	27-14	2-2-0	15-13
Feb	10-2-1	59-34	8-0-1	44-19	2-2-0	15-15
Mar	8-6-1	62-56	3-2-0	25-20	5-4-1	37-36
Apr	7-3-0	53-35	3-1-0	25-15	4-2-0	28-20

INDIANAPOLIS

Opp.	season	gf-ga	home	gf-ga	away	gf-ga
Bir	1-3-0	13-20	1-1-0	9-12	0-2-0	4-8
Cin	1-3-0	13-19	1-1-0	8-7	0-2-0	5-12
Edm	1-3-0	12-22	1-1-0	9-8	0-2-0	3-14
NE	0-3-1	16-25	0-2-1	13-19	0-1-0	3-6
Que	1-1-0	6-8	0-0-0	0-0	1-1-0	6-8
Wpg	1-5-1	18-36	1-3-0	11-22	0-2-1	7-14
Oct	2-5-1	24-34	1-4-0	15-27	1-1-1	9-7
Nov	1-9-1	30-65	1-1-1	13-14	0-8-0	17-51
Dec	2-4-0	24-31	2-3-0	22-27	0-1-0	2-4

NEW ENGLAND

Opp.	season	gf-ga	home	gf-ga	away	gf-ga
Bir	5-7-3	57-56	4-4-0	35-26	1-3-3	22-30
Cin	6-7-2	39-45	4-4-0	22-25	2-3-2	17-20
Edm	4-9-1	35-53	2-5-0	18-23	2-4-1	17-30
Ind	3-0-1	25-16	1-0-0	6-3	2-0-1	19-13
Que	11-4-1	65-54	6-2-0	30-18	5-2-1	35-36
Wpg	7-6-1	63-52	4-3-0	36-29	3-3-1	27-23
TT	1-1-0	14-11	1-1-0	14-11	0-0-0	0-0
Oct	5-3-1	40-36	1-2-0	15-14	4-1-1	25-22
Nov	6-4-3	57-46	6-1-0	35-15	0-3-3	22-31
Dec	7-3-2	53-38	5-1-0	30-18	2-2-2	23-20
Jan	4-5-0	30-34	4-3-0	25-24	0-2-0	5-10
Feb	6-7-2	52-57	4-3-0	31-26	2-4-2	21-31
Mar	5-7-1	40-44	1-6-0	17-25	4-1-1	23-19
Apr	4-5-0	26-32	1-3-0	8-13	3-2-0	18-19

QUEBEC

Opp.	season	gf-ga	home	gf-ga	away	gf-ga
Bir	11-4-0	64-50	6-1-0	29-24	5-3-0	35-26
Cin	8-5-2	46-49	4-1-2	22-20	4-4-0	24-29
Edm	10-6-0	60-51	7-1-0	36-20	3-5-0	24-31
Ind	1-1-0	8-6	1-1-0	8-6	0-0-0	0-0
NE	4-11-1	54-65	2-5-1	36-35	2-6-0	18-30
Wpg	6-6-2	49-44	3-3-1	28-21	3-3-1	21-23
TT	1-1-0	7-6	1-1-0	7-6	0-0-0	0-0
Oct	4-5-1	42-48	2-3-1	27-31	2-2-0	15-17
Nov	7-4-1	47-33	4-2-1	30-18	3-2-0	17-15
Dec	8-3-2	46-36	7-1-1	34-23	1-2-1	12-13
Jan	5-4-0	33-24	1-1-0	12-5	4-3-0	21-19
Feb	4-7-1	39-43	2-1-1	16-9	2-6-0	23-34
Mar	11-5-0	59-51	6-1-0	30-21	5-4-0	29-30
Apr	2-6-0	22-36	2-4-0	17-25	0-2-0	5-11

WINNIPEG

Opp.	season	gf-ga	home	gf-ga	away	gf-ga
Bir	8-6-0	46-46	5-2-0	24-18	3-4-0	22-28
Cin	7-7-1	68-60	5-3-0	45-33	2-4-1	23-27
Edm	7-7-0	55-63	4-3-0	28-30	3-4-0	27-33
Ind	5-1-1	36-18	2-0-1	14-7	3-1-0	22-11
NE	4-11-1	52-63	3-3-1	23-27	2-4-0	29-36
Que	6-6-2	44-49	3-3-1	23-21	3-3-1	21-28
TT	0-1-1	6-7	0-1-1	6-7	0-0-0	0-0
Oct	4-3-2	38-33	1-2-2	19-19	3-1-0	19-14
Nov	6-6-1	52-45	4-1-0	29-18	2-5-1	23-27
Dec	4-4-1	43-38	2-2-1	23-20	2-2-0	20-18
Jan	8-6-2	53-62	4-2-1	24-25	4-4-1	29-37
Feb	6-8-0	45-58	4-2-0	23-19	2-6-0	22-39
Mar	6-5-0	44-39	4-4-0	29-27	2-1-0	15-12
Apr	5-3-0	32-31	3-2-0	16-15	2-1-0	16-16

1979 All-Star Games

Edmonton Coliseum
Edmonton, Alberta
January 2, 4 and 5, 1979

WHA All-Stars

Coach: Larry Hillman (Wpg)
Goaltenders: Dave Dryden (Edm), Markus Mattsson (Wpg)
Defensemen: John Hughes, Paul Shmyr, Claire Alexander (Edm), Rob Ramage (Bir), Rick Ley (NE), Barry Long (Wpg)
Forwards: Robbie Ftorek, Mike Gartner, Peter Marsh, Rick Dudley (Cin), Wayne Gretzky, Blair MacDonald (Edm), Serge Bernier, Real Cloutier, Marc Tardif (Que), Morris Lukowich, Peter Sullivan (Wpg), Dave Keon, Gordie Howe, Mark Howe (NE)

Tardif and Cloutier did not play due to injuries.

Moscow Dynamo

Coach: Vladimir Kiselyov, Pavel Zhiburtovich (assistant)
Goaltenders: Sergei Babariko, Vladimir Polupanov
Defensemen: Vasili Payusov, Vitali Filippov, Alexander Filippov, Sergei Gimayev, Alexei Volchenkov, Vladimir Orlov, Mikhail Slipchenko
Forwards: Viktor Shkurdyuk, Vladimir Vikulov, Alexander Lobanov, Alexander Volchkov, Pavel Yezovskikh, Vladimir Popov, Alexei Frolikov, Mikhail Shostak, Vladimir Golubovich, Vladimir Semyonov, Yevgeni Kotlov, Vladimir Devyatov, Sergei Tukmachyov, Vyacheslav Anisin

Game 1 • January 2, 1979
WHA All-Stars 4, Moscow Dynamo 2

Moscow Dynamo	2	0	0 - 2
WHA All-Stars	1	1	2 - 4

1st period 1. WHA: Gretzky (Mark Howe, Shmyr) 1:35; 2. MD: Frolikov (Tukmachyov, Fillippov) 14:20; 3. MD: Semyonov (Kotlov) 18:08.
2nd period 4. WHA: Gretzky (G. Howe, Mark Howe) 16:29.
3rd period 5. WHA: Mark Howe (Gretzky, G. Howe) 7:02; 6. WHA: Sullivan 19:51.
Shots on goal

MD on Dryden	8	6	7 - 21
WHA on Babariko	12	8	10 - 30

Attendance 8,038

Game 2 • January 4, 1979
WHA All-Stars 4, Moscow Dynamo 2

Moscow Dynamo	1	1	0 - 2
WHA All-Stars	3	0	1 - 4

1st period 1. WHA: Lukowich (Ftorek, Gartner) 2:26; 2. MD: Shostak (Filippov, Shkurdyuk) 7:38; 3. WHA: Mark Howe (G. Howe, Gretzky) 9:27; 4. WHA: Gartner (Lukowich, Sullivan) 16:51.
2nd period 5. MD: Shkurdyuk (Lobanov) 19:44.
3rd period 6. WHA: Gretzky (Ley) 5:45.
Shots on goal

MD on Mattsson	4	10	8 - 22
WHA on Babariko	17	8	12 - 37

Attendance 11,220

Game 3 • January 5, 1979
WHA All-Stars 4, Moscow Dynamo 3

Moscow Dynamo	2	0	1 - 3
WHA All-Stars	3	1	0 - 4

1st period 1. WHA: Lukowich (Gartner) 1:46; 2. WHA: Ramage (MacDonald, Keon) 6:41; 3. MD: Shkurdyuk (Anisin, Volchenkov) 11:02; 4. MD: Shostak (Slipchenko, Frolikov) 11:43; 5. WHA: Sullivan 18:29.
2nd period 6. WHA: Bernier (Ley, Gartner) 14:03.
3rd period 7. MD: Semyonov (Payusov, Lobanov) 13:12.
Shots on goal

MD on Mattsson	8	2	9 - 19
WHA on Babariko	13	11	5 - 29

Attendance 15,590

No MVP selected

Moscow Dynamo also played four exhibition games during their tour of North America. The results were:

New England 4, Moscow Dynamo 1
Moscow Dynamo 4, Edmonton 1
Quebec 5, Moscow Dynamo 4
Winnipeg 6, Moscow Dynamo 4

1978-1979 Year End All-Star Teams

First Team: Goaltender: Dave Dryden, Edmonton; Defensemen: Rick Ley, New England, and Rob Ramage, Birmingham; Center: Robbie Ftorek, Cincinnati; Right Wing: Real Cloutier, Quebec; Left Wing: Mark Howe, New England.

Second Team: Goaltender: Richard Brodeur, Quebec; Defensemen: Dave Langevin, Edmonton, and Paul Shmyr, Edmonton; Center: Wayne Gretzky, Edmonton; Right Wing: Blair MacDonald, Edmonton; Left Wing: Morris Lukowich, Winnipeg.

Penalty Shots

date	player, team	goaltender, team	period	time	result
Nov 3	Rich Preston, Winnipeg	Ed Mio, Edmonton	-	-	Save
Nov 12	Real Cloutier, Quebec	Markus Mattsson, Winnipeg	1	0:43	Save
Feb 21	Steve West, Winnipeg	Al Smith, New England	-	-	Save
Mar 7	Dave Debol, Cincinnati	Markus Mattsson, Winnipeg	-	-	Save

information incomplete for 1978-79

Attendance Figures

g indicates the number of home games played

team	g	season total	avg	g	playoff total	avg	team	g	season total	avg	g	playoff total	avg
Birmingham	41	258,975	6,316	-	-	-	New England	41	286,503	6,988	5	29,797	5,959
Cincinnati	41	288,967	7,048	1	5,131	5,131	Quebec	41	362,120	8,832	2	17,664	8,832
Edmonton	41	461,347	11,252	7	85,821	12,260	Winnipeg	41	355,994	8,683	5	48,018	9,604
Indianapolis	13	82,727	6,364	-	-	-							

Total Attendance: 2,096,633 **Average Attendance:** 8,095

1978-1979 Team Thumbnails

Birmingham: It was the year of the Baby Bulls, as team owner John Bassett re-assembled his team over the summer of 1978 by signing a number of very talented players from the junior ranks. Most notable among the signees was Michel Goulet, who would lead the Bulls in goals with 28, and eventually score over 500 in the NHL with Quebec and Chicago. Fellow Baby Bulls Rick Vaive (26 goals), Louis Sleigher (26 goals), defenseman Rob Ramage and goaltender Pat Riggin turned in very solid seasons, while veterans Paul Henderson (24 goals) and J. C. Stewart (24 goals) came through with solid seasons. Bob Stephenson (23 goals) and Rick Adduono (20 goals) also met the twenty-goal mark. The team was coached by legendary minor-league fighter John Brophy, but these Bulls were not the same free-for-all mayhem-makers of 1977-78. Rick Vaive did lead the league in penalty minutes with 248, and Dave Hanson had 212, but instead of line brawls and game misconducts, the Bulls played solid hockey, winning 32 games, albeit for a 6th-place finish and out of the playoff running. With the close of the season, the Birmingham Bulls folded, one of just five teams to survive the entire seven-year run of the World Hockey Association (originating as the Ottawa Nationals).

Cincinnati: The Stingers kept the core of their team from 1977-78 together, for better or for worse. Center Robbie Ftorek was again one of the best in the league, scoring 39 goals and collecting 117 points. Jamie Hislop and Peter Marsh contributed 30 and 43 goals, respectively, while Reg Thomas had his finest season, with 32 goals and 71 points. The defense was young, dominated by first- and second-year men Craig Norwich, Barry Melrose and Chuck Luksa, with help from Bryon Baltimore and Barry Legge. Michel Dion and Mike Liut once again handled the goaltending. Floyd Smith was the team's new coach, and despite the fact the Stingers actually finished one point worse than their 1977-78 edition, the Stingers did manage a fifth-place finish and the final playoff position. Their run in the post-season was short, losing in three games to New England. With the fate of the WHA sealed in March, the Stingers knew they were destined to disband upon season's end. As a footnote to history, the final edition of the Stingers featured two future Hall of Famers: Mike Gartner scored 27 goals, while Mark Messier played in 47 games but registered just a single goal.

Edmonton: For the first time in their seven seasons in the WHA, the Oilers were the class of the league, running away with the regular-season crown with 48 wins and 98 points. Much credit goes to Wayne Gretzky, who came to the Oilers on November 2, 1978, purchased from Indianapolis along with Peter Driscoll and Ed Mio. The skinny 18-year old Gretzky showed he was very much worthy of his reputation,

finishing strong with 46 goals, 110 points, and the league's Rookie of the Year award. However, surrounding Gretzky was a strong, solid team ably coached by Glen Sather. Four other Oilers scored 30 goals (Blair MacDonald 34, Ron Chipperfield 32, Brett Callighen and Stan Weir with 31), as the Oilers led the league with 340 goals. On the blueline were Al Hamilton (healthy for the first time in years who played in all 80 games), Dave Langevin, Joe Micheletti and Paul Shmyr. Should a player get past the Edmonton defense, big Dave Dryden posed a formidable barrier. Dryden had his best season as a professional, winning 41 games with a 2.89 average, and sharing the league lead with three shutouts. In the playoffs, the Oilers fought off the Whalers in seven games, but fell to the veteran Jets in the final round. Despite the disappointing finish to a fine season, the Oilers would see greater glory in the NHL during the 1980s.

Indianapolis: The Racers were dead on their feet after 1977-78, and by all rights should have folded, but owner Nelson Skalbania had other ideas. He signed 17-year old Wayne Gretzky to play for the Racers, in the hopes he would be the savior the franchise so badly needed. To his credit, Gretzky played well for the Racers—for eight games. Still, no one went to the games as the fans had abandoned the team after a year of seeing its best talent traded away or simply let go. The financial reality was so severe Skalbania had no choice but to sell Gretzky to Edmonton for cash on November 2, 1978, but this only gave the Racers life for a few more weeks. When the cash ran out, the team folded in mid-December, 1978. During their abbreviated final season, the Racers won just 5 of 25 games and were on pace to allow over 400 goals. Fan-favorite Pat Stapleton coached the club, while Don Larway and Blaine Stoughton were the scoring stars for Indy, each with 18 points. Goaltender Ed Mio provided the only highlight of the season, a 4-0 shutout of the Nordiques in Quebec, the first time ever the Nordiques had been shut out at home during the regular season (it was also the same game in which Gretzky registered his first big-league point—an assist—on Richie Leduc's first period goal). In late November, another 17-year old kid skated a few games for the Racers: Mark Messier. In time, Gretzky and Messier would win four Stanley Cups together in Edmonton, play into the new millennium (Messier retiring from the NHL in 2004), and establish themselves as all-time greats of the game. Few people remember that both began their long and storied careers as kids, skating for a failing franchise in Indianapolis.

New England: The torch was finally passed from father to son, as Mark Howe broke through for his

finest season, leading the team in all offensive categories: 42 goals, 65 assists, and 107 points. Pop Gordie, who turned 51 during the season, had an ordinary season by his high standards, 43 points in 58 games, in which he missed long stretches of action due to a fractured ankle. Five other players reached twenty goals, with Andre Lacroix' 32 placing him second on the team. Defense was in the solid hands of perennial all-star Rick Ley, Brad Selwood, Alan Hangsleben, Marty Howe, and new to the team this season, veteran Ron Plumb. Goaltending was shared by Al Smith and John Garrett. Despite a solid lineup and quality depth, the Whalers were an ordinary 37-34-9, finishing fourth in the league. They enjoyed a run through the playoffs, knocking off Cincinnati and pushing Edmonton to seven games before falling.

Quebec: The Nordiques, always strong, turned in a good season and a second-place finish, eleven points behind Edmonton. Once again, Marc Tardif and Real Cloutier led the offense. Cloutier exploded for 75 goals and 129 points, leading the league in both categories, while Tardif collected 41 goals and 96 points. Serge Bernier bounced back from a disappointing 1977-78 and scored 36 goals and 82 points. Richie Leduc was the only other Nordique to score 30 goals, as the team's goal production slipped below 300 for the first time since 1972-73. However, the defense picked up the slack, allowing just 271 goals against, with goaltenders Jim Corsi and Richard Brodeur collecting 3 shutouts apiece. Skating on defense were J.-C. Tremblay (in his final season),

Francois Lacombe, Paul Baxter, Wally Weir, and veteran newcomer Dale Hoganson. Despite a solid all-around season, the Nordiques fell quickly in the playoffs, being swept by Winnipeg in the first round.

Winnipeg: The Jets saw Anders Hedberg and Ulf Nilsson leave over the summer of 1978, enticed by big contracts from the New York Rangers of the NHL. Bobby Hull decided to call it a day just a few games into the season, and it certainly would have been reasonable to write off Winnipeg for 1978-79 as a once-great team. However, the Jets did absorb the bulk of the players from the failed Houston franchise in July 1978, and it was this core of players that would carry Winnipeg during 1978-79. Even so, the Jets played ordinary hockey for most of the season. Tommy McVie came on as coach in March and led the Jets to an 11-6-0 finish for a 39-35-6 season and third place in the league. Former Aeros Morris Lukowich (65 goals), Rich Preston (28 goals) and Terry Ruskowski (20 goals, 211 penalty minutes) led the attack, with hold-over Jets Kent Nilsson (39 goals, 107 points), Peter Sullivan (46 goals) and Willy Lindstrom (26 goals) rounding out the attack, which produced 307 goals overall. The defense was led by Lars-Erik Sjoberg and Barry Long, with ex-Aeros Scott Campbell and Paul Terbenche; Campbell's 248 penalty minutes tied him for the league lead. In goal, late-season signee (and Indianapolis survivor) Gary Smith gave the Jets life and enough energy to outlast the up-and-coming Edmonton Oilers in the playoffs, to win their third and final WHA Championship.

Jacques Demers, Player-Coach

Coach Jacques Demers of the Quebec Nordiques found himself with just 14 able-bodied skaters available to play entering a game against Edmonton on March 18, 1979. League rules mandated a minimum of 15 skaters. With no time to call in a player from the outside, Demers "solved" his dilemma by signing himself to a 5-game tryout contract, thus officially placing himself on that night's official game roster for the Nordiques. The under-manned Nordiques beat the Oilers that evening, and Demers stayed behind the bench the entire game. The Nordiques were able to dress the required minimum of players for the games thereafter, and Demers never did see any ice time during his five-game tryout.

1978-1979 Game by Game Line Scores

Date & Teams	Scoring 1 2 3 ot F	Shots 1 2 3 ot F	Goaltenders	Goals & Other Scoring Highlights
October 13				
Cincinnati	0 1 1 - 2	4 7 9 - 20	Dion	Clark, Marsh
Edmonton	1 1 1 - 3	15 11 15 - 41	Dryden	Shmyr, Alexander, Goldsworthy (WG 18:01)
Winnipeg	0 2 2 1 5	5 10 6 1 22	Daley	Guindon, Lukowich, Hull, Moffat, Lesuk (OT 3:24)
Birmingham	1 1 2 0 4	14 15 9 4 42	Riggin	Marrin, Turkiewicz, Sleigher, Ramage
October 14				
Winnipeg	2 1 3 - 6	10 15 13 - 38	Mattsson	Sullivan 2, Hull, Campbell, Lindstrom, Nilsson
Indianapolis	2 1 0 - 3	14 8 12 - 34	G. Smith	St. Sauveur, Burgess, Driscoll
October 15				
Birmingham	1 3 5 - 9	7 15 14 - 36	Wood	Sleigher 3, Gingras 3, Crowder, Gorman, Henderson
Indianapolis	1 0 2 - 3	12 6 12 - 30	G. Smith	Leclerc, Inkpen, Larose
Cincinnati	0 3 1 - 4	11 22 9 - 42	Liut	Shutt, Gartner (first career), Marsh, Dudley
Winnipeg	1 1 1 - 3	6 16 10 - 32	Daley	Nilsson, Sullivan, Lesuk
New England	2 3 1 - 6	12 13 9 - 34	Garrett	Lyle 2, Douglas, McKenzie, Antonovich, Rogers
Quebec	2 2 1 - 5	11 12 13 - 36	Brodeur	Bernier 2, Cloutier 2, Tardif
October 17				
Cincinnati	1 1 3 0 5	12 12 12 4 40	Liut, Dion	Dudley, Hislop, Thomas, Marsh, Gartner (TG 19:58)
Quebec	1 1 3 0 5	13 10 7 9 39	Levasseur	Cloutier 2, Tardif, Brackenbury, Geoffrion
New England	0 1 1 - 2	8 9 10 - 27	A. Smith	Mty Howe, McKenzie (WG 19:08)
Edmonton	0 1 0 - 1	11 9 7 - 27	Dryden	Callighen
October 18				
Indianapolis	1 1 2 - 4	10 11 15 - 36	Mio	Leduc, Stoughton, Driscoll, Greig (Gretzky: first career point, assisting on Leduc's goal)
Quebec	0 0 0 - 0	11 17 9 - 37	Brodeur	▶ Mio: shutout (1), 37 saves
New England	1 1 2 0 4	8 11 9 5 33	Garrett	Mk Howe 2, Keon, Ley
Winnipeg	1 1 2 0 4	12 6 13 3 34	Mattsson	Lukowich 2, Sullivan, Nilsson (TG 19:41)
October 20				
Birmingham	1 0 1 - 2	5 5 4 - 14	Wood	Vaive, Hartsburg
Cincinnati	1 1 3 - 5	10 12 13 - 35	Liut	Dudley 2, Ftorek 2, Marsh
Edmonton	1 0 3 - 4	12 15 20 - 47	Dryden	Goldsworthy, Alexander, Sobchuk, Hamilton (WG 11:53)
Indianapolis	1 2 0 - 3	7 7 3 - 17	Mio	Leduc, Gretzky 2 (6:07 & 6:41 2nd, first two career goals)
October 21				
Edmonton	3 0 0 - 3	8 5 10 - 23	Walsh	Carlson, Alexander, Flett
Cincinnati	3 0 1 - 4	6 9 6 - 21	Dion	Marsh 2, Gilbert, Thomas (WG 17:48)
Quebec	0 0 1 - 1	12 3 10 - 25	Brodeur, Levasseur	Baxter
New England	2 1 4 - 7	12 12 8 - 32	A. Smith	Antonovich 2, McKenzie, Lacroix, G. Howe, Douglas, Miller
October 22				
Birmingham	6 0 2 - 8	13 11 18 - 42	Riggin, Wood	Gingras 2, Vaive 2, Henderson 2, Alley, Gorman
Quebec	3 2 0 - 5	10 11 9 - 30	Levasseur	Cloutier 2, P. Bordeleau, Lariviere, Bernier
Edmonton	2 2 2 - 6	18 8 10 - 36	Dryden	Berry, Flett, Micheletti, Guite, Goldsworthy, Semenko
Winnipeg	0 1 1 - 2	8 6 8 - 22	Daley	West, Lukowich
New England	2 4 0 - 6	9 13 10 - 32	Garrett	Mk Howe 3, G. Howe, Antonovich, Rogers
Indianapolis	1 1 1 - 3	12 10 15 - 37	Mio	Driscoll, Larose, Gretzky
October 24				
Birmingham	3 0 0 - 3	10 8 5 - 23	Riggin	Sleigher, Beaudoin, Goulet (first career goal)
Edmonton	0 1 1 - 2	9 13 12 - 34	Dryden	Chipperfield, Callighen
New England	2 0 0 - 2	7 8 8 - 23	A. Smith	G. Howe, Lacroix
Cincinnati	1 0 0 - 1	11 8 8 - 27	Liut	Marsh
October 25				
Birmingham	1 0 1 - 2	10 14 4 - 28	Wood	Goulet, Sleigher
Winnipeg	2 2 3 - 7	11 5 17 - 33	Mattsson	Lindstrom 2, Moffat, Sullivan, Gray, Lesuk, Terbenche
Cincinnati	1 0 2 - 3	17 2 11 - 30	Dion	Hislop, Thomas, Legge
Quebec	2 2 0 - 4	10 10 15 - 35	Corsi	Cloutier, Brackenbury, C. Bordeleau, Fitchner
October 26				
New England	2 0 3 - 5	10 11 11 - 32	Garrett	Miller 2, Mk Howe, Selwood, Rogers
Quebec	3 3 2 - 8	6 12 6 - 24	Corsi	Tardif 2, Cloutier 2, Bernier 2, Brackenbury, Baxter
October 27				
Indianapolis	1 0 1 - 2	7 7 11 - 25	Inness	Larway, Leduc
Birmingham	2 2 0 - 4	15 5 7 - 27	Riggin	Gorman, Stewart, Gingras, Beaudoin
Winnipeg	3 2 1 - 6	14 7 8 - 29	Daley	Nilsson 2, Preston 2, Hicks, Lindstrom
New England	1 2 1 - 4	10 8 5 - 23	A. Smith	Mk Howe, Rogers, Antonovich, Lacroix
October 28				
Quebec	1 0 2 0 3	8 3 7 4 22	Corsi	Bernier 2, C. Bordeleau
Cincinnati	1 2 0 1 4	17 11 7 4 39	Dion	Thomas, Luksa, Dudley, Gilbert (OT 9:09)
Winnipeg	1 1 0 - 2	12 12 9 - 33	Mattsson	Sullivan, Gray
Indianapolis	1 1 1 - 3	15 11 11 - 37	Mio	Leduc, Parizeau, Stoughton (WG 15:54)
October 29				
Cincinnati	2 4 1 - 7	8 9 15 - 32	Liut	Hislop 2, Debol, Norwich, Marsh, Thomas, Gartner
New England	2 1 1 - 4	12 17 12 - 41	Garrett	Miller, McKenzie, Lacroix, Mk Howe
Indianapolis	2 0 1 0 3	15 6 8 8 37	G. Smith	Stoughton, Nugent, Larose
Winnipeg	1 2 0 0 3	9 14 7 2 32	Daley	Lesuk, Nilsson, Ruskowski
Quebec	1 3 2 - 6	10 8 12 - 30	Brodeur	Cloutier 2, Tardif 2, C. Bordeleau, Brackenbury
Edmonton	1 0 1 - 2	8 14 12 - 34	Dryden, Walsh	Carlson, Micheletti
October 31				
Quebec	1 1 3 - 5	3 14 6 - 23	Brodeur	Cloutier 2, C. Bordeleau, Fitchner, Bernier (WG 16:12)
Edmonton	3 1 0 - 4	19 10 10 - 39	Dryden	Callighen, Sobchuk, Alexander, Bailey
November 1				
Birmingham	1 1 1 1 4	11 13 7 4 35	Riggin	Sleigher, Adduono, Marrin, Vaive (OT 5:48)
Cincinnati	0 1 2 0 3	9 12 12 2 35	Dion	Debol 2, Marsh

1978-1979 Game by Game Line Scores

Date & Teams	Scoring 1 2 3 ot F	Shots 1 2 3 ot F	Goaltenders	Goals & Other Scoring Highlights
November 3				
Indianapolis	1 0 2 - 3	9 8 13 - 30	G. Smith	Larose 2, Larway
New England	3 2 1 - 6	15 20 13 - 48	A. Smith	McKenzie 2, G. Howe, Mty Howe, Miller, Lacroix
Quebec	0 2 1 - 3	5 10 5 - 20	Brodeur	Hoganson, Cloutier, Geoffrion
Birmingham	0 0 2 - 2	8 12 16 - 36	Riggin	Gingras, Adduono
Winnipeg	1 1 1 0 3	7 4 12 5 28	Mattsson	Sullivan, Lukowich, Gray
Edmonton	1 2 0 1 4	12 12 13 2 39	Mio, Dryden	Sobchuk, Gretzky, MacDonald, Driscoll (OT 6:32)
November 4				
New England	0 4 2 0 6	9 13 19 4 45	A. Smith	Mk Howe 3, Selwood, G. Howe, Hangsleben
Indianapolis	2 4 0 0 6	5 14 12 4 35	Inness	Stoughton, Leduc, Block, St. Sauveur, Moretto, MacGregor
Quebec	1 2 1 - 4	10 4 7 - 21	Brodeur	Bernier, Cote, Tardif, Cloutier
Birmingham	0 1 0 - 1	10 13 5 - 28	Wood	Hartsburg
November 5				
Edmonton	0 0 0 - 0	10 8 20 - 38	Mio	▸ Corsi: shutout (1), 38 saves
Quebec	1 0 1 - 2	4 8 6 - 18	Corsi	Tremblay, Brackenbury
Indianapolis	2 0 0 - 2	5 12 5 - 22	G. Smith	Stoughton, Larway
Winnipeg	1 2 3 - 6	18 14 11 - 43	Mattsson	Ruskowski 2, Sullivan 2, Amodeo, Lindstrom
New England	1 1 2 - 4	6 7 14 - 27	A. Smith	Selwood, McKenzie, Lyle, Roberts
Cincinnati	1 3 1 - 5	13 14 10 - 37	Liut	Luksa 2, Hislop, Marsh, Ftorek
November 7				
Winnipeg	0 1 1 - 2	12 8 9 - 29	Mattsson	Lindstrom, Amodeo (WG 3:56)
Quebec	0 1 0 - 1	9 11 8 - 28	Corsi	Baxter
November 8				
Edmonton	2 2 2 - 6	20 14 11 - 45	Mio	MacDonald 3, Driscoll, Alexander, Flett
Quebec	2 1 2 - 5	15 12 10 - 37	Brodeur	Cloutier 2, Bernier, Geoffrion, Tardif
Indianapolis	0 0 0 - 0	10 4 10 - 24	Inness	▸ Liut: shutout (1), 24 saves
Cincinnati	0 3 1 - 4	6 14 14 - 34	Liut	Marsh, Forbes, Hislop, Dudley
November 9				
Edmonton	0 0 1 - 1	8 5 7 - 20	Mio, Dryden	Gretzky
New England	2 2 2 - 6	11 8 12 - 31	Garrett	Roberts 2, Rogers, Lacroix, Antonovich, Miller
Winnipeg	2 1 2 - 5	12 14 10 - 36	Daley	Lesuk, Lindstrom, Ruskowski, Lukowich, Sullivan
Birmingham	4 2 0 - 6	10 9 9 - 28	Riggin	Alley, Sleigher, Adduono, Goulet, Gorman, Henderson
November 10				
Winnipeg	0 2 0 - 2	3 3 8 - 14	Mattsson	Sullivan, Lindstrom
Cincinnati	2 0 1 - 3	11 16 8 - 35	Dion	Ftorek, Maggs, Debol (WG 4:16)
November 11				
Cincinnati	0 1 0 - 1	11 11 6 - 28	Liut	Hislop
New England	0 1 1 - 2	6 13 10 - 29	Garrett	G. Howe, Mk Howe (WG 0:47)
Edmonton	3 1 1 - 5	15 12 7 - 34	Dryden	Bailey, Sobchuk, Alexander, Driscoll, Callighen
Birmingham	2 0 1 - 3	10 10 7 - 27	Riggin, Wood	Dillon, Sleigher, Adduono
Indianapolis	0 1 1 - 2	6 6 9 - 21	G. Smith	MacGregor, Larway
Quebec	4 3 1 - 8	19 28 11 - 58	Corsi	Tardif 3, Cloutier 2, C. Bordeleau, Baxter, Bernier
November 12				
Edmonton	0 1 2 - 3	3 14 6 - 23	Mio	Driscoll, Hamilton, Gretzky
Cincinnati	2 1 2 - 5	15 9 12 - 36	Dion	Maggs 2, Dudley, Gartner, Shutt
Quebec	1 3 2 - 6	12 14 10 - 36	Corsi	Bernier 2, Dube, Tardif, Cote, Lariviere
Winnipeg	2 1 1 - 4	12 10 8 - 30	Mattsson	Lukowich 2, Guindon, Lindstrom
November 14				
New England	2 1 2 0 5	11 12 11 4 38	Garrett	Keon 2, Lacroix, Rogers, Miller
Birmingham	2 2 1 0 5	18 10 5 1 34	Riggin	Sleigher 2, Vaive 2, Henderson
November 15				
New England	2 0 2 0 4	8 8 10 4 30	Garrett	Mk Howe, Mty Howe, Rogers, Plumb
Cincinnati	0 1 3 0 4	13 16 16 3 48	Liut	Debol 2, Gilligan, Maggs
Winnipeg	0 1 1 - 2	11 7 10 - 28	Mattsson	Preston, Nilsson
Quebec	1 2 2 - 5	12 13 13 - 38	Corsi	Tardif 2, P. Bordeleau, Lacombe, Brackenbury
November 17				
Cincinnati	2 2 2 - 6	11 10 16 - 37	Dion	Ftorek 2, Hislop 2, Marsh, Baltimore
Winnipeg	3 4 3 - 10	13 14 8 - 35	Mattsson	Lukowich 4, Preston, Ruskowski, Gray, Moffat, Sullivan, Hicks
Indianapolis	0 1 0 - 1	8 10 3 - 21	G. Smith	Parizeau
Edmonton	4 1 1 - 6	14 15 8 - 37	Mio, Dryden	Gretzky 2, MacDonald, Langevin, Berry, Carlson
New England	1 0 0 - 1	15 6 7 - 28	Garrett	McKenzie
Birmingham	0 4 3 - 7	6 13 10 - 29	Wakely	Stephenson, Vaive, Turkiewicz, Goulet, Cassolato, Sleigher, Adduono
November 18				
Birmingham	1 2 0 - 3	10 6 6 - 22	Wakely	Henderson, Sleigher, Stephenson
New England	0 1 1 - 2	11 6 12 - 29	A. Smith	Mty Howe, Miller
November 19				
Cincinnati	0 1 2 - 3	9 10 13 - 32	Liut	Dudley, Gilligan, Thomas
Edmonton	1 3 2 - 6	11 15 13 - 39	Dryden	Flett 2, Berry, Alexander, Langevin, Hunter
Indianapolis	1 1 0 - 2	4 8 4 - 16	G. Smith	Stoughton, Moretto
Winnipeg	1 1 3 - 5	7 10 6 - 23	Mattsson	Lindstrom, Hicks, Gray, Preston, Lukowich
November 21				
Quebec	1 0 0 - 1	8 8 6 - 22	Corsi	Bernier
Edmonton	3 0 1 - 4	16 13 16 - 45	Dryden	Weir 2, MacDonald, Gretzky
November 22				
Birmingham	2 1 2 0 5	14 14 6 2 36	Wakely	Dillon 3, Adduono, Stephenson
Cincinnati	3 1 1 1 6	9 12 12 4 37	Liut	Gartner 2, Ftorek, Marsh, Luksa, Hislop (OT 6:02)
Winnipeg	1 1 0 - 2	11 12 11 - 34	Mattsson	Guindon, Gray
New England	3 1 1 - 5	17 10 15 - 42	Garrett	Rogers, G. Howe, Keon, Lacroix, McKenzie

1978-1979 Game by Game Line Scores

Date & Teams	Scoring 1	2	3	ot	F	Shots 1	2	3	ot	F	Goaltenders	Goals & Other Scoring Highlights
November 23												
Cincinnati	3	1	0	-	4	22	8	7	-	37	Dion	Ftorek 2, Gilbert, Gartner
Birmingham	1	1	1	-	3	6	5	12	-	23	Riggin	Sleigher, Marrin, Henderson
Winnipeg	1	2	2	-	5	8	14	11	-	33	Mattsson	Nilsson 2, Guindon, Sullivan, Ruskowski
Indianapolis	1	0	0	-	1	14	11	9	-	34	G. Smith	Stoughton
November 24												
Indianapolis	1	1	3	-	5	6	6	9	-	21	G. Smith	George 2, MacGregor 2, Leclerc
Cincinnati	1	3	4	-	8	12	13	9	-	34	Dion	Gartner 2, Dudley, Luksa, Legge, Ftorek, Marsh, Hislop
Quebec	0	3	0	0	3	9	12	7	0	28	Corsi	Tardif, P. Bordeleau, Cote
Edmonton	2	1	0	1	4	14	14	2	1	31	Dryden	Sobchuk, Carlson, Hunter, Callighen (OT 6:09)
November 25												
Birmingham	0	2	0	-	2	11	9	8	-	28	Wakely	Beaudoin, Sleigher
New England	2	2	1	-	5	13	9	10	-	32	Garrett	Mk Howe, Keon, Lacroix, Hangsleben, Rogers
Cincinnati	0	1	2	-	3	8	16	17	-	41	Liut	Thomas, Gartner, Marsh
Indianapolis	3	3	0	-	6	17	18	7	-	42	Inness	St. Sauveur 2, Morrow, Hughes, Leclerc, George
November 26												
Birmingham	1	1	1	-	3	7	14	8	-	29	Riggin	Sleigher, Goulet, Gingras
New England	5	2	2	-	9	13	12	15	-	40	Garrett	Miller 2, G. Howe 2, Mk Howe 2, Roberts, Ley, Hangsleben
Winnipeg	1	1	0	0	2	11	6	5	7	29	Mattsson	Preston, Guindon
Quebec	0	2	0	0	2	6	14	9	4	33	Brodeur	Baxter 2
November 28												
Indianapolis	1	1	0	-	2	8	10	8	-	26	Inness	Morrow, Greig
Edmonton	2	2	4	-	8	17	14	11	-	42	Mio	Weir 3, MacDonald, Sobchuk, Berry, Flett, Shmyr
November 29												
Birmingham	2	2	0	-	4	11	12	9	-	32	Wakely	Gingras, Sleigher, Adduono, Ramage
Quebec	4	3	0	-	7	17	12	10	-	39	Brodeur	Cloutier 3, Geoffrion, Leduc, Tardif, Cote
New England	1	0	1	-	2	7	5	8	-	20	Garrett	Roberts, Lacroix
Winnipeg	3	0	1	-	4	7	14	7	-	28	Mattsson	Lukowich 2, Lindstrom, Hicks
December 1												
Birmingham	0	1	2	-	3	11	17	10	-	38	Wakely	Alley 2, Marrin
Indianapolis	1	2	3	-	6	13	4	8	-	25	Inness	Larway 2, MacGregor, Stoughton, Block, Parizeau
Cincinnati	2	1	3	-	6	17	11	16	-	44	Liut	Hislop 2, Dudley, Ftorek, Gartner, Thomas
Winnipeg	1	2	2	-	5	12	14	12	-	38	Daley	Lesuk, Sullivan, Preston, Moffat, Lindstrom
New England	1	0	1	-	2	9	5	6	-	20	A. Smith	Carlson, Lacroix
Edmonton	3	3	2	-	8	11	10	4	-	25	Dryden	MacDonald 3, Weir 2, Sobchuk 2, Driscoll
December 2												
Cincinnati	0	0	0	-	0	8	4	10	-	22	Dion	▶ Corsi: shutout (2), 22 saves
Quebec	1	0	1	-	2	9	10	3	-	22	Corsi	Leduc, Geoffrion
Indianapolis	1	0	1	-	2	9	8	5	-	22	G. Smith	Greig, Leclerc
Birmingham	2	0	2	-	4	9	9	7	-	25	Wakely	Stephenson 2, Ramage, Gorman
December 3												
Cincinnati	1	2	1	-	4	7	14	12	-	33	Dion	Dudley, Gilligan, Ftorek, Thomas
Indianapolis	0	2	0	-	2	9	11	9	-	29	Inness	Stoughton, Larway
New England	1	4	2	-	7	9	13	6	-	28	Garrett	Antonovich 3, Mk Howe 2, Keon, Carlson
Edmonton	0	0	0	-	0	9	8	8	-	25	Mio	▶ Garrett: shutout (1), 25 saves
Winnipeg	1	2	0	-	3	8	7	10	-	25	Mattsson	Lukowich, Sullivan, Preston
Quebec	4	0	1	-	5	18	10	5	-	33	Brodeur	Cloutier 2, Brackenbury 2, Tardif
December 5												
New England	0	2	0	0	2	5	9	10	4	28	Garrett	Rogers, Antonovich
Cincinnati	0	1	1	0	2	9	13	12	6	40	Liut	Debol, Norwich
December 6												
Edmonton	2	1	0	-	3	13	6	7	-	26	Dryden	Gretzky 2, Berry
Quebec	1	1	4	-	6	7	7	14	-	28	Corsi	Cloutier 2, Fitchner, Geoffrion, P. Bordeleau, Leduc
December 7												
Cincinnati	0	1	1	-	2	11	8	11	-	30	Liut	Thomas, Gartner
Birmingham	0	2	2	-	4	10	14	10	-	34	Riggin	Stephenson, Gorman, Henderson, Goulet
Edmonton	2	0	1	-	3	10	6	6	-	22	Dryden	Shmyr, Semenko, Micheletti
New England	1	1	3	-	5	13	9	8	-	30	Garrett	Antonovich 2, Lacroix 2, G. Howe
Winnipeg	4	2	3	-	9	16	13	12	-	41	Mattsson	Lukowich 3, Sullivan 2, Moffat 2, Terbenche, Nilsson
Indianapolis	1	2	1	-	4	10	11	9	-	30	Inness	MacGregor 3, George
December 9												
Soviet All-Stars	2	2	3	-	7	11	10	9	-	30	Myshkin	S. Gimayev 2, I. Gimayev, Volchkov, Skvortsov, Andreyev, Kovin
New England	1	2	1	-	4	10	8	10	-	28	Garrett	Selwood, Lacroix, Mk Howe, Rogers
Cincinnati	1	1	1	-	3	20	8	13	-	41	Dion	Gartner, Gilligan, Ftorek
Quebec	1	0	3	-	4	14	9	13	-	36	Corsi	Leduc, Tardif, Cloutier, Tremblay
Edmonton	0	2	0	-	2	5	14	12	-	31	Mio	Sobchuk, Gretzky
Birmingham	3	2	1	-	6	14	10	8	-	32	Riggin	Stewart 3, Gorman, Beaudoin, Alley
December 10												
Cincinnati	0	0	0	-	0	15	8	12	-	35	Liut	▶ Riggin: shutout (1), 35 saves (Teams combined for one
Birmingham	0	0	1	-	1	6	9	8	-	23	Riggin	Henderson (WG 14:31) minor penalty in game)
Edmonton	2	1	1	-	4	8	16	9	-	33	Dryden	Sobchuk 3, MacDonald
Indianapolis	0	4	2	-	6	10	8	12	-	30	Inness	Sacharuk 2, Leclerc, Larway, Baltimore, Hughes
Quebec	2	2	0	0	4	10	10	11	6	37	Brodeur	Cloutier 2, Tardif, Leduc
Winnipeg	0	3	1	0	4	11	9	10	6	36	Daley	Preston, Moffat, Guindon, Sullivan
December 12												
Soviet All-Stars	3	2	1	-	6	6	18	11	-	35	Myshkin	Kabanov 2, Tyumenev 2, Lobanov, Skvortsov
Quebec	1	1	1	-	3	13	5	10	-	28	Corsi	Cloutier, Tardif, Bernier
Edmonton	0	2	3	-	5	9	7	10	-	26	Dryden	Gretzky 3, Micheletti, Flett
Cincinnati	1	1	0	-	2	14	9	10	-	33	Liut	Thomas, Hislop
New England	2	3	2	-	7	13	11	12	-	36	A. Smith	Lacroix 3, G. Howe, Rogers, Antonovich, Mk Howe
Indianapolis	1	2	1	-	4	9	12	11	-	32	Inness	Nugent, Parizeau, Hughes, Moretto

1978-1979 Game by Game Line Scores

Date & Teams	Scoring 1 2 3 ot F	Shots 1 2 3 ot F	Goaltenders	Goals & Other Scoring Highlights
December 14				
Soviet All-Stars	4 0 0 - 4	5 7 15 - 27	Babariko, Myshkin	Volchkov, I. Gimayev, Andreyev, Makarov
Winnipeg	2 1 0 - 3	18 8 7 - 33	Mattsson	Lukowich, Preston, Sullivan
Birmingham	1 0 1 - 2	11 9 8 - 28	Riggins	Alley 2
Quebec	1 2 0 - 3	5 11 9 - 25	Corsi	Bernier 2, Tardif
December 15 ▸ Indianapolis folds				
Soviet All-Stars	2 0 1 - 3	7 3 7 - 17	Myshkin	Kovin, S. Gimayev, Kabanov
Edmonton	2 1 2 - 5	9 1 9 - 19	Dryden	MacDonald, Chipperfield, Bailey, Sobchuk, Shmyr
December 16				
Birmingham	1 0 1 0 2	7 5 6 2 20	Riggin	Stephenson, Hughes
Cincinnati	0 1 1 0 2	11 11 11 5 38	Dion	Ftorek, Marsh
Quebec	1 0 0 - 1	14 8 9 - 31	Corsi	Cloutier
New England	1 0 1 - 2	12 10 7 - 29	A. Smith	G. Howe, Miller (WG 15:20)
December 17				
Soviet All-Stars	1 1 0 0 2	11 12 5 5 33	Myshkin	Andreyev, Kapustin
Birmingham	1 1 0 0 2	11 10 7 4 32	Riggin	Stephenson, Cassolato
Cincinnati	1 1 1 - 3	9 11 13 - 33	Liut	Hislop, Norwich, Gilligan
Winnipeg	2 2 2 - 6	11 15 12 - 38	Mattsson	Lukowich 2, Lesuk 2, Nilsson, Sullivan
New England	2 0 2 0 4	10 10 15 11 46	A. Smith	Lacroix, Keon, McKenzie, G. Howe
Quebec	1 2 1 0 4	7 17 6 3 33	Corsi	Weir, Leduc, Lacombe, Cloutier
December 19				
Edmonton	1 2 2 - 5	12 14 6 - 32	Dryden	MacDonald, Bailey, Flett, Driscoll, Gretzky
Birmingham	0 2 0 - 2	4 7 8 - 19	Riggin	Vaive, Gorman
December 20				
Soviet All-Stars	2 0 3 - 5	14 7 13 - 34	Myshkin	Lobanov, Volchkov, Skvortsov, Kapustin, Payusov
Cincinnati	2 1 0 - 3	7 10 8 - 25	Liut	Marsh, Debol, Dudley
December 22				
Quebec	1 3 1 - 5	13 9 4 - 26	Brodeur	Tardif 2, Brackenbury, Geoffrion, Leduc
Birmingham	1 0 0 - 1	9 12 8 - 29	Wakely	Gorman
Winnipeg	2 2 1 - 5	8 14 8 - 30	Mattsson	Lukowich 2 (WG 7:25), Preston, Lesuk, Nilsson
Edmonton	1 2 1 - 4	13 7 12 - 32	Dryden, Mio	Semenko, Chipperfield, Gretzky, MacDonald
December 23				
Birmingham	1 0 2 - 3	6 10 9 - 25	Riggin	Stephenson, Alley, Hartsburg
New England	0 2 2 - 4	12 5 14 - 31	A. Smith	Mty Howe, Mk Howe, Lacroix, Antonovich
Quebec	2 0 0 - 2	12 6 12 - 30	Corsi	P. Bordeleau, Cloutier
Cincinnati	2 2 2 - 6	8 10 8 - 26	Dion	Marsh 3, Dudley 2, Gartner
December 26				
Cincinnati	1 0 1 - 2	12 8 13 - 33	Liut	Ftorek, Baltimore
Birmingham	2 2 0 - 4	13 7 11 - 31	Riggin	Vaive, Hughes, Kirk, Stewart
Edmonton	1 0 2 - 3	11 10 12 - 33	Mio	Chipperfield 2, Weir
Winnipeg	3 2 0 - 5	11 9 7 - 27	Mattsson	Nilsson 2, Lesuk, Lindstrom, Sullivan
December 27				
Czechoslovakia	3 0 1 - 4	11 12 10 - 33	Crha	Salajka 2, Stransky, Holy
New England	3 4 3 - 10	13 16 10 - 39	A. Smith	Lacroix 3, McKenzie 2, Keon, Stoughton, Rogers, Mty Howe, Mk Howe
Winnipeg	1 2 0 - 3	5 10 3 - 18	Mattsson	Lukowich, Amodeo, Long
Edmonton	2 1 2 - 5	10 12 15 - 37	Dryden	MacDonald, Weir, Sobchuk, Carlson, Flett
December 28				
Czechoslovakia	0 0 0 - 0	10 13 7 - 30	Svitana	▸ Brodeur: shutout (1), 30 saves
Quebec	1 2 1 - 4	12 17 23 - 52	Brodeur	Bernier 2, Tremblay, Leduc
Birmingham	1 5 0 - 6	5 9 4 - 18	Riggin	Goulet 2, Sleigher 2, Cassolato, Adduono
Cincinnati	2 1 2 - 5	13 9 11 - 33	Dion	Gartner 2, Gilligan, Thomas, Norwich
December 29				
Birmingham	0 0 0 - 0	6 8 9 - 23	Wakely	▸ Smith: shutout (1), 23 saves
New England	1 0 4 - 5	8 9 8 - 25	A. Smith	G. Howe, Roberts, Rogers, Hangsleben, Keon
December 30				
Czechoslovakia	0 1 0 - 1	3 15 10 - 28	Crha	Stransky
Edmonton	1 2 2 - 5	15 8 10 - 33	Dryden	Chipperfield 3, Berry, Flett
Birmingham	0 1 1 - 2	13 6 11 - 30	Riggin	Vaive, Adduono
Quebec	0 1 2 - 3	6 12 18 - 26	Brodeur	Cloutier 2 (WG 14:40), Tardif
New England	1 0 0 - 1	7 4 7 - 18	A. Smith	Roberts
Cincinnati	0 1 1 - 2	5 9 8 - 22	Liut	Debol, Gartner (WG 10:43)
January 1				
Czechoslovakia	1 0 2 0 3	15 5 13 0 33	Svitana	Novak 2 (TG 19:59), Bezak
Winnipeg	1 2 0 0 3	8 14 4 6 32	Daley	Lukowich 2, Lindstrom
January 6				
Czechoslovakia	0 2 2 - 4	10 6 5 - 21	Crha	Bezak, Holan, Brunclik, Holy
Cincinnati	0 1 0 - 1	10 13 8 - 31	Dion	Melrose
January 7				
Czechoslovakia	0 1 1 - 2	9 10 11 - 30	Svitana, Crha	Holy 2
Birmingham	3 4 3 - 10	19 17 8 - 44	Riggin, Wakely	Goulet 3, Vaive 2, Dillon, Ramage, Henderson, Hanson, Stewart
Cincinnati	2 0 2 - 4	8 9 12 - 29	Liut	Ftorek, Shutt, Marsh, Dudley
New England	3 1 1 - 5	15 6 14 - 35	Garrett	Mk Howe 2, Lyle, Miller, Keon
Quebec	1 0 1 - 2	7 6 10 - 23	Corsi	Morrison, Bernier
Winnipeg	2 1 0 - 3	14 13 5 - 32	Mattsson	Ruskowski, Lukowich, Sullivan
January 9				
Edmonton	2 1 0 0 3	7 13 6 0 26	Walsh	Micheletti, Weir, Hunter
Winnipeg	2 1 0 1 4	9 7 4 3 23	Daley	Nilsson 2 (OT 6:22), Preston, Lindstrom
Quebec	2 0 2 - 4	9 7 8 - 24	Brodeur	P. Bordeleau, Lariviere, Cloutier, Fitchner (WG 19:11)
Cincinnati	1 2 0 - 3	13 10 10 - 33	Liut	Norwich, Thomas, Gilligan

1978-1979 Game by Game Line Scores

Date & Teams	Scoring 1 2 3 ot F	Shots 1 2 3 ot F	Goaltenders	Goals & Other Scoring Highlights
January 12				
Quebec	1 0 1 - 2	11 3 8 - 22	Brodeur	Leduc, Cloutier (WG 2:06 3rd)
Cincinnati	1 0 0 - 1	10 5 9 - 24	Liut	Luksa
Winnipeg	2 1 0 - 3	7 4 5 - 16	Mattsson	Preston, Lukowich, Lindstrom
Birmingham	0 0 1 - 1	12 7 18 - 37	Riggin	Goulet
January 13				
Edmonton	0 0 3 - 3	2 6 13 - 21	Dryden	Gretzky 3 (Natural hat trick in 4:40, two goals unassisted)
New England	0 0 0 - 0	15 15 7 - 37	Garrett	▶ Dryden: shutout (1), 37 saves
Winnipeg	2 0 1 - 3	12 13 7 - 32	Mattsson	Lesuk, Lukowich, Nilsson
Birmingham	0 0 1 - 1	5 5 10 - 20	Wakely	Goulet
January 14				
Birmingham	2 0 0 - 2	10 11 7 - 28	Riggin	Goulet, Adduono
Cincinnati	2 1 1 - 4	14 14 10 - 38	Liut	Ftorek, Gartner, Thomas, Debol
Winnipeg	3 0 1 - 4	9 7 7 - 23	Mattsson	Lukowich, Long, Sullivan, Nilsson
New England	0 1 1 - 2	8 8 10 - 26	A. Smith	Mty Howe, Mk Howe
January 16				
Winnipeg	0 1 0 - 1	8 7 7 - 22	Mattsson	Gray
Edmonton	1 1 1 - 3	16 12 10 - 38	Dryden	Chipperfield 2, Carlson
January 17				
Birmingham	1 3 1 - 5	4 12 6 - 22	Riggin	Cassolato, Alley, Stephenson, Henderson, Vaive
Cincinnati	3 1 4 - 8	14 10 20 - 44	Liut	Hislop 2, Gilligan, Marsh, Shutt, Ftorek, Forbes, Thomas
Edmonton	2 3 1 - 6	4 10 6 - 20	Dryden	Driscoll 2, Micheletti, MacDonald, Callighen, Chipperfield
Winnipeg	2 0 1 - 3	9 7 8 - 24	Daley, Mattsson	Eriksson 2, Sullivan
January 18				
Quebec	0 2 2 - 4	10 10 11 - 31	Corsi	Geoffrion 2, P. Bordeleau, Leduc
New England	0 0 2 - 2	8 16 12 - 36	Garrett	Rogers, Stoughton
January 19				
Birmingham	0 2 1 - 3	11 12 6 - 29	Wakely	Stewart, Hanson, Gingras, Weir, Semenko
Edmonton	2 4 5 - 11	11 14 16 - 41	Dryden	Micheletti 2, Gretzky 2, Flett, Alexander, Callighen, Shmyr, Hughes,
Cincinnati	0 2 5 - 7	9 15 17 - 41	Liut	Ftorek 4, Luksa, Marsh, Dudley
Winnipeg	2 0 0 - 2	13 11 9 - 33	Mattsson	Gray 2
January 20				
Cincinnati	0 0 1 - 1	12 13 10 - 35	Liut	Forbes
New England	1 0 2 - 3	18 4 12 - 34	A. Smith	Hangsleben, Mk Howe, Roberts
Winnipeg	0 0 1 - 1	9 13 13 - 35	Mattsson, Daley	Lukowich
Quebec	2 5 3 - 10	10 9 13 - 32	Corsi	Tardif 2, Cloutier 2, Cote 2, Geoffrion, Leduc, Dube, P. Bordeleau
January 21				
Birmingham	3 1 0 - 4	12 4 10 - 26	Riggin	Vaive, Dillon, Cassolato, Alley
Edmonton	1 2 0 - 3	8 12 12 - 32	Dryden	Chipperfield 2, Driscoll
Quebec	1 0 0 - 1	5 12 10 - 27	Brodeur	Morrison
Winnipeg	1 2 0 - 3	13 13 13 - 39	Mattsson	Guindon, Ruskowski, Preston
January 23				
New England	0 0 1 - 1	5 12 7 - 24	A. Smith	Ley
Edmonton	0 3 2 - 5	6 12 8 - 26	Dryden	Flett, MacDonald, Chipperfield, Gretzky, Weir
Quebec	4 1 2 - 7	12 7 8 - 27	Corsi, Brodeur	Bernier 2, Geoffrion, Cloutier, Cote, Tremblay, Tardif
Birmingham	1 1 3 - 5	12 11 11 - 34	Riggin, Wakely	Vaive, Gingras, Adduono, Goulet, Dillon
January 24				
Winnipeg	1 3 1 0 5	8 15 4 6 33	Mattsson	Preston 2, Moffat, Lukowich, Nilsson
Cincinnati	1 1 3 0 5	13 11 16 7 47	Liut	Hislop 2, Ftorek, Marsh, Gilligan (TG 19:44)
January 26				
Cincinnati	3 0 2 - 5	13 13 8 - 34	Liut	Ftorek 3, Thomas, Dudley
Edmonton	1 1 0 - 2	13 9 18 - 40	Dryden	MacDonald, Langevin
New England	1 1 2 - 4	9 10 10 - 29	Garrett	G. Howe, Mk Howe, Lacroix, Antonovich
Birmingham	2 2 1 - 5	12 12 3 - 27	Riggin	Ramage, Vaive, Henderson, Dillon, Goulet
January 27				
Winnipeg	2 0 2 - 4	7 11 14 - 32	Daley	Lukowich, Campbell, Moffat, Amodeo
Quebec	0 2 0 - 2	8 11 14 - 33	Corsi	Leduc, P. Bordeleau
January 28				
Cincinnati	0 0 0 - 0	11 6 9 - 26	Liut	▶ Dryden: shutout (2), 26 saves
Edmonton	0 1 2 - 3	5 10 10 - 25	Dryden	Weir, Gretzky, Chipperfield
Winnipeg	1 3 2 - 6	11 15 10 - 36	Mattsson	Sullivan 2, Lukowich, Ruskowski, Nilsson, Preston
New England	1 6 1 - 8	5 13 11 - 29	A. Smith	Miller 2, Lyle, Lacroix, Antonovich, McKenzie, Mk Howe, Stoughton
January 30				
Quebec	1 0 0 - 1	19 17 16 - 52	Brodeur	Hoganson
Birmingham	1 1 0 - 2	5 10 9 - 24	Riggin, Wakely	Henderson 2
Winnipeg	0 0 2 - 2	10 6 7 - 23	Daley	Sullivan, Lukowich
New England	1 3 1 - 5	11 11 15 - 37	A. Smith	Lyle, Antonovich, Lacroix, Ley, Stoughton
January 31				
Edmonton	2 1 0 - 3	13 12 13 - 38	Dryden	Flett, Carlson, Micheletti
Winnipeg	0 3 3 - 6	13 10 11 - 34	Mattsson	Nilsson 2, Lukowich 2, Hicks, Sullivan
February 1				
Quebec	2 1 2 - 5	17 9 8 - 34	Brodeur	Cloutier 2, Tardif, Tremblay, Bernier
Birmingham	1 2 4 - 7	6 9 20 - 35	Wakely	Ramage, Tebbutt, Hartsburg, Hanson, Stewart, Henderson, Dillon
February 2				
Edmonton	1 0 1 - 2	10 10 7 - 27	Mio	Flett, Driscoll
Winnipeg	2 1 1 - 4	8 6 7 - 21	Mattsson	Sullivan 2, Gray, Ruskowski
Quebec	0 1 0 - 1	6 12 8 - 26	Corsi	Cloutier
New England	0 1 3 - 4	23 10 19 - 52	A. Smith	Mk Howe 2, Lyle 2
February 3				
New England	1 0 1 0 2	12 10 13 - 35	A. Smith	Stoughton, Miller
Birmingham	0 0 2 0 2	10 10 14 - 34	Wakely	Vaive, Henderson

1978-1979 Game by Game Line Scores

Date & Teams	Scoring 1 2 3 ot F	Shots 1 2 3 ot F	Goaltenders	Goals & Other Scoring Highlights
February 4				
Cincinnati	1 0 0 - 1	13 16 7 - 36	Liut, Dion	Gilligan
Winnipeg	3 3 2 - 8	12 8 17 - 37	Daley	Nilsson 3, Sullivan 2, Lukowich, Ruskowski, Lesuk
Edmonton	1 1 1 - 3	8 11 7 - 26	Dryden	Hamilton 2, MacDonald
Quebec	3 0 3 - 6	14 9 9 - 32	Brodeur	Bernier 3, Leduc, Tardif, Cloutier
February 6				
Birmingham	2 0 0 - 2	9 4 4 - 17	Wakely, Riggin	Stewart, Sleigher
Edmonton	2 3 1 - 6	7 12 13 - 32	Dryden	Gretzky 2, Callighen, Chipperfield, Langevin, Semenko
New England	1 2 2 - 5	8 13 9 - 30	A. Smith	Keon 2, Plumb, Ley, Antonovich
Quebec	1 0 2 - 3	11 5 9 - 25	Corsi	Cloutier 2, Bilodeau
February 7				
Birmingham	0 0 2 - 2	7 10 13 - 30	Riggin	Sleigher, Henderson
Winnipeg	1 1 1 - 3	13 10 7 - 30	Mattsson	Lukowich 2, Long
Cincinnati	1 2 2 - 5	7 17 7 - 31	Liut, Dion	Ftorek 2, Norwich, Marsh, Clark
Edmonton	3 4 1 - 8	14 11 9 - 34	Dryden	Sobchuk 2, Chipperfield 2, Semenko, Weir, MacDonald, Callighen
February 9				
Quebec	0 0 0 - 0	7 6 6 - 19	Brodeur	▶ Dryden: shutout (3), 19 saves
Edmonton	1 0 2 - 3	4 9 11 - 24	Dryden	Weir, MacDonald, Gretzky
Winnipeg	0 0 0 - 0	7 7 4 - 18	Daley	▶ Liut: shutout (2), 18 saves
Cincinnati	3 0 1 - 4	16 12 9 - 37	Liut	Gartner, Thomas, Shutt, Hislop
February 10				
Winnipeg	0 1 1 - 2	9 15 11 - 35	Mattsson	Campbell, Sullivan
New England	1 2 4 - 7	10 10 9 - 29	A. Smith	Keon 3, Rogers, Warner, Lyle, Antonovich
February 11				
Birmingham	2 0 1 0 3	12 12 7 4 35	Riggin	Goulet, Hartsburg, Ramage
Edmonton	1 1 1 1 4	13 5 10 1 29	Dryden	MacDonald, Micheletti, Weir, Sobchuk (OT 5:25)
New England	0 1 1 - 2	7 10 6 - 23	A. Smith	Stoughton, Mty Howe
Cincinnati	2 2 1 - 5	11 12 15 - 38	Liut	Hislop, Shutt, Marsh, Parizeau, Thomas
February 13				
Quebec	0 1 0 - 1	7 7 9 - 23	Corsi	Tardif
Edmonton	3 2 1 - 6	14 17 12 - 43	Mio	Chipperfield 2, Hunter, Gretzky, Callighen, MacDonald
February 14				
Birmingham	1 3 3 - 7	7 10 12 - 29	Wakely	Stewart 2, Vaive 2, Adduono, Gingras, Gorman
New England	2 2 0 - 4	14 12 13 - 39	Garrett	Lyle 2, Stoughton, Ley
Winnipeg	3 1 1 - 5	12 7 9 - 28	Mattsson	Nilsson, Lindstrom, Eriksson, Ruskowski, Lukowich
Cincinnati	0 0 1 - 1	11 11 13 - 35	Liut	Gilligan
February 16				
Edmonton	1 3 0 - 4	1 11 9 - 21	Dryden	Flett, Shmyr, Gretzky, Sobchuk
New England	1 1 0 - 2	11 9 13 - 33	A. Smith	Keon, Lacroix
Winnipeg	0 1 0 - 1	11 19 9 - 39	Mattsson	Preston
Birmingham	0 0 2 - 2	10 4 9 - 23	Riggin	Stewart, Goulet (WG 7:46)
February 17				
Quebec	1 0 0 - 1	13 4 20 - 37	Brodeur	Tardif
New England	0 2 2 - 4	7 14 10 - 31	Garrett	Mk Howe 2, Antonovich, Warner
Winnipeg	1 0 3 - 4	12 9 11 - 32	Mattsson	Lukowich 2, Lindstrom, Ruskowski
Cincinnati	2 1 3 - 6	14 14 13 - 41	Liut	Thomas 2, Gartner 2, Ftorek, Marsh
February 18				
Edmonton	2 1 3 - 6	13 7 8 - 28	Dryden	Driscoll, MacDonald, Chipperfield, Callighen, Semenko, Carlson
Birmingham	1 2 0 - 3	11 10 13 - 34	Wakely	Stewart, Dillon, Goulet
New England	1 1 5 - 7	12 5 13 - 30	Garrett	Mk Howe 2, Miller 2, Lacroix, McKenzie, Pleau
Winnipeg	0 1 0 - 1	10 10 4 - 24	Mattsson	Lesuk
Quebec	1 0 3 - 4	6 5 7 - 18	Brodeur	Leduc, Cloutier, P. Bordeleau, Tardif
Cincinnati	1 1 0 - 2	16 17 12 - 45	Liut	Ftorek, Gilligan
February 20				
New England	0 1 1 - 2	8 4 6 - 18	Garrett	Rogers 2 Hunter
Edmonton	2 2 4 - 8	12 10 10 - 32	Dryden	Carlson 2, Chipperfield, Hamilton, Callighen, Langevin, MacDonald,
Quebec	4 3 0 - 7	11 11 14 - 36	Brodeur	Bernier 2, Tardif 2, Leduc 2, Baxter
Birmingham	1 1 1 - 3	5 10 12 - 27	Riggin, Wakely	Dillon, Gorman, Sleigher
Winnipeg	1 0 1 - 2	6 5 8 - 19	Daley	Lukowich, Nilsson
Cincinnati	1 1 3 - 5	11 6 12 - 29	Liut	Melrose, Clark, Baltimore, Forbes, Ftorek
February 21				
New England	1 0 1 - 2	6 15 13 - 34	A. Smith	Mty Howe, Lacroix
Winnipeg	1 2 2 - 5	13 13 10 - 36	Daley	West 2, Lukowich 2, Moffat
February 23				
Cincinnati	0 1 0 - 1	11 9 6 - 26	Dion	Thomas
Edmonton	0 0 3 - 3	14 13 15 - 42	Dryden	Sobchuk, Gretzky, Chipperfield
Quebec	1 3 0 0 4	9 10 3 0 22	Corsi	Bernier, Tremblay, Cloutier, P. Bordeleau
New England	0 1 3 1 5	14 9 17 4 44	Garrett	Hangsleben 2 (OT 3:03), Lyle, Roberts, Miller
Winnipeg	1 0 0 - 1	7 6 9 - 22	Daley, Mattsson	Davis Hartsburg
Birmingham	5 2 2 - 9	16 8 12 - 36	Wakely	Henderson 2, Stephenson, Vaive, Gorman, Hanson, Sleigher, Adduono
February 24				
New England	0 0 0 - 0	7 7 6 - 20	Garrett	▶ Corsi: shutout (3), 20 saves
Quebec	3 0 3 - 6	15 5 7 - 20	Corsi	Cloutier 2, Cote 2, Bilodeau, Bernier
February 25				
Birmingham	1 1 2 - 4	11 10 12 - 33	Riggin	Henderson, Sleigher, Stewart, Hartsburg
Edmonton	2 2 1 - 5	10 11 9 - 30	Dryden	Weir 2, Gretzky, MacDonald, Sobchuk
Cincinnati	1 0 0 0 1	14 6 7 2 29	Dion	Gilligan
Quebec	0 1 0 0 1	6 19 13 4 42	Brodeur	Tardif
Winnipeg	2 2 3 - 7	14 13 16 - 43	Daley	Lukowich 3, Sullivan 2, Lindstrom, Lesuk
New England	2 1 2 - 5	13 11 15 - 39	A. Smith, Garrett	Mk Howe 2, Rogers, Stoughton, Lacroix

1978-1979 Game by Game Line Scores

Date & Teams	Scoring 1 2 3 ot F	Shots 1 2 3 ot F	Goaltenders	Goals & Other Scoring Highlights
February 27				
Birmingham	1 2 2 - 5	9 14 6 - 29	Wakely	Stephenson 2, Goulet, Alley, Turkiewicz
Winnipeg	1 0 1 - 2	13 11 12 - 36	Mattsson	Sullivan, Nilsson
New England	0 1 0 0 1	6 7 11 0 24	A. Smith	Douglas
Edmonton	0 0 1 0 1	9 8 9 5 31	Dryden	Carlson
March 2				
Cincinnati	2 0 0 - 2	6 10 9 - 25	Liut	Marsh, St. Sauveur
Edmonton	2 1 2 - 5	8 18 6 - 32	Dryden	MacDonald 2, Chipperfield, Callighen, Weir
New England	2 1 1 - 4	11 8 6 - 25	A. Smith	Rogers 2, Warner, Douglas
Winnipeg	1 0 0 - 1	9 10 10 - 29	Daley	Nilsson
March 3				
Birmingham	1 0 1 - 2	14 12 6 - 32	Wakely	Henderson, Stephenson
Quebec	1 1 1 - 3	10 13 11 - 34	Brodeur	Cloutier 2, Tardif
Edmonton	2 2 2 - 6	7 10 12 - 29	Dryden	Chipperfield 3, Callighen 2, Flett
Cincinnati	2 2 0 - 4	8 16 6 - 30	Dion	Marsh 2, Gartner, St. Sauveur
March 4				
Birmingham	2 2 0 - 4	11 7 8 - 26	Riggin	Ramage, Henderson, Goulet, Alley
Quebec	1 3 1 - 5	8 8 9 - 25	Brodeur	Cloutier 3, Leduc, Bernier (WG 7:29)
Cincinnati	0 1 2 1 4	13 6 6 1 26	Liut	Ftorek, Luksa, Thomas, St. Sauveur (OT 0:17)
New England	1 1 1 0 3	13 14 13 0 40	A. Smith	Lyle, Warner, Keon
March 6				
Edmonton	1 2 0 - 3	5 15 10 - 30	Dryden	Gretzky, Callighen, Shmyr
Quebec	0 1 3 - 4	9 10 9 - 28	Brodeur	Brackenbury 2 (WG 18:19), Cloutier 2
Winnipeg	2 1 1 - 4	8 12 7 - 27	G. Smith	Preston 2, Moffat, Lindstrom
Birmingham	3 1 1 - 5	10 10 9 - 29	Wakely	Cassolato, Stephenson, Goulet, Gorman, Hughes
March 7				
Edmonton	2 0 1 - 3	9 6 9 - 24	Dryden	Weir, Gretzky, Carlson
Quebec	2 2 2 - 6	13 9 14 - 36	Brodeur	Cloutier 3, Leduc, Bernier, Lariviere
Winnipeg	3 1 1 - 5	10 4 6 - 20	Mattsson	Nilsson 3, Lukowich, Sullivan
Cincinnati	0 1 2 - 3	13 9 13 - 35	Liut	Shutt, Hislop, Parizeau
March 9				
Edmonton	2 0 2 0 4	9 13 11 6 39	Dryden	Callighen 2, Flett, Micheletti
Birmingham	1 2 1 0 4	11 7 8 4 30	Riggin	Vaive, Adduono, Ramage, Tebbutt
Quebec	1 1 1 - 3	11 7 4 - 22	Corsi	Cloutier, Fitchner, Bernier
New England	1 0 0 - 1	7 20 7 - 34	A. Smith	Ley
March 10				
Quebec	1 0 1 - 2	4 8 5 - 17	Corsi	P. Bordeleau, Cloutier
Cincinnati	1 3 1 - 5	15 13 12 - 40	Dion	Thomas 3, Hislop, Marsh
March 11				
Edmonton	0 3 1 - 4	6 13 6 - 25	Mio	MacDonald 2, Callighen, Langevin
Birmingham	0 0 0 - 0	15 4 5 - 24	Wakely	▶ Mio: shutout (2), 24 saves
New England	0 1 1 - 2	4 5 6 - 15	Garrett	Miller, Rogers (WG 13:02)
Cincinnati	0 1 0 - 1	9 9 8 - 26	Dion	St. Sauveur
Quebec	0 2 0 - 2	5 12 8 - 25	Corsi	Cloutier, Bernier
Winnipeg	2 3 2 - 7	16 15 10 - 41	Mattsson	Moffat 2, Ruskowski 2, Lukowich, MacKinnon, Nilsson
March 13				
Edmonton	0 0 1 - 1	9 10 13 - 32	Mio	Micheletti (spoiled Liut's shutout at 19:35)
Cincinnati	0 4 1 - 5	13 9 5 - 27	Liut	Marsh 2, Ftorek, Gartner, Thomas
New England	0 2 2 - 4	14 14 9 - 37	Garrett	Lyle, Pleau, Douglas, Hangsleben (WG 14:53)
Birmingham	1 2 0 - 3	9 8 11 - 28	Wakely	Vaive, Cassolato, Stewart
March 14				
Quebec	2 0 2 - 4	11 9 7 - 27	Corsi	Leduc, Brackenbury, Cote, Bernier
Winnipeg	0 2 0 - 2	4 5 13 - 22	Mattsson	Lesuk, Ruskowski
March 15				
Birmingham	1 1 1 1 4	10 10 9 3 32	Riggin	Adduono, Hanson, Stewart, Alley (OT 8:16)
New England	0 2 1 0 3	9 7 12 2 30	Garrett	Miller, Lacroix, Plumb
March 16				
Cincinnati	0 1 2 - 3	6 12 13 - 31	Dion	Thomas 2, Hislop
Winnipeg	3 1 1 - 5	10 10 10 - 30	Mattsson	Sullivan, Moffat, Nilsson, Lukowich, Preston
New England	0 3 2 0 5	10 16 10 4 40	A. Smith	Miller 2, Hangsleben, G. Howe, Douglas (TG 19:36)
Birmingham	3 1 1 0 5	10 5 10 3 28	Riggin	Goulet, Cassolato, Adduono, Beaudoin, Dillon
Quebec	0 0 1 - 1	2 4 13 - 19	Brodeur	Fitchner
Edmonton	3 1 2 - 6	11 8 9 - 28	Dryden	Chipperfield 2, Callighen, MacDonald, Semenko, Driscoll
March 18				
Birmingham	1 1 0 - 2	8 11 1 - 20	Wakely	Stewart, Goulet
Winnipeg	1 1 2 - 4	8 6 17 - 31	Mattsson	Preston, Lukowich, Lesuk, Eriksson
Cincinnati	1 0 3 - 4	10 8 9 - 27	Liut	Gilligan, Marsh, Thomas, Ftorek
New England	0 1 0 - 1	7 11 13 - 31	A. Smith	Pleau
Quebec	1 4 2 - 7	8 13 6 - 27	Corsi	Cloutier 3, Leduc 2, Fitchner, P. Bordeleau
Edmonton	1 0 1 - 2	11 5 6 - 22	Dryden	Siltanen, Flett
March 20				
Finland	1 0 3 - 4	2 5 16 - 23	Virtanen	Rinne, Villa, Peltonen, Jyrkkio
Edmonton	3 4 1 - 8	18 33 18 - 69	Dryden, Kampurri	Weir 2, Sobchuk 2, Semenko, Carlson, Siltanen, Gretzky
Birmingham	0 1 1 - 2	7 8 8 - 23	Riggin	Adduono, Henderson
Cincinnati	0 4 1 - 5	11 12 9 - 32	Liut	Gilligan, Gartner, Thomas, Forbes, Messier (first career goal)
New England	2 0 4 1 7	17 4 12 2 35	Garrett	Miller 2 (OT 3:48), Mk Howe, Hangsleben, Keon, Rogers, Lacroix
Quebec	2 1 3 0 6	8 8 10 3 29	Corsi	Cloutier 3, P. Bordeleau, Lariviere, Leduc
March 21				
Edmonton	3 4 0 - 7	7 17 9 - 33	Dryden	Carlson 2, Callighen 2, Sobchuk, Shmyr, Driscoll
Winnipeg	2 0 2 - 4	10 12 14 - 36	Mattsson, G. Smith	Nilsson 2, Preston, Sullivan

1978-1979 Game by Game Line Scores

Date & Teams	Scoring 1 2 3 ot F	Shots 1 2 3 ot F	Goaltenders	Goals & Other Scoring Highlights
March 23				
Cincinnati	1 0 0 - 1	7 12 5 - 24	Liut	Gartner
Birmingham	1 1 0 - 2	13 14 11 - 38	Wakely	Stewart, Goulet
Quebec	0 2 1 - 3	7 7 5 - 19	Corsi	Cloutier, Leduc, P. Bordeleau
New England	2 1 2 - 5	9 7 10 - 26	Garrett	Keon 2, Pleau, Warner, Rogers
Winnipeg	1 3 2 - 6	5 11 7 - 23	G. Smith	Lukowich 3, Hicks, MacKinnon, Ruskowski
Edmonton	2 2 0 - 4	16 12 12 - 40	Dryden	Hamilton, Semenko, Sobchuk, Gretzky
March 24				
Birmingham	0 3 1 - 4	3 15 11 - 29	Wakely	Stewart 2, Adduono, Sleigher
New England	2 0 1 - 3	10 15 15 - 40	Garrett	Rogers, Mk Howe, G. Howe
Quebec	1 3 1 - 5	8 9 4 - 21	Brodeur	Leduc 2, Baxter, Bilodeau, Cloutier
Cincinnati	0 0 2 - 2	12 13 13 - 38	Dion	Marsh 2
March 25				
Birmingham	1 0 1 - 2	6 6 8 - 20	Riggin	Stewart, Goulet
Quebec	1 1 1 - 3	15 6 10 - 31	Brodeur	Tardif, P. Bordeleau, Baxter (WG 17:14)
Edmonton	3 1 2 - 6	5 10 13 - 28	Dryden	Flett 3, Micheletti, Weir, Callighen
Cincinnati	3 2 0 - 5	8 15 7 - 30	Liut	Hislop, Ftorek, Marsh, Gilligan, Shutt
March 27				
New England	0 0 1 - 1	13 10 7 - 30	A. Smith	Keon
Birmingham	0 1 2 - 3	8 4 8 - 20	Wakely, Riggin	Gorman, Stewart, Alley
March 28				
Cincinnati	2 0 1 - 3	13 10 10 - 33	Liut	Ftorek, Marsh, Gilligan
Winnipeg	2 1 3 - 6	17 12 9 - 38	G. Smith	Lukowich 2, Lindstrom, Long, Preston, Guindon
Edmonton	0 0 0 - 0	6 7 13 - 26	Mio	▸ Brodeur: shutout (2), 26 saves
Quebec	0 1 2 - 3	10 6 12 - 28	Brodeur	Cote, Cloutier, Leduc
March 30				
Cincinnati	1 0 2 - 3	9 8 15 - 32	Liut	Gartner 2, Ftorek
Birmingham	1 0 1 - 2	9 7 7 - 23	Wakely	Henderson, Stewart
Edmonton	1 1 1 - 3	12 7 10 - 29	Dryden	Flett, Hunter, Callighen
New England	0 1 0 - 1	6 5 6 - 17	Garrett	Rogers
Quebec	0 1 1 - 2	11 4 5 - 20	Brodeur	Cloutier, Fitchner
Winnipeg	0 0 0 - 0	16 10 9 - 35	G. Smith	▸ Brodeur: shutout (3), 35 saves
March 31				
Cincinnati	2 1 0 - 3	8 5 6 - 19	Liut	Thomas, Hislop, Marsh
Birmingham	1 4 1 - 6	17 14 5 - 36	Wakely	Stephenson 2, Vaive 2, Alley, Cassolato
April 1				
Edmonton	2 0 3 - 5	8 6 15 - 29	Dryden	Sobchuk, Weir, MacDonald, Siltanen, Flett
New England	2 0 1 - 3	8 5 11 - 24	A. Smith	Mk Howe, Rogers, McKenzie
Winnipeg	4 3 0 - 7	14 15 12 - 41	G. Smith	Lukowich 2, Lindstrom 2, Sullivan, Preston, Terbenche
Quebec	3 0 0 - 3	9 11 6 - 26	Brodeur, Corsi	Geoffrion, Cloutier, Baxter
April 3				
Edmonton	2 2 1 - 5	9 8 8 - 25	Dryden	Weir, Gretzky, Flett, MacDonald, Driscoll
Cincinnati	1 0 0 - 1	10 10 6 - 26	Liut, Dion	Ftorek
Quebec	1 1 1 - 3	8 10 11 - 29	Corsi	Tardif, Cloutier, Weir
Birmingham	0 3 2 - 5	8 17 9 - 34	Wakely	Stephenson 2, Ramage, Vaive, Stewart
April 4				
Edmonton	2 0 0 - 2	9 3 12 - 24	Dryden	Flett, Hughes
Quebec	0 1 3 - 4	8 10 10 - 28	Brodeur	Tardif 2, Brackenbury, Fitchner
New England	2 1 1 - 4	8 8 4 - 20	A. Smith	Pleau, Keon, McKenzie, Mk Howe
Winnipeg	0 0 2 - 2	5 8 13 - 26	Mattsson, Daley	Lindstrom 2
April 6				
Birmingham	2 0 0 - 2	7 4 6 - 17	Wakely	Vaive, Cassolato
Winnipeg	0 1 0 - 1	9 13 5 - 27	G. Smith	Sullivan
New England	1 1 0 - 2	10 12 8 - 30	A. Smith	McKenzie, Lyle
Edmonton	2 4 1 - 7	11 5 11 - 27	Dryden	Gretzky 2, Micheletti, Flett, Weir, Driscoll, Carlson
April 7				
Quebec	1 1 0 - 2	7 7 7 - 21	Brodeur	Cote, P. Bordeleau
Cincinnati	1 2 3 - 6	13 13 16 - 42	Dion	Hislop 3, Parizeau, Shutt, Marsh
April 8				
Birmingham	0 2 2 - 4	5 6 11 - 22	Riggin	Adduono 2, Goulet, Stephenson
Edmonton	2 1 2 - 5	22 8 10 - 40	Dryden	Weir 2, Flett, Callighen, Sobchuk
New England	2 2 0 - 4	11 4 11 - 26	A. Smith	McKenzie, Lyle, Miller, Lacroix
Winnipeg	3 1 2 - 6	15 9 11 - 35	G. Smith	Lukowich 2, Nilsson 2, Ruskowski, Lesuk
April 10				
New England	0 2 3 - 5	11 14 13 - 38	Garrett	Miller, Warner, G. Howe, Mk Howe, Pleau
Quebec	0 1 1 - 2	5 7 11 - 23	Corsi	Leduc, Fitchner
Winnipeg	1 3 2 - 6	10 9 8 - 27	G. Smith	Lukowich 2, Preston, Ruskowski, Sullivan, Lindstrom
Edmonton	0 1 3 - 4	11 8 10 - 29	Dryden, Mio	Gretzky 3 (Natural hat trick, 3rd period), Callighen
April 11				
Birmingham	0 1 0 - 1	5 9 9 - 23	Wakely	Alley
Winnipeg	1 1 0 - 2	10 16 9 - 35	G. Smith	Sullivan, Preston
Cincinnati	3 0 3 - 6	12 11 13 - 36	Dion	Marsh, Stewart, Ftorek, Shutt, Legge, Baltimore
Quebec	0 1 1 - 2	6 9 11 - 26	Brodeur	Leduc, Lacombe
April 12				
Cincinnati	0 0 0 - 0	11 4 7 - 22	Liut	▸ Garrett: shutout (2), 22 saves
New England	1 1 2 - 4	15 18 10 - 43	Garrett	Roberts 2, Lyle, McKenzie
April 13				
Edmonton	2 1 3 - 6	11 8 11 - 30	Mio	Carlson, Callighen, Gretzky, Flett, Weir, Driscoll
Birmingham	3 1 0 - 4	10 9 10 - 29	Riggin	Hartsburg 2, Ramage, Hanson

1978-1979 Game by Game Line Scores

Date & Teams	Scoring 1 2 3 ot F	Shots 1 2 3 ot F	Goaltenders	Goals & Other Scoring Highlights
April 14				
Cincinnati	1 2 1 - 4	10 9 10 - 29	Liut	Marsh, Thomas, Forbes, Hislop
New England	0 0 0 - 0	8 10 7 - 25	Garrett	▶ Liut: shutout (3), 25 saves
Edmonton	2 1 3 - 6	13 8 9 - 30	Kampurri	Callighen 2, Goldsworthy, Chipperfield, Shmyr, Carlson
Birmingham	3 2 2 - 7	7 9 13 - 29	Wakely	Stephenson 2, Cassolato 2, Ramage, Alley, Sleigher
April 15				
Birmingham	1 3 0 0 4	8 10 5 4 27	Wakely	Stephenson, Cassolato, Gingras, Goulet
Winnipeg	2 2 0 1 5	10 12 12 6 40	G. Smith	Sullivan 2 (OT 9:00), Ruskowski, Eriksson, Preston
Cincinnati	0 1 1 - 2	9 13 11 - 33	Dion	Marsh, Stewart
Quebec	2 2 0 - 4	8 12 4 - 24	Brodeur	Bernier, Leduc, Cote, Tardif
Edmonton	1 1 2 - 4	6 7 11 - 24	Dryden	Gretzky 3, MacDonald,
New England	0 1 0 - 1	6 10 10 - 26	Garrett	Mk Howe
April 17				
New England	1 1 1 - 3	13 10 13 - 36	Garrett	Stoughton, G. Howe, Plumb (WG 18:12)
Quebec	1 0 1 - 2	9 4 11 - 24	Corsi	Leduc, Cote
April 18				
Winnipeg	2 1 0 - 3	8 6 6 - 20	Daley, Mattsson	Long, Sullivan, Nilsson
Edmonton	3 2 4 - 9	17 11 18 - 46	Mio	Chipperfield 2, Weir 2, Callighen 2, Driscoll, Gretzky, Hunter

End of Regular Season

1979 Playoffs Game by Game Line Scores

Date & Teams	Scoring 1 2 3 ot F	Shots 1 2 3 ot F	Goaltenders	Goals & Other Scoring Highlights
April 21				
Cincinnati	1 0 2 - 3	8 9 9 - 26	Liut	Parizeau, Shutt, Hislop
New England	0 2 3 - 5	13 15 11 - 39	Garrett	Mk Howe, Stoughton, Lacroix, Rogers
April 22				
New England	0 1 2 - 3	7 9 16 - 32	Garrett, A. Smith	Rogers, G. Howe, Antonovich
Cincinnati	3 2 1 - 6	13 7 8 - 28	Liut	Ftorek 3, Thomas, Marsh, Gilligan
April 23				
Winnipeg	1 5 0 - 6	8 12 10 - 30	G. Smith	Guindon 2, Moffat, Preston, Lukowich, Lindstrom
Quebec	1 1 1 - 3	14 12 5 - 31	Brodeur, Corsi	Tarfdif 2, Fitchner
April 24				
Cincinnati	1 0 0 - 1	10 11 12 - 33	Liut	Hislop
New England	1 1 0 - 2	7 18 9 - 34	A. Smith	MacKenzie, Stoughton
April 25				
Winnipeg	3 3 3 - 9	14 9 9 - 32	G. Smith, Daley	Lindstrom 2, Preston, West, Sjoberg, Lukowich, MacKinnon, Hicks,
Quebec	0 1 1 - 2	3 8 12 - 23	Corsi, Brodeur	Tardif 2 Sullivan
April 26				
New England	1 0 1 - 2	5 7 9 - 21	A. Smith	G. Howe, Pleau
Edmonton	0 3 3 - 6	9 11 9 - 29	Dryden	MacDonald 3, Carlson, Sobchuk, Weir
April 27				
Quebec	1 3 1 - 5	9 11 10 - 30	Levasseur	Cloutier, Brackenbury, Geoffrion, P. Bordeleau, Tardif
Winnipeg	2 2 5 - 9	17 11 11 - 39	G. Smith	Preston 2, Sullivan 2, West, Terbenche, Eriksson, Lukowich, Lindstrom
New England	2 1 2 - 5	9 11 7 - 27	A. Smith, Garrett	Antonovich, G. Howe, Hangsleben, Mk Howe, Pleau
Edmonton	4 2 3 - 9	15 11 13 - 39	Dryden	Callighen 3, Semenko 2, Gretzky, Flett, MacDonald, Hamilton
April 29				
Quebec	1 0 1 - 2	4 4 6 - 14	Brodeur	Tardif, Cloutier
Winnipeg	1 3 2 - 6	17 16 17 - 50	G. Smith	Lindstrom 2, Lukowich, Ruskowski, Sullivan, Nilsson
Edmonton	1 0 0 - 1	10 7 6 - 23	Dryden	Gretzky
New England	2 0 2 - 4	10 0 7 - 17	Garrett	Lyle 2, Mk Howe, Keon
May 1				
Edmonton	1 1 2 - 4	3 14 10 - 27	Dryden	Gretzky, Chipperfield, Flett, MacDonald
New England	0 4 1 - 5	13 10 7 - 30	Garrett	Douglas 2, Lyle, Lacroix, McKenzie
May 3				
New England	0 0 2 - 2	3 8 10 - 21	Garrett	McKenzie, Douglas
Edmonton	2 1 2 - 5	8 10 12 - 30	Dryden	Gretzky 3, Hunter, Shmyr
May 5				
Edmonton	0 2 2 - 4	9 12 11 - 32	Dryden, Mio	Hamilton, Sobchuk, MacDonald, Semenko
New England	4 2 2 - 8	13 13 9 - 35	Garrett	Keon 2, Antonovich 2, Plumb, Douglas, Stoughton, Lacroix
May 8				
New England	1 0 2 - 3	8 3 14 - 25	Garrett	Lacroix, Stoughton, Antonovich
Edmonton	2 4 0 - 6	11 14 4 - 29	Dryden	Gretzky 2, MacDonald, Sobchuk, Chipperfield, Flett
May 11				
Winnipeg	2 0 1 - 3	11 9 8 - 28	G. Smith	Preston 2, Lesuk
Edmonton	1 0 0 - 1	5 9 10 - 24	Dryden	Flett
May 13				
Winnipeg	0 0 3 - 3	8 8 11 - 27	G. Smith	Sullivan, Lukowich, Lindstrom (WG 15:53)
Edmonton	0 1 1 - 2	5 9 7 - 21	Dryden	Sobchuk, Hamilton
May 15				
Edmonton	4 0 4 - 8	12 5 10 - 27	Dryden	Hamilton, Driscoll, Chipperfield, Goldsworthy, MacDonald, Hunter,
Winnipeg	2 1 0 - 3	8 8 10 - 26	G. Smith, Daley	Lukowich 2, Lindstrom Callighen, Gustafsson
May 16				
Edmonton	1 1 0 - 2	5 10 7 - 22	Dryden	Gretzky, Callighen
Winnipeg	1 0 2 - 3	11 10 6 - 27	G. Smith	Preston, Lukowich, Moffat (WG 13:34)

1979 Playoffs Game by Game Line Scores

Date & Teams	Scoring 1 2 3 ot F	Shots 1 2 3 ot F	Goaltenders	Goals & Other Scoring Highlights
May 18				
Winnipeg	0 1 1 - 2	5 8 8 - 21	G. Smith, Daley	Preston, Nilsson
Edmonton	4 4 2 - 10	16 12 13 - 41	Dryden, Mio	Chipperfield 5, Sobchuk 2, Gretzky, Weir, Hughes
May 20				
Edmonton	0 1 2 - 3	11 8 11 - 30	Dryden, Mio	Chipperfield, Flett, Semenko
Winnipeg	2 3 2 - 7	10 13 11 - 34	G. Smith	Lindstrom 2, Long 2, MacKinnon, Moffat, Nilsson

Winnipeg is League Champion

The 1999 World Hockey Association Reunion
Casino Windsor Hotel • Windsor, Ontario • July 1999

The first significant reunion of players and executives of the World Hockey Association was held in July 1999 at the Casino Windsor Hotel in Windsor, Ontario. I was invited by Mr. Cory McCrindle of CBC-Windsor, who was producing a WHA retrospective for which I gave a short interview.

I had a long day of flying and driving such that when I arrived at the Casino Windsor Hotel, I had been travelling for nearly 12 hours. Tired, I gathered my bags and checked in to the hotel, then stood by the elevators, waiting for one to open. One did, and a whole stream of people exited, with a sharply-dressed gray-haired man kindly keeping the elevator door open so I could enter. My thanks to Gordie Howe for keeping that door open for me. The fun was just starting.

I met over three dozen former players and executives, surprised I could recognize them so many years later. I was able to speak with Gordie Howe for a few minutes, and had a short talk with Bobby Hull, but he was so swamped with well-wishers I never had a good chance to speak with him.

The dinner went well, and I was seated with Peter Marrin and his wife, and Frank Beaton. The events included a keynote speech by television personality Larry King, and a fascinating video retrospective including rare footage.

Dennis Murphy was there, but Gary Davidson was not. The most touching moments, however, were those involving William "Wild Bill" Hunter, the man who brought Canada to the WHA. Hunter, nearly 80 and very ill, managed to make the dinner and he was feted by everyone, many openly stating that seeing him, likely for the last time, was a main reason for attending. I chatted with Mr. Hunter for a few minutes, and I found him to be exceptionally nice, and despite his ailments, possessing a strength and confidence much to be admired. He passed away in 2002.

I left the next morning for my long flight back to Arizona. I am very happy I went and I thank Cory for his persistence in convincing me to attend, and the players, executives and everyone else for putting on such an enjoyable, superb reunion.

Left: Gordie Howe holds my book as we chatted and talked stats. **Right:** I am standing on the left, with Ron Ward, Gordie Gallant and Ralph Backstrom beside me. Gordie Gallant may have fought a lot of players in his WHA days, but he had only good things to say about his adversaries.

1978-1979 BIRMINGHAM BULLS

**Coach
John Brophy**

Summary of Games (@ Away, * Overtime)

	date	opponent	score		record	pts	gf-ga		date	opponent	score		record	pts	gf-ga
1	Oct 13	Winnipeg	*4-5	L	0-1-0	0	4-5	41	Jan 19 @ Edmonton		3-11	L	15-23-3	33	144-167
2	Oct 15 @ Indianapolis		9-3	W	1-1-0	2	13-8	42	Jan 21 @ Edmonton		4-3	W	16-23-3	35	148-170
3	Oct 20 @ Cincinnati		2-5	L	1-2-0	2	15-13	43	Jan 23	Quebec	5-7	L	16-24-3	35	153-177
4	Oct 22 @ Quebec		8-5	W	2-2-0	4	23-18	44	Jan 26	New England	5-4	W	17-24-3	37	158-181
5	Oct 24 @ Edmonton		3-2	W	3-2-0	6	26-20	45	Jan 30	Quebec	2-1	W	18-24-3	39	160-182
6	Oct 25 @ Winnipeg		2-7	L	3-3-0	6	28-27	46	Feb 1	Quebec	7-5	W	19-24-3	41	167-187
7	Oct 27	Indianapolis	4-2	W	4-3-0	8	32-29	47	Feb 3	New England	2-2	T	19-24-4	42	169-189
8	Nov 1 @ Cincinnati		*4-3	W	5-3-0	10	36-32	48	Feb 6 @ Edmonton		2-6	L	19-25-4	42	171-195
9	Nov 3	Quebec	2-3	L	5-4-0	10	38-35	49	Feb 7 @ Winnipeg		2-3	L	19-26-4	42	173-198
10	Nov 4	Quebec	1-4	L	5-5-0	10	39-39	50	Feb 11 @ Edmonton		*3-4	L	19-27-4	42	176-202
11	Nov 9	Winnipeg	6-5	W	6-5-0	12	45-44	51	Feb 14 @ New England		7-4	W	20-27-4	44	183-206
12	Nov 11	Edmonton	3-5	L	6-6-0	12	48-49	52	Feb 16	Winnipeg	2-1	W	21-27-4	46	185-207
13	Nov 14	New England	5-5	T	6-6-1	13	53-54	53	Feb 18	Edmonton	3-6	L	21-28-4	46	188-213
14	Nov 17	New England	7-1	W	7-6-1	15	60-55	54	Feb 20	Quebec	3-7	L	21-29-4	46	191-220
15	Nov 18 @ New England		3-2	W	8-6-1	17	63-57	55	Feb 23	Winnipeg	9-1	W	22-29-4	48	200-221
16	Nov 22 @ Cincinnati		*5-6	L	8-7-1	17	68-63	56	Feb 25 @ Edmonton		4-5	L	22-30-4	48	204-226
17	Nov 23	Cincinnati	3-4	L	8-8-1	17	71-67	57	Feb 27 @ Winnipeg		5-2	W	23-30-4	50	209-228
18	Nov 25 @ New England		2-5	L	8-9-1	17	73-72	58	Mar 3 @ Quebec		2-3	L	23-31-4	50	211-231
19	Nov 26 @ New England		3-9	L	8-10-1	17	76-81	59	Mar 4 @ Quebec		4-5	L	23-32-4	50	215-236
20	Nov 29 @ Quebec		4-7	L	8-11-1	17	80-88	60	Mar 6	Winnipeg	5-4	W	24-32-4	52	220-240
21	Dec 1 @ Indianapolis		3-6	L	8-12-1	17	83-94	61	Mar 9	Edmonton	4-4	T	24-32-5	53	224-244
22	Dec 2	Indianapolis	4-2	W	9-12-1	19	87-96	62	Mar 11	Edmonton	0-4	L	24-33-5	53	224-248
23	Dec 7	Cincinnati	4-2	W	10-12-1	21	91-98	63	Mar 13	New England	3-4	L	24-34-5	53	227-252
24	Dec 9	Edmonton	6-2	W	11-12-1	23	97-100	64	Mar 15 @ New England		*4-3	W	25-34-5	55	231-255
25	Dec 10	Cincinnati	1-0	W	12-12-1	25	98-100	65	Mar 16	New England	5-5	T	25-34-6	56	236-260
26	Dec 14 @ Quebec		2-3	L	12-13-1	25	100-103	66	Mar 18 @ Winnipeg		2-4	L	25-35-6	56	238-264
27	Dec 16 @ Cincinnati		2-2	T	12-13-2	26	102-105	67	Mar 20 @ Cincinnati		2-5	L	25-36-6	56	240-269
28	Dec 17	Soviet All-Stars	2-2	T	12-13-3	27	104-107	68	Mar 23	Cincinnati	2-1	W	26-36-6	58	242-270
29	Dec 19	Edmonton	2-5	L	12-14-3	27	106-112	69	Mar 24 @ New England		4-3	W	27-36-6	60	246-273
30	Dec 22	Quebec	1-5	L	12-15-3	27	107-117	70	Mar 25 @ Quebec		2-3	L	27-37-6	60	248-276
31	Dec 23 @ New England		3-4	L	12-16-3	27	110-121	71	Mar 27	New England	3-1	W	28-37-6	62	251-277
32	Dec 26	Cincinnati	4-2	W	13-16-3	29	114-123	72	Mar 30	Cincinnati	2-3	L	28-38-6	62	253-280
33	Dec 28 @ Cincinnati		6-5	W	14-16-3	31	120-128	73	Mar 31	Cincinnati	6-3	W	29-38-6	64	259-283
34	Dec 29 @ New England		0-5	L	14-17-3	31	120-133	74	Apr 3	Quebec	5-3	W	30-38-6	66	264-286
35	Dec 30 @ Quebec		2-3	L	14-18-3	31	122-136	75	Apr 6 @ Winnipeg		2-1	W	31-38-6	68	266-287
36	Jan 7	Czechoslovakia	10-2	W	15-18-3	33	132-138	76	Apr 8 @ Edmonton		4-5	L	31-39-6	68	270-292
37	Jan 12	Winnipeg	1-3	L	15-19-3	33	133-141	77	Apr 11 @ Winnipeg		1-2	L	31-40-6	68	271-294
38	Jan 13	Winnipeg	1-3	L	15-20-3	33	134-144	78	Apr 13	Edmonton	4-6	L	31-41-6	68	275-300
39	Jan 14 @ Cincinnati		2-4	L	15-21-3	33	136-148	79	Apr 14	Edmonton	7-6	W	32-41-6	70	282-306
40	Jan 17 @ Cincinnati		5-8	L	15-22-3	33	141-156	80	Apr 15 @ Winnipeg		*4-5	L	32-42-6	70	286-311

Bulls Stars of 1978-1979

Rick Vaive	**Michel Goulet**	**Louis Sleigher**	**Pat Riggin**	**Craig Hartsburg**	**Rob Ramage**
59 points led team	28 goals, 58 points	26 goals	16 wins, 1 shutout	49 points, +9 rating	48 points, +10 rating

Scoring

						Regular Season								Playoffs				
pos	#	player	gp	g	a	pts	pim	+/-	ppg	shg	sog	sc%	gp	g	a	pts	pim	+/-
C	14	Adduono, Rick	80	20	33	53	67	-2	4	1	131	0.152	-	-	-	-	-	-
LW	11	Alley, Steve	78	17	24	41	36	-5	4	0	122	0.139	-	-	-	-	-	-
D	5	Beaudoin, Serge	72	5	21	26	127	-8	1	0	89	0.056	-	-	-	-	-	-
RW	24	Cassolato, Tony	64	13	7	20	62	+1	2	0	66	0.197	-	-	-	-	-	-
RW	12	Crowder, Keith	5	1	0	1	17	-1	0	0	-	-	-	-	-	-	-	-
C	25	Dillon, Wayne	64	12	27	39	43	-3	4	0	80	0.150	-	-	-	-	-	-
D	8	Gingras, Gaston	60	13	21	34	35	+1	0	2	138	0.094	-	-	-	-	-	-
RW	7	Gorman, Dave	60	14	24	38	18	-1	2	0	74	0.189	-	-	-	-	-	-
LW	9	Goulet, Michel	78	28	30	58	65	+13	3	0	146	0.192	-	-	-	-	-	-
D	15	Hanson, Dave	53	6	22	28	212	-8	0	0	66	0.091	-	-	-	-	-	-
D	4	Hartsburg, Craig	77	9	40	49	73	+9	4	0	181	0.050	-	-	-	-	-	-
LW	19	Henderson, Paul	76	24	27	51	20	-2	6	1	190	0.126	-	-	-	-	-	-
D	3	Hughes, Brent	48	3	3	6	21	-9	1	0	40	0.075	-	-	-	-	-	-
C	16	Kirk, Gavin	30	1	5	6	16	-2	0	0	27	0.037	-	-	-	-	-	-
C	20	Marrin, Peter	20	4	11	15	18	+1	1	0	37	0.108	-	-	-	-	-	-
C	15	O'Neil, Paul	1	0	0	0	0	-1	0	0	1	0.000	-	-	-	-	-	-
D	6	Ramage, Rob	80	12	36	48	165	+10	2	1	214	0.056	-	-	-	-	-	-
G	30	Riggin, Pat	46	0	3	3	22		0	0	0		-	-	-	-	-	-
RW	23	Sleigher, Louis	62	26	12	38	46	-9	7	0	108	0.241	-	-	-	-	-	-
D	21	Stephenson, Bob	78	23	24	47	72	-15	2	0	118	0.195	-	-	-	-	-	-
C	18	Stewart, John C.	70	24	26	50	108	-3	4	0	126	0.190	-	-	-	-	-	-
D	10	Tebbutt, Greg	38	2	5	7	83	0	1	0	33	0.062	-	-	-	-	-	-
D	2	Turkiewicz, Jim	79	3	17	20	52	-15	0	0	93	0.032	-	-	-	-	-	-
RW	22	Vaive, Rick	75	26	33	59	248	+14	3	0	173	0.150	-	-	-	-	-	-
G	35	Wakely, Ernie	37	0	3	3	0		0	0	0	-	-	-	-	-	-	-
G	1	Wood, Wayne	6	0	0	0	6		0	0	0		-	-	-	-	-	-

Power Play: 51 goals scored in 259 opportunities (19.7%) with 7 short-handed goals allowed.
Penalty Killing: 69 goals allowed in 277 opportunities (75.1%) with 5 short-handed goals scored.

Goaltending

goaltender	gp	min	ga	en	so	record	gaa	sog	sv%	gp	min	ga	record	gaa
Riggin, Pat	46	2511	158	1	1	16-22-5	3.78	1322	0.880	-	-	-	-	-
Wakely, Ernie	37	2060	129	2	0	15-17-1	3.76	1073	0.880	-	-	-	-	-
Wood, Wayne	6	311	21	0	0	1-3-0	4.05	156	0.865	-	-	-	-	-

Transactions: Michel Goulet, Craig Hartsburg, Rob Ramage signed to contracts, Jun 1978 • Rick Adduono, Keith Crowder, Paul O'Neil, Pat Riggin signed to contracts, Jul 1978 • Ernie Wakely signed to contract after securing release from Winnipeg, Jul 1978 (Winnipeg had purchased his contract from defunct Houston) • Louis Sleigher signed to contract, Sep 1978 • Dave Hanson purchased from Detroit (NHL), Dec 1978

1978-1979 CINCINNATI STINGERS

**Coach
Floyd Smith**

Summary of Games (@ Away, * Overtime)

	date	opponent	score		record	pts	gf-ga		date	opponent	score		record	pts	gf-ga
1	Oct 13 @	Edmonton	2-3	L	0-1-0	0	2-3	41	Jan 12	Quebec	1-2	L	16-21-4	36	141-149
2	Oct 15 @	Winnipeg	4-3	W	1-1-0	2	6-6	42	Jan 14	Birmingham	4-2	W	17-21-4	38	145-151
3	Oct 17 @	Quebec	5-5	T	1-1-1	3	11-11	43	Jan 17	Birmingham	8-5	W	18-21-4	40	153-156
4	Oct 20	Birmingham	5-2	W	2-1-1	5	16-13	44	Jan 19 @	Winnipeg	7-2	W	19-21-4	42	160-158
5	Oct 21	Edmonton	4-3	W	3-1-1	7	20-16	45	Jan 20 @	New England	1-3	L	19-22-4	42	161-161
6	Oct 24	New England	1-2	L	3-2-1	7	21-18	46	Jan 24	Winnipeg	5-5	T	19-22-5	43	166-166
7	Oct 25 @	Quebec	3-4	L	3-3-1	7	24-22	47	Jan 26 @	Edmonton	5-2	W	20-22-5	45	171-168
8	Oct 28	Quebec	*4-3	W	4-3-1	9	28-25	48	Jan 28 @	Edmonton	0-3	L	20-23-5	45	171-171
9	Oct 29 @	New England	7-4	W	5-3-1	11	35-29	49	Feb 4 @	Winnipeg	1-8	L	20-24-5	45	172-179
10	Nov 1	Birmingham	*3-4	L	5-4-1	11	38-33	50	Feb 7 @	Edmonton	5-8	L	20-25-5	45	177-187
11	Nov 5	New England	5-4	W	6-4-1	13	43-37	51	Feb 9	Winnipeg	4-0	W	21-25-5	47	181-187
12	Nov 8	Indianapolis	4-0	W	7-4-1	15	47-37	52	Feb 11	New England	5-2	W	22-25-5	49	186-189
13	Nov 10	Winnipeg	3-2	W	8-4-1	17	50-39	53	Feb 14	Winnipeg	1-5	L	22-26-5	49	187-194
14	Nov 11 @	New England	1-2	L	8-5-1	17	51-41	54	Feb 17	Winnipeg	6-4	W	23-26-5	51	193-198
15	Nov 12	Edmonton	5-3	W	9-5-1	19	56-44	55	Feb 18	Quebec	2-4	L	23-27-5	51	195-202
16	Nov 15	New England	4-4	T	9-5-2	20	60-48	56	Feb 20	Winnipeg	5-2	W	24-27-5	53	200-204
17	Nov 17 @	Winnipeg	6-10	L	9-6-2	20	66-58	57	Feb 23 @	Edmonton	1-3	L	24-28-5	53	201-207
18	Nov 19 @	Edmonton	3-6	L	9-7-2	20	69-64	58	Feb 25 @	Quebec	1-1	T	24-28-6	54	202-208
19	Nov 22	Birmingham	*6-5	W	10-7-2	22	75-69	59	Mar 2 @	Edmonton	2-5	L	24-29-6	54	204-213
20	Nov 23 @	Birmingham	4-3	W	11-7-2	24	79-72	60	Mar 3	Edmonton	4-6	L	24-30-6	54	208-219
21	Nov 24	Indianapolis	8-5	W	12-7-2	26	87-77	61	Mar 4 @	New England	*4-3	W	25-30-6	56	212-222
22	Nov 25 @	Indianapolis	3-6	L	12-8-2	26	90-83	62	Mar 7	Winnipeg	3-5	L	25-31-6	56	215-227
23	Dec 1 @	Winnipeg	6-5	W	13-8-2	28	96-88	63	Mar 10	Quebec	5-2	W	26-31-6	58	220-229
24	Dec 2 @	Quebec	0-2	L	13-9-2	28	96-90	64	Mar 11	New England	1-2	L	26-32-6	58	221-231
25	Dec 3 @	Indianapolis	4-2	W	14-9-2	30	100-92	65	Mar 13	Edmonton	5-1	W	27-32-6	60	226-232
26	Dec 5	New England	2-2	T	14-9-3	31	102-94	66	Mar 16 @	Winnipeg	3-5	L	27-33-6	60	229-237
27	Dec 7 @	Birmingham	2-4	L	14-10-3	31	104-98	67	Mar 18 @	New England	4-1	W	28-33-6	62	233-238
28	Dec 9 @	Quebec	3-4	L	14-11-3	31	107-102	68	Mar 20	Birmingham	5-2	W	29-33-6	64	238-240
29	Dec 10 @	Birmingham	0-1	L	14-12-3	31	107-103	69	Mar 23 @	Birmingham	1-2	L	29-34-6	64	239-242
30	Dec 12	Edmonton	2-5	L	14-13-3	31	109-108	70	Mar 24	Quebec	2-5	L	29-35-6	64	241-247
31	Dec 16	Birmingham	2-2	T	14-13-4	32	111-110	71	Mar 25	Edmonton	5-6	L	29-36-6	64	246-253
32	Dec 17 @	Winnipeg	3-6	L	14-14-4	32	114-116	72	Mar 28 @	Winnipeg	3-6	L	29-37-6	64	249-259
33	Dec 20	Soviet All-Stars	3-5	L	14-15-4	32	117-121	73	Mar 30 @	Birmingham	3-2	W	30-37-6	66	252-261
34	Dec 23	Quebec	6-2	W	15-15-4	34	123-123	74	Mar 31 @	Birmingham	3-6	L	30-38-6	66	255-267
35	Dec 26 @	Birmingham	2-4	L	15-16-4	34	125-127	75	Apr 3	Edmonton	1-5	L	30-39-6	66	256-272
36	Dec 28	Birmingham	5-6	L	15-17-4	34	130-133	76	Apr 7	Quebec	6-2	W	31-39-6	68	262-274
37	Dec 30	New England	2-1	W	16-17-4	36	132-134	77	Apr 11 @	Quebec	6-2	W	32-39-6	70	268-276
38	Jan 6	Czechoslovakia	1-4	L	16-18-4	36	133-138	78	Apr 12 @	New England	0-4	L	32-40-6	70	268-280
39	Jan 7 @	New England	4-5	L	16-19-4	36	137-143	79	Apr 14 @	New England	4-0	W	33-40-6	72	272-280
40	Jan 9	Quebec	3-4	L	16-20-4	36	140-147	80	Apr 15 @	Quebec	2-4	L	33-41-6	72	274-284

Stingers Stars of 1978-1979

Peter Marsh
43 goals

Jamie Hislop
30 goals, 70 points

Mike Liut
23 wins, 3 shutouts

Robbie Ftorek
116 points

Reg Thomas
32 goals, 71 points

Mike Gartner
27 goals as rookie

Scoring

pos	#	player	gp	g	a	pts	pim	+/-	ppg	shg	sog	sc%	gp	g	a	pts	pim	+/-
						Regular Season									**Playoffs**			
D	5	Baltimore, Bryon	69	4	10	14	83	-22	1	0	60	0.067	3	0	0	0	0	0
RW	20	Clark, Gordie	21	3	3	6	2	-2	0	0	18	0.167	-	-	-	-	-	-
D	10	Davis, Kelly	18	0	1	1	20	-2	0	0	11	0.000	-	-	-	-	-	-
C	12	Debol, Dave	59	10	27	37	9	-22	2	0	141	0.071	-	-	-	-	-	-
G	30	Dion, Michel	30	0	0	0	2		0	0	0	-	-	-	-	-	-	-
D	10	Dornseif, Dave	1	0	0	0	0	-1	0	0	1	0.000	-	-	-	-	-	-
LW	9	Dudley, Rick	47	17	20	37	102	+5	3	0	106	0.160	-	-	-	-	-	-
LW	19	Forbes, Dave	73	6	5	11	83	-21	0	2	51	0.118	3	0	1	1	7	-3
C	8	Ftorek, Robbie	80	39	77	116	87	+11	14	3	260	0.150	3	3	2	5	6	+2
RW	11	Gartner, Mike	78	27	25	52	123	-18	9	0	227	0.119	3	0	0	0	2	-2
C	15	Gilbert, Ed	29	3	3	6	40	-9	1	0	60	0.050	-	-	-	-	-	-
C	16	Gilligan, Bill	74	17	26	43	54	+6	2	0	95	0.179	3	1	0	1	0	-3
RW	24	Hislop, Jamie	80	30	40	70	45	+8	9	1	183	0.164	3	2	4	6	0	+1
D	25	Legge, Barry	80	3	8	11	131	-13	0	0	104	0.029	3	0	4	4	0	-3
G	1	Liut, Mike	54	0	2	2	9		0	0	0	-	3	0	0	0	0	
D	6	Luksa, Chuck	78	8	12	20	116	0	2	0	141	0.057	3	0	0	0	7	+1
D	3	Maggs, Darryl	27	4	14	18	22	-5	2	0	63	0.063	-	-	-	-	-	-
RW	18	Marsh, Peter	80	43	23	66	95	-31	23	0	325	0.132	3	1	0	1	0	+1
C	15	Meehan, Gerry	2	0	0	0	0	-1	0	0	0	-	-	-	-	-	-	-
D	4	Melrose, Barry	80	2	14	16	222	-4	1	0	85	0.024	3	0	1	1	8	-1
C	27	Messier, Mark	47	1	10	11	58	-6	0	0	55	0.018	-	-	-	-	-	-
D	7	Norwich, Craig	80	6	51	57	73	+2	2	0	265	0.023	3	0	1	1	4	+1
C	15	Parizeau, Michel	30	3	9	12	28	-5	0	0	33	0.091	3	1	0	1	0	+1
LW	23	St. Sauveur, Claude	16	4	5	9	4	-7	3	0	26	0.154	-	-	-	-	-	-
LW	27	Shanahan, Sean	4	0	0	0	7	0	0	0	1	0.000	-	-	-	-	-	-
LW	17	Shutt, Byron	65	10	7	17	115	+1	0	0	77	0.130	3	1	1	2	14	+2
LW	2	Stewart, Paul	23	2	1	3	45	+1	0	0	6	0.333	3	0	0	0	0	0
LW	21	Thomas, Reg	80	32	39	71	22	+3	7	0	224	0.143	3	1	1	2	0	0
D	3	Watson, Bryan	21	0	2	2	56	-15	0	0	9	0.000	3	0	1	1	2	-1

Power Play: 81 goals scored in 341 opportunities (23.8%) with 5 short-handed goals allowed.
Penalty Killing: 64 goals allowed in 278 opportunities (77.0%) with 6 short-handed goals scored.

Goaltending

goaltender	gp	min	ga	en	so	record	gaa	sog	sv%	gp	min	ga	record	gaa
Dion, Michel	30	1681	93	3	0	10-14-2	3.32	735	0.873	-	-	-	-	-
Liut, Mike	54	3181	184	4	3	23-27-4	3.47	1556	0.882	3	179	10	1-2	3.35

Transactions: Mike Gartner signed to contract, May 1978 • Gordie Clark signed to contract, Aug 1978 • Bryon Baltimore purchased from Indianapolis, Nov 1978 • Gerry Meehan signed to contract, Dec 1978 • Mark Messier, Michel Parizeau and Claude St. Sauveur signed as free agents from defunct Indianapolis, Dec 1978 and Jan 1979 • Rick Dudley's contract purchased by Buffalo (NHL), Feb 1979 • Bryan Watson signed to contract, Mar 1979

1978-1979 EDMONTON OILERS

Coach
Glen Sather

Summary of Games (@ Away, * Overtime)

	date	opponent	score		record	pts	gf-ga		date	opponent	score		record	pts	gf-ga
1	Oct 13	Cincinnati	3-2	W	1-0-0	2	3-2	41	Jan 28	Cincinnati	3-0	W	23-18-0	46	163-135
2	Oct 17	New England	1-2	L	1-1-0	2	4-4	42	Jan 31 @	Winnipeg	3-6	L	23-19-0	46	166-141
3	Oct 20 @	Indianapolis	4-3	W	2-1-0	4	8-7	43	Feb 2 @	Winnipeg	2-4	L	23-20-0	46	168-145
4	Oct 21 @	Cincinnati	3-4	L	2-2-0	4	11-11	44	Feb 4 @	Quebec	3-6	L	23-21-0	46	171-151
5	Oct 22 @	Winnipeg	6-2	W	3-2-0	6	17-13	45	Feb 6	Birmingham	6-2	W	24-21-0	48	177-153
6	Oct 24	Birmingham	2-3	L	3-3-0	6	19-16	46	Feb 7	Cincinnati	8-5	W	25-21-0	50	185-158
7	Oct 29	Quebec	2-6	L	3-4-0	6	21-22	47	Feb 9	Quebec	3-0	W	26-21-0	52	188-158
8	Oct 31	Quebec	4-5	L	3-5-0	6	25-27	48	Feb 11	Birmingham	*4-3	W	27-21-0	54	192-161
9	Nov 3	Winnipeg	*4-3	W	4-5-0	8	29-30	49	Feb 13	Quebec	6-1	W	28-21-0	56	198-162
10	Nov 5 @	Quebec	0-2	L	4-6-0	8	29-32	50	Feb 16 @	New England	4-2	W	29-21-0	58	202-164
11	Nov 8 @	Quebec	6-5	W	5-6-0	10	35-37	51	Feb 18 @	Birmingham	6-3	W	30-21-0	60	208-167
12	Nov 9 @	New England	1-6	L	5-7-0	10	36-43	52	Feb 20	New England	8-2	W	31-21-0	62	216-169
13	Nov 11 @	Birmingham	5-3	W	6-7-0	12	41-46	53	Feb 23	Cincinnati	3-1	W	32-21-0	64	219-170
14	Nov 12 @	Cincinnati	3-5	L	6-8-0	12	44-51	54	Feb 25	Birmingham	5-4	W	33-21-0	66	224-174
15	Nov 17	Indianapolis	6-1	W	7-8-0	14	50-52	55	Feb 27	New England	1-1	T	33-21-1	67	225-175
16	Nov 19	Cincinnati	6-3	W	8-8-0	16	56-55	56	Mar 2	Cincinnati	5-2	W	34-21-1	69	230-177
17	Nov 21	Quebec	4-1	W	9-8-0	18	60-56	57	Mar 3 @	Cincinnati	6-4	W	35-21-1	71	236-181
18	Nov 24	Quebec	*4-3	W	10-8-0	20	64-59	58	Mar 6 @	Quebec	3-4	L	35-22-1	71	239-185
19	Nov 28	Indianapolis	8-2	W	11-8-0	22	72-61	59	Mar 7 @	Quebec	3-6	L	35-23-1	71	242-191
20	Dec 1	New England	8-2	W	12-8-0	24	80-63	60	Mar 9 @	Birmingham	4-4	T	35-23-2	72	246-195
21	Dec 3	New England	0-7	L	12-9-0	24	80-70	61	Mar 11 @	Birmingham	4-0	W	36-23-2	74	250-195
22	Dec 6 @	Quebec	3-6	L	12-10-0	24	83-76	62	Mar 13 @	Cincinnati	1-5	L	36-24-2	74	251-200
23	Dec 7 @	New England	3-5	L	12-11-0	24	86-81	63	Mar 16	Quebec	6-1	W	37-24-2	76	257-201
24	Dec 9 @	Birmingham	2-6	L	12-12-0	24	88-87	64	Mar 18	Quebec	2-7	L	37-25-2	76	259-208
25	Dec 10 @	Indianapolis	4-6	L	12-13-0	24	92-93	65	Mar 20	Finland	8-4	W	38-25-2	78	267-212
26	Dec 12 @	Cincinnati	5-2	W	13-13-0	26	97-95	66	Mar 21 @	Winnipeg	7-4	W	39-25-2	80	274-216
27	Dec 15	Soviet All-Stars	5-3	W	14-13-0	28	102-98	67	Mar 23	Winnipeg	4-6	L	39-26-2	80	278-222
28	Dec 19 @	Birmingham	5-2	W	15-13-0	30	107-100	68	Mar 25 @	Cincinnati	6-5	W	40-26-2	82	284-227
29	Dec 22	Winnipeg	4-5	L	15-14-0	30	111-105	69	Mar 28 @	Quebec	0-3	L	40-27-2	82	284-230
30	Dec 26 @	Winnipeg	3-5	L	15-15-0	30	114-110	70	Mar 30 @	New England	3-1	W	41-27-2	84	287-231
31	Dec 27	Winnipeg	5-3	W	16-15-0	32	119-113	71	Apr 1 @	New England	5-3	W	42-27-2	86	292-234
32	Dec 30	Czechoslovakia	5-1	W	17-15-0	34	124-114	72	Apr 3 @	Cincinnati	5-1	W	43-27-2	88	297-235
33	Jan 9 @	Winnipeg	*3-4	L	17-16-0	34	127-118	73	Apr 4 @	Quebec	2-4	L	43-28-2	88	299-239
34	Jan 13 @	New England	3-0	W	18-16-0	36	130-118	74	Apr 6	New England	7-2	W	44-28-2	90	306-241
35	Jan 16	Winnipeg	3-1	W	19-16-0	38	133-119	75	Apr 8	Birmingham	5-4	W	45-28-2	92	311-245
36	Jan 17 @	Winnipeg	6-3	W	20-16-0	40	139-122	76	Apr 10	Winnipeg	4-6	L	45-29-2	92	315-251
37	Jan 19	Birmingham	11-3	W	21-16-0	42	150-125	77	Apr 13 @	Birmingham	6-4	W	46-29-2	94	321-255
38	Jan 21	Birmingham	3-4	L	21-17-0	42	153-129	78	Apr 14 @	Birmingham	6-7	L	46-30-2	94	327-262
39	Jan 23	New England	5-1	W	22-17-0	44	158-130	79	Apr 15 @	New England	4-1	W	47-30-2	96	331-263
40	Jan 26	Cincinnati	2-5	L	22-18-0	44	160-135	80	Apr 18	Winnipeg	9-3	W	48-30-2	98	340-266

402

Oilers Stars of 1978-1979

   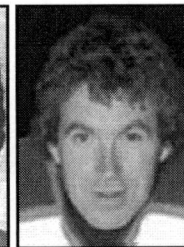  

| **Wayne Gretzky** | **Brett Callighen** | **Ron Chipperfield** | **Dave Dryden** | **Dave Langevin** | **Stan Weir** |
| 104 points with Oilers | 31 goals | 32 goals | 41 wins, League MVP | +33 rating on defense | 31 goals, +24 rating |

Scoring

						Regular Season										**Playoffs**				
pos	#	player	gp	g	a	pts	pim	+/-	ppg	shg	sog	sc%	gp	g	a	pts	pim	+/-
D	5	Alexander, Claire	54	8	23	31	16	-5	2	1	148	0.054	-	-	-	-	-	-
LW	17	Bailey, Ace	38	5	4	9	22	-8	1	0	26	0.192	2	0	0	0	4	-1
C	11	Berry, Doug	29	6	3	9	4	-9	1	0	30	0.200	-	-	-	-	-	-
C/W	18	Callighen, Brett	71	31	39	70	79	+29	12	0	161	0.193	13	5	10	15	15	+5
C	23	Carlson, Steve	73	18	22	40	50	+15	4	3	71	0.254	11	1	1	2	12	-5
C	7	Chipperfield, Ron	55	32	37	69	47	+25	6	0	181	0.177	13	9	10	19	8	+1
LW	24	Driscoll, Peter	69	17	23	40	115	+16	3	0	93	0.183	13	1	6	7	8	+4
G	28	Dryden, Dave	63	0	8	8	0		0	0	0	-	13	0	0	0	0	-
RW	19	Flett, Bill	73	28	36	64	14	+26	9	0	170	0.165	10	5	2	7	2	+3
LW	8	George, Wes	3	0	0	0	11	+1	0	0	1	0.000	-	-	-	-	-	-
RW	9	Goldsworthy, Bill	17	4	2	6	14	-3	0	0	27	0.148	4	1	1	2	11	+4
C	99	Gretzky, Wayne	72	43	61	104	19	+23	9	0	253	0.170	13	10	10	20	2	+6
LW	16	Guite, Pierre	12	1	1	2	8	-5	1	0	10	0.100	-	-	-	-	-	-
RW	16	Gustafsson, Bengt	0	-	-	-	-	-	-	-	-	-	2	1	2	3	0	+2
D	3	Hamilton, Al	80	6	38	44	38	+22	2	0	153	0.039	13	4	5	9	4	+1
D	8/20	Hughes, John	41	2	15	17	82	+22	0	0	43	0.047	13	1	0	1	35	+4
LW	12	Hunter, David	72	7	25	32	134	+7	0	0	71	0.099	13	2	3	5	42	-2
G	35	Kampurri, Hannu	2	0	0	0	0		0	0	0	-	-	-	-	-	-	-
D	26	Langevin, Dave	77	6	21	27	76	+33	3	0	130	0.046	13	0	1	1	25	-4
RW	14	MacDonald, Blair	80	34	37	71	44	+35	3	4	259	0.131	13	8	10	18	6	+1
RW	25	Mayer, James	2	0	0	0	0	-2	0	0	1	0.000	-	-	-	-	-	-
D	4	Micheletti, Joe	72	14	33	47	85	+10	3	0	155	0.090	13	0	9	9	2	+4
G	31	Mio, Ed	22	0	1	1	2		0	0	0	-	3	0	0	0	0	
D	15	Neilson, James	35	0	5	5	18	+5	0	0	13	0.000	-	-	-	-	-	-
D	2	Sandbeck, Cal	6	0	0	0	2	-2	0	0	3	0.000	-	-	-	-	-	-
LW	27	Semenko, Dave	77	10	14	24	158	-12	2	0	56	0.179	11	4	2	6	29	+3
D	6	Shmyr, Paul	80	8	39	47	119	+37	0	0	133	0.060	13	1	5	6	23	-3
D	8	Siltanen, Risto	20	3	4	7	4	+4	0	0	36	0.083	11	0	9	9	4	+6
C	10	Sobchuk, Dennis	74	26	37	63	31	+24	6	1	183	0.142	12	6	6	12	4	-4
D	8	Tajcnar, Rudy	2	0	0	0	0	-4	0	0	0	-	-	-	-	-	-	-
G	30	Walsh, Ed	3	0	0	0	0		0	0	0	-	-	-	-	-	-	-
C	21	Weir, Stan	68	31	30	61	20	+24	3	0	132	0.235	13	2	5	7	2	-4

Power Play: 70 goals scored in 276 opportunities (25.4%) with 6 short-handed goals allowed.
Penalty Killing: 62 goals allowed in 288 opportunities (78.5%) with 9 short-handed goals scored.

Goaltending

goaltender	gp	min	ga	en	so	record	gaa	sog	sv%	gp	min	ga	record	gaa
Dryden, Dave	63	3531	170	4	3	41-17-2	2.89	1544	0.890	13	687	42	6-7	3.67
Kampurri, Hannu	2	90	10	0	0	0-1-0	6.67	48	0.792	-	-	-	-	-
Mio, Ed	22	1068	71	2	1	7-10-0	3.99	482	0.853	3	90	6	0-0	4.00
Walsh, Ed	3	144	9	0	0	0-2-0	3.75	55	0.836	-	-	-	-	-

Transactions: Steve Carlson claimed off waivers, May 1978 • Jim Mayer claimed off waivers from New England, May 1978 • Claire Alexander, Dave Hunter, Jim Neilson, Risto Siltanen, Stan Weir signed to contracts, Jun 1978 • Bill Goldsworthy acquired from Indianapolis for Juha Widing, Jun 1978 • Peter Driscoll, Ed Mio and Wayne Gretzky purchased from Indianapolis, Nov 1978 • John Hughes signed as free agent from defunct Indianapolis, Dec 1978 • Wes George signed as free agent from defunct Indianapolis, Jan 1979 (George had been signed by Edmonton in Jun 1978, then traded to Indianapolis in Nov 1978) • Hannu Kampurri, Risto Siltanen, Bengt-Ake Gustafsson signed to contracts, Mar 1979 • Jari Kurri added to Edmonton's negotiating list, Mar 1979

1978-1979 INDIANAPOLIS RACERS

Coach
Pat Stapleton

Summary of Games (@ Away, * Overtime)

	date		opponent	score		record	pts	gf-ga			date		opponent	score		record	pts	gf-ga
1	Oct 14		Winnipeg	3-6	L	0-1-0	0	3-6		14	Nov 17	@	Edmonton	1-6	L	2-10-2	6	38-70
2	Oct 15		Birmingham	3-9	L	0-2-0	0	6-15		15	Nov 19	@	Winnipeg	2-5	L	2-11-2	6	40-75
3	Oct 18	@	Quebec	4-0	W	1-2-0	2	10-15		16	Nov 23		Winnipeg	1-5	L	2-12-2	6	41-80
4	Oct 20		Edmonton	3-4	L	1-3-0	2	13-19		17	Nov 24	@	Cincinnati	5-8	L	2-13-2	6	46-88
5	Oct 22		New England	3-6	L	1-4-0	2	16-25		18	Nov 25		Cincinnati	6-3	W	3-13-2	8	52-91
6	Oct 27	@	Birmingham	2-4	L	1-5-0	2	18-29		19	Nov 28	@	Edmonton	2-8	L	3-14-2	8	54-99
7	Oct 28		Winnipeg	3-2	W	2-5-0	4	21-31		20	Dec 1		Birmingham	6-3	W	4-14-2	10	60-102
8	Oct 29	@	Winnipeg	3-3	T	2-5-1	5	24-34		21	Dec 2	@	Birmingham	2-4	L	4-15-2	10	62-106
9	Nov 3	@	New England	3-6	L	2-6-1	5	27-40		22	Dec 3		Cincinnati	2-4	L	4-16-2	10	64-110
10	Nov 4		New England	6-6	T	2-6-2	6	33-46		23	Dec 7		Winnipeg	4-9	L	4-17-2	10	68-119
11	Nov 5	@	Winnipeg	2-6	L	2-7-2	6	35-52		24	Dec 10		Edmonton	6-4	W	5-17-2	12	74-123
12	Nov 8	@	Cincinnati	0-4	L	2-8-2	6	35-56		25	Dec 12		New England	4-7	L	5-18-2	12	78-130
13	Nov 11	@	Quebec	2-8	L	2-9-2	6	37-64										

Franchise folded, December 15, 1978

Wayne Gretzky Comes to the WHA

By the time Wayne Gretzky was 17 years old, he was already well-known to the hockey world as a prodigy, and after one year playing for Sault Ste. Marie of the OHA, had shown he was ready for better competition. The NHL balked at signing a 17-year old child, leaving Gretzky with one alternative: the WHA. In June 1978 he signed a personal services contract with Nelson Skalbania, who hoped the young star-to-be would vault his Racers out of the cellar, or at least keep them solvent for the upcoming season. Gretzky's career in Indianapolis lasted just eight games, and on November 2, 1978, he was sold—along with Eddie Mio and Peter Driscoll—to Edmonton. In Edmonton, Gretzky won the WHA's Rookie-of-the-Year award and of course, went on to a remarkable career in the NHL.

Wayne Gretzky's Scoring Summary with Indianapolis

No.	Date	Opponent	Summary
1	Oct 14	Winnipeg	No scoring.
2	Oct 15	Birmingham	No scoring.
3	Oct 18	Quebec	Assisted on Richie Leduc's second-period goal at 16:14. Kevin Morrison also assisted.
4	Oct 20	Edmonton	Scored at 6:07 and 6:41 of the second period against Dave Dryden. Morrison assisted on his the first goal, while Peter Driscoll and Don Larway assisted on his second goal.
5	Oct 23	New England	Assisted on Driscoll's goal at 16:56 of the first period. Scored at 3:30 of the third period, with assists to Larway and Al McLeod.
6	Oct 27	Birmingham	Assisted on Don Larway's goal at 18:49 of the first period. Gerry Leroux also assisted.
7	Oct 28	Winnipeg	No scoring.
8	Oct 29	Winnipeg	No scoring.

Racers Stars of 1978-1979

Don Larway
18 points

Blaine Stoughton
9 goals, 18 points

Ed Mio
Shutout, 3.22 average

Dave Morrow
12 pts in 10 games

Al McLeod
11 points

Claude Larose
+5 rating

Scoring

pos	#	player	gp	g	a	pts	pim	+/-	ppg	shg	sog	sc%	gp	g	a	pts	pim	+/-
D	5	Baltimore, Bryon	2	1	1	2	2	-1	0	0	4	0.250	-	-	-	-	-	-
D	24	Block, Ken	22	2	3	5	10	-11	0	0	9	0.222	-	-	-	-	-	-
LW	15	Burgess, Don	3	1	1	2	0	-4	0	0	3	0.333	-	-	-	-	-	-
LW	23	Driscoll, Peter	8	3	1	4	17	1	1	0	23	0.130	-	-	-	-	-	-
LW	14	George, Wes	9	4	2	6	23	-11	1	0	13	0.308	-	-	-	-	-	-
LW	17	Greig, Bruce	21	3	7	10	64	-5	0	0	13	0.231	-	-	-	-	-	-
C	99	Gretzky, Wayne	8	3	3	6	0	-3	0	0	17	0.176	-	-	-	-	-	-
D	21	Hughes, John	22	3	4	7	48	-16	0	0	24	0.125	-	-	-	-	-	-
D	2	Inkpen, Dave	25	1	8	9	22	-5	0	0	34	0.029	-	-	-	-	-	-
G	30	Inness, Gary	10	0	0	0	9		0	0	0	-	-	-	-	-	-	-
D	3	Irwin, Glen	24	0	1	1	124	-10	0	0	19	0.000	-	-	-	-	-	-
LW	9	Larose, Claude	13	5	8	13	0	+5	0	0	34	0.147	-	-	-	-	-	-
RW	27	Larway, Don	25	8	10	18	39	-20	2	0	56	0.143	-	-	-	-	-	-
RW	8	Leclerc, Rene	22	5	7	12	12	2	1	0	54	0.093	-	-	-	-	-	-
C	10	Leduc, Richie	13	5	9	14	14	-2	2	0	68	0.074	-	-	-	-	-	-
LW	26	Leroux, Gerry	10	0	3	3	2	-4	0	0	13	0.000	-	-	-	-	-	-
C	11	MacGregor, Gary	17	8	4	12	0	-12	1	0	45	0.178	-	-	-	-	-	-
LW	10	Magee, Dean	5	0	1	1	10	-2	0	0	6	0.000	-	-	-	-	-	-
D	6	McLeod, Al	25	0	11	11	22	0	0	0	23	0.000	-	-	-	-	-	-
C	18	Messier, Mark	5	0	0	0	0	-4	0	0	7	0.000	-	-	-	-	-	-
G	31	Mio, Ed	5	0	1	1	2		0	0	0	-	-	-	-	-	-	-
C	25	Moretto, Angelo	18	3	1	4	2	-6	1	0	12	0.250	-	-	-	-	-	-
D	4	Morrison, Kevin	5	0	2	2	0	-10	0	0	10	0.000	-	-	-	-	-	-
C	18	Morrow, Dave	10	2	10	12	29	-13	0	0	15	0.133	-	-	-	-	-	-
RW	12	Nugent, Kevin	25	2	8	10	20	-2	0	0	38	0.053	-	-	-	-	-	-
C	16	Parizeau, Michel	22	4	9	13	4	-1	0	0	25	0.160	-	-	-	-	-	-
D	5	Rollins, Jerry	7	0	1	1	7	-4	0	0	4	0.000	-	-	-	-	-	-
D	4	Sacharuk, Larry	15	2	9	11	25	-11	2	0	49	0.041	-	-	-	-	-	-
LW	20	St. Sauveur, Claude	17	4	2	6	12	-6	2	0	38	0.105	-	-	-	-	-	-
G	1	Smith, Gary	11	0	0	0	0		0	0	0	-	-	-	-	-	-	-
RW	7	Stoughton, Blaine	25	9	9	18	16	-18	3	0	78	0.115	-	-	-	-	-	-

Power Play: 16 goals scored with 7 short-handed goals allowed.
Penalty Killing: 27 goals allowed with 0 short-handed goals scored.

Goaltending

goaltender	gp	min	ga	en	so	record	gaa	sog	sv%	gp	min	ga	record	gaa
Inness, Gary	10	609	51	1	0	3-6-1	5.02	369	0.862	-	-	-	-	-
Mio, Ed	5	242	13	0	1	2-2-0	3.22	153	0.915	-	-	-	-	-
Smith, Gary	11	664	61	4	0	0-10-1	5.51	400	0.848	-	-	-	-	-

Transactions: Wayne Gretzky signed to personal services contract with Indianapolis owner Nelson Skalbania, Jun 1978 • John Hughes purchased from Houston via Winnipeg, Jul 1978 • Gary Smith signed to contract, Sep 1978 • Angelo Moretto signed to contract, Sep 1978, released Nov 1978 • Bruce Greig signed to contract, Oct 1978 • Wayne Gretzky, Ed Mio and Peter Driscoll sold to Edmonton, Nov 1978 • Don Burgess bought out and released, Nov 1978 • Bryon Baltimore sold to Cincinnati, Nov 1978 • Richie Leduc, Kevin Morrison sold to Quebec, Nov 1978 • Wes George acquired from Edmonton in Nov 1978 • Dean Magee, Mark Messier signed to contracts, Nov 1978 • Remainder declared free agents, Dec 1978

1978-1979 NEW ENGLAND WHALERS

**Coach
Bill Dineen
33-29-9**

**Coach
Don Blackburn
4-5-0**

Summary of Games (@ Away, * Overtime)

#	date	opponent	score		record	pts	gf-ga	#	date	opponent	score		record	pts	gf-ga
1	Oct 15 @	Quebec	6-5	W	1-0-0	2	6-5	41	Jan 26 @	Birmingham	4-5	L	20-15-6	46	167-146
2	Oct 17 @	Edmonton	2-1	W	2-0-0	4	8-6	42	Jan 28	Winnipeg	8-6	W	21-15-6	48	175-152
3	Oct 18 @	Winnipeg	4-4	T	2-0-1	5	12-10	43	Jan 30	Winnipeg	5-2	W	22-15-6	50	180-154
4	Oct 21	Quebec	7-1	W	3-0-1	7	19-11	44	Feb 2	Quebec	4-1	W	23-15-6	52	184-155
5	Oct 22 @	Indianapolis	6-3	W	4-0-1	9	25-14	45	Feb 3 @	Birmingham	2-2	T	23-15-7	53	186-157
6	Oct 24 @	Cincinnati	2-1	W	5-0-1	11	27-15	46	Feb 6 @	Quebec	5-3	W	24-15-7	55	191-160
7	Oct 26 @	Quebec	5-8	L	5-1-1	11	32-23	47	Feb 10	Winnipeg	7-2	W	25-15-7	57	198-162
8	Oct 27	Winnipeg	4-6	L	5-2-1	11	36-29	48	Feb 11 @	Cincinnati	2-5	L	25-16-7	57	200-167
9	Oct 29	Cincinnati	4-7	L	5-3-1	11	40-36	49	Feb 14	Birmingham	4-7	L	25-17-7	57	204-174
10	Nov 3	Indianapolis	6-3	W	6-3-1	13	46-39	50	Feb 16	Edmonton	2-4	L	25-18-7	57	206-178
11	Nov 4	Indianapolis	6-6	T	6-3-2	14	52-45	51	Feb 17	Quebec	4-1	W	26-18-7	59	210-179
12	Nov 5 @	Cincinnati	4-5	L	6-4-2	14	56-50	52	Feb 18 @	Winnipeg	7-1	W	27-18-7	61	217-180
13	Nov 9	Edmonton	6-1	W	7-4-2	16	62-51	53	Feb 20 @	Edmonton	2-8	L	27-19-7	61	219-188
14	Nov 11	Cincinnati	2-1	W	8-4-2	18	64-52	54	Feb 21 @	Winnipeg	2-5	L	27-20-7	61	221-193
15	Nov 14 @	Birmingham	5-5	T	8-4-3	19	69-57	55	Feb 23	Quebec	*5-4	W	28-20-7	63	226-197
16	Nov 15 @	Cincinnati	4-4	T	8-4-4	20	73-61	56	Feb 24 @	Quebec	0-6	L	28-21-7	63	226-203
17	Nov 17 @	Birmingham	1-7	L	8-5-4	20	74-68	57	Feb 25	Winnipeg	5-7	L	28-22-7	63	231-210
18	Nov 18	Birmingham	2-3	L	8-6-4	20	76-71	58	Feb 27 @	Edmonton	1-1	T	28-22-8	64	232-211
19	Nov 22	Winnipeg	5-2	W	9-6-4	22	81-73	59	Mar 2 @	Winnipeg	4-1	W	29-22-8	66	236-212
20	Nov 25	Birmingham	5-2	W	10-6-4	24	86-75	60	Mar 4	Cincinnati	*3-4	L	29-23-8	66	239-216
21	Nov 26	Birmingham	9-3	W	11-6-4	26	95-78	61	Mar 9	Quebec	1-3	L	29-24-8	66	240-219
22	Nov 29 @	Winnipeg	2-4	L	11-7-4	26	97-82	62	Mar 11 @	Cincinnati	2-1	W	30-24-8	68	242-220
23	Dec 1 @	Edmonton	2-8	L	11-8-4	26	99-90	63	Mar 13 @	Birmingham	4-3	W	31-24-8	70	246-223
24	Dec 3 @	Edmonton	7-0	W	12-8-4	28	106-90	64	Mar 15	Birmingham	*3-4	L	31-25-8	70	249-227
25	Dec 5 @	Cincinnati	2-2	T	12-8-5	29	108-92	65	Mar 16 @	Birmingham	5-5	T	31-25-9	71	254-232
26	Dec 7	Edmonton	5-3	W	13-8-5	31	113-95	66	Mar 18	Cincinnati	1-4	L	31-26-9	71	255-236
27	Dec 9	Soviet All-Stars	4-7	L	13-9-5	31	117-102	67	Mar 20 @	Quebec	*7-6	W	32-26-9	73	262-242
28	Dec 12 @	Indianapolis	7-4	W	14-9-5	33	124-106	68	Mar 23	Quebec	5-3	W	33-26-9	75	267-245
29	Dec 16	Quebec	2-1	W	15-9-5	35	126-107	69	Mar 24	Birmingham	3-4	L	33-27-9	75	270-249
30	Dec 17 @	Quebec	4-4	T	15-9-6	36	130-111	70	Mar 27 @	Birmingham	1-3	L	33-28-9	75	271-252
31	Dec 23	Birmingham	4-3	W	16-9-6	38	134-114	71	Mar 30	Edmonton	1-3	L	33-29-9	75	272-255
32	Dec 27	Czechoslovakia	10-4	W	17-9-6	40	144-118	72	Apr 1	Edmonton	3-5	L	33-30-9	75	275-260
33	Dec 29	Birmingham	5-0	W	18-9-6	42	149-118	73	Apr 4 @	Winnipeg	4-2	W	34-30-9	77	279-262
34	Dec 30 @	Cincinnati	1-2	L	18-10-6	42	150-120	74	Apr 6 @	Edmonton	2-7	L	34-31-9	77	281-269
35	Jan 7	Cincinnati	5-4	W	19-10-6	44	155-124	75	Apr 8 @	Winnipeg	4-6	L	34-32-9	77	285-275
36	Jan 13	Edmonton	0-3	L	19-11-6	44	155-127	76	Apr 10 @	Quebec	5-2	W	35-32-9	79	290-277
37	Jan 14	Winnipeg	2-4	L	19-12-6	44	157-131	77	Apr 12	Cincinnati	4-0	W	36-32-9	81	294-277
38	Jan 18	Quebec	2-4	L	19-13-6	44	159-135	78	Apr 14	Cincinnati	0-4	L	36-33-9	81	294-281
39	Jan 20	Cincinnati	3-1	W	20-13-6	46	162-136	79	Apr 15	Edmonton	1-4	L	36-34-9	81	295-285
40	Jan 23 @	Edmonton	1-5	L	20-14-6	46	163-141	80	Apr 17 @	Quebec	3-2	W	37-34-9	83	298-287

Whalers Stars of 1978-1979

 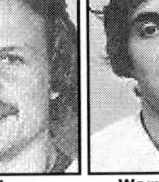     

Mark Howe
107 points

Warren Miller
26 goals, +7 rating

Mike Rogers
72 points

John Garrett
2 shutouts, 20 wins

Gordie Howe
43 points at age 51

Dave Keon
65 points

Scoring

pos	#	player	gp	g	a	pts	pim	+/-	ppg	shg	sog	sc%	gp	g	a	pts	pim	+/-
C	12	Antonovich, Mike	69	20	27	47	35	-4	3	0	151	0.132	10	5	3	8	14	+2
LW	22	Brubaker, Jeff	12	0	0	0	19	-2	0	0	0	-	3	0	0	0	12	0
LW	23	Carlson, Jack	34	2	7	9	61	-6	0	0	39	0.051	-	-	-	-	-	-
LW	11	Douglas, Jordy	51	6	10	16	15	-8	3	0	76	0.079	10	4	0	4	23	-1
G	35	Garrett, John	41	0	0	0	6		0	0	0	-	8	0	0	0	0	-
D	10	Hangsleben, Alan	77	10	19	29	148	-1	0	0	141	0.071	10	1	2	3	12	0
RW	9	Howe, Gordie	58	19	24	43	51	+9	7	0	117	0.162	10	3	1	4	4	+1
D/F	5	Howe, Mark	77	42	65	107	32	+14	13	6	314	0.134	6	4	2	6	6	-2
D	18	Howe, Marty	66	9	15	24	31	+10	1	0	135	0.067	9	0	1	1	8	-3
D	26	Inkpen, Dave	41	0	7	7	15	+10	0	0	31	0.000	5	0	1	1	4	+2
C	14	Keon, Dave	79	22	43	65	2	+4	7	0	189	0.116	10	3	9	12	2	+2
C	4	Lacroix, Andre	78	32	56	88	34	+1	7	4	172	0.186	10	4	4	8	0	-2
D	2	Ley, Rick	73	7	20	27	135	-3	0	2	113	0.062	9	0	4	4	11	-3
LW	16	Lyle, George	59	17	18	35	54	+16	1	0	113	0.150	9	3	5	8	25	+3
RW	19	McKenzie, John	76	19	28	47	115	+6	3	2	113	0.168	10	3	7	10	10	+1
RW	27	Miller, Warren	77	26	23	49	44	+7	1	0	153	0.170	10	0	8	8	28	+5
C	24	Pleau, Larry	28	6	6	12	6	-8	0	1	42	0.143	10	2	1	3	0	-5
D	6	Plumb, Ron	78	4	16	20	33	5	0	0	108	0.037	9	1	3	4	0	+2
D	7	Roberts, Gordie	79	11	46	57	113	-2	2	0	153	0.072	10	0	4	4	10	+4
C	17	Rogers, Mike	80	27	45	72	31	+5	2	0	186	0.145	10	2	6	8	2	-3
D	3	Roy, Pierre	1	0	0	0	2	0	0	0	1	0.000	-	-	-	-	-	-
D	3	Selwood, Brad	42	4	12	16	47	+2	2	0	52	0.077	-	-	-	-	-	-
G	1	Smith, Al	40	0	3	3	35		0	0	0	-	4	0	0	0	0	-
RW	21	Stoughton, Blaine	36	9	3	12	2	+4	0	0	53	0.170	7	4	3	7	4	-2
RW	25	Warner, Jim	41	6	9	15	20	-10	1	0	68	0.088	1	0	0	0	0	-2

Power Play: 53 goals scored in 259 opportunities (20.4%) with 6 short-handed goals allowed.
Penalty Killing: 63 goals allowed in 262 opportunities (76.0%) with 15 short-handed goals scored.

Goaltending

goaltender	gp	min	ga	en	so	record	gaa	sog	sv%	gp	min	ga	record	gaa
Garrett, John	41	2496	149	4	2	20-17-4	3.58	1180	0.874	8	447	32	4-3	4.30
Smith, Al	40	2396	132	2	1	17-17-5	3.31	1124	0.883	4	153	12	1-2	4.71

Transactions: Jeff Brubaker, Jordy Douglas, Jim Warner signed to contracts, Jun 1978 • Andre Lacroix acquired from Winnipeg for future considerations, Aug 1978 • Louis Levasseur traded to Quebec for Warren Miller, Sep 1978 • Dave Inkpen and Blaine Stoughton signed as free agents from defunct Indianapolis, Dec 1978 • Jack Carlson traded to Minnesota (NHL) for future considerations, Feb 1979

1978-1979 QUEBEC NORDIQUES

Coach
Jacques Demers

Summary of Games (@ Away, * Overtime)

	date	opponent	score		record	pts	gf-ga		date	opponent	score		record	pts	gf-ga
1	Oct 15	New England	5-6	L	0-1-0	0	5-6	41	Jan 21 @	Winnipeg	1-3	L	23-14-4	50	158-130
2	Oct 17	Cincinnati	5-5	T	0-1-1	1	10-11	42	Jan 23 @	Birmingham	7-5	W	24-14-4	52	165-135
3	Oct 18	Indianapolis	0-4	L	0-2-1	1	10-15	43	Jan 27	Winnipeg	2-4	L	24-15-4	52	167-139
4	Oct 21 @	New England	1-7	L	0-3-1	1	11-22	44	Jan 30 @	Birmingham	1-2	L	24-16-4	52	168-141
5	Oct 22	Birmingham	5-8	L	0-4-1	1	16-30	45	Feb 1 @	Birmingham	5-7	L	24-17-4	52	173-148
6	Oct 25	Cincinnati	4-3	W	1-4-1	3	20-33	46	Feb 2 @	New England	1-4	L	24-18-4	52	174-152
7	Oct 26	New England	8-5	W	2-4-1	5	28-38	47	Feb 4	Edmonton	6-3	W	25-18-4	54	180-155
8	Oct 28 @	Cincinnati	*3-4	L	2-5-1	5	31-42	48	Feb 6	New England	3-5	L	25-19-4	54	183-160
9	Oct 29	Edmonton	6-2	W	3-5-1	7	37-44	49	Feb 9 @	Edmonton	0-3	L	25-20-4	54	183-163
10	Oct 31 @	Edmonton	5-4	W	4-5-1	9	42-48	50	Feb 13 @	Edmonton	1-6	L	25-21-4	54	184-169
11	Nov 3 @	Birmingham	3-2	W	5-5-1	11	45-50	51	Feb 17 @	New England	1-4	L	25-22-4	54	185-173
12	Nov 4 @	Birmingham	4-1	W	6-5-1	13	49-51	52	Feb 18 @	Cincinnati	4-2	W	26-22-4	56	189-175
13	Nov 5	Edmonton	2-0	W	7-5-1	15	51-51	53	Feb 20 @	Birmingham	7-3	W	27-22-4	58	196-178
14	Nov 7	Winnipeg	1-2	L	7-6-1	15	52-53	54	Feb 23 @	New England	*4-5	L	27-23-4	58	200-183
15	Nov 8	Edmonton	5-6	L	7-7-1	15	57-59	55	Feb 24	New England	6-0	W	28-23-4	60	206-183
16	Nov 11	Indianapolis	8-2	W	8-7-1	17	65-61	56	Feb 25	Cincinnati	1-1	T	28-23-5	61	207-184
17	Nov 12 @	Winnipeg	6-4	W	9-7-1	19	71-65	57	Mar 3	Birmingham	3-2	W	29-23-5	63	210-186
18	Nov 15	Winnipeg	5-2	W	10-7-1	21	76-67	58	Mar 4	Birmingham	5-4	W	30-23-5	65	215-190
19	Nov 21 @	Edmonton	1-4	L	10-8-1	21	77-71	59	Mar 6	Edmonton	4-3	W	31-23-5	67	219-193
20	Nov 24 @	Edmonton	*3-4	L	10-9-1	21	80-75	60	Mar 7	Edmonton	6-3	W	32-23-5	69	225-196
21	Nov 26	Winnipeg	2-2	T	10-9-2	22	82-77	61	Mar 9 @	New England	3-1	W	33-23-5	71	228-197
22	Nov 29	Birmingham	7-4	W	11-9-2	24	89-81	62	Mar 10 @	Cincinnati	2-5	L	33-24-5	71	230-202
23	Dec 2	Cincinnati	2-0	W	12-9-2	26	91-81	63	Mar 11 @	Winnipeg	2-7	L	33-25-5	71	232-209
24	Dec 3	Winnipeg	5-3	W	13-9-2	28	96-84	64	Mar 14 @	Winnipeg	4-2	W	34-25-5	73	236-211
25	Dec 6	Edmonton	6-3	W	14-9-2	30	102-87	65	Mar 16 @	Edmonton	1-6	L	34-26-5	73	237-217
26	Dec 9	Cincinnati	4-3	W	15-9-2	32	106-90	66	Mar 18 @	Edmonton	7-2	W	35-26-5	75	244-219
27	Dec 10 @	Winnipeg	4-4	T	15-9-3	33	110-94	67	Mar 20	New England	*6-7	L	35-27-5	75	250-226
28	Dec 12	Soviet All-Stars	3-6	L	15-10-3	33	113-100	68	Mar 23 @	New England	3-5	L	35-28-5	75	253-231
29	Dec 14	Birmingham	3-2	W	16-10-3	35	116-102	69	Mar 24 @	Cincinnati	5-2	W	36-28-5	77	258-233
30	Dec 16 @	New England	1-2	L	16-11-3	35	117-104	70	Mar 25	Birmingham	3-2	W	37-28-5	79	261-235
31	Dec 17	New England	4-4	T	16-11-4	36	121-108	71	Mar 28	Edmonton	3-0	W	38-28-5	81	264-235
32	Dec 22 @	Birmingham	5-1	W	17-11-4	38	126-109	72	Mar 30 @	Winnipeg	2-0	W	39-28-5	83	266-235
33	Dec 23 @	Cincinnati	2-6	L	17-12-4	38	128-115	73	Apr 1	Winnipeg	3-7	L	39-29-5	83	269-242
34	Dec 28	Czechoslovakia	4-0	W	18-12-4	40	132-115	74	Apr 3 @	Birmingham	3-5	L	39-30-5	83	272-247
35	Dec 30	Birmingham	3-2	W	19-12-4	42	135-117	75	Apr 4	Edmonton	4-2	W	40-30-5	85	276-249
36	Jan 7 @	Winnipeg	2-3	L	19-13-4	42	137-120	76	Apr 7 @	Cincinnati	2-6	L	40-31-5	85	278-255
37	Jan 9 @	Cincinnati	4-3	W	20-13-4	44	141-123	77	Apr 10	New England	2-5	L	40-32-5	85	280-260
38	Jan 12 @	Cincinnati	2-1	W	21-13-4	46	143-124	78	Apr 11	Cincinnati	2-6	L	40-33-5	85	282-266
39	Jan 18 @	New England	4-2	W	22-13-4	48	147-126	79	Apr 15	Cincinnati	4-2	W	41-33-5	87	286-268
40	Jan 20	Winnipeg	10-1	W	23-13-4	50	157-127	80	Apr 17	New England	2-3	L	41-34-5	87	288-271

Nordiques Stars of 1978-1979

Serge Bernier	**Jim Corsi**	**Wally Weir**	**Real Cloutier**	**Richard Brodeur**	**Richie Leduc**
82 points, +7 rating	3 shutouts	+9 rating, 166 minutes	75 goals	3 shutouts, 25 wins	30 goals

Scoring

pos	#	player	gp	g	a	pts	pim	+/-	ppg	shg	sog	sc%	gp	g	a	pts	pim	+/-
D	4	Baxter, Paul	76	10	36	46	240	-5	6	0	125	0.080	4	0	2	2	7	-2
C	21	Bernier, Serge	65	36	46	82	71	+7	9	3	193	0.187	1	0	0	0	2	-4
LW	24	Bilodeau, Gilles	36	3	6	9	141	+2	0	0	15	0.200	3	0	0	0	25	-4
C	11	Bordeleau, Christian	16	5	12	17	0	+6	0	0	34	0.147	-	-	-	-	-	-
RW	17	Bordeleau, Paulin	77	17	12	29	44	+1	2	0	128	0.133	4	1	0	1	0	-7
RW	15	Brackenbury, Curt	70	13	13	26	155	-5	1	0	73	0.178	4	1	1	2	2	-2
G	1	Brodeur, Richard	42	0	3	3	0		0	0	0	-	3	0	0	0	0	
RW	9	Cloutier, Real	77	75	54	129	48	+23	21	0	363	0.207	4	2	2	4	4	-4
G	25	Corsi, Jim	40	0	0	0	0		0	0	0	-	2	0	0	0	0	
LW	19	Cote, Alain	79	14	13	27	23	-7	0	1	109	0.128	4	0	0	0	2	-2
LW	27	David, Richard	14	0	4	4	4	+3	0	0	11	0.000	-	-	-	-	-	-
LW	23	Devine, Kevin	5	0	0	0	6	-3	0	0	3	0.000	-	-	-	-	-	-
D	7	Dorey, Jim	32	0	2	2	17	-5	0	0	19	0.000	3	0	0	0	0	-3
LW	20	Dube, Norm	36	2	13	15	4	6	0	0	37	0.054	-	-	-	-	-	-
C	12	Fitchner, Bob	79	10	35	45	69	-3	1	0	115	0.087	4	1	3	4	0	-2
RW	16	Geoffrion, Daniel	77	12	14	26	74	-2	0	0	122	0.098	4	1	2	3	2	-6
D	33	Hoganson, Dale	69	2	19	21	17	+1	1	0	90	0.022	4	0	0	0	2	-2
D	22	Lacombe, Francois	78	3	21	24	44	+4	0	0	112	0.027	4	0	1	1	2	-4
LW	28	Lagace, Pierre	21	0	1	1	12	0	0	0	10	0.000	3	0	1	1	2	-6
D	5	Lariviere, Garry	50	5	33	38	54	-11	1	0	119	0.042	4	0	1	1	2	-12
RW	18	Leclerc, Rene	23	0	0	0	8	-2	0	0	6	0.000	4	0	0	0	0	-2
C	10	Leduc, Richie	61	30	32	62	30	-1	12	1	167	0.180	4	0	2	2	0	-1
G	30	Levasseur, Louis	3	0	0	0	0		0	0	0	-	1	0	0	0	0	
D	6	Morrison, Kevin	27	2	5	7	14	-2	1	0	45	0.044	-	-	-	-	-	-
LW	8	Tardif, Marc	74	41	55	96	98	+25	12	0	255	0.161	4	6	2	8	4	+1
D	3	Tremblay, J. C.	52	6	38	44	8	+10	0	0	86	0.070	-	-	-	-	-	-
D	2	Weir, Wally	68	2	7	9	166	+9	0	0	84	0.024	4	0	1	1	4	-8

Power Play: 67 goals scored in 272 opportunities (24.6%) with 9 short-handed goals allowed.
Penalty Killing: 63 goals allowed in 329 opportunities (80.9%) with 6 short-handed goals scored.

Goaltending

goaltender	gp	min	ga	en	so	record	gaa	sog	sv%	gp	min	ga	record	gaa
Brodeur, Richard	42	2433	126	1	3	25-13-3	3.11	1279	0.901	3	114	14	0-2	7.37
Corsi, Jim	40	2291	126	4	3	16-20-1	3.30	1242	0.899	2	66	7	0-1	6.36
Levasseur, Louis	3	140	14	0	0	0-1-1	6.00	85	0.835	1	59	8	0-1	8.14

Transactions: Dale Hoganson purchased from Birmingham, Jul 1978 • Kevin Devine purchased from Indianapolis, Sep 1978 • Warren Miller traded to New England for Louis Levasseur, Sep 1978 • Gilles Bilodeau signed to contract, Sep 1978 • Richie Leduc, Kevin Morrison purchased from Indianapolis, Nov 1978 • Christian Bordeleau announced retirement, Nov 1978 • Rene Leclerc and Kevin Morrison signed as free agents from defunct Indianapolis, Dec 1978 • Jacques Demers signs five-game tryout contract, Mar 1979 (his number is 23)

1978-1979 WINNIPEG JETS

Coach
Larry Hillman
28-27-6

Coach
Tom McVie
11-8-0

Summary of Games (@ Away, * Overtime)

	date		opponent	score		record	pts	gf-ga		date		opponent	score		record	pts	gf-ga
1	Oct 13	@	Birmingham	*5-4	W	1-0-0	2	5-4	41	Jan 20	@	Quebec	1-10	L	19-17-5	43	160-154
2	Oct 14	@	Indianapolis	6-3	W	2-0-0	4	11-7	42	Jan 21		Quebec	3-1	W	20-17-5	45	163-155
3	Oct 15		Cincinnati	3-4	L	2-1-0	4	14-11	43	Jan 24	@	Cincinnati	5-5	T	20-17-6	46	168-160
4	Oct 18		New England	4-4	T	2-1-1	5	18-15	44	Jan 27	@	Quebec	4-2	W	21-17-6	48	172-162
5	Oct 22		Edmonton	2-6	L	2-2-1	5	20-21	45	Jan 28	@	New England	6-8	L	21-18-6	48	178-170
6	Oct 25		Birmingham	7-2	W	3-2-1	7	27-23	46	Jan 30	@	New England	2-5	L	21-19-6	48	180-175
7	Oct 27	@	New England	6-4	W	4-2-1	9	33-27	47	Jan 31		Edmonton	6-3	W	22-19-6	50	186-178
8	Oct 28	@	Indianapolis	2-3	L	4-3-1	9	35-30	48	Feb 2		Edmonton	4-2	W	23-19-6	52	190-180
9	Oct 29		Indianapolis	3-3	T	4-3-2	10	38-33	49	Feb 4		Cincinnati	8-1	W	24-19-6	54	198-181
10	Nov 3	@	Edmonton	*3-4	L	4-4-2	10	41-37	50	Feb 7		Birmingham	3-2	W	25-19-6	56	201-183
11	Nov 5		Indianapolis	6-2	W	5-4-2	12	47-39	51	Feb 9	@	Cincinnati	0-4	L	25-20-6	56	201-187
12	Nov 7	@	Quebec	2-1	W	6-4-2	14	49-40	52	Feb 10	@	New England	2-7	L	25-21-6	56	203-194
13	Nov 9	@	Birmingham	5-6	L	6-5-2	14	54-46	53	Feb 14	@	Cincinnati	5-1	W	26-21-6	58	208-195
14	Nov 10	@	Cincinnati	2-3	L	6-6-2	14	56-49	54	Feb 16	@	Birmingham	1-2	L	26-22-6	58	209-197
15	Nov 12		Quebec	4-6	L	6-7-2	14	60-55	55	Feb 17	@	Cincinnati	4-6	L	26-23-6	58	213-203
16	Nov 15	@	Quebec	2-5	L	6-8-2	14	62-60	56	Feb 18		New England	1-7	L	26-24-6	58	214-210
17	Nov 17		Cincinnati	10-6	W	7-8-2	16	72-66	57	Feb 20	@	Cincinnati	2-5	L	26-25-6	58	216-215
18	Nov 19		Indianapolis	5-2	W	8-8-2	18	77-68	58	Feb 21		New England	5-2	W	27-25-6	60	221-217
19	Nov 22	@	New England	2-5	L	8-9-2	18	79-73	59	Feb 23	@	Birmingham	1-9	L	27-26-6	60	222-226
20	Nov 23	@	Indianapolis	5-1	W	9-9-2	20	84-74	60	Feb 25	@	New England	7-5	W	28-26-6	62	229-231
21	Nov 26	@	Quebec	2-2	T	9-9-3	21	86-76	61	Feb 27		Birmingham	2-5	L	28-27-6	62	231-236
22	Nov 29		New England	4-2	W	10-9-3	23	90-78	62	Mar 2		New England	1-4	L	28-28-6	62	232-240
23	Dec 1		Cincinnati	5-6	L	10-10-3	23	95-84	63	Mar 6	@	Birmingham	4-5	L	28-29-6	62	236-245
24	Dec 3	@	Quebec	3-5	L	10-11-3	23	98-89	64	Mar 7	@	Cincinnati	5-3	W	29-29-6	64	241-248
25	Dec 7		Indianapolis	9-4	W	11-11-3	25	107-93	65	Mar 11		Quebec	7-2	W	30-29-6	66	248-250
26	Dec 10		Quebec	4-4	T	11-11-4	26	111-97	66	Mar 14		Quebec	2-4	L	30-30-6	66	250-254
27	Dec 14		Soviet All-Stars	3-4	L	11-12-4	26	114-101	67	Mar 16		Cincinnati	5-3	W	31-30-6	68	255-257
28	Dec 17		Cincinnati	6-3	W	12-12-4	28	120-104	68	Mar 18		Birmingham	4-2	W	32-30-6	70	259-259
29	Dec 22	@	Edmonton	5-4	W	13-12-4	30	125-108	69	Mar 21		Edmonton	4-7	L	32-31-6	70	263-266
30	Dec 26		Edmonton	5-3	W	14-12-4	32	130-111	70	Mar 23	@	Edmonton	6-4	W	33-31-6	72	269-270
31	Dec 27	@	Edmonton	3-5	L	14-13-4	32	133-116	71	Mar 28		Cincinnati	6-3	W	34-31-6	74	275-273
32	Jan 1		Czechoslovakia	3-3	T	14-13-5	33	136-119	72	Mar 30		Quebec	0-2	L	34-32-6	74	275-275
33	Jan 7		Quebec	3-2	W	15-13-5	35	139-121	73	Apr 1	@	Quebec	7-3	W	35-32-6	76	282-278
34	Jan 9		Edmonton	*4-3	W	16-13-5	37	143-124	74	Apr 4		New England	2-4	L	35-33-6	76	284-282
35	Jan 12	@	Birmingham	3-1	W	17-13-5	39	146-125	75	Apr 6		Birmingham	1-2	L	35-34-6	76	285-284
36	Jan 13	@	Birmingham	3-1	W	18-13-5	41	149-126	76	Apr 8		New England	6-4	W	36-34-6	78	291-288
37	Jan 14	@	New England	4-2	W	19-13-5	43	153-128	77	Apr 10	@	Edmonton	6-4	W	37-34-6	80	297-292
38	Jan 16	@	Edmonton	1-3	L	19-14-5	43	154-131	78	Apr 11		Birmingham	2-1	W	38-34-6	82	299-293
39	Jan 17		Edmonton	3-6	L	19-15-5	43	157-137	79	Apr 15		Birmingham	*5-4	W	39-34-6	84	304-297
40	Jan 19		Cincinnati	2-7	L	19-16-5	43	159-144	80	Apr 18	@	Edmonton	3-9	L	39-35-6	84	307-306

Jets Stars of 1978-1979

Morris Lukowich
65 goals

Terry Ruskowski
86 points, +13 rating

Scott Campbell
248 minutes

Kim Clackson
210 minutes

Kent Nilsson
107 points

Gary Smith
8 wins in playoffs

Scoring

pos	#	player	gp	g	a	pts	pim	+/-	ppg	shg	sog	sc%	gp	g	a	pts	pim	+/-
D	2	Amodeo, Mike	64	4	18	22	29	-1	0	0	62	0.065	-	-	-	-	-	-
D	7	Campbell, Scott	74	3	15	18	248	+5	0	0	108	0.028	10	0	2	2	25	+3
D	5	Clackson, Kim	71	0	12	12	210	-6	0	0	32	0.000	9	0	5	5	28	+7
G	1	Daley, Joe	23	0	0	0	0		0	0	0	-	3	0	0	0	0	-
D	25	Davis, Bill	5	1	2	3	0	-2	0	0	4	0.250	-	-	-	-	-	-
C	19	Eriksson, Bengt	33	5	10	15	2	-5	3	0	55	0.091	10	1	4	5	0	-3
D	14	Gibson, John	9	0	1	1	5	+1	0	0	6	0.000	-	-	-	-	-	-
C	27	Gosselin, Rich	3	0	0	0	0	-1	0	0	1	0.000	-	-	-	-	-	-
LW	16	Gray, John	57	10	15	25	51	-7	6	0	91	0.110	1	0	0	0	0	0
D	6	Green, Ted	20	0	2	2	16	-7	0	0	13	0.000	-	-	-	-	-	-
LW	18	Guindon, Bob	71	8	18	26	21	-12	0	0	130	0.062	7	2	1	3	0	+2
LW	15	Hicks, Glenn	69	6	10	16	48	-2	0	0	59	0.102	7	1	1	2	4	+2
LW	9	Hull, Bobby	4	2	3	5	0	+1	1	0	12	0.167	-	-	-	-	-	-
LW	17	Lesuk, Bill	79	17	15	32	44	-14	0	0	106	0.160	10	1	3	4	6	0
RW	20	Lindstrom, Willy	79	26	36	62	22	+7	11	0	206	0.126	10	10	5	15	9	+7
D	3	Long, Barry	79	5	36	41	42	-2	0	0	180	0.028	10	2	3	5	0	0
LW	12	Lukowich, Morris	80	65	34	99	119	+26	16	0	278	0.234	10	8	7	15	21	+9
D	24	MacKinnon, Paul	73	2	15	17	70	-3	0	0	81	0.025	10	2	5	7	4	+3
G	35	Mattsson, Markus	52	0	1	1	4		0	0	0	-	-	-	-	-	-	-
LW	22	Moffat, Lyle	70	14	18	32	38	-14	0	1	89	0.157	10	3	1	4	22	0
C	11	Nilsson, Kent	78	39	68	107	8	+1	8	0	279	0.140	10	3	11	14	4	-1
RW	21	Preston, Rich	80	28	32	60	88	-5	6	1	177	0.158	10	8	5	13	15	+3
C	8	Ruskowski, Terry	75	20	66	86	211	+13	6	1	138	0.145	8	1	12	13	23	+10
D	4	Sjoberg, Lars-Erik	9	0	3	3	2	-1	0	0	15	0.000	10	1	2	3	4	+7
G	30	Smith, Gary	11	0	3	3	0		0	0	0	-	10	0	0	0	0	-
C	10	Sullivan, Peter	80	46	40	86	24	-6	9	2	220	0.209	10	5	9	14	2	+2
D	23	Terbenche, Paul	68	3	22	25	12	-1	0	0	58	0.052	10	1	1	2	4	+2
C	26	West, Steve	18	3	1	4	6	+6	1	0	24	0.125	6	2	3	5	2	+4
C	14	Yakiwchuk, Dale	4	0	0	0	0	+1	0	0	1	0.000	-	-	-	-	-	-

Power Play: 67 goals scored in 265 opportunities (25.3%) with 7 short-handed goals allowed.
Penalty Killing: 57 goals allowed in 274 opportunities (79.2%) with 5 short-handed goals scored.

Goaltending

goaltender	gp	min	ga	en	so	record	gaa	sog	sv%	gp	min	ga	record	gaa
Daley, Joe	23	1256	90	0	0	7-11-3	4.30	695	0.871	3	37	3	0-0	4.86
Mattsson, Markus	52	2990	181	3	0	25-21-3	3.63	1544	0.883	-	-	-	-	-
Smith, Gary	11	626	31	1	0	7-3-0	2.97	279	0.889	10	563	35	8-2	3.73

Transactions: Glenn Hicks, Paul MacKinnon signed to contracts, Jun 1978 • Scott Campbell, John Gray, Morris Lukowich, Rich Preston, Terry Ruskowski and Steve West signed to contracts Aug 1978 from defunct Houston • Bobby Hull announced retirement, Oct 1978 • Bengt Eriksson signed to contract, Jan 1979 • Gary Smith signed as free agent from defunct Indianapolis, Feb 1979 • John Gibson signed to contract, Mar 1979

1978-1979 Statistical Leaders

Top five in each category.

Goals: 75, Real Cloutier (Quebec), 65, Morris Lukowich (Winnipeg), 46, Wayne Gretzky (Indianapolis-Edmonton), Peter Sullivan (Winnipeg); 43, Peter Marsh (Cincinnati); Mark Howe (New England).

Assists: 77, Robbie Ftorek (Cincinnati); 68, Kent Nilsson (Winnipeg); 66, Terry Ruskowski (Winnipeg); 65, Mark Howe (New England); 64, Wayne Gretzky (Indianapolis-Edmonton).

Points: 129, Real Cloutier (Quebec); 116, Robbie Ftorek (Cincinnati); 110, Wayne Gretzky (Indianapolis-Edmonton); 107, Mark Howe (New England), Kent Nilsson (Winnipeg); 99, Morris Lukowich (Winnipeg).

Penalty Minutes: 248, Scott Campbell (Winnipeg), Rick Vaive (Birmingham); 240, Paul Baxter (Quebec); 222, Barry Melrose (Cincinnati); 212, Dave Hanson (Birmingham); 211, Terry Ruskowski (Winnipeg).

Power-play Goals: 23, Peter Marsh (Cincinnati); 21, Real Cloutier (Quebec); 16, Morris Lukowich (Winnipeg); 14, Robbie Ftorek (Cincinnati), Richie Leduc (Indianapolis-Quebec); 13, Mark Howe (New England).

Short-handed Goals: 6, Mark Howe (New England); 4, Blair MacDonald (Edmonton), Andre Lacroix (New England); 3, Steve Carlson (Edmonton), Serge Bernier (Quebec), Robbie Ftorek (Cincinnati); 2, shared by many.

Goaltending Minutes: 3531, Dave Dryden (Edmonton); 3181, Mike Liut (Cincinnati); 2990, Markus Mattsson (Winnipeg); 2511, Pat Riggin (Birmingham); 2496, John Garrett (New England).

Goals Against Average: 2.89, Dave Dryden (Edmonton); 3.11, Richard Brodeur (Quebec); 3.30, Jim Corsi (Quebec); 3.31, Al Smith (New England); 3.32, Michel Dion (Cincinnati).

Wins: 41, Dave Dryden (Edmonton); 25, Richard Brodeur (Quebec), Markus Mattsson (Winnipeg); 23, Mike Liut (Cincinnati); 20, John Garrett (New England); 17, Al Smith (New England).

Shutouts: 3, Richard Brodeur (Quebec), Jim Corsi (Quebec), Dave Dryden (Edmonton), Mike Liut (Cincinnati); 2, John Garrett (New England), Ed Mio (Indianapolis-Edmonton); 1, Pat Riggin (Birmingham), Al Smith (New England).

Totals for Players With Two or More Teams During 1978-1979

player	teams	gp	g	a	pts	pim	+/-	ppg	shg	sog	sc%
Baltimore, Bryon	Ind, Cin	71	5	11	16	85	-23	1	0	64	0.073
Driscoll, Peter	Ind, Edm	77	20	24	44	132	+17	4	0	116	0.172
George, Wes	Ind, Edm	12	4	2	6	34	-10	1	0	14	0.286
Gretzky, Wayne	Ind, Edm	80	46	64	110	19	+20	9	0	270	0.170
Hughes, John	Ind Edm	63	5	19	24	130	+6	0	0	67	0.075
Inkpen, Dave	Ind, NE	66	1	15	16	37	+5	0	0	65	0.015
Leclerc, Rene	Ind, Que	45	5	7	12	20	0	1	0	60	0.083
Leduc, Richie	Ind, Que	74	35	41	76	44	-3	14	1	235	0.149
Messier, Mark	Ind, Cin	52	1	10	11	58	-10	0	0	62	0.016
Mio, Ed	Ind, Edm	27	0	2	2	4		0	0	0	-
Morrison, Kevin	Ind, Que	32	2	7	9	14	-12	1	0	55	0.036
Parizeau, Michel	Ind, Cin	52	7	18	25	32	-5	0	0	58	0.121
St. Sauveur, Claude	Ind, Cin	33	8	7	15	16	-13	0	0	64	0.125
Smith, Gary	Ind, Wpg	22	0	3	3	0		0	0	0	-
Stoughton, Blaine	Ind, NE	61	18	12	30	18	-14	3	0	131	0.137

Totals for Goaltenders With Two or More Teams During 1978-1979

goaltender	teams	gp	min	ga	en	so	record	gaa	sog	sv%
Ed Mio	Ind, Edm	27	1310	84	2	2	9-12-0	3.85	638	0.868
Gary Smith	Ind, Wpg	22	1293	92	5	0	7-13-1	4.28	679	0.865

1978-1979 Touring Team Statistics

For games that counted in the regular season.

Soviet All-Stars

Coach: Boris Maiorov & Igor Tuzik

	date	opponent	score		record	pts
1.	Dec 9	New England	7-4	W	1-0-0	2
2.	Dec 12	Quebec	6-3	W	2-0-0	4
3.	Dec 14	Winnipeg	4-3	W	3-0-0	6
4.	Dec 15	Edmonton	3-5	L	3-1-0	6
5.	Dec 17	Birmingham	2-2	T	3-1-1	7
6.	Dec 20	Cincinnati	5-3	W	4-1-1	9

Scoring

Pos	#	Player	gp	g	a	pts	pim
LW	26	Andreyev, Alexander	-	3	3	6	-
C	8	Gimayev, Irek	-	2	3	5	-
D	4	Gimayev, Sergei	-	3	2	5	-
C	19	Kabanov, Alexander	-	3	0	3	-
RW	15	Kapustin, Igor	-	2	0	2	-
C	16	Kovin, Vladimir	-	2	1	3	-
C	10	Lobanov, Alexander	-	2	5	7	-
D	6	Makarov, Nikolai	-	1	0	1	-
D	13	Nazarov, Vyacheslav	-	0	3	3	-
D	21	Payusov, Vasili	-	1	1	2	-
RW	20	Popov, Vladimir	-	0	0	0	-
D	14	Romashin, Igor	-	0	0	0	-
LW	11	Skvortsov, Alexander	-	3	3	6	-
D	24	Slipchenko, Mikhail	-	0	0	0	-
LW	23	Tyumenev, Viktor	-	2	5	7	-
D	5	Tyzhnykh, Sergei	-	0	2	2	-
D	3	Volchenkov, Alexei	-	0	1	1	-
LW	9	Volchkov, Alexander	-	3	1	4	-
RW	7	Yemelianenko, Anatoli	-	0	1	1	-

Did Not Play: Vladimir Durdin.

Goaltending

#	Goaltender	gp	min	ga	record	gaa
22	Babariko, Sergei	2	63	3	1-0-0	2.86
1	Myshkin, Vladimir	5	307	17	3-1-1	3.32

Czechoslovakia

Coach: Stanislav Nevesely

	date	opponent	score		record	pts
1.	Dec 27	New England	4-10	L	0-1-0	0
2.	Dec 28	Quebec	0-4	L	0-2-0	0
3.	Dec 30	Edmonton	1-5	L	0-3-0	0
4.	Jan 1	Winnipeg	3-3	T	0-3-1	1
5.	Jan 6	Cincinnati	4-1	W	1-3-1	3
6.	Jan 7	Birmingham	2-10	L	1-4-1	3

Scoring

Pos	#	Player	gp	g	a	pts	pim
D	4	Adamik, Petr	-	0	2	2	-
F	19	Bezak, Marian	-	1	0	1	-
F	10	Brunclik, Bedrich	-	2	3	5	-
D	3	Hajdusek, Stanislav	-	0	0	0	-
F	17	Holan, Milos	-	1	0	1	-
F	22	Holy, Karel	-	4	2	6	-
F	23	Kokrment, Jindrich	-	0	1	1	-
F	25	Kyhos, Vladimir	-	0	3	3	-
F	14	Lukac, Josef	-	0	1	1	-

Czechoslovakia (continued)

Pos	#	Player	gp	g	a	pts	pim
D	2	Lycka, Jaroslav	-	0	1	1	-
F	15	Micka, Jindrich	-	0	0	0	-
F	18	Muller, Zdenek	-	0	1	1	-
D	9	Neliba, Jan	-	0	2	2	-
F	16	Novak, Milos	-	2	0	2	-
F	26	Penicka, Lubomir	-	0	0	0	-
D	6	Rohacik, Lubomir	-	0	1	1	-
F	11	Salajka, Bohumil	-	2	0	2	-
D	5	Sterbak, Jan	-	0	0	0	-
F	12	Stransky, Vladimir	-	2	1	3	-
D	8	Urban, Vladimir	-	0	0	0	-
D	7	Vlcek, Vladislav	-	0	0	0	-
F	21	Vlk, Jaroslav	-	0	0	0	-

Goaltending

#	Goaltender	gp	min	ga	record	gaa
1	Crha, Jiri	4	200	19	1-2-0	5.70
20	Svitana, Pavel	3	160	14	0-2-1	5.25

Finland

Lost 8-4 on March 20 at Edmonton

Scoring

Player	gp	g	a	pts	pim
Ahokainen, Seppo	1	0	0	0	0
Aro, Jorma	1	0	0	0	0
Hagman, Matti	1	0	1	1	0
Helander, Hannu	1	0	0	0	0
Hirronen, Raimo	1	0	0	0	0
Jyrkkio, Juha	1	1	0	1	2
Kaario, Matti	1	0	0	0	0
Koskilahti, Jukka	1	0	1	1	0
Kurri, Jari	1	0	0	0	0
Laine, Pekka	1	0	0	0	0
Lappanen, Reijo	1	0	0	0	0
Lehtonen, Pertti	1	0	0	0	0
Mikatolo, Jarmo	1	0	0	0	0
Peltonen, Jouni	1	1	0	1	0
Repo, Seppo	1	0	0	0	0
Rinne, Jouni	1	1	1	2	0
Saarinen, Olli	1	0	0	0	2
Suoraniemi, Seppo	1	0	0	0	0
Taimio, Tomi	1	0	0	0	0
Tuohimaa, Harri	1	0	2	2	0
Villa, Ismo	1	1	0	1	0

Goaltending

Goaltender	gp	min	ga	record	gaa
Virtanen, Jorma	1	60	8	0-1-0	8.00

Reserve: Juka Airaksinen.

Edmonton had 69 shots on goal against Finland, including a league-record 33 in the 2nd period alone. After two periods, Edmonton had outshot Finland 51-7.

Intraleague Records

Alberta-Edmonton OILERS

opponent	all-time w	l	t	gf	ga	home w	l	t	gf	ga	away w	l	t	gf	ga
Chicago	12	7	1	69	48	7	2	1	39	24	5	5	0	30	24
Cincinnati	21	13	1	134	125	14	3	1	80	59	7	10	0	54	66
Cleveland-Minnesota	9	15	1	57	80	7	4	1	37	29	2	11	0	20	51
Denver	0	1	0	3	6	0	0	0	0	0	0	1	0	3	6
Houston	12	33	1	147	190	9	14	0	88	89	3	19	1	59	101
Indianapolis	22	8	1	130	91	13	2	1	78	43	9	6	0	52	48
LA-Mich-Balt	13	8	1	86	56	9	2	0	60	28	4	6	1	26	28
Minnesota (orig.)	14	11	0	94	88	8	5	0	51	46	6	6	0	43	42
New England	24	24	5	184	175	13	10	3	99	82	11	14	2	85	93
NY-Jer-SD	16	14	0	118	114	11	4	0	76	50	5	10	0	42	64
Ott-Tor-Bir	35	22	4	258	214	21	9	0	137	99	14	13	4	121	115
Phi-Van-Cgy	16	27	3	128	169	13	8	2	78	62	3	19	1	50	107
Phoenix	6	11	1	57	62	4	4	1	40	34	2	7	0	17	28
Quebec	23	38	2	235	280	16	15	0	131	115	7	23	2	104	165
Winnipeg	31	41	3	248	314	21	14	2	141	138	10	27	1	107	176
Touring teams	5	0	0	29	11	5	0	0	29	11	0	0	0	0	0
All Time:	**259**	**273**	**24**	**1977**	**2023**	**171**	**96**	**12**	**1164**	**909**	**88**	**177**	**12**	**813**	**1114**

Chicago COUGARS

opponent	all-time w	l	t	gf	ga	home w	l	t	gf	ga	away w	l	t	gf	ga
Alberta-Edmonton	7	12	1	48	69	5	5	0	24	30	2	7	1	24	39
Cleveland	8	10	2	72	75	5	4	1	31	30	3	6	1	41	45
Houston	3	17	0	50	84	3	7	0	31	44	0	10	0	19	40
Indianapolis	3	2	1	24	24	2	0	1	16	13	1	2	0	8	11
LA-Mich-Balt	11	9	0	77	62	5	5	0	41	36	6	4	0	36	26
Minnesota	9	13	0	81	94	5	6	0	41	44	4	7	0	40	50
New England	7	13	0	65	76	4	6	0	35	38	3	7	0	30	38
NY-Jer-SD	10	9	1	81	73	7	3	0	46	28	3	6	1	35	45
Ottawa-Toronto	10	9	1	75	73	5	5	0	36	35	5	4	1	39	38
Philadelphia-Vancouver	9	8	1	62	64	5	3	1	35	32	4	5	0	27	32
Phoenix	2	4	0	19	28	1	2	0	10	13	1	2	0	9	15
Quebec	9	11	0	67	78	5	5	0	37	37	4	6	0	30	41
Winnipeg	6	15	1	56	81	6	4	1	37	36	0	11	0	19	45
All Time:	**94**	**132**	**8**	**777**	**881**	**58**	**55**	**4**	**420**	**416**	**36**	**77**	**4**	**357**	**465**

Cincinnati STINGERS

opponent	all-time w	l	t	gf	ga	home w	l	t	gf	ga	away w	l	t	gf	ga
Calgary	7	3	0	48	34	5	0	0	27	15	2	3	0	21	19
Cleveland-Minnesota	9	7	0	57	48	6	1	0	36	16	3	6	0	21	32
Denver-Ottawa	2	2	0	10	11	2	0	0	5	3	0	2	0	5	8
Edmonton	13	21	1	125	134	10	7	0	66	54	3	14	1	59	80
Houston	9	14	1	92	99	8	4	0	54	38	1	10	1	38	61
Indianapolis	19	17	1	147	121	13	5	0	87	45	6	12	1	60	76
Minnesota (orig.)	1	3	0	15	19	0	2	0	6	10	1	1	0	9	9
New England	20	24	2	167	165	13	9	2	101	84	7	15	0	66	81
Phoenix	6	6	0	55	55	4	2	0	30	19	2	4	0	25	36
Quebec	19	18	3	156	157	12	7	1	92	72	7	11	2	64	85
San Diego	6	4	2	46	52	5	1	0	22	18	1	3	2	24	34
Toronto-Birmingham	17	21	3	149	172	13	7	1	90	77	4	14	2	59	95
Winnipeg	14	21	1	126	173	6	11	1	62	86	8	10	0	64	87
Touring teams	0	3	1	13	19	0	3	1	13	19	0	0	0	0	0
All Time:	**142**	**164**	**15**	**1206**	**1259**	**97**	**59**	**6**	**691**	**556**	**45**	**105**	**9**	**515**	**703**

Cleveland CRUSADERS - Minnesota (new) FIGHTING SAINTS

opponent	all-time					home					away				
	w	l	t	qf	ga	w	l	t	qf	ga	w	l	t	qf	ga
Alberta-Edmonton	15	9	1	80	57	11	2	0	51	20	4	7	1	29	37
Chicago	10	8	2	75	72	6	3	1	45	41	4	5	1	30	31
Cincinnati	7	9	0	48	57	6	3	0	32	21	1	6	0	16	36
Denver	0	3	1	9	16	0	1	0	0	3	0	2	1	9	13
Houston	8	15	4	80	89	3	9	2	32	41	5	6	2	48	48
Indianapolis	12	8	0	75	64	8	2	0	43	28	4	6	0	32	36
LA-Mich-Balt	12	5	1	57	41	6	2	1	25	22	6	3	0	32	19
Minnesota (orig.)	10	13	1	71	85	5	7	0	27	33	5	6	1	44	52
New England	14	20	4	102	112	12	5	2	59	43	2	15	2	43	69
NY-Jer-SD	14	15	2	107	108	10	5	2	66	46	4	10	0	41	62
Ott-Tor-Bir	18	13	1	119	110	11	5	1	75	57	7	8	0	44	53
Phi-Van-Cgy	15	15	1	125	107	10	5	1	80	48	5	10	0	45	59
Phoenix	7	5	3	52	48	5	2	0	26	18	2	3	3	26	30
Quebec	16	13	2	110	106	12	4	0	69	50	4	9	2	41	56
Winnipeg	11	11	2	88	97	8	2	2	50	39	3	9	0	38	58
As Cleveland	150	144	20	1062	1036	99	49	9	586	441	51	95	11	476	599
As Minnesota	19	18	5	136	129	14	8	3	94	69	5	10	2	42	60
All Time:	169	162	25	1198	1165	113	57	12	680	510	56	105	13	518	659

Denver SPURS - Ottawa CIVICS

opponent	all-time					home					away				
	w	l	t	qf	ga	w	l	t	qf	ga	w	l	t	qf	ga
Calgary	1	1	0	4	7	0	1	0	2	6	1	0	0	2	1
Cincinnati	2	2	0	11	10	2	0	0	8	5	0	2	0	3	5
Cleveland	3	0	1	16	9	2	0	1	13	9	1	0	0	3	0
Edmonton	1	0	0	6	3	1	0	0	6	3	0	0	0	0	0
Houston	0	5	0	14	24	0	2	0	6	8	0	3	0	8	16
Indianapolis	3	1	0	13	14	1	1	0	3	8	2	0	0	10	6
Minnesota	1	2	0	12	11	0	1	0	4	5	1	1	0	8	6
New England	1	2	0	10	11	1	1	0	7	4	0	1	0	3	7
Phoenix	1	5	0	15	34	0	3	0	5	12	1	2	0	10	22
Quebec	0	1	0	3	5	0	1	0	3	5	0	0	0	0	0
San Diego	1	2	0	9	11	1	1	0	8	6	0	1	0	1	5
Toronto	0	1	0	8	11	0	1	0	8	11	0	0	0	0	0
Winnipeg	0	4	0	13	22	0	2	0	6	11	0	2	0	7	11
As Denver	13	20	1	110	142	8	12	1	73	85	5	8	0	37	57
As Ottawa	1	6	0	24	30	0	2	0	6	8	1	4	0	18	22
All Time:	14	26	1	134	172	8	14	1	79	93	6	12	0	55	79

Houston AEROS

opponent	all-time					home					away				
	w	l	t	qf	ga	w	l	t	qf	ga	w	l	t	qf	ga
Alberta-Edmonton	33	12	1	190	147	19	3	1	101	59	14	9	0	89	88
Chicago	17	3	0	84	50	10	0	0	40	19	7	3	0	44	31
Cincinnati	14	9	1	99	92	10	1	1	61	38	4	8	0	38	54
Cleveland-Minnesota	15	8	4	89	80	6	5	2	48	48	9	3	2	41	32
Denver-Ottawa	5	0	0	24	14	3	0	0	16	8	2	0	0	8	6
Indianapolis	18	10	2	124	88	10	4	0	60	41	8	6	2	64	47
LA-Mich-Balt	15	10	1	105	90	7	5	1	58	49	8	5	0	47	41
Minnesota (orig.)	19	8	1	117	77	11	3	0	70	37	8	5	1	47	40
New England	21	17	3	153	135	11	8	2	84	66	10	9	1	69	69
NY-Jer-SD	23	18	0	167	127	15	6	0	103	58	8	12	0	64	69
Ott-Tor-Bir	20	20	1	167	153	14	7	0	95	63	6	13	1	72	90
Phi-Van-Cgy	24	8	0	141	84	13	3	0	71	39	11	5	0	70	45
Phoenix	21	6	0	154	91	12	1	0	84	43	9	5	0	70	48
Quebec	15	22	2	137	153	13	6	0	87	59	2	16	2	50	94
Winnipeg	24	18	3	172	150	15	6	2	106	65	9	12	1	66	85
Touring teams	1	1	0	5	8	1	1	0	5	8	0	0	0	0	0
All Time:	285	170	19	1928	1539	170	59	9	1089	700	115	111	10	839	839

Indianapolis RACERS

opponent	all-time					home					away				
	w	l	t	qf	ga	w	l	t	qf	ga	w	l	t	qf	ga
Chicago	2	3	1	24	24	2	1	0	11	8	0	2	1	13	16
Cincinnati	17	19	1	121	147	12	6	1	76	60	5	13	0	45	87
Cleveland-Minnesota	8	12	0	64	75	6	4	0	36	32	2	8	0	28	43
Denver	1	3	0	14	13	0	2	0	6	10	1	1	0	8	3
Edmonton	8	22	1	91	130	6	9	0	48	52	2	13	1	43	78
Houston	10	18	2	88	124	6	8	2	47	64	4	10	0	41	60
Michigan-Baltimore	4	2	0	30	19	1	2	0	13	12	3	0	0	17	7
Minnesota (orig.)	1	9	0	31	46	1	4	0	13	19	0	5	0	18	27
New England	17	18	8	142	157	9	8	3	67	67	8	10	5	75	90
Phoenix	5	12	1	46	78	4	5	0	27	28	1	7	1	19	50
Quebec	12	21	1	118	148	9	7	1	68	71	3	14	0	50	77
San Diego	4	10	4	49	67	4	4	1	27	28	0	6	3	22	39
Toronto-Birmingham	17	16	2	124	126	11	6	0	69	56	6	10	2	55	70
Vancouver-Calgary	4	10	2	39	55	3	4	1	22	28	1	6	1	17	27
Winnipeg	8	25	1	95	155	5	13	0	63	86	3	12	1	32	69
Touring teams	0	2	0	6	9	0	2	0	6	9	0	0	0	0	0
All Time:	118	202	24	1082	1373	79	85	9	599	630	39	117	15	483	743

Los Angeles SHARKS - Michigan STAGS - Baltimore BLADES

opponent	all-time					home					away				
	w	l	t	qf	ga	w	l	t	qf	ga	w	l	t	qf	ga
Alberta-Edmonton	8	13	1	56	86	6	4	1	28	26	2	9	0	28	60
Chicago	9	11	0	62	77	4	6	0	26	36	5	5	0	36	41
Cleveland	5	12	1	41	57	3	6	0	19	32	2	6	1	22	25
Houston	10	15	1	90	105	5	8	0	41	47	5	7	1	49	58
Indianapolis	2	4	0	19	30	0	3	0	7	17	2	1	0	12	13
Minnesota	9	12	1	76	83	6	4	1	40	38	3	8	0	36	45
New England	5	12	1	46	72	4	4	1	21	30	1	8	0	25	42
NY-Jer-SD	10	7	1	79	75	4	5	0	38	41	6	2	1	41	34
Ottawa-Toronto	4	12	2	55	79	3	6	0	26	38	1	6	2	29	41
Philadelphia-Vancouver	7	13	0	53	75	4	6	0	23	36	3	7	0	30	39
Phoenix	2	3	1	14	26	1	1	1	4	5	1	2	0	10	21
Quebec	6	11	1	48	70	5	4	0	31	29	1	7	1	17	41
Winnipeg	6	16	0	61	95	5	6	0	39	42	1	10	0	22	53
As Los Angeles	62	88	6	495	589	35	42	1	240	275	27	46	5	255	314
As Michigan	13	27	3	107	179	12	8	2	59	70	1	19	1	48	109
As Baltimore	8	26	1	98	162	3	13	1	44	72	5	13	0	54	90
All Time:	83	141	10	700	930	50	63	4	343	417	33	78	6	357	513

Minnesota (original) FIGHTING SAINTS

opponent	all-time					home					away				
	w	l	t	qf	ga	w	l	t	qf	ga	w	l	t	qf	ga
Alberta-Edmonton	11	14	0	88	94	6	6	0	42	43	5	8	0	46	51
Chicago	13	9	0	94	81	7	4	0	50	40	6	5	0	44	41
Cincinnati	3	1	0	19	15	1	1	0	9	9	2	0	0	10	6
Cleveland	13	10	1	85	71	6	5	1	52	44	7	5	0	33	27
Denver-Ottawa	2	1	0	11	12	1	1	0	6	8	1	0	0	5	4
Houston	8	19	1	77	117	5	8	1	40	47	3	11	0	37	70
Indianapolis	9	1	0	46	31	5	0	0	27	18	4	1	0	19	13
LA-Mich-Balt	12	9	1	83	76	8	3	0	45	36	4	6	1	38	40
New England	13	7	2	79	67	10	0	1	53	30	3	7	1	26	37
NY-Jer-SD	11	15	0	94	106	7	7	0	52	48	4	8	2	42	58
Ottawa-Toronto	13	9	0	86	94	8	3	0	47	41	5	6	0	39	53
Phi-Van-Cgy	14	9	0	89	69	8	3	0	44	26	6	6	0	45	43
Phoenix	5	6	2	43	44	4	2	0	27	22	1	4	2	16	22
Quebec	12	8	1	104	85	6	4	1	50	46	6	4	0	54	39
Winnipeg	15	9	2	103	73	10	3	0	66	35	5	6	2	37	38
All Time:	154	127	12	1101	1035	92	50	4	610	493	62	77	8	491	542

New England WHALERS

opponent	all-time w	l	t	qf	ga	home w	l	t	qf	ga	away w	l	t	qf	ga
Alberta-Edmonton	24	24	5	175	184	14	11	2	93	85	10	13	3	82	99
Chicago	13	7	0	76	65	7	3	0	38	30	6	4	0	38	35
Cincinnati	24	20	2	165	167	15	7	0	81	66	9	13	2	84	101
Cleveland-Minnesota	20	14	4	112	102	15	2	2	69	43	5	12	2	43	59
Denver-Ottawa	2	1	0	11	10	1	0	0	7	3	1	1	0	4	7
Houston	17	21	3	135	153	9	10	1	69	69	8	11	2	66	84
Indianapolis	18	17	8	157	142	10	8	5	90	75	8	9	3	67	67
LA-Mich-Balt	12	5	1	72	46	8	1	0	42	25	4	4	1	30	21
Minnesota (orig.)	7	13	2	67	79	7	3	1	37	26	0	10	1	30	53
NY-Jer-SD	26	11	1	145	130	16	3	0	71	50	10	8	1	74	80
Ott-Tor-Bir	36	21	4	267	216	21	10	0	149	99	15	11	4	118	117
Phi-Van-Cgy	19	12	0	137	108	14	2	0	81	42	5	10	0	56	66
Phoenix	7	8	3	66	60	4	4	1	35	30	3	4	2	31	30
Quebec	29	34	3	236	257	18	13	1	128	107	11	21	2	108	150
Winnipeg	24	27	2	197	213	12	14	0	104	100	12	13	2	93	113
Touring teams	3	1	0	26	16	3	1	0	26	16	0	0	0	0	0
All Time:	**281**	**236**	**38**	**2044**	**1948**	**174**	**92**	**13**	**1120**	**866**	**107**	**144**	**25**	**924**	**1082**

New York RAIDERS - New York GOLDEN BLADES - Jersey KNIGHTS - San Diego MARINERS

opponent	all-time w	l	t	qf	ga	home w	l	t	qf	ga	away w	l	t	qf	ga
Alberta-Edmonton	14	16	0	114	118	10	5	0	64	42	4	11	0	50	76
Chicago	9	10	1	73	81	6	3	1	45	35	3	7	0	28	46
Cincinnati	4	6	2	52	46	3	1	2	34	24	1	5	0	18	22
Cleveland-Minnesota	15	14	2	108	107	10	4	0	62	41	5	10	2	46	66
Denver	2	1	0	11	9	1	0	0	5	1	1	1	0	6	8
Houston	18	23	0	127	167	12	8	0	69	64	6	15	0	58	103
Indianapolis	10	4	4	67	49	6	0	3	39	22	4	4	1	28	27
LA-Mich-Balt	7	10	1	75	79	2	6	1	34	41	5	4	0	41	38
Minnesota (orig.)	15	11	2	106	94	8	4	2	58	42	7	7	0	48	52
New England	11	26	1	130	145	8	10	1	80	74	3	16	0	50	71
Ott-Tor-Bir	19	12	1	141	120	12	4	0	89	60	7	8	1	52	60
Phi-Van-Cgy	20	11	1	118	91	11	5	0	60	42	9	6	1	58	49
Phoenix	14	15	2	122	116	9	6	2	71	49	5	9	0	51	67
Quebec	16	15	1	144	124	14	2	0	98	40	2	13	1	46	84
Winnipeg	10	17	2	106	137	9	6	0	66	59	1	11	2	40	78
As NY Raiders	33	43	2	303	334	23	15	1	176	144	10	28	1	127	190
As NY Golden Blades	6	12	2	47	80	4	6	0	28	36	2	6	2	19	44
As Jersey	26	30	2	221	233	18	10	1	133	103	8	20	1	88	130
As San Diego	119	106	14	923	836	76	33	10	537	353	43	73	4	386	483
All Time:	**184**	**191**	**20**	**1494**	**1483**	**121**	**64**	**12**	**874**	**636**	**63**	**127**	**8**	**620**	**847**

Ottawa NATIONALS - Toronto TOROS - Birmingham BULLS

opponent	all-time w	l	t	qf	ga	home w	l	t	qf	ga	away w	l	t	qf	ga
Alberta-Edmonton	22	35	4	214	258	13	14	4	115	121	9	21	0	99	137
Chicago	9	10	1	73	75	4	5	1	38	39	5	5	0	35	36
Cincinnati	21	17	3	172	149	14	4	2	95	59	7	13	1	77	90
Cleveland-Minnesota	13	18	1	110	119	8	7	0	53	44	5	11	1	57	75
Denver	1	0	0	11	8	0	0	0	0	0	1	0	0	11	8
Houston	20	20	1	153	167	13	6	1	90	72	7	14	0	63	95
Indianapolis	16	17	2	126	124	10	6	2	70	55	6	11	0	56	69
LA-Mich-Balt	12	4	2	79	55	6	1	2	41	29	6	3	0	38	26
Minnesota (orig.)	9	13	0	94	86	6	5	0	53	39	3	8	0	41	47
New England	21	36	4	216	267	11	15	4	117	118	10	21	0	99	149
NY-Jer-SD	12	19	1	120	141	8	7	1	60	52	4	12	0	60	89
Phi-Van-Cgy	19	15	2	145	144	12	5	1	84	62	7	10	1	61	82
Phoenix	8	5	3	74	55	6	2	0	42	26	2	3	3	32	29
Quebec	31	44	1	302	319	21	17	1	169	149	10	27	0	133	170
Winnipeg	25	33	2	217	242	16	14	0	125	100	9	19	2	92	142
Touring teams	3	0	1	23	5	3	0	1	23	5	0	0	0	0	0
As Ottawa	35	39	4	279	301	21	15	3	146	130	14	24	1	133	171
As Toronto	108	118	11	988	979	65	46	7	526	442	43	72	4	462	537
As Birmingham	99	129	13	862	934	65	47	10	503	398	34	82	3	359	536
All Time:	**242**	**286**	**28**	**2129**	**2214**	**151**	**108**	**20**	**1175**	**970**	**91**	**178**	**8**	**954**	**1244**

Philadelphia BLAZERS - Vancouver BLAZERS - Calgary COWBOYS

opponent	all-time					home					away				
	w	l	t	qf	ga	w	l	t	qf	ga	w	l	t	qf	ga
Alberta-Edmonton	27	16	3	169	128	19	3	1	107	50	8	13	2	62	78
Chicago	8	9	1	64	62	5	4	0	32	27	3	5	1	32	35
Cincinnati	3	7	0	34	48	3	2	0	19	21	0	5	0	15	27
Cleveland-Minnesota	15	15	1	107	125	10	5	0	59	45	5	10	1	48	80
Denver	1	1	0	7	4	0	1	0	1	2	1	0	0	6	2
Houston	8	24	0	84	141	5	11	0	45	70	3	13	0	39	71
Indianapolis	10	4	2	55	39	6	1	1	27	17	4	3	1	28	22
LA-Mich-Balt	13	7	0	75	53	7	3	0	39	30	6	4	0	36	23
Minnesota (orig.)	9	14	0	69	89	6	6	0	43	45	3	8	0	26	44
New England	12	19	0	108	137	10	5	0	66	56	2	14	0	42	81
NY-Jer-SD	11	20	1	91	118	6	9	1	49	58	5	11	0	42	60
Ott-Tor-Bir	15	19	2	144	145	10	7	1	82	61	5	12	1	62	84
Phoenix	11	6	1	70	58	7	2	0	44	30	4	4	1	26	28
Quebec	15	20	1	147	164	13	4	1	85	57	2	16	0	62	107
Winnipeg	16	26	2	157	187	12	9	1	88	79	4	17	1	69	108
As Philadelphia	38	40	0	288	305	24	15	0	172	144	14	25	0	116	161
As Vancouver	64	89	3	534	615	44	32	2	292	267	20	57	1	242	348
As Calgary	72	78	11	559	578	51	25	4	322	237	21	53	7	237	341
All Time:	**174**	**207**	**14**	**1381**	**1498**	**119**	**72**	**6**	**786**	**648**	**55**	**135**	**8**	**595**	**850**

Phoenix ROADRUNNERS

opponent	all-time					home					away				
	w	l	t	qf	ga	w	l	t	qf	ga	w	l	t	qf	ga
Chicago	4	2	0	28	19	2	1	0	15	9	2	1	0	13	10
Cincinnati	6	6	0	55	55	4	2	0	36	25	2	4	0	19	30
Cleveland-Minnesota	5	7	3	48	52	3	2	3	30	26	2	5	0	18	26
Denver-Ottawa	5	1	0	34	15	2	1	0	22	10	3	0	0	12	5
Edmonton	11	6	1	62	57	7	2	0	28	17	4	4	1	34	40
Houston	6	21	0	91	154	5	9	0	48	70	1	12	0	43	84
Indianapolis	12	5	1	78	46	7	1	1	50	19	5	4	0	28	27
Michigan-Baltimore	3	2	1	26	14	2	1	0	21	10	1	1	1	5	4
Minnesota (orig.)	6	5	2	44	43	4	1	2	22	16	2	4	0	22	27
New England	8	7	3	60	66	4	3	2	30	31	4	4	1	30	35
Quebec	4	11	1	58	77	1	6	1	29	33	3	5	0	29	44
San Diego	15	14	2	116	122	9	5	0	67	51	6	9	2	49	71
Toronto-Birmingham	5	8	3	55	74	3	2	3	29	32	2	6	0	26	42
Vancouver-Calgary	6	11	1	58	70	4	4	1	28	26	2	7	0	30	44
Winnipeg	10	8	0	70	71	6	3	0	42	34	4	5	0	28	37
All Time:	**106**	**114**	**18**	**883**	**935**	**63**	**43**	**13**	**497**	**409**	**43**	**71**	**5**	**386**	**526**

Quebec NORDIQUES

opponent	all-time					home					away				
	w	l	t	qf	ga	w	l	t	qf	ga	w	l	t	qf	ga
Alberta-Edmonton	38	23	2	280	235	23	7	2	165	104	15	16	0	115	131
Chicago	11	9	0	78	67	6	4	0	41	30	5	5	0	37	37
Cincinnati	18	19	3	157	156	11	7	2	85	64	7	12	1	72	92
Cleveland-Minnesota	13	16	2	106	110	9	4	2	56	41	4	12	0	50	69
Denver	1	0	0	5	3	0	0	0	0	0	1	0	0	5	3
Houston	22	15	2	153	137	16	2	2	94	50	6	13	0	59	87
Indianapolis	21	12	1	148	118	14	3	0	77	50	7	9	1	71	68
LA-Mich-Balt	11	6	1	70	48	7	1	1	41	17	4	5	0	29	31
Minnesota (orig.)	8	12	1	85	104	4	6	0	39	54	4	6	1	46	50
New England	34	29	3	257	236	21	11	2	150	108	13	18	1	107	128
NY-Jer-SD	15	16	1	124	144	13	2	1	84	46	2	14	0	40	98
Ott-Tor-Bir	44	31	1	319	302	27	10	0	170	133	17	21	1	149	169
Phi-Van-Cgy	20	15	1	164	147	16	2	0	107	62	4	13	1	57	85
Phoenix	11	4	1	77	58	5	3	0	44	29	6	1	1	33	29
Winnipeg	26	29	4	233	243	15	11	3	125	110	11	18	1	108	133
Touring teams	2	1	1	18	13	2	1	1	18	13	0	0	0	0	0
All Time:	**295**	**237**	**24**	**2274**	**2121**	**189**	**74**	**16**	**1296**	**911**	**106**	**163**	**8**	**978**	**1210**

Winnipeg JETS

opponent	all-time w	l	t	gf	ga	home w	l	t	gf	ga	away w	l	t	gf	ga
Alberta-Edmonton	41	31	3	314	248	27	10	1	176	107	14	21	2	138	141
Chicago	15	6	1	81	56	11	0	0	45	19	4	6	1	36	37
Cincinnati	21	14	1	173	126	10	8	0	87	64	11	6	1	86	62
Cleveland-Minnesota	11	11	2	97	88	9	3	0	58	38	2	8	2	39	50
Denver-Ottawa	4	0	0	22	13	2	0	0	11	7	2	0	0	11	6
Houston	18	24	3	150	172	12	9	1	85	66	6	15	2	65	106
Indianapolis	25	8	1	155	95	12	3	1	69	32	13	5	0	86	63
LA-Mich-Balt	16	6	0	95	61	10	1	0	53	22	6	5	0	42	39
Minnesota (orig.)	9	15	2	73	103	6	5	2	38	37	3	10	0	35	66
New England	27	24	2	213	197	13	12	2	113	93	14	12	0	100	104
NY-Jer-SD	17	10	2	137	106	11	1	2	78	40	6	9	0	59	66
Ott-Tor-Bir	33	25	2	242	217	19	9	2	142	92	14	16	0	100	125
Phi-Van-Cgy	26	16	2	187	157	17	4	1	108	69	9	12	1	79	88
Phoenix	8	10	0	71	70	5	4	0	37	28	3	6	0	34	42
Quebec	29	26	4	243	233	18	11	1	133	108	11	15	3	110	125
Touring teams	2	1	1	17	12	2	1	1	17	12	0	0	0	0	0
All Time:	**302**	**227**	**26**	**2270**	**1954**	**184**	**81**	**14**	**1250**	**834**	**118**	**146**	**12**	**1020**	**1120**

Seasonal Extremes
Teams that folded mid-season are not included.

Most wins, season: 53, Houston (1974-75), Houston (1975-76); 52, Winnipeg (1975-76); 50, Houston (1976-77), Quebec (1975-76), Winnipeg (1977-78)

Fewest wins, season: 18, Indianapolis (1974-75); 21, Michigan-Baltimore (1974-75); 24, Toronto (1975-76), Indianapolis (1977-78); 25, Los Angeles (1973-74)

Most wins, home: 33, Houston (1975-76), Quebec (1975-76), Houston (1976-77); 30, New England (1972-73), Winnipeg (1976-77)

Fewest wins, home: 13, Indianapolis (1974-75); 15, Michigan-Baltimore (1974-75); 16, Toronto (1975-76); 17, Chicago (1972-73), Los Angeles (1973-74), Indianapolis (1977-78)

Most wins, road: 25, Houston (1974-75); 23, Winnipeg (1975-76); 22, Winnipeg (1977-78); 20, Houston (1973-74), Houston (1975-76)

Fewest wins, road: 5, Indianapolis (1974-75), Calgary (1976-77); 6, Michigan-Baltimore (1974-75); 7, Edmonton (1975-76), Indianapolis (1977-78)

Most losses, season: 57, Indianapolis (1974-75); 53, Los Angeles (1973-74), Michigan-Baltimore (1974-75); 52, Toronto (1975-76); 51, Indianapolis (1977-78); 50, Chicago (1972-73), Vancouver (1973-74)

Fewest losses, season: 24, Houston (1976-77); 25, Houston (1973-74), Houston (1974-75); 27, Houston (1975-76), Quebec (1975-76), Winnipeg (1975-76)

Most losses, home: 26, Indianapolis (1974-75); 22, Chicago (1972-73), Los Angeles (1973-74); 21, Michigan-Baltimore (1974-75), Indianapolis (1977-78)

Fewest losses, home: 3, Houston (1976-77); 7, Houston, (1975-76), Quebec, (1975-76); 8, New England (1972-73), New England (1974-75)

Most losses, road: 32, Michigan-Baltimore (1974-75), Edmonton (1975-76), Toronto (1975-76); 31, Los Angeles (1973-74), Indianapolis (1974-75), Birmingham (1976-77), Calgary (1976-77)

Fewest losses, road: 14, Houston (1974-75); 15, Los Angeles (1972-73); 16, Houston (1973-74), Winnipeg (1975-76); 17, New England (1977-78), Winnipeg (1977-78)

Most ties, season: 9, Cleveland (1973-74), New England (1978-79); 8, Phoenix (1974-75), Indianapolis (1976-77); 7, New England (1975-76), Calgary (1976-77)

Fewest ties, season: 0, Philadelphia (1972-73), Los Angeles (1973-74), Houston (1974-75), Quebec (1974-75), Houston, (1975-76)

Most ties, home: 6, Phoenix (1975-76); 5, Quebec (1972-73), Phoenix (1974-75), Birmingham (1978-79)

Fewest ties, home: 0, shared by 14 teams; 1, shared by 15 teams.

Most ties, road: 9, New England (1978-79); 5, Los Angeles (1972-73), Cleveland (1973-74), New England (1975-76), Calgary (1976-77), Indianapolis (1976-77)

Fewest ties, road: 0, shared by 12 teams; 1, shared by 18 teams.

Most Points, Season: 106, Houston (1974-75), Houston (1975-76), Winnipeg (1975-76), Houston (1976-77); 104, Quebec (1975-76); 102, Winnipeg (1977-78)

Fewest Points, Season: 39, Indianapolis (1974-75); 46, Michigan-Baltimore (1974-75); 50, Los Angeles (1973-74); 53, Toronto (1975-76), Indianapolis (1977-78)

Player, Goaltender & Coaching Registers

Every player to have skated a shift in the World Hockey Association regular season game is listed alphabetically on the following pages, along with his yearly regular season and playoff statistics. Career totals are also listed for each player. Goaltenders are listed in a separate section, immediately following the skater listings. A coaching register follows the goaltender's register.

For the skaters, the team for which he played, games played, goals, assists, points and penalty minutes are provided, both regular season and playoffs. For goaltenders, the team for which he played, games played, minutes, goals against, shutouts, won-loss-tied record and goals against average are provided, both regular season and playoff. Also, a column for assists and penalty minutes earned by the goaltender are given as well. A total of 807 players saw action during the World Hockey Association's seven-year run.

If the player saw action in the NHL, a tagline is included beneath his WHA statistics. Other notable facts such as Olympic participation, Stanley Cups won, and so on, are given as well.

Note: the spelling of the last names of two players is uncertain: Wayne Morin is sometimes listed as Morrin, while Tom Trevelyan is sometimes listed as Trevelyn. In both cases, the spelling as seen in most contemporary sources is used here.

Bruce ABBEY
6-1 185 - 18 Aug 1951, Belmont ON

year	team	gp	g	a	pts	pim	gp	g	a	pts	pim
75-76	Cin	17	1	0	1	12					
totals		17	1	0	1	12					

Dennis ABGRALL
Dennis Harvey Abgrall
6-0 180 R 24 Apr 1953, Mooseomin SK

year	team	gp	g	a	pts	pim	gp	g	a	pts	pim
76-77	Cin	80	23	39	62	22	4	2	0	2	5
77-78	Cin	65	13	11	24	13					
totals		145	36	50	86	35	4	2	0	2	5

• Played in NHL: 1975-76, LA, 13-0-2-2-4

Thommie ABRAHAMSSON
Thommie Ulf Abrahamsson
6-2 185 L 12 Apr 1947, Leksand Sweden

year	team	gp	g	a	pts	pim	gp	g	a	pts	pim
74-75	NE	76	8	22	30	46					
75-76	NE	63	14	21	35	47	17	2	4	6	15
76-77	NE	64	6	24	30	33	5	0	3	3	0
totals		203	28	67	95	126	22	2	7	9	15

• Brother of Christer Abrahamsson • Played in NHL: 1980-81, Hart, 32-6-11-17-16

Jim ADAIR
James Albert Adair
5-11 180 L 29 Sep 1948, Brockville ON

year	team	gp	g	a	pts	pim	gp	g	a	pts	pim
73-74	Van	70	12	17	29	10					
totals		70	12	17	29	10					

• Member: Canadian National Team, 1968-69

Ray ADDUONO
Raymond Jerry Peter Adduono
5-9 160 L 21 Jan 1947, Fort William ON

year	team	gp	g	a	pts	pim	gp	g	a	pts	pim
73-74	Cle	2	0	0	0	0					
74-75	SD	78	15	59	74	23	10	5	9	14	13
75-76	SD	80	23	67	90	22	11	4	7	11	6
76-77	Min	40	4	19	23	17					
	SD	13	2	5	7	5	7	3	2	5	19
77-78	Ind	8	1	2	3	0					
totals		221	45	152	197	67	28	12	18	30	38

• Uncle of Rick Adduono

Rick ADDUONO
Rick Norman Adduono
5-10 170 L 25 Jan 1955, Fort William ON

year	team	gp	g	a	pts	pim	gp	g	a	pts	pim
78-79	Bir	80	20	33	53	67					
totals		80	20	33	53	67					

• Nephew of Ray Adduono • Played in NHL: 1975-76, 1979-80, Bos-Atl, 4-0-0-0-2

Kevin AHEARN
Kevin Joseph Ahearn
5-10 160 L 20 Jun 1948, Milton MA

year	team	gp	g	a	pts	pim	gp	g	a	pts	pim
72-73	NE	78	20	22	42	18	14	1	2	3	9
totals		78	20	22	42	18	14	1	2	3	9

• Member: United States National Team, 1970-71 • Member, United States Olympic Team, 1972

Chris AHRENS
Chris Alfred Ahrens
6-0 180 R 31 Jul 1952, San Bernardino CA

year	team	gp	g	a	pts	pim	gp	g	a	pts	pim
77-78	Edm	4	0	0	0	15					
totals		4	0	0	0	15					

• Played in NHL: 1973-78, Min, 52-0-3-3-84

Claire ALEXANDER
Arthur Claire Alexander
5-10 180 R 14 Jun 1945, Collingwood ON

year	team	gp	g	a	pts	pim	gp	g	a	pts	pim
78-79	Edm	54	8	23	31	16					
totals		54	8	23	31	16					

• Played in NHL: 1974-78, Tor-Van, 155-18-47-65-36

Jeff ALLAN
6-1 195 L 17 May 1957, Hull PQ

year	team	gp	g	a	pts	pim	gp	g	a	pts	pim
77-78	Cin	2	0	0	0	0					
totals		2	0	0	0	0					

• Played in NHL: 1977-78, Cle, 4-0-0-0-2

Steve ALLEY
6-0 185 L 19 Dec 1953, Anoka AB

year	team	gp	g	a	pts	pim	gp	g	a	pts	pim
77-78	Bir	27	8	12	20	11	5	0	1	1	10
78-79	Bir	78	17	24	41	36					
totals		105	25	36	61	47	5	1	0	1	10

• Played in NHL: 1979-81, Hart, 15-3-3-6-11 • Member, United States Olympic Team, 1976

Mike AMODEO
Michael Anthony Amodeo
5-10 190 L 22 Jun 1952, Toronto ON

year	team	gp	g	a	pts	pim	gp	g	a	pts	pim
72-73	Ott	61	1	14	15	77	5	0	1	1	10
73-74	Tor	77	0	11	11	82	12	0	2	2	26
74-75	Tor	64	1	13	14	50	3	0	1	1	4
75-76	Tor	31	4	8	12	35					
77-78	Wpg	3	1	1	2	0	7	1	3	4	19
78-79	Wpg	64	4	18	22	29					
totals		300	11	65	76	273	27	1	7	8	59

• Played in NHL: 1979-80, Wpg, 19-0-0-0-2

Ron C. ANDERSON
Ronald Chester Anderson
6-0 170 R 29 Jul 1945, Red Deer AB

year	team	gp	g	a	pts	pim	gp	g	a	pts	pim
72-73	Alb	73	14	15	29	43					
73-74	Edm	19	5	2	7	6					
totals		92	19	17	36	49					

• Played in NHL: 1967-72, Det-LA-StL-Buf, 251-28-30-58-146

Ron F. ANDERSON
Ronald Frank Anderson
6-0 185 L 15 Nov 1948, Dryden ON

year	team	gp	g	a	pts	pim	gp	g	a	pts	pim
72-73	Chi	73	3	26	29	34					
73-74	Chi	2	0	0	0	0					
74-75	Cle	39	0	9	9	10					
totals		114	3	35	38	44					

Steve ANDRASCIK
Steven George Andrascik
5-11 190 R 6 Nov 1948, Sherridan MB

year	team	gp	g	a	pts	pim	gp	g	a	pts	pim
74-75	Ind	20	2	4	6	16					
	M-B	57	4	7	11	42					
75-76	Cin	20	3	2	5	21					
totals		97	9	13	22	79					

• Played in NHL: 1972, NYR (Playoffs) 1-0-0-0-0

Paul ANDREA
Paul Lawrence Andrea
5-11 170 L 31 Jul 1941, North Sydney NS

year	team	gp	g	a	pts	pim	gp	g	a	pts	pim
72-73	Cle	66	21	30	51	12	9	2	8	10	2
73-74	Cle	69	15	18	33	14	5	1	0	1	2
totals		135	36	48	84	26	14	3	8	11	4

• Played in NHL: 1965-71, NYR-Pit-Cal-Buf, 150-31-49-80-10

Lou ANGOTTI
Louis Frederick Angotti
5-9 170 R 16 Jan 1938, Toronto ON

year	team	gp	g	a	pts	pim	gp	g	a	pts	pim
74-75	Chi	26	2	5	7	9					
totals		26	2	5	7	9					

• Played in NHL: 1964-74, NYR-Chi-Pit-Phi-StL, 653-103-186-289-228

Mike ANTONOVICH
Michael Antonovich
5-6 155 L 18 Oct 1951, Calumet MN

year	team	gp	g	a	pts	pim	gp	g	a	pts	pim
72-73	Min	75	20	19	39	44	5	2	0	2	0
73-74	Min	68	21	29	50	4	11	1	4	5	4
74-75	Min	67	24	26	50	20	12	1	4	5	2
75-76	Min	57	25	21	46	18					
76-77	Min	42	27	21	48	28					
	Edm	7	1	1	2	0					
	NE	26	12	9	21	10	5	2	2	4	4
77-78	NE	75	32	35	67	32	14	10	7	17	4
78-79	NE	69	20	27	47	35	10	5	3	8	14
totals		486	182	188	370	191	57	21	20	41	28

• Played in NHL: 1975-76, 1979-84, Min-Hart-NJ, 87-10-15-25-37

John ARBOUR John Gilbert Arbour
5-11 195 L 28 Sep 1945, Niagara Falls ON

year	team	gp	g	a	pts	pim	gp	g	a	pts	pim
72-73	Min	76	6	27	33	188	5	0	1	1	12
73-74	Min	77	6	43	49	192	11	3	6	9	27
74-75	Min	71	12	43	55	67	12	0	6	6	23
75-76	D-O	34	2	13	15	49					
	Min	7	0	4	4	14					
76-77	Min	33	3	19	22	22					
	Cgy	37	1	15	16	38					
totals		335	30	164	194	568	28	3	13	16	62

• Played in NHL: 1965-72, Bos-Pit-Van-StL, 106-1-9-10-149

Michel ARCHAMBAULT Michel Joseph Archambault
5-8 160 L 27 Sep 1950, St-Hyacinthe PQ

year	team	gp	g	a	pts	pim	gp	g	a	pts	pim
72-73	Que	57	12	25	37	36					
totals		57	12	25	37	36					

• Played in NHL: 1976-77, Chi, 3-0-0-0-0

Danny ARNDT Daniel Henry Arndt
5-11 175 L 26 Mar 1955, Saskatoon SK

year	team	gp	g	a	pts	pim	gp	g	a	pts	pim
75-76	NE	69	8	8	16	10	8	0	0	0	0
76-77	NE	46	8	14	22	11					
	Edm	1	0	0	0	0					
77-78	Bir	4	0	1	1	0					
totals		120	16	23	39	21	8	0	0	0	0

Bob ASH Robert John Ash
5-9 170 L 29 Sep 1943, Brandon MB

year	team	gp	g	a	pts	pim	gp	g	a	pts	pim
72-73	Wpg	75	3	14	17	39	13	1	3	4	4
73-74	Wpg	60	2	18	20	30	4	0	1	1	2
74-75	Ind	64	1	14	15	19					
totals		199	6	46	52	88	17	1	4	5	6

Ron ASHTON Ronald Ashton
6-2 210 L 8 May 1954, Regina SK

year	team	gp	g	a	pts	pim	gp	g	a	pts	pim
74-75	Wpg	36	1	3	4	66					
totals		36	1	3	4	66					

Duke ASMUNDSON Freeman Asmundson
6-2 195 R 17 Aug 1943, Vita MB

year	team	gp	g	a	pts	pim	gp	g	a	pts	pim
72-73	Wpg	78	2	14	16	54	12	1	3	4	4
73-74	Wpg	72	5	14	19	85	4	0	1	1	2
74-75	Wpg	38	4	15	19	53					
75-76	Wpg	72	5	11	16	19	13	3	2	5	11
totals		260	16	54	70	211	29	4	6	10	17

Steve ATKINSON Steven John Atkinson
6-0 170 R 16 Oct 1948, Toronto ON d. 2003

year	team	gp	g	a	pts	pim	gp	g	a	pts	pim
75-76	Tor	52	2	6	8	22					
totals		52	2	6	8	22					

• Played in NHL: 1968-75, Bos-Buf-Wash, 302-60-51-111-104

Ralph BACKSTROM Ralph Gerald Backstrom
5-10 170 L 18 Sep 1937, Kirkland Lake ON

year	team	gp	g	a	pts	pim	gp	g	a	pts	pim
73-74	Chi	78	33	50	83	26	18	5	14	19	4
74-75	Chi	70	15	24	39	28					
75-76	D-O	41	21	29	50	14					
	NE	38	14	19	33	6	17	5	4	9	8
76-77	NE	77	17	31	48	30	3	0	0	0	0
totals		304	100	153	253	104	38	10	18	28	12

• Played in NHL: 1956-73, Mtl-LA-Chi, 1032-278-361-639-388 • Stanley Cups: 1959, 1960, 1965, 1966, 1968, 1969 (Montreal)

Garnet BAILEY Garnet Edward Bailey "Ace"
5-11 185 L 13 Jun 1948, Lloydminster SK d. 2001

year	team	gp	g	a	pts	pim	gp	g	a	pts	pim
78-79	Edm	38	5	4	9	22	2	0	0	0	4
totals		38	5	4	9	22	2	0	0	0	4

• Played in NHL: 1968-78, Bos-Det-StL-Wash, 568-107-171-278-633 • Stanley Cups: 1972 (Boston), 1990 (Edmonton as Scout)

Ken BAIRD Kenneth Stewart Baird
6-0 190 L 1 Feb 1951, Flin Flon MB

year	team	gp	g	a	pts	pim	gp	g	a	pts	pim
72-73	Alb	75	14	15	29	112					
73-74	Edm	68	17	19	36	115	5	1	1	2	7
74-75	Edm	77	30	28	58	151					
75-76	Edm	48	13	24	37	87	4	3	1	4	16
76-77	Edm	2	1	2	3	0					
	Cgy	7	0	0	0	2					
77-78	Edm	6	2	4	6	2					
	Wpg	49	14	7	21	29	7	0	4	4	7
totals		333	91	99	190	498	16	4	6	10	30

• Played in NHL: 1971-72, Cal, 10-0-2-2-15

Blake BALL
6-3 210 L 25 Feb 1938, Berks Falls ON d. 2006

year	team	gp	g	a	pts	pim	gp	g	a	pts	pim
72-73	Cle	0	0	0	0	0	2	0	0	0	2
totals		0	0	0	0	0	2	0	0	0	2

• Played six seasons as a defensive end in the Canadian Football League in the late 1950s-early 1960s

Terry BALL Terry James Ball
5-9 165 R 29 Nov 1944, Selkirk MB

year	team	gp	g	a	pts	pim	gp	g	a	pts	pim
72-73	Min	76	6	34	40	66	5	1	2	3	4
73-74	Min	71	8	28	36	34	11	1	2	3	6
74-75	Min	76	8	37	45	36	12	3	4	7	4
75-76	Cle	23	2	15	17	18					
	Cin	36	3	14	17	12					
76-77	Bir	23	1	6	7	8					
totals		305	28	134	162	174	28	5	8	13	14

• Played in NHL: 1967-72, Phi-Buf, 74-7-19-26-26

Dave BALON David Alexander Balon
5-10 180 L 2 Aug 1938, Wakaw SK d. 2007

year	team	gp	g	a	pts	pim	gp	g	a	pts	pim
73-74	Que	22	0	0	0	2					
totals		22	0	0	0	2					

• Played in NHL: 1959-73, NYR-Mtl-Min-Van, 776-192-222-414-607
• Stanley Cups: 1965, 1966 (Montreal)

Bryon BALTIMORE Bryon Donald Baltimore
6-2 190 L 26 Aug 1952, Whitehorse YT

year	team	gp	g	a	pts	pim	gp	g	a	pts	pim
74-75	Chi	77	8	12	20	110					
75-76	D-O	41	1	8	9	32					
	Ind	37	1	10	11	30	7	0	1	1	4
76-77	Ind	55	0	15	15	63	9	0	0	0	5
77-78	Ind	22	1	7	8	47					
	Cin	28	2	9	11	23					
78-79	Ind	2	1	1	2	2					
	Cin	69	4	10	14	83	3	0	0	0	0
totals		331	18	72	90	390	19	0	1	1	9

• Played in NHL: 1979-80, Edm, 2-0-0-0-4

Butch BARBER Robert Ian Barber
5-10 170 L 31 Aug 1943, Fairview AB

year	team	gp	g	a	pts	pim	gp	g	a	pts	pim
72-73	Chi	75	4	19	23	39					
73-74	NY-J	3	0	0	0	2					
totals		78	4	19	23	41					

Bob BARLOW Robert George Barlow
5-10 175 L 17 Jun 1935, Hamilton ON

year	team	gp	g	a	pts	pim	gp	g	a	pts	pim
74-75	Phx	51	6	20	26	8					
totals		51	6	20	26	8					

• Played in NHL: 1969-71, Min, 77-16-17-33-10

Doug BARRIE Douglas Robert Barrie
5-9 175 R 2 Oct 1946, Edmonton AB

year	team	gp	g	a	pts	pim	gp	g	a	pts	pim
72-73	Alb	54	9	22	31	111					
73-74	Edm	69	4	27	31	214	4	1	0	1	16
74-75	Edm	78	12	33	45	122					
75-76	Edm	79	4	21	25	81	4	0	1	1	6
76-77	Edm	70	8	19	27	92	4	0	0	0	0
totals		351	37	122	159	620	12	1	1	2	22

• Played in NHL: 1968-72, Pit-Buf-LA, 158-10-42-52-258

Jamie BATEMAN James Bateman
6-1   185   L   16 Sep 1954, Thetford Mines PQ

year	team	gp	g	a	pts	pim	gp	g	a	pts	pim
74-75	SD	24	0	3	3	96					
75-76	SD	7	1	0	1	4					
totals		31	1	3	4	100					

Andy BATHGATE Andrew James Bathgate
5-8   170   R   28 Aug 1932, Winnipeg MB   d. 2016

year	team	gp	g	a	pts	pim	gp	g	a	pts	pim
74-75	Van	11	1	6	7	2					
totals		11	1	6	7	2					

• Played in NHL: 1952-71, NYR-Tor-Det-Pit, 1069-349-624-973-624
• Stanley Cup: 1964 (Toronto) • Member, Hockey Hall of Fame.

Paul BAXTER Paul Gordon Baxter
5-11   200   R   25 Oct 1955, Winnipeg MB

year	team	gp	g	a	pts	pim	gp	g	a	pts	pim
74-75	Cle	5	0	0	0	37					
75-76	Cle	67	3	7	10	201	3	0	0	0	10
76-77	Que	66	6	17	23	244	12	2	2	4	35
77-78	Que	76	6	29	35	240	11	4	7	11	42
78-79	Que	76	10	36	46	240	4	0	2	2	7
totals		290	25	88	113	962	30	6	11	17	84

• Played in NHL: 1979-87, Que-Pit-Cgy, 472-48-121-169-1564

Frank BEATON Alexander Francis Beaton "Seldom"
5-10   185   L   28 Apr 1953, Antigonish NS

year	team	gp	g	a	pts	pim	gp	g	a	pts	pim
75-76	Cin	29	2	3	5	61					
76-77	Edm	68	4	9	13	274	5	0	2	2	21
77-78	Bir	56	6	9	15	279	5	2	0	2	10
totals		153	12	21	33	614	10	2	2	4	31

• Played in NHL: 1978-80, NYR, 25-1-1-2-43

Norm BEAUDIN Norman Joseph Andrew Beaudin
5-9   170   R   28 Nov 1941, Montmartre SK

year	team	gp	g	a	pts	pim	gp	g	a	pts	pim
72-73	Wpg	78	38	65	103	15	14	13	15	28	2
73-74	Wpg	74	27	28	55	8	4	3	1	4	2
74-75	Wpg	77	16	31	47	8					
75-76	Wpg	80	16	31	47	38	13	2	3	5	10
totals		309	97	155	252	69	31	18	19	37	14

• Played in NHL: 1967-71, StL-Min, 25-1-2-3-4

Serge BEAUDOIN
6-2   215   L   30 Nov 1952, Montreal PQ

year	team	gp	g	a	pts	pim	gp	g	a	pts	pim
73-74	Van	26	1	11	12	37					
74-75	Van	4	0	0	0	2					
75-76	Phx	76	0	21	21	102	5	1	0	1	10
76-77	Phx	77	6	24	30	136					
77-78	Cin	13	0	1	1	10					
	Bir	64	8	25	33	105	5	1	0	1	46
78-79	Bir	72	5	21	26	127					
totals		332	20	103	123	519	10	2	0	2	56

• Played in NHL: 1979-80, Atl, 3-0-0-0

Alain BEAULE Alain Pierre Beaule
6-0   195   L   7 Apr 1946, St-Romain PQ

year	team	gp	g	a	pts	pim	gp	g	a	pts	pim
73-74	Que	78	4	36	40	93					
74-75	Que	22	4	7	11	19					
	Wpg	54	0	14	14	24					
totals		154	8	57	65	136					

John BENNETT
6-1   175   R   19 Jan 1950, Cranston RI

year	team	gp	g	a	pts	pim	gp	g	a	pts	pim
72-73	Phi	34	4	6	10	18					
totals		34	4	6	10	18					

Wendell BENNETT Wendell James Bennett
6-2   180   R   24 Mar 1950, Loon Lake SK

year	team	gp	g	a	pts	pim	gp	g	a	pts	pim
74-75	Phx	67	4	15	19	92					
totals		67	4	15	19	92					

Jim BENZELOCK James John Benzelock
5-10   190   R   21 Jun 1947, Winnipeg MB

year	team	gp	g	a	pts	pim	gp	g	a	pts	pim
72-73	Alb	26	1	1	2	10					
	Chi	43	9	12	21	23					
73-74	Chi	53	6	7	13	19	18	2	2	4	36
74-75	Chi	10	0	2	2	14					
75-76	Que	34	2	5	7	6	3	0	0	0	0
totals		166	18	27	45	72	21	2	2	4	36

Yves BERGERON
5-9   165   R   11 Jan 1952, Malartic PQ

year	team	gp	g	a	pts	pim	gp	g	a	pts	pim
72-73	Que	65	14	19	33	32					
totals		65	14	19	33	32					

• Played in NHL: 1974-77, Pit, 3-0-0-0-0

Thommie BERGMAN Thommie Lars Rudolf Bergman
6-3   200   L   10 Dec 1947, Munkfors Sweden

year	team	gp	g	a	pts	pim	gp	g	a	pts	pim
74-75	Wpg	49	4	15	19	70					
75-76	Wpg	81	11	30	41	111	13	3	10	13	8
76-77	Wpg	42	2	24	26	37					
77-78	Wpg	65	5	28	33	43					
totals		237	22	97	119	261	13	3	10	13	8

• Played in NHL: 1973-75, 1978-80, Det, 246-21-44-65-243 • Member, Sweden Olympic Team, 1972

Jean BERNIER
5-10   170   L   21 Jun 1954, St-Hyacinthe PQ

year	team	gp	g	a	pts	pim	gp	g	a	pts	pim
74-75	Que	34	1	13	14	13	9	0	1	1	2
75-76	Que	81	4	26	30	10	4	0	1	1	0
76-77	Que	72	2	13	15	23	9	0	2	2	0
77-78	Que	74	10	32	42	4	10	3	4	7	2
totals		261	17	84	101	50	32	3	8	11	4

Serge BERNIER Serge Joseph Bernier
6-1   190   R   29 Apr 1947, Padoue PQ

year	team	gp	g	a	pts	pim	gp	g	a	pts	pim
73-74	Que	74	37	49	86	107					
74-75	Que	76	54	68	122	75	15	8	8	16	6
75-76	Que	70	34	68	102	91	5	2	6	8	6
76-77	Que	74	43	53	96	97	17	14	22	36	10
77-78	Que	58	26	52	78	48	11	4	10	14	17
78-79	Que	65	36	46	82	71	1	0	0	0	2
totals		417	230	336	566	486	59	28	46	74	41

• Played in NHL: 1968-73, 1979-81, Phi-LA-Que, 302-78-119-197-234

Doug BERRY Douglas Alan Berry
6-1   190   L   3 Jun 1957, New Westminster BC

year	team	gp	g	a	pts	pim	gp	g	a	pts	pim
78-79	Edm	29	6	3	9	4					
totals		29	6	3	9	4					

• Played in NHL: 1979-81, Col, 121-10-33-43-25

Larry BIGNELL Larry Irvin Bignell
5-11   175   L   7 Jan 1950, Edmonton AB

year	team	gp	g	a	pts	pim	gp	g	a	pts	pim
75-76	D-O	41	5	5	10	43					
totals		41	5	5	10	43					

• Played in NHL: 1973-75, Pit, 20-0-3-3-2

Gilles BILODEAU "Bad News"
6-1   220   L   31 Jul 1955, St-Prime PQ   d. 2008

year	team	gp	g	a	pts	pim	gp	g	a	pts	pim
75-76	Tor	14	0	1	1	38					
76-77	Bir	34	2	6	8	133					
77-78	Bir	59	2	2	4	258	3	0	0	0	27
78-79	Que	36	3	6	9	141	3	0	0	0	25
totals		143	7	15	22	570	6	0	0	0	52

• Played in NHL: 1979-80, Que, 9-0-1-1-25

Yvon BILODEAU
6-3   210   L   18 Jan 1951, Vimy AB

year	team	gp	g	a	pts	pim	gp	g	a	pts	pim
75-76	Cgy	4	0	0	0	2					
totals		4	0	0	0	2					

Milt BLACK — Milton James Black
6-0 190 R 20 Jun 1949, Winnipeg MB

year	team	gp	g	a	pts	pim	gp	g	a	pts	pim
72-73	Wpg	77	18	16	34	31	14	1	3	4	2
73-74	Wpg	47	6	9	15	14	4	1	1	2	0
74-75	Wpg	65	4	6	10	10					
totals		**189**	**28**	**31**	**59**	**55**	**18**	**2**	**4**	**6**	**2**

Don BLACKBURN — John Donald Blackburn
6-0 175 L 14 May 1938, Kirkland Lake ON

year	team	gp	g	a	pts	pim	gp	g	a	pts	pim
73-74	NE	75	20	39	59	18	7	2	4	6	4
74-75	NE	50	18	32	50	16	5	1	2	3	2
75-76	NE	21	2	3	5	6					
totals		**146**	**40**	**74**	**114**	**40**	**12**	**3**	**6**	**9**	**6**

• Played in NHL: 1962-73, Bos-Phi-NYR-Min, 185-23-44-67-87

Bill BLACKWOOD
5-11 190 - 5 Apr 1955, Sudbury ON

year	team	gp	g	a	pts	pim	gp	g	a	pts	pim
77-78	Ind	3	0	0	0	0					
totals		**3**	**0**	**0**	**0**	**0**					

Jacques BLAIN
5-11 180 L 19 Jul 1947, Gatineau PQ

year	team	gp	g	a	pts	pim	gp	g	a	pts	pim
72-73	Que	70	1	10	11	78					
totals		**70**	**1**	**10**	**11**	**78**					

Bernie BLANCHETTE — Bernard Robert Blanchette
6-0 165 R 11 Jul 1947, N. Battleford SK   d. 2006

year	team	gp	g	a	pts	pim	gp	g	a	pts	pim
72-73	Chi	24	2	3	5	8					
	Alb	23	5	4	9	2					
totals		**47**	**7**	**7**	**14**	**10**					

Ken BLOCK — Kenneth Ritchard Block
5-10 185 L 18 May 1944, Steinbach MB

year	team	gp	g	a	pts	pim	gp	g	a	pts	pim
72-73	NY	78	5	53	58	43					
73-74	NY-J	74	3	43	46	22					
74-75	SD	36	1	11	12	12					
	Ind	37	0	17	17	18					
75-76	Ind	79	1	25	26	28					
76-77	Ind	52	3	10	13	25	9	0	2	2	6
77-78	Ind	77	1	25	26	34					
78-79	Ind	22	2	3	5	10					
totals		**455**	**16**	**187**	**203**	**192**	**9**	**0**	**2**	**2**	**6**

• Played in NHL: 1970-71, Van, 1-0-0-0-0

Greg BODDY — Greg Allan Boddy
6-2 200 R 19 Mar 1949, Ponoka AB

year	team	gp	g	a	pts	pim	gp	g	a	pts	pim
76-77	SD	18	1	2	3	19					
	Edm	46	1	17	18	41	4	1	2	3	14
totals		**64**	**2**	**19**	**21**	**60**	**4**	**1**	**2**	**3**	**14**

• Played in NHL: 1971-76, Van, 273-23-44-67-263

Mike BOLAND — Michael Anthony Boland
5-10 185 R 15 Dec 1949, Montreal PQ

year	team	gp	g	a	pts	pim	gp	g	a	pts	pim
72-73	Ott	41	1	15	16	44	1	0	0	0	12
totals		**41**	**1**	**15**	**16**	**44**	**1**	**0**	**0**	**0**	**12**

• Played in NHL: 1974-75, Phi, 2-0-0-0-0

Dan BOLDUC — Daniel George Bolduc
5-9 180 L 6 Apr 1953, Waterville ME

year	team	gp	g	a	pts	pim	gp	g	a	pts	pim
75-76	NE	14	2	5	7	14	16	1	6	7	4
76-77	NE	33	8	3	11	15					
77-78	NE	41	5	5	10	22	14	2	4	6	4
totals		**88**	**15**	**13**	**28**	**51**	**30**	**3**	**10**	**13**	**8**

• Played in NHL: 1978-84, Det-Cgy, 102-22-19-41-33

Kerry BOND — John Kerry Bond
6-0 190 L 18 Jul 1945, Sudbury ON

year	team	gp	g	a	pts	pim	gp	g	a	pts	pim
74-75	Ind	71	22	15	37	23					
75-76	Ind	15	2	0	2	9	7	1	0	1	11
totals		**86**	**24**	**15**	**39**	**32**	**7**	**1**	**0**	**1**	**11**

Christian BORDELEAU — Christian Gerard Bordeleau "Pepe"
5-8 155 L 23 Sep 1947, Noranda PQ

year	team	gp	g	a	pts	pim	gp	g	a	pts	pim
72-73	Wpg	78	47	54	101	12	12	5	8	13	4
73-74	Wpg	75	26	49	75	22	3	3	2	5	0
74-75	Wpg	18	8	8	16	0					
	Que	53	15	33	48	24	15	2	13	15	2
75-76	Que	74	37	72	109	42	5	1	1	2	4
76-77	Que	72	32	75	107	34	8	4	5	9	0
77-78	Que	26	9	22	31	28	10	1	5	6	6
78-79	Que	16	5	12	17	0					
totals		**412**	**179**	**325**	**504**	**162**	**53**	**16**	**34**	**50**	**16**

• Brother of Paulin Bordeleau • Played in NHL: 1968-72, Mtl-StL-Chi, 205-38-65-103-82 • Stanley Cup: 1969 (Montreal)

Paulin BORDELEAU — Paulin Joseph Bordeleau
5-9 155 L 29 Jan 1953, Noranda PQ

year	team	gp	g	a	pts	pim	gp	g	a	pts	pim
76-77	Que	80	42	41	83	52	16	12	9	21	12
77-78	Que	77	42	23	65	29	11	4	6	10	2
78-79	Que	77	17	12	29	44	4	1	0	1	0
totals		**234**	**101**	**76**	**177**	**125**	**31**	**17**	**15**	**32**	**14**

• Brother of Christian Bordeleau • Played in NHL: 1973-76, Van 183-33-56-89-47

Don BORGESON — Donald Gary Borgeson
5-11 175 L 20 May 1945, North Battleford SK

year	team	gp	g	a	pts	pim	gp	g	a	pts	pim
74-75	Phx	74	29	28	57	38	5	0	1	1	2
75-76	Phx	40	21	16	37	26					
	NE	31	9	8	17	4	3	1	1	2	0
totals		**145**	**59**	**52**	**111**	**68**	**8**	**1**	**2**	**3**	**2**

Henry BOUCHA — Henry Charles Boucha
6-0 185 R 1 Jun 1951, Warroad MN

year	team	gp	g	a	pts	pim	gp	g	a	pts	pim
75-76	Min	36	15	20	35	47					
totals		**36**	**15**	**20**	**35**	**47**					

• Played in NHL: 1971-77, Det-Min-KC-Col, 247-53-49-102-157 • Member, United States National Team, 1969-71 • Member, United States Olympic Team, 1972

Bruce BOUDREAU — Bruce Allan Boudreau
5-10 170 L 9 Jan 1955, Toronto ON

year	team	gp	g	a	pts	pim	gp	g	a	pts	pim
75-76	Min	30	3	6	9	4					
totals		**30**	**3**	**6**	**9**	**4**					

• Played in NHL: 1976-86, Tor-Chi, 141-28-42-70-46

Michel BOUDREAU
5-9 165 - 26 Sep 1952, Asbestos PQ

year	team	gp	g	a	pts	pim	gp	g	a	pts	pim
72-73	Phi	33	7	7	14	4	2	0	0	0	0
73-74	Van	3	1	0	1	0					
totals		**36**	**8**	**7**	**15**	**4**	**2**	**0**	**0**	**0**	**0**

Andre BOUDRIAS
5-8 165 L 19 Sep 1943, Montreal PQ

year	team	gp	g	a	pts	pim	gp	g	a	pts	pim
76-77	Que	74	12	31	43	12	17	3	12	15	6
77-78	Que	66	10	17	27	22	11	0	2	2	4
totals		**140**	**22**	**48**	**70**	**34**	**28**	**3**	**14**	**17**	**10**

• Played in NHL: 1963-76, Mtl-Min-Chi-StL-Van, 662-151-340-491-216 • Stanley Cup: 1986 (Montreal as Assistant General Manager)

Brian BOWLES — Brian Earl Bowles
5-11 180 R 18 Feb 1952, Drummondville PQ

year	team	gp	g	a	pts	pim	gp	g	a	pts	pim
75-76	Cle	3	0	0	0	0					
totals		**3**	**0**	**0**	**0**	**0**					

Kirk BOWMAN — Kirk Robert Bowman
5-9 180 L 30 Sep 1952, Leamington ON

year	team	gp	g	a	pts	pim	gp	g	a	pts	pim
73-74	LA	10	0	2	2	0					
totals		**10**	**0**	**2**	**2**	**0**					

• Played in NHL: 1976-79, Chi, 88-11-17-28-19

Bob BOYD

Robert Boyd
6-0 190 R 27 Nov 1951, Toronto ON

year	team	gp	g	a	pts	pim	gp	g	a	pts	pim
73-74	Min	41	1	14	15	14	7	0	0	0	4
74-75	Min	13	0	0	0	21					
totals		54	1	14	15	35	7	0	0	0	4

Jim BOYD

James Patrick Boyd
5-9 180 L 4 Jun 1949, Calgary AB

year	team	gp	g	a	pts	pim	gp	g	a	pts	pim
74-75	Phx	76	26	44	70	18	5	1	1	2	2
75-76	Phx	80	23	34	57	44	5	3	2	5	2
76-77	Cgy	13	0	2	2	6					
totals		169	49	80	129	68	10	4	3	7	4

Wally BOYER

Walter Boyer
5-8 170 L 27 Aug 1937, Cowan MB

year	team	gp	g	a	pts	pim	gp	g	a	pts	pim
72-73	Wpg	69	6	28	34	27	14	4	2	6	4
totals		69	6	28	34	27	14	4	2	6	4

• Played in NHL: 1965-72, Tor-Chi-Oak-Pit, 365-54-105-159-163

Dean BOYLAN

6-0 185 R 28 Jan 1951, Boston MA

year	team	gp	g	a	pts	pim	gp	g	a	pts	pim
73-74	NY-J	61	1	5	6	112					
74-75	SD	3	0	0	0	10					
totals		64	1	5	6	122					

Curt BRACKENBURY

John Curtis Brackenbury
5-10 190 L 31 Jan 1952, Kapuskasing ON

year	team	gp	g	a	pts	pim	gp	g	a	pts	pim
73-74	Chi	4	0	1	1	11					
74-75	Min	7	0	0	0	22	12	0	2	2	59
75-76	Min	59	4	9	13	254					
	Que	15	4	5	9	111	5	0	0	0	18
76-77	Que	77	16	13	29	146	17	3	5	8	51
77-78	Que	33	4	9	13	54	10	1	1	2	31
78-79	Que	70	13	13	26	155	4	1	1	2	2
totals		265	41	50	91	753	48	5	9	14	161

• Played in NHL: 1979-83, Que-Edm-StL, 141-9-17-26-226

Brian BRADLEY

Brian James Bradley
5-10 185 L 14 Dec 1944, Sudbury ON

year	team	gp	g	a	pts	pim	gp	g	a	pts	pim
72-73	NY	78	22	33	55	20					
73-74	NY-J		15	23	38	12					
74-75	SD	24	4	5	9	6	6	0	1	1	2
totals		180	41	61	102	38	6	0	1	1	2

Duane BRAY

Duane George Bray
6-2 195 L 24 Sep 1954, Flin Flon MB

year	team	gp	g	a	pts	pim	gp	g	a	pts	pim
76-77	Phx	46	2	6	8	62					
totals		46	2	6	8	62					

Gary BREDIN

Gary Blaine Bredin
6-0 185 R 25 May 1948, Edmonton AB

year	team	gp	g	a	pts	pim	gp	g	a	pts	pim
74-75	Ind	10	3	2	5	8					
	M-B	67	15	21	36	29					
75-76	D-O	16	4	3	7	2					
	SD	50	4	5	9	10					
totals		143	26	31	57	49					

Carl BREWER

Carl Thomas Brewer
5-10 185 L 21 Oct 1938, Toronto ON   d. 2001

year	team	gp	g	a	pts	pim	gp	g	a	pts	pim
73-74	Tor	77	2	23	25	42	12	0	4	4	11
totals		77	2	23	25	42	12	0	4	4	11

• Played in NHL: 1957-72, 1979-80, Tor-Det-StL, 604-25-198-223-1037 • Stanley Cups: 1962, 1963, 1964 (Toronto)

Doug BRINDLEY

Douglas Allen Brindley
5-11 175 L 8 Jun 1949, Walkerton ON

year	team	gp	g	a	pts	pim	gp	g	a	pts	pim
72-73	Cle	73	15	11	26	6	9	0	0	0	0
73-74	Cle	30	13	9	22	13	5	0	1	1	2
totals		103	28	20	48	19	14	0	1	1	2

• Played in NHL: 1970-71, Tor, 3-0-0-0-0

Arnie BROWN

Arnold Stewart Brown
5-9 180 L 28 Jan 1942, Aspley ON

year	team	gp	g	a	pts	pim	gp	g	a	pts	pim
74-75	M-B	50	3	4	7	27					
	Van	10	0	1	1	13					
totals		60	3	5	8	40					

• Played in NHL: 1961-74, Tor-NYR-Det-NYI-Atl, 681-44-141-185-738

Bob BROWN

6-1 195 R 18 Dec 1950, Toronto ON

year	team	gp	g	a	pts	pim	gp	g	a	pts	pim
72-73	Phi	4	0	0	0	2					
	NY	17	0	4	4	6					
73-74	NY-J	59	7	13	20	38					
totals		80	7	17	24	46					

Jeff BRUBAKER

Jeffery J. Brubaker
6-2 210 L 24 Feb 1958, Hagerstown MD

year	team	gp	g	a	pts	pim	gp	g	a	pts	pim
78-79	NE	12	0	0	0	19	3	0	0	0	12
totals		12	0	0	0	19	3	0	0	0	12

• Played in NHL: 1979-89, Hart-Mtl-Cgy-Tor-Edm-NYR, 178-16-9-25-512

Ron BUCHANAN

Ronald Leonard Buchanan
6-3 170 L 15 Nov 1944, Montreal PQ

year	team	gp	g	a	pts	pim	gp	g	a	pts	pim
72-73	Cle	75	37	44	81	20	9	7	3	10	0
73-74	Cle	49	18	27	45	2	5	0	0	0	2
74-75	Cle	4	2	0	2	2					
	Edm	22	6	9	15	4					
	Ind	32	16	15	31	16					
75-76	Ind	23	4	7	11	4					
totals		205	83	102	185	48	14	7	3	10	2

• Played in NHL: 1966-70, Bos-StL, 5-0-0-0-0

Brad BUETOW

Bradford Buetow
6-3 195 L 28 Oct 1950, St Paul MN

year	team	gp	g	a	pts	pim	gp	g	a	pts	pim
73-74	Cle	25	0	0	0	4					
totals		25	0	0	0	4					

Don BURGESS

Donald Rubin Burgess
6-0 170 L 8 Jun 1946, Port Edward ON

year	team	gp	g	a	pts	pim	gp	g	a	pts	pim
72-73	Phi	74	20	22	42	15	4	1	0	1	0
73-74	Van	78	30	36	66	8					
74-75	Van	62	11	18	29	19					
75-76	SD	73	14	11	25	35	11	1	7	8	4
76-77	SD	77	20	22	42	8	7	2	2	4	0
77-78	Ind	79	11	12	23	2					
78-79	Ind	3	1	1	2	0					
totals		446	107	122	229	87	22	4	9	13	4

Ron BUSNIUK

Ronald Edward Busniuk "Buzzy"
6-0 190 R 22 Sep 1947, Fort William ON

year	team	gp	g	a	pts	pim	gp	g	a	pts	pim
74-75	Min	73	2	21	23	176	12	2	1	3	63
75-76	Min	59	2	11	13	150					
	NE	11	0	3	3	55	17	0	2	2	14
76-77	NE	59	1	9	10	141					
	Edm	22	2	2	4	83	5	0	2	2	37
77-78	Edm	59	2	18	20	157	5	0	0	0	18
totals		283	9	64	73	762	39	2	5	7	132

• Played in NHL: 1972-74, Buf, 6-0-3-3-13

Bill BUTTERS

William Joseph Butters
5-10 185 R 10 Jan 1951, St Paul MN

year	team	gp	g	a	pts	pim	gp	g	a	pts	pim
74-75	Min	24	2	2	4	58	12	1	0	1	21
75-76	Min	59	0	15	15	120					
	Hou	14	0	4	4	18	17	0	3	3	51
76-77	Min	42	0	7	7	133					
	Edm	7	0	2	2	17					
	NE	26	1	8	9	65	5	0	3	3	15
77-78	NE	45	1	13	14	69					
totals		217	4	51	55	530	34	1	6	7	87

• Played in NHL: 1977-79, Min, 72-1-4-5-77

Brian BYE
Brian Eldon Bye
5-10 180 L 27 Jun 1954, Brantford ON

year	team	gp	g	a	pts	pim	gp	g	a	pts	pim
75-76	SD	1	0	0	0	0					
totals		1	0	0	0	0					

Mike BYERS
Michael Arthur Byers
5-10 185 R 11 Sep 1946, Toronto ON d. 2010

year	team	gp	g	a	pts	pim	gp	g	a	pts	pim
72-73	LA	56	19	17	36	20					
	NE	19	6	4	10	4	12	6	5	11	6
73-74	NE	78	29	21	50	6	7	2	4	6	12
74-75	NE	72	22	26	48	10	6	2	2	4	2
75-76	NE	21	4	3	7	0					
	Cin	20	3	3	6	0					
totals		266	83	74	157	40	25	10	11	21	20

• Played in NHL: 1967-72, Tor-Phi-LA-Buf, 106-42-34-76-39

Brian CADLE
6-2 165 L 13 Sep 1948, Vancouver BC d. 2015

year	team	gp	g	a	pts	pim	gp	g	a	pts	pim
72-73	Wpg	56	4	4	8	39	3	0	0	0	0
totals		56	4	4	8	39	3	0	0	0	0

Terry CAFFERY
Terrance Michael Caffery
5-9 165 R 1 Apr 1949, Toronto ON

year	team	gp	g	a	pts	pim	gp	g	a	pts	pim
72-73	NE	74	39	61	100	14	8	3	7	10	0
74-75	NE	67	15	37	52	12					
75-76	NE	2	0	0	0	0					
	Cgy	21	5	13	18	4					
totals		164	59	111	170	30	8	3	7	10	0

• Played in NHL: 1969-71, Chi, 14-0-0-0-0 • Missed all of 1973-74 season due to knee injury.

Larry CAHAN
Lawrence Henry Cahan "Hank"
6-1 215 R 25 Dec 1933, Fort William ON d. 1992

year	team	gp	g	a	pts	pim	gp	g	a	pts	pim
72-73	Chi	75	1	10	11	44					
73-74	Chi	3	0	0	0	2					
totals		78	1	10	11	46					

• Played in NHL: 1954-71, Tor-NYR-Oak-LA, 666-38-92-130-700

Brett CALLIGHEN
5-11 175 L 15 May 1953, Toronto ON

year	team	gp	g	a	pts	pim	gp	g	a	pts	pim
76-77	NE	33	6	10	16	41					
	Edm	29	9	16	25	48	5	4	1	5	7
77-78	Edm	80	20	30	50	112	5	0	2	2	16
78-79	Edm	71	31	39	70	79	13	5	10	15	15
totals		213	66	95	161	280	23	9	13	22	38

• Played in NHL: 1979-82, Edm, 160-56-89-145-132

Bryan CAMPBELL
Bryan Albert Campbell
6-0 175 L 27 Mar 1944, Sudbury ON

year	team	gp	g	a	pts	pim	gp	g	a	pts	pim
72-73	Phi	75	25	48	73	85	3	0	1	1	8
73-74	Van	76	27	62	89	50					
74-75	Van	78	29	34	63	24					
75-76	Cin	77	22	50	72	24					
76-77	Ind	8	1	4	5	6					
	Edm	66	12	42	54	18	5	3	1	4	0
77-78	Edm	53	7	13	20	12	8	3	2	5	8
totals		433	123	253	376	219	16	6	4	10	16

• Played in NHL: 1967-72, LA-Chi, 260-35-71-106-74

Colin CAMPBELL
Colin John Campbell
5-9 190 L 28 Jan 1953, London ON

year	team	gp	g	a	pts	pim	gp	g	a	pts	pim
73-74	Van	78	3	20	23	191					
totals		78	3	20	23	191					

• Played in NHL: 1974-85, Pit-Col-Van-Det, 636-25-103-128-1292

Scott CAMPBELL
Gary Scott Campbell
6-2 205 L 22 Jun 1954, Toronto ON

year	team	gp	g	a	pts	pim	gp	g	a	pts	pim
77-78	Hou	75	8	29	37	116	6	1	1	2	8
78-79	Wpg	74	3	15	18	248	10	0	2	2	25
totals		149	11	44	55	364	16	1	3	4	33

• Played in NHL: 1979-82, Wpg-StL, 80-4-21-25-243

Rychard CAMPEAU
6-0 190 R 9 Apr 1952, Montreal PQ

year	team	gp	g	a	pts	pim	gp	g	a	pts	pim
72-73	Phi	75	1	18	19	72	4	1	0	1	17
73-74	Van	7	0	0	0	2					
totals		82	1	18	19	74	4	1	0	1	17

Jim CARDIFF
Garry James Cardiff
5-9 165 L 29 Aug 1944, Dauphin MB

year	team	gp	g	a	pts	pim	gp	g	a	pts	pim
72-73	Phi	78	3	24	27	185	4	0	0	0	11
73-74	Van	78	1	21	22	188					
74-75	Van	44	0	2	2	25					
totals		200	4	47	51	398	4	0	0	0	11

Steve CARDWELL
Stephen Michael Cardwell
5-11 190 L 18 Aug 1950, Toronto O

year	team	gp	g	a	pts	pim	gp	g	a	pts	pim
73-74	Min	77	23	23	46	100	10	0	0	0	20
74-75	Cle	75	9	13	22	127	5	0	1	1	14
totals		152	32	36	68	227	15	0	1	1	34

• Played in NHL: 1970-73, Pit, 53-9-11-20-35

Wayne CARLETON
Kenneth Wayne Carleton "Swoop"
6-3 225 L 4 Aug 1946, Sudbury ON

year	team	gp	g	a	pts	pim	gp	g	a	pts	pim
72-73	Ott	75	42	49	91	42	3	3	3	6	4
73-74	Tor	78	37	55	92	31	12	2	12	14	4
74-75	NE	73	35	39	74	50	6	2	5	7	14
75-76	NE	35	12	21	33	6					
	Edm	26	5	16	21	6	4	1	1	2	2
76-77	Bir	3	1	0	1	0					
totals		290	132	180	312	135	25	8	21	29	24

• Played in NHL: 1965-72, Tor-Bos-Cal, 278-55-73-128-172

Brian CARLIN
Brian John Carlin
5-10 175 L 13 Jun 1950, Calgary AB

year	team	gp	g	a	pts	pim	gp	g	a	pts	pim
72-73	Alb	65	12	22	34	6					
73-74	Edm	5	1	0	1	0					
totals		70	13	22	35	6					

• Played in NHL: 1971-72, LA, 5-1-0-1-0

Jack CARLSON
Jack Anthony Carlson
6-3 195 L 23 Aug 1954, Virginia MN

year	team	gp	g	a	pts	pim	gp	g	a	pts	pim
74-75	Min	32	5	5	10	85	10	1	2	3	41
75-76	Min	58	8	10	18	189					
	Edm	10	1	1	2	31	4	0	0	0	4
76-77	Min	36	4	3	7	55					
	NE	35	7	5	12	81	5	1	1	2	9
77-78	NE	67	9	20	29	192	9	1	1	2	14
78-79	NE	34	2	7	9	61					
totals		272	36	51	87	694	28	3	4	7	68

• Brother of Jeff Carlson and Steve Carlson • Played in NHL: 1978-87, Min-StL, 236-30-15-45-417

Jeff CARLSON
6-3 210 R 20 Jul 1953, Virginia MN

year	team	gp	g	a	pts	pim	gp	g	a	pts	pim
75-76	Min	7	0	1	1	14					
totals		7	0	1	1	14					

• Brother of Jack Carlson and Steve Carlson

Steve CARLSON
Steven Edward Carlson
6-3 180 L 26 Aug 1955, Virginia MN

year	team	gp	g	a	pts	pim	gp	g	a	pts	pim
75-76	Min	10	0	1	1	23					
76-77	Min	21	5	8	13	8					
	NE	31	4	9	13	40	5	0	0	0	9
77-78	NE	38	6	7	13	11	13	2	7	9	2
78-79	Edm	73	18	22	40	50	11	1	1	2	12
totals		173	33	47	80	132	29	3	8	11	23

• Brother of Jack Carlson and Jeff Carlson • Played in NHL: 1979-80, LA, 52-9-12-21-23

Steve CARLYLE
5-10 180 L 10 Mar 1950, Lacombe AB

year	team	gp	g	a	pts	pim	gp	g	a	pts	pim
72-73	Alb	67	7	10	17	35					
73-74	Edm	50	2	13	15	18	5	0	1	1	4
74-75	Edm	73	2	25	27	46					
75-76	Edm	28	0	11	11	10					
totals		218	11	59	70	109	5	0	1	1	4

426

Alain CARON Alain Luc Caron "Boom-Boom"
5-9 170 R 27 Apr 1938, Dolbeau PQ d. 1986

year	team	gp	g	a	pts	pim	gp	g	a	pts	pim
72-73	Que	68	36	27	63	14					
73-74	Que	59	31	15	46	10					
74-75	Que	21	7	3	10	2					
	M-B	47	8	5	13	4					
totals		**195**	**82**	**50**	**132**	**30**					

• Played in NHL: 1967-69, Oak-Mtl, 60-9-13-22-18

Greg CARROLL Gregory John Carroll
6-0 185 L 10 Nov 1956, Edmonton AB

year	team	gp	g	a	pts	pim	gp	g	a	pts	pim
76-77	Cin	77	15	39	54	53	4	1	2	3	0
77-78	NE	48	9	14	23	27					
	Cin	26	6	13	19	36					
totals		**151**	**30**	**66**	**96**	**116**	**4**	**1**	**2**	**3**	**0**

• Played in NHL: 1978-80, Wash-Det-Hart, 131-20-34-54-44

Jean-Yves CARTIER
5-9 180 L -, Verdun PQ

year	team	gp	g	a	pts	pim	gp	g	a	pts	pim
72-73	Que	15	0	3	3	8					
totals		**15**	**0**	**3**	**3**	**8**					

Tony CASSOLATO Anthony Gerald Cassolato
5-11 185 R 7 May 1956, Guelph ON

year	team	gp	g	a	pts	pim	gp	g	a	pts	pim
76-77	SD	43	13	12	25	26	3	0	0	0	4
77-78	Bir	77	18	25	43	59	4	0	0	0	4
78-79	Bir	64	13	7	20	62					
totals		**184**	**44**	**44**	**88**	**137**	**7**	**0**	**0**	**0**	**8**

• Played in NHL: 1979-82, Wash, 23-1-6-7-4

Bob CHARLEBOIS Robert Richard Charlebois
5-11 170 L 27 May 1944, Cornwall ON

year	team	gp	g	a	pts	pim	gp	g	a	pts	pim
72-73	Ott	78	24	40	64	28	5	1	1	2	4
73-74	NE	74	4	7	11	6	7	0	0	0	4
74-75	NE	8	1	0	1	6	4	1	0	1	0
75-76	NE	28	3	3	6	0					
totals		**188**	**32**	**50**	**82**	**34**	**16**	**2**	**1**	**3**	**8**

• Played in NHL: 1967-68, Min, 7-1-0-1-0

Claude CHARTRE
6-0 180 L 21 Dec 1949, Grand Rivieres PQ

year	team	gp	g	a	pts	pim	gp	g	a	pts	pim
72-73	NY	12	2	3	5	0					
73-74	NY-J	5	0	0	0	0					
74-75	M-B	1	0	0	0	0					
totals		**18**	**2**	**3**	**5**	**0**					

Mike CHERNOFF Michael Terence Chernoff
5-10 170 L 13 May 1946, Yorkton SK d. 2011

year	team	gp	g	a	pts	pim	gp	g	a	pts	pim
73-74	Van	36	11	10	21	4					
74-75	Van	3	0	0	0	0					
totals		**39**	**11**	**10**	**21**	**4**					

• Played in NHL: 1968-69, Min, 1-0-0-0-0

Jack CHIPCHASE John Albert Chipchase
5-11 205 L 5 Apr 1945, Seaforth ON

year	team	gp	g	a	pts	pim	gp	g	a	pts	pim
72-73	Phi	3	0	0	0	2					
totals		**3**	**0**	**0**	**0**	**2**					

Ron CHIPPERFIELD Ronald James Chipperfield
5-11 180 R 28 Mar 1954, Brandon MB

year	team	gp	g	a	pts	pim	gp	g	a	pts	pim
74-75	Van	78	19	20	39	30					
75-76	Cgy	75	42	41	83	32	10	5	4	9	6
76-77	Cgy	81	27	27	54	32					
77-78	Edm	80	33	52	85	48	5	1	1	2	0
78-79	Edm	55	32	37	69	47	13	9	10	19	8
totals		**369**	**153**	**177**	**330**	**189**	**28**	**15**	**15**	**30**	**14**

• Played in NHL: 1979-81, Edm-Que, 83-22-24-46-34

Keith CHRISTIANSEN "Huffer"
5-6 155 R 14 Jul 1944, Fort Frances ON

year	team	gp	g	a	pts	pim	gp	g	a	pts	pim
72-73	Min	64	12	30	42	24	5	1	0	1	0
73-74	Min	74	11	25	36	36	10	0	1	1	2
totals		**138**	**23**	**55**	**78**	**60**	**15**	**1**	**1**	**2**	**2**

• Member, United States Olympic Team, 1972

Kim CLACKSON Kimbel Gerald Clackson
5-11 195 R 13 Feb 1955, Saskatoon SK

year	team	gp	g	a	pts	pim	gp	g	a	pts	pim
75-76	Ind	77	1	12	13	351	6	0	0	0	25
76-77	Ind	71	3	8	11	168	9	0	1	1	24
77-78	Wpg	52	2	7	9	203	9	0	1	1	61
78-79	Wpg	71	0	12	12	210	9	0	5	5	28
totals		**271**	**6**	**39**	**45**	**932**	**33**	**0**	**7**	**7**	**138**

• Played in NHL: 1979-81, Pit-Que, 106-0-8-8-370

Gordie CLARK Gordon Corson Clark
5-11 180 R 31 May 1952, St Johns NB

year	team	gp	g	a	pts	pim	gp	g	a	pts	pim
78-79	Cin	21	3	3	6	2					
totals		**21**	**3**	**3**	**6**	**2**					

• Played in NHL: 1974-76, Bos, 8-0-1-1-0

Jim CLARKE James Clarke
6-3 215 L 11 Aug 1954, Toronto ON

year	team	gp	g	a	pts	pim	gp	g	a	pts	pim
75-76	Phx	59	1	9	10	57					
totals		**59**	**1**	**9**	**10**	**57**					

Ray CLEARWATER Raymond Wesley Clearwater
5-11 175 L 10 Nov 1942, Winnipeg MB

year	team	gp	g	a	pts	pim	gp	g	a	pts	pim
72-73	Cle	78	11	36	47	41	9	1	2	3	8
73-74	Cle	68	12	23	35	47	5	0	0	0	2
74-75	Cle	66	4	18	22	51	4	1	1	2	0
76-77	Min	2	0	0	0	2					
totals		**214**	**27**	**77**	**104**	**141**	**18**	**2**	**3**	**5**	**10**

Ron CLIMIE Ronald Malcolm Climie
5-11 180 L 5 Mar 1950, Hamilton ON

year	team	gp	g	a	pts	pim	gp	g	a	pts	pim
72-73	Ott	31	12	19	31	2	4	1	0	1	2
73-74	Edm	76	38	36	74	22	5	0	0	0	0
74-75	Edm	49	15	27	42	15					
	NE	25	8	4	12	12	6	3	0	3	2
75-76	NE	65	25	20	45	17					
76-77	NE	3	0	0	0	0					
totals		**249**	**98**	**106**	**204**	**68**	**15**	**4**	**0**	**4**	**4**

Real CLOUTIER "Buddy"
5-10 170 L 30 Jul 1956, St-Emile PQ

year	team	gp	g	a	pts	pim	gp	g	a	pts	pim
74-75	Que	63	26	27	53	36	12	4	3	7	2
75-76	Que	80	60	54	114	27	5	4	5	9	0
76-77	Que	76	66	75	141	39	17	14	13	27	10
77-78	Que	73	56	73	129	19	10	9	7	16	15
78-79	Que	77	75	54	129	48	4	2	2	4	4
totals		**369**	**283**	**283**	**566**	**169**	**48**	**33**	**30**	**63**	**31**

• Played in NHL: 1979-85, Que-Buf, 317-146-198-344-119

Brian COATES Brian James Coates
6-0 195 L 22 Sep 1952, Carmen MB

year	team	gp	g	a	pts	pim	gp	g	a	pts	pim
73-74	Chi	50	10	3	13	14	17	0	3	3	35
74-75	Chi	35	12	9	21	26					
75-76	Ind	59	11	16	27	24	4	0	0	0	6
76-77	Ind	16	1	5	6	4					
77-78	Cin	42	8	10	18	18					
totals		**202**	**42**	**43**	**85**	**85**	**21**	**0**	**3**	**3**	**41**

Howie COLBORNE Howard Colborne
5-11 185 L 28 Jun 1950, Peace River AB

year	team	gp	g	a	pts	pim	gp	g	a	pts	pim
73-74	Edm	2	0	0	0	0					
totals		**2**	**0**	**0**	**0**	**0**					

Jim COLE James Cole
5-8 175 - 13 Aug 1951, Indian Head SK

year	team	gp	g	a	pts	pim	gp	g	a	pts	pim
76-77	Wpg	2	0	1	1	0					
totals		**2**	**0**	**1**	**1**	**0**					

Brian CONACHER Brian Kennedy Conacher
6-3 200 L 31 Aug 1941, Toronto ON

year	team	gp	g	a	pts	pim	gp	g	a	pts	pim
72-73	Ott	69	8	19	27	32	5	1	3	4	4
totals		**69**	**8**	**19**	**27**	**32**	**5**	**1**	**3**	**4**	**4**

• Played in NHL: 1961-72, Tor-Det, 155-28-28-56-84 • Stanley Cup: 1967 (Toronto) • Member, Canadian Olympic Team, 1964

Gary CONNELLY Gary Norman Connelly
5-11 175 R 22 Dec 1950, Noranda PQ

year	team	gp	g	a	pts	pim	gp	g	a	pts	pim
73-74	Chi	4	0	1	1	2					
totals		4	0	1	1	2					

• Nephew of Wayne Connelly

Wayne CONNELLY Wayne Francis Connelly
5-10 175 R 16 Dec 1939, Rouyn PQ

year	team	gp	g	a	pts	pim	gp	g	a	pts	pim
72-73	Min	78	40	30	70	16	5	1	3	4	0
73-74	Min	78	42	53	95	16	11	6	7	13	4
74-75	Min	76	38	33	71	16	12	8	4	12	10
75-76	Min	59	24	23	47	19					
	Cle	12	5	2	7	4	3	1	0	1	2
76-77	Cgy	25	5	6	11	4					
	Edm	38	13	15	28	18	5	0	1	1	0
totals		366	167	162	329	93	36	16	15	31	16

• Uncle of Gary Connelly • Played in NHL: 1960-72, Mtl-Bos-Min-Det-StL-Van, 543-133-174-307-156

Cam CONNOR Cameron Duncan Connor
6-2 200 L 10 Aug 1954, Winnipeg MB

year	team	gp	g	a	pts	pim	gp	g	a	pts	pim
74-75	Phx	57	9	19	28	168	5	0	0	0	2
75-76	Phx	73	18	21	39	295	5	1	0	1	21
76-77	Hou	76	35	32	67	224	11	3	4	7	47
77-78	Hou	68	21	16	37	217	2	1	0	1	22
totals		274	83	88	171	904	23	5	4	9	92

• Played in NHL: 1978-83, Mtl-Edm-NYR, 89-9-22-31-256 • Stanley Cup: 1979 (Montreal)

Mike CONROY Robert Michael Conroy
6-0 180 L 28 Aug 1951, North Bay ON

year	team	gp	g	a	pts	pim	gp	g	a	pts	pim
75-76	Cle	4	0	1	1	0					
totals		4	0	1	1	0					

Charles CONSTANTIN
6-1 180 L 30 Apr 1954, Montreal PQ

year	team	gp	g	a	pts	pim	gp	g	a	pts	pim
74-75	Que	20	2	4	6	9					
75-76	Que	41	8	7	15	77	5	0	1	1	4
76-77	Que	77	14	19	33	93	15	0	1	1	15
77-78	Que	48	2	4	6	50					
	Ind	6	2	1	3	0					
totals		192	28	35	63	229	20	0	2	2	19

Michel CORMIER Michel Paul Cormier
5-9 170 L 22 Dec 1945, Trois Rivieres PQ

year	team	gp	g	a	pts	pim	gp	g	a	pts	pim
74-75	Phx	78	36	38	74	26	5	1	0	1	2
75-76	Phx	46	21	15	36	4					
76-77	Phx	58	13	16	29	22					
totals		182	70	69	139	52	5	1	0	1	2

Alain COTE
5-11 210 L 3 May 1957, Matane PQ

year	team	gp	g	a	pts	pim	gp	g	a	pts	pim
77-78	Que	27	3	5	8	8	11	1	2	3	0
78-79	Que	79	14	13	27	23	4	0	0	0	2
totals		106	17	18	35	31	15	1	2	3	2

• Played in NHL: 1979-89, Que, 696-103-190-293-383

Roger COTE Regent Norman Cote
5-9 185 L 22 Dec 1939, Belleterre PQ

year	team	gp	g	a	pts	pim	gp	g	a	pts	pim
72-73	Alb	61	3	5	8	46					
73-74	Edm	59	0	3	3	34	2	0	0	0	0
74-75	Ind	36	0	6	6	24					
totals		156	3	14	17	104	2	0	0	0	0

Norm COURNOYER Normand Cournoyer
5-10 170 L 17 Mar 1951, Drummondville PQ

year	team	gp	g	a	pts	pim	gp	g	a	pts	pim
73-74	Cle	13	3	5	8	6					
76-77	SD	19	1	2	3	8					
totals		32	4	7	11	14					

Bart CRASHLEY William Barton Crashley
6-0 180 R 15 Jun 1946, Toronto ON

year	team	gp	g	a	pts	pim	gp	g	a	pts	pim
72-73	LA	70	18	27	45	10	6	0	2	2	2
73-74	LA	78	4	26	30	16					
totals		148	22	53	75	26	6	0	2	2	2

• Played in NHL: 1965-69, 1974-76, Det-KC-LA, 140-7-36-43-50

Glen CRITCH
- - c. 1954, NF

year	team	gp	g	a	pts	pim	gp	g	a	pts	pim
75-76	Ind	3	0	0	0	0					
totals		3	0	0	0	0					

Jim CROSS
6-1 195 - 6 Feb 1957, Edmonton AB

year	team	gp	g	a	pts	pim	gp	g	a	pts	pim
77-78	Edm	2	0	0	0	0					
totals		2	0	0	0	0					

Keith CROWDER Keith Scott Crowder
6-0 190 R 6 Jan 1959, S Porcupine ON

year	team	gp	g	a	pts	pim	gp	g	a	pts	pim
78-79	Bir	5	1	0	1	17					
totals		5	1	0	1	17					

• Played in NHL: 1980-90, Bos-LA, 662-223-271-494-1354

Paul CROWLEY
5-9 180 R 26 Dec 1955, Montreal PQ

year	team	gp	g	a	pts	pim	gp	g	a	pts	pim
75-76	Tor	4	0	0	0	0					
totals		4	0	0	0	0					

Steve CUDDIE Steve Ross Cuddie
5-10 190 R 18 Jun 1950, Toronto ON

year	team	gp	g	a	pts	pim	gp	g	a	pts	pim
72-73	Wpg	77	7	13	20	121	12	0	1	1	10
73-74	Tor	74	5	18	23	65	8	1	4	5	14
74-75	Tor	70	5	16	21	49	6	0	4	4	8
totals		221	17	47	64	235	26	1	9	10	32

John CUNNIFF John Paul Cunniff
5-9 175 L 9 Jul 1944, Boston MA d. 2001

year	team	gp	g	a	pts	pim	gp	g	a	pts	pim
72-73	NE	32	3	5	8	16	13	1	1	2	2
73-74	NE	30	7	5	12	14	5	1	1	2	6
75-76	Que	2	0	0	0	5					
totals		64	10	10	20	35	18	2	2	4	8

• Member, United States Olympic Team, 1968

Gary CUNNINGHAM
6-0 185 L 28 Aug 1950, Welland ON

year	team	gp	g	a	pts	pim	gp	g	a	pts	pim
73-74	Edm	2	0	0	0	0					
totals		2	0	0	0	0					

Rick CUNNINGHAM Richard Glen Cunningham
5-11 180 R 3 Mar 1951, Toronto ON

year	team	gp	g	a	pts	pim	gp	g	a	pts	pim
72-73	Ott	78	9	31	40	121	5	1	1	2	2
73-74	Tor	75	2	19	21	88	11	0	4	4	31
74-75	Tor	71	7	18	25	117	5	0	1	1	0
75-76	Tor	36	5	14	19	57					
76-77	Bir	63	0	8	8	75					
totals		323	23	91	114	458	21	1	6	7	33

Paul CURTIS Paul Edwin Curtis
6-0 185 L 29 Sep 1947, Peterborough ON

year	team	gp	g	a	pts	pim	gp	g	a	pts	pim
74-75	M-B	76	4	15	19	32					
totals		76	4	15	19	32					

• Played in NHL: 1969-73, Mtl-LA-StL, 185-3-34-37-161

Bob D'ALVISE Robert D'Alvise
5-11 185 L 23 Dec 1952, Etobicoke ON

year	team	gp	g	a	pts	pim	gp	g	a	pts	pim
75-76	Tor	59	5	8	13	10					
totals		59	5	8	13	10					

John DANBY — John Joseph Danby
5-10 165 R   20 Jul 1948, Toronto ON

year	team	gp	g	a	pts	pim	gp	g	a	pts	pim
72-73	NE	77	14	23	37	10	8	0	0	0	0
73-74	NE	72	2	2	4	6	7	1	0	1	0
74-75	NE	0	0	0	0	0	4	0	1	1	0
75-76	NE	1	0	0	0	0					
totals		150	16	25	41	16	19	1	1	2	0

Richard DAVID
6-2 205 L   8 Apr 1958, Notre Dame de la Sallette PQ

year	team	gp	g	a	pts	pim	gp	g	a	pts	pim
78-79	Que	14	0	4	4	4					
totals		14	0	4	4	4					

Blair DAVIDSON — Blair Murray Davidson
5-11 180 L   10 Apr 1955, Cartwright MB

year	team	gp	g	a	pts	pim	gp	g	a	pts	pim
76-77	Phx	2	0	0	0	2					
totals		2	0	0	0	2					

Bill DAVIS — William Lloyd Davis
6-1 200 L   22 Aug 1954, Lindsay ON

year	team	gp	g	a	pts	pim	gp	g	a	pts	pim
77-78	Wpg	12	0	0	0	2					
78-79	Wpg	5	1	2	3	0					
totals		17	1	2	3	2					

Kelly DAVIS
6-0 200 L   23 Sep 1958, Grand Prairie AB

year	team	gp	g	a	pts	pim	gp	g	a	pts	pim
78-79	Cin	18	0	1	1	20					
totals		18	0	1	1	20					

Butch DEADMARSH — Ernest Charles Deadmarsh
5-11 185 L   5 Apr 1950, Trail BC

year	team	gp	g	a	pts	pim	gp	g	a	pts	pim
74-75	Van	38	7	8	15	128					
75-76	Cgy	79	26	28	54	196	8	0	1	1	14
76-77	Min	35	9	4	13	51					
	Cgy	38	13	17	30	77					
77-78	Edm	20	1	3	4	32					
	Cin	45	7	6	13	86					
totals		255	63	66	129	570	8	0	1	1	14

• Played in NHL: 1970-75, Buf-Atl-KC, 137-12-5-17-155.

Barry DEAN — Barry James Dean
6-1 195 L   26 Feb 1955, Maple Creek SK

year	team	gp	g	a	pts	pim	gp	g	a	pts	pim
75-76	Phx	71	9	25	34	110					
totals		71	9	25	34	110					

• Played in NHL: 1976-79, Col-Phi, 165-25-56-81-146

Dave DEBOL — David Debol
5-11 175 R   27 Mar 1956, St Clair Shores MI

year	team	gp	g	a	pts	pim	gp	g	a	pts	pim
77-78	Cin	9	3	2	5	2					
78-79	Cin	59	10	27	37	9					
totals		68	13	29	42	11					

• Played in NHL: 1979-81, Hart, 92-26-26-52-4

Ray DELORENZI
5-10 185 R   14 Jun 1952, Sault Ste Marie ON

year	team	gp	g	a	pts	pim	gp	g	a	pts	pim
74-75	Van	3	0	0	0	0					
75-76	Cgy	39	8	12	20	4					
totals		42	8	12	20	4					

Ron DELORME — Ronald Elmer Delorme
6-3 180 R   3 Sep 1955, Cochin SK

year	team	gp	g	a	pts	pim	gp	g	a	pts	pim
75-76	D-O	22	1	3	4	28					
totals		22	1	3	4	28					

• Played in NHL: 1976-85, Col-Van, 524-83-83-166-667

Ab DEMARCO — Albert Thomas DeMarco, Jr.
6-0 190 R   27 Feb 1949, Cleveland OH

year	team	gp	g	a	pts	pim	gp	g	a	pts	pim
77-78	Edm	47	6	8	14	20	1	0	0	0	0
totals		47	6	8	14	20	1	0	0	0	0

• Played in NHL: 1969-79, NYR-StL-Pit-Van-LA-Bos, 344-44-80-124-75

Brian DERKSEN
5-10 190 L   27 Nov 1951, Borden SK

year	team	gp	g	a	pts	pim	gp	g	a	pts	pim
73-74	LA	1	0	0	0	2					
totals		1	0	0	0	2					

Andre DESCHAMPS
5-11 180 L   13 Aug 1953, Valleyfield PQ

year	team	gp	g	a	pts	pim	gp	g	a	pts	pim
76-77	Cgy	9	1	2	3	19					
totals		9	1	2	3	19					

Norm DESCOTEAUX — Joseph Normand Descoteaux
5-9 170 L   3 Jan 1948, Montreal PQ

year	team	gp	g	a	pts	pim	gp	g	a	pts	pim
72-73	Que	2	0	1	1	0					
73-74	Que	35	1	6	7	6					
totals		37	1	7	8	6					

Ken DESJARDINE — Kenneth Frederick Desjardine
6-0 180 L   23 Aug 1947, Toronto ON

year	team	gp	g	a	pts	pim	gp	g	a	pts	pim
72-73	Que	57	2	6	8	36					
73-74	Que	70	2	10	12	44					
74-75	Ind	46	0	8	8	68					
75-76	Cgy	1	0	0	0	0					
totals		174	4	24	28	148					

Kevin DEVINE
5-8 165 L   9 Dec 1954, Toronto ON

year	team	gp	g	a	pts	pim	gp	g	a	pts	pim
74-75	SD	46	4	10	14	48	10	1	0	1	14
75-76	SD	80	21	28	49	102	11	3	1	4	36
76-77	SD	81	30	20	50	114	7	1	3	4	14
77-78	Ind	76	19	23	42	141					
78-79	Que	5	0	0	0	6					
totals		288	74	81	155	411	28	5	4	9	64

• Played in NHL: 1982-83, NYI, 2-0-1-1-8

Bob DILLABOUGH — Robert Wellington Dillabough
5-11 170 L   24 Apr 1941, Belleville ON   d. 1997

year	team	gp	g	a	pts	pim	gp	g	a	pts	pim
72-73	Cle	72	8	8	16	8	9	1	0	1	0
totals		72	8	8	16	8	9	1	0	1	0

• Played in NHL: 1961-70, Det-Bos-Pit-Oak, 283-32-54-86-76

Wayne DILLON — Gerald Wayne Dillon
6-0 180 L   25 May 1955, Toronto ON

year	team	gp	g	a	pts	pim	gp	g	a	pts	pim
73-74	Tor	71	30	35	65	13	12	5	6	11	9
74-75	Tor	77	29	66	95	22	6	4	4	8	4
78-79	Bir	64	12	27	39	43					
totals		212	71	128	199	78	18	9	10	19	13

• Played in NHL: 1975-80, NYR-Wpg, 229-43-66-109-60

Bob DOBEK — Robert Andrew Dobek
6-0 180 L   4 Oct 1952, Detroit MI

year	team	gp	g	a	pts	pim	gp	g	a	pts	pim
75-76	SD	14	3	1	4	2	11	1	2	3	0
76-77	SD	58	7	17	24	17	5	0	0	0	4
totals		72	10	18	28	19	16	1	2	3	4

• Member, United States Olympic Team, 1976

Gary DONALDSON — Robert Gary Donaldson
5-9 155 L   15 Jul 1952, Trail BC

year	team	gp	g	a	pts	pim	gp	g	a	pts	pim
76-77	Hou	5	0	0	0	6					
totals		5	0	0	0	6					

• Played in NHL: 1973-74, Chi, 1-0-0-0-0

John DONNELLY
6-0 190 L   28 Sep 1948,

year	team	gp	g	a	pts	pim	gp	g	a	pts	pim
72-73	Ott	15	1	1	2	44					
totals		15	1	1	2	44					

Pat DONNELLY — Patrick Donnelly
5-10 185 R   24 Feb 1953, Detroit MI

year	team	gp	g	a	pts	pim	gp	g	a	pts	pim
75-76	Cin	23	5	7	12	4					
totals		23	5	7	12	4					

• Brother of Pete Donnelly

Jim DOREY
Robert James Dorey "Flipper"
6-1 195 L 17 Aug 1947, Kingston ON

year	team	gp	g	a	pts	pim	gp	g	a	pts	pim
72-73	NE	75	7	56	63	95	15	3	16	19	41
73-74	NE	77	6	40	46	134	6	0	6	6	26
74-75	NE	31	5	17	22	43					
	Tor	43	11	23	34	69	6	2	6	8	2
75-76	Tor	74	9	51	60	134					
76-77	Que	73	13	34	47	102	10	0	2	2	28
77-78	Que	26	1	9	10	23	11	0	3	3	34
78-79	Que	32	0	2	2	17	3	0	0	0	0
totals		431	52	232	284	617	51	5	33	38	131

• Played in NHL: 1968-72, Tor-NYR, 232-25-74-99-553

Dave DORNSEIF
6-3 205 L 12 Aug 1956, Edina MN

year	team	gp	g	a	pts	pim
77-78	Ind	3	0	1	1	0
78-79	Cin	1	0	0	0	0
totals		4	0	1	1	0

Jordy DOUGLAS
Jordan Paul Douglas
6-0 195 L 20 Jan 1958, Winnipeg MB

year	team	gp	g	a	pts	pim	gp	g	a	pts	pim
78-79	NE	51	6	10	16	15	10	4	0	4	23
totals		51	6	10	16	15	10	4	0	4	23

• Played in NHL: 1979-85, Hart-Min-Wpg, 268-76-62-138-160

Kent DOUGLAS
Kent Gemmell Douglas
5-10 210 L 6 Feb 1936, Cobalt ON   d. 2009

year	team	gp	g	a	pts	pim
72-73	NY	60	3	15	18	74
totals		60	3	15	18	74

• Played in NHL: 1962-69, Tor-Oak-Det, 428-33-115-148-631 • Stanley Cups: 1962, 1963, 1967 (Toronto)

Peter DRISCOLL
Peter John Driscoll
6-0 190 L 27 Oct 1954, Kingston ON

year	team	gp	g	a	pts	pim	gp	g	a	pts	pim
74-75	Van	21	3	2	5	40					
75-76	Cgy	75	16	18	34	127	10	2	5	7	41
76-77	Cgy	76	23	29	52	120					
77-78	Que	21	3	7	10	28					
	Ind	56	25	21	46	130					
78-79	Ind	8	3	1	4	17					
	Edm	69	17	23	40	115	13	1	6	7	8
totals		326	90	101	191	577	23	3	11	14	49

• Played in NHL: 1979-81, Edm, 60-3-8-11-97

Norm DUBE
Normand Dube
5-11 185 L 12 Sep 1951, Sherbrooke PQ

year	team	gp	g	a	pts	pim	gp	g	a	pts	pim
76-77	Que	39	15	18	33	8	14	3	12	15	11
77-78	Que	73	16	31	47	17	10	2	2	4	6
78-79	Que	36	2	13	15	4					
totals		148	33	62	95	29	24	5	14	19	17

• Played in NHL: 1974-76, KC, 57-8-10-18-54

Michel DUBOIS
Michel Jean-Claude Dubois
5-11 180 L 7 Nov 1954, Montreal PQ

year	team	gp	g	a	pts	pim	gp	g	a	pts	pim
75-76	Ind	34	2	2	4	104					
	Que	21	0	3	3	23					
76-77	Que	4	0	0	0	0	2	0	1	1	0
totals		59	2	5	7	127	2	0	1	1	0

Rick DUDLEY
Richard Clarence Dudley
6-0 190 L 31 Jan 1949, Toronto ON

year	team	gp	g	a	pts	pim	gp	g	a	pts	pim
75-76	Cin	74	43	38	81	156					
76-77	Cin	77	41	47	88	102	4	0	1	1	7
77-78	Cin	72	30	41	71	156					
78-79	Cin	47	17	20	37	102					
totals		270	131	146	277	516	4	0	1	1	7

• Played in NHL: 1972-75, 1978-81, Buf-Wpg, 309-75-99-174-292

Guy DUFOUR
5-11 160 R 9 Feb 1946, LaTuque PQ

year	team	gp	g	a	pts	pim
72-73	Que	9	3	2	5	2
73-74	Que	74	27	23	50	30
totals		83	30	25	55	32

David DUNN
David George Dunn
6-2 200 L 19 Aug 1948, Moosomin SK

year	team	gp	g	a	pts	pim	gp	g	a	pts	pim
76-77	Wpg	40	3	11	14	129	20	4	8	4	23
77-78	Wpg	66	6	20	26	79	9	1	2	3	0
totals		106	9	31	40	208	29	5	6	11	23

• Played in NHL: 1973-76, Van-Tor, 184-14-41-55-313

Rich DUPRAS
6-0 185 L 1 Jan 1950, Montreal PQ

year	team	gp	g	a	pts	pim
73-74	Tor	2	0	0	0	0
totals		2	0	0	0	0

Steve DURBANO
Harry Steven Durbano
6-1 200 L 12 Dec 1951, Toronto ON   d. 2002

year	team	gp	g	a	pts	pim	gp	g	a	pts	pim
77-78	Bir	45	6	4	10	284	4	0	2	2	16
totals		45	6	4	10	284	4	0	2	2	16

• Played in NHL: 1972-79, StL-Pit-KC-Col, 220-13-60-73-1127

Tom EARL
Warren Thomas Earl
6-0 172 R 10 Jun 1947, Niagara Falls ON

year	team	gp	g	a	pts	pim	gp	g	a	pts	pim
72-73	NE	76	10	13	23	4	15	2	3	5	10
73-74	NE	78	10	10	20	29	7	0	2	2	2
74-75	NE	72	3	8	11	20	6	1	1	2	12
75-76	NE	66	8	11	19	26	17	0	5	5	4
76-77	NE	54	9	14	23	37	1	0	0	0	0
totals		346	40	56	96	116	46	3	11	14	28

Tom EDUR
6-1 185 R 18 Nov 1954, Toronto ON

year	team	gp	g	a	pts	pim	gp	g	a	pts	pim
73-74	Cle	76	7	31	38	26	5	1	2	3	0
74-75	Cle	61	3	20	23	28	5	2	0	2	0
75-76	Cle	80	7	28	35	62	3	0	2	2	0
totals		217	17	79	96	116	13	3	4	7	0

• Played in NHL: 1976-78, Col-Pit, 158-17-70-87-67

Grant ERICKSON
Grant Charles Erickson
5-9 165 L 28 Apr 1947, Piercefield SK

year	team	gp	g	a	pts	pim	gp	g	a	pts	pim
72-73	Cle	77	15	29	44	23	9	2	1	3	2
73-74	Cle	78	23	27	50	26	5	0	2	2	0
74-75	Cle	78	12	15	27	24					
75-76	Phx	33	4	4	8	6	5	0	2	2	0
totals		266	54	75	129	79	19	2	5	7	2

Bengt ERIKSSON
Roland Bengt Eriksson
6-3 190 L 1 Mar 1954, Storatuna Sweden

year	team	gp	g	a	pts	pim	gp	g	a	pts	pim
78-79	Wpg	33	5	10	15	2	10	1	4	5	0
totals		33	5	10	15	2	10	1	4	5	0

Chris EVANS
Christopher Bruce Evans
5-9 180 L 14 Sep 1946, Toronto ON   d. 2000

year	team	gp	g	a	pts	pim	gp	g	a	pts	pim
75-76	Cgy	75	3	20	23	50	10	5	5	10	4
76-77	Cgy	81	7	27	34	60					
77-78	Bir	12	1	2	3	4					
	Que	36	0	2	2	22					
totals		204	11	51	62	138	10	5	5	10	4

• Played in NHL: 1969-75, Tor-Buf-StL-Det-KC, 241-19-42-61-143

Bill EVO
William Brian Evo
6-2 190 L 21 Feb 1954, Royal Oak MI

year	team	gp	g	a	pts	pim	gp	g	a	pts	pim
74-75	M-B	49	13	9	22	32					
75-76	Edm	8	0	4	4	0					
	Cle	40	1	5	6	32					
totals		97	14	18	32	64					

Bob FALKENBERG
Robert Arthur Falkenburg
6-0 195 L 1 Jan 1946, Stettler AB

year	team	gp	g	a	pts	pim	gp	g	a	pts	pim
72-73	Alb	76	6	23	29	44					
73-74	Edm	78	3	14	17	32	5	0	2	2	14
74-75	SD	78	2	18	20	42	10	0	1	1	4
75-76	SD	79	3	13	16	31	11	1	2	3	6
76-77	SD	64	0	6	6	34	2	0	0	0	0
77-78	Edm	2	0	0	0	0					
totals		377	14	74	88	183	29	1	5	6	24

• Played in NHL: 1966-72, Det, 54-1-5-6-26

Craig FALKMAN Craig Dean Falkman
5-11 190 R 1 Aug 1943, St Paul MN

year	team	gp	g	a	pts	pim	gp	g	a	pts	pim
72-73	Min	44	1	5	6	12					
totals		44	1	5	6	12					

• Member, United States Olympic Team, 1968

Richard FARDA
5-9 175 L 8 Nov 1945, Brno Czechoslovakia

year	team	gp	g	a	pts	pim	gp	g	a	pts	pim
74-75	Tor	66	6	25	31	2					
75-76	Tor	63	19	35	54	8					
76-77	Bir	48	9	26	35	2					
totals		177	34	86	120	12					

• Member, Czechoslovakia Olympic Team, 1972

Tony FEATHERSTONE Anthony James Featherstone
5-11 185 R 31 Jul 1949, Toronto ON

year	team	gp	g	a	pts	pim	gp	g	a	pts	pim
74-75	Tor	76	25	38	63	26	6	2	1	3	2
75-76	Tor	32	4	7	11	5					
totals		108	29	45	74	31	6	2	1	3	2

• Played in NHL: 1969-74, Oak-Cal-Min, 130-17-21-38-65

Mike FEDORKO
6-0 190 - 13 Sep 1956, Hamilton ON

year	team	gp	g	a	pts	pim	gp	g	a	pts	pim
76-77	Hou	4	0	0	0	0					
totals		4	0	0	0	0					

Norm FERGUSON Norman Gerald Ferguson
5-8 175 R 16 Oct 1945, Sydney NS

year	team	gp	g	a	pts	pim	gp	g	a	pts	pim
72-73	NY	56	28	40	68	8					
73-74	NY-J	75	15	21	36	12					
74-75	SD	78	36	33	69	6	10	6	5	11	0
75-76	SD	79	37	37	74	12	4	2	0	2	9
76-77	SD	77	39	32	71	5	7	2	4	6	0
77-78	Edm	71	26	21	47	2	5	0	0	0	0
totals		436	181	184	365	45	26	10	9	19	9

• Played in NHL: 1968-72, Oak-Cal, 279-73-66-139-72

John FISHER
5-11 185 L 21 Dec 1947, Ayr Scotland

year	team	gp	g	a	pts	pim	gp	g	a	pts	pim
72-73	Alb	39	0	5	5	0					
totals		39	0	5	5	0					

Bob FITCHNER Robert Douglas Fitchner
6-0 190 L 22 Dec 1950, Sudbury ON

year	team	gp	g	a	pts	pim	gp	g	a	pts	pim
73-74	Edm	31	1	2	3	21					
74-75	Ind	78	11	19	30	96					
75-76	Ind	52	15	16	31	112					
	Que	21	7	9	16	22	5	1	0	1	8
76-77	Que	81	9	30	39	105	17	3	3	6	16
77-78	Que	72	15	28	43	76	11	1	6	7	10
78-79	Que	79	10	35	45	69	4	1	3	4	0
totals		414	68	139	207	501	37	6	12	18	34

• Played in NHL: 1979-81, Que, 78-12-20-32-59

Reg FLEMING Reginald Stephen Fleming
5-10 190 L 21 Apr 1936, Montreal PQ d. 2009

year	team	gp	g	a	pts	pim	gp	g	a	pts	pim
72-73	Chi	74	23	45	68	95					
73-74	Chi	45	2	12	14	49	12	0	4	4	12
totals		119	25	57	82	144	12	0	4	4	12

• Played in NHL: 1959-71, Mtl-Chi-Bos-NYR-Phi-Buf, 749-108-132-240-1468 • Stanley Cup: 1961 (Chicago)

Bill FLETT William Myer Flett "Cowboy"
6-1 210 R 21 Jul 1943, Vermillion AB d. 1999

year	team	gp	g	a	pts	pim	gp	g	a	pts	pim
76-77	Edm	48	34	20	54	20	5	0	2	2	2
77-78	Edm	74	41	28	69	34					
78-79	Edm	73	28	36	64	14	10	5	2	7	2
totals		195	103	84	187	68	15	5	4	9	4

• Played in NHL: 1967-77, 1979-80, LA-Phi-Tor-Atl-Edm, 689-202-215-417-501 • Stanley Cup: 1974 (Philadelphia)

Peter FOLCO Peter Kevin Folco
6-0 185 L 13 Aug 1953, Montreal PQ

year	team	gp	g	a	pts	pim	gp	g	a	pts	pim
75-76	Tor	19	1	8	9	15					
76-77	Bir	2	0	0	0	0					
totals		21	1	8	9	15					

• Played in NHL: 1973-74, Van, 2-0-0-0-0

Rick FOLEY Gilbert Anthony Foley
6-4 225 L 22 Sep 1945, Niagara Falls ON d. 2015

year	team	gp	g	a	pts	pim	gp	g	a	pts	pim
75-76	Tor	11	1	2	3	6					
totals		11	1	2	3	6					

• Played in NHL: 1970-74, Chi-Phi-Det, 67-11-26-37-180

Len FONTAINE Leonard Joseph Fontaine
5-8 170 R 25 Feb 1948, Quebec City PQ

year	team	gp	g	a	pts	pim	gp	g	a	pts	pim
74-75	M-B	21	1	8	9	6					
totals		21	1	8	9	6					

• Played in NHL: 1972-74, Det, 46-8-11-19-10

Val FONTEYNE Valere Ronald Fonteyne
5-9 160 L 2 Dec 1933, Wetaskiwin AB

year	team	gp	g	a	pts	pim	gp	g	a	pts	pim
72-73	Alb	77	7	32	39	2					
73-74	Edm	72	9	13	22	2	5	1	0	1	0
totals		149	16	45	61	4	5	1	0	1	0

• Played in NHL: 1959-72, Det-NYR-Pit, 820-75-154-229-26

Dave FORBES David Stephen Forbes
5-10 175 L 16 Nov 1948, Montreal PQ

year	team	gp	g	a	pts	pim	gp	g	a	pts	pim
78-79	Cin	73	6	5	11	83	3	0	1	1	7
totals		73	6	5	11	83	3	0	1	1	7

• Played in NHL: 1973-79, Bos-Wash, 363-64-64-128-341

Mike FORD Mike Alfred Ford
6-1 185 R 26 Jul 1952, Ottawa ON

year	team	gp	g	a	pts	pim	gp	g	a	pts	pim
74-75	Wpg	73	12	22	34	68					
75-76	Wpg	81	13	43	56	70	12	1	12	13	8
76-77	Cgy	54	5	20	25	14					
	Wpg	22	3	14	17	20	20	3	13	16	12
77-78	Wpg	3	0	0	0	0	2	1	0	1	0
totals		233	33	99	132	172	34	5	25	30	20

Connie FOREY Conley Michael Forey
6-2 190 L 18 Oct 1950, Montreal PQ

year	team	gp	g	a	pts	pim	gp	g	a	pts	pim
73-74	Chi	1	0	0	0	0					
totals		1	0	0	0	0					

• Played in NHL: 1973-74, StL, 4-0-0-0-2 • Played in game with Chicago on March 7, 1974, but was ruled ineligible by league office the next day due to rights being owned by St. Louis of the NHL. Forey's records were subsequently expunged by league.

Dave FORTIER David Edward Fortier
5-11 190 L 17 Jun 1951, Sudbury ON

year	team	gp	g	a	pts	pim	gp	g	a	pts	pim
77-78	Ind	51	1	15	16	86					
totals		51	1	15	16	86					

• Played in NHL: 1972-77, Tor-NYI-Van, 205-8-21-29-335

Florent FORTIER
5-10 175 L 1 Jun 1955, Montreal PQ

year	team	gp	g	a	pts	pim	gp	g	a	pts	pim
75-76	Que	4	1	1	2	0	1	0	0	0	0
totals		4	1	1	2	0	1	0	0	0	0

Joe FORTUNATO
5-10 170 L 1 Jan 1955, Bari Italy

year	team	gp	g	a	pts	pim	gp	g	a	pts	pim
76-77	Edm	1	0	0	0	0					
totals		1	0	0	0	0					

Nick FOTIU Nicholas Evlampios Fotiu
6-2 200 L 25 May 1952, Staten Island NY

year	team	gp	g	a	pts	pim	gp	g	a	pts	pim
74-75	NE	61	2	2	4	144	4	2	0	2	27
75-76	NE	49	3	2	5	94	16	3	2	5	57
totals		110	5	4	9	238	20	5	2	7	84

• Played in NHL: 1976-89, NYR-Hart-Cgy-Phi-Edm, 646-60-77-137-1362

431

Rick FRASER Richard Fraser
5-10 175 R 7 Oct 1954, Sarnia ON

year	team	gp	g	a	pts	pim	gp	g	a	pts	pim
74-75	Ind	4	0	0	0	2					
totals		4	0	0	0	2					

John FRENCH John George French
5-10 165 L 25 Aug 1950, Orillia ON

year	team	gp	g	a	pts	pim	gp	g	a	pts	pim
72-73	NE	74	24	35	59	43	15	3	11	14	2
73-74	NE	77	24	48	72	31	7	4	2	6	2
74-75	NE	75	12	41	53	28	4	1	2	3	0
75-76	SD	76	25	39	64	16	11	4	7	11	0
76-77	SD	44	14	21	35	6	7	2	3	5	2
77-78	Ind	74	9	8	17	6					
totals		420	108	192	300	130	44	14	25	39	6

Robbie FTOREK Robert Brian Ftorek
5-8 155 L 2 Jan 1952, Needham MA

year	team	gp	g	a	pts	pim	gp	g	a	pts	pim
74-75	Phx	53	31	37	68	29	5	2	5	7	2
75-76	Phx	80	41	72	113	109	5	1	3	4	2
76-77	Phx	80	46	71	117	86					
77-78	Cin	80	59	50	109	54					
78-79	Cin	80	39	77	116	87	3	3	2	5	6
totals		373	216	307	523	365	13	6	10	16	10

• Played in NHL: 1972-74, 1979-85, Det-Que-NYR, 334-77-150-227-262 • Member, United States Olympic Team, 1972

Gord GALLANT Gordon Gallant
5-11 175 L 27 Oct 1950, Shediac NB

year	team	gp	g	a	pts	pim	gp	g	a	pts	pim
73-74	Min	72	7	15	22	223	11	1	2	3	67
74-75	Min	66	10	13	23	203	1	1	0	1	0
75-76	Que	64	4	15	19	297	2	0	0	0	31
76-77	Min	37	6	3	9	64					
	Bir	34	4	13	17	62					
totals		273	31	59	90	849	14	2	2	4	98

Gary GAMBUCCI Gary Allan Gambucci
5-9 175 L 27 Sep 1946, Hibbing MN

year	team	gp	g	a	pts	pim	gp	g	a	pts	pim
74-75	Min	67	19	18	37	19	12	4	0	4	6
75-76	Min	45	10	6	16	14					
totals		112	29	24	53	33	12	4	0	4	6

• Played in NHL: 1971-74, Min, 51-2-7-9-9

J.-C. GARNEAU Jean-Claude Garneau
5-9 165 L 19 Oct 1943, Quebec PQ

year	team	gp	g	a	pts	pim	gp	g	a	pts	pim
74-75	Que	17	0	5	5	27					
totals		17	0	5	5	27					

Mike GARTNER Michael Alfred Gartner
6-0 180 R 29 Oct 1959, Ottawa ON

year	team	gp	g	a	pts	pim	gp	g	a	pts	pim
78-79	Cin	78	27	25	52	123	3	0	0	0	2
totals		78	27	25	52	123	3	0	0	0	2

• Played in NHL: 1979-98, Wash-Min-NYR-Tor-Phx, 1432-708-627-1335-1158 • Member, Hockey Hall of Fame

Ron GARWASIUK Ronald Victor Garwasiuk
5-8 160 L 17 Feb 1949, St Paul AB

year	team	gp	g	a	pts	pim	gp	g	a	pts	pim
73-74	LA	51	6	13	19	100					
totals		51	6	13	19	100					

Marty GATEMAN John Martin Gateman
6-1 185 L 7 Dec 1952, Southampton ON

year	team	gp	g	a	pts	pim	gp	g	a	pts	pim
75-76	NE	12	0	1	1	6					
totals		12	0	1	1	6					

Andre GAUDETTE Andre Bernard Gaudette
5-7 165 L 16 Dec 1947, Sherbrooke PQ

year	team	gp	g	a	pts	pim	gp	g	a	pts	pim
72-73	Que	76	27	44	71	12					
73-74	Que	78	24	44	68	16					
74-75	Que	67	10	17	27	6	9	0	1	1	0
totals		221	61	105	166	34	9	0	1	1	0

Jean GAUTHIER Jean Phillipe Gauthier
6-1 205 R 29 Apr 1937, Montreal PQ d. 2013

year	team	gp	g	a	pts	pim	gp	g	a	pts	pim
72-73	NY	31	2	1	3	21					
totals		31	2	1	3	21					

• Played in NHL: 1960-70, Mtl-Phi-Bos, 166-6-29-35-150 • Stanley Cup: 1965 (Montreal)

Sam GELLARD
6-0 190 L 15 Mar 1950, Port-of-Spain Trinidad

year	team	gp	g	a	pts	pim	gp	g	a	pts	pim
72-73	Phi	5	0	0	0	0					
73-74	Van	23	7	4	11	15					
totals		28	7	4	11	15					

Jean-Guy GENDRON
5-9 165 L 30 Aug 1934, Montreal PQ

year	team	gp	g	a	pts	pim	gp	g	a	pts	pim
72-73	Que	63	17	33	50	113					
73-74	Que	64	11	8	19	42					
totals		127	28	41	69	155					

• Played in NHL: 1955-72, NYR-Bos-Mtl-Phi, 863-182-201-383-701

Danny GEOFFRION Daniel Geoffrion
5-10 185 R 24 Jan 1958, Montreal PQ

year	team	gp	g	a	pts	pim	gp	g	a	pts	pim
78-79	Que	77	12	14	26	74	4	1	2	3	2
totals		77	12	14	26	74	4	1	2	3	2

• Distant relation of Brian Morenz • Played in NHL: 1979-82, Mtl-Wpg, 111-20-32-52-99

Wes GEORGE Wesley George
6-2 220 L 26 Sep 1958, Young SK

year	team	gp	g	a	pts	pim	gp	g	a	pts	pim
78-79	Ind	9	4	2	6	23					
	Edm	3	0	0	0	11					
totals		12	4	2	6	34					

Brian GIBBONS Brian Joseph Gibbons
6-3 190 L 7 Jun 1947, St John's NF

year	team	gp	g	a	pts	pim	gp	g	a	pts	pim
72-73	Ott	73	7	35	42	62	5	1	2	3	12
73-74	Tor	78	4	31	35	84	12	2	5	7	10
74-75	Tor	73	4	22	26	105					
75-76	D-O	2	0	0	0	0					
totals		226	15	88	103	251	17	3	7	10	22

• Brother of Gerry Gibbons

Gerry GIBBONS Gerard Gibbons
6-3 185 L 7 Jan 1953, St John's NF

year	team	gp	g	a	pts	pim	gp	g	a	pts	pim
73-74	Tor	26	1	4	5	23	1	0	0	0	0
75-76	Tor	5	1	0	1	7					
totals		31	2	4	6	30	1	0	0	0	0

• Brother of Brian Gibbons

Jack GIBSON James Montegue Gibson
6-0 185 L 18 Aug 1948, Picton ON

year	team	gp	g	a	pts	pim	gp	g	a	pts	pim
72-73	Ott	59	22	12	34	48	1	1	0	1	5
73-74	Tor	61	16	9	25	60	12	1	3	4	11
75-76	Tor	2	0	0	0	0					
totals		122	38	21	59	108	13	2	3	5	16

John GIBSON
6-3 210 - 2 Jun 1959, St Catherines ON

year	team	gp	g	a	pts	pim	gp	g	a	pts	pim
78-79	Wpg	9	0	1	1	5					
totals		9	0	1	1	5					

• Played in NHL: 1980-84, LA-Tor-Wpg, 48-0-2-2-120

Ed GILBERT Edward Ferguson Gilbert
5-11 185 L 12 Mar 1952, Hamilton ON

year	team	gp	g	a	pts	pim	gp	g	a	pts	pim
78-79	Cin	29	3	3	6	40					
totals		29	3	3	6	40					

• Played in NHL: 1974-77, KC-Pit, 166-21-31-52-22

Jeannot GILBERT Jeannot Elmourt Gilbert
5-9 170 L 29 Dec 1940, Grande Baie PQ

year	team	gp	g	a	pts	pim	gp	g	a	pts	pim
73-74	Que	75	17	39	56	20					
74-75	Que	58	7	21	28	12	11	3	6	9	2
totals		133	24	60	84	32	11	3	6	9	2

• Played in NHL: 1962-65, Bos, 9-0-1-1-4

Bill GILLIGAN William Gilligan
5-11 175 R 5 Aug 1954, Beverly MA

year	team	gp	g	a	pts	pim	gp	g	a	pts	pim
77-78	Cin	54	10	14	24	59					
78-79	Cin	74	17	26	43	54	3	1	0	1	0
totals		128	27	40	67	113	3	1	0	1	0

Tom GILMORE Thomas McCracken Gilmore
5-11 190 L 14 May 1948, Flin Flon MB

year	team	gp	g	a	pts	pim	gp	g	a	pts	pim
72-73	LA	70	17	18	35	191	5	1	3	4	2
73-74	Edm	57	19	23	42	164	5	1	4	5	15
74-75	Edm	74	12	19	31	84					
totals		201	48	60	108	439	10	2	7	9	17

Dave GILMOUR David Donald Gilmour
5-9 165 L 14 Nov 1950, Kingston ON

year	team	gp	g	a	pts	pim	gp	g	a	pts	pim
75-76	Cgy	1	0	0	0	0					
totals		1	0	0	0	0					

Gaston GINGRAS Gaston Reginald Gingras
6-0 190 L 13 Feb 1959, North Bay ON

year	team	gp	g	a	pts	pim	gp	g	a	pts	pim
78-79	Bir	60	13	21	34	35					
totals		60	13	21	34	35					

• Played in NHL: 1979-89, Mtl-Tor-StL, 476-61-174-235-161 • Stanley Cup: 1986 (Montreal)

Rejean GIROUX Rejean Gerard Giroux
5-11 160 R 13 Sep 1952, Quebec PQ

year	team	gp	g	a	pts	pim	gp	g	a	pts	pim
72-73	Que	59	10	12	22	41					
73-74	Que	12	5	6	11	14					
totals		71	15	18	33	55					

Dave GIVEN David Given
6-1 185 - 19 Jul 1954, Summit NJ

year	team	gp	g	a	pts	pim	gp	g	a	pts	pim
74-75	Van	1	0	0	0	0					
totals		1	0	0	0	0					

Brian GLENWRIGHT Brian Joseph Glenwright
6-3 200 L 8 Oct 1949, Windsor ON

year	team	gp	g	a	pts	pim	gp	g	a	pts	pim
72-73	Chi	48	2	5	7	0					
73-74	Chi	15	3	2	5	0					
totals		63	5	7	12	0					

Al GLOBENSKY Alan Globensky
6-1 190 R 17 Apr 1951, Montreal PQ

year	team	gp	g	a	pts	pim	gp	g	a	pts	pim
72-73	Que	4	0	0	0	0					
74-75	Que	5	0	0	0	0	2	1	0	1	0
75-76	Que	34	1	2	3	13					
totals		43	1	2	3	18	2	1	0	1	0

Bill GOLDSWORTHY William Alfred Goldsworthy
6-1 190 R 24 Aug 1944, Kitchener ON d. 1996

year	team	gp	g	a	pts	pim	gp	g	a	pts	pim
77-78	Ind	32	8	10	18	10					
78-79	Edm	17	4	2	6	14	4	1	1	2	11
totals		49	12	12	24	24	4	1	1	2	11

• Played in NHL: 1964-78, Bos-Min-NYR, 771-283-258-541-793

Bill GOLDTHORPE William Kenneth Goldthorpe "Goldie"
5-11 185 L 20 Jun 1953, Homepayne ON

year	team	gp	g	a	pts	pim	gp	g	a	pts	pim
73-74	Min	0	0	0	0	0	3	0	0	0	25
74-75	M-B	7	0	0	0	26					
75-76	SD	14	1	0	1	30					
	D-O	12	0	0	0	31					
totals		33	1	0	1	87	3	0	0	0	25

Frank GOLEMBROSKY
6-0 190 R 3 May 1945, Calgary AB

year	team	gp	g	a	pts	pim	gp	g	a	pts	pim
72-73	Phi	8	0	0	0	0					
	Que	52	8	12	20	44					
totals		60	8	12	20	44					

Don GORDON Donald James Gordon
5-11 180 R 17 Apr 1948, Timmins ON

year	team	gp	g	a	pts	pim	gp	g	a	pts	pim
73-74	LA	29	8	6	14	24					
	Chi	23	5	4	9	9	18	4	8	12	4
74-75	Chi	42	4	5	9	10					
totals		94	17	15	32	43	18	4	8	12	4

Dave GORMAN David Peter Gorman
5-11 185 R 8 Apr 1955, Oshawa ON

year	team	gp	g	a	pts	pim	gp	g	a	pts	pim
74-75	Phx	13	3	5	8	10					
75-76	Phx	67	11	20	31	28	5	0	2	2	24
76-77	Phx	5	0	0	0	0					
	Bir	52	9	13	22	38					
77-78	Bir	63	19	21	40	93	4	1	1	2	0
78-79	Bir	60	14	24	38	18					
totals		260	56	83	139	187	9	1	3	4	24

• Played in NHL: 1979-80, Atl, 3-0-0-0-0

Rich GOSSELIN Richmond Gosselin
5-7 155 L 25 Apr 1956, St Malo MB

year	team	gp	g	a	pts	pim	gp	g	a	pts	pim
78-79	Wpg	3	0	0	0	0					
totals		3	0	0	0	0					

Michel GOULET
6-1 195 R 21 Apr 1960, Peribonqua PQ

year	team	gp	g	a	pts	pim	gp	g	a	pts	pim
78-79	Bir	78	28	30	58	65					
totals		78	28	30	58	65					

• Played in NHL: 1979-94, Que-Chi, 1089-548-604-1152-825 • Member, Hockey Hall of Fame

Bill GRATTON William Gratton
6-3 200 L 29 Feb 1948, Brantford ON

year	team	gp	g	a	pts	pim	gp	g	a	pts	pim
75-76	Cgy	6	0	1	1	2					
totals		6	0	1	1	2					

Jean-Guy GRATTON Jean-Guy Lionel Gratton
5-9 170 R 8 Mar 1949, Ste-Anne des Plaines PQ

year	team	gp	g	a	pts	pim	gp	g	a	pts	pim
72-73	Wpg	71	15	12	27	37	12	1	1	2	4
73-74	Wpg	68	12	21	33	13	2	0	0	0	0
74-75	Wpg	49	4	8	12	2					
totals		188	31	41	72	52	14	1	1	2	4

John GRAVEL Jean Michael Gravel
5-8 170 R 30 Nov 1944, St-Jerome PQ

year	team	gp	g	a	pts	pim	gp	g	a	pts	pim
72-73	Phi	8	1	3	4	0					
totals		8	1	3	4	0					

• Became the public-address announcer for the Quebec Nordiques at Le Colisee.

John GRAY John Gordon Gray
5-10 180 L 13 Aug 1949, Little Current ON

year	team	gp	g	a	pts	pim	gp	g	a	pts	pim
74-75	Phx	75	35	33	68	107	5	2	3	5	12
75-76	Phx	79	35	45	80	136	5	1	1	2	7
76-77	Phx	28	10	10	20	59					
	Hou	47	21	20	41	25	6	0	1	1	8
77-78	Hou	77	35	23	58	80	6	0	3	3	10
78-79	Wpg	57	10	15	25	51	1	0	0	0	0
totals		363	146	146	292	458	23	3	8	11	37

Ted GREEN Edward Joseph Green "Terrible"
5-11 195 R 23 Mar 1940, St Boniface MB

year	team	gp	g	a	pts	pim	gp	g	a	pts	pim
72-73	NE	78	16	30	46	47	12	1	5	6	25
73-74	NE	75	7	26	33	42	7	0	4	4	7
74-75	NE	57	6	14	20	29					
75-76	Wpg	79	5	23	28	73	11	0	2	2	16
76-77	Wpg	70	4	21	25	45	20	1	3	4	12
77-78	Wpg	73	4	22	26	52	8	0	2	2	2
78-79	Wpg	20	0	2	2	16					
totals		**452**	**42**	**138**	**180**	**304**	**58**	**2**	**16**	**18**	**62**

• Played in NHL: 1960-72, Bos, 620-48-206-254-1029 • Stanley Cups: 1970, 1972 (Boston), 1990 (Edm as Coach)

Bruce GREIG
6-3 215 L 9 May 1953, High River AB d. 2008

year	team	gp	g	a	pts	pim	gp	g	a	pts	pim
76-77	Cgy	7	1	1	2	10					
77-78	Cin	32	3	1	4	57					
78-79	Ind	21	3	7	10	64					
totals		**60**	**7**	**9**	**16**	**131**					

• Played in NHL: 1973-75, Cal, 9-0-1-1-46

Richard GRENIER
5-11 170 L 18 Sep 1952, Montreal PQ

year	team	gp	g	a	pts	pim	gp	g	a	pts	pim
76-77	Que	34	11	9	20	4					
totals		**34**	**11**	**9**	**20**	**4**					

• Played in NHL: 1972-73, NYI, 10-1-1-2-2

Gary GRESDAL Gary Edward Gresdal
6-0 195 L 15 Jan 1947, Kingston ON

year	team	gp	g	a	pts	pim	gp	g	a	pts	pim
75-76	Que	2	0	1	1	5	1	0	0	0	14
totals		**2**	**0**	**1**	**1**	**5**	**1**	**0**	**0**	**0**	**14**

Wayne GRETZKY Wayne Douglas Gretzky
5-11 165 L 26 Jan 1961, Brantford ON

year	team	gp	g	a	pts	pim	gp	g	a	pts	pim
78-79	Ind	8	3	3	6	0					
	Edm	72	43	61	104	19	13	10	10	20	2
totals		**80**	**46**	**64**	**110**	**19**	**13**	**10**	**10**	**20**	**2**

• Played in NHL: 1979-99, Edm-LA-StL-NYR, 1487-894-1963-2857-577 • Stanley Cups: 1984, 1985, 1987, 1988 (Edmonton) • Member, Hockey Hall of Fame

Don GRIERSON Donald James Grierson
6-0 185 R 18 Jun 1947, North Bay ON

year	team	gp	g	a	pts	pim	gp	g	a	pts	pim
72-73	Hou	78	22	22	44	83	3	0	0	0	6
73-74	Hou	65	11	18	29	45	14	1	5	6	23
totals		**143**	**33**	**40**	**73**	**128**	**17**	**1**	**5**	**6**	**29**

Danny GRUEN Daniel Patrick Gruen
5-11 180 L 26 Jun 1952, Thunder Bay ON

year	team	gp	g	a	pts	pim	gp	g	a	pts	pim
74-75	M-B	34	10	16	26	73					
	Wpg	32	9	12	21	21					
75-76	Cle	80	26	24	50	72	3	2	0	2	0
76-77	Min	34	10	9	19	19					
	Cgy	1	1	0	1	0					
totals		**181**	**56**	**61**	**117**	**185**	**3**	**2**	**0**	**2**	**0**

• Played in NHL: 1972-77, Det-Col, 49-9-13-22-19

Bob GUINDON Robert Pierre Guindon
5-9 160 L 19 Nov 1950, Labelle PQ

year	team	gp	g	a	pts	pim	gp	g	a	pts	pim
72-73	Que	71	28	28	56	31					
73-74	Que	71	31	39	70	30					
74-75	Que	69	12	18	30	23	15	7	6	13	10
75-76	Wpg	39	3	3	6	14	13	3	3	6	9
76-77	Wpg	69	10	17	27	19	20	4	4	8	9
77-78	Wpg	71	20	22	42	18	9	8	5	13	5
78-79	Wpg	71	8	18	26	21	7	2	1	3	0
totals		**461**	**112**	**145**	**257**	**156**	**65**	**24**	**19**	**43**	**33**

• Played in NHL: 1979-80, Wpg, 6-0-1-1-0

Pierre GUITE
6-2 190 L 17 Apr 1952, Montreal PQ

year	team	gp	g	a	pts	pim	gp	g	a	pts	pim
72-73	Que	66	10	8	18	136					
73-74	Que	72	14	20	34	106					
74-75	Que	22	14	8	22	59					
	M-B	13	5	4	9	11					
75-76	Cin	52	20	24	44	80					
76-77	Cin	27	10	8	18	32					
	Que	35	2	6	8	67	17	5	0	5	9
77-78	Que	18	4	5	9	15					
	Edm	60	12	21	33	71	5	1	1	2	20
78-79	Edm	12	1	1	2	8					
totals		**377**	**92**	**105**	**197**	**585**	**22**	**6**	**1**	**7**	**29**

Bud GULKA Walter Gulka
6-0 190 R 12 Apr 1947, Kipling SK

year	team	gp	g	a	pts	pim	gp	g	a	pts	pim
74-75	Van	5	1	0	1	10					
totals		**5**	**1**	**0**	**1**	**10**					

Bengt GUSTAFSSON Bengt-Ake Gustafsson
6-0 185 L 23 Mar 1958, Karlskoga Sweden

year	team	gp	g	a	pts	pim	gp	g	a	pts	pim
78-79	Edm	0	0	0	0	0	2	1	2	3	0
totals		**0**	**0**	**0**	**0**	**0**	**2**	**1**	**2**	**3**	**0**

• Played in NHL: 1979-89, Wash, 629-196-359-555-196

Derek HAAS
6-0 170 L 1 May 1955, Trail BC

year	team	gp	g	a	pts	pim	gp	g	a	pts	pim
75-76	Cgy	30	5	9	14	6	1	0	0	0	0
totals		**30**	**5**	**9**	**14**	**6**	**1**	**0**	**0**	**0**	**0**

Matti HAGMAN Matti Risto Tapio Hagman
6-1 185 L 21 Sep 1955, Helsinki Finland d. 2016

year	team	gp	g	a	pts	pim	gp	g	a	pts	pim
77-78	Que	53	25	31	56	16					
totals		**53**	**25**	**31**	**56**	**16**					

• Played in NHL: 1976-78, 1980-84, Bos-Edm, 237-56-89-145-36 • Member, Finland Olympic Team, 1976

Larry HALE Larry James Hale
6-1 190 L 9 Oct 1941, Summerland BC

year	team	gp	g	a	pts	pim	gp	g	a	pts	pim
72-73	Hou	68	4	26	30	65	10	1	2	3	2
73-74	Hou	69	2	14	16	35	14	3	2	5	6
74-75	Hou	76	2	18	20	40	13	0	4	4	0
75-76	Hou	77	1	14	15	32	17	0	5	5	8
76-77	Hou	67	0	14	14	18	11	0	2	2	6
77-78	Hou	56	2	11	13	22					
totals		**413**	**11**	**97**	**108**	**216**	**65**	**4**	**15**	**19**	**22**

• Played in NHL: 1968-72, Phi, 196-5-37-42-90

Del HALL Del Allison Hall
5-10 170 L 7 May 1949, Peterborough ON

year	team	gp	g	a	pts	pim	gp	g	a	pts	pim
75-76	Phx	80	47	44	91	10	5	2	3	5	0
76-77	Phx	80	38	41	79	30					
77-78	Cin	25	4	3	7	4					
	Edm	1	0	0	0	0					
totals		**186**	**89**	**88**	**177**	**44**	**5**	**2**	**3**	**5**	**0**

• Played in NHL: 1971-74, Cal, 9-2-0-2-2

Murray HALL Murray Winston Hall
5-11 175 R 24 Nov 1940, Kirkland Lake ON

year	team	gp	g	a	pts	pim	gp	g	a	pts	pim
72-73	Hou	76	28	42	70	84	10	4	4	8	18
73-74	Hou	78	30	28	58	25	14	9	6	15	6
74-75	Hou	78	18	29	47	28	13	7	3	10	8
75-76	Hou	80	20	26	46	18	17	1	4	5	0
totals		**312**	**96**	**125**	**221**	**155**	**54**	**21**	**17**	**38**	**32**

• Played in NHL: 1961-72, Chi-Det-Min-Van, 164-35-48-83-46

Al HAMILTON

Allan Guy Hamilton
6-2 195 R 20 Aug 1946, Flin Flon MB

year	team	gp	g	a	pts	pim	gp	g	a	pts	pim
72-73	Alb	78	11	50	61	124					
73-74	Edm	77	14	45	59	104	4	1	1	2	15
74-75	Edm	25	1	13	14	62					
75-76	Edm	54	2	32	34	78	4	0	1	1	6
76-77	Edm	81	8	37	45	60	5	0	4	4	4
77-78	Edm	59	11	43	54	46					
78-79	Edm	80	6	38	44	38	13	4	5	9	4
totals		454	53	258	311	492	26	5	11	16	29

• Played in NHL: 1965-72, 1979-80, NYR-Buf-Edm, 257-10-78-88-258

Ted HAMPSON

Edward George Hampson "Tick"
5-8 170 L 11 Dec 1936, Togo SK

year	team	gp	g	a	pts	pim	gp	g	a	pts	pim
72-73	Min	77	17	45	62	20	5	3	1	4	0
73-74	Min	77	17	38	55	9	11	4	4	8	8
74-75	Min	78	17	36	53	6	12	1	7	8	0
75-76	Min	59	5	15	20	14					
	Que	14	4	10	14	2	5	0	2	2	10
totals		305	60	144	204	51	33	8	14	22	18

• Played in NHL: 1959-72, NYR-Det-Oak-Cal-Min, 676-108-245-353-94

Alf HANDRAHAN

John Alfred Handrahan
5-9 185 R 27 Dec 1949, Alberton PEI

year	team	gp	g	a	pts	pim	gp	g	a	pts	pim
77-78	Cin	14	1	3	4	42					
totals		14	1	3	4	42					

Merv HANEY

5-11 185 L -, St. Lazare, MB

year	team	gp	g	a	pts	pim	gp	g	a	pts	pim
72-73	Ott	7	0	1	1	4					
totals		7	0	1	1	4					

Al HANGSLEBEN

Alan Hangsleben
6-1 195 L 22 Feb 1953, Warroad MN

year	team	gp	g	a	pts	pim	gp	g	a	pts	pim
74-75	NE	26	0	4	4	8	6	0	3	3	19
75-76	NE	78	2	23	25	62	13	2	3	5	20
76-77	NE	74	13	9	22	79	4	0	0	0	9
77-78	NE	79	11	18	29	140	14	1	4	5	37
78-79	NE	77	10	19	29	148	10	1	2	3	12
totals		334	36	73	109	437	47	4	12	16	97

• Played in NHL: 1979-82, Hart-Wash-LA, 185-21-48-69-396

Craig HANMER

6-2 210 - 6 Jan 1956, St Paul MN d. 2011

year	team	gp	g	a	pts	pim	gp	g	a	pts	pim
74-75	Ind	27	1	0	1	15					
totals		27	1	0	1	15					

John HANNA

John Jack Hanna
5-11 175 R 5 Apr 1935, Sydney NS d. 2005

year	team	gp	g	a	pts	pim	gp	g	a	pts	pim
72-73	Cle	65	6	20	26	68					
totals		65	6	20	26	68					

• Played in NHL: 1958-68, NYR-Mtl-Phi, 198-6-26-32-206

Ron HANSIS

Ronald Louis Hansis
6-2 195 R 12 Nov 1952, Brownsville TX

year	team	gp	g	a	pts	pim	gp	g	a	pts	pim
76-77	Hou	22	4	3	7	6	8	1	1	2	4
77-78	Hou	78	13	9	22	51	6	1	1	2	4
totals		100	17	12	29	57	14	2	2	4	8

Dave HANSON "Killer"

6-0 190 L 12 Apr 1954, Cumberland WI

year	team	gp	g	a	pts	pim	gp	g	a	pts	pim
76-77	Min	1	0	0	0	9					
	NE	7	0	2	2	35	1	0	0	0	0
77-78	Bir	42	7	16	23	241	5	0	1	1	48
78-79	Bir	53	6	22	28	212					
totals		103	13	40	53	497	6	0	1	1	48

• Played in NHL: 1978-80, Det-Min, 33-1-1-2-65

Nick HARBARUK

Mikolaj Nickolas Harbaruk
6-0 190 R 16 Aug 1943, Drohiczyn Poland d. 2011

year	team	gp	g	a	pts	pim	gp	g	a	pts	pim
74-75	Ind	78	20	23	43	52					
75-76	Ind	76	23	19	42	26	7	2	0	2	10
76-77	Ind	27	2	2	4	2	6	1	1	2	0
totals		181	45	44	89	80	13	3	1	4	10

• Played in NHL: 1969-74, Pit-StL, 364-45-75-120-273

Joe HARDY

Jocelyn Joseph Hardy
6-0 185 L 5 Dec 1944, Kenogami PQ

year	team	gp	g	a	pts	pim	gp	g	a	pts	pim
72-73	Cle	72	17	33	50	80	7	0	2	2	0
73-74	Chi	77	24	35	59	55	17	4	8	12	13
74-75	Chi	17	1	6	7	8					
	Ind	32	2	17	19	36					
	SD	12	2	3	5	22					
totals		210	46	94	140	201	24	4	10	14	13

• Played in NHL: 1969-71, Oak-Cal, 63-9-14-23-51

Jim HARGREAVES

James Albert Hargreaves
5-11 195 R 2 May 1950, Winnipeg MB

year	team	gp	g	a	pts	pim	gp	g	a	pts	pim
73-74	Wpg	53	1	4	5	50					
74-75	Ind	37	2	5	7	30					
	SD	41	8	10	18	45	10	1	0	1	6
75-76	SD	43	1	1	2	26	5	0	0	0	2
totals		174	12	20	32	151	15	1	0	1	8

• Played in NHL: 1970-72, Van, 66-1-7-8-105

Ted HARGREAVES

Norman Edward Hargreaves
5-11 175 L 4 Nov 1943, Weyburn SK d. 2005

year	team	gp	g	a	pts	pim	gp	g	a	pts	pim
73-74	Wpg	74	7	12	19	15	4	0	1	1	10
totals		74	7	12	19	15	4	0	1	1	10

• Member, Canada Olympic Team, 1968

Derek HARKER

Derek William Harker
6-0 185 L 7 Jan 1951, Edmonton AB

year	team	gp	g	a	pts	pim	gp	g	a	pts	pim
72-73	Alb	1	0	0	0	0					
	Phi	27	0	5	5	46					
totals		28	0	5	5	46					

Duke HARRIS

George Francis Harris
6-0 190 R 25 Feb 1942, Sarnia ON

year	team	gp	g	a	pts	pim	gp	g	a	pts	pim
72-73	Hou	75	30	12	42	14	10	1	1	2	4
73-74	Chi	64	14	16	30	20	18	6	6	12	2
74-75	Chi	54	9	19	28	18					
totals		193	53	47	100	52	28	7	7	14	6

• Played in NHL: 1967-68, Min-Tor, 26-1-4-5-4

Hugh HARRIS

Hugh Thomas Harris
6-0 190 L 7 Jun 1948, Toronto ON

year	team	gp	g	a	pts	pim	gp	g	a	pts	pim
73-74	NE	75	24	28	52	78	3	0	0	0	0
74-75	Phx	22	10	10	20	15					
	Van	58	23	34	57	19					
75-76	Cgy	30	5	9	14	19					
	Ind	41	12	28	40	23	7	2	5	7	8
76-77	Ind	46	21	35	56	21	2	0	0	0	0
77-78	Ind	19	1	7	8	6					
	Cin	45	11	23	34	30					
totals		336	107	174	281	241	12	2	5	7	8

• Played in NHL: 1972-73, Buf, 60-12-26-38-17

Jim HARRISON

Jimmy David Harrison
5-11 180 R 9 Jul 1947, Bonnyville AB

year	team	gp	g	a	pts	pim	gp	g	a	pts	pim
72-73	Alb	66	39	47	86	93					
73-74	Edm	46	24	45	69	99					
74-75	Cle	60	20	22	42	106	5	1	2	3	4
75-76	Cle	59	34	38	72	62	3	0	1	1	9
totals		231	117	152	269	360	8	1	3	4	13

• Played in NHL: 1968-72, 1976-80, Bos-Tor-Chi-Edm, 324-67-86-153-435

Dick HART

Richard Edward Hart
6-0 195 L 5 Oct 1952, Boston MA

year	team	gp	g	a	pts	pim	gp	g	a	pts	pim
76-77	Bir	4	0	0	0	0					
totals		4	0	0	0	0					

Craig HARTSBURG Craig William Hartsburg
6-1 190 L 29 Jun 1959, Stratford ON

year	team	gp	g	a	pts	pim	gp	g	a	pts	pim
78-79	Bir	77	9	40	49	73					
totals		**77**	**9**	**40**	**49**	**73**					

• Played in NHL: 1979-89, Min, 570-98-315-413-818

Mike HARVEY Michel Harvey
5-10 175 L 31 Jan 1938, Alma PQ

year	team	gp	g	a	pts	pim	gp	g	a	pts	pim
72-73	Que	40	6	13	19	14					
totals		**40**	**6**	**13**	**19**	**14**					

Ed HATOUM Edward Hatoum
5-10 185 R 7 Dec 1947, Beirut Lebanon

year	team	gp	g	a	pts	pim	gp	g	a	pts	pim
72-73	Chi	15	1	1	2	2					
73-74	Van	37	3	12	15	8					
totals		**52**	**4**	**13**	**17**	**10**					

• Played in NHL: 1968-71, Det-Van, 47-3-6-9-25

Murray HEATLEY Murray James Heatley
5-8 185 R 7 Nov 1948, Calgary AB

year	team	gp	g	a	pts	pim	gp	g	a	pts	pim
73-74	Min	71	26	32	58	23	10	1	0	1	2
74-75	Min	22	5	9	14	31					
	Ind	29	15	8	23	25					
75-76	Ind	34	2	5	7	7					
totals		**156**	**48**	**54**	**102**	**86**	**10**	**1**	**0**	**1**	**2**

Paul HEAVER Paul Gerhard Heaver
6-1 195 R 15 Feb 1955, Paddington England

year	team	gp	g	a	pts	pim	gp	g	a	pts	pim
75-76	Tor	66	2	12	14	83					
76-77	Bir	5	0	0	0	0					
totals		**71**	**2**	**12**	**14**	**83**					

Anders HEDBERG
5-11 175 L 25 Feb 1951, Ornskoldsvik Sweden

year	team	gp	g	a	pts	pim	gp	g	a	pts	pim
74-75	Wpg	65	53	47	100	45					
75-76	Wpg	76	50	55	105	48	13	13	6	19	15
76-77	Wpg	68	70	61	131	48	20	13	16	29	13
77-78	Wpg	77	63	59	122	60	9	9	6	15	2
totals		**286**	**236**	**222**	**458**	**201**	**42**	**35**	**28**	**63**	**30**

• Played in NHL: 1978-85, NYR, 465-172-225-397-144

Howie HEGGEDAL Howard Leonard Heggedal
6-0 185 L 15 Sep 1949, Lethbridge AB

year	team	gp	g	a	pts	pim	gp	g	a	pts	pim
72-73	LA	8	2	1	3	0	1	0	0	0	0
totals		**8**	**2**	**1**	**3**	**0**	**1**	**0**	**0**	**0**	**0**

Bill HEINDL William Wayne Heindl
5-9 175 L 13 May 1946, Sherbrooke PQ d. 1992

year	team	gp	g	a	pts	pim	gp	g	a	pts	pim
73-74	Cle	67	4	14	18	4	5	0	1	1	2
totals		**67**	**4**	**14**	**18**	**4**	**5**	**0**	**1**	**1**	**2**

• Played in NHL: 1970-73, Min-NYR, 18-2-1-3-0

Earl HEISKALA Earl Waldemar Heiskala
6-0 185 L 30 Nov 1942, Kirkland Lake ON

year	team	gp	g	a	pts	pim	gp	g	a	pts	pim
72-73	LA	70	12	17	29	150	5	1	1	2	4
73-74	LA	24	2	6	8	45					
totals		**94**	**14**	**23**	**37**	**195**	**5**	**1**	**1**	**2**	**4**

• Played in NHL: 1968-71, Phi, 127-13-11-24-294

Paul HENDERSON Paul Garnet Henderson
5-11 180 R 28 Jan 1943, Kincardine ON

year	team	gp	g	a	pts	pim	gp	g	a	pts	pim
74-75	Tor	58	30	33	63	18					
75-76	Tor	65	26	29	55	22					
76-77	Bir	81	23	25	48	30					
77-78	Bir	80	37	29	66	22	5	1	1	2	0
78-79	Bir	76	24	27	51	20					
totals		**360**	**140**	**143**	**283**	**112**	**5**	**1**	**1**	**2**	**0**

• Played in NHL: 1962-74, 1979-80, Det-Tor-Atl, 707-236-241-477-304

Pierre HENRY
5-10 180 L 10 Mar 1952, Montreal PQ

year	team	gp	g	a	pts	pim	gp	g	a	pts	pim
72-73	Phi	19	2	3	5	13					
totals		**19**	**2**	**3**	**5**	**13**					

Don HERRIMAN Donald Herriman
5-10 165 L 2 Jan 1946, Sault Ste Marie ON

year	team	gp	g	a	pts	pim	gp	g	a	pts	pim
72-73	Phi	78	24	48	72	63	4	1	0	1	14
73-74	NY-J	44	11	21	31	59					
74-75	Edm	33	1	2	3	21					
totals		**155**	**36**	**71**	**107**	**143**	**4**	**1**	**0**	**1**	**14**

Bill HICKE William Lawrence Hicke
5-8 165 L 31 Mar 1938, Regina SK d. 2005

year	team	gp	g	a	pts	pim	gp	g	a	pts	pim
72-73	Alb	72	14	24	38	16					
totals		**72**	**14**	**24**	**38**	**16**					

• Played in NHL: 1958-72, Mtl-NYR-Oak-Cal-Pit, 729-168-234-402-395 • Stanley Cups: 1959, 1960 (Montreal)

Pat HICKEY Patrick Joseph Hickey
6-1 180 L 15 May 1953, Brantford ON

year	team	gp	g	a	pts	pim	gp	g	a	pts	pim
73-74	Tor	78	26	29	55	52	12	3	3	6	12
74-75	Tor	74	35	34	69	50	5	0	1	1	4
totals		**152**	**61**	**63**	**124**	**102**	**17**	**3**	**4**	**7**	**16**

• Played in NHL: 1975-85, NYR-Col-Tor-Que-StL, 646-192-212-404-351

Glenn HICKS
5-10 180 L 28 Aug 1958, Red Deer AB

year	team	gp	g	a	pts	pim	gp	g	a	pts	pim
78-79	Wpg	69	6	10	16	48	7	1	1	2	4
totals		**69**	**6**	**10**	**16**	**48**	**7**	**1**	**1**	**2**	**4**

• Played in NHL: 1979-81, Det, 108-6-12-18-127

Larry HILLMAN Larry Morley Hillman
6-0 180 L 5 Feb 1937, Kirkland Lake ON

year	team	gp	g	a	pts	pim	gp	g	a	pts	pim
73-74	Cle	44	5	21	26	37					
74-75	Cle	77	0	16	16	83	5	1	3	4	8
75-76	Wpg	71	1	12	13	62	12	0	2	2	32
totals		**192**	**6**	**49**	**55**	**182**	**17**	**1**	**5**	**6**	**40**

• Brother of Wayne Hillman • Played in NHL: 1954-73, Det-Bos-Tor-Mtl-Phi-LA-Buf, 790-36-196-232-579 • Stanley Cups: 1955 (Detroit), 1967 (Toronto), 1969 (Montreal)

Wayne HILLMAN Wayne James Hillman
6-0 205 L 13 Nov 1938, Kirkland Lake ON d. 1990

year	team	gp	g	a	pts	pim	gp	g	a	pts	pim
73-74	Cle	66	1	7	8	51	5	0	0	0	16
74-75	Cle	60	2	9	11	37	5	0	2	2	2
totals		**126**	**3**	**16**	**19**	**88**	**10**	**0**	**2**	**2**	**18**

• Brother of Larry Hillman • Played in NHL: 1960-73, Chi-NYR-Min-Phi, 691-18-86-104-534 • Stanley Cup: 1961 (Chicago)

Andre HINSE Joseph Charles Andre Hinse
5-9 175 L 19 Apr 1945, Trois Rivieres PQ

year	team	gp	g	a	pts	pim	gp	g	a	pts	pim
73-74	Hou	69	24	56	80	39	14	8	9	17	18
74-75	Hou	75	39	47	86	12	11	5	4	9	8
75-76	Hou	70	35	38	73	6	17	2	3	5	2
76-77	Hou	26	2	3	5	8					
	Phx	16	2	7	9	14					
totals		**256**	**102**	**151**	**253**	**69**	**42**	**15**	**16**	**31**	**28**

• Played in NHL: 1967-68, Tor, 4-0-0-0-0

Jamie HISLOP James Donald Hislop
5-10 180 R 20 Jan 1954, Sarnia ON

year	team	gp	g	a	pts	pim	gp	g	a	pts	pim
76-77	Cin	46	7	19	26	6	4	0	1	1	5
77-78	Cin	80	24	43	67	17					
78-79	Cin	80	30	40	70	45	3	2	4	6	0
totals		**206**	**61**	**102**	**163**	**68**	**7**	**2**	**5**	**7**	**5**

• Played in NHL: 1979-84, Que-Cgy, 345-75-103-178-86

Mike HOBIN Michael Patrick Hobin
5-11 180 L 21 Feb 1954, Sarnia ON

year	team	gp	g	a	pts	pim	gp	g	a	pts	pim
75-76	Phx	9	1	1	2	2					
76-77	Phx	68	17	18	35	14					
totals		**77**	**18**	**19**	**37**	**16**					

Ted HODGSON — Theodore James Hodgson
5-11   175   R   30 Jun 1945, Hobbema AB

year	team	gp	g	a	pts	pim	gp	g	a	pts	pim
72-73	Cle	74	15	23	38	93	9	1	3	4	13
73-74	Cle	10	0	2	2	6					
	LA	23	3	9	12	22					
totals		107	18	34	52	121	9	1	3	4	13

• Played in NHL: 1966-67, Bos, 4-0-0-0-0

Ed HOEKSTRA — Edward Adrian Hoekstra
5-11   175   L   4 Nov 1937, Winnipeg MB   d. 2011

year	team	gp	g	a	pts	pim	gp	g	a	pts	pim
72-73	Hou	78	11	28	39	12	9	1	2	3	0
73-74	Hou	19	2	0	2	0					
totals		97	13	28	41	12	9	1	2	3	0

• Played in NHL: 1967-68, Phi, 70-15-21-36-6

Dale HOGANSON — Dale Gordon Hoganson "Red"
5-10   190   L   8 Jul 1949, N Battleford SK

year	team	gp	g	a	pts	pim	gp	g	a	pts	pim
73-74	Que	62	8	33	41	27					
74-75	Que	78	9	35	44	47	13	1	3	4	4
75-76	Que	45	3	14	17	18	5	1	3	4	2
76-77	Bir	81	7	48	55	48					
77-78	Bir	43	1	12	13	29	5	0	0	0	7
78-79	Que	69	2	19	21	17	4	0	0	0	2
totals		378	30	161	191	186	27	2	6	8	15

• Cousin of Paul Hoganson • Played in NHL: 1969-73, 1979-82, LA-Mtl-Que, 343-13-77-90-186

Terry HOLBROOK — Terry Eugene Holbrook
6-0   185   R   11 Jul 1950, Watford ON

year	team	gp	g	a	pts	pim	gp	g	a	pts	pim
74-75	Cle	78	10	13	23	7	5	0	1	1	0
75-76	Cle	15	1	2	3	6	3	0	0	0	0
totals		93	11	15	26	13	8	0	1	1	0

• Played in NHL: 1972-74, Min, 43-3-6-9-4

Jerry HOLLAND — Jerry Allan Holland
5-10   180   L   25 Aug 1954, Beaverlodge AB

year	team	gp	g	a	pts	pim	gp	g	a	pts	pim
77-78	Edm	22	2	1	3	14					
totals		22	2	1	3	14					

• Played in NHL: 1974-76, NYR, 37-8-4-12-6

Paul HOLMGREN — Paul Howard Holmgren
6-2   215   R   2 Dec 1955, St Paul MN

year	team	gp	g	a	pts	pim	gp	g	a	pts	pim
75-76	Min	51	14	16	30	121					
totals		51	14	16	30	121					

• Played in NHL: 1976-85, Phi-Min, 527-144-179-323-1684

Ralph HOPIAVUORI
6-1   185   L   7 Jul 1951, Kirkland Lake ON

year	team	gp	g	a	pts	pim	gp	g	a	pts	pim
72-73	Cle	31	4	5	9	44	8	0	1	1	6
73-74	Cle	13	0	2	2	6	4	0	1	1	0
74-75	Ind	28	2	8	10	21					
totals		72	6	15	21	71	12	0	2	2	6

Larry HORNUNG — Lawrence John Hornung
6-0   190   L   10 Nov 1945, Weyburn SK   d. 2001

year	team	gp	g	a	pts	pim	gp	g	a	pts	pim
72-73	Wpg	77	13	45	58	28	14	2	9	11	0
73-74	Wpg	51	4	19	23	18	4	0	0	0	0
74-75	Wpg	69	7	25	32	21					
75-76	Wpg	76	3	18	21	26	13	0	3	3	6
76-77	Edm	21	2	1	3	0					
	SD	58	4	9	13	8	6	0	0	0	0
77-78	Wpg	19	1	4	5	2					
totals		371	34	121	155	103	37	2	12	14	6

• Played in NHL: 1970-72, StL, 48-2-9-11-10

Bill HORTON — William Harley Horton
6-0   180   L   5 Sep 1946, Lindsay ON   d. 1988

year	team	gp	g	a	pts	pim	gp	g	a	pts	pim
72-73	Cle	73	2	17	19	55	9	0	1	1	10
73-74	LA	60	0	9	9	46					
74-75	Ind	59	2	9	11	30					
totals		192	4	35	39	131	9	0	1	1	10

Rejean HOULE
5-11   165   L   25 Oct 1949, Rouyn PQ

year	team	gp	g	a	pts	pim	gp	g	a	pts	pim
73-74	Que	69	27	35	62	17					
74-75	Que	64	40	52	92	37	15	10	6	16	2
75-76	Que	81	51	52	103	61	5	2	0	2	8
totals		214	118	139	257	115	20	12	6	18	10

• Played in NHL: 1969-73, 1976-83, Mtl, 635-161-247-408-395 • Stanley Cups: 1971, 1973, 1977, 1978, 1979 (Montreal)

Gordie HOWE — Gordon Howe
6-0   205   R   31 Mar 1928, Floral SK   d. 2016

year	team	gp	g	a	pts	pim	gp	g	a	pts	pim
73-74	Hou	76	31	69	100	46	13	3	14	17	34
74-75	Hou	75	34	65	99	84	13	8	12	20	20
75-76	Hou	78	32	70	102	76	17	4	8	12	31
76-77	Hou	62	24	44	68	57	11	5	3	8	11
77-78	NE	76	34	62	96	85	14	5	5	10	15
78-79	NE	58	19	24	43	51	10	3	1	4	4
totals		415	174	334	508	399	78	28	43	71	115

• Father of Marty Howe and Mark Howe • Played in NHL: 1946-71, 1979-80, Det-Hart, 1767-801-1049-1850-1685 • Stanley Cups: 1950, 1952, 1954, 1955 (Detroit) • Member, Hockey Hall of Fame

Mark HOWE — Mark Steven Howe
5-11   180   L   28 May 1955, Detroit MI

year	team	gp	g	a	pts	pim	gp	g	a	pts	pim
73-74	Hou	76	38	41	79	20	14	9	10	19	4
74-75	Hou	74	36	40	76	30	13	10	12	22	0
75-76	Hou	72	39	37	76	38	17	6	10	16	18
76-77	Hou	57	23	52	75	46	11	4	10	14	2
77-78	NE	70	30	61	91	32	14	8	7	15	18
78-79	NE	77	42	65	107	32	6	4	2	6	6
totals		426	208	296	504	198	75	41	51	92	48

• Brother of Marty Howe, son of Gordie Howe • Played in NHL: 1979-95, Hart-Phi-Det, 929-197-545-742-455 • Member, United States Olympic Team, 1972 • Member, Hockey Hall of Fame.

Marty HOWE — Marty Gordon Howe
6-1   185   L   18 Feb 1954, Detroit MI

year	team	gp	g	a	pts	pim	gp	g	a	pts	pim
73-74	Hou	73	4	20	24	90	14	1	5	6	31
74-75	Hou	75	13	21	34	89	11	0	2	2	11
75-76	Hou	80	14	23	37	51	16	4	4	8	12
76-77	Hou	80	17	28	45	103	11	3	1	4	10
77-78	NE	75	10	10	20	66	14	1	1	2	13
78-79	NE	66	9	15	24	31	9	0	1	1	8
totals		449	67	117	184	460	75	9	14	23	85

• Brother of Mark Howe, son of Gordie Howe • Played in NHL: 1979-85, Hart-Bos, 197-2-29-31-99

Harry HOWELL — Henry Vernon Howell
6-1   200   L   28 Dec 1932, Hamilton ON

year	team	gp	g	a	pts	pim	gp	g	a	pts	pim
73-74	NY-J	65	3	23	26	24					
74-75	SD	74	4	10	14	28	5	1	0	1	10
75-76	Cgy	31	0	3	3	6	2	0	0	0	2
totals		170	7	36	43	58	7	1	0	1	12

• Played in NHL: 1952-73, NYR-Oak-Cal-LA, 1411-94-324-418-1298 • Member, Hockey Hall of Fame

Fran HUCK — Anthony Francis Huck
5-7   165   R   4 Dec 1945, Regina SK

year	team	gp	g	a	pts	pim	gp	g	a	pts	pim
73-74	Wpg	74	26	48	74	68	4	0	0	0	2
74-75	Min	78	22	45	67	26	12	3	13	16	6
75-76	Min	59	17	32	49	27					
76-77	Wpg	12	2	2	4	10	7	0	2	2	6
77-78	Wpg	5	0	0	0	2					
totals		228	67	127	194	133	23	3	15	18	14

• Played in NHL: 1969-73, Mtl-StL, 94-24-30-54-38 • Member, Canadian Olympic Team, 1968

Brent HUGHES — Brenton Alexander Hughes
6-0   205   L   17 Jun 1943, Bowmanville ON

year	team	gp	g	a	pts	pim	gp	g	a	pts	pim
75-76	SD	78	7	28	35	63	10	1	5	6	6
76-77	SD	62	4	13	17	48	7	0	4	4	0
77-78	Bir	80	9	35	44	48	5	0	0	0	12
78-79	Bir	48	3	3	6	21					
totals		268	23	79	102	180	22	1	9	10	18

• Played in NHL: 1967-75, LA-Phi-StL-Det-KC, 435-15-117-132-440

437

Frank HUGHES
5-10 180 R 1 Oct 1949, Fernie BC

year	team	gp	g	a	pts	pim	gp	g	a	pts	pim
72-73	Hou	76	22	19	41	41	10	4	4	8	2
73-74	Hou	73	42	42	84	47	14	9	5	14	9
74-75	Hou	70	48	35	83	35	13	6	6	12	2
75-76	Hou	80	31	45	76	26	17	5	1	6	20
76-77	Hou	27	3	8	11	2					
	Phx	48	24	29	53	20					
77-78	Hou	11	3	2	5	2					
totals		385	173	180	353	173	54	24	16	40	33

• Played in NHL: 1971-72, Cal, 5-0-0-0-0

John HUGHES John Spencer Hughes
5-11 190 L 18 Mar 1954, Charlottetown PEI

year	team	gp	g	a	pts	pim	gp	g	a	pts	pim
74-75	Phx	72	4	25	29	201					
75-76	Cin	79	3	34	37	204					
76-77	Cin	79	3	27	30	113	4	0	0	0	8
77-78	Hou	79	3	25	28	130	6	1	1	2	6
78-79	Ind	22	3	4	7	48					
	Edm	41	2	15	17	82	13	1	0	1	35
totals		372	18	130	148	778	23	2	1	3	49

• Played in NHL: 1979-81, Van-Edm-NYR, 70-2-14-16-211

Bobby HULL Robert Marvin Hull "Golden Jet"
5-10 195 L 3 Jan 1939, Pointe Anne ON

year	team	gp	g	a	pts	pim	gp	g	a	pts	pim
72-73	Wpg	63	51	52	103	37	14	9	16	25	16
73-74	Wpg	75	53	42	95	38	4	1	1	2	4
74-75	Wpg	78	77	65	142	41					
75-76	Wpg	80	53	70	123	30	13	12	8	20	4
76-77	Wpg	34	21	32	53	14	20	13	9	22	2
77-78	Wpg	77	46	71	117	23	9	8	3	11	12
78-79	Wpg	4	2	3	5	0					
totals		411	303	335	638	183	60	43	37	80	38

• Played in NHL: 1957-72, 1979-80, Chi-Wpg-Hart, 1063-610-560-1170-640 • Stanley Cup: 1961 (Chicago) • Member, Hockey Hall of Fame

Steve HULL Steven Hull
5-10 180 R 29 Aug 1952, Ottawa ON

year	team	gp	g	a	pts	pim	gp	g	a	pts	pim
75-76	Cgy	58	11	15	26	6					
76-77	Cgy	2	0	2	2	0					
totals		60	11	17	28	6					

Dave HUNTER
5-11 195 L 1 Jan 1958, Petrolia ON

year	team	gp	g	a	pts	pim	gp	g	a	pts	pim
78-79	Edm	72	7	25	32	134	13	2	3	5	42
totals		72	7	25	32	134	13	2	3	5	42

• Played in NHL: 1979-89, Edm-Pit-Wpg, 746-133-190-323-918 • Stanley Cups: 1984, 1985, 1987 (Edmonton)

Paul HURLEY Paul Michael Hurley
5-11 180 R 12 Jul 1946, Melrose MA

year	team	gp	g	a	pts	pim	gp	g	a	pts	pim
72-73	NE	78	3	15	18	58	15	0	7	7	14
73-74	NE	52	3	11	14	21					
74-75	NE	75	3	26	29	36	6	0	1	1	4
75-76	NE	46	0	14	14	20					
	Edm	26	1	4	5	14	4	0	0	0	0
76-77	Cgy	34	0	6	6	32					
totals		311	10	76	86	181	25	0	8	8	18

• Played in NHL: 1968-69, Bos, 1-0-1-1-0 • Member, United States Olympic Team, 1968

Ron HUSTON Ronald Earle Huston
5-9 170 R 8 Apr 1945, Manitou MB

year	team	gp	g	a	pts	pim	gp	g	a	pts	pim
75-76	Phx	79	22	44	66	4	5	1	1	2	0
76-77	Phx	80	20	39	59	10					
totals		159	42	83	125	14	5	1	1	2	0

• Played in NHL: 1973-75, Cal, 79-15-31-46-8

Dave HUTCHISON David Joseph Hutchison
6-2 205 L 2 May 1952, London ON

year	team	gp	g	a	pts	pim	gp	g	a	pts	pim
72-73	Phi	28	0	2	2	34	3	0	0	0	2
73-74	Van	69	0	13	13	151					
totals		97	0	15	15	185	3	0	0	0	2

• Played in NHL: 1974-84, LA-Tor-Chi-NJ, 584-19-97-116-1550

Mike HYNDMAN Michael Anthony Hyndman
6-1 205 R 8 Dec 1945, Quebec City PQ

year	team	gp	g	a	pts	pim	gp	g	a	pts	pim
72-73	NE	59	4	14	18	21					
	LA	19	8	7	15	11	6	0	3	3	17
73-74	LA	8	0	1	1	0					
totals		86	12	22	34	32	6	0	3	3	17

David HYNES
5-9 180 L 17 Apr 1951, Cambridge MA

year	team	gp	g	a	pts	pim	gp	g	a	pts	pim
76-77	NE	22	5	4	9	4					
totals		22	5	4	9	4					

• Played in NHL: 1973-75, Bos, 22-4-0-4-2

Lee INGLIS
5-10 175 L 31 Aug 1947, Latchford ON

year	team	gp	g	a	pts	pim	gp	g	a	pts	pim
73-74	NY-J	5	0	0	0	0					
74-75	SD	5	0	2	2	0					
totals		10	0	2	2	0.					

Dave INKPEN David John Inkpen
6-0 185 R 4 Sep 1954, Edmonton AB

year	team	gp	g	a	pts	pim	gp	g	a	pts	pim
75-76	Cin	80	4	24	28	95					
76-77	Cin	48	3	14	17	61					
	Ind	32	4	12	16	20	9	0	2	2	8
77-78	Edm	19	0	1	1	16					
	Que	24	0	1	1	20					
	Ind	24	1	9	10	24					
78-79	Ind	25	1	8	9	22					
	NE	41	0	7	7	15	5	0	1	1	4
totals		293	13	76	89	273	14	0	3	3	12

Glen IRWIN Glen Mac Irwin
5-11 195 R 1 Mar 1951, Edmonton AB

year	team	gp	g	a	pts	pim	gp	g	a	pts	pim
74-75	Hou	70	2	11	13	153	13	0	2	2	8
75-76	Hou	72	3	8	11	116	5	0	0	0	9
76-77	Hou	44	2	4	6	168					
77-78	Hou	3	0	0	0	0					
	Ind	20	0	0	0	72					
78-79	Ind	24	0	1	1	124					
totals		233	7	24	31	633	18	0	2	2	17

Larry ISRAELSON
6-1 175 L 2 Aug 1952, Wetaskiwin SK

year	team	gp	g	a	pts	pim	gp	g	a	pts	pim
74-75	Van	46	12	9	21	10					
75-76	Cgy	57	10	22	32	26	3	0	0	0	0
76-77	Cgy	2	0	0	0	0					
totals		105	22	31	53	36	3	0	0	0	0

Jeff JACQUES Jeffrey Jacques
5-11 180 R 4 Apr 1953, Preston ON

year	team	gp	g	a	pts	pim	gp	g	a	pts	pim
74-75	Tor	39	12	8	20	26	6	0	4	4	2
75-76	Tor	81	17	33	50	113					
76-77	Bir	79	21	27	48	92					
totals		199	50	68	118	231	6	0	4	4	2

• Last name pronounced "Jakes"

Gary JACQUITH Gary Alan Jacquith
6-0 200 R 30 May 1948, Lynn MA

year	team	gp	g	a	pts	pim	gp	g	a	pts	pim
75-76	SD	2	0	0	0	0					
totals		2	0	0	0	0					

Mike JAKUBO Michael Paul Jakubo
6-0 190 L 7 Jul 1947, Sudbury ON

year	team	gp	g	a	pts	pim	gp	g	a	pts	pim
72-73	LA	7	0	0	0	0					
totals		7	0	0	0	0					

Gary JARRETT Gary Walter Jarrett
5-8 180 L 3 Sep 1942, Toronto ON

year	team	gp	g	a	pts	pim	gp	g	a	pts	pim
72-73	Cle	77	40	38	78	79	9	8	3	11	19
73-74	Cle	75	31	39	70	68	5	1	1	2	13
74-75	Cle	77	17	24	41	70	5	0	1	1	0
75-76	Cle	69	16	17	33	22	3	0	3	3	2
totals		298	104	118	222	239	22	9	8	17	34

• Played in NHL: 1960-72, Tor-Det-Oak-Cal, 341-72-92-164-131

Pierre JARRY — Pierre Joseph Reynald Jarry
5-11 180 L 30 Mar 1949, Montreal PQ

year	team	gp	g	a	pts	pim	gp	g	a	pts	pim
77-78	Edm	18	4	10	14	4	5	1	0	1	4
totals		18	4	10	14	4	5	1	0	1	4

• Played in NHL: 1971-78. NYR-Tor-Det-Min, 344-88-117-205-142

Rick JODZIO — Richard Joseph Jodzio
6-1 190 L 3 Jun 1954, Edmonton AB

year	team	gp	g	a	pts	pim	gp	g	a	pts	pim
74-75	Van	44	1	3	4	159					
75-76	Cgy	47	10	7	17	137	2	0	0	0	14
76-77	Cgy	46	4	6	10	61					
totals		137	15	16	31	357	2	0	0	0	14

• Played in NHL: 1977-78, Col-Cle, 70-2-8-10-71

Danny JOHNSON — Daniel Douglas Johnson
5-11 170 L 1 Oct 1944, Winnipegosis MB d. 1993

year	team	gp	g	a	pts	pim	gp	g	a	pts	pim
72-73	Wpg	76	19	23	42	17	14	4	1	5	0
73-74	Wpg	78	16	21	37	20	4	1	0	1	5
74-75	Wpg	78	18	14	32	25					
totals		232	53	58	111	62	18	5	1	6	5

• Played in NHL: 1969-72, Tor-Van-Det, 121-18-19-37-24

Jim JOHNSON — Norman James Johnson
5-9 190 L 7 Nov 1942, Winnipeg MB

year	team	gp	g	a	pts	pim	gp	g	a	pts	pim
72-73	Min	33	9	14	23	12	5	2	1	3	2
73-74	Min	71	15	39	54	30	11	1	4	5	4
74-75	Min	11	1	3	4	0					
	Ind	42	7	15	22	12					
totals		157	32	71	103	54	16	3	5	8	6

• Played in NHL: 1964-72, NYR-Phi-LA, 302-75-111-186-73

Larry JOHNSTON — Lawrence Roy Johnston
6-0 195 R 20 Jul 1943, Kitchener ON

year	team	gp	g	a	pts	pim	gp	g	a	pts	pim
74-75	M-B	49	0	9	9	93					
totals		49	0	9	9	93					

• Played in NHL: 1967-74, 1975-77, LA-Det-KC-Col, 320-9-64-73-580

Eddie JOHNSTONE — Edward LaVern Johnstone
5-9 175 R 2 Mar 1954, Brandon MB

year	team	gp	g	a	pts	pim	gp	g	a	pts	pim
74-75	M-B	23	4	4	8	43					
totals		23	4	4	8	43					

• Played in NHL: 1975-87, NYR-Det, 426-122-136-258-375

Bob JONES — Robert Charles Jones
6-0 190 L 27 Nov 1945, Espanola ON

year	team	gp	g	a	pts	pim	gp	g	a	pts	pim
72-73	LA	20	2	7	9	8					
	NY	56	11	12	23	24					
73-74	NY-J	78	17	28	45	20					
74-75	M-B	5	0	1	1	8					
75-76	Ind	2	0	0	0	0					
totals		161	30	48	78	60					

• Brother of James W. Jones • Played in NHL: 1968-69, NYR 2-0-0-0-0

James H. JONES — James Harrison Jones "Jimmy"
5-9 180 R 2 Jan 1953, Woodbridge ON

year	team	gp	g	a	pts	pim	gp	g	a	pts	pim
73-74	Van	18	3	2	5	23					
74-75	Van	63	11	7	18	39					
totals		81	14	9	23	62					

• Played in NHL: 1977-80, Tor, 148-13-18-31-68

James W. JONES — James William Jones
5-10 185 L 27 Jul 1949, Espanola ON

year	team	gp	g	a	pts	pim	gp	g	a	pts	pim
73-74	Chi	1	0	0	0	0					
totals		1	0	0	0	0					

• Brother of Bob Jones • Played in NHL: 1971-72, Cal, 2-0-0-0-0

Ric JORDAN — John Richard Jordan
6-3 200 L 31 Mar 1950, Toronto ON

year	team	gp	g	a	pts	pim	gp	g	a	pts	pim
72-73	NE	34	1	5	6	12	7	0	0	0	6
73-74	NE	34	0	3	3	14					
74-75	Que	56	6	8	14	75					
75-76	Que	54	4	7	11	75					
76-77	Cgy	5	0	0	0	4					
totals		183	11	23	34	180	7	0	0	0	6

Eddie JOYAL — Edward Abel Joyal "The Jet"
6-0 180 L 8 May 1940, Edmonton AB

year	team	gp	g	a	pts	pim	gp	g	a	pts	pim
72-73	Alb	71	22	16	38	16					
73-74	Edm	45	8	10	18	2	5	2	0	2	4
74-75	Edm	78	22	25	47	2					
75-76	Edm	45	5	4	9	6					
totals		239	57	55	112	26	5	2	0	2	4

• Played in NHL: 1962-72, Det-Tor-LA-Phi, 466-128-134-282-103

Dan JUSTIN — Daniel Sy Justin
6-1 180 L 12 Feb 1955, Palo Alto CA

year	team	gp	g	a	pts	pim	gp	g	a	pts	pim
75-76	Cin	17	0	0	0	2					
76-77	Cin	6	0	2	2	4					
totals		23	0	2	2	6					

Gord KANNEGIESSER — Gordon Cameron Kannegiesser
6-0 190 L 21 Dec 1945, North Bay ON

year	team	gp	g	a	pts	pim	gp	g	a	pts	pim
72-73	Hou	45	0	10	10	32	9	0	1	1	11
73-74	Hou	78	0	20	20	26	3	0	2	2	2
74-75	Ind	4	1	4	5	4					
totals		127	1	34	35	62	12	0	3	3	13

• Played in NHL: 1967-72, StL, 23-0-1-1-15

Al KARLANDER — Allan David Karlander
5-8 175 L 5 Nov 1946, Lac LaHache BC

year	team	gp	g	a	pts	pim	gp	g	a	pts	pim
73-74	NE	77	20	41	61	46	7	1	3	4	2
74-75	NE	48	7	14	21	2	5	0	3	3	0
75-76	Ind	79	16	28	44	36	3	0	0	0	4
76-77	Ind	65	17	28	45	23	6	2	1	3	0
totals		269	60	111	171	107	21	3	7	10	6

• Played in NHL: 1969-73, Det, 212-36-56-92-70

Dennis KASSIAN
5-11 170 L 14 Jul 1941, Vegreville AB

year	team	gp	g	a	pts	pim	gp	g	a	pts	pim
72-73	Alb	50	6	7	13	14					
totals		50	6	7	13	14					

Mike KEELER — Michael John Keeler
5-10 175 R 21 May 1950, Toronto ON

year	team	gp	g	a	pts	pim	gp	g	a	pts	pim
73-74	NE	1	0	0	0	0	1	0	0	0	0
totals		1	0	0	0	0	1	0	0	0	0

Jamie KENNEDY — James Roy Kennedy
5-9 175 R 7 Sep 1946, Dorchester NB

year	team	gp	g	a	pts	pim	gp	g	a	pts	pim
72-73	NY	52	4	6	10	11					
totals		52	4	6	10	11					

Murray KENNETT
5-10 175 L 28 Jul 1952, Kamloops BC

year	team	gp	g	a	pts	pim	gp	g	a	pts	pim
74-75	Ind	28	1	3	4	8					
	Edm	50	4	14	18	17					
75-76	Edm	28	3	4	7	14					
totals		106	8	21	29	39					

Murray KEOGAN — Murray Edward Keogan
5-10 175 L 14 Jan 1950, Biggar SK

year	team	gp	g	a	pts	pim	gp	g	a	pts	pim
74-75	Phx	78	35	29	64	68	5	0	1	1	0
75-76	Phx	8	0	2	2	4					
	Cgy	38	7	11	18	19					
totals		124	42	42	84	91	5	0	1	1	0

Dave KEON David Michael Keon
5-9 170 L 22 Mar 1940, Noranda PQ

year	team	gp	g	a	pts	pim	gp	g	a	pts	pim
75-76	Min	57	26	38	64	4					
	Ind	12	3	7	10	2	7	2	2	4	2
76-77	Min	42	13	38	51	2					
	NE	34	14	25	39	8	5	3	1	4	0
77-78	NE	77	24	38	62	2	14	5	11	16	4
78-79	NE	79	22	43	65	2	10	3	9	12	2
totals		**301**	**102**	**189**	**291**	**20**	**36**	**13**	**23**	**36**	**8**

• Played in NHL: 1960-75, 1979-82, Tor-Hart, 1296-396-590-986-117 • Stanley Cups: 1962, 1963, 1964, 1967 (Toronto) • Member, Hockey Hall of Fame

Doug KERSLAKE Douglas Robert Kerslake
5-11 200 R 23 Mar 1950, Saskatoon SK d. 2015

year	team	gp	g	a	pts	pim	gp	g	a	pts	pim
74-75	Edm	10	4	0	4	10					
75-76	Edm	13	1	1	2	4					
totals		**23**	**5**	**1**	**6**	**14**					

Veli-Pekka KETOLA
6-3 205 L 28 Mar 1948, Pori Finland

year	team	gp	g	a	pts	pim	gp	g	a	pts	pim
74-75	Wpg	74	23	28	51	25					
75-76	Wpg	80	32	36	68	32	13	7	5	12	2
76-77	Wpg	64	25	29	54	59					
	Cgy	17	4	6	10	2					
totals		**235**	**84**	**99**	**183**	**118**	**13**	**7**	**5**	**12**	**2**

• Played in NHL: 1981-82, Col, 44-9-5-14-4 • Member, Finland Olympic Team, 1968 & 1972

Kerry KETTER Kerry Kenneth Ketter
6-1 200 L 20 Sep 1947, Prince George BC

year	team	gp	g	a	pts	pim	gp	g	a	pts	pim
75-76	Edm	48	1	9	10	20					
totals		**48**	**1**	**9**	**10**	**20**					

• Played in NHL: 1972-73, Atl, 41-0-2-2-58

Steve KING Steven James King
5-9 180 R 8 Sep 1948, Toronto ON

year	team	gp	g	a	pts	pim	gp	g	a	pts	pim
72-73	Ott	69	18	34	52	28	5	0	1	1	7
73-74	Tor	67	14	22	36	26	12	0	3	3	11
totals		**136**	**32**	**56**	**88**	**54**	**17**	**0**	**4**	**4**	**18**

Gavin KIRK
5-10 165 L 6 Dec 1951, London England

year	team	gp	g	a	pts	pim	gp	g	a	pts	pim
72-73	Ott	78	28	40	68	54	5	2	3	5	12
73-74	Tor	78	20	48	68	44	12	2	4	6	4
74-75	Tor	78	15	58	73	69	6	5	6	11	2
75-76	Tor	62	29	38	67	32					
	Cgy	15	7	8	15	14	10	4	6	10	19
76-77	Bir	29	9	18	27	34					
	Edm	52	8	28	36	16	5	1	0	1	4
78-79	Bir	30	1	5	6	16					
totals		**422**	**117**	**243**	**360**	**279**	**38**	**14**	**19**	**33**	**41**

Billy KLATT William Gerald Klatt
5-11 180 R 16 Oct 1947, Minneapolis MN d. 2011

year	team	gp	g	a	pts	pim	gp	g	a	pts	pim
72-73	Min	78	36	22	58	22	5	1	3	4	5
73-74	Min	65	14	6	20	12	11	3	2	5	18
totals		**143**	**50**	**28**	**78**	**34**	**16**	**4**	**5**	**9**	**23**

Darrel KNIBBS Darrel Duane Knibbs
6-1 180 R 21 Sep 1949, Medicine Hat AB

year	team	gp	g	a	pts	pim	gp	g	a	pts	pim
72-73	Chi	41	3	8	11	0					
totals		**41**	**3**	**8**	**11**	**0**					

Keith KOKKOLA Keith Victor Kokkola
6-3 210 L 4 May 1949, Windsor ON d. 2004

year	team	gp	g	a	pts	pim	gp	g	a	pts	pim
74-75	Chi	33	0	2	2	69					
75-76	D-O	16	0	3	3	40					
76-77	Bir	5	0	0	0	21					
totals		**54**	**0**	**5**	**5**	**130**					

George KONIK George Samuel Konik
5-10 195 L 4 May 1934, Flin Flon MB

year	team	gp	g	a	pts	pim	gp	g	a	pts	pim
72-73	Min	54	4	12	16	34					
totals		**54**	**4**	**12**	**46**	**34**					

• Played in NHL: 1967-68, Pit, 52-7-8-15-26

Skip KRAKE Phillip Gordon Krake
5-11 170 R 14 Oct 1943, N Battleford SK

year	team	gp	g	a	pts	pim	gp	g	a	pts	pim
72-73	Cle	26	9	10	19	61	9	1	2	3	27
73-74	Cle	69	20	36	56	94	5	0	1	1	39
74-75	Cle	71	15	23	38	108	5	1	1	2	0
75-76	Edm	41	8	8	16	55					
totals		**207**	**52**	**77**	**129**	**318**	**19**	**2**	**4**	**6**	**66**

• Played in NHL: 1963-71, Bos-LA-Buf, 249-23-40-63-182

Reg KREZANSKI Reginald Krezanski
5-10 200 R 1 Jan 1948, New Westminster BC

year	team	gp	g	a	pts	pim	gp	g	a	pts	pim
74-75	SD	2	0	0	0	2					
totals		**2**	**0**	**0**	**0**	**2**					

Jarda KRUPICKA
5-10 170 L 15 Mar 1946, Brno Czechoslovakia

year	team	gp	g	a	pts	pim	gp	g	a	pts	pim
72-73	LA	6	1	0	1	2					
	NY	30	1	2	3	4					
totals		**36**	**2**	**2**	**4**	**6**					

Dave KRYSKOW David Roy Kryskow
5-10 175 L 25 Dec 1951, Edmonton AB

year	team	gp	g	a	pts	pim	gp	g	a	pts	pim
76-77	Cgy	45	16	17	33	47					
77-78	Wpg	71	20	21	41	16	9	4	4	8	2
totals		**116**	**36**	**38**	**74**	**63**	**9**	**4**	**4**	**8**	**2**

• Played in NHL: 1972-76, Chi-Det-Wash-Atl, 231-33-56-89-174

George KUZMICZ
6-1 200 L 24 May 1952, Montreal PQ

year	team	gp	g	a	pts	pim	gp	g	a	pts	pim
74-75	Tor	34	0	12	12	22					
75-76	Tor	1	0	0	0	0					
totals		**35**	**0**	**12**	**12**	**22**					

Gord LABOSSIERE Gordon William Labossiere
6-1 185 R 2 Jan 1940, St Boniface MB

year	team	gp	g	a	pts	pim	gp	g	a	pts	pim
72-73	Hou	77	36	60	96	56	6	1	4	5	8
73-74	Hou	67	19	36	55	30	14	7	9	16	20
74-75	Hou	76	23	34	57	40	13	6	7	13	4
75-76	Hou	80	24	32	56	18	17	2	8	10	14
totals		**300**	**102**	**162**	**264**	**144**	**50**	**16**	**28**	**44**	**46**

• Played in NHL: 1963-72, NYR-LA-Min, 215-44-62-106-75

Dan LABRAATEN
6-0 185 R 9 Jun 1951, Leksand Sweden

year	team	gp	g	a	pts	pim	gp	g	a	pts	pim
76-77	Wpg	64	24	27	51	21	20	7	17	24	15
77-78	Wpg	47	18	16	34	30	4	1	1	2	8
totals		**111**	**42**	**43**	**85**	**51**	**24**	**8**	**18**	**26**	**23**

• Played in NHL: 1978-82, Det-Cgy, 268-71-73-144-47

Francois LACOMBE
5-9 185 L 2 Feb 1948, Montreal PQ

year	team	gp	g	a	pts	pim	gp	g	a	pts	pim
72-73	Que	62	10	18	28	123					
73-74	Que	71	9	26	35	41					
74-75	Que	55	7	17	24	54	15	0	2	2	4
75-76	Cgy	71	3	28	31	62	8	0	0	0	2
76-77	Que	81	5	22	27	86	17	4	3	7	16
77-78	Que	22	1	7	8	12	10	1	4	5	2
78-79	Que	78	3	21	24	44	4	0	1	1	2
totals		**440**	**38**	**139**	**177**	**422**	**54**	**5**	**10**	**15**	**26**

• Played in NHL: 1968-71, 1979-80, Oak-Buf-Que, 78-2-17-19-54

Andre LACROIX — Andre Joseph Lacroix
5-8 175 L 5 Jun 1945, Lauzon PQ

year	team	gp	g	a	pts	pim	gp	g	a	pts	pim
72-73	Phi	78	50	74	124	83	4	0	2	2	18
73-74	NY-J	78	31	80	111	54					
74-75	SD	78	41	106	147	63	10	3	9	12	2
75-76	SD	80	29	72	101	42	11	4	6	10	4
76-77	SD	81	32	82	114	79	7	1	6	7	6
77-78	Hou	78	36	77	113	57	6	2	2	4	0
78-79	NE	78	32	56	88	34	10	4	4	8	0
totals		551	251	547	798	412	48	14	29	43	30

• Played in NHL: 1967-72, 1979-80, Phi-Chi-Hart, 325-79-119-198-44

Peter LAFRAMBOISE — Peter Alfred Laframboise
6-2 185 L 18 Jan 1950, Ottawa ON d. 2011

year	team	gp	g	a	pts	pim	gp	g	a	pts	pim
76-77	Edm	17	0	5	5	12					
totals		17	0	5	5	12					

• Played in NHL: 1971-75, Cal-Wash-Pit, 227-33-55-88-70

Jean-Guy LAGACE
5-8 175 R 5 Feb 1945, L'Abord a Plouffe PQ

year	team	gp	g	a	pts	pim	gp	g	a	pts	pim
76-77	Bir	78	2	25	27	110					
totals		78	2	25	27	110					

• Played in NHL: 1968-76, Pit-Buf-KC, 197-9-39-48-251

Pierre LAGACE
6-2 205 L 27 Oct 1957, Montreal PQ

year	team	gp	g	a	pts	pim	gp	g	a	pts	pim
77-78	Que	17	2	4	6	12	1	0	0	0	0
78-79	Que	21	0	1	1	12	3	0	1	1	2
totals		38	2	5	7	24	4	0	1	1	2

Floyd LAHACHE
5-10 175 R 17 Sep 1957, Caughnawaga PQ

year	team	gp	g	a	pts	pim	gp	g	a	pts	pim
77-78	Cin	11	0	3	3	13					
totals		11	0	3	3	13					

Bill LAING — William Laing
6-2 190 L 24 Mar 1953, Harris SK

year	team	gp	g	a	pts	pim	gp	g	a	pts	pim
74-75	Edm	43	2	4	6	32					
75-76	Edm	54	8	12	20	67					
totals		97	10	16	26	99					

Rick LALONDE — Richard Lalonde
6-0 200 R 19 Feb 1955, Ottawa ON

year	team	gp	g	a	pts	pim	gp	g	a	pts	pim
75-76	SD	2	0	0	0	0					
totals		2	0	0	0	0					

Dave LANGEVIN — David Langevin
6-2 200 L 15 May 1954, St Paul MN

year	team	gp	g	a	pts	pim	gp	g	a	pts	pim
76-77	Edm	77	7	16	23	94	5	2	1	3	9
77-78	Edm	62	6	22	28	90	5	0	2	2	10
78-79	Edm	77	6	21	27	76	13	0	1	1	25
totals		216	19	59	78	260	23	2	4	6	44

• Played in NHL: 1979-87, NYI-Min-LA, 513-12-107-119-530 • Stanley Cups: 1980, 1981, 1982, 1983 (NYI)

Rod LANGWAY — Rod Corry Langway
6-3 210 L 3 May 1957, Taiwan

year	team	gp	g	a	pts	pim	gp	g	a	pts	pim
77-78	Bir	52	3	18	21	52	4	0	0	0	9
totals		52	3	18	21	52	4	0	0	0	9

• Played in NHL: 1978-93, Mtl-Wash, 994-51-278-329-849 • Stanley Cup: 1979 (Montreal) • Member, Hockey Hall of Fame

Camille LAPIERRE
5-10 160 L 8 Feb 1951, Chicoutimi PQ

year	team	gp	g	a	pts	pim	gp	g	a	pts	pim
72-73	Phi	24	5	9	14	2	4	0	2	2	0
73-74	Van	9	0	3	3	0					
totals		33	5	12	17	2	4	0	2	2	0

Garry LARIVIERE — Garry Joseph Lariviere "Bimbo"
6-0 190 L 6 Dec 1954, St Catherines ON

year	team	gp	g	a	pts	pim	gp	g	a	pts	pim
74-75	Phx	4	0	1	1	28	1	0	0	0	0
75-76	Phx	79	7	17	24	100	5	0	2	2	2
76-77	Phx	61	7	23	30	48					
	Que	15	0	3	3	8	17	0	10	10	10
77-78	Que	80	7	49	56	78	11	3	2	5	4
78-79	Que	50	5	33	38	54	4	0	1	1	2
totals		289	26	126	152	316	38	3	15	18	18

• Played in NHL: 1979-83, Que-Edm, 219-6-57-63-167

Claude LAROSE
5-10 170 L 17 May 1955, St Jean PQ

year	team	gp	g	a	pts	pim	gp	g	a	pts	pim
75-76	Cin	79	28	24	52	19					
76-77	Cin	81	30	46	76	8	4	2	1	3	0
77-78	Cin	51	11	20	31	6					
	Ind	28	14	16	30	12					
78-79	Ind	13	5	8	13	0					
totals		252	88	114	202	45	4	2	1	3	0

• Played in NHL: 1979-82, NYR, 25-4-7-11-2

Paul LAROSE
5-8 155 R 11 Jan 1950, Noranda PQ

year	team	gp	g	a	pts	pim	gp	g	a	pts	pim
72-73	Que	28	0	7	7	7					
74-75	M-B	5	1	1	2	2					
totals		33	1	8	9	9					

Ray LAROSE
6-0 185 L 20 Nov 1941, Quebec PQ

year	team	gp	g	a	pts	pim	gp	g	a	pts	pim
72-73	Hou	68	1	10	11	25	8	0	0	0	2
73-74	NY-J	18	0	1	1	20					
totals		86	1	11	12	45	8	0	0	0	2

Don LARWAY — John Donald Larway
6-1 190 R 2 Feb 1954, Oak Lake MB

year	team	gp	g	a	pts	pim	gp	g	a	pts	pim
74-75	Hou	75	22	14	36	59	13	3	1	4	8
75-76	Hou	79	30	20	50	56	16	7	5	12	21
76-77	Hou	75	11	13	24	112	3	1	0	1	0
77-78	Hou	69	24	35	59	52	6	1	2	3	4
78-79	Ind	25	8	10	18	39					
totals		323	95	92	187	318	38	12	8	20	33

Mike LAUGHTON — Michael Frederic Laughton
6-2 200 L 21 Feb 1944, Nelson BC

year	team	gp	g	a	pts	pim	gp	g	a	pts	pim
72-73	NY	67	16	20	36	44					
73-74	NY-J	71	20	18	38	34					
74-75	SD	65	8	9	17	22	10	4	1	5	0
totals		203	44	47	91	100	10	4	1	5	0

• Played in NHL: 1967-71, Oak-Cal, 189-39-48-87-101

Brian LAVENDER — Brian James Lavender
6-0 180 L 20 Apr 1947, Edmonton AB

year	team	gp	g	a	pts	pim	gp	g	a	pts	pim
75-76	D-O	31	5	6	11	37					
totals		31	5	6	11	37					

• Played in NHL: 1971-75, StL-NYI-Det-Cal, 184-16-26-42-174

Danny LAWSON — Daniel Michael Lawson
5-11 185 R 30 Oct 1947, Toronto ON d. 2008

year	team	gp	g	a	pts	pim	gp	g	a	pts	pim
72-73	Phi	78	61	45	106	35	4	0	1	1	0
73-74	Van	78	50	38	88	14					
74-75	Van	78	33	43	76	19					
75-76	Cgy	80	44	52	96	46	9	4	4	8	19
76-77	Cgy	64	24	19	43	26					
	Wpg	14	6	7	13	2	13	2	4	6	6
totals		392	218	204	422	142	26	6	9	15	25

• Played in NHL: 1967-72, Det-Min-Buf, 219-28-29-57-61

J.-P. LEBLANC — Jean-Paul Leblanc
5-10 170 L 20 Oct 1946, S Durham PQ

year	team	gp	g	a	pts	pim	gp	g	a	pts	pim
72-73	LA	77	19	50	69	49	6	0	5	5	2
73-74	LA	78	20	46	66	58					
74-75	M-B	78	16	33	49	100					
75-76	D-O	15	1	5	6	25					
totals		248	56	134	190	232	6	0	5	5	2

• Played in NHL: 1968-69, 1975-79, Chi-Det, 153-14-30-44-87

Rene LECLERC Renald Leclerc "The Count"
5-11 170 R 12 Nov 1947, Ville de Vanier PQ

year	team	gp	g	a	pts	pim	gp	g	a	pts	pim
72-73	Que	60	24	28	52	111					
73-74	Que	58	17	27	44	84					
74-75	Que	72	18	32	50	85	14	7	7	14	41
75-76	Que	42	15	17	32	35					
	Ind	40	18	21	39	52	7	2	5	7	7
76-77	Ind	68	25	30	55	43	9	1	1	2	4
77-78	Ind	60	12	15	27	31					
78-79	Ind	22	5	7	12	12					
	Que	23	0	0	0	8	4	0	0	0	0
totals		445	134	177	311	461	34	10	13	23	52

• Played in NHL: 1968-71, Det, 88-10-11-21-105

Bob LEDUC Robert Joseph Leduc
5-10 185 L 24 May 1944, Sudbury ON

year	team	gp	g	a	pts	pim	gp	g	a	pts	pim
72-73	Ott	78	22	33	55	71	5	0	2	2	4
73-74	Tor	61	22	29	51	29	12	4	6	10	42
74-75	Tor	19	3	4	7	9					
totals		158	47	66	113	109	17	4	8	12	46

Richie LEDUC Richard Henri Leduc
5-11 170 L 24 Aug 1951, Ile Perrot PQ

year	team	gp	g	a	pts	pim	gp	g	a	pts	pim
74-75	Cle	78	35	31	66	122	5	0	2	2	2
75-76	Cle	79	36	22	58	76	3	2	1	3	2
76-77	Cin	81	52	55	107	75	4	1	3	4	16
77-78	Cin	54	27	31	58	44					
	Ind	28	10	15	25	38					
78-79	Ind	13	5	9	14	14					
	Que	61	30	32	62	30	4	0	2	2	0
totals		394	195	195	390	399	16	3	8	11	20

• Played in NHL: 1972-74, 1979-80, Bos-Que, 130-28-38-66-89

Barry LEGGE Barry Graham Legge
6-0 185 L 22 Oct 1954, Winnipeg MB

year	team	gp	g	a	pts	pim	gp	g	a	pts	pim
74-75	M-B	36	3	18	21	20					
75-76	D-O	40	6	8	14	15					
	Cle	35	0	7	7	22	3	0	1	1	12
76-77	Min	2	0	0	0	0					
	Cin	74	7	22	29	39	4	0	0	0	0
77-78	Cin	78	7	17	24	114					
78-79	Cin	80	3	8	11	131	3	0	4	4	0
totals		345	26	80	106	341	10	0	5	5	12

• Played in NHL: 1979-82, Que-Wpg, 107-1-11-12-144

Randy LEGGE Norman Randall Legge
5-11 185 R 16 Dec 1945, Newmarket ON

year	team	gp	g	a	pts	pim	gp	g	a	pts	pim
74-75	M-B	78	1	14	15	69					
75-76	Wpg	1	0	0	0	0					
	Cle	44	1	8	9	28	3	0	0	0	0
76-77	SD	69	1	9	10	69	7	0	0	0	18
totals		192	3	31	34	166	10	0	0	0	18

• Played in NHL: 1972-73, NYR, 12-0-2-2-2

Bob LEITER Robert Edward Leiter
5-9 170 L 22 Mar 1941, Winnipeg MB

year	team	gp	g	a	pts	pim	gp	g	a	pts	pim
75-76	Cgy	51	17	17	34	8	3	2	0	2	0
totals		51	17	17	34	8	3	2	0	2	0

• Played in NHL: 1962-76, Bos-Pit-Atl, 447-98-126-224-144

Richard LEMIEUX Richard Bernard Lemieux
5-8 165 L 19 Apr 1951, Temiscamingue Sur PQ

year	team	gp	g	a	pts	pim	gp	g	a	pts	pim
76-77	Cgy	33	6	11	17	9					
totals		33	6	11	17	9					

• Played in NHL: 1971-76, Van-KC-Atl, 274-39-82-121-132

Gerry LEROUX Gerald Leroux
5-7 160 L 9 Jun 1958, St Bernardin ON

year	team	gp	g	a	pts	pim	gp	g	a	pts	pim
78-79	Ind	10	0	3	3	2					
totals		10	0	3	3	2					

Bill LESUK William Anton Lesuk
5-9 185 L 1 Nov 1946, Moose Jaw SK

year	team	gp	g	a	pts	pim	gp	g	a	pts	pim
75-76	Wpg	81	15	21	36	92	13	2	2	4	8
76-77	Wpg	78	14	27	41	85	18	2	1	3	22
77-78	Wpg	80	9	18	27	48	9	2	5	7	12
78-79	Wpg	79	17	15	32	44	10	1	3	4	6
totals		318	55	81	136	269	50	7	11	18	48

• Played in NHL: 1968-75, 1979-80, Bos-Phi-LA-Wash-Wpg, 388-44-63-107-368 • Stanley Cup: 1970 (Boston)

Rick LEY Richard Norman Ley
5-9 190 L 2 Nov 1948, Orillia ON

year	team	gp	g	a	pts	pim	gp	g	a	pts	pim
72-73	NE	76	3	27	30	108	15	3	7	10	24
73-74	NE	72	6	35	41	148	7	1	5	6	18
74-75	NE	62	6	36	42	50	6	1	1	2	32
75-76	NE	67	8	30	38	78	17	1	4	5	49
76-77	NE	55	2	21	23	102	5	0	4	4	4
77-78	NE	73	3	41	44	95	14	1	8	9	4
78-79	NE	73	7	20	27	135	9	0	4	4	11
totals		478	35	210	245	716	73	7	33	40	142

• Played in NHL: 1968-72, 1979-81, Tor-Hart, 310-12-72-84-528

Bob LIDDINGTON Robert Allen Liddington
5-11 175 L 15 Sep 1948, Calgary AB

year	team	gp	g	a	pts	pim	gp	g	a	pts	pim
72-73	Chi	78	20	11	31	24					
73-74	Chi	73	26	21	47	20	18	6	5	11	11
74-75	Chi	78	23	18	41	27					
75-76	D-O	35	7	8	15	14					
	Hou	2	0	0	0	2					
76-77	Phx	80	20	24	44	28					
totals		346	96	82	178	115	18	6	5	11	11

• Played in NHL: 1970-71, Tor, 11-0-1-1-2

Len LILYHOLM "Wolfman"
5-8 170 - 1 Apr 1941, Minneapolis MN

year	team	gp	g	a	pts	pim	gp	g	a	pts	pim
72-73	Min	77	8	13	21	37	5	1	0	1	0
totals		77	8	13	21	37	5	1	0	1	0

• Member, United States Olympic Team, 1968

Mats LINDH
6-1 180 L 12 Sep 1947, Orsa Sweden

year	team	gp	g	a	pts	pim	gp	g	a	pts	pim
75-76	Wpg	65	19	15	34	12	13	2	2	4	4
76-77	Wpg	73	14	17	31	2	20	2	7	9	2
totals		138	33	32	65	14	33	4	9	13	6

Doug LINDSKOG
6-1 185 L 12 Aug 1955, Red Deer AB

year	team	gp	g	a	pts	pim	gp	g	a	pts	pim
76-77	Cgy	2	0	0	0	2					
totals		2	0	0	0	2					

Willy LINDSTROM Bo Morgan Willy Lindstrom
6-0 180 L 5 May 1951, Grums Sweden

year	team	gp	g	a	pts	pim	gp	g	a	pts	pim
75-76	Wpg	81	23	36	59	32	11	4	7	11	2
76-77	Wpg	79	44	36	80	37	20	9	6	15	22
77-78	Wpg	77	30	30	60	42	8	3	4	7	17
78-79	Wpg	79	26	36	62	22	10	10	5	15	9
totals		316	123	138	261	133	49	26	22	48	50

• Played in NHL: 1979-87, Wpg-Edm-Pit, 582-161-162-323-200 • Stanley Cups: 1984, 1985 (Edmonton)

Ken LINSEMAN
5-10 175 L 11 Aug 1958, Kingston ON

year	team	gp	g	a	pts	pim	gp	g	a	pts	pim
77-78	Bir	71	38	38	76	126	5	2	2	4	15
totals		71	38	38	76	126	5	2	2	4	15

• Played in NHL: 1978-92, Phi-Edm-Bos-Tor, 860-256-551-807-1727 • Stanley Cup: 1984 (Edmonton)

Owen LLOYD
5-11 195 L 30 Apr 1957, Vancouver BC

year	team	gp	g	a	pts	pim	gp	g	a	pts	pim
77-78	Edm	3	0	1	1	4					
totals		3	0	1	1	4					

Jacques LOCAS — Jacques Romeo Locas
5-8 170 L 7 Jan 1954, St Jerome PQ d. 2006

year	team	gp	g	a	pts	pim	gp	g	a	pts	pim
74-75	M-B	12	1	4	5	4					
	Ind	11	0	1	1	2					
75-76	Cin	80	27	46	73	70					
76-77	Cin	45	18	13	31	27					
	Cgy	22	3	4	7	2					
77-78	Cin	17	0	2	2	6					
totals		187	49	70	119	111					

Dan LODBOA — Daniel Stephen Lodboa
5-9 175 L 25 Sep 1946, St Catherines ON

year	team	gp	g	a	pts	pim	gp	g	a	pts	pim
72-73	Chi	59	15	18	33	16					
totals		59	15	18	33	16					

Mark LOMENDA — Mark Wesley Thomas Lomenda
6-0 185 R 14 Apr 1954, Esterhazy SK

year	team	gp	g	a	pts	pim	gp	g	a	pts	pim
74-75	Chi	69	16	33	49	21					
75-76	D-O	37	6	16	22	11					
	Ind	2	0	0	0	0					
76-77	Ind	56	9	12	21	14	9	3	1	4	17
totals		164	31	61	92	46	9	3	1	4	17

Barry LONG — Barry Kenneth Long
6-2 210 L 3 Jan 1949, Red Deer AB

year	team	gp	g	a	pts	pim	gp	g	a	pts	pim
74-75	Edm	78	20	40	60	116					
75-76	Edm	78	10	32	42	66	4	0	0	0	4
76-77	Edm	2	0	1	1	2					
	Wpg	71	9	38	47	54	20	1	5	6	10
77-78	Wpg	78	7	24	31	42	9	0	5	5	6
78-79	Wpg	79	5	36	41	42	10	2	3	5	0
totals		386	51	171	222	322	43	3	13	16	20

• Played in NHL: 1972-74, 1979-82, LA-Det-Wpg, 280-11-68-79-250

Ted LONG — Edward Long
6-1 185 L 26 Jan 1955, Woodstock ON

year	team	gp	g	a	pts	pim	gp	g	a	pts	pim
76-77	Cin	1	0	0	0	0					
totals		1	0	0	0	0					

Bernie LUKOWICH — Bernard Joseph Lukowich
6-0 190 R 18 Mar 1952, N Battleford SK

year	team	gp	g	a	pts	pim	gp	g	a	pts	pim
75-76	Cgy	15	5	2	7	18	10	4	3	7	8
76-77	Cgy	6	0	1	1	0					
totals		21	5	3	8	18	10	4	3	7	8

• Cousin of Morris Lukowich • Played in NHL: 1973-75, Pit-StL, 79-13-15-28-34

Morris LUKOWICH — Morris Eugene Lukowich
5-8 165 L 1 Jun 1956, Saskatoon SK

year	team	gp	g	a	pts	pim	gp	g	a	pts	pim
76-77	Hou	62	27	18	45	67	11	6	4	10	19
77-78	Hou	80	40	35	75	131	6	1	2	3	17
78-79	Wpg	80	65	34	99	119	10	8	7	15	21
totals		222	132	87	219	317	27	15	13	28	57

• Cousin of Bernie Lukowich • Played in NHL: 1979-87, Wpg-Bos-LA, 582-199-219-418-584

Chuck LUKSA — Charles Luksa
6-1 190 L 15 Feb 1954, Toronto ON

year	team	gp	g	a	pts	pim	gp	g	a	pts	pim
78-79	Cin	78	8	12	20	116	3	0	0	0	7
totals		78	8	12	20	116	3	0	0	0	7

• Played in NHL: 1979-80, Hart, 8-0-1-1-4

Larry LUND — Lawrence Lund
6-0 190 R 9 Sep 1940, Penticton BC

year	team	gp	g	a	pts	pim	gp	g	a	pts	pim
72-73	Hou	77	21	45	66	120	10	3	7	10	24
73-74	Hou	75	33	53	86	109	14	9	14	23	56
74-75	Hou	78	33	75	108	68	13	5	13	18	13
75-76	Hou	73	24	49	73	50	5	1	1	2	4
76-77	Hou	80	29	38	67	36	11	2	8	10	17
77-78	Hou	76	9	17	26	36	6	0	2	2	2
totals		459	149	277	426	419	59	20	45	65	116

• Highest WHA point total of all players not to have played in the NHL.

Len LUNDE — Leonard Melvin Lunde
6-1 195 R 13 Nov 1936, Campbell River BC d. 2010

year	team	gp	g	a	pts	pim	gp	g	a	pts	pim
73-74	Edm	71	26	22	48	8	5	0	1	1	0
totals		71	26	22	48	8	5	0	1	1	0

• Played in NHL: 1958-71, Det-Chi-Min-Van, 321-39-83-122-75

George LYLE — George Wallace Lyle
6-2 205 L 24 Nov 1953, N Vancouver BC

year	team	gp	g	a	pts	pim	gp	g	a	pts	pim
76-77	NE	75	39	33	72	62	5	1	0	1	4
77-78	NE	68	30	24	54	74	12	2	1	3	13
78-79	NE	59	17	18	35	54	9	3	5	8	25
totals		202	86	75	161	190	26	6	6	12	42

• Played in NHL: 1979-83, Det-Hart, 99-24-38-62-51

Blair MacDONALD — Blair Joseph MacDonald "BJ"
5-10 180 R 17 Nov 1953, Cornwall ON

year	team	gp	g	a	pts	pim	gp	g	a	pts	pim
73-74	Edm	78	21	24	45	34	5	4	2	6	2
74-75	Edm	72	22	24	46	14					
75-76	Edm	29	7	5	12	8					
	Ind	56	19	11	30	14	7	0	0	0	0
76-77	Ind	81	34	30	64	28	9	7	8	15	4
77-78	Edm	80	34	34	68	11	5	1	1	2	0
78-79	Edm	80	34	37	71	44	13	8	10	18	6
totals		476	171	165	336	153	39	20	21	41	12

• Played in NHL: 1979-83, Edm-Van, 219-91-100-191-65

Bruce MacGREGOR — Bruce Cameron MacGregor
5-10 180 R 26 Apr 1941, Edmonton AB

year	team	gp	g	a	pts	pim	gp	g	a	pts	pim
74-75	Edm	72	24	28	52	10					
75-76	Edm	63	13	10	23	13					
totals		135	37	38	75	23					

• Played in NHL: 1960-74, Det-NYR, 893-213-257-470-217

Gary MacGREGOR — Gary George MacGregor
5-9 170 L 21 Sep 1954, Kingston ON d. 1995

year	team	gp	g	a	pts	pim	gp	g	a	pts	pim
74-75	Chi	78	42	34	76	26					
75-76	D-O	38	16	14	30	18					
	Cle	35	5	3	8	6	3	0	0	0	4
76-77	Ind	16	0	5	5	4					
	NE	30	8	8	16	4					
77-78	Edm	37	11	2	13	29					
78-79	Ind	17	8	4	12	0					
totals		251	90	70	160	87	3	0	0	0	4

Al MacKENZIE — Alan MacKenzie
5-10 175 R 2 Feb 1952, Windsor ON

year	team	gp	g	a	pts	pim	gp	g	a	pts	pim
73-74	Chi	2	0	0	0	0					
totals		2	0	0	0	0					

Paul MacKINNON — Paul Gregory MacKinnon
6-0 190 R 6 Nov 1958, Brantford ON

year	team	gp	g	a	pts	pim	gp	g	a	pts	pim
78-79	Wpg	73	2	15	17	70	10	2	5	7	4
totals		73	2	15	17	70	10	2	5	7	4

• Played in NHL: 1979-84, Wash, 147-5-23-28-91

Bob MacMILLAN — Robert Lea MacMillan
5-10 175 L 3 Dec 1952, Charlottetown PEI

year	team	gp	g	a	pts	pim	gp	g	a	pts	pim
72-73	Min	75	13	27	40	48	5	0	3	3	0
73-74	Min	78	14	34	48	81	11	2	3	5	4
totals		153	27	61	88	129	16	2	6	8	4

• Played in NHL: 1974-85, NYR-StL-Atl-Cgy-Col-NJ-Chi, 753-228-349-577-260

Bernie MacNEIL — Stephen Bernard MacNeil
5-11 180 L 7 Mar 1950, Sudbury ON

year	team	gp	g	a	pts	pim	gp	g	a	pts	pim
72-73	LA	42	4	7	11	48	3	0	0	0	4
75-76	Cin	77	15	12	27	83					
totals		119	19	19	38	131	3	0	0	0	4

• Played in NHL: 1973-74, StL, 4-0-0-0-0

Ralph MacSWEYN — Donald Ralph MacSweyn
5-11 195 R 8 Sep 1942, Hawkesbury ON d. 1995

year	team	gp	g	a	pts	pim	gp	g	a	pts	pim
72-73	LA	78	0	23	23	39	6	1	2	3	4
73-74	LA	13	0	3	3	6					
	Van	56	2	18	20	52					
totals		147	2	44	46	97	6	1	2	3	4

• Played in NHL: 1967-72, Phi, 47-0-5-5-10

Dean MAGEE
6-1 210 - 29 Apr 1955, Banff AB

year	team	gp	g	a	pts	pim	gp	g	a	pts	pim
78-79	Ind	5	0	1	1	10					
totals		5	0	1	1	10					

• Played in NHL: 1977-78, Min, 7-0-0-0-4

Darryl MAGGS — Darryl John Maggs
6-1 195 R 6 Apr 1949, Victoria BC

year	team	gp	g	a	pts	pim	gp	g	a	pts	pim
73-74	Chi	78	8	22	30	148	18	3	5	8	71
74-75	Chi	77	6	27	33	137					
75-76	D-O	41	4	23	27	42					
	Ind	36	5	16	21	40	7	1	0	1	20
76-77	Ind	81	16	55	71	114	9	1	4	5	4
77-78	Ind	51	6	15	21	30					
	Cin	11	2	5	7	7					
78-79	Cin	27	4	14	18	22					
totals		402	51	177	228	540	34	5	9	14	95

• Played in NHL: 1971-73, 1979-80, Chi-Cal-Tor, 135-14-19-33-54

Frank MAHOVLICH — Francis William Mahovlich "The Big M"
6-1 205 L 10 Jan 1938, Timmins ON

year	team	gp	g	a	pts	pim	gp	g	a	pts	pim
74-75	Tor	73	38	44	82	27	6	3	0	3	2
75-76	Tor	75	34	55	89	14					
76-77	Bir	17	3	20	23	12					
77-78	Bir	72	14	24	38	22	3	1	1	2	0
totals		237	89	143	232	75	9	4	1	5	2

• Played in NHL: 1956-74, Tor-Det-Mtl, 1181-533-570-1103-1056 • Stanley Cups: 1962, 1963, 1964, 1967 (Toronto), 1971, 1973 (Montreal) • Member, Hockey Hall of Fame

Peter MARA — Peter John Mara
5-6 150 L 5 Jul 1947, Point Edward ON

year	team	gp	g	a	pts	pim	gp	g	a	pts	pim
74-75	Chi	57	17	21	38	16					
75-76	D-O	40	3	7	10	8					
totals		97	20	28	48	24					

Gilles MAROTTE — Jean-Gilles Marotte "Captain Crunch"
5-9 195 L 7 Jun 1945, Montreal PQ d. 2005

year	team	gp	g	a	pts	pim	gp	g	a	pts	pim
77-78	Cin	29	1	7	8	58					
	Ind	44	2	13	15	18					
totals		73	3	20	23	76					

• Played in NHL: 1965-77, Bos-Chi-LA-NYR-StL, 808-56-265-321-919

Peter MARRIN
5-10 160 R 8 Aug 1953, Toronto ON

year	team	gp	g	a	pts	pim	gp	g	a	pts	pim
73-74	Tor	31	1	4	5	4	3	0	1	1	2
74-75	Tor	4	3	1	4	0	6	0	4	4	2
75-76	Tor	64	22	16	38	16					
76-77	Bir	79	23	37	60	36					
77-78	Bir	80	28	43	71	53	5	0	3	3	2
78-79	Bir	20	4	11	15	18					
totals		278	81	112	193	127	14	0	8	8	6

Jim MARSH — Donald James Marsh
6-0 180 L 9 Jul 1951, Quesnel BC

year	team	gp	g	a	pts	pim	gp	g	a	pts	pim
76-77	Bir	1	0	0	0	0					
totals		1	0	0	0	0					

Peter MARSH — Peter William Marsh
6-0 170 L 21 Dec 1956, Halifax NS

year	team	gp	g	a	pts	pim	gp	g	a	pts	pim
76-77	Cin	73	23	28	51	52	4	2	0	2	0
77-78	Cin	74	25	25	50	123					
78-79	Cin	80	43	23	66	95	3	1	0	1	0
totals		227	91	76	167	270	7	3	0	3	0

• Played in NHL: 1979-84, Wpg-Chi, 278-48-71-119-224

Tom MARTIN — Thomas Raymond Martin
5-9 170 R 16 Oct 1947, Toronto ON

year	team	gp	g	a	pts	pim	gp	g	a	pts	pim
72-73	Ott	75	19	27	46	27	5	0	5	5	2
73-74	Tor	74	25	32	57	14	12	7	3	10	2
74-75	Tor	64	15	17	32	18	5	1	5	6	0
totals		213	59	76	135	59	22	8	13	21	4

• Played in NHL: 1967-68, Tor, 3-1-0-1-0

Larry MAVETY — Lawrence Douglas Mavety
5-11 185 R 29 May 1942, Woodstock ON

year	team	gp	g	a	pts	pim	gp	g	a	pts	pim
72-73	LA	2	1	0	1	2					
	Phi	4	0	0	0	14					
	Chi	67	9	40	49	73					
73-74	Chi	77	15	36	51	157	18	4	8	12	46
74-75	Chi	57	10	22	32	126					
	Tor	17	0	9	9	24	6	0	3	3	6
75-76	D-O	14	0	4	4	14					
76-77	Ind	10	2	2	4	8					
totals		248	37	113	150	418	24	4	11	15	52

Bryan MAXWELL — Bryan Clifford Maxwell
6-3 210 L 7 Sep 1955, Lethbridge AB

year	team	gp	g	a	pts	pim	gp	g	a	pts	pim
75-76	Cle	73	3	14	17	177	2	0	1	1	4
76-77	Cin	34	1	8	9	29	4	0	0	0	29
77-78	NE	17	2	1	3	11					
totals		124	6	23	29	217	6	0	1	1	33

• Played in NHL: 1977-85, Min-StL-Wpg-Pit, 331-18-77-95-745

Jim MAYER — James Patric Mayer
6-0 190 R 30 Oct 1954, Capreol ON

year	team	gp	g	a	pts	pim	gp	g	a	pts	pim
76-77	Cgy	21	2	3	5	0					
77-78	NE	51	11	9	20	21					
78-79	Edm	2	0	0	0	0					
totals		74	13	12	25	21					

• Played in NHL: 1979-80, NYR, 4-0-0-0-0

John MAZUR
5-10 175 L 1 Jun 1954, -

year	team	gp	g	a	pts	pim	gp	g	a	pts	pim
77-78	Hou	1	0	0	0	0					
totals		1	0	0	0	0					

Bob McANEELEY — Robert William McAneeley
5-8 175 L 7 Nov 1950, Cranbrook BC

year	team	gp	g	a	pts	pim	gp	g	a	pts	pim
72-73	Alb	51	5	7	12	24					
73-74	Edm	52	12	11	23	49	4	1	0	1	0
75-76	Edm	71	12	16	28	61	3	1	0	1	0
totals		174	29	34	63	134	7	2	0	2	0

• Brother of Ted McAneeley

Ted McANEELEY — Edward Joseph McAneeley
5-9 185 L 7 Nov 1950, Cranbrook BC

year	team	gp	g	a	pts	pim	gp	g	a	pts	pim
75-76	Edm	79	2	17	19	71	4	0	0	0	0
totals		79	2	17	19	71	4	0	0	0	0

• Brother of Bob McAneeley • Played in NHL: 1972-75, Cal, 158-8-35-43-141

Dunc McCALLUM — Duncan Selby McCallum
6-1 193 R 29 Mar 1940, Flin Flon MB d. 1993

year	team	gp	g	a	pts	pim	gp	g	a	pts	pim
72-73	Hou	69	9	20	29	112	10	2	3	5	6
74-75	Chi	31	0	10	10	24					
totals		100	9	30	39	136	10	2	3	5	6

• Played in NHL: 1965-71, NYR-Pit, 187-14-35-49-230 • Missed all of 1973-74 season due to broken leg suffered in pre-season game against Los Angeles

Ted McCASKILL — Edward Joseph McCaskill
6-1 195 L 29 Oct 1936, Kapuskasing ON d. 2016

year	team	gp	g	a	pts	pim	gp	g	a	pts	pim
72-73	LA	73	11	11	22	150	6	2	3	5	12
73-74	LA	18	2	2	4	63					
totals		91	13	13	26	213	6	2	3	5	12

• Played in NHL: 1967-68, Min, 4-0-2-2-0

Jim McCRIMMON James John McCrimmon
6-2 220 L 29 May 1953, Ponoka AB

year	team	gp	g	a	pts	pim	gp	g	a	pts	pim
73-74	Edm	75	2	3	5	106					
74-75	Edm	34	1	5	6	50					
75-76	Cgy	5	0	0	0	2					
totals		114	3	8	11	158					

• Played in NHL: 1974-75, StL, 2-0-0-0-0

Don McCULLOCH Donald McCulloch
6-2 190 L 23 Mar 1951, Little Current SK

year	team	gp	g	a	pts	pim	gp	g	a	pts	pim
74-75	Van	51	1	9	10	42					
totals		51	1	9	10	42					

Ab McDONALD Alvin Bryan McDonald
6-2 195 L 18 Feb 1936, Winnipeg MB

year	team	gp	g	a	pts	pim	gp	g	a	pts	pim
72-73	Wpg	77	17	24	41	16	14	2	5	7	2
73-74	Wpg	70	12	17	29	8	4	0	1	1	2
totals		147	29	41	70	24	18	2	6	8	4

• Played in NHL: 1957-72, Mtl-Chi-Bos-Det-Pit-StL, 762-182-248-430-200 • Stanley Cups: 1958, 1959, 1960, 1961 (Montreal)

Brian McDONALD Bryan Harold McDonald
5-11 190 R 23 Mar 1945, Toronto ON

year	team	gp	g	a	pts	pim	gp	g	a	pts	pim
72-73	Hou	71	20	20	40	78	10	3	0	3	16
73-74	LA	56	22	30	52	54					
74-75	M-B	18	3	5	8	15					
	Ind	47	14	15	29	19					
75-76	Ind	62	16	18	34	54	7	0	1	1	12
76-77	Ind	50	15	13	28	48	9	3	4	7	33
totals		304	90	101	191	268	26	6	5	11	61

• Played in NHL: 1967-71, Chi-Buf, 12-0-0-0-29

Al McDONOUGH James Allison McDonough
6-0 165 R 6 Jun 1950, St Catherines ON

year	team	gp	g	a	pts	pim	gp	g	a	pts	pim
74-75	Cle	78	34	30	64	27	5	2	1	3	2
75-76	Cle	80	23	22	45	19	3	1	0	1	2
76-77	Min	42	9	21	30	6					
totals		200	66	73	139	52	8	3	1	4	4

• Played in NHL: 1970-74, 1977-78, LA-Pit-Atl-Det, 237-73-88-161-73

Dick McGLYNN Richard Anthony McGlynn
6-2 185 R 19 Jul 1948, Medford MA

year	team	gp	g	a	pts	pim	gp	g	a	pts	pim
72-73	Chi	30	0	0	0	12					
totals		30	0	0	0	12					

• Member, United States Olympic Team, 1972

Ray McKAY Raymond Owen McKay
6-4 185 L 22 Aug 1946, Edmonton AB

year	team	gp	g	a	pts	pim	gp	g	a	pts	pim
74-75	Edm	69	8	20	28	47					
75-76	Cle	68	3	10	13	44	3	0	0	0	4
76-77	Min	42	2	9	11	28					
	Bir	19	0	1	1	11					
77-78	Edm	14	1	4	5	4	4	0	1	1	4
totals		212	14	44	58	134	7	0	1	1	8

• Played in NHL: 1968-74, Chi-Buf-Cal, 140-2-16-18-102

Brian McKENZIE Brian Stewart McKenzie
5-10 170 L 16 Mar 1951, St Catherines ON

year	team	gp	g	a	pts	pim	gp	g	a	pts	pim
73-74	Edm	78	18	20	38	66	5	0	1	1	0
74-75	Ind	9	1	0	1	6					
totals		87	19	20	39	72	5	0	1	1	0

• Played in NHL: 1970-71, Pit, 6-1-1-2-4

John McKENZIE John Albert McKenzie "Pie"
5-9 180 R 12 Dec 1937, High River AB

year	team	gp	g	a	pts	pim	gp	g	a	pts	pim
72-73	Phi	60	28	50	78	157	4	3	1	4	8
73-74	Van	45	14	38	52	71					
74-75	Van	74	23	37	60	84					
75-76	Min	57	21	26	47	48					
	Cin	12	3	10	13	6					
76-77	Min	40	17	13	30	52					
	NE	34	11	19	30	25	5	2	1	3	8
77-78	NE	79	27	29	56	61	14	6	6	12	6
78-79	NE	76	19	28	47	115	10	3	7	10	10
totals		477	163	250	413	619	33	14	15	29	32

• Played in NHL: 1958-72, Chi-Det-NYR-Bos, 691-206-268-474-917
• Stanley Cups: 1970, 1972 (Boston)

Al McLEOD Allan Sidney McLeod
5-11 195 L 17 Jun 1949, Medicine Hat AB

year	team	gp	g	a	pts	pim	gp	g	a	pts	pim
74-75	Phx	77	3	16	19	98	5	0	4	4	4
75-76	Phx	80	2	17	19	82	5	0	2	2	4
76-77	Phx	29	1	5	6	35					
	Hou	51	7	21	28	20	10	1	3	4	9
77-78	Hou	80	2	22	24	54	6	1	0	1	2
78-79	Ind	25	0	11	11	22					
totals		342	15	93	108	311	26	2	9	11	19

• Played in NHL: 1973-74, Det, 26-2-2-4-24

Mike McMAHON Michael William McMahon, Jr. "Black Mike"
5-11 180 L 30 Aug 1941, Quebec City PQ d. 2013

year	team	gp	g	a	pts	pim	gp	g	a	pts	pim
72-73	Min	75	12	39	51	87	5	0	5	5	2
73-74	Min	71	10	35	45	82	11	1	7	8	9
74-75	Min	54	5	15	20	42	7	0	1	1	0
75-76	SD	69	2	12	14	38	9	0	1	1	2
totals		269	29	101	130	249	32	1	14	15	13

• Played in NHL: 1963-72, NYR-Min-Chi-Det-Pit-Buf, 224-15-68-83-171

Rob McMANAMA Robert S. McManama
6-0 180 L 7 Oct 1951, Belmont MA

year	team	gp	g	a	pts	pim	gp	g	a	pts	pim
75-76	NE	37	3	10	13	28	12	4	3	7	4
totals		37	3	10	13	28	12	4	3	7	4

• Played in NHL: 1973-76, Pit, 99-11-25-36-28

Jim McMASTERS James Dean McMasters
5-10 195 L 20 Sep 1952, High River AB

year	team	gp	g	a	pts	pim	gp	g	a	pts	pim
72-73	Cle	76	1	7	8	37	9	0	1	1	6
73-74	Cle	9	0	0	0	4					
totals		85	1	7	8	41	9	0	1	1	6

Dale McMULLEN
5-10 175 L 13 Mar 1955, Proctor BC

year	team	gp	g	a	pts	pim	gp	g	a	pts	pim
77-78	Edm	1	0	0	0	0					
totals		1	0	0	0	0					

Mike McNAMARA
5-9 175 L 28 Mar 1949, Montreal PQ

year	team	gp	g	a	pts	pim	gp	g	a	pts	pim
72-73	Que	19	0	0	0	5					
totals		19	0	0	0	5					

Pete McNAMEE Peter Charles McNamee
5-11 200 L 11 Sep 1950, Jamaica

year	team	gp	g	a	pts	pim	gp	g	a	pts	pim
73-74	Van	3	0	0	0	0					
74-75	Van	11	2	1	3	15					
	Phx	55	9	19	28	77	5	1	0	1	2
75-76	Phx	14	1	2	3	32					
	SD	51	2	3	5	27	11	0	1	1	28
76-77	SD	41	3	6	9	38	2	0	0	0	2
totals		175	17	31	48	189	18	1	1	2	32

Gerry MEEHAN Gerry Marcus Meehan
6-2 200 L 3 Sep 1946, Toronto ON

year	team	gp	g	a	pts	pim	gp	g	a	pts	pim
78-79	Cin	2	0	0	0	0					
totals		2	0	0	0	0					

• Played in NHL: 1968-79, Tor-Buf-Van-Atl-Wash, 670-180-243-423-111

Denis MELOCHE — Denis Philippe Meloche
5-9 175 L 19 Jun 1952, Montreal PQ

year	team	gp	g	a	pts	pim	gp	g	a	pts	pim
72-73	Phi	4	1	1	2	0					
73-74	Van	41	6	13	19	18					
totals		45	7	14	21	18					

Chris MELOFF — Christopher Meloff
5-11 180 L 7 May 1952, Toronto ON

year	team	gp	g	a	pts	pim	gp	g	a	pts	pim
72-73	Ott	28	1	6	7	40					
totals		28	1	6	7	40					

Barry MELROSE — Barry James Melrose
6-0 205 R 15 Jul 1956, Kelvington SK

year	team	gp	g	a	pts	pim	gp	g	a	pts	pim
76-77	Cin	29	1	4	5	8	2	0	0	0	2
77-78	Cin	69	2	9	11	113					
78-79	Cin	80	2	14	16	222	3	0	1	1	8
totals		178	5	27	32	343	5	0	1	1	10

• Played in NHL: 1979-86, Wpg-Tor-Det, 300-10-23-33-728

Vic MERCREDI — Victor Dennis Mercredi
5-10 185 L 31 Mar 1953, Yellowknife NWT

year	team	gp	g	a	pts	pim	gp	g	a	pts	pim
75-76	Cgy	3	0	0	0	29					
totals		3	0	0	0	29					

• Played in NHL: 1974-75, Atl, 2-0-0-0-0

Barry MERRELL — Barry Lee Merrell
6-1 180 R 16 May 1945, Dauphin MB

year	team	gp	g	a	pts	pim	gp	g	a	pts	pim
76-77	Edm	10	1	3	4	0					
totals		10	1	3	4	0					

Mark MESSIER — Mark Douglas Messier
6-1 190 R 18 Jan 1961, Edmonton AB

year	team	gp	g	a	pts	pim	gp	g	a	pts	pim
78-79	Ind	5	0	0	0	0					
	Cin	47	1	10	11	58	3	0	0	0	0
totals		52	1	10	11	58	3	0	0	0	0

• Played in NHL: 1979-2004, Edm-NYR-Van, 1756-694-1193-1887-1910 • Stanley Cups: 1984, 1985, 1987, 1988, 1990 (Edmonton), 1994 (NY Rangers) • Was the last former WHA player active in the NHL and the only one to play into the new millennium • Member, Hockey Hall of Fame.

Garry METHE — Gerald Paul Methe
5-10 170 L 12 Dec 1951, Willowdale ON

year	team	gp	g	a	pts	pim	gp	g	a	pts	pim
74-75	NE	5	0	1	1	4					
totals		5	0	1	1	4					

Joe MICHELETTI — Joseph Robert Micheletti
6-0 185 L 24 Oct 1954, Hibbing MN

year	team	gp	g	a	pts	pim	gp	g	a	pts	pim
76-77	Cgy	14	3	3	6	10					
77-78	Edm	56	14	34	48	56	5	0	2	2	4
78-79	Edm	72	14	33	47	85	13	0	9	9	2
totals		142	31	70	101	151	18	0	11	11	6

• Played in NHL: 1979-82, StL-Col, 158-11-60-71-114

John MIGNEAULT — John Conn Migneault "J.C."
5-11 180 L 4 Feb 1949, Thompkins SK

year	team	gp	g	a	pts	pim	gp	g	a	pts	pim
72-73	Phi	55	10	8	18	38	4	0	0	0	0
73-74	Van	74	21	26	47	27					
74-75	Van	14	4	2	6	12					
	Phx	47	6	13	19	16	1	0	0	0	0
75-76	Phx	68	8	12	20	14	3	0	0	0	0
totals		258	49	61	110	107	8	0	0	0	0

Tom MILANI —
5-6 170 R 13 Apr 1952, Thunder Bay ON

year	team	gp	g	a	pts	pim	gp	g	a	pts	pim
76-77	Min	2	0	0	0	0					
totals		2	0	0	0	0					

Perry MILLER — Perry Elvis Miller
6-1 195 L 24 Jun 1952, Winnipeg MB

year	team	gp	g	a	pts	pim	gp	g	a	pts	pim
74-75	Wpg	67	9	19	28	133					
75-76	Min	13	1	4	5	11					
	Wpg	47	7	6	13	41					
76-77	Wpg	74	14	31	45	124	20	4	6	10	27
totals		201	31	60	91	309	20	4	6	10	27

• Played in NHL: 1977-81, Det, 217-10-51-61-387

Warren MILLER — Warren Frederick Miller
5-11 180 R 1 Jan 1954, S St Paul MN

year	team	gp	g	a	pts	pim	gp	g	a	pts	pim
75-76	Cgy	3	0	0	0	0	10	1	0	1	28
76-77	Cgy	80	23	32	55	51					
77-78	Edm	18	2	4	6	18					
	Que	60	14	24	38	50	11	0	2	2	0
78-79	NE	77	26	23	49	44	10	0	8	8	28
totals		238	65	83	148	163	31	1	10	11	56

• Played in NHL: 1979-83, NYR-Hart, 262-40-50-90-137

John MISZUK — John Stanley Miszuk
6-2 200 L 29 Sep 1940, Naliboki Poland

year	team	gp	g	a	pts	pim	gp	g	a	pts	pim
74-75	M-B	66	2	19	21	56					
75-76	Cgy	69	2	21	23	66	10	0	1	1	10
76-77	Cgy	79	2	26	28	57					
totals		214	6	66	72	179	10	0	1	1	10

• Played in NHL: 1963-70, Det-Chi-Phi-Min, 237-7-39-46-232

Lyle MOFFAT — Lyle Gordon Moffat
5-10 180 L 19 Mar 1948, Calgary AB

year	team	gp	g	a	pts	pim	gp	g	a	pts	pim
75-76	Cle	33	4	7	11	33					
	Wpg	42	13	9	22	44	13	3	3	6	9
76-77	Wpg	74	13	11	24	90	17	2	0	2	6
77-78	Wpg	57	9	16	25	39	9	5	7	12	9
78-79	Wpg	70	14	18	32	38	10	3	1	4	22
totals		276	53	61	114	244	49	13	11	24	46

• Played in NHL: 1972-75, 1979-80, Tor-Wpg, 97-12-16-28-51

Lauri MONONEN — Lauri Ilmari Mononen
6-0 190 L 22 Mar 1950, Joensuu Finland

year	team	gp	g	a	pts	pim	gp	g	a	pts	pim
75-76	Phx	75	15	21	36	19	5	1	3	4	2
76-77	Phx	67	21	29	50	10					
totals		142	36	50	86	29	5	1	3	4	2

• Member, Finland Olympic Team, 1972

Brian MORENZ —
5-10 185 L 11 May 1949, Brampton ON

year	team	gp	g	a	pts	pim	gp	g	a	pts	pim
72-73	NY	32	7	1	8	23					
73-74	NY-J	75	20	30	50	44					
74-75	SD	78	20	19	39	76	10	0	3	3	6
75-76	SD	40	6	7	13	22	11	2	1	3	11
totals		225	53	57	110	165	21	2	4	6	17

• Distant relation of Danny Geoffrion

Angelo MORETTO — Angelo Joseph Moretto "Angie"
6-3 210 L 18 Sep 1953, Toronto ON

year	team	gp	g	a	pts	pim	gp	g	a	pts	pim
78-79	Ind	18	3	1	4	2					
totals		18	3	1	4	2					

• Played in NHL: 1976-77, Cle, 5-1-2-3-2

Ron MORGAN —
5-11 190 L -, Toronto ON

year	team	gp	g	a	pts	pim	gp	g	a	pts	pim
73-74	Cle	4	0	1	1	7	2	1	0	1	0
totals		4	0	1	1	7	2	1	0	1	0

Wayne MORIN —
5-10 185 R 13 May 1955, Progress BC

year	team	gp	g	a	pts	pim	gp	g	a	pts	pim
76-77	Cgy	13	2	0	2	25					
totals		13	2	0	2	25					

Bill MORRIS — William John Morris
6-0 185 - 26 Jun 1949, Toronto ON

year	team	gp	g	a	pts	pim	gp	g	a	pts	pim
74-75	Edm	36	4	8	12	6					
totals		36	4	8	12	6					

Pete MORRIS Peter Morris
5-8 165 L 29 Jun 1955, Edmonton AB

year	team	gp	g	a	pts	pim	gp	g	a	pts	pim
75-76	Edm	75	7	13	20	34	3	0	1	1	7
76-77	Edm	3	0	1	1	7					
totals		78	7	14	21	41	3	0	1	1	7

Rick MORRIS Richard Ian Morris
5-11 175 L 5 Jul 1946, Hamilton ON

year	team	gp	g	a	pts	pim	gp	g	a	pts	pim
72-73	Chi	76	31	17	48	84					
73-74	Chi	76	17	16	33	140	18	4	3	7	42
74-75	Chi	78	15	13	28	110					
75-76	D-O	40	9	6	15	58					
	Edm	33	11	15	26	52	4	0	1	1	4
76-77	Edm	79	18	17	35	76					
77-78	Edm	5	1	1	2	7					
	Que	25	0	5	5	40					
totals		412	102	90	192	567	22	4	4	8	46

George MORRISON George Harold Morrison
6-1 175 L 24 Dec 1948, Toronto ON d. 2008

year	team	gp	g	a	pts	pim	gp	g	a	pts	pim
72-73	Min	70	16	24	40	20	5	1	1	2	2
73-74	Min	73	40	38	78	37	11	5	5	10	12
74-75	Min	76	31	29	60	30	12	5	9	14	0
75-76	Cgy	79	25	32	57	13	10	3	2	5	0
76-77	Cgy	63	11	19	30	10					
totals		361	123	142	265	110	38	14	17	31	14

• Played in NHL: 1970-72, StL, 115-17-21-38-13

Kevin MORRISON Kevin Gregory Joseph Morrison
5-11 200 L 28 Oct 1949, Sydney NS

year	team	gp	g	a	pts	pim	gp	g	a	pts	pim
73-74	NY-J	78	24	43	67	132					
74-75	SD	78	20	61	81	143	10	0	7	7	2
75-76	SD	80	22	43	65	56	11	1	5	6	12
76-77	SD	75	8	30	38	68	7	1	3	4	8
77-78	Ind	75	17	40	57	49					
78-79	Ind	5	0	2	2	0					
	Que	27	2	5	7	14					
totals		418	93	224	317	462	28	2	15	17	22

• Played in NHL: 1979-80, Col, 41-4-11-15-23

Dave MORROW
6-0 190 L 21 Apr 1957, Edmonton AB

year	team	gp	g	a	pts	pim	gp	g	a	pts	pim
78-79	Ind	10	2	10	12	29					
totals		10	2	10	12	29					

Keke MORTSON Cleland Lindsay Mortson
5-9 170 R 29 Mar 1934, Arntfield PQ d. 1995

year	team	gp	g	a	pts	pim	gp	g	a	pts	pim
72-73	Hou	69	13	16	29	95	10	0	3	3	16
77-78	Hou	6	0	1	1	7	2	0	1	1	0
totals		75	13	17	30	102	12	0	4	4	16

Wayne MOSDELL Wayne Kenneth Mosdell
6-3 185 R 4 Dec 1944, Montreal PQ

year	team	gp	g	a	pts	pim	gp	g	a	pts	pim
72-73	Phi	9	0	1	1	12					
totals		9	0	1	1	12					

Darwin MOTT Darwin Robert Mott
5-9 165 L 19 Aug 1950, Creelman SK

year	team	gp	g	a	pts	pim	gp	g	a	pts	pim
72-73	Phi	1	0	0	0	0					
totals		1	0	0	0	0					

• Brother of Morris Mott

Morris MOTT Morris Kenneth Mott
5-10 165 L 25 May 1946, Creelman SK

year	team	gp	g	a	pts	pim	gp	g	a	pts	pim
76-77	Wpg	2	0	1	1	5					
totals		2	0	1	1	5					

• Brother of Darwin Mott • Played in NHL: 1972-75, Cal, 199-18-32-50-49 • Member, Canada Olympic Team, 1968

Bob MOWAT Robert Charles Mowat
5-9 170 R 5 Oct 1949, Kamloops BC

year	team	gp	g	a	pts	pim	gp	g	a	pts	pim
74-75	Phx	53	9	10	19	34	3	0	0	0	0
totals		53	9	10	19	34	3	0	0	0	0

Wayne MULOIN John Wayne Muloin
5-8 175 L 24 Dec 1941, Dryden ON

year	team	gp	g	a	pts	pim	gp	g	a	pts	pim
72-73	Cle	70	2	13	15	64	9	1	3	4	14
73-74	Cle	76	3	7	10	39	5	1	0	1	0
74-75	Cle	78	4	17	21	5	5	0	1	1	4
75-76	Cle	27	0	5	5	12					
	Edm	10	1	1	2	0	1	0	0	0	0
totals		261	10	43	53	180	20	2	4	6	18

• Played in NHL: 1963-71, Det-Oak-Cal-Min, 147-3-21-24-93

Murray MYERS
6-0 185 R 9 Feb 1952, Yellow Grass SK

year	team	gp	g	a	pts	pim	gp	g	a	pts	pim
72-73	Phi	7	0	0	0	0					
73-74	Van	61	22	20	42	28					
74-75	Van	24	1	1	2	4					
75-76	Cin	56	14	15	29	12					
totals		148	37	36	73	44					

Mark NAPIER Robert Mark Napier
5-10 180 L 28 Jan 1957, Toronto ON

year	team	gp	g	a	pts	pim	gp	g	a	pts	pim
75-76	Tor	78	43	50	93	20					
76-77	Bir	80	60	36	96	24					
77-78	Bir	79	33	32	65	9	5	0	2	2	14
totals		237	136	118	254	53	5	0	2	2	14

• Played in NHL: 1978-89, Mtl-Min-Edm-Buf, 767-235-306-541-157
• Stanley Cups: 1979 (Montreal), 1985 (Edmonton)

Robbie NEALE Robert Alfred Neale
6-0 185 L 17 Apr 1953, Brandon MB

year	team	gp	g	a	pts	pim	gp	g	a	pts	pim
73-74	Cle	43	8	9	17	30	5	0	0	0	4
74-75	Cle	9	1	3	4	4					
	Wpg	7	0	2	2	4					
totals		59	9	14	23	38	5	0	0	0	4

Vaclav NEDOMANSKY "Big Ned"
6-2 210 L 14 Mar 1944, Hodonin Czechoslovakia

year	team	gp	g	a	pts	pim	gp	g	a	pts	pim
74-75	Tor	78	41	40	81	19	6	3	1	4	9
75-76	Tor	81	56	42	98	8					
76-77	Bir	81	36	33	69	10					
77-78	Bir	12	2	3	5	6					
totals		252	135	118	253	43	6	3	1	4	9

• Played in NHL: 1977-83, Det-NYR-StL, 421-122-156-278-88 • Member, Czechoslovakia Olympic Team, 1968 & 1972

Greg NEELD
6-0 190 L 25 Feb 1955, Vancouver BC

year	team	gp	g	a	pts	pim	gp	g	a	pts	pim
75-76	Tor	17	0	1	1	18					
totals		17	0	1	1	18					

• Lost left eye in on-ice accident in December 1973.

Jim NEILSON James Anthony Neilson
6-2 200 L 28 Nov 1940, Big River SK

year	team	gp	g	a	pts	pim	gp	g	a	pts	pim
78-79	Edm	35	0	5	5	18					
totals		35	0	5	5	18					

• Played in NHL: 1962-78, NYR-Cal-Cle, 1023-69-299-368-904

Eric NESTERENKO Eric Paul Nesterenko
6-2 200 R 31 Oct 1933, Flin Flon MB

year	team	gp	g	a	pts	pim	gp	g	a	pts	pim
73-74	Chi	29	2	5	7	8					
totals		29	2	5	7	8					

• Played in NHL: 1951-72, Tor-Chi, 1219-250-324-574-1273 • Stanley Cup: 1961 (Chicago)

Bob NEVIN Robert Frank Nevin
6-0 190 R 18 Mar 1938, S Porcupine ON

year	team	gp	g	a	pts	pim	gp	g	a	pts	pim
76-77	Edm	13	3	2	5	0					
totals		13	3	2	5	0					

• Played in NHL: 1957-76, Tor-NYR-Min-LA, 1128-307-419-726-211 • Stanley Cups: 1962, 1963 (Toronto)

Rick NEWELL Gordon Richard Newell
5-11 185 L 18 Feb 1948, Winnipeg MB

year	team	gp	g	a	pts	pim	gp	g	a	pts	pim
74-75	Phx	25	0	4	4	39	5	0	1	1	2
totals		25	0	4	4	39	5	0	1	1	2

• Played in NHL: 1972-74, Det, 6-0-0-0-0

Jim NIEKAMP James Lawrence Niekamp
6-1 185 R 11 Mar 1946, Detroit MI

year	team	gp	g	a	pts	pim	gp	g	a	pts	pim
72-73	LA	78	7	22	29	155	6	2	1	3	10
73-74	LA	76	2	19	21	95					
74-75	Phx	71	2	26	28	66					
75-76	Phx	79	4	14	18	77	5	0	1	1	0
76-77	Phx	79	1	15	16	91					
totals		383	16	96	112	484	11	2	2	4	10

• Played in NHL: 1970-72, Det, 29-0-2-2-37

Kent NILSSON
5-10 175 L 31 Aug 1956, Djugardens Sweden

year	team	gp	g	a	pts	pim	gp	g	a	pts	pim
77-78	Wpg	80	42	65	107	8	9	2	8	10	10
78-79	Wpg	78	39	68	107	8	10	3	11	14	4
totals		158	81	133	214	16	19	5	19	24	14

• Played in NHL: 1979-87, 1995, Atl-Cgy-Min-Edm, 553-264-422-686-116 • Stanley Cup: 1987 (Edmonton)

Ulf NILSSON Ulf Gosta Nilsson
5-11 175 R 11 May 1950, Nynashamn Sweden

year	team	gp	g	a	pts	pim	gp	g	a	pts	pim
74-75	Wpg	78	26	94	120	79					
75-76	Wpg	78	38	76	114	84	13	7	19	26	6
76-77	Wpg	71	39	85	124	89	20	6	21	27	33
77-78	Wpg	73	37	89	126	89	9	1	13	14	12
totals		300	140	344	484	341	42	14	53	67	51

• Played in NHL: 1978-83, NYR, 170-57-112-169-85

Lou NISTICO Louis Charles Nistico
5-7 170 L 25 Jan 1953, Thunder Bay ON

year	team	gp	g	a	pts	pim	gp	g	a	pts	pim
73-74	Tor	13	1	3	4	14					
74-75	Tor	29	11	11	22	75	6	6	1	7	19
75-76	Tor	65	12	22	34	120					
76-77	Bir	79	20	36	56	166					
totals		186	44	72	116	375	6	6	1	7	19

• Played in NHL: 1977-78, Col, 3-0-0-0-0

Joe NORIS Joseph S. Noris, Jr.
6-0 185 R 26 Oct 1951, Denver CO

year	team	gp	g	a	pts	pim	gp	g	a	pts	pim
75-76	SD	80	28	40	68	24	11	2	4	6	6
76-77	SD	73	35	57	92	30	7	2	1	3	6
77-78	Bir	45	9	19	28	6					
totals		198	72	116	188	60	18	4	5	9	12

• Played in NHL: 1971-74, Pit-StL-Buf, 55-2-5-7-22

Craig NORWICH Craig Richard Norwich
5-11 175 L 15 Dec 1955, Edina MN

year	team	gp	g	a	pts	pim	gp	g	a	pts	pim
77-78	Cin	65	7	23	30	48					
78-79	Cin	80	6	51	57	73	3	0	1	1	4
totals		145	13	74	87	121	3	0	1	1	4

• Played in NHL: 1979-81, Wpg-StL-Col, 104-17-58-75-60

Kevin NUGENT
6-5 235 R 7 Jun 1955, Little Falls MN

year	team	gp	g	a	pts	pim	gp	g	a	pts	pim
78-79	Ind	25	2	8	10	20					
totals		25	2	5	8	20					

Tim O'CONNELL
5-11 165 R 26 Oct 1953, Chicago IL

year	team	gp	g	a	pts	pim	gp	g	a	pts	pim
76-77	SD	16	0	3	3	4					
totals		16	0	3	3	4					

Fred O'DONNELL Frederick James O'Donnell
5-10 175 R 6 Dec 1949, Kingston ON

year	team	gp	g	a	pts	pim	gp	g	a	pts	pim
74-75	NE	76	21	15	36	84					
75-76	NE	79	11	11	22	81	17	2	5	7	20
totals		155	32	26	58	165	17	2	5	7	20

• Played in NHL: 1972-74, Bos, 115-15-11-26-98

Don O'DONOGHUE Donald Francis O'Donoghue
5-10 180 L 27 Aug 1949, Kingston ON d. 2007

year	team	gp	g	a	pts	pim	gp	g	a	pts	pim
72-73	Phi	74	16	23	39	43	4	0	1	1	0
73-74	Van	49	8	6	14	20					
74-75	Van	4	0	0	0	0					
75-76	Cin	20	1	8	9	0					
totals		147	25	37	62	63	4	0	1	1	0

• Played in NHL: 1969-72, Oak-Cal, 125-18-17-35-35

Gerry ODROWSKI Gerald Bernard Odrowski
5-10 190 L 4 Oct 1938, Trout Creek ON

year	team	gp	g	a	pts	pim	gp	g	a	pts	pim
72-73	LA	78	6	31	37	89	6	1	2	3	6
73-74	LA	77	4	32	36	48					
74-75	Phx	77	5	38	43	77	5	0	2	2	0
75-76	Min	37	1	12	13	10					
	Wpg	13	0	1	1	6					
totals		282	16	114	130	230	11	1	4	5	6

• Played in NHL: 1960-72, Det-Oak-StL, 309-12-19-31-111

Wally OLDS Walter Raymond Olds
6-2 200 R 17 Aug 1949, Warroad MN d. 2009

year	team	gp	g	a	pts	pim	gp	g	a	pts	pim
72-73	NY	61	5	7	12	4					
75-76	Cgy	28	0	5	5	6	9	0	2	2	4
totals		89	5	12	17	10	9	0	2	2	4

• Member, United States Olympic Team, 1972

Paul O'NEIL Paul Joseph O'Neil
6-1 185 L 24 Aug 1953, Charlestown MA

year	team	gp	g	a	pts	pim	gp	g	a	pts	pim
78-79	Bir	1	0	0	0	0					
totals		1	0	0	0	0					

• Played in NHL: 1973-76, Van-Bos, 6-0-0-0-0

Bill ORR William Lindsay Orr
5-10 180 R 12 Jun 1948, S Porcupine ON

year	team	gp	g	a	pts	pim	gp	g	a	pts	pim
73-74	Tor	46	3	9	12	16	12	1	0	1	6
totals		46	3	9	12	16	12	1	0	1	6

Danny O'SHEA Daniel Patrick O'Shea
6-1 190 L 15 Jun 1945, Toronto ON

year	team	gp	g	a	pts	pim	gp	g	a	pts	pim
74-75	Min	76	16	25	41	47					
totals		76	16	25	41	47					

• Brother of Kevin O'Shea • Played in NHL: 1968-73, Min-Chi-StL, 369-64-115-179-285 • Member, Canada Olympic Team, 1968

Kevin O'SHEA Kevin William O'Shea
6-1 200 R 28 May 1947, Toronto ON d. 2010

year	team	gp	g	a	pts	pim	gp	g	a	pts	pim
74-75	Min	68	10	10	20	42					
totals		68	10	10	20	42					

• Brother of Danny O'Shea • Played in NHL: 1970-73, Buf-StL, 134-13-18-31-85

Francois OUIMET
5-10 175 L 14 Oct 1951, Montreal PQ

year	team	gp	g	a	pts	pim	gp	g	a	pts	pim
75-76	Min	9	0	2	2	2					
76-77	Cin	16	1	8	9	10					
totals		25	1	10	11	12					

Pierre PAIEMENT
5-10 170 R 13 Sep 1950, Earlton ON

year	team	gp	g	a	pts	pim	gp	g	a	pts	pim
72-73	Phi	8	1	0	1	18					
totals		8	1	0	1	18					

• Brother of Rosaire Paiement

Rosaire PAIEMENT Joseph Wilfrid Rosaire Paiement "Rosie"
5-11 170 R 12 Aug 1945, Earlton ON

year	team	gp	g	a	pts	pim	gp	g	a	pts	pim
72-73	Chi	78	33	36	69	137					
73-74	Chi	78	30	43	73	87	18	9	6	15	16
74-75	Chi	78	26	48	74	97					
75-76	NE	80	28	43	71	89	17	4	11	15	41
76-77	NE	13	5	2	7	12					
	Ind	67	18	25	43	91	9	0	5	5	15
77-78	Ind	61	6	24	30	81					
totals		455	146	221	367	602	44	13	22	35	72

• Brother of Pierre Paiement • Played in NHL: 1967-72, Phi-Van, 190-48-52-100-343

Dick PARADISE Richard John Paradise
5-11 195 L 21 Apr 1945, St Paul MN

year	team	gp	g	a	pts	pim	gp	g	a	pts	pim
72-73	Min	77	3	15	18	189	5	0	1	1	2
73-74	Min	67	2	7	9	71	0	0	0	0	6
totals		144	5	22	27	260	12	0	1	1	8

Michel PARIZEAU Michel Gerald Parizeau "Mike"
5-10 165 L 9 Apr 1948, Montreal PQ

year	team	gp	g	a	pts	pim	gp	g	a	pts	pim
72-73	Que	75	25	48	73	50					
73-74	Que	78	26	34	60	39					
74-75	Que	78	28	46	74	69	15	2	4	6	10
75-76	Que	58	12	27	39	24					
	Ind	23	13	15	28	20	7	4	4	8	6
76-77	Ind	75	18	37	55	39	8	3	6	9	8
77-78	Ind	70	13	27	40	47					
78-79	Ind	22	4	9	13	4					
	Cin	30	3	9	12	28	3	1	0	1	0
totals		509	142	252	394	320	33	10	14	24	24

• Played in NHL: 1971-72, StL-Phi, 56-3-14-17-18

Rusty PATENAUDE Edgar Arnold Patenaude
5-9 175 R 17 Oct 1949, Williams Lake BC

year	team	gp	g	a	pts	pim	gp	g	a	pts	pim
72-73	Alb	78	29	27	56	55					
73-74	Edm	71	20	23	43	55	4	0	2	2	2
74-75	Edm	56	10	26	36	38					
75-76	Edm	77	42	30	72	88	4	1	4	5	12
76-77	Edm	73	25	16	41	57	2	0	0	0	8
77-78	Ind	73	23	19	42	71					
totals		428	159	131	290	368	10	1	6	7	22

Craig PATRICK
6-0 185 L 20 May 1946, Detroit MI

year	team	gp	g	a	pts	pim	gp	g	a	pts	pim
76-77	Min	30	6	11	17	6					
totals		30	6	11	17	6					

• Brother of Glenn Patrick • Played in NHL: 1971-79, Cal-StL-KC-Wash, 401-72-91-163-61 • Stanley Cups: 1991, 1992 (Pittsburgh, as General Manager)

Glenn PATRICK Glenn Curtiss Patrick
6-2 190 L 26 Apr 1950, New York NY

year	team	gp	g	a	pts	pim	gp	g	a	pts	pim
76-77	Edm	23	0	4	4	62	2	0	0	0	0
totals		23	0	4	4	62	2	0	0	0	0

• Brother of Craig Patrick • Played in NHL: 1973-77, StL-Cal-Cle, 38-2-3-5-72

Denis PATRY
5-8 165 R 5 Dec 1953, Asbestos PQ

year	team	gp	g	a	pts	pim	gp	g	a	pts	pim
74-75	Que	3	1	2	3	2					
totals		3	1	2	3	2					

Dennis PATTERSON Dennis Gordon Patterson
5-8 175 L 9 Jan 1950, Peterborough ON

year	team	gp	g	a	pts	pim	gp	g	a	pts	pim
76-77	Edm	23	0	2	2	2					
totals		23	0	2	2	2					

• Played in NHL: 1974-76, 1979-80, KC-Phi, 138-6-22-28-67

Jean PAYETTE Jean Laurent Payette
6-0 170 L 29 Mar 1946, Cornwall ON

year	team	gp	g	a	pts	pim	gp	g	a	pts	pim
72-73	Que	71	15	29	44	46					
73-74	Que	41	4	11	15	6					
totals		112	19	40	59	52					

Gene PEACOSH Eugene Michael Peacosh
5-11 190 L 28 Sep 1948, Sherridan MB

year	team	gp	g	a	pts	pim	gp	g	a	pts	pim
72-73	NY	67	37	34	71	25					
73-74	NY-J	68	21	32	53	17					
74-75	SD	78	43	36	79	22	10	7	5	12	4
75-76	SD	79	37	33	70	35	11	2	1	3	21
76-77	Edm	11	5	4	9	14					
	Ind	64	22	26	48	21	9	3	3	6	2
totals		367	165	165	330	134	30	12	9	21	27

Mel PEARSON George Alexander Melvin Pearson
5-10 175 L 29 Apr 1938, Flin Flon MB d. 1999

year	team	gp	g	a	pts	pim	gp	g	a	pts	pim
72-73	Min	70	8	12	20	12	5	2	0	2	0
totals		70	8	12	20	12	5	2	0	2	0

• Played in NHL: 1959-68, NYR-Pit, 38-2-6-8-25

Andre PELOFFY Andre Charles Peloffy
5-8 160 L 25 Feb 1951, Sete France

year	team	gp	g	a	pts	pim	gp	g	a	pts	pim
77-78	NE	10	2	0	2	2	2	0	0	0	0
totals		10	2	0	2	2	2	0	0	0	0

• Played in NHL: 1974-75, Wash, 9-0-0-0-0

Mike PELYK Michael Joseph Pelyk
6-1 190 L 29 Sep 1947, Toronto ON

year	team	gp	g	a	pts	pim	gp	g	a	pts	pim
74-75	Van	75	14	26	40	121					
75-76	Cin	75	10	23	33	117					
totals		150	24	49	73	238					

• Played in NHL: 1967-74, 1976-78, Tor, 441-26-88-114-566

Dwayne PENTLAND Dwayne Wilbert Pentland
5-10 180 L 8 Feb 1953, Vancouver BC

year	team	gp	g	a	pts	pim	gp	g	a	pts	pim
76-77	Hou	29	1	2	3	6	2	0	0	0	0
totals		29	1	2	3	6	2	0	0	0	0

Ross PERKINS Ross Harold Perkins
5-10 175 R 4 Nov 1946, Tisdale SK

year	team	gp	g	a	pts	pim	gp	g	a	pts	pim
72-73	Alb	71	21	37	58	19					
73-74	Edm	78	16	40	56	43	5	1	3	4	2
74-75	Edm	76	7	16	23	33					
totals		225	44	93	137	95	5	1	3	4	2

Brian PERRY Brian Thomas Perry
5-11 185 L 6 Apr 1944, Aldershot England

year	team	gp	g	a	pts	pim	gp	g	a	pts	pim
72-73	NY	74	13	20	33	30					
73-74	NY-J	71	20	11	31	19					
74-75	SD	0	0	0	0	0	6	1	2	3	6
totals		145	33	31	64	49	6	1	2	3	6

• Played in NHL: 1968-71, Oak-Buf, 96-16-29-45-24

George PESUT George Mathew Pesut
6-1 185 L 17 Jun 1953, Saskatoon SK

year	team	gp	g	a	pts	pim	gp	g	a	pts	pim
76-77	Cgy	17	2	0	2	2					
totals		17	2	0	2	2					

• Played in NHL: 1974-76, Cal, 92-3-22-25-130

Garry PETERS Garry Lorne Peters
5-10 180 – 9 Oct 1942, Regina SK

year	team	gp	g	a	pts	pim	gp	g	a	pts	pim
72-73	NY	23	2	7	9	24					
73-74	NY-J	34	2	5	7	18					
totals		57	4	12	16	42					

• Played in NHL: 1964-72, Mtl-NYR-Phi-Bos, 311-34-34-68-261 • Stanley Cup: 1972 (Boston)

Jean-Luc PHANEUF
5-8 165 R 26 Oct 1955, Montreal PQ

year	team	gp	g	a	pts	pim	gp	g	a	pts	pim
75-76	Tor	48	8	8	16	4					
76-77	Bir	30	2	7	9	2					
totals		78	10	15	25	6					

Gerry PINDER Allan Gerald Pinder
5-8 165 R 15 Sep 1948, Saskatoon SK

year	team	gp	g	a	pts	pim	gp	g	a	pts	pim
72-73	Cle	78	30	36	66	21	9	2	9	11	30
73-74	Cle	73	23	33	56	90	1	0	0	0	0
74-75	Cle	74	13	28	41	71	5	3	1	4	6
75-76	Cle	79	21	30	51	118	3	0	0	0	4
76-77	Cle	44	6	13	19	36					
77-78	Edm	5	0	1	1	0					
totals		353	93	141	234	336	18	5	10	15	40

• Played in NHL: 1969-72, Chi-Cal, 223-55-69-124-135 • Member, Canada Olympic Team, 1968

449

Ed PIZUNSKI Edward Pizunski
5-11 185 L 8 Oct 1954, Toronto ON

year	team	gp	g	a	pts	pim	gp	g	a	pts	pim
75-76	D-O	1	0	0	0	0					
totals		1	0	0	0	0					

Michel PLANTE
5-10 170 L 19 Jan 1952, Drummondville PQ

year	team	gp	g	a	pts	pim	gp	g	a	pts	pim
72-73	Phi	70	13	12	25	35	4	0	0	0	2
73-74	Van	22	3	2	5	2					
totals		92	16	14	30	37	4	0	0	0	2

Larry PLEAU Lawrence Winslow Pleau
6-1 190 L 29 Jun 1947, Lynn MA

year	team	gp	g	a	pts	pim	gp	g	a	pts	pim
72-73	NE	78	39	48	87	42	15	12	7	19	15
73-74	NE	77	26	43	69	35	2	2	0	2	0
74-75	NE	78	30	34	64	50	6	2	3	5	14
75-76	NE	75	29	45	74	21	14	5	7	12	0
76-77	NE	78	11	21	32	22	5	1	0	1	0
77-78	NE	54	16	18	34	4	14	5	4	9	8
78-79	NE	28	6	6	12	6	10	2	1	3	0
totals		468	157	215	372	180	66	29	22	51	37

• Played in NHL: 1969-72, Mtl, 94-9-15-24-27 • Member, Canada Olympic Team, 1968 • Stanley Cup: 1971 (Montreal (DNP))

Ron PLUMB Ronald William Plumb
5-10 175 R 17 Jul 1950, Kingston ON

year	team	gp	g	a	pts	pim	gp	g	a	pts	pim
72-73	Phi	78	10	41	51	66	4	0	2	2	13
73-74	Van	78	6	32	38	40					
74-75	SD	78	10	38	48	56	10	2	3	5	11
75-76	Cin	80	10	36	46	31					
76-77	Cin	79	11	58	69	52	4	1	2	3	0
77-78	Cin	54	13	34	47	45					
	NE	27	1	9	10	18	14	1	5	6	16
78-79	NE	78	4	16	20	33	9	1	3	4	0
totals		549	65	262	327	341	41	5	15	20	40

• Played in NHL: 1979-80, Hart, 26-3-4-7-14

Nick POLANO Nicholas Polano
6-0 190 L 25 Mar 1941, Sudbury ON

year	team	gp	g	a	pts	pim	gp	g	a	pts	pim
72-73	Phi	17	0	3	3	24					
totals		17	0	3	3	24					

Jan POPIEL Jan Valdemar Popiel
5-9 180 L 9 Oct 1947, Virum Denmark

year	team	gp	g	a	pts	pim	gp	g	a	pts	pim
72-73	Chi	76	31	34	65	77					
73-74	Chi	63	22	17	39	36	18	8	5	13	12
74-75	Chi	60	18	22	40	74					
75-76	D-O	1	0	0	0	2					
	Hou	67	4	7	11	59	8	1	1	2	4
76-77	Phx	28	3	2	5	8					
totals		295	78	82	160	256	26	9	6	15	16

• Brother of Poul Popiel

Poul POPIEL Poul Peter Popiel
5-10 175 L 28 Feb 1943, Sollested Denmark

year	team	gp	g	a	pts	pim	gp	g	a	pts	pim
72-73	Hou	74	16	48	64	158	10	2	9	11	23
73-74	Hou	78	7	41	48	126	14	1	14	15	22
74-75	Hou	78	11	53	64	22	13	1	10	11	34
75-76	Hou	78	10	36	46	71	17	3	5	8	16
76-77	Hou	80	12	56	68	87	11	0	7	7	10
77-78	Hou	80	6	31	37	53	6	0	2	2	13
totals		468	62	265	327	517	71	7	47	54	118

• Brother of Jan Popiel • Played in NHL: 1965-72, 1979-80, Bos-LA-Det-Van-Edm, 224-13-41-54-210

Lynn POWIS Trevor Lynn Powis "Ducky"
6-0 185 L 19 Apr 1949, Saskatoon SK

year	team	gp	g	a	pts	pim	gp	g	a	pts	pim
75-76	Cgy	21	4	10	14	2	10	5	4	9	12
76-77	Cgy	63	30	30	60	46					
77-78	Ind	14	4	6	10	2					
	Wpg	55	12	19	31	16	3	2	1	3	7
totals		153	50	65	115	66	13	7	5	12	19

• Played in NHL: 1973-75, Chi-KC, 130-19-33-52-25

Kelly PRATT Kelly Edward Pratt
5-8 175 R 8 Feb 1953, High Prairie AB

year	team	gp	g	a	pts	pim	gp	g	a	pts	pim
73-74	Wpg	46	4	6	10	50					
totals		46	4	6	10	50					

• Played in NHL: 1974-75, Pit, 22-0-6-6-15

Bill PRENTICE William John Prentice
6-0 190 L 3 Aug 1950, Lindsay ON

year	team	gp	g	a	pts	pim	gp	g	a	pts	pim
72-73	Hou	3	0	1	1	0					
73-74	Hou	55	1	2	3	35	10	0	0	0	5
74-75	Hou	17	0	3	3	19					
75-76	Ind	38	4	2	6	92					
	Que	21	2	5	7	89	5	0	0	0	17
76-77	Edm	3	0	0	0	2					
77-78	Ind	71	1	1	2	28					
totals		208	8	14	22	265	15	0	0	0	22

Rich PRESTON Richard John Preston
5-11 185 R 22 May 1952, Regina SK

year	team	gp	g	a	pts	pim	gp	g	a	pts	pim
74-75	Hou	78	20	21	41	10	13	1	6	7	6
75-76	Hou	77	22	33	55	33	17	4	6	10	8
76-77	Hou	80	38	41	79	54	11	3	5	8	10
77-78	Hou	73	25	25	50	52					
78-79	Wpg	80	28	60	88	10	8	5	13	15	
totals		388	133	152	285	237	51	16	22	38	39

• Played in NHL: 1979-87, Chi-NJ, 580-127-164-291-348

Pat PRICE Shaun Patrick Price
6-1 190 L 24 Mar 1955, Nelson BC

year	team	gp	g	a	pts	pim	gp	g	a	pts	pim
74-75	Van	68	5	29	34	15					
totals		68	5	29	34	15					

• Played in NHL: 1975-88, NYI-Edm-Pit-Que-NYR-Min-726-43-218-261-1456

Kevin PRIMEAU
6-0 180 R 3 Jan 1956, Edmonton AB

year	team	gp	g	a	pts	pim	gp	g	a	pts	pim
77-78	Edm	7	0	1	1	0	2	0	0	0	2
totals		7	0	1	1	0	2	0	0	0	2

• Played in NHL: 1980-81, Van, 2-0-0-0-0 • Member, Canada Olympic Team, 1980

Jim PRITCHARD James George Pritchard
5-9 175 L 14 Feb 1948, Winnipeg MB d. 2014

year	team	gp	g	a	pts	pim	gp	g	a	pts	pim
74-75	Chi	2	0	0	0	0					
totals		2	0	0	0	0					

Dick PROCEVIAT Richard Peter Proceviat "Pro"
6-0 180 L 25 Jun 1946, Whitemouth MB

year	team	gp	g	a	pts	pim	gp	g	a	pts	pim
72-73	Chi	56	4	14	18	33					
73-74	Chi	77	2	20	22	53	13	0	4	4	10
74-75	Chi	11	0	3	3	11					
	Ind	52	1	28	29	51					
75-76	Ind	73	7	13	20	31	7	0	0	0	2
76-77	Ind	55	2	12	14	33					
totals		324	16	90	106	265	20	0	4	4	12

Rich PUMPLE Richard Pumple
6-3 200 L 7 Feb 1948, Montreal PQ

year	team	gp	g	a	pts	pim	gp	g	a	pts	pim
72-73	Cle	78	21	20	41	45	9	3	5	8	11
73-74	Cle	17	2	2	4	16					
74-75	Ind	34	4	8	12	29					
totals		129	27	30	57	90	9	3	5	8	11

Rob RAMAGE Robert George Ramage
6-2 195 R 11 Jan 1959, Byron ON

year	team	gp	g	a	pts	pim	gp	g	a	pts	pim
78-79	Bir	80	12	36	48	165					
totals		80	12	36	48	165					

• Played in NHL: 1979-94, Col-StL-Cgy-Tor-Min-TB-Mtl-Phi, 1044-139-425-564-2226 • Stanley Cups: 1989 (Calgary), 1993 (Montreal) • Only WHA player to play with a 1990s-era expansion team (Tampa Bay)

Pekka RAUTAKALLIO Pekka Olavi Rautakallio
5-11 185 L 25 Jul 1953, Pori Finland

year	team	gp	g	a	pts	pim	gp	g	a	pts	pim
75-76	Phx	73	11	39	50	8	5	0	2	2	0
76-77	Phx	78	4	31	35	8					
totals		151	15	70	85	16	5	0	2	2	0

• Played in NHL: 1979-82, Atl-Cgy, 236-33-121-154-122

Bill REED William Ernest Reed
5-11 190 R 25 May 1954, Toronto ON

year	team	gp	g	a	pts	pim	gp	g	a	pts	pim
74-75	M-B	11	0	0	0	12					
75-76	Cgy	29	0	5	5	14					
totals		40	0	5	5	26					

Craig REICHMUTH Craig Richard Reichmuth
5-11 185 L 22 Sep 1947, Russell MB

year	team	gp	g	a	pts	pim	gp	g	a	pts	pim
72-73	NY	73	13	14	27	127					
73-74	NY-J	72	10	8	18	114					
74-75	SD	28	2	1	3	58					
	M-B	16	0	2	2	23					
totals		189	25	25	50	322					

Seppo REPO "The Fox"
5-10 180 R 21 Sep 1947, Turku Finland

year	team	gp	g	a	pts	pim	gp	g	a	pts	pim
76-77	Phx	80	29	31	60	10					
totals		80	29	31	60	10					

• Member, Finland Olympic Team, 1972

Brad RHINESS Bradford Rhiness
5-9 170 L 6 Nov 1956, Huntsville ON

year	team	gp	g	a	pts	pim	gp	g	a	pts	pim
76-77	SD	58	9	14	23	14	5	0	1	1	0
77-78	Ind	12	3	3	6	12					
totals		70	12	17	29	26	5	0	1	1	0

Steve RICHARDSON Stephen John Richardson
6-1 185 L 4 May 1949, Olds AB

year	team	gp	g	a	pts	pim	gp	g	a	pts	pim
74-75	Ind	19	1	4	5	16					
	M-B	47	8	18	26	58					
75-76	NE	6	0	0	0	0					
totals		72	9	22	31	74					

Heikki RIIHIRANTA "Hexi"
5-11 190 L 4 Oct 1948, Helsinki Finland

year	team	gp	g	a	pts	pim	gp	g	a	pts	pim
74-75	Wpg	64	8	14	22	30					
75-76	Wpg	70	1	8	9	26	4	0	4	4	5
76-77	Wpg	53	1	16	17	28					
totals		187	10	38	48	84	4	0	4	4	5

• Member, Finland Olympic Team, 1972

Ron RILEY
6-0 190 - 20 Jul 1948, Montreal PQ

year	team	gp	g	a	pts	pim	gp	g	a	pts	pim
72-73	Ott	22	0	5	5	2	2	0	0	0	0
totals		22	0	5	5	2	2	0	0	0	0

Wayne RIVERS John Wayne Rivers "Moon"
5-9 185 R 1 Feb 1942, Hamilton ON

year	team	gp	g	a	pts	pim	gp	g	a	pts	pim
72-73	NY	75	37	40	77	47					
73-74	NY-J	73	30	27	57	20					
74-75	SD	78	54	53	107	52	5	3	1	4	8
75-76	SD	71	19	25	44	24	11	4	4	8	4
76-77	SD	60	18	31	49	40	7	1	1	2	2
totals		357	158	176	334	183	23	8	6	14	14

• Played in NHL: 1961-69, Det-Bos-StL-NYR, 108-15-30-45-94

Garth RIZZUTO Garth Alexander Rizzuto
5-11 180 L 11 Sep 1947, Trail BC

year	team	gp	g	a	pts	pim	gp	g	a	pts	pim
72-73	Wpg	61	10	10	20	32	14	0	1	1	14
73-74	Wpg	41	3	4	7	8					
totals		102	13	14	17	40	14	0	1	1	14

• Played in NHL: 1970-71, Van, 37-3-4-7-16

Phil ROBERTO Phillip Joseph Roberto
6-1 190 R 1 Jan 1949, Niagara Falls ON

year	team	gp	g	a	pts	pim	gp	g	a	pts	pim
77-78	Bir	53	8	20	28	91	4	1	0	1	20
totals		53	8	20	28	91	4	1	0	1	20

• Played in NHL: 1969-77, Mtl-StL-Det-KC-Col-Cle, 385-75-106-181-464 • Stanley Cup: 1971 (Montreal)

Doug ROBERTS Douglas William Roberts
6-2 200 R 28 Oct 1942, Detroit MI

year	team	gp	g	a	pts	pim	gp	g	a	pts	pim
75-76	NE	76	4	13	17	51	17	1	1	2	8
76-77	NE	64	3	18	21	33	2	0	0	0	0
totals		140	7	31	38	84	19	1	1	2	8

• Brother of Gordie Roberts • Played in NHL: 1965-75, Det-Oak-Cal-Bos, 419-43-104-147-342

Gordie ROBERTS Gordon Roberts
5-11 185 L 2 Oct 1957, Detroit MI

year	team	gp	g	a	pts	pim	gp	g	a	pts	pim
75-76	NE	77	3	19	22	102	17	2	9	11	36
76-77	NE	77	13	33	46	169	5	2	2	4	6
77-78	NE	78	15	46	61	118	14	0	5	5	29
78-79	NE	79	11	46	57	113	10	0	4	4	10
totals		311	42	144	186	502	46	4	20	24	81

• Brother of Doug Roberts • Played in NHL: 1979-94, Hart-Min-Phi-StL-Pit-Bos, 1097-61-359-420-1582 • Stanley Cups: 1991, 1992 (Pittsburgh)

Joe ROBERTSON Joseph Dunbar Robertson
5-11 180 L 10 Mar 1948, Windsor NS

year	team	gp	g	a	pts	pim	gp	g	a	pts	pim
74-75	Ind	18	4	4	8	23					
	Min	11	1	4	5	4					
totals		29	5	8	13	27					

Francois ROCHON Francois Jean Rochon "Frankie"
5-11 180 L 18 Apr 1953, Montreal PQ

year	team	gp	g	a	pts	pim	gp	g	a	pts	pim
73-74	Chi	71	12	11	23	27	9	2	1	3	0
74-75	Chi	69	27	29	56	19					
75-76	D-O	41	11	10	21	10					
	Ind	19	6	2	8	31					
76-77	Ind	67	15	8	23	8	5	0	1	1	0
totals		267	71	60	131	95	14	2	2	4	0

John ROGERS John Alfred Rogers
5-11 175 R 10 Apr 1953, Paradise Hill AB

year	team	gp	g	a	pts	pim	gp	g	a	pts	pim
75-76	Edm	77	9	8	17	34					
totals		77	9	8	17	34					

• Played in NHL: 1973-75, Min, 14-2-4-6-0

Mike ROGERS Michael Rogers
5-9 170 R 24 Oct 1954, Calgary AB

year	team	gp	g	a	pts	pim	gp	g	a	pts	pim
74-75	Edm	78	35	48	83	2					
75-76	Edm	44	12	15	27	10					
	NE	36	18	14	32	10	17	5	8	13	2
76-77	NE	78	25	57	82	10	5	1	1	2	2
77-78	NE	80	28	43	71	46	14	5	6	11	8
78-79	NE	80	27	45	72	31	10	2	6	8	2
totals		396	145	222	367	109	46	13	21	34	14

• Played in NHL: 1979-86, Hart-NYR-Edm, 484-202-317-519-184

Jerry ROLLINS Jerry Allan Rollins
6-3 195 R 22 Mar 1955, New Westminster BC

year	team	gp	g	a	pts	pim	gp	g	a	pts	pim
75-76	Tor	52	5	7	12	185					
76-77	Bir	8	0	0	0	17					
	Phx	63	4	10	14	169					
78-79	Ind	7	0	1	1	7					
totals		130	9	18	27	378					

• Son of Al Rollins

Lorne ROMBOUGH Lorne David Rombough
5-11 190 L 2 Apr 1948, Fergus ON

year	team	gp	g	a	pts	pim	gp	g	a	pts	pim
73-74	Chi	3	1	2	3	0					
totals		3	1	2	3	0					

Bob ROSELLE Robert Roselle
6-2 185 L 17 Oct 1950, Montreal PQ

year	team	gp	g	a	pts	pim	gp	g	a	pts	pim
75-76	Ind	1	0	0	0	0					
totals		1	0	0	0	0					

Randy ROTA Randy Frank Rota
5-8 170 L 16 Aug 1950, Creston BC

year	team	gp	g	a	pts	pim	gp	g	a	pts	pim
76-77	Edm	40	9	6	15	8	5	3	2	5	0
77-78	Edm	53	8	22	30	12	5	1	1	2	4
totals		93	17	28	45	20	10	4	3	7	4

• Played in NHL: 1972-77, Mtl-LA-KC-Col, 212-38-39-77-60

Michel ROULEAU
5-10 170 L 28 Sep 1944, Hull PQ

year	team	gp	g	a	pts	pim	gp	g	a	pts	pim
72-73	Phi	6	0	1	1	15					
	Que	52	7	14	21	142					
73-74	Que	4	0	4	4	2					
74-75	Que	19	1	7	8	63					
	M-B	7	0	3	3	25					
	SD	27	5	6	11	42					
totals		115	13	35	48	289					

Dunc ROUSSEAU Duncan Franklin Rousseau
6-0 195 L 10 Feb 1945, Bissett MB

year	team	gp	g	a	pts	pim	gp	g	a	pts	pim
72-73	Wpg	75	16	17	33	19	14	3	2	5	2
73-74	Wpg	60	10	8	18	39	4	0	0	0	0
totals		135	26	25	51	114	18	3	2	5	2

Pierre ROY
6-0 175 L 12 Mar 1952, Amos PQ

year	team	gp	g	a	pts	pim	gp	g	a	pts	pim
72-73	Que	64	7	12	19	169					
73-74	Que	44	2	7	9	137					
74-75	Que	61	1	18	19	118	15	0	9	9	40
75-76	Que	78	6	30	36	258	5	1	2	3	29
76-77	Que	29	3	5	8	50					
	Cin	39	3	12	15	126	3	0	1	1	7
78-79	NE	1	0	0	0	2					
totals		316	22	84	106	860	23	1	12	13	76

Kent RUHNKE
6-1 180 R 18 Sep 1952, Toronto ON

year	team	gp	g	a	pts	pim	gp	g	a	pts	pim
76-77	Wpg	51	11	11	22	2					
77-78	Wpg	21	8	9	17	2	5	2	0	2	0
totals		72	19	20	39	4	5	2	0	2	0

• Played in NHL: 1975-76, Bos, 2-0-1-1-0

Duane RUPP Duane Edward Franklin Rupp
6-1 195 L 29 Mar 1938, MacNutt SK

year	team	gp	g	a	pts	pim	gp	g	a	pts	pim
74-75	Van	72	3	26	29	45					
75-76	Cgy	42	0	16	16	33	7	0	2	2	8
totals		114	3	42	45	78	7	0	2	2	8

• Played in NHL: 1962-73, NYR-Tor-Min-Pit, 374-24-93-117-220

Terry RUSKOWSKI Terrence Wallace Ruskowski
5-10 180 L 31 Dec 1954, Prince Albert SK

year	team	gp	g	a	pts	pim	gp	g	a	pts	pim
74-75	Hou	71	10	36	46	134	13	4	2	6	15
75-76	Hou	65	14	35	49	100	16	6	10	16	64
76-77	Hou	80	24	60	84	143	11	6	11	17	67
77-78	Hou	78	15	57	72	170	4	1	1	2	5
78-79	Wpg	75	20	66	86	211	8	1	12	13	23
totals		369	83	254	337	761	52	18	36	54	174

• Played in NHL: 1979-89, Chi-LA-Pit-Min, 630-113-313-426-1354

Bob RUSSELL Robert Russell
5-9 170 L 5 Feb 1955, Toronto ON

year	team	gp	g	a	pts	pim	gp	g	a	pts	pim
75-76	Edm	58	13	18	31	19	4	1	0	1	0
76-77	Edm	57	7	6	13	41	1	0	0	0	0
totals		115	20	24	44	60	5	1	0	1	0

Terry RYAN Terrence Clinton John Ryan
5-10 180 L 10 Sep 1952, Grand Falls NF

year	team	gp	g	a	pts	pim	gp	g	a	pts	pim
72-73	Min	76	13	6	19	13	5	0	2	2	0
totals		76	13	6	19	13	5	0	2	2	0

Al RYCROFT Allen Bruce Rycroft
5-9 170 R 9 Jan 1950, Beaver Lodge AB

year	team	gp	g	a	pts	pim	gp	g	a	pts	pim
72-73	Cle	7	0	2	2	0					
totals		7	0	2	2	0					

Blaine RYDMAN
6-2 195 L 16 Dec 1949, Weyburn SK

year	team	gp	g	a	pts	pim	gp	g	a	pts	pim
72-73	NY	2	0	0	0	4					
	Min	29	0	1	1	65	1	0	0	0	0
73-74	Min	8	0	0	0	21					
totals		39	0	1	1	90	1	0	0	0	0

Larry SACHARUK Lawrence Sacharuk
6-0 190 R 16 Sep 1952, Saskatoon SK

year	team	gp	g	a	pts	pim	gp	g	a	pts	pim
78-79	Ind	15	2	9	11	25					
totals		15	2	9	11	25					

• Played in NHL: 1972-77, NYR-StL, 151-29-33-62-42

Claude ST. SAUVEUR
6-0 170 L 2 Jan 1952, Sherbrooke PQ

year	team	gp	g	a	pts	pim	gp	g	a	pts	pim
72-73	Phi	2	1	0	1	0					
73-74	Van	70	38	30	68	55					
74-75	Van	76	24	23	47	32					
76-77	Cgy	17	0	3	3	2					
	Edm	15	5	7	12	2	5	1	0	1	0
77-78	Ind	72	36	42	78	24					
78-79	Ind	17	4	2	6	12					
	Cin	16	4	5	9	4					
totals		285	112	112	224	131	5	1	0	1	0

• Played in NHL: 1975-76, Atl, 79-24-24-48-23

Cal SANDBECK Calvin Wayne Sandbeck
6-1 220 R 28 Jan 1956, International Falls MN

year	team	gp	g	a	pts	pim	gp	g	a	pts	pim
77-78	Edm	11	1	2	3	39	5	0	0	0	10
78-79	Edm	6	0	0	0	2					
totals		17	1	2	3	41	5	0	0	0	10

Frank SANDERS Franklyn Bonn Sanders
6-3 220 R 8 Mar 1949, St Paul MN d. 2012

year	team	gp	g	a	pts	pim	gp	g	a	pts	pim
72-73	Min	78	8	8	16	94	4	0	1	1	0
totals		78	8	8	16	94	4	0	1	1	0

• Member, United States Olympic Team, 1972

Derek SANDERSON Derek Michael Sanderson
6-0 170 L 16 Jun 1946, Niagara Falls ON

year	team	gp	g	a	pts	pim	gp	g	a	pts	pim
72-73	Phi	8	3	3	6	69					
totals		8	3	3	6	69					

• Played in NHL: 1965-78, Bos-NYR-StL-Van-Pit, 598-202-250-452-911 • Stanley Cups: 1970, 1972 (Boston)

Craig SARNER Craig Brian Sarner
5-11 185 L 20 Jun 1949, St Paul MN

year	team	gp	g	a	pts	pim	gp	g	a	pts	pim
75-76	Min	1	0	0	0	0					
totals		1	0	0	0	0					

• Played in NHL: 1974-75, Bos, 7-0-0-0-0 • Member, United States Olympic Team, 1972

Dick SARRAZIN Richard Andre Sarrazin
6-0 185 R 22 Jan 1946, St Gabriel de Brandon PQ

year	team	gp	g	a	pts	pim	gp	g	a	pts	pim
72-73	NE	35	4	7	11	0					
	Chi	33	3	8	11	2					
totals		68	7	15	22	2					

• Played in NHL: 1968-72, Phi, 100-20-35-55-22

Glen SATHER Glen Cameron Sather "Slats"
5-11 180 L 2 Sep 1943, High River AB

year	team	gp	g	a	pts	pim	gp	g	a	pts	pim
76-77	Edm	81	19	34	53	77	5	1	1	2	2
totals		81	19	34	53	77	5	1	1	2	2

• Played in NHL: 1966-76, Bos-Pit-NYR-StL-Min, 656-80-113-193-724 • Stanley Cups: 1984, 1985, 1987, 1988 (Edmonton as Coach) • Member, Hockey Hall of Fame.

Ted SCHARF
Edward Wilson Scharf
5-11 185 R 3 Oct 1951, Sudbury ON

year	team	gp	g	a	pts	pim	gp	g	a	pts	pim
72-73	NY	29	2	2	4	72					
73-74	NY-J	63	4	2	6	107					
74-75	SD	67	3	1	4	94					
75-76	Ind	74	7	13	20	56	7	0	0	0	5
76-77	Edm	5	0	2	2	14					
totals		238	16	20	36	343	7	0	0	0	5

John SCHELLA
John Edward Schella
6-0 180 R 9 May 1947, Port Arthur ON

year	team	gp	g	a	pts	pim	gp	g	a	pts	pim
72-73	Hou	77	2	24	26	239	10	0	2	2	12
73-74	Hou	73	12	19	31	170	14	2	6	8	42
74-75	Hou	78	10	42	52	176	13	0	8	8	12
75-76	Hou	74	6	32	38	106	17	1	6	7	38
76-77	Hou	20	0	6	6	28	6	1	2	3	6
77-78	Hou	63	9	20	29	125	6	0	1	1	33
totals		385	39	143	182	844	66	4	25	29	143

• Played in NHL: 1970-72, Van, 115-2-18-20-224

Buzz SCHNEIDER
William Schneider
5-11 175 L 14 Sep 1954, Babbitt MN

year	team	gp	g	a	pts	pim	gp	g	a	pts	pim
76-77	Bir	4	0	0	0	2					
totals		4	0	0	0	2					

• Member, United States Olympic Team, 1976 & 1980

Jim SCHRAEFEL
James Schraefel
6-1 180 L 23 Aug 1948, Dauphin MB

year	team	gp	g	a	pts	pim	gp	g	a	pts	pim
73-74	Edm	34	1	1	2	0	5	0	3	3	0
totals		34	1	1	2	0	5	0	3	3	0

Brit SELBY
Robert Briton Selby
5-10 175 L 27 Mar 1945, Kingston ON

year	team	gp	g	a	pts	pim	gp	g	a	pts	pim
72-73	Que	7	0	1	1	4					
	NE	65	13	29	42	48	13	3	4	7	13
73-74	Tor	64	9	17	26	21	10	1	3	4	2
74-75	Tor	17	1	4	5	0					
totals		153	23	51	74	73	23	4	7	11	15

• Played in NHL: 1965-72, Tor-Phi-StL, 347-55-62-117-171

Brad SELWOOD
Bradley Wayne Selwood
6-1 190 L 18 Mar 1948, Leamington ON

year	team	gp	g	a	pts	pim	gp	g	a	pts	pim
72-73	NE	75	13	21	34	114	15	3	5	8	22
73-74	NE	76	9	28	37	91	7	0	2	2	11
74-75	NE	77	4	35	39	117	5	1	0	1	11
75-76	NE	40	2	10	12	28	17	2	2	4	27
76-77	NE	41	4	12	16	71	5	0	0	0	2
77-78	NE	80	6	25	31	88	14	0	3	3	8
78-79	NE	42	4	12	16	47					
totals		431	42	143	185	556	63	6	12	18	81

• Played in NHL: 1970-72, 1979-80, Tor-LA, 163-7-40-47-153

Dave SEMENKO
6-3 200 L 12 Jul 1957, Winnipeg MB

year	team	gp	g	a	pts	pim	gp	g	a	pts	pim
77-78	Edm	65	6	6	12	140	5	0	0	0	8
78-79	Edm	77	10	14	24	158	11	4	2	6	29
totals		142	16	20	36	298	16	4	2	6	37

• Played in NHL: 1979-88, Edm-Hart-Tor, 575-65-88-153-1175 • Stanley Cups: 1984, 1985 (Edmonton)

Dick SENTES
Richard James Sentes
5-11 180 L 10 Jan 1947, Regina SK

year	team	gp	g	a	pts	pim	gp	g	a	pts	pim
72-73	Ott	74	22	19	41	78	5	3	1	4	2
73-74	Tor	64	26	34	60	46	12	7	4	11	19
74-75	SD	74	44	41	85	52	10	0	2	2	0
75-76	Cgy	72	25	24	49	33	8	0	1	1	8
76-77	Cgy	29	10	14	24	8					
	SD	24	10	11	21	16	5	4	0	4	12
totals		337	137	143	280	233	40	14	8	22	41

Ron SERAFINI
Ronald William Serafini
5-11 185 R 31 Oct 1953, Detroit MI

year	team	gp	g	a	pts	pim	gp	g	a	pts	pim
75-76	Cin	16	0	2	2	15					
totals		16	0	2	2	15					

• Played in NHL: 1973-74, Cal, 2-0-0-0-2

Tom SERVISS
Thomas Hugh Serviss
5-10 185 R 25 May 1948, Moose Jaw SK

year	team	gp	g	a	pts	pim	gp	g	a	pts	pim
72-73	LA	73	11	26	37	32	6	0	0	0	0
73-74	LA	74	6	15	21	37					
74-75	M-B	61	12	17	29	18					
75-76	Que	71	7	19	26	12	5	0	0	0	0
76-77	Cgy	8	2	1	3	2					
totals		287	38	78	116	101	11	0	0	0	0

Sean SHANAHAN
Sean Bryan Shanahan
6-3 205 R 8 Feb 1951, Toronto ON

year	team	gp	g	a	pts	pim	gp	g	a	pts	pim
78-79	Cin	4	0	0	0	7					
totals		4	0	0	0	7					

• Played in NHL: 1975-78, Mtl-Col-Bos, 40-1-3-4-47

Bobby SHEEHAN
Robert Richard Sheehan "She-cat"
5-8 170 L 11 Jan 1949, Weymouth MA

year	team	gp	g	a	pts	pim	gp	g	a	pts	pim
72-73	NY	75	35	53	88	17					
73-74	NY-J	50	12	8	20	8					
	Edm	10	1	3	4	6	5	1	3	4	0
74-75	Edm	77	19	39	58	8					
77-78	Ind	29	8	7	15	6					
totals		241	75	110	185	45	5	1	3	4	0

• Played in NHL: 1969-72, 1975-78, Mtl-Cal-Chi-Det-NYR-Col-LA, 310-48-63-111-40 • Stanley Cup: 1971 (Montreal)

Tim SHEEHY
Timothy Kane Sheehy
6-1 185 R 3 Sep 1948, Ft Frances ON

year	team	gp	g	a	pts	pim	gp	g	a	pts	pim
72-73	NE	78	33	38	71	30	15	9	14	23	13
73-74	NE	77	29	29	58	22	7	4	2	6	4
74-75	NE	52	21	13	34	18					
	Edm	29	8	20	28	4					
75-76	Edm	81	34	31	65	17	4	2	2	4	0
76-77	Edm	28	15	8	23	4					
	Bir	50	26	21	47	44					
77-78	Bir	13	4	2	6	5					
	NE	25	8	11	19	12	13	1	3	4	9
totals		433	178	173	351	156	39	16	21	37	26

• Played in NHL: 1977-80, Det-Hart, 27-2-1-3-0 • Member, United States Olympic Team, 1972

John SHERIDAN
6-1 190 L 18 Sep 1954, Minneapolis MN

year	team	gp	g	a	pts	pim	gp	g	a	pts	pim
74-75	Ind	58	17	11	28	20					
75-76	Ind	11	1	2	3	0					
totals		69	18	13	31	20					

Jim SHERRIT
James Sherrit
5-7 170 L 29 Sep 1948, Glasgow Scotland

year	team	gp	g	a	pts	pim	gp	g	a	pts	pim
73-74	Hou	76	30	28	58	14	14	5	7	12	2
74-75	Hou	77	22	25	47	25	13	3	3	6	6
75-76	D-O	40	11	19	30	16					
totals		193	63	72	135	59	27	8	10	18	8

Glen SHIRTON
5-10 170 R 15 Jul 1947, Ingersoll ON

year	team	gp	g	a	pts	pim	gp	g	a	pts	pim
73-74	Cle	4	0	0	0	0					
totals		4	0	0	0	0					

John SHMYR
5-10 180 L 2 Jan 1945, Cudworth SK

year	team	gp	g	a	pts	pim	gp	g	a	pts	pim
72-73	Wpg	7	0	0	0	2	3	0	1	1	2
73-74	Chi	43	1	3	4	13					
74-75	Van	39	1	5	6	43					
totals		89	2	8	10	58	3	0	1	1	2

• Brother of Paul Shmyr

Paul SHMYR

5-11 175 L 28 Jan 1946, Cudworth SK d. 2004

year	team	gp	g	a	pts	pim	gp	g	a	pts	pim
72-73	Cle	73	5	43	48	169	8	1	3	4	19
73-74	Cle	78	13	31	44	165	5	0	4	4	31
74-75	Cle	49	7	14	21	103	5	2	1	3	15
75-76	Cle	70	6	44	50	101					
76-77	SD	81	13	37	50	103	7	0	2	2	8
77-78	Edm	80	9	40	49	100	5	1	3	4	11
78-79	Edm	80	8	39	47	119	13	1	5	6	23
totals		511	61	248	309	860	43	5	18	23	107

• Brother of John Shmyr • Played in NHL: 1968-72, 1979-82, Chi-Cal-Min-Hart, 343-13-72-85-528

Byron SHUTT

6-1 195 L 26 Oct 1955, Toronto ON

year	team	gp	g	a	pts	pim	gp	g	a	pts	pim
78-79	Cin	65	10	7	17	115	3	1	1	2	14
totals		65	10	7	17	115	3	1	1	2	14

Bob SICINSKI   Robert Stanley Sicinski

5-11 175 L 13 Nov 1946, Toronto ON

year	team	gp	g	a	pts	pim	gp	g	a	pts	pim
72-73	Chi	77	25	63	88	19					
73-74	Chi	69	11	29	40	8	18	6	8	14	0
74-75	Ind	77	19	34	53	12					
75-76	Ind	70	9	34	43	4	7	0	0	0	2
76-77	Ind	60	12	24	36	14	9	0	3	3	4
totals		353	76	184	260	56	34	6	11	17	6

Risto SILTANEN

5-8 185 L 31 Oct 1958, Mantta Finland

year	team	gp	g	a	pts	pim	gp	g	a	pts	pim
78-79	Edm	20	3	4	7	4	11	0	9	9	4
totals		20	3	4	7	4	11	0	9	9	4

• Played in NHL: 1979-87, Edm-Hart-Que, 562-90-265-355-266

Tom SIMPSON   Thomas Phillip Simpson "Shotgun"

5-9 190 R 15 Aug 1952, Bowmanville ON

year	team	gp	g	a	pts	pim	gp	g	a	pts	pim
72-73	Ott	57	10	7	17	44	5	1	0	1	0
73-74	Tor	74	33	20	53	27	12	4	1	5	5
74-75	Tor	70	52	28	80	48	5	1	1	2	0
75-76	Tor	73	20	21	41	15					
76-77	Bir	25	7	6	13	10					
	Edm	15	3	2	5	16					
totals		314	125	84	209	160	22	6	2	8	5

Gary SITTLER

6-1 190 L 14 Mar 1952, St Jacobs ON d. 2015

year	team	gp	g	a	pts	pim	gp	g	a	pts	pim
74-75	M-B	5	1	1	2	14					
totals		5	1	1	2	14					

Lars-Erik SJOBERG

5-8 180 L 5 Apr 1944, Falun Sweden d. 1987

year	team	gp	g	a	pts	pim	gp	g	a	pts	pim
74-75	Wpg	75	7	53	60	30					
75-76	Wpg	81	5	36	41	12	13	0	5	5	12
76-77	Wpg	52	2	38	40	31	20	0	5	5	12
77-78	Wpg	78	11	39	50	72	9	0	9	9	4
78-79	Wpg	9	0	3	3	2	10	1	2	3	4
totals		295	25	169	194	147	52	1	21	22	32

• Played in NHL: 1979-80, Wpg, 80-7-27-34-46 • Member, Sweden Olympic Team, 1968 & 1972

Peter SLATER

5-9 170 L 31 Jan 1948, Renfrew ON

year	team	gp	g	a	pts	pim	gp	g	a	pts	pim
72-73	LA	72	12	12	24	87	6	0	0	0	2
73-74	LA	19	1	1	2	2					
totals		91	13	13	26	89	6	0	0	0	2

• Brother of Terry Slater

Mike SLEEP   Michael William Sleep

6-0 180 R 13 Mar 1955, Montreal PQ d. 2014

year	team	gp	g	a	pts	pim	gp	g	a	pts	pim
75-76	Phx	9	2	0	2	0					
76-77	Phx	13	2	2	4	6					
totals		22	4	2	6	6					

Louis SLEIGHER

5-11 195 R 23 Oct 1958, Nouvelle PQ

year	team	gp	g	a	pts	pim	gp	g	a	pts	pim
78-79	Bir	62	26	12	38	46					
totals		62	26	12	38	46					

• Played in NHL: 1979-87, Que-Bos-194-46-53-99-146

Dale SMEDSMO   Dale Darwin Smedsmo

6-1 195 L 23 Apr 1951, Roseau MN

year	team	gp	g	a	pts	pim	gp	g	a	pts	pim
75-76	Cin	66	8	14	22	187					
76-77	NE	15	2	0	2	54					
	Cin	23	0	5	5	43	2	0	1	1	0
77-78	Ind	6	0	3	3	7					
totals		110	10	22	32	291	2	0	1	1	0

• Played in NHL: 1972-73, Tor, 4-0-0-0-0

Brian SMITH   Brian Desmond Smith

5-11 170 R 6 Sep 1940, Ottawa ON d. 1995

year	team	gp	g	a	pts	pim	gp	g	a	pts	pim
72-73	Hou	48	7	6	13	19	10	0	2	2	0
totals		48	7	6	13	19	10	0	2	2	0

• Brother of Gary Smith • Played in NHL: 1967-69, LA-Min, 67-10-10-20-33

Guy SMITH

6-1 180 R 2 Jan 1950, Ottawa ON

year	team	gp	g	a	pts	pim	gp	g	a	pts	pim
72-73	NE	22	3	3	6	6	11	2	0	2	4
73-74	NE	16	1	5	6	25					
totals		38	4	8	12	31	11	2	0	2	4

Rick SMITH   Richard Allan Smith

5-11 190 L 29 Jun 1948, Kingston ON

year	team	gp	g	a	pts	pim	gp	g	a	pts	pim
73-74	Min	71	10	28	38	98	11	0	1	1	22
74-75	Min	78	9	29	38	112	12	2	7	9	6
75-76	Min	51	1	32	33	50					
totals		200	20	89	109	260	23	2	8	10	28

• Played in NHL: 1968-73, 1975-81, Bos-Cal-StL-Det-Wash, 687-52-167-219-560 • Stanley Cup: 1970 (Boston)

Ross SMITH

6-0 185 L 20 Nov 1953, Fawcett AB

year	team	gp	g	a	pts	pim	gp	g	a	pts	pim
74-75	Ind	15	1	6	7	19					
totals		15	1	6	7	19					

Ron SNELL   Ronald Wayne Snell

5-10 165 R 11 Aug 1948, Regina SK

year	team	gp	g	a	pts	pim	gp	g	a	pts	pim
73-74	Wpg	70	24	25	49	32	4	0	0	0	0
74-75	Wpg	20	0	0	0	8					
totals		90	24	25	49	40	4	0	0	0	0

• Played in NHL: 1968-70, Pit, 7-3-2-5-6

Dennis SOBCHUK   Dennis James Sobchuk

6-2 175 L 12 Jan 1954, Lang SK

year	team	gp	g	a	pts	pim	gp	g	a	pts	pim
74-75	Phx	78	32	45	77	36	5	4	1	5	2
75-76	Cin	79	32	40	72	74					
76-77	Cin	81	44	52	96	38	3	0	1	1	2
77-78	Cin	23	5	9	14	22					
	Edm	13	6	3	9	4	5	1	0	1	4
78-79	Edm	74	26	37	63	31	12	6	6	12	4
totals		348	145	186	331	205	25	11	8	19	12

• Brother of Gene Sobchuk • Played in NHL: 1979-83, Det-Que, 35-5-6-11-2

Gene SOBCHUK   Eugene Sobchuk

5-9 170 L 2 Jan 1951, Lang SK

year	team	gp	g	a	pts	pim	gp	g	a	pts	pim
74-75	Phx	3	1	0	1	0	5	0	0	0	0
75-76	Cin	78	23	18	41	37					
totals		81	24	18	42	37	5	0	0	0	0

• Brother of Dennis Sobchuk • Played in NHL: 1973-74, Van, 1-0-0-0-0

Fred SPECK — Frederick Edmunstone Speck
5-9 165 L 22 Jul 1947, Thorold ON d. 2011

year	team	gp	g	a	pts	pim	gp	g	a	pts	pim
72-73	Min	47	13	16	29	52					
	LA	28	3	13	16	22	6	3	2	5	2
73-74	LA	18	2	5	7	4					
74-75	M-B	30	4	8	12	18					
totals		123	22	42	64	96	6	3	2	5	2

• Played in NHL: 1968-72, Det-Van, 28-1-2-3-2

Bill SPEER — Francis William Speer
5-11 220 L 20 Mar 1942, Lindsay ON d. 1989

year	team	gp	g	a	pts	pim	gp	g	a	pts	pim
72-73	NY	69	3	23	26	40					
73-74	NY-J	66	1	3	4	30					
totals		135	4	26	30	70					

• Played in NHL: 1967-71, Pit-Bos, 130-5-20-25-79 • Stanley Cup: 1970 (Boston)

Irv SPENCER — James Irvin Spencer
5-10 180 L 4 Dec 1937, Sudbury ON d. 1999

year	team	gp	g	a	pts	pim	gp	g	a	pts	pim
72-73	Phi	54	2	27	29	43	4	0	0	0	4
73-74	Van	19	0	1	1	6					
totals		73	2	28	30	49	4	0	0	0	4

• Played in NHL: 1959-68, NYR-Bos-Det, 230-12-38-50-127

Dan SPRING — Daniel Joseph Spring
6-0 180 R 31 Oct 1951, Rossland BC

year	team	gp	g	a	pts	pim	gp	g	a	pts	pim
73-74	Wpg	66	8	16	24	8	4	0	1	1	0
74-75	Wpg	60	19	24	43	22					
75-76	Edm	75	12	11	23	8	2	1	1	2	0
totals		201	39	51	90	38	6	1	2	3	0

Frank SPRING — Franklin Patrick Spring
6-3 215 R 19 Oct 1949, Cranbrook BC

year	team	gp	g	a	pts	pim	gp	g	a	pts	pim
77-78	Ind	13	2	4	6	2					
totals		13	2	4	6	2					

• Played in NHL: 1969-77, Bos-StL-Cal-Cle, 61-14-20-34-12

Jack STANFIELD — John Gordon Stanfield
5-11 175 L 30 May 1942, Toronto ON

year	team	gp	g	a	pts	pim	gp	g	a	pts	pim
72-73	Hou	71	8	12	20	8	9	1	0	1	0
73-74	Hou	41	1	3	4	2	7	0	0	0	2
totals		112	9	15	24	10	16	1	0	1	2

• Played in NHL: 1966, Chi (Playoffs, 1-0-0-0-0)

Pat STAPLETON — Patrick James Stapleton "Whitey"
5-8 180 L 4 Jul 1940, Sarnia ON

year	team	gp	g	a	pts	pim	gp	g	a	pts	pim
73-74	Chi	78	6	52	58	44	18	0	13	13	36
74-75	Chi	68	4	30	34	38					
75-76	Ind	80	5	40	45	48	7	0	2	2	2
76-77	Ind	81	8	45	53	29	9	2	6	8	0
77-78	Cin	65	4	45	49	28					
totals		372	27	212	239	187	34	2	21	23	38

• Played in NHL: 1961-73, Bos-Chi, 635-43-294-337-353

Billy STEELE
5-7 170 R 13 Nov 1952, Edinburgh Scotland

year	team	gp	g	a	pts	pim	gp	g	a	pts	pim
75-76	Cin	3	2	0	2	0					
76-77	Cin	81	9	22	31	21	2	0	0	0	0
totals		84	11	22	33	21	2	0	0	0	0

Ken STEPHANSON — Kenneth Stephanson
5-11 195 L 13 Nov 1941, Selkirk MB

year	team	gp	g	a	pts	pim	gp	g	a	pts	pim
72-73	Ott	77	3	16	19	93	5	1	1	2	8
73-74	Wpg	29	0	7	7	74	3	0	2	2	10
totals		106	3	23	26	167	8	1	3	4	18

Bob STEPHENSON — Robert Stephenson
6-1 190 R 1 Feb 1954, Saskatoon SK

year	team	gp	g	a	pts	pim	gp	g	a	pts	pim
77-78	Bir	39	7	6	13	33					
78-79	Bir	78	23	24	47	72					
totals		117	30	30	60	105					

• Played in NHL: 1979-80, Hart-Tor, 18-2-3-5-4

Mike STEVENS — Michael Gordon Stevens
5-11 195 L 13 Oct 1950, Winnipeg MB

year	team	gp	g	a	pts	pim	gp	g	a	pts	pim
74-75	Phx	70	2	16	18	69	5	0	1	1	0
75-76	Hou	6	0	0	0	2					
totals		76	2	16	18	71	5	0	1	1	0

John A. STEWART — John Alexander Stewart
6-0 180 L 16 May 1950, Eriksdale MB

year	team	gp	g	a	pts	pim	gp	g	a	pts	pim
75-76	Cle	79	12	21	33	42	3	0	0	0	0
76-77	Min	15	3	3	6	2					
	Bir	1	0	0	0	0					
totals		95	15	24	39	44	3	0	0	0	0

• Played in NHL: 1970-75, Pit-Atl-Cal, 258-58-60-118-158

John C. STEWART — John Christopher Stewart "JC"
5-11 170 L 2 Jan 1954, Toronto ON

year	team	gp	g	a	pts	pim	gp	g	a	pts	pim
74-75	Cle	59	4	7	11	8	1	0	0	0	0
75-76	Cle	42	2	9	11	15					
76-77	Bir	52	17	24	41	33					
77-78	Bir	48	13	26	39	52	5	1	1	2	6
78-79	Bir	70	24	26	50	108					
totals		271	60	92	152	213	6	1	1	2	6

• Played in NHL: 1979-80, Que, 2-0-0-0-0

Paul STEWART
6-1 205 L 21 Mar 1954, Boston MA

year	team	gp	g	a	pts	pim	gp	g	a	pts	pim
76-77	Edm	2	0	0	0	2					
77-78	Cin	40	1	5	6	241					
78-79	Cin	23	2	1	3	45	3	0	0	0	0
totals		65	3	6	9	288	3	0	0	0	0

• Played in NHL: 1979-80, Que, 21-2-0-2-74 • Became an NHL Referee after retirement as a player

Blaine STOUGHTON
5-10 185 R 13 Mar 1953, Gilbert Plains MB

year	team	gp	g	a	pts	pim	gp	g	a	pts	pim
76-77	Cin	81	52	52	104	39	4	0	3	3	2
77-78	Cin	30	6	13	19	36					
	Ind	47	13	13	26	28					
78-79	Ind	25	9	9	18	16					
	NE	36	9	3	12	2	7	4	3	7	4
totals		219	89	90	179	121	11	4	6	10	6

• Played in NHL: 1973-76, 1979-84, Pit-Tor-Hart-NYR, 526-258-191-449-204

Peter SULLIVAN — Peter Gerald Sullivan "Silky"
5-9 165 L 25 Jul 1951, Toronto ON

year	team	gp	g	a	pts	pim	gp	g	a	pts	pim
75-76	Wpg	78	32	39	71	22	13	6	7	13	0
76-77	Wpg	78	31	52	83	18	20	7	12	19	2
77-78	Wpg	77	16	39	55	43	9	3	4	7	4
78-79	Wpg	80	46	40	86	24	10	5	9	14	2
totals		313	125	170	295	107	52	20	32	52	8

• Played in NHL: 1979-81, Wpg, 126-28-54-82-40

Bill SUTHERLAND — William Fraser Sutherland
5-10 175 L 10 Nov 1934, Regina SK

year	team	gp	g	a	pts	pim	gp	g	a	pts	pim
72-73	Wpg	48	6	16	22	34	14	5	9	14	9
73-74	Wpg	12	4	5	9	6	4	0	0	0	4
totals		60	10	21	31	40	18	5	9	14	13

• Played in NHL: 1963-72, Mtl-Phi-Tor-StL-Det, 250-70-58-128-99

Steve SUTHERLAND — Stephen Sutherland
5-11 170 L 1 Sep 1946, Noranda PQ

year	team	gp	g	a	pts	pim	gp	g	a	pts	pim
72-73	LA	43	11	6	17	98	6	0	2	2	8
73-74	LA	72	20	12	32	182					
74-75	M-B	22	1	5	6	37					
	Que	56	14	15	29	114	13	0	3	3	34
75-76	Que	74	22	19	41	197	4	2	1	3	17
76-77	Que	36	6	9	15	34	17	0	5	5	16
77-78	Que	75	23	10	33	143	11	2	0	2	37
totals		378	97	76	173	805	51	9	6	15	112

Garry SWAIN — Garth Frederick Arthur Swain
5-9 165 L 11 Sep 1947, Welland ON

year	team	gp	g	a	pts	pim	gp	g	a	pts	pim
74-75	NE	66	7	15	22	18	6	0	3	3	41
75-76	NE	79	10	16	26	46	17	3	2	5	15
76-77	NE	26	5	2	7	6	2	0	0	0	0
totals		171	22	33	55	70	25	3	5	8	56

• Played in NHL: 1968-69, Pit, 9-1-1-2-0

Cal SWENSON — Calvin Berle Swenson
5-8 185 L 16 Apr 1948, Naicam SK d. 2014

year	team	gp	g	a	pts	pim	gp	g	a	pts	pim
72-73	Wpg	75	7	21	28	19	14	1	5	6	7
73-74	Wpg	25	5	4	9	2	1	0	0	0	0
totals		100	12	25	37	21	15	1	5	6	7

Dave SYVRET — David James Syvret
6-0 190 L 28 Oct 1954, Hamilton ON

year	team	gp	g	a	pts	pim	gp	g	a	pts	pim
75-76	Tor	50	1	11	12	14					
76-77	Bir	8	0	0	0	0					
totals		58	1	11	12	14					

Joe SZURA — Joseph Boleslaw Szura
6-3 200 L 18 Dec 1938, Fort William ON d. 2006

year	team	gp	g	a	pts	pim	gp	g	a	pts	pim
72-73	LA	72	13	32	45	25	2	0	0	0	0
73-74	Hou	42	8	7	15	4	10	0	0	0	0
totals		114	21	39	60	29	12	0	0	0	

• Played in NHL: 1967-69, Oak, 90-10-15-25-30

Rudy TAJCNAR — Rudolph Tajcnar
5-11 200 L 17 Apr 1948, Bratislava Czech. d. 2005

year	team	gp	g	a	pts	pim	gp	g	a	pts	pim
78-79	Edm	2	0	0	0	0					
totals		2	0	0	0	0					

• Member, Czechoslovakia Olympic Team, 1972

Juhani TAMMINEN
5-11 185 L 26 May 1950, Turku Finland

year	team	gp	g	a	pts	pim	gp	g	a	pts	pim
75-76	Cle	65	7	14	21	12	1	0	0	0	0
76-77	Phx	65	10	29	39	72					
totals		130	17	43	60	84	1	0	0	0	0

• Member, Finland Olympic Team, 1972

Don TANNAHILL — Donald Andrew Tannahill
5-11 180 L 21 Feb 1949, Penetang ON

year	team	gp	g	a	pts	pim	gp	g	a	pts	pim
74-75	Min	72	23	30	53	20	10	2	4	6	0
75-76	Cgy	78	25	24	49	10	10	2	5	7	8
76-77	Cgy	77	10	22	32	4					
totals		227	58	76	134	34	20	4	9	13	8

• Played in NHL: 1972-74, Van, 111-30-33-63-25

Marc TARDIF — Joseph Gerard Marquis Tardif
6-1 180 L 12 Jun 1949, Granby PQ

year	team	gp	g	a	pts	pim	gp	g	a	pts	pim
73-74	LA	75	40	30	70	47					
74-75	M-B	23	12	5	17	9					
	Que	53	38	34	72	70	15	10	11	21	10
75-76	Que	81	71	77	148	79	2	1	0	1	2
76-77	Que	62	49	60	109	65	12	4	10	14	8
77-78	Que	78	65	89	154	50	11	6	9	15	11
78-79	Que	74	41	55	96	98	4	6	2	8	4
totals		446	316	350	666	418	44	27	32	59	35

• Played in NHL: 1969-73, 1979-83, Mtl-Que, 517-194-207-401-443
• Stanley Cups: 1971, 1973 (Montreal)

Ted TAYLOR — Edward Wray Taylor
6-0 175 L 25 Feb 1942, Oak Lake MB

year	team	gp	g	a	pts	pim	gp	g	a	pts	pim
72-73	Hou	72	34	42	76	101	10	3	1	4	10
73-74	Hou	75	21	23	44	143	14	4	8	12	60
74-75	Hou	73	26	27	53	130	11	2	5	7	22
75-76	Hou	68	15	26	41	80	11	2	2	4	28
76-77	Hou	78	16	35	51	90	11	4	4	8	28
77-78	Hou	54	11	11	22	46	6	3	1	4	10
totals		420	123	164	287	598	63	18	21	39	217

• Played in NHL: 1964-72, NYR-Det-Min-Van, 166-23-35-58-181

Greg TEBBUTT — Gregory Tebbutt
6-3 215 L 11 May 1957, Vancouver BC

year	team	gp	g	a	pts	pim	gp	g	a	pts	pim
78-79	Bir	38	2	5	7	83					
totals		38	2	5	7	83					

• Played in NHL: 1979-84, Que-Pit, 26-0-3-3-35

Paul TERBENCHE — Paul Frederick Terbenche
5-10 170 L 16 Sep 1945, Port Hope ON d. 2012

year	team	gp	g	a	pts	pim	gp	g	a	pts	pim
74-75	Van	60	3	14	17	10					
75-76	Cgy	58	2	4	6	22	10	0	6	6	6
76-77	Cgy	80	9	24	33	30					
77-78	Bir	11	1	0	1	0					
	Hou	0	0	0	0	0	6	1	1	2	0
78-79	Wpg	68	3	22	25	12	10	1	1	2	4
totals		277	18	64	82	74	26	2	8	10	10

• Played in NHL: 1967-74, Chi-Buf, 189-5-26-31-28

Jean TETREAULT — Jean Rosario Tetreault
6-0 170 L 22 Jan 1953, Ste-Therese PQ

year	team	gp	g	a	pts	pim	gp	g	a	pts	pim
73-74	Van	6	1	1	2	0					
75-76	Min	3	0	0	0	0					
totals		9	1	1	2	0					

Reg THOMAS — Reginald Kenneth Thomas
5-10 170 L 21 Apr 1953, Lambeth ON

year	team	gp	g	a	pts	pim	gp	g	a	pts	pim
73-74	LA	77	14	21	35	22					
74-75	M-B	50	8	13	21	42					
75-76	Ind	80	23	17	40	23	7	1	0	1	4
76-77	Ind	79	25	30	55	34	9	7	9	16	4
77-78	Ind	49	15	16	31	44					
	Cin	18	4	2	6	36					
78-79	Cin	80	32	39	71	22	3	1	1	2	0
totals		433	121	138	159	199	19	9	10	19	8

• Played in NHL: 1979-80, Que, 39-9-7-16-6

Alex TIDEY — Alexander Mansfield Tidey
6-0 180 R 5 Jan 1955, Vancouver BC

year	team	gp	g	a	pts	pim	gp	g	a	pts	pim
75-76	SD	74	16	11	27	46	11	3	6	9	10
totals		74	16	11	27	46	11	3	6	9	10

• Played in NHL: 1976-80, Buf-Edm, 9-0-0-0-8

Gord TITCOMB — Gordon Titcomb
5-11 185 L 3 Sep 1953, Dalhousie NB

year	team	gp	g	a	pts	pim	gp	g	a	pts	pim
74-75	Tor	2	0	1	1	0					
totals		2	0	1	1	0					

John TONELLI — John A. Tonelli
6-1 190 L 23 Mar 1957, Hamilton ON

year	team	gp	g	a	pts	pim	gp	g	a	pts	pim
75-76	Hou	79	17	14	31	66	17	7	7	14	8
76-77	Hou	80	24	31	55	109	11	3	4	7	12
77-78	Hou	65	23	41	64	103	6	1	3	4	8
totals		224	64	86	150	278	34	11	14	25	28

• Played in NHL: 1978-92, NYI-Cgy-LA-Chi-Que, 1028-325-511-836-911 • Stanley Cups: 1980, 1981, 1982, 1983 (NY Islanders)

Craig TOPOLNISKY
5-11 190 R 8 Oct 1957, Edmonton AB

year	team	gp	g	a	pts	pim	gp	g	a	pts	pim
77-78	Edm	10	0	2	2	4					
totals		10	0	2	2	4					

Jean-Claude TREMBLAY
5-11 190 L 22 Jan 1939, Bagotville PQ d. 1995

year	team	gp	g	a	pts	pim	gp	g	a	pts	pim
72-73	Que	76	14	75	89	32					
73-74	Que	68	9	44	53	10					
74-75	Que	68	16	56	72	18	11	0	10	10	2
75-76	Que	80	12	77	89	16	5	0	3	3	0
76-77	Que	53	4	31	35	10	17	2	9	11	2
77-78	Que	54	5	37	42	26	1	0	1	1	0
78-79	Que	52	6	38	44	8					
totals		451	66	358	424	120	34	2	23	25	4

• Played in NHL: 1959-72, Mtl, 794-57-306-363-204 • Stanley Cups: 1965, 1966, 1968, 1969, 1971 (Montreal)

Tom TREVELYAN Thomas Arthur Trevelyan
5-11 185 L 8 Apr 1949, Toronto ON

year	team	gp	g	a	pts	pim	gp	g	a	pts	pim
74-75	SD	20	0	2	2	4					
totals		20	0	2	2	4					

Willie TROGNITZ Raymond William Trognitz
6-0 205 L 11 Jun 1953, Thunder Bay ON

year	team	gp	g	a	pts	pim	gp	g	a	pts	pim
77-78	Cin	29	2	1	3	94					
totals		29	2	1	3	94					

Jerry TROOIEN Jerold L. Trooien
6-2 195 L 10 Oct 1947, St Paul MN

year	team	gp	g	a	pts	pim	gp	g	a	pts	pim
72-73	Chi	2	0	0	0	0					
totals		2	0	0	0	0					

• Played semipro football with Madison (WI), c. 1974

Guy TROTTIER 1 Apr 1941, Hull PQ d. 2014
5-8 165 R

year	team	gp	g	a	pts	pim	gp	g	a	pts	pim
72-73	Ott	72	26	32	58	25	5	1	2	3	0
73-74	Tor	71	27	35	62	58	12	5	5	10	4
74-75	Tor	6	2	2	4	2					
	M-B	17	5	4	9	2					
totals		166	60	73	133	87	17	6	7	13	4

• Played in NHL: 1968-72, NYR-Tor, 115-28-17-45-37

Jim TROY James Earl Troy
6-2 200 R 21 Jan 1953, Boston MA

year	team	gp	g	a	pts	pim	gp	g	a	pts	pim
75-76	NE	14	0	0	0	43	2	0	0	0	29
76-77	NE	7	0	0	0	7					
77-78	Edm	47	2	0	2	124	2	0	0	0	0
totals		68	2	0	2	174	4	0	0	0	29

Jim TURKIEWICZ James Robert Turkiewicz
5-10 185 L 13 Apr 1955, Peterborough ON

year	team	gp	g	a	pts	pim	gp	g	a	pts	pim
74-75	Tor	78	3	27	30	28	6	0	2	2	6
75-76	Tor	77	9	29	38	55					
76-77	Bir	80	6	25	31	54					
77-78	Bir	78	3	21	24	45	5	1	1	2	0
78-79	Bir	79	3	17	20	52					
totals		392	24	119	143	234	11	1	3	4	6

Norm ULLMAN Norman Victor Alexander Ullman
5-10 185 L 26 Dec 1935, Provost AB

year	team	gp	g	a	pts	pim	gp	g	a	pts	pim
75-76	Edm	77	31	56	87	12	4	1	3	4	2
76-77	Edm	67	16	27	43	28	5	0	3	3	0
totals		144	47	83	130	40	9	1	6	7	2

• Played in NHL: 1955-75, Det-Tor, 1410-490-739-1229-712 • Member, Hockey Hall of Fame

Rick VAIVE Richard Claude Vaive
6-0 180 R 14 May 1959, Ottawa ON

year	team	gp	g	a	pts	pim	gp	g	a	pts	pim
78-79	Bir	75	26	33	59	248					
totals		75	26	33	59	248					

• Played in NHL: 1979-92, Van-Tor-Chi-Buf, 876-441-347-788-1445

John VAN HORLICK John Frederick Van Horlick
6-0 190 L 19 Feb 1949, Vancouver BC

year	team	gp	g	a	pts	pim	gp	g	a	pts	pim
75-76	Tor	2	0	0	0	12					
totals		2	0	0	0	12					

Gary VENERUZZO Gary Raymond Veneruzzo
5-8 165 L 28 Jun 1943, Fort William ON

year	team	gp	g	a	pts	pim	gp	g	a	pts	pim
72-73	LA	78	43	30	73	34	6	3	0	3	4
73-74	LA	78	39	29	68	68					
74-75	M-B	77	33	27	60	57					
75-76	Cin	14	3	2	5	8					
	Phx	61	19	24	43	27	5	2	0	2	7
76-77	SD	40	14	11	25	18	7	0	0	0	0
totals		348	151	123	274	212	18	5	0	5	11

• Played in NHL: 1967-72, StL, 7-1-1-2-0

Pierre VIAU
6-2 190 L 25 Jan 1952, Montreal PQ

year	team	gp	g	a	pts	pim	gp	g	a	pts	pim
72-73	Chi	4	0	0	0	0					
totals		4	0	0	0	0					

Doug VOLMAR Douglas Steven Volmar
6-1 220 R 9 Jan 1945, Cleveland Heights OH

year	team	gp	g	a	pts	pim	gp	g	a	pts	pim
74-75	SD	10	0	1	1	4					
totals		10	0	1	1	4					

• Played in NHL: 1970-73, Det-LA, 62-13-8-21-26 • Member, United States Olympic Team, 1968

Russ WALKER Russell Walker
6-2 185 R 24 May 1953, Red Deer AB

year	team	gp	g	a	pts	pim	gp	g	a	pts	pim
73-74	Cle	76	15	14	29	117	5	1	0	1	11
74-75	Cle	66	14	11	25	80	5	1	0	1	17
75-76	Cle	72	23	15	38	122	3	0	0	0	14
totals		214	52	40	92	319	13	2	0	2	42

• Played in NHL: 1976-78, LA, 17-1-0-1-41

Bob WALL Robert James Albert Wall
5-10 180 L 1 Dec 1942, Elgin Mills ON

year	team	gp	g	a	pts	pim	gp	g	a	pts	pim
72-73	Alb	78	16	29	45	20					
73-74	Edm	74	6	31	37	46					
74-75	SD	33	0	9	9	15	10	0	3	3	2
75-76	SD	68	1	20	21	32	11	1	3	4	4
totals		253	23	89	112	113	21	1	6	7	6

• Played in NHL: 1964-72, Det-LA-StL, 322-30-55-85-155

Brian WALSH Brian Gerard Walsh "Duke"
5-8 170 R 6 Nov 1954, Cambridge MA

year	team	gp	g	a	pts	pim	gp	g	a	pts	pim
75-76	Cgy	5	0	2	2	12					
totals		5	0	2	2	12					

Dave WALTER David George Walter
6-0 185 L 6 May 1952, Niagara Falls ON

year	team	gp	g	a	pts	pim	gp	g	a	pts	pim
73-74	Chi	4	0	1	1	2					
74-75	Chi	6	1	0	1	2					
75-76	SD	16	1	2	3	6					
totals		26	2	3	5	10					

Ron WALTERS Ronald Wayne Walters
6-0 175 R 9 Mar 1948, Castor AB

year	team	gp	g	a	pts	pim	gp	g	a	pts	pim
72-73	Alb	78	28	26	54	37					
73-74	LA	71	14	14	28	28					
74-75	Ind	17	2	1	3	9					
totals		166	44	41	85	74					

Mike WALTON Michael Robert Walton "Shakey"
5-10 175 L 3 Jan 1945, Kirkland Lake ON

year	team	gp	g	a	pts	pim	gp	g	a	pts	pim
73-74	Min	78	57	60	117	88	11	10	8	18	16
74-75	Min	75	48	45	93	33	12	10	7	17	10
75-76	Min	58	31	40	71	27					
totals		211	136	145	281	148	23	20	15	35	26

• Brother of Rob Walton • Played in NHL: 1965-72, 1976-79, Tor-Bos-Van-StL-Chi, 588-201-247-448-357 • Stanley Cups: 1967 (Toronto), 1972 (Boston)

Rob WALTON Robert Charles Walton
5-9 165 R 3 Sep 1949, Toronto ON

year	team	gp	g	a	pts	pim	gp	g	a	pts	pim
73-74	Min	45	8	23	31	24					
	Van	28	8	15	23	2					
74-75	Van	75	24	33	57	28					
75-76	Cgy	2	0	0	0	0					
totals		150	40	71	111	54					

• Brother of Mike Walton

Ron WARD — Ronald Leon Ward "Magic"
5-11 175 R 12 Sep 1944, Cornwall ON

year	team	gp	g	a	pts	pim	gp	g	a	pts	pim
72-73	NY	77	51	67	118	28					
73-74	Van	7	0	2	2	2					
	LA	40	14	19	33	16					
	Cle	23	19	7	26	7	5	3	0	3	2
74-75	Cle	73	30	32	62	18	5	0	2	2	2
75-76	Cle	75	32	50	82	24	3	0	2	2	0
76-77	Min	41	15	21	36	6					
	Wpg	14	4	7	11	2					
	Cgy	9	5	5	10	0					
totals		359	170	210	380	103	13	3	4	7	4

• Played in NHL: 1969-72, Tor-Van, 89-2-5-7-6

Jim WARNER — James Francis Warner
5-11 180 R 26 Mar 1954, St Paul MN

year	team	gp	g	a	pts	pim	gp	g	a	pts	pim
78-79	NE	41	6	9	15	20	1	0	0	0	0
totals		41	6	9	15	20	1	0	0	0	0

• Played in NHL: 1979-80, Hart, 32-0-3-3-10

Steve WARR
5-11 185 R 5 Jan 1951, Peterborough ON

year	team	gp	g	a	pts	pim	gp	g	a	pts	pim
72-73	Ott	72	3	8	11	79	2	0	0	0	0
73-74	Tor	0	0	0	0	0	2	0	0	0	0
totals		72	3	8	11	79	4	0	0	0	0

Bryan WATSON — Bryan Joseph Watson
5-9 175 R 14 Nov 1942, Bancroft ON

year	team	gp	g	a	pts	pim	gp	g	a	pts	pim
78-79	Cin	21	0	2	2	56	3	0	1	1	2
totals		21	0	2	2	56	3	0	1	1	2

• Played in NHL: 1963-79, Mtl-Det-Oak-Pit-StL-Wash, 878-17-135-152-2212

Jim WATSON — James Arthur Watson
6-2 195 L 28 Jun 1943, Malartic PQ

year	team	gp	g	a	pts	pim	gp	g	a	pts	pim
72-73	LA	75	5	15	20	123	4	0	1	1	2
73-74	LA	48	0	6	6	28					
	Chi	23	0	5	5	22	18	2	3	5	18
74-75	Chi	37	2	6	8	31					
75-76	Que	28	0	1	1	24					
totals		211	7	33	40	228	22	2	4	6	20

• Played in NHL: 1963-72, Det-Buf, 221-4-19-23-345

Tom WEBSTER — Thomas Ronald Webster "Hawkeye"
5-9 170 R 4 Oct 1948, Kirkland Lake ON

year	team	gp	g	a	pts	pim	gp	g	a	pts	pim
72-73	NE	77	53	50	103	89	15	12	14	26	6
73-74	NE	64	43	27	70	28	3	5	0	5	7
74-75	NE	66	40	24	64	52	3	0	2	2	0
75-76	NE	55	33	50	83	24	17	10	9	19	6
76-77	NE	70	36	49	85	73	5	1	1	2	0
77-78	NE	20	15	5	20	5					
totals		352	220	205	425	241	43	28	26	54	19

• Played in NHL: 1968-72, 1979-80, Bos-Det-Cal, 102-33-42-75-61

Stan WEIR — Stanley Brian Weir
6-1 170 L 17 Mar 1952, Ponoka AB

year	team	gp	g	a	pts	pim	gp	g	a	pts	pim
78-79	Edm	68	31	30	61	20	13	2	5	7	2
totals		68	31	30	61	20	13	2	5	7	2

• Played in NHL: 1972-78, 1979-83, Cal-Tor-Edm-Col-Det, 642-139-207-346-183

Wally WEIR — Wally Edward Weir
6-1 205 R 3 Jun 1954, Verdun PQ

year	team	gp	g	a	pts	pim	gp	g	a	pts	pim
76-77	Que	77	3	17	20	197	17	1	5	6	13
77-78	Que	13	0	0	0	47	11	1	2	3	50
78-79	Que	68	2	7	9	166	4	0	1	1	4
totals		150	5	24	29	410	32	2	8	10	67

• Played in NHL: 1979-85, Que-Hart-Pit, 320-21-45-66-625

Steve WEST — Steven Carter West
5-8 150 L 20 Mar 1952, Peterborough ON

year	team	gp	g	a	pts	pim	gp	g	a	pts	pim
74-75	M-B	50	15	18	33	4					
75-76	Hou	0	0	0	0	0	7	0	1	1	0
76-77	Hou	3	0	0	0	2	6	0	0	0	0
77-78	Hou	71	11	21	32	23	6	1	0	1	0
78-79	Wpg	18	3	1	4	6	6	2	3	5	2
totals		142	29	40	69	35	25	3	4	7	2

Pat WESTRUM — Patrick Delvan Westrum
5-10 185 L 3 Mar 1948, Minneapolis MN

year	team	gp	g	a	pts	pim	gp	g	a	pts	pim
74-75	Min	23	0	3	3	48					
75-76	Min	54	3	10	13	98					
	Cgy	9	0	2	2	23	6	0	1	1	19
76-77	Min	40	1	9	10	42					
	Bir	34	1	11	12	48					
77-78	Bir	77	2	10	12	97	3	0	1	1	0
totals		237	7	45	52	356	9	0	2	2	19

• Member, United States National Team, 1970-71

Alton WHITE — Alton James White, Jr
5-9 175 R 31 May 1945, Amherst NS

year	team	gp	g	a	pts	pim	gp	g	a	pts	pim
72-73	NY	13	1	4	5	2					
	LA	57	20	17	37	22	6	1	0	1	0
73-74	LA	48	8	13	21	13					
74-75	M-B	27	9	12	21	8					
totals		145	38	46	84	45	6	1	0	1	0

• Second player of African descent (after Willie O'Ree) to play major-league hockey in North America

Bobby WHITLOCK — Robert Angus Whitlock
5-10 175 R 16 Jul 1949, Charlottetown PEI

year	team	gp	g	a	pts	pim	gp	g	a	pts	pim
72-73	Chi	75	23	28	51	53					
73-74	Chi	52	16	19	35	44					
	LA	14	4	10	14	4					
74-75	Ind	73	31	26	57	56					
75-76	Ind	30	7	15	22	16					
totals		244	81	98	179	173					

• Played in NHL: 1969-70, Min, 1-0-0-0-0

Juha WIDING — Juha Markku Widing "Whitey"
6-1 190 L 4 Jul 1947, Uleaborg Sweden d. 1984

year	team	gp	g	a	pts	pim	gp	g	a	pts	pim
77-78	Edm	71	18	24	42	8	5	0	1	1	0
totals		71	18	24	42	8	5	0	1	1	0

• Played in NHL: 1969-77, NYR-LA-Cle, 575-144-226-370-206

Barry WILKINS — Barry James Wilkins
6-0 190 L 28 Feb 1947, Toronto ON d. 2011

year	team	gp	g	a	pts	pim	gp	g	a	pts	pim
76-77	Edm	51	4	24	28	75	4	0	1	1	2
77-78	Ind	79	2	21	23	79					
totals		130	6	45	51	154	4	0	1	1	2

• Played in NHL: 1966-76, Bos-Van-Pit, 418-27-125-152-663

Butch WILLIAMS — Warren Milton Williams
5-11 190 R 11 Sep 1952, Duluth MN

year	team	gp	g	a	pts	pim	gp	g	a	pts	pim
76-77	Edm	29	3	10	13	16					
totals		29	3	10	13	16					

• Brother of Tommy Williams • Played in NHL: 1973-76, StL-Cal, 106-14-35-49-131

Tommy WILLIAMS — Thomas Mark Williams
5-11 180 R 17 Apr 1940, Duluth MN d. 1992

year	team	gp	g	a	pts	pim	gp	g	a	pts	pim
72-73	NE	69	10	21	31	14	15	6	11	17	2
73-74	NE	70	21	37	58	6	4	0	3	3	10
totals		139	31	58	89	20	19	6	14	20	12

• Brother of Butch Williams • Played in NHL: 1961-72, 1974-76, Bos-Min-Cal-Wash, 663-161-269-430-177 • Member, United States National Team, 1958-59 • Member, United States Olympic Team, 1960

Gary WILLIAMSON — Gary Albert Williamson
5-10 175 L 25 May 1950, Montreal PQ

year	team	gp	g	a	pts	pim	gp	g	a	pts	pim
73-74	Hou	9	2	6	8	0	12	0	0	0	0
totals		9	2	6	8	0	12	0	0	0	0

Hal WILLIS Harold Willis
6-2 215 L 8 Jun 1946, Liverpool NS

year	team	gp	g	a	pts	pim	gp	g	a	pts	pim
72-73	NY	74	3	21	24	159					
73-74	LA	18	1	2	3	24					
totals		92	4	23	27	183					

Bob WINOGRAD Robert Earl Winograd
5-11 195 L 6 Jun 1950, Winnipeg MB

year	team	gp	g	a	pts	pim	gp	g	a	pts	pim
72-73	NY	52	0	12	12	23					
73-74	NY-J	7	1	0	1	0					
76-77	SD	1	0	0	0	0					
totals		60	1	12	13	23					

Jim WISTE James Andrew Wiste
5-10 185 L 18 Feb 1946, Moose Jaw SK

year	team	gp	g	a	pts	pim	gp	g	a	pts	pim
72-73	Cle	70	28	43	71	24	9	3	8	11	13
73-74	Cle	76	23	35	58	26	5	0	1	1	0
74-75	Ind	75	13	28	41	30					
75-76	Ind	7	0	2	2	0					
totals		228	64	108	172	80	14	3	9	12	13

• Played in NHL: 1968-71, Chi-Van, 52-1-10-11-8

Bob WOYTOWICH Robert Ivan Woytowich "Augie"
6-0 195 R 18 Aug 1941, Winnipeg MB d. 1988

year	team	gp	g	a	pts	pim	gp	g	a	pts	pim
72-73	Wpg	62	2	4	6	47	14	1	1	2	4
73-74	Wpg	72	6	28	34	43	4	0	0	0	0
74-75	Wpg	24	0	4	4	8					
	Ind	42	0	8	8	28					
75-76	Ind	42	1	7	8	14					
totals		242	9	51	60	140	18	1	1	2	4

• Played in NHL: 1964-72, Bos-Min-Pit-LA, 503-32-126-158-352

Randy WYROZUB William Randall Wyrozub
5-11 180 L 8 Apr 1950, Lacombe AB

year	team	gp	g	a	pts	pim	gp	g	a	pts	pim
75-76	Ind	55	11	14	25	8					
totals		55	11	14	25	8					

• Played in NHL: 1970-74, Buf, 100-8-10-18-10

Dale YAKIWCHUK Dale Alexander Yakiwchuk
6-4 205 L 17 Oct 1958, Calgary AB

year	team	gp	g	a	pts	pim	gp	g	a	pts	pim
78-79	Wpg	4	0	0	0	0					
totals		4	0	0	0	0					

Bill YOUNG William Andrew Young
6-2 195 L 5 Jul 1947, St Catherines ON

year	team	gp	g	a	pts	pim	gp	g	a	pts	pim
72-73	LA	50	14	12	26	46					
	Min	23	5	6	11	20	5	1	1	2	4
73-74	Cle	53	8	9	17	73					
	LA	16	1	3	4	4					
totals		142	28	30	58	143	5	1	1	2	4

Howie YOUNG Howard John Edward Young
6-0 200 R 2 Aug 1937, Toronto ON d. 1999

year	team	gp	g	a	pts	pim	gp	g	a	pts	pim
74-75	Phx	30	3	12	15	44					
	Wpg	42	13	10	23	42					
76-77	Phx	26	1	3	4	23					
totals		98	17	25	42	109					

• Played in NHL: 1960-71, Det-Chi-Van, 336-12-62-74-851 • Played minor-pro through 1985-86 (age 48)

Rod ZAINE Rodney Carl Zaine
5-10 175 L 18 May 1946, Ottawa ON

year	team	gp	g	a	pts	pim	gp	g	a	pts	pim
72-73	Chi	74	3	14	17	25					
73-74	Chi	78	5	13	18	17	18	2	1	3	2
74-75	Chi	68	3	6	9	16					
totals		220	11	33	44	58	18	2	1	3	2

• Played in NHL: 1970-72, Pit-Buf, 61-10-6-16-25 • Assistant General Manager, Indianapolis, 1978

Joe ZANUSSI Lawrence Joseph Zanussi
5-10 180 R 25 Sep 1947, Rossland BC

year	team	gp	g	a	pts	pim	gp	g	a	pts	pim
72-73	Wpg	73	4	21	25	53	14	2	5	7	6
73-74	Wpg	76	3	22	25	53	4	0	0	0	0
totals		149	7	43	50	106	18	2	5	7	6

• Played in NHL: 1974-77, NYR-Buf-StL, 87-1-13-14-46

Jerry ZRYMIAK
6-1 195 R 19 Oct 1948, Regina SK

year	team	gp	g	a	pts	pim	gp	g	a	pts	pim
72-73	LA	1	0	0	0	0	2	1	0	1	0
73-74	LA	27	2	8	10	8					
74-75	M-B	49	3	9	12	53					
75-76	Min	22	0	8	8	16					
	Tor	17	0	5	5	11					
76-77	Min	40	2	10	12	14					
totals		156	7	40	47	112	2	1	0	1	0

Wayne ZUK Wayne David Zuk
5-8 160 R 29 Oct 1949, Prince Albert SK

year	team	gp	g	a	pts	pim	gp	g	a	pts	pim
73-74	Edm	2	0	0	0	0					
totals		2	0	0	0	0					

Mike ZUKE Michael Zuke, Jr.
5-11 175 R 16 Apr 1954, Sault Ste Marie ON

year	team	gp	g	a	pts	pim	gp	g	a	pts	pim
76-77	Ind	15	3	4	7	2					
77-78	Edm	71	23	34	57	47	5	2	3	5	0
totals		86	26	38	64	49	5	2	3	5	0

• Played in NHL: 1978-86, StL-Hart, 455-86-196-282-220

Career Statistical Leaders

Games Played, Regular Season: 551, Andre Lacroix; 549, Ron Plumb; 519, Michel Parizeau; 511, Paul Shmyr; 486, Mike Antonovich; 478, Rick Ley; 477, John McKenzie; 476, Blair MacDonald; 468, Larry Pleau; 467, Poul Popiel.

Games Played, Playoffs: 78, Gordie Howe; 75, Marty Howe; 74, Mark Howe; 73, Rick Ley; 71, Poul Popiel; 66, Larry Pleau & John Schella; 65, Larry Hale; 64, Bob Guindon; 63, Brad Selwood & Ted Taylor; 61, Ted Green.

Goals Scored, Regular Season: 316, Marc Tardif; 303, Bobby Hull; 283, Real Cloutier; 251, Andre Lacroix; 236, Anders Hedberg; 230, Serge Bernier; 220, Tom Webster; 218, Danny Lawson; 216, Robbie Ftorek; 208, Mark Howe.

Goals Scored, Playoffs: 43, Bobby Hull; 41, Mark Howe; 35, Anders Hedberg; 33, Real Cloutier; 29, Serge Bernier, Gordie Howe & Tom Webster; 27, Marc Tardif; 26, Willy Lindstrom; 24, Bob Guindon & Frank Hughes; 21, Mike Antonovich, Murray Hall & Peter Sullivan.

Assists, Regular Season: 547, Andre Lacroix; 358, J.-C. Tremblay; 350, Marc Tardif; 344, Ulf Nilsson; 336, Serge Bernier; 335, Bobby Hull; 334, Gordie Howe; 325, Christian Bordeleau; 307, Robbie Ftorek; 296, Mark Howe.

Assists, Playoffs: 53, Ulf Nilsson; 51, Mark Howe; 47, Poul Popiel; 46, Serge Bernier; 45, Larry Lund; 43, Gordie Howe; 37, Bobby Hull; 36, Terry Ruskowski; 34, Christian Bordeleau; 33, Jim Dorey & Rick Ley.

Points Scored, Regular Season: 798, Andre Lacroix; 666, Marc Tardif; 638, Bobby Hull; 566, Serge Bernier & Real Cloutier; 523, Robbie Ftorek; 508, Gordie Howe; 504, Christian Bordeleau & Mark Howe; 484, Ulf Nilsson; 458, Anders Hedberg; 426, Larry Lund.

Points Scored, Playoffs: 92, Mark Howe; 80, Bobby Hull; 74, Serge Bernier; 71, Gordie Howe; 67, Ulf Nilsson; 65, Larry Lund; 63, Real Cloutier & Anders Hedberg; 58, Marc Tardif; 54, Poul Popiel, Terry Ruskowski & Tom Webster; 53, Peter Sullivan.

Penalty Minutes, Regular Season: 962, Paul Baxter; 932, Kim Clackson; 904, Cam Connor; 860, Pierre Roy & Paul Shmyr; 849, Gord Gallant; 844, John Schella; 805, Steve Sutherland; 778, John Hughes; 762, Ron Busniuk; 761, Terry Ruskowski.

Penalty Minutes, Playoffs: 174, Terry Ruskowski; 160, Curt Brackenbury; 147, Ted Taylor; 143, John Schella; 142, Rick Ley; 138, Kim Clackson; 132, Ron Busniuk; 131, Jim Dorey; 118, Poul Popiel; 116, Larry Lund.

Top Seasonal Performances

Goals: 77, Bobby Hull (Wpg, 1974-75); 75, Real Cloutier (Que, 1978-79); 71, Marc Tardif (Que, 1975-76); 70, Anders Hedberg (Wpg, 1976-77); 66, Real Cloutier (Que, 1976-77).

Assists: 106, Andre Lacroix (SD, 1974-75); 94, Ulf Nilsson (Wpg, 1974-75); 89, Ulf Nilsson (Wpg, 1977-78), Marc Tardif (Que, 1977-78); 85, Ulf Nilsson (Wpg, 1976-77); 82, Andre Lacroix (SD, 1976-77).

Points: 154, Marc Tardif (Que, 1977-78); 148, Marc Tardif (Que, 1975-76); 147, Andre Lacroix (SD, 1974-75); 142, Bobby Hull (Wpg, 1974-75); 141, Real Cloutier (Que, 1976-77).

Penalty Minutes: 365, Curt Brackenbury (Min-Que, 1975-76); 351, Kim Clackson (Ind, 1975-76); 297, Gord Gallant (Que, 1975-76); 295, Cam Connor (Phx, 1975-76); 284, Steve Durbano (Bir, 1977-78).

Plus/Minus: 65, Ulf Nilsson (Wpg, 1975-76); 64, Ron Plumb (Cin, 1976-77); 62, Bobby Hull (Wpg, 1975-76); 60, Anders Hedberg (Wpg, 1975-76), Anders Hedberg (Wpg, 1977-78), Lars-Erik Sjoberg (Wpg, 1977-78); 57, Ulf Nilsson (Wpg, 1976-77)

Goaltending Wins: 44, Richard Brodeur (Que, 1975-76); 41, Joe Daley (Wpg, 1975-76), Dave Dryden (Edm, 1978-79); 39, Ron Grahame (Hou, 1975-76), Joe Daley (Wpg, 1976-77); 35, Ernie Wakely (SD, 1975-76); 33, Bernie Parent (Phi, 1972-73).

Goals Against Average: 2.56, Don McLeod (Hou, 1973-74); 2.74, Michel Dion (Ind, 1975-76), Ron Grahame (Hou, 1976-77); 2.84, Gerry Cheevers (Cle, 1972-73), Joe Daley (Wpg, 1975-76), 2.84, Jacques Caron (Cin, 1976-77, 24 g.p.); 2.89, Dave Dryden (Edm, 1978-79); 2.90, Joe Daley (Wpg, 1972-73).

Same Name Game

Three pairs of players in the WHA shared a same first and last name: Ron C. and Ron F. Anderson, Jim H. and Jim W. Jones, and John A. and John C. Stewart. To add to the potential confusion, the Stewarts were teammates with Cleveland in 1975-76, and for one game in Birmingham the following season.

Four other players in the WHA shared the same name with contemporary players in the NHL. Mike Boland (Ottawa, 1972-73) shared his name with Mike Boland, who played for Kansas City and Buffalo from 1974-77. Claude Larose (Cincinnati and Indianapolis, 1975-78) was not to be confused with the Claude Larose who played with Montreal and St. Louis from 1962-78. Jim Watson (Los Angeles, Chicago and Quebec, 1972-76) had the same name as Jim Watson, the long-time Philadelphia Flyers' defenseman from 1973-82. Lastly, Tom Williams (New England, 1972-74) was a contemporary of Tom Williams, who played for the Rangers and Kings between 1971-79. All four of the WHA players also played in the NHL, often at the same time as their similarly-named counterpart.

World Hockey Association Goaltender Register

Goaltenders are listed alphabetically, with both regular season statistics (left columns) and playoff statistics (right columns). The column headers are **gp** games played, team, **min** minutes, **ga** goals against, **so** shutouts, **w** win, **l** loss, **t** tie, **gaa** goals against average, **a** assists, **pm** penalty minutes. Goaltenders who played in the NHL include a tagline with years, teams, regular season games-minutes-goal allowed-shutouts-average, then wins-losses-ties in parentheses.

Christer ABRAHAMSSON
6-2 175 Cl 12 Apr 1947, Leksand Sweden

year	team	gp	min	ga	so	w	l	t	gaa	a	pm	gp	min	ga	so	w	l	gaa	a	pm
74-75	NE	15	870	47	1	8	6	1	3.24	0	0									
75-76	NE	41	2385	136	2	18	18	2	3.42	1	6	1	1	0	0	0	0	0.00	0	0
76-77	NE	45	2484	159	0	15	22	4	3.84	0	0	2	90	5	0	0	1	3.33	0	0
totals		101	5739	342	3	41	46	7	3.58	1	6	3	91	5	0	0	1	3.30	0	0

• Brother of Thommie Abrahamsson

Yves ARCHAMBAULT
5-11 170 cL 22 Jun 1952, Montreal PQ

year	team	gp	min	ga	so	w	l	t	gaa	a	pm	gp	min	ga	so	w	l	gaa	a	pm
72-73	Phi	6	260	17	0	1	3	0	3.92	1	0	3	153	11	0	0	2	4.31	0	0
73-74	Van	5	263	27	0	1	4	0	6.16	0	0									
totals		11	523	44	0	2	7	0	5.05	1	0	3	153	11	0	0	2	4.31	0	0

Serge AUBRY
5-9 160 cL Serge Dieudonne Aubry 2 Jan 1942, Montreal PQ d. 2011

year	team	gp	min	ga	so	w	l	t	gaa	a	pm	gp	min	ga	so	w	l	gaa	a	pm
72-73	Que	52	3036	182	1	25	22	2	3.60	0	54									
73-74	Que	26	1395	90	1	11	11	2	3.87	1	8									
74-75	Que	31	1762	109	0	17	11	0	3.71	1	22									
75-76	Cin	12	549	38	1	6	4	0	4.15	1	4									
76-77	Que	21	769	51	1	6	8	0	3.98	1	0	3	18	1	0	0	0	3.33	0	0
totals		142	7511	470	4	65	56	4	3.75	4	88	3	18	1	0	0	0	3.33	0	0

• Shared shutout with Richard Brodeur, February 7, 1973

Bill BERGLUND
6-1 190 cL William Arthur Berglund 24 Sep 1948, Everett MA

year	team	gp	min	ga	so	w	l	t	gaa	a	pm	gp	min	ga	so	w	l	gaa	a	pm
73-74	NE	3	180	10	0	2	1	0	3.33	0	0									
74-75	NE	2	36	3	0	0	0	0	5.00	0	0									
totals		5	216	13	0	2	1	0	3.61	0	0									

Les BINKLEY
6-0 170 cR Leslie John Binkley 6 Jun 1934, Owen Sound ON

year	team	gp	min	ga	so	w	l	t	gaa	a	pm	gp	min	ga	so	w	l	gaa	a	pm
72-73	Ott	30	1709	106	0	10	17	1	3.72	0	0	4	223	17	0	1	3	4.57	0	0
73-74	Tor	27	1412	77	1	14	9	1	3.27	0	0	5	182	17	0	2	2	5.93	0	0
74-75	Tor	17	772	47	0	6	4	0	3.59	0	0	1	59	5	0	0	1	5.08	0	0
75-76	Tor	7	335	32	0	0	6	0	5.73	0	0									
totals		81	4228	262	1	30	36	2	3.72	0	0	10	464	39	0	3	6	5.17	0	0

• Shared shutout with Gilles Gratton, October 16, 1973 • Played in NHL: 1967-72, Pit, 196-11046-575-11-3.12 (58-94-34)

Bob BLANCHET
5-8 175 cL Robert Bertrand Blanchet 24 Feb 1954, Authier-Nord, PQ

year	team	gp	min	ga	so	w	l	t	gaa	a	pm	gp	min	ga	so	w	l	gaa	a	pm
74-75	SD	3	179	7	1	2	1	0	2.35	0	0									
75-76	SD	1	32	4	0	0	1	0	7.50	0	0									
totals		4	211	11	1	2	2	0	3.13	0	0									

• Shutout Indianapolis in his WHA and major-league debut, December 14, 1974

Frank BLUM
6-2 185 cL 29 Jun 1952, Creighton Mines, ON

year	team	gp	min	ga	so	w	l	t	gaa	a	pm	gp	min	ga	so	w	l	gaa	a	pm
72-73	Ott	2	28	3	0	0	0	0	4.78	0	0									
73-74	Tor	5	130	5	0	1	0	0	2.31	0	0									
	Wpg	0	0	0	0	0	0	0	-	0	0	2	120	15	0	0	2	7.50	0	0
totals		7	158	8	0	1	0	0	3.02	0	0	2	120	15	0	0	2	7.50	0	0

• Loaned to Winnipeg by Toronto as an emergency replacement, April 1974

Ken BRODERICK
5-11 175 cR Kenneth Lorne Broderick 16 Feb 1942, Toronto ON d. 2016

year	team	gp	min	ga	so	w	l	t	gaa	a	pm	gp	min	ga	so	w	l	gaa	a	pm
76-77	Edm	40	2301	134	4	18	18	1	3.49	3	2	3	179	10	0	1	2	3.35	0	0
77-78	Edm	9	497	42	0	2	5	0	5.07	0	0									
	Que	24	1140	83	0	9	8	1	4.37	0	0	2	48	2	0	0	1	2.50	0	0
totals		73	3938	259	4	29	31	2	3.95	3	2	5	227	12	0	1	3	3.17	0	0

• Member, Canada Olympic Team, 1964 & 1968 • Played in NHL: 1969-75, Min-Bos, 27-1464-74-1-3.03 (11-12-1)

Richard BRODEUR
5-7 160 cL 15 Sep 1952, Montreal PQ

year	team	gp	min	ga	so	w	l	t	gaa	a	pm	gp	min	ga	so	w	l	gaa	a	pm
72-73	Que	24	1288	102	0	5	14	2	4.75	0	4									
73-74	Que	30	1607	89	1	15	12	1	3.32	1	0									
74-75	Que	51	2938	188	0	29	21	0	3.90	0	5	15	906	48	1	8	7	3.18	0	0
75-76	Que	64	3967	244	2	44	21	2	3.69	3	0	5	299	22	0	1	4	4.41	0	0
76-77	Que	53	2906	167	2	29	18	2	3.45	1	0	17	1007	55	1	12	5	3.28	2	0
77-78	Que	36	1962	121	0	18	15	2	3.70	2	0	11	622	38	1	5	5	3.67	0	0
78-79	Que	42	2433	126	3	25	13	3	3.11	3	0	3	114	14	0	0	2	7.37	0	0
totals		300	17101	1037	8	165	114	12	3.64	10	9	51	2948	177	3	26	23	3.60	2	0

• Shared shutout with Serge Aubry, February 7, 1973 • Played in NHL: 1979-88, Que-Van-Hart, 385-21968-1410-6-3.85 (131-175-62)

Gary BROMLEY
Gary Bert Bromley "Bones"
5-10 160 cL 19 Jan 1950, Edmonton AB

year	team	gp	min	ga	so	w	l	t	gaa	a	pm	gp	min	ga	so	w	l	gaa	a	pm
76-77	Cgy	28	1237	79	0	6	9	2	3.83	0	2									
77-78	Wpg	39	2250	124	1	25	12	1	3.31	1	0	5	268	7	0	4	0	1.57	0	2
totals		67	3487	203	1	31	21	3	3.49	1	2	5	268	7	0	4	0	1.57	0	2

• Played in NHL: 1973-81, Buf-Van, 136-7427-425-7-3.43 (54-44-28)

Andy BROWN
Andrew Conrad Brown
5-11 185 cL 14 Feb 1944, Hamilton ON

year	team	gp	min	ga	so	w	l	t	gaa	a	pm	gp	min	ga	so	w	l	gaa	a	pm
74-75	Ind	52	2979	206	2	15	35	0	4.15	1	75									
75-76	Ind	24	1368	82	1	9	11	2	3.60	3	17									
76-77	Ind	10	430	26	0	1	4	1	3.63	0	0									
totals		86	4777	314	3	25	50	3	3.55	4	92									

• Played in NHL: 1971-74, Det-Pit, 62-3373-213-1-3.79 (22-26-9) • His last game, November 13, 1976, was last game ever in which a major-league goaltender played without a protective face mask

Ken BROWN
Kenneth Murray Brown
6-0 180 cL 19 Dec 1948, Port Arthur ON

year	team	gp	min	ga	so	w	l	t	gaa	a	pm	gp	min	ga	so	w	l	gaa	a	pm
72-73	Alb	20	1034	63	1	10	8	0	3.66	0	2									
74-75	Edm	32	1466	86	2	10	11	0	3.49	1	2									
totals		52	2500	149	3	20	19	0	3.55	1	4									

• Played in NHL: 1970-71, Chi, 1-18-1-0-3.33 (0-0-0)

Randy BURCHELL
Randall Burchell
6-1 175 cL 2 Jul 1955, Montreal PQ

year	team	gp	min	ga	so	w	l	t	gaa	a	pm	gp	min	ga	so	w	l	gaa	a	pm
76-77	Ind	5	136	8	0	1	0	0	3.53	1	0									
totals		5	136	8	0	1	0	0	3.53	1	0									

Jacques CARON
Jacques Joseph Caron
6-1 180 cL 21 Apr 1939, Noranda PQ

year	team	gp	min	ga	so	w	l	t	gaa	a	pm	gp	min	ga	so	w	l	gaa	a	pm
75-76	Cle	2	130	8	0	1	0	1	3.69	1	0									
76-77	Cin	24	1292	61	3	13	6	2	2.83	1	0	1	14	2	0	0	1	12.86	0	0
totals		26	1422	69	3	14	6	3	2.91	2	0	1	14	2	0	0	1	12.86	0	0

• Played in NHL: 1967-74, LA-StL-Van, 72-3846-211-2-3.29 (24-29-11)

Gerry CHEEVERS
Gerald Michael Cheevers
5-11 185 cL 2 Dec 1940, St. Catherines ON

year	team	gp	min	ga	so	w	l	t	gaa	a	pm	gp	min	ga	so	w	l	gaa	a	pm
72-73	Cle	52	3144	149	5	32	20	2	2.84	0	30	9	548	22	0	5	4	2.41	0	0
73-74	Cle	59	3562	180	4	30	20	6	3.03	0	30	5	303	18	0	1	4	3.56	0	0
74-75	Cle	52	3076	167	4	26	24	2	3.26	1	59	5	300	23	0	1	4	4.60	0	0
75-76	Cle	28	1570	95	1	11	14	1	3.63	0	15									
totals		191	11352	591	14	99	78	11	3.12	1	134	19	1151	63	0	7	12	3.28	0	0

• Played in NHL: 1961-72, 1976-80, Tor-Bos, 418-24394-1174-28-2.89 (230-102-74) • Stanley Cups: 1970, 1972 (Boston) • Member, Hockey Hall of Fame

Gaye COOLEY
Gaye Stewart Cooley
5-10 185 cR 8 Feb 1945, North Bay ON

year	team	gp	min	ga	so	w	l	t	gaa	a	pm	gp	min	ga	so	w	l	gaa	a	pm
75-76	NE	0	0	0	0	0	0	0	-	0	0	1	1	0	0	0	0	0.00	0	0
totals		0	0	0	0	0	0	0	-	0	0	1	1	0	0	0	0	0.00	0	0

• Recalled as an emergency replacement for 1976 playoffs.

Jim CORSI
James Corsi
5-8 175 cL 19 Jun 1954, Montreal PQ

year	team	gp	min	ga	so	w	l	t	gaa	a	pm	gp	min	ga	so	w	l	gaa	a	pm
77-78	Que	23	1089	82	0	10	7	0	4.52	1	2									
78-79	Que	40	2291	126	3	16	20	1	3.30	0	0	2	66	7	0	0	1	6.36	0	0
totals		63	3380	208	3	26	27	1	3.69	1	2	2	66	7	0	0	1	6.36	0	0

• Played in NHL: 1979-80, Que, 28-1366-83-0-3.65 (8-14-3) • Played professional soccer with Montreal (NASL), 1971-73 • Played in Italy and was sometimes a member of the Italian National Team, 1980-92.

Tom COTTRINGER
6-0 210 cL 28 Dec 1947, Niagara Falls ON

year	team	gp	min	ga	so	w	l	t	gaa	a	pm	gp	min	ga	so	w	l	gaa	a	pm
72-73	Phi	2	122	8	0	1	1	0	3.93	0	0									
totals		2	122	8	0	1	1	0	3.93	0	0									

Rich COUTU
5-8   170   cR
Richard Norman Coutu
3 May 1951, Montreal PQ

year	team	gp	min	ga	so	w	l	t	gaa	a	pm	gp	min	ga	so	w	l	gaa	a	pm
73-74	Chi	20	1207	75	0	9	10	1	3.73	0	0									
74-75	Chi	1	60	5	0	0	1	0	5.00	0	0									
75-76	Cin	3	149	17	0	0	2	0	6.85	0	0									
totals		24	1416	97	0	9	13	1	4.11	0	0									

Mike CURRAN
5-8   165   cR
Michael Curran "Lefty"
14 Apr 1944, International Falls MN

year	team	gp	min	ga	so	w	l	t	gaa	a	pm	gp	min	ga	so	w	l	gaa	a	pm
72-73	Min	43	2540	131	4	23	17	2	3.09	1	26	2	90	9	0	0	2	6.00	0	0
73-74	Min	40	2382	130	2	23	14	2	3.27	0	6	5	289	14	0	2	3	2.91	0	0
74-75	Min	26	1367	90	0	11	10	1	3.95	0	18									
75-76	Min	5	240	22	1	2	2	0	5.50	0	2									
76-77	Min	16	848	50	0	4	7	3	3.54	0	8									
totals		130	7377	423	9	63	50	8	3.44	1	60	7	379	23	0	2	5	3.64	0	0

• Member, United States Olympic Team, 1972

Joe DALEY
5-10   160   cL
Thomas Joseph Daley
20 Feb 1943, East Kildonan MB

year	team	gp	min	ga	so	w	l	t	gaa	a	pm	gp	min	ga	so	w	l	gaa	a	pm
72-73	Wpg	29	1718	83	2	17	10	1	2.90	1	10	7	422	25	0	5	2	3.55	0	0
73-74	Wpg	41	2454	163	0	19	20	1	3.99	1	4	2	119	8	0	0	2	4.03	0	0
74-75	Wpg	51	2902	175	1	23	21	4	3.99	1	6									
75-76	Wpg	62	3612	171	5	41	17	1	2.84	1	17	12	671	29	1	10	1	2.59	0	10
76-77	Wpg	65	3818	206	3	39	23	2	3.24	4	6	20	1186	71	1	11	9	3.59	0	0
77-78	Wpg	37	2075	114	1	21	11	1	3.30	2	2	5	271	13	0	4	1	2.88	1	20
78-79	Wpg	23	1256	90	0	7	11	3	4.30	0	0	3	37	3	0	0	0	4.86	0	0
totals		308	17835	1002	12	167	113	13	3.37	10	45	49	2706	149	2	30	15	3.30	1	30

• Played in NHL: 1968-72, Pit-Buf-Det, 105-5836-326-3-3.35 (34-44-19)

Michel DEGUISE
5-8   165   cL
6 Nov 1951, Sorel PQ

year	team	gp	min	ga	so	w	l	t	gaa	a	pm	gp	min	ga	so	w	l	gaa	a	pm
73-74	Que	32	1750	96	1	12	13	1	3.29	1	0									
75-76	Que	18	535	60	0	6	5	2	4.35	1	0									
totals		50	2585	156	1	18	18	3	3.62	2	0									

Gerry DESJARDINS
5-11   185   cL
Gerald Ferdinand Desjardins
22 Jul 1944, Sudbury ON

year	team	gp	min	ga	so	w	l	t	gaa	a	pm	gp	min	ga	so	w	l	gaa	a	pm
74-75	M-B	41	2282	162	0	9	28	1	4.26	1	13									
totals		41	2282	162	0	9	28	1	4.26	1	13									

• Played in NHL: 1968-74, 1975-78, LA-Chi-NYI-Buf, 331-19014-1042-12-3.29 (122-153-44)

Michel DION
5-10   170   cR
11 Feb 1954, Granby PQ

year	team	gp	min	ga	so	w	l	t	gaa	a	pm	gp	min	ga	so	w	l	gaa	a	pm
74-75	Ind	1	59	4	0	0	1	0	4.07	0	0									
75-76	Ind	31	1860	85	0	14	15	1	2.74	0	2	3	126	5	0	0	2	2.38	0	0
76-77	Ind	42	2286	128	1	17	19	3	3.36	0	0	4	245	17	0	2	2	4.16	0	0
77-78	Cin	45	2356	140	4	21	17	1	3.57	0	26									
78-79	Cin	30	1681	93	0	10	14	2	3.32	0	2									
totals		149	8242	450	5	62	66	7	3.28	0	30	7	371	22	0	2	4	3.56	0	0

• Played in NHL: 1979-85, Que-Wpg-Pit, 227-12695-898-2-4.24 (60-118-32)

Peter DONNELLY
5-8   160   cR
Peter George Donnelly
14 Jun 1948, Detroit MI

year	team	gp	min	ga	so	w	l	t	gaa	a	pm	gp	min	ga	so	w	l	gaa	a	pm
72-73	NY	47	2606	155	2	22	19	2	3.57	0	2									
73-74	Van	49	2824	179	3	22	24	0	3.80	1	9									
75-76	Que	4	129	10	0	0	1	0	4.65	0	0									
totals		100	5559	344	5	44	44	2	3.71	1	11									

• Brother of Pat Donnelly • Shutout Philadelphia in his WHA and major-league debut, October 15, 1972.

Gary DOYLE
5-8   155   cL
6 Jan 1949, Smith Falls ON

year	team	gp	min	ga	so	w	l	t	gaa	a	pm	gp	min	ga	so	w	l	gaa	a	pm
73-74	Edm	1	60	4	0	1	0	0	4.00	0	0									
totals		1	60	4	0	1	0	0	4.00	0	0									

Dave DRYDEN
6-2   185   cL
David Murray Dryden
5 Sep 1941, Hamilton ON

year	team	gp	min	ga	so	w	l	t	gaa	a	pm	gp	min	ga	so	w	l	gaa	a	pm
74-75	Chi	45	2728	176	1	18	26	1	3.87	1	4									
75-76	Edm	62	3567	235	1	22	34	5	3.95	2	2	3	180	15	0	0	3	5.00	0	0
76-77	Edm	24	1416	77	1	10	13	0	3.76	2	0									
77-78	Edm	48	2578	150	2	21	23	2	3.49	1	0	2	91	6	0	0	1	3.96	0	0
78-79	Edm	63	3531	170	3	41	17	2	2.89	8	0	13	687	42	0	6	7	3.67	0	0
totals		242	13820	808	8	112	113	10	3.51	14	6	18	958	63	0	6	11	3.95	0	0

• Played in NHL: 1961-74, 1979-80, NYR-Chi-Buf-Edm, 203-10414-555-9-3.19 (66-76-31)

Rich DUMAS
5-11   170   cL   21 Aug 1951, Granby PQ

year	team	gp	min	ga	so	w	l	t	gaa	a	pm	gp	min	ga	so	w	l	gaa	a	pm
74-75	Chi	1	1	0	0	0	0	0	0.00	0	0									
totals		1	1	0	0	0	0	0	0.00	0	0									

Ed DYCK   Edwin Paul Dyck
6-0   165   cL   29 Oct 1950, Warman SK

year	team	gp	min	ga	so	w	l	t	gaa	a	pm	gp	min	ga	so	w	l	gaa	a	pm
74-75	Ind	32	1692	123	0	3	21	3	4.36	0	6									
totals		32	1692	123	0	3	21	3	4.36	0	6									

• Played in NHL: 1971-74, Van, 49-2453-178-1-4.35 (8-28-5)

George GARDNER   George Edward Gardner
5-10   175   cL   8 Oct 1942, Lachine PQ   d. 2006

year	team	gp	min	ga	so	w	l	t	gaa	a	pm	gp	min	ga	so	w	l	gaa	a	pm
72-73	LA	49	2713	149	1	19	22	4	3.30	0	0	3	116	11	0	1	2	5.69	0	0
73-74	LA	2	120	13	0	0	2	0	6.50	0	0									
	Van	28	1590	125	0	4	21	1	4.72	0	0									
totals		79	4423	287	1	23	45	5	3.89	0	0	3	116	11	0	1	2	5.69	0	0

• Played in NHL: 1965-72, Det-Van, 66-3313-207-0-3.75 (16-30-6)

John GARRETT   John Murdock Garrett "Chi-Chi"
5-8   165   cL   15 Jun 1951, Trenton ON

year	team	gp	min	ga	so	w	l	t	gaa	a	pm	gp	min	ga	so	w	l	gaa	a	pm
73-74	Min	40	2290	137	1	21	18	0	3.59	0	10	7	372	25	0	4	2	4.03	0	0
74-75	Min	58	3294	180	2	30	23	2	3.28	0	6	12	726	41	1	6	6	3.39	0	0
75-76	Min	52	3179	177	2	26	22	4	3.34	0	6									
	Tor	9	551	33	1	3	6	0	3.59	1	0									
76-77	Bir	65	3803	224	4	24	34	4	3.53	3	21									
77-78	Bir	58	3306	210	2	24	31	1	3.81	3	26	5	271	26	0	1	4	5.76	0	0
78-79	NE	41	2496	149	2	20	17	4	3.58	0	6	8	447	32	0	4	3	4.30	0	0
totals		323	18919	1110	14	148	151	15	3.52	7	75	32	1816	124	1	15	15	4.10	0	0

• Played in NHL: 1979-85, Hart-Que-Van, 207-11763-837-1-4.27 (68-91-37)

Andre GILL   Andre Marcel Gill
5-7   175   cL   19 Sep 1941, Sorel PQ   d. 2014

year	team	gp	min	ga	so	w	l	t	gaa	a	pm	gp	min	ga	so	w	l	gaa	a	pm
72-73	Chi	33	1709	118	0	4	24	0	4.24	0	6									
73-74	Chi	13	803	46	0	4	7	2	3.44	0	0	11	614	38	0	6	5	3.71	0	0
totals		46	2512	164	0	8	31	2	3.92	0	6	11	614	38	0	6	5	3.71	0	0

• Played in NHL: 1967-68, Bos, 5-270-13-1-2.89 (3-2-0)

Russ GILLOW   Russell Howard Gillow
5-10   175   cL   2 Sep 1940, Hespeler ON

year	team	gp	min	ga	so	w	l	t	gaa	a	pm	gp	min	ga	so	w	l	gaa	a	pm
72-73	LA	38	1892	96	2	17	13	2	2.91	0	6	5	247	12	0	1	2	2.91	0	0
73-74	LA	18	1041	69	1	4	13	0	3.98	0	2									
74-75	SD	30	1653	94	1	15	11	2	3.41	1	4	3	79	5	0	0	0	3.80	0	0
75-76	SD	23	1037	74	0	1	10	2	4.28	0	0	1	20	0	0	0	0	0.00	0	0
totals		109	5713	333	4	37	47	6	3.50	1	12	9	346	17	0	1	2	2.95	0	0

Ron GRAHAME   Ronald Ian Grahame
5-11   175   cL   7 Jun 1950, Victoria BC

year	team	gp	min	ga	so	w	l	t	gaa	a	pm	gp	min	ga	so	w	l	gaa	a	pm
73-74	Hou	4	250	5	1	3	0	1	1.20	0	0									
74-75	Hou	43	2590	131	4	33	10	0	3.03	1	0	13	780	26	3	12	1	2.00	0	0
75-76	Hou	57	3343	182	3	39	17	0	3.27	1	0	14	817	54	1	6	8	3.97	0	0
76-77	Hou	39	2345	107	4	27	10	2	2.74	1	2	9	561	36	0	4	5	3.85	2	0
totals		143	8528	425	12	102	37	3	2.99	3	2	36	2158	116	4	22	14	3.23	2	0

• Played in NHL: 1977-81, Bos-LA-Que, 114-6472-409-5-3.79 (50-43-15) • Shutout Chicago in his WHA and major-league debut, December 29, 1973.

Gilles GRATTON   Gilles Andre Gratton
5-11   155   cL   29 Jun 1952, LaSalle PQ

year	team	gp	min	ga	so	w	l	t	gaa	a	pm	gp	min	ga	so	w	l	gaa	a	pm
72-73	Ott	51	3021	187	0	25	22	3	3.71	1	10	2	87	7	0	0	1	4.83	0	0
73-74	Tor	57	3200	188	2	26	24	3	3.53	4	28	10	539	25	1	5	3	2.78	0	0
74-75	Tor	53	2881	185	2	30	20	1	3.85	4	8	1	36	5	0	0	1	8.33	0	0
totals		161	9102	560	4	81	66	7	3.69	9	46	13	662	37	1	5	5	3.35	0	0

• Shared shutout with Les Binkley, October 16, 1973 • Played in NHL: 1975-77, StL-NYR, 47-2299-154-0-4.02 (13-18-9)

Chris GRIGG   Christopher Robert William Grigg
6-1   180   cL   2 Feb 1953, Ottawa ON

year	team	gp	min	ga	so	w	l	t	gaa	a	pm	gp	min	ga	so	w	l	gaa	a	pm
75-76	D-O	2	80	13	0	0	0	0	9.75	0	0									
totals		2	80	13	0	0	0	0	9.75	0	0									

Clay HEBENTON   Andrew Clayton Hebenton
5-10   185   cL   20 Feb 1953, Victoria BC

year	team	gp	min	ga	so	w	l	t	gaa	a	pm	gp	min	ga	so	w	l	gaa	a	pm
75-76	Phx	2	80	9	0	0	1	0	6.75	0	0									
76-77	Phx	56	3129	220	0	17	29	3	4.22	0	2									
totals		58	3209	229	0	17	30	3	4.28	0	2									

Paul HOGANSON
5-10 190 cR Paul Edward Hoganson
12 Nov 1949, Toronto ON

year	team	gp	min	ga	so	w	l	t	gaa	a	pm	gp	min	ga	so	w	l	gaa	a	pm
73-74	LA	27	1308	102	0	6	16	0	4.68	0	0									
74-75	M-B	32	1776	121	2	9	19	2	4.09	0	12									
75-76	NE	4	224	16	0	1	2	0	4.29	1	0									
	Cin	45	2392	145	2	19	24	0	3.64	1	4									
76-77	Cin	17	823	64	1	5	6	1	4.67	0	0									
	Ind	11	395	24	0	3	2	0	3.65	0	2	5	348	17	1	3	2	2.93	0	0
77-78	Cin	7	326	24	0	1	2	1	4.42	0	0									
totals		143	7244	496	5	44	71	4	4.11	2	18	5	348	17	1	3	2	2.93	0	0

• Cousin of Dale Hoganson • Played in NHL: 1970-71, Pit, 2-57-7-0-7.27 (0-1-0)

Bill HOLDEN
5-11 170 cR 23 Jul 1949, Toronto ON

year	team	gp	min	ga	so	w	l	t	gaa	a	pm	gp	min	ga	so	w	l	gaa	a	pm
73-74	Tor	1	10	0	0	0	0	0	0.00	0	0									
	Wpg	1	60	4	0	0	1	0	4.00	0	0									
totals		2	70	4	0	0	1	0	3.43	0	0									

• Loaned to Winnipeg by Toronto as an emergency replacement, April 1974

Leif HOLMQUIST
5-11 175 cL 22 Nov 1942, Gavle Sweden

year	team	gp	min	ga	so	w	l	t	gaa	a	pm	gp	min	ga	so	w	l	gaa	a	pm
75-76	Ind	19	1079	54	0	6	9	3	3.00	0	4									
totals		19	1079	54	0	6	9	3	3.00	0	4									

• Member, Sweden Olympic Team, 1968 & 1972

Bill HUGHES
6-1 185 cL William John Martin Hughes
7 Nov 1947, Kirkland Lake ON

year	team	gp	min	ga	so	w	l	t	gaa	a	pm	gp	min	ga	so	w	l	gaa	a	pm
72-73	Hou	3	170	11	0	0	1	1	3.88	0	2									
totals		3	170	11	0	0	1	1	3.88	0	2									

• Signed as an emergency replacement after originally being hired to work in the Houston Aeros' front office

Ed HUMPHREYS
6-1 170 cL 5 Jun 1953, Eston SK

year	team	gp	min	ga	so	w	l	t	gaa	a	pm	gp	min	ga	so	w	l	gaa	a	pm
75-76	Cgy	8	441	27	0	2	5	0	3.67	0	0	1	20	0	0	0	0	0.00	0	0
76-77	Que	22	1240	74	1	12	8	1	3.58	1	0									
totals		30	1681	101	1	14	13	1	3.60	1	0	1	20	0	0	0	0	0.00	0	0

Gary INNESS
6-0 190 cL Gary George Inness
28 May 1949, Toronto ON

year	team	gp	min	ga	so	w	l	t	gaa	a	pm	gp	min	ga	so	w	l	gaa	a	pm
77-78	Ind	52	2850	200	0	14	30	4	4.21	0	42									
78-79	Ind	10	609	51	0	3	6	1	5.02	0	9									
totals		62	3459	251	0	17	36	5	4.35	0	51									

• Played in NHL: 1974-77, 1978-81, Pit-Phi-Wash, 182-8710-494-2-3.40 (58-61-27)

Bob JOHNSON
6-1 185 cL Robert Martin Johnson
12 Nov 1948, Farmington MI

year	team	gp	min	ga	so	w	l	t	gaa	a	pm	gp	min	ga	so	w	l	gaa	a	pm
75-76	D-O	24	1334	88	0	8	14	1	3.96	0	0									
	Cle	18	1043	56	1	9	8	0	3.22	0	0	2	120	8	0	0	2	4.00	0	0
totals		42	2377	144	1	17	22	1	3.63	0	0	2	120	8	0	0	2	4.00	0	0

• Played in NHL: 1972-75, StL-Pit, 24-1059-66-0-3.74 (9-9-1)

Joe JUNKIN
5-11 180 cL Joseph Brian Junkin
8 Sep 1946, Belleville ON d. 2014

year	team	gp	min	ga	so	w	l	t	gaa	a	pm	gp	min	ga	so	w	l	gaa	a	pm
73-74	NY-J	53	3122	197	1	21	25	4	3.79	1	7									
74-75	SD	16	839	46	1	6	7	0	3.29	1	2									
totals		69	3961	243	2	27	32	4	3.68	2	9									

• Played in NHL: 1968-69, 1-8-0-0-0.00 (0-0-0)

Hannu KAMPURRI
6-0 175 cR Hannu Juhani Kampurri
1 Jun 1957, Helsinki Finland

year	team	gp	min	ga	so	w	l	t	gaa	a	pm	gp	min	ga	so	w	l	gaa	a	pm
78-79	Edm	2	90	10	0	0	1	0	6.67	0	0									
totals		2	90	10	0	0	1	0	6.67	0	0									

• Played in NHL: 1984-85, NJ, 13-645-54-0-5.02 (1-10-1)

John KIELY
6-2 190 cR John Stuart Kiely
3 Aug 1952, Ithaca NY

year	team	gp	min	ga	so	w	l	t	gaa	a	pm	gp	min	ga	so	w	l	gaa	a	pm
75-76	Cin	22	1087	78	0	6	8	1	4.31	1	6									
totals		22	1087	78	0	6	8	1	4.31	1	6									

Gary KURT
6-3   195   cL   Gary David Kurt
                            9 Mar 1947, Kitchener ON

year	team	gp	min	ga	so	w	l	t	gaa	a	pm		gp	min	ga	so	w	l	gaa	a	pm
72-73	NY	36	1881	150	0	10	21	0	4.78	1	2										
73-74	NY-J	20	1089	75	0	8	10	0	4.13	1	0										
74-75	Phx	47	2841	156	2	25	16	4	3.29	2	4		4	207	12	0	1	2	3.48	0	0
75-76	Phx	40	2369	147	1	18	20	2	3.72	4	4										
76-77	Phx	33	1752	162	0	11	19	1	5.55	3	6										
totals		176	9932	690	3	72	86	7	4.17	11	16		4	207	12	0	1	2	3.48	0	0

• Played in NHL: 1971-72, Cal, 16-838-60-0-4.30 (1-7-5)

Bruce LANDON
5-10   180   cL   Norman Bruce Landon
                            5 Oct 1949, Kingston ON

year	team	gp	min	ga	so	w	l	t	gaa	a	pm		gp	min	ga	so	w	l	gaa	a	pm
72-73	NE	30	1671	100	1	15	11	1	3.59	1	8										
73-74	NE	24	1386	82	0	11	9	2	3.55	0	24		1	40	3	0	0	0	4.50	0	0
74-75	NE	7	339	19	0	2	3	0	3.36	0	0										
75-76	NE	38	2181	126	0	14	19	5	3.47	1	0		4	197	7	0	3	0	2.13	0	0
76-77	NE	23	1118	59	1	8	8	1	3.17	0	4		3	152	11	0	1	2	4.34	0	0
totals		122	6695	386	2	50	50	9	3.46	2	36		8	389	21	0	4	2	3.24	0	0

Norm LAPOINTE
6-0   175   cL   Normand Lapointe
                            13 Aug 1955, Laval PQ

year	team	gp	min	ga	so	w	l	t	gaa	a	pm		gp	min	ga	so	w	l	gaa	a	pm
75-76	Cin	12	641	55	0	4	6	0	5.15	0	0										
76-77	Cin	52	2817	175	2	21	25	2	3.73	0	2		4	273	16	0	0	3	3.52	0	0
77-78	Cin	13	647	50	0	5	6	1	4.64	1	4										
totals		77	4105	280	2	30	37	3	4.09	1	6		4	273	16	0	0	3	3.52	0	0

Curt LARSSON
5-10   170   cL   11 Dec 1944, Nykoping Sweden

year	team	gp	min	ga	so	w	l	t	gaa	a	pm		gp	min	ga	so	w	l	gaa	a	pm
74-75	Wpg	26	1514	100	1	12	11	1	3.96	1	4										
75-76	Wpg	23	1287	83	0	11	10	1	3.87	1	6		2	110	6	0	2	0	3.27	0	0
76-77	Wpg	19	1019	82	0	7	9	0	4.83	1	4		1	20	1	0	0	0	3.00	0	0
totals		68	3820	265	1	30	30	2	4.16	3	14		3	130	7	0	2	0	3.23	0	0

Jacques LEMELIN
5-8   155   -   11 Nov 1949, Quebec PQ

year	team	gp	min	ga	so	w	l	t	gaa	a	pm		gp	min	ga	so	w	l	gaa	a	pm
72-73	Que	9	435	29	0	3	4	1	4.00	1	0										
totals		9	435	29	0	3	4	1	4.00	1	0										

Louis LEVASSEUR
5-10   160   cL   Jean-Louis Levasseur
                            16 Jun 1949, Rouyn PQ

year	team	gp	min	ga	so	w	l	t	gaa	a	pm		gp	min	ga	so	w	l	gaa	a	pm
75-76	Min	4	193	10	0	2	1	0	3.11	0	0										
76-77	Min	30	1715	78	2	15	11	2	2.73	1	4										
	Edm	21	1213	88	0	6	12	3	4.35	0	0		2	133	10	0	0	2	4.51	0	2
77-78	NE	27	1655	91	3	14	11	2	3.30	0	2		12	719	31	0	8	4	2.59	1	2
78-79	Que	3	140	14	0	0	1	1	6.00	0	0		1	59	8	0	0	1	8.14	0	0
totals		85	4916	281	5	37	36	8	3.43	1	6		15	911	49	0	8	7	3.23	1	4

• Played in NHL: 1979-80, Min, 1-60-7-0-7.00 (0-1-0)

Mike LIUT
6-2   180   cL   Michael Dennis Liut
                            7 Jan 1956, Weston ON

year	team	gp	min	ga	so	w	l	t	gaa	a	pm		gp	min	ga	so	w	l	gaa	a	pm
77-78	Cin	27	1215	86	0	8	12	0	4.25	1	0										
78-79	Cin	54	3181	184	3	23	27	4	3.47	2	9		3	179	10	0	1	2	3.35	0	0
totals		81	4396	270	3	31	39	4	3.69	3	9		3	179	10	0	1	2	3.35	0	0

• Played in NHL: 1979-92, StL-Hart-Wash, 663-38155-2219-25-3.49 (293-271-74)

Ken LOCKETT
6-0   180   cL   Kenneth Richard Lockett
                            30 Aug 1947, Toronto ON

year	team	gp	min	ga	so	w	l	t	gaa	a	pm		gp	min	ga	so	w	l	gaa	a	pm
76-77	SD	45	2397	148	1	18	19	1	3.70	0	0		5	260	19	0	1	3	4.38	0	0
totals		45	2397	148	1	18	19	1	3.70	0	0		5	260	19	0	1	3	4.38	0	0

• Played in NHL: 1974-76, Van, 55-2348-131-2-3.35 (13-15-8)

Markus MATTSSON
6-0   180   cL   Markus Rainer Mattsson
                            30 Jul 1957, Suoneiemi Finland

year	team	gp	min	ga	so	w	l	t	gaa	a	pm		gp	min	ga	so	w	l	gaa	a	pm
77-78	Que	6	266	30	0	1	3	0	6.77	0	0										
	Wpg	10	511	30	0	4	5	0	3.52	0	2										
78-79	Wpg	52	2990	181	0	25	21	3	3.63	1	4										
totals		68	3767	241	0	30	29	3	3.84	1	6										

• Played in NHL: 1979-84, Wpg-Min-LA, 92-5007-343-6-4.11 (21-46-14)

Jack McCARTAN
6-1   205   cL   Jack William McCartan
                           5 Aug 1935, St. Paul MN

year	team	gp	min	ga	so	w	l	t	gaa	a	pm	gp	min	ga	so	w	l	gaa	a	pm
72-73	Min	38	2160	129	1	15	19	1	3.58	0	19	4	213	14	0	1	2	3.94	1	0
73-74	Min	2	42	5	0	0	0	0	7.14	0	0									
74-75	Min	2	61	5	0	1	0	0	4.92	0	0									
totals		**42**	**2263**	**139**	**1**	**16**	**19**	**1**	**3.69**	**0**	**19**	**4**	**213**	**14**	**0**	**1**	**2**	**3.94**	**1**	**0**

• Member, United States Olympic Team, 1960 • Played in NHL: 1959-61, NYR, 12-680-42-1-3.71 (2-7-3)

Peter McDUFFE
5-10   180   cL   Peter Arnold McDuffe
                           16 Feb 1948, Milton ON

year	team	gp	min	ga	so	w	l	t	gaa	a	pm	gp	min	ga	so	w	l	gaa	a	pm
77-78	Ind	12	539	39	0	1	6	1	4.34	0	0									
totals		**12**	**539**	**39**	**0**	**1**	**6**	**1**	**4.34**	**0**	**0**									

• Played in NHL: 1971-76, StL-NYR-KC-Det, 57-3207-218-0-4.08 (11-36-6)

Don McLEOD
5-11   180   cL   Donald Martin McLeod "Smokey"
                           24 Aug 1946, Trail BC   d. 2015

year	team	gp	min	ga	so	w	l	t	gaa	a	pm	gp	min	ga	so	w	l	gaa	a	pm
72-73	Hou	41	2410	145	1	19	20	1	3.61	0	0	3	178	8	0	0	3	2.70	0	0
73-74	Hou	49	2971	127	3	33	13	3	2.56	3	6	14	842	35	0	12	2	2.49	0	0
74-75	Van	72	4184	233	1	33	35	2	3.34	8	14									
75-76	Cgy	63	3534	206	1	30	27	3	3.50	13	4	10	579	37	0	5	5	3.83	1	4
76-77	Cgy	67	3701	210	3	25	34	5	3.40	9	2									
77-78	Que	7	403	28	0	2	4	0	4.17	3	0									
	Edm	33	1723	102	2	15	10	1	3.55	7	2	4	207	16	1	1	3	4.64	0	0
totals		**332**	**18926**	**1051**	**11**	**157**	**143**	**15**	**3.33**	**43**	**28**	**31**	**1806**	**96**	**1**	**18**	**13**	**3.19**	**1**	**4**

Played in NHL: 1970-72, Det-Phi, 18-879-74-0-5.05 (3-10-1) • Was all-time major-league league record holder for career points by a goaltender at his retirement.

Jim McLEOD
5-8   175   cL   James Bradley McLeod
                           7 Apr 1937, Port Arthur ON

year	team	gp	min	ga	so	w	l	t	gaa	a	pm	gp	min	ga	so	w	l	gaa	a	pm
72-73	Chi	54	2996	166	1	22	25	2	3.32	1	2									
73-74	NY-J	10	517	36	0	3	7	0	4.18	0	2									
	LA	17	969	69	1	4	13	0	4.27	0	0									
74-75	M-B	16	694	53	0	3	6	1	4.58	0	0									
totals		**97**	**5176**	**324**	**2**	**32**	**51**	**3**	**3.76**	**1**	**4**									

Played in NHL: 1971-72, StL, 16-880-44-0-3.00 (6-6-4)

Paul MENARD
5-10   175   cL   Paul Leo Menard
                           22 May 1952, Chamborg PQ

year	team	gp	min	ga	so	w	l	t	gaa	a	pm	gp	min	ga	so	w	l	gaa	a	pm
72-73	Chi	1	45	5	0	0	1	0	6.67	0	0									
totals		**1**	**45**	**5**	**0**	**0**	**1**	**0**	**6.67**	**0**	**0**									

Ed MIO
5-10   180   cR   Edward Dario Mio
                           21 Jan 1954, Windsor ON

year	team	gp	min	ga	so	w	l	t	gaa	a	pm	gp	min	ga	so	w	l	gaa	a	pm
77-78	Ind	17	900	64	0	6	8	0	4.27	0	0									
78-79	Ind	5	242	13	1	2	2	0	3.22	1	2									
	Edm	22	1068	71	1	7	10	0	3.99	1	2									
totals		**44**	**2210**	**148**	**2**	**15**	**20**	**0**	**4.02**	**2**	**4**									

• Played in NHL: 1979-86, Edm-NYR-Det, 192-10428-705-4-4.06 (64-73-30)

Cam NEWTON
5-10   185   cL   Cameron Charles Newton
                           25 Feb 1950, Peterborough ON

year	team	gp	min	ga	so	w	l	t	gaa	a	pm	gp	min	ga	so	w	l	gaa	a	pm
73-74	Chi	45	2732	143	2	25	18	2	3.14	1	0	10	486	34	0	2	5	4.20	0	0
74-75	Chi	32	1905	126	0	12	20	0	3.97	0	0									
75-76	D-O	10	573	35	1	4	6	0	3.66	0	0									
	Cle	15	896	48	0	7	7	1	3.21	1	0	1	60	6	0	0	1	6.00	0	0
totals		**102**	**6106**	**352**	**2**	**48**	**51**	**3**	**3.46**	**2**	**0**	**11**	**546**	**40**	**0**	**2**	**6**	**4.39**	**0**	**0**

• Played in NHL: 1970-73, Pit, 16-814-51-0-3.76 (4-7-1)

Jack NORRIS
5-10   175   cL   Jack Wayne Norris
                           5 Aug 1942, Saskatoon SK

year	team	gp	min	ga	so	w	l	t	gaa	a	pm	gp	min	ga	so	w	l	gaa	a	pm
72-73	Alb	64	3702	189	1	28	29	3	3.06	3	2									
73-74	Edm	53	2954	158	2	23	24	1	3.21	3	0	3	111	9	0	0	2	4.86	0	0
74-75	Phx	33	1962	107	1	14	15	4	3.27	1	2	2	100	10	0	0	2	6.00	0	0
75-76	Phx	41	2412	128	1	21	14	4	3.18	2	6	5	298	17	0	2	3	3.42	0	0
totals		**191**	**11030**	**582**	**5**	**86**	**82**	**12**	**3.16**	**9**	**10**	**10**	**509**	**36**	**0**	**2**	**7**	**4.24**	**0**	**0**

• Played in NHL: 1964-71, Bos-Chi-LA, 58-3119-202-2-3.89 (20-25-4)

Ted OUIMET
6-0   170   cL   Edward John Ouimet
                           6 Jul 1947, Noranda PQ

year	team	gp	min	ga	so	w	l	t	gaa	a	pm	gp	min	ga	so	w	l	gaa	a	pm
74-75	NE	1	20	3	0	0	0	0	9.00	0	0									
totals		**1**	**20**	**3**	**0**	**0**	**0**	**0**	**9.00**	**0**	**0**									

• Played in NHL: 1968-69, StL, 1-60-2-0-2.00 (0-1-0) • Only player to play exactly one game each in WHA and in NHL

Marcel PAILLE
5-8 185 cL 8 Dec 1932, Shawinigan Falls PQ d. 2003

year	team	gp	min	ga	so	w	l	t	gaa	a	pm	gp	min	ga	so	w	l	gaa	a	pm
72-73	Phi	15	611	49	0	2	8	0	4.81	0	0	1	26	5	0	0	1	11.54	0	0
totals		15	611	49	0	2	8	0	4.81	0	0	1	26	5	0	0	1	11.54	0	0

• Played in NHL: 1957-65, NYR, 107-6342-362-2-3.42 (32-52-22)

Bernie PARENT
5-10 170 cL Bernard Marcel Parent 3 Apr 1945, Montreal PQ

year	team	gp	min	ga	so	w	l	t	gaa	a	pm	gp	min	ga	so	w	l	gaa	a	pm
72-73	Phi	63	3653	220	2	33	28	0	3.61	1	36	1	70	3	0	0	1	2.57	0	0
totals		63	3653	220	2	33	28	0	3.61	1	36	1	70	3	0	0	1	2.57	0	0

• Played in NHL: 1965-72, 1973-78, Bos-Tor-Phi, 608-35136-1493-54-2.55 (271-198-121) • Stanley Cups: 1974, 1975 (Philadelphia) • Member, Hockey Hall of Fame

Jim PARK
6-1 190 cL James Park 22 Jun 1952, Toronto ON

year	team	gp	min	ga	so	w	l	t	gaa	a	pm	gp	min	ga	so	w	l	gaa	a	pm
75-76	Ind	11	572	23	0	6	4	0	2.41	1	2	6	293	12	2	3	2	2.45	0	0
76-77	Ind	31	1727	114	1	14	12	4	3.96	1	6									
77-78	Ind	12	589	41	0	3	7	0	4.21	0	6									
totals		54	2888	178	1	23	23	4	3.70	2	14	6	293	12	2	3	2	2.45	0	0

Bob PERREAULT
5-8 180 cL Robert Perreault "Miche" 28 Jan 1931, Trois Rivieres PQ d. 1980

year	team	gp	min	ga	so	w	l	t	gaa	a	pm	gp	min	ga	so	w	l	gaa	a	pm
72-73	LA	1	60	2	0	1	0	0	2.00	0	0									
totals		1	60	2	0	1	0	0	2.00	0	0									

• Played in NHL: 1955-63, Mtl-Det-Bos, 31-1827-103-3-3.38 (8-16-7)

Jacques PLANTE
6-0 175 cL Joseph Jacques Omer Plante 17 Jan 1929, Mont Carmel PQ d. 1986

year	team	gp	min	ga	so	w	l	t	gaa	a	pm	gp	min	ga	so	w	l	gaa	a	pm
74-75	Edm	31	1592	88	1	15	14	1	3.32	1	2									
totals		31	1592	88	1	15	14	1	3.32	1	2									

• Played in NHL: 1952-73, Mtl-NYR-StL-Tor-Bos, 837-49493-1964-82-2.38 (435-247-145) • Stanley Cups: 1953, 1956, 1957, 1958, 1959, 1960 (Montreal) • Member, Hockey Hall of Fame

Cap RAEDER
6-0 175 cR Robert Raeder 8 Oct 1953, Needham MA

year	team	gp	min	ga	so	w	l	t	gaa	a	pm	gp	min	ga	so	w	l	gaa	a	pm
75-76	NE	3	100	8	0	0	1	0	4.80	0	0	14	819	31	2	7	7	2.27	0	0
76-77	NE	26	1328	69	2	12	10	1	3.12	0	2	1	60	7	0	0	1	7.00	0	0
totals		29	1428	77	2	12	11	1	3.24	0	2	15	879	38	2	7	8	3.24	0	0

Pat RIGGIN
5-9 165 cR 26 May 1959, Kincardine ON

year	team	gp	min	ga	so	w	l	t	gaa	a	pm	gp	min	ga	so	w	l	gaa	a	pm
78-79	Bir	46	2511	158	1	16	22	5	3.78	3	22									
totals		46	2511	158	1	16	22	5	3.78	3	22									

• Played in NHL: 1979-88, Atl-Cgy-Wash-Bos-Pit, 350-19872-1135-11-3.43 (153-120-52)

Wayne RUTLEDGE
6-2 205 cL Wayne Alvin Rutledge 5 Jan 1942, Barrie ON d. 2004

year	team	gp	min	ga	so	w	l	t	gaa	a	pm	gp	min	ga	so	w	l	gaa	a	pm
72-73	Hou	36	2163	110	0	20	14	2	3.05	0	11	7	422	20	0	4	3	2.84	0	0
73-74	Hou	25	1509	84	0	12	12	1	3.34	1	14									
74-75	Hou	35	2098	113	2	20	15	0	3.23	0	0									
75-76	Hou	25	1456	77	1	14	10	0	3.17	0	6	4	200	10	0	2	1	3.00	0	0
76-77	Hou	42	2512	132	3	23	14	4	3.15	3	63	2	120	4	0	2	0	2.00	0	0
77-78	Hou	12	634	47	0	4	7	0	4.45	0	2	3	131	8	0	1	2	3.66	0	2
totals		175	10372	563	6	93	72	7	3.25	4	96	16	873	42	0	9	6	2.89	0	2

• Played in NHL: 1967-70, LA, 82-4325-241-2-3.34 (28-37-9)

Nick SANZA
5-11 180 cL 5 Feb 1955, Montreal PQ

year	team	gp	min	ga	so	w	l	t	gaa	a	pm	gp	min	ga	so	w	l	gaa	a	pm
75-76	D-O	1	20	5	0	0	1	0	15.00	0	0									
totals		1	20	5	0	0	1	0	15.00	0	0									

Jim SHAW
6-1 185 cL James Morris Shaw 18 Oct 1945, Saskatoon SK

year	team	gp	min	ga	so	w	l	t	gaa	a	pm	gp	min	ga	so	w	l	gaa	a	pm
74-75	Tor	21	1055	70	0	7	9	1	3.98	0	0	5	262	18	0	2	2	4.12	0	0
75-76	Tor	16	777	63	0	4	7	1	4.86	0	0									
totals		37	1832	133	0	11	16	2	4.36	0	0	5	262	18	0	2	2	4.12	0	0

Al SMITH
6-1 195 cL 10 Nov 1945, Toronto ON d. 2002

year	team	gp	min	ga	so	w	l	t	gaa	a	pm	gp	min	ga	so	w	l	gaa	a	pm
72-73	NE	51	3059	162	3	31	19	1	3.18	3	39	15	909	49	0	12	3	3.23	1	12
73-74	NE	55	3194	164	2	30	21	2	3.08	3	33	7	399	21	1	3	4	3.16	0	0
74-75	NE	59	3494	202	2	33	21	4	3.47	0	18	6	366	28	0	2	4	4.59	0	0
77-78	NE	55	3246	174	2	30	20	3	3.22	3	4	3	120	14	0	0	2	7.00	0	0
78-79	NE	40	2396	132	1	17	17	5	3.31	3	35	4	153	12	0	1	2	4.71	0	0
totals		260	15389	834	10	141	98	15	3.25	12	129	35	1947	124	1	18	15	3.82	1	12

• Played in NHL: 1965-72, 1975-77, 1979-81, Tor-Pit-Det-Buf-Hart-Col, 233-12752-735-10-3.46 (74-99-36)

Gary SMITH
6-4 215 cL Gary Edward Smith "Axe" 4 Feb 1944, Ottawa ON

year	team	gp	min	ga	so	w	l	t	gaa	a	pm	gp	min	ga	so	w	l	gaa	a	pm
78-79	Ind	11	664	61	0	0	10	1	5.51	0	0									
	Wpg	11	626	31	0	7	3	0	2.97	3	0	10	563	35	0	8	2	3.73	0	0
totals		22	1293	92	0	7	13	1	4.28	3	0	10	563	35	0	8	2	3.73	0	0

• Brother of Brian Smith • Played in NHL: 1965-78, 1979-80, Tor-Oak-Cal-Chi-Van-Min-Wash-Wpg, 532-29619-1675-26-3.39 (173-261-74)

Danny SULLIVAN
5-8 155 - Daniel Sullivan 31 May 1947, Kimberley BC

year	team	gp	min	ga	so	w	l	t	gaa	a	pm	gp	min	ga	so	w	l	gaa	a	pm
72-73	Phi	1	60	3	0	1	0	0	3.00	0	0									
73-74	Van	1	60	7	0	0	1	0	7.00	0	0									
totals		2	120	10	0	1	1	0	5.00	0	0									

Dave TATARYN
5-9 160 cL David Nathan Tataryn 17 Jul 1950, Sudbury ON

year	team	gp	min	ga	so	w	l	t	gaa	a	pm	gp	min	ga	so	w	l	gaa	a	pm
75-76	Tor	23	1261	100	0	7	12	1	4.76	0	0									
totals		23	1261	100	0	7	12	1	4.76	0	0									

• Played in NHL: 1976-77, NYR, 2-80-10-0-7.50 (1-1-0)

Gord TUMILSON
5-8 160 cL 17 Jul 1951, Winnipeg MB

year	team	gp	min	ga	so	w	l	t	gaa	a	pm	gp	min	ga	so	w	l	gaa	a	pm
72-73	Wpg	3	138	10	0	0	2	0	4.34	0	0									
totals		3	138	10	0	0	2	0	4.34	0	0									

Frank TURNBULL
5-8 155 - 13 Jan 1953, Trenton ON

year	team	gp	min	ga	so	w	l	t	gaa	a	pm	gp	min	ga	so	w	l	gaa	a	pm
75-76	Edm	3	106	9	0	0	1	0	5.09	0	0									
77-78	Edm	1	60	6	0	0	1	0	6.00	0	0									
totals		4	166	15	0	0	2	0	5.42	0	0									

Mario VIEN
5-7 150 cR 7 Aug 1955, Cornwall ON

year	team	gp	min	ga	so	w	l	t	gaa	a	pm	gp	min	ga	so	w	l	gaa	a	pm
75-76	Tor	26	1228	105	0	4	14	3	5.13	0	0									
totals		26	1228	105	0	4	14	3	5.13	0	0									

Ernie WAKELY
5-11 160 cL Ernest Alfred Wakely 27 Nov 1940, Flin Flon MB

year	team	gp	min	ga	so	w	l	t	gaa	a	pm	gp	min	ga	so	w	l	gaa	a	pm
72-73	Wpg	49	2889	152	2	26	19	3	3.14	0	0	7	420	22	2	4	3	3.14	0	0
73-74	Wpg	37	2254	123	3	15	18	4	3.27	0	0									
74-75	Wpg	6	355	16	1	3	3	0	2.70	0	0									
	SD	35	2062	115	2	20	12	2	3.35	0	0	10	520	39	0	4	6	4.50	0	0
75-76	SD	67	3824	208	3	35	27	4	3.26	0	0	11	640	39	0	5	6	3.66	0	0
76-77	SD	46	2506	129	3	22	18	3	3.09	0	0	3	160	9	0	2	1	3.38	0	0
77-78	Cin	6	311	26	0	0	5	0	5.02	0	0									
	Hou	51	3070	166	2	28	18	4	3.24	0	0									
78-79	Bir	37	2060	129	0	15	17	1	3.76	3	0									
totals		334	19331	1064	16	164	137	21	3.30	3	0	31	1740	109	2	15	16	3.76	0	0

• Played in NHL: 1962-72, Mtl-StL, 113-6244-290-8-2.79 (41-42-17)

Ed WALSH
5-10 180 cR Edward Walsh 18 Aug 1951, Somerville MA

year	team	gp	min	ga	so	w	l	t	gaa	a	pm	gp	min	ga	so	w	l	gaa	a	pm
78-79	Edm	3	144	9	0	0	2	0	3.75	0	0									
totals		3	144	9	0	0	2	0	3.75	0	0									

Carl WETZEL
6-2 190 cL 12 Dec 1938, Detroit MI

year	team	gp	min	ga	so	w	l	t	gaa	a	pm	gp	min	ga	so	w	l	gaa	a	pm
72-73	Min	1	60	3	0	0	1	0	3.00	0	0									
totals		1	60	3	0	0	1	0	3.00	0	0									

• Played in NHL: 1964-68, Det-Min, 7-301-22-0-4.39 (1-3-1)

Bob WHIDDEN
5-10   165   cL   Robert Joseph Whidden
                            27 Jul 1946, Sudbury ON

year	team	gp	min	ga	so	w	l	t	gaa	a	pm	gp	min	ga	so	w	l	gaa	a	pm
72-73	Cle	26	1609	88	0	11	12	3	3.28	0	5									
73-74	Cle	22	1232	80	1	7	12	3	3.90	1	2									
74-75	Cle	29	1654	89	0	9	16	1	3.23	0	2									
75-76	Cle	21	1230	70	1	7	11	2	3.41	0	2									
totals		98	5725	327	2	34	51	9	3.43	1	11									

Ian WILKIE
5-9   150   cL   Ian Clair Wilkie
                           20 Jul 1949, Edmonton AB

year	team	gp	min	ga	so	w	l	t	gaa	a	pm	gp	min	ga	so	w	l	gaa	a	pm
72-73	NY	5	253	27	0	1	3	0	6.40	0	0									
73-74	LA	23	1257	82	1	11	9	0	3.91	0	2									
	Edm	5	256	9	0	3	1	1	2.11	0	0	1	41	4	0	0	1	5.85	0	0
totals		33	1766	118	1	15	13	1	4.01	0	2	1	41	4	0	0	1	5.85	0	0

Wayne WOOD
6-1   190   cL   Wayne Douglas Wood
                           5 Jun 1951, Toronto ON

year	team	gp	min	ga	so	w	l	t	gaa	a	pm	gp	min	ga	so	w	l	gaa	a	pm
74-75	Van	11	512	30	0	4	4	0	3.52	0	0									
75-76	Cgy	19	880	45	1	9	3	1	3.07	0	4									
	Tor	13	781	62	0	6	7	0	4.76	1	0									
76-77	Bir	23	1132	78	0	7	12	0	4.13	0	0									
77-78	Bir	32	1551	99	1	12	10	2	3.83	3	22	1	29	3	0	0	0	6.21	0	0
78-79	Bir	6	311	21	0	1	3	0	4.05	0	6									
totals		104	5167	335	2	27	39	4	3.97	4	32	1	29	3	0	0	0	6.21	0	0

Chris WORTHY
6-0   185   cL   Christopher John Worthy
                           23 Oct 1947, Bristol England   d. 2007

year	team	gp	min	ga	so	w	l	t	gaa	a	pm	gp	min	ga	so	w	l	gaa	a	pm
73-74	Edm	29	1452	92	1	11	12	1	3.80	0	0	3	146	8	0	1	1	3.29	0	0
74-75	Edm	29	1660	99	1	11	13	3	3.58	0	7									
75-76	Edm	24	1256	98	1	5	14	0	4.68	0	7	1	60	7	0	0	1	7.00	0	0
totals		82	4368	289	3	27	39	4	3.97	0	14	4	206	15	0	1	2	4.37	0	0

• Played in NHL: 1968-71, Oak-Cal, 26-1326-98-0-4.43 (5-10-4)

Lynn ZIMMERMAN
5-7   155   cR   Lynn Brian Zimmerman
                           13 Jul 1942, Ft Erie ON

year	team	gp	min	ga	so	w	l	t	gaa	a	pm	gp	min	ga	so	w	l	gaa	a	pm
75-76	D-O	8	495	31	0	2	5	0	3.76	0	0									
77-78	Hou	20	1166	84	0	10	9	0	4.32	0	0	4	239	21	0	1	2	5.27	0	6
totals		28	1661	115	0	12	14	0	4.15	0	0	4	239	21	0	1	2	5.27	0	6

• Served as emergency back-up goaltender for Houston during 1977 playoffs

Famous Relations

A handful of players in the WHA had more well-known brothers who played in the NHL. Denis Meloche's brother Gilles was a long-time netminder for the Seals, Barons, North Stars and Penguins. Byron Shutt's brother Steve was a linemate of Guy Lafleur during the great Montreal dynasties of the era, Gary Sittler's big brother Darryl was known to knock in a few goals for the Maple Leafs, and Norm Cournoyer was the brother of Yvon Cournoyer, also a member of the Canadiens teams of the 1960s-70s. Brian Morenz was a distant cousin of old-time great Howie Morenz, who in turn was the grandfather of Danny Geoffrion.

Career Goaltending Statistical Leaders

Minutes, Regular Season: 19,331, Ernie Wakely; 18,926, Don McLeod; 18,919, John Garret; 17,835, Joe Daley; 17,101, Richard Brodeur; 15,389, Al Smith; 13,820, Dave Dryden; 11,352, Gerry Cheevers; 11,030, Jack Norris; 10,372, Wayne Rutledge

Minutes, Playoffs: 2,949, Richard Brodeur; 2,706, Joe Daley; 2,158, Ron Grahame; 1,947, Al Smith; 1,816, John Garrett; 1,786, Don McLeod; 1,740, Ernie Wakely; 1,151, Gerry Cheevers; 958, Dave Dryden; 879, Cap Raeder

Wins, Regular Season: 167, Joe Daley; 165, Richard Brodeur; 164, Ernie Wakely; 157, Don McLeod; 148, John Garrett; 141, Al Smith; 112, Dave Dryden; 102, Ron Grahame; 99, Gerry Cheevers; 93, Wayne Rutledge

Wins, Playoffs: 30, Joe Daley; 26, Richard Brodeur; 22, Ron Grahame; 18, Don McLeod & Al Smith; 15, John Garrett & Ernie Wakely; 9, Wayne Rutledge; 8, Louis Levasseur & Gary Smith; 7, Gerry Cheevers & Cap Raeder; 6, Dave Dryden & Andre Gill; 5, Gilles Gratton

Average, Regular Season (Minimum 50 games): 2.99, Ron Grahame; 3.12, Gerry Cheevers; 3.16, Jack Norris; 3.25 Wayne Rutledge & Al Smith; 3.28, Michel Dion; 3.30, Ernie Wakely; 3.33, Don McLeod; 3.37, Joe Daley; 3.40, Mike Curran; 3.43, Louis Levasseur & Bob Whidden

Average, Playoffs (Minimum 10 games): 2.89, Wayne Rutledge; 3.19, Don McLeod; 3.23, Ron Grahame & Lou Levasseur; 3.24, Cap Raeder; 3.28, Gerry Cheevers; 3.30, Joe Daley; 3.35, Gilles Gratton; 3.60, Richard Brodeur; 3.73, Gary Smith; 3.76, Ernie Wakely

Shutouts, Regular Season: 16, Ernie Wakely; 14, Gerry Cheevers & John Garrett; 12, Joe Daley & Ron Grahame; 11, Don McLeod; 10, Al Smith; 8, Richard Brodeur & Dave Dryden; 7, Mike Curran; 6, Wayne Rutledge; 5, shared by five players.

Shutouts, Playoffs: 4, Ron Grahame; 3, Richard Brodeur; 2, Joe Daley, Jim Park, Cap Raeder & Ernie Wakely; 1, John Garrett, Gilles Gratton, Paul Hoganson & Al Smith.

Debut Shutouts

Three goaltenders made their WHA and major-league debuts with shutouts: Peter Donnelly of New York shutout Philadelphia on October 15, 1972, Ron Grahame of Houston shutout Chicago on December 29, 1973, and Bob Blanchet of San Diego shutout Indianapolis on December 14, 1974. Three other WHA goaltenders made their NHL debuts with shutouts: Bob "Miche" Perreault of Montreal shutout Chicago on December 17, 1955, Marcel Paille of New York shutout Boston on November 2, 1957, and Andre Gill of Boston shutout New York on December 23, 1967.

They Sat and Watched

Some players received the call to the WHA but never actually played in a regular-season or playoff game. Many were goaltenders, often signed on an emergency basis as a back-up. The following is a short (and probably incomplete) list of these player-spectators: Keith LeLievre (G, Chi, 1972-73); Guy DeNoncourt (G, NY, 1972-73); Randy Andreachuk (F, Wpg, 1973-74); Terry Ross (G, Wpg, 1974-75); Roger Swanson (G, Phx, 1976-77); Ron Pronchuk (D, Que, 1975-76); Richard Szabo (G, Cin, 1976-77); Pete Devlin (D, NE, 1976 playoffs); Andy Stoesz (G, Wpg, 1976 playoffs), Tom O'Toole (G, NE, 1978-79), Harvey Stewart (G, Wpg, 1978-79); John Voss (G, Cin, 1978-79).

Ron Pronchuk is credited with 1 game played for Quebec during 1975-76 in the 1976-77 Quebec Nordiques media guide (supposedly against Cincinnati), but no corroborating evidence can be found to support this, and in later editions, he is not listed on the team's all-time roster. A player named George McPhee is listed in the 1976-77 Houston Aeros media guide as having played for the team in 1972-73, but there is no corroborating evidence to support this assertion.

Coaches Register

The following pages list the complete regular season and playoff coaching records for every coach to guide a World Hockey Association club. The coaches are listed in alphabetical order, followed by their regular season coaching record and succeeded by their playoff records. The regular season record includes the year, team coached, wins, losses and ties, points, winning percentage and divisional finish.

The playoff record includes year, team coached, wins and losses and highest playoff level reached. Winners of the AVCO World Trophy are noted. A final table at the end of this section lists all the coaches' career regular season records and winning percentages.

Regular Season

Andy Bathgate b: 28 Aug 1932 Winnipeg MB

season	team	w	l	t	pts	pct	finish
1973-74	Van	21	37	1	43	.364	5-West

• Succeeded Phil Watson on November 22, 1973

John Bassett b: 5 Feb 1939 Toronto ON   d. 1986

season	team	w	l	t	pts	pct	finish
1977-78	Bir	0	3	0	0	.000	interim

• Coached team from February 5-8, 1978, while Glen Sonmor was serving a suspension

Bob Baun b: 9 Sep 1936, Lanigan SK

season	team	w	l	t	pts	pct	finish
1975-76	Tor	15	35	5	35	.318	did not finish

• Succeeded by Gilles Leger on February 15, 1976

Don Blackburn b: 14 May 1938, Kirkland Lake ON

season	team	w	l	t	pts	pct	finish
1975-76	NE	14	18	3	31	.443	did not finish
1978-79	NE	4	5	0	8	.444	4-League

• Succeeded Jack Kelley on December 26, 1975, succeeded by Harry Neale on March 10, 1976 • Succeeded Bill Dineen on March 30, 1979

Marc Boileau b: 3 Sep 1932, Pte Claire, PQ   d. 2000

season	team	w	l	t	pts	pct	finish
1976-77	Que	47	31	3	97	.599	1-East
1977-78	Que	27	30	2	56	.475	did not finish

• Relieved February 25, 1978, succeeded by Maurice Filion

John Brophy b: 20 Jan 1933, Antigonish NS   d. 2016

season	team	w	l	t	pts	pct	finish
1978-79	Bir	32	42	6	70	.438	6-League

Joe Crozier b: 19 Feb 1929, Winnipeg MB

season	team	w	l	t	pts	pct	finish
1974-75	Van	37	39	2	76	.487	4-Canadian
1975-76	Cgy	40	34	4	84	.538	3-Canadian
1976-77	Cgy	31	43	7	69	.426	5-West

• Took brief leaves-of-absence in March 1976. Harry Howell coached the team (two games) in his absence.

Jacques Demers b: 25 Aug 1944, Montreal PQ

season	team	w	l	t	pts	pct	finish
1975-76	Ind	34	35	6	74	.493	1-East
1976-77	Ind	36	37	8	80	.494	3-East
1977-78	Cin	33	39	3	69	.460	7-League
1978-79	Que	41	34	5	87	.544	2-League

• Served as bench coach for Chicago (1973-75) • Succeeded Gerry Moore on October 21, 1975

Bill Dineen b: 18 Sep 1932, Arvida PQ

season	team	w	l	t	pts	pct	finish
1972-73	Hou	39	35	4	82	.526	2-West
1973-74	Hou	48	25	5	101	.647	1-West
1974-75	Hou	53	25	0	106	.679	1-West
1975-76	Hou	53	27	0	106	.663	1-West
1976-77	Hou	50	24	6	106	.663	1-West
1977-78	Hou	42	34	4	88	.550	3-League
1978-79	NE	33	29	9	75	.528	did not finish

• Missed several games during February and March of 1978, during which Ted Taylor and Wayne Rutledge coached the team in the interim. • Succeeded as coach by Don Blackburn on April 1, 1979

Clare Drake b: 9 Oct 1928, Yorkton SK

season	team	w	l	t	pts	pct	finish
1975-76	Edm	18	28	2	38	.396	did not finish

• Relieved January 20, 1976, succeeded by Bill Hunter.

Maurice Filion b: 12 Feb 1932, Montreal PQ

season	team	w	l	t	pts	pct	finish
1972-73	Que	32	39	5	69	.454	5-East
1977-78	Que	13	7	1	27	.643	4-League

• Succeeded Maurice Richard on October 19, 1972 • Coached team in absences of Jacques Plante during 1973-74 • Succeeded Marc Boileau on February 28, 1978

Jean-Guy Gendron b: 30 Aug 1934, Montreal PQ

season	team	w	l	t	pts	pct	finish
1974-75	Que	46	32	0	92	.590	1-Canadian
1975-76	Que	50	27	4	104	.642	2-Canadian

Bill Goldsworthy b: 24 Aug 1944, Waterloo ON   d. 1996

season	team	w	l	t	pts	pct	finish
1977-78	Ind	8	20	1	17	.293	8-League

• Succeeded Ron Ingram on February 11, 1978 as player-coach. Bench coach was Rosaire Paiement

Armand (Bep) Guidolin b: 9 Dec 1925, Thorold ON   d. 2008

season	team	w	l	t	pts	pct	finish
1976-77	Edm	25	36	2	52	.413	did not finish

• Stepped down March 1, 1977, to assume full-time duties as General Manager, succeeded by Glen Sather

John Hanna b: 5 Apr 1935, Sydney NS   d. 2005

season	team	w	l	t	pts	pxt	finish
1974-75	Cle	14	18	1	29	.439	did not finish

• Relieved on January 2, 1975, succeeded by Jack Vivian

Billy Harris b: 29 Jul 1935, Toronto ON   d. 2001

season	team	w	l	t	pts	pct	finish
1972-73	Ott	35	39	4	74	.474	4-East
1973-74	Tor	41	33	4	86	.551	2-East
1974-75	Tor	23	17	1	47	.573	did not finish

• Relieved on January 14, 1975, succeeded by Bob Leduc

Camille Henry b: 31 Jan 1933, Quebec PQ   d. 1997

season	team	w	l	t	pts	pct	finish
1972-73	NY	32	43	2	66	.429	6-East
1973-74	NY	6	12	2	14	.350	did not finish

• Relieved upon demise of New York franchise, November 18, 1973

Larry Hillman b: 5 Feb 1937, Kirkland Lake ON

season	team	w	l	t	pts	pct	finish
1977-78	Wpg	50	28	2	102	.638	1-League
1978-79	Wpg	28	27	6	62	.508	did not finish

• Relieved on February 27, 1979, succeeded by Tom McVie

Harry Howell b: 28 Dec 1932, Hamilton ON

season	team	w	l	t	pts	pct	finish
1973-74	Jer	26	30	2	54	.466	6-East
1974-75	SD	43	31	4	90	.577	2-West
1975-76	Cgy	1	1	0	2	.500	interim

• Named as player-coach of Jersey franchise on November 25, 1973. Ron Ingram served as bench coach for both Jersey and San Diego • Coached Calgary on March 11 and March 23, 1976, in absence of Joe Crozier

Sandy Hucul   b: 5 Dec 1933, Eston SK

season	team	w	l	t	pts	pct	finish
1974-75	Phx	39	31	8	86	.551	4-West
1975-76	Phx	39	35	6	84	.525	2-West

Bobby Hull   b: 3 Jan 1939, Pt Anne ON

season	team	w	l	t	pts	pct	finish
1972-73	Wpg	43	31	4	90	.577	1-West
1973-74	Wpg	34	39	5	73	.468	4-West
1974-75	Wpg	4	9	0	8	.308	did not finish

• Served as player-coach during 1972-73 and 1973-74, with Nick Mickoski as bench coach • Mickoski assumed full coaching duties, March & April 1974, exact dates uncertain • Assumed coaching duties from Rudy Pilous January 19 to February 14, 1975

Bill Hunter   b: 5 May 1920, Saskatoon SK   d. 2002

season	team	w	l	t	pts	pct	finish
1972-73	Alb	14	11	1	29	.558	T4-West
1974-75	Edm	6	12	1	13	.342	5-Canadian
1975-76	Edm	9	21	3	21	.318	4-Canadian

• Succeeded Ray Kinasewich on February 7, 1973. • Succeeded Brian Shaw on March 7, 1975 • Succeeded Clare Drake on January 23, 1976

Ron Ingram   b: 5 Jul 1933, Toronto ON   d. 1988

season	team	w	l	t	pts	pct	finish
1975-76	SD	36	38	6	78	.488	3-West
1976-77	SD	40	37	4	84	.519	3-West
1977-78	Ind	16	31	4	36	.353	did not finish

• Served as bench coach for Jersey and San Diego, November 25, 1973 through end of 1974-75 season • Relieved on February 5, 1978, succeeded by Bill Goldsworthy

Jack Kelley   b: 10 July 1927, Medford MA

season	team	w	l	t	pts	pct	finish
1972-73	NE	46	30	2	94	.603	1-East
1974-75	NE	3	2	0	6	.600	1-East
1975-76	NE	14	16	3	31	.470	did not finish

• Relieved Ron Ryan on March 30, 1975 • Resigned on December 22, 1975 to return to General Manager role, succeeded by Don Blackburn

Pat Kelly   b: 8 Sep 1935, Sioux Lookout ON

season	team	w	l	t	pts	pct	finish
1976-77	Bir	24	30	3	51	.447	5-East

• Succeeded Gilles Leger on November 25, 1976

Ray Kinasewich   b: 12 Sep 1933, Smokey Lake AB

season	team	w	l	t	pts	pct	finish
1972-73	Alb	24	26	2	50	.481	did not finish

• Relieved of Alberta, February 7, 1973, succeeded by Bill Hunter

Bobby Kromm   b: 8 Jun 1928, Calgary AB   d. 2010

season	team	w	l	t	pts	pct	finish
1975-76	Wpg	52	27	2	106	.654	1-Canadian
1976-77	Wpg	46	32	2	94	.588	2-West

• Record includes one game (January 2 1977) in which Kromm "sat out" and the team was self-coached (Hull, et al)

Bob Leduc   b: 24 May 1944, Sudbury ON

season	team	w	l	t	pts	pct	finish
1974-75	Tor	20	16	1	41	.554	2-Canadian

• Succeeded Billy Harris on January 15, 1975

Gilles Leger   b: 16 Jul 1941, Cornwall ON

season	team	w	l	t	pts	pct	finish
1975-76	Tor	9	17	0	18	.346	5-Canadian
1976-77	Bir	7	16	1	15	.313	did not finish

• Succeeded Bob Baun on February 17, 1976. Resigned coaching role on November 23, 1976 to return to General Manager role. Succeeded by Pat Kelly on November 25, 1976.

Jack McCartan   b: 5 Aug 1935, St. Paul MN

season	team	w	l	t	pts	pct	finish
1973-74	Min	2	0	0	4	1.000	interim
1974-75	Min	0	1	0	0	.000	interim

• Coached in absence of Harry Neale, who was serving a suspension, January 1974

Ted McCaskill   b: 29 Oct 1936, Kapuskasing ON   d. 2016

season	team	w	l	t	pts	pct	finish
1973-74	LA	15	19	0	30	.441	did not finish

• Coached from November 18, 1973 to February 3, 1974; Succeeded, and succeeded by, Terry Slater

John McKenzie   b: 12 Dec 1937, High River AB

season	team	w	l	t	pts	pct	finish
1972-73	Phi	1	6	0	2	.167	did not finish
1973-74	Van	3	4	0	6	.429	did not finish

• Served as player-coach for Philadelphia & Vancouver, with Phil Watson as bench coach • Relinquished coaching role, November 5, 1972 • Relinquished coaching role, October 21, 1973

Tom McVie   b: 6 Jun 1935, Trail BC

season	team	w	l	t	pts	pct	finish
1978-79	Wpg	11	8	0	22	.579	3-League

• Succeeded Larry Hillman on March 2, 1979

Gerry Moore   b: 23 Nov 1941, Ottawa ON

season	team	w	l	t	pts	pct	finish
1974-75	Ind	18	57	3	39	.250	4-East
1975-76	Ind	1	4	0	2	.200	did not finish

• Relieved October 18, 1975. Succeeded by Jacques Demers.

Harry Neale   b: 9 Mar 1937, Sarnia ON

season	team	w	l	t	pts	pct	finish
1972-73	Min	10	9	0	20	.526	4-West
1973-74	Min	42	32	2	86	.566	2-West
1974-75	Min	42	32	3	87	.565	3-West
1975-76	Min	30	25	4	64	.542	team folded
	NE	5	6	1	11	.458	3-East
1976-77	NE	35	40	6	76	.469	4-East
1977-78	NE	44	31	5	93	.581	2-League

• Succeeded Glen Sonmor February 17, 1973 • Succeeded Don Blackburn on March 12, 1976

Bill Needham   b: 12 Jan 1932, Kirkland Lake ON

season	team	w	l	t	pts	pct	finish
1972-73	Cle	43	32	3	89	.571	2-East
1973-74	Cle	37	32	9	83	.532	3-East

Rudy Pilous   b: 11 Aug 1914, Winnipeg MB   d. 1994

season	team	w	l	t	pts	pct	finish
1974-75	Wpg	34	26	5	73	.562	3-Canadian

• Acceded coaching role to Bobbly Hull between January 19 and February 14, 1975

Jacques Plante   b: 17 Jan 1929, Shawinigan Falls PQ   d. 1986

season	team	w	l	t	pts	pct	finish
1973-74	Que	38	36	4	80	.513	5-East

• Took leaves of absence from duties as coach at times during 1973-74. Team was coached by Maurice Filion in the interim

Marcel Pronovost   b: 15 Jun 1930, Lac-a-la-Tortue PQ   d. 2015

season	team	w	l	t	pts	pct	finish
1972-73	Chi	26	50	2	54	.346	6-West

Jerry Rafter   b: 1942

season	team	w	l	t	pts	pct	finish
1977-78	Cin	2	3	0	4	.400	interim

• Coached team on March 19, March 22, March 29, April 2 and April 7, 1978, while Jacques Demers was serving a suspension.

Maurice Richard   b: 4 Aug 1921, Montreal PQ   d. 2000

season	team	w	l	t	pts	pct	finish
1972-73	Que	1	1	0	2	.500	did not finish

• Resigned on October 13, 1972, succeeded by Maurice Filion

Al Rollins   b: 9 Oct 1926, Vanguard SK   d. 1996

season	team	w	l	t	pts	pct	finish
1976-77	Phx	28	48	4	60	.375	6-West

Ron Ryan   b: 11 Jul 1938, Welland ON

season	team	w	l	t	pts	pct	finish
1973-74	NE	43	31	4	90	.577	1-East
1974-75	NE	40	28	5	85	.582	did not finish

• Relieved on March 29, 1975 due to medical reasons. Succeeded by General Manager Jack Kelley

Glen Sather   b: 2 Sep 1943. High River AB

season	team	w	l	t	pts	pct	finish
1976-77	Edm	9	7	2	20	.556	4-West
1977-78	Edm	38	39	3	79	.494	5-League
1978-79	Edm	48	30	2	98	.613	1-League

• Succeeded Bep Guidolin on March 3, 1977

Brian Shaw b: 8 Nov 1930   d. 1993

season	team	w	l	t	pts	pct	finish
1973-74	Edm	38	37	3	79	.506	3-West
1974-75	Edm	30	26	3	63	.534	did not finish

• Succeeded by Bill Hunter on March 5, 1975

Terry Slater b: 5 Dec 1937, Kirkland Lake ON   d. 1991

season	team	w	l	t	pts	pct	finish
1972-73	LA	37	35	6	80	.513	3-West
1973-74	LA	10	34	0	20	.227	6-West
1975-76	Cin	35	44	1	71	.444	4-East
1976-77	Cin	39	37	5	83	.512	2-East

• Succeeded by Ted McCaskill on November 18, 1973, then succeeded Ted McCaskill on February 3, 1974.

Floyd Smith b: 16 May 1935, Perth ON

season	team	w	l	t	pts	pct	finish
1978-79	Cin	33	41	6	72	.450	5-League

Glen Sonmor b: 22 Apr 1929, Moose Jaw SK   d. 2015

season	team	w	l	t	pts	pct	finish
1972-73	Min	28	28	3	59	.500	did not finish
1976-77	Min	19	18	5	43	.512	team folded
1977-78	Bir	36	38	3	75	.487	6-League

• Resigned role as coach of Minnesota February 15, 1973 to assume full-time duties as General Manager. Succeeded by Harry Neale

Pat Stapleton b: 4 Jul 1940, Sarnia ON

season	team	w	l	t	pts	pct	finish
1973-74	Chi	38	35	5	81	.519	4-East
1974-75	Chi	30	47	1	61	.391	3-East
1978-79	Ind	5	18	2	12	.240	team folded

• Served as player-coach for Chicago during 1973-75, with Jacques Demers as bench coach

Jean-Guy Talbot b: 11 Jul 1932, Cap de la Madeleine PQ

season	team	w	l	t	pts	pct	finish
1975-76	D-O	14	26	1	29	.354	team folded

Jack Vivian b: 14 May 1941, Strathroy ON

season	team	w	l	t	pts	pct	finish
1974-75	Cle	21	22	2	44	.489	2-East

• Succeeded John Hanna on January 4, 1975

Phil Watson b: 24 Apr 1914, Montreal PQ   d. 1991

season	team	w	l	t	pts	pct	finish
1972-73	Phi	37	34	0	74	.521	3-East
1973-74	Van	3	9	0	6	.250	did not finish

• Assumed coaching role from John McKenzie on November 12, 1972 • Assumed coaching role from John McKenzie on October 24, 1973 through November 22, 1973, succeeded by Andy Bathgate

Ian Wilkie b: 20 Jul 1949, Edmonton AB

season	team	w	l	t	pts	pct	finish
1972-73	NY	1	0	0	2	1.000	interim

• Coached team in absence of Camille Henry on February 21, 1973 (Henry was a "spotter" during the game, watching from different vantages and relaying information to Wilkie behind the bench)

John Wilson b: 14 Jun 1929, Kincardine ON   d. 2011

season	team	w	l	t	pts	pct	finish
1974-75	M-B	21	53	4	46	.295	5-West
1975-76	Cle	35	40	5	75	.469	2-East

Playoffs

Don Blackburn

season	team	w	l	t	pts	pct	finish
1979	NE	5	5	-	10	.500	Semifinals

Marc Boileau

season	team	w	l	t	pts	pct	finish
1977	Que	12	5	-	24	.706	AVCO Champs

Joe Crozier

season	team	w	l	t	pts	pct	finish
1976	Cgy	5	5	-	10	.500	Semifinals

Jacques Demers

season	team	w	l	t	pts	pct	finish
1976	Ind	3	4	-	6	.429	Quarterfinals
1977	Ind	5	4	-	10	.556	Semifinals
1979	Que	0	4	-	0	.000	Quarterfinals

Bill Dineen

season	team	w	l	t	pts	pct	finish
1973	Hou	4	6	-	8	.400	Semifinals
1974	Hou	12	2	-	24	.857	AVCO Champs
1975	Hou	12	1	-	24	.923	AVCO Champs
1976	Hou	8	9	-	16	.471	Finals
1977	Hou	6	5	-	12	.545	Semifinals
1978	Hou	2	4	-	4	.333	Quarterfinals

Maurice Filion

season	team	w	l	t	pts	pct	finish
1978	Que	5	6	-	10	.455	Semifinals

Jean-Guy Gendron

season	team	w	l	t	pts	pct	finish
1975	Que	8	7	-	16	.533	Finals
1976	Que	1	4	-	2	.200	Quarterfinals

Bill Harris

season	team	w	l	t	pts	pct	finish
1973	Ott	1	4	-	2	.200	Quarterfinals
1974	Tor	7	5	-	12	.583	Semifinals

Larry Hillman

season	team	w	l	t	pts	pct	finish
1978	Wpg	8	1	-	16	.889	AVCO Champs

Harry Howell

season	team	w	l	t	pts	pct	finish
1975	SD	4	6	-	8	.400	Semifinals

Sandy Hucul

season	team	w	l	t	pts	pct	finish
1975	Phx	1	4	-	2	.200	Quarterfinals
1976	Phx	2	3	-	4	.400	Preliminary

Bobby Hull

season	team	w	l	t	pts	pct	finish
1973	Wpg	9	5	-	18	.643	Finals
1974	Wpg	0	4	-	0	.000	Quarterfinals

Bill Hunter

season	team	w	l	t	pts	pct	finish
1973	Alb	0	1	-	0	.000	Tiebreaker
1976	Edm	0	4	-	0	.000	Quarterfinals

Ron Ingram

season	team	w	l	t	pts	pct	finish
1976	SD	5	6	-	10	.455	Semifinals
1977	SD	3	4	-	6	.429	Quarterfinals

Jack Kelley

season	team	w	l	t	pts	pct	finish
1973	NE	12	3	-	24	.800	AVCO Champs
1975	NE	2	4	-	4	.333	Quarterfinals

Bobby Kromm

season	team	w	l	t	pts	pct	finish
1976	Wpg	12	1	-	24	.923	AVCO Champs
1977	Wpg	11	9	-	22	.550	Finals

Bob Leduc

season	team	w	l	t	pts	pct	finish
1974	Tor	2	4	-	4	.333	Quarterfinals

Tom McVie

season	team	w	l	t	pts	pct	finish
1979	Wpg	8	2	-	16	.800	AVCO Champs

Harry Neale

season	team	w	l	t	pts	pct	finish
1973	Min	2	4	-	4	.333	Quarterfinals
1974	Min	6	5	-	12	.545	Semifinals
1975	Min	6	6	-	12	.500	Semifinals
1976	NE	10	7	-	20	.588	Semifinals
1977	NE	1	4	-	2	.200	Quarterfinals
1978	NE	8	6	-	16	.571	Finals

Bill Needham

season	team	w	l	t	pts	pct	finish
1973	Cle	5	4	-	10	.556	Semifinals
1974	Cle	1	4	-	2	.200	Quarterfinals

Ron Ryan

season	team	w	l	t	pts	pct	finish
1974	NE	3	4	-	6	.429	Semifinals

Glen Sather

season	team	w	l	t	pts	pct	finish
1977	Edm	1	4	-	2	.200	Quarterfinals
1978	Edm	1	4	-	2	.200	Quarterfinals
1979	Edm	6	7	-	12	.462	Finals

Brian Shaw

season	team	w	l	t	pts	pct	finish
1974	Edm	1	4	-	2	.200	Quarterfinals

Terry Slater

season	team	w	l	t	pts	pct	finish
1973	LA	2	4	-	4	.333	Quarterfinals
1977	Cin	0	4	-	0	.000	Quarterfinals

Floyd Smith

season	team	w	l	t	pts	pct	finish
1979	Cin	1	2	-	2	.333	Quarterfinals

Glen Sonmor

season	team	w	l	t	pts	pct	finish
1978	Bir	1	4	-	2	.200	Quarterfinals

Pat Stapleton

season	team	w	l	t	pts	pct	finish
1974	Chi	8	10	-	16	.444	Finals

Jack Vivian

season	team	w	l	t	pts	pct	finish
1975	Cle	1	4	-	2	.200	Quarterfinals

Phil Watson

season	team	w	l	t	pts	pct	finish
1973	Phi	0	4	-	0	.000	Quarterfinals

John Wilson

season	team	w	l	t	pts	pct	finish
1976	Cle	0	3	-	0	.000	Preliminary

WHA Players Who Coached in the NHL

Lou Angotti (St. Louis 1973-75, Pittsburgh 1983-84); Don Blackburn (Hartford 1979-81); Bruce Boudreau (Washington 2007-2011, Anaheim 2011-2016, Minnesota 2016-); Colin Campbell (New York Rangers 1994-98); Gerry Cheevers (Boston 1980-85); John Cunniff (Hartford 1982-83, New Jersey 1989-91); Rick Dudley (Buffalo 1989-91, Florida 2003-04); Robbie Ftorek (Los Angeles 1987-89, New Jersey 1998-2000, Boston 2001-03); Ted Green (Edmonton 1991-94); Wayne Gretzky (Phoenix 2005-2009); Craig Hartsburg (Chicago 1995-98, Anaheim 1998-2000, Ottawa 2008-09); Paul Holmgren (Philadelphia 1988-92, Hartford 1992-96); Harry Howell (Minnesota 1978-79); Rick Ley (Hartford 1989-91, Vancouver 1994-96); Barry Long (Winnipeg 1983-86); Barry Melrose (Los Angeles 1992-94, Tampa Bay 2008); Craig Patrick (New York Rangers 1980-81, 1984-85, Pittsburgh 1989-90, 1996-97); Larry Pleau (Hartford 1980-83, 1987-89); Nick Polano (Detroit 1982-85); Cap Raeder (San Jose 2002 (one game)); Glen Sather (Edmonton 1979-89, 1993-94, New York Rangers 2003-04); Bill Sutherland (Winnipeg 1979-81); Bryan Watson (Edmonton 1980-81); Tom Webster (New York Rangers 1986-87, Los Angeles 1989-92).

WHA Coaches Who Coached in the NHL

Marc Boileau (Pittsburgh 1973-76); John Brophy (Toronto 1986-89); Joe Crozier (Buffalo 1971-74, Toronto 1980-81); Jacques Demers (Quebec 1979-80, St. Louis 1983-86, Detroit 1986-90, Montreal 1992-96, Tampa Bay 1997-99); Bill Dineen (Philadelphia 1991-93); Maurice Filion (Quebec 1980-81); Armand Guidolin (Boston 1972-74, Kansas City 1974-76); Pat Kelly (Colorado 1977-79); Bobby Kromm (Detroit 1977-80); Tom McVie (Washington 1975-78, Winnipeg 1979-81, New Jersey 1983-84, 1990-92); Harry Neale (Vancouver 1979-85, Detroit 1985-86); Rudy Pilous (Chicago 1957-63); Floyd Smith (Buffalo 1971-72 (one game), 1974-76, Toronto 1979-80); Glen Sonmor (Minnesota 1978-87); Jean-Guy Talbot (St. Louis 1972-74, New York Rangers 1977-78); Phil Watson (New York Rangers 1955-60, Boston 1961-63); John Wilson (Los Angeles 1969-70, Detroit 1971-73, Colorado 1976-77, Pittsburgh 1977-80).

Harry Howell is the only person to have played in the NHL and the WHA, and to have coached in the NHL and the WHA.

All-Time Coaching Records

Regular Season				
name	**g**	**record**	**pts**	**pct**
Bill Dineen	545	318-199-28	664	.609
Harry Neale	404	208-175-21	437	.541
Jacques Demers	311	144-145-22	310	.498
Terry Slater	283	121-150-12	254	.449
Joe Crozier	237	108-116-13	229	.483
Bill Harris	197	99-89-9	207	.525
Bobby Kromm (a)	161	98-59-4	200	.621
Jean-Guy Gendron	159	96-59-4	196	.616
Glen Sather	178	95-76-7	197	.553
Ron Ingram	212	92-106-14	198	.467
Ron Ryan	151	83-59-9	175	.579
Glen Sonmor	178	83-84-11	177	.497
Bobby Hull	169	81-79-9	171	.506
Bill Needham	156	80-64-12	172	.551
Larry Hillman	141	78-55-8	164	.582
Sandy Hucul	158	78-66-14	170	.538
Marc Boileau	140	74-61-5	153	.546
Pat Stapleton	181	73-100-8	154	.425
Harry Howell	138	70-62-6	146	.529
Brian Shaw	137	68-63-6	142	.518
Jack Kelley	116	63-48-5	131	.565
John Wilson	158	56-93-9	121	.383
Maurice Filion	97	45-46-6	96	.495
Phil Watson	83	40-43-0	80	.482
Jacques Plante	78	38-36-4	80	.513
Camille Henry	97	38-55-4	80	.412
Rudy Pilous	65	34-26-5	73	.562
Floyd Smith	80	33-41-6	72	.450
John Brophy	80	32-42-6	70	.438
Bill Hunter	78	29-44-5	63	.404
Al Rollins	80	28-48-4	60	.333
Marcel Pronovost	78	26-50-2	54	.346
Bep Guidolin	63	25-36-2	52	.413
Ray Kinasewich	52	24-26-2	50	.481
Pat Kelly	57	24-30-3	51	.447
Jack Vivian	45	21-22-2	44	.489
Andy Bathgate	59	21-37-1	43	.364
Bob Leduc	37	20-16-1	41	.563
Gerry Moore	83	19-61-3	41	.247
Don Blackburn	44	18-23-3	39	.443
Clare Drake	48	18-28-2	38	.396
Gilles Leger	50	16-33-1	33	.330
Ted McCaskill	34	15-19-0	30	.441
Bob Baun	55	15-35-5	35	.318
John Hanna	33	14-18-1	29	.439
Jean-Guy Talbot	41	14-26-1	29	.354
Tom McVie	19	11-8-0	22	.579
Bill Goldsworthy	29	8-20-1	17	.293
John McKenzie	14	4-10-0	8	.286
Jack McCartan (i)	3	2-1-0	4	.667
Jerry Rafter (i)	5	2-3-0	4	.400
Ian Wilkie (i)	1	1-0-0	2	1.000
Maurice Richard	2	1-1-0	2	.500
John Bassett (i)	3	0-3-0	0	.000

Playoffs				
name	**g**	**record**	**pts**	**pct**
Bill Dineen	71	44-27	88	.620
Harry Neale	55	33-32	66	.508
Bobby Kromm	33	23-10	46	.697
Jack Kelley	21	14-7	28	.667
Marc Boileau	17	12-5	24	.706
Bobby Hull	18	9-9	18	.500
Jean-Guy Gendron	20	9-11	18	.450
Larry Hillman	9	8-1	16	.889
Tom McVie	10	8-2	16	.800
Bill Harris	17	8-9	16	.471
Ron Ingram	18	8-10	16	.444
Pat Stapleton	18	8-10	16	.444
Jacques Demers	20	8-12	16	.400
Glen Sather	23	8-15	16	.348
Bill Needham	14	6-8	12	.429
Don Blackburn	10	5-5	10	.500
Joe Crozier	10	5-5	10	.500
Maurice Filion	11	5-6	10	.455
Harry Howell	10	4-6	8	.400
Ron Ryan	7	3-4	6	.429
Sandy Hucul	10	3-7	6	.300
Bob Leduc	6	2-4	4	.333
Terry Slater	10	2-8	4	.200
Floyd Smith	3	1-2	2	.333
Brian Shaw	5	1-4	2	.200
Glen Sonmor	5	1-4	2	.200
Jack Vivian	5	1-4	2	.200
Phil Watson	4	0-4	0	.000
John Wilson	4	0-4	0	.000
Bill Hunter	5	0-5	0	.000

(a) includes game of Jan 2 1977 in which Kromm "sat out"
(i) Interim coach.

Note: Regular season coaching records are intended to be as true to the facts as possible, illustrating records for short-term interim coaches who substituted for the head coach. In a few cases, the exact dates of when the head coach was absent is not known. His coaching record includes results occurring during his absence, but a note of who replaced him during these times is included in the notes section following his record. When exact dates were known, the records above and on preceding pages dutifully reflect the exact results.

First Goals

The first WHA goal scored by each player is listed below. When the goaltender who gave up the goal is uncertain, that entry is left blank. A total of 604 players scored at least one goal in the WHA.

Name	team	date	opp.	goaltender
Abbey, Bruce	Cin	Nov 22, 1975	Que	Brodeur
Abgrall, Dennis	Cin	Oct 9, 1976	SD	Lockett
Abrahamsson, T.	NE	Oct 26, 1974	Ind	Dyck
Adair, Jim	Van	Oct 10, 1973	Wpg	Wakely
Adduono, Ray	SD	Oct 16, 1974	Phx	Kurt
Adduono, Rick	Bir	Nov 1, 1978	Cin	Dion
Ahearn, Kevin	NE	Oct 26, 1972	NY	Kurt
Alexander, Claire	Edm	Nov 8, 1978	Que	Brodeur
Alley, Steve	Bir	Mar 12, 1978	Wpg	Bromley
Amodeo, Mike	Ott	Jan 18, 1973	Min	Curran
Anderson, Ron C.	Chi	Nov 23, 1972	Ott	Binkley
Anderson, Ron F.	Alb	Oct 11, 1972	Ott	Binkley
Andrascik, Steve	Ind	Oct 26, 1974	NE	A. Smith
Andrea, Paul	Cle	Oct 25, 1972	Phi	Paille
Angotti, Lou	Chi	Dec 28, 1974	Min	Garrett
Antonovich, Mike	Min	Oct 19, 1972	Hou	D. McLeod
Arbour, John	Min	Nov 19, 1972	Chi	J. McLeod
Archambault, Michel	Que	Nov 2, 1972	Phi	Paille
Arndt, Danny	NE	Oct 24, 1975	Tor	Vien
Ash, Bob	Wpg	Oct 17, 1972	Alb	Norris
Ashton, Ron	Wpg	Dec 28, 1974	SD	Gillow
Asmundson, Duke	Wpg	Oct 12, 1972	NY	Kurt
Atkinson, Steve	Tor	Dec 26, 1975	Edm	Dryden
Backstrom, Ralph	Chi	Oct 14, 1973	Cle	Whidden
Bailey, Garnet	Edm	Oct 31, 1978	Que	Brodeur
Baird, Ken	Alb	Nov 9, 1972	LA	Gardner
Ball, Terry	Min	Nov 28, 1972	Ott	Binkley
Baltimore, Bryon	Chi	Nov 24, 1974	NE	Abrahamsson
Barber, Butch	Chi	Dec 20, 1972	Phi	Parent
Barlow, Bob	Phx	Oct 18, 1974	Hou	Grahame
Barrie, Doug	Alb	Nov 3, 1972	Hou	D. McLeod
Bateman, Jamie	SD	Nov 22, 1975	Edm	Dryden
Bathgate, Andy	Van	Dec 10, 1974	Cle	Whidden
Baxter, Paul	Cle	Dec 13, 1975	NE	Abrahamsson
Beaton, Frank	Cin	Feb 24, 1976	Tor	
Beaudin, Norm	Wpg	Oct 17, 1972	Alb	Norris
Beaudoin, Serge	Van	Feb 19, 1974	Tor	Gratton
Beaule, Alain	Que	Oct 28, 1973	Hou	D. McLeod
Bennett, John	Phi	Oct 20, 1972	Alb	K. Brown
Bennett, Wendell	Phx	Nov 10, 1974	Min	Garrett
Benzelock, Jim	Chi	Dec 13, 1972	Hou	D. McLeod
Bergeron, Yves	Que	Oct 13, 1972	Alb	Norris
Bergman, Thommie	Wpg	Feb 19, 1975	Edm	Worthy
Bernier, Jean	Que	Feb 27, 1975	Van	D. McLeod
Bernier, Serge	Que	Oct 7, 1973	NE	A. Smith
Berry, Doug	Edm	Oct 22, 1978	Wpg	Daley
Bignell, Larry	Den	Oct 16, 1975	Wpg	Larsson
Bilodeau, Gilles	Bir	Jan 4, 1977	Phx	
Black, Milt	Wpg	Oct 22, 1972	Phi	Parent
Blackburn, Don	NE	Oct 13, 1973	Chi	Newton
Blain, Jacques	Que	Oct 13, 1972	Alb	Norris
Blanchette, Bernie	Chi	Oct 22, 1972	LA	Gillow
Block, Ken	NY	Nov 3, 1972	Wpg	Wakely
Boddy, Greg	SD	Dec 7, 1976	Que	Brodeur
Boland, Mike	Ott	Dec 15, 1972	Alb	
Bolduc, Dan	NE	Mar 16, 1976	Que	Deguise
Bond, Kerry	Ind	Nov 13, 1974	Que	Brodeur
Bordeleau, Christian	Wpg	Oct 12, 1972	NY	Kurt
Bordeleau, Paulin	Que	Oct 12, 1976	SD	Lockett
Borgeson, Don	Phx	Oct 18, 1974	Hou	Grahame
Boucha, Henry	Min	Oct 29, 1975	Cin	Aubry
Boudreau, Bruce	Min	Nov 19, 1975	Cle	Cheevers
Boudreau, Michel	Phi	Dec 1, 1972	NE	Landon
Boudrias, Andre	Que	Oct 16, 1976	NE	Landon
Boyd, Bob	Min	Feb 6, 1974	Chi	Coutu
Boyd, Jim	Phx	Oct 16, 1974	SD	Gillow
Boyer, Walter	Wpg	Oct 24, 1972	Phi	Paille
Boylan, Dean	Jer	Jan 7, 1974	Van	Donnelly
Brackenbury, Curt	Min	Jan 23, 1976	SD	Wakely
Bradley, Brian	NY	Oct 14, 1972	Ott	
Bray, Duane	Phx	Jan 25, 1977	Cgy	D. McLeod
Bredin, Gary	Ind	Oct 24, 1974	Min	Garrett
Brewer, Carl	Tor	Oct 24, 1973	Van	
Brindley, Doug	Cle	Oct 15, 1972	Ott	Gratton
Brown, Arnie	Mich	Jan 4, 1975	Hou	Rutledge
Brown, Bob	NY	Oct 25, 1973	NE	A. Smith
Buchanan, Ron	Cle	Oct 11, 1972	Que	Aubry
Burgess, Don	Phi	Oct 25, 1972	Cle	Cheevers
Busniuk, Ron	Min	Nov 17, 1974	Que	Brodeur
Butters, Bill	Min	Mar 12, 1975	Van	D. McLeod
Byers, Mike	LA	Oct 17, 1972	Min	Curran
Cadle, Brian	Wpg	Oct 22, 1972	Phi	Parent
Caffery, Terry	NE	Oct 21, 1972	Que	Aubry
Cahan, Larry	Chi	Mar 28, 1973	Wpg	Daley
Callighen, Brett	NE	Dec 26, 1976	Min	Levasseur
Campbell, Bryan	Phi	Oct 25, 1972	Cle	Cheevers
Campbell, Colin	Van	Oct 20, 1973	Chi	Gill
Campbell, Scott	Hou	Nov 2, 1977	Bir	Wood
Campeau, Rychard	Phi	Nov 4, 1972	NE	Landon
Cardiff, Jim	Phi	Oct 27, 1972	LA	Gillow
Cardwell, Steve	Min	Nov 18, 1973	Edm	Norris
Carleton, Wayne	Ott	Oct 11, 1972	Alb	K. Brown
Carlin, Brian	Alb	Oct 24, 1972	Chi	J. McLeod
Carlson, Jack	NE	Feb 27, 1975	Phx	Kurt
Carlyle, Steve	Alb	Nov 11, 1972	LA	Gillow
Caron, Alain	Que	Nov 5, 1972	Chi	J. McLeod
Carroll, Greg	Cin	Nov 4, 1976	Ind	Dion
Cassolato, Tony	SD	Oct 29, 1976	Cin	Lapointe
Charlebois, Bob	Ott	Oct 11, 1972	Alb	K. Brown
Chartre, Claude	NY	Oct 22, 1972	Min	McCartan
Chernoff, Mike	Van	Nov 9, 1973	Min	Garrett
Chipperfield, Ron	Van	Oct 30, 1974	Edm	K. Brown
Christiansen, Keith	Min	Oct 22, 1972	NY	Donnelly
Clackson, Kim	Ind	Nov 27, 1975	Wpg	Daley
Clark, Gordie	Cin	Oct 13, 1978	Edm	Dryden
Clarke, Jim	Phx	Dec 18, 1975	Ind	Brown
Clearwater, Ray	Cle	Oct 25, 1972	Phi	Parent
Climie, Ron	Ott	Oct 14, 1972	NY	Kurt
Cloutier, Real	Que	Oct 22, 1974	Hou	Grahame
Coates, Brian	Chi	Oct 13, 1973	NE	Landon
Conacher, Brian	Ott	Oct 25, 1972	LA	
Connelly, Wayne	Min	Oct 13, 1972	Wpg	Daley
Connor, Cam	Phx	Oct 26, 1974	Que	Brodeur
Constantin, Charles	Que	Nov 13, 1974	Ind	A. Brown
Cormier, Michel	Phx	Oct 16, 1974	SD	Gillow
Cote, Alain	Que	Mar 28, 1978	Cin	Dion
Cote, Roger	Alb	Oct 15, 1972	Wpg	Wakely
Cournoyer, Norm	Cle	Nov 21, 1973	Wpg	Daley
Crashley, Bart	LA	Oct 17, 1972	Min	Curran
Crowder, Keith	Bir	Oct 15, 1978	Ind	G. Smith
Cuddie, Steve	Wpg	Nov 9, 1972	Ott	Gratton
Cunniff, John	NE	Oct 12, 1972	Phi	Parent
Cunningham, Rick	Ott	Nov 28, 1972	Min	McCartan
Curtis, Paul	Mich	Oct 27, 1974	Wpg	Daley
D'Alvise, Bob	Tor	Oct 14, 1975	Hou	Grahame
Danby, John	NE	Oct 23, 1972	Min	Curran
Davis, Bill	Wpg	Feb 23, 1979	Bir	Wakely
Deadmarsh, Butch	Van	Dec 18, 1974	Phx	Kurt
Dean, Barry	Phx	Oct 24, 1975	Cgy	D. McLeod
Debol, Dave	Cin	Apr 2, 1978	Ind	Inness
Delorenzi, Ray	Cgy	Nov 27, 1975	Phx	Norris
Delorme, Ron	Den	Nov 26, 1975	Cle	Cheevers
DeMarco, Ed	Edm	Dec 9, 1977	Hou	Wakely
Deschamps, Andre	Cgy	Jan 16, 1977	Phx	Hebenton
Descoteaux, Norm	Que	Oct 11, 1973	Tor	Binkley
Desjardine, Ken	Que	Oct 26, 1972	Min	Curran
Devine, Kevin	SD	Dec 22, 1974	Edm	K. Brown
Dillabough, Bob	Cle	Oct 11, 1972	Que	Aubry
Dillon, Wayne	Tor	Oct 7, 1973	Chi	Newton
Dobek, Bob	SD	Mar 11, 1976	Hou	Grahame
Donnelly, John	Ott	Oct 19, 1972	Chi	
Donnelly, Pat	Cin	Nov 29, 1975	Tor	
Dorey, Jim	NE	Dec 9, 1972	NY	Donnelly
Douglas, Jordy	NE	Oct 15, 1978	Que	Brodeur
Douglas, Kent	NY	Oct 22, 1972	Min	McCartan
Driscoll, Peter	Van	Nov 9, 1974	Wpg	Daley
Dube, Norm	Que	Feb 6, 1977	Cin	Lapointe
Dubois, Michel	Ind	Oct 14, 1975	Cgy	D. McLeod
Dudley, Rick	Cin	Oct 17, 1975	Cgy	D. McLeod
Dufour, Guy	Que	Oct 22, 1972	Ott	Gratton

Name	team	date	opp.	goaltender
Dunn, David	Wpg	Oct 24, 1976	Bir	Wood
Durbano, Steve	Bir	Nov 19, 1977	Hou	Wakely
Earl, Tom	NE	Oct 23, 1972	Min	Curran
Edur, Tom	Cle	Oct 27, 1973	Hou	Rutledge
Erickson, Grant	Cle	Oct 25, 1972	Phi	Paille
Eriksson, Bengt	Wpg	Jan 17, 1979	Edm	Dryden
Evans, Chris	Tcgy	Oct 24, 1975	Phx	Norris
Evo, Bill	Mich	Dec 29, 1974	Chi	Newton
Falkenberg, Bob	Alb	Nov 11, 1972	LA	Gillow
Falkman, Craig	Min	Nov 1, 1972	Wpg	Daley
Farda, Richard	Tor	Nov 15, 1974	Edm	Plante
Featherstone, Tony	Tor	Oct 20, 1974	Mich	Desjardins
Ferguson, Norm	NY	Oct 19, 1972	Cle	Cheevers
Fitchner, Bob	Edm	Oct 21, 1973	Chi	Newton
Fleming, Reggie	Chi	Oct 12, 1972	Hou	D. McLeod
Flett, Bill	Edm	Dec 17, 1976	Phx	Hebenton
Folco, Peter	Tor	Mar 26, 1976	Edm	Dryden
Foley, Rick	Tor	Nov 8, 1975	Min	Garrett
Fontaine, Len	Mich	Nov 21, 1974	Phx	Kurt
Fonteyne, Val	Alb	Oct 15, 1972	Wpg	Wakely
Forbes, Dave	Cin	Nov 8, 1978	Ind	Inness
Ford, Mike	Wpg	Oct 18, 1974	Edm	K. Brown
Fortier, Dave	Ind	Dec 12, 1977	Cin	Wakely
Fortier, Florent	Que	Mar 30, 1976	Edm	Dryden
Fotiu, Nick	NE	Nov 17, 1974	Mich	Desjardins
French, John	NE	Oct 16, 1972	Chi	J. McLeod
Ftorek, Robbie	Phx	Oct 16, 1974	SD	Gillow
Gallant, Gord	Min	Oct 12, 1973	Van	Archambault
Gambucci, Gary	Min	Dec 14, 1974	Phx	Kurt
Gartner, Mike	Cin	Oct 15, 1978	Wpg	Daley
Garwasiuk, Ron	LA	Nov 20, 1973	Min	Curran
Gaudette, Andre	Que	Oct 26, 1972	Min	Curran
Gauthier, Jean	NY	Nov 19, 1972	Phi	
Gellard, Sam	Van	Oct 12, 1973	Min	Curran
Gendron, Jean-Guy	Que	Oct 19, 1972	NE	A. Smith
Geoffrion, Daniel	Que	Nov 3, 1978	Bir	Riggin
George, Wes	Ind	Nov 24, 1978	Cin	Dion
Gibbons, Brian	Ott	Dec 14, 1972	NY	Wilkie
Gibbons, Gerard	Tor	Feb 27, 1976	Hou	Grahame
Gibson, Jack	Ott	Nov 28, 1972	Min	McCartan
Gilbert, Ed	Cin	Oct 21, 1978	Edm	Walsh
Gilbert, Jeannot	Que	Oct 11, 1973	Tor	Binkley
Gilligan, Bill	Cin	Dec 3, 1977	NE	A. Smith
Gilmore, Tom	LA	Oct 28, 1972	NY	
Gingras, Gaston	Bir	Oct 15, 1978	Ind	G. Smith
Giroux, Rejean	Que	Nov 2, 1972	Phi	Paille
Glenwright, Brian	Chi	Oct 24, 1972	Alb	Norris
Globensky, Alan	Que	Apr 24, 1975	Min	Garrett
Goldsworthy, Bill	Ind	Dec 6, 1977	NE	Levasseur
Goldthorpe, Bill	SD	Oct 25, 1975	Min	Curran
Golembrosky, Frank	Que	Nov 16, 1972	Min	Curran
Gordon, Don	LA	Oct 13, 1973	Hou	Rutledge
Gorman, Dave	Phx	Oct 18, 1974	Hou	Grahame
Goulet, Michel	Bir	Oct 24, 1978	Edm	Dryden
Gratton, Jean-Guy	Wpg	Oct 29, 1972	Hou	Rutledge
Gravel, John	Phi	Nov 18, 1972	Min	McCartan
Gray, John	Phx	Oct 20, 1974	Cle	Whidden
Green, Ted	NE	Oct 16, 1972	Chi	J. McLeod
Greig, Bruce	Cgy	Feb 18, 1977	Cin	Lapointe
Grenier, Richard	Que	Oct 12, 1976	SD	Lockett
Gretzky, Wayne	Ind	Oct 20, 1978	Edm	Dryden
Grierson, Don	Hou	Dec 2, 1972	NY	
Gruen, Daniel	Mich	Oct 17, 1974	Ind	A. Brown
Guindon, Robert	Que	Oct 13, 1972	Alb	Norris
Guite, Pierre	Que	Oct 21, 1972	NE	A. Smith
Gulka, Bud	Van	Jan 4, 1975	NE	A. Smith
Gustafsson, Bengt	Edm	May 15, 1979	Wpg	Daley
Haas, Derek	Cgy	Oct 14, 1975	Ind	Holmqvist
Hagman, Matti	Que	Dec 11, 1977	Cze	Dzurilla
Hale, Larry	Hou	Oct 31, 1972	Alb	Norris
Hall, Del	Phx	Oct 11, 1975	SD	Wakely
Hall, Murray	Hou	Oct 13, 1972	LA	Gardner
Hamilton, Al	Alb	Nov 7, 1972	NY	Wilkie
Hampson, Ted	Min	Oct 22, 1972	NY	Donnelly
Handrahan, Alf	Cin	Mar 1, 1978	Edm	D. McLeod
Hangsleben, Alan	NE	Oct 24, 1975	Tor	Vien
Hanmer, Craig	Ind	Dec 22, 1974	NE	A. Smith
Hanna, John	Cle	Oct 14, 1972	Alb	Norris
Hansis, Ron	Hou	Mar 6, 1977	Cin	Caron
Hanson, Dave	Bir	Dec 15, 1977	Cin	Liut
Harbaruk, Nick	Ind	Nov 24, 1974	Tor	Binkley
Hardy, Joe	Cle	Oct 15, 1972	Ott	Gratton
Hargreaves, Jim	Wpg	Oct 12, 1973	Edm	Norris
Hargreaves, Ted	Wpg	Oct 27, 1973	Min	Garrett
Harris, Duke	Hou	Oct 19, 1972	Min	McCartan
Harris, Hugh	NE	Oct 9, 1973	Que	Brodeur
Harrison, Jim	Alb	Oct 11, 1972	Ott	Binkley
Hartsburg, Craig	Bir	Oct 20, 1978	Cin	Liut
Harvey, Michel	Que	Jan 16, 1973	Ott	Gratton
Hatoum, Ed	Chi	Nov 11, 1972	Cle	Cheevers
Heatley, Murray	Min	Oct 12, 1973	Van	Archambault
Heaver, Paul	Tor	Mar 26, 1976	Edm	Dryden
Hedberg, Anders	Wpg	Oct 15, 1974	Van	D. McLeod
Heggedal, Howie	LA	Dec 17, 1973	Hou	Rutledge
Heindl, Bill	Cle	Nov 29, 1973	Que	Aubry
Heiskala, Earl	LA	Oct 15, 1972	Hou	D. McLeod
Henderson, Paul	Tor	Oct 15, 1974	NE	A. Smith
Henry, Pierre	Phi	Dec 20, 1972	Chi	Gill
Herriman, Don	Phi	Oct 22, 1972	Wpg	Wakely
Hicke, Bill	Alb	Oct 11, 1972	Ott	Binkley
Hickey, Pat	Tor	Nov 7, 1973	Hou	Rutledge
Hicks, Glenn	Wpg	Oct 27, 1978	NE	A. Smith
Hillman, Larry	Cle	Oct 13, 1973	Que	Aubry
Hillman, Wayne	Cle	Oct 31, 1973	Wpg	Daley
Hinse, Andre	Hou	Oct 13, 1973	LA	Gillow
Hislop, Jamie	Cin	Jan 11, 1977	NE	
Hobin, Mike	Phx	Jan 22, 1976	Tor	
Hodgson, Ted	Cle	Oct 25, 1972	Phi	Parent
Hoekstra, Ed	Hou	Nov 7, 1972	Chi	
Hoganson, Dale	Que	Oct 25, 1973	Chi	Newton
Holbrook, Terry	Cle	Nov 19, 1974	Tor	Shaw
Holland, Jerry	Edm	Jan 6, 1978	Wpg	Bromley
Holmgren, Paul	Min	Nov 5, 1975	Hou	Grahame
Hopiavuori, Ralph	Cle	Dec 15, 1972	Que	Aubry
Hornung, Larry	Wpg	Oct 29, 1972	Hou	Rutledge
Horton, Bill	Cle	Dec 15, 1972	Que	Aubry
Houle, Rejean	Que	Oct 9, 1973	NE	A. Smith
Howe, Gordie	Hou	Nov 3, 1973	LA	
Howe, Mark	Hou	Oct 17, 1973	Van	Archambault
Howe, Marty	Hou	Jan 12, 1974	Que	Deguise
Howell, Harry	Jer	Jan 16, 1974	NE	Landon
Huck, Fran	Wpg	Oct 18, 1973	NY	Junkin
Hughes, Brent	SD	Nov 20, 1975	Den	Johnson
Hughes, Frank	Hou	Oct 12, 1972	Chi	J. Mcleod
Hughes, John	Phx	Dec 3, 1974	SD	Gillow
Hull, Bobby	Wpg	Nov 12, 1972	LA	Gardner
Hull, Steve	Cgy	Oct 22, 1975	Den	Johnson
Hunter, David	Edm	Nov 19, 1978	Cin	Liut
Hurley, Paul	NE	Dec 31, 1972	NY	Donnelly
Huston, Ron	Phx	Oct 17, 1975	Den	Johnson
Hyndman, Mike	NE	Nov 18, 1972	Ott	Binkley
Hynes, Dave	NE	Oct 30, 1976	Bir	Garrett
Inkpen, Dave	Cin	Nov 8, 1975	SD	
Irwin, Glen	Hou	Dec 28, 1974	NE	A. Smith
Israelson, Larry	Van	Nov 5, 1974	Chi	Dryden
Jacques, Jeff	Tor	Jan 12, 1975	Hou	Rutledge
Jarrett, Gary	Cle	Oct 19, 1972	NY	Donnelly
Jarry, Pierre	Edm	Mar 3, 1978	Ind	Inness
Jodzio, Rick	Van	Apr 1, 1975	Min	
Johnson, Dan	Wpg	Oct 13, 1972	Min	Curran
Johnson, Jim	Min	Jan 1, 1973	Hou	Rutledge
Johnstone, Ed	Mich	Oct 17, 1974	Ind	A. Brown
Jones, Bob	LA	Nov 15, 1972	Hou	Hughes
Jones, James H.	Van	Feb 21, 1974	Chi	Coutu
Jordan, Ric	NE	Dec 13, 1972	Chi	Gill
Joyal, Eddie	Alb	Oct 11, 1972	Ott	Binkley
Kannegiesser, Gord	Ind	Mar 15, 1975	Balt	Hoganson
Karlander, Al	NE	Oct 25, 1973	NY	J. Mcleod
Kassian, Dennis	Alb	Oct 28, 1972	NE	Landon
Kennedy, Jamie	NY	Nov 25, 1972	Alb	K. Brown
Kennett, Murray	Ind	Nov 28, 1974	Que	Brodeur
Keogan, Murray	Phx	Oct 16, 1974	SD	Gillow
Keon, Dave	Min	Oct 15, 1975	Cle	Cheevers
Kerslake, Doug	Edm	Feb 28, 1975	Balt	Desjardins
Ketola, Veli-Pekka	Wpg	Oct 18, 1974	Edm	K. Brown
Ketter, Kerry	Edm	Oct 17, 1975	Tor	Vien
King, Steve	Ott	Oct 26, 1972	Hou	Rutledge
Kirk, Gavin	Ott	Oct 14, 1972	NY	Kurt
Klatt, Bill	Min	Nov 10, 1972	Wpg	Daley
Knibbs, Darrel	Chi	Dec 13, 1972	NE	Landon
Konik, George	Min	Oct 23, 1972	NE	Landon
Krake, Skip	Cle	Oct 15, 1972	Ott	Gratton
Krupicka, Jarda	LA	Nov 8, 1972	NY	Donnelly
Kryskow, Dave	Cgy	Jan 7, 1977	Edm	
Labossiere, Gord	Hou	Oct 19, 1972	Min	D. McLeod
Labraaten, Dan	Wpg	Oct 24, 1976	Bir	Wood

478

Name	team	date	opp.	goaltender
Lacombe, Francois	Que	Oct 13, 1972	Alb	Norris
Lacroix, Andre	Phi	Oct 22, 1972	Wpg	Wakely
Lagace, Jean-Guy	Bir	Mar 12, 1977	Ind	Dion
Lagace, Pierre	Que	Feb 2, 1978	Bir	Garrett
Laing, Bill	Edm	Mar 7, 1975	Van	D. McLeod
Langevin, Dave	Edm	Nov 5, 1976	NE	Abrahamsson
Langway, Rod	Bir	Jan 20, 1978	Edm	
Lapierre, Camille	Phi	Feb 16, 1973	NY	Donnelly
Lariviere, Garry	Phx	Nov 14, 1975	Tor	Vien
Larose, Claude	Cin	Oct 11, 1975	Cle	Cheevers
Larose, Paul	Balt	Apr 7, 1975	Hou	Rutledge
Larose, Ray	Hou	Jan 9, 1973	NE	A. Smith
Larway, Don	Hou	Oct 18, 1974	Phx	Norris
Laughton, Mike	NY	Oct 14, 1972	Ott	
Lavender, Brian	Den	Nov 9, 1975	Hou	Grahame
Lawson, Danny	Phi	Oct 19, 1972	LA	Gillow
LeBlanc, J. P.	LA	Oct 15, 1972	Hou	D. McLeod
Leclerc, Rene	Que	Oct 13, 1972	Alb	Norris
Leduc, Bob	Ott	Oct 14, 1972	NY	Kurt
Leduc, Richie	Cle	Oct 20, 1974	Phx	Kurt
Legge, Barry	Balt	Feb 25, 1975	Ind	A. Brown
Legge, Randy	Mich	Oct 29, 1974	Min	Curran
Leiter, Bob	Cgy	Dec 12, 1975	Wpg	Daley
Lemieux, Richard	Cgy	Oct 26, 1976	Bir	
Lesuk, Bill	Wpg	Oct 16, 1975	Den	Newton
Ley, Rick	NE	Oct 19, 1972	Que	Aubry
Liddington, Bob	Chi	Nov 4, 1972	LA	Gardner
Lilyholm, Len	Min	Dec 8, 1972	Chi	
Lindh, Mats	Wpg	Oct 21, 1975	Cin	
Lindstrom, Willy	Wpg	Oct 16, 1975	Den	Newton
Linseman, Ken	Bir	Oct 28, 1977	Edm	Broderick
Locas, Jacques	Mich	Nov 3, 1974	Wpg	Wakely
Lodboa, Dan	Chi	Nov 14, 1972	Phi	Paille
Lomenda, Mark	Chi	Nov 20, 1974	Ind	A. Brown
Long, Barry	Edm	Nov 10, 1974	Cle	Cheevers
Lukowich, Bernie	Cgy	Mar 6, 1976	Tor	Wood
Lukowich, Morris	Hou	Oct 21, 1976	Bir	
Luksa, Chuck	Cin	Oct 28, 1978	Que	Corsi
Lund, Larry	Hou	Oct 12, 1972	Chi	J. Mcleod
Lyle, George	NE	Oct 19, 1976	Hou	Rutledge
MacDonald, Blair	Edm	Oct 12, 1973	Wpg	Daley
MacGregor, Bruce	Edm	Nov 2, 1974	Cle	Cheevers
MacGregor, Gary	Chi	Oct 27, 1974	Min	Garrett
MacKinnon, Paul	Wpg	Mar 11, 1979	Que	Corsi
MacMillan, Bob	Min	Oct 22, 1972	NY	Donnelly
MacNeil, Bernie	LA	Oct 31, 1972	Que	Brodeur
MacSweyn, Ralph	LA	Apr 17, 1973	Hou	Rutledge
Maggs, Darryl	Chi	Oct 13, 1973	NE	Landon
Mahovlich, Frank	Tor	Oct 15, 1974	NE	A. Smith
Mara, Peter	Chi	Nov 23, 1974	NE	A. Smith
Marotte, Gilles	Cin	Nov 6, 1977	NE	A. Smith
Marrin, Peter	Tor	Dec 29, 1973	Min	
Marsh, Peter	Cin	Oct 30, 1976	Phx	
Martin, Tom	Ott	Oct 15, 1972	Cle	Whidden
Mavety, Larry	LA	Oct 22, 1972	Chi	J. McLeod
Maxwell, Bryan	Cle	Nov 7, 1975	Cgy	D. McLeod
Mayer, Jim	Cgy	Mar 16, 1977	Cin	Caron
McAneeley, Bob	Alb	Dec 1, 1972	Min	McCartan
McAneeley, Ted	Edm	Jan 6, 1976	Ind	Dion
McCallum, Dunc	Hou	Oct 13, 1972	LA	Gardner
McCaskill, Ted	LA	Oct 25, 1972	Ott	Gratton
McCrimmon, Jim	Edm	Nov 20, 1973	Cle	Cheevers
McCulloch, Don	Van	Dec 11, 1974	Hou	Grahame
McDonald, Ab	Wpg	Oct 12, 1972	NY	Kurt
McDonald, Brian	Hou	Nov 13, 1972	NE	Landon
McDonough, Al	Cle	Oct 19, 1974	Min	Garrett
McKay, Ray	Edm	Nov 15, 1974	Tor	Gratton
McKenzie, Brian	Ind	Nov 7, 1974	SD	Gillow
McKenzie, John	Phi	Nov 18, 1972	Min	McCartan
McLeod, Al	Phx	Oct 16, 1974	SD	Gillow
McMahon, Mike	Min	Oct 13, 1972	Wpg	Daley
McManama, Rob	NE	Dec 13, 1975	Cle	Whidden
McMasters, Jim	Cle	Feb 24, 1973	Chi	Gill
McNamee, Pete	Van	Nov 26, 1974	Mich	Desjardins
Meloche, Denis	Phi	Oct 22, 1972	Wpg	Wakely
Meloff, Chris	Ott	Nov 5, 1972	Alb	K. Brown
Melrose, Barry	Cin	Feb 15, 1977	Edm	Levasseur
Merrell, Barry	Edm	Oct 19, 1976	Phx	
Messier, Mark	Cin	Mar 20, 1979	Bir	Riggin
Micheletti, Joe	Cgy	Apr 1, 1977	Edm	Broderick
Migneault, John	Phi	Oct 12, 1972	NE	A. Smith
Miller, Perry	Wpg	Dec 15, 1974	NE	A. Smith
Miller, Warren	Cgy	Oct 22, 1976	Min	Curran
Miszuk, John	Mich	Nov 24, 1974	Min	
Moffat, Lyle	Cle	Nov 2, 1975	Phx	
Mononen, Lauri	Phx	Oct 17, 1975	Den	Johnson
Morenz, Brian	NY	Oct 14, 1972	Ott	
Moretto, Angelo	Ind	Nov 4, 1978	NE	A. Smith
Morgan, Ron	Cle	Apr 12, 1974	Tor	Gratton
Morin, Wayne	Cgy	Mar 6, 1977	SD	Lockett
Morris, Bill	Edm	Feb 16, 1975	Phx	Norris
Morris, Pete	Edm	Oct 14, 1975	Que	Brodeur
Morris, Rick	Chi	Nov 19, 1972	Min	Curran
Morrison, George	Min	Nov 5, 1972	Wpg	Daley
Morrison, Kevin	Jer	Dec 2, 1973	Min	Garrett
Morrow, Dave	Ind	Nov 25, 1978	Cin	Liut
Mortson, Keke	Hou	Nov 19, 1972	Cle	Cheevers
Mowat, Bob	Phx	Nov 29, 1974	Tor	Gratton
Muloin, Wayne	Cle	Jan 17, 1973	Hou	Rutledge
Myers, Murray	Van	Nov 18, 1973	Cle	Cheevers
Napier, Mark	Tor	Oct 14, 1975	Hou	Grahame
Neale, Robbie	Cle	Dec 26, 1973	Van	Donnelly
Nedomansky, V.	Tor	Oct 20, 1974	Mich	Desjardins
Nesterenko, Eric	Chi	Oct 28, 1973	LA	Gardner
Nevin, Bob	Edm	Dec 14, 1976	SD	Lockett
Niekamp, Jim	LA	Oct 25, 1972	Ott	Gratton
Nilsson, Kent	Wpg	Oct 13, 1977	Que	D. McLeod
Nilsson, Ulf	Wpg	Oct 15, 1974	Van	D. McLeod
Nistico, Lou	Tor	Dec 9, 1973	Min	Garrett
Noris, Joe	SD	Oct 23, 1975	Min	Garrett
Norwich, Craig	Cin	Nov 26, 1977	Ind	Park
Nugent, Kevin	Ind	Oct 29, 1978	Wpg	Daley
O'Donnell, Fred	NE	Nov 16, 1974	Phx	Norris
O'Donoghue, Don	Phi	Nov 2, 1972	Que	Lemelin
O'Shea, Danny	Min	Oct 19, 1974	Cle	Cheevers
O'Shea, Kevin	Min	Nov 26, 1974	Tor	
Odrowski, Gerry	LA	Oct 17, 1972	Min	Curran
Olds, Wally	NY	Nov 2, 1972	Min	Curran
Orr, Bill	Tor	Jan 10, 1974	NE	Landon
Ouimet, Francois	Cin	Oct 9, 1976	SD	Wakely
Paiement, Pierre	Phi	Oct 27, 1972	LA	Gillow
Paiement, Rosaire	Chi	Oct 16, 1972	NE	A. Smith
Paradise, Dick	Min	Nov 26, 1972	NE	Landon
Parizeau, Michel	Que	Oct 21, 1972	NE	A. Smith
Patenaude, Rusty	Alb	Oct 20, 1972	Phi	Parent
Patrick, Craig	Min	Nov 18, 1976	Que	Brodeur
Patry, Denis	Que	Mar 26, 1975	Edm	Worthy
Payette, Kevin	Que	Oct 21, 1972	NE	A. Smith
Peacosh, Gene	NY	Nov 11, 1972	NE	A. Smith
Pearson, Mel	Min	Nov 23, 1972	LA	Gardner
Peloffy, Andre	NE	Jan 22, 1978	Que	Mattsson
Pelyk, Mike	Van	Nov 26, 1974	Mich	Desjardins
Pentland, Dwayne	Hou	Mar 1, 1977	Phx	
Perkins, Ross	Alb	Oct 29, 1972	NY	Donnelly
Perry, Brian	NY	Oct 14, 1972	Ott	
Pesut, George	Cgy	Oct 9, 1976	Que	Brodeur
Peters, Garry	Jer	Mar 4, 1974	Van	Gardner
Phaneuf, Jean-Luc	Tor	Jan 6, 1976	SD	Wakely
Pinder, Gerry	Cle	Oct 14, 1972	Alb	Norris
Plante, Michel	Phi	Oct 19, 1972	LA	Gillow
Pleau, Larry	NE	Oct 12, 1972	Phi	Parent
Plumb, Ron	Phi	Oct 12, 1972	NE	A. Smith
Popiel, Jan	Chi	Oct 12, 1972	Hou	D. McLeod
Popiel, Poul	Hou	Oct 24, 1972	Que	Aubry
Powis, Lynn	Cgy	Feb 24, 1976	Edm	Dryden
Pratt, Kelly	Wpg	Oct 26, 1973	Tor	Gratton
Prentice, Bill	Hou	SApr 1, 1974	NE	Smith
Preston, Rich	Hou	Oct 26, 1974	Min	Garrett
Price, Pat	Van	Dec 27, 1974	Ind	Dyck
Proceviat, Dick	Chi	Oct 19, 1972	Ott	Gratton
Pumple, Rich	Cle	Oct 17, 1972	NY	Kurt
Ramage, Rob	Bir	Oct 13, 1978	Wpg	Daley
Rautakallio, Pekka	Phx	Oct 10, 1975	SD	Wakely
Reichmuth, Craig	NY	Oct 26, 1972	NE	A. Smith
Repo, Seppo	Phx	Oct 14, 1976	Min	Curran
Rhiness, Brad	SD	Oct 9, 1976	Cin	Hoganson
Richardson, Steve	Ind	Oct 17, 1974	Mich	Desjardins
Riihiranta, Heikki	Wpg	Oct 15, 1974	Van	D. McLeod
Rivers, Wayne	NY	Oct 15, 1972	Phi	Parent
Rizzuto, Garth	Wpg	Oct 22, 1972	Phi	Parent
Roberto, Phil	Bir	Dec 13, 1977	Hou	Wakely
Roberts, Doug	NE	Nov 22, 1975	Phx	Kurt
Roberts, Gordie	NE	Dec 13, 1975	Cle	Whidden
Robertson, Joe	Ind	Oct 27, 1974	Que	Brodeur
Rochon, Francois	Chi	Oct 11, 1973	NY	Junkin
Rogers, John	Edm	Dec 7, 1975	Cgy	D. McLeod

Name	team	date	opp.	goaltender	Name	team	date	opp.	goaltender
Rogers, Mike	Edm	Nov 18, 1974	Wpg	Wakely	Stewart, John C.	Cle	Dec 28, 1974	Phx	Kurt
Rollins, Jerry	Tor	Oct 28, 1975	Que	Brodeur	Stewart, Paul	Cin	Jan 7, 1978	NE	Levasseur
Rombough, Lorne	Chi	Jan 19, 1974	Que	Deguise	Stoughton, Blaine	Cin	Oct 7, 1976	Min	Curran
Rota, Randy	Edm	Dec 4, 1976	Ind	Park	Sullivan, Peter	Wpg	Oct 21, 1975	Cin	Lapointe
Rouleau, Michel	Que	Nov 16, 1972	Min	Curran	Sutherland, Bill	Wpg	Jan 28, 1973	Ott	Gratton
Rousseau, Dunc	Wpg	Oct 31, 1972	Chi	J. Mcleod	Sutherland, Steve	LA	Oct 13, 1972	Hou	Rutledge
Roy, Pierre	Que	Nov 8, 1972	Wpg	Wakely	Swain, Garry	NE	Oct 15, 1974	Tor	Gratton
Ruhnke, Kent	Wpg	Oct 8, 1976	Cgy	D. McLeod	Swenson, Cal	Wpg	Nov 26, 1972	Que	Lemelin
Rupp, Duane	Van	Oct 18, 1974	Chi	Newton	Syvret, Dave	Tor	Feb 15, 1976	Wpg	Daley
Ruskowski, Terry	Hou	Nov 13, 1974	Min	Garrett	Szura, Joe	LA	Oct 15, 1972	Hou	D. McLeod
Russell, Bob	Edm	Dec 19, 1975	NE	Abrahamsson	Tamminen, Juhani	Cle	Nov 22, 1975	Wpg	Larsson
Ryan, Terry	Min	Nov 24, 1972	Phi	Paille	Tannahill, Don	Min	Oct 26, 1974	Hou	Rutledge
Sacharuk, Larry	Ind	Dec 10, 1978	Edm	Dryden	Tardif, Marc	LA	Oct 30, 1973	Que	Aubry
Sandbeck, Cal	Edm	Mar 30, 1978	Hou	Wakely	Taylor, Ted	Hou	Oct 12, 1972	Chi	J. Mcleod
Sanders, Frank	Min	Nov 2, 1972	NY	Donnelly	Tebbutt, Greg	Bir	Feb 1, 1979	Que	Brodeur
Sanderson, Derek	Phi	Oct 12, 1972	NE	A. Smith	Terbenche, Paul	Van	Dec 15, 1974	Cle	Whidden
Sarrazin, Dick	NE	Oct 12, 1972	Phi	Parent	Tetreault, Jean	Van	Oct 28, 1973	Edm	Norris
Sather, Glen	Edm	Oct 17, 1976	Ind		Thomas, Reg	LA	Oct 23, 1973	Cle	Whidden
Scharf, Ted	NY	Feb 10, 1973	Cle	Cheevers	Tidey, Alex	SD	Oct 16, 1975	Ind	A. Brown
Schella, John	Hou	Feb 3, 1973	Min	Curran	Tonelli, John	Hou	Oct 25, 1975	Cin	Aubry
Schraefel, Jim	Edm	Mar 12, 1974	LA	Wilkie	Tremblay, J.-C.	Que	Oct 13, 1972	Alb	Norris
Selby, Brit	NE	Nov 12, 1972	NY	Kurt	Trognitz, Willie	Cin	Jan 20, 1978	Que	Mattsson
Selwood, Brad	NE	Oct 21, 1972	Que	Aubry	Trottier, Guy	Ott	Oct 11, 1972	Alb	K. Brown
Semenko, Dave	Edm	Dec 20, 1977	Hou	Wakely	Troy, Jim	Edm	Feb 8, 1978	Cin	Hoganson
Sentes, Dick	Ott	Oct 14, 1972	NY	Kurt	Turkiewicz, Jim	Tor	Jan 31, 1975	Van	D. McLeod
Serviss, Tom	LA	Oct 25, 1972	Ott	Gratton	Ullman, Norm	Edm	Oct 14, 1975	Que	Brodeur
Sheehan, Bobby	NY	Oct 12, 1972	Wpg	Wakely	Vaive, Rick	Bir	Oct 20, 1978	Cin	Liut
Sheehy, Tim	NE	Oct 23, 1972	Min	Curran	Veneruzzo, Gary	LA	Oct 17, 1972	Min	Curran
Sheridan, John	Ind	Dec 1, 1974	Hou	Grahame	Walker, Russ	Cle	Oct 20, 1973	Tor	Binkley
Sherrit, Jim	Hou	Nov 7, 1973	Tor	Binkley	Wall, Bob	Alb	Nov 3, 1972	Hou	D. McLeod
Shmyr, John	Chi	Dec 28, 1973	Que	Brodeur	Walter, Dave	Chi	Nov 2, 1974	Tor	Binkley
Shmyr, Paul	Cle	Oct 15, 1972	Ott	Gratton	Walters, Ron	Alb	Oct 11, 1972	Ott	Binkley
Shutt, Byron	Cin	Oct 15, 1978	Wpg	Daley	Walton, Mike	Min	Oct 12, 1973	Van	Archambault
Sicinski, Bob	Chi	Oct 15, 1972	Min	McCartan	Walton, Rob	Min	Nov 7, 1973	NY	
Siltanen, Risto	Edm	Mar 18, 1979	Que	Corsi	Ward, Ron	NY	Oct 12, 1972	Wpg	Wakely
Simpson, Tom	Ott	Dec 1, 1972	Wpg	Tumilson	Warner, Jim	NE	Feb 10, 1979	Wpg	Mattsson
Sittler, Gary	Balt	Mar 4, 1975	Tor	Binkley	Warr, Steve	Ott	Oct 14, 1972	NY	Kurt
Sjoberg, Lars-Erik	Wpg	Oct 27, 1974	Mich	Desjardins	Watson, Jim	LA	Dec 19, 1972	Hou	D. McLeod
Slater, Peter	LA	Oct 17, 1972	Min	Curran	Webster, Tom	NE	Oct 18, 1972	Hou	Rutledge
Sleep, Mike	Phx	Feb 7, 1976	Min		Weir, Stan	Edm	Nov 21, 1978	Que	Corsi
Sleigher, Louis	Bir	Oct 13, 1978	Wpg	Daley	Weir, Wally	Que	Nov 30, 1976	NE	Abrahamsson
Smedsmo, Dale	Cin	Nov 18, 1975	Que	Brodeur	West, Steve	Mich	Oct 17, 1974	Ind	A. Brown
Smith, Brian	Hou	Dec 30, 1972	Cle	Whidden	Westrum, Pat	Min	Oct 15, 1975	Cle	Cheevers
Smith, Guy	NE	Feb 20, 1973	Phi	Parent	White, Alton	NY	Oct 17, 1972	Cle	Cheevers
Smith, Rick	Min	Nov 15, 1973	Van	Gardner	Whitlock, Bobby	Chi	Oct 15, 1972	Min	McCartan
Smith, Ross	Ind	Nov 28, 1974	Que	Brodeur	Widing, Juha	Edm	Nov 18, 1977	Cin	Liut
Snell, Ron	Wpg	Nov 28, 1973	Hou	D. McLeod	Wilkins, Barry	Edm	Nov 4, 1976	Cgy	D. McLeod
Sobchuk, Dennis	Phx	Oct 28, 1974	Tor	Gratton	Williams, Butch	Edm	Oct 24, 1976	Phx	Kurt
Sobchuk, Gene	Phx	Jan 18, 1975	Edm	Worthy	Williams, Tom	NE	Oct 12, 1972	Phi	Parent
Speck, Fred	Min	Oct 13, 1972	Wpg	Daley	Williamson, Gary	Hou	Nov 18, 1973	Que	Deguise
Speer, Bill	NY	Dec 13, 1972	Que	Brodeur	Willis, Hal	NY	Dec 11, 1972	Chi	J. McLeod
Spencer, Irv	Phi	Feb 10, 1973	Que	Aubry	Winograd, Bob	Jer	Jan 6, 1974	Tor	Gratton
Spring, Dan	Wpg	Oct 18, 1973	NY	Junkin	Wiste, Jim	Cle	Oct 24, 1972	NE	A. Smith
Spring, Frank	Ind	Nov 15, 1977	NE	Levasseur	Woytowich, Bob	Wpg	Dec 3, 1972	Min	Curran
St. Sauveur, Claude	Phi	Jan 1, 1973	NY	Kurt	Wyrozub, Randy	Ind	Oct 10, 1975	Den	Johnson
Stanfield, Jack	Hou	Nov 7, 1972	Chi		Young, Bill	LA	Oct 13, 1972	Hou	Rutledge
Steele, Billy	Cin	Apr 2, 1976	Cle	Johnson	Young, Howie	Phx	Oct 30, 1974	Wpg	Larsson
Stephanson, Ken	Ott	Dec 21, 1972	LA	Gardner	Zaine, Rod	Chi	Dec 9, 1972	Que	Lemelin
Stephenson, Bob	Bir	Nov 24, 1977	Cin	Dion	Zanussi, Joe	Wpg	Oct 20, 1972	Min	Curran
Stevens, Mike	Phx	Nov 5, 1974	Ind	Dyck	Zrymiak, Jerry	LA	Mar 8, 1974	Edm	Norris
Stewart, John A.	Cle	Oct 19, 1975	Hou	Grahame	Zuke, Mike	Ind	Jan 30, 1977	NE	Abrahamsson

The following players scored two goals in their "first goal" game: Jim Adair, Ron F. Anderson, Serge Bernier, Don Borgeson, Henry Boucha, Bruce Boudreau, Michel Boudreau, Steve Cardwell, Bob Charlebois, Ray Delorenzi, Pat Donnelly, Bengt Eriksson, Wes George, Wayne Gretzky, Derek Haas, Del Hall, Duke Harris, Jamie Hislop, Mark Howe, Fran Huck, Bobby Hull, Rod Langway, Mike Laughton, Richard Lemieux, Dan Lodboa, Barry Long, Peter Marsh, Pete Morris, Eric Nesterenko (only two goals of his WHA career), Kent Nilsson, Joe Noris, Craig Norwich, Don O'Donoghue, Jean-Luc Phaneuf, Gerry Pinder, Mike Rogers, Bobby Sheehan, John Sheridan, Jim Sherrit, Bob Stephenson, Alex Tidey, Ron Ward, Jim Watson, Stan Weir, Randy Wyrozub. The following players scored three goals in their "first goal" game: Robbie Ftorek, Gaston Gingras, Joe Hardy, Ted Hodgson, Gord Labossiere, Frank Mahovlich, Keke Mortson, Tom Webster. The following players scored four goals in their "first goal" game: Christian Bordeleau, Jeff Jacques (his debut game), Matti Hagman.

The following players scored their first WHA goal in a playoff game: Alan Globensky, Bengt-Ake Gustafsson, Ralph MacSweyn and Ron Morgan. For Gustafsson and Morgan, these would be their only goals while in the WHA. Bengt-Ake Gustafsson's first goal came about as late in the WHA's existence as possible, in the fourth-to-last game of the 1979 Playoffs, May 15, 1979.

WHA Players on Stanley Cup Champion Teams

The following is a list of individuals associated with the WHA who also won at least one Stanley Cup as a player or in some other capacity (noted) while in the National Hockey League.

WHA Players:

- Ralph Backstrom (Montreal: 1959, 1960, 1965, 1966, 1968, 1969)
- Dave Balon (Montreal: 1965, 1966)
- Andy Bathgate (Toronto: 1964)
- Garnet Bailey (Boston: 1972; Edmonton: 1990 as scout)
- Christian Bordeleau (Montreal: 1969)
- Andre Boudrias (Montreal: 1986 as Assistant GM)
- Carl Brewer (Toronto: 1962, 1963, 1964)
- Wayne Carleton (Boston: 1970)
- Gerry Cheevers (Boston: 1970, 1972)
- Brian Conacher (Toronto: 1967)
- Cam Connor (Montreal: 1979)
- Kent Douglas (Toronto: 1963)
- Reg Fleming (Chicago: 1961)
- Bill Flett (Philadelphia: 1974)
- Jean Gauthier (Montreal: 1965)
- Gaston Gingras (Montreal: 1986)
- Ted Green (Boston: 1970, 1972; Edmonton: 1984, 1985, 1987, 1988 all as assistant coach; 1990 as co-coach)
- Wayne Gretzky (Edmonton: 1984, 1985, 1987, 1988)
- Bill Hicke (Montreal: 1959, 1960)
- Larry Hillman (Detroit: 1955; Toronto: 1962, 1963, 1964, 1967)
- Gordie Howe (Detroit: 1950, 1952, 1954, 1955)
- Harry Howell (Edmonton: 1990 as scout)
- Rejean Houle (Montreal: 1971, 1973, 1977, 1978, 1979)
- Bobby Hull (Chicago: 1961)
- Dave Hunter (Edmonton: 1984, 1985, 1987)
- Dave Keon (Toronto: 1962, 1963, 1964, 1967)
- Dave Langevin (NY Islanders: 1980, 1981, 1982, 1983)
- Rod Langway (Montreal: 1979)
- Bill Lesuk (Boston: 1970)
- Willy Lindstrom (Edmonton: 1984, 1985)
- Ken Linseman (Edmonton: 1984)
- Bruce MacGregor (Edmonton: 1984, 1985, 1987, 1988, 1990 as asst GM)
- Ab McDonald (Montreal: 1959, 1960; Chicago: 1961)
- John McKenzie (Boston: 1970, 1972)
- Frank Mahovlich (Toronto: 1962, 1963, 1964, 1967; Montreal: 1971, 1973)
- Mark Messier (Edmonton: 1984, 1985, 1987, 1988, 1990; NY Rangers: 1994)
- Mark Napier (Montreal: 1979; Edmonton: 1985)
- Eric Nesterenko (Chicago: 1961)
- Bob Nevin (Toronto: 1962, 1963)
- Kent Nilsson (Edmonton: 1987)
- Craig Patrick (Pittsburgh, 1991, 1992 as General Manager)
- Bernie Parent (Philadelphia: 1974, 1975)
- Garry Peters (Montreal: 1965; Boston: 1972)
- Jacques Plante (Montreal: 1953, 1956, 1957, 1958, 1959, 1960)
- Rob Ramage (Calgary: 1989; Montreal: 1993)
- Phil Roberto (Montreal: 1971)
- Gordie Roberts (Pittsburgh: 1991, 1992)
- Derek Sanderson (Boston 1970, 1972)
- Glen Sather (Edmonton: 1984, 1985, 1987, 1988 as coach, 1990 as President/GM)
- Dave Semenko (Edmonton: 1984, 1985)
- Bobby Sheehan (Montreal: 1971)
- Rick Smith (Boston: 1970)
- Bill Speer (Boston: 1970)
- Marc Tardif (Montreal: 1971, 1973)
- John Tonelli (NY Islanders: 1980, 1981, 1982, 1983)
- J.C. Tremblay (Montreal: 1965, 1966, 1968, 1969, 1971)
- Ernie Wakely (Montreal: 1965, 1968)
- Mike Walton (Toronto: 1967; Boston: 1972)
- Bryan Watson (Montreal: 1965)

Special Mention: Robbie Ftorek coached the New Jersey Devils for most of 1999-2000, but was replaced late in the season. The Devils won the 2000 Stanley Cup. Jari Kurri won five Stanley Cups with Edmonton (1984, 1985, 1987, 1988, 1990). He appeared in one official WHA game playing for the Finland touring team, March 1979.

WHA Coaches:

- Bobby Baun (Toronto: 1962, 1963, 1964, 1967)
- Jacques Demers (Montreal: 1993 as coach)
- Bill Dineen (Detroit: 1954, 1955)
- Bill Harris (Toronto: 1962, 1963, 1964)
- Rudy Pilous (Chicago: 1961 as coach)
- Marcel Pronovost (Detroit: 1950, 1952, 1954, 1955; Toronto: 1967)
- Maurice Richard (Montreal: 1944, 1946, 1953, 1956, 1957, 1958, 1959, 1960)
- Jean-Guy Talbot (Montreal: 1956, 1957, 1958, 1959, 1960, 1965, 1966)
- Phil Watson (NY Rangers: 1940; Montreal: 1944)
- John Wilson (Detroit: 1950, 1952, 1954, 1955)

Special Mention: Rudy Pilous is the only individual to win a Stanley Cup and an AVCO Cup as a non-player. He won the AVCO Cup twice as a general manager. Bill Dineen also won two AVCO Cups as a coach. Glenn Hall, assistant coach with Alberta during the first half of the 1972-73 season, won the Stanley Cup with Chicago in 1961, and with Calgary as a goaltending coach in 1989. He is also listed on the Cup as a member of the 1952 Detroit Red Wings, but he was strictly a reserve who did not play for the team during the regular season nor playoffs. Doug Harvey, assistant coach with Houston during 1972-73 and 1973-74, won six Stanley Cups with Montreal, in 1953, and then five straight from 1956-1960.

Earliest Stanley Cup Winner: Gordie Howe, Detroit, 1950. (Phil Watson, a coach in the WHA, won as a player in 1940).

Most Recent Stanley Cup Winner: Mark Messier, NY Rangers, 1994.

Individuals who won both a Stanley Cup and an AVCO Trophy as players:

- Christian Bordeleau (1 Stanley Cup, 1 ACVO Cup)
- Ted Green (2 Stanley Cups, 3 AVCO Cups)
- Larry Hillman (5 Stanley Cups, 1 AVCO Cup)
- Gordie Howe (4 Stanley Cups, 2 AVCO Cups)
- Bobby Hull (1 Stanley Cup, 2 AVCO Cups)
- Bill Lesuk (1 Stanley Cup, 1 AVCO Cup)
- Willy Lindstrom (2 Stanley Cups, 3 AVCO Cups)
- Kent Nilsson (1 Stanley Cup, 1 AVCO Cup)
- Marc Tardif (2 Stanley Cups, 1 AVCO Cup)
- J.-C. Tremblay (5 Stanley Cups, 1 AVCO Cup)

Special Mention: Larry Hillman won one AVCO Cup as a coach. Ted Green won five Stanley Cups as a coach or assistant coach. Andre Boudrias won one Stanley Cup as an assistant general manager. Larry Pleau is listed as a member of the 1971 Montreal Canadiens' Cup-winning team, but he did not play in the 1971 Playoffs.

Special Mention (Referees): Bill Friday is the only individual to referee games in the Stanley Cup Finals in the NHL, and the AVCO World Champion Finals in the WHA.

Drafts & Dispersals

1972 General Player Draft

The WHA held a draft on February 12 and 13, 1972, in Anaheim, California, in which over 1000 players were selected in nearly 100 rounds of selecting.

1973 Amateur Draft Order

1 Chicago	**5** Vancouver	**9** Houston
2 New York	**6** Edmonton	**10** Cleveland
3 Quebec	**7** Minnesota	**11** Winnipeg
4 Toronto	**8** Los Angeles	**12** New England

Cincinnati, an expansion team granted in May of 1973, was granted the 13th pick. Later in the draft, Cincinnati drafted regularly behind New England. After each round of twelve picks, a "floating" pick was granted to one of the teams, after which the next round of twelve picks would take place. No team received more than one of the floating picks.

1973 Professional Draft

The professional draft allowed for the WHA teams to select players off of other major league (NHL) and minor league rosters. Teams could select up to twenty players. It was through this draft the Houston Aeros selected Mark and Marty Howe, making the controversial claim the pair were "professionals", as they collected a $60 per week allowance from their Toronto junior squad.

1974 Amateur Draft Order

1 Vancouver	**6** San Diego	**11** Cleveland
2 Indianapolis	**7** Winnipeg	**12** Toronto
3 Cincinnati	**8** Edmonton	**13** New England
4 Michigan	**9** Quebec	**14** Minnesota
5 Phoenix	**10** Chicago	**15** Houston

The draft order was somewhat juggled due to the three new expansion teams getting a regular spot in the proceedings.

1975 Amateur Draft Order

1 Cincinnati	**6** Edmonton	**11** Toronto
2 Indianapolis	**7** Calgary	**12** San Diego
3 Baltimore	**8** Winnipeg	**13** New England
4 Denver	**9** Phoenix	**14** Quebec
5 Cleveland	**10** Minnesota	**15** Houston.

The 1975 draft once again featured fifteen teams making a regular selection. The 1975 expansion Cincinnati Stingers received the first overall choice, while the other expansion team, Denver, picked in what would otherwise have been the Chicago Cougars' slot. Baltimore participated in the draft but folded almost immediately afterwards.

1976 Amateur Draft Order

1 Toronto	**5** Cleveland	**9** Calgary
2 Edmonton	**6** Indianapolis	**10** Quebec
3 Cincinnati	**7** San Diego	**11** Winnipeg
4 New England	**8** Phoenix	**12** Houston

Cleveland moved to Minnesota and Toronto moved to Birmingham shortly after the draft.

1977 Amateur Draft Order

1 Birmingham	**4** New England	**7** Winnipeg
2 Calgary	**5** Indianapolis	**8** Quebec
3 Edmonton	**6** Cincinnati	**9** Houston

By the time the 1977 draft took place, Phoenix had already folded, and San Diego was soon to follow. Calgary participated in the draft but later folded as well. A pick that was acquired from a defunct team was used in what would have been the normal slot for that pick.

1978 Amateur Draft

No amateur draft was held in 1978 due to the uncertainty of the league's future.

1979 WHA Dispersal Draft
NHL Reclamation Draft
and NHL Expansion Draft

In preparation for the admittance of the four WHA clubs to the NHL in 1979, a series of drafts were held to determine the fates of the players. The WHA dispersal draft allowed the four WHA survivors to select players from the defunct Cincinnati and Birmingham franchises. The NHL reclamation draft allowed for the NHL teams to reclaim the players whose rights they held from the WHA. Finally, the four incoming WHA clubs/NHL expansionists participated in an expansion draft in which the players were selected from the 17 established NHL clubs. Each NHL team gave up 4 players, and the incoming WHA clubs were allowed to claim four players as priority selections, retaining their rights entering the NHL.

The lists indicate the selecting team, the selected player and his last amateur club (college or juniors) or his home country, in the case of European selectees. Numbers indicate the order in which the player was chosen. No indication is made for teams that passed on a draft opportunity.

482

1972 General Player Draft

Jr Junior, **Sr** Senior, **DNP** Did Not Play in 1971-72, **U** University, **Coll** College. Tags are included only if confusion should persist.

Calgary (Cleveland)
Preliminary: Barry Gibbs (Minnesota), Jim Harrison (Toronto), Dale Hoganson (Montreal), Jack Norris (Seattle).
Rounds 1-10: Steve Carlyle (U Alberta), Ron Homenuke (Calgary), Ross Lonsberry (Philadelphia), Jim McMasters (Calgary), Morris Mott (Queen's U), Gerry Pinder (California), Larry Romanchych (Dallas), Gregg Sheppard (Oklahoma City), Brian Walker (Calgary), Jim Watson (Calgary).
Rounds 11-20: Ron Boehm (Boston), Anatoli Firsov (USSR), Josef Golonka (Czechoslovakia), Lorne Henning (New Westminster), Skip Krake (Salt Lake City), Bernie Lukowich (New Westminster), Ray Martyniuk (Columbus), Randy Rota (Nova Scotia), Dallas Smith (Boston), Stan Weir (Medicine Hat).
Rounds 21-50: Jeff Ablett (Medicine Hat), Wayne Bell (Omaha), Dwight Bialowas (Regina), Yuri Blinov (USSR), Lyle Bradley (Salt Lake City), Gary Braun (Toledo), Ken Brown (Dallas), Jim Cardiff (San Diego), Dave Dunn (Seattle), Ed Dyck (Vancouver), Grant Erickson (Cleveland), Jan Eysselt (Czechoslovakia), Gerry Hart (Tidewater), Petr Hejma (Czechoslovakia), Ted Hodgson (Salt Lake City), Doug Horbul (Calgary), Josef Horesovsky (Czechoslovakia), Ken Ireland (New Westminster), Veli Pekka Ketola (Finland), Valeri Kharlamov (USSR), Darrell Knibbs (Muskegon), Al McDonough (Pittsburgh), Ray McKay (Buffalo), Murray MacNeil (Clinton), Ernie Moser (Tulsa), Vaclav Nedomansky (Czechoslovakia), Rod Norrish (Cleveland), Darryl Sittler (Toronto), George Swarbrick (San Diego), Joe Watson (Philadelphia).
Rounds 51-70: Grant Clay (na), Wayne Doll (Long Island), Len Frig (Dallas), Ken Gustafson (Spokane), George Hill (Calgary Sr), Les Jackson (New Westminster), Marshall Johnston (California), Gunnar Lindquist (Sweden), Barry Meisner (Omaha), Peter Muller (na), Wayne Morusyk (Oklahoma City), Tom Pinder (Saskatoon), Al Rycroft (Fort Wayne), Alois Schloder (Germany), Jim Shaw (Portland), Ed Sidebottom (Charlotte), Karl Swetberge (na), Ron Willy (Saskatoon Sr), Richard Wilson (U North Dakota), Jerry Wright (Roanoke).
Rounds 71+: Dave Amadio (Salt Lake City), Leigh Bannister (Flint), Dave Bonter (Dayton), Bill Hay (Retired), Rob Heaney (Dayton), Herb Howdle (Oklahoma City), Aleksander Maltsev (USSR), Darwin Mott (Michigan Tech), Vladimir Petrov (USSR), Morris Stefaniw (Providence), Garry Swain (Fort Wayne).

Chicago
Preliminary: Stan Mikita, Jerry Korab & Gary Smith (Chicago), Jim McKenny (Toronto).
Rounds 1-10: Ivan Boldirev (California), Roger Crozier (Buffalo), Bob Kelly (Philadelphia), Dan Lodboa (Dallas), Don Marcotte (Boston), Pit Martin (Chicago), Jim McLeod (St. Louis), Rosaire Paiement (Vancouver), Jim Pappin (Chicago), Serge Savard (Montreal).
Rounds 11-20: Chuck Arnason (Nova Scotia), Al Blanchard (Kitchener), Tom Cassidy (Kitchener), Bill Clement (Philadelphia), Chuck Goddard (DNP), John Grisdale (Tulsa), Pierre Jarry (New York), Dick Proceviat (Kansas City), Don Tannahill (Boston AHL), Bill Young (Dallas).
Rounds 21-50: Robin Burns (Hershey), Bryan Campbell (Chicago), Lyle Carter (California), Guy Charron (Detroit), Ab DeMarco (New York), Andre Dupont (St. Louis), Ron Dussiaume (Dallas), Darryl Edestrand (Pittsburgh), Tony Featherstone (Nova Scotia), Brian Glenwright (Denver), Dave Hudson (Dallas), Keith LeLeivre (U New Brunswick), Darryl Maggs (Chicago), Garry Monahan (Toronto), Bob Murray (Nova Scotia), Doug Robinson (Nova Scotia), Ron Robinson (Barrie Sr), Leon Rochefort (Detroit), Dale Rolfe (New York), Scott Seagrist (U Toronto), Bob Sicinski (Dallas), Dan Spring (Dallas), Frank Spring (Richmond), Floyd Thompson (St. Louis), Walt Tkaczuk (New York), Doug Volmar (Detroit), Tom Williams (Omaha), Murray Wilson (Nova Scotia), Roger Wilson (Dallas).
Rounds 51-70: Bob Aube (Ottawa U), Bernie Blanchette (Kansas City), Arnie Brown (Detroit), Rick Cunningham (Trenton U), Gordon Davies (U Toronto), Tom Deacon (DNP), Ron Hindson (Greensboro), Sheldon Kannegiesser (Pittsburgh), Steve Latinovich (York U), Randy Manery (Fort Worth), Dave McDowall (U Toronto), Mickey Oja (Kansas City), Marcel Paille (Providence), William Pettinger (Flint), Rick Morris, Bryan Slywchuk, Matt Thorpe (all Laurentian U), Jim Wylie (Flint), Rod Zaine (Buffalo).
Rounds 71+: Grant Cole (Orillia Sr), Ralph Maki (na), Jean Ratelle (New York).

Dayton (Houston)
Preliminary: Guy Trottier (Toronto), Andre Hinse, Larry Lund (both Phoenix), Wayne Rutledge (Denver).
Rounds 1-10: Paul Andrea (Cincinnati), Mike Corrigan (Los Angeles), Norm Gratton (Omaha), Larry Hale (Richmond), Frank Hughes (Phoenix), Gord Labossiere (Cleveland), Dunc McCallum (San Diego), John Schella, Ted Taylor (both Vancouver), Vic Venasky (Denver U).
Rounds 11-20: Gary Dornhoefer (Philadelphia), Don Grierson (Port Huron), Murray Hall (Vancouver), Bil Hogaboam (Omaha), Gord Kannegiesser (Denver), Wayne Lachance (Springfield), Maike Lampman (Denver U), Ted McAneely (Baltimore), Don McLeod (Providence), Jim Shires (St. Louis).
Rounds 21-50: John Adams (Oklahoma City), Ray Adduono (Syracuse), Jim Armstrong (New Haven), Barry Ashbee (Philadelphia), Steve Atkinson (Buffalo), Roger Bellerive (Portland), Ron Busniuk (Nova Scotia), Bob Courcy (San Diego), Ron Ellis (Toronto), Gerry Goyer (San Diego), Duke Harris (Rochester), Ed Hoekstra (Springfield), Howie Hughes (Seattle). Dennis Kassian (Salt Lake City), Larry Keenan (Philadelphia), Dave Kelly (Portland), Orest Kindrachuck, Al Lebrun (both San Diego), Frank Mahovlich (Montreal), Dale McBain (Clinton), Keith McCreary (Pittsburgh), Brian McDonald (San Diego), Billy Orr (Syracuse), Lynn Powis (Nova Scotia), Bobby Schmautz (Vancouver), Brit Selby (Kansas City), Brian Smith (DNP), John Van Horlick (Portland), Barry Wilkins (Vancouver), Larry Wright (Philadelphia).
Rounds 51-70: Bob Barlow (Phoenix), Dean Blais (U Minnesota), Kerry Bond (Phoenix), Ed Bumbacco (U Notre Dame), Jacques Caron (St. Louis), Rene Drolet (Richmond), Rocky Farr (Cincinnati), Al Genovy (Port Huron), Jim Krulicki (Tidewater), Ray Larose (Denver), Brian McBratney (Clinton), Tom Miller (Cincinnati), Rob Palmer (Denver U), Bob Plager (St. Louis), Dave Pulkkinen (Kansas City), Duane Rupp (Pittsburgh), Jack Stanfield (Rochester), Paul Terbenche (Salt Lake City), Tom Trevelyn (San Diego), Hal Willis (Seattle).
Rounds 71+: Larry Billows (Fort Wayne), Herb Boxer (Fort Worth), Bob Boyd (Phoenix), Ray Clearwater (Providence), Bob Cook (Tidewater), Leonard Cunning (Johnstown), Bill Dea (Tidewater), Alex Delvecchio (Detroit), Roy Edwards (Pittsburgh), Phil Esposito (Boston), Guyle Fielder (Salt Lake City), Jean Gauthier (Baltimore), Ed Giacomin (New York), Andre Gill (Hershey), Vic Hadfield (New York), Ed Hayes (Boston Coll), Art Jones (Portland), Bob Jones (Seattle), Cliff Koroll (Chicago), Roger Lafreniere (Denver), Randy Legge (Providence), Dick Matiussi (Baltimore), Larry McKillip (Omaha), Paul Morris (Long Island), Jim Morrison (Baltimore), Keke Mortson (Cincinnati), Lou Nanne (Minnesota), Eric Nesterenko (Chicago), Jean Nicol (Long Island), Bobby Orr (Boston), Mel Pearson (Portland), Poul Popiel (Vancouver), Ray Reeson (Omaha), Bill Saunders (Portland), Wayne Schaab (Charlotte), Con Schmidt (Oklahoma City), Tom Serviss (Flint), Larry Sokoloski (New Westminster), Bobby Taylor (Richmond), Pete Vipond (Columbus), Chris Worthy (Kansas City), Keith Wright (DNP).

Edmonton
Preliminary: Norm Ullman (Toronto), Bobby Clarke (Philadelphia), Bruce MacGregor (New York), Phil Myre (Montreal).
Rounds 1-10: Garnet Bailey (Boston), Doug Barrie (Los Angeles), Dan Bouchard (Boston AHL), Willie Brossart (Philadelphia), Reg Leach (Boston), Gilles Marotte (Los Angeles), Ross Perkins (Fort Worth), Greg Polis (Pittsburgh), Pat Quinn (Vancouver), Randy Wyrozub (Buffalo).
Rounds 11-20: Ron Anderson (Buffalo), Tom Bladon (Edmonton), Craig Cameron (Minnesota), Joe Hardy (Nova Scotia), Dave Kryskow (Dallas), Bill Lesuk (Los Angeles), Len Lunde (Retired), Lew Morrison (Philadelphia), Brian Ogilvie (Edmonton), Bob Stewart (Boston).
Rounds 21-50: Steve Andrascik (Providence), Ken Baird (Oklahoma City), Wendell Bennett (Kansas City), Jim Benzelock (Dayton), Gary Bergman (Detroit), Doug Brindley (Rochester), Brian Carlin (Springfield), Bob Falkenberg (Tidewater), John Ferguson (Retired), Val Fonteyne (Pittsburgh), Gilles Gratton (Oshawa), Del Hall (Columbus), Glenn Hall (Retired), Al Hamilton (Buffalo), Dave Johnson (Cornwall), Ed Joyal (Philadelphia), Kerry Ketter (Nova Scotia), Wayne King (Columbus), Francois Lacombe (Cincinnati), Brian Lavender (St. Louis), Barry Long (Portland), Wayne Maki (Vancouver), Brian Marchinko (Tulsa), Don Saleski (Richmond), Glen Sather (New York), John Stewart (Hershey), Ed Van Impe (Philadelphia), Ron Walters (Tidewater), Dunc Wilson (Vancouver).
Rounds 51-70: John Barber (Portland), Gary Bredin (Rochester), Ray Brownlee (Columbus), Jean-Yves Cartier (na), Roger Cote (Cleveland), John Gravel (Toledo), Terry Gray (DNP), Don Liesemer (Muskegon), Bob McAneely (Boston Coll), Gordon McCosh (Bowling Green U), Bruce Mullett (Muskegon), Edgar Patenaude (Fort Wayne), Alexander Ragulin (USSR), Barry Richardson (DNP), Jack Taggart (Cincinnati), Henry Van Drunen (Edmonton), Bob Wall (Detroit), Lorne Weighill (Dayton), Bob Whidden (Baltimore), Laurie Yaworski (U British Columbia).
Rounds 71+: Val Borisenko (DNP), Roger Bourbonnais (Retired), Tony Esposito (Chicago), John Fisher (Fort Worth), Gary Ford

(Muskegon), Wayne Hicks (Phoenix), Leif Holmquist (Sweden), Tim Horton (Pittsburgh), Bill Horton (Flint), George Hulme (Port Huron), Steve Johnson (Greensboro), Orland Kurtenbach (Vancouver), Derek Kuntz (Medicine Hat), Jean Losier (Des Moines), Jerry Mazur (Dayton), Dick Mortenson (Seattle), Hap Myers (Cincinnati), Richard Pagnutti (Fort Wayne), Robert Perani (Flint), Bob Pulford (Los Angeles), Rich Pumple (Muskegon), Henri Richard (Montreal), Pat Russell (Vancouver Jr), Mike Sauter (Dayton), L. Svensson (Sweden), Harold White (Toledo).

Los Angeles

Preliminary: Ken Dryden (Montreal), Gil Perreault (Buffalo), Matt Ravlich (Detroit), Steve Sutherland (Port Huron).
Rounds 1-10: J.P. Bordeleau, Bart Crashley, Dan Maloney (all Dallas), Norm Dennis (Kansas City), Reg Fleming (Salt Lake City), Pete Laframboise (Baltimore), Ralph MacSweyn (Richmond), Ted McCaskill, Bob Whitlock (both Phoenix), Doug Roberts (Boston AHL).
Rounds 11-20: Christian Bordeleau (Chicago), Len Fontaine (Port Huron), Butch Goring (Los Angeles), John Hanna (Seattle), Earl Heiskala (San Diego), J.-P. Leblanc (Dallas), Bob Liddington (Phoenix), Jim Niekamp (Tidewater), Noel Price (Nova Scotia), Marc Tardif (Montreal).
Rounds 21-50: Charlie Burns (Minnesota), Jerry Butler (Omaha), Mike Byers (Buffalo), Gary Croteau (California), Marv Edwards (Phoenix), George Gardner (Vancouver), Ron Garwasiuk (Providence), Tom Gilmore (Tidewater), John Gofton (Phoenix), Don Gordon (Dallas), Howie Heggedal (Toledo), Mike Jakubo (Columbus), Jean-Guy Lagace (Hershey), Claude Larose (Montreal), Real Lemieux (Los Angeles), Connie Madigan (Portland), Cesare Maniago (Minnesota), Larry Mavety (Salt Lake City), Howie Menard (Baltimore), Jack Michie (Seattle), Kevin Morrison (Rochester), Gerry Odrowski (St. Louis), Fern Rivard (Cleveland), Jim Roberts (Montreal), Peter Slater (Des Moines), Gary Veneruzzo (Denver), Mike Walton (Boston), Bryan Watson (Pittsburgh), Bert Wilson (Providence).
Rounds 51-70: Reg Bechtold (Dayton), Ken Campbell (Portland), Wayne Cashman (Boston), Terry Crisp (St. Louis), Russ Gillow (Spokane Sr), Ed Hatoum (Rochester), Rudy Hitti (Yugoslavia), Dave Hrechkosy (New Haven), Bill Inglis (Salt Lake City), Greg Jablonski (Toledo), Dennis Kearns (Vancouver), Gerry Meehan (Buffalo), John Miszuk (San Diego), Jim Nielson (New York), Bob Rivard (Baltimore), Dan Seguin (Rochester), Fred Stanfield (Boston), J.-C. Tremblay (Montreal), Don Westbrooke (Rochester).
Rounds 71+: Rich Balon (Dayton), Alain Beaule (Springfield), Jack Borotsik (Dayton), Vladimir Bouzek, Jiri Holik, Ivan Hlinka (all Czechoslovakia), Carl Brewer (St. Louis), Larry Cahan (Seattle), Guy Delparte (Johnstown), Norm Descoteaux (Verdun), Sandy Fitzpatrick (San Diego), Jean-Guy Gendron (Philadelphia), Dennis Gidluck, Gary Gilbert (both Flint), Mike Goulet (Toledo), Ron Harris (Detroit), Ken Hodge (Boston), Paul Hoganson (Fort Wayne), Gordie Howe (Retired), Doug Jarrett (Chicago), Billy Knibbs (Providence), Murray Kuntz (Cincinnati), Bernie MacNeil (Fort Wayne), Milan Marcetta (Denver), Gary MacMillan (Dayton), Gordie Nelson (Phoenix), Willie O'Ree (San Diego), Jimmy Peters (Seattle), Luc Potvin (Drummondville), Len Ronson (San Diego), Gary Sabourin (St. Louis), Alois Schloder (Germany), Pat Stapleton (Chicago), Allie Sutherland (Charlotte), Barry Boughner, Jack Criel, Ken Gratton, Bob Kelly, Nelson LeClair, Bob LePage, Peter Mara, Bob Pate, Bob Perrault, Gene Sobchuk, Ken Sutyla, Luc Tessier (all Des Moines), Ron Ullyot (Fort Wayne), Don Ward (Seattle), Jim Watson (Buffalo), Wayne Zuk (Flint).

Miami (Philadelphia)

Preliminary: Bernie Parent (Toronto), Jude Drouin (Minnesota), Derek Sanderson (Boston), Bill White (Chicago).
Rounds 1-10: Mike Bloom (St. Catherines), Terry Caffery (Cleveland), Neil Komadoski (Springfield), Yvon Lambert (Nova Scotia), Brian McSheffrey, Wayne Merrick (both Ottawa), Jean Potvin (Philadelphia), Phil Russell (Edmonton), Carol Vadnais (California), Rene Villemure (Shawinigan).
Rounds 11-20: Michel Archambault (Dallas), Rick Dudley, Jim Nicholls (both Cincinnati), Denis Dupere (Toronto), George Ferguson (Toronto Jr), Rick Foley, Simon Nolet (both Philadelphia), Don Martineau (New Westminster), Paul Shmyr (California), Claude St. Sauveur (Sherbrooke).
Rounds 21-50: Don Burgess (Greensboro), Don Caley (Phoenix), Rychard Campeau (Sorel), Gene Carr (New York), Bruce Cowick (San Diego), Wayne Elder (London), Gary Gambucci (Cleveland), Frank Golembrosky, Michel Rouleau (both Charlotte), Jack Lynch (Oshawa), Walt McKechnie (California), Brian McLay (Muskegon), Bobby Nystrom (Calgary), Craig Patrick (California), Glenn Patrick (Columbus), Ron Plumb (Oklahoma City), Michel Plante (Drummondville), Dean Prentice (Minnesota), Jean Pronovost (Pittsburgh), Paul Raymer (Peterborough), Rene Robert (Buffalo), Pierre Sigman (Syracuse), Rick Smith (Boston), Ron Stackhouse (Detroit), Gary Winchester (U North Dakota).

Rounds 51-70: Andy Bathgate (Switzerland), Serge Beaudoin (Trois Rivieres), Pat Boutette (U Minnesota-Duluth), Brian Bowles (Cornwall), Barry Chernos (Flin Flon), Richard Grenier (Verdun), Andy Hebenton (Portland), Dennis Hull (Chicago), Danny Lawson (Buffalo), Murray Myers (Calgary), Larry Mickey (Salt Lake City), Evgeny Mishakov (USSR), Bill Nyrop (U Notre Dame), Jacques Plante (Toronto), Yvon Pouliot (St-Jerome), Serge Roch (Drummondville), Bobby Rousseau (New York), Ken Schinkel (Pittsburgh), Ron Smith (Cornwall), Garry Unger (St. Louis).
Rounds 71+: Dave Arundel (U Wisconsin), John Bennett (Brown U), Yvon Blais (Cornwall), Ray Carmichael (New Westminster), Bob Dunsden (na), Pierre Henry, Denis Meloche (both Drummondville), Keith Magnusson (Chicago), Sandy McCannell (Saskatoon), Dan McCarthy (Swift Current), Boris Mikhailov (USSR), David Murphy (Hamilton), Steve West (Oshawa).

Minnesota

Preliminary: Peter Mahovlich (Montreal), Mike Curran (US Olympic), Bill Goldsworthy (Minnesota), Dale Tallon (Vancouver).
Rounds 1-10: Mike Antonovich (U Minnesota), Terry Ball (Cincinnati), Henry Boucha, Frank Sanders (both US Olympic), Andre Boudrias (Vancouver), Brian Glennie, Bill MacMillan (both Toronto), Bill Klatt (Oklahoma City), Bob Paradise (Seattle), Tom Peluso (Denver U).
Rounds 11-20: John Arbour (Minnesota), Wayne Connelly (Vancouver), Ray Cullen (Retired), Ernie Hicke (California), Jim Johnson (Los Angeles), Walt Ledingham (U Minnesota), Jack McCartan (San Diego), Bob MacMillan (St. Catherines), Mike Pelyk (Toronto), Jim Rutherford (Pittsburgh).
Rounds 21-50: Doug Acomb (Barrie Sr), Bob Ash (Omaha), Mike Baumgartner (Dallas), Ron Buchanan (Denver), Mike Christie (Denver U), Billy Collins (Detroit), Denis DeJordy (Montreal), Bernie Gagnon (DNP), Hugh Harris (Cincinnati), Phil Hoene (Springfield), Joey Johnston (California), George Konik (Retired), Dick Loe (Johnstown), Bruce McIntosh, Jim McElmury, Craig Sarner (all US Olympic), Murray McLachlan, Randy Murry (both Tulsa), Mike McMahon (Providence), George Morrison (St. Louis), Dick Paradise (Tidewater), Doug Peltier, Pokey Trachsel (both U Minnesota), Terry Ryan (Hamilton), Cliff Schmautz (Portland), Gary Simmons (Calgary Sr), Scott Smith (Regina), Fred Speck (Vancouver), Bob Vroman (Johnstown), Pat Westrum (Oklahoma City).
Rounds 51-70: Wendell Anderson (Governor of Minnesota), Andy Brown (Detroit), Keith Christianson (US Olympic), James Cahoon (U North Dakota), Jim Carter (Green Bay Packers NFL), Bob Collyard (Kansas City), Terry French (DNP), Dennis Giannini (Cleveland), John Garrett (Kansas City), Greg Hubick (U Minnesota-Duluth), Noel Jenke (Minnesota Vikings NFL), Kevin O'Shea (Buffalo), Barclay Plager (St. Louis), Jeff Roesch (na), Rod Seiling (New York), Dale Smedsmo (Bemidji Coll), Don Thompson, Jim Watt (both Michigan State), John Van Boxmeer (Guelph), Dale Yutsyk (Kansas City).
Rounds 71+: Jim Boyd (Fort Wayne), Mark Calder, Gilles Gagnon (both Michigan State), Bob Dobek (Detroit Jr), Ron Docken (Johnstown), Denis Erickson (DNP), Marty Gateman (Hamilton), Mike Stevens (U Minnesota-Duluth), Jim Young (Flint).

New England

Preliminary: Bobby Sheehan (California), Eddie Johnston (Boston), Rick Ley (Toronto), Larry Pleau (Montreal).
Rounds 1-10: Greg Boddy (Vancouver), Gerry Cheevers (Boston), Terry Harper (Montreal), Rick MacLeish (Philadelphia), Doug Mohns (Minnesota), Ron Schock (Pittsburgh), Wayne Thomas (Nova Scotia), Steve Vickers (Omaha), Tom Webster (California), Ed Westfall (Boston).
Rounds 11-20: Michel Belhumeur (Richmond), Curt Bennett (St. Louis), Gary Doak (New York), John French (Baltimore), Stan Gilbertson (California), Hilliard Graves (Baltimore), Paul Hurley, Mike Hyndman (both Boston AHL), Dick Sarrazin (Philadelphia), Tim Sheehy (US Olympic).
Rounds 21-50: Kevin Ahearn, Dick McGlynn, Tim Regan (all US Olympic) Dan Brady, Bob Brown, Bob Gryp, John Danby, Ric Jordan (all Boston U), John Bucyk (Boston), Dave Burrows (Pittsburgh), Steve Cuddie (Cincinnati), John Cunniff (Rochester), Dave Dryden, Chris Evans (both Buffalo), Larry Fullan, Jim Higgs, Dave Westner (all Cornell U), Rod Gilbert (New York), Bill Hanson (na), David Hynes (Harvard), Al Karlander (Detroit), Tom Mellor (Boston Coll), Don O'Donoghue, Tom Williams (both California), Phil Roberto (St. Louis), Michel Ruest (Syracuse), Brad Selwood (Toronto), Guy Smith (U New Hampshire), Jim Stanfield (Springfield), Steve Warr (Clarkson U).
Rounds 51-70: Ron Anderson, Don Cahoon, Dave Wisener (all Boston U), Corby Adams (Barrie Sr.), Bob Borgeson (Long Island), Joe Cavanagh (Braintree), William Corkey (na), Tom Earl (Kansas City), Gary Geldart (Cleveland), Nick Harbaruk (Pittsburgh), Rick Kessell (Hershey), Bruce Landon (Springfield), Rick McCann (Tidewater), Bob McManama (Harvard), Geoff McMullin (Colgate), Gary Milroy (Orillia Sr), Dennis O'Brien (Minnesota), Roger Pelletier

(Quebec AHL), Craig Ramsey (Buffalo), Dan Schock (Richmond).
Rounds 71+: Ralph Backstrom (Los Angeles), Robbie Ftorek, Stu Irving (both US Olympic), John Gray (New Haven), Richard Martin (Buffalo), Al Smith (Detroit), Dick Umile (U New Hampshire).

New York
Preliminary: Gerry Desjardins (Chicago), Dave Gardner, Steve Shutt, Billy Harris (all Toronto Jr).
Rounds 1-10: Don Blackburn (Providence), Ken Block (Rochester), Ken Broderick (San Diego), Jack Egers (St. Louis), Gary Peters (Boston AHL), Larry Sacharuk (Saskatoon), Dave Schultz (Richmond), Jim Schoenfeld (Niagara Falls), Rogatien Vachon (Los Angeles), Alton White (Providence).
Rounds 11-20: Chris Ahrens, Bill Barber (both Kitchener), Lou Angotti (Chicago), Norm Ferguson, Bert Marshall (both California), Ray Fortin (Nova Scotia), Anton Gale (DNP), Peter McNab (Denver U), Curt Ridley (Oklahoma City), Mike Usitalo (Michigan Tech).
Rounds 21-50: Angus Beck (Columbus), Larry Brown, Paul Curtis, Harry Howell (all Los Angeles), Claude Chartre, Pete Donnelly (both Jersey), Guy Denoncourt (Long Island), Kent Douglas (Baltimore), Bill Flett, Brent Hughes (both Philadelphia), Bob Roselle (Kansas City), John Gould (Cincinnati), Danny Grant, Tom Reid (both Minnesota), Gary Kurt (Nova Scotia), Mike Laughton (Nova Scotia), Pete Maybury (DNP), Pete McDuffe (St. Louis), Gord McRae (Tulsa), Jim Murray (Phoenix), Wally Olds (US Olympic), Bill Orban (Springfield), Gene Peacosh (Johnstown), Brian Perry (Providence), Tracy Pratt, Mike Robitaille (both Buffalo), Ian Wilkie (Boston Coll), Jim Wiste (Providence), John Wright (U Toronto).
Rounds 51-70: Reinhold Boos (Germany), Lloyd Bentley (U Wisconsin), Louis Frigon (Muskegon), Al Gousser (na), Phil Goyette (Buffalo), Bob Guindon (Fort Worth), Wayne Hillman (Philadelphia), Ron Huston (Spokane Jr), Danny Johnson (Detroit), James Kennedy (Jersey), Jacques Lemieux (DNP), Doug Manchak (Saskatoon Jr), John Nestic (St. Louis U), Billy Plager (St. Louis), Tom Polanic (Cleveland), Bill Slewidge (Lake Superior State U), Frank St. Marseille (St. Louis), Vladislav Tretiak (USSR), Ron Ward (Vancouver), Bob Winograd (Colorado Coll).
Rounds 71+: Gary Bromley (Charlotte), Paul Edorf (na), Jaroslav Jirik (Czechoslovakia), Gerald MacDonald (na), Don Marshall (Toronto), Lyle Moffat (Tulsa), Brian Morenz (Denver U), Herb Price (Jersey), Stewart Roberts (Greensboro), Bert Scott (Oklahoma City), Harry Shaw (Phoenix), Carl Sapinsky (U St. Louis), Ulf Sterner (Sweden), Vic Tisler (DNP), Bill Yeo (Sun Coast).

Ontario (Ottawa)
Preliminary: Doug Favell (Philadelphia), Dave Keon (Toronto), Brad Park (New York), Eddie Shack (Buffalo).
Rounds 1-10: Mike Amodeo (Oshawa), Bob Berry (Los Angeles), Denis Deslauriers (Shawinigan), Buster Harvey (Cleveland), Chuck Lefley (Nova Scotia), Don Lever (Niagara Falls), Nick Libett (Detroit), Bob Murdoch (Nova Scotia), Mickey Redmond (Detroit), Billy Smith (Springfield).
Rounds 11-20: Syl Apps (Pittsburgh), Fred Barrett (Cleveland), Serge Bernier (Los Angeles), Steve Cardwell (Pittsburgh), Ron Climie (Kansas City), Michel Larocque (Ottawa), Wayne Rivers (Springfield), Larry Robinson (Nova Scotia), Paul Shakes (St. Catherines), Mike Veisor (Peterborough).
Rounds 21-50: Bob Baun (Toronto), Nick Beverley, Terry O'Reilly (both Boston AHL), Wayne Carleton, Dick Redmond (both California), Gary Coalter (Omaha), Marcel Dionne (Detroit), Jim Dorey (Toronto), Tim Ecclestone (Detroit), Gary Edwards, Juha Widing (both Los Angeles), Peter Gaw (Ottawa), Bob Kirk (Oshawa), Ron Lalonde (Peterborough), Bob Leduc (Providence), Jim Lorentz (Buffalo), Johnnie Martin (Shawinigan), Chris Meloff, Glen Seperich (both Kitchener), Brian McKenzie (Hershey), Mike Murphy (St. Louis), Ken Murray (Cincinnati), Joe Noris (Pittsburgh), Murray Oliver (Minnesota), Randy Osburn (London), Doug Rombough (Cincinnati), Dick Sentes (Tidewater), Tom Simpson (Oshawa), Brian St. John (Tulsa), Tom Thompson (Toronto Jr).
Rounds 51-70: Andre Aubry (DNP), Don Awrey (Boston), Les Binkley (Pittsburgh), Doug Buhr (DNP), Brian Gibbons (Springfield), Jack Gibson (U Alberta), Larry Gould (Niagara Falls), Chris Hayes (Oklahoma City), Larry Hillman (Buffalo), Paul Laurent (Orillia Sr), Richard Longpre (U British Columbia), Joe Lundrigan (Tulsa), Tord Lundstrom (Sweden), Pat McCool, Ron Riley (both Loyola U), Bob Nevin (Minnesota), Jim O'Brien (Oakville Sr), Jan Popiel (Tulsa), Michel Poirier (Muskegon), Steve Sly (DNP).
Rounds 71+: Jim Adair (Fort Worth), Mike Boland (Springfield), Norm Dube (Sherbrooke), Jiri Holecek, Jiri Kochta (both Czechoslovakia), Kas Lysionek (U Toronto), Dennis McCord (London), Jim MacDonald (U PEI), Rich Bayes (U St. Mary's).

Québec
Preliminary: Gilles Villemure (New York), Guy Lapointe, Jacques Lemaire (both Montreal), John McKenzie (Boston).
Rounds 1-10: Larry Carriere (Loyola U), Michel Deguise (Nova Scotia), Gilles Gilbert (Cleveland), Pierre Guite (Pennsylvania U),

Jean Hamel (Drummondville), Andre Lacroix (Chicago), Serge Lajeunesse (Fort Worth), Richie Leduc (Boston AHL), Jacques Richard (Quebec Jr), Gerry Teeple (Cornwall).
Rounds 11-20: Steve Durbano (Omaha), Germain Gagnon (Nova Scotia), Rejean Giroux (Quebec Jr), Don Kozak (Edmonton), Bobby Lalonde (Vancouver), Alain Langlois (Long Island), Paul Larose (Syracuse EHL), Pierre Plante (Philadelphia), Michel Plasse (Nova Scotia).
Rounds 21-50: Norm Armstrong (Baltimore), Yves Bergeron (Shawinigan), Derek Black (Calgary), Pierre Brind'Amour (New Haven), Barry Brooks (Verdun), Pierre Bouchard, Guy Lafleur (both Montreal), Jerry Byers, Jiri Kudrasovs (both Kitchener), Brian Coates (Brandon), Reynold Comeau (Nova Scotia), Michel Dumas (Dallas), Guy Dufour (Roanoke), Pierre Farmer (Flint), Dave Fortier (Tulsa), Ed Gilbert (Hamilton), Dan Gloor (Peterborough), Bob Hurlburt (Richmond), Ron Jones (Boston AHL), Moe L'Abbe (Flint), Rene Leclerc (Tidewater), Jean Lemieux (Sherbrooke), Jim Mair (Richmond), Michel Parizeau (Philadelphia), Jean Payette (Tulsa), Andre Peloffy (New Haven), Claude Piche (Roanoke), Pierre Roy (Quebec Jr), Steve Stone (Niagara Falls), Errol Thompson (Tulsa).
Rounds 51-70: Serge Aubry (Rochester), Dave Balon (Vancouver), Red Berenson (Detroit), Richard Brodeur (Cornwall), David Foster (na), Ray Germain, Alan Globensky (both Port Huron), Lucien Grenier (Los Angeles), Jocelyn Guevremont (Vancouver), Paul Henderson (Toronto), Rejean Houle (Montreal), Adam Keller (Phoenix), J.J. Lecavalier (Quebec Jr), Serge Martel (Verdun), Brent Meeke (Niagara Falls), Gilles Meloche (California), Noel Picard (St. Louis).
Rounds 71+: Jerry Culligan (na), Ken Desjardine, Murray Heatley (both Tulsa), Rich Dupras (U Trois Rivieres), Gavin Kirk (Loyola U), Al Milnes (U Toronto), John Murray (DNP), Mark Shewchuk (Sir George Williams U), Gilbert Smith (Fort Wayne).

Winnipeg
Preliminary: Bobby Hull (Chicago), Ted Green (Boston), Ted Irvine (New York), Ernie Wakely (St. Louis).
Rounds 1-10: Ted Harris (Minnesota), Billy Heindl (Cleveland), Bryan Hextall (Pittsburgh), Dennis Hextall (Minnesota), Fran Huck (Denver), John Marks (Dallas), Rick Newell (Omaha), Chris Oddleifson (Oklahoma City), Ron Snell (Hershey), Bob Woytowich (Los Angeles).
Rounds 11-20: Wayne Chernicki (Springfield), Butch Deadmarsh (Cincinnati), Jim Hargreaves (Rochester), Bob Leiter (Pittsburgh), Brian Spencer (Tulsa), Pete Stemkowski (New York), Wayne Stephenson (St. Louis), George Surmay (Providence), Cal Swenson (Tulsa), Ken Tarnow (Fort Worth).
Rounds 21-50: Duke Asmundson (Des Moines), Norm Beaudin (Cleveland), Larry Bolonchuk (Winnipeg), Wally Boyer (Hershey), Barry Cummings (Portland), Joe Daley (Detroit), Marc Dufour (Baltimore), Billy Fairbairn (New York), Jean-Guy Gratton (Hershey), Bill Hajt (DNP), Wayne Hawrysh (Jersey), Ted Hampson (Minnesota), Larry Hornung (St. Louis), Nels Jacobson (Dayton), Larry Klewchuk (Port Huron), Alex Koglar (New Westminster), Jacques Laperriere (Montreal), Ab McDonald (Detroit), Dave Maynard (Winnipeg), Larry McIntyre (Tulsa), Bill Mikkelson (Springfield), Fred O'Donnel (Boston AHL), Gerry O'Flaherty (Tulsa), Jim Pritchard (Clinton), Glenn Resch (Muskegon), Dunc Rousseau (Baltimore), Al Simmons (Columbus), Bill Sutherland (Detroit), Lorne Worsley (Minnesota), Joe Zanussi (Fort Worth).
Rounds 51-70: Milt Black (Dallas), Brian Cadle (Columbus), Mike Chernoff (Cleveland), Steve Craft (St Boniface), Dick Duff (Retired), Connie Forey (Hershey), Bernie Germaine (Regina), Danny Helm (Columbus), Jim Ivison (New Haven), Brian Lefley (Omaha), Zeppi Lindstrom (Finland), Barry Merrell (Boston AHL), Bob Mowat (Charlotte), Neil Nicholson (Providence), Danny O'Shea (St. Louis), Art Stratton (Tidewater), Dave Shardlow (Flin Flon), Frantisek Tikal (Czechoslovakia), Bob Walton (Rochester), Ron Wilson (Cleveland).
Rounds 71+: Alexei Kosygin (USSR; pick made in jest).

1973 Amateur Draft
Listed by order of draft picks.

Round 1: Chicago: Bob Neely (Peterborough); New England: Glen Goldup (Toronto); Quebec: Andre Savard (Quebec); Toronto: Paulin Bordeleau (Toronto); Vancouver: Colin Campbell (Peterborough); Edmonton: John Rodgers (Edmonton); Minnesota: Bob Gainey (Peterborough); Los Angeles: Reg Thomas (London); Houston: Darcy Rota (Edmonton); Cleveland: Lanny McDonald (Medicine Hat); Winnipeg: Ron Andruff (Flin Flon); New England: Blake Dunlop (Ottawa); Cincinnati: Dean Talafous (U Wisconsin).
Round 2: Quebec: Blaine Stoughton (Flin Flon); Chicago: Larry Goodenough (London); New York: Al Sims (Cornwall); Quebec: Morris Titanic (Sudbury); Toronto: Pat Hickey (Hamilton); Vancouver: Brent Leavins (Swift Current); Edmonton: Jim McCrimmon (Medicine Hat); Minnesota: Rick Middleton (Oshawa); Los Angeles: Paul Sheard (Ottawa); Houston: Tom Lysiak (Medicine

Hat); Cleveland: George Pesut (Saskatoon); Winnipeg: Keith Mackie (Edmonton); New England: Mike Clarke (Calgary).

Round 3: Chicago: Francois Rochon (Sherbrooke); New York: John Wensink (Cornwall); Quebec: Eric Vail (Sudbury); Edmonton: Larry McDonald (Cornwall); Vancouver: Ed Humphreys (Saskatoon); Edmonton: Dave Lewis (Saskatoon); Minnesota: Bob Gassoff (Medicine Hat); Los Angeles: Doug Gibson (Peterborough); Houston: Vic Mercredi (New Westminster); Cleveland: Robbie Neale (Brandon); Winnipeg: Kelly Pratt (Swift Current); New England: Tom Colley (Sudbury).

Round 4: Edmonton: Bill Laing (Saskatoon); Chicago: Terry Ewasiuk (Victoria); New England: Randy Holt (Sudbury); Quebec: Jean Landry (Quebec); Toronto: Peter Marrin (Toronto); Vancouver: Jean Tetreault (Drummondville); Edmonton: Jim Moxey (Hamilton); Minnesota: Steve Langdon (London); Los Angeles: Jim Cowell (Ottawa); Houston: Don Cutts (Rensselaer); Cleveland: Russ Walker (Saskatoon); Los Angeles: Peter Crosbie (London); New England: Alan Hangsleben (U North Dakota).

Round 5: Toronto: Bob Dailey (Toronto); New England: Larry Patey (Boston U); New York: Doug Marit (Regina); Quebec: Denis Patry (Drummondville); Toronto: Louis Nistico (London); Vancouver: Jimmy Jones (Peterborough); Edmonton: Ken Houston (Chatham); Minnesota: Nelson Pyatt (Oshawa); Los Angeles: Dennis Abgrall (Saskatoon); Houston: Paul O'Neil (Boston U); Cleveland: Richard Latulippe (Quebec); Winnipeg: Randy Smith (Edmonton); New England: Cap Raeder (U New Hampshire).

Round 6: Edmonton: Dave Pay (U Wisconsin); Chicago: Keith Smith (Brown U); New York: Dennis Ververgaert (London); Quebec: Dale Cook (Victoria); Toronto: Doug Ferguson (Hamilton); Vancouver: Ian Turnbull (Ottawa); Edmonton: Yvan Buillon (Cornwall); Minnesota: John Flesch (Lake Superior State U); Los Angeles: Stuart Davidson (Cornwall); Houston: Dennis Owchar (Toronto); Cleveland: Bob Smulders (Peterborough); Winnipeg: Ron Kennedy (New Westminster); New England: Rick Chinnick (Peterborough).

Round 7: Toronto: Gerard Gibbons (St. Mary's U); Chicago: Denis Desgagnes (Sorel); New York: Lowell Ostlund (Saskatoon); Quebec: Andre Deschamps (Quebec); Toronto: Gord Titcomb (St. Catherines); Vancouver: Mike Korney (Winnipeg); Edmonton: Dwayne Pentland (Brandon); Minnesota: Tom Machowski (U Wisconsin); Los Angeles: David Lee (Ottawa); Houston: Dan Hinton (Sault Ste. Marie); Cleveland: Ron Serafini (St. Catherines); Winnipeg: Jeff Jacques (St. Catherines); New England: Steve Alley (U Wisconsin).

Round 8: Cincinnati: Norm Barnes (Michigan State); Chicago: J.P. Burgoyne (Shawinigan); New York: Frank Grandchukoff (Medicine Hat); Quebec: Bob Stumpf (New Westminster); Toronto: John Campbell (Sault Ste. Marie); Vancouver: Andre St. Laurent (Montreal RWB); Minnesota: Bob Young (Denver U); Los Angeles: Sam Clegg (Medicine Hat); Houston: Lee Palmer (Clarkson U); Cleveland: Michel Latreill (Montreal RWB); Winnipeg: Terry McDougall (Swift Current).

Round 9: Cincinnati: Mitch Brandt (Denver U); Chicago: Gord Halliday (Pennsylvania U); New York: Richard Austin (Swift Current); Quebec: Guy Ross (Sherbrooke); Toronto: Guido Tenesi (Oshawa); Vancouver: Pierre Langiere (Sherbrooke); Minnesota: Neil Korczak (Peterborough); Los Angeles: Randy Aimoe (Medicine Hat); Houston: Sean Shanahan (Providence College); Cleveland: Bruce Greig (Vancouver); Winnipeg: Russ Weichnik (Calgary).

Round 10: Cincinnati: Jack Johnson (U Wisconsin); Chicago: Mike Haramis (Laval); New York: Brian Dick (Winnipeg); 116. Quebec: Michel Belisle (Montreal RWB); Vancouver: Brian Maluick (Calgary); Minnesota: Pat Phippen (St. Paul); Houston: Yvan Dupuis (Quebec); Cleveland: Henry Durkin (Swift Current); Winnipeg: Mike Kennedy (Kitchener).

Round 11: Cincinnati: Bob Bilodeau (New Westminster).

1973 Professional Draft

This draft allowed teams to choose professional players in the NHL that were not drafted in 1972, or had been drafted but were not signed (in a sense, an intraleague draft). Its primary purpose was to allow Houston to draft Mark and Marty Howe as professionals, not as juniors, thus laying the groundwork for the subsequent signing of Gordie Howe.

Chicago Cougars: Darryl Maggs, J.P. Bordeleau, Brian Glennie, Phil Russell, Bill Clement, Rene Villemure, Richard Wilson, Claude Houde, Barry Merrell, Jean Lemieux, Jacques Royer, Ned Yettin, Rick Newell, Larry Cahan, Gary Andreatta, Dick McGlynn, Pierre Viau, Keith LeLievre, Bill Coakley.

Cincinnati Stingers: Larry Johnston, Murray Wilson, Rick Kehoe, Al McDonough, Don Kozak, Jacques Caron, John Van Boxmeer, Glen Sather, Ron Anderson, Doug Volmar, Nick Harbaruk, Tom Bladon, Pierre Bouchard, Bobby Taylor, Butch Deadmarsh, Greg

Polis, Steve Butler, Stan Gilbertson, Jake Rothwell.

Cleveland Crusaders: Peter McNab, Bob Berry, Richie Leduc, Doug Jarrett, Jim Nahrgang, Jim Murray, Bill Nyrop, Larry Sacharuk, Reynold Comeau, Stan Weir, Terry Holbrook, Norm Cherry, Bill McKenzie, George Ferguson, Ron Stackhouse, Terry O'Reilly, Chuck Ness, Bill Hajt, Mike Bartley, Randy Osburn.

Edmonton Oilers: Bill Lesuk, Brian McKenzie, Mickey Oja, Danny Maloney, Bryan Watson, Larry Wright, Chris Worthy, Bobby Schmautz, Bruce MacGregor, Rocky Farr, Willie Brossart, Brian Walker, Bill Orban, Jacques Plante, Wayne Zuk, Danny Gruen, Bob McAneely, Bernie Blanchette, Bill Hicke.

Houston Aeros: Mark Howe, Bob Murray, Tom Peluso, Rene Drolet, Vic Venasky, Mike Lampman, Wayne Thomas, Jude Drouin, Robin Burns, Marcel Dionne, Keith Magnuson, Henri Richard, Rich Preston, Marty Howe, Rick MacLeish, Pat Quinn, Michel Belhumeur, Jack Stanfield, Cleland Mortson, Ed Hoekstra.

Los Angeles Sharks: Billy Inglis, Lyle Bradley, Steve Shutt, Denis Desrosiers, Walt Ledingham, Len Fontaine, Jerry Byers, Denis Herron, John Gould, Randy Wyrozub, Gilles Villemure, Rick Dudley, Nelson Debenedet, Bernie Gagnon, Ian McKegney, Wally Sprange, Danny Grant, Howie Heggedal, Pierre Sigman, Jerry Zrymiak.

Minnesota Fighting Saints: Dave Burrows, John Garrett, Jerry Butler, Bob Gryp, Bob Boyd, Ron Busniuk, Paul Shakes, Jim Cahoon, J.P. Parise, Gary Gambucci, Jim Roberts, Randy Murray, Lou Nanne, Murray Oliver, Tom Williams, Mike Veisor, Gerry Teeple, Gord Clark, Craig Falkman, Carl Wetzel.

New England Whalers: Bill Berglund, Dan Brady, Ed Johnston, Rick Kessell, Don Lever, Doug Roberts, John Martin, Brian Stapleton, Brian Watts, Gary Winchester, Bert Wilson, Dave Dryden, Geoff McMullen.

New York Golden Blades: Mike Pelyk, Wayne Hillman, Steve Vickers, Larry McIntyre, Gary Kilpatrick, Murray Keogan, Tony Esposito, Bob Paradise, John Bennett, Steve Andrascik, Serge Lajeunesse, Pete Stemkowski, Thor Lindstrom, Lowell MacDonald, Lynn Margarit, Juha Widing, Roy Edwards, Ed Hays, Eddie Bumbacco, Jarda Krupicka.

Quebec Nordiques: Simon Nolet, Pierre Jarry, Carol Vadnais, Don Marcotte, Red Berenson, Claude Larose, Nick Beverley, Eddie Shack, Tim Ecclestone, Jean Hamel, Larry Robinson, Guy Lapointe, Gregg Sheppard, Steve Durbano, Paul Larose, Punch Cartier, Frank Golembrosky, Michel Harvey, Jacques Lemelin, Mike McNamara.

Toronto Toros: Paul Henderson, Tony Featherstone, Billy Orr, Jim McKenny, Brian St. John, John Wright, Ronnie LeBlanc, Gary Monahan, Harvey Bennett, Inge Hammarstron, Lars Erik Sjoberg, Morris Stefaniw, Ron Ramsey, Dean Blais, Ron Riley, Frank Blum, Mike Boland, Kas Lysionek, John Hutton, John Donnelly.

Vancouver Blazers: Dave Fortier, Mike Keenan, Glenn Hall, Pete McNamee, Jim Sundstrom, Bill Hogoboam, Hank Nowak, Ron Huston, Don Borgeson, John Van Horlick, Barry Wilkins, Doug Grant, Bruce Bullock, Peter Vipond, Larry Bignell Andre Boudrias, Dave Ferguson, Nick Haramis, Camille Lapierre, Pierre Paiement.

Winnipeg Jets: Mike Bloom, Steve Stirling, Gary Bromley, Gene Carr, Chuck Lefley, Doug Horbul, Phil Esposito, Ted Irvine, Luc Simard, Yvon Lambert, Pete McDuffe, Pierre Plante, John Marks, Billy Fairbairn, Dave Kryskow, Neil Komadoski, Larry Carriere, Andre Dupont, Andre Aubry.

1974 Amateur Draft
Listed by round, then alphabetically by team's city.

Round 1. Chicago: Gary MacGregor (Cornwall); Cincinnati: Don Larway (Swift Current); Cleveland: Paul Baxter (Winnipeg); Edmonton: Doug Soetaert (Edmonton); Houston: Dick Spannbauer (U Minnesota); Indianapolis: Mike Will (Edmonton); Michigan: Bill Reed (Sault Ste. Marie); Minnesota: Bruce Boudreau (Toronto); New England: Tim Young (Ottawa); Phoenix: Dennis Olmstead (U Wisconsin); Quebec: Real Cloutier (Quebec); San Diego: Brad Rhiness (Kingston); Toronto: Jim Turkiewicz (Peterborough); Vancouver (first overall): Pat Price (Saskatoon); Winnipeg: Randy Andreachuk (Kamloops);

Round 2: Chicago: Tim Burke (U New Hampshire); Cincinnati: Bryan Trottier (Swift Current); Cleveland: Charlie Simmer (Sault Ste. Marie); Edmonton: Glen Burdon (Regina); Houston: Pierre Larouche (Sorel); Indianapolis: Craig Hanmer (St. Paul); Michigan: Rick Blight (Brandon); Minnesota: Robbie Laird (Regina); New England: Mike Eruzione (Boston U); Phoenix: Dave Gorman (St. Catherines); Quebec: Charlie Constantin (Quebec); San Diego: Kevin Devine (Toronto); Toronto: Roger Lemelin (London); Vancouver: Jacques Cossette (Sorel); Winnipeg: Brian Engblom (U Wisconsin);

Round 3: Chicago: Paul McIntosh (Peterborough); Cincinnati: Dave Williams (Swift Current); Cleveland: Doug Risebrough (Kitchener); Cleveland: Bruce Affleck (Denver U); Edmonton: Clark Gillies (Regina); Houston: John Hughes (Toronto); Houston: Richard Nantais (Quebec); Indianapolis: Bill Lochead (Oshawa); New England: Peter Sturgeon (Kitchener); Phoenix: Cam Connor (Flin Flon); Quebec: Alain Daigle (Trois Rivieres); San Diego: Rick

Chartraw (Kitchener); Vancouver: Ron Greschner (New Westminster); Winnipeg: Danny Gare (Calgary);

Round 4: Cincinnati: Dave Inkpen (Edmonton); Cincinnati: Jerry Holland (Calgary); Cincinnati: Bill Evo (Peterborough); Cincinnati: Mike Palmateer (Toronto); Cleveland: John Stewart (Bowling Green); Edmonton: Mike Rogers (Calgary); Houston: Terry Ruskowski (Swift Current); Indianapolis: Bob Bourne (Saskatoon); Minnesota: John Paddock (Brandon); New England: Michel Deziel (Sorel); Phoenix: Brian Kinsella (Oshawa); Phoenix: Brad Winton (Toronto); Vancouver: Ron Chipperfield (Brandon); Winnipeg: Gord McTavish (Sudbury); Winnipeg: Ron Ashton (Saskatoon);

Round 5: Chicago: Mark Lomenda (Victoria); Chicago: Garry Lariviere (St. Catherines); Cincinnati: Brad Anderson (Victoria); Edmonton: Paul Holmgren (U Minnesota); Houston: Pete LoPresti (Denver U); Indianapolis: Mike Wong (Montreal RWB); Michigan: Barry Legge (Winnipeg); Michigan: Paul Nicholson (London); Minnesota: William Schneider (U Minnesota); New England: Peter Brown, (Boston U); Phoenix: Jim Clarke (Toronto); San Diego: Jim Warden (Michigan Tech); Toronto: Carlo Torresan (Sorel); Vancouver: Peter Driscoll (Kingston); Winnipeg: Kim McDougall (Regina);

Round 6: Chicago: Paul Evans (Kitchener); Cincinnati: Bob Murray (Cornwall); Cleveland: Jamie Hislop (U New Hampshire); Edmonton: Kevin Treacy (Cornwall); Houston: Derek Smith (Ottawa); Indianapolis: Mike Zuke (Michigan Tech); Minnesota: Dave Hanson (St. Paul); New England: Dick Lamby (Salem State U).; Phoenix: Bruce Aberhart (London); Quebec: Jean Bernier (Shawinigan); San Diego: Jamie Bateman (Quebec); San Diego: Derek Emerson (Montreal RWB); Toronto: Ron Sedlbauer (Kitchener); Vancouver: Dave Givens (Brown U); Winnipeg: Boyd Anderson (Medicine Hat);

Round 7: Chicago: Scot Jessee (Michigan Tech); Cleveland: Mike Thompson (Victoria); Edmonton: Dave Langevin (U Minnesota); Houston: Bob Sirois (Montreal RWB); Indianapolis: Pat Ribble (Oshawa); Michigan: Larry Fink (St. Catherines); Minnesota: Steve Carlson (Marquette); New England: Don McLean (Sudbury); Phoenix: Gord Buynak (Kingston); Quebec: Dave Logan (Laval); San Diego: Mike Boland (Sault Ste. Marie); Toronto: Gilles Lupien (Montreal RWB); Vancouver: Steve Jensen (Michigan Tech); Winnipeg: Rick Uhrich (Regina);

Round 8: Chicago: Emile deMoissac (New Westminster); Cincinnati: Joe Micheletti (U Minnesota); Cleveland: Tom Lindskog (U Michigan); Edmonton: Bernard Noreau (Laval); Houston: Ken Gassoff (Medicine Hat); Indianapolis: Harold Snepsts (Edmonton); Michigan: Ed Johnstone (Medicine Hat); Minnesota: Al Hillier (Flin Flon); New England: Joe Rando (U New Hampshire); Phoenix: Rob Watt (Flin Flon); Quebec: Michel Bergeron (Sorel); San Diego: Ray Maluta (Flin Flon); Toronto: Garth Malarchuk (Calgary); Vancouver: Dave Lumley (U New Hampshire); Winnipeg: Dave Rooke (Cornwall);

Round 9: Chicago: John Shewchuk (St. Paul); Cleveland: Harvey Stewart (Flin Flon); Edmonton: Tom Sundberg (St. Paul); Houston: Murray Beck (New Westminster); Indianapolis: Peter Roberts (St. Cloud State); Indianapolis: John Sheridan (U Minnesota); Michigan: Ron Pronchuk (Brandon); Minnesota: Jack Carlson (Marquette); New England: Brian Walsh (U Notre Dame); Phoenix: Andy Spruce (London); Quebec: Denis Carufel (Sorel); San Diego: Greg Holst (Kingston); Toronto: John Harper (Cornell); Vancouver: Mike Hobin (Hamilton); Winnipeg: Bob Ferguson (Cornwall);

Round 10: Chicago: Mark Trivett (Cornwall); Cleveland: Steve Colp (Michigan State); Edmonton: Cam Botting (Niagara Falls); Houston: Jerry Badiuk (Kitchener); Indianapolis: Tom Price (Ottawa); Indianapolis: Mark Toulet (Moncton U); Michigan: Paul Touzin (Shawinigan); Minnesota: Richard Moore (Montreal RWB); New England: John Nazar (Cornwall); Phoenix: Steve Short (Minnesota Jrs); Quebec: Claude Dupuis (Laval); San Diego: Mike McKegney (Kitchener); Toronto: Joe McNeil (St. Francis Xavier U); Vancouver: Mario Faubert (St. Louis U); Winnipeg: John Duncan (Cornwall);

Round 11: Chicago: Bob Chase (Cornwall); Cincinnati: David Bossy (U Notre Dame); Cleveland: Jack Brownschidle (U Notre Dame); Edmonton: Marty Mathews (Flin Flon); Houston: Jan Cascak, (St. Louis U); Indianapolis: Michel Dion (Montreal RWB); Michigan: Terry Casey (St. Catherines); Minnesota: Don Dufek (U Michigan); New England: Warren Miller (U Minnesota); Phoenix: John Taft (U Wisconsin); Quebec: Mario Lessard (Sherbrooke); San Diego: Brian Bye (Kitchener); Toronto: Jack Davies (Thunder Bay); Vancouver: John Held (London); Winnipeg: Wayne Wilhelm (Brandon);

Round 12: Chicago: Daryl Traer (Thunder Bay); Cleveland: Serge Gamelin (Sorel); Edmonton: Willy Freisen (Swift Current); Houston: Ron Wilson (St. Catherines); Indianapolis: Kevin Erickson (Calgary); Indianapolis: Jack Patterson (Kamloops); Minnesota: Reg Duncombe (New Westminster); New England: Tony White (Kitchener); Phoenix: Don Mandryk (Kitchener); Quebec: Claude Arvisais (Shawinigan); Toronto: Bill Hassard (Wexford); Vancouver: Ed Mio (Colorado College); Winnipeg: Mike Wanchuk (Regina);

Round 13: Chicago: Jim Murray (Michigan Tech); Cleveland: Glen McLeod (Sudbury); Houston: Bob Ferriter (Boston College); Indianapolis: Don Wheldon (London); Indianapolis: Gary Sargent (Fargo-Moorehead); Indianapolis: Greg Steele (Calgary); Michigan: Dave Groulx (Cornell); Minnesota: Robin Larson (U Minnesota); New England: Robbie Moore (U Michigan); Phoenix: Chuck Luksa (Kitchener); San Diego: Firmin Royer (Sorel); Vancouver: Jim Miller (Denver U); Winnipeg: John Memryk (Winnipeg);

Round 14: Chicago: Mike Dubois (Chicoutimi); Cleveland: Doug Allen (New Westminster); Houston: John McMorrow (Providence College); Indianapolis: Pierre David (Sorel); Indianapolis: Scott Mabley (Sault Ste. Marie); Indianapolis: Russ Hall (Winnipeg); Michigan: John Riley (Windsor); Minnesota: Joe Baker (St. Paul); New England: Cliff Cox (U New Hampshire); Phoenix: Mark Gaudreault (Lake Superior State); San Diego: Bob Elinesky (Clatham); Vancouver: Dave Otness (U Wisconsin); Winnipeg: Marcel Dumas (Sherbrooke);

Round 15: Chicago: Rejean Lemelin (Sherbrooke); Cleveland: Gord Stewart (Kamloops); Houston: Craig Norwich (U Wisconsin); Indianapolis: Graham Hall (Wexford); Indianapolis: Bill Best (Sudbury); Indianapolis: Mike St. Cyr (Kitchener); Minnesota: Tony Dorn (U Minnesota); New England: Dave Staffen (Ottawa); Phoenix: Kim Gellert (Lake Superior State U); San Diego: Mitch Giroux (Guelph); Vancouver: Walt Kyle (Austin);

Round 16: Houston: Kevin MacDonald (Bowling Green U); Indianapolis: Ron Tordoff (Swift Current); Indianapolis: Doug Counter (Aurora); Indianapolis: Mitch Babin (North Bay); Minnesota: Reed Larsen (U Minnesota); New England: Peter Tighe (London); Phoenix: Ron Hawkshaw (U Waterloo); San Diego: Bob Blanchet (Kitchener);

Round 17: Houston: Ian McPhee (Swift Current); Indianapolis: Yves Plouffe (Sorel); Indianapolis: Jim Chicoine (Brandon); Minnesota: Ken Yackel (St. Paul); New England: Brian Durocher (Boston U);

Round 18: Houston: Don Hay (New Westminster); Indianapolis: Brian Barker (Sorel); Minnesota: Dana Decker (Michigan Tech); New England: Colin Ahern (Tyngsboro);

Round 19: Indianapolis: Rick Fraser (Oshawa); Minnesota: John Rolstein (n.a.); New England: Dwayne Byers (Sherbrooke);

Round 20: Indianapolis: Larry Jacques (Ottawa);

Round 21: Indianapolis: Bob Volpe (Sudbury); Winnipeg: Tom Wynne (Cornwall).

1974 Expansion Draft

The Phoenix Roadrunners and Indianapolis Racers participated in an expansion draft on May 30, 1974, held in Toronto. Both teams alternated picks, with Phoenix drafting first. The team from which the player was selected is noted in parentheses.

Phoenix: Gary Kurt (San Diego); Indianapolis: Brian McKenzie (Edmonton); Phoenix: Gerry Odrowski (Michigan); Indianapolis: Bob Fitchner (Edmonton); Phoenix: Ted Hodgson (Michigan); Indianapolis: Bob Whitlock (Michigan); Phoenix: Bill Young (Michigan); Indianapolis: Bob Ash (Winnipeg); Phoenix: Rich Pumple (Cleveland); Indianapolis: Bob Sicinski (Chicago); Phoenix: Bob Jones (San Diego); Indianapolis: Rych Campeau (Vancouver); Phoenix: Bernie Blanchette (Edmonton); Indianapolis: Roger Cote (Edmonton); Phoenix: Steve King (Toronto); Indianapolis: Steve Cardwell (Minnesota); Phoenix: Dick Sarrazin (Chicago); Indianapolis: Jim Hargreaves (Winnipeg); Phoenix: Terry Ryan (Minnesota); Indianapolis: Michel Archambault (Quebec); Phoenix: Ron Anderson (Chicago); Indianapolis: Billy Orr (Toronto); Phoenix: Jack Gibson (Toronto); Indianapolis: Cal Swenson (Winnipeg); Phoenix: Jim McMasters (Cleveland); Indianapolis: Yves Bergeron (Quebec); Phoenix: Michel Plante (Vancouver); Indianapolis: Pierre Henry (Vancouver); Phoenix: Steve Warr (Toronto); Indianapolis: Ken Desjardine (Quebec); Indianapolis: Ron Morgan (Cleveland); Indianapolis: Tom Williams (New England).

1975 Amateur Draft
Listed by order of draft picks.

Round 1: Cincinnati: Claude Larose (Sherbrooke); Indianapolis: Bryan Maxwell (Medicine Hat); Baltimore: Don Ashby (Calgary); Denver: Mel Bridgeman (Victoria); Cleveland: Ralph Klassen (Saskatoon); Edmonton: Barry Dean (Medicine Hat); Calgary: Dennis McLean (Calgary); Winnipeg: Brad Gassoff (Kamloops); Phoenix: Greg Vaydik (Medicine Hat); Minnesota: Greg Hickey (Hamilton); Toronto: Rick Lapointe (Victoria); San Diego: Jamie Masters (Ottawa); New England: Terry McDonald (Edmonton); Quebec: Pierre Mondou (Montreal RWB); Houston: Rich Mulhern (Sherbrooke).

Round 2: Cincinnati: Bob Sauve (Laval); Baltimore: Don Cairns (Victoria); Baltimore: Robin Sadler (Edmonton); Cleveland: Mal

Zinger (Kamloops); Cleveland: Kelly Greenbank (Winnipeg); Edmonton: Pete Morris (Victoria); Winnipeg: Russ Anderson (U Minnesota); Phoenix: Neil Lyseng (Kamloops); Phoenix: Mike O'Connell (Kingston); Minnesota: Kim Clackson (Victoria); Toronto: Jerry Rollins (Winnipeg); San Diego: Rick Adduono (St. Catherines); New England: Danny Arndt (Saskatoon); Quebec: Doug Halward (Peterborough); Houston: Doug Jarvis (Peterborough).

Round 3: Cincinnati: Larry Hendrick (Calgary); Indianapolis: Clark Hamilton (U Notre Dame); Baltimore: Gord Laxton (New Westminster); Denver: Ron Delorme (Lethbridge); Cleveland: Ed Staniowski (Regina); Edmonton: Barry Smith (New Westminster); Calgary: Alex Pirus (U Notre Dame); Winnipeg: Glenn Richardson (Hamilton); Phoenix: Blair Davidson (Flin Flon); Minnesota: Greg Neeld (Calgary); Toronto: Paul Heaver (Oshawa); San Diego: Bob Watson (Flin Flon); New England: Matti Hagman (Finland); Quebec: Pierre Giroux (Hull); Houston: Kevin Campbell (St. Lawrence).

Round 4: Cincinnati: Norm Lapointe (Trois Rivieres); Indianapolis: Blair Mackasey (Montreal RWB); Baltimore: Rick Bourbonnais (Ottawa); Denver: Andre Leduc (Sherbrooke); Cleveland: Pete Scamurra (Peterborough); Edmonton: Stu Younger (Michigan Tech); Calgary: Rick Piche (Brandon); Winnipeg: Ted Long (Hamilton); Phoenix: Roger Swanson (Flin Flon); Minnesota: Bob Hoffmeyer (Saskatoon); Toronto: Ken Breitenbach (St. Catherines); San Diego: Don Blair (Ottawa); New England: Derek Spring (Brandon); Quebec: Ted Bulley (Hull); Houston: Dave Salvian (St. Catherines).

Round 5: Cincinnati: Paul Harrison (Oshawa); Indianapolis: Rick Bowness (Montreal RWB); Baltimore: Dale Ross (Ottawa); Denver: Nick Sanza (Sherbrooke); Cleveland: Dennis Maruk (London); Edmonton: Jim Ofrim (U Alberta); Calgary: Terry Bucyk (Lethbridge); Phoenix: Mike Sleep (New Westminster); Minnesota: Jim Minor (Regina); Toronto: Mario Vien (Cornwall); San Diego: Craig Crawford (Toronto); New England: Gary McFayden (Hull); Quebec: Andre Lepage (Montreal RWB); Houston: Paul Crowley (Sudbury).

Round 6: Cincinnati: Jack Laine (Bowling Green State); Indianapolis: Eric Sanderson (Victoria); Denver: Greg Miazga (Victoria); Cleveland: Joe Augustine (Austin); Edmonton: Bob Sunderland (Boston U); Calgary: Pat Hughes (U Michigan); Winnipeg: Nick Bobstock (n.a.); Phoenix: Dana Decker (Michigan Tech); Minnesota: Brian Shmyr (New Westminster); Toronto: Paul Woods (Sault Ste. Marie); San Diego: Alex Tidey (Lethbridge); New England: Terry Martin (London); Quebec: Jean Trottier (Laval); Houston: Bill Cheropita (St. Catherines).

Round 7: Cincinnati: Gary Carr (Toronto); Indianapolis: Doug Young (Michigan Tech); Denver: Rick Martin (London); Cleveland: Michel Lachance (Montreal RWB); Edmonton: Dave Bell (Harvard); Calgary: Greg Smith (Colorado College); Phoenix: Dale McMullen (Brandon); Minnesota: Marc Tessier (Sherbrooke); Toronto: Byron Shutt (Bowling Green State); San Diego: Rick Lalonde (Calgary); New England: John Tweedle (Lake Superior State); Quebec: Mike Backman (Montreal RWB); Houston: John Glynne (U Vermont).

Round 8: Cincinnati: Greg Clause (Hamilton); Indianapolis: Stan Jonathan (Peterborough); Cleveland: Joe Fortunato (Kitchener); Edmonton: Sid Veysey (Sherbrooke); Calgary: Doug Lindskog (U Michigan); Phoenix: Gary Morrison (U Michigan); Minnesota: Bob McNeice (New Westminster); Toronto: Jean-Luc Phaneuf (Montreal RWB); San Diego: Kelly Secord (New Westminster); New England: Mike Harazny (Regina); Quebec: Michel Brisebois (Sherbrooke); Houston: Dave Taylor (Clarkson U).

Round 9: Cincinnati: Yvon Disotell (Cornwall); Indianapolis: Larry Huras (Kitchener); Cleveland: Victor Khatulev (USSR); Edmonton: Bob Russell (Sudbury); Calgary: Paul Clarke (U Notre Dame); Winnipeg: Jim Gustafson (Victoria); Minnesota: Dave Faulkner (Regina); Toronto: Gilles Bilodeau (Sorel); San Diego: Alex Forsyth (Kingston); New England: Dave Norris (Hamilton); Quebec: Michel Hamel (Laval); Houston: Jim Maxfield (Sudbury).

Round 10: Cincinnati: Gary Burns (New Hampshire); Indianapolis: Kari Makkonen (Finland); Denver: Dave Bossy (U Notre Dame); Cleveland: Aarie Kanteenpara (Finland); Edmonton: Jean Thibodeau (Shawinigan); Calgary: Randy Koch (U Vermont); Winnipeg: Dag Bredberg (Sweden); Minnesota: Denis Daigle (Montreal RWB); Toronto: Roger Dorey (Kingston); San Diego: Don Edwards (Kitchener); New England: Paul Stevenson (Brown U); Quebec: Florent Fortier (Quebec); Houston: Chad Campbell (Denver U).

Round 11: Cincinnati: Bill Reber (U Vermont); Indianapolis: Michel Blais (Kingston); Denver: Andy Whitby (Oshawa); Cleveland: Tom McNamara (U Vermont); Edmonton: Brian Petrovek (Harvard); Calgary: Dan Tsuboushi (St. Louis U); Winnipeg: Emil Mesgaros (n.a.); Minnesota: Earl Sargent (Fargo-Moorehead); Toronto: Robert Ritchie (Sorel); San Diego: Dale Anderson (Brandon); New England: Clark Jantzie (U Alberta); Houston: Bill Oleschuk (Saskatoon).

Round 12: Cincinnati: Dave McNab (U Wisconsin); Indianapolis: Anders Steen (Sweden); Cleveland: Rick Marsh (Rensselaer);

Edmonton: Jim Montgomery (Hull); Calgary: Bill Anderson (St. Louis U); Winnipeg: Tarbjorn Nilsson (Sweden); Minnesota: Richard Dutton (Laval); Toronto: Bob Shaw (Clarkson U); San Diego: Bruce O'Grady (Sault Ste. Marie); Houston: Jim Lindquist (Brown U).

Round 13: Cincinnati: Peter Sheier (n.a.); Indianapolis: Paul Evans (Peterborough); Cleveland: Stan Shearer (n.a.); Edmonton: Terry Angel (Oshawa); Calgary: Doug Hanson (DNP); Winnipeg: Bengt Tundholm (Sweden); Minnesota: Tom Ulseth (U Wisconsin); Toronto: Wayne Morin (Kamloops); Houston: Rick St. Croix (Oshawa)

Round 14: Cincinnati: Francois Robert (Sherbrooke); Edmonton: Rick Shinske (New Westminster); Calgary: Darryl Ferner (Kamloops); Minnesota: Henry Taylor (St. Paul); Toronto: Dave Hanson (Michigan Tech); Houston: Paul Jensen (Colorado College).

1975 Intraleague Draft

Indianapolis: Bill Prentice (Houston), Al Karlander (New England); Denver: Brian Gibbons (Toronto); Cleveland: Terry Ball (Minnesota), Doug Brindley (Indianapolis); Calgary: Francois Lacombe (Quebec), Maike Laughton (San Dieg); Winnipeg: Larry Hillman (Cleveland); Minnesota: Gerry Odrowski (Phoenix); San Diego: Mike McMahon (Minnesota).

1975 Dispersal Draft

The dispersal draft was held in June 1975 to disperse the players of the Chicago and Baltimore franchises.

Denver: Barry Legge (Baltimore); Indianapolis: Pat Stapleton (Chicago); Cleveland: Danny Gruen (Baltimore); Edmonton: Dave Dryden (Chicago); Calgary: Don Ashby (Baltimore); Winnipeg: Randy Legge (Baltimore); Cincinnati: Rick Bourbonnais (Baltimore); Phoenix: Rick Blight (Baltimore); Minnesota: Dennis Owchar (Chicago); Toronto: Gord Laxton (Baltimore); San Diego: John Raynak (Baltimore); New England: Paul Hoganson (Baltimore); Quebec: Alain Caron (Baltimore); Houston: Ian McKegney (Baltimore); Denver: Dale Ross (Baltimore); Indianapolis: Mike Dubois (Chicago); Cleveland: Gil Perreault (Baltimore); Edmonton: Boris Mikhailov (Baltimore); Calgary: Duke Harris (Chicago); Winnipeg: Gary Sittler (Baltimore); Cincinnati: Rich Coutu (Chicago); Phoenix: Alexander Gusev (Baltimore); Minnesota: Ross Lonsberry (Baltimore); Toronto: Denis Herron (Baltimore); San Diego: Alton White (Chicago); New England: Dave Birch (Baltimore); Quebec: Don Saleski (Baltimore); Houston: Dave Forbes (Baltimore); Denver: Gilles Villemure (Baltimore); Indianapolis: Frank St. Marseille (Baltimore); Cleveland: Hilliard Graves (Baltimore); Edmonton: Vladimir Petrov (Baltimore); Calgary: Paul Nicholson (Baltimore); Winnipeg: Scott Garland (Baltimore); Cincinnati: Jim Pappin (Baltimore); Phoenix: Ken Lockett (Baltimore); Minnesota: Gord McDonald (Baltimore); Toronto: Doug Towler (Chicago); San Diego: Dave Walter (Chicago); New England: Bob Goodenow (Baltimore); Quebec: Jim Benzelock (Chicago); Houston: Lynn Zimmerman (Baltimore).

The following players were selected through an auction:

Cincinnati: Gary Veneruzzo (Baltimore); Minnesota: Craig Reichmuth (Baltimore); Quebec: Tom Serviss (Baltimore); Calgary: John Miszuk (Baltimore); Minnesota: Jerry Zrymiak (Baltimore); Edmonton: Billy Evo (Baltimore); Indianapolis: Reg Thomas (Baltimore); Denver: Gary Bredin (Baltimore); Quebec: Jim Watson (Chicago); Toronto: Rod Zaine (Chicago); Quebec: Ron Pronchuk (Baltimore); Calgary: Bill Reed (Baltimore); New England: Steve Richardson (Baltimore); Denver: J.P. Leblanc (Baltimore).

1975 Expansion Draft

All players selected were from Chicago's roster.

Denver: Gary MacGregor, Ralph Backstrom, Darryl Maggs, Bryon Baltimore, Keith Kokkola, Mark Lomenda, Rosaire Paiement, Francois Rochon, Bob Liddington, Jan Popiel, Rick Morris, Brian Coates, Peter Mara and Cam Newton. Chris Grigg was selected from the Cougars' Long Island affiliate of the NAHL.

1976 Amateur Draft
Listed by order of draft picks.

Round 1: Edmonton: Blair Chapman (Saskatoon); Cincinnati: Peter Marsh (Sherbrooke); Cleveland: Glen Sharpley (Hull); Indianapolis: Bob Simpson (Sherbrooke); San Diego: Dave Farrish (Sudbury); Edmonton: Bernie Federko (Saskatoon); Cincinnati: Randy Carlyle

(Sudbury); Toronto: Bjorn Johanson (Sweden); Winnipeg: Thomas Gradin (Sweden); Quebec: Rick Green (London); Toronto: Kent Nilsson (Sweden); Cincinnati: Don Murdoch (Medicine Hat).

Round 2: New England: Mike Fidler (Boston U); Cleveland: Rod Schutt (Sudbury); Indianapolis: Alex McKendry (Sudbury); Cincinnati: Greg Carroll (Medicine Hat); Winnipeg: Clayton Paschal (New Westminster); Calgary: Dave Shand (Peterborough); Quebec: Bob Manno (St. Catherines); Winnipeg: Tom Rowe (London); Toronto: Peter Lee (Ottawa); Houston: Morris Lukowich (Medicine Hat); San Diego: Romano Carlucci (Sault Ste. Marie); Toronto: Paul Gardner (Oshawa);

Round 3: San Diego: Mark Suzor (Kingston); New England: Fred Williams (Saskatoon); Cleveland: Jeff McDill (Victoria); Edmonton: Harold Philipoff (New Westminster); San Diego: Tony Horvath (Sault Ste. Marie); Edmonton: Drew Callander (Regina); New England: Dave Debol (U Michigan); Quebec: Al Glendinning (Calgary); Winnipeg: Steve Clippingdale (New Westminster); Houston: Jim Roberts (Ottawa); Toronto: Don Lemieux (Trois Rivieres); Edmonton: Brian Sutter (Lethbridge).

Round 4: Cincinnati: Barry Melrose (Kamloops); New England: Mike Kaszycki (Sault Ste. Marie); Cleveland: Rocky Maze (Edmonton); Indianapolis: Dave Dornseif (Providence College); San Diego: John Smrke (Toronto); Phoenix: Kari Makkonen (Finland); Calgary: Alain Belanger (Sherbrooke); Quebec: Maurice Barrette (Quebec); Winnipeg: Goran Lindblom (Sweden); Houston: Mike Fedorko (Hamilton); Cleveland: Vern Stenlund (London); Edmonton: Yvon Vautour (Laval);

Round 5: New England: Bill Baker (U Minnesota); New England: Mike Liut (Bowling Green State); Cleveland: Bob Miller (U.S. Olympic); Indianapolis: Jean Gagnon (Quebec); San Diego: Archie King (Hamilton); Phoenix: Juhani Wallenius (Finland); Calgary: Bruce Baker (Ottawa); Quebec: Garth MacGuigan (Montreal); Winnipeg: Doug Johnson (Lethbridge); Houston: Larry Skinner (Ottawa); Toronto: Dan Djakalovic (Kitchener); Edmonton: Tim Williams (Victoria).

Round 6: Cincinnati: Joe Oslin (U Vermont); New England: Dwight Schofield (London); Cleveland: Rob Flockhart (Kamloops); Indianapolis: Joe Kowal (Hamilton); San Diego: Rick Hodgson (Calgary); Phoenix: Doug Patey (Sault Ste. Marie); Calgary: Larry Gloeckner (Victoria); Quebec: Claude Periard (Trois Rivieres); Winnipeg: Fred Berry (New Westminster); Houston: Kevin Schamehorn (New Westminster); Toronto: Mike McEwen (Toronto); Edmonton: Gord Blumenschein (Winnipeg).

Round 7: Cincinnati: Paul Skidmore (Boston College); New England: Warren Young (Michigan Tech); Cleveland: Mark Earp (Kamloops); Indianapolis: Greg Malone (Oshawa); San Diego: Rob Tudor (Regina); Phoenix: Mark Davidson (Flin Flon); Calgary: Phil Verchota (U Minnesota); Quebec: Dennis Charbonneau (Laval); Winnipeg: Greg Craig (St. Catherines); Houston: Mike Hordy (Sault Ste. Marie); Toronto: Mike Kitchen (Toronto); Edmonton: John Tavella (Sault Ste. Marie).

Round 8: Cincinnati: Stu Ostlund (Michigan Tech); New England: Ken Morrow (Bowling Green State); Cleveland: Ron Zanussi (London); Indianapolis: Jim Kirkpatrick (Toronto); San Diego: Claude Legris (Sorel); Phoenix: Jari Takio (Finland); Calgary: Don Jackson (U Notre Dame); Winnipeg: Brian Granfield (Brandon); Houston: Larry Riggin (London); Toronto: Marc Desforges (Chicoutimi); Edmonton: Allan Dumba (Regina).

Round 9: Cincinnati: Fernand LeBlanc (Sherbrooke); New England: Ed Clarey (Cornwall); Cleveland: Charlie Skjodt (Windsor); Indianapolis: Ric Garcia (Hull); San Diego: Don Moores (Kamloops); Phoenix: Jouni Rinne (Finland); Calgary: Rob Palmer (U Michigan); Winnipeg: Anders Hakansson (Sweden); Houston: Bill Wells (Cornwall); Toronto: Brian Dillon (Oshawa); Edmonton: Jim Bedard (Sudbury);

Round 10: Cincinnati: Terry Ballingall (Flin Flon); New England: Jon Hammond (Regina); Cleveland: Larry McRae (Windsor); Indianapolis: Remi Levesque (Quebec); San Diego: Ron Roscoe (Hamilton); Phoenix: Hannu Helander (Finland); Calgary: Cal Sandbeck (Denver U); Quebec: Pierre Brossard (Cornwall); Winnipeg: Jorgen Pettersson (Sweden); Houston: Bob Pazzelli (Denver U).

1976 Intraleague Draft

Toronto: Bill Butters (Houston); Edmonton: Larry Hornung (Winnipeg), Don Borgeson (Calgary); Calgary: Jack Carlson (Edmonton), Michel Deguise (Quebec), Tom Serviss (Quebec); Minnesota: Steve Carlson (New England), Pat Westrum (Calgary), Jeff Carlson (Edmonton); Quebec: Gord Labossiere (Houston), Jerry Zrymiak (Toronto).

1976 Dispersals

All Ottawa players except for the following were declared free agents on January 20, 1976.

Ralph Backstrom and Don Borgeson: sold to New England.
Gary MacGregor and Barry Legge: sold to Cleveland.
Francois Rochon, Darryl Maggs, Mark Lomenda and Bryon Baltimore: sold to Indianapolis.

All players for the Minnesota Fighting Saints, which folded on February 27, 1976, were declared free agents on March 3, 1976.

1977 Amateur Draft
Listed by order of draft picks.

Round 1: Houston: Scott Campbell (London); Calgary: Barry Beck (New Westminster); Winnipeg: Ron Duguay (Sudbury); Edmonton: Mike Crombeen (Kingston); Indianapolis: Doug Wilson (Ottawa); Birmingham: Rod Langway (U New Hampshire); Cincinnati: Jere Gillis (Sherbrooke); Winnipeg: Miles Zaharko (New Westminster); Quebec: Lucien Deblois (Sorel); Houston: Dwight Foster (Kitchener); New England: Ron Areshenkoff (Medicine Hat).

Round 2: Birmingham: Brad Maxwell (New Westminster); Calgary: Tom Gorence (U Minnesota); Quebec: John Anderson (Toronto); New England: Moe Robinson (Kingston); Indianapolis: Wayne Ramsay (Brandon); Calgary: Doug Berry (Denver U); Cincinnati: Dave Morrow (Calgary); New England: Randy Pierce (Sudbury); Quebec: Benoit Gosselin (Trois Rivieres); Houston: Dave Semenko (Brandon);

Round 3: Birmingham: Mark Johnson (U Wisconsin); New England: John Baby (Sudbury); Edmonton: Kim Davis (Flin Flon); Cincinnati: Floyd Lahache (Sherbrooke); Cincinnati: Colin Ahern (Providence College); Winnipeg: Mark Lofthouse (New Westminster); Quebec: Tom Roulston (Winnipeg); Houston: Glen Hanlon (Brandon);

Round 4: Birmingham: Norm Dupont (Montreal); Calgary: Steve Stoyanovich (Rensselaer); Edmonton: Neil Labatte (Toronto); Edmonton: Dan Clark (Kamloops); Indianapolis: Dale McCourt (St. Catherines); Cincinnati: Jeff Allen (Hull); Winnipeg: Red Laurence (Kitchener); Quebec: Robert Picard (Montreal); Houston: Reg Kerr (Kamloops).

Round 5: Birmingham: Steve Baker (Union College); Calgary: Perry Schnarr (Denver U); Edmonton: Rocky Saganiuk (Lethbridge); New England: Brian Hill (Medicine Hat); Indianapolis: Mike Bossy (Laval); Cincinnati: Jim Trainor (Harvard); Winnipeg: Bill Stewart (Niagara Falls); Quebec: Alain Cote (Chicoutimi); Houston: Kevin McCarthy (Winnipeg);

Round 6: Birmingham: Greg Tebbutt (Regina); Calgary: Don Micheletti (U Minnesota); Edmonton: Julian Baretta (U Wisconsin); 51. New England: James Korn (Providence College); Indianapolis: Rick Vasko (Peterborough); Cincinnati: Bill Himmlewright (U North Dakota); Winnipeg: Ric Seiling (St Catherines); Quebec: Yves Guillemette (Shawinigan); Houston: Markus Mattsson (Finland);

Round 7: Birmingham: Bob Suter (U Wisconson); Calgary: Doug Butler (St. Louis U); Edmonton: Steve Hoyda (Portland); Calgary: Steve Letzgus (U Michigan); Indianapolis: Brian Drumm (Oshawa); Cincinnati: Tom Byers (Providence College); Winnipeg: Jim Hamilton (London); Quebec: Eddy Godin (Quebec); Houston: Herald Luckner (Sweden).

Round 8: Birmingham: Curt Christofferson (Colorado College); Calgary: Jack O'Callahan (Boston U); Edmonton: Ray Creasy (New Westminster); Calgary: Bob Gould (U New Hampshire); Cincinnati: Bob Boileau (Boston U); Winnipeg: Warren Holmes (Ottawa); Quebec: Pierre Lagace (Quebec); Houston: Matti Forss (Finland).

Round 9: Birmingham: Jean Savard (Quebec); Calgary: Keith Hendrickson (U Minnesota-Duluth); Edmonton: Guy Lash (Winnipeg); Calgary: Jim Harrar (U Minnesota); Cincinnati: Jim Craig (Boston U); Winnipeg: Mike Keating (St. Catherines); Quebec: Daniel Chicoine (Sherbrooke); Houston: Mike Dwyer (Niagara Falls).

Round 10: Birmingham: Ken Linseman (Kingston); Calgary: Bruce Crowder (New Hampshire); Edmonton: Owen Lloyd (Medicine Hat); Calgary: Mark Miller (U Michigan); Cincinnati: Dave Kelley (Princeton U); Winnipeg: Murray Bannerman (Victoria); Quebec: Roland Cloutier (Trois Rivieres); Houston: Miroslaw Sikora (Poland).

1977 Dispersals

All players for the Minnesota Fighting Saints (folded January 17, 1977), were declared free agents, except for the following:

Butch Deadmarsh, John Arbour and Danny Gruen: sold to Calgary
Mike Antonovich, Bill Butters, Steve Carlson, Jack Carlson, Dave Keon, John McKenzie, Louis Levasseur: sold to Edmonton

The players of the Phoenix Roadrunners (folded April 6, 1977), San Diego Mariners (folded June 1977) and Calgary Cowboys (folded August 1977) were sold to other WHA teams or made free agents upon each team's demise.

1978 Intraleague Draft

Indianapolis: Pierre Jarry (Edmonton), Don McLeod (Edmonton); Cincinnati: Jim Troy (Edmonton), Cap Raeder (New England), Steve Sutherland (Quebec); Edmonton: Matti Hagman (Quebec).

1978 Dispersals

The Houston Aeros folded July 6, 1978, when the contracts of thirteen players were purchased by the Winnipeg Jets. The remaining players of the team were then declared free agents.

Purchased by Winnipeg: John Hughes, Scott Campbell, Al McLeod, Paul Terbenche, Andre Lacroix, Cam Connor, Rich Preston, Terry Ruskowski, Don Larway, Morris Lukowich, John Gray, Steve West, Ernie Wakely.
Declared free agents: Lynn Zimmerman, Poul Popiel, John Schella, Larry Hale, Ted Taylor, Ron Hansis, Larry Lund.

All players for the Indianapolis Racers, which folded December 15, 1978, were declared free agents.

1979 Dispersal

Preceding the NHL expansion draft was a dispersal of players to the four remaining WHA clubs from the newly defunct Cincinnati and Birmingham clubs.

Cincinnati Stingers: Mike Liut, Bryon Baltimore, Bryan Watson, Dave Fortier, Reg Thomas, Dave Forbes, Kelly Davis, Michel Parizeau and Bruce Greig claimed by Edmonton. Byron Shutt claimed by Hartford. Michel Dion, Dave Dornseif, Barry Melrose, Robbie Ftorek, Bill Gilligan and Paul Stewart claimed by Quebec. Barry Legge, Craig Norwich, Peter Marsh and Jamie Hislop claimed by Winnipeg.
Birmingham Bulls: Bob Stephenson, Steve Alley, Tony Cassolato and Paul Henderson claimed by Hartford. Greg Tebbutt, Peter Marrin and John C. Stewart claimed by Quebec.

1979 NHL Reclamation Draft
June 9, 1979

The reclamation draft allowed for the NHL clubs to reclaim those players whose rights they held that were playing in the WHA. Some players were later reselected in the expansion draft, while still others were later selected by the four incoming clubs as priority selections, and thus precluded from returning to their rights-holding NHL clubs.

Atlanta Flames: Kent Nilsson from Winnipeg; **Boston Bruins:** Mark Howe from Hartford; **Buffalo Sabres:** Dave Dryden from Edmonton; **Chicago Blackhawks:** John Garrett from Hartford; Bobby Hull and Terry Ruskowski from Winnipeg; **Colorado Rockies:** Doug Berry from Edmonton; **Detroit Red Wings:** Wes George from Edmonton; George Lyle from Hartford; Glenn Hicks and Barry Long from Winnipeg; **Los Angeles Kings:** Steve Carlson from Edmonton; **Minnesota North Stars:** Ed Mio, Cal Sandbeck, Dave Semenko and Paul Shmyr from Edmonton; Greg Tebbutt from Quebec; **Montreal Canadiens:** Alan Hangsleben from Hartford; Alain Cote and Danny Geoffrion from Quebec; Peter Marsh from Winnipeg; **New York Islanders:** Dave Langevin from Edmonton;

Gary Lariviere from Quebec; Markus Mattsson from Winnipeg; Kelly Davis from Edmonton; **New York Rangers:** Jim Mayer from Edmonton; Warren Miller from Hartford; **Philadelphia Flyers:** Dennis Sobchuk from Edmonton; **Pittsburgh Penguins:** Paul Baxter from Quebec; Kim Clackson and Morris Lukowich from Winnipeg; **St. Louis Blues:** Risto Siltanen from Edmonton; Christian Bordeleau from Quebec; Scott Campbell from Winnipeg; Mike Liut from Edmonton; **Toronto Maple Leafs:** Stan Weir from Edmonton; Jordy Douglas and Rick Ley from Hartford; **Vancouver Canucks:** John Hughes from Edmonton; **Washington Capitals:** Bengt Gustafsson from Edmonton; Paul MacKinnon from Winnipeg.

1979 National Hockey League Expansion Draft
June 13, 1979, Montreal

Selection order: Winnipeg, Edmonton, Hartford, Quebec, Quebec, Hartford, Edmonton, Winnipeg. P: Priority Selection.

Edmonton Oilers
PG1. Dave Dryden; PG2. Ed Mio; P1. Wayne Gretzky; P2. Bengt Gustafsson; G1. Pete LoPresti (Minnesota); G2. Doug Favell (Colorado); 1. Cam Connor (Montreal); 2. Lee Fogolin (Buffalo); 3. Pat Price (NY Islanders); 4. Colin Campbell (Pittsburgh); 5. Larry Brown (Los Angeles); 6. Ron Areshenkoff (Buffalo); 7. Inge Hammarstrom (St Louis); 8. John Gould (Atlanta); 9. Doug Hicks (Chicago); 10. Tom Edur (Pittsburgh); 11. Wayne Bianchin (Pittsburgh); 12. Mike Forbes (Boston); 13. Doug Patey (Washington); 14. Bob Kelly (Chicago).

Hartford Whalers
PG1. John Garrett; P1. Jordy Douglas; P2. Mark Howe; G1. Norm Lapointe (Vancouver); 1. Alan Hangsleben (Montreal); 2. Nick Fotiu (NY Rangers); 3. Rick Ley (Toronto); 4. Al Sims (Boston); 5. Jean Savard (Chicago); 6. Ralph Klassen (Colorado); 7. Rick Hodgson (Atlanta); 8. Kevin Kemp (Toronto); 9. Bill Bennett (Boston); 10. Bernie Johnston (Philadelphia); 11. Brian Hill (Atlanta); 12. Dave Given (Buffalo); 13. M. F. Schurman (Philadelphia); 14. Nick Beverley (Colorado); 15. Don Kozak (Vancouver).

Quebec Nordiques
PG1. Richard Brodeur; P1. Paul Baxter; P2. Garry Lariviere; G1. Ron Low (Detroit); G2. Dave Parro (Boston); 1. Dave Farrish (NY Rangers); 2. Gerry Hart (NY Islanders); 3. Pierre Plante (NY Rangers); 4. Blair Stewart (Washington); 5. John Baby (Minnesota); 6. John Smrke (St Louis); 7. Ken Kuzyk (Minnesota); 8. Roland Cloutier (Detroit); 9. Terry Martin (Buffalo); 10. Jamie Masters (St Louis); 11. Hartland Monahan (Los Angeles); 12. Ron Andruff (Colorado); 13. Alain Cote (Montreal); 14. Lars Zetterstrom (Vancouver).

Winnipeg Jets
PG1. Markus Mattsson; P1. Scott Campbell; P2. Morris Lukowich; G1. Lindsay Middlebrook (NY Rangers); G2. Pierre Hamel (Toronto); 1. Peter Marsh (Montreal); 2. Bobby Hull (Chicago); 3. Al Cameron (Detroit); 4. Dave Hoyda (Philadelphia); 5. Jim Roberts (Minnesota); 6. Lorne Stamler (Toronto); 7. Mark Heaslip (Los Angeles); 8. Gord McTavish (St Louis); 9. Gord Smith (Washington); 10. Clark Hamilton (Detroit); 11. Jim Cunningham (Philadelphia); 12. Dennis Abgrall (Los Angeles); 13. Bill Riley (Washington); 14. Gene Carr (Atlanta); 15. Hilliard Graves (Vancouver).

Player Movement

During the World Hockey Association's first season, a total of 136 players had played previously in the National Hockey League. Below is a listing of the 80 players who played at least one game during the 1971-72 season in the NHL, and who would play at least one game in the WHA during 1972-73. If a player was with two teams during 1971-72, he will be listed under the team for which he played second.

Boston (5): Gerry Cheevers, Ted Green, John McKenzie, Garry Peters, Derek Sanderson.
Buffalo (7): Ron C. Anderson, Terry Ball, Mike Byers, Al Hamilton, Danny Lawson, Jim Watson, Rod Zaine.
California Golden Seals (12): Ken Baird, Wayne Carleton, Norm Ferguson, Frank Hughes, Garry Jarrett, Gary Kurt, Don O'Donoghue, Gerry Pinder, Bobby Sheehan, Paul Shmyr, Tom Webster, Tom Williams.
Chicago Blackhawks (4): Christian Bordeleau, Bryan Campbell, Bobby Hull, Andre Lacroix.
Detroit Red Wings (8): Brian Conacher, Joe Daley, Bob Falkenberg, Danny Johnson, Ab McDonald, Al Smith, Bill Sutherland, Bob Wall.
Los Angeles Kings (4): Doug Barrie, Brian Carlin, Jim Johnson, Bob Woytowich.
Minnesota North Stars (2): Ted Hampson, Gord Labossiere.
Montreal Canadiens (2): Larry Pleau, Jean-Claude Tremblay.
New York Rangers (3): Jim Dorey, Bruce MacGregor, Mike McMahon.
Philadelphia Flyers (7): Jean-Guy Gendron, Larry Hale, Eddie Joyal, Ralph MacSweyn, Don McLeod, Michel Parizeau, Dick Sarrazin.
Pittsburgh Penguins (4): Les Binkley, Wally Boyer, Val Fonteyne, Bill Hicke.
St. Louis Blues (8): John Arbour, Larry Hornung, Gord Kannegiesser, Jim McLeod, Gerry Odrowski, Brit Selby, Gary Veneruzzo, Ernie Wakely.
Toronto Maple Leafs (5): Jim Harrison, Rick Ley, Bernie Parent, Brad Selwood, Guy Trottier.
Vancouver Canucks (9): Wayne Connelly, George Gardner, Murray Hall, Rosaire Paiement, Poul Popiel, John Schella, Fred Speck, Ted Taylor, Ron Ward.

Some of the above were drafted by the two NHL expansion teams, New York Islanders and Atlanta Flames, before defecting to the WHA. They are:

New York Islanders: Bart Crashley, Garry Peters, Larry Hornung, Ted Hampson, John Schella, Ted Taylor, Norm Ferguson.
Atlanta Flames: Larry Hale, Frank Hughes, Rod Zaine.

Another 56 players who played in the World Hockey Association during 1972-73 had played previously in the NHL, but not during 1971-72:

Alberta: Ken Brown, Jack Norris.
Chicago: Larry Cahan, Reg Fleming, Andre Gill, Ed Hatoum, Bob Liddington, Bobby Whitlock.
Cleveland: Paul Andrea, Doug Brindley, Ron Buchanan, Bob Dillabough, Grant Erickson, John Hanna, Joe Hardy, Ted Hodgson, Skip Krake, Wayne Muloin, Jim Wiste.

Houston: Duke Harris, Ed Hoekstra, Dunc McCallum, Brian McDonald, Wayne Rutledge, Brian Smith, Jack Stanfield.
Los Angeles: Bart Crashley, Earl Heiskala, J. P. Leblanc, Ted McCaskill, Jim Niekamp, Bob Perreault, Joe Szura.
Minnesota: George Konik, Jack McCartan, George Morrison, Mel Pearson, Carl Wetzel.
New England: Terry Caffery, Paul Hurley.
New York: Ken Block, Kent Douglas, Jean Gauthier, Bob Jones, Mike Laughton, Brian Perry, Wayne Rivers, Bill Speer.
Ottawa: Bob Charlebois.
Philadelphia: Marcel Paille, Irv Spencer.
Quebec: Alain Caron, Francois Lacombe, Rene Leclerc.
Winnipeg: Norm Beaudin, Garth Rizzuto.

Another 13 players who debuted in the WHA during 1972-73 would later play in the NHL. They are:

Mike Amodeo, Mike Antonovich, Michel Archambault, Yves Bergeron, Richard Brodeur, Gilles Gratton, Bobby Guindon, Dave Hutchison, Bob MacMillan, Ron Plumb, Tim Sheehy, Claude St. Sauveur, Joe Zanussi.

By the 1978-79 season, with the WHA down to 7 (soon to be 6) teams, most players in the WHA had, or would have, NHL experience. Sorted by team are the counts of players who had or would have NHL experience, with players who never played in the NHL in parentheses:

Birmingham: 22 of 26 players had, or would have, NHL experience. (Gavin Kirk, Peter Marrin, Jim Turkiewicz, Wayne Wood)
Cincinnati: 25 of 29 players had, or would have, NHL experience. (Kelly Davis, Dave Dornseif, Bill Gilligan, Byron Shutt)
Edmonton: 26 of 31 players had, or would have, NHL experience. (Wes George, Pierre Guite, Cal Sandbeck, Rudy Tajcnar, Ed Walsh)
Indianapolis (not including players who finished the season on another WHA team): 8 of 16 players had, or would have, NHL experience. (Don Burgess, Glen Irwin, Don Larway, Gerry Leroux, Gary MacGregor, Dave Morrow, Kevin Nugent, Jerry Rollins)
New England: 23 of 25 players had, or would have, NHL experience. (Dave Inkpen, Pierre Roy)
Quebec: 26 of 27 players had, or would have, NHL experience. (Pierre Lagace)
Winnipeg: 24 of 29 players had, or would have, NHL experience. (Bill Davis, Rich Gosselin, John Gray, Steve West, Dale Yakiwchuk)

For the touring European teams, three players had, or would have, NHL experience: Jiri Crha of the Czechoslovakian team, and Matti Hagman and Jari Kurri of Finland.

A total of 452 players had both NHL and WHA experience.

Significant Games of the World Hockey Association

The following pages highlight a selection of significant games played in the World Hockey Association. The first games for each team are included, along with each team's first win, including relocated franchises. Other feats, such as any player scoring five goals, any team with 12 goals, and other notable individual or team efforts are included here as well.

October 11, 1972
Anderson and Hicke Lead Oilers Win in Inaugural Game

OTTAWA: Two goals by Ron C. Anderson and Bill Hicke paced the Alberta Oilers to a 7-4 victory over the host Ottawa Nationals in the first regular-season game ever played by the new World Hockey Association. Bob Charlebois scored two goals to lead the Nats in front of 5,006 fans at the Ottawa Civic Centre.

Oilers 7, Nationals 4

Alberta	3	3	1 -	7
Ottawa	1	1	2 -	4

1st period: 1. Alb: Anderson 1 (Harrison, Carlyle) 6:19. 2. Ott: Charlebois 1 (Meloff) 11:06. 3. Alb: Hicke 1 (penalty shot) 16:37. 4. Alb: Hicke 2 (Fisher, Fonteyne) 16:52.
2nd period: 5. Alb: Harrison 1 (McAneeley) 7:50. 6. Alb: Walters 1 (Hamilton, Fonteyne) 9:17. 7. Ott: Trottier 1 10:37. 8. Alb: Anderson 2 (Harrison, McAneeley) 17:16.
3rd period: 9. Ott: Carleton 1 (Climie) 2:02. 10. Alb: Joyal 1 (Hamilton, Wall) 2:43. 11. Ott: Charlebois 2 (Boland, Leduc) 13:12.
Shots on goal:

Alb on Binkley	14	8	9 -	31
Ott on Brown	8	12	12 -	32

October 11, 1972
Gerry Cheevers Turns in Shutout as Cleveland Defeats Quebec

CLEVELAND: Gerry Cheevers stopped 21 shots to lead the Cleveland Crusaders over the Quebec Nordiques on the opening night of the WHA. Bob Dillabough and Ron Buchanan scored the Cleveland goals, while Paul Shmyr assisted on both goals. Quebec goaltender Serge Aubry turned in a fine performance in a losing cause, stopping 32 of 34 shots put his way.

Crusaders 2, Nordiques 0

Quebec	0	0	0 -	0
Cleveland	0	1	1 -	2

1st period: No scoring.
2nd period: 1. Cle: Dillabough 1 (Erickson, Shmyr) 10:30.
3rd period: 2. Cle: Buchanan 1 (Shmyr) 14:01.
Shots on goal:

Que on Cheevers	6	9	6 -	21
Cle on Aubry	13	9	12 -	34

October 12, 1972
Hughes' Late Goal Lifts Aeros Over Cougars

HOUSTON: A late goal by Frank Hughes gave the Houston Aeros a 3-2 decision over the Chicago Cougars in the inaugural game for both teams. Larry Lund scored a goal and assisted on Hughes' tally to lead the Aeros. Reg Fleming and Jan Popiel led the Chicago offense.

Aeros 3, Cougars 2

Chicago	0	1	1 -	2
Houston	1	0	2 -	3

1st period: 1. Hou: Lund 1 (P. Popiel) 1:52.
2nd period: 2. Chi: Fleming 1 15:55.
3rd period: 3. Chi: J. Popiel 1 (Lodboa) 12:26. 4. Hou: Taylor 1 (Schella) 17:19. 5. Hou: Hughes 1 (Lund) 18:24.
Shots on goal

Chi on D. McLeod	8	12	10 -	30
Hou on J. McLeod	10	8	9 -	27

October 12, 1972
Christian Bordeleau Scores Four Goals in Jets Victory

NEW YORK: Christian Bordeleau netted four goals to lead the Jets to a 6-4 victory over the Raiders in front of 6,000 fans at New York's Madison Square Garden. Ron Ward, Bobby Sheehan and Ken Block each had three points for the New York attack.

Jets 6, Raiders 4

Winnipeg	3	1	2 -	6
New York	1	2	1 -	4

1st period: 1. Wpg: McDonald 1 (Gratton, Zanussi) 8:14. 2. Wpg: Bordeleau 1 (Sutherland, Ash) 13:20. 3. Wpg: Bordeleau 2 (Beaudin) 16:55. 4. NY: Ward 1 (Block, Bradley) 17:20.
2nd period: 5. Wpg: Asmundson 1 (Bordeleau) 14:34. 6. NY: Sheehan 1 (Ward, Block) 16:44. 7. NY: Ward 2 (Sheehan, Reichmuth) 19:51.
3rd period: 8. Wpg: Bordeleau 3 (Sutherland, Beaudin) 4:30. 9. NY: Sheehan 2 (Ferguson, Block) 14:23. 10. Wpg: Bordeleau 4 19:59.
Shots on goal

Wpg on Kurt	14	11	8 -	33
NY on Wakely	12	11	7 -	30

October 12, 1972
Larry Pleau Secures Whalers' First Win With Late Goal

BOSTON: Larry Pleau's late goal broke a 3-3 deadlock and gave the New England Whalers a win over the visiting Philadelphia Blazers in the debut game for both teams. Dick Sarrazin and John Cunniff paced the Whaler attack with two points apiece, while Derek Sanderson had two points for the Blazers.

Whalers 4, Blazers 3

Philadelphia	2	0	1 -	3
New England	1	2	1 -	4

1st period: 1. Phi: Sanderson 1 (O'Donoghue, Cardiff) 6:52. 2. Phi: Plumb 1 (Sanderson, Lacroix) 12:24. 3. NE: Williams 1 (Earl, Cunniff) 13:42.
2nd period: 4. NE: Sarrazin 1 1:29. 5. NE: Cunniff 1 (Green) 8:45.
3rd period: 6. Phi: Migneault 1 (Rouleau) 11:04. NE: Pleau 1 (Webster, Sarrazin) 17:49.
Shots on goal

Phi on Smith	12	7	10 -	29
NE on Parent	6	8	9 -	23

October 13, 1972
Fighting Saints Lose Debut on Asmundson's Late Goal

ST. PAUL: The Minnesota Fighting Saints debuted tonight, hosting the Winnipeg Jets. A late goal by Duke Asmundson spoiled the Saints' hopes for victory, giving Winnipeg its second win in as many nights. Mike McMahon had two points for Minnesota.

Jets 4, Fighting Saints 3

Winnipeg	1	1	2 -	4
Minnesota	2	1	0 -	3

1st period: 1. Wpg: Bordeleau 5 (Beaudin) 5:54. 2. Min: Connelly 1 (Pearson, Arbour) 10:00. 3. Min: Speck 1 (McMahon) 16:23.
2nd period: 4. Wpg: Johnson 1 (McDonald, Gratton) 10:05. 5. Min: McMahon 1 (Morrison, Klatt) 18:31.
3rd period: 6. Wpg: McDonald 2 (Johnson, Cuddie) 7:31. 7. Wpg: Asmundson 2 (Hornung, Bordeleau) 18:31.
Shots on goal

Wpg on Curran	8	6	13 -	27
Min on Daley	14	9	8 -	31

October 13, 1972
Sharks Drop Opener; Hale and Hall Lead Houston Edge

LOS ANGELES: Houston's Larry Hale and Murray Hall had 2 points apiece to lead the Aeros past the Los Angeles Sharks at the Los Angeles Sports Arena. Steve Sutherland scored a goal and assisted on the other Shark tally. A crowd of 10,830 was on hand to cheer the Sharks in their debut.

Aeros 3, Sharks 2

Houston	0	2	1	- 3
Los Angeles	0	1	1	- 2

1st period: No scoring.
2nd period: 1. LA: Sutherland 1 (Byers, Leblanc) 2:33. 2. Hou: Hall 1 (Labossiere, Schella) 14:40. 3. Hou: Lund 2 (Hale, Popiel) 15:59.
3rd period: 4. Hou: McCallum 1 (Hale, Hall) 5:44. 5. LA: Young 1 (Sutherland, Jones) 18:12.
Shots on goal

Hou on Gardner	11	7	9	- 27
LA on Rutledge	13	10	7	- 30

October 13, 1972
Serge Aubry and Yves Bergeron Star as Nordiques Win First

QUEBEC: Yves Bergeron had one goal and three assists, and Serge Aubry stopped all 28 shots he faced in leading the Quebec Nordiques to their first win in front of a sell-out home crowd at Le Colisee. Renald Leclerc scored twice, while Mike Harvey and Paul Larose each had two assists. The win would be the only one as a head coach for the legendary Maurice Richard, who resigned immediately after the game.

Nordiques 6, Oilers 0

Alberta	0	0	0	- 0
Quebec	3	1	2	- 6

1st period: 1. Que: Lacombe 1 (Harvey, Larose) 3:51; 2. Que: Bergeron 1 (Guite) 9:20; 3. Que: Leclerc 1 (Bergeron)
2nd period: 4. Que: Gendron 1 (Larose, Harvey) 13:08
3rd period: 5. Que: Leclerc 2 (Bergeron, Selby) 4:02; 6. Que: Tremblay 1 (Bergeron, Parizeau) 12:21
Shots on goal:

Alb on Aubry	6	16	6	- 28
Que on Norris	15	8	12	- 35

October 14, 1972
Mike Laughton and Bobby Sheehan Lead Raiders to First Win

NEW YORK: Two goals each by Mike Laughton and Bobby Sheehan paced the Raiders to an 8-goal outburst and their first win as a franchise. Ottawa made a game of it with four third-period goals, but could not overcome an early 6-1 New York lead. Mike Boland had three assists for the Nationals, who were still winless after two games in the World Hockey Association.

Raiders 8, Nationals 6

Ottawa	1	1	4	- 6
New York	4	2	2	- 8

1st period: 1. Ott: Kirk 1 (King) 3:02; 2. NY: Sheehan 3 (Ward, Ferguson) 8:24; 3. NY: Perry 1 (Block, Ferguson) 11:54; 4. NY: Ward 3 (Douglas) 12:49; 5. NY: Sheehan 4 (Perry) 14:36

2nd period: 6. NY: Bradley 1 4:23; 7. NY: Laughton 1 (White, Peacosh) 7:52; 8. Ott: Leduc 1 (Charlebois, Boland) 15:50
3rd period: 9. Ott: Warr 1 8:05; 10. NY: Laughton 2 (Rivers, Willis) 8:38; 11. Ott: Carleton 2 (Climie, Boland) 10:12; 12. NY: Morenz 1 13:14; 13. Ott: Sentes 1 (Kirk, Martin) 17:05; 14. Ott: Climie (Boland, Stephanson) 17:49
Shots on goal

Ott on Kurt	8	14	11	- 33
NY on Binkley, Gratton	14	8	8	- 30

October 15, 1972
J. P. Leblanc's Two Goals Lead Sharks to Victory

HOUSTON: The Sharks and Aeros traded wins in a home-and-home series, with the Sharks prevailing tonight at the Sam Houston Coliseum behind J. P. Leblanc's two first-period goals. Earl Heiskala and Bart Crashley had two assists to help the Sharks gain their first victory ever.

Sharks 5, Aeros 1

Los Angeles	3	1	1	- 5
Houston	1	0	0	- 1

1st period: 1. LA: Leblanc 1 (Niekamp) 9:55; 2. Hou: Harris 1 (Hoekstra, Larose) 10:29; 3. LA: Leblanc 2 (Myers, Crashley) 10:59; 4. LA: Sutherland 2 (Odrowski, Crashley) 18:59
2nd period: LA: Heiskala 1 (Veneruzzo) 7:24
3rd period: LA: Szura 1 14:22
Shots on goal

LA on McLeod	8	12	11	- 31
Hou on Gillow	12	10	8	- 30

October 15, 1972
Mike Antonovich's First Goal Propels Fighting Saints to First Win

ST. PAUL: Former University of Minnesota standout Mike Antonovich scored his first career goal at 12:22 of the third period to break a 2-2 tie, lifting Minnesota to its first franchise win. Mel Pearson and Bill Klatt also scored for Minnesota, while Bob Sicinski and Bob Whitlock scored for winless Chicago.

Fighting Saints 3, Cougars 2

Chicago	1	1	0	- 2
Minnesota	2	0	1	- 3

1st period: 1. Min: Pearson 1 (Connelly) 4:31; 2. Chi: Sicinski 1 (Proceviat, Popiel) 7:48; 3. Min: Klatt 1 (Arbour, Morrison) 8:40
2nd period: 4. Chi: Whitlock 1 (Fleming) 8:02
3rd period: 5, Min: Antonovich 1 (MacMillan, Lilyholm) 12:22.
Shots on goal

Chi on McCartan	9	9	14	- 32
Min on Gill	16	10	13	- 39

October 19, 1972
Ottawa Breaks Skid, Wins First Behind Climie's Three Points

OTTAWA: The Nationals broke into the win column for the first time ever after three losses with a convincing 6-2 win over Chicago. Ron Climie scored twice and assisted on another in leading the National attack. He was supported by Wayne Carleton and Bob Charlebois, who had 2 points each. Alas, just 850 people were in attendance at the Ottawa Civic Centre to witness the historic win.

Nationals 6, Cougars 2

Chicago	0	1	1	- 2
Ottawa	2	1	3	- 6

1st period: 1. Ott: Donnelly 1 (Charlebois) 11:32; 2. Ott: Trottier 3 (Charlebois, Leduc) 16:05
2nd period: 3. Ott: Martin 2 (King, Gibson) 4:28; 4. Chi: Proceviat 1 (Fleming) 7:22
3rd period: 5. Chi: Paiement 1 (Zaine) 2:47; 6. Ott: Climie 3 (Martin, Carleton) 6:18; 7. Ott: Carleton 5 (Climie, Boland) 7:59; 8. Ott: Climie 4 (Gibbons) 19:04
Shots on goal

Chi on Gratton	12	12	9	- 33
Ott on Gill, McLeod	8	10	14	- 32

October 22, 1972
Blanchette's Game Winner Gives Cougars First Win

LOS ANGELES: Bernie Blanchette scored 27 seconds into the third period, and it proved to be the deciding goal that gave the new Cougars their first win after four losses. Reggie Fleming had two assists, while Dick Proceviat scored an empty-net goal to seal the win.

Cougars 4, Sharks 2

Chicago	1	1	2	- 4
Los Angeles	0	1	1	- 2

1st period: 1. Chi: Whitlock 2 (Fleming) 15:45
2nd period: 2. Chi: Popiel 2 (Knibbs) 13:06; 3. LA: Mavety 1 (Leblanc, Odrowski) 19:26
3rd period: 4. Chi: Blanchette 1 (Fleming, Whitlock) 0:27; 5. LA: Crashley 2 (Sutherland) 16:16; 6. Chi: Proceviat 2 (empty net) 19:50
Shots on goal

Chi on Gillow	8	5	6	19
LA on J. McLeod	7	17	4	- 28

October 27, 1972
Blazers Come From Behind to Garner First-Ever Win

PHILADELPHIA: Two third-period goals helped the Philadelphia Blazers overcome visiting Los Angeles, holding on to gain their first-ever win. Andre Lacroix had two goals for the victors, and John Bennett assisted on

both late tallies. Bart Crashley had two goals and J. P. Leblanc three assists for the Sharks.

Blazers 5, Sharks 4

Los Angeles	3	1	0	-	4
Philadelphia	1	2	2	-	5

1st period: 1. Phi: Lacroix 3 (Campeau, Lawson) 6:07; 2. LA: Crashley 4 (Leblanc, McCaskill) 7:57; 3. LA: Crashley 5 (Leblanc, Heiskala) 9:42; 4. LA: Veneruzzo (Leblanc) 18:06
2nd period: 5. Phi: Cardiff 1 11:13; 6. Phi: Lawson 2 (O'Donoghue, Campbell) 12:52; 7. LA: Young 3 (Macsweyn, Serviss) 16:00
3rd period: 8. Phi: Paiement 1 (Bennett, O'Donoghue) 2:24; 9. Phi: Lacroix 4 (Bennett) 4:32.
Shots on goal

LA on Archambault	10	10	13	-	33
Phi on Gillow	9	10	11	-	30

November 8, 1972
Bobby Hull Makes His Debut in Jets Loss to Quebec

QUEBEC: Cleared by the courts earlier in the day to play, Bobby Hull took to the ice for the first time as his Jets invaded Le Colisee for a tilt against the Nordiques. Despite 18 shots on goal, Hull was held goalless and managed just a late assist as his Jets fell to Quebec, 3-2.

Nordiques 3, Jets 2

Winnipeg	1	0	1	-	2
Quebec	2	1	0	-	3

1st period: 1. Que: Roy 1 (Gaudette) 0:21. 2. Wpg: Rousseau 2 (Hornung) 9:03. 3. Que: Payette 4 (Harvey, Guindon) 11:28.
2nd period: 4. Que: Bergeron 3 (Tremblay, Payette) 9:57.
3rd period: 5. Wpg: Johnson 5 (Hull, McDonald) 19:55.
Shots on goal

Wpg on Aubry	16	11	17	-	44
Que on Wakely	14	8	4	-	26

November 12, 1972
Bobby Hull Scores First Two Goals in Win Over Sharks

WINNIPEG: Still getting his hockey legs under him, Bobby Hull notched his first two WHA goals, opening the scoring against Los Angeles, then cinching the victory with a late goal in the third period. Hull also had an assist on Ab McDonald's game-winning goal early in the final period.

Jets 5, Sharks 2

Los Angeles	1	0	1	-	2
Winnipeg	1	1	3	-	5

1st period: 1. Wpg: Hull 1 (Hornung) 3:18; 2. LA: MacNeil 2 (Serviss, Slater) 15:33.
2nd period: 3. Wpg: Johnson 6 (Cuddie, Ash) 13:13.

3rd period: 4. LA: Veneruzzo 8 0:41; Wpg: McDonald 5 (Hull, Hornung) 4:45; 6. Wpg: Bordeleau 11 (Cuddie, McDonald) 6:59; 7. Wpg: Hull 2 (Beaudin, Bordeleau) 16:50
Shots on goal

LA on Wakely	14	7	8	-	29
Wpg on Gardner	9	13	10	-	32

January 4, 1973
Ron Ward Tallies Five Goals as Raiders Down Nats

NEW YORK: The New York Raiders, having endured two straight shutout losses, broke out their scoring funk in a big way, as Ron Ward set the WHA record for goals in a game with five. Ward also had an assist for a six-point evening, while teammates Wayne Rivers (five assists) and Brian Bradley (two goals, three assists) had five points apiece.

Raiders 9, Nationals 4

Ottawa	0	3	1	-	4
New York	2	4	3	-	9

1st period: 1. NY: Ward 29 (Rivers, Bradley) 18:41. 2. NY: Ward 30 (Rivers, Speer) 19:16.
2nd period: 3. NY: Bradley 9 (Rivers). 4. Ott: Gibson 9 (King, Stephanson) 10:20. 5. Ott: Cunningham 3 11:17. 6. NY: Ward 31 (Winograd, Bradley) 13:46. 7. Ott: Cunningham 4 (Conacher) 16:59. 8. NY: Ward 32 (Bradley, Rivers) 19:01. 9. NY: Bradley 10 (Ward, Willis) 19:45.
3rd period: 10. NY: Kennedy 3 (Block, Jones). 11. NY: Ward 33 (Block, Rivers) 4:34. 12. Ott: Trottier 15 (Boland, Carleton) 17:19. 13. NY: Ferguson 20 (Laughton, Peacosh) 17:42.
Shots on goal

Ott on Kurt	9	11	8	-	28
NY on Gratton	6	17	17	-	40

January 30, 1973
Jim Harrison Accounts for Ten Points in Oilers Romp

EDMONTON: Jim Harrison single-handedly destroyed the New York Raiders by scoring three goals and assisting on seven others for an amazing ten-point evening, leading Alberta to an 11-3 win over New York. Teammate Doug Barrie established a personal best with five points on a goal and four assists.

Oilers 11, Raiders 3

New York	2	0	1	-	3
Alberta	3	2	6	-	11

1st period: 1. Alb: Harrison 19 (Carlin, Patenaude) 4:48. 2. Alb: Fonteyne 7 (Hamilton, Harrison) 5:40. 3. NY: Peacosh 23 (Sheehan, Ward) 7:47. 4. Alb: Hamilton 6 (Harrison, Wall) 11:05. 5. NY: Kennedy 4 (Perry, Willis) 12:43.
2nd period: 6. Alb: Wall 7 (Hicke, Harrison) 13:25. 7. Alb: Harrison 20 (Barrie, Fonteyne) 15:38.
3rd period: 8. Alb: Carlyle 3 (Harrison, Barrie) 5:06. 9. Alb: Blanchette 5

(Harrison, Barrie) 7:43. 10. Alb: Patenaude 16 (Baird) 10:48. 11. Alb: Barrie 6 (Fonteyne, Harrison) 11:40. 12. Alb: Carlyle 4 (Harrison, Barrie) 12:00. 13: Alb: Harrison 21 (Blanchette, Wall) 12:33. 14. NY: Laughton 16 (Kennedy) 17:49.
Shots on goal

NY on Norris	10	6	4	-	20
Alb on Wilkie & Kurt	11	18	23	-	52

February 11, 1973
Oilers Score Six Goals in Last Ten Minutes, Stun Saints

EDMONTON: The Fighting Saints had a 5-1 lead with less than 8 minutes to play. Then the Oilers woke up and blitzed Saints' goaltender Jack McCartan with five goals in just over six minutes, and six overall in the final frame, to gain the surprising victory. Eddie Joyal scored twice during the barrage.

Oilers 7, Fighting Saints 5

Minnesota	2	3	0	-	5
Alberta	0	1	6	-	7

1st period: 1. Min: Connelly 28 (Antonovich) 3:58; 2. Min: Klatt 22 (Christiansen, Ball) 10:44.
2nd period: 3. Min: Young 16 (Antonovich, Connelly) 3:01; 4. Min: Antonovich 18 (Young, McMahon) 6:34; 5. Min: Morrison 13 (Arbour) 15:42; 6. Alb: Baird 6 (Perkins, Wall) 16:51.
3rd period: 7. Alb: Joyal 13 (Harrison, Barrie) 11:44; 8. Alb: Barrie 8 (Perkins, Walters) 12:42; 9. Alb: Perkins 17 (Hamilton, Hicke) 13:24; 10. Alb: Joyal 14 (Wall, Walters) 16:22; 11. Alb: Harrison 27 (McAneeley, Anderson) 17:36; 12. Alb: Hamilton 8 (Harrison, Anderson) 19:42.
Shots on goal

Min on Norris, Brown	15	11	6	-	32
Alb on McCartan	4	22	17	-	43

October 10, 1973
Vancouver Wins First Behind Jim Adair's Overtime Tally

VANCOUVER: Jimmy Adair scored twice and had an assist in front of over 12,000 curious spectators at Vancouver's Pacific Coliseum, witnessing the first-ever win for the new Vancouver entrant in the WHA. Adair's second goal came in overtime to secure the win. Danny Lawson and Dave Hutchison had two points apiece for the Blazers.

Blazers 4, Jets 3 (OT)

Winnipeg	1	1	1	0	-	3
Vancouver	2	0	1	1	-	4

1st period: 1. Wpg: Gratton 1 (Asmundson) 4:18; 2. Van: Adair 1 (Ward, McKenzie) 12:43; 3. Van: Lawson 1 (Adair, Hutchison) 18:05
2nd period: 4. Wpg: McDonald 1 (Hornung, Johnson) 5:13
3rd period: 5. Van: St. Sauveur 1 (Lawson, Hutchison) 4:45; 6. Wpg: Beaudin 1 (Bordeleau) 7:14

494

Shots on goal
Wpg on Archambault 13 13 12 1 - 39
Van on Wakely   9 14 12 5 - 40

October 13, 1973
Gordie Howe Debuts with Three Assists in Win

LOS ANGELES: Gordie Howe came out of retirement and assisted on three of the four Houston goals as the Aeros defeated the Sharks in Los Angeles in front of 10,000 fans at the Sports Arena. The Sharks had taken a 3-2 lead just eight seconds into the third period on a score by Gary Veneruzzo, but the Aeros scored twice, with Howe assisting on Gord Labossiere's late game-winning goal to secure the win.

Aeros 4, Sharks 3
Houston   0 2 2 - 4
Los Angeles 0 2 1 - 3
1st period: No Scoring.
2nd period: 1. Hou: Hinse 1 (Popiel, G. Howe) 2:55. 2. LA: Gordon 1 (Thomas, Odrowski) 13:26. 3. Hou: Hughes 1 (Hinse, G. Howe) 15:57. 4. LA: Speck 1 (Tardif) 16:35.
3rd period: 5. LA: Veneruzzo 1 0:08. 6. Hou: Hughes 2 (Lund, Hinse) 9:29. 7. Hou: Labossiere 1 (G. Howe) 17:34.
Shots on goal
Hou on Gillow   12 6 6 - 24
LA on Rutledge   8 7 9 - 24

October 16, 1973
Binkley and Gratton Team to Shutout Sharks, Secure First Win for Toros

LOS ANGELES: Tom Simpson, Dick Sentes and Jack Gibson scored goals, while Les Binkley and Gilles Gratton turned aside 27 shots as Toros won their first-ever game. Binkley stopped 9 shots he faced before being struck in the head by an errant stick of his own teammate, Rick Cunningham. Gratton was called on to complete the game. The third period was "highlighted" by a bench-clearing brawl at 18:19 as players already in the penalty box attempted to climb over the barriers to continue the melee.

Toros 3, Sharks 0
Toronto   2 1 0 - 3
Los Angeles 0 0 0 - 0
1st period: 1. Tor: Simpson 3 (Gibson) 7:35. 2. Tor: Sentes 2 (Trottier, Cuddie) 12:23.
2nd period: 3. Tor: Gibson 2 (King, Gibbons) 9:32
3rd period: No scoring
Shots on goal
Tor on Gillow   13 7 3 - 23
LA on Binkley, Gratton 3 15 9 - 27

November 3, 1973
Gordie Howe Scores First WHA Goal, Aeros Defeat Sharks

HOUSTON: Gordie Howe's 787th regular season major-league goal was his first as a member of the WHA. His goal came early in the second period, assisted by Larry Lund and Gord Labossiere. Frank Hughes scored a hat trick as the Aeros built a 6-1 lead before the Sharks made a game of it with three late third-period goals.

Aeros 6, Sharks 4
Los Angeles 0 1 3 - 4
Houston   2 2 2 - 6
1st period: 1. Hou: Hughes 10 (G. Howe, Hinse) 3:34; 2. Hou: Hall 5 (Taylor, Grierson) 10:14.
2nd period: 3. G. Howe 1 (Lund Labossiere) 2:55; 4. LA: Ward 2 (Gordon, Tardif) 14:49; 5. Hou: Lund 5 (Hinse, Hughes) 16:22.
3rd period: 6. Hou: Hughes 11 6:14; Hou: Hughes 12 (Hinse, Lund) 6:52; LA: McCaskill 2 (Serviss, Niekamp) 10:06; 9. LA: Serviss 2 (McCaskill) 17:04; 10. LA: Gordon 2 (Leblanc, Veneruzzo) 19:37.
Shots on goal
LA on Rutledge   15 8 10 - 33
Hou on Gillow, Hoganson 8 13 13 - 34

November 6, 1973
Ron Climie Scores Five Goals, Oilers Rout Blades

EDMONTON: Ron Climie became the second player to score five goals in a game when he performed the feat against the New York Golden Blades. Four of Climie's goals came in the third period. Jim Harrison assisted on four of Climie's goals, while Jack Norris turned aside 31 shots for the shutout.

Oilers 8, Golden Blades 0
New York   0 0 0 - 0
Edmonton   2 2 4 - 8
1st period: 1. Edm: McDonald 3 (Gilmore, Carlyle) 15:19. 2. Edm: Climie 7 (Harrison, Hamilton) 19:39.
2nd period: 3. Edm: Perkins 3 (Baird) 10:21. 4. Edm: Carlyle 1 (McDonald, Barrie) 13:38.
3rd period: 5. Edm: Climie 8 (Harrison, McKenzie) 3:28. 6. Edm: Climie 9 (McCrimmon, Harrison) 4:01. 7. Edm: Climie 10 (Patenaude, Perkins) 7:10. 8. Edm: Climie 11 (Harrison, McKenzie) 15:29.
Shots on goal
NY on Norris   16 10 5 - 31
Edm on Junkin   9 14 17 - 40

November 25, 1973
Knights Win First Game, Defeating Quebec

CHERRY HILL: The Jersey Knights won their first game since abandoning New York a week earlier. Andre Lacroix and Brian Morenz each had a goal and an assist as the two teams combined to do all their scoring in the third period.

Knights 3, Nordiques 1
Quebec   0 0 1 - 1
Jersey   0 0 3 - 3
1st period: No scoring
2nd period: No scoring
3rd period: 1. Jer: Reichmuth 2 (Peacosh, Morrison) 3:23; 2. Jer: Morenz 3 (Lacroix, Ferguson) 5:26; 3. Que: Bernier 14 (Houle) 6:51; 4. Jer: Lacroix 10 (Morenz, Ferguson) 19:58
Shots on goal
Que on Junkin   5 9 12 - 26
Jer on Deguise   8 12 13 - 33

December 9, 1973
Toros Erupt for 8 Goals in One Period, Destroy Saints

TORONTO: Leading 2-1 going into the final period, the Toros broke open the close game with eight goals in the third period, a league record. Pat Hickey led the attack with three goals in the period, and four in the game. Tom Simpson and Dick Sentes added a pair of goals each.

Toros 10, Fighting Saints 1
Minnesota 0 1 0 - 1
Toronto   1 1 8 - 10
1st period: 1. Tor: Hickey 3 (Trottier) 14:13
2nd period: 2. Min: McMahon 6 (Ball) 11:26; 3. Tor: Simpson 13 (Carleton) 16:15
3rd period: 4. Tor: Hickey 4 (Brewer, Kirk) 1:31; 5. Tor: Hickey 5 (Brewer, Kirk) 4:10; 6. Tor: Dillon 7 (Sentes, Carleton) 5:50; 7. Tor: Sentes 7 (Trottier, Dillon) 8:58; 8. Tor: Sentes 8 (Brewer) 12:10; 9. Tor: Nistico 1 (Carleton) 14:26; 10. Tor: Hickey 6 (Martin) 15:22; 11. Tor: Simpson 14 (Sentes, Kirk) 19:35
Shots on goal
Min on Gratton   12 15 9 - 36
Tor on Garrett   7 14 18 - 39

January 27, 1974
Fighting Saints Set League Mark With 12-Goal Outburst

ST. PAUL: The Fighting Saints set a league record for goals in a single game, thrashing the Winnipeg Jets by a 12-2 score. Wayne Connelly had two goals while George Morrison had two goals and three assists as the Saints outshot the Jets 51-29 for the game.

Fighting Saints 12, Jets 2

Winnipeg	1	0	1	- 2
Minnesota	3	6	3	- 12

1st period: 1. Min: Cardwell 12 (Ball, Antonovich) 5:47; 2. Min: Walton 21 (Johnson) 15:50; 3. Wpg: Zanussi 3 (Snell, Hull) 16:03; 4. Min: Connelly 28 (Christianson, Morrison) 17:17
2nd period: 5. Min: Klatt 10 (Arbour, Gallant) 4:25; 6. Min: Connelly 29 (Morrison, Arbour) 8:08; 7. Min: Morrison 22 (Walton, Hampson) 8:28; 8. Min: Johnson (Walton, Hampson) 10:04; 9. Min: Antonovich 11 (McMahon, Hampson) 11:34; 10. Min: Morrison 23 (Connelly) 17:11
3rd period: 11. Min: Christianson 5 (Morrison, Connelly) 1:25; 12. Min: Walton 22 (Johnson, Hampson) 3:26; 13. Min: Heatley 15 (Cardwell, Antonovich) 7:44; 14. Wpg: Hornung 2 (Bordeleau, Hargreaves) 11:04
Shots on goal

Wpg on Curran	10	10	9	- 29
Min on Daley	14	21	16	- 51

April 3, 1974
George Morrison Pots Hat Trick in 43 Seconds, Saints Blast Blazers

ST. PAUL: George Morrison scored a natural hat trick in 43 seconds in the second period as the Saints beat up on the hapless Blazers, 9-0. Morrison also scored in the third period for a four-goal game.

Fighting Saints 9, Blazers 0

Vancouver	0	0	0	- 0
Minnesota	4	3	2	- 9

Ist period: 1. Min: Smith 10 (Hampson, Ball) 1:56; 2. Min: Walton 56 (Gallant, Johnson) 13:17; 3. Min: Walton 57 (Boyd) 19:09; 4. Min: Antonovich 21 (Klatt, Hampson) 19:53
2nd period: 5. Min: Morrison 37 (MacMillan, Connelly) 15:42; 6. Min: Morrison 38 (MacMillan, Connelly) 15:56; 7. Min: Morrison 39 (MacMillan, Connelly) 16:25
3rd period: 8. Min: Cardwell 23 (Christianson) 7:47; 9. Min: Morrison 40 (Antonovich) 18:57.
Shots on goal:

Van on Curran	12	16	12	- 40
Min on Gardner	18	13	8	- 39

October 16, 1974
Robbie Ftorek's Hat Trick Leads Roadrunners Win

PHOENIX: The Phoenix Roadrunners made their big-league debut with a decisive 8-2 rout of visiting San Diego, who were also making their debut after two seasons in New York and New Jersey. Robbie Ftorek led the Runner attack with a hat trick in his 16th major-league game.

Roadrunners 8, Mariners 2

San Diego	2	0	0	- 2
Phoenix	2	2	4	- 8

1st period: 1. SD: Adduono 1 (Rivers, Peacosh) 1:31. 2. Phx: Boyd 1 (Gorman, Borgeson) 8:30. 3. Phx: Harris 1

(Hughes) 10:50. 4. SD: Ferguson 1 (Morrison, Devine) 17:19.
2nd period: 5. Phx: Ftorek 1 (Young, Harris) 5:28. 6. Phx: McLeod 1 (Cormier, Sobchuk) 13:00.
3rd period: 7. Phx: Cormier 1 (Sobchuk, Stevens) 2:28. 8. Phx: Ftorek 2 (Connor) 8:51. 9. Phx: Ftorek 3 (Connor, Newell) 15:00. 10. Phx: Keogan 1 (Barlow, Hughes) 16:13.
Shots on goal

SD on Kurt	9	10	13	- 32
Phx on Gillow	11	16	8	- 35

October 17, 1974
Racers Fall to Stags in Opener

INDIANAPOLIS: Two late goals by the visiting Michigan Stags sent the Indianapolis Racers to their first loss in their debut game. Michigan was also making its debut after two seasons in Los Angeles. Marc Tardif had two points for the Stags, while Steve Richardson and Bobby Whitlock scored the two Racer goals.

Stags 4, Racers 2

Michigan	2	0	2	- 4
Indianapolis	0	1	1	- 2

1st period: 1. Mich: Johnstone 1 (Leblanc) 0:51. 2. Mich: West 1 (Tardif, Miszuk) 1:23.
2nd period: 3. Ind: Richardson 1 (Robertson, Walters) 1:18.
3rd period: 4. Ind: Whitlock 1 (Wiste, Kennett) 5:31. 5. Mich: Gruen 1 (McDonald, Fontaine) 11:35. 6. Mich: Tardif 1 (Speck) 13:16.
Shots on goal

Mich on Brown	6	11	7	- 24
Ind on Desjardins	13	11	9	- 33

October 19, 1974
Wayne Rivers Scores Twice, San Diego Wins First Game

SAN DIEGO: Wayne Rivers' second goal of the game came with 2 seconds remaining in the second period, and was the tie-breaker as San Diego won going away, defeating Houston 6-2. Rivers also had an assist, while Andre Lacroix and Ray Adduono had a goal and an assist each.

Mariners 6, Aeros 2

Houston	2	0	0	- 2
San Diego	1	2	3	- 6

1st period: 1. SD: Rivers 1 (Peacosh, Adduono) 4:48; 2. Hou: G. Howe 1 (Popiel, Preston) 9:08; 3. Hou: Schella 1 (Labossiere, Taylor).
2nd period: 4. SD: Plumb 1 17:44; 5. SD: Rivers 2 (Lacroix) 19:58
3rd period: 6. SD: Lacroix 1 (Rivers, Block) 0:57; 7. SD. Adduono 2 (Wall, Peacosh) 3:01; 8. SD: Morenz 1 (Bateman) 15:01
Shots on goal

Hou on Junkin	9	10	7	- 26
SD on Grahame	12	12	7	- 31

October 27, 1974
Racers Win First Behind Steve Andrascik's Three Points

INDIANAPOLIS: The Indianapolis Racers won their first game ever, beating visiting Quebec behind Steve Andrascik's goal and two assists. Rich Pumple had a goal and an assist, while goaltender Andy Brown stopped 27 of 30 shots and assisted on Bob Sicinski's second-period goal.

Racers 5, Nordiques 3

Quebec	1	0	2	- 3
Indianapolis	1	3	1	- 5

1st period: 1. Ind: Andrascik (Pumple, Hargreaves) 11:26; 2. Que: Parizeau (Caron, Gilbert) 16:23
2nd period: 3. Ind: Pumple (Andrascik) 2:03; 4. Ind: Robertson (Bredin, Desjardine) 5:43; 5. Ind: Sicinski (Andrascik, Brown) 14:23
3rd period: 6. Ind: Whitlock (Harbaruk, Wiste) 1:25; 7. Que: Guite (Rouleau) 7:45; 8. Que: Gaudette (Bernier) 19:53.
Shots on goal

Que on Brown	8	10	12	- 30
Ind on Brodeur	15	9	10	- 34

January 12, 1975
Jeff Jacques Scores Four Goals in Big League Debut

HOUSTON: Toronto rookie Jeff Jacques made an auspicious debut with a four-goal effort against the Houston Aeros, leading the Toros to a 7-4 victory. Three of his goals came in the third period as Toronto broke the game open with a five-goal outburst. Jacques also had an assist.

Toros 7, Aeros 4

Toronto	2	0	5	- 7
Houston	3	0	1	- 4

1st period: 1. Hou: Hinse 17 (Hughes, Lund) 2:52. 2. Tor: Simpson 30 (Hickey, Cunningham) 9:19. 3. Hou: Sherrit 13 (Popiel) 12:45. 4. Tor: Jacques 1 (Kirk) 18:41. 5. Hou: Hughes 29 (Lund, Schella) 18:58.
2nd period: No scoring.
3rd period: 6. Tor: Jacques 2 (Mahovlich, Cuddie) 5:06. 7. Tor: Jacques 3 (Henderson, Farda) 6:02. 8. Hou: Mark Howe 11 (G. Howe, Popiel) 8:07. 9. Tor: Featherstone 14 (Nedomansky, Mahovlich) 8:49. 10. Tor: Jacques 4 (Nedomansky, Mahovlich) 13:49. 11. Tor: Hickey 18 (Jacques) 18:35.
Shots on goal

Tor on Rutledge	13	9	18	- 40
Hou on Gratton	15	12	14	- 41

January 15, 1975
Andre Hinse Nets Five Goals, Aeros Handle Oilers

HOUSTON: Andre Hinse became the third player in WHA history to score five goals in a contest as he paced Houston to an easy 9-2 romp over visiting Edmonton. Gordie Howe chipped in with a goal and two assists.

Aeros 9, Oilers 2

Edmonton	0	1	1	- 2
Houston	4	1	4	- 9

1st period: 1. Hou: Hinse 18 (Lund, Hughes) 8:28. 2. Hou: Labossiere 10 (Taylor) 10:22. 3. Hou: Hinse 19 15:36. 4. Hou: Larway 12 (Ruskowski, Preston) 19:59.
2nd period: 5. Edm: Barrie 9 (Baird, Sheehan) 7:08. 6. Hou: Hinse 20 (Popiel) 13:23.
3rd period: 7. Hou: G. Howe 17 0:27. 8. Hou: Hinse 21 (G. Howe) 1:17. 9. Hou: Hinse 22 (Lund) 2:29. 10. Edm: McKay 3 (MacDonald, Kennett) 6:44. 11. Hou: Hughes 30 (Mark Howe, G. Howe) 14:20.
Shots on goal

Edm on Grahame	6	10	4	-20
Hou on Brown, Worthy	19	9	14	-42

February 8, 1975
Steve West Collects Four Assists as Blades Win First

BALTIMORE: Steve West assisted on four goals as the new Baltimore Blades won their first game since being formed two weeks earlier to replace the failed Michigan Stags. Bill Evo and Gary Veneruzzo had two goals apiece and Arnie Brown had a goal and an assist for the victorious Blades. Gordie Howe had two assists for Houston, while Poul Popiel had a goal and an assist.

Blades 6, Aeros 4

Houston	0	2	2	- 4
Baltimore	2	2	2	- 6

1st period: 1. Balt: Veneruzzo 18 (West, Brown) 2:24; 2. Balt: Evo 3 (Serviss, Leblanc) 18:38.
2nd period: 3. Hou: Popiel 6 (G. Howe, Schella) 2:25; 4. Balt: White 1 3:14; 5. Balt: Veneruzzo 19 (West, Bredin) 16:14; 6. Hou: Popiel 7 (Taylor, Labossiere) 19:10.
3rd period: 7. Hou: Mark Howe 15 (G. Howe, Hale) 4:12; 8. Balt: Evo 4 (Serviss, West) 6:34; 9. Hou: Larway 17 (Ruskowski) 6:51; 10. Balt: Brown 3 (Legge, West) 12:35.
Shots on goal

Hou on Desjardins	8	14	8	- 30
Balt on Rutledge	6	6	12	- 24

February 14, 1975
Bobby Hull Scores 50th Goal in 50 Games, Tying Rocket Richard's Feat

WINNIPEG: Bobby Hull capped a hat trick by scoring his third goal with 1:33 remaining in the game, his 50th goal in 50 games. The feat matched Maurice Richard's hallowed 50 goals in 50 games accomplishment set in 1944-45.

Jets 5, Aeros 3

Houston	2	1	0	- 3
Winnipeg	1	3	1	- 5

1st period: 1. Wpg: Hull 48 1:42. 2. Hou: Popiel 8 (Schella) 8:56. 3. Hou: Taylor 17 (Irwin, Hall) 16:46.
2nd period: 4. Hou: Mark Howe 18 (G. Howe, Popiel) 1:41. 5. Wpg: Nilsson 17 (Hull, Hedberg) 12:49. 6. Wpg: Ford 9 (Nilsson) 16:05. 7. Wpg: Hull 49 (Nilsson, Ford) 16:47.
3rd period: 8. Wpg: Hull 50 (Nilsson, Ford) 18:27.
Shots on goal

Hou on Larsson	14	10	16	- 40
Wpg on Grahame	9	19	11	- 39

March 1, 1975
Six Roadrunners Score Two Goals Apiece as Phoenix Routs Indianapolis

PHOENIX: Six Roadrunners players scored two goals apiece as the Runners whipped the Racers, 12-2. Robbie Ftorek, Dennis Sobchuk, Jim Boyd, Michel Cormier, John Gray and Bob Mowat all scored twice. Ftorek added four assists for a six-point day, while Dennis Sobchuk had three assists for five points.

Roadrunners 12, Racers 2

Indianapolis	2	0	0	- 2
Phoenix	3	6	3	- 12

1st period: 1. Phx: Sobchuk 23 (Ftorek) 0:56. 2. Phx: Ftorek 16 (Sobchuk, Gray) 1:47. 3. Ind: Fitchner 6 (Johnson, Proceviat) 3:40. 4. Phx: Boyd 17 7:29. 5. Ind: Buchanan 17 (Heatley, Proceviat) 7:46.
2nd period: 6. Phx: Sobchuk 24 (Ftorek, Niekamp) 1:24. 7. Phx: Ftorek 17 (Gray, Niekamp) 6:04. 8. Phx: Cormier 32 (Boyd, Niekamp) 11:25. 9. Phx: Cormier 33 (Boyd, Borgeson) 11:46. 10. Phx: Gray 20 (Sobchuk, Ftorek) 17:37. 11. Phx: Mowat 7 (penalty shot) 19:36.
3rd period: 12. Phx: Gray 21 (Sobchuk, Ftorek) 3:02. 13. Phx: Mowat 8 (Migneault, Keogan) 11:25. 14. Phx: Boyd 18 (Cormier, Stevens) 18:16.
Shots on goal

Ind on Norris	6	10	5	- 21
Phx on Brown	12	17	15	- 44

April 6, 1975
Hull Scores 77th Goal, Sets Major-League Mark

WINNIPEG: Bobby Hull scored his major-league record 77th goal late in the second period. San Diego's Andre Lacroix had three points on a goal and two assists to capture the league scoring title, with Hull coming in second.

Jets 5, Mariners 5

San Diego	1	2	2	0	- 5
Winnipeg	1	2	2	0	- 5

1st period: 1. Wpg: Nilsson 26 (Miller, Hull) 15:16. 2. SD: Howell 4 (Adduono) 15:37.
2nd period: 3. Wpg: Hedberg 53 (Hull, Nilsson) 8:55. 4. SD: Ferguson 36 (Lacroix) 10:56. 5. SD: Sentes 43 (Rivers, Morrison) 12:22. 6. Wpg: Hull 77 (Hedberg) 19:26.
3rd period: 7. Wpg: Hornung 7 10:12. 8. SD: Lacroix 41 (Howell, Sentes) 10:42. 9. Wpg: Ford 12 (Young, Sjoberg) 16:01. 10. SD: Sentes 44 (Lacroix, Rivers) 18:40.
OT: No scoring.
Shots on goal

SD on Larsson	10	9	13	3	- 35
Wpg on Gillow	13	8	8	8	- 37

October 11, 1975
Stingers Win Debut as Serge Aubry Stars in Goal

RICHFIELD: The Cincinnati Stingers made their debut with a 1-0 victory over the host Cleveland Crusaders. Claude Larose scored the game's only goal midway through the second period as Serge Aubry stopped all 38 Cleveland shots, including 24 in the first period alone.

Stingers 1, Crusaders 0

Cincinnati	0	1	0	- 1
Cleveland	0	0	0	- 0

1st period: No scoring.
2nd period: 1. Cin: Larose 1 (Pelyk, D. Sobchuk) 12:45.
3rd period: No scoring.
Shots on goal

Cin on Cheevers	9	12	7	- 28
Cle on Aubry	24	4	10	- 38

October 14, 1975
Derek Haas Scores Twice to Lead Calgary to First Win

CALGARY: The new Cowboys won their first game behind two goals by rookie Derek Haas, who scored in both the first and last minutes of the game. George Morrison, Danny Lawson and Larry Israelson had two points apiece to help lead the attack. Bob Fitchner and Bob Whitlock had two points each for Indianapolis.

497

Cowboys 5, Racers 3

Indianapolis	0	2	1	- 3
Calgary	2	2	1	- 5

1st period: 1. Cgy: Haas 1 (Lawson, Israelson) 0:42; 2. Cgy: Chipperfield 1 (Morrison, Sentes) 15:07
2nd period: 3. Ind: Dubois 1 4:34; 4. Cgy: Morrison 1 (Lacombe, Evans) 7:38; 5. Cgy: Harris 1 17:26; 6. Ind: Whitlock 2 (Fitchner) 19:51
3rd period: 7. Ind: Fitchner 3 (Heatley, Whitlock) 12:12; 8. Cgy: Haas 2 (Lawson, Israelson) 19:07
Shots on goal

Ind on McLeod	6	12	9	- 27
Cgy on Holmquist	10	6	7	- 23

October 17, 1975
Don Borgeson's Hat Trick Gives Spurs First Victory

PHOENIX: Don Borgeson scored a hat trick against his old teammates as the Denver Spurs won their first game, defeating the Roadrunners in Phoenix. Ralph Backstrom assisted on all three of Borgeson's goals, while goaltender Bob Johnson stopped 25 shots and also fought Roadrunners' Cam Connor toward the end of the third period.

Spurs 5, Roadrunners 4

Denver	1	2	2	- 5
Phoenix	1	0	3	- 4

1st period: 1. Phx: Hall 3 (Huston, Rautakallio) 7:25; 2. Den: Borgeson 1 (Backstrom) 13:49
2nd period: 3. Den: MacGregor 1 (Lomenda, Legge) 5:23; 4. Den: Borgeson 2 (Sherrit, Backstrom) 7:57
3rd period: 5. Phx: Mononen 1 5:03; 6. Den: Borgeson 3 (Sherit, Backstrom) 10:03; 7. Den: Bredin 1 (Liddington, Leblanc) 12:53; 8. Phx: Huston 1 (Boyd, Rautakallio) 15:24; 9. Phx: Ftorek 9 (Gray) 17:08
Shots on goal

Den on Norris	6	13	6	- 25
Phx on Johnson	8	7	14	- 29

November 13, 1975
Vaclav Nedomansky Scores Five Goals; Toros and Spurs Set League Scoring Record

DENVER: Vaclav Nedomansky became the fourth player in league history to score five goals in one game as he led the Toros to an 11-8 verdict over Denver. The 19 goals set a league mark for most total goals in one game by two teams. The Spurs also set a league record for most homes games without a win from inception, extending the streak to eight games.

Toros 11, Spurs 8

Toronto	3	3	5	- 11
Denver	2	3	3	- 8

1st period: 1. Den: Arbour 1 (Lomenda, Liddington) 7:08. 2. Tor: Kirk 7 (Mahovlich, Cunningham) 7:53. 3. Tor: Nedomansky 11 (Farda, Turkiewicz) 9:44. 4. Tor: Nedomansky 12 (Jacques, Farda)

13:20. 5. Den: MacGregor 6 (Backstrom, Maggs) 19:48.
2nd period: 6. Den: Legge 1 (Borgeson) 3:19. 7. Tor: Nedomansky 13 (Farda, Jacques) 7:58. 8. Den: Leblanc 1 (Lomenda) 10:50. 9. Tor: Nedomansky 14 15:24. 10. Den: Borgeson 7 (MacGregor, Arbour) 16:53. 11. Tor: Mahovlich 4 (Kirk, Amodeo) 17:44.
3rd period: 12. Tor: Kirk 8 (Amodeo, Cunningham) 1:18. 13. Tor: D'Alvise 3 (Napier) 3:36. 14. Tor: Amodeo 2 (Jacques) 4:36. 15. Den: Mara 3 (Lavender) 6:24. 16. Tor: Mahovlich 5 (Kirk, Napier) 8:39. 17. Tor: Nedomansky 15 (Jacques) 10:12. 18: Den: Sherrit 3 (Maggs, Arbour) 11:08. 19: Den: Bredin 4 (Bignell) 19:14.
Shots on goal

Tor on Johnson, Sanza	9	6	12	- 27
Den on Shaw	14	13	11	- 38

November 27, 1975
Wayne Connelly Scores Five Goals, Leads Saints

ST. PAUL: Wayne Connelly single-handedly defeated the Cincinnati Stingers, accounting for all five of the Saints' goals during the contest. Fran Huck assisted on four of the goals.

Fighting Saints 5, Stingers 3

Cincinnati	1	1	1	- 3
Minnesota	2	2	1	- 5

1st period: 1. Min: Connelly 7 (Huck, Boucha) 6:27. 2. Cin: G. Sobchuk 9 (Dudley, Donnelly) 11:50. 3. Min: Connelly 8 (Huck, Smith) 13:59.
2nd period: 4. Min: Connelly 9 (Huck, Antonovich) 1:38. 5. Cin: D. Sobchuk 6 (Pelyk) 5:26. 6. Min: Connelly 10 (Keon) 13:12.
3rd period: 7. Cin: Larose 14 (Hughes) 2:52. 8. Min: Connelly 11 (Huck, Antonovich) 6:35.
Shots on goal

Cin on Garrett	9	16	15	- 40
Min on Coutu	9	8	8	- 25

November 30, 1975
Ron Ward Nets Five Goals, Crusaders Come From Six Goal Deficit to Win Game

RICHFIELD: The Toronto Toros had built an 8-2 lead with just over a period to play when the Crusaders scored seven consecutive goals to take a 9-8 lead. After tying the game 9-9, Cleveland's John A. Stewart scored with 12 seconds remaining to secure the 10-9 win. Ron Ward scored five goals for the second time in his WHA career and had two assists. Jim Harrison has six assists as Cleveland sent 63 shots on the Toronto goaltenders. Toros coach Bobby Baun was so disgusted he fined his players $500 each.

Crusaders 10, Toros 9

Toronto	4	4	1	- 9
Cleveland	2	2	6	- 10

1st period: 1. Tor: Featherstone 3 (Nedomansky, Turkiewicz) 1:55. 2. Tor: Marrin

8 (Henderson, Simpson) 11:27. 3. Cle: Ward 5 (Pinder, Muloin) 12:17. 4. Tor: Cunningham 2 (Mahovlich, Kirk) 15:01. 5. Cle: Ward 6 (Pinder, Harrison) 15:37. 6. Tor: Simpson 4 (Heaver) 16:25.
2nd period: 7. Tor: Dorey 4 (Marrin, Henderson) 5:18. 8. Tor: Henderson 8 (Heaver) 9:20. 9. Tor: Marrin 7 (Henderson) 13:32. 10. Tor: Mahovlich 12 (Dorey) 15:32. 11. Cle: J. A. Stewart 5 (J. C. Stewart) 18:09. 12. Cle: Ward 7 (Maxwell, Harrison) 19:26.
3rd period: 13. Cle: Edur 2 (Harrison, Ward) 4:25. 14. Cle: Ball 2 (Tamminen, Harrison) 7:54. 15. Cle: Pinder 7 (Harrison, Ward) 8:17. 16. Cle: Ward 8 (Edur, Harrison) 8:38. 17. Cle: Ward 9 (Pinder, Shmyr) 12:12. 18. Tor: Nedomansky 21 (Featherstone, Dorey) 14:37. 19. Cle: J. A. Stewart 6 19:48.
Shots on goal

Tor on Cheevers & Whidden	12	10	7	- 30
Cle on Shaw, Vien	24	23	16	- 63

December 5, 1975
Aeros Score Three Goals in Waning Seconds to Defeat Jets; Grahame and Gordie Get the Boot, Ref Quits Mid-Game

HOUSTON: Gordie Howe scored a second-period goal and later bumped referee Ron Asselstine protesting a penalty call. The contact resulted in Howe earning the first suspension (two games) of his 28-year career. Earlier in the game, goaltender Ron Grahame had to be restrained from Asselstine protesting a goal, earning him a game misconduct. After Howe's contact, Asselstine skated off the ice and "quit", only to return 15 minutes later after pleas from both teams' coaches. Down two goals with less than 90 seconds in the contest, the Aeros blitzed Jet netminder Curt Larsson for three goals, including the game winner by Larry Hale with two seconds remaining.

Aeros 5, Jets 4

Winnipeg	3	0	1	- 4
Houston	1	1	3	- 5

1st period: 1. Wpg: Hull 16 (Hedberg) 0:59; 2. Hou: P. Popiel 4 (Hall, Taylor) 6:41; 3. Wpg: Sjoberg 1 (Miller) 9:56; 4. Wpg: Nilsson (Ford) 12:09
2nd period: 5. Hou: G. Howe 6 (Ruskowski, Larway) 5:17
3rd period: 6. Wpg: Hull 17 (Nilsson) 9:31; 7. Hou: Hall 9 (Taylor, Labossiere) 18:37; 8. Taylor 9 (Hall, Mty Howe) 19:01; 9. Hou: Hale 1 (Lund) 19:58.
Shots on goal

Wpg on Gr'me, R'ge	13	11	6	- 30
Hou on Larsson	6	19	14	- 39

December 10, 1975
Norm Ullman Scores 500th Career Goal, Tim Sheehy Scores Four Goals as Oilers Defeat Quebec

EDMONTON: Tim Sheehy scored twice in the first and second periods, and Norm Ullman scored twice in the third period, his second goal the 500th of his long career. Al Hamilton had 4 assists.

Oilers 7, Nordiques 3

Quebec	0	1	3	- 4
Edmonton	2	2	3	- 7

1st period: 1. Edm: Sheehy 12 (Patenaude, Long) 2:32; 2. Edm: Sheehy 13 (Laing) 9:28.
2nd period: 3. Edm: Sheehy 14 (Hamilton, Rogers) 7:19; 4. Que: Sutherland 9 (Gallant, Serviss) 10:10; 5. Edm: Sheehy 15 (Hamilton, Rogers) 12:44.
3rd period: 6. Que: Houle 19 (S. Bernier, Tardif) 9:25; 7. Que: C. Bordeleau 11 (Cloutier, Tardif) 9:50; 8. Edm: Ullman 9 (Baird, Hamilton) 10:42; 9. Edm: Ullman 10 (Baird, Hamilton) 14:19; 10. Que: Tardif 24 (J. Bernier, Roy) 14:53; 11. Edm: Rogers 8 15:03.

Shots on goal

Que on Dryden	8	10	7	- 25
Edm on Donnelly	15	15	11	- 43

January 31, 1976
A Hat Trick of Hat Tricks: Houle, Cloutier and Mahovlich Each Score Three

QUEBEC: Real Cloutier and Rejean Houle each scored three goals to pace Quebec's win over visiting Toronto. Not to be outdone, Frank Mahovlich scored three times for the Toros. Each of the players scored one goal in each period. Serge Bernier had five assists.

Nordiques 8, Toros 4

Toronto	1	2	1	- 4
Quebec	3	2	3	- 8

1st period: 1. Que: Houle 27 (S. Bernier, Sutherland) 0:53; 2. Tor: Mahovlich 23 (Napier, Syvret) 1:50; 3. Que: Sutherland 16 (S. Bernier, Houle) 9:53; 4. Que: Cloutier 37 (Tardif) 17:45;
2nd period: 5. Que: Cloutier 38 (Parizeau, Tardif) 3:00; 6. Tor: Henderson 16 (Farda, Nedomansky) 16:16; 7. Tor: Mahovlich 24 (Napier) 18:49; 8. Que: Houle 28 (Sutherland, S. Bernier) 19:37;
3rd period: 9. Que: Houle 29 (Tremblay, Cloutier) 3:42; 10. Tor: Mahovlich 25 (Kirk) 6:39; 11. Que: Cloutier 39 (S. Bernier, Tremblay) 11:35; 12. Que: Roy 3 (S. Bernier, Houle) 15:53.

Shots on goal

Tor on Brodeur	12	14	8	- 34
Que on Vien	14	12	14	- 40

March 12, 1976
Three More Hat Tricks: Houle, Cloutier and Lindstrom Each Score Three in Wild Shootout

WINNIPEG: Six weeks after scoring hat tricks in the same game, Rejean Houle and Real Cloutier did it again, leading Quebec to a 10-8 verdict over Winnipeg. The Jets, down 7-1 early in the second period, roared back with five goals and nearly stealing a victory. Willy Lindstrom scored three goals in the Jets' effort.

Nordiques 10, Jets 8

Quebec	6	2	2 - 10
Winnipeg	1	5	2 - 8

1st period: 1. Que: Cloutier 50 (Tardif) 1:05; 2. Que: Constantin 3 (Serviss, Gallant) 3:14; 3. Wpg: Lindstrom 18 (Ketola) 3:44; 4. Que: Houle 35 (S. Bernier) 6:06; 5. Que: Cloutier 51 (Tremblay, S. Bernier) 12:43; 6. Que: Sutherland 19 (Brackenbury, Serviss) 12:59; 7. Que: Tremblay 9 (Cloutier, Bordeleau) 15:21.
2nd period: 8. Que: Tardif 61 (Cloutier) 0:33; 9. Wpg: Lesuk (Lindh) 1:08; 10. Que: Houle 36 (S. Bernier, Bordeleau) 2:07; 11. Wpg: Lindstrom 19 (Sullivan, Hull) 4:43; 12. Wpg: Hedberg 49 (Hull, Ford) 8:05; 13. Wpg: Hedberg 50 (Nilsson, Ketola) 13:46; 14. Wpg: Lindstrom 20 (Green, Sullivan) 13:56.
3rd period: 15. Que: Cloutier 52 (Tardif, Bordeleau) 8:35; 16. Wpg: Sullivan 32 (Ketola, Bergman) 10:06; 17. Wpg: Green 5 (Bergman, Lindstrom) 14:41; 18. Que: Houle 37 (Hampson) 16:25.

Shots on goal

Que on Larsson, Daley	12	14	8 - 34
Wpg on Brodeur	14	12	14 - 40

Exciting 1976 Eastern Division Race Decided at Last Moments

The 1975-76 Eastern Division Race was not decided until the final night of the season when a Cleveland loss guaranteed the two-year old Racers the division championship. The four teams—Indianapolis, New England, Cleveland and Cincinnati—were separated by just 5 points at the close of the season. On March 25, the Whalers, Crusaders and Stingers were tied for the lead with 69 points, with the Racers a point back with 68. Cincinnati faded from the race, leaving the other three teams to fight it out for the top spot. On April 3, New England beat Indianapolis to give the Whalers 73 points, with the Racers holding at 74 points. That same night, Cleveland beat San Diego to match New England with 73 points. The next night, Indianapolis beat New England to eliminate the Whalers from first-place contention. Cleveland remained in the running

with a win over Cincinnati. The Racers and Whalers had no games remaining, while Cleveland had one game to go. A win would vault the Crusaders over the Racers and give Cleveland the divisional flag. In an emotion-filled game, the last regular season game for Cleveland as a franchise, the Crusaders lost 3-2 to San Diego, despite being outshooting the Mariners 59-21 for the game, and 20-1 in the third period.

April 4, 1976
Racers 4, Whalers 2

Indianapolis	2	1	1 - 4
New England	0	2	0 - 2

1st period: 1. Ind: MacDonald 26 (Baltimore) 14:27. 2. Ind: Maggs 9 (McDonald) 16:43.
2nd period: 3. NE: Webster 33 (Ley, Hangsleben) 1:57. 4. Ind: Parizeau 25 (Maggs, Leclerc) 4:03. 5. NE: Fotiu 3 (Selwood, Ley) 14:28.
3rd period: 6. Ind: Harbaruk 23 (Harris, Proceviat) 9:48.

Shots on goal

Ind on Landon	8	15	13 - 36
NE on Park	7	12	10 - 29

April 6, 1976
Mariners 3, Crusaders 2

San Diego	0	2	0	1 - 3
Cleveland	1	0	1	0 - 2

1st period: 1. Cle: Harrison 34 (McKey, R. Legge) 5:44.
2nd period: 2. SD: Lacroix 29 (Morrison, Ferguson) 2:44. 3. SD: Devine 21 (Adduono) 17:43.
3rd period: 4. Cle: Leduc 36 (McKay, Pinder) 7:03.
OT: 5. SD: Adduono 23 (Burgess) 7:49.

Shots on goal

SD on Newton	7	10	1	3 -21
Cle on Wakely	19	16	20	4 - 59

April 11, 1976
Marc Tardif Felled, Cowboys and Nordiques Engage in Ugly Brawl

QUEBEC: The Calgary Cowboys scored six third-period goals to defeat a furious and disheartened Quebec Nordiques squad in the second game of the 1976 quarter-finals. Nordiques' star Marc Tardif was checked and beaten by Calgary's Rick Jodzio at 6:16 of the first period, setting off a thirty-minute brawl that resulted in eleven players ejected. Calgary lost Jodzio (match penalty), Peter Driscoll, Pat Westrum, Warren Miller, and Danny Lawson (all game misconducts). Quebec lost Gord Gallant (match penalty), Bill Prentice, Pierre Roy, Curt Brackenbury, Steve Sutherland and Gary Gresdal (all game misconducts). Tardif was hospitalized with skull fractures and it was feared he would never play again. Quebec was down to three defensemen and could not keep up with the Calgary attack later in the

game. Ron Chipperfield had a goal and four assists for the Cowboys.

Cowboys 8, Nordiques 4

Calgary	2	0	6	- 8
Quebec	2	2	0	- 4

1st period: 1. Que: Tardif (Tremblay, Bernier) 3:43; 2. Cgy: Morrison (Chipperfield) 12:12; 3. Que: Bernier 15:10; 4. Cgy: Tannahill (Evans, Chipperfield) 17:51
2nd period: 5. Que: Fitchner (Bernier, Cloutier) 2:10; 6. Que: Bernier (Hoganson) 10:28
3rd period: 7. Cgy: Morrison (Powis) 3:27; 8. Cgy: Kirk (Tannahill, Chipperfield) 6:56; 9. Cgy: Lukowich (Powis) 9:24; 10. Cgy: Chipperfield (Terbenche, Kirk) 10:16; 11. Cgy: Kirk (Chipperfield, Terbenche) 15:35; 12. Cgy: Powis (Lukowich) 17:31
Shots on goal

Cgy on Brodeur	8	8	13	- 29
Que on McLeod	8	11	9	- 27

October 8, 1976
Bulls Win First in Land of Dixie

BIRMINGHAM: The brand-new Bulls impressed the opening-night audience in Birmingham with a 4-2 verdict over the Houston Aeros. Tom Simpson started the scoring, and the Bulls never trailed in the contest. Simpson had an assist, while Jean-Luc Phaneuf scored and assisted as well. Gordie Howe scored late in the game, adding Birmingham to his long list of goal-scoring locales.

Bulls 4, Aeros 2

Houston	0	1	1	- 2
Birmingham	1	2	1	- 4

1st period: 1. Bir: Simpson 1 (Phaneuf) 7:15
2nd period: 2. Bir: Phaneuf 1 (Simpson) 2:41; 3. Hou: Preston 1 (Mark Howe) 14:48; 4. Bir: Napier 1 (Kirk, Mahovlich) 15:34
3rd period: 5. Bir: Nistico 1 (Lagace) 3:31; 6. Hou: G. Howe 1 10:50
Shots on goal

Hou on Garrett	12	7	8	- 27
Bir on Grahame	6	14	7	- 27

October 26, 1976
Real Cloutier Scores Five Times, Nordiques Pound Roadrunners

QUEBEC: Real Cloutier became the sixth player in WHA history to pot five goals in a single game as he led his Nordiques to an easy 11-3 beating of the Phoenix Roadrunners. Christian Bordeleau assisted on four goals.

Nordiques 11, Roadrunners 3

Phoenix	1	2	0	- 3
Quebec	4	5	2	- 11

1st period: 1. Que: Cloutier 10 (Tardif, C. Bordeleau) 1:08. 2. Que: Sutherland 1 (Roy, S. Bernier) 1:21. 3. Que: Sutherland 2 (P. Bordeleau, C. Bordeleau) 5:14.

---

4. Phx: Ftorek 11 8:51. 5. Que: Cloutier 11 (Baxter) 11:04.
2nd period: 6. Phx: Huston 4 (Rautakallio) 0:51. 7. Phx: Liddington 3 (Cormier, Hobin) 3:45. 8. Que: Cloutier 12 (Tardif, Tremblay) 8:03. 9. Que: Brackenbury 1 (Boudrias, Roy) 8:54. 10. Que: Tardif 5 (C. Bordeleau) 16:39. 11. Que: Cloutier 13 (Fitchner) 16:55. 12. Que: S. Bernier 10 (P. Bordeleau, Sutherland) 19:08.
3rd period: 13. Que: S. Bernier 11 8:47. 14. Que: Cloutier 14 (Lacombe, C. Bordeleau) 19:47.
Shots on goal

Phx on Brodeur	9	14	7	-30
Que on Kurt, Hebenton	11	12	19	-42

December 26, 1976
Cloutier and Constantin Score Hat Tricks as Nordiques Ring Up 12 Goals Against the Jets

WINNIPEG: The Jets returned to Winnipeg after two weeks at the Izvestia Tournament in Moscow, only to be crushed by a 12-3 verdict at the hands of the Quebec Nordiques. The Nordiques spotted the Jets a 1-0 lead before scoring 7 first-period goals. Charles Constantin scored three goals while Real Cloutier had seven points on three goals and four assists. Ulf Nilsson had two points in a losing cause.

Nordiques 12, Jets 3

Quebec	7	3	2	- 12
Winnipeg	1	1	1	- 3

1st period: 1. Wpg: Hedberg 31 (Nilsson) 0:53; 2. Que: Constantin 8 (Baxter, Cloutier) 3:04; 3. Que: Sutherland 6 (P. Bordeleau) 6:23; 4. Que: Cloutier 28 (C. Bordeleau) 7:11; 5. Que: S. Bernier 26 (Cloutier, Tremblay) 9:57; 6. Que: Cloutier 29 (S. Bernier, Tremblay) 14:08; 7. Que: Roy 1 (Boudrias, Fitchner) 16:15; 8. Que: Constantin 9 (Cloutier, C. Bordeleau) 17:26
2nd period: 9. Que: C. Bordeleau 16 (Cloutier, Dorey) 8:49; 10. Wpg: Nilsson 14 (Hull, Bergman) 11:45; 11. Que: S. Bernier 27 (P. Bordeleau) 12:35; 12. Que: Constantin 10 (C. Bordeleau, Tremblay) 17:26
3rd period: 13. Que: Cloutier 30 (Boudrias, Dorey) 8:25; 14. Wpg: Ruhnke 5 (Long, Lesuk) 11:19; 15. Que: P. Bordeleau 19 (Boudrias, Weir) 16:56
Shots on goal

Que on Daley, Larsson	17	12	11	- 40
Wpg on Brodeur	7	5	12	- 24

February 1, 1977
Anders Hedberg and Perry Miller Score Four Goals Each in Winnipeg Romp

EDMONTON: The Jets' Anders Hedberg and Perry Miller scored four goals apiece as Winnipeg scored 11 consecutive times to beat the Oilers, 11-1. Miller scored three times at defense and also added two assists

---

for a six-point night. Hedberg's four-goal game initiated a three-game spurt in which he scored eleven goals and became the first player ever to score 50 goals in less than 50 games.

Jets 11, Oilers 1

Winnipeg	2	6	3	- 11
Edmonton	1	0	0	- 1

1st period: 1. Edm: Campbell (Butters, Sather) 7:15. 2. Wpg: Hedberg 41 (Nilsson, Long) 9:07. 3. Wpg: Hedberg 42 (Nilsson, Bergman) 15:15.
2nd period: 4. Wpg: Lindstrom (Sullivan) 1:02. 5. Wpg: Miller (Nilsson, Hedberg) 10:23. 6. Wpg: Lindstrom (Miller, Lindh) 11:21. 7. Wpg: Moffat (Ketola) 11:28. 8. Wpg: Hedberg 43 (Nilsson, Lesuk) 15:02. 9. Wpg: Hedberg 44 (Nilsson, Miller) 15:54.
3rd period: 10. Wpg: Miller (Guindon, Mott) 6:18. 11. Wpg: Miller (Bergman, Ketola) 10:41. 12. Wpg: Miller (Guindon) 14:54.
Shots on goal

Wpg on Levasseur	9	13	12	- 34
Edm on Daley	10	11	11	- 32

February 6, 1977
Anders Hedberg Scores Fastest 50th Goal Ever as Jets Prevail Over Cowboys

WINNIPEG: Anders Hedberg's hat trick gave him 51 goals in his 47th game, and his teams 49th game, to set the record for fastest 50 goals ever. Hedberg achieved the feat after scoring 11 goals in a three-game span and playing with a bad knee that was heavily taped.

Jets 6, Cowboys 4

Calgary	2	0	2	- 4
Winnipeg	0	4	2	- 6

1st period: 1. Cgy: Kryskow (Ford) 11:20. 2. Cgy: Driscoll (Deadmarsh) 18:02.
2nd period: 3. Wpg: Ketola 1:42. 4. Wpg: Ward (Guindon, Miller) 7:48. 5. Wpg: Hedberg 49 (Bergman, Ketola) 13:42. 6. Wpg: Sullivan (Riihiranta, Daley) 16:58.
3rd period: 7. Cgy: Evans (Driscoll) 8:24. 9. Wpg: Hedberg 50 (Lesuk, Miller) 11:21. 9. Cgy: Kryskow (Terbenche, Boyd) 17:08. 10. Wpg: Hedberg 51 (Nilsson) 19:59.
Shots on goal

Cgy on Daley	8	12	12	- 32
Wpg on Bromley	11	15	11	- 37

April 9, 1977
Racers Outlast Stingers in Three Overtimes, the Longest Playoff Game in WHA History

CINCINNATI: Indianapolis' Gene Peacosh's goal at 8:40 in the third overtime ended a five-hour battle between the Indianapolis Racers and Cincinnati Stingers. The Racers overcame three separate one-goal deficits to achieve the victory. Mark

Lomenda had a goal and two assists for the Racers.

Racers 4, Stingers 3

Indianapolis	1	1	1	0	0	1	- 4
Cincinnati	1	1	1	0	0	0	- 3

1st period: 1. Cin: Leduc 1 (Dudley, Stoughton) 4:58. 2. Ind: Lomenda 1 (Rochon, Paiement) 11:05.
2nd period: 3. Cin: Abgrall 1 (Leduc, Larose) 9:48. 4. Ind: Lomenda 2 (Peacosh, McDonald) 18:23.
3rd period: 5. Cin: Larose 1 (Roy, Carroll) 17:21. 6. Ind: Thomas 1 (Parizeau, McDonald) 18:56.
Third OT: 7. Ind: Peacosh 1 (Lomenda, McDonald) 8:40.
Shots on goal

Ind on Lapointe	12	10	5	8	12	5	-52
Cin on Hoganson	9	15	13	8	11	3	-59

November 24, 1977
Bulls Wallop Stingers in Thanksgiving Day Massacre

BIRMINGHAM: The Bulls shook off two years of torpor and came out fighting, literally and figuratively, as they pasted Cincinnati by a 12-2 margin. Newly acquired tough guys Steve Durbano, Serge Beaudoin and Frank Beaton participated in the scoring barrage, as four different Bulls players scored two goals. The win set the tone for the Bulls, who went on to rough up the league in 1977-78 and make the playoffs for the first time in three years.

Bulls 12, Stingers 2

Cincinnati	1	0	1	- 2
Birmingham	3	2	7	- 12

1st period: 1. Bir: Mahovlich 3 (Linseman, Napier) 1:35. 2. Cin: Leduc 13 3:08. 3. Bir: Henderson 6 (Marrin, Hoganson) 10:25. 4. Bir: Linseman 4 18:35.
2nd period: 5. Bir: Gorman 2 (Marrin, Henderson) 10:04. 6. Bir: Linseman 5 (Beaudoin) 17:13.
3rd period: 7. Cin: Stapleton 1 (Hislop) 3:13. 8. Bir: Cassolato 4 (Hughes, Beaudoin) 3:43. 9. Bir: Marrin 5 (Hughes, Beaudoin) 4:52. 10. Bir: Beaudoin 1 (Wood) 4:52. 11. Bir: Beaudoin 2 (Hughes, Wood) 8:08. 12. Bir: Stephenson 1 (Napier, Durbano) 10:54. 13. Bir: Cassolato 5 (Hoganson) 17:10. 14. Bir: Stephenson 2 (Beaton, Stewart) 17:33.
Shots on goal

Cin on Wood	9	10	11	- 30
Bir on Liut & Dion	6	16	14	- 36

December 7, 1977
Gordie Howe Scores His 1000th Career Goal as Whalers Beat Bulls

BIRMINGHAM: With the game still under two minutes old, Gordie Howe fired his 1000th career goal past Bulls goaltender John Garrett. Howe's 1,000 goals include 853 scored in the NHL (786 regular season, 67 playoffs) and 147 scored in the WHA (127 regular season, 20 playoffs). The

game was temporarily halted as the Birmingham crowd gave the 49-year old star a standing ovation.

Whalers 6, Bulls 3

New England	2	3	1	- 6
Birmingham	1	0	2	- 3

1st period: 1. NE: G. Howe 6 (McKenzie, Antonovich) 1:48. 2. Bir: Stephenson 4 (Linseman, Beaudoin) 5:41. 3. NE: Rogers 10 (J. Carlson, Ley) 6:38.
2nd period: 4. NE: Pleau 9 (Roberts, Ley) 6:38. 5. NE: McKenzie 10 (Antonovich, Roberts) 9:49. 6. NE: Roberts 4 (Pleau, J. Carlson) 12:21.
3rd period: 7. Bir: Linseman 7 (Stephenson, Hughes) 2:07. 8. NE: J. Carlson 4 (Rogers, Roberts) 2:41. 9. Bir: Napier 12 (Hughes, Linseman) 16:58.
Shots on goal

NE on Garrett	12	11	2	- 25
Bir on Smith	9	12	10	- 31

February 27, 1978
Jets Beat Aeros For Record 15th Straight Win

WINNIPEG: Two goals each by Kent Nilsson, Ulf Nilsson and Bobby Hull led the Winnipeg Jets past Houston, 9-6, for their league-record fifteenth straight victory. John Gray had a hat trick for Houston. The win also gave Winnipeg a perfect February at 13-0-0, to set another WHA record.

Jets 9, Aeros 6

Houston	1	1	4	- 6
Winnipeg	3	3	3	- 9

1st period: 1. Wpg: K. Nilsson 31 (Kryskow, Clackson) 3:26. 2. Wpg: Hull 40 (U. Nilsson, Dunn) 5:49. 3. Hou: Gray 23 (Lacroix, Popiel) 11:44. 4. Wpg: K. Nilsson 32 (U. Nilsson, Hull) 14:46.
2nd period: 5. Hou: Hansis 9 (Tonelli, Campbell) 1:52. 6. Wpg: Lesuk 8 (Guindon, Sullivan) 13:59. 7. Wpg: Hull 41 (K. Nilsson, Lindstrom) 16:14. 8. Wpg: Green 4 (Baird, Powis) 18:36.
3rd period: 9. Hou: Gray 24 (Larway, Lacroix) 4:42. 10. Hou: Popiel 5 (Connor, Tonelli) 10:20. 11. Wpg: U. Nilsson 28 10:33. 12. Wpg: U. Nilsson 29 (Hull, Hedberg) 11:46. 13. Hou: Gray 25 (Larway, Lund) 16:54. 14. Wpg: Baird 13 (Moffat, Powis) 17:26. 15. Hou: Lukowich 31 (Hughes, Lund) 19:31.
Shots on goal

Hou on Daley, Bromley	6	7	12	- 25
Wpg on Zimmerman	16	12	15	- 43

March 11, 1978
Bobby Hull Scores His 1000th, Jets Beat Nordiques

QUEBEC: Bobby Hull joined Gordie Howe in the exclusive 1000-goal club by hitting the mark tonight at Quebec. Hull's goals include 666 scored in the NHL (604 regular season, 62 playoffs) and 334 scored in the WHA (299 regular season, 35 playoffs). Kent Nilsson scored a hat trick to lead the Jets attack.

Jets 7, Nordiques 4

Winnipeg	2	2	3	- 7
Quebec	0	1	3	- 4

1st period: 1. Wpg: K. Nilsson 34 (Lindstrom) 1:48. 2. Wpg: K. Nilsson 35 15.38.
2nd period: 3. Que: S. Bernier 18 (P. Bordeleau, Baxter) 3:03. 4. Wpg: Hull 44 (Long) 17:27. 5. Wpg: K. Nilsson 36 (Hedberg, Hull) 19:34.
3rd period: 6. Wpg: Sullivan 14 (Lesuk, Guindon) 0:14. 7. Wpg: Baird 14 (Moffat, Powis) 1:52. 8. Que: Sutherland 19 (Miller, Boudrias) 8:04. 9. Wpg: Moffat 8 (Powis, Guindon) 13:12. 10. Que: Cloutier 44 (C. Bordeleau, Tardif) 14:45. 11. Que: C. Bordeleau 5 (Cloutier, J. Bernier) 14:56.
Shots on goal

Wpg on Brodeur	7	9	8	- 24
Que on Bromley	19	10	8	- 37

October 15, 1978
Mike Gartner Tallies First Career Goal in Stingers Victory

WINNIPEG: Mike Gartner's first career goal broke a 1-1 tie and helped Cincinnati defeat Winnipeg. Gartner retired in 1998 with 708 NHL goals, 735 overall, and was admitted to the Hall of Fame in 2001.

Stingers 4, Jets 3

Cincinnati	0	3	1	- 4
Winnipeg	1	1	1	- 3

1st period: 1. Wpg: Nilsson 2 (Hull, Terbenche) 6:43.
2nd period: 2. Cin: Shutt 1 (Gilbert, Marsh) 3:36. 3. Cin: Gartner 1 (Debol, Dudley) 11:11. 4. Wpg: Sullivan 3 (Lukowich, Clackson) 13:46. 5. Cin: Marsh 2 (Dudley, Ftorek) 16:06.
3rd period: 6. Cin Dudley 1 (Debol, Gartner) 5:43. 7. Wpg: Lesuk (Sullivan) 12:36.
Shots on goal

Cin on Daley	11	22	9	- 42
Wpg on Liut	6	16	10	- 32

October 18, 1978
Wayne Gretzky Scores First Career Point as Racers Blank Nordiques

QUEBEC: Seventeen-year old Wayne Gretzky assisted on Richie Leduc's first period goal, which proved to be the game winner as Ed Mio was perfect in nets for Indianapolis. The shutout by Mio was the first regular season shutout ever by an opposing goaltender in Quebec.

Racers 4, Nordiques 0

Indianapolis	1	1	2	- 4
Quebec	0	0	0	- 0

1st period: 1. Ind: Leduc 1 (Gretzky, Morrison) 16:14.
2nd period: 2. Ind: Stoughton 1 (McLeod) 9:28.
3rd period: 3. Ind: Driscoll 1 (Moretto) 5:34. 4. Ind: Greig 1 (Leduc, Morrison) 15:12.
Shots on goal

Ind on Brodeur	10	11	15	- 36
Que on Mio	11	17	9	- 37

October 20, 1978
Gretzky Scores First Two Career Goals in Racers Loss

INDIANAPOLIS: Wayne Gretzky's first two career goals came in a 34-second span in the second period for the Racers as he twice beat Oilers goaltender Dave Dryden. However, a third period rally by Edmonton gave the Oilers a 4-3 verdict over the Racers. Eddie Mio stopped 43 of 47 Oiler shots blasted his way.

Oilers 4, Racers 3

Edmonton	1	0	3	- 4
Indianapolis	1	2	0	- 3

1st period: 1. Edm: Goldsworthy 2 (Sobchuk, Hamilton) 7:21. 2. Ind: Leduc 2 (Larose, Stoughton) 14:21.
2nd period: 3. Ind: Gretzky 1 (Morrison) 6:07. 4. Ind: Gretzky 2 (Driscoll, Larway) 6:41.
3rd period: 5. Edm: Alexander 2 (Goldsworthy) 7:59. 6. Edm: Sobchuk 1 8:17. 7. Edm: Hamilton 1 (Hunter, MacDonald) 11:58.

Shots on goal

Edm on Mio	12	15	20	- 47
Ind on Dryden	7	7	3	- 17

October 24, 1978
Michel Goulet Scores His First as Bulls Edge Oilers

EDMONTON: Michel Goulet's first career goal was the eventual game winner as the Bulls topped the Oilers. Goulet retired in 1994 with 548 NHL goals, 576 overall. He was inducted into the Hall of Fame in 1997.

Bulls 3, Oilers 2

Birmingham	3	0	0	- 3
Edmonton	0	1	1	- 2

1st period: 1. Bir: Sleigher 5 (Alley, Stewart) 2:01. 2. Bir: Beaudoin 1 (Kirk, Henderson) 4:52. 3. Bir: Goulet 1 (Vaive, Adduono) 15:41.
2nd period: 4. Edm: Chipperfield 1 (Carlson, Flett) 16:49.
3rd period: 5. Edm: Callighen 2 (Shmyr, Sobchuk) 5:19.

Shots on goal

Bir on Dryden	10	8	5	- 23
Edm on Riggin	9	13	12	- 34

November 3, 1978
Gretzky Debuts With Oilers, Tallies Goal in Win

EDMONTON: The Oilers' newly acquired trio of Wayne Gretzky, Peter Driscoll and Ed Mio all figured in the Oilers 4-3 victory over Winnipeg. Gretzky scored an unassisted goal just 14 seconds into the second period to break a 1-1 deadlock. Driscoll's over-time goal won the game, while Mio started in the nets for Edmonton.

Oilers 4, Jets 3

Winnipeg	1	1	1	0 - 3
Edmonton	1	2	0	1 - 4

1st period: 1. Wpg: Lukowich 5 (Ruskowski, Preston) 5:04. 2. Edm: Sobchuk 4 (Callighen, Shmyr) 9:11.
2nd period: 3. Edm: Gretzky 4 0:14. 4. Edm: MacDonald 1 (Hamilton) 8:42. 5. Wpg: Gray 3 (Long, Sullivan) 14:06.
3rd period: 6. Wpg: Sullivan 7 (Lukowich, Preston) 13:52.
Overtime: 7. Edm: Driscoll 4 (Flett, Sobchuk) 6:01.

Shots on goal

Wpg on Mio, Dryden	7	4	12	5 - 28
Edm on Mattsson	12	12	13	2 - 39

January 13, 1979
Gretzky's Hat Trick Cements Stardom

SPRINGFIELD: Still just seventeen years old, Edmonton's Wayne Gretzky scored a natural hat trick in less than five minutes to break a third-period scoreless tie. Gretzky's goals were all the offense the Oilers needed in the 3-0 win, as Dave Dryden registered the shutout. Two of Gretzky's goals were unassisted.

Oilers 3, Whalers 0

Edmonton	0	0	3	- 3
New England	0	0	0	- 0

1st period: No scoring.
2nd period: No scoring.
3rd period: 1. Edm: Gretzky 18 (Hunter, Hughes) 6:55. 2. Edm: Gretzky 19 10:23. 3. Edm: Gretzky 20 11:35.

Shots on goal

Edm on Garrett	15	15	7	- 37
NE on Dryden	2	6	13	- 21

March 7, 1979
Real Cloutier's Hat Trick Gives Him 60 Goals in 60 Games

QUEBEC: The Nordiques' star goal-scorer Real Cloutier scored a hat trick against Edmonton to give him an amazing 60 goals in 60 games. His final goal came with less than a minute to play. Cloutier had barely missed scoring 50 goals in 50 games a few weeks earlier, when he had 47 after the Nordiques' 50th game.

Nordiques 6, Oilers 3

Edmonton	2	0	1	- 3
Quebec	2	2	2	- 6

1st period: 1. Edm: Weir 20 (Hamilton, Hunter) 3:49; 2. Edm: Gretzky 33 5:38; 3. Que: Cloutier 58 (Bernier, Baxter) 15:05; 4. Que: Bernier 32 (Tremblay, Tardif) 18:20
2nd period: 5. Que: Leduc 23 (Hoganson, Fitchner) 8:30; 6. Que: Cloutier 59 14:59
3rd period: 7. Que: Larievere 4 (Fitchner) 1:44; 8. Edm: Carlson 12 (MacDonald) 7:36; 9. Que: Cloutier 60 (Bernier) 19:17.

Shots on goal

Edm on Brodeur	9	6	9	- 24
Que on Dryden	17	8	14	- 39

March 20, 1979
Mark Messier Scores First Career Goal in Stingers Win

CINCINNATI: Mark Messier scored a goal and had an assist in Cincinnati's 5-2 win over Birmingham. Messier's goal was a mid-ice shot that somehow eluded Bulls goaltender Pat Riggin.

Stingers 5, Bulls 2

Birmingham	0	1	1	- 2
Cincinnati	0	4	1	- 5

1st period: No scoring.
2nd period: 1. Cin: Gilligan 15 (Gartner). 2. Bir: Adduono 17 (Vaive, Hansen) 2:23. 3. Cin: Gartner 24 (Messier, Luksa) 4:45. 4. Cin: Thomas 30 (Ftorek) 6:48. 5. Cin: Messier 1 11:53.
3rd period: 6. Bir: Henderson 23 (Ramage, Hartsburg) 1:08. 7. Cin: Forbes 5 (Gilligan, Melrose).

Shots on goal

Bir on Liut	7	8	8	- 23
Cin on Riggin	11	12	8	- 32

April 18, 1979
Oilers Clobber Jets in Last Regular-Season WHA Game

WINNIPEG: The Oilers closed out their most successful season to date with a 9-3 victory over the Jets in Winnipeg. Stan Weir had two goals and two assists, Brett Callighen two goals and an assist, Ron Chipperfield two goals, and Wayne Gretzky a goal and an assist to lead the Oiler attack. The game was not without rancor, as Morris Lukowich and Steve Carlson received match penalties for stick-swinging, while Jets coach Tom McVie tried to engage Oilers coach Glen Sather in a tangle. At the final horn, the last regular-season contest in the World Hockey Association had been played. The Oilers and Jets would meet again in the playoffs, then again the following season as members of the National Hockey League.

Oilers 9, Jets 3

Edmonton	3	2	4	- 9
Winnipeg	2	1	0	- 3

1st period: 1. Edm: Weir 30 (Hunter, Shnyr) 3:51; 2. Edm: Callighen 30 (Gretzky, Siltanen) 5:44; 3. Edm: Driscoll 20 (Hughes, Carlson) 9:52; 4. Wpg: Long 5 (Ruskowski, Sjoberg) 12:35; 5. Wpg: Sullivan 46 (Daley) 15:41
2nd period: 6. Edm: Gretzky 46 (MacDonald, Callighen) 10:07; 7. Edm: Chipperfield 31 (Hamilton, Weir) 10:22; 8. Wpg: Nilsson 39 (Long, Lukowich) 17:43
3rd period: 9. Edm: Callighen 31 (Shmyr, Sobchuk) 6:26; 10. Edm: Hunter 7 (Weir, Micheletti) 11:13; 11. Edm: Weir 31 (Sobchuk, Hunter) 11:59; 12. Edm: Chipperfield 32 (Flett, Hamilton) 13:41.

Shots on goal

Edm on Daley, M'sson	17	11	18	- 46
Wpg on Mio	8	6	6	- 20

The World Hockey Association in International Competition

The World Hockey Association participated in a number of tournaments and exhibitions involving teams from Europe, starting with the 1974 USSR Summit Challenge series. In 1975, the Jets and Toronto Toros set up training camps in Europe, followed by the Roadrunners in 1976. Starting with the 1976-77 season, the WHA regularly hosted touring teams from the USSR, Czechoslovakia, Finland and Sweden, while on occasion sending one of its teams abroad to play in tournaments. Success was variable, and controversy was not unknown when some of the squads from Europe were less than advertised, such as the 1979 Soviet Nationals. Nevertheless, the WHA was instrumental in creating bridges between North America and Europe, and paving the way for the competitions of the decades that followed.

WHA Exhibition Series
September 6 – October 8, 1974

In preparation for the upcoming Summit Challenge with the USSR, the WHA all-stars, collectively known as Team Canada, played a series of exhibitions to prepare for the Soviet squad. Team Canada played a five-game set with the Western Canada Junior All-Stars from September 6-12, winning four. The USSR series began on September 17th, with the fourth and final game in Canada on September 23rd. With a week before resuming the series in Moscow, Team Canada scored two victories over Finland and Sweden. After returning from the USSR, a tired Team Canada dropped a 3-1 decision to Czechoslovakia.

Western Canadian Junior All-Star Series

September 6:	Team Canada 7, WCJA 2	
September 7:	Team Canada 6, WCJA 5	
September 8:	WCJA 3, Team Canada 2	
September 11:	Team Canada 6, WCJA 1	
September 12:	Team Canada 8, WCJA 0	

September 26, 1974

Canada	3	1	4	-	8
Finland	0	1	2	-	3

1st Period: 1. Can: Backstrom (G. Howe, Marty Howe) 0:47; 2. Can: G. Howe (Backstrom, Marty Howe) 6:48; 3. Can: Lacroix (Hull) 11:24;
2nd Period: 4. Fin: Oksanen (Marjemeki) 16:16; 5. Can: Lacroix (Hull, Selwood) 18:23;
3rd Period: 6. Fin: Ahokainen 0:58; 7. Fin: Lindstrom 4:06; 8. Can: Houle (Hamilton, Marty Howe) 8:06; 9. Can: Mahovlich (Ley) 12:04; 10. Can: Webster (Mark Howe) 14:38; 11. Can: Mahovlich 18:47.

September 29, 1974

Canada	3	0	1	-	4
Sweden	0	1	2	-	3

1st Period: 1. Can: Hull (Lacroix, McKenzie) 1:57; 2. Can: Walton (Mahovlich, Houle) 11:20; 3. Can: G. Howe (Mark Howe, Hull) 18:38;
2nd Period: 4. Swe: Johansson (Sundquist, Brasar) 4:46;
3rd Period: 5. Swe: Lundstrom (Lindstrom, Bend) 14:02; 6. Swe: Ahlberg (Lundstrom) 15:21; 7. Can: Mahovlich (Houle, Stapleton) 17:14.

October 8, 1974

Canada	0	1	0	-	1
Czechoslovakia	2	0	1	-	3

1st Period: 1. Cze: Bubla (Hlinka) 4:07; 2. Cze: Hlinka (Eberman) 9:55;
2nd Period: 3. Can: Webster (Hull) 16:40;
3rd Period: 4. Cze: Haas (Novak) 3:16 (Goaltending information incomplete)

Preseason in Europe
Winnipeg and Toronto
September & October, 1975

The Winnipeg Jets and Toronto Toros established training camps in Europe before the 1975-76 season. Each team played an exhibition schedule against a series of European clubs.

Winnipeg: IFK Helsingfors (Fin) 7-5; Tappara (Fin) 3-3; Turku (Fin) 3-4; Swedish Nationals 6-2; AIK Stockholm (Swe) 7-3; Leksand (Swe) 8-2; Vastra Frolunda (Swe) 4-3; Czech Nationals 1-6; Czech Nationals 1-3.

Toronto: Modo (Swe) 0-6; Bjorkloven (Swe) 3-2; Skelleftea (Swe) 2-5; Timra (Swe) 1-3; Brynas (Swe) 4-7; Hammarby (Swe) 5-2; Jamtland-Harjedalen (Swe) 12-0; IFK Helsingfors (Fin) 6-2; Tappara (Fin) 5-5.

Preseason in Europe
Phoenix
September & October, 1976

The Phoenix Roadrunners held their 1976 training camp in Finland, playing an eight-game schedule..

Jokerit 8-3; TPS Finland 2-4; Finnish All-Stars 2-2; IFK Helsingfors 4-1; Finnish All-Stars 5-5; Kiekko Relpas 6-5; Assat 5-5; Karpat 7-3.

Izvestia Cup Tournament
December 16-21, 1976
Moscow, USSR

The Winnipeg Jets became the first Western professional club to compete in the Izvestia Cup Tournament, held annually in December in Moscow. The Jets were invited as a result of capturing the WHA's World Cup the previous season. However, the Jets, without defenseman Lars-Erik Sjoberg

due to an injury, could only salvage a single win in four games, tying once and losing twice.

Game 1 • December 16, 1976

Czechoslovakia	2	0	1	-	3
Winnipeg	0	1	1	-	2

1st Period: 1. Cze: Martinec (Chalupo) 4:32; 2. Cze: Lukac (Hlinka) 15:08;
2nd Period: 3. Wpg: Hedberg (Nilsson) 0:23;
3rd Period: 4. Wpg: Dunn (Hull, Ketola) 8:10; 5. Cze: Veith (Hlinka) 8:47.
Goaltenders: Cze: Kralik, Wpg: Daley.

Game 2 • December 17, 1976

Sweden	1	3	0	-	4
Winnipeg	1	1	2	-	4

1st Period: 1. Wpg: Green (Hedberg) 5:06; 2. Swe: Edberg (Lundholm) 13:44;
2nd Period: 3. Swe: Brasar 5:48; 4. Swe: Lundberg (Landeryd) 7:38; 5. Swe: Karlsson (Kallur, Anderson) 8:03; 6. Wpg: Labraaten 8:51;
3rd Period: 7. Wpg: Hedberg (Hull, Nilsson) 8:33; 8. Wpg: Hedberg (Hull, Green) 9:42.
Goaltenders: Swe: Hogosta, Wpg: Daley.

Game 3 • December 19, 1976

Winnipeg	1	0	3	-	4
USSR	1	3	2	-	6

1st Period: 1. USSR: Zhluktov (Mikhailov) 8:56; 2. Wpg: Sullivan (Labraaten) 17:43;
2nd Period: 3. USSR: Zhluktov (Alexandrov) 1:19; 4. USSR: Mikhailov (Tsygankov) 2:49; 5. USSR: Balderis (Maltsev) 5:25;
3rd Period: 6. USSR: Alexandrov (Zhluktov) 2:44; 7. Wpg: Hull (Nilsson) 3:54; 8. Wpg: Hull (Miller) 4:53; 9. USSR: Balderis (Bilyaletdinov) 8:59; 10. Wpg: Lindstrom 14:55.
Goaltenders: Wpg: Daley, USSR: Tretiak.

Game 4 • December 21, 1976

Finland	0	0	1	-	1
Winnipeg	0	2	0	-	2

1st Period: no scoring.
2nd Period: 1. Wpg: Labraaten (Miller) 12:26; 2. Wpg: Lindstrom (Bergman) 14:20;
3rd Period: 3. Fin: Peltonen 9:00.
Goaltenders: Fin: Mattsson, Wpg: Daley.

Czechoslovakian National Team
December 12-22, 1976

During the 1976-77 season, the WHA began the annual practice of hosting visiting teams from Europe. The inaugural tour was a ten-day, six-game series against the Czechoslovakian Nationals, whose squad was partially depleted with members also

playing at the Izvestia Tournament in Moscow.

Game 1 • December 12, 1976
Czechoslovakia	0	4	1	-	5
Winnipeg	0	0	6	-	6

Highlights: After spotting the Czechs to a 4-0 advantage, the Jets roared back with 5 unanswered goals in the third period. A late score by the Czechs tied the game at 5, but Peter Sullivan scored with four minutes left to secure the victory.
Goals: Cze: Bauer, Novak, Pouzar, Sykora, Melc. Wpg: Hedberg, Labraaten, Bergman, Ruhnke, Lindh, Sullivan.
Goaltenders: Cze: Dzurilla, Wpg: Daley.

Game 2 • December 13, 1976
Czechoslovakia	2	0	2	-	4
Edmonton	4	1	1	-	6

Highlights: Bill Flett scored twice, including the game winner in the second period, as Edmonton won despite a 38-20 Czech advantage in shots. Eduard Novak scored twice for the Czechs.
Goals: Cze: Bauer, Novak 2, Pouzar. Edm: Kirk, Flett 2, Beaton, Morris, Rota.
Goaltenders: Cze: Krasa and Termer, Edm: Broderick and Dryden.

Game 3 • December 15, 1976
Czechoslovakia	3	1	1	-	5
Calgary	2	2	0	-	4

Highlights: Milan Novy's late goal with less than a minute remaining secured the Czech's first win of their tour. Marian Stastny scored two goals for the Czechs, while Mike Ford scored twice for the Cowboys.
Goals: Cze: Vejvoda, Muller, M. Stastny 2, Novy. Cgy: Tannahill, Connelly, Ford 2.
Goaltenders: Cze: Dzurilla, Cgy: McLeod.

Game 4 • December 17, 1976
Czechoslovakia	0	2	0	-	2
Minnesota	0	0	2	1	- 3

Highlights: After Ron Ward scored at 19:33 of the third period to tie the game, Mike Antonovich scored at 45 seconds in overtime to pull out the victory.
Goals: Cze: Pouzar, Novak. Min: Adduono, Ward, Antonovich.
Goaltenders: Cze: Dzurilla, Min: Curran and Levasseur.

Game 5 • December 20, 1976
Czechoslovakia	1	3	0	-	4
New England	0	1	0	-	1

Highlights: Marian Stastny scored twice and the Czechs outshot New England 45-19 in an easy win for the touring squad. Mike Rogers broke Vladimir Dzurilla's shutout late in the second period.
Goals: Cze: Neliba, M. Stastny 2, Novak. NE: Rogers.
Goaltenders: Cze: Dzurilla, NE: Raeder and Abrahamsson.

Game 6 • December 22, 1976
Czechoslovakia	1	0	1	-	2
Indianapolis	1	0	2	-	3

Highlights: Rosaire Paiement's two third period goals lifted the Racers over the Czechs. A late goal by Frantisek Kaberle made the score close.
Goals: Cze: M. Stastny, Kaberle. Ind: Harris, Paiement 2.
Goaltenders: Cze: Dzurilla, Ind: Dion.

USSR National Team
December 27, 1976 - January 8, 1977

The Soviet National team arrived for an eight game exhibition tour of WHA clubs, beginning December 27, 1976. The powerful Soviet squads (Red Army and Wings) had a 5-2-1 record against NHL competition the previous year, and the WHA was not expected to improve on the record much. The Soviets handled the WHA, winning six of the eight games.

Game 1 • December 27, 1976
USSR	1	0	1	-	2
New England	3	0	2	-	5

Highlights: George Lyle scored twice as New England greeted the Soviets with a victory, outshooting them 38-33.
Goals: USSR: Maltsev, Yakushev. NE: Swain, Earl, MacGregor, Lyle 2.
Goaltenders: USSR: Tretiak, NE: Raeder.

Game 2 • December 28, 1976
USSR	1	2	4	-	7
Cincinnati	0	2	3	-	5

Highlights: Vladimir Petrov had a hat trick and led the Soviets to their first win on the tour. Cincinnati outshot the Soviets 43-31.
Goals: USSR: Alexandrov, Pervukhin, Petrov 3, Shalimov, Balderis. Cin: Stoughton, Larose, Leduc 2, Dudley.
Goaltenders: USSR: Sidelnikov, Cin: Hoganson.

Game 3 • December 30, 1976
USSR	1	8	1	-	10
Houston	1	0	0	-	1

Highlights: Vladimir Petrov and Alexander Golikov scored twice to lead the Soviets to a 10-1 thrashing of Houston. Rich Preston scored the lone Aero goal.
Goals: USSR: Krikunov, Babinov, Yakushev, Balderis, Kovin, Petrov 2, Golikov 2, Shalimov. Hou: Preston.
Goaltenders: USSR: Tretiak and Sidelnikov, Hou: Grahame and Rutledge.

Game 4 • January 1, 1977
USSR	0	3	2	-	5
Indianapolis	0	2	0	-	2

Highlights: Alexander Golikov scored the tie-breaker midway through the second period to lift the USSR over Indianapolis.
Goals: USSR: Maltsev, Kharlamov, Golikov, Lyapkin, Balderis. Ind: Harris, Block.
Goaltenders: USSR: Sidelnikov, Ind: Park and Dion.

Game 5 • January 3, 1977
USSR	0	3	3	-	6
San Diego	2	0	1	-	3

Highlights: Boris Mikhailov scored twice and Vladimir Petrov had three assists in the Soviet win.
Goals: USSR: Mikhailov 2, Yakushev, Petrov, Krikunov, Maltsev. SD: Burgess, Rivers, Shmyr.
Goaltenders: USSR: Tretiak, SD: Lockett and Wakely.

Game 6 • January 5, 1977
USSR	1	1	1	-	3
Edmonton	0	1	1	-	2

Highlights: Two goals by Alexander Yakushev, including the game winner, led the Soviets over Edmonton. Wayne Connelly scored both Edmonton goals.

Goals: USSR: Yakushev 2, Prirodin. Edm: Connelly 2.
Goaltenders: USSR: Sidelnikov, Edm: Broderick.

Game 7 • January 6, 1977
USSR	1	2	0	-	3
Winnipeg	0	1	1	-	2

Highlights: Alexander Yakushev once again led the way with two goals, as Winnipeg held tough. The Soviets outshot the Jets 31-30.
Goals: USSR: Yakushev 2, Balderis. Wpg: Hull, Long.
Goaltenders: USSR: Tretiak, Wpg: Daley.

Game 8 • January 8, 1977
USSR	1	0	0	-	1
Quebec	3	2	1	-	6

Highlights: An unlikely hero: Curt Brackenbury scored two goals as the Nordiques put an end to the Soviet winning streak. Soviet goaltender Vladislav Tretiak was removed from the game midway through the final period after giving up his 6th goal.
Goals: USSR: Mikhailov. Que: Brackenbury 2, Bernier, Tardif, C. Bordeleau, Dube.
Goaltenders: USSR: Tretiak and Sidelnikov, Que: Humphreys.

Rude Pravo Tournament
September 1977
Prague, Czechoslovakia

The Cincinnati Stingers were invited to participate in the inaugural Rude Pravo Tournament during the pre-season, 1977. The Rude Pravo Tournament was similar in format to the Soviet Union's Izvestia Tournament. Alas, the Stingers were beaten badly in four games.

	w-l	gf-ga
Czechoslovakia	3-1	26-13
USSR	3-1	24-12
Cincinnati	0-4	11-36

Scores: USSR 11, Cincinnati 4; Czech. 8, Cincinnati 2; USSR 4, Czech. 1; USSR 5, Cincinnati 2; Czech. 12, Cincinnati 3; Czech. 5, USSR 4.

Other exhibition game results: Turku (Finland) 1-6; Assat (Finland) 2-8; Finland Nationals 8-4.

Preseason in Europe
Winnipeg
September 1977

The Winnipeg Jets spent September 1977 playing an exhibition schedule against various Swedish and Finnish clubs, with a 5-3-1 record.

Timra 4-1; Skelliftea 7-2; Modo 6-2; Helsinki IFK 6-6; Leksand 2-3; Soedertalje 2-5; Orebro 9-2; Stockholm AIK 5-7; Vastra Frolunda 6-3.

Izvestia Cup Tournament
December 16-21, 1977
Moscow, USSR

The WHA continued its year-old tradition of sending its reigning league champions, the Quebec Nordiques, to compete in the Soviet Union's Izvestia Tournament. Beset with injuries to Richard Brodeur, Christian Bordeleau, Francois Lacombe and Wally Weir, the Nordiques finished the four-game tournament with three losses and a tie. The WHA did not participate in the 1978 tournament.

Game 1 • December 16, 1977

USSR	2	2	1	-	5
Quebec	0	2	1	-	3

1st Period: 1. USSR: Anisin (Balderis) 7:10; 2. USSR: Anisin 18:36;
2nd Period: 3. Que: Cloutier (Tardif, Hagman) 10:12; 4. USSR: Tsygankov (Petrov) 12:29; 5. USSR: Lutchenko (Vikulov) 12:49; 6. Que: Hagman (Cloutier, Tardif) 13:41;
3rd Period: 7. USSR: Anisin (Mikhailov) 7:02; 8. Que: Hagman (S. Bernier, Tardif) 16:09.
Goaltenders: USSR: Tretiak, Que: Broderick.

Game 2 • December 18, 1977

Sweden	0	4	2	-	6
Quebec	0	0	2	-	2

1st Period: No Scoring.
2nd Period: 1. Swe: Lundberg (Lindblom) 8:44; 2. Swe: Olsson (Salming) 13:24; 3. Swe: Lundbert (Olsson) 15:41; 4. Swe: Lundqvist (Lundholm) 16:50.
3rd Period: 5. Swe: Lundholm (Olsson) 5:44; 6. Que: Tremblay 11:03; 7. Que: Esbjorg (Salming) 13:05; 8. Que: Lariviere 19:42.
Goaltenders: Swe: Londberg; Que: Broderick & Corsi.

Game 3 • December 19, 1977

Quebec	1	5	0	-	6
Finland	2	2	2	-	6

1st Period: 1. Fin: Repo 2:37; 2. Fin: Suoraniemi (Nummelin) 6:02; 3. Que: J. Bernier (Tardif) 6:41.
2nd Period: 4. Que: Fitchner (Cloutier, Tardif) 6:15; 5. Que: Cloutier (Fitchner) 11:49; 6. Que: Tremblay (Fitchner) 12:15; 7. Que: Hagman (Lariviere) 14:06; 8. Fin: Peltonen (Koivulahti) 17:13; 9. Fin: Repo 17:34; 10. Que: Hagman (Tardif, Cloutier) 19:50.
3rd Period: 11. Fin: Tamminen (Repo) 13:05; 12. Fin: Koivulahti 14:55.
Goaltenders: Fin: Leppjanen, Que: Broderick.

Game 4 • December 21, 1977

Czechoslovakia	3	2	1	-	6
Quebec	1	0	1	-	2

1st Period: 1. Cze: Ebermann (Novak) 8:13; 2. Que: Cloutier (Fitchner) 8:21; 3. Cze: Kajkl (Machac) 11:08; 4. Cze: M. Stastny (P. Stastny) 12:45.
2nd Period: 5. Cze: P. Stastny (Novak) 11:49; 6. Cze: Novak (Martinec) 13:27.
3rd Period: 7. Que: Tardif (J. Bernier) 10:57; 8. Cze: Martinec (Hlinka) 14:52.
Goaltenders: Cze: Kralik, Que: Broderick & Corsi.

Soviet All-Stars
December 14, 1977 -
January 3, 1978

During a ten game tour, the Soviet All-Stars played each of the eight WHA teams once, with each game counting in the standings. The Soviets also played two exhibition games, December 28th against Houston and December 30th against Indianapolis.

December 28, 1977

Soviets	3	1	3	-	7
Houston	1	1	1	-	3

Highlights: Alexander Volchkov and Zinetula Biljaletdinov each scored two goals to pace the Soviets. Rich Preston had two of the Aero goals
Goals: Sov: Volchkov 2, Biljaletdinov 2, Semyonov, Yemelianenko, Makarov. Hou: Preston 2, Tonelli.
Goaltenders: Hou: Zimmerman, Sov: Babariko.

December 30, 1977

Soviets	3	1	0	-	4
Indianapolis	0	2	0	-	2

Highlights: Victor Tyumenev's two goals led the All-Stars over Indianapolis.
Goals: Sov: Volchenkov, Golubovich, Tyumenev 2. Ind: Thomas, French.
Goaltenders: Ind: Inness, Sov: Babariko.

USSR vs. Winnipeg
December 29, 1977 -
January 1, 1978
Tokyo, Japan

The Winnipeg Jets arrived in Tokyo to engage the Soviet Nationals in a three-game exhibition series. The Jets were on an eight-game winning streak when they arrived after a long flight. Tired and with no time to practice, the Jets were no match for the Soviet team, which won each game. The series was held at the 1964 Olympic swimming pool site, which was converted to a rink for the series. Today, the site is known as Yoyogi Arena, host of a selection of NHL games in recent years.

Game 1 • December 29, 1977

Winnipeg	2	3	0	-	5
USSR	2	4	1	-	7

1st Period: 1. USSR: A. Golikov (Fetisov, Maltsev) 4:14; 2. USSR: Mikhailov (Petrov, Kharlamov) 8:31; 3. Wpg: Hedberg (U. Nilsson, Long) 13:45; 4. Wpg: K. Nilsson (Lindstrom, Sullivan) 16:09;
2nd Period: 5. Wpg: Dunn (Moffatt) 3:31; 6. USSR: V. Golikov (Maltsev) 6:40; 7. USSR: Petrov (Lutchenko) 7:51; 8. Wpg: Hull 9:58; 9. USSR: Kharlamov (Petrov, Mikhailov) 11:37; 10. USSR: Tsygankov (Petrov) 14:26; 11. Wpg: Guindon (Lesuk, Dunn) 14:55;
3rd Period: 12. USSR: Anisin (Balderis) 13:28.
Goaltenders: USSR: Tretiak, Wpg: Mattsson.

Game 2 • December 30, 1977

Winnipeg	0	1	1	-	2
USSR	1	2	1	-	4

1st Period: 1. USSR: Pervukhin (Maltsev) 12:40;
2nd Period: 2. Wpg: Powis 2:53; 3. USSR: Lobanov (Alexandrov) 3:19; 4. USSR: Lobanov (Alexandrov) 8:08;
3rd Period: 5. USSR: Tsygankov (Makarov) 9:12; 6. Wpg: Kryskow (U. Nilsson) 13:30.
Goaltenders: USSR: Sidelnikov, Wpg: Bromley.

Game 3 • January 1, 1978

Winnipeg	1	0	0	-	1
USSR	0	4	1	-	5

Goals: Wpg: Powis. USSR: Kharlamov 2, Tsygankov, Petrov, Lebedev.
Goaltenders: USSR: Sidelnikov, Wpg: Bromley (Full summary not available)

USSR National Team
January 4-11, 1978

For the second season in a row, the Soviet Nationals played an exhibition schedule against WHA clubs. This time, the Soviets played a six game set, winning five of the six matches.

Game 1 • January 4, 1978

USSR	2	3	2	-	7
Edmonton	0	1	1	-	2

Highlights: A hat trick by Vladimir Petrov led the USSR attack, despite the fact Edmonton held the lead in shots, 38-25.
Goals: Petrov 3, A. Golikov, Tsygankov, Balderis, Anisin. Edm: Holland, Callighen.
Goaltenders: USSR: Tretiak, Edm: Dryden.

Game 2 • January 5, 1978

USSR	0	2	1	-	3
Winnipeg	2	2	1	-	5

Highlights: Bobby Hull had a hat trick and an assist, and Ulf Nilsson had two goals and two assists as Winnipeg downed the Soviets. Boris Alexandrov had two of the Soviet goals.
Goals: USSR: Alexandrov 2, Pervukhin. Wpg: Hull 3, U. Nilsson 2.
Goaltenders: USSR: Sidelnikov and Tretiak, Wpg: Daley.

Game 3 • January 7, 1978

USSR	3	1	2	-	6
Quebec	2	0	1	-	3

Highlights: Valeri Kharlamov had two goals, including the game winner, as the Soviets regained the advantage in wins on their tour.
Goals: USSR: Tsygankov, Balderis, Kharlamov 2, Maltsev, Anisin. Que: Inkpen, Dube, Fitchner.
Goaltenders: USSR: Tretiak, Que: Corsi.

Game 4 • January 8, 1978

USSR	1	4	4	-	9
Cincinnati	1	1	0	-	2

Highlights: An even attack led the Soviets to an easy 9-2 decision over Cincinnati. Valeri Kharlamov had three assists.
Goals: USSR: Kapustin, Mikhailov, Anisin, Gusev, Maltsev, Balderis, Vikulov, Babinov, Lobanov. Cin: Ftorek, Legge.
Goaltenders: USSR: Tretiak, Cin: Dion.

505

Game 5 • January 10, 1978

USSR	1	4	3	- 8
Indianapolis	2	0	1	- 3

Highlights: Sergei Kapustin and Alexander Golikov each scored two goals as the Soviets skated to another easy win.
Goals: USSR: A. Golikov 2, Kapustin 2, Tsygankov, Kharlamov, Anisin, Fiodorov. Ind: Maggs, Patenaude, Thomas.
Goaltenders: USSR: Sidelnikov, Ind: McDuffe.

Game 6 • January 11, 1978

USSR	4	2	1	- 7
New England	1	2	1	- 4

Highlights: Viktor Khatulev scored the game winning goal and had an assist as the Soviets closed out their tour with another decisive victory.
Goals: USSR: Alexandrov, Kapustin, Mikhailov, Anisin, Khatulev, Vikulov, Fetisov. NE: Carroll, McKenzie, Keon, G. Howe.
Goaltenders: USSR: Tretiak, NE: Levasseur.

Preseason in Europe
Edmonton
September 1978

Edmonton spent its 1978 preseason with a six game set against Swedish and Finnish clubs, with a 3-1-2 result.

Orebro 3-3; Jonkoeping 4-4; Sweden B 6-5; Sweden B 4-8; Turku 5-4; Helsinki IFK 5-2.

Moscow Dynamo
December 26-30, 1978

The Moscow Dynamo team arrived a week early and played four exhibitions against WHA competition to prepare for the upcoming three-game series against the WHA All-Stars. Controversy arose when the Soviets kept a number of star players off the squad, nearly causing the WHA to cancel its games out of protest. A financial settlement was reached, and the games proceeded.

Game 1 • December 26, 1978

Moscow Dynamo	0	0	1	- 1
New England	1	1	2	- 4

1st Period: 1. NE: Hangsleben (Selwood, Miller) 10:18;
2nd Period: 2. NE: Hangsleben (Inkpen) 7:49;
3rd Period: 3. NE: Rogers (Hangsleben, Miller) 6:15; 5. MD: Devyatov (Golubovich) 14:02; 5. NE: Keon (Antonovich, Warner) 17:02.
Goaltenders: NE: Garrett, MD: Polupanov.

Game 2 • December 27, 1978

Moscow Dynamo	0	3	1	- 4
Quebec	2	2	1	- 5

1st Period: 1. Que: Bordeleau (Bernier) 16:19; 2. Que: Tardif (Tremblay) 19:11;
2nd Period: 3. MD: Vikulov (Anisin) 4:19; 4. MD: Semyonov (Filippov) 5:47; 5. Que: Geoffrion (Tardif, Leduc) 13:37; 6. MD: Kotlov (Semyonov) 14:41; 7. Que: Bernier (Cloutier) 17:48;
3rd Period: 8. MD: Tukmachyov 2:33; 9. Que: Geoffrion (Leduc, Dorey) 18:28.
Goaltenders: Que: Brodeur and Corsi, MD: Babariko.

Game 3 • December 29, 1978

Moscow Dynamo	0	2	2	- 4
Edmonton	1	0	0	- 1

1st Period: 1. Edm: Sobchuk 10:31;
2nd Period: 2. MD: Semyonov (Kotlov) 10:52; 3. MD: Frolikov (Slipchenko, Shostak) 16:07;
3rd Period: 4. MD: Shostak 6:52; 5. MD: Volchkov 7:05.
Goaltenders: Edm: Walsh, MD: Babariko.

Game 4, December 30, 1978

Moscow Dynamo	2	1	1	- 4
Winnipeg	1	3	2	- 6

1st Period: 1. MD: Devyatov (Semyonov, Payusov) 14:51; 2. Wpg: Ruskowski (MacKinnon, Nilsson) 15:59; 3. MD: Devyatov (Semyonov, Kotlov) 19:53;
2nd Period: 4. Wpg: Long (Nilsson, Daley) 7:49; 5. Wpg: Lindstrom 16:22; 6. Wpg: Moffatt (Gray, MacKinnon) 16:59; 7. MD: Semyonov (Kotlov) 18:43;
3rd Period: 8. Wpg: Sullivan (Amodeo, Daley) 3:27; 9. Wpg: Lindstrom (Gray, Sullivan) 4:22; 10. MD: Frolikov (Slipchenko, Gimaev) 16:44.
Goaltenders: Wpg: Daley, MD: Babariko.

Sweden and Finland
Touring Teams
1977-78, 1978-79

Both Sweden and Finland sent teams to play exhibition series against the WHA during the 1977-78 and 1978-79 seasons. The games were exhibitions except for the March 1979 contest between Edmonton and Finland, which counted for both teams in the official standings.

1978 Sweden: March 21: Houston 8, Sweden 3; March 23: Indianapolis 6, Sweden 3; March 25: New England 6, Sweden 0; March 26: Sweden 5, Cincinnati 4; March 28: Birmingham 7, Sweden 4

1978 Finland: March 18: Finland 3, Birmingham 2; March 19: Houston 6, Finland 4; March 22: Finland 4, Indianapolis 3; March 25: Finland 8, Cincinnati 3; March 26: New England 7, Finland 3

1978 Sweden: December 15: Winnipeg 4, Sweden 3; December 16: Edmonton 11, Sweden 2; December 18: Quebec 7, Sweden 3

1979 Finland: March 20: Edmonton 8, Finland 4; March 21: Finland 4, Quebec 2; March 25: Winnipeg 4, Finland 3 (ot)

Gallery

Paul MacKinnon

Pierre Lagace

Roger Cote

Pete McNamee

Dean Magee

The AVCO World Trophy

All-Time Standings

	team	years	games played	record	pct	gf	ga	series won	lost	AVCO champs
1.	Winnipeg	6	70	48-22	.686	316	238	11	3	76,78,79
2.	Houston	6	71	44-27	.620	273	224	10	4	74,75
3.	New England	7	74	41-33	.554	272	256	8	6	73
4.	Quebec	5	52	26-26	.500	204	198	6	4	77
5.	Minnesota	3	29	14-15	.483	103	107	2	3	-
6.	San Diego	3	28	12-16	.429	89	111	2	3	-
7.	Ottawa-Toronto-Birmingham	4	28	11-17	.393	101	125	1	4	-
8.	Alberta/Edmonton	6	33	9-24	.273	113	141	1	5	-
9.	Indianapolis	2	16	8-8	.500	48	52	1	2	-
10.	Chicago	1	18	8-10	.444	67	72	2	1	-
11.	Cleveland	4	22	7-15	.318	62	78	1	4	-
12.	Philadelphia-Cleveland	2	14	5-9	.357	42	56	1	2	-
13.	Phoenix	2	10	3-7	.300	25	40	0	2	-
14.	Los Angeles	1	6	2-4	.333	16	23	0	1	-
15.	Cincinnati	2	7	1-6	.143	19	29	0	2	-

Appearances in the finals: Winnipeg 5 (won 3, lost 2); Houston 3 (won 2, lost 1); New England 2 (won 1, lost 1); Quebec 2 (won 1, lost 1); Edmonton 1 (won 0, lost 1); Chicago 1 (won 0, lost 1).

The AVCO World Trophy was given yearly to the league champion team, with the players' names engraved onto panels on the base of the cup. Created by Canadian sculptor D. W. Murphy, it featured a silver-plated globe suspended in clear lucite. An ornate silver cup was mounted on top, while the base featured the names of the players of the championship teams. It stood just under a meter tall and weighed approximately 35 kg. The trophy was donated to the new league along with approximately $500,000 by the AVCO Financial Services Corporation. Thus the WHA became the only major sports league to have its championship trophy bear the name of a private corporation. The AVCO Cup did not have the lore and myth that was associated with the NHL's Stanley Cup, but it was an attractive piece of hardware nevertheless. It was retired from use after the WHA ceased operations in 1979. The following is a list of the championship teams and the names of the players engraved onto the trophy:

1973 New England Whalers Jack Kelley (Coach, General Manager), Ted Green (Captain), Kevin Ahearn, Mike Byers, Terry Caffery, John Cunniff, John Danby, Jim Dorey, Tom Earl, John French, Paul Hurley, Bruce Landon, Rick Ley, Larry Pleau, Brit Selby, Brad Selwood, Tim Sheehy, Al Smith, Guy Smith, Tom Webster, Tommy Williams.

1974 Houston Aeros Bill Dineen (Coach, General Manager), Ted Taylor (Captain), Ron Grahame, Don Grierson, Larry Hale, Murray Hall, Andre Hinse, Gordie Howe, Mark Howe, Marty Howe, Frank Hughes, Gord Kannegiesser, Gord Labossiere, Larry Lund, Dunc McCallum, Don McLeod, Poul Popiel, Bill Prentice, Wayne Rutledge, John Schella, Jim Sherrit, Jack Stanfield, Joe Szura, Gary Williamson.

1975 Houston Aeros Bill Dineen (Coach, General Manager), Ted Taylor (Captain), Ron Grahame, Larry Hale, Murray Hall, Andre Hinse, Gordie Howe, Mark Howe, Marty Howe, Frank Hughes, Glenn Irwin, Gord Labossiere, Don Larway, Larry Lund, Poul Popiel, Bill Prentice, Rich Preston, Terry Ruskowski, Wayne Rutledge, John Schella, Jim Sherrit.

1976 Winnipeg Jets Rudy Pilous (General Manager), Bobby Kromm (Coach), Lars-Erik Sjoberg (Captain), Duke Asmundsson, Norm Beaudin, Thommie Bergman, Joe Daley, Mike Ford, Ted Green, Bobby Guindon, Larry Hillman, Anders Hedberg, Larry Hornung, Bobby Hull, Veli Pekka Ketola, Curt Larsson, Bill Lesuk, Mats Lindh, Willy Lindstrom, Lyle Moffat, Ulf Nilsson, Gerry Odrowski, Heikki Riihiranta, Peter Sullivan.

1977 Quebec Nordiques Maurice Filion (General Manager), Marc Boileau (Coach), Marc Tardif (Captain), Serge Aubry, Paul Baxter, Jean Bernier, Serge Bernier, Chris Bordeleau, Paulin Bordeleau, Andre Boudrias, Curt Brackenbury, Richard Brodeur, Real Cloutier, Charles Constantin, Jim Dorey, Norm Dube, Bob Fitchner, Pierre Guite, Ed Humphreys, Francois Lacombe, Garry Lariviere, Steve Sutherland, J. C. Tremblay, Wally Weir.

1978 Winnipeg Jets Rudy Pilous (General Manager), Larry Hillman (Coach), Lars-Erik Sjoberg (Captain), Mike Amodeo, Ken Baird, Gary Bromley, Kim Clackson, Joe Daley, Bill Davis, Dave Dunn, Mike Ford, Ted Green, Bobby Guindon, Anders Hedberg, Bobby Hull, Dave Kryskow, Dan Labraaten, Bill Lesuk, Willy Lindstrom, Barry Long, Markus Mattsson, Lyle Moffat, Kent Nilsson, Ulf Nilsson, Lynn Powis, Kent Ruhnke, Peter Sullivan.

1979 Winnipeg Jets John Ferguson (General Manager), Tom McVie (Coach), Lars-Erik Sjoberg (Captain), Barry Long (Captain), Scott Campbell, Kim Clackson, Joe Daley, Roland Eriksson, John Gray, Bobby Guindon, Glenn Hicks, Bill Lesuk, Willy Lindstrom, Morris Lukowich, Paul MacKinnon, Lyle Moffat, Kent Nilsson, Rich Preston, Terry Ruskowski, Gary Smith, Peter Sullivan, Paul Terbenche, Steve West.

Radio and Television Coverage

Exciting WHA action was brought to fans over the air and on television by the following individuals. First names listed are the play-by-play announcers, with commentators following. The WHA was a vanguard in one respect: two teams, the Whalers and Crusaders, employed women as commentators.

Some announcers were well-known veterans of broadcasting. Red Rush had called Chicago White Sox games before being hired by the Cougars, while Joe Tait had called Cleveland baseball and basketball before being hired by the Crusaders. Many others were rookies themselves, who would go on to long careers, such as Bob Neumeier (ESPN), Jerry Trupiano (Boston Red Sox), John Sterling (New York Yankees), Steve Albert (multiple basketball teams) and Mike Anscombe (CBC, Hockey Night in Canada). Fritz Peterson, a pitcher for the New York Yankees, and a self-described hockey fanatic, worked as a color commentator for the Raiders' home contests.

ALBERTA-EDMONTON
1972-73: Radio CJCA 930 AM, Bryan Hall; **1973-74:** Radio CFRN 1260 AM, Al McCann and Rod Phillips, with Norm Williams and Cecil "Tiger" Goldstick pre- and post-game; **1974-75:** Radio CFRN, Al McCann and Rod Phillips; **1975-76:** Radio CFRN, Al McCann and Rod Phillips; TV CITV-13; **1976-77:** Radio CFRN, Al McCann and Rod Phillips; TV CITV; **1977-78:** Radio CFRN, Al McCann and Rod Phillips; **1978-79:** Radio CFRN, Rod Phillips.

BALTIMORE
1975: Radio WBAL 1090 AM, Howard Mash with Gary Morrell.

BIRMINGHAM
1976-77: Radio WAPI 94.5 FM, Gary Sanders; **1977-78:** Radio WAPI, Gary Sanders with Tom Roberts; **1978-79:** Radio WAPI, Eli Gold.

CALGARY
1975-76 and **1976-77** Radio CFAC 960 AM, Eric Bishop, TV CFAC-2.

CHICAGO
1972-73: Radio WJJB 104.3 FM, Duane Dow, TV WSNS-44, Bud Palmer; **1973-74:** Radio WWMM 92.7 FM, WINR 106.3 FM, WGSB 1480 AM, Howard Balson and Bud Kelly, TV WSNS, Red Rush; **1974-75:** Radio WWMM, WINR, WGSB and WTAQ 1300 AM, Howard Balson and Bud Kelly, TV WSNS, Red Rush with Lorne Brown and Dan Mullalley.

CINCINNATI
1975-76: Radio WLW 700 AM, Andy Mac-Williams, TV WLWT-5 (Cincinnati), WLWD-2 (Dayton) and WLWC-4 (Columbus), Bill Brown; **1976-77:** Radio WLW, Andy MacWilliams, TV WLWT, WLWD and WLWC, Phil Samp; **1977-78:** Radio WLW, Andy MacWilliams; **1978-79:** Radio WLW, Dick Carlson.

CLEVELAND
1972-73: Radio WKYC 1100 AM, Steve Albert, TV WUAB-43, Frank Sweeney; **1973-74:** Radio WWWE 1100 AM, Steve Albert, TV WUAB, Steve Albert with Joe Tait, Gib Shanley and Sue Needham; **1974-75:** Radio WWWE, Steve Albert, TV WUAB, Steve Albert with Joe Tait and Paul Wilcox; **1975-76:** Radio WWWE, Lee Hamilton.

DENVER
1975-76: Radio KOA 850 AM, Bob Martin.

HOUSTON
1972-73: Radio KLYX 102.5 FM, Jerry Trupiano; **1973-74:** Radio KULF, Jerry Trupiano, TV KVRL-26; **1974-75:** radio KTRH 740 AM, Jerry Trupiano with Dave Lubeski and Sonny Tate, TV KHTV-39; **1975-76:** Radio KTRH, Jerry Trupiano, TV KVRL; **1976-77:** Radio KTRH, Jerry Trupiano with Jack Stanfield, TV KPRC-2; **1977-78:** Radio KTRH, Jerry Trupiano.

INDIANAPOLIS
1974-75: Radio WIBC 1070 AM, Bob Lamey, TV WTTV-4; **1975-76:** Radio WBIC, Bob Lamey, TV WTTV; **1976-77:** Radio WIBC, Bob Lamey, TV WTTV, Lee Hamilton; **1977-78:** Radio WBIC and WNON 100.9 FM, Mike Fornes and Chet Coppock; **1978-79:** Radio WIBC, Mike Fornes and Al Karlander.

LOS ANGELES
1972-73: Radio KUTE 102 FM, Gary Morrell; **1973-74:** Radio KGBS 91.7 FM, Gary Morrell and Bud Tucker.

MICHIGAN:
1974-75: Radio WWJ, Gary Morrell and Norm Plummer. TV WXON-20, Vince Doyle and Marty Pavelich (season opener only).

MINNESOTA
1972-73 through **1975-76:** Radio WLOL 1330 AM, Frank Buetel.

NEW ENGLAND
1972-73: Radio WHDH 850 AM, Dave Martin, TV WKBG-56; **1973-74:** Radio WHDH, John Moynihan, TV WKBG, John Carlson with Stan and Shirley Fischler; **1974-75:** Radio: Bill Rasmussen on the Springfield-Hartford network, TV WFSB-3; **1975-76:** Radio WTIC 1080 AM, Bob Neumeier, TV WFSB, Bill Rasmussen and Ron Ryan; **1976-77:** Radio WTIC and WSPR 1080 AM (Springfield), Bob Neumeier, TV WHCT-18, Bill Rasmussen; **1977-78:** Radio WTIC, Bob Neumeier; **1978-79:** Radio WTIC, Bob Neumeier with Larry Pleau.

NEW YORK
1972-73: Radio WCMA 570 AM, John Sterling, with Fritz Peterson (home games); **1973-74:** Radio WRVR-FM, Barry Landers.

OTTAWA
1972-73: Radio CKOY 1310 AM, Jack Dailey (English), CJRC 1150 AM, Rene LeCavallier (French).

PHILADELPHIA
1972-73: TV WHYY-12, Bob McLean and Dan Baker.

PHOENIX
1974-75: Radio KTAR 620 AM, Joe Daggett with Mike Leonard, TV KPHO-5; **1975-76:** Radio KRUX 1360 AM, Joe Daggett and Mike Leonard, TV KPHO; **1976-77:** Radio KRUX, KXTC 92.3 FM, Joe Daggett and Mike Leonard.

QUEBEC
1972-73: Radio CJRP 1060 AM, Claude Bedard, TVA television network; **1973-74:** Radio CKCV and CGRP, Claude Bedard and Guy Turbide, TV Ch 10; **1974-75:** Radio CJRP, Claude Bedard, multi-city TV network; **1975-76:** Radio CHRC 800 AM, Claude Bedard with Marc Simoneau, Various TV stations, with Jacques Moreau; **1976-77:** Radio CHRC, Claude Bedard with Marc Simoneau; **1977-78:** Radio CHRC, Claude Bedard; **1978-79:** Radio CKCV 1280 AM, Andre Cote and Michel Villeneuve.

SAN DIEGO
1974-75: Radio KOGO 600 AM, Roy Storey with Jerry Gross; **1975-76:** Radio KOGO, Roy Storey and Jerry Gross; **1976-77:** Radio KOGO, Ron Oakes.

TORONTO
1973-74: Radio: Multiple station network, Joe Spence; **1974-75:** Multiple radio station network in greater-Toronto area, Dave Wright, TV Ch 6 and 22, Mike Anscombe; **1975-76:** TV Ch 6 and 22, local cable, Mike Anscombe with Carl Brewer and Bill Bird.

VANCOUVER
1973-74: Radio CJJC 800 AM, Ron Oakes with Ed Clarke and Gary Raible; **1974-75:** Radio CJJC, Ron Oakes with Gary Raible and Bernie Pascall, TV CBC and BCTV.

WINNIPEG
1972-73 through **1978-79:** Radio CJOB 680 AM, Ken Nicolson, with Stu MacPherson (1973-74), Bob Irving (1975-77) and Ed Dearden (1975-78); TV CKND-9, Andy Arnot.

World Hockey Association 2004

The World Hockey Association was to be revived in 2004 under the leadership of Allan Howell and Nick Vaccaro, with Bobby Hull named the commissioner. The new WHA would be a "AAAA" league, presumably fitting in between the top minor leagues and the NHL, stocked by players of various experiences. The new WHA was situating itself to take advantage of the potential NHL lockout of 2004-05, filling the void and perhaps luring a number of NHL-level players to its ranks. The league held a draft in July 2004, but not long thereafter, the whole operation collapsed. No games were ever played, and the rights to the name were sold and the "WHA" then operated as a low-level "outlaw" amateur league in western Canada for a couple of years.

These press releases are reprinted here verbatim from the World Hockey Association 2004 website (which is no longer available).

Franchise fees posted by groups in four cities: The World Hockey Association Founders Committee announced that four ownership groups have posted the required franchise reservation fees for the 2004-05 season. Québec, Toronto, Hamilton, and an unnamed U.S. market are the first four franchises reserved. (Feb 20, 2004)

Miami enters WHA fold: The Founders of the World Hockey Association have accepted a Franchise Reservation for the city of Miami, Florida. This brings to six the number of franchises for the inaugural season of the WHA which begins in late November or early December of 2004. The Miami group is headed by Dan Krusz, President of Endicott Media of Boston. His partners in the franchise are all based in South Florida. This brings to six the number of franchise agreements posted for the revived WHA. Groups from Toronto, Hamilton, Québec, Minneapolis, and an as yet unnamed U.S. city have previously joined the league. (Apr 1, 2004)

Seven franchises will take to the ice in 2004-05: The founders of the World Hockey Association today announced the formation of the new league with the registration of seven ownership groups. The owner-ship groups are represented by the following individuals or groups: Jean-Paul Boily (Québec); Gino Naldini & John Marshall (Toronto); Rick Munro & Ricky Smith (Vancouver or Dallas); Jay Patel (Detroit (Pontiac)); Dan Krusz & Tim Lovell (Miami); John Tyson & John Marshall (Halifax); Mario Frankovich (Hamilton). The founders are also close to an agreement with a franchise group in Montréal. Advanced lease negotiations are proceeding in the following venues: Le Colisée Pepsi in Québec; SkyDome in Toronto;

either GM Place in Vancouver or Reunion Arena in Dallas; the Silverdome in Pontiac, MI; Miami Arena; and the Metro Centre in Halifax. In the case of Hamilton, representatives of Copps Coliseum have terminated late stage negotiations, alleging notice from the Hamilton Bulldogs exercising their right to exclusive use of the building. The WHA is in the process of referring the matter to the Competition Bureau of Canada. The City of Hamilton, Hamilton Entertainment and Convention Facilities Incorporated (HECFI), Copps Coliseum, the Hamilton Bulldogs, and the American Hockey League will be named as parties to a complaint under Sections 75, 77, and 79 of the Canadian Competitions Act. This matter is of national scope. (Apr 22, 2004)

Senticore acquires hockey franchise in Detroit World Hockey Association to Launch in November 2004: Senticore, Inc., a diversified public holding company, announced today the purchase of the Detroit hockey franchise in the new World Hockey Association. Senticore Chief Executive Officer Jay Patel says, "The acquisition of a major pro-fessional hockey franchise is a very exciting new direction for our company as we expand into the professional sports market and an outstanding opportunity to diversify our corporate holdings."

Senticore President Carl Gessner added, "Detroit is Hockeytown to the rest of North America, so it was the obvious choice when we decided to become part of the WHA." When asked about the team name, Gessner responded, "The people in Detroit know their hockey, we would like them to assist us in selecting the team name."

Hockey's Golden Jet, Bobby Hull, is the Commissioner of the new league. His son, Brett Hull, is a current star of the NHL's Detroit Red Wings. The senior Hull was the catalyst that gave instant credibility to the original WHA in 1972 when he left the Chicago Blackhawks to become hockey's first million-dollar player with the Winnipeg Jets. In a Windsor Star article in late February, the junior Hull was quoted as saying, "I'd play in the WHA. I know the commissioner. I'm sure he could get me a spot." Other NHL players, most notably Philadelphia's Jeremy Roenick, have also gone on record supporting the new league. "I hope there's a team in Detroit," said Detroit Red Wings goalie Manny Legace. "I'll be more than happy to stay here and play for them."

Six other groups have confirmed the purchase of WHA franchises for the inaugural season: Halifax, Nova Scotia; Quebec City, Quebec; Toronto, Ontario; Hamilton, Ontario; Dallas, Texas or Vancouver, British Columbia; and Miami, Florida. Other potentials franchises are under consideration and

may be approved by the WHA in the coming weeks. The WHA is set to launch their hockey season in November of this year. Amidst strong speculation of a possible lockout in the NHL, the WHA is poised to make an immediate impact in professional hockey all over North America next season.

The Detroit team plans to play its 38 game home schedule in its inaugural season in the Pontiac Silverdome, the former home to the Detroit Lions. Plans are to configure the Silverdome into an Olympic sized hockey venue with the installation of a 200 foot by 100 foot ice pad in the east end-zone. With the addition of 2,000 temporary club seats along the open side of the rink, the Silverdome will transform into an arena with a lower bowl seating capacity of 18,620. The fifty-two luxury suites coupled with the second level of seating will increase the total capacity to 23,540. For special events and the possible hosting of NCAA games, the arena bowl can accommodate up to 36,500 fans, making the Silverdome Arena the largest multiple event hockey venue in North America. (May 5, 2004)

Entry Level Draft Preview: Although it is expected Rimouski Océanic centre Sidney Crosby will be the first player chosen in the WHA Entry Level Draft on July 10, you can expect that Moscow Dynamo star Alexander Ovechkin will not be far behind. Like the original World Hockey Association the new WHA will allow 17-year-olds to play. Crosby, who turns 17 in August, could follow in the footsteps of Wayne Gretzky and Mark Messier who both turned professional in the WHA at the age of 17 with the Indianapolis Racers. Both genuine NHL stars the following season, Gretzky finished his first pro season with the Edmonton Oilers, scoring 46 goals and 110 points, while Messier went on to the Cincinnati Stingers. It is expected that players from this year's entry level draft plus those selected in the past two NHL drafts, but unsigned, could make up almost one-third of WHA rosters.

Only one year removed from high school, the Cole Harbour, Nova Scotia native would be a natural for the Halifax entry in the WHA. But his impact at the gate would also make Crosby extremely attractive in the hockey hotbeds of Toronto and Detroit. Crosby will have to choose between another year of junior with the Océanic and a lucrative year in the WHA before he becomes eligible for the NHL draft. Ovechkin and the others selected in the NHL draft will also have difficult decisions to make if they are also drafted by WHA teams. They can hope for a guaranteed NHL contract this summer and no work stoppage next fall, stay in junior, or play professionally in the WHA. The hockey operations departments in many of the WHA cities are already targeting certain junior prospects. Detroit definitely

has an interest Michigan State University blue liner A.J. Thelen. A projected first round NHL pick, Thelen scored 11 goals and added 18 assists in 41 games this past season. Left wing David Booth, a fellow Spartan, could also get the opportunity to stay close to his friends on campus. Booth played in only 29 games this season but still finished with 8 goals and 10 assists. Four University of Michigan standouts will also attract significant attention from the Detroit WHA franchise. Outstanding goaltender Al Montoya, forwards T.J. Hensick and Mike Brown, and defence-man Matt Hunwick are sure to attract attention at the draft table. Halifax will likely be targeting a number of Québec Major Junior League stars. Halifax Mooseheads goaltender Jason Churchill may get a chance to turn pro at age 19 and his teammate, forward Jan Steber should also garner attention. Bruce Graham, a 6-foot-6, 220 pound centre from the Moncton Wildcats is likely to catch the eye of the Halifax brass as will P.E.I. Rocket right wing David Laliberté. The Toronto Toros will have a couple of outstanding local puck stoppers from which to chose. David Shantz of the Mississauga Ice Dogs and Justin Peters of the Toronto St. Michael's Majors could both be drafted by the Toros. (May 16, 2004)

WHA set to play in 2004: Commissioner Bobby Hull, the Co-Founders and Board of Governors of the World Hockey Association today confirmed the new WHA will begin play in late October 2004. At a media conference in Toronto the "original six" cities were announced. Two other cities were granted inaugural year franchises pending the completion of lease negotiations. The six teams with arena leases or commitments now in place are Halifax, Nova Scotia (Metro Centre); Quebec, Quebec (Le Colisee Pepsi); Detroit, Michigan (Pontiac Silverdome); Dallas, Texas (Reunion Arena); Orlando, Florida (TD Waterhouse Center); and Jacksonville, Florida (Memorial Arena). Toronto and Hamilton, Ontario remain franchises in good standing pending the completion of lease negotiations prior to the July 10, 2004 Free Agent and Entry Level draft. Representatives from the U.S. Bank Arena in Cincinnati were also in attendance. The WHA anticipates a minimum of 10 franchises with a maximum of 12 confirmed before the draft. The World Hockey Association will play a 76 game schedule beginning October 29, 2004. Franchises will operate on a maximum salary cap of (U.S.) 15-million dollars including a 5-million dollar marquee distinction.

Named to the Board of Governors are: Mario Frankovich (Hamilton) Chairman; Rick Munro (Dallas) Vice-Chair; Jean-Paul Boily (Quebec), John Marshall (Halifax); Gino Naldini (Toronto); Jay Patel (Detroit); and Max Chambers (Jacksonville). The governor for Orlando will be appointed before the draft. The Governors also authorized league

Director of Hockey Operations Peter Young to short-list candidates for the positions of WHA League President, and WHA Referee-in-Chief. (June 9, 2004)

Moe Mantha becomes first WHA head coach: The Detroit franchise in the World Hockey Association today became the first to announce its head coach. Moe Mantha, who played more than 650 games in the National Hockey League with the Winnipeg Jets, Pittsburgh Penguins, Edmonton Oilers, and Philadelphia Flyers will coach the WHA team set to play a 38 game schedule in the Pontiac Silverdome. The 43-year-old second round NHL draft pick most recently served as Developmental Coach for the U.S. national team based in nearby Ann Arbor, Michigan. Mantha's head coaching career has also included four years in the AHL in Baltimore and Cincinnati. An assistant captain of the 1992 U.S. Olympic team in Albertville, Mantha also competed for the U.S. at the World Championships in 1982, 1985, and 1991. He was also a coach for Team USA in the 1998 World Championships. Mantha's knowledge of the collegiate and junior players from Michigan is likely to influence his selections at the World Hockey Association Draft in early July. (June 23, 2004)

Québec franchise names general manager: The Québec franchise of the World Hockey Association today announced their General Manager for the inaugural WHA season. Martin Madden, with over 30 years of hockey experience was appointed by team owner Jean-Paul Boily. A former assistant general manager and scout with the Montreal Canadiens, Madden was also with the Québec Nordiques of the NHL for ten seasons and was also employed by the New York Rangers as a scout for years. Prior to that he spent five years with NHL Central Scouting. He was also the General Manager of the Québec Remparts of the Québec Major Junior Hockey League. "His overall experience in the hockey world and his ties to Québec made Martin our number one candidate", said Boily. "This announcement initiates a very busy time in the Québec organization and should start a long and prosperous journey for this franchise".

"I'm accepting the challenge to build this Quebec team into a major force in professional hockey in not only the province but the entire league", said Madden. "I've really enjoyed the past few months working with the ownership group in recruiting the type of player who will make our team unique. This team will truly represent Québecers and give our fans a true identity". (June 29, 2004)

Franchise draft exemptions announced: Franchise owners in the World Hockey Association today announced their Draft Exemptions for the 2004-05 season. Each franchise was allowed one selection prior to the NHL/AHL Free Agent Draft on July 17,

2004. The WHA draft exemptions are: Dallas: Brett Hull (UFA, unrestricted Free Agent); Detroit: Chris Chelios (UFA); Florida: Martin St. Louis (UFA); Halifax: Glen Murray (UFA); Hamilton: Paul Kariya (UFA); Québec: Mike Ribeiro (RFA, restricted Free Agent); Toronto: Chris Phillips (RFA); Each WHA team will draft 30 NHL/AHL Free Agents on July 17th, 2004 and 30 Entry Level Players on July 18th, 2004. (July 6, 2004)

WHA breaking the ice in Halifax: Franchise owners Mr. John Marshall and Mr. Gino Naldini today announced the team name, logo and colours of the newest professional hockey team in the Maritimes. The Halifax "IceBreakers" will begin play in late October in the new World Hockey Association. WHA Commissioner Bobby Hull and Director of Hockey Operations Peter Young were joined by District Six (Westphal-Waverly) Councillor Brian Warshick and Scott Ferguson, Vice-President, Operations of Trade Centre Limited at a Media Conference in Halifax to make the announcements. The IceBreakers team colours will be silver, Maritime blue and dark green. Mr. Marshall indicated that the team is in the final stages of contract negotiations with a General Manager and Head Coach. Both have significant NHL experience and a tie to Halifax. They will be announced prior to the draft on July 17, 2004. (July 8, 2004)

Québec franchise reveals name and logo: The Québec franchise owners of the World Hockey Association announced today the name and logo of their team which will take to the ice for the 2004-05 season. "We asked all Québec hockey fans for their opinion on a team name which they could best associate with" commented Jean-Paul Boily, president of the franchise. "Several names were discussed yet from the start one seemed to come up most frequently. This preference clearly showed us that the numerous hockey fans had not forgotten their initial feelings for a team that always maintained a strong place in their hearts. Such sentiment clearly left us with no other choice but to name our team the Nordiks."

The new team's logo, was created by Québec graphic designer Alain Roberge. It represents a likeable bear that shows as much friendliness as aggressiveness to achieve his goal. The white bear represents force, robustness, and perseverance in our wintry climate. A blue circle surrounds the logo with the line forming the name "Nordics", the letter "Q" represents Québec, while the letter "o" in "Nordiks" is in the form of a puck. As well the Québec Nordiks also announced today the members of their administration.

Mr. Jean-Paul Boily, lawyer, lobbyist, and president of the VVC Exploration, was named club president. Mr. Martin Leroux of Lermaco Inc., a real estate corporation in Beauport, is the vice president and Marcel Bédard of the firm Morin Dufresne Cloutier & Bédard was named secretary-treasurer. Alain Rochon of Flamidor Inc. and Serge Cadorette, a financial consultant in Thetford-Mines were also named administrators. (July 15, 2004)

Québec franchise terminated: The Founders of the World Hockey Association announced today that the league has terminated the franchise operating agreement with Jean-Paul Boily and the Québec Nordiks. All players chosen by Québec in the July draft are now considered free agents. The Founders have determined that Mr. Boily has been unable to secure adequate financing to the satisfaction of the World Hockey Association. According to Co-Founder Allan Howell, "Mr. Boily has come to the league on numerous occasions requesting special financial concessions and we have always agreed because of our desire to have Québec as part of the WHA. The fans of Québec deserve WHA hockey and we will now explore all options to make this a reality." (Aug 27, 2004)

2004 World Hockey Association Amateur & Professional Player Draft

Amateur Draft - *Held July 17, 2004, at the Fallsview Casino Resort in Niagara Falls, Ontario. Thirty Rounds. Drafting Order: Toronto, Halifax, Detroit, Hamilton, Dallas, Quebec, Florida, Vancouver. In even numbered rounds this order was reversed.*

Round 1: 1. Toronto: Sidney Crosby C Rimouski (QMJHL). 2. Halifax: Thomas Vanek LW Minnesota (NCAA). 3. Detroit: André Benoit D Kitchener (OHL). 4. Hamilton: Corey Locke C Ottawa (OHL). 5. Toronto (from Dallas): Dion Phaneuf D Red Deer (WHL). 6. Québec: Steve Bernier RW Moncton (QMJHL). 7. Florida: Patrick O'Sullivan C Mississauga (OHL). 8. Vancouver: Brent Seabrooke D Lethbridge (WHL).

Round 2: 9. Vancouver: Eric Fehr RW Brandon (WHL). 10. Florida: Jeff Tambellini LW Michigan (NCAA). 11. Québec: Jean-François Jacques LW Baie-Comeau (QMJHL). 12. Dallas: Andrew Ladd LW Calgary (WHL). 13. Hamilton: Ryan Suter D Wisconsin (NCAA). 14. Detroit: Patrick Jarrett C Owen Sound (OHL). 15. Halifax: Dan Sisca C Sarnia (OHL). 16. Toronto: Geoff Platt C Erie (OHL).

Round 3: 17. Dallas (from Toronto): Boris Valabik D Kitchener (OHL). 18. Halifax: Tim Brent C St. Michael's (OHL). 19. Detroit: Danny Richmond D London (OHL). 20. Hamilton: Andrei Kastsitsyn RW CSKA (Russia). 21. Dallas: Al Montoya G Michigan (NCAA). 22. Québec: Lukas Kaspar RW Litvinov (Czech). 23. Florida: Hugh Jessiman RW Dartmouth (NCAA). 24. Vancouver: Braydon Coburn D Portland (WHL)

Round 4: 25. Vancouver: Kyle Greentree LW Victoria (BCHL). 26. Florida: Eric Nystrom LW Michigan (NCAA). 27. Québec: Corey Crawford G Moncton (QMJHL). 28. Dallas: Cam Barker D Medicine Hat (WHL). 29. Hamilton: Tobias Stephan G Kloten (Switzerland). 30. Detroit: Jonathan Lehun C Owen Sound (OHL). 31. Halifax: Robert Gherson G Owen Sound (OHL). 32. Toronto: Peter Tsimikalis C Ottawa (OHL)

Round 5: 33. Toronto: Kevin Klein D Guelph (OHL). 34. Halifax: David Backes RW Minnesota State-Mankato (NCAA). 35. Detroit: Robert Nilsson LW Leksands (Sweden). 36. Hamilton: Brandon Prust C London (OHL). 37. Dallas: Shea Weber D Kelowna (WHL). 38. Québec: Alexandre Picard LW Lewiston (QMJHL). 39. Florida: Anthony Stewart RW Kingston (OHL). 40. Vancouver: Derek Meech LW Red Deer (WHL).

Round 6: 41. Vancouver: Victor Oreskovich RW Green Bay (USHL). 42. Florida: Mike Richards C Kitchener (OHL). 43. Québec: Tim Ramholt D Cape Breton (QMJHL). 44. Dallas: Wojtek Wolski LW Brampton (OHL). 45. Hamilton: Kyle Wharton D Ottawa (OHL). 46. Toronto (from Detroit): Rob Schremp RW London (OHL). 47. Halifax: Paulo Colaiacovo G Barrie (OHL). 48. Toronto: Ryan Stone C Brandon (WHL)

Round 7: 49. Toronto: Adam Berti LW Oshawa (OHL). 50. Halifax: Scott Dobben LW Sault Sainte Marie (OHL). 51. Detroit: Cory Stillman C Barrie (OHL). 52. Hamilton: Alexander Ovechkin LW Dynamo Moscow (Russia). 53. Vancouver (from Dallas): Karl Gagné LW Moncton (QMJHL). 54. Québec: Marc-Antoine Pouliot C Rimouski (QMJHL). 55. Florida: Jim Howard G Maine (NCAA). 56. Vancouver: Christopher Bourque C Cushing Academy (USHSE)

Round 8: 57. Vancouver: Devan Dubnyk G Kamloops (WHL). 58. Florida: Jim Slater C Michigan State (NCAA). 59. Québec: Alexander Radulov RW Dynamo Moscow (Russia). 60. Dallas: Mike Green D Saskatoon (WHL). 61. Hamilton: Kamil Kreps C Brampton (OHL) 62. Detroit: Dominic Deblois RW Rouyn-Noranda (QMJHL). 63. Halifax: Martin St. Pierre C Guelph (WHL). 64. Toronto: Chris Campoli D Erie (OHL)

Round 9: 65. Dallas (from Toronto): Drew Stafford RW North Dakota (NCAA). 66. Halifax: Martin Vagner D Gatineau (QMJHL). 67. Toronto (from Detroit): Mike Knight C Plymouth (OHL). 68. Hamilton: Jakub Klepis C Slavia Praha (Czech). 69. Dallas: David Booth LW Michigan State (NCAA). 70. Québec: Josh Hennessy C Québec (QMJHL). 71. Florida: Stefan Meyer C Medicine Hat (WHL). 72. Dallas (from Vancouver): Ryan Getzlaf RW Calgary (WHL)

Round 10: 73. Vancouver: Aaron Rome D Moose Jaw (WHL). 74. Florida: Jeremy Colliton C Prince Albert (WHL). 75. Québec: Marek Schwarz G Sparta Praha (Czech). 76. Toronto (from Dallas): Mike Egener LW Calgary (WHL). 77. Hamilton: Chad Painchaud LW Mississauga (OHL). 78. Detroit: Mark Stuart D Colorado College (NCAA). 79. Halifax: Petr Vrana C Halifax: (QMJHL). 80. Toronto: Justin Peters G St. Michael's (OHL)

Round 11: 81. Toronto: Daniel Carcillo LW Sarnia (OHL). 82. Halifax: Jim Sharrow D Halifax (QMJHL). 83. Detroit: Patrick Ehelechner G Sudbury (OHL). 84. Dallas (from Hamilton): Steve Regier LW Medicine Hat (WHL). 85. Dallas: Nathan O'Nabigon LW Kitchener (OHL). 86. Québec: Maxim Lapierre C Prince Edward Island (QMJHL). 87. Florida: Erik Christensen C Kamloops (WHL). 88. Vancouver: Nigel Dawes LW Kootenay (WHL)

Round 12: 89. Vancouver: Dany Roussin LW Rimouski (QMJHL). 90. Florida: Patrick Eaves RW Boston College (NCAA). 91. Québec: David Laliberté RW Prince Edward Island (QMJHL). 92. Dallas: Matt Greene D North Dakota (NCAA). 93. Hamilton: B.J. Crombeen RW Barrie (OHL). 94. Detroit: Curtis McElhinney G Colorado College (NCAA). 95. Halifax: Matt Smaby D North Dakota (NCAA). 96. Toronto: Scott Lehman D St. Michael's (OHL)

Round 13: 97. Toronto: Shay Stephenson LW Red Deer (WHL). 98. Halifax: John Hecimovic RW Sarnia (OHL). 99. Detroit: Greg Moore RW Maine (NCAA). 100. Hamilton: David Bolland C London (OHL). 101. Dallas: Adam Pineault RW Boston College (NCAA). 102. Québec: Niklas Grossman D Sodertalje (Sweden). 103. Florida: Shawn Belle D Tri-City (WHL). 104. Vancouver: Maxime Talbot C Gatineau (QMJHL)

Round 14: 105. Vancouver: Dustin Byfuglien D Prince George (WHL). 106. Florida: Brian McConnell C Boston University (NCAA). 107. Québec: Doug O'Brien D Gatineau (QMJHL). 108. Dallas: Brandon Dubinsky C Portland (WHL). 109. Hamilton: Michael Tessier LW Cape Breton (QMJHL). 110. Detroit: Lee Falardeau C Michigan State (NCAA). 111. Halifax: Craig Kennedy RW Windsor (OHL). 112. Toronto: Ryan Garlock C Windsor (OHL)

Round 15: 113. Toronto: Will Colbert D Ottawa (OHL). 114. Halifax: Joey Tenute C Sarnia (OHL). 115. Detroit: Mike Brown G Saginaw (OHL). 116. Hamilton: Brian Bickell LW Ottawa (OHL). 17. Dallas: François-Pierre Guenette C Cape Breton (QMJHL). 118. Québec: Marc-André Bernier RW Halifax: (QMJHL). 119. Florida: Barry Tallackson LW Minnesota (NCAA). 120. Vancouver: Colin Fraser C Red Deer (WHL)

Round 16: 121. Vancouver: René Bourque LW Wisconsin (NCAA).122. Florida: Cory Urquhart C Prince Edward Island (QMJHL). 123. Québec David Tremblay G Gatineau (QMJHL). 124. Dallas: Brett Skinner D Denver (NCAA). 125. Hamilton: Mitch Mannu D Windsor (OHL). 126. Detroit: Mark Heatley RW Wisconsin (NCAA). 127. Halifax: Jeff Harvey G Everett (WHL). 128. Toronto: Liam Reddox LW Peterborough (OHL)

Round 17: 129. Toronto: Jean-Michel Rizk RW Saginaw (OHL). 130. Halifax: Jeffrey Doyle LW Sault Sainte Marie (OHL). 131. Detroit: Jake Dowell C Wisconsin (NCAA). 132. Hamilton: Jesse Lane LW Des Moines (USHL). 133. Dallas: Dave Steckel C Ohio State (NCAA). 134. Québec: Martin Karsums RW Montcon (QMJHL). 135. Florida: David Liffiton D Plymouth (OHL). 136. Vancouver: Jordon Parisé G North Dakota (NCAA)

Round 18: 137. Vancouver: Pierre-Olivier Beaulieu D Halifax: (QMJHL). 138. Florida: Dany Stewart LW Rimouski (QMJHL). 139. Québec: Francis Wathier LW Gatineau (QMJHL). 140. Dallas: Nathan Marsters G Rensselaer Polytechnic Institute (NCAA). 141. Hamilton: Loui Eriksson RW Frolunda (Sweden). 142. Detroit: Matt Hunwick D Michigan (NCAA). 143. Halifax: Robbie Earl LW Wisconsin (NCAA). 144. Toronto: Tyler Haskins C St. Michael's (OHL)

Round 19: 145. Toronto: Rane Carnegie RW Plymouth (OHL). 146. Halifax: Andrew Joudrey C Wisconsin (NCAA). 147. Detroit: Jason Ryznar LW Michigan (NCAA). 148. Hamilton: Dave Brown G Notre Dame (NCAA). 149. Dallas: Alexander Steen C Frolunda (Sweden). 150. Québec: Philippe Dupuis C Gatineau (QMJHL). 151. Florida: Shane Hynes RW Cornell (NCAA). 152. Vancouver: Jonathan Filewich RW Prince George (WHL)

Round 20: 153. Vancouver: Gilbert Brulé C Vancouver: (WHL). 154. Florida: Andrei Mikhnov LW Sudbury (OHL). 155. Québec: Jakub Petrulzalek RW Litvinov (Czech). 156. Dallas: Johan Fransson D Lulea (Sweden). 157. Hamilton: Johnny Boychuk RW Moose Jaw (WHL). 158. Detroit: Chris Murphy F Wexford (OHA). 159. Halifax: Mark Flood D Peterborough (OHL). 160. Toronto: Evan McGrath C Kitchener (OHL)

Round 21: 161. Toronto: Brandon Elliott D Mississauga (OHL). 162. Halifax: Matt Jones D North Dakota (NCAA). 163. Detroit:

Brian Lee D Erie (OHL). 164. Hamilton: John Mitchell C Plymouth (OHL). 165. Dallas: David Printz D AIK (Sweden). 166. Québec: Julien Ellis-Plante G Shawinigan (QMJHL). 167. Florida: John Adams D Boston College (NCAA). 168. Vancouver: Jevon Desautels LW Spokane (WHL)

Round 22: 169. Vancouver: David Jones RW Coquitlam (BCHL). 170. Florida: Patrick Wellar D Portland (WHL). 171. Québec: Nick Fugère LW Gatineau (QMJHL). 172. Dallas: Andreas Falk LW Huddinge (Sweden). 173. Hamilton: Bryan Hamm D Erie (OHL). 174. Detroit: Magnus Akerlund G Jonkoping (Sweden). 175. Halifax: Rob Hennigar C Windsor (OHL). 176. Toronto: Mark Mancari RW Ottawa (OHL)

Round 23: 177. Toronto: Anthony Butera D Mississauga (OHL). 178. Halifax: Ryan MacMurchy RW Wisconsin (NCAA). 179. Detroit: Richard Demen-Wuillaume D Frolunda (Sweden). 180. Hamilton: Jamie Tardif C Peterborough (OHL). 181. Dallas: Marcus Smith D Kitchener (OHL). 182. Québec: Alexandre Bolduc C Rouyn-Noranda (QMJHL). 183. Florida: Tyler Redenbach C Swift Current (WHL). 184.. Vancouver: Mark Rooneem Calgary (WHL).

Round 24: 185. Vancouver: D.J. King LW Lethbridge (WHL). 186. Florida: Clarke MacArthur C Medicine Hat (WHL). 187. Québec: Alexandre Picard D Cape Breton (QMJHL). 188. Dallas: Chris Zarb D Tri-City (WHL). 189. Hamilton: Ryan Deveaux RW Owen Sound (OHL). 190. Detroit: Paul Bissonnette D Saginaw (OHL). 191. Halifax: Rob Hisey C Erie (OHL). 192. Toronto: Dane Byers LW Prince Albert (WHL)

Round 25: 193. Toronto: Matt Christie C Miami (Ohio) (NCAA). 194. Halifax: Adam Keefe RW Kitchener (OHL). 195. Detroit: Mike Brown RW Michigan (NCAA). 196. Hamilton: Ryan Munce G Sarnia (OHL). 197. Dallas: David Shantz G Misssissauga (OHL). 198. Québec: Martin Houle G Cape Breton (QMJHL). 199. Florida: Kyle Brodziak C Moose Jaw (WHL). 200. Vancouver: Travis Zajac C Salmon Arm (BCHL)

Round 26: 201. Vancouver: Logan Stephenson D Tri-City (WHL). 202. Florida: Gino Guyer C Minnesota (NCAA). 203. Québec: Benoît Mondou C Shawinigan (QMJHL). 204. Dallas: Philippe Lamoureux G Lincoln (USHL). 205. Hamilton: Kyle Quincey D Misssissauga (OHL). 206. Detroit: Oscar Hedman D Modo (Sweden). 207. Halifax: Phil Kessel C U.S. National Team Developmental Program. 208. Toronto: Dylan Hunter LW London (OHL).

Round 27: 209. Toronto: Peter Sciavilla D Antigonish (MJAHL). 210. Halifax: Andrew Cogliano C St. Michael's (OHA). 211. Detroit: Lukas Mensator G Ottawa (OHL). 212. Hamilton: Ryan Donally C Windsor (OHL). 213. Dallas: Tom Gilbert D Wisconsin (NCAA). 214. Québec: Yan Stastny C Nuernberg (Germany). 215. Florida: Brett Sterling LW Colorado College (NCAA). 216. Vancouver: Wyatt Russell G Langley (BCHL).

Round 28: 217. Vancouver: Matt Schneider C Tri-City (WHL). 218. Florida: Ryan Steeves C Yale (NCAA). 219. Québec: Paul Stastny C River City (USHL). 220. Dallas: Lee Stempniak RW Dartmouth (NCAA). 221. Hamilton: Ryan Oulahen C Brampton (OHL). 222. Detroit: Matt Carle D Denver (NCAA). 223. Halifax: Bobby Ryan RW Owen Sound (OHL). 224. Toronto: Brian Ihnacak C Brown (NCAA)

Round 29: 225. Toronto: Jeff Schultz D Calgary (WHL). 226. Halifax: Brady Murray C North Dakota (NCAA). 227. Detroit: Ryan Bowness RW Oshawa (OHL). 228. Hamilton: Bret Nasby D Oshawa (OHL). 229. Dallas: Morgan Cey G Notre Dame (NCAA). 230. Québec: Andrew Andricopoulos D Québec (QMJHL). 231. Florida: Connor James LW Denver (NCAA). 232. Vancouver: Clayton Stoner D Tri-City (WHL)

Round 30: 233. Vancouver: Kyle Chipchura C Prince Albert (WHL). 234. Florida: Louis-Philippe Martin RW Baie-Comeau (QMJHL). 235. Québec: Jean-Philipp Paquet D Shawinigan (QMJHL). 236. Dallas: Matt Ryan C Guelph (OHL). 237. Hamilton: Matt Moulson LW Cornell (NCAA). 238. Detroit: Magnus Hedberg F Sandvikens IK (Sweden). 239. Halifax: Yale Lewis LW Northeastern (NCAA). 240. Toronto: Anthony Minicucci F Vaughn (OHA)

Professional Draft – *Held July 18, 2004 in Niagara Falls, Ontario. Selection Order: Quebec, Halifax, Detroit, Hamilton, Toronto, Vancouver, Dallas, Florida (order reversed in even-numbered rounds).*

Round 1: 1. Québec: Simon Gagné LW Philadelphia. 2. Halifax: Travis Green C Boston. 3. Detroit: Dany Heatley RW Atlanta. 4. Hamilton: Michael Ryder RW Montreal. 5. Toronto: Joe Thornton C Boston. 6. Vancouver: Todd Bertuzzi RW Vancouver. 7. Dallas: Eric Lindros C NY Rangers. 8. Florida: Brad Richards C Tampa Bay

Round 2: 9. Florida: Steve Shields G Florida. 10. Dallas: Scott Gomez C New Jersey. 11. Vancouver: Corey Schwab G New Jersey. 12. Toronto: Ilya Kovalchuk LW Atlanta. 13. Hamilton: Felix Potvin G Boston. 14. Detroit: Drake Berehowsky D Toronto. 15. Halifax: Craig MacDonald C Boston. 16. Québec: Yanic Perreault C Montreal

Round 3: 17. Québec: Maxime Ouellet G Washington. 18. Halifax: Chris Tamer D Atlanta. 19. Detroit: Michael Zigomanis C Carolina. 20. Hamilton: Theoren Fleury RW (DNP). 21. Toronto: Aaron Gavey C St. John's (AHL). 22. Vancouver: Lyle Odelein D Florida. 23. Dallas: Kip Miller C Washington. 24. Florida: Zac Bierk G Phoenix

Round 4: 25. Florida: Jamie Rivers D Detroit. 26. Dallas: Steve Kelly LW Los Angeles. 27. Vancouver: Tommy Albelin D New Jersey. 28. Toronto: Josh Holden C Toronto. 29. Hamilton: Trent Hunter RW NY Islanders. 30. Detroit: Chris Nielsen C Manitoba (AHL). 31. Halifax: Jeff Finley D St. Louis. 32. Québec: Stéphane Veilleux LW Minnesota

Round 5: 33. Québec: Eric Messier D Florida. 34. Halifax: Steve Passmore G Chicago. 35. Detroit: Steve Kariya LW Albany (AHL). 36. Hamilton: Bryan Marchment D Toronto. 37. Toronto: Jonathan Cheechoo RW San Jose. 38. Vancouver: Shaun Van Allen C Ottawa. 39. Dallas: Blake Sloan RW Dallas. 40. Florida: Ben Clymer RW Tampa Bay

Round 6: 41. Florida: Sean Avery C Los Angeles. 42. Dallas: Pavel Rosa RW Los Angeles. 43. Vancouver: Jiri Slegr D Boston. 44. Toronto: Brad May LW Vancouver. 45. Hamilton: Rob Zamuner LW Boston. 46. Detroit: Patrick Desrochers G Lowell (AHL). 47. Halifax: Glen Metropolit C Jokerit (Fin). 48. Québec: Joel Bouchard D NY Rangers

Round 7: 49. Québec: Simon Gamache C Nashville. 50. Halifax: Jeff Hamilton C NY Islanders. 51. Detroit: Alexander Perezhogin RW Hamilton (AHL). 52. Hamilton: Tom Fitzgerald RW Toronto. 53. Toronto: Peter Schaefer LW Ottawa. 54. Vancouver: Jarrod Skalde C Utah (AHL). 55. Dallas: Bryan Muir D Los Angeles. 56. Florida: Nicholas Dimitrakos RW San Jose

Round 8: 57. Florida: Jean-Sebastien Aubin G Pittsburgh. 58. Dallas: Tim Thomas G Providence (AHL). 59. Vancouver: Doug Gilmour C (DNP). 60. Toronto: Brad Leeb LW Toronto. 61. Hamilton: Byron Dafoe G Atlanta. 62. Detroit: Michael Henrich RW Toronto (AHL). 63. Halifax: Jason Krog C Anaheim. 64. Québec: P.J. Stock LW Philadelphia (AHL)

Round 9: 65. Québec: Denis Hamel LW Ottawa. 66. Halifax: David Ling RW Syracuse (AHL). 67. Detroit: Todd Elik C Davos (Switz). 68. Hamilton: Anson Carter C Los Angeles. 69. Toronto: Scott Hartnell C Nashville. 70. Vancouver: Dave Morissette LW (DNP). 71. Dallas: Matt Herr C Providence (AHL). 72. Florida: Rick Berry D Washington

Round 10: 73. Florida: Bob Boughner D Colorado. 74. Dallas: Ron Hainsey D Montreal. 75. Vancouver: Chris Therien D Dallas. 76. Toronto: Mathieu Garon G Montreal. 77. Hamilton: Rob Ray RW Ottawa. 78. Detroit: Dmitri Yushkevich D Yaroslavl (Russia). 79. Halifax: Peter Ferraro RW Springfield (AHL). 80. Québec: Jean-Luc Grand-Pierre D Washington

Round 11: 81. Québec: Bruno St-Jacques D Carolina. 82. Halifax: Chris Ferraro C Springfield (AHL). 83. Detroit: Brad Tiley D Milwaukee (AHL). 84. Hamilton: Scott Ferguson D Edmonton. 85. Toronto: Norm Milley RW Buffalo. 86. Vancouver: Jim Vandermeer D Chicago. 87. Dallas: Chris Armstrong D Anaheim. 88. Florida: Brandon Smith D Bridgeport (AHL)

Round 12: 89. Florida: Rob Davison D San Jose. 90. Dallas: Derrick Walser D Syracuse (AHL). 91. Vancouver: Jamie Pushor D NY Rangers. 92. Toronto: Garnet Exelby D Atlanta. 93. Hamilton: Jim Dowd C Montreal. 94. Detroit: Jason Jaspers C Phoenix. 95. Halifax: Jonathan Sim LW Pittsburgh. 96. Québec: Brandon Reid C Vancouver

Round 13: 97. Québec: Mathieu Darche LW Nashville. 98. Halifax: Harold Druken C Toronto. 99. Detroit: Martin Kariya LW Bridgeport (AHL). 100. Hamilton: Jim Cummins RW Colorado. 101. Toronto: Todd Simpson D Ottawa. 102. Vancouver: Fred Brathwaite G Columbus. 103. Dallas: Andrew Hutchinson D Nashville. 104. Florida: Karel Pilar D Toronto

Round 14: 105. Florida: Darren Rumble D Tampa Bay. 106. Dallas: Gavin Morgan C Dallas. 107. Vancouver: Kirk Muller C (DNP). 108. Toronto: Doug Doull LW Boston. 109. Hamilton: Brad Norton D Washington. 110. Detroit: Darren Van Oene LW Providence (AHL). 111. Halifax: Anders Myrvold D Detroit. 112. Québec: Joe Rullier D Manitoba (AHL)

Round 15: 113. Québec: J.F. Damphousse G Hamilton (AHL). 114. Halifax: Rory Fitzpatrick D Buffalo. 115. Detroit: Chris Hajt D Washington. 116. Hamilton: Sergei Zholtok C Nashville. 117. Toronto: Trevor Kidd G Toronto. 118. Vancouver: Mike Glumac RW Worcester (AHL). 119. Dallas: Ross Lupaschuk D Wilkes Barre/Scranton (AHL). 120. Florida: Craig Adams RW Carolina

Round 16: 121. Florida: Matt Walker D St. Louis. 122. Dallas: Pete Vandermeer LW Philadelphia (AHL). 123. Vancouver: Zach Parisé C North Dakota (NCAA). 124. Toronto: Andy Delmore D Buffalo. 125. Hamilton: John Gruden D Washington. 126. Detroit: Beat Forster D Davos (Switz). 127. Halifax: Donald Audette RW Florida. 128. Québec: Eric Bélanger C Los Angeles

Round 17: 129. Québec: Patrick Boileau D Pittsburgh. 130. Halifax: Greg Crozier LW San Antonio (AHL). 131. Detroit: Chad Wiseman RW NY Rangers. 132. Hamilton: Cliff Ronning C NY Islanders. 133. Toronto: Luke Sellars D Chicago (AHL). 134. Vancouver: Scott Upshall LW Nashville. 135. Dallas: Mike Green C NY Rangers. 136. Florida: Riku Hahl C Colorado

Round 18: 137. Florida: Trent Whitfield C Washington. 138. Dallas: Casey Hankinson RW Anaheim. 139. Vancouver: Randy Rowe LW St. John's (AHL). 140. Toronto: Steve Thomas RW Detroit. 141. Hamilton: Jan Hlavac LW NY Rangers. 142. Detroit: Seamus Kotyk G Cleveland (AHL). 143. Halifax: Jason Botterill LW Buffalo. 144. Québec: Stéphane Richer LW (DNP)

Round 19: 145. Québec: Marc Denis G Columbus. 146. Halifax: Steve Martins C St. Louis. 147. Detroit: Greg Jacina C San Antonio (AHL). 148. Hamilton: Marc Bergevin D Vancouver. 149. Toronto: David Oliver RW Detroit. 150. Vancouver: Kevin Miller RW Detroit. 151. Dallas: Craig Johnson LW Washington. 152. Florida: Jason Williams C Detroit

Round 20: 153. Florida: Brett McLean C Chicago. 154. Dallas: Shane Willis RW Tampa Bay. 155. Vancouver: D.J. Smith D Hershey (AHL). 156. Toronto: Burke Henry D Chicago. 157. Hamilton: Mike Keane RW Vancouver. 158. Detroit: Jeremy Stevenson LW Nashville. 159. Halifax: Bryan Helmer D Phoenix. 160. Québec: Alain Nasreddine D Wilkes Barre/Scranton (AHL)

Round 21: 161. Québec: Martin Grenier D Vancouver. 162. Halifax: Eric Fichaud G Hamilton (AHL). 163. Detroit: Michael Schutte D Houston (AHL). 164. Hamilton: Nolan Baumgartner D Vancouver. 165. Toronto: Shayne Corson LW Dallas. 166. Vancouver: Scott Pellerin LW St. Louis. 167. Dallas: Matt Kinch D Hershey (AHL). 168. Florida: Tyler Bouck RW Vancouver

Round 22: 169. Florida: Brad Tapper RW Binghamton (AHL). 170. Dallas: Nick Naumenko D Utah (AHL). 171. Vancouver: Mike Wilson D Springfield (AHL). 172. Toronto: Jesse Wallin D Lowell (AHL). 173. Hamilton: Dave Lowry LW Calgary. 174. Detroit: Craig Anderson G Chicago. 175. Halifax: Landon Wilson RW Pittsburgh. 176. Québec: Benoît Dusablon C NY Rangers

Round 23: 177. Québec: Steve Brulé RW Hershey (AHL). 178. Halifax: Martin Sonnenberg LW Calgary. 179. Detroit: Ryan Ready LW Worcester (AHL). 180. Hamilton: Pascal Rheaume C St. Louis. 181. Toronto: Bates Battaglia LW Washington. 182. Vancouver: Sean Pronger C Vancouver. 183. Dallas: Tom Lawson G Hershey (AHL). 184. Florida: Mikhail Kuleshov LW Colorado

Round 24: 185. Florida: Gord Dwyer LW Montreal. 186. Dallas: Curtis Foster. 187. Vancouver: Mathieu Chouinard G Los Angeles. 188. Toronto: Brendan Witt D Washington. 189. Hamilton: Andreas Lilja D Florida. 190. Detroit: Chris Hartsburg C Albany (AHL). 191. Halifax: Chris Taylor C Buffalo. 192. Québec: Marc-André Bergeron D Edmonton

Round 25: 193. Québec: Daniel Corso C Atlanta. 194. Halifax: Eric Healey C Chicago (AHL). 195. Detroit: Ted Drury C Kassel (Ger). 196. Hamilton: Travis Brigley LW Colorado. 197. Toronto: Sandy McCarthy RW NY Rangers. 189. Vancouver: Ray Schultz D Milwaukee (AHL). 199. Dallas: Mike Mottau D Cincinnati (AHL). 200. Florida: Jason Wiemer C Minnesota

Round 26: 201. Florida: Stephen Webb RW NY Islanders. 202. Dallas: Bryan Lundbohm C Milwaukee (AHL). 203. Vancouver: Michel Picard LW Grand Rapids (AHL). 204. Toronto: Jamie Hodson G Greensboro (ECHL). 205. Hamilton: Dan Blackburn G NY Rangers. 206. Detroit: Bubba Berenzweig D Utah (AHL). 207. Halifax: Paul Healey RW NY Rangers. 208. Québec: Frederic Cloutier G Houston (AHL)

Round 27: 209. Québec: Damian Surma LW Carolina. 210. Halifax: Ken Belanger LW (DNP). 211. Detroit: Craig Mills RW (DNP). 212. Hamilton: Michal Grosek LW Boston. 213. Toronto: John Tripp RW Los Angeles. 214. Vancouver: Steve Gainey LW Dallas. 215. Dallas: Kyle Wanvig RW Minnesota. 216. Florida: Bill Lindsay LW Atlanta

Round 28: 217. Florida: Bill Muckalt RW Houston (AHL). 218. Dallas: Scott Barney C Los Angeles. 219. Vancouver: Kevin Dallman D Providence (AHL). 220. Toronto: Jason Chimera LW Edmonton. 221. Hamilton: Mike Farrell RW Nashville. 222. Detroit: Patrick Traverse D Hamilton. 223. Halifax: Scott Clemmensen G New Jersey. 224. Québec: Guillaume Lefebvre LW Wilkes Barre/Scranton (AHL)

Round 29: 225. Québec: Sylvain Blouin LW Manitoba (AHL). 226. Halifax: Alex Henry D Minnesota. 227. Detroit: Serge Payer C Ottawa. 228. Hamilton: Bobby Allen D Toronto (AHL). 229. Toronto: Nathan Smith C Vancouver. 230. Vancouver: Steve McLaren LW St. Louis. 231. Dallas: Todd Harvey RW San Jose. 232. Florida: André Roy LW Tampa Bay.

Round 30: 233. Florida: Paul Elliott D San Antonio (AHL). 234. Dallas: Scott Parker RW San Jose. 235. Vancouver: Jeff Paul D Hartford (AHL). 236. Toronto: James Patrick D Buffalo. 237. Hamilton: Don McLean C Columbus. 238. Detroit: Mike Brown LW Binghamton (AHL). 239. Halifax: Brad Moran C Columbus. 240. Québec: Ramzi Abid LW Pittsburgh

The World Hockey Association 2 (WHA2)

Founded in 2003 as a developmental league by New Jersey businessman David Waronker, the WHA2 began play in November 2003 with six teams concentrated in the southeastern United States. The six teams in the WHA2 were the Lakeland Loggerheads, Macon Trax, Alabama Slammers, Miami Manatees, Orlando Seals and Jacksonville Barracudas.

2003-2004 Final Standings

	gp	record	pts	gf	ga
J'ville	59	40-18-1	91	233	175
Alabama	58	34-20-4	72	224	196
Macon	56	30-20-6	66	218	193
Miami	48	24-19-5	53	215	213
Orlando	57	27-25-5	59	198	197
Lakeland	58	13-38-7	33	181	295

Coaches

Alabama: Garry Unger; Jacksonville: Ron Duguay; Miami: Zac Boyer; Lakeland: Rick Ladouceur; Orlando: Jim Paek; Macon: Tommy Stewart.

Note: Miami was unable to play its remaining home games after February 28. Those games were cancelled and Miami only played games on the road thereafter. The top four teams by winning percentage advanced to the playoffs.

Scoring Leaders

name	g	a	pts	pim
Lawrence, Ala	26	69	95	149
Deeves, Mac	36	48	84	44
Stephens, Orl	39	43	82	24
Prentice, Ala	31	46	77	96
Miller, Jax	32	41	73	134
Zoryk, Mac	33	39	72	8
Swider, Mia	24	47	71	14
Elders, Orl	32	35	67	46
Kaebel, Jax	31	36	67	56
Federenko, Orl	24	40	64	38
Gurskis, Mac	23	35	58	24
Murphy, Mac	16	40	56	14

Goaltending
(Minimum 25 games)

name	gp	ga	record	gaa
Hevey, Jax	36	97	25-9-0	2.78
Kollar, Mac	27	76	13-8-3	3.06
Ronayne, Ala	40	129	24-12-2	3.20
Goverde, Orl	43	132	20-17-2	3.24
Faulkner, Mac	33	98	16-12-0	3.58
Poissant, Lak	36	152	6-21-1	4.89

Shutouts

Ronayne (Ala), Correia (Orl): 2 each. Goverde (Orl), Ziemski (Jax), Kollar (Mac), Hevey (Jax), Beaubien (Ala): 1 each.

Scores of Games
(ot = overtime, so = shootout)

6 Nov Macon 5 at Lakeland 2
7 Nov Jacksonville 5 at Alabama 2
8 Nov Macon 6 at Miami 10
• *Darren Cain (Mia) 3 g*
• *Eric Perricone (Mia) 3 g*
Lakeland 2 at Orlando 4
Jacksonville 2 at Alabama 1 (ot)
14 Nov Lakeland 2 at Miami 5
15 Nov Jacksonville 2 at Miami 5
16 Nov Macon 6 at Orlando 2
21 Nov Orlando 5 at Alabama 3
• *Paul Vincent (Ala) 3 g*
22 Nov Alabama 7 at Macon 8 (ot-so)
• *Ryan Prentice (Ala) 4 g*
23 Nov Alabama 5 at Lakeland 4
• *Paul Vincent (Ala) 3 g*
Miami 4 at Orlando 5 (ot)
Jacksonville 4 at Macon 3
26 Nov Alabama 4 at Lakeland 2
Orlando 3 at Miami 4
28 Nov Lakeland 4 at Alabama 5 (ot)
Miami 6 at Jacksonville 2
Orlando 4 at Macon 6
• *David Deeves (Mac) 3 g*
29 Nov Lakeland 1 at Alabama 3
Macon 3 at Jacksonville 5
Miami 2 at Orlando 6
5 Dec Jacksonville 7 at Macon 4
Miami 3 at Lakeland 4
Orlando 4 at Alabama 3
6 Dec Lakeland 4 at Macon 5
• *Steve Zoryk (Mac) 3 g*
Miami 3 at Jacksonville 5
O'do 0 at Alabama 1 (ot-so)
• *Mike Correia (Orl) 44 saves,*
• *James Ronayne (Ala) 21 sv*
7 Dec Miami 3 at Orlando 6
Jacksonville 7 at Lakeland 4
12 Dec Miami 0 at Macon 6
• *Andy Kollar (Mac) 20 saves*
Orlando 3 at Lakeland 4
Alabama 4 at Jacksonville 6
• *Paul Vincent (Ala) 3 g*
• *Mike Wirll (Jax) 3 g*
13 Dec Orlando 2 at Macon 1
Alabama 3 at Miami 4 (ot-so)
Lakeland 0 at Jacksonville 1 (ot)
• *Nate Ziemski (Jax) 18 sv*

14 Dec Jacksonville 5 at Lakeland 3
Alabama 4 at Miami 3 (ot)
• *Paul Vincent (Ala) 3 g*
18 Dec Jacksonville 5 at Macon 4 (ot)
Alabama 2 at Orlando 3
19 Dec Lakeland 4 at Alabama 6
Orlando 5 at Macon 3
Jacksonville 2 at Miami 4
20 Dec Miami 5 at Lakeland 2
Macon 6 at Alabama 4
Jacksonville 2 at Orlando 3
26 Dec Macon 3 at Alabama 9
Jacksonville 0 at Orlando 1 (ot)
• *David Goverde (Orl) 44 sv*
Lakeland 1 at Miami 2
27 Dec Macon 3 at Alabama 4 (ot-so)
Jacksonville 3 at Miami 6
• *Oak Hewer (Mia) 3 g, 2 a*
Orlando 6 at Lakeland 5 (ot)
• *Brad Federenko (Orl) 3 g*
28 Dec Miami 3 at Lakeland 5
31 Dec Alabama 4 at Jacksonville 6
Orlando 4 at L'land 5 (ot-so)
2 Jan Miami 3 at Alabama 5
Lakeland 1 at Macon 9
• *Jeff Antonovich (Mac) 3g*
• *Steve Zoryk (Mac) 2g, 3a*
• *David Deeves (Mac) 1g 4a*
Orlando 1 at Jack'ville 2 (ot-so)
3 Jan Lakeland 2 at Alabama 3
• *F. Beaubien (Ala) 26 sv*
Macon 2 at Orlando 1
Miami 4 at Jacksonville 5 (ot-so)
4 Jan Jacksonville 5 at Miami 3
• *Jamie Miller (Jax) 3 g*
Macon 3 at Lakeland 1
6 Jan Macon 1 at Jacksonville 4
• *Jamie Miller (Jax) 3 g*
8 Jan Alabama 4 at Orlando 1
• *Ryan Prentice (Ala) 3g, 1a*
9 Jan Orlando 6 at Lakeland 0
• *Mike Correia (Orl) 16 saves*
Jacksonville 5 at Macon 2
Miami 2 at Alabama 4
10 Jan Miami 7 at Alabama 3
• *Oak Hewer (Mia) 3g, 2a*
Jacksonville 1 at Orlando 4
Lakeland 1 at Macon 4

11 Jan Miami 3 at Jacksonville 5
Lakeland 2 at Orlando 1
Alabama 3 at Macon 4
15 Jan Jacksonville 0 at Alabama 2
• *James Ronayne (Ala) 36 sv*
Lakeland 1 at Orlando 4
16 Jan Jacksonville 2 at Macon 5
Alabama 1 at Miami 3
17 Jan Jacksonville 1 at Macon 4
Alabama 5 at Orlando 3
Lakeland 3 at Miami 9
• *Greg Lecolst (Mia) 3g, 1a*
18 Jan Lakeland 0 at Miami 4
• *Sean Weaver (Mia) 26 sv*
Alabama 5 at Macon 3
• *Doug Lawrence (Ala) 3g, 1a*
23 Jan Alabama 1 at Miami 5
Macon 4 at Lakeland 5 (ot)
24 Jan Orlando 3 at Miami 7
• *Oak Hewer (Mia) 3g, 1a*
Alabama 5 at Lakeland 2
Macon 2 at Jacksonville 3
25 Jan Macon 6 at Miami 7 (ot)
• *Kevin Swider (Mia) 3g, 1a*
Orlando 1 at Jacksonville 4
28 Jan Macon 2 at Orlando 3 (ot-so)
29 Jan Miami 4 at Macon 1
Alabama 3 at Lakeland 4
30 Jan Lakeland 4 at Orlando 5
Miami 2 at Macon 7
• *David Deeves (Mac) 4g, 2a*
Alabama 3 at Jacksonville 7
• *Derek Toninato (Jax) 3g, 1a*
31 Jan Alabama 2 at Macon 1
Orlando 4 at L'land 3 (ot-so)
Miami 4 at Jacksonville 5
1 Feb Jacksonville 5 at Orlando 2
3 Feb Lakeland 4 at Macon 5
6 Feb Macon 3 at Alabama 2
Orlando 3 at Miami 4 (ot-so)
Lakeland 4 at Jacksonville 2
7 Feb Macon 2 at Alabama 3
Lakeland 1 at Jacksonville 6
• *Chris Hackett (Jax) 3 g*
8 Feb Jacksonville 2 at Miami 6
• *Greg Lecolst (Mia) 3 g*
10 Feb Miami 4 at Orlando 3 (ot)
12 Feb Macon 3 at Alabama 5
Jacksonville 4 at Orlando 5

13 Feb	Jacksonville 1 at Alabama 3
14 Feb	Jacksonville 3 at Alabama 1
15 Feb	Lakeland 2 at Orlando 7
	• *Seamus Galligan (Orl) 4 g*
17 Feb	Jacksonville 8 at Lakeland 6
	• *Jamie Miller (Jax) 3 g, 1 a*
19 Feb	Alabama 7 at Orlando 6 (ot)
	• *Chad Peck (Ala) 3 g*
20 Feb	Macon 4 at Jacksonville 5
	Miami 4 at Lakeland 6
21 Feb	Miami 5 at Lakeland 6 (ot)
	Orlando 2 at Jacksonville 4
	Macon 4 at Alabama 3
22 Feb	Miami 7 at Jacksonville 3
	Macon 2 at Orlando 1
24 Feb	Alabama 3 at Jacksonville 4
26 Feb	Lakeland 2 at Alabama 5
	Macon 0 at Jacksonville 3
	• *Randy Hevey (Jax) 25 sv*
	Miami 9 at Orlando 4
28 Feb	Macon 2 at Orlando 1
	Lakeland 1 at Jacksonville 5
	Alabama 6 at Miami 5 (ot)
	• *Doug Lawrence (Ala) 6 a*
29 Feb	Alabama 3 at Macon 2 (ot)
1 Mar	Macon 7 at Lakeland 6 (ot)
4 Mar	Jacksonville 1 at Alabama 4
	Macon 5 at Orlando 4
	• *Mike Sanderson (Orl) 3 g*
5 Mar	Orlando 4 at Jacksonville 6
	• *Jason Elders (Orl) 3 g*
	Lakeland 4 at Alabama 7
	• *Jaroslav Kresac (Ala) 3 g*
7 Mar	Macon 6 at Lakeland 5 (ot)

9 Mar	Lakeland 3 at Orlando 2
11 Mar	Lakeland 5 at Orlando 8
	• *Jason Elders (Orl) 3 g*
12 Mar	Jacksonville 4 at Macon 5
	• *John Gurskis (Mac) 3 g*
	Orlando 1 at Alabama 5
13 Mar	Lakeland 5 at Alabama 9
	• *Bob Quinnell (Ala) 3 g*
14 Mar	Alabama 2 at Macon 4
	Miami 4 at Orlando 8
	Lakeland 1 at Jacksonville 6
18 Mar	Miami 7 at Lakeland 10
	• *Chris Cerrella (Lak) 3g, 3a*
	• *Kevin Swider (Mia) 3 g*
	Orlando 2 at Macon 1
19 Mar	Orlando 2 at Jacksonville 4
	Alabama 4 at Lakeland 3
20 Mar	Orlando 1 at Alabama 3
	Lakeland 1 at Jacksonville 8
	• *Kory Baker (Jax) 3 g*
21 Mar	Alabama 1 at Jacksonville 8
	• *Jamie Miller (Jax) 4g 2a*
	Macon 6 at Lakeland 2
25 Mar	Miami 6 at Orlando 5
	• *Chad Cabana (Mia) 4 g*
26 Mar	Alabama 3 at Macon 4 (ot)
	Orlando 1 at Lakeland 2
27 Mar	Orlando 1 at Macon 2
28 Mar	Jacksonville 3 at Lakeland 2
31 Mar	Alabama 3 at Jacksonville 1
1 Apr	Miami 4 at Orlando 8
2 Apr	Miami 1 at Alabama 9
	Orlando 4 at Macon 1
	Jacksonville 7 at Lakeland 2
	• *Jay McCabe (Jax) 3 g*

3 Apr	Miami 4 at Alabama 8
	Lakeland 2 at Macon 14
	• *Craig Miller (Mac) 3g, 2a*
	• *Edan Welch (Mac) 4g, 1a*
	Orlando 4 at Jacksonville 6
	• *Klage Kaebel (Jax) 3 g*
4 Apr	Alabama 2 at Jacksonville 6
	Miami 6 at Lakeland 11
	• *Chris Cerrella (Lak) 3g, 2a*
	• *Joe Seroski (Lak) 3g, 1a*
	Macon 6 at Orlando 3

End of Regular Season

Playoff Results
All series are best of three games.

6 Apr	Miami 3 at Jacksonville 2 (ot)
7 Apr	Miami 3 at Jacksonville 5
	• *Tom Perry (Mia) 3 g*
	Alabama 2 at Macon 7
8 Apr	Miami 2 at Jacksonville 3 (ot)
	Macon 4 at Alabama 2

*Jacksonville and Macon
advance to the Final Round.*

| 10 Apr | Macon 2 at Jacksonville 3 (ot) |
| 16 Apr | Jacksonville 7 at Macon 4 |

Jacksonville is League Champion

Gallery

Bill Gilligan

Guy Dufour

Norm Descoteaux

Brian Cadle

Kevin Ahearn

Nick Fotiu

Frank Golembrosky

Ed Hatoum

Gerry Leroux

Mark Messier

Bob Woytowich

Jerry Zrymiak

J. C. Migneault

Larry Israelson

Wayne Hillman

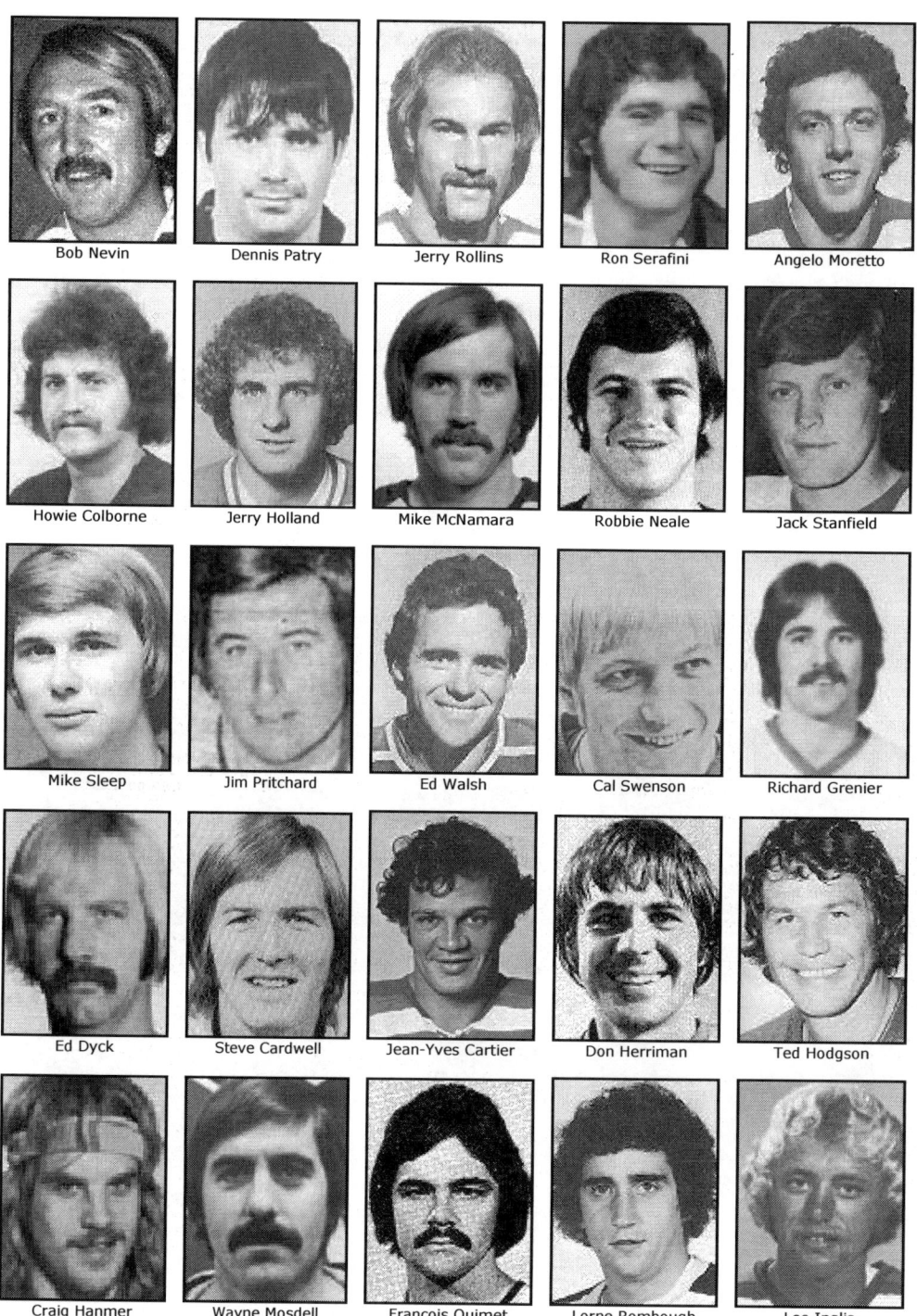

Bob Nevin   Dennis Patry   Jerry Rollins   Ron Serafini   Angelo Moretto

Howie Colborne   Jerry Holland   Mike McNamara   Robbie Neale   Jack Stanfield

Mike Sleep   Jim Pritchard   Ed Walsh   Cal Swenson   Richard Grenier

Ed Dyck   Steve Cardwell   Jean-Yves Cartier   Don Herriman   Ted Hodgson

Craig Hanmer   Wayne Mosdell   Francois Ouimet   Lorne Rombough   Lee Inglis

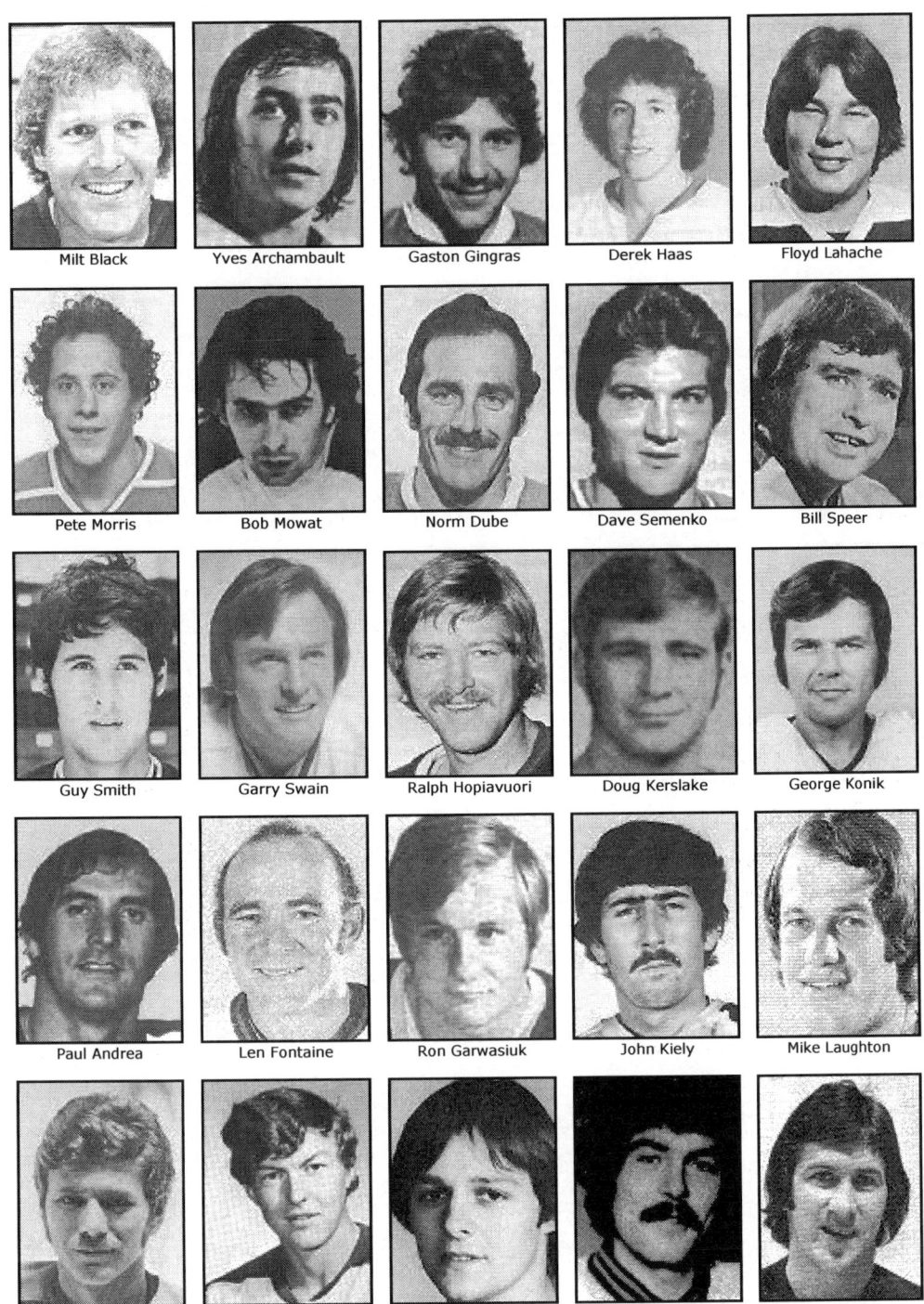

Milt Black   Yves Archambault   Gaston Gingras   Derek Haas   Floyd Lahache

Pete Morris   Bob Mowat   Norm Dube   Dave Semenko   Bill Speer

Guy Smith   Garry Swain   Ralph Hopiavuori   Doug Kerslake   George Konik

Paul Andrea   Len Fontaine   Ron Garwasiuk   John Kiely   Mike Laughton

Jarda Krupicka   Terry Holbrook   Rick Jodzio   Alf Handrahan   Don Gordon

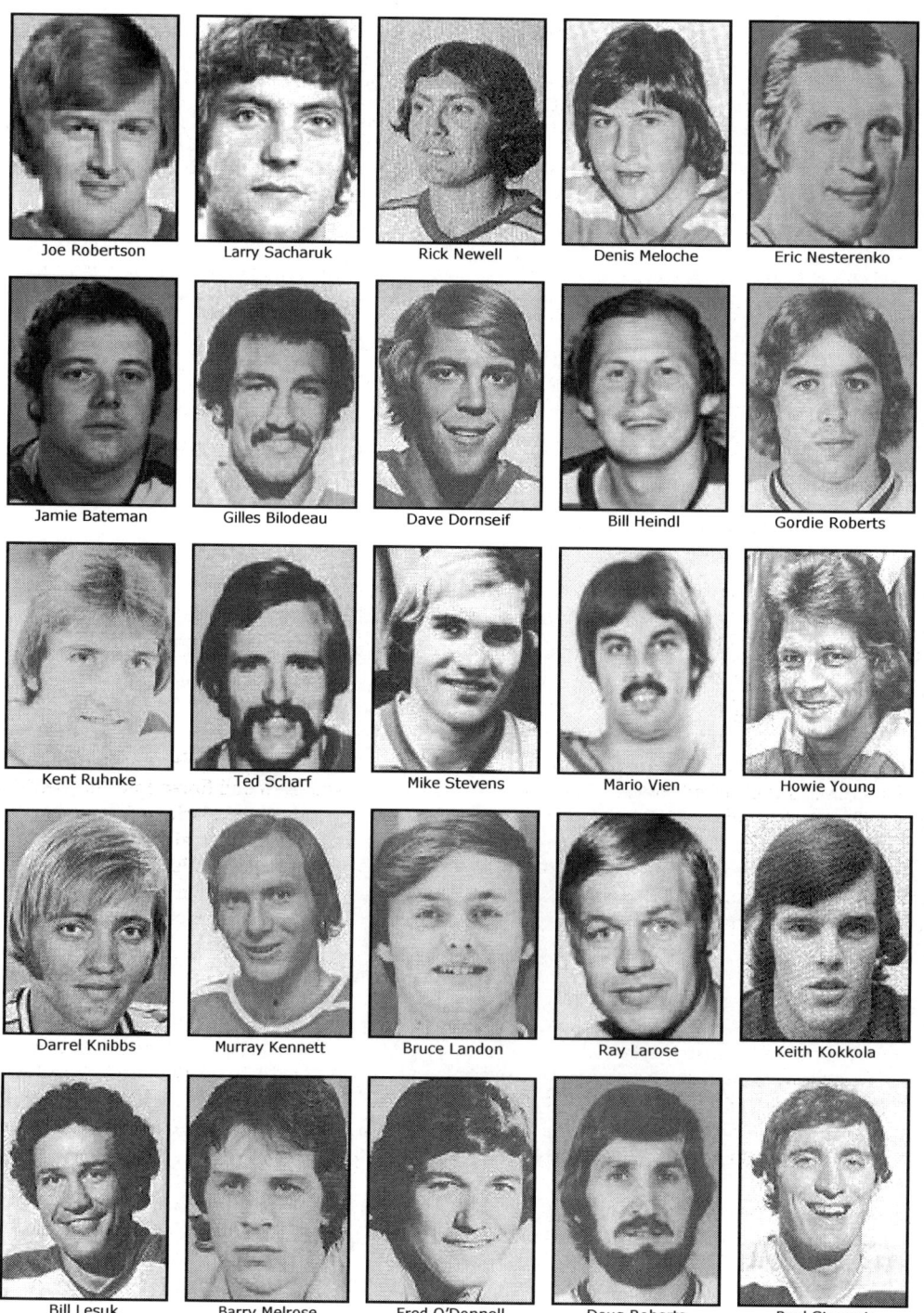

Joe Robertson   Larry Sacharuk   Rick Newell   Denis Meloche   Eric Nesterenko

Jamie Bateman   Gilles Bilodeau   Dave Dornseif   Bill Heindl   Gordie Roberts

Kent Ruhnke   Ted Scharf   Mike Stevens   Mario Vien   Howie Young

Darrel Knibbs   Murray Kennett   Bruce Landon   Ray Larose   Keith Kokkola

Bill Lesuk   Barry Melrose   Fred O'Donnell   Doug Roberts   Paul Stewart

In Memoriam

Players
Steve Atkinson
Serge Aubry
Garnet "Ace" Bailey
Blake Ball
Dave Balon
Andy Bathgate
Gilles Bilodeau
Bernie Blanchette
Carl Brewer
Ken Broderick
Mike Byers
Brian Cadle
Larry Cahan
John Cunniff
Alain Caron
Mike Chernoff
Bob Dillabough
Kent Douglas
Chris Evans
Reggie Fleming
Bill Flett
Rick Foley
George Gardner
Jean Gauthier
Andre Gill
Bill Goldsworthy
Bruce Greig
Matti Hagman
Craig Hanmer
John Hanna

Nick Harbaruk
Ted Hargreaves
Bill Heindl
Bill Hicke
Wayne Hillman
Ed Hoekstra
Larry Hornung
Bill Horton
Gordie Howe
Danny Johnson
Joe Junkin
Doug Kerslake
Bill Klatt
Keith Kokkola
Pete Laframboise
Danny Lawson
Jacques Locas
Len Lunde
Gary MacGregor
Ralph MacSweyn
Gilles Marotte
Dunc McCallum
Ted McCaskill
Don McLeod
Mike McMahon
George Morrison
Keke Mortson
Don O'Donoghue
Wally Olds
Kevin O'Shea
Marcel Paille

Bob Perreault
Jacques Plante
Jim Pritchard
Wayne Rutledge
Frank Sanders
Paul Shmyr
Gary Sittler
Lars-Erik Sjoberg
Mike Sleep
Al Smith
Brian Smith
Fred Speck
Bill Speer
Irv Spencer
Cal Swenson
Joe Szura
Rudy Tajcnar
Paul Terbenche
J.-C. Tremblay
Guy Trottier
Juha Widing
Tom Williams
Barry Wilkins
Chris Worthy
Bob Woytowich
Howie Young

Coaches
Marc Boileau
John Brophy
Armand Guidolin
Billy Harris
Doug Harvey
Camille Henry
Ron Ingram
Bobby Kromm
Marcel Pronovost
Maurice Richard
Al Rollins
Brian Shaw
Terry Slater
Glen Sonmor
Phil Watson
John Wilson

Officials
Vern Buffey
Art Skov

Builders & Executives
John Bassett
James Browitt
Bob Brownridge
Dick Carlson
Paul Deneau
Dr. Zane Feldman

John Ferguson
Ed Fitkin
Marius Fortier
Larry Gordon
Ben Hatskin
A.J. "Buck" Houle
Colleen Howe
Bill Hunter
William MacFarland
Jack McKeag
Walt Marlow
Doug Michel
Marvin Milkes
Scotty Munro
Rudy Pilous
Paul Racine
Robert Schmertz
Dave Simkin
Ed Short
Annis Stukus
Nick Trbovich

Media
Reyn Davis
Jack Lautier

Garnet (Ace) Bailey, age 53 and the Director of Professional Scouting for the Los Angeles Kings, was among the many victims on board the United Airlines Flight 175 that was commandeered and flown into the World Trade Center's South Tower, September 11, 2001. Bailey, along with Kings' Amateur Scout Mark Bavis, was returning to Los Angeles from his home in Massachusetts to prepare for the Kings' 2001 preseason training camp. Bailey was a veteran of 11 seasons in the NHL and one in the WHA. Highlights of his career include two Stanley Cups with Boston in 1970 and 1972, and a year playing alongside 18-year old Wayne Gretzky in Edmonton. Bailey had worked as a scout for the Oilers for 13 seasons after retirement as a player, before moving to a similar position with Los Angeles.

Gordie Howe passed away on June 10, 2016, age 88. His place in hockey history secure after a remarkable 25-year career with Detroit ending in 1971, and a 1972 induction into the Hockey Hall of Fame, Howe embarked on the second great phase of his career when he joined his sons with the Houston Aeros in June 1973. Howe would play six seasons in the WHA and another in the NHL, retiring a second time in 1980. In the years since, he was an ambassador for the game and active in charity. He suffered a stroke in 2014 and underwent experimental stem-cell therapy, which helped him recover to some extent. Along with Bobby Hull, Howe's role in the early WHA played a direct role in the league's survival and eventual absorption into the NHL.

Reyn Davis probably knew more about the WHA than anyone during his lifetime, covering the league for the *Winnipeg Free Press*, as well as writing many free-lance articles for *The Sporting News, The Hockey News, Hockey News-Pictorial* and many other hockey publications of the time. His weekly article in The Sporting News offered up-to-the-minute happenings in the league, and was an invaluable resource to me while researching this book.

Jack Lautier covered the Hartford Whalers for the *Hartford Times* and the *Bristol Press*. In 1996, he teamed with Frank Polnaszek to write and produce *Same Game, Different Name*, which recounted the World Hockey Association in the words of the players and executives who made the league happen. In a way, he wrote the book I had always wanted to write, a multiple first-person account of the league done in the style of Terry Pluto's landmark book *Loose Balls*, which recounted the American Basketball Association. I never viewed his book as competition; in fact, I thought our two books complemented one another well. I purchased *Same Game, Different Name* when it first came available and thought it to be a marvelous book. He was the author of seven books, mainly on the Whalers but also about the Wolf Pack of the AHL and the Boston Red Sox of Major League Baseball.

Research Methods and Notes

Research Methods

The research for this book began in October 1993. I planned to create a book that covered the WHA in as much detail as possible from a statistical standpoint. I had no real sense of what form the book would take when I started the project, but I vaguely modeled the book as though it were a massive media guide, to include each game's results and complete scoring and goaltending information. I wrote the book mainly to satisfy my own curiosity.

The game-by-game scores were taken from rolls of microfilm of the *New York Times*, *Los Angeles Times*, *Chicago Tribune*, *Washington Post* and *Arizona Republic*. This task took approximately four months to compile and sort by team, and to ensure internal accuracy. By going through the old newspapers, I also read the articles detailing the games, and the occasional expository article, to gain a flavor of the league.

Next, I compiled the individual player and goaltender statistics, using *The Hockey News*, *The Sporting News* and the individual team and league media guides. Unfortunately, but not unexpectedly, I found many discrepancies. For example, player goal totals did not sum to the team totals, which I knew to be correct. The league's media guides were the usual source of these errors, and these were often repeated unknowingly by *The Sporting News* guides. However, *The Hockey News* statistics usually were more accurate, as were those in the individual team's media guides. I was able to correct most mistakes, many of which were simply over- or under-reporting a player's goal or assist count by one or two. In a few instances, the problems were more significant:

- The 1975-76 Indianapolis Racers statistics, as reported in the 1976-77 league guide and other sources, had many errors. I tracked down a 1976 playoff program that reported the team's statistics accurately, which I use here.
- Brian Lavender's statistics for the 1975-76 Denver Spurs-Ottawa Civics were reported to be 2 goals, 0 assists, 2 points and 7 penalty minutes. However, *The Hockey News*, dated December 30, 1975, listed him with 3 goals, 6 assists and 28 penalty minutes. In one of the last games the Ottawa team played, Lavender scored 2 goals and had 7 penalty minutes. These one-game statistics were substituted for his year statistics. He also had a minor penalty in one other Ottawa content. Therefore, I give him credit for 5 goals, 6 assists, 11 points and 37 penalty minutes for 1975-76.

- The 1976 Cleveland Crusaders playoff scoring statistics as reported in most annuals were inconsistent, so I reconstructed these from scratch from the box scores. In one source, the goals scored by the players summed to five (Cleveland actually scored six), while the assists summed to thirteen. Clearly this could not be correct.

I did not have access to all of the back issues of *The Hockey News*, and I had somewhat inconvenient access to *The Sporting News* starting from January 1975, through the Phoenix Public Library, which kept the issues in bound volumes but not necessarily openly available. I purchased individual copies of *The Hockey News*, accruing nearly a hundred copies from that era over a period of time. When I needed to access *The Sporting News*, I would encamp in the library, much of that time trying to locate the bound volumes.

As a research resource, the internet was useless. The ability to "Google" for a site with "WHA Statistics" was still a fantasy for the future. However, I did participate in the rec.sport.hockey usenet group for a few years. I was able to make important contacts, people who helped me in the formative stages of the book, and some whom I list in the Author's Notes page at the front of this book.

During 1994 and 1995, I visited all of the sports memorabilia shops in Phoenix and Tucson, buying as many old Phoenix Roadrunner programs and media guides as I could find, along with other WHA-related items, such as *Left Wing and a Prayer* for 95 cents. Through advertisements in *Sports Collectors Digest* I procured other media guides and programs. Then, a huge stroke of luck: I met Ed Nudge, a collector of hockey media guides going back to the 1960s. Mr. Nudge lives in Glendale, Arizona, and he was extremely generous in allowing me to use his huge collection for my book. It was this chance meeting and his collection of guides and programs that literally brought my book to completion. Mr. Nudge and I have stayed in touch and I eventually purchased the WHA portion of his collection.

A new addition to this book is a game-by-game line score summary, detailing each game's scoring by periods, shots by period, goaltenders and goal scorers. Accuracy is important, and each player's goals should sum to his known quantity for that year. In doing so, I found many mistakes in the game summaries. As a baseline, I used those found in *The Sporting News* (now having access to the complete set of issues) but when a discrepancy would occur, I would double-check against other newspapers. I

used *Le Journal de Quebec* and the *Calgary Herald* most often, having access to most issues of that era. I also used the summaries found at the WHA-HOF website (whahof/games.php), a resource largely assembled by Curtis Walker. His resources are similar to mine, although he also had access to the *Winnipeg Free Press* and *Toronto Globe and Mail*.

The Sporting News summaries had the advantage in that they included the player's running goal count, whereas summaries in *The Hockey News* and other resources were inconsistent in doing so. I realized that although most game summaries were accurate insofar as I could determine, they were prone to errors, especially from that era. Also, it appeared that all summaries came from one source, so that an error in one newspaper would be reprinted verbatim in other newspapers, too.

Errors and discrepancies came in many flavors: (1) a simple typo, or misidentification, especially with players of a similar name. Mark and Marty Howe were often confused with one another in the summaries, as were Larry Hale and Murray Hall, for example; (2) an outright error that could be easily checked against other resources, and (3) situations where a change in scoring occurred after the summaries had been typeset and distributed to papers across Canada and the United States.

In many cases, I was able to correct these errors by checking against the team media guides, which sometimes broke a player's goals down on a team-by-team basis. I would also track the player's running goal count to identify any inconsistencies in the ordinal numbering of each goal. If there was a scoring change to a goal once summaries had been prepared and sent out, it almost certainly would not be reported after the fact in the newspapers. They don't do this today, and certainly not in the 1970s.

The following are a couple of common conundrums I encountered, and how I resolved them:

- Mike Rogers was credited with 34 goals for the 1974-75 Edmonton Oilers, when he should have had 35, while Ken Baird was credited with 31 goals, when he should have had 30. I was able to determine that a goal given to Baird (supposedly his 26th of the season) in the March 25 game against New England most likely was retroactively granted to Rogers, which would have given him the hat trick for that game. I was able to find corroborating evidence of this in the 1978-79 WHA Media Guide that listed each player's hat tricks, showing that Rogers had only two as of the end of the 1977-78 season, one during 1977-78, and none during 1975-76 or 1976-77. Furthermore, Ken Baird's running goal count resets to 26 the next night (March 26), so

the combination of clues leads to just one conclusion: Baird's goal in the March 25th game should be granted to Rogers.

- John Miszuk was credited with three goals during 1976-77, going strictly by the game summaries. However, the official records credit him with two goals that season. I found a "suspicious" goal credited to him on October 12, 1976 against Birmingham. I then checked the Calgary Herald editions of October 13 and October 14. The October 13 edition described the goal as unassisted, fired from the blue line and taking an odd bounce off goaltender Wayne Wood into the net. The October 14 edition included a sentence in which that goal was retroactively credited to Danny Lawson. This is the only instance where a scoring change was reported in a newspaper that I could find.

- Joe Noris was credited with 10 goals for the 1977-78 Birmingham Bulls, going by game summaries only, while Paul Henderson was credited with 36 goals. However, their official counts are 9 and 37, respectively. The game summary for the February 25, 1978 game shows Noris as scoring his 29th goal. That goal clearly was Henderson's which would have been his 29th. In this case, it was clearly a misprint and easy to resolve.

- Marty Howe and John McKenzie were over- and under-counted by one goal each, respectively, for the 1977-78 New England Whalers, with all other Whalers being accounted for. I was able to narrow the probable discrepancy to a March game against Birmingham. I then checked the 1978-79 Whalers Media Guide, which broke down each player's goals by team, and saw that Marty Howe (in my list) had one more goal against Birmingham than he should have, while McKenzie had one less. Thus, the goal should have been McKenzie's. In this case, I used the "overwhelming preponderance of evidence" to make this decision.

- Wayne Gretzky was credited with a goal (according to the game summary) on December 30, 1978 against the Czechs, and his running goal count continued thereafter for another month before the "correction" was made. The 1979-80 Oilers Media Guide shows only the breakdowns against each of the other WHA teams, which match perfectly with the charts, so by inference, his "extra" goal must have come against one of the touring European teams. I was able to get confirmation that he did not actually receive credit for a goal in this game, but who did is uncertain. Every other Oiler's goals are accounted for, except for Doug Berry. By inference only, this would have to be his goal, and I have listed him as such for that game.

There remain a very few cases where I simply cannot resolve the discrepancy. A couple are noted below:

- Rusty Patenaude scored 20 goals for the 1974-75 Oilers, while Bobby Sheehan scored 19 goals. However, my counts show Patenaude with 21 goals, Sheehan with 18. The 1975-76 Oilers Media Guide does not show breakdowns, and the game summaries seem to support the 21 and 18 counts, which differ from the official counts. I have no way at the moment to determine where the discrepancy lies, so I have left it alone.
- Steve Atkinson of Toronto is officially credited with two goals during 1975-76, but the game summaries give him credit for three goals, and checking against other summaries, all are consistent in crediting him with three goals. Meanwhile, teammate Paul Heaver is officially credited with two goals, but only appears once in the 1975-76 summaries. My suspicion is that Atkinson's third goal should be Heaver's, but I have no corroborating evidence, so I left the discrepancy alone.
- Thommie Abrahamsson is credited with 5 goals when he officially should have 6 for the 1976-77 New England Whalers, while Ralph Backstrom has 19 goals credited when he should have 18. All other Whaler goals are properly accounted for. However, other than narrowing down the likely game to within a two-month window, I cannot determine which of Backstrom's goals should be Abrahamsson's.

Proper Spelling of Russian Names

The names of the players from the Soviet Union were transliterated from the Cyrillic alphabet into the Western alphabet, but no standards existed at the time (1970s) regarding consistency. Thus, for example, "Alexander" could be transliterated as Aleksander or even Aleksandr, if going by a literal character-for-character transliteration. The spellings in this book reflect the preferred standards as put forth by the International Ice Hockey Federation (IIHF), dating from 2011 and 2015. Reader Alex Baranov helped in establishing the proper spellings using modern standards, an improvement over the variable ways these names were spelled in the 1970s.

Unfinished Business

Unfortunately there remain a few open questions and areas of slight confusion that I have never been able to satisfactorily rectify. The following lists a few such areas. Of course, help is always appreciated!

The San Francisco Franchise

The league granted Gary Davidson (or, equivalently, Gary Davidson granted himself) a franchise to be housed in San Francisco, at the Cow Palace south of the city. History shows that this franchise was sold to a sextet of Quebec City businessmen and moved to Quebec in February 1972, becoming the Nordiques.

Davidson himself discusses this team in his book, *Breaking the Game Wide Open*, and refers to the team as the Sharks. However, in my discussions with Len Shapiro, a former employee of the Cow Palace who dealt with Davidson and his people briefly in late 1971, he mentioned that the team was to be named the SeaHawks. Most subsequent sources refer to the team as the Sharks (and the proposed Los Angeles team as the Aces), while just one source, the 1976-77 Minnesota Fighting Saints Media Guide, refers to the team as the SeaHawks.

To me, what this team was going to be named is irrelevant. It is my opinion that Davidson had no intention of ever putting together a team for San Francisco, and held the franchise rights for the express intent of selling it for a profit, which is exactly what he did. In his book, he makes references to himself as one more comfortable running a league than a team, and one who sees holding onto, then selling for a profit, a franchise as a reasonable tactic for someone who starts such a league.

It is known that Quebec City wanted in as early as August 1971. Why they weren't granted a franchise at the November 1971 meetings is speculative, but circumstantial evidence suggests that during late 1971, there may have been some financing problems besetting the Quebec ownership group, and possibly some issues regarding Le Colisee, the planned home rink of the Quebec team. It is plausible that Davidson granted himself the rights to a franchise purely to "save" one for the Quebec group, if and when they worked out the details besetting their initial bid. For Davidson, this was a good business move: by holding a franchise in limbo, he could sell at a profit when the time arose, and clearly, Quebec City was a better bet for the league than San Francisco. Why even refer to the team as a San Francisco entrant? My best guess is purely for media exposure. I strongly believe based on the evidence I have seen that Quebec was a given for the league from the earliest days, but only got in "officially" in February 1972 after working out whatever details were obstructing their bid from the start.

The Ottawa Civics Logo and Uniform

The Civics lasted seven games during the first two weeks of January 1976. They were born as the Denver Spurs seven months earlier in May 1975 as an expansion franchise. When the team failed badly in Denver, owner Ivan Mullenix sought to sell the team through an Ottawa group known as the Founders Club. The Spurs left Denver on an extended road trip in late December 1975 and never returned. During the two weeks in which the sale of the team was attempting to be made, the nomad team called themselves the Ottawa Civics and played two "home" games in Ottawa. However, the Founders Club could not broker the deal, and Mullenix folded the team in mid-January 1976.

As far as I know, there was no Civics logo, and it is known that there was no Ottawa jersey worn by the team. During their seven games as the Civics, the team continued to wear their Spurs uniforms, sometimes without crest. A photograph from the Phoenix Gazette newspaper from January 1976, recounting a game between the Civics and Road-runners, shows the "Civics" wearing their Spurs sweaters. This was the second-to-last game ever played by the Civics. Further, I asked Ralph Backstrom about the existence of a Civics logo or uniform when I met him in 1999, and he confirmed they never wore Civics jerseys. It is possible there was a logo, perhaps on letterhead, but I have never seen an authentic, verifiable logo.

Articles in the *Ottawa Sun* newspaper from that period mention that "Civics" was meant to be a temporary name until a new one could be selected, and that there were plans to adopt a red and black color scheme at some point in the future. Given the hearty reception the team received in its first game In Ottawa, the article alludes to the possible plan to keep the orange sweaters.

The Calgary Broncos

This team was an original 1971 franchise that died when its owner, Bob Brownridge, fell ill and died soon after receiving the team. They were reborn as the Cleveland Crusaders a few months later. Calgary lasted long enough to participate in the 1972 draft, with Scotty Munro acting as the general manager. Did the team have a logo or color scheme? Apparently they did: Bill Tuele of the Edmonton Oilers said it was similar to the logo currently used by the Swift Current Broncos of the Western League. But I have yet to see an actual example that I can verify is true. I can state with confidence that the Calgary Broncos' (a.k.a. Broncs) logo was not identical to any of those used by the Swift Current Broncos. I have seen some supposed logos for this team on some auction sites, ranging from plausible (i.e. could be correct, I just can't independently verify it) to the obviously false (i.e. the old Denver Broncos NFL logo being passed off as the Calgary Broncos).

Statistical Inconsistencies

Most frustrating, there remain a number of statistical inconsistencies that I cannot resolve. All of them occur during the 1974-75, 1975-76 and 1976-77 seasons. Little things such as player power-play or short-handed goals not adding correctly to the team totals still dog me. The league and team media guides often contradict one another, and I have no way to resolve them.

Resources and Bibliography

League Media Guides

• Meade, Lee (Ed) **WHA Media Guide 1972-73.** Published by the league, Hopkins MN 1972. • Marlow, Walt (Ed) & Frank Polnaszek **WHA Media Guide, 1973-1974.** Published by the league, Newport Beach CA, 1973. • Marlow, Walt (Ed) & Frank Polnaszek **WHA Media Guide, 1974-1975.** Published by the league, Newport Beach CA, 1974. • Ornest, Leo (Ed) & Frank Polnaszek **World Hockey Association 1975-1976 Media Guide.** Published by the league, Toronto, 1975. • Ornest, Leo (Ed) & Frank Polnaszek **World Hockey Association 1976-1977 Media Guide.** Published by the league, Toronto 1976. • Clark, Gary (Ed) & Frank Polnaszek **World Hockey Association 1977-1978 Media Guide.** Published by the league, Hartford, 1977. • Hewig, John (Ed) & Frank Polnaszek **World Hockey Association 1978-1979 Media Guide.** Published by the league, Hartford, 1978.

Individual Team Media Guides, listed by season

1972-73: • **Alberta Oilers 1972-73 Media Guide.** Published by the team, Edmonton, 1972. • **Media Guide: Chicago Cougars 1972-73 Season.** Published by the team, Chicago, 1972. • **Cleveland Crusaders 1972-73 Press-Radio-TV Guide.** Published by the team, Cleveland, 1972. • **Houston Aeros 1972-73 Media Guide.** Published by the team, Houston, 1972. • **Los Angeles Sharks (1972-73) Media Guide.** Published by the team, Los Angeles, 1972. • **Minnesota Fighting Saints 1972-73 Media Guide.** Published by the team, St. Paul, 1972 • **New England Whalers 1972-73 Training Camp Guide.** Published by the team, Boston, 1972. • **New England Whalers 1972-73 Media Guide.** Published by the team, Boston, 1972. • Boyles, Bob (Ed) & Hank Lowenstein **New York Raiders 1972-3 Press Guide & Yearbook.** Published by the team, New York, 1972. • Johnson, Kevin (Ed) **Philadelphia Blazers Press Guide 1972-73.** Published by the Philadelphia World Hockey Club Inc., Philadelphia, 1972. • **Nordiques Quebec 1972-73.** Published by PSN Ltd., Quebec, 1972. • **Winnipeg Jets 1972-73** Official Yearbook. Published by the team, Winnipeg, 1972.

1973-74: • Haggerty, Michael (Ed) **Chicago Cougars 1973-74 News Media Guide.** Published by the team, Chicago, 1973. • **Cleveland Crusaders 1973-74 Press-Radio-TV Guide.** Published by the team, Cleveland, 1973. • Lerose, Don (Ed) **Edmonton Oilers Guide 1973-74.** Published by W. D. Hunter, Edmonton, 1973. • **Houston Aeros 1973-74 Media Guide "When Howe Arrived".** Published by the team, Houston, 1973. • Ferroni, Dave and Mike Lamey (Eds) **Minnesota Fighting Saints 73-74 Yearbook/Offical Guide.** Published by the team, St. Paul, 1973. • Donovan, Bob (Ed) **New England Whalers 1973/74 Fact Book.** Published by the team, Boston, 1973. • **Nordiques Quebec Annuaire** 1973-74 Yearbook. Published by the team, Quebec, 1973. • McClure, Michael (Ed) **Toronto Toros 1973-74**

Media Guide and Fact Book. Published by Analytic Communications Inc., Toronto, 1973. • Vancouver Blazer Media Guide 73/74. Published by the team, Vancouver, 1973.

1974-75: • Haggerty, Michael (Ed) Chicago Cougars 1974-75 News Media Guide. Published by the team, Chicago, 1974. • Cleveland Crusaders 1974-75 News Media Guide. Published by the team, Cleveland, 1974. • Edmonton Oilers 1974-75 News Media Guide. Published by Edmonton World Hockey Enterprises, Edmonton, 1974. • Asnes, Bill and Kevin O'Keeffe Houston Aeros 74-75 Media Guide. Published by the team, Houston, 1974. • Vargo, Joe (Ed) Indianapolis Racers 1974-75 Yearbook. Published by the team, Indianapolis, 1974. • Pelliccioni, Larry (Ed) Michigan Stags Media Guide, 1974-75. Published by the team, Birmingham MI, 1974. • Ferroni, Dave and Mike Lamey (Eds) Minnesota Fighting Saints 1974-75 Yearbook/Offical Guide. Published by the team, St. Paul, 1974. • Neumeier, Bob (Ed) New England Whalers 1974-75 Yearbook. Published by the team, Boston, 1974. • Official 1974-75 Phoenix Roadrunners Facts Book. Published by the team, Phoenix, 1974. • Les Nordiques 1974-75 Annuaire-Yearbook. Published by the team, Quebec, 1974. • DeNunzio, Gabe (Ed) San Diego Mariners 1974-75 Media Guide. Published by the team, San Diego, 1974. • Boyd, Dennis (Ed) Vancouver Blazers Illustrated Guide 1974-75. Published by the team, Vancouver, 1974. • Boyd, J. D. (Ed) Winnipeg Jets 1974-75 Media Guide. Published by the team, Winnipeg, 1974.

1975-76: • Calgary Cowboys 1975/76 Yearbook. Published by the team, Calgary, 1975. • Cincinnati Stingers 75-76 Media Guide. Published by the team, Cincinnati, 1975. • Vargo, Joe (Ed) Cleveland Crusaders Yearbook 1975-76. Published by the team, Cleveland, 1975. • Edmonton Oilers Media Guide. Published by Edmonton World Hockey Enterprises, Edmonton, 1975. • Burk, Rich (Ed) Aeros 75-76 Media Guide. Published by the team, Houston, 1975. • Marlow, Walt (Ed) Indianapolis Racers 1975/76 Yearbook. Published by Indiana Hockey, Inc. Indianapolis, 1975. • Ferroni, Dave and Mike Lamey (Eds) Minnesota Fighting Saints 1975-1976 Fact Book. Published by the team, St. Paul, 1975. • Neumeier, Bob (Ed) New England Whalers 1975-76 Yearbook and Official Guide. Published by the team, Hartford, 1975. • Official 1975-76 (Phoenix) Roadrunners Facts Book. Published by the team, Phoenix, 1975. • Les Nordiques 1975-76 Annuaire-Yearbook. Published by the team, Quebec, 1975. • DeNunzio, Gabe (Ed) San Diego Mariners 1975-1976 Media Guide. Published by the team, San Diego, 1975. • Toronto Toros Action Guide 1975-76. Published by the team, Toronto, 1975. • Winnipeg Jets Media Guide 1975/76. Published by Sports Centrepoint Enterprises, Inc., Winnipeg, 1975.

1976-77: • Birmingham Bulls Press Guide 1976-77. Published by the team, Birmingham, 1976. • Calgary Cowboys 1975-76 Media Book. Published by the team, Calgary, 1976. • Cincinnati Stingers Media Guide "A Package Called Dynamite" 1976-77. Published by the team, Cincinnati, 1976. • Wenschlag, Doug (Ed) Edmonton Oilers Media Guide, 1976-77. Published by Edmonton World Hockey Enterprises, Edmonton, 1976. • Burk, Rich (Ed) Aeros 76-77 Media Guide. Published by the team, Houston, 1976. • Marlow, Walt (Ed) Indianapolis Racers Press Guide and Yearbook, 1976-77. Published by the team, Indianapolis, 1976. • Meade, Lee (Ed) New Minnesota Fighting Saints 1976-77. Published by the team, St. Paul, 1976. • Neumeier, Bob and Dennis Randall (Eds) New England Whalers 1976-77 Yearbook and Official Guide. Published by the team, Hartford, 1976. • Official 1976-77 Phoenix Roadrunners Facts Book. Published by the team, Phoenix, 1976. • Les Nordiques 1976-77 Annuaire-Yearbook. Published by the team, Quebec, 1976. • DeNunzio, Gabe (Ed) San Diego Mariners 1976-1977 Media Guide. Published by the team, San Diego, 1976. • Coston, Norm (Ed) Winnipeg Jets Media Guide 1976-77. Published by Sports Centrepoint Enterprises, Inc., Winnipeg, 1976.

1977-78: • Hewig, John (Ed) Cincinnati Stingers Media Guide and Yearbook, 1977-78. Published by the team, Cincinnati, 1977. • Ell, Elaine (Ed) Edmonton Oilers Media Guide, 1977-78. Published by Edmonton World Hockey Enterprises, Edmonton, 1977. • Leiweke, R. Terry (Ed) Aeros '77-'78 Media Guide. Published by the team, Houston, 1977. • 1977-78 Racers' Hockey Album. Published by the team, Indianapolis, 1977. • Dennis Randall (Ed) New England Whalers 1977-78 Yearbook and Official Guide. Published by the team, Hartford, 1977. • Bell, Bob (Ed) Winnipeg Jets Media Guide 1977-78 "Playing Hockey the World Over". Published by Sports Centrepoint Enterprises, Inc., Winnipeg, 1977.

1978-79: • Gold, Eli (Ed) Birmingham Bulls 1978-79 Media Guide. Published by the team, Birmingham, 1978. • Cincinnati Stingers Media Guide, 1978-79. Published by the team, Cincinnati, 1978. • Ell, Elaine (Ed) Edmonton Oilers Media Guide, 1978-79. Published by Edmonton World Hockey Enterprises, Edmonton, 1978. • Dennis Randall (Ed) New England Whalers 1978-79 Yearbook and Official Guide. Published by the team, Hartford, 1978. • Les Nordiques 1978-79 Annuaire-Yearbook. Published by the team, Quebec, 1978. • Bell, Bob (Ed) Winnipeg Jets Hockey Club Media Guide 1978-79. Published by 8 Hockey Ventures, Inc.., Winnipeg, 1978.

1979-80: • Short, John and Elaine Ell (Eds) Edmonton Oilers Media Guide, 1979-80. Published by Edmonton World Hockey Enterprises, Edmonton, 1979. • Hewig, John (Ed) Hartford Whalers 1979-80 Yearbook & Official Guide. Published by the team, Hartford, 1979. • Quebec Nordiques Annuaire/Yearbook 1979-80. Published by the team, Quebec, 1979. • Fenson, Ken (Ed) Winnipeg Jets Media Guide, 1979-80. Published by 8 Hockey Ventures, Winnipeg, 1979.

Books, Magazines, Programs, Websites and Promotional Items

• Baldwin, Howard and Steve Milton Slim and None: My Wild Ride from the WHA to the NHL and All The Way to Hollywood Amazon/Kindle 2014 • Beisel, David Can You Name That Team? The Scarecrow Press, Metuchen NJ, 1991. • Blawie, Pamela (Ed) Cleveland Crusaders 1974-75 Game Program. Professional Sports Publications, New York, 1974. • Blueliner (Houston Aeros), Published by the team, Houston, 1973-1977 (multiple issues). • Boyles, Bob (Ed) World's First Hockey Spectacular Collector's Item Program. Published by the New York Golden Blades Hockey Club, New York, 1973. • "Blades" Baltimore Blades Souvenir Program, 1975. Published by the team, Baltimore, 1975. • Canada vs. Russia 1974 Canadian Amateur Hockey Association, Toronto, 1974. • Chidlovski, Arthur Team USSR vs. Team Canada: The Summit in 1974 www.chidlovski.com/personal/1974/index.htm • Davidson, Gary and Bill Libby Breaking the Game Wide Open Athenium, 1974 • Diamond, Dan (Ed) The Official NHL 75th Anniversary Commemorative Book. McClelland & Stevens Inc., Toronto, 1991. • Diamond, Dan and James Duplacey, Ralph Dinger, Igor Kuperman and Eric Zweig (Eds) Total Hockey Total Sports (New York) / Andrews McMeel (Kansas City), 1998. • Diamond, Dan and James Duplacey, Ralph Dinger, Igor Kuperman and Eric Zweig (Eds) Total Hockey II Total Sports (New York) / Andrews McMeel (Kansas City), 2001. • Duplacey, James Shutouts in the Spotlight The Hockey Research Journal Vol III, No III. Society of International Hockey Research, Kingston, 1997. • Eskenazi, Gerald A Thinking Man's Guide to Pro Hockey. E. P. Dutton & Co., New York, 1972. • Eskenazi, Gerald The Derek Sanderson Nobody Knows. Follett Publishing, Chicago, 1973. • Faceoff (Official magazine of the WHA). Published by the league. Multiple issues. • Fischler, Stan and Shirley Walton Fischler The Hockey Encyclopedia, MacMillan Publishers, New York, 1983. • Frayne, Trent WHA vs. Soviet Nationals. Holt Rinehart & Winston of Canada Ltd., Toronto, 1974. • Gassen, Timothy Red White & Blues: The Indianapolis Racers 1974-1979, A Personal History. Purple Cactus Media Publications, Tucson, 2007 • Gassen, Timothy, Curtis Walker et al WHAHOF.com • World Hockey Association Action Annual. Published by Edward Grusin, WHA Properties, Santa Ana, 1972. • Hockeytime (Official publication of the Stingers) Vol 1, No 1, October 25 1975. Published by the team. • Hollander, Zander and Hal Bock (Eds) The Complete Encyclopedia of Ice Hockey. Prentice Hall, Inc., Edgewood Cliffs NJ 1974. • Hollander, Zander (Ed) The Complete Encyclopedia of Ice Hockey, 4th Ed. Visible Ink Press, Detroit, 1993. • Hollander, Zander (Ed) The Complete Handbook of Pro Hockey, 1973 Edition. Signet Books, New York, 1972. • Hollander, Zander (Ed) The Complete Handbook of Pro Hockey, 1974 Edition. Signet Books, New York, 1973. • Hollander, Zander (Ed) The Complete Handbook of Pro Hockey, 1975 Edition. Signet Books, New York, 1974. • Hollander, Zander (Ed) The Complete Handbook of Pro Hockey, 1976 Edition. Signet Books, New York, 1975. • Hollander, Zander (Ed) The Complete Handbook of Pro Hockey, 1977 Edition. Signet Books, New York, 1976. • Hollander, Zander (Ed) The Complete Handbook of Pro Hockey, 1978 Edition. Signet Books, New York, 1977. • Hollander, Zander (Ed) The Complete Handbook of Pro Hockey, 1979 Edition. Signet Books, New York, 1978. • Hollander, Zander (Ed) The Complete Handbook of Pro Hockey, 1980 Edition. Signet Books, New York, 1979. • Indianapolis Racers Game Program. April 1976. Published by the team, 1976. • International Series, World Hockey Association vs. Czechoslovakia. Published by the WHA, Hartford, 1977. • International Series, World Hockey Association vs. Soviet All Stars. Published by the WHA, Hartford, 1977. • Kasiorek, Jason

WHA Oilers Page www.homeoftheoilers.orgfree.com • Marshall, James **Lake Superior Journal** www.lakesuperior.com/online/ • Mavor, Elinor (Ed) **The Roadrunners Hockey Highlights, 1974-75.** Jeffords Independent Publishing, Phoenix, 1975. • McFarland, Brian **One Hundred Years of Hockey** Deneau Publishers, Toronto, 1989. • Maclean, Norm *Hockey's Strange Love Affair* **Hockey Pictorial-World** WCC Publishing, Montreal, Feb 1977. • Maclean, Norm *1978-79 WHA Team Previews* **Hockey Pictorial.** WCC Publishing, Montreal, Oct 1978. • McGuire, Tom (Ed) **The World Almanac Guide to Pro Hockey, 1974-75.** Bantam Books, New York, 1974. • Michel, Doug and Bob Mellor **Left Wing and a Prayer.** Excalibur Sports Publications, Ottawa, 1974. • **Michigan Stags Magazine,** Published by the team, 1974 (Preseason issue). • **Phoenix Roadrunners Magazine 1975-76.** Published by the team, Phoenix, 1975. (Multiple issues) • **Phoenix Roadrunners Magazine 1976-77.** Published by the team, Phoenix, 1976. (Multiple issues) • **Justia US Law** http://law.justia.com/cases/federal/district-courts/FSupp/371/742-/2133517/ • Sanderson, Derek with Kevin Shea **Crossing The Line: The Outrageous Story of a Hockey Original** Triumph Books, 2012 • Slate, Ralph **Internet Hockey Database** www.hockeydb.com • **The Spur (Game program).** Published by the Denver Spurs, Denver, 1975. • Wallechinsky, David **The Complete Book of the Olympics.** Penguin Books, New York, 1984. • Walker, Curtis **Winnipeg Jets Memorial Site** www.curtiswalker.com/jets • Wigge, Larry and Joe Marcin (Eds) **The Sporting News 1975-76 Pro and Amateur Hockey Guide,** Compiled by Herb Elk. Published by C. C. Johnson Spink, St. Louis, 1975. • Wigge, Larry and Joe Marcin (Eds) **The Sporting News 1976-77 Pro and Amateur Hockey Guide,** Compiled by Herb Elk. Published by C. C. Johnson Spink, St. Louis, 1976. • Wigge, Larry and Joe Marcin (Eds) **The Sporting News 1977-78 Pro and Amateur Hockey Guide,** Compiled by Herb Elk. Published by C. C. Johnson Spink, St. Louis, 1977. • Wigge, Larry (Ed) **The Sporting News 1978-79 Pro and Amateur Hockey Guide,** Compiled by Herb Elk. Published by C. C. Johnson Spink, St. Louis, 1978. • Wigge, Larry (Ed) **The Sporting News 1979-80 Pro and Amateur Hockey Guide,** Compiled by Herb Elk and Frank Polnaszek. Published by C. C. Johnson Spink, St. Louis, 1979. • **Winnipeg Jets vs. Team Finland** (Game Program) Published by 8 Hockey Ventures, Winnipeg, 1979. • Ward, David **The Lost 10 Point Night: Searching for my Hockey Hero ... Jim Harrison** Amazon Publishing 2014 • Walker, Curtis **Winnipeg Jets: The WHA Years, Day by Day** 2013

Newspapers and Periodicals

• **Arizona (Phoenix) Republic:** 1974 through 1979. • **Calgary Herald:** 1972 through 1979 • **Chicago Tribune:** Various issues between 1972 and 1976 • **The Hockey News:** Multiple Issues from 1971-1980. • **Los Angeles Times:** 1972 through 1979 • **New York Times:** 1972 through 1979 • **Le Journal de Quebec:** 1972 through 1979 • **The Sporting News:** 1972 through 1979 • **Washington Post:** Various issues between 1977 and 1979 • Various issues of the **Edmonton Journal,** the **Montreal Gazette,** the **Ottawa Sun,** the **Windsor Star,** and the **Lewiston Daily Sun.**

Newspaper Articles and Reprints

• Dunn, Art *Forey Ruled Out* **Chicago Tribune,** 8 Mar 1974, Sect 3 page 2. • Eskenazi, Gerald *Hockey League Formed In Rivalry With N. H. L.* (New York Times, 14 Sept 1971) **New York Times Encyclopedia of Sports, Vol 8: Soccer and Hockey,** Gene Brown Ed, Arno Press, New York, 1979. • Eskenazi, Gerald *New Hockey Loop Picks Club Sites* (New York Times 25 Sept 1971) **New York Times Encyclopedia of Sports, Vol 8: Soccer and Hockey,** Gene Brown Ed, Arno Press, New York, 1979. • Eskenazi, Gerald *Hockey Leagues In Tune* (New York Times, 20 Feb 1974) **New York Times Encyclopedia of Sports, Vol 8: Soccer and Hockey,** Gene Brown Ed, Arno Press, New York, 1979. • Eskenazi, Gerald *Temporary Injunction Against NHL Frees Hull and Others to Play in WHA,* **New York Times,** 9 Nov 1972. • Gammons, Peter *Wild Willie Gets a New Lease on Life* **Sports Illustrated,** 28 Nov 1977 • Gutskey, Earl *Numerous NHL Stars, 3 Russians Included Among WHA Draftees,* **Los Angeles Times,** 13 Feb 1972. • Herman, Robin *NHL Governors Turn Down Merger With 6 WHA Teams* (New York Times, 10 Aug 1977) **New York Times Encyclopedia of Sports, Vol 8: Soccer and Hockey,** Gene Brown Ed, Arno Press, New York, 1979. • Herman, Robin *Salaries in Hockey Drying Up Minors* (New York Times, 21 Sept 1975) **New York Times Encyclopedia of Sports, Vol 8: Soccer and Hockey,** Gene Brown Ed, Arno Press, New York, 1979. • *Howe Displays Old Style in WHA Round Robin* **New York Times,** Page 29, 26 Sept 1973. • Keese, Parton *NHL Approves Plan to Merge With Four Clubs From WHA* **New York Times,** 23 Mar 1979. • Keese, Parton *Compensation Rule Key to NHL Pact* (New York Times, 7 Oct 1975) **New York Times Encyclopedia of Sports, Vol 8: Soccer and Hockey,** Gene Brown Ed, Arno Press, New York, 1979. • Koppett, Leonard *The League-Maker: He Weds Excess Money to Surplus Talent,* **New York Times,** 11 Nov 1973. • *Baltimore Now Site of WHA Club* (Associated Press) **Arizona Republic,** page D-1, 24 Jan 1975. • *Caught In The Draft* **Winnipeg Free Press,** 14 Feb 1972. • *The Draft, Round by Round* **The Globe and Mail (Toronto),** 14 Feb 1972. • *WHA's Dayton Team Drafts Orr, Esposito* **Los Angeles Times,** 14 Feb 1972.

Photo Credits (when known): Bill Nevers, William Torzewski, Mike Koster, Doug Davis, Bob Schmidt, Tom Cushing, Ed McCullough, Jory Levingston, Sue MacMaster, Steve Babineau, Paul Kennedy, Paul Kellogg, Les Rosner, Al Howard, Diane Carparelli, Dick Brimley, and many more.

Photographers were rarely cited in the various media guides, programs or contemporary materials. The above names are but a fraction of the many people who worked as photographers at one time or another for teams within the WHA.

All images in this book are believed to be in the public domain and are used here for their historical context. Most player and team photographs were taken by the teams for the express purpose of media exposure. If you feel an image is being used inappropriately, please contact the author at the address on the Author's Note page.

Scott Surgent is a Lecturer of Mathematics at Arizona State University in Tempe, Arizona. He is the author of **The World Hockey Association Fact Book** and has published articles in **The Journal of the Society of International Hockey Research, Total Hockey II,** and **Hockey Ink** (magazine). He is also the author of **The County Highpoints of Arizona,** and has authored or co-authored textbooks in mathematics on Introductory Logic, Calculus and Finite Mathematics. In 2012 and in 2014, he played an important role in cheering on the Los Angeles Kings to their Stanley Cup Championships, driving in from Arizona along with his wife to attend both celebration parades. He lives in Arizona with his wife, Beth and enjoys hockey, baseball, hiking, a good math problem, and the sunny climate.

39379294R00296

Made in the USA
Middletown, DE
12 January 2017